sydney
COMPACT
street directory
22nd edition

cafes restaurants shops & markets pubs & bars transport

Proudly Australian Owned Company

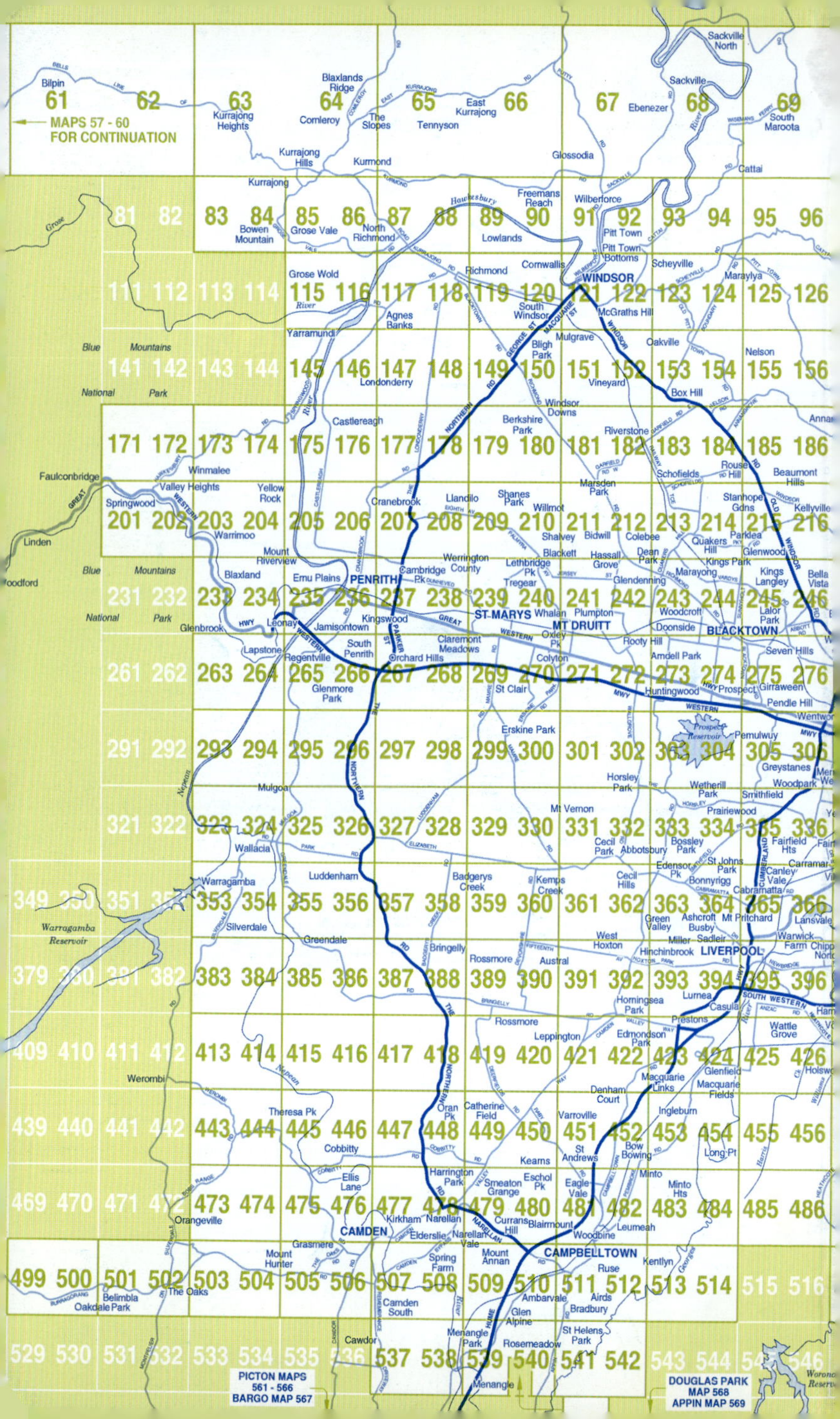

Sydney Region Map Index

Bilpin 61	62	63 Kurrajong Heights	Blaxlands Ridge 64 Comleroy The Slopes	65 Tennyson	East Kurrajong 66	67 Ebenezer	68	Sackville North Sackville 69 South Maroota	

MAPS 57 - 60 FOR CONTINUATION

Kurrajong Hills, Kurmond, Glossodia, Cattai

| 81 | 82 | 83 | 84 Bowen Mountain | 85 Grose Vale | 86 North Richmond | 87 | 88 Hawkesbury Freemans Reach | 89 Lowlands | 90 | Wilberforce 91 | 92 Pitt Town Pitt Town Bottoms | 93 | 94 | 95 | 96 |

Grose Wold, Cornwallis, Scheyville

| 111 | 112 | 113 | 114 | 115 | 116 | 117 | 118 South Windsor | 119 | 120 Windsor | 121 | 122 McGraths Hill | 123 | Maraylya 124 | 125 | 126 |

Blue Mountains, Yarramundi, Agnes Banks, Bligh Park, Mulgrave, Oakville

| 141 | 142 | 143 | 144 | 145 | 146 Londonderry | 147 | 148 | 149 | 150 | 151 Vineyard | 152 | 153 | Nelson 154 | 155 | 156 |

National Park, Castlereagh, Windsor Downs, Box Hill

| 171 | 172 | 173 | 174 | 175 | 176 | 177 | 178 | 179 Berkshire Park | 180 | 181 | 182 Riverstone | 183 | 184 | 185 | Annan 186 |

Faulconbridge, Winmalee, Valley Heights, Yellow Rock, Cranebrook, Llandilo, Shanes Park, Willmot, Marsden Park, Schofields, Rouse Hill, Stanhope Gdns, Beaumont Hills

| 201 Springwood | 202 | 203 Warrimoo | 204 | 205 | 206 | 207 | 208 | 209 | 210 Shalvey | 211 Bidwill | 212 Colebee | 213 | 214 Quakers Hill | 215 Parklea Glenwood | 216 Kellyville |

Linden, Mount Riverview

| 231 | 232 | 233 Blaxland | 234 Emu Plains | 235 PENRITH | 236 | 237 Cambridge County | 238 Werrington | 239 Lethbridge Pk Tregear | 240 Hassall Grove | 241 Dean Park | 242 Marayong | 243 Kings Park | 244 Kings Langley | 245 Bella Vista | 246 |

Blue Mountains, Woodford, Blaxland, Glendenning

| 261 | 262 | 263 | 264 Lapstone | 265 Regentville | 266 South Penrith | 267 Claremont Meadows | 268 | 269 Colyton | 270 Oxley Pk | 271 ST MARYS | 272 Plumpton | 273 Woodcroft | 274 Doonside | 275 Lalor Park | 276 BLACKTOWN |

National Park, Glenbrook, Leonay, Jamisontown, Kingswood, GREAT WESTERN HWY, MT DRUITT, Rooty Hill, Arndell Park, Seven Hills

| 291 | 292 | 293 | 294 | 295 | 296 | 297 | 298 | 299 | 300 Erskine Park | 301 | 302 | 303 | 304 | 305 Pendle Hill | 306 Wentw |

Glenmore Park, St Clair, Huntingwood, Prospect, Girraween

| 321 | 322 | 323 | 324 | 325 | 326 | 327 | 328 | 329 Horsley Park | 330 | 331 Mt Vernon | 332 Wetherill Park | 333 Pemulwuy | 334 Smithfield | 335 Greystanes | 336 Woodpark |

Mulgoa

| 349 | 350 | 351 | 352 | 353 | 354 | 355 | 356 | 357 | 358 | 359 | 360 Cecil Park | 361 Abbotsbury | 362 Bossley Park | 363 Prairiewood | 364 Fairfield Hts |

Wallacia, Warragamba

| 379 | 380 | 381 | 382 | 383 | 384 | 385 | 386 Luddenham | 387 | 388 Baggerys Creek | 389 | 390 Kemps Creek | 391 Cecil Hills | 392 Edensor St Johns Park | 393 Bonnyrigg Ashcroft | 394 Canley Vale Mt Pritchard Cabramatta | 395 Carramar |

Warragamba Reservoir, Silverdale

| 409 410 | 411 412 | 413 | 414 | 415 | 416 Greendale | 417 | 418 Bringelly | 419 Rossmore | 420 Austral | 421 West Hoxton | 422 Miller Sadleir Hinchinbrook | 423 Green Valley Busby | 424 LIVERPOOL | 425 Warwick Farm | 426 Lansvale |

Werombi

| 439 | 440 | 441 | 442 | 443 | 444 | 445 | 446 | 447 | 448 Rossmore | 449 | 450 Hornsea Park | 451 Lurnea | 452 Prestons | 453 Casula | 454 SOUTH WESTERN | 455 Wattle Grove | 456 Ham |

Theresa Pk

| 469 | 470 | 471 472 | 473 | 474 | 475 | 476 | 477 Oran Pk | 478 Catherine Field | 479 | 480 Leppington | 481 | 482 Edmondson Park | 483 | 484 Glenfield Macquarie Fields | 485 | 486 Holsw |

Cobbitty

| 499 500 | 501 502 | 503 | 504 | 505 | 506 | 507 Harrington Pk | 508 Smeaton Grange | 509 Eschol Pk | 510 Eagle Vale | 511 | 512 Minto Hts | 513 | 514 | 515 Long Pt | 516 |

Orangeville, Ellis Lane, Kirkham Narellan, Elderslie Narellan Vale, Currans Hill Blairmount, Woodbine, Leumeah, CAMDEN

| 529 530 | 531 532 | 533 | 534 | 535 | 536 | 537 | 538 Mount Hunter | 539 Grasmere | 540 Spring Farm | 541 Mount Annan | 542 CAMPBELLTOWN Ruse | 543 Kentlyn | 544 |

Belimbla Oakdale Park, The Oaks, Camden South, Ambarvale, Airds Bradbury, St Helens Park

Cawdor, Menangle Park, Rosemeadow, Menangle

PICTON MAPS 561 - 566
BARGO MAP 567

DOUGLAS PARK MAP 568
APPIN MAP 569

KEY MAP

SCALE 1:390,000

MAP SYMBOLS

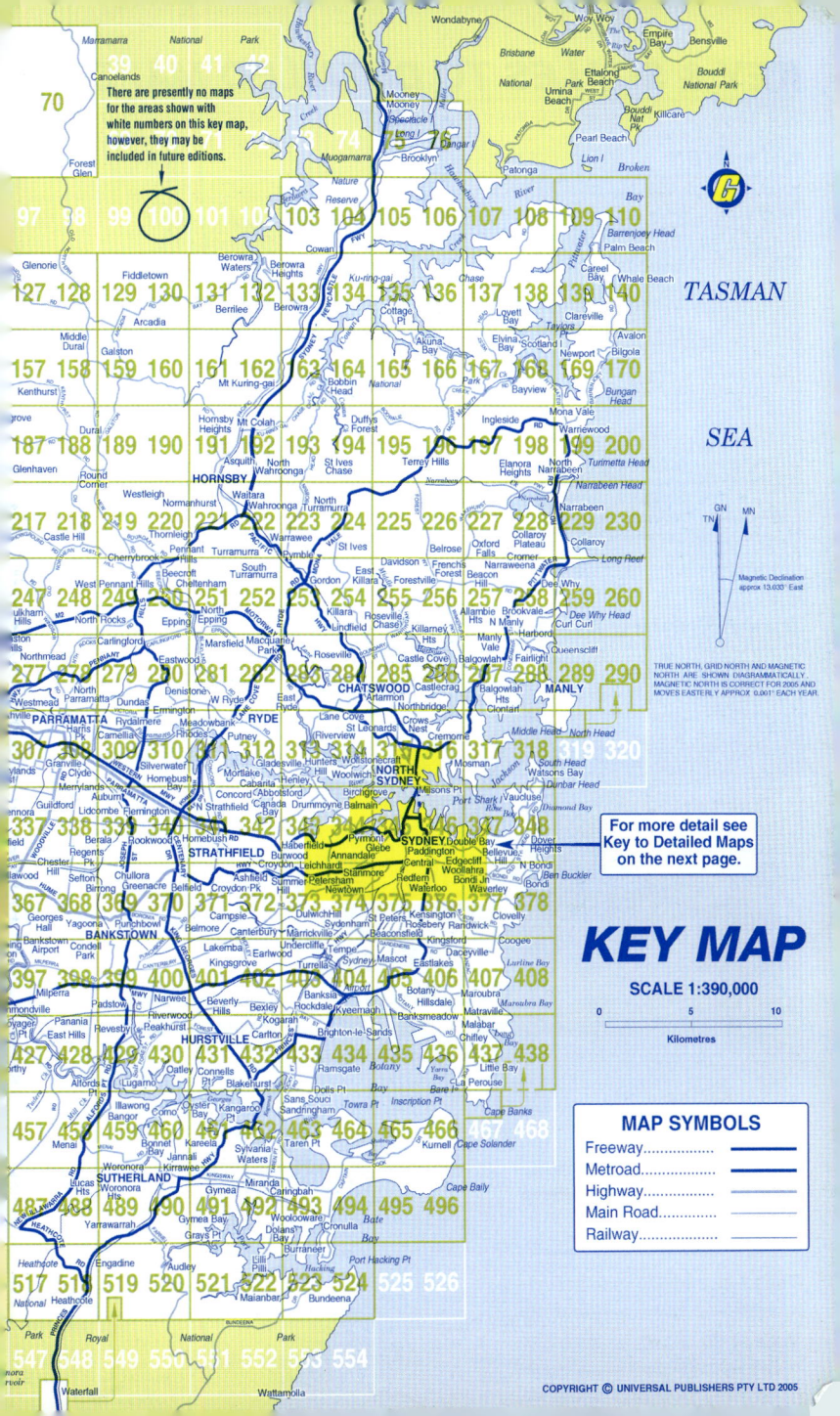

Freeway	
Metroad	
Highway	
Main Road	
Railway	

There are presently no maps for the areas shown with white numbers on this key map, however, they may be included in future editions.

TASMAN SEA

For more detail see Key to Detailed Maps on the next page.

TRUE NORTH, GRID NORTH AND MAGNETIC NORTH ARE SHOWN DIAGRAMMATICALLY. MAGNETIC NORTH IS CORRECT FOR 2005 AND MOVES EASTERLY APPROX 0.001° EACH YEAR.

Magnetic Declination approx 13.033° East

COPYRIGHT © UNIVERSAL PUBLISHERS PTY LTD 2005

KEY & SCALES TO DETAILED MAPS

City Area

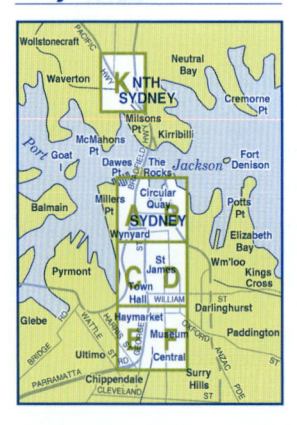

SCALE 1 : 6 250
MAPS A to F and K are City Area Maps and each map covers 625m east-west and 1 km north-south.

SCALE 1 : 20 800
MAP J is a detailed Parking map and covers 1.4km east-west and 3.4km north-south.

SCALE 1 : 20 250
MAPS 571 & 572 are detailed Homebush Bay maps and cover 3.2km east-west and 4km north-south.

Inner Suburb Area

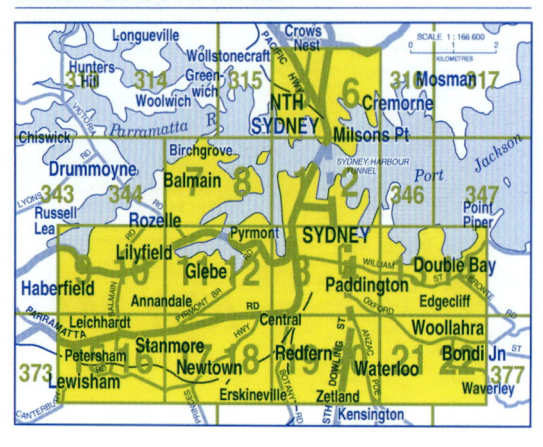

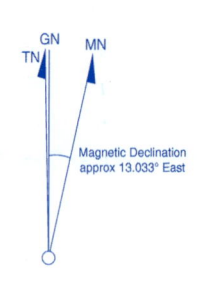

TRUE NORTH, GRID NORTH AND MAGNETIC NORTH ARE SHOWN DIAGRAMMATICALLY. MAGNETIC NORTH IS CORRECT FOR 2005 AND MOVES EASTERLY APPROX 0.001° EACH YEAR.

Magnetic Declination approx 13.033° East

Map Scales

Maps A-F and K SCALE 1 : 6 250
0   50   100   150   200   250 metres
0   0.25 kilometres

Map J SCALE 1 : 20 800
0   200   400   600   800 metres
0   0.8 kilometres

Maps 1-22 and 570 SCALE 1 : 12 500
0   100   200   300   400   500 metres
0   0.5 kilometres

Maps 57-70 SCALE 1 : 50 000
0   400   800   1 200   1 600   2 000 metres
0   2 kilometre

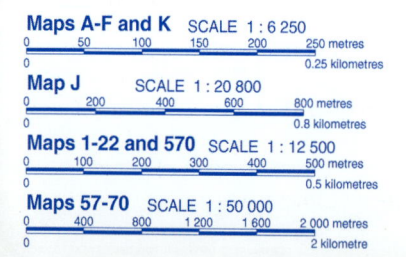

Maps 75-566 SCALE 1 : 25 000
0   200   400   600   800   1 000 metres
0   1 kilometre

Maps 567-569 SCALE 1 : 27 500
0   200   400   600   800   1 000 metres
0   1 kilometre

Maps 571 & 572 SCALE 1 : 20 250
0   200   400   600   800 metres
0   0.8 kilometres

MAP SYMBOLS

Freeway or Motorway	WARRINGAH FREEWAY
Highway or Main Traffic Route and Footbridge	PRINCES Fbr HIGHWAY
Trafficable Road	JONES AV
Un-trafficable / Proposed Road	THOMAS ST
Traffic Light, Roundabout and Red Light Camera	
No Left Turn, No Right Turn and Level Crossing	
Road and Railway Bridges	
One-way Traffic Route	
National and State Route Numbers	1 33
Metroad and Tourist Route Numbers	5 14
Proposed Freeway	Proposed Freeway
Direction of Sydney City Centre	CITY
Distance by Road from GPO	22
Railway Line, Station (distance from Central)	Dulwich Hill
Suburb Name	**EASTWOOD**
Locality Name	Audley
Walking Tracks, Horse Tracks and Cycleways	
Park, Reserve or Golf Course	
School or Hospital	
Caravan Park, Cemetery, Shopping Centre, etc	
Mall, Plaza	

Car Park	P	Point of Interest	■ Museum
Council Office	■ Cncl Off	Police Station	★
Fire Station	F	Post Office	✉
Hospital	✚	Rural Fire Service	■ RFS
Library		Shopping Centre	
Picnic Area		Speed Camera (Fixed)	
Place of Worship		Swimming Pool	

STREET MAPS overlap on each page to help in re-locating position on an adjoining page.
ADJOINING MAP NUMBERS are shown in the borders and corners of the street maps.
REFERENCE NUMBERS AND LETTERS within the borders of the street maps are the reference co-ordinates given in the indexes.

Cityside Guide

Sydney is Australia's most vibrant city. The **Cityside Guide** covers Sydney's CBD and inner city areas and includes **sightseeing** and **shopping** suggestions; **restaurant** and café recommendations; listings of Sydney's best **entertainment** venues including theatres, pubs, bars, nightclubs, cinemas, galleries, and museums; a guide to **youth hostels** and backpacker accommodation in and around the city, as well as comprehensive **public transport** info.

- **8** around the harbour
- **9** city sights
- **10** shopping & markets
- **11** culture & entertainment
- **12** restaurants & cafes
- **13** bars, clubs & pubs
- **14** city fringe
- **15** backpackers accommodation
- **16** public transport

around the harbour

Sydney Harbour and its surroundings make the City of Sydney spectacular. Sydneysiders are fortunate to have this stunning all-year-round playground at their disposal. Here you can sail from Rushcutters Bay, windsurf at Balmoral Beach, swim in harbourside pools and beaches, picnic at waterfront parks or sightsee from a ferry. Circular Quay, Sydney's ferry terminal, is the departure point for scenic cruises and ferry rides around picturesque Sydney Harbour and between harbourside suburbs.

- **Circular Quay (Map B, Ref D6)**, at the northern edge of the **Central Business District (CBD)**, is a bustling interchange connecting rail and ferry services. This busy waterfront, surrounded by some of Sydney's most famous landmarks, is the perfect place to sit back and admire the views at one of many restaurants.

- **Sydney Opera House (Map B, Ref J1)** (9250 7111) at **Bennelong Point** is both an architectural marvel and a performing arts Mecca. This unique white sail-like structure, set strikingly against the blue waters of Sydney Harbour, houses numerous restaurants and cafes, and has had frequent and diverse performances in its concert hall, theatres and forecourt. The walkways provide some of the best views of Sydney Harbour.

- **Sydney Harbour Bridge (Map 1, Ref J4)** is one of Sydney's most well known landmarks, and the view from the top is truly breathtaking (to climb call **BridgeClimb** on 8274 7777). For the not so adventurous, the southeast **Pylon Lookout** (9240 1100) contains an exhibition illustrating the construction of the bridge, which was completed in 1932.

- **The Rocks (Map B, Ref A3)** (Visitor Centre, 106 George St, 9240 8788) is our link to Sydney's colonial heritage, and has some of the best shopping Sydney has to offer. The Rocks Markets, held every weekend, is a must for those looking for something special and the Museum of Contemporary Art offers a continually changing variety of exhibitions. **Cadman's Cottage** (110 George Street, 9247 5033) is the oldest surviving building in the city, and **Campbell's Stores** (27 Circular Quay W) are the only remaining example of early nineteenth century warehouses in Sydney, currently home to many galleries and waterfront restaurants. It's also a great place to relax, having some of the best pubs in the city. The cosy **Lord Nelson Brewery Hotel** was built in 1841 and serves beer that has been brewed on the premises. After dark, The Rocks maintains its attraction, offering nightly sky viewings at the astronomy museum, **Sydney Observatory** (Watson Road, Observatory Hill, 9217 0485). Night tours must be pre-booked.

- **Fort Denison (Map 2, Ref K6)** (9247 5033) was constructed to defend Sydney during the 1850's on **Pinchgut Island**, so named because of the limited rations given to convicts once incarcerated on the island. Book a tour to explore the island's barracks, tower and gun battery. Bring along a picnic lunch or enjoy a meal from the café on the island (lunch-time tours only). Fort Denison can also be hired in the evening and is a unique venue to hold a special function (9268 1115).

- **Taronga Zoological Park (Map 316, Ref K14)** (Bradley's Head Rd, Mosman, 9969 2777) was once voted the world's best zoo. It utilises moats where possible, rather than bars and fences, to ensure its enclosures resemble the animals' natural habitat. Highlights include the nocturnal exhibit, native Australian animals and the Walkthrough Rainforest Aviary. An all-inclusive zoopass can be bought from any train station or ferry wharf, which includes return ferry and/or train travel as well as zoo entry.

- **Manly (Map 288, Ref H9)** (Manly Visitor Information Centre, Manly Wharf Forecourt, East Esplanade, 9977 1088) is a fantastic place to get a taste of Sydney's beach culture, where the bustling suburb is framed by the harbour on one side and the ocean on the other. One of Manly's main attractions is **Oceanworld** (9949 2644), an aquarium boasting the largest captive sharks in Australia, as well as other marine life, colourful coral and live shows. Enjoy free entertainment, shops and cafes at the **Manly Wharf**; stroll from harbour to beach along Manly's Corso or wander through the pretty backstreets to the surf beach and promenade. Explore Fairy Bower and secluded Shelly Beach, or visit the historic **Quarantine Station** (9247 5033) at North Head.

- **Watsons Bay (Map 318, Ref E14)** offers panoramic harbour and city views from **Wharf Beach** and is a perfect place to have a picnic or dine on fresh seafood at one of the high calibre restaurants. Watch the activity on the harbour from this relaxed vantage point, or go for a swim at nearby **Camp Cove**. Explore **South Head**, the harbour's southern entrance, and climb **The Gap's** dramatic cliffs with views of the crashing waves below.

- **Darling Harbour (Map 3, Ref C8)** (Visitor Centre, 33 Wheat Rd, 9240 8788) can be reached by foot, **monorail** or **light rail** (8584 5288). It is home to the **Sydney Aquarium** (8251 7800), which contains walk-through Perspex tunnels where sea life swims around you. Wander across **Pyrmont Bridge**, the world's oldest electrically operated swing span bridge, to the shops and eateries at the **Harbourside Shopping Centre**. Visit the adjacent **Australian National Maritime Museum** for an exploration into Australia's sea faring past. Take a relaxing stroll amid the waterfalls, bridges and Cantonese pavilions of the tranquil **Chinese Garden of Friendship** (9281 6863), before catching a film on the 3D screen at the **IMAX Theatre** (9281 3300). Chinatown, the **Powerhouse Museum**, **Sydney Fish Markets** and **Star City Casino** are also close by, making it a great place to explore.

- **Milsons Point (Map 1, Ref K1)** is a great walking destination, as well as a place to meet people or unwind. Alight at **Milsons Point Wharf**, and walk across **Bradfield Park** to admire the massive **Sydney Harbour Bridge** above you. Enjoy the views at the **North Sydney Olympic Pool** (9955 2309), then wander along Blues Point Road before venturing to nearby **McMahons Point** for a return ferry to Circular Quay. This area is spectacular at night, with possibly the best views of the city lights.

- **Cockle Bay Wharf at Darling Park (Map 3, Ref C5)** (9264 4755) on the city side of Darling Harbour contains a lively collection of eateries and bars. Restaurants such as **Chinta Ria...The Temple of Love** are exciting places to eat, and **Home** nightclub boasts one of the most incredible nightclub experiences in Sydney, carrying this feel through to the **Home Bar**. **Pontoon Bar** at the other end of Cockle Bay Wharf is extremely popular with a diverse crowd and beautiful surroundings.

city sights

Sydney city boasts a wide variety of attractions to interest both locals and tourists alike. There are numerous sights worth seeing: from the charming sandstone architecture of The Rocks to the majestic grandeur of the Queen Victoria Building; from the city's lively shopping malls to the peaceful Royal Botanic Gardens; from bustling Martin Place to elegant Macquarie Street. The NSW Visitor Info Line (132 077) and Sydney Visitor Centres (8240 8788 or Free call 1800 067 676) can also suggest places of interest.

- **Sydney Tower & Skytour (Map D, Ref A7)** (Westfield Centrepoint, 100 Market St, 9231 9300) is one of the tallest public buildings in the southern hemisphere. Its 360-degree views provide the best vantage point to familiarise yourself with Sydney and its surrounds. An observation level, coffee shop and two revolving restaurants offer magnificent views of Sydney.

- **Hyde Park (Map D, Ref E10)**, on the eastern border of the CBD, is a popular venue for city workers to take a break and have a picnic lunch or go for a jog. You can bask in the sun on the grass by the **Archibald Fountain** or sunken **Sandringham Gardens**, or watch the chess players test their skills. Stroll along the tree-covered walkways (at night lit by millions of star-like fairy lights) to the pretty poplar lined **Pool of Reflection** to admire the art deco **Anzac War Memorial**, where a photographic and military exhibition can be viewed honouring those Australians killed in battle.

- **St Mary's Cathedral (Map D, Ref H9)** (cnr Cathedral & College Sts, 9220 0400), an awesome Gothic Revival-style cathedral, was opened in 1882 and the twin southern spires originally proposed by the architect have recently been completed. Join a tour to admire the crypt's terrazzo mosaic floor, which took 15 years to complete.

- **Macquarie Street (Maps B & D)** extends from **Hyde Park** to **Bennelong Point** and by following this route many elegant examples of Georgian architecture can be seen, as can many attractions worth visiting. **Hyde Park Barracks** (8239 2311), originally designed to house convicts, is now a museum featuring changing exhibitions on Australia's history and culture. It also has a café/restaurant (9223 1155) and the venue can be hired for functions (8239 2288). **The Sydney Mint Museum** (8239 2288) contains exhibitions on Australia's currency, history and culture.

Further down Macquarie Street, rub the snout of the brass boar Il Porcellino for good luck, found at the front of Sydney Hospital, then admire the art deco fountain in the inner courtyard. **Parliament House** (9230 2111), the seat of the New South Wales parliament, has daily tours as well as an educational display on the building's development and the State's legislative history. The **State Library** (9273 1414) has two separate reading rooms, the Reference Library Reading Room and the Mitchell Library Reading Room. Both provide free services, and are worth visiting to view the periodically changing exhibitions. Free tours of the library are held on Tuesdays from 11am to 12noon and on Thursdays from 2pm to 3pm.

- **The Domain (Map D, Ref K6)**, the grassy parkland behind Macquarie Street, is a lively venue, being a public rallying point, a site of numerous and varied concerts and a favourite exercise and lunch spot for city workers. From its eastern edge near the **Art Gallery of NSW** you can view historic **Woolloomooloo Finger Wharf**, **Garden Island** and **Potts Point**. The harbour side **Andrew "Boy" Charlton Pool** is on the way to **Mrs Macquarie's Chair**, an ideal place to sit and take in the harbour side activity.

- **Royal Botanic Gardens (Map 2, Ref D15)** (9231 8111) extends over 30 lush hectares from **Mrs Macquarie's Chair** around **Farm Cove** to **Bennelong Point**. Explore Palm Grove, Sydney Tropical Centre, the National Herbarium of New South Wales and the Herb Garden, or relax in the Rose Garden's rotunda, the site of many weddings. Situated on the Macquarie Street side of the gardens, **Government House** (9931 5222), formerly the official residence of the Governor, houses collections of 19th and early 20th century furnishings.

- **Martin Place (Map C, Ref K2)**, a plaza between George and Macquarie Streets, contains the 1929 art deco **Cenotaph** where annual Anzac Day war remembrance services are held, the recently refurbished renaissance-style **General Post Office** and other grand buildings such as the Commonwealth Bank. Concerts are also held in the amphitheatre.

- **Pitt Street Mall (Map C, Ref K6)**, between King and Market Streets, is Sydney's shopping heart, surrounded by numerous department stores and shopping malls. One of the most beautiful of these is the ornate **Strand Arcade** (9232 4199), a lovingly restored Victorian-era building that houses some of Australia's premiere fashion designers and labels.

- **The State Theatre (Map C, Ref J9)** (49 Market St, 9373 6852) was completed in 1929 and is decorated in true Cinema Baroque style. It is a premier venue for concerts, theatre and special events and is home to the annual **Sydney Film Festival**.

- **Queen Victoria Building (Map C, Ref H10)** (bounded by George St, York, Market and Park Sts, 9265 6855) is a majestic Romanesque shopping arcade. Built in 1898 it was originally a fresh produce market, but now houses many fashion and gift stores, as well as cafes and other shops. The restoration of the building retained many of its original features, combining these features with an up-market, modern feel. An underground promenade connects Town Hall railway station to **Sydney Central Plaza** and Myer department store.

- **Sydney Town Hall (Map C, Ref G12)** (483 George St, 9265 9189) is an excellent example of high Victorian architecture. As Sydney's civic centre, it is the venue for concerts, balls and public meetings. It continues the tradition of being Sydney's favourite city meeting place on the front steps, due to its proximity to Town Hall Station.

shopping & markets

Sydney offers world-class shopping, with vibrant retail streets, elegant arcades, modern malls, large department stores and colourful markets in the CBD and city fringe. They offer an impressive range of high quality, locally made and imported goods, including indigenous art, handmade crafts, funky clothes and innovative jewellery. Bargains can be found at weekend markets and factory and designer seconds outlets stores selling remarkably reduced items from labels such as Marcs and Diesel.

• The Rocks (Map B, Ref A4)
Sydney's historic heart has an extensive range of quality stalls, in one of Sydney's most unique markets. The **Rocks Market** (cnr George & Playfair Sts, 9240 8717) is open every Saturday and Sunday between 10am and 5pm and is held at the northern end of George Street. There are over 150 stalls selling arts, crafts, home wares, antiques and jewellery, as well as street performers adding to the carnival atmosphere. The overhead canopy promises fantastic shopping whatever the weather.
The Aboriginal and Tribal Art Centre (117 George St, The Rocks, 9241 5998) sells Duty Free Indigenous paintings and artefacts.

• Pitt Street Mall & George Street (Map C, Ref K6)
A wide variety of specialty stores can be found on George Street, and in the many shopping centres on Pitt Street Mall, such as **Skygarden**, **Strand Arcade**, **Mid City Centre**, **Westfield Centrepoint** and **Sydney Central Plaza**.
Gowings (cnr George & Market Sts, 9287 6394) is great for basic menswear, footwear, travel goods as well as unusual gifts and lifestyle products.
Dinosaur Designs (Shop 77, Strand Arcade, 9223 2953) have a diverse range of fun and funky home wares and jewellery made from brightly coloured resin that have become a modern classic.

• Castlereagh Street, CBD (Map D, Ref B6)
Exclusive international couture and Australian designer labels can be found at the **MLC Centre** and the Castlereagh Street stores of Chanel, Louis Vuitton, Hermes and Tiffany & Co. Cartier is in **Chifley Plaza** and Emporio Armani is in **Martin Place**.
Chanel Boutique (70 Castlereagh St, 9233 4800). Classic French style.
David Jones Department Store (cnr Castlereagh & Elizabeth Sts, 9266 5544) has two buildings full of fashion, fragrances, furnishings and the fabulous Food Hall.

• Queen Victoria Building (QVB) (Map C, Ref H10)
This majestic shopping centre contains more than 200 stores selling quality souvenirs, home wares, knitwear, lingerie, cosmetics, shoes, jewellery and fashion, including chain stores **Country Road**, **Esprit** and **Lush**.
The ABC Shop (Shop 48, Level 1, 8333 1635) sells a range of merchandise associated with Australia's national broadcaster, including books, videos, music, toys and clothing.
The Body Shop (Shop G48-50, Ground Floor, 9264 1796) stocks natural beauty products.

• Harbourside, Darling Harbour (Map 3, Ref A5) (9281 3999)
This shopping centre is home to over 200 stores offering souvenirs, fashion, music, books, toys and other gifts, as well as a wide array of eateries.
Surf Dive 'N' Ski (Shop 205-207, 9281 4040) sells fashion and sports equipment that reflect Australia's beach culture.

• Chinatown (Map E, Ref F4)
This cosmopolitan part of town has everything from traditional herbalists to hip designer labels, as well as the best Chinese restaurants in Sydney.
Market City (9-13 Hay St, 9212 1388) is a bargain hunter's delight, featuring over 100 retail shops, including one whole level of factory outlets offering up to 80% off retail prices of some of the best names in fashion. Other features are an amazing food court, and entertainment at **Galaxy World** and **Reading Cinemas**.
Paddy's Market (below Market City, 1300 361 589), Thursday to Sunday, with over 800 stalls offering fresh food to fashion to electronic gadgets in Sydney's oldest, most traditional market.
Chinatown Centre Food Fair Bar (25 Dixon St, 9212 3335) is an exotic, varied and popular food outlet.

• Oxford Street, Darlinghurst (Map F, Ref G3)
Leather, gym wear, fashion, music, books and home wares are all to be found on the lower end of this popular street.
Central Station Records & Tapes (46 Oxford St, 9361 5222) sell a range of music CDs, 12-inch vinyl and LPs.

• Crown Street, Darlinghurst (Map F, Ref K9)
Scattered along Crown Street are shops selling inner-city fashion and accessories, from retro groove to basic black, interspersed with bric-a-brac and interior design stores.
Route 66 (257 Crown St, 9331 6686) has classic jeans, jackets and cowboy garb.

• Oxford Street, Paddington (Map 4, Ref H15)
Sydney's innovative fashion labels can be found at the upper end of Oxford Street, interspersed with interesting bookshops, gift and home ware stores. On Saturdays check out **Paddington Markets** (395 Oxford St, 9331 2923), the coolest markets in town.
Ariel Booksellers (42 Oxford St, 9332 4581) can supply you with quality fiction, film, art and design books.
Mambo (17 Oxford St, 9331 8034) show off a range of wild beach and street wear, reflecting our beach culture.

[Most shops open from 9.00 am – 5.30 pm weekdays, until 9.00 pm Thursday nights and 9.00 am – 4.00 pm Saturdays]

culture & entertainment

Sydney's diverse and exciting cultural scene is reflected in the remarkable range of galleries, museums, theatres and cinemas. There are many orchestras, classical and modern dance, opera and theatre companies that call Sydney home. Guides providing information on what's on include Sydney Morning Herald's Friday Metro, Beat, Drum Media, 3D World, Revolver, On the Street or alternatively check out citysearch.com.au. Tickets may be purchased through Ticketek (9266 4800 or www.ticketek.com.au) and Ticketmaster7 (131 600 or www.ticketmaster7.com.au).

MUSEUMS

· Australian Museum (Map D, Ref G14)
6 College St, Sydney, 9320 6000. Natural history museum of Australia and the Pacific.

· Australian National Maritime Museum (Map 3, Ref A3)
2 Murray St, Darling Harbour, 9298 3777. Charts Australia and the world's sea faring history and coastal lifestyle, providing tours of numerous seagoing craft.

· Powerhouse Museum (Map 3, Ref B11)
500 Harris St, Ultimo, 9217 0111. An interactive museum with exhibitions focusing on innovation, technology and learning.

· The Museum of Sydney (Map B, Ref E11)
Cnr Phillip and Bridge Sts, Sydney, 9251 5988. This state-of-the-art museum imaginatively brings Sydney's past to life on the site of the first government house.

GALLERIES

· Art Gallery of New South Wales (Map 4, Ref D2)
Art Gallery Rd, The Domain, Sydney, 9225 1744. Australia's foremost collection of Australian, Asian and European art.

· Artspace/The Gunnery (Map 4, Ref G3)
43-51 Cowper Wharf Rdy, Woolloomooloo, 9368 1899. Installations and performances.

· Australian Centre for Photography (Map 21, Ref B1)
257 Oxford St, Paddington, 9332 1455. Contemporary photography displays and courses, as well as public photographic facilities.

· Brett Whiteley Studio (Map 20, Ref C4)
2 Raper St, Surry Hills, 9225 1881. This well-known artist's works and memorabilia are displayed in his former home.

· Museum of Contemporary Art (Map B, Ref A5)
140 George St, The Rocks, 9252 4033. An adventurous and eclectic collection of modern art, Aboriginal painting and video art.

· State Library of NSW (Map B, Ref G16)
Macquarie St, Sydney, 9273 1414. Exhibitions of art, photography, drawings and unusual treasures providing an insight into Australia's culture and past.

MUSIC AND PERFORMING ARTS

· Belvoir Street Theatre (Map 19, Ref G4)
25 Belvoir St, Surry Hills, 9699 3444. Experimental and daring productions.

· Capitol Theatre (Map E, Ref H7)
13 Campbell St, Haymarket, 9320 5000. Lavishly restored 1920's lyric theatre with a starry-sky ceiling.

· Seymour Theatre Centre (Map 18, Ref G4)
Cnr Cleveland St & City Rd, Darlington, 9351 7940. A stimulating mix of theatre.

· Sydney Opera House (Map B, Ref J1)
Bennelong Point, 9250 7777. Features performances by acclaimed organisations such as Opera Australia, Australian Ballet, Sydney Theatre Company, Sydney Dance Company and Sydney Symphony Orchestra.

· The Performance Space (Map 19, Ref D5)
199 Cleveland Street, Redfern, 9698 7235. Experimental dance, movement, mime and performance arts.

· The Stables Theatre (Map 4, Ref H9)
10 Nimrod St, Darlinghurst, 9250 7799. A venue showcasing new Australian works.

· The State Theatre (Map C, Ref J8)
49 Market St, Sydney, 9373 6852. Its opulence steals the attention of audiences there to see theatre, musicals, concerts and the Sydney Film Festival in June.

· The Wharf Theatre (Map 1, Ref F7)
Pier 4, Hickson Rd, Millers Point, 9250 1700. Exciting theatre, dramatic water views and the Wharf Restaurant (9250 1761).

CINEMAS

· Academy Twin Cinema (Map 4, Ref F14)
3a Oxford St, Paddington, 9361 4453. Quality international art house.

· Chauvel Cinema (Map 21, Ref A1)
149 Oxford St, Paddington, 9361 5398. Australian cinema, independent international and movie classics at the national cinematheque.

· Dendy Cinemas Opera Quays (Map B, Ref G6)
2 Circular Quay E, Sydney, 9247 3800. Newtown (Map 17, Ref G11), 261 King St, 9550 5699. Independent Australian and international cinema.

· George St Complex (Map C, Ref G16)
505-525 George St, Sydney, 9273 7431. Blockbusters at this Hoyts & Greater Union multiplex.

· Hoyts Cinemas Fox Studios (Map 21, Ref B9)
Bent St, Moore Park, 9332 1300. Mostly mainstream movies.

· Verona Cinema (Map 4, Ref G15)
17 Oxford St, Paddington, 9360 6099. Many small theatres screen an eclectic range of films.

restaurants & cafes

Sydney's exciting eating scene offers an overwhelming choice of ethnically diverse restaurants and cafes, taking advantage of the fabulous fresh local produce. Sydney's top-end restaurants provide sublime dining experiences and often require reservations to be made weeks in advance. Your culinary memories will make them well worth both the trouble and expense.

Prices per person (GST incl.)
$	under $25
$$	$26 - $40
$$$	$41 - $55
$$$$	$56 - $65
$$$$$	$65 & over

2 courses, excluding drinks, corkage & tips

RESTAURANTS

- **Blackbird $ (Map C, Ref A11)**
The Balcony, Cockle Bay Wharf, 201 Sussex St, Sydney, 9283 7385. Funky atmosphere with great wood-fired pizzas and filling pasta.
- **Capitan Torres $$ (Map E, Ref F2)**
73 Liverpool St, Sydney, 9264 5574. Spanish sangria makes an excellent companion to the 20 plus types of tapas in this family-run rustic bar.
- **Chinta Ria...The Temple of Love $$ (Map C, Ref B9)**
The Roof Terrace, Cockle Bay Wharf, Darling Park, 9264 3211. Malaysian based menu favoured by a young crowd – one of the most beautiful restaurants in Sydney.
- **Deco $$ (Map E, Ref K3)**
Civic Hotel, 388 Pitt St, Sydney, 8080 7000. Open for dinner Tues to Sat, and lunch during the week; look for satisfying bistro food in an Art Deco setting.
- **Dragon Star $$$ (Map E, Ref D7)**
Level 3, Market City, 9 Hay St, Haymarket, 9211 8988. Wide array of delectable dishes at Sydney's largest Chinese restaurant.
- **Edna's Table $$$ (Map C, Ref F9)**
204 Clarence St, Sydney, 9267 3933. Showcases Australian bush foods, using indigenous ingredients with great effect.
- **Forty One $$$$$ (Map B, Ref D16)**
Chifley Tower, 2 Chifley Square, Sydney, 9221 2500. Summit of modern Australian cuisine accompanied by magnificent views of Sydney.
- **Fu Manchu $ (Map 4, Ref H11)**
249 Victoria St, Darlinghurst, 9360 9424. Busy atmosphere and funky décor at this popular Asian noodle bar.
- **Hard Rock Café $$$$ (Map 4, Ref D8)**
121-129 Crown St, Darlinghurst, 9331 1116. Enjoy the American-style menu whilst surrounded by rock 'n' roll memorabilia.
- **Macleay Street Bistro $$$ (Map 4, Ref K3)**
73a Macleay St, Potts Point, 9358 4891. A wine buff's BYO; take your treasured reds for the steak and mash.
- **Mezzaluna $$$$$ (Map 4, Ref J5)**
123 Victoria St, Potts Point, 9357 1988. Excellent contemporary Italian and a terrace with a spectacular city view.
- **Otto $$$$$ (Map 4, G2)**
Finger Wharf, Area 8, Cowper Wharf Rdy, Woolloomooloo, 9368 7488. This waterside hot spot attracts the in-crowd with a funky bar and sumptuous modern Italian fare.
- **Pig and The Olive Pizzeria $$ (Map 4, Ref K3)**
71a Macleay St, Potts Point, 9357 3745. Gourmet pizzas to pig out on at this popular eatery.
- **Prime Restaurant $$$$$ (Map C, Ref K3)**
GPO Building, 1 Martin Pl, Sydney, 9229 7777. For when you need a good feed, this steak house is a meat-lovers delight.
- **Rockpool $$$$$ (Map A, Ref K5)**
107 George St, The Rocks, 9252 1888. East imaginatively meets West in this striking combination of swanky design, swish service, innovative cuisine and the freshest seafood.
- **Wildfire $$$$$ (Map B, B2)**
Ground Floor, Overseas Passenger Terminal, Circular Quay West, 8273 1222. With its prime location and perfect views, Wildfire is certain to please any palette. Its menu is diverse, ranging from chilled seafood to a wood fired churrasco feast that comes to your table.
- **Yipiyiyo $$$ (Map 4, Ref C13)**
290 Crown St, Darlinghurst, 9332 3114. Sydney's best Santa Fe Style cuisine.

CAFES & FAST EATS

- **Bambini Espresso $ (Map F, Ref B4)**
299 Elizabeth St, Sydney, 9261 3331. Good for a quick lunch with gourmet baguettes and excellent coffee.
- **BBQ King $$ (Map E, Ref F4)**
18 Goulburn St, Chinatown, 9267 2433. Traditional Chinese barbecued meats. Where the chefs go for a late night bite.
- **Cafe Hernandez $$ (Map 4, Ref J8)**
60 Kings Cross Rd, Rushcutters Bay, 9331 2343. Strong Spanish coffee, interesting crowd and open 24 hours, 7 days a week.
- **Harry's Cafe de Wheels $ (Map 4, Ref G3)**
7/57 Cowper Wharf Rdy, Woolloomooloo, 9357 3074. One of Sydney's late night institutions serving the city's best pie and peas.
- **Hyde Park Barracks Cafe $$ (Map D, Ref G6)**
Queens Square, Macquarie St Sydney, 9233 1155. Soak up the history of one of Sydney's early convict quarters, while enjoying the cafe food.
- **Ippon $$ (Map E, Ref E6)**
404 Sussex St, Chinatown, 9212 7669. Choose fresh, cheap Japanese sushi from the conveyor belt.
- **Le Petit Crème $$ (Map 4, Ref G10)**
118 Darlinghurst Rd, Darlinghurst, 9361 4738. Arrive early for the Eggs Benedict weekend special and le bowl of coffee.
- **MCA Cafe $$ (Map B, Ref B6)**
MCA, Circular Quay West, 9241 4253. Stylish contemporary Australian food, with spectacular harbour views.
- **QVB Jet $ (Map C, Ref H11)**
Shop G55, Ground Floor, QVB, York St, Town Hall end, 9283 5004. Sip strong lattes, while looking like or looking at the locals. Outdoor European style seating – great for watching the passers-by whilst recharging your shopping batteries.
- **Spring $ (Map 4, Ref K2)**
65 Macleay St, Potts Point, 9331 0190. Tiny café with a buzz, sunny sidewalk scene and coffee with a kick.
- **Starbucks Coffee $ (Map D, Ref C12)**
Cnr Park & Elizabeth Sts, Sydney, 9268 0184. Perfect for a caffeine fix, with its own specially roasted coffee known worldwide. There are many other Starbucks throughout Sydney, including Wynyard, Martin Place, Cockle Bay, Haymarket, Circular Quay, George St, York St and Market St cafes.
- **The Vinyl Lounge $$ (Map 13, Ref C5)**
1/17 Elizabeth Bay Rd, Elizabeth Bay, 9326 9224. Very Funky. Very French.
- **Wedge Cafe $ (Map 13, Ref B5)**
70 Elizabeth Bay Rd, Elizabeth Bay, 9326 9015. A mecca for great coffee, good food and genuine service.
- **Zibar $$ (Map C, Ref D12)**
252 Sussex St, Sydney, 9268 0222. Quick, friendly, and known for their super large bowls of pasta.

bars, pubs & clubs

Like any great city, Sydney has a wide range of bars, pubs and nightclubs to suit all types and tastes. There are after work bars offering cheap drinks during "happy hour"; sophisticated bars in international hotels; upmarket pubs providing complimentary snacks; fun cocktail bars; noisy pubs with live music; restaurant bars where you drink and eat; large nightclubs offering pinball, pool and dancing; and dingy late-nighters where you go when there's nowhere else to go. Hours of operation do vary, with many nightclubs beginning late, around 10 pm or 11 pm, and staying open until sunrise.

CITY DRINKING

- **'The Bar' Sir Stamford (Map B, Ref G8)**
93 Macquarie St, Sydney, 8274 5447. Elegant decor at Circular Quay.
- **Cargo Bar (Map 3, Ref C2)**
52 The Promenade, King St Wharf, Sydney, 9262 1777. The latest place to go for both a cold beer and a gourmet pizza. Great atmosphere & waterside setting.
- **CBD Hotel (Map C, Ref G4)**
Cnr King and York St, Sydney, 8297 7000. Cool décor, good vibes and the best bar in the city centre.
- **Customs House Bar (Map B, Ref B11)**
Sydney Harbour Marriott, Macquarie Place, Sydney, 9259 7316. Perfect place to unwind at the end of the day with a drink under the trees.
- **Establishment Bar (Map A, Ref J12)**
252 George St, Sydney, 9240 3000. Spot the well-known faces at this ultra-hip drinking hole.
- **Blu Horizon Bar (Map A, Ref G7)**
Level 36, Shangri-La Hotel, 176 Cumberland St, The Rocks, 9250 6013. Some of Sydney's best cocktails, accompanied by views from Darling Harbour to Circular Quay.
- **Pontoon Bar (Map C, Ref A11)**
Cockle Bay Wharf, Darling Harbour, 9267 7099. The place to be seen.

PADDINGTON & DARLINGHURST BARS

- **Burdekin Hotel (Map F, Ref G3)**
2 Oxford St, Darlinghurst, 9331 3066. Join the Dugout Bar's cigar set or boogie at the main bar.
- **Elephant Bar (Map 13, Ref C14)**
The Royal Hotel, Five Ways, Paddington, 9331 2604. Sip on a drink and enjoy the sunset views over eastern Sydney.
- **Gilligan's (Map 4, Ref D12)**
Above Oxford Hotel, Taylor Square, 134 Oxford St, Darlinghurst, 9331 3467. Open from 5pm, with the wildest cocktails in Sydney.
- **Grand Pacific Blue Room (Map 4, Ref F14)**
Cnr Oxford & South Dowling Sts, Darlinghurst, 9331 7108. Classy and classic cocktails in this sophisticated setting.
- **Lizard Lounge (Map F, Ref H4)**
Exchange Hotel, 34 Oxford St, Darlinghurst, 9331 1936. Meet all types while enjoying the complimentary happy hour snacks.
- **L'otel (Map 4, Ref G10)**
114 Darlinghurst Rd, Darlinghurst, 9360 6868. A hip crowd squeezes into this small, buzzy bar to sip vodkas, see and be seen.
- **The Fringe Bar (Map 4, Ref H15)**
106 Oxford St, Paddington, 9360 3554. Popular bar with pool tables, booths and a warm and friendly atmosphere.

INNER CITY PUBS

- **Clock Hotel (Map 20, Ref B2)**
470 Crown St, Surry Hills, 9331 5333. This revamped pub now attracts an eclectic, young, inner city crowd.
- **Cricketer's Arms Hotel (Map 20, Ref E1)**
106 Fitzroy St, Surry Hills, 9331 3301. Funky music and cool beer garden.
- **Hopetoun Hotel (Map 20, Ref D1)**
Cnr Bourke & Fitzroy Sts, Surry Hills, 9361 5257. Live music every night and small underground bar.
- **Lord Nelson Brewery Hotel (Map A, Ref C2)**
Cnr Kent & Argyle Sts, 9251 4044. This cosy, historic, sandstone pub brews their own ales, keeping punters happy for more than 150 years.
- **O Bar (Map 19, Ref K3)**
Clarendon Hotel, 156 Devonshire St, Surry Hills, 9319 6062. Stylish and sleek drinking and dining.
- **Paddington Inn (Map 21, Ref D2)**
338 Oxford St, Paddington, 9380 5913. A fun, local pub, popular after Saturday's markets.
- **Palace Hotel (Map 4, Ref E16)**
122 Flinders St, Darlinghurst, 9362 5155. Several levels, pool tables and great quality modern Aussie pub food.
- **Water Bar (Map 4, Ref G2)**
W Hotel, 6 Cowper Wharf Rdy, Woolloomooloo, 9331 9000. Set on an old cargo wharf, this bar is a must for the cocktail aficionados.

NIGHTCLUBS

- **Gas Nightclub (Map E, Ref F13)**
477 Pitt St, Haymarket 9211 3088. One room on two levels featuring soul, funk and hip-hop.
- **Goodbar (Map 4, Ref F14)**
11 Oxford St, Paddington, 9360 6759. Fresh and funky sounds in this laid-back setting.
- **Home (Map C, Ref A11)**
Cockle Bay Wharf, Darling Harbour, 9266 0600. The ultimate clubbing experience in Sydney.
- **Luna Lounge (Map A, Ref J10)**
Jackson's on George, 176 George St, Circular Quay, 9247 2727. Commercial dance, house, hip-hop and hi NRG near the wharf and The Rocks.
- **Q Bar (Map F, Ref H4)**
44 Oxford St, Darlinghurst, 9360 1375. Pool tables, pinball, chill out corner, three bars and two funky dance spaces.
- **Retro (Map C, Ref C2)**
Bristol Arms Hotel, 81 Sussex St, Sydney, 9262 5491. Five levels of '70's, '80's, '90's pop, disco, indie, Britpop and techno.
- **Slip Inn (Map C, Ref C4)**
111 Sussex St, Sydney, 9299 4777. Favoured by a very cool and beautiful crowd, with 3 clubs to suit different styles.
- **SoHo (Map 4, Ref H6)**
171 Victoria St, Potts Point, 9389 3004. Different rooms, different moods, but always very sleek and sophisticated.
- **Sugareef (Map 4, Ref J8)**
20 Bayswater Rd, Potts Point, 9368 0763. Chill out to funky beats in this friendly atmosphere.
- **Tantra Bar (Map 4, Ref D12)**
169 Oxford St, Darlinghurst, 9331 7729. Popular with toned body and pierced navel set.
- **The Basement (Map B, Ref B9)**
29 Reiby Pl, Sydney 9251 2797. Well known throughout Sydney as the ultimate late night jazz and relaxed vibes spot.

city fringe

The fringes of Sydney's CBD house an array of interesting suburbs well worth exploring for their own distinct characters, whether it be the ethnic diversity of Newtown, the Italian atmosphere in Leichhardt, the bohemian nature of Surry Hills, the refined atmosphere in Woollahra or the leisurely mood of Bronte. Many suburbs, such as Glebe and Paddington, are within walking distance from the city centre, while other areas like Bondi Beach and Newtown can be reached by bus or train.

- **Newtown** (Map 374, Ref H5) is one of Sydney's most bohemian suburbs. A favoured spot of students attending the nearby **University of Sydney**, Newtown is jam-packed with cheap cafes, busy pubs, bookstores, galleries and second-hand clothes shops. Walk from the city, take a train, or catch a bus to bustling **King St**. The university campus warrants a visit to relax on the lawns and admire the original Victorian Gothic architecture of the Main Quadrangle with its intricate stonework and gargoyles.

- **Glebe** (Map 345, Ref C15) is home to Sydney's café society. Glebe Point Rd is lined with many cafes and eateries. The colourful **Badde Manors Café** (37 Glebe Point Rd, 9660 3797) is a Glebe icon, while **GNC Livewell** (55 Glebe Point Rd, 9660 8144) is a mega store for organic and macrobiotic food supplies. Bookstores are also a Glebe feature. **Gleebooks** (49 Glebe Point Rd, 9660 2333) has an eclectic range, while their second-hand store a few blocks up (191 Glebe Point Rd, 9552 2526) specialises in children's books and offers many bargains. Wander the side streets, with their rows of workers cottages and historic stately mansions. Bargain-hunt for jewellery, music, second hand clothes or unique items on Saturdays at **Glebe Markets** (Glebe Public School, Glebe Point Rd); or head to the end of Glebe Point Road to **Jubilee Park**, for stunning city views and the striking outline of the **Anzac Bridge**. Catch a bus from the city.

- **Balmain** (Map 344, Ref J5) should be visited on Saturday to explore the treasure trove of **Balmain Markets** at St Andrews churchyard, opposite **Gladstone Park**. Take a bus from Town Hall, or ferry from Circular Quay to **Darling St Wharf**, and walk up to **Balmain Village** through the historic narrow streets with their quaint sandstone cottages and Victorian terraces. Browse in the bookstores and gift shops, lunch in a café or pub or buy picnic food from a delicatessen or patisserie to take to one of Balmain's many waterfront parks. **Birchgrove Park**, **Mort Bay Park** and **Illoura Reserve** all have city skyline or Darling Harbour views.

- **Leichhardt** (Map 343, Ref J14) is Sydney's Little Italy. Scores of Italian restaurants, late-night cafes, delis, bakeries and shops line Norton and Marion Streets, giving the suburb a distinct Italian flavour, exemplified by the **Italian Forum**, a villa-like centre containing shopping and restaurants. Take a bus to **Norton Street** and embark on a culinary tour of the area. Enjoy a traditional home-style Italian cuisine or contemporary variations in one of the many eateries such as **Portofino** (166 Norton St, 9550 0782).

- **Woollahra** (Map 347, Ref A15) is Sydney's premier antiques centre. Catch the bus along Oxford Street and alight at **Queen Street**, the heart of this exclusive suburb. Hours can be spent in the fine antiques and interior design stores, galleries and shops. Explore the back streets with their grand homes and terrace houses, or walk to nearby **Centennial Park** (9339 6699) where you can laze by the lake, feed the ducks or join a nature walk. If you're feeling more energetic, you can hire a bicycle or roller blades.

- **Double Bay** (Map 347, Ref D15) is home to Sydney's society set. Take the train to **Edgecliff** or bus to this prestigious harbour side suburb and take in its village-like atmosphere. Browse in the exclusive designer boutiques or dine at a sophisticated restaurant or coffee shop. Walk up to hilly **Darling Point** and admire **Lindesay** (9363 2401), an impressive house built in 1834 that opens for exhibitions and special events. Alternatively, explore ritzy **Vaucluse** to the east where you can visit the Gothic mansion and museum **Vaucluse House** (9388 7922) and enjoy their famous Devonshire teas.

- **Bondi Beach** (Map 378, Ref E4) is synonymous with surf, sand and sun. It's now as popular for its busy **Campbell Parade** café scene and **Sunday Bondi Markets**. Take a bus or the Bondi Explorer that stops around Sydney Harbour and its shores, continuing on to Bondi Beach. There is much to do along the lively promenade: roller blade, skateboard, jog, walk the dog, eat fresh seafood on the beach, attend a play, film, dance, or enjoy a band festival at **Bondi Pavilion**. To take an invigorating walk with breathtaking ocean views, head south from Notts Avenue past Bondi Icebergs' clubhouse and along the rocky headland path to tiny **Tamarama** and **Bronte** beaches.

- **Bronte** (Map 378, Ref B8), a small, white-sand beach in a bay, is favoured by families who flock to its pretty wooded park and barbecue area on weekends. Bronte can be reached by bus from the city or by foot from Bondi Beach around the popular cliff's edge trail, with its spectacular open ocean views. Consider taking food for the barbie, as the fish and chips queue is always long. Perhaps try one of the excellent cafes across the road such as **Sejuiced** (9389 9538), which offers fresh fruit juices.

backpackers accommodation

There are many reasonably priced places for travellers on a limited budget to stay in Sydney. All types of people stay in youth and backpacker hostels, groups of young people, older people, singles or families. Some hostels attract younger and exuberant people while others have a quieter atmosphere. It is always a good idea to ring ahead so that you end up staying in the place most suitable for your needs. Listed are backpacker and youth hostels within the city, from Darlinghurst to Glebe.

Australian Backpackers (Map 4, Ref E7)
132 Bourke Street, Woolloomooloo,
9331 0822

Blue Parrot Backpackers (Map 4, Ref K4)
87 Macleay St, Potts Point,
9356 4888

Boomerang Backpackers (Map 4, Ref F8)
141 William St, Darlinghurst,
8354 0488

Captain Cook Hotel (Map 20, Ref F2)
162 Flinders Street, Paddington,
9331 6487

City Central Backpackers (Map E, Ref F10)
752 George St, Haymarket,
9212 4833

Cooee Travellers Accommodation (Map 4, Ref H8)
107 Darlinghurst Rd, Potts Point,
9331 0009

Downtown City Backpackers (Map E, Ref G5)
611 George Street, Sydney,
9211 8801

Excelsior Hotel (Map 3, Ref K16)
64 Foveaux Street, Surry Hills,
9211 4945

Fact Tree Youth Service Inc (Map 19, Ref G13)
703 Elizabeth Street, Waterloo,
9319 2708

Footprints Westend (Map E, Ref J6)
412 Pitt Street, Sydney,
9211 4588

George Street Private Hotel (Map E, Ref G7)
700a George Street, Sydney,
9211 1800

Glebe Point YHA (Map 12, Ref B12)
262 Glebe Point Road, Glebe,
9692 8418

Glebe Village Backpackers Hostel (Map 12, Ref B12)
256 Glebe Point Road, Glebe,
9660 8878

Gracelands (Map 20, Ref D7)
461 Cleveland Street, Surry Hills,
9699 1399

Great Aussie Backpackers (Map 4, Ref J6)
174 Victoria Street, Potts Point,
9356 4551

Harbour City Hotel (Map 4, Ref D5)
50 Sir John Young Crescent, Woolloomooloo
9380 2922

Hyde Park Backpackers Hostel (Map F, Ref B9)
88 Wentworth Av, Sydney,
9282 9266

Jolly Swagman Backpackers (Map 4, Ref K5)
27 Orwell Street, Potts Point
9358 6400

Kanga House (Map 4, Ref J5)
141a Victoria St, Potts Point,
9357 7897

Kangaroo Bak-Pak (Map 20, Ref D7)
665 South Dowling Street, Surry Hills
9319 5915

Maze Backpackers/CB Hotel (Map E, Ref J6)
417 Pitt Street, Sydney,
9211 5115

Nomads Forest Lodge (Map 12, Ref A16)
117 Arundel Street, Glebe,
9660 1872

Potts Point House (Map 4, Ref J5)
154 Victoria Street, Potts Point,
9368 0733

Sleeping with the Enemy (Map 3, Ref A12)
373 Bulwara Rd, Ultimo,
9211 8878

Sydney Backpackers (Map C, Ref H16)
7 Wilmot Street, Sydney,
9267 7772

Sydney Central Backpackers (Map 4, Ref J5)
16 Orwell Street, Potts Point,
9358 6600

Sydney Central YHA (Map E, Ref G11)
Cnr Pitt Street and Rawson Place, Sydney,
9281 9111

Sydney City Centre Backpackers Accommodation (Map D, Ref D1)
7 Elizabeth Street, Sydney,
9221 7528

The Funk House (Map 4, Ref K6)
23 Darlinghurst Road, Darlinghurst,
9358 6455

The Globe Backpackers Hostel (Map 4, Ref J7)
40 Darlinghurst Road, Darlinghurst,
9326 9675

The Original Backpackers Lodge (Map 4, Ref J6)
162 Victoria Street, Potts Point,
9356 3232

The Pink House Backpackers Hostel (Map 13, Ref A7)
6 Barncleuth Square, Darlinghurst,
9358 1689

Travellers Rest (Map 4, Ref J5)
156 Victoria Street, Darlinghurst,
9358 4606

V Backpackers (Map 4, Ref J5)
144 Victoria Street, Darlinghurst,
9357 4733

wake up! (Map E, Ref E13)
509 Pitt St, Sydney, 9288 7888
www.wakeup.com.au

Wattle House Travellers Accommodation (Map 11, Ref K12)
44 Hereford Street, Glebe,
9552 4997

YHA New South Wales (Map C, Ref E10)
422 Kent Street, Sydney,
9261 1111

public transport

Sydney's extensive public transport system is both convenient and clean. As many of Sydney's sights are within easy walking distance, sightseeing is generally best done on foot. Driving into the city is not recommended; the network of buses, trains, ferries, light rail and taxis will assist you to reach any destination. Ferries offer a scenic route between the city and harbourside suburbs - and they are even worth taking just for the ride. It is advisable to check prior to travelling whether any track work or diversions are taking place that may require you to allow extra travelling time.

• Getting to and around Sydney

For information on how to travel in Sydney by bus, train or ferry contact the **Transport Infoline** between 6am and 10pm daily (131 500 or www.131500.com.au). They provide details of routes, fares and timetables. To get to and from **Sydney Airport's (Map 404)** Domestic and International Flight Terminals, taxis, buses and trains are the primary options. The airport is 9 kilometres from the city centre, and although there are many taxis, the queues during peak hour can be long. State Transit offers metro route bus 400, which travels from Bondi Junction to Burwood via the airport. There are also private bus services to a number of city hotels such as Sydney Airporter (9666 9988).

Homebush Bay (Map 571), the home of the Sydney 2000 Olympic and Paralympic Games, is situated 16 kilometres from the city centre. Trains run daily from Lidcombe to Olympic Park Railway Station, which is within close walking distance of the venues at Homebush Bay. On weekdays, you can catch a train directly from Central Station to Olympic Park Station. There are also buses that travel from Lidcombe and Strathfield to Homebush Bay.

• Train Travel

CityRail: www.cityrail.info; Transport Info Line: 131 500 or www.131500.com.au. The CityRail network offers convenient and regular train services, between 4:30am and midnight daily. Central Station in the city is the main urban and country terminus. To move around the city quickly, use the underground City Circle loop, which links all the stops in the CBD. Sydney's wider rail network has 6 major lines, extending to the Blue Mountains in the west, Berowra in the north, Bondi Junction in the east and Waterfall in Sydney's south. For a full listing of the suburban lines, please refer to the CityRail Suburban Network map on the back cover of this directory. In the evening, be sure to stand in the designated 'Nightsafe' area and travel in carriages marked with a blue light, as they are near the train guard. After midnight, CityRail provides the NightRide bus service, which replaces the train service — a handy tip is to arrange for a taxi to meet you once you reach your destination. Most tickets are either single or return, however weekly and monthly tickets are offered at a cheaper rate. Contact the Transport Infoline for details.

Airport Link (8337 8417 or www.airportlink.com.au) is a fast rail link from Central Train Station to the Domestic and International Air Terminals. It operates every 7 minutes and a one-way journey takes 10 minutes. Luggage space is available. Lifts operate at Central Station.

• The Bus System

Sydney Buses: www.sydneybuses.info; Transport Infoline: 131 500 or www.131500.com.au. Sydney Buses provide a reliable service that links up effectively with the train and ferry systems. The major city bus terminals are at Circular Quay, Wynyard, the western side of the Queen Victoria Building and Central Station. The route number and destination are displayed on the front, left side and back of all buses. Single journey tickets are purchased on the bus, but TravelTen tickets, which allow you to make 10 bus trips, are more economical if you use buses frequently. Express buses are marked with an 'X' at the front, while limited stop buses are marked with an 'L' in front of the route number. Additional buses are provided for special and sporting events. Contact the Transport Infoline for details (131 500 or www.131500.com.au).

A number of private bus companies operate to and between Sydney's outlying suburbs, such as Westbus (9890 0000) and Harris Park Transport (9689 1066) in Sydney's western suburbs, Shorelink (9457 8888) and Forest Coach Lines (9450 2277) in the north, as well as many others. For details on private bus companies call the Transport Infoline on 131 500 or check their website at www.131500.com.au/private_buses.asp.

• Ferry Travel

Sydney Ferries: www.sydneyferries.info; Transport Infoline: 131 500 or www.131500.com.au. Ferries have taken passengers on scenic journeys across Sydney Harbour for more than a century. Circular Quay is the city departure point for ferries, conveniently linking them to the train and bus networks. Ferry services operate daily, travelling to the eastern suburbs, North Shore and up the river to Parramatta. Many ferry stops are also key tourist destinations, such as Darling Harbour, Manly, Watsons Bay, Balmain and Taronga Park Zoo. Sydney Ferries also offer a number of reasonably priced harbourside sightseeing cruises. A map of the Sydney Ferry Network is included in this directory on the inside back cover of this book.

Sightseeing and dining harbour cruises are also operated by Captain Cook Cruises (9206 1122 or www.captaincook.com.au) and Matilda Cruises (9264 7377 or www.matilda.com.au), who also operate the Rocket harbour Express, which stops at Darling Harbour, Circular Quay, the Opera House, Watson's Bay, Taronga Zoo and Sydney Aquarium at Darling Harbour.

• Light Rail & Monorail

Operated by Connex Sydney: 9285 5600 or www.connexsydney.com.au. **Metro Light Rail** services Capitol Square, Haymarket, Sydney Convention & Exhibition Centre, Pyrmont Bay & Star City, 24 hours per day, every day. Services continue to Lilyfield via John Street Square, Sydney Fish Market, Wentworth Park, Glebe, Jubilee Park and Rozelle Bay from 6am to 11pm Sundays to Thursdays and 6am to midnight Fridays and Saturdays. Services

public transport

generally depart every 10 to 15 minutes. **Metro Monorail** runs every 3 to 5 minutes from 8am to 10pm on Sundays, 7 am to 10 pm from Mondays to Thursdays, and 7 am to midnight on Fridays & Saturdays. It connects key sightseeing spots such as the Powerhouse Museum, City Centre, Darling Park, as well as Harbourside stop - attractions including Star City Casino and the National Maritime Museum.

• Travelling by Taxi

Efficiently organised, flexible and readily available, Sydney's taxi operators provide a fast service. To catch a cab, you can either hail one on the street (vacant cabs have an illuminated orange light on their roof), wait at a taxi rank in the queue, or telephone a company and order a cab to collect you from your location. Phone numbers for Sydney's many taxi companies are available by contacting Yellow Pages (12451), or refer to the Info Guide at the back of this book. The flag fall starts from $2.75 once the meter has started. There is a cost of $1.56 per kilometre, with a 20% surcharge between 10 pm and 6 am. A $1.45 surcharge is charged if you book by telephone. Passengers pay for all bridge and road tolls, including some return tolls.

• Disabled Access

For information to assist people with a disability to readily travel around Sydney, contact NICAN (1800 806 769), IDEAS (1800 029 904) or SCIA (1800 819 775). A number of taxis are specifically designed to enable passengers with wheelchairs to travel comfortably; they can be booked by phoning any of the major taxi companies. Information on accessible travel is also available from the Transport Infoline on 131 500 or www.131500.com.au.

• Purchasing Tickets

Sydney's public transport network offers a range of tickets including singles, returns, all day, weekly and long-term tickets. Some tickets allow you to catch a bus, ferry, and train using the same ticket. When travelling by bus, single tickets can be purchased on the bus from the driver, while for frequent travellers there are TravelTen tickets, which allow 10 journeys within the bus route sections covered by the ticket. A BusTripper ticket allows unlimited travel on the day of purchase on Sydney Buses. For occasional ferry travellers, single and return tickets can be purchased from ticket booths at ferry terminals; for more regular travellers the FerryTen ticket allows 10 rides on Sydney Ferry services. In terms of train travel, for people who only travel occasionally, single or return tickets are usually the best option, and during the day off-peak tickets are available at a discounted price. A CityHopper ticket is also available, which allows unlimited daily travel between all 11 train stations in the city area.

On buses, ferries, and trains, concession tickets are available for children, pensioners and full-time students. Family fares are also available when travelling with children. There are also a number of tickets that combine train, bus and ferry travel. The DayTripper ticket, available for purchase from any train station, ferry ticket offices, or on board a bus or ferry, allows unlimited travel on ferries, buses and trains for the day of purchase until 4am the following morning. If you require a ticket that will allow you to explore Sydney for a longer period of time, consider purchasing a 3, 5 or 7 day SydneyPass. This allows travel on any Sydney Bus (including the Sydney Explorer and Bondi Explorer, popular sightseeing bus tours), Sydney Ferries, and CityRail trains. TravelPasses are good for long term unlimited travel. They allow unlimited train, bus and ferry travel within the specified boundaries, which are indicated by the colour coded ticket. TravelPasses are available for periods of a week, a quarter or a year. Special tickets are also available for purchase that combine transport with entry to popular tourist attractions, such as Taronga Zoo or Sydney Aquarium. For more detailed information on any of these ticketing options, contact the Transport Infoline on 131500 or www.131500.com.au.

Metro Light Rail tickets can be purchased from Customer Service Operators on the Light Rail. Single tickets are available, as well as a day pass or weekly ticket. Metro Monorail tickets are available from the monorail stations. There is a standard fare, or if you are a regular user, a re-chargeable METROcard offers discounted fares. A Supervoucher Pass provides unlimited rides for the day and includes discounts and special savings on museum admission, shopping, food and car parking. For an additional cost you can add unlimited rides on the Light Rail to your ticket, or if you plan to explore Sydney for longer you can purchase a 3-day Supervoucher Pass.

• Special Events Arrangements

Sydney's range of special attractions and events can be enjoyed with the assistance of Sydney's extensive public transport system. Major sporting and entertainment events are accompanied by special transport arrangements for all major venues. The Moore Park precinct — including Sydney Cricket Ground (SCG), Aussie Stadium and the Fox Studios Complex — all have State Transit shuttle buses arranged for special events held at their major venues, leaving from Chalmers St, near Central train station. A bus station opposite the SCG at Moore Park provides speedy access to all major events held at this location. Additional bus and train services are provided for New Year's Eve celebrations to and from the CBD. CityRail and Sydney Buses also provide additional services for the Australia Day public holiday. Also refer to the Info Guide at the back of this book.

SUBURBS and LOCALITIES INDEX

Listed below are the suburbs and localities included in this directory, together with their postcodes and map references.

Suburbs and localities are differentiated in the index as follows:

        Abbotsbury   — Suburb
        Beauty Point   — Locality shown on maps
        Caravan Head   — Suburb
                              [Map reference indicates approximate location]

Note: Streets are indexed to suburbs only, not localities.

Name	Postcode	Map	Ref
Abbotsbury	2176	333	C9
Abbotsford	2046	342	H2
Abbotsford Point	2046	312	H16
Acacia Gardens	2763	214	K15
Agnes Banks	2753	117	C10
Airds	2560	512	B11
Akuna Bay	2084	166	G3
Alexandria	2015	375	D10
Alfords Point	2234	459	B1
Allambie	2100	257	G15
Allambie Heights	2100	257	E12
Allawah	2218	432	F8
Ambarvale	2560	511	A13
Annandale	2038	344	F15
Annangrove	2156	186	C4
Anzac Village	2173	396	A13
Appin	2560	569	E6
Arcadia	2159	130	C9
Arncliffe	2205	403	E7
Arndell Park	2148	273	G9
Artarmon	2064	284	J15
Ashbury	2193	372	E9
Ashcroft	2168	394	F1
Ashfield	2131	372	G4
Asquith	2077	192	B13
Auburn	2144	339	C4
Auburn North	2144	309	F16
Auburn South	2144	339	D7
Auburn West	2144	338	J7
Audley	2232	520	C7
Austral	2171	391	E7
Avalon	2107	169	H1
Avalon Beach	2107	170	D2
Avalon Heights	2107	169	H1
Avalon North	2107	139	K13
Badgerys Creek	2171	358	E7
Bald Face	2221	462	H3
Balgowlah	2093	287	G10
Balgowlah Heights	2093	287	J13
Balls Head	2060	315	C16
Balmain	2041	344	H5
Balmain East	2041	345	E4
Balmoral	2088	317	C4
Balmoral Beach	2088	317	F6
Balmoral Heights	2088	317	C5
Bangor	2234	459	G12
Banksia	2216	403	G13
Banksmeadow	2019	436	B2
Bankstown	2200	369	F14
Bankstown Airport	2200	367	G16
Bankstown South	2200	399	H7
Bankstown West	2200	368	K16
Bantry Bay	2087	286	K6
Barden Ridge	2234	488	E2
Bardwell Park	2207	402	K6

Name	Postcode	Map	Ref
Bardwell Valley	2207	403	B8
Bargo	2574	567	H7
Bass Hill	2197	368	B7
Baulkham Hills	2153	247	C11
Bayview	2104	168	G13
Beacon Hill	2100	257	H2
Beaconsfield	2015	375	F12
Beaumont Hills	2155	215	H1
Beauty Point	2088	287	A16
Beecroft	2119	250	C5
Belfield	2191	371	C11
Belimbla Park	2570	501	F9
Bell	2786	57	C9
Bella Vista	2153	246	B2
Bellevue Hill	2023	347	E14
Belmore	2192	371	D14
Belrose	2085	226	D9
Ben Buckler	2026	378	J3
Berala	2141	339	E14
Berambing	2758	60	B15
Berkshire Park	2765	180	B6
Berowra	2081	133	C12
Berowra Heights	2082	133	E6
Berowra Waters	2082	132	E4
Berrilee	2159	131	J9
Berrys Bay	2060	315	F15
Beverley Park	2217	433	B11
Beverly Hills	2209	401	D12
Beverly Hills North	2209	401	B10
Bexley	2207	402	F15
Bexley North	2207	402	D12
Bexley South	2207	432	H2
Bexley West	2207	402	E14
Bickley Vale	2570	505	H10
Bidwill	2770	211	F14
Bilgola	2107	169	J4
Bilgola Plateau	2107	169	F4
Bilpin	2758	61	C8
Birchgrove	2041	344	H1
Birkenhead Point	2047	344	C3
Birrong	2143	369	A6
Blackett	2770	241	C2
Blacktown	2148	244	G11
Blacktown North	2148	244	J11
Blacktown South	2148	274	H1
Blacktown West	2148	244	B16
Blackwattle Bay	2009	345	A11
Blair Athol	2560	511	B2
Blairmount	2559	481	A13
Blakehurst	2221	432	C14
Blaxcell	2142	338	E6
Blaxland	2774	233	H5
Blaxlands Ridge	2758	64	H4
Bligh Park	2756	150	E6
Blue Mountains National Park		264	D11
Blues Point	2060	345	H1

Name	Postcode	Map	Ref
Bobbin Head	2074	163	H12
Bondi	2026	377	J3
Bondi Beach	2026	378	E4
Bondi Junction	2022	377	C4
Bondi South	2026	378	C5
Bonnet Bay	2226	460	D12
Bonnie Vale	2230	523	D9
Bonnyrigg	2177	363	J8
Bonnyrigg Heights	2177	363	D5
Boronia Park	2111	313	C5
Bossley Park	2176	333	G6
Botany	2019	405	H14
Bow Bowing	2566	452	F13
Bowen Mountain	2753	84	B9
Box Hill	2765	154	B8
Bradbury	2560	511	E12
Bradleys Head	2088	347	D2
Breakfast Point	2137	312	C13
Brickfield Hill	2000	345	H13
Brighton-le-sands	2216	434	B1
Bringelly	2171	387	J10
Broadway	2007	3	B16
Bronte	2024	377	J8
Brooklyn	2083	76	B11
Brookvale	2100	258	C10
Brownlow Hill	2570	475	E6
Brush Farm	2122	280	G9
Bundeena	2230	523	G11
Bungan Beach	2106	169	K16
Bungan Head	2106	169	K13
Burraneer	2230	493	E16
Burwood	2134	342	B12
Burwood Heights	2136	372	A4
Busby	2168	363	H14
Cabarita	2137	342	E2
Cabarita Junction	2137	342	B3
Cabramatta	2166	365	G5
Cabramatta Heights	2166	365	B8
Cabramatta West	2166	365	A5
Cabravale	2166	365	K5
Cambridge Gardens	2747	237	H2
Cambridge Park	2747	237	G8
Camden	2570	477	E13
Camden Park	2570	508	A16
Camden South	2570	507	E14
Camellia	2142	309	B4
Cammeray	2062	316	A6
Campbelltown	2560	511	D3
Campbelltown North	2560	511	J4
Camperdown	2050	374	H3
Campsie	2194	372	C13
Campsie South	2194	372	A16

Name	Postcode	Map	Ref
Canada Bay	2046	342	E8
Canley Heights	2166	365	E1
Canley Vale	2166	366	C4
Canoelands	2157	70	J10
Canterbury	2193	372	F12
Caravan Head	2225	461	F4
Careel Bay	2107	140	B11
Caringbah	2229	492	H9
Caringbah South	2229	492	J12
Carlingford	2118	279	G3
Carlingford Heights	2118	279	C5
Carlingford North	2118	250	C13
Carlton	2218	432	G5
Carnes Hill	2171	392	C9
Carramar	2163	366	J2
Carss Park	2221	432	G14
Cartwright	2168	394	C5
Castle Cove	2069	285	J2
Castlecrag	2068	286	D10
Castle Hill	2154	217	H11
Castlereagh	2749	176	C7
Casula	2170	394	J14
Catherine Field	2171	449	J8
Cattai	2756	94	E4
Cawdor	2570	506	G9
Cecil Hills	2171	362	H4
Cecil Park	2171	332	C13
Centennial Park	2021	376	J5
Central	2000	345	J16
Charing Cross	2024	377	F7
Chatham Village	2170	425	A1
Chatswood	2067	284	J6
Chatswood West	2067	283	J10
Chatsworth	2759	269	J8
Cheltenham	2119	251	A8
Cherrybrook	2126	219	G6
Chester Hill	2162	368	D3
Chester Hill North	2162	338	B13
Chifley	2036	437	B8
Chinatown	2000	3	E11
Chippendale	2008	375	E1
Chipping Norton	2170	396	J2
Chiswick	2046	343	E2
Chowder Bay	2088	317	F13
Chullora	2190	370	C3
Church Hill	2000	345	H7
Church Point	2105	168	G6
Circular Quay	2000	345	K6
Claremont Meadows	2747	268	K3
Clarendon	2756	120	D11
Clareville	2107	169	E2
Claymore	2559	481	D10
Clemton Park	2206	402	B4
Clifton Gardens	2088	317	F14
Contarf	2093	287	E13

18 GREGORY'S STREET DIRECTORY

Name	Postcode	Map	Ref
Clovelly	2031	377	H11
Clovelly West	2031	377	F12
Clyburn Railway Station	2144	309	A15
Clyde Railway Station	2142	308	H12
Coasters Retreat	2108	139	A4
Cobbitty	2570	446	B10
Cockatoo Island	2000	314	F16
Cogra Bay	2083	76	D1
Colebee	2761	212	G13
Collaroy	2097	229	D11
Collaroy Beach	2097	229	B10
Collaroy Plateau	2097	228	H10
Colyton	2760	270	D3
Comleroy	2758	64	F11
Como	2226	460	G6
Como West	2226	460	F6
Concord	2137	341	J3
Concord East	2137	342	B5
Concord North	2138	311	E14
Concord South	2137	342	K9
Concord West	2138	341	E3
Condell Park	2200	398	E4
Connells Point	2221	431	G14
Coogee	2034	377	E14
Coogee North	2034	377	J14
Cornwallis	2756	90	J15
Cottage Point	2084	135	F8
Couridjah	2571	564	J15
Cowan	2081	104	B14
Cranebrook	2749	207	D10
Cremorne	2090	316	E10
Cremorne Junction	2090	316	F6
Cremorne Point	2090	316	F14
Cromer	2099	228	A14
Cromer Heights	2099	227	G13
Cronulla	2230	493	H13
Cronulla South	2230	523	K1
Crows Nest	2065	315	F5
Croydon	2132	342	E12
Croydon North	2132	342	H12
Croydon Park	2133	372	C7
Curl Curl	2096	258	K13
Currans Hill	2567	479	K11
Currawong Beach	2108	109	B16
Daceyville	2032	406	G5
Dangar Island	2083	76	H5
Darling Harbour	2000	345	F12
Darlinghurst	2010	346	C13
Darling Point	2027	346	J10
Darlington	2008	375	D4
Davidson	2085	255	E3
Dawes Point	2000	345	H3
Dean Park	2761	242	J1
Dee Why	2099	258	G6
Dee Why Beach	2099	259	B6
Dee Why North	2099	258	K2
Dee Why West	2099	258	F2
Denham Court	2565	422	D11
Denistone	2114	281	E12
Denistone East	2122	281	J11
Denistone West	2114	281	A13
Dharruk	2770	241	B6
Diamond Bay	2030	348	H5
Dobroyd Head	2093	288	C16
Dobroyd Point	2045	343	G11
Dolans Bay	2229	492	K16
Dolls Point	2219	463	G1
Doonside	2767	243	B11
Double Bay	2028	347	D15
Douglas Park	2569	568	C11
Dover Heights	2030	348	H11
Drummoyne	2047	343	H4
Duffys Forest	2084	195	C4
Dulwich Hill	2203	373	E8
Dundas	2117	279	G14
Dundas Valley	2117	280	B8
Dundas West	2117	279	A11
Dunheved	2760	239	F5
Dural	2158	189	D10
Eagle Vale	2558	481	G7
Earlwood	2206	402	G4
Earlwood West	2206	372	G16
Eastern Creek	2766	273	A11
Eastgardens	2036	406	F9
East Hills	2213	427	J2
East Killara	2071	254	H8
East Kurrajong	2758	66	B9
Eastlakes	2018	406	C6
East Lindfield	2070	254	K14
East Roseville	2069	285	C2
East Ryde	2113	283	B15
East Sydney	2010	4	C8
Eastwood	2122	281	E7
Ebenezer	2756	68	B13
Edensor Park	2176	363	G1
Edgecliff	2027	346	K15
Edmondson Park	2171	423	D4
Elanora Heights	2101	198	B14
Elderslie	2570	507	E4
Elizabeth Bay	2011	346	G9
Ellis Lane	2570	476	E6
Elvina Bay	2105	168	E3
Emerton	2770	240	K5
Emu Heights	2750	235	B1
Emu Plains	2750	235	G6
Enfield	2136	371	H5
Enfield South	2133	371	F6
Engadine	2233	518	G5
Englorie Park	2560	510	H10
Enmore	2042	374	F8
Epping	2121	251	D14
Epping West	2121	250	F15
Ermington	2115	310	F5
Erskine Park	2759	270	J15
Erskineville	2043	375	A9
Erskineville South	2043	374	K9
Eschol Park	2558	481	A3
Eveleigh	2015	375	D5
Fairfield	2165	336	G9
Fairfield East	2165	337	C12
Fairfield Heights	2165	336	B10
Fairfield West	2165	335	D10
Fairlight	2094	288	C6
Fairy Bower	2095	288	K11
Faulconbridge	2776	171	B14
Fiddletown	2159	129	G3
Five Dock	2046	343	B9
Flemington	2140	340	F9
Forest Glen	2157	70	J14
Forest Lodge	2037	344	J15
Forestville	2087	255	F9
Forty Baskets Beach	2093	288	B12
Fox Valley	2076	221	G16
Freemans Reach	2756	90	D6
Frenchs Forest	2086	256	J1
Frenchs Forest East	2086	257	B5
Fullers Bridge	2067	283	K8
Gallows Hill	2000	345	J6
Galston	2159	159	E7
Garden Island	2000	346	G4
Georges Hall	2198	367	H13
Georges Heights	2088	317	J9
Gilead	2560	539	H7
Girraween	2145	276	B12
Gladesville	2111	312	J7
Glebe	2037	345	C15
Glebe Island	2039	344	K9
Glebe Point	2037	11	H6
Glen Alpine	2560	510	D12
Glenbrook	2773	234	D13
Glendenning	2761	242	F6
Glenfield	2167	424	D6
Glenhaven	2156	217	J2
Glenmore	2570	503	G5
Glenmore Park	2745	266	H9
Glenorie	2157	128	A5
Glenwood	2768	215	G14
Glossodia	2756	66	E11
Goat Island	2000	345	E2
Golden Grove	2008	18	E8
Gordon	2072	253	F8
Gore Hill	2065	315	B5
Grantham Heights	2147	275	E8
Granville	2142	308	F13
Granville North	2142	308	J8
Grasmere	2570	476	B12
Grays Point	2232	491	C14
Great Mackerel Beach	2108	109	C14
Greenacre	2190	370	G10
Greendale	2745	385	H7
Greenfield Park	2176	334	B15
Green Square	2017	375	G10
Green Valley	2168	363	B11
Greenwich	2065	315	B7
Greenwich Point	2065	314	H14
Greystanes	2145	306	A7
Gronos Point	2756	93	E5
Grose Vale	2753	85	F12
Grose Wold	2753	116	B7
Guildford	2161	337	J6
Guildford East	2161	338	D7
Guildford Heights	2161	337	H5
Guildford North	2160	338	A2
Guildford West	2161	336	H4
Gundamaian	2232	521	J1
Gunnamatta Bay	2230	493	G14
Gymea	2227	491	F5
Gymea Bay	2227	491	G9
Haberfield	2045	343	D13
Hammondville	2170	396	J15
Harbord	2096	288	D1
Harbord West	2096	258	D14
Harrington Park	2567	478	J6
Harris Park	2150	308	G5
Hassall Grove	2761	212	A15
Hawkesbury Heights	2777	174	F2
Hawkesbury River Railway Station	2083	76	C11
Haymarket	2000	345	J14
Heathcote	2233	518	D12
Hebersham	2770	241	E3
Heckenberg	2168	364	B14
Henley	2111	313	A14
Hewitt	2759	270	H12
Hillsdale	2036	406	G15
Hillside	2157	127	B3
Hilltop	2145	307	A8
Hinchinbrook	2168	363	C16
HMAS Penguin	2091	317	G7
Hobartville	2753	118	C7
Holroyd	2160	307	K11
Holsworthy	2173	426	C6
Holsworthy Barracks	2173	426	E9
Homebush	2140	341	B4
Homebush Bay	2127	340	J2
Homebush West	2140	340	H10
Hookhams Corner	2077	191	F11
Hornsby	2077	221	E3
Hornsby Heights	2077	191	E5
Horsley Park	2164	302	E12
Hoxton Park	2171	392	F9
Hunters Hill	2110	313	G10
Huntingwood	2148	273	J13
Huntleys Cove	2111	313	D12
Huntleys Point	2111	313	E14
Hurlstone Park	2193	373	A12
Hurstville	2220	432	B4
Hurstville Grove	2220	431	H11
Illawong	2234	459	E6
Ingleburn	2565	453	E9
Ingleburn Village	2174	423	C8
Ingleside	2101	197	G5
Jacksons Landing	2009	12	E1
Jamisontown	2750	265	J1
Jannali	2226	460	H11
Jannali West	2226	460	F13
Kangaroo Point	2224	461	J5
Kareela	2232	461	C13
Kearns	2558	451	B15
Kellyville	2155	216	D6
Kellyville Ridge	2155	215	A2
Kemps Creek	2171	360	C8
Kensington	2033	376	B13
Kenthurst	2156	187	E5
Kentlyn	2560	513	E5
Killara	2071	254	C11
Killarney Heights	2087	255	J15
Kings Cross	2011	4	J8
Kingsford	2032	406	J5

GREGORY'S STREET DIRECTORY 19

Name	Postcode	Map	Ref
Kingsgrove	2208	401	H9
Kings Langley	2147	245	F6
Kings Park	2148	244	G4
Kingsway	2208	401	G15
Kingswood	2747	237	F12
Kingswood Park	2750	237	B4
Kirkham	2570	477	H8
Kirrawee	2232	491	A3
Kirribilli	2061	316	C16
Kissing Point	2074	252	B9
Kogarah	2217	433	E4
Kogarah Bay	2217	432	K14
Kogarah South	2177	433	C8
Kogarah West	2207	432	K15
Ku-ring-gai Chase National Pk		163	G1
Kurmond	2757	86	F5
Kurnell	2231	465	K8
Kurraba Point	2089	316	E16
Kurrajong	2758	85	G3
Kurrajong Heights	2758	63	D7
Kurrajong Hills	2758	64	B8
Kyeemagh	2216	404	A13
Kyle Bay	2221	431	K15
Lakemba	2195	401	C2
Lake Parramatta	2151	278	D8
Lakesland	2572	561	A7
Lalor Park	2147	245	F13
Lane Cove	2066	314	B2
Lane Cove North	2066	284	A12
Lane Cove West	2066	283	G15
Lansdowne	2163	367	C6
Lansvale	2166	366	H7
La Perouse	2036	436	H15
Lapstone	2773	264	G2
Lavender Bay	2060	315	J14
Leichhardt	2040	343	J14
Leightonfield Railway Station	2163	367	G1
Lemon Grove	2750	237	C9
Leonay	2750	235	A14
Leppington	2171	421	C9
Lethbridge Park	2770	240	F2
Leumeah	2560	482	D15
Lewisham	2049	373	F6
Liberty Grove	2138	311	C13
Lidcombe	2141	339	F9
Lilli Pilli	2229	522	E2
Lilyfield	2040	344	D1
Lindfield	2070	284	B2
Linley Point	2066	313	H7
Linns Hill	2570	443	F1
Little Bay	2036	437	E12
Liverpool	2170	395	C6
Liverpool North	2170	365	A16
Liverpool South	2170	395	B8
Liverpool West	2170	394	H5
Llandilo	2747	208	D4
Loftus	2232	489	J9
Loftus Heights	2232	489	K11
Londonderry	2753	148	C12
Long Bay	2036	437	G4
Long Point	2564	454	E10
Long Reef	2097	259	D2
Longueville	2066	314	E9
Loquat Valley	2104	168	K13

Name	Postcode	Map	Ref
Lovett Bay	2105	168	C2
Lucas Heights	2234	487	G8
Luddenham	2745	356	E1
Lugarno	2210	429	H1
Lugarno North	2210	430	A10
Lurline Bay	2035	407	J8
Lurnea	2170	394	F10
McCallums Hill	2195	401	D8
Macdonaldtown	2042	17	K11
McGraths Hill	2756	121	H10
McMahons Point	2060	315	F15
Macquarie Fields	2564	424	H15
Macquarie Links	2565	423	D14
Macquarie Park	2113	282	H2
Macquarie University	2109	252	B15
Maianbar	2230	523	C7
Malabar	2036	437	E7
Malabar Heights	2036	437	F8
Manahan	2200	399	B4
Manly	2095	288	J8
Manly East	2095	288	J11
Manly Vale	2093	287	J2
Manly West	2093	287	J2
Maraylya	2765	124	H5
Marayong	2148	243	J4
Marayong Heights	2148	244	B4
Marayong South	2148	244	C11
Maroota	2756	70	F3
Maroubra	2035	407	D11
Maroubra Junction	2035	407	D9
Maroubra South	2035	407	D15
Marrickville	2204	373	J13
Marrickville South	2204	373	J16
Marrickville West	2204	373	E14
Marsden Park	2765	181	H12
Marsfield	2122	281	H2
Martin Place Railway Station	2000	345	K9
Mascot	2020	405	C6
Matraville	2036	436	H6
Mays Hill	2145	307	H5
Meadowbank	2114	311	C3
Melrose Park	2114	310	J1
Melville	2759	269	J12
Menai	2234	458	G5
Menangle	2568	538	J14
Menangle Park	2563	538	J8
Merrylands	2160	307	F11
Merrylands West	2160	306	J12
Middle Cove	2068	286	C9
Middle Dural	2158	158	F7
Middle Harbour	2088	317	F1
Middle Head	2088	318	B7
Miller	2168	393	H4
Millers Point	2000	345	F5
Mill Hill	2022	377	B4
Milperra	2214	397	E8
Milperra Bridge	2170	397	E6
Milsons Point	2061	315	K16
Minchinbury	2770	271	D8
Minto	2566	482	D3
Minto Heights	2566	483	H5
Miranda	2228	492	B6
Miranda North	2228	492	E2
Mobbs Hill	2118	280	B3

Name	Postcode	Map	Ref
Model Farms	2153	247	H16
Mona Vale	2103	199	D5
Monterey	2217	433	H7
Mooney Mooney	2083	75	F1
Moorebank	2170	395	F10
Moore Park	2021	376	C6
Morning Bay	2108	138	G15
Mortdale	2223	431	B5
Mortlake	2137	312	A12
Mosman	2088	316	K10
Mount Annan	2567	479	D13
Mt Colah	2079	192	B2
Mount Druitt	2770	241	F13
Mt Hunter	2570	504	H9
Mt Irvine	2786	60	D1
Mt Kuring-gai	2080	162	K10
Mt Lewis	2200	369	K15
Mt Pleasant	2749	207	H11
Mt Pritchard	2170	364	G10
Mt Riverview	2774	234	G3
Mt Tomah	2758	59	H13
Mt Vernon	2759	331	B11
Mt Wilson	2786	58	K9
Mowbray Park	2571	561	E6
Mulgoa	2745	295	F11
Mulgrave	2756	151	H3
Museum Railway Station	2000	345	K13
Narellan	2567	478	H11
Narellan Vale	2567	478	K11
Naremburn	2065	315	E2
Narrabeen	2101	229	C6
Narrabeen Peninsula	2101	229	E1
Narraweena	2099	258	C3
Narwee	2209	400	H11
Nelson	2765	154	J9
Neutral Bay	2089	316	B10
Neutral Bay Junction	2089	316	D9
Newington	2127	310	C12
Newport	2106	169	F10
Newport Beach	2106	170	A9
Newtown	2042	374	H5
Newtown South	2042	374	G8
Normanhurst	2076	221	G11
Normanhurst West	2120	221	D9
North Balgowlah	2093	287	E5
North Bankstown	2199	369	F11
North Bondi	2026	348	E15
North Cremorne	2090	316	E6
North Cronulla	2230	494	E8
North Curl Curl	2099	258	J11
North Engadine	2233	488	G10
North Epping	2121	251	F11
North Head	2095	290	E16
North Manly	2100	258	B14
North Narrabeen	2101	228	H2
North Parramatta	2151	278	F7
North Richmond	2754	87	F11
North Rocks	2151	249	A13
North Ryde	2113	282	F10
North St Ives	2075	224	E6
North St Marys	2760	240	B7

Name	Postcode	Map	Ref
North Steyne	2095	288	J8
North Strathfield	2137	341	E7
North Sydney	2060	315	J11
North Turramurra	2074	223	G4
North Wahroonga	2076	222	H1
North Willoughby	2068	285	G8
Northwood	2066	314	G8
Oakdale	2570	500	C10
Oakhurst	2761	242	B3
Oakville	2765	153	E5
Oatlands	2117	279	C11
Oatley	2223	431	B13
Oatley West	2223	430	G11
Old Guildford	2161	337	F10
Old Mount Druitt	2770	241	B16
Old Toongabbie	2146	277	D7
Olympic Park Railway Station	2140	340	H1
Orange Grove	2040	344	B11
Orangeville	2570	443	E13
Oran Park	2570	448	H8
Orchard Hills	2748	267	J9
Osborne Park	2066	314	G4
Oxford Falls	2100	227	C14
Oxley Park	2760	270	F1
Oyster Bay	2225	461	E4
Paddington	2021	346	F16
Padstow	2211	399	E14
Padstow Heights	2211	429	C8
Padstow North	2211	399	C11
Pagewood	2035	406	E7
Palm Beach	2108	139	K2
Panania	2213	428	C3
Paradise Beach	2107	139	H11
Parklea	2768	215	B14
Parramatta	2150	308	E2
Parramatta East	2150	278	K16
Peakhurst	2210	430	G4
Peakhurst Heights	2210	430	D7
Peakhurst South	2210	430	C9
Peakhurst West	2210	430	A9
Pearces Corner	2076	222	B7
Pemulwuy	2145	305	C6
Pendle Hill	2145	276	F12
Pennant Hills	2120	220	F13
Penrith	2750	236	F13
Penshurst	2222	431	E3
Petersham	2049	373	J4
Phillip Bay	2036	436	J9
Picnic Point	2213	428	E9
Picton	2571	563	J6
Pitt Town	2756	92	H12
Pitt Town Bottoms	2756	92	B11
Pleasure Point	2171	427	F7
Plumpton	2761	242	A6
Point Piper	2027	347	D8
Port Botany	2036	436	C7
Port Hacking	2229	522	J3
Potts Hill	2143	369	E4
Potts Point	2011	346	E10
Prairiewood	2176	334	G9
Prestons	2170	393	E11
Prospect	2148	275	C14
Punchbowl	2196	400	C1

20 GREGORY'S STREET DIRECTORY

Name	Postcode	Map	Ref
Punchbowl South	2196	400	B7
Putney	2112	312	B7
Pymble	2073	253	B3
Pyrmont	2009	345	E9
Quakers Hill	2763	214	B10
Queenscliff	2096	288	F2
Queens Park	2022	377	C5
Raby	2566	451	E14
Ramsgate	2217	433	E13
Ramsgate Beach	2217	433	F14
Randwick	2031	377	C12
Randwick South	2031	407	B2
Redfern	2016	375	H4
Regents Park	2143	369	C1
Regentville	2745	265	E3
Revesby	2212	398	G11
Revesby Heights	2212	428	K6
Revesby North	2212	398	J12
Rhodes	2138	311	D10
Richmond	2753	118	C4
Richmond East	2753	119	B5
Richmond Lowlands	2753	88	E11
Riverstone	2765	182	G7
Riverview	2066	313	K6
Riverwood	2210	400	C11
Rockdale	2216	403	F14
Rodd Point	2046	343	F8
Rogans Hill	2154	218	G14
Rookwood	2141	340	D10
Rooty Hill	2766	272	E2
Rose Bay	2029	348	A8
Rose Bay North	2030	348	H8
Rosebery	2018	375	H14
Rosehill	2142	308	J7
Roselands	2196	400	G8
Roselea	2118	250	A12
Rosemeadow	2560	540	F5
Rosemount	2069	284	J3
Roseville	2069	284	J3
Roseville Chase	2069	285	F1
Rossmore	2171	389	G8
Round Corner	2158	188	F14
Rouse Hill	2155	184	E9
Royal National Park	2232	520	F6
Rozelle	2039	344	E7
Ruse	2560	512	E4
Rushcutters Bay	2011	346	G12
Russell Lea	2046	343	D4
Rydalmere	2116	309	E2
Ryde	2112	312	C2
Sackville	2756	68	D2
Sackville North	2756	68	J2
Sadleir	2168	394	B2
St Andrews	2566	481	J4
St Clair	2759	270	C11
St Helens Park	2560	541	E5
St Ives	2075	224	F12
St Ives Chase	2075	223	H3
St James Railway Station	2000	345	K10
St Johns Park	2176	364	F1
St Leonards	2065	315	C4

Name	Postcode	Map	Ref
St Marys	2760	239	E9
St Pauls	2031	377	B16
St Peters	2044	374	H15
Sand Point	2108	139	J2
Sandringham	2219	463	F4
Sandy Point	2171	428	B10
Sans Souci	2219	433	E15
Scheyville	2756	123	G5
Schofields	2762	183	F14
Scotland Island	2105	168	G1
Scotts Hill	2570	443	K5
Seaforth	2092	287	B9
Sefton	2162	368	F4
Seven Hills	2147	275	G5
Seven Hills North	2147	246	D11
Seven Hills West	2147	245	C16
Shalvey	2770	210	K15
Shanes Park	2760	209	G7
Sherwood Grange	2160	306	G13
Silverdale	2752	354	C10
Silverwater	2128	309	G13
Smeaton Grange	2567	479	F8
Smithfield	2164	335	H3
Smithfield West	2164	335	D3
Sorlie	2086	256	B3
South Coogee	2034	407	K5
South Curl Curl	2096	258	K15
South Engadine	2233	518	H7
South Granville	2142	338	F4
South Hurstville	2221	432	B9
South Maroota	2756	69	D6
South Penrith	2750	266	G3
South Steyne	2095	288	H10
South Turramurra	2074	251	J7
South Wentworthville	2145	307	B5
South Windsor	2756	120	J15
Spectacle Island	344	C1
Spit Junction	2088	317	A4
Spring Farm	2570	507	F8
Springwood	2777	201	D5
Stanhope Gardens	2768	215	B7
Stanmore	2048	374	D6
Steele Barracks	2170	425	C2
Strathfield	2135	341	E13
Strathfield South	2136	371	B6
Strawberry Hills	2010	19	K3
Summer Hill	2130	373	B4
Sun Valley	2777	202	H6
Surry Hills	2010	346	A15
Sutherland	2232	490	C2
Sydenham	2044	374	E15
Sydney	2000	345	G8
Sydney (GPO)	2001	345	J9
Sydney Olympic Park	2127	340	H1
Sylvania	2224	461	J10
Sylvania Heights	2224	461	F11
Sylvania Waters	2224	462	E11
Tahmoor	2573	566	E12
Tamarama	2026	378	E7
Taren Point	2229	462	K12
Taronga Zoological Park	2088	317	A14
Taverners Hill	2040	373	H4
Taylors Point	2107	169	C2

Name	Postcode	Map	Ref
Telopea	2117	279	F9
Tempe	2044	404	D2
Tennyson	2754	65	D12
Tennyson Point	2111	312	E10
Terrey Hills	2084	196	B7
The Basin	2108	138	G3
The Cross Roads	2170	424	B3
The Domain	2000	4	C2
The Meadows	2232	521	E9
The Oaks	2570	502	G11
Theresa Park	2570	444	H5
The Rocks	2000	345	K4
The Slopes	2754	64	J13
The Spit	2088	287	C13
The Trongate	2142	338	F2
Thirlmere	2572	565	E4
Thompsons Corner	2125	249	J5
Thornleigh	2120	220	J13
Tom Uglys Point	2221	462	F5
Toongabbie	2146	276	E8
Toongabbie West	2146	276	G7
Town Hall	2000	3	H6
Towra Point	2231	464	D4
Tregear	2770	240	D6
Tumbledown Dick	2101	196	F8
Turramurra	2074	222	G15
Turrella	2205	403	E4
Ultimo	2007	345	E14
Undercliffe	2206	403	F3
University of NSW	2052	376	G14
University of Sydney	2006	375	B1
Valley Heights	2777	202	G10
Varroville	2566	451	G5
Vaucluse	2030	348	C4
Vaucluse Heights	2030	348	D6
Victoria Cross	2060	K	E7
Villawood	2163	367	G3
Villawood East	2163	367	G4
Vineyard	2765	152	H11
Voyager Point	2171	427	E2
Wahroonga	2076	222	G6
Wahroonga South	2076	221	H16
Waitara	2077	221	J2
Waitara East	2077	222	B3
Wakehurst	2085	226	B16
Wakeley	2176	334	K13
Wallacia	2745	324	F13
Wallgrove	2164	272	G11
Wareemba	2046	343	A5
Warragamba	2752	353	E6
Warrawee	2074	222	G10
Warriewood	2102	199	A10
Warriewood Beach	2102	199	F10
Warrimoo	2774	203	F13
Warumbul	2229	521	K7
Warwick Farm	2170	365	K12
Waterfall	2233	519	C14
Waterloo	2017	375	G7
Watsons Bay	2030	318	G11
Wattle Grove	2173	396	A15
Waverley	2024	377	G7

Name	Postcode	Map	Ref
Waverley South	2024	377	H10
Waverton	2060	315	E13
Wedderburn	2560	540	C12
Wentworthville	2145	277	B14
Werombi	2570	443	F7
Werrington	2747	239	C12
Werrington County	2747	238	K7
Werrington Downs	2747	238	B4
West Gordon	2072	253	C10
West Hoxton	2171	392	B4
Westleigh	2120	220	F4
West Lindfield	2070	283	G2
Westmead	2145	307	E1
West Pennant Hills	2125	249	D4
West Pymble	2073	252	J11
West Ryde	2114	281	G14
Wetherill Park	2164	334	D2
Whalan	2770	241	B11
Whale Beach	2107	140	D6
Wheeler Heights	2097	228	F9
Wheeney Creek	2758	64	B4
White Bay	2039	344	K7
Wilberforce	2756	92	B4
Wiley Park	2195	400	G1
Willmot	2770	210	D12
Willoughby	2068	285	H11
Wilton	2571	568	K14
Windsor	2756	121	C11
Windsor Downs	2756	180	J2
Wingala	2099	258	H11
Winji Jimmi	2103	169	D14
Winmalee	2777	173	F10
Winston Hills	2153	277	C2
Wolli Creek	2205	403	J6
Wollstonecraft	2065	315	D9
Wondabyne	2256	76	H1
Woodbine	2560	481	H13
Woodcroft	2767	243	G8
Woodpark	2164	306	G14
Woollahra	2025	377	B1
Woollahra Point	2028	347	G7
Woolloomooloo	2011	346	D11
Woolooware	2230	493	E11
Woolwich	2110	314	F13
Woronora	2232	460	A15
Woronora Heights	2233	489	F4
Wynyard	2000	1	E16
Yagoona	2199	369	C11
Yanderra	2574	567	G15
Yarramundi	2753	145	H7
Yarrawarrah	2233	489	F12
Yellow Rock	2777	204	D4
Yenabilli	2230	522	J6
Yennora	2161	337	D10
Yowie Bay	2228	492	A12
Yowie Point	2228	492	A15
Zetland	2017	375	K11

GREGORY'S STREET DIRECTORY 21

STREET INDEX

[ABBREVIATIONS USED IN THE STREET INDEX]

ABBREVIATIONS FOR DESIGNATIONS

Alley	al	Corso	cso	Gate/s	gte	Outlook	out	Row	row
Approach	app	Court	ct	Gateway	gwy	Parade	pde	Serviceway	swy
Arcade	arc	Courtyard	cyd	Glade	gld	Park	pk	South	s
Avenue	av	Cove	cov	Glen	gln	Parkway	pky	Square	sq
Bend	bnd	Crescent	cr	Grange	gra	Pass	ps	Strand	sd
Boulevard	bvd	Crest	cst	Green	grn	Pathway	pwy	Street	st
Bowl	bl	Cross	cs	Grove	gr	Place	pl	Tarn	tn
Brace	br	Crossing	csg	Grovet	gr	Plaza	plz	Terrace	tce
Brae	br	Curve	cve	Haven	hvn	Pocket	pkt	Tollway	twy
Break	brk	Dale	dle	Heights	hts	Point/Port	pt	Top	top
Brook	brk	Down/s	dn	Highway	hwy	Promenade	prm	Tor	tor
Broadway	bwy	Drive	dr	Hill	hill	Quadrant	qd	Track	tr
Brow	brw	Driveway	dwy	Junction	jnc	Quay/s	qy	Trail	trl
Bypass	bps	East	e	Key	key	Ramble	ra	Turn	trn
Centre	ctr	Edge	edg	Lane	la	Reach	rch	Underpass	ups
Chase	ch	Elbow	elb	Link	lk	Reserve	res	Vale	va
Circle	cir	End	end	Loop	lp	Rest	rst	View	vw
Circuit	cct	Entrance	ent	Mall	ml	Retreat	rt	Vista	vst
Circus	crc	Esplanade	esp	Mead	md	Return	rtn	Walk	wk
Close	cl	Expressway	exp	Meander	mdr	Ridge	rdg	Walkway	wky
Common	cmn	Fairway	fy	Mews	mw	Rise	ri	Way	wy
Concourse	cnc	Freeway	fwy	Motorway	mwy	Road	rd	West	w
Copse	cps	Frontage	fr	Nook	nk	Roadway	rdy	Wynd	wyn
Corner	cnr	Garden/s	gdn	North	n	Route	rte		

ABBREVIATIONS FOR SUBURB NAMES

Where it has been necessary to abbreviate the suburb names in the street index the following conventions have been used. If any difficulty is experienced with the suburban names refer to the SUBURBS and LOCALITIES index.

Airport	Aprt	Field/s	Fd	Island	I	Paradise	Pdse	Rocks	Rks
Basin	Bsn	Flat	Fl	Junction	Jctn	Park	Pk	Saint	St
Bay	B	Forest	Frst	Lagoon	Lgn	Plain/s	Pl	South	S
Beach	Bch	Garden/s	Gdn	Lakes	L	Plateau	Plat	Terminal	Term
Bridge	Br	Grove	Gr	Lodge	Ldg	Pocket	Pkt	University	Uni
Central	Ctrl	Gully	Gly	Lookout	Lkt	Point/Port	Pt	Upper	Up
Chase	Ch	Harbor/our	Hbr	Lower	Lr	Range	Rge	Valley	Vy
Corner	Cnr	Head/s	Hd	Meadow/s	Mdw	Reach	Rch	Vale	Va
Creek	Ck	Headland	Hd	Mount	Mt	Reserve	Res	Village	Vill
Crossing	Csg	Heights	Ht	Mountain/s	Mtn	Ridge	Rdg	Waters	Wtr
Down/s	Dn	Hill/s	Hl	North	N	River	R	West	W
East	E								

NON-STANDARD ABBREVIATIONS FOR SUBURB NAMES

Banksmeadow	Bnksmeadw	Hinchinbrook	Hinchinbrk	Rosemeadow	Rsemeadow
Bankstown Airport	Bnkstn Aprt	Horningsea Park	Horngsea Pk	Royal National Park	Royal N P
Brighton-le-Sands	Btn-le-Sds	Huntingwood	Huntingwd	Rushcutters Bay	Rcuttrs Bay
Cambridge Gardens	Cmbrdg Gdn	Kings Langley	Kings Lngly	Smeaton Grange	Smeaton Gra
Cambridge Park	Cmbrdg Pk	Ku-ring-gai Chase		South Turramurra	S Turramrra
Chipping Norton	Chipping Ntn	National Park	Krngai Ch NP	South	
Claremont Meadows	Clarmnt Ms	Lethbridge Park	Lethbrdg Pk	Wentworthville	S Wntwthvle
Edmondson Park	Edmndsn Pk	Macquarie Fields	Mcquarie Fd	Stanhope Gardens	Stanhpe Gdn
Faulconbridge	Faulcnbdg	Macquarie Links	Mcquarie Lk	Warwick Farm	Warwck Frm
Freemans Reach	Freemns Rch	Macquarie Park	Mcquarie Pk	Wentworthville	Wentwthvle
Great Mackerel Beach	Gt Mckrl Bch	Mount Ku-ring-gai	Mt Krng-gai	Werrington County	Wrrngtn Cty
Greenfield Park	Greenfld Pk	Old Toongabbie	Old Tngabbie	Werrington Downs	Wrrngtn Dns
Hammondville	Hamondvle	Pitt Town Bottoms	Pitt Twn Bttms	West Pennant Hills	W Pnnant Hl
Harrington Park	Harringtn Pk	Richmond		Wollstonecraft	Wollstncraft
Hawkesbury Heights	Hawksbry Ht	Lowlands	Richmond Lwld	Woolloomooloo	Woolmloo

SPECIAL NOTE
The LANES shown in *italics* in the street index are not chartered on the street maps. For reasons of clarity it is not practical to show them.

22 GREGORY'S STREET DIRECTORY

STREETS

A

AARON
pl. Carlingford..........249 J16
pl. Plumpton...............242 A11
pl. Silverdale.............353 H12
pl. Wahroonga............222 A8
ABADAL
pl. Ingleburn...............453 H8
ABAROO
st. Ryde.......................282 E16
ABBE RECEVEUR
pl. Little Bay...............437 A12
ABBERTON
st. Jamisontown........266 C4
ABBEVILLE
cl. Prestons...............392 K12
ABBEY
av. Greenacre............370 F11
la. Parramatta...........278 F15
la. Wrrngtn Dns, off
    Abbey Row.........238 D5
pl. Cherrybrook..........219 E14
rd. Kemps Ck............330 G7
row.Wrrngtn Dns.......238 D5
st. Hunters Hill..........313 H7
st. Randwick..............377 A12
wy. Glenhaven...........218 B15
ABBOTSFORD
la. Kensington............376 E9
st. Kensington............376 F9
ABBOTSBURY
dr. Horsley Pk............332 E6
ABBOTSFORD
pde.Abbotsford..........342 H1
rd. Homebush...........341 B10
rd. Picton....................563 C1
ABBOTSFORD COVE
dr. Abbotsford...........342 K2
ABBOTT
av. Sefton...................338 F15
cr. Edensor Pk..........333 H14
la. Cammeray, off
    Abbott St............315 J4
pl. Glenorie................128 D10
pl. Ingleburn...............452 J10
pl. Artarmon..............284 K16
rd. Heathcote............518 D9
rd. N Curl Curl...........258 E10
rd. Seven Hills...........246 A14
st. Balgowlah Ht........287 G14
st. Cammeray...........315 J4
st. Coogee.................377 E14
st. Merrylands...........308 D16
ABBOTTS
rd. Kemps Ck............330 E7
ABDALE
cr. Glenwood.............215 H13
A'BECKETT
av. Ashfield................372 H4
st. Granville...............308 J9
st. Granville...............308 G9
ABEL
la. Petersham............15 H10
pl. Cronulla................493 K11
st. Canley Ht..............335 C16
st. Greenacre............370 F15
st. Jamisontown........236 D15
ABELIA
cl. Cherrybrook..........219 K5
st. Tahmoor................566 A11
wy. Blacktown..........274 F12
ABER
gr. Mount Druitt.........271 C2
ABERCORN
st. Bexley..................402 G13
ABERCROMBIE
av. Seven Hills..........275 E10
la. Sydney......................A K12
la. Cabramatta W......365 B8
st. Chippendale.........19 E8
st. Darlington.............18 E8
st. Leumeah..............482 C16
st. Redfern................19 A5
ABERDARE
pl. Cartwright.............394 E4
ABERDEEN
cct. Glenmore Pk........266 F8
pl. Stanhpe Gdn.......215 F9
rd. Busby...................363 K16
rd. St Andrews..........452 B13
st. Winston Hills.........277 C13
st. Bossley Park........334 B12
st. Cmbrdg Pk...........237 K8

ABERDOUR
av. Rouse Hill............184 K8
ABERFELDY
cr. St Andrews..........482 A1
ABERFOYLE
pl. Grasmere............475 K15
rd. Wedderburn........540 C9
rd. Wedderburn........541 J16
ABERGELDIE
st. Dulwich Hill..........373 B8
ABERMAIN
pl. Cartwright.............394 D4
ABERNATHY
cl. Kellyville...............217 B3
ABERNETHY
st. Seaforth...............286 K9
ABHAY
av. Rooty Hill............271 H3
ABICHT
cl. Kemps Ck............360 G10
ABIGAIL
la. Newtown..............17 E11
st. Hunters Hill..........313 D8
st. Seven Hills...........275 A4
ABINGDON
rd. Roseville..............284 B5
st. Chipping Ntn........490 H1
st. N Balgowlah.........287 G5
ABINGTON
cr. Glen Alpine..........510 A14
ABOUD
av. Kingsford............406 C2
ABOUKIR
st. Dover Ht...............348 G12
st. Rockdale..............403 F16
ABRAHAM
cl. Menai...................458 H11
pl. Rooty Hill............241 J12
ABRAHAMS
wy. Claymore............481 E10
ABUKLEA
rd. Eastwood.............281 G3
rd. Epping..................281 D2
rd. Marsfield..............281 G3
ACACIA
av. Glenmore Pk........265 G8
av. Greenacre...........370 D15
av. Oakdale...............500 B13
av. Prestons..............394 A15
av. Punchbowl..........400 D2
av. Ruse....................512 F7
av. Ryde....................312 D6
st. St Marys..............239 G14
ACCESS
cr. Narellan Vale........478 K11
rd. Oatlands.............279 B8
gr. Stanhpe Gdn.......215 G13
st. Belmore..............371 F16
la. Eastwood.............281 H8
la. Roseville..............284 K5
la. Greystanes..........305 K11
pl. Newington, off
    Watt Av.................310 B12
rd. Berowra..............133 D15
rd. Kirrawee.............490 H6
rd. Seaforth..............286 K7
rd. Sutherland...........490 H6
rd.n.Kirrawee.............490 H4
rd.n.Sutherland..........490 H4
st. Belmore..............371 F16
st. Cabramatta...........365 H8
st. Collaroy Plat........228 H10
st. Eastwood.............281 H8
st. Oatley..................431 A10
st. Rooty Hill............272 D4
st. Rydalmere..........279 K16
ACE
av. Fairfield...............336 F9
ACER
cl. Cherrybrook..........219 H8
gln. Castle Hill...........218 F16
ADAMSON
av. Dundas Vy..........280 B11
st. Thornleigh...........221 B8
st. Glenfield.............424 H12
ADARE
pl. Killarney Ht..........255 K15
st. Tregear...............240 F2
ADCOCH
st. Bidwill...................211 B16
ADDER
st. Beecroft..............250 G4

ACOLA
ct. Wattle Grove........396 B15
ACORN
cl. Mt Colah..............162 E13
gr. Elderslie.............507 F2
st. Emu Plains.........235 A11
wy. Acacia Gdn........214 J14
ACRES
la. Ingleburn..............453 F8
pl. Bligh Park............150 H7
rd. Kellyville.............216 D5
ACRI
st. Prestons..............393 E15
ACROPOLIS
av. Rooty Hill............271 H3
ACTINOTUS
av. Caringbah..........492 J12
ACTION
st. Greenacre............370 A9
ACTIVE
pl. Beaumont Hills....185 K14
ACTON
st. Croydon...............342 E13
st. Hurlstone Pk........372 J13
st. Sutherland...........490 F1
ACUBA
gr. Quakers Hill........214 C11
ADA
av. Brookvale............258 D12
av. Strathfield............341 A16
av. Wahroonga.........222 C13
av.s.Wahroonga........222 C14
la. Erskineville..........18 C14
la. Randwick.............377 B14
pl. Carlingford.........249 J15
pl. Doonside............243 D8
pl. Pyrmont................12 H6
pl. Ultimo....................12 J9
st. Bexley.................402 C16
st. Canley Vale.........366 E3
st. Concord..............341 H9
st. Cremorne............316 F7
st. Erskineville..........18 C14
st. Harris Park..........308 E5
st. Kingsgrove..........401 G6
st. North Ryde.........282 D9
st. Oatley................431 D11
st. Padstow...............429 F3
st. Randwick.............377 C15
ADAH
st. Guildford............338 D4
ADAIR
pl. East Killara.........254 H8
ADALUMA
av. Bangor...............459 F15
ADAM
cl. Berowra..............133 H10
dr. S Windsor..........150 J3
pl. Emu Plains.........234 K7
pl. Glenhaven..........217 J9
pl. Lalor Park..........245 E10
pl. Mcquarie Fd......424 A14
st. Campsie...........372 C10
st. Fairfield.............336 E9
st. Guildford...........338 C3
st. Ryde................282 C15
ADAMINABY
st. Heckenberg.......364 B12
ADAMS
av. Malabar..............437 F7
av. Turramurra.........223 E11
cr. St Marys..............269 K3
la. Baulkham Hl........247 D11
la. Bondi Jctn............22 K9
rd. Luddenham........356 J3
rd. Breakfast Pt.......312 B16
rd. Concord.............342 B1
rd. Curl Curl...........258 J13
rd. Frenchs Frst......256 C3
rd. Mortlake...........312 B16
ADAMSON
av. Dundas Vy.........280 B11
st. Thornleigh..........221 B8
st. Glenfield............424 H12
ADARE
pl. Killarney Ht.........255 K15
st. Tregear..............240 F2
ADCOCH
st. Bidwill.................211 B16
ADDER
st. Beecroft.............250 G4

ADDERLEY
st,e, Lidcombe.........309 J16
st.w,Auburn.............309 D13
ADDERSTONE
av. N Sydney..............6 C11
ADDERTON
rd. Carlingford...........279 H6
rd. Dundas...............279 H6
rd. Telopea..............279 H6
ADDINGTON
av. Ryde..................311 J2
ADDISCOMBE
rd. Manly Vale..........288 C4
ADDISON
av. Concord.............341 K7
av. Roseville............285 A3
gr. Bidwill................211 C16
rd. Ingleside............197 F7
rd. Manly................288 G14
rd. Marrickville.........15 J14
rd. Petersham..........15 J14
st. Balmain.................7 C7
st. Kensington..........376 D12
st. Thirlmere.............562 E8
st. Wetherill Pk.........334 E6
wy. West Hoxton......392 A13
ADDLESTONE
rd. Merrylands.........307 G14
ADDY
st. N Strathfield........341 F7
ADELAIDE
av. Campbelltown.....512 B5
av. E Lindfield.........254 K14
gr. Bella Vista..........246 G2
la. Oxley Park, off
    Adelaide St........270 G2
pde. Woollahra........22 K3
pl. Cecil Hills..........362 J4
pl. Surry Hills...........19 K3
pl. Sylvania............461 K8
st. Balgowlah Ht.....287 G14
st. Belmore...........371 F14
st. Bondi Jctn........22 K3
st. Meadowbank.....311 B2
st. Melrose Pk.......311 B2
st. Oxley Park.......269 K1
st. Rooty Hill.........242 A14
st. St Marys.........269 K1
st. Surry Hills........19 K3
st. West Ryde......281 B16
st. Woollahra........22 K3
ADELE
cl. Green Valley......363 C9
ADELINE
st. Bass Hill...........367 K7
st. Rydalmere.......279 D15
ADELLA
av. Blacktown.......243 K15
ADELONG
cl. Emu Plains.......234 K7
cl. Wakeley..........334 H13
pl. Camden S......507 B13
pl. Wahroonga.....222 C13
st. Sutherland.......490 D3
ADELPHI
cl. Doonside.........243 D8
st. Marsfield.........282 C5
st. Rouse Hill.......184 J7
ADEN
st. Quakers Hill.....214 E13
st. Seaforth.........287 B10
ADEPT
la. Bankstown......399 F6
ADEY
pl. Castle Hill.......248 D2
ADHARA
st. Erskine Park....301 A1
ADINA
av. Phillip Bay......436 K12
cl. Fairfield W......335 F12
cr. Beverly Hills....401 C12
pl. Bradbury.........511 D15
rd. Curl Curl.......258 K13
st. Miranda........491 K5
st. Seven Hills....245 K14
st. Telopea.........279 G1
wy. La Perouse...436 K13
ADLER
pde. Greystanes...306 G7
pde. Greystanes...306 G9
ADMIRALTY
dr. Breakfast Pt....312 C16
wy. Minto..........482 H7

ADNA
st. Plumpton..........242 C6
ADNUM
la. Bankstown, off
    Fetherston St...369 E16
ADOLPHUS
cl. Hinchinbrk......363 B14
st. Balmain.............8 B10
st. Canley Ht.......365 G4
st. Naremburn.....315 G2
ADOR
av. Rockdale.......403 G16
ADRIAN
av. Lurnea.........394 D8
cl. Carlingford....279 D4
pl. Balgowlah Ht..287 H14
pl. Greystanes....306 F6
st. Glenwood......215 J14
st. Mcquarie Fd..424 A14
ADRIATIC
st. Kellyville Rdg..215 A4
ADRIENNE
st. Glendenning..242 F5
ADVANCE
st. Schofields.....183 C16
ADVENTURE
pl. Caringbah....493 B1
pl. Rouse Hill....184 K10
pl. Rouse Hill....185 A10
ADY
st. Hunters Hill..313 J11
AEGEAN
ct. Kellyville Rdg..215 A4
AEOLIA
la. Randwick, off
    Aeolia St........377 B16
st. Randwick....377 C15
AEOLUS
av. Ryde........282 A13
AERO
rd. Ingleburn..453 C2
st. Btn-le-Sds..433 H1
AERODROME
rd. Cobbitty....476 K10
AFTERNOON
ct. St Clair......270 C14
AFTON
pl. Quakers Hill..214 E12
AGAR
st. Marrickville..16 E16
AGATE
cl. Eagle Vale..481 D8
AGATHA
pl. Oakhurst...241 K4
AGER COTTAGE
cr. Blair Athol..511 A4
AGINCOURT
pl. Glenwood..245 H2
rd. Marsfield..281 J2
AGIUS
st. Winston Hills..277 C1
AGNES
st. Strathfield..341 E16
AGNEW
st. Bossley Park..334 C11
AGONIS
cl. Banksia...403 G12
AGRA
pl. Riverstone..183 A4
AGRAFE
pl. Minchinbury..272 A10
AGRICULTURE
la. Camperdown..18 A2
AGRIPPA
st. Rsemeadow..540 G2
AHEARN
av. S Coogee..407 H4
AHMEDI
cl. Grose Vale..115 B4
AHMET
ct. Oakhurst..242 D2
AIKEN
rd. W Pnnant Hl..249 A7
AILSA
av. Blacktown..275 B3
cl. E Lindfield..255 B10
pl. Riverstone..182 K5
wy. Canley Vale..366 G6
AIMEE
st. Quakers Hill..214 C9

AI STREETS

AINSBURY
- rd. St Marys 269 E6

AINSLEE
- ct. Cranebrook 206 J9
- pl. Seaforth 287 A6

AINSLEY
- av. Glendenning 242 E2

AINSLIE
- cl. St Ives Ch 224 A6
- pde. Carlingford 249 H14
- pl. Condell Park 398 G2
- pl. Ruse 512 G4
- st. Fairfield W 335 F8
- st. Kingsford 407 A4

AINSWORTH
- cr. Wetherill Pk 334 H3
- st. Leichhardt 10 D12
- st. Lilyfield 10 D12

AINTREE
- cl. Casula 424 E1

AIRD
- st. Parramatta 308 B4

AIRDS
- rd. Leumeah 482 A12
- rd. Minto 482 C7

AIRDSLEY
- la. Bradbury 511 D13

AIREDALE
- av. Earlwood 402 F6

AIRLIE
- cr. Cecil Hills 362 G3
- pl. Oatlands 278 J10

AIRPORT
- av. Bnkstn Aprt 367 K16
- dr. Mascot 404 D4

AIRSTRIP
- rd. Pitt Town 93 B15

AITAPE
- cr. Whalan 240 H10
- pl. Holsworthy 426 C3

AITCHANDAR
- rd. Ryde 312 E1

AITKEN
- av. Queenscliff 288 F3

AJAX
- pl. Blacktown 245 D8
- pl. Engadine 488 J14

A J HARE
- av. Mcquarie Pk 283 C7

AJUGA
- ct. Voyager Pt 427 D5

AKMA
- cl. Bonnyrigg 363 K9

AKOONAH
- cl. Westleigh 220 F2
- pl. Peakhurst 430 C9

AKORA
- av. Baulkham Hl 247 C5
- cl. Chipping Ntn 396 F6
- st. Frenchs Frst 256 F6

AKRON
- pl. Toongabbie 275 F14

AKUNA
- av. Bangor 459 G14
- av. Bangor 459 G15
- av. Bradbury 511 A9
- av. Bradbury 511 F15
- la. Mona Vale 199 C4

ALABAMA
- av. Bexley 432 F3

ALABASTER
- pl. Eagle Vale 481 D8

ALADORE
- av. Cabramatta 365 F8

ALAINE
- pl. Cecil Park 332 D10

ALAM
- st. Campbelltown 511 K3
- st. Blacktown 244 B12
- st. Colyton 270 B6

ALAMAR
- cr. Quakers Hill 214 F16

ALAMEDA
- wy. Warriewood 198 K6

ALAMEIN
- av. Carlingford 250 A14
- av. Liverpool 394 K3
- av. Mt Annan 479 A10
- av. Narellan Vale 479 A10
- av. Narraweena 258 C4
- rd. Bossley Park 334 A5

ALA MOANA
- rd. E Kurrajong 65 A9

ALAN
- av. Hornsby 191 E10
- av. Seaforth 287 A11
- rd. Berowra Ht 133 B8
- st. Box Hill 154 B16
- st. Cammeray 316 C4
- st. Fairfield 336 G12
- st. Mount Druitt 271 B4
- st. Rydalmere 309 B2
- st. Yagoona 368 J11

ALANA
- dr. W Pnnant Hl 248 J6
- st. St Ives Ch 224 A3

ALANAS
- av. Oatlands 278 K11

ALAN BOND
- pl. Marsfield 282 B3

ALASKA
- st. Werrington 239 A11
- st. Warrimoo 203 B14
- ste.N Parramatta 278 H15
- st.s, Hornsby 221 H2

ALBERTA
- av. Cowan 104 B13
- gr. Jannali 460 G12
- st. Sydney .... F D5
- st. Sydney 3 K11

ALBERTO
- st. Lilyfield 10 F2

ALBI
- pl. Randwick 377 C14

ALBILLO
- pl. Eschol Park 481 D3

ALBION
- av. Merrylands 307 J13
- av. Paddington 4 F16
- av. Pymble 252 K1
- cl. Bossley Park 333 E9
- la. Annandale 16 E4
- la. Mosman 317 B6
- la. Paddington 4 F16
- la. St Peters 374 F14
- la. Waverley 377 G9
- la. Baulkham Hl 246 J2
- pl. Engadine 489 A8
- pl. Sydney .... E G1
- pl. Sydney 3 F8
- st. Annandale 16 E3
- st. Clovelly 377 F10
- st. Concord 342 B2
- st. Dundas 279 F13
- st. Harris Park 308 E6
- st. Leichhardt 16 E3
- st. Marrickville 373 J13
- st. Pennant Hills 220 J16
- st. Randwick 377 F10
- st. Roselands 401 A7
- st. Rozelle 344 D8
- st. Surry Hills .... F B12
- st. Surry Hills 3 J14
- st. Waverley 377 F10
- wy. Surry Hills .... F C13
- wy. Surry Hills 3 K15

ALBUERA
- rd. Epping 281 C3

ALBURY
- av. Campbelltown 512 C5
- ct. Harringtn Pk 478 G7
- st. Yagoona 368 J9

ALBYN
- la. Bexley 402 K14
- la. Strathfield 341 C15
- rd. Bexley 402 K14

ALCHIN
- st. Dharruk 241 B7

ALCOCK
- av. Casula 424 D3
- av. Casula 424 F4

ALCOOMIE
- st. Villawood 367 D3

ALDAN
- pl. St Clair 269 J14

ALDEBARAN
- st. Cranebrook 207 F6

ALDEN
- gr. Oakhurst 241 K1

ALDER
- av. Lane Cove W 283 H15
- dr. St Ives 224 A5
- gr. Menai 458 K14
- st. Clontarf 287 H15

ALDERNEY
- rd. Merrylands 307 A10
- st. Minto 482 G7

ALDERSON
- av. Liverpool 394 H9
- av. North Rocks 248 F11
- dr. Springwood 201 H1

ALDGATE
- st. Prospect 275 B12
- st. Sutherland 490 G5

ALDINGA
- pl. Bradbury 541 D1
- pl. Clarmnt Ms 268 H2
- pl. Forestville 255 H10

ALDOUS
- rd. Kemps Ck 300 G13

ALDUS
- cl. Hornsby W 161 J8

ALDRIDGE
- st. Stanhpe Gdn 215 B6

ALEPPO
- st. Quakers Hill 214 F13

ALERT
- pl. Yagoona 368 E15

ALESSANDRA
- dr. Kellyville 216 K6
- dr. Kellyville 217 A5

ALETA
- cl. Wahroonga 251 C2
- wy. Seven Hills 275 K6

ALEX
- av. Schofields 213 H6
- av. Baulkham Hl 217 A16
- pl. Bligh Park 150 H9

ALEXANDER
- av. Mosman 317 D10
- av. N Willoughby 285 F9
- av. Taren Point 462 J14
- cr. Mcquarie Fd 423 J16
- la. Surry Hills 20 C2
- la. Crows Nest, off
  Pacific Hwy 315 G7
- pde. Blacktown 273 J8
- pde. Carlingford 250 B15
- pde. Roseville 284 F6
- rd. Avalon 140 E21
- st. Alexandria 18 G13
- st. Auburn 339 A14
- st. Balmain 8 B7
- st. Bligh Park 150 B6
- st. Collaroy 229 A12
- st. Coogee 407 G2
- st. Crows Nest 315 G7
- st. Dundas Vy 280 A1
- st. Eveleigh 18 G12
- st. Manly 288 F6
- st. Paddington 21 B2
- st. Penshurst 431 G8
- st. Smithfield 335 H7
- st. Surry Hills 20 C2
- st. Sylvania 461 K11
- st. Tamarama 378 C6
- st. Yagoona 368 K9

ALEXANDRA
- av. Croydon 342 E12
- av. Westmead 277 E16
- cct. St Clair 269 J8
- cr. Bayview 169 A13
- cr. Glenbrook 264 E11
- dr. Harringtn Pk 478 K1
- dr. Camperdown 11 D16
- dr. Camperdown 17 E1
- dr. Camperdown 17 E11
- la. Glebe 11 G8
- la. Collaroy Plat 228 C9
- la. Cherrybrook 219 D9
- la. Newtown 374 H9
- la. Randwick, off
  Pine St 377 F9
- pl. Cecil Hills 362 J7
- pl. Auburn 339 C4
- pl. Ashfield 342 H14
- pl. Caringbah 492 G15
- pl. Harris Park 308 F6
- pl. Jannali 460 G13
- pl. Mcquarie Fd 424 B16
- pl. Newtown 374 G10
- pl. Padstow 399 D15
- rd. Rooty Hill 241 K14
- st. Rosehill 308 H5
- st. S Coogee 407 J5
- st. Rozelle 10 J4
- st. Sans Souci 433 B14
- st. Seven Hills 275 G3
- st. Turramurra 222 K8
- st. Wiley Park 400 J2
- st.n,Wiley Park 400 H2

ALEXIS
- pl. Rsemeadow 540 H3

ALFA
- pl. Ingleburn 453 F13

ALFORD
- rd. Beaumont Hills 215 D1
- st. Quakers Hill 243 D4

ALFORDS POINT
- pl. Alfords Point 429 C15
- rd. Illawong 459 A5
- rd. Menai 458 G10
- rd. Padstow Ht 429 C15

ALFRED
- av. Woolooware 493 J8
- la. Rozelle 10 K2
- la. Mascot, off
  Wentworth Av 405 F6
- pl. Quakers Hill 213 K8
- pl. S Turramrra 252 A8
- rd. Brookvale 258 B9
- rd. Chipping Ntn 396 E4
- rd. Forest Lodge 11 F14
- rd. Narraweena 258 B9
- st. Annandale 10 G15
- st. Bronte 377 K7
- st. Clemton Park 402 A3
- st. Cromer 228 D16
- st. Croydon 342 F11
- st. Granville 308 G10
- st. Harris Park 308 H8
- st. Hurstville 432 C6
- st. Leichhardt 10 C11
- st. Lewisham 15 B8
- st. Lilyfield 10 C11
- st. Marrickville 373 E15
- st. Mascot 405 F6
- st. Merrylands 307 H10
- st. Narraweena 258 C6
- st. Parramatta 308 H8
- st. Ramsgate Bch 433 G13
- st. Rhodes 311 D11
- st. Rhodes 311 C12
- st. Rosehill 308 H8
- st. Rozelle 10 J2
- st. Rozelle 11 A2
- st. St Peters 374 F14
- st. Sans Souci 433 G16
- st. Sydney .... B A7
- st. Sydney 1 H12
- st. Westmead 277 H16
- st. Woolwich 314 D14
- st.n,Neutral Bay 5 K9
- st.n,N Sydney 5 K9
- st.s, Milsons Point ...... K K16
- st.s, Milsons Point 5 J13

ALFREDA
- st. Coogee 377 G16

ALGERNON
- st. Oatley 461 B1

ALGIE
- cr. Kingswood 238 B14

ALGONA
- st. Bilgola 169 F7

ALI
- pde. Newington 310 B13
- pl. Glenwood 245 A1

ALIBERTI
- dr. Blacktown 273 J7

ALICANTE
- st. Minchinbury 271 G9

ALICE
- av. Newtown 374 G9
- av. Russell Lea 343 D6
- cl. Collaroy Plat 228 C9
- cl. Cherrybrook 219 D9
- la. Newtown 374 H9
- la. Randwick, off
  Pine St 377 F9
- pl. Cecil Hills 362 J7
- st. Auburn 339 C4
- st. Caringbah 492 G15
- st. Harris Park 308 F6
- st. Jannali 460 G13
- st. Mcquarie Fd 424 B16
- st. Newtown 374 G10
- st. Padstow 399 D15
- st. Rooty Hill 241 K14
- st. Rosehill 308 H5
- st. S Coogee 407 J5
- st. Rozelle 10 J4
- st. Sans Souci 433 B14
- st. Seven Hills 275 G3
- st. Turramurra 222 K8
- st. Wiley Park 400 J2
- st.n,Wiley Park 400 H2

24 GREGORY'S STREET DIRECTORY

STREETS AM

ALICE HANCOCK
cl. Castle Hill, off
Vittoria Smith Av. ...218 H13

ALICIA
la. Roselands 401 C4
pl. Kenthurst 155 J5
rd. Mt Krng-gai.........162 J12
st. Glenwood 215 C15

ALICK
st. Cabramatta 365 E10

ALINDA
cl. Middle Dural 157 K1

ALINGA
st. Cabramatta W 365 C8

ALINJARRA
rd. Tennyson 65 F11

ALINTA
cl. Thornleigh 221 C13

ALISON
cl. Cabramatta 365 D11
cl. Coogee 377 G14
rd. Centennial Pk 376 E8
rd. Coogee 377 E14
rd. Kensington 20 K16
rd. Kensington 376 E8
rd. Randwick 376 E8
st. Ashbury 372 D7
st. Croydon Pk 372 D7
st. Eastwood 281 J7
st. Roseville 284 C7
st. Russell Lea 343 E7
st. Seven Hills 245 D16

ALISTAIR
pl. Kellyville 217 C3

ALKARINGA
rd. Miranda 491 H8

ALKIRA
cct. Narraweena 257 J3
pl. Caringbah 493 C16
rd. Carlingford 249 F14
rd. St Ives 224 B15

ALKOO
av. Little Bay 437 B10

ALKOOMIE
av. Forestville 255 J9
av. S Penrith 266 K7
pl. Pymble 252 K8
st. Beverly Hills 401 B10

ALLAMBEE
cr. Beverly Hills 401 B10
st. Beverly Hills 401 B11

ALLAMBI
st. Colyton 270 G6

ALLAMBIE
av. Caringbah 492 G15
av. E Lindfield 255 A13
av. Northmead 277 E4
av. Allambie Ht 257 F9
rd. Castle Cove 285 K5
rd. Edensor Pk 333 F14
rd. Frenchs Frst 257 A7

ALLAN
av. Belmore 371 C14
av. Clovelly 377 K12
av. Ryde 311 J1
av. Turramurra 222 G14
la. Roseville Ch 285 D1
rd. Mulgoa 325 B1
st. Bexley 402 F13
st. Kangaroo Pt 461 J4
st. Lidcombe 339 F11
st. Roseville Ch 285 D1

ALLANDALE
dr. Baulkham Hl 246 H5

ALLANS
av. Petersham 15 E13

ALLARA
av. N Turramurra 223 F6
pl. Castle Hill 218 K6

ALLARD
av. Roseville Ch 285 C6
pl. Hassall Gr 211 K16
pl. Ingleburn 453 G10
st. Penrith 237 D2

ALLARS
st. Denistone W 280 J12

ALLAWAH
av. Carss Pk 432 G15
av. Elanora Ht 198 E16
av. Sefton 368 E5
av. Bangor 459 J15
av. Mt Colah 162 B15

| | Allawah Av 432 F14
la. | Carss Park, off
pl. | Greenwich 315 A7
pl. | Pymble 253 A3
st. | Blacktown 274 D2

ALLAY
st. Blacktown 243 K10

ALLDER
st. Yagoona 369 A8

ALLEGRA
av. Belmore 401 E4
la. Belmore, off
Allegra Av 401 E3

ALLEN
av. Alexandria 18 E14
av. Bilgola 170 B5
av. Alexandria 18 H13
av. Glebe 11 H8
pl. Menai 458 H14
pl. Minto 452 J16
pl. Penrith 236 J10
pl. Wetherill Pk 334 D2
pl. Blacktown 245 A9
st. Blaxland 233 K7
st. Canterbury 372 C15
st. Glebe 11 H8
st. Harris Park 308 E7
st. Hornebush 341 D7
st. Leichhardt 9 D13
st. N Strathfield 341 D7
st. Pyrmont 12 J7
st. S Hurstville 432 B10
st. S Wntwthvle 307 A6
st. Waterloo 19 D16
st. Wolli Creek 403 D1
wy. Dural 188 H13

ALLENA
cl. Georges Hall 367 K11

ALLENBY
cr. Strathfield 341 B14
la. Clontarf 287 F15
pl. Rossmore 389 F16
st. Canley Ht 365 D2
st. Clontarf 287 F14
st. Doonside 273 F1

ALLENBY PARK
pde. Allambie Ht 257 G11

ALLENDALE
st. Marayong 244 C6

ALLENGROVE
cr. North Ryde 282 H7

ALLENS
pde. Bondi Jctn 22 J9

ALLERTON
rd. Beecroft 250 D9

ALLEYNE
av. N Narrabeen 198 J16
st. Chatswood 285 E16

ALLIANCE
av. Revesby 398 E11

ALLIBONE
st. Ashbury 372 H6

ALLIEDALE
cl. Hornsby 221 G5

ALLIES
rd. Barden Rdg 488 G5

ALLIGATOR
pl. Kearns 451 B16

ALLINGHAM
st. Condell Park 398 B1

ALLINGTON
cr. Elanora Ht 198 E13

ALLIOTT
st. Bradbury 511 H11

ALLIRA
pl. Hassall Gr 211 K13

ALLISON
av. Lidcombe 339 H11
av. Auburn 338 K2
av. Lane Cove 314 G2
av. Menai 458 H12
dr. Glenmore Pk 265 J7
pde. Croydon 372 G2
pl. Kellyville 216 H4
rd. Cronulla 493 J15
rd. Guildford 337 D6

ALLISTER
st. Cremorne 316 F9

ALLMAN
av. Summer Hill 373 B4
st. Campbelltwn 511 E6

ALLOWRIE
rd. Villawood 367 B3

ALLPORT
wy. Claymore, off
Colquhoun Wy 481 C11

ALL SAINTS
cl. Cherrybrook 219 F14

ALLSOPP
av. Baulkham Hl 248 C8
dr. Cmbrdg Gdn 237 G3

ALLUM
pl. Glebe 12 C11
st. Bankstown 369 B16
st. Haberfield 343 A13
st. Yagoona 369 B16

ALLUNGA
cl. Mona Vale 169 E16

ALLWOOD
cr. Lugarno 429 H12

ALLWORTH
dr. Davidson 255 C2

ALMA
av. Campsie 371 G13
av. Erskinevle, off
Knight St 16 H15
av. Emu Heights 205 B16
pl. Rooty Hill 242 A16
pl. Thirlmere 565 D2
rd. Leppington 419 J9
rd. Mcquarie Pk 282 G1
rd. Maroubra 407 B9
rd. Padstow 429 B4
rd. Ashfield 372 G5
st. Clontarf 287 G15
st. Granville 308 A7
st. Hurstville 431 K7
st. Paddington 13 D12
st. Parramatta 308 A7
st. Pymble 253 D2
st. Rydalmere 309 J2
st. Vineyard 151 K9

ALMADA
st. Engadine 489 C9

ALMANDINE
pl. Eagle Vale 481 G5

ALMERIA
av. Baulkham Hl 246 H13

ALMETA
st. Schofields 213 J6

ALMONA
st. Glenwood 215 H11

ALMOND
pl. Casula 394 B16
pl. Casula 424 B1
st. Wentwthvle 277 A8
st. Wilton 568 K14

ALMORA
la. Mosman, off
Upper Almora St ...317 C6

ALOE
st. Quakers Hill 243 F3

ALOHA
st. Mascot 405 D3

ALONSO
cl. Rsemeadow 540 J6

ALPEN
la. Mount Druitt 241 B16

ALPHA
av. Roselands 400 K8
rd. Camden 507 B1
rd. Greystanes 305 E11
rd. Lane Cove 314 E4
rd. Northbridge 285 G15
rd. Willoughby 285 G15
st. Blacktown 244 F16
st. Chester Hill 337 H10

ALPHILL
av. Cabramatta 366 C6

ALPHIN
st. Lidcombe 339 H11

ALPHONSUS
wy. Auburn 338 K2

ALPIN
gr. Oakhurst 242 A4

ALPINE
cct. St Clair 269 G9
la. St Clair, off
Alpine Cct 269 F9
pl. Engadine 488 C12
pl. Mcquarie Fd 454 D3
wy. Glenwood 245 G1

ALPITA
st. Kareela 461 C14

ALROY
cr. Hassall Gr 212 B16

ALSACE
av. Bardwell Vy 402 K10
la. Peakhurst 430 C13

ALSON
st. Mount Druitt 271 D2

ALSOP
pl. Bligh Park 150 C7

ALSTON
dr. Berowra Ht 132 J3
st. Bexley North 402 C13
st. Glenmore Pk 266 E8
st. Kingsgrove 402 C13
wy. Roseville 284 E5

ALT
cl. West Hoxton 392 B12
cr. Davidson 225 C16
la. Queens Park 22 F12
rd. Doonside 273 E3
st. Ashfield 342 H16
st. Haberfield 343 C13
st. Queens Park 22 E12
st. Strathfield 336 C6

ALTAIR
pl. Hinchinbrk 393 D5
pl. Jamisontown 266 E2

ALTHORPE
dr. Green Valley 362 K8

ALTO
av. Seaforth 287 A4
pl. Artarmon 314 G1
st. S Wntwthvle 307 B6

ALTON
av. Concord 341 G7
la. Newtown 17 F12
st. Merrylands 307 J15
st. Woollahra 22 A2

ALTONA
av. Forestville 256 A7
pl. Blacktown 274 C3
pl. Greenacre 370 B11
pl. North Rocks 248 J16
st. Abbotsford 342 J1
st. Hornsby Ht 161 H16

ALUA
cl. North Manly 258 A13

ALVA
pl. Riverstone 183 C9

ALVERNA
st. Rooty Hill 272 D7

ALVERSTONE
st. Riverwood 400 B11

ALVIS
pl. Ingleburn 453 J10
pl. Plumpton 241 G10

ALVISIO
cl. Edensor Pk 333 G16

ALVISTON
st. Strathfield 341 E14

ALVONA
av. St Ives 254 A1

ALWYN
av. Wallacia 324 J12
av. Glenwood 215 H13

AMADIO
pl. Mt Pritchard ...364 J9

AMALFI
dr. Hornebush B ...310 J10
dr. Longueville 314 C10
st. Lurnea 394 G11

AMANDA
cl. Berowra Ht 133 A6
cl. Dean Park 213 A16
pl. Annangrove ...155 D4
pl. Ingleburn 453 D12

AMARAL
st. Narraweena 258 A5

AMARANTHUS
pl. Mcquarie Fd ...484 B5

AMARINA
av. Bass Hill 367 K5
av. Greenacre 370 G9

AMARNA
pde. Roseville 284 K1

AMAROO
av. Blaxland 234 E7
av. Castle Cove ...285 J4
av. Elanora Ht 198 B16
av. Georges Hall ...367 F12
av. Mt Colah 191 K2

av. Strathfield 371 B4
av. Wahroonga 222 C11
av. Mosman 317 F9
av. Mosman 317 E9
av. Bonnyrigg 364 B9
av. Kingswood 237 K12
av. Sylvania 461 G15

AMAROO PARK
dr. Annangrove 155 E11

AMARYLLIS
wy. Bidwill 211 D13

AMAX
av. Girraween 275 H15

AMAZON
la. St Clair, off
Amazon Pl 269 K16
pl. Kearns 481 D1
st. St Clair 269 J16
st. Seven Hills 275 E9

AMBER
cl. Bossley Park ...334 A7
cl. Parklea 215 A13
cl. Thornleigh 220 K12
la. Woolooware 493 F7
st. Bass Hill 367 F8
st. Eagle Vale 481 A7

AMBERDALE
av. Picnic Point 428 D9

AMBERLEA
cl. Castle Hill 218 J6
st. Glenwood 245 G3

AMBERWOOD
pl. Castle Hill 218 H16
pl. Menai 458 H13
st. Castle Hill 218 G15

AMBLECOTE
pl. Tahmoor 565 J8

AMBLER
cl. Emu Heights ..235 C5
pl. Narellan Vale ..478 K15

AMBLESIDE
dr. Castle Hill 247 K5
st. Collaroy Plat ...228 D12

AMBON
av. Holsworthy 426 F8
cl. Bossley Park ...334 A5
rd. Holsworthy 396 C15

AMBROSE
la. Condell Park 398 J4
st. Condell Park 398 H4
st. Glendenning 242 H5
st. Hunters Hill 313 K11

AMBROSIA
st. Mcquarie Fd 454 D6

AMBRYM
dr. Frenchs Frst 255 J2

AMBULANCE
av. Haymarket ....E E14
av. Haymarket 3 E15

AMBYNE
st. Woolooware 493 E8

AMEDE
pl. Illawong 459 K3

AMELIA
cl. Cecil Hills 362 F5
cr. Canley Ht 335 B14
gr. Pitt Town 92 H11
pl. N Narrabeen ...198 G14
st. North Ryde 282 G8
st. Waterloo 20 B16
wy. Bidwill 211 H13

AMELIA GODBEE
av. Glenhaven 218 B1

AMERICAN
ml. Rooty Hill 272 F5

AMESBURY
av. St Ives 224 B16
av. Sefton 368 F1

AMETHYST
pl. Eagle Vale 481 C7

AMHERST
st. Cammeray 315 J5
st. Guildford 337 E2

AMICITIA
cct. Old Tngabbie ...277 D7

AMIENS
av. Engadine 488 F16
av. Milperra 397 E11
av. Mosman 317 A3
av. Bossley Park ...334 A6
la. Woodcroft 243 K16
st. Clontarf 287 F14
rd. Moorebank ...395 D12

GREGORY'S STREET DIRECTORY 25

AM

STREETS

st. Gladesville 312 G12
wy. Matraville...........407 B15
AMILCAR
st. Ingleburn...........453 G12
AMINTA
cr. Hassall Gr..........211 K14
AMINYA
cr. Bradbury............541 D1
pl. Baulkham Hl 248 B10
pl. Riverview...........313 K5
pl. St Ives 224 B14
AMITAF
av. Caringbah..........492 E10
AMOR
st. Asquith..............191 H9
st. Hornsby.............191 H9
AMOS
la. Elizabeth Bay........13 A6
pl. Marayong 244 C6
pl. Sylvania.............461 K12
rd. West Hoxton......391 J7
st. Parramatta.........307 F4
st. Westmead 307 F4
AMOUR
av. Maroubra...........407 F9
st. Milperra.............398 A8
st. Revesby.............398 A8
AMOURIN
st. North Manly.......258 C13
AMPHITHEATRE
cct. Baulkham Hl 246 G9
AMRON
pl. Acacia Gdn.........214 H16
AMSTERDAM
st. Oakhurst............242 C3
AMUET
pl. Glenwood 215 B15
AMUNDSEN
st. Leumeah............482 H13
st. Tregear..............240 F7
AMUR
pl. Kearns...............451 B15
AMY
cl. Glendenning.......242 E2
la. Campsie............372 A13
la. Erskineville, off
Macdonald St.....374 K9
pl. Hornsby Ht........161 J11
pl. Narellan Vale......478 H15
rd. Peakhurst..........429 J1
st. Blakehurst..........432 A15
st. Campsie............371 J14
st. Erskineville.........374 K10
st. Marrickville........374 A9
st. Regents Pk........369 B1
st. Turrella..............403 D5
AMY HAWKINS
cct. Kellyville.............217 B1
ANAKAI
dr. Jamisontown.....236 A16
ANANA
rd. Elanora Ht..........198 F15
rd. N Narrabeen.......198 F15
ANASTASIO
rd. Liverpool............364 J15
ANATOL
pl. Pymble...............253 G4
ANCHORAGE
la. St Clair, off
Anchorage St.....270 J13
st. St Clair...............270 J13
ANCILIA
cl. Quakers Hill.......213 F7
ANCONA
av. Toongabbie........276 D7
rd. Turramurra........223 A7
ANCRUM
st. N Sydney..............5 B9
ANCURA
ct. Wattle Grove......396 B16
ANDAMAN
st. Kings Park.........244 F2
ANDAMOOKA
pl. Cartwright..........394 B4
ANDERSON
av. Blackett..............241 A3
av. Dundas..............279 B15
av. Hobartville.........118 D9
av. Liverpool............394 J3
av. Mt Pritchard.......364 E10
av. Panania..............398 B16
av. Panania..............428 B2
av. Ryde.................311 J2
av. S Turramrra.......252 A9
cl. Appin.................569 E7
la. Belmore.............401 G2
la. Concord, off
Archer St...........342 A2
la. Penrith...............237 B11
la. Ryde..................311 H2
la. Sefton, off
Torrington Av.....368 G3
pl. Cottage Pt..........135 F9
pl. S Windsor..........120 H15
rd. Concord.............342 A2
rd. Kings Lngly........246 C10
rd. Mortdale............430 G6
rd. Northmead.........278 A4
rd. Smeaton Gra......479 C5
st. Alexandria............18 J14
st. Bnksmeadw.......406 A12
st. Belmore.............401 G1
st. Bexley................432 F4
st. Chatswood.........284 J8
st. Double Bay..........14 D11
st. Kingsford...........406 H3
st. Neutral Bay............6 F6
st. Parramatta.........308 D6
st. St Helens Park....541 B6
st. Westmead 307 G4
ANDERTON
st. Marrickville........373 H11
ANDORA
pl. Glen Alpine 510 G11
ANDORRA
cl. Glendenning.......242 J4
ANDOVE
st. Belrose..............226 B14
ANDOVER
cr. Hebersham........241 F6
la. Allawah..............432 G8
st. Carlton...............432 G7
ANDRE
pl. Blacktown..........274 E10
ANDREA
cl. Bonnyrigg..........364 F5
ANDREAS
st. Petersham...........15 F6
ANDREW
av. Canley Ht...........365 C1
av. West Pymble......253 A12
cl. Mt Colah............192 C5
la. Melrose Pk.........310 J2
pl. Birrong..............368 K4
pl. Girraween..........276 D12
pl. North Rocks.......248 G15
st. Bronte................378 A8
st. Brooklyn...............75 K11
st. Clovelly..............377 K12
st. Davidson............225 D15
st. Melrose Pk.........310 J3
st. Richmond...........119 D4
st. West Ryde..........310 J3
ANDREW LLOYD
dr. Doonside............273 E5
ANDREW NASH
la. Parramatta, off
George St...........308 D2
ANDREWS
av. Ashbury.............372 G9
av. Bondi.................378 B5
av. Toongabbie........276 F10
cct. Horngsea Pk......392 F12
pl. St Helens Park....541 A8
pl. Yellow Rock.......173 G14
rd. Cranebrook.........237 B1
ANDREW THOMPSON
dr. McGraths Hl.......121 J12
pl. Colyton..............270 H9
ANDREW TOWN
pl. Richmond...........118 C5
ANDRO
pl. Werrington.........238 G10
ANDROMEDA
cr. Engadine............488 D11
dr. Cranebrook........207 F5
ANDY
st. Guildford W.......336 J3
ANDYS
ct. St Clair...............269 G11
ANEBO
st. Liverpool............394 K4
ANELLA
av. Castle Hill..........217 C12
ANEMBO
av. Georges Hall......367 J11
cr. Killara................283 F1
pl. Eastwood............281 F2
rd. Berowra.............133 D15
rd. Duffys Frst.........194 J7
st. Bradbury............511 G15
ANEMONE
pl. Kirrawee............461 A14
ANEURA
ct. Wattle Grove......396 C15
ANGARA
cct. Glenwood 245 J2
cl. Kearns...............451 C16
ANGAS
cl. Barden Rdg........488 J3
st. Meadowbank.....311 F4
st. Wrrngtn Cty.......238 H7
ANGEL
cl. Cherrybrook.......219 F15
ct. Glenwood 245 D2
la. Newtown..............17 H13
pl. Cherrybrook.......219 F15
pl. Forestville..........256 B8
pl. Sydney..................C J1
pl. Sydney...................3 G1
rd. Strathfield..........341 G16
st. Newtown..............17 G16
st. Wrrngtn Cty.......238 G6
ANGELA
st. Cecil Hills...........362 F4
ANGELINA
cr. Cabramatta........365 E10
ct. Green Valley.......362 K9
ANGELINI
av. Rozelle................10 G1
ANGELO
av. Liverpool............394 H10
st. Burwood............371 J2
st. N Sydney...............K B1
st. N Sydney................5 E5
st. Woolwich...........314 G12
ANGLE
rd. Grays Point........491 A14
rd. Leumeah............482 B14
rd.s, Leumeah...........512 C1
st. Balgowlah..........287 J8
ANGLEDOOL
av. Hinchinbrk.........392 H3
ANGLESEA
st. Bondi.................377 H4
ANGLE VALE
rd. Edensor Pk........363 D1
ANGLO
la. Greenwich..........315 B7
rd. Campsie............371 J14
rd. Greenwich..........315 B7
sq. Carlton...............432 J8
st. Chatswood W....284 F9
ANGOPHORA
av. Kingswood.........267 G2
cct. Mt Annan...........509 F3
cr. Forestville..........255 E8
ct. Voyager Pt.........427 B5
gr. Greenacre..........370 F5
pl. Alfords Point......459 B3
pl. Castle Hill...........248 E3
pl. Pennant Hills......250 J4
pl. Valley Ht............202 G9
ANGORRA
rd. Terrey Hills.........196 C6
ANGOURIE
ct. Dural.................219 B3
pl. Bow Bowing.......452 C14
ANGUS
av. Auburn..............339 B9
av. Epping...............280 E1
av. Lane Cove..........314 G2
av. Peakhurst..........430 G3
cr. Yagoona............368 H10
pl. Busby................363 K16
pl. St Andrews........482 A3
rd. Kenthurst...........188 D8
rd. Schofields...........212 H4
rd. Smeaton Gra......479 F5
st. Earlwood...........402 D6
ANICH
pl. Prestons............423 A1
ANIMBO
st. Miranda............491 K6
ANISEED
st. Prestons............393 H14
ANITA
st. Glenwood..........215 E12
ANITRA
av. Kareela.............461 D12
pl. Shalvey.............210 H15
ANJOU
cct. Cecil Hills...........362 C4
ANJUDY
cl. Casula................394 F16
ANKA
av. Old Tngabbie......276 J10
ANKALI
pl. North Manly.......258 A14
ANN
cr. Mt Pritchard.......364 H13
pl. Bligh Park..........150 F8
pl. Narellan Vale......508 J2
st. Balmain..................8 A10
st. Bondi Jctn...........22 J8
st. Earlwood...........372 G16
st. Enfield...............371 H4
st. Fairfield Ht.........335 J10
st. Faulconbdg........172 B5
st. Frenchs Frst.......256 D6
st. Lidcombe...........339 H7
st. Longueville........314 D8
st. Marrickville........373 J13
st. N Willoughby.....285 G10
st. Surry Hills...............F E12
st. Surry Hills...............3 K14
st. Willoughby.........285 G10
st. Wolli Creek........403 H7
ANNABELLA
rd. Camden.............506 K5
ANNABELLE
cr. Kellyville.............216 F5
pl. Mt Colah............162 E16
pl. Pymble..............253 A9
ANNAM
rd. Bayview............168 J15
ANNAN
pl. Baulkham Hl......246 G11
ANNANDALE
st. Annandale............16 G4
st. Darling Point........13 H6
ANNANGROVE
rd. Annangrove.......187 B7
rd. Kenthurst...........187 B7
rd. Rouse Hill..........184 H5
ANNANVALE
cct. Mt Annan...........479 D12
ANN CLARK
av. Schofields..........213 F13
ANNE
av. Seven Hills.........245 A16
cr. Blaxland.............234 C5
pl. Cecil Hills...........363 A3
pl. Cherrybrook.......219 K4
pl. Wahroonga........223 B5
pl. Wilberforce..........92 C2
st. Blacktown..........274 C4
st. Oatlands............278 K11
st. Revesby.............399 A12
st. St Marys............239 F8
wy. Mcquarie Fd.......424 F15
ANNELIESE
pl. Castle Hill...........218 C10
ANNE MARIE
cl. St Ives...............223 K16
pl. Belfield...............371 F10
pl. Carlingford.........249 E14
ANNESLEY
st. Leichhardt............10 C12
ANNETT
st. Emu Plains.........235 F12
ANNETTE
av. Ingleburn...........453 B6
av. Kogarah.............433 E5
pl. Baulkham Hl.......248 C7
pl. Belrose..............226 B16
pl. Hobartville.........118 G7
st. Cabramatta W.....365 B6
st. Oatley................431 C16
ANNE WILLIAM
dr. W Pnnant Hl.......249 F7
ANNFIELD
st. Kellyville Rdg.....215 A2
ANNIE
la. West Ryde.........281 B16
st. Hurstville...........401 J16
ANNIE LEGGETT
prm. Rhodes.............311 C9
ANNIE SPENCE
cl. Emu Heights......235 B3
ANNIVERSARY
st. Botany...............405 H16
ANN MINCHIN
wy. Minchinbury.......272 A10
ANNUAL
la. St Clair..............270 C14
ANSCHAU
cr. Windsor.............121 D8
ANSELM
st. Strathfield S.......371 A4
ANSON
pl. Castle Hill...........247 F1
ANTARES
av. Hinchinbrk.........393 D4
pl. Cranebrook........207 F5
ANTHEA
pl. Dean Park..........212 K16
ANTHONY
av. Mt Riverview......234 C1
av. Padstow............429 C3
cl. Beacon Hill.........257 H5
cl. St Ives...............254 A1
cr. Kingswood..........238 A14
dr. Rsemeadow.......540 G3
la. Matraville...........406 J15
la. West Ryde, off
Anthony Rd........281 D15
rd. Bargo.................567 J1
rd. Castle Hill...........217 J15
rd. Catherine Fd.......419 F7
rd. Denistone..........281 C12
rd. Leppington.........419 F7
rd. West Ryde.........281 D12
st. Blacktown..........245 A7
st. Carlingford.........250 B16
st. Chatswood.........285 A10
st. Croydon.............342 F16
st. Epping...............250 B16
st. Fairfield..............336 E7
st. Matraville...........406 K15
st. Yagoona............369 D8
ANTIAS
av. Pyrmont..............12 D2
ANTILL
cl. Camden S..........507 A10
cr. Baulkham Hl......247 H5
pl. Blackett..............241 C2
pl. Mt Pritchard.......364 J9
rd. Mt Pritchard.......364 H9
st. Blaxland.............234 A7
st. Picton................563 E11
st. Thirlmere...........565 B5
st. Yennora.............337 D9
wy. Airds.................511 J16
ANTIQUE
cr. Woodcroft..........243 F7
ANTOINE
st. Rydalmere.........309 G3
ANTOINETTE
av. Narellan Vale......508 E1
cl. Warrawee..........222 E13
ANTON
pl. Bonnyrigg..........363 J9
rd. Luddenham........357 F1
ANTONIA
cr. Cranebrook........207 B13
ANTONIETTA
st. Cabramatta........365 E11
ANTONIO
cl. Rsemeadow.......540 K4
st. St Johns Pk.......364 G2
ANTRIM
st. Hebersham........241 F3
ANTWERP
st. Auburn..............338 K10
st. Bankstown.........399 A6
ANULLA
pl. Wahroonga........222 A7
ANVIL
pl. Jamisontown.....236 B15
rd. Seven Hills.........276 E3
ANZAC
av. Cammeray.........315 K7
av. Collaroy............229 A15
av. Collaroy Plat.......228 J14
av. Denistone..........281 F14
av. Engadine............518 J1
av. Fairfield.............336 F13
av. Ryde.................281 F14
av. Smeaton Gra......479 C9
av. West Ryde.........281 F14
la. Campbelltown....511 E4
la. West Ryde, off
Wattle St............281 E15
mw. Holsworthy........396 B14
pde. Chifley..............437 C5
pde. Kensington.........376 E9
pde. Kingsford...........406 F1
pde. La Perouse.........436 J14

26 GREGORY'S STREET DIRECTORY

STREETS AR

pde. La Perouse 436 K14
pde. Little Bay 437 A11
pde. Malabar 437 C5
pde. Maroubra 407 A6
pde. Matraville 407 B15
pde. Moore Park 20 G4
pde. Phillip Bay 436 K13
rd. Bangor 459 B13
rd. Holsworthy 396 B14
rd. Moorebank 395 F13
rd. Wattle Grove 395 F13
sq. Campsie 371 K13
st. Canterbury 372 E16
st. Chullora 369 H10
st. Greenacre 369 H10
st. Miranda 492 D6
st. N St Marys 239 K10

ANZIO
av. Allambie Ht 257 C9

AOMA
st. Scotland I 168 H3

APACHE
gr. Stanhpe Gdn 215 C11
rd. Bossley Park 333 K10

APANIE
pl. Westleigh 220 E8

APAP
av. Castle Hill 217 C6

APARA
st. Forestville 255 F10

APERTA
pl. Beacon Hill 257 K7

APEX
av. Picnic Point 428 F7
st. Blacktown 274 D7
st. Liverpool 365 B15
st. Naremburn 315 F1

APIA
pl. Lethbrdg Pk 240 F2
st. Guildford 337 E5

APLIN
cl. St Ives Ch 223 J6
rd. Bonnyrigg Ht 363 E8

APOLLO
av. Baulkham Hl 246 K14
av. West Pymble 252 G12
cl. St Clair 269 F11
pl. Eastwood 280 E7
pl. Lane Cove W 283 F15
pl. Port Hacking 522 K3
st. Greenfld Pk 334 C13
st. Warriewood 198 H5

APPALOOSA
cct. Blairmount 481 A14

APPIAN
cct. Baulkham Hl 246 G10
wy. Burwood 371 K2

APPIN
pl. Engadine 489 D10
pl. St Marys 239 F4
rd. Ambarvale 511 B15
rd. Appin 569 F9
rd. Bradbury 511 B15
rd. Campbelltown 511 B15
rd. Gilead 540 H15
rd. Rsemeadow 540 H15
rd. St Helens Park 540 H15

APPLAUSE
st. Riverwood 400 C10

APPLE
pl. Mcquarie Fd 454 A4
st. Wentwthvle 277 B8

APPLEBEE
st. St Peters 374 J12

APPLEBOX
av. Glenwood 215 H16

APPLEBY
pl. Plumpton 242 B8

APPLECOT
la. Mt Wilson 58 H8

APPLECROSS
av. Castle Hill 218 A7

APPLEGUM
gr. Blaxlands Rdg 65 D5
pl. Mt Riverview 234 E3
pl. Prestons 393 K14

APPLETON
av. Lurnea 394 D11

APPLETREE
dr. Cherrybrook 219 J7
gr. Oakhurst 211 H16
pl. Menai 458 H13

APPS
av. N Turramurra 223 D8
pl. Narellan Vale 508 K1

APSLEY
av. Kingsford 406 H4
ct. Cranebrook 206 J9
la. Kingsford 406 H4
pl. Campbelltown 511 J8
pl. Taren Point 462 G13
st. Guildford 337 E1
st. Penshurst 431 F5

AQUA
pl. Marayong 244 B5

AQUAMARINE
dr. Eagle Vale 481 E8
st. Quakers Hill 214 H13

AQUARIUS
cr. Erskine Park 300 K1
la. Erskine Park, off Aquarius Cr 300 K1

AQUATIC
dr. Frenchs Frst 257 A7

AQUILA
la. Erskine Park, off Pegasus St 301 A2
pl. Erskine Park 301 A2

AQUILINA
dr. Plumpton 242 C11

ARA
cr. Narraweena 258 A1
pl. Hinchinbrk 393 E3

ARAB
rd. Padstow 399 C15

ARABANOO
st. Seaforth 287 C7

ARABELLA
pl. Bella Vista 246 G5
st. Longueville 314 D9
st. Northwood 314 D9

ARAFURA
av. Cranebrook 207 C10

ARAGON
st. Cecil Hills 362 D4

ARAKOON
av. Penrith 237 D7

ARALUEN
av. Moorebank 396 G6
av. St Marys 239 G14
pl. Bayview 168 F11
pl. Camden S 507 D12
pl. Castle Hill 217 E2
pl. Glenhaven 217 E2
pl. Sutherland 460 H15
rd. Lansvale 366 C10
st. Kingsford 407 A4

ARAMON
cl. Edensor Pk 363 E2

ARANA
cl. Bangor 459 J15
cl. Banksia 403 G12
cl. Georges Hall 368 A15
pl. Cabramatta W 365 C7
st. Manly Vale 287 G3

ARANDA
dr. Davidson 255 E2
dr. Frenchs Frst 255 E2

ARANDA PATH
Winmalee 173 B10

ARARAT
cl. Bossley Park 333 E9

ARBITRATION
st. Sydney B C9

ARBOR
gln. Castle Hill 217 E2

ARBOUR
gr. Quakers Hill 213 G9

ARBROATH
pl. St Andrews 482 A3

ARBUTUS
st. Canley Ht 365 E3
st. Canley Vale 365 E3
st. Mosman 317 C6

ARCADIA
av. Drummoyne 344 B3
av. Gymea Bay 491 C11
av. Woolooware 493 F7
cr. Berowra 133 C11
la. Colyton, off Arcadia Pl 270 B8
la. Coogee 377 H14
la. Glebe 11 G10
pl. Colyton 270 B8
rd. Arcadia 129 E16
rd. Chester Hill 368 D1
rd. Galston 159 D2
rd. Glebe 11 G10
st. Coogee 377 G14
st. Merrylands W 307 A12
st. Penshurst 431 C1

ARCADIAN
cct. Carlingford 279 C6
pl. Blaxlands Rdg 65 B6

ARCHBALD
av. Btn-le-Sds 403 K15

ARCHBOLD
rd. Eastern Ck 271 E12
rd. E Lindfield 254 H15
rd. Lindfield 254 H15
rd. Minchinbury 271 E12
rd. Roseville 284 J1

ARCHDALE
wky. Wahroonga 222 D7

ARCHDALL
gr. Bella Vista 246 F4

ARCHER
cl. Bossley Park 333 K8
cr. Bankstown 399 D6
ct. St Clair 270 E11
la. Windsor Dn 180 H1
pl. Maroubra 407 C8
pl. Minto 483 A3
row. Menai 458 K15
st. Blacktown 274 B6
st. Burwood 342 B12
st. Chatswood 284 J6
st. Concord 341 K2
st. Mosman 317 A8
st. Mount Druitt 271 B4
st. Roseville 284 J6
wy. West Hoxton 392 D10

ARCHIBALD
cr. Rsemeadow 540 G8
st. Belmore 401 H5
st. Granville 308 G14
st. Padstow 399 B13

ARCHITECTS
pl. St Clair 270 B10

ARCTIC
wy. Kellyville Rdg, off Atlantic Pl 214 K4

ARCTURUS
cl. Cranebrook 207 F6

ARDATH
av. Panania 428 B5

ARDEN
la. Clovelly, off Arden St 377 H12
la. Glebe 11 K9
pl. Frenchs Frst 256 G3
rd. Pymble 253 A2
st. Clovelly 377 H12
st. Coogee 377 H16
st. S Coogee 407 G3
st. Waverley 377 H12

ARDGRYFFE
st. Burwood Ht 372 A4

ARDILL
la. Warrimoo 203 B15

ARDING
st. Lane Cove N 284 B15

ARDISIA
pl. Loftus 489 K12

ARDITTOS
la. Strathfield 341 E12

ARDNO
st. Busby 363 G14

ARDRISHAIG
pl. Glenhaven 218 F6

ARDROSSAN
cr. St Andrews 451 K14
rd. Engadine 488 J11

ARDSLEY
av. Frenchs Frst 256 D3

ARDUA
pl. Engadine 488 D15

ARELEY
ct. Jamisontown 266 E5

ARGENTS
rd. Wilberforce 67 F14

ARGO
pl. Miranda 461 J16
wy. Airds 512 C11

ARGONNE
st. N Strathfield 341 C3

ARGOWAN
rd. Schofields 183 B16

ARGUIMBAU
st. Annandale 10 J13

ARGUS
la. Parramatta 308 F3

ARGYLE
av. Ryde 312 B2
cr. S Coogee 407 E6
la. Millers Pt A B3
la. Riverstone 182 F14
pl. Bonnyrigg Ht 363 B6
pl. Emu Plains 235 B9
pl. Kareela 461 B14
pl. Mcquarie Fd 423 J16
pl. Millers Pt A C2
pl. Millers Pt 1 D9
pl. W Pnnant Hl 249 A6
st. Auburn 309 D15
st. Bilgola 169 F8
st. Camden 477 B15
st. Carlton 432 J6
st. Dawes Point A D2
st. Dawes Point 1 E9
st. Millers Pt A D2
st. Millers Pt 1 E9
st. Parramatta 308 B4
st. Penshurst 431 B2
st. Picton 563 D13
st. Picton 563 E11
st. Riverstone 182 F13
st. S Windsor 120 J12
st. The Rocks A J3
st. The Rocks 1 G10
st. Wilton 568 K14
st. Wolli Creek 403 H7

ARGYLE REACH
rd. Freemns Rch 91 E12
rd. Wilberforce 91 G8

ARGYLE STAIRS
The Rocks A J3

ARGYLL
pl. Cheltenham 250 J6
rd. Winmalee 173 C12
rd. Winmalee 173 D12

ARIANA
pl. Acacia Gdn 214 J16

ARIANNA
av. Normanhurst 221 J11

ARIEL
cr. Cranebrook 207 C16
pl. Rsemeadow 540 K6

ARIELLA
pl. Edensor Pk 333 E14

ARIES
pl. Erskine Park 270 G15

ARIETTA
cct. Harringtn Pk 478 F7

ARIKA
cl. Bangor 459 G15

ARILLA
av. Riverwood 400 F11
pl. Bangor 459 J15
rd. Pymble 253 A3

ARINA
rd. Bargo 567 K12
rd. Bargo 567 K6

ARINYA
st. Kingsgrove 401 K7

ARISAIG
pl. St Andrews 451 K16

ARISTOTLE
la. Winmalee 173 H8

ARIZONA
pl. North Rocks 278 H2
pl. Riverwood 400 A12
pl. Stanhpe Gdn 215 C11

ARJEZ
pl. Marayong 244 B5

ARK
pl. Riverstone 183 A4

ARKANA
pl. Engadine 489 A8
st. Telopea 279 D7

ARKANSAS
pl. Kearns 451 C16

ARKELL
dr. Bligh Park 150 H5

ARKENA
av. Epping 250 C14

ARKLAND
st. Cammeray 316 B4

ARKLEY
st. Bankstown 399 F6

ARLENE
pl. Plumpton 241 G10

ARLEWIS
st. Chester Hill 338 B14

ARLEY
pl. North Rocks 248 K13

ARLINGTON
av. Castle Hill 217 G10
av. Riverstone 183 G9
dr. Fairlight 288 C10
st. Dulwich Hill 373 B8
st. Five Dock 342 J12
st. Rockdale 403 B13

ARMATA
ct. Wattle Grove 426 B1

ARMEN
wy. Hornsby Ht 161 G16

ARMENTIERES
av. Milperra 397 G11
wy. Matraville 407 B15

ARMIDALE
av. Hoxton Park 392 G6
cr. Castle Hill 218 J9
pl. Engadine 488 G12

ARMINE
wy. Beaumont Hills 185 J14

ARMITAGE
dr. Glendenning 242 E3
la. Mosman, off Rosherville Rd 317 D2

ARMITREE
st. Kingsgrove 401 E7
st. Kingsgrove 401 F8

ARMOUR
av. Camden S 507 B14
av. Kellyville Rdg 215 A2
av. Kellyville Rdg 215 C2

ARMSTEIN
cr. Werrington 238 F11
la. Werrington, off Armstein Cr 238 G11

ARMSTRONG
ct. Bnkstn Aprt 367 J16
ct. Bnkstn Aprt 397 J1
la. Lidcombe 339 H10
pl. Castle Hill 218 C10
pl. Dean Park 242 H1
st. Ashcroft 394 D1
st. Ashfield 372 J7
st. Cammeray 315 H4
st. Raby 451 D12
st. Seaforth 286 K4
st. Willoughby 285 E15
st.e, Willoughby 285 F16

ARMYTAGE
pl. Glen Alpine 510 E13

ARNCLIFFE
rd. Earlwood 403 C4
st. Wolli Creek 403 H7

ARNDELL
st. Camden S 507 B10
st. Windsor 121 E7
wy. Minto 482 H6

ARNDILL
av. Baulkham Hl 247 E3

ARNETT
st. Pendle Hill 306 F2

ARNHEM
pl. Leumeah 482 F9
pl. Willmot 210 C12
rd. Allambie Ht 257 B8

ARNO
tce. Glenwood 245 K4

ARNOLD
av. Camden S 507 C16
av. Green Valley 363 A11
av. Kellyville 215 J8
av. St Marys 270 A4
av. Yagoona 369 C10
la. Darlinghurst F K8
la. Panania 428 D2
pl. Darlinghurst F J6
pl. Glenwood 215 K16
pl. Glenwood 245 K1
pl. Menai 458 H11
st. Killara 254 B12
st. Leumeah 512 C2
st. N Richmond 87 C14
st. Peakhurst 430 B3
st. Queens Park 22 H13
st. Ryde 312 D5
st. Wetherill Pk 334 E6

GREGORY'S STREET DIRECTORY 27

AR STREETS

ARNOLD JANSSEN
- dr. Beaumont Hills ...185 K16
- dr. Beaumont Hills ...215 K1

ARNOTT
- cr. Warriewood ...199 D11
- rd. Wetherill Pk ...304 E13
- rd. Marayong ...244 A4

ARNOTTS
- pl. Huntingwd ...273 D12

AROA
- pl. Glenfield ...424 D13

ARONIA
- av. St Ives ...224 G9

AROONA
- rd. Oxford Falls ...227 A13

ARRABRI
- av. Warriewood ...199 B8

ARRAGONG
- st. Bangor ...459 J15

ARRAN
- pl. St Andrews ...481 J3

ARRAS
- pde. Ryde ...312 C3
- st. Prestons ...423 E2

ARRAWATTA
- cl. Edensor Pk ...333 D14

ARRIONGA
- pl. Hornsby ...191 D12

ARRIVAL
- ct. Mascot ...404 D8

ARROW
- la. Old Tngabbie ...277 F10
- la. Raby ...481 F1

ARROWFIELD
- av. Burwood ...371 H1
- dr. Wattle Grove ...396 A16

ARROWHEAD
- rd. Greenfld Pk ...333 K12

ARROWSMITH
- st. Glenwood ...215 E15

ARRUNGA
- av. Roseville ...284 G1
- rd. Arcadia ...129 C15
- st. Dundas ...279 F14

ARTARMON
- rd. Artarmon ...285 A14
- rd. Willoughby ...285 D16

ARTEGALL
- st. Bankstown ...399 A8

ART GALLERY
- rd. Campbelltown ...511 C7
- rd. Sydney ...D J1
- st. Sydney ...4 C3

ARTHUR
- av. Blacktown ...244 A11
- av. Cronulla ...494 A15
- la. Fairlight ...288 D7
- la. Lavender Bay ...K H14
- la. Lavender Bay ...5 H12
- la. Randwick ...377 A14
- st. Surry Hills ...20 C3
- st. Bonnet Bay ...460 B7
- st. Ashfield ...372 G4
- st. Auburn ...338 J5
- st. Balmain ...7 J13
- st. Bankstown ...399 B7
- st. Baulkham Hl ...247 H12
- st. Bellevue Hill ...14 H14
- st. Bexley ...402 H13
- st. Bonnet Bay ...460 C7
- st. Burwood Ht ...372 B4
- st. Cabramatta ...365 J7
- st. Carlton ...432 F6
- st. Chipping Ntn ...397 A4
- st. Concord ...341 H5
- st. Croydon ...372 B4
- st. Croydon Pk ...372 B4
- st. Dee Why ...258 F6
- st. Dover Ht ...348 F14
- st. Edgecliff ...13 E14
- st. Fairlight ...288 E7
- st. Five Dock ...343 D8
- st. Forest Lodge ...11 F13
- st. Forestville ...255 D8
- st. Granville ...308 H10
- st. Granville ...308 H8
- st. Homebush W ...340 E9
- st. Hornsby ...191 J13
- st. Killara ...254 A8
- la. Lavender Bay ...K H15
- la. Lavender Bay ...5 H17
- st. Leichhardt ...10 A13
- st. Marrickville ...373 H13
- st. Marsden Pk ...182 B14
- st. Mascot ...405 H4

ARTHUR (cont)
- st. Merrylands W ...307 A12
- st. Parramatta ...308 A6
- st. Punchbowl ...400 C4
- st. Randwick ...376 K14
- st. Redfern ...19 J6
- st. Rodd Point ...343 D8
- st. Rookwood ...340 E9
- st. Rosehill ...308 J6
- st. Rosehill ...308 H8
- st. Ryde ...282 C12
- st. Strathfield ...340 J11
- st. Surry Hills ...20 B2
- st. Surry Hills ...20 C3
- st. Warrimoo ...203 B14
- st.n.N Sydney ...K H10
- st.n.N Sydney ...5 H9

ARTHUR PHILLIP
- dr. N Richmond ...86 K13

ARTHURS
- cir. Mt Colah ...162 D9

ARTHURSLEIGH
- st. Burwood ...342 B11

ARTHUR TAYLOR
- av. Matraville ...436 G9

ARTIE
- st. Carramar ...366 G1

ARTILLERY
- cr. Holsworthy ...426 F3
- rd. Seven Hills ...245 H16
- rd. Manly ...289 B13
- rd. Holsworthy ...425 D11
- rd. Holsworthy ...426 G12
- rd. Seven Hills ...276 F2

ARTLETT
- st. Edgecliff ...13 F11

ARTORNISH
- pl. Campbelltown ...511 E6

ARU
- pl. Kings Park ...244 J2

ARUM
- pl. Mcquarie Fd ...454 D6
- wy. Cherrybrook ...219 G14

ARUMA
- av. Kellyville ...216 H8
- cl. Chipping Ntn ...396 D5
- pl. Dharruk ...241 C9

ARUNDEL
- av. Horsley Pk ...302 D14
- st. Engadine ...489 A11
- st. Forest Lodge ...11 K16
- st. Forest Lodge ...18 C1
- st. Longueville ...314 D9
- st. West Pymble ...252 G10
- wy. Cherrybrook ...219 C14

ARUNDELL
- st. Dharruk ...241 D1

ARUNDEL PARK
- dr. St Clair ...270 F14

ARUNDLE
- rd. Bass Hill ...367 J8

ARUNTA
- av. Green Valley ...363 G11
- cl. Bangor ...459 F15
- ct. Leumeah ...482 G15

ARWON
- av. Casula ...394 E16

ASAPH
- cl. Hornsby Ht ...161 E15

ASCHE
- st. Doonside ...243 B9

ASCOT
- av. Wahroonga ...222 C2
- av. Zetland ...376 A11
- dr. Chipping Ntn ...366 G13
- dr. Chipping Ntn ...366 F15
- gln. Stanhpe Gdn ...215 F6
- pl. Menai ...458 B3
- pl. S Penrith ...266 H1
- pl. Wilberforce ...92 A2
- rd. Kenthurst ...157 H9
- st. Bexley ...402 H13
- st. Canley Ht ...365 E4
- st. Kensington ...376 F11
- st. Randwick ...376 F11

ASEKI
- av. Glenfield ...424 C14

ASH
- av. Caringbah ...492 F13
- cl. Bossley Park ...333 H11
- la. Haberfield ...343 A13
- pl. Bradbury ...511 D9
- pl. Lugarno ...429 H16

ASH (cont)
- pl. Narellan Vale ...478 J14
- st. S Coogee ...407 H8
- rd. Prestons ...393 G13
- rd. Prestons ...393 J8
- st. Blacktown ...243 K15
- st. Cherrybrook ...219 G12
- st. Georges Hall ...367 F11
- st. Greystanes ...306 E4
- st. N St Marys ...239 K10
- st. Sydney ...C J1
- st. Sydney ...3 G1

ASHBURN
- cl. Baulkham Hl ...216 E15
- cl. Bella Vista ...216 D15
- la. Gladesville ...312 H11
- st. Gladesville ...312 G12

ASHBURNER
- st. Manly ...288 H11

ASHBURTON
- av. S Turramrra ...252 B10
- ct. Kellyville ...186 H16

ASHBY
- av. Yagoona ...369 C10
- st. Bargo ...567 A3
- la. Randwick ...377 D5
- st. Guildford ...338 A7
- st. Kingsgrove ...401 G13
- st. Prospect ...274 F12

ASHCOTT
- st. Kings Lngly ...245 D7

ASHCROFT
- av. Casula ...394 K14
- st. Ermington ...280 B13
- st. Georges Hall ...367 E14

ASHDOWN
- pl. Frenchs Frst ...256 F3

ASHER
- pl. Campbelltown ...511 E6
- st. Coogee ...407 G2

ASHERS
- la. Artarmon ...314 J2

ASHFIELD
- pl. Glen Alpine ...540 C2

ASHFORD
- av. Castle Hill ...217 F13
- av. Milperra ...397 J11
- cct. Currans Hill ...479 K15
- cl. Hinchinbrk ...392 H5
- st. St Clair ...270 G14
- la. St Clair, off
    Ashford Gr ...270 G14
- rd. Cherrybrook ...219 C14
- rd. Vineyard ...152 F12
- st. Ashfield ...372 J8

ASHFORDBY
- st. Chipping Ntn ...396 F1

ASHGATE
- av. Vaucluse ...348 C6

ASHGROVE
- cr. Blacktown ...274 F9
- st. St Johns Pk ...364 F1

ASHLAR
- pl. West Hoxton ...392 C12
- st. St Ives ...224 D6

ASHLEIGH MADISON
- wy. Mt Colah ...191 K4

ASHLEY
- av. W Pnnant Hl ...249 G8
- st. St Johns Pk ...364 F1
- gr. Gordon ...253 H5
- la. Hornsby ...221 F1
- la. Westmead ...277 G16
- pde. Fairlight ...288 B10
- st. Chatswood ...284 J7
- st. Hornsby ...221 F1
- st. Roseville ...285 A6
- st. Tamarama ...378 A7

ASHMEAD
- av. Castle Hill ...217 H9
- av. Revesby ...428 E8
- la. Minto ...483 B1
- st. Minto ...483 C1

ASHMONT
- st. Prestons ...393 B15

ASHMORE
- av. Pymble ...252 J2
- st. Erskineville ...375 A8

ASHTEAD
- pde. Stanhpe Gdn ...215 B5

ASHTON
- av. Chester Hill ...338 E1
- av. Earlwood ...372 J16
- av. Ermington ...310 K9
- av. Forestville ...255 K9
- av. Seaforth ...287 A12

ASHTON (cont)
- cl. Eagle Vale ...480 K9
- la. Paddington ...21 J7
- pl. Doonside ...273 F2
- Mt Pritchard ...364 J8
- st. Queens Park ...22 C11
- st. Rockdale ...433 D2

ASHTONS
- st. Georges Hall ...367 F11
- rd. Grose Wold ...116 A9

ASHUR
- cr. Greenfld Pk ...334 A15

ASHWELL
- rd. Blacktown ...274 F2

ASHWICK
- cct. St Clair ...270 G10

ASHWOOD
- cl. Menai ...458 H14
- rd. Kenthurst ...187 C3
- st. Parklea ...215 B13

ASHWORTH
- av. Belrose ...225 E14

ASPEN
- cl. Prestons ...393 J13
- st. Bossley Park ...333 H9
- st. S Penrith ...267 D5
- wy. Acacia Gdn ...215 A14

ASPINALL
- av. Minchinbury ...272 B8
- pl. Mulgrave ...121 H16
- pl. Woolwich ...314 G11

ASPLIN
- pl. Kurrajong Hl ...64 C12

ASQUITH
- av. Baulkham Hl ...247 J15
- av. Rosebery ...375 J16
- st. Oatley ...431 E12
- st. Silverwater ...309 E12

ASSETS
- st. Campsie ...371 K12

ASSISI
- pl. Rooty Hill ...272 D7

ASSUNTA
- st. Rooty Hill ...272 D7

ASTELIA
- st. Mcquarie Fd ...454 C4

ASTER
- av. Asquith ...191 K9
- av. Miranda ...492 D2
- av. Punchbowl ...399 G4
- ct. Glenmore Pk ...265 F10
- pl. Quakers Hill ...243 F5
- st. Eastwood ...281 D7
- st. Greystanes ...305 J12

ASTLEY
- av. Padstow ...429 E1
- pl. Edensor Pk ...363 G4
- rd. Casula ...424 G4

ASTOLAT
- st. Randwick ...377 C11

ASTON
- av. Lucas Ht ...487 F12
- av. S Penrith ...267 B1
- pl. Hoxton Park ...392 K6
- gdn. Bellevue Hill ...347 K11
- la. S Penrith, off
    Aston Av ...267 B1
- st. Leumeah ...482 B14
- st. Hunters Hill ...313 A7

ASTOR
- st. Moorebank ...396 E7

ASTORIA
- st. Westmead ...277 G16
- cct. Maroubra ...407 B12

ASTORIA PARK
- rd. Baulkham Hl ...246 F10

ASTRAL
- dr. Doonside ...243 G15

ASTRID
- av. Baulkham Hl ...247 E7
- cl. Cabramatta ...365 E11
- pl. Minto ...483 C1

ASTROLABE
- rd. Daceyville ...406 E3

ASTRON
- cr. Bexley North ...402 D9

ASTWIN
- st. Croydon ...342 G14

ASTWOOD
- st. Colyton ...270 D8

ATAMI
- pl. Picnic Point ...428 A7

ATCHISON
- la. Crows Nest ...315 E5
- st. St Leonards ...315 E5

ATHABASKA
- av. Seven Hills ...275 H8

ATHEL
- st. Georges Hall ...367 F11
- st. N St Marys ...240 C13

ATHELLA
- pl. Dural ...219 C7

ATHELSTANE
- av. Arncliffe ...403 D9

ATHEL TREE
- cr. Bradbury ...511 F14

ATHENA
- av. St Ives ...224 G7
- st. St Clair ...269 G11

ATHENE
- pl. Collaroy Plat ...228 K13

ATHENS
- av. Hassall Gr ...212 A16
- st. The Rocks ...A K1

ATHERTON
- cr. Auburn ...339 B12
- rd. Engadine ...489 A16
- st. Fairfield W ...335 E10

ATHLONE
- cr. Killarney Ht ...256 D15
- st. Blacktown ...273 K1
- st. Cecil Hills ...362 H9

ATHOL
- pl. Carlingford ...279 C3
- st. Frenchs Frst ...255 J1
- st. Leichhardt ...9 D12
- st. S Coogee ...407 G4

ATHOL WHARF
- rd. Mosman ...317 A15

ATKA
- st. Tregear ...240 C6

ATKINS
- av. Carramar ...336 H16
- av. Russell Lea ...343 E4
- cr. Hobartville ...118 D8
- st. Baulkham Hl ...247 E2
- pl. Barden Rdg ...488 F3
- rd. Ermington ...280 E16
- rd. Ermington ...310 E1

ATKINSON
- av. Padstow ...399 B10
- cl. Glenmore Pk ...265 J6
- la. Arncliffe ...403 C11
- la. Banksia ...403 C11
- pl. Airds ...512 F10
- rd. Taren Point ...463 A15
- st. Arncliffe ...403 B11
- st. Liverpool ...395 A7

ATLANTA
- pl. Casula ...395 A12

ATLANTIC
- dr. Brookvale ...258 F10
- pl. Beaumont Hills ...185 K14

ATLAS
- pl. Winston Hills ...277 C1
- wy. Beaumont Hills ...185 J14
- wy. Narellan Vale ...508 J2

ATNATU
- wy. Doonside ...243 F16

ATOLL
- pl. Quakers Hill ...213 F14

ATTAR
- st. Guildford ...337 K4

ATTARD
- av. Marayong ...244 D7

ATTILIO
- pl. Edensor Pk ...363 H4

ATTLEE
- pl. Baulkham Hl ...277 J1

ATTOW
- st. Winston Hills ...277 C3

ATTUNGA
- av. Earlwood ...402 F6
- av. Moorebank ...396 F11
- av. W Pnnant Hl ...249 J1
- pl. Picton ...562 H10
- pl. Bradbury ...511 B5
- pwy. Moorebank, off
    Attunga Av ...396 F10
- rd. Blaxland ...233 E4
- rd. Miranda ...492 K7
- rd. Newport ...169 K7
- rd. Roseville Ch ...255 D14
- rd. Yowie Bay ...492 K13
- st. Baulkham Hl ...247 C5

28 GREGORY'S STREET DIRECTORY

STREETS BA

st. Seven Hills 275 E4
st. Woollahra 22 F2
AUBER
gln. St Clair 300 C2
la. St Clair, off
Auber Gln 300 C2
AUBERT
st. Narellan 478 G13
AUBIN
st. Neutral Bay 6 D8
AUBREEN
st. Collaroy Plat 228 J12
AUBREY
cl. Castle Hill 248 E2
pl. Berowra 133 H9
rd. Northbridge 286 F16
st. Ingleburn 453 E7
st. S Granville 338 F3
st. Stanmore 16 C11
AUBURN
rd. Auburn 339 C11
rd. Auburn 339 D7
rd. Berala 339 C11
rd. Birrong 368 K6
rd. Regents Pk 369 A5
rd. Yagoona 368 K11
st. Hunters Hill 313 A8
st. Parramatta 307 H7
st. Sutherland 490 G4
st.s, Sutherland 490 G6
AUCKLAND
st. Bonnyrigg Ht 363 C6
st. Engadine 518 H6
AUDINE
av. Epping 280 E3
AUDLEY
la. Petersham 15 H11
rd. Royal N P 520 E2
st. Petersham 15 H11
AUDREY
pde. Condell Park 398 J5
pl. Quakers Hill 213 G8
st. Balgowlah 287 F9
st. Thirlmere 565 D2
AUGUSTA
ct. Rouse Hill 185 B9
la. Allawah 432 F9
la. Manly 288 F8
la. St Clair, off
Augusta Pl 270 J11
pl. St Clair 270 J11
rd. Fairlight 288 E7
rd. Manly 288 E7
st. Allawah 432 G9
st. Bankstown 399 A4
st. Blacktown 274 F14
st. Casula 395 A13
st. Concord 341 K1
st. Condell Park 398 H4
st. Five Dock 343 C10
st. Punchbowl 400 C9
st. Strathfield 371 A2
AUGUSTINE
st. Hunters Hill 313 B9
AUGUSTUS
la. Enmore 17 A12
st. Enmore 17 A12
wy. Ambarvale 510 K15
AUKANE
st. Green Valley 362 K11
AULD
av. Eastwood 280 J7
av. Milperra 397 B7
pl. Eagle Vale 481 B9
pl. Schofields 183 E15
AULT
pl. Illawong 459 K6
AULUBA
rd. S Turramra 252 B6
AUMUNA
rd. Terrey Hills 195 K9
AURELIA
st. Toongabbie 276 B8
AURORA
dr. St Ives Ch 224 B2
dr. Tregear 240 E7
dr. Whalan 240 F8
pl. Eveleigh 18 E12
AUSTELL
st. Stanhpe Gdn 215 D6
AUSTEN
cl. Wetherill Pk 334 G6
pl. Kellyville 215 F3
AUSTIN
av. Beverly Hills 430 K1
av. Campbelltown 511 H9
av. Croydon 372 B3
av. Homebush W 340 H7
av. N Curl Curl 259 A10
bvd. Picnic Point 428 E7
cr. Belfield 371 E11
cr. Lane Cove 314 D2
cr. Wentwthvle 277 D9
gr. Zetland 375 K9
la. Surry Hills 20 C4
pl. Orchard Hills 268 D8
st. Fairlight 288 B8
st. Illawong 459 H6
st. Lane Cove 314 D3
AUSTIN WOODBURY
pl. Toongabbie 276 H6
AUSTOOL
pl. Ingleburn 453 E1
AUSTRAL
av. Beecroft 250 C8
av. Catherine Fd 449 G7
av. Lindfield 284 B5
av. North Manly 258 B15
av. Westmead 307 E1
pde. Fairfield 336 D15
pl. St Helens Park 541 A6
st. Kogarah 433 D8
st. Malabar 437 D4
st. Mount Druitt 241 C13
st. Penshurst 431 D5
AUSTRALIA
av. Homebush B 340 J1
av. Matraville 436 F3
la. Camperdown 17 D6
la. Camperdown 17 E8
la. Woollahra 22 H4
rd. Barden Rdg 488 G2
st. Bass Hill 368 D10
st. Camperdown 17 C4
st. Croydon 342 H13
st. Hurstville 432 A9
st. Merrylands 308 A13
st. Newtown 17 E8
st. St Marys 269 K1
AUSTRALIS
av. Wattle Grove 396 B16
cl. Cranebrook 207 H6
AUSTRALORP
av. Seven Hills 275 E5
AUTUMN
gr. Glendenning 242 H4
pl. Guildford 337 C2
AUTUMN LEAF
gr. Cherrybrook 219 J15
AUTUMNLEAF
pde. St Clair 270 C13
AVA
cl. Minchinbury 272 F8
pl. Quakers Hill 213 K11
AVALON
av. Lane Cove W 283 H16
cl. Bossley Park 333 F9
cr. Glenmore Pk 266 E13
pde. Avalon 169 K1
pl. Woodbine 481 J9
st. Birrong 369 A5
st. Turramurra 223 D12
AVARYR
pl. Mcquarie Pk 283 C6
AVELINE
pl. Hassall Gr 211 K13
AVELING
st. Blakehurst 432 C16
AVENAL
la. Arncliffe 403 H9
st. Arncliffe 403 G10
st. Guildford 337 D2
AVENEL
rd. Gymea Bay 491 C8
st. Canley Vale 365 J1
AVENUE
la. Glebe 11 H8
rd. Glebe 11 H8
rd. Hunters Hill 313 E10
rd. Mosman 316 H10
AVENUE OF AFRICA
Newington 310 C10
AVENUE OF ASIA
Newington 310 C11
AVENUE OF EUROPE
Newington 310 B11
AVENUE OF OCEANIA
Homebush B 310 C11
Newington 310 C11
AVENUE OF THE AMERICAS
Newington 310 B11
AVERIL
pl. Lindfield 284 C2
AVERILL
st. Rhodes 311 E7
AVERY
av. Kirrawee 491 B4
st. Normanhurst 221 E7
wy. Narellan Vale 508 K1
AVIA
cl. Raby 451 B13
AVIAN
cr. Lane Cove N 283 G12
AVIATION
pl. Bnkstn Aprt 397 J1
AVIGNON
pl. Kellyville 216 K4
AVISFORD
st. Fairfield 336 B14
AVOCA
av. Belfield 371 E9
av. Emu Plains 236 B7
cl. West Hoxton 392 E6
la. Bondi, off
Avoca St 378 A5
la. Canley Ht, off
Birchgrove Av 364 K3
la. Randwick 407 B1
pl. Woodbine 481 K10
rd. Canley Ht 365 A3
rd. Grose Wold 115 F7
rd. Silverdale 383 A11
rd. Silverdale 383 E16
rd. Silverdale 413 A1
rd. Turramurra 222 H16
rd. Wakeley 335 A16
st. Bondi 377 K5
st. Glenbrook 264 C1
st. Kingsford 407 A5
st. Randwick 377 B16
st. Yagoona 369 D10
AVOCET
pl. Hinchinbrk 393 C2
AVON
cl. Asquith 192 D10
cl. Pymble 252 K4
grn. W Pnnant Hl 249 C5
la. Glebe 12 A9
la. St Clair, off
Avon Pl 269 J13
pl. Kirrawee 491 A10
pl. Leumeah 482 D12
pl. St Clair 269 J13
pl. Toongabbie 276 G7
pl. Windsor Dn 151 B12
rd. Bringelly 387 F5
rd. Dee Why 258 J6
rd. North Ryde 282 H9
rd. Pymble 253 B2
st. Bankstown 369 D12
st. Cammeray 316 B5
st. Canley Ht 365 A3
st. Glebe 12 A9
AVONA
av. Glebe 11 K8
cr. Seaforth 287 C11
AVONDALE
pl. Cartwright 394 E4
pl. West Pymble 252 H7
rd. Pitt Town 93 H16
rd. Scheyville 123 D1
tce. Parklea 215 A14
AVON DAM
rd. Bargo 567 G8
AVONLEA
cr. Bass Hill 368 C8
dr. Carlingford 250 C13
st. Canley Ht 335 E15
AVONLEIGH
ct. Glenwood 245 G2
wy. W Pnnant Hl 249 C3
AVRIL
ct. Glenwood 215 C16
ct. Glenwood 245 C1
ct. Kellyville 216 G3
AVRO
pl. Raby 451 G15
rd. Lane Cove N 283 G12
st. Bnkstn Aprt 367 H16
st. Mascot 404 K4
AWABA
la. Mosman, off
Killarney St 317 B4
pl. Warriewood 199 C9
st. Mosman 316 H3
st. Mosman 317 A4
AWATEA
pl. Engadine 518 F5
pl. Lethbrdg Pk 240 E2
rd. St Ives Ch 223 K2
AXAM
wy. Narellan Vale 509 A1
AXFORD
pl. Fairfield W 335 A9
AXINITE
pl. Eagle Vale 481 G9
AXON
pl. Bonnyrigg 364 B6
AYCLIFFE
av. Hebersham 241 F8
AYLES
rd. Winston Hills 246 G16
AYLESBURY
cr. Chipping Ntn 396 G2
st. Botany 405 H12
st. Newtown 17 K7
AYLETT
st. N St Marys 239 J8
AYLSFORD
st. Stanhpe Gdn 215 D8
AYLSHAM
cl. Chipping Ntn 366 G13
AYLWARD
av. Quakers Hill 214 B10
AYR
pl. Riverstone 183 C8
st. Ashbury 372 E8
st. Banksia 403 J13
AYRES
cr. Georges Hall 367 J15
cr. Leumeah 482 G10
gr. Mount Druitt 241 F15
rd. St Ives 224 D7
rd.w, St Ives 224 B7
AYRSHIRE
gdn. Picton 561 B2
pl. Narellan Vale 508 J2
st. Bossley Park 334 B11
st. Busby 363 K16
AYRTON
st. Blacktown 273 J7
AYSHFORD
st. Casula 424 B3
AZALEA
ct. Glenmore Pk 265 G8
gdn. Wahroonga 223 C6
gr. Castle Hill 217 F16
gr. Pennant Hills 250 G2
pl. Loftus 489 K9
pl. Mcquarie Fd 453 K6
pl. Panania 428 E5
st. Blacktown 274 E12
st. Greystanes 305 H11
AZILE
ct. Carlingford 279 F6
AZTEC
cl. Greenfld Pk 333 K14
AZZOPARDI
av. Glendenning 242 E5

B

BAANYA
pl. Cranebrook 207 D15
BAARTZ
tce. Glenwood 215 H16
BABBAGE
rd. Roseville 285 D3
rd. Roseville Ch 255 E16
BABBIN
av. Caringbah 492 F9
BACH
av. Emerton 240 H6
cl. Cranebrook 207 D15
pl. Bonnyrigg Ht 363 D7
pl. Engadine 518 E5
BACHELL
av. Lidcombe 340 C6
BACK
cl. Kearns 451 C16
BACKS
pl. Narellan Vale 478 H15
BADAJOZ
rd. North Ryde 282 G15
rd. Ryde 282 G15
BADANA
pl. Cromer 228 D15
BADARENE
pl. E Lindfield 255 A11
BADCOE
rd. Cromer 227 K13
BADDELEY
st. Padstow 399 B16
BADEN
av. Bass Hill 368 A6
pl. Blaxland 233 D3
rd. Neutral Bay 6 J14
st. Coogee 377 H15
st. Greystanes 306 E10
BADENOCH
av. Glenhaven 218 B6
BADEN POWELL
av. Kingswood 237 G15
pl. Lakemba 401 C4
pl. North Rocks 249 A13
pl. Winston Hills 277 F6
st. Brooklyn 75 K11
BADGALLY
rd. Blairmount 480 K11
rd. Campbelltown 481 C15
rd. Campbelltown 511 E1
rd. Claymore 480 K11
rd. Eagle Vale 480 K11
rd. The Oaks 502 D13
rd. Woodbine 481 C15
BADGER
av. Sefton 368 F5
pl. Green Valley 363 A8
BADGERY
av. Homebush 340 J11
wy. Bonnyrigg 364 C4
BADGERYS CREEK
rd. Badgerys Ck 328 G16
rd. Bringelly 388 B7
BADHAM
av. Mosman 316 H12
st. Merrylands 308 C16
st. Woolmloo, off
Crown St 4 D6
BADMINTON
rd. Croydon 372 B3
BADTO
av. Gymea 491 C4
BAECKEA
pl. Frenchs Frst 226 H15
BAGALA
st. Glenwood 215 J16
BAGDAD
st. Regents Pk 369 B2
BAGGOT
pl. Baulkham Hl 247 C2
BAGLIN
st. Bronte 377 H10
BAGO
st. Pendle Hill 276 G12
BAGUETTE
cl. Casula 394 G16
BAHAI TEMPLE
wy. Ingleside 197 G7
BAHRI
pl. Glenwood 245 K4
BAIL
wy. Glenwood 215 F13
BAILEY
av. Lane Cove N 284 A12
av. West Hoxton 391 G8
cr. N Epping 251 E8
ct. Harringtn Pk 478 J3
pde. Peakhurst 430 F1
pl. Blacktown 243 K9
st. Newtown 17 E13
st. Westmead 307 G1
BAILEYANA
ct. Wattle Grove 426 B1
BAILEYS
la. Kurrajong Hl 63 K16
BAILLEY
st. Leumeah 512 D1
BAIN
gr. Quakers Hill 214 E15
pl. Barden Rdg 488 H2
pl. Dundas Vy 280 C9
st. Glenbrook 264 A2

GREGORY'S STREET DIRECTORY 29

BA   STREETS

BAINBRIDGE
- av. Chipping Ntn......396 B5
- av. Ingleburn.........453 A12
- cr. Rooty Hill........271 H4

BAINTON
- pl. Doonside.........243 E16
- rd. Mt Pritchard.....364 K9

BAIRD
- av. Matraville.......406 H16
- av. Ryde..............312 E2
- ct. W Pnnant Hl......249 F7
- la. Matraville, off
      Baird Av.........406 H16
- la. Sefton...........368 E6
- st. Bass Hill........368 E8
- st. Sefton...........368 E8

BAKEHOUSE
- pl. The Rocks...........A K5

BAKER
- av. Newington........310 A15
- cl. Bossley Park.....333 H11
- cl. Baulkham Hl......248 A9
- la. Bundeena.........524 B10
- pl. Lindfield........284 A1
- pl. Minto............453 D15
- pl. Penshurst........431 E2
- pl. Bnksmeadw........406 B12
- rd. Blacktown........245 A15
- rd. Bundeena.........524 A9
- rd. Carlingford......279 F5
- rd. Enfield...........371 J4
- st. Galston...........159 E9
- st. Kensington.......376 B11
- st. Merrylands.......307 J16
- st. Oatley............430 H13
- st. Springwood.......202 D10
- st. Windsor...........121 D7

BAKERI
- ct. Voyager Pt.......427 B4

BAKERS
- la. Forest Lodge......17 J1
- la. Kemps Ck.........300 B12
- la. Strathfield, off
      Cooper St........341 F10
- la. Earlwood, off
      Homer St.........403 A3
- st. St Peters, off
      Mary St.........374 G14
- rd. Church Point.....168 G9

BALA
- pl. Marayong.........243 K6

BALACLAVA
- la. Alexandria........19 A16
- rd. Berowra..........133 E10
- rd. Eastwood.........281 D6
- rd. Emu Heights......235 A2
- rd. Mcquarie Pk......281 J3
- rd. Marsfield........281 J3

BALAKA
- dr. Carlingford......249 C16

BALALA
- ct. Wattle Grove....396 A16

BALANADA
- av. Chipping Ntn.....396 G6

BALANAMING
- la. Petersham........15 G11

BALANDRA
- pl. Kareela..........461 E10

BALARANG
- pl. Bangor...........459 D10

BALBEEK
- av. Blacktown........243 K11

BALBOA
- pl. Willmot..........210 C13
- st. Campbelltown.....511 A7
- st. Kurnell..........465 G8

BALDER
- st. Doonside.........243 F15

BALDI
- av. Panania..........398 C14

BALDINI
- pl. Hinchinbrk.......393 A3

BALDO
- st. Edensor Pk......333 H12

BALDRY
- st. Chatswood........285 A8

BALDWIN
- av. Asquith..........192 B10
- av. Baulkham Hl.....247 H16
- av. Glenfield........424 E10
- cl. Ellis Lane......476 C10
- st. Erskineville......17 K13
- st. Gordon............253 K5

BALL
- st. Padstow..........429 B1
- wy. Currans Hill.....479 F12

BALEMO
- pl. Bangor...........459 B12

BALFOUR
- tce. Glenmore Pk.....266 F8
- av. Caringbah........492 G3
- dr. Beaumont Hills..186 B15
- la. Bellevue Hill....347 H14
- la. Kensington.......376 D10
- la. Lindfield........254 C16
- la. Wollstncraft.....315 D8
- rd. Bellevue Hill....347 H11
- rd. Kensington......376 D12
- rd. Narwee...........400 J15
- rd. Rose Bay........347 H11
- st. Allawah..........432 G8
- st. Chippendale.......19 B4
- st. Dulwich Hill....373 D13
- st. Greenwich........314 J6
- st. Lindfield........254 C16
- st. Northmead........277 K12
- st. Wollstncraft.....315 D8

BALGA
- cl. Berowra Ht......132 K13

BALGANG
- av. Kirrawee.........491 B4

BALGOWLAH
- rd. Balgowlah........287 H6
- rd. Fairlight........288 A7
- rd. Manly............288 D6

BALI
- dr. Quakers Hill....213 H9
- pl. Berowra..........163 C1

BALIGA
- av. Caringbah........492 E10

BALIMBA
- pl. Whalan...........240 K9

BALIMO
- pl. Glenfield........424 G11

BALIN
- pl. Blacktown........274 K7

BALINTORE
- dr. Castle Hill......218 C7
- dr. Castle Hill......218 D8

BALKE
- st. Minto............452 J13

BALL
- av. Eastwood.........281 C6
- la. Colyton, off
      Ball St.........270 C3
- pl. Willmot..........210 D13
- st. Colyton..........270 C3

BALLAH
- ct. S Penrith........266 H6
- la. S Penrith, off
      Ballah Ct.......266 H6

BALLA MACHREE
- wy. Gymea Bay........491 E9

BALLANDA
- av. Lugarno..........430 B15
- pl. Bangor...........459 D12
- pl. Dural............158 E13
- st. Frenchs Frst.....256 D8

BALLANDELLA
- rd. Pendle Hill......276 E12
- rd. Toongabbie......276 E12

BALLANTRAE
- dr. St Andrews......451 K15

BALLANTYNE
- rd. Mortdale.........430 G9
- st. Mosman...........316 K9

BALLAR
- av. Gymea Bay........491 H9

BALLARAT
- av. St Clair.........270 B10
- pl. Cartwright.......394 B5
- pl. St Johns Pk......364 H1

BALLARD
- pl. Doonside.........273 E3

BALLAST POINT
- rd. Birchgrove.........7 J3

BALLENY
- pl. Tregear..........240 F5

BALLERDO PATH
- Winmalee.............173 C9

BALLINA
- av. Killarney Ht....286 B1
- cl. Hoxton Park....392 K7
- pl. Bangor...........459 B11
- pl. Bossley Park....333 F10
- st. Georges Hall...367 J13
- st. Greystanes......305 H4

BALLS HEAD
- dr. Waverton.........315 D15
- rd. Waverton.........315 D14

BALLYBUNNION
- pl. Erskine Park.....300 F2

BALLYLEANEY
- pl. Erskine Park.....300 F2

BALLYMENA
- st. Hebersham........241 F4
- wy. Kellyville.......217 C2

BALLYSHANNON
- rd. Killarney Ht....255 J13

BALMAIN
- pl. Doonside.........273 E2
- rd. Leichhardt.........10 B14
- rd. Leichhardt.........16 B1
- rd. Lilyfield..........10 B6
- rd. Lilyfield..........10 C5
- rd. McGraths Hl.....121 K13
- st. Cartwright.......394 D5
- wy. Minto.............483 A2

BALMARINGA
- av. S Turramrra......252 B5

BALMORAL
- av. Croydon Pk.......371 K9
- av. Mosman............317 C7
- cct. Cecil Hills.......362 F4
- cr. Georges Hall....367 H14
- dr. Cmbrdg Pk.......237 J9
- pl. Carlingford......279 C5
- rd. Ingleburn........453 K15
- rd. Kellyville.......215 J12
- rd. Mortdale........430 G8
- rd. Northmead........277 H11
- st. Blacktown........274 E2
- st. Hornsby...........192 A16
- st. Waitara..........222 A4

BALOG
- st. St Marys.........270 A7

BALOOK
- cr. Bradbury........511 B16

BALOWRIE
- st. Yowie Bay........492 C11

BALSON
- cl. Abbotsbury......333 A15

BALTHASAR
- cl. Rsemeadow........540 H4

BALTIC
- pl. Kellyville Rdg..215 A4
- la. Newtown...........17 D11
- st. Fairlight.........288 D7
- st. Newtown...........17 C11

BALTIMORE
- pl. Mortdale.........430 H9
- st. Belfield..........371 E11

BALYATA
- av. Caringbah........493 B12

BAMBARA
- av. Bradbury.........541 D1
- cr. Beecroft.........250 C11
- dr. Baulkham Hl.....248 C10
- rd. Frenchs Frst....256 B1
- st. Dharruk..........241 C9

BAMBI
- cl. Cranebrook......207 B10
- st. Ryde.............282 D15

BAMBIL
- pl. Blaxland.........234 E8
- rd. Berowra.........133 D16
- rd. Berowra...........163 C2
- st. Georges Hall....367 G13
- st. Greystanes......305 J10

BAMBOO
- av. Earlwood........403 H3
- wy. Stanhpe Gdn.....215 D9

BAMBRA
- av. Roselands.......400 J6

BAMBRIDGE
- la. Riverstone, off
      Pitt St.........182 J8
- st. Chester Hill....368 B5

BAMBURGH
- rd. Weromibi........443 B3

BAMENT
- pl. Minchinbury.....271 F8

BAMFIELD
- av. Yagoona.........368 F12

BAMFORD
- pl. Lalor Park......245 G10

BAMPI
- pl. Castle Cove....286 D5

BAMPTON
- av. Illawong........459 A7

BANARO
- av. Whalan..........240 K10

BANBAL
- rd. Engadine.......488 H14

BANBURY
- cr. Chipping Ntn...396 E3

BANCROFT
- av. Roseville.......284 H4
- av. W Pnnant Hl....220 B15
- la. Roseville, off
      Bancroft Av....284 H4
- rd. Abbotsbury.....333 B15
- st. Oakhurst........241 H1

BANDA
- pl. Fairfield W....335 F9

BANDAIN
- av. Kareela.........461 C14

BANDALONG
- av. West Pymble....253 B13
- cr. Bangor...........459 D11

BANDERRA
- rd. S Penrith.......237 B15

BANDO
- rd. Cronulla........494 A9
- rd. Girraween.......276 C12

BANDON
- rd. Vineyard.........152 F10

BANFF
- pl. Winston Hills..277 E3

BANGALAY
- pl. Leonay..........234 K14
- pl. Mcquarie Fd....454 G3
- st. Georges Hall...367 G11

BANGALEE
- pl. Bangor..........459 D11

BANGALLA
- av. Bradbury........511 F15
- av. Chipping Ntn...396 F4
- pde. Glenmore Pk....266 G16
- pl. Forestville.....255 H11
- rd. Concord W......311 D15
- rd. Rose Bay.......348 E12
- st. Turramurra......222 G9
- st. Warrawee........222 G9

BANGALLEY
- wy. Avalon, off
      Barrenjoey Rd..140 D13

BANGALOW
- av. Earlwood.......403 F2

BANGAR
- cl. Killarney Ht...256 A16

BANGAROO
- av. Glenmore Pk....266 G15
- st. Bangor..........459 D12
- st. N Balgowlah....287 D6

BANGOR
- bps. Bangor..........459 B15
- bps. Barden Rdg....458 H16
- bps. Menai..........458 F15
- rd. Middle Dural....128 E16
- st. Auburn..........338 J1
- st. Guildford.......337 D4

BANGU
- pl. Glenmore Pk....266 B11

BANJO
- cr. Emu Plains.....235 A8
- cr. Castle Hill.....217 D9
- pl. Springwood.....202 J1
- st. Heathcote......518 C15

BANJO PATERSON
- cl. Glenmore Pk....265 K5
- pl. Padstow Ht......429 D7

BANK
- la. Kogarah..........433 C4
- la. McMahons Pt......5 B10
- la. N Sydney..........5 B10
- st. Lidcombe.......339 G10
- st. McMahons Pt......5 B10
- st. Meadowbank.....311 A4
- st. N Sydney..........5 B10
- st. Pyrmont.........12 C3
- st. West Ryde......311 E4

BANKS
- av. Berrilee........131 D9
- av. Daceyville......406 F8
- av. Eastgardens....406 E11
- av. N Turramurra...223 E3
- av. Pagewood.......406 E11

BANKSHILL
- cr. Carlingford....280 B5

BANKSIA
- av. Banksia........403 E12
- av. Engadine........488 G16
- cl. Kings Lngly....245 J10
- cl. Lane Cove W....283 H16
- cr. Fairfield E....336 J12
- dr. Valley Ht......202 E5
- pde. Warriewood....198 G10
- pl. Arcadia.........129 G7
- pl. Canada Bay.....342 E8
- pl. Greystanes.....305 F11
- pl. Ingleburn........453 D8
- pl. Kenthurst.......156 J15
- pl. Lugarno........429 H14
- pl. Newington......310 B13
- pl. Oakdale..........500 C13
- pl. Wattle Grove...396 B16
- rd. Bellevue Hill...377 J1
- rd. Caringbah.......492 J6
- rd. Caringbah.......493 A7
- rd. Greenacre......369 H11
- rd. Mt Annan.......509 D3
- st. Botany..........405 F11
- st. Couridjah......564 F16
- st. Dee Why.........259 A8
- st. Eastwood........281 H8
- st. Normanhurst....221 D12
- st. N St Marys......240 A10
- st. Pagewood.......405 K10
- st. S Granville....338 G2
- st. Stanhpe Gdn....215 D10

BANKSIDE
- av. Earlwood.......403 F2

BANKSTOWN DISTRICT SPORTS CLUB
- dr. Georges Hall, off
      Rex Rd..........367 K12

BANN
- wy. Wentwthvle, off
      Portadown Rd..277 D11

BANNER
- rd. Kingsgrove.....402 A13

BANNERMAN
- cr. Rosebery........375 K16
- pl. Glenhaven.......187 B12
- rd. Kenthurst........187 B12
- st. Cremorne...........6 J6
- st. Ermington......310 D2
- st. Mortdale.........430 G9

BANNISTER
- pl. Mt Pritchard...364 F12
- wy. Wrrngtn Cty....238 F14

BANNOCKBURN
- av. St Andrews.....481 J2
- la. N Turramurra...223 D8
- rd. Pymble..........223 C11
- rd. Turramurra......223 C11

BANOOL
- av. St Ives.........223 H9
- av. S Penrith.......266 K1
- la. S Penrith, off
      Banool Av......266 H1

BANOOR
- st. Chester Hill....338 A16
- st. Kareela..........461 C12

BANQUO
- pl. Rsemeadow.....540 D3

BANTRY BAY
- rd. Frenchs Frst...256 G10

BANYEENA
- pl. Belrose.........226 C15

BANYULA
- pl. Killara.........253 C15
- pl. Mt Colah........162 F13

BANYULE
- ct. Wattle Grove...425 K1

BANZ
- pl. Glenfield......424 G9

30 GREGORY'S STREET DIRECTORY

STREETS BA

BAPAUME
- pde. Matraville 407 A16
- pl. Milperra 397 H10
- rd. Moorebank 395 D12
- rd. Mosman 317 A3

BAPTIST
- la. Redfern 19 K11
- st. Redfern 20 A10

BARA
- pl. Quakers Hill 243 H1

BARABA
- cl. Glenmore Pk 266 D8

BARADINE
- pl. Yarrawarrah 489 F14
- wy. Hoxton Park 392 H8

BARAGIL
- mw. Mt Annan 479 H16

BARAGOOLA
- av. Phillip Bay 436 J10
- st. Fairfield W 335 E14

BARALGA
- cr. Riverwood 400 F11

BARAMBAH
- la. Roseville 285 C5
- rd. Roseville 285 C5

BARANA
- pde. Roseville Ch 255 F16
- pl. Kareela 461 B12

BARANBALI
- av. Seaforth 287 B6
- st. Beverly Hills 401 E11
- st. Doonside 243 C14

BARANGAROO
- rd. Toongabbie 276 D7

BARARA
- pl. Fairfield W 335 F15

BARB
- pl. Blairmount 480 K14

BARBARA
- bvd. Seven Hills 245 C16
- ct. Merrylands 307 E14
- ct. Mona Vale 198 K4
- pl. Lugarno 429 K15
- st. Fairfield 336 E12

BARBARO
- la. Horsley Pk 332 A2

BARBER
- av. Eastlakes 405 K3
- av. Kingswood 237 C12
- av. Penrith 237 C12
- pl. Panania 398 C16
- pl. Glenwood 215 D15

BARBERS
- rd. Chester Hill 337 H10
- rd. Guildford 337 H10

BARBOUR
- dr. Thirlmere 565 A5

BARCELONA
- dr. Prestons 393 K15
- dr. Prestons 393 H15

BARCHAM
- ct. W Pnnant Hl 249 A9

BARCLAY
- cl. Pymble 252 K4
- rd. North Rocks 249 A14
- st. Marrickville 374 C14
- st. Quakers Hill 213 H15
- st. Waverley 377 H10

BARCOM
- av. Darlinghurst 4 G13
- av. Darlinghurst 4 J12
- av. Paddington 4 G13
- st. Merrylands W 307 B14

BARCOO
- av. Leumeah 482 B15
- cl. Erskine Park 270 G15
- la. St Clair, off
  Barcoo Cl 270 G16
- pl. St Ives 254 D4
- st. Peakhurst 430 C8
- st. Roseville 285 C4

BARCOO ISLAND
- Sylvania Wtr 462 F12

BARCOOLA
- pl. Bayview 168 C11

BARCOTE
- pl. Castle Hill 219 A8

BARD
- ct. St Clair 270 C16

BARDEN
- la. Randwick 377 A11
- rd. Barden Rdg 458 G16
- st. Arncliffe 403 F8

BARDIA
- ct. Mt Annan 479 D11
- pde. Holsworthy 396 C16
- pl. Bossley Park 334 B5
- pl. E Lindfield 254 K10
- rd. Carlingford 249 K13

BARDIN
- la. Auburn 339 F1
- rd. Newport 169 E11
- st. Glenmore Pk 266 D7

BARDOLPH
- pl. Rsemeadow 540 G8

BARDON
- cl. St Johns Pk 334 F16

BARDOO
- av. N Balgowlah 287 C4

BARDSLEY
- cct. Rouse Hill 184 J6
- gdn.N Sydney 315 J7

BARDWELL
- cr. Earlwood 402 G5
- la. Mosman, off
  Holt Av 316 J9
- rd. Bardwell Pk 402 J7
- rd. Bardwell Vy 403 A7
- rd. Mosman 316 J8
- wky.Bardwell Pk 402 J6

BARE
- av. Lurnea 394 D7
- st. Bnksmeadw 436 C1

BAREE
- pl. Warriewood 199 B8

BAREENA
- av. Wahroonga 222 D4
- dr. Balgowlah Ht 287 H14
- pl. Hamondvle 396 E14
- pl. Marsfield 251 J14
- pl. Avalon 140 E13
- st. Cabramatta 366 B5
- st. Canley Vale 366 B5
- st. Lilli Pilli 522 E4
- st. Strathfield 340 K16
- wk. Wahroonga 222 E5

BARELLAN
- av. Carlingford 280 C2
- av. Turramurra 252 K1
- st. Merrylands 306 J10

BARFF
- rd. Camperdown 18 E2
- rd. Ingleburn 453 A10

BARFIL
- cr. S Wntwthvle 306 J4

BARGO
- rd. Bargo 567 K6
- rd. Bargo 567 F7
- st. Maianbar 523 B7

BARGO RIVER
- rd. Couridjah 564 E16
- rd. Couridjah 565 E16
- rd. Couridjah 565 E16
- rd. Tahmoor 565 E16

BARHAM
- av. Heckenberg 364 A12
- av. Maianbar 523 B7
- av. Parramatta 278 J15

BARILLA
- pl. Bonnyrigg Ht 362 K6
- pl. Bonnyrigg Ht 363 A5

BARINA
- cr. Emu Plains 234 K8
- pl. Blaxland 234 D5
- rd. Riverview 314 C5

BARINA DOWNS
- rd. Baulkham Hl 246 G1
- rd. Bella Vista 246 G1

BARINGA
- av. Seaforth 287 B6
- cl. Belrose 225 K15
- cl. Green Valley 363 H11
- rd. Earlwood 402 D4
- rd. Engadine 488 H16
- rd. Mortdale 430 G9
- rd. Northbridge 285 H16
- st. Berowra Ht 133 B10
- st. Blaxland 233 F5
- st. North Ryde 282 E8

BARISTON
- av. Cremorne 316 G5

BARITE
- pl. Eagle Vale 481 F6

BARJADDA
- av. Sylvania 462 B11

BARK
- pl. Kings Lngly 245 E8

BARKALA
- pl. Westleigh 220 G4
- rd. Bayview 168 G14

BARKDUK
- av. Miranda 491 J5

BARKER
- av. Silverwater 309 J15
- cl. Camden S 506 K10
- cl. Illawong 459 F4
- dr. Castle Hill 218 J13
- la. Kingsford, off
  Houston Rd 376 F16
- la. Lewisham 15 C8
- rd. Leumeah 482 D16
- rd. Strathfield 341 A14
- st. Bossley Park 334 C11
- st. Kensington 376 E16
- st. Kingsford 376 E16
- st. Lewisham 15 B8
- st. Randwick 376 E16
- st. Rooty Hill 272 E9
- st. St Marys 269 E5

BARKERS LODGE
- rd. Mowbray Pk 562 D1
- rd. Oakdale 500 C16
- rd. Picton 563 A2

BARKL
- av. Padstow 429 C1

BARKLEY
- cl. Cherrybrook 219 C14
- st. Carramar 366 J1

BARKLY
- cl. Bonnyrigg Ht 363 G5
- dr. Windsor Dn 180 G1

BARLEY
- gln. Wrrngtn Dns ...238 B5

BARLOW
- cr. Canley Ht 364 K3
- ct. Georges Hall 367 J12
- ct. Hornsgea Pk 392 C15
- st. Dangar I 76 J7
- st. Cmbrdg Pk 237 J6
- st. Haymarket ....E F10
- st. Haymarket 3 F13

BARNABY
- pl. Ambarvale 510 K15
- pl. Mona Vale 199 B5

BARNARD
- ct. Oakhurst 241 H4
- pl. St Helens Park ..541 A8

BARNARDO
- cl. Wahroonga 221 K10

BARNARDS
- av. Hurstville 401 J16

BARNCLEUTH
- la. Potts Point 4 K6
- sq. Elizabeth Bay 13 A6
- sq. Potts Point 13 A6

BARNES
- av. Earlwood 372 F16
- cr. Menai 458 D10
- la. Blacktown 274 D6
- pl. Rouse Hill 184 K7
- rd. Frenchs Frst 257 B3
- rd. Llandilo 179 G15
- st. Girraween 276 B10
- st. Minto 453 C16

BARNET
- av. Rookwood 340 A12
- pl. Doonside 273 H2
- st. Glenbrook 234 C15

BARNETT
- la. Bondi Jctn 377 H2
- la. Darlinghurst 4 J12
- la. S Penrith, off
  Barnett St 266 F3
- pl. Cabramatta W ..365 C6
- st. Ashcroft 394 F2
- st. S Penrith 266 F3

BARNETTS
- rd. Berowra Ht 133 A10
- rd. Winston Hills ...277 C4

BARNEY
- st. Davidson 225 C15
- st. Drummoyne 343 F5
- st. N Parramatta ...278 B11

BARNFIELD
- pl. Dean Park 212 K16

BARNIER
- dr. Quakers Hill 214 B8

BARNSBURY
- gr. Bardwell Pk 402 H8
- gr. Bexley North 402 F10
- gr. Dulwich Hill 373 F10

BARNSLEY
- pl. Menai 458 J14

BARNSTAPLE
- la. Five Dock 343 A8
- rd. Five Dock 343 A9
- rd. Rodd Point 343 A9
- rd. Russell Lea 343 A9

BARNWELL
- pl. Cecil Hills 362 G3

BARODA
- la. Elizabeth Bay 13 A5
- st. Elizabeth Bay 13 A5

BAROMBAH
- rd. Epping 250 J12

BARON
- cl. Kings Lngly 245 D6

BARONBALI
- st. Dundas 279 H13

BARONESA
- la. S Penrith, off
  Baronesa Rd 237 C16
- rd. S Penrith 237 B16

BARONGA
- av. Queens Park 22 C14

BARONS
- av. Carlingford 279 D5
- cr. Hunters Hill 313 D4

BARONTA
- st. Blacktown 275 A2

BAROO
- st. Thirlmere 565 C5

BAROOGA
- av. Bradbury 511 F16

BAROOK
- pl. Mt Pritchard 364 D9

BAROONA
- pl. Seven Hills 246 B13
- rd. Northbridge 315 J1
- st. Church Point ...168 F8
- st. Dangar I 76 J7

BAROSSA
- cr. St Clair 270 D12
- ct. Baulkham Hl ...246 H4
- dr. Minchinbury 271 J9
- pl. Edensor Pk 333 D16
- pl. Mona Vale 199 B5

BARR
- st. Balmain 7 C9
- st. Camperdown 17 G1
- st. Colyton 270 F8
- st. Mortdale 430 J8
- st. North Ryde 282 H7

BARRABA
- pl. Bella Vista 246 F8

BARRABOOKA
- st. Clontarf 287 H16

BARRA-BRUI
- ct. St Ives 254 C3

BARRACE
- rd. Mosman, off
  Middle Head Rd ..317 F10

BARRACK
- cct. Mcquarie Lk ...423 E14
- la. Parramatta 308 D3
- la. Sydney ....C G2
- st. Sydney ....C G1
- st. Sydney 3 G1

BARRACKS
- st. Emu Plains 235 C10

BARRACLOUGH
- wy. Bonnyrigg 364 B4

BARRACLUFF
- av. Bondi Beach ...378 A2

BARRAKEE
- pl. Westleigh 220 G3

BARRALLIER
- wy. St Clair 270 E11

BARRARAN
- st. Gymea Bay 491 E11

BARRATT
- av. Camden S 507 B13
- st. Hurstville 432 A5
- wy. Minto 482 K1

BARRATTA
- pl. Bangor 459 C11

BARRAWARN
- pl. Castle Hill 218 B12

BARRAWINGA
- st. Telopea 279 G8

BARRE
- st. Hurlstone Pk ...373 A11

BARREMMA
- la. Lakemba 371 B14

BARREN
- cl. Green Valley ...363 A12

BARRENJOEY
- cl. Woodbine 481 H11
- cl. Avalon 140 C10
- rd. Bilgola 170 A5
- rd. Mona Vale 199 E4
- rd. Newport 169 H16
- rd. Palm Beach ...139 H2

BARRETT
- av. Thornleigh 220 J11
- pl. Cranebrook 207 F8
- pl. Randwick 377 E10
- st. Guildford 337 E15

BARRIE
- pl. Davidson 255 D1
- pl. Leumeah 512 C3
- st. East Killara 255 A8

BARRIER
- cl. Casula 424 C1
- st. Illawong 459 H3
- st. Homebush B ..310 F15

BARRIGON
- gr. Menai 458 J14

BARRINGTON
- ct. Holsworthy 426 E5
- dr. Dural 219 C4
- rd. Carlingford 279 E2
- rd. Silverdale 384 C9
- st. Bossley Park ..334 C9
- st. Ruse 512 F5

BARRON
- pl. Bossley Park ..333 G5

BARRON FIELD
- dr. Glenmore Pk ..265 K13

BARROW
- cl. Green Valley ...363 B12
- st. Silverdale 353 H16
- st. Revesby 399 A15

BARRY
- ct. Catherine Fd ..419 C2
- av. Mortdale 430 G6
- av. Rossmore 419 C2
- pl. Padstow Ht ...429 G7
- la. Neutral Bay 6 G3
- pl. Bidwill 211 C16
- pl. Cherrybrook ..219 F2
- pl. Wentwthvle ...307 C3
- rd. Chipping Ntn ...366 J16
- rd. Kellyville 185 J7
- rd. Menai 458 G13
- st. Cmbrdg Pk 237 G9
- st. Clovelly 377 G12
- st. Neutral Bay 6 F4

BARRY COE
- pl. Cranebrook ...207 G10

BARSBY
- av. Allawah 432 F7

BARSDEN
- st. Camden 506 K1

BARSENED
- st. Bonnyrigg 364 D4

BARTIL
- cl. Epping 251 E14

BARTLETT
- la. Paddington 20 G1
- st. Ermington 280 B14
- st. S Wntwthvle ...307 B7
- st. Summer Hill ...373 C6

BARTLEY
- la. Chippendale 19 B3
- st. Cabramatta ...365 H5
- st. Canley Vale ...365 H5
- st. Chippendale 19 B4

BARTOK
- gr. St Clair 300 B1
- pl. Bonnyrigg Ht ..363 D5

BARTON
- av. Haberfield 343 E14
- av. Hurlstone Pk .373 A11
- av. W Pnnant Hl .249 A8
- cr. N Wahroonga .222 G1
- dr. Artarmon 285 A16
- st. Concord 342 A1
- st. Ermington 310 E1
- st. Kogarah 433 D8
- st. Marsden Pk ..181 K13
- st. Monterey 433 D8

GREGORY'S STREET DIRECTORY 31

BA STREETS

st. N Parramatta 278 K14
st. Smithfield 336 A8
st. Strathfield S 371 C5

BARUNGA
st. Concord W 311 F15

BARWELL
av. Castle Hill 218 B15

BARWING
pl. Woronora Ht 489 F4

BARWON
av. Homebush B 310 F15
av. S Turramrra 251 K5
cr. Matraville 436 K2
ct. Wattle Grove 395 J12
pl. Campbelltown 512 A7
pl. Sylvania Wtr 462 E10
rd. Lane Cove W 313 J1
rd. Mortdale 430 H9
st. Greystanes 306 C5

BARWON PARK
rd. Alexandria 374 J12
rd. St Peters 374 J12

BARWOOD
cl. Westleigh 220 G2

BASIL
rd. Bexley 432 C1
st. Riverwood 399 J16

BASILDON
pl. Hebersham 241 F6
rd. Canley Ht 365 B4

BASILISK
pl. Whalan 240 J9

BASIN
la. Theresa Park 414 D12

BASINGSTOKE
pl. Hebersham 241 F5

BASS
av. East Hills 427 G3
cl. Hinchinbrk 363 B16
dr. Baulkham Hl 247 B11
pl. Camden S 506 J13
pl. Mt Colah 162 C11
pl. Ruse 512 F3
pl. St Ives 224 A8
pl. Willmot 210 B12
rd. Earlwood 403 B1
rd. Ingleburn 422 K10
rd. Ingleburn 423 A10
rd. Lansvale 367 B10
st. Colyton 270 E8
st. Ermington 280 C15
st. Kingsford 406 K4
st. Port Hacking 522 J2
st. Putney 312 D7

BASSELL
la. Seven Hills 245 G16

BASSETT
pl. Castle Hill 218 J11
pl. Menai 458 H13
st. Hurstville 431 E1
st. Mona Vale 199 D1

BASSIA
pl. Alfords Point 428 K13

BASTABLE
st. Croydon 372 F1

BASTILLE
cl. Padstow Ht 429 H7

BATAAN
cl. Illawong 459 J4
pl. Kings Park 244 K3
pl. Lethbrdg Pk 210 K16

BATAVIA
pl. Baulkham Hl 246 G6
pl. Illawong 459 F5
pl. Willmot 210 E14

BATCHELOR
av. Panania 398 A16
cl. Menai 458 H15

BATCHELORS WHARF
rd. Freemns Rch 90 J8

BATE
av. Allambie Ht 257 G16

BATE BAY
rd. Cronulla 494 B6

BATEHAVEN
cl. Prestons 392 K13

BATEMAN
cr. Bass Hill 367 F8
pl. Bligh Park 150 C6

BATEMANS
rd. Gladesville 312 K11

BATES
av. Blaxland 233 F9
av. Paddington 13 B13
av. S Wntwthvle 306 H7
cl. Elderslie 507 J4
dr. Kareela 461 B11
dr. Kareela 461 C14
dr. Kirrawee 461 D14
pl. Doonside 273 H1
pl. Edensor Pk 333 J14
st. Birchgrove 7 J3
st. Homebush 340 K9
st. Strathfield 340 K9
wy. Ambarvale 540 K1

BATH
rd. Kareela 461 B14
rd. Kirrawee 491 B3
rd.s, Kirrawee 491 A6
st. Monterey 433 H7

BATHO
st. Harbord 258 J15

BATHURST
la. Woollahra 22 H3
st. Berala 339 E13
st. Greystanes 305 J3
st. Gymea 461 G16
st. Leumeah 512 C3
st. Liverpool 395 D1
st. Liverpool 395 C4
st. Pitt Town 92 H15
st. Sydney C D14
st. Sydney 3 E7
st. Wakeley 334 H13
st. Warwck Frm 365 D16
st. Woollahra 22 H3

BATLOW
pl. Bossley Park 333 E13
st. Heckenberg 364 A13

BATMAN
cr. Springwood 202 C11
la. Surry Hills F E11
la. Surry Hills 3 K14
pl. St Johns Pk 364 G1
rd. Ingleburn 422 J14
wk. Parramatta, off Macquarie St 308 D3

BATT
st. Jamisontown 266 D1
st. Penrith 266 D1
st. Sefton 368 E5

BATTALION
cct. Haberfield 343 E16

BATTEN
av. Melrose Pk 310 J1
cct. S Windsor 150 F1
cr. Ermington 280 A15
pl. Doonside 273 H1

BATTENBERG
cl. Cecil Hills 362 D5

BATTERSEA
st. Abbotsford 312 H16

BATTERY
rd. Mosman 317 K6
st. Clovelly 377 J13

BATTLE
bvd. Seaforth 287 B11

BATTLEMENT
cr. Castle Hill 217 F3

BATTUNGA
pl. Engadine 489 D10

BATTY
st. Rozelle 7 F14

BATTYE
av. Beverley Pk 433 B8

BAUDIN
cl. Illawong 459 C4
cr. Fairfield W 335 D11
pl. Willmot 210 A11

BAUER
ct. Mt Annan 509 G3
rd. Cabramatta W 365 B9

BAULKHAM HILLS
rd. Baulkham Hl 247 A12

BAUMANS
rd. Peakhurst 430 G1
rd. Riverwood 400 F15

BAUXITE
pl. Eagle Vale 481 D8

BAVIN
av. Ryde 282 B16

BAX
gln. St Clair 300 B2

BAXTER
av. Kogarah 433 D3
av. Springwood 202 B1
cr. Glendenning 242 H6
dr. Old Tngabbie 277 A5
la. Kogarah 433 D3
rd. Bass Hill 367 F6
rd. Mascot 405 B5
st. S Penrith 237 A15

BAXTERS
la. Picton 563 H5

BAY
dr. Meadowbank 311 E4
la. Cronulla 523 H1
la. Ultimo 12 H14
pde. Malabar 437 F4
pl. Quakers Hill 243 K1
rd. Arcadia 130 F9
rd. Berowra Wtr 132 A6
rd. Berrilee 131 A11
rd. N Sydney K A1
rd. N Sydney 5 A6
rd. Oatley 430 G11
rd. Russell Lea 343 D3
rd. Taren Point 462 J15
rd. Waverton 5 A6
st. Birchgrove 7 H4
st. Birchgrove 7 H5
st. Botany 405 F11
st. Btn-le-Sds 433 G1
st. Coogee 407 F2
st. Croydon 342 F12
st. Double Bay 14 C10
st. Glebe 12 H13
st. Greenwich 314 K10
st. Mosman 316 K3
st. North Bondi 378 G3
st. Pagewood 405 J10
st. Pyrmont 8 J15
st. Rockdale 403 D15
st. Tempe 404 A3
st. Ultimo 12 H13
vst. Lilli Pilli 522 G1

BAYAN
pl. Bargo 567 F13

BAYARD
la. Concord, off Bayard St 312 A15
st. Concord 312 A15
st. Mortlake 312 A15

BAYBERRY
wy. Castle Hill 218 G16

BAYDON
st. Castle Hill 219 A8

BAYFIELD
rd. Arcadia 159 H2
rd. Galston 159 H2
rd. Galston 159 H7
rd. Greystanes 306 B11

BAYHAVEN
pl. Gymea Bay 491 H12

BAYLDON
pl. Glenmore Pk 266 A6

BAYLEY
rd. S Penrith 267 A6
st. Marrickville 373 E13

BAYLIS
pl. N Richmond 86 K13

BAYLY
ct. Hobartville 118 H7
st. Minchinbury 272 F9

BAYNES
st. Mount Druitt 271 A2

BAYNTON
pl. St Helens Park 541 A6

BAYSIDE
dr. Lugarno 430 B14
pl. Caringbah 492 E10
st. Lilyfield 9 G6
tce. Cabarita 312 F15

BAYSWATER
av. Hurstville Gr 431 G11
rd. Darlinghurst 13 B9
rd. Lindfield 284 D4
rd. Potts Point 4 J8
rd. Rcuttrs Bay 13 B9
st. Drummoyne 343 H1
st. St Johns Pk 364 C3

BAYTON
st. Oxley Park 270 D2

BAY VIEW
st. Lavender Bay 5 E14

BAYVIEW
av. Earlwood 403 C2
av. Mosman 317 D8
cr. Annandale 11 B6
cr. Henley 313 C14
la. Annandale 11 B6
la. Earlwood, off Bayview St 403 E2
pl. Bayview 169 B14
rd. Canada Bay 342 E10
rd. Peakhurst 430 D11
rd. Woolooware 493 D13
st. Arncliffe 403 D10
st. Bexley 402 J11
st. Bronte 378 A8
st. Concord 342 B3
st. Glebe 12 C10
st. Kogarah Bay 432 K12
st. Mt Krng-gai 163 B10
st. Northwood 314 G7
st. Pyrmont 8 G15
st. Scotland I 168 H4
st. Tennyson 312 D9

BAYVIEW HILL
la. Rose Bay 348 A7
rd. Rose Bay 348 B7

BAYVILLE
st. Balmain 344 E5

BAYWATER
dr. Homebush B 310 J8

BAZENTIN
st. Belfield 371 B11

BEACH
av. Vaucluse 318 G16
la. Coogee 377 H14
la. Emu Plains, off Beach St 235 F13
la. Mosman, off Military Rd 317 B6
rd. Bondi Beach 378 C1
rd. Collaroy 229 D14
rd. Dulwich Hill 373 E10
rd. Newport 169 H15
rd. North Bondi 348 B16
rd. Palm Beach 109 K14
st. Blakehurst 462 F1
st. Bundeena 524 A9
st. Clovelly 377 H15
st. Coogee 377 H15
st. Coogee 407 H2
st. Cronulla 524 A2
st. Curl Curl 258 J15
st. Double Bay 14 D7
st. Emu Plains 235 F13
st. Kogarah 433 D2
st. Tennyson 312 D10

BEACHCOMBER
av. Bundeena 524 A11
pl. Chipping Ntn 366 K15

BEACH PARK
av. Cronulla 493 K13

BEACON
av. Beacon Hill 257 J8
av. Glenhaven 217 J3
av. Putney 311 K5

BEACON HILL
rd. Beacon Hill 257 J7
rd. Brookvale 257 J7

BEACONIA
cl. Mona Vale 169 D16

BEACONSFIELD
av. Concord 342 A6
av. Kingsgrove 402 B7
av. West Hoxton 392 C5
la. Alexandria, off Beaconsfield St 375 F14
la. Beaconsfield, off Beaconsfield St 375 G13
la. Concord, off Beaconsfield Av 342 A6
pde. Lindfield 284 C1
rd. Chatswood W 284 C12
rd. Lane Cove N 284 C12
rd. Mortdale 430 H9
rd. Mosman 317 E9
rd. Rooty Hill 272 C5
rd. Rooty Hill 272 C7
st. Alexandria 375 F13
st. Beaconsfield 375 F13
st. Bexley 403 A16
st. Milperra 398 B12
st. Newport 169 F13
st. Revesby 398 B12
st. Silverwater 309 F13

BEACONVIEW
st. Balgowlah Ht 287 K14

BEACROFT
pl. Cranebrook 207 D13

BEAGLE
pl. Willmot 210 B12

BEAHAN
pl. Cherrybrook 219 K13

BEAL
pl. Glenmore Pk 266 A6

BEALE
cr. Fairfield W 335 C13
cr. Peakhurst 430 E6
st. Georges Hall 367 D15
st. Liverpool 395 B4

BEAMES
av. Mount Druitt 241 C16
av. Rooty Hill 272 B1
st. Lilyfield 10 C9

BEAMISH
la. Campsie 372 A13
rd. Northmead 277 J11
st. Campsie 372 A11
st. Padstow 399 D12

BEAN
pl. Bonnyrigg 364 C6

BEARD
pl. Glenorie 128 C14

BEARING
rd. Seven Hills 276 E1

BEASLEY
pl. S Windsor 150 K2

BEATHAM
pl. Milperra 397 G10

BEATRICE
cl. Berowra Ht 133 A7
st. Ashfield 372 F2
st. Auburn 339 C4
st. Balgowlah Ht 287 F14
st. Bass Hill 367 K7
st. Cecil Hills 362 K3
st. Clontarf 287 F14
st. Hurstville 431 H1
st. Lane Cove W 313 G2
st. Lidcombe 339 G12
st. North Ryde 282 H8
st. Rooty Hill 242 A13

BEATSON
la. Kingswood 237 D16

BEATTIE
av. Denistone E 281 J12
la. Surry Hills 19 H1
st. Balmain 7 F10
st. Rozelle 7 A12

BEATTY
la. Maroubra 407 C11
pde. Georges Hall 367 D13
st. Balgowlah Ht 288 A12
st. Maroubra 407 C11
st. Mortdale 430 H8
st. St Marys 270 A6

BEAU
ct. Quakers Hill 213 H7

BEAUCHAMP
av. Chatswood 284 K7
la. Surry Hills F D11
la. Surry Hills 3 K14
rd. Bnksmeadw 436 D2
rd. Hillsdale 406 F16
rd. Maroubra 407 C14
rd. Matraville 406 F16
st. Marrickville 373 E14
st. Wiley Park 400 G4

BEAUFIGHTER
st. Raby 451 F16

BEAUFORD
av. Caringbah 492 E15

BEAUFORT
cl. N Turramurra 193 E11
pl. Chullora 370 C4
rd. Blacktown 275 B7
st. Croydon Pk 372 B6
st. Guildford 337 E3
st. Northmead 277 J11

BEAUMARIS
av. Castle Hill 217 B9
cr. Mortdale 430 G10
dr. Menai 458 H9
st. Enfield 371 G3

BEAUMETZ
wy. Matraville 407 A16

BEAUMOND
av. Maroubra 407 J10

BEAUMONT
av. Denistone 281 A12
av. Glenwood 215 H13
av. N Richmond 87 F13
cr. Bayview 169 A14
dr. Beaumont Hills 185 J14
pl. Castle Hill 248 A3
rd. Killara 253 E15
rd. Mt Krng-gai 162 G3
st. Auburn 338 K8
st. Campsie 371 J16
st. Kingsgrove 402 B9

32 GREGORY'S STREET DIRECTORY

STREETS BE

Entry	Ref
st. Rose Bay	348 D12
st. Smithfield	335 B5
st. Waterloo	19 G12

BEAUMOUNT
- av. Chippendale ... 18 J4

BEAUREPAIRE
- av. Newington ... 310 A16

BEAUTY
- dr. Whale Beach ... 140 C9

BEAUTY POINT
- cr. Leonay ... 264 K2
- rd. Mosman ... 287 A9

BEAVORS
- rd. Prairiewood ... 334 J9

BEAZLEY
- pl. Baulkham Hl ... 246 K14
- st. Ryde ... 312 E3

BEBE
- av. Revesby ... 428 J2
- la. Revesby ... 428 J2

BECHARRY
- rd. Blacktown ... 243 K11

BECHERT
- rd. Chiswick ... 343 B2

BECK
- pl. Kellyville Rdg ... 215 D2
- st. Old Tngabbie ... 276 K10
- st. N Epping ... 251 J10

BECKE
- ct. Glenmore Pk ... 265 K9

BECKENHAM
- st. Canley Vale ... 366 F4

BECKET
- ct. S Penrith ... 266 K4

BECKHAUS
- st. St Johns Pk ... 364 J2

BECKMAN
- pde. Frenchs Frst ... 255 G1

BECKTON
- pl. Lilli Pilli ... 522 F2

BECKY
- av. North Rocks ... 279 A1

BECQUEREL
- pl. Lucas Ht ... 487 F13

BEDDEK
- st. McGraths Hl ... 121 H11

BEDDINGTON
- ct. Wattle Grove ... 426 C5

BEDE
- st. Lidcombe ... 339 H9
- st. Strathfield S ... 371 A4

BEDERVALE
- ct. Wattle Grove ... 426 A1

BEDFORD
- av. N Turramurra ... 223 F8
- cr. Collaroy ... 229 B16
- cr. Dulwich Hill ... 373 E13
- la. Newtown ... 17 B10
- pl. Rockdale ... 403 H15
- pl. S Coogee ... 407 H6
- pl. Sylvania ... 462 A11
- rd. Blacktown ... 244 K11
- rd. Homebush W ... 340 K6
- rd. N Epping ... 251 H11
- st. Earlwood ... 402 G2
- st. Emu Plains ... 234 K11
- st. Newtown ... 17 B11
- st. N Willoughby ... 285 F8
- st. Surry Hills ... 19 G3

BEDIVERE
- st. Blacktown ... 274 K7

BEDLEY
- pl. Cranebrook ... 207 E14

BEDNAL
- rd. Springwood ... 201 G2

BEDWIN
- rd. Marrickville ... 374 G12
- st. St Peters ... 374 G12

BEECH
- pl. Lugarno ... 429 J14
- rd. Mcquarie Fd ... 454 G1
- rd. Casula ... 423 J3
- rd. Prestons ... 393 J15
- st. Quakers Hill ... 243 F5

BEECHCRAFT
- av. Raby ... 451 F16

BEECHWOOD
- av. Greystanes ... 306 F11
- pde. Cherrybrook ... 219 G8
- pl. Bass Hill ... 367 J8

BEECHWORTH
- pl. Mt Colah ... 162 F14
- rd. Pymble ... 253 D16

BEECROFT
- rd. Beecroft ... 250 D3
- rd. Cheltenham ... 251 A12
- rd. Epping ... 251 A12
- rd. Pennant Hills ... 250 D3
- rd. Wilberforce ... 67 F15

BEE FARM
- rd. Springwood ... 201 G9

BEEF CATTLE
- rd. Richmond ... 118 J13
- rd. Richmond ... 119 A14

BEEHAG
- av. Arncliffe ... 403 E11
- st. Kyeemagh ... 404 B13

BEELA
- pl. E Kurrajong ... 67 G4

BEELAR
- st. Canley Ht ... 365 B11

BEELONG
- st. Dharruk ... 241 A6

BEEMERA
- st. Fairfield Ht ... 335 H10

BEEMRA
- st. Auburn ... 309 C15

BEERSHEBA
- pde. Holsworthy ... 426 D11

BEESON
- st. Leichhardt ... 15 B4

BEETHOVEN
- pl. Cranebrook ... 207 H9
- st. Engadine ... 518 D5
- st. Seven Hills ... 246 D12

BEGA
- av. Little Bay ... 437 B11
- cl. Prestons ... 393 A13
- pl. Bossley Park ... 333 G9
- rd. Georges Hall ... 367 J11
- rd. Jannali ... 460 H10
- rd. Northbridge ... 286 B15
- st. Marayong ... 243 J7
- st. Pendle Hill ... 276 C16
- st. St Marys ... 269 K5

BEGG
- la. Paddington ... 13 B15

BEGGS
- rd. Eastern Ck ... 272 G6
- st. Roselands ... 400 K10

BEGONIA
- av. Cabramatta ... 365 G11
- cl. Glenmore Pk ... 265 H8
- pl. Mcquarie Fd ... 454 A7
- pl. Woolooware ... 493 D9
- pl. Normanhurst ... 221 D13
- st. Pagewood ... 405 K10

BEGOVICH
- cr. Abbotsbury ... 333 A15

BEIHLER
- la. Ryde ... 282 A14

BELAH
- av. Vaucluse ... 348 H1
- gdn. Vaucluse ... 318 H16
- pl. Mcquarie Fd ... 424 E16

BEL-AIR
- ct. Penrith ... 237 B7

BELAIR
- av. Caringbah ... 493 B10
- cl. Hornsby ... 191 K15
- la. Bayview ... 169 A15
- pl. Mt Krng-gai ... 163 B10
- pl. Prairiewood ... 334 F7
- pl. Bow Bowing ... 452 D14
- st. Punchbowl ... 400 F7

BELAR
- av. Villawood ... 367 C4
- av. Villawood ... 367 E5
- rd. Camden ... 507 A8
- st. St Marys ... 239 G14

BELARADA
- cl. Bangor ... 459 B11

BELBOWRIE
- cl. Bangor ... 459 C10
- gln. Galston ... 159 G13
- gln. St Clair ... 270 B16

BELCOTE
- rd. Longueville ... 314 C10

BELEMBA
- av. Roselands ... 401 B5

BELFAST
- av. Killarney Ht ... 286 B1

BELFIELD
- la. Belfield ... 371 D9
- rd. Bossley Park ... 333 F13
- rd. Edensor Pk ... 333 G13

BELFORD
- pl. Greenacre ... 369 K10
- st. Ingleburn ... 453 A9

BELGENNY
- av. Camden ... 507 B6

BELGIAN
- st. Westmead ... 307 J3

BELGICA
- st. Tregear ... 240 C5

BELGIUM
- av. Roseville ... 284 G2
- st. Auburn ... 338 J10
- st. Lidcombe ... 340 B5
- st. Riverwood ... 400 B11

BELGRAVE
- esp. Sylvania ... 462 E8
- esp. Sylvania Wtr ... 462 C11
- la. Bronte ... 377 J7
- la. Cremorne, off
  Ben Boyd La 316 D8
- la. Neutral Bay, off
  Ben Boyd La 316 D8
- st. Bronte ... 377 J6
- st. Burwood ... 341 H16
- st. Cremorne ... 316 D8
- st. Kogarah ... 433 B5
- st. Manly ... 288 G10
- st. Petersham ... 15 J13

BELIMLA
- st. Auburn ... 309 C16

BELINDA
- cr. Glenwood ... 245 E2
- cr. N Epping ... 251 B9
- ct. Castle Hill ... 217 C10
- pl. Mays Hill ... 307 F6
- pl. Newport ... 169 G9
- rd. Alfords Point ... 459 C2
- st. Bass Hill ... 367 H8

BELL
- av. Beverly Hills ... 400 H16
- av. Hobartville ... 118 B6
- av. Kogarah Bay ... 432 J12
- av. Lindfield ... 283 H2
- av. West Ryde ... 280 G13
- av. Fairfield ... 336 H11
- av. Leumeah ... 512 E1
- la. Glebe ... 11 J10
- la. Randwick ... 377 A13
- la. Burraneer ... 523 E3
- la. Moorebank ... 396 E10
- la. Mt Pritchard ... 364 J11
- rd. Londonderry ... 148 F9
- rd. Concord ... 341 H8
- st. Glebe ... 11 H11
- st. Gordon ... 254 B7
- st. Hornsby ... 191 J11
- st. Maroubra ... 407 E9
- st. Panania ... 428 D4
- st. Riverwood ... 400 A10
- st. S Windsor ... 120 J12
- st. Thirlmere ... 565 A5
- st. Toongabbie ... 276 H5
- st. Vaucluse ... 318 G16

BELLA
- pl. Barden Rdg ... 488 H1
- st. Randwick ... 377 E9

BELLAMBI
- st. Cartwright ... 394 E4
- st. Northbridge ... 285 K15

BELLAMY
- av. Eastwood ... 281 F4
- la. Eastwood, off
  Bellamy Av 281 F4
- st. Pennant Hills ... 220 D16

BELLAMY FARM
- rd. W Pnnant Hl ... 249 E7

BELLARA
- av. N Narrabeen ... 198 G15

BELLATA
- cl. Glenbrook ... 264 D2
- pl. Hinchinbrk ... 392 J4

BELLATRIX
- la. Cranebrook ... 207 D5
  Bellatrix St 207 D5
- st. Cranebrook ... 207 E5

BELLA VISTA
- av. Warriewood ... 198 K7
- dr. Bella Vista ... 246 E3
- st. Heathcote ... 518 D11

BELLBIRD
- cl. Kurrajong Ht ... 63 F15
- cl. Canada Bay ... 342 G8
- cr. Blaxland ... 234 B7
- cr. Bowen Mtn ... 83 K9
- cr. Forestville ... 255 K12 |

Entry	Ref
ct. Quakers Hill	213 J10
dr. W Pnnant Hl	249 D7
la. Wedderburn	540 A10
pl. Cartwright	394 D4
pl. Kareela	461 C13
rd. Wedderburn	540 A11
st. Canterbury	402 D2

BELLBROOK
- av. Emu Plains ... 235 G9
- av. Hornsby ... 191 J16

BELLE ANGELA
- dr. Theresa Park ... 444 H8

BELLEDALE
- st. St Clair ... 270 E14

BELLE MARIE
- dr. Castle Hill ... 216 K9
- dr. Castle Hill ... 217 A8

BELLENDEN
- cl. Glenwood ... 215 B15
- pl. Dural ... 219 B2

BELLEREEVE
- av. Mt Riverview ... 234 B4

BELLEREVE
- pl. Leonay ... 234 J13

BELLERIVE
- cl. West Hoxton ... 392 F5

BELLETTE
- cl. Abbotsbury ... 333 A13

BELLEVALE
- ct. Stanhpe Gdn ... 215 G9

BELLEVARDE
- pde. Mona Vale ... 199 F1

BELLEVERDE
- av. Strathfield ... 371 B4

BELLEVISTA
- dr. Blacktown ... 274 B3

BELLEVUE
- av. Avalon ... 170 A3
- av. Denistone ... 281 A11
- av. Georges Hall ... 367 K13
- av. Greenwich ... 315 A6
- av. Lakemba ... 400 K1
- av. Paddington ... 13 A16
- av. West Ryde ... 281 B14
- cl. Rossmore ... 389 G5
- ct. Arncliffe ... 403 H10
- dr. Carlingford ... 249 D14
- gdn. Bellevue Hill, off
  Kendall St 377 G2
- la. Arncliffe ... 403 H11
- la. Glebe ... 12 E10
- la. Hurstville ... 432 C7
- la. Surry Hills ... F E16
- la. Surry Hills ... 3 K16
- la. West Ryde, off
  Dickson Av 281 C15
- pde. Allawah ... 432 C7
- pde. Caringbah ... 493 A6
- pde. Carlton ... 432 E9
- pde. Hurstville ... 432 C7
- pde. N Curl Curl ... 258 J9
- pde. N Curl Curl ... 258 K9
- rd. Bellevue Hill ... 14 F10
- rd. Regentville ... 235 E16
- st. Arncliffe ... 403 H11
- st. Blacktown ... 274 B4
- st. Cammeray ... 315 K5
- st. Chatswood W ... 284 B10
- st. Fairlight ... 288 C9
- st. Glebe ... 12 E10
- st. Kogarah ... 433 A6
- st. Maroubra ... 407 H10
- st. N Parramatta ... 278 D12
- st. Riverstone ... 183 C6
- st. St Peters ... 374 E16
- st. Surry Hills ... F E16
- st. Surry Hills ... 3 K16
- st. Tempe ... 404 E1
- st. Thornleigh ... 221 A14

BELLEVUE PARK
- rd. Bellevue Hill ... 377 H1

BELLFIELD
- av. Rossmore ... 389 D11

BELLINGARA
- rd. Miranda ... 461 K16
- rd. Sylvania ... 462 B13

BELLINGEN
- wy. Hoxton Park ... 392 H8

BELLINGER
- cl. Narellan Vale ... 478 G15
- pl. Sylvania Wtr ... 462 F15
- rd. Ruse ... 512 C8

BELLINGHAM
- av. Glendenning ... 242 F3
- st. Narellan ... 478 D8

BELLINI
- la. St Clair, off
  Bellini Pl 300 A2
- pl. St Clair ... 300 B2

BELLOC
- cl. Wetherill Pk ... 334 E5
- pl. Winston Hills ... 247 G16

BELLOMBI
- st. Campsie ... 372 D12

BELLONA
- av. Homebush ... 341 A5
- av. Regents Pk ... 368 H1
- st. Winston Hills ... 277 A2

BELLOTTI
- av. Winston Hills ... 277 F1

BELLS
- av. Cammeray ... 316 A6
- la. Kurmond ... 86 F5
- la. Strathfield, off
  Morwick St 341 G13
- rd. Grose Vale ... 85 B13
- rd. Oatlands ... 279 C13
- rd. Schofields ... 212 E4

BELLS LINE OF
- rd. Bell ... 57 A10
- rd. Berambing ... 60 B13
- rd. Bilpin ... 60 B13
- rd. Bilpin ... 61 A9
- rd. Blue Mtn N P ... 57 A10
- rd. Blue Mtn N P ... 59 A16
- rd. Kurmond ... 64 A16
- rd. Kurrajong ... 64 A16
- rd. Kurrajong Ht ... 63 A9
- rd. Kurrajong Hl ... 64 A16
- rd. N Richmond ... 87 C10
- rd. Kurrajong Ht ... 62 E8
- rd. Mt Tomah ... 59 H16

BELLTREE
- cr. Castle Hill ... 218 K5

BELLTREES
- cl. Glen Alpine ... 510 C11

BELLWOOD
- cl. Werrington ... 239 B11
- pl. Castle Hill ... 219 B9

BELMONT
- av. Penshurst ... 431 H6
- av. Sans Souci ... 433 F6
- av. Wollstncraft ... 315 D9
- gr. N Richmond ... 86 B13
- la. Alexandria ... 18 F16
- la. Mosman ... 317 A8
- la. Wollstncraft, off
  Shirley Rd 315 D9
- pde. Mt Colah ... 192 B5
- rd. Glenfield ... 424 D10
- rd. Mosman ... 316 H7
- st. Alexandria ... 18 G16
- st. Merrylands ... 307 E16
- st. Stanhpe Gdn ... 215 B5
- st. Sutherland ... 490 F4
- st.s. Sutherland ... 490 F6

BELMORE
- av. Belmore ... 371 D15
- av. Mount Druitt ... 241 B15
- la. Cromer ... 227 J13
- la. Enmore ... 17 B13
- la. Ryde ... 311 K2
- la. Surry Hills ... F B14
- la. Surry Hills, off
  Belmore St 3 K14
- la. Sydenham ... 374 D16
- la. Paddington ... 13 C16
- rd. Bringelly ... 418 C1
- rd. Eastern Ck ... 272 H8
- rd. Peakhurst ... 430 A7
- rd. Punchbowl ... 400 B13
- rd. Randwick ... 377 A13
- rd. Riverwood ... 400 B14
- rd. Riverwood ... 400 B16
- st. Arncliffe ... 403 G8
- st. Burwood ... 341 K15
- st. Enmore ... 17 B13
- st. Fairfield E ... 337 B13
- st. N Parramatta ... 278 E13
- st. Penrith ... 236 J9
- st. Rozelle ... 344 E8
- st. Ryde ... 311 H4
- st. Surry Hills ... F D15
- st. Surry Hills ... 3 K14
- st. Tempe ... 374 D16
- st. Villawood ... 337 B16
- st.e. N Parramatta ... 278 H12
- st.e. Oatlands ... 279 A12
- wk. Arncliffe, off
  Station St 403 G7

GREGORY'S STREET DIRECTORY 33

BE STREETS

BELROSE
ct. Bankstown.........368 H15
pl. Prospect............275 D12
BELTANA
av. Bonnyrigg..........363 K8
av. Terrey Hills.........196 F6
cl. Bangor...............459 B12
ct. Wattle Grove......425 K2
pl. Glen Alpine 510 D16
pl. Leonay...............234 K13
pl. Wahroonga........251 G1
st. Denistone 281 H13
BELUS
wy. Doonside...........243 E15
BELVEDERE
arc. Cabramatta, off
John St..............365 H7
av. Castle Hill..........217 H12
st. Mt Pritchard.......364 B11
BELVOIR
rd. Moorebank 425 B4
st. Surry Hills............19 G4
BEMBRIDGE
st. Carlton...............432 H7
BEN
pl. Beaumont Hills...185 J13
st. Marsden Pk........182 A12
BENAARA
gdn. Castle Hill...........218 A16
BENA BENA
pl. Holsworthy 426 C2
BENALLA
av. Ashfield 372 G1
av. Kellyville.............216 G7
cr. Marayong 243 K4
BENALONG
st. St Marys............239 F14
BENARES
cr. Acacia Gdn.........214 G16
BENAROON
av. St Ives 223 J10
rd. Belmore.............371 A12
rd. Lakemba............371 A12
BENAUD
cl. Menai 458 F9
ct. St Clair...............269 K16
la. St Clair, off
Benaud Ct..........269 K16
pl. Telopea..............279 H10
st. Blacktown..........274 F4
st. Greystanes.........306 A9
BENBOW
cl. Stanhpe Gdn......215 B10
BEN BOYD
la. Cremorne...........316 C8
la. Neutral Bay 316 C8
rd. Cremorne...........316 C10
rd. Neutral Bay............6 E4
BEN BULLEN
rd. Glenorie.............128 K1
BENBULLEN
wy. Castle Hill...........217 K7
BENBURY
st. Quakers Hill 214 B8
BENCOOLEN
av. Denistone 281 C14
av. West Ryde 281 C14
BENCUBBIN
st. Sadleir...............394 A1
BENDA
st. Belmore.............371 C14
BENDIGO
cl. Wakeley.............334 H13
pl. Cartwright..........394 A5
BENDTREE
wy. Castle Hill...........248 G4
BEN EDEN
st. Bondi Jctn..........377 G3
BENEDICT
cl. Cecil Hills............362 D5
ct. Holroyd..............308 A10
BENEDICTINE
pl. Cherrybrook.......219 E14
BENELONG
av. Smithfield 335 D7
cr. Bellevue Hill 347 J16
la. Cremorne...........316 E6
rd. Cremorne...........316 E6
st. Seaforth.............287 C7
BENFIELD
pde. Panania..............398 C14
BENGHAZI
rd. Carlingford.........249 K13
st. Bossley Park......334 A6
BENHAM
rd. Minto.................452 K16
st. Dulwich Hill........373 D6
BENINE
dr. Cmbrdg Pk.........238 C8
BENJAMIN
la. Glenbrook...........233 J14
pl. Currans Hill........479 K14
rd. Mt Pritchard.......364 H9
st. Bexley North 402 G9
st. Greystanes.........306 F8
BENJI
pl. Dean Park..........242 J2
BEN LOMOND
rd. Minto.................482 C2
rd. Minto Ht 483 A6
st. Bossley Park......333 D11
BENNABRA
pl. Frenchs Frst.......255 J3
BENNALONG
st. Granville 308 A13
st. Merrylands.........308 A13
BENNELONG
pl. E Kurrajong..........66 J8
pl. E Kurrajong..........66 J9
pl. Narellan 478 E15
rd. Homebush B......310 K13
rd. Homebush B......340 K1
st. Ruse..................512 H5
BENNET
pl. Maroubra...........407 D15
BENNETT
av. Carramar 366 K4
av. Darling Point........13 J3
av. Five Dock...........343 B8
av. Roselands..........401 B7
av. Strathfield S 371 E5
gr. Bidwill.................211 C15
la. Kurrajong Ht 63 F12
la. Mortlake 312 A15
la. Riverwood 400 A15
pl. Castle Hill...........218 F11
pl. Surry Hills............20 D2
rd. Colyton..............270 C9
rd. Londonderry 149 F10
rd. Riverwood 400 A15
rd. St Clair...............270 D11
rd. S Granville 338 G4
st. Bass Hill.............367 K4
st. Bondi..................377 J5
st. Burwood.............342 C11
st. Chester Hill 367 K4
st. Cremorne 6 H4
st. Curl Curl 258 F13
st. Dee Why............258 F4
st. Glenbrook...........233 H16
st. Kingsgrove.........402 B13
st. Minto.................482 K10
st. Mortlake 312 A14
st. Neutral Bay 6 H4
st. Newtown 18 C9
st. Surry Hills............20 D2
st. Wentwthvle........307 A2
st. West Ryde 281 A15
BENNETTS
rd.e, Dundas.............280 B13
rd.w, Dundas 279 H14
BENNETTS GROVE
av. Paddington 13 C16
BEN NEVIS
rd. Cranebrook........207 D14
BENNING
av. S Turramrra 252 A9
BENNISON
rd. Hinchinbrk 392 K1
BENNY
la. Yagoona 369 B13
pl. St Helens Park....541 B8
BENOWRA
pl. Davidson 225 E15
BENSBACH
rd. Glenfield 424 D13
BENSLEY
rd. Ingleburn 453 F16
rd. Mcquarie Fd.......453 K10
rd. Minto.................453 F16
BENSON
cl. Wahroonga........222 C5
la. West Ryde 281 J13
rd. Beaumont Hills...185 G15
rd. Ingleburn 452 J3
st. Carramar 366 H1
st. S Wntwthvle 307 D5
st. West Ryde 281 J13
BENSONS
la. Richmond Lwld..118 J4
BENT
la. Greenwich..........314 K9
la. Neutral Bay 6 C1
pl. Ruse..................512 G1
st. Carlton...............432 J5
st. Chester Hill 338 B16
st. Chipping Ntn......366 F14
st. Concord.............342 A4
st. Greenwich..........314 K9
st. Lindfield.............254 C16
st. Moore Park..........21 A9
st. Moore Park..........21 B7
st. Neutral Bay 6 B3
st. Paddington 21 C4
st. Petersham 16 B10
st. St Marys............239 F8
st. Sydney ....B C12
st. Sydney 1 J14
st. Villawood...........367 B4
BENTELLA
rd. Harringtn Pk.......478 H7
BENTHAM
pl. Castle Hill...........217 B6
BENTINCK
dr. Green Valley.......363 B10
BENTLEY
av. Forestville 256 B8
av. Kellyville............185 E9
gr. Menai 458 J15
la. Pendle Hill..........276 E14
rd. Colyton 270 E6
st. Balgowlah...........287 K9
st. Rooty Hill...........271 H2
st. Wetherill Pk 333 J2
BENTON
av. Artarmon 284 J15
BENTS BASIN
rd. Wallacia.............324 G14
rd. Wallacia.............354 F10
rd. Wallacia.............384 G1
BENTWOOD
tce. Stanhpe Gdn......215 D3
BENVENUE
st. Kingsford...........407 A6
BENWERRIN
av. Baulkham Hl 247 B5
av. Carss Park 432 F14
cl. East Killara.........254 H5
cr. Grasmere...........505 H4
la. Carss Park 432 F13
BERALA
st. Berala 339 E12
BERALLIER
dr. Camden S..........507 A12
BERAMBING
cr. Berambing 60 B13
BEREN
la. Cranebrook........207 D14
pl. Cranebrook........207 D15
BERENBEL
pl. Westleigh...........220 E9
BERENICE
st. Roselands..........401 A9
BERENICES
wy. Chatswood W 284 F10
BERESFORD
av. Bankstown.........369 G11
av. Baulkham Hl 248 A8
av. Beverly Hills 401 D15
av. Chatswood W 284 F12
av. Croydon Pk........372 C5
av. Greenacre 369 G10
cr. Bellevue Hill 347 G12
pde. Kingsgrove........402 B7
rd. Bellevue Hill 347 G11
rd. Caringbah 492 G3
rd. Greystanes.........305 K5
rd. Rose Bay 347 G11
rd. Strathfield 341 D11
rd. Strathfield 341 B12
rd. Thornleigh 221 C6
st. Mascot 405 E7
st. St Marys............270 A5
BERG
st. Blacktown..........274 J8
BERGALIA
cl. Prestons 393 A12
BERGER
rd. S Windsor..........150 J3
BERGIN
pl. Minchinbury.......271 J10
st. Denistone W 280 J11
BERGONIA
st. Mona Vale..........198 K3
BERILDA
av. Warrawee 222 D14
BERITH
rd. Greystanes.........306 F4
st. Auburn 339 B8
st. Collaroy Plat.......228 F11
st. Kingsgrove.........402 B10
BERKELEY
cl. Berowra Ht.........133 A10
gr. Rouse Hill 185 E2
st. Peakhurst 430 C8
st. S Wntwthvle 307 B6
st. Yanderra............567 B16
BERKLEY
rd. Padstow Ht 429 G9
wy. Rsemeadow.......540 J2
BERKSHIRE
rd. Riverstone 182 G10
BERLIET
pl. Ingleburn 453 K7
BERMILL
st. Rockdale............433 G2
BERMUDA
pl. Burraneer...........493 F13
pl. Kings Park 244 F3
BERNA
la. Canterbury 372 F15
st. Canterbury 372 F14
BERNACCI
st. Tregear..............240 C4
BERNADETTE
pl. Baulkham Hl 247 B3
pl. Fairfield..............336 E6
BERNADOTTE
st. Riverwood 400 E15
BERNARD
av. Bardwell Pk........402 G8
av. Gladesville 312 H13
la. Crows Nest, off
Emmett St..........315 H8
pl. Castle Hill...........248 C4
pl. Cherrybrook.......219 D13
pl. Mount Druitt 271 A4
rd. Padstow Ht 429 F9
st. Lidcombe...........339 H10
st. Westmead 307 F5
BERNARDO
st. Rsemeadow.......540 J8
BERNARRA
pl. Cranebrook 207 D15
BERNE
st. St Peters............374 G15
BERNERA
rd. Prestons 393 C15
rd. Prestons 423 C1
BERNICE
st. Seven Hills.........246 B11
BERNIE
av. Forestville 255 K12
st. Bundeena...........524 A10
st. Greystanes.........306 E11
BERNIE KELLY
dr. Maroubra...........407 G13
BERNIER
st. Minchinbury.......272 B8
wy. Green Valley.......363 A9
BERNOTH
pl. Edensor Pk 363 D3
BERONGA
av. Hurstville 402 B16
st. N Strathfield.......341 E5
BERONIA
ct. Cherrybrook.......219 G10
BEROWRA
pde. Berowra.............133 G13
rd. Mt Colah 192 C5
BEROWRA WATERS
rd. Berowra 133 D11
rd. Berowra Ht.........132 H4
rd. Berowra Ht.........133 A9
rd. Berowra Wtr 132 H4
BERRARA
cl. Prestons 393 C13
BERRICO
pl. Bangor...............459 C10
pl. Bargo.................567 D7
BERRIDALE
av. S Penrith............266 F5
la. S Penrith, off
Berridale Av 266 F5
pl. Heckenberg........364 A12
BERRIGAN
cl. St Clair...............270 B16
cr. Mcquarie Fd 454 D1
pl. Bossley Park 333 F9
st. Baulkham Hl 277 K3
BERRIL
pl. Glenmore Pk......266 D10
BERRILLE
rd. Narwee 400 K14
BERRILLEE
la. Turramurra 223 B14
st. Turramurra 223 B13
BERRIMA
av. Padstow 429 F5
pl. Doonside 243 C11
st. Heathcote 518 E9
BERRIMILLA
wy. Beaumont Hills...185 J15
BERRINDA
pl. Frenchs Frst.......255 K3
BERRING
av. Roselands..........400 K8
BERRIPA
cl. North Ryde 282 G14
BERRY
av. Fairlight..............288 D9
av. Naremburn 315 D3
av. N Narrabeen.......199 B14
cl. Grasmere...........475 J15
gr. Menai 459 A12
la. St Leonards 315 C7
pl. Wrrngtn Cty 238 F9
rd. St Leonards 315 C7
st. Cronulla 494 B6
st. Granville 308 H12
st. Mount Druitt 271 B2
st. N Sydney...............K C3
st. N Sydney...............K A4
st. N Sydney................5 D6
st. Prairiewood 334 K8
st. Prestons 392 H14
st. Regents Pk 369 C2
st. Rosebery 405 H2
BERRYMAN
st. North Ryde 282 K10
BERRY PARK
wy. Mt Colah 192 D5
BERT
cl. Warriewood 198 F6
BERTANA
cr. Warriewood 199 A6
BERT BAILEY
st. Moore Park..........21 B6
BERTHA
rd. Cremorne 6 J5
st. Fairfield..............336 G13
st. Merrylands.........307 J16
BERTRAM
cr. Beverley Pk........433 B8
la. Mortlake 312 A15
pl. Narellan Vale......479 C11
st. Chatswood.........285 A9
st. Concord.............312 A15
st. Eastwood............281 C5
st. Mortlake 312 A15
st. Yagoona 368 E13
BERTRAND
cl. Marsfield............282 B4
rd. N Turramurra.....223 E1
BERWICK
la. Darlinghurst...........4 D10
pl. Menai 458 J5
pwy. Winston Hills 277 F4
st. Coogee 407 F1
st. Guildford............337 D4
BERWIN
pl. Baulkham Hl 247 E8
BERYL
av. Mt Colah............162 C12
cl. Claymore 481 G9
pl. Greenacre 370 D7
pl. Rooty Hill...........242 A13
st. Westmead 307 H2
BESANT
pl. Rooty Hill...........272 A5
BESBOROUGH
av. Bexley................402 G15
BESFORD
wy. Minto.................482 K5

34 GREGORY'S STREET DIRECTORY

STREETS

BI

BESLEY
st. Cmbrdg Pk.........237 K7

BESSBROOK
wy. Wentwthvle, off
Tanderagee St 277 D10

BESSEMER
st. Blacktown 244 G10

BEST
cr. Kirrawee 490 H5
pl. Prairiewood 335 A8
rd. Middle Dural 158 C5
rd. Seven Hills........275 H2
st. Lane Cove.........313 J2
st. Woolmloo..............4 G4

BESTIC
st. Kyeemagh.........404 A14
st. Rockdale 403 E13

BESWICK
av. North Ryde........282 E6

BESZANT
st. Merrylands 308 B15

BETA
pl. Engadine 518 D3
pl. Quakers Hill 214 D13
rd. Lane Cove.........314 E4

BETH
wy. Glenwood.........215 H12

BETHAM
pl. Kirrawee 490 J8

BETHANY
ct. Baulkham Hl 216 K16
gl. Glenwood 245 H4

BETHEL
cl. Rooty Hill 271 K6
la. Paddington 4 J15
st. Toongabbie........276 F7

BETHEL STEPS
The Rocks..................B B1

BETOLA
st. Ryde..................282 C13

BETSEY
wy. Ambarvale........510 K16

BETTINA
ct. Greenacre 370 E16
pl. Dural..................188 G12
st. Merrylands W 307 A15

BETTINGTON
rd. Carlingford 279 A5
rd. Oatlands 279 B13
rd. Telopea.............279 B5
st. Millers Pt...............A A1
st. Millers Pt...............1 C9

BETTONG
cr. Bossley Park 333 F7
st. St Helens Park ..541 H1

BETTOWYND
rd. Pymble 223 C15

BETTS
av. Blakehurst........432 F12
av. Five Dock 343 C8
rd. W Pnnant Hl.......249 E10
rd. Merrylands W 306 F15
rd. Smithfield 306 F15
rd. Woodpark 306 F15
st. Kellyville Rdg 215 A1
st. Parramatta 278 F16
st. West Ryde........281 D14

BETTY
av. Winston Hills......277 F5
pl. Thirlmere 562 D16
pl. Thirlmere 565 D1
st. Blacktown 274 G8
st. Roseville 285 B4

BETTY CUTHBERT
av. Errington 310 B2

BETTY HENDRY
pde. North Ryde....282 J9

BETULA
pl. Loftus................489 J11

BEULAH
pl. Engadine 518 G3
st. Kingsford..........406 G9
st. Kirribilli..................2 D3

BEVAN
pl. Carlingford 279 J1
st. Northmead........277 J11

BEVANS
rd. Galston 160 B8

BEVERLEY
cr. Chester Hill 337 H10
av. Marsfield...........282 B7
cr. Penshurst 431 H6
cr. Roselands 401 B9

la. Darling Point.........13 K1
pl. Cherrybrook.......219 E6
pl. Curl Curl.............258 J14
pl. Wrrngtn Cty 238 D8
rd. Campbelltwn.....511 H2

BEVERLY
pl. Beverly Hills......401 A16
pl. Plumpton...........242 C11

BEVIN
av. Five Dock 342 G9

BEXLEY
rd. Bexley...............402 H12
rd. Bexley North 402 E10
rd. Campsie...........402 B1
rd. Earlwood 402 C5
st. Kingsgrove........402 C5
st. Mt Pritchard......364 C11

BEYER
pl. Currans Hill 479 H11

BIAMI
cl. Bangor...............459 C12

BIANCA
pl. Acacia Gdn 244 J1
pl. Rsemeadow......540 H5

BIARA
av. Clemton Park ...402 B3
cl. Marsfield............282 B3
pl. Turramurra 223 C8
st. Bargo.................567 C5
st. Chester Hill 338 A15

BIARGAR
av. Miranda 491 J5

BIBB
pl. West Hoxton 391 J12

BIBBALONG
la. Blacktown 273 H3

BIBBENLUKE
av. Duffys Frst 194 G7

BIBBY
st. Carlton..............432 G11
st. Chiswick 343 C2

BIBBYS
pl. Bonnyrigg..........364 B3
pl. St Johns Pk.......364 B2

BIBURY
cl. Chipping Ntn 396 D4

BICANE
cl. Edensor Pk........363 D2

BICHENO
cl. West Hoxton 392 C6

BICKELL
rd. Mosman 317 A2

BICKERTON
av. Green Valley.....362 K13

BICKLEIGH
st. Abbotsford........342 K4
st. Wareemba.........342 K4

BICKLEY
rd. S Penrith...........267 A7

BIDDY
pl. Ambarvale.........510 G14

BIDGEE
ct. Ryde..................282 E16

BIDURA
cl. Glen Alpine 510 F10

BIDURGAL
av. Kirrawee 491 C4

BIDWILL
sq. Bidwill...............211 E16

BIFFINS
rd. Cawdor.............505 D16
rd. Mt Hunter 505 D16

BIGGE
st. Liverpool...........395 E4
st. Warwck Frm 365 F16
av. Minto.................482 K6

BIG HILL
rd. The Oaks..........503 B2

BIGLAND
av. Denistone 281 B13
av. West Ryde........281 B13

BIGNELL
la. Annandale............17 D2
st. Illawong.............460 F1

BIJA
dr. Glenmore Pk.....266 B9

BIJIJI
st. Pendle Hill 276 G12

BIJOU
la. Haymarket...........E C13
la. Haymarket...........3 D15

BIKILA
st. Newington 310 B13

BILAMBEE
av. Bilgola..............169 G4
la. Bilgola...............169 H4

BILBERRY
av. Bilgola..............169 H4

BILBETTE
cr. Frenchs Frst 257 B3

BILBOA
cl. Edensor Pk........363 C1

BILBY
pl. Quakers Hill 214 E12

BILDERA
pl. Grays Point.......491 E15

BILGA
av. Bilgola..............169 H4
cr. Malabar.............437 D8
st. Kirrawee 490 K6

BILGOLA
av. Bilgola..............170 A5
st. Campbelltown...511 J6
tce. Bilgola.............170 A5

BILKURRA
av. Bilgola..............169 H4

BILLA
rd. Bangor...............459 C12

BILLABONG
av. Turramurra 223 A10
pl. Pendle Hill 276 H14
gln. Wrrngtn Dns ...238 E4
pl. Rouse Hill 185 D7
st. Pendle Hill 276 E14

BILLAGAL
pl. Blaxland 234 A6

BILLARA
av. Gymea Bay......491 D8

BILLARGA
rd. Westleigh..........220 F5

BILLAROGH
av. Dee Why 258 J2

BILL BARNACLE
av. Faulconbdg 171 G12

BILLEROY
av. Baulkham Hl 246 J7

BILLETT
st. Silverdale...........353 J13

BILLIKIN
wy. Ambarvale........511 A16
wy. Ambarvale........541 B1

BILLING
la. Greenacre, off
Glover St 370 F3

BILLINGTON
pl. Emu Plains........236 A7

BILLONG
cr. Vaucluse 348 G5
st. Neutral Bay............6 H9

BILLYARD
av. Elizabeth Bay 13 A3
av. Wahroonga.......222 F7
gr. Turramurra 222 K7
la. Wahroonga, off
Illoura Av............222 E7
pl. Carlingford 279 F4
wk. Wahroonga, off
Cleveland St......222 E7

BILMARK
pl. Btn-le-Sds.........403 K14

BILOELA
pl. Gymea Bay......491 H10
st. Villawood..........367 E3
st. Villawood..........367 F3

BILOOLO
rd. Green Valley.....363 J10

BILPIN
cl. Bangor...............459 C12
rd. Bossley Park 333 D10
st. Greystanes........305 F9

BILPIN SPRINGS
rd. Bilpin..................61 D4

BILSTON
st. Berowra............133 E9

BILWARA
av. Bilgola..............169 G4
cr. S Penrith...........266 J7

BILYANA
pl. Rouse Hill 185 C5

BIMAN
pl. Whalan..............240 K10

BIMBADEEN
av. Bradbury...........511 F16
av. Lugarno............430 A13

av. Miranda 492 D4
cr. Frenchs Frst 256 J5
st. Epping 280 G5

BIMBADGEN
pl. Bella Vista........216 B15

BIMBAI
cl. Bangor...............459 D12

BIMBERI
st. Horngsea Pk.....392 D15

BIMBI
pl. Bonnyrigg..........363 J9

BIMBIL
av. Mt Colah..........192 A4
pl. Castle Hill..........218 A12
st. Killara................283 E3
st. Blacktown 244 A14

BIMBIMBIE
av. Bayview...........168 K15

BIMBURRA
st. St Ives 223 H9

BINALONG
av. Allambie Ht 257 F14
av. Caringbah 492 F6
av. Georges Hall 367 H11
rd. Belimbla Pk.......501 D14
rd. Kenthurst..........156 H7
st. Mt Colah..........162 B16
rd. Old Tngabbie....276 H14
rd. Pendle Hill 276 H14
rd. Toongabbie.......276 H14
rd. Wentwthvle.......276 H14
rd. Yellow Rock......174 K14
st. West Pymble....252 J10

BINARA
cl. Hamondvle........396 G14

BINAVILLE
av. Burraneer.........523 E2

BINBA
pl. Brookvale..........258 C8

BINBURRA
av. Avalon 140 D13

BINDA
cr. Little Bay...........437 B10
pl. Baulkham Hl 246 K9
rd. Yowie Bay........492 A11
st. Merrylands W 307 B12

BINDAREE
pl. Kellyville............216 F2
st. Hebersham 241 F9
st. Lansvale...........367 B10

BINDEA
st. Como................460 F8
st. Jannali...............460 F8
st. Mt Pritchard......364 C10

BINDEE
cl. Glenmore Pk.....266 A7

BINDER
st. Hurstville 431 H1

BINDI
pl. Beacon Hill 257 F5

BINDON
pl. Kellyville............216 F2

BINDOOK
cr. Terrey Hills........196 D7

BINDOWAN
cl. Erskine Park.....300 D2

BINET
wy. Glenhaven.......218 D5

BINGARA
cr. Bella Vista........246 E7
dr. Sandy Point......427 K10
rd. Beecroft 250 C11
rd. Mcquarie Fd 453 C2
st. West Pymble....253 A13

BINGARRA
pl. Bargo.................567 D7

BINGHAM
pl. Edensor Pk.......333 J15

BINHAM
cl. Chipping Ntn 366 G13

BINNA BURRA
st. Villawood..........367 D2

BINNARI
rd. Hornsby Ht 191 G5

BINNAWAY
av. Hoxton Park.....392 G8

BINNEY
rd. Kings Park........244 F4
st. Caringbah 492 H15

BINNING
st. Erskineville 18 B16
st. Erskineville 18 C16

BINNIT
pl. Glenmore Pk.....266 B12

BINNOWEE
av. St Ives 223 K9
dr. Bayview...........169 A15

BINOMEA
pl. Pennant Hills 250 G2

BINYA
cl. Hornsby Ht 162 A7
pl. Como................460 H6
st. Blaxland 234 F6
st. Pendle Hill 276 G12

BINYON
cl. Wetherill Pk 334 H4

BIRALEE
cr. Beacon Hill 257 K6

BIRCH
av. Casula 394 G14
gr. Baulkham Hl 248 B12
pl. Bidwill...............211 D14
pl. Kirrawee 490 K1
pl. Mcquarie Fd 424 F16
st. Brnkstn Arpt.....368 B16
st. Condell Park....368 B16
st. East Ryde.........283 A14
st. N St Marys........240 A11

BIRCHGROVE
av. Canley Ht 364 K3
rd. Balmain 7 D2
rd. Birchgrove 7 D6

BIRD
av. Guildford...........337 K4
av. Lurnea 394 G9
la. St Clair, off
Banks Dr 269 H11
st. St Clair..............269 H11
st. St Helens Park ..541 C3
st. Ryde.................282 H16
wy. West Hoxton ...392 A10

BIRDS
la. Bondi Jctn 22 J9
la. Maraylya...........125 A14

BIRDSALL
av. Condell Park....398 H4

BIRDSVILLE
cr. Leumeah..........482 G10

BIRDWOOD
av. Belfield..............371 F9
av. Cabramatta W ...364 G7
av. Collaroy 229 C13
av. Daceyville........406 G6
av. Doonside 243 E16
av. East Killara 254 D8
av. Holsworthy 396 A13
av. Killara................254 D8
av. Lane Cove........314 D1
av. Pagewood 406 G6
av. Winmalee.........172 H13
cl. Narrabeen 228 G7
la. Georges Hall, off
Georges Cr.........367 F14
la. Lane Cove........314 D1
rd. Brnkstn Arpt.....367 G14
rd. Georges Hall 367 G14
st. Denistone E......281 J11
st. Sylvania...........461 J8

BIRGITTE
cr. Cecil Hills.........362 G7

BIRINTA
st. Narraweena.....258 A2

BIRK
pl. Bligh Park 150 G6

BIRKDALE
cct. Glenmore Pk.....266 F10
cl. Liverpool...........395 C9

BIRKLEY
la. Fairlight..............288 E8
la. Manly 288 E8
rd. Manly 288 E8

BIRMINGHAM
av. Villawood.........337 G16
rd. S Penrith...........266 F4
st. Alexandria........375 E16
st. Merrylands........307 H10

BIRNAM
av. Blacktown 243 J15
gr. Strathfield.........341 C16

BIRNIE
av. Homebush B....340 E4
av. Lidcombe.........340 C6

BIROK
av. Engadine 518 K1

BIRONG
pl. Dharruk.............241 D6

GREGORY'S STREET DIRECTORY 35

BI STREETS

BIRRAMAL
rd. Duffys Frst 194 H7
BIRR CROSS
rd. Moorebank 425 C4
BIRRELL
la. Queens Park 22 D11
st. Bondi 377 H6
st. Bondi Jctn 22 D9
st. Tamarama 377 H6
st. Waverley 22 D9
st. Waverley 377 H6
BIRRELLEA
av. Earlwood 402 E5
BIRRIGA
av. Chester Hill 368 B2
rd. Bellevue Hill 377 J1
rd. Croydon 342 G13
BIRRIMA
st. N Balgowlah 287 H5
BIRRIWA
av. Belfield 371 B8
cct. Mt Annan 479 E14
pl. Baulkham Hl 246 H6
pl. Northwood 314 G8
st. Greystanes 305 G9
BIRRONG
av. Belrose 225 H15
av. Birrong 368 K6
BIRRU
pl. Belrose 225 K14
BIRTLES
av. Pendle Hill 276 G11
BIRTLEY
pl. Elizabeth Bay 13 A6
BIRUBI
av. Gymea 491 E1
av. Pymble 223 C14
cr. Bilgola 169 E8
BIRUNNA
av. Gymea 491 G1
BISCAY
gr. Kellyville Rdg 214 K4
BISCAYNE
av. S Wntwthvle 306 K9
BISCOE
pl. Tregear 240 F8
BISDEE
pl. Engadine 489 C13
BISHOP
av. Pemulwuy 305 F7
av. Matraville, off Cemetery Av 436 G8
av. W Pnnant Hl 249 K2
cl. Green Valley 363 B12
cl. S Windsor 150 F2
cr. Bonnyrigg 364 E5
rd. Menai 458 G15
st. Cabarita 342 D1
st. Newport 169 G11
st. Petersham 15 F15
st. Revesby 399 A11
st. St Peters 374 J14
BISHOPGATE
av. Castle Hill 217 G4
la. Camperdown 17 D9
st. Camperdown 17 D9
st. Newtown 17 D9
BISHOPS
av. Randwick 377 F12
BISHOPSCOURT
pl. Glen Alpine 510 B12
BISMARCK
st. McGraths Hl 122 B14
BISMARK
rd. Northmead 278 B5
BISMIRE
st. Panania 398 A15
BITTERN
cl. Erskine Park 270 H14
cl. Hinchinbrk 393 D2
gr. Glenwood 215 F14
BIWA
cl. St Clair 269 G15
la. St Clair, off Rotarua Rd 269 F16
BIX
rd. Dee Why 258 F3
BIZET
pl. Bonnyrigg Ht 363 D7
BLACK
cl. Illawong 459 F5
st. Marrickville 374 E10
st. Vaucluse 348 D6

BLACKADDER
cl. Chiswick 343 C2
BLACKALL
st. Revesby 399 B14
BLACKASH
pl. Hornsby Ht 162 A5
BLACKBIRD
cr. Bowen Mtn 84 A9
gln. Erskine Park 271 A14
la. St Clair, off Blackbird Gln 271 A14
BLACKBURN
av. North Rocks 249 A16
av. West Hoxton 392 A10
cct. Camperdown 18 A4
pl. Gymea Bay 491 D7
rd. Wedderburn 540 A16
st. St Ives 224 F7
st. Surry Hills F B9
st. Surry Hills 3 J13
BLACKBUTT
av. Bradbury 511 F11
av. Lugarno 429 J11
av. Pennant Hills 250 K4
cir. Mt Riverview 204 E15
cr. Greystanes 306 E12
pl. Engadine 488 H16
pl. Leonay 235 A16
pl. The Oaks 502 D12
st. Bossley Park 333 G9
st. Parklea 215 A13
BLACKBUTTS
rd. Frenchs Frst 255 F2
BLACKET
pl. West Hoxton 392 B10
st. Heathcote 518 H10
BLACKETT
dr. Castle Hill 247 F3
pl. Cabramatta W 365 B4
st. Kings Park 244 D2
BLACKFORD
cr. S Penrith 266 G4
st. Fairfield E 337 D14
BLACKFRIAR
pl. Wetherill Pk 335 A1
BLACKFRIARS
la. Chippendale 19 A2
pl. Chippendale 19 A1
st. Chippendale 19 A1
BLACK LION
pl. Kensington 376 C9
BLACKMAN
cr. Horngsea Pk 392 G15
cr. S Windsor 120 K16
ct. Wrrngtn Cty 238 E5
la. Bass Hill 368 E10
la. Yagoona 368 E10
BLACKMORE
la. Redfern 19 K11
pl. Wetherill Pk 334 F6
rd. Smeaton Gra 479 B8
BLACKROCK
mw. Baulkham Hl 216 E14
BLACKS
rd. Arcadia 159 D2
rd. W Pnnant Hl 248 H7
BLACKSHAW
av. Mortdale 430 H7
BLACKSMITH
cl. Stanhpe Gdn 215 F9
ct. Bella Vista 246 F3
st. Greenfld Pk 334 D13
BLACKSTONE
st. Wetherill Pk 305 C16
BLACK SWAN
pl. Yarramundi 145 E6
BLACKTHORN
cct. Menai 458 K12
pl. Kellyville 216 A2
BLACKTOWN
rd. Blacktown 275 A2
rd. Freemns Rch 90 G3
rd. Londonderry 149 F1
rd. Prospect 275 C11
rd. Richmond 118 K8
rd. S Windsor 149 F1
BLACKWALL POINT
rd. Abbotsford 342 K2
rd. Chiswick 343 A2
BLACK WATTLE
gr. Narellan Vale 479 A14
pl. Sydney 3 D6
st. Peakhurst 430 E4

BLACKWATTLE
cct. Old Tngabbie 277 D6
la. Ultimo 12 J14
pl. Alfords Point 459 A1
pl. Cherrybrook 219 J8
pl. Sydney C B12
BLACKWATTLE CREEK
la. Darlington 18 G5
BLACKWELL
av. St Clair 270 A16
av. St Clair 300 A2
BLACKWOOD
av. Ashfield 372 F5
av. Casula 394 J15
av. Clovelly 378 A12
av. Dulwich Hill 373 E11
av. Minto 452 J15
av. Mt Krng-gai 162 J14
cl. Beecroft 250 D3
cl. Bossley Park 333 E9
cr. Mcquarie Fd 454 E1
la. Dulwich Hill, off Blackwood Av 373 E11
pl. Oatlands 278 G10
rd. Merrylands 307 C9
rd. N Curl Curl 258 K10
rd. Vineyard 152 D7
st. Belfield 371 D10
st. Miranda 491 K7
BLADES
pl. Douglas Park 568 H1
pl. Mt Annan 479 F15
BLAIKIE
rd. Jamisontown 235 J15
BLAIN
st. Toongabbie 276 F9
BLAIR
av. Croydon 342 E13
av. East Hills 427 J4
av. St Marys 239 H15
la. St Marys, off Blair Av 239 H15
pl. Cabramatta 366 A10
pl. Minto 453 C16
pl. St Ives 253 K2
st. Bondi Beach 378 C1
st. Gladesville 312 H10
st. North Bondi 378 C1
BLAIR ATHOL
dr. Blair Athol 511 A3
BLAIRGOWIE
pl. Oatlands 278 J11
BLAIRGOWRIE
cct. St Andrews 452 B16
la. Dulwich Hill, off Windsor Rd 373 D6
st. Dulwich Hill 373 D6
BLAISE
pl. Parklea 215 A12
BLAKE
av. Blakehurst 462 F3
av. Hunters Hill 314 B13
cl. Wetherill Pk 334 J6
pl. Eagle Vale 481 B9
rd. Mt Annan 479 D15
st. Balmain 8 C10
st. Dover Ht 348 D10
st. Kogarah 433 A6
st. Quakers Hill 213 K8
st. Rose Bay 348 D10
BLAKEFORD
av. Ermington 280 E15
BLAKESLEY
rd. Allawah 432 F10
rd. Carlton 432 F10
rd. S Hurstville 432 C11
st. Chatswood 285 A8
BLAMEY
av. Caringbah 492 G15
pl. Doonside 273 F1
pl. Narellan Vale 479 C10
pl. Revesby 398 J16
pl. St Ives 224 F16
rd. Holsworthy 396 A13
st. Allambie Ht 257 H16
st. Colyton 270 B5
st. North Ryde 282 J11
st. Revesby 398 H16
wy. Cherrybrook, off Tennyson Cl 219 E10
BLAMIRE
la. Marrickville 373 J14
BLANC
av. East Hills 428 A4

BLANCHE
av. Padstow 429 E2
st. Belfield 371 B9
st. Minto 482 F2
st. Oatley 431 E11
BLAND
rd. Oakville 124 E7
rd. Springwood 202 A2
st. Ashfield 372 J2
st. Bradbury 511 E8
st. Carramar 336 H16
st. Haberfield 343 A15
st. Woolmloo 4 F3
BLANDFORD
av. Bronte 377 H7
st. Collaroy Plat 228 J12
BLANE
st. Granville 308 C10
st. Minto 482 J4
BLANTYRE
cl. Thornleigh 221 C12
BLARNEY
av. Killarney Ht 286 B1
BLASHKI
av. Rookwood 340 D13
BLATTMAN
av. Oakdale 500 C12
cl. Blacktown 273 H5
st. Colyton 270 C7
BLAXCELL
pl. Harringtn Pk 478 F6
st. Granville 308 F16
st. Guildford 338 D9
st. S Granville 338 E3
BLAXLAND
av. Luddenham 356 H2
av. Newington 310 D11
av. Newington 310 D12
av. Penrith 237 B9
dr. Illawong 459 E6
la. Penrith, off Blaxland Av 237 B9
la. Ryde, off Devlin St 311 K1
pl. Glenhaven 218 B3
pl. Milperra 397 J7
rd. Bellevue Hill 347 J16
rd. Camden S 506 K12
rd. Campbelltown 511 B4
rd. Denistone 281 F10
rd. Denistone E 281 F10
rd. Eastwood 281 F10
rd. Epping 281 C1
rd. Ingleburn 423 A9
rd. Killara 253 D15
rd. Rhodes 311 D9
rd. Ryde 312 A2
st. Frenchs Frst 256 E2
st. Hunters Hill 313 B7
st. Lalor Park 245 D13
st. Matraville 437 A2
st. Silverwater 309 K8
st. Yennora 337 B10
BLAXLANDS CORNER
Lane Cove 314 F5
BLAXLANDS RIDGE
rd. Blaxlands Rdg 65 C4
BLEND
pl. Woodcroft 243 G7
BLENHEIM
av. Rooty Hill 241 J13
la. Queens Park 22 J13
pl. Glenfield 424 F9
pl. St Clair 270 F14
rd. Carlingford 279 F5
rd. Lindfield 254 D14
rd. North Ryde 283 A11
rd. Schofields 182 H15
st. Croydon Pk 371 F7
st. Queens Park 22 K11
st. Randwick 376 K14
BLENMAN
av. Punchbowl 400 A7
BLETCHLEY
pl. Hebersham 241 F5
BLICK
pde. Canterbury 372 H13
BLIGH
av. Camden S 506 J10
av. Lurnea 394 B12
cl. Georges Hall 368 C15
cr. Seaforth 286 J9
ct. St Clair 270 A11
la. Eastwood 281 F5
pl. Kellyville 215 G4
pl. Randwick 377 D11
st. Burwood Ht 371 K3
st. Chifley 437 C3
st. East Killara 254 F7
st. Eastwood 281 F5
st. Fairfield E 337 B15
st. Guildford 338 C8
st. Kirrawee 490 J7
st. Kirribilli 6 A15
st. Northbridge 286 A16
st. Riverstone 183 C11
st. Silverwater 309 H14
st. Sydney B C15
st. Sydney 1 J16
st. Villawood 337 B15
BLIGHS
rd. Cromer 227 J12
BLIND
rd. Nelson 155 A8
BLOMFIELD
rd. Denham Ct 422 G15
BLOODWOOD
pl. Bradbury 511 E9
rd. Fiddletown 130 A3
rd. Ingleside 197 F3
BLOOMFIELD
la. Surry Hills 4 D14
st. S Coogee 407 H5
st. Surry Hills 4 D14
BLOOMSBURY
av. Pymble 253 E4
BLOSSOM
pl. Quakers Hill 213 K11
BLOXSOME
la. Mosman 316 G9
BLUCHER
st. Sans Souci 463 C6
BLUE
pl. Wetherill Pk 334 D5
st. N Sydney K C11
st. N Sydney 5 F10
BLUE ANCHOR
la. Sydney A K8
BLUE BELL
cct. Kellyville 215 K3
rd. Heathcote 518 E9
BLUEBELL
cl. Glenmore Pk 265 H8
pl. Heathcote 518 E9
BLUEBERRY
ct. Narellan Vale 478 H14
dr. Colyton 270 H6
gr. Glenwood 245 C2
pl. Alfords Point 429 C16
pl. Alfords Point 459 C1
BLUEBIRD
rd. Cranebrook 207 B11
BLUEBUSH
cl. Bossley Park 333 J9
BLUE COW
av. Beaumont Hills 215 G3
BLUE CRANE
cl. W Pnnant Hl 248 F8
BLUEFISH
dr. Manly 289 A13
BLUE GUM
av. Chatswood W 284 F8
av. Gymea Bay 491 E8
av. Ingleburn 453 F5
av. Roseville 284 F8
av. S Penrith 267 B1
cr. Blaxland 234 C9
cr. Stanhpe Gdn 215 B11
dr. East Ryde 283 A15
pl. Newington, off Newington Bvd 310 B14
rd. Annangrove 156 A14
rd. Kenthurst 156 A14
rd. Wentwthvle 277 A9
BLUEGUM
av. Prestons 394 C14
cct. Old Tngabbie 277 F7
cr. Frenchs Frst 256 F4
cr. Picnic Point 428 H7
gr. Glenwood 245 J2
pl. Roseville 284 C6
rd. S Maroota 69 G1
st. Normanhurst 221 E13
wy. Menai 458 J10
BLUE GUMS
wy. Castle Hill 218 J13
BLUE HILLS
cr. Blacktown 244 B16
dr. Glenmore Pk 266 E12

36 GREGORY'S STREET DIRECTORY

STREETS BO

BLUE JAY
ct. W Pnnant Hl......249 D7
BLUE RIDGE
cr. Berowra Ht......132 K5
ct. Glenhaven......218 E2
pl. Orchard Hills......267 F5
BLUES POINT
rd. McMahons Pt......K A15
rd. McMahons Pt......5 D16
rd. N Sydney......K K10
rd. N Sydney......5 D16
BLUESTONE
dr. Glenmore Pk......266 C14
BLUETT
av. East Ryde......282 J15
cr. Doonside......243 C6
dr. Smeaton Gra......479 E7
st. Marayong......244 D7
BLUE WREN
pl. Oakdale......500 F11
BLUEWREN
cl. Glenmore Pk......265 K12
BLUFF
st. Green Valley......363 R11
BLUNDELL
cct. Kellyville......216 D2
st. Marsfield......282 A5
BLUNT
pl. Rsemeadow......540 G7
BLYTHE
av. Glenwood......215 H12
BLYTHESWOOD
av. Turramurra......222 D14
av. Warrawee......222 D14
BOAB
pl. Casula......423 K1
BOADA
pl. Winston Hills......277 G2
BOAKE
cl. Glenmore Pk......265 K7
BOALA
pl. Engadine......489 C9
BOAMBILLEE
av. Vaucluse......348 D2
BOANBONG
rd. Palm Beach......140 A4
BOARD
st. Lidcombe......339 H7
st. N Parramatta......278 B11
BOARDMAN
st. Dundas Vy......280 D10
st. Yagoona......369 F7
BOATWRIGHT
av. Lugarno......430 A8
BOBADAH
st. Kingsgrove......402 A8
BOBART
st. Parramatta......308 A5
BOBBIN
pl. Bangor......459 C13
BOBBIN HEAD
rd. Krngai Ch N P......163 J16
rd. N Turramurra......223 E7
rd. Pymble......223 E7
rd. Turramurra......223 E7
BOBIN
rd. Sadleir......364 B16
BOBS
pl. Matraville......406 K16
BOBS RANGE
rd. Orangeville......443 J16
BOBUCK
pl. St Helens Park......541 H2
BOCKING
av. Bradbury......511 K2
BOCKS
rd. Oakville......152 K7
BODALLA
cr. Bangor......459 B12
ct. Wattle Grove......426 B3
st. Fairfield Ht......335 H8
BODE
pl. Barden Rdg......458 G16
BODEN
av. Strathfield......340 J15
ct. Castle Hill......217 D9
st. Seven Hills......276 F1
BOEING
cr. Raby......451 G13
st. Btn-le-Sds......433 J1
st. St Clair......270 D16
rd. Mascot......404 J4

BOFFIN
pl. Ambarvale......510 F16
BOGALARA
rd. Old Tngabbie......276 J11
BOGAN
av. Baulkham Hl......247 G4
av. Sylvania Wtr......462 E10
pl. Ruse......512 H12
pl. Seven Hills......275 F10
pl. Wahroonga......222 A15
st. Greystanes......306 A4
st. Summer Hill......373 E3
BOGIE
la. Allawah......432 C7
la. Hurstville......432 C7
BOGONG
pl. Prairiewood......334 F7
BOGOTA
av. Neutral Bay......6 J7
BOHAN
wy. Minto......482 H6
BOHEMIA
st. Malabar......437 F6
BOHR
cr. Lucas Ht......487 H11
BOILER
cl. Blacktown......274 C14
BOKANA
pl. North Rocks......248 J16
BOKHARA
cr. Greystanes......306 C5
BOLAND
av. Springwood......201 J2
la. Marrickville......373 K10
st. Springwood......201 K2
BOLARO
av. Greystanes......305 G10
av. Gymea......491 F2
BOLD
st. Burwood......371 J1
st. Cabramatta W......364 J7
st. Granville......308 F10
BOLDERO
cr. Glenmore Pk......266 H13
BOLDREWOOD
av. Casula......424 F2
cl. Cherrybrook......219 C8
pl. Blackett......241 B3
BOLGER
st. Campbelltown......510 K7
BOLINDA
st. Busby......363 G12
BOLINGBROKE
pde. Fairlight......288 B10
BOLIVIA
st. Cabramatta......365 G8
BOLLARD
pl. Picton......563 C13
BOLTA
pl. Cromer......258 A1
BOLTON
av. Mt Colah......192 C5
av. Mt Pritchard......364 F9
pl. Pymble......253 J2
st. Guildford......337 G7
st. Prospect......275 D12
st. St Peters......374 E14
st. Sydenham......374 E14
BOLTONS
st. Horngsea Pk......392 D15
BOLWARRA
av. West Pymble......253 C14
cr. Castle Hill......248 G2
rd. N Narrabeen......198 G13
BOMADERRY
dr. Prestons......393 D16
BOMBALA
cr. Quakers Hill......243 K3
st. Pendle Hill......276 C16
BOMBARDIERE
pl. Baulkham Hl......248 B7
BOMBAY
st. Lidcombe......339 K6
BOMBELL
av. Engadine......518 F3
BOMBO
pl. Prestons......393 A16
pl. Bangor......459 C13
BOMBORA
av. Bundeena......524 B11
BON
st. Chipping Ntn......396 C5

BONA
cr. Morning Bay......138 E13
BON ACCORD
av. Bondi Jctn......377 G3
la. Bondi Jctn, off Bon Accord Av......377 G2
BONACCORDO
rd. Quakers Hill......214 B14
BONALBO
st. Kingsgrove......402 B9
BONANZA
la. Sans Souci......433 C16
pde. Sans Souci......433 C16
BONAPARTE
st. Riverwood......400 D14
BONAR
st. Arncliffe......403 G7
st. Telopea......279 F8
st. Wolli Creek......403 G7
BONA VISTA
av. Maroubra......407 H10
BOND
av. Toongabbie......276 F7
cr. Wetherill Pk......333 G4
la. Mosman......316 K4
la. N Strathfield......341 E7
pl. Illawong......459 F7
st. Hurstville......431 K4
st. Maroubra......407 H10
st. Mosman......316 K5
st. North Ryde......282 D11
st. Sydney......A J13
st. Sydney......1 G15
BONDELL
av. Gymea......491 G2
BONDI
rd. Woodbine......481 F13
pl. Bondi......377 F3
rd. Bondi Jctn......377 F3
st. Bundeena......523 J11
BONDS
rd. Peakhurst......430 E1
rd. Punchbowl......400 F7
rd. Riverwood......400 E13
rd. Riverwood......400 E16
rd. Roselands......400 E7
rd. Thirlmere......564 A3
BONEDA
cl. Annangrove......155 K16
BONGALONG
st. Naremburn......315 G3
BONHAM
st. Canley Vale......366 F2
BON MART
Winston Hills......277 G2
BONNEFIN
pl. Castle Hill......218 E16
rd. Hunters Hill......313 D8
BONNER
av. Manly......288 H5
st. Agnes Banks......117 D13
BONNET
av. Como......460 D6
BONNEY
cl. St Helens Park......541 C5
cl. St Ives Ch......224 A6
rd. Doonside......273 E4
st. Sans Souci......433 A16
BONNIE DOON
pl. Burraneer......523 E3
BONNIE FIELD
cl. Catherine Fd......449 D3
BONNIE VIEW
st. Gymea......491 D6
BONNIEVIEW
st. Woolooware......493 D12
BONNYRIGG
av. Bonnyrigg......363 K5
BONTON
rd. Springwood......202 C7
BONTOU
pl. Pymble......223 K16
st. St Ives......223 K16
BONUS
st. North Bondi......348 C15
BONZ
cl. Seven Hills......276 E1
BONZER
pl. Glendenning......242 E5
BOOBOOK
pl. Ingleburn......453 F10

BOOKER
rd. Hawksbry Ht......174 G3
BOOKS
cr. McGraths Hl......121 K12
st. Dean Park......212 H15
BOOLA
av. Yennora......337 B8
pl. Cromer......228 E13
pl. Westleigh......220 G9
BOOLARONG
av. Chipping Ntn......396 G5
rd. Pymble......223 F14
BOOLEROO
pl. Westleigh......220 G6
BOOLIGAL
rd. Terrey Hills......195 H3
BOOMERANG
av. Earlwood......402 G5
av. Lilli Pilli......522 G1
cr. Raby......451 E12
dr. Glossodia......66 D10
pl. Cmbrdg Gdn......237 F4
pl. Seven Hills......275 H2
pl. Woolmloo......D H11
rd. Collaroy Plat......228 H13
rd. Edensor Pk......363 H3
rd. Springwood......201 G3
st. Granville......308 B11
st. Haberfield......343 E6
st. Maroubra......407 G9
st. Turramurra......223 A12
BOOMI
pl. Woronora......459 K16
BOONA
rd. Terrey Hills......195 H7
BOONAH
av. Eastgardens......406 K12
la. Eastgardens......406 G12
st. Wentwthvle......276 K11
BOONAL
st. Baulkham Hl......247 A6
BOONARA
av. Bondi......378 A5
la. Bondi, off Boonara Av......378 A5
BOONDAH
pl. Kareela......461 B12
pl. Warrawee......222 H10
rd. Warriewood......199 A11
BOONGARY
st. St Helens Park......541 J1
BOONGIL
st. West Pymble......252 J8
BOONOKE
cr. Miller......393 H2
pl. Airds......512 C12
wy. Airds......512 C13
BOORABUL
av. Lindfield......283 H6
BOORAGUL
st. Beverly Hills......401 B10
BOORALEE
st. Botany......405 C12
BOORALIE
rd. Duffys Frst......195 A2
rd. Terrey Hills......196 K15
BOORALLA
dr. Edensor Pk......333 K16
BOORARA
av. Oatley......430 K16
av. Oatley......431 A15
BOOREA
av. Lakemba......371 A14
st. Blaxland......233 H6
st. Lidcombe......339 G3
BOOREE
ct. Wattle Grove......426 A2
BOOREEA
st. Blacktown......274 E2
BOORIMA
pl. Cronulla......494 A14
BOORROO
ct. Kangaroo Pt......461 J4
BOOTES
av. Hinchinbrk......393 E4
BOOTH
la. Fairfield W......335 A12
la. Annandale......11 B14
la. Cherrybrook......219 K10
pl. Minchinbury......271 F9
st. Annandale......11 A14
st. Arncliffe......403 H6
st. Balmain......7 H11

st. Camperdown......17 D1
st. Marsfield......282 C4
st. Westmead......307 H4
BOOTIE
pl. Kings Lngly......246 D10
BOOTLE
pl. Cranebrook......207 G12
BOOTLES
la. Pitt Town......92 H12
BOOTS
la. Ingleburn......453 D5
BOOYONG
av. Caringbah......492 J4
av. Lugarno......430 A13
cl. Picton......562 J8
st. Cabramatta......365 H10
BORA
pl. Toongabbie......276 H10
pl. Wilberforce......92 C1
BORAGA
st. Pemulwuy......305 E6
BORAMBIL
pl. Longueville......314 E6
pl. Oyster Bay......461 D4
st. Warrawee......222 F10
BORDEAUX
cr. Castle Hill......216 K9
cr. Castle Hill......217 A9
dr. Orchard Hills......268 H14
BORDER
cl. Eldersile......507 K1
cr. Hinchinbrk......363 A14
rd. Horsley Pk......332 H8
BORDLEY
pl. Oakhurst......242 B5
BOREC
rd. Penrith......236 F3
BOREE
pl. Bangor......459 C12
pl. Mcquarie Fd......454 F4
pl. Wrrngtn Dns......238 B3
pl. Westleigh......220 E7
st. Forestville......255 D8
st. Marsfield......282 A4
BORELLA
rd. Milperra......397 D9
BORG
pl. Prairiewood......334 E12
BORGAH
ct. Carss Park......432 F14
BORGNIS
st. Davidson......225 E16
BORLAISE
st. Willoughby......285 E14
BORNEO
ct. Bossley Park......334 B5
BORO
pl. Prestons......393 B13
BORODIN
cl. Cranebrook......207 F9
BORODINO
pl. Narellan Vale......479 A16
BOROJEVIC
st. Bonnyrigg Ht......363 A5
BOROMI
wy. Cromer......227 K11
BORONGA
av. West Pymble......252 H13
pl. Bangor......459 B11
av. Berowra Ht......133 B10
BORONIA
av. Beecroft......250 F9
av. Burwood......342 C13
av. Cheltenham......250 F9
av. Croydon......372 C3
av. Engadine......518 H2
av. Epping......280 G1
av. Hunters Hill......313 C7
av. Mt Annan......509 C3
av. Russell Lea......343 D5
av. Turramurra......252 E1
cr. Stanhpe Gdn......215 E10
cr. Mulwane......173 K6
cr. Voyager Pt......427 B5
la. Hinchinbrk......518 H12
la. Denistone E......281 F8
la. Redfern......20 B8
la. Seaforth......286 K7
la. Mosman, off Brady St......317 A5
pde. Lugarno......430 B15
pde.w.Lugarno......430 A14
pl. Cheltenham......250 J11
rd. Bellevue Hill......347 J14

GREGORY'S STREET DIRECTORY 37

BO STREETS

rd. Bossley Park......333 F10
rd. Glenorie.............127 G8
rd. Greenacre...........369 J11
rd. Ingleside............198 A4
rd. Kentlyn..............483 F12
rd. N St Marys.........239 J7
rd. N St Marys.........240 B9
st. Belfield..............371 B11
st. Concord W..........311 E14
st. Cronulla.............523 K2
st. Dee Why............259 A7
st. Ermington..........310 D4
st. Kensington.........376 E11
st. Kyle Bay............431 J15
st. Lalor Park..........245 B11
st. N Balgowlah.......287 F6
st. Redfern................19 K8
st. S Granville.........338 G2
st. S Wntwthvle.......306 K5
st. Wollstncraft.......315 D8

BORRODALE
rd. Kingsford...........406 D2

BORROWDALE
cl. Lurnea...............394 C12
cl. Narellan.............478 E14
pl. Beacon Hill..........257 F4
pl. Bligh Park...........150 C5
wy. Beaumont Hills...185 K14
wy. Cranebrook.........207 D11

BORTFIELD
dr. Chiswick............343 D1

BORTHWICK
pl. Castle Hill...........216 K10
st. Minto.................482 G7

BORU
pl. Killarney Ht........286 D2

BOSAVI
st. Glenfield............424 G14

BOSCI
rd. Ingleburn...........452 K5

BOSCO
pl. Schofields..........213 J6

BOSCOBEL
rd. Londonderry......177 G4

BOSLEY
av. Liverpool............364 K15

BOSNJAK
av. Edensor Pk........333 G15

BOSSLEY
rd. Bossley Park......333 F7
tce. Woolmloo..............4 E5

BOSTOCK
st. Richmond..........120 A5

BOSTON
cl. Hinchinbrk.........392 K1
pl. St Clair...............270 G13
pl. Toongabbie.........275 F14
wy. Beaumont Hills...216 A1

BOSWORTH
st. Richmond..........118 F5

BOTANIC
rd. Mosman............317 D8

BOTANICAL
dr. Kellyville............216 A4

BOTANY
bvd. Kings Lngly........246 A10
bvd. Seven Hills.........246 A10
cir. Matraville...........436 G8
la. Alexandria............19 B13
la. Kingsford...........406 J1
la. Mascot..............405 E6
la. St Clair...............270 C12
pl. Bondi Jctn..........377 F5
pl. Ruse..................512 G8
pl. Yagoona............368 H11
rd. Alexandria............19 A11
rd. Bnksmeadw.......435 J1
rd. Bnksmeadw.......436 C3
rd. Beaconsfield......375 F16
rd. Botany...............405 E9
rd. Mascot...............405 E5
rd. Matraville...........436 C3
rd. Port Botany.........436 C3
rd. Rosebery...........405 E5
rd. Waterloo..............19 A11
rd. Zetland..............375 F16
st. Allawah.............432 E4
st. Bondi Jctn..........377 F5
st. Kensington..........376 K16
st. Kingsford...........406 H5
st. Randwick...........406 J3

BO TREE
pl. Prestons............393 J15

BOTTLE BRUSH
av. Beaumont Hills...215 K2
dr. Faulconbdg........171 D12
pl. Colyton..............270 H6
rd. Westleigh...........220 H8

BOTTLEBRUSH
av. Bradbury............511 F10
av. Casula...............423 H2
av. Lugarno.............430 A9
cl. Picton...............561 C4
dr. Cranebrook........237 E1
gr. Acacia Gdn.........214 J15
la. Warriewood.......198 G10
la. Cranebrook, off Greygums Rd......207 E16
pl. Alfords Point......429 B15
st. Mt Annan...........509 F5

BOTTLE FOREST
rd. Heathcote..........518 J11

BOTTLES
rd. Plumpton...........241 K7

BOUCHET
cr. Minchinbury.......271 K8

BOUDDI
st. Bow Bowing.......452 C15

BOUGAINVILLE
av. Bossley Park......333 K6
ct. Maroubra...........407 C14
rd. Blackett.............241 A1
rd. Glenfield............424 E12
rd. Lethbrdg Pk.......240 G2

BOUGHTON
st. Richmond..........118 J7

BOULT
cl. Bligh Park..........150 D5

BOULTON
av. Baulkham Hl......247 E4
st. Putney...............311 K6

BOUNDARY
la. Cabramatta........365 K8
la. Cabramatta........365 J8
la. Darlington............18 E8
la. Paddington............4 J12
la. Paddington............4 K12
rd. Box Hill..............153 D13
rd. Carlingford.........279 J3
rd. Castle Cove........285 J2
rd. Cherrybrook.......219 G13
rd. Chester Hill........338 E13
rd. Cranebrook.........206 K8
rd. Faulconbdg........201 D1
rd. Glossodia.............66 G12
rd. Heathcote..........518 D14
rd. Liverpool............394 G9
rd. Lurnea...............394 G9
rd. Maraylya............124 A15
rd. Mortdale............430 G3
rd. N Epping............251 E8
rd. Northmead.........277 K11
rd. Oakville.............153 D13
rd. Oatley...............431 A8
rd. Peakhurst..........430 G3
rd. Pennant Hills......250 F1
rd. Pennant Hills......250 E1
rd. Schofields..........183 G11
rd. Sefton...............338 E13
rd. Springwood........201 D1
rd. Vineyard............153 D13
rd. Wahroonga.........222 F2
st. Alexandria............19 A10
st. Berowra.............133 E12
st. Castle Cove........285 E3
st. Clovelly..............377 J11
st. Clovelly..............378 A12
st. Croydon.............342 D15
st. Darlinghurst............4 H13
st. Darlington............18 H5
st. Granville............308 A8
st. Paddington............4 H13
st. Parramatta.........308 A8
st. Redfern................18 K10
st. Roseville............284 J5
st. Roseville Ch........285 E3
st. Thirlmere...........564 J10
st. Thirlmere...........565 A10
st. Warriewood........198 E6

BOUNTY
av. Castle Hill...........217 H10
av. Kirrawee............491 A9
cr. Bligh Park..........150 H9
pl. Old Tngabbie......277 C7

BOURKE
la. Paddington............4 K16
la. Queens Park........22 H12
la. Pymble, off Bannockburn Rd..223 C13
la. Redfern................20 B11
pl. Abbotsford.........343 A4
pl. Blairmount.........480 K13
pl. Botany...............405 F11
pl. Camden S..........506 K12
rd. Alexandria..........375 B15
rd. Mascot..............405 B3
rd. Pendle Hill..........276 G13
st. Blaxland.............233 D5
st. Darlinghurst...........4 E12
st. Liverpool............395 C5
st. Mascot..............405 B2
st. N Parramatta......278 B10
st. Pymble.............223 C13
st. Queens Park........22 H13
st. Redfern................20 B11
st. Richmond...........118 J8
st. Riverstone.........182 H5
st. Smithfield..........335 E7
st. Surry Hills..............4 D16
st. Waterloo............375 H9
st. Woolmloo..............4 E7
st. Zetland.............375 H9

BOURMAC
av. Northbridge.......286 F15

BOURNE
st. Marrickville........374 E11
st. Wentwthvle........277 A15

BOURNEMOUTH
st. Bundeena...........524 A11

BOUSSOLE
rd. Daceyville..........406 E3

BOUVARDIA
ct. Acacia Gdn.........214 J14
st. Asquith..............191 K10
st. Caringbah..........492 H16
st. Punchbowl.........400 D1
st. Russell Lea........343 C4

BOVIS
pl. Rooty Hill...........272 C6

BOW
av. Parklea..............215 A12
la. Kingsford...........406 H2

BOWAGA
av. Blaxland.............234 E7

BOWATER
cl. N Wahroonga.....222 K1

BOW BOWING
cr. Bradbury............511 H12

BOWDEN
bvd. Yagoona............369 C9
cl. Green Valley.......363 B11
cr. Connells Pt.........461 G1
la. Woollahra............22 A5
pl. Belfield...............371 E12
st. Alexandria..........375 E9
st. Cabramatta.........365 D11
st. Guildford............337 A1
st. Harris Park.........308 F8
st. Meadowbank.....311 E5
st. Merrylands W....307 B16
st. N Parramatta......278 J15
st. Ryde..................311 G2
st. Woollahra............21 K5

BOWEN
av. S Turramrra.......252 A10
cl. Cherrybrook.......219 C10
pl. Maroubra...........407 D16
pl. Seven Hills.........275 D6
st. Chatswood W....284 H13

BOWENIA
ct. Stanhpe Gdn......215 E10

BOWEN MOUNTAIN
rd. Bowen Mtn..........84 A12
rd. Grose Vale...........84 D11

BOWER
la. Manly................288 K11
st. Bankstown.........369 B14
st. Manly................288 K11
st. Plumpton............242 B10
st. Roselands..........401 D6

BOWER BIRD
ct. Kenthurst...........158 A15

BOWER-BIRD
st. Hinchinbrk.........393 B4

BOWERBIRD
av. Ingleburn...........453 F9
cr. St Clair...............269 J10

BOWERMAN
pl. Cherrybrook.......219 F15

BOWERS
pl. Leumeah............482 K11

BOWES
av. Edgecliff...............13 H12
av. Killara................253 F15
av. S Penrith............266 H2
cl. Cecil Hills...........362 J9
pl. Doonside...........273 E2

BOWIE
pl. Wetherill Pk.......334 D5

BOWLER
av. Fairfield.............336 D9

BOWLERS
av. Bexley................403 A14

BOWLING GREEN
la. Avalon...............170 A1

BOWMAN
av. Camden S..........507 B13
av. Castle Hill...........247 J4
av. Frenchs Frst.......256 D2
rd. Londonderry.......148 G13
st. Drummoyne.......343 G4
st. Mortdale............430 H8
st. Pyrmont...............12 C2
st. Richmond..........119 B5
wy. Minto................482 K1

BOWMANS
rd. Kings Park.........244 E5

BOWMER
st. Banksia.............403 D12

BOWNESS
ct. Kellyville.............186 K15
st. Collaroy Plat.......228 D9

BOWNS
rd. Kogarah............433 A6

BOWOOD
av. Bexley...............402 H14
la. St Marys, off Bowood Pl.........270 A6
pl. St Marys............270 A6
rd. Mt Vernon..........331 A6

BOWRA
cl. Bangor...............459 C12

BOWRAL
cl. Hornsby Ht........161 J7
la. Kensington, off Doncaster Av.....376 F11
rd. Blacktown..........274 F2
st. Greystanes.........305 H4
st. Kensington.........376 E11
st. North Rocks.......279 A2

BOWREY
pl. Shalvey.............211 C12

BOWTELL
av. St Johns Pk.......364 J2

BOX
av. Wilberforce..........67 J15
la. Jannali...............460 H12
pl. Mcquarie Fd.......454 H3
rd. Box Hill..............184 E1
rd. Caringbah..........462 G15
rd. Casula...............394 B16
rd. Casula...............424 B2
rd. Jannali...............460 H12
rd. Kareela..............461 B13
rd. Prestons............394 B15
rd. Rouse Hill...........184 E1
rd. Sylvania.............461 J14
rd. Sylvania Wtr.......462 G15
rd. Wakeley.............334 G14

BOXER
pl. Rooty Hill...........272 D5

BOXLEY
cr. Bankstown.........399 G6

BOXSELL
cl. Menai................458 K11

BOXWOOD
pl. Cherrybrook.......219 E10

BOYCE
av. Strathfield..........341 A11
la. Glebe...................11 H12
la. Maroubra...........407 E10
pl. Ruse..................512 H7
rd. Maroubra...........406 H8
rd. Maroubra...........407 A9
st. Glebe...................11 H12
st. Ryde..................282 E14
wy. Clarmnt Ms........268 G3

BOYD
av. Lugarno.............429 K10
av. W Pnnant Hl.......249 K3
ct. Harringtn Pk.......478 E7
la. Berala, off Sixth Av............339 D16
la. Gladesville..........313 A3
la. Glenbrook..........233 K14
la. Neutral Bay............6 D8
pl. Barden Rdg........458 G16
pl. Wrrngtn Cty.......238 E5
st. Austral..............390 E11
st. Blacktown...........244 K16
st. Cabramatta W....364 K7
st. Claymore............481 C8
st. Eagle Vale..........481 C8
st. Turramurra........222 H14

BOYER
pl. Minto.................453 A16
rd. Beacon Hill.........257 E4
rd. Beacon Hill.........257 F5

BOYLE
la. Sutherland.........490 E3
pl. Shalvey.............211 B15
st. Balgowlah..........287 K9
st. Cremorne...........316 F11
st. Croydon Pk.........372 A6
st. Ermington..........310 D4
st. Mosman............316 F11
st. Sutherland.........490 E3

BOYLES
la. Sun Valley..........203 E7

BOYLSON
pl. Cromer..............227 H13

BOYNE
av. Pendle Hill..........306 E1
pl. Baulkham Hl......246 J4
pl. Killarney Ht........256 B15
pl. Wahroonga........222 B14

BOYNTON
st. Blaxland.............233 D6

BOYS
av. Blacktown..........244 H15

BOYTHORN
av. Ambarvale..........510 J14

BOZ
pl. Ambarvale..........511 A14

BRABHAM
dr. Eastern Ck..........273 C13

BRABYN
st. Denistone E........281 F9
st. Fairfield W..........335 C8
st. N Parramatta......278 H15
st. Parramatta.........278 H15
st. Windsor.............120 K11

BRACHER
st. East Hills............427 J2

BRACK
cl. Abbotsbury........333 C12

BRACKEN
cl. Berowra.............163 C1
cl. Engadine............488 K15

BRACKEN FELL
cl. Castle Hill...........217 G10

BRACKNELL
av. Hebersham........241 F5
rd. Canley Ht...........365 A3

BRAD
pl. Kings Lngly........245 F8

BRADBURY
av. Bradbury............511 E6
av. Campbelltown....511 E6
st. Tahmoor............565 K10

BRADDOCK
pl. Baulkham Hl......247 K15

BRADDON
la. Oxley Park, off Braddon St.........240 F16
pl. Edensor Pk........363 G3
st. Blacktown...........273 K4
st. Concord.............312 A16
st. Oxley Park..........240 D15

BRADEY
av. Hamondvle........396 E15

BRADFIELD
cr. Bonnyrigg..........364 A5
hwy. Dawes Point..........A G4
hwy. Dawes Point..........1 G8
hwy. Millers Pt...............A G4
hwy. Millers Pt...............1 G8
hwy. Milsons Point.........5 K13
pl. Doonside...........273 G4
rd. Lindfield............283 F4
st. Leumeah............482 D16

BRADFORD
la. Balmain.................7 J11
st. Alexandria..........375 E16
st. Balmain.................7 J11
st. Pymble..............223 E14

BRADLEY
av. Bellevue Hill.......347 H16
av. Berala................339 D15
cr. Wiley Park..........400 H5
ct. W Pnnant Hl.......248 J7
dr. Carlingford.........249 J15
dr. Harringtn Pk.......478 J3

38 GREGORY'S STREET DIRECTORY

STREETS BR

la. Elizabeth Bay........13 B6
la. Randwick, off Bradley St..........376 K13
pl. Illawong............460 A4
pl. Liberty Gr...........311 C13
pl. Ruse.................512 H4
rd. N Richmond.........87 B13
rd. S Windsor..........150 E2
st. Drummoyne.......343 F3
st. Ingleburn...........453 C10
st. Mulgoa..............296 G1
st. Randwick...........376 K13
BRADLEYS HEAD
rd. Mosman...........317 B9
BRADLY
av. Kirribilli.................6 B12
BRADMAN
av. St Clair...............270 A15
rd. Menai................458 E9
rd. Shalvey..............211 A15
st. Greystanes.........305 J9
st. Greystanes.........306 B9
st. Merrylands.........308 B15
st. Narwee.............400 K15
BRADSHAW
av. Moorebank........395 G9
pl. Prairiewood.......334 J8
BRADY
pl. Glenmore Pk......266 A5
pl. Kellyville............216 G5
pl. Prairiewood.......334 D10
st. Croydon............342 C16
st. Merrylands.........308 B12
st. Mosman............317 A5
wy. Bonnyrigg..........364 D5
BRADYN
pl. Glenmore Pk......265 F7
BRAE
pl. Castle Hill..........248 G2
st. Bronte...............377 H9
st. Prospect...........274 H13
BRAEBURN
cr. Bella Vista..........216 C15
BRAEFIELD
pl. Castle Hill..........218 B7
BRAEKELL
pl. Kellyville............186 J15
BRAEMAR
av. Auburn.............309 E15
av. Kellyville............217 B3
av. St Andrews........451 K15
dr. S Penrith...........267 A2
pl. Roseville...........255 A16
st. Smithfield..........336 B5
BRAEMONT
av. Kellyville Rdg.....214 K2
BRAEMORE
ct. Castle Hill..........218 K6
BRAESIDE
av. Penshurst..........431 G7
av. Smithfield..........335 G5
cr. Earlwood...........402 D7
cr. Glen Alpine........510 E14
pl. Engadine...........488 J12
rd. Greystanes.........306 E6
st. Wahroonga........222 F5
BRAESMERE
rd. Panania.............427 K1
BRAHMA
cl. Bossley Park......334 A12
rd. N Richmond.........87 K6
BRAHMS
st. Seven Hills.........246 D13
wy. Clarmnt Ms........268 F3
BRAIDWOOD
av. N Epping............251 E8
dr. Prestons............392 J15
dr. Prestons............392 J16
dr. Prestons............393 A16
dr. Prestons............422 K1
st. Strathfield S.......370 H3
BRAIFIE
pl. Parklea.............214 J13
BRAIKFIELD
av. Kemps Ck..........359 J7
BRAIN
av. Lurnea...............394 D11
BRALLAS
av. St Ives Ch..........223 J6
BRALLOS
av. Holsworthy........396 D15
BRAMBLE
pl. Mcquarie Fd.......454 E5
pl. Whalan..............240 J9
BRAMHALL
av. Punchbowl.........399 J7
BRAMLEY
av. Newport............169 J11
st. Fairfield W.........335 B8
BRAMPTON
av. Stanhpe Gdn......215 C5
cl. Hinchinbrk.........363 B16
dr. Beaumont Hills...185 J13
dr. Beaumont Hills...186 A14
dr. Beaumont Hills...216 A1
pl. Greystanes.........305 J1
BRAMSTON
av. Earlwood...........402 F2
BRAMWELL
pl. Illawong............460 A3
BRAN
wy. Kellyville Rdg.....185 B16
BRANCOURT
av. Bankstown.........369 C14
av. Bankstown.........369 C16
av. Yagoona...........369 C14
BRAND
st. Artarmon...........284 K14
st. Croydon............342 D15
st. Dundas Vy.........279 J6
BRANDE
st. Belmore............371 C15
BRANDERS
la. N Richmond.........87 C6
BRANDLING
la. Alexandria............18 F13
st. Alexandria............18 F13
BRANDON
av. Bankstown.........399 C1
gr. Kellyville............217 C4
la. Bankstown, off Brandon Av........399 D2
pl. St Ives..............224 F7
st. Clovelly.............377 H11
BRANDS
la. Warriewood.......198 K8
BRANKSOME
wy. Glenmore Pk......266 F15
BRANSBY
pl. Mt Annan...........479 G13
BRANSFIELD
st. Tregear.............240 F6
BRANSGROVE
rd. Panania.............397 J13
rd. Revesby............398 A13
st. Wentwthvle........307 B3
BRANTWOOD
st. Sans Souci.........463 B5
BRASSIE
st. North Bondi.......348 C16
BRATSELL
st. Moorebank........396 C11
BRAUNBECK
st. Bankstown.........369 B15
BRAY
av. Earlwood...........402 G6
ct. North Rocks.......249 B16
gr. Menai................458 K15
la. Neutral Bay............6 A8
la. Erskineville, off Bray St..............374 J10
la. N Sydney...............6 A8
pl. Ambarvale..........510 F15
st. Drummoyne.......343 G3
st. Dundas..............280 A12
st. Erskineville.........374 K10
st. Fairfield..............336 E7
st. Mosman............316 H4
st. N Sydney...............5 K8
BRAYE
pl. Padstow Ht........429 F7
BRAYS
rd. Breakfast Pt.......341 K1
rd. Concord............341 K1
BRAYTON
cl. Prestons............392 H15
BRAZIER
st. Guildford............338 B7
BREAKFAST
rd. Marayong..........243 K7
BREAKFAST POINT
bvd. Breakfast Pt.......312 C16
BREAKWELL
la. Mortdale............431 A4
st. Mortdale............430 K5
BREAM
st. Como................460 E6
st. Coogee.............377 E15
BREASLEY
av. Yagoona...........368 J12
pl. Yagoona...........369 A11
BRECHIN
cl. Emu Plains.........235 E14
rd. St Andrews........451 K15
BRECON
ct. Castle Hill...........218 C11
BREDBO
st. Prestons............393 B13
BREDON
av. W Pnnant Hl.......218 K16
pl. Jamisontown.....266 C4
BREELLEN
cl. Tahmoor............565 F12
BREEZA
pl. Bangor..............459 B13
BREILLAT
la. Annandale............11 A8
st. Annandale............11 A8
BRELL
pl. Kingswood.........237 F9
BRELOGAIL
st. Northmead.........277 J11
BREMER
pl. Hinchinbrk.........392 K1
BREN
cl. St Clair..............269 K12
BRENAN
st. Fairfield.............335 J6
st. Lilyfield................10 F8
st. Smithfield..........335 J6
BRENDA
av. Lidcombe...........340 B7
ct. North Rocks.......248 J15
rd. Kemps Ck..........360 B11
st. Ingleburn...........453 A9
wy. Epping..............251 C15
BRENDAN
pl. Quakers Hill.......213 K9
BRENDON
pl. Carlingford.........279 J1
st. North Ryde........282 C9
BRENNAN
cl. Asquith.............192 A14
la. Newtown.............17 G12
pl. Blackett.............241 B1
pl. Minto................482 J1
st. Alexandria............19 A15
st. Yagoona............368 F10
BRENNANS
la. Russell Lea........343 D4
rd. Arncliffe.............403 J10
BRENNANS DAM
rd. Vineyard............152 C3
BRENT
st. Rozelle...................7 B15
st. Russell Lea........343 E6
BRENTFORD
rd. Wahroonga........222 B6
BRENTIN
pl. Hebersham........241 E10
BRENTWOOD
av. Hobartville.........118 G7
av. Turramurra........222 G11
av. Warrawee..........222 G11
gr. Wrrngtn Dns......237 J4
pl. Frenchs Frst.......257 A2
st. Fairfield W..........335 B8
wy. Castle Hill..........248 H3
BRERETON
av. Marrickville........373 J9
la. Marrickville, off Brereton Av........373 K10
st. Gladesville.........312 G7
BRETON
pl. Emu Heights......235 B2
BRETT
av. Balmain East..........8 G7
av. Hornsby Ht........191 E2
av. Wentwthvle........277 A10
pl. Ingleburn...........453 E11
pl. W Pnnant Hl.......249 H4
st. Kings Lngly.........245 G9
st. Revesby............428 H1
st. Tennyson...........312 E10
BREUST
pl. Punchbowl.........400 C3
BREWER
av. Liberty Gr...........311 B10
cr. S Wntwthvle......307 D5
pl. Lugarno.............430 A12
st. Concord.............342 A4
st. Marsden Pk........182 A10
BREWERS
la. Freemns Rch........91 B2
BREWON
cl. Bossley Park......333 F9
BREWONGLE
av. Penrith..............237 E4
BREWSTER
pl. Leumeah............482 F12
BREYLEY
st. Cmbrdg Pk.........237 J8
BRIAL
pl. Minto.................482 H8
BRIALY
pl. Picton................561 D4
BRIAN
rd. Appin.................569 D3
st. Merrylands W....306 H12
st. Ryde..................282 A9
BRIANA
ct. Kellyville.............217 C5
BRIAR
la. St Peters, off Henry St.............374 F14
pl. Georges Hall......367 H11
rd. Airds..................511 J13
rd. Bradbury............511 J13
st. St Ives...............224 D11
BRIARWOOD
av. Glenmore Pk......266 H12
BRIBIE
cl. Green Valley.......363 A12
BRICE
cl. Illawong.............459 K5
wy. St Helens Park....540 K7
BRICKENDON
ct. Wattle Grove......395 K16
BRICKETWOOD
dr. Woodcroft..........243 G7
BRICKFIELD
pl. Blacktown..........275 A4
pl. Sydney..................E J2
rd. Windsor.............121 B13
st. N Parramatta......278 E16
st. Parramatta.........278 E16
st. Ruse..................512 H3
BRICKPIT
lk. Homebush B......310 K13
BRICKWORKS
dr. Holroyd.............307 K11
BRIDDON
cl. Pennant Hills......220 D14
BRIDGE
la. Belmore, off Gladstone St.......371 D16
la. Drummoyne.......313 G15
la. Glebe...................12 D10
la. Sydney..................A J12
rd. Belmore.............371 D16
rd. Forest Lodge........11 H15
rd. Glebe...................12 C11
rd. Homebush.........341 A10
rd. Hornsby.............191 G14
rd. Hornsby.............191 H14
rd. Manly................288 H4
rd. Marsfield............282 A8
rd. North Ryde........282 A8
rd. Parramatta.........277 K13
rd. Queenscliff.........288 H3
rd. Ryde..................282 A8
rd. Stanmore.............17 A6
rd. Ultimo..................12 D9
rd. Westmead.........307 D3
st. Balmain.............344 E4
st. Bexley...............402 C16
st. Blaxland.............233 C5
st. Brooklyn..............76 C11
st. Cabramatta........365 K8
st. Epping...............251 A16
st. Erskineville...........18 A16
st. Erskineville...........18 B14
st. Granville............308 F10
st. Hurstville...........431 F5
st. Lane Cove..........314 A3
st. Lidcombe...........339 H8
st. Padstow............399 G15
st. Parramatta.........279 A16
st. Penshurst..........431 F5
st. Picton................563 A14
st. Picton................565 D1
st. Pymble..............253 E5
st. Rydalmere.........309 C1
st. Schofields..........183 B14
st. Sydney..................A K11
st. Sydney..................1 H14
st. Tempe...............374 C15
st. Thirlmere...........565 D1
st. Werrington.........239 C16
st. Windsor.............121 D7
st. Artarmon, off Cameron Av.......284 K15
st.w, Lidcombe, off Samuel St.........339 G8
BRIDGE END
Wollstncraft.......315 D10
BRIDGE QUARRY
pl. Glenbrook..........234 D11
BRIDGES
av. Croydon............342 F13
av. Holsworthy........396 B13
rd. Moorebank........395 H5
st. Kurnell...............465 H9
st. Maroubra...........407 F13
BRIDGE STAIRS
The Rocks.............A G3
BRIDGET
pl. Kellyville.............215 G5
BRIDGE VIEW
cct. Bella Vista..........216 B14
st. Blacktown..........274 F8
BRIDGEVIEW
av. Cammeray.........315 J4
cr. Forestville..........255 F11
cr. Mt Riverview.......204 G16
cr. Thornleigh.........221 B13
rd. Beverly Hills.......430 J2
rd. Engadine............489 D14
BRIDGEWATER
bvd. Camden S..........537 B3
BRIDLE
av. Currans Hill........479 K9
av. Oakdale.............500 G11
BRIDLEWOOD
wy. Bella Vista..........246 D1
BRIDPORT
cl. West Hoxton......392 D7
BRIENS
rd. Northmead.........277 G11
rd. Wentwthvle........277 D13
BRIER
cr. Quakers Hill.......243 G4
pl. Mt Pritchard.......364 E9
BRIERLEY
cr. Plumpton...........241 H11
pl. Eagle Vale..........480 K9
st. Mosman............316 G9
BRIERWOOD
pl. Frenchs Frst.......255 J1
BRIERY
pl. Cranebrook........207 E12
BRIGADOON
av. Glenmore Pk......266 F12
ct. Epping...............281 C3
BRIGALOW
av. Camden S..........507 B11
av. Casula...............394 E14
pl. Engadine............489 F9
pl. Westleigh...........220 E9
st. Cabramatta........365 G9
BRIGANTINE
st. Chipping Ntn......366 K15
BRIGG
rd. Epping...............281 C2
BRIGGS
pl. Doonside...........273 F4
pl. St Helens Park....541 A11
st. Camperdown.......17 F4
BRIGHT
cl. Edensor Pk.........333 J14
st. Guildford............338 A5
st. Marrickville..........16 B15
st. Ryde..................312 E3
BRIGHTMAN
cr. Bidwill................241 G1
BRIGHTMORE
la. Cremorne, off Illiliwa St...........316 E7
st. Cremorne...........316 E6
BRIGHTON
av. Btn-le-Sds..........433 K5
av. Campsie............372 A10
av. Croydon Pk.........372 B8
av. Panania.............398 C16
bvd. Bondi Beach.......378 E1

GREGORY'S STREET DIRECTORY 39

BR STREETS

bvd. North Bondi 378 E1
dr. Bella Vista 216 A14
dr. Bella Vista 216 C13
la. Croydon Pk 372 C5
la. Petersham 15 K9
la. Riverstone 183 B11
pde. Btn-le-Sds 433 K1
rd. Coogee 377 E15
rd. Peakhurst 400 F16
st. Balgowlah 287 G7
st. Botany 405 K13
st. Bundeena 523 K11
st. Croydon 372 C3
st. Croydon Pk 372 C5
st. Curl Curl 258 E13
st. Greystanes 305 K8
st. Harbord 258 E13
st. Kogarah Bay 432 J11
st. Petersham 15 F9
st. Riverstone 183 A12

BRIGID
pl. Quakers Hill 214 F15

BRINAWA
st. Mona Vale 199 A5

BRINDABELLA
dr. Horngsea Pk 392 F16
la. Narellan 478 B10
pl. W Pnnant Hl 248 J5
st. Ruse 512 H7

BRINDISI
pl. Avalon 139 H14

BRINGELLY
av. Pendle Hill 276 G14
la. Kingswood, off Bringelly Rd 237 H13
pl. Bonnyrigg Ht 363 B5
rd. Austral 391 A16
rd. Bringelly 388 E13
rd. Horngsea Pk 392 A16
rd. Kingswood 237 G16
rd. Leppington 421 A1
rd. Rossmore 389 B14
rd. West Hoxton 421 H1

BRIONY
pl. Mona Vale 198 K3

BRISBANE
av. E Lindfield 254 J14
av. Lurnea 394 D13
av. Mt Krng-gai 162 J13
av. Rodd Point 9 B1
la. Waterloo 19 G13
pl. Cromer 227 J13
rd. Campbelltown 512 B6
rd. Castle Hill 218 E14
rd. Riverstone 182 H1
rd. St Johns Pk 334 D16
rd. Vineyard 152 G14
st. Bondi Jctn 22 H9
st. Chifley 437 A5
st. Fairlight 288 C8
st. Harris Park 308 F7
st. Illawong 459 H4
st. Oxley Park 240 E16
st. St Marys 239 K15
st. Surry Hills F E7
st. Surry Hills 3 K12

BRISCOE
cr. Kings Lngly 245 C5

BRISSENDEN
av. Collaroy 229 C13

BRISTOL
av. Pymble 253 J1
av. Raby 451 G15
av. Wahroonga 221 J11
cct. Blacktown 274 B7
la. N Narrabeen 228 J2
rd. Hurstville 432 A3
st. Merrylands W 306 K15
st. N Parramatta 278 C9

BRISTOW
la. Peakhurst 430 F2

BRITANNIA
av. Burwood 341 K11
av. Merrylands 307 K13
la. Woollahra 21 J3
rd. Castle Hill 217 J12
st. Pennant Hills 250 J2

BRITTAIN
cr. Hillsdale 406 G14

BRITTANIA
pl. Bligh Park 150 E7

BRITTANY
pl. Peakhurst 430 C13

BRITTEN
cl. Cranebrook 207 H9
pl. Bossley Park 333 J12

BRITTON
cl. Elderslie 507 G2
st. Smithfield 336 B1

BRIXHAM
pl. Chipping Ntn 366 G16

BRIXTON
rd. Berala 339 E13
rd. Lidcombe 339 E13

BROAD
st. Bass Hill 368 D7
st. Cabramatta 365 D8
st. Croydon Pk 371 K8
st. Prospect 275 B11

BROAD ARROW
rd. Beverly Hills 401 A13
rd. Narwee 400 K14
rd. Riverwood 400 D15

BROADBENT
st. Kingsford 406 K5

BROADFORD
st. Bexley 402 J11
st. St Andrews 452 A12

BROADHURST
pl. Baulkham Hl 246 K12
rd. Ingleburn 453 A7

BROADLANDS
av. Glenmore Pk 266 F16

BROADLEAF
cr. Beaumont Hills 215 K1

BROADLEYS
la. Marrickville, off Malakoff St 373 K12

BROADMEADOWS
st. St Johns Pk 364 F3

BROADOAK
pl. Castle Hill 218 J7

BROADSIDE
st. Balmain East 8 D9

BROADSWORD
pl. Castle Hill 217 G5

BROADWAY
Chippendale 18 G1
Forest Lodge 18 G1
Glebe 12 J15
Punchbowl 400 E5
Ultimo 3 C16
cct. Carlingford 280 D4

BROCAS
pl. Quakers Hill 214 E13

BROCK
av. St Marys 239 H16
la. St Marys, off Brock Av 239 H16
st. Mount Druitt 271 F3

BROCKAMIN
dr. S Penrith 267 C5

BROCKLEHURST
la. Kingsgrove 402 A11

BROCKLEY
st. Lilyfield 10 H3
st. Rozelle 10 H3

BROCKMAN
av. Revesby Ht 429 A7
st. Wakeley 334 J12

BROCKS
la. Newtown 18 A9

BROCKWELL
pl. Blakehurst 432 F16

BRODERICK
st. Balmain 344 E4
st. Camperdown 17 F3

BRODIE
av. Little Bay 437 G13
cir. Baulkham Hl 248 A11
st. Baulkham Hl 248 A10
st. Paddington 4 K16
st. Rydalmere 309 B2
st. Yagoona 368 G9

BRODIE SPARK
dr. Wolli Creek 403 K5

BROE
av. Arncliffe 403 F7
av. East Hills 427 H5

BROGO
pl. Prestons 393 C13

BROKENWOOD
pl. Baulkham Hl 246 J2
pl. Cherrybrook 219 E12

BROLEN
wy. Cecil Park 331 J12

BROLGA
cr. Green Valley 363 F14
gln. St Clair 270 E12
pl. Belrose 225 F14
pl. Gymea Bay 491 G9
pl. Ingleburn 453 D8
wy. Westleigh 220 H9
wy. W Pnnant Hl 249 E7

BROMBOROUGH
rd. Roseville 284 E5

BROMFIELD
av. Prospect 275 C11
av. Toongabbie 276 E9

BROMLEY
av. Cremorne, off Kareela Rd 316 G12
av. Greenacre 370 B13
av. Pymble 253 G3
rd. Emu Heights 235 A6
st. Canley Vale 366 G5
wy. Glenhaven 218 D5

BROMLY
gr. Parklea 214 K13

BROMPTON
rd. Kensington 376 C10
st. Marrickville 374 D10

BROMUS
pl. Mcquarie Fd 454 G5

BROMWICH
pl. Menai 458 H7
st. Greystanes 306 A10

BRON
cl. W Pnnant Hl 248 H5

BRONHILL
av. East Ryde 283 B16

BRONSDON
st. Smithfield 335 B4

BRONSGROVE
cl. S Penrith 267 B7

BRONTE
av. Glenwood 215 H14
cl. West Hoxton 392 E6
cl. Wetherill Pk 334 H6
pl. Winston Hills 277 F2
pl. Woodbine 481 D14
rd. Bondi Jctn 22 J7
rd. Bondi Jctn 22 J9
rd. Bronte 377 J8
rd. Waverley 22 K11
rd. Waverley 377 E6
wy. Glenmore Pk 266 G12

BRONTE MARINE
dr. Bronte 378 B8

BRONTI
st. Mascot 405 E7

BRONZEWING
st. Ingleburn 453 F6
st. Tahmoor 565 C11
st. Tahmoor 565 J13
st. Thirlmere 565 B9
tce. Bella Vista 216 D14

BROOK
la. Crows Nest, off Brook St 315 G5
la. Fairfield Ht 335 K9
rd. Glenbrook 264 C4
rd. Seaforth 287 D8
st. Coogee 377 G16
st. Crows Nest 315 G5
st. Marayong 243 G5
st. Naremburn 315 G4

BROOKDALE
tce. Glenbrook 234 D16

BROOKE
av. Castle Hill 217 C10
st. Bass Hill 367 G8
st. Engadine 489 A16

BROOKER
av. Beacon Hill 257 E4
av. Oatlands 279 A13
st. Colyton 270 C3

BROOKES
la. Newtown 17 E9
st. Hunters Hill 314 B12
st. Thornleigh 221 D7

BROOKFIELD
av. Wrrngtn Dns 238 B5
pl. St Ives 223 H8
rd. Minto 482 H4
wy. Castle Hill 216 J8

BROOKHOLLOW
av. Baulkham Hl 216 H15

BROOKLANDS
rd. Glenbrook 264 D2

BROOKLYN
cr. Carlingford 280 D5
cr. Carlingford 280 C5
la. Double Bay 14 B10
la. Tempe, off Brooklyn St 404 C2
rd. Brooklyn 75 C11
st. Burwood 342 B15
st. Strathfield S 371 B5
st. Tempe 404 B1

BROOKPINE
pl. W Pnnant Hl 248 K3

BROOKS
la. Agnes Banks 146 K1
rd. Denham Ct 452 F1
rd. Denham Ct 452 J1
rd. Ingleburn 452 J1
st. Guildford 337 D6
st. Linley Point 313 H7
st. Mcquarie Fd 454 B3

BROOKSBANK
rd. Gilead 539 F11

BROOKS BEND
Mt Annan 479 B16

BROOKSIDE
pl. Oatlands 279 A8

BROOKS POINT
rd. Appin 569 A12

BROOKVALE
av. Brookvale 257 K10

BROOKVIEW
st. Currans Hill 479 J10

BROOM
pl. Loftus 489 J10
pl. St Andrews 452 A14

BROOMAN
st. Prestons 422 K1

BROOME
av. Centennial Pk 22 B6
pl. Bligh Park 150 C5
st. Maroubra 407 D15
st. Waterloo 20 C13
st. Waterloo 376 B7

BROOMFIELD
st. Cabramatta 365 J10
st. Canley Vale 365 K6

BROOS
rd. Oakville 152 F3

BROSNAN
pl. Castle Hill 218 J10

BROTCHIE
av. Matraville 436 G8

BROTHERS
av. Cammeray 316 C3
av. Northbridge 316 C3
pl. Narellan Vale 479 A16
st. Dundas Vy 280 A11

BROTHERSON
av. Matraville 436 G4

BROTHERTON
st. S Wntwthvle 307 B7

BROUGHAM
la. Emu Plains, off Brougham St 235 B12
la. Glebe 12 C11
la. Potts Point 4 G7
la. Woolmloo 4 G7
pl. Raby 451 E12
st. Emu Plains 235 B12
st. Potts Point 4 H7
st. Woolmloo 4 H7

BROUGHTON
av. Castle Hill 218 J14
av. Mcquarie Pk, off Main Av 283 B8
cr. Appin 569 G9
ct. Kellyville 217 A3
la. Drummoyne 343 H4
la. Glebe 12 E13
pl. Barden Rdg 488 F4
pl. Davidson 225 B16
rd. Artarmon 284 H16
rd. Strathfield 341 B11
st. Ashfield 342 H15
st. Camden 507 A3
st. Campbelltown 511 G3
st. Canterbury 372 F12
st. Concord 341 K10
st. Drummoyne 343 H5
st. Glebe 12 D11
st. Hinchinbrk 362 K16
st. Kirribilli 6 A13
st. Milsons Point 6 A13
st. Mortdale 431 A7
st. Old Guildford 337 E9
st. Paddington 13 C15
st. Parramatta 308 H2
st. Sans Souci 463 A1
st. Wilton 568 K14
st. Woolmloo 4 D6

BROULA
av. Baulkham Hl 246 H8
cl. Caringbah 492 F6
rd. Wahroonga 223 C4

BROULEE
pl. Carlingford 280 C5
pl. Engadine 518 G1
st. Prestons 423 F2

BROWALLIA
cr. Loftus 489 K10

BROWLEE
pl. Mt Pritchard 364 K10

BROWN
av. Botany 405 J11
cl. Menai 458 H15
la. Newtown 17 J10
la. Paddington 4 K13
pl. Mt Annan 509 G3
pl. Shalvey 211 B14
rd. Bonnyrigg 363 K8
rd. Bonnyrigg Ht 363 G6
rd. Maroubra 407 F15
st. Alexandria 18 G15
st. Ashfield 372 H2
st. Bronte 377 H8
st. Camperdown 17 J7
st. Chatswood 284 H10
st. Chester Hill 337 H12
st. Forestville 255 K7
st. Lewisham 15 B7
st. Lewisham 15 A9
st. Newtown 17 J10
st. N Parramatta 278 D10
st. Paddington 4 K14
st. Penrith 236 G13
st. Riverstone 182 D11
st. St Peters 374 G13
st. Smithfield 335 C6

BROWNE
pde. Warwck Frm 365 F16
pl. Baulkham Hl 247 D1
st. Campbelltown 511 F3

BROWNING
av. Campbelltown 512 B3
av. Lakemba 401 A1
cl. Mount Druitt 241 F11
cl. Wetherill Pk 334 H6
la. Hurlstone Pk 372 K11
pl. Lalor Park 245 J13
rd. N Turramurra 223 F7
st. Campsie 372 A11
st. East Hills 427 K5

BROWNLOW
ct. Wattle Grove 425 K1
pl. Ambarvale 510 G13

BROWNLOW HILL LOOP
rd. Brownlow Hl 475 C8

BROWNS
av. Austral 391 E14
av. Enmore 16 F14
la. Hunters Hill, off Ady St 313 K10
la. N Sydney K A2
la. N Sydney 5 E5
rd. Austral 421 E1
rd. Blaxland 233 G6
rd. Blaxlands Rdg 64 F8
rd. Gordon 253 F10
rd. The Oaks 502 G8
rd. Wahroonga 221 E15
rd. Wilberforce 67 F14
wy. Terrey Hills, off Booralie Rd 196 B5

BROWSE
pl. Green Valley 363 A9

BROXBOURNE
st. Westmead 307 G4

BRUBRI
st. Busby 363 H13

BRUCE
av. Belfield 371 E12
av. Caringbah 492 E15
av. Clovelly 378 A13
av. Killara 253 J10
av. Manly 288 G13
av. Panania 428 E4
la. Kingsford 406 F2
la. Newtown 17 K11
la. N Curl Curl 259 B10
la.e, Stanmore 16 D9
la.w, Stanmore 16 C9

40 GREGORY'S STREET DIRECTORY

STREETS

BU

pl. Kellyville	185	K5
rd. Glenbrook	264	A5
rd. Vineyard	152	D7
st. Ashfield	373	A2
st. Bexley	432	K15
st. Blacktown	244	K15
st. Btn-le-Sds	433	K1
st. Crows Nest	315	F8
st. Kingsford	406	F2
st. Kogarah Bay	432	H13
st. Lansvale	366	F9
st. Marrickville	373	E16
st. Merrylands W	306	G13
st. Mona Vale	199	D10
st. Rozelle	7	A12
st. Ryde	282	D13
st. Springwood	202	C10
st. Stanmore	16	C9
st. Waterloo	20	B15
st. Wollstncraft	315	F8

BRUCE BENNETTS
| pl. Maroubra | 406 | K9 |

BRUCEDALE
| av. Epping | 281 | D1 |
| dr. Baulkham Hl | 247 | D7 |

BRUCE NEALE
| dr. Penrith | 236 | D7 |

BRUCHHAUSER
| cr. Eldersie | 507 | H1 |

BRUCKNER
| pl. Clarmnt Ms | 268 | G2 |

BRUDENELL
| av. Leumeah | 481 | K16 |

BRUMBY
cl. Greendale	384	K12
cr. Emu Heights	235	C5
la. Emu Heights, off Brumby Cr	235	B5
st. Surry Hills	19	H3

BRUNDAH
rd. Tahmoor	565	D6
rd. Tahmoor	565	G5
rd. Thirlmere	565	D6

BRUNDY
| cl. W Pnnant Hl | 249 | C8 |

BRUNE
| st. Doonside | 243 | C5 |

BRUNEI
| cr. Holsworthy | 426 | D4 |

BRUNEL
| cl. Cherrybrook | 219 | K7 |

BRUNETTE
| dr. Castle Hill | 248 | B5 |

BRUNKER
rd. Chullora	369	G8
rd. Greenacre	369	G8
rd. Potts Hill	369	K7
st. Yagoona	369	A7

BRUNSWICK
av. Liberty Gr	311	B10
av. Strathfield	341	E14
ct. Colyton	270	F9
st. St Johns Pk	334	D16
pde. Ashfield	372	F4
st. Granville	308	C14
st. Merrylands	308	B14
st. Waterloo	19	H13

BRUNSWICK HEADS
| cr. Hoxton Park | 392 | H6 |

BRUNTON
| pl. Marsfield | 251 | J13 |
| st. Panania | 428 | D4 |

BRUSH
cl. Green Valley	363	B10
rd. Eastwood	280	C8
rd. West Ryde	280	H12
wy. Airds	512	F10

BRUSHBOX
cl. Glenwood	245	C2
cl. Bradbury	511	E10
pl. Cherrybrook	219	J8
pl. Newington, off Clarke St	310	B12

BRUSHFORD
| av. Castle Hill | 248 | C5 |

BRUSHWOOD
dr. Alfords Point	428	K14
dr. Alfords Point	429	A14
dr. Alfords Point	459	B2
dr. Rouse Hill	185	B7
dr. Hornsby	221	B2

BRUSSELS
| cl. Rooty Hill | 271 | J2 |
| st. Mascot | 405 | G6 |

| st. N Strathfield | 341 | C4 |
| st. S Granville | 338 | G3 |

BRUTON
| wy. Canley Vale | 366 | F5 |

BRUTUS
| wy. Rsemeadow | 540 | J3 |

BRUXNER
| pl. Doonside | 273 | K4 |

BRUZZANO
| pl. Cromer | 258 | G1 |

BRYAN
| av. Normanhurst | 221 | E9 |

BRYANT
cct. Harringtn Pk	478	J5
la. Rockdale	403	E14
pl. Fairfield W	335	D9
st. Narwee	400	K14
st. Padstow	399	C11
st. Rockdale	403	E14
wy. Claymore	481	C12

BRYCE
| av. St Ives | 254 | E1 |

BRYSON
la. Toongabbie	276	G8
st. Chatswood	284	H13
st. Toongabbie	276	G8

BUANGI
| pl. Gymea Bay | 491 | E11 |

BUCHAN
av. Edmndsn Pk	422	H5
pl. Kings Lngly	245	G6
pl. Wetherill Pk	334	F6

BUCHANAN
av. Bonnet Bay	460	B10
la. Windsor Dn	180	K4
st. Balmain	8	G14
st. Carlton	432	K8

BUCKARA
| st. Erskine Park | 300 | D2 |

BUCKERIDGE
| pl. Kellyville | 216 | G5 |

BUCKETT
| pl. Kurrajong | 85 | C2 |

BUCKHURST
| av. Point Piper | 14 | J4 |

BUCKINBAH
| pl. Lilli Pilli | 522 | F2 |

BUCKINGHAM
av. Normanhurst	221	F9
cr. Chipping Ntn	366	H15
la. Killara	253	J13
rd. Baulkham Hl	247	D5
st. Killara	253	J14
st. Canley Ht	365	G2
st. Canley Vale	365	G2
st. Kellyville Rdg	215	A3
st. Pitt Town	92	H14
st. Surry Hills	19	G5

BUCKLAND
av. Carlingford	279	H1
dr. Springwood	202	C1
la. Alexandria	18	J4
la. Newtown	17	J10
rd. Casula	395	A13
rd. St Clair	269	J8
st. Alexandria	19	A13
st. Chippendale	18	K3
st. Clarence	370	E8

BUCKLE
| av. Engadine | 488 | D15 |

BUCKLEY
cl. Revesby	398	K15
cr. Fairfield W	335	A9
rd. Marrickville	374	D14
st. Beaumont Hills	185	J16
st. Marrickville	374	C14

BUCKLEYS
| rd. Winston Hills | 276 | H2 |

BUCKNELL
| cl. Newtown | 17 | K9 |
| st. Newtown | 17 | K9 |

BUCKRA
| st. Turramurra | 223 | D11 |

BUCKRIDGE
| st. Pitt Town | 92 | J16 |

BUCKWALL
| av. Greenacre | 370 | B14 |

BUCKWELL
| dr. Hassall Gr | 211 | K15 |
| dr. Hassall Gr | 212 | B16 |

BUDAPEST
| st. Rooty Hill | 271 | J4 |

BUDBURY
| st. Harringtn Pk | 478 | F6 |

BUDD
| av. Little Bay | 437 | B12 |
| st. Drummoyne | 343 | F4 |

BUDDS
| la. Stanmore | 16 | B8 |

BUDERIM
| av. Kareela | 461 | B12 |

BUDGE
| cl. Glenmore Pk | 265 | F7 |
| la. Glenmore Pk, off Budge Cl | 265 | G7 |

BUDGEN
| av. Normanhurst | 221 | E9 |

BUDGEREE
| rd. Toongabbie | 276 | D9 |

BUDGERIGAR
| st. Green Valley | 363 | F11 |

BUD GREENSPAN
| cct. Lidcombe | 339 | J13 |

BUDINS
| rd. Kenthurst | 187 | D6 |

BUDYAN
| rd. Grays Point | 491 | B15 |

BUENA VISTA
av. Denistone	281	B11
av. Mona Vale	198	J5
av. Mosman	317	C13
rd. Winmalee	173	A14
wy. St Ives	224	F6

BUFFALO
pl. Toongabbie	275	G13
rd. Gladesville	312	G3
rd. Ryde	282	B15
wy. Beaumont Hills	186	A15

BUGATTI
| dr. Ingleburn | 453 | H9 |

BUGDEN
| av. Milperra | 397 | E11 |
| pl. Campbelltown | 511 | A7 |

BUGONG
| st. Prestons | 392 | H13 |

BUICK
| pl. Ingleburn | 453 | G10 |
| rd. Cromer | 258 | E1 |

BUIN
| pl. Glenfield | 424 | C13 |

BUIST
st. Bass Hill	368	B8
st. Sefton	368	D8
st. Yagoona	368	D8

BUJAN
| st. Glenmore Pk | 266 | C12 |

BUJARA
| pl. Bangor | 459 | D12 |

BUJWA BAY
| rd. Cowan | 104 | B12 |

BUKA
| pl. Glenfield | 424 | G9 |

BUKARI
| wy. Glenmore Pk | 266 | D8 |

BULA
| av. Clemton Park | 401 | K3 |

BULAH
| ct. Berowra Ht | 132 | J10 |
| wy. Seven Hills | 275 | K6 |

BULARA
| st. Duffys Frst | 165 | A15 |

BULBA
| rd. Engadine | 489 | F9 |

BULBERRY
| pl. Engadine | 489 | F9 |

BULBI
| av. Winmalee | 173 | A10 |
| pl. Glenmore Pk | 266 | B12 |

BULBINE
| st. Engadine | 518 | E2 |

BULBUL
| av. Green Valley | 363 | F13 |

BULGA
rd. Hornsby Ht	161	J12
st. Balmain	7	A10
la. Rozelle	7	A10

BULGALLA
| rd. Gingbah | 492 | H12 |

BULIMBA
| av. Kareela | 461 | B12 |

BULKARA
| rd. Bellevue Hill | 14 | H9 |

BULKIRA
| rd. Epping | 281 | C3 |

BULL
| pl. Harringtn Pk | 478 | C1 |
| st. Warwck Frm | 365 | J16 |

BULLARA
| cr. Narraweena | 258 | A3 |

BULLAWAI
| pl. Beecroft | 250 | E10 |

BULLDOG
| rd. Moorebank | 425 | A3 |

BULLECOURT
av. Engadine	518	F1
av. Milperra	397	G9
av,n.Mosman	317	A1
av,s.Mosman	317	A3
la. Milperra	397	H9
wk. Ultimo	3	A9
wy. Matraville	407	B15

BULLER
cct. Beaumont Hills	185	H15
la. Lane Cove	314	F1
st. Artarmon	284	J15
st. Bellevue Hill	377	A1
st. Jannali	460	H13
st. N Parramatta	278	F16
st. Parramatta	278	F16
st. S Turramrra	252	C6

BULLETIN
| pl. Sydney | B | B9 |

BULLI
st. Prestons	392	J14
rd. Old Tngabbie	276	F9
rd. Toongabbie	276	F9
rd. Wentwthvle	277	K9

BULLI APPIN
| rd. Appin | 569 | H12 |

BULLIVANT
| la. N Sydney | K | F3 |

BULLOCK
| av. Chester Hill | 337 | J12 |
| rd. Bilpin | 60 | K8 |

BULL RIDGE
| rd. E Kurrajong | 67 | B3 |

BULLS
av,w.Burraneer	523	E1
rd. Burraneer	523	E1
rd. Wakeley	334	H15

BULMANN
| av. Hornsea Pk | 392 | F16 |

BULOLO
| dr. Whalan | 240 | J10 |
| pl. Glenfield | 424 | G9 |

BULU
| dr. Glenmore Pk | 265 | K10 |

BULUMIN
| st. Como | 460 | G5 |

BULWARA
rd. Pyrmont	12	G4
rd. Pyrmont	12	H6
rd. Ultimo	3	A12

BULWARRA
av. Sefton	368	E5
av. Berowra Ht	133	D8
st. Caringbah	492	H9

BUMBERA
| st. Prestons | 392 | H15 |

BUMBORAH POINT
| rd. Matraville | 436 | F7 |
| rd. Port Botany | 436 | F7 |

BUNA
cl. Glenmore Pk	266	D12
cl. Mt Annan	479	C12
cl. N Turramurra	223	D1
cl. Ryde	282	E14
pl. Allambie Ht	257	D10
pl. Glenfield	424	H12
pl. Holsworthy	426	G9
pl. Holsworthy	426	G9

BUNARRA
| rd. Gymea Bay | 491 | F8 |

BUNBIE
| la. West Ryde | 311 | F1 |

BUNBINLA
| av. Mt Riverview | 234 | D1 |

BUNBURY
| av. Sutherland | 460 | C14 |
| rd. Mcquarie Fd | 453 | J2 |

BUNCE
| pl. Wrrngtn Cty | 238 | G5 |
| rd. Liverpool | 394 | H2 |

BUNDA
| pl. Glenmore Pk | 266 | D11 |

BUNDABAH
| av. St Ives | 224 | B9 |

BUNDAH
| st. Winmalee | 173 | A10 |

BUNDALEER
| av. Belrose | 225 | K4 |

BUNDARA
pl. Hornsby Ht	191	H5
pl. Engadine	488	K7
pl. Engadine	489	A6
pl. Prestons	392	K16
rd. Woronora Ht	488	K7
rd. Woronora Ht	489	A6

BUNDARRA
av. Mona Vale	169	E16
st. Beverly Hills	401	E13
wy. Baulkham Hl	246	E11

BUNDEEN
av,n.Wahroonga	222	C5
av,s.Wahroonga	222	B7
st. Wattle Grove	395	K12
st. Bellevue Hill	347	H15
rd. Campbelltown	511	K6
rd. Regentville	235	E16
st. Lansvale	366	G8
st. Waterfall	519	D13

BUNDEENA
dr. Bundeena	523	H9
rd. Royal N P	523	B14
rd. Woodbine	481	F12

BUNDELL
| st. Harringtn Pk | 478 | E2 |

BUNDELUK
| cr. Glenmore Pk | 266 | C12 |

BUNDEMAR
| st. Miller | 393 | H2 |
| wy. Airds | 512 | E10 |

BUNDILLA
| av. Winston Hills | 277 | F6 |
| pl. Dee Why | 258 | E4 |

BUNDOCK
la. Randwick	407	B3
la. S Coogee	407	B3
st. Kingsford	407	B3
st. Randwick	407	B3
st. S Coogee	407	B3

BUNDOON
| la. Manly | 288 | F7 |

BUNDY
| cl. Mcquarie Fd | 454 | H5 |

BUNGAL
| st. Engadine | 488 | G14 |

BUNGALOE
| av. Balgowlah | 287 | H12 |
| av. Balgowlah Ht | 287 | H12 |

BUNGALOW
av. Pymble	253	C7
rd. Bankstown	369	D16
pde. Wrrngtn Dns	238	B6
rd. Peakhurst	400	E16
rd. Plumpton	241	J10
rd. Roselands	401	A9

BUNGAN
la. Mona Vale	199	C4
la. Woodbine	481	K8
st. Mona Vale	199	B4

BUNGAN HEAD
| rd. Newport | 169 | H13 |

BUNGAREE
la. Mosman, off Beaconsfield Rd	317	E8
pl. Miller	393	H3
rd. Pendle Hill	276	F13
rd. Toongabbie	276	F13
rd. Yellow Rock	174	J14

BUNGARN
| cr. Caringbah | 493 | A12 |

BUNGARRA
| cr. Chipping Ntn | 396 | G4 |

BUNGARRIBEE
| rd. Blacktown | 274 | B2 |
| rd. Doonside | 273 | F2 |

BUNGAY
| st. Leichhardt | 10 | F14 |

BUNGENDORE
| st. Ingleside | 197 | E5 |

BUNGONIA
st. Wattle Grove	395	J12
rd. Leumeah	482	D14
st. Prestons	392	H15

BUNGOONA
| av. Elanora Ht | 198 | A16 |

GREGORY'S STREET DIRECTORY 41

BU STREETS

BUNGOWEN
av. Thornleigh 221 A7
BUNGULLA
st. Sadleir 364 A16
BUNKER
pde. Bonnyrigg 364 C5
st. Minchinbury 271 H9
st. Minto 452 H14
BUNN
la. Pyrmont 12 J5
st. Pyrmont 12 J5
BUNNAI
rd. Pemulwuy 305 E5
BUNNAL
av. Winmalee 173 B11
BUNNERONG
rd. Chifley 436 K6
rd. Daceyville 406 G4
rd. Eastgardens 406 G12
rd. Hillsdale 406 G12
rd. Kingsford 406 G4
rd. Maroubra 406 G12
rd. Matraville 436 H1
rd. Pagewood 406 G4
rd. Pagewood 406 G8
BUNNING
pl. Doonside 273 G2
BUNROY
cr. Horngsea Pk 392 F15
BUNSEN
av. Emerton 240 J4
BUNT
av. Greenacre 370 B10
BUNTING
st. Emerton 241 A6
BUNYA
cl. Baulkham Hl 246 K2
cr. Bowen Mtn 83 K10
pde. S Coogee 407 J6
pl. Glenmore Pk 265 H11
pl. Mcquarie Fd 454 G4
pl. Spring Farm 508 E1
rd. Wakeley 334 H12
rd. Bidwill 241 F1
wy. Horngsea Pk 392 F14
BUNYALA
la. Carss Park 432 F15
st. Blakehurst 432 E15
st. Carss Park 432 E14
BUNYAN
pl. Bangor 459 B12
rd. Glenbrook 234 A12
rd. Leonay 235 C14
st. Wetherill Pk 334 E6
BUNYANA
av. Wahroonga 223 B5
BUNYARRA
dr. Emu Plains 235 A9
BUNYIP BLUE GUM
rd. Faulconbdg 171 F12
BUNYULA
rd. Bellevue Hill 347 J15
BURAN
cl. Mount Druitt 241 E16
BURANDA
cr. St Johns Pk 334 C16
BURBANG
cr. Rydalmere 309 G2
BURBANK
av. East Hills 427 J6
av. Picnic Point 427 K7
pl. Baulkham Hl 216 F15
BURBONG
st. Kingsford 406 K4
BURCH
la. Mascot 405 E2
BURCHMORE
rd. Manly Vale 288 B4
BURDEKIN
st. St Ives 254 D4
ct. Wattle Grove 396 A13
la. Surry Hills 20 E4
pl. Engadine 488 J9
pl. Wilberforce 67 K16
pl. Quakers Hill 213 F6
rd. Wilberforce 67 J16
st. Wilberforce 92 H1
BURDETT
cr. Blacktown 244 A16
st. Canley Ht 365 H4
st. Hornsby 221 H1
st. Wahroonga 222 A1

BURFITT
la. Riverstone 182 F14
pde. Glenbrook 263 K1
rd. Riverstone 182 F15
st. Leichhardt 9 D14
BURFORD
st. Colyton 270 F6
st. Merrylands 307 F14
st. Minto 452 J13
BURGAN
cl. Menai 458 H13
BURGE
st. Vaucluse 348 F5
BURGESS
rd. Freemns Rch 90 D5
rd. Freemns Rch 90 F4
rd. S Penrith 267 C2
st. Beverley Pk 433 C10
st. Richmond 118 J5
BURGOYNE
la. Gordon 253 H6
la. Mt Lewis, off
    Frank St 369 K16
st. Gordon 253 H6
BURGUNDY
cl. Cecil Hills 362 E1
cl. Eschol Park 481 C5
pl. Minchinbury 271 K9
BURILLA
av. N Curl Curl 258 F10
BURING
av. Leonay 235 B16
cr. Minchinbury 271 H9
BURKE
av. Berala 339 D12
av. Wrrngtn Cty 238 H8
cr. Oatley 430 H13
cl. Mt Colah 162 B11
pl. St Johns Pk 364 H1
pl. Cronulla 493 K9
rd. Ingleburn 422 K9
rd. Lalor Park 245 F13
sq. Lansdowne 367 C5
st. Appin 569 G12
st. Blacktown 274 B6
st. Chifley 437 A4
st. Como 460 F7
st. Concord W 341 G1
st. Newport 169 K7
st. Oatley 430 H13
st. Ruse 512 F3
st. Ryde 282 F15
st. Telopea 279 G11
BURKES STEPS
Mosman 287 C14
BURKHART
pl. Minto 482 G6
BURLEIGH
av. Caringbah 493 A4
st. Burwood 342 A14
st. Lindfield 284 E3
BURLEY
cl. Illawong 459 K3
rd. Horsley Pk 302 D11
rd. Padstow 429 E1
st. Lane Cove W 284 F16
BURLEY GRIFFIN
cl. St Clair 270 B11
BURLINGTON
av. Earlwood 372 G16
la. Crows Nest 315 G7
rd. Homebush 341 B9
st. Crows Nest 315 G7
st. Monterey 433 G8
st. Northmead 277 K11
BURLINSON
st. Ultimo 12 K11
BURLISON
st. Warwck Frm 365 G13
BURMAH
rd. Denistone 281 B12
BURNE
av. Dee Why 258 F6
BURNELL
pl. Darlinghurst 4 C9
st. Drummoyne 343 F7
st. Russell Lea 343 F7
BURNETT
av. Mt Annan 509 H1
pl. Sylvania Wtr 462 C12
st. Hurlstone Pk 373 A14
st. Mays Hill 307 H6
st. Merrylands 307 C11
st. Parramatta 307 H6

st. Redfern 19 F7
wk. Denistone 281 C12
BURNHAM
av. Glenwood 215 D14
pl. N Parramatta 278 C9
st. Belfield 371 E12
BURNIE
st. Clovelly, off
    Winchester Rd 377 J11
st. Blacktown 275 B2
st. Clovelly 377 J12
BURNLEIGH
cr. Cmbrdg Gdn 237 J1
BURNLEY
av. N Turramurra 223 G7
BURNS
av. Mcquarie Fd 454 A3
cl. Rooty Hill 271 K6
cr. Chiswick 343 C2
la. Caringbah 492 H7
la. Petersham 15 K8
la. Picnic Point 428 F8
pl. Springwood 201 K12
pl. Campbelltown 512 A2
rd. Heathcote 518 C16
rd. Kellyville 215 H9
rd. Leumeah 512 A2
rd. Picnic Point 428 D8
rd. Riverstone 184 A1
st. St Ives 223 A6
st. Springwood 202 A11
st. Thirlmere 561 J12
st. Turramurra 223 A6
st. Wahroonga 222 D5
st. Wakeley 334 H16
st. Winston Hills 276 H1
rd.n.Beecroft 250 B6
rd.s.Beecroft 250 B7
st. Campsie 372 B10
st. Croydon 342 H12
st. Marsfield 282 C7
st. Petersham 15 K8
BURNS BAY
rd. Hunters Hill 313 F12
rd. Lane Cove 313 F8
rd. Lane Cove 313 J2
rd. Lane Cove W 313 F8
rd. Linley Point 313 F8
BURNSIDE
gr. Windsor Dn 180 K3
st. N Parramatta 278 F11
BURNT
st. Seaforth 286 K3
BURNT BRIDGE CREEK DEVIATION
Balgowlah 287 E8
Manly Vale 287 E8
N Balgowlah 287 E8
Seaforth 287 E8
BURR
cl. Bossley Park 334 C10
BURRA
cl. Illawong 459 K3
cl. Mt Colah 162 D16
pl. Greystanes 305 F10
pl. Artarmon 285 A15
st. Busby 363 H14
st. Pendle Hill 276 G12
BURRABIRRA
av. Vaucluse 348 D3
BURRABOGEE
rd. Old Tngabbie 276 E11
rd. Pendle Hill 276 E11
rd. Toongabbie 276 E11
BURRADDAR
av. Engadine 488 G14
BURRADOO
rd. North Rocks 279 A2
rd. Beverly Hills 401 A11
rd. Lansvale 366 D9
st. Caringbah 492 G12
st. Padstow 429 G3
BURRAGA
av. Terrey Hills 196 C5
pl. Glenmore Pk 266 B8
rd. Lindfield 284 A2
BURRAGATE
cr. Prestons 393 C15
BURRAGORANG
rd. Belimbla Pk 501 B10
rd. Bickley Vale 505 B7
rd. Brownlow Hl 505 B7
rd. Camden 506 H8
rd. Camden S 506 H8
rd. Cawdor 506 H8

rd. Glenmore 503 C4
rd. Grasmere 505 J7
rd. Mt Hunter 505 B7
rd. Oakdale 499 A8
rd. Oakdale 500 B13
rd. Ruse 512 F8
rd. The Oaks 502 J9
st. Oakdale 500 G11
st. The Oaks 502 E11
st. Woodcroft 243 F11
BURRAHPORE
la. Woolmloo 4 F7
BURRALOW
st. Frenchs Frst 256 G1
BURRALOW
rd. Kurrajong Ht 63 D14
BURRAMY
cl. Bossley Park 333 G7
BURRAN
av. Mosman 317 E3
BURRANDONG
cr. Baulkham Hl 246 J10
BURRANEER
av. St Ives 254 D3
cl. Allawah 432 C8
cr. Greenacre 369 K11
st. Leumeah 482 C15
BURRANEER BAY
rd. Caringbah 492 E10
rd. Cronulla 493 A11
rd. Woolooware 493 A11
BURRAWAL
pl. Cromer 227 K11
BURRAWALLA
rd. Caringbah 493 B6
BURRAWANG
dr. Nelson 155 D8
pl. Alfords Point 429 A13
st. Cherrybrook 219 K5
BURRAWONG
av. Mosman 317 D13
cr. Elderslie 477 F16
rd. Avalon 140 D11
BURRELL
cr. Baulkham Hl 247 E11
pde. Blacktown 273 H4
ct. Kenthurst 156 C9
st. Beverly Hills 401 F14
BURREN
st. Erskineville 18 A11
st. Eveleigh 18 A11
st. Newtown 18 A11
BURRENDONG
pl. Avalon 139 K15
rd. Leumeah 482 D12
BURRIA
pl. Winmalee 173 B10
BURRIANG
wy. Pemulwuy 305 E5
BURRILL
pl. Leumeah 482 F14
BURRIMUL
st. Kingsgrove 401 F6
BURRINGBAR
st. N Balgowlah 287 C5
BURRINJUCK
dr. Woodcroft 243 G10
pl. Miranda 491 H7
st. Leumeah 482 E13
BURROGY
la. Mosman, off
    Cardinal St 316 J5
BURROWAY
rd. Homebush B 311 A6
st. Neutral Bay 6 H5
BURROWES
gr. Dean Park 212 F16
BURROWS
av. Chester Hill 338 B13
av. Sydenham 374 D14
la. Minto, off
    Erica La 482 F2
rd. Alexandria 375 A15
rd. St Peters 375 A15
rd.s,St Peters 374 H16
st. Arncliffe 403 H8
BURRSWOOD
ct. Belrose 225 K12
BURRUNDULLA
cr. Airds 511 K15
BURSARIA
cr. Glenmore Pk 265 F10
rd. Mt Annan 509 D4

BURSILL
st. Guildford 337 H3
BURT
st. Rozelle 10 J3
BURTENSHAW
st. Panania 398 D14
BURTON
av. Chester Hill 338 D15
av. Moorebank 396 D11
av. Northmead 278 B2
la. Glebe 12 C9
la. Milsons Point, off
    Alfred St 5 K15
la. Randwick, off
    Prince St 376 K11
st. Balgowlah 287 K9
st. Concord 341 K10
st. Darlinghurst 4 D11
st. Glebe 12 B10
st. Kirribilli 5 K15
st. Linley Point 313 G7
st. Milsons Point 5 K15
st. Mosman 316 J2
st. Randwick 376 K11
st. Werrington 238 E8
st. Wrrngtn Cty 238 E8
BURU
pl. Kings Park 244 J2
BURUDA
pl. Erskine Park 270 F16
BURUNDA
st. Como 460 E6
BURUWAN
la. Annandale 11 B6
BURWOOD
pl. St Johns Pk 364 G4
rd. Belfield 371 D10
rd. Belmore 371 D13
rd. Burwood 341 K15
rd. Burwood Ht 371 J8
rd. Concord 342 B8
rd. Croydon Pk 371 J8
rd. Enfield 371 J8
BURY
rd. Guildford 337 J4
BUSACO
rd. Marsfield 252 C12
BUSBY
av. Edensor Pk 363 E1
cl. Barden Rdg 488 K1
la. Bronte, off
    Busby Pde 377 K10
la. Woolmloo ....D K13
la. Woolmloo ....A C6
pde. Bronte 377 J11
pl. Frenchs Frst 255 H4
st. Busby 393 J1
BUSCH
pl. St Helens Park 541 B5
BUSH
pl. Glenbrook 264 B4
rd. Kenthurst 125 F4
tr. Belrose 226 D6
BUSHELLS
pl. Wetherill Pk 304 B16
BUSHEY
pl. Dee Why 258 J8
BUSHLAND
av. Forestville 255 K10
cr. Carlingford 249 F16
dr. Padstow Ht 429 D8
pl. Erskine Park 270 F16
pl. Kenthurst 188 D4
BUSHLANDS
av. Gordon 253 F10
av. Hornsby Ht 191 G9
av. Hornsby Ht 191 F8
BUSHLARK
pl. Clarmnt Ms 268 J4
BUSHLEY
pl. Jamisontown 266 C2
BUSHRANGERS
hill. Newport 169 H13
BUSHVIEW
dr. Kellyville 186 K15
dr. Berowra Ht 133 B5
BUSHY
gln. Glenhaven 217 K5
BUTCHERBIRD
pl. Glenmore Pk 265 K12
BUTE
pl. St Andrews 481 K5
BUTIA
wy. Stanhpe Gdn ...215 E10

42 GREGORY'S STREET DIRECTORY

STREETS CA

BUTLER
av. Bossley Park 334 B7
av. Campsie 371 J13
cl. Menai 459 A10
cr. Bnkstn Aprt 397 K1
cr. S Penrith 237 B15
la. Hurstville 432 A6
la. S Penrith, off Butler Cr 237 C15
pl. Lalor Park 245 G14
rd. Hurstville 432 A6
rd. Mascot 405 A11
wy. S Windsor 150 F1

BUTLERS
cl. West Hoxton 392 D7

BUTLIN
av. Darlington 18 E5

BUTT
st. Surry Hills 19 H3

BUTTERCUP
pl. Mt Annan 509 E4
st. Mcquarie Fd 454 C5

BUTTERFIELD
pl. Mt Annan 509 C1
st. Blacktown 244 G11
st. Thornleigh 221 C13

BUTTIGIEG
pl. Plumpton 242 C8

BUTTSWORTH
la. Wilberforce 91 K7

BUTU WARGUN
dr. Pemulwuy 305 C4

BUVELOT
wy. Claymore 481 D13

BUXLFOLIA
ct. Voyager Pt 427 A4

BUXTON
pl. N Turramurra 223 G7
pl. Prestons 392 J14

BUYU
rd. Glenmore Pk 266 D10

BUYUMA
pl. Avalon 139 J14
st. Carlingford 280 D7

BY
st. N Parramatta 278 C11

BYAMEE
st. East Killara 254 J6

BYANBI
pl. Castle Hill 248 C6

BYDOWN
st. Neutral Bay 6 F3

BYER
st. Enfield 371 G3

BYFIELD
st. Mcquarie Pk 282 F3

BYGRAVE
st. Ryde 282 H15

BYKOOL
av. Kingsgrove 401 E8

BYLONG
pl. Ruse 512 F8

BYLOSS
st. Chester Hill 338 A13

BYNA
st. Malabar 437 E8

BYNG
la. Maroubra 407 B10
st. Maroubra 407 B11

BYNYA
rd. Palm Beach 140 B3

BYORA
cr. Northbridge 286 E14

BYRD
av. Kingsford 406 J4
pl. Tregear 240 E5
st. Canley Ht 365 C3

BYRNE
av. Drummoyne 343 D3
av. Russell Lea 343 D3
av. S Coogee 407 F7
bvd. Marayong 243 K8
cr. Maroubra 407 F14
pl. Camden 506 K8
pl. Prairiewood 334 J8
st. Ashcroft 364 E16
st. Auburn 309 B15
st. Lapstone 264 G5
st. Wentwthvle 277 C16
wy. Bradbury 511 J12
wy. Glenmore Pk 265 E11

BYRNES
av. Neutral Bay 316 B8
st. Bexley 432 H4
st. Botany 405 E11
st. Marrickville 373 K14
st. N Parramatta 278 C9
st. Rozelle 344 C7
st. S Granville 338 G2

BYRON
av. Campbelltown 512 A3
av. Ryde 282 D12
av. St Ives 224 B14
av. Wallacia 324 J13
la. Mount Druitt 241 C13
pl. Illawong 459 E5
pl. Northmead 278 B5
rd. Guildford 337 C7
rd. Leppington 421 B9
rd. Tahmoor 565 D14
rd. Tahmoor 565 E14
rd. Yennora 337 C7
st. Campsie 372 A9
st. Coogee 377 E16
st. Croydon 342 G12
st. Peakhurst 430 C7

BYRON BAY
cl. Hoxton Park 392 H6

BY THE SEA
rd. Mona Vale 199 E3

BYWONG
pl. Bonnyrigg 364 A10
pl. Sylvania 461 G14

C

CABARITA
pl. Caringbah 492 E9
rd. Avalon 139 H9
rd. Cabarita 342 D2
rd. Concord 342 B3

CABBAGE TREE
rd. Bayview 168 F16
rd. Bayview 169 A16
rd. Grose Vale 115 A3
rd. Grose Vale 115 A4
rd. Ingleside 168 C16

CABBAN
st. Mosman 317 A11

CABER
cl. Dural 219 B8

CABERNET
av. Eschol Park 481 C2
cct. Orchard Hills 268 F15

CABLE
pl. Eastern Ck 272 G7
st. Wollstncraft 315 C11

CABLES
pl. Waverley 377 F8

CABRAMATTA
av. Miller 393 F5
rd. Cremorne 316 H8
rd. Mosman 316 H8
rd. Woolooware 493 E11
rd.e, Cabramatta 366 A7
rd.w, Bonnyrigg 364 D7
rd.w, Cabramatta 365 B9
rd.w, Cabramatta W 364 C7

CABRAMURRA
st. Heckenberg 364 A14

CACIA
av. Seven Hills 245 J14

CADAC
pl. Schofields 213 K6

CADBURY
st. Quakers Hill 213 G14

CADDENS
rd. Clarmnt Ms 268 D4
rd. Kingswood 267 F3

CADDIGAL
pl. North Bondi 348 F15

CADDO
cl. Greenfld Pk 333 K14

CADELL
gln. St Clair 270 D10
la. St Clair, off Cadell Gln 270 C10

CADENCE
pl. Kareela 461 D12

CADIA
st. Kogarah 433 B2

CADIGAL
av. Pyrmont 12 E1
la. Camperdown 18 A5

CADILLAC
pl. Ingleburn 453 H9

CADMAN
cr. Castle Hill 217 H14
pl. Woodcroft 243 F6

CADOGAN
la. Marrickville 374 D12
rd. Mcquarie Fd 454 C4
st. Marrickville 374 D12

CADOW
st. Frenchs Frst 256 E1
st. Pymble 253 B9

CADWELLS
rd. Kenthurst 126 H15
rd. Kenthurst 156 H1

CAERLEON
cr. Randwick 377 D11

CAERNARVON
cl. Kirkham 477 C9

CAESAR
cl. Prairiewood 334 D12
la. St Clair, off Caesar Wy 270 C16
wy. St Clair 270 C16

CAHILL
exp. Sydney A K7
exp. Sydney 1 H12
exp. The Rocks A K7
exp. The Rocks 1 H12
la. Annandale 17 B3
la. Greenacre 370 B6
pl. Marrickville 373 F16
st. Annandale 17 B3
st. Beverly Hills 401 D14
st. Smithfield 335 F6

CAHIR
la. Marrickville 373 K12

CAHORS
rd. Padstow 399 C14

CAIN
pl. Plumpton 242 B10

CAINES
cr. St Marys 269 J7
la. St Marys, off Caines Cr 269 J7

CAINS
pl. Waterloo 19 E12

CAIRA
pl. Quakers Hill 244 A1

CAIRD
pl. Seven Hills 245 K15
st. Wentwthvle 277 C9

CAIRDS
av. Bankstown 369 D15

CAIRNES
la. Glenorie 128 D2
rd. Glenorie 128 D4

CAIRNGORM
av. Glenhaven 218 A6

CAIRNS
av. Rodd Point 343 D8
pl. Wakeley 334 H15
st. Riverwood 400 B16

CAIRO
av. Padstow 399 B15
av. Revesby 399 B15
st. Cammeray 316 A4
st. Rockdale 403 E16
st. S Coogee 407 H4

CAITHNESS
cr. Winston Hills 277 D2
st. Killara 253 K13

CALABASH
rd. Arcadia 130 F9

CALABRESE
st. Blairmount 481 A15

CALABRIA
st. Prestons 393 E13

CALABRIO
pl. Erskine Park 300 F2

CALABRO
av. Liverpool 394 H7
av. Lurnea 394 H7

CALABY
st. Toongabbie 276 H8

CALADENIA
cl. Elanora Ht 197 H13
cl. Ingleside 197 H13
st. Rooty Hill 272 C3

CALAIS
pl. Castle Hill 216 K9
pl. Erskine Park 270 H15

CALALA
st. Mount Druitt 241 C13

CALANDRA
av. Quakers Hill 214 A7

CALARIA
cl. Edensor Pk 363 D1

CALBINA
rd. Earlwood 402 C3
rd. Northbridge 315 J1

CALCA
cr. Forestville 255 K14

CALCITE
pl. Eagle Vale 481 C8

CALDARRA
av. Engadine 518 J2
pl. Westleigh 220 G2

CALDER
cl. Rydalmere 279 H15
la. Darlington 18 H5
pl. St Ives 224 B6
rd. Darlington 18 H6
rd. Rydalmere 279 D14
st. N Curl Curl 258 F10

CALDERON
la. Padstow 429 C3

CALDERWOOD
rd. Galston 160 D13

CALDWELL
la. Bexley North 402 D10
pde. Yagoona 369 B11
pl. Blacktown 274 J3
pl. Edensor Pk 333 G13
st. Darlinghurst 4 J10
st. S Windsor 150 J3

CALDY
pl. Glenhaven 217 K4

CALEDONIA
cr. Peakhurst 430 B5
la. Paddington 21 G2
st. Paddington 21 G2

CALEDONIAN
av. Winston Hills 277 D3
rd. Rose Bay 348 B9
st. Bexley 403 A15

CALEEN
st. Glenwood 245 F1

CALEY
cr. Lapstone 264 H4
dr. Mt Annan 509 D9
pl. Barden Rdg 488 G1
rd. Bradbury 511 G13
st. Chifley 437 A4

CALEYI
wy. Belrose 226 B10

CALF FARM
rd. Mt Hunter 504 D16

CALGA
av. Bronte 378 B10
av. Malabar 437 E8
av. Normanhurst 221 D12
pl. Bronte 378 B10
pl. Old Tngabbie 276 K8
pl. Sylvania 461 G14
st. Roseville Ch 285 F2

CALGAROO
cr. Kingswood 237 H16

CALIBAN
pl. Rsemeadow 540 K6

CALIDA
cr. Hassall Gr 212 A15

CALIDORE
st. Bankstown 399 A7

CALLA
gr. Pendle Hill 276 G13

CALLABONA
av. Woodcroft 243 F11

CALLAGHAN
la. Ryde, off Badajoz Rd 282 G15
st. Ryde 282 H15

CALLAGHER
st. Mount Druitt 271 D1

CALLAN
st. Rozelle 344 C7
wy. Wentwthvle 277 D10

CALLICOMA
rd. Seaforth 286 K7
st. Mt Annan 509 E5

CALLIOPE
la. Mosman, off Calliope St 316 G10
pl. Busby 363 J13
rd. Miranda 492 C7
st. Guildford 337 D4
st. Mosman 316 G10

CALLISTEMON
cl. Alfords Point 429 C15
cl. Baulkham Hl 247 C15
cl. N Epping 251 C11
gr. Greenacre 370 F6
st. Mt Annan 509 C2

CALLISTO
dr. Cranebrook 207 D11

CALLOW
la. Kingswood 237 J15
pl. Woodcroft 243 E10

CALMAR
cl. Glen Alpine 510 C14

CALMSLEY
pl. Horsley Pk 332 C5

CALOOL
cr. Belrose 225 H12
rd. Beecroft 250 D12
st. Lidcombe 339 J4

CALOOLA
av. Penrith 237 E6
cr. Beverly Hills 401 E11
cr. Penshurst 431 H7
pl. Baulkham Hl 246 J10
rd. Bargo 567 C1
rd. Wentwthvle 277 A11
st. Condell Park 398 E1

CALPAC
pl. Old Tngabbie 276 H11

CALPURNIA
wy. Rsemeadow 540 H2

CALVADOS
st. Glenfield 424 E13

CALVER
av. Mt Riverview 204 C16

CALVERT
av. Killara 253 G12
bvd. Mulgrave 121 J15
bvd. Mulgrave 151 J1
la. Marrickville, off Fernbank St 374 A13
pde. Newport 169 K11
st. Marrickville 373 K13

CALVERTS
rd. Orchard Hills 268 D11

CALYPSO
av. Mosman 316 K10
pl. Yowie Bay 491 K10
rd. Cranebrook 207 C15

CALYPTA
gr. Quakers Hill 214 F11

CAM
la. North Ryde 282 J8
st. Cmbrdg Pk 237 G9
st. North Ryde 282 J7
st. Wahroonga 222 A6

CAMARENA
av. Baulkham Hl, off Barina Downs Rd 216 H16

CAMBAGE
ct. Davidson 255 E4

CAMBALAN
st. Bargo 567 D4

CAMBERWELL
rd. Vineyard 152 F12

CAMBEWARRA
av. Castle Hill 248 B3
cr. Berowra Ht 132 K7
rd. Fairfield W 335 E10
st. Ruse 512 G7

CAMBOURNE
av. St Ives 224 H7

CAMBRAI
av. Engadine 518 H1
pl. Milperra 397 D12

CAMBRIAN
av. Voyager Pt 247 E4

CAMBRIDGE
av. Bankstown 399 A2
av. Glenfield 424 G8
av. Moorebank 425 A9
av. Narraweena 258 D2
av. North Rocks 278 H2
av. Vaucluse 348 F1
av. Windsor 120 J11
la. Cmbrdg Pk, off Cambridge St 237 F9
la. Chatswood 284 J9
la. Enmore 17 A13
la. Paddington 13 E13
pl. Narellan 478 G11
rd. Artarmon 284 K13

GREGORY'S STREET DIRECTORY 43

CA STREETS

rd. Drummoyne 313 H15
st. Berala 339 D10
st. Blacktown 244 K11
st. Cmbrdg Pk 237 G9
st. Cammeray 315 J4
st. Canley Ht 365 D3
st. Enmore 17 A13
st. Epping 251 B15
st. Fairfield W 335 E13
st. Fairfield W 335 D16
st. Gladesville 312 J7
st. Harris Park 308 E7
st. Ingleburn 453 E5
st. Lidcombe 339 D10
st. Merrylands 307 F13
st. N Willoughby 285 F8
st. Paddington 13 E13
st. Penshurst 431 D1
st. Rozelle 344 D8
st. S Turramrra 252 B8
st. Stanmore 16 F10
st. The Rocks A J4
st. Valley Ht 202 H10

CAMDEN
bps. Camden 507 A9
bps. Camden S 507 A9
bps. Elderslie 507 J4
bps. Narellan 478 F16
bps. Narellan Vale 478 F16
bps. Spring Farm 507 J4
gdn. N Turramurra 223 F2
la. Newtown 17 F16
la. Pyrmont 12 J7
rd. Campbelltown 511 C6
rd. Douglas Park 568 F7
rd. Douglas Park 568 G1
st. Enmore 374 G9
st. Fairfield Ht 335 K10
st. Newtown 17 F16
st. Penrith 236 G1
st. Sylvania 462 B13
st. Wilton 568 K15
wy. Bidwill 211 F16

CAMDEN VALLEY
wy. Casula 423 G3
wy. Catherine Fd 449 E15
wy. Currans Hill 479 A6
wy. Edmndsn Pk 392 D16
wy. Edmndsn Pk 422 F1
wy. Elderslie 477 F15
wy. Harringtn Pk 478 D10
wy. Horngsea Pk 392 D16
wy. Kirkham 477 F15
wy. Leppington 421 H5
wy. Narellan 478 D10
wy. Oran Park 449 E15
wy. Prestons 423 B2
wy. Smeaton Gra 479 A6

CAMDEN VIEW
dr. Narellan 478 C10

CAMELLIA
av. Glenmore Pk 265 F10
ct. Cherrybrook 219 G7
gr. Gymea Bay 491 C8
pl. Lalor Park 245 B10
rd. W Pnnant Hl 218 J16
st. Greystanes 306 A12

CAMELOT
cl. Kirkham 477 E8
cl. Mt Colah 162 G14
ct. Carlingford 279 A4
dr. Cranebrook 207 A12
pl. St Ives 254 A2

CAMEO
cct. Glenwood 215 C15
cr. St Clair 269 H13
pl. Eagle Vale 481 B7
pl. Kellyville 217 D4

CAMERA
st. Manly 288 F9

CAMERON
av. Artarmon 285 A15
av. Bass Hill 368 D13
av. Baulkham Hl 247 G5
av. Earlwood 402 H3
av. Manly 288 G4
av. W Pnnant Hl 249 G1
cr. Ryde 282 D16
ct. Merrylands W 306 J14
pl. Alfords Point 429 C13
pl. Parramatta 278 J15
pl. St Helens Park 541 B8
rd. Pymble 253 J3
st. Balmain 7 G4
st. Banksia 403 F13
st. Bexley 432 H4
st. Birchgrove 7 G4
st. Doonside 243 B11
st. Edgecliff 13 H12
st. Hobartville 118 G8
st. Jamisontown 266 B2
st. Lidcombe 339 F9
st. Rockdale 403 F16
st. Strathfield 371 E2

CAMILLA
wy. Ambarvale 510 K15

CAMILLE
pl. Glenhaven 187 K15
st. Sans Souci 433 C16

CAMILLERI
av. Quakers Hill 213 G7

CAMILLO
st. Pendle Hill 306 D1
st. Seven Hills 245 G14

CAMIRA
cl. Belrose 225 J14
pl. Bonnyrigg 363 J9
st. Maroubra 407 E12
st. St Marys 239 G13
st. Villawood 367 G5
st. West Pymble 252 K14

CAMIRI
st. Hornsby Ht 191 G1

CAMMARAY
rd. Castle Cove 286 D6

CAMMARLIE
st. Panania 427 J1

CAMMERAY
av. Cammeray 315 K6
rd. Cammeray 316 B5

CAMORTA
cl. Kings Park 244 H3

CAMP
la. Bondi Jctn 22 E5
st. Watsons Bay 318 E13

CAMPASPE
av. Wiley Park 400 G4

CAMPBELL
av. Cromer 228 H16
av. Dee Why 258 H1
av. Lane Cove 314 G5
av. Lilyfield 9 J5
av. Normanhurst 221 E10
av. Paddington 4 J13
cl. Minto 482 K9
cr. Glenorie 128 G1
dr. Wahroonga 222 A14
la. Clovelly, off Park La 378 A12
la. Glebe 12 C14
la. Narellan 478 E9
la. Newtown 17 D11
la. St Peters 374 K14
pde. Bondi Beach 378 D3
pde. Manly Vale 287 H2
pl. Merrylands 307 H16
rd. Alexandria 374 K14
rd. Kenthurst 156 F15
rd. St Peters 374 K14
st. Abbotsford 342 K4
st. Artarmon 314 K3
st. Auburn 309 C15
st. Balmain 7 K9
st. Berala 339 C13
st. Bexley 432 H1
st. Blacktown 244 H16
st. Clovelly 378 A12
st. Darlinghurst 4 A13
st. Eastwood 280 J10
st. Fairfield E 336 K14
st. Glebe 12 D13
st. Gymea 461 G16
st. Haymarket E G7
st. Haymarket 3 G12
st. Hunters Hill 313 K10
st. Liverpool 395 C1
st. Liverpool 395 B1
st. Luddenham 356 G3
st. Narellan 478 E8
st. Newtown 17 J8
st. Northmead 277 K8
st. N Richmond 87 B13
st. Parramatta 308 B5
st. Picton 563 G8
st. Punchbowl 400 C5
st. Ramsgate 433 D15
st. Riverstone 183 B5
st. St Peters 374 H12
st. Sans Souci 433 D15
st. S Windsor 120 H13
st. Surry Hills F B8
st. Surry Hills 4 A13
st. Thirlmere 564 K5
st. Waverley 377 G7

CAMPBELLFIELD
av. Bradbury 511 D13

CAMPBELL HILL
rd. Chester Hill 338 B15
rd. Guildford 338 B15

CAMPBELLTOWN
rd. Bow Bowing 452 C14
rd. Denham Ct 422 F15
rd. Glenfield 423 J6
rd. Ingleburn 452 C14
rd. Leumeah 481 J15
rd. Minto 482 A3
rd. St Andrews 452 C14

CAMPFIRE
ct. Wrrngtn Dns 238 E4

CAMPHORLAUREL
ct. Doonside 243 G16

CAMPI
ct. Prestons 422 K1

CAMPION
st. Wetherill Pk 334 K4

CAMPSIE
la. Canterbury, off Wonga St 372 D12
st. Campsie 371 G14
st. Campsie 371 H13
st. Wilton 568 K15

CAMPTON
av. Cmbrdg Pk 238 A10
ct. Carlingford 250 C13

CAMPUS
dr. Richmond 118 K12
dr. Richmond 119 A11

CANADA
cl. Minto 482 G5

CANADIAN
pl. Kearns 450 J16

CANAL
rd. Greystanes 306 E12
rd. Greystanes 306 E13
rd. Leichhardt 9 D9
rd. Lilyfield 9 E7
rd. St Peters 374 G15

CANARA
av. Phillip Bay 436 J11
pl. Frenchs Frst 255 F2
pl. Palm Beach 139 J2
pl. Smithfield 335 E4

CANARY
cl. St Clair 269 H10

CANARYS
rd. Roselands 400 K7

CANBERRA
av. Casula 394 J15
av. Richmond 119 K4
av. St Leonards 315 D7
av. Turramurra 223 C10
cr. Campbelltown 512 B6
cr. E Lindfield 255 B15
la. Randwick 407 B2
pwy. Casula, off Canberra Av 394 K15
rd. Sylvania 462 C9
st. Epping 251 A13
st. Hurlstone Pk 372 H13
st. Lane Cove N 284 B15
st. Oxley Park 240 A16
st. Randwick 407 C3
st. St Johns Pk 364 F1
st. St Marys 240 A16

CANDICE
cr. Stanhpe Gdn 215 B10

CANDLEBARK
cct. Glenmore Pk 265 H11

CANDLEBUSH
cr. Castle Hill 248 F5

CANDLENUT
gr. Parklea 215 B13

CANDLEWOOD
st. Bossley Park 333 G9

CANDOWIE
cr. Baulkham Hl 248 C8

CANEA
cr. Allambie Ht 257 D10

CANHAM
cl. Castle Hill 247 H1

CANIDIUS
st. Rsemeadow 540 E3

CANISIUS
cl. Pymble 223 F15

CANLEY VALE
rd. Canley Ht 365 A2
rd. Canley Vale 365 J3
rd. St Johns Pk 334 F15
rd. Wakeley 334 F15
rd. Wetherill Pk 334 C3

CANN
st. Bass Hill 368 B6
st. Bass Hill 368 B9
st. Guildford 337 D7

CANNA
pl. Quakers Hill 243 E3
pl. St Andrews 482 A1

CANNAN
cl. Cherrybrook 219 C11

CANNERY
rd. Plumpton 241 K7

CANNES
dr. Avalon 139 J13

CANNING
pl. Pitt Town 93 F8

CANNON
la. Stanmore 16 E5
st. Prospect 275 B11
st. Stanmore 16 E5

CANNONS
pde. Forestville 255 K11

CANOBOLAS
pl. Yarrawarrah 489 D13
st. Fairfield W 335 E11

CANOELANDS
rd. Canoelands 70 K5

CANONBURY
gr. Bexley North 402 G10
gr. Bexley North 402 E12
gr. Dulwich Hill 373 E12

CANOON
rd. S Turramrra 251 K5

CANOONA
av. Windsor Dn 150 E14

CANOPUS
cl. Engadine 488 D13
cl. Erskine Park 300 H1

CANOWIE
pl. Busby 363 G14

CANROBERT
st. Mosman 316 K9

CANSDALE
pl. Castle Hill 217 J7
st. Blacktown 273 H4

CANTELLO
av. Hamondvle 396 H15

CANTERBURY
rd. Bankstown 399 A9
rd. Belmore 401 B4
rd. Campsie 372 B16
rd. Canterbury 372 G13
rd. Glenfield 424 D15
rd. Hurlstone Pk 372 G13
rd. Lakemba 401 B4
rd. Mcquarie Fd 424 D15
rd. Punchbowl 399 A9
rd. Revesby 399 A9
rd. Roselands 400 H6
rd. St Johns Pk 364 H3
rd. Wiley Park 400 H6

CANTERTON
st. Hurlstone Pk 372 J12

CANTON
st. Canterbury 372 E15
st. Kings Park 244 E2

CANTOR
cr. Croydon 342 F15
la. Croydon, off Cantor St 342 F15
st. Croydon 342 F15

CANTRELL
st. Bankstown 368 G15
st. Yagoona 368 G15

CANTRILL
av. Maroubra 407 E8

CANTWELL
st. Glenwood 215 C14

CANUNGRA
pl. Elanora Ht 198 C15

CANVA
st. Canley Vale 366 D5

CANYON
dr. Stanhpe Gdn 215 B12
pl. Engadine 488 C13
rd. Baulkham Hl 248 A13

CAPE
pl. Cherrybrook 219 J6

CAPE BANKS
dr. Harringtn Pk 478 J5

CAPE BARRON
av. Green Valley 363 A14

CAPELLA
pl. Normanhurst 221 E12
rd. Hinchinbrk 393 E3
st. Erskine Park 270 H16

CAPER
pl. Quakers Hill 243 E3

CAPERTEE
st. Ruse 512 F7

CAPE SOLANDER
dr. Kurnell 466 F5

CAPITAL
pl. Sylvania 462 D9

CAPITOL HILL
dr. Mt Vernon 331 A8

CAPIZZI
pl. Kellyville 216 J8

CAPPARIS
cct. Bidwill 211 D13

CAPPER
st. Lindfield 254 G16

CAPRA
pl. Castle Hill 217 A10

CAPRERA
rd. Northmead 278 A6

CAPRI
cl. Avalon 139 J12
cl. Heathcote 518 E7
pl. Erskine Park 300 E1

CAPRICORN
av. Cranebrook 207 F15
bvd. Green Valley 363 A8
rd. Kings Lngly 245 D7

CAPTAIN COOK
dr. Caringbah 492 H2
dr. Cronulla 493 E6
dr. Kurnell 465 A15
dr. Willmot 210 B11
dr. Woolooware 493 E6

CAPTAIN HUNTER
rd. Bayview 168 E8

CAPTAIN JACKA
cr. Daceyville 406 F3

CAPTAIN PIPERS
rd. Vaucluse 348 D5

CAPTAINS
rd. Penrith 236 A11

CAPTAIN STROM
pl. Dundas Vy 279 J6

CAPUA
pl. Avalon 139 J14

CAPULET
pl. Rsemeadow 540 H4

CARA
ct. S Penrith 266 K7

CARABEELY
pl. Harringtn Pk 478 F5

CARABEEN
st. Cabramatta 365 G9

CARABELLA
rd. Caringbah 493 A5
st. Kirribilli 6 B14

CARAHERS
la. The Rocks A H6

CARAMAR
st. Dharruk 241 B8

CARANDINI
st. St Helens Park 541 B7

CARANYA
pl. Cabramatta W 365 C6

CARATEL
cr. Marayong 243 J5

CARAVAN HEAD
rd. Oyster Bay 461 A6

CARAWA
rd. Cromer 228 B16

CARAWATHA
st. Beecroft 250 E11
st. Villawood 367 C4

CARBASSE
cr. St Helens Park 540 K10

CARBEEN
av. St Ives 223 J10
rd. Westleigh 220 D8

CARBERRY
ct. Kellyville 217 A1
la. Campbelltown 511 E5

CARBETHON
cr. Beverly Hills 401 D9

44 GREGORY'S STREET DIRECTORY

STREETS CA

CARBINE
cl. Casula............424 E1
CARBONI
st. Liverpool..........395 A2
CARBOONA
av. Earlwood.........403 G3
CARCLEW
pl. Glen Alpine......510 D11
CARCOAR
cl. Erskine Park.....300 C3
CARCOOLA
av. Chipping Ntn...396 H4
cr. Normanhurst....221 F7
rd. Cromer............228 B15
rd. St Ives............224 D12
st. Campbelltwn....511 K7
st. Canley Vale......366 B4
st. Castle Hill........218 C11
CARDEN
av. Wahroonga......222 A5
CARDEW
wy. Bradbury.........511 J11
CARDIFF
st. Blacktown........244 K14
st. Engadine.........489 C15
wy. Castle Hill.......248 A3
CARDIGAN
la. Camperdown...17 A9
la. Camperdown...17 B6
la. Camperdown...17 B4
rd. Greenacre........370 A7
rd. Roseville Ch....255 E14
st. Auburn............339 A1
st. Camperdown...17 A6
st. Glebe.............12 D10
st. Guildford.........337 E3
st. Stanmore.........17 A9
CARDILLO
st. Wentwthvle.....277 E13
CARDINAL
av. Beecroft..........250 A5
av. W Pnnant Hl....249 K2
st. Mosman..........316 J6
CARDINAL CLANCY
av. Glendenning...242 G5
CARDWELL
st. Balmain...........7 J5
st. Canley Vale......365 K1
CAREDEN
av. Beacon Hill......257 J4
CAREEBONG
rd. Frenchs Frst....256 E7
CAREEL BAY
cr. Avalon............139 J11
CAREEL HEAD
rd. Avalon............140 D11
CAREFREE
rd. N Narrabeen....228 G2
CAREW
la. Marrickville.......373 K11
st. Dee Why..........258 H8
st. Mount Druitt....241 G1
st. Padstow..........429 B5
CAREX
cl. Glenmore Pk....265 H13
CAREY
la. Glenbrook........234 A13
la. Randwick, off
    Carey St 377 F11
st. Bass Hill.........367 K10
st. Liverpool.........395 C6
st. Manly.............288 H14
st. Randwick.........377 F11
CARGELLIGO
pl. Woodcroft........243 H11
CARHULLEN
st. Merrylands......308 A12
CARIBBEAN
pl. Mt Colah..........162 E13
CARIBOU
st. St Clair............270 D16
pl. Raby..............451 G14
CARIEVILLE
la. Balmain...........7 A6
st. Balmain...........7 A6
CARILLA
st. Burwood..........341 J13
CARILLON
av. Camperdown...17 H7
st. Newtown.........17 H7

CARINA
av. Hinchinbrk......393 D3
la. Oyster Bay, off
    Drummond Rd ...461 B7
pl. Castle Hill........218 J9
pl. Cranebrook......207 F7
pl. St Johns Pk....364 C1
rd. Oyster Bay......461 C6
rd. Turramurra......252 E5
CARINDA
dr. Glenhaven......187 G16
dr. S Penrith........266 K2
la. S Penrith, off
    Carinda Dr.........266 K2
st. Ingleburn.........453 A9
CARINGAL
pl. St Ives...........223 G10
st. Chipping Ntn...396 G4
CARINGBAH
rd. Caringbah.......492 F9
rd. Woolooware....493 A9
CARINGTON
st. Riverstone......182 E15
CARINYA
av. Beverly Hills...431 A1
cl. Btn-le-Sds.......403 K15
ct. Mascot...........405 D2
dr. St Marys........239 G16
cr. Allambie Ht.....257 G16
cr. E Kurrajong.....66 E7
pl. Carss Park.....432 G13
pl. Kirrawee.........490 J1
pl. Moorebank.....396 F7
rd. Girraween.......276 C10
rd. Mt Colah........191 K4
rd. Picnic Point....428 B12
rd. Pymble..........223 G14
st. Blacktown.......244 E16
CARINYAH
cr. Castle Hill.......218 A11
CARIOCA
ct. W Pnnant Hl...249 B1
wy. W Pnnant Hl...249 B1
CARISBROOK
st. Linley Point....313 H7
CARISSA
av. St Ives..........224 F8
pl. Alfords Point...458 K3
CARITTA
ct. Parklea.........214 J13
CARL
pl. Kings Lngly....246 B11
CARLEEN
cl. Werrington.....238 E10
CARLENE
av. Padstow........429 G5
CARLIE
st. Kellyville Rdg..185 A16
CARLINGFORD
rd. Carlingford......280 A2
rd. Epping...........251 A15
rd. Regents Pk....369 A2
st. Sefton..........368 G2
CARLISLE
av. Bidwill...........211 E16
av. Blackett.........241 D8
av. Colyton.........270 K7
cr. Dharruk.........241 D8
cr. Hebersham....211 D8
cr. Minchinbury...271 B6
cr. Mount Druitt..241 C16
cr. Hinchinbrk.....393 B1
cl. Mcquarie Pk...252 J16
cr. Beecroft........249 K6
cr. Kellyville........186 J16
st. Yanderra........567 B14
cr. Ashfield.........372 D4
st. Collaroy Plat...228 E11
st. Ingleburn.......453 B7
st. Leichhardt.....9 G15
st. Rose Bay......348 G10
st. Tamarama.....378 B6
CARLON
st. Harrigtn Pk....478 G6
CARLOS
rd. Artarmon......285 A14
CARLOTTA
av. Gordon.........253 G6
la. Greenwich, off
    Ffrench St........314 K9
rd. Double Bay...14 F11
st. Artarmon......314 K3
st. Greenwich....315 A9

CARLOW
cr. Killarney Ht....256 C15
st. N Sydney......5 F1
CARLOWRIE
cr. East Hills......428 A4
CARLTON
cr. Carss Park...432 H14
cr. Kogarah Bay..432 H14
cr. Summer Hill..373 B3
la. Kensington....376 F10
pde. Allawah.........432 F7
pde. Carlton..........432 F7
pde. Punchbowl....399 J8
rd. Cecil Hills......362 F7
rd. North Rocks..248 H12
rd. Thirlmere.......562 A16
rd. Thirlmere......565 A2
st. Arncliffe.........403 B11
st. Chippendale..19 B2
st. Granville........308 E11
st. Harbord........258 H16
st. Kensington...376 F10
st. Manly..........288 G7
st. Riverstone....182 J9
st. Waverley......377 H10
wy. Minto..........482 K2
CARLY
pl. Quakers Hill..214 C13
CARLYLE
cr. Cmbrdg Gdn..237 G4
rd. E Lindfield....255 B14
st. Bossley Park..334 C8
st. Enfield.........371 H3
st. Wollstncraft..315 H8
CARMAN
st. Schofields....183 C15
CARMARTHEN
st. Menai...........458 J9
CARMEL
cl. Baulkham Hl...247 C1
pl. Winston Hills..276 H1
st. Glenbrook.....233 K14
CARMELITA
cct. Rouse Hill....185 B6
CARMELO
ct. Kellyville.......217 B3
CARMEN
cr. Cherrybrook..219 J3
dr. Carlingford....249 E11
pl. Caringbah.....493 A14
pl. Freemns Rch..90 A4
st. Bankstown...369 C14
st. Guildford W..336 J2
st. Marsfield.....282 B7
st. St Ives.......224 E13
CARMICHAEL
dr. West Hoxton..392 B5
dr. West Hoxton..392 B9
dr. West Hoxton..392 C8
dr. West Hoxton..392 E7
st. Kensington...376 B10
CARMINYA
st. Carlingford....249 E11
CARNARVON
av. Glenhaven....218 C5
dr. Frenchs Frst..256 G2
rd. Bow Bowing..452 E14
rd. Riverstone....182 E11
rd. Roseville......254 K16
rd. Schofields....212 H1
st. Carlton........432 H7
st. Silverwater...309 E12
st. Wakeley......334 K11
st. Yarrawarrah..489 G13
CARNATION
av. Bankstown...399 H1
av. Casula........394 G12
av. Clarmnt Ms..238 H16
av. Old Guildford..337 F8
av. Greystanes..306 A11
CARNAVON
ct. Georges Hall..367 J13
CARNE
ct. Austral.........391 G8
pl. Oxley Park...240 D15
wy. Bidwill.........211 H14
CARNEGIE
cct. Chifley.......436 K5
pl. Blacktown....244 F9
pl. Castle Hill....247 J1
pl. Chester Hill..368 C3
st. Auburn........338 K6

CARNEY
st. Mosman, off
    Avenue Rd.......317 B8
st. Casula........394 C16
CARNIVAL
wy. Beaumont Hills..186 C16
CARNOUSTIE
pl. Glenmore Pk..266 F11
st. Rouse Hill....185 A10
CAROB
pl. Cherrybrook..219 E7
CAROL
av. Jannali.........460 F14
cr. Roselands....400 F8
CAROLE
av. Baulkham Hl..247 K10
st. Seven Hills....246 B11
CAROLES
pl. Orangeville....443 C14
CAROLINE
cr. Georges Hall..367 F10
la. Balmain........8 B1
la. Redfern.........18 K6
st. Balmain........8 B8
st. Earlwood......372 G16
st. Guildford.....338 C6
st. Kingsgrove....402 E3
st. Oyster Bay....461 A6
st. Redfern.......18 K6
st. Westmead....277 H15
wy. Minto..........482 J2
CAROLINE CHISHOLM
dr. Camden S...507 B10
dr. Winston Hills..277 A1
la. Lane Cove......313 H4
CAROLYN
av. Beacon Hill..257 J5
av. Carlingford...249 G12
ch. Orchard Hills..267 B13
cl. Castle Hill....217 J9
ct. Glenwood....215 G10
dr. Greystanes..306 F4
dr. Silverwater..309 J10
CAROMA
av. Kyeemagh...404 B14
CARONIA
av.e,Cronulla....493 J11
av.w,Cronulla....493 F10
av.w,Woolooware..493 F10
CAROONA
av. Glenwood....215 F16
cr. Carlingford...249 F11
st. Padstow.....399 A13
CAROUSEL
cl. Menai.........458 J14
cl. Cromer.......258 G2
CARPENTER
av. Rookwood...340 B12
cr. Warriewood..199 D11
CARR
cl. Coogee.......407 E1
pl. Bradbury.....511 J11
pl. Bringelly......387 F8
st. Chatswood W..284 E11
st. Coogee.......407 E2
st. Waverton.....5 A6
CARRA
av. Douglas Park..568 J12
CARRABAI
pl. Baulkham Hl..248 A11
CARRAMAR
av. Carramar....366 H4
av. North Ryde..283 B13
cr. Miranda.....492 E5
cr. Winmalee....173 F12
gr. Terrey Hills...196 D8
pl. Peakhurst...430 C9
rd. Lindfield.....283 F4
st. Berowra.....133 F11
CARRAMARR
rd. Castle Hill...218 B13
CARRANYA
rd. Riverview....314 B6
CARRARA
pl. Plumpton....241 H11
rd. Vaucluse....348 B4
CARRBRIDGE
dr. Castle Hill....218 C7
CARRE
cr. Canley Ht....335 E16

CARRICK
cl. West Hoxton..392 D7
CARRINGTON
av. Bellevue Hill..347 F13
av. Caringbah....492 F4
av. Cromer......228 B13
av. Hurstville....431 G1
av. Mortdale....431 D8
av. Mosman....316 K2
av. Strathfield...341 F13
cct. Leumeah....482 D16
dr. Centennial Pk..21 G6
la. Bellevue Hill, off
    Carrington Av ...347 F13
la. Coogee......377 E14
la. N Strathfield, off
    Carrington St....341 F8
la. Petersham....15 J9
la. Petersham, off
    Fishers Res 373 K5
pde. Curl Curl.....258 K16
pde. Harbord......258 K16
rd. Bringelly.....418 H2
rd. Castle Hill...217 D13
rd. Coogee......377 D15
rd. Guildford....337 D6
rd. Hornsby....191 F11
rd. Londonderry..148 C10
rd. Marrickville..373 K16
rd. Randwick...377 D15
rd. Wahroonga..222 F2
rd. Waverley....377 F10
sq. Campsie....371 J13
st. Auburn.......339 A3
st. Balmain......7 C11
st. Bexley......402 H16
st. Campsie....371 J13
st. Granville....308 E13
st. Lewisham..15 C7
st. Lilyfield.....10 D4
st. N Strathfield..341 F8
st. Parramatta..307 K7
st. Penshurst..431 G5
st. Revesby....398 C10
st. St Marys...269 J6
st. Seven Hills..275 K4
st. Summer Hill..373 D6
st. Sydney......A G16
st. Sydney......1 F16
st. Wahroonga..222 D2
CARRISBROOK
av. Bexley North..402 F10
av. Punchbowl...400 A1
CARROL
st. Menai.......458 J14
pl. Forestville..255 D8
CARROLL
cr. Plumpton...242 B11
la. Mosman, off
    Ourimbah Rd.....317 A5
pl. Westleigh...220 E8
rd. Woollahra..22 K5
st. Beverley Pk..433 C10
st. Lidcombe..339 G10
st. Warwck Frm..365 E13
st. Wetherill Pk..334 F5
CARROO
rd. Blaxlands Rdg..65 B1
CARROWBROOK
av. Glenwood..245 F1
CARRS
rd. Galston....159 F4
rd. Wilberforce..67 D11
CARRUTHERS
dr. Dolls Point..463 H2
dr. Hornsea Pk..392 F16
dr. Sans Souci..433 H16
st. Pearce.....431 C4
CARSHALTON
st. Croydon....372 E5
st. Croydon Pk..372 E5
CARSON
cr. Bexley North..402 C10
st. Dundas Vy..280 E10
st. Panania.....398 E15
st. Pymble.....253 E1
CARSONS
la. St Marys....239 G16
CARSTAIRS
pl. St Andrews..482 B2
CARSTONE
wy. Ambarvale..510 K16
CARTELA
cr. Smithfield..335 E4

GREGORY'S STREET DIRECTORY 45

CARTER
cr. Gymea Bay 491 E9
cr. Padstow Ht 429 E8
la. Marrickville 373 F14
la. Randwick, off Castle La 377 B10
pl. Claymore 481 B10
rd. Brookvale 258 D10
rd. Menai 458 H13
st. Belfield 371 D12
st. Bronte 377 H8
st. Cammeray 316 A5
st. Gordon 254 A7
st. Greystanes 305 H9
st. Homebush B 340 C2
st. Randwick 377 B9
st. Seven Hills 276 A4

CARTERET
av. Willmot 210 D13

CARTERS
rd. Dural 189 E3
rd. Grose Vale 84 G11

CARTHONA
av. Darling Point 14 A1

CARTIER
cr. Green Valley 363 B9
st. Bonnyrigg 363 H8

CARTLEDGE
av. Miranda 491 J6

CARTMORE
la. Surry Hills 20 B6

CARTREF
la. Mosman, off Rangers Av 316 G9

CARTWRIGHT
av. Busby 393 H1
av. Cartwright 393 H1
av. Homebush 341 B6
av. Merrylands 307 B11
av. Miller 393 H1
av. Sadleir 393 H1
cl. Glenmore Pk 265 F7
cr. Lalor Park 245 G11
st. Bonnyrigg Ht 363 G6
st. S Windsor 150 H2

CARVER
cr. Baulkham Hl 247 G6
pl. Dundas Vy 280 C8

CARVERS
rd. Oyster Bay 461 A8

CARVOSSA
pl. Bligh Park 150 J6

CARWAR
av. Carss Park 432 G13
la. Carss Park 432 G12

CARY
gr. Minto 482 C2
la. Bondi Jctn 22 K8
st. Baulkham Hl 248 B9
st. Drummoyne 344 B4
st. Emu Plains 235 E11
st. Leichhardt 15 G2
st. Marrickville 373 H16
wy. Fairfield W 337 A16

CARYSFIELD
rd. Bass Hill 368 C12
rd. Georges Hall 368 C12

CARYSFORT
st. Hurstville 432 A8

CASABLANCA
av. Beaumont Hills 186 B16

CASANDA
av. Smithfield 335 C4

CASBEN
cl. Carlingford 250 D12

CASBY
pl. Ambarvale 510 G13

CASCADE
av. Glenmore Pk 266 E14
la. Paddington 13 E13
rd. Cranebrook 207 A12
st. Paddington 13 E16
st. Seven Hills 275 C10

CASCADES
cl. West Hoxton 392 D5

CASERTA
pl. Allambie Ht 257 D8

CASEY
pl. Blackett 241 D3

CASH
pl. Prairiewood 334 E11

CASHEL
cr. Killarney Ht 255 H12
ct. Kellyville Rdg 215 A1

CASHMAN
pl. Edensor Pk 333 J14
rd. Btn-le-Sds 404 A15
st. Rozelle 10 K4

CASHMANS
la. Five Dock, off Ramsay Rd 342 K10

CASHMERE
dr. Elderslie 507 J1

CASINO
pl. Hoxton Park 393 B7
rd. Greystanes 305 G3
st. Bossley Park 333 D13
st. Eastlakes 406 A4
st. Glenwood 245 G1

CASPIAN
ct. Plumpton 242 C8
pl. Woronora Ht 489 F5

CASS
ct. Currans Hill 479 J14
pl. Cranebrook 207 E13

CASSAM
pl. Valley Ht 202 D4

CASSANDRA
av. St Ives 224 D14
cr. Heathcote 518 F9
pl. Carlingford 279 K2

CASSAR
cr. Cranebrook 207 G6
pl. Oakhurst 242 C4

CASSIA
cl. Bossley Park 333 E8
cl. St Clair 269 H9
gr. Beecroft 250 F3
la. Dee Why 258 K9
pl. Bass Hill 368 A10
pl. Eastwood 281 C5
pl. Loftus 489 J11
pl. Mcquarie Fd 454 E1
st. Dee Why 258 K9

CASSIDY
pl. Kellyville 216 A2
st. Denham Ct 422 C4

CASSILIS
st. Monterey 433 G8

CASSINA
pl. Baulkham Hl 246 G9

CASSINIA
ct. Wattle Grove 426 A2
pl. Mt Annan 509 F4

CASSINO
cl. Allambie Ht 257 D9

CASSINS
av. N Sydney 5 F1
la. N Sydney 5 F1

CASSIUS
wy. Rsemeadow 540 H3

CASSOLA
pl. Penrith 236 E2

CASTELNAU
st. Caringbah 492 G11

CASTLE
cct. Seaforth 286 K6
cct. Westleigh 220 F8
cr. Belrose 225 J14
la. Randwick, off Carter St 377 B9
pl. Castle Hill 218 B14
pl. Padstow Ht 429 H5
pl. Sylvania 461 J14
rd. Orchard Hills 267 E5
rd. Richmond 118 G11
st. Blacktown 274 C5
st. Blakehurst 462 C4
st. Castle Hill 217 K12
st. Castlereagh 176 A5
st. N Parramatta 278 C11
st. Randwick 377 B9

CASTLE CIRCUIT
cl. Seaforth 286 J5

CASTLECOVE
dr. Castle Cove 285 F4

CASTLEFERN
ct. Kellyville 186 K15

CASTLEFIELD
la. Bondi, off Castlefield St 378 A4
st. Bondi 378 A4

CASTLEFORD
tce. Stanhpe Gdn 215 D5

CASTLEGATE
pl. Castle Hill 217 A11

CASTLE HILL
rd. Castle Hill 218 H14
rd. Cherrybrook 249 D1
rd. W Pnnant Hl 249 D1

CASTLE HOWARD
rd. Beecroft 250 F9
rd. Cheltenham 250 F9

CASTLE LEA
ct. Castle Hill 219 A12

CASTLE PINES
dr. Baulkham Hl 216 K12

CASTLEREAGH
cr. Sylvania Wtr 462 D11
la. Penrith, off Castlereagh Rd 236 F7
la. Redfern 19 G7
rd. Agnes Banks 117 A14
rd. Castlereagh 205 G11
rd. Penrith 236 F7
rd. Richmond 117 H8
rd. Wilberforce 91 K1
st. Bossley Park 333 F5
st. Concord 341 H6
st. Haymarket F A8
st. Haymarket F B7
st. Haymarket 3 H11
st. Liverpool 395 C4
st. Penrith 236 H13
st. Riverstone 182 K8
st. Sydney D A16
st. Sydney 3 H11
st. Tahmoor 565 H12
st. Tahmoor 565 J10

CASTLE ROCK
cr. Clontarf 287 G15
ct. Wattle Grove 395 K14

CASTLEROCK
av. Glenmore Pk 266 H8

CASTLESTEAD
st. Concord W 311 D14

CASTLEWOOD
av. Woolooware 493 E10
dr. Castle Hill 248 H1

CASTRA
pl. Double Bay 14 F7

CASUARINA
av. Glenorie 128 C5
cct. Kingswood 267 H2
cl. The Oaks 502 E14
ct. Wattle Grove 396 C16
dr. Cherrybrook 219 G13
pl. Acacia Gdn 214 J16
pl. Mcquarie Fd 454 B5
rd. Alfords Point 429 C14
rd. Gymea Bay 491 F12

CASULA
rd. Casula 394 H15

CASURINA
pl. Narellan Vale 478 J14

CAT
pl. Seven Hills 275 B5

CATALINA
cr. Avalon 140 D14
pl. Kellyville 186 F16
pl. Raby 481 H1
st. Mascot 404 K4
st. N St Marys 239 J10

CATALPA
av. Avalon 139 J15
av. Blaxland 233 G6
cr. Turramurra 222 H16
gr. Menai 458 K13
wy. Blacktown 274 E12

CATANIA
pl. Quakers Hill 214 D9

CATARACT
pl. Leumeah 482 E13
rd. Appin 569 E14
rd. Box Hill 154 A1

CATCHPOLE
av. Hobartville 118 D6
st. St Helens Park 541 C3

CATERSON
dr. Castle Hill 217 E9

CATES
pl. St Ives 224 D8

CATHAN
st. Quakers Hill 214 E11

CATHAY
pl. Kellyville 217 A5

CATHCART
st. Fairfield 336 A16

CATHEDRAL
st. Sydney D J10
st. Sydney 4 B5
st. Woolmloo D J10
st. Woolmloo 4 B5
st. Woolmloo 4 D5

CATHERINE
av. Lurnea 394 D10
cr. Blaxland 234 C7
cr. Rooty Hill 272 C2
la. Belmore 401 H1
st. Glebe 12 B16
st. Kurrajong 85 F3
st. Leichhardt 16 D3
st. Lilyfield 10 F7
st. Punchbowl 370 B16
st. Rockdale 433 C1
st. Rozelle 10 J2
st. St Ives 224 D13
st. Werrington 238 H9
st. Windsor 121 B9

CATHERINE FIELD
rd. Catherine Fd 449 D1

CATHERINE SPENCE
pl. Cabarita 312 E16

CATHY
st. Blaxland 233 J11
wy. Seven Hills 275 K5

CATKIN
wy. Mcquarie Fd 454 G4

CATLETT
av. North Rocks 248 K16

CATO
cl. Edensor Pk 363 F3
pl. Blackett 241 D3
pl. Illawong 459 D5
wy. Casula 424 F3

CATON
pl. Quakers Hill 213 H16

CATRIONA
cl. Berowra Ht 133 A6

CATTAI
ct. Holsworthy 426 F5
rd. Cattai 94 C4
rd. Pitt Town 92 K14
rd. Pitt Town 93 A13

CATTAI CREEK
dr. Kellyville 187 A16
dr. Kellyville 216 K1
dr. Kellyville 217 C1

CATTAI RIDGE
rd. Glenorie 128 D12
rd. Maraylya 95 B13

CATTON
pl. Menai 458 J14

CAULFIELD
cr. St Johns Pk 364 E2

CAVALLARO
ct. Mount Druitt 241 D11

CAVALLI
wy. Clarmnt Ms 268 F4

CAVALRY
gr. Glenwood 245 K3

CAVAN
pl. Airds 512 B13
rd. Killarney Ht 255 K13

CAVASINNI
pl. Wetherill Pk 333 H2

CAVE
av. North Ryde 282 C9
cl. Green Valley 363 B11
rd. Strathfield 370 J2

CAVELL
av. Rhodes 311 E7

CAVENAH
wy. Kellyville Rdg 185 A16
wy. Kellyville Rdg 185 B16

CAVENDISH
av. Blacktown 275 A7
la. Stanmore 16 F12
st. Concord W 341 D1
st. Enmore 16 E11
st. Pennant Hills 220 K16
st. Stanmore 16 E11

CAVERS
st. Currans Hill 479 H8

CAVERSHAM
ct. Cherrybrook 219 F9

CAVES
la. Dulwich Hill 373 E9

CAVEY
st. Marrickville 373 K14

CAVILL
av. Ashfield 372 G2
st. Harbord 288 F2
st. Hebersham 241 F10
st. Queenscliff 288 F2

CAWARRA
pl. Fairfield 336 F7
pl. Gordon 253 E9
rd. Caringbah 492 J6
st. Eastern Ck 272 F7

CAWARRAH
rd. Middle Cove 285 J8

CAWDOR
pl. Acacia Gdn 214 H16
pl. Rsemeadow 540 D3
rd. Camden 506 H4
rd. Cawdor 506 C16
rd. Cawdor 537 A10

CAWDOR FARMS
rd. Grasmere 475 H16

CAWTHORNE
st. Hornsby Ht 191 G7

CAYDEN
av. Kellyville 216 B2

CAYLEY
av. Punchbowl 400 B6
pl. Cabramatta W 364 F6
pl. Horngsea Pk 392 F15

CECIL
av. Castle Hill 217 K14
av. Castle Hill 218 B16
av. Pennant Hills 250 J1
la. Paddington 13 G14
pl. Greenfld Pk 334 C16
rd. Cecil Park 331 G8
rd. Hornsby 192 C14
rd. Newport 169 G16
rd. Rose Bay 348 D8
st. Ashfield 373 A1
st. Caringbah 492 K16
st. Denistone E 281 H10
st. Dolans Bay 492 K16
st. Fairlight 288 E8
st. Gordon 253 G11
st. Guildford 337 G2
st. Hurstville Gr 431 H9
st. Merrylands 307 G16
st. Monterey 433 H6
st. Paddington 13 G14
st. Scotland I 168 H4
st. Wareemba 342 K6

CECILIA
pl. Castle Hill, off Vittoria Smith Av 218 J14
st. Belmore 371 E13
st. Marrickville 373 K11
st. Toongabbie 276 B7

CECIL MUNRO
av. Cronulla, off Ozone St 494 A12

CECILY
st. Belfield 371 B10
st. Lilyfield 10 G2

CEDAR
av. Bradbury 511 E14
cl. Bossley Park 333 H9
cr. N St Marys 240 A11
ct. Glenmore Pk 265 H4
gr. Castle Hill 217 D10
gr. Frenchs Frst 256 F2
la. N St Marys, off Cedar Cr 240 A12
pl. Blacktown 274 B7
pl. Ermington 280 D13
pl. Kirrawee 490 K5
pl. Newington 310 B14
pl. S Coogee 407 E6
pl. The Oaks 502 F13
rd. Casula 423 K3
rd. Prestons 394 A15
st. Greystanes 306 E4
st. Lugarno 429 G16
st. Normanhurst 221 D12

CEDAR CREEK
rd. Thirlmere 561 H11
rd. Thirlmere 561 H12

CEDAR RIDGE
rd. Blaxlands Rdg 64 K1

CEDAR WATTLE
pl. Narellan Vale 478 K14

CEDARWOOD
cl. Greystanes 306 F12
dr. Cherrybrook 219 H15
gr. Dean Park 212 F16

46 GREGORY'S STREET DIRECTORY

STREETS CH

pl. Carlingford 249 D15
pl. Cranebrook 207 F15

CEDRIC
la. Mosman, off Mulbring St 317 D9
st. Mcquarie Fd 423 K15

CELEBES
st. Kings Park 244 K2

CELEBRATION
dr. Bella Vista 216 A15
rd. Sadleir 364 B16

CELESTE
av. Castle Hill 217 B7
ct. Rooty Hill 272 A5

CELESTIAL
pl. Cranebrook 207 G5

CELIA
pl. Kings Lngly 245 G8
rd. Kellyville 185 F1
st. Granville 308 F15

CELOSIA
pl. Loftus 489 H13

CELTIS
pl. Mcquarie Fd 454 F2

CEMETERY
av. Matraville 436 G8
rd. Riverstone 182 E10

CENTAUR
st. Padstow 429 A2
st. Revesby 429 A5
st. Revesby Ht 429 A5

CENTAURI
cct. Cranebrook 207 E5

CENTAURUS
dr. Hinchinbrk 393 D4

CENTENARY
av. Hunters Hill 313 D11
av. Matraville 436 J8
av. Moorebank 395 K11
av. Old Tngabbie 277 E7
av. Old Tngabbie 277 E8
dr. Homebush W 340 F12
dr. Mosman 316 H11
dr. Strathfield 340 F12
pl. Catherine Fd 449 F4
rd. Merrylands 306 K5
rd. S Wntwthvle 307 A5

CENTENNIAL
av. Chatswood W 284 E11
av. Lane Cove 284 B16
av. Lane Cove N 284 B16
av. Lane Cove W 313 J2
av. Randwick 377 C9
ct. Mt Vernon 331 E3
dr. Campbelltown 511 A8
la. Centennial Pk 21 C10
la. Ellis Lane 476 C13
sq. Centennial Pk 21 G4
sq. Paddington 21 G4
st. Marrickville 373 K10

CENTENNIAL PARK
ct. Wattle Grove 426 A3

CENTRAL
av. Chipping Ntn 366 H15
av. Chipping Ntn 366 F16
av. Como 460 F4
av. Eastwood 280 K5
av. Eveleigh 18 J11
av. Lane Cove 314 E2
av. Lilyfield 10 C3
av. Mcquarie Pk 282 C1
av. Manly 288 H9
av. Marrickville 373 K13
av. Mosman 317 A1
av. Thornleigh 221 A13
av. Westmead 277 H16
la. Chipping Ntn 366 G14
la. Marrickville, off Victoria Rd 374 B13
pl. Baulkham Hl 247 H11
rd. Avalon 139 J15
rd. Beverly Hills 430 J1
rd. Miranda 492 A3
st. Belfield 371 D10
st. Naremburn 315 F2
st. Sydney E H1
st. Sydney 3 G9

CENTRAL PARK
dr. Bow Bowing 452 D15

CENTRE
av. Roselands 400 J7
cr. Blaxland 234 C6
la. Kingsford, off Kennedy St 406 J1
pl. Wetherill Pk 334 E1
rd. Mascot 404 C6
st. Blakehurst 462 D1
st. Leichhardt 16 D2
st. Penshurst 431 E6
st. Redfern 19 H6

CENTURY
cct. Baulkham Hl 216 G15

CEPHEUS
la. Erskine Park, off Cepheus Pl 300 F1
pl. Erskine Park 300 F1

CERAMIC
la. Manly 288 G5
wy. Woodcroft 243 E9

CEREMONIAL
dr. Richmond 118 J10
dr. Richmond 119 A10

CERES
pl. Rsemeadow 540 K5
st. Penrith 237 D2

CESSNA
pl. Raby 481 G2

CESTRUM
av. Mcquarie Fd 454 F5

CETUS
pl. Erskine Park 301 B3

CEVU
av. Willoughby 285 G13

CHABLIS
pl. Eschol Park 481 B6
pl. Minchinbury 272 B9
pl. Orchard Hills 268 F15

CHAD
pl. St Clair 299 J3

CHADD
st. Galston 160 F5

CHADDERTON
st. Cabramatta 366 E6
st. Canley Vale 366 E6

CHADLEY
ct. Cherrybrook 219 H13
pl. West Hoxton 392 A10

CHADWICK
av. Marrickville 373 D15
av. Regents Pk 339 D16
cr. Fairfield W 335 B13
st. Lucas Ht 487 J11
st. Putney 312 A9

CHADWORTH
pl. Baulkham Hl 248 B6

CHAFFEY
pl. Bonnyrigg Ht 363 E7

CHAINMAIL
cr. Castle Hill 217 E3

CHAIN-O-PONDS
cct. Mt Annan 479 A16
rd. Mulgoa 295 F9

CHAKOLA
av. Hornsby Ht 191 G4
pl. Kirrawee 461 D16

CHALCEDONY
st. Eagle Vale 481 G7

CHALDER
av. Marrickville 374 D11
la. Marrickville, off Chalder St 374 C10
st. Marrickville 374 C11
st. Newtown 17 H8

CHALET
pl. Minchinbury 272 A8
rd. Kellyville 216 E5

CHALEYER
st. N Willoughby 285 F7
st. Rose Bay 348 C13

CHALFORD
av. Canterbury 402 E1

CHALIS
la. Randwick, off Castle St 377 B9

CHALLENGER
dr. Belrose 225 H6
la. Cranebrook, off Pensax Rd 207 G14
pl. Birchgrove 7 K4
st. Voyager Pt 427 D4
wy. Cranebrook 207 G14

CHALLIS
av. Dulwich Hill 373 F12
av. Potts Point 4 J2
av. Turramurra 222 K10
st. Randwick 377 B9

CHALLONER
av. Chipping Ntn 396 E4

CHALMER
cl. St Johns Pk 364 E1

CHALMERS
av. Beacon Hill 257 H7
av. Emu Plains 235 J10
cr. Mascot 405 A3
cr. Old Tngabbie 276 J11
la. Surry Hills 19 G3
rd. Strathfield 341 B16
st. Belmore 401 C3
st. Haymarket 19 G4
st. Lakemba 401 C3
st. Redfern 19 F10
st. Surry Hills 19 G4

CHAMBERLAIN
av. Caringbah 492 G4
av. Rose Bay 348 C8
dr. Smithfield 335 B6
rd. Bexley 402 H12
rd. Guildford 337 J7
rd. Padstow 429 D5
rd. Padstow Ht 429 D6
st. Campbelltown 511 H2
st. Narwee 400 J14

CHAMBERS
av. Bondi Beach 378 B3
ct. Epping 251 B16
st. Wrrngtn Cty 238 F9

CHAMELEON
dr. Erskine Park 300 D3
la. Erskine Park, off Chameleon Dr 300 F1

CHAMPION
rd. Tennyson 312 E11
st. Glenfield 424 H10

CHAMPNESS
cr. St Marys 239 J15
la. St Marys, off Champness Cr 239 K15

CHANCERY
st. Canley Vale 366 E5

CHANDLER
av. Chippendale 18 H1
av. Cowan 104 C14
st. Rockdale 433 D2
st. Rooty Hill 271 J6

CHANDOS
la. Crows Nest, off Alexander St 315 F5
rd. Horsley Pk 303 A12
rd. Yanderra 567 C15
st. Ashfield 343 A16
st. Canley Vale 365 J2
st. Crows Nest 315 E5
st. Haberfield 343 B16
st. Manly Vale 287 J5
st. Naremburn 315 E5
st. St Leonards 315 E5

CHANEL
st. Toongabbie 276 G4

CHANG
pl. Kearns 481 B1

CHANNEL
pl. Mt Annan 479 G15
st. Dulwich Hill 373 D7

CHANNEY
cl. Bossley Park 333 H7

CHANSA
pl. Blacktown 273 K5

CHANT
av. Pagewood 406 G7

CHANTELLE
cl. N Wahroonga 192 G15

CHANTER
rd. Thirlmere 564 G9

CHAPALA
cl. St Ives 224 E8

CHAPEL
cct. Prospect 274 K13
cl. Cherrybrook 219 E14
la. Alexandria 18 K10
la. Alexandria 19 A10
la. Baulkham Hl 246 G8
la. Baulkham Hl 247 B4
la. Belmore 401 F3
la. Crows Nest, off Holterman St 315 F6
la. Marrickville 374 B10
la. Mooney Mooney 75 C2
la. Rockdale 403 D16
la. St Marys, off Champness Cr 239 J15
rd. Bankstown 369 E16
rd. Vaucluse 348 D2
rd.s, Bankstown 399 C7
st. Belmore 401 D2
st. Darlinghurst 4 C9
st. Kingsgrove 401 D2
st. Kogarah 433 C6
st. Lakemba 401 D2
st. Lilyfield 9 H4
st. Marrickville 374 C10
st. Randwick 377 C11
st. Richmond 118 E3
st. Rockdale 403 E16
st. Roselands 401 D2
st. St Marys 239 H16

CHAPEL HILL
rd. Sackville N 68 D1

CHAPERON
cr. Minto 453 B15

CHAPLAIN
pl. Bligh Park 150 J7

CHAPLIN
cr. Quakers Hill 243 H1
dr. Lane Cove W 283 F16
st. Darlinghurst 4 H11

CHAPMAN
av. Beecroft 250 B5
av. Castle Hill 217 H13
av. Chatswood 284 J11
av. Maroubra 407 G11
av. Penrith 236 H13
cct. Currans Hill 479 H9
la. Annandale 10 J15
la. Lindfield, off Tyron Rd 254 D16
la. Surry Hills 20 E3
pde. Faulconbdg 171 D13
pl. Wakeley 334 G14
rd. Annandale 11 D6
rd. Vineyard 152 H9
st. Gladesville 312 E7
st. Green Valley 363 B13
st. Gymea 491 E3
st. Gymea 491 E6
st. Strathfield 341 F10
st. Summer Hill 373 E4
st. Surry Hills 20 E3
st. Tahmoor 565 H10
st. Werrington 238 K12
st. West Hoxton 392 B11
st. West Hoxton 392 C11

CHAPPEL
av. Green Valley 363 A9
ct. Mt Annan 479 C12

CHARADE
st. Riverwood 400 C10

CHARD
rd. Brookvale 258 B10

CHARDONNAY
av. Eschol Park 481 A4
rd. St Clair 270 G11

CHARKER
dr. Harringtn Pk 478 C3

CHARKERS
st. S Penrith 266 H6

CHARLBURY
st. Chipping Ntn 396 F2

CHARLECOT
st. Dulwich Hill 373 G10

CHARLEMONT
wy. Wentwthvle 277 E11

CHARLEROI
rd. Belrose 226 A9

CHARLES
ct. North Rocks 278 F3
la. Burwood 342 B15
la. Forest Lodge 11 G15
la. Mosman, off Muston St 317 C9
la. Pemulwuy 305 F6
pl. Cherrybrook 219 H5
pl. Jannali 460 H11
pl. Mt Annan 509 F2
st. Arncliffe 403 H9
st. Balmain 8 C10
st. Baulkham Hl 247 G13
st. Blacktown 245 A8
st. Burwood 342 C15
st. Canterbury 372 E13
st. Carlingford 279 G6
st. Castlecrag 286 A11
st. Eastlakes 405 J6
st. Enmore 17 A12
st. Erskineville 18 A13
st. Fairlight 288 D8
st. Five Dock 343 A7
st. Forest Lodge 11 G15
st. Granville 308 F15
st. Guildford W 336 H3
st. Harbord 288 H2
st. Harris Park 308 E4
st. Killara 283 E2
st. Leichhardt 9 G10
st. Lilyfield 9 G7
st. Lindfield 283 E2
st. Liverpool 395 B8
st. McGraths Hl 121 J11
st. Marrickville 374 B9
st. Marsden Pk 182 A12
st. N Richmond 87 D13
st. N Sydney K B5
st. N Sydney 5 F7
st. Oatlands 279 A10
st. Oatley 431 B15
st. Parramatta 308 E4
st. Petersham 16 C4
st. Putney 311 K8
st. Redfern 20 C8
st. Riverwood 400 E16
st. Ryde 312 B5
st. St Marys 239 E5
st. Smithfield 335 B6
st. Springwood 201 F3
st. Woolmloo 4 F5

CHARLES BABBAGE
av. Currans Hill 479 G12

CHARLESCOTTE
av. Punchbowl 400 D7

CHARLES HACKETT
dr. St Marys 239 F16

CHARLES HAYMAN
la. Collaroy 229 B14

CHARLES O'NEILL
wy. Lewisham 15 D8

CHARLES STURT
dr. Wrrngtn Cty 238 F9

CHARLES TODD
cr. Wrrngtn Cty 238 E7
la. Wrrngtn Cty, off Charles Todd Cr 238 E7

CHARLESTON
av. Earlwood 402 E6

CHARLESWORTH
cl. Catherine Fd 449 G8

CHARLEYS
rd. Mt Tomah 59 J16

CHARLIE YANKOS
st. Glenwood 215 K16

CHARLISH
la. Lane Cove 313 K1

CHARLOTTE
av. Marrickville 373 K15
cl. Lurnea 394 B12
cr. Canley Vale 366 F4
gr. Bella Vista 246 G3
la. Darlinghurst F G2
la. Pennant Hills 250 J1
pl. Beacon Hill 257 F2
pl. Bligh Park 150 D4
pl. Illawong 459 G3
rd. Pennant Hills 250 J1
rd. Port Botany 436 B9
rd. Rooty Hill 271 J3
st. Ashfield 372 J1
st. Campsie 401 K1
st. Dundas Vy 280 B7
st. Lilyfield 10 C10
st. Marsden Pk 181 J12
st. Merrylands 307 C16
st. Rozelle 10 K1
wy. Minto 482 H7

CHARLTON
av. Chipping Ntn 366 E15
av. Newington, off Spitz Av 309 K15
av. Turramurra 223 E12
dr. Castle Hill 219 A13
dr. Liberty Gr 311 C15
la. Brookvale 258 B11
pl. Menai 458 E13
pl. St Clair 270 C9
pwy. Chipping Ntn, off Charlton Av 366 E14
rd. Lalor Park 245 E10
st. Abbotsford 342 J2
st. Yagoona 369 C9
wy. Glebe 11 K8

CHARLTONS CREEK
rd. Berrilee 131 D11

CHARM
pl. Peakhurst 429 K6

CHARMAINE
av. Greenacre 370 C7

GREGORY'S STREET DIRECTORY 47

CH STREETS

CHARMAN
av. Maroubra.........406 H7
CHARMER
cr. Minchinbury.......271 G8
CHARMIAN
pl. Rsemeadow........540 H3
CHARNWOOD
ct. Glen Alpine........510 E9
CHARTER
st. Sadleir.............394 B2
CHASE
av. Roseville Ch......255 E14
dr. Acacia Gdn........214 J16
CHASELING
av. Springwood.......201 G1
pl. The Oaks..........502 E10
st. Greenacre..........370 D13
CHASSELAS
av. Eschol Park.......481 A4
CHATEAU
cl. Kellyville...........185 E7
cr. St Clair.............270 B9
tce. Quakers Hill......213 G9
CHATFIELD
av. Belfield............371 C8
st. Ryde................312 D1
CHATHAM
av. Moorebank........425 A3
ct. Belrose.............226 A13
ct. Cherrybrook, off
    Glamorgan Wy...219 E9
pl. Abbotsford.........342 K2
pl. N Turramurra.....223 E6
rd. Denistone.........281 B12
rd. Eastwood..........281 B11
rd. West Ryde........281 B12
st. Botany..............405 G12
st. Canley Ht..........365 G4
st. Pitt Town...........92 H15
st. Randwick..........377 D15
CHATRES
st. St Clair.............270 F11
CHATSWOOD
av. Chatswood........285 B8
CHATSWORTH
rd. St Clair.............270 D10
st. Fairfield............336 B14
CHAUCER
cr. Leumeah...........512 B2
pl. Winmalee..........173 J9
pl. Riverstone........182 C10
st. Wetherill Pk.......334 G6
CHAUSSON
pl. Cranebrook.......207 G8
CHAUVEL
av. Holsworthy.......396 B13
av. Milperra............397 E12
cl. Wahroonga........223 B5
st. North Ryde.......282 J11
CHAVIN
pl. Greenfld Pk........333 K13
CHEAL
la. Neutral Bay........6 F1
CHEATLE
st. East Hills..........427 H2
CHECKLEY
ct. Ermington........280 B15
st. Abbotsford........342 H1
CHEDDAR
st. Blakehurst........432 D12
CHEDLEY
pl. Marayong.........208 D8
CHEERS
st. West Ryde.......280 J13
CHEERYBLE
pl. Ambarvale........510 K14
CHEESMANS
rd. Cattai...............68 K10
CHEGWYN
av. Matraville........436 H8
la. Botany, off
    Chegwyn St....405 E12
st. Botany.............405 E11
CHELLASTON
st. Camden...........507 B3
CHELMSFORD
av. Artarmon..........285 D16
st. Artarmon.........315 C1
av. Bankstown.......399 B2
st. Belmore...........401 H2
av. Botany............405 F15
st. Cronulla..........523 K3
av. Croydon..........372 C1

av. E Lindfield........254 G16
av. Epping............280 H3
av. Haberfield........343 D12
av. Lindfield..........284 E2
av. Maroubra........407 C15
av. Naremburn......315 C1
av. Willoughby......285 D16
rd. Asquith...........192 D10
st. S Wntwthvle....306 J5
st. Camperdown...17 D10
st. Newtown.........17 D10
CHELSEA
av. Baulkham Hl....247 H8
dr. Canley Ht........335 C16
pl. Colyton...........270 E6
pl. Glenfield.........424 C11
rd. W Pnnant Hls..219 K16
st. Merrylands......307 B10
st. Redfern...........20 C8
tce. Glenwood......215 H14
CHELSEA GARDEN
ct. Wattle Grove...426 B5
CHELTENHAM
av. Cmbrdg Pk.....237 K8
cl. Castle Hill.......218 E12
rd. Burwood........342 C14
rd. Cheltenham....250 H10
rd. Croydon.........342 C14
st. Chipping Ntn...366 F15
st. Rozelle...........10 J3
CHEPSTOW
dr. Castle Hill........216 J9
st. Randwick.........377 B10
CHERANA
cr. Forestville.........255 E9
pl. Kareela............461 E12
CHERIE
pl. Bass Hill..........367 F7
CHERITON
av. Castle Hill.......218 A15
CHEROKEE
av. Greenfld Pk......333 K14
pl. Raby...............451 H16
CHERRY
av. Carlingford......249 E16
ct. Marsfield.........282 A4
pl. Castle Cove.....286 D7
pl. Mcquarie Fd....454 C12
pl. Prestons..........393 H14
st. Marsden Pk.....182 A13
st. Mt Pritchard....364 E9
st. Warrawee.......222 G13
CHERRYBROOK
ch. Londonderry...178 C1
rd. Lansvale.........366 C10
rd. W Pnnant Hll..219 J15
CHERRY HAVEN
wy. Cherrybrook..219 C15
CHERRYWOOD
av. Mt Riverview..234 D3
av. Wahroonga....223 B4
pl. Menai............458 K13
st. Glenwood......245 C2
CHERTSEY
av. Bankstown....399 B3
CHERYL
cr. Newport........169 E9
la. Villawood......367 C1
pl. Castle Hill......217 C10
pl. Plumpton......242 D11
CHERYLE
av. Chester Hill....337 J10
CHESHAM
pde. Glenfield......424 E9
pl. Chipping Ntn..366 G14
pl. Plumpton......241 H8
st. St Marys......239 J14
CHESTER
av. Baulkham Hl...247 B13
av. Cmbrdg Pk....237 H10
av. Maroubra......407 C12
av. Woollahra.....22 E4
la. Zetland, off
    Joynton Av...375 H12
pl. Ermington....280 D14
pl. Narraweena..258 C2
pl. Ingleburn.....453 B7
pl. Turramurra...223 D9
st. Annandale.....17 B1
st. Annandale....17 C1
st. Blacktown....244 B15
st. Epping.........251 B14
st. Merrylands...307 F8
st. Mount Druitt.241 C14
st. Petersham....15 H12
st. Schofields....183 E12

av. E Lindfield........254 G16
st. Sylvania...........461 J13
st. Woollahra.........22 E3
CHESTERFIELD
la. Bronte.............377 J10
pde. Bronte..........377 J10
rd. Epping............280 J3
rd. S Penrith.........266 K3
CHESTER HILL
rd. Bass Hill.........368 A8
rd. Chester Hill....368 B4
CHESTERMAN
cr. Davidson.........255 B1
CHESTERTON
la. Kingswood, off
    Chindoo Cl....267 F3
ct. Cmbrdg Gdn...237 H5
CHESTNUT
av. Telopea..........279 G12
cr. Bidwill...........211 D13
cr. Prestons........393 K15
dr. Banksia........403 F12
dr. Glossodia......66 B12
gr. Kellyville.......216 H5
rd. Auburn.........339 A6
rd. Mt Colah......162 E13
st. Loftus...........489 J12
CHETWYN
pl. Wentwthvle....277 C12
CHETWYND
rd. Guildford......337 D3
rd. Merrylands..307 E16
CHEVALIER
cr. Hunters Hill...314 A14
wy. Claymore....481 B12
CHEVIOT
dr. Cobbitty......416 F6
dr. Airds..........512 A11
dr. Ashbury......372 D8
st. Mount Druitt.241 C13
CHEVROLET
pl. Ingleburn.....453 K7
CHEVRON
pl. Rouse Hill...185 F4
CHEYENNE
rd. Greenfld Pk..333 K14
CHEYNE
rd. Terrey Hills...196 F5
wk. Castlecrag.286 F12
wk. W Pnnant Hls..219 J16
CHIANTI
ct. Glenwood......246 A3
CHICAGO
av. Blacktown....244 G12
av. Maroubra....407 C14
CHICHESTER
st. Maroubra.....406 K10
CHICK
st. Roselands....400 H10
CHICKASAW
cr. Greenfld Pk...334 A16
CHIENTI
pl. Prestons.......393 H15
CHIFLEY
av. Sefton.........338 F16
la. N Wahroonga..192 G16
pl. Bligh Park....150 G8
pl. Quakers Hill..243 G4
sq. Sydney.........B D16
sq. Sydney.........1 K16
st. Smithfield....335 C2
st. Wetherill Pk..335 C2
wy. Penrith........237 B7
CHILAW
av. St Marys......269 G6
CHILCOTT
rd. Berrilee........131 D8
CHILDERS
st. Bonnyrigg Ht.363 F6
CHILDREY
pl. Castle Hill....219 A9
CHILDS
cct. Belrose.......226 C12
pl. Mt Annan....479 G15
pwy. Chipping Ntn, off
    Childs Rd....396 G1
rd. Chipping Ntn..396 F2
st. East Hills.....427 J1
st. Lidcombe....339 H7
st. Panania.......427 J1
CHILE
pl. Seven Hills..275 H4
CHILTERN
cr. Castle Hill....217 H10
rd. Guildford....337 H8

rd. Ingleside.........197 J4
rd. Willoughby.....285 F14
CHILTON
av. Oakhurst........242 D3
pde. Warrawee....222 G8
CHILVERS
pl. Rooty Hill.......272 A3
CHILWERS
rd. Thornleigh......221 A10
CHILWORTH
cl. Beecroft.........250 D7
CHINDOO
cl. Kingswood.....267 F3
la. Kingswood, off
    Chindoo Cl...267 F3
CHIOS
pl. Rooty Hill......272 A3
CHIPALEE
ct. Erskine Park..300 E2
CHIPILLY
av. Engadine......518 G1
CHIPMAN
st. Eastlakes......405 J5
CHIPP
ct. Bella Vista....246 E3
CHIPPEN
la. Chippendale..19 C4
st. Chippendale..19 B4
CHIPPENHAM
st. Chipping Ntn..366 G13
st. Chipping Ntn..366 G14
CHIPPING
pl. S Penrith......266 F4
CHIPS RAFFERTY
av. Moore Park...21 B6
CHIRCAN
st. Old Tngabbie..277 A6
CHISHOLM
av. Avalon.........139 H15
av. Clemton Park.401 J4
av. Wrngth Cty..238 F9
cr. Blaxland.......233 E9
cr. Bradbury......511 F16
dr. Windsor.......121 D16
rd. Auburn.........338 J6
rd. Catherine Fd..449 F3
rd. Sefton..........368 H1
st. Belfield.........371 B8
st. Darlinghurst..4 E14
st. Greenwich....315 A10
st. North Ryde..282 J8
st. Quakers Hill..213 H14
st. Smithfield....336 C5
st. S Turramrra..252 A5
CHISWICK
la. Woollahra.....22 B1
pl. Cherrybrook..219 C10
rd. Auburn.......338 K7
rd. Greenacre..369 K10
rd. S Granville..338 E6
st. Chiswick....343 D1
st. Strathfield S..371 E7
CHITTICK
la. Cobbitty.....446 J13
CHIVE
pl. Quakers Hill..243 G4
CHIVERS
av. Lugarno....429 K10
pl. Tahmoor....566 D8
CHOBE
wy. Glenwood.215 A16
CHOPIN
cl. Bonnyrigg Ht..363 E5
cr. Clarmnt Ms..268 G3
st. Seven Hills..246 D13
CHORLEY
av. Cheltenham.250 K7
CHOWDER BAY
rd. Mosman....317 G11
CHOWNE
pl. N Willoughby.285 G6
pl. Yennora....336 K11
CHRIS
cl. Dean Park..212 J16
st. Lansvale...367 B10
CHRISALEX
st. St Clair.....269 J8
CHRISAN
cl. Werrington.238 K10
CHRIS BANG
cr. Vaucluse..348 F6
CHRISTABEL
pl. Cecil Hills..362 F3

CHRISTEL
av. Carlingford..249 D13
CHRISTENSEN
cct. Oatley.....430 D14
CHRISTIAN
rd. Punchbowl..400 D8
CHRISTIE
la. St Leonards, off
    Christie St..315 D6
la. Surry Hills...20 A5
rd. Mcquarie Pk.252 E15
st. Liverpool....395 A8
st. Minto........452 H16
st. Prairiewood.334 E10
st. St Leonards..315 D5
St. St Marys....239 C8
st. S Penrith...236 J15
st. Werrington..239 C8
st. Windsor....121 B9
st. Wollstncraft.315 D5
CHRISTIES
la. Zetland, off
    Merton St...375 H10
CHRISTINA
pl. Kareela....461 E12
rd. Villawood..337 E16
st. Longueville.314 E7
st. Rydalmere.309 H1
CHRISTINE
av. Ryde........282 C10
cr. Lalor Park..245 H12
ct. Kellyville...217 C3
st. Northmead..277 F10
st. S Penrith...267 C3
CHRISTMAS
pl. Green Valley..363 B10
CHRISTOPHER
av. Camden....507 B6
av. Georges Hall..367 F8
pl. Beacon Hill..257 E3
pl. N Richmond..87 B16
pl. Woolooware.493 E13
st. Baulkham Hl..247 H7
CHRYSANTHEMUM
av. Lurnea....394 F12
CHUBB
pl. Rooty Hill..241 K14
CHUDLEIGH
st. Rydalmere..279 F15
CHULLORA
cr. Engadine..488 D14
CHUNOOMA
rd. N Wahroonga..222 G1
CHURCH
av. Mascot.....405 A1
av. Westmead..307 E2
la. Allawah.....432 D8
la. Castlereagh..176 B14
la. Cranebrook..206 G1
la. Darlington..18 G7
la. Glebe........11 K10
la. Mt Wilson..58 H7
la. N Sydney...5 E3
la. Randwick..377 A11
la. Surry Hills..4 D14
pl. Paddington..21 C7
rd. Denham Ct..422 E15
rd. Moorebank..395 F9
rd. Mulgoa.....325 D2
rd. Wilberforce..67 F16
rd. Wilberforce..92 B1
rd. Yagoona....369 A11
st. Appin.........569 H12
st. Appin........569 F12
st. Ashfield....342 H14
st. Balmain....7 G8
st. Birchgrove..7 G8
st. Blakehurst..462 E2
st. Burwood...342 A16
st. Cabramatta..365 J3
st. Camperdown..17 F3
st. Canterbury..372 H13
st. Castle Hill..248 B1
st. Castlereagh.176 G16
st. Chatswood..285 C9
st. Cranebrook..176 G16
st. Croydon....342 F13
st. Drummoyne..343 K3
st. Eastern Ck..272 G5
st. Elderslie...507 F1
st. Granville....308 C16
st. Greenwich..314 J12
st. Harris Park..308 C6
st. Hunters Hill..313 F11
st. Hurlstone Pk..372 H13

48 GREGORY'S STREET DIRECTORY

STREETS — CL

st. Lidcombe	339	H8
st. Lidcombe	340	H8
st. Lilyfield	9	G5
st. Mcquarie Fd	453	J2
dr. Marrickville	373	H14
st. Mt Krng-gai	163	A12
st. Newtown	17	G7
st. N Parramatta	278	B10
st. N Sydney	5	E3
st. N Willoughby	285	C9
st. Old Guildford	337	G10
st. Paddington	4	F16
st. Parramatta	308	C1
st. Parramatta	308	C4
st. Peakhurst	430	B3
st. Petersham	16	A11
st. Pitt Town	92	G15
st. Pymble	253	E2
st. Randwick	376	K12
st. Riverstone	182	J6
st. Rossmore	389	F14
st. Ryde	311	H5
st. Ryde	311	K4
st. St Peters	374	H13
st. S Windsor	120	G14
st. Waverley	377	F6
st. W Pnnant Hl	249	J4
st. Windsor	120	G14
st. Woolooware	493	E10

CHURCH HILL
| la. Gordon | 253 | H8 |

CHURCHILL
av. Kirrawee	491	A5
av. Riverwood	400	F14
av. Strathfield	341	E12
av. Wahroonga	222	C4
cr. Allambie Ht	257	D12
cr. Cammeray	316	D5
cr. Concord	341	H5
ct. Narellan Vale	479	A11
dr. Baulkham Hl	277	H2
dr. Winston Hills	277	H2
pl. Springwood	201	D1
rd. East Killara	254	E8
rd. Padstow Ht	429	F8
rd. Rose Bay	348	C8
st. Bardwell Pk	402	G9
st. Fairfield	336	A12
st. Fairfield Ht	336	A12
st. Guildford	338	D7
st. Silverwater	309	H13
st. Springwood	201	D1

CHURCH STREET
| ml. Parramatta, off Church St | 308 | C3 |

CHURCHWOOD
| wy. Castle Hill | 248 | D3 |

CHUSAN
| pl. Plumpton | 242 | C5 |

CHUTER
av. Monterey	433	G9
av. Ramsgate Bch	433	F13
av. Sans Souci	433	F16
st. McMahons Pt	5	C11

CICADA GLEN
| rd. Ingleside | 197 | K1 |

CICERO
| wy. Rsemeadow | 540 | H2 |

CIGOLINI
| pl. Kellyville | 216 | G3 |

CILENTO
| cr. East Ryde | 282 | K16 |

CINDY
| pl. Colyton | 270 | E3 |

CINI
| pl. Quakers Hill | 213 | G13 |

CINNABAR
| st. Eagle Vale | 481 | G4 |

CIPOLIN
| cl. Eagle Vale | 481 | G8 |

CIRCULAR
| qy. Sydney | B | C12 |
| qy. Sydney | 1 | J12 |

CIRCULAR QUAY
e, Sydney	B	F7
e, Sydney	2	A12
w, The Rocks	B	B3
w, The Rocks	1	J9

CIRELLA
| cl. North Manly | 258 | A13 |

CIRRUS
| pl. Bnkstn Aprt | 397 | J1 |

CISTICOLA
| st. Hinchinbrk | 363 | E16 |

CITADEL
| cr. Castle Hill | 217 | H4 |
| pl. Glenwood | 246 | C6 |

CITRINE
| cl. Bossley Park | 333 | K7 |

CITRINUS
| pl. Narellan Vale | 478 | J13 |

CITROEN
| pl. Ingleburn | 453 | G11 |

CITRON
| dr. Wattle Grove | 425 | K4 |

CITRONELLE
| pl. Oakhurst | 241 | J1 |

CITRONELLE
| cr. Cranebrook | 207 | F16 |

CITRUS
av. Hornsby	191	H12
gr. Carlingford	279	F2
st. Quakers Hill	214	H13

CITY
rd. Camperdown	18	D6
rd. Chippendale	18	D6
rd. Darlington	18	D6
rd. Newtown	18	D6

CITY VIEW
| rd. Pennant Hills | 250 | F1 |

CITY WEST LINK
Leichhardt	10	A9
Lilyfield	10	G8
Lilyfield	9	E7
Lilyfield	10	G8
Lilyfield	343	H12
Rozelle	10	G8

CIVIC
arc. Chatswood, off Victoria Av	284	K9
cr. Kogarah	433	F7
av. Pendle Hill	276	E13
dr. Bankstown	369	F15
dr. Dee Why	258	G5
la. Blacktown, off Campbell St	244	G16
la. Frenchs Frst	256	A3
la. Mosman, off Clifford St	317	A6
pl. Parramatta	308	C4
pl. Auburn	339	D3

CLACK
| rd. Chester Hill | 337 | H11 |

CLACKMANNAN
| rd. Winston Hills | 277 | E4 |

CLADDEN
| cl. Pennant Hills | 250 | J2 |

CLAFTON
| av. Northbridge | 286 | A15 |

CLAIR
| cr. Padstow Ht | 429 | C7 |

CLAIRE
| pl. Baulkham Hl | 247 | D2 |
| st. Naremburn | 315 | F1 |

CLAIRVAUX
| rd. Vaucluse | 348 | C6 |

CLANALPINE
st. Eastwood	281	A9
st. Mosman	316	K11
st. Mosman	317	A11

CLANCY
av. Mcquarie Pk	283	D6
la. Seven Hills	275	G2
st. Padstow Ht	429	E6
st. Padstow Ht	429	G6
st. Rookwood	340	A16
st. Smithfield	335	K6

CLANVILLE
| rd. Roseville | 284 | F3 |

CLANWILLIAM
st. Chatswood	285	C10
st. Eastwood	280	J11
st. N Willoughby	285	C10

CLAPHAM
rd. Regents Pk	368	G1
rd. Sefton	368	G1
st. Stanhpe Gdns	215	D5

CLAPTON
| pl. Darlinghurst | 4 | F9 |

CLARA
st. Erskineville	18	C13
st. Newtown	374	G9
st. Randwick	377	A14

CLARE
cr. Oakville	122	E13
st. Russell Lea	343	C6
st. Killarney Ht	286	C1
st. Blacktown	274	D11
st. Blacktown	274	E11
st. Cabramatta W	364	G5
st. Gladesville	312	G12

CLARENCE
st. Glebe	11	K13
st. Rozelle	7	B12
st. Surry Hills	4	E15
st. Sylvania	462	D7

CLAREMONT
av. Canley Ht	335	E16
av. Greenacre	369	G9
cct. Glen Alpine	510	D16
cr. Hinchinbrk	363	B14
cr. Windsor	120	J9
dr. Wattle Grove	425	K4
dr. Bargo	549	B2
grn. W Pnnant Hl	249	C4
pl. Castle Hill	218	E11
pl. S Penrith	266	F4
rd. Burwood Ht	372	A3
st. Balmain	7	A9
st. Campsie	371	J15
st. Merrylands	307	J15
st. Penshurst	431	F9
st. Richmond	119	A6

CLAREMOUNT
| cl. Cherrybrook | 219 | D12 |

CLARENCE
av. Dee Why	258	J5
av. Homebush B	310	F14
av. Killara	254	C13
av. Sylvania Wtr	462	D11
la. St Clair, off Clarence Rd	300	B1
st. Sydney	A	D13
pl. Double Bay	14	G15
rd. Cattai	94	G2
rd. Rockdale	403	A12
rd. St Clair	300	B1
st. Balgowlah	287	J3
st. Belfield	371	E10
st. Blacktown	243	J13
st. Burwood	342	A15
st. Canley Ht	335	F16
st. Condell Park	399	A4
st. Glenbrook	234	A14
st. Lidcombe	339	G7
st. Mcquarie Fd	423	J16
st. Matraville	436	K2
st. Merrylands	307	E11
st. North Ryde	283	B11
st. Penshurst	431	E3
st. Strathfield	341	F9
st. Sydney	C	E2
st. Sydney	3	E1
st. Wentwthvle	277	C12

CLARENDON
ct. Wattle Grove	425	J3
dr. Stanhpe Gdns	215	G9
la. Stanmore	16	F7
la.w,Stanmore	16	F7
rd. Airds	511	K15
rd. Burwood	341	K14
rd. Peakhurst	429	K2
st. Stanmore	16	E7
st. Artarmon	314	J2
st. Richmond	119	D4
st. Vaucluse	348	C6
st. Waterloo	19	H11

CLARET
| pl. Eschol Park | 481 | E3 |
| st. Bossley Park | 333 | H9 |

CLARET ASH
| gr. Menai | 458 | K14 |

CLAREVALE
| st. Edensor Pk | 333 | D16 |

CLAREVILLE
av. Sandringham	463	D5
av. Sans Souci	463	E1
cl. Belfield	371	C6
cl. Woodbine	481	G11

CLARGO
| st. Dulwich Hill | 373 | B10 |

CLARIBEL
| st. Bankstown | 399 | A8 |

CLARICE
| cr. Campbelltown | 511 | J5 |

CLARIDGE
| cl. Cherrybrook | 219 | D15 |

CLARINDA
| la. Hornsby | 191 | E10 |

CLARISSA
| pl. Ambarvale | 511 | B13 |
| pl. Castle Hill | 248 | C6 |

CLARK
pl. Minto	482	J8
rd. Kirribilli	6	A12
rd. Londonderry	149	B5
rd. Neutral Bay	6	B8
rd. N Sydney	6	A12

CLARKE
av. Hobartville	118	C8
cl. Hinchinbrk	393	A1
cl. Prairiewood	334	J7
dr. Castle Hill	218	H13
la. Bass Hill	368	D11
la. Crows Nest, off Oxley St	315	E6
la. Earlwood	402	H4
la. Panania	428	D7
la. St Leonards, off Oxley St	315	E6
pl. Castle Hill	218	E11
pl. Killara	254	F11
pl. Menai	458	F13
pl. Mt Annan	479	G16
pl. Punchbowl, off Turner St	400	C4
rd. Hornsby	221	E5
rd. Pennant Hills	250	J4
rd. Waitara	221	H5
rd. Woolwich	314	E13
st. Annandale	16	F13
st. Bass Hill	368	D13
st. Berala	339	B12
st. Chatswood W	284	E9
st. Crows Nest	315	F6
st. Earlwood	402	H4
st. Granville	308	C12
st. Guildford	337	C7
st. Narrabeen	229	A8
st. Newington	310	B12
st. Riverstone	183	F5
st. Rydalmere	279	G16
st. Sydney	F	C4
st. Sydney	3	J10
st. Vaucluse	348	G4
st. West Ryde	281	H15
st.h,Peakhurst	429	K3
sts,Peakhurst	429	K5
st.w,Narrabeen	228	J8
wy. Kenthurst	126	A16

CLARKES
rd. Ramsgate	433	D12
pde. Kirrawee	491	B4
rd. Drummoyne	343	F6
st. Russell Lea	343	F6

CLAROS
| cl. Hornsby Ht | 161 | H13 |

CLASSEN
| st. Sylvania | 462 | A13 |

CLASSERS
| pl. Currans Hill | 480 | A10 |

CLAUD
| pl. S Windsor | 150 | G3 |

CLAUDARE
| st. Collaroy Plat | 228 | H12 |

CLAUDE
| av. Cremorne | 6 | K6 |
| st. Chatswood | 284 | K10 |

CLAUDE JAMES
| cr. Regents Pk | 369 | E1 |

CLAUDIA
| st. Guildford | 338 | A4 |

CLAUDIUS
| pl. Rsemeadow | 540 | D2 |

CLAVERDON
| av. Picnic Point | 428 | G9 |

CLAVERING
| rd. Seaforth | 286 | J7 |

CLAXTON
| cct. Rouse Hill | 184 | J8 |

CLAY
| st. Balmain | 7 | D12 |

CLAYPOLE
| st. Ambarvale | 540 | E1 |

CLAYTON
la. Camperdown	17	D7
pl. W Pnnant Hl	249	A8
st. Balmain	7	J8
st. Blacktown	244	B2
st. Peakhurst	430	B2
st. Prairiewood	335	A9
st. Ryde	312	D1

CLEAL
| st. Ermington | 280 | C15 |

CLEARVIEW
| pl. Brookvale | 257 | H10 |

CLEARY
av. Belmore	371	D15
av. Forestville	256	B7
av. Edensor Pk	363	F2
la. Belmore, off Dean Av	371	E15
la. St Clair, off Cleary Pl	270	B12
pl. Blackett	241	D2
pl. Casula	424	D4
pl. St Clair	270	A12

CLEAVER
| pl. Ambarvale | 510 | K15 |

CLEEVE
| cl. Mount Druitt | 241 | E16 |
| pl. Cmbrdg Gdn | 237 | F3 |

CLEG
| st. Artarmon | 315 | B2 |

CLEGG
| pl. Glenhaven | 217 | K4 |
| pl. Prairiewood | 334 | J9 |

CLELAND
la. Ramsgate	433	D14
la. Sans Souci	433	D14
rd. Artarmon	285	B16
st. Mascot	405	H5

CLEM
| pl. Shalvey | 211 | B14 |

CLEMATIS
cl. Cherrybrook	220	A7
pl. Mcquarie Fd	454	D2
pl. Mt Annan	509	E4

CLEMENT
cl. Pennant Hills	250	G3
la. Rcuttrs Bay	13	B8
la. Sydney	A	E14
pl. Ingleburn	453	H8
st. Rcuttrs Bay	13	C8
st. Guildford	337	D6
st. Rooty Hill	242	B16
st. Rcuttrs Bay	13	B8
st. Strathfield S	371	E6

CLEMENTINA
| cct. Cecil Hills | 362 | D4 |

CLEMENTINE
| st. Parklea | 215 | A13 |

CLEMENTS
| av. Bankstown | 399 | E7 |
| pde. Kirrawee | 491 | B4 |

CLEMENTSON
| dr. Rossmore | 359 | G16 |

CLEMSON
| st. Kingswood | 237 | F15 |

CLEMTON
| av. Earlwood | 402 | C5 |
| pl. Earlwood, off Clemton Av | 402 | D5 |

CLENNAM
| av. Ambarvale | 510 | G12 |

CLENT
| st. Jamisontown | 266 | C5 |

CLEONE
| st. Guildford | 338 | A4 |

CLEOPATRA
| dr. Rsemeadow | 540 | E2 |

CLERGY
| rd. Wilberforce | 91 | K1 |

CLERKE
| pl. Kings Lngly | 246 | C11 |

CLERKENWELL
| st. Ambarvale | 510 | G15 |

CLERMISTON
| av. Roseville | 285 | A4 |

CLERMONT
av. Concord	341	F5
av. N Strathfield	341	F5
av. Ryde	282	A12
la. Concord, off Wellbank St	341	F5
la. N Strathfield, off Wellbank St	341	F5

CLEVEDON
| st. Hurstville | 431 | K2 |
| st. Botany | 405 | K13 |

CLEVELAND
av. Cromer	228	A14
av. Surry Hills	20	A6
la. Rouse Hill	185	D5
la. Chippendale	18	H3
la. Bonnet Bay	460	B9
la. Riverstone	182	C10
st. Chippendale	18	H4
st. Darlington	18	H4
st. Ermington	280	E11
st. Moore Park	20	D7
st. Redfern	19	J6
st. Strathfield S	370	K6

GREGORY'S STREET DIRECTORY 49

CL STREETS

st. Surry Hills 19 J6
st. Wahroonga 222 E7
CLEVELEY
av. Kings Lngly 245 A5
CLEY
pl. Prospect 274 K11
CLIFF
av. Northbridge 315 K2
av. N Wahroonga 222 J2
av. Peakhurst 430 B12
av. Winston Hills 277 F6
pl. Cranebrook 207 B11
rd. Collaroy 229 C14
rd. Epping 250 H15
rd. Freemns Rch 89 F6
rd. Northwood 314 H8
st. Manly 288 J11
st. Milsons Point ....K J16
st. Milsons Point 5 J13
st. Watsons Bay 318 F12
tce. Forest Lodge 11 F13
CLIFFBROOK
cr. Leonay 235 A16
pde. Clovelly 377 K14
CLIFFE
st. Picton 563 F2
st. Regents Pk 369 G2
CLIFF HAVEN
pl. Yowie Bay 491 K9
CLIFFORD
av. Canley Vale 365 K4
av. Fairlight 288 C10
av. Thornleigh 221 C15
cr. Ingleburn 453 D12
la. Canley Vale, off Clifford Av 366 A4
rd. Miranda 492 A7
st. Coogee 407 F2
st. Gordon 254 B7
st. Mosman 317 B6
st. Panania 428 B5
st. Rockdale 403 B14
CLIFF POINT
pl. Frenchs Frst 257 A2
CLIFFVIEW
rd. Berowra Ht 133 D5
CLIFT
cl. Edensor Pk 363 G2
CLIFTON
av. Burwood 342 B16
av. Glenbrook 264 C1
av. Kemps Ck 360 D1
la. Bronte, off Busby Pde 377 K11
pl. Cartwright 394 C5
pl. Cherrybrook 219 B14
rd. Clovelly 377 J12
rd. Marsden Pk 182 A16
rd. Riverstone 182 A15
res. Surry Hills ....F K13
res. Surry Hills 4 C15
st. Balmain East 8 F7
st. Blacktown 244 J15
st. Mosman 317 D12
st. Oatley 461 C1
st. Waverton 5 A8
st. West Ryde 280 J14
CLIFTONVILLE
rd. S Maroota 69 E1
CLIMUS
st. Hassall Gr 212 B15
CLINGAN
av. Lurnea 394 D9
CLINIC
cct. Narrabeen, off Snake Gulley Cl ..228 E8
CLINKER
gr. Woodcroft 243 F6
CLINTON
cl. Berowra Ht 132 J9
dr. Narellan 478 J11
st. Quakers Hill 214 B8
CLIO
la. Maroubra 407 C10
st. Sutherland 490 F1
st. Wiley Park 400 K4
CLIPPER
cl. Chipping Ntn 366 K15
CLIPSHAM
la. Gordon, off St Johns Av 253 H8
CLISBY
wy. Matraville 437 C1
CLISDELL
av. Canterbury 402 D1
st. Surry Hills 19 J4
CLISSOLD
la. Campsie 372 A12
pde. Campsie 372 A12
rd. Wahroonga 223 C6
st. Ashfield 372 J6
st. Cmbrdg Pk 238 A7
CLIVE
ct. Bayview 168 H12
rd. Eastwood 281 A7
rd. Riverstone 182 F8
st. Fairfield 336 F15
st. Revesby 428 H5
st. Roseville 285 D3
st. Roseville Ch 285 D3
CLIVEDEN
ct. Wattle Grove 426 B3
CLONCURRY
pl. Wakeley 334 G14
CLONMORE
st. Kellyville Rdg 185 C16
st. Kellyville Rdg 215 C1
CLONTARF
av. Harringtn Pk 478 K5
cl. Woodbine 481 J10
st. Seaforth 287 A5
st. Seaforth 287 A7
CLOPTON
dr. Killara 254 C8
CLORINDA
st. Rooty Hill 272 C5
CLOSE
pl. Hebersham 241 F1
st. Canterbury 372 G14
st. S Coogee 407 J6
st. Thirlmere 564 J4
st. Thirlmere 565 A5
CLOTHIER
rd. Menai 459 A11
CLOUGH
av. Illawong 459 K2
CLOUTA
pl. Emu Plains 234 J9
CLOVE
la. Randwick, off Darley La 377 B9
CLOVELLY
cct. Kellyville 215 F4
pl. Woodbine 481 F14
rd. Clovelly 377 F12
rd. Coogee 377 F12
rd. Hornsby 221 D3
rd. Randwick 377 B9
st. Clovelly 377 K13
st. Watsons Bay 318 G14
CLOVER
av. Casula 394 B16
cl. Carlingford 279 J5
pl. Mcquarie Fd 454 E6
CLOVERHILL
gr. Bella Vista 216 C16
gr. Bella Vista 246 C1
CLOVERTOP
pl. Wrrngtn Dns 238 B5
CLOWER
av. Rouse Hill 185 A8
CLUB
la. Ermington, off River Rd 310 B3
CLUBB
cr. Miranda 492 B3
st. Rozelle 344 C7
CLUCAS
rd. Dharruk 241 C10
rd. Regents Pk 369 E1
CLUDEN
cl. Toongabbie 276 H6
CLUMP
pl. Green Valley 362 K10
CLUNE
cl. Casula 424 E4
pl. Blackett 241 D2
CLUNES
la. Canterbury 372 D14
CLUNIES
pl. Bonnyrigg Ht 363 F7
CLUNIES ROSS
st. Greystanes 275 E16
st. Pemulwuy 305 E2
st. Prospect 275 E16
st. Prospect 305 E2
CLUSTER
pl. Cranebrook 207 F11
CLWYDON
cl. Belrose 226 B12
pl. Wahroonga 222 E6
CLYBURN
av. Jamisontown 266 B3
CLYDE
av. Cronulla 493 K15
av. Moorebank 396 E13
av. St Clair 269 H14
la. Kurrajong Ht 63 G15
pl. Campbelltown 511 K9
pl. Mt Hunter 504 K7
pl. Wahroonga 222 A14
rd. Dee Why 258 K6
st. Croydon Pk 372 A7
st. Granville 308 G16
st. Guildford 337 E4
st. North Bondi 348 D14
st. Randwick 377 C14
st. Rydalmere 309 D2
st. Silverwater 309 K8
st. S Granville 338 F8
st. Vineyard 152 F14
CLYDEBANK
cr. Glen Alpine 510 A13
CLYDESDALE
dr. Blairmount 480 K12
dr. Blairmount 480 K14
dr. Blairmount 481 A12
la. Richmond 118 G13
pl. Pymble 253 B2
CLYFFORD
pl. Panania 428 E6
COACH HOUSE
pl. Bella Vista 246 E2
pl. Kurrajong Ht 63 E10
rd. Kurrajong Ht 63 E10
COACHLINE
pl. Belrose 226 A11
COACHMAN
cr. Kellyville Rdg 215 A3
COACHWOOD
cl. Rouse Hill 185 B7
cr. Alfords Point 459 A2
cr. Bradbury 511 F12
cr. Picton 563 E13
pl. Lugarno 430 A16
COAL
st. Silverwater 309 J10
COALLEE
pl. S Penrith 267 A3
COAST
av. Cronulla 494 A16
COAST HOSPITAL
rd. Little Bay 437 G14
COASTVIEW
pl. Harbord 258 K16
COATES
pl. Wetherill Pk 303 J15
st. Mount Druitt 271 D4
wy. Claymore 481 A11
COATES PARK
rd. Cobbitty 416 B14
COBAC
av. Eastwood 280 J5
COBAH
rd. Arcadia 129 E12
rd. Arcadia 129 J7
rd. Fiddletown 129 J7
COBAIN
pl. Acacia Gdn 214 G15
COBAR
cl. Wakeley 334 H13
pl. Cartwright 394 A4
pl. Erskine Park 270 K16
st. Dulwich Hill 373 A9
st. Greystanes 305 H3
st. Willoughby 285 C14
wy. Mcquarie Pk 282 E4
COBARGO
rd. Gymea Bay 491 C10
COBB
av. Jamisontown 266 C1
la. Blacktown, off Campbell St 244 H16
pl. Ambarvale 511 B14
st. Frenchs Frst 256 E4
COBBADAH
av. Pennant Hills 250 J4
pl. Harbord 258 D15
COBBETT
st. Wetherill Pk 334 F3
st. Wetherill Pk 334 D4
COBBITTEE
la. Mosman, off Cobbittee St 317 G9
st. Mosman 317 G9
COBBITTY
av. Croydon Pk 371 K6
rd. Brownlow Hl 475 H2
rd. Cobbitty 447 A15
rd. Harringtn Pk 447 J13
rd. Harringtn Pk 448 D13
rd. Oran Park 448 D13
COBBITY
av. Wrrngtn Dns 237 K3
st. Seven Hills 246 C14
COBBLE
cct. West Hoxton 391 K10
COBBLER
cr. Minchinbury 271 F9
COBBLERS
cl. Kellyville 186 H16
COBBLERS BEACH
rd. Mosman 317 J6
COBBLESTONE
ct. Glenhaven 218 B4
gr. Woodcroft 243 F9
pl. Wrrngtn Dns 238 C5
wy. Castle Hill 218 J14
COBBY
pl. Bidwill 211 C14
COBCROFT
rd. Wilberforce 67 F15
COBDEN
av. Lane Cove 314 G2
la. Belmore, off Rydge St 401 G1
la. Enfield 371 H2
st. Belmore 401 H1
st. Enfield 371 H3
COBHAM
av. Melrose Pk 280 H15
la. Melrose Pk 280 H15
st. Horsley Pk 332 D2
st. Ingleburn 453 B6
st. Kings Park 244 E5
st. Maroubra 406 G10
st. Yanderra 567 B16
COBOURG
pl. Bow Bowing 452 D13
COBRA
pl. Raby 451 B14
st. Cranebrook 207 B9
COBRAN
rd. Cheltenham 251 B9
COBURG
pl. St Johns Pk 364 G1
rd. Wilberforce 67 F16
rd. Wilberforce 67 G16
COCHRAN
pl. Abbotsbury 333 B14
COCHRANE
st. Minto 482 J10
COCKATIEL
cct. Green Valley 363 F10
COCKATOO
cl. Hinchinbrk 363 A14
la. St Clair, off Cockatoo Rd 270 J14
rd. Erskine Park 270 J14
COCKBURN
cr. Fairfield E 336 J12
COCKROFT
pl. Lucas Ht 487 J11
COCKTHORPE
rd. Auburn 339 F7
COCO
dr. Glenmore Pk 266 A7
COCOS
av. Eastwood 281 A4
cl. Green Valley 363 C10
pl. Quakers Hill 213 F13
COCUPARA
av. Lindfield 283 K3
CODLIN
st. Ambarvale 510 J12
CODRINGTON
st. Darlington 18 F7
st. Fairfield 336 B15
CODY
pl. Oakhurst 242 A4
COE
pl. Riverstone 183 C8
COEN
cl. Bossley Park 333 F11
COFFEY
st. Ermington 310 B4
wy. Claymore, off Colquhoun Wy ...481 C11
COFFS HARBOUR
av. Hoxton Park 392 K9
COFTON
ct. Wrrngtn Cty 238 F6
COGAN
pl. Lane Cove 314 H5
COGGINS
pl. Mascot 404 K2
COGHILL
st. Narellan 478 E10
COGHLAN
cr. Doonside 243 A14
COHEN
av. Rookwood 339 K11
st. Fairlight 288 C8
st. Merrylands 308 C15
COILA
pl. Woodpark 306 G14
st. Turramurra 223 A10
COLAC
pl. Marayong 243 J7
COLAH
rd. Mt Colah 192 C4
st. Forest Glen 70 G16
COLANE
st. Concord W 311 E15
COLBARRA
pl. W Pnnant Hl 249 B6
COLBECK
st. Tregear 240 E5
COLBOURNE
av. Glebe 12 D12
COLBRAN
av. Kenthurst 187 A9
COLDEN
st. Picton 563 G4
COLDENHAM
dr. Picton 561 F3
wy. Airds 512 A13
COLDSTREAM
st. S Coogee 407 G5
COLE
av. Baulkham Hl 246 F12
cl. Berowra Ht 133 B4
cr. Liberty Gr 311 B10
la. Bankstown 369 D16
la. Hurstville 432 B7
pl. St Marys 269 E2
st. Brooklyn 75 G12
st. S Hurstville 432 B8
COLEBEE
cr. Hassall Gr 212 A13
pl. Narellan 478 E15
st. Schofields 213 D12
COLEBORNE
av. Mortdale 431 C8
COLECHIN
st. Yagoona 368 G13
COLEMAN
av. Bankstown 369 C15
av. Carlingford 279 J5
av. Homebush 341 A6
av. Regents Pk 369 D1
st. Mascot 405 A5
st. Merrylands 307 D7
st. S Wntwthvle 307 D7
COLENSO
cr. Daceyville 406 F3
COLERAINE
av. Killarney Ht 256 B15
st. Fairfield 336 B14
COLERIDGE
rd. Wetherill Pk 334 H5
st. Leichhardt 10 D15
st. Pymble 223 D16
st. Riverwood 399 K14
COLES
pde. Newport 169 J9
rd. Harbord 258 D15
st. Concord 341 J9
COLETTA
pl. Prestons 393 C14
COLETTE
pl. East Killara 254 G8

50 GREGORY'S STREET DIRECTORY

STREETS   CO

COLEVILE
la. Guildford........337 G5
pl. Rsemeadow......540 H8
COLEY
pl. Bligh Park.........150 H8
COLGATE
av. Balmain................8 B9
COLIN
av. Riverwood........400 A16
rd. Carlingford.......249 G13
st. Westleigh..........220 H4
st. Cammeray.........316 A4
st. Lakemba...........370 H15
COLINDIA
av. Neutral Bay..........6 C7
COLING
pl. Quakers Hill.....214 D13
COLL
pl. St Andrews........482 A3
COLLARENEBRI
rd. Hinchinbrk........392 H4
COLLAROY
av. Peakhurst.........430 G1
rd. Woodbine.........481 K10
st. Collaroy............229 A12
COLLEEN
av. Picnic Point......428 B6
cl. Cherrybrook......219 K5
COLLEGE
cr. Hornsby............221 G4
cr. St Ives..............224 C12
cr. Richmond.........118 G10
la. Bellevue Hill, off
   Cranbrook Rd......347 F12
la. Darlinghurst............F G1
la. Petersham.........16 C13
la. Rose Bay..........347 G12
rd. Campbelltown..511 J9
rd,s.Lane Cove.....314 A3
rd,s.Riverview......313 K5
st. Balmain................7 G8
st. Cmbrdg Pk......342 E16
st. Croydon............342 E16
st. Darlinghurst..........D C16
st. Darlinghurst............4 A8
st. Drummoyne.....343 J13
st. Gladesville.......312 G5
st. Liverpool..........395 F3
st. Manly................288 K12
st. Newtown............17 E15
st. Richmond..........118 H8
st. Sydney...................D C13
st. Sydney..................4 A8
COLLEN
pl. Cranebrook......207 D13
COLLESS
st. Penrith..............237 B14
COLLETT
cr. Kings Lngly.....246 C9
pde.N Parramatta..278 K15
COLLEY
pl. Hebersham......241 G3
COLLICOTT
pl. Barden Rdg......488 G2
COLLIE
ct. Wattle Grove...395 K12
pl. Bonnyrigg.......364 A8
COLLIER
av. Beverly Hills...401 A14
cl. St Helens Park..541 E7
st. Maroubra.........407 D12
COLLIMORE
av. Liverpool..........395 B2
COLLING
cr. Wrrngtn Cty.....238 F4
COLLINGS
st. Wahroonga......222 C2
COLLINGWOOD
av. Cabarita...........342 D2
av. Earlwood.........402 K3
av. Bronte..............378 A10
av. Drummoyne.....343 J1
av. Manly...............288 F6
av. Woolwich.........314 E13
COLLINS
av. Lurnea.............394 D10
av. Rose Bay........348 A10
av. Edensor Pk......363 F4
av. Capstone..........264 G5
av. Yagoona..........368 F15
ct. Rouse Hill........184 K8
st. Mt Annan.........479 H15
la. Annandale.........10 H15
la. Beaconsfield, off
    Collins St............375 F13

COLVIN
av. Carlton............432 H10
av. Kingsgrove.....401 K11
cr. Denistone E.....281 H9
pl. Frenchs Frst....256 A1
COLWELL
rd. Chatswood W..284 C12
st. Kingsgrove......401 F13
COLWYN
cl. Menai..............458 K9
rd. Minchinbury....271 E6
COLYTON
rd. Minchinbury....271 E6
COMANCHE
rd. Bossley Park...333 K12
COMANECI
av. Newington......310 B12
COMBARA
av. Caringbah.......492 K9
av. Castle Hill........247 F1
COMBE
pl. West Pymble...252 F12
COMBER
cr. Pendle Hill.......276 F13
st. Paddington..........4 H14
COMBERFORD
cl. Prairiewood....334 D10
COMBET
pl. Minchinbury....271 H9
COMBINGS
pl. Currans Hill.....480 A10
COMBLES
pde.Matraville......407 A16
COMBOYNE
av. Hoxton Park....392 H9
pl. St Clair............270 B16
COMER
st. Burwood..........341 K12
COMEROY
cr. Frenchs Frst...256 F1
COMET
cct. Beaumont Hills..185 K12
gln. St Clair..........270 E15
pl. Raby...............481 G3
pl. Springwood....172 G15
st. Ashfield...........342 J16
COMETROWE
st. Drummoyne.....343 G2
COMIN
av. Abbotsbury.....333 C10
COMLEROY
rd. Blaxlands Rdg.....64 G12
rd. Blaxlands Rdg.....65 A6
rd. Comleroy.........64 G12
rd. Kurrajong..........64 E15
COMMERCE
la. Glenbrook.......264 A1
la. Balgowlah Ht, off
    Dobroyd Rd........287 J14
COMMERCIAL
dr. Regents Pk.....338 K16
la. Merrylands, off
    Bertha St..........308 A16
rd. Kellyville.........185 B11
rd. Kingsgrove......401 J10
rd. Lalor Park........245 E12
rd. Lilyfield..............9 H6
rd. Rouse Hill......185 B11
rd. Vineyard..........152 E3
COMMISSIONERS
rd. Denistone........281 G13
COMMISSIONERS STEPS
   The Rocks............B B4
COMMODORE
cr. McMahons Pt......5 A10
st. McMahons Pt......5 B10
st. Newtown.........374 H10
COMMONS
st. Hurlstone Pk...373 A13
COMMONWEALTH
av. Mosman..........317 G11
av. N St Marys......239 H8
la. Surry Hills.........F D14
la. Surry Hills............3 K15
pde. Manly............288 E10
rd. Lindfield..........254 A15
st. Surry Hills.........F C15
st. Surry Hills............3 J15
st. Sydney................F D9
st. Sydney................3 K12
COMMUNITY
pl. Greenacre......370 C12

COMO
cl. St Clair..............269 G14
ct. Wattle Grove....395 K14
la. Cremorne..........316 C7
la. St Clair, off
    Como Cl.............269 G14
pde. Como............460 H5
pde. Como............460 H6
st. St Johns Pk....364 H3
rd. Greenacre.......370 D5
rd. Oyster Bay......461 F7
st. Blakehurst.......462 C2
st. Merrylands W....307 C13
COMPASS
av. Beaumont Hills..215 G1
COMPER
st. Bnkstn Aprt....397 K1
COMPTON
av. Lurnea...........394 E9
grn. W Pnnant Hl..249 C6
st. Bass Hill........368 B6
CONCETTINA
dr. Prestons.........392 H14
CONCISE
st. Balgowlah Ht....287 K13
CONCORD
av. Concord W.....311 C16
la. Erskineville, off
    Concord St........374 K10
la. N Strathfield, off
    Nelson Rd.........341 F7
pl. Gladesville......312 J8
st. St Johns Pk....364 H4
rd. Concord..........341 E2
rd. Concord W......341 E2
rd. N Strathfield...341 E2
rd. Rhodes...........311 D9
st. Erskineville....374 K10
CONCORDE
pl. Raby..............451 H16
pl. St Clair..........270 J12
CONDAMINE
st. Allambie Ht....257 K14
st. Balgowlah......287 K8
st. Campbelltown..511 G6
st. Manly Vale....287 K4
st. North Manly..257 K14
st,s. Balgowlah..287 J12
st,s. Balgowlah Ht..287 J12
CONDELLO
cl. Edensor Pk...333 H14
CONDER
av. Mt Pritchard..364 J12
st. Burwood.......341 J16
wy. Claymore.....481 B12
CONDOIN
la. Pemulwuy.....305 F5
CONDON
av. Panania........428 F3
st. Caringbah.....492 H9
CONDOR
cr. Blakehurst....432 A13
pl. Abbotsbury...333 B12
pl. Glenmore Pk..266 A13
pl. Quakers Hill...214 F13
CONDOVER
st. N Balgowlah..287 G5
CONEILL
pl. Forest Lodge....11 E12
CONEY
rd. Earlwood.......402 J3
CONFERTA
ct. Wattle Grove..396 B16
CONGEWOI
rd. Mosman........316 H4
rd. Mosman........316 J4
CONGHAM
rd. West Pymble..252 H12
CONGO
pl. Kearns............451 A14
CONGRESSIONAL
dr. Liverpool.......395 B9
CONIE
av. Baulkham Hl..247 G12
CONIFER
cl. Stanhpe Gdn..215 D11
pl. Greystanes....306 F10
pl. Engadine......518 F3
CONISTON
pl. Castle Hill......247 K3
st. Collaroy Plat...228 D11
CONJOLA
cr. Leumeah........482 F15
pl. Gymea Bay....491 C10

pl. Hamondvle......396 F14
pl. Woodcroft........243 F11
CONLAN
st. Bligh Park.......150 K7
CONNAUGHT
cct. Kellyville.......217 C4
st. Brookvale.......258 B8
st. Narraweena....258 B8
CONNECTICUT
av. Five Dock......343 B11
CONNELL
cl. Baulkham Hl..246 K4
rd. Oyster Bay.....461 F6
CONNELLAN
pl. Picton.............563 E9
CONNELLS POINT
rd. Connells Pt....431 K14
rd. S Hurstville...431 K14
CONNELLY
st. Penshurst.......431 C5
wy. Kellyville.......217 C5
CONNELS
cl. Cronulla........493 G11
rd. Woolooware..493 G11
CONNEMARA
av. Killarney Ht....286 C2
CONNEMARRA
st. Bexley...........432 J2
CONNER
cl. Liberty Gr......311 B10
CONNOLLY
av. Padstow Ht..429 D6
la. Beaconsfield, off
    Reserve St.......375 F12
CONNOR
pl. Illawong........459 D7
pl. Rouse Hill.....185 C7
pl. Tahmoor.......565 J9
CONRAD
rd. Kellyville Rdg..215 A7
st. North Ryde...283 B13
st. Richmond.....118 J7
st. Wetherill Pk..334 D6
CONROY
la. Revesby.......398 H15
rd. Wattle Grove..426 B3
CONSERVATORIUM
rd. Sydney............B H10
rd. Sydney.............2 B13
CONSETT
av. Bondi Beach..378 C3
st. Concord W....341 D2
st. Dulwich Hill..373 D10
CONSOLO
av. Glenwood....215 G10
CONSTANCE
av. Oxley Park...240 E15
st. Epping.........251 C12
st. Guildford......338 A3
st. Revesby.......398 K13
CONSTELLATION
cr. Carlingford....279 D4
la. Dulwich Hill, off
    Union St..........373 C8
st. Dulwich Hill..373 C8
rd. Meadowbank..311 E3
st. Ryde...............311 E3
st. Wentwthvle...277 B9
r.d.w.Meadowbank..311 B2
r.d.w.West Ryde..311 B2
CONSUL
ct. Brookvale......258 A9
r.d.n.Narraweena..258 A7
CONTAPLAS
st. Arndell Park..273 F7
CONTINUA
ct. Wattle Grove..396 C15
CONVAIR
pl. Raby.............451 E12
CONVENT
la. Marrickville...373 K12
la. Woollahra......22 K5
CONWAY
av. Cmbrdg Pk....237 H10
av. Concord W....341 C3
av. N Strathfield..341 C3
av. Randwick.....377 F11
av. Rose Bay.....348 C9
st. St Ives..........224 K2
pl. Baulkham Hl..247 K1
pl. Kings Lngly..245 F6

GREGORY'S STREET DIRECTORY 51

CO STREETS

pl. Oatlands 279 C13	**COOLABAH**	**COONANBARRA**	**COORUMBENE**	**CORAL TREE**

COOBA
pl. Mcquarie Fd......454 E2
st. Lidcombe............339 J6

COOBAH
rd. E Kurrajong......67 C3

COODE
pl. Bonnyrigg 364 B5

COOEEYANA
pde. Mt Lewis...........370 B15

COOGAN
pl. Campbelltown....511 E4
pl. Dean Park 212 H16

COOGEE
st. Blakehurst..........462 D2

COOGEE
pl. Woodbine 481 D15
st. Randwick............377 C14

COOGEE BAY
rd. Coogee 377 C15
rd. Randwick............377 C15

COOGHANS
la. Five Dock, off
    Lyons Rd W........342 K8

COOINDA
cl. Marsfield............281 J1
pl. Baulkham Hl 248 B7
pl. Bilgola 169 F5
pl. Doonside 243 A14
st. Colyton 270 G6
st. Engadine...........489 D14
st. Seven Hills 246 A14

COOK
av. Canada Bay........342 D8
av. Canley Vale 366 G3
av. Daceyville..........406 F4
cr. East Hills............427 F5
la. Bondi Jctn 22 K6
la. Mortdale, off
    Cook St............431 C7
la. St Clair, off
    Cook Pde 269 J14
la. St Marys, off
    Cook St............269 H3
la. Zetland, off
    Joynton Av.......375 J10
pde. St Clair 269 J16
pl. Lalor Park 245 C13
rd. West Hoxton 392 B11
rd. Centennial Pk 21 C11
st. Killara 253 K15
st. Marrickville 374 D10
st. Moore Park........21 C11
st. Oakhurst............241 J1
st. Oyster Bay 461 D4
st. Ruse...................512 G2
st. Baulkham Hl 247 K13
st. Caringbah..........492 J14
st. Croydon Pk........271 K7
st. Forestville 256 B10
st. Glebe..................11 J8
st. Kurnell 466 B10
st. Lewisham...........15 B7
st. Lidcombe............339 G9
st. Mortdale..............431 C7
st. North Ryde........282 C8
st. Randwick............377 A12
st. Rozelle................10 H1
st. St Marys 269 H3
st. Sutherland..........490 F4
st. Telopea..............279 J9
st. Tempe 404 A3
st. Turrella...............403 D6
st. Woolooware........493 H7
tce. Mona Vale 199 D9

COOKE
wy. Epping 250 G14

COOKNEY
pl. West Hoxton 392 C10

COOKS
av. Canterbury 372 D15
la. Canterbury, off
    Cooks Av 372 D15

COOKSEY
av. Harbord 258 H14

COOKSON
pl. Glenwood 215 C13

COOKS RIVER
av. Mascot...............404 C7

COOK TRIG
pl. N Wahroonga....192 H15

av. Greenwich..........315 A8
av. Turramurra 223 C11
cl. Thornleigh..........221 B7
cr. Forestville 256 C9
pl. Glenmore Pk......266 F12
pl. Greenwich..........315 A8
pl. Blacktown 273 A6
pl. Caringbah..........492 J3
pl. Mcquarie Fd......454 G1
pl. Turramurra 223 C11
rd. Valley Ht 202 F9
st. Beverly Hills.......401 C9

COOLAH
av. Campbelltown....511 K7
pl. Lansvale.............366 G8
wy. Hoxton Park 392 G8

COOLALIE
av. Camden S.........507 B11
pl. Allambie Ht 257 F16
cl. Kenthurst............157 B9
st. Villawood...........367 E4

COOLAMON
cl. Arcadia 130 J9
rd. Agnes Banks......146 A3

COOLANGATTA
av. Burraneer..........493 E15
al. Elanora Ht 198 D16

COOLARN
st. Chipping Ntn 396 H4

COOLAROO
cr. Lurnea 394 G7
rd. Lane Cove N......284 C13

COOLATAI
cr. Bossley Park 333 G12

COOLAWIN
rd. Avalon 169 K2
rd. Northbridge 286 F16

COOLEEN
cl. Blakehurst..........432 B13
st. Blakehurst..........432 B13

COOLEENA
rd. Elanora Ht 198 F13

COOLGARDIE
pl. Sutherland..........460 D14

COOLGUN
la. Eastwood, off
    Hillview Rd........281 A8

COOLIBAH
la. S Penrith, off
    Coolibah Pl.....266 H6
pl. S Penrith............266 G6
st. Castle Hill..........218 B11
st. Merrylands W 306 K12

COOLIBAR
st. Canley Ht 365 A1

COOLIDGE
cr. Bonnet Bay 460 A8

COOLINGA
st. Mcquarie Pk......282 H5

COOLOCK
cr. Baulkham Hl 247 C2

COOLONG
cr. St Clair...............269 H8
rd. Vaucluse............348 B1
st. Castle Hill..........217 G16

COOLOONGATTA
rd. Beverly Hills.......401 B10

COOLOWIE
rd. Terrey Hills........195 K9

COOLUM
pl. Yowie Bay..........492 C10

COOMA
ct. Wattle Grove 396 B16
dr. Greystanes........305 G3
st. Carramar 366 K15
st. Dharruk.............241 C8

COOMALIE
av. Castle Hill..........248 F2

COOMASSIE
av. Faulconbdg........201 C1

COOMBAH
pl. Engadine...........518 G7

COOMBES
dr. Penrith...............237 A6

COONABARABRAN
cr. Hoxton Park 392 J7
pl. Caringbah..........493 C14

COONAH
pde. Riverview 313 H6

COONAMBLE
st. Hoxton Park 392 G7

rd. N Wahroonga....222 E3
rd. Wahroonga........222 D7

COONANGA
rd. Avalon 140 E15

COONARA
av. W Pnnant Hl......249 A4

COONARDOO
cl. Canada Bay.......342 F9
pl. Castle Hill..........218 A12

COONAWARRA
dr. St Clair...............270 E13
dr. Terrey Hills........195 H8
st. Edensor Pk 333 D16

COONEY
cr. Artarmon 285 B15
st. North Ryde........282 G9

COONGRA
st. Busby 363 G12

COONONG
rd. Concord W........311 D15
rd. Gymea Bay........491 D12
st. Busby 363 H15
wy. Airds..................512 E10

COOPER
av. Moorebank........395 F8
av. Newington, off
    Jordan Av 310 B15
cl. Beacon Hill........257 K5
cr. Smithfield 336 C5
cr. Wahroonga........222 B15
ct. Castle Hill..........218 C10
la. Cremorne, off
    Belgrave St.....316 D8
la. Maroubra............407 C11
la. Neutral Bay, off
    Belgrave St.....316 D8
la. Paddington 13 A14
la. Penrith, off
    Cooper St........237 E3
la. Strathfield, off
    Cooper St.......341 G11
la. Surry Hills..........19 K1
la. Yagoona, off
    Cooper Rd 369 B12
pl. Currans Hill 479 H9
pl. Zetland 376 A10
rd. Birrong 369 B7
rd. Yagoona 369 B10
st. Balmain 8 C9
st. Blacktown 274 D3
st. Double Bay 14 A9
st. Engadine...........518 H5
st. Kingsford...........407 C7
st. Maroubra............407 C9
st. Marsfield............282 A5
st. Paddington 13 A13
st. Penrith 237 C3
st. Penrith 237 E3
st. Redfern 19 H7
st. Smithfield 305 H15
st. Strathfield 341 G11
st. Surry Hills..........19 J1
st. Waterloo.............19 C12

COOPERNOOK
av. E Lindfield 255 B11
av. Gymea Bay........491 G13

COOPER PARK
rd. Bellevue Hill.......347 F16

COOPWORTH
pl. Eldersie............507 K2

CORA
av. Belrose 225 J15
pl. Connells Pt 431 G15
rd. Westleigh...........220 G3
rd. Yowie Bay..........492 B12
rd. Sans Souci.........433 F16

COORABAN
rd. Milperra..............398 B6

COORABIN
pl. Riverwood 400 C12
rd. Northbridge 286 C14

COORADILLA
pl. Bradbury............541 E1

COORANG
rd. E Kurrajong......66 J5

COORI
pl. Bonnyrigg..........364 A9

COORIENGAH HEIGHTS
rd. Engadine...........488 F13

COORILLA
av. Croydon Pk........372 D9

COOROY
cr. Yellow Rock......204 K1

rd. Bella Vista..........246 H1

COOT
pl. Erskine Park.....270 K14
pl. Hinchinbrk........363 E16

COOTAMUNDRA
dr. Allambie Ht 257 E13
dr. Hornsby Ht 161 J7

COOTHA
cl. Bossley Park 334 C5

COOWARRA
dr. St Clair...............270 B16

COOYAL
pl. Glenwood 215 F16

COOYONG
cr. Toongabbie........276 D7
rd. Terrey Hills........196 A8

COPAIN
pl. S Penrith............266 H4

COPE
pl. Bass Hill............368 C12
st. Lane Cove 313 G4
st. Lane Cove W.....313 G4
st. Redfern 19 B10
st. Waterloo.............19 C12

COPELAND
av. Newtown 18 A12
la. Alexandria..........18 E15
rd. Beecroft 249 K8
rd. Emerton 240 G2
rd. Engadine...........518 G6
rd. Heathcote 518 G9
rd. Lethbrdg Pk......240 G2
rd. Wilberforce........91 K1
rd.e.Beecroft 250 F6
st. Alexandria..........18 E15
st. Erskineville.........18 E15
st. Liverpool............395 C13
st. Penrith 237 D10
st. Richmond 119 A5

COPPABELLA
cr. Bradbury............511 G15
rd. Middle Dural 158 J9

COPPERFIELD
dr. Ambarvale.........510 K16
dr. Rsemeadow......540 J5

COPPERLEAF
pl. Castle Hill..........248 H3
pl. Cherrybrook......219 H7
wy. Castle Hill..........248 G4

COPPIN
pl. Doonside 243 C5
pl. Shalvey..............211 B13

COPPINS
st. St Ives 254 B1
pl. Castle Hill..........248 A5

COPPLESTONE
pl. Castle Hill..........218 J7

COPPSLEIGH
cl. Westleigh...........220 G6

COQUET
wy. Green Valley......363 A11

CORAKI
av. Campbelltown....512 A6
cl. Bonnyrigg..........363 K8
pl. Westleigh...........220 D8
pl. Bass Hill............367 K5

CORAL
av. Kentlyn..............513 A3
av. Padstow 399 B16
cl. Avalon 140 E10
pl. Kellyville............216 G6
pl. Cherrybrook......220 A7
la. Cmbrdg Pk, off
    Coral Pl..........238 C7
pl. Cmbrdg Pk........238 C7
pl. Canley Vale 366 C2
pl. N Richmond......87 B15
pl. Quakers Hill 213 F14
pl. Woolooware......493 E9
st. Balgowlah..........287 E9
st. Marsfield............281 J1

CORALGUM
pl. Blacktown 275 A4

CORAL HEATH
av. Westleigh...........220 G8

CORALIE
st. Wareemba..........343 A4

CORAL PEA
ct. Colyton 270 H6

dr. Carlingford.........249 G11
dr. Carlingford.........249 H11

CORAMANDEL
av. Winmalee..........173 J7

CORAMBA
st. N Balgowlah......287 C5

CORANG
rd. Westleigh...........220 G6
st. Ruse...................512 C8

CORANTO
st. Wareemba..........343 A5

CORBEN
av. Moorebank........396 C11
st. Surry Hills..........F F16
st. Surry Hills..........4 A16

CORBETT
pl. Barden Rdg........488 G5
pl. Belrose 226 D13
st. Bankstown.........369 F12

CORBIERE
gr. Kellyville Rdg 215 A5
gr. Stanhpe Gdn 215 A5

CORBIN
av. Quakers Hill 214 C8
av. S Penrith............266 K5
st. Ingleburn 453 E13

CORBY
av. Concord............342 C7
pl. Chipping Ntn 366 G16

CORCORAN
st. Riverstone 182 D13

CORD
pl. Ingleburn 453 K8

CORDEAUX
cr. Sylvania Wtr......462 E14
st. Campbelltown....511 F4
st. Leppington........420 B4

CORDELIA
cr. Green Valley......363 B11
cr. Rooty Hill 271 J3
st. Rsemeadow......540 J6

CORDEN
av. Five Dock 342 H8

CORDNERS
la. Cornwallis..........90 K15

COREA
st. Miranda 461 K14
st. Sylvania 461 K12

COREE
pl. St Ives 224 B15
rd. Artarmon 284 K13

COREEN
av. Cecil Park..........331 F10
av. Loftus 489 K6
av. Peakhurst 430 H3
av. Penrith 237 A7
av. Terrey Hills........196 D4
ct. Berowra Ht........132 K3
pl. Banksia..............403 H12
pl. Blaxland.............234 E9

CORELLA
cr. Glenmore Pk......266 C13
ct. W Pnnant Hl......249 D6
dr. Green Valley......363 F10
pl. Kirrawee 491 B6
pl. Lalor Park 245 J11
st. Harbord 258 H14
wy. Westleigh...........220 J9

CORELLI
cr. Clarmnt Ms 268 G4

CORE PARK
rd. Warragamba......353 E3

CORFIELD
pl. Prestons 422 K1

CORFU
st. Woolmlloo..........4 F7

CORIN
wy. Bonnyrigg..........364 A5

CORINDA
st. St Johns Pk 364 D1

CORINDI
cl. Hoxton Park 392 J8

CORINGLE
pl. Woodcroft 243 F11

CORINNE
st. Acacia Gdn 214 G15

CORINTH
rd. Heathcote 518 E7

52 GREGORY'S STREET DIRECTORY

STREETS CR

CORIO
dr. St Clair 299 K2
la. St Clair, off Corio Dr 299 K2
rd. Prairiewood 334 J8

CORISH
cir. Bnksmeadw 406 E12
cir. Eastgardens 406 E12

CORK
pl. Bidwill 211 D16

CORKERY
cr. Allambie Ht 257 G13

CORKWOOD
pl. Acacia Gdn 215 A14

CORLETTE
wy. Bonnyrigg 364 B3

CORLISS
st. Regents Pk 369 A2

CORMACK
cct. Kellyville 217 C5
pl. Glendenning 242 E3
rd. Beacon Hill 257 J4
st. Balgowlah 287 K7

CORMISTON
av. Concord 341 K5

CORMO
cl. Elderslie 507 J3

CORMORANT
av. Hinchinbrk 393 E1
cr. Glenmore Pk 265 J13
st. Grays Point 491 D15

CORNDEW
cr. Wrrngtn Dns 238 A5
la. Wrrngtn Dns, off Corndew Cr 238 A5

CORNELIA
rd. Middle Dural 158 C5
rd. Toongabbie 276 A7
st. Wiley Park 400 F1

CORNELIAN
av. Eagle Vale 481 G5

CORNELIUS
la. Regentville, off Cornelius Pl 265 J4
pl. Kellyville 217 C3
pl. Regentville 265 H4

CORNELL
cl. Rouse Hill 185 E2
st. Blacktown 275 C2
st. Leonay 235 C15

CORNHILL
pl. Cherrybrook 219 F8

CORNICHE
dr. Homebush B 310 J9
rd. Church Point 168 G10

CORNISH
av. Beacon Hill 257 H6

CORNOCK
av. Toongabbie 276 G10

CORNUTA
cl. Narellan Vale 478 K15

CORNWALL
av. Turramurra 222 F16
pl. Bella Vista 246 H4
rd. Auburn 339 A11
rd. Ingleburn 453 A6
st. Agnes Banks 117 E15
st. N Epping 251 H11

CORNWALLIS
la. Redfern 19 A9
rd. Cornwallis 89 F9
rd. Cornwallis 120 J7
st. Eveleigh 18 K9
st. Redfern 19 A9

CORNWELL
av. Hobartville 118 C8
rd. Allambie Ht 287 J1

CORNWELLS
la. Richmond Lwld 88 H14

COROMANDEL
cl. Baulkham Hl 246 H5
rd. Ebenezer 68 D12
wy. Minto 482 H6

CORONA
av. Roseville 284 G6
rd. Fairfield W 335 C13

CORONATA
wy. Mcquarie Fd 424 D16

CORONATION
av. Cronulla 493 K16
av. Eastwood 280 K10
av. Five Dock 343 A10
av. Kings Park 244 F6
av. Mosman 317 E8
av. Peakhurst 430 D5
av. Petersham 15 K15
dr. Green Valley 363 A9
gr. Cmbrdg Gdn 237 H5
la. Cmbrdg Gdn, off Coronation Gr 237 H5
pde. Enfield 371 F7
pde. Strathfield S 371 F7
rd. Baulkham Hl 247 E10
st. Mona Vale 199 D8
st. Hornsby, off Jersey St 191 G16

CORONET
ct. North Rocks 278 J4
tce. Glenmore Pk 266 D14

CORONGA
cr. Killara 253 F15

CORREA
ct. Voyager Pt 427 D6
pl. Mcquarie Fd 454 F6

CORRELLIS
st. Harringtn Pk 478 K5

CORREY
pl. Carlingford 279 K2

CORREYS
av. Concord 341 F4
av. N Strathfield 341 F4
sq. Cabarita 312 E16

CORRIE
rd. North Manly 258 B15

CORRIEDALE
cl. Elderslie 507 J1
st. Miller 393 G2
st. Wakeley 364 K1

CORRIN
ct. Wattle Grove 396 B14

CORRY
ct. N Parramatta 278 G13
st. Bonnyrigg 363 J7

CORRYONG
st. Fairfield W 335 C8

CORRYTON
ct. Wattle Grove 425 H4
pl. Glen Alpine 510 C15

CORSAIR
cr. Cranebrook 207 A10
st. Raby 481 G1

CORUNDUM
cl. Eagle Vale 481 G4

CORUNNA
av. Leumeah 482 G16
av. North Rocks 279 A2
la. Stanmore 16 E5
rd. Eastwood 281 E4
rd. Petersham 16 B6
rd. Stanmore 16 B6

CORVUS
cl. Glenmore Pk 265 H13
rd. Hinchinbrk 393 E5

CORY
av. Padstow 399 C15
pl. Prospect 274 J11

CORYMBIA
cct. Frenchs Frst 226 G15
cct. Oxford Falls 226 G15

CORYULE
pl. Warriewood 199 B7

COSFORD
cl. Chipping Ntn 396 E1

COSGROVE
cr. Kingswood 238 A14
rd. Belfield 371 A9
rd. Strathfield S 370 J5

COSIMO
st. Ryde 282 A11
st. Toongabbie 276 H7

COSMOS
pl. Mcquarie Fd 454 E7

COSSINGTON
wy. Claymore 481 D13

COSTAIN
pl. Seven Hills 275 D6

COSTATA
ct. Voyager Pt 427 C5
pl. Mcquarie Fd 454 G2

COSTELLO
pl. Seven Hills 246 D14

COSTENS POINT
rd. Royal N P 522 E11

COSTER
st. Frenchs Frst 257 A4

COTENTIN
rd. Belrose 225 K9

COTSWOLD
av. Castle Hill 217 H10
cl. Belrose 226 B12
rd. Dural 189 E8
rd. Horsley Pk 332 K8
rd. Strathfield 371 D2
st. Westmead 307 G3

COTTAGE
la. Currans Hill 479 J9
st. Werrington 238 D11
wy. Lilyfield 10 B4

COTTAGE POINT
rd. Cottage Pt 135 E13
rd. Krngai Ch N P 165 F1

COTTAM
av. Bankstown 399 E7

COTTEE
dr. Epping 280 D4

COTTENHAM
av. Kensington 376 D16
av. Kingsford 406 D2

COTTER
la. Glebe 11 H7
pl. Greystanes 306 A4
pl. Leumeah 482 D13
pl. Quakers Hill 214 C14

COTTERILL
st. Plumpton 241 H7

COTTERS
la. Revesby Ht, off Sandakan Rd 428 K6

COTTON
gr. Stanhpe Gdn 215 C10
st. N Epping 251 J10

COTTONWOOD
cr. Mcquarie Fd 454 G2
cr. Mcquarie Pk 282 E3
gr. Menai 459 A14
pl. Castle Hill 248 H2
wy. Hornsby Ht 161 G16

COTTRELL
pl. Baulkham Hl 247 F5
pl. Fairfield W 334 K9
pl. Fairfield W 335 A9

COTULA
pl. Glenmore Pk 265 H12
pl. Mcquarie Fd 454 F4
pl. Mt Annan 509 E4

COUCAL
av. Hinchinbrk 393 E1
pl. Ingleburn 453 F9

COUGAR
pl. Raby 451 E13

COUGHLAN
rd. Blaxland 233 D12

COULL
st. Picton 563 F5
st. Picton 563 F6

COULMAN
st. Kings Park 244 E2

COULON
st. Rozelle 7 A15

COULSON
st. Erskineville 375 A10

COULTER
st. Gladesville 312 H9

COULTERS
pl. Wilton 568 K15

COULTON
la. Surry Hills 20 D4
st. Bondi 377 K5

COUNCIL
la. Fairfield, off Smart St 336 F12
pl. Sydney C F7
pl. Sydney 3 E4
st. Bondi Jctn 377 G5
st. Marrickville 374 B10
st. N Willoughby 285 E10
st. St Peters 374 H11

COUNTESS
st. Mosman 316 J5

COUNTY
av. Paddington 13 A16
dr. Cherrybrook 219 A14

COURALLIE
av. Homebush W 340 G7
av. Pymble 253 A6
rd. Northbridge 286 D14

COURANGA
st. Lilli Pilli 522 G1

COURLAND
st. Five Dock 342 H11
st. Randwick 377 D15

COURT
av. Kingsford 406 E2
la. Engadine 518 J2
pl. Menai 458 G6
rd. Double Bay 14 D11
rd. Fairfield 336 F11
st. Windsor 121 E7

COURTENAY
av. Rookwood 340 C15
rd. Rose Bay 348 D9

COURTHOUSE
st. Kellyville Rdg 215 A6

COURTLAND
av. Tahmoor 566 A12

COURTLEY
av. Kellyville Rdg 214 J2
rd. Beacon Hill 257 D6

COURTNEY
rd. Padstow 429 C5

COURTYARD
pl. Castle Hill 217 F4

COUSINS
rd. Beacon Hill 257 H5

COUTTS
cr. Collaroy 259 A1

COVE
av. Manly 288 G13
cct. Castle Cove 285 H4
cl. St Clair 269 J11
la. St Clair, off Netherton Av 269 J11
st. Birchgrove 7 F3
st. Haberfield 342 K13
st. S Turramrra 251 K7
st. Watsons Bay 318 E12

COVELEE
cct. Middle Cove 285 J9

COVENEY
st. Bexley North 402 D11

COVENTRY
cr. N Epping 251 G12
ct. Castle Hill 217 B9
pl. Mount Druitt 240 H14
pl. West Pymble 252 G8
rd. Cabramatta 365 E7
rd. Strathfield 341 B12

COVENY
st. Doonside 243 A11
st. Silverdale 353 G13

COVER
st. Auburn 339 A2
st. Birchgrove 7 H3

COVERDALE
st. Carlingford 250 C13

COW
la. Darlinghurst 4 J11
la. Hurstville 432 B7

COWAL
wy. Woodcroft 243 J9

COWAN
cl. Seven Hills 246 C12
dr. Cottage Pt 135 E10
pl. Glenmore Pk 266 A8
pl. Prairiewood 334 K9
pl. St Helens Park 540 K10
rd. Mt Colah 192 B4
rd. Mt Colah 192 C4
rd. St Ives 223 J12
st. Brooklyn 75 J11
st. Oyster Bay 461 C6

COWARD
st. Mascot 404 J2
st. Mascot 405 B2
st. Rosebery 405 E3

COWDERY
la. Strathfield 341 H11
st. Glenbrook 233 K16
wy. Currans Hill 479 J12

COWDREY
wy. Bonnyrigg 364 B4

COWDROY
av. Cammeray 316 C4

COWE
cl. Bonnyrigg Ht 363 G5

COWELL
st. Gladesville 312 J10
st. Ryde 312 A3

COWELLS
la. Ermington 280 E13

COWL
st. Greenacre 370 E8

COWLAND
av. East Hills 427 H4

COWLES
rd. Mosman 316 K8

COWLEY
cr. Prospect 274 G11

COWPASTURE
pl. Wetherill Pk 333 F3
rd. Abbotsbury 333 D15
rd. Bonnyrigg Ht 363 A4
rd. Bossley Park 333 D15
rd. Cecil Hills 362 J9
rd. Cecil Park 362 J12
rd. Edensor Pk 363 A4
rd. Green Valley 362 J9
rd. Hinchinbrk 392 G4
rd. Horngsea Pk 392 C13
rd. Horngsea Pk 392 C15
rd. Horsley Pk 333 G2
rd. Hoxton Park 392 C13
rd. Leppington 421 F5
rd. West Hoxton 392 C13
rd. Wetherill Pk 333 G2

COWPER
av. Pagewood 406 C8
cir. Quakers Hill 213 G14
ct. Milperra 397 F10
dr. Camden S 506 K11
dr. Mcquarie Pk, off Main Av 283 B9
la. Glebe 12 F13
la. Milperra 397 E11
pl. Barden Rdg 488 G3
pl. Connells Pt 431 H15
pl. Turramurra 222 H13
pl. Wetherill Pk 334 K6
st. Campsie 372 B10
st. Glebe 12 F15
st. Granville 308 F10
st. Leumeah 512 B1
st. Longueville 314 D8
st. Marrickville 16 G16
st. Marrickville 374 D9
st. Parramatta 308 D5
st. Picton 563 E10
st. Picton 563 F10
st. Randwick 376 K11

COWPER WHARF
rdy. Potts Point 4 F2
rdy. Woolmloo 4 F2

COWRA
cl. Bonnyrigg Ht 363 B7
pl. Cronulla 523 J4
pl. Leumeah 512 D3
st. Greystanes 305 H1

COWRANG
av. Terrey Hills 196 D5

COX
av. Bondi Beach 378 B2
av. Kingswood 237 C11
av. Penrith 237 C11
cr. Dundas Vy 279 K7
cr. Hobartville 118 E7
la. Toongabbie 276 C8
pl. Gymea 461 G16
pl. Ingleburn 453 C12
pl. Mortdale 431 B6
pl. Mt Pritchard 364 B11
pl. Schofields 213 E13
pl. West Hoxton 392 B10
st. Coogee 407 F3
st. Elderslie 507 G1
st. Glenbrook 263 J2
st. S Windsor 120 D16
st. Windsor 120 H12

COXS
av. Liverpool 395 A8
la. Lane Cove 314 C1
rd. East Ryde 283 A13
rd. North Ryde 282 F9

CRABB
pl. Cabramatta 365 E11

CRABBES
av. N Willoughby 285 E9

CRACKENBACK
ct. Glenhaven 218 A5

CRADDOCK
st. Wentwthvle 306 G1

CRADLE
av. Beaumont Hills 185 G15

CRAG
cr. Bowen Mtn 83 K7

GREGORY'S STREET DIRECTORY 53

CR STREETS

CRAGG
st. Condell Park.....398 H3
CRAGSIDE
pl. Glenhaven.....218 A5
CRAIG
av. Baulkham Hl.....247 H14
av. Leurneah.....512 B1
av. Manly.....288 H13
av. Moorebank.....396 D9
av. Oxley Park.....270 F2
av. Vaucluse.....348 F6
pl. Davidson.....255 E2
st. Blacktown.....274 C5
st. Punchbowl.....399 J9
st. St Ives Ch.....224 B2
st. Smithfield.....335 D7
st. Woolooware.....493 E12
CRAIGANTON
wy. Wentwthvle.....277 E10
CRAIGEND
pl. Bella Vista.....216 B13
st. Darlinghurst.....13 A9
st. Darlinghurst.....13 B9
CRAIGHOLM
st. Sylvania.....461 J12
CRAIGIE
av. Padstow.....429 D3
CRAIGLANDS
av. Gordon.....253 D9
CRAIGLEA
gdn. Carlingford.....250 D13
st. Blacktown.....274 J3
st. Guildford.....337 E6
CRAIGMORE
dr. Kellyville.....216 K1
CRAIGSLEA
pl. Canley Ht.....335 C16
CRAIGTON
pl. Glenhaven.....218 D6
CRAIK
av. Austral.....391 E2
CRAIN
ct. Harringtn Pk.....478 C1
CRAKANTHORP
la. Picton.....563 F5
CRAMER
cr. Chatswood W.....284 C13
cr. Lane Cove N.....284 C13
pl. Glenwood.....215 J14
CRAMMOND
av. Bundeena.....523 G8
bvd. Caringbah.....492 J2
pl. Minto.....453 A14
CRAMPTON
dr. Springwood.....172 E12
CRANA
av. E Lindfield.....255 A13
av. S Coogee.....407 J3
pl. Forestville.....255 J8
pl. Brownlow Hl.....475 K9
st. St Marys.....239 G16
CRANBERRY
st. Loftus.....490 A9
st. Mcquarie Fd.....454 D6
CRANBOURNE
st. Riverstone.....183 D11
CRANBROOK
av. Cremorne.....316 F9
av. Roseville.....284 J1
cl. West Hoxton.....392 D9
la. Bellevue Hill.....347 F11
   Cremorne, off
   Cranbrook Av.....316 F8
la. Cronulla.....493 H12
rd. Illawong.....460 E1
rd. Bellevue Hill.....347 F13
st. Botany.....405 F13
CRANDON
rd. Epping.....251 D16
CRANE
av. Green Valley.....363 E14
av. Haberfield.....343 D12
la. Concord.....342 B8
la. Bellevue Hill.....14 G8
pl. Cranbrook.....287 A5
pl. Double Bay.....14 G8
pl. Wetherill Pk.....335 A5
rd. Castle Hill.....218 D15
st. Concord.....342 A7
st. Homebush.....341 B8
st. Springwood.....201 E4
CRANEBUSH
rd. Castlereagh.....206 H15
rd. Cranebrook.....206 H15

CRANE LODGE
pl. Palm Beach.....140 B9
CRANFIELD
pl. Camden S.....506 K14
CRANFORD
av. St Ives.....223 K9
CRANNEY
pl. Lalor Park.....245 F14
CRANSTONS
rd. Middle Dural.....158 D3
CRATER
rd. N Balgowlah.....287 G4
CRAVEN
pl. Mt Annan.....509 H1
CRAWFORD
av. Shalvey.....210 J13
la. Emu Plains, off
   Crawford St.....235 B9
la. Tahmoor.....565 K12
pl. Beacon Hill.....257 H8
pl. Dundas Vy.....280 A6
pl. Marrickville.....373 G3
pl. Surry Hills.....F F13
rd. Btn-le-Sds.....433 H4
rd. Doonside.....243 A12
st. Mt Krng-gai.....162 J10
st. Berala.....339 D12
st. Blakehurst.....432 B13
st. Emu Plains.....235 B9
st. Old Guildford.....337 G9
swy. Liverpool.....395 E4
CRAWLEY
av. Hebersham.....241 G8
st. Merrylands.....307 J9
CRAY
pl. Parklea.....215 A11
CRAYFORD
cr. Mt Pritchard.....364 C11
CREBRA
wy. Mt Annan.....509 E3
CREDA
pl. Baulkham Hl.....248 D10
CREE
cr. Greenfld Pk.....333 K16
CREEK
rd. St Marys.....239 F15
st. Balmain.....7 F11
st. Colyton.....270 J6
st. Forest Lodge.....11 E15
st. Riverstone.....182 H9
CREEK RIDGE
rd. Freemns Rch.....66 G14
rd. Freemns Rch.....90 E1
rd. Glossodia.....66 G13
rd. Glossodia.....66 G14
rd. Glossodia.....67 A11
CREEKSIDE
pl. Casula.....423 G6
CREEKWOOD
dr. Voyager Pt.....427 B5
CREER
pl. Narraweena.....257 K4
st. Merrylands.....307 D13
st. Randwick.....407 C2
CREEWOOD
la. Concord, off
   Creewood St.....341 G7
st. Concord.....341 G7
CREGO
rd. Glenhaven.....218 D4
CREIGAN
rd. Bradbury.....511 J13
CREMA
pl. Edensor Pk.....333 J15
CREMONA
pl. Oakhurst.....242 D1
rd. Como.....460 H5
CREMORNE
la. Cremorne Pt.....316 F13
rd. Cremorne Pt.....316 F13
CREOLE
rd. Berowra.....133 C11
CRESCENT
av. Manly.....288 F7
av. Ryde.....312 C1
cl. Warrawee.....222 E8
la. Newtown.....17 E13
la. Stanmore.....16 D9
pl. Kirribilli.....6 A14
rd. Caringbah.....492 E14
rd. Ebenezer.....68 J8
rd. Mona Vale.....169 F16
rd. Newport.....169 F14

st. Fairlight.....288 E8
st. Haberfield.....9 A12
st. Holroyd.....308 B10
st. Hunters Hill.....314 A12
st. Redfern.....20 B12
st. Rozelle.....11 C1
st. Waterloo.....20 B12
CRESS
pl. Mcquarie Fd.....454 F6
pl. Quakers Hill.....243 E4
CRESSBROOK
dr. Wattle Grove.....425 K3
CRESSFIELD
av. Carlingford.....279 K4
CRESSY
av. Beaumont Hills.....215 H3
rd. East Ryde.....282 J15
rd. Mt Vernon.....331 A14
rd. North Ryde.....282 J15
rd. North Ryde.....283 A13
rd. Ryde.....312 H1
rd. Ryde.....312 E4
st. Canterbury.....372 D16
st. Rosebery.....375 H13
CREST
pl. Engadine.....488 C15
pl. Jamisontown.....266 C4
pl. Warragamba.....353 B4
CRESTA
cl. St Ives.....224 A13
CRESTANI
pl. Edensor Pk.....333 J16
CRESTBROOK
st. Seven Hills.....245 C15
CRESTREEF
dr. Acacia Gdn.....214 G15
CRESTVIEW
av. Kellyville.....216 G1
dr. Glenwood.....246 B5
pl. Cherrybrook.....219 D13
pl. Cranebrook.....207 A12
CRESTWOOD
av. Thornleigh.....221 B5
dr. Baulkham Hl.....246 J3
wk. Baulkham Hl.....247 B7
CRESWELL
st. Revesby.....398 E14
CRESWICK
pl. Dharruk.....241 D8
CRETE
pl. E Lindfield.....254 K11
st. Narraweena.....258 D6
pl. Peakhurst.....430 D7
CREWE
pl. Rosebery.....375 J14
st. Bardwell Pk.....402 J7
CREWS
rd. Seven Hills.....246 B11
CRIBBS
cl. West Hoxton.....392 E7
CRICHTON
st. Rooty Hill.....272 G1
CRICK
av. Elizabeth Bay.....13 A4
st. Chatswood.....285 B7
CRICKETERS ARMS
rd. Prospect.....274 F16
CRIEFF
st. Ashbury.....372 D9
CRIMEA
rd. Marsfield.....251 H14
st. Parramatta.....307 H7
CRIMSON
la. Ashbury.....372 H6
st. Ashbury.....372 H6
CRINAN
ct. Castle Hill.....218 D7
ct. Hurlstone Pk.....372 K11
st. Hurlstone Pk.....372 K11
CRINUM
pl. Mcquarie Fd.....454 F5
CRIPPLE
rd. Blaxland.....233 G4
CRIPPS
av. Kingsgrove.....401 G6
CRISPIN
pl. Quakers Hill.....214 B12
CRISPSPARKLE
dr. Ambarvale.....540 F1
CRITCHETT
rd. Chatswood W.....284 G12

CRITERION
cr. Doonside.....243 C6
CROATIA
av. Edmndsn Pk.....423 B4
pl. Quakers Hill.....214 A10
CROCKET
wy. Minto.....482 K5
CROCODILE
dr. Green Valley.....363 B9
CROCUS
pl. Quakers Hill.....243 F3
CROFT
av. Merrylands.....307 B11
pl. Bradbury.....511 J13
pl. Glenwood.....246 B5
CROFTS
av. Hurstville.....432 A5
la. Rockdale.....403 D15
CROISSY
av. Hunters Hill.....313 J12
CROKER
cr. Colyton.....270 D5
la. Colyton, off
   Croker Cr.....270 D5
pl. Green Valley.....362 J12
pl. Guildford W.....336 J1
CROMARTY
cr. Winston Hills.....277 C3
pl. St Andrews.....481 K5
CROMDALE
st. Mortdale.....430 J8
CROMER
pl. St Johns Pk.....364 E2
rd. Cromer.....227 J11
CROMERTY
pl. Glenhaven.....218 D5
CROMER VALLEY
la. Cromer, off
   Ada St.....341 G9
rd. Cromer.....227 B7
rd. Oxford Falls.....227 B7
CROMMELIN
cr. St Helens Park.....541 A6
CROMPTON
pl. W Pnnant Hl.....249 B3
CROMWELL
pl. Malabar.....437 D2
st. Croydon.....372 E5
st. Croydon Pk.....372 E5
st. Leichhardt.....9 H14
CRONDALL
pl. N Parramatta.....278 E10
CRONIN
st. Bonnyrigg Ht.....363 A7
CRONK
av. Penshurst.....431 H7
pl. Bonnyrigg.....364 D4
st. Penrith.....237 B14
CRONULLA
cr. Woodbine.....481 D15
pl. Allawah.....432 E4
st. Allawah.....432 E5
st. Cronulla.....493 K13
CROOKED
la. N Richmond.....87 D10
CROOKS
la. Newtown.....17 H10
CROOKSTON
dr. Camden S.....507 A13
CROOKWELL
av. Miranda.....491 J7
CROOT
st. Hurstville.....401 H15
CROPLEY
dr. Baulkham Hl.....247 C13
la. Rhodes.....311 F8
st. Rhodes.....311 E8
CROQUET
la. Mosman.....317 D10
CROSBY
av. Beaumont Hills.....215 J1
av. Hurstville.....432 D3
cr. Fairfield.....336 E7
st. Denistone W.....280 K12
st. Greystanes.....306 E3
st. Greystanes.....306 F3
CROSIO
pl. Bonnyrigg.....364 F6
CROSS
la. Double Bay.....14 E9
la. Enmore.....17 A15
la. Kogarah.....433 D4
la. Mortdale.....431 C7
la. Woolmloo.....4 H5
pl. Bligh Park.....150 K7
pl. Mt Annan.....479 G16

rd. Orchard Hills.....267 C11
rd. Regentville.....235 E16
rd. Woolooware.....493 F13
st. Balgowlah.....287 J6
st. Bankstown.....399 G2
st. Baulkham Hl.....248 B9
st. Bronte.....378 A7
st. Brookvale.....257 J11
st. Campsie.....402 B1
st. Concord.....341 G6
st. Croydon.....342 D14
st. Doonside.....243 A13
st. Double Bay.....14 B8
st. Five Dock.....342 J10
st. Forest Lodge.....11 G15
st. Glebe.....11 G15
st. Glenbrook.....264 A15
st. Guildford.....337 F6
st. Hurstville.....432 A5
st. Kemps Ck.....360 B3
st. Kogarah.....433 E4
st. Kyle Bay.....431 J16
st. Lidcombe.....339 K6
st. Merrylands.....307 A9
st. Miranda.....492 D7
st. Mortdale.....431 C6
st. Mosman.....317 C11
st. Pymble.....253 B7
st. Pyrmont.....12 F1
st. Rozelle.....7 A14
st. Ryde.....312 E6
st. Strathfield.....371 D4
st. Tahmoor.....566 D11
st. Warrimoo.....203 F11
CROSSANDRA
cl. Cranebrook.....207 F15
CROSSING
la. Concord, off
   Ada St.....341 G9
CROSSLAND
st. Merrylands.....338 C1
CROSSLANDS
rd. Galston.....160 B10
CROSSLEY
av. McGraths Hl.....122 A13
st. Ingleburn.....453 F13
CROSTON
rd. Engadine.....489 E8
CROSWELL
pl. N Parramatta.....278 E10
CROTON
pl. Mcquarie Fd.....454 C4
CROTOYE
pl. Marsfield.....281 K6
CROW
pl. Bossley Park.....333 K11
CROWBILL
pl. Erskine Park.....270 J13
CROWEA
pl. Frenchs Frst.....226 H15
CROWGEY
st. Rydalmere.....279 C16
CROWLE
rd. S Penrith.....267 A4
CROWLEY
cr. Melrose Pk.....310 K4
dr. Mcquarie Pk, off
   Main Av.....283 D7
rd. Berowra.....133 D13
CROWLEYS
la. Agnes Banks.....117 C8
CROWN
cl. Henley.....313 B13
la. Darlinghurst.....4 C8
mw. Bella Vista.....246 E4
pl. Pymble.....223 C13
st. Queenscliff.....288 F2
st. Darlinghurst.....F K9
st. Darlinghurst.....4 C12
st. Epping.....250 J16
st. Fairfield E.....337 A11
st. Glebe.....12 G14
st. Granville.....307 K8
st. Harris Park.....308 F7
st. Henley.....313 B14
st. Riverstone.....182 H4
st. St Peters.....374 J13
st. Surry Hills.....F F13
st. Surry Hills.....F K9
st. Surry Hills.....4 B16
st. Surry Hills.....20 B5
st. Woolmloo.....4 C12
tce. Bella Vista.....246 E4

54 GREGORY'S STREET DIRECTORY

STREETS — DA

CROWS NEST
- rd. Waverton 5 A5
- rd. Wollstncraft 5 A5

CROWTHER
- av. Greenwich 314 J5

CROXON
- cr. Lalor Park 245 G11

CROYDE
- st. Stanhpe Gdn 215 E6

CROYDON
- st. Croydon 372 D5
- av. Croydon Pk 372 C9
- la. Cronulla, off Cronulla Rd 493 K13
- la. Lakemba, off Croydon St N 400 K1
- rd. Bexley 402 A15
- rd. Croydon 342 F16
- rd. Hurstville 402 A15
- st. Cronulla 493 K12
- st. Lakemba 401 A2
- st. Petersham 15 J7
- st.n.Lakemba 400 K1

CROZET
- st. Kings Park 244 F3

CROZIER
- rd. Belrose 225 K5
- st. Eagle Vale 481 B9

CRUCIE
- av. Bass Hill 367 G6

CRUCIS
- la. Erskine Park, off Crucis Pl 300 J3
- pl. Erskine Park 300 J2

CRUDGE
- rd. Marayong 244 A7

CRUIKSHANK
- av. Elderslie 507 G1
- st. Stanmore 17 A5

CRUMBLY
- rd. Dural 189 H10

CRUMMOCK
- st. Collaroy Plat 228 D12

CRUMP
- st. Mortdale 431 A6

CRUSADE
- av. Padstow 399 C16
- av. Woolooware 493 C10

CRUSADER
- rd. Galston 160 E13

CRUX
- la. Mosman 316 J11
- st. Mosman 316 J10

CRYSTAL
- la.w.Petersham 16 A9
- pde. Doonside 243 E8
- pl. Kellyville 216 A3
- st. Greystanes 306 A2
- st. Newport 169 D10
- st. Petersham 16 A9
- st. Rozelle 344 D7
- st. Sylvania 461 H12
- st. Waterloo 20 B13
- st. Waterloo 376 A10
- wy. Mt Annan 479 C15
- wy. Mt Annan 479 C16

CUBBY
- cl. Castle Hill 217 B10

CUBITT
- cr. Quakers Hill 214 D12
- dr. Denham Ct 422 C7

CUDAL
- cl. Terrey Hills 196 E5
- pl. Carlingford 249 D13
- pl. Kirrawee 490 J6
- st. Turramurra 223 A9

CUDGEGONG
- rd. Rouse Hill 184 C8
- rd. Ruse 512 B8

CULBARA
- pl. Allambie Ht 257 G15

CULBURRA
- rd. Miranda 492 B1
- st. Prestons 393 C14

CULDEES
- rd. Burwood Ht 372 A3

CULGOA
- av. Eastwood 281 J5
- av. Wattle Grove 395 K13
- pl. Sylvania Wtr 462 G10
- rd. Chatswood W 284 B9

CULL
- rd. Harringtn Pk 478 E2

CULLAMINE
- dr. Duffys Frst 164 H16

CULLEN
- av. Mosman 317 C9
- av. Richmond 119 K3
- cr. Castle Hill 218 J14
- la. Maianbar 523 A8
- st. Dharruk 241 B8
- st. Minto 482 J9
- st. Smithfield 306 C15
- st. Forestville 255 B11
- st. Lane Cove W 313 H2
- st. Maianbar 523 A8

CULLENS
- av. Liverpool 394 J9
- la. Hunters Hill 313 H10
- pl. Liverpool 394 J10
- rd. Punchbowl 400 A7

CULLENYA
- cl. Berowra 133 A16

CULLIS
- pl. Woodpark 306 H14

CULLODEN
- rd. Mcquarie Pk 252 A16
- rd. Marsfield 281 A12

CULLUM
- st. Bossley Park 333 H11

CULMARA
- pl. Engadine 489 B10

CULMONE
- cl. Edensor Pk 363 F4

CULOTWA
- rd. Pymble 253 B7

CULVER
- st. Monterey 433 F16
- st. S Wntwthvle 307 A7

CULVERSTON
- av. Denham Ct 422 C5
- rd. Minto 482 C8

CULWORTH
- av. Killara 254 A12

CULWULLA
- st. S Hurstville 432 B9

CULYA
- st. Marayong 243 H6

CUMBEE
- la. Caringbah 493 B16

CUMBERLAND
- av. Castle Hill 217 J10
- av. Collaroy 259 A1
- av. Dee Why 258 F2
- cct. Georges Hall 368 C15
- cr. Lane Cove N 283 G13
- hwy.Beecroft 249 J14
- hwy.Cabramatta 365 B11
- hwy.Cabramatta W 365 D7
- hwy.Canley Ht 365 D7
- hwy.Cabramatta W 365 D7
- hwy.Fairfield W 335 D15
- hwy.Greystanes 306 H7
- hwy.Liverpool 365 B11
- hwy.Merrylands W 306 H7
- hwy.Normanhurst 221 E10
- hwy.Northmead 277 C11
- hwy.N Parramatta 278 H10
- hwy.Oatlands 278 H10
- hwy.Pennant Hills 250 A3
- hwy.Smithfield 306 H7
- hwy.S Wntwthvle 306 H7
- hwy.Thornleigh 221 E10
- hwy.Wahroonga 221 E10
- hwy.Warwck Frm 365 B11
- hwy.Wentwthvle 277 C11
- hwy.W Pnnant Hl 249 J14
- hwy.Woodpark 306 F14
- pl. Colyton 270 F8
- pl. The Rocks .....A J9
- rd. Auburn 339 A4
- rd. Greystanes 306 C6
- rd. Ingleburn 453 B13
- rd. Minto 453 B12
- sq. Newington, off Monterey St 310 D11

CUMBRA
- cct. Berowra 133 B13

CUMBORA
- cl. Erskine Park 300 F2
- pl. Oatlands 278 H10

CUMBRIAN
- cl. Northmead 278 C5

CUMMING
- av. Concord 341 F3
- av. Concord W 341 F3
- av. Quakers Hill 213 H14

CUMMINGS
- av. Pemulwuy 305 F6
- cr. Lansvale 366 H8

CUMMINS
- rd. Menangle Pk 539 B6

CUNLIFFE
- rd. East Killara 254 G7

CUNNEEN
- st. Mulgrave 121 H15

CUNNINGHAM
- cl. St Clair 270 D10
- cr. Blacktown 245 B12
- cr. Mt Annan 509 J5
- pde.Kellyville 216 J5
- pl. Camden S 506 K11
- pl. S Windsor 150 H1
- pwy.Moorebank, off Cunningham St 395 J8
- rd. Ingleburn 423 A9
- st. Haymarket .....E H6
- st. Haymarket 3 G11
- st. Matraville 437 B2
- st. Moorebank 395 J9
- st. N Sydney 5 F2
- st. Sydney .....E H6
- st. Telopea 279 G11

CUNNINGHAME
- cl. Fairfield 336 D10

CUPANIA
- cr. Bidwill 211 E13

CUPAR
- pl. St Andrews 451 K16

CUPITTS
- la. Richmond 120 B3

CURAC
- pl. Casula 424 C3

CURAGUL
- rd. N Turramurra 193 E14

CURBAN
- st. Balgowlah Ht 287 J13

CURIE
- av. Lucas Ht 487 H12

CURL CURL
- pde. Curl Curl 258 H13
- pl. Woodbine 481 J9

CURLEW
- av. Newington 310 E11
- cl. Woronora Ht 489 B3
- cl. Glenmore Pk 266 C14
- cl. Glenwood 215 E14

CURLEW CAMP
- rd. Mosman 316 J12

CURLEWIS
- st. Ashcroft 364 F15
- st. Bondi Beach 378 B1

CURRA
- cl. Frenchs Frst 255 K2
- pl. Greystanes 305 K10

CURRAGHBEENA
- rd. Mosman 316 J13

CURRAGUNDI
- rd. Belrose 226 B10

CURRAH
- pl. Como 460 G5

CURRAN
- rd. Mcquarie Fd 453 J2
- rd. Marayong 244 A8
- st. Prairiewood 335 A7

CURRANA
- st. Beverly Hills 401 C9

CURRANS HILL
- dr. Currans Hill 479 G11

CURRAWANG
- pl. Como 460 H6
- st. Cammeray 316 B4
- st. Carss Park 432 F13
- st. Concord W 311 E13

CURRAWEELA
- st. Forestville 255 K7

CURRAWONG
- av. Lane Cove W 313 H1
- av. Normanhurst 221 F12
- av. Palm Beach 140 B9
- av. Valley Ht 202 E5
- cr. Bowen Mtn 84 K8
- cr. Leonay 234 K13
- pl. Blaxland 234 E5
- pl. Berowra Ht 132 J8
- pl. Glenorie 127 K9
- pl. Glenwood 215 C16
- st. Green Valley 363 E9
- st. Ingleburn 453 E2

CURRENCY
- cl. Winston Hills 277 A3

CURRENT
- st. Padstow 429 H2

CURREY
- st. Fairfield W 335 A11

CURRIE
- av. Annangrove 186 E4
- rd. Forestville 256 C9
- rd. Oakville 122 H12

CURRINGA
- rd. Villawood 367 A3

CURRONG
- cct. Terrey Hills 196 D8
- pl. S Turramrra 252 B9
- st. S Wntwthvle 306 J7

CURRY
- cr. Artarmon 314 K2
- pl. Seven Hills 275 G8
- st. Eastern Ck 272 G2
- st. Rooty Hill 272 G2

CURT
- pl. Quakers Hill 214 A10
- rd. Ashfield 343 A16

CURTALE
- cr. Green Valley 363 C10

CURTIN
- av. Abbotsford 343 A4
- av. N Wahroonga 192 E15
- cr. Maroubra 407 E14
- dr. Penrith 237 C6
- la. Canterbury 372 F15
- pl. Concord 341 F5
- pl. Condell Park 398 G1
- pl. Narellan Vale 479 B11
- pl. Sydney J14
- pl. Sydney 1 G15
- pl. Westmead 307 F13
- st. Cabramatta 366 A5
- st. Canley Vale 366 A5

CURTIS
- av. Taren Point 462 G13
- cl. Cherrybrook 249 F1
- cr. Moorebank 396 D9
- ct. Carlingford 279 F11
- la. Catherine Fd 449 D6
- pl. Kings Park 244 F2
- pl. Balmain 7 F6
- rd. Chester Hill 338 A14
- rd. Kellyville 186 A13
- rd. Mulgrave 121 H15
- st. Banksia 403 D12
- st. Caringbah 492 G7
- st. Ryde 312 E6

CURTISS
- pl. Raby 481 E1

CURVERS
- dr. Mt Riverview 234 C1

CURZON
- rd. Padstow Ht 429 B5
- st. Ryde 282 A16
- wy. Ambarvale 511 A16

CUSACK
- av. Casula 424 G3
- cl. St Helens Park 541 C3
- pl. Blackett 241 D3
- pl. Oakville 124 C8
- st. Denistone W 280 J12
- st. Merrylands W 307 A16

CUSAK
- cl. Edensor Pk 333 H16

CUSCUS
- pl. St Helens Park 541 H2

CUSHER
- wy. Wentwthvle, off Portadown Rd 277 D11

CUSTOM HOUSE
- la. Sydney .....B D9

CUSTOMS OFFICERS STAIRS
- The Rocks 1 J8

CUTBUSH
- av. Belfield 371 C9

CUTCLIFFE
- av. Regents Pk 369 F2

CUTHBERT
- cr. Kellyville 215 H5
- cr. Edensor Pk 363 D2
- cr. Revesby 428 K7
- pl. Menai 458 F12
- pl. Newington 309 K14
- st. Queens Park 22 E11
- st. Sydney A3
- st. Sydney 3 C2

CUTHEL
- st. Campbelltown 511 K2
- st. Badgerys Ck 359 C4

CUT HILL
- rd. Cobbitty 415 B8
- rd. Cobbitty 446 D9

CUTHILL
- st. Randwick 377 B15

CUTLER
- av. St Marys 270 A1
- cct. Narrabeen 228 F6
- cl. Westleigh 220 H8
- la. St Marys, off Cutler Av 270 A2
- pde. North Ryde 282 K11
- pl. Cromer 227 K11
- pl. Clontarf 287 G15
- pl. Engadine 518 E4
- rd. Lansvale 366 E8
- st. Bondi 378 B4

CUTLER FOOTWAY
- Paddington 4 J13

CUTLER HALL
- wy. Narrabeen, off Cutler Cct 228 F7

CUVEE
- pl. Minchinbury 271 K10

CUZCO
- st. S Coogee 407 H6

CYCAS
- pl. Stanhpe Gdn 215 D10

CYCLAMEN
- pl. Mcquarie Fd 454 E5

CYGNET
- av. Green Valley 363 D14
- pl. Illawong 459 C5
- pl. Willmot 210 F12

CYGNUS
- cl. Doonside 243 E13
- pl. Cranebrook 207 G7

CYNTHEA
- rd. Palm Beach 140 A4

CYNTHIA
- av. Castle Hill 248 A5
- st. Pymble 252 K7
- wk. Pymble 252 K7

CYPERUS
- pl. Glenmore Pk 265 H14

CYPRESS
- cl. Alfords Point 458 K3
- cl. Baulkham Hl 248 B11
- cl. Lugarno 429 E6
- cl. Ryde 312 E6
- la. Blacktown, off Kildare Rd 243 K15
- pl. Liverpool 395 B9
- rd. N Sydney 5 B6
- st. Normanhurst 221 D13

CYPRIAN
- st. Mosman 317 C1

CYPRUS
- st. Mcquarie Fd 453 K4

CYRIL
- pl. Baulkham Hl 247 E11
- st. Greystanes 306 G4

CYRUS
- av. Wahroonga 222 A12

D

DABBAGE
- pl. Kurrajong Ht 63 F11

DACEY
av. Moore Park 20 D15
pl. Doonside 273 F3
DACRE
la. Malabar 437 E3
st. Malabar 437 E3
DADD
wky. Mount Druitt 240 K13
DADLEY
st. Alexandria 18 H13
DADSWELL
pl. Mt Pritchard 364 K11
DAFFODIL
pl. Glenmore Pk 265 G7
st. Eastwood 281 D7
st. Greystanes 306 C12
st. Marayong 244 B6
DAGMAR
cr. Blacktown 274 C3
DAHLIA
pl. Clarmnt Ms 238 H16
pl. Prestons 393 J14
st. Greystanes 305 G11
st. Quakers Hill 243 E2
DAIHATSU
dr. Riverwood, off Applause St 400 C10
DAIMLER
pl. Ingleburn 453 H12
DAINES
pde. Beacon Hill 257 F6
DAINTON
av. St Ives 224 D11
DAINTREE
dr. Wattle Grove 426 A4
gln. St Clair 270 D11
la. St Clair, off Daintree Gln 270 D11
pl. Dural 219 A3
pl. Kellyville 216 G2
wy. Menai 458 H10
DAINTREY
cr. Randwick 377 C16
st. Fairlight 288 D8
DAIRY
ct. Glenwood 215 E13
rd. Belimbla Pk 501 D8
DAISY
av. Penshurst 431 G6
la. Bargo 567 A5
pl. Clarmnt Ms 238 H16
pl. Lalor Park 245 C11
pl. Mcquarie Fd 454 D5
st. Chatswood 284 J8
st. Croydon Pk 372 A5
st. Dee Why 259 A8
st. Greystanes 305 H7
st. N Balgowlah 287 F6
st. Revesby 398 F10
st. Roselands 400 F8
DAKARA
cl. Pymble 252 J4
dr. Frenchs Frst 256 A2
pl. Frenchs Frst 256 B2
DAKING
st. N Parramatta 278 B10
DAKOTA
ct. Stanhpe Gdn 215 C12
dr. Bossley Park 333 K11
pl. Raby 451 B13
pl. St Clair 269 F13
DALBERTIS
st. Abbotsbury 333 A13
DALBY
pl. Chipping Ntn 366 H16
pl. Eastlakes 405 K2
DALCASSIA
st. Hurstville 431 K4
DALE
av. Chippendale 19 B4
av. Liverpool 394 F5
cl. Thornleigh 220 H12
cr. Narwee 400 G15
gr. Hebersham 241 F10
la. Mcquarie Fd 453 K2
pde. Bankstown 399 D1
pl. Cranebrook 237 D1
pl. North Rocks 248 J12
pl. Winston Hills 277 H3
st. Brookvale 258 A11
st. Fairfield 336 F13
st. Seven Hills 245 D15
DALES
cl. Blairmount 481 A14
rd. Silverdale 353 K12
DALEY
cl. Belimbla Pk 501 G16
pl. Fairfield W 335 B12
rd. Yagoona 369 B10
st. Pendle Hill 276 D16
DALGETY
rd. Millers Pt A A1
rd. Millers Pt 1 C8
tce. Millers Pt 1 C8
DALHOUSIE
st. Haberfield 343 C16
DALKEITH
la. Sans Souci 433 C13
pl. St Helens Park 511 J16
rd. Cherrybrook 219 B14
st. Busby 363 G16
st. Northbridge 285 K15
st. Ramsgate 433 C13
st. Sans Souci 433 C13
DALLAS
av. S Penrith 266 K4
pl. St Ives 224 G9
pl. Toongabbie 275 H11
DALLEY
av. Pagewood 406 B9
av. Vaucluse 348 C6
la. Pagewood, off Holloway St 406 B10
la. Redfern 20 B8
rd. Heathcote 518 G9
st. Bondi Jctn 377 G4
st. Harris Park 308 E8
st. Jamisontown 265 J2
st. Kogarah 432 K4
st. Lidcombe 340 B7
st. Queenscliff 288 E2
st. Sydney A K11
st. Sydney 1 H13
DALLEYS
rd. Naremburn 315 D3
DALLWOOD
av. Epping 250 E16
DALMAN
pl. Baulkham Hl 246 H6
pl. Sylvania 462 B10
DALMAR
pl. Carlingford 280 D5
st. Croydon 342 G12
DALMATIA
av. Edmndsn Pk 423 A4
st. Carramar 336 J15
DALMENY
av. Rosebery 375 K14
av. Rosebery 405 J1
av. Russell Lea 343 D7
dr. Prestons 393 E14
dr. Prestons 393 D16
dr. Prestons 423 E2
rd. Northbridge 286 E15
DALPRA
cr. Bossley Park 333 E12
DALPURA
pl. Bangor 459 A15
st. Cromer 228 D14
DALRAY
st. Lalor Park 245 E9
DALRYMPLE
av. Chatswood W 284 D14
av. Chatswood W 284 F13
av. Lane Cove N 284 D14
cr. Pymble 223 J16
pl. Barden Rdg 488 G2
DALSTRAITH
pl. Glen Alpine 510 D14
DALTON
av. Condell Park 398 E1
av. Eastwood 281 E9
av. Homebush 341 A7
av. Lucas Ht 487 K12
cl. Rouse Hill 185 D4
la. Mosman, off Awaba St 317 A4
pl. Fairfield W 335 A11
pl. Prestons 393 C13
rd. Mosman 317 A4
rd. St Ives Ch 223 K4
st. Colyton 270 G5
DALWOOD
av. Seaforth 287 A8
pl. Carlingford 249 E13
pl. Eschol Park 481 F3
pl. Mt Annan 509 J1
DALY
av. Concord 341 H9
av. N Wahroonga 222 K2
ct. Wrrngtn Cty 238 F7
la. Wrrngtn Cty, off Daly Ct 238 F7
rd. Faulconbdg 171 C10
st. Bilgola 169 G6
DALZIEL
av. Panania 428 C3
st. Engadine 489 D13
st. Fairfield W 335 A12
DAMASCUS
rd. Holsworthy 426 D11
DAMEELI
av. Kirrawee 491 A4
DAME MARY GILMORE
rd. Oatley 430 G11
DAMIEN
av. Greystanes 306 G5
av. S Penrith 266 K5
dr. Parklea 215 A11
DAMON
av. Epping 250 E15
cl. Glendenning 242 H4
DAMOUR
av. E Lindfield 254 J12
st. Holsworthy 396 D16
DAMPER
av. Beaumont Hills 215 H3
DAMPIER
av. Wrrngtn Cty 238 F5
cr. Fairfield W 335 C9
pl. Leumeah 482 F11
pl. Prestons 393 G7
pl. Whalan 240 J9
st. Chifley 437 A5
st. Kurnell 465 J9
DAMSEL
ct. Castle Hill 217 G4
DAN
av. Blacktown 244 B13
av. Maroubra 407 F14
cr. Castle Hill 218 F15
cr. Colyton 270 B5
cr. Lansvale 366 E9
st. Campbelltown 511 J3
st. Marsfield 282 A7
st. Merrylands 307 C10
DANA
cl. Castle Hill 247 F2
pde. Regents Pk 369 A3
DANALAM
st. Liverpool 394 K8
DANBURITE
pl. Eagle Vale 481 H4
DANBURY
cl. Marsfield 282 A6
DANBY
st. Prospect 275 A11
DANDAR
pl. Bradbury 511 C15
DANDARBONG
av. Bangor 459 B14
av. Carlingford 280 D7
DANDENONG
cl. Bossley Park 334 B6
cr. Ruse 512 H6
rd. Terrey Hills 196 E6
DANEHILL
ct. Castle Hill 217 B7
DANELLA
st. The Oaks 502 F9
DANGAR
cl. Hinchinbrk 363 B13
pl. Chippendale 19 A3
pl. Davidson 255 C2
rd. Brooklyn 76 D11
st. Chippendale 19 A4
st. Lindfield 254 F14
st. Randwick 377 A10
wy. Airds 512 A14
DANGIN
cl. Bonnyrigg 364 C9
DANIEL
av. Baulkham Hl 246 J12
cl. Cherrybrook 220 A6
la. St Clair, off Daniel Pde 269 J9
pde. St Clair 269 J9
pl. Green Valley 362 K10
st. Botany 405 G10
st. Granville 308 C11
st. Greystanes 306 D8
st. Leichhardt 9 C15
st. Wetherill Pk 334 E3
DANIELA
pl. Blacktown 273 G5
DANIELS
rd. Bidwill 211 H16
rd. Bidwill 241 G3
rd. Hassall Gr 211 H16
rd. Hebersham 241 G3
rd. Oakhurst 241 G3
st. Chippendale 18 J2
DANIEL WILLIAMS
pl. Glenbrook 234 D11
DANKS
st. Waterloo 19 J12
DANNY
rd. Lalor Park 245 D11
st. Werrington 238 H11
DANS
av. Coogee 377 G12
DANTIC
pl. Cherrybrook 219 B12
DANUBE
cr. Kearns 451 A14
pl. St Clair 270 B8
DAPHINE
la. Kingswood, off Daphine Cl 238 A14
DAPHNE
av. Bankstown 399 G3
av. Castle Hill 247 J4
cl. Cherrybrook 220 A6
cl. Kingswood 238 A14
la. Botany 405 E10
pl. Blacktown 244 K10
pl. Mcquarie Fd 454 F7
st. Botany 405 E10
st. Caringbah 492 H16
st. Merrylands 307 C10
st. West Ryde 280 H13
DAPLYN
wy. Claymore 481 A12
DAPTO
cl. Prestons 393 A14
pl. Bangor 459 A14
DARA
cr. Glenmore Pk 266 C7
D'ARAM
st. Hunters Hill 313 H10
DARANGAN
cl. Waterfall 519 D11
DARAYA
rd. Marayong 244 A8
st. Colyton 270 B6
DARCEY
rd. Castle Hill 248 E4
D'ARCY
av. Lidcombe 339 H11
wy. Minto 482 K1
wy. Minto 483 A1
DARCY
av. Appin 569 E9
pl. E Kurrajong 64 J10
rd. Wentwthvle 276 H13
rd. Wentwthvle 277 A14
rd. Westmead 277 A14
st. Casula 423 H2
st. Granville 308 K11
st. Marsfield 282 A5
st. Parramatta 308 C4
st. Stanhpe Gdn 215 F8
D'ARCY IRVINE
dr. Castle Hill 218 K12
DARDANELLES
rd. Chatswood W 284 F11
st. Mortdale 431 D8
DARE
st. Glenwood 215 C13
DAREEN
st. Beacon Hill 257 B5
st. Frenchs Frst 257 B5
DARGAN
st. Naremburn 315 E2
st. S Windsor 150 K1
st. Yagoona 368 F14
DARGHAN
la. Glebe 12 E10
st. Glebe 12 E10
DARGIE
pl. Eagle Vale 481 A9
st. Mt Pritchard 364 J10
DARICE
pl. Plumpton 242 D12
DARIUS
av. N Narrabeen 199 B15
DARK
cl. Edensor Pk 363 F3
DARKON
pl. Oakhurst 241 H2
DARLEY
ct. Rouse Hill 185 F3
la. Newtown 374 J10
la. Randwick 22 D16
pl. Darlinghurst 4 F11
rd. Bardwell Pk 402 J7
rd. Centennial Pk 22 B16
rd. Leichhardt 9 C13
rd. Manly 288 H10
rd. Randwick 376 H10
st. Darlinghurst 4 F11
st. Forestville 255 K13
st. Killarney Ht 255 K13
st. Marrickville 373 F11
st. Mona Vale 199 C2
st. Neutral Bay 5 K6
st. Newtown 374 H11
st. Sans Souci 433 B15
st. Thirlmere 562 D16
st. Thirlmere 565 D1
st.e, Mona Vale 199 E4
st.w, Mona Vale 199 B1
DARLING
av. Kentlyn 512 J7
av. Lurnea 394 D13
av. Rhodes 311 D7
av. Ruse 512 H1
av. Ruse 512 J7
dr. Haymarket E A8
dr. Haymarket 3 A8
dr. Sydney 3 A4
la. Glebe 12 D10
la. Kensington, off Darling St 376 E12
pl. Sylvania Wtr 462 E10
st. Abbotsbury 333 A13
st. Balmain 7 F8
st. Balmain East 8 C9
st. Bronte 378 A7
st. Chatswood 284 K5
st. Glebe 12 D10
st. Greystanes 306 A5
st. Homebush B 310 E15
st. Kensington 376 E12
st. Penrith 237 A14
st. Roseville 284 K5
st. Rozelle 344 D8
st. St Ives 224 F9
DARLING CAUSEWAY
Bell 57 A10
DARLINGHURST
rd. Darlinghurst 4 F13
rd. Potts Point 4 J7
DARLING ISLAND
rd. Pyrmont 8 H16
DARLING POINT
rd. Darling Point 13 H9
DARLINGTON
dr. Cherrybrook 219 C11
la. Darlington 18 D7
rd. Darlington 18 D7
rd. Newtown 18 D7
st. Stanhpe Gdn 215 D7
DARLY
pl. Dharruk 241 C8
st. Miranda 492 C6
DARMENIA
av. Greystanes 306 E11
DARMOUR
av. Allambie Ht 257 C10
DARNAY
pl. Ambarvale 540 E1
DARNLEY
st. Gordon 253 K4
DAROOK PARK
rd. Cronulla 523 H1
DARRA
pl. St Johns Pk 364 D1
DARRAGH
la. Haberfield 9 A15
la. Haberfield 343 E16
DARRAMBAL
av. Baulkham Hl 248 C10
DARRELL
pl. Oakhurst 241 K4
DARREN
ct. Glenwood 215 K16

STREETS DE

DARRI
av. N Wahroonga....222 F3
av. S Penrith........266 F2
DARRYL
pl. Gymea Bay......491 F8
DART
rd. Bringelly........388 A9
DARTBROOK
rd. Auburn..........339 F2
DARTFORD
rd. Thornleigh......221 D6
st. Mt Pritchard......364 B11
st. Stanhpe Gdn....215 D4
DARTLE
wy. Ambarvale......511 A15
DARTMOOR
cct. Emu Heights......235 A5
la. Emu Heights, off
    Dartmoor Cct.....235 B6
DART THRU
la. Croydon Pk......372 B6
DARU
pl. Glenfield........424 F10
wy. Whalan.........241 B10
DARUGA
av. Pemulwuy......305 D7
DARVALL
rd. Denistone W....280 J12
rd. Eastwood.......280 G8
rd. West Ryde......280 J12
st. Balmain...........7 J11
st. Centennial Pk....21 D9
st. St Leonards....315 E4
DARVELL
st. Bonnyrig Ht......363 G5
DARVILL
rd. Orchard Hills....268 B13
DARWIN
av. Little Bay........437 G14
cl. Wakeley........334 K13
dr. Lapstone........264 H2
pl. Barden Rdg....458 G16
pl. Campbelltown....512 E6
st. Carlingford......280 A1
st. West Ryde......281 A16
DARYL
st. Merrylands W....306 H12
wy. Claymore......481 D12
DASEA
st. Chullora.........369 G5
DASHMERE
st. Bossley Park....333 K9
DASSAULT
cl. Raby............451 F12
DATCHETT
st. Balmain...........8 F9
st. Balmain East.....8 F9
DATE
gr. Glenwood......215 J16
DAUNT
av. Matraville......406 J16
DAVENEY
wy. W Pnnant Hl....248 K2
DAVENPORT
dr. Wallacia........324 K15
DAVESTA
rd. Springwood....172 C16
DAVEY
cct. Emu Heights....235 A6
dr. Dural...........188 G7
la. Jannali.........460 K12
st. Lidcombe......339 K9
DAVID
av. Caringbah......492 H14
av. Casula.........394 G13
av. North Ryde....282 F6
la. St Ives Ch......224 A5
la. Blacktown......244 G16
la. Forest Lodge....11 J16
pl. Mt Annan......479 H15
pl. Peakhurst.....430 A3
pl. Seaforth.......286 J12
rd. Barden Rdg....488 G3
rd. Castle Hill....218 K13
rd. Castle Hill....219 A13
rd. Collaroy Plat....228 J7
rd. Emu Plains....235 F7
rd. Springwood....202 A4
rd.e. Springwood....202 B5
st. Concord........342 A4
st. Crows Nest....315 G8
st. Croydon.......342 C9
st. Dundas Vy....280 A9
st. Earlwood......403 D3

DARTLE
st. Forest Lodge....11 H16
st. Glenbrook....234 A14
st. Greenacre......370 F7
st. Marrickville....373 H12
st. Mascot.........405 H4
st. Mosman........317 D12
st. Mt Pritchard....364 G10
st. S Wntwthve....306 J9
st. Wilberforce.....91 K4
DAVIDSON
av. Concord........341 F5
av. Forestville....255 H9
av. North Rocks....278 J3
av. N Strathfield....341 F5
av. Warrawee......222 H9
cr. Maroubra......407 C15
la. Lakemba.......401 A2
la. St Clair, off
    Davidson Cl......269 K14
pde. Cremorne....316 G5
pl. Airds..........512 D11
rd. Guildford......338 C10
rd. Menai.........458 G8
st. Balmain...........7 F11
st. Greenacre....370 G2
DAVIES
av. Springwood....201 C7
av. Vaucluse.....348 G1
cl. Baulkham HI....247 G14
cl. Mt Wilson......58 K8
la. Surry Hills......20 C4
la. Picton..........561 A5
la. Picton..........563 E1
rd. Padstow......399 F13
rd. Seven Hills....275 D4
rd. Chatswood W....284 E9
rd. Leichhardt.....15 C2
rd. Marsden Pk....182 A11
st. Merrylands....307 D15
st. Mount Druitt....240 H16
st. Newington....310 D11
st. N Parramatta....278 C9
st. Surry Hills......20 B4
wy. Claymore.....481 B12
DAVIESIA
pl. Glenmore Pk....265 H14
DAVINA
cr. Cecil Hills....362 J5
DAVIS
av. Baulkham HI....248 A7
av. Epping........281 D4
la. Bankstown....369 F11
la. Pitt Twn Bttms...122 B3
la. Toowllahra.......22 H5
la. Yagoona......369 F11
pl. Bligh Park....150 D5
pl. Glenhaven....217 J1
pl. Menai.........458 K10
pl. Rooty Hill....272 C3
pl. Thirlmere....565 B1
rd. Marayong....244 C10
rd. Marayong....244 C6
rd. Wetherill Pk...304 E13
st. Dulwich Hill...373 D7
st. Richmond....120 A5
swy. Liverpool....395 D4
swy. Liverpool, off
    Northumberland St...269 D2
rd. Moorebank...395 J8
DEAKIN
av. Glenwood....215 H13
av. Haberfield...343 D15
cl. Springwood....202 E11
pl. Bonnyrig......364 C3
pl. East Killara....254 H6
pl. Kirrawee.......490 J5
pl. W Pnnant Hl....249 A8
pl. Concord......311 K15
pl. Ermington....280 E16
pl. Forestville....256 A7
pl. Silverwater...309 E13
st. West Ryde....311 A1
wy. Wahroonga...222 D3
DEAL
cl. Green Valley....363 B10
DEAN
av. Belmore......371 E15
cl. Oakdale......500 D11
cr. Ermington....280 G15
ct. Baulkham Hl....247 B14
la. Crows Nest, off
    Willoughby La....315 F7
pl. Acacia Gdn....214 J16
pl. Penrith........236 K5
st. Caringbah....492 F14
st. Granville......308 E11

DAWKINS
pl. Ambarvale......510 J12
DAWN
av. Chester Hill....368 D6
av. Mt Pritchard....364 D12
la. Lurnea........394 C6
cl. St Ives Ch....224 B2
cr. Mt Riverview....234 C1
dr. Regents Pk....339 B15
dr. Seven Hills....245 B16
st. Greystanes....305 G2
st. Peakhurst.....430 C6
DAWN FRASER
av. Homebush B....340 C12
DAWSON
av. Camden S....506 K15
av. Earlwood.....402 G3
av. Thornleigh....221 C14
la. Bass Hill......368 D10
la. Woollahra.....22 H5
ml. Mount Druitt....241 E16
pl. Bass Hill.....367 H7
pl. Menai........458 K11
pl. Ruse..........512 E5
pl. Turramurra....252 D3
rd. Mt Hunter....505 B8
st. Croydon......342 F12
st. Epping.......250 F12
st. Fairfield Ht....335 G12
st. Narembum.....315 J2
st. Rookwood....340 C12
st. Surry Hills....19 H3
DAX
pl. Prospect......274 H10
DAY
av. Hobartville....118 E9
cl. Kensington....376 C15
la. Kensington....376 E16
la. Kingsford.....406 E2
pl. Minto.........482 K9
pl. Prospect.....274 J10
rd. Cheltenham....251 A8
st. Ashcroft......394 E1
st. Chatswood....284 H9
st. Colyton......270 C4
st. Drummoyne....344 A3
st. Lansvale.....366 J7
st. Leichhardt.....15 G1
st. Marrickville....373 G16
st. Sydney........C13
st. Sydney.........D1
st. Sydney..........D7
st. Windsor......121 B10
st.n. Silverwater...310 A14
st.s. Lidcombe....339 J1
DAYDREAM
av. Hinchinbrk....393 A1
st. Warriewood...198 G4
DAYMAN
pl. Marsfield.....251 J15
DAYMAR
pl. Castle Cove....286 B5
DAYRELL
av. Mosman.....317 G9
DAYS
la. Hurstville....431 K9
rd. S Marota.....69 G1
DEADMAN
rd. Moorebank....395 J8

DEFARGE
wy. Ambarvale....541 A1
DEFOE
pl. Wiley Park....400 F2
pl. Wetherill Pk...334 G5
pl. Winston Hills....247 F16
pl. Wiley Park....400 F2
DEFRIES
av. Zetland......376 A10
st. Doonside....273 F4
DEHAVILLAND
cr. Raby.........451 H15
DEHLSEN
av. W Pnnant Hl....249 H6
DEIRDRE
dr. Riverstone....183 C7
DELA
cl. Dee Why......258 E5
st. St Ives Ch....224 A5
DELAGE
pl. Ingleburn....453 K7
DELAGOA
pl. Caringbah....492 K7

DE

av. Greystanes....306 E7
st. Strathfield S....371 B6
st. W Pnnant HI....249 K2
DEANE
pl. Bligh Park....150 G7
st. Burwood.....342 A14
st. Glenbrook....263 J1
DEANS
pl. Airds.........512 B11
DEBBIE
cct. Mount Druitt....241 H12
dr. Doonside....243 C5
la. Revesby Ht....428 J5
DEBENHAM
av. Leumeah...482 H12
DEBORAH
av. Lidcombe....340 A7
cl. Fairfield....336 E6
cl. Mt Colah....192 A4
cr. Cmbrdg Pk....237 J7
pl. Eastwood....281 F4
pl. Punchbowl....400 E7
pl. Riverstone...183 B7
rd. Annangrove...186 D3
st. Greystanes...305 H6
DEBRINCAT
av. N St Marys...239 K11
av. Tregear.....240 D9
av. Whalan.....240 D9
DE BURGH
rd. Killara......253 E15
DEBUSSY
pl. Cranebrook....207 J9
DE CASTELLA
dr. Blacktown....273 G6
DECCAN
wy. Bidwill....211 G13
DE CHAIR
av. Springwood....202 B5
rd. Narraweena....258 C7
DECKER
pl. Huntingwd....273 J12
DEE
cl. Prestons....423 F2
pl. Prospect....274 K13
DEEBAN
wk. Cronulla....493 J12
DEEBLE
st. Tennyson....312 E11
DEED
pl. Northmead....277 H7
DEEPFIELDS
rd. Catherine Fd....449 H2
DEEP POOL
wy. Mt Annan....479 D14
DEEPWATER
rd. Castle Cove....285 F4
DEERWOOD
av. Liverpool....395 B10
DEESIDE
av. Baulkham HI....246 K12
cl. S Penrith....266 K2
la. S Penrith, off
    Deeside Cl......266 K2
DEE WHY
la. N Curl Curl, off
    Headland Rd......259 C9
pde. Dee Why....258 J5
pl. Woodbine....481 H9
DELLVIEW
la. Tamarama, off
    Silva St........378 B6
st. Glenbrook....264 B2
st. Tamarama...378 C6
DELLWOOD
av. Earlwood....372 K16
st. Bankstown....399 D4
st. Chatswood W....284 E12
st. S Granville...338 E14
DELMAR
pde. Dee Why....258 G7
pde. Gladesville...312 F12
av. Birchgrove....7 H1
DELORAINE
cl. Hinchinbrk....363 A16
dr. Leonay......234 J14
DELPHINIUM
wy. Kellyville....216 D3
wy. Kellyville, off
    Delphinium Pl....216 D3
DELRAY
av. Wahroonga....223 B4

DELAIGH
av. Baulkham HI....247 C7
av. N Curl Curl....258 H10
DELAMBRE
pl. Hinchinbrk....392 K3
pl. Hinchinbrk....393 A3
DELAMERE
st. Canley Vale....335 J16
DELANEY
av. Silverdale....353 J15
dr. Baulkham HI....247 B11
DELARUE
st. Richmond....119 K5
DE LA SALLE
pl. Castle Hill....218 K10
DELAUNAY
st. Ingleburn....453 F13
DE LAURET
av. Newport....169 E7
DELAVOR
pl. Glenhaven....217 J3
DELAWARE
av. St Ives....224 C8
rd. Ermington...280 C13
rd. Horsley Pk...301 K16
st. Epping.....250 H15
DELECTA
av. Clareville....169 F1
av. Mosman....286 K15
DELFIN
dr. Wattle Grove....395 H13
DELGARNO
rd. Bonnyrig Ht....363 E8
DELGAUN
pl. Baulkham HI....246 J11
DELHI
rd. Chatswood W....283 B9
rd. Mcquarie Pk....283 B9
rd. North Ryde....283 B9
st. Lidcombe....340 A6
DELIA
av. Revesby....398 F5
pde. Engadine...518 F4
DELIVERY
dr. Randwick, off
    Hospital Rd......377 A15
DELL
pl. Georges Hall....367 H9
pl. Belrose......225 K5
st. Blacktown....274 A3
st. Woodpark....306 G16
DELLA
pl. Glendenning....242 G3
DELLER
av. Cabramatta W....365 A8
pl. Blakehurst...432 D13
DELLIT
cl. Doonside....273 C3
DELLS
la. Richmond Lwld....88 H11

GREGORY'S STREET DIRECTORY 57

DE STREETS

DELTA
- cl. Raby 451 D11
- pl. Blacktown 245 D8
- pl. Lane Cove 314 F5
- pl. Sutherland 490 B1
- rd. Lane Cove 314 F4
- row. Wrrngtn Dns ...238 E4

DELVES
- st. Mortdale 430 J5

DELWOOD
- cl. Mona Vale 199 E1

DEMAINE
- av. Bexley North 402 D9

DE MESTRE
- pl. Sydney ....A J15

DEMETRIUS
- rd. Rsemeadow 540 D3

DE MEYRICK
- av. Casula 394 E13
- av. Lurnea 394 E12

DE MILHAU
- rd. Hunters Hill 313 D11

DEMPSEY
- pl. Drummoyne 343 H2
- st. Emu Heights 235 A5
- st. North Ryde 282 E11

DEMPSTER
- cr. Regents Pk 339 B16

DENAWEN
- av. Castle Cove 285 K5

DENBERN
- st. Bossley Park 334 A8
- st. Dean Park 242 H2

DENBIGH
- cl. Castle Hill 216 J9
- cl. Harringtn Pk 478 E5
- pl. Menai 458 H9

DENBY
- st. Marrickville 374 D9

DENDROBIUM
- cr. Elanora Ht 197 J15

DENEB
- pl. Hinchinbrk 393 D5

DENEDEN
- av. Kellyville Rdg ..214 J2

DENFIELD
- cct. St Helens Park .541 A6
- la. Tahrmoor 565 J13

DENGATE
- av. Ashfield 372 J2
- st. Epping 250 F16

DENHAM
- la. Bondi, off
  Edward St 378 B4
- la. Surry Hills ......A D14
- rd. Dundas 279 E13
- rd. Kenthurst 187 B9
- st. Bondi 378 B5
- st. Bondi Beach 378 B5
- st. Darlinghurst 4 C14
- st. Rhodes 311 E8
- st. Surry Hills 4 C14

DENHAM COURT
- rd. Denham Ct 422 A13

DENIEHY
- st. Granville 309 A11

DENING
- cl. Chipping Ntn 366 E16
- st. Drummoyne 343 F2

DENINTEND
- pl. S Penrith 266 F3

DENISE
- av. Glenbrook 263 J2
- cr. Peakhurst 430 C4
- pl. Hornsby 221 E6

DENISON
- av. Lurnea 394 E13
- av. Appin 569 E8
- la. Camperdown 17 D8
- la. Concord, off
  Denison St 342 C1
- la. Newtown 17 D8
- la. Cromer 227 H13
- pl. Windsor Dn 180 K3
- rd. Dulwich Hill 373 D9
- rd. Lewisham 15 A13
- st. Arncliffe 403 E6
- st. Brksmeadow 406 C10
- st. Bondi Jctn 22 E11
- st. Camperdown 17 C4
- st. Carramar 366 K3
- st. Concord 342 C1
- st. Eastgardens 406 E13
- st. Granville 308 A7

DENISTONE
- rd. Denistone 281 D9
- rd. Eastwood 281 D9
- rd. N Parramatta ...278 G8

DENIS WINSTON
- dr. Doonside 273 F2

DENLEY
- la. St Ives 223 K12

DENMAN
- av. Caringbah 492 J7
- av. Haberfield 343 B14
- av. Wiley Park 400 H4
- av. Woolooware 493 D8
- ct. Glenwood 245 G1
- la. Glebe 12 E12
- rd. Georges Hall ...367 F11
- rd. Eastwood 280 H10
- st. Hurstville 431 J8
- st. Turramurra 222 F14

DENMARK
- rd. Riverstone 182 H10
- st. Merrylands 307 G15

DENMEAD
- st. Thirlmere 565 C10

DENNING
- st. Petersham 16 B13
- st. S Coogee 407 H4

DENNIS
- av. Wahroonga 222 B12
- av. Beverly Hills ..401 B15
- st. Campbelltown ..512 A5
- st. Colyton 270 J9
- st. Ermington 310 A1
- st. Greystanes 306 C7
- st. Lakemba 371 B16
- st. Lakemba 401 B1
- st. Lalor Park 245 E12
- st. Thirlmere 565 C7

DENNISON
- cl. Rouse Hill 185 D6

DENNISTOUN
- av. Guildford 337 A5
- av. Guildford W 336 H5
- av. Yennora 336 H5

DENNY
- rd. Picnic Point ...428 B7

DENOCI
- cl. Wetherill Pk ...304 E15

DENOS
- la. Cremorne 316 D5

DENT
- st. Hinchinbrk 363 B14
- pl. Shalvey 210 K14
- st. Brksmeadow 435 J1
- st. Epping 250 C16
- st. Jamisontown ...236 E14

DENTON
- gr. Quakers Hill ...214 A9
- la. Cabramatta, off
  Arthur St 365 J7
- pl. Wallacia 324 K15

DENTS
- pl. Gymea Bay 491 C9

DENVER
- pl. Toongabbie 275 H12
- rd. St Clair 270 G11

DENYA
- cl. Glenmore Pk ...266 E8

DENZIL
- av. St Clair 270 A9
- la. St Clair, off
  Denzil Av 269 K10

DEODAR
- wy. Blacktown 274 E12

DEODARA
- gdn. N Turramurra .223 D2

DEPARTURE
- plz. Mascot 404 D6

DEPOT
- la. Marrickville, off
  Malakoff St 373 K12
- rd. Bankstown 369 D16
- rd. Mortdale 430 F7
- st. Rooty Hill 272 D1

DEPTFORD
- av. Kings Lngly ...245 G5

DERBY
- cr. Chipping Ntn ..396 H1
- la. Camperdown 17 D6
- la. Surry Hills ......F J14
- pl. Camperdown 17 C5
- pl. Glebe 12 F16
- pl. Glossodia 66 A13
- pl. Yarrawarrah ...489 E13
- pwy. Chipping Ntn, off
  Derby Cr 366 H16
- pwy. Chipping Ntn, off
  Derby Cr 396 H1
- rd. Hornsby 222 C1
- st. Blacktown 244 C15
- st. Camperdown 17 C6
- st. Canley Ht 365 D4
- st. Epping 251 B12
- st. Kingswood 237 D13
- st. Kogarah 433 B6
- st. Merrylands 308 B16
- st. Minto 452 H16
- st. Minto Ht 483 F1
- st. Penrith 237 A12
- st. Rooty Hill 242 C15
- st. St Ives 224 C15
- st. Silverwater ...309 F11
- st. Vaucluse 318 G16

DERBYSHIRE
- av. Toongabbie 276 F9
- rd. Leichhardt 10 A10
- rd. Lilyfield 10 A8

DEREK
- pl. Hassall Gr 212 C15

DERMONT
- st. Hassall Gr 211 J14

DERNA
- av. Holsworthy ...426 E8
- cr. Allambie Ht ...257 F11
- rd. Holsworthy ...396 C16

DERNANCOURT
- av. Engadine 518 J1
- pde. Milperra 397 H11

DEROWIE
- av. Homebush 341 A7

DERRIA
- st. Canley Ht 365 D3

DERRIBONG
- cr. Bangor 459 C13
- pl. Thornleigh 221 B6
- st. Villawood 367 D4

DERRIG
- rd. Tennyson 65 F14

DERRILIN
- cl. Bangor 459 B14

DERRING
- la. Kurrajong 64 B15

DERRIWONG
- la. Dural 189 B11
- la. Dural 188 G8
- rd. Dural 189 A13

DERRY
- wy. Bonnyrigg 364 B3

DERWENT
- av. N Wahroonga ..222 K2
- ct. Wattle Grove ..395 H12
- la. Glebe 12 C14
- pde. Blacktown 274 A4
- pl. Bligh Park 150 G7
- pl. Bossley Park ..333 F5
- pl. Castle Hill ...247 K5
- pl. St Clair 300 C1
- pl. Bringelly 387 K5
- pl. Collaroy Plat .228 D11
- pl. Glebe 12 C14
- pl. Mount Druitt ..241 C12
- pl. S Hurstville ..432 B10
- rd. Rouse Hill 185 D8
- rd. St Helens Park.541 J2
- st. Thornleigh 220 G11

DESBOROUGH
- rd. Colyton 269 J5
- rd. St Marys 269 J5

DESDEMONA
- st. Rsemeadow 540 F6

DESLEY
- cr. Prospect 274 H13

DESLIE
- av. Werrington 238 F11

DESMOND
- st. Eastwood 281 H3
- st. Ingleburn 453 C10
- st. Merrylands 307 B13
- st. Merrylands W ..307 B13

DESOUTTER
- av. Bnkstn Aprt ...367 J16

DESPOINTES
- st. Marrickville ..373 K12

DETTMANN
- av. Longueville ...314 C8

DETZNER
- pl. Whalan 240 K9

DEVANEY
- av. Glenmore Pk ..265 J8
- st. Blackett 241 D2

DEVENISH
- st. Greenfld Pk ...334 B12

DEVERE
- av. Belrose 226 A13

DEVERON
- st. St Andrews ...481 K1

DE VILLIERS
- av. Chatswood W ..284 E11

DE VILNITS
- pde. Penrith 236 F10

DEVINE
- st. Erskineville ..374 K10

DEVITT
- av. Newington 310 B15
- cr. The Oaks 502 F14
- pl. Hillsdale 406 H15
- st. Blacktown 244 J16
- st. Narrabeen 229 A7

DEVLIN
- pl. Menai 458 K2
- pl. Quakers Hill .214 B12
- st. Castlereagh ..145 H14
- st. Londonderry ..177 A1
- rd. N Epping 251 C10
- st. Ashcroft 364 F15
- st. Ryde 311 K3
- wy. Bonnyrigg ...364 C6

DEVON
- cl. Bossley Park ..334 B12
- cl. Busby 363 K15
- pl. Collaroy 229 A15
- pl. Galston 159 F10
- pl. Narellan Vale .508 J2
- rd. North Rocks ..278 J2
- rd. Bardwell Pk ..402 J7
- rd. Cmbrdg Pk 237 K9
- rd. Ingleburn 452 K6
- st. N Epping 251 C11
- st. Rooty Hill 272 D3
- st. Rosehill 309 C8
- st. Wahroonga 223 C4

DEVONPORT
- st. Wakeley 334 G16

DEVONSHIRE
- rd. Kemps Ck 360 C16
- rd. Rossmore 390 B7
- st. Chatswood ...284 K11
- st. Crows Nest ...315 G8
- st. Croydon 372 B2
- st. Surry Hills ...19 H2

DEWAR
- pl. Riverstone ...183 C8
- st. St Andrews ...451 J14
- st. Campsie 371 K13

DEWBERRY
- wy. Castle Hill ..248 H3

DEWDNEY
- rd. Emu Plains ...235 H11

DEWDROP
- cl. Acacia Gdn ..214 H14
- la. Wrrngtn Dns, off
  Dewdrop Cl 238 C4

DEWEY
- ct. Maroubra 407 F14
- st. St Helens Park.540 K11

DEWHURST
- av. Castle Hill ..218 B10

DE WITT
- la. Bankstown 399 D4
- la. Fairfield W ..335 C10
- la. Willmott 210 E13
- st. Bankstown 399 D5

DEWRANG
- av. Bradbury 511 D15
- av. Elanora Ht ...198 E16
- st. Carss Park ...432 F13
- st. Lidcombe 339 J4

DEWSBURY
- st. Botany 405 E14
- swy. Liverpool ...395 E13

DEXTER
- la. Rockdale 403 B15
- pl. Plumpton 242 C10
- st. St Helens Park.541 A6

DHARUG
- cl. Mulgoa 324 A5

DHINBURRI
- wy. Pemulwuy 305 E5

DIAMANTINA
- av. Windsor Dn ...151 A16
- cl. St Clair 270 G12

DIAMOND
- av. Glenwood 215 C14
- av. Granville 308 F12
- cr. Bonnyrigg 363 G8
- ct. Newington, off
  Owens Av 310 A16
- pl. Eagle Vale ...481 C7

DIAMOND BAY
- rd. Vaucluse 348 E6

DIAMOND HILL
- dr. Kurrajong Hl ..64 B12

DIAMONTINA
- av. Kearns 451 C16

DIANA
- cr. Kellyville ...216 D3
- av. Roselands ...400 J7
- av. West Pymble .252 G12
- ct. Cecil Hills ..363 A4
- pl. S Penrith 267 B7
- st. Pendle Hill ..306 E2

DIANE
- cl. Greenacre 370 C6
- dr. Lalor Park ...245 H12
- pl. Marsfield 281 K4

DIANELLA
- cl. Kingswood 267 H2
- pl. Mt Annan 509 E4
- pl. Caringbah 492 J5
- wy. Mt Colah 162 E12

DIANNE
- dr. Berowra Ht ..132 J9
- pl. Hawksbry Ht .174 J4

DIANTHUS
- pl. Jannali 460 J10

DIBBLE
- av. Marrickville .373 D14

DIBBLER
- pl. St Helens Park.541 G2

DIBBS
- la. Alexandria 18 F15
- st. Alexandria ...18 F15
- st. Canterbury ..372 E14
- st. Centennial Pk .20 K14

DICK
- st. Balmain 7 G11
- st. Chippendale ...19 A2
- st. Harbord 258 K16
- st. Henley 313 B14
- st. Randwick 377 E12

DICKENS
- dr. Centennial Pk .21 F11
- rd. Ambarvale ...511 A14
- rd. Ambarvale ...541 A1
- rd. Wetherill Pk .334 H6
- st. Winston Hills .247 F16

DICKENSON
- st. Panania 398 D14

DICKIN
- av. Sandringham .463 D10

DICKINSON
- av. Croydon 372 C10

DICKSON
- av. Artarmon 314 J3
- av. W Pnnant Hl .249 D10
- av. West Ryde ...281 B14
- la. Bronte 377 J6
- la. S Windsor ...120 G15
- la. West Ryde ...281 C15
- la. Newtown, off
  King La 374 J10
- pl. Warriewood ..198 J6
- rd. Denham Ct ..422 F16
- rd. Leppington ..420 G6
- st. Bronte 377 J7
- st. Haberfield ..343 D15

---

58 GREGORY'S STREET DIRECTORY

STREETS DO

st. Newtown 374 H10
st. Strathfield 341 A12
DIDCOT
cl. Stanhpe Gdn 215 D4
DIDRIKSEN
av. Newington, off Henricks Av 309 K15
DIEFFENBACH
tce. Bidwill 211 E16
DIENELT
pl. Glenwood 215 B15
DIETZ
la. Oakdale 500 F4
DIFFEY
la. Yagoona 368 H11
st. Yagoona 368 H11
DIGBY
pl. Chipping Ntn 366 G16
DIGGER
cr. Gt Mckrl Bch 109 A13
DIGGERS
av. Gladesville 312 J4
la. Canley Vale, off Freeman Av 366 A3
DIGGINS
st. Beaumont Hills 186 A14
DIGHT
st. Richmond 119 B4
st. Windsor 121 B10
DILGA
cl. Bangor 459 C14
cr. Erskine Park 270 G15
st. Kings Lngly 245 G7
DILKARA
ct. Menai 459 A16
DILKE
rd. Padstow 429 F6
rd. Padstow Ht 429 F8
DILKERA
cl. Hornsby 191 C13
rd. Glenorie 127 K4
DILLON
cl. Barden Rdg 488 H2
la. Paddington 13 A12
pl. Oakhurst 242 C2
st. Paddington 4 K12
st. Ramsgate 433 D13
DILLWYNIA
dr. Glenmore Pk 265 H13
DILLWYNNIA
gr. Heathcote 518 H12
DILSTON
cl. West Hoxton 392 E6
DI MASCIO
pl. Oakhurst 211 H16
DIMBY
pl. Busby 363 G15
DIMENT
wy. Hurstville 432 A6
DINA BETH
av. Blacktown 273 J1
DIND
st. Milsons Point 5 J16
DINDIMA
pl. Bangor 459 B14
pl. Belrose 226 B14
DINE
la. Randwick 407 B1
st. Randwick 377 B16
DINGLE
st. Riverstone 183 A5
DINJERRA
cl. Bangor 459 A15
cr. Oatley 461 A1
DINMORE
pl. Castle Hill 219 A9
DINO
cl. Rooty Hill 271 J3
DINORA
st. Belmore 371 C14
DINTON
st. Prospect 274 K10
D'INZEO
pl. Hinchinbrk 393 A4
DION
pl. Plumpton 241 H8
DIONE
ct. St Clair 269 G11
DIOSMA
pl. Engadine 488 E14
DIPROSE
st. Fairfield 336 J15
DIRE STRAITS
wy. Berala 339 C15
DIRK
cl. Green Valley 363 B10
DISALVO
cl. Cabramatta W 365 C5
DISCOVERY
av. Willmot 210 C12
pl. Oyster Bay 461 D3
DISPENSARY
la. Campsie 371 K12
DISRAELI
rd. Baulkham Hl 277 J1
DISTILLERS
pl. Huntingwd 273 G12
DISTILLERY
dr. Pyrmont 12 D2
DISU
pl. Berowra 133 F10
DIVE
st. Matraville 406 J15
DIVISION
la. Coogee, off Brook St 377 G13
st. Coogee 377 G13
DIXMUDE
st. S Granville 338 G5
DIXON
av. Frenchs Frst 257 B3
cl. Illawong 459 H4
la. Revesby, off Blamey Pl 398 J16
rd. Blaxland 234 B4
st. Abbotsbury 333 C15
st. Haymarket E D3
st. Haymarket 3 E10
st. Mount Druitt 271 E5
st. Parramatta 308 B7
st. Sydney E D3
st. Sydney 3 E10
DIXSON
av. Dulwich Hill 373 B8
DOAK
av. Llandilo 178 D13
DOBBIE
pl. Glenorie 128 C5
DOBELL
cct. St Clair 270 B13
la. St Clair, off Dobell Cct 270 B13
pl. Kenthurst 158 A9
pl. St Ives 224 C9
rd. Claymore 481 C13
rd. Eagle Vale 480 K10
rd. Engadine 489 A15
st. Mt Pritchard 364 J11
DOBROYD
av. Camden 507 A9
la. Haberfield 9 B5
pde. Haberfield 9 B5
pde. Haberfield 342 K12
pde. Haberfield 343 G11
pde. Haberfield 343 D11
pde. Haberfield 343 B12
pde. Haberfield 343 C12
rd. Balgowlah Ht 287 J14
DOBROYD SCENIC
dr. Balgowlah Ht 287 K15
DOBSON
cl. Edensor Pk 363 F3
cr. Baulkham Hl 247 H10
cr. Dundas Vy 280 D10
cr. Ryde 282 C14
pl. Emu Heights 234 K6
st. Thornleigh 220 H10
DOBSON DORKING
pl. Faulconbdg 171 K12
DOBU
pl. Glenfield 424 G10
DOCHARTY
rd. Bradbury 511 J11
DOCK
rd. Birchgrove 7 J4
DOCKER
la. Chippendale 18 K2
DOCOS
cr. Bexley 432 D2
DOCTOR LAWSON
pl. Rooty Hill 272 F5
DODD
pl. Cranebrook 207 G12
DODDS
st. Naremburn 315 F3
DODFORD
rd. Llandilo 178 E14
DODS
pl. Doonside 273 F2
DODSON
av. Cronulla 493 H12
cr. Winston Hills 277 G4
DOHENY
cl. Baulkham Hl 247 B1
DOHERTY
av. Glenhaven 218 C2
st. Quakers Hill 214 F12
DOIG
av. Denistone E 281 H10
st. Wentwthvle 277 D10
DOLAN
la. Woollahra 22 F4
st. Ryde 312 E3
DOLANS
rd.s, Woolooware 493 D12
DOLE
pl. Kenthurst 156 K10
DOLGE
pl. Ambarvale 510 H15
DOLLIN
st. Colyton 270 C7
DOLLINS
rd. Blaxlands Rdg 64 J6
DOLOMITE
pl. Eagle Vale 481 E5
rd. Cranebrook 207 D14
DOLPHIN
cl. Chiswick 343 B2
cl. Clarmnt Ms 238 J16
cl. Green Valley 363 A12
cr. Avalon 140 D10
la. Coogee 377 E15
st. Coogee 377 E15
st. Randwick 377 C15
DOMAIN
ct. Bella Vista 246 J4
DOMBEY
pl. Ambarvale 510 J13
DOMENIC
cl. Hoxton Park 392 K9
DOMENICO
cl. West Hoxton 392 D4
DOMINIC
st. Woolooware 493 C12
DOMINION
cr. Mosman 317 F10
DOMINISH
cr. Camden S 506 K15
DON
cl. St Clair 269 K16
pl. Kearns 451 B15
st. Kurrajong Ht 63 E12
st. Newtown 17 D14
DONAHUE
cl. Prairiewood 334 E9
DONALBAIN
cct. Rsemeadow 540 C4
DONALD
av. Epping 281 E3
pl. Bondi Jctn 22 J10
st. Carlingford 279 J2
st. Hurstville 431 H1
st. North Ryde 283 A10
st. Old Guildford 337 E11
st. Picnic Point 428 B7
st. Yennora 337 E11
DONALDSON
st. Bradbury 511 G10
st. Pagewood 406 D8
DONATO
st. Smithfield 336 A5
DONCASTER
av. Casula 394 G16
av. Cawdor 506 D16
av. Kensington 376 E15
av. Kingsford 406 E2
av. Narellan 478 H10
av. West Pymble 252 G9
DONE
st. Arncliffe 403 G7
DONEGAL
av. Smithfield 335 E2
pl. Rouse Hill 185 D8
rd. Killarney Ht 286 B2
DONELLY
pl. Frenchs Frst 255 G1
DONGOLA
cct. Schofields 213 J5
DONINGTON
av. Georges Hall 368 C14
DON JUAN
av. Randwick 377 B15
DONLEA
wy. Mt Colah 162 E15
DON MILLS
av. Hebersham 241 F4
DONNA
pl. Acacia Gdn 214 G14
pl. Miranda 491 J1
DONNAN
st. Bexley 402 G15
DONNEGAL
ct. Castle Hill 216 J9
DONNELLAN
cct. Clovelly 377 K13
pl. Blacktown, off Campbell St 274 H1
DONNELLY
cl. Liberty Gr 311 B10
st. Balmain 7 J12
st. Crows Nest 315 F4
st. Guildford 337 B2
st. Naremburn 315 F4
st. Putney 312 C7
DONOHOES
av. Mulgoa 323 K3
DONOHUE
st. Kings Park 244 D1
DONOVAN
av. Maroubra 406 G12
pl. Bonnyrigg 364 D5
st. Eastwood 281 J8
st. Revesby Ht 428 K6
DONS
rd. Dural 189 E15
DOODSON
av. Lidcombe 339 J7
DOODY
st. Alexandria 375 D14
st. Gladesville 312 G11
DOOHAT
av. N Sydney K A2
av. N Sydney 5 E5
la. N Sydney K A3
DOOLAN
la. Balmain 7 A8
st. Dean Park 212 F16
DOOLEY
av. Bass Hill 368 C13
DOOMBEN
av. Eastwood 281 B6
cl. Casula 394 D15
DOON
dr. Sans Souci 462 K5
pl. St Andrews 482 A1
st. Marayong 243 G6
DOONKUNA
st. Beverly Hills 401 D8
DOONMORE
st. Penrith 237 A14
DOONSIDE
cr. Blacktown 243 J14
cr. Blacktown 244 B14
cr. Doonside 243 C13
cr. Woodcroft 243 C13
rd. Arndell Park 273 D9
rd. Doonside 243 C15
rd. Doonside 243 D16
DORA
cr. Dundas 279 G14
st. Blacktown 274 E6
st. Hurstville 431 G1
st. Marsfield 282 C4
DORADILLO
pl. Eschol Park 481 B4
DORADO
pl. Hinchinbrk 393 D3
st. Erskine Park 270 F16
DORAHY
st. Dundas 279 K12
DORAL
pl. Liverpool 395 A10
DORAN
av. Lurnea 394 E7
dr. Castle Hill 217 F12
st. Kingsford 406 E2
DORCAS
pl. Rsemeadow 540 J10
DORE
pl. Mt Annan 479 H15
DOREEN
cr. Baulkham Hl 247 C10
DORHAUER
la. Woollahra 21 K4
pl. Woollahra 21 J4
DORIS
av. Earlwood 402 G3
av. Miranda 461 J16
la. N Sydney 6 A9
pl. Emerton 240 K5
st. Greystanes 305 G5
st. N Sydney 6 A9
st. Ashfield, off Heighway Av 372 G2
st. Picnic Point 428 B8
DORIS HIRST
pl. W Pnnant Hl 218 K15
DORKING
rd. Cabarita 342 E1
DORLTON
st. Kings Lngly 245 E7
DORMAN
cr. Lindfield 283 H2
DORMER
cl. Elderslie 507 K2
gr. Quakers Hill 214 D14
DORMITORY HILL
rd. Scheyville 124 A6
DORNOCH
ct. Castle Hill 218 E7
st. Winston Hills 277 D3
DOROTHY
cr. Colyton 270 E5
ct. Baulkham Hl 247 D3
st. Cromer 228 C15
st. Freemns Rch 90 D2
st. Hebersham 241 F10
st. Merrylands 307 C7
st. Mt Pritchard 364 G11
st. Rydalmere 309 J3
st. Ryde 282 A10
st. Sefton 338 E13
st. Wentwthvle 276 J13
DOROTHY ALISON
st. Moore Park 21 C6
DORRE
pl. Green Valley 363 B10
DORRIE
pl. Quakers Hill 214 C13
DORRIGO
av. Hoxton Park 392 K6
av. N Balgowlah 287 B4
cl. Bangor 459 C14
cr. Bow Bowing 452 D15
la. Sans Souci 463 A5
DORRINGTON
cr. S Windsor 151 B8
pl. Glenmore Pk 266 A5
DORRIT
wy. Ambarvale 511 B15
DORRITT
st. Lane Cove 314 E3
DORSET
av. Northmead 278 C4
cl. Belrose 225 K11
cl. Elderslie 507 K1
cl. Wakeley 364 J1
dr. St Ives 223 K16
dr. St Ives 224 A14
pl. Miller 393 H3
rd. Heathcote 518 D10
rd. Northbridge 316 F1
st. Blacktown 274 G6
st. Cmbrdg Pk 237 J8
st. Epping 251 D13
DOT
la. Leichhardt 16 A4
st. Marrickville 373 G12
DOTTEREL
pl. Ingleburn 453 H6
pl. Woronora Ht 489 E5
st. Hinchinbrk 393 D1
DOUGAN
st. Ashfield 372 F6
DOUGHERTY
la. N Willoughby 285 D10
st. Rosebery 405 H3
DOUGLAS
av. Chatswood 285 D6
av. N Epping 251 F8

GREGORY'S STREET DIRECTORY 59

DO STREETS

av. Wahroonga	222	D3
bvd. Ingleburn	453	K9
cl. Green Valley	363	C11
cl. Randwick	377	F11
cl. Stanmore	16	B9
pde. Dover Ht	348	G14
pl. Miranda	461	J16
rd. Blacktown	273	E4
rd. Doonside	273	E4
rd. Kurrajong Ht	63	F13
rd. Quakers Hill	213	G13
st. Bardwell Vy	402	J9
st. Clovelly	377	F10
st. Earlwood	402	D7
st. Fairfield	336	F9
st. Faulconbdg	171	C15
st. Hobartville	118	D6
st. Merrylands	307	A9
st. N Richmond	87	E10
st. Panania	428	D5
st. Putney	311	K8
st. Randwick	377	F10
st. Redfern	19	E10
st. St Ives	224	B10
st. Springwood	201	D1
st. Stanmore	16	B9
st. Waterloo	19	E10

DOUGLAS FARM
rd. Kurrajong Ht ...63 K12

DOUGLAS HAIG
st. Oatley ...430 H12

DOUGLAS McMASTER
pl. Llandilo ...209 G2

DOUGLAS PARK
dr. Douglas Park ...568 E11
dr. Douglas Park ...568 E13
dr. Douglas Park ...568 G7

DOUGLASS
av. Carlingford ...249 J15
la. Sydney ...E E3
la. Sydney ...3 F8
st. Cromer ...228 A16
st. Sydney ...E E2
st. Sydney ...3 E9

DOULTON
av. Beacon Hill ...257 G8
dr. Cherrybrook ...219 C13

DOUNE
ct. Castle Hill ...218 E7

DOURO
pl. Airds ...511 K15
st. Marayong ...243 J7

DOUST
pl. Grasmere ...475 J16
pl. Shalvey ...211 C13
st. Bass Hill ...368 C7
st. Chester Hill ...368 C7

DOVE
cl. Woronora Ht ...489 G2
cl. Randwick ...377 F10
cl. Hinchinbrk ...363 C16
pl. Ingleburn ...453 H7
pl. St Clair ...269 H11
rd. Revesby ...399 A12

DOVECOTE
gln. Wrrngtn Dns ...237 K4

DOVEDALE
cl. Glen Alpine ...510 D10

DOVELEY
rd. Como ...460 E6

DOVER
ct. Castle Hill ...219 A11
la. Rose Bay, off
 Dover Rd ...348 C11
pl. Engadine ...489 C16
pl. West Hoxton ...392 C8
rd. Dover Ht ...348 D11
rd. Rose Bay ...348 B10
st. Botany ...405 F12
st. Marsfield ...281 K4
st. Summer Hill ...373 E4
wy. Stanhpe Gdn ...215 F7

DOW
pl. Marayong ...244 A4

DOWD
la. East Ryde ...282 K16

DOWDING
cl. Cecil Hills ...362 J8
st. Panania ...398 B14

DOWE
pl. Bligh Park ...150 D6

DOWEL
st. Chatswood ...285 A6

DOWLAND
st. Bonnyrigg Ht ...363 D7

DOWLE
pl. Camden S ...507 B16
st. Douglas Park ...568 G4

DOWLES
la. Bickley Vale ...505 J12

DOWLING
la. Kensington, off
 Ingram St ...376 A12
pl. S Windsor ...120 K15
st. Arncliffe ...403 D7
st. Bardwell Vy ...402 D7
st. Kensington ...376 A12
st. Leumeah ...482 D15
st. Queenscliff ...288 F2
st. West Hoxton ...391 J12
st. Woolmloo ...4 G7
st. Zetland ...376 A12

DOWNES
cl. Illawong ...459 K4
cr. Currans Hills ...479 G10
ct. Belfield ...371 D9
pl. Colyton ...270 D7
st. N Epping ...251 J9

DOWNEY
la. Fairfield, off
 Harris St ...336 E12
st. Bexley ...402 F16

DOWNING
av. Cmbrdg Gdn ...237 G1
av. Regents Pk ...369 E1
pl. Gladesville ...313 A11
st. Epping ...250 F14
st. Picton ...563 G2

DOWNPATRICK
rd. Killarney Ht ...255 K15

DOWNSHIRE
pde. Chester Hill ...368 C4
st. Dawes Point ...1 F8
st. Dawes Point ...1 F8

DOWRENA
pl. Berowra ...133 D10

DOWSETT
rd. Kingsgrove ...402 A12

DOYLE
cl. Wetherill Pk ...334 D4
pl. Baulkham Hl ...246 J15
pl. Gordon ...253 D12
pl. Marayong ...244 C3
rd. Padstow ...429 D1
rd. Revesby ...399 A13
st. Barden Rdge ...458 K16

DRACIC
st. S Wntwthvle ...306 J9

DRAGO
rd. Hinchinbrk ...393 D4

DRAKE
av. Caringbah ...492 K4
la. Jamisontown, off
 Drake St ...266 D5
pl. Blacktown ...275 A7
pl. Shalvey ...211 B13
st. Artarmon ...284 J14
st. Concord ...342 A1
st. Jamisontown ...266 D5
st. Panania ...398 D16

DRAKES
la. Ashfield ...372 J3

DRANSFIELD
av. Mascot ...405 F7
rd. Edensor Pk ...363 F4

DRAPER
pl. Leonay ...264 J2

DRAVA
st. Kearns ...451 B16

DRAVET
st. Padstow ...399 B11

DRAWBRIDGE
pl. Castle Hill ...217 E4

DRAYTON
av. Castle Hill ...248 A5
pl. Edensor Pk ...333 F14

DREADNOUGHT
rd. Oxford Falls ...227 A16
st. Roselands ...401 B5

DREAM HOUSE
la. Mosman, off
 Spit Rd ...287 B16

DREDGE
av. Douglas Park ...568 J14
av. Moorebank ...396 D7
pwy. Moorebank, off
 Dredge Av ...396 E7

DREMEDAY
st. Northmead ...248 B15

DRESDEN
av. Beacon Hill ...257 F7
av. Castle Hill ...247 F1

DRESS CIRCLE
rd. Avalon ...170 A4

DRESSLER
ct. Holroyd ...307 K11

DREW
pl. Belrose ...256 A1
st. Greenacre ...370 G11
st. Westmead ...307 H3

DRIFT
rd. Richmond ...117 H7

DRIFTWAY
dr. Pemulwuy ...305 F5

DRISCOLL
av. Rooty Hill ...272 B5
pl. Barden Rdg ...488 F14
st. Abbotsbury ...333 B15

DRIVER
av. Moore Park ...20 H3
av. Wallacia ...324 K13
pl. Bonnyrigg ...364 C4
st. Denistone W ...280 K13

DROMANA
rd. Marsden Pk ...181 K14

DRONE
st. Greenacre ...370 H10

DROOD
pl. Ambarvale ...510 J14

DROVER
rd. Bnkstn Aprt ...367 H16

DROVERS
wy. Lindfield ...284 C2

DRUERY
la. Hurstville ...431 K8

DRUITT
la. Sydney ...C E13
la. Sydney ...3 E7
la. Sydney ...C E11
la. Sydney ...3 E6
st. Wrrngtn Cty ...238 E9
st. Mount Druitt ...241 C11
st. Sydney ...C E12
st. Sydney ...3 E6

DRUMALBYN
rd. Bellevue Hill ...347 G13
st. Ingleburn ...453 C9

DRUMARD
av. Leumeah ...482 C14

DRUMCLIFF
av. Killarney Ht ...255 K15

DRUMMOND
la. Belmore ...401 F2
la. Warwck Frm ...365 G16
la. Beaumont Hills ...185 G15
pl. Kurrajong ...85 E3
pl. Oyster Bay ...461 A7
st. Belmore ...401 F1
st. S Windsor ...120 G15
st. Warwck Frm ...365 G16

DRUMMOYNE
av. Drummoyne ...313 G15
cr. St Johns Pk ...364 G4

DRURY
pl. Hebersham ...241 G1

DRYAD
pl. Leonay ...264 J2

DRYBERRY
av. St Clair ...269 G16

DRY DEN
pl. Wetherill Pk ...334 J6

DRYDEN
av. Carlingford ...249 E13
av. Oakhurst ...242 A5
rd. N Turramurra ...223 E7
st. Campsie ...372 B11

DRY LAKES
rd. Thirlmere ...564 A4

DRYNAN
st. Summer Hill ...373 B5

DRYSDALE
av. Picnic Point ...428 E8
cct. Beaumont Hills ...185 H14
ct. Plumpton ...242 C7
pl. Casula ...424 E2
pl. Kareela ...461 D13
pl. Elderslie ...507 J2
rd. Mt Pritchard ...364 J11

st. Claymore	481	A10
st. Eagle Vale	481	A9

DUAL
pl. Pemulwuy ...305 E6

DUARDO
st. Edensor Pk ...333 H15

DUBARDA
st. Engadine ...488 F16

DUBBO
pl. Bangor ...459 C14
st. Quakers Hill ...244 A2

DUBLIN
av. Killarney Ht ...256 C16
st. Glendenning ...242 J3
st. Smithfield ...335 D6

DUCHESS
av. Rodd Point ...343 E8
cl. Kellyville Rdg ...215 B3
wy. Minto ...482 J7

DUCK
pl. Hinchinbrk ...393 D1
st. Auburn ...309 B13

DUCKER
av. Hobartville ...118 E9

DUCKMALLOIS
av. Blacktown ...274 G5

DUCROS
st. Petersham ...15 F13

DUDLEY
av. Bankstown ...399 C4
av. Blacktown ...244 B15
av. Caringbah ...492 J11
av. Roseville ...284 J2
la. Woollahra ...22 G5
la. Tahmoor ...565 F12
rd. Guildford ...338 D10
rd. Rose Bay ...348 D8
st. Asquith ...192 B9
st. Auburn ...339 B3
st. Balgowlah ...287 F8
st. Berala ...339 D10
st. Bondi ...378 D3
st. Coogee ...407 D1
st. Haberfield ...343 E13
st. Hurstville ...431 F1
st. Kirrawee ...491 C1
st. Lidcombe ...339 D10
st. Marrickville ...373 J3
st. Mount Druitt ...241 C14
st. Paddington ...21 E1
st. Pagewood ...405 K10
st. Penshurst ...431 H7
st. Punchbowl ...400 D3
st. Punchbowl ...400 E4
st. Randwick ...377 D16
st. Rydalmere ...279 C16

DUER
pl. Cherrybrook ...219 J11

DU FAUR
st. N Turramurra ...193 F12

DUFEK
pl. Tregear ...240 B5

DUFF
pl. Castle Hill ...218 B9
rd. Cecil Park ...331 E13
st. Arncliffe ...403 D7
st. Burwood ...341 K16
st. Turramurra ...222 F15

DUFFY
av. Grose Vale ...85 D15
av. Kingsgrove ...401 K6
av. Thornleigh ...221 A10
av. Westleigh ...220 E9
st. Merrylands W ...306 J14

DUGALD
rd. Mosman ...317 D8
st. Riverstone ...183 D8

DUGGAN
cr. Connells Pt ...431 J13
st. Lalor Park ...245 E14
st. Douglas Park ...568 G5

DUGUID
st. Mascot ...405 A5

DUIGNAN
cl. Epping ...281 D3

DUKE
av. Concord ...342 D5
av. Rodd Point ...343 E8
cl. Green Valley ...362 K11
pl. Balmain East ...8 E8
rd. Wilberforce ...92 A1
st. Balmain East ...8 E7
st. Btn-le-Sds ...433 K8
st. Campsie ...372 B13
st. Canley Ht ...365 G1

st. East Hills	427	K4
st. Forestville	255	F10
st. Granville	308	E9
st. Kensington	376	D11
st. Merrylands	307	A9
st. Rooty Hill	241	H13
st. Strathfield	341	E11

DUKE OF EDINBURGH
pde. Clontarf ...287 F15

DUKES
pl. Emu Plains ...235 C11

DUKIC
st. Bonnyrigg Ht ...363 A7

DULCIE
st. Seven Hills ...245 B16

DULERAS
rd. Menai ...459 A4

DULHUNTY
cr. Cranebrook ...207 D9

DULIN
cl. Bangor ...459 B15

DULLAI
av. Pemulwuy ...305 E6

DULWICH
rd. Chatswood W ...284 F7
rd. Roseville ...284 F7
rd. Vineyard ...152 F11
st. Dulwich Hill ...373 E9

DUMARESQ
rd. Rose Bay ...348 B8
st. Campbelltown ...511 E5
st. Gordon ...253 F8

DUMAS
pl. Winston Hills ...247 E16

DU MAURIER
pl. Wetherill Pk ...335 A6

DUMBARTON
pl. Engadine ...489 A8
st. McMahons Pt ...5 B12

DUMBLE
st. Seven Hills ...275 D3

DUMFRIES
rd. St Andrews ...451 K16
st. Winston Hills ...277 E15

DUMIC
pl. Cromer ...228 E15

DUMPU
st. Holsworthy ...426 G7

DUNALLEY
st. West Hoxton ...392 D5

DUNARA
gdn. Point Piper ...14 K2

DUNBAR
av. Regents Pk ...369 C2
av. Wrrngtn Cty ...238 E8
st. Normanhurst ...221 F11
pl. Illawong ...459 D5
pl. Kellyville ...217 A2
pl. Mt Annan ...479 E16
st. Ryde ...281 K16
st. St Andrews ...452 A13
st. Silverdale ...353 H16
st. Watsons Bay ...318 G15

DUNBARS
rd. Werombi ...443 D6

DUNBIER
av. Lurnea ...394 F7

DUNBIL
ct. Bangor ...459 B15

DUNBLANE
st. Camperdwn ...17 F4

DUNCAN
cl. Glenmore Pk ...265 F9
cr. Collaroy Plat ...228 K13
la. Maroubra ...407 E11
pl. Epping ...280 J1
st. Arncliffe ...403 J8
st. Balmain ...8 A9
st. Drummoyne ...343 J5
st. Maroubra ...407 E11
st. Minto Ht ...483 J2
st. Punchbowl ...400 D5
st. Richmond ...120 B5

DUNCANSBY
cr. St Andrews ...452 B15

DUNCRAIG
dr. Kellyville ...186 K15

DUNDAS
pl. Wakeley ...334 G13
st. Coogee ...407 H3

DUNDEE
pl. St Andrews ...481 J3
st. Cmbrdg Pk ...237 H9

60 GREGORY'S STREET DIRECTORY

STREETS EA

st. Engadine.....488 J10
st. Sadleir.....364 C16
DUNDILLA
rd. Frenchs Frst.....256 D2
DUNDRA
cl. Bangor.....459 B14
DUNDRUM
gr. Kellyville Rdg.....185 C16
gr. Kellyville Rdg.....215 C1
DUNEBA
av. Kirrawee.....491 A8
av. West Pymble.....253 B12
dr. Westleigh.....220 E9
pl. Frenchs Frst.....255 K2
DUNGARA
cr. Glenmore Pk.....266 C11
cr. Stanhpe Gdn.....215 D8
dr. Pemulwuy.....305 E7
pl. Winmalee.....173 A10
DUNGARTH
la. *Emu Heights, off Dungarth Pl.....234 K6*
pl. Emu Heights.....234 K6
DUNGATE
la. Sydney.....F A2
la. Sydney.....3 H9
DUNGOG
pl. Bangor.....459 C13
DUNGOWAN
la. *Manly, off Ashburner St.....288 J10*
DUNGULLIN
wy. E Kurrajong.....66 G4
DUNHEVED
cct. St Marys.....239 F6
rd. Cmbrdg Gdn.....237 G5
rd. Cmbrdg Pk.....238 A6
rd. Wrrngtn Cty.....238 G7
rd. Wrrngtn Dns.....238 A6
DUNK
cl. Green Valley.....363 A13
pl. Kings Lngly.....245 E6
DUNKELD
av. Baulkham Hl.....246 J10
av. Hurlstone Pk.....372 J12
cl. Burraneer.....493 E15
la. Hurlstone Pk.....372 J12
pl. Dural.....219 G4
pl. St Andrews.....452 C12
DUNKIRK
av. Kingsgrove.....402 B5
DUNKLEY
ct. Rooty Hill.....272 C5
pl. Werrington.....238 K10
st. Smithfield.....335 B7
DUNLEA
rd. Engadine.....518 F3
DUNLEAVY
st. Prairiewood.....334 D11
DUNLEY
pl. Castle Hill.....219 A8
DUNLOP
av. Harringtn Pk.....478 K4
la. Roselands.....400 H6
pl. Picton.....563 E10
st. Epping.....280 E3
st. N Parramatta.....278 B12
st. Roselands.....400 J6
st. Strathfield S.....371 B6
wy. Minto.....482 J8
DUNMORE
av. Carlingford.....279 F5
cr. Casula.....394 K15
pl. Barden Rdg.....488 H4
pl. Wrrngtn Cty.....238 F4
rd. Epping.....250 K12
rd. West Ryde.....281 C16
st. Croydon Pk.....372 B7
st. Pendle Hill.....276 E15
st. Wentwthvle.....277 A16
st.n, Bexley.....402 K15
st.s, Bexley.....433 A1
DUNN
pl. Cranebrook.....207 E13
pl. Prairiewood.....334 E10
rd. Smeaton Gra.....479 D5
wy. Blacktown.....273 H6
DUNNA
la. *Glenmore Pk, off Dunna Pl.....266 C11*
pl. Glenmore Pk.....266 C11
DUNNING
av. Rosebery.....375 G16
av. Zetland.....375 G16
DUNNS
la. Burwood.....341 K13
rd. Maraylya.....124 E3
DUNOIS
st. Longueville.....314 D8
DUNOON
av. West Pymble.....253 B12
pl. Bangor.....459 B13
st. Berowra Ht.....132 J11
DUNRAVEN
wy. Cherrybrook.....219 B14
DUNROSS
pl. Beaumont Hills.....215 F2
DUNROSSIL
av. Carlingford.....250 A16
av. Casula.....394 J12
av. Fairfield E.....336 J12
DUNSHEA
pl. Guildford.....337 B3
st. Denistone W.....280 K12
DUNSMORE
st. Rooty Hill.....272 E2
DUNSTABLE
rd. Blacktown.....244 K10
DUNSTAFFENAGE
st. Hurlstone Pk.....372 K12
DUNSTAFFNAGE
pl. Erskine Park.....300 F3
DUNSTAN
av. Milperra.....397 D10
pl. Bligh Park.....150 K6
pl. Engadine.....518 E4
st. Croydon Pk.....372 D9
st. Fairfield W.....334 J10
DUNTROON
av. Epping.....250 F16
av. Roseville.....285 B3
av. Roseville Ch.....285 D2
av. St Leonards.....315 D7
la. *Hurlstone Pk, off Duntroon St.....373 B10*
st. Hurlstone Pk.....373 B11
st. Hurlstone Pk.....373 A13
DUNWELL
av. Loftus.....490 B9
DUPAS
st. Smithfield.....305 K14
DURABA
pl. Caringbah.....492 J6
pl. S Penrith.....266 J7
DURACK
cl. Edensor Pk.....363 E4
pl. Casula.....424 F2
pl. St Helens Park.....541 A7
pl. St Ives.....224 F8
DURAL
cr. Engadine.....489 E8
la. Hornsby.....221 F1
pl. Dharruk.....241 D10
st. Dural.....158 B16
st. Hornsby.....221 E1
st. Kenthurst.....188 B1
DURALI
av. Winmalee.....173 A9
rd. Glenmore Pk.....266 D12
DURANT
la. Yagoona.....369 A11
pl. Cherrybrook.....219 F16
DURANTA
cl. Casula.....423 H2
DURBAN
wy. Minto.....482 K2
DURBAR
av. Kirrawee.....491 B3
DURDANS
av. Rosebery.....375 F16
DURDEN
pl. Ambarvale.....540 E1
DURHAM
av. *St Ives, off Denley La.....223 K12*
cl. Bonnyrigg Ht.....363 C4
cl. Dural.....188 G1
cl. Mcquarie Pk.....252 J16
gr. Windsor Dn.....151 B16
la. *Dulwich Hill, off Durham St.....373 E10*
la. Springwood.....201 F3
la. Stanmore.....16 J9
pl. Sylvania.....461 J13
rd. Schofields.....212 H5
st. Allawah.....432 D6
st. Carlton.....432 D6
st. Concord.....342 E6
st. Douglas Park.....568 E7
st. Dulwich Hill.....373 E10
st. Hunters Hill.....313 F11
st. Hurstville.....432 D6
st. Minto.....452 G16
st. Mount Druitt.....271 A1
st. N Epping.....251 C9
st. Oxley Park.....240 G16
st. Rosehill.....309 E8
st. Stanmore.....16 J9
DURI
cl. Bangor.....459 B13
pl. Bonnyrigg.....364 A9
st. Malabar.....437 F8
DURIAN
pl. Wetherill Pk.....333 K3
DURKIN
pl. Peakhurst.....430 G3
DURNESS
pl. St Andrews.....452 A13
DURRAS
cl. Woodcroft.....243 F11
pl. Leumeah.....482 F15
st. Prestons.....422 K1
DURROW
av. Killarney Ht.....256 C16
DURSLEY
rd. Yennora.....336 G6
DURUMBIL
rd. Duffys Frst.....195 F3
D'URVILLE
av. Tregear.....240 F6
DURWARD
st. Dean Park.....212 G16
DUTBA
la. *Glenmore Pk, off Dutba Pl.....266 B10*
pl. Glenmore Pk.....266 B10
DUTCH
la. *St Clair, off Dutch Pl.....269 F11*
pl. Oakhurst.....242 C3
pl. St Clair.....269 G11
DUTERREAU
wy. Claymore.....481 E11
DUTRUC
st. Randwick.....377 C13
DUTTON
la. Cabramatta.....365 J7
pl. Glenmore Pk.....266 A7
rd. Beaumont Hills.....185 J16
st. Bankstown.....369 A14
st. Yagoona.....369 A14
DUVAL
st. Hebersham.....241 G2
DUXFORD
la. *Paddington, off Broughton St.....13 D15*
st. Paddington.....13 C15
DUXTON
ct. Rouse Hill.....185 D5
DWIGHT
st. Greystanes.....306 D7
DWYER
av. Blakehurst.....432 E12
av. Little Bay.....437 A12
cl. Fairfield W.....335 A13
cr. Seven Hills.....245 D15
la. Blakehurst.....432 F12
la. Woollahra.....21 J4
pl. St Helens Park.....541 A7
pl. S Penrith.....236 K16
rd. Bringelly.....387 A6
rd. Leppington.....450 C1
st. Chippendale.....E A16
st. Chippendale.....3 C16
st. Gymea.....491 G2
st. Ryde.....282 G15
DYCE
pl. St Andrews.....481 K1
DYGAL
st. Mona Vale.....199 B3
DYINDA
pl. Miranda.....492 A1
DYLAN
pl. W Pnnant Hl.....248 H7
DYMOND
rd. Bargo.....567 F5
DYMPNA
st. Cromer.....228 F13
DYSON
la. Woollahra.....22 J4
pl. Fairfield W.....335 B12
pl. Glenmore Pk.....265 K8
st. Putney.....312 A9
wy. Blackett.....241 B2
wy. Claymore.....481 B12

E

EACHAM
st. Fairfield W.....335 G8
EAGAR
la. Sydney.....E E3
la. Sydney.....3 F10
st. Sydney.....E E3
st. Sydney.....3 E10
EAGLE
pl. St Johns Pk.....334 C16
st. Ryde.....311 K3
st. Wallacia.....324 J13
wy. Glenwood.....215 F14
EAGLE CREEK
rd. Theresa Park.....443 D6
rd. Werombi.....443 D6
EAGLEHAWK
pl. W Pnnant Hl.....248 E8
st. Heckenberg.....363 K14
EAGLEMONT
cr. Campbelltown.....511 H4
EAGLES
rd. Cawdor.....506 D16
EAGLE VALE
dr. Eagle Vale.....481 B6
dr. Eschol Park.....481 B6
EAGLEVIEW
pl. Baulkham Hl.....216 J13
rd. Ingleburn.....453 C16
rd. Minto.....483 A4
EALING
pl. Quakers Hill.....214 D9
EAMES
av. Baulkham Hl.....247 C10
EARL
la. *Randwick, off Stephen St.....377 B9*
pl. Cecil Hills.....362 K5
pl. Potts Point.....4 J6
st. Beacon Hill.....257 E6
st. Canley Ht.....365 G2
st. Canley Vale.....365 G2
st. Hunters Hill.....313 B6
st. Merrylands.....338 B1
st. Mosman.....316 J5
st. Mount Druitt.....241 E13
st. Potts Point.....4 J6
st. Randwick.....377 B9
st. Roseville.....285 A2
st. Wilberforce.....91 J5
EARLE
av. Ashfield.....342 K14
st. Arncliffe.....403 C10
st. Cremorne.....316 C6
st. Doonside.....243 B12
wy. Claymore.....481 B11
EARLS
av. Riverwood.....400 E12
ct. Cherrybrook.....219 E12
ct. Roseville Ch.....255 F15
EARLWOOD
av. Earlwood.....402 J3
cr. Bardwell Pk.....402 H8
EARLY
st. Parramatta.....308 B6
EARN
pl. St Andrews.....482 A2
EARNGLEY
la. Edgecliff.....13 F10
EARNSHAW
st. Gladesville.....312 K9
EAST
av. Cammeray.....316 B3
cr. Hurstville Gr.....431 H11
dr. Bexley North.....402 C9
esp. Manly.....288 G10
la. *N Sydney, off Eden La.....5 E2*
la. Randwick.....407 B2
la. St Marys.....239 H16
pde. Campsie.....372 D12
pde. Canley Vale.....366 C2
pde. Couridjah.....564 D16
pde. Denistone.....281 B8
pde. Eastwood.....281 B8
pde. Fairfield.....336 D16
pde. Sutherland.....490 D4
rd. Riverstone.....182 F9
st. Bardwell Vy.....403 B8
st. Blakehurst.....462 D2
st. Couridjah.....564 H16
st. Five Dock.....342 K9
st. Forest Glen.....70 G15
st. Granville.....308 G11
st. Greenwich.....314 K13
st. Kurrajong Ht.....63 G12
st. Kurrajong Hl.....63 G12
st. Lidcombe.....339 J12
st. Marrickville.....16 D16
st. Parramatta.....279 B16
st. Redfern.....19 E9
tce. Bankstown.....399 G1
EAST BANK
st. Collaroy.....229 B13
EASTBANK
av. Lansvale.....366 E9
EASTBOURNE
av. Avalon.....140 C15
av. Clovelly.....378 A13
av. Wahroonga.....222 A9
rd. Darling Point.....13 K6
rd. Homebush W.....340 F10
wy. Bella Vista.....246 E5
EASTCOTE
rd. N Epping.....251 G10
EAST CRESCENT
st. McMahons Pt.....5 E16
EASTER
st. Leichhardt.....15 E5
EASTERBROOK
pl. S Penrith.....266 J5
EASTERN
av. Camperdown.....18 E3
av. Dover Ht.....348 F8
av. Kensington.....376 D16
av. Kingsford.....376 D16
av. Panania.....428 G3
av. Revesby.....428 G3
cct. Parramatta.....278 A12
rd. Doonside.....243 A15
rd. Mcquarie Pk.....282 D1
rd. Matraville.....406 K16
rd. Quakers Hill.....213 G13
rd. Rooty Hill.....272 F3
rd. Turramurra.....222 J13
rd. Wahroonga.....222 K5
EASTERN ARTERIAL
rd. East Killara.....254 E10
rd. E Lindfield.....254 E10
rd. Gordon.....254 D7
rd. Killara.....254 E10
rd. Lindfield.....254 E10
rd. St Ives.....254 C2
EASTERN DISTRIBUTOR
Darlinghurst.....4 D11
Darlinghurst.....346 C13
Moore Park.....20 D13
Moore Park.....376 B7
Paddington.....4 D11
Redfern.....376 B7
Surry Hills.....376 B7
Woolmloo.....4 D11
EASTERN VALLEY
wy. Castle Cove.....285 E4
wy. Castlecrag.....285 J15
wy. Chatswood.....285 E4
wy. Middle Cove.....285 E4
wy. Northbridge.....285 J15
wy. N Willoughby.....285 E4
wy. Roseville.....285 E4
wy. Willoughby.....285 J15
EASTGATE
av. East Killara.....254 G9
EAST KURRAJONG
rd. Comleroy.....64 J10
rd. Comleroy.....65 B9
rd. E Kurrajong.....64 J10
rd. E Kurrajong.....65 B9
EASTLEA
av. Springwood.....171 F16
gdn. Springwood.....171 F16
EASTLEWOOD
st. Narellan.....478 H10
EAST MARKET
st. Hobartville.....118 G8
st. Richmond.....118 G8
EASTMORE
pl. Maroubra.....406 H7

GREGORY'S STREET DIRECTORY 61

EA STREETS

EASTON
av. Sylvania 461 K9
rd. Berowra Ht 133 A11
st. Rozelle 10 J3
EASTVIEW
av. North Ryde 282 D8
dr. Orangeville 443 A15
dr. Orangeville 473 B1
rd. Church Point 168 F7
st. Greenwich 315 C8
EAST WILCHARD
rd. Castlereagh 176 D12
rd. Cranebrook 176 H15
EASTWOOD
av. Eastwood 281 A4
av. Epping 280 J4
la. Doonside, off
Illoura Pl 243 C14
rd. Leppington 419 K11
EASY
st. Randwick 377 A16
st. Randwick 407 A1
EATHER
av. North Rocks 248 F12
EATON
av. Normanhurst 221 G8
pl. Chiswick 343 D1
rd. Luddenham 356 K4
rd. W Pnnant Hl 249 C10
rd. W Pnnant Hl 249 G9
sq. Allambie Ht 257 B8
st. Agnes Banks 117 D12
st. Balmain 7 K10
st. Neutral Bay 6 A5
st. Rooty Hill 271 K5
st. Willoughby 285 F12
EBAL
pl. Seven Hills 275 D11
EBB
st. Quakers Hill 214 C11
EBB TIDE
st. Chipping Ntn 366 J15
EBDEN
st. Quakers Hill 214 A9
EBENEZER WHARF
rd. Ebenezer 68 A13
EBER
pl. Minchinbury 271 G10
EBLEY
st. Bondi Jctn 22 F8
EBONY
av. Carlingford 249 C15
av. North Rocks 249 C15
cl. Casula 394 F14
cr. Quakers Hill 243 D2
pl. Mcquarie Fd 454 H3
pwy. Casula, off
Ebony Cl 394 F14
row. Menai 458 K14
EBOR
pl. Hoxton Park 392 H6
rd. Palm Beach 140 A4
EBRO
pl. Kearns 481 A2
st. Seven Hills 275 F9
EBSWORTH
rd. Rose Bay 348 D9
ECCLES
av. Ashfield 372 G1
pl. Prairiewood 334 F7
st. Ermington 280 B16
wy. Stanhpe Gdn 215 D4
ECHIDNA
pl. Blaxland 233 D12
ECHO
cl. Penrith 237 C2
pl. Winston Hills 277 A1
st. Cammeray 316 A5
st. Roseville 285 C1
ECHUCA
cl. Bonnyrigg 363 K10
ECHUNGA
rd. Duffys Frst 195 F3
ECOLE
av. Winmalee 173 F5
la. Carlton 432 K8
st. Carlton 432 K8
ECONO
pl. Silverdale 353 J8
EDDIE
av. Panania 428 B3
rd. Minchinbury 271 B6

EDDY
av. Haymarket E H12
av. Haymarket 3 G14
rd. Chatswood W 284 E12
st. Merrylands W 306 G12
st. St Clair 270 F10
st. Thornleigh 220 J12
EDDYSTONE
rd. Bexley 402 J12
rd. Bexley 402 G13
EDEL
pl. Fairfield W 335 C9
EDEN
av. Croydon Pk 371 J7
av. Punchbowl 400 B8
av. S Turramrra 252 C9
dr. Asquith 192 D9
gln. St Clair 269 J14
la. N Sydney 5 D2
la. S Turramrra 252 D10
pl. Baulkham Hl 247 H16
pl. Bossley Park 333 F10
pl. Caringbah 492 E14
pl. Prestons 392 J16
st. Arncliffe 403 G9
st. Chatswood 285 D7
st. Marayong 244 B8
st. N Sydney 5 E1
st. Ryde 282 D11
st. Wolli Creek 403 G9
EDENBOROUGH
rd. Lindfield 284 B4
EDENBRIDGE
dr. Kellyville Rdg 215 B3
EDENHOLME
rd. Russell Lea 343 C4
rd. Wareemba 343 A4
st. West Pymble 252 F11
EDENLEE
st. Epping 280 H3
EDEN PARK
dr. Mcquarie Pk 282 K5
EDENSOR
rd. Bonnyrigg 364 E4
rd. Cabramatta W 364 E4
rd. Edensor Pk 333 D16
rd. Greenfld Pk 363 K1
rd. St Johns Pk 364 E4
st. Epping 251 A13
EDEN VALE
cl. St Ives 224 E8
EDGAR
cr. Belfield 371 E10
la. Tempe, off
Edgar St 404 A1
pl. Kings Lngly 245 H7
st. Auburn 339 A5
st. Bankstown 368 H15
st. Baulkham Hl 247 G13
st. Chatswood W 284 F10
st. Condell Park 398 G6
st. Condell Park 398 G8
st. Eastwood 281 D7
st. Harbord 288 K1
st. Kingsford 407 C7
st. Mcquarie Fd 424 A16
st. Revesby 398 G8
st. St Marys 269 G3
st. Strathfield 340 J13
st. Tempe 404 A1
st. Yagoona 368 H15
EDGAR BUGGY
st. Merrylands 337 H1
EDGBASTON
rd. Beverly Hills 401 A16
EDGE
st. Lakemba 400 J4
st. Wiley Park 400 J4
EDGECLIFF
pl. Engadine 488 D16
pl. Peakhurst 430 B11
rd. Edgecliff 13 K12
rd. Glenhaven 187 H13
rd. Woollahra 22 C1
rd. Woolwich 314 E14
sq. Edgecliff 13 K12
EDGECLIFFE
av. S Coogee 407 H7
bvd. Collaroy Plat 228 H9
esp. Seaforth 287 A11
EDGECOMBE
av. Moorebank 396 B7
av. Wahroonga 221 K12
rd. St Ives 224 B6

EDGECUMBE
av. Coogee 407 F2
EDGEHILL
av. Botany 405 F15
st. Carlton 432 J5
EDGELY
st. Surry Hills 20 C5
EDGEWARE
la. Enmore 17 A15
rd. Enmore 17 A15
rd. Newtown 374 G10
rd. Prospect 275 B12
EDGEWATER
dr. Baulkham Hl 216 E16
dr. Bella Vista 216 B13
dr. Bella Vista 216 E16
EDGEWOOD
av. Castle Hill 218 J14
cr. Cabarita 312 E16
pl. St Ives 224 A16
EDGEWORTH
pl. Cartwright 394 A6
EDGEWORTH DAVID
av. Hornsby 221 H2
av. Wahroonga 222 B3
av. Waitara 221 H2
EDINA
av. Waverley 377 F6
EDINBURGH
av. Carlingford 279 D4
cct. Cecil Hills 362 J4
cl. Woolooware 493 G7
cr. St Andrews 452 A13
cr. Woolooware 493 F7
dr. Revesby 428 J5
dr. Revesby Ht 428 J5
pl. Winston Hills 277 F4
rd. Castlecrag 285 H12
rd. Forestville 255 G9
rd. Marrickville 374 E10
rd. Willoughby 285 H12
st. Tahmoor 566 A16
EDISON
la. Belmore 371 G16
pde. Winston Hills 277 B5
pl. Leumeah 482 E16
st. Belmore 371 G16
EDITH
av. Concord 342 C6
av. Liverpool 364 K16
av. Mcquarie Fd 454 A2
la. Leichhardt 15 F2
la. St Peters, off
Edith St 374 H14
pl. Northmead 278 C5
pwy. Liverpool, off
Edith Av 364 J15
st. Bardwell Pk 403 B6
st. Castlecrag 286 A12
st. Girraween 276 C13
st. Hurstville 401 J16
st. Kingswood 237 J16
st. Lansdowne 367 B5
st. Leichhardt 15 F1
st. Lidcombe 339 K4
st. Marsfield 282 B8
st. Mount Druitt 271 B2
st. St Peters 374 G13
EDITH BLACK
rd. Blaxlands Rdg 65 F5
EDMONDSON
av. Austral 391 C7
av. St Marys 270 A1
cr. Carramar 366 K4
dr. Narrabeen 228 G8
st. North Ryde 282 K9
EDMUND
pl. Cecil Hills 362 E2
pl. Rsemeadow 540 J7
st. Beverly Hills 401 E16
st. Chatswood 284 K7
st. Lindfield 283 F3
st. Queens Park 377 F8
st. Riverstone 153 A13
st. Riverstone 183 C1
EDMUND BLACKET
cl. St Clair 270 C11
EDMUND HOCK
av. Avalon 170 B2
EDMUNDS
st. Carramar 366 J2
EDMUNDSON
cl. Thornleigh 220 H11

EDNA
av. Merrylands W 307 B14
av. Mt Pritchard 364 F12
av. Penshurst 431 G6
av. Springwood 202 A11
av. Toongabbie 276 C4
la. Kingswood, off
Edna St 237 J15
pl. Dee Why 258 G3
pl. Ermington 280 C13
pl. Ingleburn 453 C10
pl. Kings Lngly 245 K6
st. Bass Hill 368 D11
st. Kingswood 237 J15
st. Lilyfield 10 G11
st. N Willoughby 285 H10
st. Sans Souci 463 C4
st. Warrimoo 203 E13
st. Wiley Park 400 F1
EDROM
cl. Prestons 393 B16
cl. Prestons 423 B1
EDSEL
pl. Hassall Gr 211 J14
EDUCATION
la. Cremorne, off
Murdoch St 316 F9
EDWARD
av. Kensington 376 E16
av. Kingsford 406 E1
av. Miranda 492 E1
cl. Werrington 238 K10
dr. Pemulwuy 305 F7
la. Bondi 378 A3
la. Concord, off
Edward St 341 G9
la. Darlington 18 K6
la. Dulwich Hill 373 E6
la. Glebe 11 G7
la. Pyrmont 12 J5
pl. Canley Ht 335 B16
rd. Marayong 244 A7
st. Balmain East 8 J10
st. Bankstown 399 B6
st. Baulkham Hl 247 J5
st. Bexley North 402 B11
st. Bondi 377 K3
st. Bondi Beach 377 K3
st. Botany 405 F11
st. Camden 477 B14
st. Carlton 432 H9
st. Concord 341 G9
st. Cranebrook 207 B9
st. Darlington 18 K5
st. Glebe 11 H7
st. Gordon 253 K7
st. Guildford W 336 H2
st. Kingsgrove 402 B11
st. Kingswood 237 J16
st. Kurrajong Ht 63 G12
st. Lilyfield 10 C7
st. Lurnea 394 G11
st. Mcquarie Fd 423 K14
st. Marrickville 374 B11
st. Narraweena 258 A6
st. Northmead 277 F10
st. N Sydney 5 D5
st. Oatley 431 D10
st. Pyrmont 12 J4
st. Riverstone 182 G2
st. Ryde 312 A2
st. Strathfield S 371 D6
st. Summer Hill 373 E5
st. Sylvania 461 F12
st. The Oaks 502 F13
st. Turrella 403 F6
st. Waverton 5 D5
st. Willoughby 285 E15
st. Woollahra 22 H2
EDWARD BENNETT
dr. Cherrybrook 249 E1
EDWARD EDGAR
st. Minto 482 H5
EDWARD HOWE
pl. Narellan Vale 509 A1
EDWARDS
av. Beecroft 250 A10
la. Killara 254 C10
pl. Barden Rdg 488 G8
pl. Penrith 236 K10
rd. Box Hill 154 J15
rd. Lakemba 370 H14
rd. Middle Dural 158 J4
rd. Nelson 155 A15
rd. Richmond Lwld 88 F8
rd. Rouse Hill 155 A15
rd. Wahroonga 221 H7

EDWARDS BAY
rd. Mosman 317 D4
EDWIN
av. Avalon 140 A14
la. Cammeray, off
Edwin St 315 J6
pl. Glenwood 245 H3
pl. Liverpool 394 J8
st. Cammeray 315 J6
st. Colyton 270 G5
st. Drummoyne 343 J3
st. Fairlight 288 D8
st. Greenwich 315 A10
st. Mortlake 312 A14
st. Oatlands 279 A13
st. Regents Pk 369 B2
st. Tempe 404 A2
st.n, Croydon 342 F16
st.s, Croydon 372 E2
EDWINA
pl. Plumpton 241 J10
EDWIN FLACK
av. Homebush B 340 D1
EDWIN WARD
pl. Mona Vale 169 E16
EERAWY
rd. Allambie Ht 257 H15
EFFINGHAM
st. Mosman 317 C10
EGAN
la. Newtown 17 D14
pl. Beacon Hill 257 H4
pl. Woolmloo 4 E7
st. Bankstown 399 C1
st. Newtown 17 H8
EGANS
rd. Oakdale 500 E11
EGERSZEGI
av. Newington, off
Newington Bvd 310 B14
EGERTON
st. Silverwater 309 J11
EGGLETON
st. Blacktown 245 B6
st. Campbelltown 510 J7
EGLINGTON
st. Lidcombe 339 H12
EGLINTON
la. Glebe 11 G7
rd. Glebe 11 G7
EGRET
cl. Bella Vista 246 F1
cr. Yarramundi 145 C5
pl. Clarmnt Ms 268 H5
pl. Hinchinbrk 363 D16
pl. Ingleburn 453 H7
pl. Quakers Hill 214 E11
pl. Woronora Ht 489 E5
wy. Mt Annan 509 B1
EGYPT
st. Holsworthy 426 E10
EIDELWEISS
pl. Lugarno 430 A14
EIGER
pl. Cranebrook 207 F14
st. Seven Hills 275 C9
EIGHTEENTH
av. Austral 361 G15
st. Warragamba 353 E5
EIGHTH
av. Austral 391 A11
av. Campsie 371 H12
av. Jannali 461 A12
av. Llandilo 208 C6
av. Loftus 489 J7
av. Seven Hills 275 J4
av. Shanes Park 209 A8
EILDON
ct. Wattle Grove 396 B15
st. Wentwthvle 277 A10
EILEEN
av. Beverly Hills 401 A12
la. Campsie 372 B14
st. N Balgowlah 287 C6
st. Picnic Point 428 C8
st. Ryde 282 C14
EINSTEIN
av. Lucas Ht 487 G13
st. Winston Hills 277 C5
EIRE
wy. Kellyville Rdg 185 B16
EISENHOWER
pl. Bonnet Bay 460 A9

62 GREGORY'S STREET DIRECTORY

STREETS EL

ELABANA
cr. Castle Hill.........219 B9
wy. Castle Hill, off
Elabana Cr........219 B9

EL ADEM
rd. Holsworthy.........426 D8

ELAINE
av. Avalon..............140 C15
cr. Werrington........238 J11
pl. Hornsby.............192 D16
pl. Middle Dural.....128 C16
st. Regents Pk..........368 K2

ELAMANG
av. Kirribilli................6 C14

ELANORA
av. Blacktown.........274 E3
cl. Baulkham Hl......247 F14
cr. Cecil Hills...........362 D4
rd. Elanora Ht..........198 D14
st. Rose Bay............347 J11

ELAROO
av. La Perouse.......436 J12
av. Phillip Bay........436 J12

ELATA
ct. Wattle Grove.....396 B16
pl. Kingswood.........267 J2
wy. Bidwill...............211 E13

ELAYNE
pl. Guildford............338 B8

ELBA
wy. Glenwood.........246 A3

ELBE
pl. Kearns...............451 A15
st. Seven Hills........275 H8

ELBERTA
av. Castle Hill.........247 G2

ELBON
av. Epping...............280 D1

ELBRUS
st. Seven Hills........275 C9

ELCAR
pl. Chullora.............369 J5

ELCEDO
la. Greenwich..........315 A6

ELCHO
cl. Green Valley.....362 K13

ELDER
av. Baulkham Hl.....247 D5
la. Wrrngtn Cty, off
Elder Pl..............238 G4
pl. Alfords Point......459 B1
pl. Mcquarie Fd......454 G2
pl. Wrrngtn Cty......238 G4
rd. Dundas..............279 F14
wy. Mt Annan..........509 F1

ELDERBERRY
pl. Cherrybrook......219 K13

ELDERSHAW
rd. Edensor Pk.......333 G16

ELDERSLIE
ct. Wattle Grove.....425 K2

ELDON
av. Georges Hall....368 B15
grn. W Pnnant Hl....249 D5
la. Beecroft.............250 B7
st. Pitt Town............92 H15
st. Riverwood..........400 B16

ELDRED
st. Silverdale...........353 G13

ELDRIDGE
rd. Bankstown........399 A7
rd. Condell Park.....398 F6
rd. Greystanes.......306 C11
st. Cherrybrook......219 K5

ELEANOR
av. Belmore............401 F5
cr. Rooty Hill..........241 K15
st. Rosehill.............308 G8
wy. Cherrybrook....219 A14

ELEBANA
st. Colyton..............270 G6

ELECTRA
pl. Raby..................451 G13
st. Heathcote.........518 F9

ELEGANS
av. St Ives..............224 E15

ELEHAM
rd. Lindfield............254 C15

ELENA
la. Belmore.............401 H1

ELEVATED
rd. The Rocks............B B2
rd. The Rocks............1 J9

ELEVATION
av. Balgowlah Ht...287 K14

ELEVENTH
av. Austral..............391 B7
st. Mascot..............405 B7
st. Warragamba....353 F5

ELEY HAWKINS
dr. Warrimoo.........203 B12

ELFORD
cr. Merrylands W...306 J12

ELFRED
st. Paddington..........4 K15

ELFRIDA
st. Mosman.............317 A11

ELGA
pl. Cherrybrook......219 F16

ELGAR
cl. Bonnyrigg Ht....363 E6
pl. Narellan Vale....478 G15
pl. Seven Hills.......246 E11

ELGATA
cl. Avalon................139 J12
ct. Bradbury...........511 E16

ELGATTA
pl. Epping...............250 F13

ELGER
st. Glebe...................12 G13

ELGIN
av. St Andrews......451 K15
pl. Winston Hills....277 E3
st. Gordon..............253 K4
st. Schofields.........183 B16
st. Woolwich..........314 E13
wy. Kellyville..........217 B2

ELIAS
wy. Beaumont Hills...186 A14

ELIM
pl. Chippendale.........18 H1

ELIMATTA
rd. Mona Vale........199 A6
st. Lidcombe..........339 J3

ELIZA
av. Liberty Gr........311 B10
pl. Glenmore Pk....265 F9
st. Fairfield Ht.......335 J13
st. Newtown...........17 F11
st. W Leumeah......482 C13

ELIZABETH
av. Dulwich Hill....373 A9
cr. Kurmond............86 C1
dr. Mascot..............405 D5
cl. Appin................569 F10
cr. Kingswood.......237 F16
cr. Northmead.......278 A4
cr. Yagoona...........368 K12
dr. Abbotsbury......363 D3
dr. Ashcroft...........364 C8
dr. Badgerys Ck...328 B14
dr. Bonnyrigg........364 C8
dr. Bonnyrigg Ht...363 D3
dr. Cecil Hills.........362 F1
dr. Cecil Hills.........361 B1
dr. Edensor Pk.....363 D3
dr. Kemps Ck........361 B1
dr. Liverpool.........395 A1
dr. Luddenham.....327 B11
dr. Mt Pritchard.....364 C8
la. Campsie..........372 B15
la. Randwick, off
Elizabeth St........377 A13
st. Redfern................19 G7
st. Seven Hills.......275 F4
st. Parramatta, off
Thomas St.........308 F1
pde. Lane Cove N..284 B15
pl. Brookvale........258 A10
pl. Cronulla...........494 B14
pl. Darling Point.....13 K7
pl. N Sydney..............K B8
rd. Mt Riverview....234 C1
st. Allawah...........432 F7
st. Artarmon........284 J13
st. Ashfield...........372 F1
st. Avalon..............139 K12
st. Berala.............339 C13
st. Berowra Ht......133 A6
st. Burwood.........342 A15
st. Camden..........477 B14
st. Campsie.........401 J2
st. Croydon..........342 F16
st. Five Dock........342 H8
st. Granville........308 C13

ELIZABETH
st. Guildford.........337 F2
st. Haymarket........F A15
st. Haymarket........3 H16
st. Hurstville........431 K3
st. Kingsgrove.....402 B13
st. Liverpool.........395 E2
st. Newtown.........17 K7
st. Newtown........18 A8
st. N Richmond....87 C12
st. Paddington.....21 D3
st. Paddington.....21 E2
st. Parramatta....308 E1
st. Picton............563 F3
st. Randwick......377 A13
st. Redfern..........19 G5
st. Riverstone.....182 K9
st. Rooty Hill......242 A15
st. Rozelle..........10 K2
st. Ryde.............282 E13
st. Surry Hills.......F A15
st. Surry Hills......3 H16
st. Surry Hills......19 H6
st. Sydney..........D C16
st. Sydney............3 J6
st. Wahroonga...221 J13
st. Waterloo........19 G15
st. Wetherill Pk..334 E3
st. Windsor........121 A8
st. Zetland........375 J9
wy. Airds..........512 B13

ELIZABETH BAY
cr. Elizabeth Bay....13 B5
rd. Elizabeth Bay...13 B6
rd. Elizabeth Bay...13 C5
rd. Rcuttrs Bay......13 C5

ELIZABETH HAKE
ct. Castle Hill, off
Vittoria Smith Av..218 J13

ELIZABETH HENRIETTA
cct. Mcquarie Lk......423 F14

ELIZABETH MACARTHUR
av. Camden S.......507 B12
dr. Bella Vista......246 C2

ELK
pl. Cranebrook.....237 D1
pl. Seven Hills.....275 C9
st. Marsfield.......281 G1

ELKE
cr. Chester Hill....368 C6
wy. Toongabbie...276 A5

ELKHORN
pl. Alfords Point..429 A16

ELLA
av. Barden Rdg...488 E2
st. Artarmon.......315 C3
st. Rydalmere....309 K5
st. St Leonards..315 C3

ELLADALE
rd. Appin............569 A11

ELLALONG
cr. Cremorne, off
Ellalong Rd....316 F5
pl. Doonside......243 E10
rd. Cremorne......316 F5
rd. N Turramurra.223 F8

ELLAM
dr. Seven Hills...275 D7

ELLAMATTA
av. Mosman.......317 C10

ELLEN
st. Greenfld Pk..334 C16
pl. Ingleburn.....453 D10
st. Curl Curl......258 J15
st. Panania........428 E3
st. Randwick.....407 D2
st. Randwick......407 D3
st. Rozelle...........7 A16
st. Ryde............281 K9

ELLENDALE
cl. West Hoxton.392 C4
ct. Kenthurst......157 G14

ELLENGOWAN
dr. Whalan......240 J9

ELLEN SUBWAY
Mortdale..........431 C8

ELLERMAN
av. Kenthurst......188 D4

ELLERSLIE
dr. W Pnnant Hl..249 A6
rd. Bexley...........402 F12
rd. Bexley North..402 F12

ELLERSTON
ct. Wattle Grove..396 A16

ELLERSTONE
st. Kellyville........216 B4

ELLERY
st. St Ives Ch.....224 B1
pde. Seaforth......287 A9
pl. Caringbah.....493 A15
st. Bossley Park..334 B8

ELLESMERE
av. Hunters Hill..313 J11
av. Schofields....183 A15
ct. Wattle Grove..395 K14
rd. Gymea Bay....491 G12
st. Panania.........398 D13

ELLIM
cl. Cranebrook....207 D8

ELLIMATTA
st. Rydalmere.....279 J16

ELPHICK
av. Mascot.........405 D2

ELPHIN
st. Tahmoor........565 H9

ELPHINSTONE
pl. Davidson......225 K6
rd. S Coogee......407 F4
st. Cabarita........342 D1

ELRINGTON
pl. Cartwright.....394 C5

ELSE
pl. Springwood....201 K2

ELSEY
pl. Leumeah.......482 G11

ELSHAM
rd. Auburn..........339 E7

ELSIE
st. Burwood.......341 K13
st. Earlwood......372 G16
st. Scotland I......168 J4
wy. Parklea.......214 J14

ELSINORE
st. Merrylands....307 G15

ELSMERE
st. Kensington....376 F10

ELSMORE
pl. Carlingford....280 C3

ELSOM
st. Kings Lngly...244 K5

ELSTON
av. Denistone....281 E11
av. Narwee.........400 G14
st. Concord........342 A3
st. Condell Park..398 F5
st. Merrylands...307 C9
st. Oatlands.......279 A9
st. St Marys.......269 E2
st. Sylvania........462 E8
ELLIS BENT
rd. Greendale....385 A9

ELLISON
la. Greenwich....314 K10
pl. Emu Plains..235 G9
pl. Pymble..........253 F7
pl. Castlereagh..176 D13
rd. Springwood..172 G14

ELLISTON
pl. Barden Rdg...488 G5
st. Chester Hill..338 C14

ELLSMORE
av. Killara..........253 K15

ELLSWORTH
dr. Tregear........240 B4
st. Leumeah......482 H15

ELLWOOD
cr. Quakers Hill..213 E15
st. St Johns Pk..364 H2

ELM
av. Belrose.......225 H11
ct. Cherrybrook..219 G13
pl. Narellan Vale..479 A12
pl. North Rocks..278 E2
pl. Rydalmere...309 B5
pl. Wentwthvle..277 A8
pl. Woolooware..493 C15
rd. Auburn..........339 A7
st. Acacia Gdn..214 K14
st. Burwood Ht...371 K3
st. Greystanes..306 F9
st. Lugarno.......429 F13
st. N St Marys...239 H11
st. Villawood......366 K2
st. Villawood......367 A2

ELMBRIDGE
rd. Jamisontown..266 C2

ELMSLEA
ct. Airds.............512 C10

ELMSTREE
rd. Kellyville Rdg..215 A6
rd. Stanhpe Gdn..215 A6

ELONERA
st. Rydalmere....309 G2

ELOORA
st. Lane Cove W.313 H2

ELOUERA
cr. Moorebank...396 G7
cr. Woodbine.....481 D14
la. Clarmnt Ms...268 H1
la. Blacktown....275 B2
rd. Avalon........169 K1
rd. Cronulla......494 A10
rd. Westleigh...220 E8
st. Beverly Hills..401 C10

ELOURA
pl. Bonnyrigg....364 A7
st. Dharruk.......241 B7

ELPHICK
av. Mascot......405 D2

ELPHIN
st. Tahmoor.....565 H9

ELPHINSTONE
pl. Davidson....225 K6
rd. S Coogee....407 F4
st. Cabarita......342 D1

ELRINGTON
pl. Cartwright..394 C5

ELSE
pl. Springwood..201 K2

ELSEY
pl. Leumeah.....482 G11

ELSHAM
rd. Auburn.......339 E7

ELSIE
st. Burwood....341 K13
st. Earlwood....372 G16
st. Scotland I....168 J4
wy. Parklea.....214 J14

ELSINORE
st. Merrylands..307 G15

ELSMERE
st. Kensington..376 F10

ELSMORE
pl. Carlingford..280 C3

ELSOM
st. Kings Lngly.244 K5

ELSTON
av. Denistone..281 E11
av. Narwee......400 G14
st. Elston Av....400 G13

ELSWICK
la. Leichhardt...15 F4
la. Leichhardt...15 G1
st. Petersham..15 F10
st.n, Leichhardt..9 F10

ELTHAM
pl. Cecil Hills....362 D6
st. Heathcote...519 H11
st. Beacon Hill..257 K4
st. Blacktown..275 A9
st. Dulwich Hill..15 A13
st. Dulwich Hill..373 E7
st. Gladesville..312 H6
st. Lewisham....15 A13
st. Lewisham....373 E7

ELTON
pl. Plumpton....241 H7

ELTONS
rd. Silverdale...383 D6

ELVA
av. Killara........253 K10
av. Cabramatta W.365 B5
av. Strathfield...341 F11
av. Toongabbie.276 G8

ELVINA
av. Avalon........140 A15
av. Newport......169 D7
st. Dover Ht......348 E8
st. Greystanes..305 J6

ELVSTROM
av. Newington..310 B15

ELVY
st. Newtown......18 C8
st. Bargo..........567 A2

ELWIN
st. Peakhurst...429 J3
st. Strathfield...341 C14

ELWOOD
cr. Quakers Hill..213 E15
st. St Johns Pk..364 H2

ELWYN
cl. Mona Vale...199 A4

GREGORY'S STREET DIRECTORY 63

EL STREETS

ELY
pl. Marayong 243 J6
st. Revesby 398 G13
ELYARD
cr. West Hoxton 392 A12
st. Narellan 478 F11
EMANUEL
la. Rosebery, off Queen St 375 G13
EMERALD
dr. Eagle Vale 481 B7
pl. Cartwright 393 J5
pl. Emu Plains 235 E13
pl. Grays Point 491 C15
rd. Seven Hills 275 C7
st. Emu Plains 235 D13
st. Narrabeen 229 B1
st. W Pnnant Hl 248 J6
EMERSON
pl. Menai 458 H7
st. Leumeah 512 B2
st. Shalvey 211 A13
st. Wetherill Pk 334 J5
EMERSTAN
dr. Castle Cove 286 E6
EMERT
pde. Emerton 240 H7
st. Greystanes 306 H4
st. S Wntwthvle 306 H4
st. Wentwthvle 306 J1
EMERY
av. Yagoona 369 E10
rd. Beaumont Hills 185 J16
st. Rooty Hill 271 K3
EMEX
pl. Mcquarie Fd 454 D4
EMILIA
cl. Rsemeadow 540 G6
pl. Prestons 393 F13
EMILY
av. Emu Plains 235 H10
pl. Cherrybrook 219 G16
pl. Mcquarie Fd 454 H7
st. Breakfast Pt 312 B16
st. Hurstville 401 J15
st. Leichhardt 16 D2
st. Mortlake 312 B16
st. Mount Druitt 271 C4
st. Rozelle 10 J2
EMILY CLARKE
dr. Kellyville 217 C5
EMLYN
pl. Beaumont Hills 186 B16
EMMA
cl. Bonnyrigg 364 C5
cr. Wentwthvle 277 B9
gr. Glenwood 215 D13
pde. Winmalee 172 K13
pl. Ambarvale 510 G14
pl. Berowra 133 G9
st. Lakemba 370 J16
st. Leichhardt 10 F15
st. Mona Vale 198 J4
EMMALINE
st. Ramsgate Bch 433 G11
EMMANUEL
tce. Glenwood 215 J12
EMMAUS
rd. Ingleside 197 E3
EMMERICK
st. Lilyfield 9 K6
EMMETT
cl. Picton 563 H4
la. Crows Nest 315 G8
pl. Killarney Ht 256 C16
st. Crows Nest 315 G8
st. Tahmoor 565 J12
EMMETTS FARM
rd. Rossmore 389 F5
EMPEROR
pl. Forestville 256 C8
pl. Kenthurst 157 E14
EMPIRE
av. Blakehurst 432 C16
av. Concord 342 B5
ct. Carlingford 279 D4
la. Marrickville, off Victoria Rd 374 F10
la. Sydney A K15
pl. Illawong 459 E4
st. Haberfield 343 C14
EMPRESS
av. Rouse Hill 185 E3
la. Hurstville 432 A7
st. Hurstville 432 B7
EMPYREAN
gr. Doonside 243 F15
EMU
av. Hinchinbrk 363 C16
cl. Bossley Park 334 C10
la. Canterbury 372 D14
pl. Hornsby Ht 161 J8
rd. Glenbrook 264 D5
st. Canterbury 372 D14
st. Collaroy Plat 228 H13
st. Strathfield 371 G1
st. West Ryde 280 G11
EMU PLAINS
rd. Mt Riverview 204 F15
ENDEAVOUR
av. La Perouse 436 J14
av. St Clair 270 A12
cct. Harringtn Pk 478 J3
cl. Castle Hill 217 J9
dr. Beacon Hill 257 G4
dr. Narrabeen 228 F8
dr. Winmalee 173 H8
la. St Clair, off Endeavour Av 270 A12
la. Sans Souci 462 K3
la. Sans Souci 463 A3
pl. Riverwood 400 E14
rd. Caringbah 493 B3
rd. Daceyville 406 F3
rd. Georges Hall 367 D15
rd. Minchinbury 272 D9
st. Chatswood 284 J9
st. Ruse 512 G3
st. Sans Souci 463 A2
st. Seven Hills 275 D2
st. Sylvania 462 D9
st. Wahroonga 223 A5
st. West Ryde 281 C15
ENDERBY
cl. Hinchinbrk 362 K14
pl. Barden Rdg 458 J16
st. Tregear 240 F8
ENDGATE
gln. Wrrngtn Dns 237 K3
ENFIELD
av. N Richmond 87 C15
cl. St Johns Pk 364 H4
st. Jamisontown 266 C5
st. Marrickville 373 H10
ENGADINE
av. Engadine 518 G4
pl. Engadine 518 J3
ENGEL
av. Marsfield 281 H3
ENGESTA
av. Camden 506 K7
ENGINEERING
wk. Darlington 18 G5
ENGLAND
av. Marrickville 16 E16
rd. Ingleburn 422 J14
st. Btn-le-Sds 433 H2
wk. Lalor Park 245 D11
ENGLART
pl. Baulkham Hl 247 F7
ENGLEWOOD
wy. Glenmore Pk 266 E10
ENGLISH
av. Camden S 507 B15
av. Castle Hill 248 A4
la. Kogarah 433 B7
st. Camperdown 17 H5
st. Carlton 432 K6
st. Glenfield 424 E10
st. Kogarah 433 A7
st. Revesby 398 K14
st. Woolooware 493 D10
ENGLORIE PARK
dr. Ambarvale 510 F16
dr. Campbelltown 510 H10
dr. Englorie Park 510 F16
dr. Glen Alpine 510 F16
dr. Rsemeadow 540 C2
ENID
av. Granville 308 F12
av. Roselands 401 B8
pl. Ingleburn 453 E10
st. Denistone 281 G12
st. Greystanes 305 J8
ENID BENNETT
st. Moore Park 21 C7
ENMORE
la. Enmore 17 A14
rd. Enmore 17 A14
rd. Marrickville 16 K16
rd. Marrickville 374 E10
rd. Newtown 17 A14
ENNERDALE
cr. Collaroy Plat 228 E9
ENNIS
av. Killarney Ht 286 B1
la. Balmain 7 E12
pl. Lalor Park 245 F13
rd. Milsons Point 5 K12
st. Balmain 7 E11
ENOCH
pl. Winston Hills 277 B4
ENOGGERA
rd. Beverly Hills 401 A10
ENRIGHT
st. East Hills 427 H2
ENSIGN
pl. Castle Hill 218 A11
ENTERPRISE
av. Padstow 399 E12
cct. Prestons 393 K10
dr. Glendenning 242 E6
pl. Wetherill Pk 333 K4
rd. Cranebrook 207 A9
ENTRANCE
rd. Mcquarie Pk 283 D8
rd. Parramatta 278 B13
EOS
pl. Schofields 213 B1
EPACRIS
av. Caringbah 492 J13
av. Forestville 256 A8
cl. Mt Annan 509 B2
EPHRAIM HOWE
pl. Narellan Vale 508 K2
EPIC
pl. Villawood 337 J15
EPIDOTE
cl. Eagle Vale 481 F9
EPO
pl. Glenfield 424 F9
EPPING
av. Eastwood 280 J5
av. Epping 280 K4
cl. Cmbrdg Pk 237 J10
dr. Frenchs Frst 256 F3
rd. Double Bay 14 E12
rd. Epping 251 C16
rd. Lane Cove N 283 H14
rd. Lane Cove W 283 H14
rd. Mcquarie Pk 282 D4
rd. Marsfield 251 C16
rd. North Ryde 282 D4
EPPING FOREST
dr. Eschol Park 481 A1
dr. Kearns 481 A1
EPPLESTON
pl. West Pymble 252 J10
wk. West Pymble, off Eppleston Pl 252 J11
EPSAM
av. Stanhpe Gdn 215 D5
EPSOM
pwy. Chipping Ntn, off Epsom Rd 396 E2
rd. Chipping Ntn 396 B6
rd. Rosebery 375 H12
rd. Zetland 375 H12
EPWORTH
pl. N Narrabeen 198 F11
EQUESTRIAN
dr. Picton 563 B1
st. Glenwood 245 J3
EQUITY
la. Erskineville 18 B14
pl. Canley Vale 365 J4
ERANG
av. Kirrawee 491 A6
st. Carss Park 432 G13
ERAWAR
cl. Westleigh 190 J16
ERBY
pl. Parramatta 308 C2
ERCILDOUNE
av. Beverley Pk 433 C9
av. Kogarah 433 C9
EREBUS
cr. Tregear 240 F8
ERIC
av. Bass Hill 368 C13
av. Merrylands 307 D16
cl. Emu Plains 234 K7
cr. Lidcombe 340 A8
la. Mosman, off Earl St 316 J5
rd. Artarmon 284 H15
st. Bundeena 524 B12
st. Eastwood 280 G9
st. Harbord 258 G16
st. Lilyfield 10 B7
st. Wahroonga 223 B6
ERICA
cl. Westleigh 220 E8
cr. Georges Hall 367 H15
la. Minto 482 F2
pl. Minto 482 F2
pl. Rooty Hill 272 C4
st. Kurmond 86 E1
ERIC COOPER
dr. Castle Hill 217 B8
ERIC FELTON
st. Castle Hill, off Old Castle Hill Rd 218 C13
ERIC GREEN
dr. Mona Vale 169 C15
ERIE
la. Petersham 16 B8
pl. St Clair 269 H16
pl. Seven Hills 275 E6
st. S Granville 338 G8
ERIN
pl. Casula 423 H3
st. Quakers Hill 214 G12
ERINA
av. Five Dock 343 B8
cl. Bossley Park 333 H8
pl. S Windsor 150 D2
st. Eastwood 281 F4
ERINLEIGH
ct. Kellyville 216 D1
ERITH
st. Blacktown 275 A9
st. Botany 405 D12
st. Mosman 316 H6
ERLESTOKE
pl. Castle Hill 219 A10
ERMINGTON
la. Ermington 310 D1
la. Ermington 310 C2
la. Ermington 310 E2
st. Botany 405 J14
ERNA
av. Lansvale 366 K8
pl. Quakers Hill 214 D12
ERNEST
av. Chipping Ntn 366 H15
la. Crows Nest 315 H6
pl. Crows Nest 315 F6
st. Balgowlah Ht 287 G13
st. Cammeray 315 H7
st. Cremorne 315 H7
st. Crows Nest 315 H7
st. Glenwood 215 D13
st. Guildford 337 E6
st. Hunters Hill 313 J10
st. Lakemba 401 A4
st. Lugarno 430 A9
st. Neutral Bay 315 H7
st. Sefton 368 H3
st.n, Lakemba 400 J1
ERNST
pl. Edensor Pk 333 H12
ERNSTINE HILL
cl. Glenmore Pk 265 K7
EROLA
cir. Lindfield 283 K3
EROS
pl. Rsemeadow 540 F2
pl. Winston Hills 277 F3
ERRICA
st. Greenfld Pk 334 C13
ERRIGAL
pl. Killarney Ht 286 D1
ERRINGHI
pl. McGraths Hl 122 A13
ERROL
pl. Quakers Hill 214 F13
ERROL FLYNN
bvd. Moore Park 21 A9
ERSKINE
rd. Caringbah 462 H16
st. Chatswood 284 K11
st. Riverwood 400 C16
st. Sydney C A1
st. Sydney C D1
st. Sydney 3 E1
wy. Minto 483 A1
ERSKINE PARK
rd. Erskine Park 299 K5
rd. St Clair 270 E16
ERSKINEVILLE
la. Erskineville 18 A15
la. Newtown 17 J13
rd. Erskineville 17 H12
rd. Newtown 17 H12
ERVINE
st. Winston Hills 277 E1
ERYNE
pl. Dural 219 B7
ESCHOL PARK
dr. Eschol Park 481 C3
dr. Kearns 481 C3
ESDAILE
pl. Arncliffe 403 E9
ESHELBY
st. Green Valley 363 C11
ESHER
la. Burwood, off Burwood Rd 342 A10
mw. Wattle Grove 425 K4
st. Burwood 342 A11
st. Stanhpe Gdn 215 F7
ESK
av. Green Valley 362 J11
la. Marrickville, off Grove St 373 J15
st. Marrickville 373 J15
st. N Wahroonga 223 B1
ESKDALE
cl. Narellan Vale 508 F2
st. Minchinbury 272 C8
ESME
av. Chester Hill 338 C15
ESMOND
pl. Wakeley 334 G13
ESPALIER
pl. Minchinbury 272 B10
ESPERANCE
cr. Wakeley 334 K11
pl. Yarrawarrah 489 H13
ESPLANADE
Elizabeth Bay 13 C4
pl. Ashfield 372 H2
ESPLIN
av. Strathfield 341 H15
ESSENDON
st. St Johns Pk 364 F3
ESSEX
av. Castle Hill 217 K11
st. Blacktown 244 B13
st. Epping 281 D1
st. Guildford 337 C4
st. Killara 253 G11
st. Marrickville 16 B16
st. Minto 452 E16
st. The Rocks A G8
st. The Rocks 1 F12
ESSEY
pl. Merrylands 307 E8
ESSILIA
st. Collaroy Plat 228 H12
ESSINGTON
cr. Sylvania 461 K13
st. Wentwthvle 307 B3
wy. Glenwood, off Kosmina St 215 J16
ESSON
pl. Glenmore Pk 265 J6
ESTELLA
pl. Ambarvale 510 H15
ESTELLE
pl. Frenchs Frst 256 A3
ESTHER
la. Mosman, off Esther Rd 317 D6
la. Surry Hills 20 B4
rd. Mosman 317 D6
st. Greystanes 305 K8
st. Surry Hills 20 C4
st. Winston Hills 277 A4

64 GREGORY'S STREET DIRECTORY

STREETS FA

ESTONIAN
rd. Thirlmere 561 A16
rd. Thirlmere 564 A1
ESTRAMINA
wy. Minto 482 J7
ETA
st. Blacktown 274 C4
ETCHELL
la. Cranebrook, off
Etchell Pl 207 A10
pl. Cranebrook 207 A10
ETELA
st. Belmore 371 E15
ETERNAL
wy. Mcquarie Pk 283 B7
ETHAM
av. Darling Point 13 K4
ETHEL
av. Brookvale 258 D12
la. Allawah 432 E5
la. Eastwood 281 C7
st. Balgowlah 287 E10
st. Burwood 342 A16
st. Burwood 372 A1
st. Carlton 432 E4
st. Condell Park 398 E6
st. Eastwood 281 C7
st. Erskineville 18 C14
st. Hornsby 191 F9
st. Merrylands 307 K16
st. Randwick 407 C2
st. Seaforth 287 E10
st. Vaucluse 348 F7
ETHELL
rd. Kirrawee 461 C15
ETHERDEN
rd. Bligh Park 150 J6
ETHIE
rd. Beacon Hill 257 D8
ETHNE
av. Randwick 377 C10
ETIVAL
st. Palm Beach 140 B10
ETNA
cl. Cranebrook 207 E14
pl. Bossley Park 334 B10
ETON
ct. Cmbrdg Pk 238 A8
la. Camperdown 17 D7
la. Sutherland 490 E4
rd. Cmbrdg Pk 237 F6
rd. Lindfield 284 B5
st. Bexley 402 H14
st. Camperdown 17 D7
st. Fairfield 336 D7
st. Smithfield 335 K5
st.n, Sutherland 490 E6
st.s, Sutherland 490 E6
ETONVILLE
pde. Croydon 342 G16
ETRUSCAN
ct. Glenwood 245 K4
ETTALONG
pl. Woodbine 481 K11
rd. Greystanes 306 D4
rd. Auburn 339 A8
rd. Collaroy Plat 228 F11
ETTLESDALE
rd. Spring Farm 507 H6
ETTRICK
st. Ashbury 372 F8
EUCALYPT
rd. Springwood 202 B2
EUCALYPTS
wk. Newington 310 C13
EUCALYPTUS
cct. Mt Annan 509 E6
cl. St Ives 253 K1
cl. Warriewood 198 H10
ct. Baulkham Hl 247 F14
ct. Picnic Point 428 E8
ct. Stanhpe Gdn 215 B11
dr. Cranebrook 237 C11
dr. Mcquarie Fd 424 E16
dr. Minchinbury 272 D10
dr. Westleigh 220 F8
dr.s, Alfords Point ..459 B3
st. Peakhurst 430 H4
st. St Ives 254 A1
st. Wentwthvle 277 A9
EUCHORA
cl. Springwood 202 B1

EUCLA
cr. Malabar 437 F8
pl. Sutherland 460 C14
EUCLASE
pl. Eagle Vale 481 F8
EUCLID
st. Winston Hills 277 D5
EUCRA
st. Schofields 213 K6
EUCUMBENE
cr. Heckenberg 363 K12
dr. Woodcroft 243 H8
la. St Clair, off
Eucumbene Pl...269 J16
pl. St Clair 269 J16
EUDON
st. Doonside 243 C4
EUGENES
gln. Beaumont Hills..185 J14
EUGENIA
st. Loftus 489 K9
wy. Bidwill 211 G13
EULABAH
av. Earlwood 402 C5
EULALIA
st. West Ryde 280 H14
EULALIE
av. Randwick 377 C12
EULBERTIE
av. Warrawee 222 F12
EULDA
st. Belmore 371 B14
EULO
pde. Ryde 282 A13
EUMINA
st. Beverly Hills 401 D10
EUMUNG
st. Wattle Grove 426 A2
EUNGAI
pl. N Narrabeen 198 F15
EUPHRATES
st. Kearns 451 B14
EURABALONG
rd. Burraneer 523 E4
EURABBA
rd. Duffys Frst 195 A1
EURABBIE
gln. St Clair 270 A15
pl. Mcquarie Fd 454 E4
st. Cabramatta 365 H10
EURALLA
st. Westmead 307 F3
wy. Minto 482 J5
EUREKA
ct. Sadleir 394 C3
gr. Glenwood 215 C15
EURELLA
av. N Balgowlah 287 D4
st. Burwood 342 B13
EURIMBLA
av. Randwick 376 K15
EUROA
pl. Engadine 489 D9
EUROBIN
av. Manly 288 F4
EUROKA
rd. N Sydney 5 B8
rd. Glenbrook 264 A1
rd. Mulgoa 294 D14
st. Westleigh 220 F9
st. Ingleburn 453 B10
st. Northbridge 286 A15
st. N Sydney 5 B8
st. Waverton 5 B8
EURONG
st. Wahroonga 251 J1
st. Wahroonga 251 J1
EURYALUS
st. Mosman 286 K16
EUSTACE
pde. Killara 253 D16
st. Fairfield 335 K13
st. Fairfield Ht 335 K13
st. Manly 288 F9
EUSTON
la. Alexandria 375 C11
la. Alexandria 375 C11
rd. Auburn 338 J3
rd. Hurlstone Pk 372 K12
st. Rydalmere 309 D2

EVA
av. Green Valley 362 K11
la. Northwood 314 H9
pl. Glenfield 424 H13
pl. Northmead 277 H8
st. Condell Park 398 H5
wy. Kellyville 185 E6
st. Greystanes 305 K6
st. Northwood 314 H8
st. Riverwood 400 F9
st. Roselands 400 F9
EVALINE
st. Campsie 371 J15
st. Canterbury 372 A14
EVAN
la. Waterloo 19 J2
pl. Kings Lngly 245 A5
st. Gladesville 312 H8
st. Penrith 237 A13
st. S Penrith 266 J3
st. S Penrith 266 J4
EVANDA
st. Berowra 133 F10
EVANDALE
ct. Wattle Grove 425 J5
EVANS
av. Eastlakes 405 J2
av. Eastlakes 406 A2
av. Moorebank 396 C7
cr. Richmond 119 C3
la. Eastlakes 405 K2
la. Mosman, off
Muston St.........317 C6
la. Redfern 19 A5
la. St Leonards 315 D4
pde. Lapstone 264 G4
pl. Mt Pritchard 364 K9
rd. Carlingford 280 A7
rd. Dundas Vy 280 A7
rd. Glenhaven 217 K1
rd. Hornsby Ht 191 G4
rd. Rooty Hill 272 D6
rd. Rcuttrs Bay 13 C6
rd. Telopea 279 H10
rd. Wilberforce 67 E14
st. Balmain 7 B14
st. Bronte 377 J9
st. Como 400 H8
st. Fairfield Ht 335 H11
st. Harbord 258 H16
st. Newington 310 D11
st. Peakhurst 429 K5
st. Randwick 377 A9
st. Rozelle 7 A9
st. Sans Souci 463 B2
st. West Pymble ...252 F1
EVE
ct. Cabramatta 365 G11
ct. Winston Hills ...276 H2
pl. Arncliffe 403 J9
st. Banksia 403 J13
st. Erskineville 375 A10
st. Guildford 338 C5
st. Strathfield 371 D4
EVELEIGH
st. Redfern 19 A6
st. Redfern 19 A6
EVELYN
av. Concord 342 C7
av. Turramurra 223 B11
cl. Wetherill Pk 334 F4
ct. Berowra Ht 133 C6
pl. Belrose 226 B16
pl. Glendenning 242 F4
rd. Baulkham Hl 247 G13
st. Greenwich 314 K10
st. Mcquarie Fd 454 B6
st. S Coogee 407 E4
st. Sylvania 462 C10
st. Sylvania Wtr 462 C10
st.n, Sylvania 462 E9
EVELYN GRACE
wy. Cherrybrook 219 F8
EVENING
row. St Clair 270 C13
EVENSTAR
pl. St Clair 270 D14
EVERARD
st. Hunters Hill 313 A7
EVEREST
st. Seven Hills 275 B9
EVERETT
pl. Annangrove 155 D6
st. Maroubra 406 K8
wy. Wahroonga 222 C7

EVERGOLD
pl. Eagle Vale 481 B8
EVERGREEN
av. Bradbury 511 D15
tce. Minchinbury 272 F10
wy. Kellyville 185 E6
EVERINGHAM
rd. Sackville N 68 D1
EVERINGHAM FARM
rd. Ebenezer 68 F5
EVERITT
cr. Minchinbury 272 C10
pl. Strathfield S 371 E6
EVERLEY
rd. Auburn 338 H12
rd. Sefton 338 F11
EVERS
cl. Edensor Pk 363 F3
EVERTON
rd. Belrose 226 A15
rd. Faulconbdg 171 A16
rd. Strathfield 341 G11
st. Pymble 253 D3
EVERVIEW
av. Mosman 316 K4
EVESHAM
ct. Baulkham Hl 216 H16
pl. Chipping Ntn ...366 G13
EVESSON
la. Woollahra 22 K4
EVOE
pl. Doonside 243 A10
EWAN
st. Mascot 405 A5
EWART
la. Dulwich Hill 373 D13
st. Dulwich Hill 373 C12
wy. Claymore, off
Colquhoun Wy..481 C11
EWELL
pl. Bondi 377 J6
st. Balmain 7 B12
st. Bondi 377 J6
EWEN
st. Roselands 400 H6
EWENTON
la. Balmain 8 C11
st. Balmain 8 C11
EWING
av. Little Bay 437 E9
pl. Bligh Park 150 K7
EWOS
pde. Cronulla 494 A15
EXBURY
ct. Wattle Grove 426 B5
pl. Kellyville 216 A4
EXCALIBUR
dr. Castle Hill 217 G5
st. Mt Colah 162 E11
EXCELLER
av. Bankstown 399 F7
EXCELSIOR
av. Belfield 371 C7
av. Castle Hill 247 F2
av. Castle Hill 248 A4
pde. Marrickville 373 H16
rd. Cronulla 493 H12
rd. Mt Colah 162 E11
rd. Concord 342 B7
st. Guildford 338 B4
st. Guildford 338 B7
st. Leichhardt 15 H3
st. Merrylands 308 C16
wy. Castle Hill 247 F2
EXCHANGE
pde. Smeaton Gra...479 A9
EXELL
st. Bnksmeadw 436 A2
EXETER
gr. Kings Lngly 245 G14
pl. Bidwill 241 E1
rd. North Rocks 278 J2
rd. Homebush W..340 G9
rd. Kemps Ck 360 B6
rd. Wahroonga 222 A11
st. Camden 477 A14
EXFORD
ct. Wattle Grove 425 J2
EXHIBITION
pde. Mt Pritchard ...364 F13
pl. Haymarket ......E A3
pl. Haymarket 3 C10

EXLEY
pl. S Penrith 266 K6
rd. Wedderburn 540 A15
EXMOOR
pl. Blairmount 481 B14
EXMOUTH
rd. Yarrawarrah 489 G13
EXPERIMENT
st. Pyrmont 12 J5
EXPLORER
st. Eveleigh 18 D12
EXPLORERS
rd. Glenbrook 264 C1
rd. Glenbrook 264 C3
rd. Lapstone 264 C3
wy. St Clair 270 D11
EXTON
wy. Rsemeadow 540 J2
EYLES
av. Epping 250 C16
st. Telopea 279 H10
EYNHAM
rd. Milperra 397 F11
EYRE
av. Ingleburn 423 B10
pl. Camden S 507 B10
st. Kirrawee 460 J16
st. Mt Colah 162 C11
st. Chifley 437 A6
st. Lalor Park 245 B14
st. Smithfield 335 D1
st. Wrrngtn Cty 238 G8
EZZY
la. Chester Hill 337 F13

F

F3
Asquith 192 D16
Berowra 163 A9
Brooklyn 75 A13
Cowan 104 E13
Krngai Ch N P 192 D16
Mooney Mooney ..75 A13
Mt Colah 162 F16
Mt Krng-gai 163 A9
N Wahroonga 222 B6
Wahroonga 222 B7
F6
Waterfall 519 D16
FABIAN
pl. Mona Vale 199 A5
rd. Rsemeadow 540 G6
FABOS
pl. Croydon Pk 372 D6
pl. Smithfield 335 J7
FABRY
st. Botany 405 G13
FACER
ct. Castle Hill 217 F15
FACEY
rd. Lurnea 394 B8
FACTORY
rd. Regentville 265 E1
st. Granville 308 H15
st. Haymarket ......E C5
st. Haymarket 3 E11
st. N Parramatta ..278 C13
FADDEN
pl. N Wahroonga ..192 F14
pl. Springwood 202 D12
FAGAN
pl. Bonnyrigg 363 J10
FAGANS
rd. Arcadia 129 G11
FAHEY
la. Marrickville, off
Philpott St 374 D9
FAHY
cl. Loftus 490 B6
FAIRBAIRN
av. Clontarf 287 E12
av. East Killara 254 F8
cl. Springwood 202 E1
FAIRBURN
av. W Pnnant Hl ...249 J3
cr. Minchinbury 272 C8
rd. Wedderburn 540 D13
FAIREY
rd. S Windsor 121 B16
rd. Windsor 121 A12

FA   STREETS

FAIRFAX
rd. Bellevue Hill 14 G9
rd. Mosman 317 C2
FAIRFIELD
av. Windsor 120 J10
pl. Jamisontown 266 B1
rd. Guildford W 336 H2
rd. Woodpark 306 H16
st. Yennora 336 F7
st. Fairfield 336 G12
st. Fairfield E 336 J11
st. Old Guildford 337 A11
st. Yennora 337 A11
FAIRFORD
rd. Padstow 399 F11
FAIRFOWL
la. Dulwich Hill, off
   Fairfowl St 373 F10
st. Dulwich Hill 373 F10
FAIRGREEN
pl. Castle Hill 217 J7
FAIRHAVEN
cct. Baulkham Hl 216 J11
FAIRLIGHT
cl. Kellyville 217 B2
pl. Dharruk 241 D6
st. St Andrews 481 J1
FAIRLAND
av. Greenacre 370 C10
FAIRLAWN
av. Turramurra 223 B11
st. Lansvale 366 D10
FAIRLIGHT
av. East Killara 254 F10
av. Fairfield 336 E14
cr. Fairlight 288 B10
pl. Woodbine 481 J9
rd. Mulgoa 295 A16
st. Fairlight 288 B9
st. Five Dock 342 K14
st. Lilyfield 9 G8
st. Manly 288 C9
FAIRMONT
av. Baulkham Hl 216 J16
FAIRMOUNT
cct. Glenwood 246 A5
st. Dulwich Hill 373 D6
st. Lakemba 370 H15
st. Merrylands 307 A8
FAIRPORT
st. N Curl Curl 258 G10
FAIRS
av. Woolooware 493 E10
FAIRVIEW
av. Engadine 518 D4
av. Roselands 400 H6
av. St Ives Ch 223 K4
av. Mt Krng-gai 162 J10
rd. Cabramatta 366 C7
rd. Canley Vale 366 C7
rd. Arncliffe 403 B10
st. Concord 341 J8
st. Guildford 337 B2
FAIRWATER
cl. Breakfast Pt 312 C16
dr. Breakfast Pt 312 C16
dr. Harringtn Pk 478 D5
dr. Harringtn Pk 478 H6
FAIRWAY
av. Kogarah 433 E6
av. Mortdale 430 G8
av. Pymble 223 H14
av. Springwood 172 D13
cl. Manly Vale 288 C5
pl. Kellyville 216 E10
pl. Narellan 478 C9
pl. Parklea 215 A13
FAIRWAYS
av. Leonay 235 B15
cr. Springwood 172 B13
FAIRWEATHER
pl. Eagle Vale 481 E9
st. Bellevue Hill 347 F15
FAIRY BOWER
rd. Manly 288 J12
FAIRY DELL
cl. Westleigh 220 G9
FAIRYLAND
av. Chatswood W ... 283 J10
FAIRYWREN
cl. Glenmore Pk 265 J12
FAITH
ct. Georges Hall 367 G10
FAITHFULL
st. Airds 512 D10
st. Elderslie 477 G16

st. Richmond 119 B4
wy. Airds 512 D10
FALCON
cct. Green Valley 363 D12
cl. Greenfld Pk 334 C12
cr. Clarmnt Ms 268 J4
la. Clarmnt Ms, off
   Falcon Cr 268 J4
la. Crows Nest, off
   Sophia St 315 G7
st. Ingleburn 453 G6
st. Crows Nest 315 G7
st. Neutral Bay 315 G7
st. Newington 310 C11
st. N Sydney 315 G7
st. Gladesville 312 G6
wy. Harris Park 308 F5
FALCONER
st. West Ryde 281 G16
FALKINER
wy. Airds 512 C12
FALKIRK
cl. Kellyville 217 B2
pl. Dharruk 241 D6
st. St Andrews 481 J1
FALKLAND
cl. Winmalee 173 B12
pl. St Andrews 481 K2
FALKLANDS
av. Bossley Park 334 A8
FALL
st. Cammeray 316 C5
st. Cremorne 316 C5
st. Revesby 398 K13
FALLEN LEAF
cl. W Pnnant Hl 248 J3
FALLON
cl. Quakers Hill 214 E16
dr. Dural 219 D5
st. Rydalmere 310 A5
FALLONS
rd. Orangeville 443 G12
FALLOWFIELD
ct. Wrrngtn Dns 237 K5
la. Wrrngtn Dns, off
   Fallowfield Ct 237 K5
FALLOWS
av. Cherrybrook 219 E15
FALLS
pl. Kellyville Rdg 215 A3
st. Leichhardt 9 E10
FALMAR
pl. Woronora Ht 489 D3
FALMER
st. Abbotsbury 333 A14
FALMOUTH
rd. Quakers Hill 243 G5
FALSTAFF
pl. Rsemeadow 540 G7
FAMILY HILL
rd. Oran Park 448 B10
FAN
wy. Stanhpe Gdn 215 D10
FANE
pl. Doonside 243 B8
FANNICH
pl. St Andrews 452 B14
FANNIN
pl. Kings Lngly 245 A2
FANNING
st. Tempe 404 C3
FANNY
st. Surry Hills 20 D2
FANTAIL
cr. Erskine Park 270 K15
la. St Clair, off
   Fantail Cr 271 A15
pl. Green Valley 363 D10
st. Ingleburn 453 G10
FANTÔME
st. Voyager Pt 427 D4
FARADAY
av. Rose Bay 348 B12
la. Meadowbank 311 E3
rd. Leumeah 482 E16
rd. Padstow 429 D2
FARAH
pl. Yagoona 368 H11
FARHALL
pl. Glenhaven 218 A4
FARIOLA
st. Silverwater 309 J11

FARLEIGH
st. Ashfield 372 J6
FARLEY
pl. Londonderry 148 C10
rd. Cecil Park 332 G9
FARLOW
pl. Kingswood 237 F9
FARM
cl. Castle Hill, off
   Langshaw Cct 218 K12
rd. Kenthurst 155 J3
rd. Mulgoa 295 E14
rd. Riverstone 181 K7
wy. Springwood 202 B9
st. Gladesville 312 G6
wy. Harris Park 308 F5
FARMAN
st. Raby 451 C12
FARMER
cct. Beaumont Hills .. 186 A13
cl. Glenwood 215 F12
pl. St Clair 270 A10
rd. Clontarf 287 E11
FARMHOUSE
pl. Currans Hill 479 K11
FARMINGDALE
dr. Blacktown 274 D10
FARMRIDGE
wy. Glenhaven 218 C3
FARMVIEW
dr. Cranebrook 207 C15
rd. Erskine Park 270 E16
st. Earlwood 402 J5
FARNBOROUGH
dr. Wattle Grove ... 426 B4
rd. Dural 189 H4
FARNELL
av. Carlingford 249 E15
av. Royal N P 490 B14
rd. Yagoona 369 A10
st. Curl Curl 258 K13
st. Granville 308 B15
st. Hunters Hill 313 C6
st. Merrylands 308 B15
st. Surry Hills, off
   Sandwell St 20 D1
st. West Ryde 280 F12
FARNHAM
av. Randwick 377 D14
av. Roselands 400 F7
rd. Quakers Hill ... 214 F13
FARNINGHAM
st. Mt Pritchard ... 364 B11
FARNSWORTH
av. Campbelltown .. 511 G9
av. Silverdale 353 E9
av. Warragamba 353 E9
FARNWORTH
la. Point Piper, off
   Wyuna Rd 347 F8
FARR
st. Banksia 403 F16
st. Marrickville 374 B11
st. Rockdale 403 F16
FARRAN
la. Woollahra 22 E4
st. Lane Cove N ... 283 K13
FARRANT
pl. Carlingford 249 H15
FARRAR
av. Krngai Ch N P ... 163 J15
rd. Rookwood 340 A12
cl. Mcquarie Pk, off
   Main Av 283 D7
pl. Bonnyrigg Ht .. 363 F7
wy. Castle Hill 248 F5
st. Lalor Park 245 B12
st. St Helens Park .. 541 A8
st. Arncliffe 403 D9
st. Balgowlah Ht .. 287 J12
FARRELL
av. Darlinghurst 4 G8
rd. Fairfield W 334 K15
rd. Bass Hill 367 F7
rd. Kingsgrove 402 A13
st. Hebersham 241 F4
FARRELLS
la. Castlereagh 206 G8
la. Cranebrook 206 G8
FARRELLYS
av. Tamarama 378 A5
FARRENDON
pl. Mt Annan 509 E1
FARRER
av. W Pnnant Hl ... 248 K9
pl. Frenchs Frst ... 255 H5

pl. Oyster Bay 461 C5
pl. Sydney .... B D12
rd. Mt Irvine 60 A5
rd. Mt Wilson 59 C6
FARRIER
pl. Castle Hill 217 F5
wy. Kellyville Rdg ... 215 D2
FARRINGTON
pde. North Ryde 282 H10
st. Minchinbury 272 C10
FARROW
la. Tempe 404 B2
st. Campbelltown .. 511 E3
FARTHING
cl. Maroubra 407 D15
FARVIEW
dr. Bilgola 169 H6
FASSIFERN
pl. Cartwright 394 B4
FAUCETT
la. Woolmloo 4 D6
FAULDS
rd. Guildford W 337 A4
FAULKLAND
cr. Kings Park 244 F3
FAULKNER
st. Old Tngabbie ... 277 B7
FAUNA
pl. Kirrawee 490 J4
rd. Erskine Park ... 270 E16
st. Earlwood 402 J5
FAUNCE
st. Burwood Ht 371 K4
FAUST
gln. St Clair 270 D15
cl. Kellyville 217 A2
pl. Westmead 307 F2
st. Bankstown 368 J15
st. Yagoona 368 J15
FAVA
pl. Rooty Hill 271 K3
FAVELL
av. Rouse Hill 184 J8
st. Toongabbie 276 G9
FAVERSHAM
cr. Chipping Ntn .. 366 G15
la. Marrickville, off
   Hans Pl 374 C12
st. Marrickville 374 C12
FAWCETT
st. Balmain 7 K10
st. Glenfield 424 C12
st. Ryde 282 A11
FAWKENER
pl. Wrrngtn Cty ... 238 G6
FAWKNER
pl. Barden Rdg ... 488 H5
FAY
pl. Marsfield 281 K6
st. N Curl Curl 258 F10
FAYE
av. Blakehurst 432 D13
av. Earlwood 372 H16
av. Seven Hills 245 B16
FEARN
st. Toongabbie ... 276 H8
FEARNLEY
la. St Clair, off
   Feather St 269 G14
st. St Clair 269 G14
FEATHERWOOD
av. Cherrybrook .. 219 J5
wy. Castle Hill 248 F5
FEATON
pl. Mortdale 430 H8
FEDERAL
av. Ashfield 373 A3
pde. Brookvale ... 258 B8
pde.w.Brookvale . 258 A8
rd. Glebe 11 G6
rd. Seven Hills .. 275 D2
rd. West Ryde .. 311 C2
FEDERATION
pl. Frenchs Frst ... 256 G1
pl. Sadleir 394 C2
pl. Newtown 17 F9
wy. Moore Park .. 20 K10
FEDOTOW
pl. Rooty Hill 271 H3
FEHON
rd. Chatswood W .. 284 H12
FEILBERG
pl. Abbotsford 343 B3

FELD
av. Elderslie 507 F3
FELDSPAR
rd. Eagle Vale 481 F5
FELICIA
pl. Blacktown 244 K10
FELL
pl. Schofields 212 H1
rd. Bonnyrigg Ht .. 363 G5
FELLOWS
st. Minchinbury ... 272 C10
FELS
av. Springwood ... 202 B5
FELTON
av. Lane Cove N .. 284 B14
rd. Carlingford 279 F4
rd. Carlingford 279 B5
st. Horsley Pk 302 F16
st. Telopea 279 D7
FELUGA
pl. Acacia Gdn 214 G15
FENCHURCH
st. Prospect 275 C12
FENDER
pl. Chifley 437 C5
FENECH
pl. Quakers Hill .. 213 H7
FENNELL
st. Parramatta ... 278 B15
FENTON
av. Caringbah 493 B6
av. Maroubra 407 G12
cr. Minto 483 A2
st. Panania 427 K1
FENWICK
av. Roselands 400 J7
cl. Kellyville 217 A2
pl. Westmead 307 F2
st. Bankstown ... 368 J15
st. Yagoona 368 J15
FEODORE
dr. Cecil Hills 362 E5
FERAMIN
av. Whalan 240 J8
FERDINAND
pl. Rsemeadow .. 540 K5
st. Birchgrove ... 7 F3
st. Hunters Hill .. 313 H10
FERGERSON
av. Fairfield 336 E9
FERGUSON
av. Castle Hill .. 248 C6
av. Thornleigh .. 221 C15
av. Wiley Park .. 400 H4
cl. Menai 458 F12
la. Chatswood .. 284 J9
la. Grasmere ... 506 C1
rd. Springwood .. 201 G4
st. Forestville ... 255 F7
st. Forestville ... 255 J8
st. Maroubra 407 A10
FERGUSSON
st. Glenfield ... 424 G8
FERMI
st. Lucas Ht ... 487 G12
FERMO
pl. Engadine ... 489 C9
FERMOY
av. Bayview 169 A13
st. Marsden Pk .. 182 C14
FERN
av. Bradbury ... 511 C11
av. Wahroonga .. 222 B4
cct. Warriewood . 198 H8
cct.e.Menai 458 K14
cct.w.Menai 458 J14
gr. Bidwill 211 D15
pl. Blacktown ... 244 K9
pl. Woollahra ... 377 F3
rd. Hunters Hill .. 314 A14
st. Clovelly 377 F10
st. Pymble 253 F4
st. Randwick ... 377 G12
wk. Pymble 253 F4
FERNBANK
la. Marrickville, off
   Fernbank St .. 374 A13
pl. Cherrybrook .. 219 B13
st. Marrickville .. 374 A13
FERNBROOK
pl. Castle Hill ... 218 F4
FERNCLIFFE
rd. Glenhaven ... 218 A3

66 GREGORY'S STREET DIRECTORY

STREETS FI

FERNCOURT
av. Chatswood......285 A5
av. Roseville......285 A5

FERN CREEK
rd. Warriewood......198 G8

FERNCREEK
ct. Kellyville......186 K14

FERNDALE
av. Blaxland......233 K8
cl. Carlingford......279 C3
cl. Wentwthvle......277 D10
la. Newtown, off
   Camden St......374 H9
rd. Badgerys Ck...357 K3
rd. Beecroft......250 E9
rd. Normanhurst......221 H12
rd. Revesby......428 G4
rd. Chatswood W...284 D12
st. Ingleburn......454 A10
st. Newtown......17 D16

FERNDELL
st. Sefton......338 E12
st. S Granville......338 E12

FERNGREEN
wy. Castle Hill......248 J2

FERNGROVE
pl. Chester Hill......338 D12
pl. Canley Ht......335 D16

FERNHILL
av. Epping......250 J13
cl. Glen Alpine......510 F10
la. Grays Point......491 D14
la. Wrrngtn Dns......237 J5
rd. Hurlstone Pk...373 A11

FERNHURST
av. Cremorne......316 G4

FERNLEA
pl. Canley Ht......335 D16

FERNLEAF
cr. Beaumont Hills...185 K16
ct. Wattle Grove......396 B16

FERNLEIGH
av. Rose Bay......348 C9
cl. Cherrybrook......219 D15
cl. Ryde......312 B4
gdn. Rose Bay......348 C9
pl. Glen Alpine......510 B16
pl. N Wahrognta......192 G15
rd. Caringbah......493 B15

FERNS
la. Five Dock, off
   Lyons Rd W......342 K8

FERN TREE
cl. Hornsby......191 F13

FERNTREE
cl. Glenmore Pk...265 H11
rd. Engadine......488 E16

FERNVALE
av. West Ryde......281 C14

FERNVIEW
pl. Cranebrook......207 B7
pl. Glenwood......246 A5

FEROX
cr. S Penrith......266 G3

FEROZA
st. Riverwood......400 C10

FERRABETTA
av. Eastwood......281 J7

FERRARI
pl. Ingleburn......453 J7

FERRARO
cl. Edensor Pk......363 E2
cr. West Hoxton......391 K13

FERRERS
rd. Eastern Ck......273 E4
rd. Horsley Pk......303 D16

FERRIER
cr. Minchinbury......271 F6
dr. Menai......458 H5
pde. Clemton Park......402 B3
rd. Birrong......368 G7
rd. Sefton......368 G7
rd. Yagoona......368 G7
st. Rockdale......403 B14

FERRINGTON
cr. Liverpool......394 H4

FERRIS
st. Annandale......16 F3
st. Ermington......310 E2
st. N Parramatta......278 B11

FERRY
av. Beverley Pk......433 A11
dr. Drummoyne......343 K2

la. Glebe......12 A9
rd. Glebe......12 A10
rd. Lansvale......366 K9
st. Hunters Hill......313 J12
st. Kogarah......433 A5

FESQ
cr. Glen Alpine......510 C14
dr. Homebush B...340 H2
rd. Hunters Hill......313 E9

FESTIVAL
st. Sadleir......394 C1

FETHERSTONE
st. Bankstown......369 E16

FEWINGS
st. Clovelly......377 H12

FEWTRELL
av. Revesby Ht......428 K8

FFRENCH
st. Greenwich......314 A8

FIASCHI
pl. S Windsor......150 E3

FIAT
pl. Ingleburn......453 K7

FICUS
pl. Mcquarie Fd......454 B4
pl. Narellan Vale......478 J13

FIDDENS WHARF
rd. Killara......253 G16

FIDDICK
pl. Menai......458 G14

FIDDLEWOOD
dr. Menai......458 J15

FIELD
la. Rookwood......340 D13
la. Moorebank......395 J7
la. Mosman, off
   Clifford St......317 B6
pl. Blackett......241 A1
pl. Cranebrook......207 G10
pl. Currans Hill......479 K11
pl. Illawong......459 H5
pl. Telopea......279 G9
pl. Wahroonga......222 E11

FIELDERS
st. Seven Hills......245 F16

FIELDING
cl. Wetherill Pk......334 J6
st. Collaroy......229 B12

FIELD OF MARS
av. S Turramrra......251 K5

FIELDS
rd. Ingleburn......453 J6
rd. Mcquarie Fd......453 J6

FIFE
pl. Cecil Hills......362 H9
st. Blacktown......275 A10

FIFTEENTH
st. Austral......391 A2
av. Kemps Ck......390 A1
av. Rossmore......390 D1
st. West Hoxton......392 A4
st. Warragamba......353 E7

FIFTH
av. Austral......391 A15
av. Berala......339 D14
av. Blacktown......244 H13
av. Campsie......371 J10
av. Canley Vale......366 C3
av. Condell Park......398 E5
av. Cremorne......316 E5
av. Denistone......281 D10
av. Jannali......460 K10
av. Llandilo......207 K1
av. Loftus......489 K7
av. Mcquarie Fd......454 F5
av. Seven Hills......275 J3
av. Berkshire Pk...179 H5
av. Ashbury......372 G9
av. Granville......308 F14
av. Mascot......404 K6
av. Warragamba......353 G7

FIG
la. Pymble, off
   Peace Av......253 H1
la. Ultimo......12 J9
pl. Eastwood......281 D7
pl. Mt Pritchard......364 D8
st. Pyrmont......12 H9

FIG TREE
av. Abbotsford......342 K2
la. Telopea......279 H9
la. Bronte......377 K11
la. N Sydney......5 H1

la. Woollahra, off
   Fletcher St......377 F2
st. Lane Cove......313 J2

FIGTREE
av. Randwick......377 D9
cr. Glen Alpine......510 C14
dr. Homebush B...340 H2
rd. Hunters Hill......313 E9

FIJI
av. Lethbrdg Pk......240 E3

FILANTE
st. Kellyville Rdg...215 A4
st. Stanhpe Gdn...215 A4

FILEY
st. Blacktown......274 G9

FILLMORE
rd. Bonnet Bay......460 C10

FINCH
av. Concord......342 C7
av. East Ryde......282 K16
av. Rydalmere......309 J1
cr. Revesby......398 B10
cr. Castle Hill......217 A10
cr. Davidson......225 C15
pl. Glenwood......215 G13
dr. Greystanes......306 C3
pl. Hinchinbrk......393 E1
pl. Ingleburn......453 F10
pl. Lugarno......429 H13
st. St Clair......269 G12
st. Woronora Ht......489 F2

FINCHES
wy. Kellyville......216 K3

FINCHLEY
pl. Glenhaven......218 C2
pl. Turramurra......223 B7

FINDLAY
av. Roseville......284 F7
la. Dulwich Hill......373 E9

FINDLEY
rd. Bringelly......387 A11

FINEGAN
la. Yagoona, off
   Brodie St......368 G9

FINGAL
av. Glenhaven......217 H1
cl. Rouse Hill......184 K6
cl. Rouse Hill......185 A6

FINIAN
av. Killarney Ht......255 J14

FINISTERRE
av. Whalan......240 G8
av. Willoughby......285 G10

FINLAY
av. Beecroft......250 C10
av. Mt Pritchard......364 F14
av. Turramurra......222 D15
av. Warrawee......222 D15
st. Blacktown......274 J6

FINLAYS
av. Earlwood......403 B4
la. Earlwood, off
   Finlays Av......403 B4

FINLAYSON
st. Lane Cove......314 B1
st. S Wnthwlhle......307 A5

FINLEY
pl. Glenhaven......187 K14

FINN
cl. Cranebrook......206 K10
cr. Marayong......244 C7

FINNAN
pl. Bligh Park......150 G9

FINNEY
st. Hurstville......432 A7
st. Hurstville......432 B7
st. Old Tngabbie......276 J10

FINNIE
av. Matraville......436 H8

FINNS
la. Merrylands, off
   Merrylands Rd...307 H13
rd. Menangle......537 C14

FINO
wy. Quakers Hill......214 H13

FINSCHHAFEN
st. Holsworthy......426 D4

FINTRY
ct. Kellyville......217 A1

FINUCANE
cr. Matraville......437 B1

FIONA
av. Castle Hill......247 G1
av. Wahroonga......223 C4
cl. Padstow Ht......429 C5
pl. Ingleburn......453 D11
rd. Beecroft......250 C8
st. Belrose......226 A14
st. Mt Pritchard......364 C10
st. Woodpark......306 H16
wy. Toongabbie......276 A5

FIR
pl. Lugarno......429 J16

FIREBALL
cr. Cranebrook......207 B10
la. Cranebrook, off
   Fireball Av......207 B9

FIRENZE
st. Glenwood......245 K4

FIRESTONE
cr. Glenmore Pk......266 E11

FIRETAIL
gr. Plumpton......242 B8

FIRE TRAIL
rd. Castlereagh......176 H8
rd. Londonderry......147 A14
rd. Londonderry......176 J5

FIRMSTONE
gdn. Arncliffe......403 B10

FIRST
av. Allawah......432 C8
av. Belfield......371 G10
av. Berala......339 F15
av. Blacktown......244 H15
av. Campsie......371 G10
av. Canley Vale......366 A3
av. Eastwood......281 B8
av. Epping......280 G3
av. Five Dock......343 A10
av. Gymea Bay......491 C10
av. Hoxton Park......392 K7
av. Hoxton Park......393 A6
av. Hurstville......432 C8
av. Jannali......460 J11
av. Kentlyn......513 C7
av. Lane Cove......314 G3
av. Lindfield......254 F12
av. Loftus......490 B5
av. Mcquarie Fd......424 K16
av. Maroubra......407 G9
av. Narrabeen......226 G7
av. North Ryde......282 H12
av. N Willoughby......285 G10
av. Rodd Point......343 D9
av. Seven Hills......275 K2
av. Toongabbie......276 F8
av. Willoughby......285 G10
pl. Bligh Park......150 H9
rd. Mt Annan......479 F14
st. Marsfield......282 B6
st. Menangle Pk......539 B2
st. Revesby......398 D10
st. Berkshire Pk......180 D1
st. Ashbury......372 G9
st. Granville......308 F14
st. Kingswood......237 H16
st. Parramatta......279 A15
st. Warragamba......353 G7
wk. Chester Hill......337 J13

FIRST FARM
dr. Castle Hill......218 E11

FIRST FLEET
av. W Pnnant Hl......249 B2

FIRST ORCHARD
av. Bella Vista......246 E7

FIRTH
av. Green Valley......363 D11
av. Strathfield......341 A16
st. Arncliffe......403 C9
st. Waverley......377 H10

FIR TREE
av. West Ryde......280 H14

FISCHER
cl. Kingsford......406 K5
st. Kingsford......406 K5

FISHBOURNE
rd. Allambie Ht......257 J15

FISHBURN
cl. Lurnea......394 C12
cr. Castle Hill......217 G13
pl. Beacon Hill......257 G3
pl. Bligh Park......150 C5
pl. Narellan......478 F14
rd. Galston......160 C10
rd. Port Botany......436 A11

FISHER
av. Pennant Hills......250 F1
av. Ryde......282 F12

av. S Penrith......237 B15
av. Vaucluse......348 B4
cr. Pendle Hill......276 D15
la. Narwee......400 F14
pl. Campbelltown......511 H8
pl. Narwee......400 J14
pl. Camperdown......18 G3
pl. Dee Why......258 G6
pl. Lalor Park......245 G10
pl. Marayla......94 G12
rd.n.Cromer......258 F1
st. Balgowlah Ht......288 A14
st. Cabramatta......365 K6
st. Petersham......15 J11
st. Silverwater......309 F12
st. Yagoona......368 K8

FISHERMANS
rd. Malabar......437 F3

FISHERS
res. Petersham......15 J8

FISK
cl. Bonnyrigg Ht......363 E7

FITCH
av. Penrith......236 B10

FITTON
pl. St Helens Park......540 K8
st. Doonside......243 B8

FITZELL
pl. Brookvale......257 J10

FITZGERALD
av. Beverley Pk......433 C9
av. Edensor Pk......363 J2
av. Hamondvle......396 C14
av. Kogarah......433 C9
av. Maroubra......406 H12
av. Blackett......241 D1
av. Strathfield......370 K3
av. Maroubra......407 F13
la. Queens Park......22 H11
pl. Glenmore Pk......265 K6
rd. Ermington......280 F14
st. Newtown......17 G7
st. Queens Park......22 H11
st. Windsor......121 C8
wy. Bella Vista......246 H14

FITZGIBBON
la. Rsemeadow......540 K4

FITZPATRICK
av. Scotland I......168 G3
av.e,Frenchs Frst......256 E6
av.w,Frenchs Frst......256 C6
cr. Casula......394 G13
la. Bankstown, off
   Stanley St......399 F2
la. Bligh Park......150 H9
la. Mt Annan......479 F14
st. Marsfield......282 B6
st. Menangle Pk......539 B2
st. Revesby......398 D10

FITZROY
av. Balmain......7 C6
av. Pymble......223 D13
av. Hinchinbrk......363 A15
cl. St Johns Pk......364 G2
st. Leumeah......481 K16
st. Emu Plains, off
   Fitzroy St......235 H10
la. Newtown......17 C11
st. Newtown......18 A8
st. Pymble......223 D13
st. Surry Hills......20 E1
st. Windsor Dn......180 G2
st. Kellyville......215 F4
st. Surry Hills...F4
st. Sylvania Wtr......462 C14
st. Cromer......227 K14
st. Abbotsford......312 J16
st. Burwood......342 B16
st. Campsie......371 C1
st. Croydon......372 C1
st. Emu Plains......235 G9
st. Killara......253 G12
st. Kirribilli......5 K16
st. Marrickville......374 C12
st. Milsons Point......5 K16
st. Newtown......18 B9
st. Surry Hills......4 A16
st. Surry Hills......20 D1
st. Wilton......568 K15
wl. Bellambi......211 K16

FITZSIMMONS
av. Lane Cove N......283 G13
la. Gordon......253 E6

GREGORY'S STREET DIRECTORY 67

FI STREETS

FITZWATER
wy. Rsemeadow......540 J3

FITZWILLIAM
rd. Old Tngabbie......276 F6
rd. Toongabbie......276 F6
rd. Vaucluse......348 D1
st. Parramatta......308 C4

FIVEASH
st. St Helens Park......540 K7

FIVE WAYS
Killara......254 C12
Paddington......13 B14

FIZELL
pl. Minchinbury......271 F7

FLACK
av. Hillsdale......406 G16
rd. Edensor Pk......363 D3

FLAGSTAFF
st. Engadine......489 C8
st. Gladesville......312 J9
st. Stanhpe Gdn......215 C12

FLAGSTONE
gr. Bella Vista......246 E3

FLAHERTY
bvd. S Granville......338 G4

FLAME
cr. Mcquarie Fd......454 E3
pl. Blacktown......274 C7

FLAME TREE
pl. Cherrybrook......219 H14
st. Casula......394 B16

FLAMINGO
ct. Bella Vista......246 H2
gr. Plumpton......242 A10
pl. Pendle Hill......276 B16

FLANAGAN
av. Moorebank......396 C2

FLANDERS
av. Matraville......437 A1
av. Milperra......397 G12
av. Mt Krng-gai......162 J14

FLANNAN
ct. Kellyville......217 A2

FLAT
cl. Green Valley......363 C8
st. Leichhardt......9 E10

FLAT ROCK
dr. Naremburn......315 H1
dr. Northbridge......315 G1
rd. Gymea Bay......491 G12
rd. Kingsgrove......402 C8

FLAUMONT
av. Riverview......314 B6

FLAVEL
st. S Penrith......267 D6

FLAVELLE
st. Concord......341 H4

FLAVIUS
st. Gilead......540 E7

FLAX
pl. Mcquarie Fd......454 F6
pl. Quakers Hill......213 K10

FLEECE
cl. St Clair......270 F12

FLEET
av. Earlwood......402 E4
la. Chatswood, off
    Albert Av......284 H10
la. Mosman, off
    Orlando Av......316 G11
pl. Beacon Hill......257 G3
pl. Bligh Park......150 G6
pl. Carlton......432 F5
st. N Parramatta......278 B14
st. Parramatta......278 B14
st. Summer Hill......373 D4

FLEET STEPS
Sydney......2 G12

FLEETWOOD
st. Shalvey......211 A15

FLEMING
st. Beverly Hills......401 F14
st. Carlingford......250 A16
st. Northwood......314 G7
st. St Marys......269 K2

FLEMINGS
la. Darlinghurst......4 E16

FLEMINGTON
cl. Casula......394 F16
rd. Homebush W......340 J6
st. St Johns Pk......364 G4

FLEMMING
cl. Merrylands W......306 J12
gr. Doonside......273 E5

FLERS
av. Earlwood......402 J7
av. Allambie Ht......257 D11
wy. Matraville......407 B16

FLETCHER
av. Blakehurst......462 C4
av. Miranda......492 A6
cl. Elderslie......507 J4
cl. Old Tngabbie......277 E10
la. Woollahra, off
    Fletcher St......377 F2
pl. Davidson......225 C15
pl. Heathcote......518 B15
st. Auburn......338 K3
st. Bondi......378 B5
st. Burwood......341 H13
st. Campsie......371 K16
st. Glenbrook......233 H15
st. Marrickville......373 J13
st. Minto......452 K16
st. Northmead......277 K6
st. Revesby......398 F11
st. S Penrith......267 B3
st. Stanhpe Gdn......215 F7
st. Tamarama......378 B5
st. Vineyard......153 B9
st. Woollahra......22 J3

FLEUR
cl. W Pnnant Hl......249 H4

FLEURBAIX
av. Milperra......397 G10

FLEURS
st. Minchinbury......272 B9

FLIDE
st. Caringbah......492 G6

FLINDERS
av. Baulkham Hl......247 B11
av. Camden S......506 K12
av. Orchard Hills......269 A3
av. St Ives......224 D11
cr. Ermington......280 D16
cr. Hinchinbrk......363 A15
cr. Ingleburn......423 B10
ct. Davidson......225 B14
pl. Mt Colah......162 C13
pl. N Richmond......87 C15
pl. Earlwood......373 B16
rd. Georges Hall......367 F12
rd. North Ryde......282 C9
rd. Woolooware......493 G8
st. Darlinghurst......4 E14
st. Ermington......280 D15
st. Fairfield W......335 E11
st. Matraville......437 A2
st. Moore Park......20 F1
st. Mount Druitt......240 J16
st. Paddington......20 F1
st. Ruse......512 C3
st. Surry Hills......4 E14

FLINT
av. Penrith......236 H14
cl. West Hoxton......392 C12
cl. Illawong......460 A4
pl. Kellyville......216 D5
st. Eastgardens......406 G13
st. Hillsdale......406 G13
st. Ingleburn......453 E16
st. Kings Lngly......245 A2

FLINTLOCK
dr. St Clair......269 K12
la. St Clair, off
    Banks Dr......269 J12

FLINTON
tce. Paddington......4 K15
tce. Paddington......13 A15

FLITCROFT
pl. Glenmore Pk......265 G6

FLITTON VALLEY
cl. Frenchs Frst......256 A2

FLOOD
av. Revesby......398 J15
la. Bondi Jctn, off
    Bondi Rd......377 H4
st. Bondi......377 H4
st. Clovelly......377 J13
st. Leichhardt......15 E5

FLOODS
pl. Surry Hills......4 D16

FLORA
av. Mt Colah......192 C1
av. S Penrith......266 G2
ct. Baulkham Hl......217 A16

ct. Baulkham Hl......247 A1
st. Arncliffe......403 J7
st. Erskineville......374 K10
st. Kirrawee......491 A4
st. Mascot......405 E4
st. Narwee......400 G15
st. Oyster Bay......461 A6
st. Plumpton......242 C6
st. Roselands......401 C5
st. Sutherland......490 F3

FLORABELLA
st. Warrimoo......203 B16

FLOREAT
pl. Seven Hills......275 E5

FLORENCE
av. Collaroy......229 D14
av. Denistone......281 K11
av. Eastlakes......406 A4
av. Kurrajong......64 B16
av. Kurrajong......85 C1
av. Minto Ht......483 J6
av. Bargo......567 C2
cl. N Balgowlah......287 K6
la. Cremorne, off
    Murdoch St......316 F10
pl. Epping......250 E13
st. Cremorne......316 F10
st. Glendenning......242 D3
st. Hornsby......221 J1
st. Hurlstone Pk......372 J11
st. Mt Pritchard......364 H14
st. Oakhurst......242 D3
st. Prospect......274 G16
st. Ramsgate Bch......433 G12
st. St Peters......374 G13
st. S Wntwthvle......306 K4
st. Strathfield......341 C14
tce. Scotland I......168 J2
tce. Scotland I......168 J4

FLOREY
av. Pymble......223 E15
cr. Mt Pritchard......364 H11
cr. Springwood......202 E11
dr. Abbotsford......343 A3
pl. Barden Rdg......488 H6

FLORIAN
gr. Oakhurst......242 A2

FLORIBUNDA
av. Glenmore Pk......265 H7
rd. Kemps Ck......360 E8
wy. Kirrawee......490 J3

FLORIDA
av. Ermington......280 E11
cr. Riverwood......400 A14
pl. Seven Hills......275 D5
pl. Palm Beach......139 K1
st. Sylvania......462 C8

FLORRIE
st. Granville......308 C12

FLOSS
st. Hurlstone Pk......372 J12
st. Hurlstone Pk......373 B12

FLOWER
la. Maroubra......407 D11
st. Maroubra......407 D10

FLOWERDALE
rd. Liverpool......394 J4

FLOYD
pl. Mt Pritchard......364 H10

FLOYDS
rd. S Maroota......69 F9

FLUORITE
pl. Eagle Vale......481 D6

FLUSHCOMBE
rd. Blacktown......274 G7

FLYNN
cr. Leumeah......482 F11
pl. Bonnyrigg Ht......363 F7

FOAL
wy. Glenwood......245 J3

FOAM
st. Harbord......258 H15

FOAMCREST
av. Newport......169 J10

FOCH
av. Gymea......491 C2

FOGG
pl. Yellow Rock......204 A5

FOGGITS
wk. Hunters Hill......313 B11

FOLEY
la. Georges Hall......367 J13
pl. Castle Hill......218 K10
st. Darlinghurst......F K5

st. Darlinghurst......4 C11
st. Georges Hall......367 J14
st. Mona Vale......198 J5

FOLINI
av. Baulkham Hl......278 A2

FOLKARD
st. North Ryde......282 G8

FOLKESTONE
pde. Botany......405 E14
pl. Dural......219 B5
tce. Stanhpe Gdn......215 E5

FONDA
pl. Glendenning......242 F3

FONTAINE
st. Chatswood......285 B6

FONTAINEBLEAU
st. Sans Souci......463 A5

FONTANA
st. St Clair......300 C2

FONTENOY
rd. Mcquarie Pk......282 J1

FONTHILL
ct. Airds......512 C10

FONTI
st. Eastwood......281 G6

FOORD
av. Hurlstone Pk......372 K14

FORBES
av. Belmore......401 H2
av. Mcquarie Lk......423 G14
cl. Abbotsbury......333 C10
cr. Engadine......488 F13
la. Newtown......18 C8
la. Turramurra......222 H14
la. Warwck Frm......365 G16
pl. Allambie Ht......257 F13
pl. Leumeah......481 J16
pl. Newtown......18 C8
pl. Marayong......244 D7
st. Croydon Pk......372 C7
st. Darlinghurst......4 C12
st. Emu Plains......235 A11
st. Hornsby......221 F2
st. Liverpool......395 G1
st. Newtown......18 C8
st. Paddington......13 J16
st. Warwck Frm......365 G16
st. Windsor......121 B11
st. Woolmloo......4 F5
st. Woolmloo......4 F7

FORCETT
ct. West Hoxton......392 E8

FORD
ct. Luddenham......357 H3
la. Burwood, off
    Railway Pde......341 K16
pl. Erskine Park......270 G15
pl. Ingleburn......453 K7
pl. Maroubra......407 F14
st. Balmain......7 H9
st. Greenacre......370 G7
st. Greenwich......314 J10
st. Huntingwd......273 G13
st. North Ryde......282 D8
st. Old Tngabbie......276 H10

FORDE
pl. Currans Hill......479 J11
pl. N Wahroonga......192 F15

FORE
st. Canterbury......372 E14

FOREMAN
la. Tempe......404 C1
st. Barden Rdg......488 J1
st. Glenfield......424 E8
st. Tempe......404 C1

FORESHORE
av. Chester Hill......338 D16
rd. Bnksmeadw......435 H1
rd. Botany......405 C13

FOREST
cl. Cherrybrook......219 A14
cr. Beaumont Hills......185 K16
gln. Cherrybrook......219 E9
pl. Epping......281 C11
pl. Lansvale......366 D9
pl. Galston......159 F10

rd. Arncliffe......403 A11
rd. Baulkham Hls......248 A13
rd. Bexley......402 G16
rd. Double Bay......14 E12
rd. Gymea......491 D7
rd. Gymea Bay......491 D7
rd. Heathcote......518 K10
rd. Hurstville......431 K5
rd. Hurstville......431 K5
rd. Hurstville......432 C6
rd. Kirrawee......490 E5
rd. Kirrawee......490 H6
rd. Lugarno......429 K12
rd. Miranda......491 J8
rd. Mortdale......431 A3
rd. Peakhurst......430 E3
rd. Penshurst......431 F4
rd. Sutherland......490 E5
rd. Warriewood......198 F6
rd. Yowie Bay......491 J8
st. Forest Lodge......11 K16
st. Glebe......11 K16
av. Belrose......195 K16
dr. Cranebrook......207 B8
wy. Menai......458 H14

FORESTGROVE
dr. Menai......458 K13

FOREST GUM
pl. Greystanes......306 C3

FOREST KNOLL
Castle Hill......218 J16
av. Bondi Beach......378 B3

FORESTVILLE
av. Forestville......255 J10

FORESTWOOD
cr. W Pnnant Hl......249 G4

FORGE
pl. Narellan......478 C8
st. Blacktown......244 H9

FORK
la. Kurmond......86 D4

FORMAN
av. Glenwood......215 E15

FORMER HUME
hwy.Camden......507 A15
hwy.Camden S......507 A15

FORMOSA
st. Drummoyne......343 J3
st. Sylvania......461 K12
st. Sylvania......462 A9

FORNASIER
la. Canley Vale, off
    Canley Vale Rd...366 A3

FORREST
av. Earlwood......402 E7
av. N Wahroonga......222 F1
cr. Camden......507 B2
rd. Lalor Park......245 C13
rd. Ryde......312 F1
rd.n.East Hills......427 H4
rd.s.East Hills......427 H4
st. Chifley......437 A6
st. Ermington......280 E16
st. Haberfield......343 E14

FORRESTER
pl. Marayla......94 K13
rd. Lethbrdg Pk......240 A4
rd. N St Marys......240 A4
rd. St Marys......239 H12
rd. Tregear......240 A4
st. Kingsgrove......401 J9

FORRESTERS
cl. Woodbine......481 H11

FORRESTWOOD
pl. Prospect......274 H12

FORSHAW
av. Chester Hill......338 D16
av. Peakhurst......430 H2

FORSTER
la. West Ryde......281 F14
la. Dundas Vy......280 D9
pl. Penrith......237 B7
st. Blakehurst......432 E13
st. Concord......341 K10
st. Mascot......405 D3
st. West Ryde......281 F14

68 GREGORY'S STREET DIRECTORY

STREETS FR

FORSYTH
cl. Wetherill Pk 334 A3
la. Glebe 12 B8
pl. Oatlands 279 A14
st. Belmore 401 G6
st. Glebe 11 K9
st. Killara 253 K9
st. Kingsford 406 G1
st. Kingsgrove 401 G6
st. N Willghby 285 D10
st. West Ryde 311 G1

FORT
pl. Quakers Hill 214 E16
st. Petersham 15 H6

FORTESCUE
st. Bexley North 402 D10
st. Chiswick 343 C1

FORTH
st. Woollahra 22 B2

FORTHORN
pl. N St Marys 239 K12

FORTINBRAS
cl. Rsemeadow 540 J8

FORTRIL
av. Bankstown 399 F7

FORTUNATO
gr. Prestons 392 K14
st. Prestons 392 J14

FORTUNE
gr. Kellyville 186 G16

FORUM
cr. Baulkham Hl 246 G11
st. Heathcote 518 E7

FORWOOD
av. Turramurra 252 D4

FOSS
st. Blacktown 274 K9
st. Forest Lodge 11 G16
st. Glebe 11 G16
st. Hunters Hill 313 J11

FOSTER
av. Bellevue Hill 347 G15
cl. West Hoxton 391 K4
la. Leichhardt 15 D2
la. Surry Hills ....F B10
st. Surry Hills, off
Foster St 3 J13
st. Quakers Hill 213 K16
st. Barden Rdg 488 E1
st. Leichhardt 15 C1
st. Surry Hills ....F B9
st. Surry Hills 3 J13
st. Valley Ht 202 F6

FOSTERS
la. Bickley Vale 505 E11
la. Mt Hunter 505 E11

FOTEA
cl. Edensor Pk 333 F15

FOTHERINGHAM
la. Marrickville, off
Cowper St 374 E9
st. Enmore 16 J16

FOUCART
la. Rozelle 10 H2

FOUNDATION
pl. Pemulwuy 305 C2

FOUNDRY
rd. Seven Hills 246 E15

FOUNTAIN
av. Croydon Pk 371 G8
mw. Bella Vista 216 C13
st. Alexandria 18 H15

FOURTEENTH
av. Austral 390 H3
st. Warragamba 353 F7

FOURTH
av. Austral 390 K16
av. Berala 339 D15
av. Blacktown 244 G3
av. Campsie 371 J10
av. Canley Vale 366 G4
av. Condell Park 398 D5
av. Eastwood 281 D9
av. Jannali 460 K10
av. Lane Cove 314 G4
av. Lindfield 254 F13
av. Llandilo 177 K14
av. Llandilo 178 C16
av. Loftus 489 K6
av. Mcquarie Fd 454 C3
av. N Willoughby 285 H9
av. Seven Hills 245 C3
av. Willoughby 285 H9
rd. Berkshire Pk 179 K4

st. Ashbury 372 G8
st. Granville 308 G14
st. Mascot 404 K6
st. Parramatta 279 A16
st. Warragamba 353 F7

FOUVEAUX
cct. Harrington Pk 478 C2

FOVEAUX
av. Lurnea 394 D13
pl. Airds 511 J15
pl. Barden Rdg 488 G3
pl. Cromer 227 H12
st. Surry Hills ....F F12
st. Surry Hills 3 J16
st. Surry Hills 20 A1

FOWKES
wy. West Hoxton 392 B13

FOWLER
av. Bexley North 402 F10
cr. Maroubra 407 G8
dr. S Coogee 407 G8
la. Camperdown 17 G6
rd. Guildford 337 A4
rd. Guildford W 337 A4
rd. Illawong 459 D4
rd. Merrylands 307 B16
rd. Merrylands W 307 B16
st. Camperdown 17 G6
st. Leichhardt 10 C15
st. Seven Hills 275 D5
st.n, Woolooware 493 G13
st.s, Woolooware 493 G9

FOX
av. Erskineville 18 E16
cr. Padstow 429 B1
la. Rockdale 403 D13
pl. Beaumont Hills 215 J1
pl. Penrith 237 D3
rd. East Ryde 282 K14
rd. Holroyd 308 A10
rd. Lane Cove 314 B3
st. Malabar 437 F4
st. Narellan 478 E9
st. Riverview 314 B3
wy. Claymore 481 D11

FOXALL
rd. Kellyville 186 D8
st. Elanora Ht 198 D11

FOXGLOVE
rd. Mt Colah 162 F13

FOX GROVE
av. Casula 423 J2

FOX HILLS
cr. Prospect 275 E14

FOXLOW
st. Airds 512 D11
st. Canley Ht 335 B15

FOXS
la. Ashfield, off
Brown St 372 H3

FOXTON
st. Quakers Hill 214 D11

FOX VALLEY
rd. Denham Ct 421 J9
rd. Wahroonga 221 H16
rd. Wahroonga 222 B12

FOXWOOD
av. Quakers Hill 213 H11
cl. Silverdale 383 J3
wy. Cherrybrook 219 D13

FOY
la. Sydney ....F B6
la. Sydney 3 J11
st. Balmain 7 F12

FOYLE
av. Birrong 369 A6

FRAGAR
rd. S Penrith 267 B6

FRAM
pl. Tregear 240 G7

FRAMPTON
av. Marrickville 374 B13
av. St Clair 270 F15
la. Marrickville 374 B13
st. Lidcombe 339 J3

FRANCE
st. Canterbury 372 F16

FRANCES
av. Strathfield S 371 D5
la. Randwick, off
Frances St 377 A12
pl. Miranda 492 E2
pl. Putney 312 F11
st. Lidcombe 339 K5

st. Lindfield 284 B2
st. Merrylands 307 C8
st. Narellan 478 H10
st. Northmead 277 J9
st. Randwick 376 K12
st. S Wntwrthvle 307 C8

FRANCESCO
cr. Bella Vista 246 D8

FRANCINE
cr. Chipping Ntn 366 J15

FRANCIS
cl. Seven Hills 245 H14

FRANCIS
av. Btn-le-Sds 433 J16
av. Emu Plains 235 J9
la. Darlinghurst ....F H1
la. Emu Plains, off
Francis Av 235 J9
la. Manly, off
Raglan St 288 H8
pl. Currans Hill 479 K13
pl. Artarmon 284 J15
rd. Faulconbdg 171 C11
rd. Rooty Hill 272 A2
st. Artarmon 315 C1
st. Bondi 377 K2
st. Bondi Beach 378 B3
st. Bringelly 387 C8
st. Campsie 372 B14
st. Carlton 432 H9
st. Castle Hill 248 B1
st. Colyton 270 G4
st. Darlinghurst ....F G1
st. Darlinghurst 4 A9
st. Dee Why 258 F6
st. Earlwood 402 E3
st. Enmore 17 A15
st. Epping 280 H2
st. Fairfield 336 C15
st. Fairlight 288 E8
st. Glebe 12 F16
st. Homebush 340 K11
st. Hunters Hill 314 A13
st. Leichhardt 9 H10
st. Leichhardt 9 H12
st. Lilyfield 9 H7
st. Longueville 314 D8
st. Manly 288 E8
st. Marrickville 373 H13
st. Mascot 405 H5
st. Minto 452 J14
st. Mount Druitt 240 J16
st. Naremburn 315 C1
st. Naremburn 315 C5
st. Richmond 118 E2
st. Strathfield 340 K11

FRANCISCO
cr. Rsemeadow 540 J9

FRANCIS GREENWAY
av. St Clair 270 A9
dr. Cherrybrook 219 G12

FRANCIS MARTIN
dr. Randwick, off
Hospital Rd 377 A16

FRANCIS OAKES
wy. W Pnnant Hl 249 E9

FRANGIPANE
av. Liverpool 394 J6

FRANGIPANI
cct. Erskine Park 300 E3
pl. Caringbah 492 E13

FRANK
st. Gladesville 312 F5
st. Guildford 337 A1
st. Guildford 337 B2
st. Mount Druitt 271 C4
st. Mt Lewis 369 K16
st. Wetherill Pk 304 F15

FRANK BEAMES
la. Harris Park 308 F6

FRANKI
av. Woolwich 314 A13
la. Prospect 275 D15

FRANKIE
la. Concord 342 A10

FRANKISH
wy. W Pnnant Hl 248 G7

FRANKLIN
dr. Blackett 241 A1
pl. Bossley Park 333 E10
pl. Carlingford 249 K15
pl. Colyton 270 G7
pl. Cherrybrook 219 D16
pl. Chipping Ntn 396 B6
pl. Woolooware 493 H10
st. Chifley 437 B3
st. Leumeah 482 D15

st. Malabar 437 D3
st. Matraville 436 J2
st. Mays Hill 307 J7
st. Parramatta 307 J7

FRANKLYN
st. Concord 341 H9
st. Glebe 12 F15

FRANK OLIVERI
dr. Chipping Ntn 366 J15

FRANKSON
pl. Mona Vale 199 E2

FRANKUM
dr. Orangeville 473 C1

FRANLEE
rd. Dural 188 G14

FRASCA
pl. Kellyville 216 G4

FRASCATTI
pl. Mosman 317 E9

FRAZER
av. Eastgardens 406 F12
av. Kellyville 215 H5
pl. Mt Annan 509 G3
pl. Shalvey 210 K13
rd. Canley Vale 366 D4
rd. Cowan 104 B14
rd. Normanhurst 221 G9
rd. Springwood 172 B16
st. Auburn 338 K10
st. Homebush 340 J11
st. Homebush W 340 J11
st. Lane Cove N 283 K15
st. Randwick 377 D10
st. Rockdale 433 G2
st. Strathfield 340 J12
st. Tahmoor 565 G12
st. Wentwrthvle 277 A9
st. Westmead 307 F5

FRATERS
av. Sans Souci 463 A6

FRAZER
av. Lurnea 394 E12
dr. Birrong 368 J7
dr. Collaroy 229 B11
dr. Dulwich Hill 15 C16
dr. Lakemba 371 A13
st. Lilyfield 9 G5
st. Marrickville 15 C16

FRAZIER
cl. Liberty Gr 311 B10

FREAME
st. Wentwrthvle 276 K16

FRED
la. Lilyfield 10 G1
la. Rozelle 10 G1
st. Lewisham 373 E6
st. Lilyfield 10 G1

FREDA
pl. Hamondvle 396 C13
pl. Panania 428 A6
pl. Randwick, off
Hospital Rd 377 A16

FRED ALLEN
pl. Rooty Hill 272 B2

FREDBEN
av. Cammeray 315 J5
av. Cammeray, off
Fredben Av 315 J5

FREDBERT
st. Lilyfield 10 A5

FREDE
la. Marrickville 373 J15

FREDERICA
st. Beverly Hills 401 C14

FREDERICK
av. S Granville 338 E3
cl. Oatley 431 C12
la. Rockdale 403 C15
pl. Kurrajong Ht 63 E12
rd. Cecil Hills 362 A5
rd. Taren Point 462 J10
st. Artarmon 315 B3
st. Ashfield 372 F2
st. Bankstown 369 G12
st. Blacktown 245 A8
st. Campsie 372 B12
st. Canterbury 372 G11
st. Concord 342 B2
st. Fairfield 336 C14
st. Hornsby 221 D2
st. Killara 283 E1
st. Lalor Park 245 E9
st. Lidcombe 339 K8
st. Miranda 492 E6
st. North Bondi 348 F16
st. Oatley 431 C12
st. Pendle Hill 306 E2

st. Petersham 16 A11
st. Randwick 407 D2
st. Rockdale 403 A13
st. Ryde 312 C5
st. St Leonards 315 B3
st. Peters 374 E14
st. Sydenham 374 E14

FREDERICK SCHERGER
dr. N Turramurra 193 E11

FREDRIKA
pl. Carlingford 249 E13

FREEBODY
cl. S Windsor 150 K1

FREEDOM
cct. Kellyville Rdg 215 A5
plz. Cabramatta, off
Arthur St 365 J7

FREEMAN
av. Canley Vale 365 K2
av. Castle Hill 247 J2
av. Mcquarie Pk 283 C7
av. Oatley 430 H14
cct. Ingleburn 452 J10
ct. Newington 309 K16
pl. Carlingford 280 C4
pl. Chester Hill 338 E16
pl. Concord 342 B5
rd. Agnes Banks 117 D11
rd. Chatswood W 284 G11
rd. Heathcote 518 D11
st. Colyton 270 C5
st. Lalor Park 245 F12
st. Rookwood 340 A14
st. Warwick Frm 365 H14

FREEMANS
la. Middle Dural 128 J16

FREEMANS REACH
rd. Freemns Rch 90 D9
rd. Freemns Rch 121 C3

FREEMANTLE
pl. Wakeley 334 H15

FREEMASONS ARMS
la. Parramatta, off
George St 308 C2

FREESIA
pl. Glenmore Pk 265 H7

FREESTONE
av. Carlingford 249 C15

FREITAS
la. Lidcombe, off
Olympic Dr 339 G9

FREMANTLE
dr. Yarrawarrah 489 G13

FREMLIN
st. Botany 405 J16

FREMONT
av. Errington 280 C13
st. Concord W 311 E12

FRENCH
av. Bankstown 369 E14
av. Toongabbie 276 C5
la. Kogarah 433 D3
la. Maroubra 407 F10
pl. Currans Hill 479 K14
st. Kingswood 238 C13
st. Kogarah 433 D3
st. McMahons Pt 5 D14
st. Maroubra 407 F10

FRENCHMANS
rd. Randwick 377 C11

FRENCHS
la. Summer Hill 15 A6
rd. Willoughby 285 F14

FRENCHS FOREST
rd.e, Seaforth 287 B8
rd.e, Frenchs Frst 256 J5
rd.w, Frenchs Frst 256 F4

FRENSHAM
pl. Dural 188 G13

FRERE
pl. Cherrybrook 220 B13

FRERES
rd. Kentlyn 483 G14

FRESHWATER
cl. Woodbine 481 H10

FREYA
cr. Shalvey 210 H13
st. Kareela 461 D12

FREYCINET
cl. Dural 219 B3

FRIAR
pl. Ingleburn 453 H7

GREGORY'S STREET DIRECTORY 69

FR STREETS

FRIARBIRD
cr. Glenmore Pk 265 H12

FRICOURT
av. Earlwood 402 J2

FRIEDLANDER
pl. St Leonards, off
Nicholson St 315 E6

FRIEDMANN
pl. S Penrith 267 A5

FRIEND
av. Five Dock 342 G8
pl. Blacktown 274 D10
st. Merrylands 307 C6
wy. Mt Pritchard 364 J11

FRIENDSHIP
av. Kellyville 216 C2
pl. Beacon Hill 257 H4
pl. Bligh Park 150 C5
pl. Illawong 459 G7
rd. Port Botany 436 B10
st. Dundas Vy 280 B6
wy. Minto 482 J7

FRIESIAN
st. Busby 363 K16
wy. Picton 561 C3

FRIGATE-BIRD
av. Hinchinbrk 393 B3

FRIPP
cr. Beverly Hills 401 A15
la. Springwood 171 F16
st. Arncliffe 403 C9
st. Bardwell Vy 403 G9

FRITH
av. Normanhurst 221 J8
st. Doonside 243 D6

FROBISHER
av. Caringbah 492 K4

FROGGATT
cr. Croydon 342 E15

FROGMORE
la. Mascot 405 F6
rd. Orchard Hills 267 D7
st. Mascot 405 F6

FROME
pl. Castle Hill 217 H10
st. Fairfield W 335 G9

FROMELLES
av. Milperra 397 G10
av. Seaforth 287 A6
wy. Matraville 407 A15

FRONTIGNAN
st. Eschol Pk 481 A5

FROST
av. Matraville 436 H8
av. Narellan 478 G14
cl. St Clair 299 K2
cl. Wetherill Pk 334 H6
la. Chester Hill 368 C1
rd. Campbelltown 511 C1
st. Earlwood 402 D7

FRUTICOSA
wy. Mcquarie Fd 454 G3

FRY
pl. Quakers Hill 213 G15
st. Chatswood 285 C11

FRYAR
pl. Huntleys Cove ...313 B13

FRYER
av. Wentwthvle 276 K14
st. Mt Annan 479 D16

FUCHSIA
cr. Mcquarie Fd 454 A3
cr. Quakers Hill 243 E3
ct. Baulkham Hl 247 F14
pl. Bossley Park 333 F8

FUGGLES
rd. Kenthurst 156 K9
rd. Kenthurst 157 A10

FULBOURNE
av. Pennant Hills 220 H14

FULHAM
st. Busby 363 J12
st. Newtown 17 D16

FULLAGAR
rd. Wentwthvle 307 A3

FULLAM
rd. Blacktown 274 G6

FULLARTON
st. Telopea 279 J8

FULLER
av. Earlwood 402 F1
av. Hornsby 221 G3
pl. St Clair 270 H10

FULLERS
rd. Chatswood W 284 A9
rd. Chatswood W 284 D10
rd. Glenhaven 218 C3

FULLERTON
cct. St Helens Park ...541 D4
cr. Bligh Park 150 C6
cr. Riverwood 400 F14
pl. Glenmore Pk 265 K7
st. Woollahra 14 B16
st. Woollahra 22 B1

FULLFORD
st. Dundas Vy 280 B10

FULLWOOD
pl. Claymore 481 F11

FULTON
av. Wentwthvle 277 B12
la. Penrith 237 A11
pl. Kellyville 186 F9
pl. N Richmond 86 K14
pl. Marsden Pk 211 H6
st. Penrith 237 A11

FUNDA
cr. Lalor Park 245 F14
pl. Brookvale 257 K10

FUR
pl. Rooty Hill 241 K12

FURBER
cl. St Clair 269 J10

FURBER
la. Centennial Pk 21 D7
la. Moore Park 21 D7
pl. Davidson 225 B14
rd. Centennial Pk 21 D6

FURCI
st. St Andrews 481 J2

FURLONG
av. Edensor Pk 333 H15

FURLONG
av. Casula 424 C1
pwy. Casula, off
Furlong Av 394 C16

FURNER
av. Camden S 506 K14

FURSORB
st. Marayong 244 B7

FURY
st. Kingswood 237 H15

FUTUNA
st. Hunters Hill 314 A12

FUTURA
pl. Toongabbie 276 F5

FYALL
av. Wentwthvle 276 J14
st. Ermington 280 B13

FYFE
pl. Glenfield 424 F13
rd. Kellyville Rdg 214 J6

FYNE
cl. St Andrews 451 K12

FYSH
pl. Bidwill 211 C16

G

GABEE
pl. Malabar 437 E8

GABO
cr. Sadleir 364 A16
ct. Sadleir 394 A1
ct. Sadleir 394 B2
ct. Baulkham Hl 247 D1
pl. Gymea 491 F2

GABRIEL
cct. Blair Athol 510 J1

GABRIELLA
av. Cecil Hills 362 G7

GABRIELLE
av. Baulkham Hl 247 B8
cl. Mt Colah 162 F14

GABRIELS
la. St Marys 239 F16

GADARA
dr. S Penrith 266 F6

GADDS
la. Kurmond 65 B15

GADIGAL
av. Waterloo 20 B14
av. Waterloo 376 A7
av. Zetland 375 K10

GADSHILL
pl. Rsemeadow 540 C3

GAERLOCH
av. Tamarama 378 C7

GAGA
pl. Illawong 459 F4

GAGGIN
st. Parramatta 278 K16

GAGOOR
la. Clarrmt Ms 268 H2
la. Clarrmt Ms, off
Gagoor Cl 268 H2

GAHNIA
wy. Winmalee 172 H13

GAIETY
pl. Doonside 243 B8

GAIL
pl. Bankstown 369 B16

GAILES
st. Sutherland 460 G16

GAINFORD
av. Matraville 407 A14

GAINSFORD
dr. Kellyville 215 H5

GAIWOOD
pl. Castle Hill 248 H1

GAL
ct. Moorebank 396 B9

GALA
av. Croydon 372 C4

GALAH
cl. St Clair 269 J10

GALAHAD
cl. Mt Colah 162 E11
ct. Castle Hill 217 G7

GALASHIELS
st. St Andrews 481 J2

GALATEA
st. Plumpton 241 G8

GALAXY
pl. Raby 451 K14
rd. Luddenham 326 D8

GALBA
cl. Prestons 392 K16

GALE
pl. Oakhurst 211 J16
rd. Maroubra 406 H8
st. Concord 312 A16
st. Concord 312 B16
st. Concord 342 B1
st. Ryde 311 G4
st. Woolwich 314 E13

GALEA
dr. Glenwood 245 D2

GALEN
st. Hornsby 221 F3

GALENA
pl. Eagle Vale 481 G4

GALGA
st. Sutherland 460 D16

GALILEE
cl. Bossley Park 333 K8

GALLAGHER
st. St Helens Park ...541 B9

GALLAGHERS
rd. S Maroota 69 D1

GALLARD
st. Denistone E 281 H10

GALLEON
cl. Chipping Ntn 366 J15

GALLIMORE
av. Balmain East 8 G7

GALLIPOLI
cl. Narrabeen, off
Endeavour Dr 228 J4
la. Concord, off
Gallipoli St 342 A5
st. Bankstown 398 K7
st. Bossley Park 333 J6
st. Concord 342 A5
st. Condell Park 398 K7
st. Hurstville 432 A8
st. Lidcombe 340 C5
st. St Marys 269 F6
st. Smeaton Gra 479 F7

GALLOP
gr. Lalor Park 245 G11
st. Warwck Frm 365 G14

GALLOWAY
st. St Andrews 482 A1
st. Bossley Park 334 C12

GALLUS
pl. Rsemeadow 540 F2

GALSTON
rd. Dural 189 B6
rd. Galston 159 G11
rd. Hornsby 191 E1
rd. Hornsby Ht 191 E1

GALTON
st. Smithfield 335 C2
st. Wetherill Pk 335 C2

GALVIN
av. Kellyville 216 J5
rd. Llandilo 179 C14
st. Elderslie 507 G1
st. Maroubra 407 C10

GALWAY
av. Killarney Ht 286 B1
ct. St Clair 269 K10
pl. Smithfield 335 F2

GAMA
rd. Cranebrook 207 E10

GAMACK
ct. Rouse Hill 185 A9

GAMAY
pl. Minchinbury 272 B7

GAMBIA
pl. Cranebrook 207 E10
st. Kearns 481 C1

GAMBIER
av. Beaumont Hills ...215 G3
av. Sandy Point 427 K10
st. Bossley Park 334 B9

GAMBOOLA
wy. Airds 512 B14

GAME
st. Bonnyrigg 363 K7

GAMENYA
av. S Penrith 267 A1
st. Engadine 489 F8

GAMMA
rd. Lane Cove 314 F3

GAMMELL
st. Rydalmere 309 K3

GAMMIE
av. Matraville 436 G8

GAMUT
rd. Engadine 489 F8

GANDANGARA
st. Douglas Park 568 B8
st. Douglas Park 568 B8
pde. Greystanes 305 K12

GANDELL
cr. S Penrith 266 G5
la. S Penrith, off
Gandell Cr 266 G5

GANDER
pl. Hinchinbrk 363 E15

GANDY
la. Greenacre 370 G2

GANMAIN
cr. Milperra 397 F11
pl. Pymble 223 F15

GANNET
pl. Acacia Gdn 214 G16
pl. Hinchinbrk 393 C2
st. Woronora Ht 489 C5
st. Gladesville 313 A5
st. Raby 481 G3

GANNON
av. Dolls Point 463 G1
st. Bradbury 511 J10
la. Tempe 404 B3
st. Kurnell 466 C7
st. Tempe 404 A2

GANNONS
av. Hurstville 432 B1
rd. Caringbah 493 C7
rd.s, Caringbah 493 B15

GANORA
st. Gladesville 313 A4

GAP
rd. Watsons Bay 318 G14

GARAH
cl. Westleigh 220 E7

GARBALA
rd. Gymea 491 F1

GARBETT
pl. Doonside 273 E4

GARBUTT
pl. Oakdale 500 E11

GARDA
st. Seven Hills 275 H7

GARDEN
cl. Hinchinbrk 362 K15
cl. W Pnnant Hl 248 J9
gr. Beverly Hills 400 K16
la. Belmore 401 F3
la. Eastlakes, off
Maloney La 405 J4
la. Maroubra 407 B10
la. Warriewood 198 H10
pl. Bidwill 211 D16
pl. Bonnyrigg 364 E6
pl. Picnic Point 428 D7
pl. Warriewood 198 J10
sq. Faulconbdg 201 C1
sq. Gordon 253 A6
st. Alexandria 18 K11
st. Belmore 401 F4
st. Blacktown 245 B8
st. Eastlakes 405 J4
st. Eveleigh 18 K11
st. Kingsford 407 B10
st. Kogarah 433 A7
st. Maroubra 407 B10
st. Marrickville 374 E13
st. Mt Pritchard 364 J13
st. N Narrabeen 198 J13
st. Telopea 279 F9
st. Warriewood 198 H11
wy. Lilyfield 10 B4

GARDENER
av. Ryde 282 D16

GARDENERS
la. Kingsford 406 F2
la. West Ryde 281 A15
rd. Alexandria 375 B16
rd. Daceyville 406 B2
rd. Eastlakes 406 B2
rd. Kensington 406 B2
rd. Kingsford 406 B2
rd. Mascot 375 B16
rd. Rosebery 405 C1

GARDEN HILL
rd. Mulgoa 325 K2

GARDENIA
av. Bankstown 399 H2
av. Emu Plains 235 F9
av. Lane Cove W 313 K1
gr. Lalor Park 245 D11
pde. Greystanes 305 K12
pl. Castle Hill 248 H2
pl. Mcquarie Fd 454 E5
st. Asquith 191 K9
st. Cronulla 524 A2

GARDENSET
gr. Blacktown 274 D10

GARDENVALE
rd. Oatlands 279 C12

GARDERE
av. Curl Curl 258 H14
av. Harbord 258 H14
st. Caringbah 492 G6

GARDINER
av. Banksia 403 C12
cr. Fairfield W 335 E11
st. Badgerys Ck 358 H2
rd. Galston 159 G10
st. Bondi Jctn 22 H9
st. Minto 482 K4

GARDINIA
st. Beverly Hills 400 G15
st. Narwee 400 G15

GARDNER
st. Rooty Hill 272 B6

GARDYNE
st. Bronte 377 J8

GAREMA
cct. Kingsgrove 401 G8

GAREMYN
rd. Middle Dural 158 D3

GARETH
cl. Mt Colah 162 F11
st. Blacktown 274 H8

GARFIELD
av. Bonnet Bay 460 C9
la. Carlton, off
Shaftsbury St 432 H7
rd. Horsley Pk 331 G5
rd.e, Riverstone 182 J8

STREETS GE

Street	Suburb	Page	Ref
rd.w.Marsden Pk		181	J16
rd.w.Riverstone		182	D12
st. Carlton		432	H7
st. Five Dock		342	H10
st. McGraths Hl		122	B12
st. Oakville		122	B12
st. Wentwthvle		306	J3
st. Wentwthvle		306	K2

GARGERY
st. Ambarvale 510 F14

GARIE
cl. Woodbine 481 F12
pl. Frenchs Frst 256 J4
pl. S Coogee 407 H5

GARIGAL
pl. Mona Vale 199 B2
rd. Belrose 195 K16
rd. Belrose 225 K1

GARING
st. Richmond 120 B6

GARLAND
av. Epping 280 K2
cr. Bonnyrigg Ht...363 B3
rd. Narembum 315 F1
wy. Ambarvale 511 A15

GARLICKS RANGE
rd. Orangeville 473 A10

GARLING
av. West Hoxton ..391 J11
pl. Barden Rdg 488 G5
pl. Currans Hill ...479 J10
pl. Kings Park 244 H5
st. Lane Cove W ..283 K16
wy. Claymore 481 C10

GARMENT
st. Fairfield W 335 B8
st. Prairiewood ...335 B8

GARNER
av. Frenchs Frst ...256 G7
pl. Ingleburn 423 D16
st. St Marys 269 G2

GARNERS
av. Marrickville 374 A12
av. Marrickville 374 A12

GARNET
la. Lilyfield 10 D7
st. Killara 254 D12
gr. Glenwood 215 F13
la. Dulwich Hill ...373 C11
pl. Cartwright 393 K5
pl. Kellyville 185 F13
rd. Gymea 461 G15
rd. Kareela 461 B14
rd. Kirrawee 461 B14
rd. Miranda 461 G15
st. Bossley Park .334 B9
st. Dulwich Hill ...373 B11
st. Eagle Vale 481 F5
st. Guildford 338 C4
st. Hurlstone Pk ..373 B11
st. Killara 254 D12
st. Merrylands ...338 C4
st. Rockdale 433 F1
st. S Coogee 407 H4

GARNSEY
av. Panania 428 C5

GARONNE
st. Kearns 451 D16
st. Seven Hills 275 G7

GARRALLAN
pl. Airds 512 C10

GARRAN
la. Glebe 12 A1
st. Fairfield W 335 F11

GARRARD
la. Balmain East....8 D9
st. Granville 308 D13

GARRAWEEN
av. N Balgowlah ..287 C4

GARREFFA
cl. Edensor Pk ...333 J13

GARRETT
av. Glenhaven ...218 D3
av. S Turramurra .252 B8
av. Terrey Hills ...196 F5
pl. Shalvey 211 A15
st. Beecroft 250 F5
st. Kingsford 407 B8
st. Maroubra 407 B8
wy. Glenwood 246 B5

GARRICK
av. Hunters Hill .313 K12
la. St Clair, off St Clair Av ...269 H8
pl. Doonside 243 B7

Street	Suburb	Page	Ref
rd. St Clair		269	G8
st. St Ives		224	B10

GARRISON
rd. Bossley Park ..333 H8
wy. Glenwood 246 B5

GARRONG
rd. Lakemba 371 A15

GARRY
st. Georges Hall..367 K14

GARSWOOD
rd. Glenmore Pk ..266 F9

GARTFERN
av. Five Dock 343 A6

GARTHONS
la. Hurstville 431 J5

GARTHOWEN
av. Lane Cove 313 K2
cr. Castle Hill 218 E13

GARTMORE
av. Bankstown ...399 F5

GARTUNG
rd. Galston 159 C4

GARTY
wy. Minto 482 G2

GARVAN
rd. Heathcote ...518 C15

GARY
gr. Marayong 244 D6
st. Castle Hill 248 B3
st. Merrylands W ..306 J13

GAS
la. Millers Pt ....A C9
la. N Sydney ....K D10

GASCOGNE
st. Prestons 393 H13

GASCOIGNE
st. Birrong 368 H7
st. Yagoona 368 H8
st. Penrith 237 D9

GASCOYNE
pl. Illawong 460 B3

GASMATA
cr. Whalan 240 H10

GASPARD
pl. Ambarvale ...510 H13

GAS WORKS
rd. Wollstncraft..315 D11

GATACRE
av. Lane Cove ..314 F1

GATE
rd. Blacktown ...244 G9

GATEHOUSE
cct. Wrrngtn Dns ..238 A3

GATENBY
pl. Barden Rdg ..458 H16

GATES
rd. Luddenham ..326 F1

GATHREY
cr. Kings Lngly ...245 D5

GATLEY
ct. Wattle Grove ..426 A5

GATTO
pl. West Hoxton ..392 C7

GAUSS
pl. Tregear 240 E5

GAUTHORPE
st. Rhodes 311 D8

GAVIN
pl. Cherrybrook ..219 J9
pl. Kings Lngly ..245 K6

GAWAIN
pl. Glenhaven ..217 J5

GAWLER
pl. Bossley Park ..333 E10
pl. N Turramurra ..223 D1

GAY
st. Castle Hill ..218 D12
st. Lane Cove N ..284 D15

GAYLINE
dr. Narellan Vale ..479 B13

GAYMARK
la. Penrith 236 J10

GAZA
av. Hunters Hill ..313 E5
la. West Ryde, off Gaza Rd ..281 D15
rd. Holsworthy ..426 E7
rd. Northmead ..315 F11
rd. West Ryde ..281 D16
st. Holsworthy ..426 D10

GAZALA
rd. Holsworthy ..426 E7

Street	Suburb	Page	Ref
GAZANIA			
rd. Faulconbdg		171	E14
GAZELLE			
pl. Werrington		238	E11
st. Glenfield		424	F9

GAZI
cl. Bossley Park ..334 A6

GAZZARD
st. Birrong 368 K6

GEAKES
rd. Freemns Rch...67 A15
rd. Glossodia 67 A12
rd. Wilberforce ...67 A12

GEARS
av. Drummoyne ..343 F4

GEARY
st. Campbelltwn ..510 H7

GEDDES
pl. Cabramatta W ..365 C8
st. Balgowlah Ht...288 A13
st. Botany 405 J16

GEE
cl. Bossley Park ..334 A6

GEEBUNG
cl. Agnes Banks ..146 G4
cl. Arcadia 129 J10
ct. Voyager Pt ..427 C4
la. Engadine 518 J3
pl. Heckenberg ..364 A14
rd. Arcadia 130 A14

GEELANS
rd. Arcadia 130 A14

GEELONG
cr. St Johns Pk ..364 E3
rd. Cromer 228 D16
rd. Engadine 489 C9

GEER
av. Sans Souci ...463 B2

GEES
av. Strathfield ..371 E5

GEEVES
av. Rockdale 403 D15
pl. Pennant Hills ..220 G16
pl. Pennant Hills ..250 G1
st. Rockdale, off Geeves Av ..403 D14

GEEWAN
av. Kellyville 216 F2
pl. Clarmnt Ms ..268 K7

GEHRIG
la. Annandale ...17 C2

GELDING
st. Dulwich Hill ..373 C7

GELLING
av. Strathfield ..341 C16

GEM
pl. Greystanes ..306 C2

GEMALLA
st. Bonnyrigg ..363 K9

GEMALONG
pl. Glenmore Pk ..266 G15

GEMAS
pl. St Ives Ch ..223 J6
st. Holsworthy ..426 D1

GEMEREN
gr. W Pnnant Hl ..248 K7

GEMINI
cl. S Penrith 267 B6

GEMOORE
st. Smithfield ..335 B7

GEMSTONE
wy. Oakhurst, off Dillon Pl ..242 C2

GENDERS
av. Burwood ...371 H1
la. Burwood, off Genders Av ..371 H1

GENERAL BRIDGES
cr. Daceyville ..406 G3

GENERAL HOLMES
dr. Botany 405 D7
dr. Btn-le-Sds ..404 B16
dr. Kyeemagh ..404 B16
dr. Mascot 404 B16

GENEVA
st. Seven Hills ..275 H7
st. Engadine 489 B9
st. Cranebrook ..207 G5
st. Berowra 133 E16

GENISTA
st. Loftus 490 A10

Street	Suburb	Page	Ref
GENNER			
st. Denistone W		281	A12
GENOA			
st. Como		460	J6

GENTIAN
av. Mcquarie Fd ..454 G5
pl. Lugarno 430 A14

GENTLE
cl. Casula 424 B3
st. Lane Cove ...314 A1
st.w.Lane Cove W ..314 A1

GENTY
st. Campbelltwn ..511 H4

GEOFFREY
cl. Loftus 490 A11
st. S Turramrra ..252 C7
st. Wentwthvle ..277 A10

GEORGANN
st. Turramurra ..223 A8

GEORGE
cl. Eastlakes, off George St ..405 J4
la. N Strathfield ..341 E7
la. Paddington 21 D4
pde.Baulkham Hl ..247 G14
pl. Artarmon ..284 H16
rd. Leppington ..420 C15
rd. Wilberforce ...91 K3
st. Appin 569 J13
st. Appin 569 H14
st. Avalon 139 K11
st. Balmain 7 C13
st. Bankstown ..369 D11
st. Bardwell Vy ..402 J10
st. Bexley 402 J10
st. Blacktown ..244 H15
st. Box Hill 154 D9
st. Brooklyn 76 D7
st. Burwood ...341 J13
st. Burwood Ht ..371 K4
st. Campbelltwn ..511 G8
st. Canley Ht ...365 G1
st. Concord W ..341 C1
st. Dover Ht 348 E8
st. Eastlakes ...405 J4
st. Epping 280 G1
st. Erskineville ...18 A16
st. Gladesville ..312 G10
st. Granville ...308 D11
st. Greenwich ..314 J13
st. Guildford ..337 C3
st. Haymarket ....E E12
st. Haymarket ....E F15
st. Haymarket 3 D16
st. Hornsby 221 G1
st. Hunters Hill ..313 D11
st. Kingswood ..238 B13
st. Leichhardt ...15 D5
st. Lidcombe ..339 G9
st. Liverpool ..395 E4
st. Manly 288 E9
st. Marrickville ..373 H10
st. Miranda ...492 B7
st. Mortdale ..431 B9
st. Mount Druitt ..271 F5
st. N Strathfield ..341 D4
st. Paddington ..21 F3
st. Parramatta ..308 C2
st. Pennant Hills ..250 J1
st. Penshurst ..431 C3
st. Randwick ...377 C13
st. Redfern 19 C9
st. Riverstone ..182 H4
st. Rockdale ..403 E15
st. St Marys ...269 D2
st. Schofields ..182 H15
st. Seven Hills ..275 G3
st. S Hurstville ..432 C8
st. S Windsor ..120 E16
st. Springwood ..202 A2
st. Sydenham ..374 E14
st. Sydney ....C H16
st. Sydney 1 G3
st. Sydney 3 G6
st. Tahmoor ...565 J12
st. Tahmoor ...565 K10
st. The Rocks .....A J1
st. The Rocks 1 H8
st. Ultimo ....E C15
st. Ultimo 3 D16
st. Warwck Frm ..365 E16
st. Waterloo 19 E16
st. Waterloo 19 E16
st. Windsor ...120 H13
st. Windsor ...121 A11
st. Yagoona ...369 B7
st. Yowie Bay ..492 B7
swy.Liverpool ...395 D4

Street	Suburb	Page	Ref
GEORGE BEST			
cr. Baulkham Hl		247	F13
GEORGE BRANSBY			
rd. Harrington Pk		478	C2
GEORGE CALEY			
pl. Mt Annan		509	H2
GEORGE HUNTER			
dr. Narellan		478	H8
GEORGE JULIUS			
av. Zetland		375	K11
GEORGE MOBBS			
dr. Castle Hill		248	B5
GEORGE MUIR			
cl. Baulkham Hl		248	D10
GEORGE PING			
dr. Thirlmere		564	J6
GEORGES			
av. Berala		339	G12
av. Lidcombe		339	G12
cr. Georges Hall		367	F13
cr. Roselands		400	K9
pde. Glenfield		424	K12
rd. Vaucluse		348	G2

GEORGES RIVER
cr. Oyster Bay ..461 C4
prm.Ingleburn ...454 A11
rd. Airds 512 A9
rd. Campbelltwn ..512 A9
rd. Croydon Pk ..371 G7
rd. Jannali 460 J12
rd. Kentlyn 513 A7
rd. Lansvale ...366 G8
rd. Oyster Bay ..461 A10
rd. Ruse 512 A9

GEORGES RIVER BRIDGE
Blakehurst ...462 D13
Sylvania 462 D5

GEORGE WALLACE
st. Moore Park ...21 C6

GEORGIA
pl. Minto Ht 483 G8
pl. Quakers Hill ..214 G11
tce. Kellyville ...187 A16

GEORGIA LEE
pl. Clareville ...169 E2

GEORGIAN
av. Carlingford ..249 G15

GEORGIANA
cr. Ambarvale ..511 B11

GEORGINA
av. Elanora Ht ..198 F15
cl. Wahroonga ..221 K14
la. Newtown 18 B9
rd. Mt Vernon ..331 D12
st. Bass Hill ...368 D14
st. Bonnyrigg Ht ..363 B7
st. Newtown 18 A9

GERALD
av. Roseville 284 H2
cr. Doonside ...243 E5
rd. Illawong 459 A6
st. Cecil Hills ..362 J7
st. Greystanes ..306 F6
st. Marrickville ..374 B14

GERALDINE
av. Baulkham Hl ..247 D8

GERALDTON
pl. Yarrawarrah ..489 F12
st. Prestons 423 C1

GERANIUM
av. Mcquarie Fd ..454 F6
pl. Glenmore Pk ..265 G13

GERARD
av. Condell Park ..368 F16
cr. Cremorne ...316 F7
la. Gladesville, off Gerard St ..312 H8
pl. Glenmore Pk ..266 H15
st. Alexandria ...18 K12
st. Cremorne ..316 F7
st. Gladesville ..312 H8

GERARDA
pl. West Hoxton ..392 D8

GERBULIN
st. Glendenning ..242 F3

GERHARD
pl. Harrington Pk ..478 K3

GERLEE
pl. Quakers Hill ..214 F9

GERMAINE
av. Mt Riverview ..234 B3

GERONIMO
cl. Greenfld Pk ..334 A14

GREGORY'S STREET DIRECTORY 71

GE STREETS

GERRALE
st. Cronulla............493 K13
GERRING
st. Colyton............270 B6
GERRISH
st. Gladesville........312 K7
GERROA
av. Bayview...........169 B14
pl. Prestons...........393 A14
GERSHAM
gr. Oakhurst..........242 A4
GERSHWIN
cr. Clarmnt Ms......268 G3
GERTRUDE
av. Newport..........169 J13
rd. Ingleburn.........453 D12
st. Balgowlah Ht....287 G12
st. Beacon Hill.......257 E7
st. Wolli Creek......403 K6
GETYUNGA
rd. Oyster Bay......461 C4
GEUM
pl. Mcquarie Fd....454 F6
GHOST HILL
rd. Berambing........60 C13
GHURKA
st. Sadleir............394 B2
GIBB
av. Casula............394 J11
cl. N Parramatta....278 G12
pl. Springwood.....201 D1
st. North Ryde.....282 E8
GIBBENS
la. Camperdown.....17 E6
st. Camperdown.....17 E6
GIBBER
pl. Annangrove.....186 H4
GIBBES
la. Newtown.........17 H14
la. Banksia...........403 F16
la. Chatswood.......285 E5
st. Newtown.........17 G14
st. Regentville......265 G4
st. Rockdale.........403 F16
GIBBINS
cl. Hornsby...........191 G9
GIBBON
rd. Winston Hills..246 G15
GIBBONS
la. Arncliffe..........403 B10
la. Marayong........244 C8
st. Auburn...........339 D1
st. Eveleigh............19 A9
st. Oatlands.........279 D6
st. Redfern............19 A9
st. Telopea...........279 D6
wy. Claymore.......481 C12
GIBBS
la. Manly Vale.....287 H2
la. Newtown..........17 D10
pl. St Helens Park...541 C5
st. Auburn...........338 K5
st. Croydon.........342 E15
st. Manly Vale.....287 H3
st. Miranda..........492 A5
GIBLETT
av. Thornleigh.....220 H11
GIBRAN
pl. St Ives...........224 E16
GIBSON
av. Casula...........394 J12
av. Chatswood....284 J7
av. Padstow........399 C9
av. Werrington....238 K11
av. Horsley Pk....302 E16
pl. Blacktown......274 C5
pl. Chifley..........437 E6
pwy.Casula, off
Gibson Av......394 K12
rd. Denham Ct....452 G3
rd. Mosman........317 C6
st. Bronte...........377 H8
st. Hobartville....118 G7
st. Pagewood.....405 K10
st. Richmond......118 G7
st. Silverdale......353 G14
st. Waterloo.........19 F13
st. Waverley.......377 H8
st. Yarrawarrah..489 F11
GIDDINGS
cl. Cronulla........493 K14
lk. Harringtn Pk..478 J2
GIDEON
st. Winston Hills..276 H2

GIDGEE
st. Cabramatta....365 G9
GIDJI
rd. Miranda........491 K5
GIDLEY
cr. Claymore......481 A11
st. St Marys......239 H16
GIDYA
st. Frenchs Frst..256 F4
GIFFARD
st. Silverwater....309 J10
GIFFNOCK
av. Mcquarie Pk..282 G4
GIG
wy. Riverstone...182 H11
GILAI
pl. Allambie Ht..257 G15
GILBA
rd. Girraween....275 J11
rd. Pendle Hill...276 A12
GILBERT
cr. Kings Lngly..245 A5
pl. Frenchs Frst..256 G8
rd. Castle Hill...217 F10
rd. Glenhaven...217 J6
st. Cabramatta....365 D7
st. Colyton........270 B7
st. Dover Ht......348 E11
st. Manly..........288 G10
st. N Parramatta..278 D11
st. Sylvania......462 A12
wy. Minto..........482 K1
GILBULLA
av. Camden......507 A3
GILCHRIST
dr. Campbelltown..510 K9
st. Balmain East......8 D8
GILDA
av. Five Dock....343 A7
GILDEA
av. Bayview......168 C12
GIMI
gr. Plumpton....242 D9
GIMLET
cl. Kingswood....237 H16
cl. Kingswood....267 H1
pl. Mcquarie Pk..454 E3
GINAHGULLA
rd. Bellevue Hill......14 J7
GINAHGULLAH
av. Grose Vale......85 H9
GINDURRA
av. Castle Hill...217 C8
ct. Hamondvle..396 G14
GIOVANNA
ct. Castle Hill...217 C7
GIPPS
av. Little Bay....437 A12
cl. Turramurra..252 B3
dr. Cromer........227 G12
rd. Greystanes..305 D11
rd. Smithfield...305 D13
st. Arncliffe.......403 C8
st. Bardwell Vy..403 C8
st. Birchgrove........7 F6
st. Bradbury.....511 G14
st. Bronte.........377 H16
st. Clarmnt Ms..239 A16
st. Clarmnt Ms..268 J4
st. Concord.....341 H8
st. Drummoyne..343 F4
st. Paddington.....4 J15
st. Pyrmont......12 H5
st. Smithfield...305 D11
st. Werrington..239 A15
GIPSY
st. Bnkstn Aprt..397 K1
GIRA
pl. Dharruk......241 D8
GIRARD
st. Harbord......288 D2
GIRD
pl. Marayong...243 K6
GIRILANG
av. Vaucluse...348 E6
GIRRA
av. S Penrith....266 J1
rd. Blacktown....243 H16
st. Fairfield W..335 G10
GIRRALONG
av. Baulkhm Hl..248 A7

GIRRAWEEN
av. Como..........460 F6
av. Lane Cove N...284 A14
rd. Girraween.....275 K16
st. Kingsgrove....402 A9
GIRRILANG
rd. Cronulla......494 A8
GIRROMA
st. Carss Park...432 G13
GISSING
st. Wetherill Pk..334 F4
GIUFFRE
pl. W Pnnant Hl..249 H7
GLADE
pl. Engadine....488 K15
pl. W Pnnant Hl..249 C2
st. Balgowlah Ht..287 J13
GLADES
av. Gladesville...312 G10
GLADESVILLE
rd. Hunters Hills..313 B10
GLADIATOR
st. Raby...........451 C13
GLADSTONE
av. Hunters Hill..314 C13
av. Mosman......317 B8
av. Ryde..........312 A4
av. Warrawee....222 H11
cl. West Hoxton..392 D8
la. Kogarah, off
Gladstone St.....433 C3
la. Marrickville..374 A13
la. Newtown......17 C13
pde. Lindfield.....284 C3
pde. Riverstone..183 A10
rd. Castle Hill...217 B15
st. Balmain..........7 K10
st. Belmore......401 D1
st. Bexley........402 J16
st. Burwood.....341 J12
st. Cabramatta..365 F7
st. Canley Ht....365 F4
st. Concord......342 B7
st. Enmore.........17 A11
st. Kogarah.....433 C3
st. Lilyfield.......10 H10
st. Marrickville..374 A13
st. Merrylands..307 J12
st. Newport......169 E12
st. Newtown......17 A11
st. N Parramatta..278 E13
st. Stanmore......17 A11
st. Surry Hills......19 J2
st. Vaucluse....318 F16
GLADSWOOD
av. S Penrith.....267 B2
gdn. Double Bay.....14 F6
GLADYS
av. Frenchs Frst..256 G4
cr. Seven Hills..245 C16
st. Kingswood...237 D16
st. Rydalmere...309 J3
GLAISHER
pde. Cronulla....523 K4
GLAMIS
pl. Castle Hill....216 J10
st. Kingsgrove...401 F8
GLAMORGAN
st. Blacktown....274 H7
wy. Cherrybrook..219 F9
GLANARA
ct. Wattle Grove..426 A1
GLANDORE
st. Woolooware..493 G6
GLANFIELD
av. Yowie Bay..492 C10
GLANFIELD
st. Maroubra....406 H9
GLANMIRE
rd. Baulkham Hl..247 A9
GLANVILLE
av. Pagewood...406 G6
GLASGOW
av. Bondi Beach..378 D1
st. Holsworthy..396 B14
st. St Andrews..452 B14
st. Winston Hills..277 D4
GLASSHOUSE
rd. Beaumont Hills..215 J1
GLASSOP
la. Yagoona......368 F13
st. Balmain..........7 A8
st. Bankstown..368 A13
st. Caringbah...492 K6
st. Yagoona......368 F13

GLEAM
pl. Cranebrook..206 H8
GLEBE
cl. Appin..........569 F13
la. Glebe..........12 D13
pl. Kingswood..237 D9
pl. Penrith.......237 D9
st. St Johns Pk..364 F5
rd. Pitt Town....122 K1
st. Edgecliff......13 J13
st. Glebe..........12 D13
st. Parramatta..307 K6
st. Randwick....377 E12
GLEBE POINT
rd. Glebe..........12 C14
GLEDITSIA
cl. Narellan Vale..479 A11
GLEDSWOOD
pl. Glen Alpine..510 G12
GLEESON
av. Baulkhm Hl..247 E10
av. Condell Park..398 K6
av. Sydenham..374 D14
pl. Abbotsbury..333 C12
GLEN
la. Randwick....377 D13
la. Bondi.........378 B5
la. Glebe.........11 G11
la. Glenbrook..264 A1
la. Randwick....377 E12
pl. Currans Hill..479 K11
pl. Pendle Hill..276 C16
rd. Castle Hill..218 H14
st. Emu Heights..234 K6
st. Oatley........430 J10
rd. Roseville....284 D6
st. Belrose......225 J16
st. Blaxland....233 D5
st. Bondi.........378 B5
st. Eastwood...281 A8
st. Galston......159 F9
st. Glenbrook..264 A1
st. Granville....308 C13
st. Harbord......258 G16
st. Marrickville..373 F15
st. Milsons Point.....5 J15
st. Mosman.....316 K3
st. Paddington..13 B13
GLEN ABBEY
st. Rouse Hill..185 A9
GLENAEON
av. Belrose......226 B8
GLEN ALLAN
rd. Rossmore...390 A15
GLEN ALPINE
dr. Glen Alpine..510 D10
GLENALVON
pl. West Hoxton..392 B11
GLENANNE
pl. Tahmoor....565 F7
GLENARA
rd. Kurrajong Ht..62 H9
GLENARM
cr. Killarney Ht..256 B15
GLENARVON
st. Strathfield..371 A1
GLEN AVON
av. Beverly Hills..400 H15
GLENAVON
st. Blacktown..274 H7
pl. Glen Alpine..510 E13
GLENAVY
st. Wentwthvle..276 K15
GLEN-AYR
av. Yowie Bay..492 C10
GLENAYR
av. Bondi Beach..378 C2
av. Denistone W..280 K13
av. North Bondi..348 D16
av. West Ryde..280 K13
av. W Pnnant Hl..249 B1
la. Bondi Beach, off
Blair St......378 C1
GLENBAWN
pl. Leumeah...482 D13
pl. Woodcroft..243 H11
GLENBROOK
cr. Georges Hall..367 J10
pl. The Oaks....502 D13
rd. Blaxland....233 J14
rd. Glenbrook..233 J14
st. Jamisontown..266 J7
GLENCARRON
av. Mosman....317 C4

72 GREGORY'S STREET DIRECTORY

STREETS GO

GLENCOE
- av. Chatswood W 284 F8
- av. Oatlands 278 H10
- av. Wrrngtn Cty 238 D9
- cl. Berowra 133 G10
- rd. Woollahra 22 E1
- st. Sutherland 490 G4
- st.s. Sutherland 490 H6

GLENCORSE
- av. Milperra 397 G12

GLENCROFT
- rd. Roseville 284 A8

GLENDA
- pl. Mt Krng-gai 162 G11
- pl. North Rocks 248 J13
- pl. Plumpton 241 J8

GLENDALE
- av. Mt Pritchard 364 H14
- av. Narwee 400 J13
- av. Padstow 429 D3
- dr. Lilyfield 10 C5
- pl. W Pnnant Hl 249 A3
- pl. Jannali 460 J13
- rd. Cowan 133 K2
- rd. Turramurra 223 A8

GLEN DAVIS
- av. Bossley Park 333 E11

GLENDENNING
- rd. Glendenning 242 F11

GLENDEVIE
- st. West Hoxton 392 D6

GLENDIVER
- rd. Glenmore 503 A12
- rd. The Oaks 502 F12

GLENDON
- rd. Double Bay 14 F12

GLENDOWER
- av. Eastwood 281 H5
- pl. Gilead 540 F7
- st. Rsemeadow 540 F7

GLENEAGLES
- av. Killara 253 F15
- cr. Hornsby 192 D15
- pl. St Andrews 481 K14
- wy. Glenmore Pk 266 E9

GLENELG
- ct. Wattle Grove 395 H13
- pl. Beecroft 250 G7
- pl. St Ives Ch 223 K3
- st. Sutherland 460 F16

GLEN ELGIN
- cr. Edensor Pk 333 D15

GLENELGIN
- rd. Winmalee 173 D12

GLENELL
- st. Blaxland 233 J10

GLENELLA
- av. Beverly Hills 400 J16
- wy. Minto 482 G9

GLENESS
- pl. Glenorie 127 J3

GLENFARNE
- st. Bexley 432 G2

GLENFERN
- cl. W Pnnant Hl 248 G8
- cr. Bossley Park 334 A3
- pl. Gymea Bay 491 E8
- st. Epping 250 J16

GLENFERRIE
- av. Cremorne, off
- Iredale Av 316 F11

GLENFIELD
- dr. Currans Hill 479 K13
- rd. Casula 424 A5
- rd. Glenfield 424 A5
- rd. Glenfield 424 E7

GLENGARIFF
- av. Killarney Ht 256 A16

GLENGARRIE
- rd. Marsden Pk 211 D5

GLENGARRY
- av. N Turramurra 223 E2
- dr. Glenmore Pk 266 G12
- dr. Glenmore Pk 266 G16
- la. Carlingford 280 A2
- la. Mosman, off
- Effingham St 317 C10

GLENGYLE
- ct. Wattle Grove 425 K2

GLENHARE
- la. Glenbrook, off
- Moore St 233 K15

GLENHAVEN
- pl. Oyster Bay 461 C5
- rd. Glenhaven 218 C1
- rd. Kellyville 186 J15

GLEN HEATH
- av. Kellyville Rdg 185 A16

GLEN HELEN
- pl. Dural 219 B3

GLENHOPE
- rd. W Pnnant Hl 249 B7

GLENIDOL
- rd. Oakville 152 H4

GLEN INNES
- rd. Hinchinbrk 392 H6
- rd. Hoxton Park 392 H6

GLENISIA
- av. Georges Hall 367 J11

GLENLEA
- ct. Glenwood 215 B15
- st. Canley Ht 335 D15

GLENLEE
- cl. Mt Krng-gai 162 K13
- rd. Narellan Vale 508 F2
- rd. Gilead 509 E14
- rd. Glen Alpine 509 E14
- rd. Menangle Pk 509 E14
- rd. Spring Farm 508 E7

GLENLEIGH
- av. Mulgoa 324 C6

GLEN LOGAN
- rd. Bossley Park 333 E10

GLEN MARGARET
- av. Lurnea 394 E12

GLENMORE
- la. S Penrith, off
- Glenmore Pl 266 F4
- pky. Glenmore Pk 265 G5
- pky. Glenmore Pk 265 H9
- pky. Glenmore Pk 266 A12
- pky. Glenmore Pk 266 F11
- pl. S Penrith 266 F3
- rd. Edgecliff 13 F12
- rd. Paddington 4 J13
- rd. Paddington 13 F12
- rd. Narrembum 315 F3

GLENN
- av. Northmead 277 H9
- pl. N Richmond 87 C13
- pl. Yagoona 368 K8
- st. Dean Park 242 G1

GLENNIE
- av. Colyton 270 D8

GLENNIS
- cl. Glendenning 242 K4

GLENOAK
- wy. Cherrybrook 219 C9

GLENORA
- rd. Yarrawarrah 489 E14

GLENORE
- rd. Canterbury 402 D1

GLEN ORMOND
- av. Abbotsford 342 J3

GLEN OSMOND
- cr. Bossley Park 333 E10

GLENRIDGE
- av. W Pnnant Hl 249 B2

GLENROBEN
- pl. Mount Druitt 241 F12

GLENROCK
- av. Edgecliff 13 J11
- cr. Wahroonga 223 C5
- ct. Wattle Grove 426 A1
- pl. Glen Alpine 510 E13

GLENROE
- av. W Pnnant Hl 249 B3

GLENROSE
- pl. Belrose 225 H16

GLENROTHES
- pl. Dharruk 241 D7

GLENROWAN
- av. Kellyville 216 G6
- dr. Harringtn Pk 478 C2
- dr. St Clair 270 D12

GLENROY
- av. Middle Cove 285 J7
- st. St Johns Pk 364 F7
- pl. Glenwood 245 H3
- rd. Middle Dural 158 C9

GLENSHEE
- pl. Glenhaven 218 E6
- st. St Andrews 481 J6

GLENSIDE
- st. Balgowlah Ht 287 K13

GLENTON
- st. Abbotsbury 333 B13

GLENTREES
- av. Forestville 256 A12
- pl. Cherrybrook 219 H10

GLENUGIE
- st. Maroubra 407 E12

GLENVALE
- av. Parklea 215 A14
- cl. W Pnnant Hl 249 H6

GLENVIEW
- av. Earlwood 402 F4
- av. Revesby 398 F15
- cr. Bella Vista 216 D16
- cr. Hunters Hill 314 A13
- gr. Glendenning 242 H4
- la. Earlwood, off
- Glenview Av 402 F4
- la. Paddington 4 K12
- la. St Marys, off
- Glenview St 269 K4
- pl. Engadine 488 J14
- rd. Hunters Hill 314 B13
- rd. Mt Krng-gai 162 J11
- st. Gordon 253 K5
- st. Greenwich 315 A9
- st. Kogarah Bay 432 K12
- st. Paddington 4 K12
- st. St Marys 269 J5

GLENWALL
- st. Kingsgrove 401 G14

GLENWARI
- st. Sadleir 394 A1

GLENWOOD
- av. Coogee 377 F16
- av. Beecroft 250 A10
- wy. Castle Hill 218 G16

GLENWOOD PARK
- dr. Glenwood 215 D16
- dr. Glenwood 245 H1
- dr. Glenwood 245 D1

GLENWORTH
- pl. Theresa Park 445 B3

GLOBE
- st. The Rocks ....A K6

GLORIA
- cl. Mt Colah 162 F12
- pl. S Penrith 267 C5
- st. Merrylands W 306 J13

GLORY
- wy. Beaumont Hills 185 J13

GLOSSOP
- st. N St Marys 239 J11

GLOUCESTER
- av. Burwood 341 K13
- av. Merrylands 307 D16
- av. N Parramatta 278 E10
- av. Padstow 429 D1
- av. West Pymble 252 G13
- pl. Kensington 376 C11
- rd. Beverly Hills 401 E14
- rd. Epping 251 F13
- rd. Hoxton Park 392 H10
- st. Hurstville 431 F1
- st. Bexley 432 E2
- st. Bonnyrigg Ht 363 A5
- st. Concord 341 K1
- st. Mcquarie Fd 423 K15
- st. N Balgowlah 287 C4
- st. Rockdale 403 C14
- st. The Rocks ....A G10
- st. The Rocks ....A H6
- st. The Rocks 1 F13
- st. The Rocks 1 G11
- wk. The Rocks ....A J2

GLOVER
- av. Quakers Hill 214 E9
- la. Mosman, off
- Glover St 316 H8
- st. West Hoxton 392 C11
- st. Greenacre 370 F3
- st. Lilyfield 9 J2
- st. Mosman 316 H7
- st. N Willoughby 285 F9

GLYN
- av. Picnic Point 428 H8
- pl. Kellyville Rdg 215 A1
- st. Wiley Park 400 F2

GLYNN
- cl. Cranebrook 207 B14

GNARBO
- av. Carss Park 432 F15
- la. Carss Park, off
- Allawah Av 432 F15

GOBURRA
- pl. Engadine 518 D4

GODALLA
- rd. Freemns Rch 66 G14

GODDARD
- cr. Quakers Hill 214 C10
- st. Erskineville 375 A10
- st. Newtown 17 E14
- st. Turrella 403 F5

GODERICH
- la. Potts Point 4 J8

GODFREY
- av. Turramurra 222 H16
- av. West Hoxton 391 K4
- rd. Artarmon 285 C13
- st. Banksia 403 D11
- st. Hurstville Gr 431 F9
- st. Penshurst 431 F9

GODWIN
- st. Bexley 402 J13

GODWIT
- cl. Hinchinbrk 363 E15

GOGOL
- pl. Wetherill Pk 335 A4

GOLD
- st. Blakehurst 462 C3

GOLDEN
- gr. Beacon Hill 257 G2
- gr. Bligh Park 150 D4
- gr. Cherrybrook 219 D14
- gr. Freemns Rch 89 D5
- gr. Stanhpe Gdn 215 A10
- gr. Westleigh 220 F7
- wy. Silverdale 353 J12

GOLDEN GROVE
- av. Kellyville 216 E1
- rd. Matraville 436 F7
- st. Darlington 18 D8
- st. Newtown 18 D8

GOLDEN STAVE
- wy. Berala 339 C14

GOLDEN VALLEY
- dr. Glossodia 66 B12

GOLDERS GREEN
- av. Glenhaven 218 D5

GOLDFINCH
- pl. Bella Vista 246 F1
- pl. Grays Point 491 F14
- st. Moorebank 396 C10

GOLDIE
- av. Bondi Jctn 377 G5
- pl. Colyton 270 G4

GOLDING
- dr. Glendenning 242 G4

GOLDMAN
- la. Double Bay 14 C10
- la. Double Bay, off
- Knox St 14 D9

GOLDMARK
- cr. Cranebrook 207 G10
- cr. Cranebrook 207 G9
- la. Cranebrook, off
- Goldmark Cr 207 J9

GOLDSBOROUGH
- la. Yennora 337 C11

GOLDSMITH
- av. Campbelltown 510 H6
- av. Killarney Ht 286 D1
- av. Winston Hills 277 G1
- cl. Wetherill Pk 334 J6

GOLF
- av. Mona Vale 199 E4
- pde. Manly 288 F5

GOLF COURSE
- dr. Glen Alpine 510 E12

GOLFERS
- la. Roseville 255 A16
- pde. Pymble 253 A6

GOLF LINKS
- st. Killara 253 G14

GOLFVIEW
- dr. Wallacia 324 K13

GOLIATH
- av. Winston Hills 276 H3

GOLLAN
- av. Oatlands 278 J9

GOLSPIE
- cl. Prestons 392 H15

GONA
- pde. Narraweena 258 C6
- pl. Glenfield 424 G12
- st. Mt Annan 479 C12
- st. Holsworthy 426 E2

GONDOLA
- rd. N Narrabeen 228 H1

GONZALO
- st. Gilead 540 F7

GOOBARAH
- rd. Burraneer 523 D2

GOOD
- st. Granville 308 F10
- st. Harris Park 308 G8
- st. Parramatta 307 J4
- st. Rosehill 308 G8
- st. Westmead 307 H2

GOODACRE
- av. Fairfield W 335 B14
- av. Miranda 492 C1
- av. Winston Hills 277 G3

GOODALL
- st. Pendle Hill 276 F14

GOODCHAP
- cr. Chatswood W 284 G12
- st. Surry Hills ....F G10
- st. Surry Hills 4 A13

GOODE
- pl. Currans Hill 479 H9

GOODEN
- dr. Baulkham Hl 247 A12

GOODENIA
- ct. Voyager Pt 427 D5
- rd. Mt Annan 509 C3

GOODENOUGH
- st. Glenfield 424 H8

GOODHALL
- av. Baulkham Hl 246 J15

GOODHOPE
- la. Paddington 13 C14
- st. Paddington 13 C14

GOODIA
- wy. Bidwill 211 G13

GOODIER
- pl. Kenthurst 156 J11

GOODIN
- rd. Baulkham Hl 247 K15

GOODLANDS
- av. Thornleigh 220 J12

GOODLET
- cl. Lane Cove W, off
- Walkers Dr 283 F12
- la. Surry Hills 19 J5
- st. Ashbury 372 E7
- st. Merrylands 307 F11
- st. Surry Hills 19 J5
- st. Thirlmere 565 A3

GOODMAN
- pl. Cherrybrook 219 J6
- wy. Bonnyrigg 364 B4

GOODMANS
- tce. Surry Hills 19 J2

GOODOOGA
- cl. Hinchinbrk 392 G4

GOODRICH
- av. Kingsford 376 C15
- rd. Cecil Park 331 K11

GOODS
- rd. Oakville 152 H2

GOODSELL
- av. Minto 482 K9
- st. St Peters 374 J11

GOODSIR
- cl. Rossmore 389 J6
- st. Rozelle 7 C13

GOODSTONE
- pl. Chester Hill 368 A2

GOODWIN
- av. Ashfield 372 J8
- av. Mt Lewis 370 B15
- cr. Minto 482 H5
- st. Newport 169 G9
- st. Denistone 281 G13
- st. Narrabeen 229 A7
- st. West Ryde 281 G13
- st. Woolooware 493 G8

GOODWOOD
- st. Kensington 376 F10

GOODWYN
- rd. Berowra 133 D14

GOOLAGONG
- av. Toongabbie 276 F5
- st. Milperra 397 F11
- la. La Perouse 436 J13
- pl. Menai 458 H6

GOOLD
- st. Chippendale 19 D1

GREGORY'S STREET DIRECTORY 73

GO STREETS

GOOLGUNG
av. Baulkham Hl 248 A10
GOOLMA
pl. Hornsby 192 D13
GOOLWA
cr. Cranebrook 207 F9
GOOMERAH
cr. Darling Point 13 J4
GOONAROI
st. Villawood 367 J4
st. Villawood 367 J5
GOONDA
av. La Perouse 436 K12
GOONDAH
rd. Engadine 489 C10
st. Villawood 367 E4
GOONDARI
rd. Allambie Ht 257 G14
GOONGOONRA
cl. Jamisontown 266 A4
GOORA
st. Little Bay 437 B11
GOORARI
av. Bella Vista 246 F6
GOORAWAHL
av. La Perouse 436 J14
GOORAWAY
dr. Castle Hill 217 J7
pl. Berowra Ht 132 K5
GOOREEN
st. Lidcombe 339 K3
GOORGOOL
rd. Bangor 459 H14
GOORIWA
pl. Engadine 488 E13
GOOROA
st. Carss Park 432 G13
GOOSE
cl. Hinchinbrk 363 D15
GOOSEBERRY
la. Mosman 317 G8
pl. Glenwood 215 E14
GORADA
av. Kirrawee 491 C6
GORDON
av. Castle Hill 218 B11
av. Chatswood 284 H12
av. Coogee 377 J14
av. Ingleburn 453 F3
av. S Granville 338 F5
cr. Denistone 281 D11
cr. Lane Cove N 284 B14
cr. Stanmore 16 B10
la. Paddington 21 D3
la. Petersham 15 G11
la. Bronte 377 J10
la. Narellan Vale 478 G16
la. Windsor Dn 180 K4
rd. Auburn 339 A8
rd. Schofields 183 J14
sq. Marrickville 16 B16
st. Annandale 17 C2
st. Bankstown 369 D15
st. Blacktown 244 J15
st. Btn-le-Sds 433 K1
st. Burwood 341 J13
st. Campsie 372 C10
st. Caringbah 492 J6
st. Carramar 336 J15
st. Clontarf 287 F13
st. Eastwood 281 D6
st. Fairfield 336 J15
st. Hurstville 431 K4
st. Manly Vale 287 K2
st. Marrickville 374 D9
st. Mosman 317 D9
st. Paddington 21 D2
st. Penrith 236 G1
st. Petersham 15 F11
st. Randwick 377 B11
st. Rosebery 405 H3
st. Rozelle 11 B2
st. Rydalmere 310 A2
st. St Marys 269 K2
st. Thirlmere 565 B14
GORDON BRAY
cct. Lidcombe 339 J13
GORDONIA
gr. Baulkham Hl 247 E16
GORDON McKINNON
la. Harris Pk 308 E6
GORDON PARKER
st. Revesby 398 E10

GORDONS
la. Concord, off
  Finch Av 342 B8
GORE
av. Kirrawee 490 J8
av. Bella Vista 246 G5
la. Kirrawee 490 H8
pl. Willmot 210 D12
st. Arncliffe 403 E10
st. Greenwich 315 A8
st. Harbord 288 H2
st. Parramatta 278 K10
GORE HILL
fwy. Artarmon 315 A1
fwy. Lane Cove 314 J1
fwy. Naremburn 315 A1
GORINSKI
la. West Hoxton, off
  Harraden Dr 391 K11
pl. Menai 458 E15
pl. Parramatta 308 J1
rd. Claymore 481 E10
rd. Eagle Vale 481 E10
st. Bankstown 368 H14
st. Bondi Beach 378 D3
st. Campsie 372 C13
st. Canterbury 372 C13
st. North Bondi 348 E16
st. Strathfield S 370 J4
st. West Hoxton 391 J11
wy. Blacktown 273 H6
GORMAN
av. Panania 428 E4
cl. Cranebrook 207 D10
st. Marrickville 374 B11
st. Willoughby 285 E15
GORMLEY
st. Freemns Rch 89 F6
st. Lidcombe 339 J11
GORNALL
av. Earlwood 372 G15
GOROKA
pl. Beacon Hill 257 K8
st. Glenfield 424 F10
st. Whalan 240 H10
GORRICKS
la. Freemns Rch 90 G5
GORSE
cl. Loftus 489 K10
st. Prospect 274 G10
GORT
rd. Engadine 488 K12
GORTON
cl. Penrith 237 B7
GOSBELL
la. Paddington 13 B11
st. Paddington 13 A11
GOSBY
av. Miranda 491 J5
GOSHA
cl. Rooty Hill 271 H6
GOSHAWK
cr. Castle Hill 218 F8
pl. Green Valley 363 C12
GOSLING
av. Green Valley 363 C14
st. Emu Heights ... 234 J6
st. Greenacre 370 E14
GOSPER
la. Camperdown ... 18 C1
st. Windsor 120 H10
GOSPORT
st. Cronulla 493 J10
GOSSAMER
pl. Mcquarie Fd ... 454 E4
GOSSE
st. St Clair 270 D10
la. St Clair, off
  Gosse St 270 D10
pl. Bonnyrigg Ht .. 363 F8
GOSSELL
gr. Carlingford 249 C13
GOTHER
la. Greenwich 314 K13
GOTTENHAM
la. Glebe 12 C12
st. Glebe 12 C11
GOTTWALD
pl. W Pnnant Hl .. 249 H6
GOUDA
cl. Abbotsbury ... 333 B16
GOUGH
av. Chester Hill ... 337 K12
dr. Castle Hill 218 K13
st. Emu Plains 235 D14
st. Holroyd 307 K10
GOULBURN
st. Surry Hills .... F C12
st. Surry Hills 3 K12
st. Darlinghurst .... F C5
st. Darlinghurst 3 J11
st. Haymarket ...... E D4
st. Haymarket 3 E10
st. Kings Park 244 E6
st. Liverpool 395 F2
st. Ruse 512 C9

st. St Ives 223 K15
st. Surry Hills ....F C5
st. Surry Hills 3 J11
st. Sydney ....3 E D4
st. Sydney 3 D12
st. Warwck Frm ...365 F16
swy.Liverpool......395 F1
GOULBURN PENINSULA
pl. Sylvania Wtr 462 D14
GOULD
av. Kellyville 215 J5
av. Lewisham 15 C15
av. Narraweena 258 F11
av. St Ives Ch 224 A1
la. Lewisham 15 C13
la. West Hoxton, off
  Harraden Dr ...391 K11
pl. Menai 458 E15
pl. Parramatta 308 J1
rd. Claymore 481 E10
rd. Eagle Vale 481 E10
st. Bankstown 368 H14
st. Bondi Beach ..378 D3
st. Campsie 372 C13
st. Canterbury 372 C13
st. North Bondi ..348 E16
st. Strathfield S ..370 J4
st. West Hoxton .391 J11
wy. Blacktown 273 H6
GOULDING
rd. Ryde 282 D13
GOULDSBURY
st. Mosman 317 A7
GOURLAY
av. Balgowlah 287 K11
GOVE
av. Green Valley .363 J11
GOVER
st. Peakhurst 430 C2
GOVERNMENT
rd. Bargo 567 J2
rd. Beacon Hill .257 E7
rd. Berkshire Pk .179 H13
rd. Brooklyn 76 B11
rd. Cromer 227 K13
rd. Hinchinbrk .392 G4
rd. Hornsby 221 G2
rd. Mona Vale .198 K2
rd. Mosman 287 A16
GOVERNMENT FARM
cr. Castle Hill ..218 F8
GOVERNMENT HOUSE
dr. Emu Plains .235 D9
GOVERNOR
dr. Winston Hills, off
  Mangalore Dr ..277 A3
dr. Chipping Ntn ..396 H1
dr. Warwck Frm ..365 K15
GOVERNOR MACQUARIE
pl. W Pnnant Hl ..248 H8
GOVERNOR PHILLIP
dr. Concord 342 F6
dr. Lapstone 264 H13
dr. Mcquarie Pk ..283 B6
la. Picton 563 K2
la. Mosman 317 K6
wk. Pymble 253 E4
wy. Mcquarie Lk .423 E15
wy. Oatlands 279 A7
GOVETT
la. Randwick, off
  Govett St 376 K10
pl. Davidson 225 A15
st. Mt Pritchard ..364 C10
st. Randwick 376 K9
GOW
av. Port Hacking ..522 K3
la. Cornwallis 120 G1
st. Abbotsford 342 J2
st. Balmain 7 C5
st. Padstow 399 C9
GOWAN
ct. Carlingford ...279 B5
ct. Denham Ct ..452 A2
GOWAN BRAE
dr. Oatlands 278 K10
GOWER
st. Wetherill Pk ..334 J5
st. Ashfield 373 C2
st. Hurlstone Pk ..372 K12
st. Summer Hill ..373 C2
GOWLLAND
pde. Panania 398 D13

GOWRIE
av. Bondi Jctn 377 G3
av. Punchbowl 399 K5
st. St Ives 224 F6
cr. Westmead 307 E2
dr. Castle Hill 218 K13
la. Newtown 17 H15
pl. Cabramatta ..365 C11
pl. Cromer 227 H13
pl. Bondi Jctn 22 D6
st. Cronulla 523 K4
st. Newtown 17 H16
st. Ryde 312 A3
GOYA
pl. Old Tngabbie ..276 K6
GOYEN
av. Bexley 403 K15
pl. Padstow 429 E5
GOZO
rd. Greystanes ..305 H8
GRACE
av. Beecroft 249 K5
av. Cabramatta ..365 F9
av. Condell Park ..398 D1
av. Forestville 256 C7
av. Frenchs Frst ..256 C3
av. Lakemba 401 C3
av. Lidcombe 340 A2
av. Riverstone 183 A4
av. West Ryde 311 B2
av,n,Camellia 308 K4
dr. Centennial Pk ..21 D11
pde. Glossodia 66 B12
pde. Homebush B ..310 G15
wy. Castle Hill 218 A12
GRACEADES
pl. Bidwill 211 D16
GRACE CAMPBELL
cr. Hillsdale 406 F15
GRACELANDS
dr. Quakers Hill ..213 H7
GRACEMAR
av. Panania 428 A5
GRACEMERE
ct. Wattle Grove ..425 K1
pl. Glen Alpine ..510 F11
pde. Concord W ..341 C5
GRACILIS
wy. Bidwill 211 D16
GRADY
cr. Hassall Gr ..211 K15
GRAEME
pl. Freemns Rch ..90 E2
GRAF
av. Potts Hill ..369 E8
av. West Ryde ..281 D15
av. Yagoona 369 K8
GRAFFITI TUNNEL
Camperdown 18 C2
GRAFTON
av. Naremburn ..315 H13
cr. Dee Why 258 H3
la. Balmain 8 D11
la. Bondi Jctn, off
  Adelaide St ...377 F3
la. Chippendale ..18 J1
la. Jamisontown ..266 C2
la. Balmain 8 C11
la. Blacktown ..274 J11
st. Bondi Jctn ..22 E5
st. Cammeray ..316 C6
st. Chippendale ..18 J1
st. Cremorne ...316 C6
st. Eastlakes 406 A4
st. Greystanes ..305 H4
st. Sutherland ..490 C6
GRAHAM
av. Casula 394 D11
av. Eastwood ...281 F6
av. Harbord 258 H16
av. Lurnea 394 D11
av. Marrickville ..373 J11
av. Miranda ...461 J10
av. Pymble 253 D1
av. Rookwood ..340 E10
av. Wentwrthvlle ..276 J14
cl. Berowra Ht .133 F8
cl. Cranebrook ..207 A3
cr. Baulkham Hl ..247 J13
pl. Earlwood 402 F6
pl. Picnic Point ..428 F17
rd. Leppington ..419 J6
rd. Narwee 400 G12
rd. Rossmore ..419 J6
st. Auburn 339 C11

st. Berala 339 C11
st. Bundeena 524 A10
st. Doonside 243 B12
st. Greystanes ..306 D5
st. Lane Cove ..314 B1
st. Rozelle 11 C1
st. Silverdale 353 H14
GRAHAME
av. Glenfield 424 F8
st. Blaxland 233 H11
GRAHAM HILL
rd. Narellan 478 D8
GRAINGER
av. Ashfield 372 J2
av. Mt Pritchard ..364 H9
pl. N Curl Curl ..258 J10
pl. N Richmond ..86 K14
st. Marsden Pk ..181 K13
GRANARY
ct. Wrrngtn Dns ..238 B4
la. Wrrngtn Dns, off
  Granary Ct 238 B4
pl. Castle Hill, off
  Langshaw Cct ..218 K12
GRAND
av. Camellia 309 B5
av. Rosehill 309 B5
av. Westmead ..307 E1
av. West Ryde ..311 B2
av,n,Camellia ..308 K4
pde. Centennial Pk ..21 D11
pde. Glossodia ..66 B12
pde. Homebush B ..310 G15
wy. Castle Hill ..218 A12
GRAND FLANEUR
av. Richmond ..118 B5
GRAND HAVEN
rd. E Kurrajong ..65 D9
GRANDIS
pl. Kingswood ..267 J2
GRANDOAKS
pl. Castle Hill ..218 H16
wy. Castle Hill ..218 H16
GRANDSTAND
pde. Zetland ..375 K10
GRAND VIEW
ct. Bella Vista ..246 D8
dr. Mt Riverview ..204 G14
GRANDVIEW
av. Seven Hills ..275 F10
ct. Lugarno 429 K10
dr. Bilgola 169 G7
dr. Campbelltwn ..511 F9
dr. Newport 169 G7
la. Seaforth 287 B9
la. Bowen Mtn ..84 C12
la. Pymble 253 D3
pde. Caringbah ..493 C13
pde. Epping ...250 H16
pde. Mona Vale ..199 G1
st. Naremburn ..315 D1
st. Parramatta ..278 J16
st. Pymble 253 D3
st. S Penrith 266 J2
GRANGE
av. Marsden Pk ..211 J3
av. Schofields ..183 A16
cr. Cmbrdg Gdn ..237 G3
la. Bowen Mtn ..84 C12
la. Pymble 253 D3
la. Cmbrdg Gdn, off
  Grange Cr 237 G4
pl. Glenhaven ..218 B2
rd. Leumeah ..482 A11
GRANGEWOOD
pl. W Pnnant Hl ..248 G6
GRANITE
pl. Eagle Vale ..481 E7
pl. Hinchinbrk ..362 K15
GRANT
av. Cabramatta ..365 C9
cl. Epping 250 G15
cl. Kemps Ck ..360 G10
cr. Merrylands ..306 J10
gld. Bella Vista ..246 G2
pl. Bonnet Bay ..460 C9
st. St Ives 224 A16
st. Blacktown ..243 J10
wy. Minto 482 K7
GRANTHAM
cr. Dangar I 76 H7
la. Potts Point ..4 J2
pl. Chipping Ntn ..366 F13
rd. Seven Hills ..275 F4
st. Burwood 341 J11
st. Carlton 432 J5

STREETS GR

st. Potts Point 4 K1
st. Riverstone 153 B14
GRANTOWN
ct. Castle Hill 218 D7
GRANVILLE
st. Fairfield 336 C7
st. Fairfield Ht 336 B9
GRAPHITE
pl. Eagle Vale 481 E6
GRAPHIX
row. Alexandria 375 C15
GRASMERE
av. Northmead 278 C5
cr. Collaroy Plat 228 E10
la. Cremorne 316 C7
rd. Cremorne 316 C6
GRASSMERE
av. S Penrith 266 F2
gr. Grasmere 475 K16
rd. Killara 254 A16
st. Guildford 337 K5
GRASSY
cl. Hinchinbrk 363 A14
GRATTAN
cr. Frenchs Frst 256 F10
GRAWIN
cl. Hinchinbrk 392 H4
GRAY
av. Kogarah 433 C7
cr. Eastlakes 405 K2
cr. Yagoona 368 J10
la. Kogarah 433 C7
la. Sutherland 490 D4
pl. Bradbury 511 G11
pl. Kings Lngly 246 A9
pl. Wetherill Pk 335 A3
st. Annandale 10 K9
st. Bondi Jctn 22 J8
st. Granville 308 G9
st. Henley 313 B14
st. Kogarah 433 B5
st. Kogarah 433 C7
st. Mt Colah 192 D4
st. Randwick 377 C15
st. Sutherland 490 E4
GRAYLIND
av. W Pnnant Hl 249 G1
cl. Collaroy 229 A11
pl. Vaucluse 348 C5
GRAYLING
rd. West Pymble 252 K9
GRAYS
la. Cranebrook 207 C8
la. Waterloo 19 C11
GRAYSON
rd. N Epping 251 D10
st. Glendenning 242 G3
GRAY SPENCE
cr. W Pnnant Hl 249 B8
GRAYS POINT
rd. Grays Point 491 A14
GRAZIER
cr. Wrrngtn Dns 238 D6
pl. Minchinbury 271 F9
GREAT BUCKINGHAM
st. Redfern 19 G7
GREAT NORTH
rd. Abbotsford 342 J2
rd. Five Dock 342 J11
rd. Wareemba 343 A7
GREATREX
av. Regents Pk 369 D1
GREAT SOUTHERN
rd. Bargo 567 E1
GREAT THORNE
st. Edgecliff 13 J13
GREAT WESTERN
hwy. Annandale 16 D4
hwy. Arndell Park 273 A9
hwy. Ashfield 342 G11
hwy. Auburn 309 E14
hwy. Blacktown 274 A12
hwy. Blaxland 233 E3
hwy. Burwood 342 G11
hwy. Camperdown 17 G2
hwy. Canada Bay 342 G11
hwy. Colyton 270 A2
hwy. Concord 342 G11
hwy. Croydon 342 G11
hwy. Doonside 273 A9
hwy. Eastern Ck 273 A9
hwy. Emu Plains 234 J10
hwy. Faulconbdg 201 C1
hwy. Five Dock 342 G11
hwy. Forest Lodge 17 H2
hwy. Girraween 275 B14
hwy. Glebe 17 H2
hwy. Glenbrook 233 E3
hwy. Granville 308 D9
hwy. Greystanes 305 J1
hwy. Haberfield 373 D2
hwy. Homebush 342 G11
hwy. Homebush W 340 A2
hwy. Huntingwd 273 A9
hwy. Kingswood 237 E12
hwy. Lapstone 264 F1
hwy. Leichhardt 15 E6
hwy. Lewisham 15 E6
hwy. Lidcombe 340 A2
hwy. Mays Hill 307 A4
hwy. Minchinbury 271 B4
hwy. Mount Druitt 271 B4
hwy. Oxley Park 270 A2
hwy. Parramatta 307 A4
hwy. Pendle Hill 305 J1
hwy. Penrith 236 G10
hwy. Petersham 15 E6
hwy. Prospect 275 B14
hwy. Rooty Hill 272 B7
hwy. St Marys 269 C1
hwy. S Wntwthvle 307 A4
hwy. Springwood 201 C1
hwy. Stanmore 16 D4
hwy. Summer Hill 373 D2
hwy. Valley Ht 202 D4
hwy. Warrimoo 203 A13
hwy. Wentwthvle 307 A4
hwy. Werrington 238 D14
hwy. Westmead 307 A4
GREBE
pl. Hinchinbrk 393 E1
st. Erskine Park 270 F16
st. Ingleburn 453 G8
GRECH
st. Glenwood 245 F2
GRECIA
la. Mosman 317 C1
GRECO
pl. Rsemeadow 540 D4
GREEK
st. Glebe 12 G15
GREEN
av. Smithfield 335 K6
la. Bradbury 511 E13
la. Kogarah 433 D4
pde. Valley Ht 202 G7
pl. Peakhurst 430 B6
rd. Castle Hill 217 A5
rd. Kellyville 216 K1
rd. Kellyville 217 A3
sq. Alexandria, off Botany Rd 375 G10
st. Bnksmeadw 406 B11
st. Blacktown 274 J8
st. Brookvale 257 K11
st. Cremorne Pt 316 G13
st. Glenbrook 234 B16
st. Kogarah 433 D4
st. Maroubra 407 B9
st. Pleasure Pt 427 H7
st. Revesby 398 B10
st. Tempe 404 A3
st. Wallacia 324 K13
st. Woolooware 493 H10
GREENACRE
dr. Tahmoor 566 C13
rd. Bankstown 369 H13
rd. Connells Pt 431 K13
rd. Greenacre 369 J13
rd. S Hurstville 431 K13
GREENAWAY
av. Camden S 507 B9
GREENBANK
dr. Glenhaven 217 J4
dr. Wrrngtn Dns 238 D5
st. Hurstville 431 K7
st. Marrickville 373 H14
GREENDALE
av. Frenchs Frst 256 D2
av. Pymble 223 F14
cr. Chester Hill 338 C15
rd. Bringelly 387 A13
rd. Greendale 355 B13
rd. Wallacia 324 J13
st. Greenwich 315 B8
tce. Quakers Hill 243 J2
GREENE
av. Ryde 282 C16
GREENFIELD
av. Middle Cove 285 J7
pde. Bankstown 399 E1
pl. Forestville 256 C9
pl. Maraylya 94 A11
rd. Greenfld Pk 334 B13
rd. Prairiewood 334 B13
st. Bnksmeadw 435 K1
GREENFIELDS
pl. Theresa Park 445 A3
GREENFINCH
st. Green Valley 363 F12
GREENGATE
la. Killara 253 J10
rd. Airds 511 J16
rd. Killara 253 J11
rd. St Helens Park 511 J16
GREENHALG
rd. Cranebrook 207 D14
GREENHALGH
la. Padstow 429 E1
GREENHAVEN
dr. Emu Heights 234 K4
dr. Pennant Hills 250 G3
pl. Silverdale 354 A14
rd. Grays Point 491 A13
GREENHILL
av. Normanhurst 221 D12
cl. Castle Hill 218 B10
cr. St Ives Ch 223 J4
dr. Glenwood 245 K3
GREEN HILLS
dr. Rouse Hill 185 A9
dr. Silverdale 383 J2
GREENHILLS
av. Moorebank 395 H10
av. Moorebank 395 G13
av. S Penrith 236 H16
rd. Holsworthy 425 F10
st. Croydon 372 D5
st. Croydon Pk 372 D5
GREENKNOWE
av. Elizabeth Bay 13 A5
GREENLANDS
av. Peakhurst 430 G1
rd. Lane Cove N 284 C14
GREENLEAF
st. Wentwthvle 277 A7
GREENLEE
st. Berala 339 C15
GREENLEES
av. Concord 342 B5
GREENMEADOWS
cr. Toongabbie 276 E6
GREENMOUNT
wy. Mt Colah 192 D5
GREENOAKS
av. Bradbury 511 D13
av. Cherrybrook 219 H15
av. Darling Point 13 J7
GREEN POINT
rd. Oyster Bay 461 A7
GREENS
av. Oatlands 279 B12
dr. Cammeray 316 B5
rd. Paddington 4 G16
rd. Warrimoo 202 K13
GREENSBOROUGH
av. Rouse Hill 185 B8
GREENSLOPE
st. S Wntwthvle 306 H5
GREENSTEAD
la. Randwick 377 B13
GREENTREE
pl. Wilberforce 92 A1
GREENVALE
gr. Hornsby 221 F6
pl. Castle Hill 248 D5
st. Fairfield W 335 D12
GREEN VALLEY
rd. Busby 363 A10
rd. Green Valley 363 A10
GREENVALLEY
av. St Ives 224 D4
GREENVIEW
pde. Berowra 163 D2
GREENWAY
av. Shalvey 211 A14
cr. Windsor 120 K8
dr. Kirribilli 5 K12
dr. Pymble 252 J7
dr. S Penrith 267 A1
dr. West Hoxton 392 A10
dr. West Pymble 252 J7
la. Springwood 202 A3
la. The Rocks A K3
pde. Revesby 398 F11
pl. Horsley Pk 331 G1
st. Gymea 491 G1
st. Ruse 512 G1
GREENWELL
rd. Prestons 392 K15
GREENWICH
cl. St Johns Pk 364 F5
pl. Kellyville 216 D1
rd. Greenwich 315 A6
wk. Campbelltown 511 A8
wy. Kellyville Rdg 215 C3
GREENWOOD
Blacktown 274 D12
av. Bankstown 399 C1
av. Narraweena 258 B3
av. S Coogee 407 G4
cl. Hamondvle 396 H15
gr. Blacktown 244 D15
la. Enfield 371 H2
pl. Harbord 258 H16
pl. St Helens Park 541 C2
rd. Kellyville 216 F3
GREER
st. Bonnyrigg Ht 363 E8
GREG
pl. Dean Park 212 J16
GREGGS
rd. Kurrajong 85 C5
GREGORACE
pl. Bonnyrigg 363 J6
GREGORY
av. Baulkham Hl 247 A11
av. Croydon 342 G15
av. N Epping 251 E12
av. Oxley Park 270 F3
cr. Beverly Hills 401 A15
la. Earlwood 402 K4
pl. Harris Park 308 H5
rd. Leppington 419 E6
st. Ermington 310 F5
st. Fairfield W 335 B13
st. Glendenning 242 E2
st. Granville 308 E16
st. Greystanes 306 E3
st. Maroubra 407 H6
st. N Richmond 87 B14
st. Putney 312 D7
st. Rsemeadow 540 H4
st. Roseville 284 J2
st. S Coogee 407 H6
st. Strathfield S 371 A5
st. Yagoona 368 E12
tce. Lapstone 264 H4
GREGSON
pl. Quakers Hill 214 E8
GREG TAYLOR
av. Matraville 436 K8
GREIG
pl. Engadine 518 D4
pl. Seven Hills 246 E13
GRENACHE
pl. Eschol Park 481 A5
GRENADA
st. Fairfield W 335 B11
GRENFELL
av. N Narrabeen 228 J2
st. Blakehurst 432 C15
GRENVILLE
av. Cabarita 342 E1
av. Caringbah 493 A4
st. Pitt Town 92 G14
GRESHAM
av. W Pnnant Hl 249 G8
st. Cowan 104 B13
st. Sydney B B12
st. Sydney 1 J14
GRETA
pl. Cartwright 394 D4
pl. Hebersham 241 G3
GRETCHEN
av. Earlwood 402 E5
GRETEL
st. Greenfld Pk 334 D15
GRETNA
cl. West Hoxton 392 E6
pl. St Andrews 482 A2
GRETTA
pl. Kellyville 186 J16
GREVILLE
st. Chatswood W 284 C13
st. Chatswood W 284 D9
st. Clovelly 377 G11
st. Randwick 377 G11
GREVILLEA
av. St Ives 224 D14
av. Warriewood 198 G9
cl. Bossley Park 333 E8
cr. Greystanes 305 E11
cr. Hornsby Ht 191 G5
cr. Mcquarie Fd 454 G4
cr. Prestons 394 A14
cr. Stanhpe Gdn 215 D11
dr. St Clair 270 A15
gr. Baulkham Hl 247 D16
gr. Heathcote 518 J11
gr. Narellan Vale 478 K14
la. St Clair, off Grevillea Dr 270 A15
pl. Kenthurst 156 K15
pl. S Coogee 407 E6
pwy. Valley Ht 202 E5
rd. Chester Hill 368 C1
st. Collaroy Plat 228 H11
GREX
av. Minchinbury 271 D7
GREY
st. Carlton 432 F4
st. Emu Plains 235 A11
st. Glenbrook 264 C2
st. Silverwater 309 J14
GREYCAIRN
pl. Woollahra 22 E3
GREYCLIFFE
av. Pennant Hills 220 F16
av. Vaucluse 348 B2
st. Queenscliff 288 G4
GREYFRIAR
pl. Kellyville 216 B5
GREY GUM
pl. Narellan Vale 478 H14
rd. Mt Colah 191 K2
wk. Newington, off Lewis Wy 310 C13
GREYGUM
av. Rouse Hill 184 K7
cl. Sackville 67 J5
pl. Gymea Bay 491 F11
tce. Old Tngabbie 277 E6
GREYGUMS
rd. Cranebrook 207 B13
GREYSTANES
rd. Greystanes 305 G8
GREYSTOKE
st. Collaroy Plat 228 D9
GREYSTONES
rd. Killarney Ht 255 K14
GREYWOOD
st. Cherrybrook 219 C11
GRIBBENMOUNT
rd. Galston 159 H8
GRIBBLE
pl. Blacktown 244 E15
GRIDE
pl. Ambarvale 511 B14
GRIER
csg. Mulgrave 121 J15
GRIEVE
cr. Milperra 397 E11
GRIFFIN
av. Bexley 432 J3
pde. Illawong 459 J2
pl. Doonside 273 F3
pl. Glebe 12 A7
pl. Kenthurst 157 K5
rd. Dee Why 259 A12
rd. N Curl Curl 259 A12
st. Manly 288 E9
st. Surry Hills 20 B1
GRIFFINS
rd. Tennyson 65 E11
st. Pemulwuy 305 F6
GRIFFITH
av. North Bondi 348 C16
av. Roseville Ch 285 F2
cl. Galston 159 G10
st. Ashfield 372 J10
st. Hurlstone Pk 372 J10
GRIFFITHS
av. Bankstown 399 H1
av. Camden S 507 B16
av. McGraths Hl 121 K12
av. Punchbowl 399 H1
av. West Ryde 311 G1
la. West Ryde 281 G16
pl. Eagle Vale 480 K11
st. Balgowlah 287 J7
st. Blacktown 274 K1

GREGORY'S STREET DIRECTORY 75

GR STREETS

Street	Page	Grid
st. Ermington	310	C2
st. Fairlight	288	A7
st. N St Marys	239	J9
st. Oatley	431	A9
st. Sans Souci	463	B2
st. Tempe	404	A2
st. Wentwthvle	307	B3
st. Woolmloo	4	F4

GRIGG
av. N Epping	251	D11
cl. Ellis Lane	476	C11
st. Oatley	431	D10

GRIGOR
| pl. Allambie Ht | 257 | D12 |

GRIMES
la. Carlingford	280	D5
pl. Bonnyrigg	364	B8
pl. Davidson	225	B15

GRIMLEY
| cl. Penrith | 237 | F2 |
| la. Penrith, off Grimley Cl | 237 | F2 |

GRIMMET
| av. Rouse Hill | 184 | K7 |

GRIMMETT
ct. St Clair	269	K16
la. St Clair, off Grimmett Ct	269	K16
st. Greystanes	305	H8

GRIMMOND
| av. Ashfield | 372 | K3 |

GRIMSON
| cr. Liverpool | 365 | B16 |
| la. Liverpool, off Grimson Cr | 365 | B16 |

GRIMWIG
| cr. Ambarvale | 510 | H12 |

GRIMWOOD
| st. Granville | 308 | B11 |

GROGAN
| st. Croydon | 342 | E11 |

GRONO
| pl. McGraths Hl | 121 | K13 |

GRONO FARM
| rd. Wilberforce | 67 | K16 |
| rd. Wilberforce | 93 | F1 |

GROOTE
| av. Hinchnbrk | 363 | A15 |

GROSE
av. Lurnea	394	B13
av. N St Marys	239	J8
la. Bowen Mtn	84	E15
la. Grose Vale	84	E15
pl. Camden S	507	B9
pl. Ruse	512	G8
pl. Seven Hills	275	F10
rd. Blue Mtn N P	171	D3
rd. Faulconbdg	171	B16
st. Camperdown	17	G5
st. Glebe	12	G16
st. Little Bay	437	A13
st. Parramatta	278	C15
st. Richmond	118	G6

GROSE FARM
| la. Camperdown | 18 | A3 |

GROSE RIVER
| rd. Grose Wold | 116 | E8 |

GROSE VALE
rd. Grose Vale	84	J9
rd. Kurrajong	85	A6
rd. N Richmond	87	A14

GROSE VALE COMMUNITY CENTRE
| rd. Grose Vale | 85 | A11 |

GROSE VALLEY
| ct. Faulconbdg | 171 | D11 |

GROSE WOLD
| rd. Grose Vale | 85 | C15 |
| rd. Grose Wold | 115 | H5 |

GROSVENOR
cr. Cronulla	493	G13
cr. Summer Hill	373	C3
la. Bondi Jctn	22	H6
la. Cremorne	6	H1
la. Lindfield, off Grosvenor Rd	284	D3
la. Brookvale	258	B4
la. W Pnnant Hl	249	D2
rd. Lindfield	283	J5
rd. S Hurstville	432	C11
st. Bondi Jctn	22	J5
st. Cremorne	316	D8
st. Croydon	342	D16

st. Kensington	376	D13
st. Neutral Bay	316	C8
st. N Wahroonga	192	F16
st. Sydney	A	G11
st. Sydney	1	F14
st. Wahroonga	222	F5
st. Woollahra	22	J5

GROUNDSEL
| av. Mcquarie Fd | 454 | E5 |

GROUT
| pl. Menai | 458 | K11 |
| pl. Rouse Hill | 184 | K5 |

GROVE
av. Hurstville Gr	431	E7
av. Narwee	400	G11
av. Penshurst	431	E7
la. Eastwood	281	G7
la. Lilyfield	10	F5
pl. Prospect	275	A10
st. Birchgrove	7	G4
st. Bondi	377	K5
st. Casula	394	H11
st. Dulwich Hill	373	D9
st. Earlwood	402	H2
st. Eastwood	281	G8
st. Guildford	337	F3
st. Lilyfield	10	E5
st. Marrickville	373	J15
st. St Peters	374	F14

GROVER
av. Cromer	227	K15
cr. Mulgoa	296	D11
st. Lapstone	264	G4

GROVES
| av. Mulgrave | 151 | H2 |
| rd. Minto Ht | 483 | G2 |

GROVEWOOD
| pl. Castle Hill | 218 | J6 |

GRUMMAN
la. St Clair, off Grumman Pl	270	E15
pl. Raby	451	D15
pl. St Clair	270	E15

GRUNER
| pl. Mt Pritchard | 364 | J11 |
| wy. Claymore | 481 | D11 |

GUAM
| pl. Kings Park | 244 | F2 |

GUARDIAN
av. Beaumont Hills	185	H11
cr. Bligh Park	150	E8
pde. Beacon Hill	257	F3

GUELPH
| st. Regents Pk | 368 | J2 |

GUERIE
| st. Marayong | 244 | C3 |

GUERIN
| la. Bass Hill | 367 | K4 |
| rd. Doonside | 243 | G4 |

GUERNSEY
av. Minto	452	K16
pl. Busby	363	J16
pl. Guildford	337	D7
wy. Stanhpe Gdn	215	F10

GUESS
| av. Wolli Creek | 403 | H5 |

GUEUDECOURT
| av. Earlwood | 402 | J1 |

GUIHEN
| st. Annandale | 17 | C1 |

GUILDFORD
la. Cmbrdg Pk, off Guildford Rd	237	J10
pl. Leumeah	482	C16
rd. Cmbrdg Pk	237	J11
rd. Guildford	337	G5
rd.w.Guildford	337	A3
rd.w.Guildford W	337	A3

GUILFOYLE
| av. Double Bay | 14 | B8 |
| st. Berala | 339 | C12 |

GUINEA
| st. Kogarah | 433 | A4 |

GUINEVIERE
| ct. Castle Hill | 217 | G4 |

GUIREN
| pl. Toongabbie | 276 | G6 |

GUISE
av. Casula	394	C15
pwy.Casula, off Guise Av	394	D16
rd. Bradbury	511	F10

GULIA
| st. Mona Vale | 198 | G1 |

GULL
pl. Erskine Park	270	H14
pl. Hinchinbrk	363	E16
pl. Lugarno	429	H12
pl. Prospect	274	J11
st. Little Bay	437	G14

GULLALIE
| cir. Blaxland | 233 | K6 |

GULLIVER
| st. Brookvale | 258 | A9 |

GULLY
| pl. Berowra | 133 | F10 |
| rd. Valley Ht | 202 | G3 |

GULLY GULLY
| rd. Mooney Mooney | 75 | D2 |

GUM
| st. Greystanes | 306 | E4 |
| st. Riverstone | 182 | K3 |

GUMBLETON
| pl. Narellan Vale | 508 | H1 |

GUM BLOSSOM
| dr. Westleigh | 220 | H9 |

GUMBOOYA
| av. Baulkham Hl | 246 | H7 |
| st. Allambie Ht | 257 | H14 |

GUMBUYA
cr. Roselands	401	D6
pl. Avalon	140	A13
pl. Glen Alpine	510	D13
st. Cronulla	523	J2
st. Marsfield	281	G2
st. Northbridge	286	A16

GUMLEAF
| cl. Hornsby Ht | 162 | A9 |

GUMLEAF
| pl. W Pnnant Hl | 249 | G3 |

GUM NUT
| cl. Kellyville | 186 | C15 |

GUMNUT
cl. Blaxland	233	F4
cl. Bidwill	211	D15
pl. Cherrybrook	219	F12
pl. Mcquarie Fd	454	E1
rd. Cherrybrook	219	F11

GUMNUT BABY
| wk. Faulconbdg | 171 | D14 |

GUMTREE
| la. Double Bay | 14 | C10 |
| wy. Smithfield | 335 | G7 |

GUNARA
| tce. Glenmore Pk | 265 | K10 |

GUNBALANYA
| av. Beecroft | 250 | C4 |

GUNBOWER
| rd. Bowen Mtn | 84 | B10 |

GUNDAGAI
| cr. Wakeley | 334 | F14 |

GUNDAH
| rd. Mt Krng-gai | 162 | J5 |

GUNDAIN
| la. Kirrawee, off Gundain Rd | 461 | D16 |
| rd. Kirrawee | 461 | D16 |

GUNDAMAIAN ROAD SERVICE
| trl. Royal N P | 521 | H4 |

GUNDAROO
| st. Villawood | 367 | E4 |

GUNDARY
| cl. Prestons | 422 | J1 |

GUNDAWARRA
| cl. Kenthurst | 157 | G9 |
| st. Lilli Pilli | 522 | G1 |

GUNDIBRI
| st. Busby | 363 | H14 |

GUNDIMAINE
| av. Neutral Bay | 6 | J9 |

GUNDOWRINGA
| pl. Airds | 512 | A10 |

GUNDY
| pl. Westleigh | 220 | F10 |

GUNELL
| pl. Cranebrook | 207 | F13 |

GUNGAH BAY
| rd. Oatley | 430 | J12 |

GUNGARLIN
| dr. Horngsea Pk | 392 | F14 |

GUNGAROO
| pl. Beverly Hills | 401 | B10 |

GUNGARTEN
| cl. Kellyville | 216 | C1 |

GUNGURRU
| st. Kingswood | 267 | H2 |

GUNJULLA
| pl. Avalon | 139 | J16 |

GUNN
| rd. St Helens Park | 540 | K9 |
| rd. Lalor Park | 245 | F10 |

GUNNAMATTA
| cr. Cronulla | 493 | G13 |
| rd. Woolooware | 493 | G13 |

GUNNEDAH
| rd. Hoxton Park | 392 | H7 |

GUNNERS
| mw. Hollsworthy | 426 | F4 |

GUNNING
| cl. Prestons | 393 | D16 |

GUNSYND
| av. Casula | 394 | G15 |
| st. Kellyville Rdg | 215 | A5 |

GUNTAWONG
| rd. Rouse Hill | 183 | K9 |

GUNYA
| pl. Hebersham | 241 | E10 |
| st. Regents Pk | 369 | A2 |

GUNYAH
cr. Roselands	401	D6
pl. Avalon	140	A13
pl. Glen Alpine	510	D13
st. Cronulla	523	J2
st. Marsfield	281	G2
st. Northbridge	286	A16

GUNYAH PATH
| Winmalee | 173 | A9 |

GURGAR
| pl. Harringtn Pk | 478 | G2 |

GURIN
| av. Killara | 253 | E14 |

GURLEY
| pl. Bonnyrigg | 363 | J10 |

GURNER
av. Austral	361	A15
av. Kemps Ck	360	E13
la. Paddington	13	D14
pl. Kellyville	216	G5
st. Paddington	13	D14

GURNEY
cr. Fairfield W	335	A12
cr. Seaforth	286	J8
rd. Chester Hill	337	G12

GURRAWILLIE
| st. Villawood | 367 | J3 |

GURRIER
| av. Miranda | 492 | C4 |

GURRIGAL
| st. Mosman | 316 | K6 |

GURU
| pl. Glenmore Pk | 266 | C6 |

GUTHEGA
cl. Woodcroft	243	H9
cr. Heckenberg	364	A12
pl. Bossley Park	334	C8

GUTHRIE
| av. Cremorne | 6 | J6 |

GUY
| pl. Emu Heights | 205 | A15 |
| pl. Rooty Hill | 271 | K5 |

GUYONG
| st. Lindfield | 283 | H6 |

GUYRA
| cr. Bossley Park | 333 | F11 |
| rd. Hinchnbrk | 392 | G5 |

GUYS
| pl. St Johns Pk | 364 | C1 |

GWANDALAN
cr. Berowra	133	A16
pl. Emu Plains	235	E12
pl. Edensor Pk	363	F2
pl. Padstow	399	C12
st. Emu Plains	235	E11

GWAWLEY
| pde.Miranda | 462 | E16 |

GWEA
| av. Daceyville | 406 | F4 |

GWEN
cr. Warrimoo	203	C11
pl. Padstow Ht	429	B6
pl. W Pnnant Hl	249	E10

GWENDALE
| cr. Eastwood | 281 | D5 |

GWYDIR
| av. Matraville | 436 | K1 |
| av. N Turramurra | 193 | D14 |

av. Quakers Hill	213	K7
pl. Campbelltown	512	A8
pl. Engadine	488	E12
st. Greystanes	306	A4
st. Hornebush B	310	G14
wy. Glenhaven	218	D6

GWYN
| st. St Ives | 224 | G10 |
| st. Doonside | 243 | D9 |

GWYNELLEN
| pl. Cherrybrook | 219 | D8 |

GWYNN
| cl. Emu Plains | 235 | A10 |

GWYNNE
| st. Ashcroft | 364 | D16 |

GWYNN HUGHES
| rd. Bargo | 567 | A6 |

GYMEA
| pl. Jamisontown | 266 | D5 |

GYMEA BAY
rd. Gymea	491	E3
rd.s,Gymea	491	D8
rd.s,Gymea Bay	491	D9

GYMKHANA
| pl. Glenwood | 245 | J3 |

GYMNASIUM
| rd. Mcquarie Pk | 252 | B15 |

GYMPIE
| pl. Wakeley | 334 | H13 |

GYPSUM
| pl. Eagle Vale | 481 | H6 |

GYRA
| pl. Dharruk | 241 | B6 |

H

HABERFIELD
| rd. Haberfield | 373 | D1 |

HACKETT
pl. North Rocks	248	F15
rd. Abbotsbury	363	A2
st. Ultimo	3	A11
wy. Blacktown	273	H6

HACKING
| av. Wrrngtn Cty | 238 | F6 |
| dr. Narellan Vale | 478 | F16 |

HACKNEY
| st. Greystanes | 306 | B4 |

HADDENHAM
| st. Chipping Ntn | 366 | H15 |

HADDIN
| cl. Turramurra | 222 | H13 |
| pl. Kirkham | 477 | C8 |

HADDON
pl. Bonnyrigg Ht	363	H5
cl. Glenwood	215	C16
rd. Revesby	398	K14
st. Picton	563	F12

HADDON RIG
| pl. Airds | 512 | D12 |
| pl. Miller | 393 | G2 |

HADENFIELD
| av. Mcquarie Pk | 282 | A1 |

HADLEIGH
| av. Collaroy | 259 | B1 |

HADLEY
| pl. Jamisontown | 266 | D5 |

HADLOW
| cl. Beaumont Hills | 185 | K15 |

HADRIAN
| av. Blacktown | 275 | A8 |

HAERSE
| av. Chipping Ntn | 396 | B5 |

HAFEY
| rd. Kenthurst | 157 | J6 |

HAFLINGER
| cl. Emu Plains | 235 | C13 |

HAGEN
| pl. Glenfield | 424 | G13 |
| pl. Whalan | 241 | A8 |

HAGUE
| gr. Oakhurst | 242 | C2 |

HAHN
| st. Lucas Ht | 487 | H12 |

HAIG
av. Daceyville	406	F4
av. Denistone E	281	J11
av. Georges Hall	367	D15
av. Summer Hill	15	A7
la. Maroubra	407	B10
la. Woolmloo	4	C6
st. Bexley	432	D1

76 GREGORY'S STREET DIRECTORY

STREETS HA

st. Chatswood 285 D7
st. Maroubra 407 B10
st. Mt Pritchard 364 G8
st. Roseville 285 C1
st. Wentwthvle 307 C2
HAIGH
av. Belrose 225 H15
av. Roselands 400 J7
pl. Castle Hill 218 F15
HAINES
av. Carlingford 249 C13
gr. Mt Annan 509 H1
pl. Menangle 538 G16
HAINING
st. Cmbrdg Pk 237 K7
HAINSWORTH
st. Westmead 277 J14
HAIR
cl. Greenfld Pk 334 C12
HAITE
cl. West Pymble 252 F9
HAKEA
av. Belrose 225 F16
av. Frenchs Frst 255 F1
cl. Casula 394 F13
cr. Galston 159 D10
ct. St Clair 269 G8
pl. Baulkham Hl 247 C15
pl. Epping 280 E4
pl. Mcquarie Fd 454 G4
st. Engadine 489 C13
st. Mt Annan 509 F3
st. Stanhpe Gdn 215 C10
wy. Acacia Gdn 214 H14
HALCROWS
rd. Cattai 68 K16
rd. Cattai 95 F1
rd. Glenorie 95 F1
HALCYON
av. Kellyville 216 A3
av. Padstow 399 D12
av. Wahroonga 222 H8
av. Winmalee 172 K11
ct. Harringtn Pk 478 G5
st. Gladesville 312 K6
HALDANE
cr. Lane Cove 314 G2
la. Lane Cove 314 G2
st. Asquith 192 A10
HALDIS
pl. Plumpton 241 H7
HALDON
la. Lakemba 401 B4
st. Lakemba 401 A1
st.n, Lakemba 401 A1
HALE
cr. S Windsor 150 K2
pl. Fairfield Ht 336 B11
rd. Mosman 316 H6
st. Botany 405 C12
HALELUKA
cr. Plumpton 242 D10
HALES
pl. Blackett 241 A4
HALESMITH
rd. Mona Vale 169 D14
HAL HAMMOND
pl. Belrose 226 B13
HALIFAX
av. Roselands 400 G10
ct. St Clair 270 E15
la. St Clair, off Halifax Ct 270 E16
st. Raby 451 D15
HALINDA
st. Whalan 240 K7
HALL
av. Collaroy Plat 228 G12
av. Thornleigh 221 A11
cr. Padstow 429 F5
cr. Padstow Ht 429 F5
dr. Menai 458 E12
pde. Lakemba 401 B3
pl. Eagle Vale 481 A10
pl. Fairfield W 334 K10
pl. Guildford W 336 K1
pl. Minto 452 J13
rd. Hornsby 221 E4
st. Auburn 339 E1
st. Belmore 371 G14
st. Bondi Beach 378 A1
st. Chifley 437 B8
st. Pitt Town 92 H8
st. St Marys 269 E5
st. S Turramrra 252 A6
st. West Ryde 281 B14
HALLAM
av. Lane Cove W 283 H16
wy. Cherrybrook, off Tennyson Cl 219 D9
HALLEN
pl. West Hoxton 392 B13
rd. Cherrybrook 219 J12
HALLEY
av. Bexley 402 G15
st. Five Dock 343 A6
HALLORAN
av. Davidson 225 C16
st. Lilyfield 10 F6
HALLS
la. E Kurrajong 67 C2
la. Woollahra 21 H3
rd. Arcadia 159 B2
rd. Galston 159 B2
HALLSTROM
cl. Northbridge 286 G16
pl. Mona Vale 199 C2
pl. Wetherill Pk 333 J2
HALMAHERA
cr. Lethbrdg Pk 240 J1
HALSALL
st. Granville 308 D10
HALSLEY
st. Hassall Gr 211 K15
HALSTEAD
st. S Hurstville 431 K10
HAM
st. S Windsor 120 F15
st. S Windsor 120 H16
HAMBIDGE
pl. Bow Bowing 452 D14
HAMBLEDON
av. Baulkham Hl 247 E3
av. Castle Hill 247 E3
cct. Harringtn Pk 478 G1
cct. Harringtn Pk 478 G2
rd. Quakers Hill 213 J12
rd. Schofields 214 A5
wy. West Hoxton 392 B12
HAMBLY
st. Botany 405 J12
st. Fairfield W 335 D13
HAMBRIDGE
rd. Bargo 567 D3
rd. Bargo 567 B4
HAMBRO
av. Glenwood 215 E13
HAMEL
cl. Milperra 397 H11
cr. Earlwood 402 K1
rd. Matraville 407 A16
rd. Mt Pritchard 364 B10
HAMELIN
pl. Illawong 459 D6
HAMER
st. Epping 250 E13
st. Kogarah Bay 432 H12
HAMERSLEY
pl. Bow Bowing 452 C14
st. Fairfield W 335 F10
HAMILTON
av. Earlwood 402 H3
av. Holsworthy 396 B13
av. Matraville, off Cemetery Av 436 H8
av. Naremburn 315 H4
cr. Ryde 311 G5
cr.w, Ryde 311 G4
dr. Centennial Pk 21 G8
la. Naremburn 315 H4
pde. Pymble 253 B8
pl. Narellan 478 G12
rd. Fairfield 335 H13
rd. Fairfield Ht 335 H13
rd. Fairfield W 335 A11
rd. Kentlyn 513 C4
st. Allawah 432 G7
st. Arncliffe 403 A10
st. Bardwell Vy 403 A10
st. Coogee 377 G14
st. Granville 308 J10
st. Lidcombe 339 G9
st. N Strathfield 341 D6
st. Riverstone 183 A4
st. Riverview 314 A4
st. Rose Bay 348 C10
st. Rozelle, off Merton St 344 E7
st. S Wntwthvle 307 B5
st. Sydney A K14
st. Vineyard 152 F12
st.e, N Strathfield 341 D6
wy. Beaumont Hills 185 J14
HAMISH
ct. Beaumont Hills 186 B16
HAMLET
cl. St Clair 300 C1
cr. Rsemeadow 540 J7
la. Mosman, off Raglan St 317 B9
HAMLEY
rd. Mt Krng-gai 162 K6
HAMLIN
st. Quakers Hill 214 J13
HAMMAL
wy. Minto 482 J5
HAMMENT
pl. Glenbrook, off Great Western Hwy 234 B16
HAMMERLI
wy. Shalvey 210 J12
HAMMERS
rd. Northmead 277 H8
rd. Old Tngabbie 277 E8
HAMMERSLEY
rd. Grays Point 491 A13
HAMMERSMITH
rd. Homebush W 340 H6
HAMMON
av. Doonside 243 G16
HAMMOND
av. Croydon 342 G12
av. Normanhurst 221 F8
ct. Baulkham Hl 247 C14
pl. Campbelltown 511 F8
pl. Mascot 405 C9
pl. Narwee 400 H10
HAMPDEN
av. Cremorne 6 K1
av. Darling Point 13 J3
av. Marrickville 373 G16
av. Wahroonga 223 B6
pl. Raby 451 H13
rd. Abbotsford 343 A4
rd. Artarmon 284 J14
rd. Lakemba 370 J14
rd. Pennant Hills 250 H2
rd. Russell Lea 343 A4
rd. S Wntwthvle 306 J5
rd. Wareemba 343 A4
st. Ashfield 372 F4
st. Belrose 226 B12
st. Beverly Hills 401 C15
st. Hurlstone Pk 373 B12
st. Mosman 317 B3
st. North Rocks 278 H1
st. N Sydney K J2
st. N Sydney 5 J5
st. Paddington 13 F13
HAMPSHIRE
av. W Pnnant Hl 249 C2
av. West Pymble 252 K15
ct. Cherrybrook, off Glamorgan Wy 219 E9
la. Camperdown 17 E4
pl. Seven Hills 275 F5
pl. Wakeley 334 J15
st. Camperdown 17 E3
st. Cronulla 493 J16
HAMPSON
av. Maroubra 407 E8
HAMPSTEAD
rd. Auburn 309 C15
rd. Campbelltown 511 A8
rd. Dulwich Hill 373 C7
rd. Homebush W 340 H10
HAMPTON
cl. Castle Hill 248 A3
cr. Prospect 274 K13
ct. Wattle Grove 426 C3
rd. Sylvania Wtr 462 C13
st. Balmain 7 C7
st. Canley Vale 366 A1
st. Croydon Pk 372 A8
st. Fairfield 336 C15
st. Fairfield 336 B16
st. Hurstville Gr 431 G10
HAMPTON COURT
rd. Carlton 432 H8
HAMRUN
cct. Rooty Hill 271 K5
HANBURY
cl. S Penrith 267 D5
st. Greystanes 306 F7
HANCEY
av. North Rocks 248 E14
HANCKEL
rd. Oakville 153 E1
HANCOCK
dr. Cherrybrook 219 D7
st. Bexley 402 D15
st. Rozelle, off Belmore St 344 E8
HANCOTT
st. Ryde 282 B13
HAND
av. Penrith 236 K13
HANDCOCK
la. Greenwich, off Greenwich Rd 315 A9
HANDEL
av. Emerton 240 J6
st. Bonnyrigg Ht 363 D7
HANDLE
st. Bass Hill 367 K10
HANDLEY
av. Bexley North 402 F11
av. Thornleigh 221 B15
av. Turramurra 223 C10
la. Marrickville 374 C9
pl. Raby 451 G13
st. Auburn 338 J5
st. Marrickville 374 C9
HANDOUB
pde. Dee Why 259 C9
pde. N Curl Curl 259 C9
HANDS
la. Surry Hills F C10
la. Surry Hills 3 J13
HANGER
pl. Narellan 478 G13
HANIGAN
st. Penshurst 431 E6
HANKINS
ct. Greenacre 370 E6
HANKS
st. Ashbury 372 J9
st. Ashfield 372 J9
HANLAN
st. Cranebrook 207 A9
HANLEY
st. Stanhpe Gdn 215 E6
HANLON
cl. Minto 453 A14
HANLONS
rd. Bilpin 61 E6
rd.n, Bilpin 61 F5
HANLY
st. Lansdowne 367 A7
HANNA
av. Lurnea 394 F12
pl. Oakhurst 241 J3
st. Botany 405 H16
HANNABUS
pl. Mulgrave 151 J1
HANNAFORD
st. Campbelltown 511 H8
HANNAH
av. Kellyville 217 C1
pl. Mt Annan 479 D16
st. Beecroft 249 K6
st. Westmead 307 G4
wy. Pemulwuy 305 F7
HANNAH BELLAMY
pl. W Pnnant Hl 249 E5
HANNAM
pl. Englorie Park 510 J10
st. Bardwell Vy 403 C6
st. Darlinghurst 4 E15
st. Turrella 403 C6
HANNAN
st. Maroubra 406 J9
HANNANS
rd. Narwee 400 C13
rd. Riverwood 400 C13
HANNON
st. Botany 405 G14
HANNONS
av. Peakhurst 430 E4
HANOVER
av. N Epping 251 G8
st. Cecil Hills 362 D6
st. Rozelle 7 B14
st. Wilberforce 91 J2
HANS
pl. Casula 424 H1
pl. Marrickville 374 C12
HANSARD
st. Zetland 375 H12
HANSEN
av. Earlwood 402 F2
av. Galston 159 D9
HANSENS
rd. Minto Ht 482 J13
HANSFORD
pde. Bilgola 169 E4
HANSLOW
st. Surry Hills F K16
HANSON
st. Fairfield 337 A13
st. Fairfield E 337 A13
HANWELL
swy. Liverpool 395 E3
HANWOOD
pl. Edensor Pk 363 C1
HAPP
st. Auburn 339 B3
HARAH
cl. Bonnyrigg 363 K9
HARAN
st. Mascot 405 C2
HARBER
st. Alexandria 375 A14
st. St Peters 374 K14
HARBORD
rd. Brookvale 258 E12
rd. Dee Why 258 E12
rd. Harbord 258 E14
rd. N Curl Curl 258 E12
rd. North Manly 258 E14
rd. Woodbine 481 J11
st. Granville 308 K11
HARBOUR
la. Middle Cove 285 K8
st. Clontarf 287 G16
st. Cronulla 523 K3
st. Haymarket E C2
st. Haymarket 3 D8
st. Mosman 316 K7
st. Sydney E C2
st. Sydney 3 D8
HARBOUR MASTERS STEPS
The Rocks B B14
HARBOURNE
la. Kingsford, off Harbourne Rd 376 G16
rd. Kingsford 406 G1
HARBOUR VIEW
cr. Lavender Bay K H16
cr. Lavender Bay 5 H12
st. Clontarf 287 F11
HARBOURVIEW
cr. Abbotsford 343 A2
la. Woollahra 22 H4
HARCOURT
av. Campsie 371 H13
av. East Hills 427 J4
cl. Castle Hill 218 K7
gr. Glenwood 245 G3
pde. Rosebery 375 G16
pl. Eagle Vale 481 A8
st. East Killara 254 E7
HARCUS
st. Merrylands 307 D13
HARDEN
av. Northbridge 285 J15
cr. Georges Hall 367 H12
la. Northbridge 285 J15
rd. Artarmon 285 B15
st. Canley Ht 335 A16
HARDIE
av. Summer Hill 373 C4
la. Mascot 405 E6
st. Darlinghurst 4 G11
st. Mascot 405 E6
st. Neutral Bay 6 D2
HARDIMAN
av. Randwick 377 C16
HARDING
la. Bexley 402 H12
pl. Bonnet Bay 460 B9
pl. Minto 482 G5

GREGORY'S STREET DIRECTORY 77

HA STREETS

HARDWICKE
- st. Riverwood......430 C1
- st. The Oaks......502 G14

HARDY
- av. Riverwood......400 C13
- la. Riverwood......400 B13
- pl. Casula......424 F4
- st. Ashbury......372 H10
- st. Ashfield......372 H10
- st. Blackett......241 A3
- st. Dover Ht......348 E14
- st. Eschol Park......481 B6
- st. Fairfield......336 C11
- st. Hurlstone Pk......372 H10
- st. North Bondi......348 E14

HARE
- st. Glenbrook......233 K15

HAREBELL
- cl. Carlingford......280 D5

HAREDALE
- st. Ambarvale......540 D2

HAREFIELD
- cl. N Epping......251 H10

HAREWOOD
- pl. Cecil Hills......362 J8
- pl. Warriewood......199 D11

HARFORD
- av. East Hills......427 K3
- st. Jamisontown......236 E15
- st. North Ryde......282 K13

HARGRAVE
- la. Darlinghurst......F H2
- la. Darlinghurst......F J2
- la. Paddington......13 F14
- rd. Auburn......339 D7
- st. Lalor Park......245 B12
- st. Darlinghurst......F H2
- st. Darlinghurst......4 B9
- st. Kingswood......237 F13
- st. Leumeah......512 D1
- st. Paddington......13 F14

HARGRAVES
- av. Punchbowl......400 E8
- pl. Maroubra......407 D15
- pl. Wetherill Pk......304 D16
- st. Allambie Ht......257 J15

HARGREAVES
- st. Condell Park......398 D2

HARKEITH
- st. Mona Vale......199 D3

HARKNESS
- av. Glenorie......128 C5
- rd. Oakville......153 D9
- st. Woollahra......22 G4

HARLAND
- st. Ashfield......372 K8
- st. Fairlight......288 B7

HARLECH
- cl. Menai......458 K8
- st. Castle Hill......218 K11

HARLEY
- cr. Condell Park......398 B3
- cr. Eastwood......280 K4
- pl. Kellyville......216 D4
- rd. Avalon......140 E16
- st. Alexandria......375 D9
- st. Sylvania......461 H11
- st. Yanderra......567 B16

HARLOW
- av. Hebersham......241 F8

HARLOWE
- pl. Bronte......378 A7

HARMAN
- st. Inglebum......453 A11

HARMER
- st. Greenacre......370 G10
- st. Woolmloo......4 F5

HARMONY
- st. Ashbury......372 D9

HARMSTON
- av. Frenchs Frst......257 A5

HARNESS
- pl. Wrrngtn Dns......238 A4

HARNETT
- av. Marrickville......373 G14
- av. Mosman......316 H11
- pl. Chatswood W......284 C11
- st. N Sydney......K G2
- st. N Sydney......5 H5
- st. Woolmloo......4 H3

HARNEY
- st. Marrickville......373 G11

HARNLEIGH
- av. Woolooware......493 D8
- av.s.Woolooware......493 D9

HAROLD
- av. Hobartville......118 E8
- av. Pennant Hills......250 J1
- av. Scotland I......168 J5
- pl. Dee Why......258 F2
- pl. Blacktown......244 K14
- st. Campsie......372 A13
- st. Fairfield......336 C14
- st. Guildford......337 J2
- st. Inglebum......453 H8
- st. Mcquarie Fd......424 D16
- st. Matraville......436 G2
- st. Mt Lewis......369 K15
- st. Newtown......17 H15
- st. Parramatta......278 C14

HARP
- st. Belmore......401 G4
- st. Campsie......401 G4

HARPER
- cl. Tahmoor......565 K13
- gr. Mt Annan......479 J15
- pl. Frenchs Frst......255 F4
- pl. Kellyville......216 F4
- st. Merrylands......307 J15
- st. N Epping......251 F11
- wy. Inglebum......453 A10
- wy. Menai, off
  Forest Gln Wy......458 J14

HARPUR
- cl. Glenmore Pk......265 J6
- cr. S Windsor......150 E2
- pl. Casula......424 E4
- pl. Lalor Park......245 E11
- st. Fairfield W......335 B13

HARRABROOK
- av. Five Dock......342 K12

HARRADANCE
- pl. Liverpool......394 J9

HARRADEN
- dr. West Hoxton......391 K11
- dr. West Hoxton......391 K12

HARRADINE
- cr. Bligh Park......150 E5

HARRAH
- pl. Bradbury......511 J12

HARRICKS
- pl. Bonnyrigg......364 B5

HARRIER
- av. Green Valley......363 C12
- av. Raby......481 F2
- pl. Clarmnt Ms......268 J5
- pl. Woronora Ht......489 E2

HARRIET
- wky. Revesby......428 H2

HARRIET
- av. Castle Hill......247 G1
- pl. Currans Hill......480 A12
- st. Marrickville......374 A15

HARRIETT
- cl. Glenmore Pk......265 F11
- la. Glenmore Pk, off
  Harriett Cl......265 F10

HARRIETTE
- st. Neutral Bay......6 H8
- st. Neutral Bay......6 F7

HARRINGTON
- av. Castle Hill......217 A9
- av. Kellyville......217 K7
- av. Warrawee......222 H10
- st. Enmore......16 G13

HARRIOTT
- la. The Rocks, off
  Globe St......1 H11
- pky. Harrington Pk......478 F3
- st. Cabramatta W......364 J7
- st. Elderslie......477 F16
- st. Enmore......16 G13
- st. The Rocks......A H10
- st. The Rocks......A J6
- st. The Rocks......1 G13

HARRIOTT
- st. Waverton......5 A6
- st. Waverton......5 A5

HARRIS
- ct. Five Dock......342 G10
- la. Willoughby......285 F14
- la. Fairfield, off
  Hamilton Rd......336 E13
- la. Jamisontown, off
  Harris St......236 C15
- pl. Baulkham Hl......247 F5
- pl. West Hoxton......392 C11
- rd. Dural......189 D15
- rd. Five Dock......342 G11
- rd. Normanhurst......221 E9
- rd. Wentwrthvle......277 D11
- st. Balmain......7 A11
- st. Condell Park......398 G7
- st. Fairfield......336 C13
- st. Granville......308 F8
- st. Guildford......337 C3
- st. Harris Park......308 F7
- st. Inglebum......453 E7
- st. Jamisontown......236 B15
- st. Merrylands......307 C16
- st. N St Marys......239 H13
- st. Paddington......13 H15
- st. Parramatta......308 F7
- st. Pyrmont......12 F1
- st. Rosebery......405 G3
- st. Sans Souci......462 J5
- st. Ultimo......E A13
- st. Ultimo......3 A10
- st. Warriewood......198 J5
- st. Willoughby......285 F14
- st. Windsor......121 C14
- st. Woolooware......493 F12

HARRISON
- av. Bonnet Bay......460 B10
- av. Concord W......311 D12
- av. Eastwood......280 H8
- av. Harringtn Pk......478 K4
- av. Maroubra......407 G8
- la. Cremorne......6 K3
- pl. Minto......482 H4
- st. Kentlyn......513 C8
- st. Kentlyn......513 D5
- st. Ashcroft......394 E2
- st. Cremorne......6 H3
- st. Greenwich......314 J13
- st. Marrickville......373 H11
- st. Old Tngabbie......277 F9
- st. Revesby......398 F15

HARRISONS
- la. Glenorie......128 F5

HARROD
- st. Prospect......275 A12

HARROW
- av. Lansvale......366 C9
- la. Stanmore......16 J10
- rd. Auburn......339 B11
- rd. Auburn......339 C7
- rd. Berala......339 B11
- rd. Bexley......403 A14
- rd. Cmbrdg Pk......238 B9
- rd. Glenfield......424 D13
- rd. Glenfield......424 G9
- rd. Kogarah......433 C1
- st. Stanmore......16 H10
- st. Marayong......243 H6
- st. Sylvania......462 C7

HARROWER
- pl. Glenmore Pk......265 K6

HARRY
- av. Lidcombe......339 K5
- pl. Bella Vista......246 D7
- st. Eastlakes......405 J5

HARRY KNOX
- pl. Harbord......258 F13

HARRY LAWLER
- rd. Cranebrook......207 C15

HARSLETT
- cr. Beverley Pk......433 A10

HARST
- pl. Belrose......226 A10

HARSTON
- av. Mosman......316 K3

HART
- dr. Wentwthvle......277 A14
- dr. Warrick Frm......365 H16
- pl. Kellyville......216 G8
- st. St Clair......270 C9
- rd. S Windsor......150 G2
- st. Balmain East......8 C9
- st. Dundas Vy......280 A8
- st. Lane Cove N......283 K13
- st. Redfern......19 B5
- st. Smithfield......335 E3
- st. Surry Hills......19 J2
- st. Tempe......404 B3
- st. Warrick Frm......365 H16

HARTAM
- st. Kings Lngly......245 F5

HARTFORD
- av. Glen Alpine......510 D15

HARTHOUSE
- rd. Ambarvale......510 G16

HARTIGAN
- av. Emu Plains......235 F9
- wy. Bradbury......511 J12

HARTILL-LAW
- av. Bardwell Pk......402 J5
- av. Earlwood......402 J5

HARTINGTON
- st. Granville......308 E13
- st. Rooty Hill......242 C14

HARTLAND
- st. Northmead......277 K5

HARTLEY
- cl. Bligh Park......150 K7
- cl. N Turramurra......223 E1
- rd. Ruse......512 F8
- rd. Wrrngtn Cty......238 H8
- rd. Currans Hill......479 F12
- rd. Seven Hills......275 G1
- rd. Smeaton Gra......479 B7
- st. Rozelle......7 B11

HARTNETT
- pl. Doonside......273 E1

HARTOG
- av. Fairfield W......335 D11
- av. Willmot......210 C12
- dr. Wrrngtn Cty......238 H14
- la. Wrrngtn Cty, off
  Henry Lawson Av......238 H5
- pl. Illawong......459 F5

HARTREE
- pl. Cherrybrook......220 A10

HARTWELL
- st. St Clair......270 J10

HARTZELL
- pl. Bnkstn Aprt......367 K16

HARVARD
- cct. Rouse Hill......185 D4
- st. Sutherland......490 D11
- st. Gladesville......312 J8

HARVEST
- av. Castle Hill, off
  Langshaw Cct......218 K12
- dr. Wrrngtn Cty......238 C4
- dr. Wrrngtn Dns......238 C4

HARVEY
- av. Moorebank......396 E7
- av. Padstow......429 D5
- cct. St Clair......270 B13
- la. St Clair, off
  Harvey Cct......270 B13
- rd. Cherrybrook......219 G16
- rd. Menai......458 E10
- rd. Toongabbie......276 B9
- pwy.Moorebank, off
  Harvey Av......396 D7
- rd. Ingleside......197 C6
- st. Kings Park......244 C2
- st. Little Bay......437 G14
- st. Mcquarie Fd......424 B16
- st. Parramatta......308 G2
- st. Pyrmont......12 F1
- st,e. Seaforth......287 A9
- st,w.Seaforth......287 A9

HARWELL
- pl. Colyton......270 H9

HARWOOD
- av. Chatswood......285 D7
- av. Mt Krng-gai......163 B11
- cct. Glenmore Pk......265 J4
- pl. Pyrmont......12 K4
- st. St Helens Park......541 A10
- pl. Seaforth......287 A6
- st. Pyrmont......12 J4
- st. Seven Hills......275 J6

HASCOMBE
- la. St Clair, off
  Hascombe Wy......270 F13
- wy. St Clair......270 F13

HASLEM
- dr. Rookwood......340 A14

HASLEWOOD
- pl. Hinchnbrk......363 B16

HASLUCK
- pl. Glenmore Pk......265 J6
- rd. Bonnyrigg......363 H7

HASSALL
- st. Camellia......308 H4
- st. Elderslie......477 G14
- st. Harris Park......308 F4
- st. Harris Park......308 H4
- st. Parramatta......308 E4
- st. Smithfield......335 C3
- st. Westmead......307 G2
- st. Wetherill Pk......335 C3

HASSARATI
- pl. Casula......423 J1

HASSELBURGH
- rd. Tregear......240 F8

HASSELL
- st. St Ives......224 D6

HASSETT
- cl. Menai......458 G9
- la. St Clair, off
  Hassett Pl......269 K16
- pl. Rouse Hill......184 J8
- st. St Clair......269 K16

HASTINGS
- av. Chifley......437 A7
- av. Greystanes......306 A3
- la. Surry Hills......20 B6
- la. Marrickville, off
  Livingstone Rd......373 J11
- pde. Bondi Beach......378 E1
- pde. North Bondi......378 E1
- pl. Campbelltown......511 K9
- pl. Sylvania Wtr......462 D10
- rd. Beverley Pk......433 C12
- rd. Castle Hill......218 H7
- rd. Glenhaven......218 H7
- rd. Warrawee......222 G10
- rd. Botany......405 F12
- st. Lidcombe......339 G6
- st. Marrickville......373 J11

HATCHINSON
- cr. Jamisontown......265 K2

HATFIELD
- pl. Hebersham......241 F6
- pl. Canley Ht......365 C4
- st. Blakehurst......462 C1
- st. Lane Cove N......283 K13
- st. Mascot......405 D5

HATHAWAY
- rd. Lalor Park......245 G10

HATHERN
- st. Leichhardt......15 B5

HATHERTON
- rd. Lethbrdg Pk......240 C3
- rd. Tregear......240 C3

HATHOR
- st. Doonside......243 F15

HATTAH
- wy. Bow Bowing......452 E12

HATTERSLEY
- st. Arncliffe......403 E11
- st. Banksia......403 E12

HATTON
- la. Ryde, off
  Gladstone Av......312 A3
- pl. Barden Rdg......488 H3
- st. Ryde......312 B3

HAUGHTON
- st. Wattle Grove......426 B4
- st. Carramar......336 H16
- st. Linley Point......313 G8

HAULTAIN
- st. Minto......452 K13

HAVANNAH
- pl. Illawong......459 E5

HAVARD
- pl. Ashcroft......394 E1

HAVELOCK
- av. Coogee......407 F1
- av. Engadine......488 D14
- st. McGraths Hl......122 B12
- st. S Turramrra......252 C5

HAVEN
- ct. Cherrybrook......219 B12
- ct. Dural......188 C13
- st. Merrylands......307 B10
- st. Plumpton......242 A10

HAVENDALE
- av. Penshurst......431 H5

HAVEN VALLEY
- wy. Lansvale......366 C10

HAVENWOOD
- pl. Blacktown......274 A8

HAVERHILL
- av. Hebersham......241 E8

HAVILAH
- av. Wahroonga......221 K10
- ct. Wattle Grove......426 A1
- la. Lindfield......254 D15
- pl. Carlingford......279 J1
- rd. Lindfield......254 D15
- st. Chatswood......285 A8

HAVISHAM
- wy. Ambarvale......511 A15

STREETS HE

HAWAII
av. Lethbrdg Pk 240 F2

HAWDON
av. Wrrngtn Cty 238 E8
cl. Eldersnle 507 H3

HAWEA
pl. Belrose 226 A16

HAWICK
ct. Kellyville 187 A16

HAWK
cl. Green Valley 363 D12
pl. Erskine Park 270 E16
rd. Penshurst 431 B3

HAWKE
la. Kings Lngly 245 K9
pl. Kings Lngly 245 K9

HAWKEN
st. Newtown 374 G10

HAWKER
cl. Raby 451 D16
pl. West Hoxton 392 C12
st. Kings Park 244 C2

HAWKES
av. Newington, off
Newington Bvd ...310 A15

HAWKESBURY
av. Dee Why 258 J4
cr. Brooklyn 75 G12
esp. Sylvania Wtr 462 F13
rd. Hawksbry Ht 175 A4
rd. Springwood 202 B2
rd. Westmead 307 E4
rd. Winmalee 173 H7
st. Fairfield W 335 C14
st. Homebush B......310 G14
st. Pitt Town 92 H9

HAWKESWORTH
pde. Kings Lngly 245 A5
pl. Cherrybrook 219 K7

HAWKEY
cr. Camden 507 B5

HAWKHURST
st. Marrickville 373 J10

HAWKINS
av. Luddenham 356 H1
av. Bexland 233 E10
pl. Wilberforce 92 A3
rd. Tahmoor 565 J16
st. Artarmon 284 J14
st. Blacktown 275 A6

HAWKRIDGE
pl. Dural 219 B5

HAWKSLEY
st. Waterloo, off
Bourke St 375 J9

HAWKSVIEW
st. Guildford 337 C1
st. Merrylands 307 C16

HAWLEY
ct. St Ives 224 C8

HAWTHORN
cl. Cherrybrook 219 K6
ct. Penrith 237 C8
st. Loftus 489 H11
st. St Johns Pk 364 G2

HAWTHORNE
av. Chatswood W 284 B10
av. Rookwood 340 C14
pde. Haberfield 15 A2
pl. Mcquarie Fd 454 F2
rd. Bargo 567 F3
rd. Bargo 567 F7
st. Leichhardt 15 C1
st. Ramsgate Bch......433 F12

HAY
av. Caringbah 492 J7
st. St Clair 269 J14
la. Caringbah, off
Hay Av 492 J7
la. Randwick, off
Hay St 376 K16
pl. Quakers Hill 244 A4
st. Wakeley 334 K12
st. Ashbury 372 D9
st. Collaroy 229 C14
st. Croydon Pk 372 D7
st. Haymarket ......E D7
st. Haymarket ......E J8
st. Haymarket 3 E12
st. Leichhardt 16 B4
st. Liverpool 395 C6
st. Randwick 376 K16
st. Vaucluse 348 D7
st. West Ryde 281 A15

HAYBERRY
la. Crows Nest, off
Bernard La 315 H8
st. Crows Nest 315 G8

HAYBURN
av. Rockdale 403 D16

HAYDEN
la. Darlinghurst 4 G10
ct. Botany 405 G16
pl. Darlinghurst 4 G11
st. Engadine 518 E5

HAYDN
cl. Bonnyrigg Ht 363 E6
st. Seven Hills 246 E13

HAYDOCK
la. Revesby 398 J15

HAYES
av. Kellyville 216 K3
av. Northmead 277 H9
av. S Wntwthvle 307 D7
cl. Harringtn Pk 478 F7
pl. Bonnet Bay 460 C10
pl. Minto 452 K13
rd. Rosebery 375 G15
rd. Seven Hills 275 C4
rd. Wilberforce 67 A10
st. Balgowlah 287 K5
st. Lidcombe 339 G12
st. Neutral Bay 6 E10

HAYLE
st. St Ives 224 H8
tce. Stanhpe Gdn 215 C6

HAYLEN
st. Blackett 241 B2
pl. Edensor Pk 363 G1

HAYLEY
gr. Blacktown 273 G6
st. Cherrybrook 219 J5

HAYMAN
av. Hinchnbrk 393 A1
st. N Richmond 87 C14

HAYMET
st. Blaxland 233 H11
st. Kirrawee 490 J6

HAYNES
av. Seven Hills 245 C15
ct. Penrith 237 B10

HAYTER
pde. Camden S 506 J15

HAYTERS
rd. Werombi 413 A15

HAYWARD
st. Kingsford 406 H4

HAYWOOD
cl. Wetherll Pk 335 A3
st. Greystanes 305 J1
st. Epping 250 D16

HAZEL
cl. Lurnea 394 C10
ct. Cranebrook 207 B13
ct. Burraneer 493 F15
pl. Ingleburn 453 E11
st. Bass Hill 367 E10
st. Georges Hall 367 E10
st. Girraween 276 A16
st. Lansdowne 367 E10

HAZELBANK
pl. N Sydney 5 E2
pl. N Sydney 5 A3
pl. Wollstncraft 5 A3

HAZELDEAN
av. Hebersham 241 F10
ct. Kenthurst 157 D2

HAZELGLEN
pl. Panania 398 C15

HAZELMEAD
rd. Asquith 192 B9

HAZELTON
av. Quakers Hill Rdg 214 K2

HAZELWOOD
pl. Epping 250 J15

HEADLAND
rd. Castle Cove 285 H4
rd. N Curl Curl 258 F9

HEALD
rd. Ingleburn 452 K7

HEALEY
av. Newington 310 A16

HEANEY
cl. Mt Colah 162 E14

HEAPY
st. Blacktown 274 F9

HEARD
av. Tregear 240 G2
st. Denistone E 281 H10

HEARN
st. Leichhardt 16 D3

HEARNE
cl. Eastlakes 405 K2
ct. Bligh Park 150 H5
st. Mortdale 430 H5

HEARNSHAW
st. North Ryde 282 K9

HEART
st. Blacktown 244 C15

HEATH
cl. East Killara 254 G6
la. Heathcote 518 G12
la. Hunters Hill 313 F11
rd. Ryde 281 K12
rd. Heathcote 518 K10
rd. Blakehurst 432 D13
rd. Kellyville 186 D7
rd. Leppington 420 E6
st. Asquith 191 K12
st. Auburn 338 K6
st. Bankstown 369 F13
st. Bexley North 402 E12
st. Concord 311 K16
st. Five Dock 343 G9
st. Granville 338 G1
st. Kingswood 238 B12
st. Merrylands 307 G16
st. Mona Vale 199 F3
st. Prospect 274 G10
st. Punchbowl 400 A6
st. Randwick 377 C15
st. Ryde 281 K12
st. Turrella 403 C6

HEATHCLIFF
cr. Balgowlah Ht......287 K14

HEATHCOTE
rd. Engadine 518 C1
rd. Hamondvle 426 F1
rd. Heathcote 518 C1
rd. Holsworthy 427 H11
rd. Lucas Ht 487 A12
rd. Moorebank 395 H7
rd. Pleasure Pt 427 B6
rd. Sandy Point 427 H11
rd. Voyager Pt 427 B6
rd. Picton 563 F9
st. Rockdale 403 B13

HEATHER
cl. Baulkham Hl 247 E6
pl. Acacia Gdn 214 G15
pl. Hornsby Ht 161 G11
pl. Wilberforce 92 A2
rd. Winmalee 173 E8
st. Caringbah 492 J15
st. Collaroy Plat 228 E12
st. Girraween 276 A16
st. Leonay 234 J15
st. Loftus 489 J10
st. Yagoona 368 E13

HEATHERBRAE
pl. Castle Hill 218 E12

HEATHERFIELD
ct. Catherine Fd 449 E1

HEATHER GLEN
rd. Yellow Rock 173 F15

HEATHERWOOD
cl. Winmalee 173 B12

HEATHFIELD
st. Airds 512 A11

HEATLEY
st. Abbotsbury 333 D14

HEATON
av. Clontarf 287 E11

HEAVEY
st. Werrington 238 F10

HEBBLEWHITE
av. Bonnyrigg 364 A6

HEBBURN
pl. Cartwright 394 D4

HEBE
st. Kellyville 186 J15
st. Greenacre 370 J12

HEBER
st. Prospect 274 K13
st. Hurstville 431 H1

HEBRIDES
av. Mcquarie Lk 423 G13
pl. St Andrews 482 A4

HECKENBERG
av. Busby 393 K2
av. Heckenberg 364 A16
av. Sadleir 364 A16
rd. Glenorie 128 K7

HECTOR
rd. Willoughby 285 D14
st. Bass Hill 368 C10
st. Chester Hill 368 D6
st. Greystanes 306 E6
st. Illawong 459 K6
st. Sefton 338 E16

HEDDA
st. Oakhurst 241 K4

HEDGER
av. Ashfield 342 G15

HEDGES
av. Strathfield 370 J2
st. Fairfield 336 F8

HEDLEY
st. Greystanes 306 E9
st. Marayong 244 C10
st. Riverwood 430 B1

HELY
ct. Wrrngtn Cty 238 F5

HEMERS
rd. Dural 189 H15

HEMINGWAY
cr. Fairfield 336 D6

HEMMINGS
st. Penrith 237 B9

HEMPHILL
av. Mt Pritchard 364 F10

HEMSBY
st. Doonside 243 E5

HEMSWORTH
av. Northmead 277 H9

HENDERSON
av. Panania 428 B4
cr. Jamisontown 266 B3
rd. Alexandria 18 E13
rd. Alexandria 18 E13
rd. Bexley 402 F14
rd. Eveleigh 18 E13
rd. Ingleburn 453 D1
rd. Mcquarie Fd 453 F4
st. Bondi 377 K4
st. Denistone E 281 F9
st. Merrylands 307 J9
st. Turrella 403 D5

HENDLE
cl. Baulkham Hl 246 J5

HENDON
grn. W Pnnant Hl 249 C4

HENDRA
cl. St Johns Pk 364 E1
st. Warwck Frm 395 K1

HENDREN
pl. Colyton 270 G6

HENDRENS
rd. Ebenezer 68 D13

HENDY
av. Collaroy 229 A14
av. Coogee 407 D3
av. Panania 428 F1
av. S Coogee 407 D3

HENLEY
av. Belrose 225 K13
cl. Castle Hill 248 F3
cl. Hornsby Ht 191 F9
st. St Clair 270 G10
st. Lane Cove W 284 F16
st. Sefton 368 F3
st. Drummoyne 343 H5
st. Lane Cove W 283 J16
st. Rosebery 405 F2

HENLEY MARINE
dr. Drummoyne 343 J6
dr. Five Dock 343 B12
dr. Rodd Point 343 E9
dr. Russell Lea 343 E9

HENNESSY
st. Croydon 342 C16

HENNESSY
cr. Shalvey 211 A13

HENNING
av. Kingsford 407 D7
av. Maroubra 407 D7
av. S Coogee 407 D7

HENNINGS
la. Newtown 17 K11

HELIODOR
pl. Eagle Vale 481 G8

HELIOS
cr. Doonside 243 E14

HELIOTROPE
av. Blacktown 274 E12

HELISSIO
pl. Castle Hill 217 B8

HELLES
av. Moorebank 395 D10

HELMAN
pl. Ingleburn 452 J11

HELM COTTAGE
st. Blair Athol 511 A3

HELMSLEY
gr. Castle Hill 216 J9

HELP
st. Chatswood 284 H9

HELSTON
st. Stanhpe Gdn 215 E7

HELVETIA
av. Berowra 163 D2
la. Earlwood 402 J3

GREGORY'S STREET DIRECTORY 79

HE STREETS

HENRICKS
av. Drummoyne 313 G16
av. Newington 309 K15
pl. Beacon Hill 257 J8
HENRIETTA
cl. Cecil Hills 362 D3
dr. Narellan Vale 508 F2
la. Double Bay 14 B10
la. Manly, off Raglan St 288 H9
st. Chippendale 19 B3
st. Double Bay 14 B10
st. Waverley 377 G8
HENRY
av. Sylvania 461 H13
av. Ultimo 12 J9
la. Lewisham 15 B10
la. St Leonards 315 E5
la.n, Lewisham 15 B10
pl. Narellan Vale 508 K2
pl. Plumpton 241 G10
rd. Riverwood 399 J15
rd. Vineyard 152 B2
st. Ashfield 342 J13
st. Balmain 7 C13
st. Baulkham Hl 247 K8
st. Carlton 432 J5
st. Cecil Hills 362 H7
st. Dee Why 259 A9
st. Five Dock 342 H9
st. Gordon 253 J8
st. Guildford 337 H7
st. Leichhardt 9 K9
st. Lewisham 15 B10
st. Lidcombe 339 J10
st. Lilyfield 9 K8
st. Old Guildford 337 E7
st. Parramatta 308 F1
st. Penrith 237 A10
st. Picton 563 C15
st. Punchbowl 370 C16
st. Queens Park 22 K15
st. Randwick 407 D2
st. Ryde 312 C5
st. St Peters 374 E15
st. Strathfield 371 G1
st. Sydenham 374 E15
st. Tempe 374 D16
st. Turrella 403 E5
HENRY COX
dr. Mulgoa 324 C1
HENRY KENDALL
av. Padstow Ht 429 C6
cl. Heathcote 518 C15
cr. Mascot 405 D2
HENRY LAWSON
av. Abbotsford 342 J3
av. McMahons Pt 5 E16
av. Wrrngtn Cty 238 E6
dr. Bnkstn Aprt 397 C1
dr. East Hills 427 F5
dr. Georges Hall 367 C16
dr. Lansdowne 367 B6
dr. Milperra 397 C1
dr. Padstow 429 F6
dr. Padstow Ht 429 A9
dr. Panania 428 B9
dr. Peakhurst 430 A3
dr. Picnic Point 428 B9
dr. Revesby Ht 429 A9
rd. Peakhurst 430 D4
HENSHAW
cl. Bonnyrigg 364 F6
HENSON
la. Ultimo 12 K12
st. Btn-le-Sds 403 K16
st. Marrickville 373 F15
st. Merrylands 307 D12
st. Summer Hill 373 B7
st. Toongabbie 276 H8
HENSTOCK
rd. Arcadia 129 C12
HENTIC
ct. Wrrngtn Cty 238 H5
HENTY
pl. Bonnyrigg 363 H7
pl. Quakers Hill 214 B9
rd. Ingleburn 422 K13
st. Yagoona 368 G9
HENVILLE
pl. Bass Hill 367 G7
HENZE
cr. Clarmnt Ms 268 G4
HEPBURN
av. Carlingford 280 C2
av. Gladesville 312 H8
rd. North Rocks 248 H12
HEPHER
rd. Campbelltown 481 B15
HERA
pl. St Clair 269 G11
pl. Winston Hills 277 D1
HERAKLES
pl. Doonside 243 F16
HERALD
pl. Beaumont Hills 185 K14
sq. Sydney A K8
HERB ELLIOTT
av. Homebush B 340 G1
HERBER
pl. Wahroonga 222 C11
HERBERT
av. Newport 169 C7
av. Wahroonga 222 B2
la. Newtown 17 J12
la. West Ryde, off Herbert St 281 F16
pl. Narellan 478 G15
pl. Smithfield 336 C2
rd. Edgecliff, off New McLean St 13 J12
st. Artarmon 315 B2
st. Bankstown 399 C7
st. Cmbrdg Pk 238 A10
st. Dulwich Hill 373 F9
st. Kemps Ck 359 K11
st. Malabar 437 D4
st. Manly 288 E6
st. Marsden Pk 182 A12
st. Merrylands 308 B13
st. Mortlake 312 B16
st. Newtown 17 J12
st. Oatley 431 C16
st. Pyrmont 8 F15
st. Regentville 265 F4
st. Rockdale 403 A12
st. St Leonards 315 B2
st. Summer Hill 373 B6
st. West Ryde 281 F15
HERBERTO
la. Glebe 11 K10
HERBERTON
av. Hunters Hill 313 F11
HERBORN
pl. Minto 452 K14
HERCULES
av. Padstow 429 C2
cl. Cranebrook 207 E6
cl. Raby 451 H14
la. Dulwich Hill 373 D11
pl. Bligh Park 150 E7
rd. Btn-le-Sds 433 K4
st. Ashfield 372 J3
st. Chatswood 285 B9
st. Dulwich Hill 373 D11
st. Fairfield E 337 A15
st. Surry Hills 19 J1
HEREFORD
pl. Minto Ht 482 J13
pl. S Wntwthvle 306 H6
pl. West Pymble 252 H14
st. Busby 393 J1
st. Forest Lodge 11 F15
st. Glebe 11 J13
st. Hobartville 118 E6
wy. Picton 561 B3
HEREWARD
hwy. Blacktown 274 H3
st. Maroubra 407 G11
HERFORD
st. Botany 405 J16
HERING
av. Emerton 240 K6
HERITAGE
cl. Castle Hill, off Langshaw Cct 218 K12
ct. Castle Hill 248 E4
ct. Dural 219 B6
ct. Glenmore Pk 265 G5
dr. Illawong 459 E4
pl. Glenwood 245 F3
wy. Glen Alpine 510 C13
HERITAGE HEIGHTS
cct. St Helens Park 541 A5
HERITAGE PARK
dr. Castle Hill 218 F9
HERLEY
av. Rossmore 390 E4
HERMES
pl. Emu Plains 235 F8
HERMIES
av. Milperra 397 G11
HERMINGTON
st. Epping 280 E1
HERMITAGE
av. Kellyville 185 F9
cr. Cartwright 394 C4
ct. Orchard Hills 268 E5
la. West Ryde, off Hermitage Rd 281 F16
pl. Eschol Park 481 A4
pl. Minchinbury 271 K9
rd. Kurrajong Hl 63 K14
rd. West Ryde 281 F16
HERMOSA
ct. Castle Hill 217 D9
HERMOYNE
st. West Ryde 280 G13
HERON
av. Georges Hall 367 K13
cr. St Clair 270 B14
ct. Castle Hill 218 D8
pl. Dee Why 258 H2
pl. Grays Point 491 F14
pl. Hinchinbrk 393 C1
pl. Ingleburn 453 F7
pl. Yarramundi 145 D4
HERRICK
cl. West Hoxton 392 E5
st. Blacktown 275 A8
st. Wetherill Pk 334 D4
HERRING
rd. Mcquarie Pk 282 D3
rd. Marsfield 282 A6
HERRON
wk. Mosman, off Raglan St 316 H14
HERSEY
st. Blaxland 233 H11
HERSHON
st. St Marys 269 K6
HERSTON
rd. St Johns Pk 364 C2
HERTZ
pl. Emerton 240 J4
HERVEY
st. Georges Hall 367 E13
HESELTINE
pl. Rooty Hill 272 B4
HESPERUS
st. Pymble 252 K7
HESSEL
pl. Emu Heights 234 J7
HESSION
rd. Nelson 155 A14
rd. Oakville 124 A12
HESTEN
la. Rockdale, off Gloucester St 403 C14
la. Rockdale, off Walz St 403 C15
HESTER
st. Castlereagh 146 D15
wy. Beaumont Hills 186 A15
HESWELL
av. Morning Bay 138 G14
HEVINGTON
rd. Auburn 339 E7
HEVRELL
ct. Glenwood 215 D14
HEWETT
la. Penrith, off Warwick St 236 J13
HEWIN
cl. Liberty Gr 311 B10
HEWISON
av. Green Valley 363 C11
wy. Minto 482 H8
HEWIT
av. Glebe 12 A14
HEWITT
av. Greystanes 306 F11
av. Wahroonga 221 K11
lk. Harringtn Pk 478 G2
pl. Minto 482 J9
st. Colyton 270 G9
st. Greenacre 370 F9
HEWLETT
st. Bronte 377 K7
st. Granville 308 C11
HEWS
ct. Belrose 226 C13
pde. Belrose 226 A13
HEXHAM
pl. Wetherill Pk 304 A15
HEXTOL
st. Croydon Pk 371 H9
HEYDE
av. Strathfield 341 B13
HEYDON
av. Warrawee 222 F11
st. Enfield 371 J3
st. Mosman 317 A5
HEYSEN
av. Ermington 310 B5
cl. Pymble 253 F1
pl. Casula 424 H2
st. Abbotsbury 333 B11
HEYSON
wy. Claymore 481 F11
HEYWARD
cl. Jamisontown 266 C2
HEYWOOD
cl. Hinchinbrk 362 K16
ct. Bella Vista 246 H3
gln. Stanhpe Gdn 215 G8
HEZLET
st. Chiswick 343 E1
HEZLETT
rd. Kellyville 186 C11
HIBBERTIA
pl. Westleigh 220 G8
HIBBERTS
la. Freemns Rch 90 D3
HIBBLE
st. West Ryde 311 A2
HIBERNIA
pl. Harringtn Pk 478 G5
HIBERTIA
pl. Mt Annan 509 E2
HIBISCUS
av. Carlingford 249 C16
cl. Acacia Gdn 214 J14
cl. Alfords Point 429 B13
cr. Mcquarie Fd 454 D2
ct. St Clair 270 B15
pl. Cherrybrook 219 F11
st. Greystanes 305 G11
HICKETTS
av. Glebe 11 K7
HICKEY
cl. Abbotsbury 333 C11
la. Darlinghurst 13 A9
pl. Mt Annan 479 F15
HICKEYS
la. Penrith 237 A5
HICKLER
gr. Bidwill 211 C14
HICKORY
cl. Alfords Point 459 C2
mw. Wattle Grove 396 C16
pl. Acacia Gdn 214 J14
pl. Dural 219 B6
pl. Mcquarie Fd 424 G16
pl. St Clair 270 G11
st. Greystanes 306 D4
HICKS
av. Mascot 405 G6
av. S Turramrra 252 A4
pl. Kings Lngly 245 J8
HICKSON
cct. Harringtn Pk 478 H3
rd. Dawes Point 1 D8
rd. Millers Pt A B4
rd. Millers Pt 1 D10
rd. Millers Pt 1 D8
rd. Sydney A B4
rd. Sydney 1 D10
rd. The Rocks B A1
rd. The Rocks 1 H8
st. Botany 405 E10
HICKSON STEPS
Dawes Point 1 G6
HIDES
st. Glenfield 424 H11
HIGGERSON
av. Engadine 518 F5
HIGGINBOTHAM
rd. Gladesville 312 G3
rd. Ryde 312 G3
HIGGINS
la. Penrith 236 K11
pl. Westleigh 220 J2
st. Condell Park 398 D1
st. Penrith 237 A11
HIGGS
la. Turramurra, off William St 222 H14
pl. Cranebrook 207 C10
st. Coogee 407 D2
st. Randwick 407 D2
HIGH
la. Millers Pt A B3
la. Moorebank 395 G7
la. Waverley, off High St 377 G8
st. Balmain 7 A10
st. Bankstown 399 B5
st. Berowra 133 E11
st. Cabramatta W 365 A8
st. Campbelltown 511 F8
st. Canterbury 372 E16
st. Caringbah 492 G8
st. Carlton 432 F4
st. Chatswood 285 D6
st. Concord 341 J5
st. Dee Why 258 E4
st. Edgecliff 13 K13
st. Epping 281 B1
st. Gladesville 313 A3
st. Glenbrook 234 B13
st. Granville 308 D7
st. Gymea 491 D6
st. Harris Park 308 D7
st. Hornsby 221 G1
st. Hunters Hill 313 C5
st. Kensington 376 F14
st. Kirribilli 6 A11
st. Kogarah 433 A7
st. McGraths Hl 121 J11
st. Manly 288 J12
st. Marrickville 373 K15
st. Mascot 405 B5
st. Millers Pt A B3
st. Millers Pt 1 D10
st. Milsons Point 6 A11
st. Mt Krng-gai 163 B11
st. N Sydney 6 A11
st. N Willoughby 285 F10
st. Penrith 236 H10
st. Penrith 236 D7
st. Penrith 237 D11
st. Randwick 377 A15
st. Strathfield 371 B3
st. Waverley 377 G8
st. Willoughby 285 F10
st. Willoughby 285 G15
st. Woolooware 493 H8
HIGHBRIDGE
rd. Killara 253 F13
HIGHBROOK
pl. Castle Hill 218 K7
HIGHBURY
st. Croydon 372 E2
HIGHCLAIRE
pl. Glenwood 245 H3
HIGHCLERE
av. Banksia 403 H13
av. Burwood 371 H1
av. Punchbowl 370 D16
cr. North Rocks 279 A2
pl. Castle Hill 218 H8
HIGHCLIFF
la. Earlwood 403 E3
rd. Earlwood 403 E3
HIGHERDALE
av. Miranda 492 C4
HIGHETT
pl. Glenhaven 218 A2
HIGHFIELD
cr. Strathfield 371 E4
la. Lindfield 254 A16
pl. Beaumont Hills 186 B15
rd. Guildford 338 D9
rd. Lindfield 283 H1
rd. Quakers Hill 214 A14
HIGHGATE
cct. Kellyville 185 E6
pl. Cherrybrook 219 D13
pl. Glenwood 246 B4
rd. Lindfield 254 D15
st. Auburn 309 B14
st. Bexley 402 F13
st. Strathfield 371 D1
HIGHGROVE
ct. Cecil Hills 362 G3
HIGH HOLBORN
st. Surry Hills 20 A6

80 GREGORY'S STREET DIRECTORY

STREETS HO

HIGHLAND
av. Bankstown.........369 A15
av. Roselands..........400 F7
av. Toongabbie........276 C5
av. Yagoona 369 A15
cr. Earlwood 403 C3
rd. Peakhurst 430 G1
rdg. Middle Cove.......285 K8
st. Guildford............337 K2
HIGHLANDS
av. Gordon 253 G5
av. Wahroonga..........222 B4
cr. Blacktown 274 B2
wy. Rouse Hill 185 E3
HIGHPOINT
dr. Blacktown 274 B8
dr. N Wahroonga.....192 G15
pl. Como 460 E5
HIGHRANGE
tce. Bella Vista..........216 C13
HIGHS
rd. W Pnnant Hl.......219 A15
HIGH SCHOOL
dr. Winmalee...........173 H7
HIGHVIEW
av. Faulconbdg........171 E14
av. Greenacre 369 J13
av. Manly Vale 287 K4
av. Neutral Bay 6 D4
av. Penrith...............237 B6
av. Queenscliff.........288 G2
cl. N Epping............251 C10
cr. Oyster Bay 461 B6
la. Neutral Bay 6 D4
st. Blacktown 274 C7
HIGHWORTH
av. Bexley................402 H14
HILAND
cr. Smithfield 336 A6
HILAR
av. Carlingford.........279 E4
HILARY
cr. Dundas.............279 K13
st. Winston Hills......276 G1
HILDA
av. Casula................394 H12
av. Scotland I 168 G4
rd. Baulkham Hl 247 A11
st. Bass Hill.............367 K6
st. Blaxland.............234 B5
st. Prospect 274 K12
HILDEGARD
pl. Baulkham Hl 247 B2
HILDER
rd. Balgowlah Ht......287 H12
rd. Ermington..........310 B4
st. Elderslie............477 J14
wy. Claymore 481 D12
HILDERLEIGH
cl. Faulconbdg........171 B13
HILES
la. Alexandria............19 B16
st. Alexandria............19 B16
HILL
av. Hobartville 118 C9
la. Campsie 372 B14
la. Carlton...............432 K5
la. Coogee 377 G15
rd. Birrong 368 J6
rd. Homebush B......340 B2
rd. Lidcombe...........340 B2
rd. Lurnea 394 C11
rd. W Pnnant Hl.......249 B5
st. Arncliffe 403 D7
st. Balgowlah 288 A9
st. Baulkham Hl 247 J9
st. Berowra..............133 E13
st. Cabramatta 365 H7
st. Camden 477 B16
st. Campsie 372 A14
st. Carlton...............432 J5
st. Coogee 377 G15
st. Dulwich Hill.........373 D8
st. Fairlight..............288 A9
st. Five Dock...........342 K6
st. Glenbrook 234 B15
st. Hurstville 432 C6
st. Leichhardt............10 B13
st. Marrickville 373 F15
st. N Sydney...............K F9
st. N Sydney...............5 G9
st. Picton................563 D11
st. Queenscliff..........288 G2
st. Roseville 284 G4
st. Strathfield S.......371 E5
st. Surry Hills.............4 D15
st. Wareemba 342 K6
st. Warriewood 199 C9
st. Wentwthvle........277 A15
st. Woolooware.......493 F11
HILLARD
st. Wiley Park..........370 G16
HILLARY
cl. Eastlakes............406 A3
pde. Matraville...........437 C2
st. Greystanes.........306 D9
st. West Pymble......252 F11
HILLAS
av. Kellyville.............216 G4
HILLBAR
la. Glenbrook 234 B15
HILL CLIMB
dr. Annangrove 155 H11
HILLCOT
st. Hurlstone Pk......372 J10
HILLCREST
av. Ashfield 372 J7
av. Bardwell Vy........402 H10
av. Epping 250 H14
av. Gladesville 312 K11
av. Greenacre 369 K14
av. Hurstville 431 H8
av. Hurstville Gr.......431 E10
av. Mona Vale...........199 H1
av. Moorebank 396 C11
av. Mt Lewis............369 J16
av. Oatley 431 E10
av. Penrith...............237 B6
av. Penshurst 431 E10
av. Strathfield S 371 E6
av. Villawood...........367 B3
av. Winston Hills......277 D2
dr. St Ives 224 D8
la. Emu Heights, off
Hillcrest Rd 235 A2
la. Tempe 374 B16
pl. North Manly.......288 C1
rd. Berowra.............133 D10
rd. Emu Heights 235 A2
rd. Pennant Hills.......220 G16
rd. Quakers Hill 214 A15
rd. Wedderburn.......541 F15
rd. Yarramundi........145 A8
st. Homebush 341 B7
st. Punchbowl..........400 D5
st. Tempe 374 C16
st. Wahroonga 222 J6
st. Wiley Park..........400 D5
HILLCROSS
st. Lugarno.............429 K14
HILL END
rd. Doonside 243 C13
HILLEND
pl. Wakeley.............334 G14
HILLGATE
av. Castle Hill...........219 B11
HILLIARD
dr. Castle Hill...........218 J12
HILLIER
cl. Camden S 507 B16
cl. Camden S 537 B1
rd. Liverpool............395 A3
st. Concord W.........341 E4
st. Edensor Pk 363 C2
st. Merrylands.........307 E9
HILLIGER
rd. S Penrith............267 C2
HILLINA
wy. Mcquarie Fd.......454 H4
HILLMAN
av. Rydalmere 309 J1
HILLMONT
av. Thornleigh 221 B13
HILLOAK
ct. Castle Hill...........218 K6
wy. Menai 458 H13
HILLPINE
av. Kogarah 433 C9
pl. Terrey Hills.........196 D4
HILLS
av. Epping 250 E16
st. Bnksmeadw 435 K1
HILLSBOROUGH
ct. Cherrybrook.......219 D12
wy. Baulkham Hl 216 K16
HILLSIDE
av. Clemton Park 401 K4
av. St Ives Ch 224 A5
av. Vaucluse............348 C7
cct. Cranebrook........207 D8
cr. Epping 281 A3
cr. Glenbrook..........234 E16
dr. Harringtn Pk.......478 C3
la. Blacktown 275 B2
la. Carlingford.........249 G11
pde. Mt Colah 162 B16
pl. Glen Alpine 510 G10
pl. W Pnnant Hl.......249 J9
rd. Blacktown 274 B4
rd. Newport.............169 J7
st. Chatswood W 284 F8
st. Roseville 284 F8
HILLSLOPE
rd. Newport.............169 H7
HILL TOP
rd. Tennyson.............65 D14
HILLTOP
av. Blacktown 274 A3
av. Currans Hill 480 A9
av. Marrickville 403 E1
av. Mt Pritchard 364 F13
av. Padstow Ht 429 G7
cr. Campbelltown 511 F9
cr. Fairlight.............288 C9
cr. Fairlight.............288 A9
ct. Castle Hill...........217 B10
rd. Avalon 139 G16
rd. Merrylands.........307 C8
rd. Penrith...............237 C6
st. Kingsgrove.........402 A5
HILLVIEW
av. Bankstown 369 J15
av. S Penrith............266 J1
cr. Warriewood 198 F6
la. Eastwood...........281 A8
la. Sans Souci.........433 C14
pde. Lurnea 394 B11
pl. Glendenning.......242 H4
pl. Narellan 478 H13
rd. Eastwood...........281 A7
rd. Kellyville.............185 F5
st. Auburn 339 A10
st. Hornsby Ht 161 H12
st. Narellan 478 H13
st. Roselands..........401 D4
st. Sans Souci.........433 B14
HILLY
st. Mortlake 312 A13
HILMA
st. Collaroy Plat.......228 K14
HILMER
st. Frenchs Frst.......256 G6
HILSDEN
st. Rooty Hill...........272 B5
HILTON
av. Roselands..........400 J9
av. Sydenham 374 E16
cr. Casula...............394 G16
cr. Casula...............424 G1
pl. Kenthurst...........157 G8
rd. Cmbrdg Gdn 237 H4
rd. Springwood 202 C6
st. Greystanes.........306 E9
HILTON PARK
rd. Tahmoor............565 H6
rd. Tahmoor............565 J7
HILTS
rd. Strathfield 341 F10
HILVERSUM
cr. Belrose 226 B4
HILWA
st. Villawood...........367 C2
HIMALAYA
cr. Seven Hills.........275 B8
HINCHEN
st. Guildford...........338 A6
HINCHINBROOK
dr. Hinchinbrk 363 A15
HINCKS
st. Glenorie...............96 H15
st. Kingsford...........406 J4
HIND
pl. Chipping Ntn......396 C4
HINDEMITH
av. Emerton.............240 J6
HINDER
cl. Abbotsbury 333 B11
HINDLE
tce. Bella Vista..........246 F4
HINDMARSH
av. Camden S..........537 B2
rd. Liverpool............365 A15
st. Cranebrook 207 D8
HINDSON
pl. Belrose 226 B15
HINEMOA
av. Normanhurst 221 J11
st. Panania..............428 C5
HINES
pl. Mt Annan...........509 E1
HINGERTY
pl. S Penrith............266 K6
HINKLER
av. Bargo.................567 K6
av. Caringbah 492 G5
av. Condell Park.......398 C2
av. Ryde.................281 J16
av. S Turramrra 251 K6
av. Warwck Frm 365 E15
cr. Lane Cove N.......283 G12
ct. Drummoyne.......343 G1
la. Warwck Frm 365 G15
pl. Doonside 273 F4
pwy. Warwck Frm, off
Hinkler Av...........365 F15
st. Btn-le-Sds..........433 H1
st. Ermington..........280 A15
st. Greenwich..........314 J6
st. Maroubra...........406 G11
st. Smithfield 335 E2
HINTON
cl. St Johns Pk 364 J2
gln. N St Marys.........239 J8
la. N St Marys, off
Hinton Gln..........239 J8
pl. Chipping Ntn......366 E14
HINXMAN
rd. Castlereagh 176 B4
HIPWOOD
st. Kirribilli..................6 B12
st. N Sydney 6 B12
HIRST
pl. Fairfield W..........335 A12
st. Arncliffe 403 C8
st. Bardwell Vy........403 C8
HISHION
pl. Georges Hall 367 K14
HISPANO
pl. Ingleburn 453 J8
HITTER
av. Bass Hill.............368 B7
av. Casula...............394 K11
av. Mt Pritchard.......364 H13
HIXON
st. Stanhpe Gdn 215 C5
HIXSON
st. Bankstown 399 D5
HOAD
pl. Greystanes.........306 B11
pl. Menai 458 F7
pl. Shalvey..............211 A13
HOADLEY
pl. Arndell Park 273 H10
HOBART
av. Campbelltown....512 B5
av. E Lindfield..........254 K15
pl. Illawong.............459 G5
pl. Wakeley.............334 H15
st. Oxley Park..........240 A14
st. Richmond 119 C4
st. Riverstone 153 B16
st. Riverstone 182 H3
st. St Marys 240 A14
HOBBITS
gln. Wrrngtn Dns 237 J4
HOBBS
st. Bligh Park 150 J6
st. Kingsgrove.........401 H11
st. Lewisham 15 C10
HOBBY
cl. S Penrith............266 G5
la. S Penrith, off
Hobby Cl............266 G5
HOBLER
av. West Hoxton 392 B10
HOBSON
pl. Plumpton...........242 C10
HOCKING
av. Earlwood 403 A4
la. Earlwood, off
Hocking Av.........403 A4
pl. Erskine Park.......300 K1
HOCKLEY
rd. Eastwood...........280 F6
HODDLE
av. Bradbury............511 E9
av. Campbelltown....511 E9
cr. Davidson 255 E2
pl. West Hoxton 392 A11
st. Paddington 13 C13
HODGE
st. Hurstville 431 J1
HODGES
pl. Currans Hill........479 G11
st. Kings Lngly........245 A3
HODGKINSON
cr. Panania..............428 E1
HODGSON
av. Cremorne...........316 F12
av. Cremorne Pt 316 F12
cl. Wedderburn........540 C10
cr. Baulkham Hl 247 D13
rd. Glenbrook 264 C4
st. Randwick...........377 B11
HODKIN
pl. Ingleburn 453 A11
HOFF
st. Mt Pritchard.......364 K11
HOFFMAN
la. Newtown 17 E12
pl. Oakhurst............242 C4
HOFFMANN
pwy. Springwood 201 D1
HOFFMANS
la. Balmain 7 J9
HOGAN
av. Bass Hill.............367 F7
av. Green Valley.......362 K8
av. Sydenham 374 E14
gr. Castle Hill...........216 K9
gr. Castle Hill...........217 A9
la. Panania..............428 D2
pl. Kingswood..........267 E2
pl. Mt Annan...........479 E15
pl. Quakers Hill 214 C12
st. Balgowlah Ht......287 K12
HOGANS
dr. Bargo.................567 D1
dr. Bargo.................567 B3
HOGARTH
av. Dee Why............258 F5
HOGBEN
st. Kogarah 433 C5
HOGUE
pl. Mt Annan...........509 D1
HOLBEACH
av. Tempe 404 B4
HOLBECHE
rd. Arndell Park 273 E8
HOLBORN
av. Dee Why............258 G3
st. Ambarvale..........510 G12
HOLBOROW
st. Croydon.............372 D5
st. Croydon Pk........372 D5
HOLBORROW
av. Hobartville 118 B7
HOLBROOK
av. Kirribilli..................2 F1
ct. Stanhpe Gdn 215 D12
st. Bossley Park 333 G10
HOLBURN
cr. Kings Lngly........245 G8
HOLCROFT
pl. Cherrybrook.......219 K7
HOLDEN
av. Epping 250 G13
st. Ashbury 372 H10
st. Ashfield 372 J6
st. Canterbury 372 H10
st. Chester Hill 337 K11
st. Maroubra...........406 H11
st. Northwood.........314 G7
st. Redfern................19 B6
st. Toongabbie........276 G8
HOLDIN
st. Bonnyrigg..........364 A7
HOLDSWORTH
av. Rcuttrs Bay..........13 C6
av. St Leonards 315 C7
dr. Mt Annan...........479 A12
dr. Narellan Vale......479 A12
la. Newtown 18 C10
la. Paddington 4 G14
rd. Neutral Bay 6 C6
st. Merrylands.........307 C14
st. Neutral Bay 6 B6
st. Newtown 18 C10
st. Woollahra 21 K1
HOLFORD
cr. Gordon 253 D8
rd. Cabramatta W 365 B6

GREGORY'S STREET DIRECTORY 81

HO STREETS

HOLKER
st. Homebush B......309 K9
st. Silverwater.........309 K9
HOLKER BUSWAY
Homebush B......310 F12
HOLKHAM
av. Randwick...........376 K11
HOLLAND
av. Rockdale............403 B12
cr. Casula...............394 J14
cr. Frenchs Frst.......256 E5
ct. Glenmore Pk.......266 F15
pl. Lakemba............370 J14
pl. Telopea..............279 J11
rd. Bellevue Hill 14 J16
rd. Glenhaven..........187 H13
st. Birrong 369 B5
st. Chatswood.........285 B11
st. Cronulla.............493 H12
st. N Epping............251 E10
st. St Peters............374 K14
st. Springwood 202 A2
HOLLANDS
av. Marrickville 373 G12
HOLLEY
la. Beverly Hills.......430 J3
rd. Beverly Hills.......430 J2
HOLLIDAY
av. Berowra.............133 C11
av. Berowra Ht.........133 C11
la. Auburn 339 E2
HOLLIER
pl. Baulkham Hl 247 D10
rd. Picton................561 C4
st. Cmbrdg Pk.........238 A6
HOLLINGS
cr. Heathcote 518 G9
pl. Plumpton...........241 G9
HOLLINGSHED
la. Mascot, off Johnson St........405 E6
st. Mascot 405 E6
HOLLINSWORTH
rd. Marsden Pk........211 J11
HOLLIS
av. Denistone E........281 E8
la. Newtown 18 B9
st. Wentwthvle........277 B9
st. Wentwthvle........277 C9
HOLLISTER
pl. Carlingford.........249 G14
HOLLOWAY
la. Pagewood, off Holloway St........406 B10
pl. Curl Curl 258 F12
st. Pagewood..........405 K10
HOLLOWFORTH
av. Neutral Bay 6 H10
HOLLOWS
pl. Bonnyrigg..........363 H8
HOLLY
av. Chipping Ntn......396 D5
av. Ryde..................312 G3
rd. Cherrybrook.......219 H12
st. Caringbah 493 A11
st. Castle Cove........285 F3
HOLLYDALE
pl. Prospect............275 B10
HOLLYDENE
cr. Edensor Pk........333 D16
HOLLYLEA
rd. Leumeah............481 K13
HOLLYWOOD
av. Bondi Jctn 22 K8
cr. Willoughby.........285 F11
dr. Lansvale 366 G8
rd. Newport.............169 J12
st. Merrylands.........307 A8
st. Monterey 433 G10
st. S Wntwthvle 307 A8
HOLMAN
pl. St Helens Park....541 B3
st. Canley Ht 335 A16
HOLMEGATE
cr. Cranebrook........207 G11
HOLMES
av. Ashbury.............372 E8
av. Clontarf.............287 E14
av. Oatlands 279 D12
av. Sefton................338 F15
cr. Richmond...........119 K5
rd. Minto.................482 C2
st. Colyton 270 D6
st. Kingsford...........407 A6
st. Lalor Park..........245 G13
st. Turramurra 222 F15
HOLMESDALE
st. Marrickville 374 A10
HOLMLEA
pl. Engadine............488 F11
HOLMWOOD
av. Strathfield S.......371 C5
la. Newtown, off King La..............374 J10
st. Newtown 374 H9
HOLROYD
rd. Merrylands.........307 B11
HOLST
cl. Bonnyrigg Ht......363 E7
HOLSTEIN
cl. Emu Heights 235 B3
HOLSTON
st. Casula................395 A12
HOLT
av. Cremorne...........316 G8
av. Mosman 316 G8
av. N Wahroonga.....192 G16
cr. Marrickville 403 H1
ct. Penrith...............237 C6
pl. Dundas Vy 280 B11
rd. Sylvania 461 J11
rd. Sylvania 462 A11
rd. Taren Point 462 G12
st. Ashcroft.............364 F16
st. Doonside 243 C8
st. Double Bay 13 K10
st. McMahons Pt 5 D11
st. Newtown 17 E15
st. Newtown 17 F15
st. North Ryde 282 F6
st. Stanmore.............16 E11
st. Surry Hills.............F B16
st. Surry Hills............19 J1
HOLTERMAN
pl. Cartwright..........393 J6
HOLTERMANN
st. Crows Nest........315 G6
HOLTS POINT
pl. Sylvania Wtr.......462 F10
HOLWAY
st. Eastwood...........280 H7
HOLWOOD
av. Ashfield 372 K8
HOLYWOOD
wy. Glenmore Pk......266 H8
HOMANN
av. Leumeah............512 A1
HOMEBUSH
rd. Homebush 341 D13
rd. Strathfield 341 D16
rd. Strathfield S........371 C5
st. St Johns Pk 364 H4
HOMEBUSH BAY
dr. Concord W.........311 C16
dr. Homebush..........341 A3
dr. Homebush B......340 J5
dr. Rhodes..............311 C16
HOMEDALE
av. Bexley North 402 E12
av. Concord.............341 G6
cr. Connells Pt 431 J12
rd. Bankstown.........399 G7
st. Springwood........201 H4
HOMELANDS
av. Carlingford.........279 G7
HOMELEA
av. Panania..............397 K15
HOMEPRIDE
av. Warwck Frm 365 D14
HOMER
la. Earlwood 402 J3
pl. Caringbah 493 B16
pl. Wetherill Pk 335 A5
st. Earlwood 402 H4
st. Kingsgrove.........401 K7
st. Winston Hills......277 E1
HOMESTEAD
av. Chipping Ntn......366 G12
av. Collaroy 229 B13
cct. Mcquarie Lk.......423 G14
ct. Bella Vista 246 G2
rd. Bonnyrigg Ht.......363 H5
rd. Orchard Hills......267 B9
HOMEWOOD
av. Hornsby.............221 E6
HONDA
rd. Neutral Bay 6 J7
HONEMAN
cl. Huntingwd.........274 B12
HONEYCUP
cl. Westleigh...........220 G8
HONEYEATER
cr. Blaxland.............233 E11
la. St Clair, off Honeyeater Pl.....270 K13
pl. Erskine Park.......270 K13
pl. Hinchinbrk.........363 E15
pl. Ingleburn...........453 F9
pl. Woronora Ht......489 F2
tce. Glenwood 215 F14
HONEYMYRTLE
rd. Kellyville.............215 K3
HONEYSUCKLE
av. Glenmore Pk......265 G9
pl. Kellyville.............216 E1
pl. Leonay...............234 K14
st. Jannali...............460 J9
HONEYTREE
pl. Baulkham Hl 246 J3
HONITON
av.e,Carlingford.........279 K6
av.w,Carlingford........279 J6
HONOR
st. Ermington..........310 D4
HONOUR
av. Fairfield.............336 G14
HOOD
av. Earlwood 402 E4
av. Rodd Point 9 A1
cl. Wetherill Pk 334 H6
la. Old Tngabbie......277 F8
pl. Vaucluse............348 B3
st. Miranda 491 K7
st. Old Tngabbie......277 F8
st. Yagoona 368 E10
HOOK
cl. Hinchinbrk 363 A16
pl. Wakeley.............334 H12
HOOP
pl. Spring Farm.......508 E1
HOOPER
la. Randwick...........377 E10
st. Clovelly..............377 E9
st. Randwick...........377 E9
HOOP PINE
pl. W Pnnant Hl.......218 J15
HOOVER
pl. Bonnet Bay 460 E11
pl. Cromer 228 D14
HOP-BUSH
pl. Mt Annan...........509 F3
HOPE
av. North Manly.......258 A15
cr. Bossley Park......334 C6
pl. Beaumont Hills....215 G1
pl. McGraths Hl.......122 A12
st. Blaxland.............233 F7
st. Ermington..........310 F3
st. Harringtn Pk.......478 F6
st. Penrith...............237 B12
st. Pymble 253 E1
st. Regents Pk 369 B3
st. Rosehill 308 J6
st. Seaforth.............287 E9
st. Seven Hills.........245 F15
st. Strathfield S 371 A8
st. Warwck Frm 365 K16
HOPE FARM
rd. Cattai 68 E14
HOPETOUN
av. Chatswood.........284 J12
av. Denistone E.........281 F10
av. Mosman 317 D2
av. Vaucluse............348 E4
av. Watsons Bay......318 F16
la. Camperdown 17 E7
la. Paddington 13 E16
mw. Vaucluse............348 D3
st. Camperdown 17 E7
st. Hurlstone Pk......373 A13
st. Paddington 13 E16
st. Petersham 16 B10
HOPEWELL
la. Paddington 4 H15
st. Paddington 4 H15
HOPKINS
ct. Rouse Hill 185 D4
pl. Austral..............391 C8
pl. Forestville 255 G9
pl. N Turramurra 193 E14
st. Wentwthvle.........277 C12
st. Wetherill Pk 334 G4
HOPMAN
av. Menai 458 G7
cr. Shalvey..............210 J14
st. Greystanes.........306 A10
HOPPING
rd. Ingleburn 453 A11
HOPPYS
la. Kingsgrove.........401 H11
HOPSON
av. Camden S..........507 C13
st. Douglas Park 568 G5
HORACE
st. St Ives 254 B1
st. Waverton...........315 D12
HORANS
la. Grose Vale 84 F6
HORATIO
pl. Plumpton...........241 H9
st. Rsemeadow.......540 J6
HORBLING
av. Georges Hall 368 C15
HORBURY
la. Newtown 17 D12
st. Sans Souci.........433 E16
HORDERN
av. Petersham 16 A7
av. Putney 311 K7
la. Mosman 317 B5
pde. Croydon............372 F1
pl. Camperdown 17 B5
pl. Mosman 317 A5
st. Newtown 17 H8
HORDERNS
la. Bundeena...........523 H9
pl. Potts Point.............4 H4
HORIZON
pl. Cranebrook........206 J8
HORIZONS
pl. Kellyville............216 B3
HORLER
av. Vaucluse............348 E2
HORN
cl. Abbotsbury........333 B14
HORNBY
av. Sutherland 460 E15
st. Wilton................568 K15
HORNE
cl. Bargo.................567 A4
pl. Blackett..............241 B2
HORNER
av. Mascot 405 G5
HORNET
pl. Raby..................451 H16
st. Greenfld Pk........334 B15
HORNING
pde. Manly Vale.........287 J4
st. Kurnell...............465 H10
HORNINGSEA PARK
dr. Horngsea Pk......392 E14
dr. Horngsea Pk......392 F16
HORNS
av. Gymea Bay.........491 D12
HORNSBY
st. Hornsby.............221 H3
HORNSEY
cl. Bonnyrigg Ht......363 B6
rd. Homebush W......340 G10
st. Burwood............341 J14
st. Rozelle................11 B2
HORNSEYWOOD
av. Penrith...............236 K14
HORSELL
av. Arncliffe.............403 D8
HORSEMAN
pl. Currans Hill........480 A11
HORSESHOE
cct. St Clair..............299 H2
HORSFALL
st. Ermington...........280 B16
HORSFIELD
rd. Bilpin 61 D7
HORSHAM
pl. Chipping Ntn......366 H15
HORSLEY
av. N Willoughby 285 E10
rd. Horsley Pk 302 E16
rd. Milperra.............398 A11
rd. Panania..............398 A11
rd. Panania..............398 A15
rd. Revesby.............398 A15
HORSNELL
la. Mosman, off Civic La..............317 A6
HORST
pl. Mona Vale..........199 A2
HORTICULTURE
dr. Richmond 118 F11
HORTON
la. Bass Hill.............368 D13
la. Yagoona 368 D13
st. Bass Hill.............368 E13
st. Marrickville 374 A9
st. Mt Pritchard.......364 A11
st. Yagoona 368 E13
wy. Parklea 214 J14
HORWOOD
av. Baulkham Hl 247 J14
av. Killara 283 D2
pl. Kings Lngly........245 B3
pl. Parramatta 308 C3
HOSIER
pl. Bligh Park 150 C6
HOSKING
av. West Hoxton......392 C8
cr. Glenfield 424 D10
pl. Sydney..................D B1
pl. Sydney 3 J1
st. Balmain East...........8 G10
st. Cranebrook........207 C11
wy. Bonnyrigg 364 C5
HOSKINS
av. Bankstown.........399 D6
HOSPITAL
la. Crows Nest, off Willoughby La....315 F6
la. Marrickville, off Stanley St 373 J11
rd. Concord W..........311 E13
rd. Randwick...........377 A15
rd. Sydney..................D H5
rd. Sydney 4 B2
HOTHAM
av. Beaumont Hills...185 H15
pde. Artarmon 314 H2
rd. Gymea 491 C5
rd. Kirrawee 461 D16
st. Chatswood W 284 H7
HOTSON
av. Matraville...........436 J8
HOTSPUR
cl. Rsemeadow.......540 H8
HOUGH
st. Bondi Jctn 22 D9
st. Colyton 270 J9
HOUISON
pl. Parramatta, off Horwood Pl........308 C3
st. Westmead 307 G2
HOURGLASS
gln. St Clair..............270 D14
HOURIGAN
la. Potts Point.............4 H6
HOUSMAN
av. Kellyville.............215 J5
st. Wetherill Pk 334 E6
HOUSTON
la. Kensington.........376 F16
la. Kingsford...........406 F1
pl. Mt Pritchard.......364 E8
rd. Kensington.........376 F16
rd. Kingsford...........406 F1
rd. Yagoona 369 A8
st. Gymea...............491 G5
HOUTMAN
av. Willmot..............210 D12
HOVEA
ct. Voyager Pt.........427 C5
pl. Glenmore Pk......265 J9
pl. Kirrawee 491 A10
pl. Mcquarie Fd.......454 D4
wy. Mt Annan...........509 E3
HOVELL
rd. Ingleburn 422 J14
st. Narellan 478 F12
HOVEY
av. St Ives 254 D1
HOWARD
av. Dee Why............258 H6
av. Northmead.........277 K10
cl. Green Valley.......363 A8
la. Lindfield.............254 G15
la. Randwick, off Howard St..........407 B1
pl. Castle Hill...........248 D4

82 GREGORY'S STREET DIRECTORY

STREETS IA

pl. Hebersham 241 F7
pl. Hunters Hill 313 E11
pl. N Epping 251 G11
pl. Randwick 407 D1
rd. Minto Ht 483 K6
rd. Padstow 399 C16
st. Canterbury 372 D15
st. Greystanes 306 E5
st. Lansvale 366 K11
st. Lindfield 254 G16
st. Randwick 407 B1
st. Strathfield 340 J13
st. Telopea 279 J7
st. Ultimo 12 K16

HOWARTH
rd. Lane Cove N 284 G16

HOWATT
st. Villawood 367 C2

HOWE
av. Horngsea Pk 392 F16
pl. Canley Ht 365 A4
pl. Kings Lngly 245 H6
st. Campbelltown 511 F4
st. Malabar 437 F5
st. Westmead 307 G4

HOWELL
av. Lane Cove 313 K3
av. Matraville 406 K16
cl. Newport 169 J8
cr. S Windsor 150 J1
pl. Lane Cove 314 A2
rd. Londonderry 149 B13

HOWES
cl. Westleigh 220 J1
rd. E Kurrajong 65 C10
rd. E Kurrajong 66 K7
rd. E Kurrajong 67 A6

HOWIE
av. Woolooware 493 J10

HOWITT
pl. Bonnyrigg 364 B8

HOWLETT
cl. Chipping Ntn 396 D4

HOWLEY
st. Five Dock 343 C9

HOWSE
cr. Cromer 227 J14

HOWSON
av. Turramurra 252 A2

HOXLEY
st. Stanhpe Gdn 215 D4

HOXTON PARK
rd. Cartwright 393 G6
rd. Hinchinbrk 393 A6
rd. Hoxton Park 393 A6
rd. Liverpool 395 A6
rd. Lurnea 394 F5

HOYA
pl. Cherrybrook 220 A7

HOYLE
av. Castle Hill 217 D14
dr. Dean Park 242 G1
pl. Greenfld Pk 334 A14
pl. S Penrith 267 A6

HOYS
rd. Lansvale 366 E9

HUBER
av. Cabramatta 365 G6

HUBERT
st. Condell Park 398 H6
st. Fairfield 335 K14
st. Harbord 258 E14
st. Leichhardt 9 G10
st. Lilyfield 9 G7

HUCKSTEPP
swy. Liverpool 395 D4

HUDDART
av. Normanhurst 221 F10
la. Randwick 376 K9

HUDDLESTON
st. Colyton 270 G7

HUDSON
av. Castle Hill 217 A14
av. Willoughby 285 F13
cl. S Turramrra 252 D5
pde. Avalon 139 G16
pde. Birrong 369 A6
pde. Clareville 169 D2
pl. Bargo 567 C4
pl. Ingleburn 453 J8
pl. Mulgrave 151 H1
rd. Frenchs Frst 257 B6
st. Annandale 10 J10
st. Homebush 341 A8
st. Hurstville 432 A3
st. Lewisham 15 A10
st. Redfern 19 A5
st. Seven Hills 275 J6
st. S Granville 338 F1
st. Wentwthvle 307 C2
wy. Currans Hill 479 G11

HUEGILL
wy. Blacktown 273 H5

HUEN
pl. Tahmoor 565 G9

HUETT
pl. Berowra 133 G10

HUGH
av. Dulwich Hill 373 A9
av. Peakhurst 430 E2
pl. Greystanes 306 E9
pl. Kings Lngly 245 F8
st. Ashfield 372 H4
st. Belmore 371 A12

HUGHES
av. Castle Hill 217 G14
av. Ermington 310 F1
av. Hobartville 118 B7
av. Maroubra 407 D16
av. Mascot 405 D2
av. Mulgrave 121 K16
av. Penrith 237 C7
la. Potts Point 4 J5
pl. Chester Hill 368 A2
pl. E Lindfield 255 A12
pl. Potts Point 4 J5
rd. Glenorie 129 B2
st. Cabramatta 365 E6
st. Earlwood 402 H6
st. Kings Lngly 246 B10
st. Leumeah 481 J15
st. Londonderry 148 B9
st. Petersham 16 C5
st. Potts Point 4 J5
st. West Ryde 311 D1
st. Woolooware 493 E9

HUGHES STEPS
Mosman 286 K15
Mosman 287 A15

HUGO
pl. Quakers Hill 214 F13
st. Redfern 19 A6

HUIE
st. Cabramatta 365 E10

HULL
av. Lurnea 394 E9
pl. Moorebank 395 H4
pl. Seven Hills 275 C5
rd. Beecroft 250 B1
rd. W Pnnant Hl 220 A15

HULLICK
la. East Hills 427 G5

HULLS
rd. Leppington 450 E1

HUMBER
pl. Ingleburn 453 J8

HUMBERSTONE
av. Gymea 491 G1

HUME
av. Castle Hill 218 A16
av. Ermington 280 B16
av. St Ives 224 E10
cr. Wrrngtn Cty 238 G7
dr. West Hoxton 392 A12
hwy.Ashfield 372 E2
hwy.Bankstown 369 C12
hwy.Bargo 567 G16
hwy.Bass Hill 368 B9
hwy.Blairmount 481 B14
hwy.Burwood Ht 371 C5
hwy.Cabramatta 366 B10
hwy.Campbelltown 481 B15
hwy.Canley Vale 366 B10
hwy.Carramar 366 B10
hwy.Casula 424 B3
hwy.Chullora 370 B6
hwy.Claymore 481 B15
hwy.Croydon 372 E2
hwy.Denham Ct 422 K16
hwy.Douglas Park 568 B15
hwy.Eagle Vale 481 B15
hwy.Enfield 371 D5
hwy.Gilead 509 H16
hwy.Glen Alpine 510 A8
hwy.Glenfield 423 B15
hwy.Greenacre 369 C12
hwy.Greenacre 370 B6
hwy.Ingleburn 423 B15
hwy.Lansdowne 367 D5
hwy.Lansvale 366 B10
hwy.Liverpool 395 A9
hwy.Menangle 539 B16
hwy.Menangle Pk 509 H16
hwy.Mt Annan 510 A8
hwy.Raby 481 B15
hwy.St Andrews 481 B15
hwy.Strathfield S 371 D5
hwy.Summer Hill 373 A3
hwy.Varroville 451 J15
hwy.Villawood 367 E5
hwy.Warwck Frm 365 F16
hwy.Woodbine 481 B15
hwy.Yagoona 369 C12
hwy.Yanderra 567 G16
la. Crows Nest 315 F6
pl. Appin 569 F9
pl. Frenchs Frst 256 C1
pl. Mt Colah 162 D12
rd. Cronulla 493 K7
rd. Ingleburn 422 J14
rd. Lapstone 264 H3
rd. Smithfield 305 F13
st. Campbelltown 511 J7
st. Chifley 437 B3
st. Crows Nest 315 F6
st. Homebush B 310 G16
st. Kellyville Rdg 215 A1
st. Narellan 478 F11
st. Wollstncraft 315 E7

HUMPHREY
pl. Kirribilli 6 A14
st. Lidcombe 339 F10
st. Rosebery 405 H3

HUMPHREYS
av. Casula 394 H12
wy. Claymore 481 E12

HUMPHRIES
la. Blacktown, off Sunnyholt Rd 244 H15
la. Hurstville, off The Avenue 432 A6
rd. Bonnyrigg 364 E6
rd. Mt Pritchard 364 D9
rd. St Johns Pk 364 H3
rd. Wakeley 335 A15

HUNGERFORD
dr. Glenwood 245 F1

HUNT
av. Dural 189 E10
la. Lakemba 401 D3
pl. Wrrngtn Cty 238 G8
st. Croydon 342 G15
st. Enfield 371 J4
st. Glenbrook 263 K1
st. Guildford W 336 H4
st. N Parramatta 278 B10
st. Schofields 183 C15
st. Surry Hills F D7
st. Surry Hills 3 K12

HUNTER
av. Lurnea 394 B13
av. Matraville 436 J2
av. St Ives 254 C1
cr. N Sydney K B12
cr. N Sydney 5 E10
la. Greenacre 370 E6
la. Hornsby 191 H16
la. Hornsby 221 H1
la. Mosman, off Hunter Rd 317 D5
la. Penshurst 431 D6
la. Woolwich, off Gale St 314 F13
pl. Castle Hill 218 C10
rd. Mosman 317 D6
st. Abbotsford 342 H1
st. Auburn 309 E15
st. Blacktown 273 H5
st. Camden S 507 B9
st. Campbelltown 511 K9
st. Condell Park 398 J4
st. Dover Ht 348 G9
st. Emu Plains 235 G12
st. Fairfield 336 C12
st. Heathcote 518 G10
st. Homebush B 310 G15
st. Hornsby 221 H1
st. Kirrawee 491 A8
st. Lewisham 15 D10
st. McGraths Hl 121 K14
st. N Balgowlah 287 D6
st. Parramatta 308 A3
st. Penshurst 431 D6
st. Riverstone 182 K9
st. Riverwood 400 A14
st. St Clair 269 K9
st. Strathfield 371 D2
st. Sydney A J15
st. Sydney 1 H16
st. Tahmoor 565 H11
st. Warriewood 199 D10
st. Waterloo 19 H15
st. Woolwich 314 F13
st.n, Mona Vale 199 D10
st.s, Warriewood 199 D11
wy. Faulconbdg 171 E14

HUNTERFORD
cr. Oatlands 279 A8

HUNTINGDALE
av. Lansvale 366 C9
av. Miranda 461 J15
av. Narwee 400 G14
cir. Castle Hill 218 F7
dr. Denham Ct 422 B10
dr. Glenmore Pk 266 G10
wy. Thornleigh 220 K10

HUNTINGDON
pde. Cmbrdg Gdn 237 J3
pl. Berowra 133 E9

HUNTINGTON
st. Crows Nest 315 G6

HUNTINGWOOD
dr. Huntingwd 273 D12

HUNTLEY
dr. Blacktown 274 E10
pl. Cartwright 394 D5
st. Alexandria 375 B11

HUNTLEY GRANGE
rd. Springwood 172 A15

HUNTLEYS POINT
rd. Huntleys Pt 313 D14

HUNTS
av. Eastwood 281 F5
la. Epping, off Bridge St 251 B16

HUNTSMORE
rd. Minto 482 C6

HUON
cr. Holsworthy 426 D2
pl. Bella Vista 246 G5
pl. Glenfield 424 F13
pl. Illawong 459 D4
st. Cabramatta 365 H10
st. N Wahroonga 223 B2

HURDIS
av. Frenchs Frst 256 K5

HURKETT
pl. Bossley Park 333 H11

HURLEY
cr. Matraville 437 B2
st. Campbelltown 511 C5
st. Toongabbie 276 G6

HURLSTONE
av. Glenfield 424 D12
av. Hurlstone Pk 372 J14
av. Summer Hill 373 B7

HURNDELL
la. Panania 428 C2

HURON
pl. Jamisontown 266 A2
pl. Seven Hills 275 E6

HURRICANE
dr. Raby 481 F1

HURST
pl. Glenorie 127 G13

HURSTVILLE
rd. Hurstville 431 F10
rd. Hurstville Gr 431 F10
rd. Oatley 431 C11
st. St Johns Pk 364 J3

HUSKISSON
st. Gymea Bay 491 C11
st. Prestons 393 B12

HUSKY
la. East Hills 427 K4

HUSSELBEE
st. Blaxland 233 H12

HUSTON
pde. N Curl Curl 259 A10

HUTCH
wy. Minto 482 H5

HUTCHENS
av. Mt Pritchard 364 K9

HUTCHESON
st. Rozelle 10 J5

HUTCHINS
cr. Kings Lngly 246 A7

HUTCHINSON
la. Annandale 10 J10
pl. Surry Hills 20 E1
st. Annandale 11 A9
st. Auburn 309 D16
st. Bardwell Pk 402 H9
st. Granville 308 E12
st. St Peters 374 H12
st. Surry Hills 4 E16
wk. Zetland 376 A10

HUTCHISON
av. Kellyville 216 K5

HUTHNANCE
pl. Camden S 506 K15

HUTTON
st. Canterbury 372 H14
st. Hurlstone Pk 372 H14

HUXLEY
dr. Winston Hills 277 G4
pl. Colyton 270 E6
pl. Wetherill Pk 334 F5
st. West Ryde 311 A1

HUXTABLE
av. Lane Cove N 284 G14

HYACINTH
av. Mcquarie Fd 454 E5
st. Asquith 191 J10
st. Greystanes 305 K12

HYALIN
pl. Eagle Vale 481 F7

HYAM
st. Balmain 7 G13

HYATT
cl. Rouse Hill 185 E4

HYATTS
rd. Oakhurst 241 K4
rd. Plumpton 241 J10

HYDE
av. Glenhaven 217 K1
av. Killarney Ht 286 D2
cl. Illawong 459 F3
pde. Campbelltown 511 B8

HYDE BRAE
st. Strathfield 341 A12

HYDE PARK
ct. Wattle Grove 426 A3
rd. Berala 339 D13

HYDRA
pl. Erskine Park 300 G1

HYDRAE
st. Revesby 428 K4

HYDRANGEA
ct. Acacia Gdn 214 J15
pl. Mcquarie Fd 454 B5

HYDRUS
st. Cranebrook 207 E4

HYLAND
av. W Pnnant Hl 249 G8
pl. Minchinbury 271 H8
rd. Greystanes 305 B12

HYMAN EIZENBERG
dr. Ingleside 197 G9

HYMEN
st. Peakhurst 429 J3

HYNDES
pl. Davidson 225 E16

HYNDMAN
pde. Woolooware 493 E11

HYNDS
rd. Box Hill 154 C14

HYNES
pl. Elderslie 507 F3
st. Lansdowne 367 B8

HYTHE
pl. Glen Alpine 510 B13
st. Drummoyne 313 H16
st. Mount Druitt 241 D13

HYTON
pl. Cranebrook 207 F13

I

IAGO
pl. Rsemeadow 540 G6

IAN
av. Canley Vale 366 B5
av. N Curl Curl 259 C10
cr. Chester Hill 337 K11
la. N Curl Curl, off Ian Av 259 C10
la. Rose Bay, off Ian St 348 B9
pde. Concord 342 B4
pl. Casula 424 D3
st. Glossodia 66 D11
st. Greystanes 306 E9
st. Kingsford 407 A6

GREGORY'S STREET DIRECTORY 83

IA STREETS

st. Lalor Park		245 F14
st. North Ryde		283 B11
st. Rose Bay		348 B10

IANDO
wy. Currans Hill 479 H11

IANDRA
st. Concord W 311 E15

IAN SMITH
dr. Milperra 397 K10

IBBOTSON
st. Tahmoor 565 G10

IBERIA
st. Padstow 399 E15

IBEX
st. Earlwood 402 H5

IBIS
pl. Bella Vista 246 F1
pl. Grays Point 491 F15
pl. Hinchinbrk 393 B1
pl. Ingleburn 453 H7
pl. St Clair 270 E13
rd. Lalor Park 245 J10
wy. Mt Annan 479 C14

IBSEN
pl. Wetherill Pk 335 A4

ICARUS
pl. Quakers Hill 214 D16

ICASIA
la. Woollahra 377 F3

ICE
st. Darlinghurst 4 H13

ICETON
st. Burwood 341 J16

IDA
av. Lurnea 394 E10
av. Mosman 287 A16
av. Edensor Pk 333 F16
pl. Blacktown 244 C15
pl. Cecil Hills 362 G5
pl. Hornsby 191 G9
pl. Hurlstone Pk 372 J11
pl. Putney 312 C7
pl. Sandringham 463 A3
pl. Sans Souci 463 A3

IDAHO
pl. Riverwood 399 K12

IDALINE
st. Collaroy Plat 228 K12

IDLEWILD
rd. Glenorie 70 H5
rd. Maroota 70 H5

IDRIESS
cr. Blackett 241 D4
pl. Casula 424 D3
pl. Edensor Pk 363 K2

IGNATIUS
av. N Richmond ...87 C14
rd. Lindfield 283 K2

IKARA
av. Kellyville 216 H8
cr. Moorebank 396 F8
pl. Peakhurst 430 F2
st. St Ives 224 B14

IKIN
st. Jamisontown ..266 C4

ILFORD
av. Ashfield 342 K15
pl. Abbotsbury 333 A15
rd. Frenchs Frst 256 K3

ILFRACOMBE
av. Burwood 341 J12

ILIFFE
st. Bexley 432 C1

ILIKAI
pl. Dee Why 258 G2

ILKA
st. Lilyfield 10 F11

ILKINIA
av. Engadine 489 A12

ILLABO
st. Quakers Hill ..244 A1

ILLALONG
av. N Balgowlah ..287 D4
av. Granville 308 B12

ILLARANGI
st. Carlingford 280 C7

ILLAROO
pl. Mona Vale 199 B3
rd. Hoxton Park ...393 C9
rd. Prestons 393 C9
st. Bangor 459 H12

ILLAWARRA
cl. Woodcroft 243 E11
dr. St Clair 300 C1
la. Allawah 432 F9
la. Illawarra St 373 K13
pde. Beverly Hills ..401 E14
rd. Earlwood 403 E2
rd. Holsworthy 426 G11
rd. Holsworthy 426 H6
rd. Leumeah 482 F14
rd. Marrickville 374 A12
st. Allawah 432 G8
st. Appin 569 H13
st. Homebush B 310 H15
st. Mosman 316 J12

ILLAWONG
av. Caringbah 492 G14
av. Penrith 237 C5
av. Riverview 314 B5
av. Tamarama 378 A6
cr. Greenacre 370 C9
rd. Leumeah 482 B14
st. Lugarno 430 A15

ILLEROY
av. Killara 254 B8

ILLIWA
la. Cremorne 316 F6
st. Cremorne 316 E6

ILLINGA
pl. Lugarno 430 B16

ILLINGWORTH
rd. Yellow Rock ..204 H2

ILLINOIS
rd. Five Dock 343 B12

ILLOCA
pl. Toongabbie ..276 G9

ILLOURA
av. Wahroonga ..222 E7
la. Wahroonga ..222 E7
pl. Doonside 243 B14
pl. Nelson 155 F8

ILLUTA
dr. Engadine 488 C13

ILLYARIE
cl. Castle Hill 218 G15

ILMA
av. Kangaroo Pt ...461 H4
cl. McGraths Hl ...121 K10
cl. Condell Park ...398 G7
st. Marsfield 281 H1

ILSA
st. Hebersham ...241 F10

ILUKA
av. Elanora Ht ...198 C15
cl. Manly 288 F4
cl. Wakeley 334 H16
cl. Cronulla 523 K3
cl. Hebersham ...241 F10
st. St Ives 224 E16
pl. S Coogee 407 F4
rd. Mosman 317 D13
rd. Palm Beach ..139 H2
rd. Revesby 398 E15
rd. Riverwood 400 E13
st. Rose Bay 347 J11

ILUMBA
pl. Bangor 459 H13

ILYA
av. Bayview 168 G31

IMBARA
ct. Newport 169 E10

IMBER
ct. Kings Lngly ..245 K7

IMHOFF
st. Kenthurst 156 H9

IMITA
cl. Mt Annan 479 C11

IMLAY
av. Carlingford ..249 D14
av. Barden Rdg ..488 G2

IMMARNA
av. Pitt Hills 522 F3
pl. Oatlands 279 C8
pl. Penshurst 431 D3
pl.w.Penshurst ...431 C3

IMPALA
av. Werrington ..238 E11

IMPERIAL
arc. Sydney 3 H3
av. Bondi 378 A5
av. Emu Plains ..235 H10
av. Gladesville ..313 B3

la. Emu Plains, off		
Imperial Av		235 J9
pl. Mosman		317 G11

IMPLEXA
cl. Wattle Grove ..426 B2

IMUNGA
pl. Bradbury 511 G15

INALA
av. Kyle Bay 432 A15
pl. Carlingford 280 E7
pl. N Narrabeen ..198 G12

INALLS
la. Richmond 117 H3

INBERRA
rd. Bilpin 61 A7

INCA
cl. Greenfld Pk ..333 K15

INCENSE
pl. Casula 393 J16
pl. Casula 423 J1

INCH
pl. Minto 452 K16

INDAAL
pl. St Andrews ..481 K6

INDERI
pl. Grays Point ..491 E15

INDI
st. Heckenberg ..363 K13

INDIANA
av. Belfield 371 E11
av. Belfield 371 E11

INDIGO
av. Kellyville 216 A3
ct. Voyager Pt ..427 D5
wy. Blacktown ..274 F11

INDRA
av. Baulkham Hl ..248 B9

INDURA
rd. N Narrabeen ..198 G12

INDUS
pl. Kearns 481 B1
st. Erskine Park ..301 B2

INDUSTRY
rd. Mulgrave 151 K1
rd. Vineyard 151 K1
st. Regents Pk ..339 A16

INDY
cl. Cranebrook ..207 F8

INELGAH
rd. Como 460 G6

INFANTRY
pde. Holsworthy ..426 E3

INGA
pl. Quakers Hill ..214 E9

INGAL
wy. Cabramatta, off
John St 365 J7

INGALARRA
cl. Cronulla 494 A15
cl. Wahroonga ..222 C4

INGARA
av. Miranda 492 E1
ct. Erskine Park ..300 D2

INGHAM
av. Five Dock ..343 B10
cl. Casula 394 D16

INGLEBAR
av. Allambie Ht ..257 C11

INGLEBAR
cl. Bangor 459 H13
cl. Villawood 367 H5

INGLEBURN
rd. Ingleburn ...453 A8
rd. Leppington ..421 K7

INGLEBY
st. Oatlands 279 C8

INGLESIDE
rd. Ingleside ...198 B6

INGLETHORPE
av. Kensington ..376 D14

INGLEWOOD
cl. Baulkham Hl ..216 E16
pl. Grays Point ..491 C15

INGLIS
av. St Marys 269 H4
st. Harringtn Pk ..478 F8
la. St Marys, off
Inglis Av 269 H4
rd. Ingleburn 452 G9

INGOLDS
la. Clarendon ...120 A4

INGOOLA
cl. Moorebank ..396 F7

INGRAM
av. Milperra 397 E9
la. Crows Nest, off
Chandos St 315 F5
rd. Wahroonga ..222 A6
rd. Wahroonga ..222 A7
st. Kensington ..376 B12

INGRID
pl. Hassall Gr ...211 K13
pl. Kareela 461 E11

INKERMAN
la. Emu Heights, off
Inkerman Rd ..235 A1
rd. Denistone ..281 G11
rd. Emu Heights ..235 A1
st. Granville 308 B7
st. Mosman 316 J3
st. Parramatta ..308 B7

INMAN
rd. Cromer 228 G15
st. Maroubra 407 J9

INNES
av. Hornsby 221 F14
cr. Mount Druitt ..241 A16
rd. Werrington ..238 G11
rd. Greenwich ..314 J5
st. Campbelltown ..511 H5
st. Five Dock ..342 K8
st. Thirlmere ...562 F16
st. Thirlmere ...565 F1

INNESDALE
rd. Arncliffe 403 K7
rd. Wolli Creek ..403 K7

INNIS
pl. Kurrajong Hl ..64 C11

INNISFAIL
rd. Wakeley 334 J13

INNOVATION
rd. Mcquarie Pk ..252 E16

INSIGNIA
st. Sadleir 394 B1

INSPIRATION
pl. Berrilee 131 E13

INSTITUTE
rd. Westmead ..277 F14

INTER-TERMINAL ACCESS
rd. Bnksmeadw ..436 C4
rd. Port Botany ..436 C4

INTREPID
pl. Greenfld Pk ..334 C14

INVERALLAN
av. West Pymble ..253 A9

INVERARY
dr. Kurmond 86 J3
st. Concord 341 H8

INVERELL
av. Hinchinbrk ..392 H4

INVERGOWRIE
av. Glen Alpine ..510 J5
dr. W Pnnant Hl ..249 A3

INVERNESS
av. Frenchs Frst ..257 A5
av. Penshurst ..431 C2
cct. Cecil Hills ..362 E5
cr. Glenhaven ..218 C5
dr. Cranebrook ..207 F16
dr. Wilberforce ..67 J15
gr. Greenacre ..370 G5
pl. Westleigh ..220 F7
st. Bargo 567 F3

INVESTIGATOR
pl. Newington ..310 C14

INWOOD
cl. Castle Hill ..218 K13

IOLANTHE
st. Campbelltown ..511 G2

IONA
av. North Rocks ..278 G2
av. West Pymble ..252 K9
la. Paddington ..4 G15
pl. Bass Hill 368 A10
pl. St Andrews ..452 A16
st. Blacktown ..273 K1

IONIAN
wy. Kellyville Rdg ..214 K4

IOWA
cl. St Clair 269 G13

IPEL
cl. St Clair 269 G16

IPOH
st. Holsworthy ..426 F11

IPSWICH
av. Glenwood ..215 G12

IRAGA
av. Peakhurst ..430 H2
pl. Forestville ..256 C7

IRAKING
av. Moorebank ..396 A7

IRALBA
av. Emu Plains ..235 A9

IRAMIR
pl. Warriewood ..198 K6

IRAS
pl. Rsemeadow ..540 E2

IRBY
pl. Quakers Hill ..243 K2

IREDALE
av. Cremorne ...316 F11
la. Cremorne, off
Hodgson Av ...316 F12
st. Newtown 374 J9

IRELAND
st. Burwood 371 J1
st. St Clair 269 H10

IRELANDS
rd. Blacktown ..243 J13

IRENE
cr. Eastwood ..281 H4
cr. Kingsgrove ..401 K15
la. Panania 428 A6
pl. Ingleburn ...453 E11
st. Kogarah 433 D9
st. Panania 428 A6
st. S Penrith 267 C3
st. Wareemba ..342 K5

IRETON
st. Malabar 437 D4

IRIS
av. Riverwood ..399 K10
cl. Glenmore Pk ..265 G7
cl. Blacktown ..245 C8
st. Beacon Hill ..257 A4
st. Frenchs Frst ..257 A4
st. Guildford W ..336 G2
st. North Ryde ..282 D8
st. Paddington ..20 G1
st. Sefton 368 G4

IRMA
pl. Oakhurst 241 H4

IRON
st. N Parramatta ..278 C10

IRON BARK
gr. Bella Vista ..246 H3
wy. Colyton 270 H6

IRONBARK
av. Camden 507 A8
av. Casula 394 E14
cct. Minchinbury ..272 C10
cl. Alfords Point ..429 C16
cr. Blacktown ..273 K7
cr. Mcquarie Fd ..454 F1
dr. Cranebrook ..207 F16
dr. Wilberforce ..67 J15
gr. Greenacre ..370 G5
pl. Westleigh ..220 F7
st. Bargo 567 F3

IRONMONGER
av. Rouse Hill, off
Grimmet Av ...184 K7

IRONSIDE
av. St Helens Park ..541 C2
st. St Johns Pk ..364 D1

IRONWOOD
pl. Newington ..310 C14

IRRABELLA
pl. Erskine Park ..300 C2

IRRARA
st. Croydon 342 E14

IRRAWONG
rd. N Narrabeen ..198 F15

IRRIBIN
st. Marayong ..243 H6

IRRIGATION
rd. Merrylands ..306 J9
rd. S Wntwthvle ..306 J9

IRRUBEL
rd. Caringbah ..493 B6
rd. Newport 169 E10

IRRUKA
cl. Cranebrook ..207 H11

IRVINE
cr. Ryde 312 D3
pl. Bella Vista ..246 B1
pl. Ruse ....512 H6 |

84 GREGORY'S STREET DIRECTORY

STREETS JA

st. Bankstown 399 B6
st. Elderslie 477 K16
st. Kingsford 406 J6
IRVING
st. Parramatta 308 K1
wy. Doonside 273 E3
IRWIN
cr. Bexley North 402 F9
ct. Narellan Vale 478 K16
pl. Wentwthvle 307 B3
st. N Parramatta 278 C10
st. Werrington 238 J9
IRWINE
rd. Caringbah 493 B16
IRWINS
rd. E Kurrajong 66 G5
ISA
cl. Bossley Park 334 B10
pl. Cartwright 393 K5
ISAAC
pl. Quakers Hill 213 J8
pl. Ruse 512 D4
st. Peakhurst 430 B6
ISAAC SMITH
pde. Kings Lngly 245 B4
rd. Castlereagh 176 B7
st. Daceyville 406 E3
ISABEL
av. Vaucluse 348 E6
cl. Cherrybrook 219 D8
st. Belmore 371 F15
st. Cecil Hills 362 E1
st. Ryde 282 B16
ISABELLA
cl. Bella Vista 246 G2
la. Queens Park 22 J12
st. Balmain 7 C9
st. Camperdown 17 E2
st. N Parramatta 278 E14
st. Queens Park 22 J11
st. Revesby 398 K16
st. Werrington 238 H10
ISABELLE
st. Seven Hills 275 J6
ISAR
st. Seven Hills 275 G8
ISCA
pl. Glenmore Pk 266 G12
ISCHIA
st. Cronulla 524 A4
ISIS
la. Kingsford 406 J4
pl. Quakers Hill 243 G5
st. Fairfield W 335 D8
st. Wahroonga 222 B7
ISLA
pl. Belrose 225 K11
ISLAY
st. Winston Hills 277 B3
ISLER
st. Gladesville 313 A11
ISLES
pl. Plumpton 241 H11
ISLINGTON
cr. Greenacre 369 J10
dr. Stanhpe Gdn 215 D5
st. Cranebrook 207 C10
ISMAY
av. Homebush 341 C6
ISMONA
av. Newport 169 J8
ISOBEL
cl. Mona Vale 199 A3
ISOBELL
av. W Pnnant Hl 249 D8
ITHACA
cl. St Johns Pk 334 E16
rd. Elizabeth Bay 13 C4
st. Emu Plains 235 C9
ITHIER
la. Quakers Hill 213 H13
IVAN
st. Greystanes 306 C6
st. Minchinbury 271 G7
IVANHOE
pl. Mcquarie Pk 282 D4
pl. Oatlands 278 H11
rd. Croydon 342 F14
st. Ingleburn 453 B10
st. Marrickville 373 J15
st. St Johns Pk 364 H1
IVERS
pl. Minto 483 A2
IVERYS
la. Newtown 18 C10
IVES
av. Liverpool 394 H9
ct. St Clair 300 C2
la. Crows Nest, off Willoughby La 315 F5
IVEY
st. Lindfield 284 A3
IVOR
st. Lidcombe 340 A4
IVORY
la. Leichhardt 15 F2
pl. Jamisontown 266 B4
pl. Richmond 117 J6
IVY
av. McGraths Hl 121 K11
la. Bilpin 61 F5
la. Darlington 18 J5
la. Oatlands, off Hunterford Cr 279 A8
la. Randwick, off Ivy St 407 C1
pl. Cherrybrook 219 H11
pl. Kenthurst 187 J1
st. Botany 405 F10
st. Canterbury 372 E15
st. Chatswood W 284 F13
st. Darlington 18 H5
st. Greenacre 370 E7
st. Liverpool 395 B7
st. Randwick 407 C1
st. Ryde 282 F15
st. Toongabbie 276 B5
st. Wollstncraft 315 E10
IWAN
pl. Beaumont Hills 216 B1
IWUNDA
rd. Guildford 338 D9
rd. Lalor Park 245 E12
IXION
la. Cammeray, off Amherst St 315 K5
st. Winston Hills 277 C1

J

JABEZ
st. Marrickville 374 C9
JABIRU
cl. Mona Vale 169 E16
pl. Blacktown 274 B9
pl. Castle Hill 217 A10
pl. Ingleburn 453 F10
pl. Woronora Ht 489 F2
st. Green Valley 363 D14
JACANA
cl. Wahroonga 223 C3
gr. Heathcote 519 A10
pl. Ingleburn 453 F6
pl. W Pnnant Hl 248 F8
wy. Glenmore Pk 265 K13
wy. Plumpton 242 A9
JACARANDA
av. Baulkham Hl 247 K10
av. Blaxland 233 G5
av. Bradbury 511 E13
av. Lugarno 430 B14
cr. Casula 394 F13
ct. Fairfield E 337 A15
dr. Georges Hall 367 F11
dr. Parramatta 278 A12
pl. Beecroft 250 F3
pl. Doonside 243 G16
pl. Manly Vale 287 J5
pl. S Coogee 407 F5
rd. Blaxlands Rdg 65 C4
rd. Caringbah 492 K10
st. Cabarita 342 E3
tce. Glenmore Pk 266 G16
JACEVA
pl. Cattai 94 D4
JACINTA
av. Beecroft 250 D4
pl. Picton 561 F4
JACKA
st. St Marys 270 A2
JACKAMAN
st. Bondi 377 K6
JACKARANDA
rd. N St Marys 240 A9
JACK DAVIS
pl. Bargo 567 B5
JACKEY
dr. Camden S 537 B3
JACKLIN
rd. Ebenezer 68 J7
JACK McLURE
pl. Northbridge 285 K14
JACK McNAMEE
pl. Kellyville 217 D1
JACK O'SULLIVAN
rd. Moorebank 396 B7
JACK RUSSELL
rd. Berrilee 131 H10
JACKS
ct. Currans Hill 479 G13
JACKSON
av. Miranda 492 B5
cl. Menai 458 F13
cr. Chester Hill 338 D16
cr. Denistone E 281 G10
cr. Pennant Hills 220 F12
pl. Cabramatta W 365 B8
pl. Earlwood 403 E4
pl. Kellyville 215 K5
rd. Lalor Park 245 C10
rd. Luddenham 357 F2
st. Balgowlah 287 J9
st. Ermington 310 B3
st. Marsden Pk 182 A14
JACKSONS
rd. Warriewood 199 A13
JACK WILLIAMS
dr. Penrith 236 F3
JACLYN
st. Ingleburn 453 C9
JACOB KING
pl. Emu Plains 235 G9
JACOBS
av. Asquith 192 B11
cl. Menai 458 G15
cl. N Epping 251 F9
pl. Bligh Park 150 D6
st. Bankstown 369 F15
JACOBSON
av. Kyeemagh 404 B14
JACQUELENE
cl. Bayview 168 E8
JACQUELINE
cr. Greenacre 370 C10
pl. Kurmond 86 E1
pl. Moorebank 396 F13
JACQUES
av. Peakhurst 430 B2
la. Balmain 7 D8
pl. Minchinbury 271 H7
st. Balmain 7 D8
st. Chatswood 285 C9
st. Kingsford 406 H3
JACQUI
cct. Baulkham Hl, off Camarena Av 216 H16
JACQUIE
st. Cabramatta 365 E9
JACQUINOT
ct. Moorebank 425 B4
pl. Glenfield 424 E12
rd. Moorebank 425 B4
JADCHALM
st. W Pnnant Hl 249 J3
JADE
ct. Georges Hall 367 J11
pl. Eagle Vale 481 C8
pl. St Clair 269 J13
pl. Seven Hills 275 C7
pl. W Pnnant Hl 249 H5
JAEGER
pl. Woronora Ht 489 B4
JAF
pl. Blairmount 481 B14
JAFFA
rd. Dural 188 J13
st. Fairfield W 335 F13
JAGELMAN
rd. Badgerys Ck 358 D9
JAGGERS
pl. Ambarvale 511 A11
JAGO
pl. Toongabbie 276 G5
st. Greenwich 314 K11
JAGUNGAL
pl. Heckenberg 364 C14
JAKARI
cr. Whalan 240 H12
JAKOB
wy. Glenwood 215 H10
JAMAICA PARK
rd. Ellis Lane 476 B8
JAMBEROO
av. Baulkham Hl 246 K8
av. Terrey Hills 196 D6
la. Double Bay 14 E9
pl. Bangor 459 J12
JAMES
av. Lurnea 394 C11
cl. Menai 459 A12
la. Balmain East 8 H8
la. Paddington 13 D13
la. Sydney C D15
la. Sydney 3 E8
la. Waitara 221 H3
la. Woollahra 21 H4
pl. Castle Hill 217 G15
pl. Darlinghurst 4 D12
pl. Hillsdale 406 G14
pl. N Sydney 5 F3
rd. Brooklyn 76 A11
st. Allambie Ht 257 K16
st. Balmain 7 F11
st. Baulkham Hl 247 J11
st. Blakehurst 432 D16
st. Bondi Jctn 377 F5
st. Canterbury 372 F11
st. Carlingford 279 H4
st. Chatswood W 284 G10
st. Enmore 374 G9
st. Fairfield E 337 A12
st. Five Dock 342 H8
st. Glossodia 66 C13
st. Guildford W 336 H4
st. Hornsby 221 H3
st. Hunters Hill 313 D9
st. Ingleburn 453 E4
st. Leichhardt 9 J9
st. Lidcombe 339 J9
st. Lilyfield 9 J8
st. Manly 288 E9
st. Melrose Pk 311 A3
st. Mosman 317 B1
st. Northwood 314 G8
st. Petersham 15 K12
st. Punchbowl 399 H7
st. Redfern 19 D5
st. Redfern 19 G5
st. Riverstone 183 A10
st. Seven Hills 275 C4
st. S Windsor 120 G14
st. Strathfield S 371 C6
st. Summer Hill 373 B7
st. Sydney C D16
st. Sydney 3 E9
st. Wallacia 325 D16
st. Waterloo 19 D16
st. Woollahra 21 H4
wy. Mt Annan 479 D16
JAMES BAILEY
dr. Harringtn Pk 478 D1
JAMES BARNETT
gln. St Clair 270 B11
la. St Clair, off James Barnett Gln 270 B11
JAMES BELLAMY
pl. W Pnnant Hl 249 E6
JAMES BERES BRIDGE
Silverdale 384 C3
JAMES COOK
dr. Castle Hill 218 H13
dr. Kings Lngly 245 A3
JAMES COOK ISLAND
Sylvania Wtr 462 D12
JAMES CRAIG
rd. Rozelle 11 D4
JAMES FLYNN
av. Harringtn Pk 478 G7
JAMES HENTY
dr. Dural 219 A6
JAMES KING
la. Mosman, off Union St 317 C11
JAMES MACARTHUR
ct. N Parramatta 278 G12
JAMES MEEHAN
st. Windsor 121 B14
wy. Mcquarie Lk 423 E14
JAMES MILEHAM
dr. Kellyville 186 H16
dr. Kellyville 216 F1
JAMESON
la. Sans Souci 463 A2
JAMES RANDALL
pl. Glenbrook 234 C12
JAMES ROWLAND
av. N Turramurra 193 E11
JAMES RUSE
cl. Windsor 121 A8
dr. Camellia 308 K4
dr. Granville 308 J11
dr. N Parramatta 278 C9
dr. Oatlands 278 C9
dr. Oatlands 279 A16
dr. Parramatta 308 K4
dr. Rosehill 308 J11
JAMES WHEELER
pl. Collaroy Plat 228 C9
JAMIESON
av. Baulkham Hl 247 G6
av. Fairlight 288 C7
av. N Curl Curl 258 J10
cl. Horsley Pk 332 C1
la. Fairfield E 337 A14
la. Greenacre 370 E13
pde. Collaroy 229 B15
pl. Glendenning 242 G10
sq. Forestville 256 A9
st. Emu Plains 235 A10
st. Granville 308 E11
st. Revesby 428 K1
st. Silverwater 310 D10
wy. Thornleigh 220 K10
JAMISON
pl. Barden Rdg 488 H1
rd. Jamisontown 235 J13
rd. Kingswood 237 D15
rd. S Penrith 237 A14
st. Blaxland 234 A5
st. Luddenham 356 H2
st. Ruse 512 F8
st. Sydney A E13
st. Sydney 1 F14
JAN
av. Lurnea 394 C9
pl. Greystanes 305 J7
pl. Quakers Hill 213 K8
st. Picton 561 E3
JANACEK
pl. Bonnyrigg Ht 363 D4
JANALI
av. Bonnyrigg 364 A10
JANAMBA
av. Kellyville 216 F4
JANAN
cl. Kellyville 216 D2
JANDIGA
pl. Winmalee 173 A11
JANE
ct. Narellan Vale 508 H2
ct. Narellan Vale 508 J2
pl. Cecil Hills 363 B3
pl. Dural 188 H7
pl. Heathcote 518 H9
st. Balmain 7 K10
st. Blacktown 274 K1
st. Penrith 236 F8
st. Randwick 406 K1
st. Smithfield 335 B5
JANE JARVIS
wy. Mcquarie Lk 423 G13
JANELL
cr. Carlingford 279 K4
JANET
av. Newington 309 K16
av. Thornleigh 220 J13
st. Bass Hill 368 A11
st. Drummoyne 343 F5
st. Merrylands 307 C7
st. Mount Druitt 271 D5
st. Russell Lea 343 F5
JANETTE
pl. Oakdale 500 E12
JANICE
av. Padstow 429 G5
av. Smithfield 335 H5
dr. Tahmoor 566 A11
pl. Cherrybrook 219 C12
pl. Narraweena 258 C3
st. Seven Hills 245 B16
JANITA
cr. Mt Colah 162 D14
pl. Bossley Park 333 H11

GREGORY'S STREET DIRECTORY 85

JA STREETS

JANNALI
- av. Jannali 460 F16
- av. Sutherland 490 F1
- cr. Jannali 460 K10

JANNARN
- gr. Seven Hills 246 A13

JANOA
- pl. Chiswick 343 A2

JANPIETER
- rd. Box Hill 154 G3
- st. Marsylya 125 A14

JANSZ
- pl. Fairfield W 335 C11

JAPONICA
- pl. Loftus 490 A10
- rd. Epping 250 E13

JAPURA
- pl. Kearns 450 K15
- pl. St Clair 270 J10

JAQUES
- av. Bondi Beach 378 C3

JAQUETTA
- cl. Cecil Hills 362 E2

JARANDA
- st. Berowra 133 F10

JARDIN
- wy. Mount Druitt 241 E11

JARDINE
- ct. N Willoughby 285 G7
- dr. Edmndsn Pk 422 G3

JARI
- cl. St Clair 269 F15

JARLEY
- pl. Ambarvale 510 G15

JARNDYCE
- av. Ambarvale 511 A13

JAROCIN
- av. Glebe 11 K14

JARRA
- cr. Glenmore Pk 266 A9

JARRAH
- av. Bradbury 511 F13
- av. Prestons 394 C15
- cl. Alfords Point 459 C1
- pl. Bossley Park 333 F8
- pl. Castle Hill 248 F1
- pl. Doonside 243 G16
- pl. Faulconbdg 171 E13
- pl. Frenchs Frst 255 F2

JARRETT
- la. Leichhardt, off
  Jarrett St 373 J3
- st. Clemton Pk 402 A3
- st. Leichhardt 15 H4

JARVIE
- av. Petersham 15 E15
- la. Marrickville, off
  Northcote St 373 K11

JARVIS
- pl. Hebersham 241 G3
- st. Thirlmere 565 A6

JARVISFIELD
- rd. Picton 561 D4
- rd. Picton 563 K1

JASMINE
- av. Padstow Ht 429 D7
- av. Quakers Hill 243 E2
- cl. Arcadia 130 H3
- cl. Glenmore Pk 265 G9
- cr. Cabramatta 365 G10
- cr. Cherrybrook 219 K12
- pl. Castle Hill 248 G1
- pl. Greystanes 305 B11
- pl. Sylvania 462 B13
- rd. Normanhurst 221 J8
- st. Botany 405 G10
- st. Bidwill 211 E15
- tce. Bidwill 211 E15
- wy. Castle Hill 248 G1

JASNAR
- st. Greenfld Pk 334 C15

JASON
- av. S Penrith 266 J6
- la. S Penrith, off
  Jason Av 266 J5
- pl. North Rocks 248 J16
- st. Greystanes 306 C6
- st. Miranda 461 J16

JASPER
- ct. Prestons 392 H14
- pl. Ambarvale 540 F2
- pl. Baulkham Hl 247 A8
- rd. Baulkham Hl 247 D9
- st. Greystanes 306 D9
- st. Quakers Hill 214 G12

JAUNCEY
- pl. Hillsdale 406 H14

JAVA
- pl. Beaumont Hills .. 185 J13
- pl. Quakers Hill 214 B11

JAVELIN
- la. St Clair, off
  Javelin Row 270 F15
- pl. Raby 451 G15
- row. St Clair 270 F15

JAY
- av. Belfield 371 D10
- pl. Oxley Park 240 F16
- pl. Rooty Hill 271 K4
- st. Lidcombe 339 F10

JAYELEM
- cr. Padstow 399 G3

JAYNE
- st. West Ryde 280 G11

JEAN
- av. Miranda 461 J16
- st. Fairfield E 337 A16
- st. Greenacre 370 F3
- st. Kingswood 237 D15
- st. North Rocks 278 B8
- st. Rydalmere 309 H4
- st. Seven Hills 245 D16

JEANETTE
- av. Mona Vale 198 H3
- st. East Ryde 283 B15
- st. Padstow 399 E15
- st. Regentville 265 J4
- st. Seven Hills 245 E16

JEANNERET
- av. Hunters Hill 314 A13

JEAN WAILES
- av. Rhodes 311 C10

JED
- pl. Marayong 244 A8

JEDDA
- pl. Mona Vale 199 E1
- rd. Lurnea 394 B9
- rd. Prestons 393 E8

JEENGA
- pl. Sylvania 461 G15

JEFFERIES
- pl. Prairiewood 334 J8

JEFFERSON
- av. St Ives 224 C7
- cr. Bonnet Bay 460 D11
- gr. Kenthurst 157 C14

JEFFERY
- av. N Parramatta .. 278 D10

JEFFREY
- av. Greystanes 306 D6
- st. St Clair 299 K2
- st. Canterbury 372 G13
- st. Kirribilli 6 B16
- st. Kurnell 466 E8

JEFFREYS
- st. Kirribilli 6 B16

JELENA
- cl. Bossley Park ... 333 G12

JELLICOE
- av. Kingsford 407 A4
- st. Balgowlah Ht .. 288 A14
- st. Caringbah 492 G11
- st. Concord 342 A5
- st. Condell Park .. 398 J2
- st. Hurstville Gr .. 431 G10
- st. Lidcombe 340 B5

JELLIE
- pl. Oakhurst 242 C4

JELLINGAL
- rd. Engadine 489 B12

JEM
- pl. Blacktown 275 A9

JENDI
- av. Bayview 168 J12

JENKINS
- av. Penrith 237 D10
- la. Crows Nest, off
  Brook St 315 G5
- st. S Wntwthvle, off
  Hereford Pl 306 H6
- pl. Carlingford ... 279 H4
- st. Berala 339 B14
- st. Cammeray ... 315 H5
- st. Chatswood W .. 284 G10
- st. Collaroy 229 A11
- st. Douglas Park .. 568 C7
- st. Dundas 280 B13
- st. Millers Pt .... A C10

JENKYN
- pl. Bligh Park 150 E5

JENNA
- cl. Allambie Ht .. 287 G1
- cl. Rooty Hill 271 K2

JENNER
- rd. Dural 219 B7
- st. Baulkham Hl .. 247 J10
- st. Little Bay 437 G14
- st. Minto 482 J4
- st. Seaforth 287 A9
- wy. Minto 482 H7

JENNIE
- pl. Carlingford .. 249 C14

JENNIFER
- av. Allambie Ht .. 257 F14
- av. Blacktown ... 273 K2
- av. Baulkham Hl .. 247 A14
- pl. Cherrybrook . 219 K4
- pl. Smithfield ... 335 G8
- st. Little Bay 437 B13
- st. Ryde 282 K13

JENNINGS
- av. Bass Hill 367 G7
- rd. Faulconbdg .. 171 D6
- st. Heathcote ... 518 D14
- st. Alexandria ... 18 F14
- st. Matraville ... 406 G16

JENNY
- pl. Rooty Hill ... 272 C2

JENOLA
- la. Woolooware .. 493 C9

JENOLAN
- cl. Hornsby Ht .. 161 J9
- st. Wattle Grove .. 395 H13
- st. Leumeah 482 D14

JENSEN
- av. Vaucluse 348 G4
- pl. Engadine 518 F4
- pl. S Coogee 407 H7
- pl. Colyton 270 H8
- pl. Condell Park .. 398 E2
- st. Fairfield W .. 335 A11

JEREMY
- wy. Castle Hill .. 362 H9

JERILDERIE
- av. Kellyville 216 G7

JEROME
- av. Winston Hills .. 247 E16

JERRARA
- st. Engadine ... 488 J13

JERRAWA
- pl. Glenhaven .. 187 J14

JERRYS
- pl. Wallacia 354 K13
- st. Wallacia 355 C3

JERSEY
- av. Mortdale 431 B4
- gln. St Clair 270 A13
- la. Five Dock, off
  Barnstaple Rd .. 343 A8
- la. Hornsby 191 G15
- pde. Minto 482 H9
- pl. Cromer 227 H14
- pl. Glenhaven .. 218 B1
- pl. Artarmon ... 284 J16
- pl. Blackett 241 A5
- pl. Bringelly ... 388 K14
- pl. Dharruk 241 A5
- pl. Emerton ... 240 J4
- pl. Greystanes . 306 H9
- pl. Hebersham . 241 A5
- pl. Maroubra .. 406 J15
- pl. Matraville . 406 J15
- pl. Merrylands . 306 H10
- pl. Oakhurst ... 241 H5
- pl. Oakhurst ... 242 A5
- pl. Plumpton ... 241 H5
- pl. Plumpton ... 242 A5
- pl. Schofields . 212 J7
- pl. S Wntwthvle . 306 H9
- rd. Strathfield . 341 G15
- rd. Woollahra ... 21 G3
- st. Busby 393 J1
- st. Hornsby ... 191 G15
- st. Marrickville .. 373 H13
- st. Mt Colah ... 192 A5
- st. Richmond ... 119 A5
- st. Turramurra .. 222 J15
- st.n. Asquith .. 191 H13
- st.n. Hornsby . 191 H13

JERSEYWOLD
- av. Springwood .. 201 H3

JERVIS
- dr. Illawong 459 A7
- st. Ermington .. 310 F2
- st. Fairfield 336 F8
- st. Prestons ... 392 K16

JERVOIS
- av. Centennial Pk .. 21 E9

JESMOND
- av. Dulwich Hill .. 373 B10
- av. Vaucluse ... 318 G16
- dr. Beecroft ... 250 A4
- st. Surry Hills ..... F K14
- st. Surry Hills 4 C15

JESSICA
- gdn. St Ives 224 G5
- pl. Mt Colah ... 162 D15
- pl. Plumpton .. 241 J7
- pl. Prestons 393 G9
- rd. Rsemeadow .. 540 K4

JESSIE
- st. Smithfield . 335 G8
- st. Westmead . 277 J14

JESSON
- la. Surry Hills .. 20 B4
- st. Surry Hills . 20 B3

JESSOP
- pl. Westmead ... 307 E3

JESSUP
- pl. Glenmore Pk .. 265 E9

JET
- pl. Eagle Vale . 481 E9

JETTY
- rd. Putney 312 B9

JEWEL
- st. Quakers Hill .. 214 H13

JEWELL
- cl. Hamondvle .. 426 G1

JEWELSFORD
- rd. Wentwthvle .. 306 G2

JIBBON
- pl. Woodbine .. 481 G12
- st. Cronulla ... 524 A3

JILL
- st. Marayong .. 244 A9

JILLAK
- cl. Glenmore Pk .. 266 A11

JILLIAN
- pl. Mcquarie Fd .. 424 F15

JILLIBY
- cl. Belrose 225 K15

JILLONG
- st. Rydalmere . 279 J14

JIMADA
- av. Frenchs Frst .. 257 A4

JIMBI
- pl. Glenmore Pk .. 266 B8

JIMBOUR
- ct. Wattle Grove .. 425 J4

JIMBUCK
- cl. Glenmore Pk .. 266 B11

JIM RING
- la. Birrong, off
  Rodd St 369 A5

JIM SIMPSON
- la. Blacktown, off
  Main St 244 G15

JINATONG
- st. Miranda .. 491 J2

JINCHILLA
- rd. Terrey Hills .. 196 C6

JINDABYNE
- av. Baulkham Hl .. 248 A8
- cct. Woodcroft .. 243 G12
- cr. Peakhurst .. 430 C9
- st. Bossley Park .. 333 E11
- st. Frenchs Frst . 256 F1
- st. Heckenberg . 363 K13

JINDALEE
- pl. East Killara .. 254 J8
- rd. Riverwood .. 400 D11

JINDALL
- cct. Glenhaven .. 218 A1

JINDALLA
- cr. Hebersham . 241 D9

JINGARA
- pl. Sylvania ... 461 G14

JINIWIN
- pl. Ambarvale .. 510 K11

JINKINS
- pl. Ambarvale .. 510 H14

JINNA
- rd. Peakhurst . 430 D10

JIPP
- st. Penrith ... 237 A14

JIRANG
- pl. Glenmore Pk .. 266 A8

JIRI
- pl. Engadine .. 518 G4

JIRRAMBA
- ct. Glenmore Pk .. 266 B7

JIRRANG
- cl. Mount Druitt .. 241 E16

JOADJA
- cr. Glendenning .. 242 G5
- st. Prestons 393 F8

JOALAH
- av. Blaxland .. 234 E9
- cl. St Ives 224 D16
- cr. Berowra Ht .. 133 B10
- rd. Duffys Frst .. 194 H3

JOAN
- la. Belmore 401 G3
- la. Baulkham Hl . 247 K9
- la. Currans Hill .. 479 K13
- la. Greystanes . 305 J6
- la. Mount Druitt .. 271 A3
- st. Chester Hill .. 368 C5
- st. Hurstville .. 431 H1

JOANIE
- pl. Glendenning .. 242 F2

JOANNA
- st. S Penrith .. 266 K5

JOANNE
- cl. Cherrybrook .. 219 E6
- cl. Sefton 368 H3
- st. Bilgola 169 E7

JOCARM
- av. Condell Park .. 398 F1

JOCELYN
- av. Marrickville .. 373 F11
- bvd. Quakers Hill .. 213 J7
- bvd. Quakers Hill .. 214 A7
- la. N Curl Curl .. 258 G9
- st. Chester Hill .. 368 B4
- st. N Curl Curl .. 258 G9

JOCELYN HOWARTH
- st. Moore Park 21 B5

JOCKBETT
- st. Agnes Banks .. 117 F16
- st. Agnes Banks .. 147 F2
- st. Londonderry .. 147 F2

JOCKEY
- cl. Casula 394 F16

JODIE
- pl. Quakers Hill .. 244 A2

JODY
- pl. St Clair ... 299 K2

JOEL
- pl. Kings Lngly .. 246 C10

JOFFRE
- cr. Daceyville .. 406 G4
- st. Gymea Bay .. 491 D7
- st. S Hurstville .. 432 B10

JOHANNA
- pl. Schofields .. 213 H5

JOHN
- av. Mcquarie Fd .. 454 A3
- la. Glebe 11 K14
- la. Randwick, off
  John St 376 J10
- la. Cecil Hills .. 362 E2
- rd. Cherrybrook .. 219 C13
- st. Ashfield 342 G15
- st. Avalon 140 C12
- st. Bardwell Vy .. 403 B7
- st. Baulkham Hl .. 247 H13
- st. Beecroft 250 B10
- st. Bexley 402 F15
- st. Blacktown . 274 C5
- st. Burwood .. 341 K13
- st. Cabramatta . 365 D6
- st. Cabramatta W .. 365 A6
- st. Camden 477 A14
- st. Canterbury . 372 F12
- st. Concord 341 J8
- st. Cronulla ... 523 K2
- st. Croydon 342 G15
- st. Erskineville .. 18 A13
- st. Glebe 11 K13
- st. Granville .. 308 B13
- st. Hunters Hill .. 313 B9
- st. Hurstville .. 431 J2
- st. Kogarah Bay .. 432 J11
- st. Leichhardt . 10 F15

86 GREGORY'S STREET DIRECTORY

st. Lidcombe 339 J4
st. McMahons Pt 5 B11
st. Marsden Pk 181 K11
st. Mascot 405 B2
st. Merrylands 308 B13
st. Newtown 374 H11
st. Petersham 16 A14
st. Punchbowl 399 H7
st. Pyrmont 12 E2
st. Queens Park 22 K15
st. Queens Park 377 E8
st. Randwick 376 J10
st. Rooty Hill 271 J5
st. Rydalmere 309 H3
st. St Marys 269 E3
st. Schofields 182 H14
st. Strathfield S 371 A5
st. Tempe 374 C16
st. The Oaks 502 E12
st. Waterloo 19 C14
st. West Ryde 280 G11
st. Windsor 121 G8
st. Woollahra 21 J5

JOHN ALBERT
cl. Kellyville 216 H7

JOHN BATMAN
av. Wrrngtn Cty 238 G5

JOHN BOY
pl. Blacktown 273 J7

JOHN CRAM
pl. Penrith 236 K11

JOHN DAVEY
av. Cronulla 494 B7

JOHN DWYER
rd. Lalor Park 245 F12

JOHN DYKES
av. Vaucluse 348 G1

JOHN EWART
st. Moore Park 21 C6

JOHN FORREST
av. Sutherland 460 D14

JOHN HARGREAVES
av. Moore Park 20 K8
av. Moore Park 21 A7

JOHN HINES
av. Minchinbury 270 K5
av. Minchinbury 271 A5

JOHN HOPKINS
dr. Camperdown 17 J4

JOHN HUGHES
pl. Wahroonga 222 B6

JOHN HUNTER
gr. Mt Annan 479 H16

JOHN KIDD
dr. Blair Athol 511 C2

JOHN McDONALD
wy. Brownlow Hl 474 B1

JOHN McLENNON
cct. Harringtn Pk 478 D2

JOHN MEILLON
st. Moore Park 21 B7

JOHN MILLER
st. Ryde 282 H16

JOHN NORTHCOTT
pl. Surry Hills 19 K4

JOHN OXLEY
av. Werrington 238 G7
av. Wrrngtn Cty 238 G7
dr. Davidson 255 E4
dr. Frenchs Frst 255 E4

JOHN RADLEY
av. Dural 219 B8

JOHNS
av. Normanhurst 221 G7

JOHN SAVAGE
cr. W Pnnant Hl 219 J16

JOHNSON
av. Camden S 506 K10
av. Dulwich Hill 373 A9
av. Kenthurst 156 A7
av. Mcquarie Pk 283 B8
av. Melrose Pk 280 J16
av. Seven Hills 245 K14
cl. Bonnet Bay 460 A9
la. Mascot 405 E6
pl. Ruse 512 H4
pl. Springwood 172 G16
rd. Campbelltown 481 B16
rd. Campbelltown 511 B1
rd. Galston 159 D10
st. Alexandria 375 G11
st. Beaconsfield 375 G11
st. Chatswood 285 A11
st. Harbord 258 E15
st. Hunters Hill 313 B10
st. Lindfield 283 F3
st. Mascot 405 E6

JOHNSONS
rd. Bilpin 61 K6

JOHNSTON
av. Cammeray 316 D4
av. Kirrawee 490 K7
av. Kogarah Bay 432 H12
av. Lurnea 394 C13
cr. Lane Cove N 283 K15
la. Annandale 11 A16
la. Lane Cove W 313 H3
la. Marrickville 373 J16
pde. Maroubra 407 D7
pde. Maroubra 407 E7
pde. S Coogee 407 E7
rd. Bargo 567 G8
rd. Bass Hill 367 F7
rd. Eastwood 280 F6
st. Annandale 16 H3
st. Balmain East 8 G9
st. Earlwood 402 E8
st. Pitt Town 92 H9
st. Windsor 121 C8

JOHNSTONE
st. Guildford W 336 K5
st. Peakhurst 429 K4

JOHN SULMAN
la. St Clair, off
John Sulman Pl 270 B11
pl. St Clair 270 B11

JOHN TEBBUT
pl. Richmond 118 E4

JOHN TIPPING
gr. Penrith 236 F10

JOHN VERGE
pl. Wolli Creek 403 J5

JOHN WALL
la. Yagoona 369 E11

JOHN WARREN
av. Glenwood 215 J16

JOHORE
pl. E Lindfield 254 J12
rd. Holsworthy 426 F10

JOINER
pl. Bonnyrigg 364 D6

JOKIC
st. Bonnyrigg Ht 362 K7

JOLLY
st. Castlereagh 176 E8

JOLY
pde. Hunters Hill 313 C11

JONATHAN
pl. Miranda 491 J1
st. Greystanes 306 C7

JONATHON
pl. Cherrybrook 219 J7
pl. Frenchs Frst 256 B4

JONES
av. Kingsgrove 402 C8
av. Monterey 433 H9
ct. Currans Hill 479 G13
la. Kingswood, off
Jones St 237 H16
la. Pyrmont 12 H8
la. Redfern 19 D8
la. Rosebery, off
Hayes Rd 375 G15
pl. Mt Pritchard 364 D11
rd. Eastwood 280 G6
rd. Kenthurst 187 G1
st. Beacon Hill 257 C5
st. Blacktown 274 J5
st. Concord 342 A6
st. Croydon 342 G14
st. Engadine 518 F1
st. Kingswood 237 H16
st. Pyrmont 12 E2
st. Pyrmont 12 H9
st. Ryde 282 D15
st. Ultimo 3 A13
st. Ultimo 3 B15
st. Ultimo 12 K12
st. Wentwthvle 306 F2

JONES BAY
rd. Pyrmont 12 H1

JONES STREET
ml. Ultimo 3 A14

JONQUIL
pde. Kellyville 216 H6
pl. Alfords Point 459 A3
pl. Glenmore Pk 265 G10

JOORILAND
rd. The Oaks 502 C16

JOPLING
cr. Lalor Park 245 B11
st. North Ryde 283 A12

JORDAN
av. Beverly Hills 401 A12
av. Glossodia 66 E14
av. Newington 310 B15
cl. Mt Colah 162 E16
la. Valley Ht 202 H10
pl. Kearns 451 A15
pl. Kellyville 216 G4
rd. Moorebank 425 B1
rd. Wahroonga 221 K16
st. Fairfield W 335 C9
st. Gladesville 312 H9
st. Rosehill 308 H8
st. Seven Hills 245 F15
st. Wentwthvle 307 C1

JORDANA
pl. Castle Hill 248 E4

JORDANS
la. Matraville 436 J4

JORDON
st. Cmbrdg Pk 238 A7

JORGENSEN
av. St Clair 270 D10

JORJA
pl. Kellyville 216 D1

JOSEPH
cl. Liberty Gr 311 B10
cr. Sefton 368 F6
la. Yagoona 369 E10
rd. Leppington 420 B9
st. Ashfield 372 J5
st. Avalon 140 A13
st. Berala 339 G16
st. Blacktown 274 E6
st. Blakehurst 432 C15
st. Cabramatta 365 D5
st. Cabramatta 365 C8
st. Cabramatta W 365 C8
st. Chipping Ntn 396 C5
st. Kingswood 237 H11
st. Lane Cove 314 G3
st. Lidcombe 339 G16
st. Lidcombe 339 H10
st. Lilyfield 10 D6
st. Regents Pk 369 G2
st. Richmond 118 K7
st. Rozelle 7 B16
st. Rydalmere 279 E15

JOSEPH BANKS
ct. Mt Annan 509 G4
dr. Kings Lngly 245 H7

JOSEPHINE
cr. Cherrybrook 219 J4
cr. Georges Hall 367 F10
cr. Moorebank 396 C11
st. Merrylands W 306 H13
st. Riverwood 400 C14
wy. Glendenning, off
Tony Pl 242 F1

JOSEPHSON
st. Paddington 20 F2

JOSHUA
rd. Freemns Rch 66 K14
rd. Freemns Rch 67 A14
wy. Cranebrook 207 E13
wy. Dean Park, off
Medea Pl 212 F15

JOSHUA MOORE
dr. Horngsea Pk 392 C14

JOSQUIN
wy. Clarmnt Ms 268 F4

JOSSELYN
pl. Concord 342 B3

JOUBERT
st.n, Hunters Hill 313 F9
st.s, Hunters Hill 313 E11

JOWARRA
pl. Bow Bowing 452 E13
wy. Merrylands W 306 K11

JOWETT
pl. Ingleburn 453 J8

JOWYN
pl. Kirrawee 491 C3

JOY
av. Earlwood 402 J4
la. Earlwood, off
Joy Av 402 J4
st. Gladesville 313 A4
st. Mt Pritchard 364 G10

JOYCE
av. Picnic Point 428 D8
dr. Mascot 405 B6
pl. Dural 219 C7
st. Fairfield 336 A13
st. Glenwood 245 D2
st. Pendle Hill 276 E14
st. Punchbowl 399 J9

JOYCELYN
cl. Hornsby Ht 161 J12

JOYLYN
rd. Annangrove 155 E12

JOYNER
av. Newington 309 K16
st. Westmead 307 J4

JOYNT
av. Milperra 397 F10

JOYNTON
av. Zetland 375 J11

JUBA
cl. St Clair 269 J16

JUBILEE
av. Beverley Pk 433 A8
av. Carlton 432 J7
av. Pymble 252 K1
av. Warriewood 198 F5
la. Lewisham, off
Jubilee St 15 B10
la. Parramatta 308 D6
pl. Balmain 8 D10
pl. Balmain East 8 D10
st. Lewisham 15 B9
st. Wahroonga 222 C2

JUDD
av. Hamondvle 396 H16
st. Banksia 403 C12
st. Berkshire Pk 179 H11
st. Cronulla 493 K9
st. Mortdale 431 D9
st. Oatley 431 D10
st. Penshurst 431 D9

JUDE
av. Kogarah Bay 432 H11

JUDGE
la. Randwick, off
Coogee Bay Rd 377 C15
la. Woolmloo 4 F7
pl. Randwick, off
Judge St 377 C15
pl. Woolmloo 4 G6
st. Randwick 377 C15
st. Woolmloo 4 G7

JUDGES
la. Waverley, off
Bronte Rd 377 F8

JUDITH
av. Cabramatta 365 C10
av. Mt Colah 192 B3
av. Mt Riverview 234 D2
av. Seven Hills 275 D5
cl. Werrington 238 J11
pl. Cromer 228 C15
st. Baulkham Hl 247 K11
st. Berala 339 B13
st. Chester Hill 368 D2
st. Pendle Hill 306 C1
st. Seaforth 286 K2

JUDITH ANDERSON
dr. Doonside 243 B9

JUDSON
rd. Thornleigh 221 C8

JUGIONG
st. West Pymble 252 G10

JUKES
cl. Barden Rdg 488 H6

JULAR
pl. Jamisontown 266 D6

JULIA
cl. Cherrybrook 220 A13
cl. West Hoxton 391 K4
gr. Castle Hill 217 C7
st. Ashfield 342 K16

JULIAN
cl. Kellyville 216 B2
pl. Arcadia 130 A16
pl. Glenwood 245 A1
pl. Sefton 368 F5
st. Mosman 316 H3
st. Willoughby 285 E14
wy. Claymore 481 E11

JULIANA
cr. Baulkham Hl 246 H5
pl. Bligh Park 150 E8
wy. Cherrybrook 219 A14

JULIANNE
pl. Canley Ht 365 C4

JULIE
av. Clemton Park 402 A4
cr. St Clair 269 H8
ct. Beaumont Hills 216 B1
st. Blacktown 274 E7
st. Marsfield 282 B8

JULIET
cl. Rsemeadow 540 H4

JULIETT
la. Marrickville 16 K16
la. Marrickville 374 E8
st. Enmore 16 K16
st. Marrickville 16 K16
st. Marrickville 374 F8

JULIETTE
av. Punchbowl 370 B16

JULIUS
av. North Ryde 283 C10
rd. Rsemeadow 540 J2
st. Fairfield W 335 C13

JULL
pl. St Helens Park 541 A9

JUMAL
pl. Smithfield 306 D15

JUMBUNNA
pl. Terrey Hills 196 C7

JUNCTION
la. N Sydney K H11
la. Wahroonga 223 A4
la. Woolmloo 4 E5
rd. Baulkham Hl 247 C16
rd. Beverly Hills 400 H16
rd. Heathcote 518 G10
rd. Leumeah 482 G16
rd. Moorebank 396 A10
rd. Peakhurst 430 H1
rd. Riverstone 153 E16
rd. Ruse 512 E8
rd. Schofields 183 E14
rd. Summer Hill 373 B6
rd. Wahroonga 222 E3
rd. Winston Hills 247 C16
st. Auburn 309 C13
st. Cabramatta 365 K9
st. Forest Lodge 11 H16
st. Gladesville 312 J10
st. Granville 308 D8
st. Marrickville 373 K15
st. Miranda 492 D3
st. Mortdale 431 B4
st. Old Guildford 337 D8
st. Ryde 311 H4
st. Silverwater 309 C13
st. Strathfield S 371 B5
st. Woollahra 22 J5
st. Woolmloo 4 F5
st. Yennora 337 D8

JUNE
pl. Glenhaven 218 B1
pl. Gymea Bay 491 C9
st. Bankstown 399 C4
st. Blacktown 274 H8
st. Seven Hills 245 C15

JUNEE
cl. Bossley Park 333 G9
cr. Kingsgrove 402 B6
st. Marayong 243 K8

JUNIA
av. Toongabbie 276 B8

JUNIOR
st. Leichhardt 15 H3

JUNIPER
dr. Breakfast Pt 312 C15
pl. Baulkham Hl 248 B11
pl. Prestons 393 K15
pl. Sylvania 462 A9
wy. Blacktown 274 E12
wy. Mcquarie Fd 454 H4

JUNO
pde. Greenacre 370 E11

JUPITER
ct. Cranebrook 207 F15
la. Cranebrook, off
Pensax Rd 207 F14
rd. Kellyville 216 C2
st. Gladesville 312 K9
st. Lansvale 366 J8
st. Winston Hills 277 C1

JUPP
pl. Eastwood 281 E4

JURA
cl. Cranebrook 207 E15
cr. Winmalee 173 E12
pl. St Andrews 481 J1
pl. Seven Hills 275 C8

GREGORY'S STREET DIRECTORY 87

JU — STREETS

JURDS
la. Ryde 281 K9
JURY
wy. Minto 482 J7
JUSTIN
pl. Quakers Hill 214 F12
st. Lilyfield 10 F4
st. Smithfield 335 J5
JUSTINE
av. Baulkham Hl 247 C8
cl. Bargo 567 B4
JUSTIS
dr. Harringtn Pk 479 A4
JUSTUS
st. North Bondi 348 C15
JUVENIS
av. Oyster Bay 461 C3

K

KABAN
st. Doonside 243 D14
KABARLI
rd. Lalor Park 245 E13
KABLE
rd. Bradbury 511 G13
st. Windsor 121 C7
KABU
ct. Glenmore Pk 266 B6
KABUL
cl. St Clair 269 K16
la. St Clair, off
  Kabul Cl 269 K16
KADER
st. Bargo 567 A5
st. Bargo 567 D6
KADIERA
cl. Wallacia 325 A15
KADIGAL
pl. Beacon Hill 257 D6
KADINA
pl. Quakers Hill 214 B16
KAFFIR
cl. Cherrybrook 219 E7
KAGA
pl. Marsfield 281 K5
KAGA PATHWAY
Blaxland 233 G13
KAHIBAH
rd. Mosman 317 F10
rd. Mosman 317 F9
KAIN
av. Matraville 437 C1
cl. Bonnyrigg 364 C6
KAIRAWA
dr. S Hurstville 432 C10
KALA
cct. St Clair 269 H14
la. St Clair, off
  Kala Cct 269 H14
KALAMBO
pl. St Clair 270 H11
KALANA
cl. Moorebank 396 H7
KALANG
av. Killara 254 C9
av. St Marys 239 F15
la. Yowie Bay 492 C10
rd. Edensor Pk 333 D16
rd. Edensor Pk 363 D2
rd. Elanora Ht 198 D14
rd. Greystanes 306 B6
rd. Kenthurst 187 F6
rd. Mt Colah 191 K5
rd. Seven Hills 275 G4
KALAUI
st. N Balgowlah 287 E4
KALBARRI
cr. Bow Bowing 452 C13
KALDOW
la. Grose Vale 85 E16
la. Grose Wold 85 E16
KALESKI
st. Moorebank 395 G9
KALGAL
st. Frenchs Frst 255 J1
KALGOORLIE
pl. Cartwright 393 K5
st. Sutherland 460 D14
st. Leichhardt 9 F13
st. Willoughby 285 D13

KALIANNA
cr. Beacon Hill 257 H8
KALIMNA
dr. Baulkham Hl 247 A6
gr. Minchinbury 272 C8
st. Moorebank 396 F7
KALINDI
la. St Clair, off
  Kalindi Pl 270 H11
pl. St Clair 270 H11
KALINYA
st. Newport 169 E12
KALKADA
av. Gymea Bay 491 E11
KALLANG
pde. Wahroonga 221 J16
KALLAROO
rd. Riverview 314 C7
rd. Terrey Hills 195 K7
st. Mosman 316 K11
KALLAWATTA
gr. McGraths Hl 122 B10
KALLISTA
av. St Ives 254 E1
KALMIA
pl. Miranda 491 K5
KALOE
pl. Marayong 244 B3
KALOONA
ct. Kirrawee 460 J16
KALORA
av. Dee Why 258 J1
av. Fairfield W 335 G14
KALUA
pl. Glenmore Pk 266 B6
KALUGA
st. Busby 363 H13
KALUMNA
cl. Cherrybrook 219 F12
KALUNA
av. Smithfield 336 B5
st. Putney 312 A8
KALUNGA
la. Rooty Hill 242 D16
la. Rooty Hill 272 C1
KALYAN
av. Bradbury 511 F16
KAMAROOKA
cr. W Pnnant Hl 249 G5
KAMBAH
cr. W Pnnant Hl 249 A8
KAMBALA
cr. Fairfield W 335 F14
pl. Bellevue Hill 347 F15
st. Bellevue Hill 14 J7
KAMBALDA
cr. Yarrawarrah 489 E13
KAMBER
rd. Terrey Hills 196 C12
KAMBORA
av. Davidson 255 D1
av. Frenchs Frst 255 D1
KAMERUKA
rd. Northbridge 285 K14
KAMILAROI
rd. Bayview 169 A14
KAMILAROY
rd. West Pymble 253 A12
KAMIRA
av. Villawood 367 C1
ct. Villawood 367 C1
dr. Lilli Pilli 522 F3
KAMIRI
st. Seaforth 287 B5
KAN
cl. St Clair 269 H15
KANA
cl. Cranebrook 207 E6
KANADAH
av. Baulkham Hl 246 J8
KANANDAH
rd. Engadine 488 C13
KANANGRA
av. Baulkham Hl 247 B4
cr. Balgowlah 287 E11
cr. Cherrybrook 219 J7
cr. Clontarf 287 E11
cr. Eldersle 477 H16
cr. Ruse 512 F5
cr. Wattle Grove 426 B4
rd. Terrey Hills 196 F7

KANANGUR
av. Gymea 491 H1
KANANOOK
av. Bayview 168 H10
KANDARA
cl. Middle Dural 157 H1
KANDOS
st. Glenwood 245 F1
KANDRA
rd. Beacon Hill 257 H8
KANDY
av. Epping 251 A12
KANE
pl. Casula 424 D3
st. Guildford 337 F4
KANERUKA
pl. Baulkham Hl 246 K8
KANGAROO
cl. Green Valley 363 A12
la. Manly, off
  Carlton St 288 G7
rd. Emu Plains 235 A11
rd. Collaroy Plat 228 J13
rd. Tahmoor 565 B13
st. Manly 288 F7
KANGAROO POINT
rd. Kangaroo Pt 461 J7
KANILI
av. Baulkham Hl 247 B15
KANIMBLA
cr. Bilgola 169 H7
st. Ruse 512 F8
KANINA
pl. Cranebrook 207 B13
KANINI
cl. Cromer 227 K16
KANNAN
cr. Kirrawee 461 D15
KANNING
av. Gymea Bay 491 E8
KANO
cl. Bonnyrigg 364 C8
KANOONA
av. Homebush 341 A7
av. St Ives 223 J11
st. Caringbah 492 F8
KANOWAR
av. East Killara 254 J6
KANSAS
pl. Toongabbie 275 H12
KANUKA
st. Bossley Park 333 F8
KANYA
st. Frenchs Frst 256 F8
KAPALA
av. Bradbury 511 E16
KAPITI
st. St Ives Ch 223 J2
KAPOVIC
st. Edensor Pk 363 F1
KAPUNDA
pl. Belrose 226 A14
KAPUTAR
ct. Holsworthy 426 C5
pl. Prairiewood 334 F7
KAPYONG
st. Belrose 226 A15
KARA
cr. Bayview 168 K13
la. Peakhurst 430 B10
la. Randwick, off
  Howard St 407 B1
st. Lane Cove N 284 E16
st. Randwick 407 B1
st. Sefton 368 E3
KARABAH
pl. Frenchs Frst 257 C4
tce. Warrimoo 203 C15
KARABAR
st. Fairfield Ht 335 H9
KARABI
cl. Glenmore Pk 266 C10
KARABIL
cr. Baulkham Hl 248 C8
KARA KAROOK
st. Maianbar 523 B8
KARALEE
cl. Marsfield 281 K1
rd. Galston 160 J7
KARALTA
cr. Belrose 225 G14

KARAMARRA
rd. Engadine 488 J13
KARANA
pl. Chatswood W 284 C10
KARANGI
pl. Illawong 460 B4
rd. Whalan 241 A9
KARANI
av. Guildford W 336 G3
KARDA
pl. Gymea 491 F1
KARDELLA
av. Killara 254 D11
ct. Condell Park 368 H16
la. Killara 254 E11
KARDINIA
rd. Mosman 317 D13
KAREELA
av. Penrith 237 E6
cr. Greenacre 370 B13
la. Cremorne Pt 316 F12
la. Penrith, off
  Kareela Av 237 E5
rd. Baulkham Hl 247 B16
rd. Chatswood W 284 B8
rd. Cremorne Pt 316 F12
rd. Cremorne, off
  Hodgson Av 316 F12
st. Doonside 243 B15
KAREELAH
rd. Hunters Hill 313 G12
KAREEMA
st. Balgowlah 287 F10
KAREENA
rd.n.Miranda 492 E5
rd.s,Miranda 492 E7
KARELLA
av. Villawood 367 B2
KAREN
av. Picnic Point 428 D8
ct. Baulkham Hl 247 A10
ct. Cranebrook 206 J8
dr. Faulconbg 171 D15
dr. Ingleburn 453 D12
dr. Mount Druitt 270 K1
pl. Silverdale 353 B11
rd. Rossmore 419 E3
st. St Ives 224 F9
KARIBOO
cl. Mona Vale 199 E1
KARILLA
av. Lane Cove N 284 C15
KARIMBLA
rd. Miranda 491 J4
KARINA
cr. Belrose 226 D15
KARINGAL
av. Carlingford 279 E3
cr. Frenchs Frst 256 E6
ct. Glenmore Pk 266 G16
pl. Marsfield 281 K1
pl. Bradbury 511 J12
pl. Greenacre 370 B14
rd. Riverview 314 C7
st. Kingsgrove 401 J9
st. Seaforth 287 B7
KARINI
cl. Green Valley 363 H11
KARINYA
pl. Kellyville 216 C2
pl. Wahroonga 221 H6
KARIOLA
st. Lane Cove N 284 C15
KARIUS
st. Glenfield 424 H9
KARIWARA
st. Dundas 279 G13
KARLOO
cl. Moorebank 396 H6
pde. Newport 169 H15
st. Turramurra 223 B10
KARLOON
rd. W Pnnant Hl 249 H9
KARNAK
st. Denistone E 281 F9
KARNE
st. Narwee 400 G13
st. Riverwood 400 G13
st. Roselands 400 G13
KARNU
pl. Kareela 461 D14

KARONGA
st. Epping 250 D15
KAROO
av. E Lindfield 255 A13
cr. Hornsby Ht 161 F15
pl. Malabar 437 D8
KAROOL
av. Earlwood 372 H16
KAROOLA
cr. Caringbah 492 F4
rd. Brooklyn 76 D11
st. Busby 363 J14
st. Narraweena 258 C2
KAROOM
av. St Ives 223 H9
KAROON
av. Canley Ht 335 B15
KARRABA
rd. Sefton 368 G6
KARRABAH
rd. Auburn 309 C16
KARRABEE
av. Huntleys Cove 313 B13
st. Dee Why 258 E7
KARRABUL
pl. Bossley Park 333 F6
rd. Airds 511 H16
rd. St Helens Park 541 G3
KARRANGA
av. Killara 254 B11
KARREE
pl. Heathcote 518 E10
KARRI
pl. Alfords Point 429 A14
pl. Bradbury 511 E10
pl. Parklea 215 B13
KARRIL
av. Beecroft 249 K12
KARRONG
st. Clarmnt Ms 268 G2
KARUAH
pl. Engadine 488 K8
pl. Penrith 237 C5
rd. Turramurra 222 J11
st. Campbelltown 511 K7
st. Doonside 243 B7
st. Greenacre 370 E11
st. Greystanes 306 C7
st. Strathfield 340 H13
KARUK
st. Glenmore Pk 266 D10
KARWARRA
pl. Peakhurst 430 C8
KASCH
st. Tahmoor 565 D12
KASHMIR
av. Quakers Hill 214 D7
KASIE
la. St Clair, off
  Kasie Pl 299 J3
pl. St Clair 299 K3
KASTELAN
st. Blacktown 273 J3
KATANDRA
rd. Avalon 139 J16
KATANNA
rd. Wedderburn 540 D14
KATAVICH
cr. Bonnyrigg Ht 363 C4
KATE
cl. Cherrybrook 219 J4
pl. Quakers Hill 213 K7
st. Turramurra 252 E2
KATELLA
ct. Airds 512 B14
KATER
pl. Croydon Pk 372 A5
KATH
pl. Kings Lngly 245 C4
KATHERIN
rd. Baulkham Hl 247 E11
KATHERINE
cl. Cranebrook 207 D4
pl. Castle Hill 248 C1
st. Cecil Hills 362 J3
st. Chatswood, off
  Victoria Av 284 H10
st. Leumeah 482 F12

88 GREGORY'S STREET DIRECTORY

STREETS KE

KATHLEEN
av. Castle Hill...........217 F11
av. Lurnea...............394 D10
la. Emu Plains, off Kathleen St..........235 B9
pde. Picnic Point.........428 D7
pl. Thirlmere............565 C6
st. Emu Plains..........235 A9
st. North Ryde.........282 H8
st. Wiley Park...........400 J2
KATHRYN
pl. Gymea Bay..........491 F8
pl. Lalor Park...........245 C13
KATHY
cl. Pymble...............223 B14
wy. Dean Park...........212 F15
KATIA
st. N Parramatta......278 F12
KATINA
st. Turramurra.........223 A11
KATINKA
st. Bonnyrigg...........364 D7
KATNOOK
pl. W Pnnant Hl.......249 A2
KATO
av. Newington..........310 A15
KATOA
cl. N Narrabeen.......198 J13
pl. Marsfield............282 A3
KATRINA
av. Mona Vale..........198 J2
cl. Hobartville..........118 E7
cr. Cabramatta W....364 H6
ct. Normanhurst.......221 J11
pl. Baulkham Hl......247 G13
pl. Ermington...........280 D14
pl. Roselands...........401 E4
st. Seven Hills..........245 K12
KATTA
cl. Hornsby..............191 J7
KAUAI
pl. Kings Park..........244 H3
KAURI
av. Berowra.............163 D1
ct. Castle Hill............218 J14
pl. Blaxland..............234 B8
st. Blacktown...........244 A15
st. Cabramatta.........365 G10
KAVENAGH
cl. Prairiewood........335 A8
KAVIENG
av. Whalan..............241 A8
KAWANA
cl. Epping................250 H13
ct. Bella Vista...........246 E7
pl. Bangor................459 J14
pl. Erskine Park........270 G16
st. Bass Hill..............367 K6
st. Frenchs Frst........255 G3
KAY
cl. Cherrybrook........220 A11
cl. Jamisontown.......266 B2
cl. Mona Vale...........198 H3
la. Jamisontown, off Kay Cl................266 B2
st. Blacktown...........274 H7
st. Carlingford..........280 C4
st. Granville.............308 K10
st. Old Guildford......337 F7
KAYLEY
pl. Glenhaven...........218 D3
KAYLYN
pl. Mount Druitt.......241 G12
KAYS
av.e,Marrickville.........373 F13
av.w,Dulwich Hill........373 E12
KAZANIS
ct. Werrington..........239 A12
KEA
cl. Acacia Gdn..........214 G15
KEADY
wy. Wentwthvle.........277 E11
KEARNEY
ct. Baulkham Hl.......247 A2
pl. Bonnyrigg...........363 J8
rd. S Maroota.............69 G8
KEARNS
av. Kearns...............451 C16
la. Yagoona.............369 D11
pl. Horngsea Pk......392 C14
KEARY
st. Willoughby..........285 F12

KEATES
av. Padstow Ht.........429 E6
KEATING
pl. Denham Ct..........422 G16
st. Lidcombe............339 J7
st. Maroubra............407 C7
wy. Narellan Vale......508 G1
KEATO
av. Hamondvle.........396 F16
KEATS
av. Riverwood..........400 C13
av. Rockdale............403 C16
av. Ryde..................282 D12
cl. Wetherill Pk........334 H5
pl. Heathcote...........518 C16
pl. Ingleburn............453 C12
pl. Winston Hills......277 G1
rd. N Turramurra......223 E7
st. Carlingford..........250 B16
KEDA
cct. N Richmond..........87 D16
KEDDIE
pl. Riverstone..........183 C9
KEDRON
av. Beecroft..............250 C8
pl. St Johns Pk........334 E15
st. Glenbrook...........233 K13
KEDUMBA
cr. N Turramurra......223 F2
KEECH
rd. Castlereagh.........176 E12
KEEDEN
pl. Bonnyrigg...........364 A7
KEEGAN
av. Glebe....................12 B11
pl. Forestville...........256 A12
rd. Bass Hill.............367 G8
KEELE
st. Como.................460 E5
st. Stanhpe Gdn.......215 E5
st. Vaucluse.............318 F15
KEELENDI
rd. W Pnnant Hl.......250 A1
KEELER
st. Carlingford..........280 A2
KEELO
st. Quakers Hill........243 D4
KEENAN
la. Chester Hill.........368 C2
st. Mona Vale...........199 B3
KEENE
st. Baulkham Hl.......247 F10
KEERA
st. Quakers Hill........243 F5
KEESING
cr. Blackett...............241 D4
st. Edensor Pk.........363 G3
KEEVIN
st. Roselands...........401 A7
KEEYUGA
rd. Huntleys Pt.........313 F13
KEGWORTH
st. Leichhardt.............15 B3
KEIGHRAN
pl. Cherrybrook........219 E6
pl. Minto..................482 H8
KEIGHRAN MILL
dr. Blair Athol...........511 A4
KEILEY
st. Marsfield.............281 K5
KEINO
av. Newington..........310 A15
KEIR
av. Hurlstone Pk......372 K14
KEIRA
av. Greenacre...........370 F4
cl. Terrey Hills..........196 D5
pl. Beecroft..............249 K12
pl. Ruse...................512 F4
KEIRAN
la. Bondi Jctn............22 F9
st. Bondi Jctn............22 F9
KEIRLE
rd. Kellyville Rdg......215 A4
st. North Manly........258 B14
KEITH
ct. Cherrybrook........219 F6
la. Dulwich Hill.........373 D12
pl. Baulkham Hl.......247 E11
st. Clovelly...............377 K12
st. Dulwich Hill.........373 D12
st. Earlwood............373 A16
st. Lindfield..............284 G1

st. Peakhurst...........430 E1
st. S Penrith.............266 J2
KEITH SMITH
av. Mascot...............404 J6
KELBRAE
cl. Castle Hill............247 J1
KELBURN
pl. Airds...................512 B13
rd. Roseville.............284 F2
KELD
pl. Blacktown...........244 D15
KELDIE
st. Forestville...........255 K6
KELHAM
st. Glendenning........242 G7
KELLAWAY
pl. Wetherill Pk........304 G15
st. Doonside.............243 B7
st. East Ryde............282 J16
KELLER
pl. Casula.................395 A12
KELLERMAN
dr. St Helens Park....540 K9
dr. St Helens Park....541 B4
KELLETT
pl. Rcuttrs Bay.............4 K7
st. Potts Point..............4 J7
wy. Potts Point.............4 K7
KELLICAR
rd. Campbelltown....510 H8
KELLICK
st. Waterloo...............19 F13
KELLOGG
rd. Rooty Hill............242 E13
KELLOWAY
av. Camden..............507 A7
KELLS
la. Darlinghurst............4 D11
rd. Ryde...................312 D1
KELLY
cl. Baulkham Hl.......247 A2
cl. Mount Druitt.......241 E15
la. Brooklyn...............75 F12
la. Matraville............436 G2
la. Padstow, off Watson Rd..........399 D14
pl. Mt Pritchard........364 H14
st. Austral................390 F15
st. Henley................313 B14
st. Matraville............436 G1
st. Punchbowl..........400 B3
st. Sylvania..............461 K13
st. Ultimo..................12 H14
wy. Mcquarie Pk, off A J Hare Av.........283 C7
KELLYS
esp. Longueville.........314 F7
esp. Northwood..........314 F7
wy. Oxford Falls.........226 H10
KELMSCOTT
la. St Clair, off Kelmscott Wy......270 G14
wy. St Clair...............270 F14
KELPA
pl. Allambie Ht.........257 D12
KELRAY
pl. Asquith...............192 A13
KELSALL
pl. Barden Rdg.........488 G5
st. Doonside............273 E4
KELSEY
st. Arncliffe..............403 F7
KELSO
cl. Bonnyrigg Ht......363 C6
cr. Moorebank..........395 K7
la. Blacktown...........274 H1
la. Randwick............377 A12
pl. St Andrews.........452 A15
st. Burwood Ht.........372 A3
st. Engadine.............489 A8
KELTON
pl. Engadine.............488 K8
KELVEDON
la. Marsden Pk.........182 B11
KELVIN
ct. Oatlands.............279 A10
gr. Winston Hills.......277 F6
la. Picnic Point.........428 B8
pde. Picnic Point........428 B7
pl. Busby.................363 H16
rd. St Ives................224 D16
st. Ashbury..............372 F8

KELVIN PARK
dr. Bringelly.............388 G12
KEMBLA
av. Chester Hill.........368 D1
cr. Ruse...................512 F4
st. Arncliffe..............403 D8
st. Croydon Pk.........371 F7
st. Dharruk..............241 C8
st. Wakeley..............334 H14
KEMBLE
la. Mosman.............317 A8
pl. Bilgola................169 F8
KEMERTON
la. St Clair, off Kemerton St........269 J11
st. St Clair................269 J10
KEMIRA
pl. Cartwright...........394 D5
KEMMEL
cl. Bossley Park.......334 B10
KEMMIS
st. Randwick............377 D11
KEMP
av. Kirrawee.............490 K8
av. Matraville............436 J2
pl. Bonnyrigg...........364 D5
pl. Glenorie..............126 E5
pl. Minto..................482 G9
pl. Tregear...............240 E7
st. Granville.............308 G10
st. Mortdale.............431 A6
st. Tennyson............312 E9
KEMPBRIDGE
av. Seaforth..............287 E9
KEMPE
pde. Kings Lngly.........246 B10
KEMPSEY
cl. Dee Why.............258 H3
la. Jamisontown, off Kempsey St.........266 D5
pl. Bossley Park.......333 D13
st. Blacktown...........274 J2
st. Jamisontown......266 D5
wy. Hoxton Park........392 G9
KEMPT
st. Bonnyrigg...........363 K6
KENARF
cl. Kingswood..........238 A14
KENBURN
av. Cherrybrook........219 G10
KENDAL
cr. Collaroy Plat........228 E11
KENDALL
dr. Casula.................394 H16
dr. Casula.................424 F2
dr. Casula.................424 C3
la. Surry Hills.............20 D3
la. The Rocks..............A K3
pl. Kareela...............461 C13
pl. Kellyville.............186 G12
rd. Castle Cove.........285 F3
st. Cabarita..............342 D1
st. Campbelltown.....512 A4
st. Ermington............310 B2
st. Fairfield W...........335 B13
st. Granville.............308 J11
st. Harris Park..........308 E5
st. Mortdale.............430 J7
st. Penrith................237 C11
st. Pymble...............253 A9
st. Riverstone..........182 E14
st. Rydalmere...........310 B2
st. Sans Souci..........463 A3
st. Surry Hills.............20 D3
st. Thirlmere............562 D11
st. West Pymble.......252 J10
st. Woollahra...........377 G2
KENDALL INLET
Cabarita..............312 E15
KENDEE
st. Sadleir................364 C15
KENDELL
st. Stanhpe Gdn.......215 F8
KENEALLY
cr. Edensor Pk.........333 H16
wy. Casula.................424 G3
KENELDA
av. Guildford.............338 A2
KENFORD
cct. Stanhpe Gdn.......215 D4
KENGE
pl. Ambarvale...........510 G15
KEN HALL
pl. Agnes Banks.......117 C12

KENIBEA
pl. Dee Why.............258 H1
KENILWORTH
cr. Cranebrook.........207 A6
la. Bondi Jctn, off Flood La..............377 H3
rd. Dundas Vy..........280 B6
rd. Lindfield..............254 C14
st. Bondi Jctn...........377 G3
st. Croydon..............342 F15
st. Miller..................393 F2
KENJI
pl. Blacktown...........273 J7
KENLEY
rd. Normanhurst......221 E9
KENMARE
rd. Londonderry.......148 C11
KENNA
pl. Cromer...............227 K12
pl. Gymea................491 C6
KENNEDIA
pl. Mt Annan............509 C2
KENNEDY
av. Belmore..............371 C14
cr. Bonnet Bay.........460 D8
dr. S Penrith.............236 J15
gr. Appin..................569 G9
la. Gladesville..........313 A3
la. Kingsford............376 J16
pde. Lalor Park...........245 G14
pl. Bayview..............168 D8
pl. St Ives.................224 G16
st. Appin..................569 F12
st. Appin..................569 G9
st. Gladesville..........313 A3
st. Guildford.............338 C8
st. Kingsford............376 J16
st. Liverpool.............394 H3
st. Panania...............428 F6
st. Picnic Point.........428 F8
st. Revesby..............428 F6
st. Ruse...................512 F2
st. Woolmloo...............4 D7
wy. Bonnyrigg...........364 D6
KENNELLY
st. Colyton...............270 F8
KENNETH
av. Baulkham Hl.......247 F11
av. Kirrawee.............490 J2
av. Panania...............428 E1
cr. Dean Park...........242 H2
la. Kingsford, off Kennedy St..........376 J16
pl. Dural...................219 D5
rd. Balgowlah...........288 A5
rd. Fairlight...............288 A5
rd. Manly..................288 A5
rd. Manly Vale..........287 J4
rd. Manly Vale..........288 A5
st. Longueville.........314 D9
st. Mcquarie Fd........424 A16
st. Ryde...................312 D4
st. Tamarama...........378 C6
KENNETH SLESSOR
dr. Glenmore Pk.......265 J6
KENNETT
pl. Glenfield.............424 D10
KENNIFF
st. Rozelle..................10 K1
KENNINGTON
av. Quakers Hill........214 C12
KENNINGTON OVAL
Auburn...............339 A12
KENNY
av. Casula.................394 G13
av. Chifley................437 B8
av. St Marys.............240 A14
cl. St Helens Park....541 C3
la. Marayong............244 D6
pl. Dundas Vy..........279 H5
pl. Fairfield W..........334 K10
rd. Pagewood...........406 F9
KENNY HILL
rd. Currans Hill.........510 C1
KENOMA
pl. Arndell Park........273 H9
KENS
rd. Frenchs Frst........255 H2
rd. Yarramundi.........145 B1
KENSINGTON
dr. Harringtn Pk........478 C1
la. Kogarah, off Kensington St......433 B5
la. Summer Hill.........373 D2
la. Waterloo...............19 G14

GREGORY'S STREET DIRECTORY 89

KE STREETS

KE
- mw. Waterloo 19 H14
- pl. Cecil Hills 362 D7
- rd. Kensington 376 D13
- st. Summer Hill 373 D2
- st. Chippendale 19 C1
- st. Kogarah 433 B5
- st. Punchbowl 400 B9
- st. Waterloo 19 H14

KENSINGTON PARK
- rd. Schofields 183 B13

KENT
- av. Croydon Pk 371 K6
- av. Roselands 400 J7
- cl. Newtown 17 D11
- la. Newtown 17 D11
- la. Turramurra 223 E10
- pl. Beverly Hills 430 J1
- pl. Bossley Park 333 H11
- pl. Colyton 270 E4
- pl. E Kurrajong 67 J4
- pl. Heathcote 518 D11
- rd. Clarmnt Ms 268 J9
- rd. Marsfield 282 B6
- rd. Mascot 404 K3
- rd. Mascot 405 A1
- rd. Narellan Vale 478 H16
- rd. North Ryde 282 B6
- rd. Orchard Hills 268 J9
- rd. Rose Bay 347 K11
- rd. Tahmoor 566 F7
- rd. Turramurra 223 E9
- st. Baulkham Hl 247 C7
- st. Belrose 401 E1
- st. Blacktown 244 D13
- st. Collaroy 229 A14
- st. Epping 250 H12
- st. Glenbrook 234 B14
- st. Hamondvle 396 G14
- st. Millers Pt ...... A C1
- st. Millers Pt 1 D10
- st. Minto 482 G3
- st. Newtown 17 D16
- st. Regents Pk 339 B16
- st. Rockdale 403 E14
- st. Sydney ...... C D2
- st. Sydney 3 E1
- st. Waverley 377 H10
- st. Winmalee 172 H14

KENTHURST
- pl. Chester Hill 368 B5
- rd. Dural 188 E11
- rd. Kenthurst 188 B1
- rd. Kenthurst 188 E11
- st. St Ives 224 A10

KENTIA
- ct. Stanhope Gdn 215 C9
- pde. Cherrybrook 219 F7
- pl. Alfords Point 429 B13

KENTMERE
- st. Stanhope Gdn 215 B5

KENTOLEEN
- rd. Blaxlands Rdg 65 G5

KENTRIDGE
- pl. Bella Vista 216 C14

KENTUCKY
- dr. Glossodia 65 K12
- rd. Riverwood 400 A12

KENTVILLE
- av. Annandale 11 B7
- la. Annandale 11 B7

KENTWELL
- av. Castle Hill 218 A14
- av. Concord 341 H7
- av. Thornleigh 220 J10
- cr. Stanhope Gdn 215 G8
- dr. S Windsor 151 A7
- rd. Allambie Ht 257 G16
- rd. North Manly 258 A16
- st. Baulkham Hl 247 E12

KENTWOOD
- pl. Narellan 478 G11

KENWARD
- av. Chester Hill 338 A14

KENWICK
- la. Beecroft 250 D7

KENWOOD
- rd. Wedderburn 540 B11

KENWORTHY
- st. Rydalmere 279 E14

KENWYN
- cl. St Ives 224 J8
- cl. Bonnyrigg Ht 362 K7
- rd. Hurstville 432 D4

KENYON
- cr. Doonside 243 D6
- la. Fairfield 336 E12

KE
- rd. Bexley 432 D2
- st. Fairfield 336 D12

KENYONS
- rd. Merrylands W 307 A13

KEON
- pl. Quakers Hill 214 F11

KEPOS
- la. Redfern 20 A11
- st. Redfern 20 A11

KEPPEL
- av. Concord 341 H8
- av. Riverwood 400 A16
- cct. Hinchinbrk 362 K14
- rd. Ryde 282 E12
- st. Kings Lngly 245 E6

KERELA
- av. Wahroonga 221 H16

KEREMA
- pl. Glenfield 424 C13

KERILEE
- cl. Bella Vista 246 H1

KERIN
- av. Five Dock 342 K7

KERLE
- cr. Castle Hill 218 J14

KERR
- av. Bundeena 523 G8
- cl. Narraweena 258 D3
- gr. Pagewood 406 G7
- pde. Auburn 339 E3
- rd. Ingleburn 453 D3
- st. Appin 569 E10
- st. Hornsby 191 E11

KERRAN
- cl. Cmbrdg Pk 238 A11
- la. Cmbrdg Pk, off
  Kerran Cl 238 A11

KERRAWAH
- av. St Ives 223 K7

KERRIBEE
- pl. Carlingford 249 H10

KERRIDGE
- pl. Forest Lodge 18 A1

KERRIE
- av. Regents Pk 369 K3
- pl. Panania 397 K16
- st. Peakhurst 430 B4
- st. Hornsby 191 J9
- st. Oatlands 278 J12
- st. Woodpark 306 H16

KERRINEA
- rd. Sefton 368 F3

KERRS
- rd. Berala 339 F10
- rd. Castle Hill 247 J1
- rd. Lidcombe 339 F10
- rd. Mt Vernon 330 G12

KERRUISH
- av. Homebush W 340 G8

KERRY
- av. Epping 250 F11
- av. Springwood 202 A5
- cl. Beacon Hill 257 H5
- cl. Roselands 401 C8
- pl. Oakdale 500 D13
- rd. Blacktown 243 J16
- rd. Schofields 212 K4

KERSLAKE
- av. Regents Pk 369 C3
- gr. Menai 458 H15

KERSTIN
- st. Quakers Hill 213 H9

KERULORI
- cl. Hornsby Ht 161 H12

KERWICK
- st. Baulkham Hl 247 B3

KERWIN
- cir. Hebersham 241 F1

KERYN
- pl. Cabramatta 365 E10

KESAWAI
- pl. Holsworthy 426 D2

KESSELL
- av. Homebush W 340 H10

KESTER
- cr. Oakhurst 241 K3

KESTON
- av. Mosman 317 A8
- la. Mosman, off
  Keston Av 317 A8

KESTREL
- av. Hinchinbrk 393 B3
- cr. Erskine Park 270 K13

KE
- la. St Clair, off
  Kestrel Cr 270 K13
- pl. Bnkstn Aprt 397 J1
- pl. Bella Vista 216 D14
- pl. Ingleburn 453 G5
- pl. Woronora Ht 489 C5
- wy. Yarramundi 145 C6

KESWICK
- av. Castle Hill 247 K5
- st. Dee Why 259 A8
- st. Georges Hall 367 H14

KETHEL
- rd. Cheltenham 250 J7

KETTLE
- la. Ultimo 12 H15
- st. Redfern 19 H9

KETURAH
- cl. Glenwood 245 E2

KEVIN
- av. Avalon 140 A14
- av. Scotland I 168 J3
- pl. Thirlmere 565 A2
- st. Wentwthvle 277 D10

KEVIN COOMBS
- av. Homebush B ...... M 310 E14

KEW
- cl. Belrose 225 K13
- pl. Dharruk 241 B7
- pl. St Johns Pk 364 G3
- wy. Airds 511 H16

KEW GARDENS
- ct. Wattle Grove 426 A3

KEWIN
- av. Mt Pritchard 364 D8

KEWOL
- pl. Port Hacking 522 J2

KEY
- ct. Baulkham Hl 246 J12

KEYNE
- st. Prospect 275 A12

KEYPORT
- cr. Glendenning 242 G4

KEYS
- st. Westleigh 220 J1
- pde. Milperra 397 B9
- pl. Liverpool 394 K4

KEYSOR
- rd. Kingsgrove 401 F7

KEYWORTH
- dr. Blacktown 275 A7

KHANCOBAN
- st. Heckenberg 363 K13

KHARTOUM
- av. Gordon 253 J7
- av. Gordon 253 J8
- rd. Mcquarie Pk 282 G3

KIA
- pl. Ambarvale 511 B13

KIAH
- cl. Bayview 168 J16
- cl. Hornsby Ht 191 G4
- cl. Baulkham Hl 247 A5
- cl. Bonnyrigg 364 B9
- cl. Greystanes 306 B7
- pl. Miranda 491 H5

KIAKA
- cr. Jamisontown 266 D6

KIALBA
- rd. Campbelltown 481 H16

KIAMA
- cl. Terrey Hills 196 E6
- cl. Emu Plains 234 K9
- st. Greystanes 305 J2
- st. Miranda 462 B15
- st. Padstow 429 F3
- st. Prestons 392 K14

KIAMALA
- cr. Killara 254 C14

KIANDRA
- cl. Terrey Hills 196 E5
- pl. Heckenberg 364 A15
- pl. Wakeley 334 F14

KIANGA
- pl. Prestons 422 J1

KIAORA
- la. Double Bay 14 C11
- rd. Double Bay 14 E10

KIARA
- cl. Bangor 459 K14
- pl. N Sydney 6 C11
- st. Marayong 244 C2

KIATA
- cr. Doonside 243 H14

KIBAH
- st. Busby 363 J13

KIBBLE
- pl. Narellan 478 C8

KIBER
- dr. Glenmore Pk 266 C12
- dr. Glenmore Pk 266 E11

KIBO
- rd. Regents Pk 339 C16

KIDD
- cl. Bidwill 211 G16
- cr. Currans Hill 479 H13
- pl. Minto 453 B14
- st. Richmond 119 K5

KIDMAN
- la. Paddington 4 H15
- st. Blaxland 233 H13
- st. Coogee 377 F16
- st. Glenwood 215 H15

KIDMANS
- tce. Woolmloo, off
  Junction La 4 E5

KIDNER
- cl. Castle Hill 218 J13

KIEREN
- dr. Blacktown 273 G5

KIERNAN
- cr. Abbotsbury 363 B2

KIEV
- st. Merrylands 307 C11

KIEWA
- pl. Bayview 168 J16
- pl. Kirrawee 460 K15
- pl. St Marys 239 H3

KIEWARRA
- st. Kingsgrove 401 F7

KIHILLA
- rd. Auburn 309 C16
- st. Fairfield Ht 335 H9

KIKORI
- cr. Whalan 241 A9
- pl. Glenfield 424 F10

KILBENNY
- st. Kellyville Rdg 185 D16

KILBORN
- pl. Menai 458 G12

KILBRIDE
- av. Dharruk 241 C5
- st. Hurlstone Pk 372 H13

KILBURN
- cl. Beacon Hill 257 K9

KILBY
- pl. Illawong 459 J6
- st. Kellyville Rdg 185 B15

KILCARN
- pl. Wakeley 334 G14

KILDARE
- av. Killarney Ht 286 D2
- la. Coogee, off
  Beach St 377 J14
- rd. Blacktown 244 B16
- rd. Doonside 243 D14

KILGOUR
- ct. Glen Alpine 510 F9

KILIAN
- st. Winston Hills 246 J16

KILKEE
- av. Kingsgrove 402 B6

KILKENNY
- av. Killarney Ht 256 B3
- av. Smithfield 335 E2
- rd. S Penrith 266 K2

KILLALA
- av. Killarney Ht 255 J13

KILLALOE
- av. Pennant Hills 250 C1

KILLANOOLA
- st. Villawood 367 G4

KILLARA
- av. Killara 254 A14
- av. Kingsgrove 402 B6
- av. Panania 398 A15
- av. Riverwood 400 A14
- cr. Winmalee 173 F4
- pl. Dharruk 241 C7

KILLARNEY
- av. Blacktown 274 A1
- av. Glenmore Pk 266 H8
- cl. Castle Hill 248 E2
- dr. McGraths Hl 121 J11

KE
- dr. Killarney Ht 256 A15
- la. Mosman, off
  Killarney St 317 B4
- st. Mosman 317 A3

KILLAWARRA
- pl. Wahroonga 222 E2
- rd. Duffys Frst 195 A6

KILLEATON
- st. St Ives 223 H10

KILLEEN
- st. Auburn 338 H8
- st. Balmain 8 D9
- st. Balmain East 8 D9
- st. Wentwthvle 307 B2

KILLINGER
- av. Liverpool 394 J1

KILLOOLA
- st. Concord W 311 E12
- st. Concord W 311 D13

KILLURAN
- cr. Emu Heights 234 K5

KILLYLEA
- wy. Wentwthvle 277 E11

KILMARNOCK
- rd. Engadine 488 J10

KILMINSTER
- la. Woollahra 22 B2

KILMORE
- st. Kellyville Rdg 185 C16

KILMOREY
- st. Busby 363 G15

KILMORY
- pl. Mt Krng-gai 162 K14

KILN
- pl. Woodcroft 243 F9

KILNER
- la. Camperdown 17 B4

KILPA
- pl. St Ives 254 A3

KILTO
- cr. Glendenning 242 F11
- cr. Glendenning 242 G9
- pl. Blaxlands Rdg 64 K6
- pl. Blaxlands Rdg 65 A6

KIM
- av. Regents Pk 369 A3
- cl. Cabramatta 365 E11
- cl. Thirlmere 564 J4
- pl. Ingleburn 453 E12
- pl. Quakers Hill 214 E16
- pl. Toongabbie 276 G9
- st. Gladesville 312 K3

KIMBA
- cl. Westleigh 220 G6

KIMBAR
- pl. Yarrawarrah 489 E14

KIMBARRA
- av. Baulkham Hl 248 A8
- av. Camden 507 A4
- rd. Berowra Ht 133 D6
- rd. Pymble 252 K2

KIMBER
- la. Forest Lodge 11 H16
- la. Haymarket ...... E D5
- la. Haymarket 3 E11

KIMBERLEY
- av. Lane Cove 314 F1
- cr. Fairfield W 335 F9
- ct. Bella Vista 246 E8
- gr. Rosebery 375 K14
- la. Hurstville 431 K3
- la. Windsor Dn 181 A1
- pde. Gymea Bay 491 J9
- rd. Carlingford 250 B13
- rd. Hurstville 432 A2
- st. East Killara 254 H5
- st. Guildford 338 B2
- st. Leumeah 482 E10
- st. Rooty Hill 241 K15
- st. Vaucluse 348 F7

KIMBRIKI
- rd. Ingleside 196 H11

KIMO
- pl. Marayong 244 B3
- st. N Balgowlah 287 F5
- st. Roseville 284 B5

KIMPTON
- st. Banksia 403 C12

KIMS
- av. Lugarno 429 K16

KINALDY
- cr. Kellyville 186 K16

STREETS

KI

KINARRA
av. Kellyville......216 F4

KINCHEGA
cr. Glenwood......215 E15
ct. Holsworthy......426 C5
rd. Wattle Grove......426 C5
pl. Bow Bowing......452 D14

KINCRAIG
ct. Castle Hill......218 D7

KINCUMBER
pl. Engadine......489 B10
rd. Bonnyrigg......363 J9

KINDEE
av. Bonnyrigg......363 K9

KINDELAN
rd. Winston Hills......246 H16

KINDER
st. Lalor Park......245 F10

KINDILAN
pl. Miranda......492 E5

KINDILEN
cl. Rouse Hill......185 D6

KING
av. Balgowlah......287 K9
la. Balmain......7 D7
la. Marrickville, off
   Renwick St......373 J16
la. Mascot, off
   Sutherland St......405 F5
la. Moorebank......395 G8
la. Newtown......374 J9
la. Penrith, off
   King St......237 C9
la. Randwick......377 A11
la. Rockdale, off
   King St......403 D15
rd. Rockdale......403 E14
rd. Waverton......5 A4
rd. Wollstncraft......5 A4
sq. Kings Lngly......245 C3
st. Camden S......506 K11
st. Fairfield W......335 A13
st. Hornsby......192 A15
st. Hornsby......192 C15
st. Ingleside......197 J7
st. Prairiewood......335 A8
st. Wahroonga......222 D15
st. Wilberforce......67 H16
st. Wilberforce......91 K4
sq. Bidwill......211 G15
st. Alexandria......374 H8
st. Appin......569 F11
st. Ashbury......372 F9
st. Ashfield......372 G4
st. Auburn......309 D14
st. Balmain......7 D7
st. Berowra......133 E12
st. Bondi......377 A3
st. Campbelltown......511 G3
st. Canterbury......372 F10
st. Concord W......311 C16
st. Croydon......342 D15
st. Dundas Vy......280 C9
st. Eastlakes......405 J5
st. Enfield......371 F4
st. Glenbrook......233 J14
st. Guildford W......336 H1
st. Heathcote......518 F10
st. Hunters Hill......313 E11
st. Kogarah......433 A4
st. Maianbar......522 K9
st. Manly Vale......287 G3
st. Marrickville......374 B10
st. Mascot......405 A4
st. Mt Krng-gai......163 A13
st. Naremburn......315 G2
st. Narrabeen......229 A5
st. Newport......169 F10
st. Newtown......17 G12
st. Newtown......374 K8
st. Parramatta......307 K5
st. Penrith......237 C10
st. Randwick......376 J10
st. Riverstone......182 H6
st. Rockdale......403 D15
st. Rossmore......390 C15
st. St Marys......269 H1
st. St Peters......374 H8
st. S Hurstville......432 C10
st. Sydney......C D4
st. Sydney......A A5
st. Sydney......3 E2
st. Tahmoor......565 G11
st. Turramurra......222 H12
st. Waverton......315 D11
st. Wilberforce......91 J4
st. Wollstncraft......5 A4

st. Wollstncraft......315 D11
st.w.Appin......569 E11

KINGARTH
st. Busby......363 G13

KINGCOTT
pl. Annangrove......186 H5

KINGDOM
pl. Kellyville......215 H4

KINGDON
pde. Long Point......454 E13

KING EDWARD
av. Bayview......169 B13
st. Croydon......342 D11
st. Pymble......253 E3
st. Rockdale......403 B15
st. Roseville......285 B5

KINGFISHER
av. Bossley Park......333 F7
av. Hinchinbrk......363 C15
cr. Grays Point......491 F14
dr. Duffys Frst......195 C1
pl. Glendenning......242 H5
pl. W Pnnant Hl......249 D6
st. Ingleburn......453 H8
wy. St Clair......270 F13
wy. Warriewood......198 H10

KING GEORGE
st. Lavender Bay......5 E13
st. McMahons Pt......5 E13

KING GEORGES
rd. Beverly Hills......401 A10
rd. Blakehurst......432 A9
rd. Hurstville......431 F3
rd. Penshurst......431 F3
rd. Roselands......400 K7
rd. S Hurstville......432 A9
rd. Wiley Park......400 G1

KINGHORNE
rd. Bonnyrigg Ht......363 H6

KING MAX
st. Mosman......317 C10

KINGMORE
pl. Glenmore......233 K15

KINGS
av. Roseville......284 F6
la. Btn-le-Sds......433 K4
la. Darlinghurst......F K4
la. Darlinghurst......4 C10
pl. Beverly Hills......401 F15
pl. Carlingford......279 B6
pl. Kingsgrove......401 F15
pl. Btn-le-Sds......433 H3
pl. Castle Hill......217 C8
pl. Denistone E......281 G10
pl. Five Dock......342 G9
pl. Ingleburn......453 G4
pl. Vaucluse......348 G3

KINGS BAY
av. Five Dock......342 G9

KINGSBURY
cl. Kingswood, off
   Kingsbury Pl......238 C12
pl. Jannali......460 K13
pl. Kingswood......238 C13
st. Croydon Pk......371 G6

KINGSCLARE
st. Leumeah......481 K15
st. Leumeah......482 B16
st. Leumeah......512 A1

KINGSCLEAR
cl. Alexandria......18 G13
rd. Alexandria......18 G13

KINGSCOTE
pl. Kingswood......267 H3

KINGSCOTT
pl. Castle Hill......218 J8

KINGS CROSS
st. Darlinghurst......4 H8
st. Potts Point......4 H8
st. Rcuttrs Bay......13 A9

KINGSDALE
av. Kellyville......217 A1

KINGSFIELD
av. Glenmore Pk......266 F14

KINGSFORD
av. Eastwood......281 J6
av. Five Dock......343 A11
av. S Turramrra......251 K7
st. Blacktown......245 C10
st. Ermington......280 A14
st. Maroubra......406 G10
st. Smithfield......335 F3

KINGSGROVE
av. Bexley North......402 A9
av. Kingsgrove......402 A9
rd. Belmore......401 H3
rd. Kingsgrove......401 K9

KINGSHILL
rd. Mulgoa......295 F13

KINGSLAND
rd. Berala......339 C16
rd. Regents Pk......369 C2
rd. Strathfield......371 E1
rd.n,Bexley North......402 F9
rd.s,Bexley......402 H12

KINGSLANGLEY
rd. Greenwich......314 J6

KINGSLEA
pl. Canley Ht......335 E15

KINGSLEY
cl. S Windsor......120 H15
cl. Wahroonga......222 A9
gr. Kingswood......238 B12
la. Kingswood, off
   Kingsley Gr......238 C12
la. Queens Park......22 J12
st. Blackett......241 B4

KINGS LYNN
ct. W Pnnant Hl......249 G5

KINGSMERE
dr. Glenwood......245 H3

KINGS PARK
cct. Five Dock......342 G9
rd. Five Dock......342 G9

KINGSTON
av. Concord......312 A15
cl. Panania......428 F3
cl. W Pnnant Hl......249 A8
ct. Camperdown......17 B10
ct. Newtown......17 A10
pl. Abbotsbury......363 C1
rd. Airds......511 J14
rd. Camperdown......17 A10
rd. Mt Annan......479 G14
rd. Newtown......17 A10
st. Botany......405 E13
st. Haberfield......343 D15

KINGSVIEW
wy. Glenwood, off
   Citadel Pl......246 C7

KINGSWAY
   Beverly Hills......401 G14
av. Caringbah......492 H5
cl. Cronulla......493 J11
cl. Dee Why......258 H4
dr. Gymea......491 D3
  Kingsgrove......401 G14
pl. Miranda......492 C4
pl. Woolooware......493 E9

KINGSWOOD
rd. Engadine......489 A12
rd. Orchard Hills......267 H12

KINGTON
la. Cranebrook, off
   Pendock Rd......207 F14
pl. Cranebrook......207 F14
rd. Minchinbury......272 E8

KINGUSSIE
av. Castle Hill......218 B7

KING WILLIAM
st. Greenwich......314 K9

KINKA
rd. Duffys Frst......195 C7
rd. Terrey Hills......195 C7

KINKUNA
st. Busby......363 G13

KINLEY
pl. Baulkham Hl......247 H10

KINMONT
rd. S Penrith......267 C7

KINNANE
cr. Acacia Gdn......214 H14

KINNARD
av. Kellyville......217 A1

KINNEAR
st. Harringtn Pk......478 F2
st. Harringtn Pk......478 D2

KINROSS
cl. Wattle Grove......426 A5
cl. Engadine......518 F4
rd. Revesby......428 G5
st. St Andrews......452 A15
st. Riverstone......183 C9

KINROSS PATH
   Winmalee......173 E12

KINSDALE
la. Killarney Ht......255 H12

KINSEL
av. Kingsgrove......401 H14
dr. Bexley......402 J15

KINSELA
st. Illawong......460 B4

KINSELLA
ct. Kellyville......186 K16

KINSELLAS
dr. Lane Cove W, off
   Whitfield Av......283 F12

KINSON
cr. Denistone......281 C11

KINTORE
st. Dulwich Hill......373 D10
st. Wahroonga......222 G4

KINTYRE
pl. St Andrews......481 K4
st. Cecil Hills......362 D3

KIOGLE
la. Wahroonga, off
   Kiogle St......221 H16
st. Wahroonga......221 H16

KIOLA
pl. Castle Hill......218 A11
rd. Northbridge......285 K15
st. Smithfield......336 A4

KIOLOA
wy. Merrylands W......306 J11

KIORA
av. Mosman......317 C2
cr. Yennora......392 H13
st. Prestons......392 H13
st. Miranda......492 A4
st. Panania......398 C16

KIPPAX
la. St Clair, off
   Kippax Pl......269 K15
pl. Menai......458 F8
st. St Clair......269 K15
st. Shalvey......211 A15
st. Greystanes......305 J9
st. Surry Hills......F A16
st. Surry Hills......3 H16

KIPPIST
av. Minchinbury......271 B6

KIRA
av. Tregear......240 D5

KIT
pl. Rooty Hill......272 B5

KITA
rd. Berowra Ht......133 A8

KITAVA
pl. Glenfield......424 H10

KITCHEN
pl. West Hoxton......392 D11

KITCHENER
av. Concord......342 C2
av. Earlwood......402 J2
av. Regents Pk......369 B2
ct. Holsworthy......426 G3
pl. Carlingford......249 J16
pl. Chatswood......284 J9
st. Artarmon......284 H15
st. Cherrybrook......220 B14
st. Balgowlah......287 G6
st. Caringbah......492 K6
st. Kogarah......433 A4
st. Maroubra......407 B11
st. Oatley......431 E13
st. St Ives......224 D5

KITCHING
wy. Currans Hill......479 H13

KIRKHAM
la. Elderslie......477 E6
la. Kirkham......477 E6
rd. Wattle Grove......425 J5
rd. Auburn......338 J12
st. Beecroft......250 F8
st. Narellan......478 E9

KIRKMAN
la. Chester Hill......337 K12
rd. Blacktown......274 D2

KIRKOSWALD
av. Mosman......317 D3

KIRK PATRICK
la. Petersham......15 J7

KIRKPATRICK
av. West Hoxton......391 J5
st. N Turramurra......193 F13
wy. Berowra Wtr......132 F2

KIRKSTONE
rd. Collaroy Plat......228 D12

KIRKTON
pl. Beaumont Hills......215 F2
pl. Edensor Pk......333 F16

KIRKWALL
av. Castle Hill......216 J10

KIRKWOOD
av. N Epping......251 C10
ct. Castle Hill......248 J2
rd. Cronulla......494 B7
st. Seaforth......286 K2

KIRRA
pl. Wilberforce......91 K1
pl. Allambie Ht......257 F12

KIRRANG
av. Villawood......367 B2
st. Beverly Hills......401 C10
st. Cromer......227 K16
st. Wareemba......343 A6

KIRRAWEE
st. Kirrawee......490 K6

KIRRIBILLI
av. Kirribilli......2 B1

KIRRIFORD
wy. Carlingford......249 J10

KIRRILY
pl. Bass Hill......367 F7
wy. Castle Hill......248 G3

KIRSTY
cr. Hassall Gr......212 B14

KIRTON
st. Stanhpe Gdn......215 C6

KISDON
cr. Prospect......274 J12

KISHANLAL
cl. Glenwood......215 B16

KISSING POINT
rd. Dundas......279 A14
rd. Dundas......280 A12
rd. Dundas Vy......279 A14
rd. Ermington......280 C12
rd. N Parramatta......279 A14
rd. Oatlands......279 A14
rd. S Turramrra......252 B9
rd. Turramurra......222 G16

KISTA DAN
av. Tregear......240 D5

KIT
pl. Rooty Hill......272 B5

KITA
rd. Berowra Ht......133 A8

KITAVA
pl. Glenfield......424 H10

KITCHEN
pl. West Hoxton......392 D11

KITCHENER
av. Concord......342 C2
av. Earlwood......402 J2
av. Regents Pk......369 B2
ct. Holsworthy......426 G3
pl. Carlingford......249 J16
pl. Chatswood......284 J9
st. Artarmon......284 H15
st. Cherrybrook......220 B14
pde. Bankstown......369 E15
st. Artarmon......284 H15
st. Cherrybrook......220 B14
st. Balgowlah......287 G6
st. Caringbah......492 K6
st. Kogarah......433 A4
st. Maroubra......407 B11
st. Oatley......431 E13
st. St Ives......224 D5

KITCHING
wy. Currans Hill......479 H13

GREGORY'S STREET DIRECTORY 91

KI STREETS

KITE
cl. Green Valley 363 D12
pl. Ingleburn 453 H8
st. Emu Plains 235 G8

KITSON
pl. Minto 453 A16
wy. Casula 424 E3

KITTANI
st. Killara 253 E14
st. Kirrawee 491 B6

KITTY
pl. Bligh Park 150 E7

KITTYHAWK
cr. Raby 481 F2

KITTYS
st. Mcquarie Pk 282 H5

KIWI
cl. St Clair 269 G16
cl. Lethbrdg Pk 240 F1

KIWONG
st. Yowie Bay 492 A10

KLEINS
rd. Northmead 277 H1

KLEIST
pl. Emerton 240 J4

KLEMM
st. Bnkstn Aprt 367 J16

KLIM
wy. Blacktown 273 H6

KNAPSACK
pl. Jamisontown 266 D3
st. Glenbrook 234 F16

KNAPTON
st. St Johns Pk 364 D3

KNEALE
cl. Edensor Pk 333 G14

KNIGHT
av. Kings Lngly 245 C3
av. Panania 398 A15
cl. Kingswood 238 B13
la. Erskineville, off
Knight St. 374 J7
la. Newtown 17 D11
pl. Bligh Park 150 G8
pl. Castlecrag 286 E11
pl. Castle Hill 248 D4
pl. Minto 453 B15
rd. Arncliffe 403 C10
st. Erskineville 374 K9
st. Homebush 341 D9
st. Lansvale 366 K6
wy. Castle Hill 248 D3

KNIGHTON
pl. S Penrith 267 B7

KNIGHTS
rd. Galston 159 J8

KNIGHTSBRIDGE
av. Belrose 226 A12
av. Glenwood 245 G3
pl. Castle Hill 217 F6

KNOCK
cr. Beverly Hills 430 J2

KNOCK FARRELL
rd. Glenorie 128 F7

KNOCKLAYDE
st. Ashfield 342 J14

KNOLL
av. Turrella 403 G6

KNOLTON
pl. Oakhurst 241 H3

KNOT
pl. Hinchinbrk 393 C2

KNOTWOOD
av. Mcquarie Fd 454 F7

KNOWLES
av. Matraville 437 A5
av. North Bondi 348 K16
pl. Bossley Park 334 C9

KNOWLMAN
av. Pymble 253 G3

KNOX
av. Epping 281 D2
la. Double Bay 14 C9
rd. Normanhurst 221 F9
rd. Rouse Hill 185 C6
rd. Doonside 243 A9
st. Ashfield 372 H3
st. Belmore 371 B13
st. Chippendale 18 H1
st. Clovelly 377 G12
st. Double Bay 14 C9
st. Glenmore Pk 265 K5
st. Lindfield 283 E3

st. Pendle Hill 276 G11
st. St Marys 269 K3

KOALA
av. Ingleburn 453 F5
cl. St Ives 253 J2
gln. Cranebrook 237 C1
la. Avalon 170 A2
pl. Hornsby Ht 191 F1
pl. Kellyville 216 H4
rd. Blaxland 233 F4
rd. Greenacre 370 G15
rd. Lilli Pilli 522 E4
rd. Punchbowl 370 F16
wy. Horsley Pk 332 B8

KOBADA
pl. Sylvania 461 G14
rd. Dover Ht 348 E8

KOBINA
av. Glenmore Pk 266 A6
av. Glenmore Pk 266 A7

KOCHIA
la. Lindfield 254 E16

KODALA
la. Glenbrook 233 K13
wy. Bangor 459 H14

KOEL
pl. Ingleburn 453 H6
pl. Woronora Ht 489 D3
st. Hinchinbrk 393 C4

KOHLENBERG
cl. Emu Plains 235 B11

KOKERA
st. Hunters Hill 314 A11

KOKODA
av. Wahroonga 223 C6
cct. Mt Annan 479 D11
cr. Beacon Hill 257 F8
pl. Bossley Park 333 K6
pl. Glenfield 424 H10
st. Abbotsford 343 A3
st. North Ryde 282 K11

KOLODONG
dr. Quakers Hill 244 A1

KOLONGA
pl. Frenchs Frst 256 G7

KOLOONA
dr. Emu Plains 234 K8
st. Berowra 133 F10
st. Berowra Ht. 133 F8

KOLORA
rd. Ebenezer 68 A11

KOMIATUM
st. Holsworthy 426 E3

KOMIRRA
dr. Cranebrook 207 D5

KOMMER
pl. St Marys 239 D4

KONA
cl. Berowra 133 F10

KONDA
av. Bayview 168 J15
pl. Bangor 459 J14

KONDAH
av. Chatswood W 284 E8
st. Merrylands 306 H10

KOOBILYA
st. Seaforth 287 C7

KOEEMBA
rd. Beverly Hills 401 D11

KOOKABURRA
cl. Bayview 168 J16
cr. Glenmore Pk 266 D13
gr. Galston Downs 215 D4
la. Kingsgrove 402 B10
la. St Clair, off
Kookabura Pl 270 K14
pl. Blaxland 234 D5
pl. Erskine Park 270 K14
pl. Grays Point 491 F15
pl. W Pnnant Hl 248 J6
rd. Hornsby Ht 191 E1
rd. Prestons 392 K15
rd.n.Prestons 393 A12
st. Greystanes 306 C3
st. Ingleburn 453 F7

KOOLA
av. East Killara 254 E8

KOOLOONA
cr. Bradbury 511 F14
cr. West Pymble 253 A14

KOOLOORA
av. Harbord 288 H1

KOOMBALAH
av. S Turramrra 252 C9

KOOMOOLOO
cr. Shalvey 210 G14

KOONAWARRA
av. Lindfield 283 J3
st. Villawood 367 J4

KOONGARRA
rd. Roseville Ch 285 F1

KOONOONA
av. Villawood 367 A2

KOONYA
av. Bankstown 399 B3
cct. Caringbah 492 H1

KOORA
av. Wahroonga 222 B10

KOORABAN
st. Waterfall 519 D13

KOORABAR
rd. Bangor 459 H15

KOORABEL
av. Gymea 491 D5
la. Gymea, off
Koorabel Av 491 E5
pl. Baulkham Hl 247 A13
rd. Lalor Park 245 D12
st. Lugarno 430 A13

KOORALA
st. Manly Vale 288 A4

KOORANA
cl. Baulkham Hl 247 D5
rd. Tahmoor 566 F7

KOORANGA
pl. Normanhurst 221 H8

KOORANGI
av. Elanora Ht 198 B16

KOORAWATHA
st. Hornsby Ht 161 E15

KOOREELA
st. Kingsgrove 402 A9

KOORINDA
av. Kensington 376 E14
av. Villawood 367 B2

KOORINE
st. Engadine 488 G12

KOORINGA
cr. Emu Plains 235 A8

KOORINGA
st. Blair Athol 511 B2
rd. Chatswood 285 C6

KOORINGAI
av. Phillip Bay 436 H11

KOORINGAL
av. Thornleigh 221 A6
dr. Agnes Banks 146 B4

KOORONG
pl. Bangor 459 H14
st. Berowra 133 E9
st. Marsfield 282 A3

KOOROOL
av. Lalor Park 245 J12

KOOROOMA
pl. Sylvania 462 D7

KOOTINGAL
st. Greystanes 306 B7

KOOWONG
av. Mosman 317 A1

KOOYONG
av. Mt Colah 192 D3
rd. Riverview 313 J5
st. Pymble 253 C9
st. St Johns Pk 364 G2
wy. Shalvey 210 J14

KORANGI
rd. Pymble 223 F14

KORBEL
pl. Georges Hall 367 H10

KORIMUL
cr. S Penrith 266 H7
la. S Penrith, off
Korimul Cr 266 H7

KORINYA
pl. Castle Cove 286 D6

KOROKAN
rd. Lilli Pilli 522 G3

KORTUM
pl. Auburn 339 A4

KOSCIUSKO
pl. Bow Bowing 452 D13
pl. Heckenberg 363 K11
st. Bossley Park 334 B7

KOSMALA
cl. Newington 310 C12

KOSMINA
st. Glenwood 215 J16

KOTA BAHRU
rd. Holsworthy 426 F11

KOTARA
pl. Miranda 492 E2

KOVACS
st. Rooty Hill 271 K5

KOWAN
rd. Mooney Mooney .. 75 D2

KOWARI
st. St Helens Park ... 511 H16

KRAHE
rd. Wilberforce 67 C15

KRECKLER
cr. Lalor Park 245 G11

KRESSER
gr. Canterbury 372 E15

KRISTA
pl. Tahmoor 566 A9

KRISTEN
pl. W Pnnant Hl 249 B6

KRISTINE
av. Baulkham Hl 247 K9
cl. Cherrybrook 219 E6
dr. Mona Vale 198 H1
st. Winmalee 173 E7

KRISTY
ct. Kellyville 216 G4
ct. Berowra 133 C13

KROOMBIT
st. Dulwich Hill 373 B10
rd. Tahmoor 566 F7

KRUGER
la. Erskine Park, off
Kruger Pl 300 K1
pl. Erskine Park 300 K1

KRUI
st. Fairlight 288 B9

KUALA
cl. Dean Park 242 G1

KUBOR
cr. Whalan 241 A13
st. Glenfield 424 G13

KUDILLA
st. Engadine 488 G12

KUHN
st. Blair Athol 511 B2

KUKUNDI
dr. Glenmore Pk 266 C6

KULA
ct. Baulkham Hl 246 J7
cl. Bangor 459 H14

KULALYE
pl. Belrose 226 A10

KULGOA
av. Ryde 282 A14
cr. Terrey Hills 195 E6
la. Bellevue Hill 14 G10
rd. Bellevue Hill 14 H11
rd. Pymble 253 H4
st. Lalor Park 245 H10
st. Leumeah 481 J15

KULGUN
av. Auburn 339 B11

KULINIA
st. Engadine 488 H11

KULLAH
pde. Lane Cove N 283 K14

KULLAROO
av. Bradbury 511 H14
av. Castle Hill 217 K7

KULLEROO
cr. Clarmnt Ms 268 H1

KULLI
pl. Engadine 489 C10

KUMA
pl. Glenmore Pk 266 E12

KUMALI
cl. Allambie Ht 257 H14

KUMARINA
av. Bradbury 511 H14

KUMARRA
st. Duffys Frst 194 J1

KUMBARA
cl. Glenmore Pk 266 D10

KUMBARDANG
av. Miranda 492 B2

KUMQUAT
wy. Glenwood 215 E13

KUMULLA
rd. Miranda 492 F1

KUNARI
pl. Mona Vale 199 A1

KUNDABUNG
st. Belimbla Pk 501 B16

KUNDI
st. Blaxland 234 D7

KUNDIBAH
rd. Elanora Ht 198 F15

KUNDUL
pl. Engadine 488 K9

KUNGALA
rd. Beecroft 250 A1
st. St Marys 239 F15
st. Villawood 367 F4

KUNGAR
rd. Caringbah 492 F13

KUNIPIPI
st. St Clair 269 G8

KUNYAL
pl. Greystanes 306 B6

KUPPA
rd. Ryde 282 B13

KURA
pl. Seven Hills 275 H8

KURALJI
cl. Glenmore Pk 266 D7

KURAMA
cr. Whalan 241 A9

KURANDA
av. Padstow 399 F14

KURARA
cl. Terrey Hills 196 C6

KU-RING-GAI
av. Turramurra 222 K14
cr. Bow Bowing 452 C14

KU-RING-GAI CHASE
rd. Krngai Ch N P .. 163 E16
rd. Mt Colah 192 C6

KURMOND
rd. Freemns Rch 90 B3
rd. Kurmond 64 J16
rd. Kurmond 65 A16
rd. N Richmond 87 K1
rd. Wilberforce 66 K16
rd. Wilberforce 67 A16
st. Jamisontown ... 266 D4

KURNELL
rd. Cronulla 493 J10
rd. Woolooware 493 J10
st. Botany 405 J13
st. Btn-le-Sds 433 H3

KUROKI
st. Penshurst 431 F7

KURPUN
pl. Glenmore Pk 266 A11

KURRABBA
rd. Neutral Bay 5 K7
rd. N Sydney 5 K7

KURRABI
rd. Allambie Ht 257 C8

KURRAGHEIN
av. Rcuttrs Bay 13 B8

KURRAGLEN
pl. Comleroy 64 F13

KURRAJONG
av. Georges Hall 367 J10
av. Mount Druitt 241 A14
cct. Mt Annan 509 E5
cr. Blacktown 274 E8
rd. Casula 394 E14
rd. Frenchs Frst 256 F1
rd. Greystanes 305 E12
rd. Horngsea Pk 392 F13
rd. Hoxton Pk 392 F10
rd. Kurrajong 64 B16
rd. Lurnea 394 E14
rd. N St Marys 240 A13
rd. Prestons 393 G13
rd. Richmond 117 K1
st. Cabramatta 365 G8
st. Pennant Hills ... 250 K4
st. Sutherland 460 E16

KURRAMATTA
pl. Cronulla 493 G12

KURRARA
st. Lansvale 366 F8

92 GREGORY'S STREET DIRECTORY

STREETS

LA

KURRAWA
av. Coogee 407 H1
KURRAWONG
la. Mosman, off
Warringah La.......317 C3
KURREWA
pl. Kareela 461 C10
KURRI
st. Lane Cove N........284 D15
st. Loftus 489 K11
KURTS
rd. Bilpin 61 G7
KURU
st. N Narrabeen 198 J14
KURUK
pl. Turramurra 252 E5
KURWIN
st. Engadine 488 H10
KUTA
pl. Quakers Hill 213 H9
KUTMUT
st. Glenmore Pk 266 D9
KUTS
av. Newington 310 B13
KUTTABUL
pl. Elanora Ht 198 F12
KUYORA
pl. N Narrabeen 198 G12
KWANI
pl. Narraweena 258 B2
KYALITE
st. Glenwood 245 F1
KYANITE
pl. Eagle Vale 481 G5
KYARRA
tce. Glenmore Pk 266 H12
KYD
pl. Wetherill Pk 334 G3
KYDRA
cl. Prestons 393 B16
cl. Prestons 423 B1
KYEEMA
pde. Belrose 225 H15
pl. Bow Bowing 452 C16
pl. Doonside 243 H16
pl. Picton 561 D2
KYEEMAGH
av. Mascot 404 E12
KYLE
av. Glenhaven 218 D2
pde. Connells Pt 431 J14
pl. Kyle Bay 431 J15
st. Arncliffe 403 H8
KYLEANNE
pl. Dean Park 242 H1
KYLIE
av. Killara 254 B9
cr. W Pnnant Hl 249 B11
pde. Punchbowl 399 K9
pl. Camden S 507 B13
pl. Frenchs Frst 256 F8
pl. Ingleburn 453 D10
wy. Casula 424 F2
KYLIE TENNANT
cl. Glenmore Pk 265 J7
KYMEA
pl. Hebersham 241 E9
KYNASTON
av. Randwick 376 K12
KYNGDON
st. Cammeray 315 H4
KYOGLE
pl. Frenchs Frst 256 F8
pl. Grays Point 491 B14
pl. Hoxton Park 393 A4
rd. Bass Hill 367 K5
rd. Northbridge 285 K14
st. Eastlakes 405 K5
st. Maroubra 407 E12
KYONG
st. Lane Cove N........284 C16
KYRA
pl. Rooty Hill 241 J14
KYRE
cr. Emu Plains 234 K8
KYWONG
av. Castle Hill 218 B1
av. Pymble 253 F2
rd. Berowra 133 B16
st. Elanora Ht 198 D13
st. Telopea 279 F7

L

LA BOHEME
av. Caringbah 492 D11
LABRADOR
st. Rooty Hill 272 C5
LABUAN
rd. Wattle Grove 396 B15
LACEBARK
wy. Castle Hill 248 G2
LACEPEDE
pl. Hinchinbrk 392 K3
LACEY
pl. Blacktown 275 A3
st. Kogarah Bay 432 J11
st. Surry Hills 20 A11
LACHAL
av. Kogarah 433 D6
LACHLAN
av. Harringtn Pk 478 D6
av. Mcquarie Pk 282 E3
av. Sylvania Wtr 462 F10
av. West Pymble 252 H9
dr. Winston Hills 277 A2
dr. Carlingford 279 J7
la. Warwck Frm 365 H16
la. Berowra 133 B15
la. Campbelltown 511 G9
la. Silverdale 354 B10
la. Bossley Park 333 G6
st. Liverpool 365 F16
st. Liverpool 365 D16
st. Revesby 399 A9
st. St Marys 269 C11
st. Warwck Frm 365 F16
st. Warwck Frm 365 D16
st. Waterloo 20 A14
LACK
st. Werrington 238 F10
LACKENWOOD
ct. Galston 159 E9
LACKEY
av. Currans Hill 479 J11
st. Fairfield 336 D14
st. Merrylands 338 B1
st. N Parramatta 278 D9
st. St Peters 374 H12
st. S Granville 338 E1
st. Summer Hill 373 C4
LACKS
pl. Blair Athol 511 A3
LACOCKE
wy. Airds 511 J15
LACROZIA
la. Darlinghurst 4 H13
LACY
pl. Mt Annan 479 H16
LADBROKE
st. Milperra 398 A8
LADBURY
av. Penrith 236 B10
LADY
ct. Stanhpe Gdn 215 D9
st. Mt Colah 191 K5
LADY CARRINGTON
dr. Royal N P..........520 D8
LADY CUTLER
av. Bankstown 369 G15
LADY DAVIDSON
cct. Forestville 255 K6
LADY GAME
dr. Chatswood W 283 J6
dr. Killara 253 B15
dr. Lindfield 283 G1
dr. West Pymble 253 B15
LADY JAMISON
dr. Glenmore Pk 265 F8
LADY PENRHYN
cl. Lurnea 394 B12
dr. Beacon Hill 257 G2
dr. Bligh Park 150 C4
LADY WOODWARD
pl. Miller 393 J3
LAE
pl. Allambie Ht 257 C8
pl. Glenfield 424 H10
pl. Narellan Vale 478 K10
pl. Narellan Vale 479 A10
pl. Whalan 240 K8
st. Holsworthy 426 C3

LAGANA
pl. Wetherill Pk 334 A4
LAGGAN
av. Balmain 344 E4
LAGO
pl. St Clair 269 G15
LAGONDA
av. Killara 254 A9
dr. Ingleburn 453 H12
LAGOON
dr. Blaxland 233 H13
dr. Glenbrook 233 H13
rd. Pitt Town 122 H1
rd. Pitt Twn Bttms 122 G2
st. Narrabeen 229 A4
LAGOON FLATS
pl. Cawdor 506 D16
LAGOON VIEW
rd. Cromer 258 D1
LAGUNA
cl. Glenmore Pk 266 E10
cl. Glen Alpine 510 A14
rd. Bilgola 169 J5
rd. Northbridge 286 F16
st. Caringbah 492 F8
st. Vaucluse 348 E5
LAING
av. Killara 254 A9
pl. West Hoxton 392 A10
LAIRD
st. Mcquarie Lk 423 E13
LAITOKI
rd. Terrey Hills 196 B7
LAKE
cl. Collaroy Plat 228 D11
st. N Parramatta 278 F10
wy. Narellan 478 B9
LAKELAND
cct. Harringtn Pk 478 E8
rd. Cattai 94 A6
LAKEMBA
st. Belmore 371 C15
st. Lakemba 371 A16
st. Wiley Park 400 G2
LAKE PARK
rd. N Narrabeen 199 B15
LAKER
st. Blacktown 274 H6
LAKES
dr. Kellyville Rdg 214 K3
dr. Penrith 206 G16
dr. Thirlmere 564 E3
LAKESIDE
av. Monterey 433 F9
cr. North Manly 288 D3
dr. Minchinbury 272 G9
dr. Mt Hunter 504 B16
rd. Eastwood 281 A6
rd. Narrabeen 228 K7
st. Currans Hill 479 J9
LAKESLAND
rd. Lakesland 561 A6
LAKEVIEW
cl. Baulkham Hl 216 J16
ct. Harringtn Pk 478 E4
pde. Warriewood 199 C10
pl. Glen Alpine 540 D1
LAKEWOOD
cr. Casula 395 K1
dr. Woodcroft 243 F10
tce. Glenmore Pk 266 E13
LALANDA
cl. Cranebrook 207 F5
LALCHERE
st. Curl Curl 258 K12
LALICH
av. Bonnyrigg 364 A9
LALOKI
st. Seven Hills 275 H7
LALOR
cr. Engadine 488 K10
dr. Springwood 202 D11
rd. Quakers Hill 213 K13
st. Cabramatta 365 E11
st. Glenfield 424 F9
LALS
pde. Fairfield E..........337 A16
LA MASCOTTE
av. Concord 342 C6
LAMATTINA
pl. Green Valley 362 J8

LAMB
cl. Wetherill Pk 334 F6
cr. Merrylands 337 K1
st. Lidcombe 507 H1
st. Bellevue Hill 347 F15
st. Glendenning 242 F5
st. Lilyfield 10 F4
st. Marsden Pk 182 A11
st. Oakhurst 242 C5
st. Plumpton 242 C5
LAMBE
pl. Cherrybrook 219 H13
st. West Hoxton 392 A13
LAMBERT
av. Ermington 310 B3
av. Plumpton 242 D8
cr. Baulkham Hl 246 K16
rd. Leumeah 482 C16
rd. Mt Pritchard 364 H11
rd. Bardwell Pk 402 K7
st. Cammeray 316 C15
st. Camperdown 17 E2
st. Cremorne 316 C15
st. Erskineville 18 A15
st. West Ryde 280 G12
st. Yagoona 369 E8
LAMBETH
pl. Illawong 459 G6
rd. Schofields 183 C13
st. Panania 428 B4
st. Picnic Point 428 B8
LAMBIE
pl. Ruse 512 G8
LAMBIE DEW
dr. Camperdown 17 K4
LAMBS
rd. Artarmon 315 C1
LAMERTON
st. Oakhurst 242 A3
LAMETTE
st. Chatswood 285 B7
LAMINGTON
pl. Bow Bowing 452 C13
LAMMING
pl. St Marys 269 K7
LAMOND
cmn.Camden S 537 B1
dr. Turramurra 222 G13
LAMONERIE
st. Toongabbie 276 E10
LAMONT
cl. Kellyville 216 B3
cl. Cartwright 393 K5
dr. S Windsor 150 E2
st. Parramatta 308 D1
st. Wollstncraft 315 F9
LAMORNA
av. Beecroft 249 K10
LAMROCK
av. Bondi Beach 378 A2
av. Glossodia 66 J10
av. Russell Lea 343 D7
pl. Bondi Beach, off
Lamrock Av 378 C4
st. Emu Plains 236 A7
LAMSON
pl. Greenacre 370 C6
LANA
cl. Kings Park 244 G2
LANAI
pl. Beacon Hill 257 H5
LANARK
av. Earlwood 402 H3
ct. Castle Hill 218 D8
st. St Andrews 451 J16
LANCASHIRE
la. Gymea 491 F3
LANCASTER
av. Beecroft 250 A3
av. Cecil Hills 362 F2
av. Melrose Pk 310 J2
av. Punchbowl 399 J4
av. Punchbowl 399 H6
av. St Ives 224 C14
cr. Collaroy 259 B1
cr. Kingsford 406 H5
rd. Marsfield 281 K2
la. Seaforth 286 K16
rd. Dover Ht 348 F9
st. Blacktown 274 A2
st. Ingleburn 453 A5
wy. W Pnnant Hl 248 J4
LANCASTRIAN
rd. Mascot 404 J4

LANCE
av. Blakehurst 432 E14
cr. Greystanes 306 E8
la. Millers Pt..........A B5
LANCELEY
av. Carlingford 249 G15
pl. Abbotsbury 333 C11
pl. Artarmon 315 A3
LANCELOT
ct. Castle Hill 217 F5
st. Allawah 432 F7
st. Bankstown 399 A3
st. Blacktown 274 G8
st. Concord 341 K2
st. Condell Park 398 H3
st. Five Dock 342 H9
st. Mt Colah 162 F13
st. Punchbowl 400 A5
LANCEWOOD
rd. Dural 188 F6
LANCIA
dr. Ingleburn 453 E12
LANDAIS
la. Emu Heights, off
Landais Pl........235 B3
pl. Emu Heights 235 B4
LANDENBURG
pl. Greenwich 314 K11
LANDERS
av. Blacktown 244 F13
la. Darlington 18 H6
la. Darlington 18 G7
st. Leumeah 481 K16
LANDERS
rd. Lane Cove N......284 C16
st. Werrington 239 A12
LANDON
st. Fairfield E..........336 K14
LANDOR
av. Barden Rdg 488 H1
LANDRA
av. Mt Colah 192 D1
LANDS
la. Newtown 17 C9
LANDSCAPE
av. Forestville 256 C10
st. Baulkham Hl 247 F9
LANDSDOWNE
cr. Hornsby Ht 161 K9
rd. Lansdowne 367 D6
LANDY
av. Penrith 237 C3
cl. Edensor Pk 363 E3
cl. Menai 458 E13
pl. Beacon Hill 257 J8
pl. Kellyville 215 H6
rd. Lalor Park 245 D10
st. Matraville 437 C2
LANE
av. Newington 310 A15
gr. Schofields 213 C1
pl. Minto 453 A15
st. Wentwthvle 307 A3
LANE COVE
rd. Ingleside 197 K5
rd. Mcquarie Pk 282 E9
rd. North Ryde 282 E9
rd. Ryde 282 A16
LANE W58
rd. Northbridge 286 A16
LANFORD
av. Killarney Ht 255 H12
LANG
av. Pagewood 406 B9
cr. Blackett 241 A2
cr. Glenmore Pk 265 K8
rd. Casula 394 J14
rd. Centennial Pk 21 D11
rd. Eastwood 373 B14
rd. Kenthurst 155 K4
rd. Moore Park 20 J10
rd. S Windsor 150 G2
st. Croydon 342 F13
st. Mosman 316 J5
st. Padstow 429 B5
st. Smithfield 336 B7
st. Sydney ....A G12
st. Sydney 1 F14
LANGDALE
av. Revesby 399 A13
pl. Collaroy Plat 228 E10

GREGORY'S STREET DIRECTORY 93

LANGDON
av. Campbelltown 511 G2
rd. Baulkham Hl 246 J16
rd. Winston Hills 276 J1
LANGER
av. Caringbah 492 J16
av. Dolans Bay 492 J16
st. Banksia 403 E13
LANGFORD
rd. Dural 188 G4
LANGFORD SMITH
cl. Kellyville 216 K2
LANGHAM
pl. Davidson 225 E15
LANGHOLM
ct. Kellyville 217 B3
LANGLAND
st. Wetherill Pk 334 F6
LANGLANDS
rd. Annangrove 155 J16
LANGLEE
av. Waverley 377 H6
la. Bronte, off Brown St 377 H7
LANGLEY
av. Cremorne 316 G7
av. Glenmore Pk 265 J8
la. Glenmore Pk, off Langley Av 265 J8
pl. Blackett 241 D2
pl. Richmond 117 J7
st. Darlinghurst 4 D11
wy. Rsemeadow 540 J2
LANGMEAD
rd. Silverdale 354 C12
LANGSHAW
cct. Castle Hill 218 K12
pl. Connells Pt 431 J13
LANGSTON
pl. Epping 251 B16
LANGSWORTH
wy. Five Dock 342 K11
LANGTRY
av. Auburn 339 B4
LANHAMS
rd. Wedderburn 541 F15
rd. Winston Hills 277 B2
LANSBURY
st. Edensor Pk 363 F3
LANSDOWNE
cr. Oatley 430 J14
la. Surry Hills 20 A4
pde. Oatley 430 H14
rd. Canley Vale 366 C4
rd. Orchard Hills 268 F9
st. Arncliffe 403 A10
st. Bardwell Vy 403 A10
st. Concord 342 A9
st. Eastwood 281 D6
st. Greenwich 314 K6
st. Merrylands 337 J1
st. Parramatta 307 H6
st. Parramatta 308 B6
st. Penshurst 431 E7
st. Surry Hills 20 A5
LANTANA
av. Collaroy Plat 228 F9
av. Narrabeen 228 F9
dr. Faulconbdg 171 E13
rd. Engadine 488 H14
st. Mcquarie Fd 454 D4
LANYON
ct. Wattle Grove 426 A2
pl. Newport 169 D10
LA PEROUSE
st. Fairlight 288 B8
LAPIS
cr. Bardwell Vy 403 A9
LAPISH
av. Ashfield 372 G3
LAPSTONE
cr. Blaxland 233 G12
pl. Leonay 265 A3
LAPWING
wy. Plumpton 242 A10
LARA
cl. Illawong 459 H4
pl. Frenchs Frst 256 E1
LA RAMBLA
cr. Campbelltown 511 A8
LARAPINTA
cr. St Helens Park 541 H1
cr. St Helens Park 541 H3
pl. Glenhaven 187 D14
LARBERT
av. Wahroonga 222 J8
pl. Prestons 392 J13
LARCHMONT
av. East Killara 254 F9
pl. W Pnnant Hl 249 H9
LARCOM
rd. Beaumont Hills 215 K2
LARCOMBE
st. Regents Pk 369 D1
LARIEN
cr. Birrong 369 A7
cr. Yagoona 369 A7
LARISSA
av. W Pnnant Hl 249 G3
rd. Allambie Ht 257 C9
LARK
pl. Green Valley 363 E11
pl. Greystanes 306 C3
pl. Ingleburn 453 H8
pl. Wallacia 324 K13
st. Belmore 371 G15
LARKARD
st. North Ryde 282 H7
LARKEN
av. Baulkham Hl 247 A14
LARKHALL
av. Earlwood 402 H3
la. Earlwood, off Larkhall Av 402 H3
LARKHILL
av. Riverwood 400 D16
LARKIN
la. Roseville 284 G5
pl. Camden 477 B15
pl. E Kurrajong 66 F6
st. Camperdown 17 H1
st. Riverwood 400 E11
st. Roseville 284 G5
st. Tahmoor 565 J12
st. Waverton 315 E13
LARKSPUR
pl. Heathcote 518 E9
LARKVIEW
av. Chester Hill 337 K14
LARMAR
pl. West Hoxton 391 K12
LARMER
pl. Narraweena 258 D2
LARNACH
pl. Elderslie 477 G15
LARNE
pl. Killarney Ht 255 K14
st. Prestons 423 E2
LARNOCK
av. Pymble 253 J2
LARNOOK
cl. Oatlands 279 B14
LAROOL
av. Lindfield 284 B4
av. Oatley 431 B13
cr. Castle Hill 218 B13
cr. Thornleigh 221 A8
pl. Engadine 489 A12
rd. Terrey Hills 196 A9
LAROSE
av. Matraville 437 A2
LAROW
pl. Bonnyrigg 364 A10
LARRA
cr. North Rocks 248 F12
ct. Wattle Grove 425 J2
pl. Dundas Vy 279 J8
pl. Glen Alpine 510 C16
st. Yennora 337 B9
LARRY
pl. Annangrove 155 F2
LASA
st. Cabramatta 366 C8
LASBURN
cr. Carlingford 279 G2
LASCELLES
av. Greenacre 370 E14
la. Greenacre 370 E14
rd.n,Narraweena 258 A4
rd.s,Narraweena 258 A6
st. Cecil Hills 362 G8
LASSETER
av. Chifley 437 A7
LASSETTER
pl. Ruse 512 F2
LASSWADE
st. Ashbury 372 E8
LATAN
wy. Stanhpe Gdn 215 B10
LATHAM
pl. Canley Vale 366 D6
tce. Newington 310 C11
LATIMER
rd. Bellevue Hill 347 J14
LATINA
cct. Prestons 393 F13
LATONA
av. Vineyard 152 E6
la. Pymble 252 K7
st. Pymble 252 K8
st. Winston Hills 277 B1
LA TROBE
cl. Barden Rdg 488 H1
LATROBE
rd. West Hoxton 392 E8
LATTY
st. Fairfield 336 F15
LATVIA
av. Greenacre 370 D8
LATYNINA
wk. Newington, off Newington Bvd 310 C11
LAUDER
st. Doonside 243 E6
LAUDERDALE
av. Fairlight 288 A9
st. West Hoxton 392 F6
LAUMA
av. Greenacre 370 A9
LAUNCELOT
av. Croydon Pk 371 J7
LAUNDESS
av. Panania 398 B14
LAURA
cl. Bargo 567 C5
pl. St Clair 270 J12
st. Gladesville 313 B3
st. Merrylands 307 E7
st. Newtown 374 G10
st. Seaforth 287 A12
LAURANTUS
swy.Liverpool 395 D3
LAUREL
av. Turramurra 222 H12
ch. Forestville 255 G10
cl. Hornsby 191 H10
cr. Revesby 399 A11
ct. Glenmore Pk 265 H5
gr. Menai 458 K13
pl. Lalor Park 245 B10
pl. Liverpool 394 J9
pl. Mcquarie Fd 454 G1
rd.e, Ingleside 198 C6
rd.w,Ingleside 198 B4
st. Carramar 366 J3
st. N Willoughby 285 D11
st. Willoughby 285 D11
LAUREN
av. Castle Hill 248 C2
pl. Cherrybrook 220 A3
pl. Plumpton 241 G9
LAURENCE
av. Bundeena 523 H9
av. Turramurra 222 K10
rd. Londonderry 149 C13
st. Greystanes 306 D7
st. Hobartville 118 D9
st. Manly 288 D10
st. Pennant Hills 220 D14
st. Sans Souci 433 D15
LAURIE
pl. Belrose 226 E12
rd. Dural 189 J8
rd. Manly Vale 288 B5
LAURIETON
rd. Hoxton Park 392 H10
LAURINA
av. Earlwood 372 H16
av. Engadine 489 B16
av. Fairfield E 337 A15
wy. Glenwood 245 B2
LAURISTON
pl. Glen Alpine 510 F10
pl. St Clair 270 G14
LAVARACK
st. Ryde 282 C12
LAVENDER
av. Bexley 402 D16
av. Kellyville 216 J7
av. Punchbowl 399 H4
cl. Casula 423 J2
cl. Glenmore Pk 265 H9
cr. Lavender Bay K C15
cr. Lavender Bay 5 F12
ct. St Helens Park 541 A8
pl. Alfords Point 459 A1
pl. Blacktown 245 B9
pl. Fairfield W 335 B10
st. Five Dock 342 H11
st. Lavender Bay K C14
st. Lavender Bay 5 F11
st. McMahons Pt K C14
st. McMahons Pt 5 F11
st. Milsons Point K C14
st. Milsons Point 5 F11
st. Narellan 478 F13
LAVER
av. Menai 458 G7
pl. Greystanes 305 K11
st. Shalvey 210 K13
LAVERACK
cr. S Granville 338 G4
LAVIN
cr. Wrrngtn Cty 238 E7
LAVINGTON
av. Chipping Ntn 366 E15
pwy.Chipping Ntn, off Lavington Pwy 366 E14
st. Yagoona 368 J8
LAVINIA
pl. Ambarvale 511 B13
st. Merrylands 338 C2
st. Riverstone 183 B10
st. Seven Hills 275 H9
st. S Granville 338 C2
LA'VISTA
gr. Castle Hill 217 C6
LAVONI
st. Mosman 317 D5
LAW
cr. Tregear 240 C3
st. North Rocks 279 A3
LAWFORD
st. Fairfield W 335 F11
st. Greenacre 370 F4
LAWLER
st. Panania 428 B6
LAWLEY
cr. Pymble 252 J3
st. Bossley Park 334 C7
LAWN
av. Bradbury 511 D9
av. Clemton Park 402 B3
av. Lane Cove W 313 K1
LAWNDALE
av. North Rocks 249 A15
LAWRENCE
cr. Lucas Ht 487 H12
la. Alexandria 18 G16
rd. Blaxlands Rdg 64 K4
rd. Blaxlands Rdg 65 A4
rd. Kenthurst 157 D3
st. Alexandria 18 H16
st. Chatswood 285 C8
st. Fairfield 336 D7
st. Harbord 288 F1
st. Peakhurst 430 C2
st. Seven Hills 275 G8
st. West Ryde 280 G11
LAWRENCE HARGRAVE
rd. Warwck Frm 365 E14
LAWRENCE HARGREAVES
dr. Mascot 404 J11
LAWRY
pl. Shalvey 211 B14
st. Greystanes 306 A9
LAWS
la. Strathfield S 371 C6
LAWSON
av. Camden S 506 K13
av. Marrickville 15 F16
la. Bondi Jctn 22 E9
la. Naremburn 315 E4
la. Paddington 13 D12
pde. St Ives 224 D12
pl. Barden Rdg 488 G1
pl. Castle Hill 218 A9
pl. Cherrybrook 220 B12
pl. Manly 288 F8
rd. Badgerys Ck 329 C16
rd. Ingleburn 423 A9
rd. Springwood 202 C2
sq. Redfern 19 B7
st. Balmain 7 B9
st. Bondi Jctn 22 F9
st. Campbelltown 512 A5
st. Eastwood 280 F9
st. Emu Plains 235 F10
st. Ermington 310 B2
st. Eveleigh 19 A7
st. Fairfield 336 E14
st. Lalor Park 245 B11
st. Matraville 437 B1
st. Paddington 13 B12
st. Panania 398 A13
st. Penrith 236 K10
st. Redfern 19 A7
st. Sans Souci 463 A4
LAWTON
pl. Oakhurst 242 A4
LAYBUTT
rd. Lalor Park 245 F10
LAYCOCK
av. Cronulla 493 K13
pl. Bonnyrigg 364 C6
rd. Hurstville Gr 431 F6
rd. Penshurst 431 F6
st. Bexley North 402 C11
st. Cranebrook 207 A13
st. Mascot 405 B2
st. Neutral Bay 6 D1
LAYDEN
av. Engadine 518 H4
LAYTON
av. Blaxland 233 H7
ct. Harringtn Pk 478 E1
st. Camperdown 17 E2
st. Wentwthvle 276 H16
wy. Beaumont Hills 185 K15
LAZIO
pl. Prestons 393 D15
LEA
av. N Willoughby 285 D11
av. Russell Lea 343 B7
rd. Bringelly 388 B9
st. Croydon 372 C1
st. Quakers Hill 244 A3
LEABONS
la. Seven Hills 275 B4
LEACH
rd. Guildford W 336 H4
LEACOCKS
la. Casula 424 F4
LEADENHAM
pl. Chipping Ntn 366 H16
LEADER
st. Padstow 429 B3
LEAFY
gr. Plumpton 242 C9
LEAGAY
cr. Frenchs Frst 257 B4
LEAH
av. Picnic Point 428 E6
cl. Smithfield 335 F8
LEAL
ct. Pymble 253 J3
LEAMINGTON
av. Newtown 18 B11
la. Newtown 18 B11
rd. Dundas 279 F12
LEANE
pl. Cranebrook 207 G10
LEANNE
pl. Quakers Hill 214 B15
LEAR
cl. St Clair 270 D15
pl. Rsemeadow 540 J7
LEARMONTH
av. Balgowlah 287 K8
st. Haberfield 9 A7
st. Rooty Hill 272 D3
LEAT
pl. Blacktown 244 D15
LEATHERWOOD
ct. Baulkham Hl 247 C16
LEAVESDEN
pl. Sylvania 461 K7
LEAWARRA
st. Engadine 488 G11
LEAWILL
pl. Gladesville 312 J4
LE CLOS
la. Marrickville 374 A12

94 GREGORY'S STREET DIRECTORY

STREETS LI

LEDBURY
pl. Chipping Ntn......396 H2

LEDGER
cl. Casula...............394 G15
pwy.Casula, off
　Ledger Cl..........394 G15
rd. Merrylands.........307 J8

LEE
av. Beverly Hills........401 D14
av. Ryde..................311 K1
cl. Edenscr Pk..........333 H13
la. Sydenham, off
　Yelverton St......374 F15
pl. Illawong..............458 K7
pl. Killarney Ht.........256 D15
pl. St Ives Ch..........224 B1
rd. Beacon Hill.........257 H6
rd. Cherrybrook........220 B15
rd. Winmalee..........173 C11
st. Chippendale.......E C16
st. Chippendale.........3 C16
st. Condell Park........398 F3
st. Emu Plains..........235 J6
st. Haymarket..........E C16
st. Haymarket...........3 D1
st. Randwick...........407 C1
st. Seven Hills..........245 G14

LEE AND CLARK
rd. Kemps Ck..........360 B15

LEEDER
av. Penshurst...........431 G6

LEEDHAM
pl. Riverwood..........400 A10

LEEDS
cl. Castle Hill............217 J9
cl. Turramurra..........222 F16
st. Merrylands.........307 F10
st. Rhodes...............311 E7
st. Stanhpe Gdn......215 D4

LEE HOLM
rd. St Marys............239 E7

LEEMING
st. Mt Krng-gai........163 A12

LEEMON
st. Condell Park........398 E3

LEES
av. Croydon Pk........371 G8
av. Blacktown..........274 J5
cl. Sydney..................3 A4
cl. Sydney..................3 H2
pl. Beaumont Hills...185 K15
pl. Kingsgrove.........401 D8

LEESWOOD
cl. Wattle Grove......425 K4

LEETON
av. Coogee..............377 F14
cr. Panania...............398 E16
st. Merrylands.........306 J10

LEGANA
st. West Hoxton......392 F6

LEGENDRE
pl. Hinchinbrk..........393 A4

LEGGE
st. Roselands...........401 D4

LEGGO
st. Badgerys Ck.......358 F6

LE HANE
plz. Caringbah..........492 K14

LEHMANN
av. Glenmore Pk......265 K4
av. Liverpool............394 H1

LEHN
rd. Leumeah............427 H4

LEICESTER
av. Strathfield..........341 H10
pl. Miller..................393 G3
sq. Blacktown..........274 A3
st. Bexley................432 E1
st. Chester Hill.........368 C1
st. Epping...............250 E14
st. Leumeah............482 E11
st. Marrickville.........374 E10
st. Narellan.............478 K11
st. Wakeley.............364 J1
wy. St Clair..............270 F13

LEICHHARDT
av. Fairfield W..........335 C9
av. Glebe....................11 J7
cr. Sylvania..............462 A12
la. Waverley, off
　Leichhardt St....377 G9
st. Ingleburn............422 J14
st. Bronte................377 H9

st. Chifley.................436 K6
st. Darlinghurst...........4 H12
st. Glebe...................11 J7
st. Horngsea Pk.......392 D14
st. Lalor Park............245 D14
st. Leichhardt............10 B16
st. Ruse..................512 G4
st. Waverley............377 H9

LEIDICH
pl. Kurrajong Ht........63 H12
la. Kurrajong Hl........63 H12

LEIGH
av. Concord.............341 J6
av. Roselands..........400 G10
cr. Claymore............481 D9
pl. Ashcroft..............364 E15
pl. Kings Lngly.........246 B9
pl. Riverwood..........400 F10
pl. S Windsor...........150 J2
pl. W Pnnant Hl........249 D9
st. Merrylands.........307 C16

LEIGHDON
st. Bass Hill..............368 D14

LEIGHTON
pl. Hornsby...............192 B14
st. Rooty Hill............272 F4

LEIHA
pl. Tahmoor.............565 H8

LEILA
st. Berala.................339 G13

LEILANI
cl. Casula................394 F15
st. Kellyville Rdg......215 A5

LEINSTER
av. Killarney Ht.........256 D16
st. Paddington...........21 B3

LEIST
wy. Claymore, off
　Dutterreau Wy...481 E11

LEISURE
cl. Mcquarie Pk.......282 J1

LEITCH
av. Londonderry......149 A14

LEITH
pl. St Andrews.........482 A2
rd. Pennant Hills......220 E16
st. Ashbury.............372 D7
st. Croydon Pk........372 D7

LEITZ
st. Liverpool............395 A1

LELAND
pl. Penrith...............236 F1

LELIA
av. Freemns Rch.......90 D2

LE MAIRE
av. Lethbrdg Pk.......240 D3

LEMAIRES
la. Glenbrook..........233 G15

LE MERTON
pl. Rooty Hill...........271 J2

LEMKO
pl. Penrith...............236 G3

LEMM
st. Birchgrove.............8 A4

LEMNOS
av. Milperra..............397 D12
st. N Strathfield.......341 D7

LEMON
cl. Prairiewood........334 H7
gr. Glenwood..........215 D13
pl. Cherrybrook......219 D10

LEMON GROVE
rd. Penrith...............237 A9

LEMONGROVE
av. Carlingford........249 F16

LEMONGUM
pl. Alfords Point......459 C2
pl. Quakers Hill.......214 A7

LEMON TREE
cl. Frenchs Frst.......256 H1
pl. Minto................482 J4

LEMONWOOD
pl. Castle Hill..........248 F4

LEN
cl. Plumpton...........242 A11

LENA
av. Allambie Ht.......257 C9
pl. Kearns..............451 B16
st. Merrylands.......307 E9
st. Tregear.............240 F4
st. Granville...........308 D12

st. Mt Pritchard......364 E8
st. Sandringham.....463 E5

LENNA
la. Jannali..............460 H14

LENNARTZ
st. Croydon Pk.......371 G7

LENNOX
pl. Barden Rdg......488 G1
st. St Andrews.......481 K1
pl. West Hoxton....392 A12
pl. Wetherill Pk......305 C16
st. Banksia............403 G14
st. Bellevue Hill......347 G16
st. Colyton............270 F6
st. Glenbrook.........233 J16
st. Gordon.............253 K5
st. Mosman...........317 A12
st. Newtown.............17 E11
st. Normanhurst....221 D8
st. Northmead........277 K5
st. Old Tngabbie...276 H11
st. Parramatta.......308 B6
st. Richmond.........118 H6
st. Rockdale..........403 G14

LENNOX BRIDGE
　Glenbrook............234 E11

LENORE
la. Erskine Park......300 C4
pl. Lidcombe..........340 B6
st. Russell Lea........343 G6

LENTARA
st. Georges Hall......367 F13
av. Bayview...........168 G12

LENTHALL
st. Kensington........376 B13

LENTHEN
la. Botany.............405 H15

LENTON
av. Fairfield W........335 C12
cr. Oakhurst..........241 K4
pde. Waterloo..........19 F12
pl. North Rocks......248 E16

LEO
av. Lurnea.............394 C9
cr. Greystanes.......306 G6
pl. Erskine Park......300 G2
pl. Hebersham......241 J3
pl. Telopea...........279 F7
rd. Pennant Hills....220 D16
st. Hunters Hill......313 A7
st. Mt Pritchard....364 F8

LEOFRENE
av. Marrickville......373 K14

LEON
av. Georges Hall......367 G10
av. Roselands..........400 G8
pl. Ingleburn..........453 J9

LEONARD
av. Greystanes........306 G6
av. Kingsford.........406 D2
cr. Earlwood..........403 B1
la. Colyton, off
　Leonard Pl....270 D6
pl. Bonnyrigg.........363 K8
pl. Colyton............270 D5
pl. Marsfield..........282 B5
st. Bankstown.......399 F3
st. Blacktown........244 A12
st. Colyton...........270 C5
st. Hornsby..........221 A7
st. Thirlmere........565 A7
st. Waitara..........221 H3
st. Waitara..........221 J3

LEONARDS
wy. Beaumont Hills..185 K16

LEONAY
pde. Leonay..........235 A16
st. Sutherland......460 C16

LEONE
av. Baulkham Hl....247 B1

LEONELLO
pl. Edensor Pk.....333 H14

LEONG
pl. Baulkham Hl....247 E8

LEONIE
cr. Berala............339 B14
pl. Hassall Gr......212 B15

LEONORA
av. Kingsford.......406 J6
st. St Ives...........224 J2
st. Hornsby Ht....161 K12
st. Earlwood.......402 F5

LEONTES
cl. Rsemeadow....540 J8

LEOPARDWOOD
pl. Mcquarie Fd....454 F1

LEOPOLD
pl. Cecil Hills........362 G5
st. Ashbury.........372 E7
st. Croydon Pk....372 E7
st. Merrylands....307 J9
st. Rooty Hill......241 J14

LEPP
la. Leppington.....420 H10

LERIDA
av. Camden........507 B3

LERWICK
st. St Andrews....452 A14

LES BURNETT
la. Harris Park.....308 E7

LESLEY
av. Carlingford.....279 D2
av. Revesby........428 H2
cl. Elanora Ht......198 F13
cr. Mortdale.......430 K4

LESLIE
cr. Wrrngtn Cty...238 F6
rd. Bexley..........432 C1
rd. Glenbrook.....234 C16
st. Bass Hill........368 B11
st. Blacktown.....274 A5
st. North Ryde...282 D6
st. Roselands....401 C6
st. Tempe.........374 C16
st. Winmalee.....173 F6
wk. Narrabeen...228 G8

LESNIE
av. Matraville.....436 K8

LES SHORE
pl. Castle Hill....218 C13

LESSING
st. Emerton......240 H7
st. Hornsby.....191 K13

LESTER
pl. Abbotsford..342 K3
rd. Greystanes.306 D8
rd. Revesby.....399 A13
st. Lurnea......394 F6

LESWELL
la. Woollahra......22 E4
st. Bondi Jctn....22 E4
st. Bondi Jctn....22 E4
wy. Newington..310 C13

LETHBRIDGE
st. Werrington..238 J11
st. Penrith......237 A12
st. St Marys....239 J15

LETI
pl. Marayong...244 B4

LETITIA
st. Oatley........431 B15
st. Oatley........431 C12

LETTER BOX
la. Illawong......460 C2

LEUMEAH
av. Baulkham Hl...246 A6
cl. W Pnnant Hl...220 A16
rd. Leumeah.....482 D13
st. Cronulla.....493 K16

LEUNA
av. Wahroonga...251 K3

LEURA
cl. Bossley Park...333 E13
cr. N Turramurra..193 F13
pl. Prospect.......275 C11
rd. Auburn........338 K3
rd. Double Bay....14 E10

LEVEL CROSSING
rd. Vineyard......151 J9

LEVEN
st. Northmead...278 C5
st. St Andrews..481 K1

LEVENDALE
st. West Hoxton...392 D7

LEVER
st. Rosebery.....405 F2

LEVERTON
st. St Ives.......224 E14

LE VESINET
dr. Hunters Hill..314 A14

LEVETT
av. Beverly Hills..401 A14

LEVEY
st. Chippendale....19 A3
st. Wolli Creek....403 K7
st. Wolli Creek....404 A7

LEVICK
rd. Greystanes...306 F9
st. Cremorne.....316 F6

LEVUKA
st. Cabramatta...366 A8

LEVY
av. Matraville.....436 H8
cl. Hamondvle...426 G1
st. Glenbrook.....233 J14
st. Pendle Hill....306 F1
st. Putney..........312 B7
wk. Zetland.......376 A10

LEWERS
st. Abbotsbury...333 A14

LEWIN
cr. Bradbury.....511 H13
cr. Chipping Ntn..396 E5
st. Blaxland.......234 A5
st. Springwood...201 E2

LEWINS
av. Rhodes........311 C11
cl. Warriewood...198 J6
ct. Castle Hill....248 C4
la. Cmbrdg Gdn, off
　Lewis Rd.....237 G5
la. N Strathfield...341 F6
la. Tahmoor.....565 K12
pl. Bonnyrigg Ht.363 C5
pl. Panania......428 C4
rd. Cmbrdg Gdn...237 F5
rd. Liverpool.....395 A1
st. Appin.........569 E10
st. Avalon........140 C13
st. Balgowlah Ht..287 G13
st. Bexley........402 G16
st. Bradbury.....511 E8
st. Cronulla......493 K14
st. Dee Why......258 E5
st. Epping........280 G1
st. Lapstone......264 G5
st. Merrylands...307 B7
st. Regents Pk...369 E3
st. Schofields...183 C15
st. Silverdale.....353 G12
st. S Wntwthvle..307 B7
wy. Newington.310 C13

LEWISHAM
st. Dulwich Hill..373 E9

LEXCEN
pl. Marsfield.....282 B4

LEXIA
cl. Mona Vale....199 A5

LEXINGTON
av. Eastwood....280 F6
dr. St Clair.......270 H13
dr. Bella Vista....216 A15
dr. Bella Vista....246 B11
la. St Clair, off
　Lexington Av...270 H14
pl. Maroubra.....407 D13

LEYBURN
st. Stanhpe Gdn...215 E7

LEYLAND
gr. Zetland........375 K10
pl. Ingleburn....453 G11

LEYLANDS
pde. Belmore....401 D2
pde. Lakemba....401 D2

LEYS
av. Lilyfield..........10 E11

LEYSDOWN
av. North Rocks...249 B15

LEYTE
av. Lethbrdg Pk...240 D2

LIBERA
av. Padstow......399 D13

LIBERATOR
st. Raby..........451 C15
st. St Clair.......270 E14

LIBERATOR GENERAL SAN MARTIN
dr. Krngai Ch N P..167 A9

LIBERTY
rd. Huntingwd...273 D11
st. Belmore.....401 G3
st. Enmore........16 K13
st. Enmore........17 A12
wy. Kellyville....185 F6
wy. Old Tngabbie..277 C6

GREGORY'S STREET DIRECTORY 95

LI STREETS

LIBRA
pl. Erskine Park 300 K2

LIBRARY
pl. Lane Cove, off Longueville Rd 314 D2
rd. Camperdown 18 E3

LIBYA
cr. Allambie Ht 257 F11
pl. Marsfield 252 B13

LICHEN
pl. Westmead 307 J3

LIDBURY
st. Berala 339 B12

LIDCO
st. Arndell Park 273 F9

LIDDLE
st. N St Marys 239 J8

LIDELL
pl. Bonnyrigg Ht 363 B7

LIDO
av. N Narrabeen 228 J1

LIDWINA
pl. Cromer 228 A16

LIEGE
st. Russell Lea 343 E5

LIEUTENANT BOWEN
dr. Bowen Mtn 83 K13
rd. Bowen Mtn 83 K10

LIFFEY
pl. Woronora 460 B15

LIGAR
st. Fairfield Ht 335 H11

LIGATO
pl. Liverpool 364 J16

LIGHT BODY
wy. Narellan Vale 508 G1

LIGHTCLIFF
av. Lindfield 254 F15

LIGHT HORSE
pde. Holsworthy 426 E4

LIGHTNING
st. Raby 481 G3

LIGHTNING RIDGE
rd. Hinchinbrk 392 H3

LIGHTWOOD
st. Ambarvale 510 G15
wy. Beaumont Hills ..185 K16

LIGNITE
pl. Eagle Vale 481 E9

LIGUORI
wy. Pennant Hills 250 H2

LIGURIA
st. Maroubra 407 H7
st. S Coogee 407 H7

LIHON
st. Lane Cove W 313 G3

LILAC
pl. Eastwood 281 G7
pl. Jamisontown 266 B4
pl. Quakers Hill 213 K10
pl. Loftus 490 A12
pl. Punchbowl 400 D1

LILIAN
la. Campsie 371 H14
st. Campbelltown 511 H5
st. Campsie 371 J13

LILIAN FOWLER
pl. Marrickville 374 D12

LILLA
pl. Quakers Hill 214 D12
rd. Pennant Hills 250 E2

LILLAS
pl. Minto 482 J1

LILLE
pl. Milperra 397 H11

LILLEY
st. St Clair 269 G14

LILLIAN
cr. Revesby 398 H14
pl. Annangrove 155 C1
st. Riverwood 399 J15
st. Berala 339 F13

LILLIE
st. N Curl Curl 258 H11

LILLIHINA
av. Cromer 258 B1

LILLI PILLI
av. Beverley Pk 433 B8
cl. Peakhurst 430 E4
st. Epping 250 G15

LILLI PILLI POINT
rd. Lilli Pilli 522 E4

LILLIS
st. Cammeray 315 K7

LILLY PILLY
ct. Beaumont Hills, off Lilly Pilly Pl 185 J14
st. Beaumont Hills ..185 J14

LILLYVICKS
cr. Ambarvale 510 J13

LILY
av. Riverwood 399 K10
av. Warriewood 198 J9
ct. Glenmore Pk 265 H9
ct. Narellan Vale 479 A15
la. Allawah 432 D5
la. Warriewood 198 J9
pl. Lalor Park 245 H13
st. Auburn 339 B4
st. Burwood Ht 371 K4
st. Croydon Pk 371 K4
st. Hurstville 432 D5
st. North Ryde 282 D8
st. Wetherill Pk 334 G6

LILYDALE
av. Peakhurst 430 E5
st. Marrickville 373 J11

LILYFIELD
cl. Catherine Fd 449 F2
rd. Lilyfield 9 F6
rd. Rozelle 11 A3

LILYVALE
cl. Bella Vista 246 D6

LIMA
cl. Clarmnt Ms 268 J1
la. Clarmnt Ms, off Lima Cl 268 J2
pl. Erskine Park 270 H15
st. Greenacre 370 G14

LIME
gr. Carlingford 279 F4
st. Cabramatta W 364 J7
st. Quakers Hill 243 E3
st. Sydney ....C A1
st. Sydney 3 C1

LIME KILN
rd. Lugarno 430 A16

LIMONITE
pl. Eagle Vale 481 D7

LIMPOPO
cr. Seven Hills 275 F9

LINARA
cct. Glenmore Pk 265 J11

LINCLUDEN
pl. Airds 512 C10
rd. Oatlands 278 J10

LINCOLN
av. Castlecrag 285 K10
av. Collaroy 229 A16
av. Riverstone 183 C10
cl. Asquith 191 K7
cr. Bonnet Bay 460 F9
cr. Sydney 4 F1
cr. Woolmloo 4 F1
dr. Cmbrdg Pk 237 J9
gr. Harringtn Pk 478 G7
la. Cmbrdg Pk, off Lincoln Dr 238 A9
la. Stanmore 16 K9
pl. Castle Hill 218 B16
pl. Edgecliff 14 A13
pl. Cecil Park 331 H7
rd. Georges Hall 368 C15
rd. Horsley Pk 331 K6
st. St Ives 224 A10
st. Belfield 371 G12
st. Campsie 371 G13
st. Dulwich Hill 373 G10
st. Eastwood 281 G3
st. Lane Cove W 313 F1
st. Miller 393 F4
st. Minto 482 E2
st. Stanmore 16 J9
tce. Marsden Pk 182 B14

LIND
av. Oatlands 279 A9
st. Minto 482 J4

LINDA
av. Bass Hill 367 E6
av. Oatley 430 K8
av. Merrylands 308 A15
st. Belfield 371 C10
st. Fairfield Ht 335 G12
st. Hornsby 191 H16
st. Seven Hills 246 A13

LINDE
rd. Glendenning 242 H4

LINDEL
pl. Lindfield 284 B11

LINDEMAN
cr. Green Valley 363 A13

LINDEN
av. Belrose 225 K5
av. Punchbowl 400 A5
av. Pymble 252 K2
av. Woollahra 22 F1
cl. Pymble 253 A3
cr. Cranebrook 207 D7
cr. Lugarno 429 J12
dr. Freemns Rch 89 H4
gr. Ermington 310 F1
la. Surry Hills 4 D14
pl. Seven Hills 245 H14
st. Mascot 405 G4
st. Mount Druitt 241 B15
st. Sutherland 460 D15
st. Sutherland 490 D4
st. Toongabbie 276 C8
wy. Bella Vista 246 E1
wy. Castlecrag 286 F11

LINDESAY
st. Campbelltown 511 E6
st. Leumeah 511 K3

LINDFIELD
av. Concord 342 C6
av. Killara 254 C14
av. Lindfield 254 C14
av. Winmalee 173 E4
pl. Dean Park 212 F16

LINDISFARNE
cr. Carlingford 279 C13

LINDLEY
av. Mcquarie Fd 424 B15
av. Narrabeen 228 J8
sq. Bidwill 211 E15

LINDRIDGE
pl. Colyton 270 A7
st. S Penrith 267 A7

LINDRUM
st. Belrose 226 E14

LINDSAY
av. Darling Point 14 A1
av. Ermington 310 B5
av. Smithfield 335 C5
av. Summer Hill 373 B5
cr. Pymble 223 E15
st. S Penrith 267 A6
la. Darlinghurst 4 K11
la. Mosman 316 H8
la. Doonside 243 D11
la. Glossodia 66 B11
la. Mt Pritchard 364 J11
la. Richmond 118 D5
rd. Faulconbdg 171 J11
st. Baulkham Hl 247 F11
st. Burwood 371 H2
st. Campsie 372 C10
st. Caringbah 492 F12
st. Casula 424 F4
st. Neutral Bay 6 D3
st. Panania 398 C14
st. Philip Bay 436 K11
st. Rockdale 433 F2
st. Wentwthvle 277 A14

LINDSAY GORDON
pl. Heathcote 518 D15

LINDSELL
pl. Tahmoor 565 G12

LINDSEY
pl. Eldersle 507 J1

LINDUM
st. St Johns Pk 334 F16
st. Kurnell 465 B16

LINDWALL
ct. Menai 458 F9
ct. St Clair 269 K15
la. St Clair, off Lindwall Ct 269 K15
pl. Rouse Hill 184 K7
st. Shalvey 211 A15

LINEATA
pl. Glenmore Pk 265 H13

LINEY
av. Clemton Park 401 K4

LINFORD
pl. Beaumont Hills ..216 A2

LINGARD
st. Randwick 377 B13

LINGAYEN
av. Lethbrdg Pk 240 E2

LINGELLEN
st. Berowra Ht 133 A7

LINIFOLIA
mw. Wattle Grove 396 B16

LINIGEN
pl. St Ives 224 G6

LINK
act. Menai 459 A10
rd. Bnkstn Aprt 367 F15
rd. Hornsby 191 G9
rd. Mascot 404 D5
rd. St Ives 224 B11
rd. Zetland 376 A12
st. Manly Vale 287 J4

LINKMEAD
av. Clontarf 287 E11

LINKS
av. Cabramatta 365 C10
av. Concord 341 G4
av. Cronulla 494 B7
av. Milperra 397 C10
av. Roseville 285 C1
la. Concord 341 G4
st. St Marys 239 E2
wy. Narellan 478 B10

LINKSLEY
av. Glenhaven 217 J5

LINKSVIEW
av. Leonay 235 B15
pl. Comleroy 64 F12
rd. Springwood 172 C12

LINLEY
av. Girraween 276 B15

LINLEY
cl. Carlingford 279 B4
la. Linley Point, off Burns Bay Rd 313 G6
pl. Cecil Hills 362 G9
pl. Linley Point 313 G8
wy. Ryde 312 A4

LINN
st. Campbelltown 511 A8

LINNE
pl. Hinchinbrk 392 K1

LINNET
pl. Quakers Hill 214 D12
st. Winmalee 173 J6

LINSLEY
st. Gladesville 312 H10

LINTHORN
av. Croydon Pk 371 G8

LINTHORNE
st. Guildford 338 A3

LINTHORPE
la. Newtown 17 H12
st. Newtown 17 J12

LINTINA
av. Tahmoor 565 K13

LINTON
av. Revesby 398 J14
av. West Ryde 281 G16
la. West Ryde 281 G16
rd. Currans Hill 479 H8
st. Baulkham Hl 248 B13
st. Stanhpe Gdn ..215 B6

LINUM
pl. Mt Annan 509 F3
st. Mcquarie Fd 454 E6

LINWOOD
av. Bexley 403 A14
st. Guildford W 336 J4

LION
la. Randwick, off Oberon St 407 B2
st. Croydon 372 E3
st. Randwick 407 B2

LIONEL
av. North Ryde 283 A12
st. Georges Hall 367 D14
st. Ingleburn 453 D7

LIONS
av. Lurnea 394 E7

LIPARI
pl. Acacia Gdn 214 H15

LIPSIA
pl. Carlingford 279 E2

LIPSOM
av. Bondi Jctn, off James St 377 G5

LIQUIDAMBER
dr. Narellan Vale 478 K12

LISA
cl. Narellan 478 H12
cl. Westleigh 220 E7
cr. Castle Hill 217 G10
pl. Bilgola 169 F3
pl. Leonay 234 K14
st. Quakers Hill 214 C16

LISA VALLEY
cl. Wahroonga 221 F15

LISBON
ct. Castle Hill 247 H3
rd. Kenthurst 157 H14
st. Fairfield E 337 B12
st. Mount Druitt ..241 C12
st. Sylvania 461 J10

LISGAR
av. Baulkham Hl 247 C6
la. Hornsby 221 D1
rd. Hornsby 221 D1
st. Merrylands 338 C1
st. S Granville 338 C1

LISLE
ct. W Pnnant Hl 249 G9
st. Narrabeen 229 B1

LISMORE
av. Dee Why 258 H3
cl. Bossley Park 333 D13
st. Blacktown 274 J2
st. Eastlakes 406 A4
st. Hoxton Park 392 K7
st. Pendle Hill 276 D13

LISSANTHE
st. Mt Annan 509 F6

LISSON
pl. Minto 452 K14

LISTER
av. Cabramatta W 365 B7
av. Ermington 310 A3
av. Little Bay 437 G14
av. Rockdale 403 D16
av. Seaforth 287 A5
pl. Rooty Hill 241 J14
st. N Wahroonga 222 H2
st. Winston Hills 277 E5

LISZT
pl. Cranebrook 207 G8

LITCHFIELD
pl. St Helens Park 541 D4

LITERATURE
pl. Blackett 241 C2

LITHGOW
av. Yagoona 369 E9
st. Campbelltown 511 F5
st. Russell Lea 343 E6
st. St Leonards 315 D6
st. Wollstncraft 315 D6

LITORIA
pl. Glenmore Pk 265 H13

LITTIMER
wy. Ambarvale 510 K16

LITTLE
la. Lane Cove 314 E2
rd. Bankstown 369 A16
rd. Yagoona 369 A16
st. Austral 390 F11
st. Balmain 7 F10
st. Cmbrdg Pk 238 B7
st. Camden 506 K3
st. Dee Why 258 G6
st. Dulwich Hill 373 E7
st. Granville 308 C11
st. Lane Cove 314 E2
st. Marayong 244 A9
st. Maroubra 407 F11
st. Mosman 317 C5
st. Parramatta 308 E4
st. Smithfield 335 K3
st. Yellow Rock 174 H16

LITTLE ADA
st. Canley Vale 366 E3

LITTLE ALBION
st. Surry Hills ....F E13
st. Surry Hills 3 K14

LITTLE ALFRED
st. N Sydney 5 K10

LITTLE ARTHUR
st. Balmain 7 C8

LITTLE BAY
rd. Chifley 437 A9
rd. Little Bay 437 A9

LITTLE BEATTIE
st. Balmain 7 D10

LITTLE BLOOMFIELD
st. Surry Hills 4 C14

96 GREGORY'S STREET DIRECTORY

STREETS

LO

LITTLE BOURKE
st. Surry Hills......4 D14
LITTLEBOY
st. Kings Lngly......245 A5
LITTLE BRIGHTON
st. Petersham......15 G9
LITTLE BUCKINGHAM
st. Surry Hills......19 H5
LITTLE BURTON
st. Darlinghurst......F K5
LITTLE BYRNE
st. Camden......506 K3
LITTLE CHAPEL
st. St Marys......239 H15
LITTLE CHURCH
st. Ryde......311 K3
st. Windsor......121 B9
LITTLE CLEVELAND
st. Redfern......20 C7
LITTLE COLLINS
st. Surry Hills......20 A2
LITTLE COMBER
st. Paddington......4 G14
LITTLE COMMODORE
st. Newtown, off Pearl St......374 H10
LITTLE CORMISTON
av. Concord......341 K5
LITTLE DARLING
st. Balmain......7 E8
LITTLE DOWLING
st. Paddington......4 F16
LITTLE EDWARD
st. Balmain East......8 H10
st. Pyrmont......12 J4
LITTLE EVELEIGH
st. Eveleigh......18 K7
st. Eveleigh......19 A7
st. Redfern......19 A7
LITTLEFIELDS
rd. Luddenham......325 J1
rd. Mulgoa......295 D16
LITTLE FOREST
rd. Lucas Ht......487 D9
LITTLE HAY
st. Haymarket......E D6
st. Haymarket......3 E11
LITTLE HUNTER
st. Sydney......A J14
LITTLE JANE
st. Penrith......236 H9
LITTLE LLEWELLYN
st. Balmain......7 E9
LITTLE MONTAGUE
st. Balmain......7 E10
LITTLE MORT
st. Randwick......376 K10
LITTLE MOUNT
st. Pyrmont......12 G4
LITTLE NAPIER
st. Paddington......4 F15
LITTLE NICHOLSON
st. Balmain East......8 F9
LITTLE NORTON
la. Surry Hills......F H16
st. Surry Hills......F H16
st. Surry Hills......4 B16
LITTLE OXFORD
st. Darlinghurst......4 C12
LITTLE PIER
st. Haymarket......E A4
st. Haymarket......3 D10
LITTLE QUEEN
st. Chippendale......E C16
st. Newtown......18 B7
LITTLE QUEENS
la. Vaucluse......348 B5
LITTLE REGENT
st. Chippendale......E C16
st. Chippendale......3 D16
LITTLE RILEY
st. Surry Hills......F G13
st. Surry Hills......F G16
st. Surry Hills......4 A14
st. Surry Hills......20 A3
LITTLE SELWYN
st. Paddington......4 F16
LITTLE SMITH
st. Surry Hills......F F11

LITTLE SPRING
st. N Sydney......K F6
st. N Sydney......5 G7
st. Sydney......B A12
LITTLE STEPHEN
st. Balmain......7 H10
LITTLE STEWART
st. Paddington......21 B2
LITTLE SURREY
st. Darlinghurst......4 H10
LITTLE TARONGA
wy. Faulconbdg......171 B13
LITTLE THEODORE
st. Balmain......7 D9
LITTLETON
st. Riverwood......400 C15
LITTLE TURRIELL BAY
rd. Lilli Pilli......522 H2
rd. Port Hacking......522 H2
LITTLE WALKER
st. N Sydney......K H10
st. N Sydney......5 H9
LITTLE WEST
st. Darlinghurst......4 J10
LITTLE WILLANDRA
rd. Cromer......228 A16
LITTLE WONGA
rd. Cremorne......316 F5
LITTLE WYNDHAM
st. Alexandria......19 A11
LITTLE YOUNG
st. Cremorne......316 E5
st. Redfern......19 J7
LITTON
st. Emu Heights......235 A4
LIVERPOOL
la. Darlinghurst......F K3
la. Darlinghurst......4 C10
rd. Ashfield......372 C2
rd. Burwood Ht......372 C2
rd. Cabramatta......366 E8
rd. Canley Vale......366 E8
rd. Croydon......372 C2
rd. Enfield......371 K3
rd. Strathfield......371 A4
rd. Strathfield S......371 A3
rd. Summer Hill......373 B3
st. Bundeena......523 H10
st. Cabramatta......365 K10
st. Darlinghurst......F C3
st. Darlinghurst......4 C10
st. Dover Ht......348 C12
st. Ingleburn......453 A6
st. Liverpool......394 G10
st. Lurnea......394 G10
st. Paddington......4 J13
st. Pitt Town......92 H14
st. Rose Bay......348 C12
st. Sydney......E D1
st. Sydney......3 F9
LIVINGSTONE
av. Dharruk......241 C6
av. Windsor......121 G6
LIVINGSTONE
av. Baulkham Hl......247 J14
av. Botany......405 G15
av. Ingleburn......453 C12
av. Pymble......253 A8
la. Botany, off Livingstone Av......405 G13
la. Burwood, off Livingstone St......341 K15
pl. Mt Colah......162 D12
pl. Newport......169 G12
rd. Lidcombe......339 F8
st. Marrickville......15 H16
st. Marrickville......373 G13
st. Petersham......15 H16
st. Burwood......341 K15
st. McGraths Hl......122 C13
wy. Thornleigh......220 K10
LIVISTONA
la. Palm Beach......139 K1
LIVORNO
gr. Glenwood......246 A4
LIZARD
cl. Green Valley......363 A12
LIZZIE WEBBER
dr. Birchgrove......7 K4
LLANBERIS
dr. Menai......459 A4
LLANDAFF
st. Bondi Jctn......22 K8
st. Bondi Jctn......377 F4

LLANDILO
av. Strathfield......341 E16
rd. Berkshire Pk......179 H5
rd. Llandilo......179 A16
LLANFOYST
st. Randwick......377 B14
LLANGOLLAN
av. Enfield......371 J5
LLANKELLY
pl. Potts Point......4 K6
LLEWELLYN
av. Villawood......367 E1
la. Lindfield, off Llewellyn St......284 E2
st. Marrickville......374 F9
st. Balmain......7 D9
st. Lindfield......284 D2
st. Marrickville......374 F9
st. Oatley......431 A15
st. Rhodes......311 E8
LLOYD
av. Cremorne......316 F4
av. Hunters Hill......313 K11
av. Yagoona......369 E9
pl. Casula......424 C4
pl. Bexley......402 H11
pl. Blacktown......230 G12
pl. Greystanes......306 D6
pl. Oatley......430 G12
pl. Sans Souci......433 B13
st. Alexandria......19 A11
LLOYD GEORGE
av. Baulkham Hl......247 J16
av. Concord......341 H9
LLOYD REES
dr. Lane Cove W......313 F1
LLOYDS
av. Carlingford......279 J4
wy. Bargo......567 A4
LOADER
av. Beverly Hills......401 A16
LOBB
cr. Beverley Pk......433 A9
LOBELIA
cr. Quakers Hill......243 F4
pl. Gymea......491 C6
pl. Chatswood W......283 J11
st. Mcquarie Fd......454 B6
LOBLAY
pl. Bilgola......169 F4
LOCH
av. Centennial Pk......21 J12
la. Campsie......371 J14
la. Campsie......371 H13
st. Harbord......258 J15
LOCHALSH
st. St Andrews......451 K12
LOCH AWE
dr. Carlingford......250 A15
LOCHBURIE
wy. Mcquarie Lk......423 E13
LOCHEE
av. Minto......452 G16
LOCH ETIVE
pl. Narraweena......258 A4
LOCHIEL
pl. Georges Hall......367 H14
rd. Engadine......488 H12
LOCHINVAR
pde. Carlingford......249 H14
rd. Revesby......428 G4
st. Winmalee......173 C12
LOCHINVER
pl. St Andrews......452 B15
LOCH LOMOND
cr. Burraneer......523 D4
LOCH MAREE
av. Thornleigh......221 B12
pl. Connells Pt......431 H16
pde. Kingsford......407 C4
pl. Vaucluse......348 B2
st. Ringwood......407 B8
st. Maroubra......407 B8
LOCH NESS
pl. Hornsby......221 A1
LOCHNESS
cr. Engadine......488 J12
LOCHTON
pl. Beaumont Hills......215 G2
LOCHVIEW
cr. Mt Annan......479 E14
LOCHVILLE
st. Wahroonga......222 C4
st. Wahroonga......222 E4

LOCK
av. Padstow......399 F16
la. Forest Lodge......11 H16
rd. Wilberforce......67 B16
st. Blacktown......274 J6
st. Girraween......276 B15
st. Ryde......282 J15
LOCKE
st. Wetherill Pk......334 F4
LOCKER
av. Lurnea......394 C9
LOCKERBIE
rd. Thornleigh......221 C8
LOCKHART
av. Balmain, off Elliott St......344 E4
av. Castle Hill......217 K10
ct. Harringtn Pk......478 E4
pl. Berowra......226 A9
LOCKHEED
cct. St Clair......270 E16
st. Raby......481 G3
LOCKINVAR
pl. Hornsby......191 C16
LOCKLEY
pde. Roseville Ch......285 G13
LOCKSLEY
av. Merrylands......307 J14
cl. Wahroonga......221 K11
pl. Bexley......432 D2
st. Killara......254 B12
st. Woolooware......493 H7
LOCKUNDY
la. Hurstville......431 G1
LOCKWOOD
av. Frenchs Frst......255 H1
av. Greenacre......370 C5
gr. Bidwill......211 B16
st. Asquith......191 K12
st. Merrylands......307 F11
LODDON
cl. Bossley Park......333 G5
cr. Campbelltown......511 J8
LODER
cr. S Windsor......150 F2
la. Punchbowl......400 A4
pl. Glen Alpine......510 B15
LODESTONE
pl. Eagle Vale......481 H6
LODGE
av. Old Tngabbie......277 C7
la. Harbord......258 J16
la. Mosman, off Rangers Av......316 G9
pl. Chester Hill......368 A4
pl. Wetherill Pk......335 A5
rd. Cremorne......316 G3
st. Balgowlah......287 J6
st. Forest Lodge......12 A15
st. Glebe......12 A15
st. Hornsby......191 J10
LODGES
rd. Elderslie......478 A16
rd. Narellan......478 D15
LODGEWORTH
pl. Castle Hill......216 K8
LODI
cl. West Hoxton......392 D5
LODORE
pl. Northmead......278 B6
LOFBERG
rd. West Pymble......253 A10
LOFT
pl. Kellyville Rdg......215 D2
LOFTS
av. Roselands......401 D5
LOFTUS
av. Loftus......489 J13
av. Sutherland......490 B8
cr. Homebush......341 A8
la. Sydney......B D10
la. Bringelly......388 C14
rd. Darling Point......13 G7
rd. Mcquarie Fd......454 C7
rd. Pennant Hills......250 C1
st. Yennora......337 A8
st. Ashfield......373 A1
st. Bundeena......524 A9

st. Campsie......371 H13
st. Campsie......371 H14
st. Concord......342 B10
st. Dulwich Hill......373 E10
st. Fairfield E......337 A14
st. Glenfield......424 H13
st. Leichhardt......9 B15
st. Marsden Pk......181 J13
st. Merrylands......308 A13
st. Narrabeen......229 B2
st. Regentville......265 F4
st. Riverstone......182 H2
st. Sydney......B C11
st. Sydney......1 J13
st. Turrella......403 E5
LOFTY
cr. Bossley Park......334 B9
pl. Cranebrook......207 F9
pl. Ruse......512 F6
LOGAN
av. Haberfield......373 D1
st. Loftus......490 A11
LOGANS
pl. Quakers Hill......214 D8
LOGIE
rd. Kenthurst......186 K11
LOIRE
pl. Kearns......451 A14
pl. St Clair......270 J10
LOIS
cr. Jamisontown......266 B2
la. Minto......452 F16
la. Pennant Hills......220 C15
pl. Merrylands......307 E11
st. Baulkham Hl......278 A1
LOLA
pl. Miranda......461 K16
rd. Dover Ht......348 G14
LOLITA
av. Forestville......255 E9
LOLOMA
pl. Rooty Hill......241 K13
st. Cabramatta......366 B8
LOMANDRA
cct. Castle Hill......217 D6
cr. Mt Annan......509 C2
ct. Voyager Pt......427 D6
pl. Alfords Point......429 A15
pl. S Coogee......407 E5
LOMANI
st. Busby......363 G16
LOMATIA
la. Springwood......201 K1
LOMAX
st. Epping......280 E4
LOMBARD
la. Glebe......12 A11
pl. Bella Vista......246 H2
pl. Prospect......275 C12
st. Balgowlah......287 H7
st. Fairfield......335 G13
st. Fairfield W......335 G13
st. Glebe......12 B11
st. Northmead......277 J7
LOMBARDO
st. Prestons......393 D13
LOMOND
cr. Winston Hills......277 C4
cr. Wattle Grove......395 K15
pl. Castle Hill......218 E7
st. Guildford W......336 J5
st. Wakeley......334 J12
LONACH
cl. Baulkham Hl......247 A2
LONARD
av. Wiley Park......400 E4
LONDON
cr. Cecil Hills......362 D7
la. Campsie, off London St......371 K12
pl. Grose Wold......116 B6
rd. Berala......339 E12
rd. Lidcombe......339 E12
st. Blacktown......243 K13
st. Campsie......371 K12
st. Enmore......17 A12
LONDONDERRY
dr. Killarney Ht......256 B14
rd. Londonderry......117 K12
rd. Richmond......118 E10
LONE PINE
av. Chatswood W......284 F12
av. Milperra......397 D11
pde. Matraville......407 B16
pl. N Balgowlah......287 B4

GREGORY'S STREET DIRECTORY 97

LO STREETS

LONG
- av. East Ryde.........283 A14
- cl. Green Valley......363 B10
- cl. Menai................458 G6
- dr. Mcquarie Pk......252 A16
- dr. Mcquarie Pk......282 A1
- st. Hobartville.........118 C6
- st. Smithfield..........305 E14
- st. Strathfield.........371 D3

LONG ANGLE
- rd. Yellow Rock......173 F16

LONGBOW
- cl. Old Tngabbie.....277 E9

LONGDON
- cl. S Penrith..........267 D5
- la. S Penrith, off
  Longdon Cl......267 C5

LONGDOWN
- st. Newtown..............17 J8

LONGFELLOW
- st. Wetherill Pk......335 A6

LONGFIELD
- st. Cabramatta.......366 A6

LONGFORD
- st. Roseville..........284 C6

LONG HAI
- rd. Moorebank.......395 C16
- rd. Moorebank.......425 C1

LONGHURST
- rd. Minto..............453 A14
- rd. Minto................482 J4

LONGLEAT
- la. Kurmond.............86 A2
- rd. Kurmond.............86 D1

LONGLEY
- pl. Castle Hill........217 C6
- wy. S Windsor.........150 F2

LONGLEYS
- rd. Badgerys Ck......358 B4
- rd. Luddenham........357 G4

LONGPORT
- st. Lewisham............15 A9

LONGREACH
- pl. Bella Vista........246 G1

LONG REEF
- cr. Woodbine.........481 H9

LONGS
- la. The Rocks...........A A6

LONGSTAFF
- av. Chipping Ntn....396 E5
- la. Chipping Ntn.....396 E5
- wy. Claymore.........481 E11

LONG TAN
- pl. Scheyville.........123 D8

LONGUEVILLE
- rd. Lane Cove........314 E1

LONGVIEW
- pl. Baulkham HI......216 J13
- pl. Mulgoa............295 J4
- st. Balmain..............344 E5
- st. Eastwood..........281 H5
- st. Five Dock.........342 J11

LONGWORTH
- av. Eastlakes.........405 K3
- av. Point Piper........347 F8
- cr. Castle Hill........219 A10
- la. Point Piper, off
  Longworth Av...347 F8

LONICERA
- pl. Cherrybrook......219 K14

LONSDALE
- av. Berowra Ht........133 B6
- av. Pymble.............252 K4
- av. W Pnnant HI.....249 H5
- st. Lilyfield...............10 E9
- st. St Marys...........269 G4

LOOKES
- av. Balmain East........8 G8

LOOKOUT
- av. Blaxland...........234 C8
- av. Dee Why..........259 B9
- dr. Mt Pritchard.....364 F14

LOOMBAH
- av. E Lindfield........254 J13
- av. S Penrith..........266 G1
- rd. Dover Ht..........348 F16
- st. Bilgola..............169 B6

LOORANA
- rd. Leumeah...........482 B15
- rd. Roseville Ch......285 E2

LOPEZ
- la. Bankstown.........399 F1

LOQUAT VALLEY
- rd. Bayview............168 J13

LORAINE
- av. Caringbah........492 G14

LORANDO
- av. Sefton..............338 F16

LORANTHUS
- cr. Bidwill..............211 F13

LORD
- av. Dundas Vy........279 K9
- pl. Barden Rdg........488 F3
- st. Orchard Hills.....267 D9
- st. Belrose............226 D15
- st. Botany..............405 E9
- st. Cabramatta W..364 K7
- st. Haberfield.........373 E2
- st. Mt Colah..........192 C6
- st. Narellan............478 F11
- st. Newtown..........374 H11
- st. N Sydney..............5 D8
- st. Rockdale...........403 E15
- st. Roseville...........284 H4
- wy. Glenwood........215 J16

LORD CASTLEREAGH
- cct. Macquarie Lk...423 E14

LORD ELDON
- dr. Harringtn Pk.....478 D2

LORD HOWE
- dr. Green Valley.....363 A11
- dr. Hinchinbrk........363 A13
- st. Dover Ht..........348 F13

LORDS
- av. Asquith............192 A9
- rd. Leichhardt..........15 B3

LOREE
- tce. Kellyville.........217 C4

LORENZO
- cr. Rsemeadow.......540 K4

LORETTA
- av. Como...............460 H5
- pl. Belrose............225 K14
- pl. Glendenning......242 J3

LORIKEET
- av. Ingleburn.........453 F10
- cl. Woronora Ht.....489 C4
- cr. Green Valley....363 D9
- pl. St Clair............270 G13
- st. Glenwood.........215 D15
- wy. W Pnnant HI....249 D7

LORING
- pl. Quakers Hill.....214 B11

LORKING
- st. Canterbury........372 E16

LORNA
- av. Blakehurst.......432 C15
- av. North Ryde......282 H7
- la. Stanmore...........16 C8

LORNA LEIGH
- la. Longueville.......314 E7

LORNE
- av. Kensington......376 E13
- av. Killara..............253 K12
- av. S Penrith..........266 K6
- pr. Bossley Park....333 D11
- st. Girraween.........276 A15
- st. Prospect...........274 K10
- st. Summer Hill.....373 C5

LOROY
- cr. Frenchs Frst.....255 G1

LORRAINE
- av. Bardwell Vy......403 A10
- av. Padstow Ht.......429 H7
- pl. Merrylands W...307 B15
- pl. Oatlands..........278 J12
- st. N Strathfield.....341 C5
- st. Peakhurst.........430 E6
- st. Seven Hills......245 J15

LORRINA
- cl. W Pnnant HI.....249 K1

LOSCOE
- st. Fairfield..........336 E8

LOSTOCK
- pl. Leumeah..........482 E13

LOT
- la. Hunters Hill......313 H10

LOTHIAN
- st. Winston Hills....277 F4

LOTOS
- la. Petersham.........15 G8
- st. Petersham.........15 G8

LOTTIE LYELL
- av. Moore Park........21 A6

LOTUS
- cl. Baulkham HI.....246 J4
- pl. Mcquarie Fd....454 D6

LOUDEN
- av. Illawong...........460 B2
- st. Canada Bay......342 D10

LOUDON
- av. Haberfield........343 D12

LOUGH
- av. Guildford..........337 K7
- la. Guildford..........337 K7

LOUGHLIN
- st. Rozelle...............7 C16

LOUIE
- la. Revesby, off
  Louie St.........399 C11
- st. Padstow...........399 B11

LOUIS
- av. Newington, off
  Newington Bvd..310 B12
- st. Granville..........308 B14
- st. Merrylands......308 B14
- st. Redfern..............19 A6

LOUISA
- dr. Birchgrove..........7 F3
- st. Auburn.............339 E5
- st. Earlwood..........402 G2
- st. Oatley..............431 E11
- st. Summer Hill....373 B4

LOUISE
- av. Baulkham HI.....247 B9
- av. Chatswood W...284 A9
- av. Ingleburn.........453 C4
- pl. Bonnyrigg........364 B5
- pl. Cecil Hills.........362 J4
- st. Dean Park........242 H1
- st. Jannali............460 G13
- wy. Cherrybrook....219 C15

LOUISE LOVELY
- la. Moore Park........21 B6

LOUISE SAUVAGE
- pwy.Newington.....310 C14

LOUISIANA
- pl. Riverwood......400 B13

LOURDES
- av. Lindfield..........254 E13

LOUTH
- pl. Hoxton Park....392 F7

LOVAT
- av. Earlwood........372 K16
- st. West Pymble...252 H11

LOVE
- av. Emu Plains....235 H11
- la. Guildford.........337 G5
- la. Picton..............563 G1
- st. Blacktown........244 A10

LOVEGROVE
- dr. Quakers Hill...213 H14

LOVELL
- rd. Denistone E......281 E8
- rd. Eastwood.........281 E8

LOVELY
- pl. St Helens Park..541 B5

LOVERIDGE
- st. Alexandria...........19 A16

LOVERING
- pl. Newport............169 K12

LOVES
- av. Oyster Bay......461 B9

LOVETT
- pl. Manly Vale.......288 A3
- st. Thornleigh........220 J13

LOVILLE
- av. Peakhurst......430 D10
- av. Seven Hills....245 C15

LOVONI
- st. Cabramatta......366 B10

LOW
- st. Hurstville........401 H16
- st. Mt Krng-gai....163 A12
- st. Smithfield........336 A4

LOWAN
- pl. Kellyville.........216 K1
- pl. Woronora Ht...489 D5

LOWANA
- av. Kirrawee.........491 B5
- av. Merrylands.....307 E10
- av. Roseville........284 G2
- av. Seven Hills....246 C12
- st. Beverly Hills...401 B13
- st. Villawood.......367 G5

LOWANNA
- av. Baulkham HI....247 B4
- dr. S Penrith.........266 G7
- pl. Hornsby..........221 C1
- st. Belrose............225 K16
- st. Scotland I.......168 J4

LOWE
- cr. Elderslie.........477 H15
- rd. Hornsby...........192 B16
- st. Clovelly...........378 A14
- st. Merrylands......307 K15

LOWER ALMORA
- st. Mosman...........317 D6

LOWER AVON
- st. Glebe..............12 B10

LOWER BEACH
- st. Balgowlah........287 H10

LOWER BLIGH
- st. Northbridge.....286 A14

LOWER BOYLE
- st. Mosman...........316 G11

LOWER CAMPBELL
- cr. Casula.............394 H12

LOWER CARRIAGE
- la. Haymarket.........E C16

LOWER CLIFF
- av. Northbridge....316 A12

LOWER DARLING POINT
- rd. Edgecliff..........13 H10

LOWER FORT
- st. Dawes Point........A F2
- st. Dawes Point........1 F9
- st. Millers Pt..........A F2
- st. Millers Pt..........1 F9

LOWER MOUNT
- st. Wentwthvle.....277 A13

LOWER PLATEAU
- rd. Bilgola............169 E5

LOWER PUNCH
- st. Mosman..........317 C5

LOWER ST GEORGES
- cr. Drummoyne.....313 K16

LOWER SERPENTINE
- rd. Greenwich........314 J14

LOWER SPOFFORTH
- wk. Cremorne, off
  Lower Boyle St...316 F11

LOWER WASHINGTON
- dr. Bonnet Bay......460 B8
- dr. Bonnet Bay......460 E10

LOWER WYCOMBE
- rd. Neutral Bay........6 F10

LOWERY
- cl. Emu Plains.....234 K10

LOWES
- dr. Cobbitty.........416 H6

LOWING
- cl. Forestville.......255 K8

LOWRY
- av. West Hoxton...391 G7
- cr. St Ives............253 K2
- pl. Prairiewood....334 K9
- pl. Woronora Ht...489 B6
- rd. Lalor Park......245 J10
- st. Mt Lewis........370 A16

LOWTHER PARK
- av. Warrawee.......222 G12

LOXTON
- pl. Bossley Park...333 E11
- pl. Forestville......256 B6

LOXWOOD
- av. Cmbrdg Pk.....238 C8

LOY
- pl. Quakers Hill....243 K3

LOYALTY
- rd. North Rocks....278 K2
- sq. Balmain..............7 H1

LOZANO
- pl. Bossley Park...333 K10

LUCAN
- pl. Minchinbury....271 K8

LUCAS
- av. Malabar..........437 F6
- av. Moorebank.....396 E8
- av. Russell Lea....343 B3
- cct. Kellyville.......215 G4
- rd. Burwood.........342 C14
- rd. East Hills........427 K5
- rd. Lalor Park......245 F15
- rd. Seven Hills....245 F15
- st. Camperdown....17 G5
- st. Cronulla..........524 A2

- st. Emu Plains.....235 C12
- st. Guildford........337 B3
- wy. Ingleburn......453 A10

LUCASVILLE
- rd. Glenbrook......234 B16

LUCE
- pl. St Andrews....481 K6

LUCENA
- cr. Lethbrdg Pk...240 D2

LUCERNE
- av. S Wntwthvle..306 K6
- st. Belrose..........371 B13

LUCETTE
- pl. Castle Hill......216 K9
- pl. Castle Hill......217 A9

LUCIA
- av. Baulkham HI..247 C9
- av. St Ives..........224 F11

LUCIDUS
- pl. Glenmore Pk..265 H14

LUCILLE
- cr. Casula............394 H12

LUCINDA
- av. Bass Hill.......367 E7
- av. Georges Hall..367 E7
- av. Springwood...201 F1
- av. Wahroonga....222 A11
- av.s.Wahroonga...222 A13
- gr. Winston Hills..277 A2
- pl. Mona Vale......169 D15
- rd. Greystanes....306 G8
- rd. Marsfield........282 A7

LUCIUS
- pl. Rsemeadow....540 C3
- st. Bondi Beach...378 B4

LUCKNOW
- rd. North Ryde....283 C10
- st. Willoughby.....285 D15

LUCRETIA
- av. Longueville.....314 E9
- rd. Seven Hills....275 E7
- rd. Toongabbie....275 H10

LUCULIA
- av. Baulkham HI..247 D14

LUCY
- av. Lansvale........366 K8
- cl. Hornsby........191 J10
- ct. Ashfield..........342 H14
- st. Ashfield..........342 H14
- st. Kingswood......237 D16
- st. Merrylands W..306 J13

LUDDENHAM
- rd. Luddenham....327 H12
- rd. Orchard Hills..269 E16
- rd. Orchard Hills..299 C5

LUDGATE
- st. Concord..........341 J5
- st. Fairfield..........336 D5
- st. Roselands.......401 K5

LUDLOW
- rd. Castle Hill.....218 D16
- st. Stanhpe Gdn..215 E6

LUDMILA
- cl. Carlingford......279 F3

LUDWIG
- sq. Bidwill...........211 G14

LUE
- pl. Airds............512 B10

LUELLA
- pl. Rooty Hill......241 J13

LUFF
- pl. Ingleburn......453 A11
- st. Botany...........405 G14

LUGANO
- av. Burraneer.......523 E2
- av. Springwood....201 F3
- ct. Springwood....201 F2

LUGAR
- st. Bronte...........377 H9

LUGAR BRAE
- av. Bronte...........377 H9

LUGARD
- st. Penrith..........236 F2

LUGARNO
- av. Leumeah.......482 C15
- pde. Lugarno......429 J15
- pl. The Oaks......502 A12

LUKAS
- av. Kenthurst......158 B16

LUKE
- av. Burwood........342 C11
- pl. Rooty Hill......272 B1
- st. Hunters Hill...313 D10

98 GREGORY'S STREET DIRECTORY

STREETS MA

LUKER
st. Elderslie.........507 F2
LUKES
la. Baulkham Hl......247 D5
LUKIN
pl. Newington, off
Baker Av..........310 A16
LUKIS
av. Richmond.........119 B6
av. Richmond.........119 K5
LULAND
st. Botany...........405 D12
LUMEA
pl. Dharruk..........241 C9
LUMEAH
av. Elanora Ht.......198 D16
av. Punchbowl........400 D8
rd. Lindfield........284 C3
st. Merrylands.......308 A15
LUMLEY
st. Granville........308 E12
LUMSDAINE
av. East Ryde........313 B1
dr. Harbord..........288 K2
st. Picton...........563 F6
LUMSDEN
st. Cammeray.........316 A5
LUNAR
av. Heathcote........518 E14
LUND
st. Denistone........281 G13
LUNDY
av. Kingsgrove.......402 B7
LUNN
ct. Cabramatta.......365 H10
LUONGO
cl. Prestons.........393 B13
LUPIN
av. Fairfield E......337 B16
av. Riverwood........399 K10
av. Greystanes.......306 A11
LUPP
la. Lane Cove........314 A2
LUPTON
pl. Hornsgea Pk......392 F14
pwy.Warrimoo.........203 C15
rd. Bargo............567 K14
LURGAN
st. Wentwthvle.......277 D10
LURLINE
st. Maroubra.........407 J9
LURNEA
av. Georges Hall.....367 G13
cr. Forestville......255 H9
LURR
pl. Bonnyrigg........364 A7
LUSKIN
pl. Bossley Park.....333 K9
LUSS
ct. Glenhaven........218 E6
LUSTY
pl. Moorebank........396 F6
st. Wolli Creek......403 J5
st. Wolli Creek......403 H5
LUTANA
pl. Baulkham Hl......248 B8
LUTANDA
cl. Pennant Hills....220 C15
LUTHER
rd. Winmalee.........172 K12
LUTON
pl. Colyton..........270 E5
st. St Ives..........224 A9
rd. Blacktown........244 K10
LUTTRELL
st. Glenmore Pk......265 K7
st. Glenmore Pk......265 J9
st. Hobartville......118 D10
wy. Minto............482 K5
LUWASA
pl. Kellyville.......217 B4
LUXFORD
rd. Bidwill..........211 A14
rd. Emerton..........240 G6
rd. Hassall Gr.......241 K1
rd. Lethbrdg Pk......240 G6
rd. Londonderry......148 K5
rd. Mount Druitt.....241 G14
rd. Oakhurst.........241 K1
rd. Shalvey..........211 A14
rd. Tregear..........240 G6
rd. Whalan...........240 G6

LUXOR
pde. Roseville.......284 K1
LUYTEN
cl. Cranebrook.......207 E6
LUZON
av. Lethbrdg Pk......240 D12
LYALL
av. Dean Park........212 K16
st. Leichhardt.......9 D12
LYCETT
av. Kellyville.......215 F3
av. West Hoxton......391 J11
cr. Hornsby Ht.......191 H1
cr. S Wntwthvle......307 E5
pl. Belrose..........226 A13
LYDHAM
av. Rockdale.........403 A12
pl. Castle Hill......219 A10
LYDIA
pl. Hassall Gr.......211 J11
LYELL
pl. Bow Bowing.......452 C15
pl. Cartwright.......394 A5
st. Bossley Park.....334 C7
LYGON
pl. Castle Hill......217 J11
wy. Cranebrook.......207 G13
LYLA
pl. Narwee...........400 G14
LYLE
av. Lindfield........283 K5
av. Girraween........276 A15
st. Hurstville.......401 H15
st. Ryde.............281 K9
LYLY
rd. Allambie Ht......257 H13
LYMERSTON
st. Tempe............404 C1
LYMINGE
rd. Croydon Pk.......371 K8
LYMINGTON
st. Bexley...........402 H16
LYMM
st. Belrose..........225 J13
LYMOORE
av. Thornleigh.......221 C9
LYON
av. Punchbowl........399 K7
av. S Turramra.......252 A5
cl. Killara..........253 J12
pl. Cecil Hills......362 G3
st. Mascot...........405 F4
LYNBARA
av. St Ives..........254 A1
LYNBRAE
av. Beecroft.........250 C10
LYNBROOK
ct. Castle Hill......217 B10
LYNCH
av. Caringbah........492 G13
av. Enmore...........374 F9
av. Queens Park......22 D12
cl. Carlingford......279 G3
la. Marrickville.....374 F9
rd. Faulconbdg.......171 D10
rd. Glenbrook........264 B2
st. Dover Ht.........348 E12
st. Strathfield......341 G13
wy. Belrose..........226 C10
wy. Cherrybrook, off
Purchase Rd......219 D10
LYNDIA
st. Ingleburn........453 C10
LYNDLEY
st. Busby............363 G15
LYNDON
st. Fairfield........336 E15
wy. Beecroft.........250 A4

LYNE
la. Alexandria........18 G13
rd. Cheltenham.......250 K11
st. Alexandria........18 G13
LYNEHAM
pl. W Pnnant Hl......249 A8
LYNESTA
av. Bexley North.....402 D10
av. Fairfield W......335 B12
LYNETTE
av. Carlingford......249 H13
cl. Hornsby Ht.......191 H1
cr. S Wntwthvle......307 E5
pl. Belrose..........226 A13
LYNNE
dr. Hornsby..........221 F6
LYNN RIDGE
av. Gordon...........253 E10
LYNROB
pl. Thornleigh.......220 G11
LYNSTOCK
av. Castle Hill......218 D12
LYNTON
ct. Glenwood.........215 H13
grn. W Pnnant Hl.....249 D5
LYNVALE
cl. Lane Cove N......284 G14
LYNWEN
av. Banksia..........403 H12
wy. Banksia..........403 G12
LYNWOOD
av. Cromer...........258 E2
av. Dee Why..........258 E2
av. Doonside.........243 J14
av. Killara..........254 A11
av. Narraweena......258 E2
cl. Pennant Hills....220 F14
pl. Castle Hill......217 J9
rd. St Helens Park...541 H3
st. Blakehurst.......432 C13
LYNX
pl. Cranebrook.......207 G5
pl. Quakers Hill.....214 C9
LYON
av. Punchbowl........399 K7
av. S Turramra.......252 A5
cl. Killara..........253 J12
pl. Cecil Hills......362 G3
st. Mascot...........405 F4
LYONPARK
rd. Mcquarie Pk......282 F4
LYONS
av. Cabramatta.......365 D10
la. Sydney...........F E4
la. Sydney...........3 K10
rd. Cherrybrook......219 D9
rd. Drummoyne.......343 K1
rd. St Clair.........270 B10
rd. Camperdown......17 F1
rd. Drummoyne.......343 E5
rd. Five Dock.......343 A8
rd. Russell Lea.....343 E5
rd.w.Canada Bay.....342 E7
rd.w.Five Dock......342 J8
st. Dover Ht........348 E12
st. Strathfield.....341 G13
wy. Minto...........482 A2
LYPTUS
wy. Plumpton........241 G9
LYRA
la. Seven Hills.....246 D7
pl. Hinchinbrk......393 D4
LYREBIRD
cr. Green Valley....363 D10
ct. St Clair........269 H11
ct. Kenthurst.......158 A16
dr. St Clair, off
Banks Dr........269 H12
pl. Ingleburn.......453 F9
pl. St Ives Ch......223 K1
LYSAGHT
rd. Wedderburn......540 B16
LYSANDER
av. Rsemeadow......540 H9
LYTE
pl. Prospect........275 A12
LYTHAM
st. Glenmore Pk.....266 G8
LYTON
st. Blacktown.......244 B14

LYTTON
la. Riverstone......182 D8
pl. Campbelltown...511 K2
rd. Riverstone......182 F9
st. Cammeray........315 K7
st. Wentwthvle......307 B3

M

M2
mwy.Baulkham Hl.....246 J15
mwy.Beecroft.......250 A9
mwy.Carlingford....249 A13
mwy.Cheltenham.....251 F12
mwy.Epping.........250 A10
mwy.Mcquarie Pk....283 A5
mwy.Marsfield......251 F12
mwy.N Epping.......251 F12
mwy.North Rocks....248 B14
mwy.North Ryde.....283 A5
M4
Auburn.............309 C12
Blacktown..........273 C14
Clarmnt Ms.........269 B7
Eastern Ck.........272 C11
Emu Plains.........235 A12
Glenbrook..........234 H15
Granville..........308 C8
Greystanes.........306 E3
Harris Park........308 C8
Homebush...........341 A1
Homebush B.........340 A1
Homebush W.........340 A1
Huntingwd..........273 C14
Jamisontown........265 G1
Lapstone...........234 H15
Leonay.............234 H15
Lidcombe...........340 A1
May Hill...........307 B4
Merrylands.........307 B4
Minchinbury........271 C10
N Strathfield......341 K7
Orchard Hills......267 D8
Parramatta.........308 C8
Prospect...........275 B16
St Clair...........270 A8
Silverwater........309 C12
S Penrith..........266 D6
S Wntwthvle........307 B4
M5
Beverly Hills......400 A11
Casula.............423 C15
Hamondvle..........396 C12
Liverpool..........393 K16
Lurnea.............393 K16
Milperra...........397 B14
Moorebank..........396 C12
Narwee.............400 A11
Padstow............399 B11
Panania............398 B12
Prestons...........423 G5
Revesby............398 B12
Riverwood..........400 A11
M5 EAST
fwy. Arncliffe.....403 K9
fwy. Bardwell Pk...402 J8
fwy. Bardwell Vy...402 J8
fwy. Beverly Hills.401 C11
fwy. Kingsgrove....401 C11
fwy. Mascot........403 K9
MAAS
st. Cromer.........258 C1
MABEL
st. Hurstville.....431 K7
st. Kingsgrove.....402 B12
st. Willoughby.....285 D12
MABUHAY
gr. Mount Druitt...241 D12
McADAM
pl. Lalor Park.....245 H11
MACADAMIA
st. Prestons.......393 K15
McALEER
st. Leichhardt.....15 D6
McALISTER
av. Cronulla.......494 A13
av. Engadine.......518 G3
la. Chippendale....19 B8
rd. Galston........160 D4
McANALLY
la. Randwick, off
Carrington Rd...377 D16
McANDREW
cl. Lurnea.........394 F12

McARDLE
st. Ermington......280 B14
MACARTHUR
av. Crows Nest.....315 J7
av. Pagewood.......406 C8
av. Revesby........398 J16
av. Strathfield....371 C3
cct. Camden S......507 B16
cct. Camden S......537 B16
cr. Westmead.......307 E3
dr. Holsworthy.....426 F7
dr. St Clair.......270 A10
pde. Dulwich Hill..373 E11
pl. Ruse...........512 G1
rd. Elderslie......477 F16
st. Spring Farm....507 G5
st. Douglas Park...568 C3
st. Ermington......310 E1
st. Fairfield E....337 C15
st. Homebush B.....310 F15
st. Parramatta.....308 F3
st. St Ives........254 D1
st. Sylvania.......462 A14
st. Ultimo.........12 J13
wy. Bidwill........211 F15
McARTHUR
st. Guildford......337 J2
MACARTYE
av. Chatswood W....284 E9
cr. Hebersham......241 E3
st. Ermington......310 D3
st. Miranda........461 K16
MACAULAY
la. Stanmore........16 G5
la.w.Stanmore.......16 F5
rd. Stanmore........16 H6
st. Wetherill Pk...334 E4
McAULAY
av. Bankstown......399 D3
st. Leichhardt......9 G14
McAULEY
cl. Heathcote......518 C15
cr. Emu Plains.....235 F8
pl. Waitara........221 K5
McAULIFFE
pl. Silverdale.....353 J13
MACBETH
st. St Clair.......270 C16
McBETH
wy. Rsemeadow......540 K2
McBRIAN
pl. Wakeley........334 F15
McBRIDE
av. Hunters Hill...313 J10
McBRIEN
pl. Davidson.......255 E4
pl. Frenchs Frst...255 E4
McBURNEY
av. Mascot.........405 E8
la. Kirribilli......6 D16
la. Mascot.........405 E7
rd. Baulkham Hl...248 B8
rd. Cabramatta.....365 E5
st. Naremburn......315 H3
McCABE
cl. Prairiewood....334 K9
cl. St Clair.......269 K16
st. St Clair, off
McCabe Cl.....269 K16
McCAHONS
pl. Chatswood......285 F6
pl. Menai..........458 F9
pl. Rouse Hill.....184 K7
st. Greystanes.....305 K11
McCALL
av. Camden S.......507 B14
av. Croydon Pk.....371 J7
McCALLUM
av. East Ryde......313 C2
st. Roselands......401 D6
McCANN
av. Berrilee.......131 K9
McCANN
pl. Hassall Gr.....212 B14
pl. Leppington.....420 C2
rd. Rossmore.......419 G1
rd. Rossmore.......420 C2
st. Yellow Rock....204 G5
wy. Minto..........482 K1
McCARRS CREEK
rd. Church Point...168 C10
rd. Krngai Ch N P..166 G14
rd. Krngai Ch N P..166 G16
rd. Terrey Hills...196 F7

GREGORY'S STREET DIRECTORY 99

MA STREETS

McCARTHY
la. Annandale...........17 A3
la. Concord............341 J4
la. Woolmloo ....D K13
pl. Woolmloo.............4 C7
st. Fairfield W..........334 K10
st. Richmond..........119 K5
McCARTHYS
la. Castlereagh........206 D11
McCARTNEY
cr. St Clair..............270 A16
la. St Clair, off McCartney Cr.....270 A16
pwy. Warwck Frm, off McCartney St.....365 E14
st. Warwck Frm 365 E14
McCAULEY
cr. Glenbrook..........234 F16
la. Alexandria...........19 B16
st. Alexandria............19 A16
st. Matraville...........436 E3
McCLEAN
st. Blacktown..........243 J12
st. Georges Hall 367 K11
McCLEER
st. Rozelle..............344 D7
McCLEERS
la. Drummoyne.......343 H5
McCLELLAND
st. Chester Hill 368 A5
st. N Willoughby 285 G9
McCLYMONTS
rd. Kenthurst...........125 C12
rd. Maraylya............125 C12
McCOMBE
av. Rouse Hill 185 B10
McCONVILLE
la. Beaconsfield, off Connolly La........375 G11
McCORMACK
la. Revesby............398 G16
pl. Denham Ct.........452 F5
st. Arndell Park 273 E8
McCOURT
st. Wiley Park.........370 H16
McCOWEN
rd. Ingleside............197 D3
McCOY
la. Btn-le-Sds..........433 J2
st. Toongabbie........276 A5
st. Toongabbie........276 B4
McCRAE
dr. Camden S..........506 K12
pl. Blackett.............241 C3
McCREA
cl. Edensor Pk 363 G4
McCREADY
pl. Berowra.............133 H11
McCREDIE
dr. Horngsea Pk......392 F13
rd. Guildford W 336 H3
rd. Smithfield 336 E3
McCROSSIN
av. Birrong..............368 J7
McCUBBENS
la. Sutherland, off Old Princes Hwy.490 E3
McCUBBIN
pl. Casula...............424 E2
pl. Mt Pritchard.......364 J12
pl. Plumpton...........242 C7
wy. Claymore...........481 F10
McCULLOCH
rd. Blacktown..........243 J13
st. Riverstone 183 C6
st. Russell Lea 343 E7
McCUSKER
cr. Cherrybrook.......219 D11
MACDONALD
av. Lalor Park..........245 G11
av. Lurnea..............394 E7
cr. Bexley North 402 E11
la. Paddington 4 K13
rd. Ingleburn...........423 A14
st. Erskineville.........375 A9
st. Lakemba...........370 J15
st. Paddington 4 K13
st. Ramsgate 433 D14
st. Sans Souci.........433 D14
st. Vaucluse............348 G5
McDONALD
av. Auburn 339 B10
av. Baulkham Hl 277 J1
cr. Strathfield 341 G16
la. Bankstown.........399 E2
la. N Sydney..............K F11
la. Potts Point.............4 K2
pl. McGraths Hl.......122 A14
pl. Rooty Hill...........241 K12
st. Balmain 7 J9
st. Berala 339 E12
st. Cronulla..............494 A11
st. Harbord 258 D16
st. Illawong.............459 K4
st. Leichhardt...........16 A1
st. Mortlake 312 A15
st. North Rocks.......249 B16
st. Potts Point............4 K2
wy. Greenacre 370 G5
MACDONNELL
av. Fairfield W..........335 F11
McDONNELL
st. Raby..................451 C12
McDOUGALL
av. Baulkham Hl 247 F4
la. Castle Hill..........218 C15
st. Kensington.........376 B11
st. Kirribilli...................6 A12
MACDUFF
wy. Rsemeadow.......540 K2
MACEDON
pl. Warriewood 199 C10
st. Bossley Park......334 B10
McELHONE
pl. Surry Hills............20 E2
st. Woolmloo.............4 G7
st. Woolmloo.............4 H4
McELIVER
wy. Minto.................482 J5
McENCROE
st. Strathfield S.......371 A4
MACERI
pl. Edensor Pk 333 J15
McEVOY
cl. Hamondvle 396 F14
rd. Padstow 399 F14
st. Alexandria............19 A16
st. Waterloo..............19 A16
McEWAN
av. Winston Hills......277 G3
cct. Mt Annan...........479 F15
McFADYEN
st. Botany 405 E13
McFALL
pl. Rooty Hill...........271 K3
st. Botany 405 D12
MACFARLANE
pde. Sylvania............461 H13
st. Davidson 225 A16
McFARLANE
dr. Minchinbury.......271 F8
st. Merrylands.........307 G12
McGANN
pl. Cranebrook.........207 E14
McGARVIE
st. Paddington 21 F2
McGEE
pl. Baulkham Hl 248 C10
pl. Fairfield W..........334 K10
McGETTIGAN
la. Panania..............398 E15
McGILL
pl. Menai 458 E14
st. Lewisham 15 A10
McGILVRAY
pl. Rouse Hill 184 K6
McGIRR
pde. Warwck Frm 365 F15
pl. Abbotsford.........343 A3
st. Padstow 399 B16
McGOVERN
cr. Merrylands W 307 A13
McGOVETT
pl. Menai 458 K12
McGOWAN
av. Marrickville 403 H1
st. Putney 312 C10
McGOWEN
av. Malabar 437 E5
cr. Liverpool............395 C8
McGRATH
av. Earlwood 402 F1
av. Five Dock...........342 K8
pl. Currans Hill........479 H12
rd. McGraths Hl.......121 K14
McGRATHS
la. Kensington, off Doncaster Av 376 F12
MACGREGOR
st. Croydon............342 E14
McGREGOR
st. Kingsgrove.........401 H13
st. North Ryde 282 G6
McGUIRK
wy. Rouse Hill 185 A8
McHALE
la. Sefton................338 E15
wy. Nelson 154 J13
McHATTON
pl. Hassall Gr 211 J15
st. N Sydney..............5 C4
st. Waverton..............5 C4
McHENRY
rd. Cranebrook........207 C14
McILVENIE
st. Canley Ht 365 C3
McILWAINS
st. Ashcroft.............364 E15
McILWRAITH
st. Wetherill Pk 334 A3
MACINA
pl. St Clair...............269 H13
McINNES
pl. Ingleburn 453 B11
MACINTOSH
st. Mascot 405 D4
st. Melrose Pk.........310 K3
McINTOSH
av. Padstow Ht 429 G6
la. Kurrajong............64 D14
la. Neutral Bay 6 B1
la. Newtown 17 E12
rd. Beacon Hill.........257 J4
rd. Dee Why............258 E5
rd. Narraweena.........257 J4
st. Chatswood.........284 H9
st. Fairfield..............336 G15
st. Gordon 253 K8
st. Kings Park 244 D2
st. The Oaks............502 D12
MACINTYRE
cr. Ruse..................512 C8
cr. Sylvania Wtr.......462 D13
McINTYRE
av. Btn-le-Sds..........403 K15
av. St Clair...............269 G16
la. Gordon 253 G7
la. St Clair, off McIntyre Av 269 G16
pl. Castle Hill...........217 K7
st. Gordon 253 F7
st. Oatley 430 J12
McIVER
av. West Hoxton 362 B16
pl. Maroubra...........407 D14
MACK
st. Wentwthvle........306 H2
MACKANESS
cl. Five Dock...........342 G8
MACKAY
pl. Leumeah............482 H12
rd. S Granville 338 G4
st. Ashfield 342 G16
st. Caringbah 492 J7
st. Emu Plains.........235 C11
wy. Rouse Hill 184 J6
McKAY
av. Moorebank 396 D7
dr. Silverdale...........353 H15
pl. Minchinbury.......271 K7
rd. Hornsby Ht 161 E15
rd. Palm Beach.........139 K4
st. Dundas Vy 280 B9
st. Toongabbie........276 G5
McKEARNS
pl. Arncliffe.............403 H9
McKECHNIE
st. Epping 250 C16
McKEE
rd. Theresa Park......444 D7
st. Ultimo 12 K13
McKELL
av. Casula................394 K12
cl. Bonnyrigg 363 K6
st. Birchgrove.............7 J6
MACKELLAR
cir. Springwood 202 H1
pl. Campbelltown....512 B4
rd. Hebersham 241 E2
st. Casula................424 G3
st. Emu Plains.........235 K7
McKELLAR
cr. S Windsor..........150 H2
MACKEN
cl. Edensor Pk 363 E3
cr. Oatley 430 J13
st. Liverpool............365 B16
st. Oatley 430 J13
McKENDRICK
pl. Warrimoo 202 J13
McKENNY
wy. Narellan Vale......508 H1
McKENSIE
pl. McGraths Hl.......121 K12
MACKENZIE
av. Glenmore Pk......265 G5
bvd. Seven Hills.........275 F8
pl. Kearns 481 B2
st. Bondi Jctn 22 H9
st. Canley Vale 366 B4
st. Concord W..........341 E2
st. Homebush.........341 A11
st. Lavender Bay.........K D13
st. Lavender Bay 5 F11
st. Leichhardt............10 C14
st. Lilyfield................10 C14
st. Lindfield.............254 E14
st. Revesby.............399 A13
st. Rozelle...................7 B16
st. Strathfield 341 A11
McKENZIE
av. Chifley 437 C10
cr. Wilberforce..........67 G16
la. Earlwood 402 G3
pl. Menai 458 E9
st. Campsie 371 H16
wk. Cmbrdg Pk, off Cambridge St.....237 J9
McKEON
st. Maroubra...........407 G11
McKEOWN
st. Prairiewood 334 H7
McKERN
st. Campsie 371 J16
st. Wentwthvle........307 A1
McKEVITTE
av. East Hills............427 J2
MACKEY
st. Surry Hills.............F F11
st. Surry Hills.............F H12
MACKEYS
st. Horngsea Pk 392 E14
McKIBBIN
st. Canley Ht 365 A2
MACKIE
la. Mosman 316 H5
MACKILLOP
cr. St Helens Park....540 K10
dr. Baulkham Hl 247 A3
pl. Erskine Park.......270 E16
McKILLOP
pl. Dundas Vy 279 J7
rd. Beacon Hill.........257 K6
MACKIN
cl. Barden Rdg........488 F7
McKINLEY
av. Bonnet Bay 460 C11
pl. Cherrybrook.......219 J9
MACKINNON
av. Padstow 399 B12
st. St Helens Park....541 A9
McKINNON
av. Five Dock...........343 A7
McKINNONS
rd. Wilberforce..........67 B14
MACKLIN
st. Pendle Hill..........276 D15
MACKS
gln. Beaumont Hills...185 K16
MACKSVILLE
st. Hoxton Park.......392 K8
McKYE
st. Waverton............315 E11
McLACHLAN
av. Artarmon 314 J1
av. Darlinghurst.........13 B11
av. Rcuttrs Bay..........13 B11
wy. Darlinghurst.........13 A11
McLAREN
gr. St Clair..............270 E13
pl. Ingleburn 453 J7
st. Blackett..............241 B4
st. Carramar 366 K1
st. N Sydney..............K G1
st. N Sydney...............5 E4
McLAUGHLAN
pl. Paddington 4 K15
McLAUGHLIN
cct. Bradbury............511 J9
MACLAURIN
av. East Hills............427 G4
pde. Roseville...........284 G5
st. Penshurst 431 H8
MACLEAN
la. Camden S..........537 C1
st. Woolmloo.............4 G4
McLEAN
av. Chatswood W 284 E9
cr. Mosman 317 C1
rd. Campbelltown....511 K4
st. Auburn 339 A3
st. Emu Plains..........235 E12
st. Ingleside............198 A8
st. Liverpool............394 H1
MACLEAY
av. Wahroonga........223 C4
cr. St Marys............269 J5
ct. Harringtn Pk........478 F6
pl. Earlwood 402 F3
pl. Sylvania Wtr.......462 C11
st. Bradbury............511 F13
st. Elizabeth Bay..........4 K5
st. Greystanes.........306 A3
st. North Bondi 348 E14
st. Potts Point.............4 K5
st. Ryde.................282 E13
st. S Coogee 407 G6
McLENNAN
av. Randwick...........377 C11
McLEOD
av. Lindfield.............284 H1
av. Roseville.............284 H1
rd. Middle Dural 158 C1
st. Hurstville 432 B3
st. Mosman 316 H13
MAC MAHON
pl. Menai 458 H11
MACMAHON
st. Hurstville 432 A5
st. N Willoughby 285 E8
McMAHON
av. Liverpool............365 A15
cl. Penrith...............237 D7
gr. Glenwood 215 C14
rd. Yagoona 368 J11
McMAHONS
rd. Blaxlands Rdg......64 G5
rd. Lane Cove..........314 F6
rd. Longueville 314 F6
rd. Wilberforce..........67 F9
McMAHONS PARK
rd. Kurrajong.............85 C1
McMANUS
pl. Lugarno 430 A14
st. Kellyville.............217 C3
st. McMahons Pt 5 D15
MACMILLAN
st. Seaforth.............287 A8
McMILLAN
av. Baulkham Hl 277 K1
av. Sandringham 463 E2
rd. Artarmon 284 K16
st. Heckenberg........364 B12
st. Yagoona 369 D9
McMINN
pl. Narellan Vale......478 G16
McMULLEN
av. Carlingford.........250 A13
av. Castle Hill...........218 D14
McMURDO
av. Tregear..............240 F6
McNAIR
av. Kingsford...........406 K3
MACNAMARA
av. Concord.............341 H6
pl. Appin.................569 F14
McNAMARA
av. Richmond...........120 A6
rd. Cromer 227 J13
McNAUGHTON
st. Jamisontown 236 B15
McNEILLY
pl. Marrickville 373 H14
McPHEE
pl. Bligh Park 150 B5
st. Chester Hill 338 D15

100 GREGORY'S STREET DIRECTORY

STREETS MA

MACPHERSON
rd. Londonderry 149 A8
st. Bronte............377 J10
st. Cremorne.........316 G5
st. Hurstville........401 H15
st. Mosman 316 G5
st. Warriewood.......198 G7
st. Waverley..........377 G3
McPHERSON
av. Punchbowl........399 K5
la. Carlton............432 G9
la. Meadowbank, off
 McPherson St 311 F2
la. Zetland, off
 Joynton Av 375 J9
pl. Illawong..........459 J3
pl. Ruse..............512 H6
rd. Smeaton Gra.....479 F10
st. Bnksmeadw 435 K1
st. Bnksmeadw 436 D1
st. Carlton...........432 G8
st. Revesby..........398 K15
st. Wakeley..........334 H12
st. West Ryde.......311 F2
McQUADE
av. S Windsor.......120 G12
MACQUARIE
av. Camden..........507 A5
av. Campbelltown ...511 J6
av. Kellyville.........215 G4
av. Leumeah.........512 C3
av. Penrith...........237 A9
cct. Holsworthy 426 C9
dr. Cherrybrook......219 H9
dr. Mcquarie Pk.....282 C1
gr. Tahmoor, off
 Macquarie Pl 565 F9
la. Parramatta.......308 D3
pl. Denistone E......281 J10
pl. Glossodia..........66 C12
pl. Mortdale..........431 B8
pl. Sydney..............B B11
pl. Tahmoor..........565 F10
rd. Auburn...........339 D1
rd. Earlwood.........403 B2
rd. Greystanes.......305 G11
rd. Ingleburn.........453 E4
rd. Mcquarie Fd.....453 G4
rd. Pymble...........253 H2
rd. Rouse Hill........184 C11
rd. Springwood.......201 D3
rd. Vaucluse..........348 G2
rd. Wilberforce........91 K2
st. Annandale.........16 D4
st. Chatswood........285 A5
st. Chifley............437 A6
st. Cromer...........227 H12
st. Fairfield..........336 A12
st. Greenacre........370 D13
st. Gymea............461 H16
st. Homebush B.....310 F14
st. Leichhardt........16 D4
st. Liverpool.........395 E1
st. Liverpool.........395 D4
st. Liverpool.........395 C6
st. Parramatta.......308 A3
st. Rosebery.........405 J2
st. Roseville.........285 A5
st. S Windsor........120 G15
st. Sydney..............D F5
st. Sydney..............4 A3
st. Warwck Frm.....365 E16
st. Windsor..........121 A11
tce. Balmain............7 E6
MACQUARIEDALE
rd. Appin.............569 C10
rd. Appin.............569 A7
MACQUARIE GROVE
rd. Camden..........477 A11
rd. Cobbitty.........447 F15
rd. Harringtn Pk....447 F15
rd. Kirkham..........477 A9
MACQUARIE LINKS
dr. Macquarie Lk....423 D16
MACQUEEN
pl. Mt Riverview....234 D4
McRAE
pl. N Turramurra...223 D7
rd. Sans Souci.......433 G16
st. Petersham........15 H15
McRAES
av. Penshurst........431 E7
McTAGGART
pl. N Turramurra...193 E12

MACTIER
av. Milperra........397 F12
st. Narrabeen......228 J8
st. Narrabeen......229 A8
MACULATA
cr. Mcquarie Fd....454 D3
pl. Kingswood.....267 J1
McVEY
pl. Rooty Hill......241 K12
McVICARS
la. Lidcombe.......339 H10
McVICKER
st. Moorebank.....396 D10
McWILLIAM
dr. Douglas Park...568 D5
MADAGASCAR
dr. Kings Park.....244 F2
MADANG
av. Whalan........240 J12
pl. Glenfield........424 G14
rd. Belrose.........226 B3
rd. Ingleside.......226 B3
rd. Terrey Hills....226 B3
st. Holsworthy....426 D4
wy. Matraville......407 C16
MADDECKS
av. Moorebank....396 C8
MADDEN
la. Blacktown......245 D8
MADDENS
rd. N Richmond....87 D6
MADDISON
cl. Redfern..........20 C9
cl. Redfern..........20 C10
MADDOCK
cl. Dulwich Hill...373 C7
MADDOX
ct. Alexandria.....375 C10
MADDY
wy. Stanhpe Gdn..215 C9
MADEIRA
av. Kings Lngly...245 D7
pl. Surry Hills......19 J2
st. Sylvania........462 B7
wy. Minto............482 K2
MADELEINE
cl. Mt Colah........162 F14
pl. Sackville.........68 C4
MADELINE
av. Northmead....278 A5
st. Belfield.........371 B8
st. Fairfield.......335 G14
st. Fairfield W.....335 G14
st. Hunters Hill...313 H10
st. Strathfield S..371 A7
MADIGAN
dr. Wrrngtn Cty...238 F6
gr. Thirlmere......565 C4
MADISON
av. Carlingford....280 C5
cct. St Clair........269 F13
la. St Clair, off
 Madison Cct ...269 G12
pl. Bonnet Bay....460 D11
pl. Kellyville.......216 C2
pl. Schofields......213 H5
wy. Allambie Ht..256 K8
MADOLINE
st. Springwood...201 J2
MADONNA
st. Winston Hills..246 G15
MADRERS
av. Kogarah.......433 D9
MADRID
pl. Glendenning..242 G3
MADSON
pl. Bonnyrigg.....364 B6
MAE
cr. Panania........398 B13
MAEVE
av. Kellyville.......216 J3
MAFEKING
av. Lane Cove.....314 F1
MAGARRA
pl. Seaforth.......287 D10
MAGDALA
rd. North Ryde....283 B12
MAGDALENE
st. St Marys.......269 J1
tce. Wollli Creek...403 J5
MAGGI
st. Birrong.........369 A5

MAGEE
la. Glenfield......424 D10
pl. Killarney Ht..256 D15
st. Ashcroft......364 F16
MAGELLAN
av. Lethbrdg Pk...240 G5
st. Fairfield W.....335 D9
MAGENTA
la. Paddington.......4 F15
MAGGA DAN
av. Tregear........240 C5
MAGGIOTTO
pl. Mt Prichard....364 K10
MAGIC
gr. Mosman 317 A11
MAGIC PUDDING
pl. Faulconbdg....171 F11
MAGILL
st. Randwick.....376 K16
MAGNA
wy. Oakhurst, off
 Alpin Gr........242 A4
MAGNETIC
av. Hinchinbrk...393 A1
MAGNEY
av. Regents Pk...369 A3
la. Woollahra....377 F2
pl. Bella Vista....246 F4
st. Woollahra....22 G4
MAGNOLIA
av. Baulkham Hl..247 F14
av. Epping.........250 E12
av. Villawood, off
 Wisteria Pl 337 A15
cl. Casula........423 K2
ct. Frenchs Frst..256 H1
dr. Breakfast Pt..311 B14
dr. Picton.........561 B3
ct. Schofields....214 A6
pl. Mcquarie Fd..453 K6
st. Greystanes...306 C13
st. Kirrawee.....460 J15
st. N St Marys..240 B9
MAGNUM
pl. Minto..........482 E9
MAGOWAR
rd. Girraween...275 J13
rd. Pendle Hill...276 A14
MAGPIE
cl. Glenwood.....215 E14
cl. Glenmore Pk..265 J12
cl. Ingleburn.....453 H5
rd. Green Valley..363 D8
MAGRA
pl. Kings Lngly..245 C5
MAGRATH
pl. Emu Plains..235 E8
MAGREE
cr. Chipping Ntn..396 E5
MAGUIRES
rd. Maraylya....124 E10
MAGYAR
pl. Oakhurst....242 D2
MAHAN
wy. Minto........483 A1
MAHER
cl. Beecroft......249 K11
cl. Chiswick.....343 C2
la. Hurstville, off
 Maher St......432 A7
st. Hurstville....431 J8
MAHNKEN
av. Revesby.....399 A13
MAHOGANY
bvd. Warriewood ..198 G10
cl. Alfords Point..429 C14
cl. Cranebrook..237 F7
cl. Glenwood....215 J16
ct. Castle Hill...218 K7
ct. Mcquarie Fd..454 E2
st. Prestons.....393 H14
wy. Greenacre....370 F5
MAHON
st. West Ryde...281 H14
MAHONEY
la. Edgecliff.......13 E9
MAHONGA
st. Tahmoor.....565 K10
MAHONS CREEK
rd. Yarramundi..145 B2
MAHONY
rd. Riverstone....182 K5
rd. Wentwthvle..277 B11

MAHRATTA
av. Wahroonga...222 B11
MAI
pl. Hebersham..241 D10
MAIANBAR
rd. Royal N P.....522 B15
MAIDA
rd. Epping.........281 C2
st. Five Dock......342 G8
st. Lilyfield.........10 E4
MAIDEN
la. Surry Hills......4 D8
st. Greenacre....370 E11
MAIDOS
pl. Quakers Hill..214 D11
MAIDSTONE
pl. Glenmore Pk..266 E12
st. Picton..........563 F11
st. Stanhpe Gdn..215 E4
MAILEY
cct. Rouse Hill....184 J5
pl. Shalvey.......211 B15
MAIN
av. Mcquarie Pk..283 C6
la. Merrylands...307 H12
st. Blacktown....244 H16
st. Earlwood......402 D4
st. Horngsea Pk..392 E11
st. Mt Annan.....479 D13
MAINERD
av. Bexley North...402 F11
MAINO
cl. Green Valley..363 H11
MAINSBRIDGE
av. Liverpool......394 H4
MAIN SOUTHERN
rd. Camden........506 E10
rd. Cawdor........506 E10
MAINTENANCE
la. Richmond.....118 F13
MAISMONDE
pl. Carlingford....280 E6
MAITLAND
av. Kingsford.....406 C2
pl. Baulkham Hl..216 H14
pl. Kirrawee......491 B7
st. Davidson.....255 D3
st. Killara.........253 H12
wy. Airds...........511 H15
MAJESTIC
dr. Stanhpe Gdn..215 D10
MAJOR
rd. Merrylands...307 E11
st. Coogee........377 J15
st. Mosman 317 A12
st. Punchbowl...400 C8
MAJORS
la. Concord, off
 Brewer St 341 K4
MAJORS BAY
rd. Concord.......341 J1
MAJURA
cl. St Ives Ch....194 B16
MAKIM
st. N Curl Curl..258 F9
MAKINSON
st. Gladesville..312 K9
MALA
cr. Blacktown...244 B12
st. Smithfield...335 B3
MALABAR
rd. Dural..........188 E15
rd. Maroubra....407 F12
rd. S Coogee.....407 F4
st. Canley Vale..366 B1
st. Fairfield.......335 K15
la. S Penrith, off
 Malabine Pl ...266 H7
pl. S Penrith......266 H7
MALACHITE
rd. Eagle Vale...481 A8
MALACOOTA
rd. Northbridge..286 B16
MALAHIDE
rd. Pennant Hills..220 E16
MALAKOFF
st. Marrickville..373 K12
MALAKUA
st. Whalan.......240 K11
MALAWA
pl. Bradbury.....511 C15

MALBARA
cr. Frenchs Frst...255 K2
MALBEC
pl. Eschol Park...481 C3
MALCOLM
av. Mt Pritchard..364 F9
av. Werrington....238 H10
la. Erskineville.....18 B16
st. Blacktown....274 J5
st. Erskineville....18 B16
st. Mascot........405 H4
st. Narrabeen....229 C1
wy. Rsemeadow...540 K2
MALDON
st. S Penrith.....266 F5
MALEY
gr. Glenwood.....215 K15
st. Guildford......337 C5
MALGA
av. Roseville Ch..255 E16
MALIBU
cl. Bundeena.....524 B11
MALING
av. Ermington....310 C3
MALINYA
cl. Moorebank....396 F11
rd. Allambie Ht..257 H14
MALIYAWUL
st. Lilyfield...........9 F3
st. Lilyfield........343 H10
MALLACOOTA
cl. Prestons......393 B16
cl. Prestons......423 A1
pl. Woodcroft....243 F10
st. Wakeley......334 H12
MALLAM
rd. Picton........561 C3
MALLARD
dr. Oatley.......430 E12
st. Woronora Ht..489 B3
MALLAWA
rd. Duffys Frst...194 J1
MALLEE
cl. Narellan Vale...478 H16
ct. Holsworthy....426 D5
st. Mcquarie Fd..454 E2
st. Cabramatta...365 J9
st. N St Marys...240 B12
st. Quakers Hill..243 J1
MALLENY
st. Ashbury.......372 E9
MALLET
cl. Kingswood....267 H1
MALLETT
la. Camperdown...17 F6
st. Annandale.....17 D2
st. Camperdown...17 D2
MALLEY
av. Earlwood......402 D5
MALLORY
dr. Bow Bow......242 J1
st. Concord......341 J1
MALLOW
pl. Cabramatta W..365 B4
MALO
rd. Whale Beach..140 C8
MALONE
cr. Dean Park....242 K1
MALONEY
la. Eastlakes......405 J4
st. Blacktown....273 K3
st. Mascot........405 H6
st. Mascot........405 J5
st. Rosebery.....405 J5
MALONGA
av. Kellyville......216 G3
MALORY
av. West Pymble..252 H9
cl. Wetherill Pk..334 E4
MALOUF
pl. Blacktown....243 J9
st. Canley Ht.....365 B3
st. Colyton......270 B4
st. Guildford W..336 H2
MALSBURY
rd. Hornsby......221 G8
rd. Normanhurst..221 G8
MALTA
pl. Rooty Hill....241 H3
st. Fairfield E....337 B14
st. Fairfield E....337 C14
st. N Strathfield..341 D6
MALTI
wy. Parklea......214 J13

GREGORY'S STREET DIRECTORY 101

MA STREETS

MALTON
grn. W Pnnant Hl 249 D5
rd. Beecroft 250 G5
rd. Cheltenham 251 A7
rd. N Epping 251 E9
st. Stanhpe Gdn 215 E5
MALUA
st. Dolls Point 463 G1
MALUKA
pl. Kingsgrove 401 H14
MALVERN
av. Baulkham Hl 247 A13
av. Chatswood 284 K8
av. Croydon 372 D1
av. Manly 288 G6
av. Merrylands 307 J14
av. Roseville 285 C3
av. Roseville Ch 285 D3
cl. St Johns Pk 364 F3
cr. Strathfield 341 F16
rd. Glenwood 215 B16
rd. Miranda 492 D4
st. Panania 428 C5
MALVINA
st. Ryde 312 E1
MALVOLIO
st. Rsemeadow 540 F5
MAMBLE
pl. S Penrith 267 B7
MAME
pl. Kearns 451 A15
MAMIE
av. Seven Hills 245 B16
MAMMONE
cl. Edensor Pk 333 J14
MAMRE
cr. Airds 512 A14
la. St Clair, off
Mamre Rd 269 F10
rd. Kemps Ck 330 A2
rd. Orchard Hills 269 F14
rd. St Clair 269 F14
rd. St Marys 269 G6
MANAHAN
st. Condell Park 398 D2
MANAM
pl. Glenfield 424 J9
MANAR
pl. Prestons 392 J16
MANARA
pl. Seven Hills 275 F5
MANCHESTER
rd. Auburn 338 K1
rd. Gymea 491 F4
rd. Gymea 491 F6
st. Dulwich Hill 373 C7
st. Merrylands 307 G10
wy. Currans Hill 479 G11
MANDA
pl. Rooty Hill 272 A6
MANDALAY
pl. Pymble 253 F5
MANDALONG
cl. Orchard Hills 299 F6
tce. Glenmore Pk 266 F12
MANDARIN
st. Fairfield E 337 C15
wy. Glenwood 215 F11
MANDEMAR
av. Homebush W 340 F7
MANDIBLE
st. Alexandria 375 F10
MANDINA
pl. Bringelly 389 A5
MANDOLONG
la. Mosman 317 D6
rd. Mosman 317 B6
st. Bonnyrigg Ht 363 A6
MANDOO
dr. Doonside 243 E15
MANDOON
rd. Girraween 275 J14
MANDUR
pl. Caringbah 492 H12
MANEROO
rd. Allambie Ht 257 F13
MANETTE
pl. Ambarvale 510 J11
MANEY
st. Rozelle 11 B1
MANGALOO
st. Berowra Ht 133 A8

MANGALORE
dr. Winston Hills 277 B3
MANGARIVA
av. Emerton 240 G6
av. Lethbrdg Pk 240 G6
MANGIRI
rd. Beecroft 250 C3
MANGROVE
la. Taren Point 463 B15
MANHATTAN
ct. Carlingford 280 D5
MANIFOLD
cr. Glenmore Pk 265 K4
rd. Blackett 241 C1
MANILA
rd. Lethbrdg Pk 240 G5
MANILDRA
av. Carlingford 279 D2
st. Earlwood 402 F6
st. Prestons 393 E15
MANILLA
pl. Woronora 459 K16
rd. Hoxton Park 392 H6
MANINS
av. Kingsgrove 401 K7
MANION
av. Rose Bay 347 J12
MANLY
la. Fairlight, off
Birkley Rd 288 E8
la. Manly, off
Birkley Rd 288 E8
pl. Kings Lngly 245 D5
pl. Woodbine 481 H9
rd. Balgowlah 287 C11
rd. Clontarf 287 C11
rd. Seaforth 287 C11
MANN
pl. St Helens Park 541 A6
st. Chatswood 285 E6
st. Glenbrook 233 K16
MANNA
ct. Mt Riverview 204 E15
pl. Bossley Park 333 G9
pl. Kingswood 237 H16
wy. Silverdale 353 K16
MANNA GUM
rd. Narellan Vale 479 A14
MANNERIM
pl. Castle Cove 286 B6
MANNIKIN
dr. Woronora Ht 489 B4
pl. Mount Druitt 241 E12
MANNING
av. Strathfield S 371 D5
cl. McGraths Hl 121 K12
dr. Carlingford 280 E5
pde. Dundas Vy 279 K10
pl. Currans Hill 479 F12
pl. Rookwood 340 C13
pl. Seven Hills 275 F10
rd. Camperdown 18 B2
rd. Double Bay 14 C11
rd. Gladesville 313 A12
rd. Hunters Hill 313 A12
rd. Killara 253 D16
rd. North Ryde 282 H11
rd. Sackville N 68 D1
rd. Woollahra 22 F1
st. Campbelltown 511 K9
st. Homebush B 310 G14
st. Kingswood 237 J16
st. N Balgowlah 287 B3
st. Oyster Bay 461 A7
st. Potts Point 4 K4
st. Prospect 274 F16
st. Queens Park 22 G13
st. Rozelle 344 C7
st. Warwck Frm 365 J16
MANNIX
ct. Harringtn Pk 478 D1
la. Warwck Frm 365 G15
pde. Warwck Frm 365 G15
pl. Quakers Hill 214 B9
st. Bonnyrigg Ht 363 F8
MANNOW
av. West Hoxton 392 B6
MANNS
av. Greenwich 314 K12
av. Neutral Bay 6 E9
pl. Greenwich, off
O'Connell St 314 K14
rd. Wilberforce 93 G5

MANOOKA
cr. Bradbury 511 C15
pl. Kareela 461 D14
pl. Warriewood 199 A7
rd. Currans Hill 480 A9
MANOR
gln. Wrrngtn Dns 238 D5
pl. Baulkham Hl 247 F7
rd. Hornsby 191 C13
rd. Ingleside 197 J5
st. Kellyville Rdg 215 D1
MANOR HILL
rd. Miranda 461 J14
MANORHOUSE
bvd. Quakers Hill 213 F9
MANSFIELD
av. Caringbah 492 K8
la. Glebe 11 J10
rd. Galston 159 J4
st. Girraween 276 B16
st. Glebe 11 J10
st. Rozelle 7 B15
st. Wetherill Pk 334 J5
wy. Kellyville 217 C5
MANSION
ct. Quakers Hill 213 G9
la. Potts Point 4 K7
rd. Bellevue Hill 347 F14
st. Marrickville 403 H1
MANSION POINT
rd. Grays Point 491 E16
MANSON
pl. Clovelly 377 G11
rd. Strathfield 341 G10
st. S Wntwthvle 307 C5
st. Telopea 279 G11
MANTA
pl. Chiswick 343 A2
MANTAKA
st. Blacktown 275 A2
MANTALINI
st. Ambarvale 510 H14
MANTILLUS
gr. Baulkham Hl 246 H4
MANTON
av. Newington 310 D11
MANTURA
ct. Winston Hills 276 H1
MANUELA
pl. Curl Curl 258 E12
MANUKA
av. Baulkham Hl 247 D15
cir. Cherrybrook 219 G11
cr. Bass Hill 368 A10
st. Wentwthvle 277 C12
MANUS
pl. Glenfield 424 G9
MANWARING
av. Maroubra 407 D16
MAPITI
pl. Acacia Gdn 214 G16
MAPLE
av. Pennant Hills 220 F15
av. The Oaks 502 F9
cl. Canada Bay 342 F9
cr. Ermington 280 D13
ct. Greenacre 370 B14
gr. Kellyville Rdg 215 B1
gr. Narellan 478 C10
la. N St Marys, off
Maple Rd 240 B11
pl. Belrose 225 J14
pl. Mcquarie Fd 424 E16
pl. Wentwthvle 277 A9
rd. Casula 423 J2
rd. N St Marys 239 J8
rd. W Pnnant Hl 218 J16
st. Bowen Mtn 83 K7
st. Cabramatta 365 G8
st. Caringbah 492 J15
st. Dural 188 H12
st. Greystanes 306 E4
st. Lugarno 429 H15
MAPLELEAF
dr. Padstow 429 G2
MAPLES
av. Killara 254 A11
MARA
cl. Bonnyrigg 363 J10
cr. Mooney Mooney 75 E1
MARAGA
pl. Doonside 243 F16
MARAKET
av. Blaxland 234 D9

MARALINGA
av. Elanora Ht 198 B16
pl. W Pnnant Hl 249 G6
MARAMBA
cl. Kingsgrove 401 F7
MARAMPO
st. Marayong 243 H5
MARANA
rd. Earlwood 402 C3
rd. Northbridge 315 K1
st. Blacktown 274 F5
MARANATHA
cl. W Pnnant Hl 248 G7
st. Rooty Hill 271 K6
MARANIE
av. St Marys 269 K5
MARANOA
pl. Wahroonga 223 C4
st. Auburn 338 J11
MARANTA
st. Hornsby 191 F11
MARANUI
av. Dee Why 258 F4
MARATHON
av. Darling Point 13 K7
av. Newington 310 B13
la. Darling Point 13 K7
mw. Double Bay 14 B7
rd. Darling Point 13 K6
MARAU
pl. Yellow Rock 204 G1
MARBLE
cl. Bossley Park 334 A8
MARCEAU
dr. Concord 342 D6
MARCEL
av. Coogee 377 F12
av. Randwick 377 F12
cr. Blacktown 274 K2
pl. Baulkham Hl 247 K7
MARCELLA
st. Bankstown 399 G4
st. Bankstown 399 G5
st. Kingsgrove 401 K5
st. N Epping 251 D9
MARCELLUS
pl. Rsemeadow 540 H6
MARCH
pl. Earlwood 403 B5
st. Bellevue Hill 347 F15
st. Richmond 118 F4
wy. Kellyville Rdg 215 A6
MARCHMONT
pl. Airds 512 B10
MARCIA
la. Hurlstone Pk, off
Duntroon St 373 A12
st. Hurlstone Pk 373 A12
st. Toongabbie 276 A6
MARCIANO
cl. Edensor Pk 363 G4
MARCO
av. Panania 397 J16
av. Revesby 398 D16
MARCOALA
pl. St Ives 224 D10
MARCONI
pl. Little Bay 437 B13
rd. Bossley Park 333 H10
rd. Bossley Park 333 H7
st. Winston Hills 277 C5
MARCUS
pl. Frenchs Frst 255 K3
st. Asquith 191 K7
st. Kings Park 244 E3
MARCUS CLARK
wy. Hornsby 191 E12
MARCUS CLARKE
cr. Glenmore Pk 265 J8
MARDEN
st. Artarmon 314 H1
st. Georges Hall 367 G12
MARDI
ct. Kellyville 217 D2
st. Girraween 276 A14
MARDY
ct. Parklea 214 J13
MARE
cl. Harringtn Pk 478 F1
MAREE
av. Cabramatta W 365 C4
pl. Blacktown 243 K9
pl. Condell Park 398 F1

MARELLA
av. Kellyville 216 H2
MARETIMO
st. Balgowlah 287 F10
MARGA
rd. Gymea Bay 491 H9
MARGARET
av. Hornsby Ht 191 E2
cr. Lugarno 429 K16
ct. Shalvey 210 K13
la. Newtown 17 D16
la. Stanmore 16 D5
la. Sydney A G13
pl. Lane Cove N 283 G13
pl. Paddington 4 K16
st. Abbotsford 343 C3
st. Ashfield 342 H16
st. Beacon Hill 257 E7
st. Belfield 371 E9
st. Dulwich Hill 373 E11
st. Fairfield 335 G14
st. Fairfield W 335 G14
st. Fairlight 288 D10
st. Granville 308 D10
st. Greenacre 370 G3
st. Kingsgrove 401 J12
st. Kogarah 433 D9
st. Mays Hill 307 G7
st. Minto 482 G2
st. Newtown 17 D16
st. Northmead 278 A4
st. N Sydney 6 A10
st. Petersham 16 B5
st. Picton 563 G3
st. Redfern 19 A9
st. Riverstone 183 G8
st. Roseville 285 B3
st. Rozelle 344 D6
st. Russell Lea 343 C3
st. Ryde 312 E5
st. St Marys 269 G5
st. Seven Hills 275 F4
st. Stanmore 16 B5
st. Strathfield 341 F13
st. Sydney A F14
st. Sydney 1 F15
st. Woolwich 314 D13
tce. Silverdale 354 B16
wy. Cecil Hills 362 H4
MARGARETA
cl. Guildford 337 D3
MARGATE
st. Botany 405 G14
st. Ramsgate 433 D12
st. Sans Souci 433 E14
MARGO
pl. Schofields 213 J5
MARGOT
pl. Castle Hill 217 H16
MARGUERETTE
st. Ermington 310 D3
MARGUERITE
av. Mt Riverview 234 D2
cr. W Pnnant Hl 220 A15
MARI
cl. Glenmore Pk 266 D9
MARIA
la. Newtown, off
Darley St 374 J10
pl. Blacktown 274 E5
pl. Oakdale 500 D12
st. Petersham 15 G13
st. Strathfield S 371 D7
MARIALA
ct. Holsworthy 426 D5
MARIA LOCK
gr. Oakhurst 242 D4
MARIAM
cl. Cherrybrook 219 B15
MARIAN
ct. Baulkham Hl 247 B1
la. Enmore 17 B14
st. Enmore 17 B14
st. Eveleigh 19 A8
st. Guildford 337 H4
st. Killara 254 A13
st. Redfern 19 A8
st. S Coogee 407 F3
MARIANA
cl. St Ives 224 D14
cr. Lethbrdg Pk 240 G3
MARIANI
cl. Bossley Park 333 G11

102 GREGORY'S STREET DIRECTORY

STREETS MA

MARIE
av. Glenwood 245 F3
cl. Bligh Park 150 H6
cr. Mona Vale 198 J3
la. Belmore 371 E16
st. Belmore 401 D1
st. Castle Hill 247 J2
st. Lurnea 394 E10
st. Wentwthvle 277 A10
MARIEANNE
pl. Minchinbury 271 D7
MARIEBA
rd. Kenthurst 157 A6
MARIE DODD
cr. Blakehurst 462 D3
MARIE PITT
pl. Glenmore Pk 265 H5
MARIGOLD
av. Marayong 244 B7
cl. Glenmore Pk 265 G10
la. Glenmore Pk, off Marigold Cl 265 F10
pl. Revesby 398 B11
st. Revesby 398 B11
MARIKO
pl. Blacktown 273 J7
MARILLIAN
av. Waitara 221 H5
MARILYN
st. North Ryde 282 G8
MARIN
pl. Glendenning 242 F5
pl. Merrylands 307 C11
pl. Prestons 393 A16
MARINA
cl. Bossley Park 333 K9
cl. Mt Krng-gai 162 K6
cr. Cecil Hills 362 K3
cr. Greenacre 369 H12
cr. Gymea Bay 491 E13
pl. Belrose 225 J15
rd. Baulkham Hl 246 J12
st. Kingsgrove 401 J12
MARINE
cr. Hornsby Ht 191 D8
dr. Chiswick 343 B2
dr. Oatley 430 G15
esp. Cronulla 494 C7
pde. Avalon 140 E16
pde. Double Bay 14 B6
pde. Homebush B 310 K9
pde. Manly 288 K10
pde. Maroubra 407 G12
pde. Watsons Bay 318 F15
rd. Avalon 140 F14
MARINEA
st. Arncliffe 403 G10
st. Arncliffe 403 F11
MARINELLA
st. Manly Vale 287 H5
MARINER
cr. Abbotsbury 333 C15
rd. Illawong 459 C3
MARINNA
rd. Elanora Ht 198 E14
MARION
cr. Lapstone 264 H5
st. Auburn 339 E5
st. Bankstown 369 A16
st. Bnkstn Aprt 367 H15
st. Blacktown 274 H2
st. Cecil Hills 362 G5
st. Condell Park 368 C16
st. Georges Hall 367 H15
st. Gymea 491 G3
st. Haberfield 373 E1
st. Harris Park 308 E6
st. Leichhardt 15 G1
st. Parramatta 308 D6
st. Seven Hills 245 D16
st. Strathfield 340 J14
st. Thirlmere 565 D3
MARIPOSA
rd. Bilgola 169 H6
MARIST
pl. Parramatta 278 C16
MARJORIE
cl. Casula 423 H2
cr. Maroubra 406 H7
pl. Kellyville 217 B2
st. Roseville 284 G1
st. Sefton 368 H1
MARJORIE JACKSON
pky. Homebush B 310 H13
MARJORY
pl. Baulkham Hl 248 A10
MARJORY THOMAS
pl. Balgowlah 288 A7
MARK
la. Roselands 401 C7
la. St Marys, off Mark St 270 A5
la. Sydney C D5
la. Sydney 3 E3
pl. Bilgola 169 F4
pl. Cherrybrook 219 F8
rd. Nelson 154 H9
rd. Rossmore 419 K4
st. Dundas Vy 280 D10
st. Hunters Hill 313 B9
st. Lidcombe 339 J9
st. Merrylands 306 K10
st. Mount Druitt 271 C3
st. St Marys 270 A5
MARKELL
pl. Liverpool 394 J5
MARKET
la. Manly 288 G10
la. Merrylands, off Baker St 307 J16
row. Sydney C G10
row. Sydney 3 F5
st. Appin 569 G10
st. Clarmnt Ms 269 B1
st. Condell Park 398 K4
st. Drummoyne 343 H6
st. Moorebank 395 G9
st. Naremburn 315 G2
st. Parramatta 308 C1
st. Randwick 377 C10
st. Randwick 377 D9
st. Riverstone 182 J7
st. Rockdale 403 D15
st. Smithfield 335 G5
st. Sydney C D8
st. Sydney 3 E4
st. Tahmoor 565 G12
st. West Ryde 281 D15
st.e, Naremburn 315 H2
MARKETOWN
la. Riverstone, off Garfield Rd E 182 J8
MARKET PLACE
st. Horngsea Pk 392 E11
MARKEY
st. Guildford 338 D5
MARKHAM
av. Penrith 237 D11
cl. Mosman 317 E10
ct. Acacia Gdn 214 H16
la. Ashfield 372 H2
st. Holsworthy 426 C4
MARKOVINA
st. Edensor Pk 333 F16
MARKS
av. Seven Hills 245 H14
la. Bass Hill 368 A5
la. Chester Hill 368 A5
la. Tamarama 378 D6
st. Bass Hill 368 A5
st. Canley Ht 364 K2
st. Canley Ht 365 A2
st. Chester Hill 368 A5
st. Chester Hill 368 B5
st. Naremburn 315 H3
MARKWELL
pl. Agnes Banks 117 E11
MARL
pl. Eagle Vale 481 F7
MARLBOROUGH
av. Harbord 258 C15
la. Glebe 12 B11
pl. St Ives 223 J7
rd. Homebush W 340 G8
rd. Willoughby 285 G15
st. Drummoyne 343 H1
st. Fairfield Ht 336 B9
st. Glebe 12 B12
st. Leichhardt 9 G16
st. Smithfield 336 B9
st. Surry Hills 20 A5
MARLEE
rd. Engadine 489 E9
st. Hornsby 191 H8
st. N Balgowlah 287 G5
MARLENE
cr. Greenacre 370 F1
pl. Belmore 401 F6
st. Freemns Rch 90 A3
MARLEY
cr. Bonnyrigg Ht 363 B3
st. Ambarvale 511 A14
MARLIS
av. Revesby 398 E11
MARLO
rd. Cronulla 494 A9
MARLOCK
pl. Alfords Point 429 C13
pl. Mcquarie Fd 454 D4
st. Kingswood 267 H1
MARLOO
pl. St Helens Park 541 H3
MARLOW
av. Denistone 281 F13
la. Denistone 281 F12
pl. Campbelltown 511 H9
pl. Kellyville Rdg 214 K3
pl. Kellyville Rdg 215 A3
rd. Artarmon 285 C13
MARLOWE
st. Campsie 372 A15
st. Wetherill Pk 334 K4
MARMADUKE
st. Burwood 342 A14
MARMION
la. Abbotsford 312 K16
la. Camperdown 17 B8
rd. Abbotsford 312 K16
st. Birrong 369 B5
st. Camperdown 17 B8
wy. Beaumont Hills 185 J14
MARMORA
st. Harbord 258 G16
MARNE
la. St Clair, off Marne Pl 269 G16
pl. St Clair 269 G15
st. Vaucluse 348 G5
MARNIE
gr. Kings Lngly 245 K8
MARNOO
pl. Belrose 226 C15
MARNPAR
rd. Seven Hills 246 A13
MAROA
cr. Allambie Ht 287 G1
MARONG
st. Panania 398 D16
MARONI
pl. St Clair 269 F14
MAROOBA
pl. Engadine 488 G11
rd. Northbridge 285 K15
MAROOK
st. Carlingford 280 E6
MAROOPNA
rd. Yowie Bay 492 A10
MAROUBRA
cr. Woodbine 481 F13
la. Maroubra 407 B10
rd. Maroubra 406 H9
rd. Maroubra 407 G10
MARPLE
av. Villawood 367 F1
MARQUESA
cr. Lethbrdg Pk 240 F3
MARQUET
st. Rhodes 311 C9
MARRA
pl. Sylvania 462 E8
MARRAKESH
pl. Arcadia 129 B12
MARRETT
wy. Cranebrook 207 F9
MARRICKVILLE
av. Marrickville 373 G12
la. Marrickville 374 A13
rd. Dulwich Hill 373 F10
rd. Marrickville 373 F10
MARRIOTT
gr. Castle Hill 217 D10
rd. Bonnyrigg 363 F9
rd. Bonnyrigg Ht 363 F9
st. Redfern 19 K11
st. Redfern 20 A7
MARRON
pl. Beecroft 250 A12
MARROO
st. Bronte 377 J11
MARS
la. Gladesville 313 A3
pl. Lansvale 366 H8
rd. Lane Cove W 283 E16
st. Epping 280 D2
st. Gladesville 312 K10
st. Padstow 429 B3
st. Revesby 428 J3
wy. Glenwood 215 C13
MARSALA
st. Mosman 287 A15
MARSANNE
pl. Eschol Park 481 C2
MARSCAY
st. Kellyville Rdg 215 A5
MARSDEN
av. Elderslie 507 H1
av. Kellyville 215 G4
cl. Bossley Park 334 D11
cr. Bligh Park 150 E5
cr. Peakhurst 430 E1
la. Riverstone 182 C9
rd. Barden Rdg 458 G16
rd. Carlingford 280 B4
rd. Dundas Vy 280 B4
rd. Liverpool 395 A1
rd. Riverstone 182 E9
rd. St Marys 270 A7
rd. West Ryde 280 F11
st. Camperdown 17 F3
st. Granville 308 B7
st. Lidcombe 339 J9
st. Parramatta 308 B5
st. Ruse 512 G2
MARSH
av. Woolooware 493 J8
pde. Casula 394 K14
pl. Cranebrook 207 D10
pl. Lane Cove 314 G3
pl. The Oaks 502 F14
rd. Silverdale 353 F15
st. Arncliffe 403 J8
st. Condell Park 398 F2
st. Granville 308 H11
st. Wakeley 364 K1
st. Wolli Creek 403 K8
MARSHALL
av. Bargo 567 F10
av. Moorebank 396 E12
av. Newington 310 A16
av. St Leonards 315 C6
av. Warrawee 222 D13
cl. Hornsby Ht 161 J10
cr. Beacon Hill 257 H9
la. Panania 398 B16
la. Petersham 16 C13
la. St Leonards, off Berry Rd 315 C6
pl. North Ryde 282 K8
rd. Dundas Vy 279 H9
rd. Kirrawee 461 C16
rd. Mt Riverview 234 B4
rd. Telopea 279 H9
st. Balmain 7 K8
st. Bankstown 399 E6
st. Bnkstn Aprt 368 B16
st. Kogarah 433 D7
st. Manly 288 H13
st. Paddington 4 F14
st. Petersham 16 B13
st. Surry Hills 20 D2
MARSILEA
cl. Mt Annan 509 B1
MARTEN
cl. Prestons 392 J16
MARTENS
cct. Kellyville 215 G3
la. Cremorne, off Waters La 316 D8
la. Mosman, off Raglan St 317 C9
la. Neutral Bay, off Waters La 316 D8
pl. Abbotsbury 333 B11
wy. Claymore 481 B10
MARTHA
av. Northmead 277 K6
cr. Cranebrook 207 D11
la. Cranebrook, off Martha Cr 207 D10
st. Granville 308 K11
st. Hunters Hill 313 K11
st. Yagoona 369 A10
wy. Ambarvale 510 K15
MARTI
pl. Hebersham 241 E10
MARTIN
av. Arncliffe 403 G6
av. Pagewood 406 C8
bvd. Plumpton 241 K11
cr. Milperra 397 C10
cr. Woodpark 306 H14
gr. Colyton 270 G9
gr. Werombi 413 A14
la. Roseville 284 H3
pl. Dural 188 G12
pl. Mortdale 431 A8
pl. Mt Annan 479 H14
pl. Sydney C K2
pl. Sydney 3 G1
rd. Badgerys Ck 329 D16
rd. Centennial Pk 21 A14
rd. Galston 159 H9
rd. Moore Park 20 J14
rd. Oakville 124 E6
st. Blakehurst 432 A14
st. Emu Plains 235 C10
st. Haberfield 343 B12
st. Harbord 288 D1
st. Heathcote 518 F11
st. Hunters Hill 313 E9
st. Lidcombe 340 A8
st. Mulgoa 265 D4
st. Paddington 21 B3
st. Regentville 265 D4
st. Roselands 400 F9
st. Ryde 282 D14
st. St Leonards 315 F4
MARTINA
st. Plumpton 241 J11
MARTINDALE
av. Baulkham Hl 247 F5
ct. Wattle Grove 395 K16
MARTINE
av. Camden S 507 B11
MARTIN LUTHER
la. Allambie Ht 257 A10
pl. Allambie Ht 257 B10
MARTINO
cl. Prestons 422 H1
MARTINS
av. Bondi 377 J2
la. Carlingford 279 G6
la. Freemns Rch 90 J2
MARTLEY
la. Cranebrook, off Martley Wy 207 F14
wy. Cranebrook 207 F14
MARTON
cr. Kings Lngly 245 G8
MARULAN
wy. Prestons 392 H15
MARUM
st. Ashcroft 364 F14
MARVELL
rd. Wetherill Pk 334 E6
MARVILLE
av. Kingsford 406 H6
MARWOOD
dr. Beecroft 250 C10
MARX
av. Beverley Pk 433 B9
pl. Quakers Hill 243 K1
MARY
av. Cranebrook 206 H8
cr. Liverpool 394 H9
la. Bundeena 523 K10
la. Surry Hills F C14
la. Surry Hills 3 J15
pde. Rydalmere 309 C1
pl. Bligh Park 150 F7
pl. Castle Hill, off Vittoria Smith Av 218 H14
pl. Paddington 4 J15
pl. Surry Hills 4 D15
st. Auburn 339 A3
st. Beacon Hill 257 E6
st. Beecroft 250 E7
st. Blacktown 244 A11
st. Bundeena 524 A9
st. Burwood 342 A14
st. Drummoyne 343 F5
st. Ermington 310 H3
st. Glebe 11 J6
st. Granville 308 E11
st. Hunters Hill 313 C10
st. Jannali 460 G12
st. Lidcombe 339 J8
st. Lilyfield 9 H4
st. Lilyfield 9 J7
st. Longueville 314 C9
st. Mcquarie Fd 424 E15

GREGORY'S STREET DIRECTORY 103

MA STREETS

st. Merrylands 337 E1
st. Newtown 17 G11
st. Northmead 278 A3
st. N Parramatta 278 D11
st. Regents Pk 368 J2
st. Rhodes 311 D10
st. Riverwood 399 K14
st. Rooty Hill 241 K15
st. Rozelle 10 J4
st. St Peters 374 F14
st. Schofields 182 H14
st. Surry Hills F B14
st. Surry Hills 3 J15
st. The Oaks 502 E11
st. Turrella 403 D6
st. Wetherill Pk 334 J6
st. Wiley Park 400 J4

MARY ANN
st. Ultimo 3 A14
st. Ultimo 12 K14

MARY ANN DYSON
rd. Appin 569 G10

MARY ANNE
cl. Mt Annan 509 F2
pl. Cherrybrook 219 E11

MARY BROWN
pl. Blair Athol 511 A2

MARYFIELDS
dr. Blair Athol 510 J1

MARY GILMORE
pl. Heathcote 518 C15

MARY-HELEN
ct. Baulkham Hl 247 A1

MARY HOWE
pl. Narellan Vale 508 J2

MARY IRENE
pl. Castle Hill 248 F2

MARYL
av. Roselands 401 B8

MARY MARGARET
la. Mosman 317 D13

MARY ROSE
st. Green Valley 362 K9

MARYVALE
av. Liverpool 394 G4

MARY WALL
cr. Berowra 133 G9

MARY WOLLSTONECRAFT
la. Milsons Point 5 K16

MASCOT
dr. Eastlakes 405 J3

MASEFIELD
pl. Woolooware 493 C12

MASER
st. Cranebrook 207 F10

MASERATI
dr. Ingleburn 453 G11

MASHMAN
av. Kingsgrove 401 K11
av. Wentwthvle 306 J1

MASIKU
pl. Glendenning 242 F4

MASLIN
cr. Quakers Hill 214 A11

MASON
av. Cheltenham 250 H9
av. Hobartville 118 D6
dr. Harringtn Pk 478 H4
la. Bondi, off Jackaman St 377 K6
pl. Barden Rdg 488 F7
pl. Bonnyrigg 364 D6
rd. Box Hill 154 C13
st. Camperdown 17 E2
st. Denistone E 281 G10
st. Maroubra 406 H8
st. Merrylands 307 D13
st. Mount Druitt 240 H16
st. Parramatta 278 H16
st. Thirlmere 564 J4
st. Thirlmere 565 A4

MASONS
dr. N Parramatta 278 H8
la. N Parramatta 278 H7

MASSA
la. Clarmnt Ms, off Massa Pl 268 J3
pl. Clarmnt Ms 268 J3

MASSEY
la. Gladesville 312 J9
pl. St Ives Ch 223 K6
st. Cammeray 315 H4
st. Carlton 432 G11
st. Gladesville 312 J9
wy. Glenmore Pk 265 H5

MASSIE
st. Ermington 310 F3

MASTERFIELD
st. Rossmore 389 C16

MASTERS
pl. Girraween 276 B14
pl. Penrith 236 J10

MATARA
wy. Glenwood 215 F13

MATARO
cl. Edensor Pk 333 C16
pl. Eschol Park 481 E3

MATHERS
pl. Menai 458 G15

MATHESON
av. Chatswood 285 C11
av. Mt Pritchard 364 F11
av. N Richmond 87 D15
gr. Hassall Gr 211 J15

MATHEW
la. Belmore 371 A12
pl. West Hoxton 392 D10

MATHEWS
pl. Menai 458 F12
st. Davidson 225 A15

MATHEWSON
st. Eastgardens 406 G13

MATHIESON
st. Annandale 17 B3

MATHINNA
cct. West Hoxton 392 D6

MATHIS
pl. Ingleburn 453 J6

MATIKA
pl. Lethbrdg Pk 210 G15

MATILDA
gr. Beaumont Hills 185 K15
st. Rozelle 10 G1
wy. Glenwood 245 K5

MATINGARA
wy. Wallacia 354 K2

MATLOCK
pl. Glenwood 215 B16

MATONG
pl. Gymea Bay 491 G10
st. Gordon 254 A7

MATORA
la. Cremorne 316 D5

MATRA
pl. Raby 451 H13

MATRUM
st. Holsworthy 426 E6

MATSON
cr. Miranda 492 C7

MATTERSON
la. Redfern 20 B7

MATTHES
st. Yennora 337 B11

MATTHEW
av. Heckenberg 363 K13
cl. Galston 160 J10
cl. Mt Annan 509 D1
cl. St Ives 224 F10
cr. Blacktown 274 D4
la. Crows Nest, off Atchison St 315 H5
pde. Blaxland 233 J9
pl. Bella Vista 246 F2
rd. Lidcombe 339 F10
st. Beverley Pk 433 A12
st. Crows Nest 315 G5
st. Hunters Hill 313 D10
st. Merrylands 307 C15
wy. W Pnnant Hl 219 A16

MATTHEW FLINDERS
pl. Burraneer 523 D3

MATTHEWS
av. East Hills 427 K4
av. Lane Cove 313 K2
la. Picton 563 H10
sq. Ingleburn 453 E8
st. Carramar 336 J16
st. Emu Heights 235 A5
st. Greenacre 370 G11
st. Punchbowl 400 D4

MATTS
av. Panania 398 C14
la. Revesby 398 H15

MAUBEUGE
st. S Granville 338 G6

MAUD
cl. Cecil Hills 362 G7
la. Marrickville 374 B14
st. Blacktown 274 H8
st. Fairfield Ht 335 G12
st. Fairfield W 335 G14
st. Granville 308 E12
st. Lidcombe 339 K6
st. Randwick 376 K16

MAUDE
st. Regents Pk 369 B3

MAUGHAM
cr. Wetherill Pk 334 G3

MAUGHAN
st. Lalor Park 245 E13

MAUNDER
av. Girraween 276 B14
av. St Ives 224 C8
pl. Warragamba 353 E8
st. Regents Pk 369 D2

MAUREEN
pl. Blacktown 274 B3

MAURICE
la. St Clair, off Maurice St 270 A9
st. Marsden Pk 182 B14
st. St Clair 270 A9

MAURIE FIELDS
st. Moore Park 21 C7

MAURITIUS
av. Georges Hall 368 C15

MAVICK
cr. Leumeah 511 K1

MAVIS
av. Peakhurst 430 H4
st. Greystanes 305 G7
st. North Ryde 282 D9
st. Revesby 398 J9
st. Rooty Hill 272 D1

MAVOR
cr. Frenchs Frst 256 C8

MAWARRA
av. Miranda 491 J5
cl. Forestville 255 G8
cr. Kellyville 216 E3
cr. Marsfield 251 H15

MAWBANNA
cl. West Hoxton 392 E5

MAWSON
av. Beecroft 250 D10
cr. Ermington 310 C1
ct. Wrrngtn Cty 238 F8
dr. Cartwright 393 J5
la. Chifley, off Mawson Pde 437 B7
pde. Chifley 437 B7
pl. Pitt Town 92 J15
rd. Tregear 240 C5
st. Bardwell Vy 403 C7
st. Leumeah 482 J10
st. Punchbowl 399 J4
st. St Ives 224 C7

MAX
st. Kurrajong Ht 63 F12

MAX ALLEN
dr. Lindfield 283 G8

MAXIM
la. West Ryde, off Maxim St 281 D16
pl. St Marys 239 G10
st. West Ryde 281 D16

MAXINE
rd. Greystanes 306 G9

MAXWELL
av. Maroubra 407 G11
av. Milperra 397 E14
cl. Illawong 459 D1
la. Glebe 11 G10
la. Pagewood, off Maxwell Rd 406 G9
pde. Frenchs Frst 256 C9
pl. Blaxland 233 F6
pl. Narellan 478 J8
pl. W Pnnant Hl 249 C9
rd. Glebe 11 F9
rd. Pagewood 406 G9
st. Blacktown 274 D3
st. Mcquarie Fd 424 A14
st. Mona Vale 198 J3
st. S Penrith 266 F2
st. S Turramrra 252 C8

MAXWELLS
av. Ashcroft 364 F16
av. Sadleir 394 B3

MAXWELTON
pl. Narraweena 258 C5

MAY
av. Rossmore 389 C12
la. Dulwich Hill, off Union St 373 C10
la. Eastwood 281 C7
la. Neutral Bay 6 G1
la. St Peters 374 J11
pl. Illawong 459 H6
pl. St Andrews 482 A3
rd. Dee Why 258 D7
rd. Narraweena 258 D7
st. Bardwell Pk 403 A7
st. Dulwich Hill 373 B10
st. Eastwood 281 B7
st. Fairfield 336 J14
st. Glenbrook 234 D16
st. Hornsby 191 J16
st. Lilyfield 10 C5
st. Merrylands 308 D15
st. St Peters 374 H12
st. Turramurra 252 D2
st. Wentwthvle 277 A10
wk. Lalor Park 245 G11

MAYA
cl. Bossley Park 333 K12

MAYBANKE
ct. Mona Vale 169 D15

MAYBERRY
cr. Liverpool 395 A2

MAYBROOK
av. Cromer 227 J14

MAYBUSH
ct. Schofields 213 H5
pl. Cherrybrook 219 J14
wy. Castle Hill 248 F1

MAYCOCK
st. Denistone E 281 H10

MAYDA
pl. Beaumont Hills 186 A15

MAYES
st. Annandale 16 G1

MAYFAIR
av. Kellyville 185 E8
cr. Beverly Hills 401 A13
pl. E Lindfield 255 D12
rd. Mulgoa 295 A7
st. Auburn 338 K14

MAYFARM
rd. Brownlow Hl 505 D3
rd. Mt Hunter 505 E4

MAYFIELD
av. Pymble 253 A2
av. Woolwich 314 F13
st. Wentwthvle 277 C13

MAYGAR
cl. Milperra 397 D13

MAY GIBBS
pl. Frenchs Frst 256 G3
wy. Frenchs Frst 256 H3

MAYLIE
cl. Ambarvale 510 H13

MAYMAN
row. Menai 458 J12

MAYNE
la. Abbotsford 342 J3
st. Wilberforce 91 K3

MAYO
pl. Killarney Ht 256 D16
rd. Llandilo 179 B16

MAYOR
st. Kogarah Bay 432 H13

MAYTONE
av. Killara 254 C8

MAYVIC
st. Greenacre 370 G7

MAZARI
gr. Stanhpe Gdn 215 A10

MAZARIN
st. Riverwood 400 D14

MAZE
av. Ryde 312 C2
cr. Darlington 18 E5
la. Chippendale 18 H3

MAZEPA
av. S Penrith 267 D1
pl. Lidcombe 340 B7

MEACHER
st. Mount Druitt 241 D12

MEAD
dr. Chipping Ntn 366 J14
pl. Chipping Ntn 366 K14
st. Banksia 403 F13

MEADE
st. Allawah 432 E9

MEADOW
cl. Beecroft 250 F10
cr. Meadowbank 311 D4
la. Wollstncraft, off Rocklands Rd 315 E10
pl. Kellyville 216 E1
pl. Miranda 461 J15
rd. Schofields 212 G8
st. Concord 341 J7

MEADOWBANK
la. West Ryde 311 A1

MEADOWLAND
rd. Peakhurst 400 F16

MEADOWLANDS
Blacktown 274 D12

MEADOWS
pl. Castle Hill 218 J14
rd. Cabramatta W 364 F8
rd. Mt Pritchard 364 D12
rd. N Richmond 65 H16
st. Merrylands 308 B15
wy. Minto 482 J4

MEADOWVIEW
wy. Wrrngtn Dns 237 J5

MEADWAY
cl. Pymble 253 J4

MEAGER
av. Padstow 399 G16

MEAGHER
av. Maroubra 407 E14
st. Chippendale 19 B3

MEAKEM
st. Hurstville 431 J5

MEAKIN
cr. Chester Hill 338 D16
st. Merrylands 307 F15

MEALIA
la. Edgecliff 13 F11

MEANDER
cl. West Hoxton 392 D6

MEARES
rd. McGraths Hl 121 K13

MEARS
av. Randwick 377 B15

MEATH
pl. Blacktown 243 J15
pl. Killarney Ht 256 E16

MEATWORKS
av. Oxford Falls 227 B14

MECHANIC
st. Newtown 17 H10

MECKIFF
av. North Rocks 278 J3
cl. Menai 458 E9

MEDCALFE
pl. Edensor Pk 363 E3

MEDEA
pl. Dean Park 212 F15

MEDHURST
rd. Gilead 539 F10

MEDIATI
av. Kellyville 216 G7

MEDICH
pl. Bringelly 388 E10

MEDICI
pl. Glenwood 246 A4

MEDIKA
pl. Kirrawee 461 D15

MEDLEY
av. Liverpool 365 A14

MEDLOW
dr. Quakers Hill 243 H1

MEDORA
la. Cabarita 312 E16
st. Cabarita 312 D16

MEDUSA
st. Mosman 287 A16

MEDWAY
rd. Bringelly 387 K11
rd. Bringelly 388 A12
st. Bexley 402 H14

MEDWIN
pl. Quakers Hill 214 C11

MEEGAN
pl. Colyton 270 F8

104 GREGORY'S STREET DIRECTORY

STREETS — ME

MEEHAN
- av. Hamondvle 396 D13
- av. Wrrngtn Cty 238 J5
- la. Georges Hall 367 H9
- la. Matraville 437 D3
- la. Wrrngtn Cty, off Meehan Av 238 H5
- pl. Baulkham Hl 247 F3
- pl. Campbelltown 511 E8
- pl. Harringtn Pk 478 E5
- pl. Kirrawee 490 H7
- rd. Cromer 228 C15
- st. Granville 308 A8
- st. Matraville 437 C1
- st. West Hoxton 392 A12
- tce. Harringtn Pk 478 F5

MEEKATHARRA
- pl. Yarrawarrah 489 H12

MEEKS
- cr. Faulcnbdg 171 A15
- la. Kingsford 406 G1
- la. Marrickville, off Meeks Rd 374 A14
- la. Marrickville, off Meeks Rd 374 B13
- rd. Marrickville 374 A14
- st. Kingsford 406 G1

MEELA
- st. Blacktown 273 K3

MEGALONG
- av. N Willoughby 285 H8
- av. Campbelltown 512 A7

MEGAN
- pl. Bankstown 399 F4
- av. Smithfield 335 F2
- av. Galston 160 F10
- st. Telopea 279 D6

MEIG
- pl. Marayong 244 D9

MEITNER
- pl. Lucas Ht 487 J12

MEKEO
- pl. Glenfield 424 G13

MEKONG
- pl. Kearns 481 B1

MELALEUCA
- av. Fairfield E 337 A16
- cl. Castle Hill 248 G4
- cr. Carlingford 280 A6
- dr. Mcquarie Fd 454 F3
- dr. St Ives 224 D15
- gr. Greenacre 370 F6
- la. Kingswood, off Melaleuca Pl 267 F2
- la. Mosman, off Mandolong Rd 317 B6
- pl. Alfords Point 429 B15
- pl. Kingswood 267 G2
- pl. Prestons 393 J16
- rd. Narellan Vale 478 H14
- st. Newport 169 K13

MELALUCA
- st. Stanhpe Gdn 215 D10

MELANESIA
- av. Lethbrdg Pk 240 G3

MELANIE
- pl. Bella Vista 246 F6
- st. Bankstown 369 C13
- st. Hassall Gr 211 K15
- st. Yagoona 369 C13

MELBA
- av. Chifley 437 B7
- dr. East Ryde 282 K15
- pl. Casula 424 G1
- st. St Helens Park 541 D3
- st. Labor Pk 245 C10

MELBOURNE
- av. Mona Vale 199 D9
- av. Baulkham Hl 247 J16
- cl. E Lindfield 254 K13
- rd. Riverstone 182 G1
- rd. St Johns Pk 364 D3
- st. Concord 341 J9
- st. Fairlight 288 B8
- st. Oxley Park 270 G1

MELDON
- pl. Stanhpe Gdn 215 G9

MELDRUM
- av. Miranda 492 C1
- av. Mt Pritchard 364 A11
- av. Ryde 282 G15
- wy. Claymore 481 D12

MELFORD
- st. Hurlstone Pk 372 J13

MELHAM
- av. Panania 398 D14

MELIA
- ct. Castle Hill 218 J14
- pl. Mcquarie Fd 424 F16

MELINDA
- cl. Beaumont Hills 185 J15

MELINGA
- pl. Revesby 428 G4

MELINZ
- pl. Quakers Hill 214 F12

MELISSA
- cl. Cherrybrook 219 F7
- pl. Kings Park 244 G6
- pl. W Pnnant Hl 248 K7
- st. Auburn 338 G14

MELITA
- rd. Cmbrdg Pk 237 H8

MELKARTH
- pl. Doonside 243 E16

MELKIN
- end, Gordon 253 J6

MELLA
- cl. West Hoxton 392 C5

MELLFELL
- rd. Cranebrook 207 F10

MELLICK
- st. Fairfield W 335 F13

MELLIODORA
- wy. Mcquarie Fd 454 F3

MELLOR
- pl. Bonnyrigg Ht 363 A7
- pl. Hebersham 241 F9
- pl. West Ryde 311 F1

MELNOTTE
- av. Roseville 284 A5

MELODY
- la. Collaroy 229 A15
- la. Coogee 377 K13
- la. Coogee 377 E16
- la. Toongabbie 276 B5

MELROSE
- av. Lakemba 400 K3
- av. Quakers Hill 243 G2
- av. Sylvania 461 K9
- av. Wiley Park 400 K3
- ct. Abbotsford 343 A2
- cr. Chiswick 343 A2
- la. Woollahra 21 F4
- pde. Clovelly 377 K13
- pl. Bossley Park 333 E12
- pl. Brooklyn 75 F11
- pl. Chester Hill 338 C16
- pl. Croydon Pk 372 A7
- pl. Epping 280 J2
- pl. Homebush 341 D11
- pl. Lane Cove N 284 A12
- pl. Mosman 316 J6

MELTON
- rd. Glenorie 127 H9
- st.n, Silverwater 309 G14
- st.s, Auburn 309 G15

MELUCA
- cr. Hornsby Ht 191 D1

MELVILLE
- av. Cabramatta 366 A6
- av. Strathfield 340 H15
- ci. Berowra 133 C16
- cl. Hinchinbrk 393 A1
- cl. Harringtn Pk 478 H3
- la. Newtown 17 E12
- pl. Barden Rdg 488 F2
- pl. Minchinbury 272 E9
- pl. Rooty Hill 272 A4
- rd. St Clair 269 J12
- st. Ashbury 372 F8
- st. Parramatta 308 H1
- st. Ryde 281 J15
- st. West Ryde 281 H15

MELVIN
- st.n, Beverly Hills 401 A14
- st.s, Beverly Hills 401 B15

MELWOOD
- av. Forestville 255 J12
- la. Killarney Ht 255 K14

MEMA
- pl. Quakers Hill 243 H3

MEMBREY
- st. Granville 308 F16

MEMMANG
- pl. Kirrawee 461 D15

MEMORIAL
- av. Ingleburn 453 B4
- av. Kellyville 216 E8

MENA
- av. Lansvale 367 A8
- st. Belfield 371 C11
- st. N Strathfield 341 C4
- wy. Bidwill 211 D13

MENAI
- rd. Bangor 459 A13
- rd. Bangor 459 H13
- rd. Menai 458 H12
- rd. Woronora 460 A13

MENANGLE
- rd. Camden 507 A3
- rd. Campbelltown 511 A6
- rd. Douglas Park 568 C2
- rd. Gilead 509 K16
- rd. Glen Alpine 510 C10
- rd. Menangle 538 H16
- rd. Menangle Pk 538 J11
- rd. Menangle Pk 539 B7
- st. Picton 563 G4
- st.w, Picton 563 F3

MENDANA
- st. Lethbrdg Pk 240 F4

MENDELEEF
- av. Lucas Ht 487 F12

MENDELSSOHN
- av. Emerton 240 H5

MENDI
- pl. Engadine 489 F7

MENDOS
- cl. Milperra 397 G12

MENIN
- cl. Milperra 397 G12
- rd. Matraville 407 A16
- rd. Oakville 153 B7

MENINDEE
- av. Leumeah 482 K13
- wy. Woodcroft 243 H10

MENSA
- pl. Castle Hill 218 K9
- pl. Jamisontown 266 D6

MENTHA
- pl. Mcquarie Fd 454 B4

MENTMORE
- av. Rosebery 375 G16

MENTONE
- av. Cronulla 494 A13

MENUS
- pl. Rsemeadow 540 H2

MENZIES
- arc. Sydney 1 F16
- cct. St Clair 270 A12
- la. St Clair, off Menzies Cct 270 A13
- pl. Edensor Pk 333 H13
- rd. Marsfield 281 G1

MEPUNGA
- st. Concord W 341 F2

MERA
- st. Guildford 337 C4

MERAUKE
- st. Whalan 240 J11

MERCATOR
- cr. Willmot 210 E14

MERCEDES
- pl. Kareela 461 D11
- rd. Ingleburn 453 H13

MERCER
- st. Beverly Hills 400 K16
- st. Castle Hill 218 E15
- st. Castle Hill 218 D15

MERCHANT
- st. Mascot 405 E7
- st. Stanmore 16 G12

MERCURY
- pl. Kings Lngly 246 B8
- st. Beverly Hills 400 J14
- st. Narwee 400 J14

MERCUTIO
- pl. Gilead 540 F8

MERCY
- av. Chester Hill 337 K12

MERDLE
- pl. Ambarvale 540 F1

MEREDITH
- av. Hornsby Ht 191 B8
- av. Kellyville 216 H4
- av. Rhodes 311 D7
- cl. Fairfield 336 E6
- cr. St Helens Park 541 B8
- dr. Frenchs Frst 256 F7
- rch. Westleigh 220 H7
- st. Bankstown 369 D16
- st. Blaxland 233 E9
- st. Epping 280 F6
- st. Homebush 341 B11
- st. Strathfield 341 B11
- wy. Cecil Hills 362 C11

MEREIL
- st. Campbelltown 511 K3

MERELYN
- rd. Belrose 226 B16

MERELYNNE
- av. W Pnnant Hl 248 K8

MEREVALE
- pl. Oakhurst 241 J4

MERIDIAN
- pl. Bella Vista 216 A15
- pl. Doonside 243 H16
- st. Eastlakes 405 J2

MERIEL
- st. Sans Souci 463 A5

MERINDA
- av. Baulkham Hl 248 B8
- av. Epping 250 F11
- pl. Bonnyrigg 364 B8
- st. Lane Cove N 283 J14
- st. St Marys 239 F14

MERINDAH
- rd. Baulkham Hl 247 A7
- wy. Kurrajong 64 E13

MERINO
- cct. St Clair 270 D12
- cr. Airds 511 H15
- dr. Elderslie 507 H1
- dr. Sylvania 462 B13
- st. Miller 393 G2

MERION
- ct. Glenmore Pk 266 G9

MERITON
- st. Gladesville 312 G12

MERLE
- st. Bass Hill 368 D7
- st. N Epping 251 C8
- st. Sefton 338 F13

MERLEN
- cr. Yagoona 369 B9

MERLEY
- rd. Strathfield 341 A13

MERLIN
- cl. Mt Colah 162 D8
- ct. Castle Hill 217 H4
- pl. Emu Heights 235 C12
- st. Blacktown 274 G8

MERLOT
- pl. Edensor Pk 333 C16

MERMAID
- av. Maroubra 407 H8

MERNAGH
- st. Ashcroft 364 E15

MEROO
- cl. Wakeley 334 J13
- st. Auburn 338 J11
- st. Blacktown 244 D16

MERRANG
- ct. Wattle Grove 425 J6

MERREDIN
- cl. Yarrawarrah 489 F13

MERRENBURN
- av. Naremburn 315 G3

MERRETT
- cr. Greenacre 370 C9

MERRI
- av. Peakhurst 430 D9
- pl. St Johns Pk 364 F2

MERRIC
- ct. Oakhurst 242 A4

MERRICK
- av. Lakemba 371 A14
- ri. N Richmond 87 A13
- wy. Glenhaven 217 K6

MERRIDONG
- rd. Elanora Ht 198 F13

MERRILEE
- cr. Frenchs Frst 255 K3

MERRILONG
- av. Mt Krng-gai 163 B10
- st. Castle Hill 247 G3

MERRIMAN
- cl. Elderslie 507 H2
- pl. Airds 512 B11
- st. Kyle Bay 432 A15
- st. Millers Pt ...... A A1
- st. Millers Pt 1 C9

MERRIN
- st. St Helens Park 541 E2

MERRINA
- st. Hebersham 241 E9

MERRINDAL
- cl. Cranebrook 207 E7

MERRINGTON
- pl. Woolwich 314 F14

MERRIS
- pl. Milperra 397 H10
- st. Kingsgrove 401 H6

MERRIT
- pl. Mcquarie Fd 454 G4

MERRIVALE
- la. Turramurra 223 F12
- rd. Pymble 223 D16
- st. St Ives 223 D16

MERRIVILLE
- rd. Kellyville Rdg 215 B2

MERRIWA
- av. Hoxton Park 392 G7
- pl. Cherrybrook 219 D10
- pl. Yarrawarrah 489 E14
- st. Gordon 253 E7

MERROO
- cr. Kurrajong 64 B13

MERRYL
- av. Old Tngabbie 276 J8

MERRYLANDS
- rd. Greystanes 306 F10
- rd. Merrylands 307 B11
- rd. Merrylands W 307 B11

MERRYN
- cl. Cobbitty 448 A13
- la. Harringtn Pk 448 A13

MERRYVALE
- rd. Minto 482 C2

MERRYVILLE
- ct. Wattle Grove 425 K2

MERRYWEATHER
- cl. Minto 483 A2

MERSEY
- cl. Bossley Park 333 F5
- pl. Kearns 450 J16
- rd. Bringelly 387 G3
- st. Woronora 460 A16

MERTON
- av. Cmbrdg Gdn 237 G2
- la. Stanmore 16 C11
- st. Dean Park 242 G1
- st. Kogarah Bay 432 K11
- st. Petersham 16 C10
- st. Rozelle 7 A13
- st. Stanmore 16 C10
- st. Zetland 375 J10
- st.n, Sutherland 490 E1
- st.s, Sutherland 490 E6

MERTZ
- pl. Leumeah 482 J11

MERU
- pl. St Clair 269 F7

MERVILLE
- st. Concord W 311 E12

MERYLA
- st. Burwood 342 A12
- st. Couridjah 564 E16

MERYLL
- av. Baulkham Hl 247 F10

MESA
- wy. Stanhpe Gdn 215 C11

GREGORY'S STREET DIRECTORY 105

ME — STREETS

MESSINA
- cct. Prestons 393 E15
- cr. Bonnyrigg Ht......362 K7
- st. Parklea 214 J13

MESSINES
- av. Milperra 397 H11
- pl. Matraville 407 B16

MESSITER
- st. Campsie 372 C16

META
- st. Caringbah 492 K2
- st. Croydon 342 G16
- st. Ryde 282 H14

METCALF
- av. Carlingford 249 G16

METCALFE
- av. Moorebank 396 D9
- la. Lidcombe 339 F8
- st. Cammeray 315 J6
- st. Maroubra 407 C8

METELLA
- cr. Belfield 371 G13
- rd. Toongabbie 275 E14

METEOR
- pl. Raby 451 D16

METEREN
- cl. Milperra 397 E13

METHIL
- st. St Andrews 452 A12

METHUEN
- av. Mosman 317 F10
- pde. Riverwood 400 E12

METHVEN
- st. Mount Druitt 241 D13

METROPOLITAN
- rd. Enmore 17 B14

METTERS
- pl. Wetherill Pk 334 B2

METZ
- pl. Plumpton 241 G7

METZLER
- pl. Gordon 253 G5

MEURANTS
- la. Glenwood 245 B1
- la. Ramsgate 433 D12

MEWS
- la. Marrickville 373 G15

MEWTON
- rd. Maraylya 94 J15

MEY
- cl. Cecil Hills 362 G4

MEYERS
- av. Hunters Hill 313 F6
- rd. Sefton 368 F1

MEYMOTT
- av. Coogee 407 D1
- st. Randwick 407 D1

MEZEN
- pl. St Clair 299 J1

MIA
- tce. Stanhpe Gdn 215 F8

MIA
- pl. Clareville 169 F2
- pl. Marayong 244 C3

MIAMBA
- av. Carlingford 279 D1

MIAMI
- cl. Greenfld Pk 333 K13
- pl. Cranebrook 207 H11
- rd. Frenchs Frst 256 G7
- st. Glenwood 215 H12

MIA MIA
- st. Girraween 276 D12

MIANGA
- av. Engadine 518 J2

MIAX
- pl. Dharruk 241 B8

MICA
- pl. Eagle Vale 481 A8

MICAWBER
- st. Ambarvale 511 A14

MICHAEL
- av. Belfield 371 F12
- cl. Luddenham 356 H2
- cl. Cranebrook 207 B14
- cr. Ingleburn 453 C10
- st. N Richmond 87 B14
- st. North Ryde 282 D7

MICHAELS
- cr. Punchbowl 399 H5

MICHELGA
- cct. Prestons 393 B13

MICHELE
- av. Cmbrdg Pk 237 H7
- ct. Regents Pk 339 B16
- la. Kingsgrove, off
  Bykool Av 401 E8
- pl. Camden S 507 C11
- pl. Turramurra 222 K7
- rd. Cromer 228 H16

MICHELL
- rd. Thirlmere 564 E6

MICHELLE
- dr. Wentwthvle 277 C10
- pl. Dural 188 G13
- pl. Marayong 244 A6

MICHIGAN
- av. Asquith 192 B11
- rd. Riverwood 399 K12
- rd. Seven Hills 275 E6

MIDDLE
- la. Kingsford 406 G1
- la. Oxford Falls 227 A12
- st. Kingsford 406 G1
- st. McMahons Pt 5 E16
- st. Marrickville 16 C15
- st. Randwick 406 G1

MIDDLEBROOK
- ri. Bella Vista 216 D16

MIDDLE HARBOUR
- dr. Belrose 225 F14
- rd. E Lindfield 254 F16
- rd. Lindfield 284 E1

MIDDLE HEAD
- rd. Mosman 317 C9

MIDDLEHOPE
- st. Bonnyrigg Ht......363 A6

MIDDLEMISS
- st. Lavender Bay ......K G13
- st. Lavender Bay 5 H11
- st. Mascot 405 F4
- st. Rosebery 405 F4

MIDDLETON
- av. Castle Hill 217 G13
- av. Cranebrook 207 E9
- av. Richmond 119 J4
- av. Richmond 119 J6
- dr. Bidwill 211 B15
- dr. Picton 561 C4
- rd. Chester Hill 337 G12
- rd. Cromer 228 E14
- rd. Leumeah 512 B2
- st. Petersham 16 C13

MID-DURAL
- rd. Galston 159 A7
- rd. Middle Dural 158 J7

MIDELTON
- av. Bexley North 402 F10
- av. North Bondi 348 E15

MIDIN
- cl. Glenmore Pk 266 C9
- cl. Mount Druitt 241 F15

MIDLANDS
- tce. Stanhpe Gdn 215 F8

MIDLOTHIAN
- av. Beverly Hills 401 A12
- rd. St Andrews 452 A12

MIDSON
- rd. Beecroft 250 F11
- rd. Eastwood 280 H1
- rd. Epping 280 H1
- rd. Oakville 123 K13

MIDWAY
- dr. Maroubra 407 C13
- pl. Lethbrdg Pk 240 F3

MIDWINTER
- row. St Clair 270 D14

MIFSUD
- cr. Oakhurst 241 H3
- st. Girraween 276 A10

MIGGS
- pl. Ambarvale 511 A10

MIKADO
- wy. Doonside 243 F16

MIKARIE
- pl. Kirrawee 461 D15

MIKKELSEN
- av. Tregear 240 F7

MILA
- pl. Marayong 243 J6

MILAK
- pl. Whalan 240 H12

MILAN
- st. Prestons 393 F16

MILANO
- pl. Edensor Pk 363 F1

MILBA
- rd. Caringbah 493 C6

MILBURN
- pl. St Ives Ch 194 B16
- rd. Gymea 491 E2
- rd. Quakers Hill 214 C12

MILDARA
- pl. Edensor Pk 333 D15
- pl. W Pnnant Hl 249 A2

MILDRED
- av. Hornsby 191 H13
- av. Manly Vale 287 H4
- st. Warrawee 222 D14
- st. Wentwthvle 306 J1

MILDURA
- pl. Prestons 393 E14
- st. Killara 253 G14

MILE END
- rd. Rouse Hill 184 K9
- rd. Rouse Hill 185 A8

MILEHAM
- av. Baulkham Hl 247 H5
- av. Castle Hill 247 H5
- st. S Windsor 120 G16
- st. Windsor 121 A11
- wy. Minto 482 H6

MILENA
- av. Glenwood 245 G3

MILES
- st. Bnkstn Aprt 367 K16
- st. Brookvale 258 D12
- st. Chester Hill 338 C16
- st. Mascot 405 D1
- st. Surry Hills 20 B4

MILES FRANKLIN
- av. Glenmore Pk 265 K6

MILFORD
- av. Panania 428 A5
- dr. Rouse Hill 185 C7
- dr. Rouse Hill 185 D3
- dr. Cherrybrook 219 A13
- pl. Turramurra 252 F5
- pl. Ellis Lane 476 A9
- rd. Londonderry 148 F10
- rd. Miranda 492 D3
- rd. Peakhurst 400 F16
- rd. Randwick 377 B14
- wy. Wentwthvle 277 C11

MILGA
- wy. Avalon 140 E13

MILGATE
- la. Campbelltown 511 E4

MILGUY
- av. Castle Hill 247 F1

MILHAM
- av. Eastwood 281 F5
- cr. Forestville 255 D8
- st. St Marys 269 J4

MILI
- pl. Kings Park 244 J2

MILITARY
- dr. Lilyfield 10 A1
- la. Cremorne 6 H2
- rd. Cremorne 316 C9
- rd. Dover Ht 348 F8
- rd. Guildford 337 G4
- rd. Matraville 436 G8
- rd. Merrylands 307 J16
- rd. Mosman 316 H6
- rd. Neutral Bay 6 F7
- rd. North Bondi 378 G1
- rd. Vaucluse 348 F7
- rd. Watsons Bay 318 G14
- rd. Yennora 337 C8

MILK
- av. Vaucluse 348 E2

MILL
- dr. North Rocks 248 F12
- dr. Hurlstone Pk 373 A12
- la. The Rocks ......B A2
- pl. St Clair 270 E10
- rd. Campbelltown 481 H14
- rd. Kurrajong 64 D15
- rd. Kurrajong Hl 63 K14
- rd. Liverpool 395 C6
- st. Bnksmeadw 406 D12
- st. Carlton 432 G4
- st. Currans Hill 479 J10
- st. Hurlstone Pk 373 A12
- st. Pyrmont 8 G15
- st. Riverstone 182 J6

MILLAR
- cr. Dural 188 H12
- st. Drummoyne 343 G5

MILLARD
- cr. Plumpton 241 G9

MILLBROOK
- pl. Cherrybrook 219 E12

MILLCROFT
- wy. Beaumont Hills 215 F2

MILLEN
- st. Kingswood 238 A13

MILLENNIUM
- ct. Matraville 436 H7
- ct. Silverwater 309 G11

MILLER
- av. Ashfield 372 G3
- av. Bexley North 402 F11
- av. Dundas Vy 280 E10
- av. Hornsby 191 H14
- la. Cammeray 315 K5
- la. Petersham 15 F16
- la. Pyrmont 12 F4
- pl. Menai 458 F10
- pl. Mt Prichard 364 J10
- pl. Tahmoor 565 G9
- rd. Bass Hill 367 J6
- rd. Chester Hill 337 J11
- rd. Chester Hill 367 J6
- rd. Glenorie 126 F2
- rd. Miller 393 G4
- rd. Villawood 367 J6
- st. Bondi 378 A4
- st. Cammeray 315 J6
- st. Crows Nest 315 J6
- st. Haberfield 343 C13
- st. Kingsgrove 402 B5
- st. Kingsgrove 402 C6
- st. Lavender Bay ......K C14
- st. Lavender Bay 5 F11
- st. Merrylands 307 H13
- st. Mount Druitt 271 C3
- st. N Sydney ......K D10
- st. N Sydney ......K C14
- st. N Sydney ......K D6
- st. N Sydney 5 F11
- st. N Sydney 5 G7
- st. Petersham 15 F15
- st. Pyrmont 12 F4
- st. S Granville 338 F4
- st. S Penrith 236 H15
- wy. Claymore 481 D11
- wy. Kellyvle Rdg 215 E2

MILLERS
- rd. Cattai 94 B7
- wy. W Pnnant Hl 248 H7

MILLET
- row. Wrrngtn Dns 238 E5

MILLETT
- rd. Mosman 316 J10
- st. Hurstville 431 F1

MILLEWA
- av. Wahroonga 222 C6
- av. Warrawee 222 C6
- la. Wahroonga, off
  Millewa Av 222 D6

MILL HILL
- rd. Bondi Jctn 22 D8

MILLHOUSE
- pl. Bella Vista 216 B14

MILLICENT
- st. Greystanes 305 J1

MILLIE
- st. Guildford 337 E6

MILLIGAN
- la. Cranebrook, off
  Milligan Rd 207 C13
- rd. Cranebrook 207 C13

MILLING
- av. Vaucluse 348 E2
- st. Hunters Hill 313 A8

MILL POND
- rd. Botany 405 D8

MILLS
- av. Asquith 191 K7
- av. North Rocks 249 A16
- ct. Burwood 342 C12
- la. Chatswood 284 K9
- la. Winmalee 173 J7
- pl. Beacon Hill 257 D7
- rd. Glenhaven 187 F14
- rd. Londonderry 148 G15
- st. Croydon 372 B8
- st. Lidcombe 339 J7
- st. Merrylands 307 A10

MILLSTREAM
- gr. Dural 219 A3
- rd. Wrrngtn Dns 237 K5

MILLWOOD
- av. Chatswood W 284 A8
- av. Narellan 478 C9
- st. McMahons Pt 5 D14

MILNE
- av. Kingswood 237 G15
- av. Matraville 406 H16
- cl. Wetherill Pk 335 A7
- ct. Castle Hill, off
  Western Rd 218 H13
- la. Merrylands, off
  Terminal Pl 307 J13
- la. Tempe, off
  Lymerston St 404 D1
- pl. Narellan Vale 478 K10
- st. Ryde 282 G16
- st. Tahmoor 565 F12

MILNER
- av. Hornsby 221 C4
- av. Kirrawee 490 H6
- av. Wollstncraft 315 C9
- la. Mosman, off
  Milner St 317 A10
- rd. Artarmon 284 J16
- rd. Guildford 337 H7
- rd. Peakhurst 400 F16
- st. Mosman 317 A9

MILPARINKA
- av. Glenwood 245 F1
- cl. Hoxton Park 392 F7

MILPERA
- cl. Cromer 228 B16

MILPERRA
- rd. Bnkstn Aprt 397 G6
- rd. Milperra 397 G6
- rd. Revesby 397 G6

MILRAY
- av. Wollstncraft 315 B11
- st. Lindfield 254 D15

MILROY
- av. Kensington 376 B10
- st. North Ryde 282 E8

MILSON
- la. The Rocks ......A G11
- pde. Normanhurst 221 D9
- pde. Thornleigh 221 D9
- rd. Cremorne Pt 316 F13
- rd. Doonside 243 E12
- st. Woodcroft 243 E12

MILSOP
- pl. Mortdale 431 B4
- st. Bexley 432 H4

MILSTED
- rd. Terrey Hills 196 E5

MILTON
- av. Eastwood 280 G7
- av. Mosman 317 B11
- av. Woollahra 22 F2
- av. Wetherill Pk 334 K5
- cr. Leumeah 512 B2
- cr. Prestons 392 H13
- la. Ashfield, off
  Norton St 372 F3
- la. Burwood, off
  Neich Pde 342 A11
- pl. Frenchs Frst 256 D8
- pl. Greystanes 306 C11
- rd. N Turramurra 223 C3
- rd. Riverstone 182 D10
- st. Ashbury 372 F5
- st. Ashfield 372 F4
- st. Ashfield 372 F5
- st. Bankstown 369 G14
- st. Burwood 342 A11
- st. Carlingford 280 B7
- st. Chatswood 285 B7
- st. Colyton 270 H7
- st. Granville 308 C10
- st. Leichhardt 10 D14
- st. Lidcombe 339 F8
- st. Riverstone 182 F13
- st. Rydalmere 309 J4
- st. Thirlmere 562 C15
- st.n.Ashfield 372 F2
- wy. Shalvey 210 J14

MILVAY
- pl. Ambarvale 511 B15

MIMA
- st. Sefton 368 G2

MI MI
- st. Oatley 431 A12

106 GREGORY'S STREET DIRECTORY

STREETS MO

MIMIKA
av. Whalan 240 J12
MIMOS
st. Denistone W 281 A13
MIMOSA
av. Toongabbie 276 C5
cct. Breakfast Pt 312 D16
cl. St Clair 270 B15
gr. Glenwood 245 G2
rd. Bossley Park 334 A10
rd. Greenacre 369 J12
rd. Greenfld Pk 334 A12
rd. Turramurra 252 E3
st. Bargo 567 D5
st. Bexley 402 E14
st. Frenchs Frst 255 F3
st. Granville 308 G16
st. Heathcote 519 A10
st. Oatley 431 A14
st. S Hurstville 432 A11
st. Westmead 307 H3
MIMULUS
la. Regents Pk 369 B2
pl. Caringbah 492 E13
pl. Mcquarie Fd 454 G4
MINA
rd. Menai 458 G9
rd. Menai 458 H10
MINAGO
pl. Castle Hill 218 A7
MINAHAN
pl. Plumpton 241 G9
MINA ROSA
st. Enfield 371 G4
MINARTO
la. N Narrabeen 228 K2
MINCHIN
av. Hobartville 118 D9
dr. Minchinbury 271 J7
MINCHINBURY
st. Eastern Ck 272 D7
tce. Eschol Park 481 A6
MINDA
pl. Whalan 240 H11
MINDANAO
av. Lethbrdg Pk 240 F3
MINDAR
st. Como 460 H7
MINDARIBBA
av. Rouse Hill 185 D7
MINDARIE
st. Lane Cove N 283 J14
MINDONA
wy. Woodcroft 243 J11
MINDORO
pl. Lethbrdg Pk 240 G5
MINELL
ct. Harringtn Pk 478 E1
MINER
gln. Erskine Park 271 A11
pl. Ingleburn 453 F7
MINERAL SPRINGS
rd. Picton 563 G11
MINERVA
cr. Beaumont Hills 186 A14
pl. Prestons 392 K13
rd. Wedderburn 540 B11
st. Kirrawee 490 H5
MINGA
st. Ryde 282 F15
MINIMBAH
rd. Northbridge 286 D14
MINJ
pl. Glenfield 424 J9
MINKARA
rd. Bayview 168 E15
MINKI
wy. Glenwood 215 C15
MINMAI
rd. Chester Hill 337 F13
rd. Mona Vale 198 G2
MINNA
cl. Belrose 225 H1
st. Burwood 371 H1
MINNAMORRA
av. Earlwood 403 A5
MINNAMURRA
av. Miranda 492 F3
av. Pymble 253 C8
cct. Prestons 393 B16
cct. Prestons 423 A1
gr. Dural 219 A3
pl. Pymble 253 C9
rd. Northbridge 286 D15
MINNEAPOLIS
cr. Maroubra 407 C13
MINNEK
cl. Glenmore Pk 266 C11
MINNESOTA
av. Five Dock 343 B11
av. Riverwood 400 A13
MINNIE
st. Belmore 371 A12
MINNS
rd. Gordon 253 J6
MINOGUE
cr. Forest Lodge 11 E13
cr. Forest Lodge 11 E14
MINORCA
wy. Minto 482 H7
MINSTREL
pl. Rouse Hill 185 C6
MINT
cl. Casula 423 J1
cl. St Clair 269 G11
la. St Clair, off Mint Cl 269 G11
pl. Quakers Hill 243 F4
MINTARO
av. Strathfield 371 C2
MINTER
st. Canterbury 372 G13
MINTO
av. Haberfield 343 E12
cl. Bonnyrigg Ht 363 C4
pl. Erskine Park 270 J15
rd. Minto 453 A14
st. Hebersham 241 D9
MINTOFF
pl. Dean Park, off Raupach St 212 F16
MINTON
av. Dolls Point 463 E1
MINUET
ct. Glenwood 245 C1
MINYA
av. Kingsford 406 D2
MIOWERA
av. Carss Park 432 E15
rd. Chester Hill 337 F14
rd. Northbridge 286 F15
rd. N Turramurra 223 G6
MIRAGE
av. Raby 481 E1
MIRAMBENA
cl. Cherrybrook 220 A13
MIRAMONT
av. Riverview 314 A6
MIRANDA
cl. Cherrybrook 219 J3
pl. Rsemeadow 540 K6
rd. Miranda 492 C2
rd. Miranda 492 C5
st. S Penrith 267 C5
MIRANG
pl. Engadine 488 J9
MIRBELIA
ct. Voyager Pt 427 C5
pde. Elanora Ht 197 J12
pde. Ingleside 197 J12
pl. Caringbah 493 B6
MIRCA
pl. Appin 569 C7
MIRETTA
pl. Castle Hill 247 J3
MIRI
cr. Holsworthy 426 D2
ct. St Ives 223 K16
MIRIAM
cl. Smithfield 336 B7
ct. Baulkham Hl 247 C2
rd. Denistone 281 D12
rd. West Ryde 281 D12
st. Bass Hill 368 C10
st. Wilton 568 K15
MIRIMAR
av. Bronte 378 B7
MIROOL
st. Denistone W 280 K13
st. West Ryde 280 K13
MIRRA
pl. Cromer 228 D14
MIRRABOOK
pl. Heathcote 518 F10
MIRRABOOKA
av. Strathfield 341 B11
cr. Little Bay 437 A11
ct. Emu Heights 234 K5
st. Bilgola 169 E5
MIRRADONG
pl. Kirribilli 2 E3
MIRRAL
rd. Caringbah 492 G15
rd. Lilli Pilli 522 G1
MIRRI
pl. Glenmore Pk 266 B10
MIRROOL
st. N Narrabeen 198 G16
st. N Narrabeen 228 G2
st. N Wahroonga 192 E15
MISIMA
pl. Glenfield 424 J10
MISSENDEN
rd. Camperdown 17 G3
rd. Newtown 17 J6
MISSISSIPPI
cr. Kearns 451 A15
rd. Seven Hills 275 D9
MISSOURI
pl. Riverwood 400 A13
st. Kearns 451 A14
MISTLETOE
av. Clarmnt Ms 238 J16
av. Mcquarie Fd 454 B6
st. Loftus 489 K11
MISTRAL
av. Mosman 316 K11
pl. Shalvey 210 J13
st. Greenfld Pk 334 C13
MISTY
gln. Wrrngtn Dns 238 B4
MITALA
st. Newport 169 D10
MITCHAM
rd. Bankstown 369 B15
st. Punchbowl 400 A7
MITCHELL
av. Jannali 460 F12
cl. Tahmoor 565 K13
cr. Turramurra 222 C16
cr. Warrawee 222 C16
dr. Glossodia 66 D12
dr. West Hoxton 392 B12
la. Alexandria 18 G15
la. Mosman, off Mitchell Rd 317 B3
la.e, Glebe 12 F13
la.w, Glebe 12 E13
pl. Douglas Park 568 F12
pl. Kenthurst 188 E7
rd. Alexandria 18 G16
rd. Alexandria 375 B10
rd. Brookvale 258 C12
rd. Cronulla 494 A10
rd. Darling Point 13 K4
rd. Dural 190 A9
rd. Erskineville 375 B10
rd. Moorebank 395 J9
rd. Mosman 317 B3
rd. Palm Beach 140 A3
rd. Pitt Town 93 B11
rd. Rose Bay 348 D8
rd. Strathfield 340 G12
st. Arncliffe 403 E8
st. Bondi Beach 378 D1
st. Camden 477 A15
st. Campbelltown 511 J7
st. Carramar 336 H16
st. Centennial Pk 21 E7
st. Chifley 437 A3
st. Condell Park 398 F3
st. Croydon Pk 371 G5
st. Enfield 371 G5
st. Ermington 280 D16
st. Fairfield E 336 H16
st. Fairfield E 337 A16
st. Five Dock 343 B7
st. Glebe 12 D16
st. Greenwich 314 J13
st. Lalor Park 245 C13
st. McMahons Pt 5 C13
st. Marrickville 374 C11
st. Naremburn 315 E5
st. North Bondi 378 D1
st. Putney 312 B8
st. St Leonards 315 E5
st. St Marys 269 H3
st. S Penrith 236 H14
wy. Eveleigh 18 K10
MITCHELL PARK
rd. Cattai 94 F3
MITCHELLS
ps. Blaxland 233 K9
ps. Glenbrook 234 F10
rd. Sackville N 68 D1
MITTABAH
rd. Asquith 191 J8
rd. Hornsby 191 J8
MITTIAMO
st. Canley Ht 365 B1
MITUMBA
rd. Seven Hills 275 C10
MIVO
st. Holsworthy 426 D1
MIYAL
pl. Engadine 518 H2
MOALA
st. Concord W 311 E15
MOANI
av. Gymea 491 D4
MOAT
st. Kellyville Rdg 215 B3
MOATE
av. Btn-le-Sds 433 K2
MOBBS
la. Carlingford 280 E6
la. Epping 280 E6
MOCATTA
av. Pymble 253 E3
MOCKRIDGE
av. Newington 310 C12
MODEL FARMS
rd. Baulkham Hl 247 H16
rd. Baulkham Hl 277 H1
MODERN
av. Canterbury 402 E1
MOFFAT
pl. Minto 482 H9
MOFFATT
dr. Lalor Park 245 H10
wy. Beaumont Hills 185 J14
MOFFATTS
dr. Dundas Vy 279 J10
MOFFITT
cr. Edensor Pk 333 G15
MOFFITTS
la. Ellis Lane 476 C6
MOGILA
st. Seven Hills 275 E4
MOGO
ct. Prestons 392 J13
pl. Glenmore Pk 266 B11
MOHAVE
pl. Bossley Park 334 A12
MOHAWK
cr. Greenfld Pk 334 A16
pl. Erskine Park 271 A16
MOIR
av. Northmead 277 J6
pl. Bidwill 211 B16
st. Smithfield 335 E3
MOIRA
av. Denistone W 281 A14
av. West Ryde 281 A14
cr. Coogee 377 F13
cr. Randwick 377 F13
cr. St Marys 269 J4
la. St Marys, off Moira Cr 269 K3
pl. Frenchs Frst 256 F10
st. Sutherland 460 H16
MOJO
pl. Greenfld Pk 333 K13
MOKARI
st. N Richmond 87 C14
MOKERA
av. Kirrawee 461 A15
MOLES
rd. Wilberforce 67 A9
MOLESWORTH
la. Longueville 314 E7
MOLISE
av. Kellyville 186 H16
st. Prestons 393 D15
MOLLE
pl. Narellan Vale 478 G16
MOLLER
av. Birrong 369 A6
MOLLISON
cr. Ermington 280 A16
MOLLOY
av. S Coogee 407 G7
ct. Mortdale 430 F6
pl. Minchinbury 272 C9
MOLLS
la. Mowbray Pk 561 J8
MOLLUSO
cl. Wakeley 334 G15
MOLLYMOOK
st. Prestons 393 B13
MOLONG
rd. Gymea Bay 491 E12
st. N Curl Curl 259 B11
st. Quakers Hill 243 K1
wy. Bidwill 211 E13
MOLONGLO
rd. Seven Hills 275 E10
MOLYNEAUX
av. Kings Lngly 245 J7
MOMBRI
st. Merrylands 307 K12
MONA
la. Darling Point 13 F8
rd. Darling Point 13 G9
rd. Menai 458 K11
rd. Riverwood 400 E15
st. Allawah 432 E7
st. Auburn 339 A2
st. Bankstown 399 E1
st. Mona Vale 199 C1
st. S Granville 338 G1
st. Wahroonga 222 J7
MONACO
av. Kellyville 185 F8
pl. Prestons 393 C15
pl. Quakers Hill 214 E13
MONAGHAN
st. Minto 482 H2
MONAHAN
av. Banksia 403 E13
MONARCH
cct. Glenmore Pk 266 C13
cl. Rouse Hill 185 E5
pl. Quakers Hill 213 K8
MONARO
av. Kingsgrove 401 H12
cl. Bossley Park 333 K9
pl. Beacon Hill 258 A5
pl. Emu Plains 234 K7
pl. Heckenberg 364 A15
st. Homebush B 310 G16
st. Seven Hills 246 C13
MONASH
av. East Hills 427 H4
av. East Killara 254 G10
av. Gt Mckrl Bch 109 A13
av. Holsworthy 396 B13
cr. Clontarf 287 E14
gdn. Pagewood 406 F7
pde. Croydon 342 E12
pde. Dee Why 259 B9
pl. Bonnyrigg 364 A6
rd. Blacktown 273 J1
rd. Doonside 273 G1
rd. Gladesville 312 H5
rd. Menai 458 J6
st. Wentwthvle 306 J3
MONASTERY
pl. Cherrybrook 219 F15
MONA VALE
pl. Woodbine 481 J10
rd. Belrose 225 B3
rd. Ingleside 197 B9
rd. Krngai Ch N P 224 F3
rd. Mona Vale 198 G3
rd. Pymble 253 F4
rd. St Ives 224 C10
rd. Terrey Hills 195 H16
rd. Warriewood 198 B6
MONCKTON
pl. Glenfield 424 H11
MONCRIEFF
cl. St Helens Park 541 C3
dr. East Ryde 282 K15
pl. Milperra 397 E10
rd. Lalor Park 245 C9
MONCUR
av. Belmore 401 H4
la. Woollahra 21 J3
st. Marrickville 373 G14
st. Woollahra 21 J3
MONDIAL
pl. West Ryde 281 H13
MONDOVI
cl. Prestons 393 H16

GREGORY'S STREET DIRECTORY 107

MO STREETS

MONDS
la. Picton 563 E1
MONET
ct. Kellyville..........216 A4
MONFARVILLE
st. St Marys..........269 H5
MONFORD
pl. Cremorne........316 E8
MONGA
pl. Prestons.........392 J15
MONGON
pl. St Helens Park....541 H3
MONI
wy. Doonside........243 F15
MONICA
av. Hassall Gr........211 K16
cl. Lurnea............394 D6
pl. Jamisontown.....265 K3
pl. Tahmoor..........565 H8
MONIE
av. East Hills..........427 G4
MONIER
sq. Villawood........367 G1
MONITOR
rd. Merrylands.......307 F12
MONK
av. Arncliffe..........403 G6
MONKEY
rd. The Oaks........502 B7
MONKS
la. Alexandria........18 D13
la. Erskineville......18 D13
st. Mt Hunter........504 H5
MONMOUTH
av. East Killara.....254 F9
st. Randwick.........377 B10
MONOMEETH
pl. Miranda..........462 A16
st. Bexley............402 J15
MONRO
av. Kirrawee........491 A2
MONROE
st. Blacktown........274 H4
st. Ermington........280 E12
MONS
av. Maroubra.......407 A8
av. West Ryde......311 C1
rd. N Balgowlah.....287 B4
rd. Wentwthvle......277 E13
rd. Westmead.......277 E13
rd. Canterbury......372 D16
st. Condell Park....398 J9
st. Lidcombe........340 B5
st. Revesby..........398 J9
st. Russell Lea.....343 D5
st. S Granville......338 G3
st. Vaucluse........348 G5
MONSERRA
rd. Allambie Ht.....257 F13
MONTAGUE
cl. Green Valley....363 A13
rd. Rsemeadow....540 G4
rd. Cremorne........316 G5
st. Balmain..........7 E9
st. Fairfield Ht......335 H9
st. Greystanes......306 C7
st. Illawong..........459 C6
st. North Manly.....258 A14
MONTAH
av. Killara............254 C9
MONTANA
av. North Rocks....278 G2
cr. Riverwood......399 K12
st. Stanhpe Gdn...215 B11
wy. Mcquarie Fd...454 H4
MONTAUBAN
av. Seaforth........287 A7
MONT CLAIR
la. Darlinghurst....4 F11
MONTEBELLO
cl. Green Valley...362 K14
MONTECLAIR
av. Liverpool.......395 A10
MONTEITH
la. Turramurra......222 D15
pl. Baulkham Hl...247 D6
st. Turramurra......222 D15
st. Warrimoo........222 D15
MONTEL
pl. Acacia Gdn....215 A16
MONTELIMAR
pl. Wallacia........325 A13

MONTELLA
pl. Prestons........393 F14
MONTERAY
tce. Glenmore Pk...266 F14
MONTEREY
pde. Ermington....280 E1
pl. Cherrybrook...219 D11
rd. Bilgola...........169 H6
st. Monterey........433 F9
st. Newington......310 D12
st. St Ives............224 D6
st. S Wntwthvle ...307 A7
MONTERRA
av. Peakhurst......430 D8
MONTGOMERY
av. Revesby........398 K16
av. S Granville....338 E6
pl. Bonnyrigg......363 J9
rd. Carlingford.....250 B15
st. Kogarah.........433 C4
st. Miranda.........492 C3
st. Narellan Vale..479 A11
MONTI
pl. N Richmond....87 C13
MONTORE
rd. Minto............482 C4
MONTPELIER
dr. The Oaks.....502 D16
st. Neutral Bay....6 B5
MONTREAL
av. Killara..........283 E1
MONTROSE
av. Fairfield E....337 B14
av. Merrylands...307 K14
pl. St Andrews...451 K12
rd. Abbotsford....342 K1
rd. Winmalee.....173 B12
st. Quakers Hill..211 K14
st. Turramurra...222 E16
MONTVIEW
pde. Hornsby Ht..191 E1
wy. Glenwood, off
 Crestview Dr ...246 B6
MOOCULLA
st. Russell Lea...343 B6
MOODIE
la. Cammeray....316 K8
st. Cammeray....315 K8
st. Rozelle..........344 D8
MOODY
cr. Rooty Hill......272 C4
MOOKARA
pl. Port Hacking..522 H1
MOOKI
st. Miranda........492 C6
MOOLA
pde. Chatswood W..284 D13
pde. Lane Cove N..284 D13
MOOLAH
rd. Terrey Hills...196 C6
MOOLANA
pde. S Penrith...266 G7
rd. Bnksmeadw..405 K15
MOOLANDA
av. W Pnnant Hl..249 C10
MOOMBARA
av. Peakhurst....430 H3
cr. Port Hacking..522 J3
MOOMIN
pl. Busby..........363 J15
st. Lalor Park....245 H10
MOONA
av. Baulkham Hl..246 K7
av. Matraville.....436 H4
pde. Wahroonga..221 H16
rd. Kirrawee......460 J15
st. Hornsby.......191 H8
MOONAH
cl. St Ives Ch...194 B15
cl. West Hoxton..392 E6
pl. St Clair........270 B15
pl. Mcquarie Fd..454 D4
rd. Alfords Point..428 K13
rd. Alfords Point..429 A13
MOONARIE
pl. Cromer........228 A15
MOONBEAM
cl. St Clair........270 D13
MOONBI
cl. Greenfld Pk..334 C15
cr. Frenchs Frst..256 F2
pl. Kareela.......461 E10
rd. Penrith........237 D3

MOONBIE
st. Summer Hill...373 C6
MOONBIRA
pl. Airds............512 C12
st. Naremburn....315 E3
MOONDANI
av. Beverly Hills, off
 Moondani Rd...401 A10
rd. Beverly Hills...401 A10
MOONDO
st. Greenacre.....370 F11
MOONEY
av. Blakehurst....432 A14
av. Earlwood......402 F2
pl. Ruse............512 C8
st. Lane Cove N..284 A12
st. Strathfield S...371 B5
MOONLIGHT
pl. Prairiewood...334 E10
MOON POINT
rd. Illawong.......459 D4
MOONS
av. Lugarno......429 F14
MOONSHINE
av. Cabramatta W..364 G6
MOONSTONE
pl. Eagle Vale...481 E6
MOONYEAN
pl. Cromer........228 C16
MOORA
st. Chester Hill...338 A15
MOORAL
av. Punchbowl...400 A9
MOORAMBA
av. Riverview......314 A5
rd. Dee Why......258 F7
MOORAMIE
av. Kensington...376 E15
MOORANYAH
cl. Woodcroft.....243 H11
MOORE
av. Lindfield.......283 F1
cr. Faulconbdg...171 D14
cr. Faulconbdg...171 C15
la. Campsie......372 B10
la. East Hills......427 J4
la. Harbord........288 G1
la. Leichhardt....10 F12
la. Rozelle........7 D16
pl. Bligh Park....150 E5
pl. Currans Hill..479 J12
pl. Doonside.....243 D5
pl. Harbord........288 G1
pl. Oakdale.......500 D11
rd. Springwood..202 B1
st. Bnksmeadw..406 C11
st. Bardwell Pk..402 J8
st. Bexley..........402 A16
st. Blaxland.......234 B6
st. Bondi...........377 K4
st. Cabarita......342 D1
st. Campbelltown..481 J16
st. Campbelltown..511 G4
st. Campbelltown..511 F5
st. Campsie......372 B10
st. Canley Vale..366 F4
st. Clontarf......287 G15
st. Coogee.......377 J14
st. Drummoyne..343 F3
st. Glenbrook.....233 J15
st. Hurstville......402 A16
st. Lane Cove W..283 H15
st. Lansdowne...367 B4
st. Leichhardt....10 C5
st. Leumeah......481 J16
st. Liverpool......395 A3
st. Roseville......285 B2
st. Rozelle.........7 C14
st. St Clair.......269 K11
st. Strathfield...341 J10
st. Sutherland...490 D3
st. Vaucluse.....318 G15
stw. Leichhardt..10 A11
MOOREBANK
av. Moorebank..395 E10
cr. Whalan........240 H12
pl. Allambie Ht...257 E11
MOORECOURT
av. Springwood..201 G3
MOOREFIELD
av. Hunters Hill..313 G11
cl. Kogarah......433 E6
cl. Kogarah......433 C4
MOOREFIELDS
la. Beverly Hills, off
 Moorefields Rd...401 A10
rd. Beverly Hills..401 B9

rd. Kingsgrove....401 B9
rd. Roselands.....401 B9
MOOREHEAD
av. Silverdale......353 H15
MOOREHOUSE
cr. Edensor Pk...363 H1
MOORE-OXLEY
rd. Douglas Park..568 F10
bps. Bradbury......511 D6
bps. Campbelltown..511 D6
bps. Leumeah.....511 H4
MOORE PARK
rd. Moore Park.....20 G2
rd. Paddington.....20 G2
MOORES
av. Earlwood......402 F2
la. Alexandria......19 B15
av. Glenorie.......128 J3
wy. Glenmore.....503 E4
wy. The Oaks....503 E4
MOORESFIELD
la. Ellis Lane.....476 D8
MOORES STEPS
 Sydney..........B G5
MOORFOOT
rd. St Andrews...451 J15
MOORGATE
la. Chippendale..18 J1
st. Chippendale..18 K1
st. Toongabbie...276 H7
MOORHEN
st. Ingleburn......453 G5
MOORHOUSE
av. St Ives........254 D4
MOORILLA
av. Carlingford...249 G11
st. Dee Why.....258 E8
MOORINA
av. Matraville....436 H4
cl. Greenfld Pk..334 D14
st. Pymble.......223 G14
MOORLAND
rd. Tahmoor.....566 B10
rd. Tahmoor.....566 C9
MOORLANDS
rd. Ingleburn....452 J8
MORAGO
wy. Airds.........512 E10
MORAN
cct. Mcquarie Pk..283 D8
cl. Bonnyrigg Ht..363 E8
pl. Currans Hill...479 J12
st. Mosman.....316 K12
wy. Minto........482 H8
MORANDOO
pl. Elanora Ht..198 F14
MORANT
st. Edensor Pk..363 H2
MORAR
st. St Andrews..452 C12
MORAY
pl. Sylvania....461 G10
st. Richmond...118 J8
st. Winmalee...173 F13
MORDEN
st. Cammeray..315 K6
MOREE
av. Westmead..307 E1
pl. Bossley Park..333 E10
st. Gordon.......253 F8
MOREHEAD
av. Mount Druitt..241 G11
st. Redfern......19 H14
st. Waterloo....19 H14
MORELLA
av. Sefton........368 E6
pl. Castle Cove..286 C6
rd. Mosman.....317 D12
rd. Whale Beach..140 B6
MOREN
st. Blacktown....274 F7
MORESBY
av. Glenfield....424 C13
cr. Whalan.......240 H12
MORESTONE
pl. Windsor Dn..180 K1
MORETON
av. Kingsgrove..401 J12
cl. Hinchinbrk....363 C5
rd. Illawong.....459 C5
rd. Minto ht.....483 G6
st. Concord.....342 B9
st. Douglas Park..568 G6

st. Douglas Park..568 G7
st. Lakemba......401 C1
MORETON BAY
av. Spring Farm..508 F1
sq. Bidwill.........241 F1
MORETON PARK
rd. Douglas Park..568 F10
rd. Menangle....538 K16
MOREY
pl. Kings Lngly..245 C3
MORGAN
av. Matraville.....436 G8
cl. Prairiewood..334 E12
la. Bankstown, off
 West Tce.......399 F1
st. Beaumont Hills..185 H14
st. Bligh Park....150 H8
st. Glendenning..242 J4
st. Strathfield....370 K2
st. Belrose.......226 B8
st. Mt Annan...479 D15
st. Oxford Falls..226 E8
st. Beverly Hills..401 C14
st. Botany........405 J11
st. Earlwood....402 G5
st. Ingleburn....453 E13
st. Kingsgrove..401 G12
st. Merrylands..307 F7
st. Miller..........393 G4
st. Petersham..15 E14
st. Thornleigh..220 G12
MORIAC
st. Warriewood..198 K6
MORIAL
la. Pymble, off
 Peace Av........253 H1
MORIARTY
rd. Chatswood W..284 H13
MORIL
av. Mt Riverview..204 E14
MORILLA
rd. E Kurrajong..67 A3
MORINDA
gr. Acacia Gdn..215 A16
st. Mt Annan...509 C3
MORISON
dr. Lurnea.......394 B11
la. Panania......428 B6
MORLEY
av. Hamondvle..396 G15
av. Kingswood..237 K12
av. Rosebery...375 G14
cl. Baulkham Hl..246 H4
la. Kingswood, off
 Kingsley Gr...238 B12
st. Sutherland..490 E5
MORNA
pl. Kareela......461 E11
pl. Quakers Hill..214 D15
pl. Turramurra..252 F5
st. Greenfld Pk..334 C13
MORNINGBIRD
cl. St Clair.......270 D13
la. St Clair, off
 Morningbird Cl...270 D13
MORNINGTON
av. Castle Hill..247 H1
pl. Hinchinbrk..393 B2
MORO
av. Padstow....399 D3
MOROBE
st. Whalan.....240 H12
MORONA
av. Wahroonga..251 G2
MORONEY
av. Castle Hill..217 B7
cl. Blacktown..273 G5
MOROTAI
av. Riverwood..400 A7
cr. Castlecrag..285 K13
rd. Revesby Ht..428 E5
st. Whalan.....240 J11
MORPHETT
st. Kingswood..238 B14
MORREL
pl. Kingswood..267 H11
MORRELL
cr. Quakers Hill..213 H8
st. Woollahra...21 C11
MORRICE
st. Lane Cove...314 C6
MORRIS
av. Croydon Pk..372 G6
av. Kingsgrove..401 J13

av. Thornleigh 220 H11
av. Wahroonga 223 A3
cl. Menai 458 D10
gr. Kellyville 217 A5
gr. Zetland 375 K10
la. Burwood 341 J16
la. St Marys, off Morris St 270 A3
pl. Ingleburn 453 G11
pl. Maroubra 407 D13
st. Dundas Vy 280 E8
st. Merrylands 307 D14
st. Regents Pk 369 A3
st. St Marys 269 J2
st. Seven Hills 245 H15
st. Smithfield 335 K6
st. Summer Hill 373 C5

MORRISEY
wy. Rouse Hill 185 F3

MORRISON
av. Chester Hill 368 D4
av. Engadine 488 J16
pl. Pennant Hills 220 C13
rd. Gladesville 312 E8
rd. Putney 312 A6
rd. Ryde 311 J3
rd. Tennyson 312 E8
st. Glenmore Pk 265 J9

MORRISSEY
rd. Erskineville 17 K16

MORSE
pl. Blaxland 233 G6
st. Fairfield E 337 A16

MORSHEAD
av. Carlingford 250 B13
cr. S Granville 338 G4
dr. Connells Pt 431 G13
dr. Hurstville Gr 431 F13
dr. Hurstville Gr 431 G13
dr. S Hurstville 431 J13
rd. Narellan Vale 479 B12
st. Colyton 270 C5
st. North Ryde 282 K8

MORT
cl. Barden Rdg 488 G3
la. Randwick 377 A10
la. Surry Hills 20 D6
pl. Glenmore Pk 265 E10
st. Balmain 7 H8
st. Blacktown 245 A14
st. Granville 308 D9
st. Randwick 376 K9
st. Surry Hills 20 C6

MORTAIN
av. Allambie Ht 257 C9

MORTIMER
cl. Cecil Hills 362 F2
la. Emu Plains, off Mortimer St 235 H9
st. Emu Plains 235 G9
st. Minto 482 K2
st. Yanderra 567 B16

MORTIMER LEWIS
dr. Huntleys Cove 313 C13
gr. St Clair 270 B11
la. St Clair, off Mortimer Lewis Cr 270 B11

MORTLAKE
la. Concord, off Archer St 342 B2
st. Concord 342 B1

MORTLEY
av. Haberfield 343 E11

MORTON
av. Carlingford 249 D12
av. Dulwich Hill 15 B15
cl. Wakeley 334 H12
ct. Wattle Grove 426 B3
la. Wollstncraft, off Sinclair St 315 F8
la. Woollahra 21 K4
rd. Lalor Park 245 E13
st. Lilyfield 9 G4
st. N Richmond 87 B12
st. Parramatta 308 H2
st. Wollstncraft 5 A1
tce. Harringtn Pk 478 E5

MORTS
rd. Mortdale 431 A5

MORUBEN
rd. Mosman 317 B5

MORUYA
av. Sylvania Wtr 462 G12
cl. Prestons 392 K15
cr. Greystanes 305 H5

MORVAN
st. Denistone W 281 A13
st. West Ryde 281 A13

MORVEN
ct. Castle Hill 218 C7
st. Old Guildford 337 F9

MORVEN GARDENS
la. Greenwich 314 K5

MORWICK
st. Strathfield 341 G13

MOSELEY
st. Carlingford 279 H2

MOSELLE
pl. Eschol Park 481 C5

MOSELY
av. S Penrith 266 F3
st. Strathfield 341 G11

MOSES
st. Windsor 120 K9

MOSMAN
pl. Barden Rdg 488 H6
sq. Mosman, off Military Rd 317 A6
st. Mosman 316 H12

MOSS
gln. Cranebrook 207 B12
la. Mosman 287 A16
pl. Galston 159 E8
pl. St Helens Park 540 K10
pl. Westmead 307 J3
st. Chester Hill 337 K11
st. Northmead 277 H7
st. Sans Souci 463 B5
st. West Ryde 281 A16

MOSSBERRY
st. Blair Athol 511 A3

MOSSFIELD
la. Marayong 244 A7

MOSSGIEL
st. Fairlight 288 E7

MOSSGLEN
st. Minto 482 J3

MOTH
cl. Cranebrook 207 B10
pl. Raby 481 G1

MOTTLE
gr. Woodcroft 243 F7

MOTU
pl. Glenfield 424 F13

MOULAMEIN
tce. Glenwood 215 E15

MOULTON
av. Newington 310 D11

MOUNSLOW
av. Castle Hill 217 A10

MOUNT
av. Roselands 400 G6
cl. Cranebrook 207 B12
la. Coogee, off Dolphin St 377 F15
st. Arncliffe 403 D10
st. Bonnyrigg Ht 363 B4
st. Coogee 377 F14
st. Coogee 377 F16
st. Georges Hall 368 B13
st. Glenbrook 234 E16
st. Hunters Hill 313 G11
st. Hurlstone Pk 372 J10
st. Mt Colah 192 A5
st. Mount Druitt 241 F16
st. N Sydney K A7
st. N Sydney K F8
st. N Sydney 5 E8
st. N Sydney 5 G8
st. Pyrmont 12 F2
st. Redfern 20 D8
st. Strathfield 371 F2
st. Wentwthvle 277 A11
st. West Ryde 281 J14

MT ADELAIDE
st. Darling Point 13 K6

MOUNTAIN
av. Yarramundi 115 F15
cr. Mt Pritchard 364 G10
la. Ultimo 12 J14
st. Engadine 488 D13
st. Epping 250 F14
st. Ultimo 12 J15

MOUNTAIN VIEW
av. Glen Alpine 510 E15
cl. Kurrajong Hl 64 C11
cl. Vineyard 152 F4
cr. W Pnnant Hl 249 F8

pl. Narellan 478 B9
rd. Berowra 133 C15

MOUNTAINVIEW
cr. Penrith 237 A9

MT ANNAN
dr. Mt Annan 479 J16
dr. Mt Annan 509 E5

MT ANNAN CHURCH
rd. Currans Hill 479 K14

MT AUBURN
rd. Auburn 339 C10
rd. Berala 339 C10

MT BANKS
ri. Bella Vista 216 C16

MOUNTBATTEN
st. Oatley 431 E10

MT BETHEL
cct. Brownlow Hl 444 F13

MT CARMEL
pl. Engadine 488 E12

MT DRUITT
pl. Mount Druitt 241 B16
rd. Mount Druitt 271 A3

MOUNTFORD
av. Greystanes 305 K1
av. Guildford 337 H4

MOUNTFORT
st. Lalor Park 245 B13

MT HUON
cct. Glen Alpine 510 F9

MT IDA
st. Gordon 254 B5

MT IRVINE
rd. Bilpin 60 J4
rd. Bilpin 61 A6
rd. Mt Irvine 60 D4

MT LAGOON
rd. Bilpin 61 G5

MT LEWIS
av. Mt Lewis 370 B16
av. Punchbowl 370 B16

MT MORRIS
la. Woolwich, off Mt Morris St 314 G12
st. Woolwich 314 H12

MT OLYMPUS
bvd.e, Wolli Creek, off Brobie Spark Dr 403 K5
bvd.w, Wolli Creek, off Magdalene Tce 403 J5

MT PLEASANT
av. Burwood 341 J12
av. Frenchs Frst 256 B2
av. Mona Vale 199 E2
av. Normanhurst 221 G13

MOUNTSIDE
av. Mt Colah 192 D3

MT SION
pl. Glenbrook 234 A11

MT STREET
wk. Pyrmont 8 E16
wk. Pyrmont 12 E1

MT SUGARLOAF
dr. Glen Alpine 510 B15
dr. Glen Alpine 540 B1

MT TOOTIE
rd. Bilpin 61 A5

MT VERNON
la. Glebe 12 B15
pde. Blakehurst 462 D1
rd. Mt Vernon 331 A16
st. Glebe 12 A15

MOUNTVIEW
av. Beverly Hills 400 H14
av. Chester Hill 337 K11
av. Doonside 243 D14
av. Narwee 400 H14
pl. Bilgola 169 E8

MT WILLIAM
st. Gordon 253 G6

MT WILSON
rd. Blue Mtn N P 58 C16
rd. Mt Wilson 58 C16

MOURNE
cl. Killarney Ht 256 A16

MOUTRIE
pl. Castle Hill 218 E13

MOVERLY
rd. Kingsford 407 B7
rd. Maroubra 407 B7
rd. S Coogee 407 F7

MOWATT
st. Narellan 478 G13

MOWBRAY
cl. Castle Hill 218 J6
pl. Willoughby 285 H13
rd. Artarmon 284 J13
rd. Chatswood 284 J13
rd. Willoughby 285 F13
rd.w, Chatswood W 284 D14
rd.w, Lane Cove N 283 F12
st. Prestons 393 A13
st. Sylvania 462 D8
wy. Rsemeadow 540 J3

MOWBRAY PARK
rd. Mowbray Pk 561 B7

MOWER
pl. S Windsor 150 J1

MOWLA
av. Jamisontown 266 A3

MOWLE
st. Westmead 307 G2

MOXHAM
la. Cranebrook, off Moxham St 207 D9
st. Cranebrook 207 D9
st. N Parramatta 278 C10

MOXHAMS
rd. Northmead 277 H6
rd. Winston Hills 277 G5

MOXON
rd. Punchbowl 399 H7

MOY
cl. Prestons 423 E2

MOYA
cr. Kingsgrove 401 K11

MOYARTA
st. Hurstville 431 H2

MOYES
st. Marrickville 373 H14

MOYRAN
pde. Grays Point 491 A16

MOZART
pl. Bonnyrigg Ht 363 E7
pl. Cranebrook 207 G8
st. Seven Hills 246 D13

MRS MACQUARIE
dr. Frenchs Frst 256 H2

MRS MACQUARIES
rd. Sydney 2 F15

MUBO
cr. Holsworthy 426 C3

MUCCILLO
st. Quakers Hill 214 F14

MUDGEE
pl. St Clair 270 E14

MUDIE
pl. Blackett 241 C4

MUDIES
rd. St Ives 223 H8

MUD ISLAND
rd. Sackville N 68 F1

MUELLER
pl. Tregear 240 F5
wy. Mt Annan 509 G3

MUIR
pl. St Andrews 452 A13
pl. Wetherill Pk 304 F13
rd. Chullora 369 G5
rd. Yagoona 369 G5

MUIRBANK
av. Hunters Hill 313 J12

MUIRFIELD
cr. Glenmore Pk 266 F8

MUJAR
pl. Winmalee 173 C9

MULAWA
pl. Frenchs Frst 255 H2

MULBERRY
st. Loftus 489 J10

MULBRING
st. Mosman 317 D9

MULDOON
cct. Mcquarie Pk, off Freeman Av 283 D7

MULGA
pl. Kirrawee 460 K14
pl. Mcquarie Fd 454 D1
rd. Oatley 431 A12
st. N St Marys 240 C11
st. Punchbowl 399 K4

MULGARA
pl. Bossley Park 333 F7
pl. St Helens Park 511 H16

MULGI
st. Blacktown 274 G8

MULGOA
rd. Glenmore Pk 265 F4
rd. Jamisontown 236 C15
rd. Mulgoa 265 B9
rd. Mulgoa 295 C6
rd. Penrith 236 C15
rd. Regentville 265 F4
rd. Wallacia 324 J12

MULGOWRIE
cr. Balgowlah Ht 287 J15

MULGRAVE
rd. Mulgrave 121 G16

MULGRAY
av. Baulkham Hl 247 E10
av. Maroubra 407 E10

MULHERON
av. Baulkham Hl 247 A12

MULHOLLANDS
rd. Mowbray Pk 561 D7
rd. Mowbray Pk 562 A7
rd. Thirlmere 561 D7
rd. Thirlmere 562 A7

MULL
pl. St Andrews 481 J2

MULLA
rd. Yagoona 369 C13

MULLANE
av. Baulkham Hl 247 B12

MULLENDERREE
st. Prestons 392 J16
st. Prestons 392 H16

MULLENS
rd. N Richmond 87 A1
st. Balmain 7 E12
st. Rozelle 7 D14

MULLER
av. West Hoxton 392 D5

MULLEY
pl. Belrose 225 H12

MULLIGAN
cl. St Clair 270 D10
la. St Clair, off Mulligan Cl 270 C10
st. Bossley Park 334 B9

MULLINGER
la. S Windsor 120 G14

MULLINS
st. Sydney C G10
st. Sydney 3 F5

MULLION
cl. Hornsby Ht 191 H4

MULLOO
la. Cranebrook, off Mulloo Pl 207 J10
pl. Cranebrook 207 J10

MULLUMBIMBY
av. Hoxton Park 392 H5

MULQUEENEY
la. Newtown 17 E12

MULVIHILL
st. West Ryde 311 F1

MULWARREE
av. Randwick 376 K11

MULYAN
av. Carlingford 280 D6
st. Como 460 G8

MUMFORD
rd. Cabramatta W 365 B9

MUNCASTER
pl. Cranebrook 207 F12

MUNDAKAL
av. Kirrawee 490 J6

MUNDAMATTA
st. Villawood 367 H6

MUNDARA
pl. Narraweena 258 C5

MUNDARDA
pl. St Helens Park 541 G3

MUNDARRAH
st. Clovelly 377 J13

MUNDAY
pl. Currans Hill 479 H13
st. Warwck Frm 365 J15

MUNDERAH
st. Wahroonga 222 D9

MUNDIN
st. Doonside 243 C9

MU STREETS

MUNDON
pl. W Pnnant Hl......249 G10
MUNDOWI
rd. Mt Krng-gai...... 162 G6
MUNDOWIE
pl. Clarmnt Ms......268 J2
MUNDOWY
pl. Bradbury......511 C16
MUNDURRA
pl. Kellyville......216 E2
MUNDY
st. Emu Plains......235 D9
MUNEELA
pl. Yowie Bay......492 C11
MUNGADAL
wy. Airds......512 E10
MUNGARRA
av. St Ives......223 H10
pl. W Pnnant Hl......248 J7
MUNGERIE
rd. Beaumont Hills...185 G12
MUNMORA
pl. Oxley Park......240 E15
MUNMORAH
rd. Riverwood......400 E15
MUNN
pl. Toongabbie......276 H7
st. Millers Pt............A A2
MUNNI
st. Newtown......17 H16
st. Woolooware......493 D11
MUNNUMBA
av. Belrose......226 B13
MUNOORA
st. Seaforth......287 A9
MUNRO
st. Baulkham Hl......248 A6
st. Canley Vale......366 E5
st. Eastwood......281 A4
st. Greystanes......305 D11
st. Lane Cove W......284 A16
st. McMahons Pt.......5 B13
st. Sefton......338 F15
MUNROE
pl. Harmondvle......396 E15
MUNROS
la. Glenorie......128 G8
MUNYANG
st. Heckenberg......364 A13
MURA
la. Baulkham Hl......247 B6
MURABAN
pl. Belrose......226 B12
rd. Dural......189 K4
MURCH
pl. Eagle Vale......481 A11
MURCHISON
st. St Ives......224 B8
st. Sylvania......461 K12
MURDOCH
cr. Lugarno......429 J10
la. Guildford......337 F3
la. Cronulla......494 C7
st. Guildford......337 F3
MURIEL
av. Epping......281 E2
av. Rydalmere......309 C2
la. Hornsby......191 J4
la. Hornsby......221 J2
st. Faulconbdg......171 C13
st. Hornsby......221 J2
wy. Glenwood......215 J15
MURINGO
wy. Blacktown......274 D11
MURNDAL
cct. Wattle Grove......425 H4
MURONGA
pl. Kirrawee......461 D16

MURPHY
av. Liverpool......394 K5
dr. Mcquarie Pk, off
Main Av............283 C8
pl. Blackett......241 B3
st. Blaxland......233 H12
st. Merrylands W......307 A15
st. Revesby......398 K16
wy. Minto......482 K1
wy. Minto......483 A1
MURPHYS
la. Croydon, off
Young St............342 E14
MURRABIN
av. Matraville......436 G3
MURRALAH
pl. Lane Cove......313 J3
MURRALIN
la. Sylvania......462 B8
MURRALONG
av. Five Dock......342 K11
rd. Mt Colah......162 A15
MURRAMI
av. Caringbah......493 B5
MURRANDAH
av. Camden......507 A4
MURRAY
av. Springwood......201 F1
pl. Wattle Grove......395 J12
la. Lane Cove N......284 E15
la. Marrickville......373 E13
pl. Blacktown......274 H5
pl. Beecroft......250 G9
pl. Harbord......288 H1
pl. Pagewood......406 G8
pl. Bronte......377 J8
st. Camden......477 A16
st. Campbelltown......511 K8
st. Croydon......372 C1
st. Greenacre......370 E3
st. Lane Cove......314 E15
st. Lidcombe......339 F11
st. Maroubra......407 H9
st. Marrickville......374 F11
st. Merrylands......307 G15
st. Northmead......277 K7
st. N Parramatta......278 J14
st. Pyrmont......12 K6
st. Russell Lea......343 D5
st. St Marys......269 K6
st. Smithfield......335 K8
st. Sydney......12 K6
st. Waterloo......20 B15
st. West Ryde......281 A14
MURRAY FARM
rd. Beecroft......249 K11
rd. Carlingford......249 E12
MURRAY ISLAND
Sylvania Wtr......462 E11
MURRAY JONES
dr. Bnkstn Aprt......397 J6
MURRAY PARK
rd. Kenthurst......187 A2
MURRAY ROSE
av. Homebush B......340 G1
MURRAYS
rd. Tennyson......65 E12
MURRELL
pl. Dural......219 A5
st. Ashfield......372 K3
MURRILLS
cr. Baulkham Hl......247 K15
MURRIRERIE
rd. North Bondi......348 C15
MURRIWONG
gr. Ebenezer......68 D6
MURRONG
la. La Perouse......436 J12
MURROOBAH
rd. Wallacia......324 K14
MURRUA
rd. N Turramurra......193 E13
MURRUMBA
pl. Castle Hill......217 K8
st. East Killara......254 K6
MURRUMBIDGEE
av. Sylvania Wtr......462 F13
st. Bossley Park......333 H6
st. Heckenberg......364 A15
MURRUMBURRAH
st. Wakeley......334 H14
MURTHA
st. Arndell Park......273 J9

MURU
av. Winmalee......173 A11
dr. Glenmore Pk......266 B11
la. Glenmore Pk, off
Muru Dr............266 C11
MURUBA
av. Carlingford......279 E3
MURULLA
pl. Airds......511 J15
MURWILLUMBAH
av. Hoxton Park......393 A6
MUSCAT
gr. Glenwood......215 D14
pl. Eschol Park......481 C2
pl. Orchard Hills......268 D9
MUSCATEL
wy. Orchard Hills......268 F12
MUSCHARRY
rd. Londonderry......148 C10
MUSCIO
st. Colyton......270 C4
MUSCIOS
rd. Glenorie......128 J12
MUSEUM
pl. Penrith......236 F8
MUSGRAVE
av. Centennial Pk......22 B16
av. Queens Park......22 B16
cr. Fairfield W......335 E9
pl. Ruse......512 F6
pl. Mosman......316 H13
st. Turramurra......223 E12
MUSGROVE
cr. Doonside......243 E8
MUSSELBURGH
rd. Strathfield......341 A15
MUSSON
la. Richmond......118 G4
MUSTANG
av. St Clair......270 F11
dr. Raby......451 D16
MUSTON
la. Sutherland, off
Flora St............490 K1
pl. Glenhaven......187 K16
st. Mosman......317 C17
MUSWELLBROOK
rd. Hoxton Park......392 G9
rd. Glenwood......245 G1
MUTCH
av. Kyeemagh......404 A14
MUTTAMA
rd. Artarmon......284 K13
rd. Wahroonga......251 J1
MUTUAL
dr. Old Tngabbie......277 C7
rd. Mortdale......431 A5
MYAHGAH
mw. Mosman, off
Vista St............317 A6
rd. Mosman......317 A7
MYALL
av. Vaucluse......348 A11
av. Wahroonga......222 E11
cr. Strathfield......340 H12
pl. Leumeah......482 F14
pl. Casula......424 C1
st. Auburn......338 K11
st. Belmore......371 F16
st. Cabramatta......365 H8
st. Concord W......311 F16
st. Doonside......243 D15
st. Merrylands......307 E16
st. Oatley......430 K13
st. Pagewood......405 H9
st. Prestons......393 K14
st. Prospect......274 C11
st. Rydalmere......309 G1
st. Stanmore......16 E11
MYALLIE
av. Baulkham Hl......247 C16
MYALORA
st. Russell Lea......343 C6
MYAMBA
rd. Collaroy......229 A16
MYCUMBENE
av. E Lindfield......255 A15
MYDDLETON
av. Fairfield......336 C9
MYDELL
st. Kingsgrove......401 F9
MYEE
av. Strathfield......340 J15
cr. Baulkham Hl......246 F11
st. Old Tngabbie......276 K7

rd. Mcquarie Fd......453 H2
st. Lakemba......401 A3
st. Merrylands......307 H15
MYERLA
cr. Connells Pt......431 H16
MYERS
st. Roselands......401 D5
st. Sans Souci......463 A1
st. Five Dock......342 G9
MYLER
pl. Minto......452 K15
MYLES
MYNAH
cl. St Clair......270 E12
MYOLA
rd. Newport......169 J12
pl. N Turramurra......193 F12
rd. Liverpool......395 C7
swy.Liverpool......395 D5
st. Seven Hills......245 K13
wy. Quakers Hill......214 B12
MYORA
cl. Green Valley......363 H10
MYPOLONGA
dr. Gymea Bay......491 H10
MYRA
av. Ryde......282 B15
cl. Dulwich Hill......373 C11
pl. Ingleburn......453 C10
pl. Oatley......431 B15
rd. Dulwich Hill......373 C11
st. Frenchs Frst......257 B4
st. Plumpton......242 C7
st. Wahroonga......222 A4
MYRNA
rd. Strathfield......341 A15
MYRTLE
rd. Warriewood......198 G10
cl. Voyager Pt......427 C4
gr. Bella Vista......246 G6
la. Chippendale......18 H2
la. Stanmore......16 G8
la.w.Stanmore......16 H7
pl. St Ives......224 B10
rd. Bankstown......369 G14
rd. Clarmnt Ms......268 J3
rd. Greenfld Pk......334 E13
rd. Prairiewood......334 E13
st. Botany......405 H9
st. Chippendale......18 J2
st. Chippendale......19 A3
st. Crows Nest......5 F7
st. Granville......308 G16
st. Kensington......376 B12
st. Leichhardt......15 E3
st. Loftus......489 J13
st. Marrickville......374 A15
st. Minto Ht......483 F1
st. Normanhurst......221 E13
st. N Balgowlah......287 F6
st. N Sydney......5 D1
st. Oatley......430 K12
st. Oatley......431 A13
st. Pagewood......405 H9
st. Turramurra......223 C8
MYRTLE CREEK
av. Tahmoor......566 B8
MYRTUS
cr. Bidwill......211 F13
MYSON
dr. Cherrybrook......219 E13
MYUNA
cl. Westleigh......220 E7
cl. Seven Hills......275 C7
pl. Camden S......507 C10
pl. Port Hacking......522 H2
rd. Dover Ht......348 F10

N

NAALONG
pl. Cranebrook......207 H11
pl. Wallacia......355 C3
NABIAC
av. Belrose......225 H12
av. Gymea Bay......491 G8
pl. Westleigh......220 G10
NABILLA
rd. Palm Beach......139 H2
NADA
st. Old Tngabbie......276 K7

NADENE
pl. Pymble......253 C7
NADER
pl. Hornsea Pk......392 E16
NADIA
pl. Guildford......338 B7
NADIE
pl. Kings Lngly......245 K7
NADINE
cl. Cherrybrook......219 J4
NADZAB
rd. Holsworthy......426 F9
NAGLE
av. Maroubra......406 K11
av. Springwood......172 E12
cl. Menai......458 H6
pl. N Turramurra......193 F12
st. Liverpool......395 C7
swy.Liverpool......395 D5
st. Seven Hills......245 K13
wy. Quakers Hill......214 B12
NAILON
pl. Mona Vale......199 C1
NAIRANA
dr. Marayong......244 B4
NAIRN
st. Kingsgrove......402 B9
NAIROBI
pl. Toongabbie......275 E13
NALAURA
cl. Beecroft......250 B6
NALLADA
pl. Beecroft......250 B12
pl. Alfords Point......429 C14
NALONG
st. St Clair......270 F10
NALYA
av. Baulkham Hl......246 K7
la. Berowra Ht......132 J5
rd. Berowra Ht......132 J6
rd. Narraweena......258 B1
NAMAN
cl. Bossley Park......334 B5
NAMARA
pl. Engadine......518 G6
NAMATJIRA
av. Londonderry......148 C9
cl. Eagle Vale......481 A10
pl. Chifley......437 B9
pwy.Winmalee......172 K10
NAMBA
rd. Duffys Frst......194 H4
NAMBOUR
pl. Engadine......489 E9
NAMBRUK
cl. Cranebrook......207 E7
NAMBUCCA
pl. Clarmnt Ms......268 K1
pl. Padstow Ht......429 G8
rd. Terrey Hills......196 C5
st. Ruse......512 C6
st. Turramurra......223 C8
NAMBUCCA HEADS
cr. Hoxton Park......392 H9
NAMBUNG
pl. Bow Bowing......452 D13
NAME
la. Dulwich Hill......373 E7
NAMOI
cct. Wattle Grove......395 H13
la. Georges Hall, off
Surrey Av............368 B16
pl. E Lindfield......255 B14
pl. Ruse......512 B9
pl. Sylvania Wtr......462 D13
pl. Toongabbie......275 F10
rd. Matraville......436 K11
rd. Northbridge......316 B1
st. Greystanes......305 K4
st. N Epping......251 E10
NAMONA
st. N Narrabeen......199 A14
NAMUR
st. S Granville......338 G5
NANA GLEN
pl. Hoxton Park......392 J9
NANARDINE
la. Waterfall......519 D13
NANBAREE
rd. Ryde......282 E16
NANCARROW
av. Ryde......311 F4
la. Ryde......311 F4

STREETS NE

NANCE
av. Cabramatta 365 D9
la. Croydon Pk 372 B6
NANCY
pl. Ambarvale 510 F15
pl. Galston 159 H8
st. North Bondi 348 D15
st. Pendle Hill 306 C1
st. St Marys 269 J3
NANCYE
st. Randwick 377 C16
NANDEWAR
pl. Airds 512 A10
NANDI
av. Frenchs Frst 256 J4
NANDINA
tce. Avalon 139 K15
NANETTE
pl. Castle Hill 217 H11
NANGANA
rd. Bayview 168 J14
NANGAR
pl. Emu Plains 235 A8
st. Fairfield W 335 E12
NANOWIE
av. Wahroonga 221 J12
st. Narwee 400 H13
NANT
st. Bnksmeadw 436 C1
NANTUCKET
pl. Rouse Hill 185 A9
NAOI
av. Pemulwuy 305 F6
pl. Glenmore Pk 266 A11
NAOLI
la. St Clair, off Naoli Pl 269 G14
pl. St Clair 269 G13
NAOMI
ct. Cherrybrook 219 K4
st.n, Baulkham Hl 248 A16
st.s, Baulkham Hl 278 A1
NAPIER
av. Emu Plains 235 K8
av. Lurnea 394 C13
cr. North Ryde 282 G7
la. Emu Plains, off Napier St 235 K8
pl. Bossley Park 334 C8
pl. Ingleburn 453 F13
st. Canterbury 372 E16
st. Dover Ht 348 F11
st. Drummoyne 343 K1
st. Engadine 518 G6
st. Lindfield 284 B3
st. Malabar 437 E6
st. Mays Hill 307 J5
st. N Strathfield 341 F7
st. N Sydney K B4
st. N Sydney 5 E6
st. Paddington 4 F15
st. Parramatta 307 J5
st. Petersham 15 G15
st. Rooty Hill 242 C14
NAPOLEON
rd. Greenacre 370 D15
st. Mascot 405 F4
st. Riverwood 400 D14
st. Rosebery 405 F4
st. Rozelle 7 A14
st. Sans Souci 463 C5
st. Sydney A C13
st. Sydney 1 D15
NAPOLI
st. Padstow 399 A9
st. Revesby 399 A9
NAPPER
av. Riverwood 400 C16
st. S Coogee 407 H5
NAPULYA
st. Duffys Frst 165 A14
NAPUNYAH
wy. St Clair 270 A16
NARA
pl. St Ives 224 D7
NARABANG
wy. Belrose 225 H1
NARAMBI
cl. Berowra Ht 132 J10
NARANG
pl. St Marys 239 G10
NARANGA
av. Engadine 518 G5
NARANGANAH
av. Gymea Bay 491 F12
NARANGHI
av. Telopea 279 E9
st. Busby 363 G13
NARANI
cr. Earlwood 402 D2
cr. Northbridge 286 C16
NARCISSUS
av. Quakers Hill 243 D3
NARDANGO
rd. Bradbury 511 C16
NARDI
tce. Orchard Hills 267 E5
NARDOO
rd. Willoughby 285 D13
st. Ingleburn 453 B7
st. Ingleburn 453 C6
wy. Mt Annan 479 C14
NARDU
la. S Penrith, off Nardu Pl 266 H7
pl. S Penrith 266 H7
NAREE
ct. Glenwood 245 E2
rd. Frenchs Frst 256 D4
NAREEN
pde. N Narrabeen 228 K1
NARELLAN
cr. Bonnyrigg Ht 363 C7
rd. Blairmount 510 C1
rd. Campbelltown 510 C1
rd. Currans Hill 479 B10
rd. Mt Annan 479 B10
rd. Narellan 478 J9
rd. Narellan Vale 478 J9
rd. Smeaton Gra 479 B10
NARELLE
av. Castle Hill 248 C2
av. Pymble 253 G4
av.e, Castle Hill 248 C3
cr. Greenacre 370 C8
pl. Silverdale 354 A11
st. Mount Druitt 271 A3
st. North Bondi 348 D14
st. N Epping 251 D10
NARENA
cl. Beecroft 250 F3
NARETHA
la. Green Valley 363 F10
NARGONG
rd. Allambie Ht 257 G13
NARIEL
pl. Peakhurst 430 D9
st. St Marys 239 G13
NARLA
rd. Bayview 168 F12
NAROO
rd. Terrey Hills 196 G5
NAROOMA
av. S Penrith 266 F6
cl. Panania 428 G3
dr. Prestons 393 C16
pl. Gymea Bay 491 C9
rd. Northbridge 286 C15
NARRABEEN
pl. Glenmore Pk 266 B5
rd. Leumeah 482 F12
st. Narrabeen 229 A5
NARRABEEN PARK
pde. Mona Vale 199 D9
pde. N Narrabeen 199 D14
pde. Warriewood 199 D14
NARRABRI
st. Quakers Hill 243 K3
NARRABURRA
cl. Mt Colah 191 K6
NARRAGA
pl. Gymea Bay 491 D8
NARRAMORE
st. Kingsgrove 402 A14
NARRAN
ct. Woodcroft 243 H10
pl. Glenmore Pk 266 C6
NARROMINE
pl. Bonnyrigg Ht 363 C5
wy. Mcquarie Pk 282 E4
NARROW
la. Paddington, off Broughton St 13 D15
NARROY
rd. N Narrabeen 228 J1
NARRUN
cr. Dundas 279 F11
NARRYNA
pl. Glen Alpine 510 B16
NARTEE
pl. Wilberforce 92 B1
NARVA
pl. Seven Hills 275 G6
NARWEE
av. Narwee 400 H14
NASH
la. Carramar 366 H3
pl. Blacktown 244 B12
pl. Currans Hill 479 G13
pl. North Ryde 283 B12
st. S Penrith 267 A4
NASHS
la. Concord 312 A15
NASSAU
cl. Bossley Park 333 K6
NATAL
pl. Seven Hills 275 H4
NATALIE
cl. Casula 423 K2
cl. Hornsby Ht 191 G3
cr. Fairfield W 335 E12
ct. Glenhaven 218 D2
pl. Oakhurst 242 D2
NATASHA
pl. Picton 561 G3
NATCHEZ
cr. Greenfld Pk 333 K15
NATHAN
cr. Dean Park 212 H15
la. Mosman, off Harbour St 316 K6
la. Mosman, off Vista St 316 K6
la. Willoughby 285 F15
pl. Engadine 518 E3
st. Coogee 377 E15
st. Mulgoa 296 F1
NATHANIEL
pde. Kings Lngly 245 E7
NATHIA
st. Glenwood 215 B16
NATIONAL
av. Loftus 490 A12
la. Rozelle 7 A14
st. Cabramatta 365 K10
st. Leichhardt 15 F4
st. Rozelle 7 A14
st. Warwck Frm 365 J16
NATIONAL PARK
rd. Holsworthy 426 H6
rd. Holsworthy 427 E16
NATTAI
cl. Thornleigh 221 B6
pl. Banksia 403 H12
st. Couridjah 564 G13
st. Couridjah 565 A14
st. Loftus 490 B10
st. Ruse 512 B9
st. Seven Hills 246 C13
NATUNA
pl. Lethbrdg Pk 240 K1
st. N Narrabeen 198 J13
NAUGHTON
av. Lansdowne 367 D7
st. Greenacre 370 G7
NAURU
cr. Lethbrdg Pk 240 J1
NAUTICA
sq. Chiswick 343 B2
NAVAHO
st. Bossley Park 334 A10
NAVAJO
cl. Stanhpe Gdn 215 D11
NAVINS
la. Zetland, off Elizabeth St 375 H10
NAVUA
rd. Grose Wold 116 C8
NAVY
pl. Schofields 213 D12
st. Schofields 213 C11
NAYING
dr. Pemulwuy 305 F5
NAYLA
cl. Bardwell Vy 403 C7
NAYLOR
pl. Ingleburn 453 A11
NEA
cl. Glenmore Pk 266 C8
dr. Pemulwuy 305 E5
st. Chatswood 284 J12
NEAGLE
la. Colyton, off Neagle St 270 E7
st. Colyton 270 E7
NEAL
pl. Appin 569 F13
pl. Minto 482 H8
NEALE
av. Cherrybrook 219 E15
av. Forestville 256 A11
ct. Castle Hill 217 A9
st. Belmore 371 C13
st. St Marys 269 E1
wy. Berrilee 131 E12
NEALES
la. Penrith 237 A10
NEBO
pl. Cartwright 394 C5
NEBULA
gln. N St Marys 239 K7
NECROPOLIS
cct. Rookwood 340 A11
dr. Rookwood 339 K10
dr. Rookwood 340 C11
dr. Rookwood 340 B11
NECTARBROOK
dr. Brownlow Hl 444 H12
dr. Brownlow Hl 474 E1
NEEDLEBRUSH
cl. Alfords Point 459 B1
NEEDLEWOOD
cl. Rouse Hill 185 A7
gr. Padstow Ht 429 D8
NEENAN
pl. Erskine Park 270 H16
NEERIM
cl. Berowra 133 E9
rd. Castle Cove 285 J3
NEERINI
av. Smithfield 336 A8
NEETA
av. Cmbrdg Pk 238 C8
NEEWORRA
rd. Northbridge 286 D15
NEICH
pde. Burwood 342 A11
rd. Glenorie 126 J1
rd. Maraylya 124 G1
NEICHS
la. Concord 342 A10
NEIL
pl. Canley Ht 365 D1
st. Bundeena 524 B8
st. Epping 280 F2
st. Holroyd 307 H11
st. Hornsby 221 E6
st. Merrylands 307 H11
st. North Ryde 283 A12
NEILD
av. Darlinghurst 13 B12
av. Paddington 13 B12
NEILSON
av. Peakhurst 430 G2
cl. Glenmore Pk 265 J6
cr. Bligh Park 150 G8
st. Granville 308 G16
wy. Blackett 241 B2
NEIRBO
av. Hurstville 431 J6
NEIWAND
av. Kellyville 215 H6
NELL
pl. Ambarvale 511 A14
NELLA
st. Padstow 429 F4
NELLA DAN
av. Tregear 240 C5
NELLELLA
st. Blakehurst 432 B14
NELLIE
st. Lalor Park 245 D9
NELLIE STEWART
dr. Doonside 243 D5
NELLIGEN
cl. Prestons 393 C14
NELLO
pl. Wetherill Pk 334 C4
NELSON
av. Belmore 401 G3
av. Bronte 378 A9
av. Padstow 399 C9
la. Annandale 11 C14
la. Riverstone 182 F13
la. Waterloo 19 E11
la. Woollahra 22 C3
pde. Hunters Hill 314 C14
pl. Petersham 15 G11
rd. Box Hill 184 D2
rd. Cattai 94 G3
rd. Earlwood 403 B2
rd. Killara 254 D13
rd. Lindfield 254 E15
rd. Nelson 154 F16
rd. N Strathfield 341 F7
rd. Yennora 337 A9
st. Annandale 17 A3
st. Bondi Jctn 22 D5
st. Chatswood 284 H13
st. Dulwich Hill 373 E7
st. Engadine 488 J14
st. Fairfield 336 C11
st. Fairfield Ht 336 A11
st. Gladesville 312 H4
st. Gordon 253 K7
st. Kenthurst 158 B15
st. Minto 452 G15
st. Minto 452 J14
st. Mount Druitt 271 B4
st. Penshurst 431 D5
st. Randwick 407 C1
st. Riverstone 182 G13
st. Rozelle 7 A13
st. Sans Souci 462 J4
st. Thornleigh 221 C11
st. Turrella 403 F5
st. Woollahra 22 C3
NEMBA
st. Hunters Hill 313 F10
NEMESIA
av. Caringbah 493 A12
st. Greystanes 305 K11
NENAGH
st. North Manly 258 C16
NENTOURA
pl. Forestville 255 G10
pl. N Turramurra 193 D15
NEOSHO
wy. Maroubra 407 D13
NEOTSFIELD
av. Dangar I 76 J7
NEPEAN
av. Camden 507 B7
av. Normanhurst 221 F12
av. Penrith 236 A10
pl. Sylvania Wtr 462 E10
st. Campbelltown 512 A8
st. Cranebrook 206 J12
st. Douglas Park 568 C8
st. Emu Plains 235 E14
st. Fairfield W 335 C14
st.s, Leonay 235 C16
wy. Yarramundi 145 F9
NEPEAN GARDENS
pl. Glenbrook 264 G1
NEPEAN GORGE
dr. Mulgoa 323 K1
NEPEAN TOWERS
av. Glen Alpine 510 B16
NEPTUNE
cr. Bligh Park 150 E6
cr. Green Valley 363 A12
pl. W Pnnant Hl 249 B8
rd. Newport 169 J8
st. Coogee 407 H3
st. Dundas Vy 280 A8
st. Padstow 429 A5
st. Padstow 429 B5
st. Raby 451 F16
st. Revesby 428 J5
NERADA
st. Blacktown 274 C2
NERANG
av. Terrey Hills 196 D5
cct. S Penrith 266 H6
cl. W Pnnant Hl 249 J1
la. Cronulla, off Nerang Rd 494 A10
rd. Cronulla 494 A10
st. Ryde 282 G14
st. Wahroonga 222 B16
tce. Yellow Rock 204 K2
NEREID
rd. Cranebrook 207 E10

GREGORY'S STREET DIRECTORY 111

NE STREETS

NERI
pl. Jamisontown 266 A4
NERIBA
cr. Whalan 240 H8
NERIDA
pl. Shalvey 210 H13
rd. Kareela 461 E10
NERIDAH
av. Belrose 226 B10
av. Mt Colah 192 D3
st. Chatswood 285 A10
NERINE
wy. Bidwill 211 D13
NERINGAH
av.n.Wahroonga 222 D6
av.s.Wahroonga 222 C7
NERLI
st. Abbotsbury 333 C11
wy. Claymore 481 B11
NERRIGA
ct. Prestons 392 K13
NESBITT
pl. Prairiewood 335 A7
st. Woolmloo..............4 H3
NESS
av. Dulwich Hill 373 C13
pl. Winston Hills 277 D3
NESTOR
la. Lewisham 15 D6
st. Winston Hills 277 D7
NET
rd. Avalon 140 A13
NETHERBY
st. Wahroonga 221 K6
NETHERBYES
wy. Narellan Vale ...508 G2
NETHERCOTE
cl. Prestons 393 C16
cl. Prestons 423 C1
NETHERTON
av. St Clair 269 J11
NETTLETON
av. Riverwood 400 C14
NETTLETREE
pl. Casula 393 K16
pl. Casula 423 K1
NEUTRAL
av. Birrong 369 A4
rd. Hornsby 221 F5
st. N Sydney 5 K9
NEVADA
av. Colyton 270 F8
cr. Punchbowl 399 H6
NEVELL
la. Cranebrook, off
  Nevell Pl..........207 E14
pl. Cranebrook 207 D14
NEVERFAIL
pl. Oatley 461 A1
NEVIL
wy. Casula 424 E2
NEVILLE
ct. Castle Hill 248 E5
la. Bankstown, off
  Greenfield Pde...399 D1
la. Marrickville 16 A13
rd. Riverstone 182 H12
st. Bass Hill 368 D12
st. Colyton 270 C7
st. Lidcombe 339 F9
st. Marayong 244 C11
st. Marrickville 16 A13
st. Marrickville 373 K9
st. N Willoughby 285 F8
st. Oatley 431 C14
st. Ryde 282 B10
st. Smithfield 335 C7
st. Yagoona 368 D12
NEVILLE McNAMARA
dr. N Turramurra 193 E11
NEVIN
cl. Menai 459 A9
NEVIS
cr. Seven Hills 275 C9
pl. Castle Hill 218 D8
NEVORIE
cr. Maroubra 406 J8
NEW
la. Mosman 317 B11
pl. Narellan Vale 508 J1
st. Ashfield 372 A6
st. Auburn 339 A10
st. Balgowlah Ht.....287 J11

st. Balgowlah Ht.....287 J11
st. Bondi 377 J2
st. Burwood 342 B11
st. Longueville 314 E7
st. N Parramatta 278 B13
st. Windsor 121 B8
st.e.Lidcombe........339 H9
st.w,Balgowlah.......287 F11
st.w,Balgowlah Ht..287 F11
st.w,Clontarf..........287 F11
st.w,Lidcombe 339 H8
NEWARK
cr. Lindfield 284 C1
pl. St Clair 270 G13
NEW BEACH
rd. Darling Point 13 F8
NEWBERY
la. Panania, off
  Tower St..........428 B1
NEWBIGIN
cl. North Ryde 283 D10
NEWBOLT
st. Wetherill Pk 334 F5
NEWBRIDGE
pl. Glenbrook 264 G1
rd. Chipping Ntn....396 B6
rd. Liverpool 395 E5
rd. Moorebank 396 B6
NEWBURY
av. Stanhope Gdn ..215 E7
pl. Eagle Vale 480 K10
NEWBY
pl. Collaroy Plat......228 F12
pl. Oakhurst 242 A4
NEW CAMBRIDGE
st. Fairfield W........335 D12
NEW CANTERBURY
rd. Dulwich Hill 373 A10
rd. Hurlstone Pk 373 A10
rd. Lewisham 15 A15
rd. Petersham 15 A15
NEWCASTLE
st. Five Dock 342 J8
st. Rose Bay 348 B11
st. Wakeley 334 H15
NEWCOMBE
pl. Lurnea 394 D11
pl. Toongabbie 276 G5
st. Maianbar 522 K9
st. Paddington 21 D3
st. Sans Souci 433 B16
NEWEENA
pl. Avalon 140 D10
NEWELL
st. Frenchs Frst 256 J4
st. Homebush B....310 G14
NEW ENGLAND
av. Homebush B....310 F15
dr. Kingsgrove........401 G14
wy. Castle Hill 217 H7
NEWEY
av. Padstow 399 D13
la. Padstow, off
  Newey Av........399 D13
NEW FARM
rd. W Pnnant Hl....219 J16
NEWHAM
dr. Cmbrdg Gdn 237 G2
pl. Chipping Ntn....366 G13
NEWHAVEN
av. Blacktown 274 G5
pl. St Ives 224 B12
NEW ILLAWARRA
rd. Barden Rdg......487 D12
rd. Bexley North 402 E10
rd. Lucas Ht 487 D12
NEWINGTON
bvd. Newington 310 B14
ml. Blaxland, off
  View St............233 F6
rd. Marrickville 16 A13
rd. Petersham 16 A13
rd. Silverwater 310 B9
NEW JERSEY
rd. Five Dock 343 B11
NEW JERUSALEM
rd. Oakdale............500 J3

st. Woollahra 22 G9
st. Woollahra 377 C6
NEWLANDS
la. Wollstncraft 5 A1
pl. Baulkham Hl 247 G4
st. Wollstncraft 315 E9
NEWLEAF
cl. Wrrngtn Dns 237 J4
NEW LINE
rd. Castle Hill 218 K4
rd. Cherrybrook 219 A6
rd. Dural 189 A16
rd. Glenhaven 218 K4
rd. W Pnnant Hl 249 H1
NEWLYN
st. St Ives 224 H10
NEW McLEAN
st. Edgecliff.............13 H11
NEWMAN
la. Newtown 17 G14
rd. Glenorie 95 G9
rd. Minto Ht 483 D9
st. Bass Hill 368 C6
st. Blacktown 274 C2
st. Merrylands.......307 F13
st. Mortdale 431 B7
st. Newtown 17 F13
NEWMARCH
pl. Bligh Park 150 C6
NEWMEN
cl. Wetherill Pk 334 E4
NEWMOON
pl. St Clair 270 C13
NEWNES
cl. Glenwood 245 F1
NEWNHAM
st. Dean Park 212 F15
NEW NORTH ROCKS
rd. North Rocks 249 A16
NEW ORLEANS
cr. Maroubra 407 D14
NEWPORT
cl. Woodbine 481 H11
pl. Oatlands 279 B13
rd. Yellow Rock 204 C1
st. Cmbrdg Pk.......237 J8
wy. Stanhope Gdn ..215 D5
NEWRY
pl. Hinchinbrk 392 K2
pl. Quakers Hill 244 A3
wy. Wentwthvle, off
  Ferndale Cl......277 D11
NEWS
rd. Werombi 443 A12
NEWS DIRECT
rd. Alexandria 375 C14
NEWSOME
la. Merrylands.......307 D7
NEW SOUTH HEAD
rd. Bellevue Hill 347 E10
rd. Double Bay 14 B11
rd. Edgecliff.............13 F9
rd. Point Piper 14 B11
rd. Rose Bay 348 A10
rd. Vaucluse 348 D5
NEWSTAN
pl. Cartwright........394 C4
NEWTIMBER
cct. St Clair 270 D9
NEWTON
av. Richmond 119 K6
cl. Liberty Gr........311 B10
la. Alexandria 18 F13
la. Mosman, off
  Medusa St......287 A16
la. Sydney ....C D4
la. Sydney 3 E2
pde. Forestville 256 A8
rd. Blacktown 274 B1
rd. Strathfield 341 A15
rd. Wetherill Pk 333 G3
st. Alexandria 18 E13
st. Guildford W 306 J16
st. Little Bay.........437 G14
st. N Epping 251 G10
st.n.Silverwater 309 D12
st.s.Auburn 309 D13
wy. Winmalee.........173 H8

NEY
st. Mascot 405 H6
st. Sans Souci 463 C4
NIANBILLA
pl. Frenchs Frst 255 H2
NIANGALA
cl. Belrose 195 J16
pl. Frenchs Frst 256 F1
NIANGLA
av. Carlingford.......279 F4
NIARA
st. Ryde 282 F16
NIAS
pl. Schofields 183 A16
NIBLICK
av. Roseville 285 C1
cr. Oatlands 279 B11
st. Arncliffe 403 J10
st. North Bondi 348 C16
NIBLO
st. Doonside 243 D9
NICE
pl. Seven Hills 275 H5
NICHOL
pde. Strathfield 341 F14
NICHOLAS
av. Campsie 372 A16
av. Concord 342 B6
av. Forestville 256 B10
cl. Bella Vista 246 F7
cl. Bonnyrigg 364 B7
cr. Cecil Hills 362 K5
ct. Normanhurst 221 J12
st. Blacktown 274 E4
st. Lidcombe..........340 A5
st. N Sydney 6 A8
NICHOLI
pl. Alfords Point 459 A3
pl. Cherrybrook 219 D7
st. Kellyville Rdg ...215 B1
NICHOLII
cr. Kenthurst 156 G16
pl. Mcquarie Fd....454 D3
NICHOLL
av. Haberfield 373 D1
pde. Enmore..............16 F13
st. Warwick Frm ...365 G14
wy. Minto 482 H5
NICHOLS
av. Beverly Hills 401 A15
av. Revesby 398 F13
pde. Mt Riverview 234 E2
pl. Kingswood 237 F10
st. Surry Hills............4 D16
NICHOLSON
av. Leumeah 482 A16
av. St Ives 254 D4
av. Thornleigh 220 H10
cr. Kings Lngly 245 H7
la. Wollstncraft, off
  Nicholson St...315 F7
pde.Cronulla 493 J15
pl. Crows Nest, off
  Nicholson St...315 F7
pl. St Leonards, off
  Cristie St.........315 D5
pl. Windsor Dn......180 H4
pl. Wollstncraft, off
  Nicholson St...315 F7
st. Balmain East 8 F7
st. Burwood 341 G16
st. Chatswood........284 K8
st. North Manly 258 B13
st. Penshurst 431 B1
st. St Leonards 315 E6
st. Strathfield 341 G16
st. Tempe 404 A3
st. Wollstncraft 315 E6
st. Woolmloo...........4 F3
NINA GRAY
av. Rhodes 311 D7
NINDI
cr. Glenmore Pk 266 C6
NICKLEBY
wy. Ambarvale 510 K16
NICKSON
la. Surry Hills..........20 C5
st. Surry Hills..........20 B6
NICOBAR
st. Kings Park 244 K3
NICOL
av. Maroubra 407 F10
la. Berala 339 C12
la. Maroubra 407 F10
NICOLAIDIS
cr. Rooty Hill 272 A3

NICOLE
pl. Winmalee..........173 D5
NICOLL
av. Earlwood 402 G3
av. Ryde 311 K1
la. Burwood 342 A11
la. Ryde, off
  Lee Av............311 K1
st. Roselands 400 K5
NICOLSON
cct. Menai 458 G14
NIELA
gr. Baulkham Hl ...246 F12
NIELD
av. Balgowlah 287 H10
av. Greenwich.......315 A5
av. Rodd Point 343 E8
NIELLO
cl. Castle Hill 248 G1
NIELSEN
av. Carlton 432 J8
NIEMUR
rd. St Marys 239 H2
NIEUPORT
av. Milperra 397 E12
NIGEL
pl. Mcquarie Fd....424 A15
pl. Padstow 399 F15
pl. Rooty Hill 271 K4
NIGEL LOVE
cr. Mascot 405 B10
NIGER
pl. Kearns 481 C1
NIGHTINGALE
dr. Blaxland 233 G9
sq. Glossodia.........66 D10
NIGHTMIST
gr. St Clair 270 D15
la. St Clair, off
  Nightmist Gr...270 E15
NILAND
cr. Blackett 241 B2
pl. Edensor Pk 363 J3
wy. Casula 424 G2
NILE
av. Seven Hills 275 F7
cl. Marsfield..........251 K13
pl. Kearns 481 A1
st. St Clair 270 B9
st. Fairfield Ht 335 H10
NILLERA
av. Terrey Hills 196 C6
NILSON
av. Hillsdale 406 F15
NILSSON
la. Botany 405 F11
NIMBEY
av. Narraweena 258 B6
NIMBIN
av. Hoxton Park 393 B7
pl. Yarrawarrah 489 E14
st. N Balgowlah.....287 C11
NIMBRIN
st. Turramurra 252 D4
NIMOOLA
rd. Engadine..........489 D9
NIMROD
pl. Tregear 240 E4
st. Darlinghurst......4 H10
NINA
pl. Kurrajong Ht 63 E12
pl. Oakhurst 241 H1
st. Revesby 398 K12
NINETEENTH
av. Hoxton Park 392 G7
st. Warragamba 353 E9
NINEVEH
cr. Greenfld Pk......334 A15
NINNIS
st. Leumeah 482 H11
NINTH
av. Austral 391 A10
av. Belfield 371 H13
av. Campsie 371 H13
av. Jannali 461 K12
av. Llandilo 207 K8
av.n,Loftus 490 A8
av.s,Loftus 489 H11
rd. Berkshire Pk ...180 C10

112 GREGORY'S STREET DIRECTORY

STREETS NO

st. Mascot 405 A7
st. Warragamba 353 F5

NIOBE
la. Turramurra 252 E1

NIOKA
pl. Bankstown 369 H13
pl. Bell 57 B9
pl. Caringbah 492 F6
pl. St Ives Ch 223 K4
rd. Narrabeen 228 H7
rd. Penrith 237 C3
st. Gladesville 312 F8
st. Oatlands 279 B7

NIPIGON
rd. Seven Hills 275 G6

NIRIMBA
av. Narwee 400 G13
av. N Epping 251 E9
cr. Heathcote 518 J9
dr. Quakers Hill 213 H12
dr. Schofields 213 H12

NIRRANDA
st. Concord W 341 F1

NIRVANA
st. Pendle Hill 276 E12

NITH
pl. St Andrews 451 J14

NITHDALE
st. Pymble 223 D15

NITHSDALE
la. Sydney F D4
la. Sydney F B5
la. Sydney 3 J10
st. Sydney F C5
st. Sydney 3 J11

NIVEN
pl. Belrose 226 D13

NIX
av. Malabar 437 F7

NIXON
av. Ashfield 372 H2
la. Strathfield 341 J11
pl. Bonnet Bay 460 B8
pl. Cherrybrook 219 G6
rd. Thirlmere 562 B14
st. Emu Plains 235 E9
st. Glenwood 215 J14

NOAKES
pde. Lalor Park 245 F13

NOBBS
la. Surry Hills 20 D5
rd. Yagoona 369 A9
st. S Granville 338 F2
st. Surry Hills 20 D4

NOBEL
pl. Castle Hill 217 K13
pl. Winston Hills 277 D5

NOBLE
av. Greenacre 370 B10
av. Mt Lewis 370 A16
av. Punchbowl 370 A16
av. Strathfield 371 C4
cl. Kings Lngly 245 D7
cl. Menai 458 G8
la. St Clair, off Noble Pl 269 K15
pl. St Clair 269 K15
pl. Telopea 279 F9
st. Allawah 432 D7
st. Canley Vale 366 F2
st. Concord 342 A2
st. Five Dock 343 C8
st. Hornsby 221 E4
st. Mosman 316 K8
st. Rodd Point 343 C8
wy. Rouse Hill 184 J7

NOCK
la. Mosman, off Avenue Rd 317 A9

NOCKOLDS
av. Punchbowl 370 A16

NODDY
pl. Hinchinbrk 363 F16

NOEL
st. Georges Hall 367 H14
st. Marayong 244 D11

NOELA
pl. Oxley Park 270 D2

NOELENE
st. Fairfield W 335 G11

NOELINE
av. Mcquarie Fd 454 B2
st. Hurstville 401 G16

NOFFS
pl. Bonnyrigg Ht 363 F6

NOLA
la. Roseville, off Nola Rd 284 G6
pl. Baulkham Hl 247 D1
rd. Roseville 284 G5
st. Marsfield 282 C4

NOLAN
av. Clovelly 377 G11
av. Engadine 518 K1
cr. Naremburn 315 D2
cr. Westmead 307 F2
pl. Balgowlah Ht 287 J14
pl. Mt Pritchard 364 K10
pl. Seven Hills 245 K14
st. Casula 424 E4
wy. Harringtn Pk 478 H2

NOLLAND
pl. Kenthurst 156 K8

NOLLANDS
rd. Fiddletown 129 J4

NOLLER
pde. Parramatta 308 G4

NOMAD
gr. St Clair 270 E15
pl. Raby 481 H2

NOOAL
st. Newport 169 E10

NOOK
av. Neutral Bay 6 A5
la. Neutral Bay 6 A5
la. West Ryde 281 F16
pl. Leonay 235 A16

NOOLINGA
rd. Bayview 168 J10

NOONAN
rd. Ingleburn 453 B1

NOONBINNA
cl. Northbridge 286 A14
cr. Northbridge 286 B14

NOONGAH
pl. Canada Bay 342 E8
st. Bargo 567 C7

NOORA
av. Little Bay 437 A10
pl. Marayong 244 C2
st. Lidcombe 339 H5

NOORAL
st. Bargo 567 E8

NOORONG
av. Frenchs Frst 256 G1
cl. Baulkham Hl 247 C5

NORA
ct. Rouse Hill 184 K9
ct. Rouse Hill 185 A9

NORBAR
la. Kingsford 376 J16

NORE
pl. Minto 482 K4

NOREE
pl. Wrrngtn Dns 238 A3

NORFOLK
av. Beverly Hills 401 D15
av. Collaroy 229 A16
av. Fairfield W 335 B10
la. Matraville, off Franklin St 436 J2
la. Paddington 13 E15
pde. Matraville 436 J2
pl. Carlingford 279 B3
pl. Miranda 492 D6
pl. N Richmond 87 H13
rd. Cmbrdg Pk 237 H10
rd. Epping 251 D14
rd. Greenacre 370 E6
rd. Longueville 314 B9
rd. N Epping 251 D10
st. Blacktown 244 C13
st. Ingleburn 453 C6
st. Killara 253 G11
st. Liverpool 395 C5
st. Mount Druitt 240 K16
st. Newtown 17 G14
st. Paddington 13 E15
swy. Liverpool 395 C5
wy. North Ryde 282 J13

NORHAM
mw. Castle Hill 216 H9

NORIKA
pl. Toongabbie 276 E10

NORMA
av. Belmore 401 F5
av. Eastwood 281 G7
cl. Bargo 567 A2
cr. Cheltenham 250 K7
pl. Merrylands 307 E15
rd. Palm Beach 140 C4

NORMAC
rd. Girraween 276 A11
st. Roseville Ch 285 G1

NORMAN
av. Auburn 339 A12
av. Dolls Point 463 F1
av. Hamondvle 396 F15
av. Thornleigh 221 A4
cr. Claymore 481 C12
pl. Bligh Park 150 K7
st. Allawah 432 F9
st. Berala 339 D10
st. Concord 341 H1
st. Condell Park 398 H2
st. Darlinghurst F J4
st. Darlinghurst 4 B10
st. Five Dock 343 C10
st. Merrylands 307 B8
st. Peakhurst 430 F5
st. Prospect 274 G13
st. Punchbowl 400 B6
st. Rozelle 344 E6
swy. Hamondvle 396 F15

NORMANBY
rd. Auburn 339 B1
st. Fairfield E 337 A14

NORMAN DUNLOP
cr. Minto 482 J4

NORMANDY
rd. Allambie Ht 257 C10
tce. Leumeah 482 F11

NORMAN HALL
cl. Castle Hill 219 A12

NORMANHURST
rd. Normanhurst 221 G10
st. Elvina Bay 168 C4

NORMAN LINDSAY
cr. Faulconbdg 171 H11

NORMAN MAY
dr. Lidcombe 339 J13

NORMANS
rd. Silverdale 354 C15

NORMIC
av. Blaxland 234 A8
la. Blaxland 234 A8

NORMURRA
av. N Turramurra 223 F5

NORN
cl. Greenfld Pk 334 D14

NORRIE
pl. Oakhurst 242 A2
st. Yennora 337 A8

NORRIS
pl. Narellan Vale 478 K16
wy. Wentwthvle, off Portadown Rd 277 D11

NORSEMAN
cl. Green Valley 363 J11
pl. Yarrawarrah 489 F13

NORTH
av. Cammeray 315 K3
av. Leichhardt 16 E1
av. Rossmore 389 J14
av. Westmead 277 E15
cir. Blaxland 233 H6
cr. Lilyfield 10 E1
pde. Auburn 339 E3
pde. Campsie 372 A12
pde. Guildford 337 G7
pde. Hunters Hill 313 H10
pde. Mount Druitt 241 C16
pde. Rooty Hill 272 A1
rd. Denistone E 281 K10
rd. Eastwood 281 G5
rd. N Curl Curl 258 K10
rd. Ryde 281 K11
st. Auburn 339 A6
st. Balmain 7 E7
st. Fairfield 336 E15
st. Gymea 491 E4
st. Leichhardt 9 G11
st. Marrickville 16 C14
st. Mt Colah 162 B16
st. Penrith 237 A9
st. Schofields 182 H15
st. Thirlmere 565 A1
st. Thirlmere 565 B2
st. Windsor 121 F7
tce. Bankstown 369 F16

NORTHAM
av. Bankstown 399 A8
av. Newington, off Spitz Av 309 K14
dr. North Rocks 279 A3
st. Belrose 225 K15

NORTHAMPTON DALE
rd. Appin 569 A14

NORTH ARM
rd. Middle Cove 285 K7

NORTH AVALON
rd. Avalon 140 D14

NORTHBROOK
pl. Illawong 459 D5
st. Bexley 432 H1

NORTHBURY
ct. Glen Alpine 510 C11

NORTHCLIFF
st. Milsons Point 5 J16

NORTHCLIFFE
av. Brookvale 258 A7
av. Narraweena 258 A7

NORTHCOTE
av. Caringbah 492 J12
av. Fairlight 288 A9
av. Killara 254 A10
la. Glebe 11 G6
rd. Glebe 11 G6
rd. Greenacre 370 A8
rd. Hornsby 192 A16
rd. Lindfield 254 E14
st. Auburn 339 A2
st. Canterbury 372 C16
st. Earlwood 402 C2
st. Haberfield 343 A13
st. Marrickville 373 K11
st. Mortlake 312 A14
st. Naremburn 315 D4
st. Rose Bay 348 E9
st. St Leonards 315 D4
st. Sans Souci 433 B15

NORTHCOTT
av. Kingsgrove 401 J11
la. Parramatta 278 B15
rd. Blacktown 245 C10
rd. Cromer 227 G12
rd. Lalor Park 245 C10
st. North Ryde 282 D10
st. S Wntwthvle 306 J8
wy. Cherrybrook, off Tennyson Cl 219 E10

NORTH COURT
rd. Russell Lea 343 D5

NORTH EAST
cr. Lilli Pilli 522 G3

NORTHEND
av. S Penrith 266 G3

NORTHERN RIVERS
av. Homebush B 310 F14

NORTH FORT
rd. Manly 290 B13

NORTH HARBOUR
st. Balgowlah 287 J11

NORTH HEAD SCENIC
dr. Manly 289 A16

NORTHLAND
rd. Bellevue Hill 14 H16
rd. Bellevue Hill 22 J1

NORTH LIVERPOOL
rd. Bonnyrigg 363 K11
rd. Bonnyrigg Ht 363 A8
rd. Green Valley 363 A8
rd. Heckenberg 363 K11
rd. Mt Pritchard 363 K11

NORTHMEAD
av. Northmead 277 J9

NORTHRIDGE
av. Bella Vista 216 C16
av. Bella Vista 246 D1

NORTH ROCKS
rd. Carlingford 249 H13
rd. N Parramatta 278 B9
rd. North Rocks 249 A16
rd. North Rocks 278 B9

NORTHROP
st. Raby 451 C13

NORTH STEYNE
Manly 288 H5
rd. Woodbine 481 D15

NORTHUMBERLAND
av. Mt Colah 192 C1
av. Stanmore 16 H5
ct. Castle Hill 217 B9
dr. Caringbah 493 B1
la. Clovelly, off Warner Av 378 B12
la.e. Stanmore 16 J5
la.w. Stanmore 16 H5
rd. Auburn 309 E16
st. Blacktown 274 H6
st. Bonnyrigg Ht 363 A7
st. Clovelly 378 B12
st. Liverpool 395 D4
st. Woolwich 314 D12
swy. Liverpool 395 D4

NORTH VANDERVILLE
st. The Oaks 502 E9

NORTHVIEW
pl. Mt Colah 192 A3
rd. Palm Beach 109 K15

NORTH WEST ARM
rd. Grays Point 491 B11
rd. Gymea 491 B9
rd. Gymea Bay 491 B9

NORTHWOOD
cl. Mona Vale 199 A2
la. Camperdown 17 F7
pl. Dundas Vy 280 D8
pl. Kellyville 216 J8
rd. Lane Cove 314 F6
rd. Longueville 314 F6
rd. Northwood 314 F6
st. Camperdown 17 F7
wy. Cherrybrook 219 E11

NORTON
av. Chipping Ntn 366 F13
av. Dover Ht 348 E8
av. Springwood 171 K16
ct. Berowra Ht 133 A7
la. Kingsford, off Barker St 376 J16
la. Lane Cove N 284 G15
pl. Glenmore Pk 265 E10
pl. Minto 483 A1
rd. North Ryde 282 G13
st. Ashfield 372 F3
st. Croydon 372 D3
st. Glebe 12 D14
st. Kingsford 376 J16
st. Leichhardt 9 J8
st. Lilyfield 9 J8
st. Surry Hills 20 B1

NORTONS BASIN
rd. Wallacia 323 K12

NORVAL
pl. Illawong 459 G5
st. Auburn 339 C6

NORVEGIA
av. Tregear 240 C4

NORVIC
pl. Seven Hills 275 D9

NORWEST
bvd. Baulkham Hl 216 G16
bvd. Bella Vista 246 B2

NORWICH
la. Rose Bay 348 B11
pl. Cherrybrook 219 A13
rd. Ingleburn 453 B5
rd. Rose Bay 348 A11

NORWIN
pl. Stanhpe Gdn 215 G9

NORWOOD
av. Beecroft 250 B12
av. Carlingford 250 B12
av. Lindfield 284 C3
la. Marrickville 15 K16
pl. Baulkham Hl 246 K3
rd. Vineyard 152 F13
st. Burwood 341 H15
st. Sandringham 463 D4

NOTE
st. Hunters Hill 313 B6

NOTLEY
st. Mount Druitt 241 E12

NOTT
la. Longueville 314 E8
pl. Mt Annan 479 F14

NOTTING
la. Cottage Pt 135 F10

NOTTINGHAM
av. Castle Hill 217 K10
cr. Chipping Ntn 366 F13
pl. Ryde 312 B4
pl. Yowie Bay 492 B12
pwy. Chipping Ntn, off Nottingham Cr 366 H13
st. Old Tngabbie 277 E9

GREGORY'S STREET DIRECTORY 113

NO STREETS

NOTTINGHILL
rd. Berala 339 F13
rd. Lidcombe 339 F13
rd. Regents Pk 369 F1
NOTTLE
st. Ashfield 373 A4
NOTTS
av. Bondi Beach 378 D5
NOUMEA
av. Bankstown 399 E5
st. Lethbrdg Pk 240 K1
st. Shalvey 210 K16
NOVA
pl. Mount Druitt 241 H12
pl. S Penrith 267 D4
NOVAR
st. St Johns Pk 364 H1
NOVARA
cr. Como 460 H10
cr. Jannali 460 H10
NOWILL
st. Condell Park 398 H6
st. Rydalmere 309 J5
NOWLAND
pl. Abbotsbury 333 B14
st. Seven Hills 246 B14
wy. Bradbury 511 J12
NOWRA
cl. Prestons 423 B2
la. Campsie 372 D12
st. Gymea Bay 491 C11
st. Campsie 372 D12
st. Greystanes 305 H2
st. Marayong 244 B3
st. Merrylands 308 D15
NOWRANIE
st. Windsor Dn 151 A15
st. Summer Hill 373 D5
NOYANA
av. Grays Point 491 A15
NUGENT
pl. Prairiewood 334 E12
NULANG
rd. Forestville 255 E8
st. Old Tngabbie 276 K8
NULGARRA
av. Gymea Bay 491 E11
pl. Bradbury 511 E15
st. Frenchs Frst 256 D8
st. Northbridge 285 H16
NULLA
st. Vaucluse 348 C6
NULLABOR
pl. Yarrawarrah 489 G12
NULLABURRA
rd. Newport 169 H10
rd.s,Caringbah 493 B7
rd.s,Caringbah 493 B7
NULLAGA
wy. Clarmnt Ms 268 H2
NULLA NULLA
st. Turramurra 222 K13
NULLAWARRA
av. Concord 341 G1
av. Concord W 311 F14
NUMA
rd. North Ryde 282 F13
st. Birchgrove 314 K16
NUMANTIA
rd. Engadine 518 G7
NUNANA
pl. Frenchs Frst 255 H1
NUNATAK
la. Tregear 240 E6
NUNDA
cl. Pennant Hills 220 B14
NUNDAH
pl. Woronora 460 A15
st. Lane Cove N 284 E16
st. St Johns Pk 334 F16
NUNDLE
st. Smithfield 335 F1
NUNGA
pl. Baulkham Hl 246 E10
pl. Marayong 243 K6
NUNGEROO
av. Jamisontown 266 A3
NUNKERE
cr. Rouse Hill 185 D6
NURLA
av. Little Bay 437 B10

NURMI
av. Newington 310 C12
NURRAGI
pl. Belrose 225 G15
st. Villawood 367 J5
NURRAN
rd. Vaucluse 348 B2
NURSEL
pl. Tregear 240 C4
NURSERY
pl. Belrose 226 A10
st. Hornsby 221 E2
NURSES
dr. Randwick 377 A16
wk. The Rocks .... A K6
NUTMANS
rd. Grose Wold 116 B11
NUTMEG
cl. Casula 424 A2
st. Westmead 307 H2
NUTT
rd. Londonderry 177 F8
NUTWOOD
la. Windsor Dn 151 A13
NUWARRA
rd. Chipping Ntn 396 F4
rd. Moorebank 396 D12
NYALLA
pl. Castle Hill 247 G3
NYAN
st. Chifley 437 B9
NYARA
st. Mt Krng-gai 162 J12
NYARDO
pl. Jannali 460 H10
NYARI
rd. Kenthurst 157 A3
wy. Narraweena 258 B3
NYDEGGAR
av. Glenwood 215 D14
NYINYA
av. Gymea 491 G4
NYLETA
st. Doonside 243 D13
NYMAGEE
st. Glenwood 215 E16
NYMBOIDA
av. Hoxton Park 392 J8
cr. Ruse 512 D6
cr. Sylvania Wtr 462 D13
st. Greystanes 306 A2
st. S Coogee 407 G6
NYNGAN
pl. Miranda 462 D16
st. Hoxton Park 392 H7
st. Quakers Hill 244 A2
wy. Mcquarie Pk 282 E4
NYORA
av. Smithfield 336 B8
st. Chester Hill 368 C3
st. Killara 254 C10
NYORIE
pl. Frenchs Frst 256 B2
NYRANG
rd. Kirrawee 490 J5
rd. Allambie Ht 257 F16
st. Lidcombe 339 H4

O

OADBY
st. Chipping Ntn 396 G1
OAG
cr. Kingswood 267 E2
OAK
dr. Georges Hall 367 F11
la. N St Marys, off
    Oak St 240 A10
la. N Sydney .... K A6
la. N Sydney 5 E7
la. Potts Point 4 K1
pl. Banksia 403 F12
pl. Bradbury 511 G13
pl. Mt Pritchard 364 D10
rd. Kirrawee 490 K6
rd.n,Kirrawee 460 K16
st. Ashfield 372 K2
st. Clovelly 377 K13
st. Greystanes 306 F9
st. Lugarno 429 J16
st. Normanhurst 221 D12
st. N Narrabeen 199 A14
st. N St Marys 240 A10

OAKBORNE
rd. Liverpool 395 B9
OAKDALE
av. Kogarah 433 E6
pl. Baulkham Hl 246 J4
pl. Cartwright 394 E5
OAKES
av. Eastwood 281 F6
rd. North Bondi 348 F15
rd. Carlingford 249 F9
rd. Old Tngabbie 277 A6
rd. W Pnnant Hl 249 F9
rd. Winston Hills 277 A6
st. Westmead 307 H2
OAKHAM
st. Sylvania 461 J13
wy. Stanhpe Gdn 215 B6
OAKHILL
dr. St Ives 224 F11
dr. Castle Hill 218 J8
OAKLAND
av. Baulkham Hl 248 A13
la. Wrrngtn Dns, off
    Oakland Pde 237 K5
pde. Wrrngtn Dns 237 K5
OAKLANDS
av. Beecroft 250 F9
av. Summer Hill 373 B3
OAKLEA
pl. Canley Ht 335 C15
OAKLEAF
st. Glenwood 245 C1
OAKLEIGH
av. Banksia 403 J13
av. Milperra 397 F11
av. S Granville 338 E6
av. Thornleigh 220 J11
OAKLEY
rd. Long Point 454 B7
rd. Mcquarie Rd 454 B7
rd. North Bondi 348 D16
OAKMONT
av. Glenmore Pk 266 G9
wy. Rouse Hill 185 C9
OAKRIDGE
ct. Kenthurst 156 H2
OAKS
av. Cremorne 316 C7
av. Dee Why 258 H6
av. Mowbray Pk 561 B7
rd. Thirlmere 561 B7
rd. Thirlmere 561 F16
rd. Thirlmere 564 F1
st. Cronulla 523 K2
st. Thirlmere 564 J3
st. Thirlmere 565 A3
OAK SIDE
dr. Minchinbury 272 E10
OAK TREE
pl. Kellyville 217 D2
OAKTREE
gr. Prospect 274 H11
pl. Penshurst 431 D1
OAKURA
st. Rockdale 403 C14
OAKVILLE
rd. Oakville 122 G15
rd. Willoughby 285 F12
OAKWOOD
dr. Busby 363 H16
dr. Hornsby Ht 162 A8
pl. Kellyville 216 H5
rd. Toongabbie 275 F14
st. Sutherland 460 D15
st. Sutherland 490 C1
wy. Menai 458 H10
OAKY
rd. Luddenham 326 B7
OATES
av. Gladesville 312 J5
pl. Belrose 226 B9
pl. Leumeah 482 J11
rd. Mortdale 430 J7
OATLANDS
cr. Oatlands 279 A8
st. Wattle Grove 426 B3
st. Wentwthvle 276 G16

OATLEY
av. Oatley 431 B14
av. Oatley 431 C11
cct. Harringtn Pk 478 K3
pde. Oatley 431 B14
pl. Padstow Ht 429 C6
rd. Paddington 21 A3
st. Kingsgrove 401 H6
OATLEY PARK
av. Oatley 430 G12
OATWAY
pde. North Manly 258 C15
OBA
pl. Toongabbie 275 E12
OBADIAH
pl. S Penrith 266 H4
OBAN
cl. Windsor Dn 180 H3
pl. St Andrews 481 K2
st. Schofields 183 B16
OBELISK
av. Mosman 317 K7
OBERON
cr. Gordon 253 G9
cr. S Penrith 267 C4
la. Randwick, off
    Oberon St 407 B2
rd. Ruse 512 F6
st. Blakehurst 462 C1
st. Coogee 407 F3
st. Georges Hall 367 J10
st. Randwick 407 C2
OBI
la. Toongabbie 275 E11
O'BRIEN
la. Marrickville, off
    Byrnes St 373 K13
la. Windsor 121 C9
pde. Liverpool 365 A14
rd. Barden Rdg 488 G3
rd. Londonderry 148 C10
rd. Mt Annan 479 F14
rd. Bondi Beach 378 A2
st. Chatswood 284 H8
st. Mount Druitt 241 E11
O'BRIENS
la. Darlinghurst 4 D9
rd. Cattai 68 J9
rd. Hurstville 431 J6
OBSERVATORY
ri. Bella Vista 246 D1
OCCUPATION
rd. Kyeemagh 404 A14
OCEAN
av. Double Bay 13 K11
av. Newport 169 J9
gr. Collaroy 229 B15
la. Bondi, off
    Bennett St 377 J4
la. Clovelly, off
    Warner Av 378 B12
la. Manly 288 F8
la. Mortdale 431 B4
la. Pagewood 405 K10
pl. Illawong 459 H4
pl. Palm Beach 139 K1
pl. Woodbine 481 K9
rd. Manly 288 F8
rd. Palm Beach 109 K16
rd. Bnksmeadw 405 K10
st. Beverley Pk 433 C7
st. Bondi 377 J5
st. Clovelly 378 B13
st. Cronulla 493 K8
st. Edgecliff 13 K12
st. Kogarah 433 A6
st. Kogarah 433 C7
st. Narrabeen 229 A6
st. Pagewood 405 K10
st. Penshurst 431 C5
st. Woollahra 13 K12
st.n, Bondi 377 J4
OCEANA
av. Narraweena 258 C5
st.e, Dee Why 258 D7
OCEAN GROVE
av. Cronulla 493 K12
OCEANIA
cr. Newport 169 K13
OCEAN VIEW
rd. Harbord 258 H16
st. Woolooware 493 E11
wy. Belrose 226 C10

OATLEY

OCEANVIEW
av. Dover Ht 348 F7
av. Vaucluse 348 F7
O'CONNELL
av. Killarney Ht 286 C1
av. Matraville 407 A15
cl. Lurnea 394 D14
st. Clarmnt Ms 268 C1
st. Greenwich 314 K14
st. Kingswood 268 C1
st. Monterey 433 G6
st. Newtown 17 J8
st. N Parramatta .. 278 B12
st. Parramatta 308 A4
st. Smithfield 335 H6
st. Sydney .... B B14
st. Sydney 1 J15
st. Vineyard 152 G11
O'CONNOR
la. Beaconsfield, off
    Queen St 375 G11
la. Marrickville, off
    Llewellyn St .. 374 F10
st. Chippendale 19 A2
st. Eastlakes 405 K5
st. Guildford 337 C1
st. Haberfield 343 D16
wy. Haberfield 343 E16
O'CONNORS
rd. Beacon Hill 257 F7
OCTAGON
rd. Darling Point .. 13 J9
OCTAGONAL
av. Castle Hill 217 B7
OCTAVIA
av. Rsemeadow 540 F3
st. Narrabeen 229 B2
st. Toongabbie 276 A8
ODAWARRA
cl. Fairlight 288 D7
O'DEA
av. Kyeemagh 404 D13
av. Waterloo 375 J9
av. Zetland 375 J9
rd. N Richmond 87 A12
rd. Mt Annan 479 D16
ODELIA
cr. Plumpton 241 G10
O'DELL
st. Vineyard 153 A9
ODELL
ct. Kellyville Rdg . 185 C15
ODEON
pl. Heathcote 518 G8
ODETTE
rd. Dural 189 F12
ODNEY
pl. Castle Hill 219 A10
O'DONNELL
av. Greenacre 369 H11
st. North Bondi 348 F16
st. North Bondi 348 D16
O'DOWD
cl. Edensor Pk 333 H16
st. Waverley 377 G7
OERTER
av. Newington 309 K15
O'FARRELL
rd. Penrith 236 K11
OFFENBACH
av. Emerton 240 H5
OFFERTON
wy. Cranebrook 207 F13
OFT
pl. Blacktown 274 G9
OGDEN
cl. Abbotsbury 333 A8
st. St Clair 270 H13
st. Redfern 19 K7
st. St Clair, off
    Ogden Cl 270 H13
wy. Oakville 122 K12
OGILVIE
pl. Blackett 241 C4
st. East Hills 427 H2
OGILVY
rd. Clontarf 287 H16
st.n, Peakhurst 430 A7
st.s, Peakhurst ... 430 A6
OGMORE
av. Blackheath 399 B4
O'GRADY
pl. Kellyville 216 D2

114 GREGORY'S STREET DIRECTORY

STREETS — OR

O'HAGON
st. Chester Hill 368 A3

O'HARA
st. Marrickville 373 K14

O'HARAS CREEK
rd. Middle Dural 158 B3

O'HARES
rd. Wedderburn 540 A9
rd. Wedderburn 541 E16

OHIO
pl. Erskine Park 271 A16
pl. Kearns 451 A15
pl. Quakers Hill 214 D9

OHLFSEN
rd. Minto 453 A15

O'KEEFE
cr. Eastwood 281 G6
av. Annangrove 156 B11

O'KEEFES
la. Kogarah, off
Kensington St 433 B5
pl. Hornglsea Pk 392 C14

OKLAHOMA
av. Toongabbie 275 H12

OKRA
pl. Quakers Hill 243 E4

OLA
pl. Oakhurst 241 J3

OLBURY
pl. Airds 512 B13

OLD
la. Cremorne, off
Waters La 316 D8
st. Tempe 404 B4

OLDAKER
st. Doonside 243 C5

OLD BARRENJOEY
rd. Avalon 170 A3

OLD BATHURST
rd. Blaxland 233 J7
rd. Emu Heights 235 A6
rd. Emu Plains 235 A6

OLD BEECROFT
rd. Cheltenham 251 A11

OLD BELLS LINE OF
rd. Kurrajong 64 D16
rd. Mt Tomah 59 H15
rd. Mt Tomah 59 J16

OLD BEROWRA
rd. Hornsby 191 G9

OLD BRIDGE
rd. Windsor 121 D7

OLDBURY
ct. Wattle Grove 426 A2
rd. West Hoxton 392 B12
st. Stanhpe Gdn 215 E8

OLD BUSH
rd. Engadine 489 D14

OLD CANTERBURY
rd. Ashfield 373 A8
rd. Dulwich Hill 373 A8
rd. Lewisham 15 A10
rd. Summer Hill 373 A8

OLD CASTLE HILL
rd. Castle Hill 218 D14

OLD CHURCH
la. Prospect 275 B11

OLD EAST KURRAJONG
rd. E Kurrajong 66 H7
rd. Glossodia 66 G12

OLD FERRY
rd. Illawong 459 F4
rd. Penrith 236 C8

OLDFIELD
ct. St Clair 269 K16
la. St Clair, off
Oldfield Ct 269 K14
pl. Menai 458 G8
rd. Seven Hills 275 G3
st. Greystanes 305 G9

OLD FIFTEENTH
av. West Hoxton 392 F4

OLD FOREST
rd. Lugarno 429 K14

OLD FORT
rd. Mosman 317 K6

OLD GLENFIELD
rd. Casula 424 A4
rd. Glenfield 424 A4

OLD GLENHAVEN
rd. Glenhaven 187 J14

OLDHAM
av. Wrrngtn Cty 238 H4
cr. Dolls Point 433 E16

OLD HAWKESBURY
rd. McGraths Hl 122 A12
rd. Vineyard 152 C1
rd. Vineyard 152 E6

OLD HILL
lk. Homebush B 310 C16

OLD HUME
hwy.Camden 507 A5

OLD ILLAWARRA
rd. Barden Rdg 488 F2
rd. Barden Rdg 488 F4
rd. Holsworthy 426 E16
rd. Illawong 458 G8
rd. Illawong 459 A6
rd. Lucas Ht 487 G11
rd. Menai 458 G8

OLD JERUSALEM
rd. Oakdale 500 H10

OLD KENT
rd. Greenacre 369 J14
rd. Greenacre 370 D15
rd. Kentlyn 512 F5
rd. Mt Lewis 369 J14
rd. Ruse 512 F6

OLD KURRAJONG
rd. Casula 394 G14
rd. Richmond 118 C1

OLD LEUMEAH
rd. Leumeah 482 A13

OLD LIVERPOOL
rd. Lansvale 366 B10

OLD LLANDILO
rd. Llandilo 179 B16

OLD MENANGLE
rd. Campbelltown 511 C7

OLD NORTHERN
rd. Baulkham Hl 247 H9
rd. Canoelands 70 G15
rd. Castle Hill 218 C15
rd. Dural 188 G16
rd. Dural 189 A14
rd. Forest Glen 70 G15
rd. Glenhaven 218 E3
rd. Glenorie 128 B2
rd. Maroota 70 H2
rd. Middle Dural 158 H1

OLD PEATS FERRY
rd. Cowan 104 C14

OLD PITT TOWN
rd. Box Hill 153 K4
rd. Nelson 154 F8
rd. Oakville 153 H2
rd. Pitt Town 92 K15
rd. Pitt Town 93 A15

OLD PITTWATER
rd. Brookvale 257 J10

OLD POST OFFICE
rd. Cattai 68 K15

OLD PRINCES
hwy.Engadine 518 G5
hwy.Sutherland 490 E13

OLD PROSPECT
rd. Greystanes 306 D5
rd. S Wntwthvle 306 D5
rd. S Wntwthvle 307 A4

OLD RACECOURSE
cl. Picton 561 G2

OLD RAZORBACK
rd. Cawdor 506 D16

OLD SACKVILLE
rd. Wilberforce 67 E16

OLD SAMUEL
st. Mona Vale 198 G1

OLDSMOBILE
pl. Ingleburn 453 K8

OLD SOUTH HEAD
rd. Bellevue Hill 377 F3
rd. Bondi 377 F3
rd. Bondi Beach 348 B16
rd. Bondi Jctn 377 F3
rd. Dover Ht 348 B16
rd. North Bondi 348 B16
rd. Rose Bay 348 B16
rd. Vaucluse 348 E5
rd. Watsons Bay 318 G15
rd. Woollahra 377 F3

OLD STOCK ROUTE
rd. Oakville 122 F15
rd. Pitt Town 93 F13

OLD SYDNEY
rd. Seaforth 287 C10

OLD TAREN POINT
rd. Taren Point 462 J11

OLD WALLGROVE
rd. Eastern Ck 302 B3
rd. Horsley Pk 301 G9

OLD WINDSOR
rd. Bella Vista 246 A1
rd. Glenwood 215 E3
rd. Kellyville 215 E3
rd. Kings Lngly 246 D8
rd. Old Tngabbie 277 B7
rd. Seven Hills 246 F14
rd. Stanhpe Gdn 215 E3
rd. Toongabbie 276 G2
rd. Winston Hills 246 F14

O'LEA
st. Kellyvile Rdg 215 B1

OLEA
pl. Mcquarie Fd 454 C4

OLEANDER
av. Baulkham Hl 246 K14
av. Lidcombe 339 F11
cr. Riverstone 182 K4
ct. Peakhurst 430 E1
la. N St Marys, off
Oleander Rd 240 A12
pde. Caringbah 493 B10
rd. N St Marys 239 J10
rd. Wahroonga 222 B4
st. Greenacre 370 G9
st. Greystanes 306 A11

OLGA
cl. Bossley Park 334 C5
cl. Belrose 225 E14
pl. Cecil Hills 362 H7
rd. Leumeah 482 G12
rd. Blacktown 243 K10
st. Chatswood 285 B9
st. Greystanes 306 G8

OLIN
cl. Cranebrook 207 B13

OLINDA
cr. Carlingford 279 D1
st. St Ives 254 C1

OLIPHANT
st. Mt Pritchard 364 H11

OLIVE
la. Neutral Bay, off
Holt Av 6 F1
la. Turramurra 222 H13
pl. Mcquarie Fd 454 G1
st. Artarmon 285 A16
st. Asquith 191 K12
st. Baulkham Hl 247 H11
st. Condell Park 398 J6
st. Fairfield 336 C16
st. Kingsgrove 402 B5
st. Liverpool 395 D6
st. Minto Ht 483 F8
st. Paddington 13 B15
st. Ryde 281 K10
st. Seven Hills 275 G3
st. Wentwthvle 276 J13

OLIVE LEE
st. Quakers Hill 213 J7

OLIVER
av. Rookwood 339 K12
la. Roseville, off
Oliver Rd 284 G4
rd. Chatswood W 284 G11
rd. Roseville 284 G3
st. Bexley North 402 C10
st. Curl Curl 258 G16
st. Harbord 288 D2
st. Heathcote 518 D10
st. Mascot 405 D3
st. Queenscliff 288 E2
st. Riverstone 183 A6
wy. Mona Vale 199 A4

OLIVERI
cl. Edensor Pk 363 H1
cr. Green Valley 363 G10
pl. Schofields 213 J6

OLIVET
st. Glenbrook 233 K12

OLIVIA
cl. Kellyville 217 A6
cl. Rsemeadow 540 F6
la. Surry Hills 20 C5

OLIVIERI
pl. Ryde 282 C12

OLLIE
pl. Castle Hill 218 J11

OLLIER
cr. Prospect 274 F12

OLLIVER
cr. St Clair 270 B9

OLOLA
av. Castle Hill 218 D16
av. Vaucluse 348 B3

O'LOUGHLIN
st. Surry Hills 19 H1

OLPHERT
av. Vaucluse 348 F3

OLSEN
pl. Harrngtn Pk 478 J4
st. Guildford 338 D9

OLSSON
cl. Hornsby Ht 161 J11

OLWEN
pl. Quakers Hill 214 C8

OLWYN
pl. Earlwood 403 G2

OLYMPIA
rd. Naremburn 315 D1

OLYMPIC
bvd. Homebush B 310 E15
ct. Bradbury 511 D8
cr. Carlingford 279 D2
dr. Lidcombe 339 H5
dr. Milsons Point 1 K1
pde. Bankstown 399 D1
pde. Mt Riverview 204 C16
pl. Doonside 243 E7

OLYMPUS
dr. St Clair 269 G11
st. Winston Hills 276 K1

OMAGH
pl. Killarney Ht 256 B14

OMAHA
ct. Belfield 371 E12

O'MALLEY
cl. Glenfield 424 E13

OMAR
cl. Illawong 459 F3
la. Greenwich 314 J6
pl. Winston Hills 277 F2

OMAROO
av. Doonside 243 B14

OMARU
av. Miranda 491 H2
cr. Bradbury 511 F16
st. Beverly Hills 400 H16

OMATI
st. Whalan 240 J8

OMDURMAN
st. Harbord 288 D1

O'MEALLY
st. Prairiewood 334 E11

O'MEARA
st. Carlton 432 K9

OMEGA
av. Lapstone 264 H5
ct. Prestons 392 K14
la. St Clair, off
Omega Pl 270 E16
pl. Greenacre 370 A12
pl. St Clair 270 E16

OMEO
st. St Clair 269 K9

OMNIBUSES
la. Ultimo 3 C13
rd. Kingsgrove 401 J8

ONA
cl. Bossley Park 333 K11

ONDIEKI
ct. Blacktown 273 H5

ONDINE
pl. Kareela 461 E10

ONEATA
la. Lakemba 401 A1
st. Lakemba 401 A2

O'NEIL
wk. Mosman 317 D7

O'NEILE
cr. Lurnea 394 D6

O'NEILL
av. Newington 310 B14
la. Btn-le-Sds 433 H4
la. Lilyfield 10 E4
rd. Menai 458 F8
st. Btn-le-Sds 433 H5
st. Granville 308 E16
st. Guildford 337 F2
st. Guildford 337 F4

ONSLOW
av. Camden 507 B6
av. Elizabeth Bay 13 A3
la. Canterbury, off
Onslow St 372 D15
la. Gordon 254 B5
pl. Elizabeth Bay 13 A3
st. Leumeah 482 B14
st. Rose Bay 348 E13
st. Sylvania 462 A14
st. Canterbury 372 D15
st. Granville 308 H10
st. Rose Bay 348 C12
st. St Clair 269 K10
st. Seven Hills 275 K4

ONTARIO
av. Roseville 284 E4
st. St Clair 269 H15
cl. Illawong 459 D5
cl. Seven Hills 275 E6

ONUS
av. Hobartville 118 F8
la. Richmond Lwld 118 F2

ONYX
cl. Bossley Park 333 K8
pl. Eagle Vale 481 A7
st. Artarmon 285 B14

OORANA
av. Phillip Bay 436 J12

OORIN
rd. Hornsby Ht 191 H4

OPAL
cl. S Penrith 267 B1
la. Northmead 278 A5
pl. Bossley Park 333 K8
pl. Cartwright 393 H6
pl. Eagle Vale 481 H7
pl. Greystanes 306 B2
st. Gymea 461 F16
st. Northmead 278 A5
st. Padstow Ht 429 F8
st. Rooty Hill 242 A12

OPALA
st. Belrose 225 J15

OPEL
pl. Ingleburn 453 J10

OPHELIA
pl. Oakhurst 241 K1
st. Rsemeadow 540 J6

OPHIR
gr. Mount Druitt 271 A4
pl. Illawong 459 F4

OPREY
cl. Minto 452 J14

OPUS
pl. Cranebrook 207 E16

ORALLO
av. Blacktown 244 F14

ORAMZI
rd. Girraween 275 K11

ORAN
pl. Fairfield W 335 E12

ORANA
av. Hornsby 191 J9
av. Kirrawee 490 J2
av. Penrith 237 D6
av. Pymble 253 F2
av. Seven Hills 275 C3
cr. Blakehurst 432 D16
cr. Peakhurst 430 D7
la. Merrylands 307 H14
pde. Homebush B 310 F15
pl. Greenacre 369 J11
pl. Liverpool 394 J3
pl. Telopea 279 E8
rd. Kenthurst 156 F5
rd. Mona Vale 199 G2
rd. North Ryde 282 F8

ORANGE
av. Clarmnt Ms 238 G13
av. Castle Hill 218 C16
gr. Frenchs Frst 255 J2
la. Hurstville 432 C5
la. Randwick, off
Clovelly Rd 377 C9
st. Seven Hills 275 G7
st. Eastwood 281 F8
st. Greystanes 305 H5
st. Greystanes 305 J5
st. Hurstville 432 C3

GREGORY'S STREET DIRECTORY 115

OR STREETS

ORANGE GROVE
rd. Cabramatta 365 B12
rd. Liverpool 365 B12
rd. Warwck Frm 365 B12

ORANGERY
pl. Bella Vista 246 G4

ORANGEVILLE
st. Marsden Pk 181 K11

ORARA
ct. Wattle Grove 395 J13
pl. Plumpton 242 C10
rd. Allambie Ht 257 J15
st. Chatswood 285 D6
st. Waitara 221 J3

ORATAVA
av. W Pnnant Hl 249 D7

ORBELL
st. Kingsgrove 401 G12

ORCAM
la. Rooty Hill 272 E5

ORCHARD
av. Castle Hill, off
Gough Dr 218 K13
cl. Winston Hills 277 G1
cr. Ashfield 372 G3
gr. Oakhurst 242 A2
pl. Glenwood 215 E12
pl. Ingleburn 453 D8
rd. Bass Hill 368 A7
rd. Beecroft 250 B10
rd. Brookvale 258 B11
rd. Busby 363 G13
rd. Chatswood 284 J12
rd. Chatswood 284 J9
rd. Chester Hill 368 A4
rd. Colyton 270 A8
rd. Fairfield 336 F16
rd. Richmond 118 F10
st. Balgowlah 287 K9
st. Baulkham Hl 247 K12
st. Croydon 342 E14
st. Epping 280 D2
st. Pennant Hills 221 A15
st. Pymble 223 D15
st. Thornleigh 221 A15
st. Warriewood 198 F9
st. West Ryde 281 F14

ORCHARDLEIGH
st. Old Guildford 337 C10
st. Yennora 337 C10

ORCHARDS
dr. Breakfast Pt 312 B15

ORCHID
cl. Colyton 270 H6
cl. Quakers Hill 214 A10
pl. Mcquarie Fd 454 C5
pl. W Pnnant Hl 248 G8
rd. Old Guildford 337 C8
st. Loftus 489 K12

ORD
cl. Bossley Pk 333 G5
cr. Sylvania Wtr 462 E14
pl. Leumeah 482 G11

ORDAK
av. Gymea Bay 491 D8

ORDE
pl. Prospect 274 H13

ORDER
pl. Redfern 19 E7

ORE
la. Erskine Park 300 G5
pl. Eagle Vale 481 G6

OREADES
wy. Bidwill 211 D16

O'REGAN
dr. Ryde 312 B3

OREGON
st. Blacktown 243 J14

O'REILLY
cl. Menai 458 F9
st. Parramatta 307 K5
wy. Rouse Hill 184 J8

ORELIA
wy. Minto 482 J6

ORFORD
pl. Illawong 459 B7

ORIANA
dr. Illawong 459 A6

ORIELTON
rd. Smeaton Gra 479 A8
st. Narellan 478 E8

ORIENT
av. Cronulla 524 A2
rd. Greendale 385 C9

rd. Padstow 429 E2
st. Gladesville 312 H5

ORIENTAL
st. Bexley 402 K13

ORIGMA
st. Forest Glen 70 G16

ORINOCO
cl. Seven Hills 275 B3
st. Pymble 253 C5

ORIOLE
pl. Green Valley 363 D9
pl. Ingleburn 453 D9
pl. Glenmore Pk 265 G12
st. Aburora Ht 489 D2

ORION
cl. Castle Hill 218 J9
pl. Leonay 234 J15
rd. Lane Cove W 283 F15
st. Bardwell Vy 403 A9
st. Engadine 488 D12
st. Rooty Hill 272 B2

O'RIORDAN
st. Alexandria 375 D16
st. Beaconsfield 375 D16
st. Mascot 405 B5

ORISON
st. Georges Hall 367 H13

ORISSA
la. Cammeray 316 A3
st. Campsie 371 K15
wy. Doonside 243 H16

ORKNEY
pl. Prestons 423 E2

ORLANDER
av. Glenmore Pk 266 K15

ORLANDO
av. Mosman 316 G11
cr. Voyager Pt 427 C4
pl. Edensor Pk 333 E14
rd. Cromer 228 H14

ORLEANS
cct. Cecil Hills 362 E4
cr. Toongabbie 275 E12
wy. Castle Hill 216 J8
wy. Kellyville 216 J8

ORLETON
la. Wrrngtn Cty, off
Orleton Pl 238 D7
pl. Wrrngtn Cty 238 D7

ORLICK
st. Ambarvale 510 G16

ORMISTON
av. Gordon 253 F9
av. N Sydney 5 K8
av. West Hoxton 392 C11

ORMOND
gdn. Coogee 377 F16
st. Ashfield 373 B2
st. Bondi Beach 378 B4
st. Paddington 13 B16

ORMONDE
av. Epping 251 D16
cl. Glenmore Pk 266 F12
pde. Hurstville 432 A6
rd. E Lindfield 255 B14
rd. Roseville Ch 255 E15

ORMSBY
pl. Wetherill Pk 333 K2

ORNELLA
av. Glendenning 242 F4

ORO
pl. Glenfield 424 G14

ORONGA
av. Baulkham Hl 248 B8

ORONTES
la. Burwood 341 J16

O'ROURKE
cr. Eastlakes 405 J2

OROYA
pde. Roseville 285 A2

ORPHANS SCHOOL CREEK
la. Camperdown 17 J2

ORPHEUS
cl. Green Valley 363 B12

ORPINGTON
st. Ashfield 373 A2
st. Bexley 402 G12
st. Bexley North 402 G11

ORR
pl. Davidson 255 D3
st. Bondi 377 H2
st. Gladesville 312 H10

ORRCON
pde. Glendenning 242 F6

ORRS
la. Strathfield 341 G12

ORSINO
pl. Rsemeadow 540 G5

ORTH
st. Kingswood 237 H13

ORTON
av. Concord 311 K15
pl. Currans Hill 479 J12
st. Barden Rdg 488 G6
st. Kings Lngly 245 E4

ORTONA
pde. Como 460 J6
pl. Lindfield 284 D4

ORWELL
la. Potts Point 4 K5
st. Blacktown 274 E11
st. Blacktown 274 E9
st. Potts Point 4 J5

OSBERT
pl. Acacia Gdn 214 H16

OSBORN
rd. Normanhurst 221 G12

OSBORNE
av. Dundas Vy 279 K9
av. Putney 311 H6
la. Woollahra 22 B1
pl. Lane Cove 314 G5
rd. Greenwich 314 G5
rd. Lane Cove 314 G5
rd. Manly 288 H12
rd. Marayong 244 A8
st. Chipping Ntn 396 F5
pl. St Helens Park 541 B6

OSCAR
pl. Acacia Gdn 214 H14
st. Chatswood 285 A9
st. Greenwich 315 A8

OSGATHORPE
rd. Gladesville 312 G7

OSGOOD
av. Marrickville 373 E14
st. Guildford 338 A2

O'SHANNASSY
st. Mt Pritchard 364 F10

OSHEA
cl. Edensor Pk 363 F1

O'SHEAS
la. Surry Hills 4 C16
la. Surry Hills 20 C1

OSLO
st. Marsfield 281 J1

OSMOND
pl. Currans Hill 479 J14
gr. Hassall Gr 212 A15

OSMUND
la. Bondi Jctn 22 D5

OSPREY
av. Glenmore Pk 266 D13
av. Green Valley 363 D12
cl. Maroubra 407 D14
pl. Illawong 459 F6
pl. Clarmnt Ms 268 H4
tce. Bella Vista 216 D16

OSROY
av. Earlwood 403 D3

OSSARY
st. Mascot 404 K1

OSTEND
st. Bankstown 399 A5
st. Condell Park 398 K5
st. Lidcombe 340 C5
st. S Granville 338 F6

O'SULLIVAN
av. Maroubra 406 J11
la. Queens Park 22 E12
pl. Kellyville 216 D2
rd. Bellevue Hill 347 H11
rd. Leumeah 482 A15
rd. Rose Bay 347 H11

OSWALD
cl. Warrawee 222 E13
pl. Rsemeadow 540 J7
la. Campsie, off
Redman St 372 C13
st. Canterbury, off
Redman St 372 C13

la. Darlinghurst 13 A10
st. Darling Point 13 F8
st. Campsie 372 C13
st. Edgecliff 13 F9
st. Guildford 337 C6
st. Mosman 316 H10
st. Randwick 377 D14

OSWALD PARK
pl. Kurrajong 64 D14

OSWELL
st. Rockdale 403 A12

OSWIN
la. Rockdale 403 C13

OTAGO
cl. Glenorie 128 C1
pde. Yowie Bay 492 A8
pl. Northmead 248 C15
st. Vineyard 152 H12

OTAKI
pl. St Ives Ch 223 J3

OTHELLO
av. Rsemeadow 540 H6
pl. St Clair 270 D15
st. Blakehurst 432 B15

OTTAWA
cl. Cranebrook 207 H10
st. Kearns 481 A2
st. Toongabbie 275 E12

OTTER
la. Erskine Park, off
Otter Pl 301 A1
pl. Erskine Park 301 A1

OTTEY
av. Newington 310 A14

OTTLEY
st. Quakers Hill 244 A3

OTTO
st. Merrylands W 307 A16

OTTWAY
cl. St Ives 224 D9

OTWAY
cl. Wetherill Pk 334 J5
pl. Illawong 459 C5

OULTON
av. Concord W 311 C12
av. Rhodes 311 C12
st. Prospect 274 G10

OURIMBAH
rd. Mosman 316 H4

OUSE
cl. West Hoxton 392 C6

OUSLEY
pl. Milperra 397 E9

OUTLOOK
av. Emu Heights 235 A6
av. Mt Riverview 204 G15
cct. Menai 458 G9
st. Blacktown 274 E11

OUTRAM
pl. Currans Hill 479 J14
st. Chippendale 19 D2

OVAL
la. Glenbrook 234 A16
la. Kingsford 376 J15
st. Old Tngabbie 276 K8

OVENS
cl. Horngsea Pk 392 F15
dr. Wrrngtn Cty 238 G6
pl. St Ives Ch 224 A3

OVER
pl. Shalvey 210 K15

OVERETT
av. Kemps Ck 359 G1

OVERTON
av. Chipping Ntn 366 F14
cct. Berowra 133 C16
rd. Comleroy 64 F11

OWEN
av. Baulkham Hl 247 G12
av. Kyeemagh 404 C13
la. Ultimo 12 K16
pl. Illawong 459 D7
pl. S Windsor 150 F3
rd. Georges Hall 367 J15
st. E Lindfield 254 G15
st. Gladesville 312 H5
st. Glendenning 242 H8
st. Lindfield 254 G15
st. North Bondi 348 C14
st. N Willoughby 285 G10
st. Punchbowl 400 C5
st. Thirlmere 562 D14
st. Ultimo 12 K16
st. Wentwthvle 277 B13

OWEN JONES
row. Menai 458 G15

OWENS
av. Newington 309 K16
pl. Cranebrook 207 F10

OWEN STANLEY
av. Allambie Ht 257 E10
av. Beacon Hill 257 D9
rd. Glenfield 424 F13
st. Mt Annan 479 C11

OWL
cl. Green Valley 363 D11
pl. Ingleburn 453 D9
pl. St Clair 269 H11

OXFORD
av. Bankstown 399 B4
av. Castle Hill 217 K10
cl. Belrose 226 C13
la. Cmbrdg Pk 237 H8
la. Mount Druitt 241 C15
la. Newtown 17 D10
pl. St Ives 224 A7
pl. Ingleburn 453 D6
rd. Strathfield 341 C13
sq. Darlinghurst 4 B11
sq. Surry Hills 4 B11
st. Belrose 371 D15
st. Berala 339 E10
st. Blacktown 244 J16
st. Bondi Jctn 22 E6
st. Burwood 341 H15
st. Cmbrdg Pk 237 G7
st. Centennial Pk 21 D2
st. Chipping Ntn 366 G16
st. Darlinghurst ......F G3
st. Darlinghurst 4 A10
st. Epping 251 B15
st. Gladesville 312 J7
st. Guildford 337 J2
st. Lidcombe 339 E10
st. Merrylands 307 E14
st. Mortdale 431 A8
st. Newtown 17 C10
st. Paddington 4 F13
st. Petersham 15 H13
st. Riverstone 182 K8
st. Rozelle 344 D8
st. St Marys 269 A6
st. Smithfield 335 J8
st. Surry Hills ....F G3
st. Surry Hills 4 A10
st. Sutherland 490 D2
st. Woollahra 21 K6

OXFORD FALLS
rd. Beacon Hill 257 C1
rd. Oxford Falls 257 C1
rd.w,Oxford Falls 226 H12

OXFORD ST
ml. Bondi Jctn 22 C7

OXLEY
av. Castle Hill 247 H4
av. Jannali 460 G11
av. Panania 428 E2
av. St Ives 224 E10
dr. Mt Colah 162 B10
gr. Tahmoor 566 A11
la. Centennial Pk 21 A14
pl. Frenchs Frst 256 D1
rd. Ingleburn 423 A10
st. Bradbury 511 C7
st. Camden 477 A15
st. Campbelltwn 511 C7
st. Crows Nest 315 E5
st. Ermington 280 C16
st. Fairfield 336 B14
st. Glebe 11 K5
st. Lalor Park 245 C14
st. Matraville 437 C1
st. St Leonards 315 D7

OYAMA
av. Manly 288 F13

OYSTER BAY
rd. Como 460 K8
rd. Oyster Bay 461 A8

OZARK
pl. Cranebrook 207 F10
st. Seven Hills 275 B9

OZONE
pde. Dee Why 259 B9
st. Cronulla 494 K13
st. Harbord 258 C15

116 GREGORY'S STREET DIRECTORY

STREETS

PA

P

PACER
st. Riverstone......182 G10

PACEY
av. North Ryde......282 K12

PACHA
pl. Shalvey......210 G14

PACIFIC
av. Penshurst......431 F6
av. Tamarama......378 B7
cr. Maianbar......523 B7
hwy.Artarmon......284 H15
hwy.Asquith......192 A9
hwy.Berowra......133 E14
hwy.Brooklyn......75 B13
hwy.Chatswood......284 H6
hwy.Chatswood W..284 H6
hwy.Cowan......104 D13
hwy.Crows Nest......5 D3
hwy.Gordon......253 J10
hwy.Greenwich......315 A5
hwy.Hornsby......221 G2
hwy.Killara......253 J10
hwy.Lane Cove......314 G3
hwy.Lane Cove N ...284 H15
hwy.Lindfield......284 G2
hwy.Mooney Mooney..75 B13
hwy.Mt Colah......162 F16
hwy.Mt Krng-gai...162 F16
hwy.N Sydney......K B2
hwy.N Sydney......5 G8
hwy.Pymble......253 B1
hwy.Roseville......284 G2
hwy.St Leonards......315 A5
hwy.Turramurra......222 H13
hwy.Wahroonga......222 C8
hwy.Waitara......221 G2
hwy.Warrawee......222 C8
hwy.Waverton......5 D3
hwy.Wollstncraft......5 D3
la. Manly......288 G5
la. Penshurst......431 F6
la. St Clair, off
    Pacific Rd......270 H15
pde. Dee Why......258 G6
pde. Manly......288 F6
pl. Palm Beach......140 B2
rd. Erskine Park....270 H15
rd. Palm Beach......139 J1
rd. Quakers Hill......213 F14
st. Blakehurst......462 C2
st. Bronte......378 A9
st. Caringbah......492 F9
st. Clovelly......377 J11
st. Greystanes......306 E7
st. Kingsgrove......401 K7
st. Manly......288 G5
st. Watsons Bay....318 E13

PACIFIC PALMS
cct. Hoxton Park......392 G6

PACIFIC PARK
dr. S Maroota......69 B6

PACKARD
av. Castle Hill......217 E16
cl. Ingleburn......453 G11
pl. Horngsea Pk....392 C13

PACKENHAM
pl. Mt Annan......509 F1

PACKSADDLE
st. Glenwood......215 F16

PADBURY
st. Chipping Ntn....396 G2

PADDINGTON
la. Paddington......21 G1
st. Paddington......21 F1

PADDISON
av. Gymea......491 G4

PADDOCK
cl. Casula......394 B16

PADDY
st. Kellyville Rdg ...185 A16
st. Kellyville Rdg ...215 A1

PADDY MILLER
av. Currans Hill....479 H13

PADEMELON
av. St Helens Park..541 F3

PADSTOW
pde. Padstow......399 E16
rd. Rozelle......10 G1

PADUA
cl. Prestons......393 D14
pl. Hebersham......241 G4

PADULLA
pl. Castle Cove......286 C5

PAGANINI
cr. Clarmnt Ms......268 G3

PAGE
av. Ashfield......342 J13
av. Illawong......459 D3
av. N Wahroonga...192 F14
cl. Minto......452 J14
ct. Carlingford......249 G15
la. Canterbury......402 C2
pl. Cabramatta W..364 H15
pl. Moorebank......396 D9
rd. North Ryde......283 C14
st. Canterbury......402 C2
st. Pagewood......405 K11
st. Wentwthvle......277 A12

PAGES
rd. St Marys......269 D3

PAGES WHARF
rd. Sackville N......68 J4

PAGET
cl. Winmalee......173 G12
st. Richmond......118 H7

PAGODA
cr. Quakers Hill......214 B9

PAILS
pl. Shalvey......210 K12

PAINE
av. Moorebank......396 D11
dr. Bligh Park......150 J8
st. Kogarah......433 A4
st. Maroubra......406 H10

PAINS
pl. Currans Hill......479 H10
rd. Hunters Hill......313 C3

PAINTERS
pde. Dee Why......258 E7

PAINTS
la. Chippendale......18 H2

PAISLEY
cl. St Andrews......482 A2
cl. Carlingford......249 J16
cl. Burwood......342 B14
cl. Croydon......342 B14
cl. Croydon......372 E1
st. Cecil Hills......362 K3
st. Mortlake......312 A13
st. Petersham......15 J8
st. Baulkham Hl....247 D8
st. Ashfield......372 G5
st. Kellyville Rdg ...215 A4
st. Petersham......15 H9
st. Stanhpe Gdn...215 A4

PALAMARA
pl. Chester Hill......337 H10

PALANA
cl. West Hoxton......392 F5

PALARA
pl. Dee Why......258 J1

PALAU
cr. Lethbrdg Pk......240 G1

PALAWAN
av. Kings Park......244 J2

PALENA
ct. St Clair......269 F15
la. St Clair, off
    Rotarua Rd......269 F14

PALERMO
pl. Allambie Ht......257 C9
st. Campbelltown..511 A8

PALFREY
cr. Emu Heights......235 C3

PALING
st. Beacon Hill......257 K4
st. Cremorne......316 F9
st. Lilyfield......10 F11
st. Thornleigh......220 K14

PALINGS
la. Sydney......C J1
la. Sydney......3 G1

PALISADE
st. Bonnyrigg......364 D6

PALISANDER
pl. Castle Hill......218 G12

PALLAMANA
pde. Beverly Hills..401 B12

PALLISTER
st. Kings Lngly......246 B10

PALM
av. Breakfast Pt......312 C13
av. North Manly......288 D2
cl. Green Valley......362 J13
ct. Narellan Vale...479 A13
ct. Woodbine......481 J11
gr. Beverly Hills......400 K5
gr. Normanhurst......221 D13
pl. Bidwill......211 J11
rd. Newport......169 J11
st. Cabramatta......275 K12
st. St Ives......224 D5
tce. N Narrabeen....228 H3

PALM BEACH
rd. Palm Beach......109 J16

PALMER
av. Strathfield......371 A2
cl. Illawong......459 E2
cr. Bexley......403 A14
la. Darlinghurst......4 D10
la. Parramatta, off
    Palmer St......278 D16
pl. Blacktown......274 H3
pl. Emu Plains......235 C13
st. Artarmon......284 J14
st. Balmain......7 G10
st. Belmore......371 H16
st. Cammeray......315 G1
st. Campsie......371 H16
st. Darlinghurst......4 D12
st. Guildford W......336 K3
st. Ingleburn......453 C8
st. Parramatta......308 D1
st. Sefton......368 E6
st. S Coogee......407 J6
st. Windsor......121 F7
st. Woolmloo......4 E7
wy. Bonnyrigg......364 D5

PALMERSTON
av. Baulkham Hl.....247 K15
av. Bronte......377 H7
av. Glebe......12 B11
av. Seaforth......287 B11
rd. Fairfield W......335 D12
rd. Hornsby......192 B16
rd. Mount Druitt....241 A16
rd. Waitara......222 B2
st. Canley Ht......365 H3
st. Canley Vale......365 H3
st. Kogarah......433 C2
st. Vaucluse......318 F16

PALMETTO
cl. Stanhpe Gdn...215 E9

PALMGROVE
rd. Avalon......169 K3

PALMYRA
av. Lethbrdg Pk......240 B12
av. St Marys......210 B12
av. Shanes Park...209 G10
av. Willmot......210 B12

PALOMAR
pde. Harbord......288 E1
pde. Yagoona......369 C11

PALOMINO
cl. Eschol Park......481 B4
cl. Emu Heights......235 D2

PALONA
cr. Engadine......488 F15
st. Marayong......244 A4

PALYA
pl. Narraweena......258 E3

PAMBULA
av. Prestons......393 D16
av. Revesby......398 G16
cr. Woodpark......306 G14
rd. Forestville......255 J7
rd. Engadine......489 A12

PAMELA
av. Peakhurst......430 D10
av. Bayview......168 J12
cr. Berala......339 E13
cr. Bowen Mtn......83 K12
la. Leonay, off
    Pamela Pde....235 B14
pde. Leonay......235 B14
pde. Leonay......235 C14
pde. Marayong......244 A4
pl. Concord......342 A3
pl. Girraween......276 A12
pl. Kenthurst......157 E9
pl. North Ryde......282 H9

PAM GREEN
pl. Doonside......273 G1

PAMPAS
cl. Clarmnt Ms......238 H15

PAMSHAW
pl. Bidwill......211 C15

PAN
cr. Greystanes......306 E7

PANAMA
cl. Illawong......459 G5

PANANIA
av. Panania......398 A15

PANAVIEW
cr. North Rocks....279 C11

PANDALA
pl. Woolooware......493 C9

PANDANUS
ct. Stanhpe Gdn...215 D10

PANDORA
cr. Greystanes......306 E7
cr. Tahmoor......566 A12
st. Greenacre......370 D11

PANETH
st. Lucas Ht......487 H13

PANETTA
av. Liverpool......394 J8

PANGARI
cr. Dharruk......241 B5

PANGEE
st. Kingsgrove......402 A7

PANICUM
pl. Glenmore Pk...265 G12

PANIMA
pl. Newport......169 F14

PANK
pde. Blacktown......243 J12

PANKLE
st. S Penrith......266 H5

PANMURE
st. Rouse Hill......184 K9

PANORA
av. North Rocks....248 H16

PANORAMA
av. Cabramatta......365 C11
av. Leonay......264 K1
av. Woolooware......493 F9
cr. Freerns Rch......90 A3
cr. Frenchs Frst......256 E7
cr. Mt Riverview....234 C14
la. Seaforth......287 B11
pde. Blacktown......274 K13
pde. Panania......428 D1
pde. Seaforth......287 C10
rd. Kingsgrove......401 K5
rd. Lane Cove......314 H4
rd. Penrith......237 B6
st. Bargo......567 D6
st. Penshurst......431 E9

PANTHER
pl. Penrith......236 D12

PANTON
cl. Glenmore Pk...266 F9

PAPALIA
cl. Edensor Pk......333 K16

PAPEETE
av. Lethbrdg Pk......240 G1

PAPER BARK
pl. Mcquarie Fd......454 E1

PAPERBARK
cct. Casula......423 J3
cl. Glenmore Pk...265 H10
cr. Beaumont Hills..186 A16
cr. Beaumont Hills..216 A1
dr. Alfords Point...429 B16
pl. Bondi Beach......378 E2
pl. Lilyfield......10 E1
pl. Ashfield......372 F5
pl. Caringbah......492 H7
pl. Clovelly, off
    Park St........378 A12
la. Erskineville......18 D14
la. Glebe......12 F12
la. Gordon......253 H7
la. Greenwich......315 B7
la. Mosman, off
    Lower Almora St.317 D6
la. Newtown......18 A10
la. Sydenham......374 D15
la. Waitara......221 K3
la. Waterloo......19 F12
pde. Bondi......377 H5
pde. Pagewood......406 F8
pde. Parramatta......307 J1
pl. Caringbah......492 H7
rd. Alexandria......18 J14
rd. Auburn......339 B8
rd. Baulkham Hl....248 B11
rd. Berala......339 A15

PARAKEET
gr. Glenmore Pk....266 C14
pl. W Pnnant Hl....248 E9

PARAMOUNT
cl. Belrose......226 D12
cr. Kellyville......185 E8

PARANA
av. Revesby......428 G1

PARAPET
pl. Glenhaven......217 K6
st. Fairfield......336 D6

PARBURY
la. Dawes Point......1 G7
la. Ultimo......12 K12

PARC GUELL
dr. Campbelltown..510 K8

PARDALOTE
pl. Glenmore Pk...265 H12
st. Glenwood......215 C15
st. Ingleburn......453 F7
wy. W Pnnant Hl....249 D7

PARDEY
st. Kingsford......406 J6

PARE
cl. Loftus......490 A11

PARER
av. Condell Park....398 C2
st. Kings Park......244 E1
st. Maroubra......406 G11
st. Melrose Pk......310 J2
st. Springwood......202 D12

PARINGA
pl. Bangor......459 F14

PARIS
av. Earlwood......403 A2
cr. Miranda......461 K15
cr. Toongabbie......276 C4
st. Balgowlah......287 J7
st. Carlton......432 G11

PARISH
st. Pemulwuy......305 F6

PARK
av. Ashfield......372 F5
av. Avalon......140 A14
av. Beecroft......250 F4
av. Bexley......403 A14
av. Blaxland......233 J6
av. Burwood......341 K12
av. Cammeray......316 B7
av. Chatswood W..284 E10
av. Concord......341 K9
av. Cremorne......316 B7
av. Denistone......281 C13
av. Drummoyne......344 A4
av. Glebe......11 H9
av. Gordon......253 H7
av. Hurstville......431 F10
av. Kingswood......237 H12
av. Manly......288 F9
av. Mosman......316 H10
av. Neutral Bay......316 B8
av. Oatley......430 G11
av. Penshurst......431 E9
av. Punchbowl......370 F16
av. Randwick......377 D10
av. Roseville......285 A2
av. Springwood......201 K1
av. Tahmoor......566 C8
av. Waitara......221 K4
av. Westmead......217 H16
av. West Ryde......281 C13
pl. Pymble......253 D2
pl. Bondi Beach......378 E2
pl. Lilyfield......10 E1
pl. Ashfield......372 F5
pl. Caringbah......492 H7
pl. Clovelly, off
    Park St........378 A12
la. Erskineville......18 D14
la. Glebe......12 F12
la. Gordon......253 H7
la. Greenwich......315 B7
la. Mosman, off
    Lower Almora St.317 D6
la. Newtown......18 A10
la. Sydenham......374 D15
la. Waitara......221 K3
la. Waterloo......19 F12
pde. Bondi......377 H5
pde. Pagewood......406 F8
pde. Parramatta......307 J1
pl. Caringbah......492 H7
rd. Alexandria......18 J14
rd. Auburn......339 B8
rd. Baulkham Hl....248 B11
rd. Berala......339 A15

GREGORY'S STREET DIRECTORY 117

PA
STREETS

rd. Burwood 341 J13
rd. Cabramatta 365 J6
rd. Carlton 432 G9
rd. Cowan 104 B14
rd. Dundas 279 G13
rd. East Hills 427 G4
rd. Five Dock 343 A10
rd. Homebush 341 A7
rd. Homebush W 340 K6
rd. Hunters Hill 313 C6
rd. Hurstville 431 K3
rd. Kenthurst 157 K6
rd. Kogarah Bay 432 J11
rd. Leppington 420 J12
rd. Liverpool 395 A2
rd. Luddenham 325 C13
rd. Maianbar 522 K9
rd. Marrickville 15 K16
rd. Marrickville 373 K9
rd. Marsden Pk 181 J13
rd. Naremburn 315 D2
rd. Panania 427 G4
rd. Regents Pk 339 A15
rd. Riverstone 181 J9
rd. Rydalmere 309 G3
rd. St Leonards 315 B7
rd. Sans Souci 433 D14
rd. Seven Hills 246 A16
rd. Springwood 202 D8
rd. Sydenham 374 D15
rd. Vineyard 152 A3
rd. Wallacia 325 B13
rd.n,Moore Park 21 A8
rd.s,Moore Park 21 A9
rd.s,Mulgrave 151 J4
row. Bradbury 511 E13
st. Arncliffe 403 E7
st. Bexley North 402 C12
st. Camden 507 A1
st. Campsie 372 B13
st. Carlton 432 K7
st. Clovelly 378 A12
st. Collaroy 229 A10
st. Croydon Pk 371 K9
st. Curl Curl 258 H13
st. Emu Plains 235 F9
st. Epping 280 F2
st. Erskineville 18 D13
st. Glenbrook 234 A16
st. Homebush B 310 H16
st. Ingleburn 453 C8
st. Kingsgrove 402 C12
st. Kogarah 433 A7
st. Merrylands 308 B16
st. Mona Vale 199 A2
st. Mortdale 431 D8
st. Mulgoa 325 C3
st. Narrabeen 229 A10
st. Northmead 277 G10
st. Peakhurst 430 B4
st. Petersham 15 E6
st. Pyrmont 8 H16
st. Riverstone 182 J7
st. Rossmore 390 C5
st. Rozelle 344 D8
st. Sutherland 490 D4
st. Sydney C J12
st. Sydney 3 G6
st. Tahmoor 565 G9
st. Woronora 489 J1

PARKCREST
pl. Kenthurst 156 H1

PARKER
av. Earlwood 402 C5
av. West Pymble 252 F9
cl. Beecroft 250 F9
la. Haymarket E F10
la. Haymarket 3 F13
la. Padstow 399 F16
rd. Londonderry 149 E14
st. Canley Vale 335 J15
st. Fairfield 335 J15
st. Granville 308 J9
st. Guildford 337 D5
st. Haymarket E G10
st. Haymarket 3 F13
st. Kings Lngly 246 A10
st. Kingswood 237 D15
st. McMahons Pt 5 D15
st. Northbridge 286 B14
st. Rockdale 403 C14

PARKERS
la. Erskineville, off Victoria St 17 K16

PARKERS FARM
pl. Casula 423 H4

PARKES
av. Werrington 239 A11
cr. Blackett 241 A1
dr. Centennial Pk 21 G6
rd. Artarmon 315 A1
rd. Collaroy 228 J16
rd. Collaroy Plat 228 G12
rd. Cromer 228 J16
st. Ermington 310 D1
st. Guildford W 337 A2
st. Harris Park 308 D5
st. Heathcote 518 F10
st. Kirribilli 6 C16
st. Manly Vale 288 B4
st. Naremburn 315 H3
st. Parramatta 308 D5
st. Ryde 281 G15
st. Thornleigh 221 A13
st. West Ryde 281 G15

PARKFIELDS
pl. Beverly Hills 401 F12

PARKHAM
la. Surry Hills 20 D5
pl. Surry Hills 20 D5
rd. Oatlands 279 C7
st. Chester Hill 337 H11
st. Surry Hills 20 C5

PARKHILL
av. Leumeah 482 E14
cr. Cherrybrook 220 A11
st. Croydon Pk 371 K6

PARKHOLME
cct. Englorie Park 510 J10

PARKHURST
av. Panania 428 F4

PARKIN
rd. Colyton 270 C6

PARKINSON
av. S Turramrra 252 A4
gr. Minchinbury 272 C9
st. Kings Lngly 245 E6

PARKLAND
av. Mcquarie Fd 424 A16
av. Pendle Hill 276 D14
av. Punchbowl 400 D7
av. Rydalmere 279 H16
pl. Thornleigh 220 J10
rd. Carlingford 249 F16
rd. Mona Vale 198 J1
st. Blacktown, off Outlook St 274 E11
wy. Warriewood 198 J7

PARKLANDS
av. Heathcote 519 A10
av. Lane Cove N 284 D16
av. Leonay 265 A2
rd. Glenbrook 264 B3
rd. Mt Colah 192 C1
rd. North Ryde 282 E5

PARKLAWN
la. N St Marys, off Parklawn Pl 239 K11
pl. N St Marys 239 K11

PARKLEA
cl. Dural 190 A13
dr. Parklea 214 K13
pde. Canley Ht 335 C15
pl. Carlingford 279 J2

PARK RIDGE
cct. Kellyville 217 A3

PARKRIVER
cl. Mulgoa 323 C3

PARKSIDE
av. Miranda 491 K2
av. Wrrngtn Dns 238 C5
cr. Campbelltown 511 A8
ct. Currans Hill 479 J10
dr. Kogarah Bay 432 H13
dr. Lalor Park 245 F12
dr. Sandringham 463 D3
dr. S Hurstville 432 C13
la. Chatswood 284 K11
la. Westmead 307 J2
pl. Mt Pritchard 364 H14
tce. Cabarita 312 E15

PARKTREE
pl. Narellan 478 H13

PARK VIEW
gr. Blakehurst 432 C16

PARKVIEW
av. Belfield 371 F11
av. Glenorie 128 C6
av. Picnic Point 428 F9
av. S Penrith 236 J16
dr. Homebush B 310 J16
la. Fairlight, off Parkview Rd 288 E9
la. Manly, off Parkview Rd 288 E9
pl. N Wahroonga 192 G15
pl. Westleigh 220 H8
rd. Abbotsford 343 C3
rd. Chiswick 343 C3
rd. Fairlight 288 E8
rd. Russell Lea 343 C3
st. Miranda 492 D7
st. Stanhpe Gdn 215 C4
wy. Acacia Gdn 214 J16

PARKWOOD
cl. Castle Hill 218 K8
dr. Menai 459 A12
gr. Emu Heights 234 K3
gr. West Pymble 253 A13
pl. North Rocks 279 B2
st. Plumpton 242 C9

PARLAND
cl. Illawong 459 D1

PARLIAMENT
rd. Mcquarie Fd 454 A2
tce. Bardwell Vy 402 J11
tce. Bexley 402 J11

PARMA
cr. St Helens Park 541 F3
pl. Carlingford 249 F14

PARMAL
av. Padstow 399 F16

PARNELL
av. Quakers Hill 214 D16
cl. Minto 483 A2
st. East Killara 254 J7
st. Strathfield 341 G12

PARNI
pl. Frenchs Frst 256 D7

PARNOO
av. Castle Cove 285 J4

PAROO
av. Sylvania Wtr 462 F14
ct. Wattle Grove 395 J13
pl. Hornsby Ht 191 H4
pl. Seven Hills 275 G8
pl. S Turramrra 252 B7
st. Greystanes 306 B5
st. Ruse 512 D6

PARR
av. N Curl Curl 258 H9
cl. Bossley Park 333 G9
pde. Beacon Hill 257 J3
pde. Faulconbdg 171 D14
pde. Narraweena 258 B3
pl. Marayong 243 H5

PARRAMATTA
rd. Annandale 16 C4
rd. Ashfield 343 A15
rd. Auburn 309 B13
rd. Burwood 341 H10
rd. Camperdown 17 C3
rd. Canada Bay 342 E11
rd. Concord 341 H10
rd. Croydon 342 E11
rd. Five Dock 342 E11
rd. Forest Lodge 17 C3
rd. Forest Lodge 18 D1
rd. Glebe 18 D1
rd. Granville 308 G10
rd. Haberfield 373 C1
rd. Homebush 341 B8
rd. Homebush W 339 J1
rd. Leichhardt 15 C6
rd. Lewisham 15 C6
rd. Lidcombe 339 J1
rd. N Strathfield 341 B8
rd. Petersham 15 C6
rd. Silverwater 309 B13
rd. Stanmore 16 C4
rd. Strathfield 341 B8
rd. Summer Hill 15 C6
st. Cronulla 493 K15

PARRAWEEN
st. Cremorne 316 F8

PARRAWEENA
av. Baulkham Hl 248 B7
rd. Caringbah 462 J16
rd. Miranda 462 C16

PARRELLA
gr. Glendenning 242 F3

PARRISH
pl. Mt Colah 162 C15

PARRIWI
rd. Mosman 317 B2

PARROO
cl. St Clair 299 J2

PARROT
rd. Green Valley 363 F11

PARRY
av. Narwee 400 K12
cl. Bonnyrigg 364 B8
st. Pendle Hill 276 C14
st. Putney 312 B6
st. Ryde 312 B6
wy. Glenmore Pk 265 J6

PARSLEY
rd. Vaucluse 348 E2

PARSON
pl. Harringtn Pk 478 F6

PARSONAGE
rd. Castle Hill 247 F1
st. Ryde 311 G5

PARSONS
av. S Penrith 266 F2
av. Strathfield 341 E15
pl. Barden Rdg 488 H2
st. Ashcroft 364 D15
st. Rozelle 7 D16

PARTANNA
av. Matraville 436 G4

PARTHENIA
st. Caringbah 493 A16
st. Dolans Bay 492 K16

PARTRIDGE
av. Castle Hill 217 F13
av. Hinchinbrk 393 C1
av. Miranda 492 B6
av. Yennora 336 K10

PARUKALA
pl. N Narrabeen 199 B15

PARUNA
pl. Cromer 228 A15

PARYS
cl. Menai 458 K10

PASADENA
pl. St Clair 270 J12
st. Monterey 433 G10

PASCHA
pl. Kareela 461 F9

PASCO
pl. Hinchinbrk 392 K3

PASHLEY
st. Balmain 7 F10

PASKIN
st. Kingswood 237 H14

PASLEY
rd. Georges Hall 368 B15

PASSEFIELD
st. Liverpool 395 A7

PASSEY
av. Belmore 371 D13

PASSIONFRUIT
wy. Glenwood 215 E13

PASSY
av. Hunters Hill 313 K12

PASTUREGATE
av. Cmbrdg Gdn 237 J4
av. Wrrngtn Dns 237 J4

PATAK
rd. Ingleside 167 K16

PATANGA
rd. Frenchs Frst 257 A5

PATCHING
cl. Minto 482 K4

PAT DEVLIN
cl. Chipping Ntn 396 K5

PATE
av. East Ryde 313 B1

PATEN
st. Revesby 398 E14

PATENT
sq. Holroyd 308 A10

PATER
st. Bnksmeadw 406 A13

PATERNOSTER
row. Pyrmont 12 H4

PATERSON
av. Kingsgrove 401 K11
av. Lurnea 394 C13
cr. Fairfield W 335 B12
pl. Colyton 270 H8
rd. Springwood 172 F15
rd. Yellow Rock 203 A2
st. Camden S 507 B9
st. Campbelltown 512 A6
st. Carlingford 250 B16
st. Matraville 436 J1

PATEY
st. Dee Why 258 H7

PATHERTON
pl. Narellan Vale 478 H15

PATIENCE
av. Yagoona 369 E8

PATON
pl. Balgowlah 288 A5
st. Kingsford 406 K4
st. Merrylands W 306 H12
st. Merrylands W 307 A12
st. Rookwood 340 B11

PATONGA
cl. Woodbine 481 J8
pl. Engadine 489 A11

PATONS
la. Orchard Hills 299 A6

PATRICIA
av. Mt Pritchard 364 D12
ct. Castle Hill 248 B3
pl. Cherrybrook 220 A4
st. Belfield 371 B10
st. Blacktown 274 F10
st. Cecil Hills 362 H6
st. Chester Hill 368 B2
st. Colyton 270 F5
st. Marsfield 282 A7
st. Mays Hill 307 G6
st. Rydalmere 309 J3

PATRICK
av. Castle Hill 217 J12
pl. Berowra Ht 133 B5
pl. Currans Hill 479 G10
st. Avalon 139 K11
st. Beacon Hill 257 E8
st. Blacktown 274 F2
st. Campbelltown 511 E4
st. Casula 424 F3
st. Greystanes 306 C8
st. Hurstville 431 H1
st. N Willoughby 285 E8
st. Punchbowl 400 E8

PATRICK O'POSSUM
pl. Faulconbdg 171 G13

PATRINE
pl. Bella Vista 246 E6

PATRIOT
pl. Rouse Hill 185 D8

PATSY
pl. Kings Park 244 E2

PATTEN
av. Merrylands 307 J15
pl. Kings Lngly 245 D4

PATTERN
pl. Woodcroft 243 G7

PATTERSON
av. Kellyville 216 H7
av. West Pymble 252 H12
cl. Padstow 429 H5
la. Avalon, off Central Rd 170 C1
la. Concord 341 J7
la. Surry Hills 4 D14
rd. Heathcote 518 C16
rd. Lalor Park 245 D11
st. Concord 341 G8
st. Double Bay 14 D11
st. Ermington 310 B1
st. North Bondi 348 C15
st. Rydalmere 309 K1
st. Tahmoor 565 H10

PATTERSONS
la. Grose Vale 85 A8

PATTISON
av. Hornsby 221 H3
av. Waitara 221 H3

PATTON
la. Willoughby 285 D13

PATTYS
pl. Jamisontown 265 K1

PATU
pl. Cherrybrook 219 D12

PATYA
cl. Epping 250 J14
ct. Kellyville 186 F16
pl. N Richmond 87 D16

PAUL
av. St Ives 224 F14
cl. Camden 507 B2
cl. Cranebrook 207 C15
cl. Hornsby Ht 161 J13
cl. Mona Vale 199 E2
cr. Canley Ht 335 F16
cr. S Wntwthvle 306 H8
ct. Baulkham Hl 247 G15

118 GREGORY'S STREET DIRECTORY

STREETS PE

la. Bondi Jctn, off Paul St 377 G4	pl. Sylvania Wtr......462 F12	**PEMBURY**	**PENNYS**
la. Coogee 407 G2	rd. Baulkham Hl 246 G8	av. North Rocks.....249 B15	la. Potts Point.............4 J8
pl. Carlingford 279 J2	st. Belmore 371 C15	cl. Denham Ct.........422 C9	**PENOLA**
st. Auburn 339 A3	st. Belmore 371 C16	rd. Minto.................482 B6	ct. Baulkham Hl 247 A2
PEAKE	st. Canley Ht 365 E4	**PEMELL**	st. Rookwood 339 K13
av. Rhodes............311 C8	st. Dover Ht 348 F9	la. Newtown 17 C14	**PENPRASE**
pde. Peakhurst 430 E3	st. Glenbrook 233 J16	st. Newtown 17 C15	la. Miranda 491 K3
PEAKER	st. Holroyd............308 A10	**PENDANT**	st. Riverstone 182 D11
la. Woollahra 21 K3	st. Kirribilli................2 D11	av. Blacktown 274 J8	**PENRHYN**
PEAL	st. Quakers Hill 214 D11	**PENDERGAST**	av. Beecroft 249 K7
pl. Warriewood 199 E14	st. Ruse................512 D8	av. Minto.................482 J7	av. Pymble 253 C6
PEARCE	st. Wilton 568 K16	**PENDERLEA**	pl. Castle Hill 217 K7
av. Newington 310 C13	**PEELER**	dr. W Pnnant Hl.....248 K6	rd. Bnksmeadw 435 K4
av. Peakhurst 430 E2	pl. Milperra..........397 D10	**PENDEY**	**PENRITH**
la. Hurlstone Pk, off Fernhill St 373 A10	**PEERLESS**	av. Northbridge 285 G16	av. Collaroy Plat 228 D13
pl. Emu Plains......235 E11	cl. Ingleburn.........453 G11	st. Willoughby......285 G16	st. Jamisontown 236 D16
rd. Narellan Vale ...508 F1	**PEFFER**	**PENDLE**	**PENRITH VALLEY BRIDGE**
rd. Quakers Hill 213 J13	st. Panania............428 C1	wy. Pendle Hill......306 D1	Emu Plains 235 F16
st. Baulkham Hl ...247 K6	**PEGAR**	**PENDLEBURY**	Jamisontown 235 F16
st. Double Bay 114 E7	pl. Marayong 243 H5	pl. Abbotsbury 333 D11	**PENROSE**
st. Ermington 280 A16	**PEGASUS**	**PENDLEY**	av. Belmore 401 G5
st. Liverpool 395 A6	av. Hinchinbrk 393 D5	cr. Quakers Hill 214 C12	av. Cherrybrook ...219 J10
st. S Coogee 407 H5	la. Erskine Park, off Weaver St 301 A3	**PENDOCK**	av. East Hills.........428 A5
wk. Rockdale.........403 F15	st. Erskine Park 301 A2	la. Cranebrook, off Pendock Rd.....207 F14	cl. Prestons 392 K14
PEARL	**PEGGOTTY**	rd. Cranebrook......207 F14	cr. S Penrith 237 A15
av. Belmore 371 E13	av. Ambarvale......511 A15	**PENDRILL**	pl. Frenchs Frst 256 G9
av. Chatswood W ..284 G12	**PEGGY**	st. Glebe 11 H7	pl. Menai 458 H6
av. Epping 281 C4	ct. Glendenning 242 K3	**PENELOPE**	st. Lane Cove 313 G3
cl. Erskine Park 270 H16	st. Mays Hill 307 G6	cr. Arndell Park 273 D9	st. Lane Cove W 313 G3
cl. Woodbine 481 K10	**PEGLER**	la. Cranebrook, off Milligan Rd.....207 C13	st. Minto.................483 A2
la. Newtown 374 H10	av. S Granville 338 E5	rd. Cranebrook......207 C13	**PENRUDDOCK**
pl. Seven Hills 275 B7	la. S Granville 338 E4	**PENELOPE LUCAS**	st. S Windsor 150 K2
st. Hurstville 431 H4	wy. Ambarvale.......511 A16	la. Rosehill 308 J8	**PENSACOLA**
st. Newtown 374 H10	**PEITA**	**PENFOLD**	pl. Casula..............395 A11
st. West Ryde 311 B1	cr. Mona Vale 198 J2	cl. Edensor Pk 333 E15	**PENSAX**
PEARL BAY	**PEKE**	pl. Sydney................D A1	la. Cranebrook, off Pensax Rd.....207 G14
av. Mosman 287 A15	pl. Rooty Hill 272 D5	pl. Sydney................3 H1	rd. Cranebrook......207 F14
PEARRA	**PELARGONIUM**	st. Eastern Ck.......272 E7	**PENSHURST**
wy. Clarmnt Ms.....268 H1	cr. Mcquarie Fd 454 G6	**PENGILLY**	av. Neutral Bay..........6 H8
PEARSON	**PELICAN**	st. Riverview 314 A5	av. Penshurst 431 G6
av. Gordon 253 G6	la. St Clair, off Swamphen St......271 A13	**PENGUIN**	la. Penshurst 431 E5
cr. Harringtn Pk.....478 G7	pl. Hinchinbrk 393 C1	pde. Hinchinbrk 393 C1	rd. Narwee............400 J13
la. Gladesville 312 J10	pl. Woronora Ht ...489 D6	pl. Tregear 240 B4	rd. Roselands 401 A15
pl. Baulkham Hl ...247 B15	rd. Schofields 213 E3	st. Beverly Hills 401 A15
st. Balmain East 8 H9	st. Erskine Park 271 A13	st. Chatswood 285 C5
st. Bligh Park 150 H5	st. Gladesville 312 K6	st. N Willoughby ...285 D9
st. Gladesville 312 J11	st. Surry Hills ....F H6	dr. Breakfast Pt 312 C13	st. Penshurst 431 C1
st. Kingswood.......237 K13	st. Surry Hills 4 B11	rd. Valley Ht 202 F4	st. Roseville 285 C5
st. S Wntwthvle 307 C6	**PELLATT**	**PENINSULAR**	st. Willoughby......285 D9
PEARTREE	pl. Emu Plains......235 F9	rd. Grays Point 491 E15	**PENTECOST**
cct. W Pnnant Hl....249 C5	**PELLEAS**	**PENKIVIL**	av. Pymble 223 G13
PEAT	st. Blacktown 275 A9	st. Bondi 377 J4	av. St Ives 223 C12
cl. Eagle Vale 481 D7	**PELLIGRINO**	st. Willoughby......285 D13	av. Turramurra 223 C12
st. Brooklyn............75 F12	gr. Rouse Hill 185 D2	**PENMON**	av. Hinchinbrk 392 K2
PEBBLEWOOD	**PELLION**	cl. Menai 458 H9	**PENTLAND**
ct. W Pnnant Hl....248 K1	st. Blaxland 233 E16	**PENN**	av. Roselands 400 G6
PEBBLY HILL	**PELLISIER**	cr. Quakers Hill 213 G15	st. Quakers Hill 213 K14
rd. Cattai 94 E8	pl. Putney 312 A9	**PENNA**	**PENTLANDS**
rd. Maraylya............94 E11	rd. Putney 312 B9	pl. Bonnyrigg Ht...363 C4	dr. Winmalee........173 E11
PEBWORTH	**PELLITT**	**PENNANT**	**PENTONVILLE**
pl. S Penrith 267 A8	la. Dural 188 G11	av. Denistone 281 G11	pde. Castle Hill 216 K10
PAYNE	**PECAN**	st. Casula.............394 B16	av. Gordon 253 G10	pde. Castle Hill 217 B10
st. Oakhurst 211 J16	cl. Cherrybrook 220 A9	**PELMAN**	pde. Carlingford......280 C1	**PENZA**
st. S Penrith 237 C16	cl. St Clair 269 G16	av. Belmore 371 E14	pde. Epping 280 C1	pl. Quakers Hill 214 C10
PAYTEN	pl. Casula 394 B16	av. Greenacre 370 F14	st. Castle Hill........218 B14	**PEONY**
av. Roselands 400 F8	**PECK**	**PELORUS**	st. N Parramatta ...278 J15	pl. Quakers Hill 243 F3
ct. Kogarah Bay ...432 H11	la. Bardwell Pk.....402 J6	dr. Voyager Pt 427 D5	st. Parramatta......278 J15	**PEPLER**
ct. Menangle Pk 539 A6	**PECKHAM**	**PELSART**	wy. Castle Hill........218 C13	rd. Cabramatta W ..365 B7
st. Putney 312 A6	av. Chatswood W ..284 G7	av. Penrith............237 D2	**PENNANT HILLS**	**PEPLOW**
PAYTON	**PECKS**	av. Willmot............210 D12	pde. Carlingford......279 A7	pl. Doonside 273 E3
ct. Narellan Vale ...509 A2	rd. Kurrajong Ht 63 E11	**PEMBERTON**	pde. Carlingford......279 A7	**PEPPER**
st. Canley Ht 366 B5	rd. N Richmond......87 A12	la. Parramatta 308 J1	pde. Normanhurst ...221 A13	la. Clovelly, off Thorpe St.........377 K14
PEACE	**PECOS**	rd. Botany 405 H15	rd. N Parramatta ...278 D13	pl. Pennant Hills ...220 H16
av. Peakhurst 430 D7	cl. St Clair 299 J2	st. Parramatta......308 J2	rd. Oatlands 279 A7	**PEPPERCORN**
cr. Pymble 253 H1	cl. Seven Hills 275 D7	st. Strathfield 340 H14	rd. Pennant Hills...220 H16	av. Fiddletown 129 J1
st. St Clair 299 H1	**PEDDER**	**PEMBREW**	rd. Thornleigh 221 A13	av. Fairfield E........337 A15
PEACH	cl. Woodcroft 243 G10	cr. Earlwood 403 C3	rd. Wahroonga.....221 A13	av. Mt Hunter 505 B8
ct. Carlingford 249 G16	cl. Wattle Grove ...396 A14	**PEMBROKE**	st. W Pnnant Hl....249 J7	av. Narellan 478 G14
gdn. Glenwood 215 H3	st. Glenbrook 264 C5	av. Earlwood 402 F3	**PENNICOOK**	**PEPPERCRESS**
PEACH TREE	**PEDIT**	av. Summer Hill....373 B3	la. Pennant Hills, off Hillcrest Rd.....220 G16	dr. Frenchs Frst 256 H1
la. Kirrawee 490 J2	pl. Cherrybrook 219 C12	av. Turramurra 252 F5	**PENNINGTON**	la. Oatlands, off Hunterford Cr 279 A8
rd. Mcquarie Pk.....282 G3	**PEDRICK**	cr. Belrose 226 A13	av. Georges Hall ...367 K14	**PEPPERFIELDS**
PEACHTREE	pl. Dundas Vy 280 B11	cr. Leumeah.........482 B14	av. Georges Hall ...367 K14	pl. Cranebrook......207 B8
av. Wentwthvle.....277 B8	**PEDVIN**	rd. Marsfield.........251 G15	**PENNSYLVANIA**	pl. Glenwood 245 H2
la. Penrith, off Peachtree Rd.....236 E7	pl. Annangrove 155 K9	rd. Minto................452 H16	rd. Riverwood 400 A13	rd. Hornglsea Pk ...392 F13
rd. Penrith............236 E7	**PEEBLES**	st. Ashfield 373 A2	**PENNY**	rd. Kirrawee 460 K16
wy. Menai 458 H10	av. Kirrawee 461 A15	st. Blacktown 273 J5	cr. Holsworthy 395 E1	st. Mt Hunter 504 B16
PEACOCK	rd. Fiddletown 129 H1	st. Bronte.............377 K10	la. Liverpool.........365 E16	**PEPPERS**
cl. Green Valley....363 F11	st. Winston Hills ..277 K4	st. Cmbrdg Pk.....237 F10	la. Thirlmere........565 B3	cl. Old Tngabbie....277 F8
pde. Frenchs Frst 255 G1	**PEEK**	st. Epping 251 C15	la. Arndell Park.....274 B11	**PEPPERFIELDS**
rd. Bardwell Pk.....402 K7	pl. Chester Hill 338 A14	st. Epping 251 E15	**PENNYBRIGHT**	pl. Grasmere........476 A12
st. Seaforth..........287 A8	**PEEL**	st. Surry Hills 19 G5	pl. Kellyville.........216 C2	**PEPPRIDGE**
wy. Claymore........481 A11	pde. Comleroy........64 F12	st. Sylvania 462 C9	av. Oakhurst 242 D1
wy. Currans Hill.....479 G11	pl. Baulkham Hl ...277 J2		

GREGORY'S STREET DIRECTORY 119

PE STREETS

PEPPERINA
pl. Carlingford 249 H11
PEPPERMINT
cl. Prestons 394 C14
cr. Kingswood 267 G1
cr. Mcquarie Fd 454 G3
gr. Engadine 518 D2
gr. Panania 428 E5
PEPPERMINT GUM
pl. Westleigh 220 F7
PEPPERTREE
dr. Erskine Park 270 G15
gr. Quakers Hill 214 C14
la. St Clair, off Swallow Dr 270 K16
pl. Castle Hill 216 K11
PEPPIN
cl. St Clair 270 B13
cr. Airds 512 D9
la. St Clair, off Peppin Cl 270 B13
pl. Elderslie 507 H1
PERA
pl. Fairfield W 335 C9
PERABO
cl. Bossley Park 333 F9
PERAK
st. Mona Vale 199 E2
PERCEVAL
cl. Abbotsbury 333 A11
PERCHERON
st. Blairmount 480 K14
PERCIVAL
av. Appin 569 E8
la.e, Stanmore 16 G5
la.w, Stanmore 16 F5
rd. Caringbah 492 J16
rd. Greystanes 306 C16
rd. Smithfield 336 C1
rd. Stanmore 16 F5
st. Bexley 432 H3
st. Carlton 432 H3
st. Clarendon 120 B4
st. Lilyfield 10 G9
st. Maroubra 406 J7
st. Penshurst 431 E3
PERCY
st. Auburn 339 G2
st. Bankstown 399 F3
st. Fairfield Ht 335 H10
st. Gladesville 312 J7
st. Greystanes 306 D9
st. Haberfield 373 E1
st. Ingleburn 453 D10
st. Marayong 244 C10
st. Rozelle 10 J1
PEREGRINE
cl. Green Valley 363 E11
PEREIRA
st. Newington, off Newington Bvd 310 A15
PERENTIE
rd. Belrose 226 D13
rd. Oxford Falls 226 D12
PERFECTION
av. Kellyville Rdg 215 C2
av. Stanhpe Gdn 215 C8
PERI
cl. Woodcroft 243 J11
ct. Wattle Grove 395 K15
PERIDOT
cl. Eagle Vale 481 E5
pl. Glenwood 215 F13
PERIGEE
cl. Doonside 243 F14
PERIMETER
rd. Mascot 404 C12
rd. Mascot 404 E4
PERINA
cl. Bangor 459 E14
cl. Casula 424 C3
PERISHER
rd. Beaumont Hills 185 H15
st. Horngsea Pk 392 C15
PERKINS
av. Newington 310 A14
dr. Kellyville 215 J5
pl. Bonnyrigg Ht 363 E8
st. Bligh Park 150 K7
st. Denistone W 280 K12
st. Rooty Hill 272 B1
wy. Maroubra 407 C12
PERMANENT
av. Earlwood 372 H15
PERMIAN
dr. Cartwright 394 D4
PERON
pl. Willmot 210 D14
PERONNE
av. Clontarf 287 E11
cl. Milperra 397 D12
pde. Allambie Ht 257 J16
wy. Matraville 407 A15
PEROUSE
rd. Randwick 377 B15
PERRETT
st. Rozelle 7 D14
PERREY
st. Collaroy Plat 228 H13
PERRI
la. Haberfield 343 C15
PERRIN
av. Plumpton 241 H6
PERRITT
pl. S Penrith 236 K15
PERRUMBA
pl. Bradbury 511 G16
PERRY
av. Springwood 201 G2
cr. Engadine 518 F4
ct. Harringtn Pk 478 E5
la. Campsie 372 B15
la. Lilyfield 9 G6
la. Lilyfield 9 J7
la. Lilyfield, off Mary St 343 K12
la. Paddington 13 B16
rd. Arcadia 129 J8
st. Bossley Park 334 B5
st. Campsie 372 B15
st. Dundas Vy 280 C9
st. Kings Lngly 245 H8
st. Lilyfield 9 H6
st. Lilyfield 9 K6
st. Marrickville 16 G16
st. Marrickville 374 D9
st. Matraville 436 F2
st. North Rocks 248 F15
st. Surry Hills 19 H5
st. Wentwthvle 307 A1
wy. Auburn 338 K2
PERRYMAN
pl. Cronulla 494 A11
PERRYS
av. Bexley 432 F3
PERSEUS
cct. Kellyville 186 G16
cl. Cranebrook 207 G7
PERSHORE
la. Cranebrook, off Pendock Rd 207 G13
rd. Cranebrook 207 G13
PERSIC
st. Belfield 371 C10
PERSIMMON
wy. Glenwood 215 E14
PERSOONIA
av. Agnes Banks 146 J3
cl. Mt Annan 509 B1
PERTAKA
pl. Narraweena 258 B1
PERTARINGA
wy. Glenorie 128 A6
PERTH
av. Campbelltown 512 C4
av. E Lindfield 254 K14
cl. West Hoxton 392 D6
st. Kirrawee 461 A14
st. Oxley Park 270 E1
st. Riverstone 152 F15
st. Vineyard 152 F15
PERU
pl. Illawong 459 K3
PESSOTTO
pl. Wakeley 334 F14
PETER
av. Camden 507 B6
cl. Hornsby Ht 161 J12
cr. Greenacre 370 B7
ct. Jamisontown 266 A2
pde. Old Tngabbie 277 B6
pl. Bligh Park 150 K8
pl. Gymea Bay 491 F9
st. Baulkham Hl 247 E11
st. Blacktown 244 J14
st. Glossodia 66 C13
PETER BROCK
dr. Oran Park 448 D12
PETER FINCH
av. Moore Park 20 K8
PETERLEE
pl. Hebersham 241 E7
rd. Canley Ht 365 B3
PETER MEADOWS
rd. Kentlyn 483 A15
rd. Leumeah 482 J14
PETER PAN
av. Wallacia 324 K14
gln. St Clair 270 D11
la. St Clair, off Peter Pan Gln 270 D11
PETERS
pl. Maroubra 407 E14
PETERS CORNER
Randwick 377 A12
PETERSEN
cr. Tregear 240 C4
PETERSHAM
la. Petersham 16 A5
rd. Marrickville 373 K13
st. Bonnyrigg Ht 363 C7
st. Petersham 16 A5
PETERSON
pl. North Rocks 248 K14
PETER WILSON
st. Glenwood 245 J1
PETESA
dr. Kellyville 217 D3
PETITE
la. Springwood 201 K3
PETITH
la. Hurstville 401 H16
PETRARCH
av. Vaucluse 348 E5
PETREL
pl. Hinchinbrk 393 C1
pl. Tregear 240 B4
pl. Woronora Ht 489 E4
PETRIE
cl. Bidwill 211 D15
pl. Georges Hall 368 C15
PETRIKAS
la. Tennyson 65 G10
PETRINA
cr. Baulkham Hl 248 B13
PETRIZZI
pl. Baulkham Hl 247 E8
PETTIT
av. Lakemba 371 A13
PETTY
av. Yagoona 368 K11
PETUNIA
av. Bankstown 399 G3
pl. Mcquarie Fd 454 E4
st. Marayong 244 A6
PEUGEOT
dr. Ingleburn 453 J9
PEVENSEY
st. Canley Vale 365 J4
st. Castle Hill 216 H9
PHAR LAP
cl. Casula 394 E16
la. St Clair, off Phar Lap Pl 270 E12
pl. St Clair 270 E11
PHARLAP
st. Bossley Park 333 J8
PHEASANT
st. Canterbury 402 E2
PHEASANTS
rd. Wedderburn 540 D9
PHELPS
cr. Bradbury 511 E7
la. Surry Hills 20 D3
st. Canley Vale 365 K4
st. Surry Hills 20 C3
PHILBY
pl. Bonnyrigg 363 H8
PHILIP
la. West Pymble 252 J10
ml. West Pymble 252 J10
pl. Carlingford 249 F13
pl. Cherrybrook 220 B4
rd. Leppington 420 D7
rd. Mona Vale 169 G16
st. Blacktown 244 B11
st. Bondi 377 K5
st. Strathfield 341 H11
st. Woolooware 493 J9
PHILIPPA
cl. Cecil Hills 362 E2
ct. Kellyville 217 C1
PHILLIP
av. Cabramatta 365 F9
av. Seaforth 287 B7
cr. Btn-le-Sds 403 K15
la. Newtown 17 C12
la. Parramatta, off Phillip St 308 C2
la. Penshurst 431 B3
la. Putney 312 A8
la. St Marys, off Champness Cr 239 K15
la. Sydney B F13
pky. Colebee 212 E16
pky. Dean Park 212 E16
pky. Glendenning 212 E16
pky. Oakhurst 212 E16
pky. Rooty Hill 242 D14
pky. Rooty Hill 272 E1
pl. McGraths Hl 121 J12
rd. Putney 311 K6
rd. St Ives Ch 194 B16
st. Balmain 7 F8
st. Birchgrove 7 F8
st. Blakehurst 432 C15
st. Campbelltown 511 J6
st. Glebe 12 E12
st. Guildford W 336 J4
st. Kingswood 237 F11
st. Liverpool 394 H2
st. Newtown 17 B12
st. Oatlands 278 K10
st. Oyster Bay 461 B8
st. Panania 428 B5
st. Parramatta 308 C2
st. Petersham 16 C4
st. Redfern 19 C10
st. Riverwood 400 C15
st. Roselands 401 C5
st. St Marys 239 H14
st. Seven Hills 245 E16
st. S Coogee 407 G6
st. Stanmore 16 C4
st. Sydney B D15
st. Sydney D D4
st. Sydney 1 K16
st. Sydney 3 K2
st. Waterloo 19 C10
PHILLIPA
pl. Bargo 567 B5
PHILLIPS
av. Canterbury 372 D13
av. Regents Pk 339 C16
la. Marrickville 373 F15
la. Neutral Bay 6 C6
rd. Kogarah 433 D10
st. Alexandria 18 J13
st. Auburn 339 A4
st. Cabarita 342 E2
st. Neutral Bay 6 C7
st. Rookwood 340 C12
PHILLIPSON
la. Springwood 172 A15
PHILO
cl. Rsemeadow 540 E2
PHILPOTT
st. Marrickville 16 H16
st. Marrickville 374 D9
PHINEY
rd. Ingleburn 453 E1
PHIPPS
rd. Maraylya 94 C10
st. Oatley 461 D1
PHLOX
cl. Lalor Park 245 C10
PHOEBE
st. Balmain 7 A7
PHOENIX
av. Beaumont Hills 215 G2
av. Beaumont Hills 215 H3
av. Concord W 311 E12
av. Ingleburn 453 A9
av. Stanhpe Gdn 215 A11
cl. Castle Hill 218 K9
cr. Casula 395 A11
cr. Erskine Park 270 H15
la. St Clair, off Phoenix Cr 270 J15
pl. Illawong 459 G3
pl. Narellan Vale 479 B14
st. Lane Cove 314 E1
PHYLLIS
av. Picnic Point 428 G5
av. Thornleigh 221 B12
cr. Guildford 337 D3
la. N Curl Curl, off Phyllis St 259 C10
st. Minto 482 G2
st. Mt Pritchard 364 G12
st. N Curl Curl 259 C10
PHYSICS
rd. Camperdown 18 B4
PIAF
cl. Bonnyrigg Ht 363 C4
PIANOSA
pl. Glenwood 245 K3
PIBRAC
av. Warrawee 222 G10
PICASSO
cr. Old Tngabbie 276 K6
la. Emu Plains, off Picasso Pl 236 A7
pl. Emu Plains 236 A7
PICCADILLY
pl. Maroubra 407 A9
st. Riverstone 183 A6
st. Riverstone 183 B8
PICCOLO
wy. Shalvey 210 H14
PICHOLA
pl. Castle Hill 218 E15
PICKEN
la. Blacktown 244 F13
st. Silverwater 309 K8
PICKERING
la. Woollahra 22 B2
PICKERING PATH
Winmalee 173 A14
PICKERSGILL
st. Kings Lngly 245 H7
PICKETS
la. Currans Hill 479 K10
pl. Currans Hill 479 K10
PICKETT
av. Minto 453 A15
PICKFORD
av. Eastwood 281 F7
PICKWICK
wy. Ambarvale 540 K1
wy. Ambarvale 541 A1
PICKWORTH
av. Balgowlah 287 G8
pl. Menai 458 J6
PICNIC
gln. Springwood 201 H6
gr. Ingleburn 454 A8
pl. Clarmnt Ms 238 K16
PICNIC POINT
rd. Panania 428 D5
rd. Picnic Point 428 C8
PICOT
pl. Blackett 241 C1
PICRITE
cl. Pemulwuy 305 A2
cl. Prospect 305 A2
PICTON
av. Picton 563 F5
cl. Bonnyrigg Ht 362 K7
rd. Picton 563 H11
rd. Wilton 568 K16
st. Mascot 405 H6
st. Quakers Hill 244 A1
PICTOR
st. Erskine Park 300 K3
PIDCOCK
st. Camperdown 17 D4
PIDDING
rd. Ryde 312 G1
PIER
st. Haymarket E A4
st. Haymarket 3 B10
st. Prospect 274 H11
st. Sydney E A4
st. Sydney 3 B10
PIERCE
pl. Bonnet Bay 460 D10
st. Mount Druitt 241 F13
st. Newtown 17 A10
st. Prairiewood 334 H7
PIERRE
cl. Mt Colah 192 C3
PIERSON
la. Canterbury 372 G13
PIESLEY
st. Prairiewood 334 K9
PIGEON
cl. Hinchinbrk 393 C4

120 GREGORY'S STREET DIRECTORY

STREETS PO

PIGGOTT
wy. Ingleburn 452 K10
PIGOTT
la. Marrickville 373 E15
st. Dulwich Hill 373 D8
PIKE
rd. Hornsby Ht 191 F2
st. Rydalmere 309 E4
PIKES
la. Eastern Ck 272 J11
la. Newtown 17 E11
PILBARA
pl. Grays Point 491 A14
PILBARRA
pl. Cartwright 394 A4
PILCHER
av. Castle Hill 218 J12
st. Strathfield S 370 K7
PILCHERS
la. Burwood, off Belmore St 342 A15
PILDRA
av. St Ives 223 J14
pl. Frenchs Frst 256 E8
PILE
pl. N Sydney 6 A10
st. Dulwich Hill 373 G9
st. Gladesville 312 G13
st. Marrickville 373 H9
st.n, Bardwell Pk 402 K8
st.s, Bardwell Vy 403 A9
PILGRIM
av. Marrickville 373 D14
av. Strathfield 341 F11
PILLARS
pl. Matraville 436 J1
PILLIGA
cr. Bossley Park 333 G12
ct. Wattle Grove 426 C3
pl. Bangor 459 E14
PIMA
cl. Greenfld Pk 334 B16
PIMELEA
pl. Rooty Hill 272 B3
PIMELIA
ct. Voyager Pt 427 C5
st. Tahmoor 565 H8
PINANG
pl. Whalan 240 K7
PINAROO
cr. Bradbury 511 C16
pl. Gymea Bay 491 H8
pl. Lane Cove N 283 J14
PINCOMBE
cr. Harringtn Pk 478 F8
PINDARI
av. Camden 506 K4
av. Carlingford 279 F3
av. Castle Cove 285 H3
av. Loftus 490 B10
av. Mosman 287 A16
av. St Ives 254 A2
cr. S Wntwthvle 306 H7
dr. S Penrith 266 J7
pl. Bardwell Vy 403 C7
pl. Bayview 168 K13
rd. Dover Ht 348 F14
rd. Peakhurst 430 C9
st. Hornsby Ht 191 G2
st. North Ryde 282 F8
st. Winmalee 173 A9
PINDARUS
wy. Rsemeadow 540 H3
PINDOS
pl. Emu Heights 235 B5
PINDRIE
pl. Belrose 225 H16
st. Yowie Bay 492 C9
PINDURO
pl. Cromer 227 H13
PINE
av. Bradbury 511 C13
av. Brookvale 258 C9
av. Earlwood 403 H2
av. Five Dock 343 B7
av. Narraweena 258 C7
av. Russell Lea 343 B7
av. Wareemba 343 B7
cr. Bella Vista 246 E5
cr. Bidwill 211 G13
la. Bondi Jctn, off Hollywood Av 377 F3
la. Chippendale 18 H3
la. Engadine 518 J2
la. Engadine, off Mianga Av 518 J2
la. Manly 288 G6
la. Newtown 18 A11
la. Rydalmere 309 H1
pl. Chippendale 18 J3
pl. Grose Vale 84 J13
pl. Narraweena 258 C7
pl. Riverstone 182 K4
rd. Auburn 339 A6
rd. Casula 423 K1
rd. Casula 423 J1
rd. Casula 424 D2
rd. Fairfield 336 H7
rd. Yennora 336 H7
sq. Leichhardt 16 B1
st. Cammeray 316 A3
st. Chippendale 18 J3
st. Lugarno 429 J15
st. Manly 288 F6
st. Manly 288 E6
st. Marrickville 373 F11
st. Newtown 18 B10
st. Normanhurst 221 D13
st. North Ryde 282 F7
st. Randwick 377 D9
st. Rozelle 7 D14
st. Rydalmere 309 G1
st.e, Cammeray 316 B4
PINE CREEK
cct. St Clair 299 H1
PINECREST
st. Winmalee 173 E5
PINEDALE
pl. Kurrajong Ht 63 E10
PINE HILL
av. Double Bay 14 D12
PINEHURST
av. Glenmore Pk 266 G10
av. Rouse Hill 185 B9
PINELEIGH
rd. Lalor Park 245 K13
PINERA
cl. Hornsby 221 B2
PINERIDGE
cr. Silverdale 383 A11
cr. Silverdale 413 A4
PINES
av. Little Bay 437 G15
pde. Gymea 491 G7
PINE TREE
gr. Minchinbury 272 D9
PINETREE
av. Cranebrook 237 E1
dr. Carlingford 249 H13
PINE VALLEY
rd. Galston 160 D13
PINEVIEW
av. Manly Vale 287 H3
av. Roselands 400 G8
pl. Dural 219 B7
PINNACLE
st. Miranda 491 H4
st. Sadleir 394 B1
wy. Glenwood 215 G16
PINNER
cl. N Epping 251 G11
PIN OAK
gr. Menai 458 J15
pl. Narellan Vale 479 A12
PINOT
pl. Minchinbury 271 G7
st. Eschol Park 481 D2
PINTA
pl. Cromer 228 B15
PINTO
la. St Clair, off Pinto Pl 270 E12
pl. St Clair 270 E11
PINUS
av. Glenorie 128 F12
PIONEER
av. Thornleigh 221 B11
dr. Menai 459 A12
gr. Wrrngtn Dns 238 C5
la. Wrrngtn Dns, off Pioneer Gr 238 D5
pl. Castle Hill 218 F13
rd. Cronulla 493 J16
st. Seven Hills 245 E15
st. Wentwthvle 276 H13
PIPER
cl. Kingswood 267 E3
cl. Milperra 397 C10
la. Annandale 11 A12
la. Kingswood, off Piper Cl 267 F2
pl. Minchinbury 271 H8
st. Annandale 10 J11
st. Lilyfield 10 D9
st. West Hoxton 392 C9
st.n, Annandale 11 B12
st.s, Annandale 11 A12
wy. Minto 482 K2
wy. Narellan 478 G13
PIPERITA
cl. Mt Colah 191 K3
pl. Winmalee 173 E8
PIPERS
la. Silverdale 384 A4
PIPERSBROOK
cr. Bella Vista 216 C16
PIPET
pl. Hinchinbrk 393 C3
PIPINO
pl. Dee Why 258 H1
PIPIT
pl. Ingleburn 453 H8
PIPON
cl. Green Valley 362 K11
PIPPA
st. Seven Hills 246 A11
PIPPEN
pl. Rooty Hill 242 A12
st. Harringtn Pk 478 F6
PIPPITA
pl. Bangor 459 F14
st. Lidcombe 340 D6
PIPPITTA
st. Marayong 244 B2
PIQUET
pl. Toongabbie 276 D5
PIRA
pl. Forestville 255 F8
PIRIE
cl. Wakeley 334 J14
st. Liverpool 395 D5
PIRIWAL
cl. Bangor 459 D14
PIROL
pl. Dean Park 242 K1
PIRON
pl. Woronora Ht 489 C6
PIRRAMA
rd. Pyrmont 8 F16
PISA
pl. Plumpton 241 G8
PISCES
la. Erskine Park, off Pisces Pl 300 H1
pl. Erskine Park 300 H1
PITAPUNGA
cl. Woodcroft 243 G11
PITCAIRN
av. Lethbrdg Pk 210 F16
PITLOCHRY
pl. St Andrews 452 A15
PITMAN
av. Hornsby Ht 161 F15
PITT
la. N Richmond 87 F14
la. Parramatta, off Steele St 307 K5
la. Rockdale 403 E15
rd. N Curl Curl 258 G10
st. Badgerys Ck 358 G4
st. Balgowlah 287 J6
st. Canley Ht 335 G16
st. Concord 341 H7
st. Granville 307 K8
st. Haymarket E F13
st. Haymarket 3 F15
st. Holroyd 307 J12
st. Hunters Hill 313 E11
st. Kirribilli 6 A16
st. Loftus 490 C9
st. Manly Vale 287 J5
st. Mays Hill 307 K8
st. Merrylands 307 J12
st. Mortdale 431 B9
st. Parramatta 308 A4
st. Randwick 377 C14
st. Redfern 19 E10
st. Richmond 119 B5
st. Riverstone 182 J7
st. Rockdale 403 E15
st. Springwood 201 E4
st. Sydney C K16
st. Sydney 1 H16
st. Sydney 3 H6
st. Tahmoor 565 H13
st. Waterloo 19 E11
st. Waterloo 19 F15
st. Windsor 121 F7
PITTMAN
pl. Bella Vista 246 D7
rd. Kurrajong Ht 62 G10
PITTMAN STEPS
pl. Blair Athol 511 B4
PITT-OWEN
av. Arncliffe 403 F9
PITT TOWN
rd. Kenthurst 157 A13
rd. McGraths Hl 121 J12
rd. Maraylya 125 B2
rd. Pitt Town 122 F7
PITT TOWN BOTTOMS
rd. Pitt Town 92 A8
rd. Pitt Twn Bttms 122 A3
PITT TOWN DURAL
rd. Maraylya 94 A14
rd. Pitt Town 93 E12
PITT TOWN FERRY
rd. Wilberforce 92 D2
PITT VIEW
st. Scotland I 168 J2
PITTWATER
rd. Bayview 168 J10
rd. Bayview 169 B12
rd. Brookvale 258 A12
rd. Church Point 168 F7
rd. Collaroy 229 A6
rd. Dee Why 258 F7
rd. East Ryde 283 B11
rd. East Ryde 313 C2
rd. Gladesville 312 J9
rd. Hunters Hill 313 A7
rd. Mcquarie Pk 283 A6
rd. Manly 288 G8
rd. Mona Vale 199 C6
rd. Narrabeen 229 A6
rd. North Manly 258 A13
rd. N Narrabeen 229 A2
rd. North Ryde 283 B11
rd. Queenscliff 288 D2
rd. Warriewood 199 A16
PITURI
pl. Alfords Point 429 A14
wy. Kellyville Rdg 215 A1
PIUS
la. Marsden Pk 211 J2
PIVETTA
st. Revesby 399 A14
PLAINS VIEW
cr. Mt Riverview 204 H14
PLANA
cr. Springwood 202 B2
PLANE
st. Prestons 393 J14
PLANE TREE
dr. Narellan Vale 479 A13
dr. Stanhpe Gdn 215 D10
PLANT
la. Mortlake 312 B16
st. Balgowlah 287 E10
st. Carlton 432 H11
PLANTE
wk. Lalor Park 245 G12
PLANTHURST
rd. Carlton 432 F10
PLASSER
cr. N St Marys 240 A13
PLASSEY
rd. Mcquarie Pk 283 D7
PLASTO
st. Greenacre 370 F15
PLATEAU
cl. Hornsby Ht 161 H15
pde. Blaxland 233 C6
rd. Avalon 169 K4
rd. Bilgola 169 F6
rd. Collaroy Plat 228 J15
rd. Springwood 201 D1
PLATFORM
st. Lidcombe 340 A6
PLATO
pl. Wetherill Pk 335 A6
PLATTS
av. Belmore 401 H3
PLAYER
st. St Marys 269 D3
PLAYFAIR
av. Moore Park 21 B10
rd. Mt Colah 192 D1
rd. N Curl Curl 258 H11
st. The Rocks A K2
PLAYFORD
rd. Padstow Ht 429 E8
PLEASANT
av. E Lindfield 255 A13
av. Erskineville 374 K9
ct. Carlingford 279 G5
pl. Leonay 234 K16
pl. Yarramundi 145 F8
st. Bossley Park 334 B10
wy. Blakehurst 462 B1
PLEASURE POINT
rd. Pleasure Pt 427 G9
PLIMSOLL
la. Belmore, off Plimsoll St 401 H1
st. Belmore 401 H1
st. McGraths Hl 122 A11
st. Sans Souci 462 J4
PLOUGH INN
rd. Leumeah 481 K13
PLOUGHMAN
cr. Wrrngtn Dns 238 A4
cr. Wrrngtn Dns 238 A5
PLOVER
cl. St Clair 270 B14
gln. Bella Vista 246 F1
la. St Clair, off Plover Cl 270 B14
pl. Ingleburn 453 G10
st. Grays Point 491 F15
st. Newington 310 D12
st. Plumpton 241 K9
PLOWMAN
rd. Currans Hill 479 K8
rd. Minto 453 C15
st. North Bondi 348 D16
PLUKAVEC
cct. Prestons 393 C13
PLUM
cl. Casula 424 B2
gdn. Glenwood 215 D13
PLUME
cl. Mcquarie Fd 454 A3
PLUMER
rd. Rose Bay 347 G12
PLUMPTON
rd. Glendenning 242 C7
rd. Plumpton 242 C7
PLUMTREE
ct. W Pnnant Hl 248 K4
PLUNKETT
cr. Kingswood 267 F1
cr. Mount Druitt 241 G11
la. Drummoyne 343 H4
pl. Gladesville 312 K12
rd. Mosman 317 E8
st. Drummoyne 343 G5
st. Kirribilli 2 F2
st. Marsfield 281 K2
st. St Leonards 315 D5
st. Woolmloo 4 F4
PLUTO
ct. Glenwood 215 C14
pl. Cranebrook 207 G7
PLYMOUTH
av. Chester Hill 338 C14
av. North Rocks 278 H3
cl. Wahroonga 222 G7
cr. Kings Lngly 246 C8
st. Enfield 371 G3
PLYMPTON
rd. Carlingford 250 C12
rd. Epping 250 C12
wy. Glenhaven 218 E5
POA
pl. Glenmore Pk 265 H12
POATE
la. Centennial Pk 21 D5
pl. Davidson 225 B15
rd. Centennial Pk 21 C6
rd. Moore Park 21 C6
POBJE
av. Birrong 368 K6
POBJOY
pl. Bnkstn Aprt 397 K1
POCKET
cl. Ambarvale 540 G1
POCKLEY
av. Roseville 284 F5

GREGORY'S STREET DIRECTORY 121

PO STREETS

PODARGUS
pl. Ingleburn 453 G8
PODMORE
pl. Hillsdale 406 G14
POETS
gln. Wrrngtn Dns 238 E6
la. Wrrngtn Dns, off
  Poets Gln 238 E6
POGSON
dr. Cherrybrook 219 K9
POIDEVIN
la. Wilberforce 91 J1
POINCIANA
cl. Greystanes 306 E12
cl. Mt Colah 192 B2
row. Menai 458 J15
POINSETTIA
av. North Rocks 279 B1
POINT
av. Chiswick 343 B2
la. Northwood 314 H9
rd. Lilyfield, off
  Central Av 344 A7
rd. Mooney Mooney ..75 D1
rd. Northwood 314 H9
st. Lilyfield 10 B6
st. Pyrmont 8 F15
POINT PIPER
la. Paddington 21 H2
POKOLBIN
pl. Edensor Pk 363 E2
POLAR
st. Tregear 240 E7
POLARIS
pl. Rooty Hill 272 B2
POLDING
cl. Macquarie Pk, off
  Main Av 283 D7
la. Drummoyne 343 H4
pl. Telopea 279 G10
rd. Lindfield 283 J2
st. Bossley Park 334 C6
st. Drummoyne 343 G4
st. Fairfield Ht 335 G8
st. Fairfield W 335 G8
st. Smithfield 335 G8
st. Wetherill Pk 334 C6
st.n. Fairfield 336 F9
POLE
la. Crows Nest, off
  Hume St 315 F6
la. St Leonards, off
  Oxley St 315 E6
POLK
pl. Bonnet Bay 460 C10
POLLACK
st. Blacktown 274 B5
POLLARD
pl. Sutherland 490 G6
POLLOCK
st. Georges Hall 367 H12
POLLUX
cl. Erskine Park 301 A1
POLLY
pl. Plumpton 241 H10
POLO
av. Mona Vale 199 E3
cr. Girraween 276 A11
rd. Jamisontown 236 A16
rd. Prestons 392 J16
rd. Rossmore 419 H4
st. Kurnell 466 D7
st. Revesby 398 G15
POLONIA
av. Plumpton 242 D11
POLONIUS
st. Rsemeadow 540 J5
POLWARTH
cl. Bradbury 511 D13
st. Miller 393 F3
POLWORTH
cl. Elderslie 507 J2
POLYBLANK
pde. North Bondi 348 C14
pde. Rose Bay 348 C14
POLYGON
cr. Earlwood 372 K16
POMADERRIS
cct. Mt Annan 509 F6
POMARA
gr. Narellan Vale 508 G2
POMEGRANATE
pl. Glenwood 215 F13

POMEROY
st. Homebush 341 C6
st. N Strathfield 341 C6
POMO
cl. Greenfld Pk 334 A16
POMONA
st. Greenacre 370 H12
st. Pennant Hills 220 K15
POMROY
av. Earlwood 373 B16
PONDAGE
lk. Homebush B 310 D15
PONDEROSA
pde. Warriewood 198 G5
pl. Lugarno 430 A12
PONDS
rd. Prospect 275 A15
wy. Airds 511 J16
PONSFORD
av. Rouse Hill 184 K5
PONSONBY
pde. Seaforth 287 A10
PONTIAC
pl. Ingleburn 453 J7
PONTO
pl. Kings Lngly 245 J8
PONTVILLE
cl. West Hoxton 392 D8
PONYARA
rd. Beverly Hills 401 C13
PONYTAIL
dr. Stanhpe Gdn 215 B10
POOH
la. Glenbrook 233 H15
la. Fairfield W 335 C11
POOLE
cl. Kellyville 216 B4
st. Kingsgrove 402 B8
st. Longueville 314 E10
st. Wrrngtn Cty 238 J6
st. West Hoxton 392 C12
POOLEY
st. Ryde 282 G15
POOLMAN
st. Abbotsford 342 H1
POPE
pl. Campbelltown 512 B2
pl. Fairfield W 334 K11
rd. Mount Druitt 241 A15
st. Ryde 312 A1
POPIO
wy. Woodcroft 243 H11
POPLAR
av. Sans Souci 463 B2
cr. Bradbury 511 C13
ct. Castle Hill 218 E16
la. Narraweena 258 C7
pl. Kirrawee 490 K1
pl. Lugarno 429 J14
pl. Picton 561 B3
pl. Westleigh 220 G9
st. N St Marys 240 B11
st. Surry Hills ....F G5
st. Surry Hills 4 A11
wy. Acacia Gdn 214 K14
POPONDETTA
pl. Glenfield 424 H12
rd. Bidwill 211 C16
rd. Blackett 211 C16
rd. Dharruk 241 A6
rd. Emerton 240 H8
rd. Whalan 240 H8
POPOV
av. Newington 310 B13
POPPERWELL
dr. Menai 458 H11
POPPLE
cl. Casula 394 C15
POPPLEWELL
pl. S Coogee 407 F7
POPPY
st. Clarrnt Ms 238 J16
st. Greystanes 306 A12
st. Macquarie Fd 454 B6
PORLOCK
wy. Canley Vale 366 E5
PORPOISE
cr. Bligh Park 150 H7
pl. Willmot 210 C13
PORRENDE
st. Narellan 478 C6
PORST
pl. Guildford 338 B3

PORT
dr. Kings Lngly 245 D5
rd. Wentwthvle 277 D11
PORTADOWN
rd. Glenbrook, off
  Great Western
  Hwy 234 E15
st. Kellyville Rdg 214 J1
PORTEOUS
st. Edensor Pk 363 H3
PORTER
av. Marrickville 373 H9
pl. Blackett 241 B3
rd. Engadine 489 A16
st. Bondi Jctn 22 K10
st. Bondi Jctn 377 F5
st. Minto 453 C14
st. Ryde 311 H5
PORT ERRINGHI
rd. Ebenezer 68 E8
PORTERS
la. St Ives 224 A13
rd. Kenthurst 158 A10
PORT HACKING
rd. Miranda 492 C1
rd. Sylvania 462 B10
rd.s. Caringbah 492 H16
rd.s. Dolans Bay 522 H1
rd.s. Port Hacking 522 H1
PORTIA
cl. Rsemeadow 541 A4
rd. Toongabbie 275 K8
PORTICO
pde. Toongabbie 276 B5
PORTLAND
cl. Illawong 459 F6
cr. Maroubra 407 D14
pl. Kellyville Rdg 215 A6
st. Croydon Pk 371 G7
st. Dover Ht 348 F11
st. Enfield 371 G7
st. Waterloo 19 H12
PORTLAND HEAD
rd. Ebenezer 68 F6
PORT MACQUARIE
rd. Hoxton Park 392 H9
PORTMADOC
dr. Menai 459 A10
PORTMAN
la. Zetland, off
  Merton St 375 H10
st. Zetland 375 H10
PORTSEA
pl. Castle Hill 217 J7
PORTSMOUTH
st. Cronulla 493 J16
PORTVIEW
rd. Burraneer 523 E3
rd. Greenwich 315 B7
POSSUM
cl. Mooney Mooney ..75 C2
wy. Parklea, off
  Candlenut Gr 215 B13
POST HARVEST
rd. Richmond 118 F10
POST OFFICE
la. Chatswood, off
  Victor St 284 J10
la. Croydon, off
  Paisley Rd 372 D1
la. Kogarah 433 B5
la. Merrylands 307 H13
la. Mosman, off
  Upper Almora St .317 B7
la. Pymble 253 C2
rd. Castlereagh 176 A4
rd. Ebenezer 68 B12
rd. Glenorie 128 B8
st. Carlingford 279 H3
st. Pymble 253 C2
POTOROO
st. St Helens Park ...511 H16
POTTER
av. Earlwood 372 F16
cl. Wetherill Pk 303 H16
st. Old Tngabbie ...276 J9
st. Quakers Hill 214 F12
st. Russell Lea 343 D7
st. Waterloo 20 A13
st. Waterloo 376 A7
POTTERY
cct. Woodcroft 243 E9
la. Richmond 119 A5

POTTINGER
st. Dawes Point 1 F8
POTTS
st. Beverly Hills 401 E9
st. Hobartville 118 D9
st. Homebush 340 K7
st. Kingsgrove 401 E9
st. Ryde 312 E5
POULET
st. Matraville 406 J16
POULTER
av. Engadine 488 G13
POULTON
av. Beverley Pk 432 K10
pde. Frenchs Frst 257 A2
POULTRY
pl. Richmond 118 H13
POUND
av. Frenchs Frst 255 F2
cl. Hamondvle 396 G16
la. Ashfield, off
  Frederick St 372 G1
rd. Hornsby 221 G2
POWDER WORKS
rd. Elanora Ht 198 D12
rd. Ingleside 197 J7
rd. N Narrabeen ...198 H14
POWDRILL
rd. Prestons 394 B9
POWELL
cl. Edensor Pk 333 H15
cl. Liberty Gr 311 B11
la. Coogee, off
  Melody St 377 E16
pl. Cherrybrook 219 F13
rd. Rose Bay 347 G11
rt. Westleigh 220 H5
st. Blaxland 233 G12
st. Coogee 377 E16
st. Glenbrook 233 G12
st. Hobartville 118 E6
st. Homebush 341 C8
st. Killara 253 K11
st. Neutral Bay 6 H6
st. Waterloo 19 G16
st. Yagoona 369 E9
POWELLS
la. Brookvale 258 B11
la. Richmond Lwld..88 F9
rd. Bilpin 60 F11
rd. Brookvale 258 B12
POWER
av. Alexandria ..19 A15
cl. Eagle Vale ..481 A10
pl. Kings Lngly ..245 G6
pl. Menai 458 F12
pl. Doonside 243 B10
st. Glendenning ...242 G9
st. Plumpton 242 C8
st. Prairiewood ...334 H7
st. St Marys 239 G10
POWERS
pl. Bass Hill 368 C13
rd. Seven Hills ..276 E2
POWHATAN
st. Greenfld Pk .334 A13
POWIE
cl. Clarrnt Ms ..268 J3
POWYS
av. Bardwell Pk ..402 K6
cct. Castle Hill ..217 C9
cl. S Penrith 267 C7
POZIERES
av. Matraville ..407 A16
av. Milperra ...397 D11
pde. Allambie Ht ..257 J14
st. Woolooware ..493 J7
PRAHA
pl. Kellyville ..215 K3
PRAHRAN
av. Davidson ..255 D2
av. Frenchs Frst ..255 G4
dr. Engadine ..518 C9
PRAIRIE
gln. Clarrnt Ms ..268 C15
PRAIRIE VALE
rd. Bankstown ..369 H15
rd. Bossley Park ..333 E12
rd. Mt Lewis 369 H15
rd. Prairiewood ..334 B11
PRAIRIEVEALE
rd. S Hurstville ..432 B12

PRATIA
ct. Voyager Pt 427 D5
pl. Glenmore Pk 265 G12
PRATO
ct. Glenwood 245 K5
PRATTEN
av. Ryde 282 C16
la. Punchbowl 399 J5
st. Kemps Ck 360 K4
PRECISION
pl. Vineyard 152 A4
PREDDYS
rd. Bexley 402 E13
rd. Bexley North 402 E13
PRELI
pl. Quakers Hill 214 C11
PRELL
st. Airds 512 B10
PREMIER
la. Darlinghurst 4 F8
la. Rooty Hill 272 C1
st. Canley Vale ...366 D3
st. Gymea 491 E7
st. Gymea 491 F3
st. Kogarah 433 C4
st. Marrickville ...373 H16
st. Neutral Bay ...6 D4
st. Toongabbie ...276 C5
PRENTICE
la. Strathfield ...371 A3
la. Willoughby ..285 F15
st. Bnkstn Aprt ..398 A1
PRENTIS
la. Ebenezer 68 D10
PRESCOT
pde. Milperra ..397 D12
PRESCOTT
av. Cromer 258 E3
av. Dee Why ...258 E3
av. Narraweena ..258 E3
cct. Quakers Hill ..214 C13
PRESIDENT
av. Caringbah ..492 D7
av. Gymea 491 B5
av. Kirrawee ..491 B5
av. Kogarah ...433 D2
av. Miranda ..491 H6
av. Monterey ..433 D4
av. Sutherland ..490 F4
rd. Kellyville ..216 G6
st. Croydon Pk ..371 K7
PRESLAND
av. Revesby ..398 F13
PRESTIGE
av. Bella Vista ..246 D6
av. Roselands ..401 C4
PRESTON
av. Bellevue Hills ..14 G7
av. Double Bay ..14 G7
av. Engadine ..518 E3
av. Five Dock ...342 J7
la. Engadine ..518 J3
pl. Roseville ..284 G1
rd. Old Tngabbie ..276 J10
st. Jamisontown ..236 D14
wy. Claymore ..481 D15
PRESTWICK
av. Rouse Hill ..185 A10
tce. Glenmore Pk ..266 G8
PRETORIA
av. Mosman ..317 F9
pde. Hornsby ..221 A1
rd. Seven Hills ..275 H5
st. Lilyfield ..10 D9
PRIAM
st. Chester Hill ..338 C16
PRICE
av. Belmore ..401 G6
la. Agnes Banks ..117 B12
la. Bankstown ..369 F12
la. Riverwood ..400 B7
la. Merrylands ..307 C13
st. Ryde 282 A15
st. S Penrith ..266 F5
st. Wetherill Pk ..334 G6
PRICES
cct. Woronora ..459 K16
rd. Douglas Park ..568 H7
PRIDDIS
st. Warwck Frm ..365 J16
st. Westmead ..307 G11
wy. Bonnyrigg ..364 B4

122 GREGORY'S STREET DIRECTORY

STREETS

QU

PRIEST
pl. Barden Rdg.....458 K16
PRIESTLEY
cl. St Ives.....224 B14
PRIMA
pl. Arndell Park.....273 C7
PRIME
dr. Seven Hills.....276 D1
PRIMROSE
av. Frenchs Frst.....256 G6
av. Rosebery.....375 H16
av. Rydalmere.....309 K5
av. Ryde.....311 J2
av. Sandringham.....463 E3
cct. Clarmnt Ms.....268 G1
pl. Loftus.....490 B7
pl. Windsor.....121 A8
PRIMULA
st. Lindfield.....283 J2
PRINCE
la. Mosman, off
Union St.....317 B11
la. Randwick, off
Prince St.....376 K10
rd. Killara.....253 J15
rd. Blacktown.....244 A15
st. Canley Ht.....365 G1
st. Canley Vale.....365 G1
st. Cronulla.....494 B16
st. Glenbrook.....233 G15
st. Granville.....308 F9
st. Mosman.....316 H6
st. Mosman.....316 H7
st. Newtown.....374 G9
st. N Parramatta.....278 D11
st. Oatlands.....279 A12
st. Picnic Point.....428 G7
st. Picton.....563 F8
st. Randwick.....376 K12
st. Rozelle.....11 A1
st. Springwood.....202 A1
st. Wrrngtn Cty.....238 F19
PRINCE ALBERT
rd. Sydney.....D G6
st. Sydney.....4 A4
st. Mosman.....317 B12
PRINCE ALFRED
pde. Newport.....169 C7
PRINCE CHARLES
pde. Kurnell.....465 E7
rd. Belrose.....226 C16
rd. Frenchs Frst.....256 A2
PRINCE EDWARD
av. Earlwood.....372 J16
av. Earlwood.....373 A16
cir. Daceyville.....406 F6
cir. Pagewood.....406 F6
pde. Hunters Hill.....314 C13
rd. Seaforth.....287 A5
st. Carlton.....432 J8
st. Gladesville.....313 A12
st. Malabar.....437 D3
PRINCE EDWARD PARK
rd. Woronora.....460 A16
PRINCE GEORGE
pde. Hunters Hill.....314 C13
PRINCE HENRY
av. Little Bay.....437 G15
PRINCE OF WALES
dr. Matraville.....436 B13
dr. Phillip Bay.....436 B13
dr. Port Botany.....436 B13
dr. West Pymble.....253 A11
PRINCES
av. Vaucluse.....348 G2
hwy.Arncliffe.....403 D14
hwy.Banksia.....403 D14
hwy.Beverley Pk.....433 A8
hwy.Blakehurst.....432 E15
hwy.Carlton.....432 H11
hwy.Carss Park.....432 E15
hwy.Engadine.....489 C16
hwy.Engadine.....518 D15
hwy.Gymea.....491 B3
hwy.Heathcote.....518 D15
hwy.Kirrawee.....490 J3
hwy.Kirrawee.....491 B3
hwy.Kogarah.....433 C6
hwy.Kogarah Bay.....432 H11
hwy.Rockdale.....403 D16
hwy.Rockdale.....433 B5
hwy.St Peters.....374 E16
hwy.Sutherland.....490 C9
hwy.Sydenham.....374 E16
hwy.Sylvania.....461 F16
hwy.Tempe.....374 E16

hwy.Waterfall.....519 D11
hwy.Wolli Creek.....403 K6
hwy.Yarrawarrah.....489 C16
la. Kogarah.....433 B6
la. Newport.....169 E11
pl. McMahons Pt.....5 D13
strm.Seaforth.....286 K11
rd. Schofields.....183 B14
rd.e,Auburn.....339 A14
rd.e,Regents Pk.....339 A14
rd.w,Auburn.....338 G14
st. Bexley.....402 K10
st. Burwood.....342 C12
st. Guildford W.....336 J3
st. Hunters Hill.....313 B5
st. McMahons Pt.....5 D13
st. Marrickville.....373 E15
st. Mortdale.....431 D9
st. Newport.....169 E11
st. Penshurst.....431 F8
st. Putney.....311 J6
st. Riverstone.....153 A14
st. Ryde.....312 A4
st. Turramurra.....223 D11
PRINCESS
av. Kellyville.....217 C4
av. N Strathfield.....341 F8
av. Rodd Point.....343 E8
av. Rosebery.....375 G13
la. N Strathfield, off
Queens La.....341 F8
la. Carlton.....432 K5
st. Ashbury.....372 G10
st. Btn-le-Sds.....433 K2
st. Canley Vale.....366 D3
st. Canterbury.....372 G10
st. Hurlstone Pk.....372 G10
st. Lidcombe.....340 B6
st. Rose Bay.....348 E10
st. Werrington.....238 K10
PRINCESS MARY
st. Beacon Hill.....257 K5
st. St Marys.....269 F1
PRINCETON
av. Oatlands.....279 B8
PRINCE WILLIAM
dr. Seven Hills.....276 F3
PRINDLE
st. Oatlands.....279 A10
PRING
st. Woolmloo.....4 H4
PRINGLE
av. Bankstown.....399 A4
av. Belrose.....225 K13
av. Frenchs Frst.....256 A2
dr. Woollahra, off
Old South
Head Rd.....377 G2
rd. Hebersham.....241 G10
rd. Plumpton.....241 G10
PRION
st. Hinchinbrk.....393 C2
PRIOR
av. Cremorne.....6 K7
cl. Illawong.....459 K13
st. Winston Hills.....246 G16
PRIORY
cl. Cherrybrook.....219 F14
cl. St Ives Ch.....224 B2
rd. Baulkham Hl.....247 A12
pde. Cmbrdg Gdn.....237 J2
rd. Waverton.....5 C5
PRISCILLA
pl. Baulkham Hl.....247 D3
pl. Quakers Hill.....213 J7
PRITCHARD
av. Hamondvle.....396 E15
la. Annandale.....10 K8
pl. Glenmore Pk.....265 K9
pl. Peakhurst.....430 F4
rd. Mcquarie Fd.....453 K3
st. Annandale.....10 K8
st. Auburn.....339 B3
st. Marrickville.....16 H16
st. Mt Pritchard.....364 G8
st. Thornleigh.....220 H23
st.e,Wentwthvle.....277 A16
st.w,Wentwthvle.....276 K16
PRIVATE
rd. Northwood.....314 H8
PRIVET
wy. Blacktown.....274 E12
PROBATE
st. Narembrn.....315 G2
PROBERT
la. Camperdown.....17 D8
st. Camperdown.....17 D8
st. Newtown.....17 D8

PROCTER
cl. Abbotsbury.....333 A14
PROCTOR
av. Kingsgrove.....402 A5
pde. Chester Hill.....368 B3
pde. Sefton.....368 E3
pl. Berowra.....163 D2
wy. Claymore.....481 D11
PROCYON
pl. Cranebrook.....207 G5
PRODUCTION
av. Kogarah.....433 D11
av. Warragamba.....353 E10
pl. Jamisontown.....266 D1
rd. Taren Point.....462 K14
PROGRESS
av. Eastwood.....281 A8
cct. Prestons.....393 J11
pl. Cranebrook, off
Pendock La.....207 F14
rd. Eveleigh.....18 E12
st. Tahmoor.....566 A12
wy. Cranebrook.....207 F14
PROSPECT
av. Cremorne.....316 G6
av. Canley Vale.....366 D2
hwy.Prospect.....275 A13
hwy.Seven Hills.....245 H16
hwy.Seven Hills.....275 G2
la. Carlton.....432 K5
pl. Como.....460 F4
pl. Canley Vale.....366 D3
pl. Peakhurst.....430 G2
pl. Summer Hill.....373 A4
pl. Blacktown.....274 C4
pl. Campbelltown.....511 A8
pl. Carlton.....432 K5
st. Erskineville.....18 K15
st. Greenwich.....314 K14
st. Leichhardt.....16 B1
st. Newtown.....17 H9
st. Paddington.....4 J15
st. Rosehill.....308 G7
st. Surry Hills.....20 D2
st. Waverley.....377 A15
PROSPER
la. Rozelle.....7 A15
pl. Condell Park.....398 F6
st. Rozelle.....7 A15
PROSPERITY
pde. Warriewood.....198 H6
PROSPERO
la. Rsemeadow.....540 K5
PROSS
st. Ambarvale.....540 G1
PROSSER
av. Padstow.....429 F7
PROTEA
pl. Cherrybrook.....219 C7
PROTEUS
pl. Kellyville.....216 G3
PROTHERO
pl. Pagewood.....406 D8
PROUT
la. West Hoxton, off
Harraden Dr.....391 J17
pl. Quakers Hill.....214 E11
st. Cabramatta.....366 B9
st. West Hoxton.....391 K10
wy. Claymore.....481 A11
PROVIDENCE
dr. Bella Vista.....246 F6
la. Darlinghurst.....F K7
pl. Darlinghurst.....F K7
st. Ryde.....312 D3
PROVINCE
st. Abbotsbury.....333 D11
PROVINCIAL
rd. Lindfield.....254 A16
rd. Auburn.....339 B5
PROVINS
la. Cranebrook, off
Milligan Rd.....207 C14
wy. Cranebrook.....207 C13
PROVOST
mw.Holsworthy.....426 F3
PROYART
av. Milperra.....397 G2
PRUNE
st. Wentwthvle.....277 B8
PRUNELLA
pl. Faulcnbdg.....171 E15
PRUNUS
cl. Glenmore Pk.....265 G11

PRYCE
cl. Kellyville.....186 K16
pl. Rooty Hill.....272 C6
PRYOR
st. Rydalmere.....279 D15
st. Springwood.....202 D3
PUEBLO
st. Greenfld Pk.....333 K13
PUGH
av. Pemulwuy.....305 F7
PUKARA
pl. Cromer.....258 C1
PULBROOK
pde. Hornsby.....192 A15
PULHAM
pl. Chipping Ntn.....366 F14
PULLMAN
pl. Emu Plains.....235 C7
PULPIT
la. Mosman.....286 J16
st. Tahmoor.....566 A12
PUNCH
la. Mosman.....317 B5
pl. Glenbrook.....264 E11
st. Artarmon.....315 B1
st. Balmain.....7 C5
st. Mosman.....317 B5
PUNCHBOWL
rd. Belfield.....371 B10
rd. Belmore.....371 B11
rd. Lakemba.....370 H15
rd. Punchbowl.....400 C3
rd. Wiley Park.....400 C3
PUNCTATA
cl. Voyager Pt.....427 B5
PUNICEA
wy. Mcquarie Fd.....454 H14
PUNKA
pl. Glenmore Pk.....266 D7
PUNT
rd. Emu Plains.....236 B7
rd. Gladesville.....312 J13
rd. Pitt Town.....92 G8
PUP
rd. Bilpin.....61 J6
PURCELL
cr. Lalor Park.....245 E13
rd. Londonderry.....148 H12
st. Eldersle.....477 F16
PURCHASE
rd. Cherrybrook.....219 D9
st. Parramatta.....308 G4
PURDIE
la. Pendle Hill.....276 E14
PURDY
st. Minchinbury.....271 C5
PURKIS
st. Camperdown.....17 E2
PURLEY
cl. Bonnyrigg Ht.....363 A7
cl. Cronulla.....493 K12
PURRI
av. Baulkham Hl.....246 E10
PURSELL
av. Mosman.....287 B16
PURSER
av. Castle Hill.....217 K15
PURTON
st. Stanhpe Gdn.....215 D6
PURVES
st. Glebe.....12 A14
PURVINES
rd. Yellow Rock.....204 A3
PUSAN
pl. Belrose.....226 A15
PUTARRI
av. St Ives.....223 J14
PUTLAND
cl. Kirrawee.....490 K8
pl. Vineyard.....153 A8
st. Clarmnt Ms.....269 A1
st. St Marys.....269 E1
PUTNEY
pde. Putney.....312 C10
PUTTY
rd. E Kurrajong.....66 K4
rd. E Kurrajong.....67 A3
rd. Wilberforce.....67 D12
rd. Wilberforce.....91 J2
PYALLA
st. Northbridge.....285 H16

PYE
av. Northmead.....278 C6
rd. Acacia Gdn.....214 F15
rd. Bringelly.....386 K10
rd. Quakers Hill.....214 A15
st. Westmead.....307 G2
PYES
rd. Dural.....219 F2
PYKETT
pl. Dural.....219 A5
PYLARA
pl. Busby.....363 H15
PYMBLE
av. Pymble.....253 A6
av. Winmalee.....173 F5
st. Dharruk.....241 C7
PYRAMID
av. Padstow.....399 C14
st. Emu Plains.....235 B9
PYRAMUS
cct. Rsemeadow.....540 H9
pl. St Clair.....270 D16
PYREE
st. Bangor.....459 D14
PYRENEES
wy. Beaumont Hills.....185 J13
PYRITE
pl. Eagle Vale.....481 H5
PYRL
rd. Artarmon.....285 B15
PYRMONT
st. Ashfield.....372 J5
st. Pyrmont.....12 G2
st. Sydney.....3 A8
st. Ultimo.....3 A8
PYRMONT BRIDGE
rd. Annandale.....17 C3
rd. Camperdown.....17 C3
rd. Pyrmont.....12 F7

Q

QANTAS
dr. Mascot.....405 A4
QUAAMA
cl. Prestons.....393 B16
QUADRANT
cl. Pymble.....252 J4
la. Sadleir.....364 B16
QUAIL
pl. Hinchinbrk.....393 C2
pl. Ingleburn.....453 D8
pl. Woronora Ht.....489 C6
rd. Blacktown.....274 B9
st. Coogee.....377 H13
st. Cranebrook.....207 C16
QUAKERS
rd. Marayong.....243 C13
rd. Marayong.....243 K4
rd. Mosman.....316 K1
rd. Mosman.....317 A1
rd. Quakers Hill.....243 C3
QUAKERS HILL
pky. Acacia Gdn.....214 F14
pky. Quakers Hill.....213 H12
pky. Quakers Hill.....243 C3
QUALLEE
pl. Engadine.....488 G16
QUAMBI
pl. Edgecliff.....14 B13
QUAMBY
cct. Wattle Grove.....425 J6
QUANDONG
av. Burwood.....371 J2
st. Concord W.....341 G1
st. Concord W.....341 F1
QUARRION
pl. Woronora Ht.....489 D4
QUARRY
ct. Yagoona.....369 B8
la. Dural.....189 F14
Quarry St.....12 B9
la. Ultimo.....12 J10
rd. Bossley Park.....333 F6
rd. Dundas Vy.....280 K13
rd. Dural.....189 C14
rd. Greystanes.....275 F16
rd. Hornsby.....191 E16
rd. Prospect.....275 F16
rd. Ryde.....281 K5
rd. The Oaks.....501 K11
st. Glebe.....12 K11

GREGORY'S STREET DIRECTORY 123

QU — STREETS

Type	Name	Suburb	Ref
st.	Naremburn		315 J3
st.	Paddington		13 K16
st.	Tempe		404 A3
st.	Ultimo		12 H10
st.	Woollahra		13 J16

QUARRY MASTER
dr. Pyrmont 12 D3

QUARTER
row. Mooney Mooney, off Chapel La.........75 D2

QUARTER MASTER
row. Mcquarie Lk..........423 F13

QUARTERS
pl. Currans Hill............480 A11

QUARTER SESSIONS
- rd. Appin 569 C16
- rd. Church Point.........168 E7
- rd. Glenfield 423 G9
- rd. Westleigh 220 G10

QUARTZ
pl. Eagle Vale 481 G8

QUAY
- st. Haymarket ....E B8
- st. Haymarket 3 D13

QUEANBEYAN
av. Miranda 462 A15

QUEBEC
- av. Killara 283 E1
- rd. Chatswood W......283 J9
- st. Toongabbie.........275 F12

QUEEN
- la. St Marys, off Queen St........239 H15
- rd. Paddington 21 E1
- st. Arncliffe 403 G8
- st. Ashfield 372 J10
- st. Auburn 339 C2
- st. Auburn 339 E4
- st. Beaconsfield 375 F13
- st. Botany 405 J12
- st. Burwood 342 D13
- st. Campbelltown.....511 F3
- st. Campbelltown.....511 E4
- st. Canley Ht 365 G1
- st. Canley Vale 365 G1
- st. Chippendale..........19 B3
- st. Concord W..........341 D1
- st. Croydon 342 D13
- st. Croydon Pk..........371 F6
- st. Glebe 12 G14
- st. Granville 308 E12
- st. Guildford W 336 H3
- st. Hurlstone Pk........372 J10
- st. Kurrajong Ht.........63 G13
- st. Marrickville 374 A14
- st. Mosman 317 B10
- st. Narellan 478 F10
- st. Newtown 18 C8
- st. N Strathfield 341 E6
- st. Petersham 15 J5
- st. Randwick 377 D15
- st. Revesby...............398 F14
- st. Riverstone 182 D13
- st. Rosebery 375 G14
- st. St Marys 239 G16
- st. Woollahra 21 G4

QUEEN ELIZABETH
dr. Bondi Beach..........378 D3

QUEENS
- av. Avalon 140 A13
- av. Kogarah 433 B6
- av. McMahons Pt 5 C13
- av. Mt Wilson 58 H9
- av. Parramatta 308 E2
- av. Rcuttrs Bay 13 B8
- av. Vaucluse 348 A6
- ct. Castle Hill 217 B8
- la. Beaconsfield, off William St.....375 F13
- la. Mortdale 431 D7
- la. N Strathfield, off Princess Av ...341 F8
- pde. Newport.............169 K12
- pde.e,Newport..........169 H12
- pl. Balmain..................7 K9
- rd. Asquith 192 B9
- rd. Btn-le-Sds..........433 J8
- rd. Canada Bay 342 E10
- rd. Connells Pt 431 F16
- rd. Five Dock 342 E10
- rd. Hurstville 432 A4
- rd. Westmead 277 H15
- sq. Sydney 3 K3
- st. Sydney ....A K10

QUEENSBOROUGH
rd. Croydon Pk..........372 C7

QUEENSBURY
- av. Kellyville............216 J4
- rd. Padstow Ht.........429 H7
- rd. Penshurst 431 A2

QUEENSCLIFF
- dr. Woodbine 481 H10
- rd. Queenscliff 288 E3

QUEENS HILL
dr. Luddenham........326 C7

QUEENS PARK
rd. Queens Park 22 E13

QUEENSWAY
Blacktown........274 H4

QUEEN VICTORIA
- st. Bexley...................402 J16
- st. Drummoyne.........344 A2
- st. Kogarah 433 A2

QUENDA
pl. St Helens Park....541 G1

QUENTIN
- pl. Oatlands 279 B9
- st. Bass Hill 368 B11

QUEST
- av. Carramar 366 J4
- av. Miranda 491 K8
- av. Yowie Bay..........491 K8
- la. Belmore, off Dean Av 371 E15
- st. Naremburn 315 F2
- st. Greystanes 305 J6

QUIBEREE
st. Miranda 462 B16

QUIG
pl. Narellan Vale 508 G1

QUIGG
- la. Lakemba............401 C4
- pl. Orchard Hills 267 F3
- st. Lakemba............371 A16
- st. Lakemba............401 B1

QUILP
av. Ambarvale..........510 K11

QUILPIE
st. North Manly 258 C13

QUINDALUP
pl. Bella Vista 246 H2

QUINE
la. Punchbowl..........400 C3

QUINION
av. Ambarvale..........510 J16

QUINLAN
pde. Manly Vale........287 H2

QUINN
- av. Seven Hills 245 H15
- av. Prairiewood 334 E11
- st. Castlereagh........176 G9
- st. S Wntwthvle 306 K4

QUINTANA
av. Baulkham Hl 246 J13

QUINTON
la. Manly, off Birkley Rd 288 E7
st. Manly 288 F8

QUIRK
- rd. Balgowlah..........288 A6
- rd. Manly Vale........288 B4
- st. Dee Why............258 G8
- st. Rozelle.................11 A1

QUIROS
av. Fairfield W..........335 D9

QUIST
av. Lurnea 394 C9

QUOKKA
pl. St Helens Park....541 D2

QUOTA
- av. Chipping Ntn......396 A5
- pl. Edensor Pk 333 J15

R

RABAT
cl. Cranebrook........207 G6

RABAUL
- av. Whalan 240 J10
- cl. Bossley Park 333 J6
- rd. Bnkstn Aprt.......367 D16
- rd. Georges Hall 367 D16
- rd. N Curl Curl........258 K10
- wy. Matraville..........407 B16

RABBETT
st. Frenchs Frst........256 E5

RABETT
cr. Horngsea Pk 392 F13

RABY
- la. Randwick 377 F10
- rd. Catherine Fd......450 E5
- rd. Leppington..........450 E5
- rd. Raby...................481 E1
- rd. St Andrews 481 E1
- rd. Varroville 450 G10

RACECOURSE
- av. Menangle Pk......538 K6
- av. Menangle Pk......539 A7
- pl. Eastlakes...........406 A2
- pl. S Penrith 236 J14
- rd. Clarendon 119 J4
- rd. S Penrith 236 H16

RACEMOSA
cl. Kemps Ck 360 B9

RACHAEL
- cl. Silverwater........310 A11
- pl. Glenwood 215 B16
- pl. Glenwood 245 B1

RACHEL
- av. W Pnnant Hl......249 E8
- cr. Mt Pritchard 364 G11
- cl. Minto.................482 K6
- la. Belmore, off Rachel St 371 E15

RACO
cl. Edensor Pk 333 J14

RADALJ
cl. Rooty Hill 271 K2

RADBURN
rd. Hebersham 241 E4

RADCLIFFE
- pl. Kellyville 216 H4
- st. Ingleburn 453 A11

RADFORD
- av. Bondi Jctn.........377 F5
- pl. Castle Hill 218 C10
- pl. Gordon 253 G7
- pl. Oakhurst 242 B2

RADIATA
av. Baulkham Hl 247 F14

RADIO
av. Balgowlah Ht......287 H13

RADISSON
pl. Kellyville 185 E8

RADLEY
- pl. Cherrybrook......219 E16
- rd. Seven Hills 245 B15

RADNOR
- pl. Campbelltown....511 H9
- pl. Smithfield 335 D1
- rd. S Turramrra 252 C8
- st. Bargo................567 D4
- st. Galston 160 E5

RAE
- av. Moorebank 396 D12
- la. Randwick 377 C12
- pl. Currans Hill 479 J11
- pl. Woolmloo...........4 H6
- st. Randwick 377 C13
- st. Seven Hills 245 D15

RAEBURN
av. Castlecrag.........285 K11

RAEMOT
la. Baulkham Hl 247 J11

RAFFERTY
wy. Quakers Hill 213 K14

RAFFO
la. Harbord 258 E15

RAFTER
cr. Abbotsbury 363 A1

RAFTREE
st. Padstow Ht.........429 J7

RAGLAN
- av. Ingleburn 453 A9
- la. Waterloo..............19 F12
- pde. Castle Hill.......216 J9
- rd. Auburn 339 A13
- rd. Miranda 491 H7
- st. Darlington...........18 G7
- st. Drummoyne........313 J10
- st. Malabar 437 E5
- st. Manly 288 F8
- st. Mosman 316 J13
- st. Mosman 317 C8
- st. Turramurra 223 D12
- st. Waterloo..............19 C11

RAHT
pl. Doonside 273 H3

RAIDELL
pl. N Epping 251 F10

RAIL
pl. Chipping Ntn.....396 C6

RAILSIDE
av. Bargo................567 E4

RAILWAY
- av. Eastwood 281 B6
- av. Lavender Bay.......K E16
- av. Seven Hills 276 A3
- cr. Stanmore 16 G9
- cr. Strathfield 341 H12
- cr. Wahroonga 222 D7
- cr. Burwood 341 J13
- la. St Clair, off Dobell Cct 270 C14
- pde. Peakhurst 430 C12
- pl. Kareela 461 E11
- pl. St Clair 270 C14
- st. Coogee 407 F2
- st. Kingsford 406 H2
- st. Randwick 406 H2
- st. Randwick 407 C3
- st. S Coogee 407 F2
- st. S Wntwthvle 307 D6

RAINE
- av. Liverpool..........394 H8
- av. North Rocks 248 G11
- la. St Clair, off
- pl. Barden Rdg.......458 H16
- pl. Padstow 399 A15
- pde. Douglas Park..568 F6
- pde. Eastwood 281 B7
- st. Woollahra 377 G2

RAINFORD
st. Surry Hills 20 B3

RAINHAM
cct. West Hoxton 391 K11

RAIN RIDGE
rd. Kurrajong Ht......63 D12

RAJ
pl. Mount Druitt 241 H13

RAJOLA
pl. North Rocks 248 F13

RALEIGH
- av. Caringbah 493 A3
- cl. St Clair 270 J12
- ct. St Ives Ch 224 A7
- pl. Bonnyrigg Ht...363 A6
- rd. Milperra 397 D12
- st. Artarmon 284 J13
- st. Blakehurst........462 E2
- st. Cammeray 315 K5
- st. Coogee 377 E13
- st. Dover Ht 348 F13
- st. Guildford..........337 J2

RALFE
st. Tahmoor 565 K14

RALPH
- pl. Mount Druitt 241 F15
- st. Alexandria 375 F16
- st. Cabramatta 366 D7
- st. Sydenham 374 D15
- st. Westmead 307 G3

RALSTON
- av. Belrose 225 H11
- pl. Palm Beach 139 J3
- rd. Palm Beach 139 K3
- st. Lane Cove N....284 F15

RAMBLER
pl. Ingleburn 453 K9

RAMEAU
wy. Clarmnt Ms......268 G4

RAMILLIES
wy. Beaumont Hills...185 K15

RAMLEH
st. Hunters Hill 313 D5

RAMONA
- pl. Hurlstone Pk......373 A13
- st. Kogarah 433 A5

RAMOSUS
st. Quakers Hill 213 J13

RAMSAY
- av. Bidwill.............211 F13
- av. West Pymble....252 F7
- cl. Narellan Vale....479 C10
- cl. Five Dock 342 K10
- cl. Kemps Ck 359 D16
- pde. Panania 428 D7
- pd. Picnic Point....428 D7
- rd. Five Dock 343 A12
- rd. Haberfield 343 B13
- st. Picton 563 G1
- wy. Claymore 481 E12

RAMSEY
st. Kings Lngly.....245 H7

124 GREGORY'S STREET DIRECTORY

STREETS   RE

RAMSGATE
av. Bondi Beach......378 E1
av. North Bondi......378 G3
rd. Kogarah Bay......433 A13
rd. Ramsgate............433 D13
rd. Ramsgate Bch.....433 D13
rd. Sans Souci.........433 A13
st. Botany................405 G12

RAMU
cl. Sylvania Wtr.......462 D15
pl. Whalan...............240 J10

RANCE
rd. Werrington..........239 B13

RANCH
av. Glenbrook..........264 B5

RANCOM
st. Botany................405 H15

RAND
av. Pymble...............253 C5

RANDAL
cr. North Rocks........248 F14

RANDALL
av. Minto..................453 B16
ct. Collaroy Plat.......228 H15
st. Agnes Banks.......117 D12
st. Marrickville........373 G13

RANDELL
av. Lilli Pilli..............522 F2

RANDLE
la. Newtown...............18 B11
la. Surry Hills.............E K16
la. Surry Hills.............19 H1
st. Granville..............308 B11
st. Newtown...............18 B10
st. Surry Hills............19 G1

RANDOLPH
la. Wahroonga, off Billyard Av............222 H7
st. Campbelltown.....511 K5
st. Guildford............338 D7
st. Rosebery............405 H3
st. S Granville.........338 F7
st. Wahroonga.........222 H7

RANDWICK
cl. Casula................394 D15
st. Randwick...........377 B11

RANELAGH
cr. Chatswood........285 C10

RANFURLEY
rd. Bellevue Hill........14 J16

RANGE
pl. Engadine.............488 C14
rd. W Pnnant HI........249 B9
st. Chatswood W.....284 D9

RANGER
rd. Croydon.............342 G14

RANGERS
av. Mosman.............316 G9
la. Cremorne...............6 H2
la. Cremorne...............6 J2
rd. St Helens Park....541 H4
rd. Yagoona.............368 G8

RANGERS RETREAT
rd. Frenchs Frst......256 F8

RANGIHOU
cr. Parramatta..........308 G3

RANI
pl. Kareela...............461 D9

RANIERI
pl. Hoxton Park........392 K8

RANKIN
pl. Doonside...........273 F1

RANLEIGH
cct. Kellyville Rdg...214 K2

RANMORE
rd. St Marys............269 K4

RANNOCH
pl. Thornleigh..........221 C12
st. St Andrews........451 K14

RANSLEY
st. Penrith...............236 E12

RAPER
st. Newtown..............17 H8
st. Surry Hills............20 C4

RAPHAEL
dr. Hornsby Ht.........191 F3
pl. Old Tngabbie......277 A7
st. Greenfld Pk........364 B1
st. Lidcombe............339 K9

RAPLEYS LOOP
rd. Werombi............443 D1
rd. Werombi............443 H3

RASCHKE
st. Cmbrdg Pk........237 G10

RASP
cl. West Hoxton......392 B13

RASPA
pl. Quakers Hill.......213 K10

RATA
pl. Sutherland.........460 C16

RATCLIFFE
st. Ryde..................312 D2

RATHANE
rd. Royal N P..........521 J7

RATHMORE
cct. Glendenning.....242 J3
ct. Kellyville...........216 D2

RATHOWEN
pde. Killarney Ht.....256 B14

RAUPACH
st. Dean Park........212 F16

RAUSCH
st. Toongabbie........276 G6

RAVEL
st. Seven Hills........246 D12

RAVEN
gr. Bidwill...............211 D13
pl. Ingleburn...........453 H6
pl. S Windsor..........150 D3
st. Gladesville........312 G9

RAVENGLASS
pl. Cranebrook.......207 F12

RAVENHILL
rd. Turramurra........252 E6
st. Kings Lngly.......245 B4

RAVENNA
st. Strathfield..........371 A1

RAVENSBOURNE
cct. Dural................219 B4
wy. Dural................219 B4

RAVENSWOOD
av. Gordon..............253 J9
av. Randwick..........377 E11
ri. Bella Vista.........216 C13
st. Canley Vale......366 G4

RAVENSWORTH
pl. Airds.................512 B10

RAVENUE
la. Stanmore............16 H9

RAVINE
av. Blaxland...........233 J6
cl. Cranebrook......207 B11

RAW
av. Bankstown.......369 E14
sq. Strathfield........341 F12

RAWDON
pl. Airds.................512 A15

RAWHITI
st. Roseville..........284 F3

RAWSON
av. Bexley..............432 G3
av. Drummoyne....343 J4
av. Loftus..............490 C8
av. Penrith............236 H14
av. Queens Park.....22 D11
av. Sutherland.......490 C8
cr. Hornsga Pk....392 F15
la. Pymble...........223 D13
la. Haymarket........E F11
la. Haymarket........3 F14
la. Mascot, off Rawson St.......405 E3
la. Mosman.............317 C4
la. Newtown............17 D15
la. Queens Park.....22 D11
la. Sans Souci.......433 B16
pde. Caringbah......493 A13
pl. Cromer..............227 J14
pl. Haymarket..........E F11
pl. Haymarket.........3 F14
rd. Berowra...........133 C14
rd. Fairfield W.......335 F11
rd. Greenacre........369 K9
rd. Guildford..........337 K8
rd. Rose Bay..........348 C8
rd. S Wntwthvle....306 J4
st. Auburn.............309 B15
st. Croydon Pk.....371 H7
st. Epping.............251 A15
st. Haberfield.......343 D14
st. Lidcombe.........340 A7
st. Mascot.............405 E3
st. Mosman............317 B4
st. Neutral Bay........6 K7
st. Newtown...........17 E15
st. Rockdale.........403 B16

st. Sans Souci......433 B16
st. Stanhpe Gdn...215 B6
st. Wiley Park.......400 F4

RAWTON
av. Northmead.......277 H8

RAY
av. Vaucluse.........348 C5
la. Erskineville......18 A13
pl. Kings Lngly....245 C5
pl. Minto...............453 B15
pl. Penrith............237 C5
pl. Woodpark......306 G14
rd. Epping.............251 A13
st. Blakehurst.......462 B4
st. Turramurra.....222 H13
st. Vaucluse.........348 G7

RAYBEN
st. Glendenning....242 H8

RAYFORD
cl. Bossley Park....333 J8

RAYM
rd. Kenthurst........187 C7

RAY MACDONALD
dr. Emu Plains.......235 G5

RAYMENT
av. Kingsgrove......401 J14

RAYMOND
av. Campbelltown..511 K5
av. Drummoyne.....313 F16
av. Matraville........436 E2
av. Menai..............458 K15
av. Northmead......277 J9
av. Roselands.....400 J10
av. Warrawee.......222 H9
la. Springwood.....201 K3
pl. Engadine........518 F5
pl. Epping............251 F15
rd. Bilgola............169 E8
rd. Neutral Bay........6 E4
rd. Neutral Bay........6 F6
rd. Springwood....201 K6
rd. Bankstown......399 F1
rd. Blacktown......245 A7
rd. Eastwood.......281 G3
rd. Freemns Rch....90 E2
rd. Glenbrook......264 A1
rd. Granville........308 D7
rd. Harris Park....308 D7
rd. Oatley............430 H14
rd. Thornleigh.....221 E7
rd. w Cranebrook.207 G13

RAYNER
av. Narraweena...258 D2
pl. Bonnyrigg.......364 A8
rd. Whale Beach..140 E9
st. Lilyfield..........10 A7

RAYNOR
av. Abbotsford....342 K3
av. Baulkham HI..247 D6
st. Mount Druitt..241 C13

RAYWOOD
cl. Glenwood.......245 B2

REA
st. Greenacre......370 E9

REACH
cl. Abbotsbury....333 B15

READ
la. Bronte............377 J7
la. W Pnnant HI..249 F7
st. Blakehurst.....462 C1
st. Bronte............377 J7
st. Eastwood......280 H11
wy. Claymore......481 B11

READFORD
pl. Ryde...............282 B13

READING
av. East Killara...254 F7
av. Kings Lngly..246 B9
rd. Btn-le-Sds.....404 A16
st. Glenbrook.....233 G15

REAGHS FARM
rd. Minto.............482 E7

REALM
st. Arncliffe........403 D7

REARDEN
av. Kings Lngly..245 K9

REARWIN
pl. Bnkstn Aprt...397 K1

REBECCA
ct. Rouse Hill....184 K8
pde. Winston Hills...276 J3
pl. Cherrybrook..219 H4
pl. Ingleburn.......453 D10
st. Greenacre......370 F7
st. Colyton..........270 D8

REBELLION
pl. Mcquarie Lk....423 E13

RECONCILIATION
rd. Pemulwuy.....305 B2
rd. Prospect......304 K10

RECREATION
av. Penrith........236 C8
av. Roseville.....284 J4
dr. Barden Rdg...488 C5
dr. Wollstncraft..315 D11
pl. Busby..........363 H12
av. Ashfield......342 K15

REDAN
la. Mosman.......317 C7
st. Mosman.......317 C7

REDBANK
la. N Richmond.....86 F10
pl. Northmead......277 G9
pl. Picton.............563 B14
rd. Killara............253 K16
rd. Kurrajong.......86 A7
rd. Northmead....277 H11
rd. Northmead....277 G9
rd. N Richmond.....86 A7

REDBUSH
ct. Rouse Hill.....185 C8
gr. Menai.............458 K15

RED CEDAR
dr. Mt Colah.......162 E14
ct. Winmalee......173 G6

REDDALL
st. Campbelltown..511 G5
st. Manly..............288 J11

REDDAN
av. Penrith........237 C13

REDDEN
dr. Kellyville......216 A2
pl. Kellyville......216 C3

REDDINGTON
dr. St Clair.......270 E12

REDDISH
cr. Hebersham....241 E7
wy. Cranebrook...207 G13

REDDY
la. Edgecliff...........13 E10
st. Edgecliff...........13 F10

REDFERN
la. Redfern............19 G8
rd. Bnkstn Aprt....397 K1
st. Gymea..............461 H16
st. Pitt Town.........93 A12
st. Minto...............482 F3
st. Blaxland.........234 B7
st. Granville........338 F1
st. Ingleburn........453 E3
st. Redfern...........19 C8
st. Wetherill Pk...335 A1

REDFIELD
rd. East Killara....254 H7

RED GABLES
pl. Box Hill..........124 C14

REDGRAVE
st. W Pnnant HI..248 K9
st. Normanhurst...221 H12

REDGROVE
av. Beecroft.......250 E10

RED GUM
dr. Bowen Mtn.....83 K7

REDGUM
av. Cronulla........523 J3
av. Killara..........254 D11
cr. Pennant Hills...220 D13
cct. Glendenning..242 J5
dr. Beaumont Hills...186 A16
dr. Lugarno........429 K9
dr. Padstow........429 G2
dr. Frenchs Frst..256 B2

REDHEAP
rd. Faulcnbdg.....172 A5

RED HOUSE
cr. McGraths HI...121 J13

REDIN
pl. Connells Pt...431 H14

REDLEAF
av. Wahroonga...222 D8
cl. Galston..........159 F9

la. Wahroonga, off Redleaf Av.....222 D8

RED LION
st. Rozelle.........344 E8

REDMAN
av. Illawong......459 J7
cl. Belmore........371 E14
pde. Belmore......371 F5
pl. W Pnnant HI..248 K2
rd. Dee Why........258 C6
st. Campsie.........372 B14
st. Canterbury....372 B14
st. Seaforth.......287 B8

REDMAYNE
rd. Horsley Pk....302 G13

REDMILL
cl. Cheltenham....250 J10

REDMOND
av. Baulkham HI..246 K15
st. Leichhardt.....16 C3

REDMYRE
rd. Strathfield....341 G12
rd. Strathfield....341 C14

REDNAL
st. Mona Vale....169 D14

REDPA
cl. West Hoxton...392 F5

REDSHAW
st. Ryde..............312 E1

REDSTONE
pl. St Clair.........299 H1

REDWOOD
av. Berowra......133 C16
cl. Castle Hill....218 D8
cr. Clarmnt Ms...238 G16
pl. Forestville....256 F7
pl. Mcquarie Fd..424 E15
rd. Padstow Ht..429 E7
rd. Engadine......488 G15
st. Blacktown....244 K7

REE
pl. Bidwill.........211 C16
pl. St Clair.........299 K2

REED
cl. Lane Cove W, off Whitfield Av.....283 F12
la. Cremorne, off Florence La.....316 F10
pl. Fairfield W....335 C9
st. Shalvey........211 B13
st. Cremorne.....316 F11
st. Croydon.......342 D16

REEDE
st. Turrella........403 D5

REEDY
rd. Cattai...........94 G6
rd. Horsley Pk...302 F10
rd. Marayya......204 G6

REEF
st. Bundeena.....524 A11
st. Quakers Hill..213 G14

REELY
st. Pymble.........223 C12

REEN
rd. Prospect.....273 K15
rd. Prospect.....274 A16

REES
av. Belmore......401 H4
cl. Eagle Vale...480 K10
st. Mays Hill.....307 G6

REEVE
cr. Doonside.....243 D9
dr. Barden Rdg..488 G7
pl. Camden S....507 A13
st. Waterloo......19 E13

REEVES
av. Epping.........251 D16
cr. Bonnyrigg....364 C4

REFALO
pl. Quakers Hill..213 H7

REFINERY
dr. Pyrmont........8 B14
dr. Pyrmont.......12 D1

REFRACTORY
ct. Holroyd........307 K10

REGAL
av. Kings Lngly..245 D6
ct. North Rocks..278 J3
st. Regents Pk..338 J15

REGAN
ct. Jamisontown..266 B4
pl. Rooty Hill......272 A4
st. Hurstville......401 G15
st. Rsemeadow..540 J5

GREGORY'S STREET DIRECTORY 125

RE STREETS

REGATTA
av. Caringbah 492 H16
la. Leonay, off
   Regatta Pl 264 K2
pl. Leonay 265 A2
rd. Canada Bay 342 E10
rd. Five Dock 342 E11
wy. Cabarita 312 F16

REGENCY
ct. Oatlands 279 A8
gr. Woodcroft 243 F8

REGENT
cr. Moorebank 396 A9
la. Kogarah 433 D3
la. Newtown 17 E12
la. Paddington 21 C3
la. Putney 311 J5
pl. Castle Hill 217 C8
pl. Illawong 459 G3
st. Redfern 19 B7
st. Berala 339 B16
st. Bexley 432 E1
st. Chippendale ...... E D1
st. Chippendale 19 C4
st. Dee Why 258 G4
st. Kogarah 433 B3
st. Leichhardt 9 E15
st. Paddington 21 C4
st. Petersham 15 J11
st. Putney 311 J6
st. Redfern 19 B9
st. Regents Pk 339 B16
st. Riverstone 182 K10
st. Rozelle 10 G1
st. Summer Hill 373 C5

REGENTVILLE
rd. Glenmore Pk 265 F5
rd. Jamisontown 236 C16
rd. Mulgoa 265 B5

REGIMENT
gr. Winston Hills 277 A3

REGIMENTAL
dr. Camperdown 17 K2
sq. Sydney ...... C G2
sq. Sydney 3 G1

REGINA
av. Brookvale 258 C9
st. Guildford W 306 K16

REGINALD
av. Belmore 401 F2
pl. Merrylands W 307 B15
st. Bexley 402 J12
st. Chatswood W 284 E10
st. Mosman 316 G10
st. Wareemba 342 K5

REGIS
gr. Rouse Hill 185 D3

REGREME
rd. Picton 561 B3
rd. Picton 563 G1

REGULUS
la. Erskine Park, off
   Regulus St 300 H2
st. Erskine Park 300 F2

REIBA
cr. Revesby 399 A10

REIBY
dr. Baulkham Hl 247 G5
la. Newtown 17 D14
pl. Bradbury 511 H11
pl. McGraths Hl 122 A12
pl. Sydney ...... B B8
rd. Hunters Hill 313 F9
st. Newtown 17 D14

REID
av. Castle Hill 247 K5
av. Clemton Park 402 A3
av. Greenacre 370 D7
av. Matraville 436 K8
av. Narraweena 258 C6
av. N Curl Curl 258 J10
av. Wentwthvle 277 C16
av. Woolmloo 4 G6
av. Winmalee 173 D10
dr. Chatswood W 283 K9
pl. Chipping Ntn 396 C6
pl. Illawong 459 A7
st. Winmalee 173 C11
st. Ermington 310 C1
st. Lindfield 254 C15
st. Merrylands 308 D16
st. Seaforth 287 C9
st. Werrington 238 K9

REILEYS
rd. Winston Hills 277 F6

REILLY
la. Sydenham 374 E15
st. Liverpool 395 A9
st. Lurnea 394 C8

REIMS
st. Russell Lea 343 E5

REIN
rd. Greystanes 306 G8

REINA
st. North Bondi 348 D15

REINDEER
la. Werrington, off
   Reindeer Pl 238 G11
pl. Werrington 238 F11

RELIANCE
av. Yagoona 368 E16
cr. Willmot 210 C13
pl. Illawong 459 G5
wy. Airds 511 J16

REMBRANDT
dr. Baulkham Hl 247 G10
dr. Middle Cove 285 K8
st. Carlingford 280 A1

REMEMBRANCE
av. Warwck Frm 365 H15
dwy.Bargo 567 G7
dwy.Bargo 567 G9
dwy.Camden S 537 B3
dwy.Cawdor 537 B3
dwy.Menangle 537 B3
dwy.Picton 561 D4
dwy.Picton 563 F16
dwy.Picton 563 K1
dwy.Tahmoor 565 G16
dwy.Yanderra 567 E16

REMI
st. Bankstown 369 G12

REMLY
st. Roselands 401 B5

REMUERA
st. Willoughby 285 H13

REMUS
pl. Winston Hills 276 K1

RENA
st. S Hurstville 432 C10

RENARD
cl. Illawong 460 B3

RENATA
pl. Hassall Gr 211 J15

RENAULT
pl. Ingleburn 453 J9

RENE
pl. Cecil Hills 362 E1
pl. Doonside 243 B9
st. East Ryde 313 C2

RENEE
cl. Glenhaven 218 C3

RENFORD
cl. Menai 458 F15

RENFREW
st. Guildford W 337 A5
st. St Andrews 452 C12

RENMARK
pl. Engadine 518 H8
st. Engadine 518 H7

RENN
st. Kogarah Bay 432 H12

RENNELL
pl. Green Valley 362 K8
st. Kings Park 244 H2

RENNIE
rd. Woodbine 481 K12
st. Redfern 20 C8
st. Wetherill Pk 333 K5

RENNY
la. Paddington 21 B1
st. Paddington 21 B2

RENOIR
st. Old Tngabbie 276 K6

RENOWN
av. Miranda 492 E2
av. Oatley 431 D10
av. Wiley Park 400 G3
dr. Baulkham Hl 248 C12
dr. Canada Bay 342 D9

RENSHAW
av. Auburn 339 A10
st. Warwck Frm 365 E15

RENTOUL
st. Glenfield 424 H12

RENWAY
av. Lugarno 429 H11

RENWICK
cl. Blaxland 234 D8
la. Leichhardt, off
   Norton St 15 K4
st. Alexandria 18 F14
st. Drummoyne 343 K2
st. Leichhardt 15 K1
st. Marrickville 373 H15
st. Redfern 19 C9

REPON
pl. Belfield 371 D8

REPPAN
av. Baulkham Hl 248 B11

RESEARCH PARK
dr. Mcquarie Pk 282 E1

RESERVE
av. Blaxland 233 K7
cct. Currans Hill 479 K10
la. Annandale 16 H2
la. Chatswood W 284 D8
la. Mona Vale 198 J1
la. Randwick 407 B2
rd. Artarmon 315 A2
rd. Casula 394 H14
rd. Clarmnt Ms 239 A16
rd. Freemns Rch 66 J15
rd. Kurnell 466 E8
rd. St Leonards 315 A2
rd. St Leonards 315 C5
st. Abbotsford 312 J16
st. Alexandria 375 F12
st. Annandale 16 G1
st. Beaconsfield 375 F12
st. Denistone 281 E13
st. Hunters Hill 313 B10
st. Neutral Bay 6 E26
st. Penrith 236 H11
st. Rydalmere 279 C15
st. Seaforth 287 A3
st. Smithfield 335 H8
st. West Ryde 281 E13

RESERVOIR
av. Greenacre 369 G10
rd. Ryde 281 J13
la. Surry Hills ...... F J12
rd. Bargo 567 J11
rd. Blacktown 274 D9
rd. Mt Pritchard 364 F13
rd. Prospect 274 C15
rd. Prospect 275 B16
rd. Pymble 253 B1
st. Little Bay 437 A12
st. Surry Hills ...... F B10
st. Surry Hills 3 J13

RESOLUTE
av. Gt Mckrl Bch 109 A14

RESOLUTION
av. Willmot 210 G13
dr. Caringbah 493 B3
pl. Rouse Hill 184 K9
pl. Rouse Hill 185 A10

RESOURCES
rd. Richmond 118 G12

RESTHAVEN
rd. Bankstown 369 J15
rd. S Hurstville 432 A12

RESTIO
cct. Voyager Pt 427 B5

RESTON
av. Hebersham 241 F4
gra. Bella Vista 246 G1

RESTORMEL
st. Woolooware 493 G6

RESTWELL
rd. Bossley Park 333 F9
rd. Bossley Park 333 J9
rd. Prairiewood 334 B8
st. Bankstown 399 E3

RETIMO
wy. Hornsby Ht 161 J14

RETIRO
st. St Ives Ch 224 A4

RETREAT
dr. Penrith 236 E11
st. Alexandria 19 C16

REUBEN
st. Winston Hills 276 K3

REUSS
st. Birchgrove 7 F4
st. Glebe 12 A14
st. Leichhardt 15 G3

REVESBY
pl. Revesby 398 J16

REVINGSTONE
st. Prairiewood 334 J7

REX
pl. Rooty Hill 241 K14
rd. Georges Hall 367 J12
rd. Georges Hall 367 K14
st. West Ryde 311 B1

REXHAM
pl. Chipping Ntn 366 F15

REXROTH
pl. Huntingwd 273 E11

REYCROFT
av. Quakers Hill 213 F7

REYES
la. Merrylands, off
   Merrylands Rd 307 H13

REYNALDO
pl. Rsemeadow 540 J8

REYNELL
st. Eastern Ck 272 E7

REYNELLA
cl. Edensor Pk 363 E1

REYNOLDS
av. Bankstown 369 D15
av. Hobartville 118 F8
av. Rozelle 7 F13
cr. Beacon Hill 257 E4
pl. Galston 160 H9
rd. Londonderry 148 D3
st. Balmain 7 C12
st. Cremorne 316 F7
st. Old Tngabbie 276 J6
st. Pymble 223 E14
st. Toongabbie 276 J6

RHINE
cl. Kearns 481 B2
st. St Clair 270 B10

RHOADES
la. Auburn 338 K7
la. Auburn 339 A7

RHODES
av. Guildford 337 H6
av. Naremburn 315 G3
pl. Harringtn Pk 478 E1
pl. Kellyville 216 F6
st. Hillsdale 406 G16
st. West Ryde 311 F1

RHONDA
av. Frenchs Frst 256 D9
av. Narwee 400 G11
cl. Wahroonga 222 D10
cl. Concord 342 B6
cl. Plumpton 241 H6
st. Pendle Hill 306 D1
st. Revesby 399 A15

RHONNDA
st. Smithfield 335 H1

RHYL
st. Auburn 338 H1

RHYS
pl. Edensor Pk 363 F8

RIALTO
av. Cremorne Pt 316 G14
la. Manly 288 H10
st. Heathcote 518 F7
st. Kellyville 217 B4

RIBBON GUM
cl. Alfords Point 459 C3
pl. Picton 561 B3

RICE
pl. Oxley Park 270 E2
pl. Shalvey 211 C13

RICH
cl. Bligh Park 150 A6
pl. Jamisontown 266 E3
st. Marrickville 374 C10

RICHARD
av. Campbelltown 512 A4
av. Earlwood 402 K5
cl. North Rocks 278 D1
cr. Bardwell Pk 402 H8
cr. Bardwell Vy 402 H8
cr. Cecil Hills 362 E3
la. Bardwell Pk 402 H8
rd. Leppington 420 C4
rd. St Ives 224 B13
st. Scotland I 168 G3
st. Colyton 270 D7
st. Greenwich 314 J13
st. Newtown 17 K7
st. Panania 428 F4
st. Richmond 118 J6

RICHARD ARTHUR
wk. Mosman, off
   Ballantyne St 316 K9

RICHARD JOHNSON
cr. Ryde 311 F3
sq. Sydney ...... B B15
sq. Sydney 1 J16

RICHARD PORTER
wy. Pymble 253 B1

RICHARDS
av. Drummoyne 343 G5
av. Eastwood 280 J8
av. Marrickville 403 H1
av. Peakhurst 430 B2
av. Riverstone 182 G6
av. Surry Hills 20 C2
cl. Berowra 133 G10
la. Surry Hills 20 C2
rd. Concord 342 B6
rd. Riverstone 181 K6
rd. Wakeley 334 G12
st. Blaxland 233 J10

RICHARDSON
av. Padstow Ht 429 C6
cr. Regents Pk 339 C16
cr. Hebersham 241 E2
pl. Bella Vista 246 K3
pl. Glenmore Pk 265 J6
pl. North Ryde 283 E10
rd. Narellan 478 E10
rd. Narellan Vale 478 F16
rd. Spring Farm 508 D6
st. Fairfield 335 K14
st. Merrylands 307 D9
st. Thirlmere 562 C14
st,e. Lane Cove 314 G5
st.w,Lane Cove 314 E5
wk. Hillsdale 406 H15

RICHARDSONS
cr. Marrickville 403 K1

RICHLAND
st. Kingsgrove 401 J8

RICHLANDS
pl. Prestons 392 K12

RICHMOND
av. Ashfield 342 J15
av. Auburn 338 J8
av. Cremorne 316 G5
av. Dee Why 258 J5
av. Padstow Ht 429 G6
av. St Ives 224 F4
av. Sylvania Wtr 462 C10
av. Willoughby 285 D16
cl. St Johns Pk 364 D3
cr. Campbelltown 511 K7
cr. Cecil Hills 362 E7
ct. Hunters Hill 313 B11
ct. Castle Hill 219 A11
la. Cmbrdg Pk, off
   Richmond Rd 237 F8
rd. Berkshire Pk 180 F1
rd. Blacktown 244 C11
rd. Cmbrdg Pk 237 G7
rd. Clarendon 120 C5
rd. Colebee 212 C10
rd. Dean Park 242 F1
rd. Doonside 243 G7
rd. Glendenning 242 F1
rd. Hassall Gr 212 C10
rd. Homebush W 340 F9
rd. Kingswood 237 F8
rd. Marayong 243 G7
rd. Marsden Pk 211 J2
rd. Penrith 237 F6
rd. Plumpton 212 C10
rd. Quakers Hill 243 A3
rd. Rose Bay 348 B10
rd. Seaforth 286 K15
rd. Windsor 120 C5
rd. Windsor Dn 180 F1
rd. Woodcroft 243 G7
st. Banksia 403 E14
st. Croydon 342 F13
st. Denistone E 281 H10
st. Earlwood 402 G2
st. Merrylands 307 D9
st. Rockdale 403 G14
st. S Wntwthvle 307 A8

RICHMOUNT
st. Cronulla 493 J15

RICHTER
cr. Davidson 255 D3

RICKABY
st. Clarendon 119 K13
st. S Windsor 150 C1

126 GREGORY'S STREET DIRECTORY

STREETS — RO

RICKARD
- av. Bondi Beach....378 A3
- av. Mosman....317 A3
- rd. Bankstown....369 E15
- rd. Berowra....133 D14
- rd. Bossley Park....334 B9
- rd. Chipping Ntn....397 D4
- rd. Leppington....421 B1
- rd. N Narrabeen....228 G1
- rd. Oyster Bay....461 E5
- rd. Quakers Hill....213 K16
- rd. S Hurstville....431 K11
- rd. Strathfield....371 B3
- rd. Warrimoo....203 E12
- st. Auburn....339 A6
- st. Balgowlah....287 H8
- rd. Carlingford....280 B3
- st. Concord....342 A1
- st. Denistone E....281 J12
- st. Five Dock....343 C10
- st. Guildford....337 J5
- st. Merrylands....307 H9
- st. Punchbowl....400 D3
- st. Ryde....281 J12
- st. Turrella....403 C6

RICKARDS
- rd. Agnes Banks....146 C11
- rd. Castlereagh....146 A13
- rd. Castlereagh....146 C11

RICKETTY
- st. Mascot....404 J1

RICKMAN
- st. Kings Lngly....245 E4

RIDDELL
- cl. Glenmore Pk....265 K8
- cr. Blackett....241 B4
- la. Bellevue Hill, off Riddell St....377 H1
- st. Bellevue Hill....347 G16
- st. West Hoxton....392 C8

RIDDLES
- la. Pymble....253 H1

RIDER
- bvd. Rhodes....311 C12
- pl. Minto....453 B14

RIDGE
- la. N Sydney....5 G2
- la. Surry Hills....20 H7
- pl. Richmond....118 H7
- rd. Surry Hills....20 C7
- rd. Arcadia....129 H9
- rd. Engadine....488 D12
- sq. Leppington....420 H10
- st. Chester Hill....368 A4
- st. Epping....250 D14
- st. Glenwood....215 G16
- st. Gordon....253 D8
- st. Merrylands....307 A11
- st. N Sydney....5 G1
- st. S Penrith....266 G1
- st. Surry Hills....20 C6

RIDGECROP
- dr. Castle Hill....217 F2

RIDGEHAVEN
- pl. Baulkham Hl....216 G16
- pl. Baulkham Hl....246 G1
- pl. Bella Vista....246 G1
- pl. Silverdale....353 J14

RIDGELAND
- av. Killara....253 F12

RIDGEMARK
- gr. Bella Vista....246 D2

RIDGEMONT
- cl. Cherrybrook....219 D15
- cl. W Pnnant Hl....248 K10
- pl. Kings Park....244 G2

RIDGES
- la. Richmond....88 B15
- la. Richmond Lwld....88 B15

RIDGETOP
- dr. Glenmore Pk....266 B13
- dr. Glenmore Pk....266 F15
- pl. Dural....219 F4

RIDGE VIEW
- cl. Winmalee....173 D4
- pl. Narellan....478 C9

RIDGEVIEW
- cr. Erskine Park....300 E2
- cl. Oakhurst....242 D3
- wy. Cherrybrook....219 E11

RIDGEWAY
- cl. West Hoxton....392 F7
- cr. Quakers Hill....213 H15
- cr. Sun Valley....202 K5
- cr. Sun Valley....203 A5

RIDGEWELL
- st. Roselands....401 A6

RIDGEWOOD
- pl. Dural....219 C5

RIDLEY
- pl. Blacktown....275 A6

RIESLING
- pl. Eschol Park....481 B3

RIFLE RANGE
- rd. Bligh Park....150 H6
- rd. Northmead....278 B1
- rd. S Windsor....150 D3

RIGA
- av. Greenacre....370 A8

RIGEL
- pl. Glendenning....242 F5

RIGELSFORD
- st. Mt Annan....479 E16

RIGG
- pl. Bonnyrigg....364 B7

RIGNEY
- av. Kingsford....406 K3
- la. Cranebrook, off Rigney Pl....207 D10
- la. Kingsford, off Rigney Av....407 A3
- pl. Cranebrook....207 C9
- st. Harringtn Pk....478 F6

RIGNOLD
- st. Doonside....243 C9
- st. Seaforth....286 K7

RIGO
- pl. Glenfield....424 D13

RIKARA
- pl. Frenchs Frst....256 A2

RIKKARA
- pl. E Kurrajong....67 G5

RILEY
- av. W Pnnant Hl....249 E8
- la. Burwood....342 A11
- la. Quakers Hill....213 E16
- rd. Leppington....420 D14
- st. Darlinghurst....F K4
- st. Darlinghurst....4 C10
- st. N Sydney....5 C7
- st. Oatley....430 H11
- st. Penrith....236 H9
- st. Surry Hills....F H10
- st. Surry Hills....F G16
- st. Surry Hills....19 K5
- st. Surry Hills....20 A3
- st. Woolmloo....4 C7

RIMA
- pl. Hassall Gr....211 K16

RIMFIRE
- cl. Bossley Park....334 A8

RIMINI
- pl. Prestons....393 D15

RIMMINGTON
- st. Artarmon....284 H16

RIMU
- st. Cherrybrook....219 J6

RING
- st. Belmore....371 D14
- st. Sefton....368 G1

RINGAROOMA
- cct. West Hoxton....392 D6

RINGROSE
- av. Greystanes....306 F6

RINGTAIL
- cr. Bossley Park....333 H7

RIO
- wk. Seven Hills....275 J4

RIO GRANDE
- dr. Kearns....480 K1
- dr. Kearns....481 A1

RIPLEY
- gld. Bella Vista....246 F3
- pl. Hassall Gr....212 A16

RIPON
- rd. Moorebank....425 B2
- wy. Rosebery....375 K15

RIPPLE
- cl. Greenfld Pk....334 C13
- st. Kareela....461 E10

RIPPON
- av. Dundas....279 C15

RISBEY
- pl. Bligh Park....150 J9

RISCA
- pl. Quakers Hill....214 B9

RISDONI
- wy. Mcquarie Fd....424 D16

RISORTA
- av. St Ives....254 E1

RITA
- av. Faulconbdg....171 K8
- pl. Oakhurst....241 J5
- st. Merrylands....307 E6
- st. Narwee....400 H15
- st. Thirlmere....565 C3

RITCHARD
- av. Coogee....377 E12

RITCHIE
- la. Mosman, off Upper Almora St....317 B6
- rd. Silverdale....354 B13
- rd. Yagoona....369 A11
- rd. Rosehill....308 G8
- st. Sans Souci....433 C15

RIVAL
- pl. Shalvey....210 H12
- st. Kareela....461 C11

RIVATTS
- dr. Yarramundi....145 F6

RIVENDELL
- wy. Wrrngtn Dns....237 J5
- wy. Glenhaven....217 K4

RIVENOAK
- av. Padstow....429 E3

RIVER
- av. Carramar....366 H2
- av. Chatswood W....283 J9
- av. Villawood....367 A1
- cr. Freemns Rch....89 H5
- la. Chatswood W, off River Av....283 J8
- la. Drummoyne....313 G16
- la. Emu Plains, off River Rd....235 H12
- la. Wollstncraft....315 E7
- rd. Elderslie....507 E3
- rd. Emu Plains....235 D16
- rd. Ermington....310 A5
- rd. Greenwich....314 G6
- rd. Lane Cove....314 G6
- st. Leonay....235 D16
- st. Northwood....314 G6
- st. Oatley....431 B12
- st. Osborne Park....314 G6
- st. Parramatta....278 A13
- st. St Leonards....315 D7
- st. Sutherland....460 C14
- st. Tahmoor....566 D7
- st. Tahmoor....566 D9
- st. Wollstncraft....315 D7
- st. Woronora....489 H1
- st. Yarramundi....115 K16
- rd.w.Camellia....308 J4
- rd.w.Lane Cove....314 B3
- rd.w.Longueville....314 B3
- rd.w.Parramatta....308 J4
- rd.w.Riverview....314 B3
- st. Birchgrove....7 E4
- st. Blakehurst....462 C12
- st. Earlwood....402 G2
- st. Silverwater....309 J9
- st. Strathfield S....371 A4

RIVERDALE
- av. Marrickville....373 K14

RIVERGLEN
- pl. Illawong....459 K6

RIVERGUM
- wy. Rouse Hill....185 A6

RIVERHAVEN
- pl. Oyster Bay....461 B6

RIVER HEIGHTS
- rd. Pleasure Pt....427 J8

RIVERHILL
- av. Forestville....255 J10

RIVERINA
- av. Homebush B....310 G16

RIVERINE
- ct. Warriewood....198 J7

RIVER OAK
- cct. Kellyville....215 K3
- cct. Kellyville....216 A4
- wy. Westleigh....220 J8

RIVERPARK
- dr. Liverpool....395 E7

RIVERPLAINS
- la. Mt Riverview....204 H14

RIVERS
- st. Bellevue Hill....347 G16

RIVERSDALE
- av. Connells Pt....431 G15
- dr. Glen Alpine....510 B13
- pl. Mt Annan....479 J15

RIVERSFORD
- cl. Menangle....538 J16

RIVERSIDE
- av. Picnic Point....427 K7
- av. Putney....311 H5
- cr. Dulwich Hill....373 D13
- cr. Marrickville....373 D14
- cr. Airds....512 A11
- cr. Lugarno....429 H14
- dr. Mcquarie Pk....283 B2
- dr. North Ryde....283 F9
- dr. Sandringham....463 B6
- dr. Sans Souci....463 B6
- dr. Yarramundi....145 F10
- rd. Chipping Ntn....397 A1
- rd. Croydon Pk....371 K9
- rd. Emu Heights....205 A15
- rd. Lansvale....366 K8
- rd. Royal N P....520 E5

RIVERSTONE
- pde. Riverstone....182 G2
- pde. Vineyard....152 E12
- rd. Riverstone....183 A11

RIVERTOP
- cl. Normanhurst....221 F12

RIVER VIEW
- rd. Pleasure Pt....427 J7

RIVERVIEW
- av. Connells Pt....431 K14
- av. Dangar I....76 G8
- av. Kyle Bay....431 K16
- av. Woolooware....493 H8
- av. Mt Riverview....204 H14
- pde. Leonay....264 K1
- pde. North Manly....288 C2
- pl. Oatlands....278 K8
- pl. Avalon....139 H13
- pl. Earlwood....373 C15
- pl. Fairfield....336 F16
- pl. Kentlyn....513 C2
- pl. Oyster Bay....460 K6
- pl. Riverview....314 E10
- st. Chiswick....343 C1
- st. Concord....342 C2
- st. N Richmond....87 E14
- st. Riverview....313 J5
- st. West Ryde....281 B15

RIVETT
- pl. Doonside....273 H1
- rd. North Ryde....283 C10

RIVIERA
- av. Avalon....139 J13
- av. North Rocks....249 A15
- pl. Glenmore Pk....266 E9

RIX
- av. Hamondvle....396 D14
- pl. Camden S....507 D13

RIXON
- rd. Appin....569 F8
- st. Bass Hill....368 B8

ROA
- pl. Blacktown....274 J9

ROACH
- av. Thornleigh....220 J10
- st. Arncliffe....403 E10
- st. Marrickville....373 H15

ROAD 1
- Kurnell....466 E12

ROAD 2
- Kurnell....466 E12

ROAD 3
- Kurnell....466 D12

ROAD 4
- Kurnell....466 D12

ROAD 6
- Kurnell....466 C12

ROAD 7
- Kurnell....466 D9

ROAD 9
- Kurnell....466 B11

ROAD 12
- Kurnell....466 A10

ROAD 13
- Kurnell....466 A10

ROAD 16
- Kurnell....466 B14

ROAD 17
- Kurnell....466 C9

ROAD A
- Kurnell....466 E9

ROAD B
- Kurnell....466 E9

ROAD D
- Kurnell....466 D9

ROAD E
- Kurnell....466 D10

ROAD G
- Kurnell....466 E10

ROAD J
- Kurnell....466 A10

ROAD L
- Kurnell....466 A10

ROAD M
- Kurnell....466 B11

ROAD N
- Kurnell....466 B12

ROAD Q
- Kurnell....466 B13

ROAD U
- Kurnell....466 A14

ROAD V
- Kurnell....466 A14

ROAD W
- Kurnell....466 A15

ROATH
- pl. Prospect....274 G12

ROB
- pl. Vineyard....152 A3

ROBARDS
- pl. Stanhpe Gdn....215 G10

ROBB
- av. Bexley....432 K1
- st. Revesby....398 G15

ROBBIE
- cr. Carlingford....249 F16

ROBBINS
- rd. Box Hill....154 F16
- st. Fairfield W....335 C14

ROBBS
- pl. Dundas Vy....279 K7

ROBECQ
- av. Cheltenham....251 A7

ROBENS
- st. Catherine Fd....419 B6

ROBERT
- av. North Manly....258 A13
- av. Russell Lea....343 D7
- la. Marrickville....373 H12
- la. St Peters, off Mary St....374 G14
- la. Wolli Creek....403 K7
- rd. Cherrybrook....219 B15
- st. Artarmon....284 J15
- st. Ashfield....372 J5
- st. Ashfield....372 K5
- st. Belmore....401 H4
- st. Canterbury....372 F13
- st. Gordon....253 J8
- st. Greenwich....314 J12
- st. Harbord....258 F14
- st. Holroyd....307 K9
- st. Kingsgrove....401 H4
- st. Marrickville....373 H12
- st. Marsden Pk....182 C12
- st. N Richmond....87 B15
- st. N Willoughby....285 G11
- st. Penrith....237 A8
- st. Petersham....16 B6
- st. Riverstone....182 A12
- st. Rozelle....7 D16
- st. Ryde....311 G3
- st. Sans Souci....433 C15
- st. Smithfield....336 A3
- st. Telopea....279 D9
- st. Telopea....279 E9
- st. Willoughby....285 G11

ROBERTA
- cr. Greystanes....305 J8

ROBERT MOCKLER
- la. Manly Vale....288 A2

ROBERTS
- av. Mortdale....430 F7
- av. Mt Pritchard....364 K12
- av. Randwick....377 E11
- av. Wahroonga....252 D11
- cl. Liberty Gr....311 B11
- la. Camperdown....17 F7
- la. Hurstville....432 D5
- la. Lane Cove W, off Whitfield Av....283 F12
- pde. Hawksbry Ht....174 H3
- pl. McGraths Hl....121 K11
- rd. Casula....424 F2
- rd. Greenacre....370 F16

GREGORY'S STREET DIRECTORY 127

RO STREETS

rd. Greenacre 370 F9
rd. Strathfield S 370 F9
rd. Werombi 443 A9
st. Cabarita 342 D1
st. Camperdown 17 F7
st. Jannali 460 H13
st. Rose Bay 348 D10
st. St Peters 374 G14
st. Strathfield 341 H11
wy. Claymore 481 E10
ROBERTS CREEK
rd. Blaxlands Rdg 66 A4
rd. E Kurrajong 66 A8
ROBERTSON
av. Seven Hills 245 J15
cl. Holsworthy, off Chauvel Av 396 B13
cr. Mt Lewis 370 B16
la. Kirribilli 6 B16
la. Sutherland, off Adelong St 490 D2
pl. Bella Vista 246 G3
pl. Jamisontown 266 D1
pl. Watsons Bay 318 G14
rd. Bass Hill 368 C9
rd. Centennial Pk 21 A13
rd. Chester Hill 368 C6
rd. Moore Park 21 A13
rd. Newport 169 H9
rd. N Curl Curl 259 B10
rd. Scotland I 168 G3
st. Campsie 372 B16
st. Greenwich 314 J10
st. Guildford 338 D4
st. Guildford 338 C9
st. Guildford W 337 A2
st. Kogarah 433 A4
st. Kurrajong 85 E4
st. Merrylands 338 D4
st. Narrabeen 229 A6
st. Parramatta 308 E2
st. Sutherland 490 D2
ROBERTSWOOD
av. Blaxland 234 B5
ROBERT TUDAWALI
pl. Moore Park 21 C6
ROBEY
st. Maroubra 407 A10
st. Mascot 405 A5
st. Matraville 407 A10
ROBILLIARD
st. Mays Hill 307 H6
ROBIN
av. S Turramrra 252 D8
cr. S Hurstville 432 A10
pl. Caringbah 492 J9
pl. Glenmore Pk 265 J13
pl. Ingleburn 453 G8
pl. Roselands 400 H9
st. Carlingford 250 A15
st. Hinchinbrk 363 D16
ROBINA
st. Blacktown 274 H3
st. St Ives Ch 223 K2
ROBINIA
av. Fairfield E 337 A15
pl. Alfords Point 429 C14
ROBINSON
cl. Hornsby Ht 191 G3
cl. Lurnea 394 D14
dr. Centennial Pk 22 B10
la. Eastlakes, off Robinson St 405 K4
la. Woollahra 22 F4
pl. Baulkham Hl 247 C12
pl. S Turramrra 252 A8
pwy. Denistone 281 B10
pwy. Eastwood 281 B10
rd. Bringelly 388 F15
rd. Cranebrook 207 E11
st. Belfield 371 B9
st. Campbelltown 510 J7
st. Chatswood 285 B9
st. Croydon 342 F15
st. Eastlakes 405 J4
st. E Lindfield 254 J12
st. Greenacre 370 E3
st. Minchinbury 271 F7
st. Monterey 433 H7
st. Riverstone 182 K10
st. Ryde 312 F2
st. Wiley Park 400 E2
st. Wiley Park 400 F4
st. Woolmloo 4 D7
st. Woolooware 493 J8
ROBIN VALE
pl. Baulkham Hl 247 G11
ROBSHAW
rd. Marayong 244 C4
ROBSON
cr. St Helens Park 541 B2
rd. Kenthurst 187 A11
ROBVIC
av. Kangaroo Pt 461 H7
ROBYN
av. Belfield 371 E11
av. Frenchs Frst 256 K3
av. S Penrith 266 J2
cr. Mt Pritchard 364 H14
la. Panania 428 B1
pl. Northmead 277 H8
pl. Tahmoor 565 F10
rd. Winmalee 173 J6
st. Blacktown 243 K12
st. Peakhurst 430 C10
st. Revesby 398 K14
st. Woodpark 306 G16
ROBYNE
pl. W Pnnant Hl 249 D10
ROCCA
st. Ryde 281 K10
ROCCO
pl. Green Valley 362 J10
ROCHDALE
cct. Stanhpe Gdn 215 D7
ROCHE
gr. Shalvey 211 C13
la. Northbridge 316 B1
pl. Merrylands W 306 J11
ROCHER
av. Hunters Hill 313 C11
ROCHERLEA
cl. West Hoxton 392 C4
ROCHES
av. Bayview 169 B13
ROCHESTER
gr. Castle Hill 217 B10
st. Botany 405 F13
st. Camperdown 17 H6
st. Homebush 341 C11
st. Strathfield 341 C11
ROCHFORD
st. Erskineville 17 J16
st. Erskineville 374 K9
st. St Clair 269 H9
wy. Cherrybrook 219 B15
ROCK
la. Glebe 11 G12
st. Yagoona 368 G10
ROCK BATH
rd. Palm Beach 140 B3
ROCKDALE
st. Banksia 403 D13
st. Rockdale 403 D13
ROCKDALE PLAZA
dr. Rockdale 433 C1
ROCK FARM
av. Dundas 279 E11
ROCKFORD
rd. Tahmoor 565 J14
ROCKLANDS
la. Wollstncraft 5 A1
rd. Crows Nest 5 A2
rd. Wollstncraft 5 A2
ROCKLEA
cr. Sylvania 461 F12
ROCKLEIGH
st. Croydon 342 E13
wy. Epping 251 C14
ROCKLEY
av. Baulkham Hl 247 A9
st. Bondi 378 A4
st. Castlecrag 286 C13
ROCKLILY
av. Westleigh 220 G8
ROCKTON
pl. Prestons 393 C15
ROCKWALL
cr. Potts Point 4 K3
la. Potts Point 4 K3
pl. Potts Point 4 K3
pl. W Pnnant Hl 249 B6
ROCK WALLABY
wy. Blaxland 233 D12
ROCKY
la. Mosman 317 A3
ROCKY HALL
pl. Wilberforce 67 C8
ROCKY MAIN
dr. Holsworthy 426 K7
ROCKY POINT
rd. Beverley Pk 433 C8
rd. Kogarah 433 C8
rd. Ramsgate 433 C8
rd. Sans Souci 463 A3
ROD
st. Belmore 401 H3
RODBOROUGH
av. Crows Nest 315 J7
rd. Frenchs Frst 257 B6
RODD
la. Five Dock 343 A8
rd. Five Dock 343 A8
st. Birrong 368 H5
st. Sefton 368 E4
RODEN CUTLER
cr. N Turramurra 193 E11
RODENS
la. Millers Pt A A1
la. Millers Pt 1 C9
RODEO
dr. Green Valley 362 K9
RODERIGO
cl. Rsemeadow 540 G5
RODGERS
av. Kingsgrove 402 A12
av. Panania 428 E3
st. Kingswood 237 F12
ROD LAVER
dr. Homebush B 340 J4
dr. Homebush B 340 H5
RODLEY
av. Penrith 236 F11
la. Penrith, off Rodley Av 236 G10
RODMAN
av. Maroubra 407 E15
RODNEY
av. Beecroft 250 B3
cr. Beverly Hills 401 B16
pl. Ingleburn 453 D11
pl. W Pnnant Hl 249 B8
st. Dover Ht 348 G11
st. East Ryde 283 B15
RODWELL
pl. Kellyville 216 E4
ROE
st. North Bondi 348 C14
ROEBOURNE
st. Yarrawarrah 489 H13
ROEBUCK
cr. Willmot 210 E12
pl. Illawong 459 A6
rd. Werrington 238 E11
st. Cabramatta 366 D8
ROENTGEN
st. Lucas Ht 487 J12
ROFE
cr. Hornsby Ht 191 F7
pl. Grasmere 505 J1
pl. Turramurra 252 H2
st. Leichhardt 15 J2
ROGAL
pl. Mcquarie Pk 282 K1
ROGAN
cr. Wakeley 334 F13
ROGER
av. Castle Hill 248 C1
cr. Mt Riverview 234 D3
pl. Blacktown 275 C6
st. Brookvale 258 A11
ROGER BOWMAN
la. Chester Hill 337 G12
ROGERS
av. Haberfield 343 B16
av. Liverpool 365 A14
pl. Campbelltown 511 J8
st. Kingsgrove 401 C8
st. Merrylands 307 J16
st. Roselands 401 C8
st. Wentwthvle 276 H16
wy. Mt Annan 479 D15
ROHAN
pl. N Richmond 87 A13
st. Naremburn 315 F3
ROHINI
st. Turramurra 222 H13
ROKEBY
rd. Abbotsford 342 K1
ROKER
st. Cronulla 494 A14
ROKEVA
st. Eastwood 281 F6
ROLAND
av. Liverpool 394 G5
av. Northmead 248 B15
av. Wahroonga 222 C15
la. Warrawee 222 C15
st. Bossley Park 334 B5
st. Greystanes 306 D11
ROLESTONE
av. Kingsgrove 401 H7
ROLF
la. St Peters 374 F14
ROLFE
st. Manly 288 F5
st. Rosebery 405 E2
ROLLA
wy. Beaumont Hills 185 K14
ROLTON
av. Newington, off Henricks Av 309 K15
ROMA
av. Blacktown 244 F14
av. Kensington 376 D13
av. Mt Pritchard 364 F11
av. Padstow Ht 429 E7
av. Wallacia 324 K14
ct. W Pnnant Hl 248 J8
la. Blacktown 244 F12
pl. Ingleburn 453 C10
pl. Sylvania 462 A12
rd. St Ives 224 F7
st. N Epping 251 E10
ROMAINE
av. Wrrngtn Cty 238 D8
ROMANA
sq. Prestons 393 F15
ROMANI
av. Hurstville 432 C2
av. Riverview 314 B7
pde. Matraville 437 B1
st. N Parramatta 278 F12
wy. Matraville 407 B16
ROMANO
cl. Edensor Pk 333 H15
ROME
pl. Shalvey 211 A14
st. Canterbury 372 F15
ROMEO
cr. Rsemeadow 540 H4
pl. Dural 219 A6
ROMFORD
rd. Epping 250 J12
rd. Frenchs Frst 256 K4
rd. Kings Park 244 K6
ROMILLY
pl. Ambarvale 540 D2
st. Riverwood 400 D15
ROMINA
rd. Winmalee 173 G10
ROMLEY
cr. Oakhurst 242 C1
rd. Kurnell 464 A11
ROMNEY
cr. Miller 393 H3
pl. Wakeley 334 K16
rd. St Ives Ch 224 A6
wy. Airds 512 A13
ROMSEY
st. Waitara 221 J4
ROMSLEY
rd. Jamisontown 266 C2
ROMULUS
st. Winston Hills 277 A1
RON
pl. Plumpton 241 H10
RONA
cl. Berowra Ht 132 K10
st. Peakhurst 430 D6
RONALD
av. Dundas 279 K14
av. Earlwood 372 H15
av. Greenwich 314 J4
av. Harbord 258 J16
av. Lane Cove 314 H3
av. Narraweena 258 A4
av. Ryde 281 K9
pl. Guildford 337 D1
st. Birchgrove 8 C4
st. Blacktown 243 K12
st. Campbelltown 511 K3
st. Carramar 366 J2
st. Hornsby 221 F6
st. Padstow 399 B12
RONDELAY
dr. Castle Hill 247 H3
RON FILBEE
pl. Maroubra 407 H8
RON MACE
dr. Minchinbury 272 D9
RON SCOTT
cct. Greenacre 370 F5
ROOKE
ct. Kellyville 186 H15
la. Hunters Hill 313 K11
st. Hunters Hill 314 A12
ROOKIN
pl. Minchinbury 271 J10
ROOKWOOD
rd. Bankstown 369 F10
rd. Potts Hill 369 F10
rd. Yagoona 369 F10
ROONY
av. Abbotsbury 333 A12
ROOSEVELT
av. Allambie Ht 257 D12
av. Riverwood 400 A12
av. Sefton 338 F15
la. Allambie Ht, off Roosevelt Av 257 D12
pl. Bonnet Bay 460 A10
ROOTS
av. Luddenham 356 G3
ROOTY HILL
rd.n, Oakhurst 242 C4
rd.n, Plumpton 242 B11
rd.n, Rooty Hill 242 B14
rd.s, Eastern Ck 272 F4
rd.s, Rooty Hill 272 D2
ROPE
st. Dundas Vy 280 B10
ROPER
av. S Coogee 407 G5
cr. Sylvania Wtr 462 E14
la. Hornsby 191 G13
pl. East Killara 254 H10
rd. Colyton 270 H5
ROPES CREEK
rd. Mount Druitt 271 A2
RORKE
st. Beecroft 250 B6
RORY
ct. Glenwood 215 H10
ROSA
cr. Castle Hill 218 D14
pl. West Hoxton 392 C8
st. Acacia Gdn 214 H14
st. Croydon 342 D16
st. Oatley 431 D12
ROSAKI
cl. Edensor Pk 333 E16
ROSALIE
av. Camden 507 A6
cr. Greenacre 370 C7
ROSALIND
cr. Campbelltown 511 K4
rd. Marayong 244 B7
st. Cammeray 315 J6
st. Crows Nest 315 J6
st. Greystanes 305 J7
ROSAMOND
st. Hornsby 191 F11
ROSANNAH
wy. Cranebrook 207 E13
ROSCOE
st. Bondi Beach 378 B1
ROSCOMMON
cr. Killarney Ht 286 B2
rd. Arcadia 129 F14
ROSCREA
av. Randwick 377 D10
ROSE
av. Bexley 402 C16
av. Collaroy Plat 228 D9
av. Concord 341 K6
av. Connells Pt 431 F16
av. Mt Pritchard 364 D9
av. Neutral Bay 6 A2
cir. Winmalee 173 E9
cr. Glossodia 65 K13
cr. Mosman 316 H12
cr. N Parramatta 278 E10
cr. Regents Pk 369 A1
ct. Bidwill 211 D16
dr. Mt Annan 479 F16
la. Annandale 11 C10
la. Cmbrdg Gdn, off Rose Pl 237 G2
pl. Cmbrdg Gdn 237 G2
pl. Lalor Park 245 C12

128 GREGORY'S STREET DIRECTORY

STREETS RO

st.	Annandale	11	A9		**ROSELEA**			av.w. Rossmore	389	C13	
st.	Ashfield	372	H5	wy.	Beecroft	249	J13	cr.	Rossmore	419	E3
st.	Auburn	309	D16		**ROSELLA**			**ROSSMOYNE**			
st.	Baulkham Hl	247	G13	cl.	Blaxland	234	E5	la.	Ellis Lane	476	C8
st.	Birchgrove	7	G2	gr.	Bidwill	211	D13	**ROSS PHILLIPS**			
st.	Botany	405	F10	la.	Darlinghurst	4	D8	la.	Padstow, off		
st.	Bronte	377	J9	pl.	Cranebrook	207	C15		Alice St	399	D15
st.	Campbelltown	481	G16	st.	Dural	190	A7	**ROSS SMITH**			
st.	Chatswood	284	K7	st.	Prestons	423	A11	av.	Mascot	404	K11
st.	Chippendale	18	H3	wy.	W Pnnant Hl	249	E7	cr.	Kings Lngly	245	G4
st.	Cronulla	524	A3		**ROSEMARY**			st.	Fairfield	335	G13
st.	Croydon Pk	371	K6	cr.	Glenmore Pk	265	G10	st.	Fairfield W	335	G13
st.	Darlington	18	E7	pl.	Blacktown	244	K9	**ROSITANO**			
st.	Darlington	18	F7	pl.	Cherrybrook	219	F10	pl.	Rooty Hl	271	H4
st.	Epping	281	C2	pl.	Mcquarie Fd	454	D2	**ROSLEEN**			
st.	Hurstville	432	B6	row.	Menai	458	K14	pl.	Baulkham Hl	247	E10
st.	Liverpool	395	A8		**ROSEMEAD**			**ROSLYN**			
st.	Newtown	17	J9	rd.	Hornsby	221	B1	av.	Btn-le-Sds	433	J5
st.	Pendle Hill	306	F1		**ROSEMEADOW**			av.	Northmead	277	H9
st.	Petersham	15	K15	dr.	Cabarita	342	F2	av.	Panania	428	E1
st.	Punchbowl	400	A5		**ROSEMEATH**			av.	Roseville	284	F2
st.	Sefton	368	G8	av.	Kingsgrove	402	A5	av.	Croydon	342	D12
st.	Smithfield	335	C7		**ROSEMONT**			st.	Cronulla	524	A2
st.	Wilberforce	91	K4	av.	Emu Plains	235	H9	**ROSTREVOR**			
st.	Winmalee	173	D9	av.	Mortdale	431	D7	la.	Elizabeth Bay	13	A7
st.	Yagoona	368	F10	av.	Smithfield	335	H7	pl.	Cherrybrook	219	C13
tce.	Paddington	4	F14	av.	Woollahra	14	B15	st.	Ashbury	372	D8
ROSEA				la.	Thirlmere	565	C2	st.	Elizabeth Bay	13	A7
pl.	Glenmore Pk	265	H12	la.	Gymea Bay	491	G13	st.	Lane Cove N	284	D15
ROSEANNE				pl.	Potts Point	4	K7	st.	Liverpool	394	J1
av.	Roselands	400	H10	pl.	Punchbowl	400	E3	st.	Potts Point	4	K7
ROSEBANK				pl.	Punchbowl	400	E4	st.	Rcuttrs Bay	13	A7
av.	Dural	188	G12	pl.	Wiley Park	400	E4	**ROSLYNDALE**			
av.	Epping	250	K14		**ROSEMOUNT**			av.	Woollahra	14	D15
cr.	Kingsgrove	401	E8	av.	Pennant Hills	220	G15	**ROSS**			
cr.	Hurstville	431	J6	av.	Summer Hill	373	B7	av.	Kingsgrove	401	G6
cr.	Darlinghurst	4	J9		**ROSEN**			cr.	Blaxland	233	D7
st.	Glebe	12	B12	st.	Epping	250	J14	pl.	Kellyville	185	F1
st.	Panania	398	D13		**ROSENEATH**			pl.	Minto	452	K13
ROSE BAY				pl.	Baulkham Hl	247	G6	pl.	N Wahroonga	222	K1
av.	Bellevue Hill	347	E11	pl.	Engadine	518	F6	pl.	St Marys	239	H14
ROSEBERRY					**ROSENTHAL**			pl.	Wetherill Pk	303	H15
st.	Balgowlah	287	K6	av.	Lane Cove	314	D1	st.	Bankstown	399	E3
st.	Balmain	7	C11	la.	Lane Cove, off			st.	Blacktown	274	J4
st.	Manly Vale	287	K6		Rosenthal Av	314	D1	st.	Brooklyn	75	H11
st.	Merrylands	337	F1	la.	Sun Valley	203	B7	st.	Camperdown	17	C6
st.	Riverstone	153	C14	st.	Doonside	273	E2	st.	Chipping Ntn	396	C5
ROSEBERY					**ROSE PAYTEN**			st.	Currans Hill	479	J8
av.	Rosebery	375	J15	dr.	Leumeah	482	A11	st.	Dulwich Hill	373	A10
pl.	Mosman	316	K4	dr.	Minto	482	A11	st.	Epping	280	B1
pl.	Balmain	7	H12		**ROSES RUN**			st.	Forest Lodge	11	H13
rd.	Guildford	337	H7		Westleigh	220	G7	st.	Gladesville	312	G10
rd.	Kellyville	217	K4		**ROSETTA**			st.	Glenbrook	264	A1
st.	Heathcote	518	F12	av.	East Killara	254	E11	st.	Naremburn	315	E4
st.	Mosman	316	J5	av.	Killara	254	E11	st.	Newport	169	J10
st.	Penshurst	431	B2	cl.	Cranebrook	207	D11	st.	N Curl Curl	258	J10
ROSEBRIDGE				cl.	N Richmond	87	G13	st.	Parramatta	278	C16
av.	Castle Cove	285	T3	la.	Beverly Hills, off			st.	Seaforth	287	C10
ROSEBUD					Rosetta St	401	A12	st.	Seven Hills	275	K6
la.	Paddington	4	G15	la.	Cranebrook, off			st.	Waverton	315	D12
ROSEBY					Rosetta Cl	207	D11	st.	Windsor	121	D8
st.	Drummoyne	344	B4	pl.	Glenfield	424	E13		**ROSSELL**		
st.	Leichhardt	15	H3		**ROSSER**			st.	Lethbrdg Pk	240	E1
st.	Marrickville	403	C11	la.	Rozelle	7	E14		**ROTTNEST**		
ROSECREA				st.	Balmain	7	E13	av.	Hinchinbrk	362	A16
ct.	Glenmore Pk	266	F15	st.	Rozelle	7	E13		**ROTUMA**		
ROSECRAFT				rd.	Ryde, off			st.	Oakhurst	211	J16
					O'Regan Dr	312	C4		**ROUGHLEY**		
ROSEDALE				st.	Stanmore	16	H8	rd.	Kenthurst	157	K5
av.	Bankstown	369	G10		**ROSETTI**				**ROUNCE**		
av.	Fairlight	288	A9	st.	Wetherill Pk	334	H4	av.	Forestville	256	A6
av.	Greenacre	369	G10		**ROSSFORD**				**ROUND TABLE**		
av.	Penrith	237	C14	av.	Jannali	460	J13	cl.	Mt Colah	162	E9
cr.	Croydon Pk	371	K6		**ROSEVILLE**				**ROUSE**		
dr.	W Pnnant Hl	248	K3	av.	Roseville	284	H4	la.	N Richmond	87	G7
rd.	Gordon	253	J6	av.	Kellyville	217	B4	pl.	Illawong	459	H5
rd.	Pymble	223	K16	la.	Roseville, off			rd.	Rouse Hill	184	F11
rd.	St Ives	223	K16		Roseville Av	284	G4		**ROWALLAN**		
st.	Canley Ht	335	B15	tce.	Roseville	266	G12	av.	Castle Hill	217	K13
st.	Dulwich Hill	373	C7		**ROSEWALL**			dr.	Harringtn Pk	478	D2
ROSEGREEN				dr.	Menai	458	G6	rd.	Mona Vale	199	B6
ct.	Glendenning	242	H3	pl.	Shalvey	210	J13		**ROWANBRAE**		
ROSEGUM				st.	Greystanes	306	B10	cr.	Baulkham Hl	216	D15
pl.	Alfords Point	429	B15	st.	N Willoughby	285	E10	cr.	Bella Vista	216	D15
pl.	Quakers Hill	213	K7	st.	Willoughby	285	E10		**ROWANY**		
ROSEHILL					**ROSEWATER**			cl.	Bonnyrigg	363	H9
cl.	Casula	394	D15	cct.	Breakfast Pt	312	C14		**ROWE**		
cl.	Parramatta	308	A7		**ROSEWOOD**			av.	Lurnea	394	E7
st.	Redfern	19	A8	av.	Carlingford	249	E16	cl.	Wetherill Pk	334	F6
ROSELAND				av.	Prestons	393	J14	la.	Quakers Hill	243	B2
av.	Roselands	400	J8	av.	Prestons	393	K14	la.	Bondi Jctn	22	G6
ROSELANDS				av.	Greystanes	306	F11	la.	Eastwood	281	B8
av.	Frenchs Frst	255	H3	pl.	Mcquarie Fd	454	E1	la.	Paddington	4	J14
dr.	Roselands	400	J8	pl.	Cherrybrook	219	K13	la.	Sydenham	374	D15
				row.	Menai	458	K12	la.	Baulkham Hl	247	D15
				st.	Parklea	215	A12	la.	Doonside	273	H3
				st.	Bellevue Hill	347	G16				
				st.	Berowra	133	E10				
					ROSSMORE						
				av.	Punchbowl	400	C5				
				av.e. Rossmore	389	H14				

pl.	Greystanes	305	J9
pl.	Eastwood	280	H9
st.	Eastwood	281	B8
st.	Five Dock	342	G9
st.	Harbord	288	E2
st.	Manly	288	F10
st.	Roseville Ch	285	D1
st.	S Hurstville	432	A12
st.	Sydneham, off		
	Henry St	374	D16
st.	Sydney	D	
st.	Sydney	3	H2
st.	Woollahra	22	H5
ROWELL			
st.	Granville	308	G10
st.	North Ryde	282	J10
st.	Revesby Ht	428	K7
ROWENA			
pl.	Cherrybrook	219	C9
pl.	Potts Point	4	H5
rd.	Narraweena	258	D2
st.	Greystanes	305	J7
ROWLAND			
av.	Bondi	378	C6
av.	Kurmond	64	H16
st.	Revesby	428	H3
ROWLEY			
la.	Camperdown	17	B8
la.	Eveleigh	18	F11
la.	Eveleigh	375	C6
st.	Airds	511	J15
rd.	Guildford	338	A7
rd.	Russell Lea	343	C5
st.	Btn-le-Sds	404	A15
st.	Burwood	341	J11
st.	Camperdown	17	A9
st.	Eveleigh	18	F12
st.	Eveleigh	375	C6
st.	Pendle Hill	276	E16
st.	Seven Hills	245	F16
st.	Smithfield	335	F4
ROWLEYS POINT			
rd.	Lansvale	366	J11
ROWLISON			
pde. Cammeray	316	B3
ROWNTREE			
st.	Balmain	7	E7
st.	Birchgrove	7	E7
st.	Quakers Hill	213	G16
ROWOOD			
rd.	Prospect	275	B14
ROXANA			
rd.	Kurrajong	64	D16
ROXBOROUGH PARK			
rd.	Baulkham Hl	247	F6
rd.	Castle Hill	247	F6
ROXBURGH			
cr.	Stanhpe Gdn	215	F7
pl.	Bella Vista	246	H3
ROXBY			
gr.	Quakers Hill	214	D8
pl.	Hinchinbrk	362	J14
ROY			
st.	Marayong	244	C8
st.	Kingsgrove	401	J5
ROYAL			
av.	Baulkham Hl	247	G8
av.	Birrong	368	J3
av.	Plumpton	242	C5
pl.	Bardwell Pk	402	K8
pl.	Greystanes	306	H10
pl.	St Clair	270	E10
row. Menai	459	A14
st.	Chatswood	285	C7
st.	Maroubra	406	J9
ROYALA			
cl.	Prestons	393	D16
ROYAL GEORGE			
dr.	Harringtn Pk	478	C12
ROYALIST			
rd.	Mosman	316	K11
ROYAL OAK			
dr.	Alfords Point	459	A3
pl.	W Pnnant Hl	248	J4
ROYCE			
av.	Croydon	342	D12
st.	Greystanes	306	C10
ROYCROFT			
av.	Newington	309	K15
pl.	Edensor Pk	363	C2
ROYENA			
wy.	Blacktown	274	E2
ROYERDALE			
pl.	E Kurrajong	67	C6

GREGORY'S STREET DIRECTORY 129

RO STREETS

ROYLSTON
la. Paddington 13 F13
st. Fairfield W 335 D13
st. Paddington 13 F14
ROYSTON
cl. Pymble 223 D16
pde. Asquith 192 A10
pde. Mt Colah 192 A10
st. Darlinghurst 4 J9
ROY WATTS
rd. Glenfield 423 J7
RUBIDA
wy. Mcquarie Fd 424 D16
RUBIE
la. Malabar, off Nix Av 437 F7
RUBINA
st. Merrylands W 307 B12
RUBY
ct. Kellyville 185 F7
pl. Seven Hills 275 D8
rd. Gymea 461 F16
st. Carramar 366 G1
st. Guildford 337 J2
st. Hurstville 431 G3
st. Marrickville 373 K15
st. Mosman 317 B12
st. Yagoona 368 G11
wy. Claymore 481 C12
RUCKLE
pl. Doonside 273 E5
RUDD
cl. Casula 424 G3
cl. Edensor Pk 363 F3
pde. Campsie 371 K14
pl. Blackett 241 C4
pl. Doonside 243 B8
rd. Leumeah 481 J16
st. East Ryde 283 A16
st. Narellan 478 F12
RUDDERS
la. Eastern Ck 273 B12
RUDELLE
cr. Yagoona 369 B9
RUDGE
pl. Ambarvale 511 A15
RUDHAM
pl. Chipping Ntn 366 H15
RUDOLF
rd. Seven Hills 275 F7
RUDYARD
st. Winston Hills 247 G16
RUFUS
av. Glenwood 215 E15
RUGBY
cr. Chipping Ntn 396 F1
pl. Sydney A K8
pwy. Chipping Ntn, off Rugby Cr 396 G1
rd. Marsfield 281 G2
st. Cmbrdg Pk 238 B7
st. Wrrngtn Cty 238 B7
RULANA
st. Acacia Gdn 214 H16
RULE
st. Cmbrdg Pk 237 H9
RULES
pl. Horngsea Pk 392 F16
RULWALLA
pl. Gymea 491 C7
RUM CORP
la. Windsor 120 J9
RUMKER
st. Picton 563 D10
st. Picton 563 D12
RUMPOLE
la. N Strathfield 341 E7
RUMSAY
la. Rozelle 7 F13
st. Rozelle 7 F14
RUMSEY
cr. Dundas Vy 279 K11
RUNCORN
av. Hebersham 241 E8
st. St Johns Pk 334 F16
RUNDLE
pl. Gladesville 312 K5
rd. Busby 363 F14
rd. Green Valley 363 F14
st. S Granville 338 F3
RUNIC
la. Maroubra 406 K7
RUNNYMEDE
wy. Carlingford 249 H11
RUNYON
av. Greystanes 306 G5
RUPARI
pl. Belrose 225 F15
RUPERT
st. Bass Hill 368 A11
st. Ingleburn 453 B10
st. Merrylands W 307 B14
st. Mt Colah 192 A6
RUPERTSWOOD
av. Bellevue Hill 14 K9
rd. Rooty Hill 271 H5
RUSDEN
ml. Mt Riverview 234 C1
rd. Blaxland 234 A7
rd. Mt Riverview 234 A7
RUSE
pl. Campbelltown 511 H9
pl. Illawong 459 E4
st. Harris Park 308 F5
st. North Ryde 282 C7
RUSH
pl. Quakers Hill 243 E4
st. Woollahra 21 H3
RUSHALL
st. Pymble 223 C14
RUSHDEN
wy. Stanhpe Gdn 215 E4
RUSHES
pl. Minto 453 B14
RUSHTON
pl. Casula 394 K16
RUSKIN
cl. Wetherill Pk 334 F6
RUSKIN ROWE
Avalon 169 H2
RUSSELL
av. Baulkham Hl 277 J1
av. Dolls Point 463 C1
av. Frenchs Frst 256 D4
av. Lindfield 284 E1
av. Sans Souci 463 C1
av. Valley Ht 202 H11
av. Wahroonga 221 J7
cl. Green Valley 363 B13
cr. Westleigh 220 H2
ct. Maroubra 407 E13
la. Allawah 432 D9
la. Lindfield 254 F16
la. Oakdale 500 C16
la. Sans Souci 463 C1
la. Strathfield 341 G14
pl. Camperdown 18 B2
rd. N Parramatta 279 A7
st. Blacktown 274 G4
st. Campbelltown 511 J5
st. Clontarf 287 F11
st. Denistone E 281 F8
st. Emu Heights 235 C7
st. Emu Plains 235 B12
st. Granville 308 F11
st. Greenacre 370 E7
st. Lilyfield 10 E9
st. Mt Pritchard 364 H11
st. Northmead 248 B14
st. Oatley 431 D14
st. Riverwood 400 B10
st. Russell Lea 343 C6
st. Strathfield 341 G13
st. The Oaks 502 E10
st. Vaucluse 318 G16
st. Wollstncraft 315 C8
st. Woollahra 22 G3
RUSTIC
pl. Woodcroft 243 G7
RUTAR
pl. Abbotsbury 333 B10
RUTH
pl. Cherrybrook 219 J4
pl. Minto 482 G2
pl. Panania 398 D15
st. Canley Ht 365 A2
st. Marsfield 281 K5
st. Merrylands W 307 C12
st. Naremburn 315 E1
st. Winston Hills 277 A4
RUTHERFORD
av. Burraneer 523 E4
av. Lucas Ht 487 G12
st. Blacktown 274 A3
RUTHERGLEN
av. Hobartville 118 D8
av. Northmead 278 C1
dr. St Andrews 481 K2
pl. Minchinbury 271 J10
RUTHVEN
av. Milperra 397 D9
la. Bondi Jctn 22 D6
st. Bondi Jctn 22 D8
RUTLAND
av. Baulkham Hl 247 F4
av. Castlecrag 285 K11
pl. N Wahroonga 222 J2
st. Allawah 432 F8
st. Blacktown 274 J7
st. Surry Hills 19 G2
RUTLEDGE
cr. Quakers Hill 214 C8
st. Eastwood 280 H10
st. West Ryde 280 F10
RUZAC
st. Campbelltown 511 J5
RYAN
av. Beverly Hills 401 B16
av. Cabramatta 365 D9
av. Hornsby Ht 191 G6
av. Maroubra 407 E8
av. Mosman 317 D6
cl. St Andrews 452 C14
cr. Riverstone 183 A6
la. East Hills, off Park Rd 427 G5
la. Forest Lodge 11 E15
la. St Leonards 315 F5
la. Yagoona 369 D10
pl. Beacon Hill 257 J9
pl. Emu Plains 235 B9
pl. Illawong 459 E4
pl. Mount Druitt 270 K2
rd. Padstow 399 F16
st. Bnkstn Aprt 367 J16
st. Dundas Vy 280 B11
st. Lilyfield 10 G4
st. St Marys 269 J2
st. Thirlmere 564 J4
st. Thirlmere 564 J6
RYDAL
av. Castle Hill 247 J5
pl. Collaroy Plat 228 E11
pl. Cranebrook 207 E11
st. Prospect 274 G12
RYDE
pl. St Johns Pk 364 G5
rd. Gladesville 312 J6
rd. Gordon 253 B14
rd. Hunters Hill 313 C8
rd. Pymble 253 B14
rd. West Pymble 253 B14
st. Epping 280 G1
RYDER
ct. Rouse Hill 184 K9
rd. Greenfld Pk 334 D14
st. Darlinghurst 4 C13
st. Glenwood 215 E13
RYDGE
la. Belmore, off Rydge St 401 G1
st. Belmore 401 G1
RYE
av. Bexley 402 F14
st. Stanhpe Gdn 215 D7
RYEDALE
la. West Ryde, off Wattle St 281 F15
rd. Denistone 281 E13
rd. Eastwood 281 D9
rd. West Ryde 281 E13
RYELAND
cl. Elderslie 507 J3
pl. Airds 512 A12
st. Miller 393 F2
RYLAND
cl. Wakeley 334 K15
RYMILL
pl. Bundeena 523 K11
pl. Leumeah 482 J11
rd. Tregear 240 B4
RYNAN
av. Edmndsn Pk 422 G3
RYRIE
av. Cromer 228 D15
av. Forestville 255 F10
rd. Earlwood 402 C3
rd. N Parramatta 278 K6
st. Mosman 317 A2
st. North Ryde 282 H10
RYRIES
pde. Cremorne 316 G4

S

SABA
st. Fairfield W 335 G10
SABER
st. Woollahra 22 H5
SABINA
pl. St Ives 224 F8
st. Mosman 317 D3
SABRE
cr. Holsworthy 426 F3
pl. Raby 451 E16
SABRINA
gr. Plumpton 241 J8
SABUGAL
rd. Engadine 488 D13
SACKVILLE
rd. Ebenezer 68 C9
rd. Sackville 68 C9
rd. Wilberforce 67 J16
st. Bardwell Vy 402 K10
st. Bexley 402 K10
st. Blacktown 245 A13
st. Canley Ht 365 H4
st. Canley Vale 365 H4
st. Fairfield 336 A15
st. Hurstville 401 G16
st. Ingleburn 453 A10
st. Lalor Park 245 A13
st. Maroubra 407 J10
SACKVILLE FERRY
rd. Sackville N 68 B4
rd. Sackville N 69 A1
rd. S Maroota 69 C3
SACOYA
av. Bella Vista 246 G6
SADDINGTON
st. St Marys 269 E2
st. S Turramrra 252 A8
SADDLE
cl. Currans Hill 480 A9
row. Holsworthy 426 E4
SADDLEBACK
cl. Hinchinbrk 363 B16
SADDLER
wy. Glenmore Pk 266 G13
SADLEIR
av. Ashcroft 394 D1
av. Heckenberg 364 C14
av. Sadleir 394 D1
SADLIER
av. Milperra 397 D9
cr. Fairfield W 335 A10
cr. Petersham 15 G11
wk. Mosman, off Awaba St 317 A4
SAFORD
st. Forestville 256 A5
SAGARS
rd. Dural 188 A11
SAGE
av. Oyster Bay 461 C8
st. Mount Druitt 270 K3
st. St Ives 253 K2
SAGER
pl. East Ryde 282 K16
SAGGART FIELD
rd. Minto 482 C1
SAGGAS
st. Springwood 171 D16
SAIALA
rd. East Killara 254 G7
SAID
tce. Quakers Hill 214 H14
SAIDOR
rd. Whalan 241 A13
SAIL
pl. Illawong 459 B7
SAILORS BAY
rd. Northbridge 285 G15
SAINSBURY
st. St Marys 269 G1
ST AGNES
av. Rooty Hill 272 F6
wy. Blair Athol 511 C2
ST AIDANS
av. Oatlands 279 A11
av. Oatlands 279 A12
ST ALBANS
rd. Kingsgrove 401 H7
rd. Schofields 183 C14
st. Abbotsford 342 J1
ST ANDREWS
bvd. Casula 395 A11
cl. Belrose 226 E14
dr. Glenmore Pk 266 F11
dr. Pymble 252 J4
gte. Elanora Ht 198 D12
pl. Cronulla 493 J11
rd. Leppington 420 J15
rd. Raby 451 G8
rd. St Andrews 451 K13
rd. Varroville 451 C3
st. Balmain 8 B9
st. Rydalmere 279 E14
wy. Rouse Hill 185 B8
ST ANN
st. Merrylands 307 F14
ST ANNE
pl. Blair Athol 510 K2
ST ANNES
cl. Belrose 226 B12
sq. Strathfield S 371 A5
st. Ryde 312 A3
ST ANTHONY
cl. Kings Park 244 E5
ST AUBINS
pl. Glen Alpine 510 F12
ST BARBARAS
av. Manly 289 A16
ST BARNABAS
st. Ultimo 12 J16
ST BARTHOLOMEWS
pl. Prospect 275 B15
ST CATHERINE
cl. Blair Athol 510 K2
st. Mortdale 431 B6
ST CLAIR
av. St Clair 269 H9
st. Belmore 371 E14
ST CLARE
pl. Blair Athol 510 J2
ST DAVID
av. Dee Why 258 G5
ST DAVIDS
rd. Haberfield 343 C16
rd. Varroville 451 G3
ST ELMO
pde. Kingsgrove 401 H12
st. Mosman 317 C13
ST ERMES
ct. Wahroonga, off Isis St 222 A7
ST GEORGE
cr. Sandy Point 428 A14
ST GEORGES
cr. Cecil Hills 362 E7
cr. Drummoyne 344 A2
pde. Allawah 432 C7
pde. Earlwood 402 K4
pde. Hurstville 432 C7
rd. Bexley 402 D14
rd. Penshurst 431 D4
ST GILES
av. Greenwich 315 B8
ST HELENA
la. Eastlakes 405 K4
pde. Eastlakes 405 K5
ST HELENS
av. Mt Krng-gai 162 J14
cl. West Hoxton 392 E8
ST HELENS PARK
dr. St Helens Park 541 C5
ST HELIERS
rd. Silverdale 353 G16
ST HILLIERS
rd. Auburn 339 G1
ST IVES
av. Hunters Hill 314 A12
ST JAMES
arc. Sydney 3 J3
av. Baulkham Hl 247 E7
av. Earlwood 402 J4
av. Glebe 11 K13
av. Menangle 538 G16
la. Glebe 12 A13
la. Turramurra 222 H12
pl. Appin 569 E13
pl. Narellan 478 H12
pl. Seven Hills 276 D1
rd. Bondi Jctn 22 C8
rd. Sydney D D6
rd. Sydney 3 K3
rd. Varroville 451 D4
rd. Vineyard 152 D10

STREETS SA

ST JEROME
cl. Blair Athol 510 J1
ST JOHN
st. Balmain 8 B9
st. Lewisham 15 B7
st. Newtown 17 G16
ST JOHNS
av. Auburn 339 A12
av. Gordon 253 F9
cl. Brookvale 258 A8
la. Gordon, off
  St Johns Av 253 H8
pl. Narellan 478 B10
rd. Auburn 339 A12
rd. Blaxland 233 F10
rd. Bradbury 511 C14
rd. Busby 363 K14
rd. Busby 363 K15
rd. Cabramatta 365 E4
rd. Cabramatta W 365 A4
rd. Campbelltown 511 H12
rd. Canley Ht 365 A4
rd. Forest Lodge 11 J16
rd. Glebe 11 J16
rd. Heckenberg 363 K14
rd. Heckenberg 363 K15
rd. Maraylya 95 C12
rd. Maraylya 95 D8
rd. St Johns Pk 364 H3
wk. Gordon 253 F9
ST JUDE
cr. Belmore 401 H3
ST KILDA
la. Woolmloo, off
  Bourke St 4 E8
st. Bexley North 402 C10
st. Kingsgrove 402 C10
st. St Johns Pk 364 F3
ST LAWRENCE
av. Kearns 451 A16
st. Greenwich 314 A13
ST LUKE
cl. Blair Athol 510 J10
st. Randwick 377 D15
SAINTLY
ct. Castle Hill 217 B7
ST MALO
av. Hunters Hill 314 A14
ST MARIA
pl. Blair Athol 510 H1
ST MARK
cl. Blair Athol 510 J1
ST MARKS
av. Castle Hill 217 K9
la. Randwick 377 C10
rd. Darling Point 13 J8
rd. Randwick 377 D13
ST MARTINS
cr. Blacktown 274 K5
ST MARYS
av. Bondi Jctn 377 G5
la. Camperdown 17 C10
la. Newtown 17 C10
rd. Berkshire Pk 180 A13
rd. Sydney ....D H7
rd. Sydney 4 B4
st. Balmain East 8 H10
st. Camperdown 17 C10
st. Newtown 17 C10
st. West Hoxton 392 D9
ST MATTHEWS
la. Baulkham Hl, off
  Rose St 247 G13
ST MERVYNS
av. Point Piper 14 J4
ST MICHAELS
rd. Baulkham Hl 247 D4
pl. Vaucluse 348 B5
ST MONICA
wy. Blair Athol 510 J1
ST NEOT
av. Potts Point 4 K1
ST PAUL
pl. Blair Athol 510 K2
ST PAULS
av. Castle Hill 217 A10
av. Kellyville 216 J8
cl. Burwood 341 K16
cr. Emu Plains 235 D9
cr. Liverpool 394 G5
la. Cobbitty 446 J11
la. Chester Hill 337 H12
pl. Chippendale 19 C5
rd. N Balgowlah 287 C6

st. Randwick 377 B16
wy. Blacktown 274 A6
ST PETER
cl. Hinchinbrk 392 K2
pl. Blair Athol 510 K2
ST PETERS
la. Darlinghurst 4 E8
la. Redfern 19 D10
st. Darlinghurst 4 E8
st. St Peters 374 H13
ST SIMON
pl. Blair Athol 480 J16
pl. Castle Hill 218 E9
ST STEPHEN
rd. Blair Athol 480 J16
ST THOMAS
rd. Mulgoa 295 D11
st. Bronte 377 K11
st. Clovelly 377 K11
ST VINCENT
rd. Bexley 432 D1
ST VINCENTS
rd. Greenwich 314 K8
rd. Greenwich 315 A7
SAIPAN
av. Lethrdg Pk 240 H1
SALADILLO
gr. Wallacia 325 A16
SALADINE
av. Punchbowl 399 H4
SALAMANDER
gr. Baulkham Hl 246 K2
pl. Mt Lewis 370 A15
rd. Raby 451 E12
st. St Clair 269 F15
SALAMAUA
cr. Holsworthy 426 D3
pl. Glenfield 424 G12
rd. Whalan 241 A13
SALECICH
pl. Bonnyrigg 364 E6
SALEM
cl. St Clair 269 G13
SALERNO
cl. Emu Heights 235 B5
la. Emu Heights, off
  Salerno Cl. 235 B4
pl. Blairmount 481 A13
pl. St Ives Ch 223 J5
st. Forestville 256 A6
SALERWONG
pl. Ryde 282 E12
SALES
av. Silverdale 353 J15
SALFORD
dr. Beaumont Hills ..215 A4
pl. Kellyville 215 A4
st. Ingleburn 453 E5
st. St Clair 269 G13
st. Stanhpe Gdn 215 D8
SALIGNA
wy. Mcquarie Fd 424 E16
SALIGNUS
pl. Narellan Vale 478 J14
SALINA
st. W Pnnant Hl 249 H7
SALISBURY
av. Bexley 402 H14
rd. Glenfield 424 C11
rd. Kemps Ck 360 E1
st. West Hoxton 392 B11
SALISBURY DOWNS
dr. W Pnnant Hl 249 A2
SALIX
pl. Engadine 488 H16
SALLAWAY
pl. W Pnnant Hl 249 B1
rd. Galston 159 B8
rd. Galston 159 C9
rd. Middle Dural 159 B8
SALLEE
gln. Kingswood 267 F2
la. Kingswood, off
  Sallee Gln 267 F2
SALLY
pl. Glendenning 242 E4
pl. Kellyville 217 C2
SALMON
cl. Asquith 192 C8
rd. S Windsor 150 F2
SALT
st. Concord 342 D4
SALTASH
st. Yagoona 368 F15
SALTBUSH
pl. Bossley Park 333 J9
SALTER
av. Minto 452 K14
ct. Denistone E 281 H9
ct. Harringtn Pk 478 E6
rd. Bossley Park 333 K9
st. Gladesville 313 A12
SALTERS
rd. Wilberforce 67 G14
SALT PAN
rd. Peakhurst 429 J1
SALTPETRE
cl. Eagle Vale 481 H5
SALVANA
pl. Claymore 481 C11
SALVESTRO
pl. Bella Vista 246 G6
SALVIA
av. Bankstown 399 H2
cl. Cherrybrook 219 F10
SAMANTHA
cr. Glendenning 242 J4
pl. Smeaton Gra 479 E9
SAMANTHA RILEY
dr. Beaumont Hills ..215 A4
SAMARAI
pl. Beacon Hill 257 H4
rd. Whalan 241 A12
SAMES
cl. Mona Vale 198 K3
SAM JOHNSON
wy. Lane Cove W ...283 G15
SAMMUT
cr. Chipping Ntn 396 D4
st. Smithfield 305 F14
SAMOA
av. Picnic Point 428 D8
pl. Lethbrdg Pk 240 H1
SAMORA
av. Cremorne 316 A9
SAMPSON
cr. Acacia Gdn 214 F16
ct. Quakers Hill 214 F16
pl. Rsemeadow 540 J4
SAMUEL
la. Tempe, off
  Samuel St 374 C16
la. Camperdown 17 B7
ct. Airds 512 B14
pl. Quakers Hill 214 A8
pl. St Clair 269 K11
st. Bligh Park 150 J8
st. Lidcombe 339 G8
st. Mona Vale 198 H3
st. Peakhurst 430 B5
st. Ryde 281 K16
st. Surry Hills ....F F10
st. Surry Hills 4 A13
st. Tempe 374 C16
st. Wiley Park 400 J3
SAMUEL FOSTER
dr. S Penrith 267 A4

st. Penshurst 431 C3
st. Riverwood 400 F14
st. Silverwater 309 H13
st. S Hurstville 432 A9
st. Watsons Bay 318 F15
st. Waverley 377 G6
SAMUEL MARSDEN
rd. Orchard Hills 269 A10
SAMUELS
av. Jannali 461 A9
SANANANTA
av. Allambie Ht 257 D11
rd. Holsworthy 396 D16
SANBROOK
la. Newtown 17 A10
SAN CRISTOBAL
dr. Green Valley 363 A8
SANCTUARY
av. Avalon 140 A15
cl. Cherrybrook 219 F14
dr. Beaumont Hills ..185 G15
dr. Windsor Dn 180 F1
pl. Chipping Ntn 366 K14
SANCTUARY PARK
dr. Plumpton 242 A9
SANCTUARY POINT
rd. W Pnnant Hl 248 F8
SANDY
cl. Wrrngtn Dns 238 B3
la. Thirlmere 561 G11
rd. Burraneer 493 E15
SANDY BAY
rd. Clontarf 287 E12
SANDY HOLLOW
la. Ebenezer 68 D8
SANFORD
st. Glendenning 242 F3
SANGRADO
st. Seaforth 287 A10
SAN MARINO
dr. Prestons 393 E14
SAN MICHEL
cr. Ryde, off
  O'Regan Dr. 312 B4
SAN MICHELLE
av. Baulkham Hl 247 G14
SANONI
av. Sandringham 463 E2
SAN REMO
av. Gymea 491 E2
pl. Dural 189 C5
rd. Baulkham Hl 247 B10
SAN STEFANO
cr. Ryde, off
  O'Regan Dr. 312 B4
SANTA
pl. Bossley Park 334 C11
SANTA MARINA
av. Waverley 377 F8
SANTANGELO
cl. Edensor Pk 363 G3
SANTA ROSA
av. Ryde 282 B11
SANTIAGO
pl. Seven Hills 275 H4
SANTLEY
cr. Kingswood 237 H13
SANTON
pl. Cranebrook 207 F12
SANTOS
pl. Toongabbie 275 F11
SAOKI
ct. Quakers Hill 214 B11
SAPIUM
wy. Mcquarie Fd 454 F3
SAPPHIRE
cct. Quakers Hill 214 G12
la. Eagle Vale 481 C7
st. Greystanes 306 A1
SAPPHO
rd. Warwck Frm 365 K13
st. Canley Ht 365 B1
SARACEN
rd. Beecroft 250 E10
SARAH
cr. Baulkham Hl 247 F7
pl. Appin 569 E10
pl. Bossley Park 334 C9
pl. Cecil Hills 362 J4
pl. Illawong 459 D8
pl. Minchinbury 271 G8
st. Enmore 17 B16
st. Mascot 405 A5
wy. Minto 482 J3
SARAH DURACK
av. Homebush B 340 G4
SARAH HOLLANDS
dr. Horngsea Pk 392 D14

st. Putney 312 D7
st. Woodpark 306 G16
SANDRIDGE
st. Bondi 378 C5
SANDRINGHAM
av. Cmbrdg Pk 237 J10
dr. Carlingford 279 D5
dr. Cecil Hills 362 G4
st. Dolls Point 463 H1
st. St Johns Pk 364 D4
st. Sans Souci 433 C16
SANDS
st. Sydney ....C D14
st. Sydney 3 E7
SANDSTOCK
pl. Woodcroft 243 F7
SANDSTONE
av. Glenmore Pk 266 F15
SANDWELL
st. Surry Hills 20 D1

GREGORY'S STREET DIRECTORY 131

SA — STREETS

SARAH JANE
av. Beaumont Hills....185 K12
SARAHS
wk. Mosman....317 E13
SARAH WEST
pl. Mt Annan....509 G1
SARDAM
av. Cranebrook....206 H8
SARDAN
cr. Fairfield....336 F8
SARDINIA
av. Glenwood....245 J3
pl. Birchgrove....7 G4
SARDONYX
av. Hobartville....118 E9
SARDYGA
st. Plumpton....242 A7
SARGENTS
rd. Ebenezer....67 J13
rd. Minchinbury....271 B7
SARIC
av. Georges Hall....368 C16
SARISSA
wy. Mcquarie Fd....454 H4
SARK
gr. Minto....482 F8
SARNER
rd. Greenwich....315 A7
SARNIA
cr. Killara....253 G11
SARRE
pl. Prospect....274 G12
SARSFIELD
cct. Bexley North....402 E9
st. Blacktown....244 K14
SARTOR
cr. Bossley Park....333 G11
SASSAFRAS
cl. Bradbury....511 G12
la. Cabramatta....365 H8
st. Vaucluse....318 E16
st. Parklea....215 B13
SASSAFRAS GULLY
rd. Springwood....201 G5
SATARA
av. Cabramatta W....365 B6
SATELBERG
st. Holsworthy....426 D4
SATINASH
st. Parklea....215 A13
SATINWOOD
cl. Alfords Point....429 B14
SATTERLEY
av. Turramurra....252 D4
SATURN
pl. Doonside....243 D15
SAUNDERS
av. Liverpool....365 B16
la. Quakers Hill....243 C2
la. Yagoona....368 K11
rd. Menai....458 H14
rd. Raby....451 D12
rd. Errmington....310 E4
rd. Oakville....122 G8
st. N Parramatta....278 E12
st. Pyrmont....12 E3
SAUNDERS BAY
rd. Caringbah....492 K12
SAURINE
st. Bankstown....368 H15
SAUTERNE
cr. Minchinbury....272 A8
SAUTERNES
pl. Eschol Park....481 D5
SAUVAGE
pl. Doonside....273 F5
pl. Newington....310 A16
SAUVIGNON
cl. Eschol Park....481 B4
SAVA
pl. Bonnyrigg....364 A10
SAVANNAH
la. St Clair, off
Fantail Cr....271 A15
pl. Erskine Park....271 A15
SAVERY
cr. Blacktown....274 C8
cr. Fairfield W....335 C12
SAVIC
pl. Bonnyrigg Ht....363 C7

SAVOY
av. East Killara....254 H6
cr. Chester Hill....368 B3
ct. W Pnnant Hl....249 H9
SAWELL
st. Bossley Park....333 K10
SAWMILL
la. Mona Vale....199 A3
SAWTELL
cl. Hoxton Park....392 K6
SAWYER
cr. Lane Cove W, off
Whitfield Av....283 F12
la. Artarmon....314 K2
SAXBY
st. Girraween....276 C14
wy. Blacktown....273 G5
SAXON
dr. Cecil Hills....362 E8
ct. Wentwthvle....277 C9
st. Belfield....371 D9
st. Wy. Airds....512 A13
SAXONVALE
rd. Edensor Pk....333 E14
rd. Baulkham Hl....246 H3
rd. Bella Vista....246 H3
SAXONY
dr. Horsley Pk....332 G6
SAYERS
st. N Balgowlah....287 E4
SAYONARA
pl. Greenfld Pk....334 E14
SAYWELL
la. Btn-le-Sds....433 K2
rd. Mcquarie Fd....453 J1
rd. Mcquarie Fd....454 A2
st. Chatswood....284 K12
st. Marrickville....374 D12
SCADDAN
st. Quakers Hill....214 E9
SCAHILL
st. Campsie....372 B16
SCAIFE
st. Padstow....429 B4
SCALES
pde. Balgowlah Ht....287 H12
SCANLEN
wy. Ingleburn....452 K10
SCAPOLITE
pl. Eagle Vale....481 E7
SCARAB
st. Bnkstn Aprt....397 K1
SCARANISH
wy. Mcquarie Lk....423 G13
SCARBOROUGH
cl. Mt Annan....479 B13
cl. Lurnea....394 C12
cl. Narellan....478 E16
ct. W Pnnant Hl....249 A1
rd. North Bondi....378 G3
la. Kogarah....433 E8
pl. Beacon Hill....257 G2
st. Bundeena....523 J10
st. Monterey....433 G9
wy. Cherrybrook....219 A14
SCARCELLA
pl. Edensor Pk....333 J15
SCARFE
st. Fairfield W....335 F13
SCARR COTTAGE
av. Blair Athol....511 A1
SCARSBOROUGH
cr. Bligh Park....150 C5
SCARUS
pl. Rsemeadow....540 F3
SCARVELL
av. McGraths Hl....121 J13
SCENIC
cct. Cranebrook....237 C1
cir. Blaxland....234 A5
cr. Mt Riverview....204 G15
cr. S Hurstville....432 A13
gr. Glenwood....246 A5
SCHAEFER
tce. Glenwood....215 K16
SCHERELL
st. Shalvey....211 A14
st. Dharruk....241 B7
SCHEYVILLE
rd. Maraylya....124 B5
rd. Oakville....122 K8
rd. Scheyville....123 B8

SCHILLER
pl. Emerton....240 K6
SCHLEICHER
st. St Marys....269 D3
SCHOEFFEL
gr. Horngsea Pk....392 F13
SCHOFIELD
av. Earlwood....402 F4
av. Rockdale....433 D2
pde. Pennant Hills....220 D12
pl. Menai....458 J11
rd. Pitt Town....122 K3
rd. Scheyville....123 A4
st. Riverwood....400 A10
SCHOFIELDS
rd. Rouse Hill....185 A13
rd. Schofields....183 G16
SCHOFIELDS FARM
rd. Schofields....183 F13
SCHOOL
cl. Villawood....337 G16
la. Earlwood, off
William St....402 H4
la. Five Dock....342 J10
pde. Doonside....243 C13
pde. Marrickville....373 F13
pde. Padstow....429 C2
pde. Westmead....307 E4
rd. Galston....159 D8
st. Balmain East....8 G7
SCHOOL HOUSE
la. Glenbrook, off
Mann St....233 K16
rd. Regentville....265 H4
SCHUBERT
pl. Bonnyrigg Ht....363 E5
wy. Clarmnt Ms....268 G4
SCHULTZ
st. Balmain....7 A9
st. St Marys....269 K4
SCHUMACK
st. North Ryde....282 J11
SCHWEBEL
la. Glenorie....127 G3
st. Marrickville....373 J14
SCIARRA
cr. Acacia Gdn....244 J1
SCIENCE
rd. Camperdown....18 B2
rd. Richmond....118 G12
SCINTILLA
gr. Doonside....243 H15
SCIPIO
st. Yagoona....368 D15
SCOBIE
pl. Mt Annan....479 B13
st. Doonside....273 F1
SCONE
pl. Doonside....243 A11
SCORPIUS
pl. Cranebrook....207 F5
SCOT
st. Bargo....567 C3
SCOTCHEY
st. Prairiewood....334 F12
SCOTNEY
pl. Collaroy Plat....228 K13
pl. Quakers Hill....213 H10
SCOTT
cr. Roseville....285 D4
ct. Cherrybrook....249 F1
la. Kogarah....433 D7
la. Maroubra....407 F13
pl. Baulkham Hl....247 D5
pl. Kirrawee....460 J16
pl. St Ives....224 G8
pl. Colyton....270 H8
st. Bankstown....400 A3
st. Belfield....371 D9
st. Bronte....377 J1
st. Campbelltown....512 B3
st. Croydon....342 G12
st. Fairfield E....337 F12
st. Five Dock....342 H9
st. Kogarah....433 D7
st. Liverpool....395 E4
st. Maroubra....407 F13
st. Marsfield....282 C5
st. Mortdale....430 K6
st. Narellan....478 H12
st. Punchbowl....399 J2
st. Pyrmont....12 F1
st. Springwood....202 A5

st. Toongabbie....276 E11
st. Willoughby....285 E16
SCOTTS-DALE
cct. West Hoxton....392 E5
cct. West Hoxton....392 D5
SCOTTSDALE
st. Stanhope Gdn....215 B12
SCOTTS FARM
rd. Grose Wold....115 E9
SCOULLER
la. Marrickville....374 E9
st. Marrickville....374 E9
SCOUT
pl. Sydney....B E8
SCOUTS
la. Paddington....21 F1
SCRIBBLY
pl. Mcquarie Fd....454 F4
SCRIBBLY GUM
cl. Hornsby Ht....161 K9
cl. Voyager Pt....427 B4
la. Mona Vale, off
Waratah St....199 A3
pl. Alfords Point....459 B3
SCRIBBLYGUM
cct. Rouse Hill....184 K7
cct. Rouse Hill....185 A7
SCRIVENER
la. Springwood....202 E3
st. Warwck Frm....395 J3
SCRIVIN
st. Leumeah....482 A16
SCROGGIES
rd. Thirlmere....561 A12
SCRUBWREN
pl. Glenmore Pk....265 J12
SCULLIN
pl. N Wahroonga....192 G14
pl. Penrith....237 C6
SCULLY
pl. Mt Annan....479 F15
st. Seaforth....287 A10
SCYLLA
rd. Oyster Bay....461 A6
SEA
st. Hunters Hill....313 H10
av. Mona Vale....199 F4
SEABORG
av. Lucas Ht....487 J12
SEABROOK
av. Grays Point....491 B11
av. Russell Lea....343 E7
cr. Doonside....273 G3
SEAEAGLE
cr. Green Valley....363 C11
SEAFORD
cct. Kellyville Rdg....214 K3
SEAFORTH
av. Oatley....430 J10
av. Woolooware....493 F11
cr. Seaforth....287 A10
st. Bexley....402 K16
SEDDON
pl. Campbelltown....511 K3
st. Bankstown....399 F6
SEDDON HILL
rd. Harbord....258 J16
SEDGEMAN
av. Menai....458 G7
SEDGER
rd. Kenthurst....187 G4
SEDGMAN
cr. Shalvey....210 J14
st. Greystanes....306 A10
SEDGWICK
st. Leumeah....482 A16
st. Leumeah....512 K10
st. Smeaton Gra....479 E10
SEE
la. Kingsford....406 E1
st. Kingsford....406 E1
st. Meadowbank....311 F9
SEEANA
pl. Belrose....225 K10
SEEBREES
st. Manly Vale....287 J3
SEELAND
pl. Padstow Ht....429 B6
SEFTON
rd. Thornleigh....220 J8
rd. Westleigh....220 J8
SEGEFIELD
pl. Casula....395 B12

SEASIDE
pde. S Coogee....407 J7
SEA SPRAY
ct. Chipping Ntn....366 K15
SEATON
av. Wahroonga....222 A4
cr. Cranebrook....207 G13
st. Stanhpe Gdn....215 E6
SEATTLE
cl. St Clair....270 J11
SEAVIEW
av. Harbord....258 J14
av. Newport....169 H10
pde. Belrose....226 C15
pde. Collaroy....229 D15
st. Ashfield....372 K7
st. Balgowlah....287 G10
st. Clovelly....377 G11
st. Cronulla....493 K9
st. Dulwich Hill....373 F9
st. Mt Krng-gai....163 B10
st. Summer Hill....373 A7
st. Waverley....377 H7
SEBASTIAN
av. Rsemeadow....540 F6
dr. Dural....219 A2
SEBASTOPOL
rd. Emu Heights....235 A1
st. Enmore....16 G14
SECANT
st. Liverpool....395 D1
SECOND
av. Berala....339 E15
av. Blacktown....244 H14
av. Campsie....371 G10
av. Canley Vale....366 B3
av. Condell Park....398 D4
av. Eastwood....281 C9
av. Epping....280 G3
av. Five Dock....343 H4
av. Gymea Bay....491 D10
av. Jannali....460 J11
av. Kentlyn....513 B7
av. Kingswood....237 H14
av. Lane Cove....314 G4
av. Lindfield....254 F13
av. Llandilo....208 K9
av. Loftus....490 A5
av. Mcquarie Fd....454 A1
av. Maroubra....407 G9
av. Narrabeen....228 J4
av. North Ryde....282 H13
av. Seven Hills....275 H2
av. Toongabbie....276 F8
av. West Hoxton....362 D16
av. West Hoxton....392 C6
av. Willoughby....285 H11
rd. Berkshire Pk....180 B2
st. Ashbury....372 G9
st. Granville....308 G13
st. Parramatta....279 A15
st. Warragamba....353 G6
wk. Chester Hill....337 J13

132 GREGORY'S STREET DIRECTORY

STREETS SH

SEGENHOE
pl. Richmond 118 C5
st. Arncliffe 403 G11
SEGERS
av. Padstow 399 D16
SEIDEL
av. Picnic Point 428 G7
pl. Abbotsbury 333 C13
SEINE
ct. St Clair 270 H10
pl. Kearns 451 C16
pl. Miranda 461 K15
SELBORNE
st. Burwood 342 C12
SELBY
av. Dee Why 258 E6
pl. Blacktown 274 D5
pl. Minto 482 K10
pl. St Johns Pk 364 G3
SELDON
st. Quakers Hill 213 F7
SELEMS
pde. Revesby 398 H15
SELF
pl. Shalvey 211 B13
SELINA
pl. Cherrybrook 219 D7
pl. Glenwood 245 E2
SELKIRK
av. Cecil Park 331 E12
pl. Bligh Park 150 B7
pl. Camden S 507 B12
st. St Andrews 452 B13
st. Winston Hills 277 D4
SELLERS
la. Greenacre 370 D12
SELLWOOD
st. Btn-le-Sds 434 A1
SELMA
pl. Oakhurst 242 A2
SELMON
st. Sans Souci 433 D14
SELMS
pl. Minto 452 J16
SELWA
pl. Kareela 461 C12
SELWAY
av. Moorebank 396 D10
SELWYN
av. Cmbrdg Gdn 237 G2
cl. Pennant Hills 220 D14
pl. Cartwright 393 K6
pl. Fairfield W 335 E10
pl. Quakers Hill 243 J3
st. Artarmon 285 B13
st. Paddington 20 F1
st. Pymble 223 B15
st. Wollstncraft 315 D9
SEMAAN
st. Werrington 238 H10
SEMANA
pl. Winmalee 173 G12
st. Whalan 241 B13
SEMILLON
cr. Eschol Park 481 D2
SEMPLE
st. Ryde 282 C15
SENIOR
st. Canley Vale 366 C3
SENNAR
la. Erskine Park, off Sennar Rd 271 A16
rd. Erskine Park 271 A16
SENTA
rd. Londonderry 177 J12
SENTINEL
av. Kellyville 216 H3
cl. Horngsea Pk 392 F16
st. Glenwood 215 C16
SENTRY
dr. Parklea 215 A13
dr. Stanhpe Gdn 215 A10
SEPIK
pl. Kearns 451 C16
st. Holsworthy 426 G7
SEPPELT
pl. Edensor Pk 333 D15
st. Eastern Ck 272 F8
SEPTIMUS
av. Punchbowl 399 K7
st. Chatswood 285 B9
st. Erskineville 17 K13

SEQUOIA
cl. West Pymble 252 H11
gr. Menai, off Fern Cct W 458 J14
SERA
st. Lane Cove 314 C2
SERAM
pl. Kings Park 244 D2
SERCIAL
pl. Eschol Park 481 C3
SERGEANT LARKIN
cr. Daceyville 406 G3
SERGEANTS
la. St Leonards, off Chandos St 315 D5
SERI
pl. Bossley Park 333 K10
SERINA
av. Castle Hill 248 C3
SERMELFI
dr. Glenorie 127 K1
SERPENTINE
cr. N Balgowlah 287 E7
la. Bowen Mtn 84 D11
pde. Vaucluse 348 E4
pl. Eagle Vale 481 B7
rd. Hunters Hill 314 C12
rd. Kirrawee 491 A9
st. Bossley Park 333 G5
st. Merrylands W 306 J11
SERVICE
av. Ashfield 372 K9
la. Five Dock 343 A8
SESQUICENTENARY
sq. Sydney C G2
SESTO
pl. Bossley Park 333 G8
SETA
cl. St Clair 299 H2
SETON
pl. Rouse Hill 185 D4
rd. Moorebank 395 K8
SETTLERS
bvd. Liberty Gr 311 C14
cl. Castle Hill 218 F11
cr. Bligh Park 150 H7
gld. Wrrngtn Dns 238 B4
wy. Westleigh 220 G7
SEVEN HILLS
rd. Baulkham Hl 247 A11
rd. Bella Vista 246 E9
rd. Seven Hills 246 A14
rd.s, Seven Hills 275 D6
wy. Baulkham Hl 246 F9
SEVENOAKS
cr. Bass Hill 367 G7
pl. Jannali 461 A13
SEVENTEENTH
av. Austral 361 F16
av.e, West Hoxton 391 K1
SEVENTH
av. Austral 391 A12
av. Berala 339 D14
av. Campsie 371 H11
av. Jannali 460 K12
av. Llandilo 207 J4
av. Loftus 490 A7
av. Seven Hills 275 K3
st. Granville 308 G15
st. Mascot 405 A7
st. Warragamba 353 G4
SEVEN WAYS
Bondi Beach 348 C16
North Bondi 348 C16
SEVERN
pl. Kearns 450 K16
rd. Bringelly 387 G3
rd. Woronora 489 H1
st. Maroubra 407 H11
st. St Marys 239 G6
SEVIER
av. Rhodes 311 C10
SEVILLE
pl. Glenwood 215 F12
pl. Kenthurst 157 J11
st. Fairfield E 337 A13
st. Lane Cove 314 B3
st. N Parramatta 278 B10
SEWELL
av. Padstow Ht 429 E7
av. Seven Hills 246 A13
st. Ryde 311 H1
SEXTANS
pl. Cranebrook 207 H6

SEXTON
av. Castle Hill 217 G13
la. Cammeray, off West St 315 H6
SEYMOUR
cl. Wahroonga 221 H16
la. Marrickville, off Frampton Av 374 A13
pde. Belfield 371 C10
pl. Bossley Park 333 E11
pl. Paddington 20 F1
st. Croydon Pk 372 B6
st. Drummoyne 343 J1
st. Dundas Vy 280 A7
st. Hurstville Gr 431 G11
wy. Kellyville 216 K3
wy. Kellyville 217 A4
SEYTON
pl. Rsemeadow 540 C3
SHAARON
ct. Banksia 403 F12
la. Banksia, off Shaaron Ct 403 F12
SHACKEL
av. Brookvale 258 C8
av. Clovelly 378 A13
av. Concord 341 J6
av. Gladesville 312 G12
av. Kingsgrove 401 K5
av. Old Guildford 337 E7
rd. Bangor 459 D14
SHACKLETON
av. Birrong 368 J5
av. Tregear 240 F4
SHADDOCK
av. Pymble 253 B10
av. Villawood 367 F2
SHADE
pl. Lugarno 429 K9
SHADFORTH
pl. Paddington 4 K16
rd. Mt Wilson 59 A8
st. Mosman 316 J11
st. Paddington 4 K15
st. Wiley Park 400 G1
SHADFORTH BRIDGE
Silverdale 384 H1
SHADLOW
cr. St Clair 269 H10
SHADWELL
cr. Kings Lngly 246 A7
SHAFT
st. Silverwater 309 K10
st. Silverwater 309 K9
SHAFTESBURY
rd. Burwood 342 B15
st. Carlton 432 H7
SHAFTSBURY
av. Castlereagh 175 K5
rd. Denistone W 281 A10
rd. Eastwood 280 K7
rd. West Ryde 281 A10
SHAKESPEARE
dr. St Clair 270 C15
dr. Winmalee 173 J8
pl. Sydney B G15
st. Campbelltown 512 A3
st. Campsie 372 A11
st. Wetherill Pk 334 G5
SHALOM
cl. Old Guildford 337 F8
wy. Mcquarie Pk 283 C7
SHAMROCK
cl. Winmalee 173 D10
ct. St Clair 269 K10
pde. Killarney Ht 286 D1
pl. Glendenning 242 H3
st. Smithfield 335 F2
SHAND
cl. Illawong 459 G4
cr. Turramurra 252 G2
SHANDLIN
pl. S Penrith 267 A7
SHANE
pl. Bella Vista 246 E5
pl. Kurrajong Ht 63 E11
st. Colyton 270 E4
SHANE PARK
rd. Shanes Park 209 H9
SHANKE
cr. Kings Lngly 245 C3
SHANNON
av. Killarney Ht 256 C15
av. Merrylands 307 E10
gln. St Clair 270 A12
la. St Clair, off Menzies Cct 270 A13
pl. Kearns 481 A2
rd. Bringelly 387 J1
rd. Mt Colah 162 B16
st. Greenacre 370 F7
st. Lalor Park 245 G9
st. St Ives 224 E11
SHANUK
st. Frenchs Frst 255 G1
SHARAN
pl. Forestville 255 G8
SHARI
av. Picnic Point 428 G5
av. Picnic Point 428 G6
SHARLAND
av. Chatswood W 284 F14
pl. Smithfield 335 C3
SHARLEEN
ct. Bella Vista 246 C6
SHARMAN
cl. Harringtn Pk 478 H8
SHARN
st. Kurnell 466 E8
SHARON
cl. Bossley Park 333 J11
cl. Hornsby 192 A16
pl. Engadine 488 E15
pl. Rooty Hill 271 J6
st. Holsworthy 426 D12
SHARP
cl. Castle Hill 218 A9
st. Belmore 401 G1
st. Matraville 406 K15
SHARPE
pl. Camden S 507 B15
SHARREE
wy. Acacia Gdn 214 K15
SHARROCK
av. Glenwood 215 J13
SHARWEN
pl. Blaxland 234 B5
SHAUGHNESSY
st. Oakhurst 242 C4
SHAULA
cr. Erskine Park 300 H2
la. Erskine Park, off Shaula Cr 300 H2
SHAUN
dr. Glenwood 215 J15
SHAW
av. Earlwood 402 E6
av. Kingsford 376 C16
cl. Barden Rdg 488 G1
la. Bexley North 402 E9
la. Sefton 368 F2
pl. Fairfield W 335 D13
pl. Prospect 274 G12
pl. Rooty Hill 242 A12
rd. Ingleburn 452 K7
st. Beverly Hills 401 B15
st. Bexley North 402 A10
st. Cmbrdg Pk 238 B11
st. East Ryde 283 A14
st. Kingsgrove 402 A10
st. Kogarah 433 C8
st. North Bondi 348 B14
st. Petersham 15 J14
SHAWNEE
st. Greenfld Pk 334 A13
SHAWS
pl. Yarramundi 145 B7
SHAYNE
ct. Oakdale 500 D13
SHEAFFE
pl. Davidson 225 A16
SHEAHAN
av. Guildford 338 D7
pwy. Warwck Frm, off Sheahan St 365 H15
st. Warwck Frm 365 H15
SHEARER
la. Padstow 399 C15
la. St Clair, off Shearer St 270 F12
pl. Elderslie 477 H16
st. St Clair 270 F12
SHEARING
pl. Bonnyrigg 364 C5
SHEARS
wy. Minto 482 J5

SHEARWATER
av. Woronora Ht 489 D4
cr. Yarramundi 145 E6
dr. Glenmore Pk 266 A13
dr. Warriewood 198 H10
rd. Hinchinbrk 393 E2
SHEATHER
av. St Ives 254 D1
pl. Campbelltown 511 H8
SHEATHERS
la. Camden 506 E2
la. Cawdor 506 E2
la. Grasmere 506 E2
SHEBA
cr. S Penrith 267 C1
SHEDWORTH
st. Marayong 244 B5
SHEEHAN
st. Eastwood 281 H7
st. Wentwthvle 276 H14
SHEEHY
av. Rookwood 340 B16
av. Rookwood 370 B1
st. Glebe 12 A7
SHEFFIELD
st. Auburn 339 A1
st. Kingsgrove 401 J9
st. Merrylands 307 G11
SHEILA
pl. Kellyville 216 F6
SHELBY
rd. St Ives Ch 223 K5
SHELDON
pl. Bellevue Hill 14 J8
SHELL
rd. Burraneer 493 E15
SHELLBANK
av. Mosman 316 H2
pde. Cremorne 316 G3
SHELLCOTE
rd. Greenacre 370 C6
SHELLCOVE
rd. Neutral Bay 6 H5
SHELLEY
cr. Blacktown 273 G6
pl. Wetherill Pk 334 K6
rd. N Turramurra 223 E8
rd. Wallacia 324 J13
st. Campbelltown 512 B3
st. Campsie 372 A10
st. Enfield 371 H3
st. Sydney A A16
st. Sydney C B1
st. Sydney 3 D1
st. Winston Hills 277 F2
SHELLEYS
la. Marrickville, off Llewellyn St 374 F10
la. Thirlmere 561 G15
SHELLY
cr. Beaumont Hills 185 J16
SHELSLEY
pl. S Penrith 267 A7
SHELTON
av. Winmalee 173 E7
la. Richmond 119 A5
SHENSTONE
rd. Riverwood 429 J1
SHENTON
av. Bankstown 399 B4
SHE-OAK
gr. Narellan Vale 478 J14
SHEOAK
cl. Cherrybrook 219 G11
pl. Alfords Point 459 A2
pl. Bossley Park 333 G8
pl. Colyton 270 J6
pl. Glenmore Pk 265 H11
SHEPHARD
st. Marayong 244 D7
SHEPHERD
av. Padstow Ht 429 G7
la. Ashfield 372 G5
la. Baulkham Hl 248 A7
la. Chippendale 18 J2
la. Darlington 18 J5
pde. Bardwell Vy 403 B8
rd. Artarmon 285 A13
st. Ashfield 372 G5
st. Chippendale 18 J3
st. Colyton 270 E8
st. Darlington 18 H6
st. Kurnell 466 B9
st. Lalor Park 245 D10

GREGORY'S STREET DIRECTORY 133

SH STREETS

st. Liverpool...395 D8
st. Maroubra...406 K8
st. Marrickville...374 B10
st. Ryde...311 H2
st. St Marys...269 K7

SHEPHERDS
dr. Cherrybrook...219 E10
rd. Freemns Rch...66 F16
rd. Freemns Rch...90 B2

SHEPPARD
la. Emu Plains, off Sheppard Rd...235 J9
rd. Emu Plains...235 H11
rd. Narraweena...258 D4

SHER
pl. Prospect...275 A11

SHERACK
pl. Minto...453 A14

SHERARS
av. Strathfield...341 H16

SHERBORNE
pl. Glendenning...242 G2

SHERBROOK
rd. Asquith...192 A12
rd. Hornsby...221 K1

SHERBROOKE
av. Double Bay...14 F7
rd. West Ryde...311 D2
st. Darlinghurst...4 D11
st. Rooty Hill...242 A16

SHEREDAN
rd. Castlereagh...176 D11

SHERIDAN
cl. Milperra...398 A7
pl. Manly...288 F7
st. Granville...308 F16
wy. Mt Annan...479 E16

SHERIFF
st. Ashcroft...394 D1

SHERLOCK
av. Panania...428 A1

SHERMAN
st. Greenacre...370 B5

SHERRIDON
cr. Quakers Hill...214 C16

SHERRINGHAM
la. Cranebrook, off Sherringham Rd.207 E13
la. Cranebrook, off Pendock St...207 F13
rd. Cranebrook...207 D12

SHERRITT
pl. Prairiewood...334 H8

SHERRY
pl. Minchinbury...271 G7
st. Mona Vale...199 B5

SHERWIN
av. Castle Hill...217 K14
st. Henley...313 B15
wy. Minto...482 J6

SHERWOOD
av. Springwood...201 F2
av. Yowie Bay...492 B11
cct. Penrith...237 D10
cl. Pennant Hills...250 E2
cr. Narraweena...258 C2
ct. Carlingford...249 E13
la. Penrith, off Sherwood Cct...237 D10
pl. North Ryde...282 J14
pl. St Ives...254 A2
rd. Merrylands W...306 K14
st. Kensington...376 C12
st. Kurrajong...85 D3
st. Old Tngabbie...277 D9
st. Revesby...398 G13

SHETLAND
rd. Blairmount...481 A13

SHIEL
pl. St Andrews...452 B13

SHIELDS
la. Pennant Hills...220 H15
rd. Colyton...270 F7
st. Marayong...244 C3

SHIELS
ct. Glenmore Pk...265 E10

SHIERS
av. Mascot...404 J6

SHINFIELD
av. St Ives...223 J13

SHINNICK
dr. Oakhurst...241 H4

SHIPHAM
st. Concord...342 A3

SHIPLEY
av. N Strathfield...341 F6

SHIPROCK
rd. Port Hacking...523 A3

SHIPTON
pl. Dean Park...242 F1

SHIPWAY
st. Marsfield...251 J14

SHIPWRIGHT
pl. Oyster Bay...461 A6

SHIRAZ
cl. Edensor Pk...363 E1
pl. Eschol Park...481 D2
pl. Minchinbury...271 K7

SHIRLEY
av. Roselands...400 J10
cl. Narraweena...258 E3
cr. Matraville...436 J4
la. Campsie, off Canterbury Rd...372 A16
la. Matraville, off Jordons La...436 J3
la. Wollstncraft...315 D9
rd. Crows Nest...315 E8
rd. Miranda...462 G16
rd. Roseville...284 C7
rd. Wollstncraft...315 B11
rd. Wollstncraft...315 E8
st. Alexandria...375 F15
st. Bexley...432 G1
st. Blacktown...245 A15
st. Carlingford...279 K3
st. Epping...250 D16
st. Padstow...429 A1
st. Rosehill...309 B9

SHIRLEY STRICKLAND
av. Homebush B...340 H4

SHIRLOW
st. Marrickville...374 D13

SHOAL
pl. Illawong...459 C5

SHOALHAVEN
rd. Sylvania Wtr...462 C11
rd. Sylvania Wtr...462 C13
st. Homebush B...310 H15
st. Ruse...512 D6
st. Wakeley...334 K12

SHOEMAKER
pl. Bonnyrigg...364 C6

SHOEMARK
pl. Narellan...478 F15

SHOPLANDS
rd. Annangrove...155 F4

SHORE
br. Avalon...139 H10
cl. Illawong...459 C3
rd. Chiswick...343 C2
st. Warwck Frm...366 A16

SHOREHAM
cr. Chipping Ntn...366 G15

SHORE LINE
av. Rhodes...311 C9

SHORLAND
av. Jannali...460 K13

SHORT
av. Bundeena...523 G9
la. Emu Plains, off Short St...235 E9
la. Neutral Bay, off Byrnes Av...316 B8
la. Rose Bay, off Hamilton St...348 C11
la. S Hurstville, off Short St...432 B11
la. Woollahra, off Fletcher St...377 G2
pl. Surry Hills...4 D15
rd. Riverwood...400 A16
st. Auburn...309 B13
st. Balmain...7 F8
st. Banksia...403 F12
st. Bankstown...399 G8
st. Birchgrove...7 F8
st. Blaxland...233 G8
st. Brookvale...258 B13
st. Campbelltown...511 E3
st. Canterbury...372 D16
st. Carlton...432 H5
st. Chatswood...285 D5
st. Croydon...342 F11
st. Double Bay...14 C9
st. Drummoyne...343 F3
st. Dulwich Hill...373 E7
st. Emu Plains...235 E9
st. Enfield...371 H4
st. Enmore...16 J16
st. Enmore...374 F9
st. Forest Glen...70 H14
st. Forest Lodge...17 J1
st. Gladesville...313 A5
st. Heathcote...518 E13
st. Hunters Hill...313 D10
st. Hurlstone Pk...373 A11
st. Kogarah...433 C6
st. Leichhardt...9 K15
st. Lidcombe...339 J6
st. Lindfield...254 F16
st. Liverpool...395 C5
st. Manly...288 H9
st. Mosman...316 K6
st. North Manly...258 B13
st. N St Marys...239 J8
st. N Sydney...5 D8
st. Oatley...430 H11
st. Oyster Bay...461 B9
st. Parramatta...278 F15
st. Randwick...377 B14
st. Redfern...19 D6
st. Rooty Hill...242 C15
st. Rosehill...308 J8
st. St Peters...374 J12
st. S Hurstville...432 B11
st. Springwood...201 G4
st. Summer Hill...373 B4
st. Surry Hills...4 D14
st. Tahmoor...565 G12
st. Thornleigh...221 A15
st. Waterloo...19 G16
st. Watsons Bay...318 F13
st. Waverley...377 F7
st. Wentwthvle...277 B15
st. Woolooware...493 E8
st.e, Homebush...341 C7
st.w, Homebush...341 B8

SHORTER
av. Beverly Hills...400 G10
av. Narwee...400 G10
la. Darlinghurst...4 E10
la. Narwee...400 H10
la. Roselands...400 H10

SHORTLAND
av. Lurnea...394 B12
av. Strathfield...340 H12
av. Strathfield...341 A12
cl. N Richmond...87 F15
pl. Doonside...273 E2
pl. Ruse...512 H5
st. Canley Vale...366 E4
st. Lidcombe...339 J6
st. Telopea...279 G10
st. Wrrngtn Cty...238 G8

SHOULTS
la. Padstow...399 E16

SHOWFREIGHT
wy. Berala...339 D14

SHOWGROUND
rd. Castle Hill...217 J13
rd. Homebush B...340 G1

SHRIKE
gln. Erskine Park...270 K11
pl. Ingleburn...453 H6

SHROPSHIRE
cl. Wakeley...334 K16
st. Miller...393 G3

SHUTE
wy. Casula...424 E3

SHUTTLEWORTH
av. Raby...451 F13

SIANDRA
av. Fairfield...336 D5
av. Shalvey...210 H14
dr. Kareela...461 B11

SIBBICK
st. Chiswick...343 C6
st. Russell Lea...343 C6

SIBELIUS
cl. Seven Hills...246 E12

SIBLEY
cl. Abbotsbury...333 C11

SICILIA
st. Prestons...393 F14

SICKLES
dr. Grasmere...475 J15

SIDDELEY
pl. Raby...451 F16

SIDDINS
av. Pagewood...406 F7

SIDNEY
cl. Quakers Hill...213 K7
pl. Casula...424 E3

SIDON
pl. Mt Pritchard...364 H15

SIDWELL
av. Shalvey...210 J14

SIEBEL
st. Blacktown...243 K11

SIEMENS
cr. Emerton...240 J3

SIENA
cl. Prestons...393 D13

SIENNA
gr. Woodcroft...243 F6

SIERRA
pl. Baulkham Hl...246 F14
pl. Seven Hills...275 B10
rd. Engadine...488 C12

SIGLINGEN
st. Emerton...240 J7

SIKES
pl. Ambarvale...510 H12

SILAS
wy. Ambarvale...511 A16

SILDOR
ct. Kenthurst...188 A1

SILEX
rd. Mosman...317 C12

SILICA
cr. Eagle Vale...481 B8
rd. Bargo...567 E15
rd. Yanderra...567 E15

SILK
pl. Prestons...393 K14
rd. Springwood...202 D1

SILKS
la. N Richmond...87 A1
rd. Kurmond...64 K16
rd. Kurmond...65 A16

SILKWOOD
gr. Quakers Hill...214 D14

SILKY
cl. Bossley Park...333 E8

SILKY OAK
pl. Castle Hill...248 E4

SILKY-OAK
gr. Elderslie...507 F2

SILKYOAK
gr. Greenacre...370 G6
pl. Glenwood...245 J1

SILLWOOD
pl. West Hoxton...392 A12

SILVA
rd. Springwood...202 A2
st. Tamarama...378 B6

SILVEN PARK
wy. Silverdale...353 K12

SILVER
cr. Westleigh...220 G3
la. Marrickville, off Calvert St...373 K13
la. St Peters...374 H14
st. Marrickville...374 A12
st. Randwick...376 K13
st. St Peters...374 G13
st. Silverwater...309 K9

SILVER BEACH
rd. Kurnell...466 A8

SILVERBURN
av. Richmond...118 A6

SILVERDALE
rd. Orangeville...473 A6
rd. Silverdale...353 K10
rd. Silverdale...353 F16
rd. The Oaks...502 G7
rd. Wallacia...324 A16
rd. Wallacia...354 A1
rd. Warragamba...353 K10
rd. Werombi...413 A15

SILVEREYE
cl. Glenmore Pk...265 H13
ct. Woronora Ht...489 C4
pl. Hinchinbrk...363 F15

SILVERFERN
cr. W Pnnant Hl...248 K2

SILVERLEAF
row. Menai...458 J15

SILVER MIST
cr. Castle Hill, off Barker Dr...218 J13

SILVERTON
st. Glenwood...215 F16

SILVERTOP
cl. Glenwood...245 H1
cl. Westleigh...220 F7

SILVERWATER
cr. Lansvale...366 E10
cr. Miranda...462 B16
rd. Auburn...309 H16
rd. Dundas...280 A15
rd. Ermington...280 A15
rd. Rydalmere...309 K10
rd. Silverwater...309 K10

SILVERWOOD
av. Luddenham...356 A6
rd. Brownlow Hl...475 E11

SILVIA
st. Hornsby...191 G13

SIMBLIST
rd. Port Botany...436 B11

SIMEON
pl. Liberty Gr...311 B11
rd. Orchard Hills...267 D8
st. Clovelly...377 G10

SIMEON PEARCE
dr. Randwick, off Easy St...377 A16

SIMLA
rd. Denistone...281 B12
st. Lidcombe...340 B4

SIMMAT
av. Condell Park...398 F6

SIMMONDS
la. Avalon, off Edmund Hock Av..170 B2
pl. W Pnnant Hl...249 A6
st. Kings Lngly...246 A9

SIMMONS
rd. Kingsgrove...401 J13
st. Balmain East...8 F7
st. Enmore...17 C14
st. Enmore...17 C16
st. Newtown...17 C14
st. Revesby...398 J15
st. Warwck Frm...365 F13

SIMMS
rd. Glendenning...242 D2
rd. Oakhurst...242 C2
rd. Oakhurst...242 D2

SIMON
av. Bonnyrigg...364 A8
cl. Illawong...459 D7
pl. Hornsby Ht...191 E8
st. Winston Hills...246 G15
wk. Pagewood...406 A11

SIMONE
cr. Casula...394 G14
cr. Strathfield...341 A11
pl. Peakhurst...430 C4

SIMPSON
av. Baulkham Hl...247 C13
av. Burwood...342 B13
av. Casula...394 G13
cl. Narrabeen...228 G8
la. Lidcombe...339 F9
pl. Kings Lngly...245 D4
pl. Leumeah...482 H11
rd. Bonnyrigg Ht...363 E5
rd. Bundeena...523 G9
st. Artarmon...315 A1
st. Auburn...339 F1
st. Baulkham Hl...278 A1
st. Belrose...226 E13
st. Bondi...377 K2
st. Bondi Beach...377 K2
st. Dundas Vy...279 J10
st. Greystanes...306 B9
st. Mosman...317 A13
st. Putney...311 J4

SIMPSON HILL
rd. Mount Druitt...270 J3

SIMS
gr. Maroubra...407 D13
la. Maroubra...407 D13
pl. St Johns Pk...364 J2
st. Darlinghurst...4 F14

SINAI
av. Milperra...397 H10

SINCLAIR
av. Blacktown...274 K4
av. Thornleigh...220 K11
rd. Ashcroft...394 E1
st. Wollstncraft...5 B1

134 GREGORY'S STREET DIRECTORY

STREETS SO

SINDEL
cl. Bonnyrigg.........363 K7
st. West Ryde........280 J13
SINDONE
pl. Caringbah.........492 J3
SINFIELD
st. Ermington.........280 B15
SINGER
pl. Ingleburn.........453 E15
SINGH
la. Chester Hill.......368 C2
SINGLE
la. S Penrith, off
    Single Rd.........267 B4
rd. S Penrith.........267 A4
SINGLE RIDGE
rd. The Slopes........64 H12
SINGLES RIDGE
rd. Winmalee........173 A13
rd. Yellow Rock......203 G1
SINGLETON
av. East Hills.........428 A3
av. Kellyville Rdg....215 B5
av. Wrrngtn Cty.....238 E5
cl. Kirrawee..........491 B7
rd. Wilberforce........91 J3
st. Earlwood..........402 F5
st. Hornsgea Pk......392 D14
SINNOTT
st. Fairfield E.........336 K16
SIOBHAN
pl. Mona Vale........198 J2
SIOUX
cl. Greenfld Pk.......334 A15
SIOVI
rd. Londonderry......177 J12
SIR BERTRAM STEVENS
dr. Royal N P.........520 E7
SIR HENRYS
pde. Faulconbdg......201 A1
pde. Springwood......201 A1
SIRIUS
av. Mosman..........316 K12
cct. Narellan.........478 E15
cr. Ebenezer..........68 F8
pde. Beacon Hill.....257 G3
pl. Berkshire Pk.....179 H14
pl. Engadine.........488 D12
pl. Riverwood........400 C13
rd. Bligh Park........150 D5
rd. Lane Cove W.....283 F16
rd. Voyager Pt........427 A4
rd. Voyager Pt........427 B4
st. Cremorne Pt......316 F13
st. Dundas Vy.......280 C8
st. Fairfield W........335 B10
st. Ruse..............512 H4
SIRIUS COVE
rd. Mosman..........317 A12
SIR JOHN JAMISON
cct. Glenmore Pk....265 D9
SIR JOHN YOUNG
cr. Sydney.............4 D5
cr. Woolmloo..........4 D5
SIR JOSEPH BANKS
dr. Kurnell............465 J12
st. Bankstown.......369 G14
st. Botany............405 G15
SIROCCO
pl. Bella Vista........216 C14
SIROIS
st. Toongabbie......276 J5
SIR REGINALD ANSETT
dr. Mascot...........405 A7
SIRRIUS
cl. Beaumont Hills...215 J4
SIR THOMAS MITCHELL
dr. Davidson.........255 B1
rd. Bondi Beach......378 B3
rd. Chester Hill......367 K3
rd. Villawood........367 K3
SIR WARWICK FAIRFAX
dr. Harringtn Pk.....478 G3
SISKIN
st. Quakers Hill.....214 E11
SISTERS
cr. Drummoyne......343 K4
la. Edgecliff..........14 A13
SITAR
pl. Plumpton.........241 H9
SITELLA
pl. Ingleburn........453 D9

SITTELLA
pl. Glenmore Pk....265 J12
SIWA
st. Holsworthy......426 F7
SIWARD
pl. Rsemeadow......540 F4
SIXTEENTH
av. Austral............391 F2
av.e,West Hoxton..391 K2
SIXTH
av. Austral............390 J14
av. Berala............339 D15
av. Campsie.........371 K10
av. Condell Park....398 E5
av. Denistone........281 D11
av. Jannali...........460 K9
av. Llandilo..........208 C3
av. Loftus............489 K7
av. Mcquarie Fd....454 G6
av. Seven Hills......275 J3
av. West Hoxton....391 A14
st. Berkshire Pk.....179 H6
st. Granville.........308 G15
st. Mascot...........404 K7
st. Warragamba....353 G5
SIXTH MILE
la. Roseville.........284 G4
SKAIN
pl. Seven Hills Pk...392 C13
SKARRATT
av. Glenbrook.......233 J13
st.n,Silverwater.....309 E12
st.s, Auburn.........309 D14
SKATE
st. Cranebrook......207 A10
SKELTON
st. Leichhardt........16 C1
SKENE
pl. Belrose..........225 K9
SKENES
av. Eastwood........280 G6
SKERRETT
la. Doonside........243 C13
SKILLCORN
av. Jannali...........460 G9
SKINNER
av. Riverwood......400 F10
pde. Roseville.......284 J1
SKINNERS
av. Dolls Point......463 H1
SKIPTON
la. Prestons........393 H15
wy. Stanhpe Gdn...215 B6
SKONE
st. Condell Park....398 J6
SKYE
cl. Merrylands W...306 K13
cl. Kellyville.........216 K1
pl. Engadine........488 J12
pl. Prospect.........274 G10
pl. St Andrews.....481 K2
pl. Winston Hills...277 B3
SKYFARMER
dr. Raby.............481 F2
SKYHAWK
av. Raby.............481 F1
SKYLARK
cct. Bella Vista......246 F1
cr. Erskine Park....270 H14
SKYLINE
st. Frenchs Frst....256 K3
rd. Mt Tomah.......59 H15
st. Greenacre.......370 K13
SKYROS
la. Emu Heights, off
    Skyros Pl........235 B5
pl. Emu Heights...235 B5
SLADDEN
rd. Engadine.......489 B15
SLADE
av. Castle Hill.....218 J13
av. Lindfield......254 F14
rd. Bardwell Pk....402 H7
rd. Bardwell Pk....402 F8
rd. Prospect........274 G12
rd. Bexley North...402 F8
rd. Ingleside......196 G11
st. Narellan.........478 H9
st. Naremburn.....315 G3
st. Rozelle............7 A12
SLADES
rd. Couridjah......564 E10

SLAPP
st. Merrylands.......307 E8
SLATER
rd. Ingleburn........452 J8
SLATTERY
pl. Eastlakes........406 B2
wy. Eastlakes........406 C3
SLAVIN
st. S Penrith.........267 D6
SLEIGH
pl. Wetherill Pk......303 H15
SLENDER
av. Smithfield.......335 J8
SLESSOR
la. Blackett..........241 C3
la. Heathcote......518 D14
rd. Casula...........424 F5
SLIGAR
av. Hamondvle.....396 E16
SLIGO
cl. Killarney Ht....255 J14
pl. Prestons........423 E2
SLIM
cl. Cabramatta......365 D11
pl. Wenthwtvle.....277 A12
SLIP
st. Sydney............C C3
st. Sydney............3 D2
SLOANE
cr. Allambie Ht.....287 J1
cr. Manly Vale.......287 J1
st. Marrickville......374 D13
st. Haberfield.......373 D3
st. Marrickville......374 D13
st. Newtown.........17 D15
st. Summer Hill.....373 D3
SLOE
pl. Prestons.........393 K15
SLOOP
st. Seven Hills......275 B5
SLOPER
av. Hobartville......118 F8
SLOPES
rd. Comleroy.........64 H12
rd. Comleroy.........65 A11
rd. Kurmond..........64 K14
rd. Kurmond..........65 A11
rd. Richmond........87 D6
rd. The Slopes.......64 H12
rd. The Slopes.......65 A11
SLOUGH
av. Silverwater.....309 K11
SLUMAN
st. Denistone W....281 A11
SMAIL
la. Ultimo............12 J15
st. Ultimo............12 J15
SMALL
cr. Glenmore Pk....265 F7
ln. Petersham.......15 G11
la. Woollahra, off
    Fletcher St.......377 F2
rd. Illawong.........459 D4
st. Marayong........244 D4
st. Northbridge.....285 F16
st. Putney...........311 J4
st. Willoughby......285 F16
st. Woollahra.......377 F2
SMALLS
st. Arcadia..........129 J16
rd. Brownlow Hl....475 G15
rd. Grasmere.......475 G15
rd. Ryde............282 B11
SMALLS CREEK
wy. Beaumont Hills...185 K12
SMALLWOOD
av. Homebush......341 A8
rd. Glenorie.........96 H3
rd. McGraths Hl...121 K13
SMART
av. Camden S......507 B15
cl. Minto............482 K4
st. Fairfield........336 E10
st. Fairfield Ht.....336 B9
SMARTS
cr. Burraneer.......493 F14
SMEATON GRANGE
rd. Smeaton Gra....479 A8
SMEE
av. Roselands......400 F8
SMEETON
rd. Londonderry...177 A9

SMERDON
pl. Kenthurst.......126 G15
SMIDMORE
st. Marrickville....374 F11
SMIKE
pl. Ambarvale.....510 H16
SMITH
av. Allambie Ht....257 J14
av. Hobartville.....118 E10
av. Hurlstone Pk...373 A14
cr. Liverpool.......394 J5
dr. Mcquarie Pk....283 B8
gr. Shalvey..........211 C13
la. Five Dock, off
    Ramsay Rd.....342 K11
la. Newtown........17 F14
pl. Mt Annan......509 D1
pl. Artarmon......285 B14
rd. Castlereagh....175 G6
rd. Oakville........122 J14
st. Annandale.....10 J1
st. Balmain..........7 E13
st. Bexley...........402 J13
st. Chatswood....285 E5
st. Eastgardens...406 F13
st. Emu Plains....235 J6
st. Epping..........251 C16
st. Granville.......308 D10
st. Hillsdale........406 F13
st. Kentlyn........513 B6
st. Kingsford......406 K6
st. Kingswood....267 E1
st. Lindfield.......254 E15
st. Manly..........288 G6
st. Marrickville....374 D10
st. Parramatta....308 D4
st. Pendle Hill....306 E1
st. Regents Pk...369 E2
st. Rozelle..........7 E13
st. Ryde...........282 B16
st. St Marys......269 D3
st. S Penrith......237 A16
st. Summer Hill...373 B4
st. Surry Hills......F F11
st. Surry Hills......4 A14
st. Taren Point....462 J12
st. Tempe..........404 C2
st. Wentwthvle....306 E1
st. Woollahra.....21 G4
st. Yagoona........368 E10
SMITHERS
st. Chippendale....19 A3
SMITHFIELD
av. Coogee.........377 G15
rd. Edensor Pk....363 J4
rd. Fairfield W....335 A9
rd. Greenfld Pk....334 C15
rd. Prairiewood...335 A9
rd. Smithfield.....335 F7
rd. Wakeley.......334 C15
SMITHS
av. Cabramatta...365 C10
av. Hurstville......401 J15
la. Erskineville, off
    Victoria St.....374 K9
la. Freemns Rch...90 K3
la. Glenorie.......127 E14
SMITHYS
pl. Richmond.....118 F12
SMOOTHY
pl. Arndell Park....273 H10
SMYTHE
st. Merrylands....307 K13
SMYTHES
st. Concord........342 A3
SNAILHAM
cr. S Windsor.....150 J1
SNAKE GULLEY
cl. Narrabeen.....228 E8
SNAPE
st. Kingsford......406 H6
st. Maroubra......406 H6
SNAPPER
cl. Green Valley...362 K12
SNAPPERMAN
la. Palm Beach, off
    Iluka Rd........139 J3
SNELL
av. West Hoxton...392 B12
SNIPE
cl. Hinchinbrk....363 E15
pl. Ingleburn.....453 H7
wy. Mt Annan....479 B15

SNOWBIRD
la. Erskine Park, off
    Snowbird Pl......300 K1
la. Erskine Park, off
    Snowbird Pl......301 A1
pl. Erskine Park....301 A1
SNOWDEN
av. Sylvania......461 K10
cl. Cecil Hills....362 F3
pl. St Ives Ch....224 C1
st. Jamisontown...266 B1
SNOWDON
av. Carlingford....279 B4
cr. Smithfield.....335 D1
SNOWDRIFT
st. St Clair.........270 D13
SNOW GUM
pl. Alfords Point....429 C12
SNOWGUM
st. Acacia Gdn....214 K14
st. Acacia Gdn....215 A14
SNOWSILL
av. Revesby.......399 B9
SNOWY
cl. St Clair........269 H15
pl. Heckenberg...364 A12
pl. Sylvania Wtr....462 D10
st. Seven Hills...275 E10
SNOWY BAKER
st. Moore Park....21 B5
SNUG
st. West Hoxton...392 E8
SNUGGLEPOT
dr. Faulconbdg....171 D15
SOBRAON
rd. Marsfield......282 A4
SODBURY
st. Chipping Ntn...396 F2
SOFA
st. Marayong......244 B6
SOFALA
av. Riverview......314 A4
st. Riverwood....400 B11
SOFTWOOD
av. Beaumont Hills...215 K2
SOL
dr. Rooty Hill....272 A2
SOLANDER
av. West Hoxton....392 B13
cl. Turramurra....252 D4
dr. St Clair........269 F13
la. Daceyville, off
    Cook Av........406 F3
pl. Mt Annan.....509 G3
pl. Daceyville...406 F3
rd. Kings Lngly....245 K9
st. Kurnell........466 A9
st. Monterey.....433 H6
st. Ruse...........512 H9
st. Matraville.....436 G1
SOLAR
av. Baulkham Hl....246 F9
pl. Glenwood......215 B14
SOLARIS
dr. Doonside.....243 H16
SOLDIERS
av. Harbord.......258 D16
pl. Woodbine.....481 K10
st. Jannali.........460 F9
SOLENT
cct. Baulkham Hl...216 F14
cct. Baulkham Hl...216 F16
SOLERO
pl. Eschol Park....481 C9
SOLIANO
st. Gilead..........540 E6
SOLING
cr. Cranebrook....207 A9
SOLITAIRE
ct. Stanhpe Gdn....215 B11
SOLITARY
pl. Ruse............512 H7
SOLO
cr. Fairfield......336 D5
pl. Shalvey.......210 J12
st. Kareela.......461 D11
SOLOMON
av. Kings Park...244 F2
st. Greenacre....370 D6
SOLVEIG
cr. Kareela.......461 D12

GREGORY'S STREET DIRECTORY 135

SO STREETS

SOLWAY
rd. Bringelly 388 A10
SOMERCOTES
cl. Glen Alpine 510 F9
ct. Wattle Grove 425 H5
SOMERS
st. Bonnyrigg 363 J6
SOMERSET
av. Narellan 478 G9
av. N Turramurra 223 G4
ct. Wattle Grove 426 A4
dr. North Rocks 278 J2
st. Epping 251 C12
st. Hurstville 432 B1
st. Kingswood 237 E1
st. Marsfield 251 E12
st. Minto 482 E2
st. Mosman 316 J10
st. Pitt Town 92 J15
st. Stanhpe Gdn 215 F7
wy. Castle Hill 248 B3
SOMERVILLE
av. Ashfield 372 F4
pl. Manly Vale, off
Sunshine St 287 K4
rd. Hornsby Ht 191 F2
st. Arncliffe 403 F10
SOMME
cr. Milperra 397 H12
st. Kearns 450 J16
wy. Matraville 407 B15
SOMMERVILLE
rd. Rozelle 11 J2
SOMOV
pl. Tregear 240 C4
SONDER
pl. Leumeah 482 H10
SONIA
pl. Hassall Gr 212 B14
SONIVER
rd. N Curl Curl 259 B11
SONJA
cl. Cabramatta 365 F9
st. Picton 561 F4
SONTER
st. Quakers Hill 213 H8
SONYA
cl. Jamisontown 266 B2
SOPER
pl. Penrith 236 K10
SOPHIA
cr. North Rocks 248 E14
la. Croydon, off
Croydon Rd 342 H12
la. Surry Hills 20 A1
st. Blair Athol 511 C1
st. Crows Nest 315 G6
st. Surry Hills ....F B16
st. Surry Hills 3 J16
SOPHIE
av. Ingleside 197 G5
st. Cecil Hills 363 A3
st. Glenwood 245 B1
st. Telopea 279 J9
SOPWITH
av. Raby 481 G1
pl. Bnkstn Aprt 397 K1
SORBELLO
cl. Kenthurst 157 J14
SORELL
rd. Barden Rdg 488 H2
SORENSEN
cr. Blackett 241 B2
SORENSON
cr. Glenmore Pk 266 A6
SORLIE
av. Northmead 248 B16
cl. Doonside 243 E8
rd. Frenchs Frst 256 D5
rd. Frenchs Frst 256 A3
SORRELL
la. N Parramatta 278 D13
st. N Parramatta 278 D16
st. Parramatta 278 D16
SORRENTO
cct. Kellyville 186 H15
dr. Glenwood 215 C13
pl. Burraneer 523 D3
pl. Erskine Park 300 E2
SORRIE
st. Balmain 7 G10
SORTIE
pt. Castlecrag 286 B12

SOUDAN
la. Newtown 18 A9
la. Paddington 13 G14
la. Randwick, off
Soudan St 377 B15
st. Bexley North 402 D13
st. Merrylands 308 A13
st. Randwick 377 B16
SOULT
st. Sans Souci 463 C5
SOUTER
pl. Hebersham 241 E2
st. Kogarah Bay 432 J13
SOUTH
av. Double Bay 14 A9
av. Petersham 15 H9
av. Westmead 277 D15
cr. Lilyfield 10 D2
la. Double Bay 14 A9
pde. Auburn 339 C1
pde. Campsie 372 A13
pde. Canterbury 372 A13
pde. Old Guildford ..337 G8
st. Drummoyne 343 H3
st. Edgecliff 13 F10
st. Ermington 309 J3
st. Glenmore Pk 266 J9
st. Granville 308 F12
st. Gymea 491 F4
st. Kogarah 433 C5
st. Marrickville 373 G12
st. Marsden Pk 211 D9
st. Rydalmere 309 D3
st. Schofields 212 E3
st. Strathfield 341 A16
st. Tempe 404 C4
st. Thirlmere 565 B2
tce. Bankstown 399 J1
tce. Bankstown 399 G1
tce. Punchbowl 399 J1
SOUTHBOURNE
wy. Mona Vale 199 A2
SOUTH CREEK
rd. Collaroy Plat 228 C11
rd. Cromer 228 E14
rd. Dee Why 258 H5
rd. Shanes Park 209 F5
SOUTH DOWLING
la. Darlinghurst 4 F16
st. Moore Park 20 C16
st. Paddington 4 F16
st. Redfern 20 C16
st. Surry Hills 20 E7
st. Waterloo 20 C16
SOUTHDOWN
pl. Airds 512 A13
pl. Elderslie 507 H3
pl. Horsley Pk 332 H6
pl. Miller 393 F3
SOUTHEE
cct. Oakhurst 241 H2
rd. Hobartville 118 B7
SOUTHERN
fwy. Waterfall 519 D16
st. Oatley 460 K1
SOUTHERN CROSS
cl. Kensington, off
Houston La 406 G2
dr. Eastlakes 406 A6
dr. Kensington 376 A15
dr. Mascot 405 G8
dr. Rosebery 376 A15
la. Kingsford, off
Houston Rd 406 F2
wy. Allambie Ht 257 F14
SOUTHLEIGH
av. Castle Hill 217 H16
SOUTH LIVERPOOL
rd. Busby 363 C14
rd. Green Valley ..363 C14
rd. Heckenberg ...364 A14
rd. Hinchinbrk 363 C14
SOUTH PACIFIC
av. Mt Pritchard ..364 F14
SOUTH STEYNE
Manly 288 H10
SOUTHSTONE
cl. S Penrith 266 K6
SOUTH VANDERVILLE
st. The Oaks 502 E11
SOUTHWAITE
cr. Glenwood 215 E12

SOUTH WESTERN
mwy. Beverly Hills 400 A11
mwy. Casula 423 G5
mwy. Edmndsn Pk 423 G5
mwy. Hamondvle 396 C12
mwy. Liverpool 393 K16
mwy. Lurnea 393 K16
mwy. Milperra 397 B14
mwy. Moorebank 396 C12
mwy. Narwee 400 A11
mwy. Padstow 399 B11
mwy. Panania 398 B12
mwy. Prestons 423 G5
mwy. Revesby 398 B12
mwy. Riverwood 400 A11
SOUTHWOOD
pl. W Pnnant Hl 248 G6
SOVEREIGN
av. Carlingford 279 B3
av. Kellyville Rdg ...185 A16
av. Kellyville Rdg ...185 B16
pl. S Windsor 121 A14
SPA
pl. Prospect 274 H12
SPAGNOLO
pl. Prestons 423 A1
SPAINS WHARF
rd. Neutral Bay 6 H10
SPALDING
cr. Hurstville Gr 431 G12
SPARK
la. Wolli Creek 403 J4
la,n. Wolli Creek 403 K4
st. Earlwood 402 G2
SPARKES
av. Mortdale 430 J5
la. Camperdown ...17 H1
st. Camperdown ...17 H1
SPARKLE
av. Blacktown 274 A5
SPARKS
la. Greenacre 370 F8
rd. Jamisontown ..266 B3
st. Eastlakes 405 G6
st. Mascot 405 G6
SPARMAN
cr. Kings Lngly 245 H9
SPARROW
la. Green Valley ...363 F12
SPARTA
cl. Bossley Park ...333 J8
SPEARMAN
st. Chatswood 284 K5
st. Roseville 284 K5
SPEARWOOD
af. Acacia Gdn 215 A15
SPEDDING
rd. Hornsby Ht 191 E9
SPEED
av. Russell Lea 343 E7
st. Liverpool 395 D7
SPEEDWELL
pl. S Windsor 151 B1
SPEERS
cr. Oakhurst 241 J3
rd. North Rocks ...278 B6
SPEETS
pl. Oakville 123 E16
SPEKE
pl. Bligh Park 150 E7
SPELLING
st. Picton 563 C8
SPENCE
pl. Belrose 225 F14
st. St Helens Pk ...540 K9
rd. Berkshire Pk ...179 D10
st. Revesby 428 J1
SPENCER
ct. Baulkham Hl ...248 A9
la. Alexandria 19 A11
la. Fairfield, off
Nelson St 336 E11
la. Rose Bay, off
Hamilton St 348 C10
pl. Illawong 459 F3
pl. Lane Cove N ...284 E14
rd. Cecil Hills 362 F5
rd. Cremorne 316 G8
rd. Killara 253 F13
rd. Londonderry ...147 N14
rd. Mosman 316 G8
st. Berala 339 C15
st. Eastwood 280 H7
st. Fairfield 336 F12

st. Five Dock 342 F10
st. Gladesville 312 E7
st. Regentville 265 G3
st. Rooty Hill 241 J13
st. Rose Bay 348 C10
st. Sefton 368 D7
st. Summer Hill 373 D5
wy. Minto 482 K1
SPERRING
av. Oakhurst 242 E2
SPEY
pl. St Andrews 451 K16
st. Winston Hills ...277 E3
SPICA
av. Padstow 398 K16
av. Revesby 398 K16
SPICER
av. Hamondvle 396 G15
la. Woollahra 21 K1
rd. Silverdale 354 C12
rd,n.Oxford Falls ..227 A15
rd,s.Oxford Falls ..226 J16
st. Woollahra 21 K2
SPICKER
pl. Beacon Hill 257 F5
SPINEBILL
pl. Ingleburn 453 G6
SPINEL
st. Eagle Vale 481 F6
SPINKS
rd. Freemns Rch ...65 J15
rd. Glossodia 66 A13
rd. Llandilo 178 B13
rd. N Richmond 65 J15
SPINOSA
pl. Glenmore Pk ...265 H13
SPIRE
av. Narellan 478 B10
SPIRETON
pl. Pendle Hill 276 F11
SPIT
rd. Mosman 317 A5
SPITFIRE
dr. Raby 481 F3
SPITZ
av. Newington 309 K15
SPOFFORTH
av. Rouse Hill 184 J6
la. Cremorne, off
Florence La 316 F10
st. Cremorne 316 G10
st. Ermington 310 E3
st. Mosman 316 G10
SPOONBILL
av. Blacktown 274 B9
av. Woronora Ht ...489 E2
la. St Clair, off
Spoonbill St ...270 K12
st. Erskine Park ...270 K12
st. Hinchinbrk 393 D2
wy. Mt Annan 479 C15
SPOONER
av. Cabramatta W ..365 B8
pl. North Ryde 282 J8
SPORING
av. Kings Lngly 245 G5
SPORTSGROUND
pde. Appin 569 E9
SPOTTED GUM
gr. Greystanes 306 C4
rd. Westleigh 220 F8
SPOTTEDGUM
pl. Rouse Hill 184 K5
SPRIGG
pl. Mt Colah 162 D16
SPRIGGS
st. Fairlight 288 B7
SPRING
cl. Chatswood 284 K9
cl. Kellyville 216 G6
cl. N Curl Curl 258 K11
st. Abbotsford 342 H1
st. Arncliffe 403 F11
st. Beecroft 250 C3
st. Birchgrove 7 F5
st. Bondi Jctn 22 F7
st. Chatswood 284 K10
st. Concord 342 A4

st. Double Bay 14 B6
st. Dural 188 J13
st. Eastwood 281 G8
st. Fairfield E 337 C14
st. Kurrajong Ht ...63 F12
st. N Sydney ....K F7
st. N Sydney 5 G8
st. Paddington 4 J15
st. Padstow 429 B1
st. Pagewood 405 K11
st. Springwood 202 A8
st. Sydney ....B A13
st. Sydney 1 H15
SPRING CREEK
rd. Glenmore 503 H16
rd. Mt Hunter 504 F15
SPRINGDALE
mw. Bella Vista ..216 D14
rd. East Killara 254 F10
rd. Killara 254 C12
rd. Wentwthvle ...276 H16
ri. Bella Vista 216 C14
SPRINGFERN
pl. Valley Ht 202 E5
SPRINGFIELD
av. Blacktown 244 F13
av. Potts Point 4 J8
av. Roselands 400 F7
cr. Bella Vista 246 F7
cr. Springwood 172 C16
ct. Wattle Grove ...425 J4
la. Penrith, off
Springfield Pl ...237 E9
pl. Potts Point, off
Springfield Av ..4 J5
rd. Airds 512 D10
rd. Penrith 237 D9
rd. Catherine Fd ..449 D6
rd. Hornsby Ht 191 E8
rd. Padstow 429 C3
rd. Old Guildford ..337 G8
SPRING GARDEN
la. Granville, off
Milton St 308 D10
st. Granville 308 D10
SPRING GULLY
pl. Wahroonga 222 D1
SPRING HILL
cir. Currans Hill ...479 K16
SPRINGMEAD
dr. Denham Ct 422 A10
SPRING MILL
av. Rouse Hill 185 B9
SPRING PARK
cct. Breakfast Pt ..312 B16
ct. Breakfast Pt ...312 B16
SPRINGROVE
la. Kurrajong Hl ..63 J9
SPRINGS
rd. Spring Farm ..507 H6
SPRINGSIDE
st. Rozelle 344 C10
SPRINGVALE
av. Frenchs Frst ..256 A3
SPRINGWOOD
av. Springwood ...201 J4
cl. Springwood ...201 J4
rd. Agnes Banks ..117 A12
rd. Yarramundi ...116 E13
SPROULE
rd. Illawong 459 K6
st. Lakemba 401 K3
SPRUCE
gr. Menai 458 K14
st. Blacktown 274 B7
SPRUSON
st. Camperdown ..17 H5
st. Neutral Bay 6 J14
SPUMANTE
cl. Eschol Park ...481 C5
SPUR
st. Loftus 519 J11
pl. Glenorie 70 F14
st. Warrimoo 203 F9
SPURGIN
st. Wahroonga ...222 C2
SPURWAY
dr. Baulkham Hl ..216 N16
st. Dundas 280 A12
st. Ermington 310 D1
SPURWOOD
cl. Dural 188 D10
cl. Kenthurst 188 D10

136 GREGORY'S STREET DIRECTORY

STREETS ST

rd. Turramurra 223 D8
rd. Warrimoo 203 E15
SQUEERS
pl. Ambarvale 510 J15
SQUILL
pl. Arndell Park 273 F10
SQUIRE
pl. Castle Hill 217 G6
st. Ryde 311 G2
SQUIRES
rd. Springwood 202 E10
SRAID NA'H ALBAINN
Mosman, off Cross St 317 D11
STABLE SQUARE
pl. Richmond 118 F12
STABLE VIEW
pl. Narellan 478 B9
STACEY
st. Bankstown 369 G10
st. Bankstown 399 G6
st. Cronulla 523 J3
st. Fairfield W 335 G11
st. Greenacre 369 G10
st. Punchbowl 399 G6
st.s, Bankstown 399 G5
st.s, Punchbowl 399 G5
STACK
st. Balmain East 8 E8
st. Narrabeen 228 G8
STADDON
cl. St Ives 224 C6
STAFF
av. Glenwood 215 D14
STAFFORD
la. Paddington 13 C15
la. Stanmore 16 K9
pl. N Turramurra 223 G4
rd. Artarmon 285 A12
st. Cabramatta 365 C11
st. Double Bay 14 E7
st. Kingswood 237 E14
st. Minto 482 F2
st. Paddington 13 C15
st. Penrith 237 A13
st. S Granville 338 E8
st. Stanmore 16 K9
wy. Beaumont Hills 216 A1
STAGG
pl. Ambarvale 510 F16
STAHLS
rd. Oakville 153 A2
STAINSBY
av. Kings Lngly 246 A9
cl. Turramurra 252 A2
STALEY
ct. W Pnnant Hl 249 C1
STALLION
gln. Glenwood 245 J4
STALWART
st. Prairiewood 334 J7
STAMFORD
av. Cabarita 342 D1
av. Ermington 280 D12
cl. West Hoxton 392 E8
STAN
st. N Willoughby 285 G10
STANBROOK
st. Fairfield Ht 335 K9
STANBURY
pl. Quakers Hill 214 A12
st. Gladesville 312 F8
STANDARD
wy. Minto 482 H7
STANDISH
av. Oakhurst 241 H3
st. Greenwich 314 J7
STANFORD
cct. Rouse Hill 185 D4
wy. Airds 511 H15
STANHOPE
pky. Kellyville Rdg 214 G7
pky. Parklea 215 A8
pky. Quakers Hill 214 B7
pky. Schofields 214 B7
pky. Stanhpe Gdn 215 A8
rd. Killara 254 A14
rd. Theresa Park 445 C12
row. Bella Vista 246 G3
st. Auburn 338 J3
STANIER
cl. Cherrybrook 219 K7
STANLEA
pde. Wiley Park 400 G2
STANLEY
av. Kurrajong Ht 63 F14
av. Mosman 317 C5
av. W Pnnant Hl 249 G5
cl. St Ives 224 A12
la. Arncliffe, off Stanley St 403 F9
la. Darlinghurst D K16
la. Darlinghurst 4 C8
la. Ermington 310 B2
la. Hunters Hill 313 H11
la. Kogarah, off Regent St 433 C3
la. Queens Park 22 H11
la. St Ives 224 A12
la. Stanmore 16 B9
pl. Illawong 459 H5
rd. Epping 251 E15
rd. Hunters Hill 313 H11
rd. Ingleburn 453 B7
rd. Lidcombe 339 F7
st. Arncliffe 403 F9
st. Bankstown 399 F2
st. Blacktown 274 G7
st. Burwood 341 J15
st. Campsie 372 A15
st. Chatswood 285 C11
st. Concord 342 A8
st. Croydon Pk 371 J7
st. Darlinghurst D G16
st. Darlinghurst 4 B8
st. Fairfield Ht 335 H12
st. Kogarah 433 C2
st. Leichhardt 10 B15
st. Marrickville 373 J11
st. Merrylands 307 C10
st. Mona Vale 199 G3
st. Newport 169 K12
st. Peakhurst 430 F4
st. Putney 312 B9
st. Queens Park 22 G11
st. Randwick 377 B10
st. Redfern 20 C9
st. St Ives 224 A12
st. St Marys 269 H5
st. Shanes Park 209 K1
st. Silverwater 309 J13
st. Stanmore 16 B9
st. Tempe 404 B2
st. Woollahra 22 E3
STANMORE
la. Stanmore 16 G9
rd. Enmore 16 B12
rd. Petersham 16 B12
rd. Stanmore 16 B12
STANNARDS
pl. N Sydney 6 D13
STANNIX PARK
rd. Ebenezer 67 G9
rd. Wilberforce 67 D10
STANNUM
cl. Hinchinbrk 392 H5
STANSBURY
st. Emu Plains 235 E11
STANSELL
av. Jannali 460 J10
st. Gladesville 312 J8
STANSFIELD
av. Bankstown 399 K1
STANTON
dr. W Pnnant Hl 249 C9
la. Mosman, off Spit Rd 317 B3
pl. Emu Plains 236 B6
rd. Haberfield 373 D1
rd. Mosman 317 B3
rd. Mosman 317 E3
rd. Seven Hills 246 B15
st. Liverpool 394 H3
STANWAY
av. Springwood 201 E4
STANWELL
cr. Ashcroft 394 E2
STAPLES
pl. Glenmore Pk 265 F8
st. Kingsgrove 402 B10
STAPLETON
av. Sutherland 490 F2
la. St Marys, off Stapleton Pde 239 J16
pde. St Marys 269 J1
pl. Pymble 223 G16
st. Pendle Hill 276 E14
st. Wentwthvle 276 E14
STAPLEY
st. Kingswood 237 E16
STAPYLTON
st. Winmalee 173 D5
STAR
cr. Pennant Hills 220 B15
cr. W Pnnant Hl 220 B15
ct. Cmbrdg Gdn 237 F4
la. Rooty Hill 272 B2
st. Eastwood 281 H6
st. Picton 563 C9
STARFIGHTER
av. Raby 481 F1
STARK
st. Coogee 377 D16
STARKEY
dr. Bnkstn Aprt 397 F5
st. Forestville 256 A13
st. Hurlstone Pk 373 B13
st. Killarney Ht 256 A14
STARLEAF
wy. Mcquarie Fd 454 H3
STARLIGHT
pl. Beaumont Hills 186 B16
pl. Richmond 118 D5
pl. St Clair 270 C13
STARLING
st. Green Valley 363 F12
st. Lilyfield 10 G10
st. Rozelle 7 C15
STARR
av. Padstow 429 E5
cl. Camden 507 A9
pl. Blacktown 274 A5
STARTOP
pl. Ambarvale 510 J14
STATEN
pl. Carlingford 280 D6
STATHAM
av. Faulconbdg 171 C16
av. North Rocks 278 K2
st. Belfield 371 G11
STATION
av. Concord W 341 C1
la. Hurstville 432 E7
la. Narwee 400 J13
la. Newtown 17 E14
la. Penrith 236 G11
la. Penshurst, off The Strand 431 F6
la. Wahroonga, off Coonabarra Rd 222 D7
pl. Eveleigh 18 F12
rd. Auburn 309 F16
rd. Belmore 371 C16
rd. Menangle Pk 539 A5
rd. Seven Hills 245 K15
rd. Toongabbie 276 A2
st. Arncliffe 403 E9
st. Ashfield 372 J2
st. Blaxland 233 F7
st. Camden 477 B15
st. Concord 341 G6
st. Couridjah 564 E15
st. Douglas Park 568 F6
st. Dundas 279 D14
st. Engadine 518 J2
st. Fairfield 335 K10
st. Fairfield Ht 335 K10
st. Glenbrook 263 K2
st. Guildford 337 G6
st. Homebush 341 D9
st. Hornsby 221 G1
st. Kogarah 433 B4
st. Marrickville 373 J14
st. Menangle 538 H16
st. Mortdale 431 A7
st. Naremburn 315 C1
st. Newtown 17 D12
st. Newtown 17 F15
st. Penrith 236 H10
st. Petersham 15 E6
st. Picton 563 G8
st. Pymble 253 E2
st. Regents Pk 368 K1
st. Rooty Hill 242 D16
st. St Marys 239 H14
st. Schofields 183 C15
st. S Wntwthvle 307 A3
st. Springwood, off Jerseywold Av 201 J3
st. Thirlmere 564 H9
st. Thirlmere 565 A6
st. Thornleigh 221 A14
st. Warwck Frm 365 H14
st. Wentwthvle 307 A3
st. West Ryde 281 C16
st.e, Harris Park 308 D4
st.e, Parramatta 308 D4
st.e, Tempe 404 B3
st.s, Emu Plains 235 K7
st.w, Harris Park 308 D7
st.w, Tempe 404 A3
STAUNER
pl. Quakers Hill 213 H13
STAVE
pl. Kellyville Rdg 215 D2
pl. Stanhpe Gdn 215 D2
STEAD
cl. Edensor Pk 363 H2
pl. Casula 424 F5
STEAMER
pl. Currans Hill 480 A12
STEDHAM
gr. Oakhurst 241 J4
STEEL
la. Surry Hills 19 K3
st. Blacktown 244 H10
st. S Granville 338 E7
st. Surry Hills 19 K3
STEELE
av. Revesby Ht 428 K8
pl. Bligh Park 150 F5
pl. Bonnyrigg 364 A6
st. Mays Hill 307 K6
st. Parramatta 307 K6
STEEPLE
wy. Narellan 478 B10
STEERFORTH
wy. Ambarvale 510 K16
wy. Ambarvale 511 A16
STEFAN
la. Doonside 243 C12
STEFANIE
pl. Bonnyrigg 364 A11
STEFIE
pl. Kings Lngly 245 G8
STEIN
pl. Cecil Hills 362 K5
pl. Glenmore Pk 265 F8
rd. Harringtn Pk 478 J4
STEINTON
st. Manly 288 H8
STELLA
cl. East Killara 254 E6
dr. Green Valley 362 K9
pl. Blacktown 274 F8
st. Collaroy Plat 228 J12
st. Fairfield Ht 335 H12
STENHOUSE
dr. Mt Annan 509 F2
STENNETT
rd. Ingleburn 452 E9
STEPHANIE
la. Belmore 371 G16
la. Belmore 401 G1
pl. Bella Vista 246 F5
pl. N Turramurra 223 G5
st. Padstow 399 E15
STEPHANO
pl. Rsemeadow 540 C3
STEPHEN
av. Matraville 436 G9
av. Ryde 281 K11
cl. Castle Hill 218 F16
la. Mt Wilson 59 A7
la. Paddington 13 C12
la. Randwick 377 B10
pl. Roselands 401 B9
rd. Botany 405 K12
rd. Engadine 518 G6
st. Balmain 8 A10
st. Beacon Hill 257 E7
st. Blacktown 245 A10
st. Bondi 377 J5
st. Chatswood 285 C12
st. Hornsby 191 J13
st. Newtown 17 K8
st. N Richmond 87 B14
st. Paddington 13 B13
st. Penshurst 431 A2
st. Randwick 377 B10
st. Woolmloo 4 G5
STEPHENS
la. Padstow 399 E16
STEPHENSON
pl. Currans Hill 479 J14
st. Birrong 368 J4
st. Leumeah 512 D1
st. Roselands 400 J6
st. Winston Hills 277 E5
STERLAND
av. North Manly 258 A14
STERLING
cct. Camperdown 11 D16
cct. Camperdown 11 E16
cct. Camperdown 17 E1
rd. Minchinbury 271 C6
STERLINI
cl. Blacktown 274 D10
STERN
pl. Roselands 400 K7
STEVENAGE
rd. Canley Ht 365 B3
rd. Hebersham 241 E5
STEVENS
av. Miranda 491 K1
cr. Smithfield 336 C5
la. Marrickville, off Philpott St 374 D9
rd. Glenorie 128 G2
rd. Ingleburn 422 J11
rd. Menangle 538 J16
st. East Hills 428 A2
st. Ermington 310 C1
st. Panania 428 A2
st. Pennant Hills 220 G14
st.e, Pennant Hills 220 J15
STEVENSON
av. Newington, off Heidelberg Av 310 B14
st. Lane Cove 314 F6
st. S Penrith 266 K1
st. S Penrith 267 A1
st. Wetherill Pk 334 G4
STEVEYS FOREST
rd. Oakdale 499 H7
STEWARD
st. Lilyfield 9 K7
STEWART
av. Blacktown 244 E12
av. Curl Curl 258 H12
av. Hamondvle 396 F15
av. Hornsby 191 E11
av. Matraville 406 J16
av. Peakhurst 430 B3
cl. Cheltenham 251 A11
dr. Castle Hill 248 C2
dr. Mcquarie Pk, off Smith Dr 283 C8
la. Bankstown 399 E1
la. Sydenham, off Park Rd 374 E16
pl. Balmain 7 E10
pl. Glenmore Pk 265 J7
pl. Paddington 21 D4
pl. Strathfield 341 E12
pwy. Hamondvle, off Stewart Av 396 G16
st. Arncliffe 403 D9
st. Artarmon 285 A13
st. Balmain 7 E11
st. Campbelltown 511 G7
st. Eastwood 280 K10
st. Ermington 280 C11
st. Glebe 11 J7
st. Harringtn Pk 478 G8
st. North Bondi 348 D14
st. Paddington 21 B2
st. Paddington 21 D3
st. Parramatta 308 F2
st. Randwick 407 C1
st. S Windsor 150 H3
STEWARTS
la. Wilberforce 67 B13
STILES
av. Padstow 399 B9
st. Croydon Pk 371 H6
st. Windsor 121 G8
STILLER
pl. Greenacre 369 J12
STILT
av. Cranebrook 207 H10
cl. Hinchinbrk 363 D16
STILTON
la. Picton 563 C16
STIMPSON
cr. Grasmere 505 J3
STIMSON
st. Guildford 337 D3
st. Smithfield 336 A6
STINGRAY
cl. Raby 451 C13
st. Cranebrook 207 B10

GREGORY'S STREET DIRECTORY 137

ST STREETS

STINSON
- cr. Bnkstn Apart....367 J16
- la. Marrickville, off Warren Rd 373 J15
- pl. Forestville 256 A7

STIPA
- pl. Mt Annan 509 D4

STIRGESS
- av. Curl Curl 258 G12

STIRLING
- av. Kirrawee 461 A15
- av. North Rocks......248 J16
- ct. Castle Hill 219 A11
- pl. Chatswood........285 D8
- pl. Belrose 225 K12
- st. Glenfield 424 E10
- st. Cmbrdg Pk........237 K9
- st. Cecil Hills 362 D7
- st. Glebe 12 K11
- st. Redfern 19 D6

STOCK
- av. Kingswood 237 H15
- pl. Winston Hills 276 H1

STOCKADE
- la. Emu Plains, off Stockade St.....235 D10
- st. Woodcroft 243 E8
- st. Emu Plains 235 D10

STOCKALLS
- pl. Minto 452 K16

STOCKDALE
- cr. Abbotsbury 333 C12

STOCK FARM
- av. Bella Vista 246 F2

STOCKHOLM
- av. Hassall Gr........211 H13

STOCKMAN
- rd. Wrrngtn Dns 238 D5
- rd. Currans Hill 479 K9

STOCKTON
- av. Moorebank 396 C7

STOCKWOOD
- st. S Penrith 266 G4

STODDART
- pl. Dee Why 258 F3
- rd. Prospect 275 A13
- st. Roselands 400 K6

STOKE
- av. Marrickville 373 H9
- cr. S Penrith 266 G5

STOKES
- av. Alexandria 375 E9
- av. Acquith 192 B11
- pl. Lindfield 254 B16
- pwy.Springwood 201 H1
- rd. Couridjah 565 C16
- rd. Tahmoor 565 D15
- st. Lane Cove N....284 F15

STOKOE
- st. Warwck Frm 365 F14

STOLLE
- cl. Menai 458 J7
- st. Shalvey 210 K14

STONE
- pde. Davidson 225 C14
- rd. Wrrngtn Dns.....238 C3
- st. Earlwood 402 G2
- st. Glendenning 242 F2
- st. Lidcombe 339 E10
- st. Meadowbank ...311 F2
- tce. Kurrajong Hl 63 H15

STONE BRIDGE
- dr. Glenbrook 234 B12

STONEBRIDGE
- pl. Gymea Bay.....491 C7

STONE COTTAGE
- ct. Castle Hill 248 D2
- pl. Blair Athol 511 A2

STONECROP
- pl. N Turramurra ..193 E15

STONEHAVEN
- av. Kellyville Rdg ...214 J2
- pde. Cabramatta 365 D11
- pl. Castle Hill 218 A7
- rd. Mt Colah........162 D14

STONELEA
- ct. Dural 188 G13

STONE PINE
- wy. Bella Vista 246 G4

STONE QUARRY
- dr. Picton 562 G10

STONEQUARRY
- pl. Picton 563 F9

STONES
- rd. Ebenezer 68 E9

STONEX
- la. Turramurra 222 H14

STONEY CREEK
- rd. Beverly Hills 401 C16
- rd. Bexley 402 A14
- rd. Kingsgrove.......401 C16
- rd. Narwee 430 J2

STONNY BATTER
- st. Minto 482 E7

STONYBROOK
- tce. Bella Vista 216 C15

STONY CREEK
- rd. Shanes Park 209 K9

STOREY
- av. West Hoxton ...391 G13
- st. Maroubra 406 J7
- st. Putney 311 J5

STORNOWAY
- av. St Andrews 451 J15

STORY
- pl. Quakers Hill ...213 H15

STOTT
- cl. Bonnyrigg 363 G8

STOTTS
- av. Bardwell Pk....402 G8

STOULTON
- wy. Cranebrook 207 G13

STOUT
- rd. Mount Druitt ...241 A15

STOW
- cl. Edensor Pk 363 K2
- pl. Illawong 459 G3

STOWE
- ct. Wattle Grove ..426 A5

STRABANE
- av. Killarney Ht 256 C15

STRACHAN
- ct. Kellyville 217 A2
- la. Kingsford, off Houston Rd....406 F1
- st. Kingsford 406 F1

STRADBROKE
- av. Green Valley ..363 A13

STRAITS
- av. Guildford 338 E10

STRAND
- arc. Sydney 3 G3
- la. Penshurst 431 F6

STRAND PASSAGE
- la. Lindfield, off Strickland Av.....284 E3
- la. St Clair, off Strickland Pl....270 G16

STRANG
- pl. Bligh Park 150 F6
- pwy. Castle Hill 218 E14

STRANRAER
- dr. St Andrews 481 K3

STRAPPER
- cl. Casula 394 F16

STRASSMANN
- cr. Lucas Ht 487 G12

STRATFORD
- av. Denistone 281 E12
- cl. Asquith 192 E10
- dr. Belrose 225 K10
- pl. St Ives 254 A3
- rd. North Rocks...278 J2
- rd. Tahmoor 565 H16
- st. Cammeray 316 C4

STRATH
- pl. Kenthurst 157 F5

STRATHALBYN
- dr. Oatlands 278 H11

STRATHALLEN
- av. Northbridge ...315 K1

STRATHAM
- st. Belrose 225 K12

STRATHCARRON
- av. Castle Hill 218 B7

STRATHDARR
- st. Miller 393 F11

STRATHDON
- cr. Blaxland 233 F12
- la. Emu Heights, off Strathdon Rd...205 B15
- rd. Emu Heights ..205 A15

STRATHEDEN
- av. Beaumont Hills ...185 J14

STRATHFIELD
- av. Strathfield 341 F14
- cl. St Johns Pk 364 G5
- sq. Strathfield 341 G12

STRATHFILLAN
- wy. Kellyville..........186 K16

STRATHLORA
- st. Strathfield 341 A16

STRATHMORE
- la. Glebe 11 K7
- pde. Chatswood 284 K6
- pl. Glen Alpine ...510 F13

STRATHROY
- cl. Cabarita 312 E16

STRATHWALLEN
- cl. Mcquarie Lk ...423 E14

STRATHWOOD
- cl. Pymble 253 G2

STRATTON
- cr. Milperra 397 D11
- rd. N Turramurra ..193 F11

STRAUSS
- cl. Bonnyrigg Ht...363 F5
- pl. Seven Hills 246 E12
- st. St Clair 300 A2

STRAWBERRY
- rd. Casula 424 E1
- wy. Glenwood 215 F12

STREAM
- st. Darlinghurst ......D K15

STREAMDALE
- gr. Warriewood ...198 J6

STREATFIELD
- rd. Bellevue Hill ...347 E16

STREBER
- pl. Hornsby 191 D12

STREETON
- av. Mt Pritchard ...364 J12
- pl. Casula 424 C4
- pl. Plumpton 242 C7

STRETHAM
- av. Picnic Point....428 G6

STRETTON
- la. Illawong 460 A7
- wy. Claymore 481 F11

STRIATA
- wy. Mcquarie Fd ...454 G4

STRICKLAND
- av. Cromer 227 H13
- av. Lindfield 284 E2
- av. Maroubra 407 C15
- cr. Ashcroft 364 D15
- la. Lindfield, off Strickland Av.....284 E3
- la. St Clair, off Strickland Pl....270 G16
- pl. Edensor Pk 363 C2
- pl. Erskine Park ...270 F16
- rd. Wentthvle 276 K14
- rd. Guildford 338 C9
- st. Bass Hill 368 B8
- st. Heathcote 518 G11
- st. Rose Bay 348 D11

STRICTA
- pl. Frenchs Frst ...226 G16

STRINGER
- pl. Oatlands 279 E12
- rd. Kellyville 185 G2

STRINGYBARK
- av. Cranebrook ...237 E1
- cl. Westleigh 220 F7
- pl. Alfords Point...429 C12
- pl. Bradbury 511 E10
- pl. Castle Hill 248 G3
- pl. Lugarno 430 B16

STROKER
- st. Canley Ht 365 C1

STROMBOLI
- pl. Bilgola 169 F3

STROMBOLI STRAIT
- Homebush B......310 J9

STROMEFERRY
- cr. St Andrews ...481 J5

STROMLO
- pl. Ruse 512 H1
- st. Bossley Park ..334 D9

STRONE
- av. Wahroonga ...221 K13

STRONG
- pl. Richmond 119 A6

STROUD
- cl. Belrose 226 B12
- st. North Ryde ..282 G13

- st. Warwck Frm 365 K16
- wy. Bonnyrigg 364 D5

STROUTHION
- ct. Green Valley ...363 F14

STRUAN
- st. Tahmoor 566 A9

STRUEN MARIE
- st. Kareela 461 C10

STRUTHERS
- la. Cronulla 524 A1

STRZELECKI
- cl. Wakeley 334 G15

STRZLECKI
- dr. Horngsea Pk ...392 E13

STUART
- av. Normanhurst ..221 D11
- av. Springwood ...201 H3
- cl. Illawong 460 G1
- ct. Blakehurst 462 B4
- cr. Drummoyne ...343 H1
- la. Blakehurst 432 D15
- la. Wahroonga, off Illoura Av 222 E7
- pl. Tahmoor 565 F9
- rd. Dharruk 241 B5
- rd. Horngsea Pk ...391 K16
- rd. West Hoxton ..391 K16
- st. Blakehurst 432 C16
- st. Burwood 342 C11
- st. Canley Vale ...366 A2
- st. Collaroy 229 A9
- st. Concord W 341 D2
- st. Granville 308 E16
- st. Jamisontown ..236 C15
- st. Kogarah 433 C5
- st. Longueville ...314 C9
- st. Manly 288 G12
- st. Newport 169 F12
- st. Padstow 399 F12
- st. Ryde 282 E13
- st. Wahroonga ...222 D6
- wk. Mosman, off Bloxsome La....316 G9

STUART MOULD
- cr. Lalor Park 245 D10

STUBBS
- pl. Bonnyrigg 364 C6
- st. Auburn 309 E14
- st. Beverley Pk ...432 K10
- st. Silverwater 309 E14

STUCKEY
- pl. Narellan Vale ..478 G15

STUDDY
- cr. Bligh Park 150 D5

STUDENTS
- la. Mt Riverview ..204 D16

STUDLEY
- ct. Narellan 478 B10
- st. Carramar 366 J3
- st. Londonderry ..148 B14

STUKA
- cl. Raby 451 D12

STURDEE
- la. Lovett Bay 168 B2
- pde. Dee Why 258 F2
- st. North Ryde ...282 K10
- st. Wentthvle 306 H1

STURGESS
- pl. Eagle Vale 481 A9

STURT
- av. Georges Hall ...368 A15
- la. Kingsford 406 J3
- pl. Camden S 507 A12
- pl. Castle Hill 218 D9
- pl. Mt Colah 162 C11
- pl. St Ives 224 A11
- pl. Windsor Dn....151 B5
- rd. Ingleburn 423 A9
- rd. Woolooware...493 J7
- st. Campbelltown ..511 G6
- st. Darlinghurst 4 E14
- st. Frenchs Frst ...256 C1
- st. Kingsford 406 G3
- st. Lalor Park 245 D13
- st. Smithfield 336 E2
- st. Telopea 279 G10

STUTT
- st. S Windsor 150 G2
- st. Kings Park 244 D2

STUTZ
- pl. Ingleburn 453 G13

STYLES
- cr. Minto 482 G6
- pl. Merrylands ...307 F14
- st. Leichhardt 10 D16

STYPANDRA
- pl. Springwood ...201 K2

SUAKIN
- dr. Mosman 317 F10
- st. Pymble 253 D6

SUBWAY
- la. Homebush 341 C9
- rd. Banksia 403 D11
- rd. Rockdale 403 D11

SUCCESS
- av. Kellyville 216 H1
- st. Greenfld Pk 334 D13

SUDBURY
- st. Belmore 371 E14

SUE
- pl. Mt Colah 162 G13

SUEZ CANAL
- The Rocks...........A K4

SUFFOLK
- av. Collaroy 229 A15
- cl. St Ives 224 D9
- la. Paddington 13 D15
- la. Colyton 270 E5
- pl. Elderslie 507 J1
- st. Tahmoor 566 E8
- st. Blacktown 244 C13
- st. Ingleburn 453 B7
- st. Miller 393 G2
- st. Paddington 13 D15
- st. Windsor 121 C9

SUGAR HOUSE
- rd. Canterbury, off Hutton St....372 H14

SUGARLOAF
- cr. Castlecrag 285 K10
- rd. Ingleside 198 C14

SUGARWOOD
- gr. Greenacre 370 F6

SULLIVAN
- av. Lurnea 394 C7
- st. Blacktown 273 K5
- st. Fairfield W 335 A12

SULLIVANS
- rd. Douglas Park ..568 G1

SULLY
- st. Randwick 407 D1

SULMAN
- pl. Doonside 273 F3
- pl. Menangle 538 G16
- rd. Cabramatta W ..365 B5

SULTANA
- gr. Glenwood 215 D15

SULU
- wy. Glenfield 424 E11

SUMBA
- pl. Blairmount ...481 A12

SUMBRAY
- av. Kemps Ck 359 J3

SUMMER
- rd. Faulconbdg ..171 B13

SUMMERCROP
- dr. Wrrngtn Dns ..237 K4

SUMMERFIELD
- av. Quakers Hill ..214 B15
- av. Quakers Hill ..214 E15
- cct. Cmbrdg Gdn ..237 H2

SUMMERHAZE
- cl. Hornsby Ht ...161 H15

SUMMER HILL
- la. St Clair, off Summer Hill Pl...270 C10
- pl. St Clair 270 C10
- st. Lewisham 15 A11

SUMMERS
- av. Hornsby 191 F13
- st. Bradbury 511 D3
- st. Dundas Vy 279 K11

SUMMERSTONE
- wy. Ambarvale.....510 A16

SUMMERVILLE
- cr. N Willoughby ..285 F9

SUMMERWOOD
- wy. Beecroft 250 A7

SUMMIT
- av. Dee Why 259 B9
- ct. Marsfield 281 A6
- ct. Glenwood 215 G16

STREETS SY

gln. Cranebrook........207 B11
la. Cranebrook, off Summit Gln.........207 B11
pl. Baulkham Hl.......246 F11
pl. Strathfield..........341 C16
st. Earlwood............402 E5
st. Mt Riverview......204 G14

SUMNER
st. Hassall Gr..........212 B15
st. Sutherland..........460 F15

SUNART
pl. St Andrews.........481 J5

SUNBEAM
av. Burwood.............371 J2
av. Croydon.............342 H13
av. Kogarah.............433 D10
la. Campsie.............401 K2
pl. Ingleburn...........453 K7

SUNBIRD
cl. Hinchinbrk..........393 B4
tce. Glenmore Pk.......266 A12

SUNBLEST
cr. Mount Druitt.......240 K15

SUNBURY
st. Sutherland..........460 D15

SUNCREST
av. Newport.............169 G15
pl. Doonside............243 H15

SUNCROFT
av. Georges Hall.......368 D15

SUNDA
av. Whalan..............241 B13

SUNDALE
pl. Chester Hill........368 C2

SUNDERLAND
av. Castle Hill..........217 A10
av. Rose Bay, off New South Head Rd.............347 K10
cr. Bligh Park...........150 J6
dr. Raby..................451 F15

SUNFLOWER
dr. Clarmnt Ms.........268 H1

SUNHAVEN
st. Beecroft..............250 A11

SUNHILL
pl. North Ryde.........282 F7

SUNLAND
cr. Mt Riverview......204 G16

SUNLEA
av. Mortdale.............430 J5
cr. Belfield...............371 C8
pl. Allambie Ht.........257 B8

SUNNDAL
cl. St Clair...............269 H15

SUNNING
pl. Summer Hill........373 C3

SUNNINGDALE
Blacktown..........274 D11
dr. Glenmore Pk.......266 E9
dr. Glenmore Pk.......266 F10
pl. Rouse Hill, off Glen Abbey St.....185 A9

SUNNY
cr. Punchbowl..........399 J6
pl. St Johns Pk........334 E15

SUNNYDALE
pl. Narellan, off Links Wy............478 B10

SUNNYHOLT
rd. Acacia Gdn.........215 A16
rd. Blacktown...........244 J15
rd. Glenwood...........215 A16
rd. Kings Lngly.........244 K8
rd. Kings Park..........244 K8
rd. Parklea..............215 A16
rd. Stanhpe Gdn......215 D12

SUNNYMEADE
cl. Asquith..............192 C10
rd. Berkshire Pk.......179 E9

SUNNY RIDGE
rd. Winmalee...........172 K12

SUNNYRIDGE
pl. Bayview.............168 J11
rd. Arcadia..............129 E8

SUNNYSIDE
av. Caringbah...........492 J6
av. Lilyfield...............10 G3
cr. Castlecrag...........285 K11
cr. N Richmond..........87 E15
dr. Ellis Lane............476 D5
pl. Blakehurst...........462 C2
st. Gladesville..........312 K11

SUNNYVALE
rd. Middle Dural......158 K10

SUNRAY
cr. St Clair...............270 D14

SUNRIDGE
pl. W Pnnant Hl........248 K3

SUNRISE
pl. Horngsea Pk.......392 C14
pl. Kellyville.............216 H3
rd. Palm Beach.........109 J16

SUNSET
av. Bankstown..........399 B5
av. Cabramatta W.....365 C5
av. Cronulla..............523 J2
av. Elderslie..............507 F2
av. Hornsby Ht.........161 G12
av. Lurnea................394 C7
av. S Penrith.............266 F1
bvd. Winmalee...........173 E5
la. Seaforth..............286 K11
pl. Earlwood.............402 H5
pl. Frenchs Frst........256 K4
pl. North Rocks.........278 G3

SUNSHINE
av. Penrith................237 A7
pde. Peakhurst..........430 C11
st. Manly Vale..........287 J3

SUNTER
wy. Castle Hill...........217 K6

SUNTOP
pl. Glenmore Pk.......266 H14

SUN VALLEY
pl. Carlingford..........279 F2
rd. Sun Valley...........202 J6
rd. Sun Valley...........202 K9
rd. Sun Valley...........203 A6

SUNVILLE
ct. Blacktown...........274 B8

SUPERBA
av. Cronulla..............494 C6
la. Mosman, off Superba Pde.......317 C6
pde. Mosman.............317 C6

SUPERIOR
av. Seven Hills..........275 F7

SUPPLY
av. Beacon Hill..........257 G2
av. Lurnea................394 C12
cl. Narellan..............478 E16
ct. Kellyville.............216 H1
pl. Bligh Park...........150 E4
rd. Lilyfield.................10 A2
st. Dundas Vy..........280 B7
st. Ruse...................512 H3

SUPPORT
rd. Kingsford............407 B4

SURADA
av. Riverview............314 B7

SURF
la. Cronulla..............493 K12
rd. Cronulla..............493 K12
rd. N Curl Curl..........259 A11
rd. Palm Beach.........140 B7
rd. Whale Beach.......140 B7
rd. Whale Beach.......140 C6

SURFERS
pde. Harbord.............258 E16

SURFSIDE
av. Avalon................170 C2
av. Clovelly...............377 K12

SURFVIEW
rd. Mona Vale...........199 G4

SURGEONS
ct. The Rocks.............A K5

SURPRISE
cr. Bligh Park...........150 C7

SURREY
av. Castle Hill...........217 K9
av. Collaroy..............258 K1
av. Georges Hall.......368 B15
la. Darlinghurst............4 J9
la. Waterloo................19 F11
pl. Kareela...............461 B13
rd. Turramurra..........223 D9
st. Blacktown...........274 G6
st. Darlinghurst............4 H10
st. Epping.................251 B13
st. Guildford.............337 G3
st. Marrickville.........374 A9
st. Minto..................452 G16
st. Stanmore...............16 G9
st. Waterloo................19 F11

SURVEY
pl. St Ives.................224 B16

SURVEYOR
av. Heathcote...........518 D13

SURVEYOR ABBOT
dr. Glenbrook...........234 C11

SURVEYORS CREEK
rd. Glenmore Pk.......266 E9

SUSAN
av. Padstow Ht.........429 D6
la. Annandale.............11 B16
la. Clovelly, off Fern St.................377 G12
pde. Castle Hill..........217 K16
pl. Eastwood.............281 G6
pl. Gymea Bay...........491 F9
pl. Minto..................482 G3
st. Annandale..............17 B2
st. Auburn................339 D5
st. Camperdown..........17 H5
st. Newtown...............17 J7
st. S Wntwthvle.........306 H8

SUSANNE
la. Cmbrdg Pk, off Susanne Pl..........238 C7
pl. Cmbrdg Pk...........238 C7

SUSELLA
cr. N Richmond..........87 A12

SUSSEX
la. Sydney....................A C15
pl. Narellan..............478 H12
pl. Seven Hills..........275 E5
rd. Kellyville.............216 B4
rd. St Ives.................254 A2
st. Cabramatta.........365 G10
st. Epping.................251 C12
st. Haymarket..............E E3
st. Haymarket..............3 E7
st. Minto..................482 E1
st. Sydney....................A C13
st. Sydney....................E E3
st. Sydney....................1 D15
st. Sydney....................3 D1

SUSSMAN
av. Bass Hill.............368 C13
cr. Smithfield...........336 C5

SUTCLIFFE
pl. Barden Rdg.........488 G4
st. Kingsgrove..........401 H12

SUTHERLAND
av. Kings Lngly.........245 D6
av. Paddington...........13 F14
av. Ryde...................311 H3
av. Wahroonga..........222 F8
cr. Darling Point.........14 B4
la. Chippendale, off O'Connor St..........19 A2
la. Cremorne, off Ben Boyd La........316 D7
la. Merrylands..........307 J13
la. Sutherland..........490 D2
rd. Beecroft..............250 F5
rd. Chatswood W.....284 G12
rd. Cheltenham.........251 A9
rd. Jannali................460 F14
rd. Londonderry.......148 J16
rd. N Parramatta......278 E11
st. Canley Ht............365 B3
st. Cremorne.............316 C7
st. Granville..............308 H12
st. Lane Cove............314 B1
st. Mascot................405 F6
st. Paddington...........13 F14
st. Rosebery.............405 F6
st. St Peters..............374 F14
st. Sutherland...........490 D3
st. Yagoona..............369 D8

SUTTIE
rd. Bellevue Hill..........14 H16
rd. Double Bay............22 G1
rd. Woollahra.............22 G1

SUTTON
av. Earlwood.............402 K5
grn. W Pnnant Hl.......249 C4
la. Balmain, off Sutton St.................7 F11
la. Darlinghurst, off Wisdom La.............4 E9
pl. Minto..................453 C15
pl. St Ives.................224 B16
rd. Ashcroft...............364 D16
rd. Cmbrdg Pk...........238 B8
st. Balmain..................7 F10
st. Blacktown...........274 H4
st. Five Dock............343 A9
st. Hornsby..............191 F9

SUTTOR
av. Moore Park............21 B9
av. Ryde...................311 J4
pl. Baulkham Hl.......247 E4
rd. N Parramatta......278 K6
st. Alexandria.............18 F15
st. Silverwater..........309 G12
st. Woolmloo................4 C7

SUVA
cr. Greenacre...........369 K14
pl. Lethbrdg Pk........240 G1

SUWARROW
st. Fairlight...............288 D7

SUZANNE
cl. Berowra Ht..........133 A6
rd. Mona Vale...........198 J2
st. Seven Hills..........275 J6

SVENSDEN
pl. Ingleburn............453 B12

SVERGE
st. Mosman..............316 K12

SWAFFHAM
rd. Minto..................482 A6

SWAGER
pl. Canley Ht............335 E16

SWAGMAN
la. Wrrngtn Dns, off Swagman Pl.......238 D4
pl. Wrrngtn Dns.......238 D4

SWAIN
st. Moorebank..........395 H9
st. Sydenham...........374 D14

SWAINE
dr. Wilton.................568 K16

SWALES
pl. Colyton...............270 J9

SWALLOW
dr. Erskine Park........270 G16
dr. Erskine Park........270 J14
la. St Clair, off Swallow Dr.........270 J14
pl. Hinchinbrk..........363 D15
pl. Ingleburn............453 G9
st. Jamisontown.......236 B16

SWALLOW REACH
pl. Ebenezer...............68 E8

SWALLOW ROCK
dr. Grays Point.........491 C15

SWAMP
rd. Tempe.................404 D4

SWAMPHEN
la. St Clair, off Swamphen St......271 A14
st. Erskine Park........271 A13

SWAN
av. Strathfield...........341 G10
cct. Green Valley........363 C14
ct. Harringtn Pk........478 D4
pl. Ingleburn............453 D9
pl. Jamisontown.......266 D4
pl. Lalor Park...........245 J11
pl. Pennant Hills.......220 D16
rd. Edensor Pk..........333 G16
st. Gladesville...........312 K5
st. Lilli Pilli...............522 E3
st. Revesby..............398 H15
st. Rydalmere...........279 F16
st. Woolooware.........493 G9

SWANE
st. Ermington............310 F2

SWANLEY
st. Mt Pritchard........364 C11

SWANN
pl. Kellyville..............215 F4

SWANNELL
av. Chiswick..............343 D2

SWANNS
la. Allawah................432 G9

SWANSEA
ct. Glenwood............215 J14
pl. West Hoxton........392 E5

SWANSON
la. Erskineville............18 C15
st. Erskineville............18 B14
st. Eveleigh................18 B14
wy. Claymore.............481 B11

SWANSTON
st. St Marys..............269 H2

SWEENEY
av. Plumpton.............241 G10

SWEETHAVEN
rd. Bossley Park........333 J10
rd. Edensor Pk..........333 J13
rd. Greenfld Pk..........333 J13
st. Bankstown...........399 E1

SWEETWATER
gr. Orchard Hills........268 H12

SWETE
st. Lidcombe.............339 K8

SWETTENHAM
rd. Minto..................482 B3

SWIFT
gln. Erskine Park........270 K11
pl. Hinchinbrk..........393 C3
pl. Ingleburn............453 F6
pl. Wetherill Pk.........334 K6
st. Guildford..............337 F5

SWINBORNE
cr. Wetherill Pk.........335 A4

SWINBOURNE
st. Bnksmeadw.........405 J13
st. Botany.................405 J13

SWINDON
cl. Turramurra..........222 J16
pl. Chipping Ntn.......366 E16

SWINSON
rd. Blacktown............274 G3

SWIVELLER
cl. Ambarvale............540 F1

SWORDFISH
av. Raby...................481 G2

SWORDS
pl. Mount Druitt.......271 A1

SYBIL
la. Btn-le-Sds...........433 H4
st. Beverley Pk.........432 K10
st. Eastwood.............280 G8
st. Guildford W.........306 J16
st. Newport...............169 H7

SYCAMORE
av. Casula.................394 F14
cr. Quakers Hill.........243 D3
gr. Menai..................458 J13
st. N St Marys...........240 B9

SYD EINFELD
dr. Bondi Jctn.............22 E5
dr. Woollahra..............22 E5

SYDENHAM
la. Marrickville, off Shirlow St............374 D13
rd. Brookvale.............258 B11
rd. Marrickville.........373 K9

SYDNEY
arc. Sydney....................3 G3
gte. Waterloo................19 K15
la. Erskineville............18 B14
la. Marrickville.........374 B14
pl. Ruse...................512 G1
pl. Woolmloo................4 H5
rd. Balgowlah............287 F9
rd. E Lindfield...........254 J14
rd. Fairlight................288 B8
rd. Hornsby Ht..........191 E4
rd. Manly..................288 B8
rd. Seaforth..............287 D10
rd. Warriewood.........199 E13
rd. Warwck Frm........365 D16
st. Artarmon.............285 C14
st. Blacktown............245 A15
st. Chatswood...........285 C12
st. Concord...............341 H8
st. Erskineville............18 C14
st. Marrickville.........374 C13
st. N Willoughby.......285 C12
st. Panania...............398 B15
st. Randwick.............377 A11
st. Riverstone...........182 H4
st. St Marys..............270 B2
st. Willoughby...........285 C14

SYDNEY HARBOUR BRIDGE
Dawes Point..............1 H3

SYDNEY HARBOUR TUNNEL
Milsons Point.........2 A4
Sydney....................B H1
Sydney....................2 A4

SYDNEY JOSEPH
dr. Seven Hills..........246 B13

SYDNEY LUKER
rd. Cabramatta W......365 C6

SYDNEY-NEWCASTLE
fwy. Asquith..............192 D16
fwy. Berowra.............163 A9
fwy. Brooklyn..............75 A13
fwy. Cowan...............104 E13
fwy. Krngai Ch N P....192 D16

GREGORY'S STREET DIRECTORY 139

fwy. Mooney Mooney..75 A13
fwy. Mt Colah............162 F16
fwy. Mt Krng-gai........162 F16
fwy. N Wahroonga.......222 B7
fwy. Wahroonga.........222 B7
SYDNEY PARK
rd. Alexandria..........375 A11
rd. Erskineville.........374 K11
SYDNEY STEEL
rd. Marrickville........374 E12
SYKES
pl. Colyton..............270 E4
pl. Mount Druitt......271 A1
SYLVA
av. Miranda..............491 J4
SYLVAN
av. E Lindfield..........255 B12
gr. Glenhaven...........187 K16
gr. Picnic Point.........428 C12
la. Sylvania..............461 J9
pl. Leonay................264 K2
st. Galston................159 E10
st. Sylvania..............461 J10
SYLVANIA
av. Springwood.........201 G3
rd.n,Miranda.............491 H4
rd.n,Sylvania.............461 H16
rd.s,Gymea Bay.........491 G8
rd.s,Miranda..............491 G7
SYLVAN RIDGE
dr. Illawong..............459 C1
SYLVANUS
st. Greenacre...........370 H11
SYLVESTER
av. Roselands...........400 J8
SYLVIA
av. Carlingford..........249 F12
pl. Frenchs Frst........256 F4
pl. Greystanes..........305 H8
st. Blacktown............273 H1
st. Chatswood W.....284 D10
st. Rydalmere...........309 K5
SYLVIA CHASE
sq. Sydney....................4 C5
sq. Woolmloo................4 C5
SYM
av. Burwood..............341 K15
la. Burwood, off Livingstone St....341 K15
SYMONDS
av. Parramatta..........278 J15
rd. Colebee...............213 A16
rd. Dean Park............242 K2
rd. Londonderry.......148 F7
wky.Denistone...........281 D11
SYMONS
pl. West Hoxton.......392 B11
st. Fairfield...............336 D16
SYNCARPIA
wy. Winmalee............173 E8
SYRUS
pl. Quakers Hill........213 H8
SYSTRUM
st. Ultimo.....................3 B12

T

TABALI
st. Whalan...............241 A11
TABALUM
rd. Balgowlah Ht......287 J16
TABARD
pl. Illawong..............459 D5
TABELL
cl. Hornsby Ht.........191 F8
TABER
pl. Bradbury.............511 G11
st. Menangle Pk.......539 A3
TABERS
rd. Orangeville..........473 E10
TABITHA
pl. Plumpton.............241 H6
TABLETOP
cct. Horngsea Pk......392 C15
TABOOBA
st. Wentwthvle.........277 A9
TABOR
st. Glenbrook...........233 K14
TABORA
st. Forestville...........255 K13
TABOURIE
st. Leumeah.............482 F15
TABRETT
st. Banksia...............403 E12
TADMORE
rd. Cranebrook.........206 K1
TAFFS
av. Lugarno..............430 A10
TAFT
pl. Bonnet Bay.........460 F11
TAGGARTS
la. Darlinghurst............4 C13
TAGU
pl. Kings Park..........244 K3
TAGUDI
pl. Bangor................459 E12
TAGULA
pl. Glenfield.............424 H10
TAHITI
av. Lethbrdg Pk........240 H2
pl. Kings Lngly.........245 C6
TAHLEE
cl. Castle Hill............218 J8
cr. Leumeah.............482 A15
st. Burwood..............342 B16
st. Burwood..............372 B2
TAHMOOR
rd. Tahmoor.............566 A10
TAHOE
pl. Erskine Park........271 A15
TAILBY
rd. Campbelltown.....510 H7
TAIN
pl. Schofields...........183 B16
TAIO
pl. Kings Lngly.........245 E8
TAIRORA
st. Whalan...............241 A10
TAIT
la. Russell Lea.........343 E5
st. Russell Lea.........343 E5
st. Smithfield...........336 A1
TAIWAN
pl. Sylvania..............462 A12
TAIYUL
rd. N Narrabeen........198 H14
TALARA
av. Glenmore Pk.......266 A8
la. Gymea.................491 E2
rd.n,Gymea...............491 D3
rd.s,Gymea...............491 D6
st. Pemulwuy............305 E6
TALASEA
st. Whalan...............241 A11
TALAVERA
rd. Mcquarie Pk........282 F1
rd. Marsfield.............252 C13
TALBINGO
pl. Heckenberg.........364 D13
pl. Ruse...................512 H6
pl. Woodcroft...........243 H9
TALBOT
cl. Menai.................458 E15
ct. Wattle Grove.......395 K16
pl. Ingleburn............453 G13
pl. Woolmloo...............4 F7
rd. Guildford.............337 H4
rd. Yagoona.............368 K8
st. Riverwood...........400 D16
st. St Peters.............374 E16
TALBRAGAR
st. Ruse...................512 D7
TALC
pl. Eagle Vale...........481 B7
TALEEBAN
rd. Riverview............314 B5
TALFOURD
la. Glebe....................12 B12
st. Glebe....................12 C12
TALGAI
av. Wahroonga.........251 H1
TALGARA
pl. Beacon Hill..........257 J8
TALIA
cl. Kingswood..........267 J3
TALINGA
av. Georges Hall.......368 A15
pl. Cherrybrook........219 B12
pl. Lilli Pilli...............522 G2
st. Carlingford..........280 B3
TALISMAN
av. Castle Hill...........247 H3
TALKOOK
pl. Baulkham Hl.......246 K6
TALLAGANDRA
dr. Quakers Hill........243 D3
TALLARA
pl. Busby..................363 J15
pl. Terrey Hills..........196 F5
TALLAROOK
cl. Mona Vale...........199 D1
pl. Bangor................459 F12
TALLAWALLA
st. Beverly Hills........401 C12
TALLAWARRA
av. Padstow.............429 G2
pl. Narrabeen...........229 A5
rd. Leumeah.............482 A15
TALLAWONG
av. Blacktown...........273 H4
rd. Rouse Hill...........184 A9
TALLAWUNG
pl. Kenthurst............156 E11
TALLGUMS
av. W Pnnant Hl........249 J2
TALLINN
gr. Rooty Hill............271 K5
TALLONG
pl. Caringbah...........492 F13
pl. Turramurra.........223 D11
st. Prestons.............393 B13
TALLOW
pl. Glenwood............245 J2
pl. S Coogee............407 E5
TALLOWOOD
av. Casula.................394 F14
cr. Bossley Park.......333 E8
ct. Plumpton.............242 B8
gdn.Blaxland.............234 B8
gr. Beaumont Hills...186 A16
pl. Cranebrook.........207 B8
wy. Frenchs Frst.......256 F1
TALLOW WOOD
cl. Wilberforce...........93 E3
TALLOW-WOOD
av. Narellan Vale......479 A13
TALLOWWOOD
av. Cherrybrook........219 F11
av. Lugarno..............429 K9
cl. Alfords Point.......429 C15
cr. Bradbury.............511 F12
TALL SHIPS
av. W Pnnant Hl........249 A1
TALL TIMBERS
rd. Winmalee............173 E12
TALL TREES
av. Castle Hill, off Barker Dr............218 J13
TALLWOOD
av. Eastwood............281 K8
dr. North Rocks.........278 G3
pl. St Clair...............270 D9
TALMIRO
st. Whalan...............241 A11
TALOFA
pl. Castle Hill............218 C8
TALOMA
av. Lurnea................394 E6
la. S Penrith.............237 A16
st. Picnic Point.........428 G6
st. S Penrith.............237 A15
TALOOMBI
st. Cronulla..............493 H16
TALPA
cl. Thornleigh..........221 A5
TALUS
st. Naremburn..........315 D3
TALWONG
st. Hornsby Ht.........161 K11
TAMAR
ct. Glenhaven...........218 D5
pl. Fairfield W..........335 B10
pl. N Wahroonga.......223 A1
st. Marrickville.........373 F13
st. Sutherland..........490 C1
TAMARA
cl. Oakdale..............500 D12
pl. Beaumont Hills...186 C16
rd. Faulconbdg.........171 E13
TAMARAMA
st. Tamarama..........378 A6
TAMARAMA MARINE
dr. Tamarama..........378 B7
TAMARIN
ct. Kellyville.............217 A4
TAMARIND
dr. Acacia Gdn..........214 J15
dr. Acacia Gdn..........215 A15
pl. Alfords Point.......429 B16
TAMARISK
cr. Cherrybrook........219 H6
TAMARIX
cr. Banksia...............403 G12
st. Greystanes..........305 E11
TAMARO
av. Whalan...............241 A10
TAMBA
pl. Port Hacking.......522 H2
TAMBAROORA
cr. Marayong............243 H6
pl. W Pnnant Hl........248 G7
TAMBOON
av. Turramurra.........252 F2
TAMBORINE
rd. Beaumont Hills...215 J1
TAMBOURA
av. Baulkham Hl.......247 B14
TAMBOURINE BAY
rd. Lane Cove...........314 C3
rd. Riverview............314 A6
TAMBOY
av. Carlingford..........279 C1
TAMBU
st. St Ives................224 F10
TAMINA
pl. S Penrith.............267 C6
TAMINGA
rd. Green Valley........363 H10
st. Bayview..............168 H11
TAMMAR
pl. St Helens Park....541 F3
TAMPLIN
rd. Guildford.............337 B5
TAMWORTH
cr. Hoxton Park........392 G6
pl. Allambie Ht.........257 D13
pl. Engadine.............488 G13
TANA
pl. Kings Park...........244 H2
TANAMI
cl. Belrose...............225 J12
cl. Wakeley, off Mallacoota St......334 J12
pl. Bow Bowing........452 C15
TANBARK
cct. Wrrngtn Dns.......238 C4
pl. Dural..................219 B7
TANCRED
av. Kyeemagh...........404 C13
TANDARA
av. Bradbury.............511 C16
TANDERAGEE
st. Wentwthvle.........277 D10
TANDERRA
av. Carlingford..........279 J2
pl. Curl Curl.............258 J14
st. Colyton...............270 F6
st. Wahroonga.........222 C10
TANGALOA
cr. Lethbrdg Pk........240 J2
TANGARA
st. Eveleigh................18 H11
TANGARRA
st. Croydon Pk.........371 F6
st.e, Croydon Pk.......371 H6
TANGERINE
dr. Quakers Hill........214 G12
st. Fairfield E...........337 A14
TANGLEWOOD
cl. Glenmore Pk.......266 F10
pl. W Pnnant Hl........248 H5
wy. Hornsby Ht.........161 H15
TANGO
av. Dee Why.............258 F8
TANIA
av. S Penrith.............267 C3
cl. Hornsby Ht..........161 K8
st. Greystanes..........305 H5
TANK STREAM
wy. Sydney...................B A12
TANNA
pl. Prestons.............393 K15
TANN-DARBY
ct. Glenwood............215 K16
TANNER
av. Allawah...............432 G9
av. Carlton................432 G9
la. Carlton................432 G8
pl. Minchinbury........271 H7
TANNERS
wy. Kellyville.............216 J1
TANTALLON
av. Arncliffe..............403 G10
la. Arncliffe..............403 G11
rd. Lane Cove N.......284 A15
TANTANGARA
pl. Woodcroft...........243 E11
st. Heckenberg.........363 K14
TANTANI
av. Green Valley........363 G11
TANYA
pl. Tahmoor.............566 A13
TAO
cl. St Clair................269 H15
TAPI
gln. St Clair...............300 A3
TAPIOLA
av. Hebersham.........241 E4
TAPLAN
st. Como..................460 F7
TAPLEY
wy. Ambarvale...........511 B15
TAPLIN
pl. Camden S...........506 K15
TAPP
pl. Bidwill.................211 B15
TAPPEINER
ct. Baulkham Hl.......217 A16
TARA
cl. Yennora..............336 K11
pl. Lugarno..............430 A13
rd. Blacktown...........273 J1
st. Kangaroo Pt........461 H7
st. Merrylands..........308 D15
st. Sylvania..............461 H7
st. Woollahra.............21 K1
TARAGO
pl. E Lindfield...........255 B11
pl. Prestons.............392 J15
TARAKAN
cr. Northbridge........285 J14
pl. Narraweena.........257 K4
rd. Moorebank..........425 A4
st. Holsworthy.........396 D16
TARALGA
st. Old Guildford.......337 G9
st. Prestons.............392 H14
TARANA
cl. Casula.................394 C16
cr. Baulkham Hl.......246 J9
cr. Dharruk..............241 B7
TARANAKI
av. Lethbrdg Pk........240 H2
pl. Northmead..........248 B16
TARANTO
pl. Prestons.............393 D16
rd. Marsfield.............252 B13
TARAWA
rd. Lethbrdg Pk........240 H3
TARBAN
st. Gladesville..........313 B11
TARBERT
pl. St Andrews.........481 J3
TARCOOLA
pl. Ellis Lane............476 C6
pl. Engadine.............488 D13
TAREE
av. N Balgowlah........287 B5
cr. Greystanes..........305 J5
pl. Dharruk..............241 B8
pl. Hoxton Park........392 J9
TARELLA
pl. Cammeray, off Amherst St..........315 J5
TAREN
rd.s,Caringbah..........492 E11
TAREN POINT
rd. Caringbah...........492 G5
rd. Taren Point.........462 H15
TARGO
rd. Beverley Pk.........433 B13
rd. Girraween...........276 B16
rd. Toongabbie.........276 C8
TARI
wy. Glenfield............424 E11
TARINGA
av. Kellyville.............216 A3
st. Ashfield..............342 J15

140 GREGORY'S STREET DIRECTORY

STREETS TE

TARINGHA
st. Blaxland 233 D6
TARLINGTON
pde. Bonnyrigg 364 A5
pl. Prospect 275 C15
pl. Smithfield 305 D12
TARO
pl. Quakers Hill 243 F4
st. Blakehurst 462 D1
TARONGA
pde. Caringbah 492 K5
pl. Mona Vale 199 D3
st. Blacktown 274 E8
st. Como 460 F6
st. Hurstville 401 K15
wy. Faulconbdg 171 A13
TAROO
pl. Forestville 255 G11
TAROOK
av. S Turramrra 252 A5
TAROONA
st. St Marys 239 G14
TARPAN
pl. Emu Heights 235 B2
TARPEIAN
wy. Sydney B H5
TARPLEE
av. Hamondvle 396 F15
TARRA
cr. Dee Why 258 J2
TARRABUNDI
dr. Glenmore Pk 266 C7
TARRAGEN
av. Hobartville 118 C7
TARRAGUNDI
rd. Epping 250 J12
TARRANT
av. Bellevue Hill 14 G10
cl. Picton 563 F12
pl. Doonside 243 E16
TARRANTS
av. Eastwood 280 J9
TARRILLI
pl. Kellyville 216 E4
st. Beverly Hills 401 B12
TARRO
av. Revesby 428 G1
cl. Hornsby 191 H7
TARUN
pl. Dharruk 241 B6
TARWIN
av. Glenwood 215 H12
TASKER
av. Clemton Park 402 A3
av. Peakhurst 430 A4
TASMA
pl. Airds 512 C11
TASMAN
av. Lethbrdg Pk 240 H2
cr. Killara 254 C10
ct. Castle Hill 218 D10
la. Bundeena 524 B11
pde. Fairfield W 335 C11
pl. Mcquarie Pk 282 J1
pl. S Windsor 150 E3
rd. Avalon 140 D16
rd. Mulgoa 325 G4
st. Bondi 377 K6
st. Cmbrdg Pk 237 H6
st. Dee Why 259 A9
st. Hinchinbrk 363 B15
st. Kurnell 465 G9
st. Phillip Bay 436 J12
TATE
cr. Horngsea Pk 392 F16
pl. Lugarno 429 J16
st. Panania 428 C4
TATES
la. Kurrajong 85 B5
TATHIRA
cr. Merrylands W 306 J11
TATHRA
av. Prestons 393 D16
ct. Dural 219 B3
pl. Bow Bowing 452 D12
pl. Castle Hill 218 D16
pl. Forestville 255 G8
pl. Gymea Bay 491 C8
TATIARA
cr. N Narrabeen 198 G14
TATLER
pl. Woronora Ht 489 B4
TATTERSALL
pl. Emu Plains 235 D14
rd. Kings Park 244 H6
TATTLER
pl. Hinchinbrk 363 E16
TAUBMAN
dr. Horngsea Pk 392 E14
TAUNTON
la. Pymble, off Taunton St 253 D2
rd. Hurstville 432 A1
st. Blakehurst 432 D12
st. Pymble 253 D2
TAUPO
rd. Glenorie 128 C1
TAURUS
pl. Gilead 540 F7
st. Erskine Park 300 K2
TAVISTOCK
rd. Homebush W 340 F10
rd. Kemps Ck 360 B7
rd. S Hurstville 432 A12
st. Auburn 338 J4
st. Croydon Pk 371 G7
st. Drummoyne 343 H2
TAWA
st. Ashfield 342 J15
TAWARRI
cr. Kyle Bay 431 J16
TAWMII
pl. Castle Hill 218 H9
TAWNY
cl. Glenwood 215 E15
TAWORRI
st. Doonside 243 C15
TAY
la. Kensington 376 E9
pl. St Andrews 481 K6
pl. Winston Hills 277 E4
pl. Woronora 489 G2
st. Kensington 20 K16
TAYLEE
pl. Rouse Hill 185 D6
TAYLER
rd. Valley Ht 202 E4
TAYLOR
av. Banksia 403 E12
av. Lugarno 429 K15
av. Melrose Pk 310 H1
av. Turramurra 252 E3
cl. Miranda 492 B5
ct. Springwood 202 D11
la. Artarmon 315 A2
la. Glebe 12 B9
la. N Strathfield, off Carrington St 341 G8
pl. Ermington 280 A14
pl. Kings Lngly 245 H8
pl. Pennant Hills 220 F12
pl. Theresa Park 445 A11
rd. Cranebrook 177 D15
sq. Darlinghurst 4 D13
st. Annandale 17 C1
st. Condell Park 398 H3
st. Darlinghurst 4 E14
st. Fairfield 336 E16
st. Five Dock 342 D10
st. Glebe 12 B8
st. Gordon 254 A6
st. Greystanes 305 K10
st. Kogarah 433 A4
st. Lakemba 371 B16
st. Lakemba 401 C1
st. Lidcombe 339 J9
st. Maroubra 406 H11
st. N Curl Curl 259 B10
st. Paddington 21 H1
st. Queens Park 22 K13
st. Queens Park 377 F7
st. Waterloo 20 C16
st. W Pnnant Hl 248 K5
wy. Claymore 481 B10
TAYLORS
dr. Lane Cove N 283 F13
la. Lane Cove N 284 F16
rd. Badgerys Ck 328 E16
rd. Badgerys Ck 358 E4
rd. Dural 189 G3
rd. Silverdale 353 G16
TAYLORS POINT
rd. Clareville 169 D2
TAYNISH
av. Camden S 507 B14
TAYWOOD
av. Winston Hills 277 G4
st. Woolooware 493 F8
TEAGAN
pl. Blacktown 274 B6
TEA GARDENS
av. Kirrawee 491 C1
TEAGUE
st. Girraween 276 A10
st. Toongabbie 276 A10
TEAK
cl. Bossley Park 333 F8
pl. Cherrybrook 219 H7
pl. Miranda 462 C16
st. St Clair 269 G10
wy. Acacia Gdn 214 K14
wy. Prestons 393 K14
TEAKLE
st. Summer Hill 373 B5
TEAL
pl. Blacktown 273 K7
pl. Hinchinbrk 363 C15
pl. Ingleburn 453 H9
pl. Woronora Ht 489 C5
TEALE
pl. Parramatta 278 G15
rd. E Kurrajong 66 J2
rd. E Kurrajong 67 A2
TEA TEA
wk. Newington, off Newington Bvd 310 B13
TEA TREE
cr. Mcquarie Fd 424 F16
gln. Jamisontown 266 A3
pl. Bossley Park 333 H9
pl. Kirrawee 460 K15
wy. Colyton 270 H7
TEA-TREE
pl. Mt Annan 509 E5
TEATREE
pl. Beaumont Hills 216 A1
TEAWA
cr. Glenwood 215 G13
TEBBUTT
st. Leichhardt 15 C5
st. Windsor 121 A9
TECHNOLOGY
dr. Appin 569 D15
la. Camperdown 18 C2
pl. Mcquarie Pk 252 E16
TECOMA
dr. Glenorie 128 C2
st. Heathcote 518 K12
TEDDICK
pl. Cherrybrook 219 G6
TEDMAN
pde. Sylvania 461 H12
TEDWIN
av. Kensington 376 C14
st. Mt Pritchard 364 C11
TEELE
rd. Harringtn Pk 478 F2
TEEMER
st. Tennyson 312 E9
TEESWATER
pl. Airds 512 A13
TEGGS
la. Chippendale 19 B3
TEKAPO
rd. Glenorie 128 C3
TEKLA
st. W Pnnant Hl 249 K2
TELAK
cl. N Willoughby 285 H7
TELEGRAPH
rd. Eastern Ck 272 J5
rd. Pymble 253 C1
TELFER
pl. Westmead 307 H4
rd. Castle Hill 218 G14
wy. Castle Hill 218 G15
TELFORD
la. Willoughby 285 J11
pl. N St Marys 239 J11
pl. Prairiewood 335 B8
st. Leumeah 512 C1
TELL
cl. Abbotsbury 333 B16
TELLICHERRY
cct. Beaumont Hills 185 J13
TELOPEA
av. Caringbah 492 F12
av. Homebush W 340 G6
av. Strathfield 371 D4
cl. Glenmore Pk 265 J9
la. Redfern 20 A9
pl. Mcquarie Fd 454 G3
st. Collaroy Plat 228 G12
st. Mt Annan 509 B2
st. Mt Colah 192 D3
st. Punchbowl 370 D16
st. Redfern 19 K9
st. Telopea 279 G9
st. Wollstncraft 315 B10
TELOWIE
ct. Dural 219 C4
TEME
pl. Jamisontown 266 A3
TEMI
pl. Marayong 243 G6
TEMMA
pl. West Hoxton 392 D8
TEMORA
rd. Glenhaven 187 G16
st. Prestons 393 E14
TEMPE
st. Earlwood 403 H3
st. Greenacre 370 D11
TEMPI
pl. Dharruk 241 C7
TEMPLAR
st. Blacktown 274 K7
TEMPLE
la. Stanmore 16 E8
st. Stanmore 16 C8
TEMPLEMAN
cr. Hillsdale 406 G13
TEMPLETON
cr. Baulkham Hl 247 E5
cr. Moorebank 396 C9
rd. Elderslie 507 H1
wy. Airds 512 C13
TENBY
st. Blacktown 274 H9
TENCH
av. Jamisontown 235 G14
pl. Glenmore Pk 265 F5
wy. West Hoxton 392 A11
TENELLA
st. Canley Ht 335 A16
TENGAH
cr. Mona Vale 199 E2
TENILBA
rd. Northbridge 285 J14
TENISON
av. Cmbrdg Gdn 237 H5
ct. Baulkham Hl 247 B2
TENISON WOODS
dr. Rookwood 339 K13
TENNANT
pl. Blackett 241 A3
pl. Edensor Pk 363 J3
pl. Illawong 459 C7
rd. Werrington 239 B15
st. Casula 424 F3
TENNENT
pde. Dulwich Hill 373 A14
pde. Hurlstone Pk 373 A14
TENNESSEE
pl. Riverwood 400 A13
TENNIS COURT
la. Mosman, off Countess St 316 J4
TENNYSON
av. Turramurra 222 K8
dr. Cherrybrook 219 D9
pde. Guildford W 306 K15
pl. Sylvania 462 C14
rd. Breakfast Pt 312 A13
rd. Concord 312 B16
rd. Cromer 258 E1
rd. E Kurrajong 65 G11
rd. Gladesville 312 F8
rd. Greenacre 370 B7
rd. Mortlake 312 A13
rd. Ryde 312 F8
rd. Tennyson 65 D16
rd. Tennyson 87 H1
rd. Tennyson 312 E11
st. Campsie 372 A10
st. Dulwich Hill 373 C13
st. Enfield 371 H3
st. Granville 309 B11
st. Parramatta 308 J1
st. Wetherill Pk 334 J7
st. Winston Hills 277 G1
TENT
st. Kingswood 267 E1
TENTERDEN
rd. Botany 405 G11
TENTERFIELD
av. Hinchinbrk 392 J5
st. N Strathfield 341 E5
TENTH
av. Austral 391 B9
av. Loftus 490 B9
av. Oyster Bay 461 B11
st. Warragamba 353 F5
TEPKO
rd. Terrey Hills 196 C6
TERALBA
rd. Btn-le-Sds 433 J4
rd. Leumeah 482 A15
TERAMA
st. Bilgola 169 F8
TERANGLE
cl. Prestons 393 A13
TERAWEYNA
cl. Woodcroft 243 G10
TERESA
pl. Cromer 228 A16
st. Birrong 369 B5
TERGUR
cr. Caringbah 492 F3
TERMEIL
st. Prestons 392 K16
TERMINAL
ct. Bnkstn Aprt 397 J2
pl. Merrylands 307 J12
TERMINUS
la. Petersham, off Terminus St 15 K9
rd. Seven Hills 275 H1
rd. Seven Hills 275 G1
st. Castle Hill 218 C15
st. Liverpool 395 D5
st. Petersham 15 J9
TERN
pl. Erskine Park 300 F1
pl. Hinchinbrk 393 C2
pl. Tregear 240 C4
pl. Woronora Ht 489 B3
pl. Yarramundi 145 C4
TERNEN
st. Balmain East 8 E9
TERONE
pl. Bossley Park 333 G8
TERPENTINE
pl. Yagoona 369 C9
TERRA
ct. Glenmore Pk 266 E7
st. Thornleigh 221 C10
TERRACE
av. Sylvania 461 K10
dr. Cranebrook 207 E15
la. Dulwich Hill 373 C11
rd. Dulwich Hill 373 C11
rd. Freemns Rch 89 A5
rd. Killara 253 C16
rd. N Richmond 87 F12
TERRACOTTA
cl. Woodcroft 243 E9
TERRAL
pl. Kings Lngly 246 A8
TERRANORA
pl. Bangor 459 F10
wy. Woodcroft 243 G11
TERRA NOVA
pl. Tregear 240 D6
TERRELL
av. Wahroonga 221 K16
TERRENE
st. Regents Pk 369 B1
TERRIE
pl. Kellyville 216 G4
TERRIGAL
av. Turramurra 222 K15
pl. Engadine 489 B13
pl. Woodbine 481 K8
rd. Terrey Hills 196 C7
st. Marayong 243 H5
TERROL
cr. Mona Vale 199 F4
TERRY
av. Seven Hills 245 B15
la. Arncliffe 403 G11
rd. Box Hill 154 B15

GREGORY'S STREET DIRECTORY 141

TE STREETS

rd. Denistone....281 F11	Linley Point....313 F8	**THE CIRCLE**	Sylvania....461 E12	**THE LEE**
rd. Dulwich Hill....373 C8	Merrylands....308 D15	Bilgola....169 J3	Thornleigh....220 K13	Middle Cove....285 K10
rd. Eastwood....280 G8	Mount Druitt....271 B1	Jannali....461 A10	**THE FAIRWAY**	**THELMA**
rd. Rouse Hill....184 H10	Mt Wilson....58 G9	Narraweena....258 C6	Chatswood W....283 K9	av. Panania....398 D13
rd. Theresa Park....444 K9	Newport....169 F14	Oatlands....279 A8	Elanora Ht....198 D14	st. Greystanes....305 H7
rd. West Ryde....281 F13	N Sydney....6 B10	**THE CITADEL**	**THE FRESHWATER**	st. Lurnea....394 G6
st. Arncliffe....403 G11	Petersham....15 G8	Castlecrag....286 C11	Mt Annan....479 B16	st. Marsfield....281 H2
st. Balmain....344 E6	Randwick....377 B12	**THE CLEARWATER**	**THE GLADE**	**THE LOOP**
st. Blakehurst....432 A14	Riverstone....182 D10	Mt Annan....479 B14	Belrose....226 D16	rd. Putney....311 G6
st. Connells Pt....431 G16	Rose Bay....348 G13	**THE CLOISTERS**	Galston....159 F10	rd. Ryde....311 G6
st. Greenacre....370 F4	Valley Ht....202 D4	Cherrybrook....219 E15	Kirkham....477 G4	**THE McKELL**
st. Greystanes....306 C9	Voyager Pt....427 C6	St Ives....224 E8	Wahroonga....222 B9	av. Waterfall....519 E13
st. Kyle Bay....431 G16	Waitara....221 H4	**THE CLOSE**	W Pnnant Hl....249 C4	**THE MALL**
st. Rozelle....344 D6	Warrimoo....203 B13	Hunters Hl....313 G11	wk. Wahroonga....222 C9	Bankstown....369 F16
st. Surry Hills....F A16	Yagoona....368 H12	Strathfield....340 J12	**THE GLEN**	Punchbowl....400 G6
st. Surry Hills....3 H16	**THE BARBETTE**	**THE COAL**	Beecroft....250 B4	S Hurstville....432 B11
st. Tempe....374 D16	Castlecrag....286 C13	rd. Bickley Vale....506 E8	cr. Springwood....201 J4	Turramurra....223 D9
TERRYBROOK	**THE BARBICAN**	rd. Camden....506 E8	rd. Bardwell Vy....403 A8	Warrimoo....203 C15
rd. Llandilo....208 A7	Castlecrag....286 C12	rd. Camden S....506 E8	**THE GRAND**	Wiley Park....400 G6
TERRYMONT	**THE BARRICADE**	rd. Cawdor....506 E8	pde. Btn-le-Sds....404 B16	**THE MEADOWS**
rd. Warrimoo....203 C12	Castlecrag....286 D12	rd. Grasmere....506 E8	pde. Btn-le-Sds....433 J9	Kirkham....477 F6
TESSA	**THE BARTIZAN**	**THE COMENARRA**	pde. Monterey....433 J9	**THE MEADOWS FIRE**
st. Chatswood W....284 G8	Castlecrag....286 C11	pky. S Turramrra....251 K2	pde. Ramsgate Bch....433 G16	trl. Royal N P....521 C5
TETBURY	**THE BASTION**	pky. Thornleigh....221 B13	pde. Sans Souci....433 G16	**THE MEWS**
cl. Cmbrdg Pk....238 C9	Castlecrag....286 B12	pky. Turramurra....252 D5	pde. Sutherland....490 B1	Kirkham....477 G6
TEUMA	Hornsby....221 B4	pky. Wahroonga....221 B13	pde. Sutherland....490 D1	Oatlands....278 K8
pl. Glendenning....242 F5	**THE BATTLEMENT**	pky. West Pymble....252 D5	**THE GRANDSTAND**	**THE NINE WAYS**
TEVIOT	Castlecrag....286 B12	**THE CORSO**	St Clair....270 A15	Kingsford....406 H2
av. Abbotsford....312 K15	**THE BOARDWALK**	Manly....288 G10	**THE GRANGE**	**THE NOOK**
pl. St Andrews....452 A15	Homebush B....310 K10	Maroubra....407 J9	Cherrybrook....219 E14	West Ryde....281 F16
st. Richmond....118 H7	**THE BOOMERANG**	**THE COTTELL**	Kirkham....477 F5	**THE NORTHERN**
TEWINGA	Freemns Rch....90 B5	wy. Baulkham Hl....247 G9	Mona Vale....198 H2	rd. Bringelly....388 B8
rd. Birrong....369 A4	**THE BOULEVARD**	**THE CREEL**	Mowbray Pk....302 H16	rd. Cobbitty....448 B6
TEWKESBURY	Harringtn Pk....478 E2	Lansvale....366 E10	**THE GREENWAY**	rd. Cranebrook....207 G16
av. Darlinghurst....4 G10	**THE BOULEVARDE**	**THE CRESCENT**	Duffys Frst....195 C1	rd. Glenmore Pk....266 J16
st. Chipping Ntn....396 F3	Btn-le-Sds....433 K3	Annandale....11 B5	Elanora Ht....198 D13	rd. Harringtn Pk....448 A10
THACKER	Cammeray....316 A3	Auburn....339 B1	**THE GROVE**	rd. Llandilo....207 H7
cl. Gymea....491 G5	Canley Vale....335 J15	Avalon....170 B3	Belrose....226 D16	rd. Londonderry....149 D15
st. Gymea....491 G4	Caringbah....492 B3	Beecroft....250 G8	Fairfield....336 A15	rd. Luddenham....356 G2
THACKERAY	Cheltenham....250 K9	Berala....339 D11	Mosman....317 C4	rd. Mulgoa....296 D14
cl. Wetherll Pk....335 A6	Dulwich Hill....15 A14	Beverly Hills....401 F11	Padstow Ht....429 H8	rd. Narellan....478 B2
st. Camellia....309 G5	Epping....280 J2	Chatswood W....284 F9	Penrith....237 B6	rd. Oran Park....448 A10
st. Winston Hills....277 E1	Fairfield....335 J15	Cheltenham....250 G8	Roseville....284 B3	rd. Orchard Hills....267 A9
THALIA	Fairfield E....335 J10	Dee Why....258 J7	Woollahra....22 C3	rd. S Penrith....267 A9
st. Hassall Gr....211 K14	Fairfield W....335 J13	Fairfield....336 F13	Oatlands, off	**THEO**
THALLON	Gymea....491 F1	Forest Lodge....11 C8	Hunterford Cr....279 A8	st. Liverpool....365 B15
st. Carlingford....279 J3	Kirrawee....460 G15	Homebush....341 A9	wy. Normanhurst....221 H10	**THE OAKS FIRE**
THAMES	Kirrawee....461 A16	Homebush B....310 J10	**THE GULLY**	trl. Blue Mtn N P....263 B15
pl. Kearns....481 B2	Lakemba....400 K1	Homebush W....340 G9	rd. Berowra....133 F13	**THEODORE**
pl. Seven Hills....275 D7	Lewisham....15 A14	Hurstville Gr....431 F12	**THE HAVEN**	pl. Rooty Hill....271 H2
rd. Bringelly....388 C11	Lidcombe....339 G11	Kingsgrove....401 F1	Orchard Hills....267 G14	st. Balmain....7 D9
st. Balmain....7 J8	Lilyfield....10 D5	Linley Point....313 G8	**THE HERMITAGE**	**THE OLD OAKS**
st. Merrylands W....306 H11	Malabar....437 E5	Manly....288 D10	W Pnnant Hl....248 G6	rd. Brownlow Hl....505 H6
st. Woronora....460 B15	Miranda....492 B1	Marayong....244 C5	**THE HIGH**	rd. Grasmere....505 H6
THANE	Newport....169 J11	Mosman....317 A6	rd. Blaxland....234 A8	**THE OUTLOOK**
cl. Rsemeadow....540 D3	N Turramurra....193 E11	Narrabeen....228 F7	**THE HIGH TOR**	Bilgola....169 H5
st. Pendle Hill....276 H12	Petersham....15 A14	N Narrabeen....198 J15	Castlecrag....286 F11	Harringtn Pk....477 F4
st. Wentwthvle....276 H13	Punchbowl....400 E4	Pennant Hills....250 H1	**THE HIGHWATER**	Hornsby Ht....191 D4
THARAWAL	Sans Souci....462 K3	Penrith....237 A9	Mt Annan....479 D14	Kirkham....477 F4
la. Waterfall....519 D12	Smithfield....335 J10	Rozelle....11 B4	**THE HILLS**	**THE OUTPOST**
st. Thirlmere....564 G8	Strathfield....341 F16	Russell Lea....343 D7	cr. Seven Hills....275 E2	Castlecrag....286 A14
THARKINENA	Sutherland....460 G15	Toongabbie....275 F11	**THE HORSLEY**	Northbridge....286 A14
cl. Cranebrook....207 J10	Warrimoo....203 C14	Vaucluse....348 E1	dr. Fairfield....336 G11	**THE PALISADE**
THEA	Wiley Park....400 G4	Woronora....489 G2	dr. Fairfield E....336 G11	Castlecrag....286 A13
pl. Rooty Hill....272 B5	Yagoona....369 A12	Yagoona....369 A12	dr. Horsley Pk....302 H16	**THE PALMS**
THEA DARE	**THE BRIARS**	**THE CRESENT**	dr. Smithfield....336 B5	Blacktown....274 D12
dr. Castle Hill....219 A13	Mowbray Pk....561 J4	North Ryde....282 H12	dr. Villawood....367 A3	**THE PARADE**
THE APPIAN	**THE BROADWAY**	**THE CREST**	dr. Wetherll Pk....334 A5	Drummoyne....343 E4
wy. Avalon....139 H14	Enfield....371 E3	Frenchs Frst....256 D1	**THEILE**	Dulwich Hill....373 C12
wy. Bankstown....369 F16	Penrith....236 H11	Hornsby Ht....161 E14	av. Newington....309 K15	Enfield....371 H3
wy. Mt Vernon....331 D5	Strathfield....371 E3	Killara....254 E11	**THE IRONBARKS**	Russell Lea....343 E4
wy. S Hurstville....432 A12	Strathfield S....371 E3	**THE CROFT**	Mowbray Pk....562 A2	Telopea....279 H9
THE ARC	Wahroonga....221 H16	wy. W Pnnant Hl....249 H6	**THE KINGSWAY**	**THE PARAPET**
av. Blair Athol....511 K4	**THE BULWARK**	**THE DRIFTWAY**	Roseville Ch....255 E15	Castlecrag....286 A12
THE ARCADE	Castlecrag....286 C12	Agnes Banks....117 F13	St Marys....239 B15	**THE PARKWAY**
Arncliffe....403 G8	**THE CARRIAGEWAY**	Londonderry....149 B3	Wentwthvle....277 A16	Beaumont Hills....185 H13
THE AVENUE	Glenmore Pk....265 E10	S Windsor....149 B3	Werringtn....239 B15	Bradbury....511 D13
Annandale....16 K3	North Rocks....278 D6	**THE DRIVE**	**THE KNOLL**	Bradbury....511 D8
Ashfield....372 G2	**THE CASCADES**	Concord W....311 E16	Avalon....169 K2	**THE PIAZZA**
Balmain East....8 J6	Mt Annan....479 D8	Harbord....258 K16	Blakehurst....462 G10	Homebush B....310 J10
Bankstown....368 H12	Oatlands....278 K8	North Ryde....282 G11	Galston....159 G10	**THE PINNACLE**
Bundeena....524 A9	Oatlands....279 A8	**THE ENTRANCE**	Lansvale....366 F10	Bilgola....169 J3
Canley Vale....366 B1	**THE CAUSEWAY**	Earlwood....402 F1	Miranda....491 J14	**THE PLATEAU**
Collaroy....229 A12	Beverley Pk....433 A13	**THE ESPLANADE**	**THE KRAAL**	Lansvale....366 F9
Condell Park....368 G16	Maroubra....407 G10	Botany....405 E15	dr. Blair Athol....510 J3	**THE PLAZA**
Eastwood....281 A8	Strathfield S....371 D6	Cronulla....524 A4	dr. Blair Athol....511 A2	Rose Bay....348 D13
Gladesville....312 H6	**THE CENTRE**	Drummoyne....343 G1	dr. Blair Athol....511 A4	**THE POINT**
Glenmore Pk....265 F6	Forestville....256 A10	Drummoyne....343 E3	**THE LAKES**	S Wntwthvle....306 H7
Granville....308 D15	**THE CHASE**	Frenchs Frst....256 C1	dr. Glenmore Pk....266 A8	rd. Woolwich....314 F12
Heathcote....518 J9	Orchard Hills....267 E14	Guildford....337 F4	**THE LAMBETH**	**THE PONDS**
Hunters Hl....313 F10	Sun Valley....202 G4	Mona Vale....169 D14	wk. Bundeena....524 A8	Mt Annan....479 B15
Hurlstone Pk....372 K10	Valley Ht....202 G4	Mosman....317 D4	**THE LANES**	Mt Annan....479 C15
Hurstville....432 A3	Kingsgrove....402 A11	Narrabeen....228 H7	Kirkham....477 G3	
Leichhardt....16 D1	rd. Turramurra....223 A9	S Hurstville....432 B12		

142 GREGORY'S STREET DIRECTORY

STREETS

TI

THE POSTERN
Castlecrag 285 K12
THE PROMENADE
Cheltenham 250 J9
Chiswick 343 B2
Old Guildford 337 D9
Sans Souci 433 A16
Sydney 1 C16
Sydney 3 C1
Sylvania 461 G10
Yennora 337 G9
THE QUARTERDECK
Middle Cove 286 A7
Mt Annan 479 B15
THE RAMPART
Castlecrag 286 A13
Hornsby 221 C3
THE RAPIDS
Mt Annan 479 C15
THE REDOUBT
Castlecrag 286 B13
THERESA
st. Blacktown 274 C5
st. Greystanes 306 F6
st. Smithfield 336 B10
THERESA VIEW
rd. Theresa Park 444 A5
THERESE
cct. Baulkham Hl 247 C3
THE RETREAT
Bringelly 388 G3
THE RIDGE
Frenchs Frst 256 D1
Lansvale 366 D10
THE RIDGEWAY
Ebenezer 68 E6
THE RIVER
rd. Picnic Point 428 J7
rd. Revesby 428 A5
rd. Revesby Ht 428 A5
THE RIVULET
Mt Annan 509 C1
THE ROAD
Penrith 237 B7
THE ROCKS
sq. The Rocks .... A K2
THE ROYAL
pl. Blair Athol 511 A9
THERRY
rd. Ambarvale 511 A10
rd. Campbelltown 510 K10
rd. Englorie Park 510 K10
st. Avalon 139 K13
st. Bligh Park 150 K7
st. Drummoyne 343 H5
st. Rookwood 340 F15
st.e. Strathfield S 371 B5
st.w. Strathfield S 371 A5
THE SANCTUARY
Westleigh 220 H9
dr. Leonay 264 J1
THE SCARP
Castlecrag 286 D11
THE SERPENTINE
Bilgola 170 A6
Kensington 376 C10
THESEUS
cct. Rsemeadow 540 J10
THE SEVEN WAYS
Rockdale 403 C16
THESIGER
cl. Bonnyrigg 363 J7
THE SPRINGS
Mt Annan 479 B16
Mt Annan 509 B1
THE STABLES
la. Darlinghurst .... F H2
THE STRAIGHT
rd. Mulgoa 325 B10
THE STRAND
Croydon 372 C1
Dee Why 259 A7
Gladesville 313 A6
Mortdale 431 A6
Penshurst 431 F6
Rockdale 403 E16
Whale Beach 140 C7
THE TAR
Mosman, off
 Wolseley Rd 317 D9
THE TERRACE
Abbotsford 312 J15
Birchgrove 7 G3

Warrimoo 203 B12
Windsor 121 A9
Windsor 121 C7
Oatlands, off
 Governors Wy 279 A8
THE TOR
wk. Castlecrag 286 F10
THE TRONGATE
Granville 308 F16
S Granville 338 F2
THE UPPER SANCTUARY
dr. Leonay 234 J16
THE VALE
Belrose 225 K13
la. Chatswood, off
 Thomas St 284 H10
la. Crows Nest, off
 Huntingdon St 315 H6
st. Darlington 18 K5
st. Haymarket .... E C10
st. Haymarket 3 D13
la. St Marys, off
 Thomas St 269 A6
pl. Bligh Park 150 F6
rd. Freemns Rch 66 K13
rd. Freemns Rch 67 A14
rd. Galston 159 C6
st. Londonderry 178 A6
st. Appin 569 E11
st. Ashfield 372 E1
st. Birchgrove 7 E5
st. Campbelltown 511 J2
st. Chatswood 284 H10
st. Coogee 407 E2
st. Croydon 372 E1
st. Darlington 18 J5
st. Fairfield 336 C13
st. Granville 308 E15
st. Haymarket .... E B11
st. Haymarket 3 D14
st. Hornsby 221 J2
st. Hurstville 401 E16
st. Kingsgrove 401 K5
st. Lewisham 15 C8
st. McMahons Pt 5 C12
st. Merrylands 307 J9
st. Merrylands 308 E15
st. Newtown 17 G13
st. North Manly 258 B3
st. Northmead 277 J7
st. Parramatta 308 F1
st. Picnic Point 428 G8
st. St Marys 269 H6
st. Seven Hills 246 B11
st. Strathfield 371 E2
st. Ultimo 3 A15
st. Woolooware 493 J10
st.w. Currans Hill 479 H10
THOMAS BELL
av. Wrrngtn Cty 238 H6
THOMAS BOLAND
pl. Springwood, off
 Jerseywold Av 201 J3
THOMAS CLARKE
st. Westmead 307 H3
THOMAS FRANCIS
wy. Rouse Hill 184 K8
THOMAS HOLT
dr. Mcquarie Pk 282 J6
THOMAS KELLY
cr. Lalor Park 245 G12
THOMAS LAYCOCK
pl. Bringelly 388 J9
THOMAS MAY
pl. Westmead 307 J3
THOMAS MITCHELL
dr. Barden Rdg 488 F7
THOMAS NELSON
pl. Glenbrook 234 C11
THOMAS ROSE
dr. Rsemeadow 540 K3
THOMAS TELFORD
pl. Glenbrook 234 B11
THOMAS WILKINSON
av. Dural 219 A5
THOMOND
st. Hurstville 401 G16
THOMPSON
av. Artarmon 285 A16
av. Hobartville 118 D6
av. Illawong 459 J3
av. Maroubra 407 E15
av. Moorebank 396 B8
av. Newington 309 K15
av. St Marys 269 K2
cl. W Pnnant Hl 250 B1
cr. Glenwood 215 E12

dr. Terrey Hills 196 C11
la. Belmore 401 F2
la. Bondi Jctn 22 C9
la. East Hills 427 G5
la. Five Dock 342 K10
pl. Baulkham Hl 247 D7
pl. Camden S 507 A15
pl. Darlinghurst 4 E10
pl. Minto 482 H8
sq. Windsor 121 D7
st. Arncliffe 403 H5
st. Bundeena 523 H9
st. Drummoyne 343 G3
st. Earlwood 372 K6
st. Gladesville 312 K4
st. Marrickville 374 B11
st. Mosman 317 B12
st. Scotland I 168 G3
st. Scotland I 168 G4
st. Tamarama 378 B7
st. Turrella 403 G5
st. Wetherill Pk 334 G4
st. Wolli Creek 403 H5
THOMPSONS
la. Yagoona 369 B23
THOMSON
av. Beverly Hills 430 J1
av. Lucas Ht 487 J11
av. Springwood 172 C12
la. Darlinghurst 4 E10
st. Darlinghurst 4 E11
THOR
pl. Hebersham 241 G4
THORA
st. Greystanes 305 H6
THORBY
av. Leichhardt 10 E16
THORLEY
st. S Windsor 150 A6
THORN
av. Harringtn Pk 478 J4
pl. Mt Pritchard 364 D9
pl. North Rocks 248 F14
st. Hunters Hill 313 E5
st. Liverpool 395 A8
st. Pennant Hills 220 F12
st. Revesby 398 E13
st. Ryde 311 G3
wy. Penrith 237 D2
THORNBILL
cr. Glenmore Pk 265 J13
wy. W Pnnant Hl 249 D8
wy. Yarramundi 145 C6
wy. Yarramundi 145 E7
THORNBURY
pl. Bella Vista 246 K13
pl. Minto 483 A2
THORNCRAFT
pde. Campsie 371 J16
THORNCROFT
cl. Bargo 567 B3
THORNE
av. Pendle Hill 276 G14
st. Edgecliff 13 K14
st. Ingleburn 453 B12
THORNEY
rd. Fairfield W 335 B13
THORNFLAT
rd. Cranebrook 207 F12
THORNHILL
cr. Wrrngtn Dns 238 B6
pl. Cherrybrook 219 C14
THORNLEIGH
av. Concord 341 G8
st. Thornleigh 221 A14
THORNLEY
pl. Glenbrook 234 A1
st. Prospect 305 A1
st. Drummoyne 344 A4
st. Leichhardt 15 J2
st. Marrickville 403 K1
THORNTON
av. Bass Hill 368 C13
av. Carlingford 279 E2
pl. Kangaroo Pt 461 H7
st. Canada Bay 342 D9
st. Darling Point 13 J2
st. Fairlight 288 D8
st. Rozelle 7 A10
THORP
rd. Woronora 489 J3
THORPE
av. Cherrybrook 219 J11
av. Liberty Gr 311 B11
st. Abbotsbury 363 B1
st. Newington 310 A14

rd. Kingsgrove 401 J14
st. Clovelly 377 K13
st. Colyton 270 G7
wy. Blacktown 273 H6
THORSBY
pl. Emu Plains 235 E9
THOW
pl. Currans Hill 479 G12
THREDBO
st. Heckenberg 364 C13
THRELFALL
st. Eastwood 281 G5
THRELKELD
dr. Cattai 94 A5
THRIFT
cl. W Pnnant Hl 249 A7
st. Colyton 270 B7
THROSBY
cl. Barden Rdg 488 F6
la. Narellan Vale 508 G1
st. Casula 394 C16
st. Fairfield Ht 335 H11
wy. Ambarvale 511 B12
THRUPP
st. Neutral Bay 6 F8
THUDDUNGRA
dr. Duffys Frst 194 K4
THUNDERBOLT
dr. Raby 451 C13
THURBON
av. Peakhurst 430 H1
THURLGONA
rd. Engadine 488 F13
THURLOW
st. Redfern 20 C9
st. Redfern 20 C9
st. Riverwood 400 C15
THURN
pl. Elderslie 507 F4
THURNBY
st. Newtown 17 C13
st. Chipping Ntn 396 G1
THUROONG
cr. Cranebrook 207 D5
THURSDAY
pl. Green Valley 362 K8
THURSO
pl. St Andrews 452 A12
THURSTON
st. Penrith 237 B8
THURWOOD
av. Jamisontown 266 D2
THYME
st. Quakers Hill 243 F5
THYRA
rd. Palm Beach 140 A6
TIA
pl. Hoxton Park 392 J10
pl. Ruse 512 D9
TIANIE
pl. Rouse Hill 185 D7
wy. Parklea, off
 Fairway St 215 A14
TIARA
pl. Granville 307 K8
TIARRI
av. Terrey Hills 196 H3
TIBBETT
pl. Kellyville 216 E5
TIBER
pl. Heathcote 518 E7
pl. Kearns 451 B16
st. Seven Hills 275 D8
TIBOOBURRA
pl. Hoxton Park 392 K7
st. Engadine 489 B12
TICH
pl. Doonside 243 C5
TICHBORNE
dr. Quakers Hill 213 J14
TICKLE
dr. Tahmoor 565 G5
TICKNER
st. Castlereagh 146 B14
TIDESWELL
st. Ashfield 373 C2
TIDSWELL
st. Mount Druitt 271 E2
st. St Marys 270 A3
TIERNAN
av. North Rocks 248 J14

GREGORY'S STREET DIRECTORY 143

TI STREETS

TIERNEY
- av. Eastgardens 406 G13
- ct. Kurmond 64 J15
- rd. The Slopes 64 J15

TIFFANY
- pl. Rooty Hill 271 K2

TIGG
- pl. Ambarvale 511 A10

TIGRIS
- st. Kearns 450 K16

TILBA
- av. Balmain 7 A6
- pl. Woodpark 306 G14
- pl. Yarrawarrah 489 F14
- pl. Mulgoa 295 H15
- st. Berala 339 D11

TILBURY
- av. Stanhpe Gdn 215 C6

TILDEN
- st. Plumpton 242 C11

TILEY
- la. Cammeray, off
   Tiley St 316 B4
- st. Cammeray 316 B4

TILFORD
- st. Zetland 375 J10

TILIA
- wy. Acacia Gdn 215 A16

TILLEARD
- dr. Winston Hills 277 C3

TILLETT
- pde. Lansdowne 367 C5

TILLEY
- st. Dundas Vy 279 J10

TILLFORD
- gr. Rooty Hill 272 C6
- rd. Kenthurst 187 F6
- rd. Royal N P 522 D9

TILLOCK
- st. Haberfield 9 B10
- st. Pennant Hills 220 G13
- st. Thornleigh 220 H13

TILPA
- pl. Hoxton Park 392 F7

TIMARU
- gr. S Penrith 266 J7
- pl. Kirrawee 491 B8
- rd. Terrey Hills 196 E4
- st. Glenorie 128 B2
- st. Turramurra 222 K16

TIMBARA
- ct. Wattle Grove 395 K12

TIMBARAM
- wy. Woodcroft 243 E10

TIMBARRA
- pl. Sutherland 460 C16
- rd. St Ives Ch 194 A15
- rd. Westleigh 220 G10

TIMBER
- gr. Glenhaven 217 K5
- wy. Wrrngtn Dns 238 D4
- la. Wrrngtn Dns, off
   Timber Gr 238 D4

TIMBERLEA
- cl. Bradbury 511 E14

TIMBERLINE
- av. W Pnnant Hll 249 F6
- av. W Pnnant Hll 249 G7

TIMBERTOP
- av. Carlingford 249 H11
- wy. Beecroft 250 J5

TIMBILLICA
- pl. Prestons 393 C15

TIMBRELL
- dr. Five Dock 393 D10

TIMBREY
- cct. Barden Rdg 488 E1

TIMBROL
- av. Rhodes 311 C8

TIMESWEEP
- dr. St Clair 270 C13

TIMGALEN
- av. S Penrith 237 A16

TIMMS
- cl. Edensor Pk 363 F4
- st. Hebersham 241 E2

TIMMS HILL
- rd. Kurrajong 85 F2

TIMOR
- cl. Kirrawee 490 K8
- st. Kings Park 244 F1

TIMOTHY
- av. Castle Hill 248 E1
- cl. Cherrybrook 219 D7
- la. Belmore 401 G3
- pl. Edensor Pk 363 G2
- rd. Londonderry 178 B8
- st. Hurstville 431 J3

TIMOTHY LACEY
- la. The Oaks 502 E8

TIMS
- cr. Guildford W 336 H1

TIM WHIFFLER
- pl. Richmond 118 A6

TINA
- av. Lethrdg Pk 210 G15

TINAKILL
- av. Engadine 488 K11

TINAM
- av. Whalan 240 K11

TINANA
- pl. Bidwill 211 F16
- st. Haberfield 343 B16

TINARRA
- cr. Erskine Park 300 C2
- cr. Erskine Park 300 D2

TINCOMBE
- st. Canterbury 372 G13

TINDAL
- wy. Mt Annan 479 H16

TINDALE
- la. Woollahra 377 F2
- rd. Artarmon 284 K14
- st. Penrith 236 J11

TINDALL
- av. Liverpool 395 F1
- st. Campbelltown ...511 A6

TINDELL
- av. Camden S 537 B1
- st. Marayong 243 H6

TINDER
- st. Bligh Park 150 H5

TINDIVANAM
- av. Vaucluse 348 B4
- la. Cabarita 342 E1

TINEARRA
- cr. Carlingford 250 A13
- cr. Cremorne 316 F4
- cr. Engadine 488 J16

TINGHA
- av. S Penrith 266 E6
- cl. Hinchinbrk 392 G4
- st. Chatswood 284 K11
- st. Engadine 488 F12

TINGIRA
- pl. Forestville 255 K12

TINTAGEL
- pl. Glenhaven 217 J6
- pl. Turramurra 222 G15

TINTERN
- av. Carlingford 279 E9
- av. Telopea 279 E9
- rd. Ashfield 373 A5

TINTO
- pl. Acacia Gdn 244 K1

TIPANI
- pl. Erskine Park 300 E2

TIPPER
- av. Bronte 378 A10

TIPPERARY
- av. Killarney Ht 256 D14

TIPPET
- pl. Quakers Hill 214 C8

TIPPING
- pl. Ambarvale 510 H15

TIPTREE
- av. Strathfield 341 E16

TIPTREES
- av. Carlingford 279 H5
- la. Carlingford 279 J5

TIRAGE
- pl. Minchinbury 272 B10

TIRANNA
- pl. Oyster Bay 461 C4

TIREE
- av. Hunters Hill 314 B13

TIRRABEENA
- pl. Bangor 459 E12

TIRTO
- st. Barden Rdg 488 F8

TISANE
- av. Frenchs Frst 256 G2

TISHER
- pl. Ambarvale 511 A14

TITANIA
- la. Cranebrook, off
   Titania Pl 207 E10
- la. Randwick, off
   Lion St 407 B2
- la. Randwick, off
   Rainbow La 407 A1
- pl. Cranebrook 207 F10
- pl. Rsemeadow 540 J10
- st. Randwick 407 B2

TITAS
- rd. Blaxlands Rdg ...66 D1

TI TREE
- cr. Berowra 163 C1
- pl. Wilberforce 67 J14

TITUS
- pl. Acacia Gdn 244 K1

TIVERTON
- wy. Airds 512 E9

TIVOLI
- av. Rose Bay 348 B7
- ct. Wattle Grove ...426 C3
- esp. Como 460 J6
- pl. Doonside 243 B9
- st. Mosman 317 C3
- st. Paddington 21 F3

TIVY
- pl. Marayong 243 H6

TIZZANA
- rd. Ebenezer 68 C11
- rd. Ebenezer 68 E6
- rd. Sackville 68 C4

TOBERMORY
- av. St Andrews 481 J2

TOBIAS
- pl. Kings Lngly 245 A4

TOBIN
- av. Camden S 537 B1
- pl. Marayong 243 H6

TOBRUK
- av. Allambie Ht 257 F11
- st. Balmain 7 E12
- st. Belmore 371 F16
- cr. Carlingford 250 A13
- st. Engadine 488 J16
- st. Liverpool 394 J4
- st. St Ives Ch 223 J4
- pl. Bossley Park ...334 A6
- rd. Narellan Vale ..479 A11
- st. North Ryde 282 K11
- st. N St Marys 239 J10

TOBY
- cr. Panania 398 A13
- mw. Bella Vista 246 G3
- pl. Kings Lngly 246 B10

TOBYS
- bvd. Mt Pritchard ...364 G13

TOCAL
- ct. Wattle Grove ...426 A1

TOD
- pl. Minchinbury ...271 G9

TODD
- cir. Old Tngabbie .277 B6
- ct. Peakhurst 400 H16
- ct. Wattle Grove ..395 H12
- la. St Clair, off
   Banks Pl 269 K13
- pl. Bossley Park ..333 J6
- pl. Cherrybrook ..219 J11
- pl. Illawong 459 J5
- pl. Leumeah 482 G11
- pl. Mt Annan 509 F1
- row. St Clair 269 J12
- st. Kingsgrove 402 A12
- st. Merrylands W 307 A12

TODMAN
- av. Kensington 376 D12
- av. Kensington 376 D9
- av. West Pymble ..252 H9
- la. St Clair, off
   Todman Pl 270 E12
- pl. St Clair 270 E11
- rd. Strathfield 341 B14
- rd. Warwick Frm ...365 J14

TOELLE
- st. Rozelle 344 C7

TOGGERAI
- st. Appin 569 F13

TOGIL
- st. Canley Vale 366 E2

TOKANUE
- pl. St Ives Ch 223 J3

TOKARA
- st. Allambie Ht 257 G15

TOKAY
- ct. Edensor Pk 363 D1
- pl. Eschol Park 481 E2

TOLEDO
- pl. Baulkham Hl 246 J13

TOLL
- rd. N Parramatta ..278 A10

TOLLAND
- st. Prestons 393 B15

TOLLAUST
- la. Mcquarie Fd 252 D13

TOLLEY
- pl. Edensor Pk 333 F14

TOLLGATE
- cr. Windsor 121 C9

TOLLHOUSE
- wy. Windsor 121 C9

TOLMER
- st. Bossley Park ...334 C5

TOLOL
- av. Miranda 491 H2

TOM
- st. Ermington 310 F3
- wy. Casula 424 H2

TOMAGO
- ct. Wattle Grove ..425 K3

TOMAH
- pl. Bossley Park ..334 B10
- pl. Ruse 512 G5
- pl. Sylvania 461 K8
- pl. Westleigh 220 G9
- pl. Carlingford ...280 C4
- ct. Kurrajong Ht ...63 F11
- st. St Ives Ch 224 B1

TOM DRURY
- pl. Minchinbury ..272 E8

TOM HAYDON
- st. Moore Park 21 D8

TOMINTOUL
- wy. Glenhaven 218 A6

TOMKI
- st. Carramar 366 J1

TOMKINS
- la. Camperdown ...17 E6

TOMKINSON
- st. Bexley North ..402 E11

TOMKO
- pl. Parklea 214 J13

TOMPSON
- rd. Panania 428 E3
- rd. Revesby 428 E3

TOMS
- la. Engadine 518 K1

TOM SCANLON
- cl. Kellyville 216 E1

TOM UGLYS BRIDGE
- Blakehurst 462 E5
- Sylvania 462 E5

TONBRIDGE
- st. Ramsgate 433 F14
- st. Sans Souci 433 F14

TONGA
- cl. Greenacre 370 C14
- cl. St Clair 270 D8
- cr. Smithfield 336 B6
- rd. Lethbrdg Pk ..240 H2

TONGARIRO
- tce. Bidwill 211 F15

TONGARRA
- cl. Bangor 459 G10
- pl. Westleigh 220 F6

TONI
- cr. Ryde 282 D15
- pl. Baulkham Hl 247 F9

TONITTO
- av. Peakhurst 430 E5

TONKIES
- pl. Menai 459 A11

TONKIN
- cr. Schofields 213 H6
- cr. Cronulla 493 K13

TONY
- cr. Padstow 399 B16
- pl. Glendenning ..242 F1

TOOCOOYA
- la. Hunters Hill ...313 J12
- rd. Hunters Hill ..313 J12

TOOGOOD
- la. Erskineville 17 J14

TOOHEY
- av. Westmead 307 D2
- cr. Bexley 402 D15
- rd. Wetherill Pk ..333 H4

TOOHEYS
- la. Lidcombe 339 H8

TOOLANG
- rd. St Ives 223 J6

TOOLE
- st. Doonside 243 F8

TOOLONG
- pl. Hornsgea Ht ..392 G15

TOOMA
- pl. Heckenberg ..364 A15

TOOMEVARA
- st. Kogarah 433 D7

TOOMEY
- cr. Quakers Hill ...213 J7

TOOMUNG
- cct. Clarmnt Ms ..268 G2

TOONA
- pl. Bossley Park ..333 H8

TOONGABBIE
- rd. Girraween 275 H14
- rd. Toongabbie ..275 H15
- rd. Toongabbie ..276 B9

TOONGARAH
- rd. Roseville 284 D6
- rd. Waverton 5 C6

TOORADIN
- pl. W Pnnant Hl ..250 A2

TOORAH
- rd. Londonderry ..149 H9

TOORAK
- av. Beverly Hills ..401 A15
- av. Taren Point ...462 J13
- st. St Johns Pk ..364 E4
- cr. Emu Plains ...234 K9
- ct. Cherrybrook ..219 D10
- pl. Avalon 140 G4

TOORONGA
- rd. Terrey Hills ..195 F5
- tce. Beverly Hills ..401 C14

TOOTH
- av. Newington ...309 K15
- la. Camperdown ...17 E6

TOOTHILL
- la. Lewisham, off
   Old Canterbury Rd ..15 B10
- st. Lewisham 15 A11

TOOTHS
- pl. Camperdown ...17 E7

TOPAROA
- cl. Casula 394 F16

TOPAZ
- cr. Seven Hills ...275 B7
- pl. Bankstown ...399 E6
- pl. Bossley Park ..334 A7
- pl. Eagle Vale 481 B7

TOPE
- pl. Ambarvale ...510 J15

TOPEKA
- gln. St Clair 270 H13
- la. St Clair, off
   Topeka Gln 270 H13

TOPHAM
- rd. Smeaton Ga ..479 B6

TOPIN
- pl. Moorebank ...396 C5

TOPLICA
- pl. Canley Ht 365 B4

TOPNOT
- av. Hinchinbrk ...393 C4

TOPPER
- pl. Englorie Park ...510 J10

TOPPING
- st. Panania 398 A16

TOR
- rd. Dee Why 258 F3

TORA
- pl. Dharruk 241 A6
- pl. Forestville 255 K12

TORBERT
- av. Quakers Hill ..214 F10

TORCH
- st. Voyager Pt 427 C4

TORICELLI
- av. Whalan 241 A11

TORKINGTON
- rd. Londonderry ..147 G5

144 GREGORY'S STREET DIRECTORY

STREETS TR

TORNADO
cr. Cranebrook......207 B10
la. Cranebrook, off
  Tornado Cr......207 B10
pl. Raby......451 E16

TORNAROS
av. Penrith......237 A13

TOROKINA
av. St Ives......224 C15

TORONTO
cr. Cromer......227 J12
pde. Jannali......460 F16
pde. Sutherland......490 F1

TORQUAY
tce. Glenmore Pk......266 G14

TORQUIL
av. Carlingford......250 A15

TORRANCE
cr. Quakers Hill......214 C12

TORRENS
cl. Wattle Grove......396 A14
pl. Cherrybrook......219 F12
pl. Cromer......228 C16
st. Kearns......481 A2
st. Blakehurst......432 F16
st. Canley Ht......365 E3
st. Canley Vale......365 E3
st. Matraville......437 B3
st. Merrylands W......306 K13
st. Punchbowl......400 B8
st. St Ives......254 H1

TORRES
cl. Emu Plains......234 K11
cl. Whalan......241 A10
cl. Kings Lngly......245 D3
st. St Ives......224 A8
st. Kurnell......465 H8

TORRINGTON
av. Sefton......368 G3
rd. Marsfield......281 H3
rd. Maroubra......407 H9
rd. Strathfield......341 F14

TORRS
st. Baulkham Hl......247 J14

TORTON
cl. Penrith......236 J13

TORULOSA
pl. Winmalee......173 F8

TORUMBA
av. Bayview......168 E11
cl. Bangor......459 E11

TORVER
pl. Collaroy Plat......228 D10

TORWOOD
st. St Johns Pk......334 E16
st. Sans Souci......433 B14
st. Warrimoo......203 A10

TOSCANA
st. Prestons......393 E13

TOSCANO
ct. Erskine Park......300 F2

TOSH
la. Zetland, off
  Dunning Av......375 H11

TOSICH
cl. Bonnyrigg Ht......363 F5

TOTALA
pl. Elanora Ht......198 F12

TOTEM
la. Balgowlah......287 J8

TOTNESS
ct. Castle Hill......216 H9

TOTTENHAM
st. Blakehurst......462 F2
st. Granville......308 D8
st. N Balgowlah......287 F5

TOUCAN
cr. Plumpton......241 H7

TOULOUSE
st. Cecil Hills......362 C4

TOURMALINE
st. Eagle Vale......481 F8
st. Narrabeen......229 B1

TOURNAY
st. Peakhurst......430 H2

TOUT
rd. Bidwill......211 F12
rd. Marsden Pk......211 F12

TOWARRI
cl. Belrose......226 C16

TOWER
ct. Castle Hill......217 B9
st. Berowra......133 E12

rd. Bnkstn Aprt......397 E5
res. Castlecrag, off
  Edinburgh Rd......286 C11
st. Coogee......377 K13
st. Glenwood......215 C15
st. Manly......288 F9
st. Panania......428 A2
st. Revesby......428 E2
st. Vaucluse......348 G5

TOWERS
pl. Arncliffe......403 E9
st. Arncliffe......403 E9
st. Cabramatta......365 C9

TOWN
st. Hobartville......118 E7
tce. Glenmore Pk......265 J10

TOWNER
av. Milperra......397 D10
gdn. Pagewood......406 F7
st. Galston......160 H6

TOWN HALL
la. Auburn, off
  Queen St......339 D3

TOWNS
pl. Millers Pt......1 D8
rd. Vaucluse......348 C7
st. Gladesville......312 G8

TOWNSEND
av. Frenchs Frst......255 H4
cct. Beaumont Hills......185 G16
rd. N Richmond......86 J4
st. Condell Park......398 E3
st. Guildford......337 J3

TOWNSON
av. Leumeah......482 F11
av. Minto......482 G8
pl. Marsden Pk......212 D9
pl. Schofields......212 D9
st. Blakehurst......462 D2

TOWNSVILLE
rd. Wakeley......334 K14

TOWNVIEW
rd. Mt Pritchard......364 J9

TOWRADGI
pl. Bangor......459 G10
st. Narraweena......257 K3

TOWRA POINT
rd. Kurnell......463 K12

TOWRI
cl. St Ives......224 C15
pl. Marsfield......251 H16

TOWSON
la. Bexley......402 C16

TOXANA
st. Richmond......118 J4

TOXTETH
la. Glebe......11 H11
st. Glebe......11 G11

TOYER
av. Sans Souci......463 A3
st. Tempe......374 B16

TRABB
pl. Ambarvale......510 J12

TRACEY
av. Carlingford......249 F13
cl. Normanhurst......221 H7
la. Chippendale......18 H3
pl. Orchard Hills......268 G8
st. Revesby......398 D11

TRACK
st. Clarendon......120 B15

TRACY
st. Rooty Hill......242 A15

TRADE
st. Newtown......17 B10
st. Newtown......17 B10

TRADEWINDS
pl. Kareela......461 E10

TRAFALGAR
av. Lindfield......284 F1
av. Roseville......284 F1
la. Annandale......11 B14
la. Concord, off
  Trafalgar Pde......341 K4
pde. Concord......341 J4
pl. Marsfield......252 A13
pl. Northmead......278 C6
rd. Emu Heights......235 A2
st. Annandale......16 K3
st. Belmore......401 F4
st. Btn-le-Sds......433 K3
st. Bronte......378 A10
st. Crows Nest......315 J6
st. Engadine......488 J14
st. Enmore......17 A11

st. Glenfield......424 E10
st. Peakhurst......430 C2
st. Petersham......15 H10
st. Riverstone......182 F13
st. Stanmore......16 C10

TRAHLEE
rd. Bellevue Hill......14 H9
rd. Londonderry......148 B10
rd. Londonderry......148 D10

TRAILL
cl. Mt Annan......479 J16

TRAINER
av. Casula......394 F16

TRALEE
av. Killarney Ht......256 A16

TRAM
la. Randwick, off
  Church St......376 K12

TRAMINER
gr. Orchard Hills......268 G13
pl. Eschol Park......481 E3
pl. Minchinbury......272 B8

TRAMORE
pl. Killarney Ht......256 B16

TRAMWAY
arc. Rockdale, off
  Frederick St......403 B15
arc. Rockdale, off
  Princes Hwy......403 C15
av. Camellia......308 J4
av. Parramatta......308 J4
dr. Currans Hill......479 J12
la. Concord, off
  Frederick St......342 B2
la. Randwick......377 A10
la. Rosebery......405 F1
st. Denistone W......280 J13
st. Rosebery......405 F1
st. Tempe......404 A2
st. West Ryde......280 J13

TRANMERE
st. Drummoyne......343 J3

TRANQUILITY
ct. Bella Vista......246 F6

TRANSVAAL
av. Double Bay......14 D9

TRAPPERS
wy. Avalon......139 H10

TRAVERS
rd. Curl Curl......258 J13

TRAVIS
pl. Menai......458 K6

TRAWALLA
st. Hebersham......241 E9

TRAYNOR
cr. Kogarah......433 E6

TREACY
st. Hurstville......432 B6

TREADGOLD
pl. Leichhardt......15 D4
st. Milperra......397 F10

TREATT
av. Padstow......429 A1

TREATTS
rd. Lindfield......254 B15

TREBARTHA
st. Bass Hill......368 C9

TREBBIANO
pl. Eschol Park......481 B4

TREBLE
cl. Harmondvle......396 D13

TREBOR
rd. Pennant Hills......250 F1

TREBORTH
pl. Menai......459 B9

TREEDALE
dr. Vineyard......153 C10

TREELANDS
av. Ingleburn......453 C8
cl. Galston......160 J4

TREES
wy. Rooty Hill......271 K6

TREE TOP
cct. Quakers Hill......214 B13

TREE TOPS
av. S Penrith......267 A1
pl. Valley Ht......202 E6

TREETOPS
pl. Cherrybrook......219 A13

TREEVIEW
pl. Epping......251 A12
pl. North Rocks......248 K15

TREGENNA
cl. St Ives......224 E11

TREHARNE
cl. Marsfield......282 B4

TRELAWNEY
st. Croydon Pk......371 H9
st. Eastwood......280 K11
st. Eastwood......281 A9
st. Thornleigh......221 C11
st. Woollahra......14 A15

TRELOAR
av. Mortdale......430 C3
cr. Chester Hill......338 A13
pl. Edensor Pk......363 C2
pl. Menai......458 D12

TREMA
pl. Mt Annan......509 D3

TREMAIN
av. Kellyville......216 E4

TREMERE
st. Concord......342 D6

TREMLOW
cr. Ambarvale......511 B11

TRENT
av. Ambarvale......511 B14
pl. Hassall Gr......211 J14
pl. N Richmond......87 C12
rd. North Rocks......278 F1
st. S Penrith......266 H4

TRENTBRIDGE
rd. Belrose......225 J12

TRENTHAM
av. Douglas Park......568 J12

TRENTHAM PARK
ct. Wattle Grove......425 K5

TRENTINO
rd. Turramurra......222 K7

TRENTON
rd. Guildford......337 D5

TRENTWOOD
pk. Avalon......139 J16

TRESALAM
st. Mt Pritchard......364 H15

TRESCO
st. St Marys......239 G7

TRESIDDER
av. Roseville......406 C1

TRESS
st. Blacktown......274 K5

TRESSIDER
av. Haberfield......9 A16
av. Haberfield......343 E16

TREUER
la. Yagoona, off
  The Crescent......369 A12
pde. Yagoona......368 F14

TREVALGAN
pl. St Ives......224 F5

TREVALSA
pl. Burraneer......523 D3

TREVANION
st. Five Dock......343 A8

TREVANNA
st. Busby......363 H13

TREVELLYAN
st. Cronulla......523 J1

TREVELYAN
st. Botany......405 J13

TREVENA
la. Enfield......371 J3

TREVENAR
st. Ashbury......372 F7

TREVES
st. Merrylands......307 G12

TREVILYAN
av. Rose Bay......375 K16

TREVITHICK
st. Riverstone......182 J10

TREVITT
rd. North Ryde......282 D6

TREVLYN
wy. Acacia Gdn......244 K1

TREVONE
st. Padstow......399 G16

TREVOR
st. Castle Hill......217 G15
rd. Newport......169 H12
st. Lilyfield......10 D6

TREVORS
la. Cherrybrook......220 A3

TREVOR TOMS
dr. Acacia Gdn......214 K16

TREWILGA
av. Earlwood......372 J16

TREZISE
pl. Quakers Hill......213 K16

TRIABUNNA
av. West Hoxton......392 E5

TRIAL
pl. Illawong......459 D5

TRIANGLE
la. Richmond......88 C16
la. Richmond Lwld......88 C16

TRICKETT
rd. Woolooware......493 G11

TRIDA
pl. Emu Plains......235 G11

TRIDENT
cl. Raby......481 H1

TRIGALANA
pl. Frenchs Frst......256 E1

TRIGG
av. Carlingford......279 J1

TRIGGS
st. St Marys......239 E2

TRIGLONE
la. Mona Vale......199 B3

TRIGON
rd. Abbotsbury......362 G1

TRILLER
pl. Ingleburn......453 F10
st. Green Valley......363 D10

TRINA
cr. Canterbury......402 E1
pl. Hassall Gr......211 K16

TRINDER
av. Kingswood......237 F15

TRINERVIS
wy. Mcquarie Fd......454 H4

TRINEURA
ct. Wattle Grove......396 B15

TRINITY
pl. Dawes Point......A G2
pl. Dawes Point......1 F9
av. Kellyville......216 H5
dr. Cmbrdg Gdn......237 G2
la. Cmbrdg Gdn, off
  Trinity Dr......237 G5
pl. Cherrybrook......219 F14
pl. Kings Lngly......245 H5

TRIPOD
st. Concord......342 C5

TRIPOLI
av. Carlingford......249 K14
pl. Eagle Vale......481 H4
rd. Fairfield W......335 F13

TRIPP
pwy. Warwck Frm, off
  Tripp St......365 E14
st. Warwck Frm......365 E14

TRIS
pl. Kings Lngly......246 B9

TRISH
pl. Castle Hill......248 F3

TRISTAN
cl. Oakhurst......242 D2
ct. Castle Hill......217 G4

TRISTANIA
ct. Baulkham Hl......247 C15
gr. Greenacre......370 F5
gr. Menai......459 A14
pl. West Pymble......252 G11
st. Mt Annan......509 C3
wy. Beecroft......250 F3
wy. Winmalee......173 F7

TRISTRAM
pl. Beacon Hill......257 F5
st. Errmington......310 B4

TRITEN
la. Ingleburn......453 G11

TRITON
av. Greenfld Pk......334 D15
pl. S Penrith......267 C4

TRITTONS
la. Lakemba......370 H15

TRIUMPH
pl. Ingleburn......453 G11

TRIVET
st. Horsley Pk......303 G13

TRIVETTS
la. Balmain......7 H8

TROBRIAND
cr. Glenfield......424 H11

GREGORY'S STREET DIRECTORY 145

TR STREETS

TROON
ct. Glenmore Pk 266 E11
pl. Pymble 252 J4
pl. St Andrews 481 K5
TROOPERS
mw. Holsworthy 426 F4
TROPIC-BIRD
cr. Hinchinbrk 393 C3
TROTT
st. Parramatta 278 C15
TROTWOOD
av. Ambarvale 510 H15
TROUT
pl. St Clair 269 H16
TROUTON
st. Balmain 7 K6
TROUVE
st. Lane Cove 314 B3
TROY
la. Campsie 401 K2
pl. Winston Hills 277 D1
rd. Heathcote 518 F7
st. Campsie 401 K1
st. Emu Plains 235 D13
TRUDY
pl. Hassall Gr 211 J14
TRUEMAN
pl. North Rocks 278 J3
TRUK
pl. Kings Park 244 J3
TRUMAN
av. Bonnet Bay 460 C8
av. Cromer 227 J13
av. Riverwood 400 B14
pl. Bonnet Bay 460 C8
rd. Horsley Pk 331 H4
st. Hurstville 431 K9
st. S Hurstville 431 K9
TRUMBLE
av. Ermington 310 C3
pl. Rouse Hill 184 K8
TRUMFIELD
la. Mosman 316 H13
TRUMPER
pl. Menai 458 F9
st. Ermington 310 E2
wy. Rouse Hill 184 J6
TRURAN
cl. Hornsby 221 E4
TRURO
pde. Padstow 429 G1
pl. Dural 188 A12
TRUSCOTT
av. Matraville 407 C16
la. Panania 427 K1
pl. Bidwill 211 C15
pl. East Killara 254 G9
st. North Ryde 282 J10
st. Panania 427 K1
TRYAL
pl. Willmot 210 C11
TRYON
av. Wollstncraft 315 C12
la. Chatswood, off Orchard Rd 284 J12
la. Lindfield 254 E16
pl. Lindfield, off Pacific Hwy 284 D1
rd. E Lindfield 254 G15
rd. Lindfield 254 E16
st. Chatswood 284 J12
TSAR
cl. Cecil Hills 362 J5
TUABILLI
st. Pemulwuy 305 E6
TUAM
pl. Killarney Ht 255 H11
st. Concord 342 D6
TUART
cir. Narellan Vale 478 J15
pl. Narellan Vale 478 J15
TUART PARK
la. Narellan Vale 478 J15
TUCABIA
av. Georges Hall 367 H10
st. S Coogee 407 G7
TUCANA
st. Erskine Park 300 G2
TUCKER
la. Bass Hill, off Tucker St 368 D11
pl. Edensor Pk 363 G2
rd. Casula 424 D4
st. Bass Hill 368 D11
st. N Sydney 5 G1
st. Ryde 312 A1
st. Wiley Park 400 H4
TUCKERMAN
rd. Ebenezer 68 A7
TUCKS
rd. Seven Hills 276 E2
rd. Toongabbie 276 F6
TUCKWELL
pl. Mcquarie Pk 283 A2
rd. Castle Hill 217 G10
TUCSON
gr. Stanhpe Gdn 215 B11
TUDAR
rd. Bonnet Bay 460 D10
rd. Sutherland 460 D10
TUDOR
av. Blacktown 275 A6
av. Cherrybrook 219 K9
cl. Belrose 226 C12
cr. Cecil Hills 362 E7
pl. Carlingford 279 B5
pl. Glenfield 424 C11
pl. St Ives Ch 224 B6
pl. Surry Hills 20 B3
st. Belmore 401 J1
st. Campsie 401 J1
st. Surry Hills 20 A3
TUFF HILL
la. S Maroota 69 C1
TUFFY
av. Sans Souci 463 B6
TUGA
pl. Glenmore Pk 266 A11
TUGGERAH
cl. St Clair 300 C1
pl. Woodcroft 243 H11
st. Leumeah 482 E14
TUGLOW
pl. Leumeah 482 C14
TUGRA
cl. Glenmore Pk 266 C10
TUKARA
rd. S Penrith 267 A6
TUKIDALE
cl. Elderslie 507 J2
TULA
pl. Tregear 240 F6
TULICH
av. Dee Why 258 H2
av. Prestons 393 A15
TULIP
cl. Alfords Point 459 A2
gr. Fairfield W 335 B9
pl. Quakers Hill 243 D3
pl. St Clair 269 G10
st. Chatswood 284 J8
st. Greystanes 306 A12
st. North Ryde 282 C8
TULIPWOOD
dr. Colyton 270 H7
TULLAMORE
av. Killarney Ht 256 A14
TULLANE
pl. Kellyville Rdg 214 K2
TULLAROAN
st. Kellyville Rdg 185 C16
st. Kellyville Rdg 215 C1
TULLET
st. Camden S 537 C2
TULLIMBAR
rd. Cronulla 494 A8
st. Croydon Pk 371 F7
TULLOCH
av. Concord W 311 E12
cl. Casula 394 G15
la. St Clair, off Tulloch Pl 270 D11
pl. Baulkham Hl 246 J3
pl. Edensor Pk 333 E15
pl. St Clair 270 E11
st. Blacktown 243 K10
TULLOH
la. Willoughby, off Tulloh St 285 F14
st. Willoughby 285 F15
TULLOONA
st. Mount Druitt 241 C12
TULLY
av. Liverpool 394 H10
pl. Quakers Hill 214 D14
TULONG
av. Oatlands 279 B13
pl. Kirrawee 491 A9
TULSA
ct. Quakers Hill 214 F11
TULUKERA
pl. Bangor 459 G10
TUMBARUMBA
cr. Heckenberg 364 C13
TUMBRIDGE
cr. Cmbrdg Pk 238 C8
TUMBURRA
st. Ingleside 197 D6
TUMMUL
pl. St Andrews 452 B15
TUMUT
cl. Bankstown 399 B5
la. St Clair, off Tumut Pl 269 J15
pl. Bossley Park 333 J5
pl. Heckenberg 363 K15
pl. St Clair 269 J16
pl. Seven Hills 275 E10
pl. Sylvania Wtr 462 D11
st. Ruse 512 G8
TUNA
pl. St Clair 269 H16
TUNBRIDGE
pl. Cherrybrook 219 H5
pl. Jannali 461 A13
st. Busby 363 G14
st. Mascot 405 E4
TUNCOEE
rd. Villawood 367 A4
TUNCURRY
st. Bossley Park 333 E12
TUNGARRA
rd. Girraween 276 B10
TUNGOO
pl. St Helens Park 511 J16
TUNIS
pl. Quakers Hill 214 C9
TUNKS
pl. Barden Rdg 488 G3
st. Northbridge 286 B16
st. Ryde 282 B14
st. Waverton 315 D11
TUNLEY
pl. Kings Lngly 245 B3
TUNNACK
cl. West Hoxton 392 E7
TUNNEL
pl. Horsley Pk 333 B9
TUNSTALL
av. Kensington 376 C16
av. Kingsford 376 C16
TUNUNDA
pl. Eschol Park 481 A3
TUOHY
la. Marrickville 373 K13
TUPELO
gr. Menai 458 J12
wy. Acacia Gdn, off Hydrangea Ct 214 J15
TUPIA
pl. Kings Lngly 245 H6
st. Botany 405 G16
TUPPEL
wy. Airds 512 C12
TUPPER
st. Enmore 16 H15
TURBO
rd. Kings Park 244 F5
TURBOTT
av. Harringtn Pk 478 H4
TURELLA
cl. Belrose 225 K14
st. Glenbrook 264 D2
TURF
pl. Quakers Hill 214 G16
TURI
cl. Bangor 459 F12
TURIMETTA
av. Leumeah 482 B16
st. Mona Vale 199 B6
TURIN
pl. Prestons 393 F16
TURLINJAH
cl. Prestons 393 A13
TURNBERRY
cr. Glenmore Pk 266 F11
wy. Rouse Hill 185 B8
TURNBULL
av. Kemps Ck 359 J5
av. Wilberforce 67 G16
av. Wilberforce 92 C1
st. Winmalee 173 J6
TURNER
av. Baulkham Hl 247 D13
av. Concord 342 A1
av. Haberfield 9 A11
av. Haberfield 343 E13
av. Ryde 312 C2
cl. Bligh Park 150 G5
la. Punchbowl 400 B4
la. Woolmloo 4 D6
pl. Casula 424 D4
rd. Berowra Ht 133 A7
rd. Currans Hill 479 D3
rd. Smeaton Gra 479 D3
st. Balmain 7 D7
st. Blacktown 244 K8
st. Bronte 378 A7
st. Colyton 270 J8
st. Dee Why 258 H1
st. Ermington 310 D2
st. Guildford 337 E6
st. Punchbowl 400 B5
st. Redfern 19 C8
st. Riverwood 399 K16
st. Ryde 311 K2
st. Thirlmere 565 C3
TURON
av. Baulkham Hl 247 B8
av. Kingsgrove 401 J11
pl. Ruse 512 C9
TUROSS
av. Sylvania Wtr 462 F12
cl. Prestons 393 D16
pl. Leumeah 482 G14
st. Seven Hills 275 E10
TURPENTINE
av. Peakhurst 430 E4
cl. Alfords Point 429 C16
gr. Blaxlands Rdg 65 A3
TURQUOISE
cr. Bossley Park 333 K7
pl. Eagle Vale 481 A7
st. Quakers Hill 214 G13
TURRA
st. S Turramrra 252 C5
TURRAMURRA
av. Turramurra 222 J13
TURRELLA
rd. Yarrawarrah 489 E13
st. Turrella 403 E5
TURRET
pl. Castle Hill 217 F4
pl. Glenmore Pk 266 D6
TURRIELL BAY
rd. Caringbah 492 G16
rd. Lilli Pilli 492 F16
TURRIELL POINT
rd. Port Hacking 522 H2
TURTLE
cct. Green Valley 363 B9
la. Erskineville 17 K16
la. Newtown 17 D10
rd. Caringbah 492 D11
TURTON
av. Belmore 401 J5
av. Clemton Park 401 J5
la. Belmore, off Turton Av 401 J5
la. Clemton Park, off Turton Av 401 J5
pl. Castle Hill 217 H15
TURUGA
pl. Bangor 459 F11
st. Turramurra 223 A14
TURUNEN
av. Silverdale 353 H12
TURVEY
rd. Blacktown 274 F3
st. Padstow 399 A10
st. Revesby 398 K10
TUSCAN
av. Kellyville 186 H15
av. Kellyville 186 H16
pl. Beacon Hill 257 G7
pl. Casula 395 A13
wy. Cherrybrook 220 A5
wy. Glenwood 245 K4
TUSCANY
gr. S Penrith 267 B6
TUSCULUM
ct. Wattle Grove 425 J5
la. Potts Point 4 J4
rd. Valley Ht 202 D5
st. Potts Point 4 K4
TUSMORE
st. Punchbowl 400 A9
TUTOR
cl. Winmalee 173 G7
TUTT
cr. Chiswick 343 D2
TUTUS
st. Balgowlah Ht 288 A12
TWAIN
st. Winston Hills 277 E1
TWEED
ct. Wattle Grove 395 K13
pl. Ruse 512 C9
pl. St Clair 270 E10
pl. Sylvania Wtr 462 D10
TWEEDMOUTH
av. Rosebery 405 G1
TWELFTH
av. Austral 391 B6
av. Rossmore 390 B5
st. Warragamba 353 F4
TWENTIETH
av. Hoxton Park 393 A6
st. Warragamba 353 E8
TWENTYEIGHTH
av. Austral 391 J1
TWENTYFIFTH
av. West Hoxton 391 H16
TWENTY FOURTH
st. Warragamba 353 B6
TWENTYFOURTH
av. West Hoxton 391 H14
TWENTYNINTH
av. Austral 391 G9
TWENTYSECOND
av. West Hoxton 391 K5
TWENTYSEVENTH
av. West Hoxton 391 J1
TWENTYSIXTH
av. West Hoxton 391 H16
TWENTY THIRD
st. Warragamba 353 C8
TWENTYTHIRD
av. West Hoxton 391 H8
TWICKENHAM
av. Cmbrdg Pk 238 B7
cl. Normanhurst 221 D9
TWIN
rd. North Ryde 282 E11
TWINGLETON
av. Ambarvale 510 H16
TWIN TOWERS
wk. Mosman, off Macpherson St 316 G7
TWYFORD
av. Earlwood 403 A3
TWYNAM
pl. Horngsea Pk 392 F15
rd. Davidson 255 C1
TYAGARAH
la. Cromer 228 A15
pl. Cromer 228 A15
st. Putney 312 E7
st. Ryde 312 E7
TYALGUM
av. Panania 428 G2
TYALLA
av. Frenchs Frst 256 D8
cl. Casula 394 G14
TYARAN
pl. Bangor 459 E12
TYCANNAH
pl. Bangor 459 H9
rd. Northbridge 286 F14
TYGH
st. Lapstone 264 G5
TYLER
cr. Abbotsford 343 A3
pl. Bonnet Bay 460 D10
st. Campbelltown 511 H2
TYLERS
rd. Bargo 567 A10
rd. Bargo 567 F9
TYNE
cl. Baulkham Hl 246 J5
cr. N Richmond 87 A13
ct. St Clair 299 K1
pl. Prospect 274 G13
TYNESIDE
av. N Willoughby 285 G7

146 GREGORY'S STREET DIRECTORY

STREETS — VA

TYPHOON
- pl. Raby 451 E16

TYRELL
- cr. Fairfield W. 335 G9
- st. Gladesville 312 G9

TYRINGHAM
- cl. Hoxton Park 392 J8

TYRONE
- av. Forestville 256 B11
- pl. Blacktown 275 A8

TYRRELL
- st. Rockdale 403 A13

TYRWHITT
- st. Maroubra 407 F14

TYSON
- pl. Emu Plains 235 D14
- pl. North Rocks 278 J3
- rd. Bringelly 387 G11
- rd. Wilton 568 K16

U

UDALL
- av. Five Dock 342 J8

UHRIG
- rd. Homebush B. 340 D2

UHRS
- la. Rhodes 311 E7

UKI
- av. Picnic Point 428 G5

ULA
- cr. Baulkham Hl 247 K11

ULANDI
- pl. Baulkham Hl 277 J4

ULINGA
- pl. Engadine 488 G14

ULLADULLA
- pl. Prestons 393 B14
- pl. Kareela 461 B13

ULLATHORNE
- la. Drummoyne 343 H6
- la. Drummoyne 343 H5

ULM
- av. Mascot 405 A12
- av. S Turramrra 251 K6
- pl. Doonside 273 F4
- pl. Orchard Hills 268 C6
- st. Ermington 280 A14
- st. Lane Cove N. ...283 J13
- st. Maroubra 406 G11

ULMARRA
- av. Camden S. 507 B10
- pl. E Lindfield 255 D11

ULOLO
- av. Hornsby Ht 191 D1

ULONGA
- av. Greenwich 314 K5
- pl. Toongabbie 276 E9

ULOOLA
- pl. Gymea Bay 491 E11

ULPHA
- pl. Cranebrook 207 E12

ULRIC
- la. Northbridge 316 B2

ULSTER
- st. Cecil Hills 362 E6
- st. Paddington ......21 D1 (?) E4
- st. Peakhurst 430 A7

ULTIMO
- rd. Haymarket ....E A11
- rd. Haymarket ....E E9
- rd. Haymarket 3 C14
- st. Ultimo ....E A11
- st. Ultimo 3 C14
- st. Caringbah 492 K10

ULUNDRI
- dr. Castle Hill 218 A9

ULVERSTONE
- st. Fairfield 336 F14

UMBRIA
- st. Prestons 393 E15

UMINA
- pl. Woodbine 481 J10

UNA
- la. Campsie, off
  Una St. 372 A15

UNARA
- la. Campsie 372 A14
- st. Campsie 372 A15

UNCLE WATTLEBERRY
- cr. Faulconbdg 171 F11

UNDERCLIFF
- st. Harbord 288 G2
- st. Neutral Bay 6 E5

UNDERCLIFFE
- la. Earlwood 403 G3
- rd. Earlwood 403 F2
- st. Earlwood 403 F2

UNDERDALE
- la. Meadowbank, off
  Railway Rd 311 E4

UNDERWOOD
- av. Botany 405 E11
- la. Paddington 21 E1
- la. Sydney ....A J10
- la. Sydney 1 G13
- rd. Barden Rdg 488 H4
- rd. Homebush 341 A4
- rd. Prairiewood 334 K8
- st. St Clair 270 E9
- st. Minto 482 G7
- st. Paddington 13 B16
- st. Paddington 21 D1
- st. Sydney ....A K10

UNDINE
- st. Maroubra 407 K9
- st. Russell Lea 343 F6

UNDULA
- pl. Belrose 225 J13

UNGARRA
- st. Rydalmere 279 J14

UNICORNE
- cr. Oakhurst 242 A2

UNION
- la. Carlton 432 K5
- la. Dulwich Hill 373 C9
- la. Erskineville, off
  Union St. 374 K9
- la. Fairlight, off
  William St. 288 D8
- la. Newtown 17 H15
- la. Paddington 13 D16
- la. Penrith 236 G10
- la. Pyrmont 12 K4
- la. Windsor 121 C8
- rd. Auburn 339 A5
- rd. Penrith 236 F10
- st. Arncliffe 403 F8
- st. Balmain East 8 F9
- st. Dulwich Hill 373 C9
- st. Eastwood 280 G7
- st. Erskineville 17 J16
- st. Erskineville 374 J9
- st. Granville 308 B10
- st. Kogarah 432 K4
- st. Lidcombe 340 A8
- st. McMahons Pt ...5 B10
- st. Mosman 317 B11
- st. Newtown 17 J16
- st. N Sydney 5 B10
- st. Paddington 13 D16
- st. Parramatta 308 E3
- st. Pyrmont 12 H3
- st. Riverstone 152 J12
- st. Riverwood 399 K14
- st. Tempe 404 B1
- st. Toongabbie 276 B8
- st. Vineyard 152 J12
- st. Waterloo 19 F11
- st. Waverton 5 B10
- st. West Ryde 311 D2

UNITED
- la. Parramatta 308 C3

UNIVERSAL
- av. Georges Hall ...367 G12
- la. Eastlakes, off
  Universal St. 405 K3
- la. Eastlakes 405 J3
- la. Mortdale 431 A7

UNIVERSITY
- av. Camperdown ...18 E2
- av. Mcquarie Pk 282 C1
- la. Camperdown ...18 E2
- pl. Miranda 491 J4

UNSTED
- cr. Hillsdale 406 G14

UNSWORTH
- st. Abbotsbury 333 A16

UNWIN
- la. Earlwood, off
  Unwin St. 403 H3
- rd. Cabramatta W. .365 B7

- rd. Wahroonga 221 H7
- rd. Waitara 221 H7
- st. Bexley 402 C16
- st. Canterbury 372 G12
- st. Earlwood 403 H3
- st. Rosehill 309 A8

UNWINS
- la. Hunters Hill 313 B5

UNWINS BRIDGE
- rd. St Peters 374 E14
- rd. Sydenham 374 E14
- rd. Tempe 374 B16

UPFIELD
- la. Catherine Fd 449 D5
- st. Edensor Pk 363 H2

UPPER
- rd. Forest Lodge 11 E14

UPPER ALMORA
- st. Mosman 317 B7

UPPER AVENUE
- rd. Mosman 316 J11

UPPER BEACH
- st. Balgowlah 287 F10

UPPER CARRIAGE
- la. Haymarket ....E E14

UPPER CLIFF
- av. Northbridge 316 A1
- rd. Northwood 314 H7

UPPER CLIFFORD
- av. Fairlight 288 B9

UPPER CLONTARF
- st. Seaforth 287 A3

UPPER FAIRFAX
- rd. Mosman 317 B2

UPPER FORT
- st. Millers Pt ....A E5
- st. Millers Pt 1 E11

UPPER GILBERT
- st. Manly 288 F9

UPPER GREYCLIFF
- st. Queenscliff, off
  Greycliff St. 288 H3

UPPER MINIMBAH
- rd. Northbridge 286 E14

UPPER PITT
- st. Kirribilli 2 C1
- st. Kirribilli 6 B16

UPPER RAILWAY
- pde. Condell Pk 398 G4

UPPER SERPENTINE
- rd. Greenwich 314 J13

UPPER SPIT
- rd. Mosman 287 B16

UPPER WASHINGTON
- dr. Bonnet Bay 460 D9
- dr. Bonnet Bay 460 D10

UPTON
- la. Bonnyrigg 364 A5
- st. S Penrith 236 K16
- st. Stanhpe Gdn ...215 B6

UPWARD
- st. Leichhardt 15 C5

UPWEY
- ct. Mt Krng-gai....162 H7
- st. St Johns Pk 364 J2
- st. Prospect 274 G10

URALBA
- av. Caringbah 492 F10
- pl. N Wahroonga ..192 E14
- rd. Oatlands 279 B14

URALLA
- pl. Padstow 429 D3
- pl. S Coogee 407 E4
- pl. Dural 189 D4
- rd. E Kurrajong 66 K10
- st. Hebersham 241 E9

URAMBI
- pl. Engadine 488 G14

URANA
- pl. Leumeah 482 F15
- rd. Yarrawarrah 489 D12
- st. Villawood 367 D2

URANUS
- rd. Padstow 429 A1
- rd. Revesby 428 K1

URARA
- rd. Avalon 140 E14

URBANE
- st. Leonay 235 D15

URDALA
- pl. Sutherland 490 C1

UREN
- pl. Bligh Park 150 E6
- pl. Merrylands 308 A16
- st. S Penrith 237 C16

URIAH
- av. Ambarvale 510 K13

URQUHART
- st. Riverwood 400 D15

URSULA
- pl. Cecil Hills 362 C2
- st. Winston Hills ..276 G1

URUNGA
- pde. Miranda 492 B4
- pl. Punchbowl 400 D3
- pl. Wiley Park 400 D3
- pr. Bossley Park 333 F10
- st. N Balgowlah 287 B4

USHER
- cl. Abbotsbury 333 A13
- cr. Sefton 368 E5

UTAH
- pl. Erskine Park 270 K15
- pl. Toongabbie 275 H12

UTE
- pl. Bossley Park 333 K10

UTHER
- av. Bradbury 511 G12
- st. Surry Hills 19 K1

UTINGU
- pl. Bayview 168 K15

UTYANA
- pl. Frenchs Frst ...256 G11

UTZON
- ct. St Clair 270 A10
- rd. Cabramatta W. .365 B5

UWORRA
- rd. Wilberforce 67 B8

V

VAIRYS
- cr. Merrylands 337 J1

VALADON
- pl. Baulkham Hl, off
  Camarena Av 216 H16

VALDA
- av. Arncliffe 403 J8
- av. Baulkham Hl ...247 C2
- pl. Ingleburn 453 D10
- pl. Marsfield 281 K5
- st. Bexley 402 G2
- st. Blacktown 274 F6
- st. Merrylands W. 306 H13
- st. W Pnnant Hill ..249 H1

VALDER
- av. Hobartville 118 C8

VALE
- cr. Dee Why 258 F4
- cct. Narellan Vale ..478 K10
- cct. Narellan Vale ..479 A10
- ct. Canley Vale 366 A4
- la. Peakhurst 430 B10
- rd. Thornleigh 221 A4
- st. Cabramatta 366 C7
- st. Cammeray 315 J4
- st. Canley Vale 366 C7
- st. Clovelly 377 H11
- st. Gordon 253 F7
- st. Woodpark 306 K13

VALEDICTION
- rd. Kings Park 244 J5

VALENCIA
- cr. Toongabbie 275 F11
- st. Dural 188 J12
- st. Greenacre 370 E10

VALENTI
- cr. Kellyville 216 C4

VALENTIA
- av. Lugarno 429 H11
- av. Woolwich 314 G12

VALENTINE
- av. Parramatta 308 D5
- av. Winston Hills ..277 C2
- pl. Rsemeadow 540 G6
- st. Blacktown 274 F6
- st. Haymarket ....E D12
- st. Haymarket 3 E14
- st. Yagoona 368 F11

VALERIA
- st. Toongabbie 276 B6

VALERIE
- av. Baulkham Hl ...246 F12
- av. Chatswood W. 284 A9

VALES
- la. Auburn 339 D2

VALETTA
- ct. Blacktown 274 G6

VALEWOOD
- st. Marsfield 281 K4

VALINDA
- cr. Campbelltown .512 A5

VALIS
- rd. Glenwood 215 B16
- rd. Glenwood 245 B1

VALLANCE
- st. St Marys 239 F5

VALLEN
- pl. Quakers Hill 214 D13

VALLEY
- cr. Bayview 168 J12
- cl. Casula 423 K2
- gln. W Pnnant H. ..249 A5
- la. Lindfield 254 F16
- la. Warriewood 198 G6
- st. Balgowlah Ht ..287 J12
- st. Campbelltown .512 A6
- st. Eastwood 280 G5
- st. Epping 280 G5
- st. Forestville 255 G11
- st. Hornsby 221 A1
- st. Lindfield 254 F16
- st. Padstow Ht 429 F8
- st. Springwood 201 G5
- st. Valley Ht 202 D4
- st. Balmain 7 G10
- wy. Glossodia 65 K10
- wy. Gymea Bay 491 G9
- wy. Tennyson 65 K10

VALLEYFIELD
- ct. Wattle Grove .395 K15

VALLEY PARK
- cr. N Turramurra ..223 E5

VALLEY RIDGES
- rd. Bilpin 60 E12

VALLEY VIEW
- cct. Warriewood ..198 J7
- cr. Roseville 284 B6
- cr. Engadine 489 A14
- cr. N Epping 251 C10
- dr. Narellan 478 B9
- dr. Frenchs Frst ..257 A3

VALLEYVIEW
- cr. Greenwich .....314 A6 (?) A...
- cr. Wrrngtn Dns ..237 K5
- pl. Kellyville 186 K15

VALLINGBY
- av. Hebersham 241 E4

VALMA
- pl. Colyton 270 G4

VALMAY
- av. Picnic Point 428 E9

VALOUR
- wy. Kellyville Rdg .215 A6

VALPARAISO
- av. Toongabbie 275 F12

VALVE HOUSE
- rd. Warragamba ...353 C5

VAL WHEELER
- dr. Kurrajong Ht 63 C10

VAN BENTUM
- st. Blacktown 273 H6

VAN BUREN
- cct. Bonnet Bay 460 D9

VANCE
- st. Dean Park 212 H16

VANCOUVER
- av. Toongabbie 275 E12
- av. Fairfield W. 335 C10

VAN DIEMAN
- cr. Fairfield W. 335 C10
- rd. Caringbah 492 F7
- rd. St Clair 299 J3

VAN DIEMEN
- av. Willmot 210 B11

VAN DYKE
- la. Punchbowl 400 D4

VANE
- st. Cranebrook 206 J2

VANESSA
- av. Baulkham Hl ...247 D9
- ct. Glenwood 245 J15
- pl. Mcquarie Fd ...424 F15

GREGORY'S STREET DIRECTORY 147

VA STREETS

st. Beverly Hills	401	E13
st. Kingsgrove	401	E13
VANGELI		
st. Arndell Park	273	H9
VAN HEE		
st. Concord	342	A1
VANIMO		
pl. Eastwood	281	D4
VANNAN		
la. Padstow	399	C14
VANNON		
cct. Currans Hill	479	J9
VANNY		
pl. Maroubra	407	F9
VANSTON		
pde. Sandringham	463	E4
VANTAGE		
cr. Kellyville	216	H2
la. Peakhurst	430	C10
pl. Thornleigh	221	A4
VARDEN		
wy. Ambarvale	541	A1
VARDYS		
rd. Blacktown	245	A6
rd. Kings Lngly	245	A6
rd. Kings Park	244	E5
rd. Lalor Park	245	F8
VARGA		
pl. Hassall Gr	212	C15
VARIAN		
st. Mount Druitt	241	C15
VARIDEL		
av. Belfield	371	F10
VARNA		
st. Clovelly	377	G10
st. Mt Colah	192	A4
VARNDELL		
pl. Dundas Vy	280	D9
VARUNA		
st. Doonside	243	E16
VASEY		
cl. St Ives Ch	224	B2
VASSALLO		
pl. Glendenning	242	E3
VASTA		
av. Mooreback	396	E13
VAUCLUSE		
pl. Glen Alpine	510	C2
rd. Vaucluse	348	A3
VAUDAN		
st. Kogarah Bay	433	A13
VAUGHAN		
av. Pennant Hills	220	E14
av. Revesby	398	J14
dr. Mcquarie Pk, off Main Av	283	D7
pl. Middle Dural	128	E15
pl. Redfern	20	D8
st. Auburn	339	C8
st. Blakehurst	432	D16
st. Lidcombe	339	C8
VAUTIN		
rd. Marsden Pk	211	J7
VAUXHALL		
st. Ingleburn	453	G12
VEAL		
gr. Plumpton	242	B11
VEALE		
wy. Bella Vista	246	H4
VEGA		
cr. Bnkstn Aprt	367	J16
cr. Hinchinbrk	393	D5
pl. Revesby	428	J5
VELA		
pl. Erskine Park	301	A2
VELLA		
cr. Blacktown	273	K6
VENDETTA		
rd. Winmalee	173	C15
VENESS		
cct. Narellan Vale	478	J16
VENETIA		
st. Kangaroo Pt	461	J10
st. Sylvania	461	J10
VENETIAN		
rd. N Narrabeen	228	J1
VENETTA		
rd. Glenorie	128	A14
VENEZIA		
st. Prestons	393	E14
VENICE		
pl. Guildford W	336	J3

VENN		
av. Lalor Park	245	B11
VENO		
st. Heathcote	518	G11
VENTURA		
av. Miranda	492	C3
av. Narwee	400	G13
dr. Hornsby Ht	161	J15
pl. Warriewood	199	C8
rd. Northmead	248	B16
VENTURE		
cr. Yagoona	369	B10
VENUS		
cl. Cranebrook	207	G6
pl. Kings Lngly	245	C6
pl. Lansvale	366	H8
st. Gladesville	312	K8
VERA		
st. Mona Vale	199	A3
wy. Doonside	243	G15
VERDELHO		
pl. Glenorie	126	H3
VESTA		
st. Sutherland	460	F16
VESUVIUS		
st. Seven Hills	275	B8
VETERANS		
pde.Collaroy Plat	228	G11
pde.Narrabeen	228	G11
VEZEY		
pl. Blacktown	274	B5
VIALOUX		
av. Paddington	13	C12
VIALS		
la. Paddington	21	E2
VIA MARE		
Cronulla	524	A1
VIANNEY		
cr. Toongabbie	276	E5
VIBURNUM		
rd. Loftus	489	H11
VICAR		
av. Coogee	377	G16
VICAR PARK		
la. Luddenham	356	F11
VICARS		
av. North Bondi	348	F16
pl. Wetherill Pk	334	B3
VICKERS		
av. Mascot	404	K7
pl. Raby	451	D15
VICKERY		
av. Carlingford	279	J1
av. Rose Bay	347	K10
st. Seven Hills	275	C6
st. Sutherland	460	E16
VICKY		
av. Castle Hill	217	G9
pl. Glendenning	242	E1
VICLIFFE		
av. Campsie	402	A1
VICTA		
pl. Minchinbury	271	K2
VICTOR		
av. Kemps Ck	359	G11
av. Panania	428	F5
av. Picnic Point	428	E8
cl. Baulkham Hl	247	C12
pl. Illawong	459	G4
pl. Raby	451	F15
rd. Brookvale	258	D9
rd. Dee Why	258	D7
rd. Narraweena	258	D7
st. Chatswood	284	J10
st. Greystanes	306	B8
st. Lewisham	15	D14
st. Marayong	244	D10
st. Punchbowl	399	J8
st. S Turramrra	252	A8
st. Strathfield	341	E14
st. Woollahra	22	G6
wy. Cranebrook	207	C14
VERNONIA		
av. Kellyville	216	A4
VERON		
rd. Bexley	402	H11
st. Schofields	213	A2
st. Fairfield E	336	K12
st. Wentwthvle	307	B1
VERONA		
av. Mt Pritchard	364	G11
st. Auburn	339	D1
st. N Narrabeen	228	K2
st. Paddington	4	G15
st. Strathfield	371	A3

VERONA RANGE		
Como	460	J5
VERONICA		
cr. Seven Hills	245	K11
pl. Cherrybrook	219	F10
pl. Loftus	490	A7
pl. Narellan Vale	479	B15
st. Chester Hill	368	C2
VERRELL		
st. Wetherill Pk	335	B1
VERRILLS		
gr. Oakhurst	241	H4
VESCEY		
st. Waterloo	19	F11
VESPER		
VESPERMAN		
VICTORIA		
av. Castle Hill	217	C12
av. Chatswood	284	H10
av. Chatswood	284	K9
av. Concord W	341	C1
av. Mortdale	431	C7
av. N Willoughby	285	D8
av. Penshurst	431	C7
av. West Pymble	252	H12
av. Woollahra	21	H4
cr. Auburn	338	J4
cs. N Sydney	5	G8
la. Beaconsfield, off Beaconsfield St	375	F13
la. Malabar	437	D3
la. Marrickville	374	B13
la. Putney	311	J5
la. Rydalmere	309	H3
la. Waverley, off Victoria St	377	F7
la. Werrington	239	A12
pde. Manly	288	H10
pl. Drummoyne	313	F16
pl. McMahons Pt	5	D12
pl. Paddington	21	D1
pl. Richmond	117	K6
rd. Bellevue Hill	14	J6
rd. Drummoyne	343	J1
rd. Dundas	279	A16
rd. Ermington	309	K2
rd. Gladesville	312	H6
rd. Glebe	11	G9
rd. Henley	313	A13
rd. Huntleys Pt	313	A13
rd. Mcquarie Fd	423	K15
rd. Marrickville	374	D10
rd. Marrickville	374	A14
rd. Minto	452	F15
rd. Parramatta	278	D16
rd. Pennant Hills	249	K2
rd. Punchbowl	400	B5
rd. Punchbowl	400	B9
rd. Rooty Hill	241	K14
rd. Rozelle	7	A16
rd. Rozelle	11	E3
rd. Rydalmere	309	C1
rd. Ryde	311	G1
rd. Thirlmere	565	A2
rd. Wedderburn	540	C14
rd. W Pnnant Hl	249	G2
rd. West Ryde	281	A15
sq. Ashfield	373	A6
st. Ashfield	372	K9
st. Beaconsfield	375	G13
st. Botany	405	K12
st. Cmbrdg Pk	237	J11
st. Darlinghurst	4	F13
st. Dulwich Hill	373	E7
st. Epping	281	A1
st. Erskineville	17	K16
st. Granville	308	E9
st. Greenwich	314	K13
st. Jannali	460	G13
st. Kingswood	237	J11
st. Kogarah	433	C3
st. Lewisham	15	A11
st. Lewisham	373	E7
st. Lilyfield	10	F3
st. McMahons Pt	5	C12
st. Malabar	437	E3
st. Merrylands	307	G9
st. Mount Druitt	270	J1
st. Newtown	17	H9
st. Paddington	21	D2
st. Picton	563	G8
st. Potts Point	4	H7
st. Queens Park	22	K14
st. Queens Park	377	F7
st. Randwick	377	B13
st. Redfern	19	J7
st. Revesby	398	J14
st. Riverstone	152	F16
st. Riverstone	153	A13
st. Roseville	284	J5
st. St Peters	374	J14
st. Smithfield	335	G3
st. Strathfield	341	C15
st. Turrella	403	E6
st. Warrimoo	203	B13
st. Watsons Bay	318	E12
st. Waverley	377	F7
st. Werrington	238	D12
st. Wetherill Pk	333	J1
st. Wetherill Pk	334	F1
st.e,Burwood	342	A13
st.e, Lidcombe	339	H11
st.w,Burwood	341	K13
st.w,Lidcombe	339	G10
wy. Kogarah	433	A3
VICTORIA PARK		
pde. Zetland	375	K10
VICTORY		
av. Belfield	371	D8
av. Camden	507	A3
av. Mulgoa	325	C9
av. Canley Vale	366	F7
bd. Davidson	225	H3
pl. Concord	341	J4
rd. Oatley	430	K16
st. Asquith	192	B10
st. Belmore	401	F3
st. Clovelly	378	A14
st. Dover Ht	348	E11
st. Engadine	488	E14
st. Fairfield E	336	K12
st. Rose Bay	348	E11
st. S Penrith	236	J15
VIDAL		
st. Wetherill Pk	334	D5

VIDILINI		
la. Northmead	277	H9
VIDLER		
pl. Mt Annan	479	F15
VIENNA		
st. Seven Hills	275	C5
VIEW		
av. Chatswood W	284	G9
av. Ingleside	198	B3
st. Annandale	11	A14
st. Arncliffe	403	F10
st. Blaxland	233	F7
st. Cabramatta	365	C11
st. Camden	477	B16
st. Chatswood W	284	G9
st. Concord	342	C4
st. Cowan	104	B14
st. Cremorne	316	C6
st. Earlwood	402	K4
st. Forestville	256	C10
st. Gymea	491	G5
st. Hurstville Gr	431	G11
st. Linley Point	313	A17
st. Marrickville	373	G15
st. Miranda	491	G5
st. Peakhurst	430	B12
st. Picton	563	F7
st. Queens Park	22	K13
st. Sefton	368	F4
st. Telopea	279	G8
st. Tempe	404	A4
st. W Pnnant Hl	249	B5
st. Woollahra	22	H3
st. Woolwich	314	G12
VIEW PARK		
st. Prospect	275	B10
VIGNES		
st. Ermington	280	B15
VIKING		
st. Campsie	402	A1
VILLAGE		
cr. Penrith	237	C10
dr. Breakfast Pt	312	C15
rd. Carlingford, off Martins La	279	G6
wy. Wattle Grove	426	B1
VILLAGE GREEN		
pde. St Ives	223	K12
VILLAGE HIGH		
rd. Vaucluse	348	F1
VILLAGE LOWER		
rd. Vaucluse	348	E3
VILLAWOOD		
pl. Villawood	367	C1
rd. Villawood	367	C1
VILLERS BRETT		
Engadine	489	A13
VILLIERS		
av. Mortdale	431	B4
la. Rockdale	403	C13
pl. Cromer	228	H14
pl. Oxley Park	240	E16
rd. Cecil Park	332	F16
rd. Padstow Ht	429	F7
st. Kensington	376	D12
st. Merrylands	307	C16
st. Parramatta	278	C16
st. Rockdale	403	A11
VIMIERA		
rd. Eastwood	281	C5
rd. Marsfield	251	H16
VIMY		
la. Earlwood	403	A1
st. Bankstown	399	E3
st. Earlwood	403	A1
VINCENNES		
av. Tregear	240	D3
VINCENT		
av. Emu Plains	235	J9
av. Liverpool	365	A15
av. Mulgoa	325	C9
cr. Canley Vale	366	F7
pl. Cranebrook	206	J3
pl. Kurrajong	85	H2
st. Balmain	8	A11
st. Baulkham Hl	247	H14
st. Blacktown	274	C3
st. Canterbury	372	H11
st. Marrickville	374	C13
st. Merrylands	307	D8
st. Mount Druitt	271	C2
st. St Marys	269	D3
VINCENTIA		
st. Marsfield	281	K3

148 GREGORY'S STREET DIRECTORY

STREETS

WA

VINCENTS
av. Arncliffe...........403 F11

VINCENZ
la. Mosman............316 K4

VINE
gr. Darlington........18 J4
la. Condell Park....398 G3
la. Darlington..........18 J4
st. Ashfield............342 G15
st. Darlington..........18 J4
st. Fairfield............336 G14
st. Hurstville.........432 C3
st. Redfern..............19 A5
st. Schofields........182 E16
s.t.w.Marsden Pk....211 K1

VINEGAR HILL
rd. Kellyville Rdg...185 B16

VINES
av. Forestville........256 A6
av. Minto...............482 K5
dr. Richmond.........118 E11

VINEY
st. N St Marys.......239 J9

VINEYARD
av. Smithfield........336 B5
rd. Mulgoa.............296 C16
st. Mona Vale........199 A5
st. Rydalmere.......279 D15
wy. Breakfast Pt....312 C15

VINEYS
la. Dural...............189 C12
la. Dural...............189 C12

VINTAGE
pl. Minchinbury.....272 A8

VIOLA
av. Warriewood....198 G10
pl. Glenmore Pk...265 H8
pl. Greystanes......305 J12
pl. Heathcote.......518 K9
pl. Lalor Park.......245 C10
pl. Rsemeadow....540 F6
pl. Punchbowl.....399 K6
pl. Punchbowl.....400 A8
wy. Mt Annan.......509 F3

VIOLET
av. Forestville......256 A11
av. Liverpool.......365 A15
ct. Quakers Hill...214 A10
la. Greystanes....306 G5
la. Balgowlah Ht...287 F9
la. Bronte...........377 J9
la. Chatswood......284 J7
st. Croydon Pk....371 K5
st. Miranda........461 J16
st. Revesby.......398 E10
st. Roselands....400 G8
st. Surry Hills.....20 C4
swy. Punchbowl, off
Violet Av......365 A15

VIRET
st. Hunters Hill...314 A11

VIRGIL
av. Chester Hill..338 A16
st. Sefton...........368 E1
st. Bronte..........377 K9
st. Greystanes....306 D7

VIRGINIA
av. Bardwell Vy..403 A9
av. Baulkham Hl..247 B9
pl. Forestville....256 A7
pl. Riverwood...400 B13
pl. W Pnnant Hl..249 B11
st. Blacktown....244 A11
st. Guildford W..306 J15
st. Kensington..376 B12
st. Rosehill........308 G7

VIRGINIUS
st. Padstow.......429 B8

VIRGO
pl. Erskine Park..300 G2

VIRIA
ct. Glenhaven...218 C3

VIRTLE
rd. S Maroota...69 G11

VIRTUE
st. Condell Park..398 H5

VISCOUNT
cl. Raby.............451 F13
rd. Warwick Frm..365 C13

VISCOUNT VAMPIRE
pl. Richmond, off
Davis St........120 B5

VISION VALLEY
rd. Arcadia.......130 A13

VISTA
av. Balgowlah Ht..287 H15
av. Bayview..........169 A14
av. Peakhurst......430 C11
cl. Hornsby..........191 H9
cl. Kings Park.....244 G2
cr. Chester Hill...338 C13
la. Bellevue Hill..347 J14
la. Greenwich....315 A10
la. Penrith, off
Vista St........236 F10
pde. Mt Riverview..204 J13
pl. Kurrajong Ht..63 E11
pl. Narellan.......478 C10
st. Belrose..........226 C14
st. Caringbah....492 G8
st. Greenwich....315 A10
st. Mosman.......316 K7
st. Oatlands......278 J9
st. Penrith........236 F10
st. Pymble........223 H16
st. Sans Souci..462 J3

VISTA HEIGHTS
rd. Miranda.......461 K16

VITTORIA SMITH
av. Castle Hill...218 J14

VIVALDI
cl. Clarmnt Ms..268 G4
pl. Beaumont Hills..216 C1

VIVIAN
cr. Berala........339 E11
st. Bellevue Hill..347 G15
st. Bexley..........432 G1
st. Manly..........288 J12
st. Scotland I....168 G4

VIVIEN
pl. Castle Hill..218 C12

VIVIENNE
av. Lakemba...371 A13
st. Kingsgrove.401 J12
st. Woodpark..306 G15

VIVYAN
cl. Denistone..281 H12

VLATKO
dr. West Hoxton..392 C11

VOGAN
st. Mt Riverview..234 E3

VOLANS
la. Erskine Park, off
Volans Pl........300 J1
pl. Erskine Park..300 J2

VOLLERS
la. Freemns Rch..90 K1

VOLMER
st. Oatlands.....279 C7

VOLTA
pl. Winston Hills..277 B5

VOLTAIRE
rd. Winston Hills..277 F2

VOLUNTEER
rd. Kenthurst...188 A4

VONN
av. Smithfield..335 B3

VON NIDA
pl. Menai........458 J5

VORE
st. Silverwater..309 H13

VOYSEY
cl. Quakers Hill..213 D15

VUKAS
pl. Bonnyrigg Ht..363 C7

VUKO
pl. Warriewood..199 C11

VULCAN
cl. Raby..........451 H15
st. Guildford...337 C3
wy. Currans Hill..479 G10

W

W121
la. Chatswood..285 C12

W22
la. N Willoughby..285 D8

WABASH
av. Cromer.....228 A13

WABBA
st. Marayong..243 J6

WACKETT
st. Bnkstn Aprt..398 B2
st. Maroubra..406 H11

WADDELL
cr. Hornsby Ht..161 J9

WADDS
av. Cabramatta..366 D8

WADE
cl. Illawong........459 J5
la. Gordon.........253 H7
la. Putney..........311 A6
pl. Kings Lngly...246 B9
pl. Surry Hills....F13
st. Surry Hills....4 A14
rd. N Parramatta..278 K6
st. Campsie......401 K1
st. Maroubra.....407 A13
st. Putney..........311 A6
st. Telopea........279 G10
st. Toongabbie..276 E5

WADSLEY
cr. Connells Pt..431 H16

WAGGA WAGGA
st. Prestons......393 B15

WAGNER
la. Bonnyrigg Ht..363 G5
pl. Cranebrook..207 G9
pl. Seven Hills..246 D12

WAGONGA
cl. Prestons......393 C16

WAGSTAFF
st. Edensor Pk...363 D2

WAGTAIL
cr. Ingleburn.....453 E9
pl. Castle Hill...216 K10
pl. Castle Hill...217 A10
pl. Erskine Park..270 K13

WAHROONGA
av. Wahroonga..222 G5
pl. W Pnnant Hl..248 G6
rd. Winmalee....173 F4

WAIKANDA
cr. Whalan.......240 H9

WAIKATO
pl. Kearns........450 J16

WAIMEA
av. Woollahra..22 B3
rd. Lindfield.....284 G2
st. Burwood....342 B14
st. N Balgowlah..287 D4

WAINE
la. Cabarita.....312 E16
la. Cabarita.....342 E1
st. Harbord.....288 D1
st. Surry Hills..F H6
st. Surry Hills..4 B11

WAINES
cr. Rockdale...403 D14

WAINEWRIGHT
av. West Hoxton..391 K11

WAINWRIGHT
av. Padstow....429 G5
la. Kingswood..237 G12
mw. Bella Vista..246 F2
rd. Mount Druitt..241 A14
rd. Whalan.....241 A14
st. Guildford..337 D1

WAIPORI
st. St Ives Ch..223 J3

WAIROA
av. Bondi Beach..378 E2
av. North Bondi..378 E2
la. Canterbury..372 D12
st. Campsie....372 D12
st. Canterbury..372 D12

WAITAKI
st. Lethbrdg Pk..240 F1

WAITANGI
pl. Glenorie.....128 C2

WAITARA
av. Waitara....221 K3
pde. Hurstville Gr..431 K1
pl. Dharruk...241 D8

WAITE
av. Balmain.....8 B10

WAITOVU
st. Mosman....317 D5

WAIWERA
av. North Manly..258 C16
st. Lavender Bay..K B16
st. Lavender Bay..5 E13

WAKE
pl. Kings Park..244 J3

WAKEFIELD
pl. Orchard Hills..267 F5
st. North Manly..258 B16

WAKEFORD
rd. Blaxland......233 F12
rd. Strathfield...371 E1

WAKEHURST
pky. Cromer......227 E6
pky. Elanora Ht..228 B3
pky. Frenchs Frst..256 H6
pky. Ingleside.....227 E6
pky. N Narrabeen..228 B3
pky. Oxford Falls..227 B15
pky. Seaforth.....286 K3

WAKELIN
av. Mt Pritchard..364 J11
wy. Claymore....481 D12

WAKELY
av. Quakers Hill..214 D7
pl. Forestville....256 A5

WAKOOKA
av. Elanora Ht..198 C16

WALANA
cr. Warriewood..198 F3

WALAR
st. East Killara..254 K6

WALBURGA
cl. Bradbury.....511 J10

WALCHA
cl. Mt Krng-gai..162 G3
la. S Penrith, off
Walcha Pl....266 H6
pl. S Penrith.....266 G6
wy. Hoxton Park..392 G5

WALDEN
rd. N Parramatta..278 F10

WALDER
rd. Hamondvle..396 E15

WALDO
cr. Peakhurst...430 C3

WALDON
rd. Belrose......225 K5

WALDRON
la. Sandringham, off
Norwood St..463 D4
pl. Cmbrdg Pk..238 A6
rd. Chester Hill..368 A1
rd. Sefton........368 E2
st. Sandringham..463 D5

WALENORE
av. Kingsford...406 H10
st. Newtown....374 H9

WALER
pl. Blairmount..481 A13

WALES
cl. Illawong......459 G5
la. Greenacre..370 G14
pl. Kings Lngly..245 B3
st. Greenacre..370 G15

WALGETT
cl. Hinchnbrk...392 H4

WALKER
av. Edgecliff....13 F11
av. Gymea.......491 F7
av. Haberfield..343 A14
av. Mascot.....405 E4
av. Narrabeen..228 J8
av. Peakhurst..430 H3
av. St Ives.....224 E6
cl. Silverdale..353 H15
la. Lavender Bay..K G13
la. Lavender Bay..5 H11
la. Paddington..4 A15
pde. Riverstone..181 K10
pl. Church Point..168 C9
pl. N Epping....251 F9
pl. Wetherill Pk..334 A1
rd. Port Hacking..522 J2
st. Belmore....371 C12
st. Canada Bay..342 D10
st. Clovelly....378 A13
st. Five Dock..342 D10
st. Lavender Bay..K F14
st. Lavender Bay..5 G11
st. Merrylands..307 G16
st. N Sydney..K D10
st. N Sydney....5 H9
st. Putney......312 C8
st. Quakers Hill..213 K10
st. Quakers Hill..213 G7
st. Redfern.....19 H10
st. Rhodes....311 D9
st. S Windsor..120 J16
st. Springwood..202 H1
st. Turrella....403 F5
st. Waterloo...19 H12
st. Werrington..239 A13
wy. Minto.......482 H5

WALKERS
cr. Emu Plains..234 K10
dr. Lane Cove N..283 F12
st. St Clair....300 A1

WALKOM
av. Forestville..256 B9

WALL
av. Asquith.....192 A7
pl. Panania....398 C13
pl. Bonnyrigg..364 C5

WALLABA
pl. Greystanes..305 H10

WALLABY
cl. Blacktown..273 J5
cl. Bossley Park..333 F7
gr. Winmalee..173 K5

WALLACE
av. Hunters Hill..313 A8
av. Hurlstone Pk..373 A11
cl. Hornsby Ht..161 J10
la. Balmain....8 C10
la. Hurlstone Pk..372 K11
la. Kingsford, off
Wallace St..406 J2
pde. Lindfield..254 B16
pl. Mt Pritchard..364 J9
rd. Vineyard..152 C7
st. Ashfield....373 A2
st. Balmain....8 C10
st. Bexley......432 G3
st. Blacktown..244 J15
st. Burwood...342 B6
st. Concord....342 B6
st. Eastwood..280 H8
st. Granville..308 C10
st. Greenwich..314 J13
st. Kingsford..406 H2
st. Marrickville..373 F16
st. Sefton......368 G5
st. Waverley..377 G10
st. Willoughby..285 D12

WALLAGA
av. Leumeah..482 G16
wy. Woodcroft..243 G10

WALLALONG
cr. West Pymble..252 G11

WALLAMI
st. Caringbah..492 G16

WALLAN
cl. Glenmore Pk..266 B6
pl. Plumpton..242 D9
st. Pemulwuy..305 E7

WALLANGRA
rd. Dover Ht..348 E13

WALLARINGA
av. Neutral Bay..6 G10
st. Mt Colah..162 B15

WALLAROO
st. Killara.....253 K11

WALLAROY
cr. Woollahra..14 D13
rd. Woollahra..14 E14
rd. Woollahra..22 D2
st. Concord W..311 D14

WALLAWA
av. Engadine..488 H15

WALLCLIFFE
ct. Wattle Grove..425 H6

WALLENDBEEN
av. Port Hacking..523 A2
pl. Bardwell Vy..403 C7

WALLGROVE
rd. Cecil Park..332 E13
rd. Eastern Ck..302 G2
rd. Horsley Pk..302 H15

WALLINA
av. Belrose....225 H14

WALLINGA
cr. Airds......512 A13

WALLINGTON
rd. Mosman..317 D2

WALLIS
av. Matraville..436 K8
av. Strathfield..371 B3
cir. Cecil Hills..362 J6
gln. Cranebrook..207 F9
la. Woollahra..22 D1
pde. North Bondi..378 F1
st. St Ives....224 B15
st. Willmot..210 B11
st. Leumeah..482 G14
st. Maianbar..522 K9
st. Woollahra..22 C1
st. Woollahra..22 C4

GREGORY'S STREET DIRECTORY 149

WA STREETS

WALL PARK
av. Blacktown 275 C2
av. Seven Hills 275 C2
WALLUMATTA
rd. Newport 169 D8
rd.n,Caringbah 493 B8
rd.s,Caringbah 493 B8
WALMAN
av. Lurnea 394 B10
WALMER
st. Ramsgate 433 E14
st. Sans Souci 433 E14
WALMSLEY
cl. Prairiewood 334 K9
WALNUT
gr. Cherrybrook 219 H7
st. Greystanes 306 E5
WALPA
pl. Quakers Hill 213 G7
WALPOLE
cl. Wetherill Pk 334 J3
pl. Wahroonga 222 D11
st. Holroyd 307 K10
st. Merrylands 307 F9
WALRUS
pl. Raby 451 D15
WALSH
av. Castle Hill 248 E2
av. Croydon Pk 371 F8
av. Glebe 11 J12
av. Maroubra 406 H11
cl. Edensor Pk 333 H13
cl. Illawong 459 E7
la. Greenacre 369 J10
pl. Kingswood 267 F1
st. Eastwood 281 H7
st. N Narrabeen 199 B13
WALSHE
gr. Bidwill 211 B15
WALTER
cl. Bligh Park 150 D5
pl. Greystanes 306 E12
pl. Northmead 278 D4
rd. Ingleside 168 E14
rd. Ingleside 198 C2
st. Balmain 7 C8
st. Bondi Jctn 22 G9
st. Croydon 372 E1
st. Granville 308 D11
st. Kingswood 237 K12
st. Leichhardt 9 B16
st. Mortdale 431 A5
st. Paddington 21 B2
st. Roselands 401 B5
st. Sans Souci 433 E15
st. Wetherill Pk 334 H1
st. Willoughby 285 E16
WALTERS
av. Glenbrook 234 E16
rd. Arndell Park 274 A10
rd. Berala 339 D14
rd. Blacktown 274 B4
st. Arncliffe 403 E8
st. Auburn 339 A2
wy. Castle Hill, off
Kerle Cr 218 J14
WALTHAM
st. Artarmon 315 A2
st. Coogee 407 G1
wy. Glenwood 215 C13
WALTHER
av. Bass Hill 367 E7
WALTON
cl. Pymble 253 F5
cr. Abbotsford 342 K1
la. Abbotsford 312 K15
la. Picton 563 F3
pl. Emu Plains 235 B12
pl. Minchinbury 271 F6
st. Blakehurst 432 C14
WALUMETTA
dr. Wollstncraft 315 D10
WALWORTH
av. Newport 169 H13
ct. Newport 169 H12
rd. Horsley Pk 302 E11
WALZ
la. Rockdale, off
Walz St 403 C15
st. Rockdale 403 C15
WAMBIRI
pl. Cromer 227 K14
WAMBOOL
pl. Brooklyn 76 C11
st. Turramurra 222 J16

WAMINDA
av. Campbelltown 511 J8
WANAARING
tce. Glenwood 215 E16
WANAKA
pl. Belrose 226 A16
pl. Glenorie 128 C3
WANARI
rd. Terrey Hills 196 E7
WANAWONG
dr. Thornleigh 220 J12
rd. Avalon 139 K12
WANDA
cr. Berowra Ht 133 C7
pl. Woodbine 481 D15
st. Merrylands W 307 B14
st. Strathfield S 371 E7
WANDANA
av. Baulkham Hl 247 C4
WANDARRA
cr. Bradbury 511 D15
WANDARRI
rd. Kenthurst 157 E10
WANDEARAH
av. Avalon 139 J12
WANDEEN
av. Beecroft 250 F5
pl. St Ives Ch 223 K3
rd. Clareville 169 D2
WANDELLA
av. Hunters Hill 313 F12
av. Northmead 278 C2
av. Roseville 284 K4
pl. Glen Alpine 510 E14
rd. Allambie Ht 257 G16
rd.n,Miranda 491 K4
rd.s,Miranda 491 K5
WANDERERS
wy. Hornsby 221 G3
WANDOBAH
st. Engadine 489 E8
WANDOO
av. Ryde 311 K4
gln. Kingswood 237 H16
pl. Bradbury 511 E10
WANDSWORTH
st. Parramatta 308 G1
WANGAL
pl. Five Dock 342 K12
WANGALLA
rd. Riverview 314 C5
WANGANELLA
cl. Mt Colah 162 B15
rd. St Ives Ch 223 K3
st. Balgowlah 287 G10
st. Balgowlah 287 G8
st. Miller 393 F4
wy. Airds 512 E10
WANGANUI
rd. Kirrawee 491 B8
WANGARA
st. Doonside 243 B15
st. Mona Vale 199 A3
WANGAROA
cr. Lethbrdg Pk 240 E1
WANGEE
rd. Greenacre 370 E12
rd. Lakemba 370 K14
WANGI
av. Cronulla 523 J4
WANGOOLA
wy. Minto 482 K3
WANILL
pl. Berowra 133 E10
WANINGA
rd. Hornsby Ht 161 J8
WANJINA
pl. North Rocks 278 H2
WANNITI
rd. Belrose 225 H14
WANNYL
rd. Kirrawee 490 J5
WANSEY
rd. Randwick 376 J14
WANSTEAD
av. Earlwood 403 G2
WANT
st. Caringbah 492 K14
st. Mosman 317 B9
st. Rosebery 405 H2
WARABIN
st. Waterfall 519 D12

WARAGAL
av. Rozelle 344 E6
WARANA
rd. Cecil Park 331 E14
WARANDOO
st. Gordon 254 C6
st. Hornsby 221 G6
WARATAH
av. Casula 394 J11
av. Randwick 377 A14
cr. Mcquarie Fd 453 G1
ct. Narellan Vale 478 K12
la. Canterbury 372 C14
la. Sutherland 490 E4
pde. Narraweena 258 B6
pl. Glenorie 127 K10
rd. Berowra 133 D14
rd. Botany 405 H16
rd. Engadine 518 E3
rd. Ingleside 197 H6
rd. Ingleside 198 A6
rd. Kentlyn 483 C13
rd. Palm Beach 109 J14
rd. Turramurra 252 E3
rd. Warrimoo 202 K11
rd. W Pnnant Hl 218 J16
st. Arncliffe 403 D10
st. Balgowlah 288 A8
st. Bexley 432 D2
st. Blakehurst 432 B15
st. Bowen Mtn 83 K13
st. Burwood Ht 372 A6
st. Canterbury 372 D14
st. Chatswood 284 J6
st. Cronulla 493 K14
st. Croydon Pk 372 A6
st. Eastwood 281 H8
st. Ermington 310 H3
st. Granville 308 B10
st. Haberfield 9 A10
st. Haberfield 343 D12
st. Harbord 258 F14
st. Kirrawee 490 G1
st. Kyle Bay 432 B15
st. Leichhardt 10 B14
st. Mona Vale 199 A2
st. North Bondi 348 F15
st. N Strathfield 341 E6
st. Oatley 431 A12
st. Oatley 431 A14
st. Old Guildford 337 E9
st. Punchbowl 400 C2
st. Rooty Hill 272 E4
st. Rcuttrs Bay 13 C8
st. St Marys 239 F14
st. Stanhpe Gdn 215 D10
st. Sutherland 490 G1
WARAWARA
cct. Schofields 213 E11
WARAYAMA
pl. Rozelle 344 C6
WARBLER
av. Ingleburn 453 F10
cl. Hinchinbrk 363 E15
la. St Clair, off
Warbler St 271 A12
st. Erskine Park 270 K14
WARBRICK
st. Concord 342 A5
WARBROON
ct. Bella Vista 246 H2
WARBURTON
cr. Wrrngtn Cty 238 E4
la. Earlwood 402 D4
pde. Earlwood 402 E3
st. Chifley 437 A5
st. Condell Park 398 F1
st. Gymea 491 E3
st. Marrickville 373 J14
WARBY
st. Campbelltown 511 G2
WARCOO
av. Gymea Bay 491 G12
WARD
av. Canterbury 372 D14
av. Darlinghurst 4 K9
av. Elizabeth Bay 13 A7
av. Potts Point 4 K9
av. Rushcutters B 4 K9
cl. Prairiewood 334 J7
cr. Oyster Bay 461 F5
la. Concord 342 D6
pl. Dural 188 H13
pl. Hinchinbrk 362 J16
pl. Northmead 277 H8
st. Bass Hill 368 E9

st. Concord 342 D6
st. Eastwood 280 J6
st. Epping 250 G16
st. Kurnell 465 F8
st. N Sydney K F3
st. N Sydney 5 G6
st. Pymble 253 A7
st. Willoughby 285 E12
st. Yagoona 368 E9
wy. Minto 482 K1
WARDANG
rd. Hinchinbrk 362 J16
WARDELL
cl. Earlwood 403 B1
dr. Barden Rdg 488 H2
dr. S Penrith 267 C4
la. Blaxland 233 E10
la. Dulwich Hill, off
Keith St 373 E12
pl. Agnes Banks 117 C12
rd. Dulwich Hill 15 E16
rd. Dulwich Hill 373 G9
rd. Earlwood 403 A3
rd. Lewisham 373 G9
rd. Marrickville 373 D13
rd. Petersham 373 G9
st. Arncliffe 403 G10
wy. Minto 482 J6
WARDIA
st. Glenwood 245 E1
WARDINGTON
ri. Bella Vista 246 H2
WARDLE
cl. Currans Hill 479 F12
WARDROP
st. Greenwich 315 A9
WARE
st. Fairfield 336 E12
st. Fairfield Ht 336 B10
WAREEMBA
av. Thornleigh 221 A4
pl. Lilli Pilli 492 F16
st. Wareemba 343 A5
WAREHAM
cr. Frenchs Frst 256 D3
WAREJEE
st. Kingsgrove 402 A8
WAREKILA
cl. Berowra Ht 133 D8
rd. Beacon Hill 257 H8
WARESLEY
la. Cranebrook, off
Waresley Wy 207 G14
wy. Cranebrook 207 F14
WARFIELD
pl. Cecil Hills 362 J9
WARGON
cr. Glenmore Pk 266 A10
WARHAM
la. Marrickville 374 A11
WARI
av. Glenmore Pk 266 D10
pl. Pemulwuy 305 F5
WARIALDA
st. Kogarah 433 A3
st. Merrylands W 307 B13
wy. Hinchinbrk 392 H5
WARILDA
av. Engadine 489 B10
la. Beverly Hills 401 C13
st. Villawood 367 F4
WARILI
rd. Frenchs Frst 255 K2
WARILLA
pl. Riverview 314 A6
WARIN
pl. Glenmore Pk 266 C12
WARING
av. Caringbah 492 D15
cr. Plumpton 242 C10
st. Marsfield 282 B2
WARINGA
cr. Glenmore Pk 266 A6
WARK
av. Pagewood 406 G6
WARKS HILL
rd. Kurrajong Ht 63 E10
WARLENCOURT
av. Milperra 397 F12
WARMAN
st. Dundas Vy 280 C11
st. Pendle Hill 276 C14

WARNDON
la. Cranebrook, off
Warndon Rd 207 E13
rd. Cranebrook 207 E13
WARNE
cr. Beverly Hills 400 K11
pl. Marrickville 373 G16
st. Pennant Hills 220 G15
WARNER
av. Clovelly 378 A12
av. S Turramrra 252 A5
pl. Greystanes 306 D12
st. Gladesville 312 E6
WARNERS
av. Bondi Beach 378 D1
av. North Bondi 348 B16
av. Willoughby 285 J12
WARNING
pl. Ruse 512 F7
WARNOCK
rd. Agnes Banks 117 C11
st. Guildford W 336 H3
WAROOGA
av. Baulkham Hl 246 E10
WAROON
rd. Cromer 228 C15
WARRA
st. Wentwthvle 276 K13
WARRABA
rd. N Narrabeen 198 H13
st. Como 460 F7
st. Hurstville 402 A15
WARRABINA
av. St Ives 224 C9
WARRABRI
pl. West Pymble 252 H11
WARRADALE
rd. Silverdale 353 F9
rd. Warragamba 353 F9
WARRAGAL
rd. Turramurra 222 J16
WARRAGAMBA
cr. Bossley Park 333 H5
cr. Jamisontown 266 A3
cr. Leumeah 482 G13
WARRAH
pl. Greystanes 305 G10
rd. Yowie Bay 492 A9
st. Chatswood 285 C5
WARRAMUNGA
st. St Marys 239 H16
WARRAN
pl. Castle Hill 218 B12
WARRANA
st. Botany 405 J13
WARRANE
pl. Castle Cove 285 E3
rd. Chatswood 285 G7
rd. N Willoughby 285 G7
rd. Roseville Ch 285 D1
WARRANGARREE
dr. Woronora Ht 489 C3
WARRANGI
st. Turramurra 223 A15
WARRAROON
rd. Riverview 314 D5
WARRAROONG
st. Beverly Hills 401 C13
WARRATTA
pl. Oatlands 279 B13
WARRAWEE
av. Castle Cove 285 K5
av. Warrawee 222 F9
pl. Beverly Hills 401 C13
WARRAWIDGEE
rd. Chester Hill 337 F13
WARRAWONG
st. Eastwood 280 H11
st. Glenmore Pk 266 H15
WARREGO
av. Sylvania Wtr 462 D12
ct. Wattle Grove 395 K12
pl. East Killara 254 E9
pl. Greystanes 306 B4
rd. Berowra Ht 133 D8
st. N St Marys 239 J10
WARRELL
ct. Rooty Hill 272 B4
WARREN
av. Bankstown 399 F7
av. Bankstown 399 G7
av. Grays Point 491 A15
av. Kogarah 433 E5

STREETS WE

la. Marrickville, off Church St 373 H14
pde. Punchbowl 400 E5
pl. Silverdale 353 J9
pl. Wakeley 334 H12
rd. Bellevue Hill 14 J15
rd. Marrickville 373 G14
rd. Smithfield 336 B2
rd. Woodpark 306 E16
rd. Woodpark 306 F16
st. Quakers Hill 244 B2
st. Ryde 282 B10
swy. Liverpool 395 E3

WARREN BALL
av. Newtown 18 A9

WARRENTON
la. St Clair, off Warrenton St 270 J12
st. St Clair 270 J11

WARRI
cl. Narraweena 258 A6

WARRICK
la. Blacktown 244 H15

WARRIEWOOD
rd. Warriewood 199 A8
st. Woodbine 481 H11

WARRIGAL
dr. Westleigh 220 H5
gln. Wrrngtn Dns 238 E5
la. Canterbury, off Warrigal St 372 D13
rd. Blaxlands Rdg 65 C1
rd. Frenchs Frst 256 G2
st. Blacktown 244 A10
st. Canterbury 372 D13
st. Jannali 460 G9

WARRIGO
st. Sadleir 364 B15

WARRIMOO
av. St Ives 223 G9
av. St Ives Ch 223 K4
dr. Quakers Hill 243 J1

WARRINA
av. Baulkham Hl 246 K6
av. Parramatta 278 A13
pl. Glendenning 242 G5
pl. Greystanes 305 H10
pl. Londonderry 148 B11
rd. Bradbury 511 C16
rd. Caringbah 492 G12
st. Berowra Ht 133 C9

WARRING
av. Emu Plains 235 H10

WARRINGA
rd. Cammeray 316 A6
st. Bass Hill 368 E14
st. Yagoona 368 E14

WARRINGAH
fwy. Cammeray 315 G4
fwy. Crows Nest 315 G4
fwy. Naremburn 315 G4
fwy. N Sydney K K6
fwy. N Sydney 5 J6
la. Mosman 317 C3
rd. Beacon Hill 257 B5
rd. Dee Why 258 A6
rd. Forestville 255 F16
rd. Frenchs Frst 256 C8
rd. Mosman 317 C3
rd. Narraweena 258 A6
st. N Balgowlah 287 D3

WARRINGTON
av. Caringbah 493 A6
av. East Killara 254 F7
av. Epping 281 A2

WARRIOR
pl. St Marys 239 F9

WARROWA
av. West Pymble 252 J7

WARRUGA
cr. Berowra Ht 133 C8
pl. N Narrabeen 198 H13
pl. Riverview 313 J6

WARRUMBUNGLE
pl. Bow Bowing 452 D12
st. Fairfield W 335 E11

WARRUNG
rd. St Helens Park 541 E2

WARSAW
st. N Strathfield 341 C5

WARSOP
st. Kurnell 464 C16

WARUDA
av. Kirribilli 2 D2
pl. Huntleys Cove 313 D12
st. Bankstown 368 E14
st. Kirribilli 2 C2
st. Yagoona 368 E14

WARUMBUI
av. Baulkham Hl 246 H8
av. Miranda 492 A1

WARUMBUL
rd. Royal N P 520 K10

WARUNG
av. Frenchs Frst 255 F2
st. Georges Hall 368 D15
st. McMahons Pt 5 E16
st. Yagoona 368 D15

WARWICK
av. Cabramatta 365 C10
av. Cammeray 316 B5
cl. Berowra 133 E9
cl. Blaxland 234 A9
cr. Canterbury 402 E1
la. Hurstville 401 F16
la. Stanmore 16 H9
pde. Castle Hill 217 J15
pl. Wahroonga 221 K15
rd. Dundas Vy 280 A6
rd. Merrylands 307 F12
st. Hurstville 401 E16
st. Killara 253 H11
st. Minto 482 F1
st. North Ryde 283 B11
st. Penrith 236 J13
st. Punchbowl 399 J5
st. St Marys 269 F3
st. Stanmore 16 H9
st. Sylvania 461 K13
st. Warwck Frm 365 J15

WARWILLA
av. Wahroonga 222 C6
wk. Wahroonga, off Warwilla Av 222 D7

WARWILLAH
rd. Russell Lea 343 C5

WASCOE
st. Glenbrook 233 H14

WASDALE
st. Collaroy Plat 228 E12

WASHINGTON
av. Cromer 228 A13
av. Riverwood 400 B13
dr. Bonnet Bay 460 A10
dr. Bonnet Bay 460 E11
pl. Castle Hill 247 E1
st. Bexley 432 K2
st. Bexley 433 A1
wy. Cecil Park 332 A12

WASSALL
la. Alexandria 18 J13

WASSELL
st. Chifley 437 A4
st. Dundas 279 K12
st. Matraville 437 A4

WATCH HOUSE
rd. Prospect 304 K1

WATER
la. Carlton 432 K5
la. Emu Plains, off Water St 235 D10
la. Mosman 317 A12
st. Annandale 17 B2
st. Auburn 339 D7
st. Bardwell Pk 402 K6
st. Belfield 371 C8
st. Birchgrove 7 E4
st. Blakehurst 432 E16
st. Cabramatta W 365 A8
st. Caringbah 493 B13
st. Emu Plains 235 C10
st. Hornsby 191 J15
st. Lidcombe 339 D7
st. Sans Souci 462 K5
st. Strathfield S 371 C7
st. Wahroonga 222 F6
st. Wallacia 324 J11
st. Wentwthvle 277 B15
st. Werrington 238 K15
st. Werrington 239 A15

WATERFALL
av. Forestville 256 A13
cr. Bella Vista 216 D16
cr. Bella Vista 246 D1
cr. Cranebrook 207 B12
rd. Heathcote 518 F10
rd. Mt Wilson 58 J9
rd. Oatley 430 H10

WATERFORD
pl. Killarney Ht 255 J14
st. Kellyville Rdg 185 C15
wy. Glenmore Pk 266 E14

WATERFRONT
dr. Lilyfield, off Military Dr 10 A1
wy. Harringtn Pk 478 D5

WATERGUM
cl. Rouse Hill 185 C8
dr. Warriewood 198 G11
pl. Alfords Point 459 C1
pl. Warriewood 198 G10
wy. Greenacre 370 F5

WATERHOUSE
av. St Ives 254 D1
dr. Silverdale 353 K10
pl. Airds 511 J14
pl. Camden S 507 C10
st. Abbotsbury 333 C12

WATER LILY
tce. Bidwill 211 E14

WATERLOO
av. Castle Hill 217 K11
pl. Glenfield 424 E9
rd. Greenacre 370 C15
rd. Mcquarie Pk 251 J13
rd. Mcquarie Pk 282 E2
rd. Mcquarie Pk 283 A6
rd. Marsfield 251 J13
rd. Mt Lewis 370 C15
rd. N Epping 251 G11
st. Narrabeen 229 B4
st. Rozelle 344 D8
st. Surry Hills F F16
st. Surry Hills 19 K2

WATER RESERVE
rd. N Balgowlah 287 F5

WATERS
la. Cremorne 316 E8
la. Neutral Bay 316 E8
la. Richmond Lwld 88 E9
rd. Cremorne 6 J1
rd. Cremorne 316 E8
rd. Glenbrook 264 B2
rd. Naremburn 315 E2
rd. Naremburn 315 D3
rd. Neutral Bay 6 J1

WATERSIDE
av. Maroubra 407 J8
cr. Carramar 366 H4
cr. Earlwood 372 J15
gr. Warriewood 198 J7
gr. Woodcroft 243 G9
pde. Peakhurst 430 D11

WATERSLEIGH
la. Cremorne 316 E7

WATERTON
av. Matraville 436 J2

WATERVIEW
av. Caringbah 492 E12
cr. Blaxland 233 H12
st. Balmain 8 A9
st. Carlton 432 F11
st. Five Dock 342 K10
st. Mona Vale 199 E1
st. Oyster Bay 461 C7
st. Putney 311 J6
st. Seaforth 286 K3

WATERWORTH
dr. Mt Annan 479 A15
dr. Narellan Vale 478 G16
dr. Narellan Vale 508 F1
pl. St Helens Park 541 B4

WATFORD
cl. N Epping 251 G9

WATKIN
av. Earlwood 403 A3
la. Concord, off Watkin St 312 A16
la. Newtown 17 K10
st. Bexley 403 A16
st. Concord 342 A1
st. Hurlstone Pk 372 J11
st. Newtown 17 K10
st. Rockdale 403 A16

WATKINS
cr. Currans Hill 479 H13
rd. Avalon 140 F14
rd. Baulkham Hl 247 E15
st. Bondi 377 H3

WATKIN TENCH
pde. Pemulwuy 305 F8

WATKIN WOMBAT
wy. Faulconbdg 171 H12

WATKISS
st. Glenwood 215 H16

WATLING
av. West Hoxton 392 A14
wy. Claymore 481 B11

WATSFORD
rd. Campbelltown 511 F2

WATSON
av. Ashbury 372 E6
av. Hornsby 191 F12
av. N Wahroonga 192 F16
dr. Penrith 237 C7
la. Balmain 7 H9
la. Narwee, off Broad Arrow Rd 400 F15
pl. Doonside 243 B5
pl. Minto 453 A13
pl. Northmead 278 C4
rd. Lapstone 264 F2
rd. Millers Pt A E3
rd. Millers Pt 1 E10
rd. Mt Annan 479 G14
rd. Padstow 399 D14
st. Bondi 377 K5
st. Ermington 310 D1
st. Glenbrook 264 A4
st. Hamondvle 396 E14
st. Neutral Bay 6 E1
st. Paddington 21 E3
st. Pennant Hills 220 D14
st. Putney 311 J7
st. Rosehill 308 H8

WATSONIA
st. Emu Plains 235 H8

WATT
av. Newington 310 B12
av. Ryde 282 B16
pde. Lansdowne 367 C6
pl. Emu Plains 235 E9
st. Leumeah 512 C1
st. Rooty Hill 272 B2

WATTING
st. Abbotsbury 333 B11

WATTLE
av. Carramar 366 H2
av. Fairlight 288 C7
av. Mcquarie Fd 453 K4
av. N St Marys 239 K11
av. Villawood 367 A1
cr. Glossodia 66 B11
cr. Pyrmont 12 G7
gr. Minchinbury 272 C10
la. Asquith, off Amor St 191 K10
la. Hurlstone Pk, off New Canterbury Rd 372 K10
la. N St Marys 239 K11
la. Ultimo 12 K13
la. West Ryde 281 G15
pl. Carlingford 249 F15
pl. Rooty Hill 272 D3
pl. Turramurra 252 D2
pl. Ultimo 3 A16
pl. Ultimo 12 K16
rd. Brookvale 258 C12
rd. Casula 423 H2
rd. Ingleside 197 K8
rd. Jannali 460 H14
rd. Jannali 460 J9
rd. North Manly 258 C12
rd. Ruse 512 E8
rd. Sutherland 460 H15
rd. W Pnnant Hl 218 J16
st. Asquith 191 K10
st. Bankstown 369 J16
st. Bargo 567 G4
st. Blacktown 243 J14
st. Bowen Mtn 84 A10
st. Enfield 371 G5
st. Greystanes 306 E4
st. Haberfield 343 A13
st. Killara 254 B10
st. Peakhurst 430 H4
st. Punchbowl 370 B16
st. Rydalmere 309 G1
st. Springwood 202 E8
st. Ultimo 3 A15
st. Ultimo 12 G9
st. West Ryde 281 F14
wk. Newington, off Newington Bvd 310 B13
wy. Cherrybrook 219 G10

WATTLEBIRD
cr. Glenmore Pk 266 A13
pl. Glenwood 245 B1

WATTLE CREEK
dr. Theresa Park 445 A10

WATTLE GREEN
pl. Narellan Vale 478 J13

WATTLE GROVE
dr. Wattle Grove 396 A16

WATTON
rd. Carlingford 249 F12
st. Quakers Hill 214 F16

WATTS
gr. Blacktown 273 H5
pl. Cherrybrook 220 A11
pl. Prairiewood 335 B8
pl. West Hoxton 392 C10
rd. Kemps Ck 359 G13
rd. Ryde 281 K9
st. Canada Bay 342 E9
st. North Rocks 249 A16

WAU
pl. Glenfield 424 J10
pl. Holsworthy 426 C3
pl. Whalan 240 K8

WAUCHOPE
rd. Hoxton Park 392 H10

WAUGH
av. N Parramatta 278 G13
cr. Blacktown 273 H3

WAUGOOLA
la. Gordon 254 B5
st. Gordon 254 A5

WAUHOPE
cr. S Coogee 407 F4

WAVEHILL
av. Windsor Dn 180 J1

WAVELL
av. Carlingford 250 A15
pde. Earlwood 403 D4

WAVERLEY
cr. Bondi Jctn 377 F3
la. Belmore, off Plimsoll St 401 H1
st. Belmore 401 H1
st. Bondi Jctn 22 K7
st. Bondi Jctn 377 F4
st. Fairfield W 335 D8
st. Randwick 377 B11

WAVERLY
pl. Illawong 459 K5

WAVERTON
av. Waverton 5 B6
la. Waverton 5 B6

WAY
cl. Carlingford 250 B13
st. Kingsgrove 402 B11
st. Tempe 374 B16

WAYCOTT
av. Kingsgrove 402 B13

WAYELLA
st. West Ryde 280 J12

WAYFIELD
rd. Dural 218 F2
rd. Glenhaven 218 F2

WAYGARA
av. Green Valley 363 H11

WAYGROVE
av. Earlwood 402 F3

WAYLAND
av. Lidcombe 339 H13

WAYMAN
pl. Merrylands 307 G13

WAYNE
av. Lugarno 430 A11
cr. Condell Park 398 F5
cr. Greystanes 306 F13
st. Dean Park 242 J2

WAYS
tce. Pyrmont 8 G16

WAZIR
st. Bardwell Vy 403 C8

WEALTHEASY
st. Riverstone 182 B9

WEARDEN
rd. Belrose 226 C15
rd. Frenchs Frst 226 C15
rd. Frenchs Frst 257 B1

WEARNE
av. Pennant Hills 220 E14
rd. Bonnyrigg 363 K10
st. Canterbury 402 C1

WEATHERBOARD RIDGE
rd. Blaxlands Rdg 65 F4

WEATHERBY
av. Cmbrdg Pk 238 A10

WEAVER
la. Erskine Park, off Weaver St 301 B2
pl. Minchinbury 271 G7

GREGORY'S STREET DIRECTORY 151

WE — STREETS

pl. Woronora Ht......489 C5	la. E Lindfield, off	WENTON	WESCOE
st. Erskine Park......300 K2	Wellington Rd......255 A12	av. Liberty Gr......311 B11	pl. Cranebrook......207 F11
st. Erskine Park......301 K1	la. Lavender Bay......5 E13	WENTWORTH	WESLEY
st. Ryde......312 F6	la. McMahons Pt......5 E13	av. Bnksmeadw......406 A8	cct. Mcquarie Pk, off
WEAVERS	la. Waterloo......19 G12	av. Blakehurst......432 B15	Main Av......283 D9
rd. S Maroota......69 E1	pl. Bondi......377 J4	av. Eastgardens......406 A8	pl. Cherrybrook......220 A5
WEBB	pl. N Turramurra......193 E11	av. East Kilara......254 F8	pl. Greystanes......306 D12
av. Hornsby......221 F2	rd. Auburn......338 G8	av. Eastlakes......405 E7	pl. Hornsea Pk......392 C13
av. Liberty Gr......311 B11	rd. Auburn......339 C9	av. Glenfield......424 C11	st. Elanora Ht......198 D11
cl. Edensor Pk......333 H16	rd. Rookwood......340 F14	av. Hillsdale......406 A8	st. Greenacre......370 F3
cl. Illawong......459 J5	rd. Rookwood......340 K16	av. Mascot......405 E7	st. Oatlands......279 C8
la. Blackett......241 D1	rd. Strathfield......340 F14	av. North Rocks......278 F3	st. Telopea......279 C8
pl. Bligh Park......150 J7	WEETA	av. Pagewood......406 A8	WESSEL
pl. Minto......482 H7	st. Picton......561 D3	pde. Pendle Hill......276 G14	cl. Hinchinbrk......363 A15
st. Croydon......342 D15	WEETALIBAH	av. Surry Hills......F C7	WESSEX
st. McMahons Pt......5 C12	rd. Northbridge......286 E15	av. Surry Hills......3 J12	la. Wentwthvle......277 C9
st. Merrylands......307 E7	WEETAWA	av. Sydney......F C7	pl. Raby......451 H12
st. N Parramatta......278 H15	rd. Northbridge......286 D15	av. Sydney......3 J12	WESSON
st. Parramatta......278 H15	rd. Bilgola......169 J3	av. Toongabbie......276 D9	rd. W Pnnant Hl......249 G1
st. Riverwood......399 J16	WEE WAA	av. Waitara......222 A2	WEST
st. Werrington......238 K12	cl. Hoxton Park......392 J7	av. Wentwthvle......276 G14	av. Darlinghurst......4 J12
tce. Westleigh......220 G7	WEGG	av. Wentwthvle......277 B16	cir. Blaxland......233 J6
WEBBER	pl. Ambarvale......511 A14	dr. Camden S......507 A13	cl. Illawong......459 B7
pl. Kings Lngly......245 A2	WEHLOW	dr. Liberty Gr......311 C13	cir. Hurstville Gr......431 F10
pl. Prairiewood......335 A8	st. Mount Druitt......271 D1	pde. Yennora......337 B10	dr. Bexley North......402 C10
st. Greenacre......370 G11	WEIGAND	pl. Belrose......226 C16	esp. Manly......288 F10
st. Sylvania......415 K12	av. Bankstown......369 C15	pl. Point Piper......14 K1	la. Carlton......432 J5
WEBBS	WEIL	pl. Point Piper......347 E8	la. Darlinghurst......4 H12
av. Ashfield......372 J1	av. Croydon Pk......371 H8	rd. Burwood......341 H16	la. N Sydney......5 D1
av. Auburn......338 J5	WEIPA	rd. Eastwood......280 J9	la. Randwick......407 B2
la. Burwood......342 A11	cl. Green Valley......363 J11	rd. Ingleburn......423 B9	la. St Marys......239 G15
st. Ashfield......342 K16	WEIR	rd. Orchard Hills......266 K12	pde. Chatswood W......284 F8
WEBER	rd. Forestville......256 B6	rd. Orchard Hills......267 A12	pde. Courtilgah......564 D16
cr. Emerton......240 H6	cr. Lurnea......394 F10	rd. Strathfield......371 H1	pde. Denistone......281 D12
WEBSTER	pl. Kings Lngly......246 A10	rd. Vaucluse......348 C3	pde. Eastwood......281 B8
av. Peakhurst......430 B6	rd. Penrith......236 D8	rd. Vaucluse......348 B3	pde. Riverstone......182 J9
cl. Lurnea......394 E10	rd. Warragamba......353 F8	rd.n.Homebush......341 A5	pde. Roseville......284 F8
st. Milperra......397 D16	WEISEL	rd.s.Homebush......341 A6	pde. Thirlmere......564 G12
st. Pendle Hill......276 B16	pl. Willmot......210 D12	st. Auburn......309 C16	pde. West Ryde......281 E15
st. Picton......563 G7	WEJA	st. Bardwell Vy......403 C7	pl. Camden S......506 K14
WEDDELL	cl. Prestons......422 J1	st. Birrong......368 J4	prm.Manly......288 G10
av. Tregear......240 E4	WELBY	st. Caringbah......492 J14	st. Auburn......338 J6
WEDDERBURN	st. Eastwood......281 E8	st. Croydon Pk......372 A7	st. Balgowlah......287 H10
rd. St Helens Park......541 F4	tce. Acacia Gdn......214 G14	st. Dolans Bay......492 J14	st. Balgowlah......287 H8
rd. Wedderburn......540 B9	WELCH	st. Dover Ht......348 G15	st. Blacktown......274 H4
rd. Wedderburn......541 F11	av. Greenacre......370 A10	st. Ermington......310 C1	st. Blakehurst......432 E11
WEDDIN	cl. Minto......452 K15	st. Glebe......12 F12	st. Brookvale......258 D9
pl. Ruse......512 F7	st. North Manly......258 B14	st. Granville......308 K11	st. Cammeray......315 H6
WEDDLE	WELCOME	st. Greenacre......370 H7	st. Canley Vale......366 B4
av. Abbotsford......343 B3	st. Wakeley......334 H13	st. Greenacre......370 J12	st. Carlton......432 E11
av. Chiswick......343 B3	WELD	st. Manly......288 H10	st. Crows Nest......315 H6
WEDGE	st. Prestons......393 G8	st. Paddington......21 F3	st. Croydon......342 J12
pl. Beaumont Hills......215 H3	WELDER	st. Parramatta......308 D5	st. Darlinghurst......4 G14
pl. Lurnea......394 C7	rd. Seven Hills......246 F15	st. Petersham......15 F8	st. Darlinghurst......4 H12
WEDGEWOOD	WELDON	st. Point Piper......14 K2	st. Five Dock......342 K9
cr. Beacon Hill......257 G8	la. Woollahra......21 K2	st. Point Piper......347 E8	st. Glenbrook......233 G14
rd. The Oaks......502 J1	st. Burwood......372 A2	st. Randwick......22 C16	st. Guildford......337 J5
WEDMORE	WELFARE	st. Randwick......377 A11	st. Hurstville......432 B7
la. Emu Heights, off	av. Beverly Hills......400 K12	st. Tempe......404 B3	st. Kingswood......237 G16
Wedmore Rd......235 A5	av. Narwee......400 K12	wy. Vaucluse......348 D3	st. Lewisham......15 E10
rd. Emu Heights......235 A5	st. Homebush W......340 J6	WENTWORTH PARK	st. Lurnea......394 C9
wy. Canley Vale......366 D5	WELHAM	av. Cmbrdg Pk......238 B7	st. Naremburn......315 J3
WEEDON	st. Beecroft......250 E8	rd. Glebe......12 E9	st. N Sydney......5 E3
av. Paddington......13 A16	WELL	WEONGA	st. Paddington......4 G14
rd. Artarmon......285 A14	st. Ryde......311 G5	rd. Dover Ht......348 F10	st. Parramatta......279 A16
WEEKES	WELLAND	WERAMBIE	st. Petersham......15 E10
av. Rookwood......340 B12	cl. Jamisontown......236 B15	st. Woolwich......314 H11	st. Petersham......15 D7
la. Newtown......17 F11	WELLARD	WERINGA	st. Pymble......253 D6
rd. Clontarf......287 H15	pl. Bonnyrigg......364 A7	av. Cammeray......316 B4	st. S Hurstville......432 B7
WEEKS	WELLBANK	WERNA	st. Strathfield......371 B1
pl. Narellan Vale......508 J1	st. Concord......341 J5	pl. Hornsby......221 F4	st. Waterloo......19 E13
WEELSBY PARK	st. N Strathfield......341 E6	WERNICKLE	tce. Bankstown......399 F1
dr. Cawdor......505 E16	WELLE	cl. Prairiewood......335 A9	WESTACOTT
WEEMALA	cl. St Clair......299 H1	WEROMBI	la. Canley Vale, off
av. Doonside......243 B14	WELLER	rd. Brownlow Hl......475 G9	Railway Pde......366 A3
av. Kirrawee......490 J2	pl. Rydalmere......279 F16	rd. Ellis Lane......476 B11	WESTALL
av. Riverwood......399 K16	av. West Hoxton......392 A7	rd. Grasmere......506 C1	cl. Abbotsbury......333 C12
cr. Bradbury......511 H14	st. Fairfield......335 K14	rd. Orangeville......444 A10	WESTBANK
rd. Duffys Frst......195 A3	WENDLEBURY	rd. Theresa Park......445 A12	av. Emu Plains......235 H11
rd. Northbridge......286 F16	rd. Chipping Ntn......396 G3	rd. Werombi......443 D2	WEST BOTANY
rd. Pennant Hills......220 F16	WENDOUREE	WEROMBIE	st. Arncliffe......403 H11
rd. Terrey Hills......195 A3	st. Busby......363 G14	rd. Mt Colah......192 B4	st. Kogarah......433 F4
st. Baulkham H......277 K3	WENDOVER	WERONA	st. Rockdale......403 G16
st. Chester Hill......338 B16	st. Doonside......243 B10	av. Abbotsbury......342 J3	WESTBOURNE
WEEM FARM	WENDRON	av. Clarmnt Ms......268 J3	av. Thirlmere......565 B3
rd. Grose Vale......84 G16	st. St Ives......224 G9	av. Gordon......253 H7	la. Petersham......16 B7
WEENA	WENDY	av. Killara......253 H7	la. Stanmore......16 B7
rd. Kurrajong Hl......64 A16	av. Georges Hall......367 F10	av. Padstow......429 G3	rd. Lindfield......284 D4
WEENAMANA	av. Normanhurst......221 F11	av. Punchbowl......400 E8	st. Artarmon......315 A5
pl. Padstow......429 G2	cl. Cabramatta......365 E9	pl. Dharruk......241 D8	st. Bexley......432 E3
WEENEY	cl. Glenwood......215 D13	rd. E Kurrajong......67 B3	st. Carlton......432 J9
st. Beverly Pk......433 C11	pl. Toongabbie......276 G8	rd. Riverview......314 C6	st. Drummoyne......343 H11
WEERONA	WENKE	st. Pennant Hills......220 H15	st. Petersham......16 B7
pl. Caringbah......492 D14	cr. Yagoona......368 H10	WERRIBEE PARK	st. St Leonards......315 A5
	av. Ingleburn......453 A8	pl. Glen Alpine......510 A15	st. Stanmore......16 B7
	av. Kellyville......216 K3	WERRINGTON	WESTBROOK
	WELLINGTON	rd. Werrington......239 B9	av. Wahroonga......223 A5
			rd. Bickley Vale......505 F13

152 GREGORY'S STREET DIRECTORY

STREETS WI

rd. Cawdor.............505 F13
rd. Mt Hunter..........504 K8
st. Beverly Hills.......401 F13
WESTBURY
rd. Grose Vale...........84 H10
st. Chipping Ntn......396 E3
WESTCHESTER
av. Casula...............395 A12
WESTCOMBE
pl. Rooty Hill...........272 B2
WESTCOTT
pl. Oakhurst............241 J1
st. Eastlakes............405 J5
WEST CRESCENT
st. McMahons Pt........5 D15
WESTELLA
av. Roselands..........401 B7
WEST END
la. Ultimo.................12 H14
WESTERLY
wy. Glenmore Pk......266 F13
WESTERN
av. Blaxland.............234 A5
av. Camperdown.......18 B5
av. North Manly.......258 C16
cr. Blacktown..........274 D5
cr. Gladesville.........312 G10
cr. Gladesville.........312 H8
cr. Westleigh...........220 H1
mwy.Auburn............309 C12
mwy.Blacktown.........273 C14
mwy.Clarmnt Ms.......269 B7
mwy.Eastern Ck........272 C11
mwy.Emu Plains.......235 A12
mwy.Glenbrook.........234 H15
mwy.Granville...........308 C8
mwy.Greystanes.......306 E3
mwy.Harris Park.......308 C8
mwy.Homebush.........341 A7
mwy.Homebush B......340 A1
mwy.Homebush W.....340 A1
mwy.Huntingwd........273 C14
mwy.Jamisontown.....265 G1
mwy.Lapstone..........234 H15
mwy.Leonay............234 H15
mwy.Lidcombe.........340 A1
mwy.Mays Hill..........307 B4
mwy.Merrylands.......307 B4
mwy.Minchinbury.....271 C10
mwy.N Strathfield.....341 A7
mwy.Orchard Hills.....267 D8
mwy.Parramatta........308 C8
mwy.Prospect...........275 B16
mwy.St Clair............270 A8
mwy.Silverwater........309 C12
mwy.S Penrith..........266 D6
mwy.S Wntwthvle......307 B4
rd. Castle Hill...........218 H13
rd. Kemps Ck...........359 K13
rd. Mcquarie Pk.......282 C1
wy. Chatswood W....284 G10
WESTERN DISTRIBUTOR
Pyrmont.............12 E5
Sydney.................A C16
Sydney.................1 D16
Sydney.................3 D6
WESTFIELD
dr. Eastgardens.......406 F11
pl. Blacktown, off Flushcombe Rd..244 G16
st. Earlwood...........402 E3
WESTHALL
wy. Claymore...........481 B10
WEST HEAD
rd. Krngai Ch N P....167 E13
rd. Terrey Hills.........196 G4
WEST HILL
pl. Green Valley.......362 J11
st. McGraths Hl.......121 K11
WESTLAKE
pl. Balgowlah..........287 G7
WESTLAND
cl. Raby..................451 G13
WESTLEIGH
dr. Westleigh...........220 D6
la. Neutral Bay............6 F4
st. Neutral Bay............6 F5
WEST LINK
rd. Eveleigh...............18 G12
WEST MARKET
st. Richmond..........118 F5
WESTMEATH
av. Killarney Ht........286 D1
WESTMINSTER
av. Carlingford.........279 D5
av. Dee Why............258 H4

dr. Castle Hill...........218 K10
dr. Castle Hill...........219 A12
rd. Gladesville.........312 J6
st. Bexley................402 J11
st. Rooty Hill...........242 A16
st. Schofields..........183 C13
wy. Rsemeadow.......540 J2
WESTMONT
dr. S Penrith............267 B1
WESTMOOR
gr. Wrrngtn Dns......238 A5
WESTMORE
dr. W Pnnant Hl.......249 C11
WESTMORELAND
av. Collaroy.............259 A1
la. Glebe...................12 B14
rd. Leumeah............482 F9
rd. Minto.................482 F9
st. Glebe...................12 B15
WESTON
av. Narwee..............400 H11
la. Rooty Hill...........242 C16
pl. West Hoxton......392 A10
rd. Hurstville...........431 K1
st. Balmain East..........8 H9
st. Dulwich Hill........373 D7
st. Fairfield.............336 G13
st. Harris Park.........308 F6
st. Panania.............428 C1
st. Revesby.............428 E1
st. Rosehill.............308 F6
WEST PORTLAND
rd. Sackville..............67 K5
WESTRINGIA
pl. Gymea Bay.........491 J10
pl. Mcquarie Fd.......454 D3
WESTVILLE
pl. Westmead.........307 E2
WESTWARD
av. Shalvey..............210 J12
st. Kareela..............461 C11
WEST WILCHARD
rd. Castlereagh........176 A7
WESTWOOD
av. Belmore.............401 H2
st. Bossley Park......334 D10
st. Pennant Hills......220 G13
st. Prairiewood........334 D10
wy. Bella Vista.........246 D2
WETHERILL
cr. Bligh Park..........150 B5
st. Croydon.............372 E2
st. Croydon.............372 E3
st. Leichhardt............10 A16
st. Narrabeen..........229 A9
st. Smithfield...........335 A6
st. Wetherill Pk.......335 A6
st.n, Silverwater.......309 J15
st.s, Lidcombe..........309 J16
WETSTONE
wy. Dural.................219 C6
WEWAK
pl. Allambie Ht........257 F13
pl. Bossley Park......333 K5
rd. Holsworthy........396 C16
WEXFORD
gr. Kellyville Rdg.....185 C16
pl. Killarney Ht........255 K13
WEYLAND
st. Punchbowl.........399 J7
WEYMOUTH
av. Auburn..............338 J9
WEYNTON
la. Annandale............11 A7
mw. Bella Vista.........246 G5
st. Annandale............11 B8
WHADDON
av. Dee Why............258 E6
WHALAN
pl. Gymea...............491 G1
pl. Whalan..............240 K10
rd. E Kurrajong..........66 E7
WHALANS
rd. Greystanes.........305 G8
WHALE
pl. Woodbine...........481 K9
WHALE BEACH
rd. Avalon...............140 D12
rd. Palm Beach........140 B2
rd. Whale Beach......140 B7
WHALING
rd. N Sydney...............5 K9
WHARF
rd. Birchgrove.............7 K2
rd. Cremorne Pt, off Cremorne Rd......316 G15

rd. Ermington..........280 H15
rd. Gladesville.........312 H13
rd. Kogarah Bay......432 J14
rd. Lansvale............367 A10
rd. Lilyfield................10 A4
rd. Longueville........314 B9
rd. Melrose Pk.........280 H15
rd. Vaucluse............318 F16
st. Brooklyn..............75 F11
st. Marrickville........403 E1
st. Pyrmont.................8 J15
WHARF HOUSE STEPS
The Rocks.............B B1
WHATELEY
la. Newtown.............17 H11
st. Newtown.............17 J11
WHATMORE
la. Waverton, off Bay Rd...............315 E12
st. Waverton...........315 D12
WHEAT
pl. Horngsea Pk......392 E15
rd. Sydney..................C A11
rd. Sydney..................3 C6
WHEATLEIGH
st. Crows Nest........315 G4
st. Naremburn........315 G4
WHEATLEY
pl. Harringtn Pk.......478 G7
rd. Hawksbry Ht......174 E7
rd. Yarrawarrah.......489 E15
st. St Johns Pk.......364 J2
WHEEDON
st. Glenwood..........215 H14
WHEELER
av. Camden S..........507 C16
av. Lurnea..............394 C10
la. N Sydney...............K A6
la. Surry Hills, off Brumby St............19 H3
pde. Dee Why...........258 K8
pl. Minto.................453 B16
st. Carlton...............432 K8
st. Lalor Park...........245 C13
st. Narrabeen..........228 F9
WHEENY CREEK
rd. Cattai...................69 A11
WHELAN
av. Chipping Ntn......396 A5
av. Rookwood.........340 E14
la. Paddington..........21 G3
WHELLER
st. Bossley Park......334 D8
WHERRITT
cl. Picton................563 F10
WHIBLEY
av. Glenwood..........215 J13
WHIDDON
cl. Denham Ct.........422 C8
WHIMBREL
av. Hinchinbrk.........393 D1
pl. Woronora Ht......489 E4
wy. Glenmore Pk......266 B13
WHIPBIRD
av. Ingleburn...........453 G9
la. St Clair, off Whipbird Pl........270 J14
pl. Castle Hill...........219 B10
pl. Erskine Park.......270 J14
pl. Green Valley.......363 E9
WHISSON
cl. Abbotsbury........333 D12
WHISTLER
av. Ingleburn...........453 F10
cr. Erskine Park.......270 K14
la. St Clair, off Whistler Cr.........271 A14
st. Green Valley.......363 E9
st. Manly.................288 G9
WHITAKER
rd. Rossmore...........389 F7
st. Old Guildford......337 C9
st. Yennora.............337 C9
WHITBAR
wy. Cherrybrook.......219 B12
WHITBECK
la. Cranebrook, off Whitbeck Pl........207 G11
pl. Cranebrook........207 F11
WHITBREAD
pl. North Rocks.......278 C7
WHITBY
rd. Kings Lngly........245 F7
wy. Bembaring...........59 K15

WHITCROFT
pl. Oxley Park.........270 D2
pl. Thornleigh.........220 K10
WHITE
av. Bankstown.........399 C4
av. Maroubra...........407 D15
la. Paddington..........13 C15
pde. St Marys...........270 A3
pl. Bossley Park......334 C5
pl. Castle Hill...........217 J13
pl. Rooty Hill...........272 D3
pl. S Windsor..........120 K16
rd. Pagewood..........406 G6
st. Artarmon...........284 H16
st. Artarmon...........284 J16
st. Balgowlah..........287 G9
st. Balmain.................7 A6
st. Brookvale...........257 K12
st. Jannali...............460 H12
st. Lilyfield................10 G12
st. Randwick...........377 A9
st. Strathfield..........341 J11
wy. Casula...............424 F3
WHITE CEDAR
dr. Castle Hill...........217 F16
WHITECHAPEL
cl. Ambarvale..........510 K16
WHITE CLIFFS
av. Hoxton Park.......392 F8
WHITE CROSS
rd. Winmalee...........173 E4
WHITEFRIARS
wy. Winston Hills......276 H1
WHITEGATES
av. Peakhurst..........430 C8
rd. Londonderry......178 B4
WHITE GUM
pl. Greystanes.........306 C4
pl. Kellyville............185 H8
WHITEHALL
rd. Kenthurst...........187 A5
st. Kellyville Rdg.....215 B2
WHITEHAVEN
av. Quakers Hill.......213 H9
pl. Castle Hill...........217 H16
rd. Northmead.........277 H6
st. St Ives...............224 F7
WHITEHEAD
ct. Glendenning.......242 F8
WHITEHEART BRIDGE
Beaumont Hills...215 E2
WHITEHORSE
st. Newtown.............17 F15
WHITELEY
cl. Casula...............424 C4
WHITELY
gr. Harringtn Pk.......478 H2
WHITEMAN
av. Bella Vista.........246 H2
la. Ellis Lane...........476 C11
WHITEMORE
av. Georges Hall......367 H11
WHITES
av. Caringbah..........492 G15
la. Darlinghurst...........4 G11
rd. Glenorie.............128 C8
rd. Shanes Park.......209 F5
WHITES CREEK
la. Annandale............16 E3
WHITESIDE
st. North Ryde.........282 E5
WHITES RIDGE
rd. Annangrove.......156 B14
WHITEWOOD
pl. Caringbah..........492 K10
WHITFIELD
av. Ashbury.............372 F7
av. Lane Cove N.......283 F12
av. Narwee..............400 K16
pde. Hurstville Gr.....431 H12
pl. Picton................563 E6
WHITFORD
rd. Green Valley.......363 E12
rd. Hinchinbrk.........393 C5
WHITING
st. Artarmon...........314 J2
st. Leichhardt.............9 E12
st. Regents Pk.........369 E1
WHITING BEACH
rd. Mosman............317 A13
WHITLAM
av. Edensor Pk........333 H13
sq. Darlinghurst..........F F3

sq. Darlinghurst...........4 A10
sq. Surry Hills..............F F3
sq. Surry Hills..............4 A10
sq. Sydney..................F F3
WHITLEY
pl. Abbotsbury........332 K14
WHITLING
av. Castle Hill...........217 K15
WHITMONT
cr. St Ives Ch..........224 B1
WHITMORE
rd. Maraylya..............94 A12
rd. Maraylya..............94 A13
WHITNEY
st. East Killara.........254 K8
st. Mona Vale..........198 H2
WHITSUNDAY
cct. Green Valley.......362 J11
WHITTAKER
st. Mortlake............312 A13
WHITTALL
st. Russell Lea........343 E7
WHITTELL
st. Surry Hills............20 C4
WHITTIER
st. Quakers Hill.......213 G16
WHITTLE
av. Balgowlah..........287 E10
av. Milperra.............397 F9
WHITTON
pl. Bligh Park..........150 H5
pl. Doonside............273 E3
rd. Chatswood W....284 G11
st. Heathcote..........518 F12
WHITWORTH
pl. Raby..................451 F16
st. Westmead.........307 F5
WHORLONG
st. St Helens Park....541 A7
WHYALLA
cl. Wakeley.............334 J13
pl. Prestons............393 H8
WIAK
rd. Jannali...............460 H10
WIANAMATTA
dr. Cartwright..........394 A5
WIBLEN
st. Silverwater.........309 J12
WICK
pl. St Andrews........481 K5
WICKFIELD
cct. Ambarvale..........511 A12
WICKHAM
la. Avalon...............170 B2
st. Arncliffe.............403 H9
WICKLOW
pl. Killarney Ht........255 K14
pl. Rouse Hill..........185 B6
st. Bidwill................211 C16
WICKS
av. Marrickville.........373 E14
la. Kogarah, off South St.............433 B4
rd. Mcquarie Pk.......282 F11
rd. North Ryde........282 F11
WIDE BAY
cct. Bidwill...............211 F14
WIDEMERE
rd. Wetherill Pk.......304 K14
WIDEVIEW
rd. Berowra Ht.........133 C7
WIDGIEWA
rd. Northbridge.......286 D14
WIGAN
rd. Dee Why............258 E3
st. Stanhpe Gdn......215 E7
WIGENS
av. Como.................460 D5
WIGGAN
pl. Cranebrook........207 C10
WIGGINS
av. Beverly Hills.......430 K1
pl. Concord.............342 B1
st. Botany...............405 J15
WIGGLES
wy. Bidwill...............211 D16
WIGGS
rd. Punchbowl.........399 J9
rd. Riverwood.........399 J9
WIGHT
st. Bnksmeadw.......406 D12

GREGORY'S STREET DIRECTORY 153

WI STREETS

WIGMORE
gr. Glendenning...242 G3
WIGNELL
pl. Mt Annan...479 G16
WIGRAM
la.e, Glebe...11 H13
la.w, Forest Lodge...11 E15
rd. Annandale...11 D15
rd. Faulconbdg...201 A2
rd. Forest Lodge...11 D15
rd. Glebe...11 D15
rd. Hinchinbrk...392 K2
st. Harris Park...308 E8
WILBAR
av. Cronulla...493 J11
WILBERFORCE
av. Rose Bay...348 B11
rd. Revesby...398 K14
rd. Revesby...399 A15
rd. Wilberforce...91 J7
st. Ashcroft...394 F2
WILBOW
pl. Bligh Park...150 H7
WILBUNG
rd. Illawong...459 F5
WILBUR
la. Greenacre...370 K13
st. Greenacre...370 E12
WILBY
st. Chipping Ntn...396 F1
WILCANNIA
wy. Hoxton Park...392 F8
wy. Mcquarie Pk...282 D3
WILCO
av. Cabramatta W...365 A7
WILCOCK
st. Carramar...366 H1
st. Regents Pk...338 K16
WILCOX
la. Marrickville, off Black St...374 F10
WILD
la. Maroubra...406 G9
st. Maroubra...406 G9
st. Picton...563 E12
WILDARA
av. W Pnnant Hl...249 G9
WILDE
av. Killarney Ht...256 B16
av. Parramatta...308 E1
pl. Wrrngtn Cty...238 J5
st. Carramar...366 J3
WILDEN
cl. Jamisontown...236 B14
WILDFLOWER
pl. Dural...219 B7
pl. Kellyville...216 G3
WILDING
st. Edensor Pk...363 G2
st. Marsfield...282 B5
WILDMAN
av. Liverpool...365 A14
WILD ORANGE
pl. Mcquarie Fd...424 F16
WILDROSE
st. Kellyville...216 H6
WILDTHORN
av. Dural...188 F1
WILDWOOD
wy. Dural...219 D6
WILES
pl. Cmbrdg Pk...238 A10
WILEY
av. Greenacre...370 F16
ct. Wrrngtn Cty...238 E8
la. Wiley Park...400 G2
pl. Guildford W...336 G1
st. Chippendale...18 K3
st. Waverley...377 G7
WILFIELD
av. Vaucluse...348 F7
WILFORD
la. Newtown...17 D13
st. Newtown...17 D13
WILFRED
av. Campsie...371 K13
av. Chatswood W...284 D10
la. Campsie...371 J13
pl. Jamisontown...266 A2
st. Lidcombe...339 D8
WILFRID
st. Mcquarie Fd...424 A15

WILGA
av. Dulwich Hill...373 E12
cl. Casula...394 G14
la. Concord W...341 E1
pl. Mcquarie Fd...454 E4
pl. Marsfield...281 K5
rd. Caringbah...492 F12
st. Blacktown...273 H4
st. Bondi...378 C5
st. Burwood...342 A13
st. Concord W...341 F1
st. Elanora Ht...197 K11
st. Fairfield...336 E15
st. Ingleside...197 K11
st. N St Marys...240 B12
st. Punchbowl...399 K5
st. Regents Pk...369 C1
st. W Pnnant Hl...249 K1
WILIMA
pl. Frenchs Frst...256 F7
WILKES
av. Artarmon...284 K15
av. Matraville...437 B2
av. Moorebank...396 D11
cr. Tregear...240 E9
WILKIE
cr. Doonside...243 C8
WILKINS
av. Beaumont Hills...215 G2
av. Beaumont Hills...215 G3
pl. Leumeah...482 J11
st. Bankstown...368 J15
st. Bardwell Vy...403 C6
st. Turrella...403 C6
st. Yagoona...368 J15
WILKINSON
av. Kings Lngly...245 B3
cr. Ingleburn...452 H10
la. Marrickville...374 C14
la. Telopea...279 F8
pl. Cranebrook...207 H10
pl. Hornsby...192 A14
rd. Bexley North...402 G10
st. Elderslie...477 F15
WILKINSON AXIS
Camperdown...18 B2
WILKSCH
la. Naremburn...315 E2
WILL
cl. Glendenning, off Vicky Pl...242 E1
WILLABURRA
rd. Woolooware...493 D13
WILLAN
dr. Cartwright...394 B4
WILLANDRA
pde. Heathcote...518 F10
rd. Beacon Hill...257 H4
rd. Cromer...258 A1
rd. Narraweena...257 H4
st. Lane Cove N...283 J14
st. Miller...393 F3
st. Ryde...311 J3
wy. Airds...512 E10
WILLARA
av. Merrylands...307 E9
WILLARONG
rd. Caringbah...492 H5
rd. Mt Colah...191 K6
rd.s, Caringbah...492 D15
WILLAROO
av. Kellyville...216 F3
av. Woronora Ht...489 B5
WILLARRA
la. Point Piper, off Wunulla Rd...347 G7
WILLAWA
av. Penrith...237 D7
la. Penrith, off Kareela Av...237 E6
st. Balgowlah Ht...287 J15
WILLEE
st. Strathfield...371 G2
WILLEROO
av. Rooty Hill...272 E4
dr. Windsor Dn...151 A16
dr. Windsor Dn...180 J3
st. Lakemba...401 A4
WILLETT
pl. Ambarvale...510 G15
st. Yagoona...368 F12
WILLFOX
st. Condell Park...398 H7

WILLIAM
av. Camden...507 A3
cl. Liberty Gr...311 B11
dr. Rookwood...340 A10
la. Alexandria...375 F13
la. Earlwood...402 D4
la. Pemulwuy...305 F6
la. Redfern...19 A9
la. Woolmloo...4 F7
la. Ryde, off William St...312 A3
pl. North Rocks...278 F4
pwy. Caringbah...492 D15
rd. Riverwood...399 K15
st. Alexandria...375 F13
st. Annandale...11 D10
st. Ashfield...372 K6
st. Avalon...140 A14
st. Balmain East...8 H10
st. Bankstown...368 K15
st. Beaconsfield...375 F13
st. Blacktown...244 B14
st. Botany...405 H11
st. Brooklyn...76 D11
st. Brookvale...258 A13
st. Cmbrdg Pk...238 B8
st. Chatswood...284 J6
st. Concord...342 B1
st. Darlinghurst...D H13
st. Double Bay...14 B7
st. Earlwood...402 G4
st. Epping...281 A1
st. Ermington...280 F14
st. Fairfield...336 E13
st. Fairlight...288 D8
st. Five Dock...342 F11
st. Granville...308 A12
st. Henley...313 B14
st. Holroyd...307 K10
st. Hornsby...221 D1
st. Kingsgrove...401 J5
st. Leichhardt...9 E11
st. Lewisham...15 B9
st. Lidcombe...339 G9
st. Lurnea...394 G7
st. Marrickville...16 B14
st. Merrylands...308 A12
st. North Manly...258 A13
st. Northmead...278 B3
st. N Parramatta...278 D11
st. N Richmond...87 D12
st. N Sydney...K B12
st. N Sydney...5 E10
st. Paddington...21 D1
st. Randwick...376 J10
st. Redfern...19 E7
st. Richmond...118 K6
st. Riverstone...152 K14
st. Riverstone...183 A1
st. Rockdale...403 H14
st. Rose Bay...348 C13
st. Roseville...284 J6
st. Ryde...312 A2
st. St Marys...269 J4
st. Schofields...182 H15
st. Seven Hills...275 H3
st. S Hurstville...431 K10
st. Strathfield S...371 C6
st. Tempe...404 C1
st. The Oaks...502 E11
st. Turramurra...222 H13
st. Wallacia...325 E16
st. Werrington...238 D10
st. Wilberforce...91 J3
st. Woolmloo...D H13
st. Woolmloo...4 B7
st. Yagoona...368 K15
st.e, Roseville...285 B5
st.s, Condell Park...398 J3
WILLIAM CAMPBELL
av. Harringtn Pk...478 D5
av. Harringtn Pk...478 F7
WILLIAM COX
dr. Richmond...118 A6
WILLIAM DEANE
cct. Blaxland, off Hope St...233 G7
WILLIAM DOWLE
pl. Grasmere...475 K13
WILLIAM EDWARD
st. Longueville...314 C9
WILLIAM FAHY
pl. Camden S...507 B9
WILLIAM HENRY
st. Ultimo...3 A11
st. Ultimo...12 H12

WILLIAM HOWE
pl. Narellan Vale...508 F2
WILLIAM HOWELL
dr. Glenmore Pk...265 K10
WILLIAM MAHONEY
st. Prestons...393 K14
WILLIAM MANNIX
av. Currans Hill...479 H9
av. Currans Hill...479 J8
WILLIAMS
av. Richmond...119 K5
cl. Hoxton Park...392 K6
la. Paddington...4 F16
pde. Campsie...371 J12
pde. Dulwich Hill...373 C9
rd. North Rocks...248 E14
WILLIAMSON
av. Seven Hills...245 J15
cr. Warwck Frm...365 E13
rd. Ingleburn...452 E8
WILLIAM THOMPSON
wy. Baulkham Hl...247 F13
WILLIAMTOWN
ct. Glenhaven...218 E6
WILLINGTON
st. Turrella...403 D6
WILLIS
av. Guildford...338 C7
av. Pennant Hills...220 H15
av. St Ives...224 E9
la. Kingsford...406 H2
pl. Winston Hills...277 F1
rd. Castle Cove...286 D7
st. Kensington...376 H16
st. Kingsford...406 H2
st. Lansvale...366 K7
st. Oakdale...500 D11
st. Rooty Hill...272 A6
st. Wolli Creek...403 H6
WILLISON
rd. Carlton...432 G3
WILLMOT
av. Toongabbie...276 F7
st. Bossley Park...334 C10
WILLMOTT
av. Winston Hills...277 H2
pl. Glenmore Pk...265 E9
rd. E Kurrajong...65 J8
WILLOCK
av. Miranda...492 A3
WILLORING
cr. Jamisontown...236 B15
la. Jamisontown, off Willoring Cr...236 B14
WILLOUGHBY
cct. Grasmere...475 K14
la. Crows Nest, off Falcon St...315 F6
rd. Crows Nest...315 F6
rd. Naremburn...315 F1
rd. Naremburn...315 F6
rd. St Leonards...315 F6
rd. Willoughby...285 E14
rd. Willoughby...315 F1
st. Colyton...270 G8
st. Epping...280 D2
st. Guildford...338 C6
st. Kirribilli...6 A14
wy. Rsemeadow...540 J2
WILLOW
cl. East Killara...254 G7
cl. Epping...250 D15
cl. Lansvale...366 K9
cr. Ryde...281 K13
ct. Bradbury...511 G11
dr. Baulkham Hl...248 B11
gr. Plumpton...242 A9
la. Earlwood...402 G1
pl. Bass Hill...368 C11
pl. Kirrawee...490 J5
rd. N St Marys...239 K10
st. Casula...423 K2
st. Greystanes...306 E4
st. Lugarno...429 J16
wy. Forestville...256 A13
wy. Leonay...265 B2
WILLOWBROOK
pl. Castle Hill...218 H8
pl. Sylvania...462 B11
pl. Tennyson...65 J11
WILLOWDENE
av. Luddenham...356 C5
WILLOW GLEN
rd. Kurrajong...85 A4

WILLOWGUM
cr. Cranebrook...207 D7
WILLOWIE
cl. Hornsby Ht...191 E1
rd. Castle Cove...286 A5
WILLOWLEAF
cl. Glenwood...245 D1
pl. W Pnnant Hl...248 H5
WILLOW TREE
av. Emu Plains...235 K8
cr. Belrose...226 B14
WILLOWTREE
av. Glenwood...215 B15
st. Normanhurst...221 E12
WILLS
av. Castle Hill...218 C16
av. Chifley...437 A6
av. Waverley...377 G10
cr. Daceyville...406 F4
gln. St Clair...270 E11
pl. Camden S...507 A11
pl. Guildford...337 J4
rd. Long Point...454 E7
rd. Mcquarie Fd...454 E7
rd. Woolooware...493 G10
rd. Woolooware...493 G9
st. Lalor Park...245 B12
WILLUNGA
av. Earlwood...402 D6
cr. Forestville...255 G10
pl. W Pnnant Hl...249 A1
rd. Berowra...133 G11
WILLYAMA
av. Fairlight...288 A9
la. Fairlight...288 A9
st. Dharruk...241 C7
WILMA
pl. Hassall Gr...211 K14
WILMAR
av. Berala...339 D15
WILMETTE
pl. Mona Vale...199 D2
WILMOT
st. Sydney...C H16
st. Sydney...3 G8
WILMOTT
ct. Camden S...537 B1
WILONA
av. Greenwich...315 B8
av. Lavender Bay...K D13
av. Lavender Bay...5 F11
WILSHIRE
av. Carlingford...249 D12
av. Cronulla...523 J1
rd. Agnes Banks...147 B2
rd. Londonderry...147 B2
st. Surry Hills...20 B5
WILSON
av. Beaumont Hills...215 J2
av. Belmore...401 E3
av. Ingleside...197 K10
av. Regents Pk...339 C16
av. Baulkham Hl...247 H16
cr. Narellan...478 C11
gr. Thirlmere...565 C5
la. Belmore...401 E3
la. Darlington...18 E9
la. Jamisontown...235 K13
la. Longueville...314 E9
la. Newtown...18 B10
la. Padstow Ht...429 F6
pde. Heathcote...518 G13
pde. Royal N P...518 G13
pl. Bonnet Bay...460 A9
pl. Ruse...512 F6
pl. St Marys...269 D4
rd. Acacia Gdn...214 F15
rd. Acacia Gdn...215 A16
rd. Bonnyrigg Ht...363 C10
rd. Green Valley...363 C10
rd. Hinchinbrk...393 B4
rd. Pennant Hills...250 D1
rd. Quakers Hill...214 F15
st. Botany...405 J15
st. Cammeray...316 A4
st. Chatswood...284 H8
st. Darlington...18 E9
st. Eveleigh...18 E9
st. Harbord...258 E16
st. Kogarah...433 D8
st. Maroubra...407 K9
st. Narwee...400 F15
st. Newtown...17 G12
st. Newtown...17 H11
st. North Ryde...282 D7
st. Panania...398 B16

154 GREGORY'S STREET DIRECTORY

STREETS

WO

st. St Marys	269	D4
st. Strathfield	340	J16
st. Woolmloo	4	F3
wy. Blaxland	233	G4
wy. Blaxland	233	H7

WILSONS
rd. Arncliffe 403 B9

WILSONS RD LOWER
Bardwell Vy.....403 A8

WILSONS RD UPPER
Bardwell Vy.....403 B9

WILTON
cl. Castle Hill.....217 K16
cl. Gordon.....253 G4
pl. Georges Hall.....367 G9
rd. Appin.....569 B16
rd. Cherrybrook, off
Doonside.....243 B9
rd. Wilton.....568 K16
st. Narellan.....478 F12
st. Surry Hills.....19 J5
st. Wilton.....568 K16
wy. Bonnyrigg.....363 K5

WILTONA
cl. Girraween.....275 K10

WILTSHIRE
cl. Liberty Gr.....311 B11
ct. Cherrybrook, off
Glamorgan Wy.....219 E9
pl. Turramurra.....222 J8
pl. The Slopes.....64 K11
st. Miller.....393 H13
st. Minto.....482 E3

WIMBLEDON
av. N Narrabeen.....228 J3
ct. Wattle Grove.....426 B5

WIMBOW
pl. S Windsor.....150 E3

WINANI
cl. Belrose.....225 J13

WINBOURNE
pl. Airds.....511 K15
rd. Brookvale.....258 B10
rd. Mulgoa.....295 C16
rd. Mulgoa.....325 C2
st. West Ryde.....280 F11
st. West Ryde.....280 G13
ste, West Ryde.....280 G11

WINBURN
av. Kellyville.....376 D15

WINBURNDALE
rd. Wakeley.....334 F14

WINCHCOMBE
av. Haberfield.....343 C15
pl. Castle Hill.....218 E13

WINCHESTER
av. Lindfield.....283 J5
la. Clovelly, off
Winchester Rd.....377 J11
rd. Clovelly.....377 J12
st. Carlton.....432 J7

WINCHMORE
st. Merrylands.....307 G16

WINDAM
pl. Westleigh.....220 D8

WINDAMERE
rd. Woodcroft.....243 F10

WINDARRA
cr. Wahroonga.....221 K7
pl. Castle Hill.....217 D6
pl. Cromer.....258 B1
st. Narwee.....400 H12

WINDERMERE
av. Cmbrdg Pk.....237 J10
av. Miranda.....492 C3
av. Northmead.....278 B3
cr. Panania.....398 D14
dr. Collaroy Plat.....228 D10
rd. Epping.....250 J12

WINDERS
la. Revesby.....398 H15

WINDEYER
av. Gladesville.....313 A10
av. St Helens Park.....541 J1
av. N Parramatta.....279 A8
st. Thirlmere.....565 C2
st. Woolmloo.....4 H5

WINDHOVER
cl. Bella Vista.....246 E6
ct. Menai.....458 E15

WINDMILL
cl. Seven Hills.....275 C6
pde. Currans Hill.....479 K9

pl. Wrrngtn Dns	237	K3
st. Dawes Point	A	C1
st. Dawes Point	1	E9
st. Millers Pt	A	B1
st. Millers Pt	A	C1
st. Millers Pt	1	D9

WINDMILL STEPS
Millers Pt.....A C1

WINDORRA
av. Glenmore Pk.....266 G13

WINDRUSH
av. Belrose.....225 J11
cct. St Clair.....269 J15
la. St Clair, off
Windrush Cct.....269 K14

WINDSOR
av. Carlingford.....279 B6
av. Croydon Pk.....371 J8
ct. Castle Hill.....219 A11
dr. Mcquarie Pk.....282 D2
la. Dulwich Hill, off
Weston St.....373 E6
rd. Paddington.....13 F15
pde. N Narrabeen.....228 K2
rd. Bargo.....567 C4
rd. St Ives Ch.....223 J5
rd. Baulkham HI.....247 G9
rd. Beaumont Hills.....215 E2
rd. Box Hill.....184 C1
rd. Castle Hill.....247 E1
rd. Cecil Hills.....362 K3
rd. Cronulla.....493 J16
rd. Dulwich Hill.....373 C8
rd. Kellyville.....217 A14
rd. Kellyville Rdg.....185 A11
rd. McGraths Hl.....121 G10
rd. Merrylands.....307 G12
rd. Northmead.....277 K7
rd. Padstow.....429 D2
rd. Richmond.....119 C7
rd. Riverstone.....184 C1
rd. Rouse Hill.....184 C1
rd. Vineyard.....152 A1
rd. Willoughby.....285 J13
rd. Windsor.....121 G10
st. Mcquarie Fd.....423 K16
st. Matraville.....436 K1
st. Paddington.....13 F16
st. Paddington.....21 G1
st. Richmond.....118 J5
wy. West Pymble.....253 A12

WINDWARD
av. Mosman.....317 F9
pde. Chiswick.....343 A2

WINES
st. Emu Plains.....235 G9

WINESHOP
av. Oakdale.....500 J12

WINFORD
dr. Mulgrave.....121 K15

WING
pde. Homebush B.....310 A15
pde. Newington.....310 A15

WINGADAL
pl. Point Piper.....14 H1

WINGADEE
pl. Windsor Dn.....150 F16
st. Lane Cove N.....284 B16

WINGARA
gr. Belrose.....225 H15
st. Chester Hill.....338 A15

WINGARIE
pde. Berowra Ht.....133 C7

WINGATE
av. Eastwood.....281 A6
av. West Hoxton.....391 J11
av. Guildford W.....336 H1
rd. Mulgrave.....121 J14

WINGELLO
rd. Miranda.....492 B3
rd. Guildford.....337 F6

WINGHAM
cl. Hoxton Park.....392 H10

WINGROVE
av. Epping.....250 G12

WINIFRED
av. Caringbah.....492 F6
av. Epping.....281 C3
cr. Blacktown.....245 A16
st. Condell Park.....398 H5

WINIFRED FALLS FIRE
trl. Royal N P.....521 A11

WINJEEL
av. Richmond.....119 K3

| pl. Winkin | | |
| av. Gymea Bay | 491 | E11 |

WINKURRA
st. Kensington.....376 B10

WINNA
pl. Glenmore Pk.....266 B7

WINNALEAH
st. West Hoxton.....392 C7

WINNALL
pl. Ashcroft.....364 E14

WINNICOOPA
rd. Blaxland.....233 F4

WINNIE
st. Cremorne.....316 E7

WINNIFRED
rd. McGraths Hl.....121 K10

WINNIPEG
st. Seven Hills.....275 G6

WINNOW DOWN
la. Cobbitty.....446 A16

WINNUNGA
rd. Dural.....158 D10
rd. Lilli Pilli.....522 G3
rd. Middle Dural.....158 D10

WINPARA
cl. Tahmoor.....565 H8

WINSFORD
av. Hebersham.....241 E5

WINSLEA
av. Frenchs Frst.....257 B4

WINSLOW
av. Castle Hill.....217 C6
av. Stanhope Gdn.....215 D11
cl. Kirribilli.....6 B13
cl. Kirribilli.....2 J12
st. Connells Pt.....431 H15

WINSOME
av. N Balgowlah.....287 E6
pl. Plumpton.....241 J9

WINSPEAR
av. Bankstown.....369 C16

WINSTANLEY
pl. Mt Pritchard.....364 K9

WINSTON
av. Bass Hill.....368 C6
av. Cammeray.....316 D4
av. Earlwood.....372 G15
av. Guildford W.....336 H1
cl. Badgerys Ck.....358 D3
pl. Baulkham Hl.....248 A8
pl. Narellan Vale.....479 B11
pl. Sylvania.....462 A10
st. Asquith.....192 A11
st. Marsfield.....282 B5
st. Penrith.....236 H14

WINTAROO
cr. St Helens Park.....541 G1

WINTEN
dr. Glendenning.....242 G3

WINTER
av. Kellyville.....216 A4
av. Neutral Bay.....6 A3
pl. Blacktown.....274 J9
pl. Oatley.....431 B14
rd. Springwood.....203 B2
st. Telopea.....279 F11

WINTERCORN
row. Wrrngtn Dns.....237 J4

WINTERGREEN
pl. W Pnnantt Hl.....248 J3

WINTHINGTON
pky. Denistone.....281 C11

WINTON
av. Edensor Pk.....333 J14
av. Northmead.....248 C15
cl. Wedderburn.....540 F12
st. Appin.....569 F9
st. Warrawee.....222 G12

WIRANDA
cl. Windsor Dn.....151 A14

WIRE
la. Camden S.....507 A16
la. Cawdor.....506 E14
la. Freemns Rch.....88 K5
la. N Richmond.....88 K5

WIREGA
av. Kingsgrove.....401 G7

WIRILDA
wy. Blacktown.....274 E11

WIRRA
cl. Edensor Pk.....333 F16
st. St Ives.....224 D16
pl. Glenorie.....128 C4

| WIRRABARA | | |
| rd. Dural | 188 | H11 |

WIRRALEE
st. S Wntwthvle.....306 K7

WIRRALIE
av. Baulkham Hl.....247 A7

WIRRAWAY
pl. Doonside.....273 F4
pl. Raby.....451 D12

WIRREANDA
cl. Warrawee.....222 E13
rd. Ingleside.....197 B8
rd.n, Ingleside.....197 C6

WIRRILDA
wy. Forestville.....256 A12

WIRRINA
pl. N Narrabeen.....198 H13

WIRRINDA
rd. Mt Krng-gai.....162 H6

WIRRINGULLA
av. Elvina Bay.....168 C3

WIRRINYA
pl. Grasmere.....505 H4

WIRRUNA
st. Blacktown.....244 A10

WIRUNA
cr. Narwee.....400 K14
cr. Newport.....169 G14

WISBEACH
st. Balmain.....7 B11
st. Balmain.....7 C10

WISDOM
la. Darlinghurst.....4 E8
rd. Greenwich.....314 K5
st. Annandale.....10 J12
st. Connells Pt.....431 H15
st. Maroubra.....407 A11
st. Rozelle.....7 A12

WISEMAN
rd. Castle Hill.....247 G1

WISEMANS FERRY
rd. Cattai.....68 J16
rd. S Maroota.....69 E2

WISHART
rd. Kemps Ck.....359 E15
st. Eastwood.....281 F7

WISTARIA
pl. Baulkham Hl.....247 F15
pl. Blacktown.....245 A9
st. Dolans Bay.....492 J16

WISTERIA
cr. Glenmore Pk.....265 G10
cr. Cherrybrook.....219 K6
cr. Stanhpe Gdn.....215 C11
pl. Fairfield E.....337 A15

WISTON
gdn. Double Bay.....14 B6

WITCHHAZEL
pl. Casula.....424 A1

WITCOM
st. Cranebrook.....207 C11

WITHAM
pl. Chipping Ntn.....366 H14

WITHECOMBE
st. Rozelle, off
Belmore St.....344 E8

WITHERS
la. Kurrajong Ht.....63 G11
la. Surry Hills.....20 A2
rd. Abbotsbury.....333 B11
rd. Surry Hills.....20 B2
rd. Kellyville.....185 K11
rd. Rouse Hill.....184 J4
st. Arncliffe.....403 D11
st. Chiswick.....343 D11
wy. Claymore.....481 D12

WITHNELL
cr. St Helens Park.....541 B9

WITHYBROOK
pl. Sylvania.....462 A12

WITLEY
cl. St Marys.....269 K7

WITNEY
st. Prospect.....274 K9

WITONGA
cr. Baulkham Hl.....248 C10

| WITT | | |
| cl. Edensor Pk | 333 | J12 |

WITTAMA
dr. Glenmore Pk.....266 C7

WITTENOOM
pl. Yarrawarrah.....489 H13

WOBURN
pl. Glenmore Pk.....266 E10

WOBURN ABBEY
ct. Wattle Grove.....425 K5

WODROW
pl. Rooty Hill.....241 K13

WOIDS
av. Allawah.....432 D7
av. Carlton.....432 D7
av. Hurstville.....432 D7

WOKARI
st. Engadine.....489 C10

WOLARA
av. Glenmore Pk.....266 D8

WOLAROI
cr. Revesby.....399 B10
cr. Tamarama.....378 B7

WOLBAH
pl. Cromer.....228 A11

WOLDHUIS
st. Quakers Hill.....214 E15

WOLF
cl. St Clair.....269 H15

WOLFE
rd. East Ryde.....283 B14

WOLGER
rd. Mosman.....316 K8
rd. Ryde.....282 A14
st. Como.....460 F8

WOLI
pl. Malabar.....437 F8

WOLKA
rd. Bilpin.....60 F10

WOLLABI
cr. Glenmore Pk.....266 A11

WOLLATON
gr. Oakhurst.....241 H2

WOLLEMI
cl. Kellyville Rdg.....215 B1
ct. Wattle Grove.....426 B3
pl. Dural.....219 A4
pl. Kurrajong Ht.....63 C10

WOLLI
av. Earlwood.....402 E7
av. Earlwood.....402 D8
pl. Greenacre.....370 F9
st. Kingsgrove.....402 B10

WOLLI CREEK
pl. Arncliffe.....403 A10
pl. Banksia.....403 A10
pl. Bardwell Vy.....403 A10

WOLLOMBI
rd. Bilgola.....169 J5
rd. Northbridge.....286 F16

WOLLOMOMBI
wy. Hoxton Park.....392 H6

WOLLONDILLY
pl. Sylvania Wtr.....462 G14

WOLLONGONG
rd. Arncliffe.....403 B10

WOLLSTONECRAFT
av. Avalon.....140 B15

WOLLUN
st. Como.....460 G8

WOLLYBUTT
rd. Engadine.....488 H12

WOLSELEY
cr. Point Piper.....347 E7
cr. Zetland.....375 K9
la. Ingleburn.....453 K11
la. Coogee.....407 H3
rd. Lindfield.....254 B15
rd. McGraths Hl.....122 C11
rd. Mosman.....317 D9
rd. Oakville.....122 C11
rd. Point Piper.....14 J1
rd. S Coogee.....407 H4
st. Bexley.....433 A3
st. Drummoyne.....313 D6
st. Fairfield.....335 K15
st. Fairfield.....336 B15
st. Guildford.....338 D4
st. Haberfield.....342 K13
st. Jamisontown.....265 K2
st. Merrylands.....338 D4
st. Rooty Hill.....242 A13

GREGORY'S STREET DIRECTORY 155

WO — STREETS

WOLSLEY
av. Riverstone 183 B12
WOLSTEN
av. Turramurra 223 A10
WOLSTENHOLME
av. Greendale 385 H6
st. Gymea 491 F2
WOLUMBA
st. Chester Hill 338 B13
WOLVERTON
av. Chipping Ntn 366 E15
pwy.Chipping Ntn, off
  Wolverton Av 366 E14
WOMBAT
wy. Parklea 215 B12
WOMBERRA
pl. S Penrith 266 H3
WOMBEYAN
ct. Wattle Grove 395 H12
pl. Leumeah 482 D14
st. Forestville 255 K7
WOMBIDGEE
av. St Clair 269 H8
WOMBOYNE
av. Kellyville 216 F3
WOMERAH
av. Darlinghurst 4 J11
la. Darlinghurst 4 K10
st. Turramurra 222 K15
WOMRA
cr. Glenmore Pk 266 A11
la. Glenmore Pk, off
  Womra Cr 266 B10
WONAWONG
st. Belimbla Pk 501 F14
WONDABAH
pl. Carlingford 249 H13
WONDAKIAH
dr. Wollstncraft 315 D11
WONDERLAND
av. Tamarama 378 B6
WONGA
la. Canterbury 372 C12
pl. Ingleburn 453 F7
pl. Cremorne 316 E4
rd. Lalor Park 245 J11
rd. Lurnea 394 F8
rd. Lurnea 394 F9
rd. Miranda 491 K9
rd. Mt Colah 192 D2
rd. Picton 563 F16
rd. Yowie Bay 491 K9
st. Canterbury 372 D13
st. N Balgowlah 287 C4
st. Strathfield 371 G1
WONGAJONG
cl. Castle Hill 218 F10
WONGALA
av. Elanora Ht 198 C16
cr. Beecroft 250 F5
cr. Pennant Hills 250 F2
WONGALARA
pl. Woodcroft 243 H12
WONGALEE
av. Wahroonga 251 H1
WONGAWILLI
st. Courdijah 564 G16
WONGA WONGA
st. Turramurra 222 K12
WONIORA
av. Wahroonga 222 D6
rd. Blakehurst 432 C9
rd. Hurstville 431 J5
rd. S Hurstville 431 C9
WONNAI
pl. Clarmnt Ms 268 G1
WONOONA
pde.e,Oatley 431 C11
pde.w,Oatley 431 A11
WONSON
st. Wilton 568 K16
WOODALE
cl. Green Valley 362 J8
cl. Mt Annan 479 G14
la. Cronulla 493 K15
la. Randwick 377 C12
pl. Emu Plains 235 F13
st. Ashfield 372 J2
st. Bexley 432 G2
st. Chatswood W 284 D9
st. Eastwood 281 F3
st. Fairfield 336 C8
st. Forest Lodge 11 F15
st. Lane Cove W 313 G2

st. Manly 288 H12
st. Picton 563 E13
st. Randwick 377 C12
st. Richmond 119 K3
st. Tempe 404 C2
st. Thornleigh 221 A14
st. Waverton 315 E13
WOODBERRY
rd. Winston Hills 277 B3
WOODBINE
av. Normanhurst 221 G7
cr. Ryde 282 C15
st. N Balgowlah 287 D4
st. Yagoona 369 C10
WOODBRIDGE
pl. Bella Vista 216 C15
rd. Menangle 538 B16
WOODBROOK
gr. Glenmore Pk 265 G4
rd. Casula 395 B11
WOODBURN
ct. Panania 428 D1
ct. Glenbrook 234 B15
pl. Glenhaven 187 H15
rd. Berala 339 D12
rd. Kurrajong 85 E2
rd. Lidcombe 339 E10
st. Redfern 19 B5
WOODBURY
rd. St Ives 224 C8
st. Marrickville 373 H11
st. North Rocks 248 H16
WOODCHESTER
cl. Castle Hill 217 H8
WOODCLIFF
pde. Lugarno 430 B14
WOODCOCK
pl. Lane Cove W 283 F16
WOODCOURT
rd. Berowra Ht 133 B6
st. Ambarvale 540 F2
st. Marrickville 373 G11
WOODCREST
av. Ingleburn 453 G9
pl. Cherrybrook 219 J14
WOODCROFT
dr. Woodcroft 243 F8
WOODD
rd. Denham Ct 452 G2
WOODEND
cir. Springwood 202 E1
WOODFIELD
av. Bundeena 523 F10
bvd. Caringbah 492 K2
pl. Castle Hill 248 H2
pl. Lalor Park 245 E12
WOODFORD
ct. Jamisontown 266 C5
cr. Heathcote 519 K12
la. Lindfield 284 C1
rd. Rockdale 403 C12
st. Longueville 314 F7
WOODFULL
ct. Rouse Hill 185 A9
WOODGATE
cr. Cranebrook 207 E12
WOODGLEN
pl. Cherrybrook 219 C8
WOODGROVE
av. Castle Hill 219 B11
av. Cherrybrook 219 B11
WOODHILL
st. Castle Hill 248 B2
WOODHOUSE
dr. Ambarvale 511 A12
WOODI
cl. Glenmore Pk 266 B9
WOODLAKE
ct. Wattle Grove 395 K16
WOODLAND
av. Oxley Park 270 E2
cr. Narellan 478 J9
pl. Newington, off
  Wenden Av 310 C12
rd. Annangrove 186 B1
rd. Bradbury 541 C1
rd. Chester Hill 337 K12
rd. St Helens Park 541 C1
st. Coogee 377 G13
st. Marrickville 374 B10
st. Riverstone 153 C14
st.n,Balgowlah 287 J8
st.s,Balgowlah 287 H11
st.s,Balgowlah Ht 287 H13

WOODLANDS
av. Blakehurst 462 C4
av. Bossley Park 333 K11
av. Breakfast Pt 312 B14
av. Lugarno 430 A16
av. Narwee 400 K11
av. Pymble 253 G2
dr. Glenmore Pk 265 J13
la. Glenmore Pk, off
  Woodlands Dr 265 J13
rd. Ashbury 372 G6
rd. E Lindfield 254 J16
rd. Forestville 255 J9
rd. Liverpool 364 K16
rd. Taren Point 462 J12
rd. Wilberforce 67 H14
st. Baulkham Hl 248 A15
WOODLARK
pl. Castle Hills 219 B11
pl. Glenfield 424 F14
st. Rozelle 10 H1
WOODLAWN
av. Earlwood 402 E7
dr. Toongabbie 276 D5
WOODLEAF
cl. W Pnnant Hl 249 M15
WOODLEY
cr. Glendenning 242 F4
st. St Peters 374 K14
WOODMAN
pl. Abbotsbury 333 B16
WOODPARK
rd. Guildford W 306 E14
rd. Smithfield 305 G13
rd. Smithfield 306 E14
rd. Woodpark 306 E14
WOOD RIDGE
pl. Baulkham Hl 247 B10
WOODRIDGE
av. N Epping 251 H9
WOODRIFF
st. Penrith 236 G13
st.n, Penrith 236 J10
WOODRUSH
ct. Dural 219 C6
WOODS
av. Cabramatta 365 D9
av. Woollahra 22 C4
cl. Huntingwood 273 K12
la. Darlinghurst 4 D9
pl. N Epping 251 G8
st. Riverstone 183 B7
WOODSIDE
av. Blacktown 243 J15
av. Hurlstone Pk 373 A10
av. Kellyville 216 H5
av. Lindfield 254 D15
av. West Hoxton 392 D9
av.e,Burwood 341 J16
av.w,Strathfield 341 G15
pl. Cranebrook 207 B6
pl. Forestville 256 B8
WOODS RESERVE
rd. Grose Wold 115 A11
WOODSTOCK
av. Dharruk 241 A7
av. Glendenning 242 E12
av. Hebersham 241 E11
av. Mount Druitt 241 E11
av. Plumpton 241 E11
av. Rooty Hill 242 C12
av. Whalan 241 A7
la. Bondi Jctn, off
  Paul St 377 G3
rd. Carlingford 249 H15
rd. Bondi Jctn 377 G3
st. Botany 405 G13
st. Guildford 337 J3
st. St Johns Pk 364 F4
WOODSTREAM
cr. Kellyville 217 D4
cr. Kellyville 217 D3
WOODVALE
av. N Epping 251 G12
cl. Plumpton 241 K11
cl. St Ives 254 B2
pl. Castle Hill 218 D11

WOODVIEW
la. Oxley Park, off
  Woodview Rd 270 F2
rd. Oxley Park 270 F2
WOODVILLE
av. Wahroonga 222 E8
la. Hurstville, off
  Barratt St 432 A5
rd. Chester Hill 337 E15
rd. Fairfield E 337 E15
rd. Granville 308 A15
rd. Guildford 337 K6
rd. Merrylands 308 A15
rd. Old Guildford 337 E15
rd. Villawood 367 G3
rd. Glenbrook 233 J16
st. Hurstville 432 A5
WOODWARD
av. Caringbah 492 K11
av. Strathfield 341 E14
cr. Miller 393 J2
pl. St Ives 254 F1
rd. Hunters Hill 313 H11
st. Cromer 227 J12
st. Ermington 280 B16
st. Villawood 367 E15
WOODY
av. Morning Bay 138 E16
WOOL
pl. Miller 393 F4
WOOLCOTT
av. Wahroonga 221 K6
st. Earlwood 372 G16
st. Newport 169 G11
st. Waverton 5 A9
st. Waverton 315 E12
WOOLEY
la. Marrickville 373 H14
WOOLGEN PARK
rd. Leppington 420 G13
WOOLGOOLGA
av. Hoxton Park 392 J9
st. N Balgowlah 287 B4
WOOLISIA
pl. Baulkham Hl 247 G15
WOOLLEY
la. Glebe 11 K13
la. Glebe 12 A13
WOOLLSIA
ct. Voyager Pt 427 C6
WOOLLYBUTT
pl. Mcquarie Fd 454 E2
WOOLMERS
ct. Wattle Grove 425 H5
pl. Glen Alpine 510 D14
WOOLNOUGH
pl. Cartwright 394 B5
WOOLOOWARE
rd.n,Wooloware 493 F8
rd.s,Burraneer 493 E16
rd.s,Wooloware 493 E12
WOOLPACK
st. Elderslie 477 G16
WOOLRYCH
cr. Davidson 255 C1
WOOLSHED
pl. Currans Hill 480 A10
WOOLWASH
rd. Airds 512 A15
WOOLWICH
rd. Hunters Hill 313 K12
WOOLWONGA
pl. Bow Bowing 452 D14
WOOLWORTHS
wy. Bella Vista 246 B1
WOOLYBUTT
pl. Mt Riverview 204 E15
WOOMBA
ct. Hornsby Ht 161 H12
WOOMBYE
ct. Berowra Ht 132 K6
WOOMERA
rd. Little Bay 437 A10
WOOMERA PATH
Winmalee 173 B9
WOONAH
st. Little Bay 437 B10
st. Miranda 492 C6
WOONGARRA
wy. Glenhaven 218 D3
WOONGARRA
av. Chipping Ntn 396 B5

WOONONA
av. Wahroonga 222 C6
av.n,Wahroonga 222 C4
av.s,Wahroonga 222 C7
rd. Northbridge 286 B16
WOORAIL
av. Kingsgrove 402 C7
WOORAK
cr. Miranda 491 J1
rd. Palm Beach 139 H2
WOORANG
st. Eastwood 281 J7
st. Milperra 398 C7
WOORARRA
av. Elanora Ht 228 D1
av. N Narrabeen 228 G1
WOOTTEN
st. Colyton 270 B5
WORBOYS
pl. N St Marys 239 H15
WORCESTER
pl. Turramurra 222 J8
rd. Cmbrdg Pk 237 K11
rd. Rouse Hill 184 E6
st. Collaroy 229 B14
WORDIE
pl. Padstow 399 E10
WORDOO
st. St Marys 239 H9
WORDSWORTH
av. Concord 341 J7
av. Leumeah 512 C2
pl. Sylvania 462 B14
st. Wetherill Pk 334 K5
WORKMAN
pl. Leonay 235 D15
WORKS
pl. Milperra 397 K8
WORLAND
st. Yagoona 368 K13
WORONORA
av. Leumeah 482 B15
cr. Como 460 E5
cr. Como 460 E6
pde. Oatley 431 A12
pl. St Clair 270 B16
rd. Engadine 518 E1
WORROBIL
st. N Balgowlah 287 D6
WORSLEY
st. East Hills 427 H2
WORTH
la. Blaxland 233 E9
st. Chullora 369 K5
st. Penrith 236 F10
WORTHING
av. Castle Hill 218 A14
pl. Cherrybrook 219 K11
WORTLEY
av. Belmore 371 E16
st. Balmain 7 F12
WOYLIE
pl. St Helens Park 541 F14
WRAY
st. Fairfield Ht 336 A10
WRAYSBURY
pl. Oakhurst 241 H4
WREN
ct. Castle Hill 219 B9
ct. Woronora Ht 489 D6
pl. Clarmnt Ms 268 J4
pl. Greystanes 306 D3
pl. Lugarno 429 H13
pl. Thirlmere 565 C5
pl. Winmalee 173 A3
pl. Wooloware 493 E13
st. Condell Park 398 E1
tce. Plumpton 242 A9
WRENCH
pl. Kenthurst 157 H11
st. Cmbrdg Pk 238 A10
WRENTMORE
st. Fairfield 336 C12
WRIDE
st. Maroubra 407 F10
WRIGHT
st. Georges Hall 367 F14
st. Heathcote 518 D15
la. Surry Hills F13
av. Bligh Park 150 H7
pl. Narellan Vale 479 A16
st. Blacktown 244 A9

156 GREGORY'S STREET DIRECTORY

STREETS YA

st. Croydon ... 342 E15
st. Fairfield W ... 335 B12
st. Glenbrook ... 263 K3
st. Hurstville ... 432 B3
st. Merrylands ... 307 C9
st. Merrylands ... 308 C16
st. Sydenham, off Gleeson Av ... 374 D15

WRIGHTLAND
pl. Arndell Park ... 273 D7

WRIGHTS
av. Berala ... 339 B14
av. Marrickville ... 373 G14
rd. Castle Hill ... 217 A6
rd. Drummoyne ... 343 J1
rd. Kellyville ... 216 G8

WRIGHTSON
wy. Douglas Park ... 568 E2

WROXHAM
st. Prestons ... 393 C16

WUDGONG
st. Mosman ... 316 K6
wk. Mosman, off Cowles Rd ... 316 K6

WULUMAY
cl. Rozelle ... 344 D6

WULWORRA
av. Cremorne Pt ... 316 G15

WUNDA
rd. Concord W ... 311 D16
rd. Mosman ... 316 K8

WUNULLA
rd. Point Piper ... 14 K3
rd. Point Piper ... 347 F9
rd. Rose Bay ... 347 F9

WURLEY
av. Kingsford ... 406 E2

WURUMA
pl. Warriewood ... 199 A7

WYADRA
av. Harbord ... 258 F14
av. North Manly ... 258 C14

WYAGDON
st. Neutral Bay ... 6 A1

WYALONG
cl. Wakeley ... 334 G15
st. Burwood ... 342 B15
st. Panania ... 398 D15
st. Willoughby ... 285 D15

WYANBAH
rd. Cronulla ... 493 K9

WYANDOTTE
pl. Seven Hills ... 275 F6

WYANG
gln. Cranebrook ... 207 A6
pl. Engadine ... 489 B11

WYANGA
la. Beverly Hills, off Tooronga Tce ... 401 C13
rd. Elanora Ht ... 198 F14

WYANGALA
cct. Woodcroft ... 243 J10
cr. Leumeah ... 482 E14
cr. Leumeah ... 482 G10
pl. Miranda ... 491 H7

WYANNA
gr. Yennora ... 337 A8
st. Berowra Ht ... 132 J11

WYARAMA
st. Allambie Ht ... 257 D8

WYARGINE
st. Mosman ... 317 D4

WYATT
av. Belrose ... 225 H10
av. Burwood ... 372 A1
av. Earlwood ... 402 C6
av. Padstow ... 429 D5
av. Regents Pk ... 369 C1
cl. Wetherill Pk ... 335 A7
la. Burwood ... 371 K1
pde. Narwee ... 400 J13
pl. Doonside ... 243 C6
pl. Greystanes ... 306 E13
pl. Leumeah ... 482 D16

WYATTVILLE
dr. West Hoxton ... 392 C11
dr. West Hoxton ... 392 B12

WYBALENA
pl. Jannali ... 460 G9
rd. Hunters Hill ... 314 A13

WYBORN
la. Merrylands ... 306 K10

WYBURN
av. Carlingford ... 249 G16

WYCH
av. Lurnea ... 394 D7

WYCHBURY
av. Croydon ... 342 E11
la. Croydon ... 342 E11

WYCHWOOD
pl. Castle Hill ... 217 J9

WYCOMBE
av. Btn-le-Sds ... 433 J5
av. Monterey ... 433 J5
la. Neutral Bay ... 6 F9
rd. Neutral Bay ... 6 G5
rd. Neutral Bay ... 6 G9
st. Birrong ... 368 G10
st. Doonside ... 243 B10
st. Epping ... 250 G12
st. Yagoona ... 368 G10

WYE
cl. St Clair ... 299 H2
st. Blacktown ... 274 H9
st. Prospect ... 274 H9

WYEE
pl. Greystanes ... 305 H10
pl. Malabar ... 437 E8
st. Kogarah Bay ... 432 J13

WYEENA
cl. N Wahroonga ... 222 K2

WYENA
rd. Pendle Hill ... 276 C16

WYHARBOROUGH
pl. Canley Ht ... 335 B16
pl. Canley Ht ... 365 B1

WYLAH
pl. Woronora Ht ... 489 E2

WYLDE
cr. Abbotsbury ... 333 C16
st. Potts Point ... 2 K15
st. Potts Point ... 4 K1
st. Telopea ... 279 F9

WYLDS
rd. Arcadia ... 128 J14
rd. Arcadia ... 129 A15
rd. Glenorie ... 128 J14
rd. Middle Dural ... 128 J14

WYLDWOOD
cr. Baulkham Hl ... 247 J6

WYLEENA
pl. Punchbowl ... 399 K6

WYLIE
st. Kirrawee ... 490 J1

WYLLIE
pl. Cherrybrook ... 219 F6

WYLMAR
av. Burraneer ... 493 F14

WYMAH
cr. Berowra Ht ... 132 H8

WYMARKS
la. Ebenezer ... 68 B9

WYMSTON
la. Wareemba, off Hill St ... 342 K6
pde. Abbotsford ... 342 J4
pde. Five Dock ... 342 J4
pde. Five Dock ... 342 J7
pde. Wareemba ... 342 J4

WYNDARRA
pl. Northwood ... 314 G7

WYNDHAM
av. Leumeah ... 482 F10
av. Mt Wilson ... 58 G8
la. Alexandria ... 19 B13
pl. Baulkham Hl ... 247 C8
st. Alexandria ... 19 A11

WYNDORA
av. Harbord ... 258 D15

WYNGATE
cr. Forestville ... 256 B10

WYNN
cl. Edensor Pk ... 333 F16
st. Eschol Park ... 481 C6

WYNNE
av. Burwood ... 341 K14

WYNNES ROCKS
rd. Mt Wilson ... 58 H10

WYNNSTAY
av. Enfield ... 371 G4

WYNWARD
pl. Barden Rdg ... 488 G2

WYNYARD
av. Bass Hill ... 367 K8
av. Rossmore ... 389 D9
la. Sydney ... A H16
st. Guildford ... 338 A4
st. Sydney ... C G1
st. Sydney ... 3 G1

WYOMEE
av. West Pymble ... 252 H8

WYOMING
av. Oatlands ... 278 J9
av. Valley Ht ... 202 G5
pl. Riverwood ... 400 A12
rd. Dural ... 188 E1

WYONG
rd. Cremorne ... 316 H3
rd. Duffys Frst ... 194 H6
rd. Mosman ... 316 H3
st. Canley Ht ... 365 E4
st. Oatley ... 431 B16

WYPERFELD
pl. Bow Bowing ... 452 C16

WYRALLA
av. Epping ... 280 G2
rd. Miranda ... 491 H6
rd. Yowie Bay ... 492 A8

WYREEMA
av. Padstow ... 399 A16
st. Merrylands ... 307 A11

WYUNA
av. Harbord ... 258 E15
cr. Padstow ... 429 G2
pl. Oatlands ... 279 D13
rd. Point Piper ... 347 E8
rd. West Pymble ... 253 B15
st. Beverley Pk ... 432 J10

WYVERN
av. Chatswood W ... 284 G7
av. Roseville ... 284 G7
st. Epping ... 250 J15

X

XENIA
av. Carlton ... 432 E5

Y

YABSLEY
av. Ashbury ... 372 F6
av. Marrickville ... 373 K11

YACHTSMAN
dr. Chipping Ntn ... 366 J15

YACHTSMANS PARADISE
Newport ... 169 F16

YACHTVIEW
av. Newport ... 169 D9

YAGOONA
cl. Bangor ... 459 F13
la. Yagoona ... 369 A12

YAKIMA
av. Bossley Park ... 333 K10

YALA
rd. Bangor ... 459 E13

YALANGA
pl. Riverview ... 314 B5

YALDING
av. Carlingford ... 249 C16
av. North Rocks ... 249 C16

YALE
cl. North Rocks ... 249 A13
pl. Blacktown ... 274 K6
st. Epping ... 250 H15

YALGAR
rd. Kirrawee ... 461 A16

YALKIN
rd. Oakhurst ... 242 D2

YALLAH
st. Belimbla Pk ... 501 D12

YALLAMBEE
ct. Baulkham Hl ... 246 G8
pl. Terrey Hills ... 196 D7
rd. Berowra ... 133 A16
rd. Riverview ... 314 C5

YALLAMBI
st. Picton ... 561 D3

YALLARA
st. St Helens Park ... 541 G2

YALLAROI
pde. Dangar I ... 76 J6
rd. Narraweena ... 258 B2

YALLEROI
av. West Pymble ... 252 K9

YALLOCK
pl. Prospect ... 274 E15

YALLUM
ct. Wattle Grove ... 425 H5

YALLUMBA
cl. Forestville ... 255 K8

YALTA
st. Sadleir ... 364 C15

YALUMBA
pl. Edensor Pk ... 363 E1

YALUNGA
pl. St Ives ... 224 B15

YALWAL
ct. Prestons ... 392 H13

YAMBA
cl. Marsfield ... 281 J4
la. Blacktown ... 274 J1
pl. Bossley Park ... 333 G10
pl. S Coogee ... 407 F4
rd. Bellevue Hill ... 14 H12
rd. Como ... 460 G7
st. N Balgowlah ... 287 C5

YAMMA
st. Sefton ... 368 G1

YAMPI
pl. Cartwright ... 394 A5
st. Leumeah ... 482 F10

YANAGANG
st. Waterfall ... 519 C13

YANAGIN
pl. W Pnnant Hl ... 249 A1

YANCANNIA
tce. Glenwood ... 215 E16

YANCHEP
pl. Yarrawarrah ... 489 G13

YANCO
av. Jamisontown ... 236 A15
cl. Frenchs Frst ... 255 K4
gln. Glenwood ... 215 F15
st. Merrylands ... 306 J10

YANDA
pl. Greystanes ... 306 A5

YANDARLO
st. Croydon Pk ... 371 H8

YANDEL'ORA
cct. Mt Annan ... 509 H5

YANDERRA
av. Bangor ... 459 E13
cl. Hamondvle ... 396 H14
gr. Cherrybrook ... 219 J11
rd. Bargo ... 567 B15
rd. Duffys Frst ... 195 D1
rd. Yanderra ... 567 B15
st. Condell Park ... 398 D5

YANDIAH
pl. Castle Hill ... 218 C9

YANDINA
av. Winmalee ... 172 J11

YANGALLA
st. Marsfield ... 281 H1

YANGOORA
cl. Bangor ... 459 F13
rd. Belmore ... 371 A14
rd. Lakemba ... 370 K14

YANGTZE
pl. Kearns ... 480 K2
pl. Kearns ... 481 A2

YANILLA
av. Wahroonga ... 251 G2

YANINA
pl. Bangor ... 459 E13
pl. Frenchs Frst ... 256 A1

YANKO
av. Bronte ... 377 J9
cl. Woronora ... 459 K16
rd. West Pymble ... 252 H10
rd. West Pymble ... 253 A13

YANNINA
av. Hornsby Ht ... 191 H5

YANTARA
pl. Woodcroft ... 243 J8

YARA
av. Rozelle ... 344 D6
cl. Bangor ... 459 G14

YARAAN
av. Epping ... 281 A3

YARABAH
av. Gordon ... 253 H9

YARALLA
cr. Thornleigh ... 221 B8
la. Newtown ... 18 A9
pl. Baulkham Hl ... 246 K6
pl. Engadine ... 489 C11
rd. Putney ... 311 J8
st. Concord ... 341 E2
st. Concord W ... 341 E2
st. Newtown ... 18 A9

YARALLAH
pl. Beverly Hills ... 401 C13

YARBON
st. Wentwthvle ... 276 K13

YARDLEY
av. Narwee ... 400 F14
av. Riverwood ... 400 F14
av. Waitara ... 221 J5

YARENBOOL
wy. Bangor, off Yangoora Cl ... 459 F13

YARGO
rd. Winston Hills ... 277 A2

YARINGA
rd. Castle Hill ... 218 A8

YARLUKE
rd. Blaxlands Rdg ... 65 B3

YARMOUTH
pl. Smeaton Gra ... 479 B9

YARPOLE
av. W Pnnant Hl ... 218 K16

YARRA
cl. Kearns ... 481 B1
pl. Glenmore Pk ... 266 A12
pl. Prestons ... 392 K15
pl. St Johns Pk ... 364 F4
rd. Phillip Bay ... 436 J11
st. N St Marys ... 239 J9

YARRABEE
av. Bangor ... 459 F13
pl. Bilgola ... 169 E4
pl. Colyton ... 270 G8
rd. Baulkham Hl ... 277 J3

YARRABIN
cr. Berowra ... 133 C13
rd. Kenthurst ... 187 F8
st. Belrose ... 225 J15

YARRABUNG
av. Thornleigh ... 221 A8
rd. St Ives ... 224 C16
rd. St Ives ... 224 D14

YARRABURN
av. W Pnnant Hl ... 249 A2

YARRA BURRA
st. Gymea Bay ... 491 C11

YARRAGA
pl. Yowie Bay ... 492 C9

YARRALUMLA
av. St Ives Ch ... 194 A16
dr. Carlingford ... 279 A4

YARRAM
st. Lidcombe ... 339 H5

YARRAMAN
av. Frenchs Frst ... 256 F9
cl. Quakers Hill ... 213 K8
rd. Grose Wold ... 116 C8

YARRAMUNDI
dr. Dean Park ... 212 G16
la. Agnes Banks ... 117 C6
la. Richmond ... 117 C6
rd. Richmond ... 118 F11

YARRAN
cl. Mona Vale ... 169 D16
ct. Wattle Grove ... 426 B1
pl. Mcquarie Fd ... 454 D3
rd. Bargo ... 567 C1
rd. Oatley ... 431 A16
st. Punchbowl ... 400 A4
st. Pymble ... 253 C8

YARRANABBE
rd. Darling Point ... 13 J1
rd. Darling Point ... 13 J4

GREGORY'S STREET DIRECTORY 157

YA STREETS

YARRANDALE
st. Stanhpe Gdn 215 B7
YARRANDI
pl. Longueville 314 F7
YARRANGOBILLY
st. Heckenberg......363 K11
YARRARA
la. Pymble 252 J8
la. West Pymble......252 J8
rd. Pennant Hills 220 H15
rd. Pymble 253 A7
rd. Terrey Hills 195 J14
rd. Thornleigh 220 H15
rd. West Pymble......252 J10
YARRA VISTA
ct. Yarrawarrah 489 G14
YARRAWA
st. Prestons 393 B9
YARRAWIN
wy. Airds......512 D10
YARRAWONGA
cl. Pymble 253 H3
st. S Windsor 120 E16
YARREN
av. Btn-le-Sds......403 K16
YARRENNAN
av. West Pymble......253 A10
YARROWEE
rd. Strathfield 370 K1
YARRUNGA
st. Prestons 393 A10
YARWOOD
la. Woollahra, off
    Fletcher St......377 G2
rd. Bligh Park 150 H5
st. Marsfield......281 K1
YASMAR
av. Haberfield 343 C15
YASS
cl. Bossley Park 333 E11
cl. Frenchs Frst 255 K4
cl. Prestons 392 K16
pl. Quakers Hill 244 B2
YATALA
rd. Mt Krng-gai......162 J6
YATAMA
st. Seaforth......287 C7
YATAY
cl. Plumpton 242 D5
YATE
av. Mt Riverview 204 E14
cl. Kingswood......267 J4
pl. Mcquarie Fd......454 E3
la. Marayong 243 J6
pl. Narellan Vale 478 K15
YATES
av. Dundas Vy 280 A9
cr. Padstow 429 F4
rd. Bangor 459 H13
YATHONG
rd.n,Caringbah 493 A7
rd.s,Caringbah 493 A16
YATTENDEN
cr. Baulkham Hl 247 H12
YAWL
pl. Seven Hills 275 B5
YAWUNG
av. Baulkham Hl 246 H8
st. Dundas 279 G13
YEATS
av. Killarney Ht 256 D16
st. Wetherill Pk 334 K4
YEELANNA
pl. Kingswood......267 G2
YEEND
st. Birchgrove......8 A4
st. Merrylands......307 G9
YELL
pl. St Andrews 481 J5
YELLAMBIE
st. Yowie Bay 492 A13
YELLOW
pl. Clarmnt Ms......238 G15
YELLOW GUM
cl. Glenmore Pk......265 F11
YELLOWGUM
av. Rouse Hill 185 A6
gr. Glenwood 215 H16
YELLOW ROCK
rd. Yellow Rock......204 G2
YELVERTON
st. Sydenham 374 E15

YENDA
av. Queens Park 22 J13
YENGO
ct. Holsworthy 426 E5
YENNA
pl. Glenmore Pk......266 B7
YENNORA
av. Yennora 337 A9
st. Campbelltown......511 K6
YEO
av. Ashfield 372 K7
la. Bexley......402 H13
la. Neutral Bay 6 F1
pl. Menai 459 A12
st. Cremorne 6 D1
st. Neutral Bay 6 D1
st. Yagoona 368 J9
YEOMANS
rd. N Richmond......86 H7
YERAMBA
av. Caringbah 493 A15
cr. Berowra 133 C14
pl. Rydalmere 279 E15
st. Turramurra 252 D3
YERAN
st. Sylvania......462 C9
YERANDA
pl. Kenthurst......187 K8
YEREVAN
pl. Belrose 226 A12
YERONA
st. Prestons 423 B1
YERONG
pl. Castle Hill 218 B8
st. Ryde......311 H3
YERONGA
cl. St Johns Pk 364 F1
YERRAWAR
pl. Springwood 201 H4
YERRICK
rd. Lakemba......371 A13
rd. Lakemba......371 A14
YERRIEBAH
pl. Rouse Hill 185 C5
YERRINBOOL
cl. Prestons 392 K12
YERROULBIN
st. Birchgrove 314 K16
YERTON
av. Hunters Hill 313 J12
YETHOLME
av. Baulkham Hl 246 K9
YETHONGA
av. Lane Cove W 313 J1
YEW
pl. Casula......424 A2
pl. Quakers Hill 214 E13
YILKI
cl. Cranebrook 207 E8
YILLOWRA
st. Auburn 309 C15
YIMBALA
st. Rydalmere 279 J15
YINDELA
st. Davidson 255 F3
YINDI
pl. Doonside 243 G14
YINNELL
pl. Castle Hill 218 C8
YIRAK
la. Como 460 G4
YIREMBA
pl. Forestville 255 F10
YIRGELLA
av. East Killara 254 G10
YIRRA
rd. Mt Colah 192 A5
YODALLA
av. Emu Plains......235 G11
la. Emu Plains, off
    Yodalla Av......235 G11
YONDELL
av. Springwood 201 G9
YOOGALI
st. Merrylands 306 J10
tce. Blaxland 234 D7
YOORAMI
rd. Beverly Hills 401 D12
YOORANA
pl. Castle Hill 219 A8

YORK
av. Five Dock 342 J11
cl. Yowie Bay 492 B12
cr. Petersham 16 A9
la. Glebe 11 J13
la. Queens Park 22 C10
la. Sydney ......A F15
la. Sydney 3 F1
pl. Bondi Jctn 22 C7
pl. Kensington 376 C11
pl. Rozelle......344 E6
rd. Bondi Jctn 22 C8
rd. Ingleburn 453 A4
rd. Jamisontown 236 F16
rd. Kellyville......216 G2
rd. Kellyville......216 J6
rd. Queens Park 22 C10
rd. Riverstone 82 D10
rd. S Penrith......266 E4
st. Beecroft 250 D6
st. Belmore 401 D2
st. Berala 339 B13
st. Casula......424 A3
st. Condell Park......398 K1
st. Emu Plains......235 K9
st. Epping 251 E12
st. Fairfield 336 D14
st. Gladesville 312 G11
st. Glebe 11 J14
st. Glenbrook 234 B14
st. Kingsgrove......401 K9
st. Marrickville 374 C9
st. Merrylands 307 H15
st. Oatlands 279 B9
st. Rockdale......403 E14
st. Sydney......A F12
st. Sydney 1 F15
st. Tahmoor 565 J13
tce. Bilgola 169 G8
YORKSHIRE
ct. Catherine Fd......449 G1
YORKTOWN
pde. Maroubra 407 C12
YORLIN
pl. Rouse Hill 185 C5
YORREL
cl. Alfords Point......429 A15
YOSEFA
av. Warrawee 222 F11
YOUL
pl. Bligh Park 150 E5
YOUNG
av. Camden S......537 C2
cr. Frenchs Frst 256 B3
la. Annandale......16 G3
la. Cremorne......316 D8
la. Neutral Bay 316 D8
la. Redfern......19 J9
st. Redfern......19 K9
pde. Eastwood......281 C9
pl. Eagle Vale 481 A10
pl. S Hurstville 431 K11
rd. Carlingford......279 K1
st. Annandale 16 F4
st. Balmain 7 B7
st. Chatswood 284 J12
st. Colyton 270 J8
st. Cremorne......316 D6
st. Cremorne......316 D8
st. Croydon......342 E15
st. Kings Lngly 245 E8
st. Mt Krng-gai......163 C11
st. Mt Pritchard......364 E9
st. Neutral Bay 6 G1
st. Neutral Bay 316 D8
st. N Strathfield......341 G9
st. Paddington 13 A16
st. Parramatta......307 J8
st. Penshurst......431 C1
st. Randwick......406 K1
st. Redfern......19 J10
st. Sydney......B D12
st. Sydney 1 K14
st. Sylvania 461 H10
st. Tempe......404 B3
st. Vaucluse 348 F5
st. Wahroonga......222 H9
st. Warrawee 222 H9
st. Waterloo 19 H15
st. N Strathfield, off
    Parramatta Rd......341 F9
YOUNGER
av. Earlwood 372 K15
YOUTH
la. Burwood, off
    Deane St......342 A14

YOWAN
cl. Bangor 459 G13
YOWIE
av. Caringbah 492 F12
YPRES
rd. Moorebank 395 E12
YUGILBAR
av. Villawood......367 D3
YUKKA
st. Regents Pk 369 D3
YUKON
cl. Kearns......481 A2
pl. Quakers Hill 214 C9
YULAN
pl. Narellan Vale 479 A13
YULE
pl. Glenfield 424 G9
rd. Dulwich Hill......15 B16
YULONG
av. Terrey Hills 196 E7
st. Bangor 459 F13
YULUMA
cl. Bangor 459 F13
YULUNGA
pl. Bradbury......511 C14
YUMA
pl. Bossley Park 333 K12
YUNGA
rd. Glenmore Pk......266 C9
YUNGABURRA
st. Villawood......367 E5
YUNGANA
pl. Bangor 459 F13
YUROKA
st. Glenmore Pk......266 D7
st. Glenmore Pk......266 D8
YURONG
la. Darlinghurst ......D K14
la. Darlinghurst 4 C7
pky. Woolmloo ......D J13
pky. Woolmloo 4 C6
st. Darlinghurst ......D J16
st. Darlinghurst ......F J2
st. Darlinghurst 4 B10
YURREEL
cl. Bangor 459 H13
YURUGA
av. Caringbah 492 H12
av. Doonside 243 B15
pl. Allambie Ht 257 D13
pl. Lindfield......283 J3
rd. Dural 188 D12
st. Beverly Hills 400 G16
YURUNGA
st. Telopea 279 E8
YVES
pl. Minchinbury 272 B10
YVETTE
st. Baulkham Hl 247 K12
YVONNE
av. Hawksbry Ht 174 H2
cr. Bass Hill......367 G8
cr. Georges Hall 367 G8
pl. Castle Hill......248 C2
pl. N Richmond......87 B14
st. Cabramatta W 364 H6
st. Greystanes......306 G4
st. Seven Hills 246 A11

Z

ZADRO
av. Bossley Park 333 H8
ZAHEL
st. Mosman 316 H4
ZAHRA
pl. Quakers Hill 214 D13
ZAMBESI
rd. Seven Hills 275 F9
ZAMBEZI
pl. Kearns 450 K16
pl. Kearns 451 A16
ZAMIA
st. Redfern 19 K10
ZAMMIT
av. Quakers Hill 213 K10
ZANCO
rd. Marsfield......282 A2
ZANE
cl. Bella Vista 246 E6
ZANITH
wy. Kellyville......186 K15

ZAPPIA
pl. Edensor Pk......363 J1
ZARA
cl. Cecil Hills 362 H7
rd. Willoughby......285 D13
ZARITA
av. Waverley 377 F6
ZARLEE
st. Fairfield W......335 F13
ZATOPEK
av. Newington, off
    Newington Bvd......310 B13
ZEALANDER
st. Sandringham 463 D5
ZEBRA
pl. Quakers Hill 214 B7
ZEEHAN
cl. West Hoxton 392 F8
ZELA
st. Mortdale 430 A7
ZELDA
av. Wahroonga......222 K3
ZELENY
rd. Minchinbury 271 A6
ZENITH
cl. Wakeley 334 K16
ct. Glenwood 245 G1
ZEOLITE
pl. Eagle Vale 481 D9
ZEPPELIN
st. Raby 451 E13
ZERAFA
pl. Quakers Hill 214 A11
ZERMATT
av. Seven Hills 275 D11
ZETA
rd. Lane Cove 314 E4
ZEYA
cl. St Clair 269 H16
ZIERIA
pl. Belrose 225 G15
ZIG ZAG
la. Crows Nest, off
    Albany St......315 F6
ZILLAH
st. Guildford......338 C4
st. Merrylands 338 C4
ZINNIA
wy. Blacktown......274 E11
ZIONS
av. Malabar 437 F6
ZIRCON
pl. Bossley Park 334 A8
pl. Eagle Vale 481 F9
ZODIAC
pl. Erskine Park 270 K1
ZOE
cl. Yennora 336 K11
pl. Mount Druitt 241 G15
ZOELLER
st. Concord......342 C5
ZOLA
av. Ryde......282 B9
ZOLYOMI
la. Blacktown, off
    First Av......244 J15
ZONNEBEKE
cr. Milperra......397 H11
ZORIC
cl. Prestons 423 B1
ZOUCH
rd. Denham Ct......422 F9
ZULFI
pl. Cherrybrook......219 B14
ZULLO
ct. Castle Hill......217 B11
ZUNI
cl. Bossley Park 333 K11
ZUTTION
av. Beverly Hills 401 A12
la. Tempe, off
    Union St......404 B2

158 GREGORY'S STREET DIRECTORY

INFORMATION INDEX

AIRPORTS / AIRFIELDS

Bankstown 397 F4
Bankstown Heliport 367 H15
Camden 476 G8
Holsworthy
　Military Reserve 456 E2
Hoxton Park 362 G13
Palm Beach Seaplane ..109 K12
Parramatta Heliport 309 A9
Richmond
　(RAAF Base) 119 G5
Sydney Harbour
　Seaplanes 347 J9
Sydney (Kingsford Smith)
　Domestic 404 J5
　Heliport 405 C9
　International 404 E8
The Oaks 502 B14

CARAVAN, TOURIST & MOBILE HOME PARKS

BARGO
　Avon Caravan Village
　Avon Dam Rd 567 J10
BASS HILL
　Bass Hill Tourist Park
　713 Hume Hwy 368 A9
BUNDEENA
　Bonnie Vale Camping Ground
　Bundeena Dr 523 D9
　Bundeena Caravan Park
　Scarborough St 523 J10
CANLEY VALE
　Lansdowne
　61 Hume Hwy 366 H6
CARINGBAH
　Cronulla Carapark
　cnr Kingsway &
　Gannons Rd S 493 C9
CATTAI
　Riverside Ski Park
　307 Cattai Rd 93 J6
DURAL
　Dural Village Park
　269 New Line Rd 188 K15
EBENEZER
　Hawkesbury Waters
　Leisure Park
　Port Erringhi Rd 68 F8
　Kallawatta Park
　Coromandel Rd 68 E11
ELDERSLIE
　Poplar Park
　Macarthur Rd 477 E16
EMU PLAINS
　Nepean River
　Mackellar St 236 B6
FAIRFIELD WEST
　320 Polding St 335 C7
HEATHCOTE
　Heathcote Tourist Park
　Princes Hwy 518 F13
INGLEBURN
　Denham Court
　505 Campbelltown Rd ..422 F14
KURNELL
　Silver Beach Resort
　288 Prince
　Charles Pde 465 F8
LEPPINGTON
　Casa Paloma
　105 Camden
　Valley Wy 421 G5
　Four Lanterns
　1481 Camden
　Valley Wy 421 E6
MACQUARIE PARK
　Lane Cove River
　Plassey Rd 283 E7
MARSDEN PARK
　Town & Country
　140 Hollinsworth Rd ...211 H11
MIRANDA
　Harts
　215 Port Hacking Rd ..462 B16

NORTH NARRABEEN
　Lakeside
　Lake Park Rd 199 C15
OAKDALE
　Burragorang Rd 500 F11
PARKLEA
　Parklea Garden Village
　30 Majestic Dr 215 C11
PITT TOWN
　Perry Place
　Caravan & Water Ski Park
　Hall St 93 B4
PITT TOWN BOTTOMS
　Hawkesbury Riverside
　Tourist Park
　505 Pitt Town
　Bottoms Rd 92 B8
ROCKDALE
　Sheralee
　88 Bryant St 403 J15
ROUSE HILL
　OK Caravan Corral
　51 Terry Rd 184 J12
SACKVILLE
　Sackville Gardens
　Tizzana Rd 68 C4
SANS SOUCI
　Grand Pines Tourist
　Park Ramsgate Beach The
　289 The Grand Pde ...433 G14
SOUTH MAROOTA
　Pacific Park Ski Gardens
　Wisemans Ferry Rd ...69 A6
TERREY HILLS
　319 Mona Vale Rd 196 A13
VINEYARD
　A-Vina
　217 Commercial Rd ..153 A7
WALLACIA
　cnr Silverdale Rd &
　Alwyn Av 324 H12
WILBERFORCE
　Windsor Riverside
　Putty Rd 91 J7
WORONORA
　1 Menai Rd 460 A14

CLUBS

18 FOOT SAILING
　76 McDougall St
　Kirribilli 6 C13
ABRUZZI SPORTS
　Lot 11 Elizabeth St
　Wetherill Park 334 D3
AKLA (GRANVILLE CSC)
　Onslow St
　Granville 308 H10
AMERICAN
　131 Macquarie St
　Sydney ....B F12
ARNCLIFFE RSL
　71a Wollongong Rd ...403 E8
ARNCLIFFE SCOTS
　SPORTS & SOCIAL
　29 Burrows St 403 G8
ASHFIELD CATHOLIC &
　COMMUNITY
　7 Charlotte St 372 J2
ASHFIELD RSL
　374 Liverpool Rd......372 F3
ASQUITH RUGBY LEAGUE
　11 Alexandria Pde
　Waitara 221 K3
ASSYRIAN SPORTS &
　CULTURAL
　52 Stanbrook St
　Fairfield Heights 335 K9
AUBURN RSL
　33 Northumberland Rd ..339 E1
AUBURN SOCCER SPORTS
　5-7 Northumberland Rd ..339 E2
AUSTRALASIAN PIONEERS
　61 York St
　Sydney ....C F12
AUSTRALIAN
　165 Macquarie St
　Sydney ....B F15
AUSTRALIAN
　18 FOOTERS LEAGUE
　77 Bay St
　Double Bay 347 B11
AUSTRALIAN JOCKEY
　Alison rd
　Randwick 376 G10

AUSTRALIAN OPERA FRIENDS
　480 Elizabeth St
　Surry Hills 19 H4
AUSTRIAN CLUB SYDNEY
　20 Grattan Cr
　Frenchs Forest 256 F10
AVALON BEACH RSL
　1 Bowling Green La
　Avalon 170 B1
BALGOWLAH RSL MEMORIAL
　30 Ethel St
　Seaforth 287 E10
BALMAIN LEAGUES
　138 Victoria Rd
　Rozelle 344 E7
BANKSTOWN DISTRICT
　SPORTS
　8 Greenfield Pde 399 E1
BANKSTOWN POLISH
　9 East Tce 399 G1
BANKSTOWN RSL
　Kitchener Pde 369 E15
BANKSTOWN TROTTING
　RECREATIONAL
　178 Eldridge Rd 398 E7
BARGO SPORTS CLUB
　3584
　Remembrance Dwy ..567 H11
BASS HILL RSL
　330 Hector St 368 C9
BAULKHAM HILLS SPORTING
　6 Renown Rd 248 C12
BELFIELD RSL
　2 Persic St 371 C11
BELMORE RSL
　427 Burwood Rd 401 F1
BERALA-CARRAMAR
　TENNIS & RECREATION
　181 Chisholm Rd
　Auburn 338 J7
BEROWRA RSL & CITIZENS
　997 Pacific Hwy 133 F13
BEXLEY RSL
　24 Stoney Creek Rd ..402 J14
BLACKTOWN CITY RUGBY
　LEAGUE & SPORTS CLUB
　122-128 Rooty Hill Rd N
　Rooty Hill 242 B14
BLACKTOWN CITY SOCCER
　162 Prospect Hwy
　Seven Hills 245 J15
BLACKTOWN RSL
　Second Av 244 G14
BLACKTOWN WORKERS
　55 Campbell St 274 G1
BLACKTOWN WORKERS
　SPORTS CLUB
　Reservoir Rd 274 C10
BONDI DIGGERS
　MEMORIAL & SPORTING
　5 Military Rd
　North Bondi 378 G2
BONDI ICEBERGS
　1 Notts Av
　Bondi Beach 378 D5
BONDI JUNCTION-
　WAVERLEY RSL
　1 Gray St
　Bondi Junction 22 J8
BOOMERANG ITF SEAFARERS
　84a Wentworth Av
　Mascot 405 G7
BOTANY BAY YACHT
　Endeavour St
　Sans Souci 462 J2
BOTANY RSL
　1421 Botany Rd 405 F11
BOWLERS CLUB OF NSW
　95 York St
　Sydney ....C G7
BRIGHTON-LE-SANDS
　AMATEUR FISHING
　Bestic St
　Kyeemagh 403 K14
BRIGHTON-LE-SANDS RSL
　351 Bay St 433 K3
BRONTE RSL
　113 Macpherson St
　Waverley 377 K10
BRONTE SURF
　LIFE SAVING
　Bronte Beach 378 A8
BULLDOGS LEAGUES
　28 Bridge Rd
　Belmore 371 E16
BUNDEENA RSL
　71 Loftus St 524 A9
BURWOOD RSL
　96 Shaftesbury Rd ...342 B15

CABRAMATTA RUGBY LEAGUE
　24 Sussex St 365 J10
CABRA VALE EX-ACTIVE
　SERVICEMENS
　1 Bartley St
　Canley Vale 365 K4
CAMDEN LAKESIDE COUNTRY
　50 Raby Rd
　Catherine Field 450 F7
Campbelltown CATHOLIC
　20 Camden St 511 C6
Campbelltown RSL
　6 Lithgow St 511 E5
Campbelltown TENNIS
　16 Old Leumeah Rd
　Leumeah 482 B12
CAMPSIE RSL
　25 Anglo Rd 371 K13
CANLEY HEIGHTS RSL
　26 Humphries Rd
　Wakeley 334 K16
CANTERBURY-HURLSTONE
　PARK RSL
　20 Canterbury Rd
　Hurlstone Park 372 K11
CARINGBAH BUSINESS &
　SPORTS
　32 Banksia Rd 492 J7
CARINGBAH RSL
　28-30 Banksia Rd 492 K7
CASTELLORIZIAN
　440 Anzac Pde
　Kingsford 406 G1
CASTLE COVE COUNTRY
　60 Deepwater Rd 285 J5
CASTLE HILL COUNTRY
　Windsor Rd
　Baulkham Hills 216 H13
CASTLE HILL RSL
　77 Castle St 217 K12
CASTLE PINES COUNTRY
　Spurway Dr
　Baulkham Hills 216 K13
CATHOLIC
　199 Castlereagh St
　Sydney ....D A13
CENTRO SOCIALE ITALIANO
　South St
　Schofields 212 K4
CHATSWOOD
　11 Help St 284 H9
CHATSWOOD RSL
　446 Victoria Av 284 H10
CHELTENHAM
　RECREATION CLUB
　60-74 The Crescent ..251 A9
CHESTER HILL-
　CARRAMAR RSL
　cnr Proctor Pde &
　Chester Hill Rd 368 B2
CITY OF SYDNEY RSL
　565 George St
　Sydney ....E G2
CITY TATTERSALLS
　198 Pitt St
　Sydney ....D A9
CLOVELLY RSL & AIR FORCE
　263 Clovelly Rd 377 G12
CLUBHOUSE
　North Manly 257 K16
CLUB HURSTVILLE SPORTS
　311a Forest Rd 432 C6
CLUB PACEWAY
　147 Station St
　Penrith 236 F12
CLUB SEVEN HILLS
　Best Rd 275 H3
COLLAROY SERVICES BEACH
　1058 Pittwater Rd 229 C12
COMBINED SERVICES RSL
　5 Barrack St
　Sydney ....C F3
COMMERCIAL TRAVELLERS
　ASSOCIATION
　MLC Centre, Martin Pl
　Sydney ....D B3
CONCORD RSL
　Nirranda St 311 H16
CONCORD RYDE SAILING
　Waterview St
　Putney 311 J8
COOGEE LEGION
　266a Coogee Bay Rd ..377 G16
COOGEE RANDWICK RSL
　Byron St
　Coogee 407 C1
COOKS RIVER MOTOR BOAT
　18-20 Holbeach Av
　Tempe 404 B4

CORONATION
　86 Burwood Rd
　Burwood 342 A12
COVE SPORTS
　325a Eastern Valley Wy
　Middle Cove 285 F5
CROATIAN
　cnr Canterbury &
　Punchbowl Rds
　Punchbowl 399 J7
CROATIAN (JADRAN HAJDUK)
　130 Edensor Rd
　Bonnyrigg 364 C3
CRONULLA
　cnr Elouera &
　Hume Rds 494 A7
CROWS NEST RSL
　38 Gerrale St 494 A13
CROWS NEST CLUB
　118 Willoughby Rd ...315 F6
CROYDON PARK
　EX-SERVICEMENS
　55 Seymour St 372 B6
CRUISING YACHT CLUB
　OF AUSTRALIA
　1 New Beach Rd
　Darling Point 13 G7
CUMBERLAND COMMUNITY
　Civic Av
　Pendle Hill 276 E13
CYPRUS COMMUNITY
　CENTRE OF NSW
　58 Stanmore Rd
　Enmore 16 J14
CYPRUS HELLENE
　150 Elizabeth St
　Sydney ....F C4
DALMACIJA SYDNEY
　CROATIAN
　16 Myoora Rd
　Terrey Hills 195 K13
DEEPWATER MOTOR BOAT
　Webster St
　Milperra 397 C16
DEE WHY RSL
　932 Pittwater Rd 258 H4
DEPT OF GOVERNMENT
　TRANSPORT SOCIAL CLUB
　19-25 Regent St
　Chippendale 19 D1
DIGGERS ON THE PARK
　Ivanhoe Park Raglan St
　Manly 288 F8
DOBROYD AQUATIC
　Rodd Park
　Rodd Point 343 G8
DOUBLE BAY SAILING
　79 Bay St 347 B11
DRUMMOYNE ROWING
　Henley Marine Dr 344 A5
DRUMMOYNE RSL
　162 Victoria Rd 343 K2
DRUMMOYNE RUGBY
　169 Victoria Rd 343 J2
DRUMMOYNE SAILING
　2 St Georges Cr 344 B3
DUNDAS SPORTS &
　RECREATION
　9 Elder Rd 279 F14
DUNDAS VALLEY RUGBY
　UNION FOOTBALL
　35 Quarry Rd 280 A10
DURAL COUNTRY
　662a Old Northern Rd ..188 K4
EARLWOOD-BARDWELL
　PARK RSL
　Hartill-law Av
　Bardwell Park 402 J6
EARLWOOD EX-SERVICEMENS
　32 Fricourt Av 402 K2
EASTERN SUBURBS DISTRICT
　RUGBY UNION FOOTBALL
　Grimley Hall, O'Sullivan Rd
　Rose Bay 347 J14
EASTERN SUBURBS LEAGUES
　93 Spring St
　Bondi Junction 22 H7
EASTERN SUBURBS LEGION
　213 Bronte Rd
　Waverley 377 F8
EASTERN SUBURBS
　TENNIS CLUB
　cnr Brook & Bream St
　Coogee 377 G15
EASTWOOD CLUB
　6A Hillview Rd 281 A8
EASTWOOD RUGBY CLUB
　146 Vimiera Rd
　Marsfield 281 H2

GREGORY'S STREET DIRECTORY 159

INFORMATION

CLUBS

ELANORA COUNTRY
Elanora Rd
Elanora Heights............198 B13

EMU PLAINS SPORTING &
RECREATION
Leonay Pde
Leonay 235 A14

ENFIELD RSL
236 Liverpool Rd............371 H2

ENGADINE RSL
1029 Old Princes Hwy .518 J3

FAIRFIELD RSL
14 Anzac Pde..................336 G13

FIVE DOCK RSL
66 Great North Rd..........342 K11

FOGOLAR FURLAN
VENETO CLUB
cnr Hollywood Dr &
Wharf Rd
Lansvale 367 A10

FORESTVILLE RSL
22 Melwood Av.............255 J10

GALLIPOLI MEMORIAL
12 Loftus St
Sydney ....B D10

GEA HELLENIC ESTIA LTD
140-142 McEvoy St
Alexandria 375 D9

GEORGES RIVER SAILING
Sanoni Av
Sandringham..................463 F2

GERMAN AUSTRIAN SOCIETY
OF AUSTRALIA
73 Curtin St
Cabramatta..................366 A5

GERMAN CONCORDIA
231 Stanmore Rd
Stanmore 16 E11

GLADESVILLE BOWLING &
SPORTS CLUB
cnr Ryde Rd &
Halcyon St 312 K6

GLADESVILLE RSL &
COMMUNITY
2 Linsley St..................312 J10

GLENMORE HERITAGE VALLEY
690 Mulgoa Rd
Mulgoa........................265 C14

GLENORIE RSL
3 Post Office Rd 128 B4

GRANVILLE RSL
Memorial Dr..................308 G12

GREEK COMMUNITY
206 Lakemba St
Lakemba........................400 K1

GREEK MACEDONIAN CLUB
ALEXANDER THE GREAT
160 Livingstone Rd
Marrickville....................373 J11

GREYHOUND SOCIAL
140 Rookwood Rd
Yagoona........................369 F7

GROSVENOR
40 Flinders St
Darlinghurst 4 E14

GUILDFORD RUGBY LEAGUE
Tamplin Rd....................337 B4

HAKOAH
61 Hall St
Bondi Beach 378 C6

HARBORD DIGGERS
MEMORIAL
Evans St........................288 K1

HEATHCOTE SERVICES &
CITIZENS
24 Oliver St..................518 F12

HELLENIC HOUSE CLUB
Level 2, 251 Elizabeth St
Sydney ....D B16

HENRY LAWSON
Henry Lawson Av
Werrington County 238 E6

HOMEBUSH RSL
26 Pomeroy St..............341 C6

HORNSBY RSL
4 High St......................221 G1

HUBERTUS COUNTRY
Adams Rd
Luddenham................327 F16

HUBERTUS LIVERPOOL RIFLE
cnr Badgerys Creek Rd &
Elizabeth Dr
Badgerys Creek............328 H15

HUNGARIAN (MAGYAR)
SOCIAL
706 Smithfield Rd
Edensor Park................363 K3

HUNTERS HILL CLUB
14 Madeline St............313 J10

HUNTERS HILL CROQUET
cnr Matthew St &
Gladesville Rd 313 D10

HUNTERS HILL RSL
cnr Ady &
Alexandra Sts..............313 K11

HURSTVILLE RSL
1 Ormonde Pde............432 A6

ILLAWARRA CATHOLIC
13 Woodville St
Hurstville....................432 A5

INGLEBURN RSL
70 Chester Rd..............453 E10

INTERNATIONAL NIPPON CLUB
229 Macquarie St
Sydney ....D F4

JET SPORTS
Holbeach Av
Tempe........................404 B5

JOHN EDMONDSON VC
MEMORIAL
185 George St
Liverpool......................395 E3

JOURNALISTS
36 Chalmers St
Surry Hills 19 G1

KELLYVILLE COUNTRY
Mungerie Rd
Beaumont Hills............185 H13

KENSINGTON WAR MEMORIAL
2 Goodwood St..........376 E10

KIEV SPORTS
32 Broomfield St
Cabramatta..................366 A5

KINGSGROVE RSL
4 Brocklehurst La........401 K11

KINGSWOOD SPORTS
Santley Cr....................237 J13

KING TOMISLAV CROATIAN
223 Edensor Rd
Edensor Park..............333 E15

KIRRIBILLI CLUB
11 Harbour View Cr
Milsons Point ....K J16

KOGARAH BAY SAILING
Princes Hwy
Blakehurst 462 G2

KOGARAH RSL
254 Railway Pde 432 K6

KURING-GAI MOTOR YACHT
1 Cottage Point Rd
Cottage Point..............135 G9

KURNELL CATAMARAN CLUB
cnr Prince Charles Pde &
Ward St......................465 F8

KURNELL COMMUNITY
SPORTS & RECREATION
Captain Cook Dr..........466 A10

KYEEMAGH RSL
Tancred Av 404 B13

LAKEMBA RETURNED
SOLDIERS
60 Quigg St 401 B2

LAKEMBA SERVICES
MEMORIAL
26 Quigg St 401 B1

LANE COVE
1 Birdwood Av............314 E1

LANE COVE COUNTRY
River Rd......................314 G6

LANE COVE TENNIS
Kenneth St
Longueville..................314 E6

LANSVALE UNITED SPORTS
21 Shortland St
Canley Vale................366 E4

LEICHHARDT-LILYFIELD
SOLDIERS SAILORS AIRMEN
38 Short St..................10 A15

LEMNIAN ASSOCIATION OF
NSW
44 Albert St
Belmore 371 F14

LE MONTAGE
38 Frazer St
Lilyfield......................343 J11

LIDCOMBE CATHOLIC
WORKMENS
24 John St..................339 J8

LIDCOMBE RSL
Joseph St....................339 J9

LITHUANIAN
16 East Tce
Bankstown..................399 G1

LIVERPOOL CATHOLIC
5 Hoxton Park Rd
Prestons....................393 F7

LONGUEVILLE SPORTING
cnr Kenneth St & River Rd
Longueville 314 E6

MALABAR RSL
Ireton St......................437 E3

MANDARIN
396 Pitt St
Haymarket..................E K5

MANLY 16FT SKIFF
SAILING CLUB
cnr East Esp &
Stuart St....................288 G12

MANLY CIVIC
2 West Pm 288 G10

MANLY FISHING &
SPORTING ASSOCIATION
270 Pittwater Rd..........288 F4

MANLY RUGBY UNION CLUB
52 Raglan St..............288 G8

MANLY-WARRINGAH
MASTER BUILDERS
18 Fisher Rd
Dee Why 258 F6

MANLY-WARRINGAH
RUGBY LEAGUE
563 Pittwater Rd
Brookvale 258 D9

MANLY-WARRINGAH SOCCER
101 South Creek Rd
Dee Why....................228 F16

MARCONI
Marconi Rd
Bossley Park..............333 H10

MAROUBRA RSL
946 Anzac Pde............407 B11

MAROUBRA SEALS
SPORTS & COMMUNITY
212 Marine Pde..........407 G12

MARRICKVILLE
ANZAC MEMORIAL
21 Garners Av............374 A12

MARRICKVILLE DISTRICT
HARDCOURT TENNIS
Henson Park
Centennial St..............374 A9

MARRICKVILLE RSL
359 Illawarra Rd..........373 J14

MASCOT RSL
1271 Botany Rd..........405 D6

MATRAVILLE RSL
Norfolk Pde 436 J2

MEKONG PANTHERS
117 John St
Cabramatta................365 H7

MERRYLANDS RSL
14 Military Rd............307 H13

MIDDLE HARBOUR 16FT
SKIFF CLUB
The Spit Lower Parriwi Rd
Mosman......................287 D14

MIDDLE HARBOUR
YACHT CLUB
The Spit Lower Parriwi Rd
Mosman......................287 D14

MIRANDA BUILDERS &
BUSINESSMENS
601 Kingsway 491 K3

MIRANDA RSL
615 Kingsway............491 K3

MONASH COUNTRY
Powder Works Rd
Ingleside....................197 H9

MOONEY MOONEY WORKERS
SPORTS & RECREATION
5 Kowan Rd................75 D2

MOOREBANK SPORTS
Heathcote Rd
Hammondville............426 G2

MORTDALE RSL
25 Macquarie Pl..........431 B8

MOSMAN RETURNED
SERVICEMENS
719 Military Rd..........317 B7

MOSMAN ROWING CLUB
3 Centenary Dr
Mosman....................316 H11

MT DRUITT WORKERS
247 Woodstock Av
Dharruk......................241 B9

MT PRITCHARD &
DISTRICT COMMUNITY
(MOUNTIES)
101 Meadows Rd........364 E8

NARRABEEN RSL
116 Naree Rd
North Narrabeen 198 G15

NEPEAN MOTORSPORTS
CLUB
Rickards Rd
Castlereagh..................146 D11

NEPEAN ROWING
Bruce Neale Dr
Penrith 236 D7

NEWTOWN RSL
52 Enmore Rd 17 E13

NINEVEH
673 Smithfield Rd
Edensor Park 364 A2

NORTH BONDI RSL
120 Ramsgate Av........378 G3

NORTHBRIDGE SAILING
Clive Park....................286 G13

NORTHERN SUBURBS
RUGBY FOOTBALL
80 Christie St
St Leonards..................315 D6

NORTH RICHMOND PANTHERS
Beaumont Av..............87 G13

NORTH RYDE RSL
cnr Magdala &
Pittwater Rds..............283 C13

NORTH SYDNEY
88 Berry St..................K J3

NORTH SYDNEY ANZAC
cnr Miller & Ernest Sts
Cammeray..................315 J7

NORTH SYDNEY LEAGUES
12 Abbott St
Cammeray..................315 J4

NSW CRICKETERS
11 Barrack St
Sydney ....C G3

NSW GUN
131 Booralie Rd
Duffys Forest 195 B3

NSW HARNESS RACING
CLUB LTD
Ross St
Forest Lodge................11 G12

NSW LEAGUES
165 Phillip St
Sydney ....D D4

NSW MASONIC
169 Castlereagh St
Sydney ....D A11

NSW RUGBY
Rugby PI
Sydney ....A K8

NSW SPORTS
10 Hunter St
Sydney ....A J14

OAKDALE WORKERS
Burragorang Rd 500 A13

OATLEY RSL
23 Letitia St................431 C13

PADDINGTON-
WOOLLAHRA RSL
226 Oxford St..............13 A16

PADSTOW RSL
24 Howard Rd............399 D16

PALM BEACH RSL
1087 Barrenjoey Rd......139 K2

PALM BEACH SURF
31-32 Ocean Rd..........139 K1

PANANIA EAST HILLS RSL
28 Childs St
Panania 427 H1

PANTHERS WORLD OF
ENTERTAINMENT
Mulgoa Rd
Penrith 236 D12

PARRAMATTA LEAGUES
15 O'Connell St............287 B15

PARRAMATTA MASONIC
163 George St..............308 G4

PARRAMATTA RETURNED
EX-SERVICEMANS
Macquarie St 308 A3

PARRAMATTA RUGBY UNION
2a Amos St
Parramatta..................307 K4

PENRITH GAELS CULTURAL &
SPORTING ASSOCIATION
75 Richmond Rd
Kingswood 237 G9

PENRITH RSL
cnr Castlereagh &
Lethbridge Sts............236 J11

PENSHURST RSL
58a Penshurst St..........431 E5

PETERSHAM RSL
7a Regent St................373 K5

PITT TOWN DISTRICT SPORTS
139 Old Pitt Town Rd ...123 D2

PITTWATER AQUATIC
Esplanade
Mona Vale..................169 D14

PITTWATER RSL
82 Mona Vale Rd
Mona Vale 198 J4

POLISH
73 Norton St
Ashfield 372 J4

POLONIA SPORTS CLUB
28 Bungalow Rd
Plumpton....................242 A11

PORT HACKING OPEN SAILING
224 Attunga Rd
Yowie Bay..................492 C13

PORTUGUESE MADEIRA SYDNEY
SOCIAL & SPORTS
1 Denby St
Marrickville..................374 D9

PUNCHBOWL & DISTRICT
RETURNED SERVICEMEN &
EX-SERVICEMENS
1 The Broadway 400 D4

QUEENS
137 Elizabeth St
Sydney ....D C8

RAMSGATE RSL MEMORIAL
cnr Ramsgate Rd &
Chuter Av 433 F14

RANDWICK LABOUR
135 Alison Rd 376 K13

RANDWICK RUGBY
104 Brook St
Coogee......................377 G16

REDFERN RSL
157 Redfern St..............19 B7

REVESBY HEIGHTS
EX-SERVICEMENS
1 Donovan St..............428 K6

REVESBY WORKERS
26 Brett St..................398 H16

RICHMOND
6 East Market St..........118 J4

RIVERSTONE SCOFIELDS RSL
Market St
Riverstone..................182 K7

RIVERWOOD LEGION &
COMMUNITY
32 Littleton St..............400 C15

RIVERWOOD SPORTS &
RECREATION
283 Belmore Rd..........400 B15

ROCKDALE BUSINESSMENS
34 Bay St....................403 D15

ROCKDALE RSL
45 Bay St....................403 E16

ROCKDALE TENNIS
71 Chapel St................433 E1

ROOTY HILL RSL
cnr Sherbrooke Rd &
Railway St 241 J16

ROSE BAY RSL
Vickery Av..................347 K10

ROSEVILLE RETURNED
SERVICEMENS MEMORIAL
64 Pacific Hwy............284 G5

ROSNAY GOLF CLUB
5 Weymouth Av
Auburn........................338 J9

ROYAL AUTOMOBILE
89 Macquarie St
Sydney ....B G8

ROYAL MOTOR YACHT
Broken Bay
46 Prince Alfred Pde
Newport 169 B8
New South Wales
21 Wunulla Rd
Point Piper..................347 F8
Port Hacking
228 Woolooware Rd
Burraneer....................493 F16

ROYAL PRINCE ALFRED YACHT
16 Mitala St
Newport 169 C10

ROYAL PRINCE EDWARD
YACHT
160 Wolseley Rd
Point Piper..................347 F8

ROYAL SYDNEY
YACHT SQUADRON
33 Peel St
Kirribilli 6 F16

160 GREGORY'S STREET DIRECTORY

INFORMATION

HOSPITALS

RUGBY
Rugby Pl
Sydney .... B A8
RUSSIAN CLUB THE
7 Albert Rd
Strathfield 341 G11
RYDE EASTWOOD LEAGUES
117 Ryedale Rd
West Ryde 281 F14
RYDE EX-SERVICES
724 Victoria Rd 311 K3
ST GEORGE BUSINESS &
SOCIAL
8 Crofts Av
Hurstville 432 A5
ST GEORGE LEAGUES
124 Princes Hwy
Beverley Park 433 A9
ST GEORGE MASONIC
86 Roberts Av
Mortdale 430 G7
ST GEORGE MOTOR BOAT
2 Wellington St
Sans Souci 462 J4
ST GEORGE ROWING
1 Levey St
Wolli Creek 404 A6
ST GEORGE SAILING
Riverside Dr
Sans Souci 463 B7
ST JOHNS PARK PANTHERS
80 Brisbane Rd 334 E15
ST MARYS BAND
411 Great
Western Hwy 239 G16
ST MARYS RSL
EX SERVICEMENS
Mamre Rd 269 G5
ST MARYS RUGBY LEAGUE
Boronia Rd 239 J7
SERBIAN CENTRE
Simpson Rd
Bonnyrigg Heights ... 363 E4
SERBIAN CULTURAL
256 Cowpasture Rd
West Hoxton 392 H2
SHARKS INTERNATIONAL
Captain Cook Dr
Woolooware 493 F5
SILVERWATER
cnr Silverwater Rd &
Clyde St 309 K8
SLOVENIAN
2 Elizabeth St
Wetherill Park 334 E3
SMITHFIELD RSL
Smithfield Rd 335 J5
SOUTHERN DISTRICT RUGBY
233 Belgrave Esp
Sylvania Waters 462 D15
SOUTHERN SPORTS &
RECREATIONAL
Rawson St
Sutherland 490 C8
SOUTH HURSTVILLE RSL
72 Connells Point Rd...432 B11
SOUTH SYDNEY GRAPHIC
ARTS
182 Coward St
Mascot 405 D2
SOUTH SYDNEY JUNIOR
RUGBY LEAGUE
558a Anzac Pde
Kingsford 406 H3
SOUTH SYDNEY LEAGUES
265 Chalmers St
Redfern 19 F10
SPANISH
88 Liverpool St
Sydney .... E G2
STRATHFIELD RECREATION
4A Lyon St 341 G13
SUTHERLAND DISTRICT
TRADE UNION
57 Manchester Rd
Gymea 491 F3
SUTHERLAND SHIRE
SAILING CLUB
Kurnell 465 E8
SUTHERLAND UNITED
SERVICES
7 East Pde 490 E2
SYDNEY
9 Rowe St .... D A4
SYDNEY AMATEUR SAILING
Kareela Rd
Cremorne Point 316 G13

SYDNEY AUSSIE RULES
SOCIAL
28 Darlinghurst Rd
Potts Point 4 K6
SYDNEY AUSTRALIAN
FOOTBALL
Driver Av
Moore Park 20 K3
SYDNEY CRICKET &
SPORTS GROUND TRUST
Driver Av
Moore Park 20 K7
SYDNEY FLYING SQUADRON
18 Foot Sailing Club
76 McDougall St
Kirribilli 6 C13
SYDNEY LABOUR &
COMMUNITY
464 Bourke St
Surry Hills 20 D2
SYDNEY MARKET INDUSTRIES
Parramatta Rd
Homebush West 340 J7
SYDNEY OLYMPIC SPORTING
64 Tennent Pde
Hurlstone Park 373 B14
SYDNEY PISTOL
Cape Banks
La Perouse 437 F16
SYDNEY ROWING CLUB
613 Great North Rd
Abbotsford 312 J15
TATTERSALLS
181 Elizabeth St
Sydney .... D B4
TEACHERS CLUB
33 Mary St
Surry Hills .... F C11
THE BRIARS SPORTING
30a George St
Burwood 341 K13
THE EPPING CLUB
45 Rawson St
Epping 251 A16
THE GALSTON CLUB
21-23 Arcadia Rd
Galston 159 G10
THE NEUTRAL BAY
Barry St
Neutral Bay 6 F5
THE PARRAMATTA
37 Hunter St
Parramatta 308 B3
TRASANDINOS SPORTING
418 Gardeners Rd
Rosebery 405 F1
TWIN CREEKS GOLF &
COUNTRY CLUB
Luddenham Rd
Luddenham 299 C12
UKRAINIAN CULTURAL &
SOCIAL
11 Church St
Lidcombe 339 H8
UNION CLUB SYDNEY
25 Bent St
Sydney .... B E14
UNIVERSITY & SCHOOLS
60 Phillip St
Sydney .... B F12
UPPER HAWKESBURY POWER
BOAT
George St
Windsor 121 G5
URUGUAYAN SOCIAL &
SPORTING
56 Whitford Rd
Hinchinbrook 393 C3
UTS HABERFIELD ROWING
Dobroyd Pde
Haberfield 343 G10
VAUCLUSE AMATEUR 12
FOOT SAILING
Wharf Rd 318 E15
VAUCLUSE YACHT
Marine Pde
Watsons Bay 318 F14
WARRAGAMBA WORKERS &
SPORTING
Eighteenth St 353 F6
WENTWORTHVILLE LEAGUES
Smith St 306 H2
WESTERN SUBURBS
AUSTRALIAN FOOTBALL
40 Hampton St
Croydon Park 372 A8

WESTERN SUBURBS INDOOR
CRICKET
Blackstone St
Wetherill Park 305 C16
WESTERN SUBURBS LEAGUES
115 Liverpool Rd
Ashfield 373 A3
10 Old Leumeah Rd
Leumeah 482 B13
WESTERN SUBURBS SOCCER
4 William St
Five Dock 342 G9
WEST HARBOUR
RUGBY FOOTBALL
28A George St
Burwood 341 K14
WEST PENNANT HILLS
SPORTS
103 New Line Rd 219 G15
WILLOUGHBY LEGION
EX-SERVICES
26 Crabbes Av 285 E9
WINDSOR LEAGUES
Rifle Range Rd
Bligh Park 150 D4
WINDSOR RSL
Argyle St
South Windsor 120 K13
WOOLLAHRA SAILING
Vickery Av
Rose Bay 347 K10
WORONORA RIVER RSL &
CITIZENS
118 Prince Edward Park Rd
Woronora 489 J2
YARRA BAY SAILING
Yarra Rd
Phillip Bay 436 H11
YWCA (HEADQUARTERS)
5 Wentworth Av
Sydney .... F E3

HOSPITALS

ALLOWAH CHILDRENS
PRIVATE
8 Perry St
Dundas Valley 280 E8
ALWYN REHABILITATION
PRIVATE
1 Emu St
Strathfield 341 G16
AUBURN HOSPITAL &
COMMUNITY HEALTH
SERVICES
Norval St 339 D7
BALMAIN
29 Booth St 7 H11
BANKSTOWN-LIDCOMBE
Eldridge Rd
Bankstown 398 K7
BLACKTOWN
Blacktown Rd 274 K2
BRAESIDE
340 Prairie Vale Rd
Prairiewood 334 F8
CALVARY
91 Rocky Point Rd
Beverley Park 433 C9
CAMDEN
Menangle Rd 507 A3
CAMPBELLTOWN
Therry Rd 511 B10
CANTERBURY
Canterbury Rd
Campsie 401 J1
CARRINGTON CENTENNIAL
FOR CONVALESCENTS
90 Werombi Rd
Camden 476 B15
CASTLECRAG PRIVATE
150 Edinburgh Rd 286 B12
CHILDRENS HOSPITAL AT
WESTMEAD, THE
Hawkesbury Rd
Westmead 277 J13
CONCORD REPATRIATION
GENERAL
Hospital Rd
Concord West 311 F12
CUMBERLAND
1 Hainsworth St
Westmead 277 K13
DALCROSS PRIVATE
28 Stanhope Rd
Killara 254 B13

DALWOOD CHILDRENS HOME
21 Dalwood Av
Seaforth 286 K7
DAME EADITH WALKER
DIALYSIS TRAINING CENTRE
Nullawarra Av
Concord West 311 J13
DELMAR PRIVATE
58 Quirk St
Dee Why 258 H8
EASTERN SUBURBS PRIVATE
8 Chapel St
Randwick 377 C12
EVESHAM CLINIC PRIVATE
3 Harrison St
Cremorne 6 H3
FAIRFIELD
cnr Polding St &
Prairie Vale Rd
Prairiewood 334 F8
GARRAWARRA CENTRE FOR
AGED CARE
Princes Hwy
Waterfall 519 C16
GREENWICH
97 River Rd 314 K7
HAWKESBURY DISTRICT
HEALTH SERVICE
Day St
Windsor 121 C10
HILLS PRIVATE, THE
499 Windsor Rd
Baulkham Hills 247 E4
HIRONDELLE PRIVATE
10 Wyvern Av
Chatswood West 284 H7
HMAS PENGUIN
Naval Depot
Mosman 317 G7
HOLROYD PRIVATE
123 Chetwynd Rd
Guildford 337 D1
HORNSBY DAY SURGERY
CENTRE
1a Northcote Rd 192 B16
HORNSBY & KU-RING-GAI
COMMUNITY HEALTH
SERVICES
Palmerston Rd 192 B16
HUNTERS HILL PRIVATE
9 Mount St 313 G11
HURSTVILLE COMMUNITY
PRIVATE
37 Gloucester Rd 431 H4
JEAN COLVIN PRIVATE
9 Loftus Rd
Darling Point 13 H7
KAREENA PRIVATE
86 Kareena Rd N
Caringbah 492 F4
LADY DAVIDSON
Bobbin Head Rd
Turramurra 193 G11
LANGTON CENTRE
cnr 591 Dowling &
Nobbs Sts
Surry Hills 20 E5
LIVERPOOL
cnr Goulburn &
Elizabeth Sts 395 G2
LONGUEVILLE PRIVATE
47 Kenneth St 314 E7
LOTTIE STEWART
40 Stewart St
Dundas 280 D11
MACARTHUR PRIVATE
92 Dumaresq St
Campbelltown 511 F6
MACQUARIE
Wicks Rd
North Ryde 282 H11
MANDALAY PRIVATE
2 Addison Rd
Manly 288 F14
MANLY HOSPITAL &
COMMUNITY HEALTH SERVICES
Darley Rd 288 K13
MANLY WATERS PRIVATE
17 Cove Av
Manly 288 G13
MATER MISERICORDIAE
PRIVATE
Rocklands Rd
North Sydney 5 B1
METROPOLITAN
REHABILITATION PRIVATE
275 Addison Rd
Petersham 373 K7

MINCHINBURY COMMUNITY
PRIVATE
cnr Great Western Hwy &
Rupertswood Rd
Rooty Hill 271 H5
MONA VALE HOSPITAL &
COMMUNITY HEALTH
SERVICES
Coronation St 199 D8
MOSMAN PRIVATE
1 Ellamatta Av 317 C10
MOUNT DRUITT
75 Railway St 241 H14
MT WILGA PRIVATE
2 Manor Rd
Hornsby 191 E12
NEPEAN
Somerset St
Kingswood 237 D13
NEPEAN PRIVATE
Barber Av
Kingswood 237 E12
NERINGAH HOPE HEALTHCARE
GROUP
4 Neringah Av S
Wahroonga 222 C7
NORTH SHORE PRIVATE
Westbourne St
St Leonards 315 B4
NORTHSIDE CLINIC PRIVATE,
THE
2 Greenwich Rd
Greenwich 315 A4
PARRAMATTA HEALTH
SERVICE
158 Marsden St 308 B2
PENINSULA PRIVATE
12 McDonald St
Harbord 258 D15
POPLARS PRIVATE
66 Norfolk Rd
Epping 251 D12
PRESIDENT PRIVATE
369 President Av
Kirrawee 491 C5
PRINCE OF WALES
PRIVATE THE
Barker St
Randwick 377 A16
PRINCE OF WALES THE
cnr High & Avoca Sts
Randwick 377 A15
QUEEN VICTORIA
MEMORIAL HOME
Thirlmere Wy
Picton 562 H12
RACHEL FORSTER
150 Pitt St
Redfern 19 D9
RIVENDELL CHILD
ADOLESCENT & FAMILY UNIT
Hospital Rd
Concord West 311 H11
ROMA PRIVATE
9 Willaim St
Randwick 376 J10
ROYAL FAR WEST
CHILDRENS HEALTH SCHEME
18 Wentworth St
Manly 288 H10
ROYAL HOSPITAL FOR WOMEN
Barker St
Randwick 377 A16
ROYAL NORTH SHORE
Reserve Rd
St Leonards 315 B5
ROYAL PRINCE ALFRED
Missenden Rd
Camperdown 17 J5
ROYAL REHABILITATION
CENTRE, SYDNEY
227 Morrison Rd
Ryde 312 C4
Coorabel
227 Morrison Rd
Ryde 312 B6
Weemala
259 Morrison Rd
Ryde 312 A5
ROYAL SOUTH SYDNEY
COMMUNITY HEALTH
COMPLEX
7 Joynton Av
Zetland 375 J11
ROZELLE
cnr Church & Glover Sts
Lilyfield 343 G10

GREGORY'S STREET DIRECTORY 161

RYDE HOSPITAL & COMMUNITY HEALTH SERVICES
Denistone Rd
Eastwood 281 E10
SACRED HEART PALLIATIVE CARE & REHABILITATION
279 Victoria St
Darlinghurst 4 F13
ST GEORGE
Belgrave St
Kogarah 433 B6
ST GEORGE PRIVATE & MEDICAL CENTRE
1 South St
Kogarah 433 C5
ST JOHN OF GOD PRIVATE
13 Grantham St
Burwood 341 J11
Richmond
177 Grose Vale Rd
North Richmond 116 J4
ST JOSEPHS
Normanby Rd
Auburn 339 C2
ST LUKES PRIVATE
18 Roslyn St
Potts Point 13 A7
ST VINCENTS
406 Victoria St
Darlinghurst 4 G12
ST VINCENTS CARITAS CENTRE
299 Forbes St
Darlinghurst 4 E12
SCOTTISH THE
2 Cooper St
Paddington 13 A13
SOUTH PACIFIC PRIVATE
18 Beach St
Harbord 258 J16
STRATHFIELD PRIVATE
3 Everton Rd 341 H12
SUTHERLAND HOSPITAL & COMMUNITY HEALTH SERVICES
cnr Kingsway & Kareena Rd N
Caringbah 492 F5
SYDNEY ADVENTIST PRIVATE
185 Fox Valley Rd
Wahroonga 221 G14
SYDNEY CHILDRENS
High St
Randwick 377 A15
SYDNEY DIALYSIS CENTRE
37 Darling Point Rd
Darling Point 13 H9
SYDNEY EYE HOSPITAL
Macquarie St ....D G3
SYDNEY HOME NURSING SERVICE
36 Boyce St
Glebe 11 J11
SYDNEY HOSPITAL
Macquarie St ....D G3
SYDNEY PRIVATE, THE
Victoria St
Ashfield 372 K5
SYDNEY SOUTHWEST PRIVATE
40 Bigge St
Liverpool 395 F1
THE WENTWORTH PRIVATE CLINIC
23-27 Lytton St
Wentworthville 307 B1
TRESILLIAN
2 Second Av
Willoughby 285 H12
TRESILLIAN FAMILY CARE CENTRES
McKenzie St
Belmore 371 J16
UNITED DENTAL
2 Chalmers St
Surry Hills ....E K16
UNITED GARDENS PRIVATE SURGERY
11a Moonbie St
Summer Hill 373 C5
WANDENE PRIVATE
7 Blake St
Kogarah 433 A6
WAR MEMORIAL
125 Birrell St
Waverley 377 F6
WENTWORTH AREA HEALTH SERVICE
Governor Phillip Campus
Glebe Pl
Penrith 237 D9
WESLEY PRIVATE
91 Milton St
Ashfield 372 E5
WESTMEAD
cnr Darcy & Hawkesbury Rds 277 G14
WESTMEAD PRIVATE
cnr Mons & Darcy Rds
Wentworthville 277 E13
WESTSIDE PRIVATE
55 Burwood Rd
Concord 342 B9
WOLPER JEWISH PRIVATE
8 Trelawney St
Woollahra 347 B16

HOTELS & MOTELS

Aarons Hotel
Haymarket ....E C10
ABA Motel
Sylvania 462 B8
Abcot International Motor Inn
Sylvania 461 G15
Airport Sydney International Motor Inn
Wolli Creek 403 K7
Alexander the Great Motel
Vineyard 152 B2
A Line Hotel
Glebe 12 G16
All Seasons Premier Menzies Hotel
Sydney ....A H15
Angel Motel
Narellan 478 F9
Apia Hotel
Camperdown 17 G2
Appin Hotel 569 F10
Artarmon Motor Inn 284 H15
Ascot Motor Inn
Wahroonga 222 A7
Ashfields Philip Lodge Motel
Ashfield 373 B1
Astoria Hotel
Potts Point 4 K6
Avillon Hotel Sydney
Sydney ....E J3
Banksia Motel
Bass Hill 367 J7
Barclay Hotel
Potts Point 4 J8
Bargo Country Lodge 567 H11
Bass Hill Tourist Park & Motel 368 A9
Bellbird Motel
Kurmond 64 F16
Berowra Heights Hotel Motel 133 A9
Blacket Hotel
Sydney ....C H4
Boyles Sutherland Hotel
Sutherland 490 E3
Buena Vista Hotel
Mosman 317 B9
Burwood Motel 371 J2
Cambridge Park Inn International
Surry Hills ....F J9
Camden Country Club Motel 507 A15
Camden Valley Golf Resort
Camden 449 K12
Camden Valley Inn
Cawdor 507 A16
Camelot Inn
Darlinghurst 4 H11
Camperdown Towers Motel
Camperdown 17 F6
Camperdown Travelodge .17 G3
Capitol Square Hotel
Haymarket ....E G7
Carlton Crest Hotel Sydney
Haymarket ....E B12
Carnarvon Manor
Neutral Bay 6 H7
Carss Park Motel
Blakehurst 432 E16
Castlereagh Inn
Sydney ....D B11
C B Hotel
Haymarket ....E J6
Centra Camperdown 17 G3
Central Park Hotel
Sydney ....D B12
Central Railway Motel
Redfern 19 G6
Checkers Resort
Terrey Hills 195 K14
Citigate Sebel Sydney
Surry Hills ....F C11
City Crown Lodge International
Surry Hills ....F K12
Clarion Suites Southern Cross Darling Harbour
Sydney ....E D4
Colonial Hotel/Motel
Werrington 238 H11
Colonial Motels
Richmond 118 F4
Comfort Inn Pacific International Sydney
Haymarket ....E E10
Coogee Bay Boutique Hotel
Coogee 407 G1
Coogee Bay Hotel
Coogee 377 G16
Coogee Sands Motor Inn
Coogee 377 H15
Coolibah Hotel
Merrylands West 306 K12
Corus Hotel Sydney ....A F14
Cosy Private Hotel
Haymarket ....E J6
Country Comfort
Blakehurst 432 E13
Lane Cove 314 G1
Country Comfort Sydney Central
Haymarket ....E D13
Courtyard by Marriott
Macquarie Park 282 J4
Parramatta 308 D6
Cranbrook International
Rose Bay 347 F10
Cremorne Point Manor ..316 G15
Crescent on Bayswater
Potts Point 4 J8
Crest Hotel
Potts Point 4 H7
Cronulla Motor Inn
Woolooware 493 H10
Crowne Plaza Coogee Beach
Coogee 407 G1
Crowne Plaza Darling Harbour
Sydney ....C D12
Crowne Plaza Norwest Sydney
Baulkham Hills 216 K14
Dive Hotel
Coogee 407 G1
Drummoyne Manor 343 H1
Dural Hotel & Motel 189 A15
El Toro Motor Inn
Warwick Farm 365 D15
Engadine Motor Inn 518 H7
Ermington Hotel/Motel ..310 A2
Esron Motel
Randwick 377 D16
Establishment Hotel
Sydney ....A J12
Evesham Private Hotel
Manly 288 H10
Fountainebleau Inn
Casula 394 K12
Four Points by Sheraton
Sydney ....C C6
Four Seasons Hotel Sydney
The Rocks ....A J8
Gardenia Motor Inn
Bass Hill 368 B10
Gateway Motel
Vineyard 153 C13
Gemini Hotel
Randwick 377 A13
Gladesville Motel 312 J11
Glebe Private Hotel
Glebe 11 J14
Golf View Hotel/Motel
Guildford 337 K8
Grand Hotel
Sydney ....A K15
Greenwich Inn Hotel
Artarmon 315 A15
Grey Gums Hotel/Motel
Jamisontown 266 A1
Greystanes Inn Hotel/Motel 306 D10
Hampton Court Hotel
Potts Point 4 J8
Harbour Rocks Hotel
The Rocks ....A K4
Haven Inn
Glebe 12 A10
Hawkesbury Campus Conference Centre & Motel
Richmond 118 F11
Heathcote Inn
Hotel Motel 518 G11
Heritage Hotel Motel
Wilberforce 91 K6
Hills Lodge Boutique Hotel
Castle Hill 217 A14
Hilton
Sydney ....C J10
Holiday Inn
Potts Point 4 H7
Holiday Inn Darling Harbour
Haymarket ....E C5
Holiday Inn Penrith Panthers
Penrith 236 D12
Holiday Inn Rooty Hill 241 K16
Holiday Inn Sydney Airport
Mascot 405 B3
Hotel 10
Greenacre 369 K8
Hotel Bakpak Westend
Haymarket ....E J6
Hotel Coronation
Sydney ....C J12
Hotel Ibis
Thornleigh 221 B12
Hotel Ibis Sydney Airport
Mascot 405 B4
Hotel Ibis World Square
Sydney ....E K4
Hotel Inter-Continental
Sydney ....B F10
Hughenden Hotel
Woollahra 21 G4
Hunts Motel
Casula 424 A3
Hyde Park Inn
Sydney ....F B1
Hyde Park Plaza Hotel
Darlinghurst ....F G2
James Ruse Hotel/Motel
Kellyville Ridge 215 D1
Jamison Hotel Motel
South Penrith 237 A16
Jolly Knight Motel
Casula 394 H16
Jonah's Motel
Palm Beach 140 B5
Killara Inn 254 A15
Kingsview
Potts Point 4 K6
Kirribilli Hotel
Milsons Point 6 A14
Lansdowne Motor Inn
Lansvale 366 F7
Liberty Plains Motor Inn
Lidcombe 339 H6
Lidcombe Motor Inn 339 J9
Liverpool Motel 395 C6
Lochinvar Motel
Kellyville Ridge 215 D1
Lodge Motel
Edgecliff 13 F9
Log Cabin Motor Inn
Penrith 236 C8
Lucas Heights Motel & Function Centre 487 K10
Macarthur Inn
Leumeah 482 A11
Maclin Lodge Motel
Campbelltown 511 H1
Manly Lodge 288 H11
Manly Pacific Sydney 288 H8
Manly Paradise Motel 288 H9
Manor House Boutique Hotel
Darlinghurst 4 F16
Marco Polo Motor Inn
Summer Hill 373 E3
Mariners Court Motel
Potts Point 4 H4
Markets Hotel-Motel
Homebush West 340 J7
Merchant Court Hotel
Sydney ....C J8
Mercure Hotel
St Leonards 315 A5
Mercure Hotel Lawson City West
Ultimo 3 A13
Mercure Hotel Sydney on Broadway
Ultimo ....E C16
Mercure Hotel Ultimo, Sydney
Ultimo 12 J9
Mercure Sydney Airport
Wolli Creek 404 A7
Meriton Rialto
Sydney ....C K14
Meriton Tiffany
Bondi Junction 22 H6
Meriton World Tower
Sydney ....E H3
Metro Motor Inn
Ashfield 373 B2
Chippendale 19 A3
Double Bay 13 K11
Haberfield 343 B16
Miranda 492 B4
Ryde 311 G2
MGSM Executive Hotel & Conference Centre
Macquarie Park 252 D15
Milperra Palms 398 B12
Mona Vale Motel 199 C7
Motel Formula One
Campbelltown 481 K11
Wentworthville 306 J3
Motel Formule 1
Darlinghurst 4 G8
Mascot 405 B6
Casula 394 K11
Enfield
Strathfield South 370 J3
Motel Voyager
Minchinbury 272 D8
Mt Kuring-gai Motel 162 H13
Nepean Shores Riverside Conference Centre
Jamisontown 235 J13
Nepean Shores Riverside Resort & Conference Centre
Emu Plains 235 J14
New Inn Motel
Richmond 118 F4
Newport Arms
Newport 169 E12
Newport Mirage 169 E12
Noah Lodge
Redfern 19 C5
North Sydney Harbourview Hotel ....K G12
Novotel Brighton Beach
Brighton-le-sands 434 A2
Novotel Century Sydney
Haymarket ....E B4
Novotel Hotel Ibis
Homebush Bay 340 G1
Oakford Darling Harbour ...C D11
Old Sydney Holiday Inn
The Rocks ....B A1
Overlander Hotel/Motel
Cambridge Park 237 F5
Pacific International Hotel
Bankstown 369 F14
Parramatta 308 D5
Palm Court Motor Inn
Haberfield 373 E2
Palms Hotel Motel, The
Greenacre 370 A7
Park Regis Hotel
Sydney ....D A12
Parramatta Central Hotel
Harris Park 308 E6
Parramatta City Motel 308 B5
Pasadena on Pittwater
Church Point 168 F6
Penrith Hotel/Motel 237 A10
Penrith Valley Inn 236 D8
Pentura on Pitt
Sydney ....C K15
Philip Lodge Motel
Ashfield 372 K4
Picton Village Motel 563 K2
Plumpton Motor Inn
Glendenning 242 K3
Pop-In Motel
Casula 424 A3
Prospect Hotel/Motel 275 E15
Quality Hotel S C
Sydney ....F B9
Quay Grand Suites
Sydney ....B G6
Quay West Suites Sydney
The Rocks ....A H8
Radisson Hotel
Sydney ....E E1
Radisson Kestrel Hotel on Manly Beach
Manly 288 J10

162 GREGORY'S STREET DIRECTORY

Radisson Plaza Hotel
Sydney ....B A14
Randwick Lodge 377 B15
R G on Capitol Square
Sydney...........................E J7
Richards on the Park
Canley Vale.................366 A3
Richmond Inn
Hotel/Motel.................118 H5
Rooftop Motel
Glebe 12 B12
Roslyn Gardens Motor Inn
Elizabeth Bay 13 C6
Royal Hotel (Ryde)........312 A2
Ryde Motor Inn
West Ryde..................280 J15
Rydges
Cronulla.....................494 A11
Rydges Bankstown
Bass Hill 368 B9
Rydges Jamison
Sydney ....A G13
Rydges North Sydney
North Sydney 5 H4
Rydges Parramatta
Rosehill.......................308 J7
St George Tavern Hotel &
Accomodation
Rockdale 403 D16
Sans Souci Motor Inn....433 C15
Saville 2 Bond St
Apartment Hotel
Sydney ....A J13
Saville Park Suites
Sydney...........................F H3
Savoy Double Bay Hotel ..347 B13
Seaview Motel
Manly.........................288 G5
Sebel Pier One Sydney, The
Dawes Point...................1 H5
Sebel Resort &
Spa Hawkesbury
Windsor.....................120 H9
Shangri-la Hotel
The Rocks......................A G7
Sheraton on the Park
Sydney ....D C9
Sheridan Hotel/Motel
Guildford West............336 G3
Silver Beach Resort
Kurnell 465 G8
Sir Stamford
Double Bay 347 B13
Sir Stamford at Circular Quay
Sydney ....B F9
Sleep-Inn Express Motel
Greenacre...................370 D5
Somerset Darling Harbour.C D11
Sovereign Inn
Crows Nest.................315 G8
Spanish Inn Motor Lodge
Strathfield...................371 C4
Stamford Airport Hotel
Mascot.......................405 A5
Stamford Grand North Ryde
Macquarie Park...........282 C3
Stamford Plaza
Double Bay.................347 B12
Sullivans Hotel
Paddington.....................4 G15
Sunnybrook Hotel
Warwick Farm.............366 A10
Sutherland Inn Motel.....490 H5
Sydney Boulevard Hotel
Woolloomooloo..............4 E7
Sydney Central
Private Hotel ....F B7
Sydney Central YHA
Haymarket......................E F11
Sydney Harbour Marriott
Sydney ....B B10
Sydney Huntley Inn
Gladesville 312 J11
Sydney Marriott
Sydney...........................F G1
Sydney Park Inn
Darlinghurst...................F G1
Sydney Park Lodge Hotel
Moore Park 20 D9
Tahmoor Inn
Hotel/Motel.................565 J14
Taren Point Hotel/Motel
Miranda......................462 H16
The Blaxland Accommodation &
Conference Complex
Ryde 281 K15
The Clovelly
Clovelly 377 K13
The Falls Resort
Oxford Falls 257 C2
The Grace Hotel
Sydney ....C F5
The Grosvenor
Waterloo 19 H11
The Observatory Hotel
Millers Point...................A C6
The President Hotel
Belrose.......................226 B13
The Russell Hotel
The Rocks......................A K6
The Stafford
The Rocks......................A J4
The Wahroonga Spanish Motel
Wahroonga.................222 A6
The Wentworth
Sydney ....B D15
Town & Country Motel
Strathfield South 371 E4
Tradewinds Hotel
Maroubra 407 B10
Travelodge
Bankstown 399 E1
Blacktown..................274 C10
Sydney.........................D D4
Travelodge Macquarie North
Ryde
Macquarie Park...........252 E16
Travelodge Manly/Warringah
Brookvale 258 D9
Travelodge Wentworth Av
Sydney..........................F D5
University Motor Inn Broadway
Glebe 12 D16
Valentine on George
Haymarket......................E E12
Vibe Rushcutters
Rushcutters Bay............13 D9
Vineyard Hotel/Motel.....153 D13
Wake Up
Haymarket......................E E13
Waldorf Apartment Hotel, The
Sydney...........................E F2
Warwick Farm
Grandstand Motel........366 A13
Wesley Lodge Motel
Westmead..................277 H15
Westin Sydney Hotel
Sydney ....C K3
Westside Inn Motel
Ashfield 373 B3
Wild Orchid Private Hotel
Haymarket......................E J9
Windsor Motel..............121 E7
Windsor Terrace Motel ..121 E7
Winston Hotel/Motel
Winston Hills 277 A1
Woolloomooloo Bay Hotel
Woolloomooloo..............4 F3
Wooloomooloo Waters
Apartment Hotel
Woolloomooloo..............4 H4
W Sydney
Woolloomooloo..............4 G2
Y on the Park
Sydney...........................F F3

MOTOR REGISTRIES

BANKSTOWN
Shop 4a Bankstown
Shopping Centre 369 F16
BEVERLY HILLS
cnr Cambridge St &
Stoney Creek Rd 401 C16
BLACKTOWN
85 Flushcombe Rd 274 G1
BONDI JUNCTION
88 Ebley St 22 J8
BOTANY
5 Lord St 405 F9
BURWOOD
Shops 1 & 2,
25 Belmore St.............341 K15
CAMDEN
Albert Baker Arcade,
167 Argyle St..............477 A16
Campbelltown
cnr Tindall St &
Menagle Rd 511 A6
CAMPSIE
Shop 43, Campsie Centre,
Amy St........................372 A14
CASTLE HILL
18 Anella Av................217 D12
CHATSWOOD
313 Victoria Av............285 A9
CITY
19 York St
Sydney ....A F15
CITY SOUTH
Centennial Plaza,
260 Elizabeth St
Surry Hills ....F B12
ENGADINE
Engadine Court,
101 Caldarra Av 518 J2
FAIRFIELD
32 Harris St 336 E13
FIVE DOCK
cnr Ramsay Rd &
Henley Marine Dr 343 A12
FRENCHS FOREST
Shop 12, Forest
Way Shopping Centre..256 D5
GLADESVILLE
230 Victoria Rd 312 J9
HORNSBY
324 Pacific Hwy 191 G14
HURSTVILLE
8 Woodville St.............432 A5
INGLEBURN
Shop 9, Centennial
House, cnr Oxford &
Ingleburn Rds.............453 C6
LIDCOMBE
cnr Swete & Mills Sts ..339 K7
LIVERPOOL
357 Hume Hwy...........395 B8
MANLY
239 Pittwater Rd 288 F5
MAROUBRA JUNCTION
832 Anzac Pde
Maroubra 407 A9
MERRYLANDS
12 McFarlane St..........307 H12
MIRANDA
Shop 7-9, Kiora Mall,
Kiora Rd 492 A3
MOUNT DRUITT
23 Luxford Rd.............241 F14
NORTH RYDE
Shop 2,
Macquarie Centre
Macquarie Park...........282 F2
NORTH SYDNEY
154 Pacific Hwy.............K B3
PARRAMATTA
Shop 6
197-205 Church St......308 C3
PADSTOW
11 Cahors Rd..............399 D14
PENRITH SOUTH
81 York Rd
Jamisontown..............266 E1
RICHMOND
173 Windsor St...........118 H4
ROCKDALE
Rockdale Plaza,
1 Rockdale Plaza Dr.....433 E2
RYDE
cnr Blaxland &
North Rds...................281 K13
ST CLAIR
Shop 20,
St Clair Shopping Cntr,
cnr Endeavour &
Bennett Rds................270 C12
SILVERWATER
1 River St 309 J9
THORNLEIGH
1 Central Av................221 A13
WARRIEWOOD
Shop 4, Warriewood
Shopping Centre,
Jackson Rd.................198 K12
WETHERILL PARK
Unit 1, Greenway Plaza,
1183 The Horsley Dr ...334 D4

PARKS, RESERVES & OVALS

Abbotsford Cove
Foreshore Park
Abbotsford 343 A1
Abbott Park
Chester Hill 367 K1
Abel Reserve
Revesby 398 H16
Acacia Park
Dundas Valley.............279 K9
Eastwood...................281 J8
Prestons 394 B15
Acacia Reserve
Oatley........................431 A10
Ace Reserve
Fairfield 336 G8
Acron Oval
St Ives........................224 G11
Adams Park
Canley Vale................365 K3
Adam St Ground
Curl Curl....................258 K12
Ador Av Reserve
Rockdale 403 G16
Adventure Park
Ryde 282 A14
A E Watson Reserve
Bexley 402 J15
Agnes Banks
Nature Reserve 146 F8
Airey Park
Homebush.................340 J10
Airport Reserve
Bankstown Airport.......397 F6
Aitken Reserve
Queenscliff.................288 F3
Akuna Av Oval
Bangor 459 G14
Alamein Park
Liverpool 394 K3
Alan Ashton Foreshore Reserve
Picnic Point 428 B13
Alan Davidson Oval
Homebush.................340 J10
Albert Brown Park
Ermington 280 E11
Albert Delardes
Memorial Reserve
Illawong 459 J2
Albert Park
Earlwood 403 B4
Alberts Bush
Killara........................283 D3
Albert St Park
Guildford West............306 H16
Alcheringa Reserve
Miranda.....................491 J8
Alderson Park
Merrylands 307 C7
Aleta End
Wahroonga.................251 G2
Alexandria Park...............19 A14
Alfred Henry Whaling
Memorial Reserve
Baulkham Hills............247 G4
Algie Park
Haberfield 343 C14
Alice Park
Bankstown 369 C13
Alison Park
Randwick 377 A12
Alison Playground
Dulwich Hill 373 C11
Allambie Heights Oval....257 C11
Allambie Rd Reserve
Edensor Park 333 G13
Allan Border Oval
Mosman.....................317 A7
Allan Small Park
East Killara.................254 J6
Allard Corner
Roseville Chase...........255 G16
Allder Park
Sefton 368 E4
Allenby Park
Allambie Heights 257 E9
Allen Park
Killara........................253 C15
Allen Robertson Reserve
Kings Langley 245 A5
Allison Park
Chiswick.....................343 B2
Allman Park
Ashfield 373 A4
Allsopp Oval
Cambridge Park 237 H7
Allum Park
Greenacre...................370 E11
Alma Reserve
Padstow 429 G5
Alpha Park
Blacktown..................244 F16
Alpha Rd Park
Greystanes 305 F12
Alroy Park
Plumpton 242 B6
Alston Reserve
Macquarie Park...........282 K1
Amalfi Park
Lurnea........................394 F9
Amaroo Reserve
Georges Hall 367 F13
Ambleside Reserve
Collaroy Plateau 228 D12
Ambrose Hallen Park
Toongabbie 276 F9
Amour Park
Revesby 398 F16
Amundsen Reserve
Leumeah 482 J10
Anana Reserve
Elanora Heights...........198 E16
Anderson Park
Rydalmere..................309 K1
Ryde...........................311 F5
Andrew Campbell Reserve
Prospect.....................304 J4
Andrew Thompson Park
Erskine Park................270 G16
Andrew Town Park
Richmond 118 D5
Andromeda Fields
Cranebrook.................207 G6
Anembo Reserve
Duffys Forest 194 J8
Angelo St Reserve
Woolwich 314 G11
Angle Park
Chipping Norton..........366 E12
Angophora Park
Forestville...................255 F9
Angophora Reserve
Avalon........................169 G3
Bilgola 169 G3
Angus Memorial Park
Rooty Hill 272 C2
Anita Cobby Reserve
Blacktown...................274 A5
Annangrove Park 186 E2
Ann Cashman Reserve
Balmain..........................7 C10
Annie Prior Reserve
Glenhaven 187 G16
Annie Wyatt Park
Palm Beach 140 B3
Ann Thorn Park
Ryde 311 G3
Ansell Park (Private)
Clarendon...................120 F8
Anzac Avenue Reserve
Collaroy......................228 K14
Anzac Oval
Engadine 488 F15
Anzac Park
Cammeray..................315 K7
West Ryde 281 F15
A P Austin Field
Arncliffe.....................403 K11
Apex Community Park
Ingleburn....................453 J5
Apex Park
Bradbury 511 D8
Liverpool 395 C2
Mona Vale..................199 G4
Riverview...................314 B4
Apex Reserve
Bankstown 369 G11
Appin AIS
Sportsground 569 D9
Appin Park....................569 F10
Applegum Reserve
Glenmore Park............265 G7
Aquatic Park
Longueville 314 D11
Aquatic Reserve
Frenchs Forest 256 J8
Aquilina Reserve
Rooty Hill 242 J15
Ararat Reserve
Frenchs Forest 256 G10
Arcadia Park 130 A10
Arcadia St Park
Merrylands West.........307 A12
Ardill Park
Warrimoo...................203 C12
Argyle Bailey Memorial Park
Ebenezer 68 D13
Argyle Place Park
Millers Point..................A E2
A R Hurst Reserve
Sylvania......................461 F10

GREGORY'S STREET DIRECTORY 163

PARKS INFORMATION

Arlington Recreation Reserve
Dulwich Hill 373 C9
Armitage Reserve
Chiswick 313 D16
Arncliffe Park 403 E7
Arnett Park
Guildford 337 B1
Arrowsmith Park
Hurstville 431 H5
Arrunga Gardens
Wentworthville 277 C12
Artarmon Oval 285 C16
Artarmon Park 315 B1
Artarmon Reserve ... 285 B16
Arthur Byrne Reserve
Maroubra 407 G13
Arthur Loundy Reserve
Bass Hill 367 C1
Arthur McElhone Reserve
Elizabeth Bay 13 B3
Arthur (Paddy) Gray Reserve
Glebe 11 J13
Arthur Park
Punchbowl 399 H5
Arthur Phillip Reserve
Northmead 277 G10
Arthur Walker Reserve
Concord West 311 H16
Arthur Whitling Castle
Hill Memorial Pk 218 D14
Ashcroft Reserve
Georges Hall 367 E14
Ashfield Park 373 B11
Ashford Reserve
Milperra 397 G6
Ashley Brown Reserve
Lalor Park 245 J12
Ashton Park
Mosman 317 C15
Asquith Park 192 A7
A S Tanner Reserve
Monterey 433 C2
Astrolabe Park
Pagewood 406 E4
Atchison Reserve
Macquarie Fields 423 K14
Atkinson Reserve
Gladesville 312 K5
Atlas Reserve
Narellan Vale 508 H2
Attunga Reserve
Bilgola 169 K6
Newport 169 K6
Auburn
Botanic Gardens 338 H6
Auburn Community
Picnic Area 338 G7
Auburn Park 309 D16
Auluba Reserve
South Turramurra 252 B6
Austin Park
Homebush West 340 G7
Austral Bringelly Lions Park
West Hoxton 392 F4
Australia Rd Reserve
Barden Ridge 488 G2
Australis Park
Wattle Grove 425 K3
Avenel Park
Canley Vale 365 J1
Avery Park
Fairfield West 335 E13
Baden Powell Reserve
Bradbury 511 H11
Badgally Reserve
Claymore 481 B12
Badgerys Creek Park .. 358 F1
Bain Playground
Stanmore 16 J7
Baird Reserve
Matraville 436 H1
Baker Park
Coogee 407 E1
Bald Face Point Reserve
Blakehurst 462 A5
Bales Park
Chatswood 285 C10
Balgowlah Oval
Balgowlah 287 F8
Balmaringa Reserve
South Turramurra 252 B5
Balmoral Oval
Mosman 317 F8
Balmoral Park
Mosman 317 F8
Bancroft Park
Roseville 284 K4
Bancroft Rd Reserve
Abbotsbury 333 B15

Band Hall Reserve
Birrong 368 K7
Bangalow Reserve
Mona Vale 199 D1
Bangor Park
Auburn 338 H1
Coogee 407 D3
Banjo Paterson Park
Gladesville 312 J13
Banksia Field
Arncliffe 403 J11
Banksmeadow Park
Banksmeadow 435 J1
Botany 435 J1
Banks Reserve
Camden South 506 K12
Kings Langley 245 J9
Bankstown
Memorial Park 399 E2
Bankstown Oval 399 D2
Bannockburn Park
Pymble 223 C15
Banool Reserve
North Ryde 283 D12
Bantry Reserve
Seaforth 287 A2
Baraply Park
Dundas Valley 280 B7
Barbara Long Park
Liverpool 395 A3
Barden Ridge Oval
Barden Ridge 488 E6
Bardia Park
Holsworthy 426 C1
Bardon Park
Coogee 377 F15
Bardo Park
Auburn 339 F1
Bardwell Valley Parklands
Bexley 402 E13
Bareena Park
Balgowlah Heights .. 287 H14
Canley Vale 366 D5
Bargo Community Park .567 D4
Barker Reserve
Camden South 507 A10
Bark Huts Reserve
Belfield 371 C6
Barnetts Rd Reserve
Berowra Heights ... 132 G10
Barney & Bligh Reserve
The Rocks .... B A3
Baronesa Park
South Penrith 237 B16
Barra Brui Oval
St Ives 254 C2
Barracluff Park
North Bondi 348 B16
Barralier Park
The Oaks 502 F12
Barratt Reserve
Camden South 507 C14
Barra Wood
St Ives 224 C14
Bartlett Park
Ermington 280 G16
Barton Park
Banksia 403 K12
North Parramatta . 278 J13
Barwell Park
Bexley 432 G3
Basil Cook Reserve
Epping 250 E15
Bass Reserve
Macquarie Fields . 454 E3
Bates Dr Oval
Kirrawee 461 E15
Bates Reserve
Elderslie 507 K3
Bathurst Park
Greystanes 305 J4
Batten Park
Lane Cove North ... 284 A14
Battersea Park
Abbotsford 312 H16
Baythorn Reserve
Ambarvale 510 J16
Bayview Park
Bayview 169 C13
Concord 342 G5
Greenwich 314 K10
Beach Reserve
Mona Vale 199 G5
Beacon Hill Reserve... 257 H6
Beale Reserve
Peakhurst 430 E6
Beaman Park
Earlwood 373 D15

Beare Park
Elizabeth Bay 13 C3
Beatty Reserve
Georges Hall 367 C13
Beatty St Reserve
Mortdale 430 H8
Beauford Avenue Reserve
Caringbah 492 E15
Beaumont Park
Kingsgrove 402 C7
Beauty Point Reserve
Padstow Heights .. 429 E9
Bede Spillane Gardens
Croydon 342 G14
Bedlam Bay Regional Park
Henley 312 K14
Beeby Park
Mona Vale 199 D6
Beecroft Park 250 E9
Beecroft Village Green .250 F7
Begnall Park
Belfield 371 A9
Belgenny Oval
Camden 507 B6
Belgenny Reserve
Camden 507 C7
Bellamy Creek Reserve
West Pennant Hills .249 E6
Bellamy Farm Reserve
West Pennant Hills .249 D9
Bella Vista Oval
Bella Vista 246 K4
Bellbird Hill Reserve
Kurrajong Heights ...63 G14
Bellevue Park
Bellevue Hill 377 J1
Leumeah 482 F10
Bellevue Reserve
Georges Hall 368 B13
Bell Park
Hurstville 431 K9
West Ryde 280 G12
Bell St Reserve
Thirlmere 565 C6
Belmore Park
North Parramatta . 278 D12
Sydney .... E K10
Belrose Oval 256 B1
Bendall Reserve
Ruse 512 G2
Ben Lomond Reserve
Minto 482 K6
Bennelong Park
Putney 311 J8
Bennett Park
Riverwood 400 F10
St Marys 239 J16
Ben Prior Park
Casula 394 J15
Bensley Reserve
Macquarie Fields . 454 B7
Bents Basin
State Recreation Area
Greendale 384 F10
Silverdale 384 F10
Benwerrin Reserve
Grasmere 505 F2
Berger Road Reserve
South Windsor 150 J2
Berkshire Park ... 179 J7
Bernie Amos Oval
Westmead 277 H13
Berowra Oval 133 E13
Berowra Park 133 F12
Berowra Valley Regional Park
Berowra 132 J12
Berowra Heights .. 132 G6
Berrilee 132 C6
Cherrybrook 220 D2
Dural 190 E5
Galston 161 C2
Hornsby 191 A12
Hornsby Heights .. 191 B3
Hornsby Heights .. 191 H6
Mt Colah 191 H2
Mt Kuring-gai 162 E2
Pennant Hills 220 D2
Westleigh 220 D2
Berrico Playground
Bargo 567 C7
Berriwerri Reserve
Marsfield 251 H12
Bertuex Reserve
Minchinbury 271 K10
Berry Island Reserve
Wollstonecraft 315 B12
Berryman Reserve
Warwick Farm 365 H15

Berry Park
Mt Colah 192 D5
Berry Reserve
Narrabeen 228 K4
Bert Saunders Reserve
Doonside 243 G14
Best Rd Park
Seven Hills 275 J3
Beswick Park
Liverpool 394 G4
Betts Park
Huntleys Point ... 313 E13
Betty Morrison Reserve
Newport 169 J14
Beveridge Park
Chipping Norton ..397 C6
Beverley Job Park
Narraweena 258 D5
Beverly Grove Park
Kingsgrove 401 F10
Beverly Hills Park ...401 F12
Bexley Park 402 G14
Bicentenary Reserve
Ingleburn 452 K11
Bicentennial Equestrian Pk
Camden 506 H1
Bicentennial Park
Annandale 11 D7
Glebe 11 F6
Homebush Bay 311 A15
Bicentennial Reserve
Illawong 459 A6
Willoughby 285 F16
Biddigal Reserve
Bondi Beach 378 F3
Bidjigal Reserve
Baulkham Hills .. 248 D8
Castle Hill 248 D8
Northmead 248 D14
North Rocks 248 D14
West Pennant Hills .248 D8
Bidwill Reserve 211 F15
Bigge Park
Liverpool 395 F3
Bilarong Reserve
North Narrabeen .. 228 F2
Bill Anderson Park
Kemps Creek 360 D2
Billa Rd Oval
Bangor 459 C10
Bill Boyce Reserve
Homebush 341 B7
Bill Colbourne Reserve
Doonside 243 D7
Bill Delauney Reserve
Revesby Heights .. 428 J9
Bill Mitchell Park
Tennyson Point ... 312 F9
Bill Morrison Park
Moorebank 395 G5
Bill Peters Reserve
Ashfield 372 G2
Bill Swift Reserve
Blacktown 244 K13
Bill Wakeham Reserve
Illawong 460 H1
Bill Watson Reserve
North Rocks 278 F2
Bill Wood Reserve
Glenhaven 217 K3
Billy Goat Hill Reserve
Blacktown 244 K14
Billy Hughes Park
North Wahroonga .. 192 F15
Bilpin Oval 61 E5
Bimbi Reserve
Denistone 281 G13
Binalong Park
Old Toongabbie ... 276 J8
Binamittalang Garden
Bexley 402 H12
Binder Reserve
Hurstville 401 G16
Bingara Reserve
Macquarie Fields . 453 H2
Birchgrove Park 7 H2
Birdwood Park
Narrabeen 199 D16
Birdwood Reserve
Georges Hall 367 G15
Birriwa Reserve
Mount Annan 479 E14
Birrung Park
Balmain 7 K12
Blackburn Gardens
Double Bay 347 D11
Blackbutt Park
Pymble 223 G15
Blackbutt Reserve
Killara 253 D14

Blackman Park
Lane Cove West ... 313 F2
Blackmore Park
Leichhardt 343 H13
Black Muscat Park
Chipping Norton .. 366 J13
Blacktown Showground ..244 D14
Blackwall Point Reserve
Chiswick 313 D16
Blackwattle Bay Park
Glebe 11 K5
Blain Reserve
Raby 481 H1
Blair Oval
St Marys 239 D13
Blair Park
Croydon 342 E13
Blanche Barkl Reserve
Punchbowl 400 A3
Blamfield Oval
Ashcroft 364 H16
Bland Oval
Riverwood 400 E12
Blankers-Koen Park
Newington 310 A15
Blaxland Common
Silverwater 310 D8
Blaxland Crossing Reserve
Wallacia 324 J11
Blaxland Dr Reserve
Illawong 459 A6
Blaxland Oval 233 F10
Blaxland
War Memorial Park .. 233 E4
Blenheim Park
Coogee 407 G3
North Ryde 283 A16
Blick Oval
Canterbury 372 G10
Bligh Park
Seaforth 287 A3
Blinman Park
Glenfield 424 C10
Blue Gum Reserve
Eastwood 281 A6
Blue Hills Oval
Glenmore Park ... 266 F13
Blue Hills Park
Glenmore Park ... 266 G14
Blue Mountains National Park
Bowen Mountain.. 83 A10
Glenbrook 263 B3
Mulgoa 323 A1
Bluff Reserve
Glenbrook 264 C6
Elderslie 507 G2
Bobbie Vile Reserve
Macquarie Fields . 453 K4
Bob Prenter Reserve
Drummoyne 313 G16
Bob Smith Reserve
Warriewood 199 A12
Booralee Park
Botany 405 G9
Booral Reserve
North Ryde 282 D11
Booth Park
Beecroft 250 F7
Booth Reserve
Marsfield 282 E5
Boothtown Reserve
Greystanes 305 F14
Borgnis Reserve
Belrose 225 D15
Boronia Park
Epping 250 K16
Hunters Hill 313 D6
St Marys 240 D11
Bosnjak Park
Edensor Park 333 J16

164 GREGORY'S STREET DIRECTORY

Bossley Rd Bush Reserve
Bossley Park 333 J7
Botany Bay National Park
Kurnell 466 F8
La Perouse 436 J15
Little Bay 437 A13
Boundary Rd Reserve
Glossodia 66 G9
Boundary Reserve
Peakhurst 430 H4
Bounty Reserve
Bligh Park 150 B6
Bow Bowing Park 452 D16
Bow Bowing Reserve
Bradbury 511 H12
Bowen Mountain Park 83 K10
Bowman Reserve
Camden South 507 B14
Boyd Reserve
Currans Hill 479 K9
Boyd St Reserve
Blacktown 275 A1
Boyla Reserve
Gladesville 312 H11
Bradbury Park 511 D7
Bradfield Park
Milsons Point 5 K16
Bradley Av Reserve
Bellevue Hill 347 H16
Bradley Bushland Reserve
Mosman 317 E10
Bradley Reserve
Liberty Grove 311 C13
Wahroonga 251 J2
Bradshaw Park
Busby 363 G16
Miller 393 H2
Brady Park
Claymore 481 C9
Braemar Park
Eastwood 280 J7
Braeside Reserve
Glen Alpine 510 E14
Brallos Park
Holsworthy 396 D15
Brays Bay Reserve
Rhodes 311 E10
Breen Park
Caringbah 492 H8
Bremner Park
Gladesville 312 E7
Brenan Park
Smithfield 335 F7
Brennan Park
Waverton 315 E10
Brereton Park
East Ryde 283 C16
Bressington Park
Homebush 341 B3
Brewongle Walkway
Blacktown 274 D6
Brick Pit Reserve
Frenchs Forest 256 H6
Bridge St Reserve
Penshurst 431 F5
Bridgeview Reserve
Beverly Hills 430 J1
Brigade Park
Ryde 282 D16
Brightmore Reserve
Mosman 316 E5
Brighton Street Park
Petersham 373 K4
Bright Park
Guildford 338 C5
Brimbecom Park
Balgowlah 287 H11
Brindley Park
Airds 512 B13
Bringelly Park 388 B11
Brinsley Park
Pitt Town 92 K15
Brisbane Field
Holsworthy 426 D8
Brisbane Water
National Park
Wondabyne 76 K1
Broadarrow Reserve
Maroubra 407 F12
Broadford Street Reserve
Bexley 402 J11
Broken Bay
National Fitness Camp 107 G1
Bromley Reserve
Greenacre 370 B12
Bronte Park 378 A8
Brooklyn Park 75 J11
Brookvale Park 258 B8

Broughton Reserve
Currans Hill 479 K11
Brownes Farm Reserve
Hoxton Park 393 A7
Brownlee Reserve
Birchgrove 8 B3
Browns Field
Wahroonga 222 A15
Browns Forest
St Ives 223 H15
Browns Rd Reserve
The Oaks 502 G8
Browns Reserve
Croydon Park 371 H9
Bruce Cole Reserve
Winston Hills 246 H16
Bruce Reserve
Panania 428 E4
Brunswick Park
Liberty Grove 311 C14
Brush Farm Park
Eastwood 280 G9
Bryce Oval
St Ives 254 F1
Buchanan Oval,
Newington College
Stanmore 16 E14
Buckle Reserve
Menai 458 E10
Buckley Park
Winston Hills 276 H1
Buffalo Creek Reserve
Hunters Hill 313 C3
Bugler Playground
Enmore 17 B11
Bullock Park
Pymble 253 D6
Bullock Reserve
Chester Hill 337 J12
Bunbury Curran Park
Glenfield 424 D14
Macquarie Fields 424 D14
Bundara Reserve
North Ryde 283 B9
Bundeena Oval 523 H10
Bundeena Reserve
Bundeena 523 K9
Woodbine 481 F13
Bundock Park
Clovelly 378 B13
Bungan Head Reserve
Newport 170 A13
Bungarribee Creek Reserve
Arndell Park 273 H7
Blacktown 273 H7
Doonside 273 H7
Burke Reserve
Matraville 437 B4
Burke St Reserve
Oatley 430 H13
Burnie Park
Clovelly 377 J12
Burns Bay Reserve
Riverview 313 J5
Burraneer Park
Woolooware 493 C12
Burra Reserve
Parramatta 307 H7
Burrendah Reserve
Raby 451 G12
Burrows Group
West Pymble 252 K10
Burrows Park
Clovelly 378 B13
Ryde 312 D2
Buruwang Park
Newington 310 B13
Burwood Park 341 K12
Bushells Place
The Rocks B A1
Bushranger Reserve
East Killara 254 E7
Butler Park
South Penrith 237 B15
Buttercup Reserve
Mount Annan 509 E4
Byrne Reserve
St Andrews 451 J16
Byron Park
Ryde 282 D12
Cabarita Park 312 F15
Caber Park
Winston Hills 277 E4
Cabra-Vale Park
Cabramatta 365 J5
Caddies Creek Park
Kellyville 185 E7
Cadi Park
Pyrmont 8 D16

Caffyn Park
Dover Heights 348 E11
Cahill Park
Wolli Creek 403 K6
Calanagara Park
Carlingford 279 G7
Caldew Reserve
Macquarie Park 252 J16
Caley Park
Macquarie Fields 454 F2
Caleys Reserve
St Ives 224 B3
St Ives Chase 224 B3
Calga Reserve
Waverley 378 B10
Calgaroo Native Garden
West Pennant Hills 249 F2
Calga St Reserve
Roseville Chase 285 F1
Caloola Rd Reserve
Wentworthville 276 K12
Cambridge Park 237 H7
Camden Apex Park 506 K2
Camden Rugby Park
Camden South 506 H14
Camden Showground 476 K16
Cameron Park
Holsworthy 426 C2
Turramurra 222 J13
Wattle Grove 426 C2
Cammeray Park 316 B7
Campbell Hill Pioneer Reserve
Guildford 338 C11
Campbell Oval
Canterbury 372 G10
Campbell Park
Chiswick 343 C3
West Pennant Hills 219 K16
Campbell Reserve
Blacktown 244 C12
Harrington Park 478 G3
Campbelltown
Showground 511 H3
Camperdown Memorial
Rest Park 17 F10
Camperdown Park 17 D5
Canally Reserve
Airds 512 G9
Canal Rd Park
Greystanes 306 E13
Canberra Rd Oval
Sylvania 462 C9
Canidius Reserve
Rosemeadow 540 F3
Cann Park
La Perouse 436 K14
Canterbury Park 372 G10
Captain Cook Memorial
Park No 1
Blacktown 274 J2
Captain Cook Oval
Woolooware 493 D6
Carara Reserve
West Ryde 281 H14
Caravan Head
Bushland Reserve
Oyster Bay 461 D4
Careden Reserve
Beacon Hill 257 J4
C A Redmond Field
Rockdale 403 J16
Careel Bay Ovals
Palm Beach 140 B10
Careel Headland Reserve
Avalon 140 G12
Carina Bay Reserve
Como 460 K6
Caringbah Oval 492 H8
Carlingford
Memorial Park 280 A4
Carlson Park
Willoughby 285 F10
Carmen Park
Cherrybrook 219 J3
Carmichael Park
Pyrmont 12 E2
Caroline Chisholm Park
Winston Hills 276 K1
Carolyn St Park
Greystanes 306 G4
Carpenter Cr Reserve
Warriewood 199 E11
Carrawood Park
Carramar 366 J4
Carrington Park
Wahroonga 222 E2
Carroll Park
Casula 395 A14

Carrs Bush
Galston 159 H4
Carss Bush Park
Carss Park 432 G15
Carters Island Nature Reserve
Kurnell 463 J9
Carysfield Park
Bass Hill 368 B10
Casement Reserve
Castlecrag 286 B13
Casey Reserve
Blackett 241 C2
Castle Cove Park 285 G3
Castle Glen Reserve
Castle Hill 217 H5
Castle Haven Reserve
Castlecrag 286 C12
Castle Hill Heritage Park 218 F8
Castle Hill Lions Park 217 J6
Castle Hill Showground 217 E11
Castlereagh Nature Reserve
Berkshire Park 178 G10
Castle Rock Reserve
Clontarf 287 H16
Castlewood Village Green
Castle Hill 248 H1
Casuarina Park
Winston Hills 276 K3
Casuarina Rd Oval
Alfords Point 429 B13
Casuarina Reserve
Forestville 255 K11
Cathedral Reserve 59 B7
Catherine Field Reserve 449 F3
Catherine Park
Scotland Island 168 H2
Cattai Bridge Reserve
Cattai 94 E2
Cattai Farm
Picnic Ground 93 J1
Cattai National Park 68 F15
Cattai National Park 95 B5
Cattle Duffers Flat
Picnic Point 428 E12
Cavanagh Reserve
Lalor Park 245 C11
C D Hensley Field
Hillsdale 406 E12
Cec Blinkhorn Memorial Oval
Oxley Park 270 E2
Cedar Grove Reserve
Castle Hill 217 D10
Cedars Park
Claremont Meadows 238 G16
Centenary Park
Campbelltown 511 J5
Croydon 342 F13
Centennial Parklands
Centennial Park 21 H10
Central Gardens
Merrylands West 306 H11
Central Park
Concord 341 H5
Longueville 314 E6
Maroubra 407 C8
Central Tree Reserve
Glenmore Park 266 A10
C F Williams Reserve
Lugarno 429 H12
Chadwick Reserve
Lidcombe 339 H6
Chain of Ponds Reserve
Ebenezer 67 H11
Strathfield 371 A2
Chambers Park
Chiswick 343 E1
Chaplin Oval
Lane Cove West 283 G16
Chapman Gardens
Kingswood 237 J14
Charles Heath Reserve
Five Dock 342 F10
Charles Herbert Reserve
Northmead 277 J5
Charles Kemp
Recreational Reserve
Ebenezer 68 E7
Charles Kernan Reserve
Darlington 18 H7
Charles Kiernan Reserve
Darlington 18 H7
Charles Moore Reserve
Mount Annan 509 F4
Charles Park
Smithfield 335 C6
Charles Throsby Reserve
Currans Hill 479 J9
Charlie Bali Reserve
Doonside 243 A15

Charlotte Breen Memorial Park
Kurnell 464 E15
Charlton Park
Liberty Grove 311 C15
Chattan Park
North Narrabeen 228 K3
Chauvel Park
Chipping Norton 396 D3
Ched Towns Reserve
Glenmore Park 265 J10
Cheltenham Oval 250 G10
Cherrybrook Park
Cabramatta 366 D11
Cherrywood Reserve
Wahroonga 223 B4
Chester Park
Blacktown 244 B15
Childs Park
Chipping Norton 366 H13
Childs Reserve
Glenfield 424 G12
Chilworth Recreation Reserve
Beecroft 250 D8
Chisholm Park
Canley Heights 364 J3
Chiswick Park
Woollahra 22 A1
Choma Park
Bossley Park 334 C9
Chopin Park
Plumpton 242 A11
Chopin Reserve
Seven Hills 246 D13
Christie Park
Macquarie Park 252 E14
Christison Park
Vaucluse 348 G3
Churchill Reserve
Narellan Vale 479 A10
Padstow Heights 429 D8
Churchills Wharf Reserve
Sackville 68 B5
Church Point Reserve 168 F6
Church St Native Flora Reserve
Blakehurst 432 E16
Cintra Park
Concord 342 D9
Civic Park
Auburn 339 D7
Pendle Hill 276 D13
Clareville Beach Reserve
Clareville 169 D1
Clareville Reserve
Sandringham 463 D4
Clarke Reserve
Bella Vista 246 F6
Padstow 429 F1
Vaucluse 348 G4
Clarkes Point Reserve
Woolwich 314 F14
Clark Oval
Kearns 451 C15
Clark Park
Milsons Point K G16
Clark Reserve
Oakville 123 C14
Claude Cameron Grove
Wahroonga 223 A4
Claydon Reserve
Kogarah Bay 433 B13
Claymore Park 481 B13
Cleland Park
Artarmon 285 A16
Clementson Park
Bondi Junction 22 F8
Clemton Park
Kingsgrove 401 G7
Cleopatra Reserve
Ambarvale 540 F2
Clerkenwell Reserve
Ambarvale 510 G16
Cliff Reserve
North Wahroonga 222 K1
Clifton Gardens Reserve
Mosman 317 D12
Clinchs Pond Reserve
Moorebank 395 H8
Clissold Reserve
Emu Heights 234 K3
Clive Park
Northbridge 286 G14
Clontarf Reserve 287 E14
Clyde Park
Moorebank 396 E13
Clyne Reserve
Millers Point 1 C8
Cobbitty Walk 446 H16
Cockayne Reserve
Castle Hill 217 F14

GREGORY'S STREET DIRECTORY 165

PARKS INFORMATION

Park	Location	Map Ref
Cohen Park	Annandale	10 J9
Col Barratt Reserve	Narellan	478 B9
Colbee Park	Oakville	122 C14
Coleman Park	Bankstown Airport	367 D16
	Berala	339 G12
Cole Park	Moorebank	396 F7
College St Playground	Balmain	7 H7
Collimore Park	Liverpool	395 B2
Colonial Reserve	Bligh Park	150 F7
Colquhoun Park	South Granville	338 E2
Col Sutton Park	Baulkham Hills	246 H12
Colvin Park	Denistone East	281 J9
Comenarra Playing Field	Turramurra	252 D15
Comleroy Rd Reserve	Blaxlands Ridge	65 C2
Commemoration Flat Picnic Area	Kurnell	466 F5
Commercial Rd (Netball) Reserve	Kellyville	185 G9
Commercial Rd Reserve	Kellyville	185 D9
Community Hall Park	Mt Riverview	204 D16
Como Pleasure Grounds		460 J3
Concord Oval		342 C10
Condor C Reserve	Connells Point	432 A13
Connells Point Reserve		431 G16
Connie Lowe Reserve	Rouse Hill	184 J7
Coogee Beach Plaza	Coogee	407 H1
Coogee Oval		377 G16
Cooinoo Reserve	Enfield	371 F5
Cooke Park	Belfield	371 B8
Cook Park	Cabramatta West	364 G7
	Kyeemagh	404 C14
	St Marys	269 E3
	Sandringham	463 E5
	Sans Souci	433 G16
	Sans Souci	463 B6
	Sydney	D H12
Cook Reserve	Ruse	512 G3
Cooks Paddock	Paddington	21 D1
Coolaroo Park	Lane Cove North	284 C13
Cooleena Reserve	Elanora Heights	198 F13
Coolibah Reserve	Bardwell Valley	403 B7
Coolock Cr Reserve	Baulkham Hills	247 E2
Coolong Reserve	Castle Hill	217 G16
Coonong Creek Bushland	Gymea Bay	491 F9
Cooper Park	Bellevue Hill	22 H2
	Woollahra	22 H2
Cooper St Reserve	Engadine	518 H5
Copperfield Reserve	Ambarvale	510 H13
Coralie Reserve	Wareemba	343 A5
Coral Sea Park	Maroubra	407 C12
Corbin Reserve	Quakers Hill	214 D15
Cor Brouwer Reserve	Eastern Creek	272 F7
Corea Oval	Miranda	461 K14
Cornucopia Reserve	Glenwood	215 C14
Coronation Park	Minto	482 F3
Coronation Playground	Surry Hills	19 E4
Coronation View Point	Greenwich	314 H13
Corryton Park	Wattle Grove	425 J2
Cortelle Reserve	Castlecrag	286 A12
Corunna Reserve	Leumeah	482 G15
Costa Park	Busby	393 H1
Cowan Creek Reserve	North Turramurra	223 H4
	St Ives Chase	223 H4
Cowan Park	Chipping Norton	396 G5
Cowells La Reserve	Ermington	280 E15
Cox Park	Carlingford	279 K5
Cox Reserve	Revesby Heights	429 A7
Craig St Reserve	Punchbowl	399 J9
Craik Park	Austral	391 B7
Crammond Park	Stanmore	16 D10
Cranebrook Park		206 H9
Cremorne Reserve	Cremorne Point	316 H16
Crest Sporting Complex	Georges Hall	368 A12
Crestwood Reserve	Baulkham Hills	246 K6
Cripple Creek Reserve	Blaxland	234 A2
Croft Playground	Marrickville	373 D14
Croker Park	Five Dock	342 K12
Cromer Park	Cromer	228 F16
Cromwell Park	Malabar	437 F2
Cronulla Reserve	Cronulla	494 A13
Crookston Reserve	Camden South	506 K14
Croot Park	Hurstville	432 B2
Crosslands Reserve	Hornsby Heights	131 K16
Crossman Reserve	Wallacia	325 A13
Crown of Newport Reserve	Newport	169 G6
Crown Reserve	Picton	563 C11
Croydon Park		372 C8
Cudal Reserve	Ryde	312 C6
Cumberland Park	Newington	310 D11
Cumberland State Forest	West Pennant Hills	249 E2
Cunninghams Reach Park	Linley Point	313 F7
Curagul Field	North Turramurra	193 E14
Currans Hill Park		479 H10
Curry Reserve	Elderslie	477 F15
Curtis Oval	Dundas Valley	280 B10
Cut Hill Reserve	Cobbitty	446 D8
Cutting Reserve	Padstow	429 H1
C V Kelly Park	Girraween	276 A10
Cynthea Reserve	Palm Beach	140 A4
Daisy St Park	Greystanes	305 H7
Dalrymple Hay Nature Reserve	St Ives	223 H15
Dalton Reserve	Condell Park	398 E1
Dangar Oval		347 K11
Daniel St Park	Greystanes	306 D7
Dan Mahoney Reserve	Dundas	278 H13
Dan Parklet	Lansvale	366 E8
Darcy Smith Oval	Emu Plains	235 F11
Dardabong Reserve	Terrey Hills	195 J11
Dark Gully Park	Palm Beach	140 A6
Darks Common	Lapstone	264 E4
Darling St Park	Greystanes	306 A3
Darnley Oval	Gordon	254 C5
Darook Park	Cronulla	523 H4
Darri Reserve	Gladesville	312 H10
Daruk Park	Casula	394 E15
Darvall Park	Denistone	281 B12
Davey Sq Reserve	Strathfield	341 B12
David Carty Reserve	Fairfield East	336 H12
David Frater Reserve	Parramatta	308 D1
David Hamilton Reserve	Eastwood	280 J7
David Joel Reserve	Bellevue Hill	347 D12
David Scott Reserve	Epping	280 H2
David Thomas Reserve	Manly Vale	287 J1
Davison Reserve	Parklea	215 A13
Davis Park	Claymore	481 C10
Davy Robinson Park	Chipping Norton	397 A6
Dawes Point Reserve	The Rocks	1 J7
Deakin Park	Silverwater	309 H14
Dean Reserve	Strathfield South	371 B6
Dearin Reserve	Newport	169 F12
Deborah Wicks Walkway	Blacktown	273 K1
Deep Creek Reserve	Elanora Heights	228 C2
Deepwater Park	Milperra	397 D14
Deerbush Park	Prairiewood	334 F11
Deer Park	Royal National Park	521 J2
Deerubbun Park	Cornwallis	120 K7
Deerubbun Reserve	Mooney Mooney	75 C5
Dee Why Park		258 J2
Dee Why West Recreation Reserve	Cromer	227 F9
Degotardi Park	St Ives	254 B3
Demetrios Reserve	Rosemeadow	540 E3
Dence Park	Epping	251 E16
Denistone Park		281 F11
DEnzil Joyce Oval	North Curl Curl	258 F11
Des Creagh Reserve	Avalon	140 D16
Deverall Park	Condell Park	398 D5
Devils Hole Creek Reserve	Bowen Mountain	83 G3
Devon Park	Cambridge Park	237 K9
	Seven Hills	275 G5
Diamond Bay Reserve	Vaucluse	348 F6
Dickson Park	Bondi	377 K3
Digger Black Reserve	Ingleburn	453 F12
Dillon St Reserve	Paddington	13 B12
Dimeny Park	Claymore	481 C12
Dingley Dell	St Ives	224 D13
Discovery Park	Kings Langley	245 D4
	Liverpool	395 C10
Dobell Rd Reserve	Engadine	489 A15
Dog Kennel Reserve	Huntingwood	273 J11
Dolphin Park	Avalon	140 C9
Dominey Reserve	Bexley	432 F2
Don Dawson Oval	Cabramatta	365 H11
Don Moon Memorial Park	Camden	507 A4
Don Moore Reserve	North Rocks	248 K14
Donnans Reserve	Bexley	402 J13
Donnelly Park	Connells Point	431 J16
	Putney	312 C7
Donovan Park	Eastwood	281 J8
Don Stewart Park	Epping	280 D4
Don't Worry Oval	Windsor	120 K10
Doris Fitton Park	North Sydney	K J3
Doris Sargeant Park	Old Toongabbie	276 J11
Dorothy Park	Bankstown	399 J2
Dorothy Radford Reserve	St Clair	269 J9
Douglas Park Sportsground		568 G8
Douglas Smith Memorial Park	Glenbrook	263 K2
Doug Rennie Field	Kingswood	237 H14
Dover Heights Reserve		348 G8
Dover Park	Blakehurst	462 F2
Downes Park	Wallacia	324 K14
Downes Reserve	Currans Hill	479 G9
Dowsett Park	Kingsgrove	402 A12
Doyle Gardens	Hurstville	401 E16
Doyle Ground	North Parramatta	278 H6
	Parramatta	278 G15
Dr Charles McKay Reserve	Mount Druitt	271 H2
Dr H J Foley Rest Park	Glebe	12 B13
Drivers Triangle	Moore Park	20 F2
Drummoyne Park		343 G2
Drysdale Reserve	Elderslie	507 H3
Duck River Reserve	Granville	308 H15
Dudley Page Reserve	Dover Heights	348 F10
Dudley Park		339 D8
Duff Reserve	Point Piper	347 E7
Dukes Oval	Emu Plains	235 F10
Dumaresq Reserve	Rose Bay	348 B8
Dunbar Park	Avalon	170 B1
	Marsfield	282 A3
Dunbar St Reserve	Silverdale	353 H16
Dunbier Park	Liverpool	395 C7
Duncan Park	Epping	280 J1
	Seven Hills	275 G5
Dundas Park		
Dundas Valley		280 A10
Dundee Park	Winston Hills	277 D4
Dunholm Reserve	Macquarie Park	252 H16
Dunningham Park	Cronulla	494 A11
Dunningham Reserve	Coogee	377 J15
Dunrossil Park	Carlingford	250 B15
Dural Park		189 H16
Dural State Forest	Dural	219 B1
Duri Reserve	Malabar	437 G8
Durrant Oval	Warwick Farm	365 G12
Dwyer Oval	Warwick Farm	365 E13
Eagle Creek Reserve	Eschol Park	481 B5
Eagle Farm Reserve	Eagle Vale	481 F6
Eagleview Reserve	Minto	483 B4
Earl Reserve	Beacon Hill	257 G7
Earlwood Park		402 G3
East Gordon Park	Gordon	254 C5
East Hills Park		427 F6
Eastlakes Reserve		405 K3
Eastlea	Lidcombe	339 J13
East Lindfield Park		255 C11
Easton Park	Rozelle	10 K3
Eastwood Park		281 A7
Ebenezer Park		68 B11
Eccles Park	Ermington	310 B1
Eccles Reserve	Belfield	371 D12
Echo Point Park	Roseville Chase	285 H1
Edenborough Park	Lindfield	284 A4
Edgecombe Park	Moorebank	396 C7
Edinburgh Rd Reserve	Castlecrag	286 D10
Edna Hunt Sanctuary	Epping	281 B4
Edna Reserve	Ingleburn	453 C11
Edward Bennett Oval	Cherrybrook	219 G15
Edwards Park	Concord	342 A14
Edwin Wheeler Oval	Sadleir	394 B3
Egan Reserve	Beacon Hill	257 H4
E G Waterhouse National Camellia Gardens	Caringbah	492 E7
Eileen Cammack Soccer Fields	South Penrith	266 J4
Eileen Mahoney Reserve	Epping	280 H1
Elder Reserve	Mount Annan	509 F1
Eldrinoge Green	Wahroonga	223 A3
Eldridge Reserve	Condell Park	398 J6
Elizabeth Chaffey Reserve	Castle Hill	217 D7
Elizabeth Farm Reserve	Rosehill	308 H15
Elizabeth Jonsson Reserve	Mount Druitt	241 F11
Elizabeth Macarthur Park	Telopea	279 F9
Elizabeth Macarthur Reserve	Camden South	507 C10
Elizabeth Park	Narellan Vale	478 H16
	Northbridge	286 G16
	Scotland Island	168 H3
Elizabeth Throsby Reserve	Currans Hill	479 K11
Eliza Park	Liberty Grove	311 C16
Elkington Park	Balmain	7 B6
Ellen Dale Reserve	Rooty Hill	241 H13
Ellerman Park	Dural	188 G13
Ellery Park	Mosman	287 B12
Elliott Reserve	Belfield	371 E8
Ellison Reserve	Werrington County	238 G9
Ellis Park	Miller	363 G10
Ellis Reserve	Ellis Lane	476 K11
Elms Reserve	Woollahra	22 B3
Elouera Nature Reserve	Ashcroft	394 G14

166 GREGORY'S STREET DIRECTORY

INFORMATION

PARKS

Elouera Reserve
  Macquarie Park..........282 E2
Eloura Nature Reserve
  Liverpool..........394 D3
E L S Hall Park
  Marsfield..........282 C6
Elvina Park
  Elvina Bay..........168 B3
Elyard Reserve
  Narellan..........478 G10
Embrasure Reserve
  Castlecrag..........286 B12
Emerson St Reserve
  Wetherill Park..........334 J4
Emily McCarthy Park
  South Coogee..........407 G4
Emma Edwards Reserve
  Hurstville..........431 K1
Empress Reserve
  Hurstville..........432 C8
Emu Park
  Emu Plains..........235 F10
Endeavour Park
  Kings Langley..........245 F5
Engadine Park..........488 F15
Engesta Reserve
  Camden..........506 K6
Epacris Reserve Number 1
  Forestville..........256 B9
Epping Park
  North Epping..........251 D11
Epworth Park
  Elanora Heights..........198 E11
Equestrian Park
  Sans Souci..........463 D2
Eric Green Reserve
  Newport..........170 A7
Eric Mobbs Memorial Park
  Carlingford..........280 A4
Eric Primrose Reserve
  Rydalmere..........309 K6
Eric Wood Reserve
  Kenthurst..........158 B16
Ernie Smith Recreation Park
  Moorebank..........396 B9
Erskineville Oval..........18 E16
Erskineville Park..........18 D15
Esdkale Reserve
  Mount Annan..........479 G12
Esperance Reserve
  Wakeley..........334 K12
Esplanade Park
  Fairlight..........288 A10
Etchell Reserve
  Minto..........482 G8
Ethel Pyers Reserve
  Greenacre..........370 G12
Ettiesdale Reserve
  Spring Farm..........507 H6
Eugenie Byrne Park
  Warragamba..........353 G13
Eureka Cr Reserve
  Sadleir..........394 B3
Euroka Clearing
  Blue Mountains
  National Park..........263 K15
Euston Park
  Hurlstone Park..........372 K12
Evan Jones Playground
  Leichhardt..........10 G16
Evatt Park
  Bexley..........432 D1
  Lugarno..........429 J13
Everett Park
  Liverpool..........394 J8
Everley Park
  Sefton..........338 F12
Eve Sharp Reserve
  Stanmore..........16 K13
Eve St Wetlands
  Arncliffe..........403 J11
Ewen Park
  Hurlstone Park..........373 A14
Ewenton Park
  Balmain..........8 D10
Excelsior Reserve
  Baulkham Hills..........248 A12
Explosives Reserve
  Castle Cove..........286 F5
Fagan Park
  Galston..........159 G6
Fairfax Reserve
  Harrington Park..........478 G4
Fairfield Heights Park..........336 A10
Fairfield Oval..........336 G14
Fairfield Park..........336 G15
Fairfield Rd Park
  Yennora..........336 F6

Fairfield Showground
  Prairiewood..........334 G10
Faulkland Cr Reserve
  Kings Park..........244 G2
Fay St Ground
  North Curl Curl..........258 F11
Fearnley Park
  Beecroft..........250 B6
Federal Park
  Annandale..........11 D8
Federation Forest
  Mount Druitt..........270 J3
Ferdinand St Reserve
  Hunters Hill..........313 J9
Ferndale Park
  Chatswood West..........284 D12
Fern Rd Reserve
  Hunters Hill..........314 A14
Fiddens Wharf Oval
  Lindfield..........283 E4
Fieldhouse Park
  Ambarvale..........511 A13
Field of Mars Reserve
  East Ryde..........312 K2
Field Park
  Chipping Norton..........396 G6
Fifth Av Reserve
  Macquarie Fields..........454 G5
Figtree Bay Reserve
  Chiswick..........343 C1
Fig Tree Park
  Eschol Park..........481 F3
Findlay Park
  Mt Pritchard..........364 E13
Fingleton Reserve
  Bondi Junction..........377 F3
First Fleet Park
  The Rocks..........B A6
Firth Park
  Ashcroft..........394 F2
Fishers Ghost Reserve
  Bradbury..........511 D9
Fitzgerald Park
  Homebush..........341 G14
Fitzpatrick Park
  Picnic Point..........428 C13
Fitzroy Gardens
  Potts Point..........4 K6
Fiveash Reserve
  St Helens Park..........541 A7
Five Dock Park..........343 B9
Flagstaff Reserve
  Rosemeadow..........540 G8
Flat Rock Gully Reserve
  Naremburn..........315 H1
Fleming Park
  Naremburn..........315 F1
Fleming Playground
  Newtown..........17 E11
Flinders Field
  Macquarie Fields..........454 F6
Flinders Park
  North Ryde..........282 C8
Flinders Slopes
  Lansdowne..........367 C10
Flinders Square
  Georges Hall..........367 G14
Flockhart Park
  Croydon Park..........371 J9
Flood Reserve
  Revesby..........399 A9
Flora Park
  Prairiewood..........334 F10
Flora Reserve
  Curl Curl..........259 A14
Florence Cotton Park
  Hornsby..........221 C2
Florence Park
  Newport..........169 B7
Flynn Reserve
  St Helens Park..........541 F4
Flynns Reserve
  Bexley..........402 C6
Foley Reserve
  Georges Hall..........367 J14
Follies Park
  East Lindfield..........255 B15
Fontenoy Park
  Macquarie Fields..........282 J1
Forbes Creek Reserve
  Engadine..........488 J13
Ford Park
  Strathfield South..........371 C7
Forest Park
  Epping..........281 C1
Forest Park Reserve
  Harrington Park..........478 E1

Forest Redgum Reserve
  Glenmore Park..........265 F6
Forestville Park..........256 E9
Forestville War Memorial
  Playing Fields..........255 J11
Forman Av Reserve
  Glenwood..........215 G14
Formica Park
  Busby..........363 J15
Forrester Park
  Eastwood..........281 D4
Forrester Reserve
  Kingsgrove..........401 J9
Forshaw Field
  Sylvania Waters..........462 D15
Forsyth Park
  Neutral Bay..........5 J4
Foundation Park
  The Rocks..........A K2
Founders Way
  St Ives..........254 G2
Fowler Rd Park
  Merrylands West..........307 B16
Fowler Reserve
  Newtown..........17 G15
  Wallacia..........324 H13
Foxglove Oval
  Mt Colah..........162 F13
Fox Park
  Collaroy..........229 D14
France Petanque Club
  North Narrabeen..........228 H3
Francis Park
  Blacktown..........244 E14
Francis St Park
  Enmore..........17 A16
Frappell Reserve
  Narwee..........400 G13
Fraser Park
  North Wahroonga..........222 H1
Freame Park
  Mays Hill..........307 G6
Freda Park
  Hammondville..........396 B12
Fred Caterson Reserve
  Castle Hill..........217 D8
Fred Hollows Reserve
  Randwick..........377 D12
Fred Hutley Reserve
  Naremburn..........315 H4
Fred Spurway Park
  Eastwood..........280 F5
Fred Vassel Fields
  Kings Langley..........245 C6
Freeburn Park
  Luddenham..........356 H2
Freeman Oval
  Warwick Farm..........365 F12
Freemans Reach Park..........90 G3
French Reserve
  Currans Hill..........479 K14
Frenchs Forest
  Showground..........256 A14
Freres Crossing Reserve
  Kentlyn..........483 G16
Freshwater Park
  Strathfield..........340 H16
Freshwater Reserve
  Harbord..........288 J2
Freya St Reserve
  Kareela..........461 D9
Friars Park
  Pymble..........223 F15
F Robertson Reserve
  Dundas..........279 C13
Frog Hollow
  Centennial Park..........21 E11
Frogmore Park
  Turramurra..........222 G16
Frost Reserve
  Narellan..........478 G14
Frys Reserve
  Kogarah..........433 B2
F S Garside Park
  Granville..........308 H10
Fuchs Reserve
  Elderslie..........507 K1
Fullers Park
  Chatswood West..........284 A8
Fullers Rd Reserve
  Castle Hill..........217 G3
  Chatswood West..........284 E10
Fullwood Reserve
  Claymore..........481 F10
  Eagle Vale..........481 F10
Furber Park
  Berowra Waters..........132 E3
Gabo Park
  Sadleir..........394 A1

Gaden Park
  Woollahra..........22 D3
Gaiarine Gardens
  Pagewood..........405 J10
Galaringi Reserve
  Carlingford..........280 A5
Gale St Reserve
  Woolwich..........314 F12
Gallard Reserve
  Greystanes..........306 G7
Galston Recreation Ground
  Kenthurst..........159 D14
Gandangara Park
  Casula..........394 E16
Gannan Park
  Ryde..........282 F14
Gannons Park
  Peakhurst..........430 B8
Gap Park
  Watsons Bay..........318 H15
Gardenia Pde Park
  Greystanes..........306 B13
Gardiner Park
  Banksia..........403 C11
Gard Park
  Ashcroft..........364 F16
Garigal National Park
  Davidson..........224 H11
  East Killara..........254 J9
  Forestville..........256 E12
  Frenchs Forest..........255 G6
  Ingleside..........196 E14
  Ingleside..........227 B2
  Killarney Heights..........255 H13
  St Ives..........224 K6
  Terrey Hills..........196 E14
Garnet Jackson Reserve
  Botany..........405 K12
Gayline Reserve
  Mount Annan..........479 C13
Gazzard Park
  Yagoona..........369 A11
George Alder Reserve
  Quakers Hill..........214 A13
George Caley Reserve
  Mount Annan..........509 G2
George Christie Playing Field
  Wahroonga..........251 F2
George Green Oval
  Yagoona..........369 D11
George Harley Reserve
  Eastwood..........280 K4
George Kendall Riverside Park
  Ermington..........310 D5
Georges Heights Oval
  Mosman..........317 F10
Georges River National Park
  Alfords Point..........428 J14
  Illawong..........459 E1
  Lugarno..........429 C10
  Padstow Heights..........429 C10
Georges River
  Nature Reserve
  Airds..........512 G9
  Glenfield..........424 J12
  Ingleburn..........454 A9
  Kentlyn..........484 A9
Georges River Parkway Reserve
  Airds..........512 B14
Georges River Softball Complex
  Panania..........397 G15
George W I Brown Reserve
  Quakers Hill..........213 G13
Giba Park
  Pyrmont..........8 F15
Gibbs Park
  Sadleir..........364 C16
Gifford Park
  Penshurst..........431 C1
Gilbert Barry Reserve
  Marrickville..........373 F11
Gilchrist Oval
  Campbelltown..........511 A6
Gilgandra Reserve
  North Bondi..........348 C15
Gillespie Field
  Warrawee..........222 G9
Gilles Reserve
  Beacon Hill..........257 J5
Gilligans Island
  Darlinghurst..........4 E13
Gillman Reserve
  Yagoona..........368 F12
Gimes Park
  Casula..........394 J10
Ginger Meggs Park
  Hornsby..........191 A16

Gipps Park
  Smithfield..........335 C5
Gipps Rd Oval
  Greystanes..........305 D14
Giriwa Picnic Ground
  Oatley..........430 H10
Girrahween Park
  Earlwood..........402 K5
Girraween Park
  Toongabbie..........276 A9
Glades Bay Park
  Gladesville..........312 G11
Gladesville Reserve
  Henley..........313 C13
Gladstone Park
  Balmain..........7 J10
Glenbrook
  Native Plant Reserve..........234 A15
Glenbrook Oval..........234 A15
Glenbrook Park..........234 B16
Glendale Park
  Castle Hill..........217 K7
Glendenning Reserve..........242 H3
Glenfield Park..........424 D11
Glenhaven Reserve..........188 A16
Glenlee Reserve
  Narellan Vale..........508 F1
Glenorie Park..........128 B3
Glen Regent Reserve
  Casula..........424 F4
Glen Reserve
  Eastwood..........281 A8
Glenrock Reserve
  Picton..........563 G12
Glenroy Park
  Claymore..........481 C13
Glenwood Way Reserve
  Castle Hill..........248 G1
Glossodia Park
  Freemans Reach..........66 F15
Goanna Park
  Greystanes..........305 D14
Goddard Park
  Concord..........341 K9
Golden Grove Park
  Kings Langley..........245 B4
Golden Grove Reserve
  Beacon Hill..........257 F4
Golden Jubilee Field
  North Wahroonga..........223 B1
Gollan Park
  Doonside..........243 C14
  South Coogee..........407 G6
Goodacre Reserve
  Fairfield West..........335 B14
Gooden Reserve
  Baulkham Hills..........247 A16
Gordon Glen..........253 F7
Gordon Lewis Oval
  Appin..........569 D8
Gordon Park..........254 A6
Gordon Parker Reserve
  Milperra..........397 C7
Gore Creek Reserve
  Northwood..........314 H7
Gore Hill Oval
  St Leonards..........315 B5
Gore Hill Park
  St Leonards..........315 B5
Goroka Park
  Beacon Hill..........257 D8
Gosling Park
  Greenacre..........369 K10
Gough Reserve
  Ashfield..........372 K9
Gough Whitlam Park
  Earlwood..........403 H2
Governor Phillip Park
  Palm Beach..........109 K14
  Windsor..........121 F6
Governor Phillip Reserve
  Gordon..........254 D6
Gowlland Reserve
  Panania..........398 D13
Gow Park
  Mulgoa..........295 F15
Graf Park
  Yagoona..........369 D10
Grandin Park
  Lidcombe..........339 J12
Grange Av Reserve
  Schofields..........212 F7
Granny Smith Memorial Park
  Eastwood..........281 J6
Grantham Reserve
  Seven Hills..........275 E4
Grant Park
  Enfield..........371 H4

GREGORY'S STREET DIRECTORY 167

PARKS INFORMATION

Grant Reserve
 Coogee 407 H2
Granville Park
 Merrylands 308 A14
Granville
Soldiers
 Memorial Park 308 G12
Grasmere Reserve
 Cremorne 316 E6
Grays Point Oval 491 A14
Greco Reserve
 Rosemeadow 540 E5
Greenacre Heights Reserve
 Greenacre 369 J14
Green Ban Park
 Erskineville 17 J13
Greenhalgh Reserve
 Quakers Hill 213 F14
Greenlees Park
 Concord 342 A5
Green Park
 Darlinghurst 4 G12
Green Point Reserve
 Oyster Bay 460 K5
 Watsons Bay 318 D13
Greenup Park
 Castle Hill 248 D1
Greenway Park
 Cherrybrook 219 G8
Greenway Reserve
 Camden South 507 B9
 Revesby 398 F11
Greenwich Park 314 H13
Greenwich Point Reserve
 Greenwich 314 H14
Greenwood Park
 North Ryde 282 D7
Gregson Park 58 J9
Grey Box Gum Reserve
 Auburn 339 B12
Greygums Oval
 Cranebrook 207 B15
Gribble Reserve
 Blacktown 244 E15
Griffith Park
 Collaroy 229 D16
 Longueville 314 H13
Griffiths Reserve
 Camden South 507 B16
Grotto Pt Reserve
 Balgowlah Heights .. 317 J2
Grove Park
 Hurstville Grove 431 H9
Guildford Park 337 H2
Guilfoyle Park
 Regents Park 369 B1
Gumbooya Reserve
 Allambie Heights ... 257 H14
Gundangarra Reserve
 Mount Annan 509 D2
Gundungurra Park
 Belimbla Park 501 D14
Gundungurra Reserve
 Narellan Vale 508 G2
Gungah Bay Reserve
 Oatley 430 J3
Gunnamatta Park
 Cronulla 493 J15
Gwandalan Reserve
 North Ryde 283 C13
Gwarra Reserve
 Forestville 255 H8
Gwawley Oval
 Sylvania Waters ... 462 H14
Gwendale Park
 Eastwood 281 D5
Gymea Baths Reserve
 Gymea Bay 491 G11
Gymea Bay Oval 491 D9
Hadfield Reserve
 Lugarno 429 K15
Hagan Reserve
 Airds 511 K16
Haigh Park
 Moorebank 395 J4
Hall Drive Bushland Reserve
 Menai 458 F11
Halliday Park
 Five Dock 342 K7
Halls Reserve
 Tahmoor 565 G9
Hallstrom Park
 Willoughby 285 F16
Ham Common
Bicentenary Park
 Richmond 119 E7
Hamilton Park
 Turramurra 252 F1

Hamilton Reserve
 Bilgola 169 J5
Hammond Park
 Ashfield 342 J14
Hammondville Park .. 426 K2
Hampshire Reserve
 Wakeley 334 J16
Hanna Laycock Reserve
 Bexley North 402 C13
Hannan Reserve
 Rozelle 11 B1
Hanna Park
 North Richmond 87 H14
Hanna Reserve
 Raby 481 G3
 Oakhurst 241 K2
Harbord Park 258 F14
Harbour View Park
 Woollahra 22 G3
Harcourt Reserve
 Campsie 371 H11
Harden Reserve
 Georges Hall 367 H12
Haredale Reserve
 Ambarvale 540 D2
Hargrave Park
 Warwick Farm 365 F14
Hargraves Reserve
 Leumeah 512 D1
Harley Park
 Mt Riverview 204 G14
Harnett Park
 Mosman 316 G12
Harold Bull Reserve
 Lakemba 401 D3
Harold Corr Oval
 Cambridge Park 238 C10
Harold Fraser Oval
 Kogarah Bay 432 G12
Harold Moon Reserve
 Auburn 338 J2
Harold Noakes Reserve
 The Oaks 502 F13
Harold Read Park
 Girraween 275 K15
Harold Reid Reserve
 Middle Cove 286 B8
Harold Reserve
 Scotland Island 168 J5
Harold West Reserve
 Carlingford 279 K1
Harrington Green
 Elderslie 477 H14
Harrington Park 478 D4
Harris Creek Oval
 Hammondville 426 J4
Harry Carr Reserve
 Baulkham Hills 247 F10
Harry Dennison Park
 Rooty Hill 242 C14
Harry Gapes Reserve
 Merrylands 338 D2
Harry Lawler Park
 Penrith 237 C11
Hartford Reserve
 Glen Alpine 540 D1
Hartleys Oval
 Canley Vale 366 D4
Hart Park
 Warwick Farm 365 H16
Harvey Brown Reserve
 Blair Athol 511 A3
Harvey Dixon Reserve
 Peakhurst 429 J4
Harvey Park
 Marayong 243 K5
Hassell Park
 St Ives 224 E6
Hastings Park
 Castle Hill 218 K5
Haviland Park
 Warragamba 353 D6
Hawkesbury Park
 North Richmond 87 H14
Hawkesbury Reserve
 Sylvania Waters ... 462 G11
Hawkesbury Showground
 Richmond 119 H9
Hawthorne Canal Reserve
 Leichhardt 343 F15
Hayes Park
 Galston 159 D14
Hayes Reserve
 Ryde 311 H5
Hayter Reserve
 Camden South 506 J14
Hazel Ryan Oval
 North Rocks 278 C7
Hazlett Oval
 Macquarie Fields .. 454 A6

H C Press Park
 Castle Cove 286 F6
H D Robb Reserve
 Castle Cove 285 K3
Headen Park
 Thornleigh 220 K11
Headland Park
 Meadowbank 311 E5
Heathcote National Park . 518 A4
Heathcote Oval 518 G13
Heather King Park
 Cabramatta 366 D7
Heathfield Reserve
 Raby 481 G3
Heber Park
 Hebersham 241 K2
Heffron Park
 Maroubra 406 J13
Helene Park
 Meadowbank 311 F5
Helen St Reserve
 Lane Cove North . 284 G15
Helles Park
 Moorebank 395 D9
Henley Park
 Concord 341 J6
 Enfield 371 H5
Henningham Playground
 Greenwich 314 K7
Henri Dunant Reserve
 Ryde 282 C12
Henry Lawson Park
 Abbotsford 342 H2
Henry Lawson Reserve
 Como 460 F5
Henry Mitchell Reserve
 Acacia Gardens ... 214 F15
Henry Turner Reserve
 Yowie Bay 492 B13
Henty Park
 Yagoona 368 G9
Herbert Crabtree Reserve
 Bass Hill 368 D9
Herbert Rumsey Reserve
 Dundas Valley 279 J7
Heritage Dr Reserve
 Illawong 459 E3
Heritage Park
 Windsor 121 A7
Hermitage Foreshore Reserve
 Rose Bay 348 A6
Heron Park
 Chipping Norton .. 367 A14
Hewitt Park
 Bilgola 169 K5
Hews Pde Mini Fields
 Belrose 226 A14
Hews Reserve
 Belrose 226 A13
Heydon Park
 Hunters Hill 313 C11
 Rosemeadow 540 H6
Haynes Reserve
 Earlwood 372 G15
Hickeys Park
 Penrith 237 A4
Highfield Park
 Claymore 481 C11
High St Reserve
 Mascot 405 B4
Hilder Reserve
 Elderslie 477 H15
Hillcrest Park
 Moorebank 396 C10
Hillier Oval
 Liverpool 395 B5
Hillside Park
 Glenbrook 234 E16
Hills Reserve
 Surry Hills FG13
Hind Park
 Chipping Norton .. 397 D6
Hinkler Park
 North Manly 288 F3
Hinsby Park
 Annandale 11 B12
Hitchcock Park
 Avalon 140 C11
H J Mahony Memorial Reserve
 Marrickville 403 A2
Hodgson Park
 Longueville 314 C8
Hogan Park
 Annandale 11 D13
Hogben Park
 Kogarah 433 C1
Holland Reserve
 Kenthurst 187 G11

Hollier Reserve
 Emu Plains 235 C13
Hollis Park
 Newtown 18 B10
Holloway Park
 Greenwich 315 A11
Hollylea Reserve
 Leumeah 481 K12
Holman Park
 Hornsby 191 K16
Holmlea Pl Reserve
 Engadine 488 F11
Holroyd Apex Park
 Greystanes 306 F11
Holroyd Gardens Park
 Holroyd 307 K10
Holt Park
 North Ryde 282 F6
Homelands Reserve
 Telopea 279 G7
Homepride Park
 Warwick Farm 365 C16
Homestead Park
 Chipping Norton .. 366 G12
Honeysuckle Reserve
 Jannali 460 H9
Hopeville Park
 Hornsby 191 D8
Hopman St Reserve
 Greystanes 306 B10
Horbury Hunt Place
 Bellevue Hill 347 D11
Hordern Park
 Palm Beach 140 A2
Horlyck Reserve
 South Granville 338 F2
Hornsby Park 191 D15
Horsley Park 302 E15
Horton Reserve
 Burwood 372 A1
Hoskins Park
 Dulwich Hill 373 D8
Hospital Farm Reserve
 Northmead 277 K21
Howell Oval
 Penrith 236 E13
Howe Park
 Windsor 121 A7
Howley Park
 Drummoyne 313 E15
Howse Park
 Concord 312 A16
Howson Oval
 Turramurra 252 A1
Hoxton Park Reserve ... 393 B5
Hoy Park
 Lansvale 366 E10
Hubert Hunt Reserve
 Eastwood 281 F6
Hudson Park Oval
 Strathfield 340 G11
Hugh Bamford Reserve
 North Bondi 348 G16
Hughes Park
 Earlwood 402 E2
Hugh St Reserve
 Belmore 371 B12
Hume Oval
 Picton 563 F1
Hume Park
 Silverwater 309 H14
Humphries Reserve
 Strathfield 371 C3
Hunter Fields
 Emu Plains 235 F11
Huntingdale Cir Res
 Castle Hill 218 G7
Huntington Reserve
 Emu Plains 235 E14
Huntleys Point Reserve . 313 F12
Hunt Park
 Lakemba 401 D3
Hunt Reserve
 Mt Colah 162 F15
Hurley Park
 Campbelltown ... 511 G7
Hurstville Natural Heritage Pk
 Mortdale 430 B8
Hurstville Oval 431 K3
Hyacinth Reserve
 Macquarie Fields . 454 E5
Hycraft Reserve
 Five Dock 342 G9
Hyde Park
 Sydney .... D E10
Hyland Rd Reserve
 Greystanes 305 C12
Hyndes Park
 West Lindfield ... 283 J6

Iando Reserve
 Currans Hill 479 J13
Ibbotson St Reserve
 Tahmoor 565 G10
Icely Park
 Richmond 119 D4
Ida Kennedy Park
 Green Valley 363 G13
Ilberry Park
 Neutral Bay 6 F1
Illawarra Reserve
 Leumeah 482 F14
Illoura Park
 Earlwood 402 F7
Iluka Park
 Palm Beach 139 H3
 Ingleburn Reserve 454 B9
Ingleside Park 198 D8
Inman Park
 Cromer 228 G15
Innisfail Reserve
 Wakeley 334 K13
International Peace Park
 Seven Hills 275 D1
Inveresk Park
 Strathfield 341 B12
Invergowrie Reserve
 Glen Alpine 510 D15
Ireland Park
 Liverpool 394 G3
Irelands Bridge Reserve
 Lansvale 366 B11
Irene Park
 Eastwood 281 G4
Irish Town Grove
 Turramurra 223 D11
Iron Bark Reserve
 Colyton 270 H6
Ironbark Ridge
 Rouse Hill 184 G8
Irrawong Reserve
 Warriewood 198 G11
Ismay Reserve
 Homebush 341 G6
Issy Wheiner Reserve
 Balmain 7 H8
Ivanhoe Park
 Manly 288 F9
Ivanhoe Reserve
 Marsfield 251 J13
Ivor Wyatt Reserve
 St Ives 224 B12
Jacka Park
 Harbord 258 G16
Jackett Park
 Burwood 341 H16
Jack Ferguson
Recreation Area
 Greystanes 305 D14
Jack Haynes Reserve
 Newtown 18 A10
Jack Nash Reserve
 Currans Hill ... 479 G22
Jack O'Brien Reserve
 Redfern 20 A11
Jack Shanahan Park
 Dulwich Hill 373 D12
Jackson Park
 Croydon Park ... 371 F7
 Woodbine 481 J7
Jacksons Rd Reserve
 North Narrabeen . 199 B12
Jack Vanny Memorial Park
 Maroubra 407 A12
James Greenwood Reserve
 Castle Hill 218 E10
James Henty Reserve
 Dural 219 B5
James Hoskin Reserve
 Eastwood 280 E6
James Meehan Park
 Macquarie Fields . 454 C1
James Meehan Reserve
 Dee Why 259 A5
James Morgan Reserve
 Cromer 258 E1
James Park
 Hornsby 192 C15
 Lurnea 394 F7
James Ruse Park
 Ruse 512 G12
James Watkinson Reserve
 Pyrmont 8 G16
Jamieson Park
 Avalon 140 B14
 Casula 394 K15
 Narrabeen 228 E6
Jamison Park
 South Penrith 236 G14

168 GREGORY'S STREET DIRECTORY

INFORMATION

PARKS

Jannali Oval 460 F14
Jannali Reserve
Bonnet Bay 460 D12
Jardine Park
Casula 394 H14
Jarvie Park
Marrickville 373 K11
Jasper Reserve
Kenthurst 187 K8
Jegorow Reserve
Haberfield 342 K12
Jelba Reserve
Bangor 459 J11
Jellicoe Park
Pagewood 406 F8
Jemina Jenkins Park
Kearns 481 B2
Jenkins Park
Penrith 237 D10
Jenkins Reserve
Dundas 280 B12
Jenola Park
Woolooware 493 C8
Jensen Park
Regents Park 368 J1
Jerome Dowling Reserve
Eastlakes 406 A3
Jessie Stewart Reserve
Concord 342 A5
Jessie Street Gardens
Sydney B C9
J F Laxton Reserve
Dulwich Hill 373 C9
Jim Crowgey Reserve
Rydalmere 279 D15
Jim Ring Reserve
Birrong 368 J3
Jim Scott Park
South Penrith 266 J4
Jim Walsh Park
Eastwood 281 E6
Jindabyne Reserve
Frenchs Forest 256 F2
Jinkers Green
Killara 283 E1
Jirramba Reserve
Toongabbie 276 B7
J J Melbourne Hills
Memorial Reserve
Terrey Hills 196 D11
Joe Broad Reserve
Mt Pritchard 364 K12
Joe McAleer Park
Glendenning 242 J5
John Curtin Reserve
Mascot 405 B5
Winston Hills 277 H4
John Dwyer Park
Caringbah 493 B9
John Fisher Park
Wingala 258 G11
John Knowles Park
Merrylands West 306 H12
John Miller Park
Ryde 282 G16
John Mountford Reserve
Narwee 400 K11
John Oxley Reserve
Kirkham 477 H3
John Paton Reserve
Summer Hill 373 B4
John Peat Reserve
Camden 507 C3
John Pope Reserve
Ashfield 342 J13
John Rider Reserve
Minto 482 J10
John Roche Prak
Northbridge 316 B1
John Shore Park
Maroubra 407 G12
Johnson Oval,
Newington College
Stanmore 16 E13
Johnson Park
Dulwich Hill 373 C8
Johnstone Reserve
Revesby 398 F14
Johnston Park
Canley Vale 366 B3
John Tebbutts Observatory
Windsor 121 G7
John Victor
McMahon Reserve
Forest Lodge 11 D13
John Wearn Reserve
Carlingford 249 E16
John Whitton
Memorial Place
Glenbrook 234 J10
Jonathan Brooker Reserve
Woodbine 481 J10
Jones Park
Parramatta 307 J6
Jones St Reserve
Ryde 282 E15
Joseph Banks
Native Plants Reserve
Kirrawee 461 E14
Joseph Frank Park
Blacktown 244 C15
Josephine Park
Moorebank 396 D12
Joseph Knox Park
Pendle Hill 276 G11
Joshua Moore Park
Sadleir 394 C3
J Peters Field
Ruse 512 E5
Jubilee Park
Glebe 11 F7
Mortdale 431 B9
Parramatta 308 D5
Judges Park
Penrith 236 H11
Jupp Reserve
Eastwood 281 D4
Kanangra Reserve
Kingswood 237 F8
Kanbyugal Reserve
Woodbine 481 F14
Kangaroo Point Reserve 461 J4
Kanimbla Reserve
Bilgola 169 J7
Karabi Reserve
Merrylands 307 F9
Kareela Oval
Kirrawee 461 E16
Kareela Reserve
Doonside 242 K15
Kareena Park
Caringbah 492 E8
Karuah Oval
Turramurra 222 J11
Katandra Bushland Sanctuary
Mona Vale 198 E1
Kate Bird Park
Baulkham Hills 246 J5
Kathleen Reserve
North Ryde 282 G9
Katoa Reserve
Warriewood 198 J13
Kawana Reserve
Bass Hill 367 K6
Kayess Park
Minto 452 H13
Keene Park
Toongabbie 276 B9
Keep Reserve
Castlecrag 286 A13
Keirle Park
Manly 288 E4
Keith McKinnon Park
Ermington 280 A15
Keith Smith Park
Croydon 372 C3
Keith Willis Reserve
Winston Hills 277 F2
Kelly Playground
Newtown 18 A9
Kellyville Park 216 E9
Kellyville Rotary Park 216 G6
Kelso Park
Moorebank 396 A7
Panania 397 H16
Kelso Park North
Sporting Complex
Panania 397 F15
Kempt Field
Hurstville 432 D6
Kendall Green
West Pymble 253 A9
Kendall St Reserve
Sans Souci 463 A4
Kendrick Park
Tempe 404 A4
Kenley Park
Normanhurst 221 E9
Kennedy Park
Bayview 168 D7
Kennett Park
Glenfield 424 B13
Kenny Reserve
Bradbury 511 H14
Kensington Green
Harrington Park 478 C1
Kensington Reserve
Waterloo 19 H14
Kenthurst Park 158 A5
Kentlyn Reserve 513 B7
Kent Oval
North Turramurra 223 E9
Kentucky Reserve
Bankstown Airport 397 D4
Kessell Square
Strathfield 340 J12
Kesterton Park
North Sydney 6 E13
Kevin Wheatley Reserve
Airds 512 B11
Kiah Reserve
Clareville 169 D3
Kia Reserve
Campbelltown 511 A2
Kibo Reserve
Regents Park 339 D16
Killara Park 254 E9
Killara Reserve
Panania 398 A14
Killarney Heights Oval 256 A15
Kilpack Park
Carlingford 280 B1
Kilparra Park
Dangar Island 76 G8
Kimberley Park
Rooty Hill 242 A14
Kimberley Reserve
Vaucluse 348 E6
Kinch Reserve
Condell Park 398 C5
King George V Memorial Park
The Rocks A H2
King George V Park
Rhodes 311 F7
King George V
Recreation Centre
The Rocks A G4
King Park
Merrylands 307 F13
Wakeley 334 K14
King Reserve
Manly Vale 287 J3
Kingsbury Reserve
Kingsgrove 402 A8
Kingsdene Oval
Carlingford 279 D5
Kingsford Smith Oval
Longueville 314 D9
Kingsgrove Av Reserve
Kingsgrove 402 C8
Kingsgrove Park 402 B15
Kingsland Rd Reserve
Bexley 402 H13
Kings Park
Denistone East 281 H9
Five Dock 342 G9
Kingswood Rd Oval
Engadine 489 D9
Kinka Reserve
Terrey Hills 195 E5
Kinnear Park
Harrington Park 478 E2
Kinta Park
Fairfield 336 A12
Kirby Park
Gordon 253 F5
Kirkham Park
Elderslie 477 J13
Kirrawee Oval 490 H6
Kissing Point Oval
South Turramurra 252 C6
Kissing Point Park
Putney 311 J9
Kissing Point Village Green
South Turramurra 252 B7
Kitchener Park
Mona Vale 199 C5
Kittys Creek Reserve
East Ryde 283 C15
Klensendorlffe Reserve
Macquarie Fields 454 D4
Knapsack Park
Glenbrook 234 D14
Knight Park
Yennora 337 D10
Knights Field
Castle Hill 217 F7
Knox Park
Miller 393 F1
Knudsen Reserve
Riverstone 182 E10
Koala Reserve
Greenacre 370 J13
Koala Walk Reserve
Ingleburn 453 G6
Kobada Park
Chatswood 283 J9
Kogarah Jubilee Oval
Carlton 433 A8
Kogarah Park
Carlton 433 A8
Kokoda Reserve
Mount Druitt 240 J13
Kookaburra Reserve
Kingsgrove 402 A10
Koolangarra Reserve
Bonnet Bay 460 D8
Koola Park
East Killara 254 E7
Kooringa Reserve
Raby 451 J13
Korpie Reserve
Melrose Park 310 K4
Koshigaya Park
Campbelltown 511 C6
Kotara Park
Marsfield 281 K6
Kotori Field
Londonderry 148 D3
Kruse Park
Tregear 240 E8
Kulgoa Reserve
Ryde 282 B13
Kundibah Park
Elanora Heights 198 F14
Ku-ring-gai Bicentennial Park
West Pymble 252 K11
Ku-ring-gai Chase
National Park 192 G3
Brooklyn 75 H14
Ku-ring-gai
Wildflower Garden 224 D1
Kurraba Pt Reserve
Neutral Bay 6 H13
Kurung Reserve
Holroyd 307 K9
Kyeemagh Boat
Ramp Reserve 404 C12
Kyeemagh Reserve 404 A13
Kyle Williams
Recreation Reserve
Blakehurst 462 B1
Kyngmount Reserve
Minto 482 J8
Kywung Reserve
Macquarie Park 283 B6
Lachlan Macquarie Park
Dundas Valley 280 C11
Lachlan Reserve
Centennial Park 21 G13
Lack Reserve
Ambarvale 510 F16
Lady Penhryn Park
Kings Langley 245 F4
Lagoon Park
Manly 288 F4
Lake Malabar
Maroubra 407 D16
Lake Parramatta Reserve
North Parramatta 278 E7
Lakeside Park
North Narrabeen 199 A15
Wattle Grove 396 A16
Lakewood City Reserve
Bonnet Bay 460 A8
Lalich Av Reserve
Bonnyrigg 364 B10
Lambert Park
Leichhardt 373 F1
West Ryde 280 G11
Lambert Reserve
Peakhurst 430 D8
Lambeth Park
Picnic Point 428 A9
Lambeth St Reserve
Picnic Point 428 B9
Lamrock Reserve
Kingswood 238 B15
Lance Hutchinson Oval
Riverwood 400 D12
Lance Stoddert Reserve
Kyeemagh 403 K14
Landa Park
Ashcroft 394 G1
Sadleir 394 B3
Lane Cove
Bushland Park 314 H5
Lane Cove National Park
East Ryde 283 C15
Killara 283 A1
Lindfield 283 E5
Macquarie Park 283 A1
Marsfield 252 A11
North Ryde 283 F10
Wahroonga 251 F1
West Pymble 252 G15
Langlands Oval
Annangrove 186 E4
Lang Park
St Marys 239 G16
Sydney A F11
Lansdowne Park
Villawood 367 E8
Lansvale Reserve 366 K5
Lapstone Oval 264 G2
Larchmont Pl Reserve
West Pennant Hills 249 H9
Larkins Reserve
Rodd Point 343 E8
Larool Playground
Thornleigh 221 A8
Larry J Peck Oval
Ruse 512 E5
Latham Park
South Coogee 407 E7
Laurel Park
Ryde 312 E2
Lauriston Park
Rosebery 405 F3
Lawrence Hargrave Park
Elizabeth Bay 13 B6
Lawry Plunket Reserve
Mosman 317 D8
Lawson Reserve
Camden South 506 K13
Lawson Square
Merrylands 307 D13
Leacock Regional Park
Casula 394 J16
Casula 424 J2
Leahvera Reserve
Scotland Island 168 F3
Leemon Reserve
Greenwich 314 J12
Lee Park
Greenacre 370 F8
Winmalee 173 F12
Lees Park
Ashbury 372 D10
Leeton St Park
Merrylands 306 K10
Le Gay Brereton Park
Mosman 316 H2
Lehmanns Oval
Liverpool 394 G1
Leichhardt Oval
Lilyfield 343 J10
Leichhardt Park
Lilyfield 343 J9
Lennox Park
Blaxland 233 J10
Lennox Reserve
Lansvale 366 J5
Len Reynolds Reserve
Sans Souci 462 K1
Leonard Reserve
Roselands 401 E5
Leone Av Reserve
Baulkham Hills 217 B16
Leon Lachal Reserve
Eastlakes 405 J3
Leo Reserve
Greenacre 369 K11
Leo Smith Reserve
Ramsgate 433 F11
Leppington Oval 421 A10
Lessing Park
Hornsby 191 K13
Les Tegel Oval
Catherine Field 449 G4
L'Estrange Park
Mascot 405 G5
Leumeah Park 482 E11
Lewis Hoad Reserve
Forest Lodge 11 E13
Lidcombe Oval 339 G5
Lieutenant Cantello Reserve
Hammondville 397 A15
Light Horse Park
Liverpool 395 E5
Lighthouse Reserve
Vaucluse 348 H2
Lillian Rd Reserve
Riverwood 399 J15
Lilli Pilli Oval
Caringbah 492 H16
Lilli Pilli Point Reserve
Lilli Pilli 522 G4
Lime Kiln Bay
Bushland Sanctuary
Oatley 430 G10
Lincoln Park
Cambridge Park 237 K8

GREGORY'S STREET DIRECTORY 169

PARKS

INFORMATION

Linden Reserve
Castlecrag 286 F11
Lindfield Oval
East Lindfield 254 H14
Lindfield Park............59 G6
Lindsay Reserve
Forestville 256 A7
Linear Park
Pernulwuy 305 E7
Lin Gordon Reserve
Thirlmere 564 J11
Links Creek Reserve
Killara 253 F13
Linley Point Reserve
Lane Cove 313 H6
Lionel Watts Park
Frenchs Forest 255 J1
Lion Park
Lurnea 394 F6
Lions Park
Riverstone 182 K7
West Ryde 281 A14
Lions Park & Gardens
Tahmoor 566 A11
Liquidamber Reserve
Narellan Vale 478 K11
Lisa C Reserve
Castle Hill 217 H9
Lisgar Gardens
Hornsby 221 D2
Little Digger Park
East Roseville 284 K2
Little Reserve
Camden 506 K4
Padstow 399 D15
Little Salt Pan Reserve
Padstow Heights 429 A5
Little Tasker Park
Campsie 372 E12
Liverpool Showground
Prestons 393 J11
L M Graham Reserve
Manly 288 D6
Lockwood Park
Greenacre 370 D5
Lofberg Oval
West Pymble 252 K11
Loftus Oval 490 C12
Loftus Park
Liberty Grove 311 C16
Londonderry Park 148 C10
London Reserve
St Ives 254 F4
Long Island Nature Reserve
Brooklyn 75 G9
Long St Park
Smithfield 335 J2
Looking Glass Bay Park
Gladesville 312 C12
Lorikeet Sanctuary
Warrawee 222 E13
Lorraine Cibilic Reserve
Woodbine 481 J11
Lough Playing Field
Double Bay 22 G1
Louisa Lawson Reserve
Marrickville 373 H15
Lovedale Place
Rhodes 311 F11
Lovetts Reserve
Lane Cove West 313 F3
Lowe Cr Reserve
Elderslie 477 H16
Low Reserve
Smithfield 336 B3
Loyal Henry Park
Roseville 284 D5
Lucas Reserve
Cronulla 494 C6
Lucknow Park
Marsfield 251 C14
Lucy Cobcroft Park
Oxley Park 270 G2
Luddenden
Showground 326 F16
Ludovic Blackwood Memorial
Sanctuary
Beecroft 250 C2
Ludowici Reserve
Lane Cove 313 J3
Lukes Lane Reserve
St Clair 269 K13
Lumeah Reserve
Elanora Heights 228 C1
Lynch Creek Reserve
Yarramundi 145 F13

Lyndhurst Reserve
Huntleys Point 313 H12
Lynelle Park
Eastwood 281 H3
Lyne Park
Rose Bay 347 K10
Lynn Park
Denistone West 280 J11
Lynwood Park
Blacktown 245 A9
St Helens Park 541 J3
Lysaght Park
Chiswick 343 D13
Lytton St Park
Wentworthville 307 B1
Macarthur Park
Camden 507 C2
McBurney Reserve
Baulkham Hills 248 B9
McCarrs Creek Reserve
Ingleside 168 A13
McCarthy Park
Lurnea 394 D9
McCarthy Reserve
Rockdale 403 G16
McCauley Park
Ryde 282 F14
McCoy Park
Toongabbie 276 C3
McCredie Park
Guildford 337 B5
McGilroy Park
East Killara 254 F9
McGirr Park
Cartwright 394 A4
McGowan Reserve
Lugarno 429 H11
McIlwaine Park
Rhodes 311 E9
McKay Reserve
Palm Beach 139 K3
McKell Park
Brooklyn 76 E11
Darling Point 347 A8
McKell Playground
Alexandria 18 K14
Mackey Park
Marrickville 403 K1
McKillop Park
Harbord 288 K1
Macks Place
Lindfield 254 F15
McLaughlin Oval
Riverwood 399 J10
McLean Reserve
Bass Hill 368 A11
Macleay Reserve
Bradbury 511 G13
McLeod Reserve
Bankstown 369 D12
McMahons Park
Kurrajong 85 B7
McMillan Park
Chipping Norton 396 A6
McNeilly Park
Marrickville 373 H13
McQuade Park
Windsor 120 K9
Macquarie Fields Park ..454 C3
Macquarie Fields Reserve
Freemans Reach 121 C6
Macquarie Place Park
Sydney ....B C11
Macquarie Rd Reserve
Macquarie Fields 453 H4
McRaes Reserve
Penshurst 431 E7
Maddison Park
Pymble 223 F13
Magdala Park
North Ryde 283 D14
Magura Park
Mt Riverview 234 E2
Maiandar Reserve 523 C6
Maitland Reserve
Davidson 255 E3
Major Mitchell Reserve
Blaxland 234 D8
Majors Bay Reserve
Concord 311 H16
Maley Park
Guildford West 336 K2
Mallee Reserve
Gladesville 312 E6
Malta Park
Fairfield East 337 B13
Maluga Passive Park
Birrong 368 H6

Manaleuka Park
Raby 451 D13
Manly Dam Reserve
Allambie Heights 287 F1
Manly District Park
North Manly 258 A16
Manly Oval 288 G9
Manly-Warringah
War Memorial Park
Allambie Heights 257 B13
Manly West Park
Balgowlah 288 A5
Manna Gum Reserve
Narellan Vale 478 K14
Mannell Reserve
Bankstown 368 K16
Mannix Park
Heckenberg 364 C14
Manns Point Park
Greenwich 315 A14
Manooka Reserve
Bradbury 511 C15
Mansion Point Reserve
Grays Point 491 F15
Manuka Park
Bass Hill 368 A10
Marayiya Park 124 G4
Marayong Oval 244 B7
Marconi Oval
Bossley Park 333 H9
Marconi Park
Bossley Park 333 J10
Marden Reserve
Georges Hall 367 G12
Maria Iori Park
Rouse Hill 185 D4
Marine Park
Avalon 170 D3
Bilgola 170 D3
Marion Reserve
Yagoona 368 F15
Marjorie Park
Eastwood 281 J8
Marlene Reserve
Greenacre 370 G1
Marramarra National Park
Canoelands 70 D7
Forest Glen 70 D9
Marr Playground
Petersham 16 A12
Marsden Park
Campbelltown 511 B7
Marsfield Park 251 K15
Martin Knight Reserve
Kellyville 216 F3
Martin Reserve
North Ryde 283 B13
Marton Park
Kurnell 466 A9
Maru Reserve
Merrylands 307 H8
Mary Brookes Park
Playing Fields
St Helens Park 541 C7
Mary Howe Reserve
Narellan Vale 508 H2
Mary MacKillop Park
St Marys 269 F2
Mary Wade Reserve
Woodbine 481 G11
Mascot Memorial Park ..405 D3
Mascot Oval 405 C3
Mascot Park 405 C3
Maserati Reserve
Ingleburn 453 G10
Masonic Schools Oval
Baulkham Hills 247 C13
Mason Park
Homebush 341 B5
South Windsor 120 G13
Mater Gardens
Crows Nest 5 C1
Matheson Park
Kurrajong 64 D15
Matraville Park
Maroubra 406 J15
Matthews Park
Greenacre 370 G8
Maundrell Park
Petersham 16 B11
Maurice Bolton Reserve
Blacktown 274 K1
Maurice Hughes Reserve
Castle Hill 218 B12
Maurice O'Connell Reserve
Guildford 337 J7
Mawarra Cr Reserve
Kellyville 216 E3

Mawson Park
Campbelltown 511 F4
Max Ruddock Reserve
Winston Hills 277 B1
Maxwell Reserve
Bankstown 368 J15
May Cowpe Reserve
Rooty Hill 271 J4
Mays Hill Reserve 307 J5
Maze Park
West Ryde 280 J14
Meadowbank
Memorial Park 311 D4
Meadowbank Park 311 B4
Meere Park
Lurnea 394 C13
Melaleuca Reserve
Narellan Vale 478 J14
Melody Gardens
Seven Hills 246 D12
Melrose Park
Quakers Hill 243 G2
Melville Reserve
Homebush 340 H11
Memorial Av Reserve
St Ives 224 A9
Memorial Oval
Ingleburn 453 C3
Memorial Park
Kurrajong 85 E2
Matraville 407 B15
Memorial Playing Fields
Brighton-le-sands 433 H4
Memory Park
Mosman 316 K9
Menai Park 458 J12
Menangle River Reserve
Menangle 538 J11
Mercer St Reserve
Castle Hill 218 D15
Mereil Reserve
Campbelltown 511 K3
Merino Reserve
Airds 511 K15
Elderslie 507 H2
Merrett Playground
Waverton 315 E13
Merrylands
Memorial Park 307 G12
Merrylands Park 307 G11
Merrylands Remembrance Park
Merrylands West ...307 A11
Meryll Av Reserve
Baulkham Hills 247 G11
Metcalfe Park
Moorebank 396 D9
Metella Reserve
Toongabbie 275 E13
Metzlers End
Gordon 253 G6
Meyer Reserve
Oatley 430 J13
Michael Simpson Reserve
Baulkham Hills ...246 K11
Middle Creek Reserve
Cromer 228 A6
Middle Head Oval
Mosman 317 J6
Middleton Park
Yagoona 368 F10
Midge Reserve
Marsfield 251 J13
Midlothian Reserve
St Andrews 452 B12
Mihajlovic Park
Green Valley 363 D9
Mihkelson Reserve
Eastwood 281 D5
Mildura Reserve
Campsie 372 B9
Milford Dr Reserve
Rouse Hill 185 E4
Milkmaids Reserve
North Turramurra 223 F7
Miller Park 393 G5
Miller Reserve
Ermington 310 E2
Millers Reserve
Manly Vale 287 K1
Mill Park
Liverpool 395 C9
Mills Park
Asquith 192 D11
Mills Reserve
Beacon Hill 257 D7
Mill St Reserve
Riverstone 182 H6
Millwood Park
Lindfield 284 E3

Milperra Reserve 397 J10
Milson Park
Wentworthville 277 D13
Milton Park
Macquarie Fields 453 G3
Mimosa Rd Oval
Turramurra 252 F4
Minchinbury Cellars,
Row of Olive Trees
Minchinbury 272 A8
Minchinbury Reserve ...271 J7
Minga Reserve
Ryde 282 F15
Minkara Reserve
Bayview 168 F12
Minnamurra Av Reserve
Pymble 253 C8
Mirambeena Regional Park
Lansdowne 367 A6
Miranda Park 491 J2
Mission Fields
Centennial Park 21 F14
Mitchell Cr Oval
Cattai 95 B6
Mitchell Reserve
Blacktown 275 A5
M J Bennett Reserve
Westmead 307 E2
Mobbs La Reserve
Epping 280 F4
Model Farms Reserve
Baulkham Hills 277 J2
Model Farms Siding Reserve
Northmead 278 A3
Mollets Reserve
Hurstville 401 H15
Molly Moore Park
Chipping Norton ...396 G4
Mona Park
Auburn 338 J2
Monarch Field
Macquarie Fields ..453 K5
Monash Park
Gladesville 312 J6
Monash Reserve
East Hills 427 J5
Mona Vale
Headland Reserve 199 H3
Moncur Reserve
Woollahra 21 J2
Monfarville Reserve
St Marys 269 G6
Monro Park
Cronulla 493 K13
Montague Gardens
Stanmore 16 G11
Montague Park
Drummoyne 343 J5
Monteith Reserve
Baulkham Hills ..247 D6
Montgomery Reserve
Padstow 428 K1
Montrose Reserve
Abbotsford 343 A1
Montview Park & Oval
Hornsby Heights .161 E16
Monty Bennett Oval
Wentworthville ..306 H3
Moolanda Av Reserve
West Pennant Hills 249 C9
Moorefield Reserve
Kogarah 433 E5
Moore Park
Beverley Park ..433 A9
Busby 363 H14
Eastwood 281 D5
Merrylands 307 D15
Moore Park 20 D1
Moore Reserve
Oatley 431 F11
West Pennant Hills 249 C5
Moorfield Hills Reserve
Dural 219 A3
Morgan Park
Palm Beach 140 B5
Morgan Park
Miller 393 G4
Morgan Power Reserve
Kings Langley .245 B6
Moriac Reserve
Warriewood 198 K6
Mornington Reserve
Hunters Hill 314 B12
Morreau Reserve
Rooty Hill 272 H4
Morrison Bay Park
Putney 312 C8

170 GREGORY'S STREET DIRECTORY

INFORMATION

PARKS

Morris St Park
Merrylands 307 E14
Mort Bay Park
Birchgrove 7 K5
Mortdale Memorial Park ..431 A8
Mortlock Park
Cammeray 316 C3
Morton Park
Lewisham 373 G7
Morunga Park
North Richmond 87 B10
Mosman Park
Mosman 317 A7
Mount Annan
Botanic Garden 509 G7
Mountbatten Park
West Pymble 253 B13
Mount Druitt Park
Bonnyrigg 270 K3
Mount Druitt
Town Centre Reserve ..241 G15
Mt Kuring-gai Oval 162 J14
Mt Lewis Park 370 A16
Mt Pritchard Oval 364 E7
Mt Royal Reserve
Strathfield 341 A14
Mt Sion Park
Glenbrook 234 A11
Mt Wilberforce Lookout Reserve
West Pennant Hills ..249 J4
Mowbray Park
Lane Cove West 283 G11
Moxham Park
Northmead 277 J4
Mubo Park
Holsworthy 426 D3
Mulgoa Nature Reserve
Glenmore Park 265 C9
Mulgoa Park 295 C15
Muller Reserve
Hillsdale 406 G13
Munal Reserve
Merrylands 307 E11
Mundurama Reserve
Ambarvale 540 E2
Munn St Reserve
Millers Point ....A A2
Munro Park
Lurnea 394 E11
Northbridge 315 J1
Munro St Park
Greystanes 305 D10
Murragan Reserve
Hinchinbrook 363 D15
Murray Farm Reserve
Carlingford 249 E12
Muston Park
Chatswood 285 D6
Mutch Park
Pagewood 406 D9
Myall Reserve
North Ryde 283 B10
Myles Dunphy
Bushlands Reserve
Oatley 431 B13
Myrtle St Fields
Claremont Meadows ..268 H2
Nagle Park
Maroubra 406 J10
Namatjira Park
Rooty Hill 272 E1
Nanbaree Reserve
Balgowlah Heights ..287 J12
Napoli Reserve
Padstow 399 A10
Nareen Reserve
North Narrabeen 198 J16
Narellan Park 478 B7
Naremburn Park 315 D2
Narnia Park
Alfords Point 459 A2
Narroy Park
North Narrabeen 198 H16
Navua Reserve
Grose Wold 116 G10
Neal Park
Hornsby 191 K16
Neat Reserve
Campsie 371 H14
Nemesia St Park
Greystanes 305 K12
Neptune Park
Revesby 428 K5
Nerang Park
Ryde 282 G14
Ness Park
Marrickville 373 G12
Neville Park
Bass Hill 368 D12

Newington Old Boys Oval
Stanmore 16 F13
Newington Reserve
Silverwater 310 A10
Newington Road Playground
Enmore 16 G15
Newland Reserve
Milperra 397 E10
Newlands La Reserve
Wollstonecraft 315 E9
Newlands Park
St Leonards 315 D7
Newport Heights Reserve
Bilgola 169 E5
Newport Park 169 H11
New Reserve
Narellan Vale 508 J1
Nichols Reserve
Lane Cove 314 A1
Nield Park
Rodd Point 343 E8
Nielsen Park
Vaucluse 348 A1
Nineveh Soccer Field
Edensor Park 364 A2
Noel Seiffert Reserve
Sans Souci 463 D11
Nolan Reserve
Chatswood West 284 A10
Noorumba Reserve
Gilead 540 F10
Nore Reserve
Minto 482 K5
Norfolk Reserve
Greenacre 370 E6
Norford Park
Sefton 338 G14
Norman Griffiths Oval
West Pymble 253 A11
Normanhurst Park 221 E7
Norman May Park
Lidcombe 339 J14
Norman Park
Auburn 339 B9
Norman Peek Reserve
Penrith 237 B8
Norm Neilson Reserve
Greenacre 370 F11
North Arm Reserve
Castle Cove 285 J6
North Caringbah Oval
Caringbah 492 J4
Northcote Park
Greenacre 370 D9
Northcote Reserve
Sans Souci 433 A15
North Epping Oval 251 J9
Northern Oval
Macquarie Park 252 D11
Northern Winter Sportfield
Macquarie Park 252 E12
North Harbour
Aquatic Reserve
Balgowlah Heights ..288 D15
North Harbour Reserve
Balgowlah 287 J10
Northmead Reserve 278 B4
North Narrabeen Reserve
Warriewood 199 D12
North Pymble Park
Pymble 223 D14
North Rocks Park
Carlingford 249 F15
North Ryde Common
Ryde 282 F12
North Ryde Park 283 B12
North Sydney Oval 5 H2
North Turramurra Oval ..223 E4
Norton Russell Reserve
Newtown 17 B11
Norwest Hilltop Park
Bella Vista 216 C15
Nott Oval
Narellan 478 F11
Nugent Park
Chester Hill 368 B2
Nundah Reserve
North Ryde 283 C12
Nunook Reserve
Marsfield 281 H3
Nurraginey Reserve
Doonside 242 J11
Nurra Reserve
Ambarvale 510 K14
Oakdene Park
Fairfield 336 H16
Oakes Reserve
Old Toongabbie 277 A4

Oakleigh Park
Thornleigh 220 G11
Oak Park
Cronulla 524 A3
Oakville Reserve 122 G15
Oatley Heights Park
Mortdale 430 G10
Oatley Park 430 F11
Oatley Pleasure Grounds ..431 D14
Oatley Point Reserve
Oatley 461 D1
Oatley Reserve
Paddington 21 A2
O'Brien Park
Condell Park 398 J2
Observatory Park
Millers Point ....A D3
Pennant Hills 250 D2
Ocean View Park
Maroubra 407 D15
O'Connor Reserve
Rozelle 7 A16
Octavia Reserve
Rosemeadow 540 F3
O'Dea Reserve
Camperdown 17 B6
O H Reid Memorial Park
Chatswood West 284 A10
Old Boys Union Fields
North Parramatta ...278 G6
Old Bush Rd Oval
Engadine 489 D14
Old Saleyards Reserve
North Parramatta ...278 H13
Old School Park
Gymea Bay 491 F10
Olds Park
Penshurst 430 K3
Old Wharf Reserve
Clareville 139 G14
Ollie Webb Reserve
Parramatta 308 A6
Olola Av Reserve
Castle Hill 218 D16
Olson Reserve
Oakhurst 241 J5
Olympic Park
Ryde 312 E5
O'Neill Park
Yagoona 369 A9
Only Park
Moorebank 396 E11
Onslow Park
Camden 476 J15
Opala Reserve
Belrose 225 K15
Oppy Reserve
Quakers Hill 213 G10
Orana Park
Seven Hills 275 B3
Orange Green
North Turramurra ..223 F6
Orara Park
Wattle Grove 395 J12
Orchard Park
Mt Colah 163 J13
Orchid St Oval
Loftus 489 K11
O'Regan Reserve
Baulkham Hills 248 A10
Origlass Park
Balmain 8 B1
Osborne Park
Lane Cove 314 G6
Oswald Reserve
Rosemeadow 540 J8
Oswald Scholes Reserve
Bexley North 402 E13
Otto Losco Reserve
Northmead 277 G6
Outlook Park
Eastwood 281 B10
Outram Reserve
Currans Hill 479 J14
Owen Earle Oval
Richmond Lowlands 88 J15
Oxford Falls Peace Park ..227 B16
Oxley Reserve
Mt Colah 162 C12
Oyster Bay Oval 461 D7
Oyster Cove Reserve
Waverton 315 D12
Paciullo Park
Liverpool 394 H6
Padstow Park 399 G15
Paine Park
Moorebank 396 J7
Paine Reserve
Randwick 406 K2

Palestine Park
Winston Hills 276 J4
Palmgrove Park
Avalon 169 K3
Pannerong Reserve
Rose Bay 348 B10
Panorama Reserve
Cabramatta 365 B11
Paperbark Grove
Centennial Park 21 E7
Parabianga Reserve
Wentworthville 277 C13
Parker St Reserve
Penrith 237 D8
Parkes Avenue
Sporting Complex
Werrington 239 B10
Parkes Reserve
Canley Vale 366 F2
Parkhill Reserve
Leumeah 482 F12
Parklands Oval
Mt Colah 162 A16
Parkside Dr Reserve
Kogarah Bay 432 H13
Parkside Gardens
Wattle Grove 426 B4
Parraweena Av Reserve
Castle Hill 248 B7
Parriwi Park
Mosman 287 C15
Parr Reserve
Narraweena 257 K3
Parry Park
Lakemba 370 G15
Ryde 312 C6
Parsley Bay Reserve
Vaucluse 348 E2
Parsons Park
Wentworthville 276 K12
Paruna Reserve
Como 460 E4
Passfield Park
Minto 453 B16
Passmore Reserve
Manly Vale 288 B2
Paterson Park
Quakers Hill 214 F10
Pathalla Reserve
Scotland Island 168 J3
Pat Hynes Park
North Narrabeen ...229 A1
Pat Kontista Reserve
Leppington 421 A9
Pat O'Connor Reserve
Canterbury 372 E16
Patricia Gardiner Reserve
Lindfield 283 G1
Patterson Oval
Cambridge Park 237 H6
Pat Zikan Reserve
Blacktown 274 G9
Paul Keating Park
Bankstown 369 F15
Paul Wallenberg Garden
Woollahra 22 D2
Pavich Reserve
Mona Vale 199 E2
Payten Reserve
Woodbine 481 J11
Peace Park
Ashbury 372 H7
Peakhurst Park 430 D2
Pearce Park
Liverpool 394 K6
Pearce Reserve
Kings Langley 245 K8
Peel Park
Gladesville 312 G8
Lakemba 371 C15
North Richmond 86 J12
Pemberton Reserve
Sans Souci 433 F14
Pembroke Park
Marsfield 251 F15
Minto 482 E8
Pendle Hill Park
Girraween 276 A16
Pennant Hills Park 250 K7
Penrith Football Stadium ..236 E13
Penrith Showground ..236 F11
Penrose Park
South Penrith 237 A15
Penshurst Park 431 F3
Peppercorn Park
Frenchs Forest 256 H2
Mt Hunter 505 A8
Peppermint Reserve
Kingswood 267 G1

Peppertree Reserve
Erskine Park 270 J16
Peppin Park
Airds 512 F9
Percival Park
Rose Bay 348 A9
Perentie Park
Belrose 226 F13
Peter Depena Reserve
Sandringham 463 F2
Peter Hislop Park
Auburn 338 G12
Peter Kearns Memorial Oval
St Clair 269 H12
Peter Lowe Reserve
Kingsgrove 401 H13
Peter Moore Field
Belmore 371 H15
Peter Pan Park
Hammondville 426 K1
Petersham Park 373 H4
Peterson Park
Chipping Norton 397 D5
Peter Van Hasselt Park
Shalvey 210 G13
Phillip Park
Sydney ....D H12
Phillips Park
Lidcombe 340 B6
Lurnea 394 E8
P H Jeffrey Reserve
North Parramatta ...278 K14
Picken Oval
Croydon Park 372 B8
Pickering Park
Peakhurst 430 D7
Picton Showground ...563 G6
Pidding Park
Ryde 312 G1
Pierre De Coubertin
Newington 310 C11
Piggott Park
Minto 483 B2
Pilgrim Reserve
Strathfield 340 K11
Pimelea Picnic Area
Abbotsbury 333 D4
Pindari Reserve
Bayview 168 J13
Camden 507 A6
Pine Grove
Centennial Park 21 K11
Pine Tree Park
Carlingford 249 H13
Pioneer Field
South Hungarian Association
Oakhurst 242 C3
Pioneer Memorial Park
Liverpool 365 E16
Pioneer Park
Marsfield 281 K1
Pioneers Memorial Park
Leichhardt 10 A11
Pioneers Park
Malabar 437 E1
Pittwater Rugby Park
Warriewood 199 D13
Plateau Park
Bilgola 169 G4
Collaroy Plateau 228 J11
Playford Park
Padstow 399 C13
Pleasure Point Reserve ..427 J6
Plumpton Park 241 K8
Plumpton Park 242 A8
Point Gilchrist Park
Bexley North 402 C10
Pollard Park
Kirrawee 490 K4
Pope Paul VI Reserve
Glebe 11 G5
Poplar Park
St Marys 240 B12
Popondetta Park
Emerton 240 J2
Popplewell Park
South Coogee 407 H6
Portal Waterhole
Blue Mountains
National Park 264 B11
Porter Reserve
Newport 169 K8
Porters Park
Macquarie Park 283 A6
Portius Park
North Ryde 283 A15
Potter Field
Colyton 270 C8

GREGORY'S STREET DIRECTORY 171

PARKS — INFORMATION

Park	Location	Ref
Pottery Green	Lane Cove	314 E2
Potts Park	Yagoona	369 F6
Poulton Park	Hurstville Grove	431 J11
Powell Park	Cartwright	393 G6
	Kurrajong Heights	63 F14
Powells Creek Reserve	Concord West	341 C2
Powhatan Street Reserve	Greenfield Park	334 A13
Pratten Park	Ashfield	372 H5
Preston Park	Engadine	518 J4
Price Reserve	North Parramatta	278 H7
Primrose Park	Cremorne	316 D5
Primula Oval	Lindfield	283 J2
Prince Alfred Park	Surry Hills	19 F3
Prince Edward Park	Cabarita	342 F3
	Sutherland	489 K3
Princes Park		338 G13
	Lindfield	283 J2
Prior Av Reserve	Cremorne	6 K7
Progress Park	Auburn	338 H8
	Narwee	400 H14
	North Narrabeen	198 K13
Progress St Reserve	Tahmoor	566 A12
Propsting Reserve	Greenwich	315 B7
	St Leonards	315 B7
Prospect Park	Smithfield	275 C12
Prospect View Park	Smithfield	335 H8
Prout Park	Mt Pritchard	364 G12
Pryor Park	East Ryde	283 A14
Pughs Lagoon Reserve	Richmond	118 C12
Pullen Reserve	Yagoona	369 B13
Pulpit Point Reserve	Hunters Hill	314 B15
Punchbowl Park	Holsworthy	426 F3
Punch Park	Balmain	7 F12
Punt Park	Mortlake	312 A12
Purcell Park	Matraville	436 F3
Putney Park		312 B10
Pye Av Reserve	Northmead	278 D3
Pye Hill Reserve	Cecil Hills	362 H5
Pymble Soldiers Memorial Park		253 G3
Pyrmont Point Park	Pyrmont	8 F14
Quakers Hill Park		213 J11
Quandong Reserve	Macquarie Park	282 K3
Quarantine Reserve	Abbotsford	342 G1
Quarry Reserve	Hurstville	431 J9
	Maroubra	407 E8
	North Manly	258 D13
Queen Elizabeth Park	Concord	341 K7
Queen Elizabeth Reserve	Lindfield	283 F2
Queens Park		22 H14
Queen St Reserve	Narellan	478 H13
Queens Wharf Reserve	Parramatta	308 G3
Quinn Playground	Petersham	16 A5
Quirk Reserve	Bradbury	511 E15
Quota Park	Chipping Norton	396 A4
RAAF Memorial Park	Mount Druitt	241 C10
Rabbett Reserve	Frenchs Forest	256 E4

Park	Location	Ref
Rainbow Farm Reserve	Carlingford	249 H11
Rance Oval	Werrington	239 A11
Rapenea Community Forest	Dundas Valley	279 J8
Rasdall Park	Narwee	400 K14
Rawson Park	Mosman	317 D10
Ray Marshall Reserve	South Granville	338 G7
Ray O'Keefe Reserve	Bondi Beach	378 G4
Ray Oxford Reserve	Turrella	403 G5
Ray Park	Epping	250 E12
Rea Reserve	Drummoyne	313 J14
Reconciliation Park	Redfern	19 D5
Red Bank Reserve	Picton	563 D12
Reddy Park	Hornsby	221 E3
Redfern Oval		19 F10
Redfern Park	Minto	482 K3
	Redfern	19 F9
Red Hill Reserve	Oxford Falls	257 E1
Redin Place Reserve	Connells Point	431 H14
Reeve Reserve	Camden South	507 A13
Refalo Reserve	Glenwood	246 A4
Refinery Square	Pyrmont	12 D1
Regan Park	Moorebank	396 E6
Regatta Park	Emu Plains	236 A8
Reg Coady Reserve	Haberfield	343 B12
Regimental Park	Killara	253 K12
Reid Murray Reserve	St Andrews	452 A14
Reid Park	Mosman	316 H10
Reliance Reserve	Yagoona	368 F15
Remount Park	Holsworthy	426 F3
Renown Park	Oatley	431 E9
Renton Park	Moorebank	396 E11
Resolution Park	Kings Langley	245 D5
Rest Park	Brooklyn	75 C11
Reub Hudson Oval	North Curl Curl	258 F11
Rex Reserve	Georges Hall	367 J12
Reynolds Park	Toongabbie	276 H4
Rhodes Park	Concord West	311 E11
Rho-ker Reserve	Duffys Forest	194 K3
Richard Healey Reserve	Davidson	255 K4
Richard Murden Reserve	Haberfield	343 G13
Richard Podmore Reserve	Narwee	400 G12
Richards Cl Reserve	Berowra	133 G10
Richard Webb Reserve	West Pennant Hills	249 B7
Deakin Place	West Pennant Hills	249 A9
Richie Benaud Oval		
Richie Roberts Reserve	Curl Curl	259 A12
Richmond Park	Gordon	253 J4
	Richmond	118 H5
Rickaby Park	South Windsor	150 D1
Riddle Reserve	Bayview	168 H10
Ridgeline Reserve	Pemulwuy	305 D5

Park	Location	Ref
Ridge Park	Oxley Park	270 E2
Ridgeview Park	Riverstone	182 K4
Rifle Range Park	Moorebank	395 C11
Riley Park	Airds	512 C11
Ringrose Park	Wentworthville	306 H2
Riverglade Reserve	Gladesville	313 B12
Riverine Park	Arncliffe	403 K10
River Reserve	Eldersile	507 D3
River Road Reserve	Emu Plains	236 A9
Riverstone Park		182 H9
Riverwood Park		399 J14
Rizal Park	Rooty Hill	241 J12
	Rosemeadow	540 H3
R M Campbell Reserve	Bankstown	369 G14
Roberta Street Park	Greystanes	305 J6
Robert Brown Reserve	Prospect	274 E13
Robert Dunn Reserve	Mona Vale	199 E8
Robert Gardner Reserve	Narwee	400 G12
Robert Green Oval	Luddenham	356 G3
Robert Park	Cherrybrook	219 C14
Robert Pymble Park	Pymble	253 D2
Robertson Park	Watsons Bay	318 F14
Roberts Park	Greenacre	370 D14
Roberts Reserve	Five Dock	343 D8
Robertswood Park	Blaxland	234 C5
Robin Place Reserve	Caringbah	492 K10
Robinson Park	Jamisontown	266 C3
Robin Thomas Reserve	Parramatta	308 F4
Robson Park	Haberfield	343 E11
Rockdale Bicentennial Park		433 G3
Rockdale Park		403 G15
Rock Farm Reserve	Dundas	279 E12
Rodd Park	Rodd Point	343 G8
Rodney Reserve	Dover Heights	348 G11
Rofe Park	Hornsby Heights	191 G7
	Turramurra	222 G3
Roger Sheeran Oval	Macquarie Park	252 D12
Ron Darcey Oval	Miller	393 J4
Ron Dine Reserve	Camden South	506 J11
Ron Gosling Reserve	Bardwell Park	403 A6
Ron Hill Park	Toongabbie	276 E6
Ron Routley Oval	Concord	311 J16
Rooty Hill Central Park		272 D2
Rose Bay Park		347 F10
Rosedale Oval	Warwick Farm	365 K16
Rosedale Reserve	Croydon Park	372 A9
Roselea Park	Beecroft	249 J12
Rosella Prak	Harris Park	308 E7
Rosemeadow Reserve		541 A2
Rose Park	Sefton	368 G6
Rosevale Reserve	Narellan	478 J12
Roseville Chase Oval		255 D15
Roseville Park		254 H16
Rosewood Oval	Waitara	221 H5

Park	Location	Ref
Rosford Street Reserve	Smithfield	305 D16
Rosherville Reserve	Mosman	317 C2
Roslyn Park	Cherrybrook	219 D13
Rossmore Park		389 F15
Ross Park	Bangor	459 E14
Rotary Cowpasture Reserve	Camden	477 D16
Rotary Park	Condell Park	398 C2
	Eastwood	281 G5
	Kenthurst	158 B15
	Kirrawee	490 J4
	Ramsgate	433 F13
	Rhodes	311 F11
	Riverwood	400 C11
	St Ives	224 A12
	Warwick Farm	365 G15
Rotary Playground	Bondi Junction	22 F14
Rothwell Park	Concord	342 A6
Rouse Hill Regional Park	Riverstone	184 B3
	Rouse Hill	184 G7
Rowland Park	Daceyville	406 G5
Rowland Reserve	Bayview	169 C14
Rowley Park	Lansvale	367 K10
Roxborough Park Rose Garden	Castle Hill	247 H4
Royal National Park	520 A3
Rozelle Common		10 K2
RSL Memorial Park	Picton	563 G2
Rubie Reserve	Malabar	437 F7
Ruddock Park	Westleigh	220 G7
Rudd Park	Belfield	371 F10
Rupertswood Park	Mount Druitt	271 E3
Ruse Park	Bankstown	399 F6
Rushcutters Bay Park	Darling Point	13 D8
	Rushcutters Bay	13 D8
Russell Park	Drummoyne	343 E3
Rutherford Park	Burraneer	523 D5
Ruth Park	Merrylands West	307 C12
R Whack Allen Field	Ingleburn	453 B4
Ryan Park	Chester Hill	337 J12
Ryan Playground	Enmore	16 G13
Rydalmere Park		309 F2
Ryde Park		312 B2
Sackville Memorial Park	Sackville North	68 D1
Sadleir Park		394 C1
Saggart Reserve	St Andrews	481 K2
Saiala Oval	East Killara	254 J6
Sailors Bay Park	Castlecrag	286 C13
St Aloysius Oval	North Willoughby	285 H8
St Andrews Oval	University of Sydney	18 A6
St Andrews Park		452 B16
St Crispens Green	Killara	283 D2
St Helens Park Reserve		541 D4
St Ives Memorial Park	North Turramurra	223 K13
	St Ives	224 J1
St Ives Village Green		223 K11
St James Park	Glebe	11 K13
St Johns Oval	University of Sydney	17 J3
St Johns Park	Parramatta	308 C3
	St Johns Park	364 C2
St Leonards Park	North Sydney	5 J1

Park	Location	Ref
St Lukes Park	Concord	342 C9
St Malo Reserve	Huntleys Point	313 F9
St Matthews Farm Reserve	Cromer	228 D14
St Pauls Cobbitty Reserve	Cobbitty	446 G15
St Pauls Oval	University of Sydney	18 C5
St Peters Park	North Sydney	K C12
St Pius X College Playing Fields	Oxford Falls	227 A16
St Thomas Rest Park	Crows Nest	315 H5
Salamaua Park	Holsworthy	426 D3
Sales Park	Luddenham	356 G3
Salmon Playground	Newtown	17 F15
Salmon Reserve	Punchbowl	399 K4
Salt Pan Reserve	Padstow	399 H13
Samuel King Park	North Turramurra	223 E4
Samuel Lee Place	Concord	342 A6
Samuel Marsden Reserve	Orchard Hills	269 B8
Samuel Park	Vaucluse	348 E4
Sananda Park	Holsworthy	396 D16
Sandakan Park	North Turramurra	193 F12
Sando Park	Croydon Park	371 J9
Sandra St Park	Woodpark	306 H16
Sandringham Gardens	Sydney	D F11
Sandstone Ridge	Centennial Park	21 K8
Sandy Brennan Reserve	Penrith	236 D7
Sandy Point Reserve		428 A13
Sangrado Park	Seaforth	286 K10
Sanity Reserve	Warrawee	222 H8
Sans Souci Park		462 K6
Santa Rosa Park	Ryde	282 B10
Sarah Rose Reserve	Mount Annan	509 H1
Satelberg Park	Holsworthy	426 F3
Saunders Park	St Clair	270 A13
Sawmillers Reserve	McMahons Point	5 B14
Scarborough Park	Monterey	433 E10
Scarborough Playing Field	West Pymble	252 K12
Scattergood Reserve	St Helens Park	541 J1
SCEGS War Memorial Playing Fields	Northbridge	285 H14
Schell Park	Liverpool	365 A15
Scheyville National Park		123 D2
Schofields Park		183 D14
Scott Park	Sans Souci	463 C5
Scott Reserve	Roselands	400 E7
Scriven Reserve	Leumeah	482 K16
Scylla Bay Reserve	Como	460 J4
Seaforth Oval		286 J3
Seaforth Park	Bexley	403 A16
Searle Park	Telopea	279 G8
Second Ponds Oval	Rouse Hill	184 K4
Seddon Park	Glenfield	424 B12
Sedgwick Reserve	Currans Hill	479 G11
Selkirk Park	Killara	254 A13

172 GREGORY'S STREET DIRECTORY

Sensory Garden
Lilyfield 343 H9
Septimus Reserve
Camden 507 A7
Sequoia Cl Park
West Pymble 252 H11
Settlers Park
Putney 311 H6
Seven Little Australians Park
Lindfield 254 G13
Seville Reserve
North Rocks 278 H3
Seymour Reserve
Hurstville Grove 431 F11
Seymour Shaw Park
Miranda 492 A2
Shane Park Reserve 209 F5
Shaw Park
Cambridge Park 238 B10
Shaw Playground
Riverview 314 E7
Shaw Reserve
Randwick 406 J1
Sheldon Forest
Pymble 252 J2
Shell Park
Greenwich 314 K12
Shelly Beach Park
Manly 289 B10
Shelly Park
Cronulla 494 A16
Shepherd Street Park
Colyton 270 C8
Sherwin Park
Canley Vale 366 E1
North Parramatta 278 F13
Sherwood Park
Quakers Hill 213 J12
Shields Playground
Leichhardt 343 G15
Shiel Reserve
Ambarvale 511 A14
Shiprock Aquatic Reserve
Port Hacking 523 B3
Shipwrights Bay Reserve
Blakehurst 462 D4
Shortland Brush
Lansdowne 367 A5
Sickles Creek Reserve
Grasmere 475 J13
Sidings Park
Punchbowl 399 K1
Sidney Smith Park
Westmead 307 G3
Sid Sharpe Oval
Oakdale 500 A13
Sid Teale Memorial Grove
North Parramatta 278 G14
Sierra Pl Reserve
Baulkham Hills 246 G14
Signal Hill Reserve
Vaucluse 318 H16
Silkstone Park
Breakfast Point 312 C14
Silva Plana Sportsfield 58 G9
Silver Jubilee Park
Bardwell Valley 402 K9
Silverwater Park 309 K7
Simmons Point Reserve
Balmain East 8 G6
Simmos Beach
Recreation Reserve
Macquarie Fields 454 J5
Simpson Reserve
Canterbury 372 F14
Sir David Martin Reserve
Darling Point 13 H5
South Turramurra 252 B6
Sirius Cct Reserve
Narellan 478 F15
Sirius Cove Reserve
Mosman 316 K12
Sir Joseph Banks Park
Botany 405 D13
Sir Phillip Game Reserve
Lindfield 283 J3
Sir Robert Menzies Park
Wahroonga 221 J16
Sir Thomas Mitchell Reserve
Dundas Valley 280 A8
S J Harrison Reserve
Earlwood 402 G6
Skarratt Park
Lapstone 234 H15
Skate Park
Engadine 518 H6
Skenes Av Reserve
Eastwood 280 H6

Skillinger Park
Busby 363 J16
Slade Rd Reserve
Bardwell Park 402 H7
Smalls Reserve
Grasmere 475 H16
Smart Av Reserve
Camden South 507 B16
Smeeton Reserve
Currans Hill 480 A9
Smithfield Park 336 B5
Smith Park
Castlereagh 176 A5
East Hills 427 J2
Richmond 118 E2
Smith Reserve
Kingsgrove 401 J11
Smiths Creek Reserve
Campbelltown 512 E1
Leumeah 512 E1
Ruse 512 E1
Smoothey Park
Wollstonecraft 315 B9
Snape Park
Maroubra 406 J7
Snapperman Beach Reserve
Palm Beach 139 H1
Snowy Park
Heckenberg 364 A15
Snowy Reserve
Seven Hills 275 E10
Solander Playing Fields
Woolooware 493 D4
Soldiers Memorial Park
East Killara 254 H12
Somerset Park
Marsfield 251 H13
Somerville Park
Eastwood 281 C4
Sophia Doyle Reserve
Baulkham Hills 247 A10
Soudan St Playground
Paddington 13 H14
South Creek Park
St Marys 239 E13
Southlands Oval
South Penrith 266 J4
South Maroota Reserve 69 G5
South Park
Chipping Norton 366 D14
South Sydney Rotary Park
Eveleigh 18 D13
Spain Reserve
Castle Hill 218 D9
Spectacle Island
Nature Reserve
Mooney Mooney 75 G4
Spence Park
Penrith 237 B13
Spencer St Reserve
Berala 339 C15
Springfield Gardens
Potts Point 4 J5
Springfield Park
Old Guildford 337 E8
Spring Reserve
Spring Farm 508 A6
Spring St Reserve
Dural 188 K13
Stafford Walk
Earlwood 403 C1
Stanhope Reserve
Stanhope Gardens 215 E8
Stanley Park
Blaxlands Ridge 66 H6
Stanmore Reserve 16 F9
Stan Moses Reserve
Sans Souci 463 D5
Stan Thomson Reserve
St Andrews 452 B13
Stanwell Oval
Ashcroft 394 F3
Stapleton Park
Avalon 139 K14
Starr Reserve
Camden 506 J9
Startop Reserve
Ambarvale 510 J14
Steamroller Park 430 F12
Steel Park
Marrickville South 403 F1
Stevens Park
Beverley Park 433 B9
Stevens Reserve
Bankstown 399 G2
Oatley 430 J11
Stewart Park
Marsfield 251 J16

Stewart St Reserve
Parramatta 308 F2
Steyne Park
Double Bay 347 A12
Stockdale Cr Reserve
Abbotsbury 333 C13
Stockmans Drift
Mount Annan 479 J15
Stoney Range Reserve
Camden South 507 D16
Stony Range Flora Reserve
Dee Why 258 F8
Storey Park
Five Dock 343 A8
Hornsby 191 H10
Stotts Reserve
Bexley North 402 G8
Strathfield Park 371 C1
Strathfield Square 341 G12
Streeton Lookout
Freemans Reach 89 E7
Stringybark Reserve
Lane Cove North 284 E15
Stromeferry Reserve
St Andrews 481 J4
Stromlo Reserve
Ruse 512 F4
Strong Park
Lansvale 366 K11
Stuart Park
Blakehurst 432 D16
Stuart St Reserve
Padstow 399 G13
Sturt Reserve
Georges Hall 367 K15
Telopea 279 H11
Styles St Playground
Leichhardt 10 F16
Summerhayes Park
Winmalee 173 C8
Summit Reserve
Mt Riverview 204 H15
Sunderland Park
Raby 451 F15
Sunnyside Reserve
Caringbah 492 J6
Surf Reserve
North Curl Curl 259 A11
Surgeon White Reserve
St Ives 224 G13
Surrey Reserve
Georges Hall 368 B15
Surveyors Creek
Public Reserve
Glenmore Park 266 E12
Surveyors Creek
Softball Facility
Glenmore Park 266 F7
Sutcliff Reserve
Georges Hall 367 K15
Sutherland Park 490 C1
Sutton Reserve
Earlwood 372 H14
Swain Gardens
Lindfield 254 E13
Swallow Rock Reserve
Grays Point 491 D16
Sydney Field
Holsworthy 426 D6
Sydney Harbour
National Park
Balgowlah Heights 288 B13
Clontarf 317 H1
Manly 289 B13
Mosman 317 H10
Vaucluse 347 K2
Watsons Bay 318 G13
Clarke Island 347 B6
Fort Denison 2 K6
Rodd Island 343 J7
Shark Island 347 H5
Sydney University Park
Brownlow Hill 475 F2
Sylvania Heights Reserve
Sylvania 461 H14
Syme Park
Moorebank 396 D10
Symonds Reserve
Ingleburn 453 J9
Tablet House Steps
Pyrmont 12 D1
Tahmoor Park 566 C7
Tahmoor Regional
Sporting Centre 565 D10
Tahmoor Sportsground 565 D10
Tait St Park
Smithfield 336 B1
Talavera Reserve
Marsfield 252 C13

Talinga Park
Carlingford 280 B4
Tallawang Rd Reserve
Forestville 255 D8
Tallawong Oval
Blacktown 273 H2
Taloma Park
South Penrith 237 A15
Talus Reserve
St Leonards 315 D3
Tambourine Bay Reserve
Riverview 314 A7
Tamplin Fields
Hobartville 118 D8
Tancred Av Reserve
Kyeemagh 404 C13
Tandarra Reserve
Shalvey 210 J13
Tania Park
Balgowlah Heights 287 K15
Tantallon Oval
Lane Cove North 284 A15
Taplin Park
Drummoyne 343 G1
Taren Point Reserve
Sylvania Waters 462 H11
Tarlington Reserve
Bonnyrigg 364 C4
Tasker Park
Canterbury 372 E13
Taunton Reserve
Blakehurst 432 D12
Taylor Reserve
East Hills 427 J2
Ted Burge Sportsground
Merrylands 307 A8
Ted Horwood Reserve
Baulkham Hills 248 C11
Ted Schwebel Park
Glenorie 128 C6
Tempe
Recreation Reserve 404 B4
Tench Reserve
Jamisontown 235 G14
Penrith 235 G14
Regentville 265 D1
Tennyson Park
Lane Cove 314 A3
Tennyson Point 312 D10
Terone Park
Bossley Park 334 B8
Terrey Hills
Playing Fields 196 E6
Terrigal Reserve
Terrey Hills 196 C7
Terry Lamb Reserve
Belmore 371 G16
Terry St Reserve
South Hurstville 432 C12
The Breakaway Oval
Freemans Reach 91 E14
The Charles McLaughlin
Recreation Reserve
Baulkham Hills 246 K3
The Clive Evatt Reserve
Turramurra 222 K6
The Crescent Village Green
Woronora 489 H2
The Domain
Sydney 4 D1
The Elizabeth Piazza
Pyrmont 8 E16
The Eric Mobbs
Recreation Reserve
Castle Hill 248 D6
The Esplanade
Cronulla 494 B15
The Glade Reserve
Wahroonga 222 C9
The Glen Bushland Reserve
Bonnet Bay 460 E9
The Green
Blakehurst 432 A15
The Harry Noble Reserve
Erskineville 18 D15
The Ironbarks
Blue Mountains
National Park 263 H11
The James Hilder Reserve
Surry Hills F G9
The Kingsway Playing Fields
Werrington 239 C13
The Knoll
Northbridge 286 F14
The Lakes of
Cherrybrook 219 H9
The Lilian Fraser Garden
Pennant Hills 220 E15

Thella-Kenway Reserve
Bankstown 368 H16
The Lookout
Turramurra 222 J14
The Nolan Oval
Rydalmere 279 K15
The Rampart
Hornsby 221 C5
The Reg Bartley Oval
Rushcutters Bay 13 C7
The Rooty Hill
Rooty Hill 272 F4
The Saltpan Reserve
Brooklyn 75 G12
The Spit Reserve
Mosman 287 C14
The Walter Read Reserve
Paddington 21 B1
The Water Holes Reserve
(Historic Precinct)
Mount Druitt 270 K3
The William Cowan Oval
St Ives 223 J11
Thew Reserve
Strathfield 371 A2
The Zig Zag
Balmain East 8 F7
Third Settlement Reserve
Winston Hills 277 B5
Thirlmere Lakes
National Park 564 A8
Thirlmere
Memorial Park 565 B3
36th Battalion Park
Leichhardt 10 C14
Thomas Acres Reserve
Ambarvale 540 H1
Thomas Atkins Walk
Macquarie Fields 454 A5
Thomas Bourke Reserve
Blairmount 481 B13
Thomas Clarkson Reserve
Eagle Vale 481 C7
Thomas Extrem Reserve
Baulkham Hills 247 C11
Thomas Hogan Reserve
Bondi 377 K2
Thomas Moore Park
Chipping Norton 396 B4
Thomas Park
Blaxland 233 J6
Thomas Thompson Park
Cherrybrook 219 J14
Thomas Wemyss Park
Ermington 280 C14
Thomas Williams Reserve
North Parramatta 278 E12
Thompson Park
Artarmon 284 K16
Thompson Reserve
Milperra 397 G12
Thompsons Bay Reserve
Illawong 460 D2
Thorley Park
Smithfield 335 K6
Thornleigh Park 221 C16
Thornleigh Reserve
Narellan Vale 479 B13
Thornton Playground
Bellevue Hill 347 H14
Thornton Reserve
Bass Hill 368 C12
Thorpe Park
Hurstville 401 H16
Padstow Heights 429 H8
Throsby Reserve
Ambarvale 511 A12
Thurina Park
Villawood 367 H5
Ticket of Leave Park
Killara 253 G16
Timbergetters Reserve
Winston Hills 277 D1
Timbertop Reserve
Prospect 274 J13
Timbrell Park
Five Dock 343 C11
Tindale Reserve
Carlton 432 H6
Tindal Reserve
Mount Annan 479 G16
Tindarra Reserve
North Ryde 282 C7
Tingira Reserve
Rose Bay 348 A10
Titalka Park
Moorebank 395 D12
Tobin Park
Telopea 279 F7

GREGORY'S STREET DIRECTORY 173

PARKS — INFORMATION

Park	Map Ref
Tobruk Reserve	
Narellan Vale	479 B11
Waterloo	19 G13
Toby Reserve	
Panania	398 B13
Toby Toe Retreat	
St Ives	224 D8
Todd Park	
Blakehurst	432 E15
Tom Kenny Reserve	
Marrickville	373 E13
Tom Uren Park	
Guildford West	336 G2
Tonbridge St Reserve	
Ramsgate	433 F12
Tonga Park	
Seven Hills	276 A5
Tonkin Park	
Cronulla	493 J12
Toolang Playing Field	
St Ives Chase	223 J6
Toongarri Reserve	
Avalon	139 J16
Topin Park	
Moorebank	396 C15
Torry Burn Reserve	
Baulkham Hills	247 D8
Towards Park	
Macquarie Fields	454 E4
Tower Reserve	
Castlecrag	286 C11
Townson Oval	
Minto	482 H5
Towra Point Aquatic Reserve	
Kurnell	464 G5
Towra Point Nature Reserve	
Kurnell	464 D8
Toyer Reserve	
Sans Souci	463 B3
Tracey Reserve	
Revesby	398 D11
Trafalgar Park	
Newport	169 F12
Trafalgar Reserve	
Marsfield	252 A14
Treelands Walk	
Ingleburn	453 E9
Treetop Park	
Oatlands	279 A7
Tregear Reserve	240 D7
Trenerry Reserve	
Coogee	407 J3
Trewartha Park	
Lurnea	394 C10
Trim Park	
Gladesville	312 J10
Tristram Reserve	
Ermington	310 C4
Trobriand Park	
Glenfield	424 H9
Trotwood Reserve	
Ambarvale	510 J14
Troubador Park	
Kings Langley	246 D9
Truman Reserve	
Cromer	227 J12
Trumper Oval	
Paddington	13 G12
Trumper Park	
Paddington	13 G12
Trumper Park Playground	
Paddington	13 G12
Tucker Reserve	
Bass Hill	368 D12
Tuckwell Park	
Macquarie Park	283 A14
Tunks Farm	283 B3
Tunnel Gully Reserve	
Lapstone	264 F1
Turiban Reserve	
Wahroonga	222 J6
Turnbull Oval	
North Richmond	87 G12
Turnbull Reserve	
Box Hill	154 B16
Turramurra	
Memorial Park	222 K10
Turramurra Oval	222 J11
Turrella Reserve	
Earlwood	403 C4
Turrett Reserve	
Castlecrag	286 A13
Turrumburra Park	
Lane Cove West	284 B16
Twin Creeks Reserve	
Turramurra	252 B1
Wahroonga	252 B1
Twin Gums Reserve	
Lalor Park	245 J10
Two Turners Reserve	
Lindfield	284 C3
Tyagarah Park	
Ryde	312 D6
Tynan Park	
Ermington	280 D12
Tyrell Park	
Ryde	282 H16
Uhrs Pt Reserve	
Rhodes	311 F6
Ulmarra Park	
North Ryde	283 H11
Ulolo Av Reserve	
Hornsby Heights	191 E1
Ulundri Dr Reserve	
Castle Hill	218 B9
University Basin Reserve	
Campbelltown	510 H6
University of Sydney Ovals	18 A14
Upjohn Park	
Rydalmere	279 K14
Utz Reserve	
Drummoyne	313 H15
Vale Brook Reserve	
Eschol Park	481 B3
Valentia Street Reserve	
Woolwich	314 G12
Valentine Sports Park	
Glenwood	245 K2
Vale of Ah Reserve	
Vale Reserve	
Narellan Vale	478 K10
Valerie Park	
Eastwood	281 C9
Valley Reserve	
Campbelltown	511 K6
Valley View Reserve	
Narellan	478 B8
Warriewood	198 J7
Van Dieman Park	
Willmot	210 B11
Van Montfoort Cricket Oval	
Glenwood	215 F15
Varna Park	
Waverley	377 G10
Vasta Park	
Moorebank	396 E13
Vaucluse Park	348 C3
Vesta Reserve	
Milperra	397 E12
Vice Chancellors Oval	
Eveleigh	18 A11
Vic Huxley Oval	
Collaroy Plateau	228 J11
Victor Brazier Park	
Guildford	338 B7
Victoria Park	
Camperdown	18 F3
Minto	452 G14
Picton	563 G6
Queens Park	22 K14
St Marys	269 F1
Victoria Rd Reserve	
Castle Hill	217 A7
Victoria St Park	
Wetherill Park	335 A2
Victoria Wharf Reserve	
Watsons Bay	318 E13
Victory Reserve	
Engadine	488 K14
View St Reserve	
West Pennant Hills	249 A4
Village Green	
Bella Vista	246 F3
Breakfast Point	312 C15
Liberty Grove	311 C14
West Pymble	252 J11
Villiers Reserve	
Padstow Heights	429 G6
Vimiera Reserve	
Epping	281 D4
Vineyard Creek Reserve	
Dundas	279 E10
Vineyard Park	152 B3
Viret St Reserve	
Hunters Hill	314 A10
Virginius Reserve	
Padstow	429 A2
Voyager Park	
Voyager Point	427 C4
Wabash Reserve	
Cromer	228 D13
Wahroonga Park	222 D6
Waitara Park	221 K3
Wakehurst Rugby Park	
Belrose	226 A5
Walder Park	
Wetherill Park	304 H9
Wallis Reserve	
Strathfield	371 B1
Wall Reserve	
Panania	398 C12
Wallumatta Nature Reserve	
North Ryde	282 K14
Walsh Av Reserve	
Croydon Park	371 F8
Walshaw Park	
Bass Hill	368 D8
Walter Gors Park	
Dee Why	258 J5
Wambiri Place Reserve	
Cromer	227 K14
W A McInnes Reserve	
North Strathfield	341 C4
Waminda Reserve	
Campbelltown	512 C4
Leumeah	512 C4
Wanda Reserve	
Cronulla	494 D6
Wandoo Reserve	
Ryde	311 K3
Wangal Centenary Bushland Reserve	
Mortlake	311 K11
Wanstead Reserve	
Earlwood	403 G1
Waratah Park Reserve	
Sutherland	490 D6
Waratah Park Wildlife Reserve	
Duffys Forest	194 G4
Ward Park	
Surry Hills	20 A4
Warimoo Oval	203 H11
War Memorial Park	
Leichhardt	10 E11
Pitt Town	92 H15
Warmul Oval	
Greystanes	305 D15
Warners Park	
Castlecrag	285 K13
Warragamba Park	
Mulgoa	323 J10
Warraroon Reserve	
Longueville	314 D5
Warrawong Reserve	
Eastwood	280 J11
Warren Park	
Marrickville South	403 H1
Warren Try Reserve	
Merrylands	307 F15
Warriewood Escarpment	
Ingleside	198 D5
Warrimoo Oval	
St Ives Chase	224 A3
Warrina St Oval	
Berowra	133 D9
Warumbul Picnic Area	
Royal National Park	522 A6
Warwick Farm Recreation Reserve	365 H12
Wascoe Park	
Glenbrook	233 G14
Waterfall Oval	519 E13
Waterfall Reserve	58 J8
Waterfront Park	
Breakfast Point	312 D15
Waterloo Oval	
Waterloo	19 F15
Waterloo Park	
Marsfield	252 A14
Waterloo	19 F14
Waterworth Park	
Earlwood	403 J3
Waterworth Reserve	
Narellan Vale	479 B14
Wattawa Reserve	
Condell Park	398 G1
Wattlebird Bushland Reserve	
Caringbah	493 A13
Wattle Grove Park	396 A16
Watt Park	
McMahons Point	K D16
Watts Park	
Ryde	281 K8
Waverton Park	
Waverton	315 E13
Weaver Park	
Mosman	316 F9
Webbs Av Playing Fields	
Auburn	338 H5
Wedgewood Reserve	
Allambie Heights	257 H9
Weekley Park	
Stanmore	16 G7
Weir Reserve	
Penrith	236 D6
Weldon Park	
Curl Curl	258 G12
Wellings Reserve	
Balgowlah	287 K11
Wentworth Common	
Homebush Bay	310 J12
Wentworth Park	
Ultimo	12 F9
Wentworth Reserve	
Homebush	341 A6
Werrell Reserve	
Abbotsford	312 K15
Werribee Park	
Glen Alpine	510 B15
Werrington Creek Park	
Cambridge Park	238 C10
Westbourne St Reserve	
Bexley	432 F1
West Denistone Park	
Denistone West	280 K13
West Pennant Hills	
West Epping Park	250 F15
Western Sydney Regional Park	
Horsley Park	332 K5
Westland Memorial Park	
Ingleburn	453 G4
Westminster Park	
Gladesville	312 J5
West Pennant Hills Village Green	
Castle Hill	248 J1
Wetherill Park	334 J2
Wetlands	
Homebush	341 B4
Wetlands Reserve	
Camden	477 C16
Whalan Reserve	240 F10
Whale Beach Reserve	
Whale Beach	140 C6
Wheat Park	
Sadleir	364 B16
Wheeler Park	
Lalor Park	245 D13
Narrabeen	228 K7
Whelan Reserve	
Paddington	21 F5
Whiddon Reserve	
Croydon Park	371 G9
Whitbread Park	
Bexley North	402 E10
White Bay Park	
Balmain	8 A11
Whiteley Park	
Stanmore	16 J7
Whitemore Reserve	
Georges Hall	367 G11
Whiteoak Reserve	
Brighton-le-sands	403 J15
White Oval, Kings School	
North Parramatta	278 K7
Whites Creek Valley Park	
Annandale	10 J8
Leichhardt	10 J8
Whitlam Park	
Busby	363 J12
Whitton & Martin Sts Reserve	
Heathcote	518 F12
Whitton Park	
Glenbrook	233 K15
W H Wagener Oval	
Ashbury	372 F6
Widemere Reserve	
Greystanes	305 H12
Wilberforce Park	92 B2
Wild Flower Sanctuary	
Warragamba	353 E7
Wildlife Sanctuary	
North Rocks	279 A4
Wiley Park	400 E5
Wilga Park	
Macquarie Park	282 E3
Wilkes Park	
Moorebank	396 D11
William Campbell Reserve	
Harrington Park	478 E7
William Harvey Reserve	
Rouse Hill	185 C8
William Howe Reserve	
Narellan Vale	508 J3
William Joyce Reserve	
Baulkham Hills	246 H11
William Lawson Park	
Prospect	274 J10
William Lewis Park	
Wahroonga	222 B12
Williams Park	
Chipping Norton	396 E5
North Bondi	378 K11
Williams Reserve	
Dundas	279 F14
William Woods Reserve	
Appin	569 F13
Willis Park	
Castle Cove	285 G5
Oakdale	500 E13
Willoughby Park	
North Willoughby	285 H10
Willow Park	
Hornsby	221 J2
Lansvale	367 A9
Wills Ground	
Earlwood	373 B14
Willunga Reserve	
Hurstville Grove	431 H12
Wilson Cr Reserve	
Narellan	478 C11
Wilson Oval	
St Marys	269 F4
Wilson Park	
Llandilo	208 H5
Silverwater	310 A7
Wilton Reserve	
Narellan	478 E11
Wilton Park	
Palm Beach	139 K2
Windarra Reserve	
Narwee	400 J12
Windmill Park	
Glenmore Park	266 H13
Windsor Downs Nature Reserve	150 E11
Wingala Reserve	
North Curl Curl	258 J8
Winji Jimmi Park	
Mona Vale	169 D13
Winjoy Reserve	
Dundas	279 D14
Winnal Reserve	
Green Valley	363 D13
Winnererremy Bay Foreshore Reserve	
Mona Vale	169 C15
Winsor Park	
Greenacre	369 J9
Wiremill Park	
Chiswick	343 B1
Wirrimbirra Sanctuary	
Bargo	567 C1
Wise Reserve	
Riverwood	400 F11
Withers Rd Reserve	
Kellyville	185 E10
Wollemi National Park	
Blaxlands Ridge	65 F1
Wolseley St Reserve	
South Granville	338 D4
Wonga Rd Reserve	
Yowie Bay	492 B10
Woodbury Reserve	
Glossodia	66 A12
Woodcroft Field	243 F11
Woodfarm Reserve	
Doonside	243 A7
Woodford Bay Bicentennial Reserve	
Longueville	314 F8
Northwood	314 F8
Woodlands Park	
Wilberforce	67 J15
Wood Park	
Bankstown	369 G11
Ingleburn	453 E9
Woodriff Gardens	
Penrith	236 B8
Woodside Park	
Hinchinbrook	362 G15
Woods St Reserve	
North Epping	251 G7
Woodstock	
Burwood	342 A16
Wood St Reserve	
Epping	281 E3
Woodville Park	
Hurstville	432 C5
Woodville Reserve	
Villawood	367 D5
Woodward Park	
Liverpool	395 A6
Woolcott Park	
Newport	169 G11
Woollahra Oval	
Rose Bay	347 K13
Woollahra Playing Fields	
Rose Bay	347 K12
Woolooware Oval	493 F10
Woolway Park	
Meadowbank	311 E2

174 GREGORY'S STREET DIRECTORY

- Woolwich Foreshore Reserve 314 D12
- Woomera Reserve Little Bay 437 A10
- Woorarra Lookout Reserve Elanora Heights 228 D1
- Woronora Heights Oval 489 C4
- Worrell Park Ruse 512 E5
- Wright Reserve Georges Hall 367 F14
- Wright Reserve Quakers Hill 214 A16
- W V Scott Memorial Park Austral 391 B16
- Wyanda Reserve Dharruk 241 A6
- Wyangala Reserve Leumeah 482 G13
- Wyargine Reserve Mosman 317 E3
- Wyatt Park Lidcombe 339 G5
- Wyatt Reserve Belrose 226 A9
- Wylde Park Greenfield Park 334 A13
- Wynyard Park Sydney A G15
- Yamble Reserve Ryde 282 A12
- Yarra Bay Bicentennial Park Phillip Bay 436 H10
- Yarranabbe Park Darling Point 13 H3
- Yarran St Reserve Pymble 253 B8
- Yarra Recreation Reserve Phillip Bay 436 J10
- Yarrawarrah Reserve 489 F14
- Yatama Park Clemton Park 402 A4
- Yattenden Park Baulkham Hills 247 J13
- Yellomundee Regional Park Yellow Rock 174 K8
- Yena Picnic Area Kurnell 466 H9
- Yeo Park Ashfield 373 A8
- Yeramba St Reserve Turramurra 252 D3
- Yinnell Reserve North Ryde 283 C11
- York Park Berala 339 C12
- York St Park Tahmoor 565 K9
- Yurrah Reserve Macquarie Park 282 K2
- Yurulbin Park Birchgrove 315 A16

PLACES OF INTEREST

- Addington Museum 813 Victoria Rd Ryde 311 H2
- Ahimsa Sanctuary Day Rd Cheltenham 251 B7
- Animal & Plant Quarantine Station Eastern Creek 272 F10
- Animal Welfare League Herley Av Rossmore 390 E3
- ANSTO Technology Park New Illawarra Rd Lucas Heights 487 H13
- Anzac Bridge Western Distributor Rozelle 12 A3
- Anzac War Memorial Hyde Park F E1
- Appin Mine Memorial Garden 569 E8
- Aquamagic Cockle Bay Sydney 3 C6
- Archibald Fountain Hyde Park D E8
- Archives Repository of NSW 143 O'Connell St Kingswood 268 F3
- Arms of Australia Inn (Museum) cnr Gardenia Av & Great Western Hwy Emu Plains 235 H9
- Auburn Botanic Gardens cnr Chisholm & Chiswick Rds 338 H6
- Audley Royal National Park 520 C7
- Australiana Park Camden Valley Wy Catherine Field 450 A11
- Australian Army Museum of Military Engineering Moorebank 425 B3
- Australian Aviation Museum cnr Henry Lawson Dr & Milperra Rd Bankstown 397 G5
- Australian Koi Farm 83 Jersey Rd Bringelly 388 K16
- Australian Museum 6 College St Darlinghurst D H14
- Australian Technology Park Eveleigh 18 H11
- Australia Square 264 George St Sydney A K14
- Aviation Museum 11 Stewart St Harrington Park 478 G8
- Bahai Temple 173 Mona Vale Rd Ingleside 197 G8
- Balmain Watch House Darling St 8 B9
- Bare Island Museum & Fort Anzac Pde La Perouse 436 J16
- Barrenjoey Lighthouse Barrenjoey Rd Palm Beach 109 J2
- Bass & Flinders Memorial 524 A4
- Belgenny Farm RMB 8 Elizabeth Macarthur Av Camden South 507 E12
- Bethlehem Monastery Narellan Rd Campbelltown 510 H2
- Bicentennial Park Australia Av Homebush 311 A15
- Blacktown City Bicentennial Museum Blacktown 182 K7
- Blue Pool Glenbrook 263 K4
- Bobbin Head Ku-ring-gai Chase National Pk 163 H12
- Bondi Pavillion Queen Elizabeth Dr Bondi Beach 378 E3
- Botanical Gardens Regreme Rd Picton 563 F1
- Bowman Cottage 370 Windsor St Richmond 118 F3
- Bridgeclimb 5 Cumberland St The Rocks A J1
- Brislington (Medical & Nursing Museum) cnr Marsden & George Sts Parramatta 308 B2
- Brush Farm House Eastwood 280 F9
- Burnside Heritage Centre 9 Blackwood Pl Oatlands 278 G10
- Burnside St Andrews Farm Emerald Hill Poll Hereford Stud St Andrews Rd Leppington 450 H1
- Bushrangers Cave Silverdale 384 D12
- Bus & Truck Museum of NSW 1B Gannon St Tempe 404 A2
- Butterfly Farm 446 Wilberforce Rd Wilberforce 91 J7
- Cables Water Ski Park Panther Pl Penrith 236 B13
- Cadmans Cottage 110 George St B A3
- Camden Historical Museum 40 John St 477 A15
- Camden Park House Elizabeth Macarthur Av Camden South 508 A16
- Cammeray Suspension Bridge 315 K2
- Campbelltown City Bicentennial Art Gallery Art Gallery Rd 511 C7
- Campbelltown Steam Museum Gilead 509 H16
- Canterbury Sugar Works Sugar House Rd 372 H14
- Cape Baily Lighthouse Kurnell 496 F4
- Captain Cooks Landing Place Captain Cook Dr Kurnell 466 C5
- Carisbrook House & Museum 334 Burns Bay Rd Lane Cove 313 G5
- Carss Cottage Carss Park 432 H16
- Castle Hill RSL Sub-Branch Memorial 218 D14
- Castlereagh Wesleyan Church & Cemetery Castlereagh Rd Castlereagh 205 H11
- Casula Powerhouse Arts Centre 1 Casula Rd Casula 395 A15
- Cataract Dam Cataract Dam Rd Appin 569 K16
- Cenotaph Martin Pl Sydney C J2
- Centennial Parklands Centennial Park 21 H10
- Central Gardens Merrylands West 306 H11
- Centrepoint Pitt St Sydney D A7
- Chinatown Dixon St E D5
- Chinese Garden of Friendship Darling Harbour E B9
- Circular Quay B D6
- Coastal Environment Centre Lake Park Rd North Narrabeen 199 C15
- Cockle Bay Wharf at Darling Park 201 Sussex St Sydney C A11
- Collingwood House cnr Hume Hwy & Congressional Dr Liverpool 395 C9
- Commodore Heights 108 J7
- Concord Heritage Museum 5 Wellbank St 342 A4
- Concord Pavilion of Honour Concord 342 A7
- Cook Obelisk Kurnell 466 D6
- Crusaders The Gorge Outdoor Recreation Centre Crusader Rd Galston 160 G14
- CSIRO Research Station Badgerys Creek 328 F8
- Cumberland State Forest Castle Hill Road West Pennant Hills 249 E2
- Customs House 31 Alfred St Sydney B D9
- Darling Harbour 3 B8
- Darling Harbour Passenger Terminal 13 Sussex St Sydney 1 C14
- Darlinghurst Court & Old Gaol Oxford St 4 E13
- Dee Why Lagoon Wildlife Refuge 258 K3
- Dobroyd Head Scenic Area Balgowlah Heights 288 B14
- Domain cnr Hospital & Art Gallery Rds Sydney 4 K6
- Don Bank Museum 6 Napier St North Sydney K B5
- 6 Napier St North Sydney 5 E7
- Dr H J Foley Memorial Glebe 12 B13
- Dunmore House Dunmore St Pendle Hill 276 F15
- Early Pioneers of the District Monument Greendale 355 C15
- Ebenezer Uniting Church Coromandel Rd 68 E12
- Eden Gardens & Garden Centre 283 A3
- Edgar Gornall Wildflower Gardens Edgecliff Bvd Narrabeen 228 J9
- E G Waterhouse National Camellia Gardens President Av Caringbah 492 E7
- El Alamein Fountain Kings Cross 4 K6
- El Caballo Blanco Camden Valley Wy Catherine Field 450 B11
- Elizabeth Bay House 7 Onslow Av 13 A3
- Elizabeth Farm 70 Alice St Rosehill 308 H6
- Elizabeth Macarthur Agricultural Institute Menangle 537 H9
- Endeavour Light La Perouse 437 J15
- Entertainment Centre Sydney 35 Harbour St Haymarket E B5
- Eryldene Heritage House & Camellia Garden 17 McIntosh St Gordon 253 K9
- Experimental Farm Cottage 9 Ruse St Harris Park 308 F5
- Explorers Memorial Memorial Av Penrith 236 D8
- Fagan Park Rural Museum Arcadia Rd Galston 159 G7
- Fairfield City Farm 31 Darling St Abbotsbury 332 J13
- Fairfield City Museum & Gallery 632 The Horsley Dr Smithfield 335 K5
- Featherdale Wildlife Park 217 Kildare Rd Doonside 243 H14
- Federation Pavilion Centennial Park 22 A10
- Fernbrook Garden & Gallery 2 Queen St Kurrajong Heights 63 F13
- Ferry Wharves (Sydney Harbour) Sydney B D5
- 1st Train Stopping at Merrylands 307 J13
- Fitzroy Bridge Windsor 121 E8
- Fleurs Radio Observatory Field Station Kemps Creek 330 A12
- Fort Macquarie Cannon Mays Hill 307 J5
- Fox Studios Australia cnr Lang Rd & Driver Av Moore Park 21 C5
- Fragrance Garden Sydney D J12
- Galston Gorge 160 J16
- Gardens of Many Nations Fagan Park Galston 159 F6
- Garrison Church Arglye Place Dawes Point A F2
- Gilroy House Manly 288 J13
- Gladesville Bridge 313 G14
- Gladwyn 96 Queens Rd Hurstville 432 A4
- Gledswood Homestead & Winery 900 Camden Valley Wy Catherine Field 450 D9
- Golden Ridge Animal Farm 686 Old Northern Rd Dural 188 J2
- Government House Macquarie St Sydney B K4
- GPO 1 Martin Pl Sydney C J2
- Great Synagogue & Am Rosenblum Jewish Museum 166 Castlereagh St Sydney D B11
- Great War Memorial Mt Hunter 504 K8
- Green Point Astronomical Observatory Oyster Bay 460 K5
- Greycliffe House Vaucluse 348 A2
- Hambledon Cottage 63 Hassall St Harris Park 308 G5
- Harbourside Darling Dr Sydney 3 A5
- Harrington Park Homestead 478 H2
- Hawkesbury Heritage Farm Rose St Wilberforce 91 K6
- Hawkesbury Museum & Tourist Information Centre 7 Thompson Sq Windsor 121 D7
- Hawkesbury Natural Horsemanship Centre Sargents Rd Wilberforce 67 G13
- Hawkesbury River Railway Bridge 76 D5
- Hazelhurst Arts Centre cnr Kingsway & Talara Rd N Gymea 491 D3
- Hills Centre,The Carrington Rd Castle Hill 217 F12
- Hills District Historical Museum Old Castle Hill Rd Castle Hill 218 D14
- Historic Coast Hospital Cemetery Little Bay 437 E15
- HMAS Parramatta Memorial George St Parramatta 308 G4
- HMAS Sydney Mast Bradleys Head Rd Mosman 347 C2
- Hordern Pavilion Driver Av Moore Park 20 K9
- Hornby Lighthouse Watsons Bay 318 F9
- Horseworld Stadium Maraylya 125 B14
- Housing Surrounding this Park Westmead 307 E2
- Hurstville Historical Museum 319 Forest Rd 431 H5
- Hyde Park Sydney D E10
- Hyde Park Barracks Queens Sq, Macquarie St Sydney D G6
- Information Centre Great Western Hwy Glenbrook 234 B16
- Jacksons Falls 235 F2
- James Beres Bridge Silverdale 384 C3
- Japanese Gardens cnr Chisholm & Chiswick Sts Auburn 338 J6
- Jellybean Pool 263 K7
- Joan Sutherland Performing Arts Centre 597 High St Penrith 236 F9

GREGORY'S STREET DIRECTORY 175

John Tebbutts Observatory
Palmer St
Windsor 121 G8
Justice & Police Museum
cnr Phillip & Albert Sts
Sydney B F8
K13 Memorial
Carlingford 279 H5
Kalkari Visitor Centre
Ku-ring-gai Chase
National Pk 163 F16
Keith Anderson Memorial
Rawson Park
Mosman 317 D10
King St Wharf
Sydney 3 C1
Kings Cross
Darlinghurst 4 J8
Kirinari
Box Rd
Sylvania 461 F13
Kirkham Stables
Homestead 477 F7
Kirribilli House
Kirribilli Av 2 F3
Knapsack Viaduct 234 G13
Koala Park Sanctuary
84 Castle Hill Rd
Pennant Hills 249 H2
Kokoda Track Memorial
Centrepiece
Rhodes 311 E11
Ku-ring-gai Wildflower Garden
420 Mona Vale Rd
St Ives 224 D1
Lancer Barracks Heritage
Precinct
Smith St
Parramatta 308 D4
Lansdowne Bridge 366 K4
La Perouse Monument 436 H14
La Perouse Museum
Anzac Pde 436 J14
Lapstone Hill 234 H10
Lapstone Zig Zag 234 G15
Lavendar Bay Gallery
Walker St
North Sydney K F13
Law Courts D E5
Lennox Bridge
Mitchells Ps
Lapstone 234 E11
Lieutenant Cantello Memorial
Lieutenant Cantello Reserve
Hammondville 397 A16
Lime Kiln Bay
Bushland Sanctuary
Oatley 430 G10
Lindesay
1a Carthona Av
Darling Point 347 A9
Linnwood Horse Museum
Byron Rd
Guildford 337 C5
Liverpool Regional Museum
cnr Hume Hwy &
Congressional Dr 395 B8
Long Bay Correctional Centre
Anzac Pde
Malabar 437 C6
Loxley on Bellbird Hill
993 Bells Line of Road
Kurrajong Hills 63 J15
Luna Park
Milsons Point 5 J16
Macarthur Bridge 507 D6
Macarthurs Homestead
Elizabeth Macarthur Av
Camden South 507 E13
Macleay Building
Gosper La,
University of Sydney
Camperdown 18 C1
Macquarie Field House
Quarter Sessions Rd
Glenfield 423 H12
Macquarie House
Ferguson La
Grasmere 476 F15
Macquarie Lighthouse
Vaucluse 348 H2
Macquarie Place B B11
Mamre Homestead Tea Rooms
Mamre Rd
Orchard Hills 269 E10
Manly Amusement Pier 288 F11
Manly Art Gallery & Museum
West Esp 288 F10
Manly Dam 287 F2
Manly Waterworks
West Esp 288 E10
Manly Wharf
East Esp 288 F11
Martin Place
Sydney C K2
Mary MacKillop Place Museum
7 Mount St
North Sydney 5 E8
Memorial Garden
Eastern Rd
Schofields 213 F13
Metro Monorail C K9
MLC Centre
19 Martin Pl
Sydney D B4
Model Park
R53 Luddenham Rd
Luddenham 327 H11
Model Steam Trains
Darvall Park
West Ryde 281 D14
Mount Annan Botanic Garden
Mount Annan Dr 509 G7
Mount Portal 264 F7
Mrs Macquaries Chair 2 H10
Museum
Camden Aerodrome
Cobbitty 476 J11
Museum of Applied Arts &
Sciences Powerhouse Museum
500 Harris St
Ultimo 3 A11
Museum of Contemporary Art
Maritime Services Building,
140 George St
The Rocks B A5
Museum of Fire
Castlereagh Rd
Penrith 236 G8
Museum of Sydney
37 Phillip St B D11
National Maritime Museum
Shipyard
Balls Head Dr
Waverton 315 E15
National Park Office
Glenbrook 264 A6
National Parks &
Wildlife Information Centre
110 George St
The Rocks B A3
National Trust of Australia
Observatory Hill
Millers Point A D7
Native Gardens
Picnic Point 428 C12
Nativity House Christmas
Museum Gallery
136 Garfield Rd
Horsley Park 331 F5
Nepean Observatory
University of Western
Sydney, Great Western Hwy
Werrington 238 E14
Newport Memorial 169 F12
Nicholson Museum
Main Quadrangle,
University of Sydney
Camperdown 18 D2
Notre Dame
Mulgoa Rd
Mulgoa 294 H4
NSW Fire Brigade Operational &
Support Complex
Amarina Av
Greenacre 370 G8
NSW School House Museum
Coxs Rd
North Ryde 282 F9
Nutcote The Home of May Gibbs
5 Wallaringa Av
Neutral Bay 6 G10
Obelisk
Macquarie Place Park
Sydney B C10
Oceanworld Manly
West Esp 288 F10
Old Government House
Parramatta Park
Parramatta 308 A2
Old Post Office
Community Art Centre
Great Western Hwy
St Marys 269 H1
Old School House
Arthur Phillip High School
cnr Macquarie & Smith Sts
Parramatta 308 D3
Opal Access Museum
1a Warks Rd
Kurrajong Heights 63 F12
Over The Road
70 Mulhollands Rd
Mowbray Park 562 E2
Oxford Square
Darlinghurst F J5
Padstow War Memorial 399 E15
Panthers World of
Entertainment
Mulgoa Rd
Penrith 236 D12
Parliament House
Macquarie St D G2
Peats Ferry Bridge 75 D7
Penrith Regional Gallery &
The Lewers Bequest
86 River Rd
Emu Plains 235 G13
Penrith Whitewater Stadium
McCarthys La
Castlereagh 206 D11
Pier One
Hickson Rd
Millers Point 1 G6
Pitt Street Mall
Sydney C K7
Police HQ
cnr College & Stanley Sts
Darlinghurst D G16
Pool of Reflection
Hyde Park
Sydney D E15
Powerhouse Museum
500 Harris St
Ultimo 3 A11
Prospect Reservoir 304 B5
Pyrmont Bridge
Sydney 3 B4
Q Theatre
cnr Railway & Belmore Sts
Penrith 236 J9
Quarantine Station (tours)
North Head Scenic Dr
Manly 318 H1
Queens Square
Sydney D E5
Queen Victoria Building
455 George St
Sydney C H9
Quondong Visitor
Information Centre
15 Old Menangle Rd
Campbelltown 511 C7
Railway Square
Haymarket E E13
Randwick District
Memorial 377 B15
Richmond Bridge 87 H15
Richmond Villa Museum
12 Lithgow St
Campbelltown 511 F5
Rockend Cottage
Punt Rd
Gladesville 312 J14
Rose Seidler House
71 Clissold Rd
Wahroonga 223 C3
Rouse Hill Estate
980 Windsor Rd
Rouse Hill 184 F6
Royal Blind Society of NSW
Enfield 371 J5
Royal National Park
Rock Carvings 524 F7
Royal National Park
Visitor Centre
Farnell Av 520 E1
RSPCA Animals Shelter
Rookwood Rd
Chullora 369 G4
St Andrews Cathedral
cnr George & Bathurst Sts
Sydney C G14
St Bartholomews Church
Ponds Rd
Prospect 275 A15
St Benedicts Monastery
121 Arcadia Rd
Arcadia 129 H12
St Johns Cathedral
187 Church St
Parramatta 308 C3
St Johns Church
Menangle Rd
Camden 507 B1
St Mary Magdalene
Anglican Church
cnr Great Western Hwy &
Magdalene St
St Marys 269 J1
St Marys Cathedral
cnr College & Cathedral Sts
Sydney D H9
St Michaels Cave
Avalon 140 F15
St Stephens Church
Macquarie St D F2
St Thomas Historic Church
St Thomas Rd
Mulgoa 295 E12
St Thomas Rest Park
250 West St
Crows Nest 315 H5
Sandakan Memorial
North Turramurra 193 F12
Sandringham Gardens D F11
Santas Cottage
35 George St
The Rocks 1 H8
Scenic Hills Riding Ranch
Lot 1 Campbelltown Rd
Varroville 452 B7
Schoenstatt Shrine
230 Fairlight Rd
Mulgoa 324 B1
Scotland Australia Cairn
Rawson Park
Mosman 317 D10
Scots Church
Jamison St A F14
Searles Monument
Henley 313 B16
Shadforth Bridge
Silverdale 384 G1
S H Ervin Gallery
National Trust Centre,
Observatory Hill
Millers Point A D8
Silvicultural Demonstration Area
Berkshire Park 178 H10
Sir Joseph Banks Memorial
Kurnell 466 D5
Skywalk on Sydney Tower
Pitt St
Sydney D A7
Solander Monument
Kurnell 466 E5
South Head Signal Station
Vaucluse 348 H1
Sphinx War Memorial
Ku-ring-gai Chase
National Pk 193 G9
State Archives
The Rocks
2 Globe St A K5
State Library of NSW
Macquarie St B H16
Stony Range Flora Reserve
Pittwater Rd
Dee Why 258 F8
Strand Arcade
412 George St
Sydney C J5
Strickland House
Vaucluse 348 A3
Supreme Court
Queens Sq
Sydney D E5
Susannah Place
58 Gloucester St
The Rocks A J5
Sutherland Entertainment Centre
30 Eton St N 490 F2
Sydney Aquarium at
Darling Harbour
1 Wheat Rd
Sydney C A7
Sydney Central
Railway Station E H13
Sydney Childrens Museum
cnr Pitt & Walpole Sts
Holroyd 307 J10
Sydney Conservatorium of
Music
Conservatorium Rd B J11
Sydney Convention Centre
Darling Dr 3 A6
Sydney Cove B E2
Sydney Cove Terminal B C2
Sydney Cricket Ground
(Sportspace Tours)
Driver Av
Moore Park 21 A6
Sydney Exhibition Centre
Darling Dr 3 A8
Sydney Fish Market
cnr Bank St &
Pyrmont Bridge Rd
Pyrmont 12 F6
Sydney Holocaust Museum
Gallery & Library
398 Cleveland Av
Surry Hills 20 A6
Sydney Jewish Museum
148 Darlinghurst Rd
Darlinghurst 4 G11
Sydney Observatory
Observatory Hill, Watson Rd
Millers Point A D4
Sydney Olympic Park
Homebush Bay 340 F2
Sydney Olympic Park
Sports Centre
(Hall of Champions)
Olympic Bvd
Homebush Bay 340 H4
Sydney Opera House
Bennelong Point B J1
Sydney Showground
1 Showground Rd
Homebush Bay 310 G15
Sydney Square C G13
Sydney Tower & Skytour
Pitt St
Sydney D A7
Sydney Town Hall
483 George St C G12
Sydney Tramway Museum
Pitt St
Loftus 490 C9
Sydney Tropical Centre
Royal Botanic Gardens,
Mrs Macquaries Rd
Sydney B K15
Sydney Visitor Centre &
Heritage Gallery
106 George St
The Rocks B A2
Sydney Visitors Centre
Darling Harbour
33 Wheat Rd C A11
Taronga Zoological Park
Bradleys Head Rd
Mosman 317 A14
Teen Ranch Holiday Camp
Cobbitty Rd
Cobbitty 446 J15
The Gap
Watsons Bay 318 G14
The Macquarie Arms
99 George St
Windsor 121 D7
The Mint (Historic House)
10 Macquarie St
Sydney D G4
The Old St Thomas Chapel
cnr Camden Valley Wy &
Wilson Cr
Narellan 478 E10
The Rocks
George St 1 K8
Thirlmere Rail Heritage Centre
Barbour Rd 565 A4
Thomas V Cross Memorial
Forest Rd
Lugarno 429 K12
Tingira Memorial
Rose Bay 348 A10
Tipperary Falls
Hunters Hill 313 E6
Tudor Gatehouse The
Parramatta 308 B2
University of Sydney
Parramatta Rd
Camperdown 18 B5
Valley View Park Range
Trail Rides
299 Grose Vale Rd
Grose Vale 86 D15
Vaucluse House
Wentworth Rd 348 C3
Vision Valley
Recreation Centre
Vision Valley Rd
Arcadia 130 C12
Waratah Park
Wildlife Reserve
13 Namba Rd
Duffys Forest 194 G4
War Memorial
Bundeena 523 K9

176 GREGORY'S STREET DIRECTORY

St Leonards Park
North Sydney 5 E4
St Leonards Park
North Sydney 5 E4
St Leonards Park
North Sydney 5 E4
Wentworthville 276 K16
West Pymble 253 A11
Warragamba Dam
Farnsworth Av............353 B5
Wascoe Siding
Miniature Railway
Grahame St
Blaxland 233 G10
Watsons Bay Naval Depot &
Memorial Chapel.........318 F11
Watsons Bay School
Historical Site
Old South Head Rd......318 G14
Westpac Museum
6 Playfair St
The Rocks....................A K1
Willandra Art Centre
770 Victoria Rd
Ryde 311 J3
Windsor Bridge............121 D6
Wollondilly Heritage Centre
45 Edward St
The Oaks 502 G13
World War 1 Honour Roll
National Park 520 D5
World War 1 Memorial
Mascot Memorial Park
Mascot......................405 E3
1 Broadway
Punchbowl................400 D4
World War 1 Monument
Werombi Rd
Theresa Park..............445 C13
World War 2 Memorial
Berowra Heights 133 B9
World War 2 Monument
Aerodrome Rd
Cobbitty.....................476 K9
Yaralla House
Concord West............311 J13
Yarra Bay House
La Perouse 436 H12
YMCA Yarramundi
Youth Camp 116 B14

SHOPPING COMPLEXES - MAJOR

Ashfield Shopping Mall..372 H3
Auburn Home
Mega Mall 309 C13
Bangor........................459 D13
Bankstown Square........369 G16
Bass Hill Plaza..............367 K8
Bayside Plaza...............433 K2
Birkenhead Point..........344 B4
Bonnyrigg Plaza...........364 A3
Bridgepoint..................317 A5
Broadway 12 H16
Burwood Plaza.............341 K14
Campbelltown Mall 511 D5
Campsie Centre............372 A14
Caringbah....................492 G8
Caringbah SupaCenta....492 H2
Carlingford Court 280 A2
Carlingford Village.........280 A3
Carnes Hill Marketplace..392 F10
Castle Mall...................218 C15
Castle Towers 218 C14
Casula Mall...................394 F15
Cherrybrook 219 G9
Chifley Plaza.....................B E15
Chullora Marketplace.....370 E5
Clocktower Square...........A J3
Cockle Bay Wharf at
Darling Harbour..............C A11
Cosmopolitan 347 B13
Cronulla Plaza..............493 K11
Crows Nest Plaza 315 F5
Eagle Vale Marketplace ..481 F5
Eastgate 22 H8
Eastlakes 406 A2
East Ocean Arcade ....E E7
Eastwood Centre...........281 B8
Edgecliff 13 H11
Emerton Village............240 K5
Engadine Court 518 J2
Fairfield Chase 336 F12
Fairfield Forum.............336 E11
Forestway....................256 D5
Galeries Victoria...............C J11
Glasshouse.......................D A5
Glenquarie Town Centre ..424 C16
Glenrose.......................225 J16
Gordon Centre 253 G7
Greenfield.....................334 A13
Greenway 308 C3
Harbourside 3 A5
Homebase....................275 A13
Home Central...............399 D7
Homemaker City 399 D7
Homemaker City
Castle Hill 217 C14
Homemaker
Collection Norwest 216 A14
Homemakers Supa Centa
Moore Park 20 D16
Hunter Connection............A K16
Hurstville Supa Centre ...432 B6
Illawong Village.............459 J4
Ingleburn Fair 453 D5
Kien Hay Centre ....E E7
Kingsgate..........................4 H8
Kogarah Town Centre....433 B4
Leichhardt Market Place ..373 G1
Lemon Grove................284 J9
Lennox Centre 235 E10
Macarthur Square 510 K8
Macquarie Centre..........282 F1
Mandarin Centre 284 J10
Market City........................E C8
Marketown 182 J8
Marrickville Metro 374 F10
Megacenta Liverpool 365 C12
Menai Marketplace.........458 J11
Menai Metro 458 K11
Metcentre ....A H13
Mid City Centre.................C K6
Miller 393 J2
Minchinbury Hometown..271 D5
Minto Mall 482 H4
MLC Centre.......................D B4
Mount Annan
Marketplace................479 E12
Narellan Town Centre 478 G10
Neeta City.....................336 F11
Nepean Square 236 G12
Neutral Bay Village 6 J1
Newtown Plaza 17 F13
Northbridge Plaza..........285 J15
North Sydney
Shoppingworld..............K F5
Norton Plaza...................16 A2
Norwest Marketown 216 G15
Paddys Markets
Flemington 340 J7
Paddys Markets
Market City ....E C8
Parklea Markets 215 F11
Parkway Plaza...............221 A13
Penrith Plaza................236 G9
Piccadilly Centre...............D A9
Plumpton Marketplace...241 K6
Quadrangle
Shopping Village 285 K12
Quakers Court...............243 J3
Queen Victoria Building .....C H9
Richmond Marketplace..118 H6
Riverwood Plaza 400 B16
Rockdale Plaza..............433 E1
Roselands 400 H8
Royal Randwick 377 A14
St Clair 270 C12
St Ives Village 223 K12
Seven Hills....................275 F2
Shopsmart
Outlet Centre...............241 G15
Skygarden ....D A6
Southgate.....................462 B9
Southpoint 406 H14
South Terrace Plaza.......369 G16
Station Street Plaza 239 H14
Stockland 334 D7
Stockland Imperial Arcade..D A6
Stockland Mall
Baulkham Hills............247 H10
Stockland Mall
Maroubra...................407 A9
Stockland Mall
Merrylands 307 H12
Strand Arcade ....C J5
Strathfield Plaza 341 G12
Surry Hills 20 A7
Sussex Arcade...................E F6
Sydney Central Plaza.........C J7
Sydney Markets 340 J7
Sylvania Waters 462 F13
The Interchange............284 H10
The Valley Plaza 363 D13
Top Ryde......................312 A1
Totem 287 J8
Town Hall Arcade.............C G13
Town Hall Square ....C F14
Village 239 F16
Warriewood..................198 K12
Warringah Mall 257 J12
Wentworthville Mall.......277 A16
Wentworthville
Shopping Plaza 307 A4
Westfield Bondi Junction ..22 J6
Westfield Burwood........342 A13
Westfield Centrepoint........D A7
Westfielf Chatswood.......284 J10
Westfield Eastgardens 406 F11
Westfield Hornsby.........221 J1
Westfield Hurstville 432 B5
Westfield Liverpool.........395 E2
Westfield Miranda 491 K4
Westfield Mount Druitt ..241 D15
Westfield North Rocks...249 B14
Westfield Parramatta.......30 B4
Westpoint.....................244 F15
Winston Hills Mall 246 K16
Wintergarden Plaza...........B B13

SPORTING VENUES

Alexandria
Basketball Stadium......375 E11
Ambarvale
Sports Complex 510 K12
Andrews Rd Baseball Complex
Penrith 237 C1
Anne Clark Netball Centre
Lidcombe 339 F5
Anzac Rifle Range
Malabar......................437 H2
Appin AIS
Sportsground 569 D9
Arlington Recreation Reserve
Dulwich Hill 373 C9
Aussie Stadium
Moore Park 21 A4
Australian Tennis Academy
Frenchs Forest 257 C2
Avalon
Recreation Centre........170 B1
Bankstown Basketball Stadium
Condell Park 398 C4
Bankstown City
Sports Complex 399 A5
Bankstown Football
Centre 399 F5
Bankstown Oval 399 D2
Bargo Sportsground.......567 E8
Baulkham Hills Netball Assn
Kellyville 185 G9
Bellingara Netball Courts
Miranda.....................461 K15
Belmore Sportsground ..371 G16
Bensons Lane
Sporting Complex
Richmond Lowlands ...118 J1
Bernie Mullane
Sports Complex
Kellyville 216 J2
Bill Spilstead Complex
for Canine Affairs
(Dog Showground)
Orchard Hills...............299 E2
Blacktown Equestrian Centre
Marsden Park 212 B5
Blacktown
International Ice 244 H15
Blacktown Olympic Park-
Sydney
Rooty Hill 272 G1
Blake Rimmer Diamond
Chipping Norton..........397 B3
Botany Athletic Centre
Hillsdale 406 E12
Broken Bay Sports &
Recreation Centre........107 E1
Brookvale Oval..............258 B9
Cabramatta
Sportsground 365 G12
Calabria Community Club
Prairiewood 334 D8
Campbelltown Sportsground
Leumeah 482 B12
Campbelltown Sports Stadium
Leumeah 482 B13
Canterbury Ice 372 D12
Canterbury Velodrome
Earlwood 403 J3
Caringbah Oval 492 H8
Centennial Parklands
Equestrian Centre
Moore Park 21 B10
Centennial Stadium
Minto 482 E3
Chatswood Oval............284 J11
Chatswood War Memorial
Athletic Field
Lane Cove West 283 F11
Clive Rogers Equestrian Ground
Warriewood 199 C13
Concord Oval................342 C10
Coogee Oval 377 G16
Cromer Park.................228 F16
Dangar-Cranbrook
Sportsground
Rose Bay....................347 K12
David Phillips Sports Field
Daceyville 406 E5
Drummoyne Oval..........343 G2
Dudley Chesham
Sportsground
The Oaks 502 C13
Eastern Creek
International Raceway ..273 C15
Endeavour Sports Reserve
Fairfield 335 G15
Eschol Park
Sports Complex 481 D4
Fairfield Showground
Prairiewood 334 G10
Forshaw Field
Sylvania Waters 462 D15
Frank Downing Sports Ground
Putney........................312 D8
Gabbie Stadium
Seven Hills..................245 J14
Gipps Rd Sporting Complex
Greystanes 305 A13
Greystanes
Sportsground 305 J10
Guildford West
Sportsground 336 F4
Harold Laybutt Sporting
Complex
Arndell Park................274 B11
Hawkesbury Equestrian Centre
Richmond 119 G10
Hawkesbury Indoor Stadium
South Windsor............150 G1
Hills Basketball Stadium
Castle Hill 217 D10
Holroyd Sportsground...308 B9
Howell Oval
Penrith 236 E13
Hurstville Oval..............431 K3
Ingleside Valley Equestrian
Centre
Ingleside.....................197 E3
Jacqui Osmond
Softball Centre
Warwick Farm.............365 J12
Jim Campbell Sportsfield
Macquarie Park...........252 C12
Joshua Allen Diamond
Chipping Norton..........397 B2
Kevin Betts Stadium
Mount Druitt 241 H15
King Tomislav Croatian Oval
Edensor Park 333 E15
Kogarah Jubilee Oval
Carlton 433 A8
Lambert Park
Leichhardt 373 F1
Leichhardt Oval.............343 J10
Lidcombe Velodrome 339 G5
Little Bay Sports Field 437 C9
Liverpool City Hockey Centre
Moorebank.................396 A10
McKay Sportground........21 C14
Macquarie Ice
Macquarie Park...........282 F1
Makepeace
Athletic Field 336 H14
Marcellin Sports Fields ..407 A12
Marconi Oval
Bossley Park...............333 H9
Mark Leece Sporting Complex
St Clair 270 C10
Melita Stadium
South Granville 338 G11
Merrylands Park............307 D11
Merrylands Velodrome ..307 D11
Mileham St Netball Complex
South Windsor............120 G16
Mt Pritchard
Sportsground 364 E8
National Equestrian
Sports Centre
Menangle Park............509 C13
Nepean Raceway
Castlereagh.................146 D10
Nepean Rugby Union Oval
Penrith 237 B2
Northbridge Oval...........316 C1
Northern Beaches
Gymnastics Centre
North Narrabeen 199 A15
North Sydney
Indoor Sports Centre
Crows Nest.................315 F6
North Sydney Oval 5 H2
NSW Catholic
Lawn Tennis Assn
Haberfield 343 F15
NSW Lawn Tennis Assn Courts
(White City)
Paddington..................13 E12
Old Kings Oval
Parramatta..................278 A16
Oran Park Motorsport....448 E11
Oriole Stadium
Auburn 338 H3
Parramatta City
Raceway.....................309 A10
Parramatta Granville
Sportsground 309 A10
Parramatta Stadium 278 B16
Penrith City Archers
Werrington 239 C11
Penrith Ice Palace
Jamisontown..............265 K1
Penrith Park.................236 E12
Penrith Sports Stadium
Cambridge Park 238 C10
Penrith Whitewater Stadium
Castlereagh.................206 D11
Peter Kearns Memorial Oval
St Clair 269 H12
Petersham Park 373 H4
Pittwater Rugby Park
Warriewood................199 D13
Pratten Park
Ashfield 372 H5
Princess Anne Equestrian Area
St Ives.........................194 J16
Raby Sports Complex....451 C14
Redfern Oval..................19 F10
Reg Bartley Oval The
Rushcutters Bay............13 C7
Rockdale Womens
Sports Fields...............403 H15
Roper Rd Soccer Field
Colyton.......................270 H5
Ross Gwilliam Sportsfield
Macquarie Park...........252 D12
St George Soccer Stadium
Banksia 403 K12
St Josephs College
Sportsground 313 B7
St Marys
Indoor Shooting
Centre 239 H9
Serbian Centre
Bonnyrigg Heights.......363 E4
Seymour Shaw Park
Miranda......................492 A2
Soldiers Hockey Field 460 F12
Somerville Park
Eastwood 281 C4
State Sports Centre
Homebush Bay 340 H4
Sydney Academy of Sport
Cromer.......................227 G7
Sydney Athletic Field
Moore Park.................376 E9
Sydney Cricket Ground
Moore Park 21 A6
Sydney International
Archery Park
Homebush Bay 310 J11
Sydney International
Equestrian Centre
Horsley Park 332 K2
Sydney International
Regatta Centre
Castlereagh.................206 B13
Sydney International
Shooting Centre
Cecil Park 361 D5

GREGORY'S STREET DIRECTORY 177

INFORMATION

SPORTING VENUES

Sydney International
Tennis Centre
Homebush Bay 340 H4
Sydney & Marconi
Clay Target Complex
Lucas Heights 486 J8
Sydney Olympic Park
Aquatic Centre
Homebush Bay 340 G2
Sydney Olympic Park
Athletic Centre
Homebush Bay 340 F2
Sydney Olympic Park
Hockey Centre
Homebush Bay 340 G4
Sydney Shooters Association
Rifle Range
Silverdale..................383 H13
Sydney Showground
Homebush Bay 310 G15
Sydney University Ovals ..18 A4
Telstra Stadium
Homebush Bay 340 E1
T G Millner Sportsground
Marsfield..................281 H1
The Ridge
Barden Ridge 488 C1
The Western Weekender
Sports Stadium
North St Marys 239 J6
Thirlmere Sportsground 564 K3
Thornleigh Indoor
Recreational Centre ..221 C10
Tiger-Wests Athletics Club
Lidcombe 339 F4
Toyota Park
Woolooware 493 E5
Trumper Oval
Paddington................13 G12
Warragamba
Sportsground 353 F9
Warwick Farm
Polo Field..................366 C14
Waverley Oval 377 H4
Weigall Sportsground......13 D10
Western Sydney
International Dragway
Eastern Creek............303 C3
Whitlam Leisure Centre
Liverpool 395 A6
Windsor Polo Club
Richmond 88 A16
Windsor Sporting Complex
South Windsor............150 C3
Womens Athletic Field
Chifley......................437 A8
Woodlands Baseball Complex
St Helens Park 541 G2
Wran Leisure Centre
Villawood 367 E4

TERTIARY & OTHER INSTITUTIONS

ACADEMY OF INFORMATION
TECHNOLOGY
Level 1, 841 George St
Ultimo ....E C14
ACTORS COLLEGE OF
THEATRE & TELEVISION
505 Pitt St
Sydney......................E F12
APM TRAINING INSTITUTE
33 Chandos St
St Leonards 315 D5
AQUINAS ACADEMY
152 Gloucester St
Sydney......................A G10
AUSTRALASIAN COLLEGE OF
NATURAL THERAPIES
57 Foveaux St
Surry Hills ....F C16
AUSTRALIAN CATHOLIC
UNIVERSITY
Mackillop Campus
40 Edward St
North Sydney 5 D7
Main Campus (Mt St Mary)
179 Albert Rd
Strathfield..................341 A13
AUSTRALIAN COLLEGE OF
APPLIED PSYCHOLOGY
414-418 Elizabeth St
Surry Hills 19 H2

AUSTRALIAN COLLEGE OF
PHYSICAL EDUCATION
Australia Centre, & Figtree Dr
Homebush Bay 340 H2
AUSTRALIAN FILM,
TELEVISION &
RADIO SCHOOL
cnr Epping & Balaclava Rds
Macquarie Park..........282 A1
AUSTRALIAN GRADUATE
SCHOOL OF ENGINEERING
INNOVATION
Locomotive Workshop,
Australian Technology Park,
Garden St
Eveleigh 18 J9
AUSTRALIAN INSTITUTE OF
POLICE MANAGEMENT
Collins Beach Rd
Manly 288 J15
AUSTRALIAN INTERNATIONAL
CONSERVATORIUM OF MUSIC
31 Allen St
Harris Park 308 E7
AUSTRALIAN & NEW
ZEALAND COLLEGE OF
ANAETHETISTS
Suite 603, 180 Ocean St
Edgecliff 13 J12
AUSTRALIAN PACIFIC COLLEGE
ADC Building, 189 Kent St
Sydney......................A C11
BANKSTOWN
COMMUNITY COLLEGE
457 Chapel Rd
Bankstown 369 E16
BILLY BLUE ENGLISH SCHOOL
Level 9, Northpoint Centre,
cnr Miller St & Pacific Hwy
North Sydney ....K D5
BILLY BLUE SCHOOL
OF GRAPHIC ARTS
221 Miller St
North Sydney ....K E2
BLACKTOWN DISTRICT
COMMUNITY COLLEGE
cnr Kildare Rd &
Lancaster St..............244 D16
CANCES
National Innovation Centre,
Australian Technology Park
Eveleigh 18 K9
CANISIUS
102 Mona Vale Rd
Pymble......................223 G15
CATHOLIC THEOLOGICAL
Albert Rd
Strathfield..................341 C12
CENTRAL QUEENSLAND
UNIVERSITY
Level 5, Imperial Arcade,
85 Castlereagh St
Sydney......................D B6
CHRISTIAN CITY CHURCH
Ministry Training College
Wakehurst Pky
Oxford Falls 227 A16
COLLEGE OF LAW
2 Chandos St
St Leonards 315 D5
233 Macquarie St
Sydney......................D F4
DEAF EDUCATION NETWORK
Level 8, Strathfield
Plaza, 11 The Boulevard
Strathfield..................341 G12
DOROTHY WATTS
VOCATIONAL
TRAINING CENTRE
49 Blackbutts Rd
Frenchs Forest 256 A2
DUNMORE LANG COLLEGE
Macquarie University
130 Herring Rd
Macquarie Park..........282 D2
EMMAUS BIBLE COLLEGE
25 Ray Rd
Epping 251 A14
GOLDEN KEY NATIONAL
HONOUR SOCIETY
102 Darlington Rd
Darlington..................18 E7
HILLS DISTRICT
COMMUNITY COLLEGE
129 Showground Rd
Castle Hill 217 G12

HORNSBY KU-RING-GAI
COMMUNITY COLLEGE
45 Hunter St
Hornsby 191 H16
INSEARCH LANGUAGE CENTRE
& INSTITUTE OF COMMERCE
Level 2, 187 Thomas St
Haymarket..................E D11
INTERNATIONAL COLLEGE OF
TOURISM & HOTEL
MANAGEMENT
151 Darley St
Manly 288 K12
JAPANESE LANGUAGE
INSTITUTE
109 Pitt St
Sydney......................A K16
KVB INSTITUTE OF
TECHNOLOGY
99 Mount St
North Sydney ....K G8
L.I.F.E BIBLE COLLEGE
2 Bridge Rd
Westmead 307 D4
MACARTHUR
COMMUNITY COLLEGE
Willan Dr
Cartwright 394 B5
MACLEAY COLLEGE
Level 1, 175 Liverpool St
Sydney......................F D3
MACQUARIE CHRISTIAN
STUDIES INSTITUTE
Union Building,
Macquarie University
Macquarie Park..........252 D16
MACQUARIE COMMUNITY
COLLEGE
263b Marsen Rd
Carlingford 280 B3
MACQUARIE
GRADUATE SCHOOL
51-57 Pitt St
Sydney......................B A11
MACQUARIE GRADUATE
SCHOOL OF MANAGEMENT
(MGSM)
Talavera Rd
Macquarie Park..........252 D15
MACQUARIE UNIVERSITY
Balaclava Rd
Macquarie Park..........252 C15
Peter Board Campus
Wicks Rd
Macquarie Park..........282 K7
MANLY WARRINGAH
COMMUNITY COLLEGE
Narrabeen Sports High School
1525 Pittwater Rd
North Narrabeen 199 A15
MARTIN COLLEGE
161 Macquarie St
Parramatta................308 D3
MERCURY BUSINESS COLLEGE
3 Waverley St
Bondi Junction..........22 K7
METROPOLITAN
BUSINESS COLLEGE
Level 5, Margaret St
Sydney......................A E14
MORLING COLLEGE (BAPTIST)
120 Herring Rd
Macquarie Park..........282 D3
MOSMAN EVENING COLLEGE
Gladstone Av
Mosman 317 B8
MT ELIZA BUSINESS SCHOOL
Level 1, 63 York St
Sydney......................C F2
NSW BUSINESS &
ENGLISH COLLEGES
Wembley House, 841
George St
Ultimo ....E C14
OPEN TRAINING &
EDUCATION NETWORK
EXTERNAL STUDIES
Strathfield
Wentworth Rd 341 H12
PATRICIAN BROTHERS
TRAINING CENTRE
134 Eastern Rd
Wahroonga................222 J6
RENWICK COLLEGE
367 North Rocks Rd
North Rocks 249 B14

ROBERT MENZIES COLLEGE
Macquarie University
136 Herring Rd
Macquarie Park..........282 D2
ROYAL AUSTRALASIAN
COLLEGE
OF PHYSICIANS, THE
145 Macquarie St
Sydney......................B F13
SAE TECHNOLOGY COLLEGE
55-57 Wentworth Av
Surry Hills ....F C6
ST ANDREWS COLLEGE
cnr Carillon Av &
Missenden Rd
Camperdown..............17 J6
ST GEORGE &
SUTHERLAND COMMUNITY
COLLEGE
131 Sutherland Rd
Jannali 460 F13
ST PATRICKS BUSINESS
COLLEGE
cnr Devonshire & Riley Sts
Surry Hills 20 A3
SALVATION ARMY COLLEGE
OF FURTHER EDUCATION
School for Biblical &
General Studies
32a Barnsbury Gr
Bexley North 402 G9
School for Officer Training
120 Kingsland Rd N
Bexley North 402 G10
SEMINARY OF THE
GOOD SHEPHERD
50 Abbotsford Rd
Homebush..................341 B10
SHILLINGTON COLLEGE
Level 2, 50 Margaret St
Sydney......................A G14
SOUTHERN CROSS COLLEGE
40 Hector St
Chester Hill 338 D14
SYDNEY BIBLE BAPTIST
COLLEGE
214 Pennant Hills Rd
Oatlands 279 B7
SYDNEY COLLEGE OF
TRADITIONAL CHINESE
MEDICINE
92 Norton St
Leichhardt..................373 K1
SYDNEY COMMUNITY
COLLEGE
cnr Victoria Rd & Gordon St
Rozelle 11 B1
Intensive Language Centre
cnr Cleveland & Chalmers Sts
Surry Hills 19 F4
SYDNEY INSTITUTE OF
BUSINESS & TECHNOLOGY
Library Building, Macquarie
University
Macquarie Park..........252 C16
SYDNEY INSTITUTE OF
TECHNOLOGY
Annandale Campus
cnr Johnston St &
The Crescent
Annandale..................11 C7
TABOR COLLEGE
10 Kiama St
Miranda 462 B15
TAFE NSW-NORTHERN
SYDNEY INSTITUTE
Bradfield College
192 Pacific Hwy
Crows Nest................5 C1
Brookvale College
154 Old Pittwater Rd ..257 J13
Crows Nest College
Rodborough Av..........315 J7
Hornsby College
205 Pacific Hwy 191 F15
Meadowbank College
cnr See St &
Constitution Rd 311 F2
North Sydney College
213 Pacific Hwy
Artarmon 315 A4
Ryde College
250 Blaxland Rd 281 K15
TAFE NSW-SOUTHERN
SYDNEY INSTITUTE
Bankstown College
500 Chapel Rd 369 E13
Bankstown College Annex
Chullora 369 K5

Gymea College
cnr Kingsway &
Hotham Rd................491 D3
Lidcombe College
East St......................339 K15
Loftus College
Rawson Av 490 C7
Padstow College
Raine Rd....................399 B14
St George College
cnr Princes Hwy &
President Av
Kogarah 433 D5
TAFE NSW-SOUTH WESTERN
SYDNEY INSTITUTE
Campbelltown College
Narellan Rd................510 K4
Granville College
136 William St 308 C12
Liverpool College
College St 511 G3
Macquarie Fields College
Victoria Rd................424 D15
Miller College
cnr Hoxton Park &
Banks Rds..................393 F6
Wetherill Park College
The Horsley Dr..........334 K3
TAFE NSW-SYDNEY INSTITUTE
Design Centre
110 Edgeware Rd
Enmore......................374 F9
Eora College
333 Abercrombie St ..18 G7
Petersham College
West St
Petersham 373 H6
Petersham College Main
Campus
27 Crystal St..............16 B5
Randwick Campus
cnr Darley Rd & King St376
J10
Ultimo College
George St ....E C14
Ultimo College
Mary Ann St..............3 B14
TAFE NSW-
WESTERN SYDNEY INSTITUTE
Baulkham Hills College
cnr Old Northern Rd &
Edward St..................247 H5
Blacktown College
cnr Main St &
Newton Rd................274 J1
Building Industry Skills Centre
cnr Showground &
Victoria Rds
Castle Hill..................217 B11
Mount Druitt College
cnr Mount St &
North Pde 241 F16
Nepean College-
Kingswood Campus
cnr Second Av &
O'Connell St
Kingswood................238 D15
Nepean College-
Penrith College
117 Henry St..............236 J9
Nirimba College
Eastern Rd
Schofields..................213 C11
Richmond College
Ceremonial Dr 118 J10
THE COLLEGE OF
SOMATIC STUDIES
20 Hudson Av
Castle Hill..................217 A12
THE POWER GROUP COLLEGE
Level 2, 2 Crofts Av
Hurstville....................432 A5
UNISEARCH LTD
Rupert Myers Building
University of NSW
Kensington................376 H16
UNITED THEOLOGICAL
COLLEGE
16 Masons Dr
North Parramatta 278 H9
UNIVERSITY OF NSW
College of Fine Arts
Selwyn St
Paddington................4 G16
Coogee Campus
Battery St
Clovelly......................377 J13

178 GREGORY'S STREET DIRECTORY

INFORMATION

THEATRES & CINEMAS

Kensington Campus
Anzac Pde
Kensington 376 H15
Little Bay Campus
Prince Henry Hospital .437 D9
Randwick Campus
King St 376 J10
UNIVERSITY OF SYDNEY
Burren St Campus
(Australian Graduate School of Management)
144 Burren St
Newtown 18 A11
Camperdown Campus
Parramatta Rd
Camperdown 18 C4
Cumberland Campus
(Health Sciences & Nursing)
East St
Lidcombe 339 K16
Darlington Campus
City Rd
Darlington 18 F5
Mallett St Campus
(Faculty of Nursing)
88 Mallett St
Camperdown 17 F5
St James Campus
(Law School)
173 Phillip St
Sydney ....D D5
Sancta Sophia College
8 Missenden Rd
Camperdown 17 H3
Surry Hills Campus
(Faculty of Dentistry)
2 Chalmers St
Surry Hills ....E K16
Sydney College of the Arts
Balmain Rd
Lilyfield 10 D2
Sydney Conservatorium of Music
Conservatorium Rd ....B J11
Westmead Hospital, Dental Clinic School
cnr Darcy & Hawkesbury Rds
Westmead 277 F14
UNIVERSITY OF TECHNOLOGY SYDNEY
City Blackfriars Campus
Blackfriars St
Chippendale 18 K1
City Campus
cnr Quay St & Ultimo Rd
Haymarket ....E A8
City Campus, Broadway
1 Broadway
Ultimo 3 B15
Kuring-gai Campus
Eton Rd
Lindfield 284 A7
St Leonards Campus,
Centenary
Reserve Rd 315 C5
St Leonards Campus,
Dunbar
cnr Pacific Hwy &
Westbourne St 315 A15
St Leonards Campus,
Research Labrotories
Westbourne St 315 B4
St Leonards Campus,
West Wing
Reserve Rd 315 B4
UNIVERSITY OF WESTERN SYDNEY
Bankstown Campus
Bullecourt Av
Milperra 397 J10
Campbelltown
Campus 510 F5
Hawkesbury
Blacktown Campus,
Eastern Rd
Schofields 213 E13
Hawkesbury Campus
Bourke St
Richmond 118 G11
Nepean, Parramatta Campus
cnr Victoria Rd &
James Ruse Dr 309 A1
Penrith Campus
cnr O'Connell St &
Second Av
Kingswood 238 A15
Penrith Campus
Great Western Hwy
Werrington 238 H13

Westmead Precinct
Hawkesbury Rd 277 G15
WESLEY INSTITUTE FOR MINISTRY-THE ARTS
Mary St
Drummoyne 343 G5
WESTPAC COLLEGE
30 Ingleside Rd
Ingleside 198 D4
WHITEHOUSE SCHOOL OF FASHION & INTERIOR DECORATION
Level 3, 53 Liverpool St
Sydney ....E E2
WILLIAM BLUE INTERNATIONAL
Hotel Management School
21 Miller St
North Sydney ....K E2
WINDSOR INSTITUTE OF COMMERCE
127 Liverpool St
Sydney ....F B3
WIVENHOE VOCATION
229 Macquarie Grove Rd
Cobbitty 477 B2

THEATRES & CINEMAS

AVALON
United Cinemas
Avalon Cinema Centre
39 Old Barrenjoey Rd ..170 B2
BANKSTOWN
Hoyts Cinemas
Westfield Shoppingtown
cnr Jacob St &
The Mall 369 F15
BASS HILL
Greater Union Cinemas
Drive-In
Johnston Rd 367 J9
BELROSE
Glen Street Theatre
Glen St 225 J16
BEVERLY HILLS
United Cinemas
Beverly Hills Cinemas
449 King Georges Rd ..401 C15
BLACKTOWN
Greater Union Cinemas
Twin Drive In
Cricketers Arms Rd 274 F16
Hoyts Cinemas
Westpoint Marketown ..244 F16
BONDI JUNCTION
Bondi Plaza Cinema
500 Oxford St 22 K6
BROOKVALE
Hoyts Cinemas
Warringah Mall
cnr Old Pittwater Rd &
Condamine St 257 K13
BURWOOD
Greater Union Cinemas
Westfield,
100 Burwood Rd 342 A13
Campbelltown
Dumaresq Street Twin Cinemas
4 Dumaresq St 395 D5
Greater Union Cinemas
Macarthur Square,
Kellicar Rd 510 J8
Town Hall Theatre
303 Queen St 511 D6
CASTLE HILL
Greater Union Cinemas
Megaplex 16
Castle Towers,
Old Northern Rd 218 C14
Hills Centre
Carrington Rd 217 F12
Pavilion Theatre
Doran Dr 217 E11

CHATSWOOD
Hoyts Cinemas
Mandarin
cnr Victor St &
Albert Av 284 J10
Hoyts Cinemas
Westfield
cnr Albert Av &
Anderson St 284 J10
Zenith Theatre
cnr Railway &
McIntosh Sts 284 H9
COLLAROY
United Cinemas
Collaroy Cinemas
1097 Pittwater Rd 229 B13
CREMORNE
Hayden Orpheum
Picture Palace
380 Military Rd 316 G7
CRONULLA
Arts Theatre
Surf Rd 493 K12
United Cinemas
Cronulla Cinema Centre
2 Cronulla St 493 K11
DARLINGHURST
Movie Room
112 Darlinghurst Rd 4 H9
Stables Theatre
10 Nimrod St 4 H9
DARLINGTON
Seymour Theatre Centre
(Downstairs, Everest, York)
cnr Cleveland St &
City Rd 18 G4
DOUBLE BAY
Greater Union Cinemas
377 New South
Head Rd 347 B13
EASTGARDENS
Hoyts Cinemas
Westfield Shoppingtown
cnr Wentworth Av &
Bunnerong Rd 406 F11
ELIZABETH BAY
Darlinghurst Theatre
19 Greenknowe Av 13 B5
ENMORE
Enmore Theatre
130 Enmore St 17 C14
ERSKINEVILLE
PACT Youth Theatre
107 Railway Rd 18 C14
The Edge Theatre
cnr King & Bray Sts ..374 J10
FAIRFIELD
World Cinemas
cnr Station &
Nelson Sts 336 E11
GLEBE
Footbridge Theatre
Sydney University,
Parramatta Rd 18 C1
Broadway Shopping Centre
Bay St 12 H5
Valhalla Cinema Glebe
166d Glebe Point Rd 12 A12
GLENBROOK
Glenbrook Theatre
Great Western Hwy 234 A16
HAYMARKET
Capitol Theatre
13 Campbell St ....E H7
Entertainment Centre Sydney
35 Harbour St ....E B5
Reading Cinemas
Market City
Level 3, Market
City Shopping Centre,
9 Hay St ....E C8
HOMEBUSH BAY
Sydney Superdome
Sydney Olympic Park,
cnr Olympic Blvd &
Edwin Flack Av 310 E16
HORNSBY
Hornsby Odeon Cinema
155 Pacific Hwy 221 G1
HURSTVILLE
Greater Union Cinemas
Westfield Shoppingtown
cnr Cross & Park Rds ..432 B5
KILLARA
Marian Street Theatre
2 Marian St 254 A13

KENSINGTON
Fig Tree Theatre
University of NSW
Gate 4, High St 376 F14
NIDA Theatre
215 Anzac Pde 376 F14
Parade Theatre
215 Anzac Pde 376 F14
KOGARAH
Mecca Movie City
28 Station St 433 B3
LEICHHARDT
Palace Cinemas
Norton St Cinema
99 Norton St 16 A2
LIDCOMBE
Reading Cinemas
Auburn
100 Parramatta Rd ...339 J1
LIVERPOOL
Greater Union Cinemas
Westfield Shoppington,
Northumberland 395 D5
MACQUARIE PARK
Greater Union Cinemas
Megaplex Macquarie
Macquarie Centre 282 F1
Lighthouse Cinemas
Macquarie University ..252 C15
MANLY
Manly Twin Cinemas
43 East Esp 288 G10
MERRYLANDS
Hoyts Cinemas
Shopping Centre,
cnr McFarlane &
Treves Sts 307 G12
MIRANDA
Greater Union Cinemas
Westfield Shoppingtown,
Kiora St 492 B4
MOORE PARK
Hoyts Cinemas
Cinema Paris at Fox Studios
Bent St 21 A9
Hoyts Cinemas
Fox Studios, Australia
Bent St 21 B9
MOSMAN
Greater Union Cinemas
9 Spit Rd 317 B5
MOUNT DRUITT
Hoyts Cinemas
Westfield, Carlisle Av ...241 D15
NEWTOWN
Dendy Cinemas
261 King St 17 H11
New Theatre
542 King St 374 J9
Newtown Theatre
354 King St 17 F13
NORTH SYDNEY
Independent Theatre
269 Miller St 5 G3
PADDINGTON
Chauvel Cinemas
Paddington Town Hall,
cnr Oxford St &
Oatley Rd 21 A1
Palace Cinemas
Academy Twin Cinemas
3a Oxford St 4 F14
Palace Cinemas
Verona Cinema
17 Oxford St 4 G14
PARRAMATTA
Riverside Theatres Parramatta
cnr Church &
Market Sts 308 C1
Village Cinemas
Parramatta 8
Westfield Shoppingtown,
Church St 308 C4
PENRITH
Hoyts Cinemas
Penrith Plaza
cnr Jane & Riley Sts ...236 G9
Joan Sutherland
Performing Arts Centre
597 High St 236 F9
Q Theatre
cnr Railway &
Belmore Sts 236 J9
PRAIRIEWOOD
Hoyts Cinemas
Wetherill Park
Stockland Town Centre,
Polding St 334 E7

RANDWICK
Ritz Theatre
43 St Pauls St 377 C16
REDFERN
Performance Space, The
199 Cleveland St 19 E5
RICHMOND
Regent Twin Cinema
149 Windsor St 118 H5
ROCKDALE
Guild Theatre
cnr Railway &
Waltz Sts 403 C15
ROSEVILLE
Roseville Cinemas
112 Pacific Hwy 284 F4
RYDE
Argyl Theatre
cnr Argyl Av &
Blaxland Rd 312 B2
SURRY HILLS
Belvoir Street Theatre
25 Belvoir St 19 J4
The Kirk
422 Cleveland St 20 A6
Tom Mann Theatre
136 Chalmers St 19 G3
SUTHERLAND
Sutherland
Entertainment Centre
30 Eton St N 490 F2
SYDNEY
City Recital Hall Angel Place
Angel Pl ....C K1
Dendy Cinemas
Opera Quays
2 Circular Quay E ....B G4
Genesian Theatre Company
420 Kent St ....C F10
Greater Union Cinemas
George St
505–525 George St ...CG16
Harbour City Cinemas
6 Harbour St ....E D2
Hoyts Cinemas
George St
Greater Union
Entertainment Complex,
505 George St CG16
Metro Theatre
624 George St ....E H1
Pilgrim Theatre
262 Pitt St ....C K13
State Theatre, The
49 Market St ....C J8
Sydney Conservatorium of Music
Conservatorium Rd ....B J11
Sydney Opera House
Bennelong Point ....B J1
Theatre Royal
MLC Centre, King St ...D A4
WARRIEWOOD
United Cinemas
Warriewood Cinemas
4 Vuko Pl 199 C11
WOOLLOOLI
Hunters Hill Theatre
13 Margaret St 314 D13

PUBLISHING DATES

1st Edition	1967
2nd Edition	1968
3rd Edition	1975
4th Edition	1977
5th Edition	1978
6th Edition	1985
7th Edition	1989
8th Edition	1990
9th Edition	1991
10th Edition	1992
11th Edition	1993
12th Edition	1994
13th Edition	1995
14th Edition	1996
15th Edition	1998
16th Edition	1999
17th Edition	2000
18th Edition	2001
19th Edition	2002
20th Edition	2003
21st Edition	2004
22nd Edition	2005

MAP A

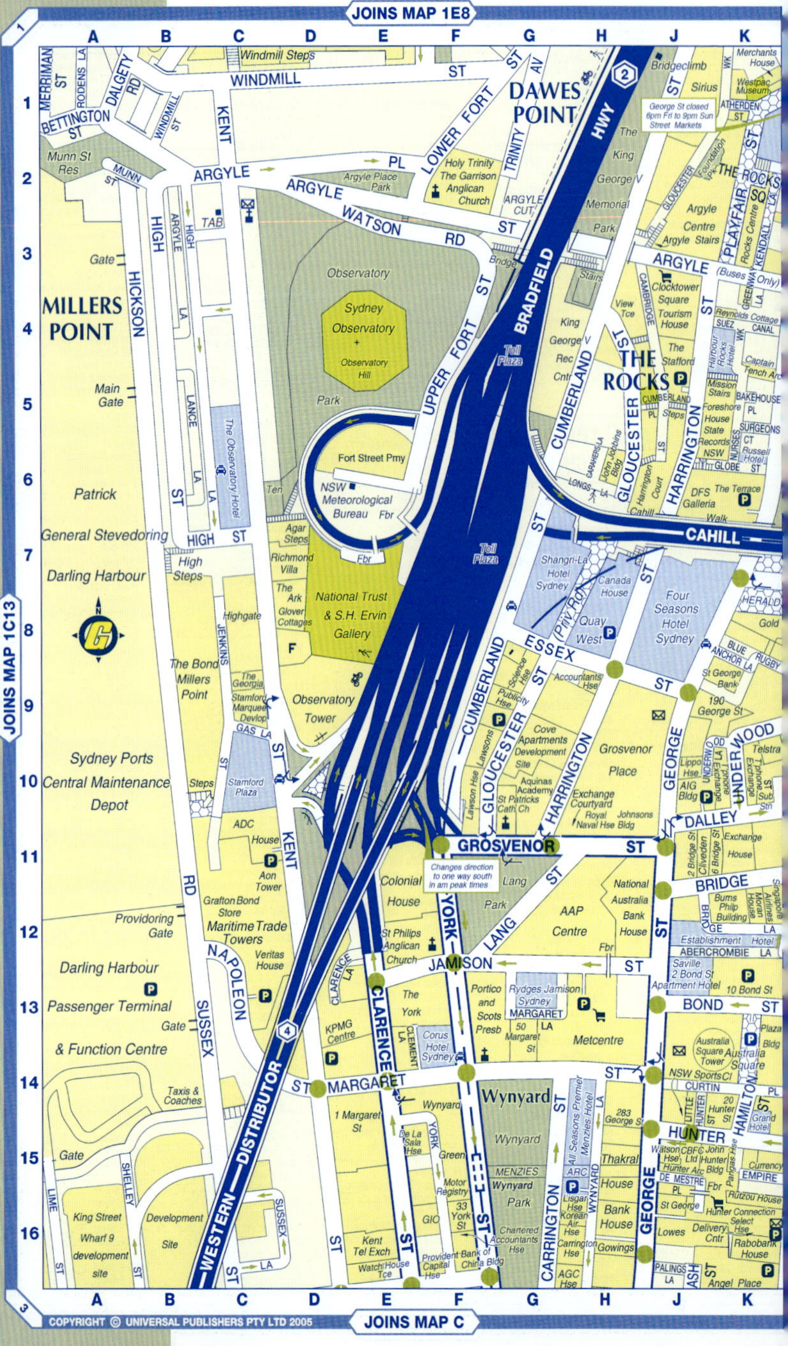
JOINS MAP 1E8
JOINS MAP 1C13
JOINS MAP C
A
B
C
D
E
F
G
H
J
K
1
2
3
4
5
6
7
8
9
10
11
12
13
14
15
16
MILLERS POINT
DAWES POINT
THE ROCKS
Windmill Steps
WINDMILL
ST
MERRIMAN ST
RODENS LA
DALGETY RD
BETTINGTON ST
WINDMILL ST
KENT
Munn St Res
MUNN ST
ARGYLE
PL
ARGYLE
Argyle Place Park
WATSON
RD
LOWER FORT
TRINITY
AV
Holy Trinity
The Garrison
Anglican Church
ARGYLE CUT
ST
Bridge
HWY
The King George V Memorial Park
Bridgeclimb
Sirius
Merchants House
Westpac Museum
ATHERDEN ST
George St closed 6pm Fri to 9pm Sun Street Markets
GLOUCESTER
Foundation Pk
THE ROCKS SQ
Argyle Centre
Argyle Stairs
PLAYFAIR
Rocks Centre
KENDALL LA
ARGYLE
(Buses Only)
TAB
HIGH
ARGYLE
Gate
HICKSON
Observatory
Sydney Observatory
Observatory Hill
Park
UPPER FORT
BRADFIELD
Toll Plaza
Stairs
King George V Rec Cntr
CUMBERLAND
Clocktower Square
Tourism House
CAMBRIDGE
View Tce
The Stafford
Reynolds Cottage
SUEZ CANAL
Harbour Rocks Hotel
Captain Tench Arc
Mission Stairs
BAKEHOUSE
Foreshore House
State Records NSW
SURGEONS CT
Russell Hotel
GLOBE ST
NURSES WK
CUMBERLAND PL
Steps
HARRINGTON
John Jobbins Bldg
CARAHERS LA
LONGS LA
Harrington Court
Cahill Walk
DFS Galleria
The Terrace
CAHILL
Main Gate
LANCE
LA
The Observatory Hotel
Fort Street Pmy
NSW Meteorological Bureau
Fbr
Ten
Patrick
General Stevedoring
Darling Harbour
HIGH ST
High Steps
Agar Steps
Richmond Villa
The Ark
Glover Cottages
National Trust & S.H. Ervin Gallery
Shangri-La Hotel Sydney
Canada House
Quay West
Four Seasons Hotel Sydney
HERALD
Gold
BLUE ANCHOR LA
RUGBY
St George Bank
190 George St
JENKINS
Highgate
The Bond
Millers Point
The Georgia
Stamford Marquee Develop
GAS LA
F
Observatory Tower
ESSEX
Science Hse
Publicity Hse
Accountants Hse
Cove Apartments Development Site
Lawsons Hse
Aquinas Academy
St Patricks Cath Ch
Exchange Courtyard
Royal Naval Hse
Johnsons Bldg
Grosvenor Place
GEORGE
Lippo Hse
AIG Bldg
UNDERWOOD
Telstra
Phone Exchange
Sub Stn
Sydney Ports Central Maintenance Depot
Steps
Stamford Plaza
ADC House
Aon Tower
GROSVENOR
ST
DALLEY
Changes direction to one way south in am peak times
Lang Park
AAP Centre
National Australia Bank House
2 Bridge St
Cliveden
6 Bridge St
Exchange House
BRIDGE
Burns Philp Building
Moran House
Singapore Airlines
BRIDGE LA
Establishment Hotel
ABERCROMBIE LA
Saville 2 Bond St Apartment Hotel
10 Bond St
RD
Providoring Gate
Grafton Bond Store
Maritime Trade Towers
Veritas House
Colonial House
St Philips Anglican Church
YORK
LANG
JAMISON
ST
Darling Harbour Passenger Terminal & Function Centre
Gate
SUSSEX
NAPOLEON
CLARENCE LA
The York
KPMG Centre
Portico and Scots Presb
Rydges Jamison Sydney
MARGARET LA
50 Margaret St
Metcentre
BOND ST
Plaza Bldg
Australia Square Tower
Australia Square
NSW Sports Cl
CURTIN PL
20 Hunter St
Grand Hotel
HAMILTON
CLARENCE
CLEMENT LA
Corus Hotel Sydney
DISTRIBUTOR
WESTERN
Taxis & Coaches
ST MARGARET ST
1 Margaret St
Wynyard
De La Sala Hse
Wynyard
Green
Motor Registry
33 York St
MENZIES
Wynyard Park
All Seasons Premier Menzies Hotel
283 George St
HUNTER
LITTLE HUNTER ST
Watson Hse
CBFC Ltd
John Hunter Bldg
Hunter Arc
Currency
DE MESTRE PL
EMPIRE
Rutzou House
Hunter Connection
Gate
LIME ST
SHELLEY ST
King Street Wharf 9 development site
Development Site
SUSSEX
LA
ST
Kent Tel Exch
Watch House Tce
GIO
Provident Capital Hse
Chartered Accountants Hse
Bank of China Bldg
ARC
Lisgar Hse
Korean Air Hse
Carrington Hse
AGC Hse
CARRINGTON
WYNYARD LA
Thakral House
Bank House
Gowings
GEORGE
St George
Lowes
Delivery Cntr
Select Hse
Rabobank House
PALINGS LA
ASH ST
Angel Place

MAP B

JOINS MAP 1J8
JOINS MAP 2B8
JOINS MAP 2C13
JOINS MAP D
A B C D E F G H J K
1 2 3 4 5 6 7 8 9 10 11 12 13 14 15 16
Sydney Cove
Circular Quay
Ferry Wharves
Sydney Opera House
Tarpeian Way Gate
Bennelong Lawn
Opera House Gate
Tarpeian Precinct
Government House
Govt House Delivery Gate
Northern Depot
Northern Depot Gate
Parade Ground
Macquarie Precinct
Govt House Gate
Sydney Conservatorium of Music
Greenway Building
Western Forecourt
South Foyer Terrace
Royal Botanic Gardens
Grass Plots
Rose Garden
Pioneer Garden
Sydney Tropical Centre
Herb Garden
Museum of Contemporary Art
First Fleet Park
Sydney Cove Overseas Passenger Terminal
Sydney Visitor Cntr
Cadmans Cottage
Old Sydney Holiday Inn
Bushells Place
Wharf Hse Steps
Bethel Steps
Barney & Bligh Res
GEORGE ST
HICKSON RD
CIRCULAR QUAY W
ELEVATED RD
CIRCULAR QUAY E
SYDNEY HARBOUR TUNNEL
TARPEIAN
EXP
Cahill Walk
Raised Viewing Area
Circular Quay
ALFRED ST
Gateway (AXA Building)
Jessie Street Gdns
Sydney Harbour Marriott
Obelisk Macquarie Place Park
Customs House Sq
Sydney Customs House
AMP Sydney Cove Building
AMP Plaza
AMP Centre Tower
Justice & Police Museum
Sir Stamford at Circular Quay
Transport House
SYDNEY
Hotel Inter-Continental Sydney
The Quay
Royal Automobile Club
ALBERT ST
CONSERVATORIUM RD
MACQUARIE ST
PHILLIP ST
YOUNG ST
LOFTUS ST
PITT ST
BRIDGE ST
MACQUARIE PL
Education Department Building
Department of Lands Building
Royal Exchange Building
Museum of Sydney
Governor Phillip Tower
Governor Macquarie Tower
Chief Secretarys Building
The Astor
Hudson Hse
American Cl
History Hse
BMA House
Domain House
Aurora Place
Dorchester Hse
Macquarie Apartments
Morshead Fountain Gate
Palace Gdn Gate
Rose Gdn Gate
Kiosk
CAHILL
BENT ST
SPRING ST
GRESHAM ST
O'CONNELL ST
BLIGH ST
PHILLIP ST
SHAKESPEARE PL
Wintergarden Plaza
O'Connell House
Norwich House
Union Club
The Wentworth Sydney
Chifley Tower
Chifley Plaza
Chifley Square
Hambros House
Australian Club
State Library of NSW
HUNTER ST
CASTLEREAGH ST
ELIZABETH ST
HOSPITAL RD
ANZ Bank
70 Pitt St
72 Pitt St
74 Pitt St
Pitt Telephone Exchange
Castlereagh Cntr
QBE Bldg
55 Hunter St
Goodsell Building
City Mutual Bldg
Radisson Plaza Hotel
Richard Johnson Square

MAP C

JOINS MAP A
JOINS MAP E
JOINS MAP 3C5
A B C D E F G H J K
1 2 3 4 5 6 7 8 9 10 11 12 13 14 15 16
King Street Wharf 9 Development Site
Development Site
ERSKINE ST
SUSSEX LA
Watch House Tce
Provident Capital Hse
Bank of China Bldg
AGC Hse
Bank of New Zealand House
PALINGS LA
ASH ST
Angel Place
Societe Generale House
City Recital Hall
ANGEL PL
Colonial Mutual Life Bldg
Lumley Technology House
Medibank Hse
Accountancy Hse
Logical House
AWA Bldg
Shaw Hse
WYNYARD ST
WYNYARD LA
Portside (Nth Residential Tower)
Portside Retail Units
Portside (Sth Residential Tower)
Energy Aust Power Stn
Lumley House
Corporation Cntr
Garland Hawthorn Brae Chambers
Carrington
REGIMENTAL SQUARE
BARRACK LA
Westpac
Australasia Chambers
Challis Hse
Ernst & Young Building
SFV Hse
United Airlines Hse
Barrack House
NAB
Cenotaph
MARTIN
BARRACK ST
SESQUICENTENARY SQUARE
GPO
Macquarie Bank
CUTHBERT ST
The Chelsea
333 Kent Street
NEWTON LA
Red Cross House
RSL
James Hardie House
Sомare Haus
Priv. Rd
Aust Retailers Assoc.
Savings Bank of NSW Bldg
The Landmark Bldg
Westin Sydney Hotel
No.1 Martin Place
Cosco Hse
Clarence Hse
24 York Street
363 George St
NRMA House
Wharf
Medina Grand Harbourside
The Beehive
ING Centre
EGO Hse
Griffin Hse
Charles Plaza
ANZ Bank Bldg
Knight Frank
Tank Stream Arc
KING ST
DISTRIBUTOR
WESTERN DISTRIBUTOR
SLIP ST
SUSSEX ST
KENT ST
CLARENCE ST
YORK ST
GEORGE ST
PITT ST
Street
Reid Hse
77 King Street
400 George Street
Sydney Arcade
Kings-leigh
Savoy
The Rex Dvlpmnt Site
Trafalgar Dvlpmnt Site
Broughton House
The Grace Hotel
King York Hse
Substn
Joshua Berger Bldg
Shorter Hse
Minnamurra
Endeavour Credit Union House
Carlton Hse
36 York St
King George Chambers
Fletcher Jones Bldg
Georges Radio Hse
Strand Arcade
Proposed Australia's Animal World
Four Points by Sheraton Hotel Sydney
Windsor on Kent
P & O Australia
Royston Hse
Old Kent Hse
Ikon Hse
Charles Bldg
PSA Hse
State Chamber of Commerce
York House
56-58 York St
60 York St
363 George St
Mid City Centre
Dymocks Building
Load Dock
Sydney Aquarium
383 Kent Street Development Site
AME Hse
COUNCIL PL
Bowlers Club of NSW
Forestry House
HCF House
SYDNEY
Sydney Central Plaza
Darling Harbour (Aquarium) Wharf 28
Escalator Under
PYRMONT BRIDGE
Allianz Centre
Kelco Hse
Bentley's Hse
Clarence Corporate Cntr
44 Market St
Australian Collection
George & Market Sts Bldg
Myer
The Tower Apts
MARKET ST
Darling Park
Gowings
State Theatre
City Centre
Wharf
Bay
Cockle
RD
WHEAT
BT Tower
The Berkeley
Workcover NSW
St Martins Tower
Queen Victoria Building
Dudley Hse
Simpson Hse
Fairfax
Tower 1 IBM Cntr
Lexington
Alliance Francaise
Cachet Dvlpmnt Site
Comaltech Hse
Marble Arch
Capital Centre & Hilton Sydney Hotel
Marina
Crescent Garden
DARLING PARK
Astoria Tower
Genesian Th
The University Cntr
MARKET ROW
SU Hse
Exit
MULLINS ST
222 Clarence St
The Galeries Victoria
Galeries Victoria
Monorail
447 Kent St
YHA
Clarence Kent Hse
Trafalgar Sq
145 York St
Hong Kong Hse
Citigroup Centre
Town Hall
National
Darling Park Stage 3 Proposed Tower 3
Tower 2 PWC
DRUITT PL
NSW Crime Commission
Somerset
A-One Hse
Kent Inst
Lift
Substn
BLACKWATTLE PL
DRUITT ST
PARK ST
The Quadrant
Wanderers on Kent
Town Hall House
Cncl Off
Sydney Town Hall
Woolworths Metro
Park House
Pittsway Arc
Pilgrim
Uniting
Crowne Plaza Darling Harbour
New Haven
Kentbridge Hse
SYDNEY SQUARE
Town Hall Square (Underground)
Manchester Unity Bldg
309 Pitt Street
Defence
IMAX Theatre
Intl Hse
Chalmers Hse
SANDS ST
DRUITT LA
Standards
RCA House
St Andrews House
St Andrews Cathedral
Town Hall
321 Pitt Street
Plaza
Polding Hse
Ped Ent
The Vintage
Australia
WEA Hse
507 Kent St
Town Hall Square
Energy Australia
Rialto
International House
BATHURST ST
Cross City Tunnel Under Construction
Millennium Tower
Maestri Towers 2
Medina Grand
ABM Hse
Bible Hse
MBF Centre
Development Site
Maestri Towers 1
Theosophy Hse
The Pavilion
Sydney Water Corporation
Darling
Rudolf Steiner Hse
JAMES LA
Ent
Village Greater Union Hoyts Entertainment Centre
HSBC Cntr
Pentura Hotel
Druids Hse
The Princeton
Darling Harbour
Walk
HARBOUR ST
DAY ST
Flying Angel Hse
Judges House
WILMOT ST
Telstra Plaza Bldg
Tumbalong Park
JAMES ST
LM Hse
Windsor Plaza
Meriton
The George
ALBION PL
Victoria Bldg
Century Tower
CENTRAL ST

JOINS MAP B
A B C D E F G H J K
1 2 3 4 5 6 7 8 9 10 11 12 13 14 15 16
Pitt Telephone Exchange
Q B E Building
Castlereagh Centre
City Freehold House
84 Pitt St
The Aston Apartments
PENFOLD
HOSKING PL
ANZ
United O'seas Bank Bldg
Henry Davis York Bldg
5 Elizabeth St Chifley Arc
7 Elizabeth St
9 Elizabeth St
BNP Bldg
Savings Bank Building
Goodsell Building
Colonial Centre
126 Phillip St Development
Macquarie Chambers
Park Hse
Hengrove Hall
Agriculture Hse
St Stephens Uniting
Westpac Building
State Library of NSW
Parliament House
Phillip Precinct
The
Fountain & Amphitheatre
Martin Place Shopping Circle (underground)
Martin Pl
PL
Commonwealth Bank Building
Commercial Travellers' Association
Colonial Building
Overseas Union Bank Bldg
Reserve Bank of Australia
Sydney Hospital & Sydney Eye Hospital
DL8
DL9
DL10
Heritage Building
NSW Leagues Club
University Chambers
St James Hall
Uni of Sydney St James Campus
BNP Paribas Centre
Castlereagh Chmbrs
Atanaskovic Hartnell
Cullinan Hse Bldg
The Law Society Bldg
Windeyer Chambers
Selborne Chambers
William Bland Cntr
Nat Dispute Cntr
Wentworth Chambers
Beanbah Chambers
NSW Supreme Court & Federal Court of Australia
MLC Centre
Theatre Royal
LEES
The Mint (Historic House)
HOSPITAL RD
Central Avenue
DL6
DL5
DL4
DL18
DL17
Bank of America Centre
Ashington Court
Culwulla Chambers
OCBC Building
Skygarden
The Trust Bldg
ADC Elizabeth
County Cntr
St James Centre
KING ST
Old Supreme Court Building
St James Anglican (1819)
Law Courts
QUEENS SQ
MACQUARIE ST
PHILLIP
ELIZABETH
CASTLEREAGH
Hyde Park Barracks
ART GALLERY RD
Stockland
Imperial Arcade
David Jones
Elizabeth St Store
ST JAMES RD
PRINCE
Land & Property Information Offices
Domain
Domain Depot
Westfield Centrepoint & Sydney Tower
Domain Parking Stn
Pedestrian Ent
St James
ALBERT
Chessboard
Stn Ent
Moving Footway (Under)
DL16
DL15
DL13
ST MARYS RD
Rowlandson Hse
Queens Club
Philip Court
Highmount Hse
David Jones Market St Store
City Tattersalls Club Centre
Archibald Fountain
St Marys Cathedral
St Marys Cathedral College
Sheraton on the Park
Piccadilly Tower
Piccadilly Centre
Grand United Bldg
Citisite House
Hyde
CATHEDRAL ST
Tattersalls Bldg
St James Trust Bldg
Great Synagogue
Pitt Street Plaza
Legion Hse
Angus & Son Bldg
NSW Masonic Club
Stockland House
Australian Consolidated Press
50 Park St
60 Park St
Cathedral Square
Basketball Court
Cook & Phillip Centre
Boomerang
Domain Walk
PKY
PCYC
Park
Sandringham Gardens
WOOLLOOMOOLOO
Cook & Phillip Park
Pond
Fragrance Garden Place
YURONG
Cross City Tunnel
Under Construction Due for Completion - 2005
Park Regis
Victoria Tower & Catholic Club
201 Elizabeth St
WILLIAM ST
BUSBY LA
McCARTHY LA
Scientology
St Georges Presb
Porter House
Credit Union
227 Elizabeth
Australian Museum
DARLINGHURST
Hertz Car Rental
YURONG LA
Park
Bathurst Hse
Telstra House
Pool of Reflection
Sydney Grammar School
NSW Fire Brigade
Worker Bldg
Hellenic House
STREAM
STANLEY LA
RILEY ST
City South Telephone Exchange
Museum
Anzac War Memorial
COLLEGE
STANLEY
COLLEGE LA
FRANCIS LA
Ret Vill
JOINS MAP F
JOINS MAP 4 C4
COPYRIGHT © UNIVERSAL PUBLISHERS PTY LTD 2005

MAP E

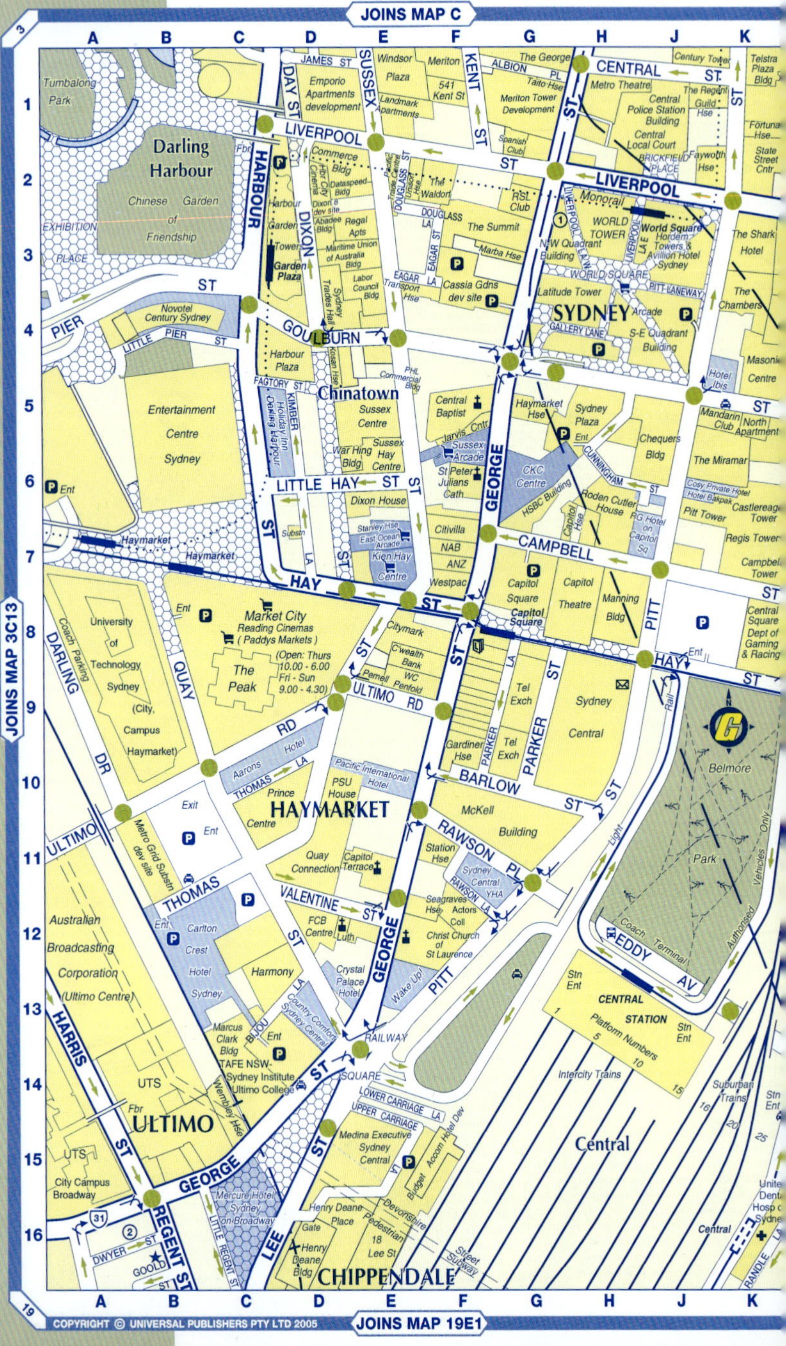
JOINS MAP C
JOINS MAP 3C13
JOINS MAP 19E1
A B C D E F G H J K
1 2 3 4 5 6 7 8 9 10 11 12 13 14 15 16
Tumbalong Park
Darling Harbour
Chinese Garden of Friendship
EXHIBITION PLACE
PIER ST
LITTLE PIER ST
Novotel Century Sydney
Entertainment Centre Sydney
HARBOUR ST
Harbour Garden Towers
Garden Plaza
Harbour Plaza
DAY ST
JAMES ST
Emporio Apartments development
Windsor Plaza
Landmark Apartments
Meriton 541 Kent St
KENT ST
SUSSEX ST
ALBION PL
The George
Taito Hse
Meriton Tower Development
Spanish Club
CENTRAL ST
Metro Theatre
Central Police Station Building
Central Local Court
The Regent Guild Hse
Century Tower
Telstra Plaza Bldg
Fortuna Hse
State Street Cntr
BRICKFIELD PLACE
Faywoth Hse
LIVERPOOL ST
LIVERPOOL
Commerce Bldg
Dataspeed Bldg
Dixon's dev site
Abadee Bldg
Regal Apts
Maritime Union of Australia Bldg
Labor Council Bldg
Sydney Trades Hall
DIXON ST
DOUGLASS ST
DOUGLASS LA
The Waldorf
RSL Club
The Summit
Marba Hse
EAGAR ST
EAGAR LA
Transport Hse
Cassia Gdns dev site
Monorail
WORLD TOWER
World Square
Hordern Towers & Avillion Hotel Sydney
N-W Quadrant Building
LIVERPOOL LANE
WORLD SQUARE
PITT LANEWAY
Latitude Tower
SYDNEY
Arcade
GALLERY LANE
S-E Quadrant Building
The Shark Hotel
The Chambers
Masonic Centre
Hotel Ibis
GOULBURN
FACTORY ST
Chinatown
KIMBER LA
Holiday Inn Darling Harbour
Kosan Hse
PHL Commercial Bldg
Sussex Centre
Sussex Hay Centre
War Hing Bldg
Central Baptist
Jarvis Cntr
Sussex Arcade
St Peter Julians Cath
Haymarket Hse
Sydney Plaza
Chequers Bldg
Mandarin Club
North Apartment
The Miramar
CKC Centre
HSBC Building
CUNNINGHAM ST
Cosy Private Hotel
Hotel Bakpak
Roden Cutler House
Castlereagh Tower
Pitt Tower
RG Hotel on Capitol Sq
Regis Tower
LITTLE HAY ST
Dixon House
Substn
Stanley Hse
East Ocean Arcade
Kien Hay Centre
Citivilla
NAB
ANZ
Westpac
GEORGE
CAMPBELL
Capitol Square
Capitol Theatre
Manning Bldg
Campbell Tower
Central Square
Dept of Gaming & Racing
Haymarket
HAY ST
PITT ST
Market City
Reading Cinemas
(Paddys Markets)
(Open: Thurs 10.00 - 6.00 Fri - Sun 9.00 - 4.30)
The Peak
University of Technology Sydney (City Campus Haymarket)
Coach Parking
DARLING DR
QUAY ST
Citymark
C'wealth Bank
WC Penfold
Pemell
ULTIMO RD
Tel Exch
PARKER LA
PARKER ST
Gardiner Hse
Sydney Central
Rail
Belmore Park
Vehicles Only
Authorised
Aarons Hotel
THOMAS LA
Pacific International Hotel
PSU House
Prince Centre
HAYMARKET
BARLOW ST
McKell Building
RAWSON PL
Station Hse
Sydney Central YHA
RAWSON LA
Light Rail
ULTIMO
Metro Grid Substn dev site
Exit
Ent
THOMAS
Quay Connection
Capitol Terrace
VALENTINE ST
FCB Centre
Luth
Seagraves Hse
Actors Coll
Christ Church of St Laurence
Carlton Crest Hotel Sydney
Harmony
Crystal Palace Hotel
Wake Up!
PITT
Australian Broadcasting Corporation (Ultimo Centre)
HARRIS ST
Marcus Clark Bldg
BLOW LA
Country Comfort Sydney Central
TAFE NSW-Sydney Institute Ultimo College
Wembley Hse
RAILWAY SQUARE
LOWER CARRIAGE LA
UPPER CARRIAGE LA
Coach Terminal
EDDY AV
Stn Ent
CENTRAL STATION
Platform Numbers
Intercity Trains
Suburban Trains
Central
UTS
Fbr
ULTIMO
UTS
City Campus Broadway
GEORGE
Mercure Hotel Sydney on Broadway
Medina Executive Sydney Central
Accom Hotel Dev
Budget
Henry Deane Place
Devonshire Pedestrian Street Subway
18 Lee St
Gate
Henry Deane Bldg
LEE ST
CHIPPENDALE
REGENT ST
LITTLE REGENT ST
DWYER ST
GOOLD ST
United Dental Hosp of Sydney
RANDLE LA
31
2

MAP F

MAP J FOLLOWS

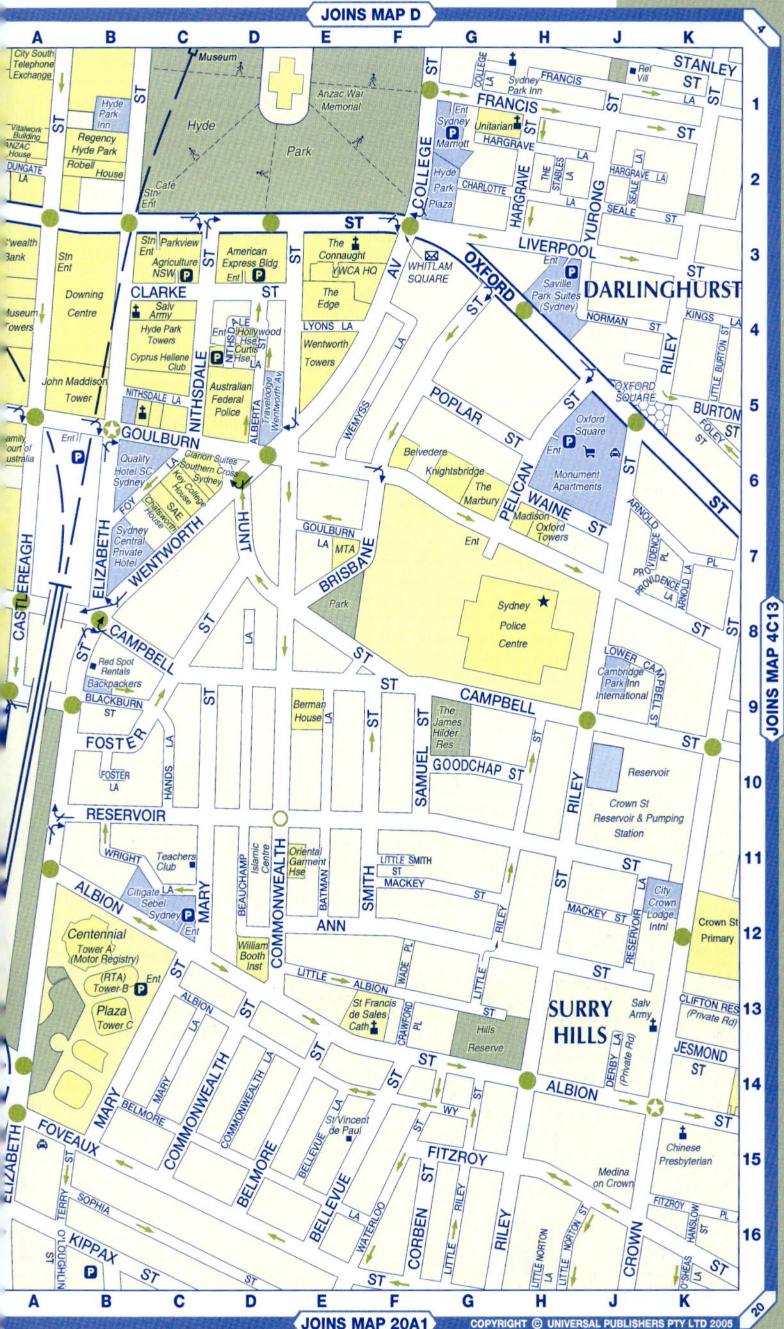

MAP J
PREVIOUS MAP F

CITY PARKING STATIONS

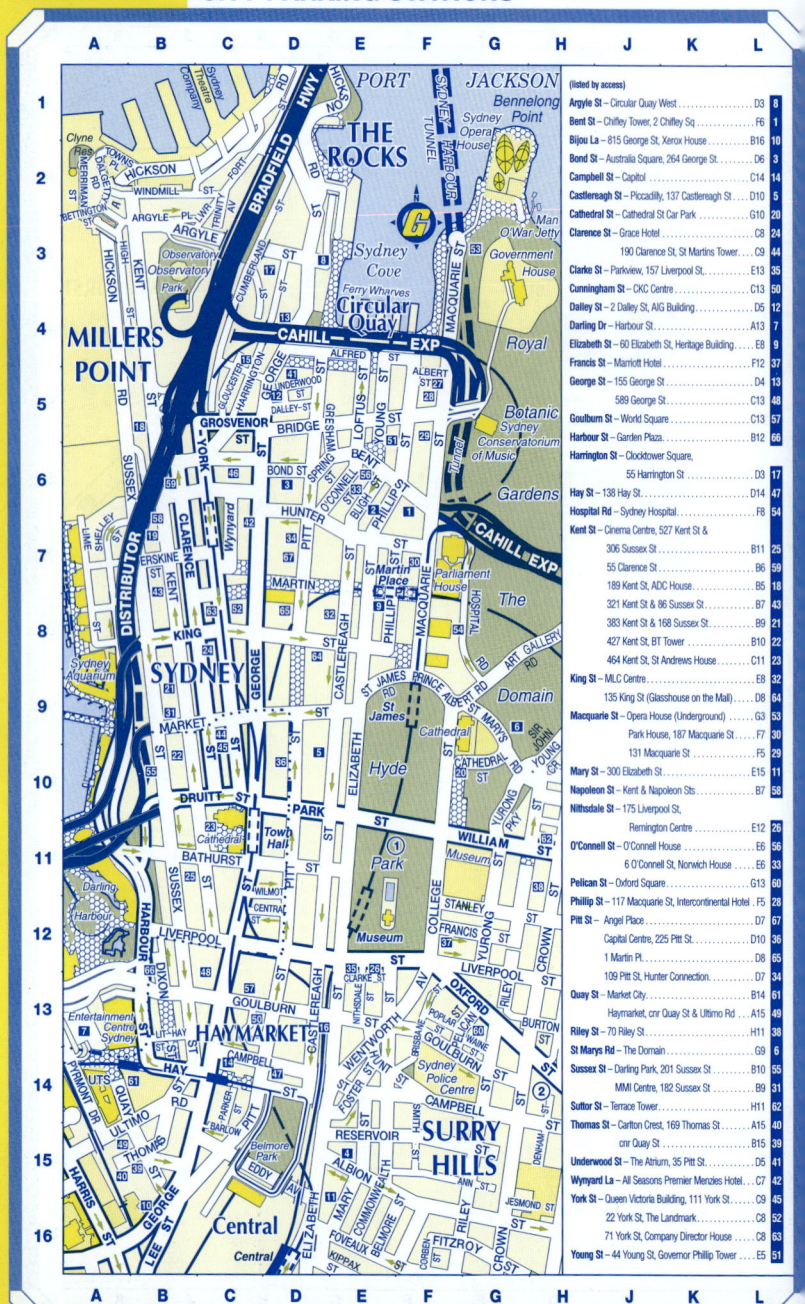

(listed by access)

Street	Location	Grid	#
Argyle St	Circular Quay West	D3	8
Bent St	Chifley Tower, 2 Chifley Sq	F6	1
Bijou La	815 George St, Xerox House	B16	10
Bond St	Australia Square, 264 George St	D6	3
Campbell St	Capitol	C14	44
Castlereagh St	Piccadilly, 137 Castlereagh St	D10	5
Cathedral St	Cathedral St Car Park	G10	20
Clarence St	Grace Hotel	C8	24
	190 Clarence St, St Martins Tower	C9	44
Clarke St	Parkview, 157 Liverpool St	E13	35
Cunningham St	CKC Centre	C13	50
Dalley St	2 Dalley St, AIG Building	D5	12
Darling Dr	Harbour St	A13	
Elizabeth St	60 Elizabeth St, Heritage Building	E8	9
Francis St	Marriott Hotel	F12	37
George St	155 George St	D4	13
	589 George St	C13	48
Goulburn St	World Square	C13	57
Harbour St	Garden Plaza	B12	66
Harrington St	Clocktower Square, 55 Harrington St	D3	43
Hay St	138 Hay St	D14	47
Hospital Rd	Sydney Hospital	F8	54
Kent St	Cinema Centre, 527 Kent St &		
	306 Sussex St	B11	25
	55 Clarence St	B6	59
	189 Kent St, ADC Building	B5	2
	321 Kent St & 86 Sussex St	B7	45
	383 Kent St & 168 Sussex St	B9	21
	427 Kent St, BT Tower	B10	51
	464 Kent St, St Andrews House	C11	23
King St	MLC Centre	E8	32
	135 King St (Glasshouse on the Mall)	D8	64
Macquarie St	Opera House (Underground)	G3	7
	Park House, 187 Macquarie St	F7	30
	131 Macquarie St	F5	29
Mary St	300 Elizabeth St	E15	11
Napoleon St	Kent & Napoleon Sts	B7	58
Nithsdale St	175 Liverpool St, Remington Centre	E12	26
O'Connell St	O'Connell House	E6	56
	6 O'Connell St, Norwich House	E6	4
Pelican St	Oxford Square	G13	22
Phillip St	117 Macquarie St, Intercontinental Hotel	F5	28
Pitt St	Angel Place	D7	67
	Capital Centre, 225 Pitt St	D10	36
	1 Martin Pl	D8	65
	109 Pitt St, Hunter Connection	D7	27
Quay St	Market City	B14	33
	Haymarket, cnr Quay St & Ultimo Rd	A15	19
Riley St	70 Riley St	H11	38
St Marys Rd	The Domain	G9	6
Sussex St	Darling Park, 201 Sussex St	B10	55
	MMI Centre, 182 Sussex St	B9	34
Sutter St	Terrace Tower	H11	62
Thomas St	Carlton Crest, 169 Thomas St	A15	40
	cnr Quay St	B15	63
Underwood St	The Atrium, 35 Pitt St	D5	41
Wynyard La	All Seasons Premier Menzies Hotel	E7	42
York St	Queen Victoria Building, 111 York St	C9	46
	22 York St, The Landmark	C8	52
	71 York St, Company Director House	C8	63
Young St	44 Young St, Governor Phillip Tower	E5	51

MAP K

MAP 1 FOLLOWS

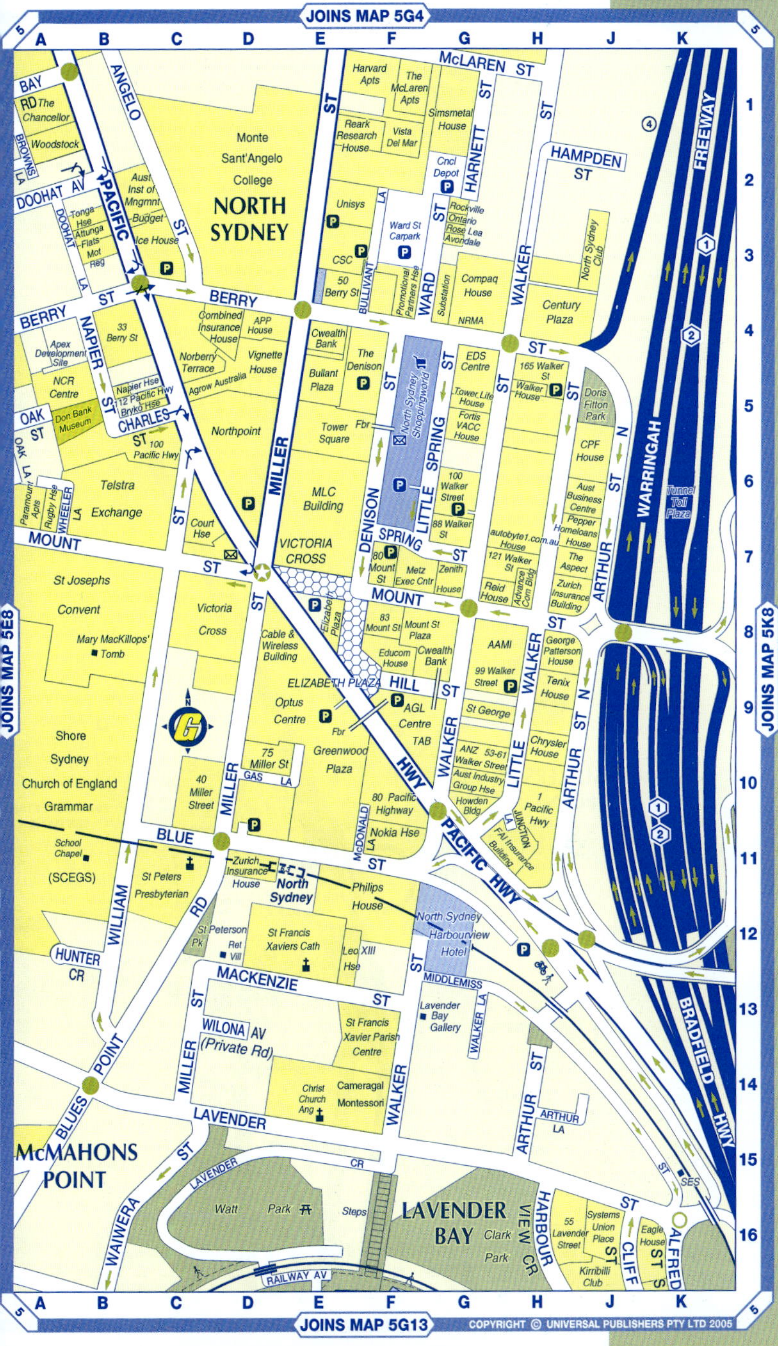

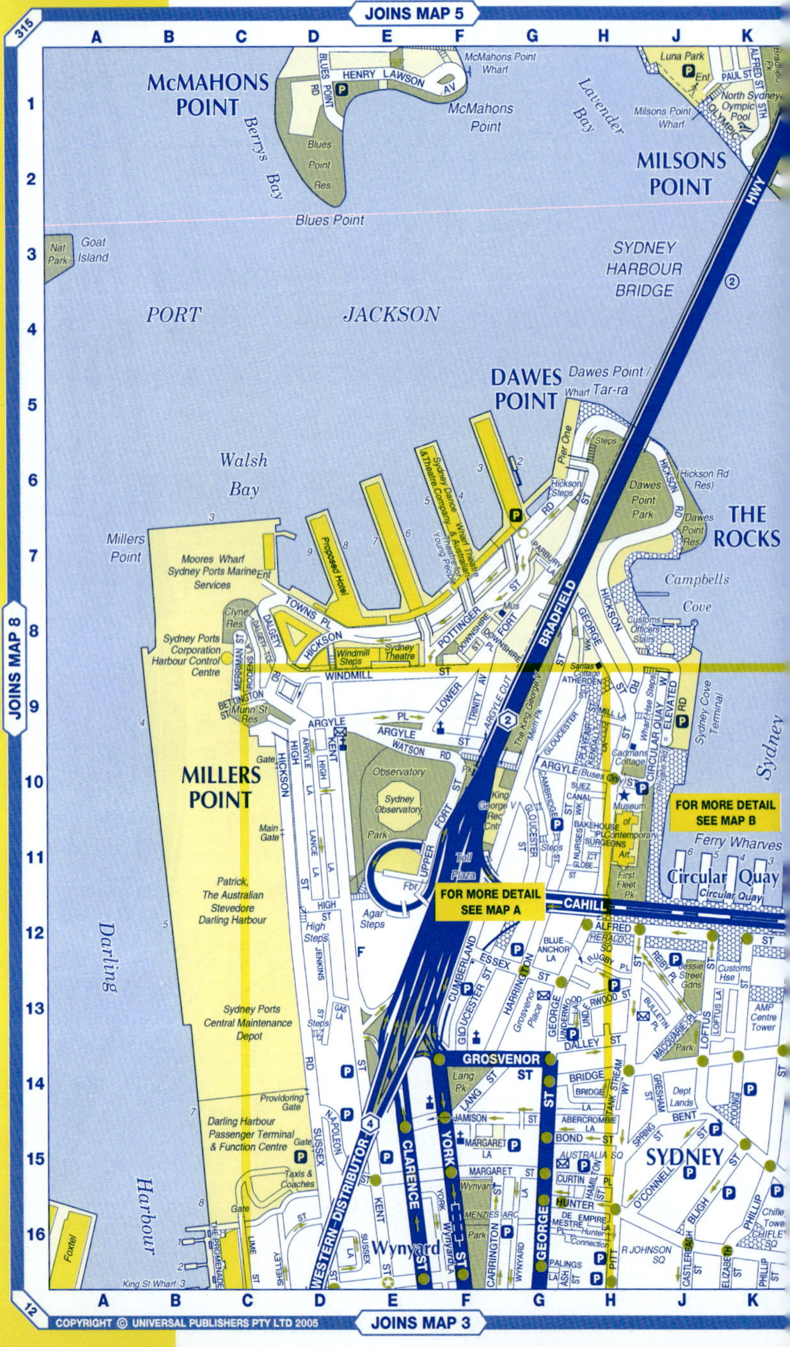
JOINS MAP 5
JOINS MAP 8
JOINS MAP 3
315
12
McMAHONS POINT
Berrys Bay
Blues Point Res
Blues Point
HENRY LAWSON AV
BLUES POINT RD
McMahons Point Wharf
McMahons Point
Lavender Bay
Luna Park
Milsons Point Wharf
North Sydney Olympic Pool
MILSONS POINT
HWY
Nat Park
Goat Island
PORT
JACKSON
SYDNEY HARBOUR BRIDGE
DAWES POINT
Dawes Point / Tar-ra Wharf
Walsh Bay
Millers Point
Moores Wharf Sydney Ports Marine Services
Pier One
Hickson Steps
Dawes Point Park
Hickson Rd Res
Dawes Point Res
THE ROCKS
Campbells Cove
Sydney Dance Company & Australian Theatre for Young People
Wharf Theatre
Proposed Hotel
TOWNS PL
HICKSON RD
Clyne Res
Sydney Ports Corporation Harbour Control Centre
Windmill Steps
Sydney Theatre
WINDMILL ST
BRADFIELD
Customs Officers Stairs
Munn St Res
ARGYLE PL
WATSON RD
LOWER FORT ST
ARGYLE CUT
The King George V Mem Pk
Cadmans Cottage
Sydney Cove Terminal
MILLERS POINT
Observatory Park
Sydney Observatory
King George V Rec Cntr
Museum of Contemporary Art
FOR MORE DETAIL SEE MAP B
Ferry Wharves
Circular Quay
First Fleet Pk
Toll Plaza
FOR MORE DETAIL SEE MAP A
CAHILL
Patrick, The Australian Stevedore Darling Harbour
Agar Steps
High Steps
Darling
Sydney Ports Central Maintenance Depot
ALFRED ST
Jessie Street Gdns
Customs Hse
AMP Centre Tower
GROSVENOR ST
Lang Pk
Providoring Gate
Darling Harbour Passenger Terminal & Function Centre
Taxis & Coaches
WESTERN DISTRIBUTOR
CLARENCE ST
YORK ST
GEORGE ST
Dept Lands
SYDNEY
Harbour
Foxtel
THE PROMENADE
King St Wharf
Wynyard
R JOHNSON SQ
Chifley Tower
CHIFLEY SQ

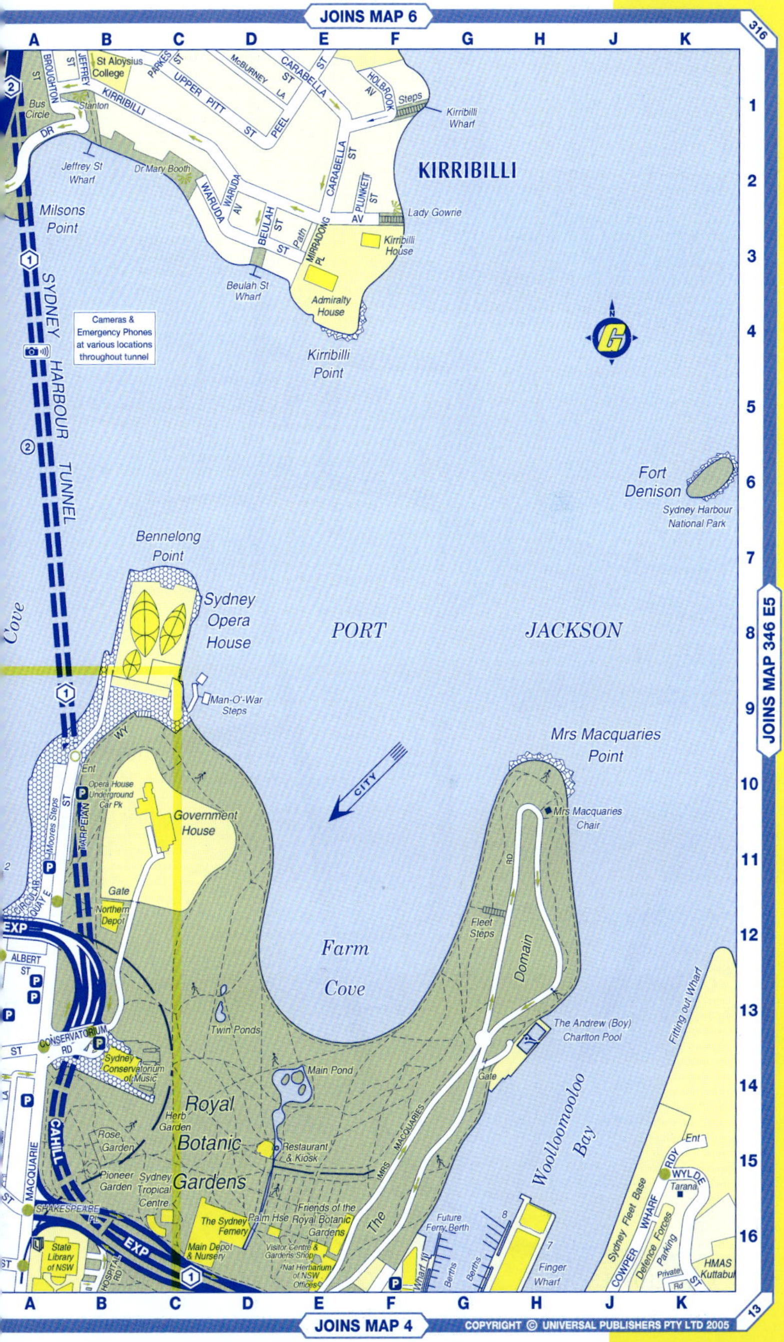
JOINS MAP 6
316
A B C D E F G H J K
1 2 3 4 5 6 7 8 9 10 11 12 13 14 15 16
KIRRIBILLI
St Aloysius College
BROUGHTON ST
JEFFREY ST
PARKES ST
McBURNEY LA
CARABELLA ST
HOLBROOK AV
UPPER PITT ST
KIRRIBILLI
PEEL
Bus Circle
Stanton
DR
Steps
Kirribilli Wharf
Jeffrey St Wharf
Dr Mary Booth
WARUDA AV
WARUDA ST
CARABELLA ST
PLUNKETT ST
AV
Lady Gowrie
Milsons Point
BEULAH ST
Path
MIRRADONG PL
Kirribilli House
Beulah St Wharf
Admiralty House
Kirribilli Point
SYDNEY HARBOUR TUNNEL
Cameras & Emergency Phones at various locations throughout tunnel
Fort Denison
Sydney Harbour National Park
Bennelong Point
Sydney Opera House
Cove
PORT
JACKSON
Man-O'-War Steps
WY
CITY
Mrs Macquaries Point
Ent
Opera House Underground Car Pk
Government House
Mrs Macquaries Chair
TARPEIAN ST
Moores Steps
CIRCULAR QUAY E
Gate
Northern Depot
RD
EXP
ALBERT ST
Fleet Steps
Farm Cove
Domain
Twin Ponds
CONSERVATORIUM RD
ST
Sydney Conservatorium of Music
The Andrew (Boy) Charlton Pool
Fitting out Wharf
Main Pond
Gate
Royal Botanic Gardens
Herb Garden
Rose Garden
Restaurant & Kiosk
Woolloomooloo Bay
Pioneer Garden
Sydney Tropical Centre
MRS MACQUARIES
Ent
RDY
WYLDE
Tarana
CAHILL
MACQUARIE
SHAKESPEARE PL
The Sydney Fernery
Palm Hse
Friends of the Royal Botanic Gardens
The
Future Ferry Berth
8
Sydney Fleet Base
COWPER WHARF
Defence Forces Parking
State Library of NSW
HOSPITAL RD
Main Depot & Nursery
Visitor Centre & Gardens Shop
Nat Herbarium of NSW Offices
Wharf
Berths
Berths
7
Finger Wharf
Private
Rd
ST
HMAS Kuttabul
EXP
JOINS MAP 346 E5
JOINS MAP 4
13

MAP 3

JOINS MAP 1
JOINS MAP 12
JOINS MAP 19
8
18
A B C D E F G H J K
1 2 3 4 5 6 7 8 9 10 11 12 13 14 15 16
Darling Harbour
Darling Harbour (King St) Wharf
King Street Wharf
Pyrmont Bay Wharf
Australian National Maritime Museum
Australia's Animal World (under const)
Sydney Aquarium
Darling Harbour (Aquarium) Wharf
Charter Boat Wharves
Harbourside
PYRMONT BRIDGE
Cockle Bay
Darling Harbour Marina
Cockle Bay Amphitheatre
Convention
Sydney Convention Centre
IMAX Theatre
Darling Park
FOR MORE DETAIL SEE MAP C
Wynyard
Town Hall
Queen Victoria Building
Galeries Victoria
Sydney Arcade
Strand Arc
Mid City Cntr
Glasshouse Skygarden
Imperial Arc
Westfield Centrepoint
Sydney Tower
St James Arc
City Centre
Piccadilly Centre
MLC Centre
Cmwlth Bank
GPO
Martin Pl
Archibald Fountain
Hyde Park
Pool of Reflection
Museum
Anzac War Memorial
Cross City Tunnel
Under Construction
Cncl Off Town Hall
Sydney Sq
St Andrews Cathedral
Energy Australia
Sydney Water
Police Court
World Square
SYDNEY
Tumbalong Park
Chinese Garden
EXHIBITION PLACE
Sydney Exhibition Centre
Garden Plaza
Chinatown
Entertainment Centre Sydney
Haymarket
HAYMARKET
Market City The Peak
Uni of Technology Sydney
FOR MORE DETAIL SEE MAP E
Capitol Square
Sydney Central
Belmore Park
Coach Terminal
CENTRAL STATION
Intercity Trains
Suburban Trains
Central
Devonshire Street Pedestrian Subway
Centennial Plaza (RTA)
SURRY HILLS
Islamic Cntr
ULTIMO
Powerhouse Museum
Harwood Building
The Sydney Art Gallery
TAFE NSW - Sydney Institute - Ultimo College
Australian Broadcasting Corporation
TAFE NSW - Syd Inst
Broadway
UTS
CHIPPENDALE
BROADWAY
GEORGE ST
HARRIS ST
WATTLE ST
HAY ST
LIVERPOOL ST
PARK ST
DRUITT ST
MARKET ST
KING ST
BATHURST ST
GOULBURN ST
CAMPBELL ST
SUSSEX ST
KENT ST
CLARENCE ST
YORK ST
PITT ST
CASTLEREAGH ST
ELIZABETH ST
WESTERN DISTRIBUTOR
HARBOUR ST
ERSKINE ST
MARTIN PL
ST JAMES RD
PIER ST
QUAY ST
RAILWAY SQ
LEE ST
REGENT ST

JOINS MAP 2
JOINS MAP 13
JOINS MAP 20
346
21
A B C D E F G H J K
1 2 3 4 5 6 7 8 9 10 11 12 13 14 15 16
Royal Botanic Gardens
State Library of NSW
Parliament House
Sydney Hospital & Sydney Eye Hospital
Mint (Historic House)
Hyde Park Barracks
Land & Property Info Offices
Phillip Precinct
The Domain
Restaurant & Kiosk
Art Gallery of NSW
Crescent Precinct
Domain Car Park
Moving Footway (Under)
St Marys Cathedral
St Marys Cathedral College
FOR MORE DETAIL SEE MAP D
Fragrance Garden
Cook & Phillip Park
Australian Museum
Sydney Grammar School
Due for Completion - June 2005
East Sydney
CAHILL EXP
DISTRIBUTOR
Toll Plaza
WILLIAM ST
Finger Wharf
Woolloomooloo Bay
Wharf 10
Wharf 11
Sydney Fleet Base
Embarkation (Defence Forces Parking)
HMAS Kuttabul
POTTS POINT
St Vincents College
Plunkett St Pmy & Syd Dist Education High
WOOLLOOMOOLOO
Daffodil Pk
Kings Cross
Fitzroy Gardens
El Alamein Fountain
Springfield Gardens
Hills Stairs
Butlers Stairs
Horderns Stairs
McElhone Stairs
KINGS CROSS TUNNEL
SCEGGS
Theatre
Cinema
Darlinghurst Pmy
DARLINGHURST
National Art Sch
TAFE NSW - Syd Inst
Green Park
St Vincents Caritas Cntr
St Vincents Hospital
St Vincents Private Hospital
St Vincents Clinic
Sacred Heart Palliative Care & Rehab
Speed Cameras & Emergency Phones throughout tunnel
Darlinghurst Court House
Cmnty Health Cntr
Museum
FOR MORE DETAIL SEE MAP F
Sydney Police Centre
Reservoir
Crown St Pmy
Cutler Footway
Global Galleries
PADDINGTON
Uni of NSW College of Fine Arts
Victoria Barracks
OXFORD ST
SOUTH DOWLING ST
EASTERN DISTRIBUTOR
COPYRIGHT © UNIVERSAL PUBLISHERS PTY LTD 2005

MAP 5

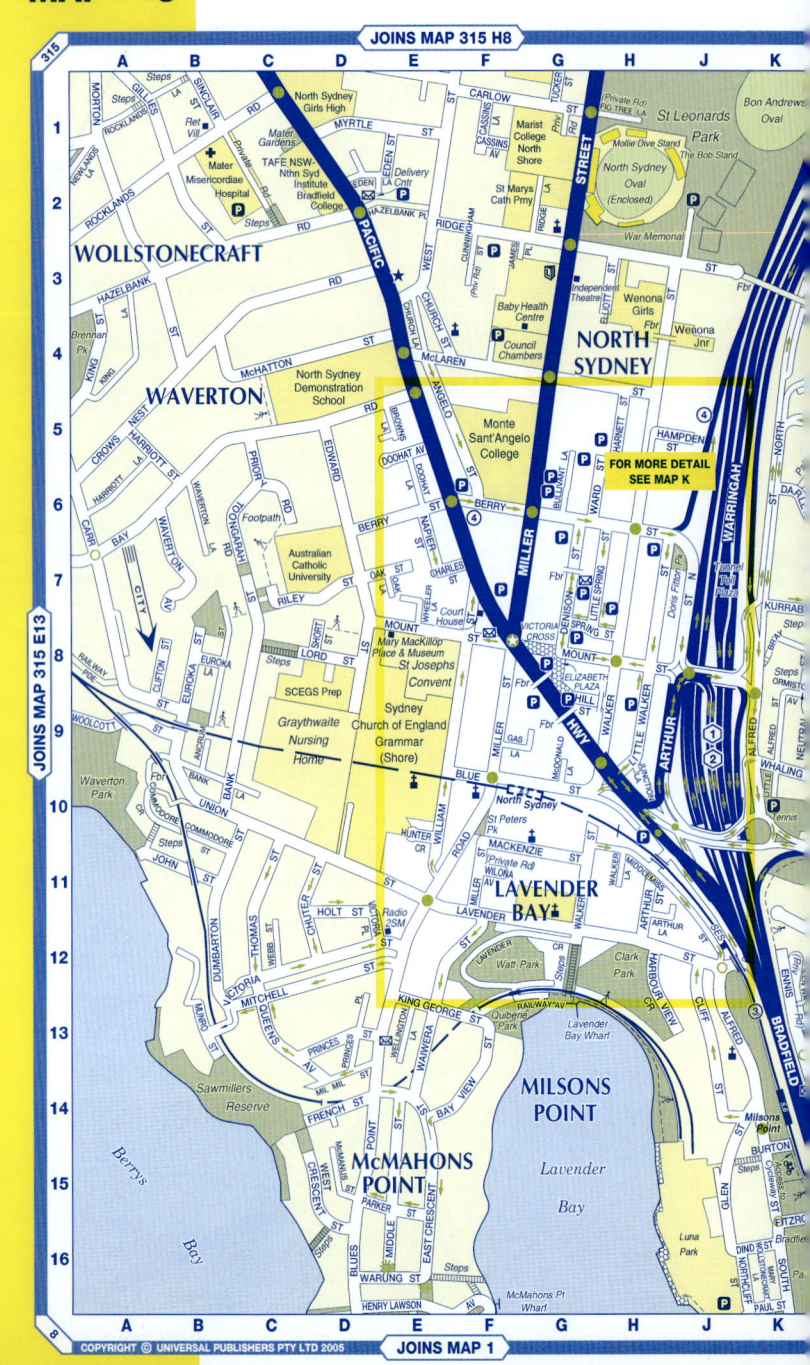

JOINS MAP 316 C8
JOINS MAP 316 F13
JOINS MAP 2
316
346
A B C D E F G H J K
1 2 3 4 5 6 7 8 9 10 11 12 13 14 15 16
NEUTRAL BAY
CREMORNE
KIRRIBILLI
MILITARY ROAD
10
No Left Turn
Mon - Fri 6-10 am
From Rangers Rd
into Military Rd
Forsyth Centre
Forsyth Park
Anderson Park
Milson Park
Neutral Bay Pmy
Ilberry Pk
The Neutral Bay Club Tennis
Nursing Home
Prior Av Res
Cremorne Res
Marina
Australian Customs
Neutral Bay Wharf
Nutcote
Kurraba Wharf
Former HMAS Platypus Site
Ent
Kesterton Pk
North Sydney Wharf
18ft Sailing Club
Ensemble Theatre
Wrixton Pk
Loreto Kirribilli
St Aloysius Junior College
St Aloysius College
Royal Sydney Yacht Squadron
Wudyong Pt
Kurraba Pt Res
The Hodgson
Spains
Kurraba Pt
Neutral Bay
Careening Cove
Shell Cove
PORT JACKSON
James Milson Nurs Home & Ret Vill
Ret Vill
Syn
Willow Tree Pk
Yarringa Park
THE AVENUE (Priv Rd)
Footpath
Steps
Path
Fbr
YEO ST
GROSVENOR LA
WATERS RD
HAMPDEN AV
RANGERS RD
CHEAL LA
YOUNG ST
MAY LA
OLIVE LA
HARDIE ST
LINDSAY ST
HIGHVIEW AV
HIGHVIEW LA
BOYD ST
BEN BOYD RD
RAYMOND RD
WESTLEIGH LA
WESTLEIGH ST
BARRY ST
BYDOWN ST
WYCOMBE RD
SHELLCOVE RD
BURROWAY RD
BERTHA RD
GUTHRIE AV
CLAUDE AV
POWELL ST
BANNERMAN ST
HARRISON ST
HARRISON LA
BENNETT ST
MILITARY LA
PREMIER ST
SPRUSON ST
MONTPELIER ST
HOLDSWORTH ST
HOLDSWORTH RD
PHILLIPS ST
PHILLIPS LA
COLINDIA AV
AUBIN ST
UNDERCLIFF ST
RESERVE ST
ANDERSON ST
HARRIETTE ST
HARRIETTE LA
THRUPP ST
PENSHURST AV
KURRABA RD
MANNS AV
WYCOMBE LA
LOWER WYCOMBE RD
HAYES ST
WALLARINGA AV
SPAINS WHARF RD
HOLLOWFORTH AV
BILLONG ST
GUNDIMAINE AV
HONDA RD
BOGOTA AV
PRIOR AV
MILSON RD
BADEN RD
MERLIN ST
McINTOSH LA
WYAGDON ST
ALFRED ST N
ROSE AV
WINTER AV
BENT ST
BENT LA
LAYCOCK ST
WATSON ST
NOOK AV
RAWSON ST
BRAY LA
CLARK RD
NICHOLAS ST
DORIS ST
MARGARET LA
HIGH ST
ADDERSTONE AV
KIARA CL (Priv Rd)
HIPWOOD ST
McDOUGALL ST
BRADLY AV
STANNARDS PL
WINSLOW ST
WINSLOW LA
WILLOUGHBY ST
CRESCENT ST
HUMPHREY LA
CARABELLA ST
ELAMANG AV
BLIGH ST
JEFFREYS ST
ROBERTSON LA
UPPER PITT ST
PITT ST
PARKES ST
McBURNEY LA
PEEL ST
FREEWAY
HIGHWAY

MAP 7

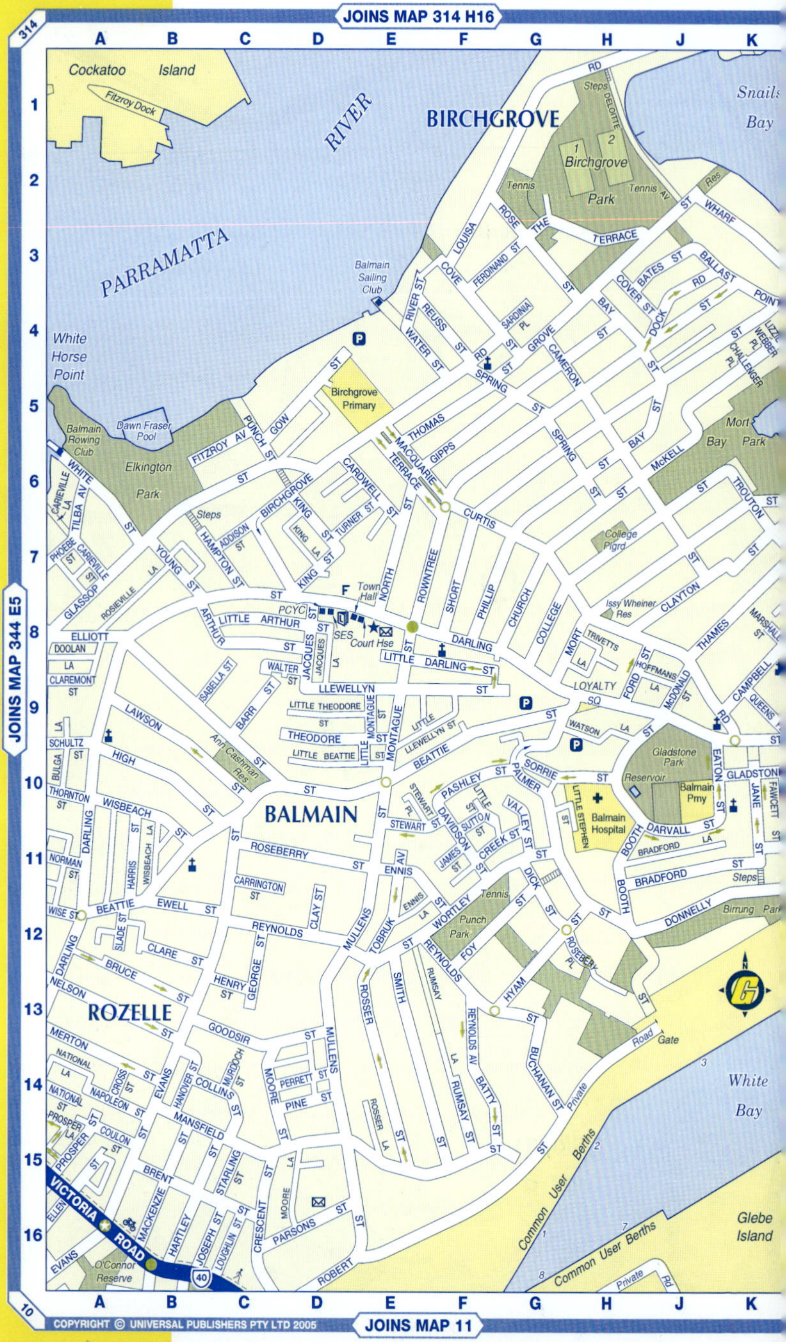
JOINS MAP 314 H16
JOINS MAP 344 E5
JOINS MAP 11
Cockatoo Island
Fitzroy Dock
PARRAMATTA
RIVER
BIRCHGROVE
BALMAIN
ROZELLE
Snails Bay
Birchgrove Park
Tennis
Balmain Sailing Club
White Horse Point
Balmain Rowing Club
Dawn Fraser Pool
Elkington Park
Birchgrove Primary
Mort Bay Park
College Plgrd
Issy Wheiner Res
Town Hall
PCYC
SES
Court Hse
Ann Cashman Res
Gladstone Park
Reservoir
Balmain Pmy
Balmain Hospital
Punch Park
Birrung Park
White Bay
Glebe Island
Common User Berths
Private Road
Gate
Steps
O'Connor Reserve
VICTORIA ROAD
40
DARLING ST
MONTAGUE ST
EVANS ST
MULLENS ST
BEATTIE ST
REYNOLDS AV
BUCHANAN ST
CURTIS RD
ROSEBERRY ST
LOUISA RD
ELLIOTT ST
ROBERT ST

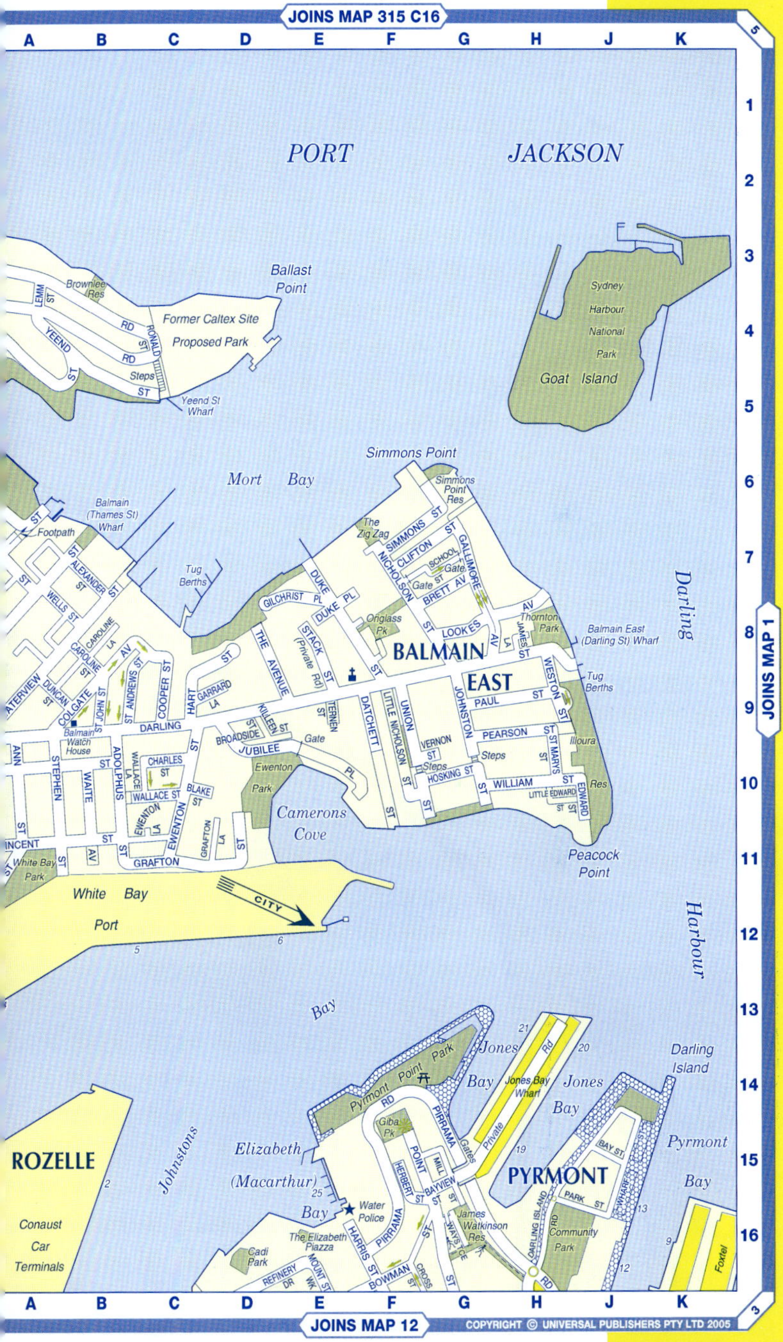
JOINS MAP 315 C16
JOINS MAP 1
JOINS MAP 12
PORT JACKSON
Ballast Point
Former Caltex Site
Proposed Park
Brownlee Res
LEMM ST
YEEND ST
RONALD ST
RD
Steps
Yeend St Wharf
Sydney Harbour National Park
Goat Island
Simmons Point
Mort Bay
Simmons Point Res
Balmain (Thames St) Wharf
Footpath
Tug Berths
The Zig Zag
SIMMONS ST
CLIFTON ST
NICHOLSON ST
GALLIMORE AV
SCHOOL
Gate
BRETT AV
GILCHRIST PL
DUKE PL
DUKE ST
Origlass Pk
LOOKES AV
JAMES LA
Thornton Park
Balmain East (Darling St) Wharf
Darling Harbour
BALMAIN EAST
ALEXANDER ST
WELLS ST
CAROLINE ST
CAROLINE LA
THE AVENUE
STACK ST (Private Rd)
GARRARD LA
HART ST
COOPER ST
ST ANDREWS ST
ST JOHN ST
COLGATE AV
DUNCAN ST
WATERVIEW ST
Balmain Watch House
DARLING ST
BROADSIDE ST
KILLEEN ST
JUBILEE PL
Gate
TERNEN ST
DATCHETT ST
LITTLE NICHOLSON ST
UNION ST
JOHNSTON ST
PAUL ST
WESTON ST
Tug Berths
VERNON ST
PEARSON ST
ST MARYS ST
Steps
HOSKING ST
WILLIAM ST
LITTLE EDWARD ST
EDWARD ST
Illoura Res
Peacock Point
ANN ST
STEPHEN ST
WAITE AV
ADOLPHUS ST
WALLACE LA
WALLACE ST
CHARLES ST
BLAKE ST
EWENTON LA
EWENTON ST
GRAFTON LA
GRAFTON ST
Ewenton Park
Cameron's Cove
VINCENT ST
White Bay Park
White Bay Port
CITY
Bay
Johnstons Bay
ROZELLE
Conaust Car Terminals
Elizabeth (Macarthur) Bay
Water Police
Pyrmont Point Park
PYRMONT
PIRRAMA RD
Giba Pk
POINT ST
HERBERT ST
MILL ST
BAYVIEW ST
HARRIS ST
The Elizabeth Piazza
Cadi Park
REFINERY DR
MOUNT ST
BOWMAN ST
CROSS ST
WAYS TCE
James Watkinson Res
Jones Bay
Jones Bay Wharf
Private Rd
DARLING ISLAND RD
Community Park
BAY ST
PARK ST
WHARF ST
Darling Island
Pyrmont Bay
Foxtel
A B C D E F G H J K
1 2 3 4 5 6 7 8 9 10 11 12 13 14 15 16

MAP 9

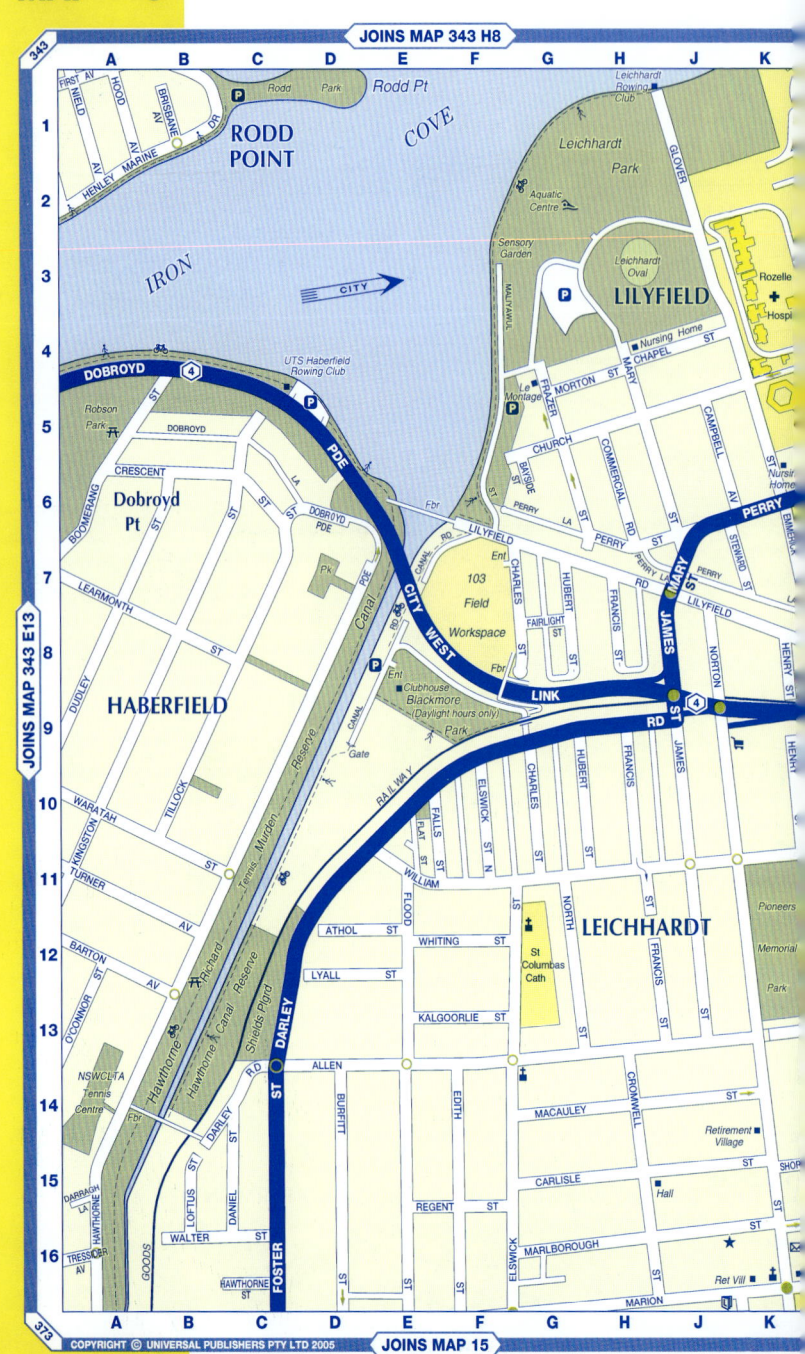

JOINS MAP 344 C8
JOINS MAP 11
JOINS MAP 16
COPYRIGHT © UNIVERSAL PUBLISHERS PTY LTD 2005
A B C D E F G H J K
1 2 3 4 5 6 7 8 9 10 11 12 13 14 15 16
7
17
ROZELLE
LILYFIELD
ANNANDALE
University of Sydney
Sydney College of the Arts
Office
Swim Pool (Private)
Rozelle Hospital
Govt Library
Writers' Centre
Outpatients
Aldersgate House Ret Vill & Nursing Home
Orange Grove Plaza
Orange Grove Primary
Oval
Rozelle Common
Cmnty Cntr
Easton Park
Rozelle Goods Yard
Lilyfield
Whites Creek Valley Park
Cohen Park
Channel
Viaduct
Whites Stormwater
Leichhardt Bus Depot
Sydney Secondary College Leichhardt Campus
Gates
War Memorial Park
Rubbish Tip (Weekends Only)
Ent
36th Battalion Pk
Footpath
Leichhardt Lilyfield SS A Club
SES Cncl Off
Leichhardt Primary
St Fiacres Cath
Evan Jones Plgrd
Styles St
Annandale Neighbourhood Centre
Nursing Home
Gate
VICTORIA RD
BALMAIN RD
CITY WEST LINK
JOHNSTON ST
CATHERINE ST
CARRINGTON ST
THE BOULEVARDE
O'NEILL ST
JUSTIN ST
LAMB ST
RYAN ST
MAIDA ST
ALBERTO ST
GROVE ST
SUNNYSIDE AV
BROCKLEY ST
FOUCART ST
DENISON ST
COOK ST
PERCY ST
EVANS ST
CHARLOTTE ST
ELIZABETH ST
ALFRED ST
BURT ST
CHELTENHAM ST
EASTON ST
MARYON ST
ALICE ST
ALBERT ST
HUTCHESON ST
CASHMAN ST
BELMORE ST
RED LION ST
ELLEN ST
KENNIFF ST
MATILDA ST
REGENT ST
WOODLARK ST
ANGELINI AV
FRED ST
PADSTOW ST
CECILY ST
JOSEPH ST
TREVOR ST
GARNET AV
HALLORAN ST
LILYFIELD RD
EDWARD ST
RAYNER ST
ERIC ST
HELENA ST
POINT ST
MAY ST
FREDBERT ST
CENTRAL WY
COTTAGE WY
GARDEN
GLENDALE DR
SUPPLY
WHARF
NORTH
PARK DR
SOUTH
KIRKBRIDE WY
PRETORIA ST
RUSSELL ST
LONSDALE ST
BRENAN ST
PERCIVAL ST
STARLING ST
GLADSTONE ST
PRITCHARD ST
PRITCHARD LA
BREILLAT ST
HUTCHINSON ST
GRAY ST
HUDSON ST
RAILWAY PDE
PIPER ST
CHARLOTTE ST
LEYS AV
ALFRED ST
AINSWORTH ST
ILKA ST
MOORE ST
MOORE ST W
MOORE LA
ANNESLEY ST
HILL ST
WARATAH ST
MACKENZIE ST
MILTON ST
FOWLER ST
COLERIDGE ST
STANLEY ST
STYLES ST
THORBY AV
NORTH AV
PALING ST
EDNA ST
WHITE ST
WISDOM ST
YOUNG ST
GILLIES ST
SMITH ST
ARGUIMBAU ST
BOOTH ST
COLLINS ST
ALFRED ST
JOHN ST
EMMA ST
BUNGAY ST
WHITES CREEK LA
MAYES ST
RESERVE ST
ANNANDALE ST
CHAPMAN LA
DERBYSHIRE RD
GOODS RD
BEAMES ST
ETHERILL
LEICHHARDT ST
SKELTON ST

JOINS MAP 7
JOINS MAP 10
JOINS MAP 17
344
16
A B C D E F G H J K
1 2 3 4 5 6 7 8 9 10 11 12 13 14 15 16
ROZELLE
ANNANDALE
GLEBE
FOREST LODGE
Glebe Point
Glebe Island
Rozelle Bay
Glebe Pt
Rozelle Goods Yard
CITY WEST LINK
THE CRESCENT
VICTORIA RD
JAMES CRAIG (Private Road) RD
SOMMERVILLE RD
Common User Berths
Silos
Gate
Waterways
CITY
O'Connor Res
Hannan Res
PRINCE ST
QUIRK ST
ALFRED ST
HORNSEY ST
GORDON ST
BURT ST
LILYFIELD RD
ROBERT ST
CRESCENT ST
MANEY ST
GRAHAM ST
ELLEN ST
CHARLOTTE ST
ELIZABETH ST
Rozelle Bay
BAYVIEW CR
RAILWAY PDE
BURUWAN
KENTVILLE AV
WEYNTON ST
PRITCHARD
BREILLAT
HUTCHINSON ST
ROSE ST
Steps
ANNANDALE
Annandale North Primary
PIPER ST
Hinsby Pk
JOHNSTON ST
VIEW ST
TRAFALGAR
BOOTH ST
NELSON
WELLS ST
SUSAN
TAYLOR
COLLINS ST
CHESTER ST
WILLIAM ST
CHAPMAN RD
Pavilion
Bicentennial Park
Federal Park
Wet Lands
Johnstons Creek
Stormwater Channel
Jubilee Park
Oval
Jubilee Park
Reserve
Pope Paul VI Reserve
Harold Park Paceway
Grandstand
Club
Ent
Rec Res
Viaduct
CONEILL PL
MINOGUE CR
PCYC
Lewis Hoad Res
Hogan Park
John Victor McMahon Res
Fbr
WIGRAM RD
STERLING
ALEXANDRA DR
Orphan School Creek
(Private Rd)
PYRMONT BRIDGE RD
BRIDGE RD
ROSS ST
MAXWELL RD
St Scholasticas College
Ent
Deliveries
RAILWAY
TUNNEL
ARCADIA RD
TOXTETH RD
BOYCE ST
GLEN ST
ROCK LA
NORTHCOTE RD
FEDERAL RD
EGLINTON RD
EDWARD ST
Buddhist Temple
PENDRILL ST
ALEXANDRA RD
AVENUE RD
ALLEN ST
COTTER LA
Youth Hostel
GLEBE POINT RD
LEICHHARDT ST
MARY ST
STEWART ST
OXLEY ST
Blackwattle Bay Park
HICKETTS
COOK
CHARLTON
AVONA
FORSYTH
MANSFIELD ST
BELL
CHURCH
HERBERTO
WALSH AV
Arthur (Paddy) Gray Res
WOOLLEY
HEGARTY
JOHN ST
YORK
HEREFORD ST
Steps
Cmnty Health Cntr
Forest Lodge Pmy
ALBERT
ARTHUR ST
CLIFF TCE
UPPER
ALFRED ST
CHARLES
CROSS
WOOD ST
CREEK ST
HEREFORD
FOSS ST
JUNCTION
KIMBER LA
LOCK LA
DAVID ST
SHORT
ST JOHNS
AAPT
Youth Hostel
BAKERS
ARUNDEL
(covered)

JOINS MAP 8
JOINS MAP 3
JOINS MAP 18
A B C D E F G H J K
1 2 3 4 5 6 7 8 9 10 11 12 13 14 15 16
Conaust Car Terminals
Johnstons Bay
Old Glebe Island Br permanently open to shipping
ANZAC BRIDGE
Blackwattle Bay
Sydney University Women's Rowing Club
Sydney Secondary College Blackwattle Bay Campus
PYRMONT
ULTIMO
Wentworth Park
Greyhound Track
Oval
Soccer
Star City Casino
Lyric Theatre
Pyrmont Bay Marina
Pyrmont Bay Park
Wharf 7 Plaza
Wharf 10
Aust Maritime Museum
Australian National Maritime Museum
Pyrmont Bay
Light Rail
Tablet House Steps
Refinery Square
Gatehouse
John St Sq
Carmichael Pk
Tennis
Maybanke Courts
Steps
Citywest Office Park
TEN Channel 10 TV Studios
Fish Market
Sydney Fish Market
Wentworth Park
Convention
Grand Mercure
Novotel Hotel
Motor Museum
The Sydney Art Gallery
Fig La Pk
Ultimo Pmy
Sports House
Main Ent
Cmnty Cntr
City of Sydney Depot
TAFE NSW
Glebe
Valhalla Theatre
Cmnty Health Cntr
St James Pmy
Dr H J Foley Rest Pk
Ret Vill
Ct Hse
Town Hall
Glebe Primary
Broadway Cin
Shopping Centre
Unilodge Hotel
Diabetes Australia
WESTERN DISTRIBUTOR
PYRMONT BRIDGE RD
BRIDGE RD
HARRIS ST
WATTLE ST
BROADWAY
GLEBE POINT RD
COPYRIGHT © UNIVERSAL PUBLISHERS PTY LTD 2005

MAP 13

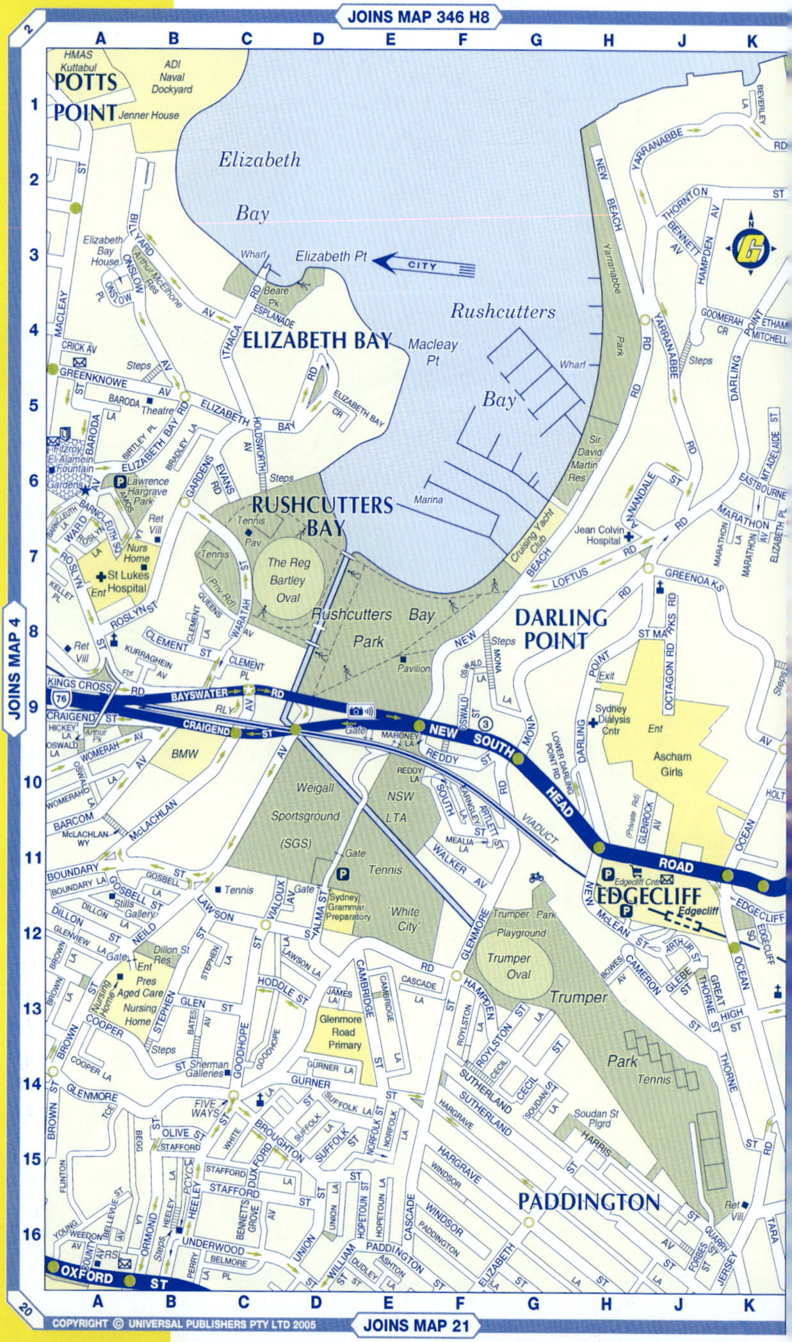
JOINS MAP 346 H8
JOINS MAP 4
JOINS MAP 21
A B C D E F G H J K
1 2 3 4 5 6 7 8 9 10 11 12 13 14 15 16
POTTS POINT
HMAS Kuttabul
ADI Naval Dockyard
Jenner House
Elizabeth Bay
Elizabeth Pt
CITY
Wharf
Beare Pk
ESPLANADE
ELIZABETH BAY
Macleay Pt
Rushcutters Bay
Marina
Elizabeth Bay House
Arthur McElhone Res
ONSLOW
BILLYARD AV
MACLEAY ST
CRICK AV
GREENKNOWE AV
BARODA
Theatre
ELIZABETH BAY RD
Fitzroy El-Alamein Fountain Gardens
Lawrence Hargrave Park
Ret Vill
Nurs Home
St Lukes Hospital
Ent
ROSLYN ST
KINGS CROSS RD
BAYSWATER RD
CRAIGEND ST
RUSHCUTTERS BAY
Tennis
Pav
The Reg Bartley Oval
Rushcutters Bay Park
Pavilion
Sir David Martin Res
Cruising Yacht Club
Jean Colvin Hospital
NEW BEACH RD
Yarranabbe Park
YARRANABBE RD
THORNTON ST
BENNETT AV
HAMPDEN AV
GOOMERAH CR
ETHAM
MITCHELL
DARLING POINT RD
EASTBOURNE
MARATHON RD
ANNANDALE ST
LOFTUS RD
GREENOAKS
DARLING POINT
ST MARKS RD
OCTAGON RD
Sydney Dialysis Cntr
Ascham Girls
NEW SOUTH HEAD ROAD
VIADUCT
EDGECLIFF
Edgecliff Cntr
Edgecliff
OCEAN ST
BMW
McLACHLAN AV
Weigall Sportsground (SGS)
NSW LTA
Gate
Tennis
Sydney Grammar Preparatory
'White City'
Trumper Park
Playground
Trumper Oval
GLENMORE RD
BOUNDARY ST
GOSBELL ST
Stills Gallery
Dillon St Res
Pres Aged Care Nursing Home
Nursing Home
Steps
Sherman Galleries
GLEN ST
HODDLE ST
CAMBRIDGE ST
Glenmore Road Primary
GURNER ST
FIVE WAYS
BROUGHTON ST
SUFFOLK ST
NORFOLK ST
HARGRAVE ST
SUTHERLAND ST
Soudan St Plgrd
PADDINGTON
UNDERWOOD ST
OXFORD ST
Ret Vill
QUARRY ST
JERSEY RD

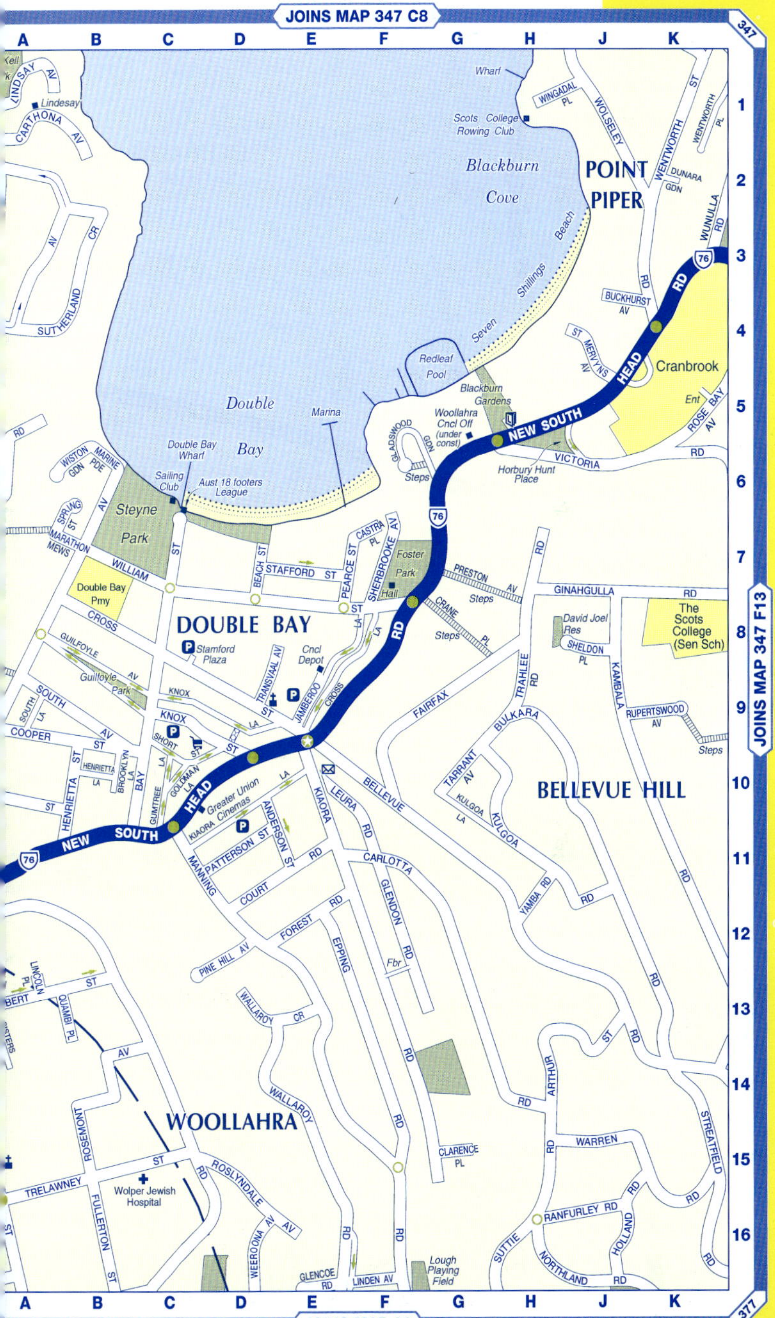
JOINS MAP 347 C8
347
A B C D E F G H J K
1 2 3 4 5 6 7 8 9 10 11 12 13 14 15 16
JOINS MAP 347 F13
377
Blackburn Cove
Double Bay
POINT PIPER
DOUBLE BAY
BELLEVUE HILL
WOOLLAHRA
Wharf
Scots College Rowing Club
WINGADAL PL
WOLSELEY RD
WENTWORTH ST
WENTWORTH PL
DUNARA GDN
WUNULLA RD
Seven Shillings Beach
BUCKHURST AV
MERVYNS AV
ST
Redleaf Pool
Marina
Blackburn Gardens
Woollahra Cncl Off (under const)
Cranbrook
Ent
ROSE BAY AV
NEW SOUTH HEAD RD
76
VICTORIA RD
Horbury Hunt Place
GLADSWOOD GDN
Steps
Double Bay Wharf
Sailing Club
Aust 18 footers League
Steyne Park
LINDSAY AV
Lindesay
CARTHONA AV
SUTHERLAND AV
CR
RD
WISTON GDN
MARINE PDE
SPRING ST
MARATHON MEWS
AV
WILLIAM ST
Double Bay Pmy
CROSS
GUILFOYLE AV
Guilfoyle Park
SOUTH AV
SOUTH LA
COOPER ST
HENRIETTA ST
HENRIETTA LA
BROOKLYN LA
BAY
GUMTREE LA
GOLDMAN LA
KNOX
KNOX LA
SHORT ST
P
Stamford Plaza
BEACH ST
STAFFORD ST
PEARCE ST
CASTRA PL
SHERBROOKE AV
Foster Park
Hall
Cncl Depot
TRANSVAAL AV
JAMBEROO LA
CROSS ST
LA
PRESTON AV
CRANE PL
GINAHGULLA RD
David Joel Res
SHELDON PL
The Scots College (Sen Sch)
KAMBALA RD
RUPERTSWOOD AV
FAIRFAX RD
TRAHLEE RD
BULKARA RD
TARRANT AV
KULGOA LA
KULGOA RD
YAMBA RD
BELLEVUE RD
KIAORA RD
LEURA RD
CARLOTTA
GLENDON RD
Fbr
Greater Union Kiaora Cinemas
KIAORA LA
PATTERSON ST
ANDERSON ST
MANNING RD
COURT RD
FOREST RD
EPPING RD
PINE HILL AV
WALLAROY CR
WALLAROY RD
LINCOLN PL
BERT ST
QUAMBI PL
SISTERS
ROSEMONT AV
ROSLYNDALE AV
WEEROONA AV
TRELAWNEY ST
FULLERTON ST
Wolper Jewish Hospital
GLENCOE RD
LINDEN AV
Lough Playing Field
CLARENCE PL
ARTHUR RD
WARREN RD
STREATFIELD RD
RANFURLEY RD
HOLLAND RD
NORTHLAND RD
SUTTIE RD
ST

JOINS MAP 22

JOINS MAP 9
JOINS MAP 373 E5
JOINS MAP 373 H9
343
373
A B C D E F G H J K
1 2 3 4 5 6 7 8 9 10 11 12 13 14 15 16
LEICHHARDT
HABERFIELD
Taverners Hill
SUMMER HILL
LEWISHAM
PETERSHAM
DULWICH HILL
MARRICKVILLE
PARRAMATTA
(GREAT
WESTERN
HIGHWAY)
ROAD
TEBBUTT
ST
FOSTER
NEW
CANTERBURY
ROAD
Lambert Park
Market Place
Kegworth Primary
Fort Street High
Petersham Oval
Ozanam Village
St Thomas Cath Boys High
St Thomas Becket Cath Pmy
Nursing Home
TAFE
Petersham Pmy
Tennis
Skate Rink
Locke Haven Ret Vill
Reservoir
Catholic
Lewisham Primary
Morton Park
Metro Rehab
Former Everleigh Hospital
Wilkins Primary
Croquet Club
Marrickville Park
Nurs Home
Cmnty Health Cntr
Brighton St Park
Nursing Home
Ret Vill
RSL
Cncl Off
Lewisham
Petersham
Fbr
Ent
Hawthorne Canal
MARION ST
HAWTHORNE ST
HAWTHORNE PDE
PERCY ST
LORD ST
BURFITT ST
EDITH ST
DAY ST
CARY ST
REUSS ST
ROSEBY ST
RENWICK ST
ROFE ST
THORNLEY ST
EXCELSIOR ST
JUNIOR ST
ELSWICK ST
ELSWICK LA
SEALE ST
MYRTLE ST
IVORY
EDITH LA
DAVIES ST
LORDS RD
KEGWORTH ST
BEESON ST
HATHERN ST
UPWARD ST
GEORGE ST
TREADGOLD ST
FLOOD ST
McALEER ST
ALBERT ST
EASTER ST
NATIONAL ST
JARRETT ST
QUEEN ST
FORT ST
KIRK PATRICK LA
CROYDON ST
BRIGHTON ST
BURNS LA
BURNS ST
PALACE LA
FISHERS RES
CARRINGTON LA
TERMINUS
SOUTH AV
SEARL ST
THE AVENUE
LITTLE
LOTOS ST
LOTOS LA
WENTWORTH ST
STATION ST
ANDREAS ST
NESTOR LA
CARRINGTON ST
PARK ST
WEST ST
DOVER ST
FRENCHS LA
HAIG AV
COOK ST
BROWN ST
ST JOHN ST
BARKER ST
BARKER LA
ALFRED ST
GROSVENOR CR
SMITH ST
LONGPORT ST
WILLIAM ST
THOMAS ST
CHARLES ST
O'NEILL WY
RAILWAY
HUDSON ST
McGILL ST
HENRY ST
HENRY LA
JUBILEE ST
LA N
HOBBS ST
HUNTER ST
TCE
TRAFALGAR ST
NELSON PL
ABEL LA
CR
SADLIER
GORDON ST
GORDON LA
BALANAMING LA
AUDLEY ST
SMALL LA
FISHER ST
REGENT ST
OLD CANTERBURY RD
TOOTHILL ST
TOOTHILL LA
SUMMER HILL ST
VICTORIA ST
BOULEVARDE
CHESTER ST
JAMES
ROSFORD AV
OXFORD ST
BELGRAVE ST
SHAW
ALBERT
DENISON ST
ELTHAM ST
THE
GOULD LA
GOULD AV
VERNON ST
ALLANS AV
DUCROS ST
MARIA ST
MORGAN ST
NAPIER ST
JARVIE AV
BISHOP ST
MILLER LA
MILLER ST
LIVINGSTONE RD
ADDISON
CORONATION AV
ROSE ST
McRAE ST
MORTON ST
FRAZER ST
FAIRFOWL ST
WARDELL RD
YULE ST
LAWSON AV
SYDENHAM RD
PARK
NORWOOD LA
31
54
6
5
7

JOINS MAP 10

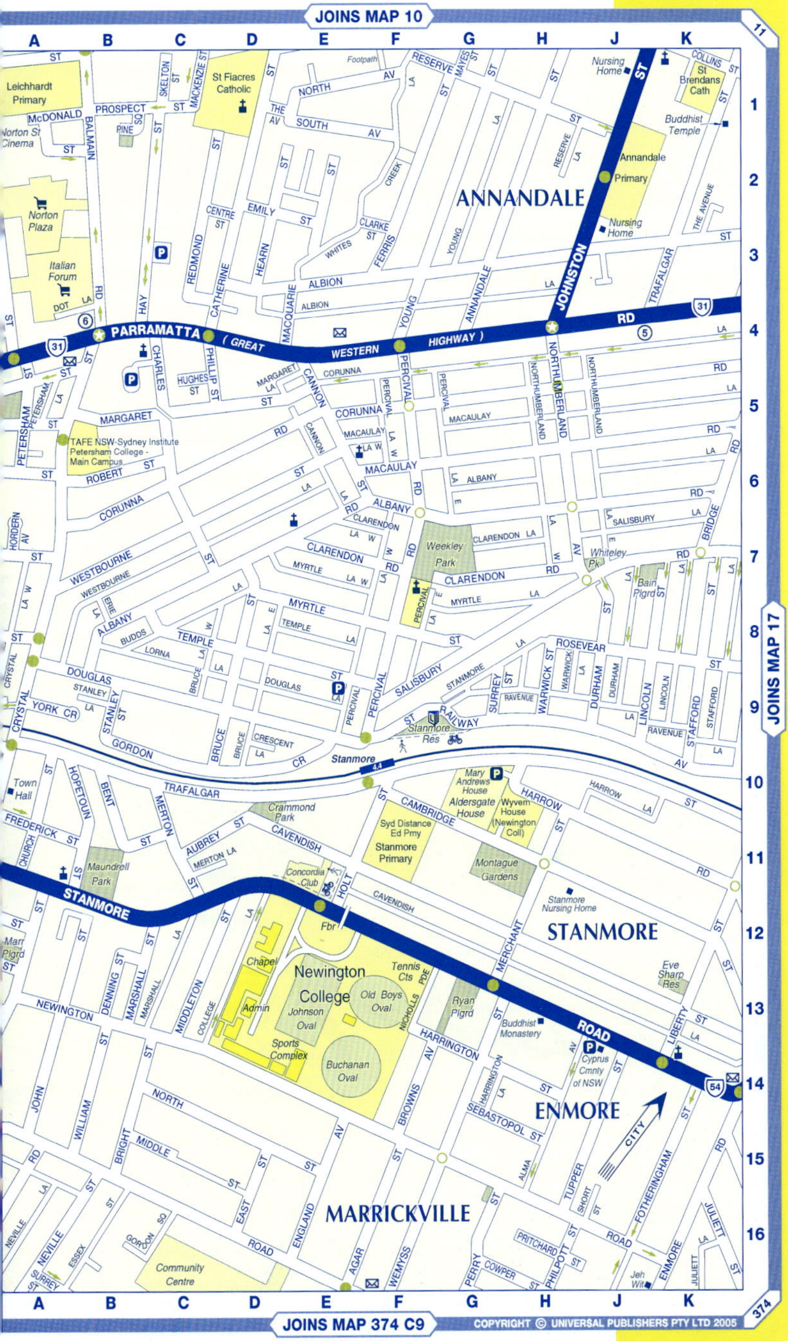

JOINS MAP 17

JOINS MAP 374 C9

JOINS MAP 11
JOINS MAP 16
JOINS MAP 374 H9
10
374
A B C D E F G H J K
1 2 3 4 5 6 7 8 9 10 11 12 13 14 15 16
ANNANDALE
CAMPERDOWN
NEWTOWN
ENMORE
Macdonaldtown
Buddhist Temple
Camperdown Park
O'Dea Reserve
Bridge Rd
Tennis
Uni of Sydney
Chinese Consulate
Queen Mary Building
Sancta Sophia College
St Johns Oval
St Johns College
Royal Prince Alfred Hospital
King George V Building
St. Andrews College
CSIRO
Williams
State Coroners Court
Rhodes Hse
Centra
Travelodge
Camperdown Memorial Rest Park
St Stephens Cemetery
Dendy Cinema
Athena
Bugler Plgrd
Subway
Town Hall
Newtown
PCYC
Green Ban Pk
RSL
Theatre
Newtown Theatre
Newtown High School of the Performing Arts
Fowler Res
Newtown Primary
Salmon Plgrd
Francis Park
Cmnty Hlth
Stormwater
Channel
PARRAMATTA RD
PYRMONT BRIDGE ROAD
GREAT WESTERN
KING ST
ENMORE ROAD
ERSKINEVILLE RD
CITY RD
MISSENDEN RD
CARILLON AV
AUSTRALIA ST
CHURCH ST
STATION ST
WILSON ST
BROWN ST
SALISBURY RD
CAMDEN ST
ROSS ST
31
54

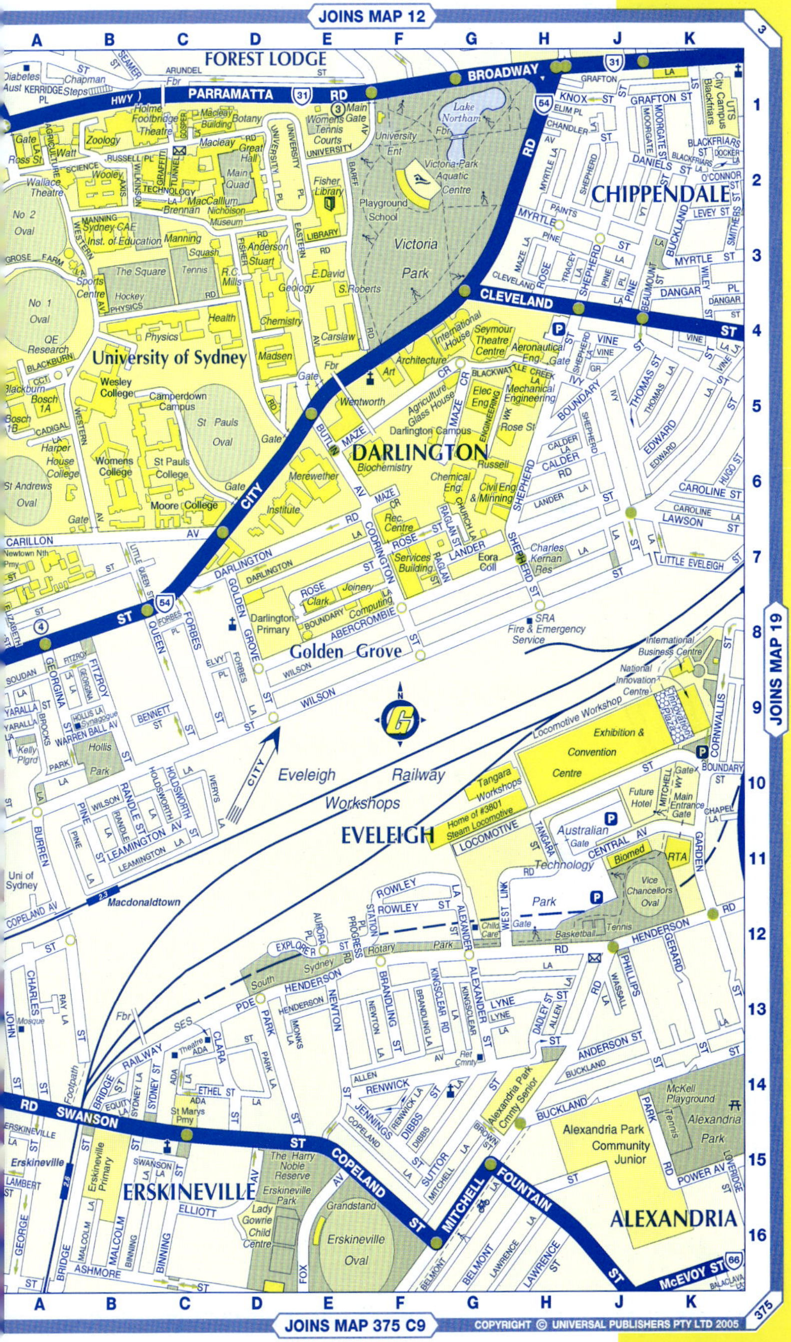
JOINS MAP 12
JOINS MAP 19
JOINS MAP 375 C9
FOREST LODGE
CHIPPENDALE
DARLINGTON
EVELEIGH
ERSKINEVILLE
ALEXANDRIA
University of Sydney
Golden Grove
Victoria Park
Eveleigh Railway Workshops
Macdonaldtown
Exhibition & Convention Centre
Australian Technology Park
National Innovation Centre
International Business Centre
Erskineville Oval
Alexandria Park
Alexandria Park Community Junior
PARRAMATTA RD
BROADWAY
CITY RD
CLEVELAND ST
SWANSON ST
COPELAND ST
MITCHELL
FOUNTAIN
McEVOY ST
Lake Northam
Victoria Park Aquatic Centre
Wesley College
Womens College
St Pauls College
St Andrews Oval
St Pauls Oval
Moore College
Darlington Primary
Erskineville Primary
Seymour Theatre Centre
The Harry Noble Reserve
Erskineville Park
Tangara Workshops
Home of #3801 Steam Locomotive
Future Hotel
Vice Chancellors Oval

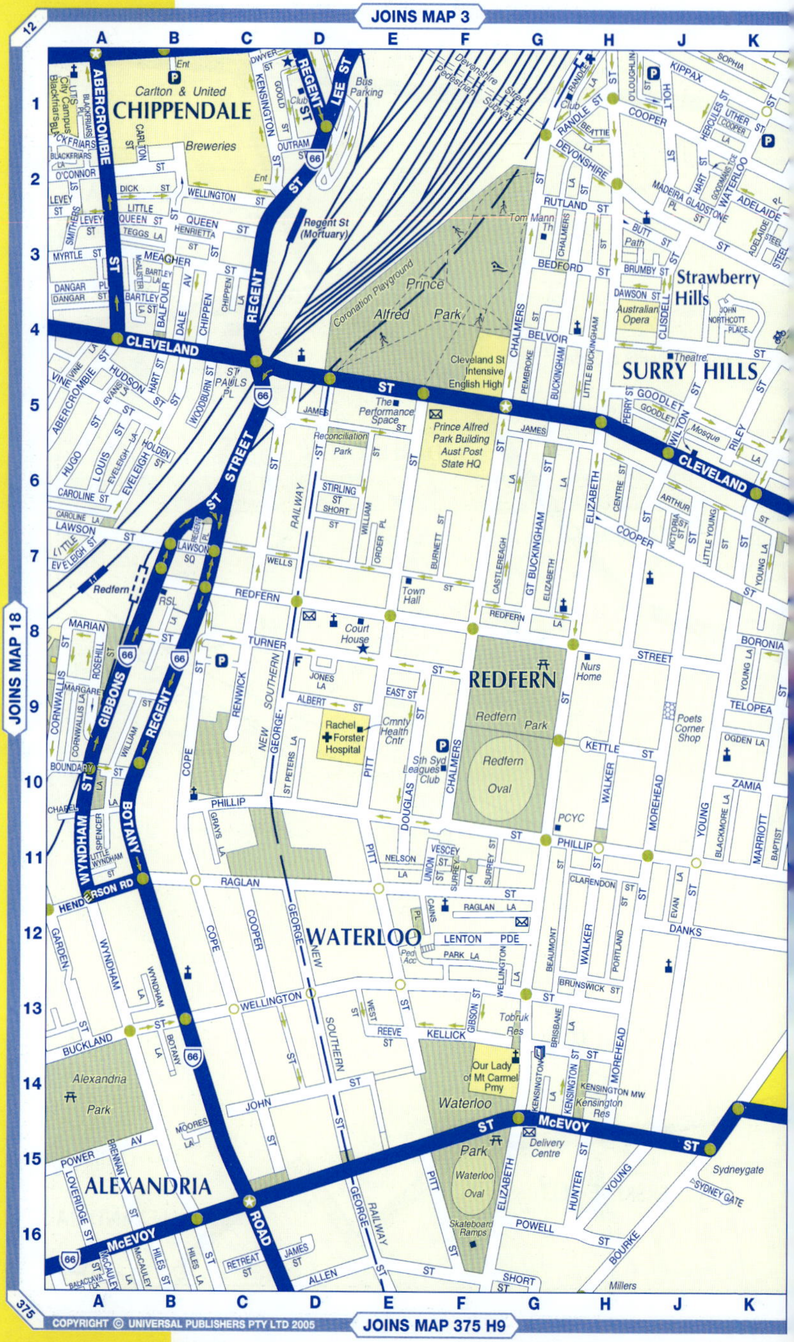
JOINS MAP 3
JOINS MAP 18
JOINS MAP 375 H9
12
375
A B C D E F G H J K
1 2 3 4 5 6 7 8 9 10 11 12 13 14 15 16
CHIPPENDALE
Carlton & United Breweries
UTS City Campus Blackfriars
ABERCROMBIE ST
BLACKFRIARS ST
O'CONNOR ST
LEVEY ST
SMITHERS ST
LEVEY ST
MYRTLE ST
DANGAR PL
DANGAR ST
CARLTON ST
DICK ST
LITTLE QUEEN ST
QUEEN ST
TEGGS LA
HENRIETTA ST
WELLINGTON ST
MEAGHER ST
BARTLEY LA
BARTLEY ST
BALFOUR ST
DALE AV
CHIPPEN ST
KENSINGTON ST
GOOLD ST
DWYER ST
OUTRAM ST
Club
REGENT ST
LEE ST
Bus Parking
Regent St (Mortuary)
Devonshire Street Pedestrian Subway
CLEVELAND ST
ST PAULS PL
VINE ST
ABERCROMBIE ST
HUDSON ST
HART ST
EVANS LA
WOODBURN ST
HUGO ST
LOUIS ST
EVELEIGH LA
EVELEIGH ST
HOLDEN ST
CAROLINE ST
CAROLINE LA
LAWSON ST
LITTLE EVELEIGH ST
LAWSON SQ
Redfern
RSL
MARIAN ST
ROSEHILL ST
MARGARET ST
CORNWALLIS ST
CORNWALLIS LA
GIBBONS ST
WILLIAM ST
REGENT ST
BOUNDARY LA
CHARLES ST
WYNDHAM ST
SPENCER ST
LITTLE WYNDHAM ST
BOTANY RD
HENDERSON RD
66
Coronation Playground
Prince Alfred Park
Tom Mann Th
Cleveland St Intensive English High
The Performance Space
JAMES ST
Reconciliation Park
Prince Alfred Park Building Aust Post State HQ
STIRLING ST
SHORT ST
WILLIAM ST
ORDER PL
BURNETT ST
RAILWAY ST
WELLS ST
REDFERN ST
TURNER ST
Court House
JONES LA
ALBERT ST
EAST ST
Rachel Forster Hospital
Cmnty Health Cntr
Sth Syd Leagues Club
NEW SOUTHERN
GEORGE ST
ST PETERS LA
PITT ST
DOUGLAS ST
CHALMERS ST
RENWICK ST
COPE ST
PHILLIP ST
GRAYS LA
Town Hall
REDFERN
Redfern Park
Redfern Oval
PCYC
CASTLEREAGH ST
GT BUCKINGHAM ST
ELIZABETH ST
REDFERN LA
Nurs Home
KETTLE ST
WALKER ST
MOREHEAD ST
PHILLIP ST
NELSON LA
VESCEY ST
UNION ST
SURREY ST
RAGLAN ST
RAGLAN LA
WATERLOO
LENTON PDE
PARK LA
Ped Acc
CAINS PL
WELLINGTON ST
CLARENDON ST
PORTLAND ST
BEAUMONT ST
BRUNSWICK ST
WELLINGTON ST
WEST ST
REEVE ST
KELLICK ST
GIBSON ST
Tobruk Res
Our Lady of Mt Carmel Prmy
Waterloo Park
Waterloo Oval
Skateboard Ramps
KENSINGTON ST
KENSINGTON MW
Kensington Res
BRISBANE ST
McEVOY ST
Delivery Centre
HUNTER ST
YOUNG ST
POWELL ST
BOURKE ST
SHORT ST
Millers
Sydneygate
SYDNEY GATE
JOHN ST
MOORES LA
BUCKLAND ST
GARDEN ST
WYNDHAM ST
WYNDHAM LA
BOTANY LA
Alexandria Park
POWER AV
BRENNAN ST
LOVERIDGE ST
ALEXANDRIA
McEVOY ST
BALACLAVA ST
McCAULEY LA
McCAULEY ST
HILES ST
HILES LA
RETREAT ST
JAMES ST
ALLEN ST
ROAD
COOPER ST
DANKS ST
EVAN LA
YOUNG ST
BLACKMORE LA
MARRIOTT ST
BAPTIST ST
ZAMIA ST
OGDEN LA
TELOPEA ST
BORONIA ST
YOUNG LA
Poets Corner Shop
STREET
RANDLE ST
RANDLE LA
BEATTIE LA
DEVONSHIRE ST
O'LOUGHLIN ST
HOLT ST
COOPER ST
KIPPAX ST
SOPHIA ST
HERCULES ST
UTHER ST
COOPER ST
MADEIRA PL
GLADSTONE ST
HART ST
GOODMANS LA
WATERLOO ST
ADELAIDE PL
ADELAIDE ST
STEEL ST
RUTLAND ST
CHALMERS ST
BUTT ST
Path
BEDFORD ST
BRUMBY ST
DAWSON ST
Australian Opera
CLISDELL ST
Strawberry Hills
JOHN NORTHCOTT PLACE
BELVOIR ST
PEMBROKE ST
BUCKINGHAM ST
LITTLE BUCKINGHAM ST
Theatre
SURRY HILLS
PERRY ST
GOODLET ST
GOODLET LA
WILTON ST
Mosque
RILEY ST
JAMES ST
ELIZABETH ST
CENTRE ST
ARTHUR ST
VICTORIA ST
LITTLE YOUNG ST
COOPER ST
YOUNG LA

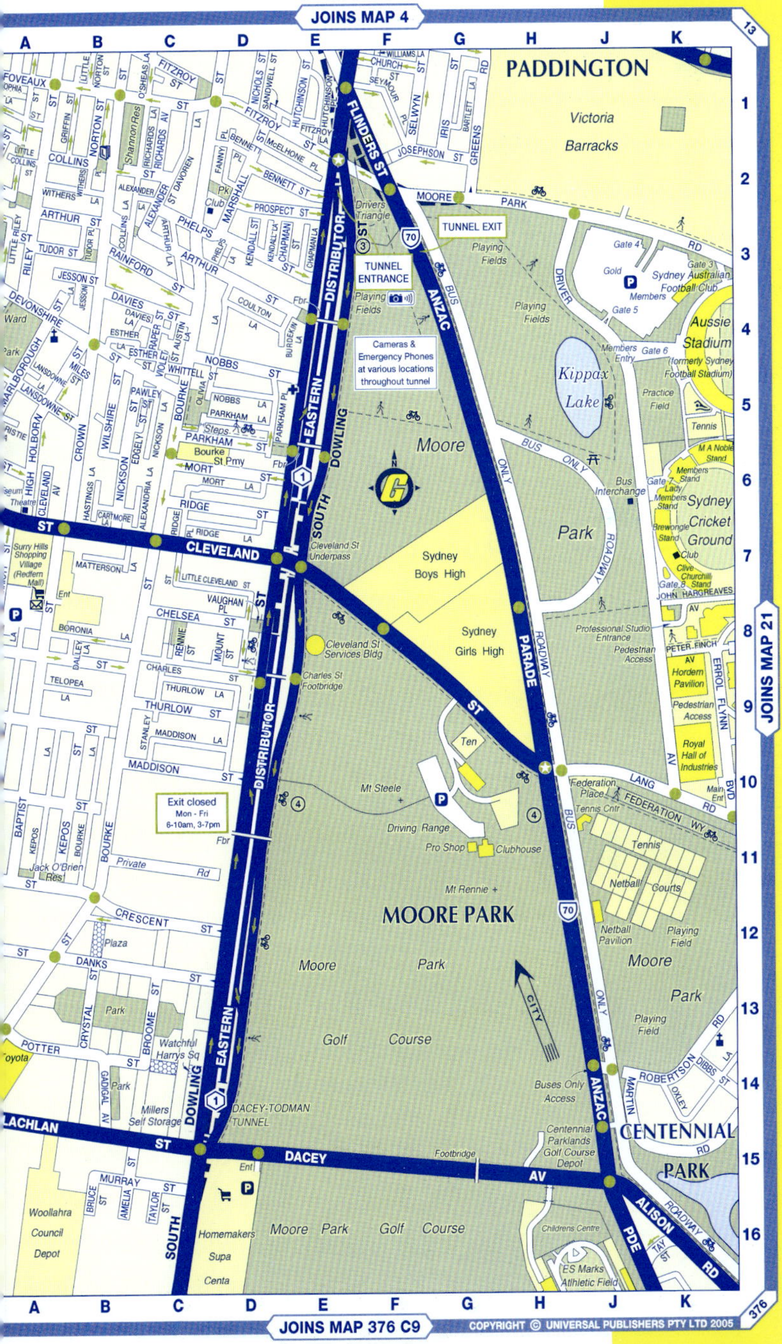
JOINS MAP 4
JOINS MAP 21
JOINS MAP 376 C9
13
376
A B C D E F G H J K
1 2 3 4 5 6 7 8 9 10 11 12 13 14 15 16
PADDINGTON
Victoria Barracks
MOORE PARK
Moore Park
Moore Park Golf Course
CENTENNIAL PARK
Kippax Lake
Aussie Stadium (formerly Sydney Football Stadium)
Sydney Cricket Ground
Sydney Australian Football Club
Sydney Boys High
Sydney Girls High
Cleveland St Services Bldg
Cleveland St Underpass
Charles St Footbridge
Drivers Triangle
TUNNEL EXIT
TUNNEL ENTRANCE
Cameras & Emergency Phones at various locations throughout tunnel
Exit closed Mon - Fri 6-10am, 3-7pm
DACEY-TODMAN TUNNEL
Surry Hills Shopping Village (Redfern Mall)
Homemakers Supa Centa
Woollahra Council Depot
Watchful Harrys Sq
Millers Self Storage
Jack O'Brien Res
Plaza
Park
Driving Range
Pro Shop
Clubhouse
Mt Steele
Mt Rennie
Ten
Federation Place
Tennis Cntr
Tennis
Netball Courts
Netball Pavilion
Playing Field
Playing Fields
Practice Field
Hordern Pavilion
Royal Hall of Industries
Professional Studio Entrance
Pedestrian Access
Bus Interchange
Buses Only Access
Centennial Parklands Golf Course Depot
Childrens Centre
ES Marks Athletic Field
Footbridge
Members Entry
Gate 4
Gate 5
Gate 6
Gate 7
Gate 8
Gate 3
M A Noble Stand
Members Stand
Lady Members Stand
Brewongle Stand
Clive Churchill Stand
Club
CLEVELAND ST
FLINDERS ST
ANZAC PARADE
EASTERN DISTRIBUTOR
SOUTH DOWLING ST
MOORE PARK RD
DACEY AV
LACHLAN ST
ALISON RD
LANG RD
FEDERATION WY
DRIVER AV
ROBERTSON RD
MARTIN RD
BUS ONLY ROADWAY
CITY
PADDINGTON
FITZROY ST
NOBBS ST
PARKHAM ST
BOURKE ST
CRESCENT ST
DANKS ST
POTTER ST
MURRAY ST
CHELSEA ST
THURLOW ST
MADDISON ST
CROWN ST
RIDGE ST
MORT ST
ARTHUR ST
COLLINS ST
DEVONSHIRE ST
JOSEPHSON ST
PETER FINCH AV
ERROL FLYNN BVD
JOHN HARGREAVES AV

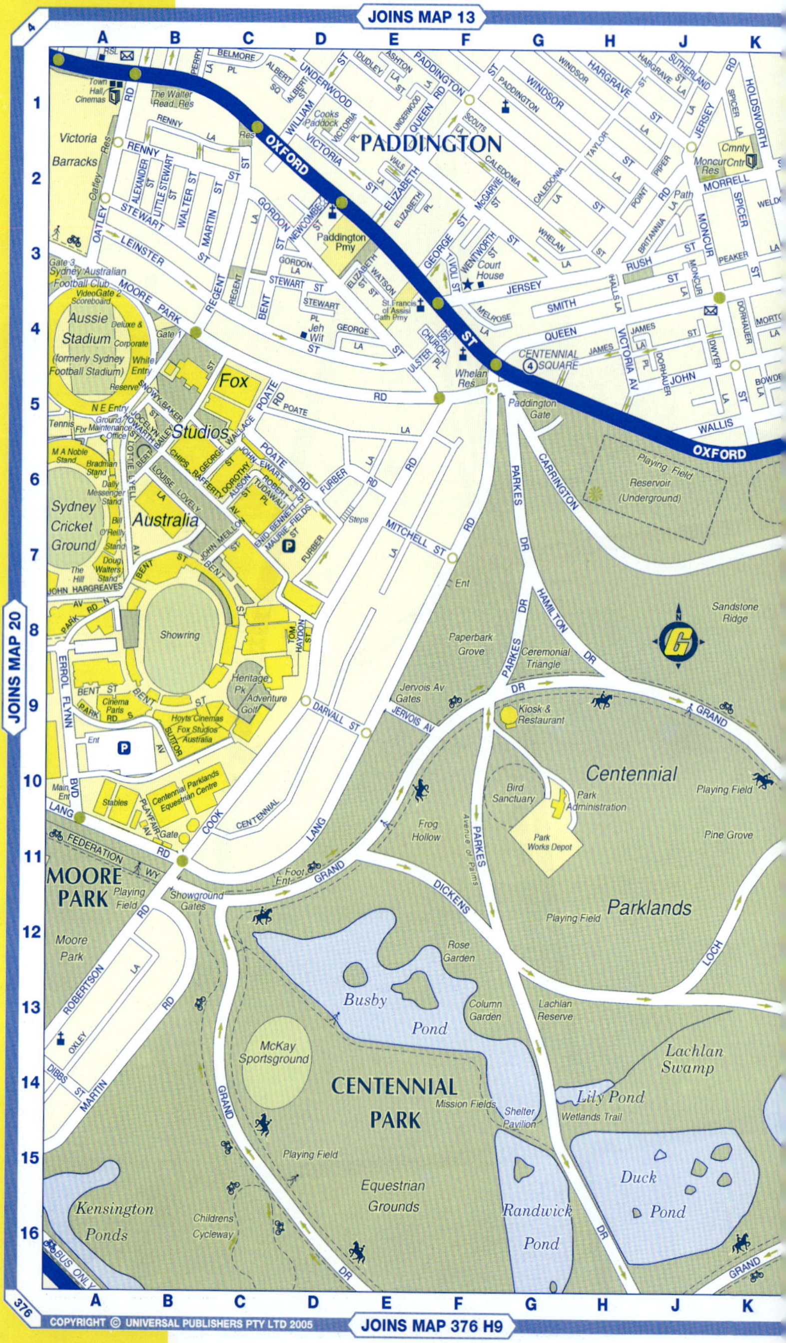

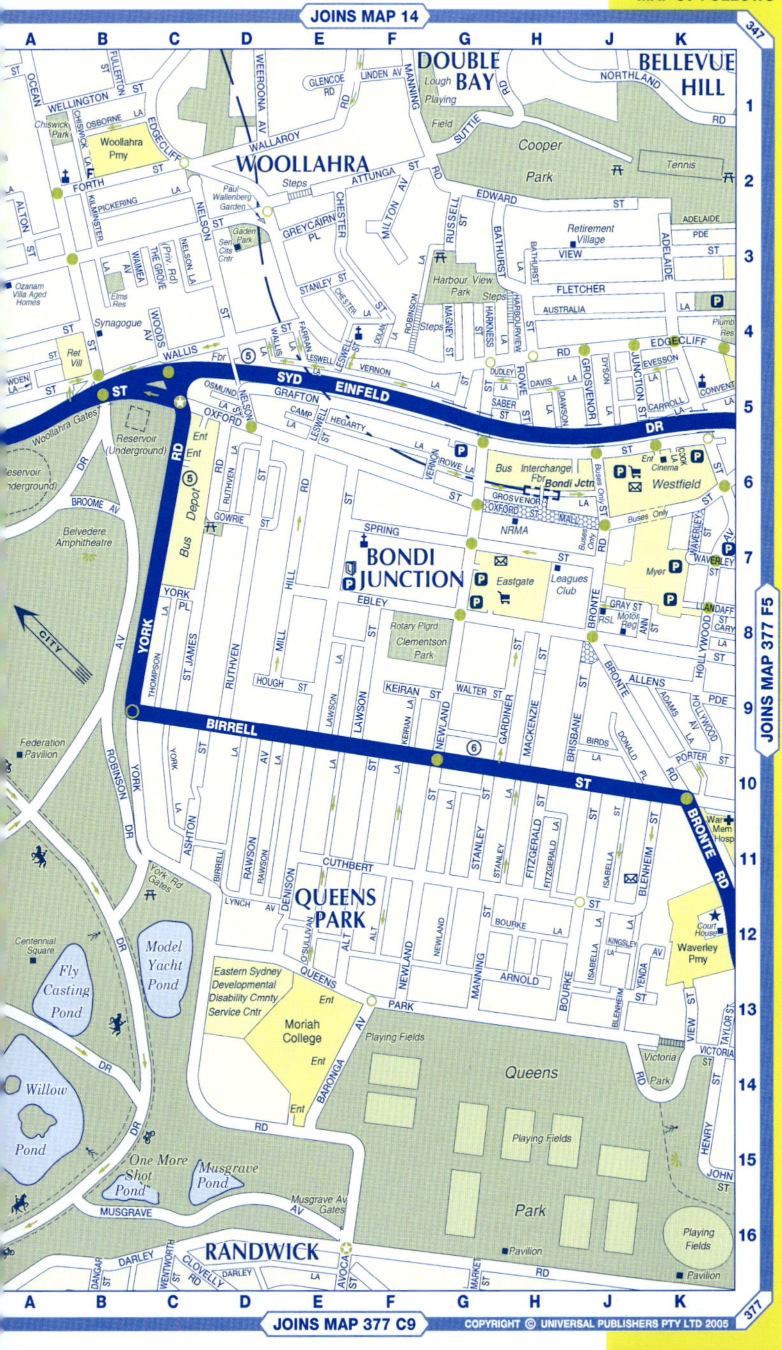

JOINS MAP 14
347
A B C D E F G H J K
1 2 3 4 5 6 7 8 9 10 11 12 13 14 15 16
DOUBLE BAY
BELLEVUE HILL
WOOLLAHRA
BONDI JUNCTION
QUEENS PARK
RANDWICK
Lough Playing Field
Cooper Park
Tennis
Retirement Village
Harbour View Park
Woollahra Pmy
Chiswick Park
Paul Wallenberg Garden
Gaden Park
Sen Cits Cntr
Ozanam Villa Aged Homes
Elms Res
Synagogue
Ret Vill
Plumb Res
Reservoir (Underground)
Woollahra Gates
Bus Depot
Belvedere Amphitheatre
Bus Interchange
Bondi Jctn
Westfield
Cinema
NRMA
Eastgate
Leagues Club
Myer
RSL
Motor Reg
Rotary Plgrd
Clementson Park
Federation Pavilion
York Rd Gates
Centennial Square
Model Yacht Pond
Fly Casting Pond
Willow Pond
One More Shot Pond
Musgrave Pond
Musgrave Av Gates
Eastern Sydney Developmental Disability Cmnty Service Cntr
Moriah College
Playing Fields
Queens Park
Pavilion
Victoria Park
War Mem Hosp
Court House
Waverley Pmy
SYD EINFELD DR
YORK RD
BIRRELL ST
BRONTE RD
OXFORD ST
EDGECLIFF RD
WALLAROY
WALLIS ST
ATTUNGA ST
EDWARD ST
FLETCHER
NORTHLAND RD
ADELAIDE PDE
ALLENS PDE
CUTHBERT
QUEENS PARK RD
DARLEY RD
MUSGRAVE AV
CITY
JOINS MAP 377 F5
JOINS MAP 377 C9
377

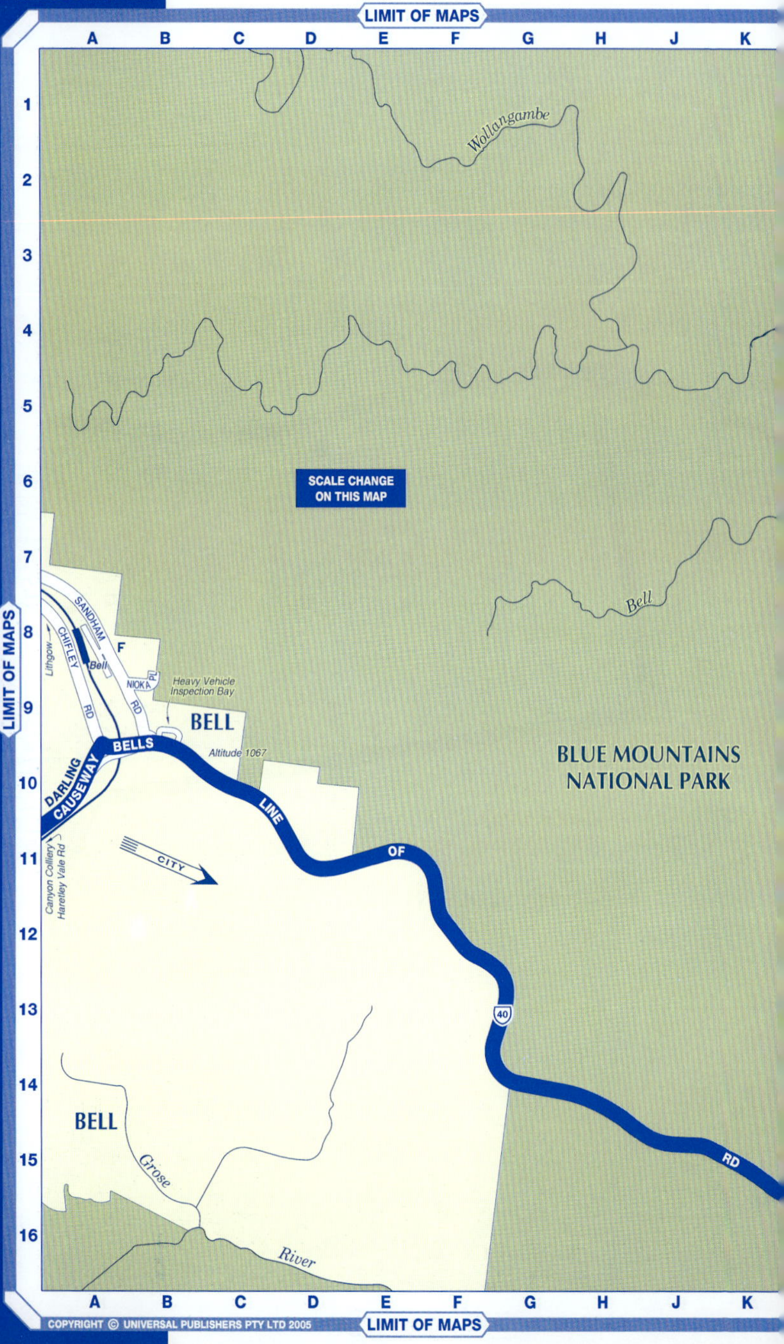

MAP 57
PREVIOUS MAP 22

Wollangambe

SCALE CHANGE ON THIS MAP

Bell

BELL
BLUE MOUNTAINS NATIONAL PARK

SANDHAM
CHIFLEY
Lithgow
Bell
NIOKA
Heavy Vehicle Inspection Bay
BELLS
Altitude 1067
DARLING CAUSEWAY
Canyon Colliery
Hareley Vale Rd
CITY
LINE OF
40
RD

BELL
Grose River

COPYRIGHT © UNIVERSAL PUBLISHERS PTY LTD 2005
LIMIT OF MAPS

MAP 58

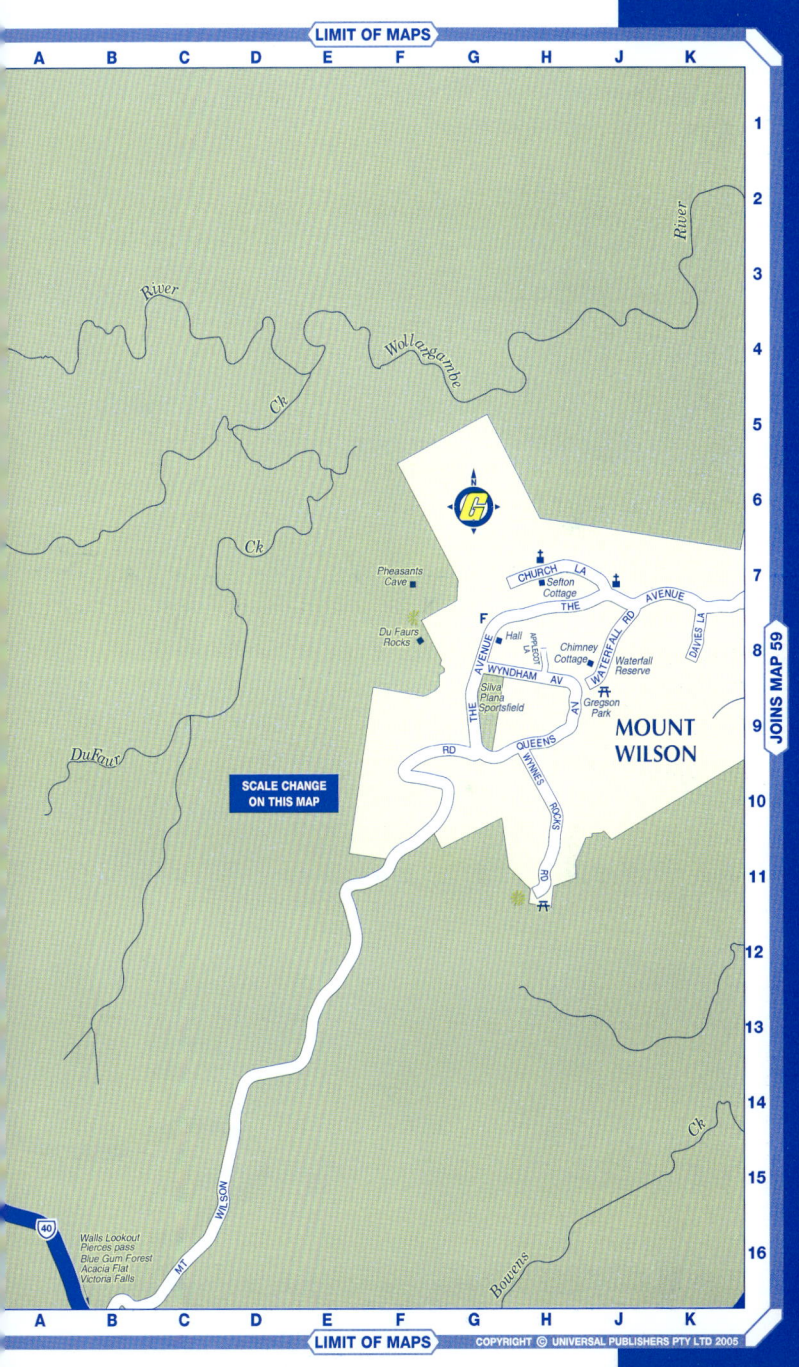

MOUNT WILSON

- Pheasants Cave
- Du Faurs Rocks
- Sefton Cottage
- Church La
- The Avenue
- Hall
- Applecott La
- Chimney Cottage
- Waterfall Reserve
- Wyndham Av
- The Avenue
- Silva Plana Sportsfield
- Waterfall Rd
- Davies La
- Gregson Park
- Queens Av
- Wynnes Rocks Rd

Du Faur
Wollangambe River
Ck

Walls Lookout
Pierces pass
Blue Gum Forest
Acacia Flat
Victoria Falls

Mt Wilson Rd
Bowens Ck

SCALE CHANGE ON THIS MAP

LIMIT OF MAPS
JOINS MAP 59

MAP 59

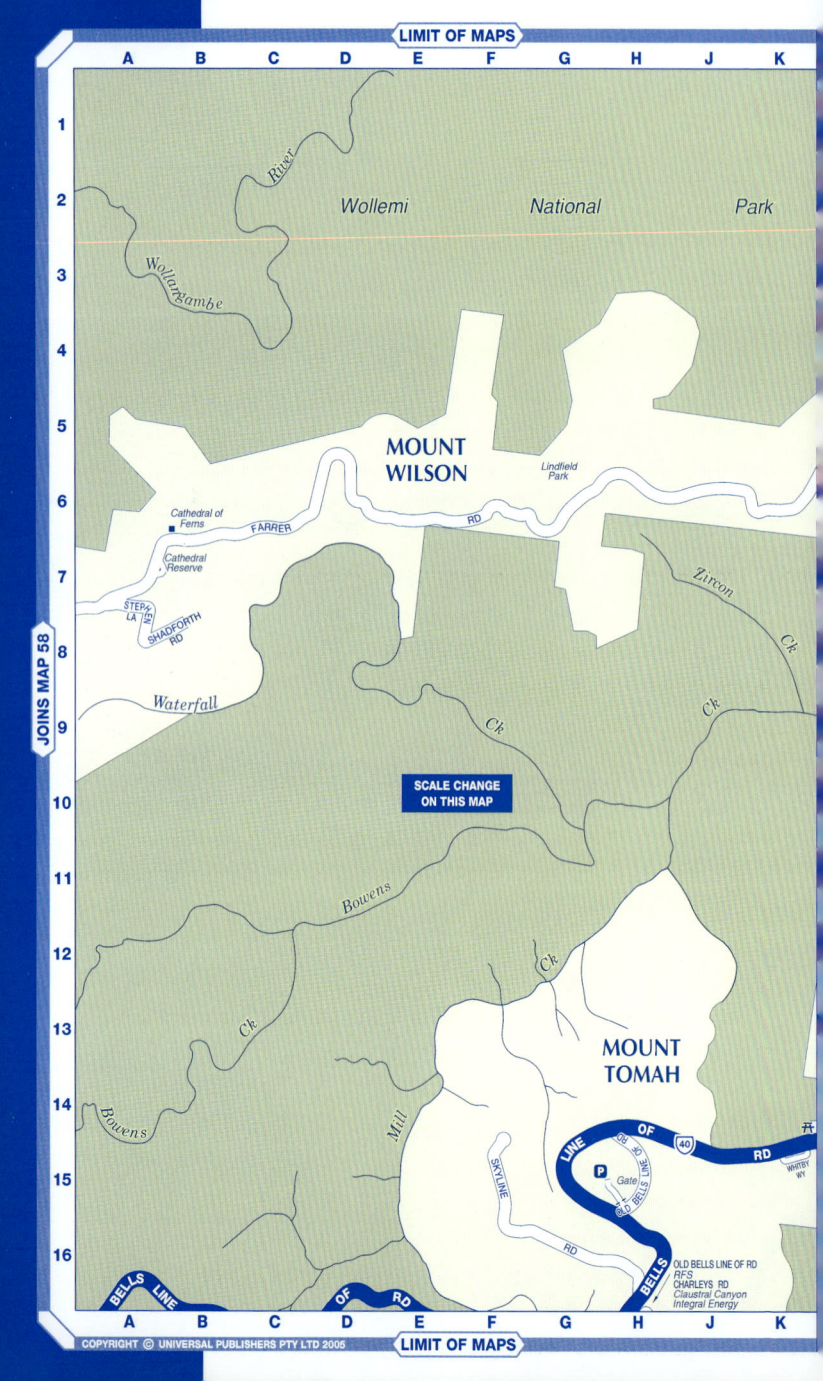

Wollemi National Park

Wollangambe River

MOUNT WILSON

Lindfield Park

Cathedral of Ferns
FARRER RD
Cathedral Reserve
STEPHEN LA
SHADFORTH RD

Zircon Ck

Waterfall Ck

SCALE CHANGE ON THIS MAP

Bowens Ck

MOUNT TOMAH

Bowens Ck

Mill Ck

SKYLINE RD

BELLS LINE OF RD (40)
OLD BELLS LINE OF RD
Gate
WHITBY WY

OLD BELLS LINE OF RD
RFS
CHARLEYS RD
Claustral Canyon
Integral Energy

BELLS LINE OF RD

LIMIT OF MAPS

JOINS MAP 58

COPYRIGHT © UNIVERSAL PUBLISHERS PTY LTD 2005

MAP 60

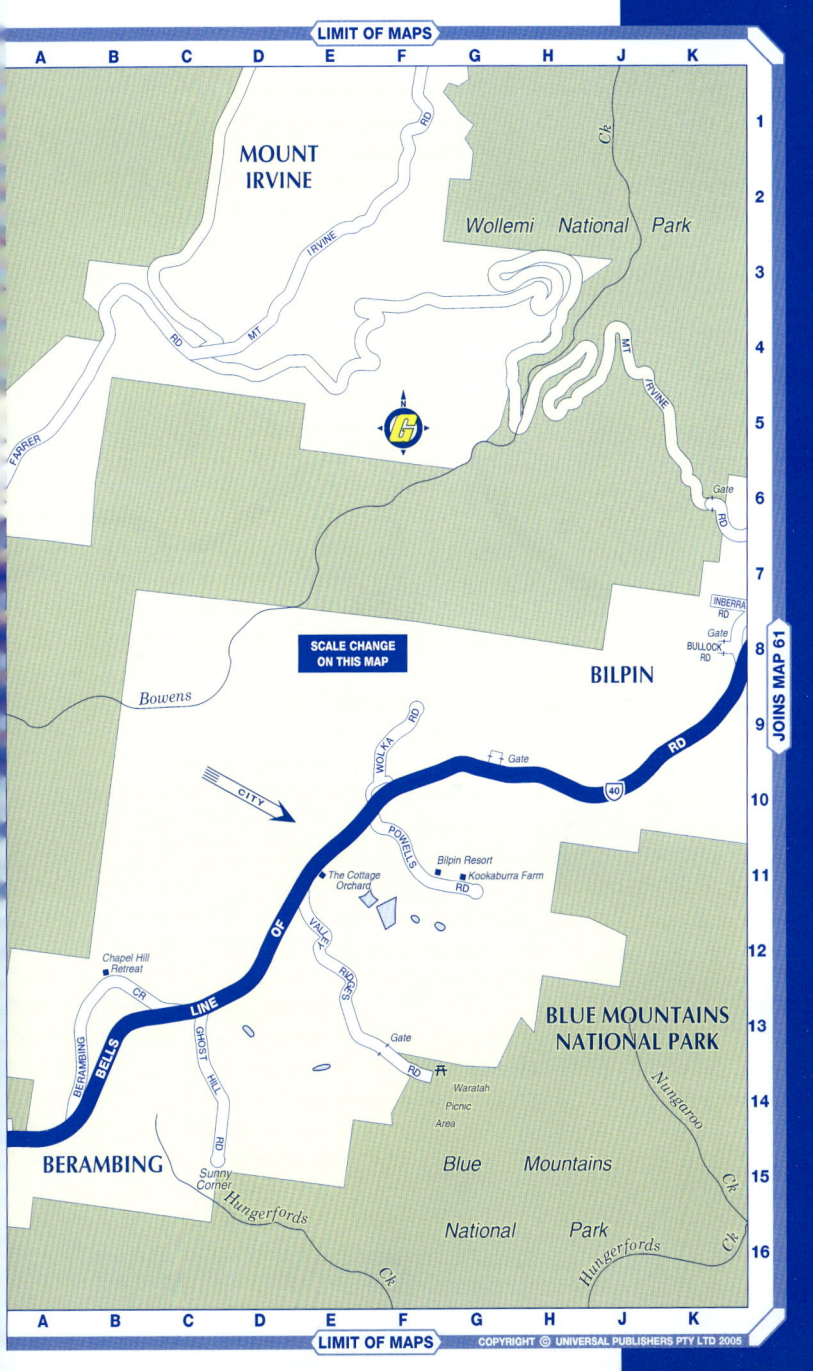

MAP 61

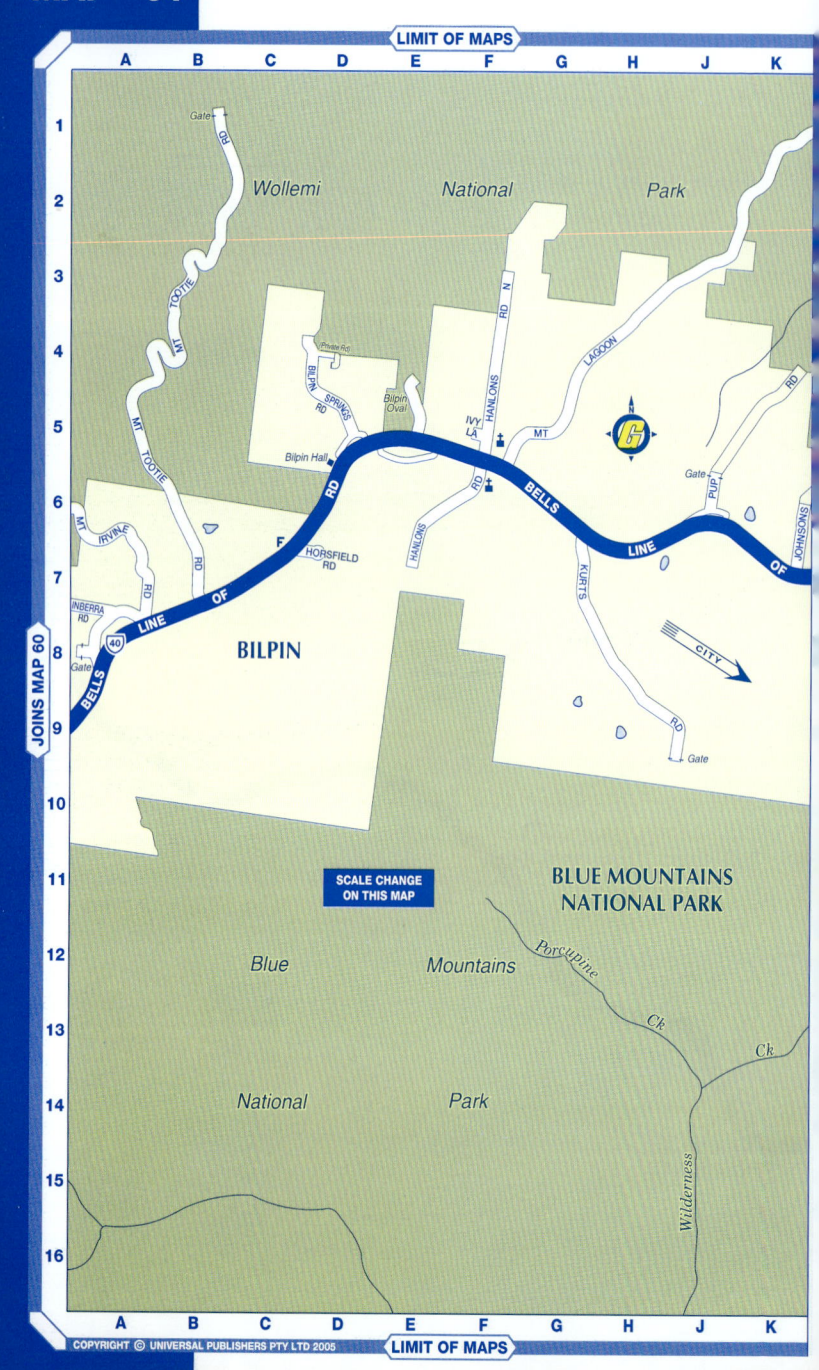

MAP 62

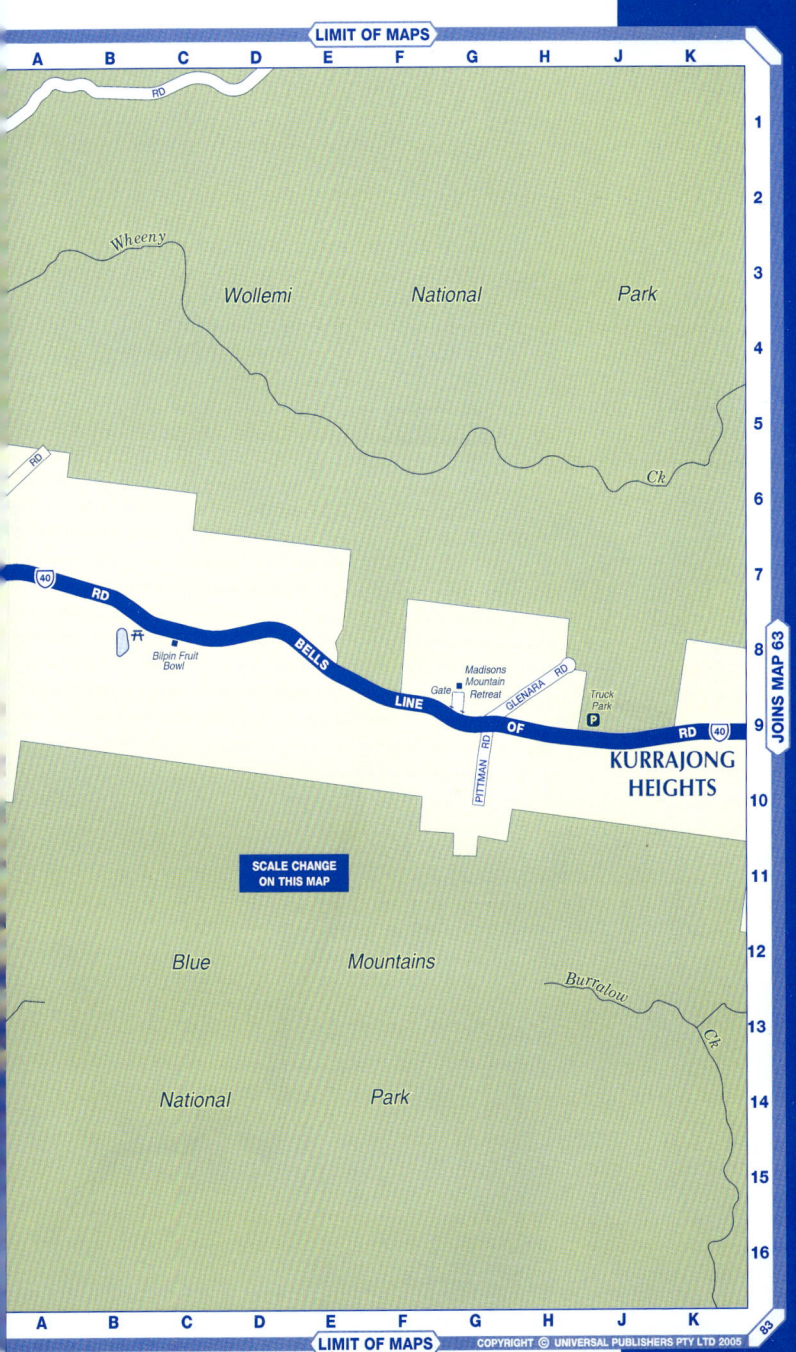

- Wheeny
- Wollemi National Park
- Ck
- RD
- BELLS LINE OF RD
- Bilpin Fruit Bowl
- Madisons Mountain Retreat
- Gate
- PITTMAN RD
- GLENARA RD
- Truck Park
- KURRAJONG HEIGHTS
- SCALE CHANGE ON THIS MAP
- Blue Mountains National Park
- Burralow Ck

LIMIT OF MAPS

JOINS MAP 63

COPYRIGHT © UNIVERSAL PUBLISHERS PTY LTD 2005

MAP 63

MAP 64

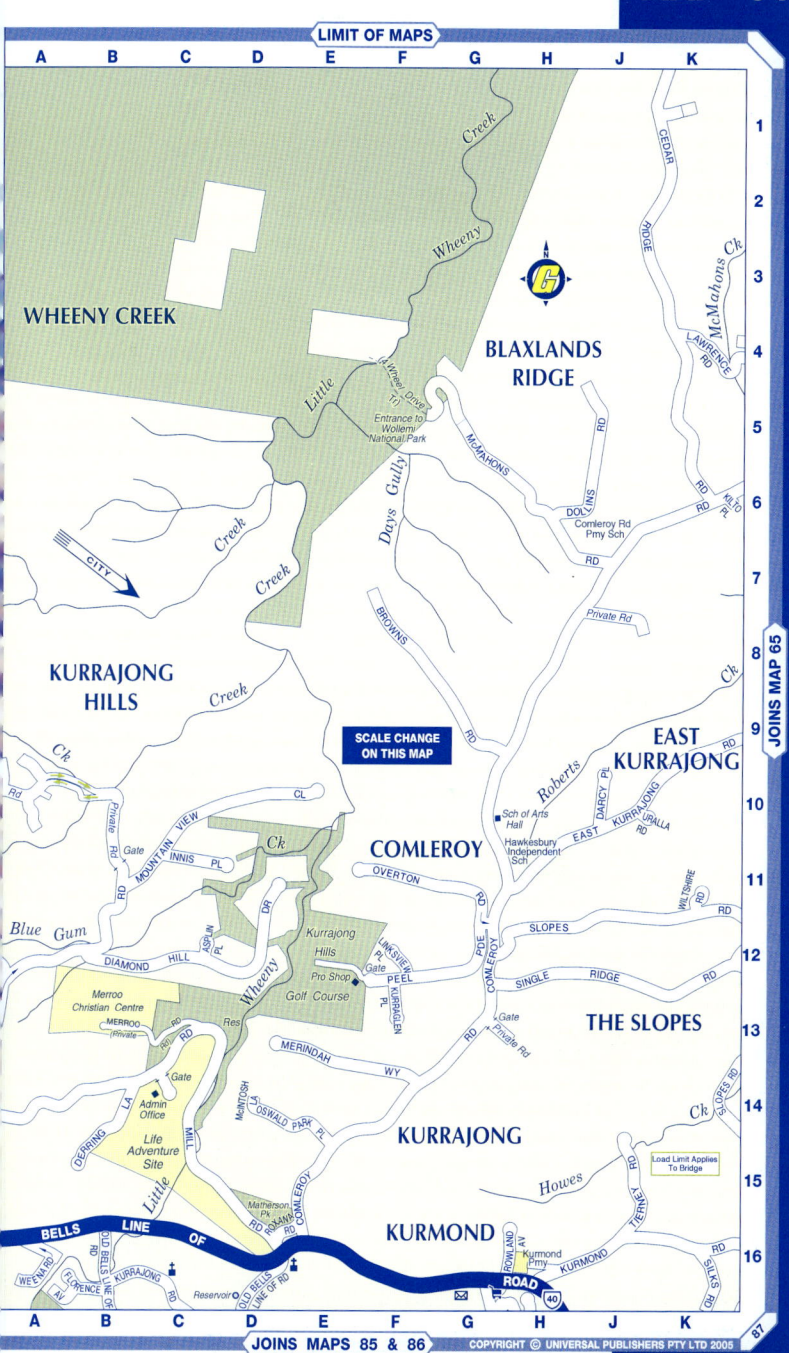

Locations
- WHEENY CREEK
- BLAXLANDS RIDGE
- KURRAJONG HILLS
- COMLEROY
- EAST KURRAJONG
- THE SLOPES
- KURRAJONG
- KURMOND

Notable features
- Entrance to Wollemi National Park
- Comleroy Rd Pmy Sch
- Sch of Arts Hall
- Hawkesbury Independent Sch
- Kurrajong Hills Pro Shop Golf Course
- Merroo Christian Centre
- Admin Office
- Life Adventure Site
- Matherson Pk
- Reservoir
- Kurmond Pmy
- Load Limit Applies To Bridge
- SCALE CHANGE ON THIS MAP

Roads and streets
- Wheeny Creek
- Little Creek
- Days Gully
- McMahons Rd
- Dolins Rd
- Kelso Pl
- Lawrence Rd
- Cedar Ridge
- McMahons Ck
- Browns Rd
- Private Rd
- Roberts Ck
- Darcy Pl
- East Kurrajong Rd
- Uralla Rd
- Wiltshire Rd
- Overton Rd
- Comleroy Rd
- Slopes Rd
- Single Ridge Rd
- Linksley Pde
- Peel Pl
- Kurraglen Pl
- Mountain View Rd
- Innis Pl
- Aspin Pl
- Diamond Hill Dr
- Wheeny Dr
- Blue Gum Rd
- Private Rd
- Merindah Wy
- McIntosh La
- Oswald Park
- Merroo Rd
- Gerring La
- Mill Rd
- Little Comleroy Rd
- Bells Line Of Road
- Old Bells Line Of Rd
- Kurrajong Rd
- Florence Rd
- We'ena Rd
- Rowland Av
- Kurmond Rd
- Tetney Rd
- Sills Rd
- Howes Rd
- Slopes Rd
- CL

Map edges
- LIMIT OF MAPS (top)
- JOINS MAP 65 (right)
- JOINS MAPS 85 & 86 (bottom)
- CITY (arrow)

COPYRIGHT © UNIVERSAL PUBLISHERS PTY LTD 2005

MAP 65

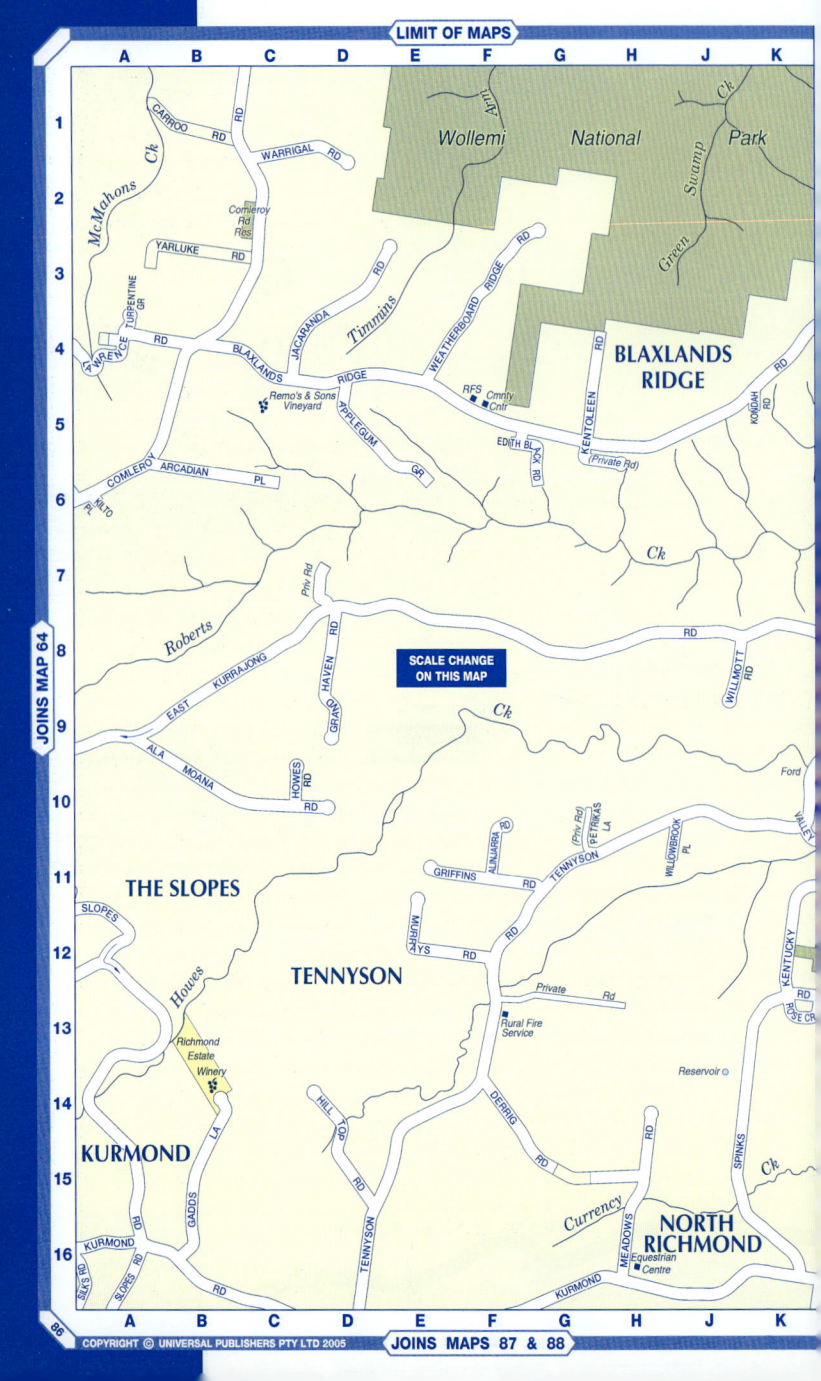

Wollemi National Park
Green Swamp Ck

BLAXLANDS RIDGE

THE SLOPES

TENNYSON

KURMOND

NORTH RICHMOND

McMahons Ck
Carroo Rd
Warrigal Rd
Comleroy Rd Res
Yarluke Rd
Turpentine Gr
Lawrence Rd
Jacaranda Rd
Timmins Rd
Weatherboard Ridge Rd
Kentoleen Rd
Korigh Rd
Blaxlands Ridge
Remo's & Sons Vineyard
Applegum Gr
RFS
Cmnty Cntr
Edith Black Rd
(Private Rd)
Comleroy Pl
Arcadian Pl
Rialto
Ck
Roberts Rd
Priv Rd
East Kurrajong Rd
Grady Haven Rd
Willmott Rd
SCALE CHANGE ON THIS MAP
Ck
Ala Moana
Howes Rd
Ford
Griffins Rd
Alinarra Rd
Priv Rd
Petriks La
Willowbrook Pl
Tennyson Rd
Murrays Rd
Kentucky Rd
Rose Cr
Private Rd
Rural Fire Service
Slopes Rd
Howes La
Richmond Estate Winery
Hill Rd
Derrig Rd
Reservoir
Spinks Ck
Gadds La
Tennyson Rd
Currency
Meadows
Equestrian Centre
Kurmond Rd
Sks Rd
Slopes Rd

JOINS MAP 64
JOINS MAPS 87 & 88
LIMIT OF MAPS

COPYRIGHT © UNIVERSAL PUBLISHERS PTY LTD 2005

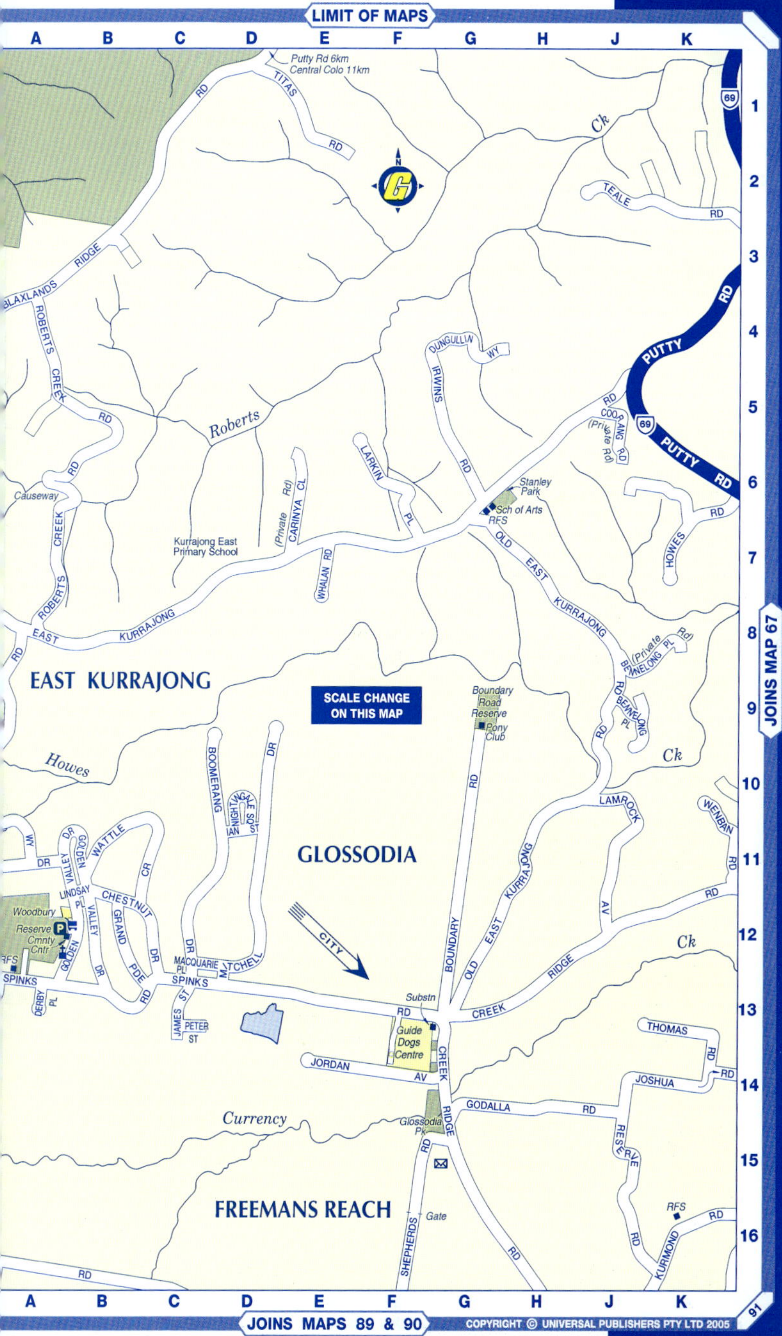
LIMIT OF MAPS
A B C D E F G H J K
1 2 3 4 5 6 7 8 9 10 11 12 13 14 15 16
Putty Rd 6km
Central Colo 11km
TITAS RD
BLAXLANDS RIDGE RD
ROBERTS CREEK RD
Causeway
Roberts
Ck
TEALE RD
PUTTY RD
69
DUNGULLIN WY
IRWINS RD
LARKIN PL
CARINYA CL
(Private Rd)
WHALAN RD
COORANG RD
(Private Rd)
Stanley Park
Sch of Arts
RFS
OLD EAST KURRAJONG RD
Kurrajong East Primary School
EAST KURRAJONG RD
HOWES RD
BENELONG PL
(Private Rd)
BENELONG PL
JOINS MAP 67
EAST KURRAJONG
SCALE CHANGE ON THIS MAP
Boundary Road Reserve
Pony Club
Howes
Ck
BOOMERANG DR
NIGHTINGALE SQ
IAN ST
LAMROCK AV
WENBAN RD
GLOSSODIA
WATTLE CR
GOLDEN VALLEY DR
WY
DR
LINDSAY PL
CHESTNUT DR
GRAND PDE
VALLEY DR
Woodbury Reserve
Cmnty Cntr
RFS
SPINKS RD
MACQUARIE PL
MITCHELL DR
CITY
BOUNDARY RD
OLD EAST KURRAJONG RD
RIDGE RD
Ck
DERBY PL
JAMES ST
PETER ST
Substn
Guide Dogs Centre
CREEK RIDGE RD
JORDAN AV
THOMAS RD
JOSHUA RD
GODALLA RD
RESERVE RD
Currency
Glossodia Pk
FREEMANS REACH
SHEPHERDS RD
Gate
RFS
KURMOND RD
RD
JOINS MAPS 89 & 90

MAP 67

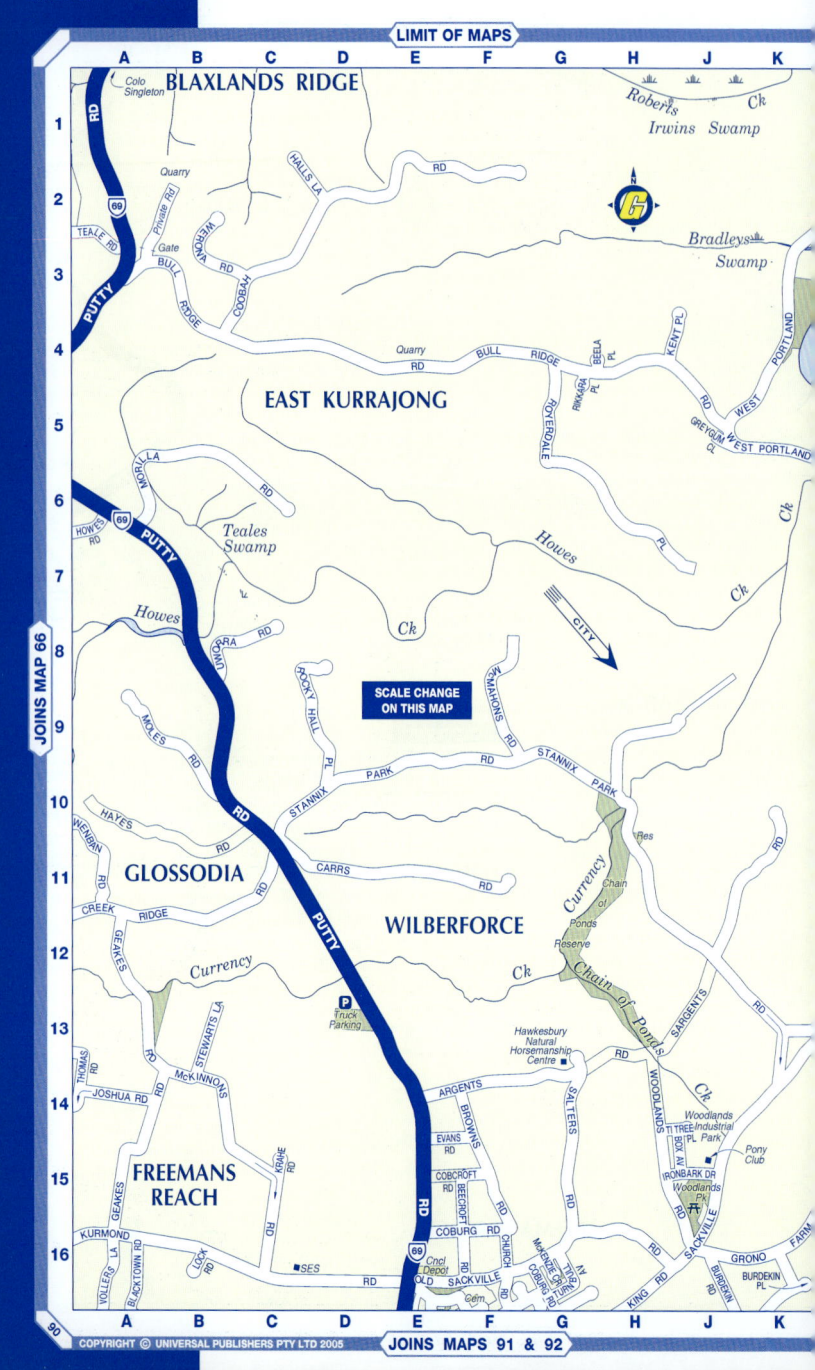

BLAXLANDS RIDGE

Roberts Ck
Irwins Swamp
Bradleys Swamp

EAST KURRAJONG

WEST PORTLAND

Teales Swamp

Howes Ck

SCALE CHANGE ON THIS MAP

CITY

GLOSSODIA

WILBERFORCE

Currency Chain of Ponds Reserve

Hawkesbury Natural Horsemanship Centre

Woodlands Industrial Park
Pony Club
Woodlands Pk

FREEMANS REACH

SACKVILLE

JOINS MAP 66
JOINS MAPS 91 & 92
LIMIT OF MAPS

COPYRIGHT © UNIVERSAL PUBLISHERS PTY LTD 2005

MAP 68

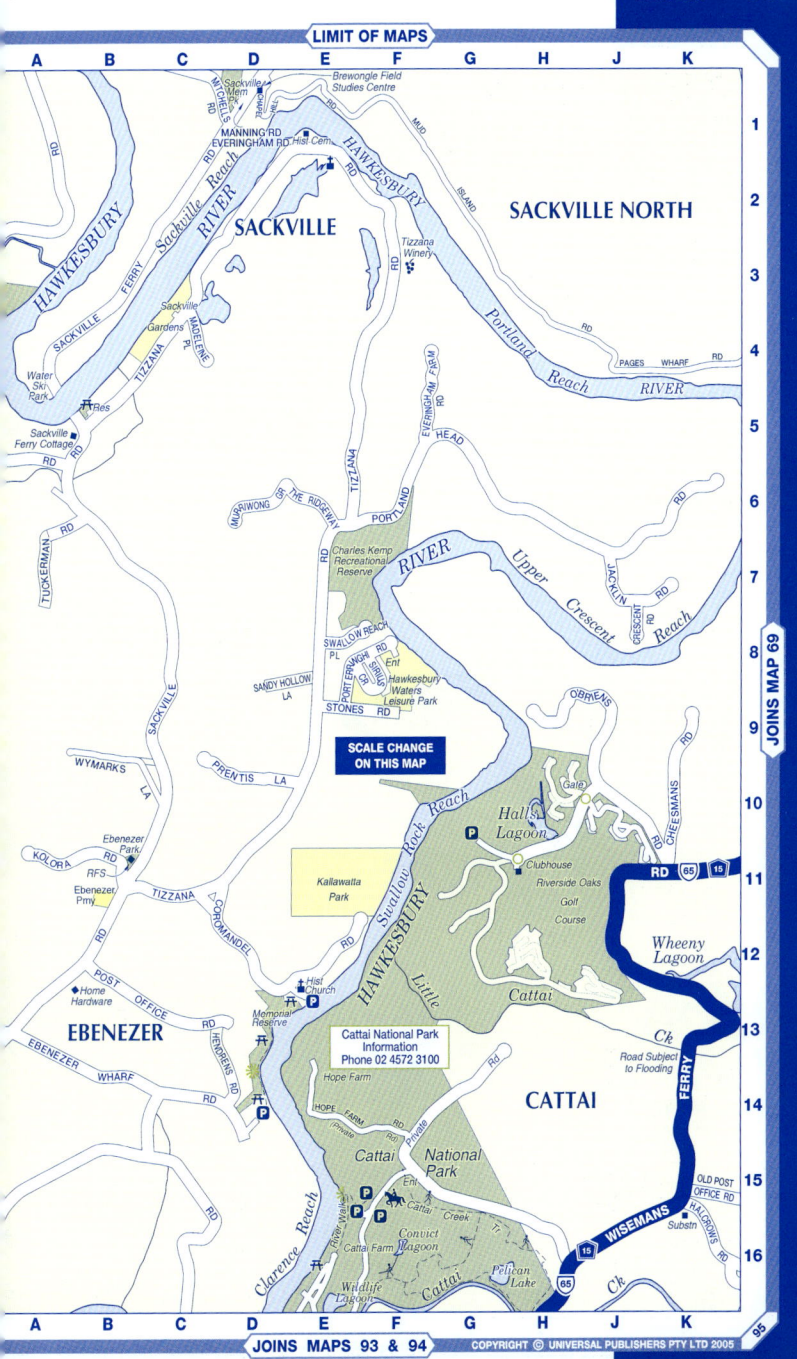

MAP 69

LIMIT OF MAPS

SACKVILLE NORTH

Sackville Ferry 6km
CLIFTONVILLE RD
WEAVERS RD
Old Northern Rd 5km
Wisemans Ferry 17km

TUFF LA
GALLAGHERS RD
SACKVILLE FERRY RD
DAYS RD
BLUEGUM RD
WISEMANS FERRY RD
PAGES WHARF
Bonnie View
Pacific Park Water Ski Gdns
Kiosk
Gate
PACIFIC PARK DR
(Private Rd) Gate
Motocross Track
Lower Crescent Reach
HAWKESBURY R.

SOUTH MAROOTA

Palls Res
Sth Maroota Pre-School
KEARNEY RD

SCALE CHANGE ON THIS MAP

RFS
FLOYDS RD
WISEMANS FERRY RD
WHEENY CREEK RD
CHILVERS LA
VIRTLE RD

Wheeny Lagoon
Little Cattai

Broadwater Swamp

CATTAI

OLD POST OFFICE RD
HALCROWS RD
Fair Ck
Kellys Ck
Blue Gum

JOINS MAP 68

JOINS MAPS 95 & 96

COPYRIGHT © UNIVERSAL PUBLISHERS PTY LTD 2005

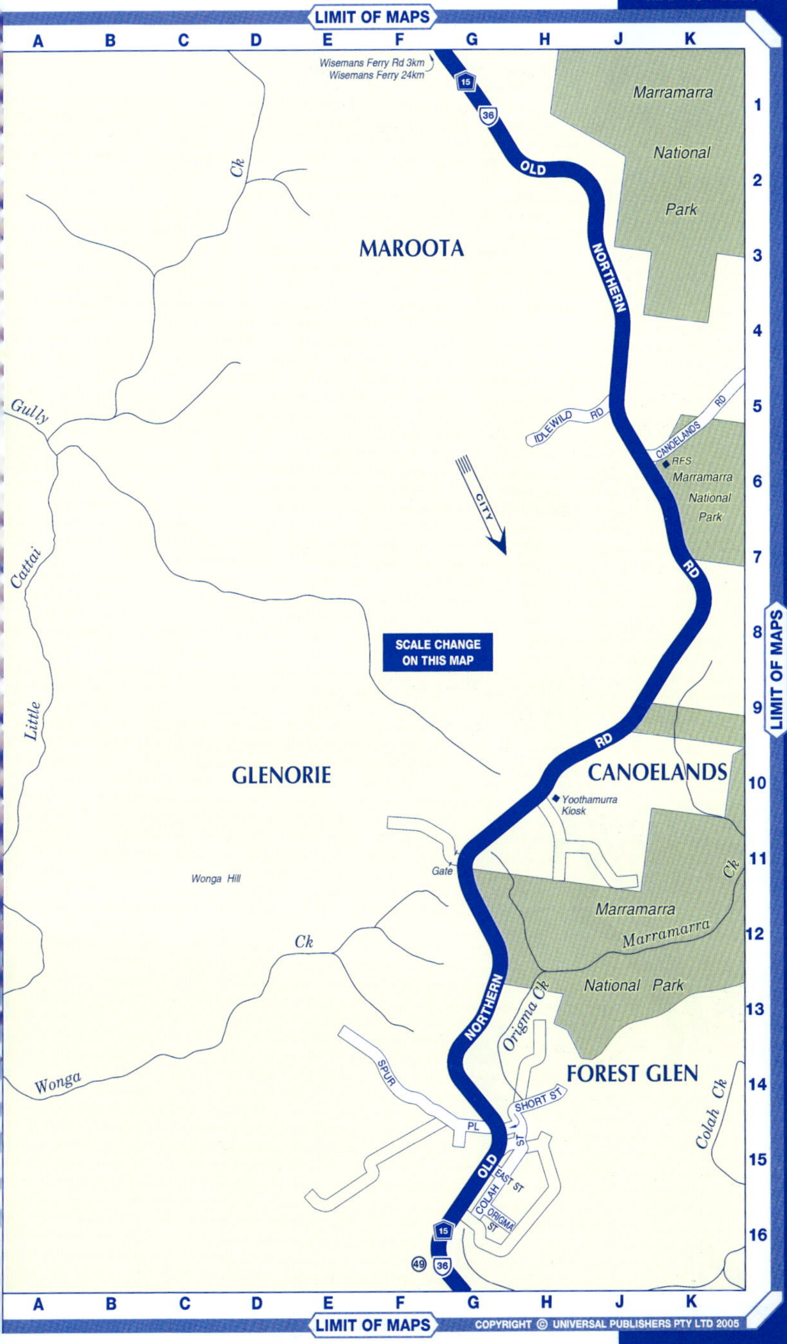

MAP 70
MAP 75 FOLLOWS

Marramarra National Park

MAROOTA

Wisemans Ferry Rd 3km
Wisemans Ferry 24km

OLD NORTHERN RD

IDLEWILD RD

CANOELANDS RD

RFS Marramarra National Park

CITY

SCALE CHANGE ON THIS MAP

GLENORIE

CANOELANDS

Yoothamurra Kiosk

Gate

Wonga Hill

Ck

Marramarra National Park

Wonga

SPUR

Origma Cr

FOREST GLEN

SHORT ST

PL

OLD NORTHERN RD

COLAH EAST ST

ORIGMA ST

Colah Ck

Little Cattai Ck

Gully

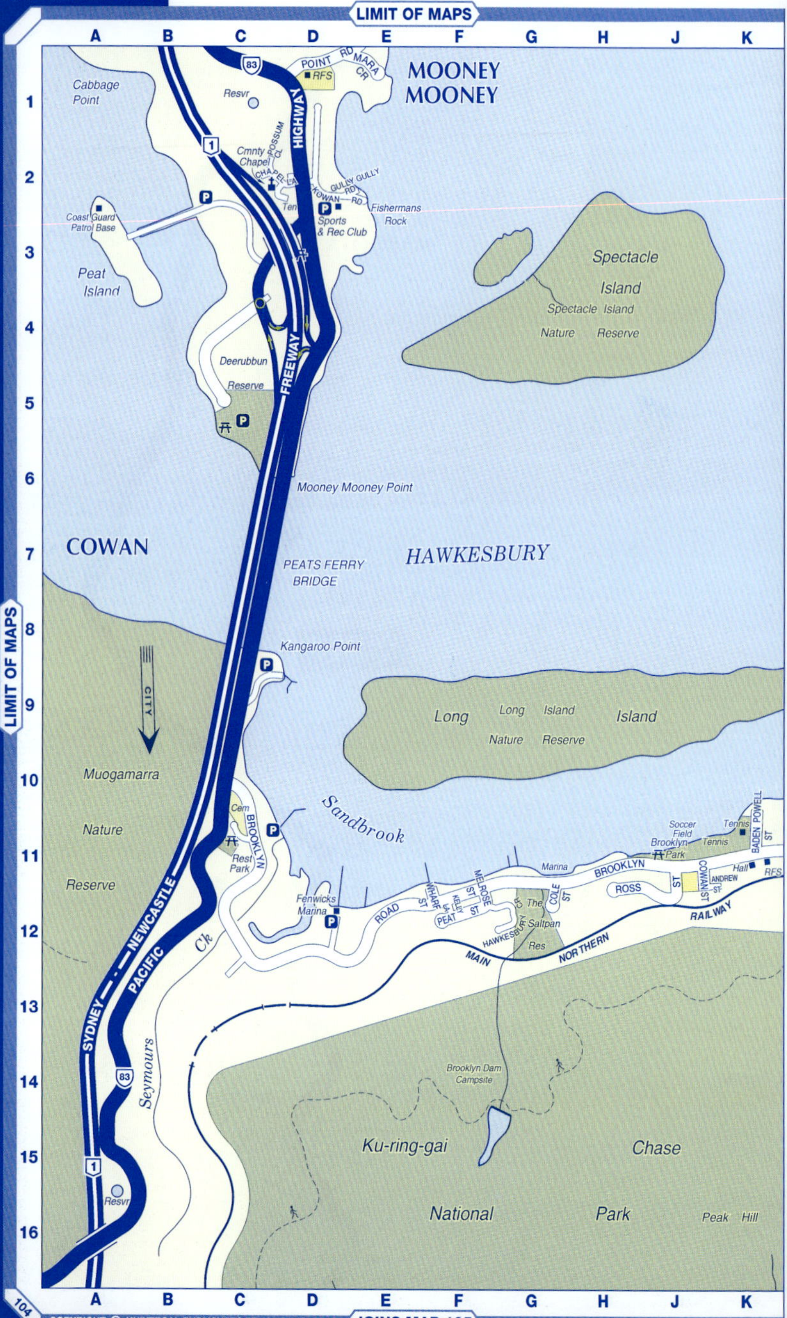
LIMIT OF MAPS
A B C D E F G H J K
1 2 3 4 5 6 7 8 9 10 11 12 13 14 15 16
MOONEY MOONEY
Cabbage Point
Resvr
POINT RD
MARA CR
RFS
HIGHWAY
83
1
POSSUM CL
Cmnty Chapel
CHAPEL LA
GULLY GULLY RD
KOWAN RD
Ten
Sports & Rec Club
Fishermans Rock
Coast Guard Patrol Base
Peat Island
Spectacle Island
Spectacle Island Nature Reserve
Deerubbun Reserve
FREEWAY
Mooney Mooney Point
COWAN
HAWKESBURY
PEATS FERRY BRIDGE
Kangaroo Point
CITY
Long Island
Long Island Nature Reserve
Muogamarra Nature Reserve
Sandbrook
Cem
BROOKLYN
Rest Park
Fenwicks Marina
ROAD
WHARF ST
MELROSE ST
KELLY ST
PEAT LA
HAWKESBURY CR
The Saltpan
Res
COLE ST
Marina
BROOKLYN
ROSS
ST
COWAN ST
ANDREW ST
Hall
RFS
RAILWAY
MAIN NORTHERN
Soccer Field
Brooklyn Park
Tennis
BADEN POWELL ST
SYDNEY - NEWCASTLE
PACIFIC
Ck
Seymours
Brooklyn Dam Campsite
Ku-ring-gai National Park Chase
Peak Hill
LIMIT OF MAPS
JOINS MAP 105

MAP 76
MAP 83 FOLLOWS

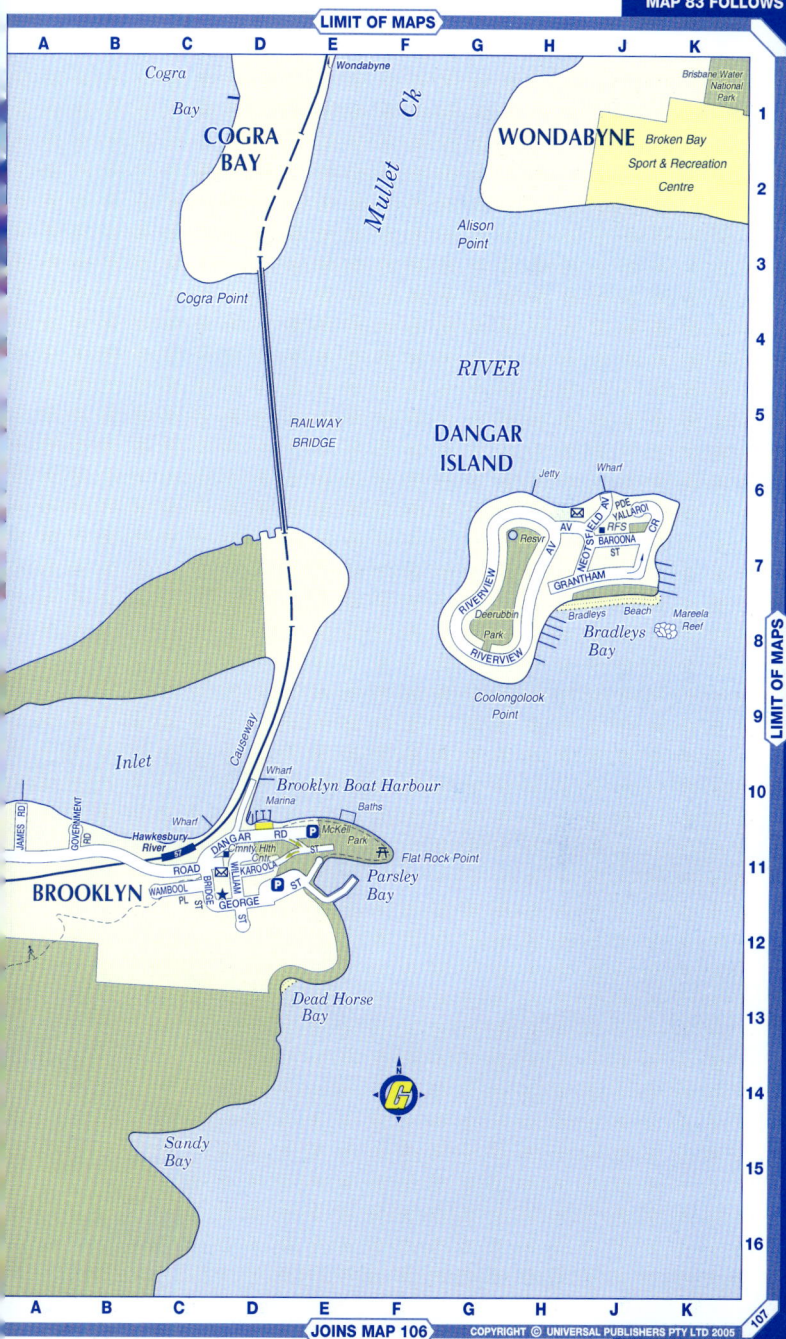

LIMIT OF MAPS

- Cogra Bay
- **COGRA BAY**
- Wondabyne
- Mullet Ck
- **WONDABYNE** Broken Bay Sport & Recreation Centre
- Brisbane Water National Park
- Cogra Point
- Alison Point
- RIVER
- RAILWAY BRIDGE
- **DANGAR ISLAND**
- Jetty
- Wharf
- RIVERVIEW AV
- Resvr
- POE
- VALLAROI
- NEOTSFIELD AV
- RFS
- BAROONA ST
- GRANTHAM CR
- Deerubbin Park
- RIVERVIEW
- Bradleys Beach
- Bradleys Bay
- Mareela Reef
- Coolongolook Point
- Inlet
- Wharf
- Brooklyn Boat Harbour
- Marina
- Baths
- McKell Park
- Flat Rock Point
- Wharf
- Hawkesbury River
- DANGAR RD
- Trinity Hlth Cntr
- KAROOLA ST
- Parsley Bay
- **BROOKLYN**
- JAMES RD
- GOVERNMENT RD
- BRIDGE ST
- WAMBOOL PL
- GEORGE ST
- MINTON ST
- Dead Horse Bay
- Sandy Bay

JOINS MAP 106

COPYRIGHT © UNIVERSAL PUBLISHERS PTY LTD 2005

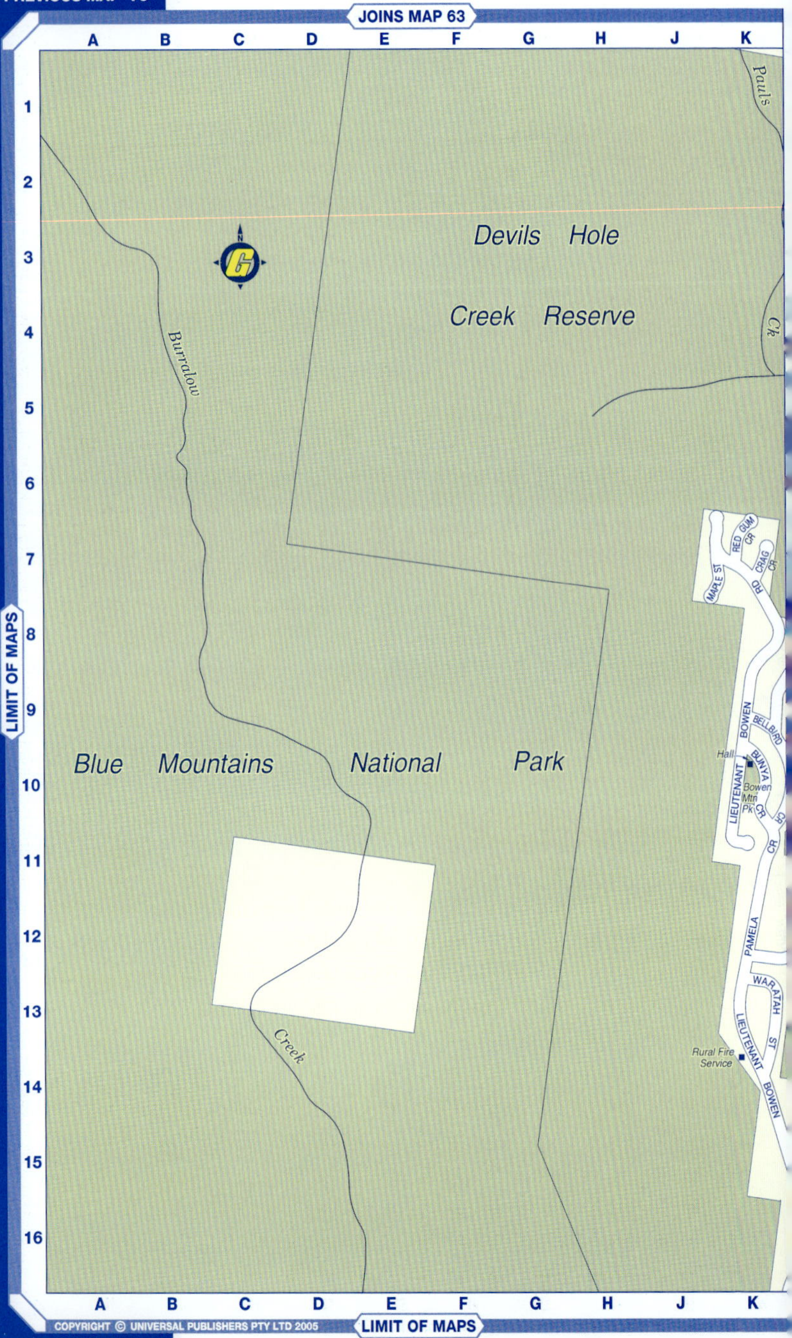

MAP 83
PREVIOUS MAP 76

JOINS MAP 63

Devils Hole

Creek Reserve

Burralow

Blue Mountains National Park

Creek

Pauls Ck

RED GUM CR
MAPLE ST
CRAG RD
BELLBIRD
BOWEN
BUNYA CR
LIEUTENANT
Hall
Bowen Mtn Pk
BOWEN ST
PAMELA
WARATAH
LIEUTENANT BOWEN
Rural Fire Service

LIMIT OF MAPS

LIMIT OF MAPS

COPYRIGHT © UNIVERSAL PUBLISHERS PTY LTD 2005

MAP 84

KURRAJONG HEIGHTS

KURRAJONG HILLS

KURRAJONG

BOWEN MOUNTAIN

GROSE VALE

- Baggers La
- Little Wheeny Ck
- Devils Hole Ck
- Willow Glen Rd
- Horans La
- Pattersons La (Private Rd)
- Grose Vale Rd
- Westbury Rd
- Carters Rd
- Bowen Mountain Rd
- Serpentine Rd
- Grandview Rd
- Gunnover
- Wattle St
- Bowen Mountain Rd
- Blackbird Cr
- Rawong Cr
- Cabbage Tree Pine Rd Pl
- Enniskillen Orchard
- Bellbird Ck
- Grose La
- Weem Rd
- Ck
- Private Rd / Gate
- CITY

JOINS MAP 63
JOINS MAP 85
LIMIT OF MAPS
COPYRIGHT © UNIVERSAL PUBLISHERS PTY LTD 2005

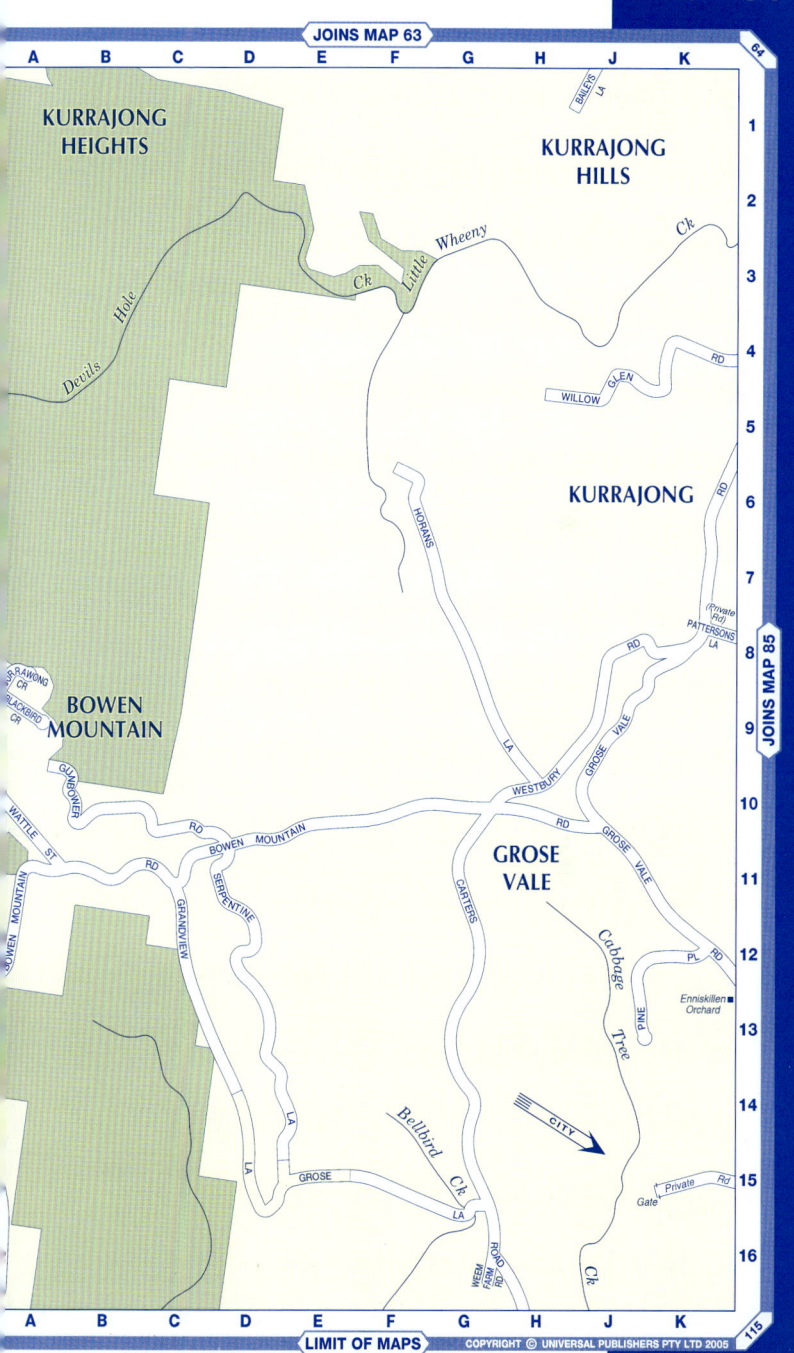

MAP 85

JOINS MAP 64 (top)
JOINS MAP 115 (bottom)
JOINS MAP 84 (left)
JOINS MAP 83 (top left)

Key locations and features:

Kurrajong area:
- Little Wheeney Ck
- Florence Av
- McMahons Park / Soccer
- Mamahons Park Rd
- Old Bells Line of Rd
- Kurrajong Rd
- Woodburn Rd
- Bells Line of Road
- Vincent Rd
- Reservoir
- Country Womens Association
- Memorial Pk
- RFS
- Kurrajong & District Cmnty Nurs Home
- Kurrajong Pmy
- Tennis
- Bickett Rd
- Timms Hill Rd
- Lenords St
- Sherwood St
- Drummond St
- Catherine St
- Robertson St
- KURRAJONG
- Willow Glen Rd
- Cem
- Grose Vale Rd
- Tates La
- Greggs
- Redbank Creek
- Kuype Christian
- Pattersons La (Private Rd)
- Bells Road
- Ginahgullah Av
- Bells Rd

Grose Vale / Grose Wold area:
- GROSE VALE
- Grose Vale Rd
- Bells Rd
- Enniskillen Orchard
- Community Centre
- Grose Vale Community Centre
- RFS
- Private Rd
- Cabbage Tree
- Grose Wold Rd
- Duffy Av
- Phillip La
- Kaldow
- GROSE WOLD
- Grose Vale Conference Centre
- Charley Road

COPYRIGHT © UNIVERSAL PUBLISHERS PTY LTD 2005

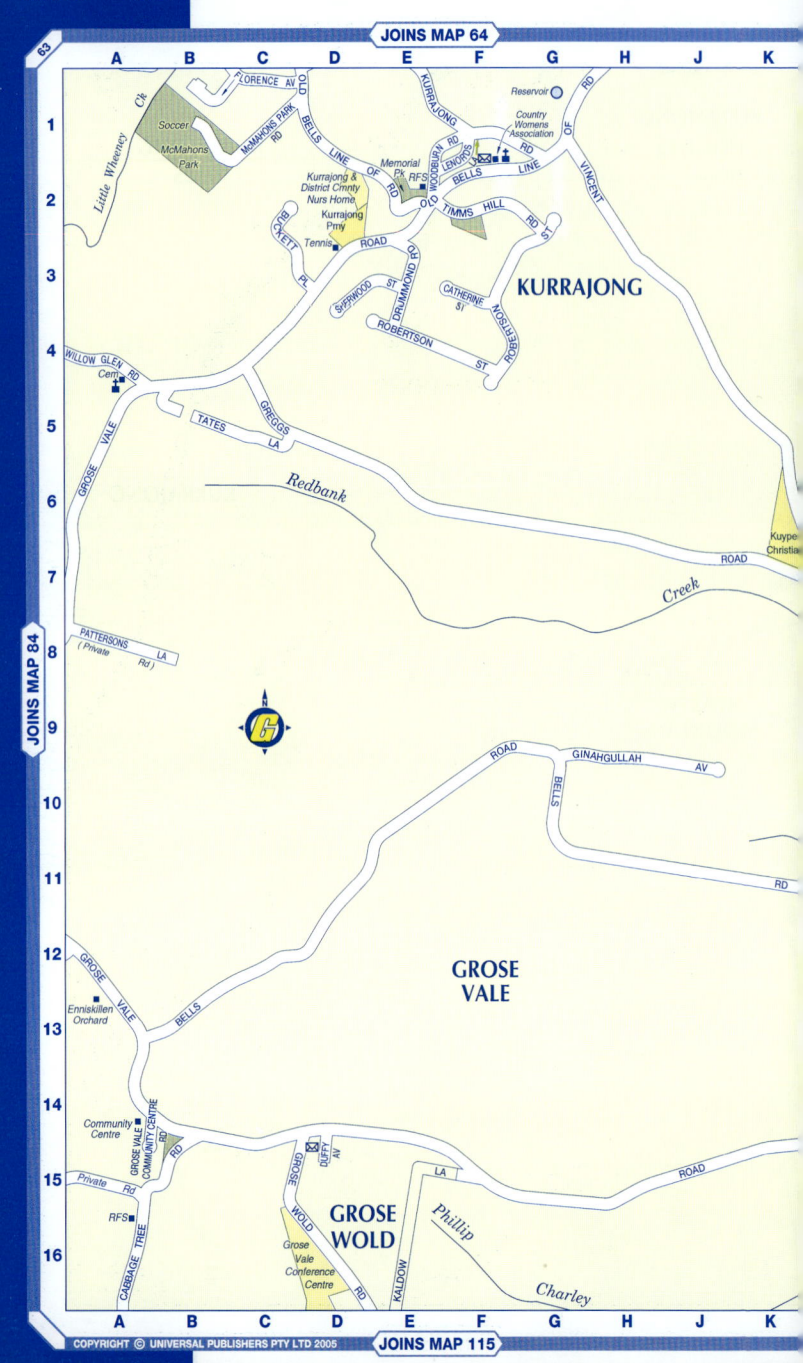

MAP 86

KURMOND

NORTH RICHMOND

Streets and features:
- Longleat La – A2/B2
- Jacqueline Pl – D1
- Elizabeth Av – E1
- Erica St – D1/D2
- Fork La – C4
- Bells La – E2/F3
- Bells Line Of Road – E1/K8
- Eureka Steakhouse – F2
- Maxwells Table – G3
- Inverary Dr – H3/H4
- Yeomans Rd – G6/G7
- Redbank Rd – A7
- Redbank La – E9/E10
- Belmont Rd – B13/C12
- Bells Rd – B14
- Grose Vale Rd – B14/K16
- Grose Vale – C14
- Valley View Park Range (Trail Rides) – D15
- Peel Park – J12
- O'Dea Pl – K12
- Pecks Rd – J13
- Arthur Phillip Dr – J13/J14
- Batus Pa – K13
- Tilton Pl – K14
- Granger Pl – K14
- Townsend Rd – J14
- Nepean Stud Farm – K16

JOINS MAP 64 (top)
JOINS MAP 87 (right)
JOINS MAP 116 (bottom)

COPYRIGHT © UNIVERSAL PUBLISHERS PTY LTD 2005

JOINS MAP 65
JOINS MAP 86
JOINS MAP 117
64
116
A B C D E F G H J K
1 2 3 4 5 6 7 8 9 10 11 12 13 14 15 16
TENNYSON
NORTH RICHMOND
RICHMOND
KURMOND RD
TENNYSON RD
KURMOND
MULLENS RD
SILKS LA
SLOPES RD
CROOKED LA
BRANDERS LA
MADDENS RD
ROUSE LA
DOUGLAS ST
BRAHMA
CITY
Colo High
Gate
Enfield Hill
Rural Press
St Philips Cemetery
BELLS LINE OF ROAD
40
68
One Lane Bridge
CROOKED
Sewage Treatment Works
Creek
Redbank
Fbr
O'DEA PL
MERRICK PL
SUSELLA CR
MORTON ST
BRADLEY RD
PECKS
TYNE CR
ROHAN PL
TYNE
FULTON PL
GRAINGER PL
ELIZABETH
TRENT PL
WILLIAM ST
Cmnty Cntr
Hall
Jeh Wit
CAMPBELL
MONTI ST
CHARLES ST
Pmy
ST
ROAD
GLENN PL
MOKARI ST
HAYMAN ST
IGNATIUS AV
PL
STEPHEN CR
YVONNE PL
MICHAEL ST
GREGORY ST
CORAL PL
ARNOLD ST
ROBERT ST
RD
CHRISTOPHER PL
VALE
GROSE
Water Filtration Plant & Training Centre
Reservoirs
Res
ENFIELD AV
SUNNYSIDE CR
MATHESON AV
CCT
KEDA CCT
Morunga Pk
PATYA PL
KEDA
Hawkesbury
RIVERVIEW ST
FLINDERS PL
PITT LA
SHORTLAND CL
Park
TERRACE
Tennis
Turnbull Oval
BEAUMONT
ROSETTA CL
NORFOLK PL
AV
Nth Richmond Business Park
North Richmond Panthers
Hanna Group
Hanna Park
HAWKESBURY
RICHMOND BRIDGE
Fbr
40
KURRAJONG RD
66
OLD KURRAJONG RD
OLD
ROAD

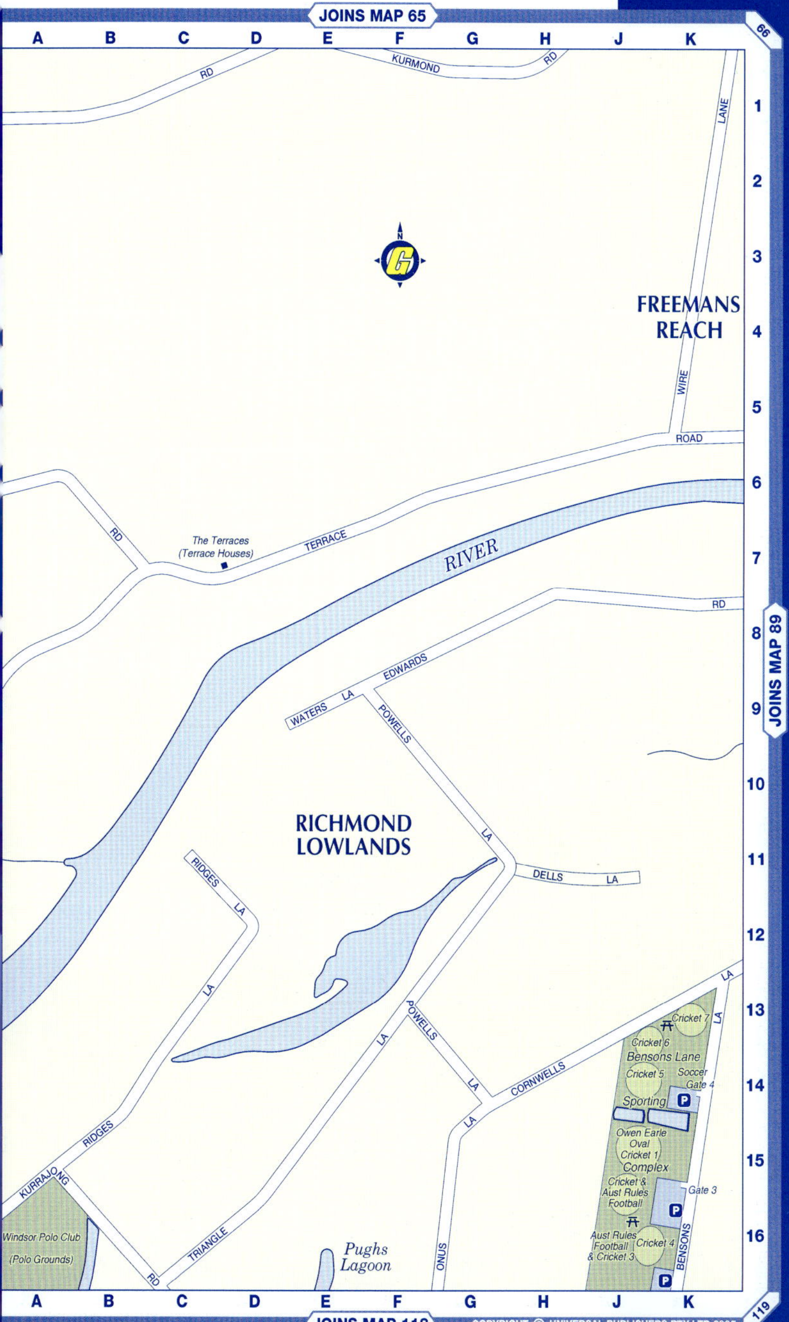

MAP 88

FREEMANS REACH

RICHMOND LOWLANDS

- Kurmond Rd
- Wire Lane
- Road
- Terrace
- The Terraces (Terrace Houses)
- River
- Rd
- Waters La
- Edwards
- Powells La
- Ridges La
- Dells La
- Powells La
- Cornwells La
- Onus La
- Triangle Rd
- Kurrajong Rd
- Ridges La
- Bensons Lane
- Pughs Lagoon
- Windsor Polo Club (Polo Grounds)

Owen Earle Oval Sporting Complex:
- Cricket 7
- Cricket 6
- Cricket 5
- Soccer, Gate 4
- Cricket 1
- Cricket & Aust Rules Football
- Gate 3
- Aust Rules Football & Cricket 3
- Cricket 4

JOINS MAP 65 / JOINS MAP 89 / JOINS MAP 118

JOINS MAP 66

A B C D E F G H J K
1 2 3 4 5 6 7 8 9 10 11 12 13 14 15 16
65
KURMOND
ROAD
WIRE
LA
ROAD
GOLDEN GR
LINDEN
DR
RIVER CL
TERRACE
TERRACE
ROAD
GORMLEY ST
CLIFF
ROAD
HAWKESBURY
Streeton Lookout
ROAD
EDWARDS
CORNWALLIS
ROAD
LANE
RICHMOND LOWLANDS
CORNWELLS
BENSONS LA
RICHMOND
Bakers Lagoon
118

JOINS MAP 88

JOINS MAP 119

MAP 90

JOINS MAP 67

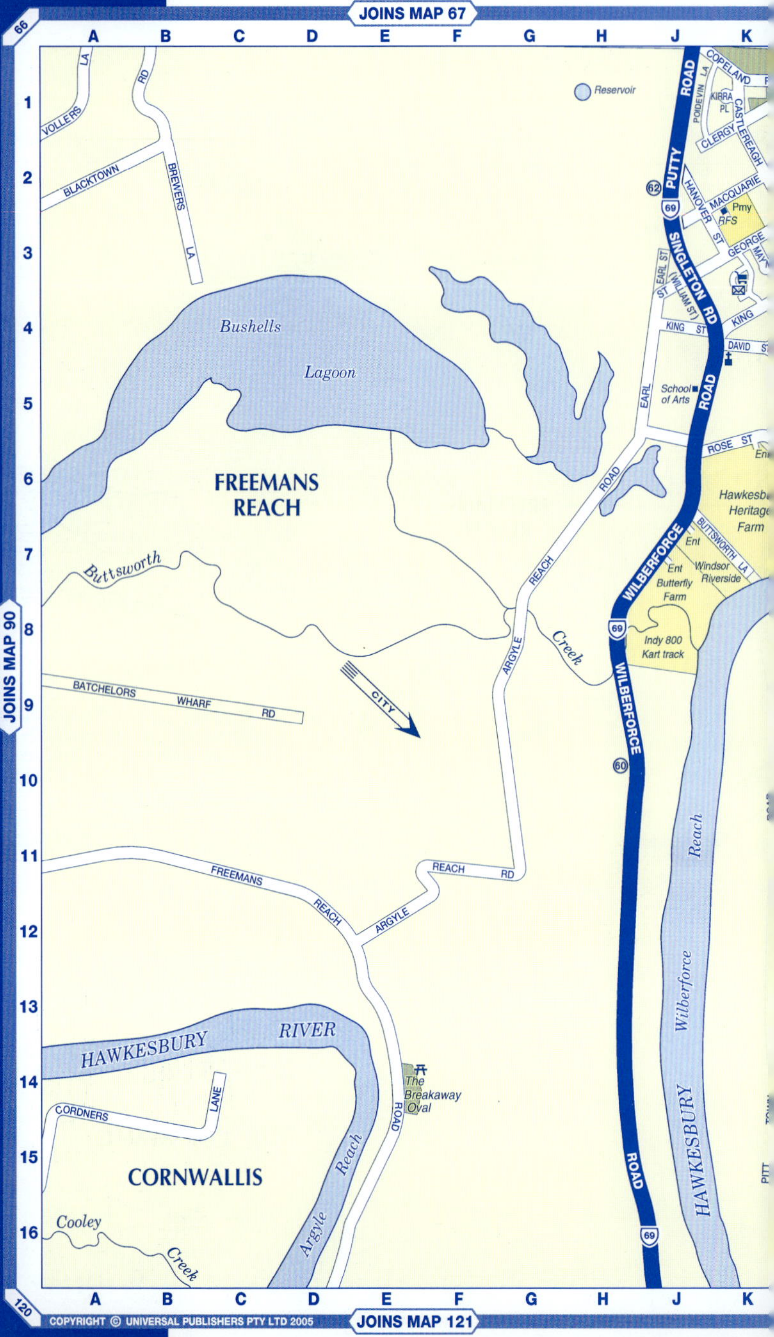

JOINS MAP 121
JOINS MAP 90
66
120

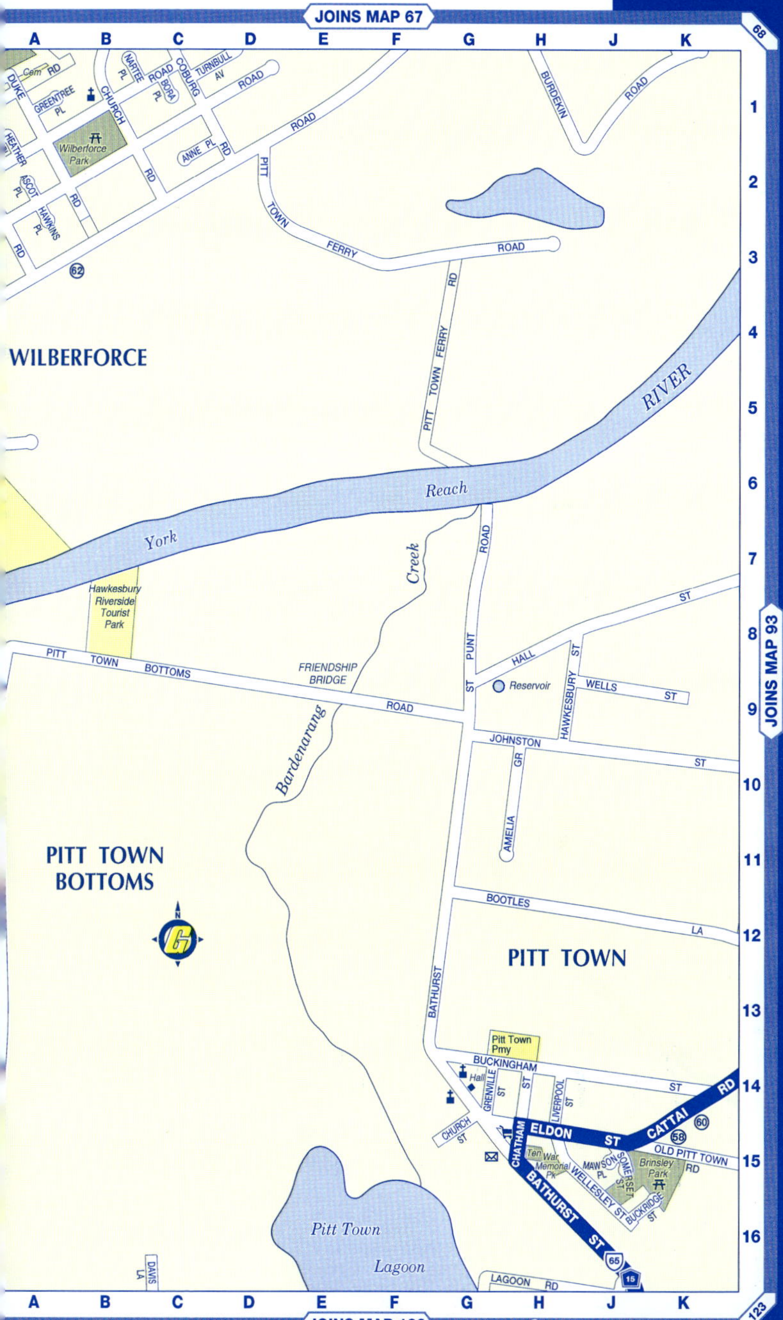
JOINS MAP 67
68
A B C D E F G H J K
1 2 3 4 5 6 7 8 9 10 11 12 13 14 15 16
Cem RD
DUKE
GREENTREE PL
CHURCH
NARTEE PL
ROAD
BORA PL
COBURG
TURNBULL AV
ROAD
HEATHER
ASCOT PL
Wilberforce Park
ANNE PL
RD
RD
HAWKINS PL
RD
RD
62
ROAD
PITT TOWN FERRY ROAD
BURDEKIN
ROAD
RD
PITT TOWN FERRY
WILBERFORCE
RIVER
York Reach
Creek
ROAD
Hawkesbury Riverside Tourist Park
PITT TOWN BOTTOMS ROAD
FRIENDSHIP BRIDGE
PUNT ST
HALL
ST
ST
Reservoir
HAWKESBURY
WELLS ST
JOHNSTON ST
GR
AMELIA
Bardenarang
PITT TOWN BOTTOMS
BOOTLES LA
PITT TOWN
BATHURST
Pitt Town Pmy
BUCKINGHAM
Hall
GRENVILLE ST
ST
LIVERPOOL ST
ST
CATTAI RD
60
ELDON ST
58
CHURCH ST
CHATHAM
OLD PITT TOWN RD
Ten War Memorial Pk
MAWSON PL
SOMERSET ST
Brinsley Park
WELLESLEY ST
BUCKRIDGE ST
BATHURST ST
65
15
Pitt Town Lagoon
DAVIS LA
LAGOON RD
JOINS MAP 93
JOINS MAP 122
123

COPYRIGHT © UNIVERSAL PUBLISHERS PTY LTD 2005

JOINS MAP 68

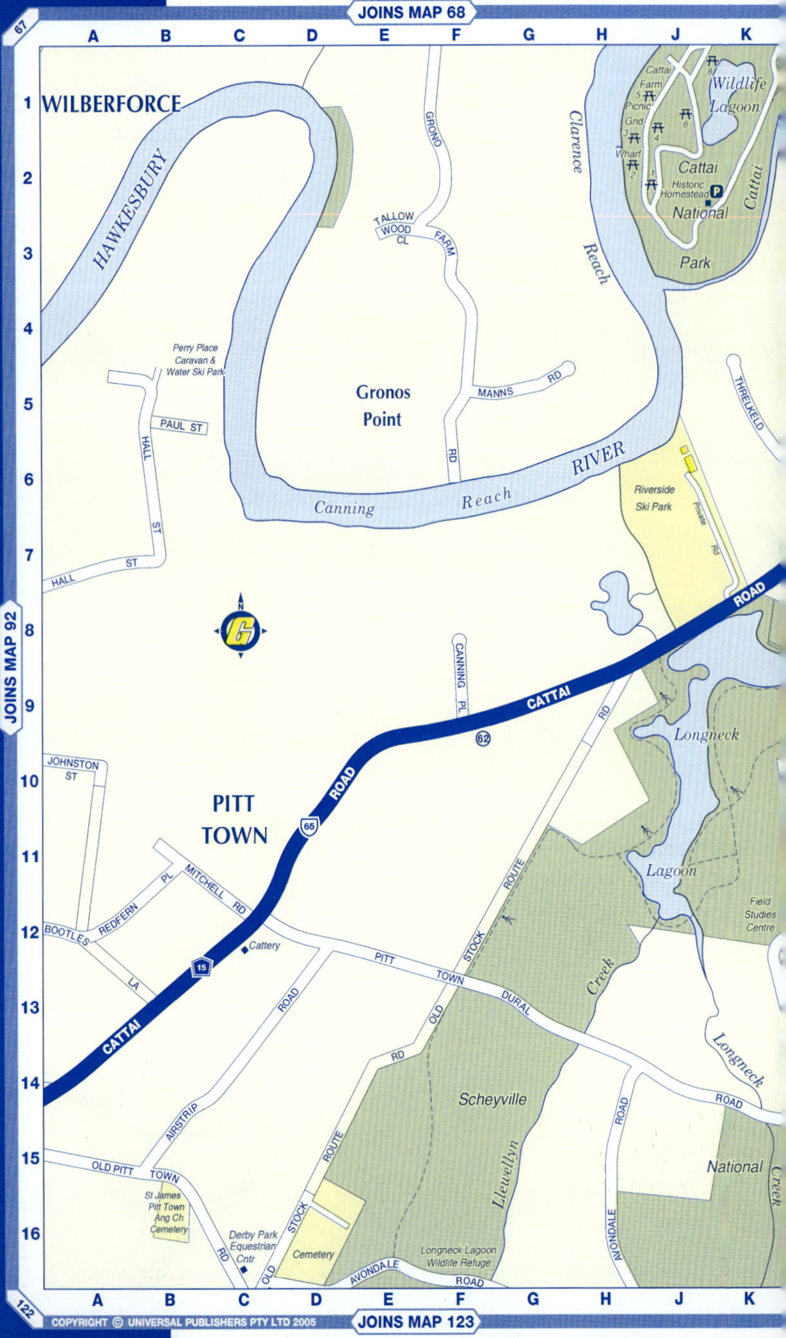

JOINS MAP 92

JOINS MAP 123

JOINS MAP 68

A B C D E F G H J K
1 2 3 4 5 6 7 8 9 10 11 12 13 14 15 16
69
Cattai Creek Track
Creek
WISEMANS FERRY RD
ROAD
Cattai Bridge Reserve
CATTAI BRIDGE
Cattai Primary
15
65
64
54
CLARENCE RD
NELSON RD
MITCHELL PARK
Cattai National Park Information: Phone 02 4572 3100
Park Ent
Cattai National Park
Mitchell Park
CATTAI
CATTAI
JACEVA PL
DR
THRELKELD
LAKELAND RD
MILLERS ROAD
ROAD
REEDY
PEBBLY HILL
ROAD
FISHER
CITY
MARAYLYA
PHIPPS ROAD
GREENFIELD PL
Gate
WHITMORE ROAD
PEBBLY HILL ROAD
Rural Fire Service
PITT TOWN DURAL ROAD
PITT TOWN DURAL RD
FORRESTER PL
MEWTON ROAD
BOUNDARY ROAD
SCHEYVILLE ROAD
NEICH ROAD
SCHEYVILLE
Park
125

JOINS MAP 95

JOINS MAP 124

COPYRIGHT © UNIVERSAL PUBLISHERS PTY LTD 2005

MAP 95

JOINS MAP 69

CATTAI

HALCROWS

Fair Ck

Cattai

Mt Halcrow

Field Studies Centre

Reedy Wetlands

Cattai National Park

Creek

CITY

Mitchell Park

REEDY ROAD ST JOHN'S RD

Cattai

NEWMAN

JOINS MAP 94

MARAYLYA

FORRESTER PL

ST JOHNS RIDGE

52 One Lane Bridge

Road Subject to Flooding

ROAD

PITT TOWN DURAL RD

CATTAI

BOUNDARY RD

KENTHURST

Creek

The Long Swamp

JOINS MAP 125

COPYRIGHT © UNIVERSAL PUBLISHERS PTY LTD 2005

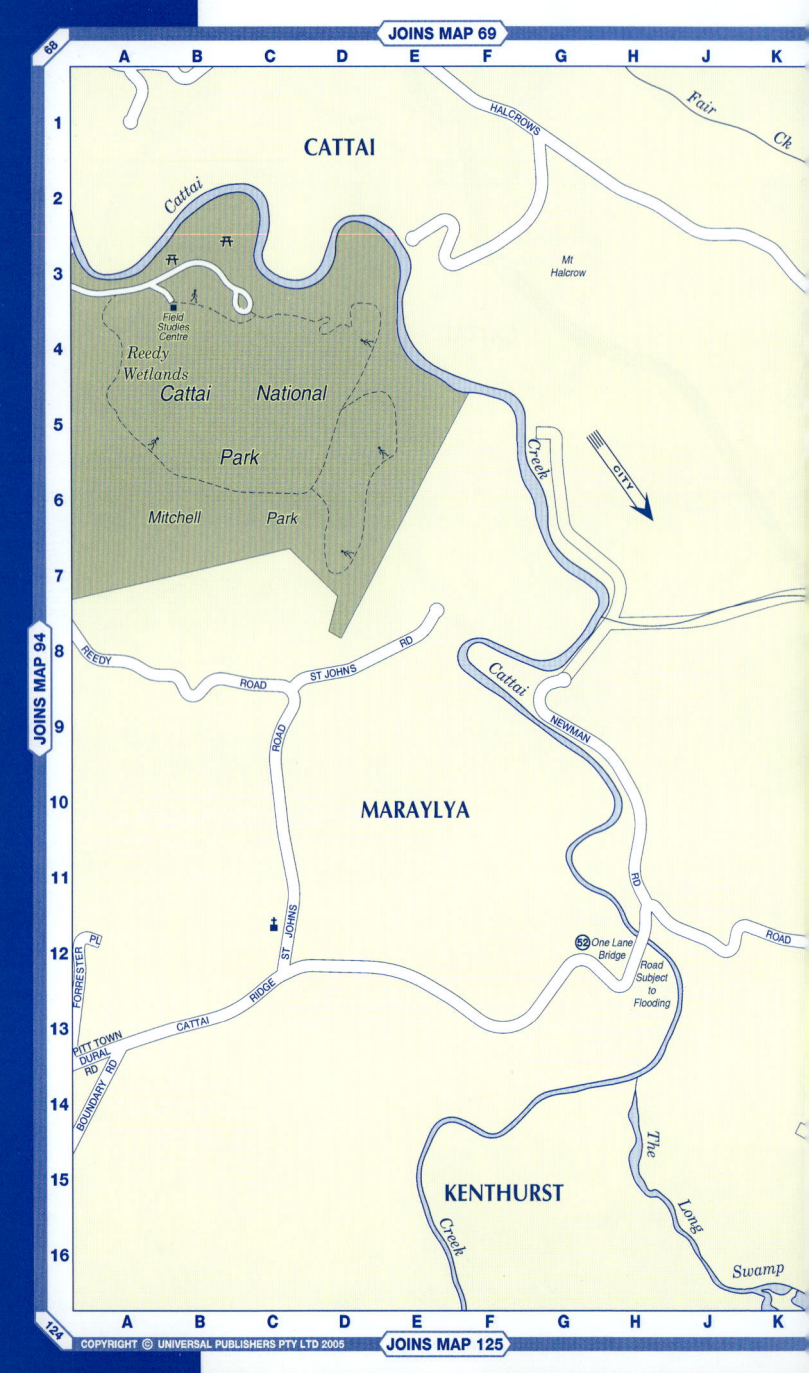

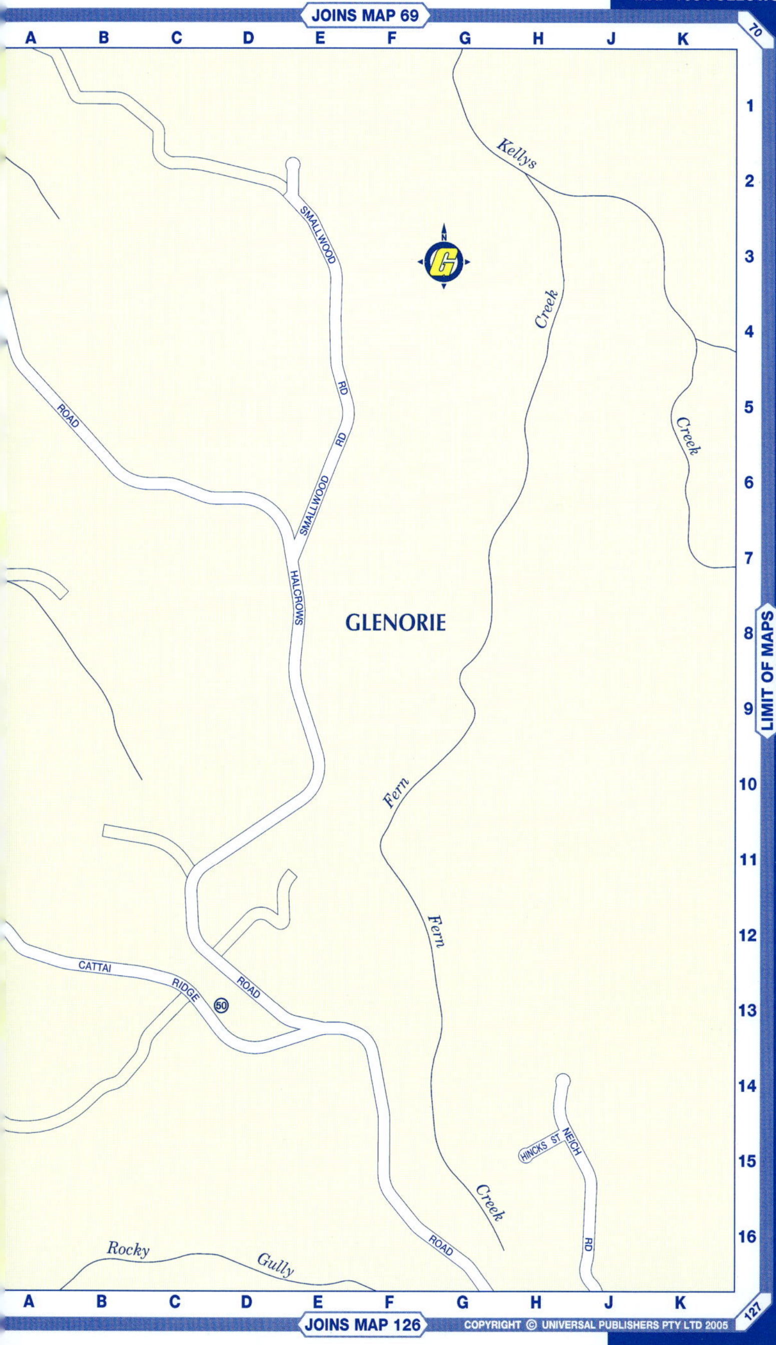

MAP 96
MAP 103 FOLLOWS

GLENORIE

MAP 103
PREVIOUS MAP 96

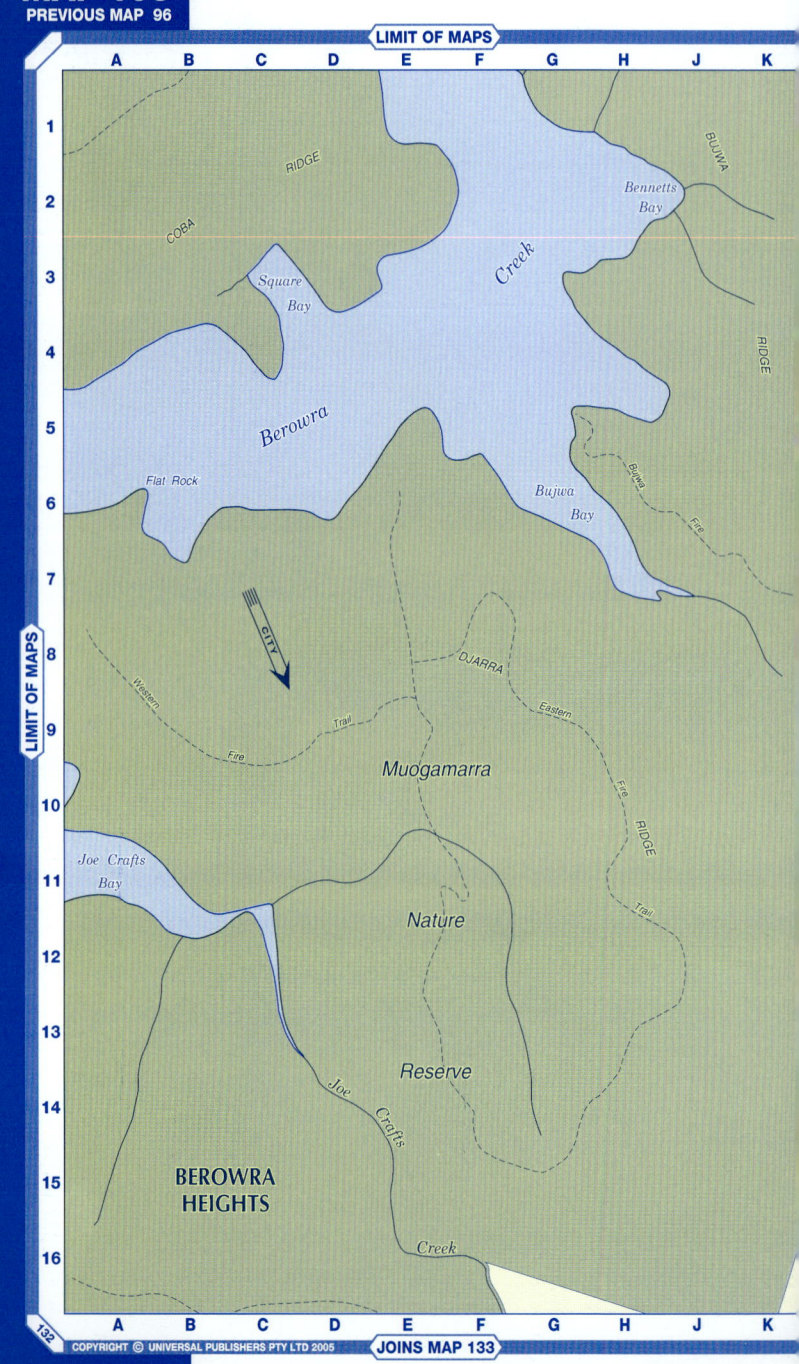

LIMIT OF MAPS

Berowra Creek
Bennetts Bay
BUJWA RIDGE
COBA RIDGE
Square Bay
Flat Rock
Bujwa Bay
Bujwa Fire
Western Fire Trail
DJARRA
Eastern Fire Trail
RIDGE
Muogamarra Nature Reserve
Joe Crafts Bay
Joe Crafts Creek
BEROWRA HEIGHTS

JOINS MAP 133

MAP 104

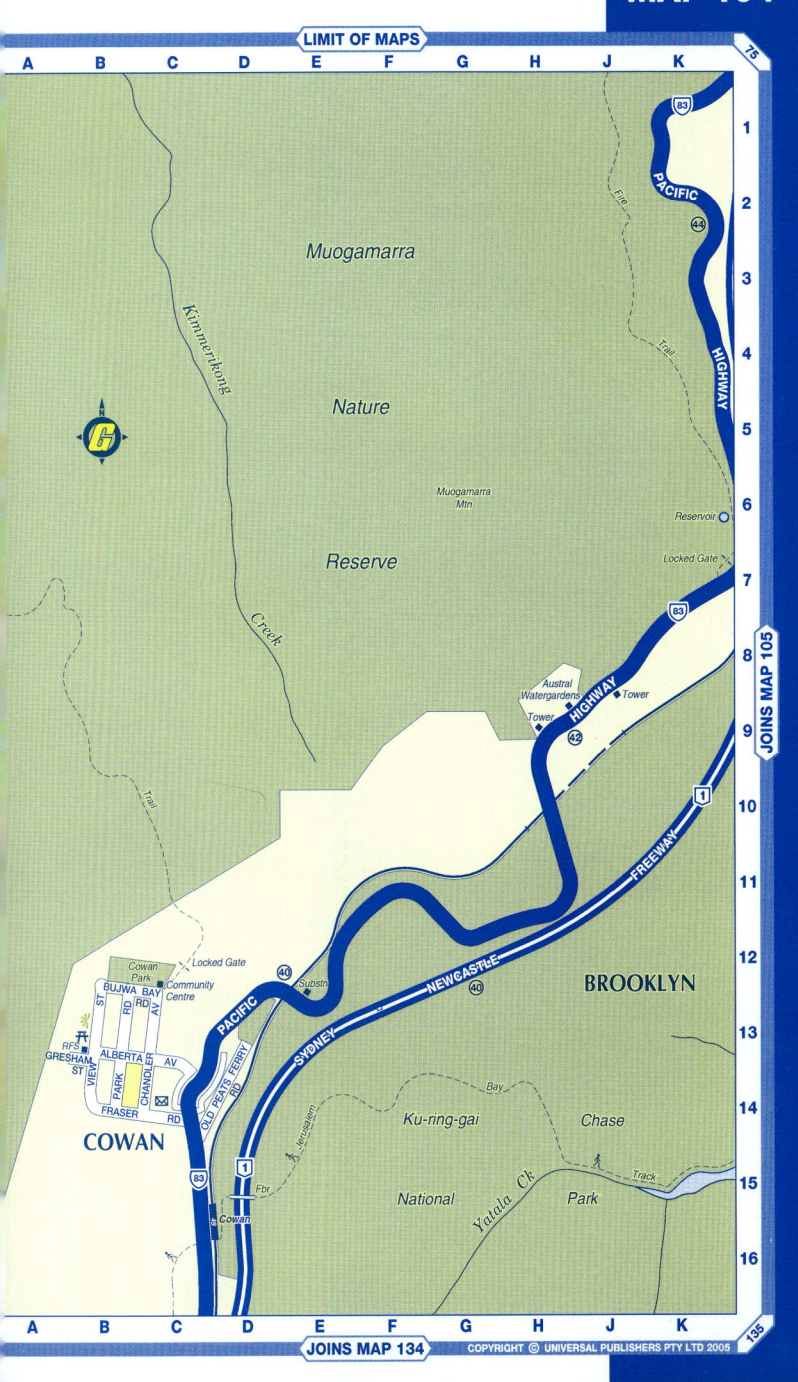

MAP 105

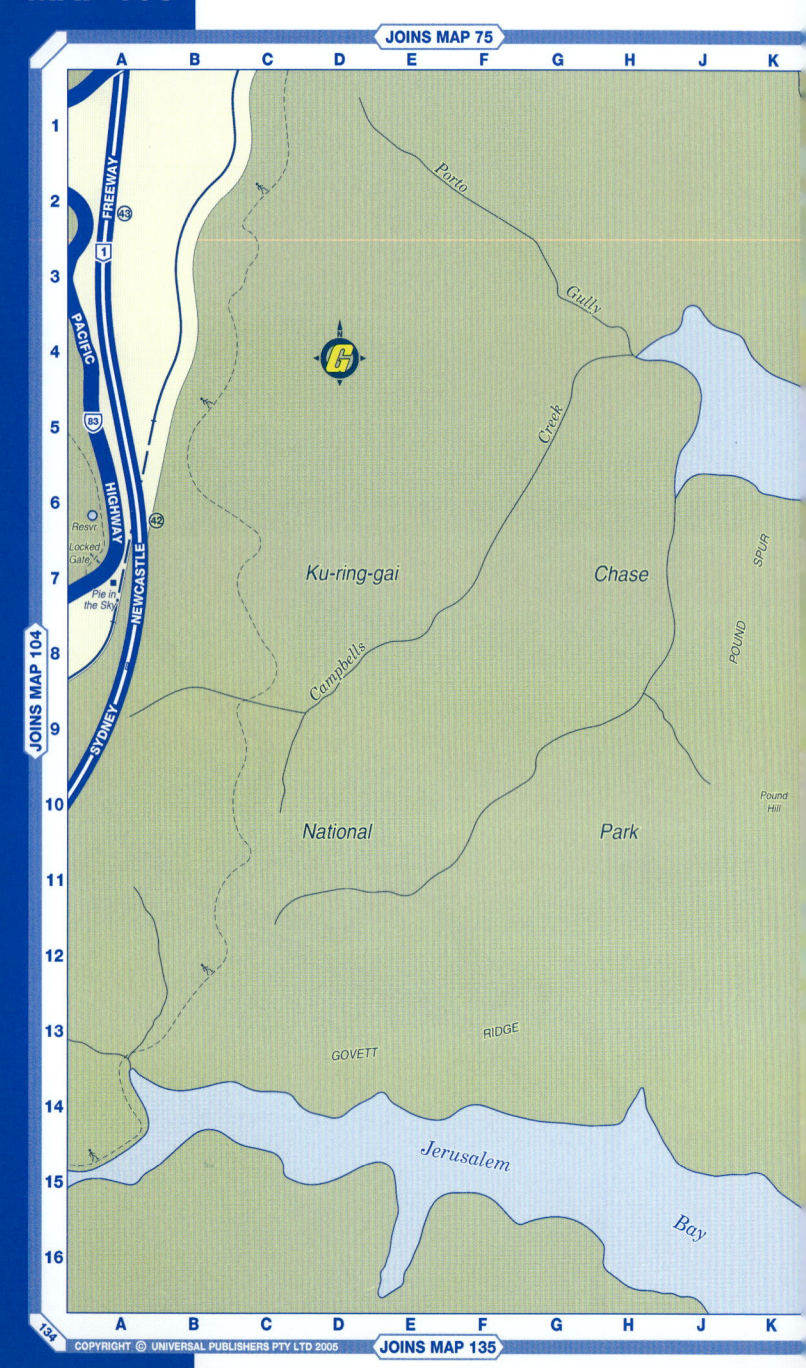

MAP 106

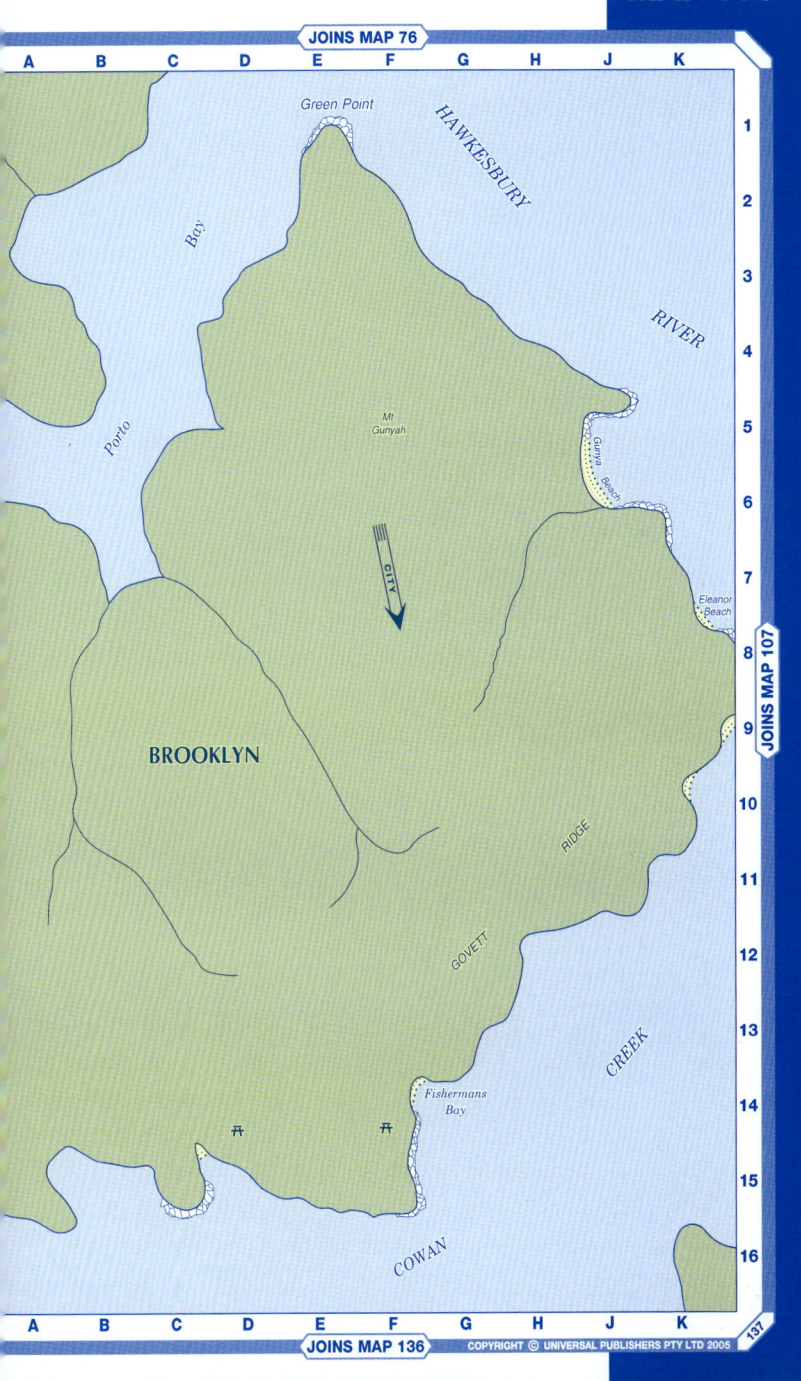

JOINS MAP 76

Green Point
HAWKESBURY
Porto Bay
Mt Gunyah
Gunya Beach
RIVER
CITY
Eleanor Beach
BROOKLYN
GOVETT RIDGE
CREEK
Fishermans Bay
COWAN

JOINS MAP 107

JOINS MAP 136

MAP 107

- Broken Bay Sport and Recreation Centre
- Broken Bay National Fitness Camp
- Pacific Head
- Little Patonga Beach
- Walker Pt
- Juno Pt
- HAWKESBURY
- Eleanor Beach
- National Park
- Eleanor Bluffs
- COWAN CREEK
- Challenger Head
- Challenger Mtn
- Little Pittwater Bay
- Ku-ring-gai Chase National Park
- Challenger
- America Bay
- Refuge Bay

LIMIT OF MAPS
JOINS MAP 106
JOINS MAP 137
COPYRIGHT © UNIVERSAL PUBLISHERS PTY LTD 2005

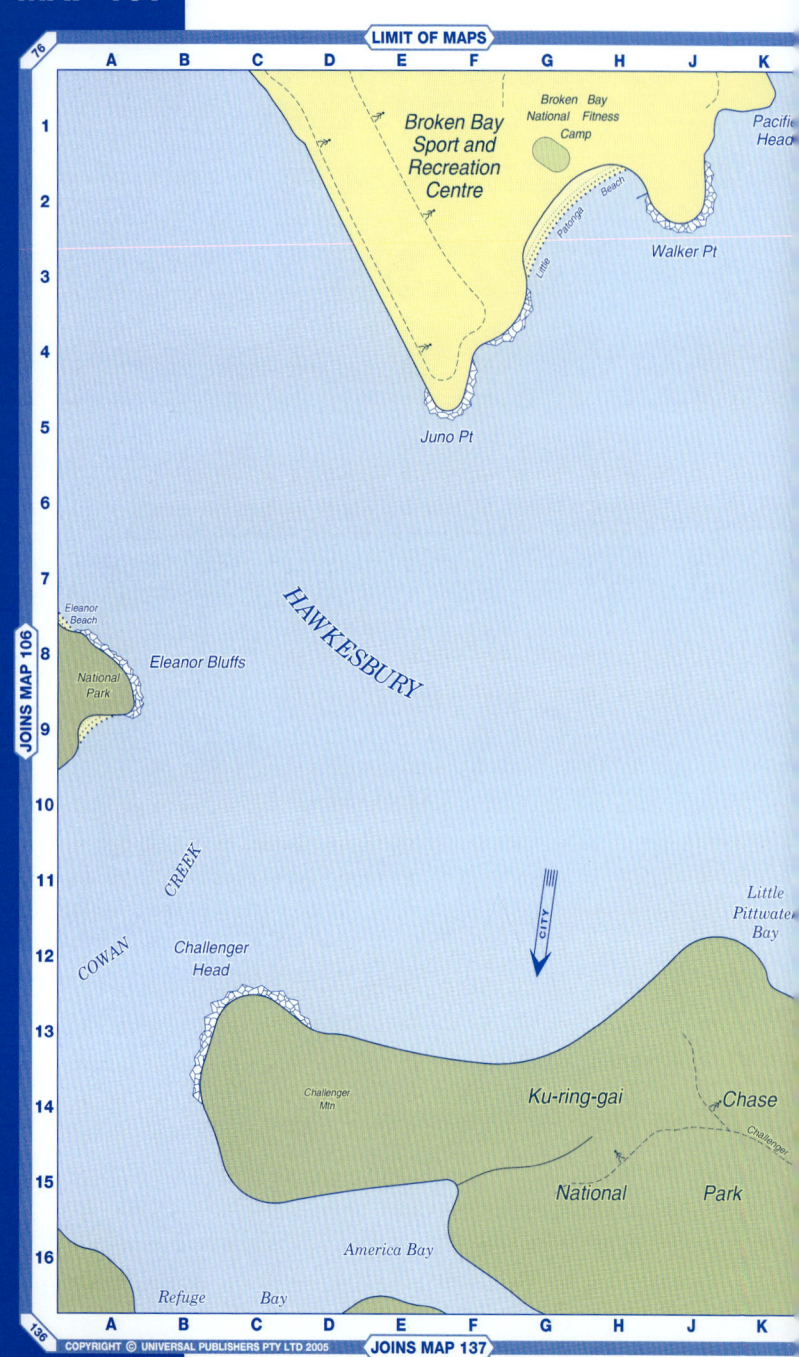

MAP 108

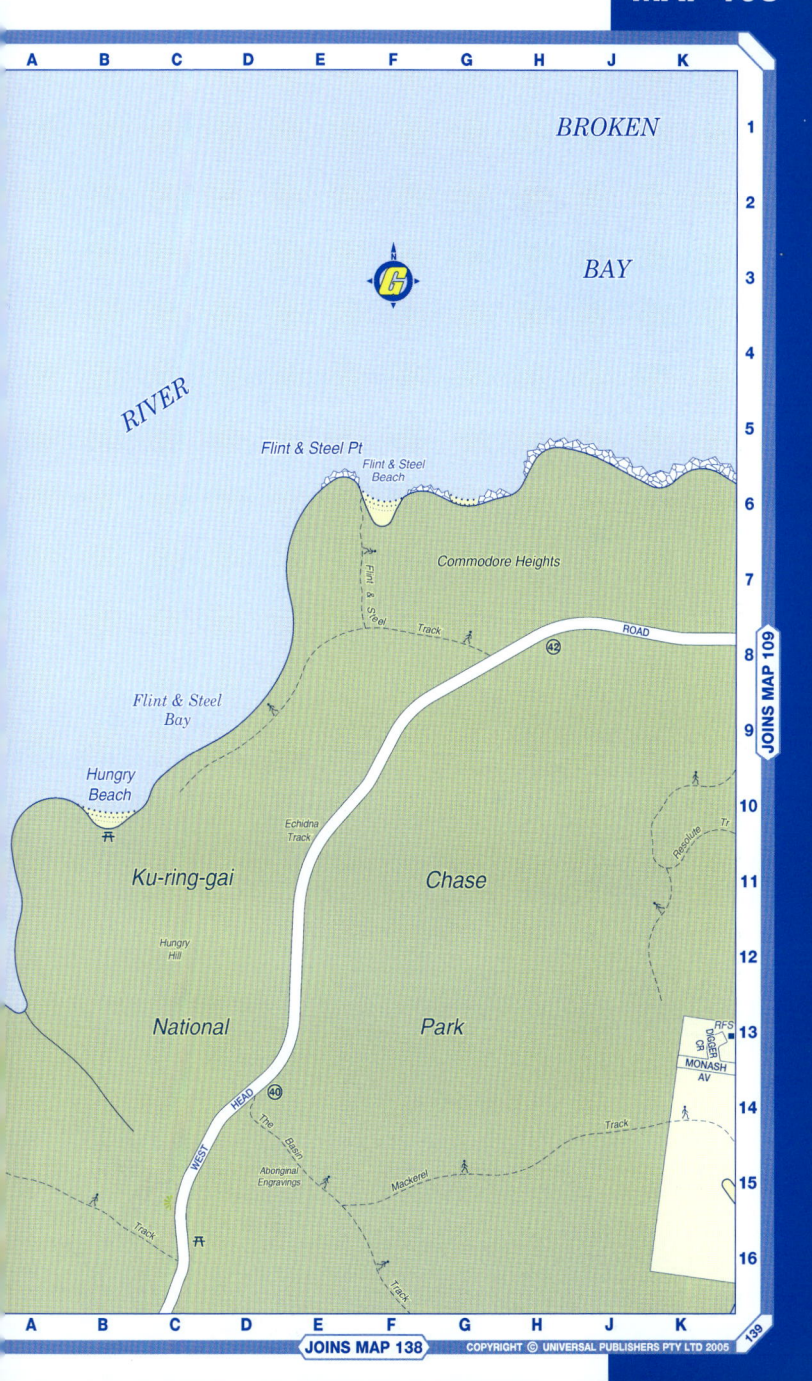

BROKEN BAY

RIVER

Flint & Steel Pt
Flint & Steel Beach
Flint & Steel Track
Commodore Heights
ROAD (42)

Flint & Steel Bay

Hungry Beach

Echidna Track

Ku-ring-gai

Chase

Resolute Tr

Hungry Hill

National

Park

RFS
Diger Cr
MONASH AV

WEST HEAD (40)

The Basin
Aboriginal Engravings
Mackerel Track

Track

JOINS MAP 109
JOINS MAP 138

MAP 109

BROKEN BAY

- Commodore Heights
- WEST HEAD RD (43)
- Resolute Picnic Area
- West Head Lookout
- West Head
- Ku-ring-gai Chase National Park
- Shark Pt
- Barrenjoey
- Resolute Track
- Resolute Beach
- Seaplane Wharf
- Barrenjoey Boathouse
- *PITTWATER*
- Great Mackerel Beach
- Mackerel Beach Wharf
- DIGGER CR
- RFS
- MONASH AV
- ROSS SMITH PDE
- RESOLUTE AV
- **GREAT MACKEREL BEACH**
- Palm Beach Golf Course
- Governor Phillip Park
- Palm Beach SLSC
- BEACH RD
- Clubhouse
- WAIGATTI RD
- RD (40)
- NORTHVIEW RD
- OCEAN RD
- Observation Pt
- **PALM BEACH**
- Jetty
- Currawong Beach
- **CURRAWONG BEACH**
- Palm Beach Public Wharf
- Snapperman Beach
- BARRENJOEY RD
- PACIFIC RD
- SUNRISE RD

JOINS MAP 108

JOINS MAP 139

COPYRIGHT © UNIVERSAL PUBLISHERS PTY LTD 2005

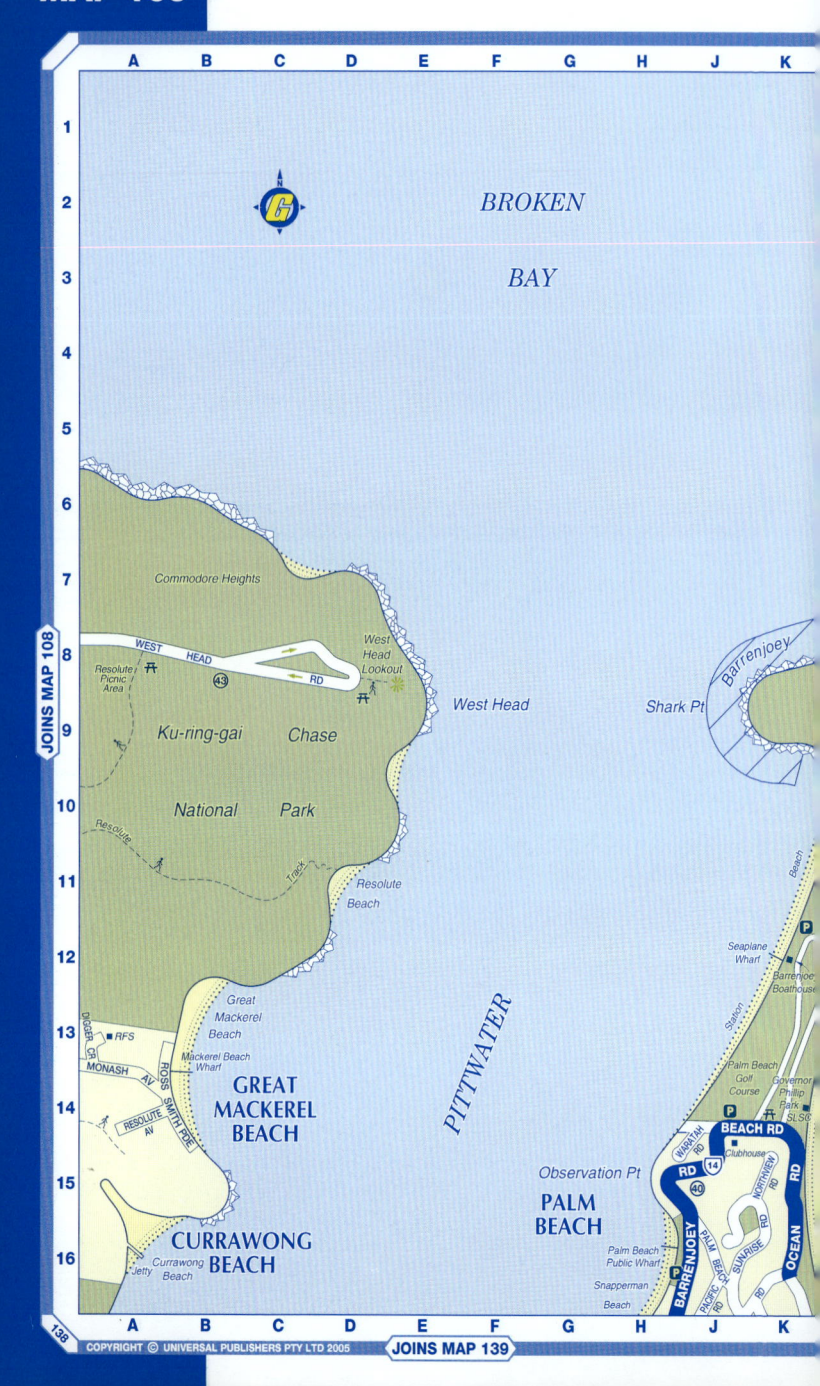

MAP 110
MAP 115 FOLLOWS

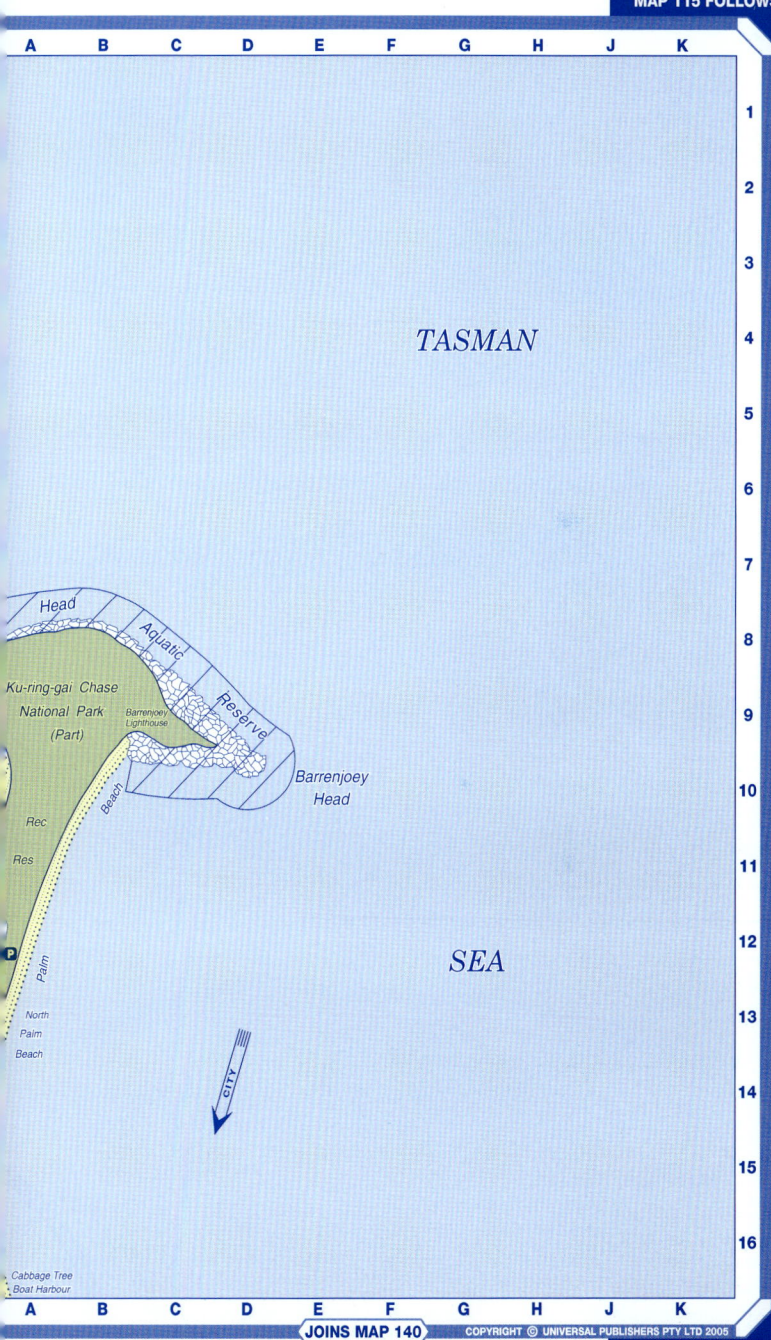

TASMAN

SEA

Head
Aquatic Reserve
Ku-ring-gai Chase National Park (Part)
Barrenjoey Lighthouse
Barrenjoey Head
Beach
Rec Res
Palm
North Palm Beach
Cabbage Tree Boat Harbour

CITY

JOINS MAP 140

MAP 115
PREVIOUS MAP 110

JOINS MAP 85

JOINS MAP 145

GROSE VALE

- Rural Fire Service (A3)
- Cabbage Tree Rd
- Cabbage Tree Rd (Private)
- Ahmedi Cl
- Grose Vale Conference Centre
- Grose View Pmy
- Kaldow La
- Grose Rd / Grose Wold Rd
- Rural Fire Service (E5)
- Phillip Charley
- Trooper
- Stinsons
- Nutmans
- Jonora Alpaca Stud
- Avoca Rd
- Scotts Farm Rd
- Ck
- Woods Reserve
- Tragedy Ck
- Grose
- Scotts
- CITY →
- Grace Lodge Christian Conference Centre
- Mountain Av
- Rural Fire Service (J15)
- Springwood
- River

LIMIT OF MAPS

COPYRIGHT © UNIVERSAL PUBLISHERS PTY LTD 2005

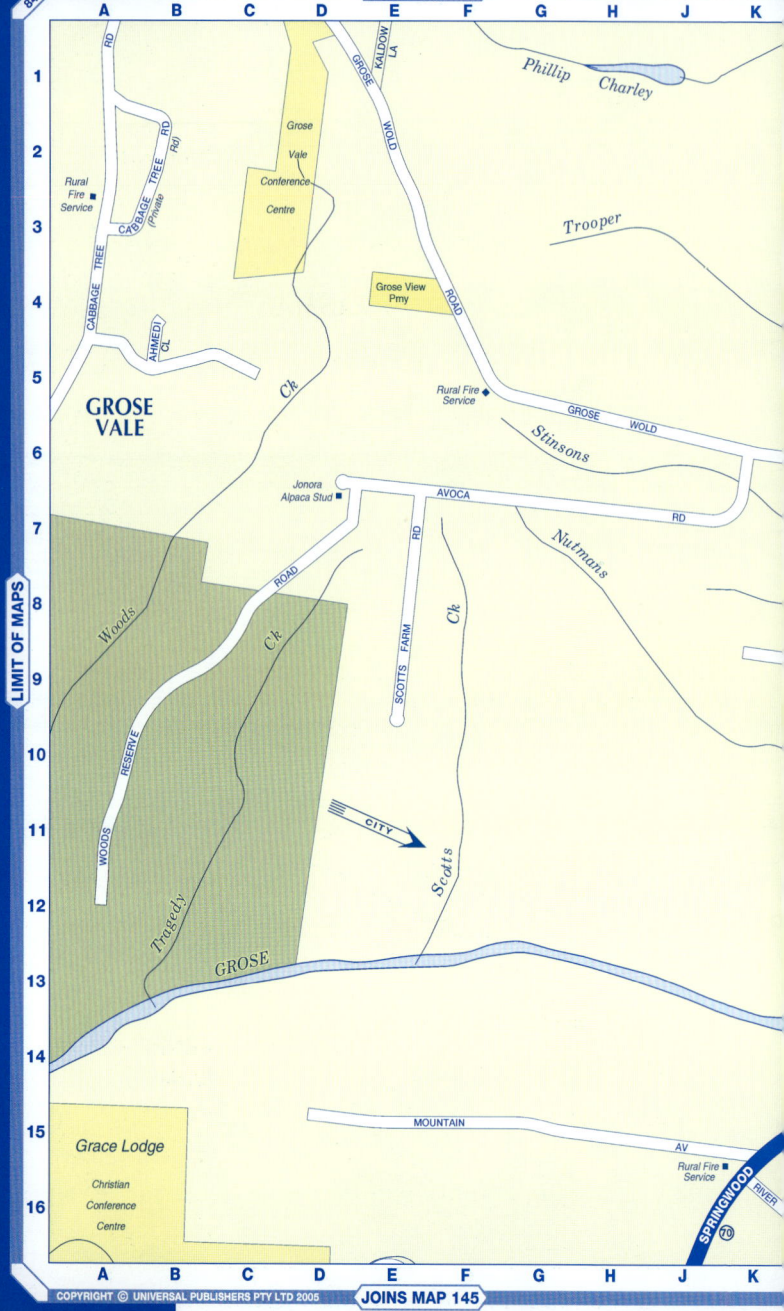

MAP 116

JOINS MAP 86

GROSE VALE

NORTH RICHMOND

- Nepean Stud Farm

"Belmont Park" St John of God Private Hospital

Belmont Park

Clarks Island

Hawkesbury R.

Steading Ck
Phillip Ck
Charley Ck

GROSE WOLD

London Pl
Yarraman Rd
Navua Rd
Ashtons Rd
Macquarie Vale Pre School
Grose River Rd
Grose River

Gate Close at 8pm
Navua Reserve

Evergreen Turf

Office/Pro Shop
Grose River
Nutmans
Golf Course

YMCA Youth Camp
Yarrundi Road
Springwood Road
Tilmunda Sand, Soil & Gravel
Australia House
68

YARRAMUNDI BRIDGE

Nepean River

AGNES BANKS

Yarramundi Lagoon

Castlereagh Rd
Sand Pit

YARRAMUNDI

JOINS MAP 146

COPYRIGHT © UNIVERSAL PUBLISHERS PTY LTD 2005

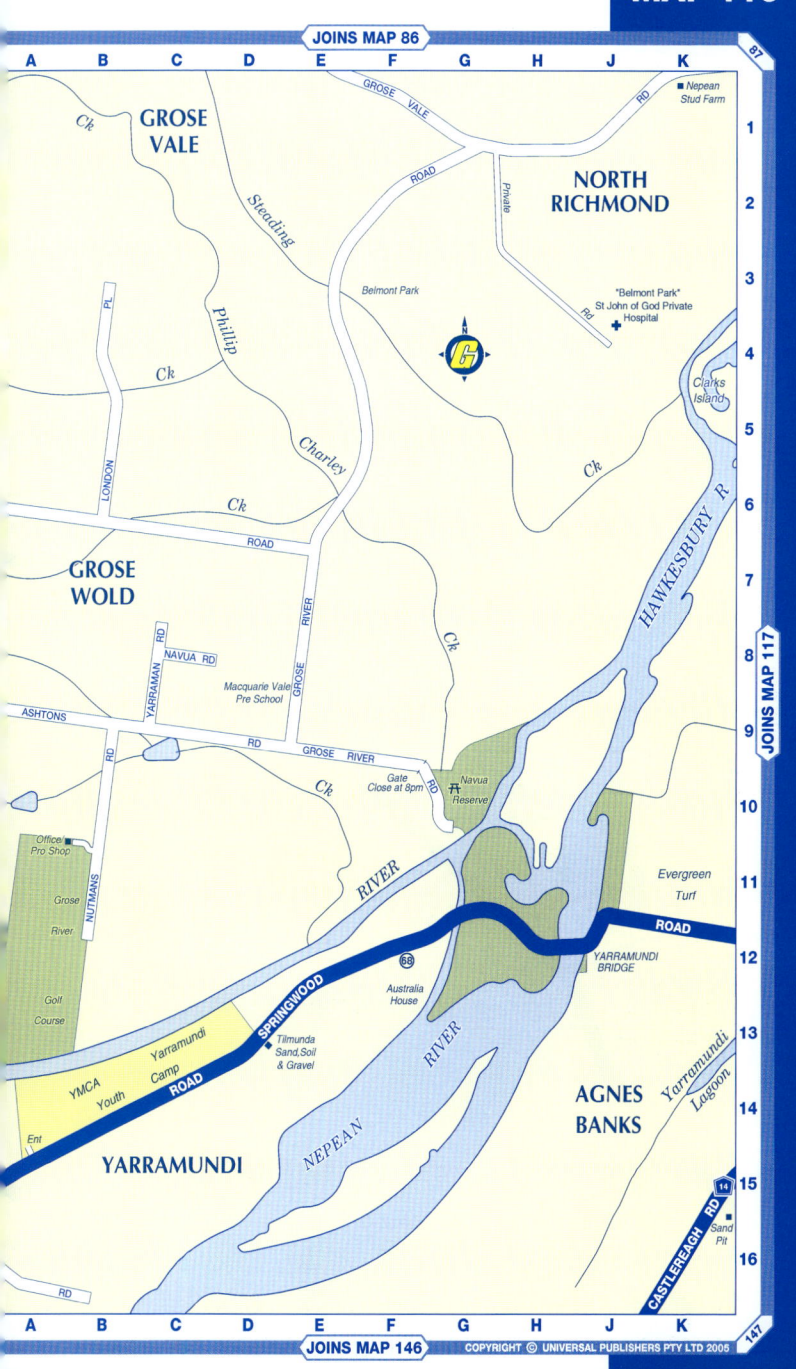

MAP 117

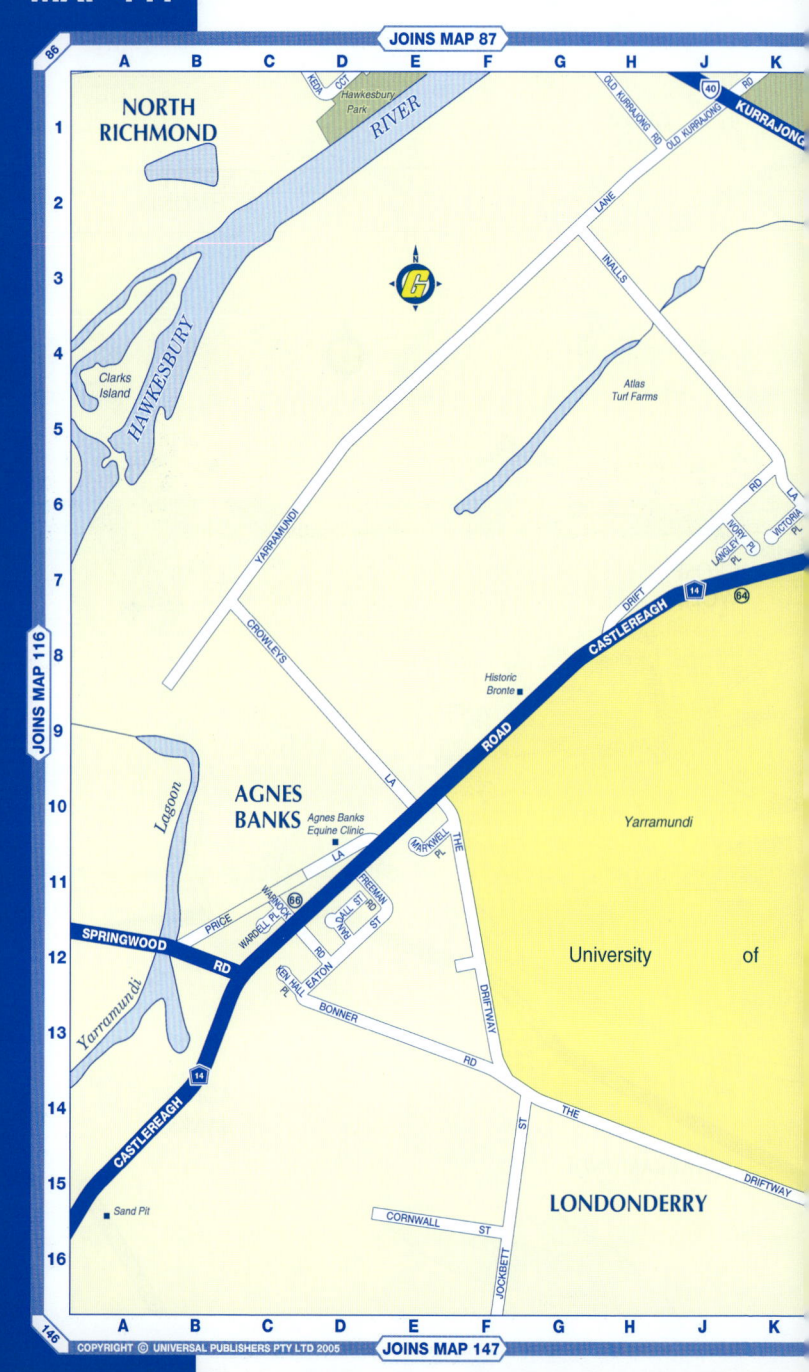

JOINS MAP 87

NORTH RICHMOND

Hawkesbury Park

HAWKESBURY RIVER

Clarks Island

KURRAJONG

OLD KURRAJONG RD

LANE

INALLS

Atlas Turf Farms

LANGLEY PL
IVORY PL
VICTORIA PL
RD
LA

YARRAMUNDI

CROWLEYS

DRIFT

CASTLEREAGH ROAD

Historic Bronte

LA

THE DRIFTWAY

Yarramundi

AGNES BANKS
Agnes Banks Equine Clinic

MAXWELL PL

FREEMAN

PRICE
WARDELL PL
HANCOCK
CALL ST
ST
RD

SPRINGWOOD RD

BEN PL
EATON RD

BONNER RD

University of

Yarramundi

CASTLEREAGH

Sand Pit

CORNWALL ST

JOCKBETT ST

THE DRIFTWAY

LONDONDERRY

JOINS MAP 147

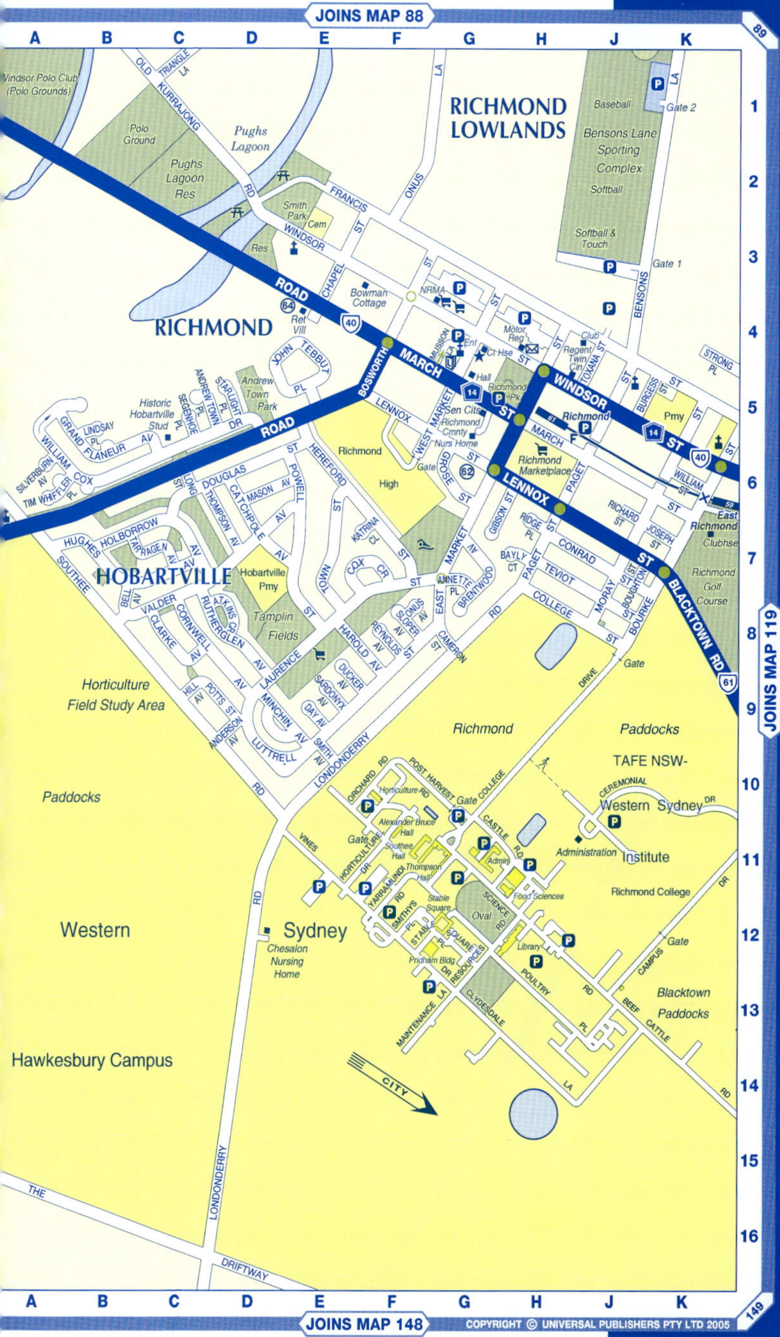
JOINS MAP 88
JOINS MAP 119
JOINS MAP 148
89
149
A B C D E F G H J K
1 2 3 4 5 6 7 8 9 10 11 12 13 14 15 16
RICHMOND LOWLANDS
RICHMOND
HOBARTVILLE
Windsor Polo Club (Polo Grounds)
Polo Ground
Pughs Lagoon
Pughs Lagoon Res
Smith Park
Cem
Res
Ret Vill
Bowman Cottage
NRMA
Baseball
Gate 2
Bensons Lane Sporting Complex
Softball
Softball & Touch
Gate 1
Motor Reg
Club
Regent Twin Cin
Ent
Ct Hse
Hall
Richmond Pk
Sen Cits
Richmond Cmnty
Nurs Home
Richmond
Richmond Marketplace
Pmy
East Richmond
Clubhse
Richmond Golf Course
Andrew Town Park
Historic Hobartville Stud
Richmond High
Gate
Hobartville Pmy
Tamplin Fields
Horticulture Field Study Area
Paddocks
Richmond
Paddocks
TAFE NSW-
Western Sydney Institute
Administration
Richmond College
Gate
Horticulture Rd
Alexander Bruce Hall
Southee Hall
Thompson Hall
Stable Square
Oval
(Admin)
Food Sciences
Library
Pridham Bldg
Western Sydney
Chesalon Nursing Home
Hawkesbury Campus
Blacktown Paddocks
CITY
WINDSOR ROAD
MARCH ST
WINDSOR ST
LENNOX ST
BLACKTOWN RD
BOSWORTH ST
LONDONDERRY RD
THE DRIFTWAY
COLLEGE DRIVE
OLD KURRAJONG RD
TRIANGLE LA
FRANCIS ST
CHAPEL ST
ONUS LA
BENSONS LA
JOHN TEBBUTT PL
WEST MARKET ST
EAST MARKET ST
HEREFORD ST
GROSE ST
GIBSON ST
RIDGE PL
PAGET ST
CONRAD ST
TEVIOT ST
COLLEGE ST
MORAY ST
BOUGHTON ST
BOURKE ST
RICHARD ST
JOSEPH ST
WILLIAM ST
BURGESS ST
TOXANA ST
STRONG PL
MUSSON LA
BAYLY CT
CAMERON ST
BRENTWOOD AV
ANNETTE PL
ANDREW TOWN PL
STARLIGHT DR
SEGENHOE PL
LINDSAY PL
GRAND FLANEUR AV
WILLIAM COX AV
SILVERBURN PL
TIM WHIFFLER PL
DOUGLAS ST
LONG ST
THOMPSON AV
CATCHPOLE AV
MASON AV
POWELL ST
TOWN ST
KATRINA CL
COX CR
HOLBORROW AV
TARRAGEN AV
HUGHES AV
SOUTHEE RD
BELL AV
VALDER AV
CLARKE AV
CORNWELL AV
ATKINS CR
RUTHERGLEN AV
HILL AV
POTTS ST
ANDERSON AV
LAURENCE AV
MINCHIN AV
LUTTRELL
HAROLD AV
REYNOLDS AV
ONUS SLOPER AV
DUCKER AV
SARDONYX AV
DAY AV
SMITH AV
POST HARVEST RD
ORCHARD RD
VINES
HORTICULTURE DR
YARRAMUNDI RD
SMITHYS PL
STABLE SQUARE
RESOURCES DR
CASTLE RD
SCIENCE RD
POULTRY RD
MAINTENANCE LA
CLYDESDALE LA
CEREMONIAL DR
CAMPUS DR
BEEF CATTLE RD
40
64
14
62
61
59

MAP 119

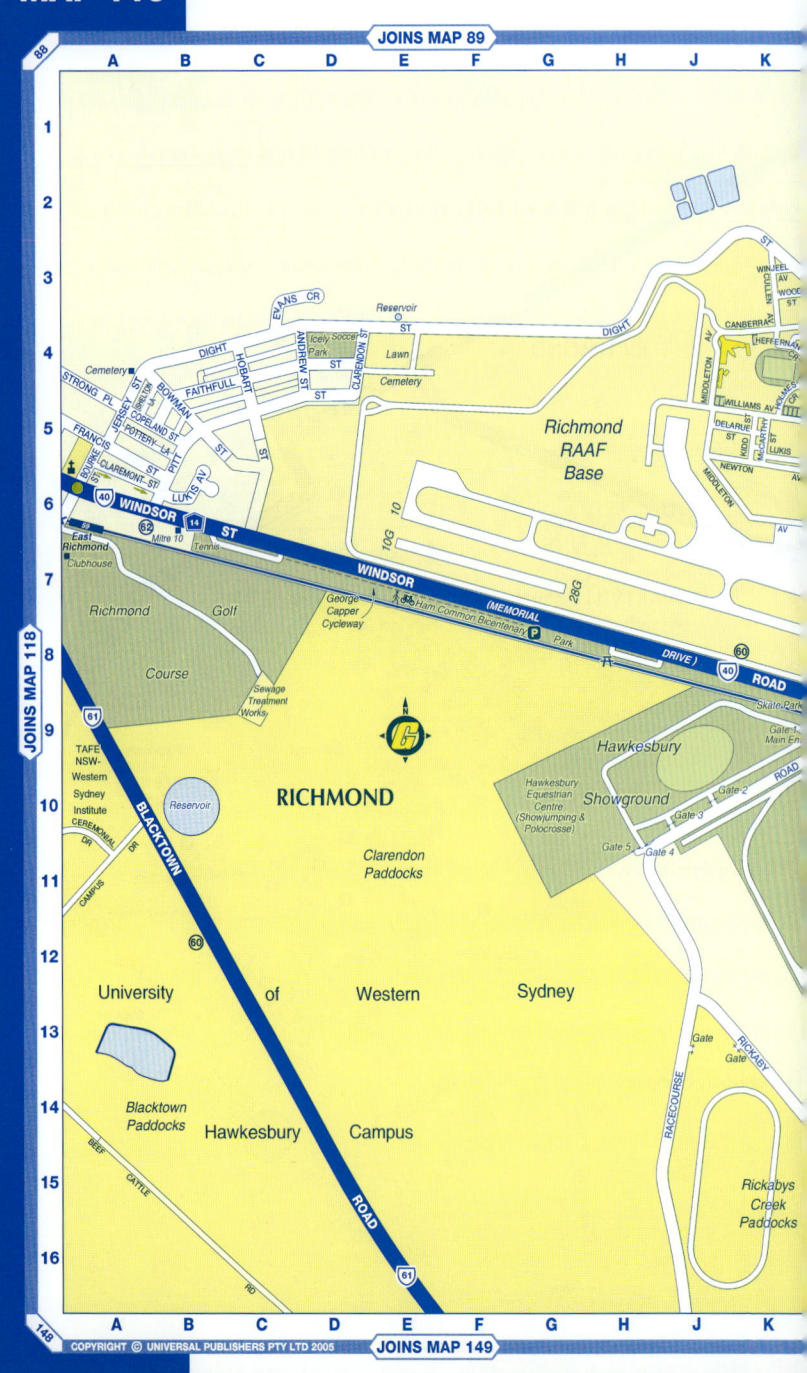

MAP 120

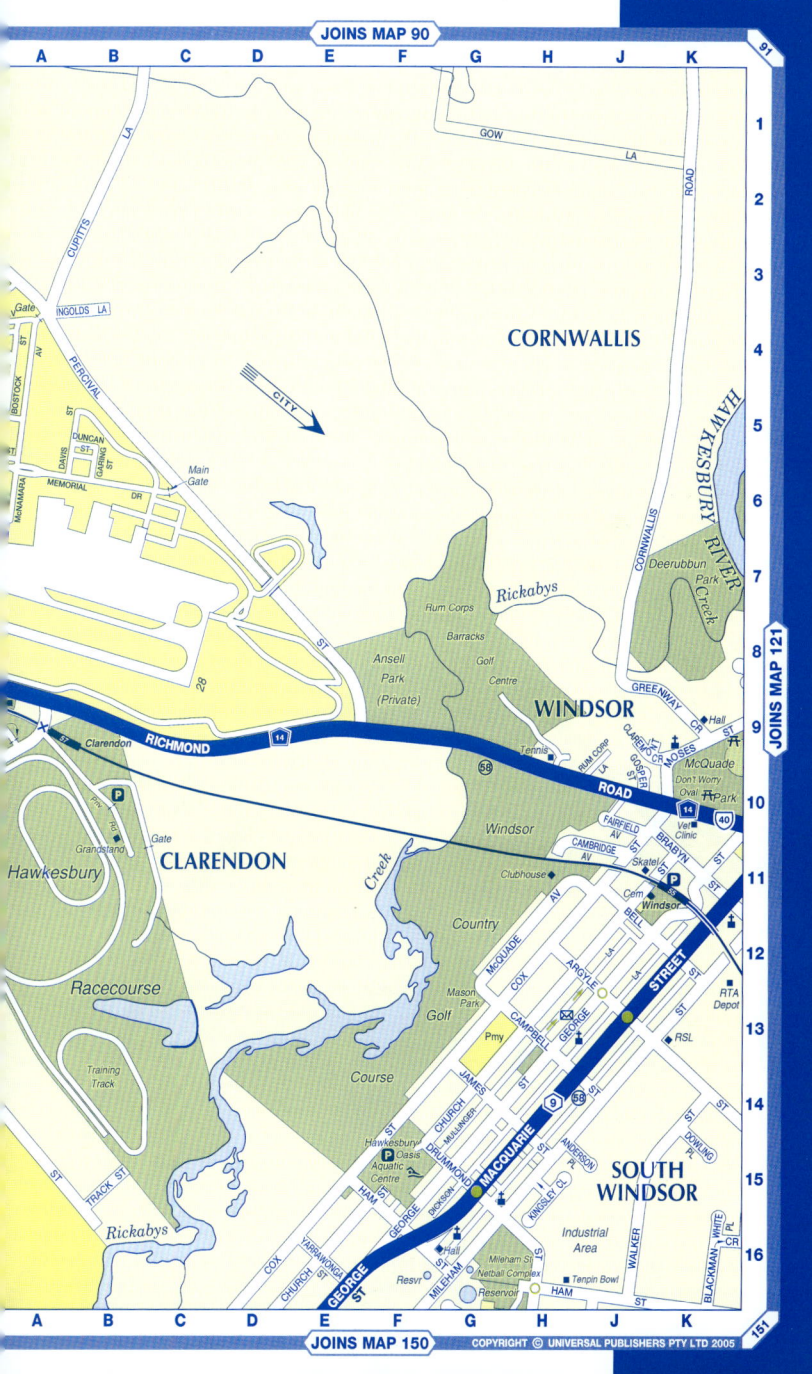

CORNWALLIS

WINDSOR

CLARENDON

SOUTH WINDSOR

Hawkesbury Racecourse

MAP 121

MAP 122

MAP 123

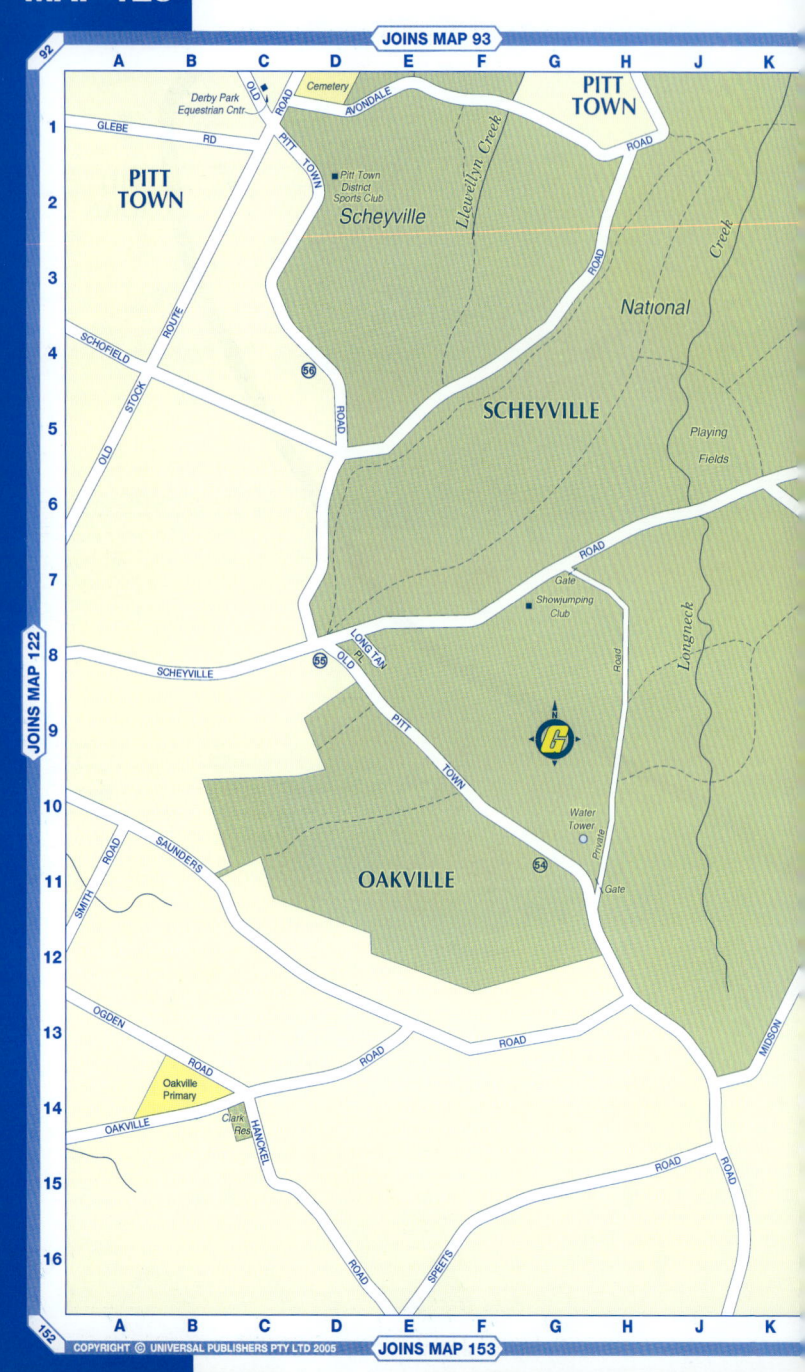

JOINS MAP 94

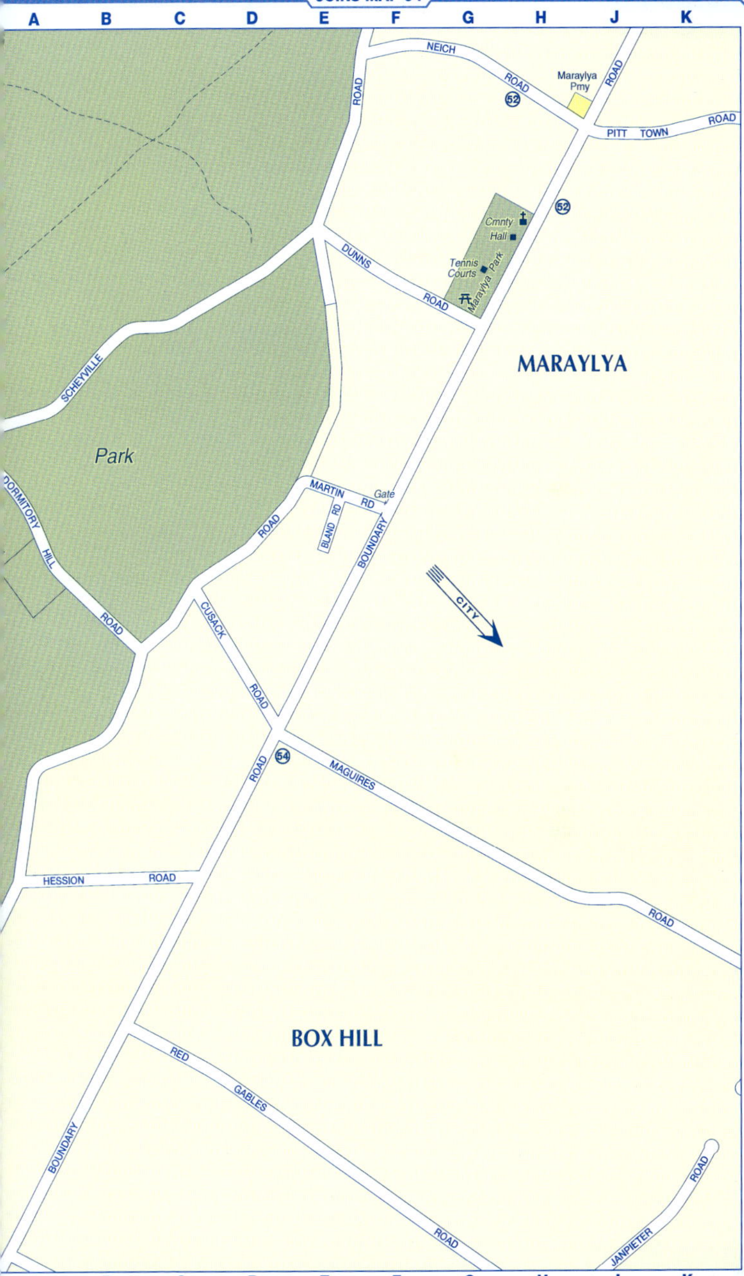

JOINS MAP 125

JOINS MAP 154

MAP 125

JOINS MAP 95

- Cattai Ck
- Pitt Town Road
- Bush Rd
- Idle Acres
- MARAYLYA
- CITY
- Road
- Gate
- Private
- Gate
- Flood Evacuation Route
- Road
- McClymonts
- Maguires Rd
- Jupiter Rd
- Birds La
- Horseworld Stadium
- Cattai Ck
- BOX HILL
- Lillian Rd

JOINS MAP 124
JOINS MAP 155

COPYRIGHT © UNIVERSAL PUBLISHERS PTY LTD 2005

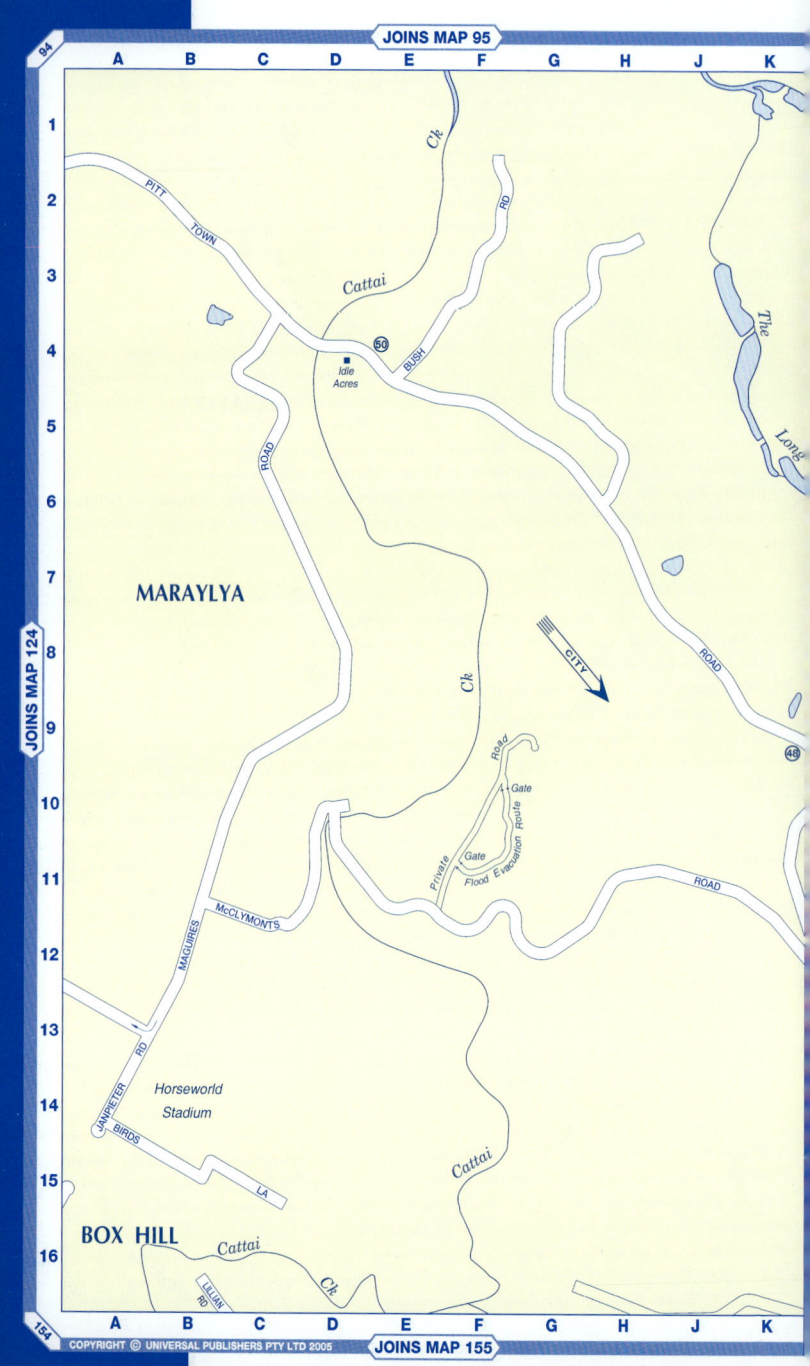

MAP 126

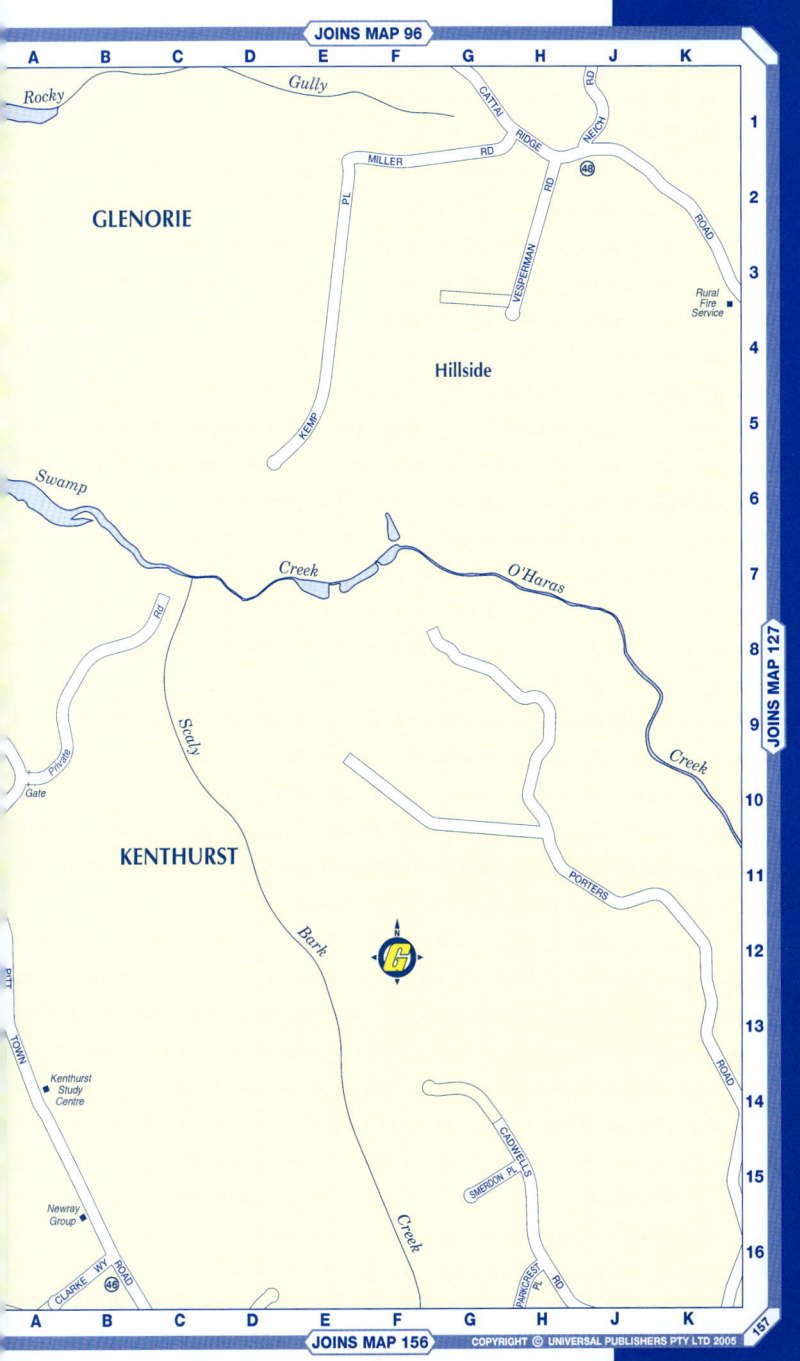

GLENORIE

Rocky Gully
Miller Rd
Cattai Ridge Rd
Neich Rd
Kemp Pl
Vesperman Rd

Hillside

Rural Fire Service

Swamp Creek
O'Haras Creek

KENTHURST

Private Rd
Gate
Scaly
Bark
Porters Rd
Pitt Town Rd
Kenthurst Study Centre
Cadwells Rd
Smerdon Pl
Newray Group
Clarke Wy
Princes Pl
Creek

JOINS MAP 96
JOINS MAP 127
JOINS MAP 156

MAP 127

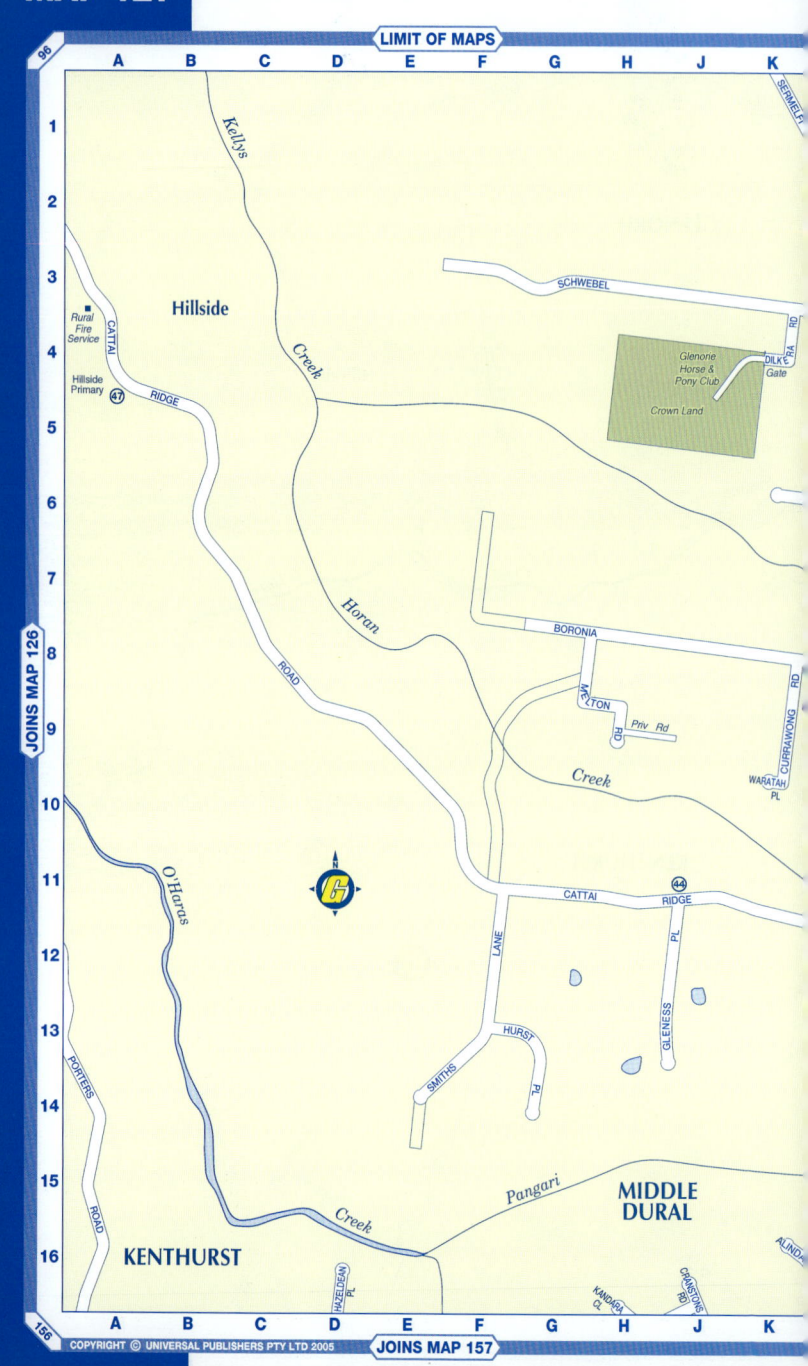

MAP 128

GLENORIE

MAP 129

LIMIT OF MAPS

FIDDLETOWN

GLENORIE

- Heckenberg Rd
- Hughes Rd
- Colah Creek
- Reserve
- Peebles Rd
- Nollands Rd
- Northholm Grammar
- Private Rd
- Banksia (Gravel Road) Pl
- Sunnyridge Rd
- Cobah Rd
- Perry Rd
- Ridge Rd
- Geebung Cl
- Calabash Rd
- Arcadia Health Cntr
- Henstock Rd
- Marrakesh Pl
- Fagans Rd
- St Benedicts Monastery
- Nursery
- Arcadia Road
- Community Hall
- Pmy
- Linga Longa Nursery
- Aprilunga Rd
- Roscommon Rd
- Wylds Rd
- Halls Rd
- Blacks Rd
- Smalls Rd

JOINS MAP 128

JOINS MAP 159

COPYRIGHT © UNIVERSAL PUBLISHERS PTY LTD 2005

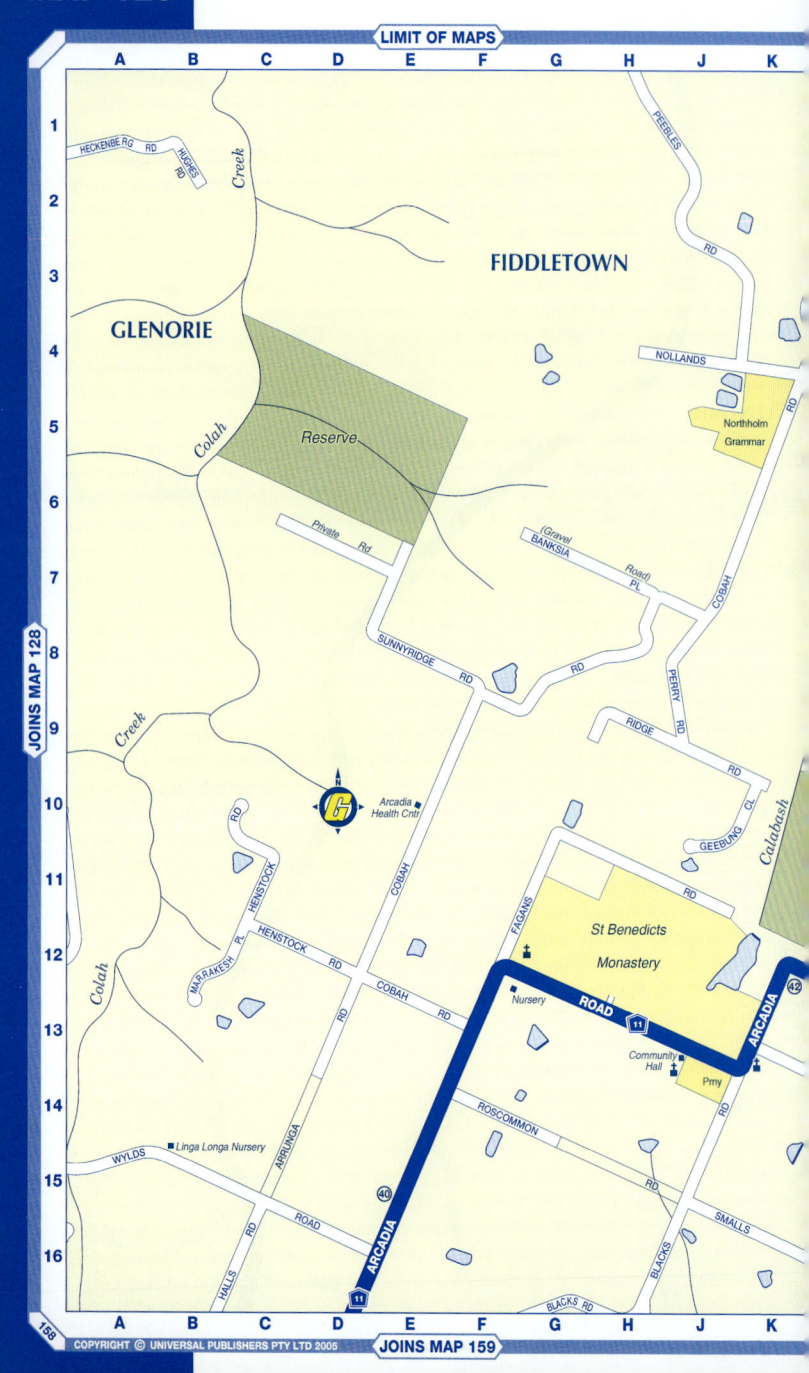

MAP 130

MAP 131

- Banks Creek
- ARCADIA
- BERRILEE
- Berrilee Pmy
- BANKS AV
- CHILCOTT ROAD
- MCCALLUMS AV
- Crosslands
- ROAD (44)
- JACK RUSSELL RD
- Gate
- BAY (45)
- CHARLTONS CREEK RD
- NEALE WY
- INSPIRATION PL
- Still Valley Park
- Berowra Regional
- GALSTON
- Charltons Creek
- Crosslands Convention & Field Study Centre
- Camp Windeyer
- Private Rd
- CROSSLANDS RD
- Gate

JOINS MAP 130 (left)
JOINS MAP 161 (bottom)
LIMIT OF MAPS (top)

LIMIT OF MAPS
103
A B C D E F G H J K
1 2 3 4 5 6 7 8 9 10 11 12 13 14 15 16
JOINS MAP 133
JOINS MAP 162
163
NOTE:
This road is unsuitable for caravans & semi-trailers
Recreation Reserve
Recreation Reserve
Recreation Reserve
Benowie Track
Dusthole Bay
Marina
Berowa Waters Marina East
KIRKPATRICK WY
RFS
BEROWRA WATERS RD
BAY Creek ROAD
Furber Park
BEROWRA WATERS
CREEK
Benowie
The Woolwash
CITY
ALSTON DR
COREEN CL
TURNER
GOORAWAY PL
BLUE RIDGE CR
NALYA LA
NALYA RD
WOOMBYE CL
AMANDA CL
ELIZABETH ST
ROAD
CAMBEWARRA CR
KITA RD
BEROWRA HEIGHTS
CURRAWONG RD
WYMAH CR
Aboriginal Carvings
DIANNE PL
CLINTON CL
BERKELEY CL
Berowra Valley Regional Park
Banggarai Ck
Track
Walking
BALGA CL
NARAMBI CL
BULAH CL
RONA CL
BARNETTS RD
DUNOON ST
WYANNA ST
Barnetts Road Res
Berowra Valley Regional Park
Berowra Valley
MT KURING-GAI Regional Park
(Great North Walk)
Sams Creek
BEROWRA
BEROWRA
Track
Footbridge
Calna Ck
Walking
Benowie
SOMERVILLE ROAD
Crosslands Reserve
HORNSBY HEIGHTS
GWANDALAN CR
11
40
42
38
P
COPYRIGHT © UNIVERSAL PUBLISHERS PTY LTD 2005

MAP 133

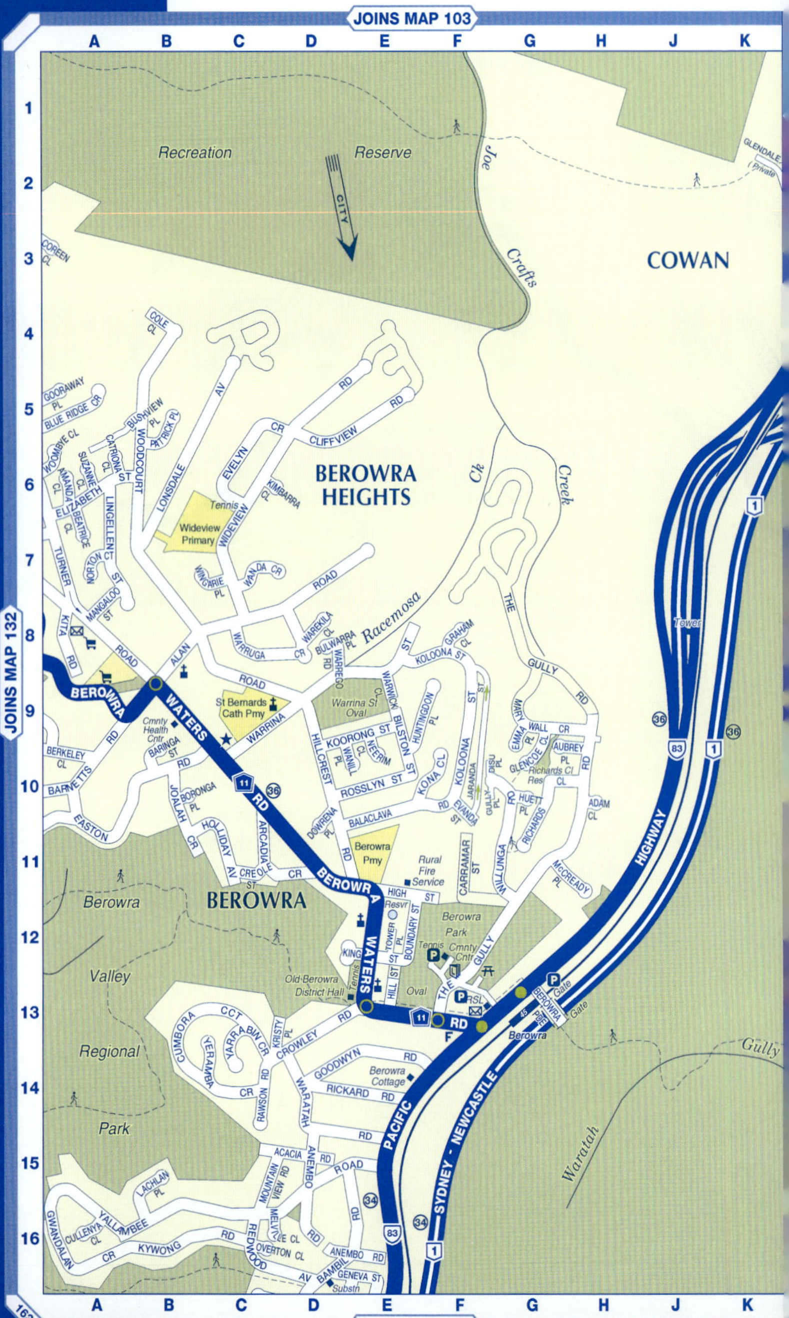

JOINS MAP 163

MAP 134

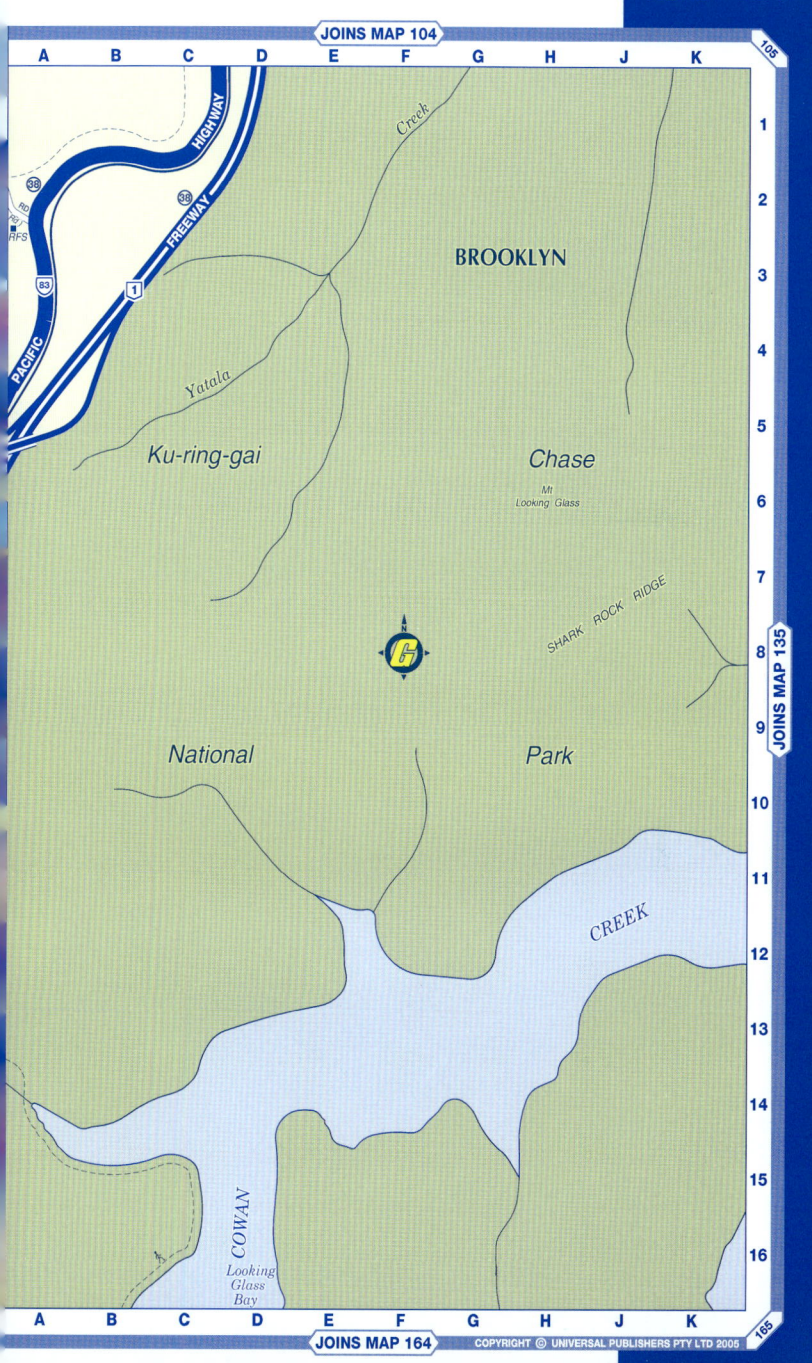

MAP 135

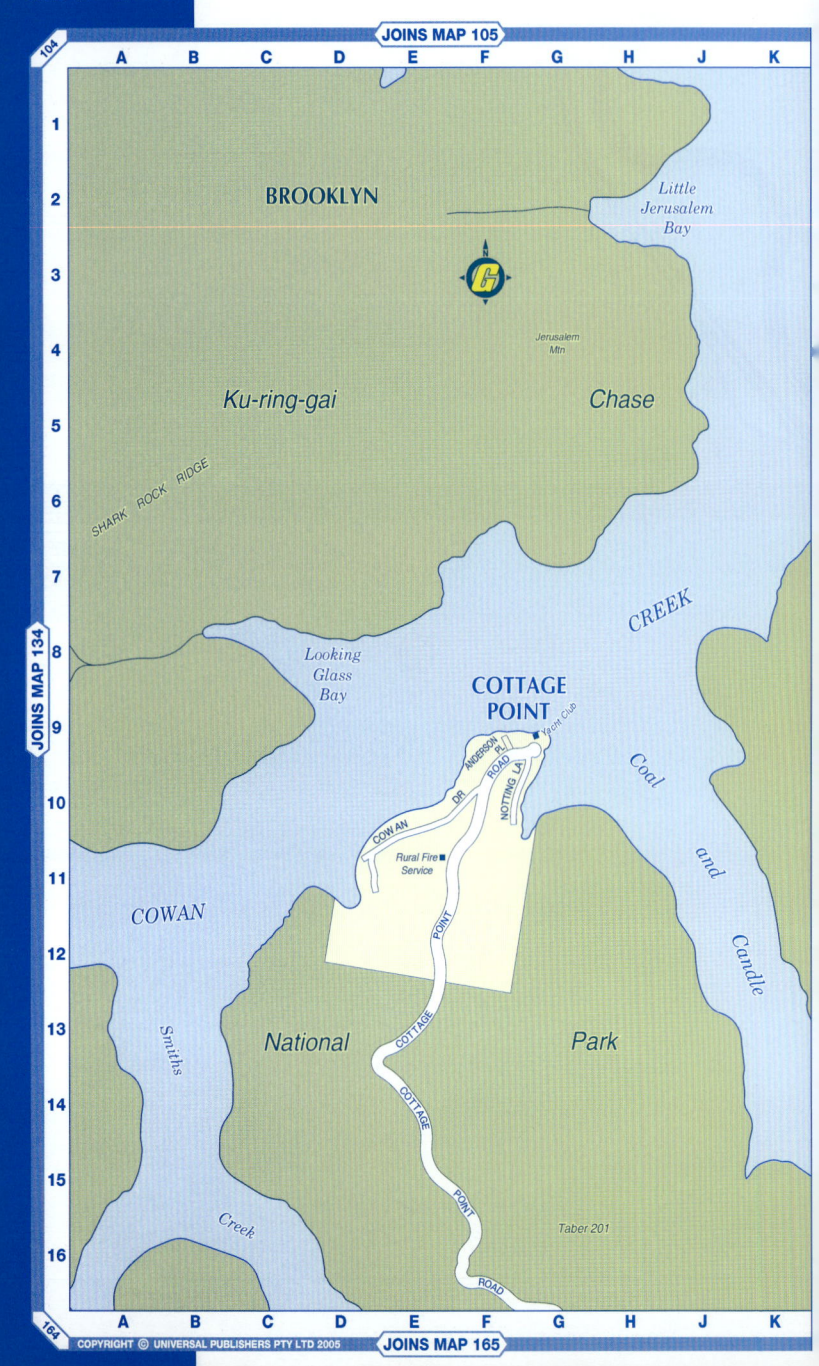

BROOKLYN

Little Jerusalem Bay

Jerusalem Mtn

Ku-ring-gai   *Chase*

SHARK ROCK RIDGE

CREEK

Looking Glass Bay

COTTAGE POINT

Yacht Club

ANDERSON PL
COWAN DR
ROAD
NOTTING LA

Rural Fire Service

Coal

COWAN

COTTAGE POINT

National   *Park*

and

Smiths

Candle

COTTAGE POINT ROAD

Creek

Taber 201

JOINS MAP 105 (top)
JOINS MAP 165 (bottom)
JOINS MAP 134 (left)

MAP 136

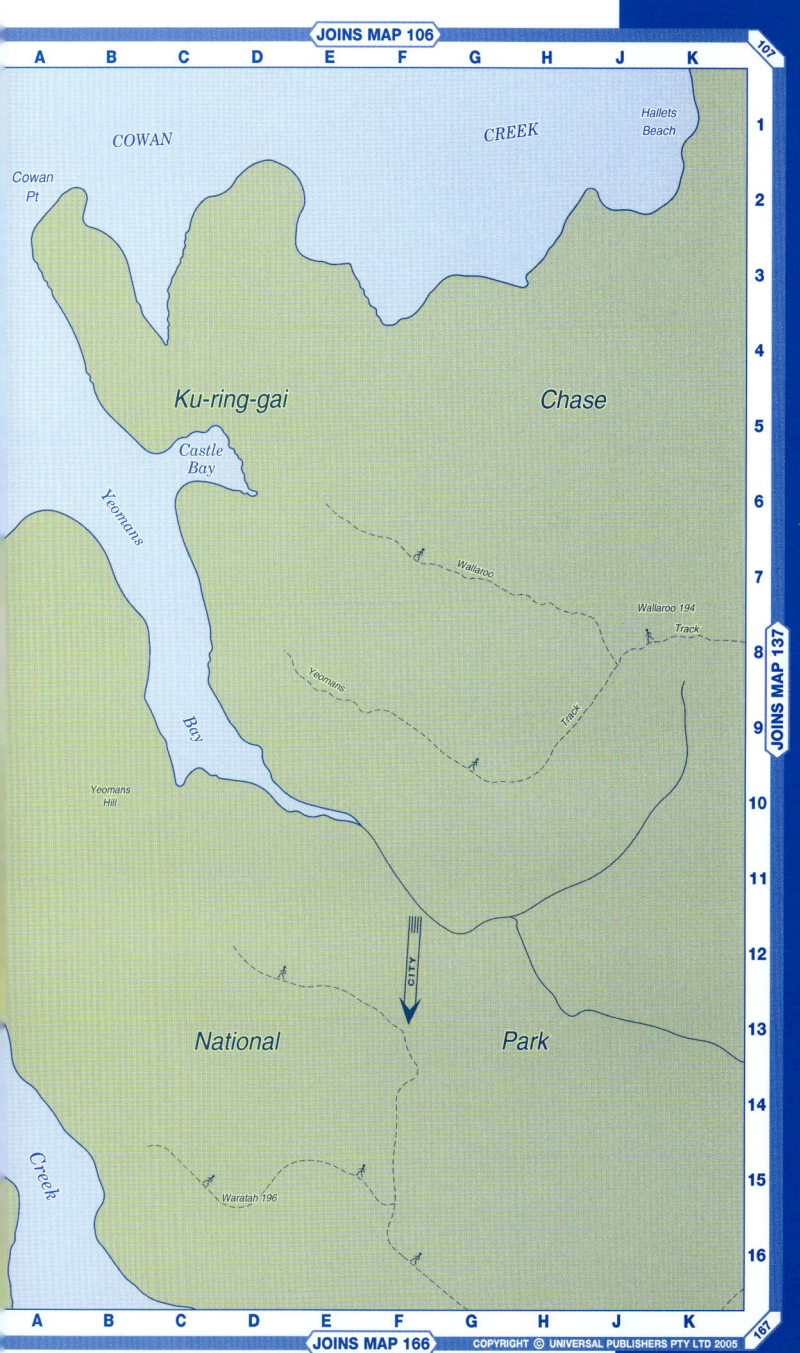

MAP 137

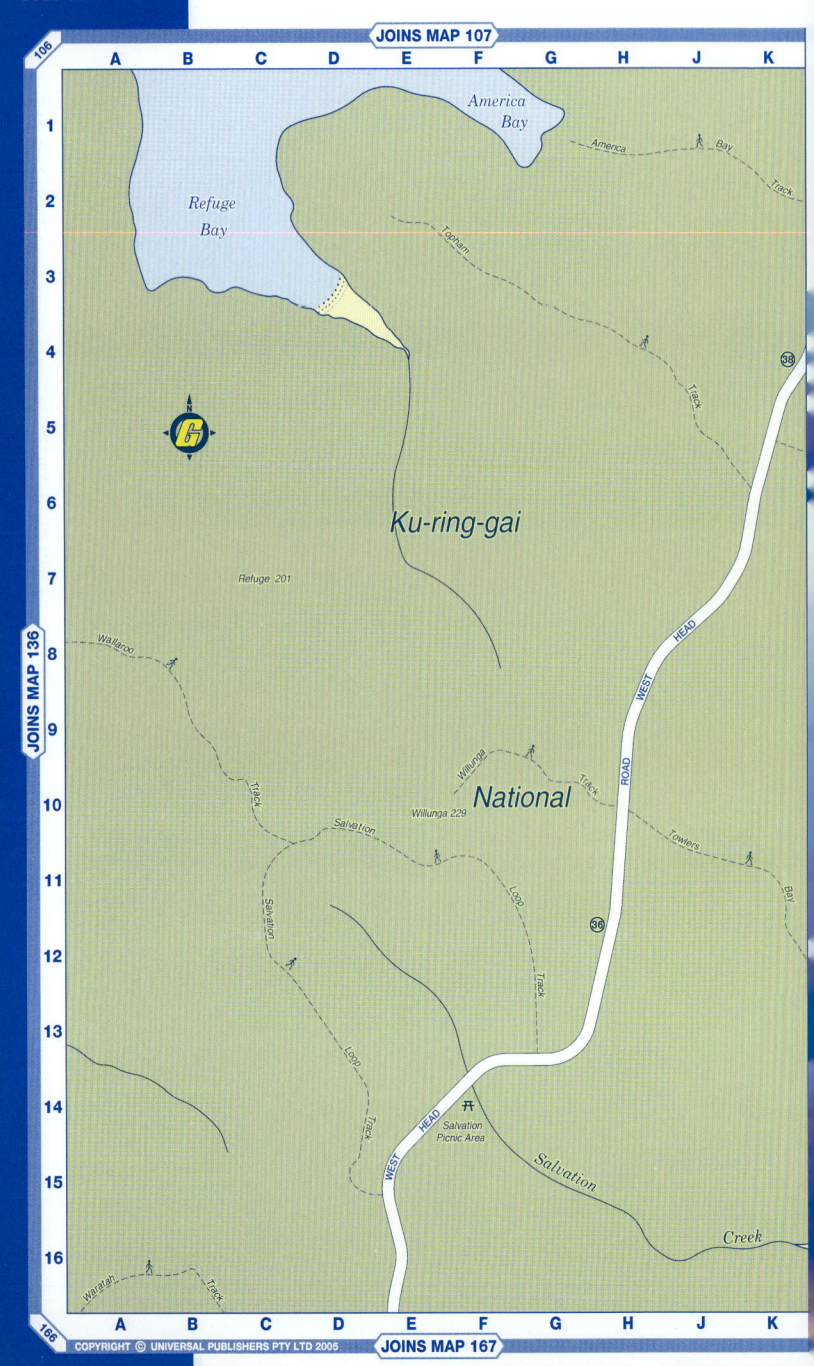

America Bay
Refuge Bay
Topham
America Bay Track
Ku-ring-gai
Refuge 201
Wallaroo
Track
Salvation
Willunga Track
Willunga 229
National
Towers Bay
Loop Track
WEST HEAD ROAD
Salvation Loop Track
Salvation Picnic Area
Salvation Creek
Waratah Track

JOINS MAP 107 (top)
JOINS MAP 167 (bottom)
JOINS MAP 136 (left)

MAP 138

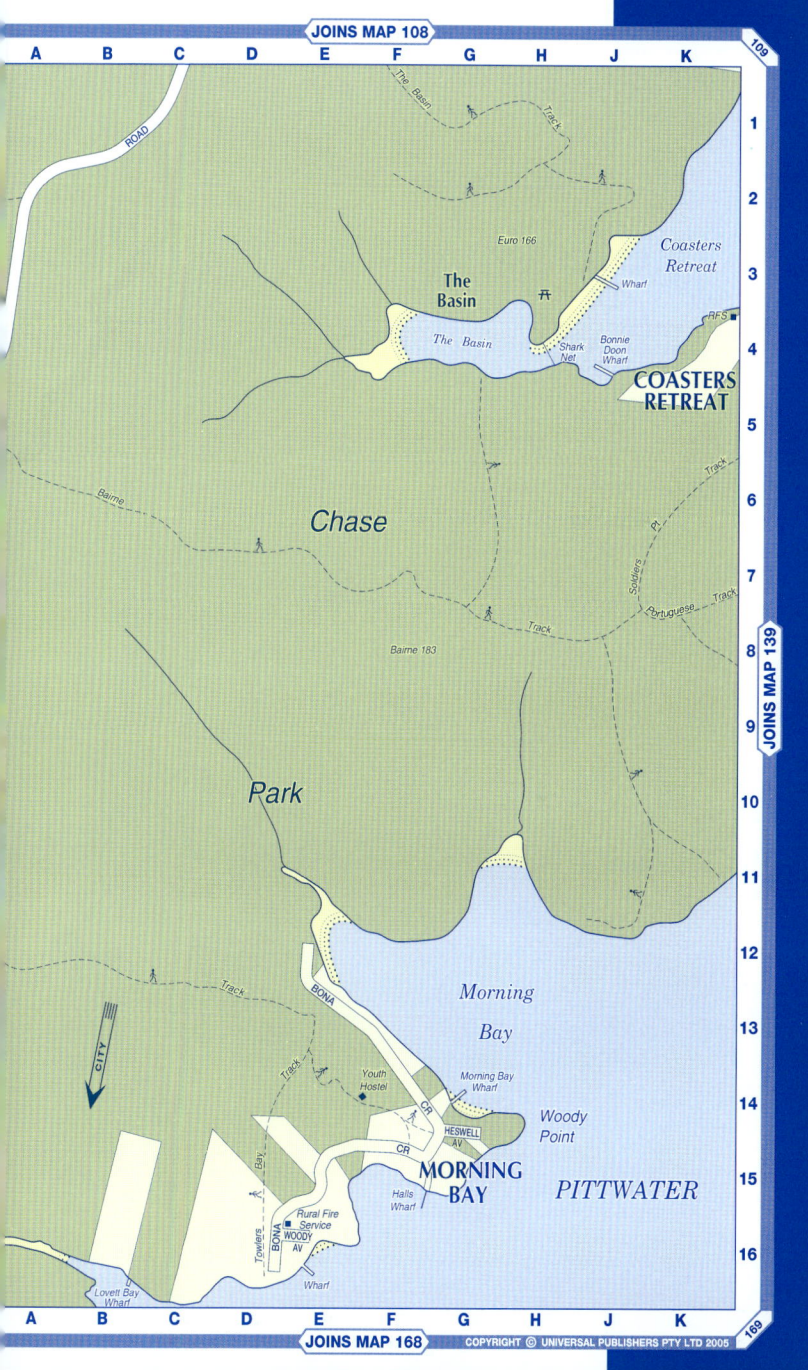

JOINS MAP 108

The Basin

Coasters Retreat

Euro 166

The Basin

Shark Net

Wharf

Bonnie Doon Wharf

RFS

COASTERS RETREAT

Bairne

Chase

Soldiers Pt

Track

Portuguese Track

Bairne 183

Park

CITY

Track

BONA

Morning Bay

Youth Hostel

Morning Bay Wharf

CR

HESWELL AV

Woody Point

CR

Bay

MORNING BAY

PITTWATER

Halls Wharf

Towlers

Rural Fire Service

BONA

WOODY AV

Lovett Bay Wharf

Wharf

JOINS MAP 168

JOINS MAP 139

MAP 139

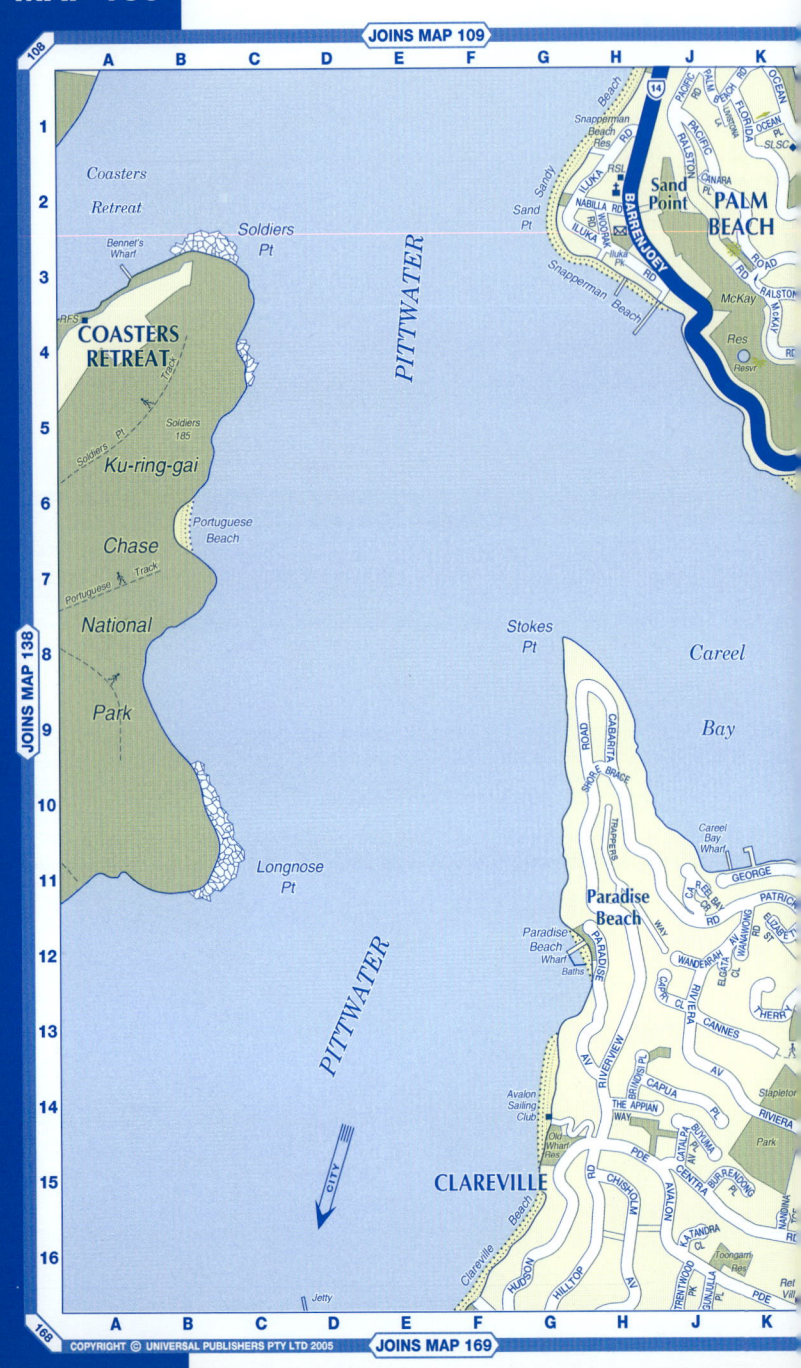

MAP 140
MAP 145 FOLLOWS

JOINS MAP 110

WHALE BEACH

- Cabbage Tree Boat Harbour
- Rock Baths
- Wiltshire
- Hordern Park
- Mitchell Rd
- Pacific Rd
- Whale Beach Rd
- Rock Bath Rd
- Annie Wyatt Pk
- Ebor Rd
- Banksia
- Cynthea Rd
- Bynya Rd
- Norma Rd
- Cynthea Res
- McKay Reserve
- Morella Rd
- Dark Gully Pk
- Kidds
- Whale Beach
- Memorial
- Whale Beach H88
- SLSC
- Thyra Rd
- Surf Rd
- The Strand
- Malo Rd
- Rock Baths
- Little Head
- Dolphin Bay
- Careel Head
- Beau
- Dolphin Pk
- Lane Lodge
- Dolphin Cr
- Rayner Rd
- Etna
- Drawing
- Newena Pl
- Coral Rd
- Barrenjoey Rd
- Careel Bay Ovals (Avalon Soccer Club)
- Careel Head Rd
- Albert Rd
- Alexander Rd

CAREEL BAY

- Careel Bay
- Careel Cr
- Hitchcock Park
- Burrawong Rd
- Whale Beach Rd
- Careel Headland Reserve
- Bangalley Head
- St
- Queens St
- Joseph St
- Toorak
- John Pl
- Nursing Home
- Tennis
- Binburra
- Milga Rd
- Gunyah Pl
- Lewis
- Net Rd
- Av
- Bareena Rd
- Watkins Rd
- Marine Rd
- William Av
- Edwin Av
- North Avalon Rd
- Catalina Cr
- Urara Rd
- Park Av
- Kevin
- Elvina Av
- Jamieson Pk
- Coonanga Rd
- Tasman Rd
- Harley Rd
- St Michael's Cave
- Sanctuary Av
- Wollstonecraft
- Eastbourne Av
- Elaine Av
- Barrenjoey High
- Ten
- Central
- Maria Regina Pmy
- Av
- Rec Res
- Des Creagh Reserve
- Avalon Beach
- Marine
- Hole in the Wall

AVALON

TASMAN SEA

JOINS MAP 170

COPYRIGHT © UNIVERSAL PUBLISHERS PTY LTD 2005

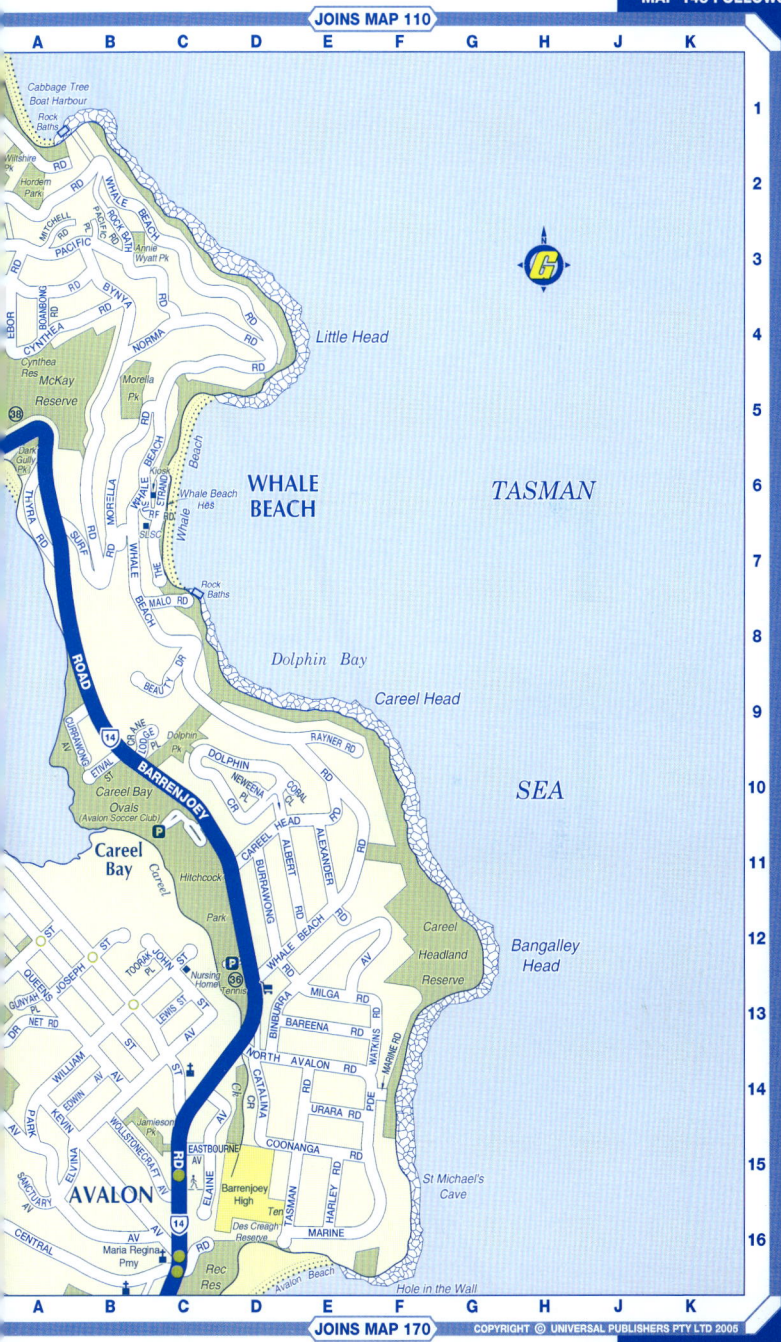

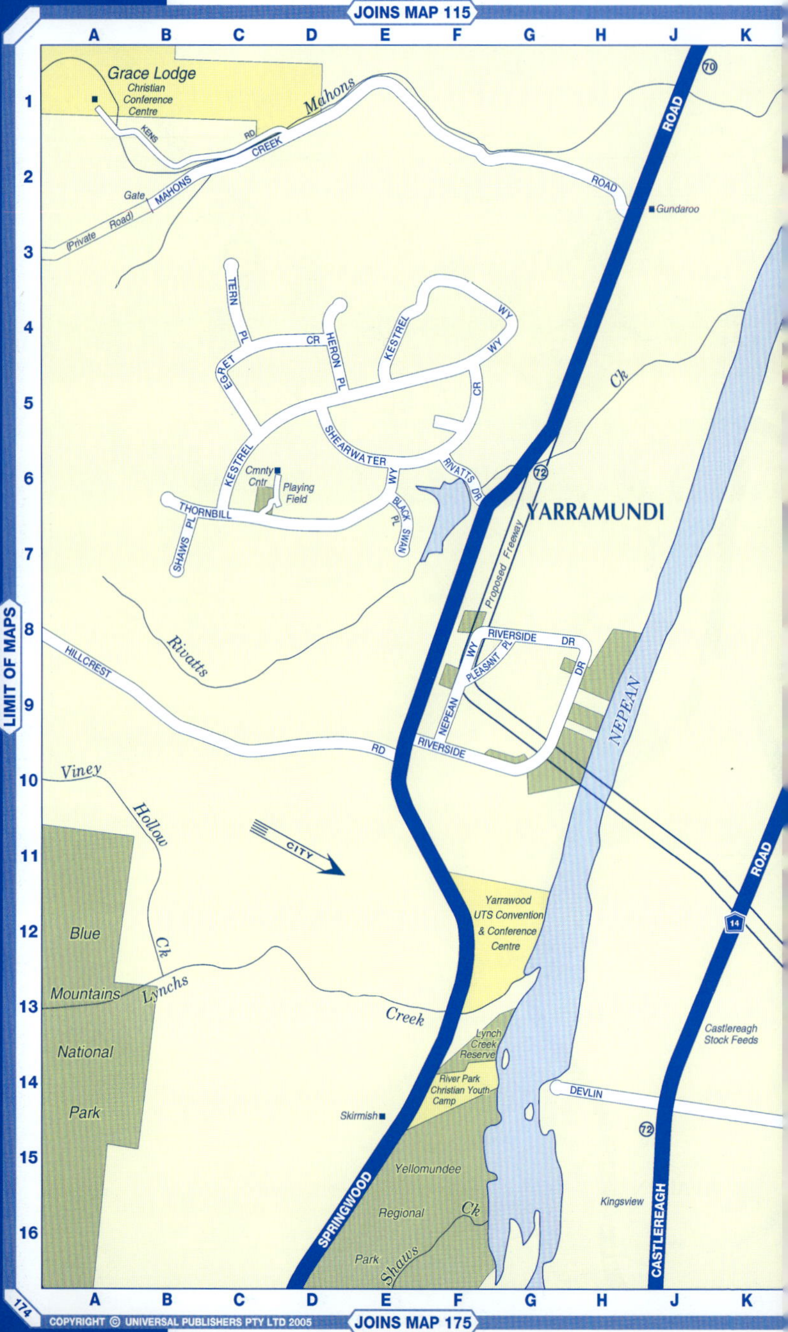
JOINS MAP 115
A B C D E F G H J K
1 2 3 4 5 6 7 8 9 10 11 12 13 14 15 16
LIMIT OF MAPS
Grace Lodge
Christian
Conference
Centre
KENS
RD
Mahons
CREEK
MAHONS
Gate
(Private Road)
ROAD
Gundaroo
70
TERN
PL
CR
HERON
PL
EGRET
KESTREL
WY
WY
CR
SHEARWATER
WY
RIVATTS
DR
Ck
72
YARRAMUNDI
KESTREL
Cmnty
Cntr
Playing
Field
THORNBILL
SHAWS
PL
BLACK
SWAN
PL
Proposed Freeway
RIVERSIDE
DR
WY
PLEASANT
PL
DR
NEPEAN
HILLCREST
Rivatts
NEPEAN
RIVERSIDE
RD
Viney
Hollow
CITY
Ck
ROAD
14
Yarrawood
UTS Convention
& Conference
Centre
Blue
Mountains
National
Park
Lynchs
Creek
Lynch
Creek
Reserve
River Park
Christian Youth
Camp
Skirmish
DEVLIN
72
Castlereagh
Stock Feeds
Yellomundee
Regional
Park
Ck
Shaws
SPRINGWOOD
Kingsview
CASTLEREAGH
JOINS MAP 175

MAP 146

AGNES BANKS

- RIVER RD
- COOLAMON RD
- KOORINGAL DR
- BROOKS LA
- PERSOONIA AV
- GEEBUNG CL
- CASTLEREAGH ROAD
- RICKARDS RD
- Plant Nursery
- Penrith Valley Ranges
- Agnes Banks Nature Reserve
- Ent Gate
- Nepean Raceway (Nepean Motorsports Club)

CASTLEREAGH

- Proposed
- TICKNER ST
- HESTER ST
- Freeway
- Castle Lodge Greyhound Complex
- DEVLIN RD
- POST OFFICE RD
- FIRE TRAIL RD

JOINS MAP 116 (top)
JOINS MAP 176 (bottom)
JOINS MAP 147 (right)

COPYRIGHT © UNIVERSAL PUBLISHERS PTY LTD 2005

MAP 147

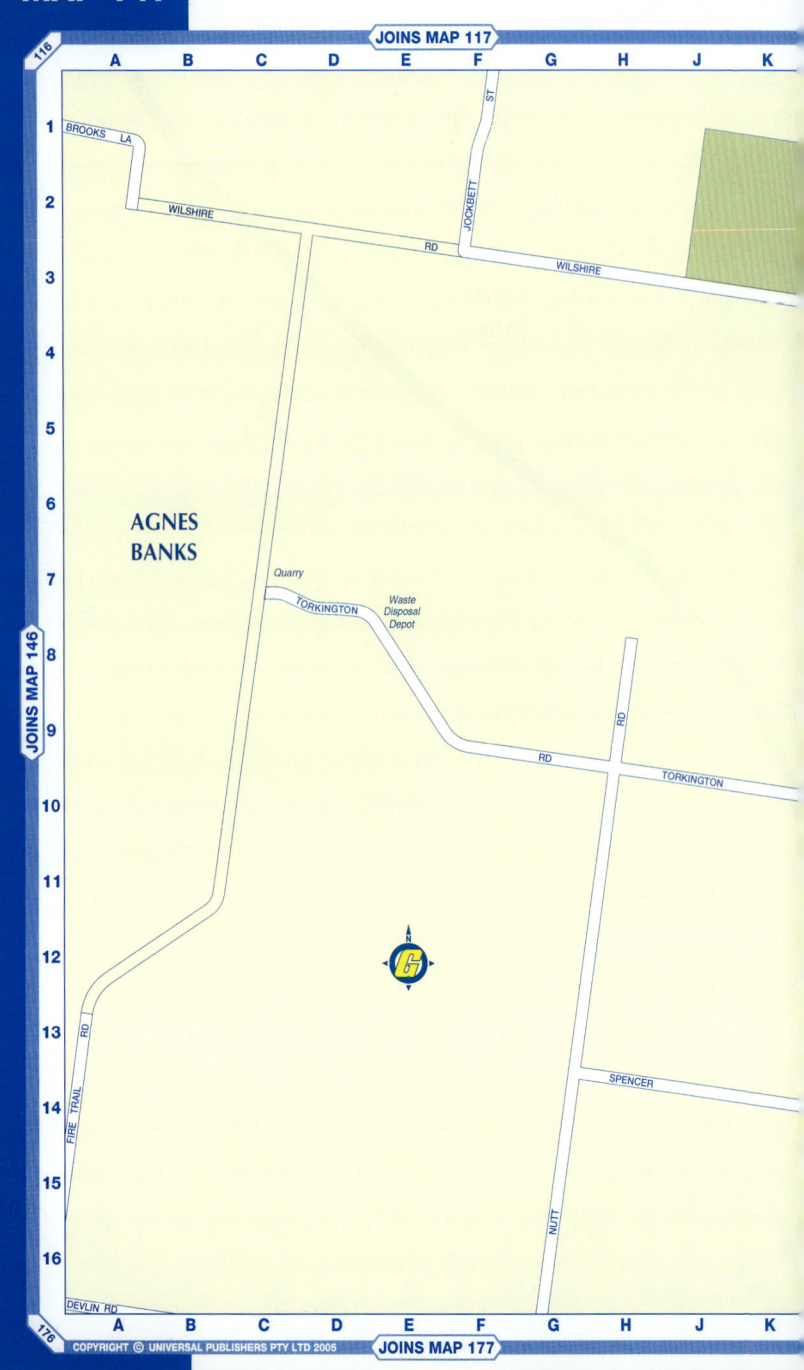

JOINS MAP 117

- Brooks La
- Wilshire Rd
- Jockbett St
- Wilshire Rd

AGNES BANKS

- Quarry
- Torkington Rd
- Waste Disposal Depot
- Torkington Rd
- Fire Trail Rd
- Spencer
- Nutt
- Devlin Rd

JOINS MAP 146
JOINS MAP 177

COPYRIGHT © UNIVERSAL PUBLISHERS PTY LTD 2005

MAP 148

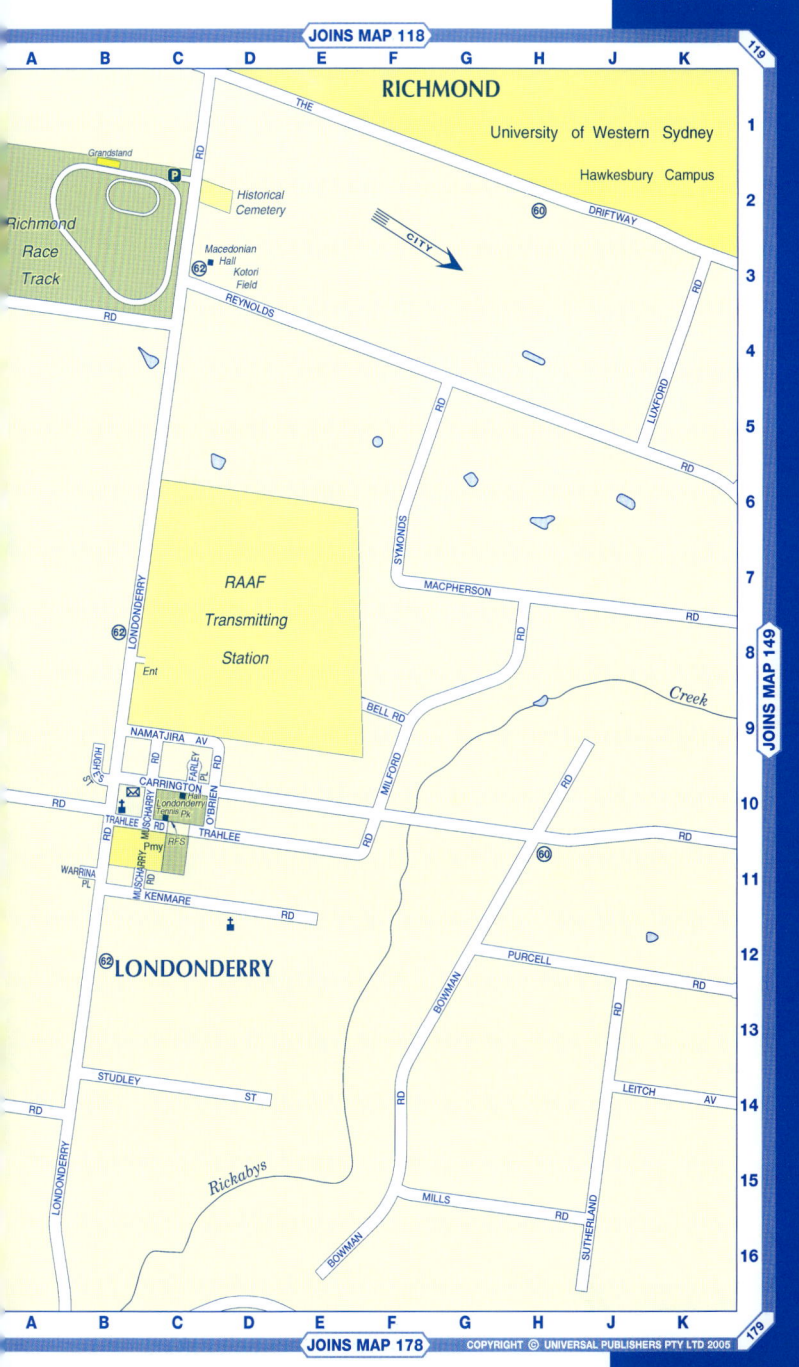

RICHMOND

University of Western Sydney
Hawkesbury Campus

Richmond Race Track
Grandstand
Historical Cemetery
Macedonian Hall
Kotori Field
REYNOLDS RD
THE DRIFTWAY
CITY
LUXFORD RD
SYMONDS RD
MACPHERSON RD
RAAF Transmitting Station
Ent
BELL RD
MILFORD RD
Creek
NAMATJIRA AV
CARRINGTON RD
Hall
Londonderry Tennis Pk
O'BRIEN
FARLEY PL
TRAHLEE RD
MUSSHARRY RD
Pmy
RFS
WARRINA PL
KENMARE RD
LONDONDERRY
PURCELL RD
BOWMAN RD
STUDLEY ST
LEITCH AV
Rickabys
MILLS RD
SUTHERLAND RD
LONDONDERRY RD

JOINS MAP 118
JOINS MAP 178
JOINS MAP 149

COPYRIGHT © UNIVERSAL PUBLISHERS PTY LTD 2005

MAP 149

JOINS MAP 119

RICHMOND

University of Western Sydney
Hawkesbury Campus

Clarendon Paddocks

Rickabys Creek Paddocks

Blacktown Paddocks

Hawkesbury City Waste Management Facility

Reserve

Rickabys Hill

LONDONDERRY

Rickabys

Camp Elim Conference Cntr

John Morony Correctional Complex

Waste Services Depot

Castlereagh Landfill

Arran Lodge Kennels

Restricted Entry Gate

Depot

Roads/labels: BEEF CATTLE RD, BLACKTOWN RD, RACECOURSE RD, THE DRIVEWAY, CLARK RD, REYNOLDS RD, MACPHERSON RD, CARRINGTON RD, PURCELL RD, HOWELL RD, LAURENCE RD, LEITCH AV, PARKER RD, BENNETT RD, TOORAH RD, THE NORTHERN ROAD

JOINS MAP 148 / JOINS MAP 179

COPYRIGHT © UNIVERSAL PUBLISHERS PTY LTD 2005

MAP 150

JOINS MAP 121

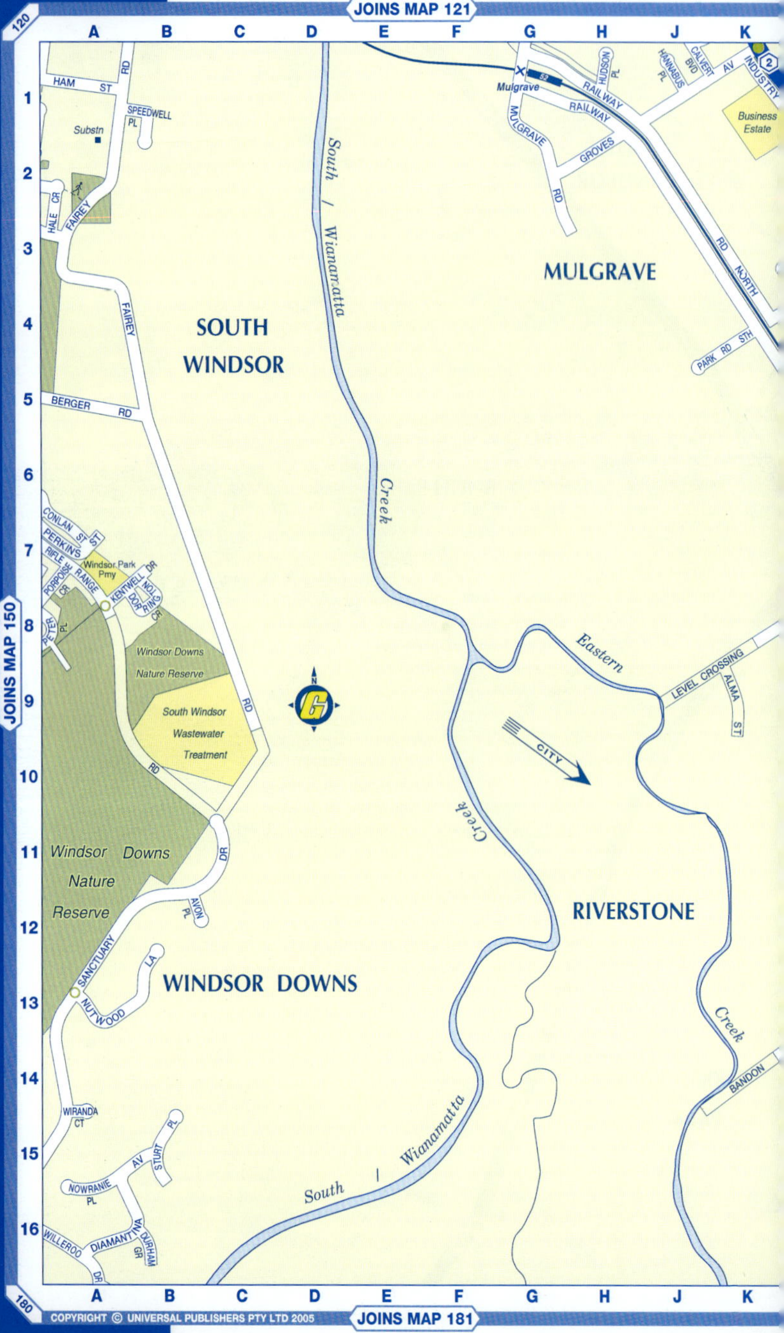

JOINS MAP 150

JOINS MAP 181

JOINS MAP 122

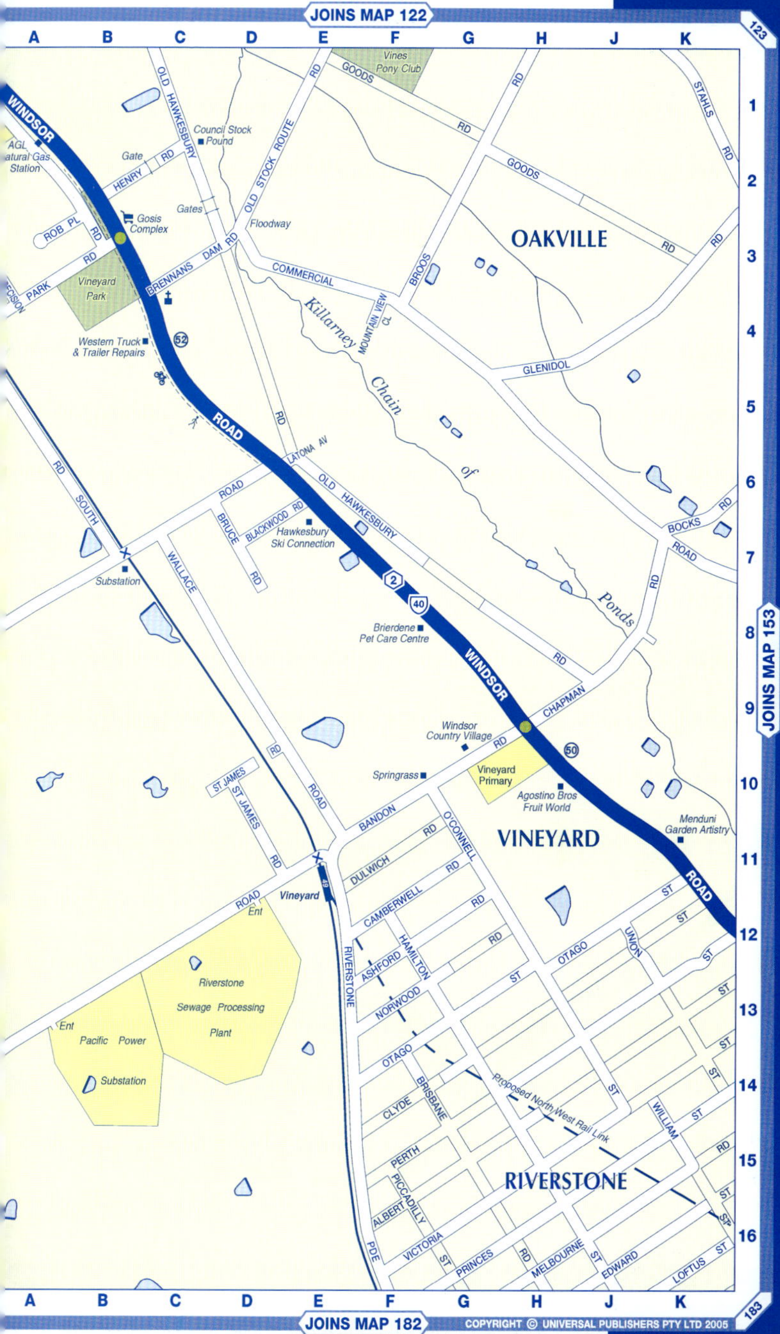

JOINS MAP 182

MAP 153

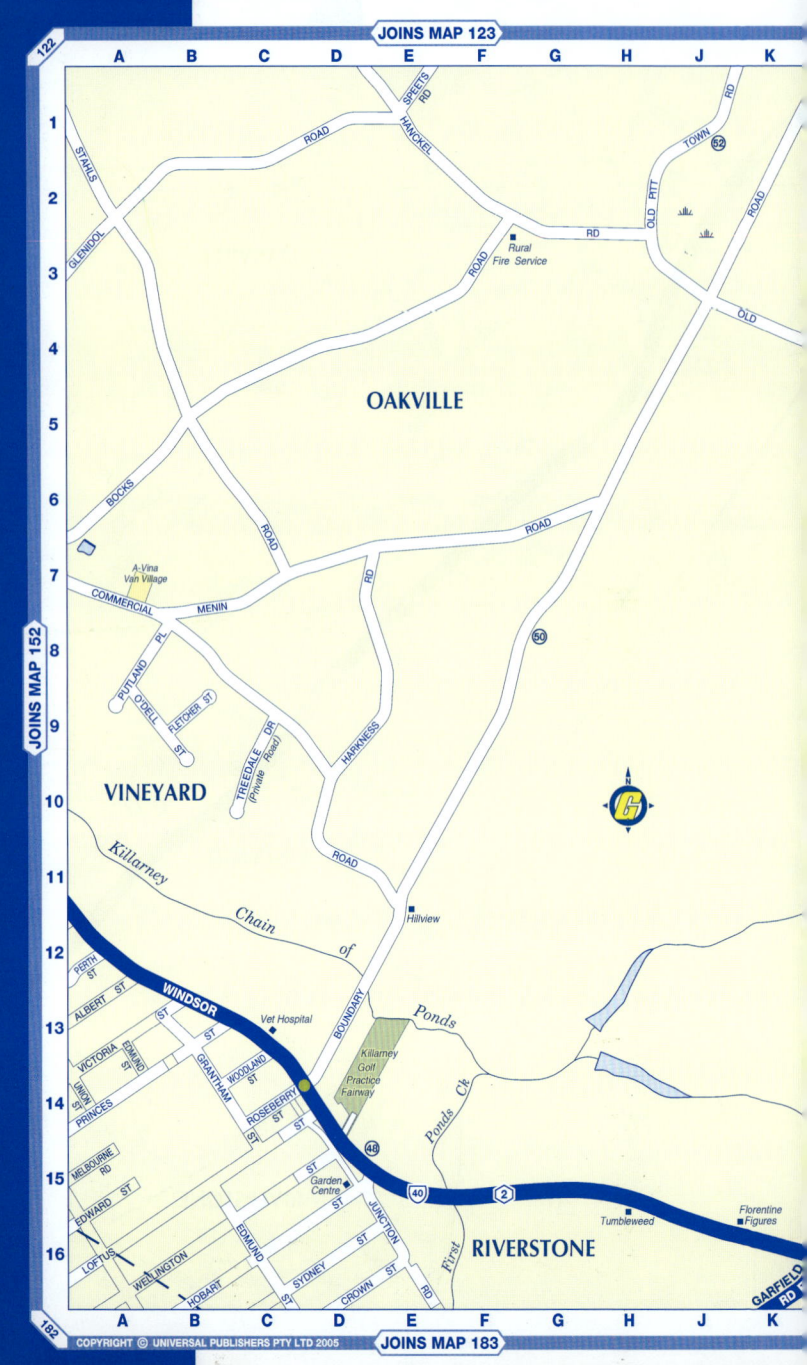

OAKVILLE

VINEYARD

RIVERSTONE

Streets and features visible:
- Stahls Road
- Glendol Road
- Speets Rd
- Hanckel Road
- Old Pitt Town Road
- Old Pitt Rd
- Rural Fire Service
- Bocks Road
- Menin Road
- Commercial Road
- A-Vina Van Village
- Putland Pl
- O'Dell St
- Fletcher St
- Treedale Dr (Private Road)
- Harkness Rd
- Killarney Chain of Ponds
- Hillview
- Boundary Road
- Windsor Road
- Perth St
- Albert St
- Victoria St
- Edmund St
- Union St
- Princes St
- Melbourne St
- Edward St
- Loftus St
- Wellington St
- Hobart St
- Grantham St
- Woodland St
- Roseberry St
- Sydney St
- Crown St
- Edmund St
- Junction St
- First St
- Vet Hospital
- Killarney Golf Practice Fairway
- Garden Centre
- Ponds Ck
- Tumbleweed
- Florentine Figures
- Garfield Rd

JOINS MAP 123 (top)
JOINS MAP 183 (bottom)
JOINS MAP 152 (left)
JOINS MAP 122 (top-left)
JOINS MAP 182 (bottom-left)

MAP 154

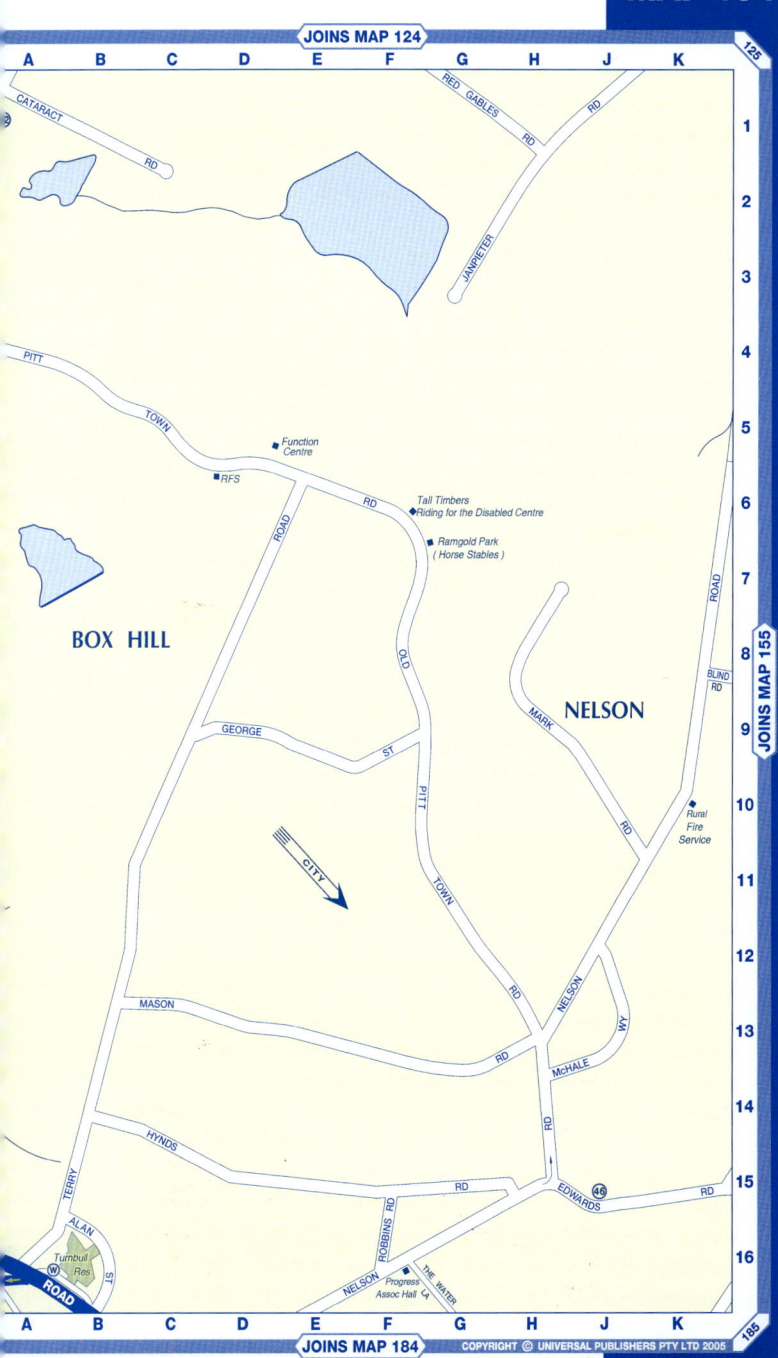

JOINS MAP 124

CATARACT RD
RED GABLES RD
JANPETER RD
PITT TOWN ROAD
Function Centre
RFS
RD
Tall Timbers
Riding for the Disabled Centre
Ramgold Park
(Horse Stables)

BOX HILL

OLD PITT TOWN RD
GEORGE ST
MARK RD
NELSON
BLIND RD
ROAD

CITY

Rural Fire Service

MASON RD
NELSON WY
McHALE RD

HYNDS RD
TERRY ST
ALAN ST
Turnbull Res
ROBBINS RD
NELSON RD
Progress Assoc Hall
THE WATER LA
EDWARDS RD (46)
ROAD

JOINS MAP 184
JOINS MAP 155
COPYRIGHT © UNIVERSAL PUBLISHERS PTY LTD 2005

MAP 155

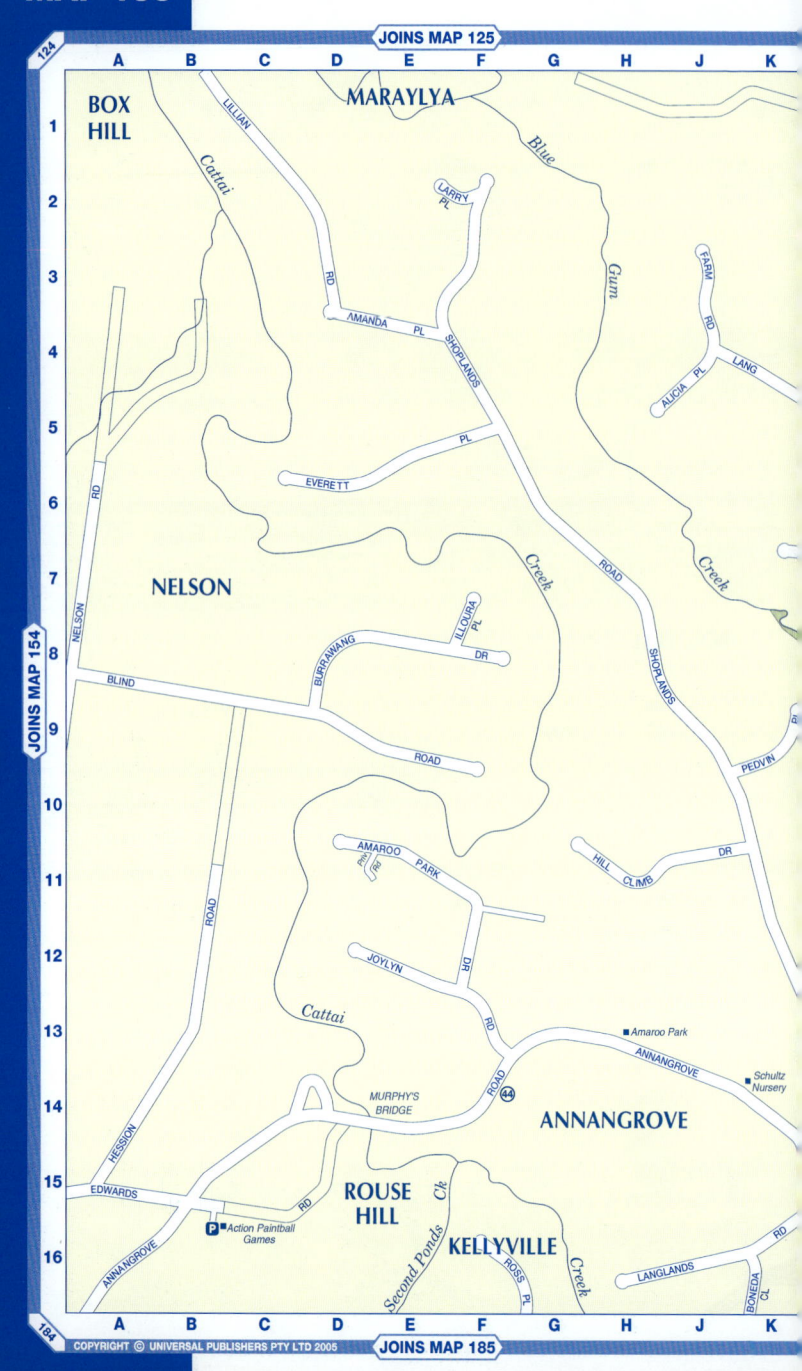

JOINS MAP 125

BOX HILL

MARAYLYA

- Lillian Rd
- Cattai Rd
- Larry Pl
- Amanda Pl
- Shoplands
- Alicia Pl
- Farm Rd
- Lang
- Everett Pl
- Blue Gum Creek

NELSON

- Nelson Rd
- Blind Rd
- Burrawang
- Illoura Pl
- Dr
- Shoplands Road
- Pedvin
- Creek
- Road
- Amaroo Park
- Phils Rd
- Hill Climb Dr
- Joylyn Dr
- Cattai
- Amaroo Park
- Annangrove Road
- Schultz Nursery
- Murphy's Bridge
- (44)

ANNANGROVE

- Hession Rd
- Edwards
- Action Paintball Games
- Annangrove Rd

ROUSE HILL

KELLYVILLE

- Second Ponds Ck
- Ross Pl
- Langlands Rd
- Boneda Ct
- Creek

JOINS MAP 185

COPYRIGHT © UNIVERSAL PUBLISHERS PTY LTD 2005

MAP 156

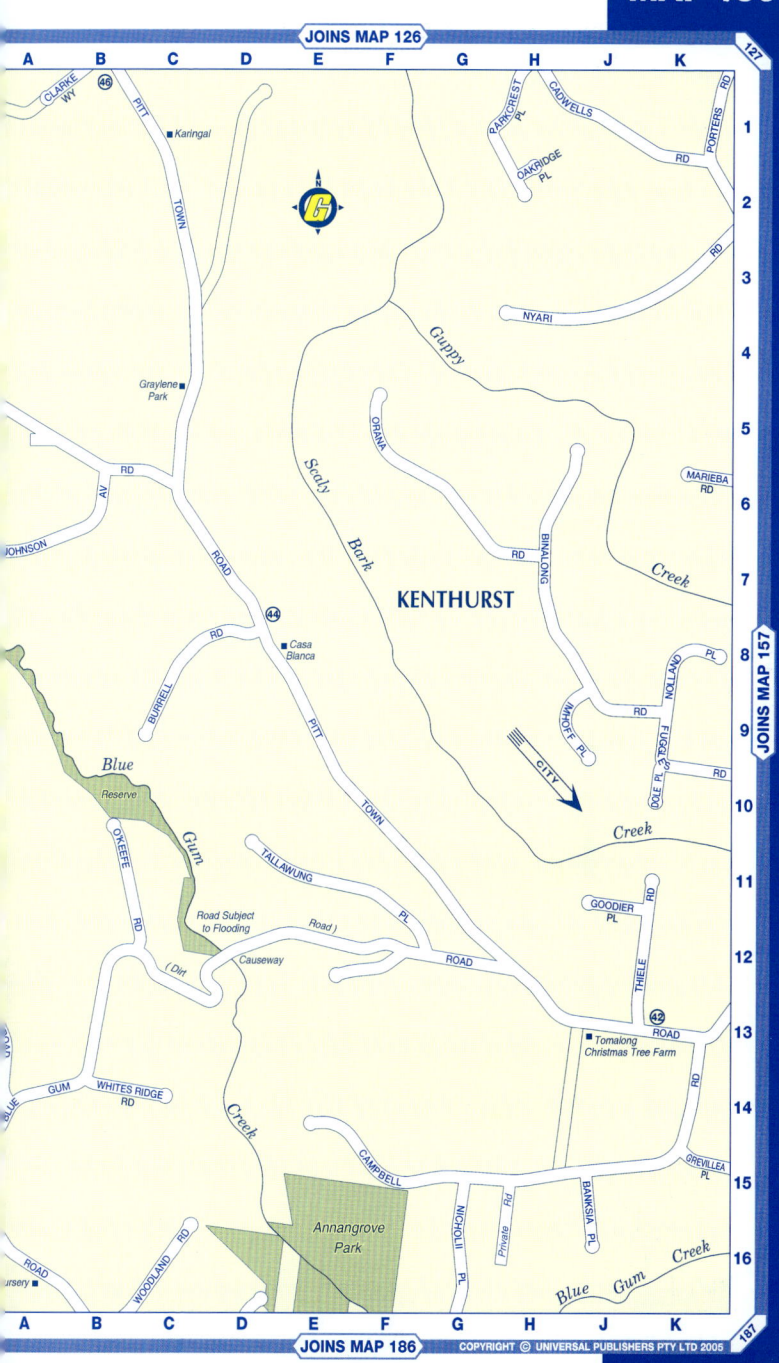

KENTHURST

MAP 157

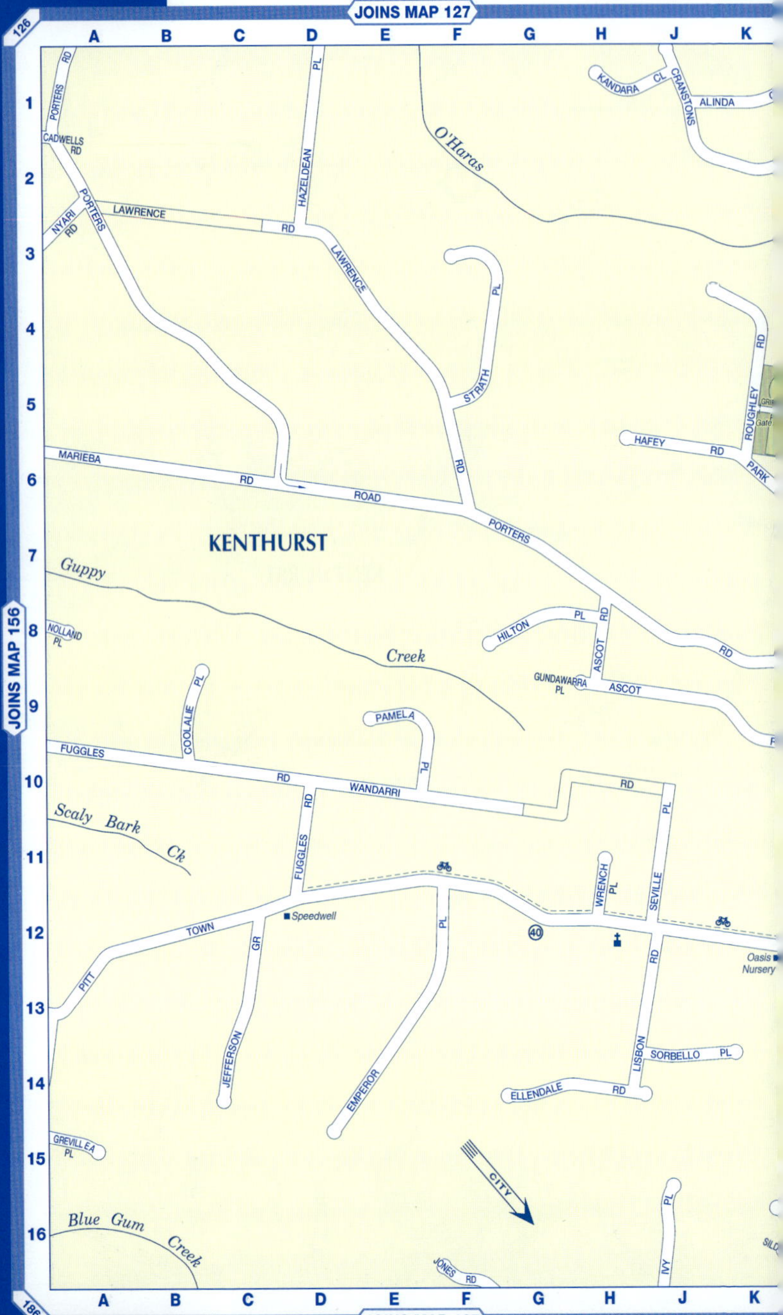
JOINS MAP 127
JOINS MAP 156
JOINS MAP 187
126
186
A B C D E F G H J K
1 2 3 4 5 6 7 8 9 10 11 12 13 14 15 16
KENTHURST
PORTERS RD
CADWELLS RD
NYARI RD
LAWRENCE RD
HAZELDEAN PL
O'Haras
KANDARA CL
CRANSTONS
ALINDA
STRATH PL
ROUGHLEY RD
HAFEY RD
PARK
Gate
MARIEBA RD
ROAD
PORTERS RD
Guppy Creek
NOLLAND PL
HILTON PL
ASCOT RD
GUNDAWARRA PL
ASCOT
COOLALIE PL
PAMELA PL
FUGGLES RD
WANDARRI RD
Scaly Bark Ck
FUGGLES RD
WRENCH PL
SEVILLE PL
Speedwell
TOWN
PITT
GR
40
Oasis Nursery
LISBON RD
SORBELLO PL
ELLENDALE RD
JEFFERSON
EMPEROR
GREVILLEA PL
CITY
Blue Gum Creek
JONES RD
IVY PL

MAP 158

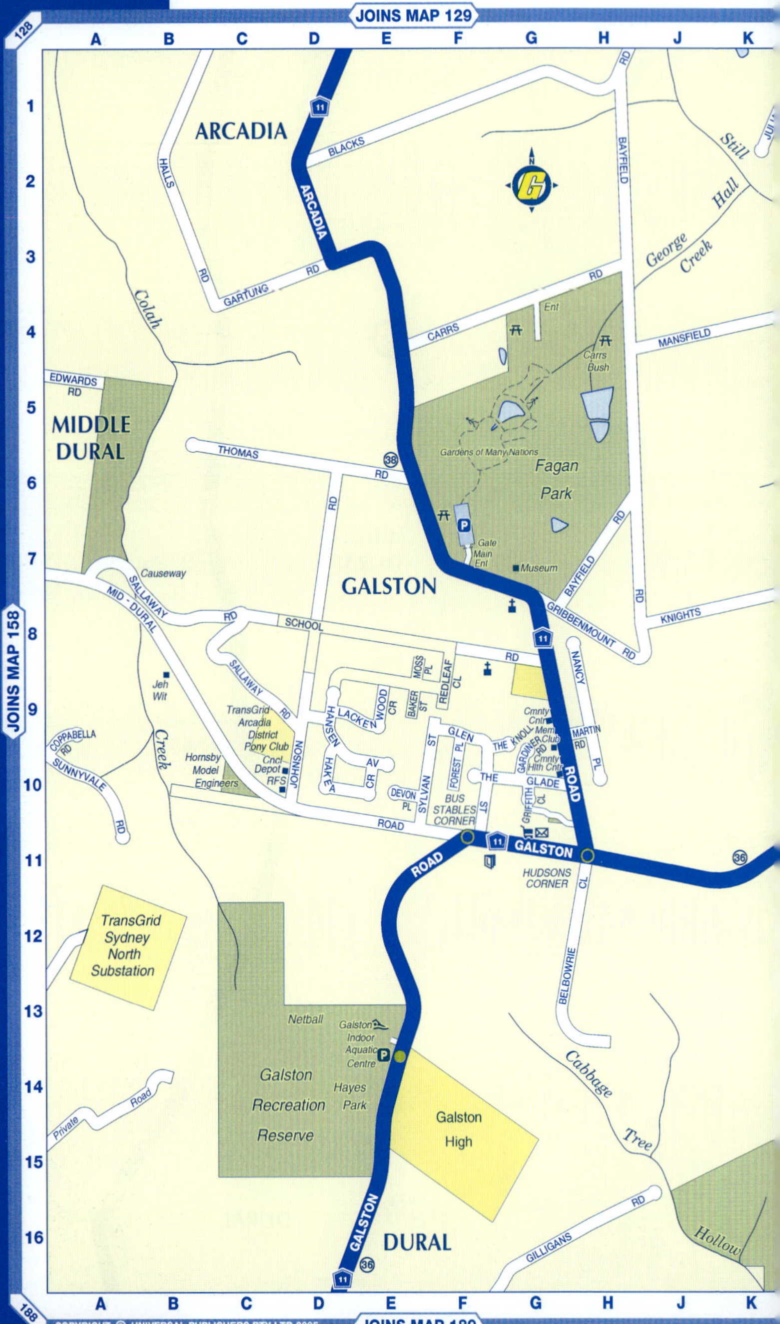
JOINS MAP 129
JOINS MAP 158
JOINS MAP 189
128
188
A B C D E F G H J K
1 2 3 4 5 6 7 8 9 10 11 12 13 14 15 16
ARCADIA
MIDDLE DURAL
GALSTON
DURAL
HALLS RD
BLACKS
ARCADIA
GARTUNG RD
Colah
CARRS RD
BAYFIELD RD
MANSFIELD
Still Hall
George Creek
Ent
Carrs Bush
Gardens of Many Nations
Fagan Park
Gate Main Ent
Museum
EDWARDS RD
THOMAS RD
Causeway
SALLAWAY RD
MID - DURAL
SCHOOL RD
GRIBBENMOUNT RD
KNIGHTS
NANCY PL
MARTIN RD
MOSS PL
REDLEAF CL
BAKER ST
LACKEN WOOD CR
HANSEN AV
HAKEA CR
Jeh Wit
Creek
TransGrid Arcadia District Pony Club
Cncl Depot
RFS
JOHNSON
Hornsby Model Engineers
COPPABELLA RD
SUNNYVALE RD
SYLVAN ST
GLEN FOREST PL
THE GLADE
THE KNOLL
GARDINER RD
GRIFFITH CL
DEVON PL
BUS STABLES CORNER
Cmnty Cntr
Mem Club
Cmnty Hlth Cntr
ROAD
GALSTON ROAD
HUDSONS CORNER
BELBOWRIE CL
TransGrid Sydney North Substation
Netball
Galston Indoor Aquatic Centre
Galston Recreation Reserve
Hayes Park
Galston High
Private Road
Cabbage Tree
Hollow
GILLIGANS RD
11
36
38

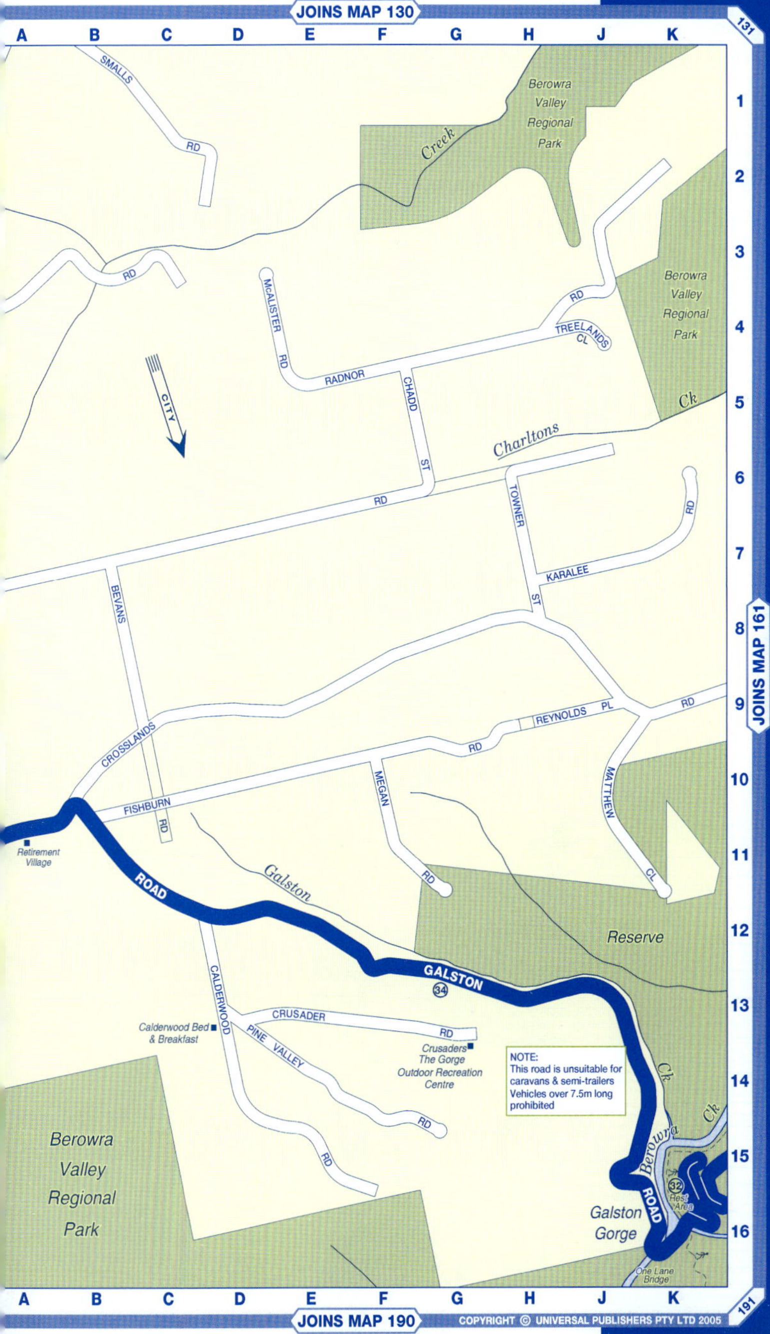
JOINS MAP 130
A B C D E F G H J K
131
1 2 3 4 5 6 7 8 9 10 11 12 13 14 15 16
SMALLS RD
Berowra Valley Regional Park
Creek
RD
McALISTER RD
RADNOR
CHADD ST
RD
TREELANDS CL
Berowra Valley Regional Park
Ck
CITY
Charltons
RD
TOWNER ST
RD
KARALEE
BEVANS
JOINS MAP 161
REYNOLDS PL
RD
RD
CROSSLANDS
MEGAN RD
MATTHEW CL
FISHBURN RD
Retirement Village
ROAD
Galston
Reserve
GALSTON
34
CALDERWOOD
CRUSADER RD
Calderwood Bed & Breakfast
PINE VALLEY RD
Crusaders The Gorge Outdoor Recreation Centre
NOTE: This road is unsuitable for caravans & semi-trailers Vehicles over 7.5m long prohibited
Ck
Ck
Berowra
Berowra Valley Regional Park
RD
32
Rest Area
ROAD
Galston Gorge
One Lane Bridge
191
JOINS MAP 190

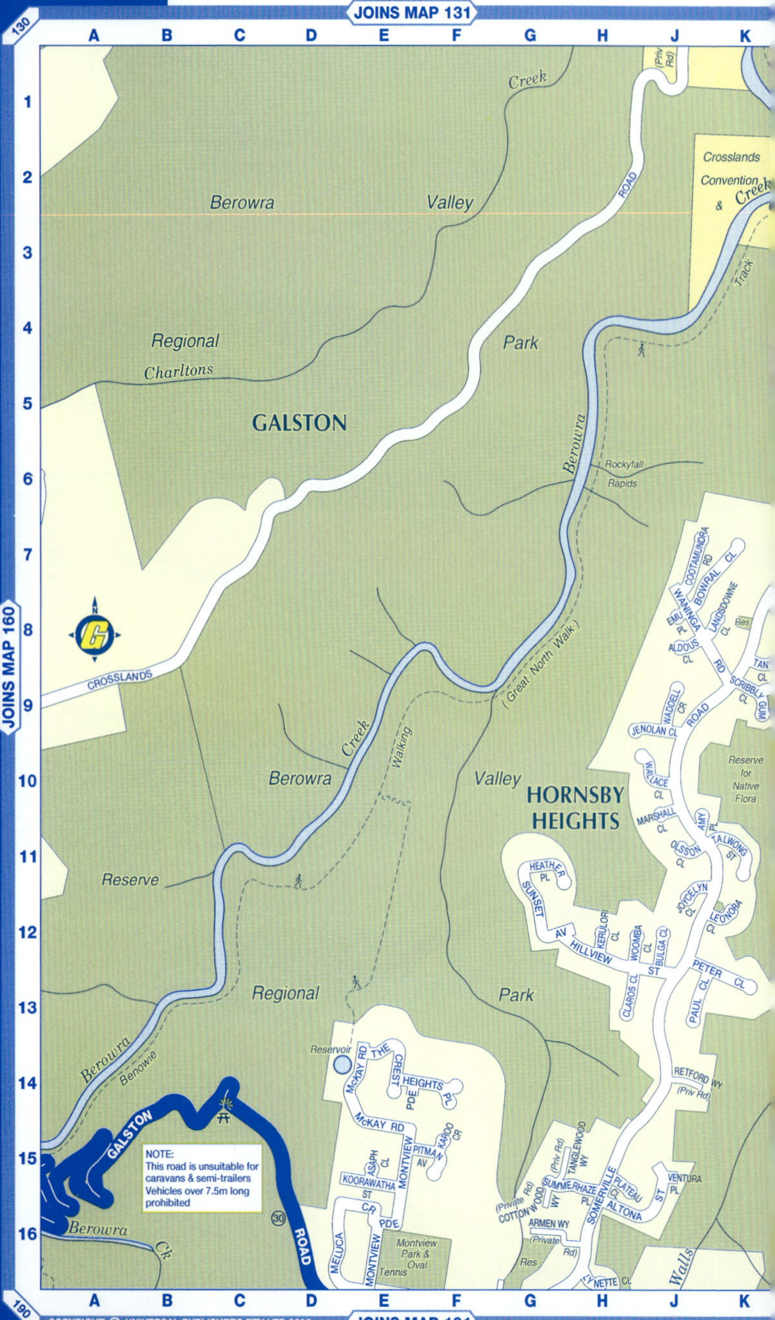
JOINS MAP 131
JOINS MAP 160
JOINS MAP 191
130
190
A B C D E F G H J K
1 2 3 4 5 6 7 8 9 10 11 12 13 14 15 16
GALSTON
HORNSBY HEIGHTS
Berowra Valley Regional Park
Berowra Valley Regional Reserve
Berowra Valley Regional Park
Charltons Creek
Crosslands Convention & Creek
Track
Berowra Creek
Rockyfall Rapids
(Great North Walk)
Walking
Berowra Ck
Benowie
Walls
CROSSLANDS ROAD
GALSTON ROAD
30
(Priv Rd)
NOTE:
This road is unsuitable for caravans & semi-trailers
Vehicles over 7.5m long prohibited
Reservoir
Res
Reserve for Native Flora
Montview Park & Oval
Tennis
COOTAMUNDRA RD
BOWRAL CL
WANINGA
LANDSDOWNE CL
EMU PL
ALDOUS CL
SCRIBBLY GUM CL
TAN CL
WADDELL CR
JENOLAN CL
ROAD
WALLACE CL
MARSHALL CL
AMY PL
TALWONG ST
OLSSON CL
HEATHER PL
SUNSET AV
HILLVIEW
KERULORI CL
WOOMBA CL
BULGA CL
JOYCELYN CL
LEONORA CL
ST
CLAROS CL
PETER CL
PAUL CL
RETFORD WY
(Priv Rd)
McKAY RD
THE CREST
HEIGHTS PL
PDE
PITMAN AV
KAROO CR
ASAPH CL
KOORAWATHA ST
MONTVIEW CR
MONTVIEW PDE
MELUCA
TANGLEWOOD WY
(Priv Rd)
SUMMERHAZE PL
WY
SOMERVILLE
PLATEAU CL
ALTONA ST
VENTURA PL
(Private Rd)
COTTONWOOD
ARMEN WY
(Private Rd)
NETTE CL

MAP 162

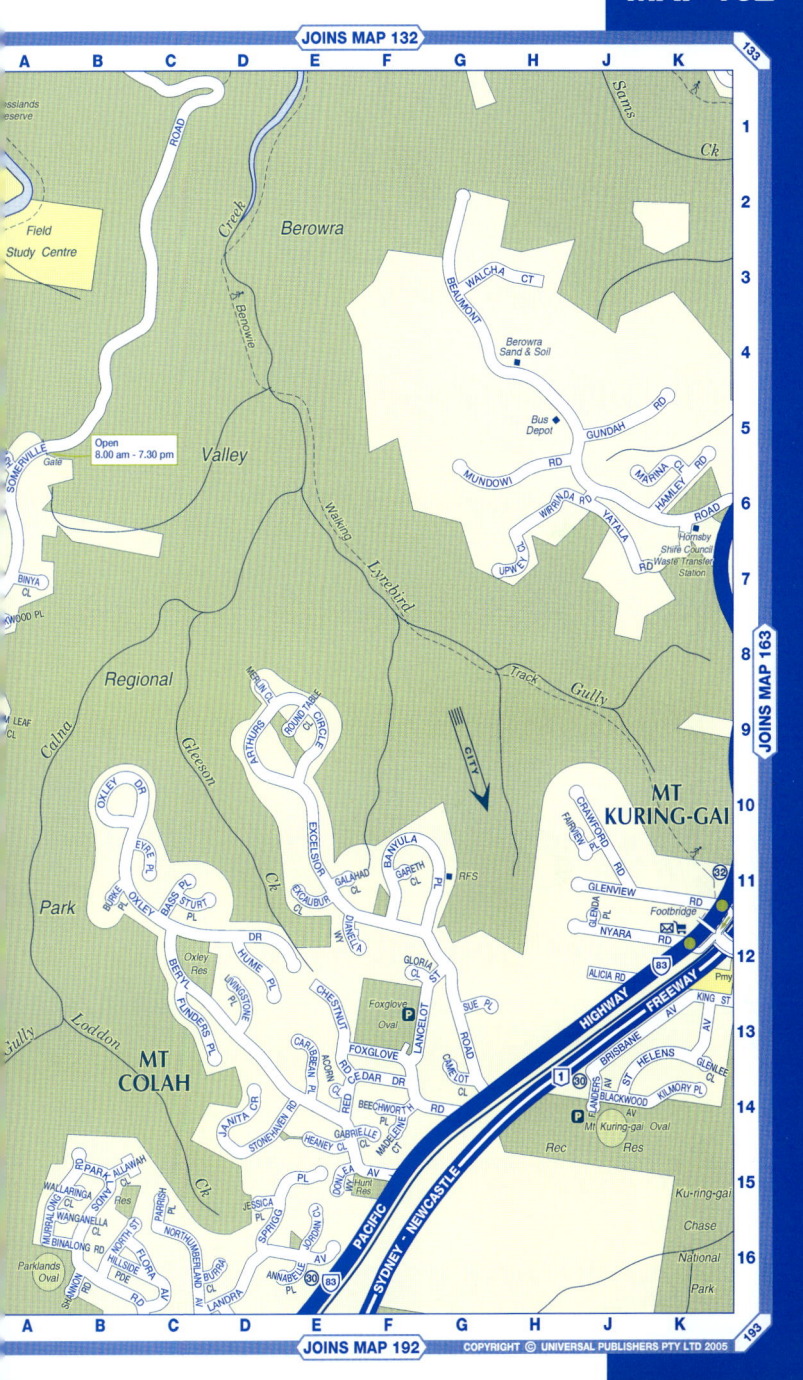

JOINS MAP 133

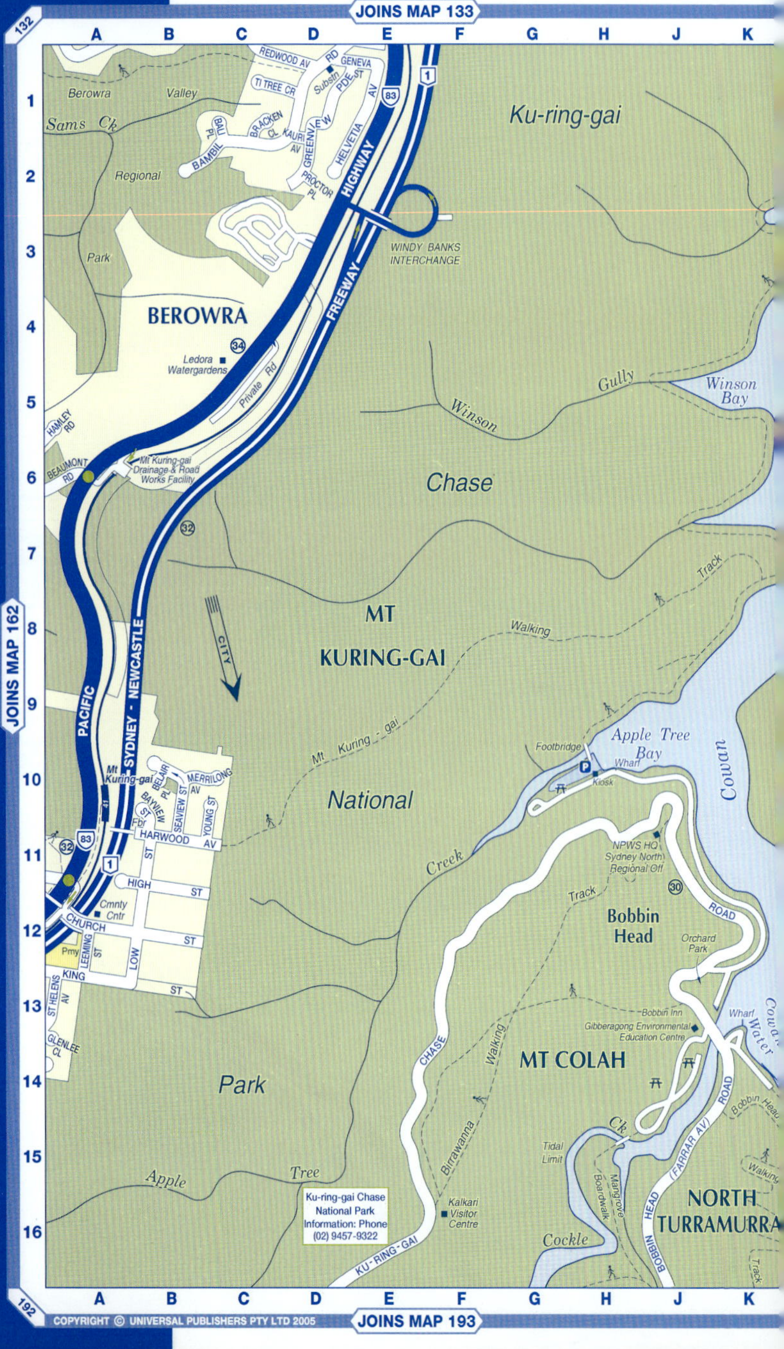

JOINS MAP 193

MAP 164

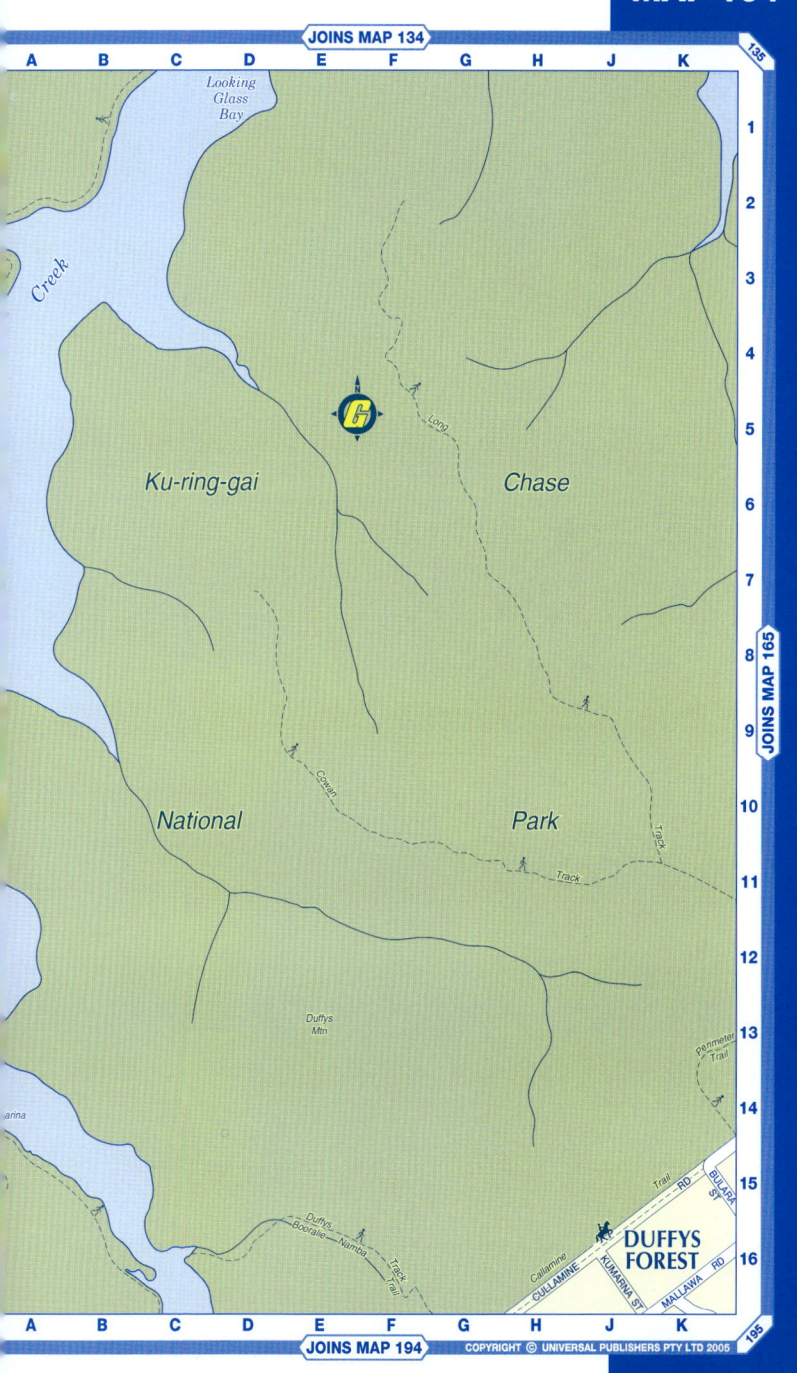

Looking Glass Bay

Creek

Ku-ring-gai Chase National Park

Long

Coral

Track

Duffys Mtn

Perimeter Trail

Marina

Duffys Boorale Namba Track Trail

Cullamine

DUFFYS FOREST

Bulara St
Kumarra St
Mallawa Rd

JOINS MAP 134
JOINS MAP 165
JOINS MAP 194

COPYRIGHT © UNIVERSAL PUBLISHERS PTY LTD 2005

MAP 165

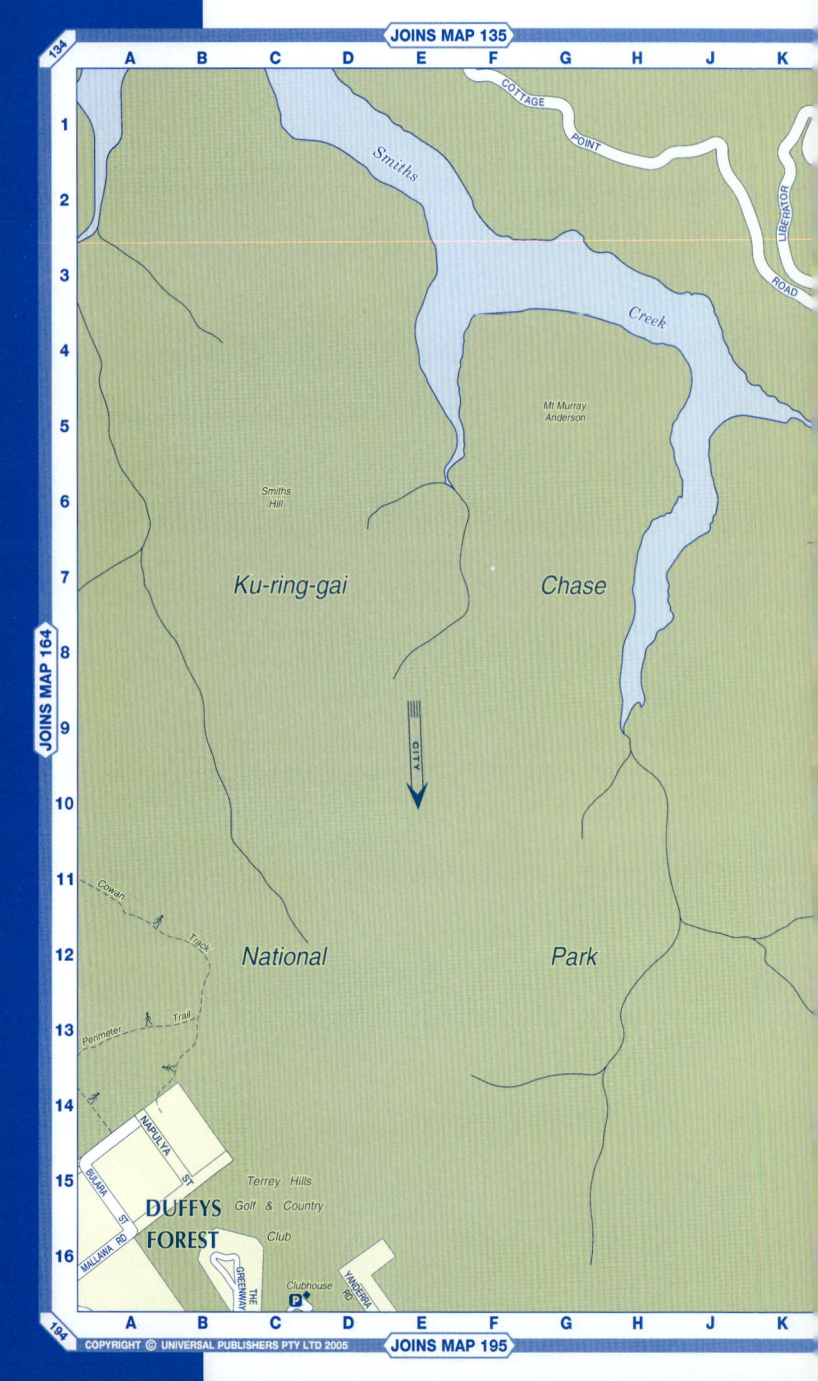

JOINS MAP 136
A B C D E F G H J K
137
1 2 3 4 5 6 7 8 9 10 11 12 13 14 15 16
Coal
and
Candle
Creek
GENERAL
Illawong
Bay
Swim
Encl
SAN
MARTIN
Gate
LIBERATOR
GENERAL
SAN
MARTIN
Akuna
Bay
Marina
Akuna Bay
DRIVE
Gate
Ku-ring-gai
Chase
Mt
Akuna
National
Park
Track
McCARRS
CREEK
ROAD
28
Centre
DRIVE
Toll
Booth
McCARRS
CREEK
RD
JOINS MAP 167
JOINS MAP 196
197

MAP 167

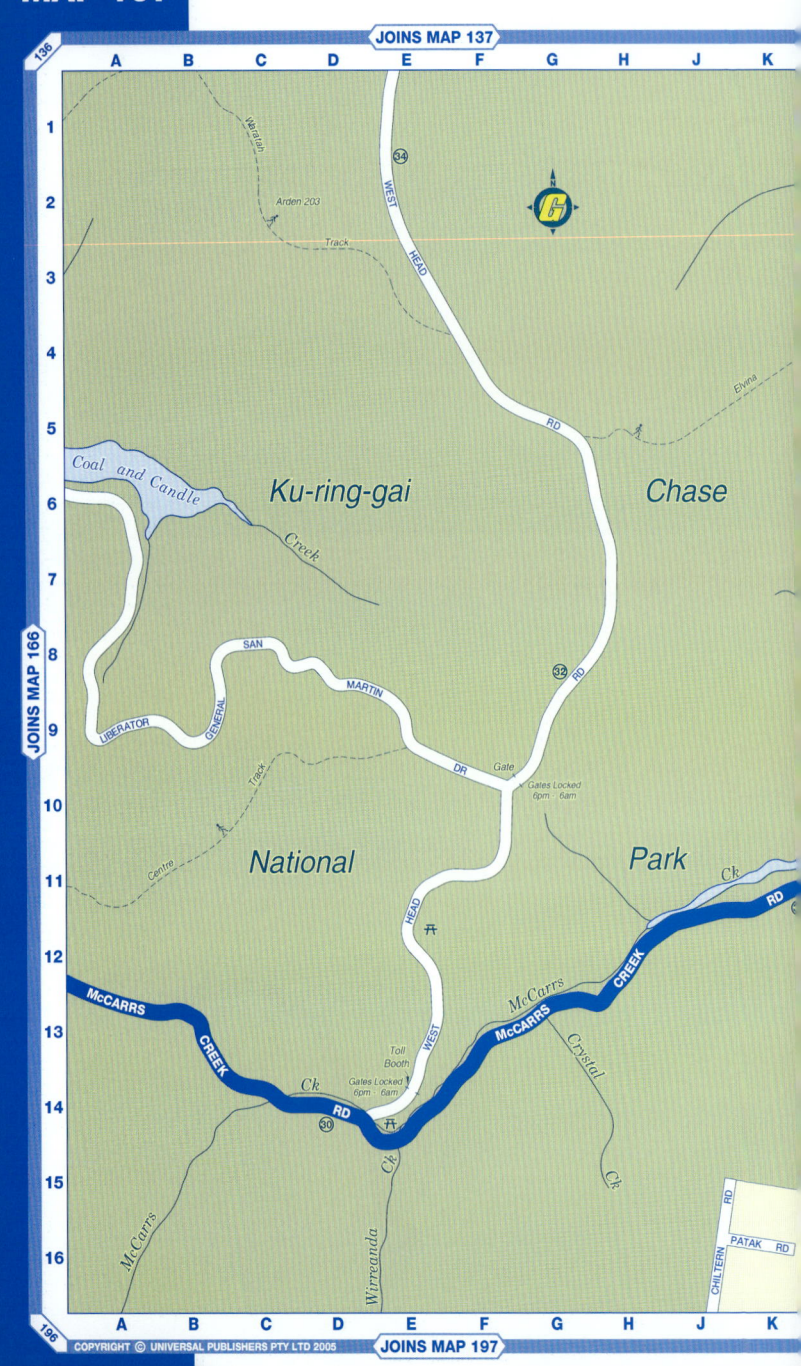

Ku-ring-gai Chase National Park

- Coal and Candle Creek
- Waratah
- Arden 203
- West Head Rd (34)
- Elvina
- Liberator
- General San Martin Dr
- Gate (32) Rd
- Gates Locked 6pm–6am
- Centre Track
- West Head Rd
- Toll Booth
- Gates Locked 6pm–6am
- McCarrs Creek Rd (30)
- McCarrs Ck
- Crystal Ck
- Wirreanda Ck
- Chiltern Rd
- Patak Rd

JOINS MAP 137
JOINS MAP 166
JOINS MAP 197

MAP 168

JOINS MAP 139
138
JOINS MAP 168
JOINS MAP 199
198

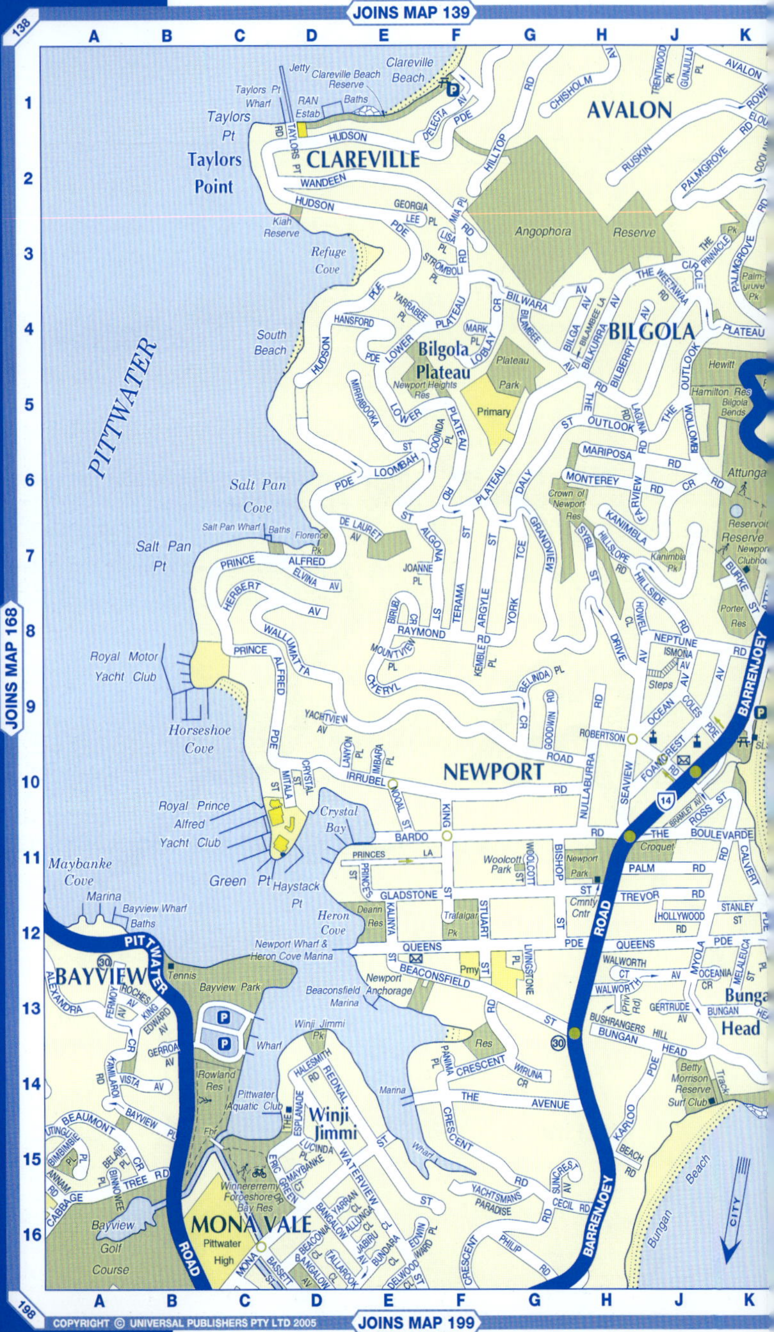

MAP 170

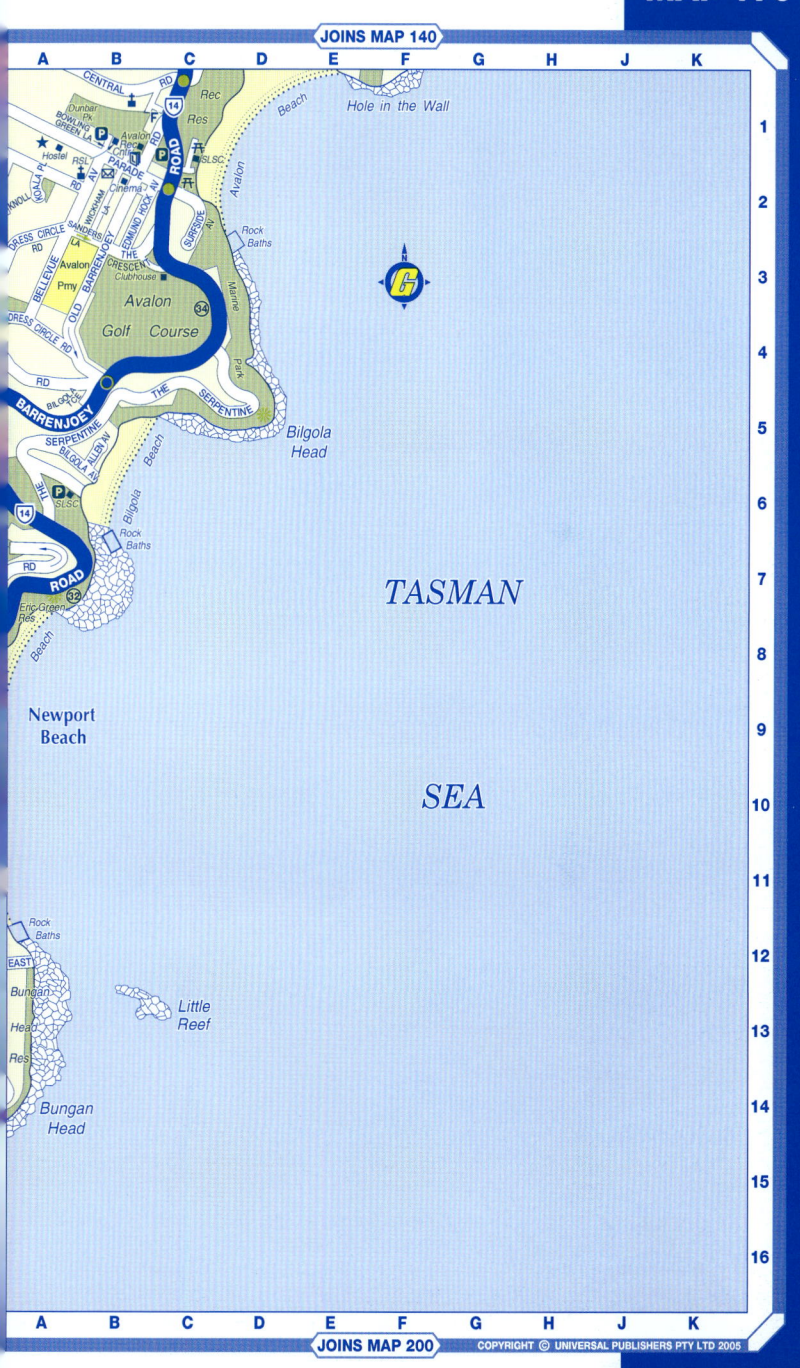

Hole in the Wall
Avalon Beach
Rock Baths
Avalon Golf Course
Bilgola Head
Bilgola Beach
Rock Baths
Newport Beach
Rock Baths
Bungan Head
Little Reef

TASMAN SEA

JOINS MAP 140
JOINS MAP 200

COPYRIGHT © UNIVERSAL PUBLISHERS PTY LTD 2005

MAP 171

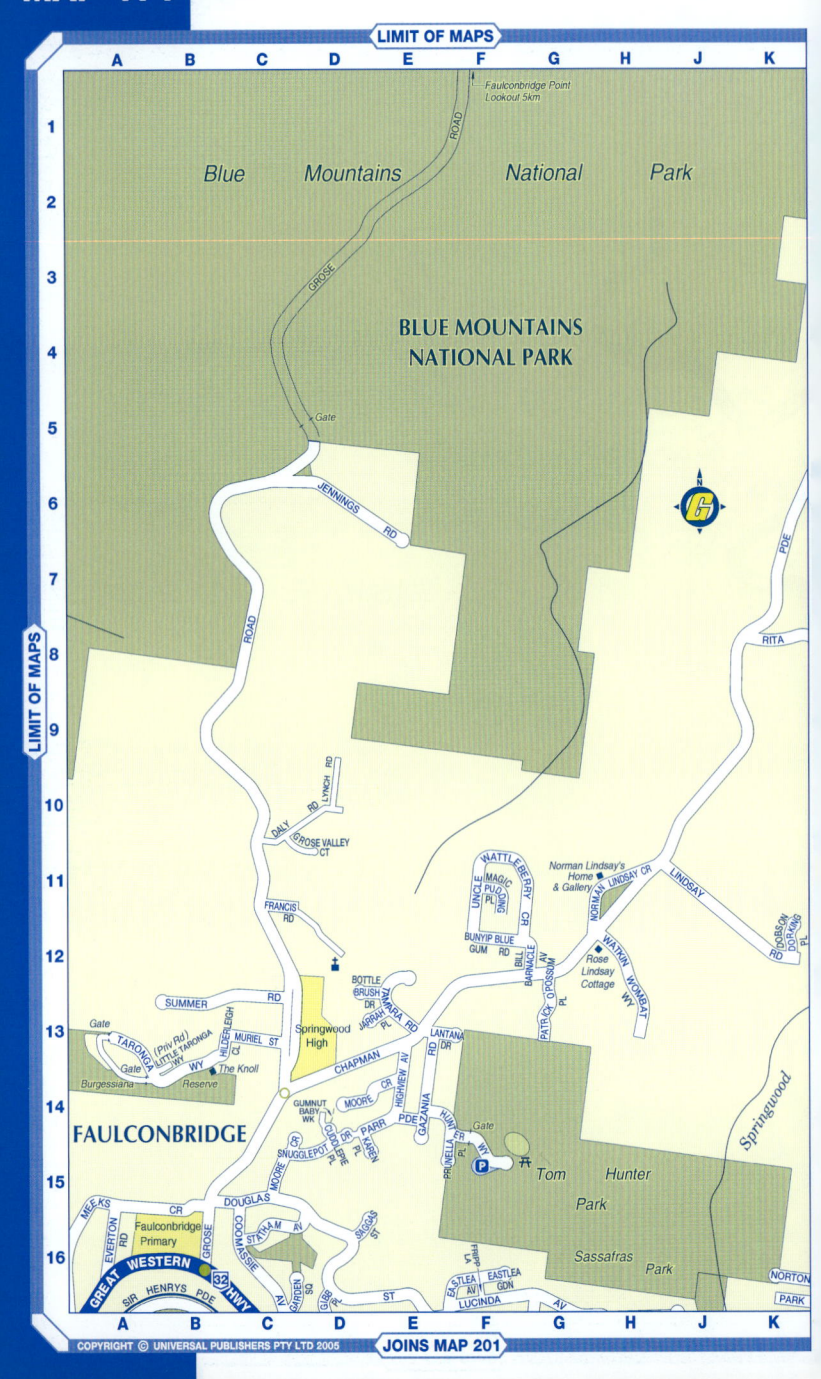

LIMIT OF MAPS

Columns: A B C D E F G H J K
Rows: 1–16

Blue Mountains National Park

Faulconbridge Point Lookout 5km

BLUE MOUNTAINS NATIONAL PARK

GROSE ROAD

Gate

JENNINGS RD

RITA PDE

LYNCH RD
DALY RD
GROSE VALLEY CT

FRANCIS RD

NATTLEBERRY CR
UNCLE MAGIC PUG PL
OMG
BUNYIP BLUE GUM RD
BILL BARNACLE AV
POSSUM PL
PATRO
NORMAN LINDSAY CR
Norman Lindsay's Home & Gallery
LINDSAY
DOBSON RD

BOTTLE BRUSH DR
JARRAH PL
TAMARA RD
WATKIN WOMBAT WY
Rose Lindsay Cottage

SUMMER RD
HILDERLEIGH
(Priv Rd) LITTLE TARONGA WY
TARONGA CL
MURIEL ST
CHAPMAN
Springwood High
LANTANA DR
Gate
The Knoll Reserve
Burgessiana
GUMNUT BABY WK
MOORE CR
HIGHVIEW AV
GAZANIA PDE
HUNTER
PRIMULA
P
Tom Hunter Park

FAULCONBRIDGE

SNUGGLEPOT CR
MOORE
PARR PDE
KAREN
Springwood

MEEKS
EVERETT RD
Faulconbridge Primary
DOUGLAS
GROSE
COOMASSIE
STATHAM AV
GARDEN SQ
GIBB
SIGGS ST
EASTLEA
EASTLEA GDN
LUCINDA AV
Sassafras Park
NORTON PARK

GREAT WESTERN HWY 32
SIR HENRYS PDE

JOINS MAP 201

COPYRIGHT © UNIVERSAL PUBLISHERS PTY LTD 2005

LIMIT OF MAPS
A B C D E F G H J K
1 2 3 4 5 6 7 8 9 10 11 12 13 14 15 16
BLUE MOUNTAINS NATIONAL PARK
Blue Mountains National Park
Creek
REDHEAP RD
ANN ST
AV
CITY
St Columba's High
Private Road
St Thomas Aquinas
SPRINGWOOD
WINMALEE
PAULWOOD AV
YANDINA AV
ROAD
HALCYON AV
MURU AV
PINDARI ST
BULBI AV
BUNDAH ST
NAMATJIRA PWY
DUNGARA PL
MURU AV
JANDIGA PL
SUNNY RIDGE RD
LUTHER RD
EMMA PDE
GAHNIA WY
THOMSON AV
LINKSVIEW AV
CRAMPTON
NAGLE AV
DR
ROAD
FAIRWAY
FAIRWAYS CR
BIRDWOOD AV
KENT ST
Altitude 310m
FESQ PWY
Springwood Golf Course
Cemetery
Clubhouse
ELLISON RD
COMET PL
Ellison Pmy
HUNTLEY GRANGE RD
PHILLIPSON LA
Springwood Hospital
DAVESTA RD
CR
HAWKESBURY
Nurs Home
PATERSON RD
JOHNSON PL
MACKELLAR CIR
SPRINGFIELD AV
MOORE
FRASER RD
BAXTER AV
RD
BLAND RD
AV
AV
Resvr
BUCKLAND DR
Priv Rd
Buckland Convalescent Hospital & Buckland Village
JOINS MAP 173
JOINS MAP 202
203

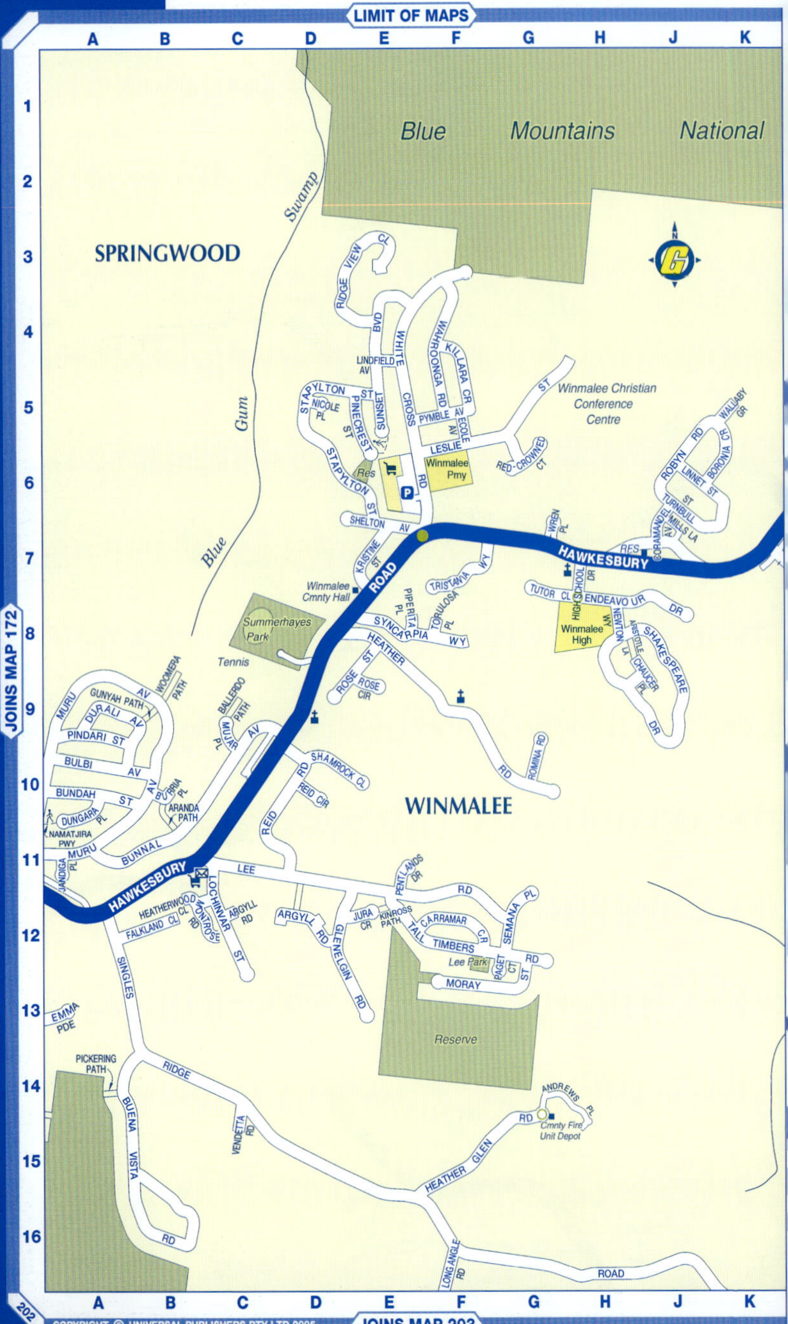

MAP 174

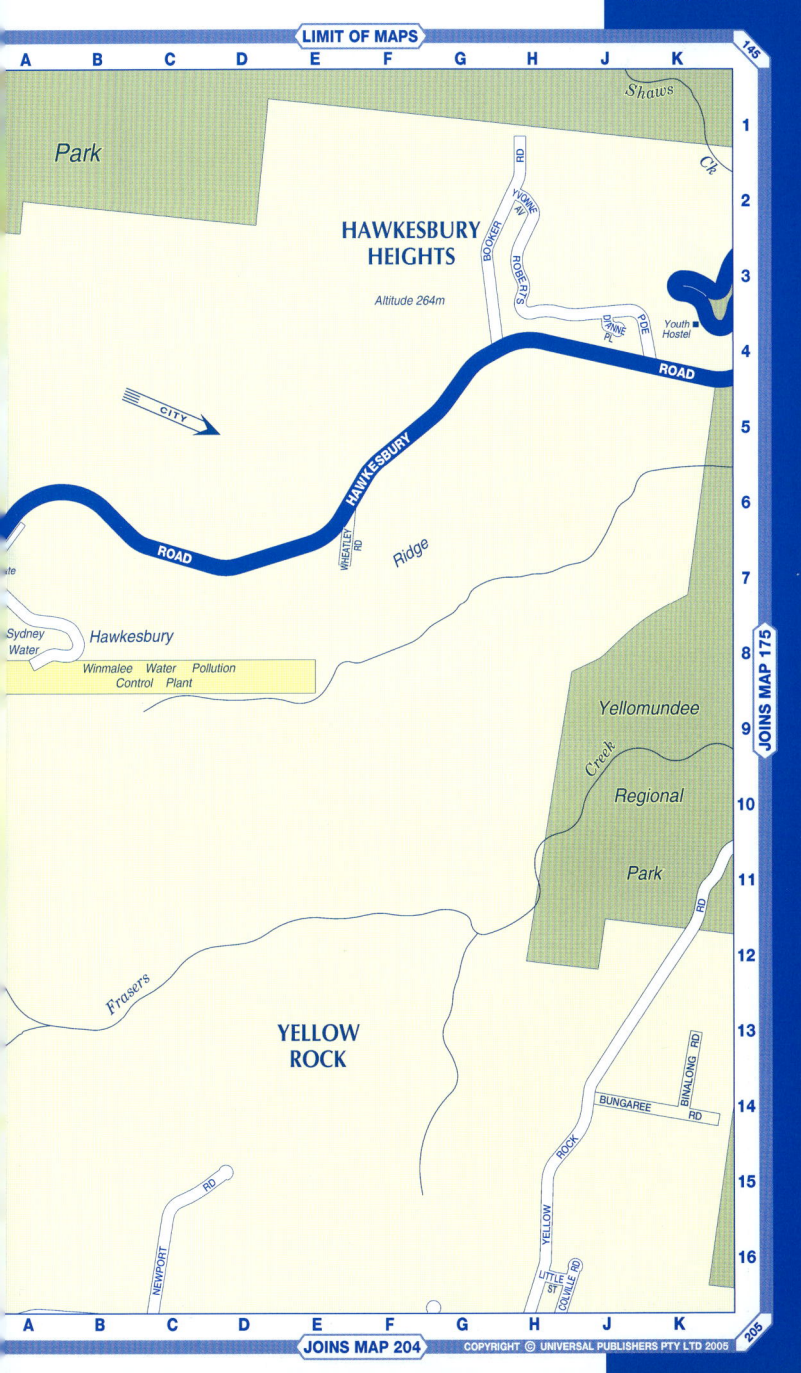

Park

HAWKESBURY HEIGHTS
Altitude 264m

Shaws Ck

BOOKER RD
YVONNE AV
ROBERTS PDE
DIANNE PL
Youth Hostel

HAWKESBURY ROAD
CITY
WHEATLEY RD
Ridge

Sydney Water — Hawkesbury
Winmalee Water Pollution Control Plant

Yellomundee Creek Regional Park

Frasers

YELLOW ROCK

YELLOW ROCK RD
BINALONG RD
BUNGAREE RD
NEWPORT RD
LITTLE ST
COXVILLE RD

LIMIT OF MAPS
JOINS MAP 175
JOINS MAP 204

COPYRIGHT © UNIVERSAL PUBLISHERS PTY LTD 2005

MAP 175

JOINS MAP 145

JOINS MAP 174 / *JOINS MAP 205*

- Shaws Ck
- YARRAMUNDI
- SPRINGWOOD ROAD
- HAWKESBURY ROAD
- Hawkesbury
- HAWKESBURY HEIGHTS — Altitude 264m
- NEPEAN RIVER
- CASTLEREAGH ROAD (14)
- Castlereagh Pmy
- SHAFTSBURY AV
- Gate
- Castlereagh Hall
- SMITH RD
- Castlereagh Equestrian Centre
- Yellomundee Regional Frasers Park
- Ck
- NEPEAN
- YELLOW ROCK RD
- Yellow Rock
- YELLOW ROCK
- Yellomundee Regional Park
- RIVER
- (64)
- (14) CASTLEREAGH ROAD

204 COPYRIGHT © UNIVERSAL PUBLISHERS PTY LTD 2005

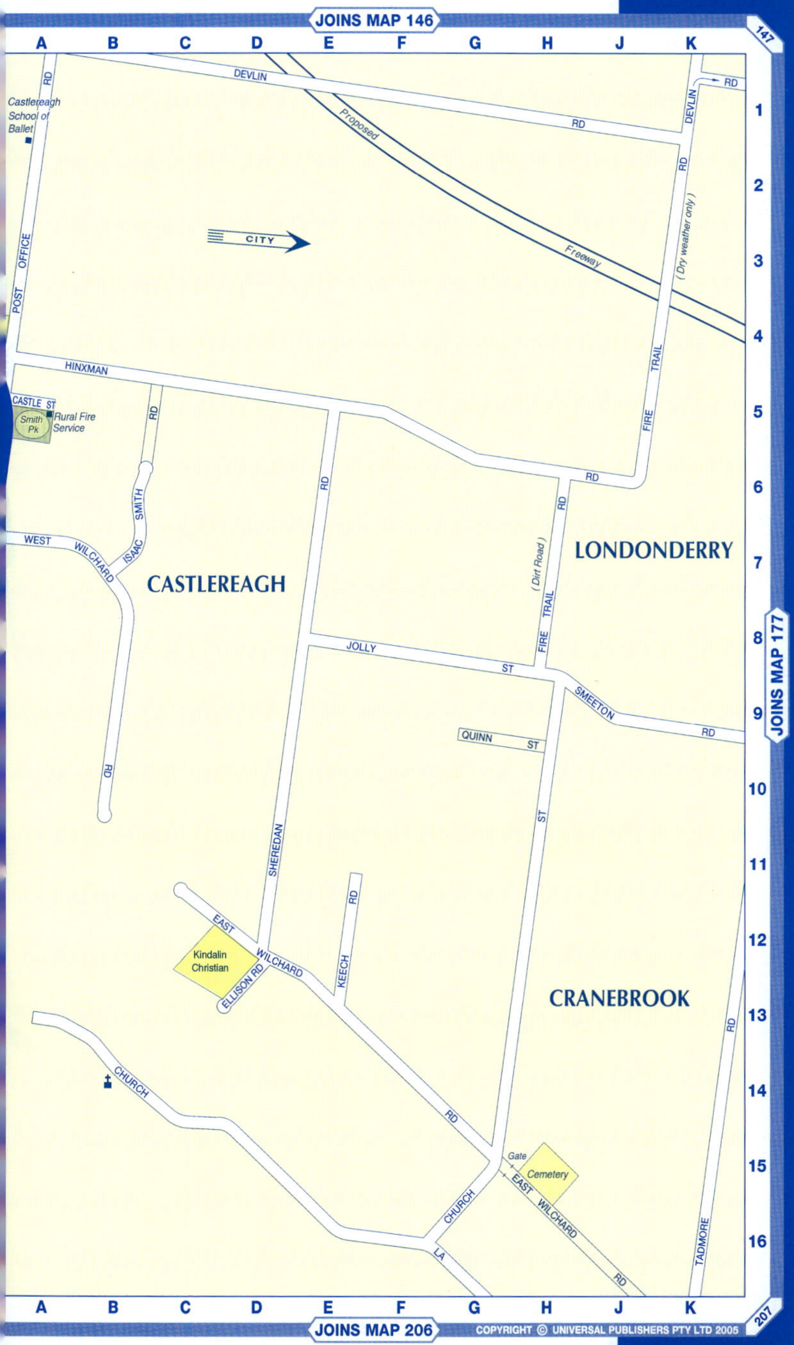
JOINS MAP 146
147
A B C D E F G H J K
1 2 3 4 5 6 7 8 9 10 11 12 13 14 15 16
DEVLIN RD
RD
Castlereagh School of Ballet
Proposed Freeway
DEVLIN RD
RD
(Dry weather only)
CITY
POST OFFICE RD
HINXMAN
CASTLE ST
Smith Pk
Rural Fire Service
RD
FIRE TRAIL
RD
RD
SMITH
ISAAC
WEST WILCHARD
RD
CASTLEREAGH
RD
(Dirt Road)
FIRE TRAIL
LONDONDERRY
JOLLY ST
SMEETON RD
QUINN ST
ST
SHEREDAN
RD
EAST WILCHARD RD
Kindalin Christian
ELLISON RD
KEECH RD
CRANEBROOK
CHURCH
Gate
Cemetery
EAST WILCHARD RD
CHURCH LA
TADMORE RD
JOINS MAP 177
JOINS MAP 206
207

MAP 177

JOINS MAP 147

DEVLIN RD

BOSCOBEL RD

LONDONDERRY

Rickabys Creek

NUTT RD

SMEETON RD

SMEETON RD

TADMORE RD

CRANEBROOK

Ent

St Pauls Grammar

Rickabys

SIONI RD

SENTA RD

LONDONDERRY

TAYLOR

Palms Galore Nursery

Cranebrook Native Nursery

CRANEBROOK

Airservices Australia

THE NORTHERN

FOURTH

JOINS MAP 176
JOINS MAP 207

COPYRIGHT © UNIVERSAL PUBLISHERS PTY LTD 2005

MAP 178

JOINS MAP 148

Cherrybrook Creek
CH
WHITEGATES RD
CITY →
THE NORTHERN ROAD
Waste Services Depot
TIMOTHY RD
THOMAS RD
Test Safe Australia
ndonderry ny Club
neral Resources Core Library
BERKSHIRE PARK
Silvicultural Demonstration Area
Castlereagh Nature Reserve
SPINKS RD
DOAK AV
DODFORD RD
Proposed Freeway
LLANDILO
TERRYBROOK RD
AV
FOURTH AV
THIRD AV
AV

JOINS MAP 208

JOINS MAP 179

COPYRIGHT © UNIVERSAL PUBLISHERS PTY LTD 2005

MAP 179

LONDONDERRY
THE NORTHERN ROAD
Reservoir
Waste Services Depot
Castlereagh Landfill
Depot
Castlereagh
Nature
Reserve
LLANDILO
Reserve

LLANDILO
FOURTH
FIFTH
SIXTH
ROAD
RFS Hall
Berkshire Pk
Guard Dog Training Centre
SUNNYMEADE RD
JUDD ST
SPENCE RD
GOVERNMENT RD
GALVIN RD
SIRIUS
BARNES RD
South
STANLEY
OLD LLANDILO RD
LLANDILO MAYO RD

JOINS MAP 149
JOINS MAP 178
JOINS MAP 209

MAP 180

JOINS MAP 150

WINDSOR DOWNS

- Archer La
- Wavehill
- Morestone
- Sanctuary Dr
- Barkly
- Fitzroy La
- Oban Cl
- Willeroo Dr
- Denison Pl
- Burnside Gr
- Nicholson Pl
- Buchanan La
- Gordon Pl
- Willeroo Dr

Richmond Road (61)

Road (32)

BERKSHIRE PARK

- Road
- First Rd
- Second
- Third
- St Marys Rd
- Pfn Rd
- Berkshire Park Bird Farm
- Ninth Rd

South Wianamatta Creek

→ CITY

MARSDEN PARK

Wianamatta Creek

St Marys
Cemetery
Low Level Causeway
Floodgate

SHANES PARK

Stony Creek St

JOINS MAP 210
JOINS MAP 181
COPYRIGHT © UNIVERSAL PUBLISHERS PTY LTD 2005

MAP 181

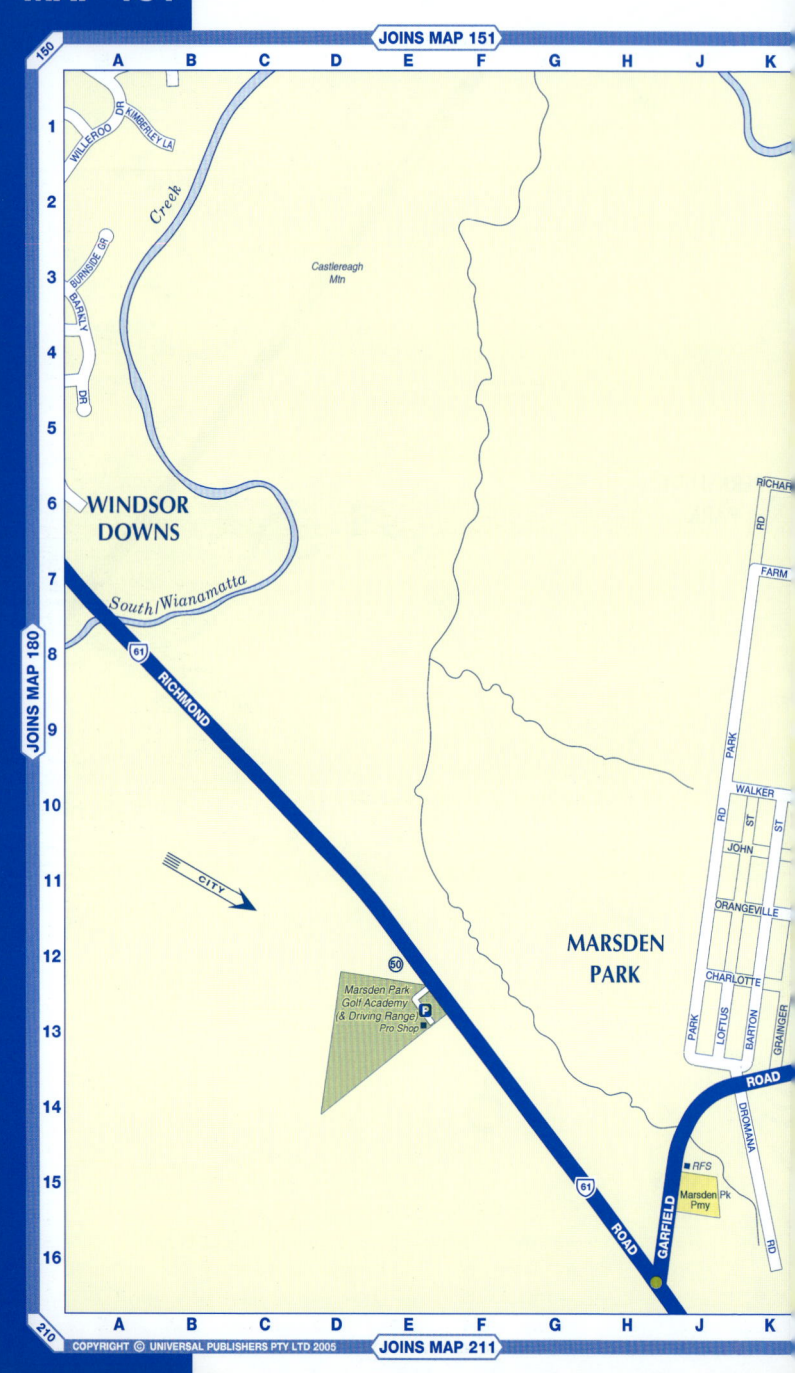

JOINS MAP 151
JOINS MAP 180
JOINS MAP 211

WINDSOR DOWNS

Castlereagh Mtn

Creek

South Wianamatta

RICHMOND ROAD

CITY

MARSDEN PARK

Marsden Park Golf Academy (& Driving Range) Pro Shop

RFS
Marsden Pk Pmy

WILLEROO DR, KIMBERLEY LA, BURNSIDE GR, BARKLY DR

RICHARD RD, FARM, PARK RD, WALKER, ST, JOHN ST, ORANGEVILLE, CHARLOTTE, PARK, LOFTUS, BARTON, GRAINGER, DROMANA, GARFIELD ROAD

JOINS MAP 152
JOINS MAP 183
JOINS MAP 212
153
213
A B C D E F G H J K
1 2 3 4 5 6 7 8 9 10 11 12 13 14 15 16
RIVERSTONE
SCHOFIELDS
Eastern
Creek
Bells
Ck
GARFIELD ROAD WEST
GARFIELD RD EAST
PRINCES ST
MELBOURNE
PICCADILLY
RIVERSTONE
EDWARD
LOFTUS
WELLINGTON
HOBART
SYDNEY
GEORGE
CROWN
BOURKE
KING
CHURCH
MILL
PITT
PARK
MARKET
BRISBANE RD
HAMILTON
OLEANDER
GUM
PINE
CR
Ridgeview Pk
MAHONY RD
AILSA PL
DINGLE
Substn
Mill St Res
Lions Pk
Mus
RSL
Riverstone
PDE
OXFORD
CASTLEREAGH
ELIZABETH
HUNTER
REGENT
ROBINSON ST
GLADSTONE PDE
TCE
RAILWAY
WEST
TREVITHICK ST
CARLTON
Tennis
Riverstone Park
RICHARDS (Private Rd)
Roadmaster
AV
DENMARK
CREEK
BERKSHIRE
PACER ST
Riverstone Trotting Track
GIG WY
RD
ST
LYTTON
MARSDEN
WEALTHEASY ST
AVENUE
LA
CLIVE RD
EAST RD
CLEVELAND
CHAUCER
MILTON
YORK
THE
DELEWARE
MARSDEN LA
LYTTON
PDE
PENPRASE
Cemetery
Ent
CEMETERY RD
Knudsen Res
BREWER ST
KELVEDON
DAVIES
LAMB
BEN
HERBERT
CHARLES
CHERRY
ROBERT
BROWN ST
CARNARVON
Causeway
Road Subject to Flooding
NEVILLE
ROAD
LYNDHURST
QUEEN ST
CORCORAN ST
ARGYLE
NELSON
TRAFALGAR
MILTON
NELSON LA
BURFITT
KENDALL
CARINGTON
CLIFTON
BLENHEIM RD
MARY ST
JOHN ST
NORTH
GEORGE ST
WILLIAM ST
JACKSON
ARTHUR
MAURICE ST
LINCOLN TCE
FERMOY
Hamrun Assoc
CLIFTON RD
VINE ST
EAST
FELL PL
GRANGE AV

MAP 183

RIVERSTONE

SCHOFIELDS

Joins Map 153 (top)
Joins Map 182 (left)
Joins Map 213 (bottom)

Grid columns: A B C D E F G H J K
Grid rows: 1–16

Streets and features:
- Wellington, William, Hobart, Sydney, Crown, Hamilton, Jeh Wit, Singh Pk, Agra Pl, Grace, Majory Rd, Ailsa Pl, Dingle, Piccadilly, Ryan Cr, Oliver, Campbell, Bellevue St, Riverstone Sports Cntr, McCulloch, Cath, Market, Lions Pk Museum, Garfield Rd East, Edmund St, Junction Rd, First, Potts, Garfield Rd East, New Holland, Clarke St, Proposed North West Rail Link, City
- Casuarina School, Castlereagh, Woods, Debroe, Piccadilly, Dugall, Oxford, Elizabeth, Hunter, Regent, Robinson, James St, Gladstone, Riverstone, Brighton La, Coverdale Christian, Riverstone Pmy, Riverstone High, Denar, Inverness Rd, Kene, Poe, Lincoln Av, Riverstone Rd, Margaret St, Arlington, Guntawong
- Brighton, Bligh, Wolsley, Park, Cranbourne, Chester St, Boundary Rd, Buddhist Temple, Kensington, Lambeth Rd, Westminster, Schofields Rd, Gordon Rd, Princes Rd, St Albans, Schofields Pmy, Schofields Park, Junction, Farm Rd
- Bridge, Omnty Cntr, Carman, Station, Lewis, Audi, Gil, Ellesmere Av, Nias Pl, Grange, Schofields, Oban, Elgar, Rose, Argowan, Hunt, Advance, Schofields Rd, Alex Av, Oak Rd, Railway, West, Poe, RFS

COPYRIGHT © UNIVERSAL PUBLISHERS PTY LTD 2005

MAP 184

BOX HILL

Rouse Hill Regional Park

- Country Bear Child Care Centre
- Deeth Family Florist
- Visitors Centre
- Rouse Hill Estate
- Scottholme
- Storage King
- Nathan Repairs
- Second Ponds Oval
- Rouse Hill Preschool Kindergarten

ROUSE HILL

- Rouse Hill Regional Park
- Ironbark Ridge
- Rouse Hill Cattery
- Rouse Hill Anglican College
- Causeway
- Proposed Stabling Facility
- Shale Quarry
- Castlebrook Lawn Cemetery and Crematorium
- Recreation Reserve
- Tebbutts Open Range

KELLYVILLE RIDGE

JOINS MAP 154 (top)
JOINS MAP 214 (bottom)
JOINS MAP 185 (right)

Roads: Windsor Road, Burns Road, Nelson Road, Box Road, Annangrove Road, Withers Road, Worcester Road, Cudgegong Road, Tallawong Road, Macquarie Road, Rouse Road, Terry Road, Schofields Road, Hambledon Road, Second Ponds Creek, The Water La

COPYRIGHT © UNIVERSAL PUBLISHERS PTY LTD 2005

JOINS MAP 155
JOINS MAP 184
JOINS MAP 215
154
214
ROUSE HILL
KELLYVILLE RIDGE
BEAUMONT HILLS
Second Ponds Ck
Cattai Creek
Smalls Creek
Caddies Creek
Second Ponds Oval
Rouse Hill Recycled Water Plant
Hudson Timber & Hardware
Rouse Hill Primary
Aberdoon Homestead
William Harvey Res
Commercial Rd Reserve
Commercial Rd Netball Reserve
Withers Rd Reserve
Mini Bike Track
The Mean Fiddler
Kellyville Country Club Golf Course
Proposed Pmy Sch
St Gregorys Armenian
Kellyville Country Club
Castlebrook Lawn Cemetery and Crematorium
Mungerie Park
Proposed Mungerie Park Station
Merriville
Neighbourhood Centre Site
WINDSOR ROAD
COMMERCIAL ROAD
WITHERS RD
WELLGATE AV
MILE END RD
STRINGER RD
HILLVIEW RD
BARRY RD
BRUCE PL
WHITE GUM PL
SCHOFIELDS RD
SANCTUARY DR
HOTHAM AV
PARKWAY
MUNGERIE RD
GUARDIAN
COPYRIGHT © UNIVERSAL PUBLISHERS PTY LTD 2005

MAP 186

JOINS MAP 156

ANNANGROVE

Annangrove Park
Annangrove Pmy
Nursery
Nursery
Tennis
Langlands Oval
RFS
Aristocat Boarding Cattery
Sleepy Haven Boarding Cattery
Annangrove Australian Miniature Pony Stud

KENTHURST

WHITEHALL RD

Creek
Blue Gum Ck
NICHOLI PL
WOODLAND RD
DEBORAH RD
ANNANGROVE RD
CURRIE AV
GIBBER RD
KINGCOTT RD

Cattai Creek

CITY

HEATH RD
FOXALL RD
FULTON PL
COLBRAN AV
LOGIE RD
ROBSON RD

KELLYVILLE

HEZLETT RD
KENDALL PL
CURTIS RD

GLENHAVEN BRIDGE
ONE LANE BRIDGE UNSUITABLE FOR HEAVY VEHICLES LOAD LIMIT APPLIES

Cattai Creek Conservation Area

GUM NUT CL
Kellyville Zone Substation
Temp Access
SAMANTHA
RILEY
PATYA
MILEHAM
PERSEUS CCT
TUSCAN
ASHBURTON
JAMES
MILEHAM
COBBLERS
CARLISLE CR
GRETA
GLENHAVEN RD
HOOPE
HEBE
SORRENTO DR
GREEN
BUSHHEN
CATTAI CK
VALLEYVIEW WY
ZANITH
CASTLEFERN
BOWNESS
STRATHALLAN
ROYCE
RISELLA

Beaumont Pmy PL
MAYDA PL
MINERVA CR
ELIAS
BRAMPTON
BUFFALO WY
HIGHFIELD PL
BALFOUR
CAMISH
CASABLANCA
CARMEL
TAMARA
JULIE
BALYN
PARKWAY
PAPERBARK
REDWOOD
DR

JOINS MAP 216
JOINS MAP 187
COPYRIGHT © UNIVERSAL PUBLISHERS PTY LTD 2005

MAP 187

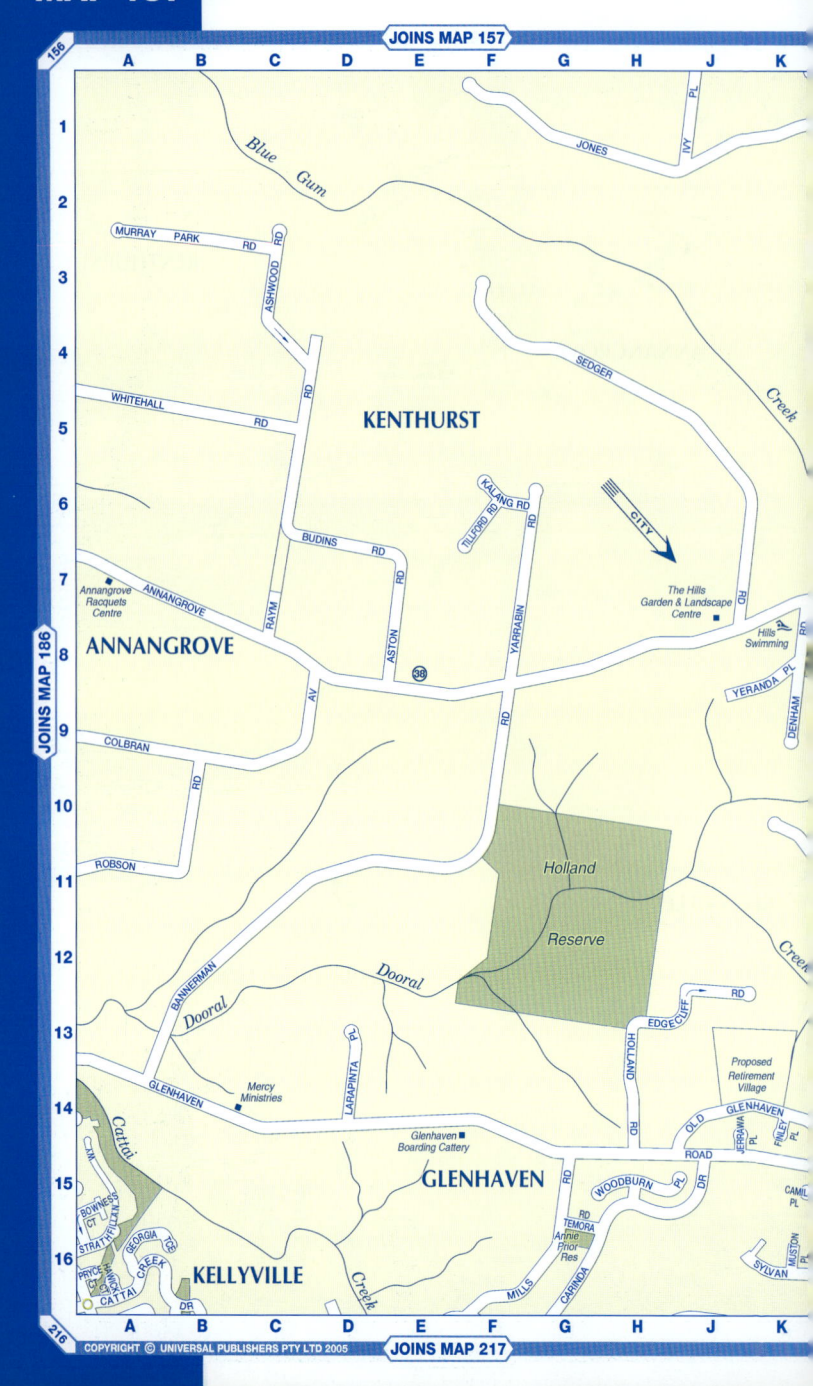

JOINS MAP 158
JOINS MAP 189
JOINS MAP 218
159
219
A B C D E F G H J K
1 2 3 4 5 6 7 8 9 10 11 12 13 14 15 16
DURAL
Round Corner
DURAL ST
SANDPIPER PL
RD
Kenthurst Pmy
Retirement Villas
KENTHURST RD
Ronald Coles Gallery
Telstra Exchange
RD
WYOMING
WILDTHORN AV
DURHAM CL (Private Rd)
RD
Golden Ridge Animal Farm
Boarding Kennels
OLD NORTHERN RD
LANGFORD RD
O'Haras
ELLERMAN AV
BUSHLAND PL
Nursery
Dural Country Club
Sydney Equest Cntr
Dural Garden Centre
LANCEWOOD
MITCHELL PL
JANE PL
DAVEY RD
RD
Fire Control Cntr & RFS
ANGUS RD
CWA
Gate
Tennis Centre
St Madeleines Pmy
Marian Cath Coll
Hills Grammar
DERRIWONG RD
Function Centre
Hargraves Nurseryland
Dural Pmy
Fbr
Melody Farm
SPURWOOD CL
ROAD
Cabbage Tree Nursery
SAGARS
Dural Sport & Leisure Cntr
WIRRABARA RD
Creek
DERRIWONG (Dirt Road) RD
PELLITT LA
Ellerman Park
Dural Rec Cntr
TRURO PL
PL
YURUGA RD
BETTINA PL
MARTIN PL
ROSEBANK AV
MILLAR CR
MAPLE ST
VALENCIA ST
JAFFA RD
Spring St Res
SPRING ST
THE VILLAGE PL
HAVEN
Retirement Village
MICHELLE PL
FRENSHAM PL
STONELEA CT
Priv Rd
Dural Mall
Vet Clinic
RD
Reservoir
FRANLEE RD
MALABAR RD
Tennis
OLD NORTHERN
ENHAVEN RD
Cmnty Cntr
Glenhaven Res
AV
Glenhaven Pmy
RD
GILMOUR CL
Lorien Novalis
Georges Ck
36
15
34

MAP 189

JOINS MAP 159

JOINS MAP 188 / *JOINS MAP 219*

Key labels visible on map:
- Canine Lodge
- Susan Park
- Carters Rd
- Gilligans Rd
- Taylors Rd
- Farnborough Rd
- Muraban Rd
- Langlands
- Uralla
- Swanes Nursery
- San Remo Pl
- Sydney Equestrian Centre
- Reservoir
- Galston Road
- The Porter Scenic Lookout
- Pitt Rd
- Cotswold Rd
- Laurie Av
- Gallery
- Squash
- Cemetery
- Function Cntr
- Hargraves Nurseryland
- Carters Rd
- Crumbly Rd
- Dural Pwy
- Footbridge
- Melody Farm
- Nursery
- Dural Antiques
- DURAL
- Hunt
- Derriwong (Old Road)
- Dembridge Rd
- Snombree Rd
- Hall
- Redfield College
- Vineys Rd
- Odette Rd
- Uniting Church Cem
- Northern Rd
- Dural Flower Farm
- Tunks
- Valenga St
- Jaffa Rd
- Derriwong Rd
- Old Rd
- Quarry Rd
- Dural Business Park
- Pacific Hills Chr Sch
- Quarry La
- Reservoirs
- Dural Irrigation
- Parson Rd
- Harris Rd
- Big Rd
- Hemers Rd
- New Line Rd
- Dural Golf Driving Range
- New Line Business Park
- Rural Fire Service
- Dural Park
- Tennis
- Quarry Rd
- Delivery Cntr

© COPYRIGHT UNIVERSAL PUBLISHERS PTY LTD 2005

MAP 190

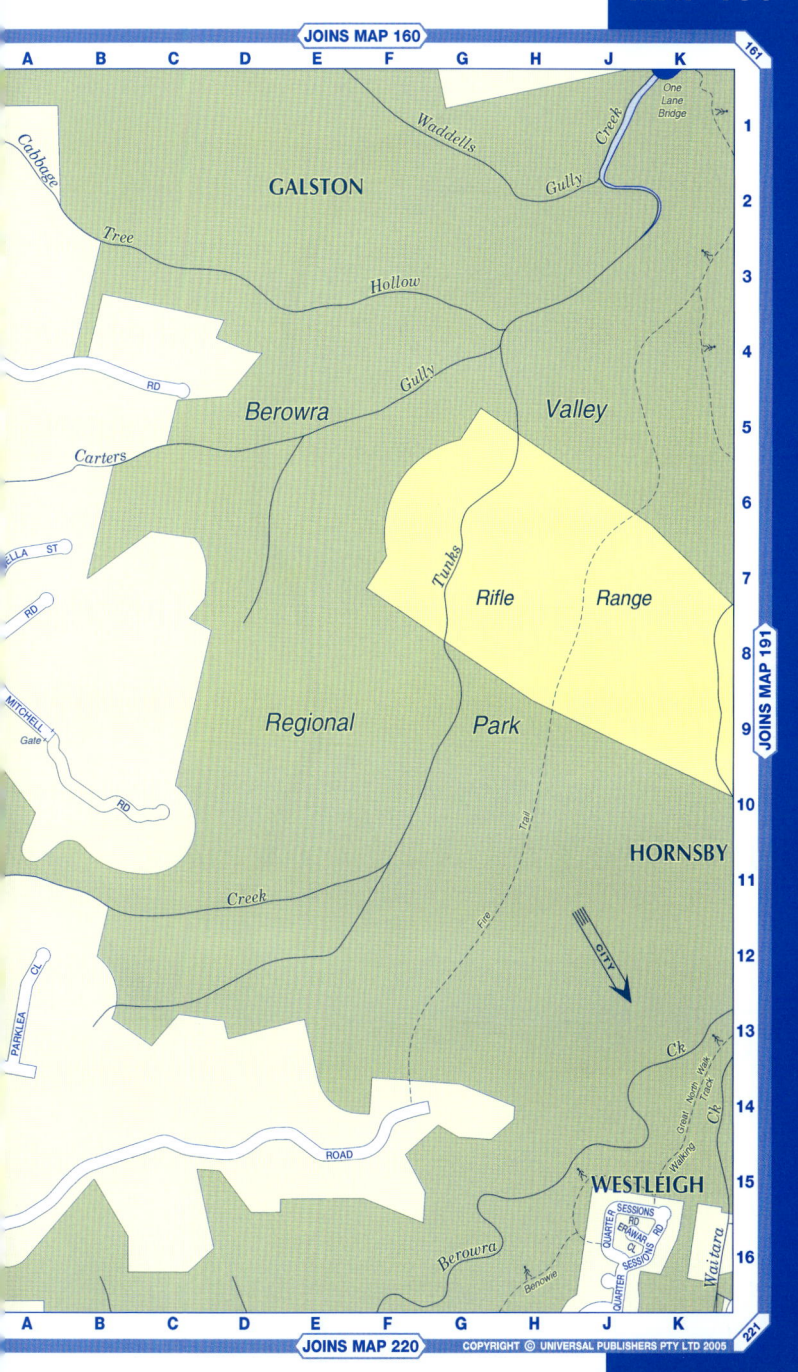

MAP 191

JOINS MAP 161
JOINS MAP 190
JOINS MAP 221
160
220
DURAL
Berowra Valley Regional Park
HORNSBY HEIGHTS
Hookhams Corner
HORNSBY
Rifle Range
Old Mans Valley
Hornsby Park
Great North Walk
Benowie Walking Track
Berowra Ck
Old Mans Ck
Waitara Ck
Walls Gully
GALSTON RD
PACIFIC HWY
GEORGE ST
JERSEY RD
BRIDGE RD
DURAL ST
Montview Park & Oval
Hornsby Hts Pmy
Fire Control Cntr & RFS
Cmnty Cntr
Rofe Park
Tennis Courts
Pmy
Hopeville Pk
Mt Wilga Hospital
Storey Park
Hall
Petanque
Reservoirs
Ret Vill
Asquith Boys High
Lessing Pk
Motor Registry
TAFE NSW
Hornsby Aquatic Centre
Ginger Meggs Pk
Tenpin Bowl
PCYC
Cncl

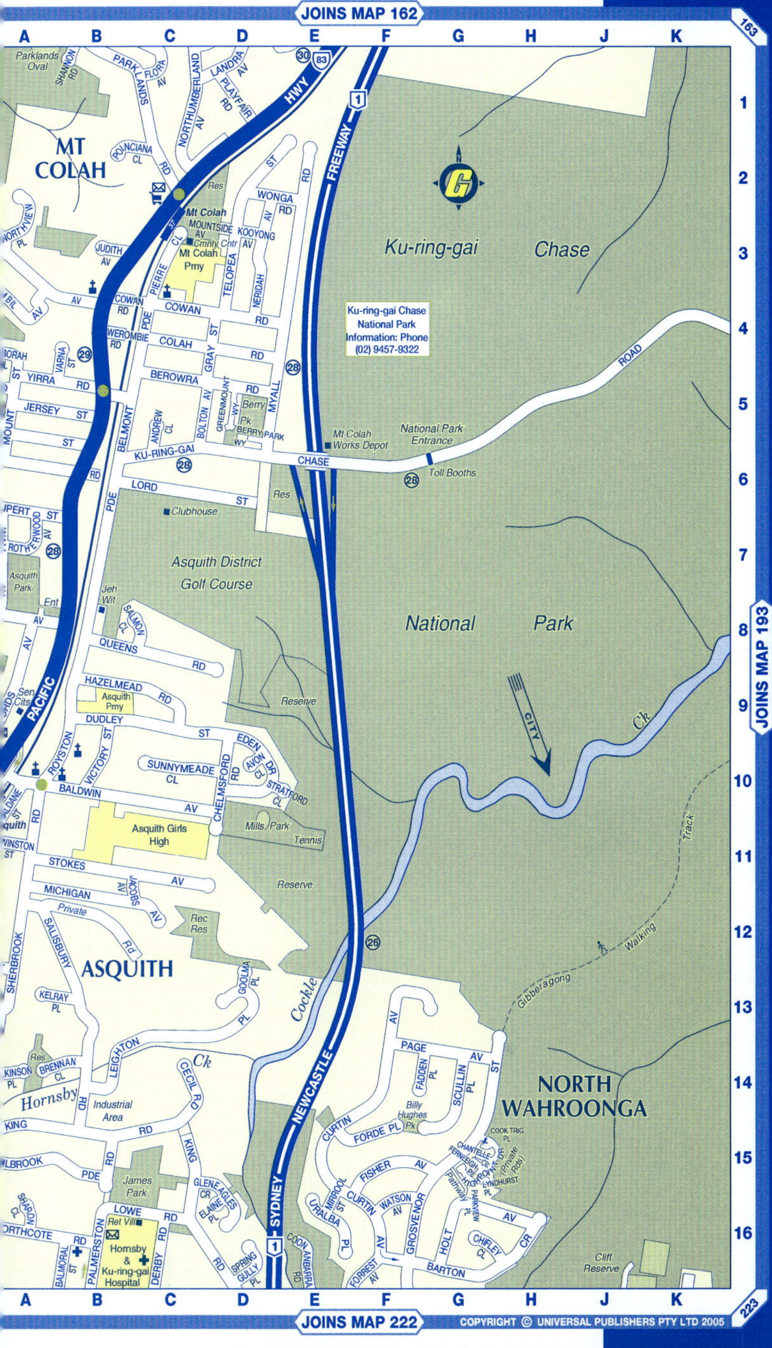
JOINS MAP 162
JOINS MAP 193
JOINS MAP 222
163
223
A B C D E F G H J K
1 2 3 4 5 6 7 8 9 10 11 12 13 14 15 16
MT COLAH
ASQUITH
NORTH WAHROONGA
Ku-ring-gai Chase
National Park
Ku-ring-gai Chase National Park Information: Phone (02) 9457-9322
PACIFIC HWY
FREEWAY
SYDNEY NEWCASTLE
KU-RING-GAI CHASE ROAD
National Park Entrance
Toll Booths
Mt Colah Works Depot
Asquith District Golf Course
Clubhouse
Mt Colah Pmy
Asquith Pmy
Asquith Girls High
Hornsby & Ku-ring-gai Hospital
Ret Vill
James Park
Billy Hughes Pk
Mills Park
Tennis
Reserve
Rec Res
Industrial Area
Cockle Ck
Hornsby Ck
Gibberagong Walking Track
Cliff Reserve
Parklands Oval
Asquith Park
Berry Pk
Cmnty Cntr
Sen Cits
Jeh Wit
CITY
BELMONT PDE
BALDWIN AV
STOKES AV
MICHIGAN AV
DUDLEY ST
QUEENS RD
HAZELMEAD RD
SUNNYMEADE CL
CHELMSFORD RD
EDEN DR
STRATFORD CL
ROYSTON
VICTORY ST
LORD ST
BEROWRA RD
COLAH RD
COWAN RD
WONGA RD
TELOPEA
KOOYONG AV
NERIDAH RD
MYALL
BOLTON AV
ANDREW CL
GREENMOUNT WY
GRAY ST
PIERRE CL
MOUNTSIDE AV
NORTHUMBERLAND AV
LANDRA AV
PLAYFAIR RD
PARKLANDS
FLORA AV
POINCIANA CL
JUDITH AV
YIRRA RD
JERSEY ST
SALISBURY
KELRAY PL
LEIGHTON PL
GOOLMA PL
BRENNAN CL
CECIL RD
KING RD
PALMERSTON RD
LOWE RD
DERBY RD
GLENEAGLES CR
ELAINE PL
SPRING GULLY PL
COONANBARRA RD
PAGE ST
FADDEN PL
SCULLIN PL
CURTIN AV
FORDE PL
FISHER AV
WATSON AV
GROSVENOR
URALBA PL
MIRROOL ST
HOLT AV
BARTON
FORREST AV
CHIFLEY CL
PARKVIEW PL
LYNDHURST PL
COOK TRIG PL
CHANTELLE CL
FERNLEIGH PL
HIGHLAND DR

MAP 193

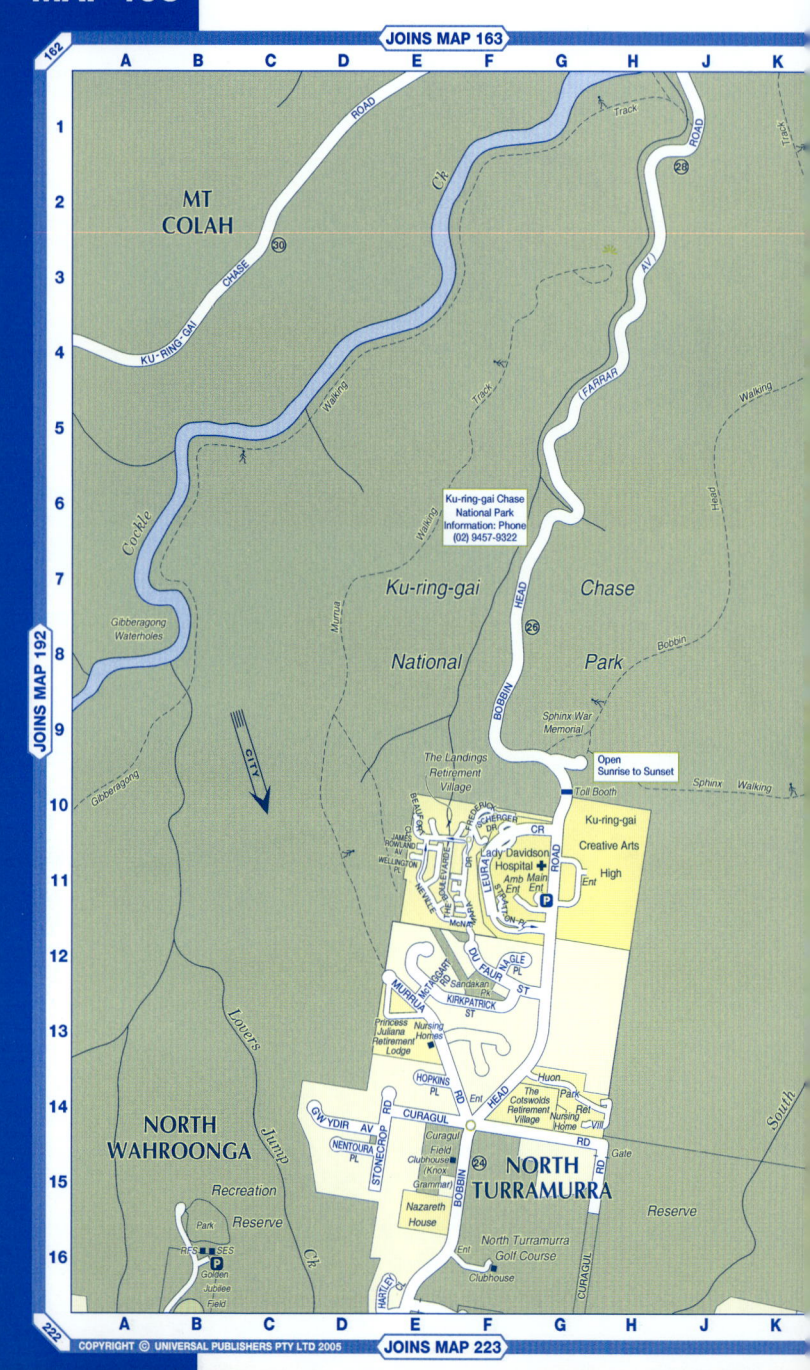

MAP 194

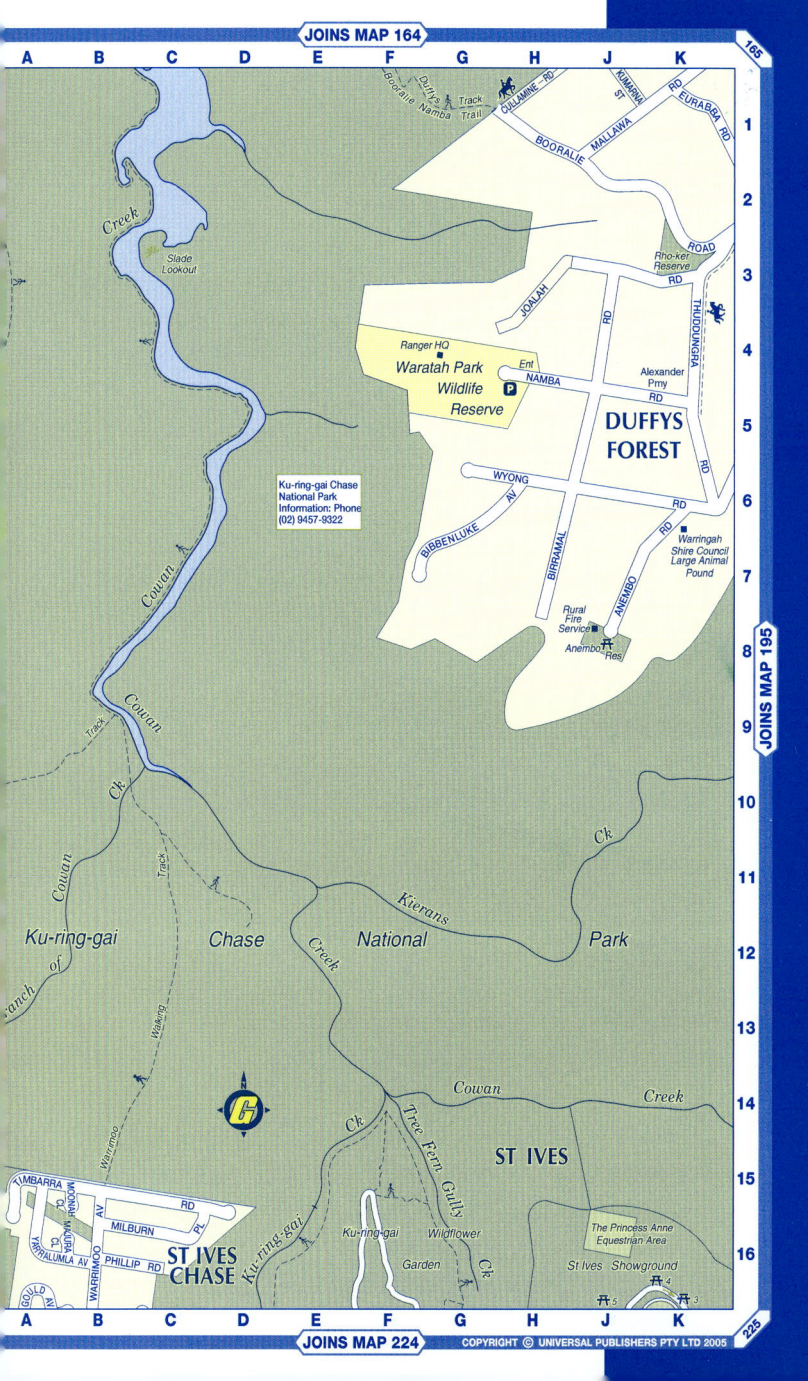

MAP 195

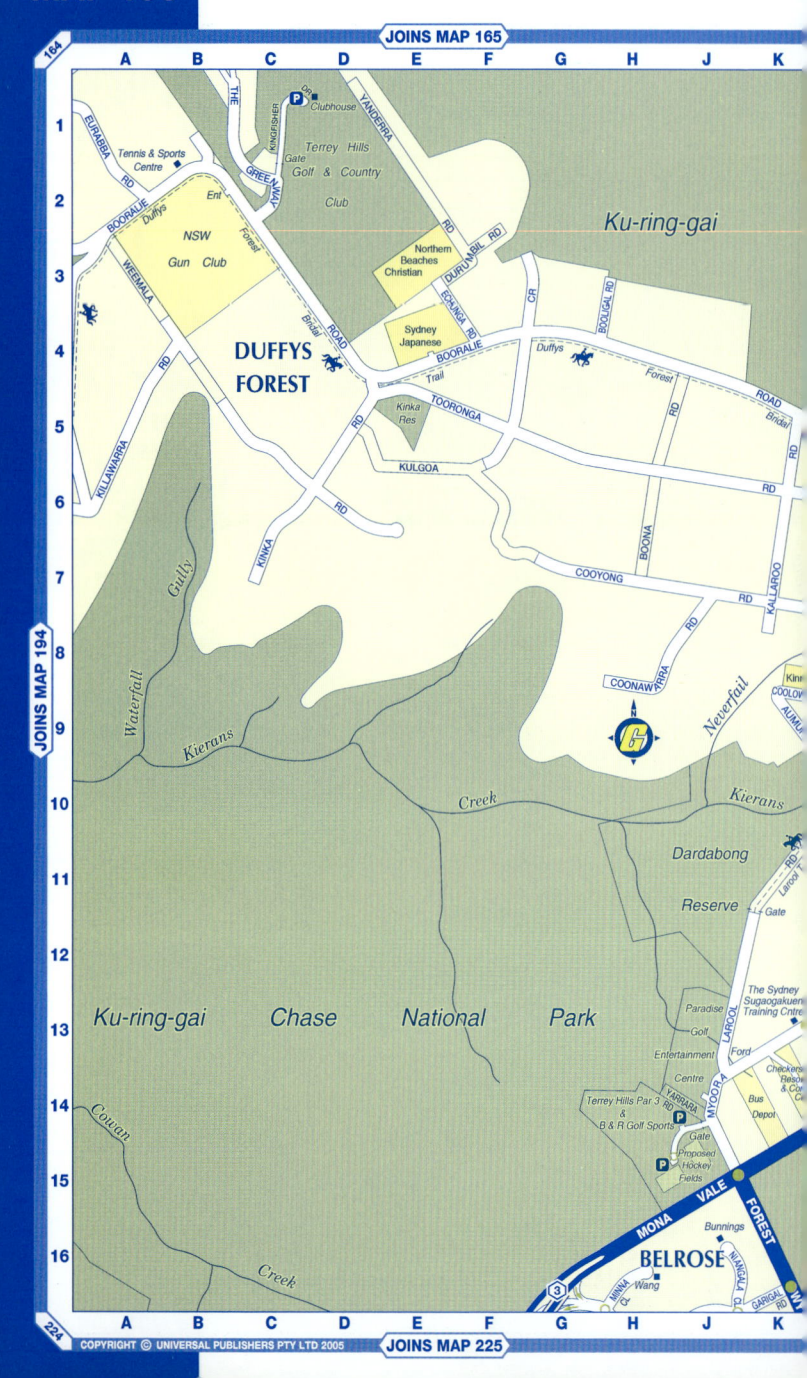

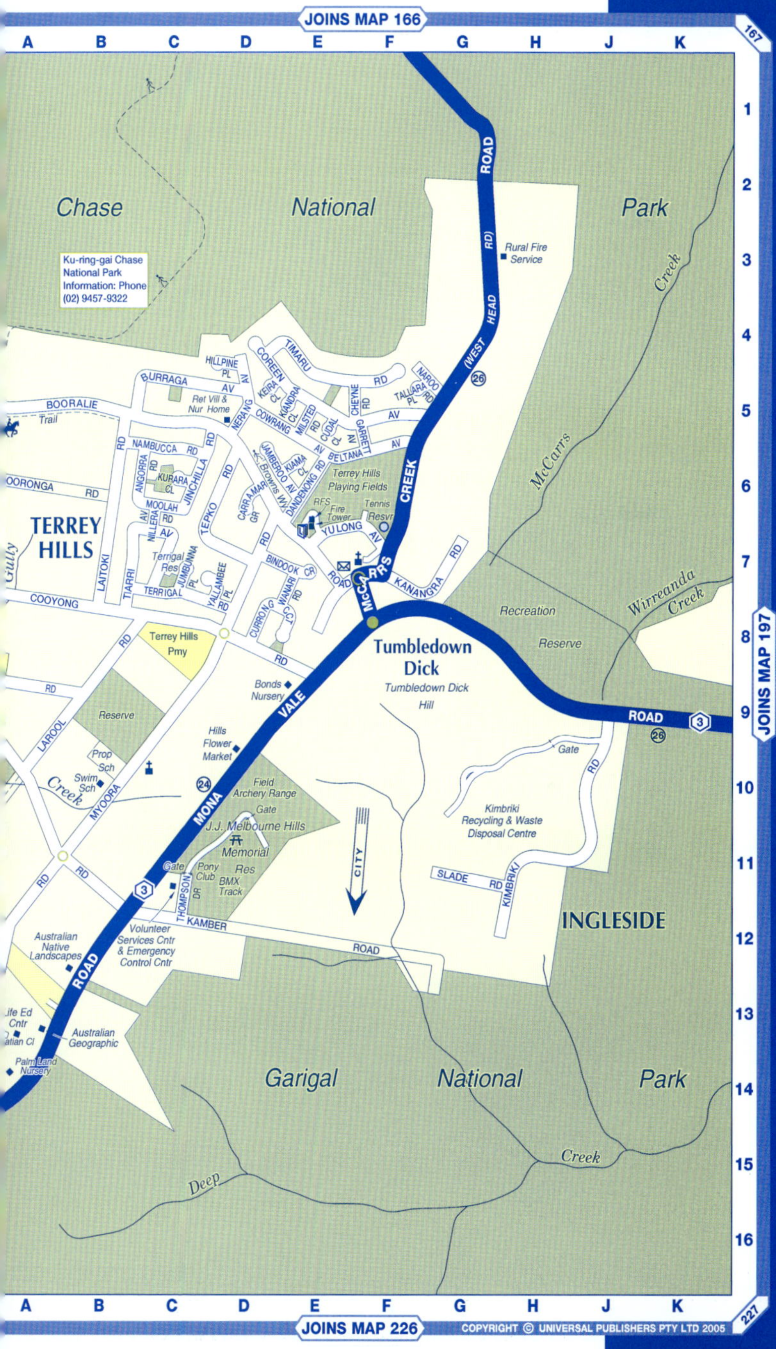

JOINS MAP 166
A B C D E F G H J K
1 2 3 4 5 6 7 8 9 10 11 12 13 14 15 16
167
Chase
National
Park
Ku-ring-gai Chase
National Park
Information: Phone
(02) 9457-9322
ROAD
(WEST HEAD RD)
Rural Fire
Service
Creek
HILLPINE PL
COREEN
TIMARU
BURRAGA AV
Ret Vill &
Nur Home
NERANG
KEIRA CL
KIANDRA CL
COWRANG
MILSTED RD
CUDAL CL
CHEYNE RD
GARRETT AV
NAROO RD
TALLARA PL
BOORALIE
Trail
NAMBUCCA RD
BELTANA AV
ANGORRA RD
KURARA CL
JINCHILLA
JAMBEROO AV
Browns Wy
KIAMA CL
DANDENONG RD
Terrey Hills
Playing Fields
RFS
Fire
Tower
Tennis
Resvr
CREEK
McCarrs
OORONGA RD
MOOLAH RD
TEPKO RD
CARRAMAR GR
YULONG AV
TERREY
HILLS
NILLERA AV
Terrigal
Res
JUMBUNNA PL
RD
BINDOOK CR
ROAD
McCARRS
KANANGRA RD
LAITOKI
TIARRI
TERRIGAL
YALLAMBEE PL
WANARI RD
CURRONG CCT
Wirreanda
Creek
Recreation
Reserve
COOYONG
Terrey Hills
Pmy
Tumbledown
Dick
Tumbledown Dick
Hill
RD
Bonds
Nursery
VALE
ROAD
JOINS MAP 197
Reserve
LAROOL
Hills
Flower
Market
Gate
Prop
Sch
Swim
Sch
Creek
MYOORA
MONA
Field
Archery Range
Gate
J.J. Melbourne Hills
Memorial
Res
CITY
Kimbriki
Recycling & Waste
Disposal Centre
Gate
Pony
Club
BMX
Track
THOMPSON DR
SLADE RD
KIMBRIKI
INGLESIDE
KAMBER
ROAD
Australian
Native
Landscapes
Volunteer
Services Cntr
& Emergency
Control Cntr
Life Ed
Cntr
Australian
Geographic
Palm Land
Nursery
Garigal
National
Park
Creek
Deep
JOINS MAP 226
227

JOINS MAP 167

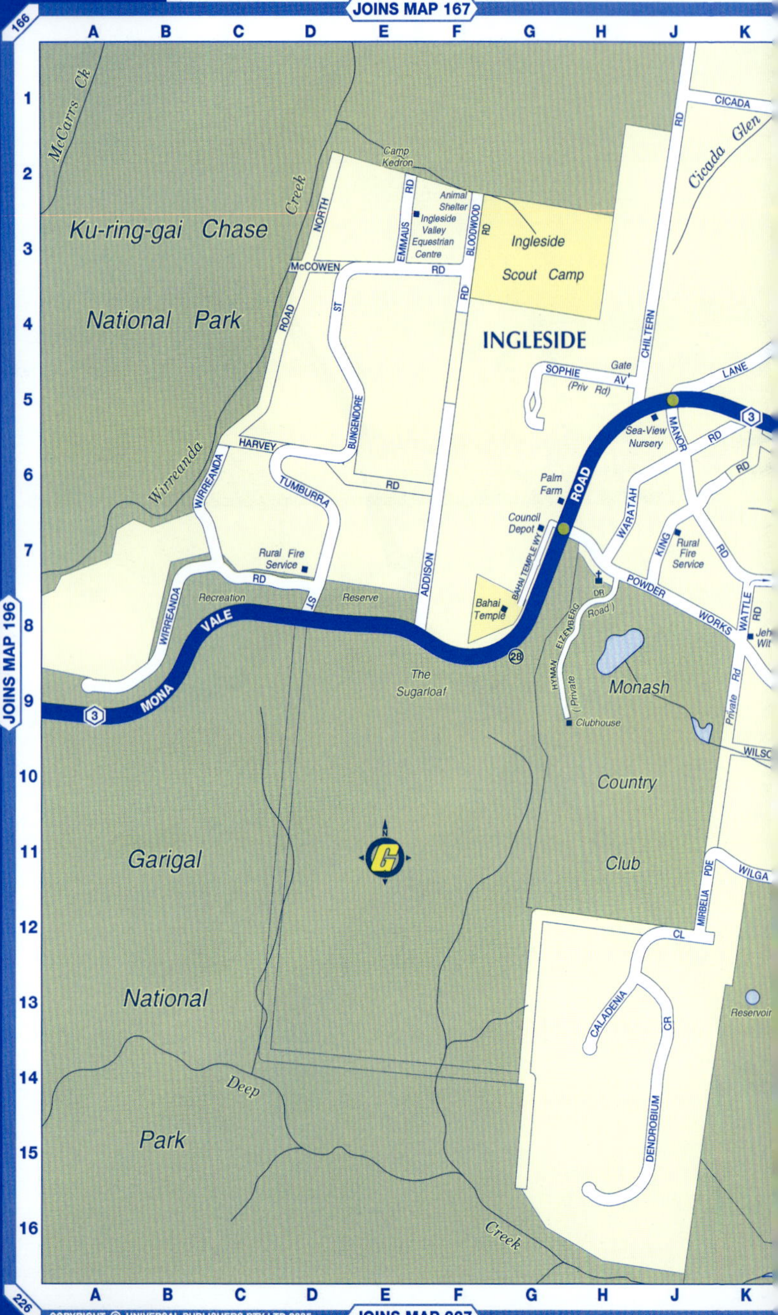

JOINS MAP 196

JOINS MAP 227

JOINS MAP 168
JOINS MAP 199
JOINS MAP 228
169
229
BAYVIEW
Bayview Golf Course
MONA VALE
WARRIEWOOD
ELANORA HEIGHTS
NORTH NARRABEEN
Peninsula Gardens Village
Katandra Bushland Sanctuary
Electricity Substation
Mona Vale Cemetery
Warriewood Escarpment
Narrabeen
CITY
Mater Maria College
Ingleside Park
Rec Res
Reservoir
Westpac Coll Training Cntr
Foley's Hill
Delivery Centre
Ponderosa Business Centre
Flower Power
Elanora Conference Centre
Garden Works
Elanora Country Club
Clubhouse
Epworth Park
Irrawong Res
Irrawong Walk
Ret Vill & Nursing Home
Warriewood Wetlands
Wetland Walk
Boardwalk
Swamp Forest Walk
Mullet
Warriewood
Narrabeen Sports High
Peninsula Industrial
Cmnty Cntr
Cooleena Res
Kundibah Pk
Anana Res
Elanora Heights Pmy
Narroy Park
Nareen Res
Lumeah Res
Katoa Res
Moriac Res
Valley View Res
Progress
Fbr Park
Sub Stn
RSL
MONA VALE ROAD
CABBAGE TREE RD
SAMUEL ST
PONDEROSA PDE
MACPHERSON ST
BOUNDARY ST
FOREST RD
INGLESIDE RD
POWDER WORKS RD
GARDEN ST
JACKSONS RD
WARRIEWOOD RD
PITTWATER RD
ALLEYNE AV
COPYRIGHT © UNIVERSAL PUBLISHERS PTY LTD 2005

MAP 199

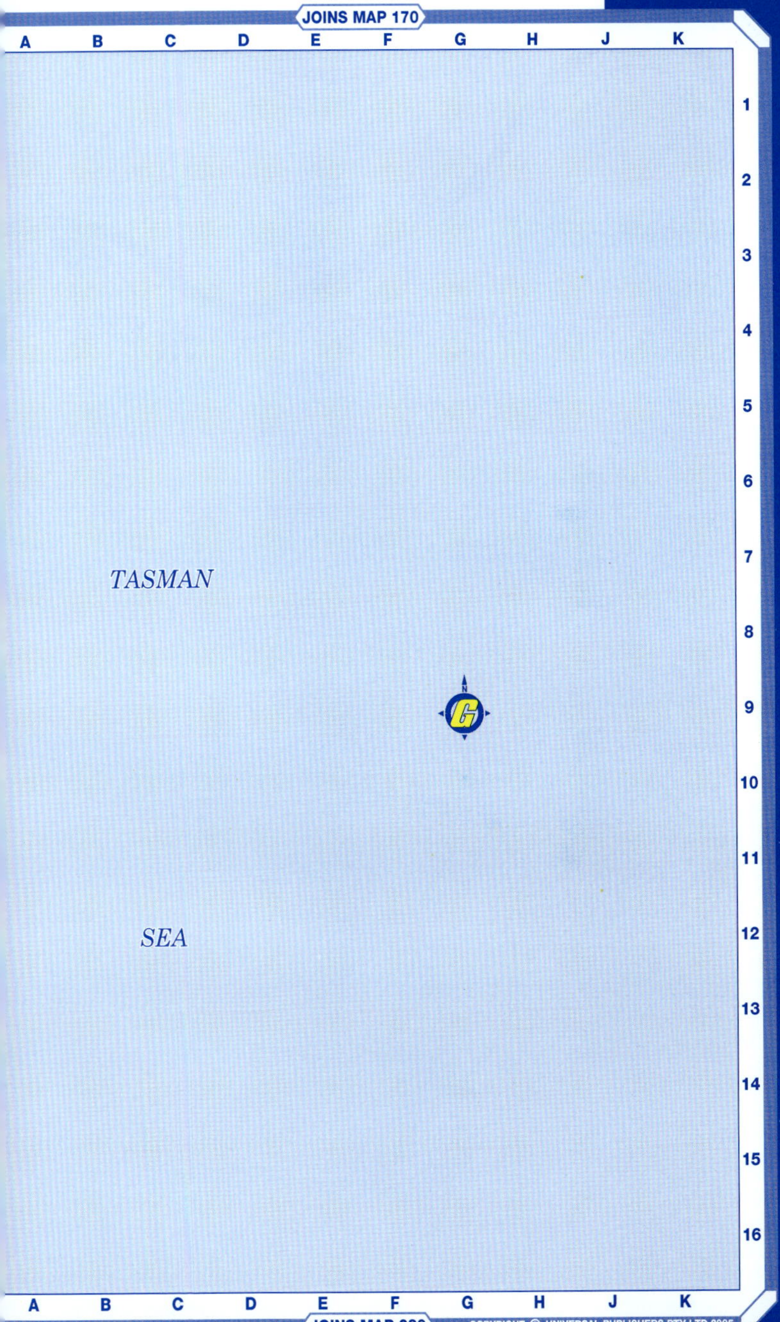

MAP 200

TASMAN

SEA

JOINS MAP 171
LIMIT OF MAPS
FAULCONBRIDGE
SPRINGWOOD
BLUE MOUNTAINS NATIONAL PARK
Jackson Park
Davies Park
Recreation Reserve
Sassafras Gully Reserve
Blue Mountains National Park
Wiggins Park
Picnic Point Res
Fairy Dell Reserve
Birdwood Gully Park
Buttenshaw Park
Clarinda Falls
Altitude 371m
Rifle Club
Lawsons
GREAT WESTERN HIGHWAY
MACQUARIE RD
VALLEY RD
FARM RD
SASSAFRAS GULLY RD
Glenbrook
Magdala
Sassafras Track
Wiggins Track
Gully
Creek
Springwood Ck

MAP 202

MAP 203

JOINS MAP 173

SPRINGWOOD

Long Angle Rd
Singles Ridge
Paterson, Winter Rd
Fitzgerald
Ridgeway
SUN VALLEY
Sun Valley Rd
Rosenthal La
Boyles La / Cr
Rd

Creek
Wayande

Torwood St
Spur St
Cross St
Cr
Terrymont Grn
Rd
Warrimoo Oval
Tennis
Recreation Reserve

The Terrace
Railway
Riley, Hawkins
Ardill, Warrimoo Pde
U'pass 68
GREAT WESTERN Rickard
John Wycliffe Christian
Waratah Rd
Underpass
Victoria St
The Boulevarde
Resvr
A W Bewley Bridge
Railway
Edna St
WARRIMOO
Albert St
Altitude 273m
Avenue
Arthur St
The Mill
Ardill, Karabah Tce
Lupton Pathway
Spurwood Rd
Blue Mountains National Park
Florabella
Warrimoo Pmy
Hwy 32
Pde

Florabella Pass

JOINS MAP 202 / JOINS MAP 233

COPYRIGHT © UNIVERSAL PUBLISHERS PTY LTD 2005

MAP 204

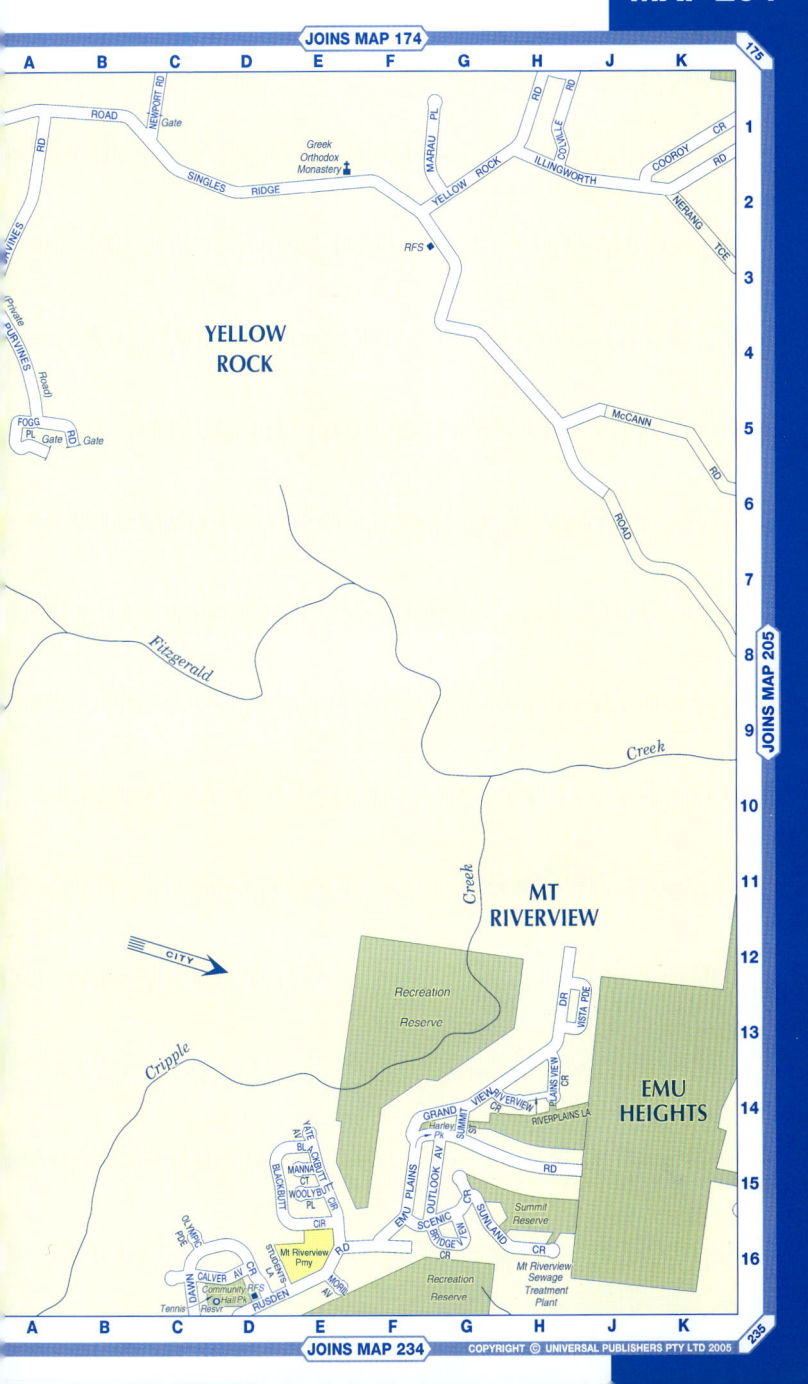

YELLOW ROCK

- Newport Road
- Singles Ridge
- Vines Road
- Purvines Road (Private)
- Fogg Pl
- Marau Pl
- Yellow Rock Rd
- Illingworth Rd
- Colville Rd
- Cooroy Cr
- Nerang Tce
- McCann Road
- Greek Orthodox Monastery
- RFS

Fitzgerald Creek

MT RIVERVIEW

EMU HEIGHTS

- Recreation Reserve
- Cripple Creek
- CITY →
- Vista Pde
- Riverplains La
- Riverview Cr
- Grand View
- Summit
- Harley
- Emu Plains
- Outlook Av
- Scenic Ridge Cr
- Sunland Cr
- Road
- Mt Riverview Pmy
- Community Hall
- Tennis
- Dawn
- Calver Av
- Rusden
- Students La
- Mori Av
- Blackbutt Pl
- Woolybutt Pl
- Manna Ct
- Acacia Av
- Yate
- Olympic Pde
- Summit Reserve
- Mt Riverview Sewage Treatment Plant
- Recreation Reserve

JOINS MAP 174 (top)
JOINS MAP 234 (bottom)
JOINS MAP 175 (right top)
JOINS MAP 205 (right middle)
JOINS MAP 235 (right bottom)

COPYRIGHT © UNIVERSAL PUBLISHERS PTY LTD 2005

MAP 205

JOINS MAP 175

YELLOW ROCK

Cooroy Cr
Illingworth Rd
Nerang Tce
McCann Rd
Singles Ridge Rd

Yellomundee Regional Park

NEPEAN RIVER

CASTLEREAGH

Cranebrook
Penrith Lakes Quarry
Gate 13
Lake
Castlereagh Road

Fitzgerald
Park Ck

EMU HEIGHTS

Stratton Rd
Riverside Rd
Guy Pl
Alma Rd
Private

McCanns Island

Private Road
CSR Readymix
Cem
Lake
P
Grandstand
Finish Observatory
Fbr
Gate A
Gate B
Gen Entry
CASTLEREAGH

Quarry
Quarry
PENRITH

JOINS MAP 204
JOINS MAP 235

COPYRIGHT © UNIVERSAL PUBLISHERS PTY LTD 2005

MAP 206

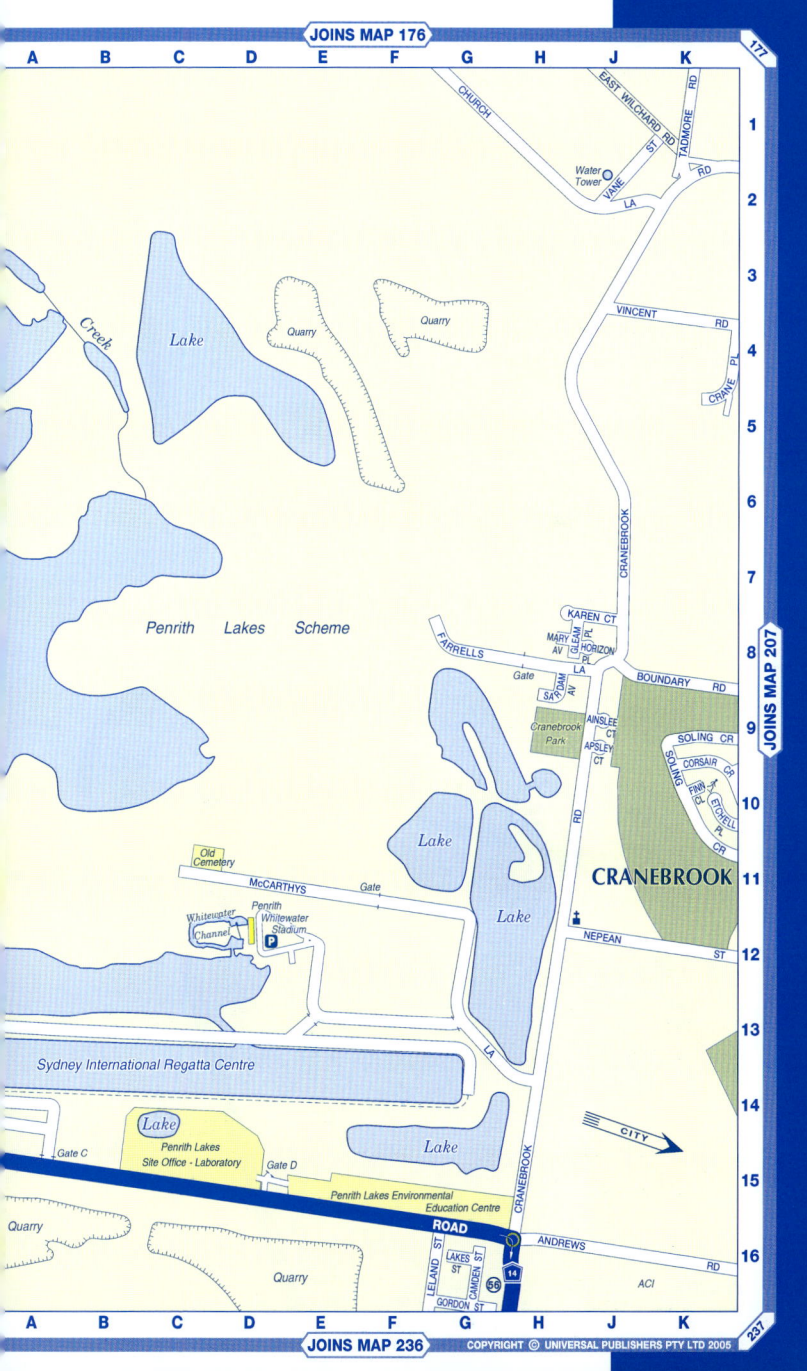

JOINS MAP 176

- Church La
- East Wilchard Rd
- Vane St
- Tadmore Rd
- Water Tower
- Vincent Rd
- Crane Pl
- Creek
- Lake
- Quarry
- Quarry
- Cranebrook Rd
- Penrith Lakes Scheme
- Karen Ct
- Farrells La
- Mary Av
- Gleam Pl
- Horizon
- Sam Pl
- Adam Av
- Gate
- Boundary Rd
- Ainslee Ct
- Soling Cr
- Cranebrook Park
- Apsley Ct
- Corsair Cr
- Finn Pl
- Etchell Pl
- Lake
- **CRANEBROOK**
- Old Cemetery
- McCarthys Gate
- Whitewater Channel
- Penrith Whitewater Stadium
- Lake
- Nepean St
- Sydney International Regatta Centre
- La
- CITY
- Lake
- Penrith Lakes Site Office - Laboratory
- Gate C
- Gate D
- Penrith Lakes Environmental Education Centre
- Quarry
- ROAD
- Leland St
- Camden St
- Gordon St
- Andrews Rd
- ACI
- Quarry

JOINS MAP 236

JOINS MAP 207

COPYRIGHT © UNIVERSAL PUBLISHERS PTY LTD 2005

MAP 207

JOINS MAP 177
JOINS MAP 206
JOINS MAP 237
176
236
A B C D E F G H J K
1 2 3 4 5 6 7 8 9 10 11 12 13 14 15 16
Cranebrook Native Nursery
CRANEBROOK RD
Airservices Australia
FIFTH
THE NORTHERN ROAD
9
Ent
VINCENT RD
SEVENTH
Henry Fulton Pmy
KATHERINE LA (Private Rd)
CENTAURI CL
HYDRUS ST
CCT
LALANDA CL
ANDROMEDA DR
ANTARES PL
GENEVA RD
LYNX PL
CELESTIAL PL
PROCYON PL
SEXTANS PL
CITY
CRANE PL
GLN
WYANG
WOODSIDE GLN
KENILWORTH CR
KOMIRRA RD
THURONG PL
BELLATRIX
HERCULES CL
LUYTEN CL
ARCTURUS CL
SCORPIUS PL
ALDEBARAN
KANA CL
Andromeda Fields
RABAT CL
AUSTRALIS CL
CASS CR
VENUS CL
CYGNUS PL
PERSEUS CL
PLUTO PL
CASSAR CR
CARINA PL
ST
LINDEN CR
NUMBRUK CL
MERRINDAL CL
LINDEN
Golf Driving Range
Corpus Christi Pmy
WILLOWGUM CR
GRAYS LA
Samuel Terry Pmy
FOREST GLEN DR
TALLOWOOD PL
PEPPERCORN PL
BARRETT PL
CHAUSSON PL
LISZT PL
Boarding Kennels & Cattery
MOZART CR
NINTH
ELLIM
HILLSIDE CCT
YILKI CL
HINDMARSH ST
INDY PL
BORODIN CL
GOLDMARK DR
BEETHOVEN PL
BOUNDARY ROAD
ENTERPRISE RD
EDWARD ST
OZARK PL
DULHUNTY CT
GOOLWA CR
LOFTY PL
MIDDLETON AV
McGarritys Hill
MARRETT WY
WAGNER PL
BRITTEN CL
DEBUSSY PL
SOLING
HANLAN ST
COBRA ST
RIGNEY PL
GORMAN PL
MOXHAM ST
WALLIS GLN
GAMBIA PL
MELLFELL
OWENS PL
CORSAIR
SKATE ST
FIREBALL
BAMBI CL
ARAFURA AV
ISLINGTON ST
TORNADO CR
STINGRAY ST
MOTH CL
WIGGAN PL
CRANEBROOK
GAMA PL
TITANIA PL
MASER ST
BARRY COE PL
LEANE PL
FIELD PL
WILKINSON PL
OTTAWA CL
STILT AV
THARKINNA CL
MULLOO PL
ETCHELL PL
HIGGS PL
WITCOM CR
MARSH PL
MARTHA
NEREID RD
CLUSTER PL
IRRUKA PL
SOLING CR
BLUEBIRD RD
RAVINE CL
ROSETTA CL
CALLISTO
Res
ROBINSON RD
FERNVIEW PL
CLIFF PL
BORROWDALE ST
MELLFELL RD
WHITBECK PL
Reservoir
MIAMI PL
NAALONG PL
STILT
CAMELOT DR
SUMMIT GLN
WATERFALL
MOUNT CL
Cmnty Health Cntr
HOSKING
WESCOE PL
RYDAL PL
THORNFLAT RD
SANTON PL
HOLMEGATE
DODD PL
CR
WAY
NEPEAN ST
CRESTVIEW PL
CASCADE RD
MOSS GLN
Braddock Pmy
Cranebrook High
SHERRINGHAM RD
ULPHA PL
WOODGATE CR
PAVEY PL
BRIERY PL
MUNCASTER PL
RAVENGLASS PL
HYTON PL
STOULTON WY
BOOTLE PL
SEATON
LAYCOCK
OLIN CL
GREYGUMS RD
KANINA PL
MILLIGAN RD
PENELOPE PL
HEFFERMAN RD
JOSHUA WY
CASS PL
DUNN PL
GUNELL PL
COLLITT CR
OFFERTON WY
PERSHORE RD
REDDITCH WY
LYGON WY
GRAHAM CL
HAZEL CL
ANTONIA CR
Res
COLLEN PL
ROSANNAH WY
WARNDON RD
MICHAEL GLYNN CL
PROVINS WY
VERNON WY
BEACROFT PL
GREENHALGH RD
SHERRINGHAM
PENDOCK
PROGRESS WY
WARESLEY WY
CHALLENGER WY
NEVELL PL
McGANN PL
BEDLEY PL
KINGTON PL
MARTLEY
Reserve
McHENRY
DOLOMITE
ETNA CL
EIGER WY
PENSAX RD
JUPITER CT
Greygums Oval
FARMVIEW
PAUL CL
CALYPSO
BEREN PL
BAANYA LA
NEVIS
JURA CL
RD
CAPRICORN AV
ROSELLA PL
HARRY LAWLER RD
BACH CL
BERNARRA PL
DR
CROSSING
CEDARWOOD PL
CITRONELLE CT
P
QUAIL ST
TERRACE DR
Skateboard Ramp
ARIEL
CR
BOTTLEBRUSH AV
OPUS PL
PINETREE
IRONBARK DR
ANDREWS RD
Substation
PENRITH
Oval
KOALA GLN
SCENIC CCT
ELK PL
MAHOGANY CL

MAP 208

MAP 209

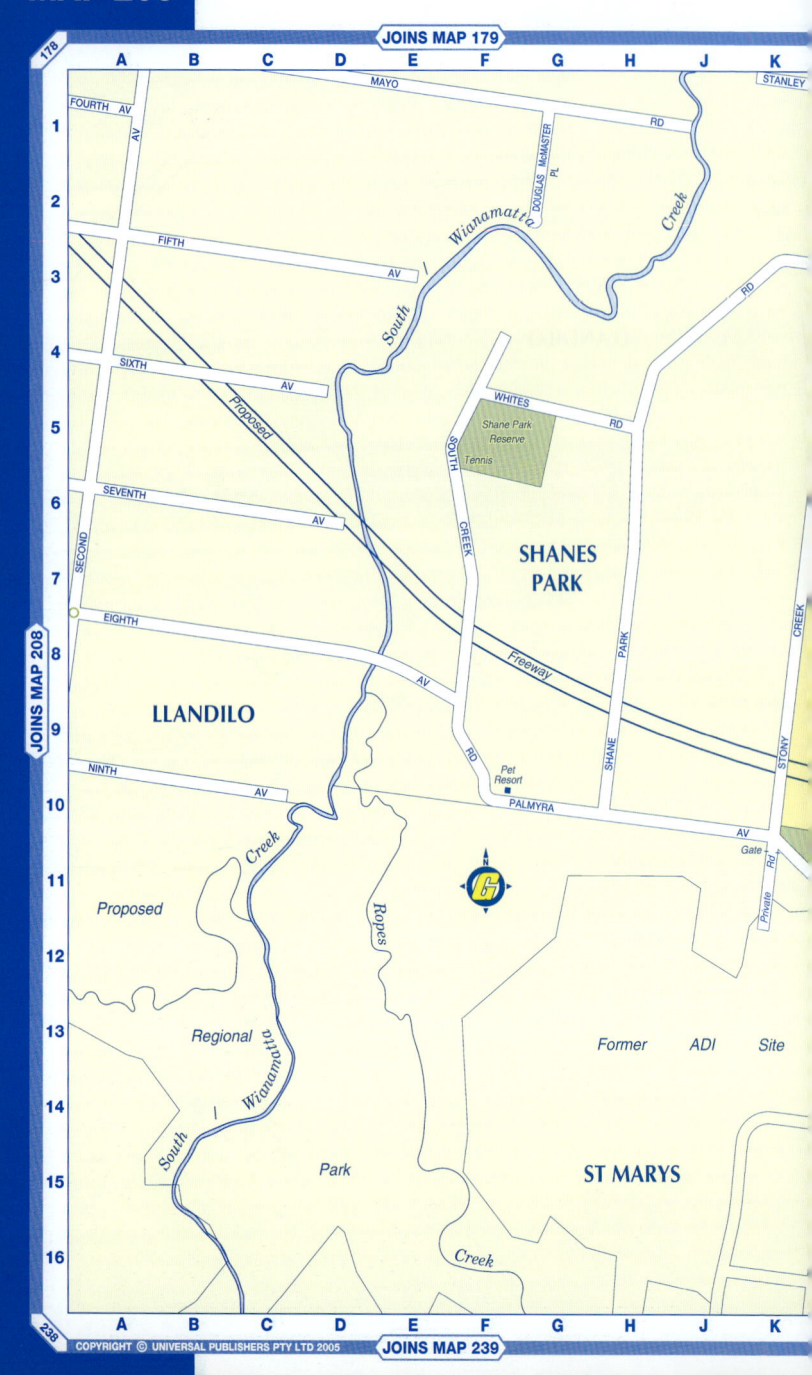

MAP 210

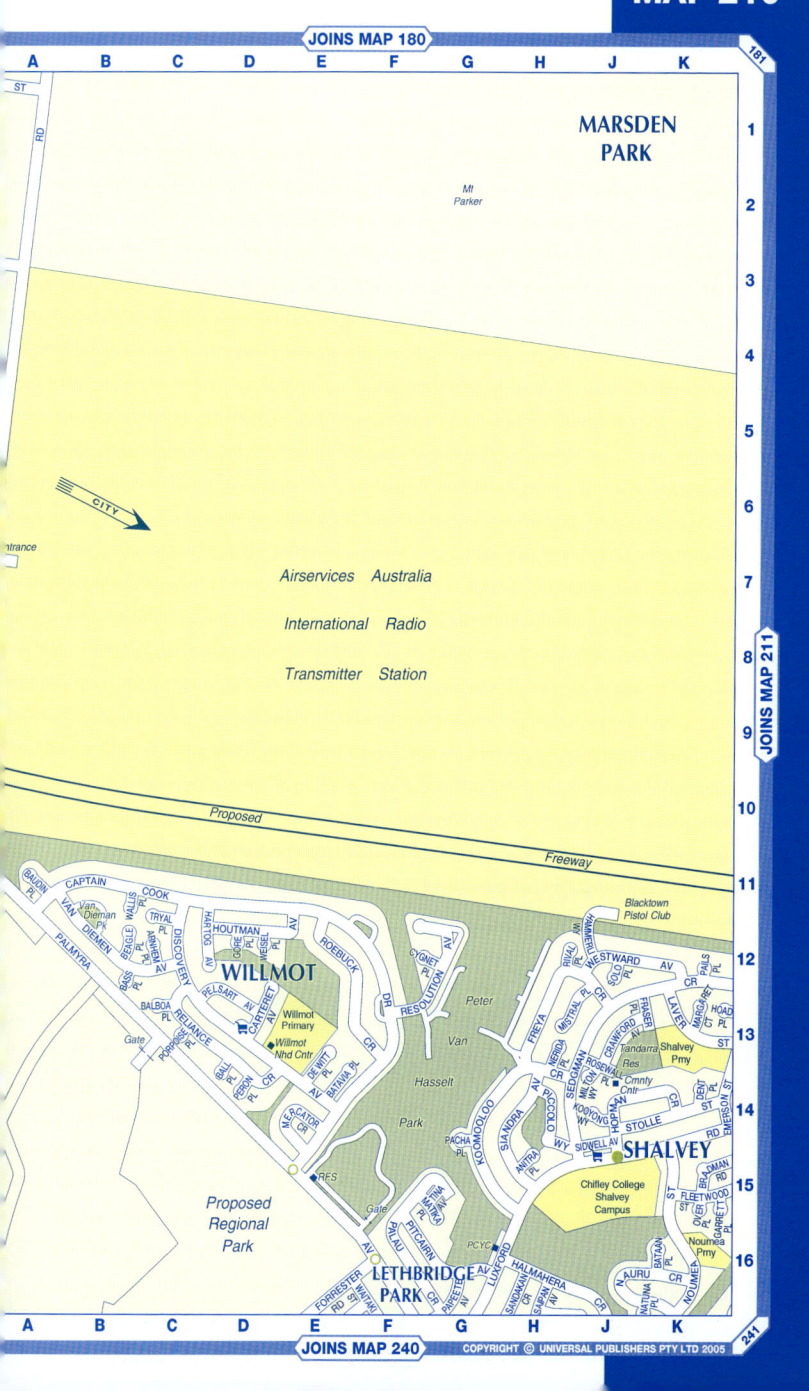

MARSDEN PARK

Mt Parker

CITY

Airservices Australia

International Radio

Transmitter Station

Proposed Freeway

WILLMOT

Willmot Primary
Willmot Nhd Cntr

Peter Van Hasselt Park

Blacktown Pistol Club

Tandarra Res
Shalvey Pmy
Cmnty Cntr

SHALVEY

Chifley College Shalvey Campus

Noumea Pmy

Proposed Regional Park

PCYC

LETHBRIDGE PARK

JOINS MAP 180
JOINS MAP 211
JOINS MAP 240

COPYRIGHT © UNIVERSAL PUBLISHERS PTY LTD 2005

MAP 211

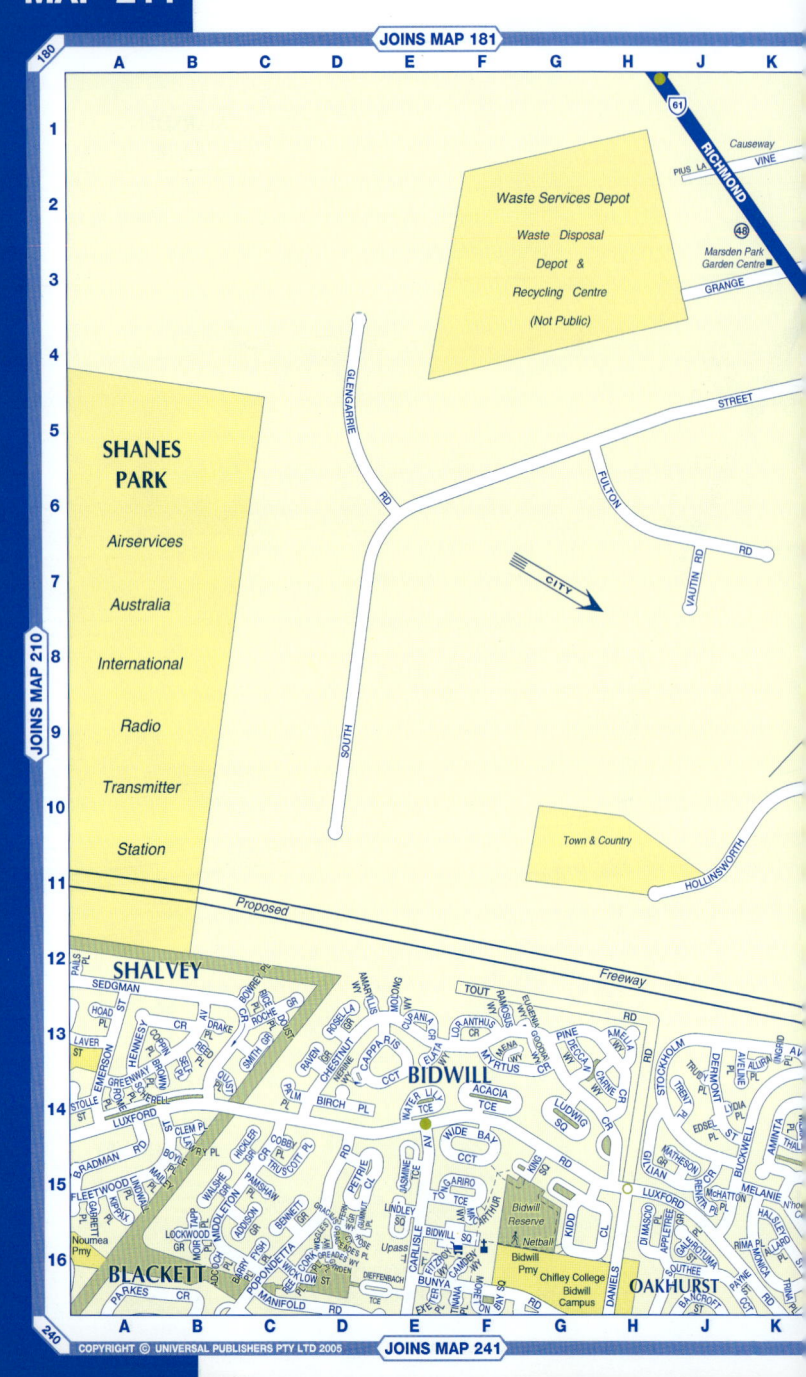

JOINS MAP 181

Waste Services Depot
Waste Disposal Depot & Recycling Centre
(Not Public)

Causeway
VINE
RICHMOND
PIUS LA
Marsden Park Garden Centre
GRANGE
STREET
GLENGARRIE RD
FULTON RD
VAUTIN RD
CITY
SOUTH HILL
SHANES PARK
Airservices Australia International Radio Transmitter Station

JOINS MAP 210

Town & Country
HOLLINSWORTH

Proposed Freeway

SHALVEY
BIDWILL
BLACKETT
OAKHURST
Bidwill Reserve
Bidwill Pwy
Chifley College Bidwill Campus

JOINS MAP 241

COPYRIGHT © UNIVERSAL PUBLISHERS PTY LTD 2005

MAP 212

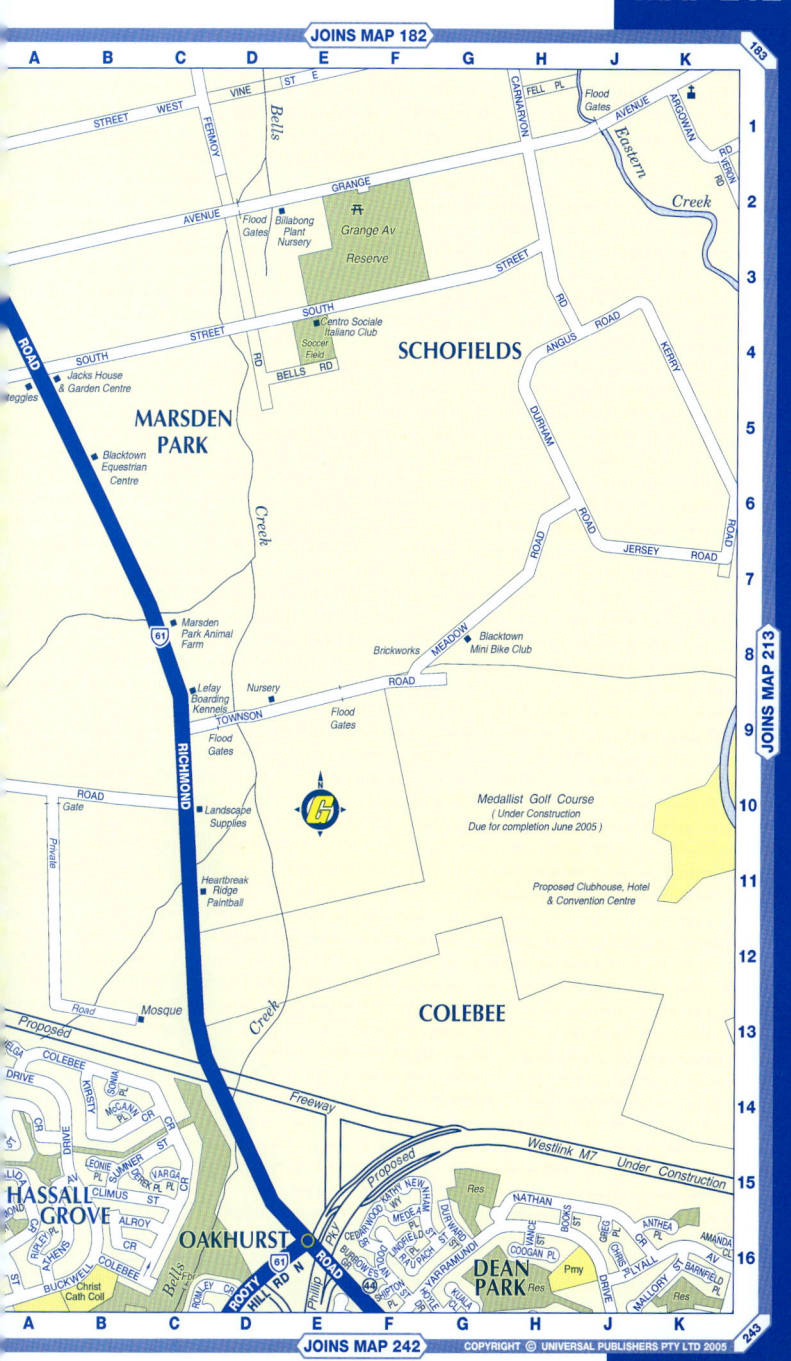

JOINS MAP 182

SCHOFIELDS

MARSDEN PARK

- Grange Av Reserve
- Billabong Plant Nursery
- Centro Sociale Italiano Club
- Soccer Field
- Jacks House & Garden Centre
- Blacktown Equestrian Centre
- Marsden Park Animal Farm
- Lefay Boarding Kennels
- Brickworks
- Blacktown Mini Bike Club
- Flood Gates
- Nursery
- Landscape Supplies
- Heartbreak Ridge Paintball

Medallist Golf Course
(Under Construction
Due for completion June 2005)

Proposed Clubhouse, Hotel & Convention Centre

COLEBEE

- Mosque

HASSALL GROVE

OAKHURST

DEAN PARK

- Christ Cath Coll
- Res
- Pmy
- Res

Streets/Features visible: STREET WEST, VINE ST, FERMOY, BELLS ST, CARNARVON, FELL PL, Flood Gates, AVENUE, ARGOWAN RD, Eastern Creek, GRANGE, AVENUE, SOUTH STREET, BELLS RD, ANGUS ROAD, DURHAM ROAD, KERRY ROAD, JERSEY ROAD, RICHMOND ROAD, TOWNSON, MEADOW ROAD, ROAD, Freeway, Proposed, Westlink M7 Under Construction, COLEBEE DRIVE, KIRSTY, McCANN ST, LEONIE PL, SUMNER, DEREK PL, VARGA PL, CLIMUS, ALROY CR, ATHENS, BUCKWELL, COLEBEE CR, RIPLEY PL, CEDARWOOD WY, KATHY NEW, BURGOYNE, MEDE, INGREA PL, SHIPTON PL, NATHAN, BOOKS, COOGAN PL, YARRAMUNDI, CHRIS PL, ANTHEA PL, AMANDA AV, LYALL, BARNFIELD, MALLORY DRIVE, PHILLIP RD, ROOTY HILL RD N

JOINS MAP 242
COPYRIGHT © UNIVERSAL PUBLISHERS PTY LTD 2005
JOINS MAP 213

MAP 213

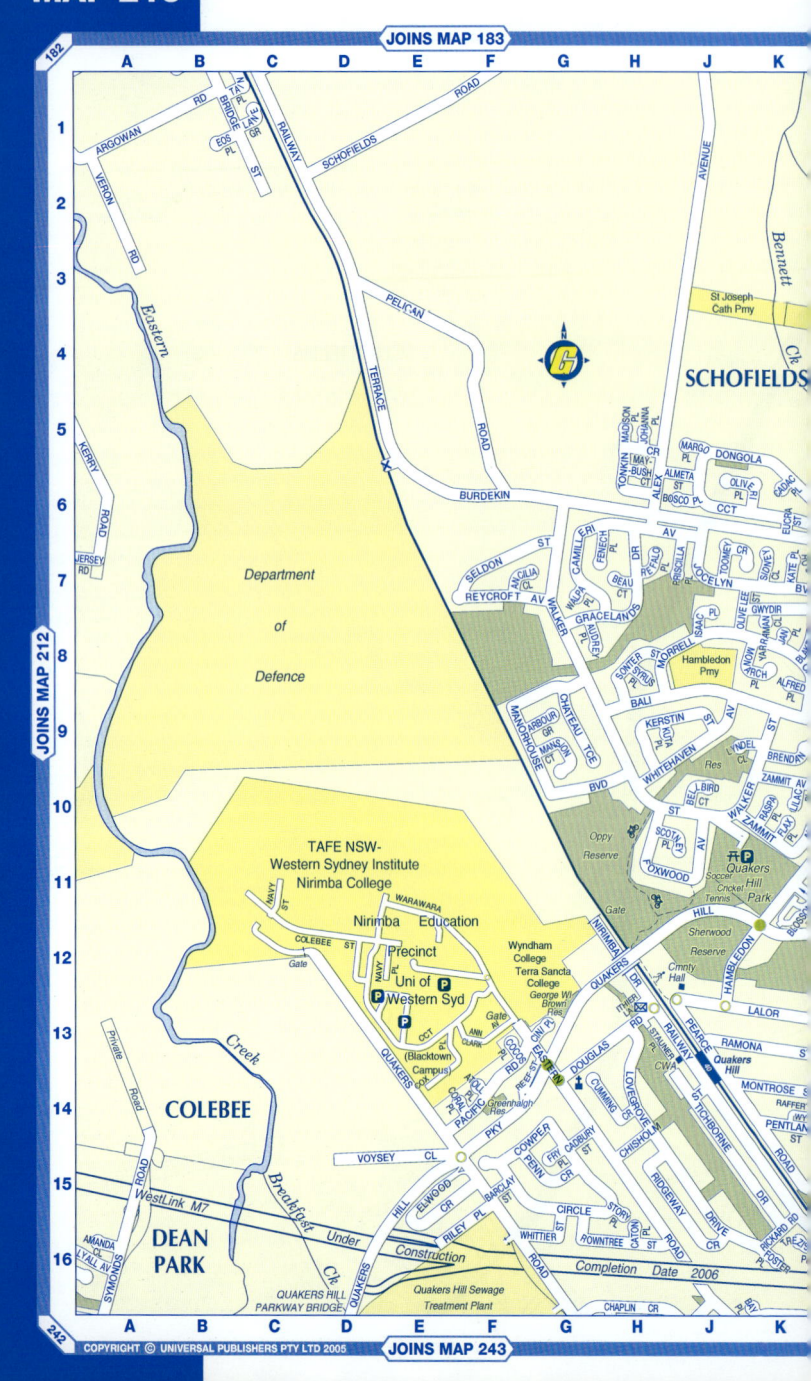

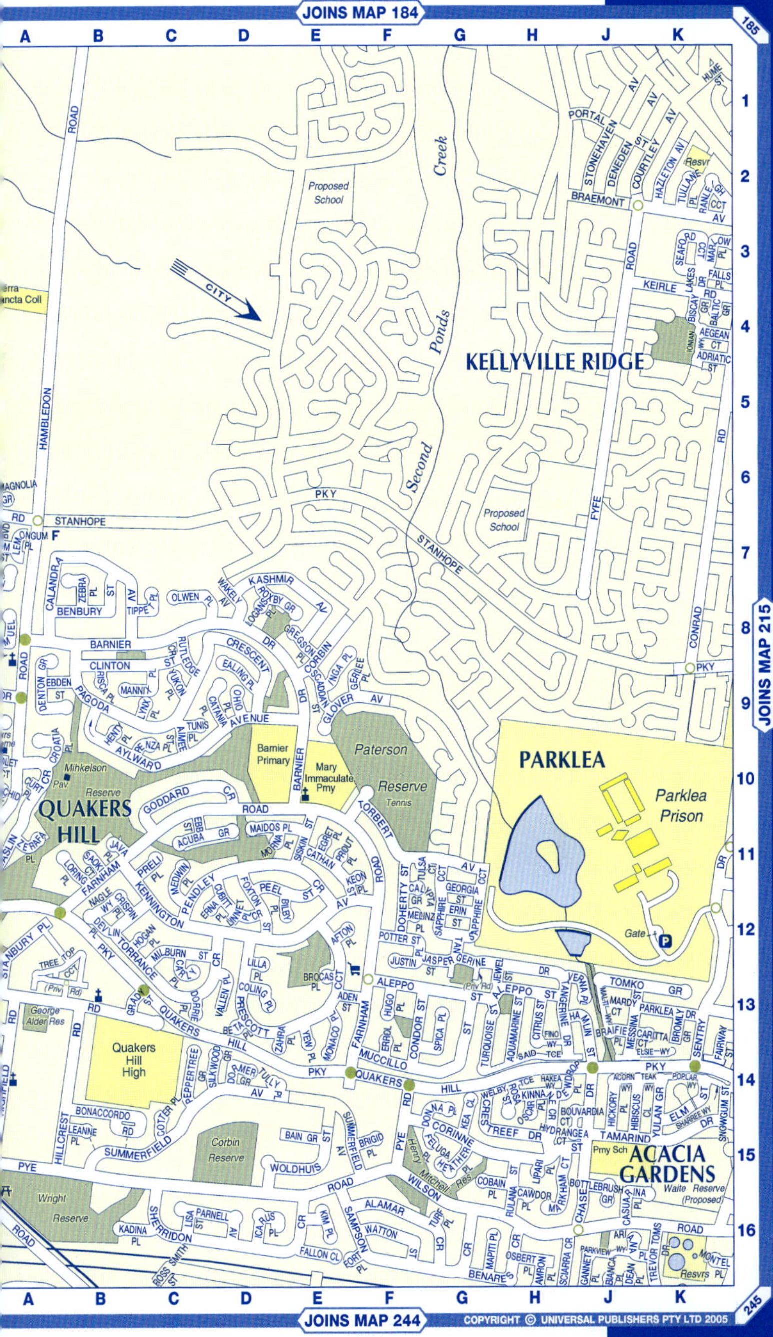
JOINS MAP 184
JOINS MAP 215
JOINS MAP 244
185
245
A B C D E F G H J K
1 2 3 4 5 6 7 8 9 10 11 12 13 14 15 16
KELLYVILLE RIDGE
PARKLEA
QUAKERS HILL
ACACIA GARDENS
Second Ponds Creek
Proposed School
Parklea Prison
Gate
Paterson Reserve
Tennis
Mary Immaculate Pmy
Barnier Primary
Mihkelson Reserve
Pav
Quakers Hill High
Corbin Reserve
Wright Reserve
George Alder Res
Henry Mitchell Res
Pmy Sch
Waite Reserve (Proposed)
Resvr
Resvrs
HAMBLEDON ROAD
STANHOPE PKY
QUAKERS HILL PKY
PYE ROAD
FYFE ROAD
CONRAD RD
AVENUE
CRESCENT
TORBERT ROAD
GODDARD CR
FARNHAM ROAD
CITY

MAP 215

JOINS MAP 185

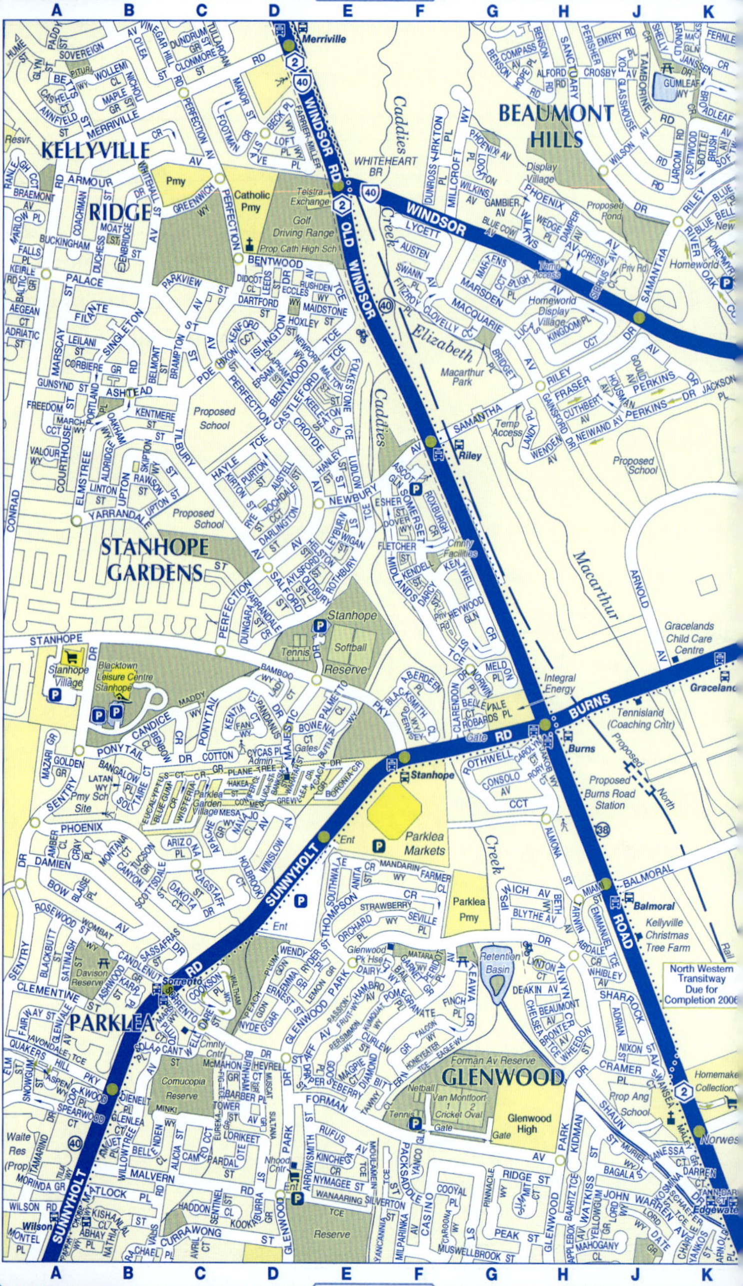

JOINS MAP 214

JOINS MAP 245

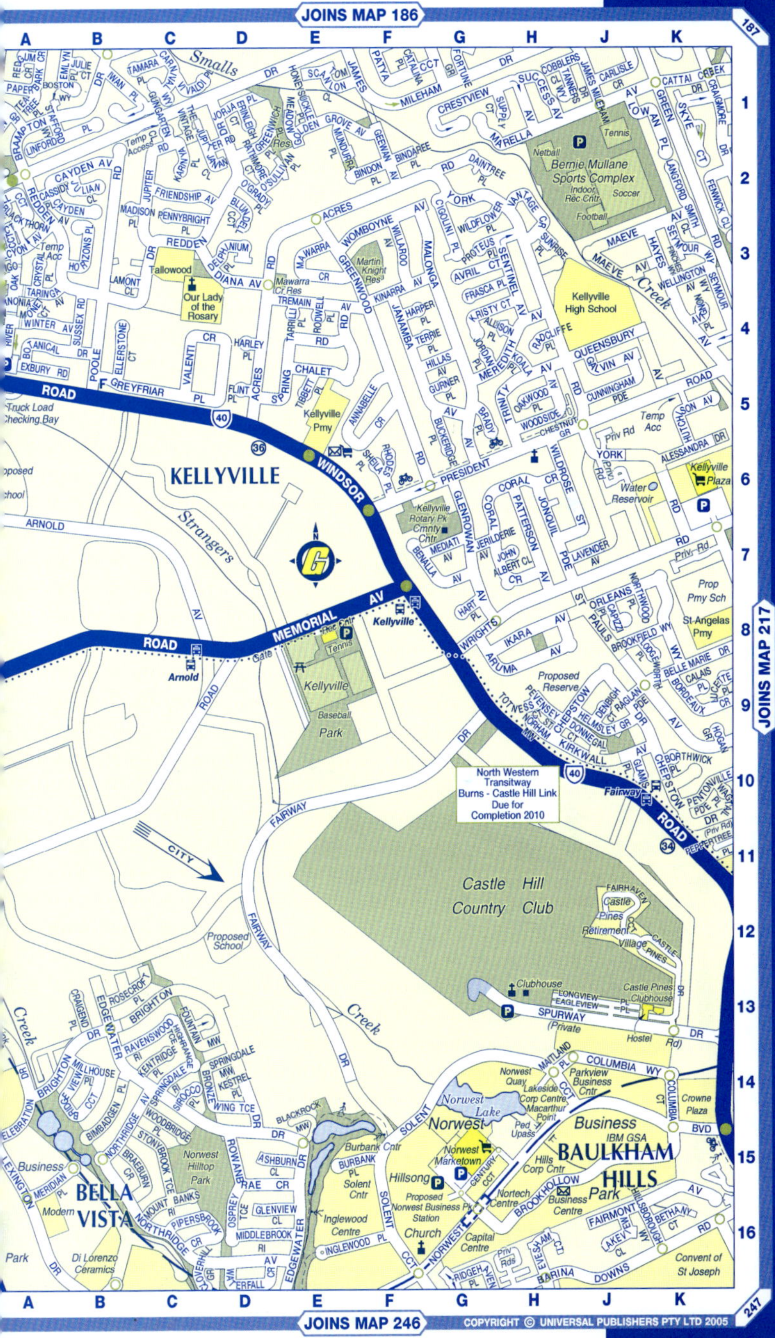
JOINS MAP 186
JOINS MAP 217
JOINS MAP 246
187
247
KELLYVILLE
BELLA VISTA
BAULKHAM HILLS
Business Park
Castle Hill Country Club
Bernie Mullane Sports Complex
Kellyville High School
Our Lady of the Rosary
Tallowood
Kellyville Pmy
Kellyville Rotary Pk Cmnty Cntr
Kellyville Baseball Park
Kellyville Plaza
Water Reservoir
Prop Pmy Sch
St Angelas Pmy
Proposed Reserve
North Western Transitway Burns - Castle Hill Link Due for Completion 2010
Castle Pines Retirement Village
Clubhouse
Castle Pines Clubhouse
Norwest Lake
Norwest
Norwest Quay
Lakeside Corp Centre
Macarthur Point
Norwest Marketown
Hillsong
Proposed Norwest Business Pk Station
Church
Capital Centre
Nortech Centre
Hills Corp Cntr
Business Centre
IBM GSA
Parkview Business Cntr
Crowne Plaza
Convent of St Joseph
Burbank Cntr
Solent Cntr
Inglewood Centre
Norwest Hilltop Park
Di Lorenzo Ceramics
Modern
Proposed School
Truck Load Checking Bay
WINDSOR ROAD
MEMORIAL AV
FAIRWAY DR
ARNOLD
CITY
Strangers Creek
Smalls Creek
Maeve Creek
Arnold
Kellyville
Fairway
SPURWAY DR (Private)
Hostel Rd
Temp Acc
40
36
34
A B C D E F G H J K
1 2 3 4 5 6 7 8 9 10 11 12 13 14 15 16

JOINS MAP 187

186

JOINS MAP 216

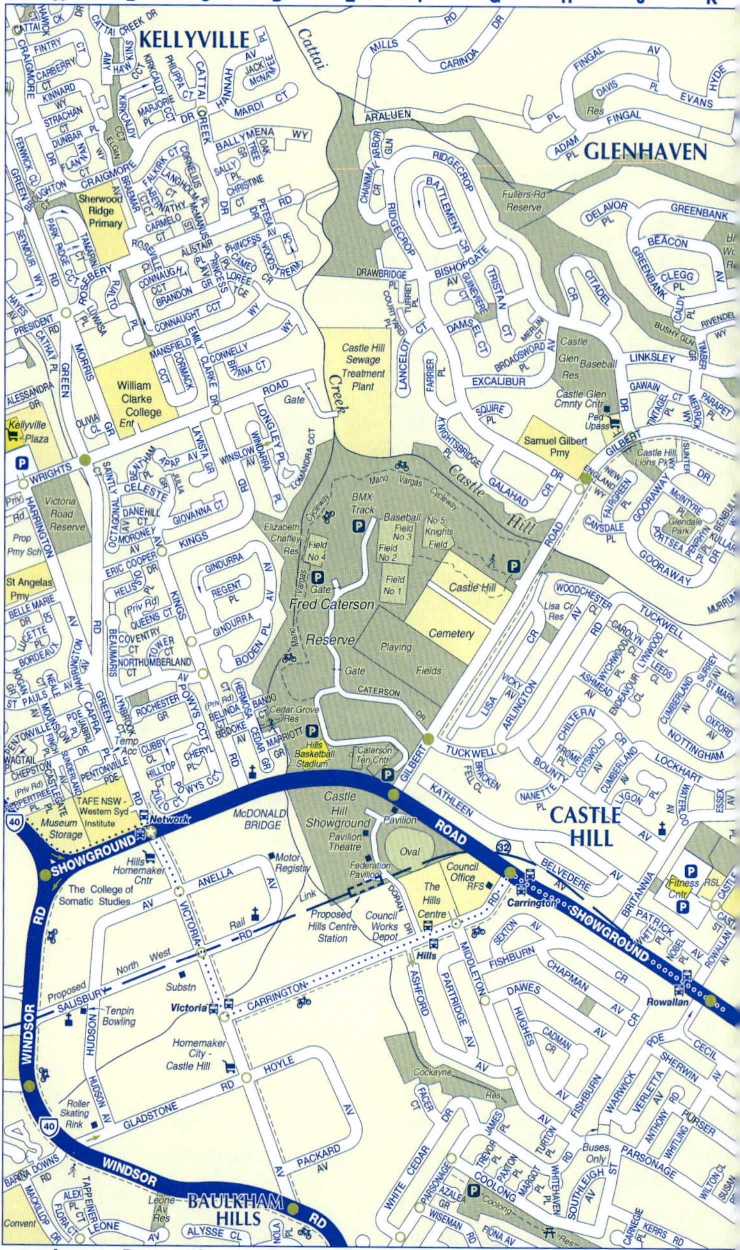

246

JOINS MAP 247

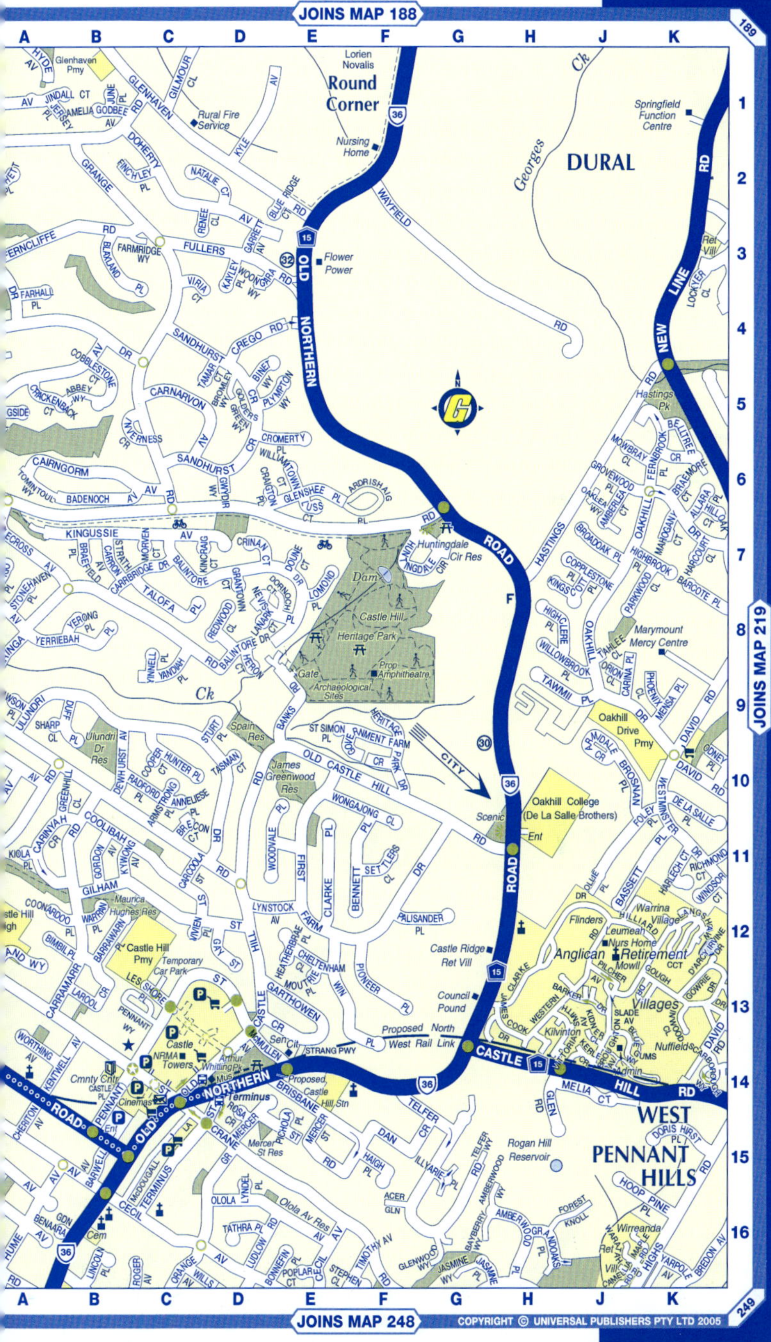
JOINS MAP 188
JOINS MAP 219
JOINS MAP 248
189
249
A B C D E F G H J K
1 2 3 4 5 6 7 8 9 10 11 12 13 14 15 16
Round Corner
DURAL
WEST PENNANT HILLS
Lorien Novalis
Rural Fire Service
Nursing Home
Springfield Function Centre
Georges Ck
Flower Power
OLD NORTHERN ROAD
NEW LINE RD
WAYFIELD RD
Hastings Pk
Huntingdale Cir Res
Dam
Castle Hill Heritage Park
Gate
Prop Amphitheatre
Archaeological Sites
Marymount Mercy Centre
Oakhill Drive Pmy
Oakhill College (De La Salle Brothers)
Scenic
Ent
Spain Res
James Greenwood Res
Ulundri Dr Res
Maurice Hughes Res
Castle Hill Pmy
Temporary Car Park
Castle Ridge Ret Vill
Council Pound
Proposed North West Rail Link
Anglican Retirement Villages
Warrina Village
Flinders
Leumeah
Nurs Home
Mowll
Kilvinton
Nuffield
Admin
CASTLE HILL RD
Castle
NRMA Towers
Arthur Whitling Pk
Mus
Terminus
Proposed Castle Hill Stn
Cmnty Cntr
Cinemas
Sen Cit
Mercer St Res
Rogan Hill Reservoir
Olola Av Res
Cem
Wirreanda
Ret Vill
Glenhaven Pmy
CITY

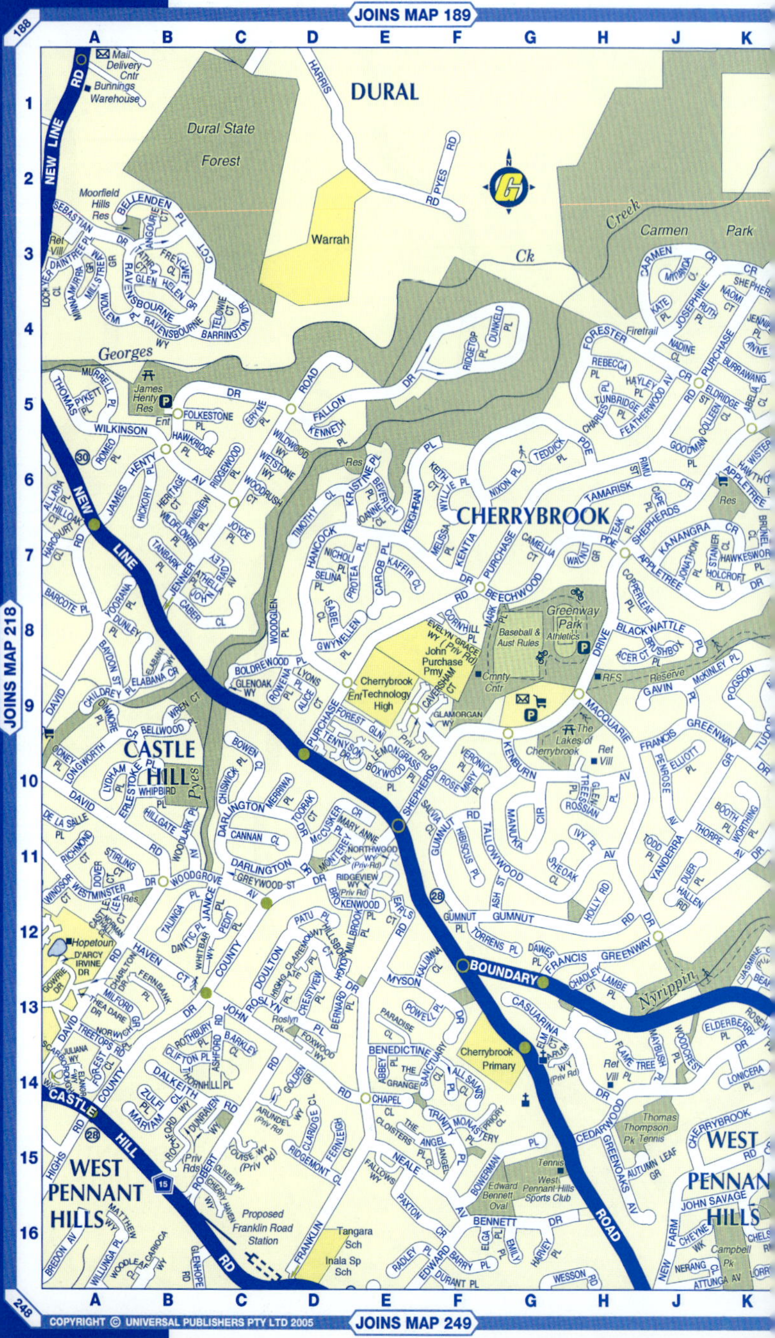
JOINS MAP 189
JOINS MAP 218
JOINS MAP 249
188
248
A B C D E F G H J K
1 2 3 4 5 6 7 8 9 10 11 12 13 14 15 16
DURAL
Dural State Forest
Warrah
Mail Delivery Cntr
Bunnings Warehouse
NEW LINE RD
HARRIS RD
PYES RD
Creek
Carmen Park
Ck
Moorfield Hills Res
Ret Vill
Georges
James Henty Res
Res
CHERRYBROOK
Greenway Park
Baseball & Aust Rules
Athletics
Cmnty Cntr
RFS
Reserve
The Lakes of Cherrybrook
Ret Vill
Cherrybrook Technology High
John Purchase Pmy
CASTLE HILL
Pyes
Hopetoun
BOUNDARY RD
Nyrippin
Cherrybrook Primary
Thomas Thompson Pk Tennis
Tennis
West Pennant Hills Sports Club
Edward Bennett Oval
CASTLE HILL RD
WEST PENNANT HILLS
WEST PENNANT HILLS
Proposed Franklin Road Station
Tangara Sch
Inala Sp Sch
Campbell Pk
Roslyn Pk
FOLKESTONE PL
WILKINSON
HAWKRIDGE PL
RIDGEWOOD
WOODRUSH CT
WETSTONE WY
WILDWOOD WY
FALLON DR
KENNETH PL
RIDGETOP PL
DUNKELD PL
KERRS
TEDDICK PL
NIXON PL
WYLLIE PL
KEITH CT
KEIGHRAN
TAMARISK CR
SHEPHERDS DR
KANANGRA CR
APPLETREE DR
BEECHWOOD DR
PURCHASE RD
MACQUARIE DRIVE
BLACKWATTLE
GREENWAY DR
FRANCIS
KENBURN AV
TALLOWWOOD AV
GUMNUT RD
CASUARINA RD
CEDARWOOD DR
DARLINGTON DR
WOODGROVE AV
COUNTY DR
JOHN RD
CHAPEL CL
BENEDICTINE
BENNETT DR
EDWARD
FRANKLIN
ROBERT RD
DAVID RD
HAVEN CT
CHERRYBROOK RD
JOHN SAVAGE CR
AUTUMN LEAF GR
GREENOAKS AV

MAP 220

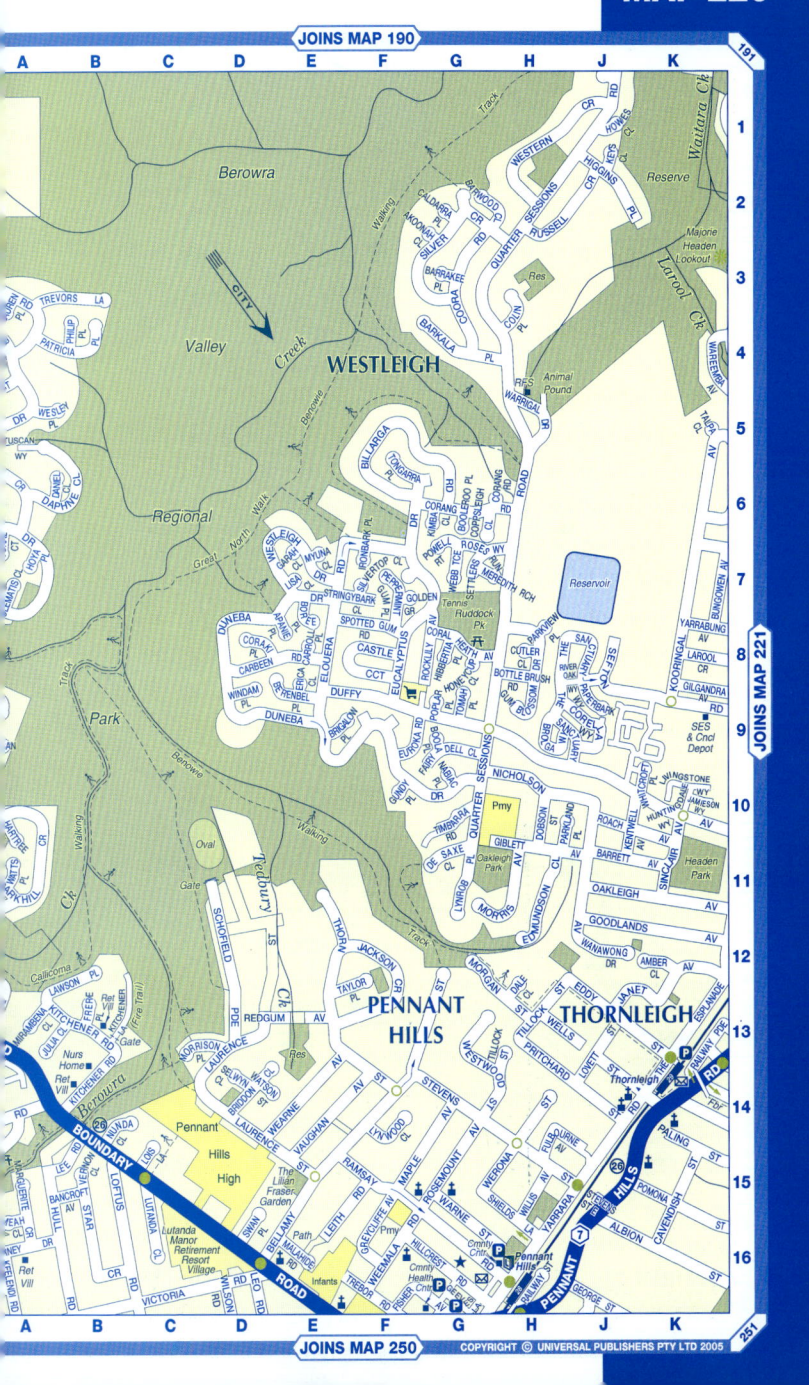

WESTLEIGH

PENNANT HILLS

THORNLEIGH

MAP 221

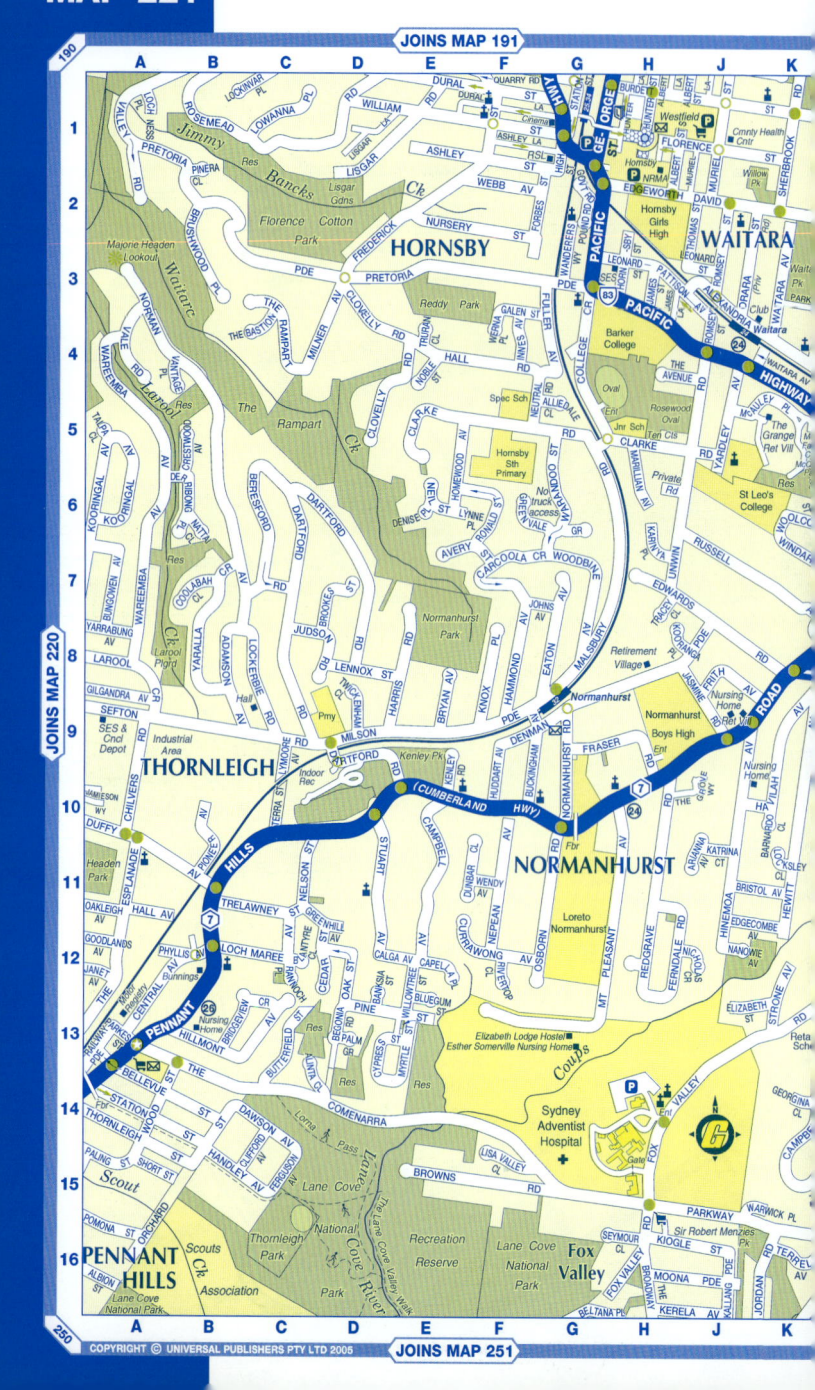

JOINS MAP 192

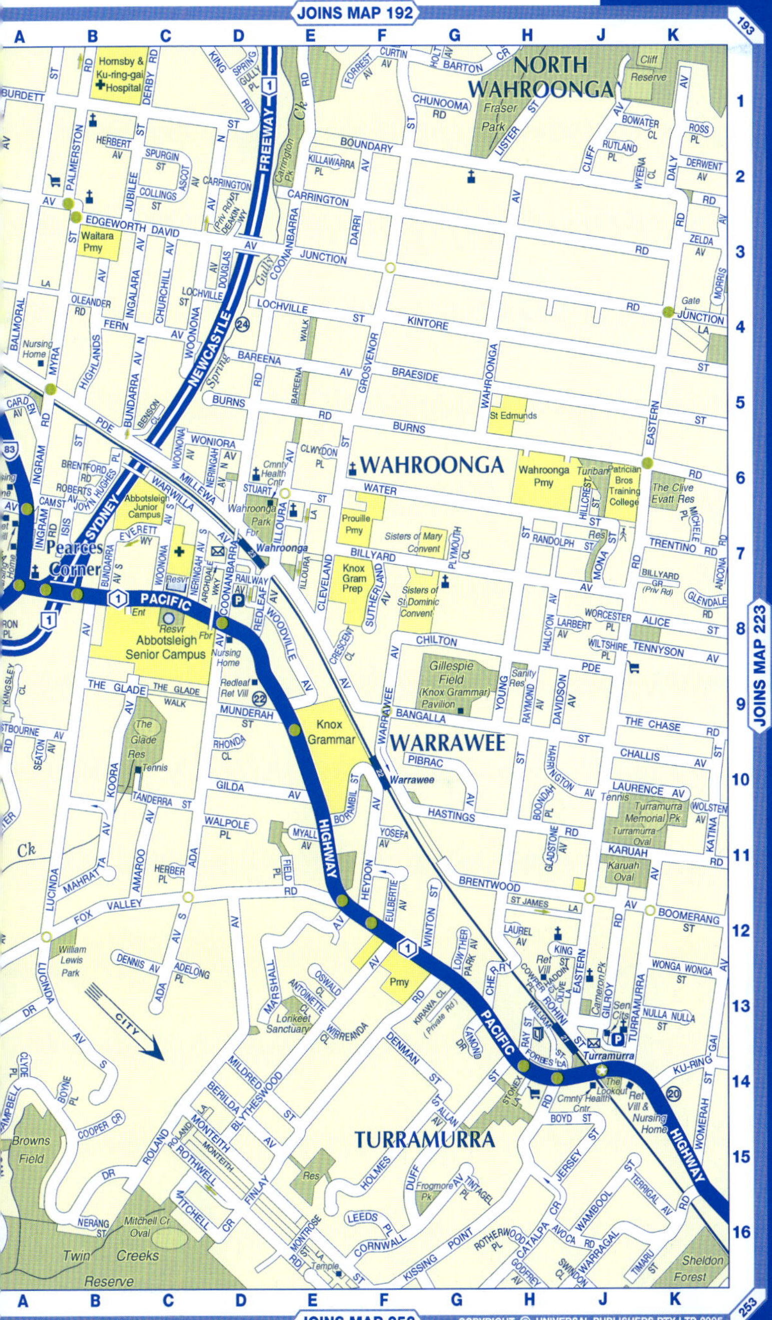

JOINS MAP 223

JOINS MAP 252

JOINS MAP 193
JOINS MAP 222
JOINS MAP 253
192
252
A B C D E F G H J K
1 2 3 4 5 6 7 8 9 10 11 12 13 14 15 16
NORTH WAHROONGA
WAHROONGA
NORTH TURRAMURRA
TURRAMURRA
ST IVES CHASE
PYMBLE
Recreation Reserve
Golden Jubilee Field
Lovers Jump Creek
Recreation Reserve
North Turramurra Golf Course
Guides of NSW
Creek
Eldinhope Green
Rose Seidler House
Samuel King Park
North Turramurra Oval
Glengarry State Training Centre
Cowan Creek Reserve
Claude Cameron Grove
Cherrywood Res
Turramurra Nth Pmy
Orange Green
Toolang Playing Field
Rec Res
Milkmaids Res
Cowan Creek Reserve
Kent Oval
Kent Pathway
Irish Town Grove
South Branch
Pymble Golf Course
Clubhouse
The William Cowan Oval
St Ives Village Green
Skate Facility
Cmnt Cntr
VILLAGE GREEN
St Ives Memo Pk
Maddison Res
Pymble Pmy
North Bannockburn Park
Pymble Park
Friars Field
Blackbutt Pk
Canisius College
Reservoir
Browns Forest
Dalrymple Hay Nature Reserve
Sacred Heart Cath Sch Pymble
Sheldon Forest
PACIFIC HWY
MONA VALE RD
ESK ST
ROSS PL
TAMAR PL
DERWENT AV
HUON ST
BOUNDARY RD
ZELDA AV
JACANA CL
MORRIS
JUNCTION LA
GLADYS AV
CHERRYWOOD AV
DELRAY AV
FIONA AV
DEVON ST
MARANOA PL
MACLEAY ST
BROULA RD
GLENROCK AV
BUNYANA AV
KINTORE ST
ENDEAVOUR ST
ANNE PL
CHAUVEL CL
BRAESIDE ST
WESTBROOK
HAMPDEN
ERIC ST
AZALEA GDN
CLISSOLD
KOKODA
BURNS RD
FINCHLEY PL
TRENTINO RD
ANCONA
GLENDALE RD
ALICE
GEORGANN ST
TENNYSON AV
CUDGEE ST
CHASE
THE
CHALLIS AV
COILA ST
BILLABONG AV
KARLOO ST
WOLSTEN AV
KATINA
KARUAH RD
EVELYN
FAIRLAWN
BOOMERANG ST
WONGA WONGA ST
KU-RING-GAI
TURUGA ST
WOMERAH ST
WARRANGI
BOBBIN
BERRILLEE ST
KATHY CL
SELWYN
BANNOCKBURN RD
RESERVOIR
BUNGALOW AV
MERRIVALE
ROYSTON CL
COLERIDGE ST
TELEGRAPH
STATION ST
HARTLEY CL
BUNA CL
ROAD
BERTRAND
CURAGUL RD
GAWLER PL
DEODARA GDN
GLENGARRY AV
KEDUMBA
CAMDEN GDN
BANKS AV
MILTON RD
SOMERSET
STAFFORD PL
STEPHANIE PL
VALLEY PARK CR
HEAD
NORMURRA AV
MIOWERA
SOMERSET
ALLARA AV
CHATHAM PL
BROWNING
BURNLEY AV
BUXTON PL
BOBBIN
DRYDEN RD
KEATS RD
ELLALONG
BEDFORD
SHELLEY RD
APPS
BURNS
McRAE PL
BANNOCKBURN LA
SPURWOOD RD
NAMBUCCA ST
BIARA PL
ROAD
THE CHESTER
MALL
KENT RD
SURREY
KENT LA
HANDLEY AV
SANDFORD
MURDOCH AV
CANBERRA AV
TALLONG PL
CARINGAL PL
COOLABAH AV
COOLABAH PL
PRINCES
BUCKRA
ADAMS
MUSGRAVE ST
AVALON ST
RAGLAN ST
CHARLTON
MERRIVALE
PENTECOST AV
REELY ST
BOURKE ST
FITZROY LA
RAWSON CR
CROWN
RUSHALL
BIRUBI AV
STATION RD
REYNOLDS ST
BRADFORD ST
BETTOWYND
NITHDALE ST
ORCHARD ST
FLOREY AV
LINDSAY CL
CANISIUS CL
GANMAIN
BOOLARONG
KORANGI
GREENDALE AV
CARINYA RD
MOORINA RD
FAIRWAY AV
STAPLETON PL
RIDDLES LA
PEACE AV
KULGOA RD
DALRYMPLE CR
VISTA ST
ROSEDALE
BONTOU RD
ANNIE MARIE
GOULBURN
WARRIMOO RD
MARLBOROUGH PL
TOOLANG
MUDIES AV
BROOKFIELD PL
BANOOL AV
KAROOM AV
BIMBURRA
MUNGARRA AV
CARBEEN
BENAROON
KILLEATON
KANOONA AV
COLLINS
CRANFORD
BINNOWEE AV
KERRAWAH AV
SHINFIELD AV
PUTARRI AV
PILDRA AV
DENLEY LA
COWAN
LYREBIRD
KAPITI ST
TOKANUE PL
OTAKI PL
WAIPORI
WANDEEN
ROBINA
WANGANELLA
DALTON
TOBRUK AV
FAIRVIEW AV
GREENHILL
NIOKA PL
WARRIMOO
SALERNO PL
WINDSOR PL
BRALLAS AV
GEMAS PL
ALPIN CL
MASS
SHELL

JOINS MAP 194

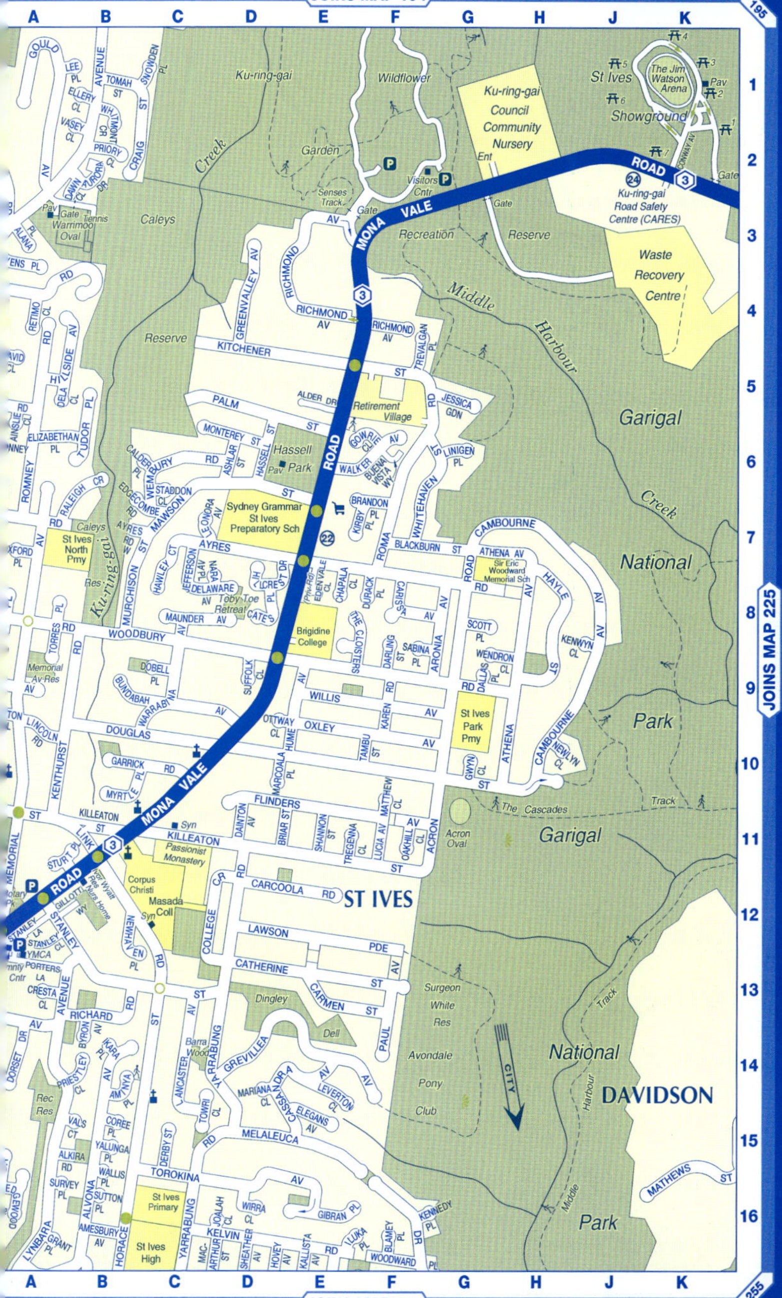

JOINS MAP 225

JOINS MAP 254

MAP 225

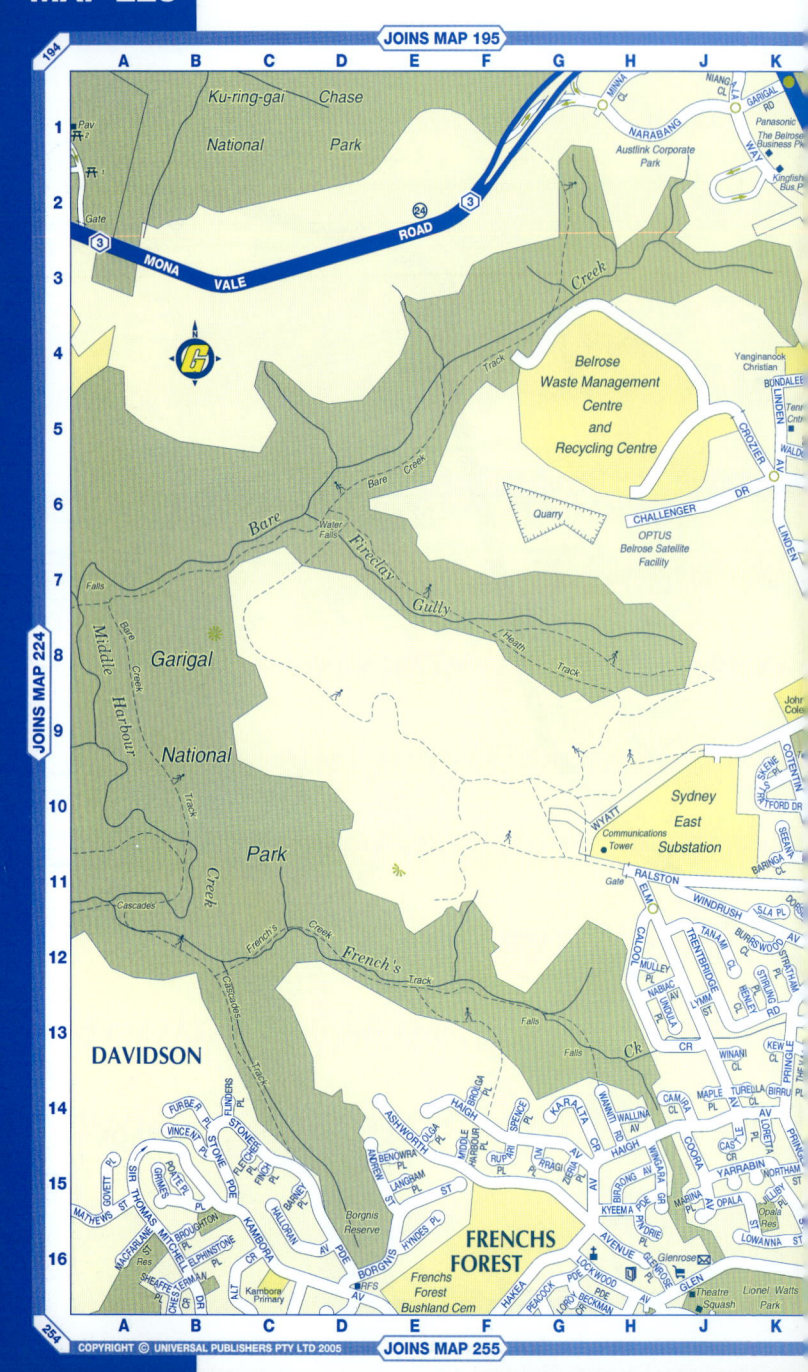

MAP 226

TERREY HILLS
INGLESIDE

Garigal National Park

BELROSE

OXFORD FALLS

MAP 227

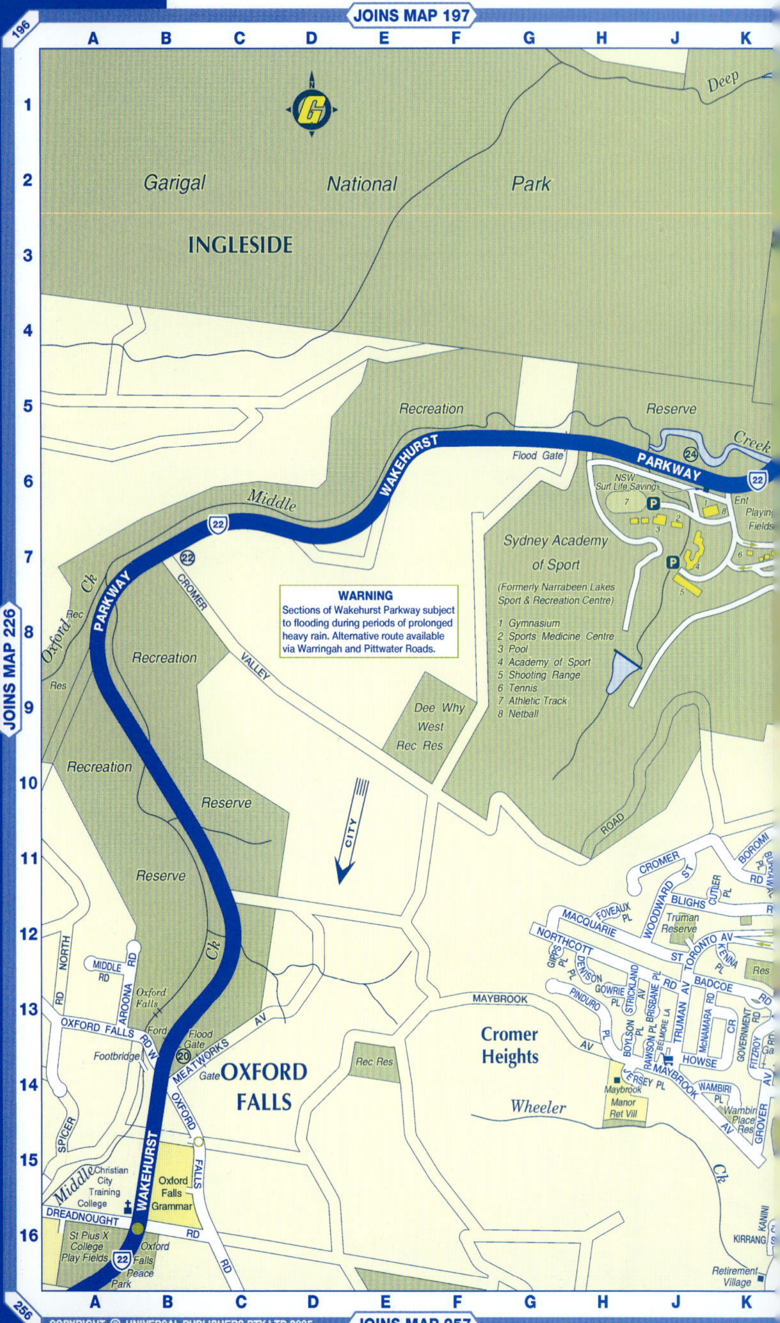

JOINS MAP 197
JOINS MAP 226
JOINS MAP 257
196
256
Garigal National Park
INGLESIDE
Deep Creek
Recreation Reserve
WAKEHURST PARKWAY
Flood Gate
Middle
Oxford Ck
Rec Res
CROMER
VALLEY
ROAD
WARNING
Sections of Wakehurst Parkway subject to flooding during periods of prolonged heavy rain. Alternative route available via Warringah and Pittwater Roads.
NSW Surf Life Saving
Ent
Playing Fields
Sydney Academy of Sport
(Formerly Narrabeen Lakes Sport & Recreation Centre)
1 Gymnasium
2 Sports Medicine Centre
3 Pool
4 Academy of Sport
5 Shooting Range
6 Tennis
7 Athletic Track
8 Netball
Dee Why West Rec Res
CITY
Recreation
Reserve
Ck
NORTH RD
MIDDLE RD
AROONA RD
Oxford Falls
OXFORD FALLS RD
Ford
Flood Gate
Footbridge
MEATWORKS AV
Gate
OXFORD FALLS
OXFORD FALLS RD
Rec Res
Cromer Heights
Wheeler
Ck
SPICER
Christian City Training College
Oxford Falls Grammar
DREADNOUGHT RD
St Pius X College Play Fields
Oxford Falls Peace Park
MAYBROOK AV
CROMER
WOODWARD ST
CUTLER PL
BLIGHS
BOROMI
Truman Reserve
FOVEAUX PL
MACQUARIE
NORTHCOTT
ST
TORONTO AV
KENNA PL
Res
GIPPS PL
DENISON PL
GOWRIE PL
STRICKLAND AV
BRISBANE PL
RD
BADCOE RD
PINDURO PL
BOYLSON PL
RAWSON PL
BELMORE LA
TRUMAN AV
McNAMARA RD
CR
GOVERNMENT RD
FITZROY
HOWSE
JERSEY PL
MAYBROOK
Maybrook Manor Ret Vill
WAMBIRI PL
Wambiri Place Res
AV
GROVER
KIRRANG
KANINI
Retirement Village

JOINS MAP 198
JOINS MAP 229
JOINS MAP 258
199
259
A B C D E F G H J K
1 2 3 4 5 6 7 8 9 10 11 12 13 14 15 16
ELANORA HEIGHTS
NORTH NARRABEEN
NARRABEEN
WHEELER HEIGHTS
COLLAROY PLATEAU
CROMER
COLLAROY
Narrabeen
Lakes
Pipeclay Pt
Jamieson Park
WAKEHURST PARKWAY
Recreation Reserve
Deep Creek Reserve
Lumeah Reserve
Woorarra Lookout Reserve
Narroy Park
Bilarong
France Petanque Club
Reserve
Chattan Park
Rec Res
Berry Res
Rec Cntr
Cmnty Arts Cntr
Middle Ck Res
Sailing Club
RSL Veterans Retirement Villages
Colooli Theatre
Med Cntr
Nursing Home
Day Care Centre
Chapel
Off WK
Wheeler Park
Steps
Edgar Gornall Wildflower Garden
McLean Lookout
Cromer Golf Course
Clubhouse
Reserve South Ck
St Rose Cath
Augusta Cntr
Wheeler Heights Pmy
Vic Huxley Oval
Plateau Park
Nurs Home
Ambleside Res
Austlink & eState Bus Pk
Wabash Res
Energy Australia
Warringah Council Depot
Collaroy Plateau Pmy
Anzac Avenue Res
St Matthews Farm Reserve
Pavilion
Cromer Pmy
Nthn Beaches Sec Coll Cromer Campus
Pavilion
Inman Park
Clubhouse
Cromer Park
M W Soccer Ground
James Morgan Res
The Pittwater House Schools
28 Field Battery 7 Field Regiment
Res
Pk
TORONTO
WABASH
WASHINGTON
GROVER
CLEVELAND
CARRINGTON
WOOLBAH PL
WOORARRA AV
WEEROONA AV
MIRROOL ST
RICKARD
GONDOLA
NARROY
LIDO
NAREEN
ALLEYNE AV
PDE
BRISTOL LA
VERONA ST
MINARTO LA
WINDSOR PDE
GRENFELL AV
CAREFREE RD
PALM TCE
WIMBLEDON AV
VENETIAN RD
ELANORA RD
AMAROO AV
WAKOOKA AV
NARRABEEN ST
ROBERTSON ST
DEVITT ST
GOODWIN ST
LAKESIDE RD
THE ESPLANADE
NIOKA RD
LINDLEY AV
MACTIER ST
WALKER AV
CLARKE ST
WETHERILL ST
PARK
EDGECLIFFE
ACACIA ST
GREVILLEA
TELOPEA
HALL
PARKES
LANTANA AV
WHEELER PL
JAMES
BOWNESS ST
ALICE
ROSE
GREYSTOKE ST
ENNERDALE
WINDERMERE PL
TORVER PL
LANGDALE RD
GRASMERE CR
BERITH ST
VETERANS
FULLER
CLAUDARE
ESSILIA
STELLA
BLANDFORD AV
AUBREEN
IDALINE
CARLISLE ST
KENDAL CR
ETTALONG
RYDAL PL
HEATHER ST
LAKE ST
DERWENT ST
CONISTON
SOUTH CREEK
KIRKSTONE
AMBLESIDE
CRUMMOCK ST
WASDALE
PENRITH
NEWBY PL
BOOLA PL
DYMPNA
MIDDLETON RD
THEW PDE
GILMORE AV
PERREY ST
BOOMERANG RD
EMU ST
KANGAROO RD
DAVID RD
ATHENE PL
HILMA
DUNCAN
SCOTNEY CR
ANZAC
HENDY AV
MELODY LA
SUFFOLK AV
LINCOLN AV
NORFOLK AV
MIAMBA AV
WESTMORELAND
ORLANDO RD
VILLIERS PL
RANDALL CT
PLATEAU RD
CAMPBELL AV
MICHELE RD
PARKES RD
SOUTH CREEK RD
INMAN
FISHER
DUMIC PL
SOUTH CREEK
GROVER AV
DALPURA ST
BADANA
MIRRA PL
HOOVER PL
RYRIE ST
DOROTHY ST
JUDITH PL
WAROON
GEELONG RD
ALFRED ST
MEEHAN RD
CARCOOLA
PINDA PL
CARAWA
MILPERA PL
LILLIHINA AV
WILLANDRA RD
TYAGARAH PL
DOUGLASS PL
MOONYEAN PL
MAAS ST
TORRENS PL
DAVISON ST
TENNYSON RD
LITTLE
CUTLER
THE CRESCENT
BIRDWOOD
COLOOLI CL
SNAKE GULLEY CL
ENDEAVOUR
EDMONDSON
LESLIE
STACK
WOODS
SIMPSON CL
FIRST
SECOND AV

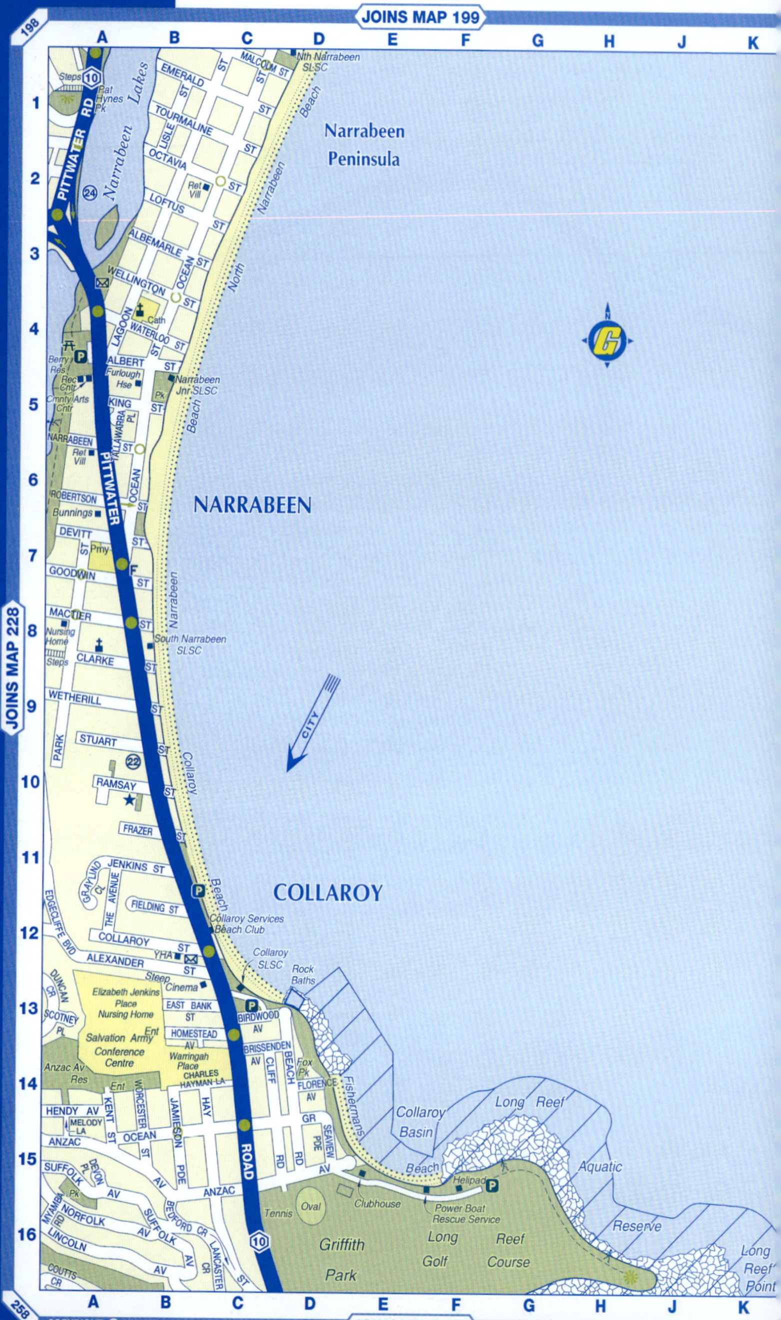
JOINS MAP 199
JOINS MAP 228
JOINS MAP 259
198
258
A B C D E F G H J K
1 2 3 4 5 6 7 8 9 10 11 12 13 14 15 16
Narrabeen Peninsula
NARRABEEN
COLLAROY
CITY
Narrabeen Lakes
Nth Narrabeen SLSC
North Narrabeen Beach
Steps
Pat Hynes Pk
PITTWATER RD
MALCOLM ST
EMERALD ST
TOURMALINE ST
LISLE ST
OCTAVIA ST
Ret Vill
LOFTUS ST
ALBEMARLE ST
WELLINGTON ST
OCEAN ST
Cath
LAGOON ST
WATERLOO ST
ALBERT ST
Furlough Hse
Narrabeen Jnr SLSC
Pk
Berry Res
Rec Cntr
Cmnty Arts Cntr
KING ST
TALLAWARRA PL
NARRABEEN ST
Ret Vill
PITTWATER
OCEAN ST
ROBERTSON
Bunnings
DEVITT ST
Pmy
GOODWIN ST
MACTIER ST
Nursing Home
Steps
CLARKE ST
South Narrabeen SLSC
Narrabeen
WETHERILL ST
PARK
STUART ST
Collaroy
RAMSAY ST
FRAZER ST
JENKINS ST
GRAYLIND CL
THE AVENUE
FIELDING ST
EDGECLIFFE BVD
Beach
Collaroy Services Beach Club
COLLAROY ST
YHA
ALEXANDER ST
Collaroy SLSC
Rock Baths
DUNCAN CR
Steep
Cinema
Elizabeth Jenkins Place Nursing Home
EAST BANK ST
SCOTNEY PL
Salvation Army Conference Centre
Ent
HOMESTEAD AV
BIRDWOOD AV
BRISSENDEN AV
CLIFF RD
BEACH RD
Fox Pk
Anzac Av Res
Warringah Place
CHARLES HAYMAN LA
FLORENCE AV
Fishermans Beach
Collaroy Basin
Long Reef
Ent
WORCESTER ST
KENT ST
JAMIESON PDE
HAY
HENDY AV
MELODY LA
ANZAC AV
OCEAN GR
SEAVIEW PDE
ROAD
AV
SUFFOLK
DEVON PL
Pk
AV
ANZAC
Helipad
Aquatic Reserve
NORFOLK AV
MYAMBA RD
SUFFOLK AV
BEDFORD CR
LANCASTER CR
ST
Tennis
Oval
Clubhouse
Power Boat Rescue Service
LINCOLN AV
COUTTS CR
Griffith Park
Long Reef Golf Course
Long Reef Point

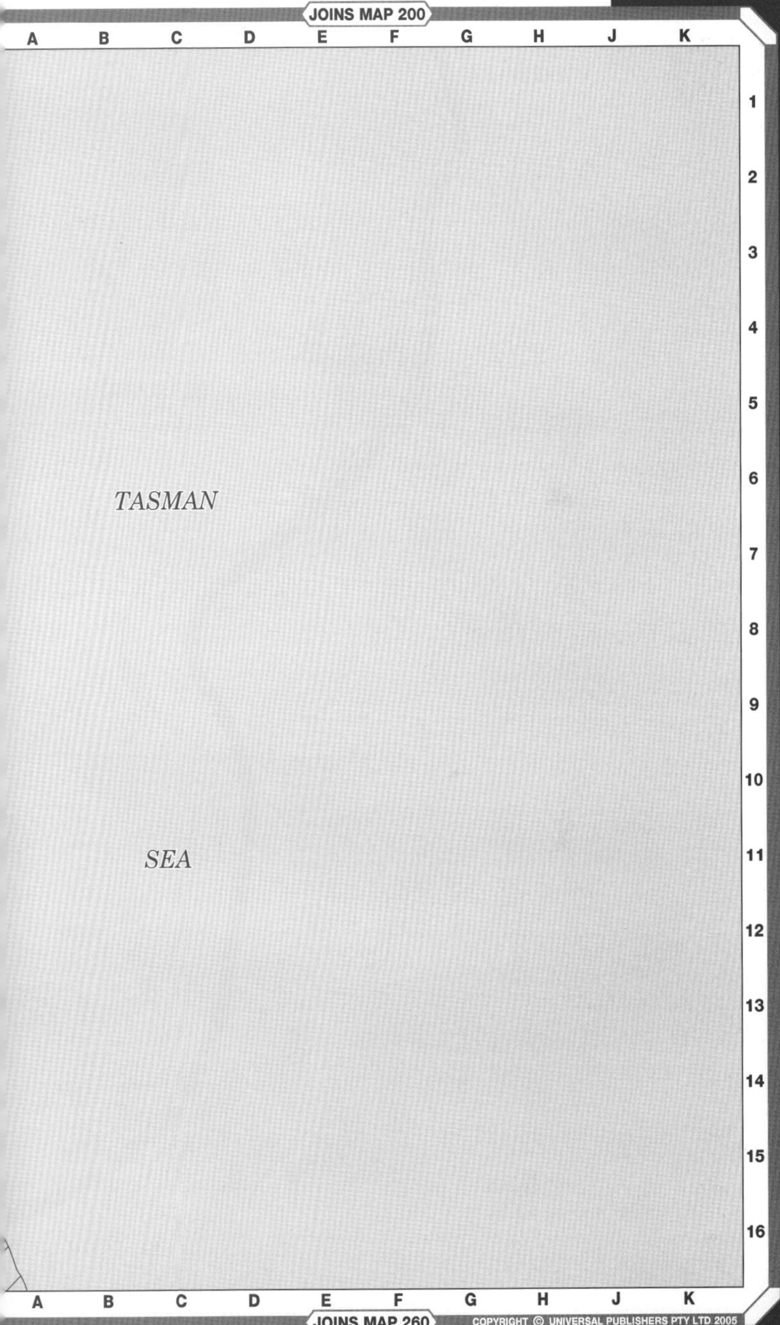

MAP 230

MAP 233 FOLLOWS

JOINS MAP 200

TASMAN

SEA

JOINS MAP 260

MAP 233

PREVIOUS MAP 230

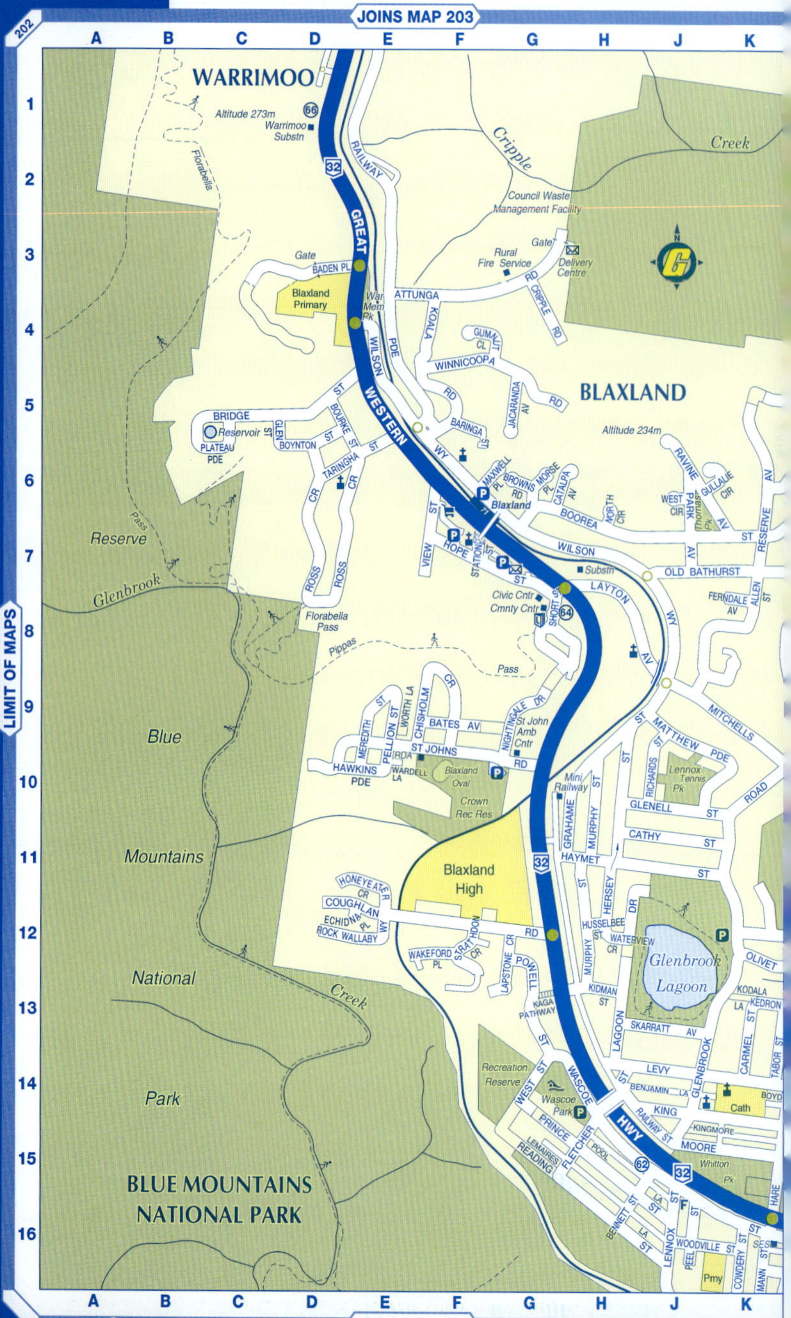

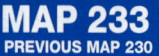

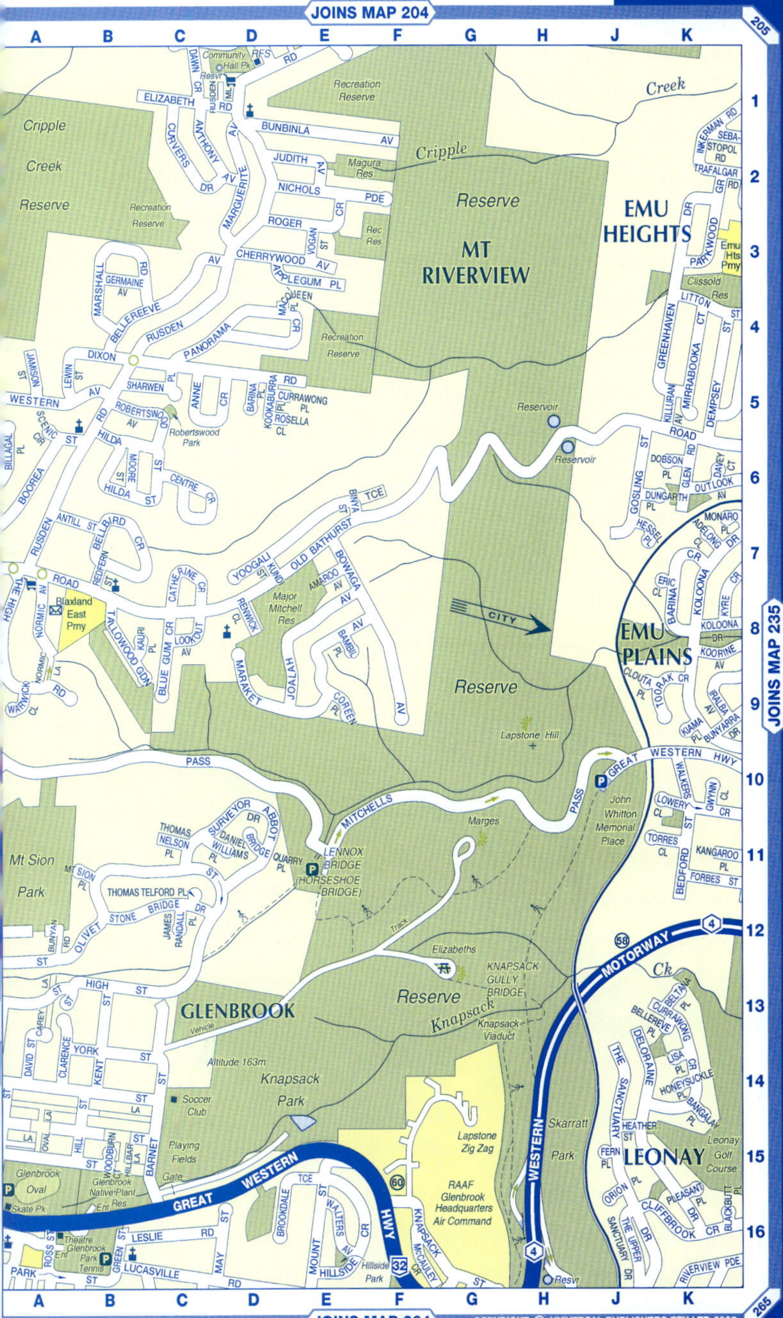
JOINS MAP 204
205
A
B
C
D
E
F
G
H
J
K
1
2
3
4
5
6
7
8
9
10
11
12
13
14
15
16
JOINS MAP 235
JOINS MAP 264
265
MT RIVERVIEW
EMU HEIGHTS
EMU PLAINS
GLENBROOK
LEONAY
Cripple Creek Reserve
Recreation Reserve
Reserve
Creek
Cripple
Magura Res
Rec Res
Community Hall Pk
RFS
Resvr
ELIZABETH
RUSDEN RD
DAWN CR
CURVERS
ANTHONY
DR
AV
MARGUERITE
BUNBINLA AV
JUDITH AV
NICHOLS PDE
ROGER CR
VOGAN ST
CHERRYWOOD AV
APPLEGUM PL
MACQUEEN PL
CR
MARSHALL
GERMAINE AV
RD
BELLEREEVE
RUSDEN
PANORAMA
DIXON
JAMISON ST
LEWIN ST
WESTERN
AV
SHARWEN
PL
ANNE CR
BARINA PL
KOOKABURRA
RD
CURRAWONG PL
ROSELLA CL
ROBERTSWOOD AV
Robertswood Park
SCENIC CIR
ST
HILDA
MOORE ST
HILDA ST
CENTRE CR
BILLAGAL PL
BOOREA
RUSDEN
ANTILL ST
BELLBIRD CR
REDFERN
ROAD
THE HIGH
NORMIC AV
Blaxland East Pmy
TALLOWOOD GDN
KAURI PL
BLUE GUM CR
CATHERINE CR
LOOKOUT AV
RENWICK CL
YOOGALI ST
KUNDI
OLD BATHURST
BINYA ST
TCE
BOWAGA
AMAROO AV
Major Mitchell Res
AV
BAMBIL PL
JOALAH
MARAKET
COREEN PL
AV
NORMIC LA
WARWICK CL
RD
Reservoir
Reservoir
CITY
Lapstone Hill
EMU HEIGHTS
Emu Hts Pmy
PARKWOOD
Clissold Res
LITTON ST
GREENHAVEN
CT
MIRRABOOKA
ST
DEMPSEY
KILLURAN AV
ROAD
DOBSON PL
GLEN RD
DAVEY CT
OUTLOOK AV
DUNGARTH PL
GOSLING ST
HESSEL PL
INKERMAN RD
SEBASTOPOL RD
TRAFALGAR GR
RD
MONARO PL
ADELONG DR
CR
ERIC CL
BARINA
KOLOONA
KYRE CR
KOLOONA DR
KOORINE AV
CLOUTA PL
TOORAK CR
IRALBA AV
KIAMA PL
BUNYARRA DR
PASS
GREAT WESTERN HWY
WALKERS
GWYNN CL
LOWERY CL
CR
TORRES CL
BEDFORD ST
KANGAROO PL
FORBES ST
John Whitton Memorial Place
PASS
MITCHELLS
Marges
LENNOX BRIDGE (HORSESHOE BRIDGE)
QUARRY PL
ABBOTT
SURVEYOR DR
THOMAS NELSON PL
DANIEL WILLIAMS PL
BRIDGE
ST
Mt Sion Park
MT SION PL
THOMAS TELFORD PL
STONE BRIDGE DR
JAMES RANDALL PL
OLIVET
BUNYAN RD
ST
Track
Elizabeths
KNAPSACK GULLY BRIDGE
Reserve
Knapsack
Knapsack Viaduct
MOTORWAY
4
58
Ck
BELTANA PL
CURRAWONG
BELLEREVE PL
DELORAINE
THE SANCTUARY
LISA PL
CR
HONEYSUCKLE PL
BANGALAY PL
HEATHER ST
FERN PL
ORION PL
PL
PLEASANT PL
DR
CLIFFBROOK CR
Leonay Golf Course
BLACKBUTT PL
THE UPPER DR
SANCTUARY DR
RIVERVIEW PDE
Skarratt Park
WESTERN
Resvr
HIGH ST
CAREY ST
DAVID ST
CLARENCE ST
YORK ST
KENT ST
ST
Vehicle
Altitude 163m
Knapsack Park
Soccer Club
Playing Fields
Gate
LA
OVAL LA
HILL ST
WOODBURN CT
HILLBAR CT
BARNET ST
Glenbrook Oval
Skate Pk
Glenbrook Native Plant Res
Ent
GREAT WESTERN HWY
TCE
BROOKDALE
ST
WALTERS AV
CR
60
KNAPSACK ST
MCCAULEY CR
Lapstone Zig Zag
RAAF Glenbrook Headquarters Air Command
Theatre
Glenbrook Park
Tennis
ROSS ST
GREEN ST
LESLIE RD
LUCASVILLE RD
MAY ST
MOUNT ST
HILLSIDE
Hillside Park
32
PARK ST
ST

JOINS MAP 205
JOINS MAP 234
JOINS MAP 265
204
264
EMU HEIGHTS
PENRITH
EMU PLAINS
LEONAY
JAMISONTOWN
REGENTVILLE
Jacksons Falls
Emu Plains Correctional Centre
Emu Heights Primary
Clissold Reserve
Emu Green
Substation
CSI
(Private Rd)
Gate
RAY MACDONALD DR
Winnebago
Emu Plains
Altitude 30m
Nepean High
Arms of Aust Mus
Reserve
Substn
Cemetery PL
Emu Cmnty Cntr
Tennis
Dukes Oval
Hall
Darcy Smith Oval
Park
Hunter Fields
Ret Vill & Nurs Home
Emu Plains Pmy
Cath
Leonay Oval
Playing Fields
Clubhouse
Emu Sports Club
Leonay Golf Course
Leonay Pmy
Hollier Res
Huntington Res
Regional Gallery
NEPEAN
Rowing Course
Championship
Tench Reserve
Nepean Shores Riverside Resort & Conference Cntr
Art Gallery
Jamison Golf Resort
Inswim Aquatic Cntr
PENRITH VALLEY BRIDGE
Tench Res
MOTORWAY
GREAT WESTERN HWY
WESTERN
OLD BATHURST RD
RUSSELL ST
INKERMAN RD
SEBASTOPOL RD
HILLCREST RD
TRAFALGAR RD
PARKWOOD GR
BALACLAVA RD
BRETON PL
TARPAN PL
ANNIE SPENCE CL
HOLSTEIN RD
PALFREY PL
MERLIN PL
HAFLINGER CL
LITTON ST
DEMPSEY ST
MATTHEWS ST
WEDMORE RD
PALOMINO RD
LANDAIS PL
SALERNO CL
SKYROS PL
DARTMOOR CCT
PINDOS PL
BRUMBY CR
AMBLER CL
DAVEY CT
OUTLOOK AV
BROMLEY RD
MONARO PL
ADELONG PL
KYRE CR
NANGAR PL
BANJO DR
KOLOONA CR
PULLMAN PL
KITE ST
DAVID RD
SMITH ST
LEE ST
RAILWAY ST
MACKELLAR ROAD
RAILWAY ROW
STATION ST
KOORINE AV
IRALBA AV
BUNYARRA DR
PYRAMID ST
RYAN PL
ITHACA ST
PYRAMID ST
KATHLEEN ST
ARGYLE PL
CRAWFORD ST
JAMIESON ST
GOVERNMENT HOUSE DR
BARRACKS ST
STOCKADE ST
WATER ST
MARTIN ST
GREAT WESTERN CR
GWYNN CL
WALKERS CR
KANGAROO PL
ACORN ST
GREY ST
KOHLENBERG CL
MACKAY ST
DUKES PL
FORBES ST
BROUGHAM ST
WALTON PL
LUCAS ST
GOUGH ST
PALMER PL
TROY ST
MUNDY ST
PAULS CR
SHORT ST
NIXON ST
WATT PL
MAGRATH ST
PELLATT PL
THORSBY PL
HARTIGAN AV
GARDENIA ST
McAULEY CR
HERMES PL
BELLBROOK AV
MORTIMER ST
WATSONIA ST
FITZROY PL
ELLISON PL
JACOB KING PL
WINES ST
ROSEMONT AV
LAWSON ST
PARK ST
CARY ST
PEARCE PL
STANSBURY ST
GWANDALAN ST
GWANDALAN PL
STREET
McLEAN ST
EMERALD ST
EMERALD PL
WOOD PL
BEACH ST
ANNETT ST
HUNTER ST
YODALLA AV
TRIDA PL
DEWDNEY RD
SHEPPARD AV
LOVE AV
EMILY AV
WESTBANK AV
WARRING AV
IMPERIAL AV
CHALMERS AV
FRANCIS AV
VINCENT AV
YORK RD
NAPIER ST
WILLOW TREE AV
ROAD
TATTERSALL RD
TYSON PL
NEPEAN ST
NEPEAN PL
BRECHIN CL
PAMELA PDE
PAMELA PL
BUNYAN RD
CORNELL ST
WORKMAN PL
URBANE ST
LINKSVIEW AV
FAIRWAYS PL
BURING AV
NEPEAN AV
RIVER RD
BLACKBUTT PL
NOOK PL
CLIFFBROOK CR
RIVERVIEW PDE
LEONAY PDE
BELLEVUE RD
CROSS RD
BUNDARRA RD
FACTORY RD
JAMISON RD
WILSON LA
TENCH AV
BLAIKIE RD
44
56
57
58
4

JOINS MAP 206
JOINS MAP 237
JOINS MAP 266
207
267
A B C D E F G H J K
1 2 3 4 5 6 7 8 9 10 11 12 13 14 15 16
Penrith Lakes Scheme
Quarry
ACI
GORDON ST
Storage King
LELAND
CAMDEN
LUGARD ST
ROAD
CITY
CASSOLA PL
LEMKO PL
BOREC
JACK WILLIAMS DR
Penrith Valley Business Park
Penrith Sewage Treatment Works
Kennards Hire
Boundary Ck
Weir
McCarthy Catholic
Nepean River
RIVER
Global Self Storage
COOMBES DR
DEAN PL
COREEN AV
Penrith Trade Centre
PEACHTREE
RD
Weir Reserve
Penrith Skatel
Gate
Rowing Club
Sandy Brennan Res
BRUCE NEALE DR
Fitness World
Electricity Substation
CASTLEREAGH
STANTON
AVOCA AV
PICASSO PL
LAMROCK
(GREAT WESTERN HWY)
PUNT RD
VICTORIA BRIDGE
WEIR RD
HIGH
Regatta Park
Reserve Rd
Indoor Sports Complex
MUSEUM DR
Pura Milk
Museum of Fire
Army Reserve
OLD FERRY RD
MEMORIAL AV
Rowing and Kayak Sprint Course
River Road
Woodriff Gardens
Tennis
Coreen Av Commuter Parking
Penrith
Army Regiment
Gate
RECREATION AV
JANE ST
BELMORE ST
Cncl Off
Performing Arts Centre
Penrith Cinemas Plaza
Cmnty Health Cntr
TAFE NSW
ST (GREAT
HENRY WSTN HWY) ST
NEPEAN
FITCH AV
LADBURY
CAPTAINS RD
Proposed Golf Course
JOHN TIPPING GR
UNION
DE VILNITS PDE
VISTA ST
WORTH
Mountainview Retreat Ret Vill
RODLEY AV
STATION
THE BROADWAY
Judges Park
PCYC
RSL
LETHBRIDGE
TINDALE ST
O'FARRELL
HIGGINS ST
Peach Tree
Aqua Golf
Putt Putt Golf
Panthers World of Entertainment
Nurs Home
RETREAT
Penrith Paceway Function Cntr
Showground
Club Paceway
RESERVE ST
Nepean Square
DERBY
RANSLEY
Trash & Treasure Market Open Sun
PANTHER PL
Penrith Playing Field
Gates
Penrith Stadium
Ent ST
Tenpin Bowl
STAFFORD
PENRITH
Cables Water Ski Park
Park
Howell Oval
STATION
WOODRIFF
BROWN
CASTLEREAGH
WINSTON ST
RAWSON AV
CHAPMAN AV
FLINT AV
TORTON PL
WARWICK
HORNSEY WOOD AV
EVAN
JIPP ST
DARLING ST
HAND AV
Driving Range
Clubhouse
RD
Aged Care Cntr
JAMISON
DENT ST
RD
RACECOURSE PL
MITCHELL ST
VICTORIA ST
KENNEDY DR
CHRISTIE ST
MILLER ST
PERRITT PL
Penrith South Pmy
BAXTER ST
UPTON ST
WILDEN CL
WELLAND CL
ANVIL PL
HARRIS
WILLORING
PRESTON ST
Jamison Town Service Cntr
STUART ST
Jamison
SOUTH PENRITH Park
McNAUGHTON
Bus Depot
HARFORD ST
Jamison Golf Resort
YANCO AV
ANAKAI
POLO PL
SWALLOW ST
MULGOA
Dick Smith
BATT
ABEL ST
Industrial Area
REGENTVILLE
PENRITH
YORK
Skate Park
Netball
RACECOURSE
BANOOL AV
SMITH
Res
GREENHILLS AV
PARKVIEW AV
DWYER PL
SANDRA PL
Surveyors Ck
14
44
54
55

JOINS MAP 207

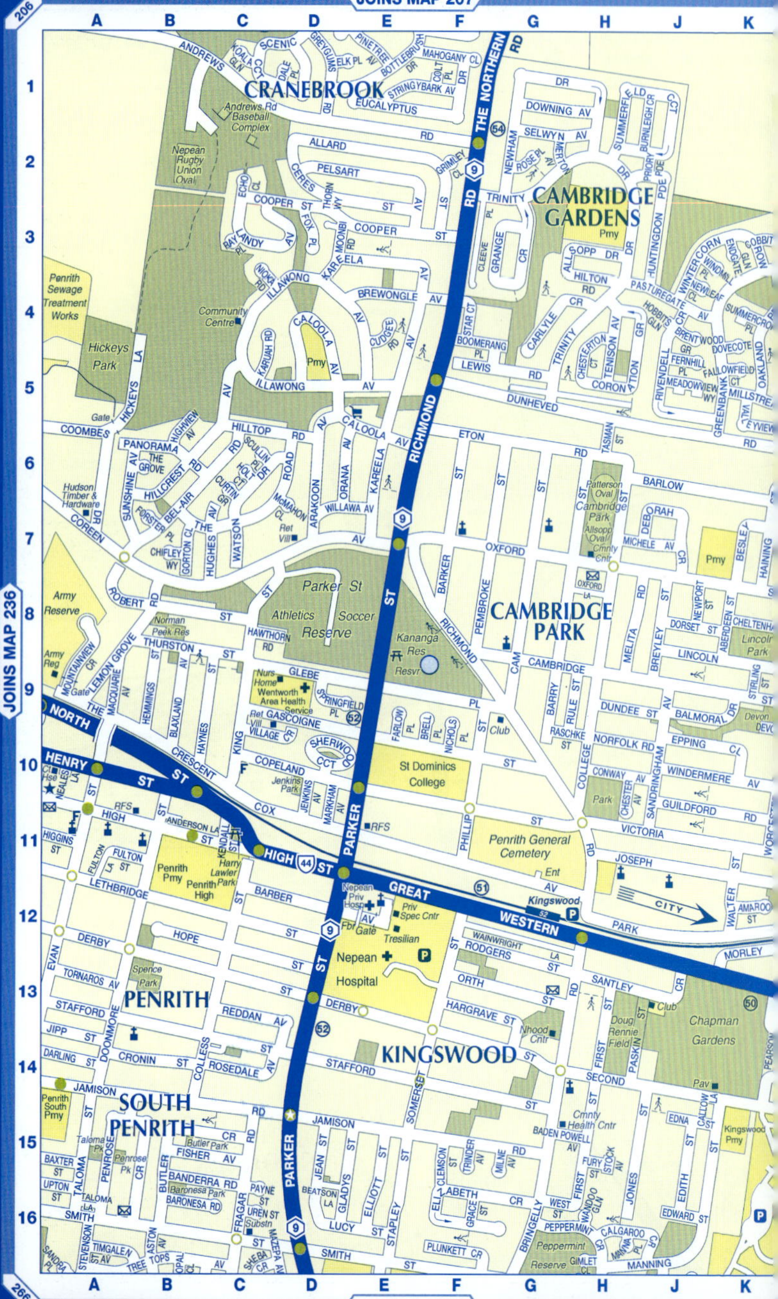

JOINS MAP 267

MAP 238

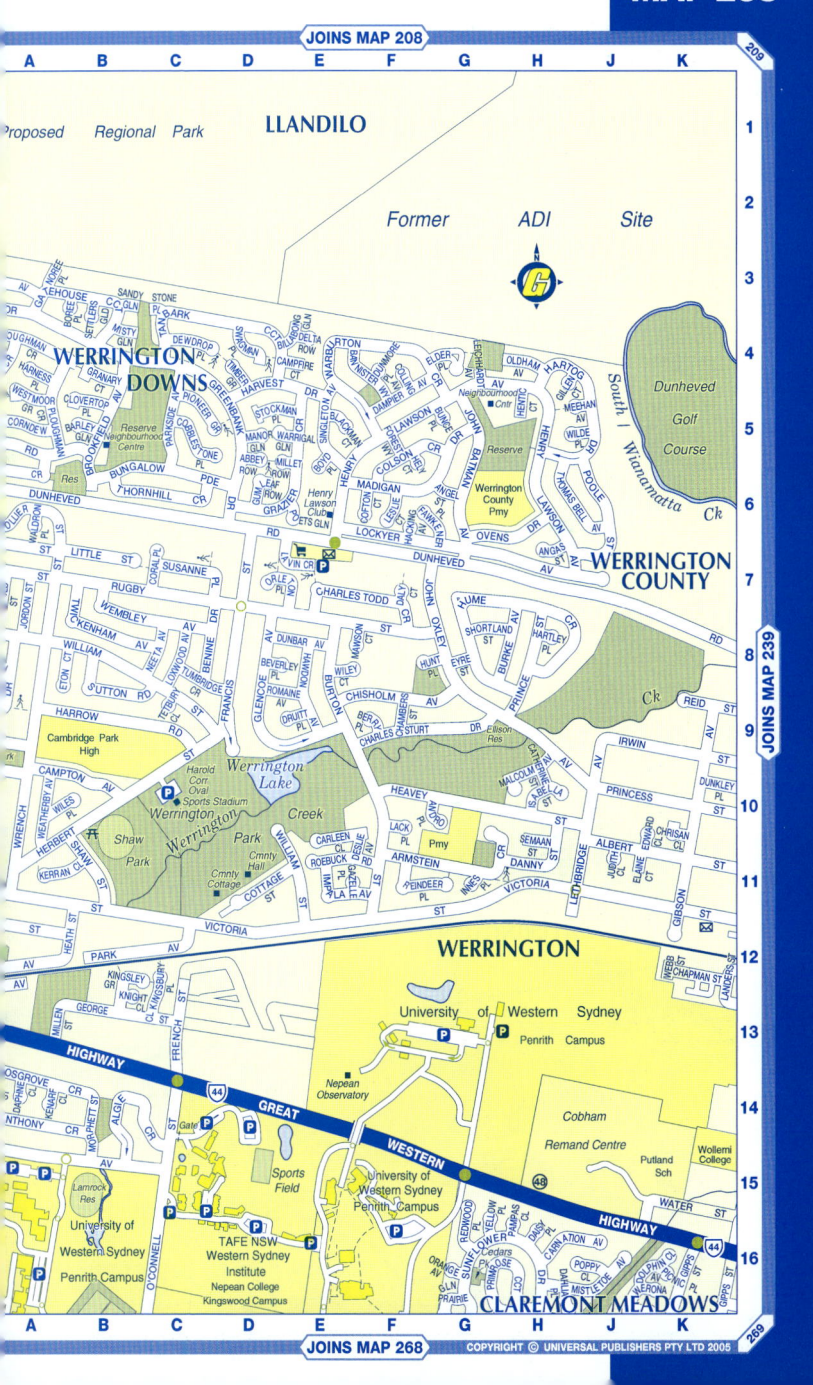

MAP 239

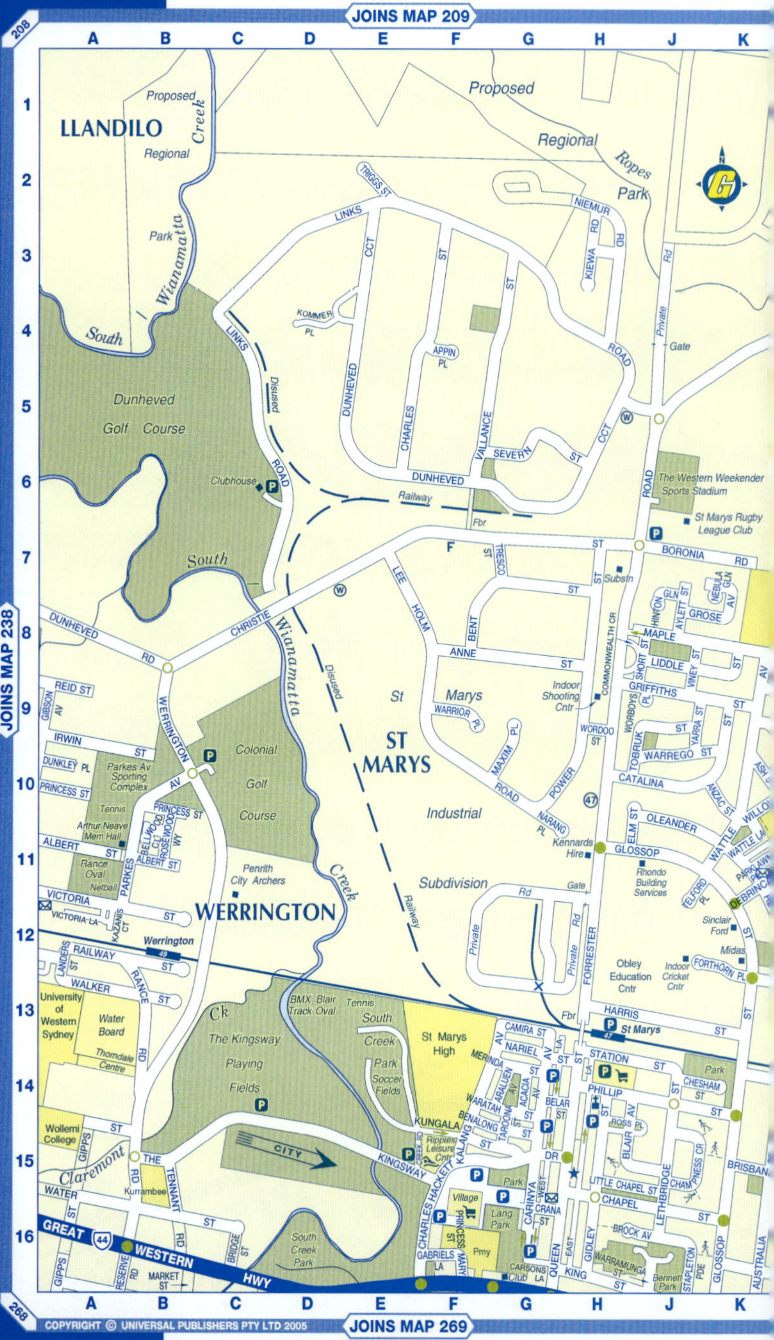

JOINS MAP 209
JOINS MAP 238
JOINS MAP 269
208
268
A B C D E F G H J K
1 2 3 4 5 6 7 8 9 10 11 12 13 14 15 16
LLANDILO
Proposed Regional Park
Proposed Regional Ropes Park
South Creek
Wianamatta Creek
Dunheved Golf Course
Clubhouse
LINKS RD
TRIGGS ST
KOMMER PL
DUNHEVED CCT
CHARLES ST
APPIN PL
VALLANCE ST
SEVERN ST
NIEMUR RD
KIEWA RD
Private Rd
Gate
Disused Railway
Fbr
DUNHEVED RD
CHRISTIE ST
The Western Weekender Sports Stadium
St Marys Rugby League Club
BORONIA RD
LEE HOLM
TRESCO ST
BENT ST
ANNE ST
Substn
COMMONWEALTH CR
St Marys Industrial Subdivision
ST MARYS
WARRIOR PL
MAXIM PL
Indoor Shooting Cntr
WORDOO ST
POWER ST
NARANG PL
Kennards Hire
GLOSSOP ST
FORRESTER RD
HINTON GLN
AYLETT ST
NEBULA GLN
GROSE AV
MAPLE ST
SHORT ST
LIDDLE ST
VINEY ST
GRIFFITHS ST
WORBOYS PL
YARRA ST
TOBRUK ST
WARREGO ST
CATALINA ST
ANZAC ST
ELM ST
OLEANDER ST
WATTLE LA
WILLOW
Rhondo Building Services
TELFORD PL
Sinclair Ford
Midas
Obley Education Cntr
Indoor Cricket Cntr
FORTHORN PL
HARRIS ST
St Marys
REID ST
GIBSON AV
IRWIN ST
DUNKLEY PL
PRINCESS ST
Parkes Av Sporting Complex
Tennis
Arthur Neave Mem Hall
ALBERT ST
BELLWOOD CT
ROSEWOOD WY
Rance Oval
Netball
PARKES AV
WERRINGTON RD
Colonial Golf Course
Penrith City Archers
WERRINGTON
VICTORIA ST
VICTORIA LA
KAZANIS CT
Werrington
RAILWAY ST
LANDERS ST
WALKER ST
RANCE RD
University of Western Sydney
Water Board
Thorndale Centre
Wollemi College
GIPPS ST
CLAREMONT
THE KINGSWAY
WATER ST
Kurrambee
TENNANT RD
BRIDGE ST
RESERVE RD
MARKET ST
GREAT WESTERN HWY
44
49
47
The Kingsway Playing Fields
BMX Blair Track Oval
Tennis
South Creek Park
Soccer Fields
St Marys High
CITY
KINGSWAY
Ripples Leisure Cntr
KUNGALA
CREEK RD
South Creek Park
CAMIRA ST
NARIEL ST
MERINDA AV
ARALUEN AV
ACACIA AV
WARATAH ST
BENALONG ST
TAROONA ST
KALANG ST
BELAR ST
DR
STATION ST
PHILLIP ST
ROSS PL
BLAIR AV
CHESHAM ST
Park
LITTLE CHAPEL ST
CHAPEL ST
CHAMPNESS CR
LETHBRIDGE ST
BRISBANE
Village
Lang Park
CARINYA AV
WEST LA
CRANA ST
CHARLES HACKETT DR
PRINCESS MARY ST
GABRIELS LA
Pmy
CARSONS LA
Club
QUEEN ST
EAST LA
GIDLEY ST
KING ST
BROCK AV
WARRAMUNGA ST
Bennett Park
STAPLETON PDE
GLOSSOP ST
AUSTRALIA

MAP 240

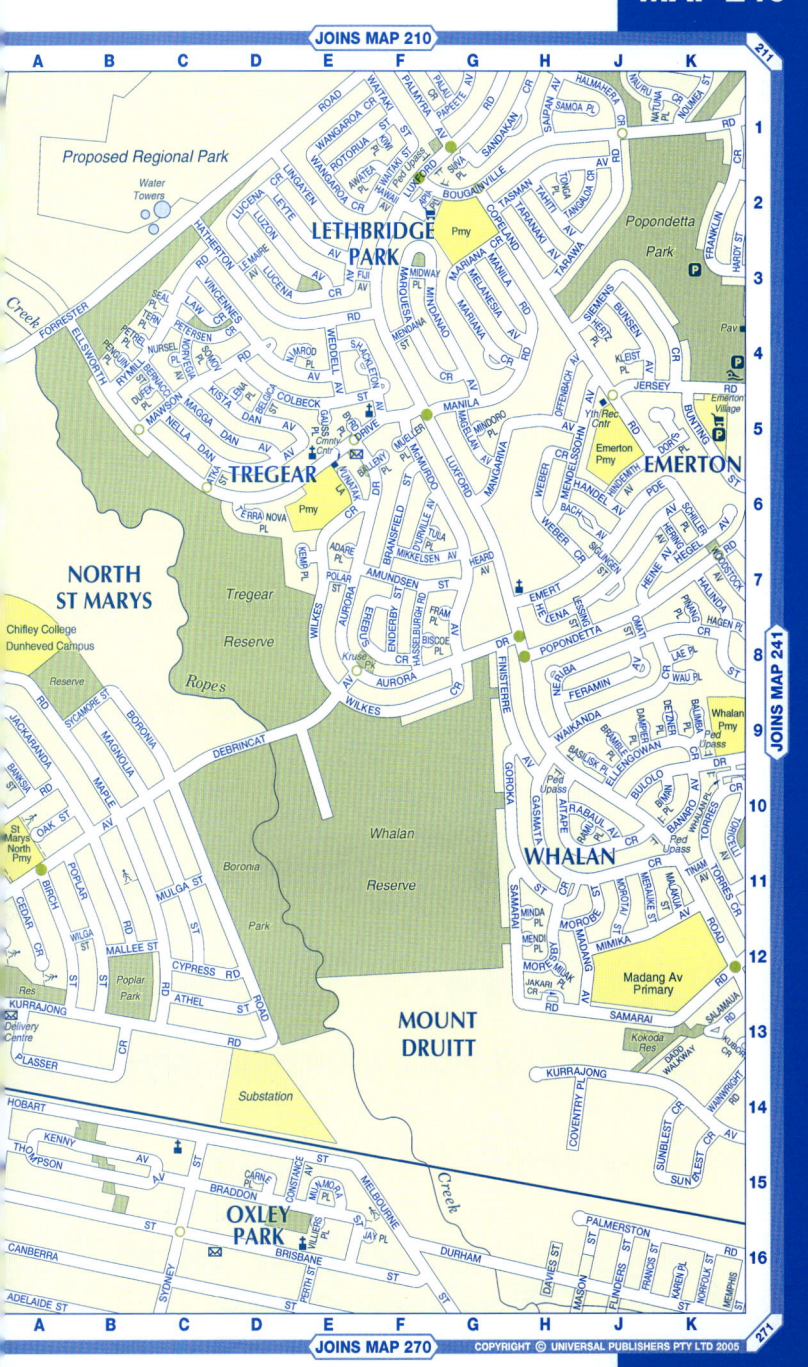

MAP 241

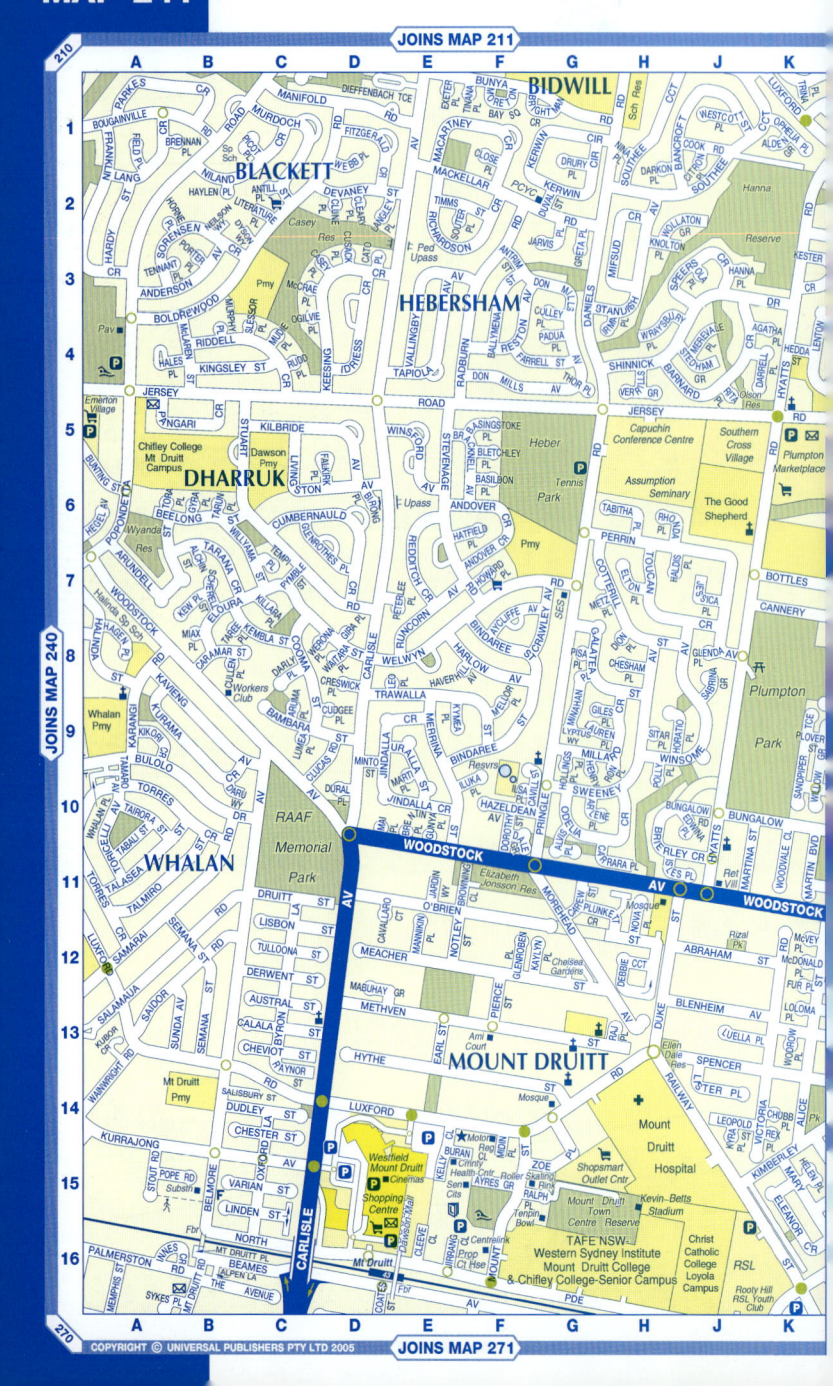

JOINS MAP 212

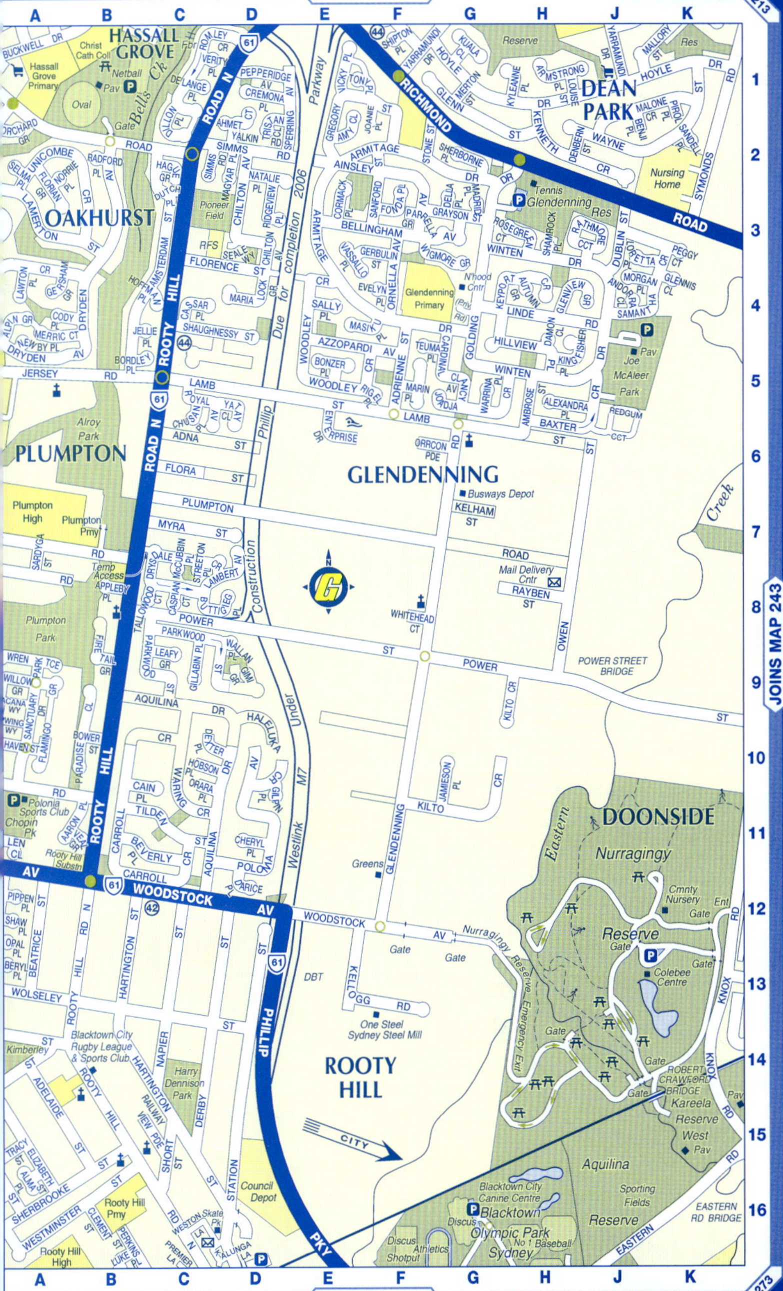

JOINS MAP 243

JOINS MAP 272

MAP 243

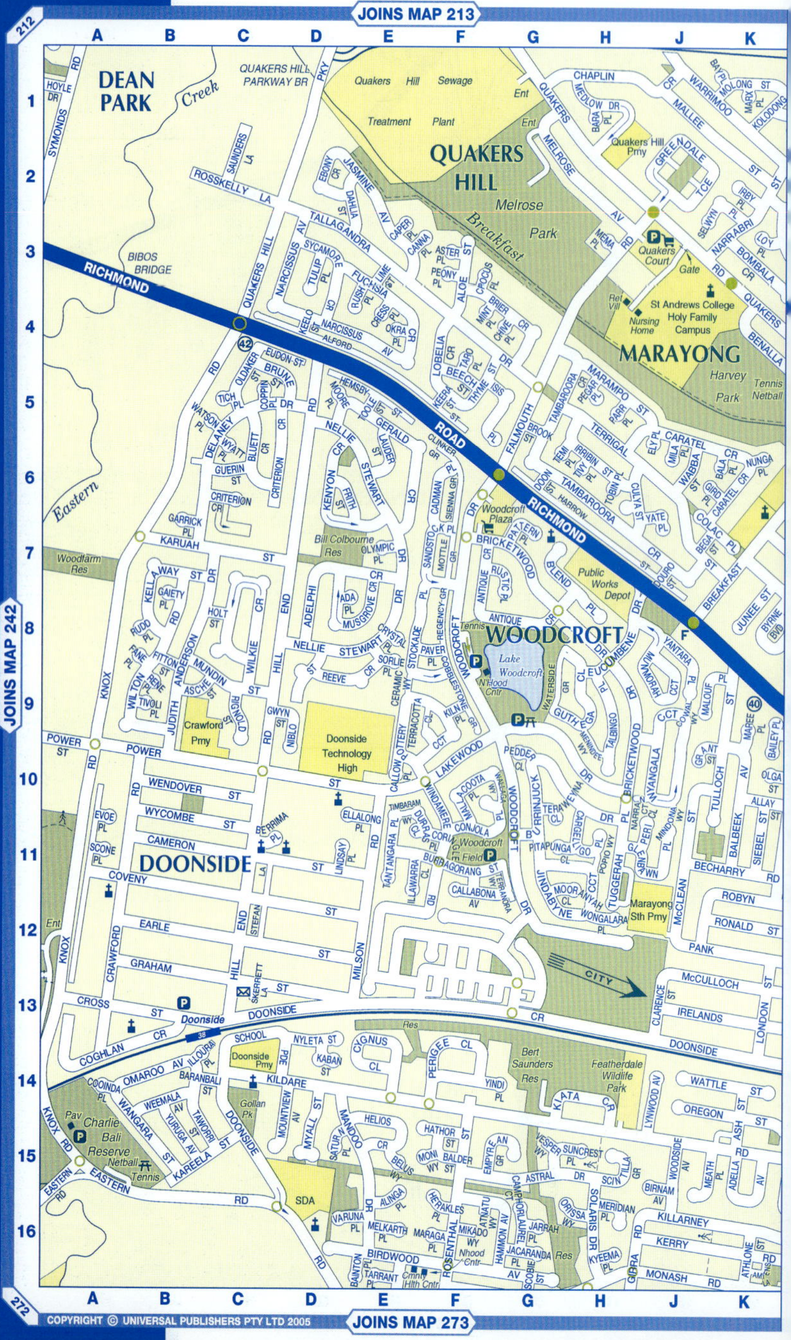

JOINS MAP 213
JOINS MAP 242
JOINS MAP 273
212
272
A B C D E F G H J K
1 2 3 4 5 6 7 8 9 10 11 12 13 14 15 16
DEAN PARK
QUAKERS HILL
MARAYONG
WOODCROFT
DOONSIDE
QUAKERS HILL PARKWAY BR
Quakers Hill Sewage Treatment Plant
Melrose Park
Breakfast Creek
Eastern Creek
BIBOS BRIDGE
RICHMOND ROAD
Quakers Hill Pmy
Quakers Court
St Andrews College Holy Family Campus
Nursing Home
Ret Vill
Gate
Harvey Park
Tennis Netball
Woodcroft Plaza
Public Works Depot
Lake Woodcroft
N'Hood Cntr
Bill Colbourne Res
Woodfarm Res
Crawford Pmy
Doonside Technology High
Woodcroft Field
Marayong Sth Pmy
Doonside
Doonside Pmy
Gollan Pk
Bert Saunders Res
Featherdale Wildlife Park
Charlie Bali Reserve
Pav
Netball
Tennis
SDA
Nhood Cntr
Cmnty Hlth Cntr
CITY
KNOX RD
POWER ST
WENDOVER ST
WYCOMBE ST
CAMERON
COVENY
EARLE
GRAHAM
CROSS ST
COGHLAN CR
DOONSIDE CR
SCHOOL
KILDARE
EASTERN RD
QUAKERS HILL PKY
TALLAGANDRA
ROSSKELLY LA
NELLIE ST
STEWART
KARUAH
LAKEWOOD
BRICKETWOOD
FALMOUTH
TAMBAROORA
BREAKFAST
JUNEE ST
McCLEAN
BECHARRY RD
PANK
McCULLOCH ST
IRELANDS
WATTLE ST
OREGON ST
KILLARNEY
KERRY
MONASH RD
BIRDWOOD
HELIOS
HATHOR ST
ASTRAL DR
SOLARIS DR
MERIDIAN
CHAPLIN
MELROSE
WARRIMOO
MALLEE
GREENDALE
NARRABRI
BOMBALA
BENALLA
CARATEL
YANTARA
MALOUF
TULLOCH
BALBEEK
ROBYN
RONALD ST
40
42
38

JOINS MAP 214
JOINS MAP 245
JOINS MAP 274
215
275
A
B
C
D
E
F
G
H
J
K
1
2
3
4
5
6
7
8
9
10
11
12
13
14
15
16
ACACIA GARDENS
KINGS PARK
BLACKTOWN
Westlink M7 Under Construction Due for completion 2006
North Western Transitway Completion Date 2006
Faulkland Crescent Reserve
Marayong Hts Pmy
Marayong Hse Nhood Cntr
Marayong
Kings Park
Ind Cricket Cntr
Hardware & General
Coca-Cola Amatil
Rexroth
Marayong Oval
Tennis
Ashlar Golf Course
Clubhouse
Marayong Pmy
Heartland Holden
Blacktown North Pmy
Blacktown Girls High
Blacktown Boys High
Business & Delivery Cntr
Indoor Rock Climbing
Bill Swift Res
Ret Vill
Pav
Campbell Res
Blacktown Showground
Cncl Nursery
Francis Park
Joseph Frank Park
Chester Park
Blacktown West Pmy
Jeh Wit
Gribble Res
CWA
Ct Hse
Bus Only
Blacktown
NRMA Westpoint Centre
Cinemas
Westpoint (Under Construction)
Tennis
Alpha Pk
Cncl Off
RSL
PCYC
Tenpin Bowl
Ice Rink
Billy Goat Hill Res
TAFE NSW
RSL Mem Gdns
Orbital
Resvrs
Vardys
Turner
Bessemer
Sackville
Devitt
SUNNYHOLT ROAD
RICHMOND RD
LYTON ST
LANCASTER ST
BALMORAL ST
THIRD AV
RAILWAY RD
VARDYS RD
BESSEMER ST
FORGE ST
GARLING RD
BINNEY RD
TATTERSALL RD
MADAGASCAR DR
DONOHUE ST
SAMPSON PL
FAULKLAND CR
CAMORTA CL
WELLESLEY CR
BLACKETT ST
COBHAM AV
HARVEY RD
TURBO RD
CORONATION AV
SHEDWORTH ST
ROBSHAW RD
NOWRA DR
DAVIS RD
PERCY ST
NOEL ST
BUTTERFIELD ST
CHICAGO AV
FIFTH AV
FOURTH AV
SECOND AV
FIRST AV
GEORGE ST
MAIN ST
DEVITT ST
CAMBRIDGE ST
DUNSTABLE RD
BEDFORD RD
KILDARE RD
DOONSIDE CR
RAILWAY PDE
VIRGINIA ST
ARTHUR AV
PHILIP ST
NORFOLK ST
KENT ST
SPRINGFIELD AV
STEWART AV
CARNEGIE PL
GATE RD
STEEL ST
ROMFORD RD
VALEDICTION RD
CHARLES ST
PETER ST
SARSFIELD ST
HAROLD ST
GORDON ST
CLIFTON ST
BRUCE ST
OXFORD ST
WALLACE ST
BOYD ST
SYDNEY ST
ALLAWAH ST
CARINYA ST
MEROO ST
WALTERS RD
HEART PL
FLUSHCOMBE RD
CAMPBELL ST
PATRICK ST
ALPHA ST
DAVID ST
WARRICK LA
PRINCE ST
BOYS AV
BAKER ST
SHIRLEY ST
JANE ST
Ck
38
36
35

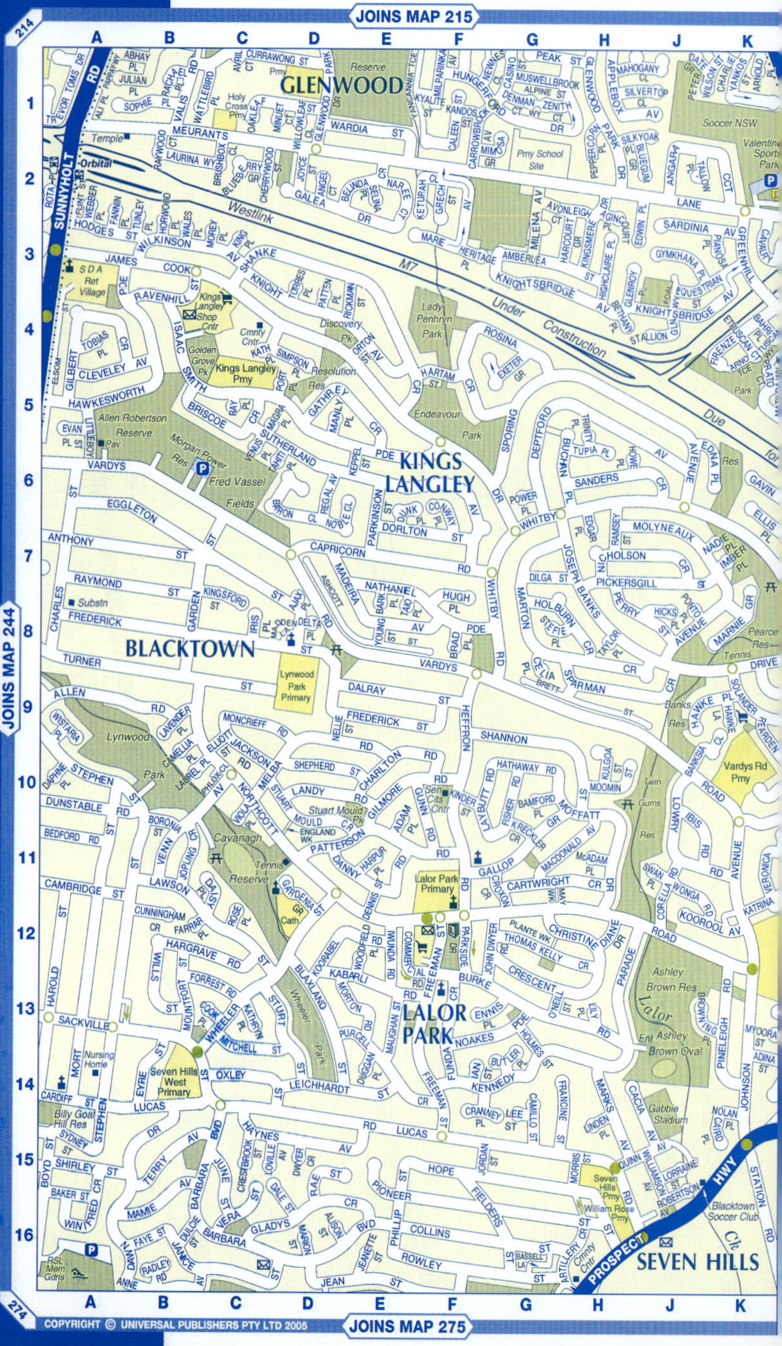
JOINS MAP 215
JOINS MAP 244
JOINS MAP 275
214
274
A
B
C
D
E
F
G
H
J
K
1
2
3
4
5
6
7
8
9
10
11
12
13
14
15
16
GLENWOOD
KINGS LANGLEY
BLACKTOWN
LALOR PARK
SEVEN HILLS
SUNNYHOLT RD
Orbital
Westlink
M7
Under Construction
Due
PROSPECT HWY
Reserve
Holy Cross Pmy
Temple
Pmy School Site
Soccer NSW
Valentine Sports Park
SDA Ret Village
Kings Langley Shop Cntr
Cmnty Cntr
Golden Grove Pk
Kings Langley Pmy
Resolution Res
Discovery Pk
Lady Penhryn Park
Endeavour Park
Allen Robertson Reserve
Pav
Morgan Power Res
Fred Vassel Fields
Substn
Lynwood Park Primary
Lynwood Park
Cavanagh Reserve
Tennis
Stuart Mould Pk
Sen Cits Cntr
Lalor Park Primary
Twin Gums Res
Vardys Rd Pmy
Pearce Res
Banks Res
Ashley Brown Res
Ashley Brown Oval
Gabbie Stadium
Wheeler Park
Nursing Home
Seven Hills West Primary
Billy Goat Hill Res
RSL Mem Gdns
Seven Hills Pmy
William Rose Pmy
Blacktown Soccer Club
Cmnty Cntr
TREVOR TOMS DR
ABHAY PL
JULIAN PL
SOPHIE PL
RACHAEL PL
VALIS ST
WATTLEBIRD RD
CURRAWONG ST
GLENWOOD PARK DR
MEURANTS LANE
WARDIA ST
HUNGERFORD DR
PEAK ST
MUSWELLBROOK
ALPINE ST
DENMAN AV
ZENITH CT
MAHOGANY CL
SILVERTOP CL
SILKYOAK PL
LANE
SARDINIA AV
GREENHILL
CAVALRY
GYMKHANA PL
EQUESTRIAN ST
KNIGHTSBRIDGE AV
STALLION
FIRENZE
ARNO
HODGES ST
WILKINSON
JAMES
COOK ST
RAVENHILL
SHANKE
KNIGHT
TORRES PL
PATTEN PL
RICKMAN ST
ORTON AV
ROSINA
EXETER GR
HARTAM ST
SPORTING
DEPTFORD
BUCHAN
TUPIA PL
SANDERS
EDNA PL
GAVIN
ELLIS PL
TOBIAS PL
CLEVELEY AV
HAWKESWORTH
ISAAC SMITH
BRISCOE
VENUS
SUTHERLAND
GATHREY
MANLY PL
KEPPEL ST
PDE
POWER PL
WHITBY
MOLYNEAUX
NICHOLSON
PICKERSGILL
DILGA ST
JOSEPH BANKS
MARTON
HOLBURN
PERRY
HICKS PL
PONTO
AVENUE
MARNIE
VARDYS
EGGLETON
ANTHONY ST
CAPRICORN RD
DORLTON ST
CONWAY
DUNK PL
PARKINSON
RAYMOND ST
KINGSFORD ST
MADEIRA
ASHCOTT
NATHANIEL
HUGH PL
FREDERICK
TURNER
ALLEN RD
DALRAY ST
FREDERICK ST
SHANNON
HEFFRON
WHITBY RD
CHARLES
GARDEN
DELTA PL
BRAD PL
TAYLOR PL
SPARMAN
DRIVE
WISTARIA PL
LAVENDER PL
CAMELLIA
LAUREL PL
PHLOX CL
ELLIOTT ST
JACKSON RD
MONCRIEFF RD
NELLIE ST
CHARLTON
HATHAWAY RD
KULGOA ST
MOOMIN
BANKSIA
HAWKE PL
SOLANDER
REARDEN
DAPHNE PL
STEPHEN
DUNSTABLE RD
BEDFORD RD
BORONIA ST
VENN ST
JOPLING CR
NORTHCOTT
MELBA
STUART
SHEPHERD ST
LANDY
MOULD
PATTERSON
GILMORE
ADAM PL
NINNIS RD
KINDER ST
LAYBUTT RD
FISHER PL
BAMFORD PL
KRECKLER CR
MOFFATT
MACDONALD AV
McADAM PL
LOWRY
IBIS RD
SWAN PL
WONGA
CORELLA RD
KOOROOL AV
VERONICA
KATRINA
CAMBRIDGE ST
LAWSON
DAISY PL
ROSE PL
GARDENIA ST
HARPUR PL
DANNY
DENNIS ST
GALLOP
CROXON
CARTWRIGHT CR
MAY WK
CUNNINGHAM CR
FARRAR PL
HARGRAVE RD
WILLS
FORREST RD
COOK PL
WHEELER
KATHRYN
KOORABEL
BLAXLAND
WOODFIELD RD
IWUNDA RD
COMMERCIAL RD
FREEMAN ST
PARKSIDE DR
JOHN DWYER RD
PLANTE WK
THOMAS KELLY
CRESCENT
CHRISTINE
DIANE DR
PARADE
ROAD
BROWNING PL
PINELEIGH RD
JOHNSON
MYOORA ST
HAROLD
SACKVILLE
MORT ST
MOUNTFORT ST
MITCHELL ST
KABARLI
MORTON
PURCELL
DUGGAN
MAUGHAN ST
FUNDA
ENNIS PL
NOAKES
HOLMES ST
BUTLER
KENNEDY
FRANCINE
MARKS
CACIA AV
CARDIFF ST
LUCAS
EYRE
OXLEY
LEICHHARDT ST
CRANNEY PL
LEE ST
CAMILLO ST
LINDEN PL
NOLAN PL
CAIRD PL
SYDNEY ST
SHIRLEY ST
BOYD ST
TERRY
HAYNES
CRESTBROOK ST
LOVILLE AV
DWYER CR
RAE ST
HOPE
JORDAN ST
FIELDERS
MORRIS ST
QUINN
WILLIAMSON AV
LORRAINE ST
ROBERTSON
STATION RD
BAKER ST
WINIFRED CR
MAMIE
JUNE ST
BARBARA BVD
VERA
DALE ST
GLADYS
PIONEER
CR
PHILLIP ST
COLLINS
ROWLEY
BASSELL LA
ARTILLERY CR
FAYE ST
DULCIE
JANICE
RADLEY RD
DAWN
ANNE
MARION ST
ALISON ST
JEANETTE ST
JEAN ST

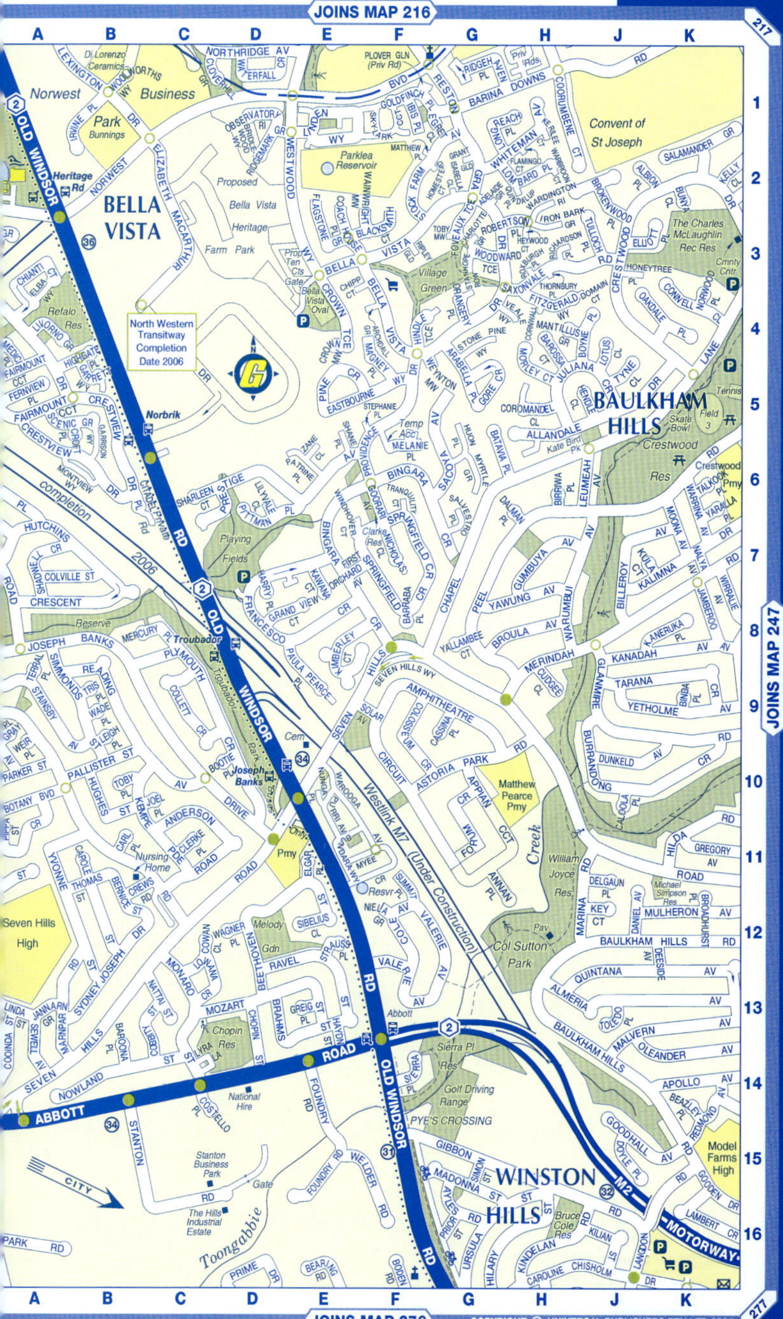
JOINS MAP 216
JOINS MAP 247
JOINS MAP 276
217
277
A B C D E F G H J K
1 2 3 4 5 6 7 8 9 10 11 12 13 14 15 16
BELLA VISTA
BAULKHAM HILLS
WINSTON HILLS
Norwest
Business
Park
Bunnings
Di Lorenzo Ceramics
Heritage Rd
Proposed
Bella Vista
Heritage
Farm Park
North Western Transitway Completion Date 2006
Norbrik
Parklea Reservoir
Village Green
Bella Vista Oval
Convent of St Joseph
The Charles McLaughlin Rec Res
Cmnty Cntr
Refalo Res
Crestwood Res
Crestwood Pmy
Skate Bowl
Field 3
Tennis
Kate Bird Pk
Temp Acc
Clarke Res
Playing Fields
Reserve
Troubador
Joseph Banks
Cem
Pmy
Nursing Home
Seven Hills High
Melody Gdn
Chopin Res
Resvr
Matthew Pearce Pmy
William Joyce Res
Michael Simpson Res
Col Sutton Park
Pav
Creek
Westlink M7 (Under Construction)
completion 2006
Sierra Pl Res
Golf Driving Range
PYE'S CROSSING
Abbott
National Hire
Stanton Business Park
The Hills Industrial Estate
Toongabbie
Gate
Bruce Cole Res
Model Farms High
CITY
MOTORWAY
M2
OLD WINDSOR RD
ABBOTT ROAD
SEVEN HILLS WY
NORWEST BVD
NORTHRIDGE AV
BARINA DOWNS RD
BELLA VISTA DR
ELIZABETH MACARTHUR DR
WESTWOOD WY
CROWN TCE
HINDLE TCE
ORANGERY RD
FITZGERALD RD
CRESTWOOD DR
CHAPEL LANE
BAULKHAM HILLS RD
JOSEPH BANKS DR
PLYMOUTH AV
MERCURY ST
READING AV
PALLISTER ST
SYDNEY JOSEPH DR
SEVEN HILLS RD
AMPHITHEATRE CCT
ASTORIA PARK RD
VALERIE AV
SOLAR AV
COLUMBIA CR
FRANCESCO CR
PAULA PEARCE PL
SPRINGFIELD CR
BINGARA CR
EASTBOURNE WY
MERINDAH RD
KANADAH AV
TARANA AV
YETHOLME AV
DUNKELD AV
BURRANDONG CR
GREGORY AV
MULHERON AV
QUINTANA AV
ALMERIA AV
MALVERN AV
OLEANDER AV
APOLLO AV
GOODHALL AV
GIBBON RD
MADONNA ST
KINDELAN RD
CHISHOLM ST
LANGDON RD
LAMBERT CR
FOUNDRY RD
WELDER RD
STANTON RD
NOWLAND AV
BEETHOVEN ST
MOZART ST
BRAHMS ST
CHOPIN ST
MONARO CR
PRIME DR
BEARING RD
BODEN RD
PARK RD
CRESCENT RD
HUTCHINS CR
COLVILLE ST
CITADEL Private Rd
SALAMANDER GR
COORUMBENE CT
WHITEMAN AV
ROBERTSON PL
WOODWARD CT
SAXONVALE

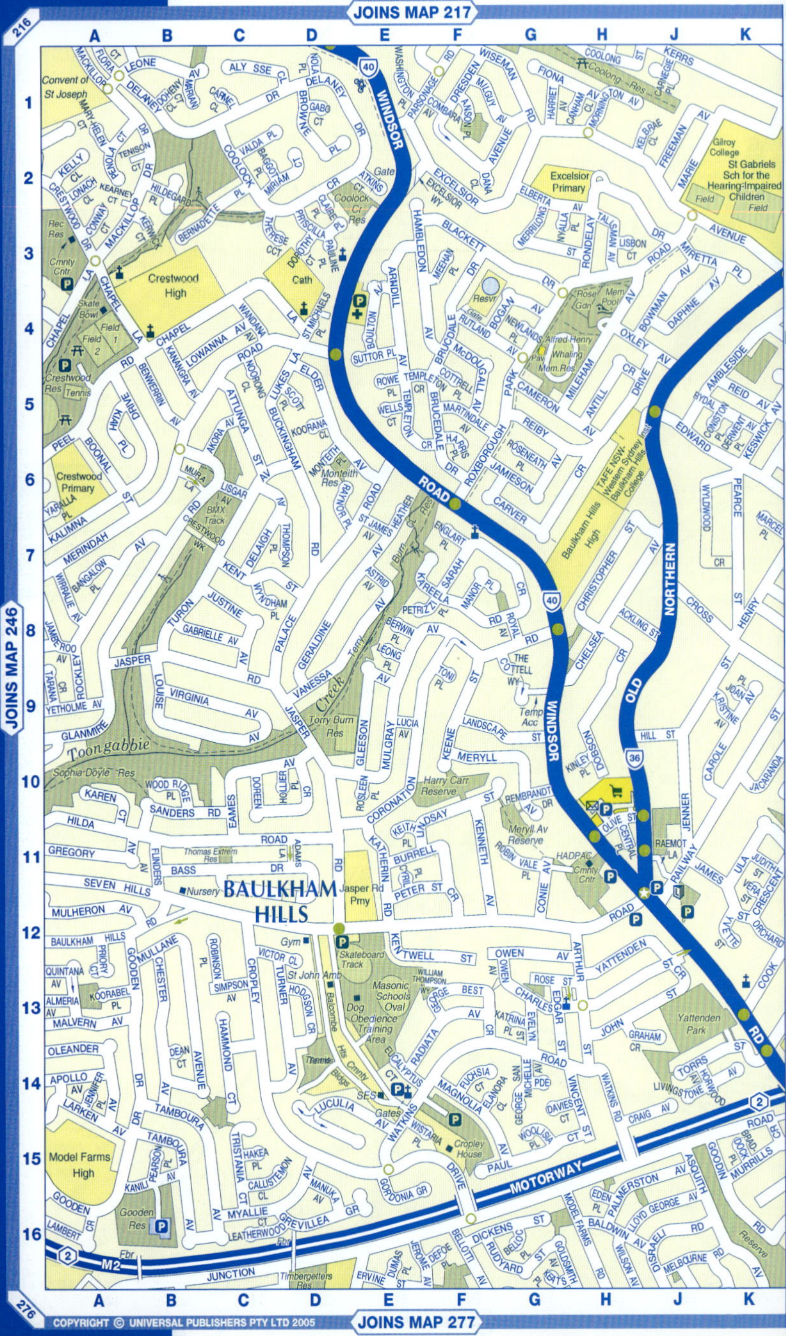
JOINS MAP 217
JOINS MAP 246
JOINS MAP 277
216
276
A B C D E F G H J K
1 2 3 4 5 6 7 8 9 10 11 12 13 14 15 16
BAULKHAM HILLS
WINDSOR ROAD
OLD NORTHERN RD
MOTORWAY
M2
Convent of St Joseph
Crestwood High
Crestwood Primary
Cath
Excelsior Primary
Gilroy College
St Gabriels Sch for the Hearing-Impaired Children
Field
Rec Res
Cmnty Cntr
Skate Bowl
Crestwood Res
Tennis
Coolock Cr Res
Resvr
Rose Gdn
Mem Pool
Pav
Alfred Henry Whaling Mem.Res.
TAFE NSW-Western Sydney Inst Baulkham Hills College
Baulkham Hills High
Monteith Res
BMX Track
CRESTWOOD WK
Toongabbie Creek
Torry Burn Res
Sophia Doyle Res
Harry Carr Reserve
Meryll Av Reserve
Temp Acc
HADPAC Cmnty Cntr
Thomas Extrem Res
Nursery
Jasper Rd Pmy
Gym
Skateboard Track
St John Amb
Masonic Schools Oval
Dog Obedience Training Area
Balcombe Hts Cmnty Bldgs
SES
Gates
Cropley House
Yattenden Park
Model Farms High
Gooden Res
Timbergetters Res
Coolong Res
JUNCTION RD
SEVEN HILLS RD
BAULKHAM HILLS RD
CHAPEL LA
MERINDAH RD
JASPER RD
CORONATION RD
SEVEN HILLS RD
ATHUR ST
YATTENDEN CR
WATKINS RD
MURILLS
COPYRIGHT © UNIVERSAL PUBLISHERS PTY LTD 2005

MAP 248

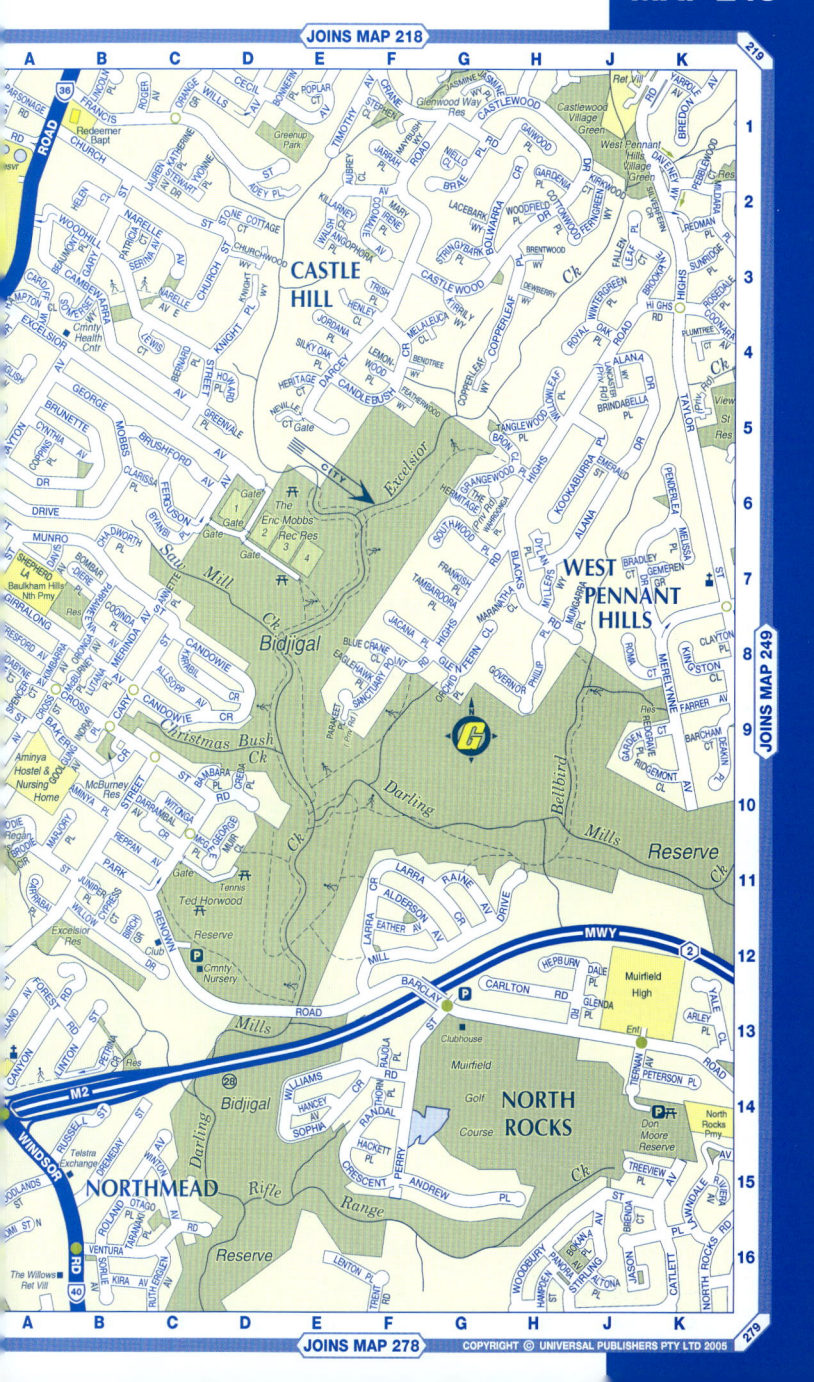

MAP 249

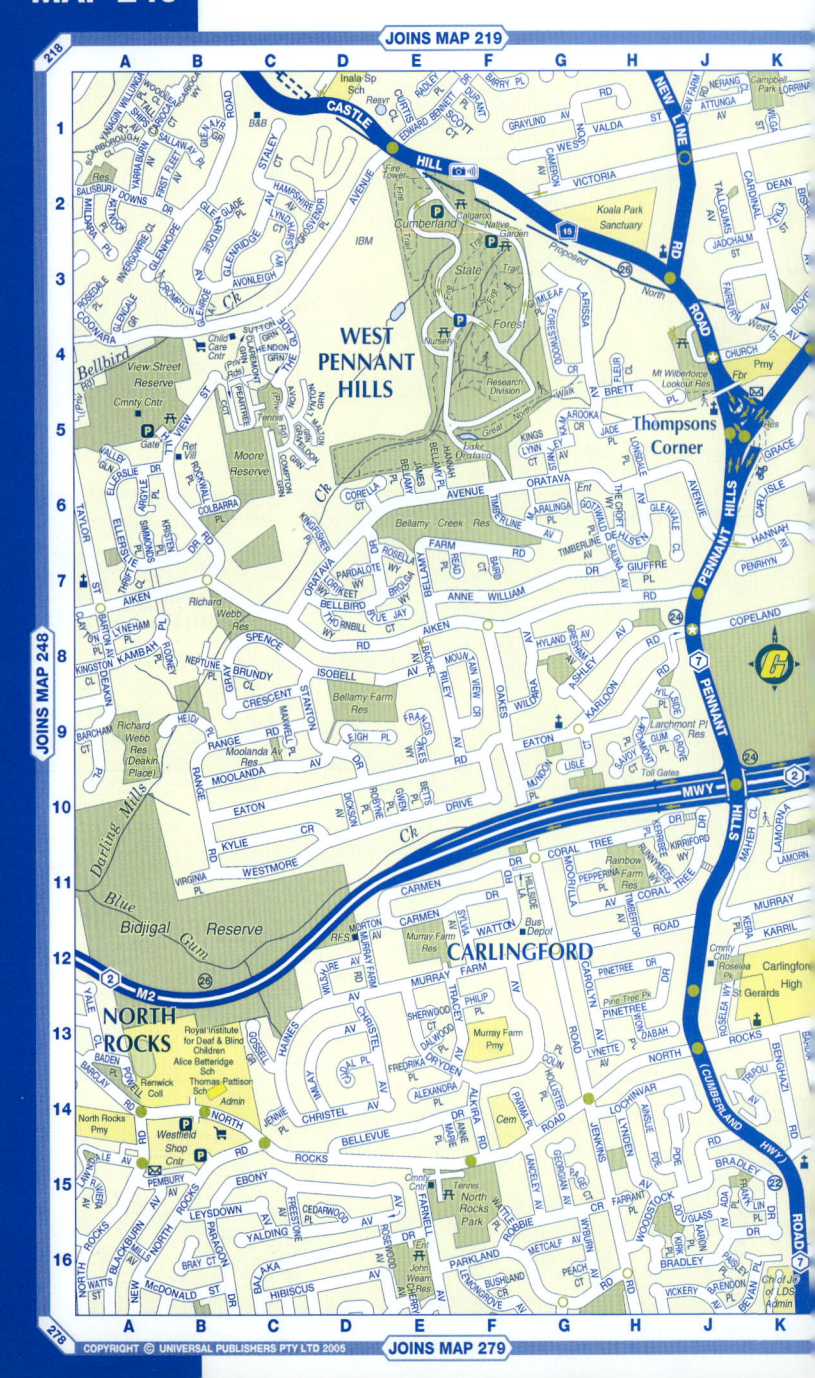

JOINS MAP 220
JOINS MAP 251
JOINS MAP 280
221
281
A
B
C
D
E
F
G
H
J
K
1
2
3
4
5
6
7
8
9
10
11
12
13
14
15
16
PENNANT HILLS
BEECROFT
CHELTENHAM
EPPING
BOUNDARY RD
BEECROFT ROAD
CUMBERLAND HWY
M2
MOTORWAY
CARLINGFORD RD
Lane Cove National Pk
Pennant Hills Park
Pennant Hills Golf Course
Recreation Reserve
Observatory Park
Ludovic Blackwood Mem Sanctuary
Mt St Benedict College
Devlins Ck
Beecroft Ck
Cheltenham Girls High
Cheltenham Oval
Epping Heights Pmy
Epping West Pmy
Roselea Primary
Karonga Sch
Beecroft Pmy
Beecroft Nursing Home
Chesalon Nursing Home
West Epping Park
Boronia Park
Dunrossil Pk
Fearnley Park
Booth Park
Basil Cook Res
Chilworth Rec Res
Beecroft
Cheltenham
Pennant Hills
Arden
Ten Croquet Club
Band Hall
Netball
Clubhouse
YMCA
Hall
Tennis
Res
Rec Res
Fbr
Cmnty Health Cntr
Cmnty Cntr
Nurs Home
Beecroft Village Grn
CITY
COPYRIGHT © UNIVERSAL PUBLISHERS PTY LTD 2005

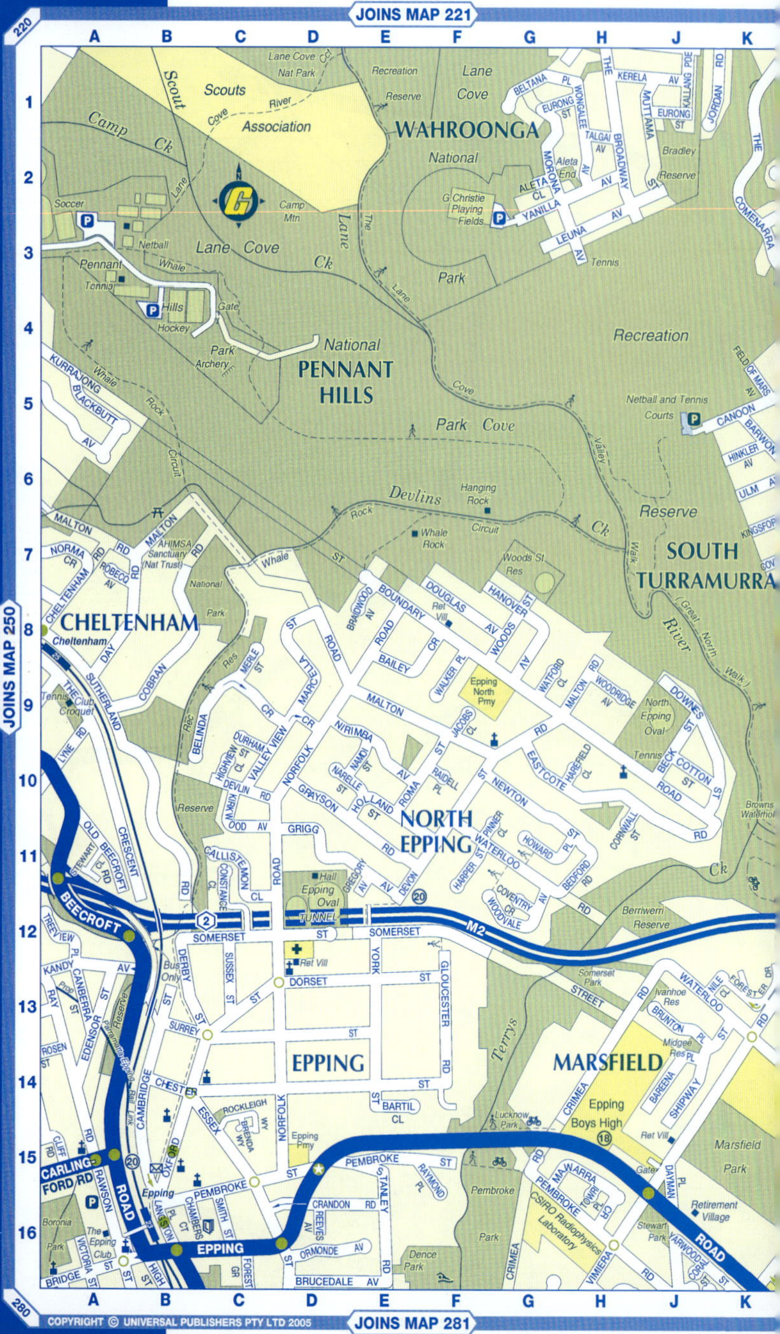
JOINS MAP 221
JOINS MAP 250
JOINS MAP 281
220
280
A B C D E F G H J K
1 2 3 4 5 6 7 8 9 10 11 12 13 14 15 16
WAHROONGA
PENNANT HILLS
SOUTH TURRAMURRA
CHELTENHAM
NORTH EPPING
EPPING
MARSFIELD
Lane Cove River Scouts Association
Lane Cove Nat Park
Recreation Reserve
Lane Cove National Park
Lane Cove Recreation Reserve
Camp Ck
Scout
Camp Mtn
Soccer
Netball
Pennant Tennis
Pennant Hills Hockey
Park Archery
Gate
Whale Rock Circuit
Devlins Ck
Hanging Rock
Whale Rock
Woods St Res
G Christie Playing Fields
Bradley Reserve
Aleta End
Tennis
Netball and Tennis Courts
Great North Walk
Valley Walk
River
Browns Waterhole
AHIMSA Sanctuary (Nat Trust)
National Park
Cheltenham
Tennis Club Croquet
Rec Res
Reserve
North Epping Oval
Epping North Pmy
Ret Vill
Hall Epping Oval
TUNNEL
M2
Berriwerri Reserve
Somerset Park
Ivanhoe Res
Midgee Res
Epping Boys High
Lucknow Park
Marsfield Park
Retirement Village
Stewart Park
Pembroke Park
CSIRO Radiophysics Laboratory
Dence Park
Epping Pmy
Boronia Park
The Epping Club
Epping
Bus Only
Parramatta-Epping Rail Link
Terrys
BEECROFT RD
CARLINGFORD RD
RAWSON ROAD
EPPING ROAD
SOMERSET ST
DORSET ST
SURREY ST
CHESTER ST
PEMBROKE ST
CRANDON RD
ORMONDE AV
BRUCEDALE AV
BRIDGE ST
MALTON RD
NORMA CR
ROBECCO AV
CHELTENHAM RD
SUTHERLAND RD
THE CRESCENT
LYNE RD
DAY RD
COBRAN RD
KURRAJONG AV
BLACKBUTT AV
BOUNDARY RD
BRADWOOD AV
DOUGLAS AV
HANOVER ST
WOODS AV
WATFORD CL
WOODRIDGE AV
DOWNES ST
COTTON ST
BECK ROAD
CORNWALL ST
EASTCOTE RD
HAREFIELD CL
NEWTON ST
HOWARD PL
BEDFORD RD
WATERLOO RD
PINNER CL
HARPER ST
COVENTRY CR
WOODVALE AV
MALTON RD
JACOBS CL
WALKER PL
BAILEY CR
MARCELLA ST
NORFOLK RD
NIRIMBA AV
NAMOI ST
NARELLE ST
HOLLAND ST
ROMA ST
RAIDELL PL
GRAYSON RD
GREGORY AV
DEVON ST
GRIGG AV
MERLE ST
BELINDA CR
DURHAM ST
VALLEY VIEW CR
HIGHVIEW CL
DEVLIN RD
KIRKWOOD AV
CALLISTEMON CL
CONSTANCE CL
OLD BEECROFT RD
STEWART CL
BEECROFT CRESCENT
TREEVIEW PL
KANDY AV
CANBERRA ST
RAY ST
EDENSOR ST
ROSEN ST
CLIFF RD
CAMBRIDGE ST
DERBY ST
SUSSEX ST
ESSEX ST
OXFORD ST
ROCKLEIGH WY
BRENDA WY
YORK ST
GLOUCESTER RD
BARTIL CL
STANLEY RD
RAYMOND PL
REEVES AV
FOREST GR
SMITH ST
CHAMBERS CT
LANGSTON PL
HIGH ST
VICTORIA ST
CRIMEA RD
PEMBROKE ST
MANARRA RD
TOWRI CR
VIMIERA RD
DAYMAN PL
YARWOOD CR
CORAL ST
WATERLOO RD
NILE CL
FORESTER
BRUNTON PL
BAREENA ST
SHIPWAY ST
BELTANA PL
EURONG ST
WONGALEE AV
TALGAI AV
BROADWAY
KERELA AV
MUTTAMA
KALLANG PDE
JORDAN RD
THE COMENARRA
MORONA AV
ALETA CL
YANILLA AV
LEUNA AV
FIELD OF MARS AV
CANOON RD
BARWON
HINKLER AV
ULM AV
KINGSFORD
2
20
18

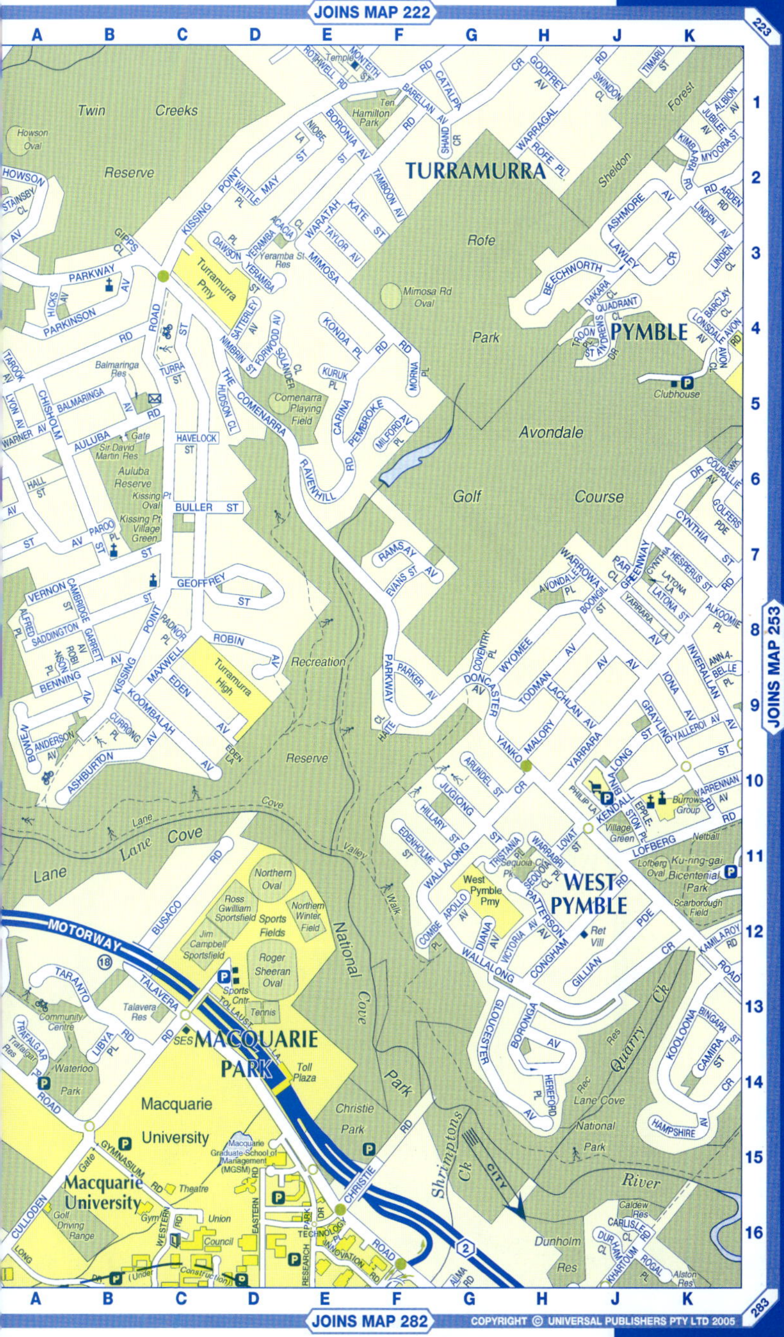
JOINS MAP 222
JOINS MAP 253
JOINS MAP 282
223
283
A
B
C
D
E
F
G
H
J
K
1
2
3
4
5
6
7
8
9
10
11
12
13
14
15
16
TURRAMURRA
PYMBLE
WEST PYMBLE
MACQUARIE PARK
Macquarie University
Twin Creeks Reserve
Howson Oval
Rofe Park
Sheldon Forest
Avondale Golf Course
Clubhouse
Mimosa Rd Oval
Ten Hamilton Park
Temple
Turramurra Pmy
Turramurra High
Yeramba St Res
Comenarra Playing Field
Balmaringa Res
Sir David Martin Res
Auluba Reserve
Kissing Pt Oval
Kissing Pt Village Green
Gate
Recreation Reserve
Lane Cove
Lane Cove Valley Walk
Lane Cove National Park
Northern Oval
Ross Gwilliam Sportsfield
Sports Fields
Northern Winter Field
Jim Campbell Sportsfield
Roger Sheeran Oval
Sports Cntr
Tennis
Talavera Res
Community Centre
Trafalgar Res
Waterloo Park
SES
Toll Plaza
Christie Park
Macquarie Graduate School of Management (MGSM)
Theatre
Gym
Union
Council
Golf Driving Range
Under Construction
West Pymble Pmy
Sequoia Cl Pk
Ret Vill
Village Green
Burrows Group
Lofberg Oval
Ku-ring-gai Bicentenial Park
Scarborough Field
Netball
Quarry Ck
Shrimptons Ck
Rec
River
Caldew Res
Dunholm Res
Alston Res
MOTORWAY
18
2
CITY
HOWSON AV
STAINSBY CL
GIPPS CL
PARKWAY AV
HICKS AV
PARKINSON RD
TAROOK AV
LYON AV
CHISHOLM
BALMARINGA AV
WARNER AV
AULUBA RD
HALL ST
PAROO PL
VERNON ST
CAMBRIDGE ST
ALFRED PL
SADDINGTON ST
GARRETT AV
ROBINSON PL
BENNING AV
BOWEN AV
ANDERSON AV
ASHBURTON AV
CURRONG PL
KOOMBALAH AV
KISSING POINT RD
RADNOR PL
MAXWELL ST
EDEN AV
EDEN LA
ROBIN AV
GEOFFREY ST
BULLER ST
HAVELOCK ST
TURRA ST
ROAD
DAWSON PL
YERAMBA PL
YERAMBA ST
ACACIA CL
SATTERLEY AV
NIMBRIN ST
FORWOOD AV
SOLANDER CL
THE COMENARRA PARKWAY
HUDSON CL
WATTLE PL
MAY ST
NIOBE LA
BORONIA AV
WARATAH ST
KATE ST
TAYLOR AV
MIMOSA RD
KONDA PL
KURUK PL
CARINA RD
PEMBROKE AV
MILFORD PL
MORNA PL
RAVENHILL RD
ROTHWELL RD
MONTEITH ST
BARELLAN AV
CATALPA CR
SHAND CR
TAMBOON AV
GODFREY AV
WARRAGAL RD
ROFE PL
SWINDON CL
TIMARU ST
ALBION AV
JUBILEE AV
KIMBARRA RD
MYOORA ST
ARDEN RD
LINDEN AV
LINDEN CL
ASHMORE AV
LAWLEY CR
BEECHWORTH RD
DAKARA CL
QUADRANT CL
TROON PL
ST ANDREWS DR
BARCLAY CL
LONSDALE AV
AVON RD
RAMSAY AV
EVANS ST
PARKWAY
PARKER AV
HATE PL
COVENTRY PL
DONCASTER AV
WYOMEE AV
TODMAN AV
LACHLAN AV
YANKO CR
MALORY AV
YARRARA RD
WARROWA AV
AVONDALE PL
BOONGIL ST
GREENWAY PAR CL
YARRARA LA
CYNTHIA ST
HESPERUS ST
LATONA LA
LATONA ST
COURALLIE AV
GOLFERS PDE
ALKOOMIE PL
ANNABELLE PL
INVERALLAN AV
IONA AV
GRAYLING ST
YALLEROI AV
YARRENNAN AV
LONG ST
KENDALL ST
PHILIP LA
EPPLESTON PL
LOFBERG RD
ARUNDEL ST
JUGIONG ST
HILLARY ST
EDENHOLME ST
WALLALONG CR
TRISTANIA PL
WARRABRI PL
LOVAT ST
SEQUOIA CL
PATTERSON AV
APOLLO AV
DIANA AV
VICTORIA AV
CONGHAM DR
GILLIAN PDE
COMBE PL
GLOUCESTER AV
BORONGA AV
HEREFORD PL
KOOLOONA CR
BINGARA RD
CAMIRA ST
HAMPSHIRE AV
KAMILAROY ROAD
CARLISLE RD
DURHAM CL
KHARTOUM RD
ROGAL PL
BUSACO RD
TARANTO RD
TALAVERA RD
TOLLAUST LA
LIBYA PL
TRAFALGAR PL
WATERLOO ROAD
CULLODEN RD
LONG
GYMNASIUM RD
GATE
WESTERN RD
EASTERN RD
RESEARCH PARK DR
TECHNOLOGY PL
INNOVATION RD
CHRISTIE RD
ALMA RD
ROAD

JOINS MAP 223
JOINS MAP 252
JOINS MAP 283
222
282
A B C D E F G H J K
1 2 3 4 5 6 7 8 9 10 11 12 13 14 15 16
PYMBLE
Pymble Ladies College
GORDON
WEST PYMBLE
PACIFIC
HIGHWAY
MONA VALE RD
ROAD
RYDE
Gordon Golf Course
Blackbutt Recreation Reserve
Blackbutt Reserve
Blackbutt Ck
Lane Cove National Park
Lane Cove River
DE BURGHS BRIDGE
Killara Golf Course
Links Creek Res
Falls Ck
Rudder Ck
Stony Creek
Richmond Park
Bullock Park
Government Laboratory
Army Depot
Creswell O'Reilly Lookout
Town Hall
Ped Sub
Pymble
Gordon
Sheldon Forest
Pymble Soldiers Mem Pk
Gordon East Pmy
Gordon West Pmy
Killara Pmy
Beaumont Road Pmy
Ravenswood Girls
Kirby Pk
Council Depot
Metzlers End
Council Office
Cem
Substation
Tennis
Kendall Green Tennis
Norman Griffiths Oval
Cmnty Hall
Ku-ring-gai Bicentennial Pk
Yarran St Res
Minnamurra Res
Clubhouse
Eryldene
Gowrie Village Roden Cutler Lodge & Nurs Home
Nursing Home
Retirement Village
Telstra Exchange
Croquet Regimental Park
Ticket of Leave Pk
Allen Pk
Upass
CITY
COPYRIGHT © UNIVERSAL PUBLISHERS PTY LTD 2005

JOINS MAP 224

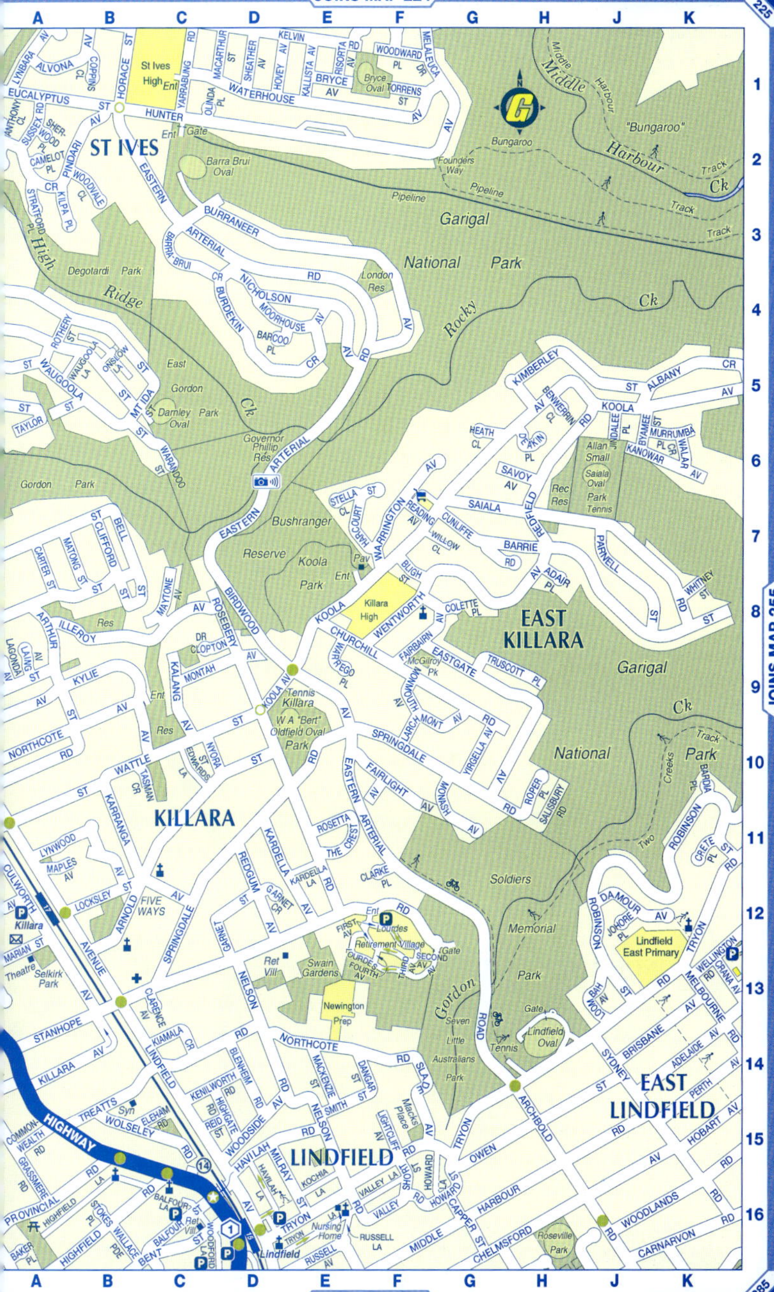

JOINS MAP 255

JOINS MAP 284

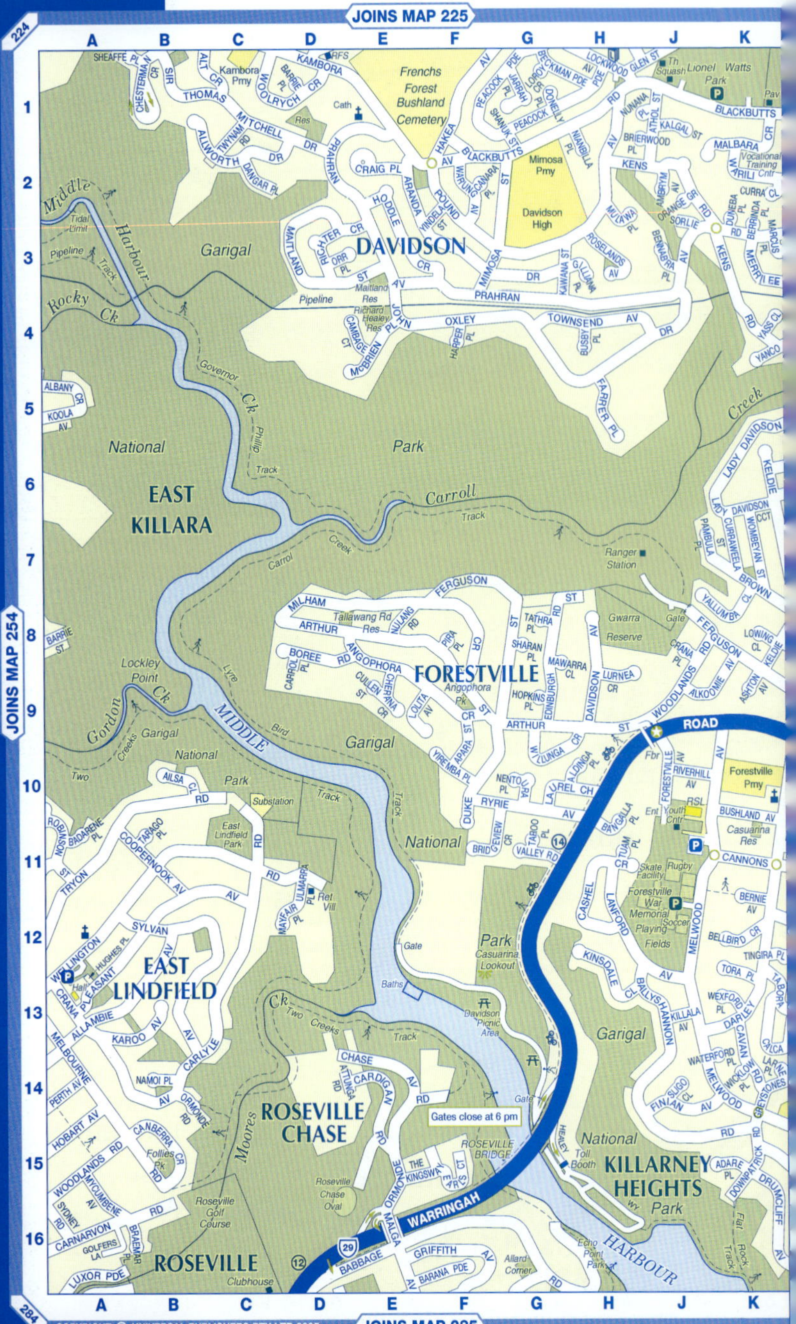
JOINS MAP 225
224
A B C D E F G H J K
1 2 3 4 5 6 7 8 9 10 11 12 13 14 15 16
JOINS MAP 254
JOINS MAP 285
284
DAVIDSON
EAST KILLARA
FORESTVILLE
EAST LINDFIELD
ROSEVILLE CHASE
ROSEVILLE
KILLARNEY HEIGHTS
Frenchs Forest Bushland Cemetery
Mimosa Pmy
Davidson High
Lionel Watts Park
Kambora Pmy
National Park
Garigal National Park
Middle Harbour
Rocky Ck
Governor Phillip Track
Carroll Track
Carrol Creek
Ranger Station
Gwarra Reserve
Lockley Point
Gordon Creeks
Two Creeks Track
Lyre Bird Track
MIDDLE HARBOUR
Tallawang Rd Res
Angophora Pk
Forestville Pmy
Casuarina Res
Forestville War Memorial Playing Fields
Skate Facility
Rugby
Soccer
Youth Cntr
RSL
Vocational Training Cntr
East Lindfield Park
Substation
Ret Vill
Baths
Gate
Casuarina Lookout
Davidson Picnic Area
Gates close at 6 pm
ROSEVILLE BRIDGE
Roseville Chase Oval
Roseville Golf Course
Clubhouse
Follies Pk
Allard Corner
Echo Point Park
Toll Booth
Flat Rock Track
Pipeline
Tidal Limit
Maitland Res
Richard Healey Res
WARRINGAH ROAD
BLACKBUTTS RD
PRAHRAN AV
MIMOSA DR
TOWNSEND AV
OXLEY DR
FERGUSON ST
FERGUSON RD
ARTHUR ST
RYRIE AV
BUSHLAND AV
CANNONS
MELWOOD AV
KINSDALE CL
BALLYSHANNON
WOODLANDS RD
DUKE ST
DAVIDSON AV
HAKEA AV
PEACOCK PDE
LOCKWOOD AV
GLEN ST
MITCHELL RD
THOMAS ST
KAMBORA AV
WOOLRYCH CR
CRAIG PL
RICHTER CR
MAITLAND ST
JOHN PL
MILHAM ST
BOREE RD
ANGOPHORA CR
SYLVAN AV
COOPERNOOK AV
TRYON RD
WELLINGTON
PLEASANT AV
ALLAMBIE AV
KAROO AV
CARLYLE RD
ORMONDE RD
CHASE AV
CARDIGAN RD
HOBART AV
MELBOURNE RD
WOODLANDS RD
CARNARVON RD
LUXOR PDE
GOLFERS LA
BRAEMAR
BABBAGE RD
GRIFFITH AV
BARANA PDE
MALGA AV
LADY DAVIDSON CCT
YALLUMBA CL
BROWN ST
KEN ST
ROSELANDS AV
HEALEY WY
DOWNPATRICK RD
DRUMCLIFF AV
ADARE PL
29
12
14

JOINS MAP 226
JOINS MAP 257
JOINS MAP 286
227
287
A B C D E F G H J K
1 2 3 4 5 6 7 8 9 10 11 12 13 14 15 16
BELROSE
Sorlie
FRENCHS FOREST
ALLAMBIE HEIGHTS
FOREST WAY
WARRINGAH RD
FRENCHS FOREST RD WEST
FRENCHS FOREST RD EAST
WAKEHURST PARKWAY
Treacy Education Centre
Cmnty Cntr Belrose Oval
Peppercorn Pk
Jindabyne Reserve
The Forest High
Cmnty Health Cntr
Frenchs Forest Pmy
Sky Channel
ABC Film Studio
Industrial Area
Capital Business Park
Aurora Business Pk
Forestridge Business Pk
Sullage Depot
Warringah Aquatic Centre
Rugby Soccer Baseball
Lindsay Res
Epacris Res
Sen Cits Hall
Cath
Playing Fields
Forestville Park
Austrian Club
Armenian Cmnty Cntr
Ararat Reserve
Autistic Childrens Centre
St Davids Ret Vill
Forestville Ret Vill
Tredinnick Ret Vill
Garigal National Park
Bates Creek
Cook Street Track
The Bluff Track
The Bay Track
Manly Creek
Manly-Warringah War Memorial Park
(Manly Dam Reserve)
Pipeline
CITY
Bantry Bay
Prohibited Area
Wakehurst Golf Course
Killarney Hts High
Killarney Heights Oval
Killarney Hts Pmy
Reserve
Motor Reg
Brick Pit

MAP 257

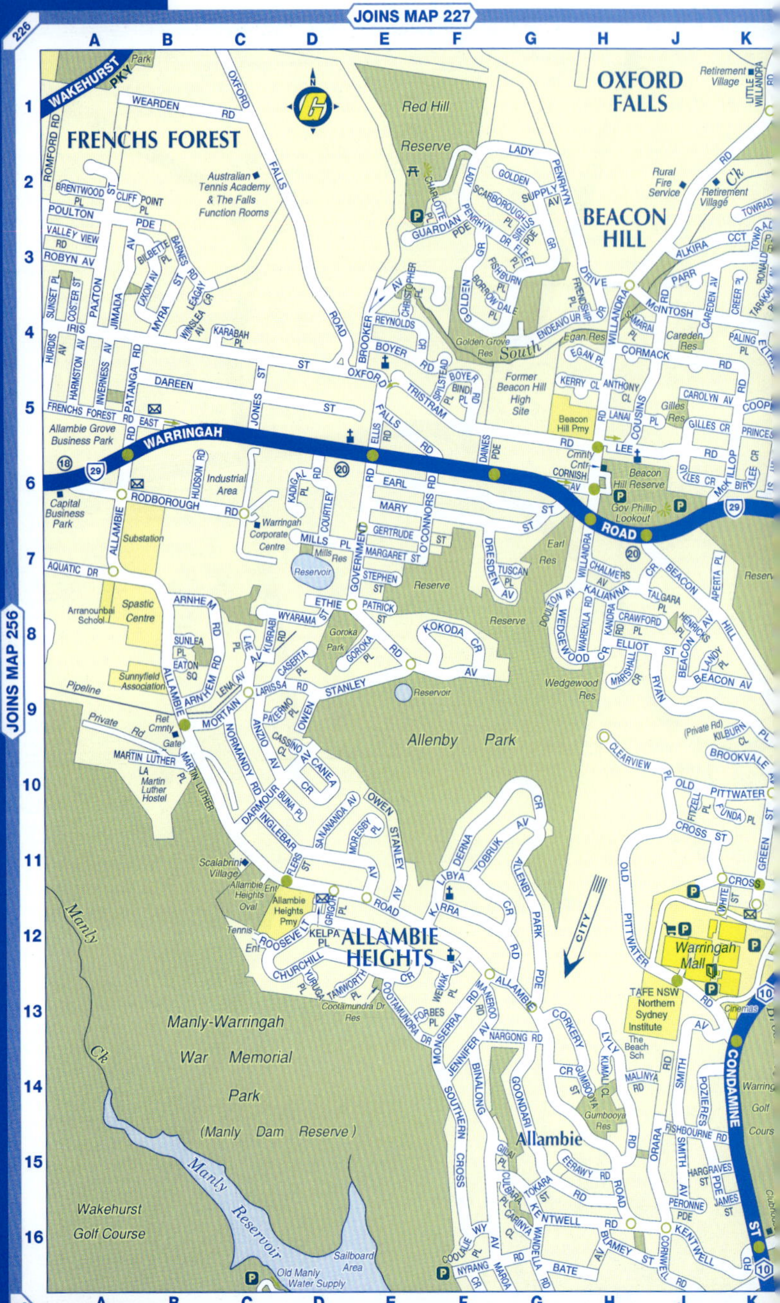
JOINS MAP 227
JOINS MAP 256
JOINS MAP 287
226
286
A B C D E F G H J K
1 2 3 4 5 6 7 8 9 10 11 12 13 14 15 16
FRENCHS FOREST
OXFORD FALLS
BEACON HILL
ALLAMBIE HEIGHTS
Allambie
WAKEHURST PKY
Park
WEARDEN RD
ROMFORD RD
OXFORD FALLS ROAD
Red Hill Reserve
Australian Tennis Academy & The Falls Function Rooms
BRENTWOOD PL
CLIFF ST
POINT PL
POULTON PDE
VALLEY VIEW RD
ROBYN AV
SUNSET PL
COSTER ST
PAXTON
JIMADA AV
BILBETTE PL
BARNES RD
DIXON AV
MYRA ST
LEAGAY CR
WINSLEA AV
KARABAH PL
HURDIS AV
HARMSTON AV
INVERNESS AV
PATANGA RD
IRIS
DAREEN
FRENCHS FOREST RD EAST
JONES ST
Allambie Grove Business Park
WARRINGAH ROAD
Capital Business Park
RODBOROUGH RD
HUDSON RD
Industrial Area
Warringah Corporate Centre
KADIGAL PL
COURTLEY RD
Substation
AQUATIC DR
ALLAMBIE RD
Arranounbai School
Spastic Centre
ARNHEM RD
SUNLEA PL
EATON SQ
Sunnyfield Association
Pipeline
Private Rd
Ret Cmnty
Gate
MARTIN LUTHER LA
Martin Luther Hostel
MARTIN LUTHER PL
MORTAIN AV
LENA AV
NORMANDY RD
ANZIO AV
LAE PL
KURRABI RD
WYARAMA ST
ETHIE ST
CASERTA PL
LARISSA RD
PALERMO PL
OWEN PL
CASSINO CL
CANEA CR
DARMOUR RD
INGLEBAR AV
BUNA PL
SANANANDA AV
MORESBY PL
OWEN STANLEY AV
STANLEY RD
FLERS ST
GRIGOR PL
Scalabrini Village
Allambie Heights Oval
Allambie Heights Pmy
Tennis
Ent
ROOSEVELT AV
KELPA PL
CHURCHILL CR
YURUGA PL
TAMWORTH PL
Cootamundra Dr Res
COOTAMUNDRA DR
FORBES PL
WEWAK PL
MONSERRA RD
MANEROO RD
JENNIFER AV
NARGONG RD
BINALONG AV
SOUTHERN CROSS WY
COOLALIE PL
NYRANG CR
MAROA RD
GILBAI PL
CULBARA PL
CARINYA CL
TOKARA ST
KENTWELL RD
WANDELLA RD
BATE AV
BLAMEY ST
GOONDARI RD
GUMBOOYA ST
Gumbooya Res
EERAWY RD
CORKERY CR
LYLY RD
KUMALI CL
MALINYA RD
ORARA RD
SMITH AV
POZIERES AV
FISHBOURNE RD
HARGRAVES ST
PERONNE PDE
JAMES PDE
KENTWELL RD
CORNWELL RD
CONDAMINE ST
Manly-Warringah War Memorial Park (Manly Dam Reserve)
Manly Ck
Manly Reservoir
Wakehurst Golf Course
Sailboard Area
Old Manly Water Supply
Allenby Park
ALLENBY PARK PDE
KOKODA CR
DERNA CR
TOBRUK AV
LIBYA
KIRRA RD
ALLAMBIE RD
CITY
Reservoir
Goroka Park
GOROKA PL
Mills Res
MILLS PL
GOVERNMENT RD
MARGARET ST
GERTRUDE
STEPHEN ST
PATRICK ST
EARL
MARY
O'CONNORS RD
DRESDEN AV
TUSCAN PL
Reserve
Earl Res
Wedgewood Res
BROOKER AV
ELLIS RD
CHRISTOPHER PL
REYNOLDS
BOYER RD
TRISTRAM RD
SPILSTEAD CL
BINDI PL
CHARLOTTE PL
GUARDIAN PDE
LADY PENRHYN DR
GOLDEN SUPPLY AV
SCARBOROUGH PL
SIRIUS PDE
FLEET PL
FISHBURN PL
BORROWDALE PL
GOLDEN GROVE
Golden Grove Res
South
Former Beacon Hill High Site
DAINES PDE
FRIENDSHIP PL
ENDEAVOUR DR
Egan Res
EGAN PL
KERRY CL
ANTHONY CL
LANAI PL
COUSINS RD
Beacon Hill Pmy
Cmnty Cntr
CORNISH AV
LEE
Beacon Hill Reserve
Gov Phillip Lookout
DRIVE
WILLANDRA RD
SAMARAI PL
McINTOSH
CORMACK
Rural Fire Service
Retirement Village
LITTLE WILLANDRA RD
ALKIRA CCT
PARR AV
CAREDEN AV
Careden Res
CREER PL
TOWRADGI
TARAKAN
PALING PL
CAROLYN AV
Gilles Res
GILLES CR
COOPER
PRINCES
McKILLOP RD
BIRALEE CR
CHALMERS AV
KALIANNA
DOULTON AV
WEDGEWOOD CR
WAREKILA RD
KANDRA RD
CRAWFORD PL
TALGARA PL
HENRICKS AV
ELLIOT ST
MARSHALL CR
RYAN
BEACON HILL
LANDY PL
BEACON AV
APERTA PL
(Private Rd)
KILBURN CL
BROOKVALE AV
CLEARVIEW PL
OLD PITTWATER RD
FITZELL PL
FUNDA PL
CROSS ST
GREEN ST
WHITE ST
Warringah Mall
TAFE NSW Northern Sydney Institute
The Beach Sch
Cinemas
Warringah Golf Course

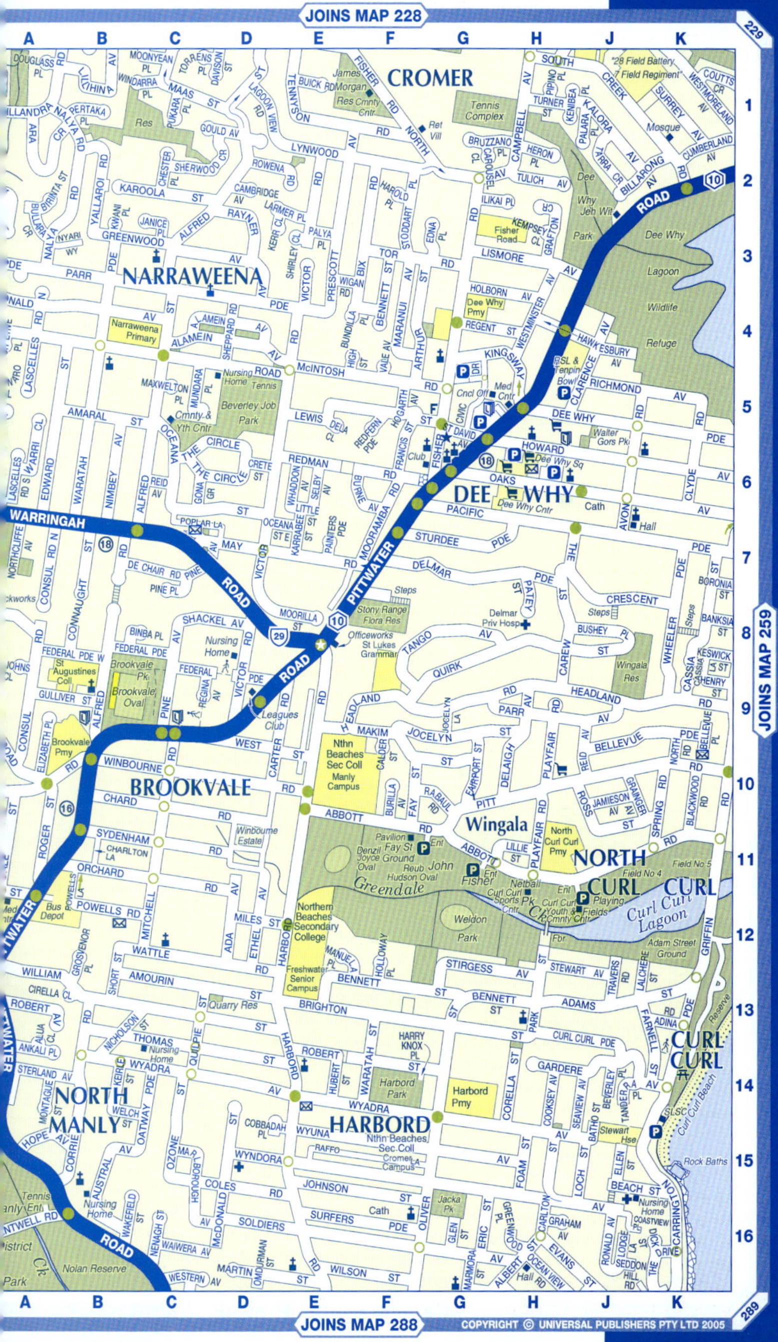

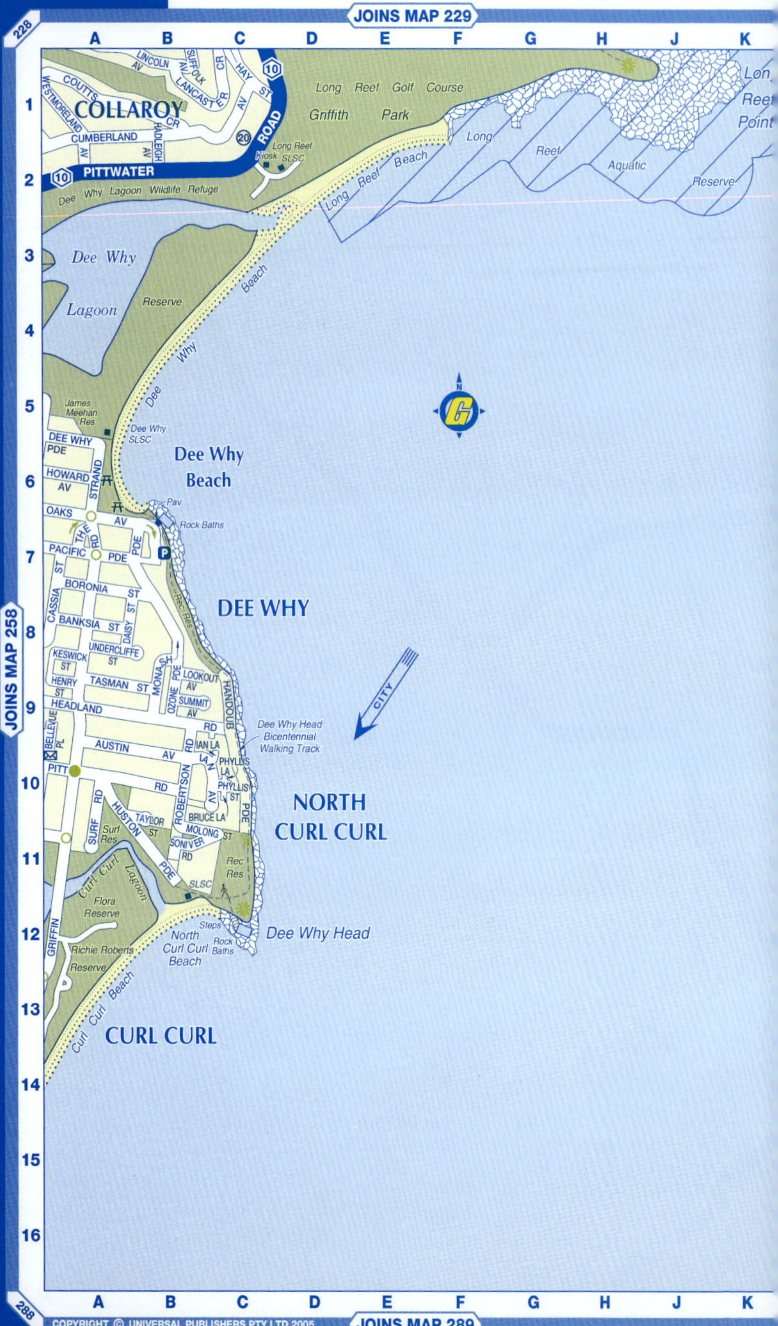
JOINS MAP 229
228
A B C D E F G H J K
1 2 3 4 5 6 7 8 9 10 11 12 13 14 15 16
COLLAROY
LINCOLN AV
SUFFOLK AV
LANCASTER CR
HAY ST
COUTTS CR
WESTMORELAND
CUMBERLAND AV
HADLEIGH AV
PITTWATER ROAD
Long Reef Kiosk SLSC
Long Reef Golf Course
Griffith Park
Long Reef Aquatic Reserve
Long Reef Point
Long Reef Beach
Dee Why Lagoon Wildlife Refuge
Dee Why Lagoon
Reserve
Dee Why Beach
James Meehan Res
Dee Why SLSC
Dee Why Beach
DEE WHY PDE
HOWARD AV
STRAND
OAKS AV
THE RD
PACIFIC PDE
Pav
Rock Baths
BORONIA ST
CASSIA ST
DAISY ST
BANKSIA ST
Rec Res
DEE WHY
UNDERCLIFFE ST
KESWICK ST
HENRY ST
TASMAN ST
MONASH PDE
OZONE PDE
LOOKOUT AV
SUMMIT AV
HANDOUB RD
HEADLAND RD
BELLEVUE PL
IAN LA
AUSTIN AV
PITT RD
ROBERTSON RD
PHYLLIS LA
PHYLLIS ST
Dee Why Head Bicentennial Walking Track
CITY
NORTH CURL CURL
BRUCE LA
MOLONG ST
SONIVER RD
TAYLOR ST
HUSTON PDE
SURF RD
Surf Res
Rec Res
SLSC
Curl Curl Lagoon
Flora Reserve
Steps
Rock Baths
Dee Why Head
North Curl Curl Beach
GRIFFIN
Richie Roberts Reserve
Curl Curl Beach
CURL CURL
JOINS MAP 258
288
JOINS MAP 289

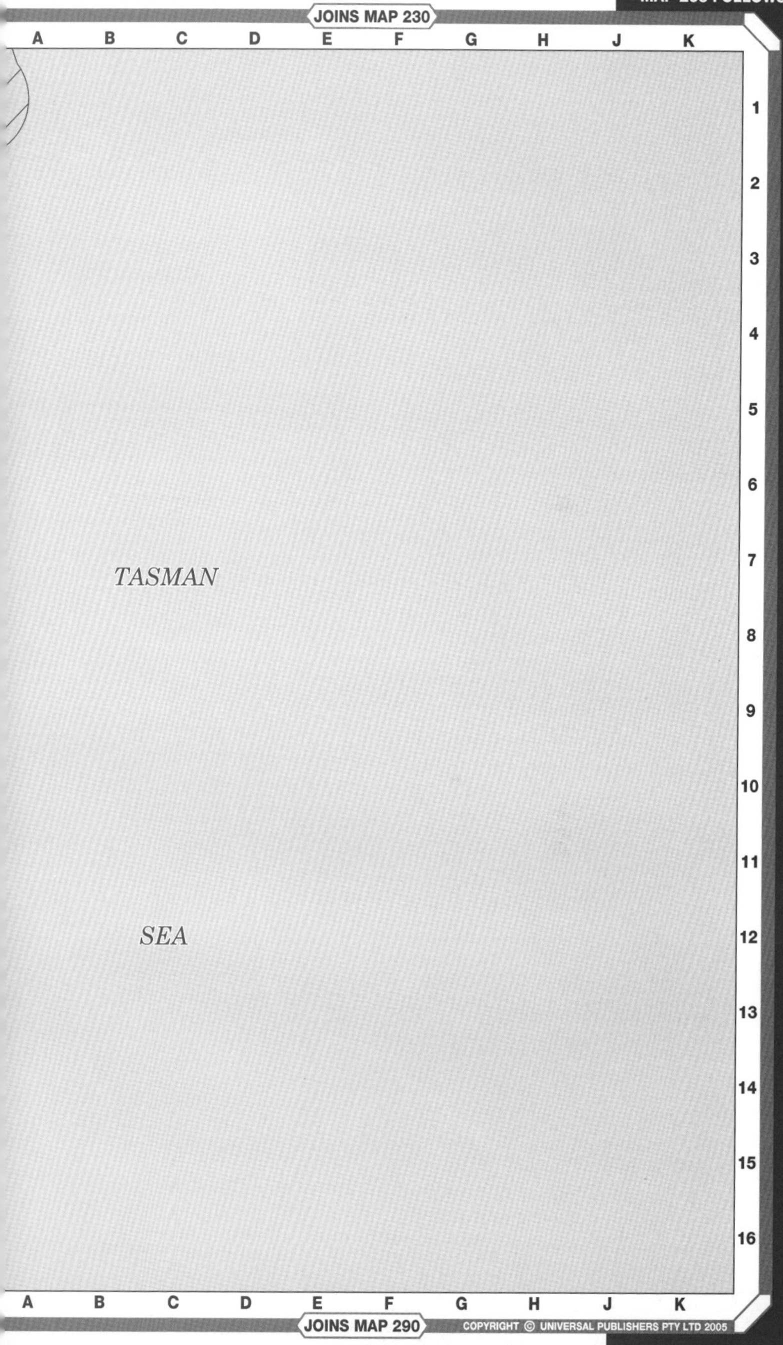

MAP 260
MAP 263 FOLLOWS

TASMAN

SEA

MAP 263
PREVIOUS MAP 260

JOINS MAP 233

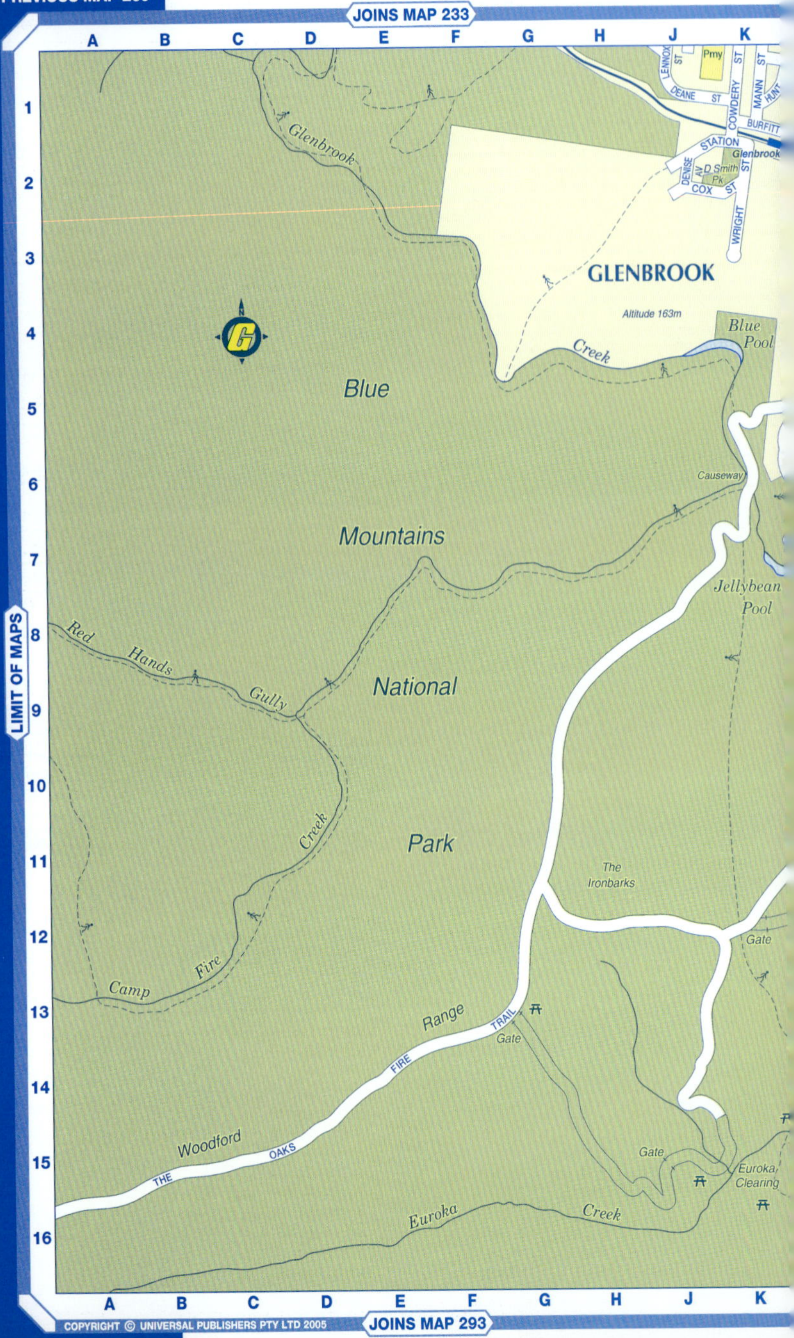

GLENBROOK
Altitude 163m

Blue Pool

Causeway

Jellybean Pool

Blue Mountains National Park

Glenbrook Creek

Red Hands Gully

Camp Fire Creek

The Ironbarks

Gate

Range Fire Trail

Gate

The Oaks Fire Trail

Woodford

Euroka Clearing

Euroka Creek

LIMIT OF MAPS

JOINS MAP 293

COPYRIGHT © UNIVERSAL PUBLISHERS PTY LTD 2005

MAP 264

JOINS MAP 235

234

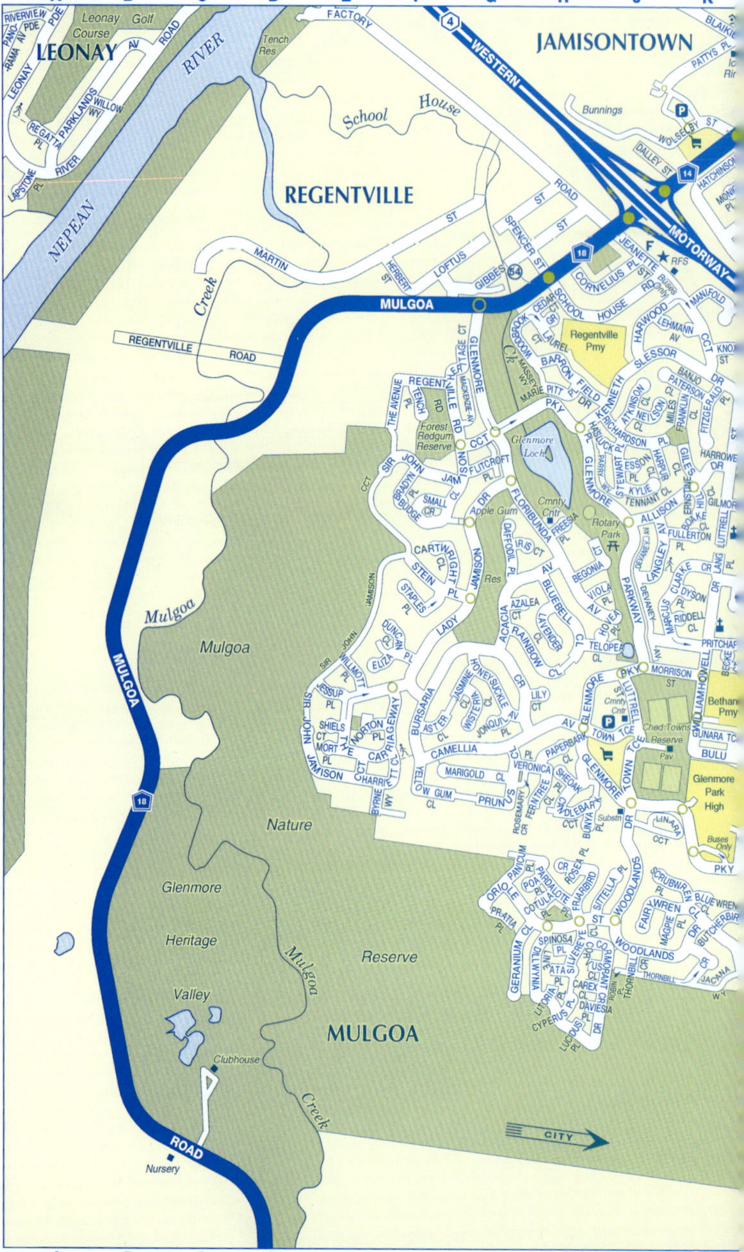

294

JOINS MAP 295

JOINS MAP 264

JOINS MAP 236
JOINS MAP 267
JOINS MAP 296
237
297
SOUTH PENRITH
GLENMORE PARK
Penrith Golf & Recreation Club
Mulgoa Nature Reserve
Defence Restricted Area
WESTERN MOTORWAY
THE NORTHERN ROAD
Penrith Trade Cntr
Jamison Park
Netball
Postal Cntr
Mot Reg & Veh Insp Stn
Robinson Park
Jamisontown Pmy
Southlands
Jim Scott Pk
Nhood Cntr
Jamison High
York Pmy
Eileen Cammack Soccer Fields
Southlands Oval
Pav
Glenmore Park Pmy
Caroline Chisholm College
Central Tree Res
Surveyors Creek Softball Facility
Cmnty Cntr
Primary
Clubhouse
Gate
Vics Produce & Pet Cntr
Truck Parking Bay
Windmill Park
Blue Hills Oval
Blue Hills Pk
Blue Hills Fbr
Wetland
Primary School Site
Jilondalee
Private Rd
Surveyors Creek
Public Res

MAP 267

JOINS MAP 237
236
A B C D E F G H J K
1 2 3 4 5 6 7 8 9 10 11 12 13 14 15 16
JOINS MAP 266
296
JOINS MAP 297
KINGSWOOD
SOUTH PENRITH
ORCHARD HILLS
SANDRA PL
STEVENSON ST
TIMGALEN AV
TREE TOPS
ASTON
OPAL CL
WESTMONT DR
AV
RD
SMITH ST
SMITH
ST
PARKER
ROAD
Kingswood South Pmy
TENT ST
PLUNKETT CR
Kingswood High
Peppermint Reserve
GIMLET CL
MANNING
MALLET
MARLOCK ST
CR
CCT
YATE PL
MACULATA PL
CL
ST
WALSH PL
PEPPERMINT
YEELANNA PL
AV
GUNGURRU ST
MORREL PL
GILJA GLN
DIANELLA PL
GRANDIS PL
CASUARINA
ELATA PL
KINGSCOTE PL
TALIA CL
MELALEUCA PL
ANGOPHORA
SALLEE GLN
CHINDOO CL
CADDENS
QUIGG PL
GAMENYA AV
BLUE GUM AV
GREENWAY
GLADSWOOD AV
SHEBA CR
MAZEPA AV
BURGESS RD
OAG
HOGAN PL
PIPER CL
CR
INVERNESS RD
BRAEMAR DR
HILL
LIGER
IRENE ST
KILKENNY RD
FLETCHER ST
CHRISTINE ST
CHESTERFIELD RD
DR
Pk
FRAGAR
TANIA AV
BRINGELLY
MAXWELL
Rotary Pk
COALLEE PL
SINGLE RD
DALLAS AV
NASH ST
OBERON CR
Prep Sch
SAMUEL
CROWLE RD
WARDELL
TRITON PL
MIRANDA ST
NOVA PL
DR
ASPEN ST
JOANNA ST
FOSTER DR
GLORIA PL
Reservoirs
NARDI TCE
WAKEFIELD PL
BLUE RIDGE PL
FRIEDMANN PL
BAYLEY RD
CORBIN AV
Reserve
Mary Mackillop Cath
HANBURY CL
CASTLE
Garden Barn
54
DAMIEN AV
HOYLE PL
LINDSAY CR
BAYLEY RD
TUSCANY GR
BROCKAMIN DR
LONGDON CL
SLAVIN ST
Telstra Exchange
GEMINI CL
WARDELL RD
TUKARA
KINMONT RD
TAMINA PL
FLAVEL ST
SHELSLEY PL
SHANDLIN PL
LINDRIDGE ST
MAMBLE PL
DIANA PL
POWYS CL
BRONSGROVE RD
KNIGHTON CL
BICKLEY GR
FROGMORE
Orchard Hills Pmy
PINDARI DR
TIMARU
PEBWORTH PL
Penrith Christian Cmnty
SIMEON RD
RD
KINGSWOOD
NORTHERN
4
50
WESTERN
LORD RD
RD
THE
9
Jeh Wit
HOMESTEAD
52
CROSS RD
RD
HOMESTEAD
Vics Produce & Pet Cntr
WENTWORTH
CAROLYN CH
Penrith Anglican College
KINGSWOOD
RD
WENTWORTH
THE CHASE
THE HAVEN
Reservoirs
Private Rd
Defence Restricted Area

MAP 268

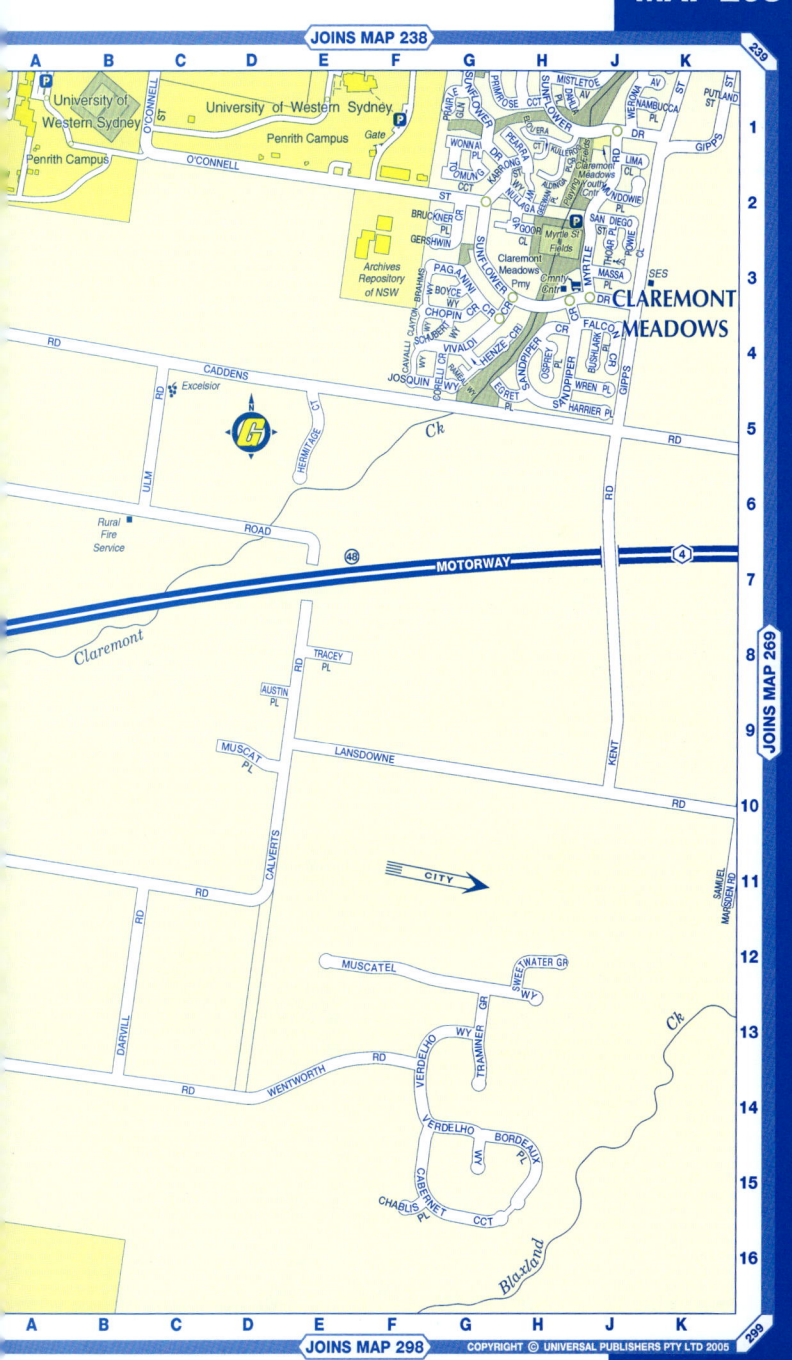

CLAREMONT MEADOWS

- University of Western Sydney, Penrith Campus
- Archives Repository of NSW
- Rural Fire Service
- Motorway (48) (4)
- Claremont Ck
- Blaxland Ck

Streets and places:
- O'Connell St
- Caddens Rd
- Hermitage Ct
- Ulm Rd
- Excelsior
- Bruckner Pl
- Gershwin
- Paganini Cr
- Chopin
- Schubert
- Brahms
- Canalli
- Clayton
- Corelli Cr
- Boyce Wy
- Josquin
- Vivaldi
- Henze Cr
- Sandpiper
- Osprey Pl
- Bushlark
- Wren Pl
- Egret Pl
- Harrier Pl
- Falco Cr
- Myrtle
- Sunflower
- Primrose Cct
- Mistletoe
- Werna
- Nambucca
- Putland
- Gipps
- Lima Cl
- Dowdie
- San Diego
- Massa
- SES
- Claremont Meadows Cmnty Cntr
- Myrtle Sh Fields
- Wonna Dr
- Karrong Wy
- Pebra
- Vera
- Kuleyo
- Nullaga
- Abrica
- Goor Cl
- Tracey Pl
- Austin Pl
- Muscat Pl
- Lansdowne
- Kent Rd
- Calverts Rd
- Darvill Rd
- Wentworth Rd
- Muscatel Wy
- Sweetwater Gr
- Traminer Gr
- Verdelho Wy
- Bordeaux Pl
- Cabernet Cct
- Chablis Pl
- Samuel Marsden Rd
- CITY →

JOINS MAP 238 (north)
JOINS MAP 239 (east)
JOINS MAP 269 (east)
JOINS MAP 298 (south)

COPYRIGHT © UNIVERSAL PUBLISHERS PTY LTD 2005

MAP 269

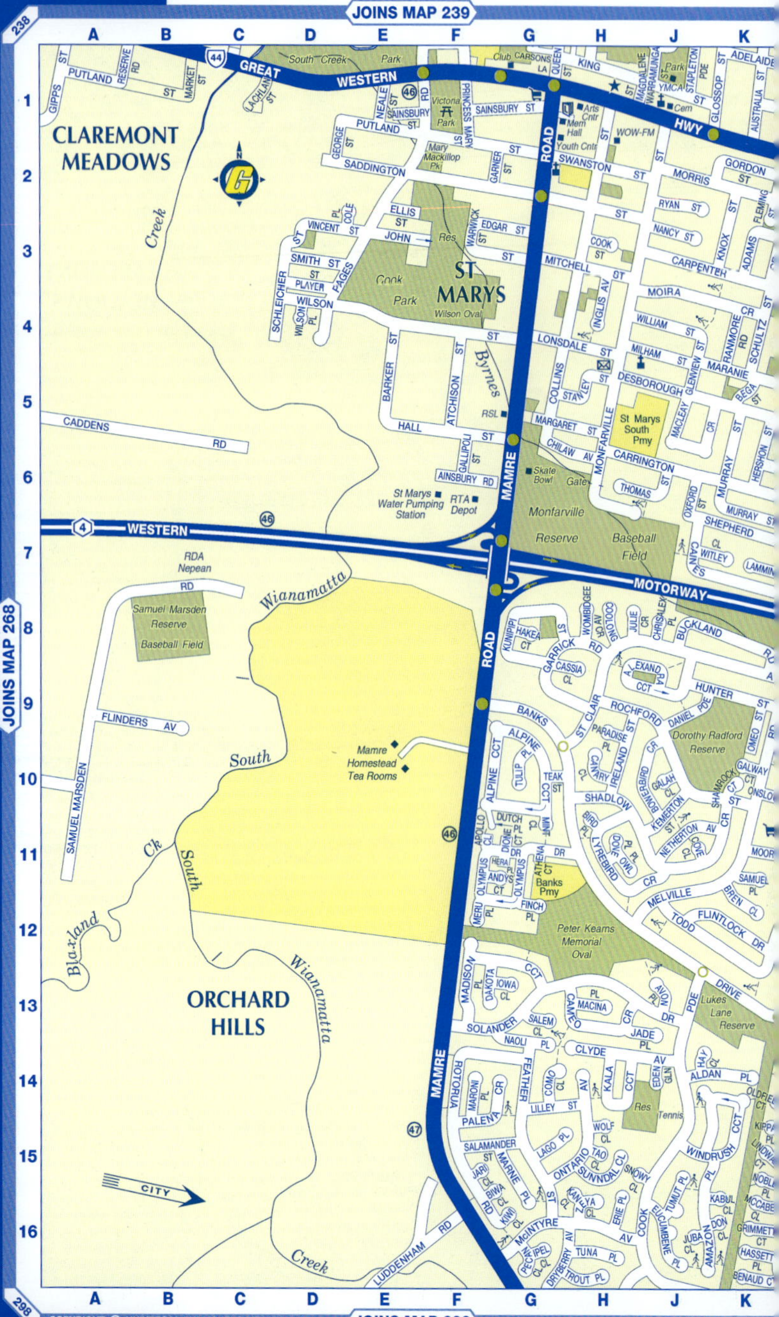

JOINS MAP 239
JOINS MAP 268
JOINS MAP 299
238
298
A B C D E F G H J K
1 2 3 4 5 6 7 8 9 10 11 12 13 14 15 16
CLAREMONT MEADOWS
ST MARYS
ORCHARD HILLS
GREAT WESTERN HWY
WESTERN MOTORWAY
MAMRE ROAD
QUEEN ST
South Creek Park
Victoria Park
Mary Mackillop Pk
Cook Park
Wilson Oval
Res
Arts Cntr
Mem Hall
Youth Cntr
WOW-FM
YMCA
Cem
Park
Club
CARSONS LA
RSL
Skate Bowl
Gate
Monfarville Reserve
Baseball Field
St Marys South Pmy
St Marys Water Pumping Station
RTA Depot
RDA Nepean
Samuel Marsden Reserve
Baseball Field
Mamre Homestead Tea Rooms
Dorothy Radford Reserve
Banks Pmy
Peter Kearns Memorial Oval
Lukes Lane Reserve
Tennis
Creek
South Creek
Wianamatta
South
Blaxland Ck
Byrnes
CADDENS RD
FLINDERS AV
SAMUEL MARSDEN
LUDDENHAM RD
PUTLAND ST
RESERVE RD
MARKET ST
GIPPS ST
LACHLAN ST
NEALE ST
SAINSBURY ST
PRINCESS MARY ST
GEORGE ST
SADDINGTON ST
GARNER ST
SWANSTON ST
KING ST
MAGDALENE ST
WARRAMUNGA ST
STAPLETON PDE
GLOSSOP ST
ADELAIDE ST
AUSTRALIA ST
GORDON ST
MORRIS ST
RYAN ST
NANCY ST
FLEMING ST
KNOX ST
ADAMS ST
CARPENTER ST
MOIRA
WILLIAM ST
MILHAM ST
GLENVIEW ST
RANMORE RD
SCHULTZ ST
MARANIE ST
DESBOROUGH RD
BEGA ST
VINCENT ST
COLE PL
ELLIS ST
JOHN ST
EDGAR ST
WARWICK ST
SMITH ST
FAGES
PLAYER
WILSON
SCHLEICHER ST
WILSON PL
MITCHELL ST
COOK ST
INGLIS AV
LONSDALE ST
COLLINS ST
STAWLEY ST
BARKER ST
ATCHISON ST
HALL ST
GALLIPOLI ST
AINSBURY RD
MARGARET ST
CHILAW AV
MONFARVILLE ST
CARRINGTON ST
THOMAS
MACLEAY CR
MURRAY ST
HERSHON ST
OXFORD ST
SHEPHERD ST
WITLEY CL
CAINES
LAMMING
KUNIPIPI
HAKEA CT
GARRICK RD
WOMBIDGEE AV
COOLONG CR
JULIE CR
CHRISALEX PL
BUCKLAND RD
CASSIA CL
ALEXANDRA CCT
HUNTER ST
ROCHFORD ST
DANIEL PDE
ST CLAIR
BANKS DR
ALPINE PL
ALPINE CCT
TULIP PL
TEAK ST
TEAK CCT
PARADISE PL
CANARY CL
IRELAND
BOWERBIRD
GALAH
SHADLOW
KEMERTON
SHAMROCK
GALWAY CT
OMEO ST
ONSLOW
NETHERTON AV
COVE CL
DUTCH
APOLLO CL
DIONE PL
MINI PL
HERA PL
ANDYS CT
OLYMPUS
ATHENA CT
BIRD PL
LYREBIRD
DOVE PL
OWL PL
MELVILLE CR
SAMUEL PL
BREN CL
MOORE
FINCH PL
MERU PL
TODD
FLINTLOCK DR
DRIVE
MADISON PL
DAKOTA
IOWA CL
AVON PL
MACINA
CAMEO CR
JADE PL
SALEM CL
SOLANDER
NAOLI PL
CLYDE AV
LUKES PDE
HAY CL
ALDAN PL
ROTORUA
MARONI PL
FEATHER ST
COMO CL
KALA CCT
EDEN GLN
LILLEY ST
PALENA
SALAMANDER ST
JARI CL
BIWA CL
KIWI CL
MARNE PL
LAGO PL
WOLF CL
TAO CL
ONTARIO
SUNNDAL CL
SNOWY CL
KANEYA
ZEYA CL
ERIE PL
COOK AV
EUCUMBENE PL
TUMUT PL
WINDRUSH CCT
KABUL CL
JUBA CL
DON CL
AMAZON
OLDFIELD CT
KIPPAX PL
LINDWALL CT
NOBLE PL
McCABE CL
GRIMMETT CT
HASSETT PL
BENAUD CL
McINTYRE
PECAN PL
IPEL CL
DRYBERRY AV
TUNA PL
TROUT PL
44
46
4
47
CITY

JOINS MAP 240
JOINS MAP 271
JOINS MAP 300
241
301
A
B
C
D
E
F
G
H
J
K
1
2
3
4
5
6
7
8
9
10
11
12
13
14
15
16
OXLEY PARK
MOUNT DRUITT
COLYTON
ST CLAIR
ERSKINE PARK
GREAT WESTERN HWY
WESTERN MOTORWAY
CANBERRA ST
MELBOURNE ST
PERTH ST
SYDNEY ST
DURHAM ST
VICTORIA ST
ROPES CREEK
Ropes Creek
MASON
FLINDERS ST
ALBERT ST
NORFOLK ST
BAYNES ST
Jeh Wit
Fbr
EDMONDSON AV
CUTLER AV
JACKA ST
Oxley Park Pmy
St Marys Gen Cem
RICE PL
BAYTON ST
CROFT PL
NOELA PL
WHITE
Jeh Wit
WOODLAND AV
Ridge Park
Cec Blinkhorn Mem Oval
CRAIG ST
Lucy Cobcroft Pk
WOODVIEW RD
GREGORY AV
RYAN PL
SAGE ST
Ten
Mt Druitt
Federation Forest
SIMPSON HILL RD
The Water Holes Res (Historic Precinct)
Park Remembrance Gardens
OPHIR GR
BALL ST
BROOKER ST
MUSCIO ST
DAY ST
WHITE PDE
TIDSWELL ST
CINDY PL
SHANE ST
Colyton High
GOLDIE
VALMA PL
FRANCIS ST
EDWIN ST
DALTON ST
KENT
SYKES PL
MALOUF ST
DAN
MARK AV
MORSHEAD ST
WOOTTEN ST
BLAMEY
FREEMAN ST
CROKER CR
LUTON PL
SUFFOLK PL
DOROTHY CR
STREET
PATRICIA ST
Roper Road Soccer Field
JOHN HINES AV
Creek
ROPER RD
Life Education Centre
Iron Bark Reserve
IRON BARK
SHEOAK
ORCHID
BLUEBERRY DR
CREEK ST
LEONARD PL
BENTLEY
CHELSEA PL
HUXLEY PL
LENNOX
ELEBANA ST
COOINDA
HENDREN PL
ALLAMBI ST
CORAL PEA CT
BRUSH
BOTTLE
TANDERRA ST
BURFORD
ALAM ST
GERRING ST
GILBERT ST
THRIFT ST
DARAYA
PARKIN
DOLLIN
NEVILLE ST
HOLMES ST
Substn
Bennett Road Pmy
ROAD
TULIPWOOD
TEA TREE WY
MILTON ST
MARSDEN
BALOG
BOWOOD
BERESFORD
BLATTMAN
DOWNES ST
RICHARD ST
REBECCA
NEAGLE ST
SHIELDS RD
HUDDLESTON ST
FRANKLIN PL
THORPE
JENSEN
PATERSON ST
TURNER ST
KIPLING
CARLISLE AV
LINDRIDGE PL
ARCADIA PL
ORCHARD
Potter Field
Shepherd St Park
SHEPHERD
ASTWOOD
BASS
BARR
NEVADA AV
MEEGAN PL
YARRABEE PL
ALBANY LA
WILLOUGHBY
GILMOUR
SCOTT RD
YOUNG ST
ROPER
CUMBERLAND PL
KENNELLY
HEWITT
GLENNIE ST
BRUNSWICK CL
MARTIN GR
HOUGH ST
DENNIS ST
HARWELL PL
ANDREW
THOMPSON
SWALES PL
DANUBE
OLLIVER
NILE PL
CLAIR
MAURICE ST
MACARTHUR
FRANCIS GREENWAY
CHATEAU
BALLARAT
RHINE
HART PL
CHARLTON PL
SUMMER HILL PL
BENNETT
NEWTIMBER
TALLWOOD PL
CHATSWORTH
UNDERWOOD RD
MILL PL
ROYAL PL
NALONG ST
CCT
EDDY ST
ASHWICK
SALFORD ST
HENLEY GR
CCT
FULLER PL
SEINE
CTRA
JAPURA PL
HARTWELL CT
LOIRE
AUGUSTA
CADELL GLN
JORGENSEN
CUNNINGHAM WY
MULLIGAN CL
GOSSE CT
REDFERN GLN
GLN
TWEED PL
MUSTANG
WILLS
FARMER
LYONS AV
Mark Leece Sporting Complex
ARCHITECTS
EDMUND
BLACKETT
JOHN
SULMAN
UTZON CT
BURLEY
GRIFFIN
MORTIMER LEWIS
JAMES BARNETT
DAINTREE
BENNETT
EXPLORERS
BARRALLIER
ARCHER
PHAR LAP
PINTO PL
CHATRES
CHARDONNAY RD
HICKORY
SANDALWOOD
DENVER
KALINDI
KALAMBO
COLUMBUS
WARRENTON ST
LAURA PL
RALEIGH
SEATLE CL
GLN
MINER
SHRIKE GLN
SWIFT GLN
SPOONBILL ST
WARBLER
BLIGH CT
ENDEAVOUR
MENZIES
CLEARY
St Clair High
St Clair Pmy
BOTANY
Motor Reg
Cmnty Health Cntr
BAROSSA
PETER PAN
TULLOCH
BROLGA
WOODNOTE
REDDINGTON AV
DIAMANTINA CL
Clairgate Pmy
MERINO
GLENROWAN
MYNAH CL
LEICESTER
SHEARER ST
FLEECE CL
PASADENA PL
ANCHORAGE
DR
ROAD
KESTREL
JERSEY
HARVEY
DOBELL
PEPPIN CL
TIMESWEEP
NEWMOON
AUTUMNLEAF
STARLIGHT
MORNINGBIRD
MCLAREN
IBIS PL
KINGFISHER
LORIKEET
BOSTON
NEWARK
COLORADO
TOPEKA
OGDEN CL
LEXINGTON
SWALLOW CR
HONEYEATER
CROWBILL PL
PELICAN
WAGTAIL
WHISTLER
BANKS
Saunders Pav
Park Athletics
EVENROW
RAINBOW
AFTERNOON
MIDWINTER
SNOWDRIFT
EVENSTAR
SUNRAY
MOONBEAM
BELLEDALE CL
COONAWARRA
HASCOMBE WY
MUDGEE
LIBERATOR
CONCORDE
ARUNDEL PARK
KELMSCOTT WY
LAURISTON
GULL PL
SKYLARK
WHIPBIRD
KOOKABURRA
COOT PL
PLOVER
HERON
ANNUAL LA
HOURGLASS GLN
GRUMMAN
JAVELIN
BLENHEIM
FRAMPTON AV
ASHFORD
ARIES
BITTERN
CALAIS
PACIFIC
COCKATOO
ZODIAC PL
FANTAIL
UTAH PL
EURABBIE GLN
MOONAH
BRADMAN
GRANDSTAND
GREVILLEA
HIBISCUS
MIMOSA
OTHELLO PL
FAUST
NIGHTMIST
LOCKHEED
COMET
HALIFAX
NOMAD
DILGA
BARCOO
FORD
LIMA
PHOENIX
MINTO
PEARL CL
CCT
MCCARTNEY
BLACKWELL
NAPUNYAH
COMBOYNE
BELBOWRIE
BERRIGAN
NORA
TONGA
COOWARRA
SHAKESPEARE
CAESAR
MACBETH
LEAR
BARD
PYRAMUS
CARIBOU
BOEING
OMEGA
ERSKINE PARK RD
FAUNA
HAWK
DORADO
MACKILLOP PL
BURUDA
Substn
PEPPERTREE
BUSHLAND
STRICKLAND
GREBE
SWALLOW DR
KAWANA
NEEMAN
CAPELLA
Cmnty Hall
N'hood Cntr
James Erskine Pmy
Peppertree Reserve
SENNAR RD
COBAR
44
4
42

MAP 271

JOINS MAP 241

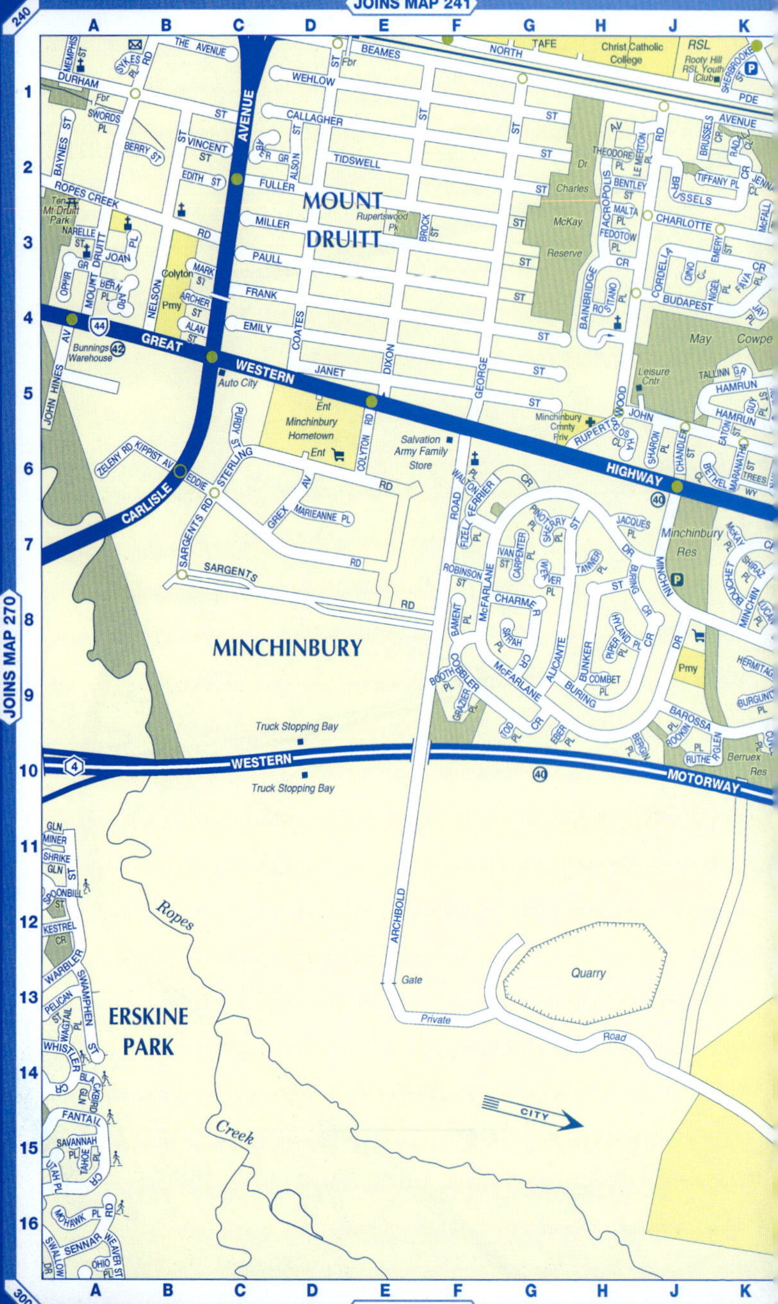

JOINS MAP 270

JOINS MAP 301

JOINS MAP 242

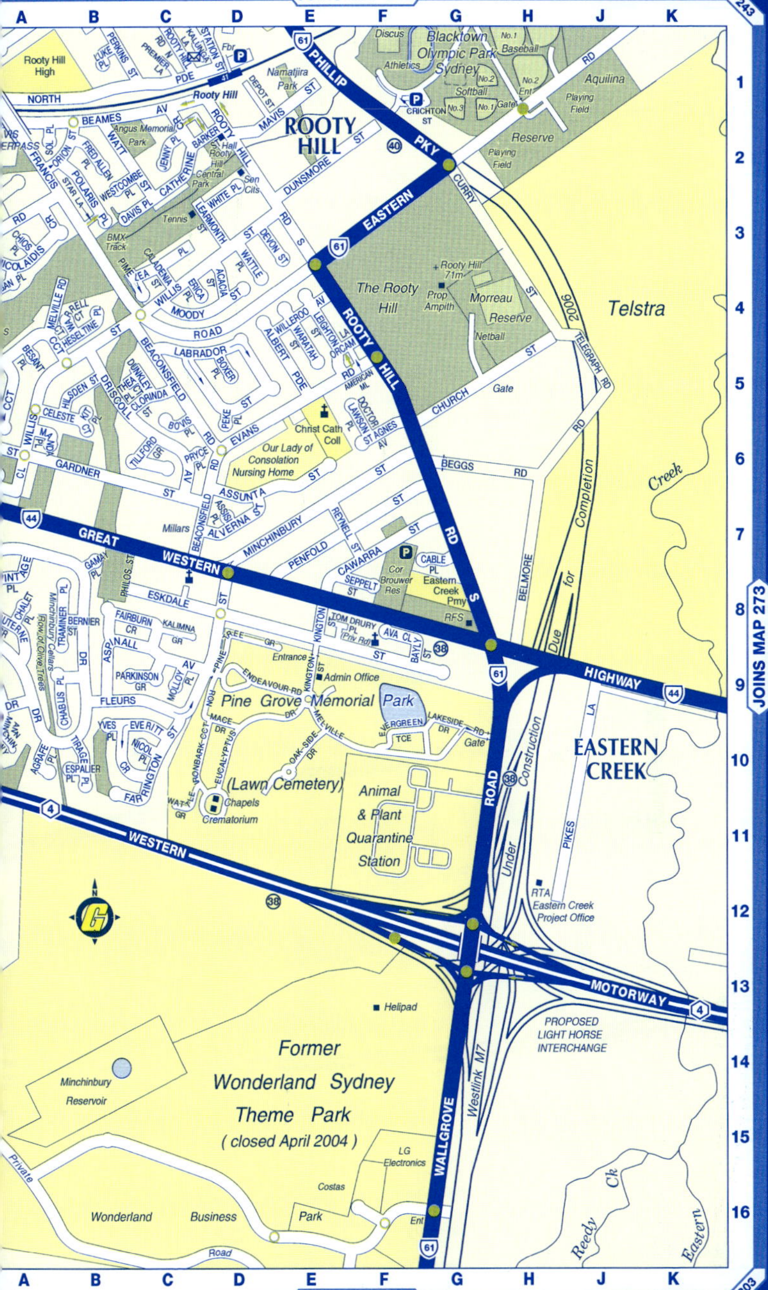

JOINS MAP 273

JOINS MAP 302

MAP 273

JOINS MAP 243
JOINS MAP 272
JOINS MAP 303
242
302
A B C D E F G H J K
1 2 3 4 5 6 7 8 9 10 11 12 13 14 15 16
DOONSIDE
Telstra
CITY
Eastern
Bungarribee
Creek
ARNDELL PARK
EASTERN CREEK
HUNTINGWOOD
GREAT WESTERN HIGHWAY
WESTERN
44
4
36
DOONSIDE RD
BIRDWOOD
BUNGARRIBEE
ALLENBY
MONASH
TARA
RD
SYLVIA
ROAD
SEABROOK
BUNNING PL
SULMAN PL
WINSTON
DENIS
ASHTON PL
ROSENTHAL
SHORTLAND PL
BALMAIN PL
BOWES PL
PEPLOW PL
ALT PL
IRVING WY
WHITTON PL
BALLARD PL
BONNEY PL
DE FRIES PL
KELSALL ST
GARBETT PL
HINKLER PL
ULM PL
WIRRAWAY PL
BRIGGS PL
DOUGLAS
ANDREW LLOYD DR
BUCKLE PL
FLEMMING GR
BRUXNER PL
BRADFIELD
TALLAWONG AV
BURRELL
WILGA ST
CANSDALE ST
HUNTER ST
PEMBROKE
LLOYD
KASTELAN
MEELA ST
MALONEY
BRADDON
Weeron Pk
Tallawong Oval
School Site
DELLIT PL
ROWE PL
BARNETT PL
RAHT
WAUGH
BIBBALONG LA
SAUVAGE
MORONEY CL
DANIELA PL
DE CASTELLA DR
KIEREN
SHELLEY CR
HAYLEY GR
WATTS GR
VAN BENTUM DR
BLATTMAN CL
ONDIEKI CT
HACKETT WY
GOULD
THORPE WY
DUNN WY
KUM WY
HUEGILL WY
Tyndale Christian
WALLABY CL
ALIBERTI
MARIKO PL
JOHN BOY PL
AYRTON ST
ALEXANDER PDE
KENJI PL
TEAL PL
IRONBARK
WRIGHTLAND PL
CONTAPLAS ST
HOLBECHE
PRIMA PL
PENELOPE CR
McCORMACK ST
LIDCO ST
NOMA PL
VANGELI ST
SQUILL PL
SMOOTHY PL
HOADLEY PL
MURTHA ST
Dog Kennel Res
Beaurepaires
DR
LIBERTY RD
REXROTH PL
HUNTINGWOOD DR
ARNOTTS PL
Gate
Arnotts
Integral Energy
HEALEY
DISTILLERS PL
FORD ST
CCT
DECKER PL
WOODS
RUDDERS LA
BRABHAM
FERRERS
RD
ARDC
Gate 1
Gate 2
Helipad
Eastern Creek International Raceway
Service Centre
Eastern Creek International Karting Raceway
Res

JOINS MAP 244

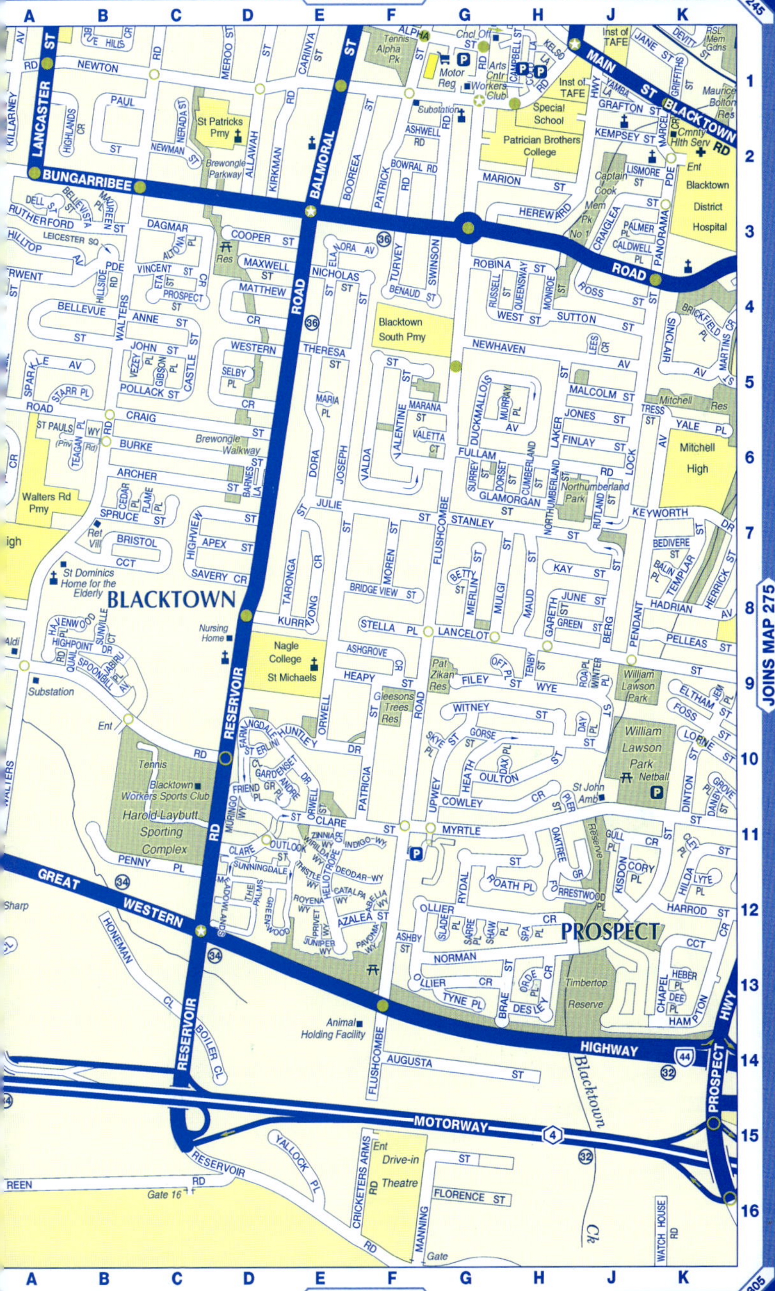

JOINS MAP 275

JOINS MAP 304

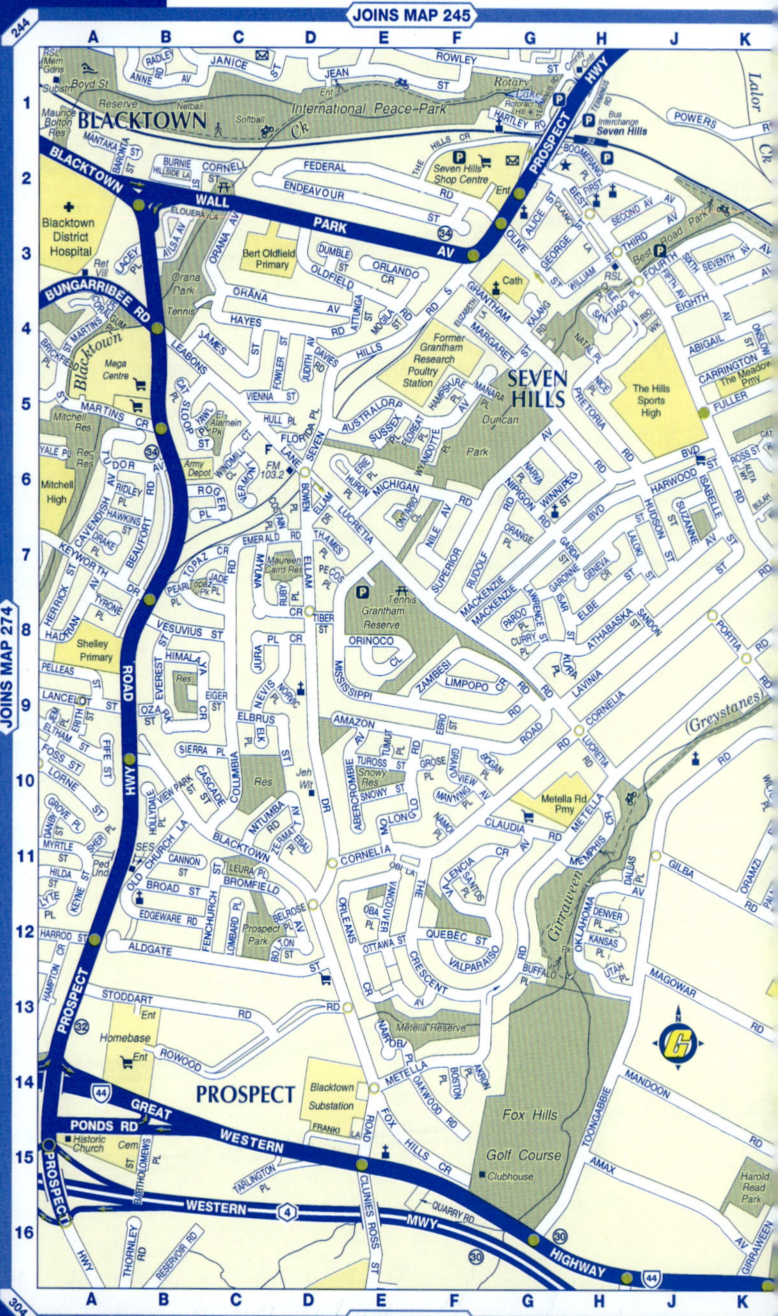

JOINS MAP 305

JOINS MAP 246
247

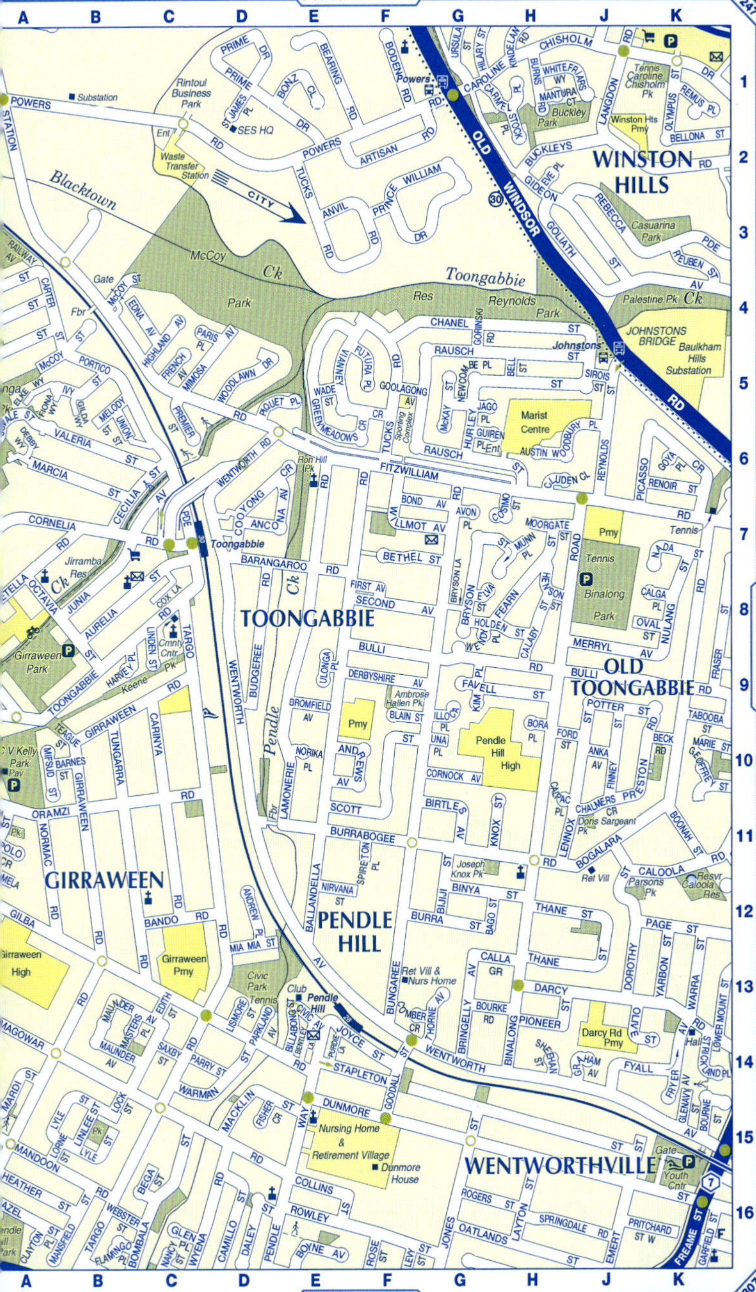

JOINS MAP 277
JOINS MAP 306
307

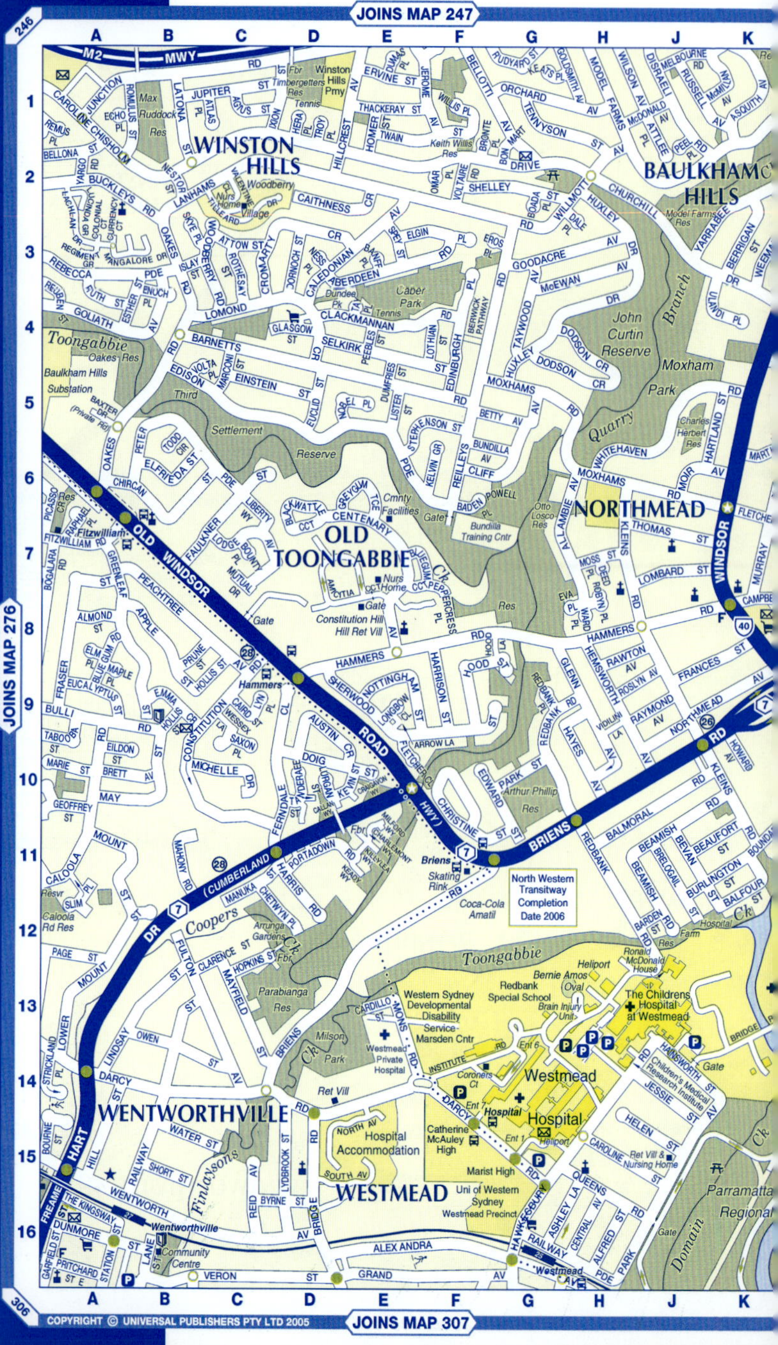
JOINS MAP 247
JOINS MAP 276
JOINS MAP 307
246
306
A
B
C
D
E
F
G
H
J
K
1
2
3
4
5
6
7
8
9
10
11
12
13
14
15
16
M2 MWY
WINSTON HILLS
BAULKHAM HILLS
NORTHMEAD
OLD TOONGABBIE
WENTWORTHVILLE
WESTMEAD
Winston Hills Pmy
Max Ruddock Res
Woodberry Nurs Home Village
Keith Willis Res
Caber Park
Dundee Pk
John Curtin Reserve
Moxham Park
Quarry
Charles Herbert Res
Toongabbie
Oakes Res
Baulkham Hills Substation
Third Settlement Reserve
Cmnty Facilities
Bundilla Training Cntr
Otto Losco Res
Nurs Home
Constitution Hill Hill Ret Vill
Hammers
OLD WINDSOR ROAD
WINDSOR
CUMBERLAND HWY
BRIENS RD
NORTHMEAD RD
Arthur Phillip Res
Briens Skating Rink
Coca-Cola Amatil
North Western Transitway Completion Date 2006
Coopers Ck
Arrunga Gardens
Parabianga Res
Milson Park
Westmead Private Hospital
Western Sydney Developmental Disability Service-Marsden Cntr
Redbank Special School
Bernie Amos Oval
Heliport
Ronald McDonald House
The Childrens Hospital at Westmead
Brain Injury Unit
Children's Medical Research Institute
Westmead Hospital
Hospital Accommodation
Catherine McAuley High
Marist High
Uni of Western Sydney Westmead Precinct
Ret Vill
Ret Vill & Nursing Home
Caloola Rd Res
Fitzwilliam
Finlaysons
Wentworthville
Community Centre
Westmead
Parramatta Regional
Domain
HART DR
DARCY RD
HAWKESBURY RD
ALEXANDRA AV
GRAND AV
VERON ST
WENTWORTH
THE KINGSWAY
DUNMORE ST
HAMMERS RD
MOXHAMS RD
CHURCHILL DR
CAITHNESS CR
ABERDEEN
CLACKMANNAN
BARNETTS RD
EINSTEIN ST
GOODACRE AV
DODSON CR
SHELLEY
ORCHARD RD
TENNYSON
JUPITER ST
ERVINE ST
THACKERAY ST
COPYRIGHT © UNIVERSAL PUBLISHERS PTY LTD 2005

JOINS MAP 248

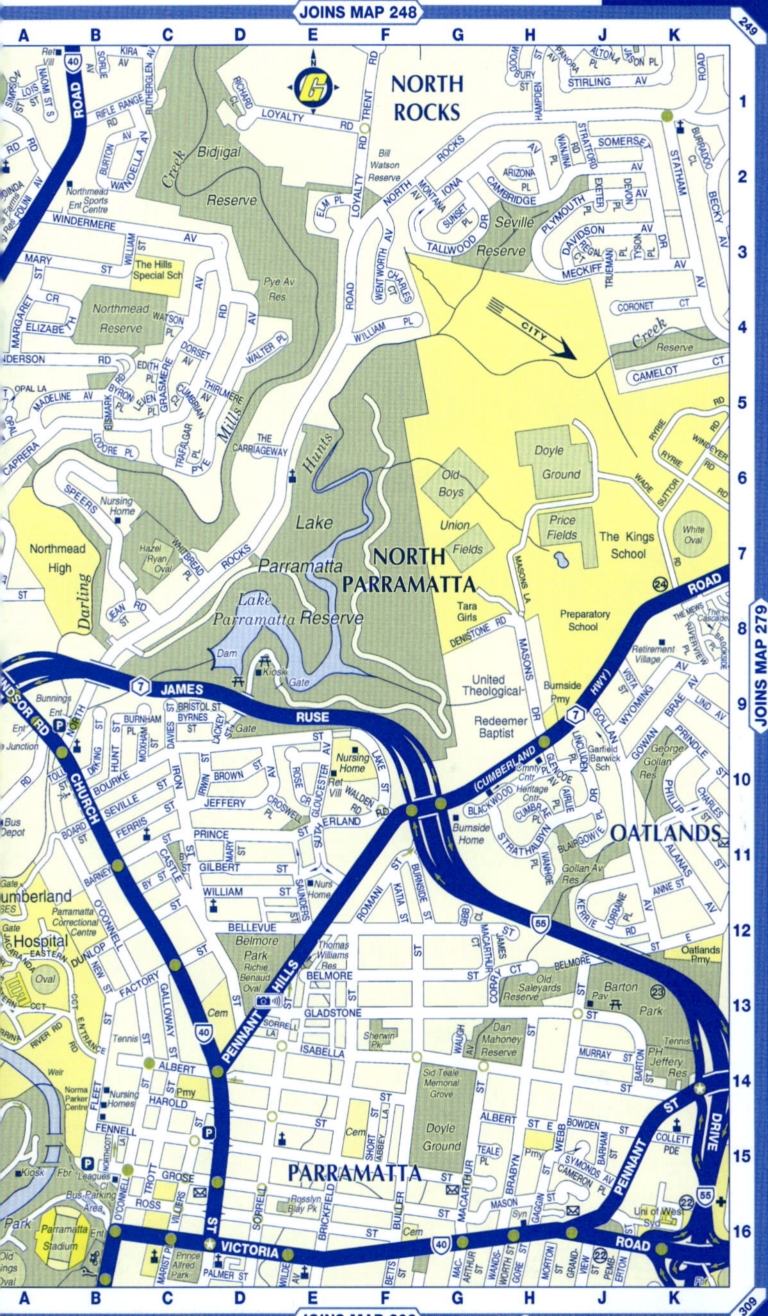

JOINS MAP 308

MAP 279

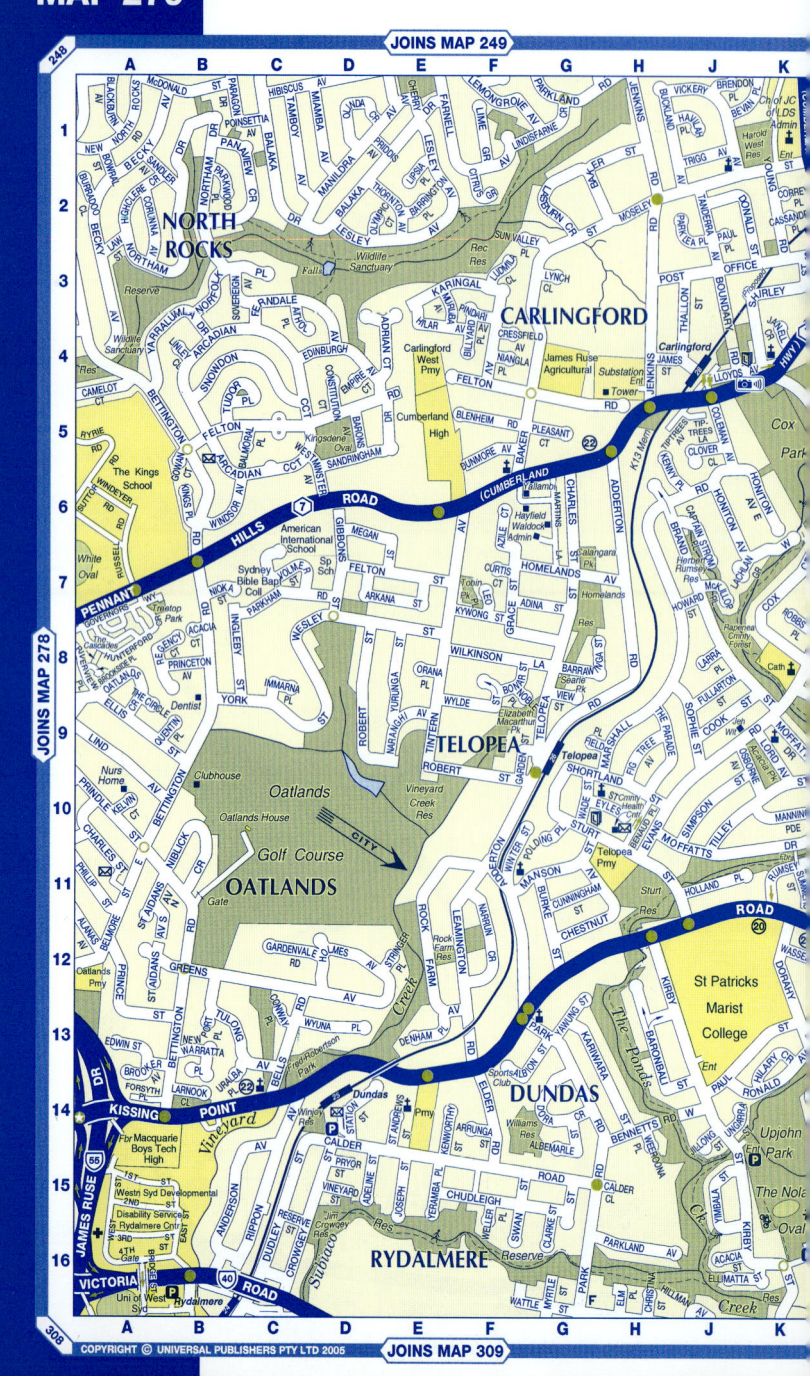

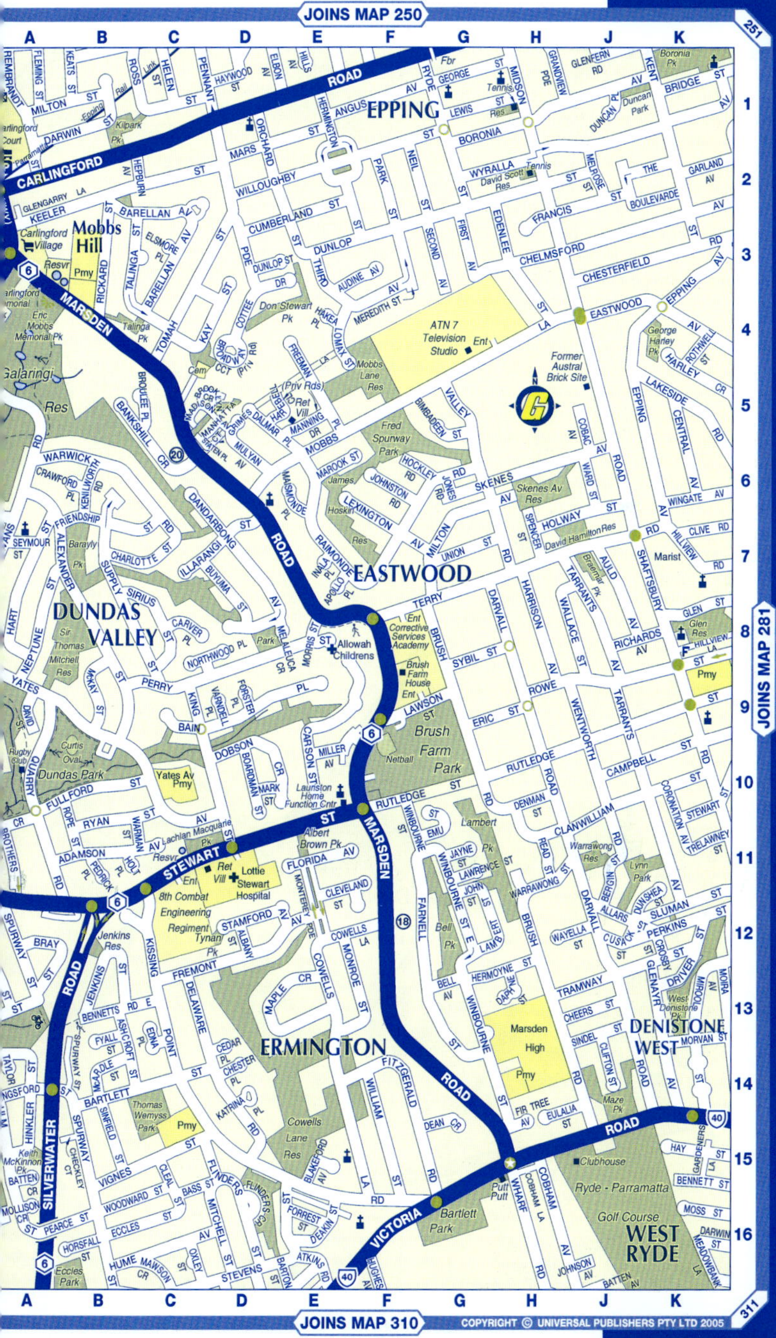
JOINS MAP 250
JOINS MAP 281
JOINS MAP 310
251
311
A B C D E F G H J K
1 2 3 4 5 6 7 8 9 10 11 12 13 14 15 16
EPPING
EASTWOOD
DUNDAS VALLEY
ERMINGTON
DENISTONE WEST
WEST RYDE
Mobbs Hill
CARLINGFORD ROAD
MARSDEN ROAD
STEWART ST
VICTORIA ROAD
SILVERWATER ROAD
ATN 7 Television Studio
Former Austral Brick Site
Carlingford Village
Don Stewart Pk
Fred Spurway Park
Mobbs Lane Res
Eric Mobbs Memorial Pk
Galaringi Res
Sir Thomas Mitchell Res
Dundas Park
Curtis Oval
Rugby Club
Yates Av Pmy
Lachlan Macquarie Pk
Albert Brown Pk
Lottie Stewart Hospital
8th Combat Engineering Regiment
Tynan Pk
Jenkins Res
Allowah Childrens
Ent Corrective Services Academy
Brush Farm House
Brush Farm Park
Netball
Laurieston Home Function Cntr
Lambert Pk
Bell Pk
Marsden High
Pmy
Warrawong Res
Lynn Park
West Denistone Pk
Maze Pk
Ryde - Parramatta Golf Course
Clubhouse
Bartlett Park
Putt Putt
Cowells Lane Res
Thomas Wemyss Park
Keith McKinnon Pk
Eccles Park
Skenes Av Res
David Hamilton Res
Braemar Pk
Marist
Glen Res
George Harley Pk
Duncan Park
Boronia Pk
David Scott Res
Tennis
Kilpark Pk
Talinga Pk
Barayly Pk
James Hoskin Res
Ret Vill
COPYRIGHT © UNIVERSAL PUBLISHERS PTY LTD 2005

MAP 281

JOINS MAP 252
JOINS MAP 283
JOINS MAP 312
253
313
A B C D E F G H J K
1 2 3 4 5 6 7 8 9 10 11 12 13 14 15 16
Macquarie University
Aust Film TV & Radio School
Macquarie Centre
Cinemas
NRMA
Ice Skating Rink
Motor Reg
Macquarie University Railway Station (Underground) (Under Constr)
Morling College
Willandra Ret Vill
Ret Vill
Nursing Home
Dunholm Res
Fontenoy Park
Alston Res
Yurrah Res
Elouera Res
Macquarie Corporate Park
MACQUARIE PARK
Talavera Business Park
Macquarie Park Railway Station (Underground) (Under Constr)
Waterloo Business Park
Eden Pk Centre
North Ryde Link Business Park
Aust Radio Network
Nat Standards Comm
Centrecourt Business Park
Wilga Park
Dunbar Park
The Ranch
Booth Res
Ped O'pass
Datacom
Austrans
Substn
Hockey Field
Macquarie Uni Block E Language Studies
Alto Parts
Kent Road Pmy
ELS Hall Park
Shrimptons Ck
Greenwood Park
Tindarra Res
Holt Pk
Flinders Pk
Kathleen Res
Museum
Cmnty Cntr
Holy Spirit Cath
North Ryde Pmy
NORTH RYDE
North Ryde Golf Course
Clubhouse
Santa Rosa Park
Education Dept
Spastic Cntr
Yamble Reserve
RYDE
Booral Res
Byron Pk
Resvr
North Ryde Common
Truscott St Pmy
Macquarie Hospital
Admin
Arndell Spec Sch
Wallumatta Nature Reserve
Pryor Park
Gannan Park
Nerang Pk
Ryde East Pmy
Kulgoa Res
Adventure Park
Jones St Res
Brigade Pk
Minga Res
John Miller Park
Pidding Park
Tyrell Pk
Field of Mars Cemetery
Field of Mars Reserve
Strangers Ck
EPPING ROAD
LANE COVE ROAD
M2 MWY
Freeway
CITY
TALAVERA RD
WATERLOO RD
KHARTOUM RD
LYON PARK RD
GIFFNOCK AV
COOLINGA ST
BYFIELD ST
HERRING RD
WINDSOR DR
LACHLAN AV
COTTONWOOD CR
FONTENOY RD
TASMAN PL
LEISURE CL
TUCKWELL PL
PAUL ST
DAVID AV
PARKLANDS AV
BESWICK AV
TREVITT RD
MILROY AV
WILSON ST
MICHAEL ST
KENT RD
SCOTT ST
BOOTH ST
DORA ST
LUCINDA AV
PATRICIA ST
DOROTHY ST
EASTVIEW RD
NORTHCOTT ST
CHRISTINE AV
ZOLA AV
WARREN AV
FAWCETT ST
SANTA ROSA AV
SMALLS RD
COSIMO ST
AEOLUS AV
WOLGER RD
KUPPA AV
HANCOTT ST
TUNKS ST
QUARRY RD
BRUCE ST
MACLEAY ST
STUART ST
KEPPEL RD
ELIZABETH ST
FISHER AV
SALERWONG PL
WICKS RD
NUMA RD
BERRIPA CL
STROUD ST
META ST
NERANG ST
MELDRUM ST
BYGRAVE ST
CALLAGHAN ST
MILNE ST
BADAJOZ RD
JOHN MILLER ST
BIRD ST
CRESSY RD
KELLAWAY ST
MONCRIEFF DR
MELBA DR
ELLIOTT AV
FOX RD
HARFORD ST
JOPLING ST
BLENHEIM RD
TOBRUK RD
KOKODA ST
CUTLER PDE
CHAUVEL ST
SCHUMACK ST
BLAMEY ST
EDMONDSON ST
HENDRY PDE
ROWELL ST
TRUSCOTT ST
FARRINGTON ST
RYRIE ST
BETTY ST
COLLINS ST
CHISHOLM ST
MORSHEAD ST
MARSHALL ST
HEARNSHAW ST
STURDEE ST
BERRYMAN ST
AVON RD
PAMELA ST
KATHLEEN ST
AMELIA ST
MARILYN ST
FOLKARD ST
COONEY RD
BEATRICE ST
LORNA ST
ALLENGROVE CR
ARKARD ST
BARR ST
CAM ST
SPOONER PL
MANNING RD
THE DRIVE
NORTON
THE CRESENT
FIRST AV
SECOND AV
THIRD AV
NORFOLK RD
SHERWOOD (Priv Rd)
WAL
MYRA AV
BUFFALO RD
SEMPLE ST
WOODBINE ST
GREENE AV
CAMERON CR
GARDENER AV
KELLS RD
JONES AV
BAMBI ST
DOBSON CR
TONI ST
ADAM ST
EILEEN ST
MARTIN CR
BOYCE ST
McCauley Pk
BUNA CT
MINGA ST
DWYER ST
BURKE ST
POOLEY ST
NIARA ST
PIDDING RD
MALVINA ST
AITCHANDAR RD
IVY ST
BIDGEE RD
NARBAREE RD
ABAROO RD
MARMOO ST
WATT AV
BAVIN AV
PRATTEN AV
SMITH RD
CURZON ST
POPE ST
ISABEL ST
PRICE ST
READFORD PL
BETOLA ST
BYRON AV
KEATS AV
GOULDING RD
LAVARACK ST
OLIVIERI PL
ARTHUR ST
EDEN ST
BOND AV
DEMPSEY ST
TWIN RD
FLINDERS RD
BRENDON ST
CAVE AV
COOK ST
MAVIS ST
ADA AV
FORD ST
TULIP ST
JULIE ST
BURNS RD
RUSE ST
EDITH ST
BRIDGE RD
BRIAN ST
NEVILLE ST
BERTRAND CL
ALAN BOND PL
WARING ST
KATOA CL
BIARA CL
ZANCO RD
TREHARNE CL
LEXCEN PL
WILDING ST
WINSTON AV
COOPER ST
BLUNDELL ST
DARCY RD
LEONARD PL
ADELPHI RD
NOLA ST
FITZPATRICK AV
BEVERLEY CR
CARMEN ST
DAN AV
HOLT AV
McGREGOR ST
NAPIER CR
PINE ST
SUNHILL PL
BARINGA RD
GIBB ST
ORANA ST
PINDARI ST
COVE
NTH
WHITESIDE ST
KITTYS

JOINS MAP 253
JOINS MAP 282
JOINS MAP 313
252
312
KILLARA
West Lindfield
CSIRO
National Measurement Laboratory
MACQUARIE PARK
Macquarie Park Cemetery and Crematorium
Lane Cove River National Park
Lane Cove National Park
NORTH RYDE
CHATSWOOD WEST
EAST RYDE
LANE COVE WEST
Universal Publishers
Eden Pk Centre
Eden Gardens
Tunks Farm National Park
Tuckwell Park
De Burghs Bridge
Toll Booth
Killara Golf Course
Cmnty Cntr
Jinkers Green
St Crispens Green
Alberts Bush
Queen Elizabeth Res
Fiddens Wharf Oval
Recreation Reserve
Rec Res
Nat Park
Naamaroo Conference Centre
Porters Ck Cncl Depot
Waste Transfer Stn
Kywung Res
Delhi Road Railway Station Underground (Under Constr.)
Global Television Studios
Microsoft
Riverside Corporate Pk
Binary Centre
Precinct Corp Cntr
Works Depot
Zoo
Kiosk
Northern Suburbs Memorial Gardens Crematorium
Chatswood War Memorial Athletic Field
Mowbray Park
Mowbray Pmy
Tennis
Yinnell Res
Nundah Res
Nth Ryde Park
Banool Res
RSL
Gwandalan Res
Martin Res
Magdala Park
Boobajool Res
Pryor Park
Portius Park
Brereton Park
Lane Cove National Park
Lane Cove Substn
Lane Cove Industrial Estate
Lane Cove West Pmy
Batten
Gate Closed 7 - 9 am Mon-Fri
Tunnel Completion date 2007
Stringybark
CITY
EPPING RD
DELHI RD
M2 MWY
LANE COVE RD
PITTWATER RD
LUCKNOW
FULLERS BR
Ulmarra Pk
Blenheim Park
Tennis World
Myall Res
Bundara Res

JOINS MAP 254
JOINS MAP 285
JOINS MAP 314
255
315
A B C D E F G H J K
1 2 3 4 5 6 7 8 9 10 11 12 13 14 15 16
LINDFIELD
ROSEVILLE
CHATSWOOD
LANE COVE NORTH
ARTARMON
PACIFIC HWY
MILLWOOD AV
FULLERS RD
BOUNDARY ST
MOWBRAY RD
CENTENNIAL (Under Construction) ROAD
Lindfield
Roseville
Chatswood
Artarmon
Lindfield Primary
Two Turners Res
Edenborough Park
Film Australia
Greenhalgh Theatre
University of Technology Sydney (Kuring-gai Campus)
Lane Cove National Park
Blue Gum Ck
Sugarbag Ck
Rec Res
Loyal Henry Park
Blue Gum Park
Hotham Street Res
C'wealth Acoustic Laboratories & Ultrasonic Inst.
O.H. Reid Memorial Park
Swaines Ck
Chatswood Golf Course
Clubhouse
Cmnty Coll
Chatswood High
Fullers Rd Res
Ferndale Park
Campbell Park
Coolaroo Park
Dalrymple Park
Turrumbarra Park
Stringybark Res
Helen St Res
Roseville Park
Roseville Coll
Bancroft Pk Cmnty Art Cntr
Little Digger Pk
Beauchamp Park
Chatswood Chase
Chatswood Park
Parkland
Artarmon Day Care Cntr
Thompson Pk
Nursing Home
Ret Vill
Sen Cits
Cinema
RSL
Lexus
Day Cinema
Club
Cncl Off
Fbr
TV Tower
Tennis
Construction

JOINS MAP 255

254

A B C D E F G H J K

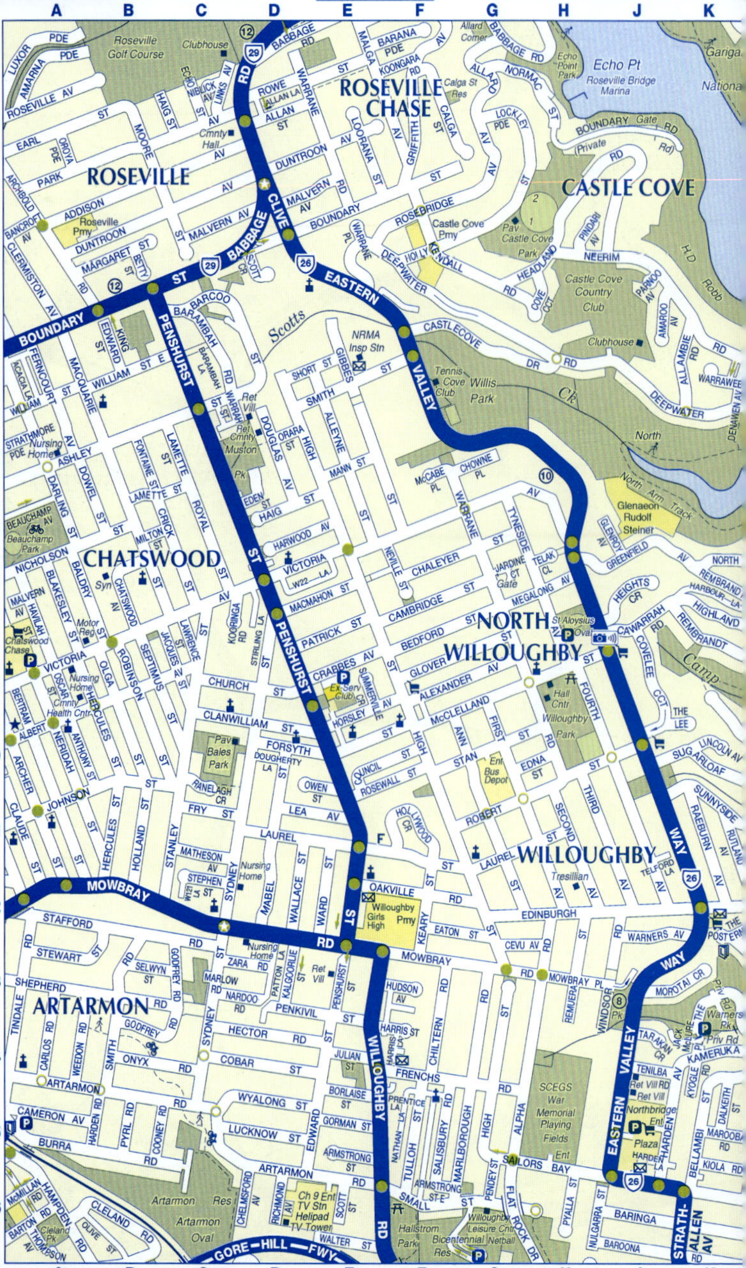

1 2 3 4 5 6 7 8 9 10 11 12 13 14 15 16

JOINS MAP 284

314

JOINS MAP 315

JOINS MAP 256
JOINS MAP 287
JOINS MAP 316
257
317
A B C D E F G H J K
1 2 3 4 5 6 7 8 9 10 11 12 13 14 15 16
KILLARNEY HEIGHTS
Garigal National Park
Prohibited Area
Bantry Bay
Garigal
Timber Getters Track
National
Old Bullock Track
The Bluff
Park
Seaforth Oval
View Walking Track
Wakehurst Golf Course
Reservoirs
Bantry Res
WAKEHURST PARKWAY
Killarney Pt
Flat Rock Walking Track
Magazine Track
Flat Rock Beach
MIDDLE HARBOUR
Yeoland Pt
Explosives Reserve
HC Press Pk
CITY
Reserve
North Arm Track
SEAFORTH
Castle Cove
Sugarloaf Bay
Swimming Enclosure
Pickering Pt
Dalwood Home
Harold Reid Reserve
The Sugarloaf
MIDDLE COVE
Foreshore Track
Sugarloaf Pt
Crag Cove
CASTLECRAG
Edinburgh Rd Res
Sugarloaf Ck
Sangrado Pool
Sangrado Pk
Powder Hulk Bay
Seaforth Sailing Club
MIDDLE
Tower Res
Linden Res
Embrasure Res
Castle Haven Res
Corteille Res
Casement Res
Turrett Res
Keep Res
Sailors Bay Park
Mowbray Pt
Sailors Bay
Seaforth Bluff
Sailors Bay Boathouse & Northbridge Sailing Club
HARBOUR
Northbridge Baths
The Knoll
Clive Park
MOSMAN
Beauty Pt
Foreshore Walk
NORTHBRIDGE
Long Bay
Beauty Point
Quakers Hat
Clubhouse
Northbridge Golf Course
Northbridge Oval
Elizabeth Pk
Hughes Steps

MAP 287

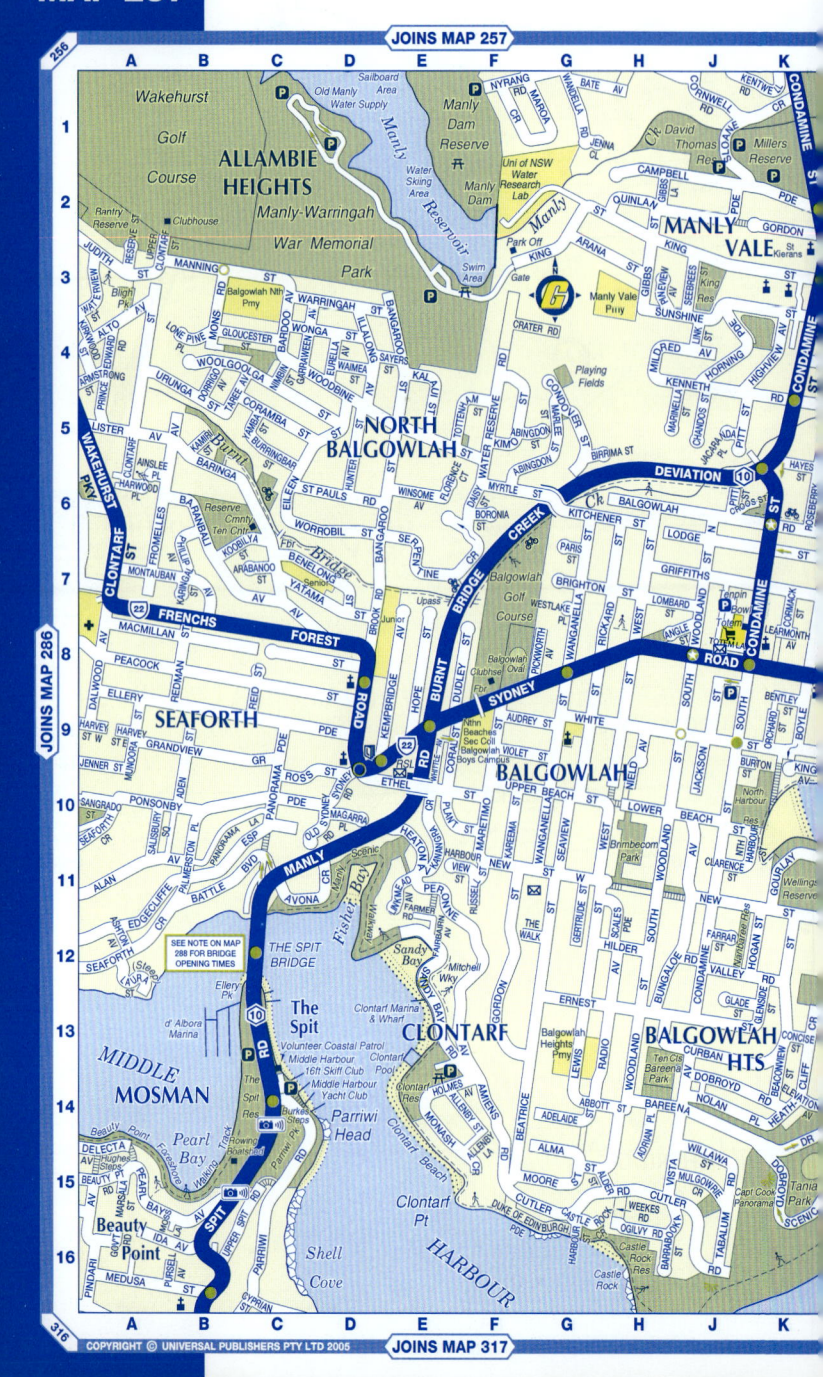

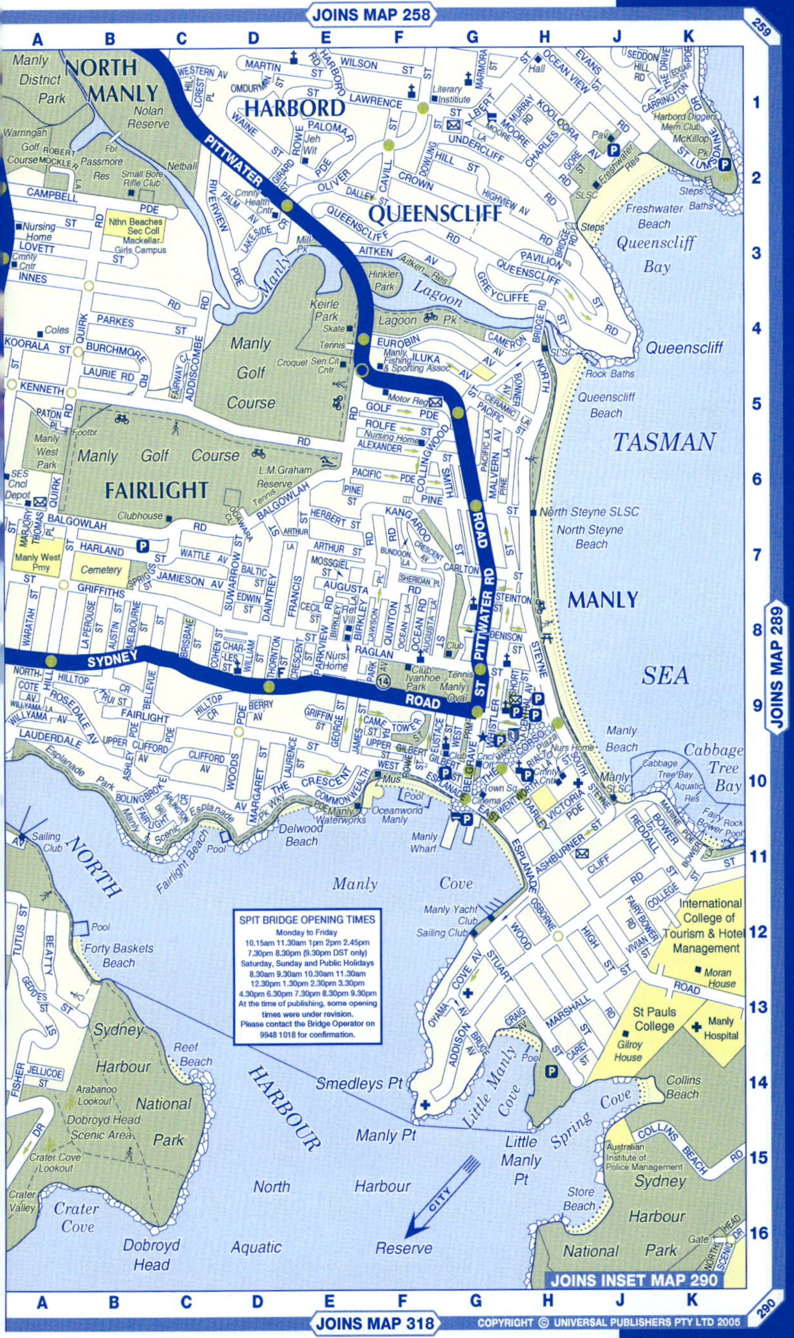
JOINS MAP 258
JOINS MAP 289
JOINS MAP 318
JOINS INSET MAP 290
259
290
A B C D E F G H J K
1 2 3 4 5 6 7 8 9 10 11 12 13 14 15 16
NORTH MANLY
HARBORD
QUEENSCLIFF
FAIRLIGHT
MANLY
Manly District Park
Nolan Reserve
Warringah Golf Course
Passmore Res
Small Bore Rifle Club
Nthn Beaches Sec Coll Mackellar Girls Campus
Manly Lagoon
Keirle Park
Hinkler Park
Lagoon Pk
Manly Golf Course
Manly West Park
L.M.Graham Reserve
Manly West Pmy
Cemetery
Freshwater Beach
Queenscliff Bay
Queenscliff Beach
Rock Baths
North Steyne SLSC
North Steyne Beach
Manly Beach
Cabbage Tree Bay
TASMAN SEA
Manly Wharf
Manly Cove
Oceanworld Manly
Delwood Beach
Fairlight Beach
Manly Yacht Club
Sailing Club
International College of Tourism & Hotel Management
Moran House
St Pauls College
Gilroy House
Manly Hospital
Collins Beach
Spring Cove
Little Manly Cove
Little Manly Pt
Manly Pt
Smedleys Pt
Store Beach
Australian Institute of Police Management
Sydney Harbour National Park
NORTH HARBOUR
Forty Baskets Beach
Reef Beach
Arabanoo Lookout
Dobroyd Head Scenic Area
Crater Cove Lookout
Crater Cove
Crater Valley
Dobroyd Head
North Harbour Aquatic Reserve
CITY
PITTWATER RD
SYDNEY ROAD
SPIT BRIDGE OPENING TIMES
Monday to Friday
10.15am 11.30am 1pm 2pm 2.45pm
7.30pm 8.30pm (9.30pm DST only)
Saturday, Sunday and Public Holidays
8.30am 9.30am 10.30am 11.30am
12.30pm 1.30pm 2.30pm 3.30pm
4.30pm 6.30pm 7.30pm 8.30pm 9.30pm
At the time of publishing, some opening times were under revision.
Please contact the Bridge Operator on 9948 1018 for confirmation.

MAP 289

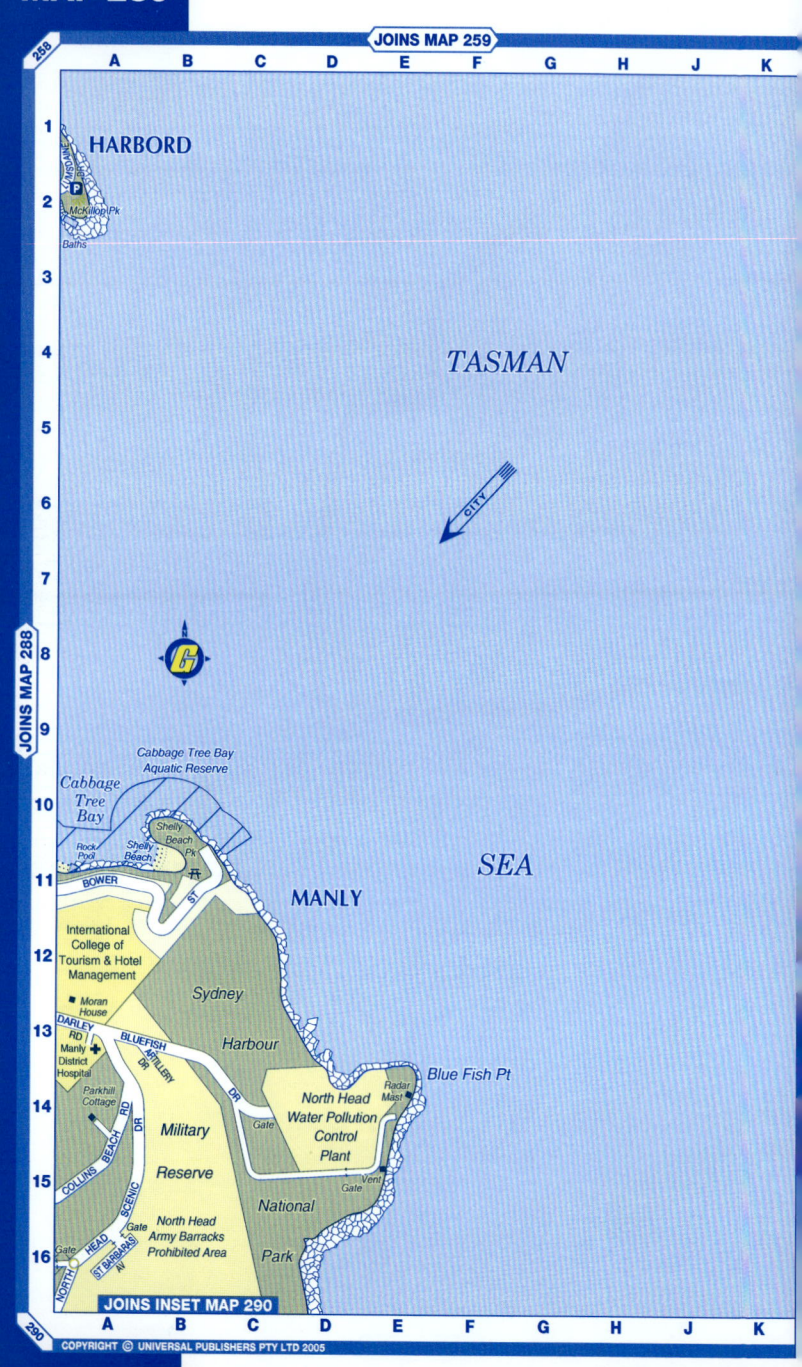

HARBORD

McKillop Pk
Baths

TASMAN

SEA

Cabbage Tree Bay Aquatic Reserve

Cabbage Tree Bay

Shelly Beach
Rock Pool
Shelly Bch Pk

BOWER ST

MANLY

International College of Tourism & Hotel Management

Moran House

Sydney Harbour

DARLEY RD
Manly District Hospital

BLUEFISH DR
ARTILLERY DR

Parkhill Cottage

Military Reserve

North Head Water Pollution Control Plant

Blue Fish Pt
Radar Mast

Gate
Vent
Gate

COLLINS BEACH RD
SCENIC DR

National Park

Gate
North Head Army Barracks Prohibited Area

Gate
NORTH HEAD
ST BARNABAS AV

JOINS MAP 259
JOINS MAP 288
JOINS INSET MAP 290

COPYRIGHT © UNIVERSAL PUBLISHERS PTY LTD 2005

MAP 290
MAP 293 FOLLOWS

JOINS MAP 260

INSET

JOINS MAP 289

North Head Army Barracks Prohibited Area

Military Reserve

North Fort Artillery Museum

Sydney Harbour National Park

TASMAN SEA

North Head Scenic Area

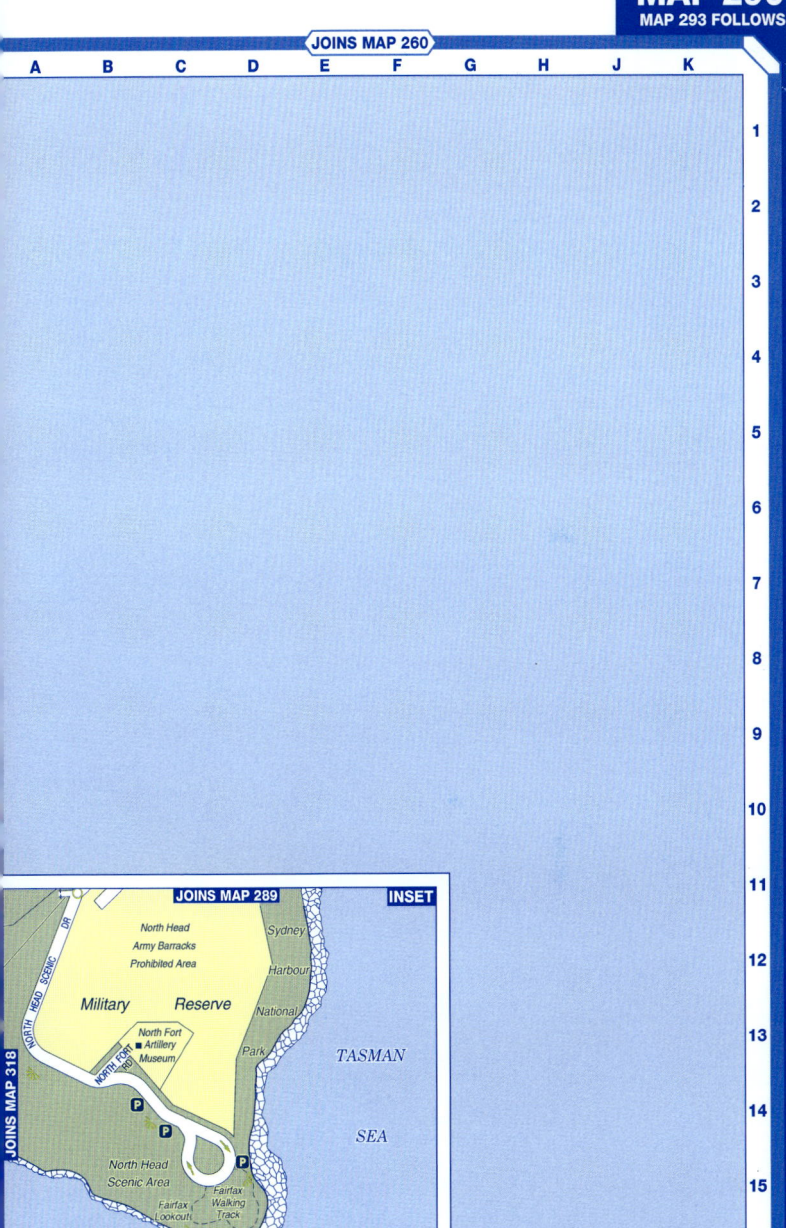

Fairfax Lookout

Fairfax Walking Track

North Head

NORTH HEAD SCENIC DR

NORTH FORT RD

JOINS MAP 318

COPYRIGHT © UNIVERSAL PUBLISHERS PTY LTD 2005

MAP 293
PREVIOUS MAP 290

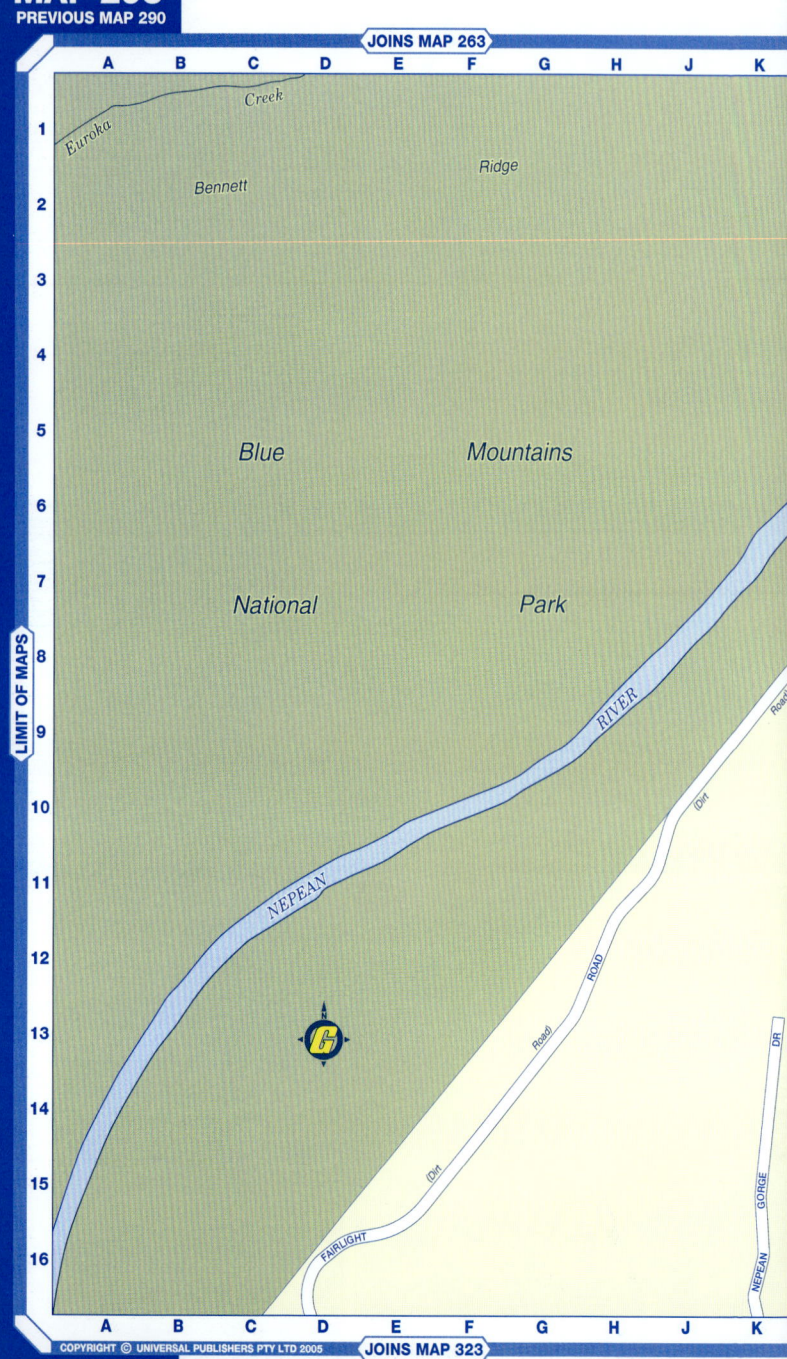

JOINS MAP 263

Euroka Creek

Bennett Ridge

Blue Mountains

National Park

NEPEAN RIVER

FAIRLIGHT (Dirt) Road

Road (Dirt)

NEPEAN GORGE DR

LIMIT OF MAPS

JOINS MAP 323

COPYRIGHT © UNIVERSAL PUBLISHERS PTY LTD 2005

MAP 294

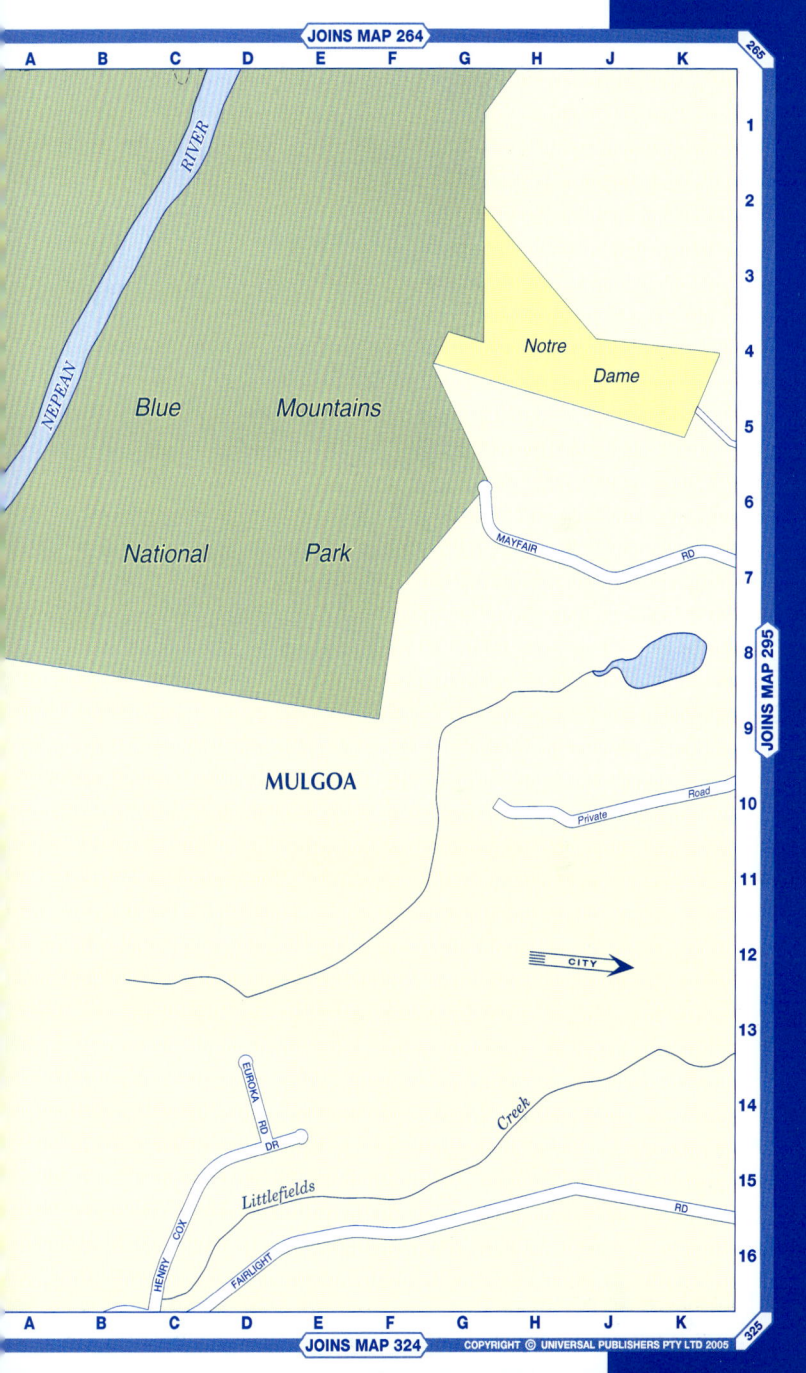

- Nepean River
- Blue Mountains National Park
- Notre Dame
- Mayfair Rd
- Private Road
- MULGOA
- CITY →
- Euroka Rd
- Littlefields Rd
- Henry Cox Dr
- Fairlight
- Creek

JOINS MAP 264 (top)
JOINS MAP 295 (right)
JOINS MAP 324 (bottom)

COPYRIGHT © UNIVERSAL PUBLISHERS PTY LTD 2005

MAP 295

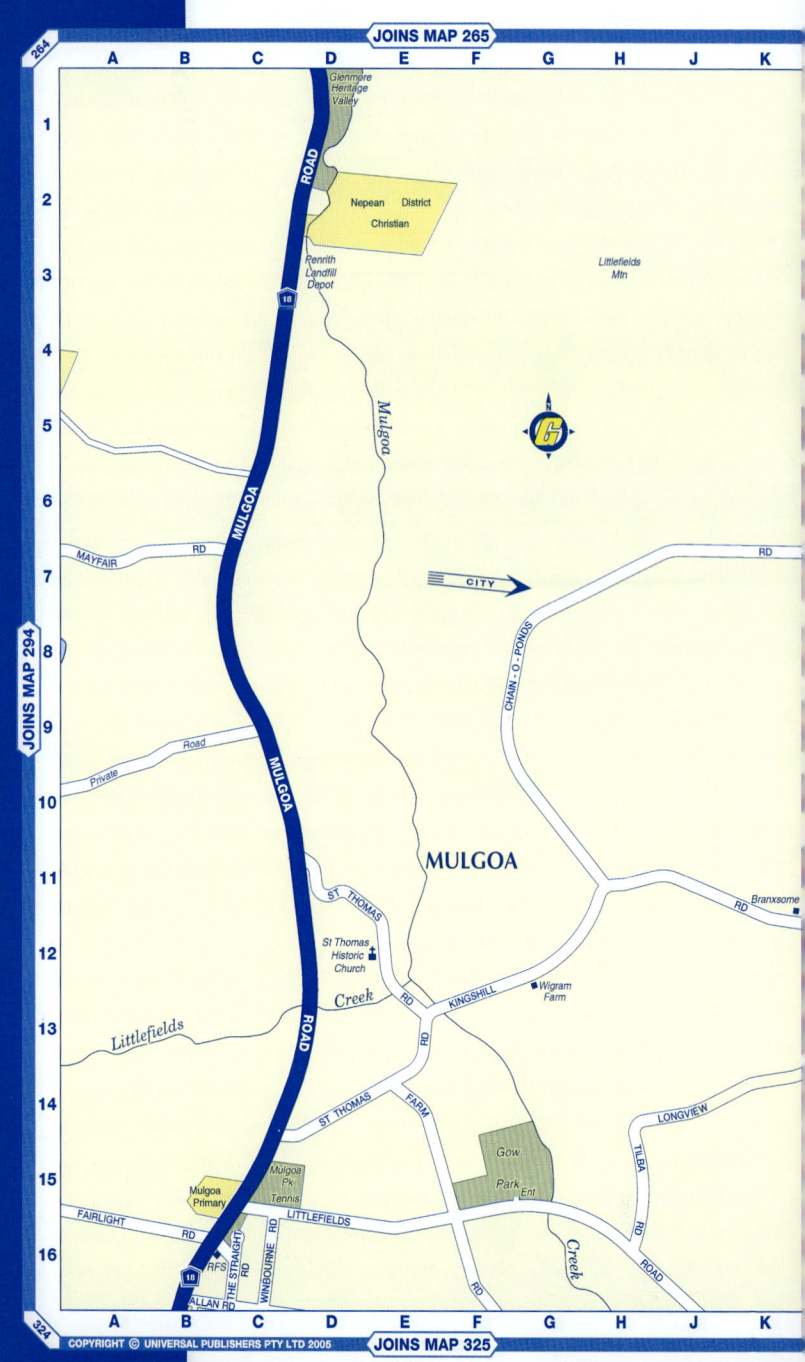

JOINS MAP 265 / JOINS MAP 325 / JOINS MAP 294 / 264 / 324

Glenmore Heritage Valley
Nepean District Christian
Penrith Landfill Depot
Littlefields Mtn
Mulgoa
MAYFAIR RD
MULGOA ROAD
CITY
CHAIN-O-PONDS
Private Road
MULGOA
Branxsome RD
ST THOMAS
St Thomas Historic Church
Creek
KINGSHILL RD
Wigram Farm
Littlefields
ST THOMAS FARM RD
LONGVIEW
Gow Park Ent
TILBA RD
Mulgoa Primary
Mulgoa Pk Tennis
FAIRLIGHT RD
LITTLEFIELDS
Creek
ROAD
RFS
THE STRAIGHT
WINBOURNE RD
ALLAN RD

COPYRIGHT © UNIVERSAL PUBLISHERS PTY LTD 2005

MAP 296

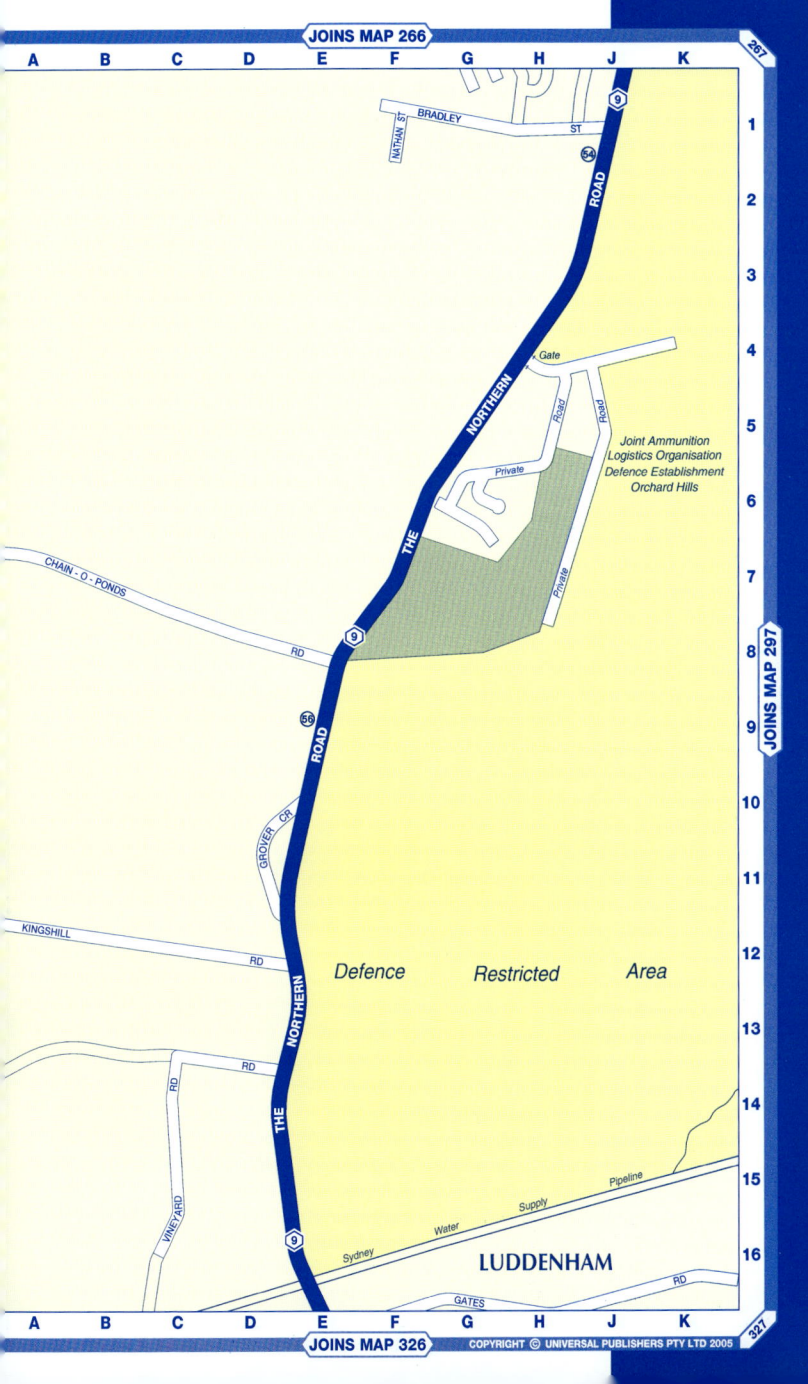

JOINS MAP 266

NATHAN ST — BRADLEY ST

THE NORTHERN ROAD

Gate
Road
Road
Private

Joint Ammunition
Logistics Organisation
Defence Establishment
Orchard Hills

Private

CHAIN - O - PONDS RD

GROVER CR

KINGSHILL RD

Defence   Restricted   Area

RD

VINEYARD

Pipeline
Water Supply
Sydney
LUDDENHAM
GATES RD

JOINS MAP 326

MAP 297

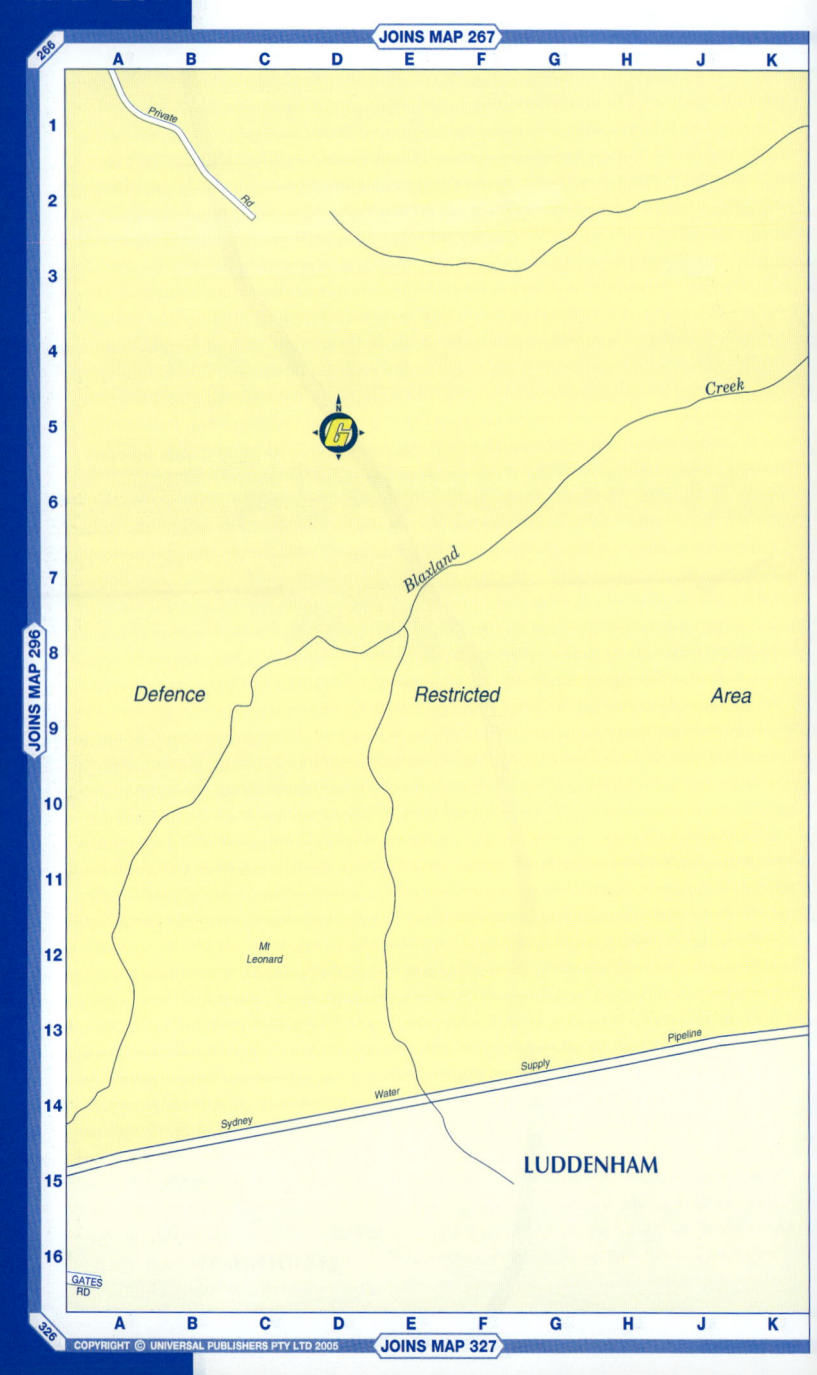

Private Rd

Creek

Blaxland

Defence Restricted Area

Mt Leonard

Pipeline
Supply
Water
Sydney

LUDDENHAM

GATES RD

MAP 298

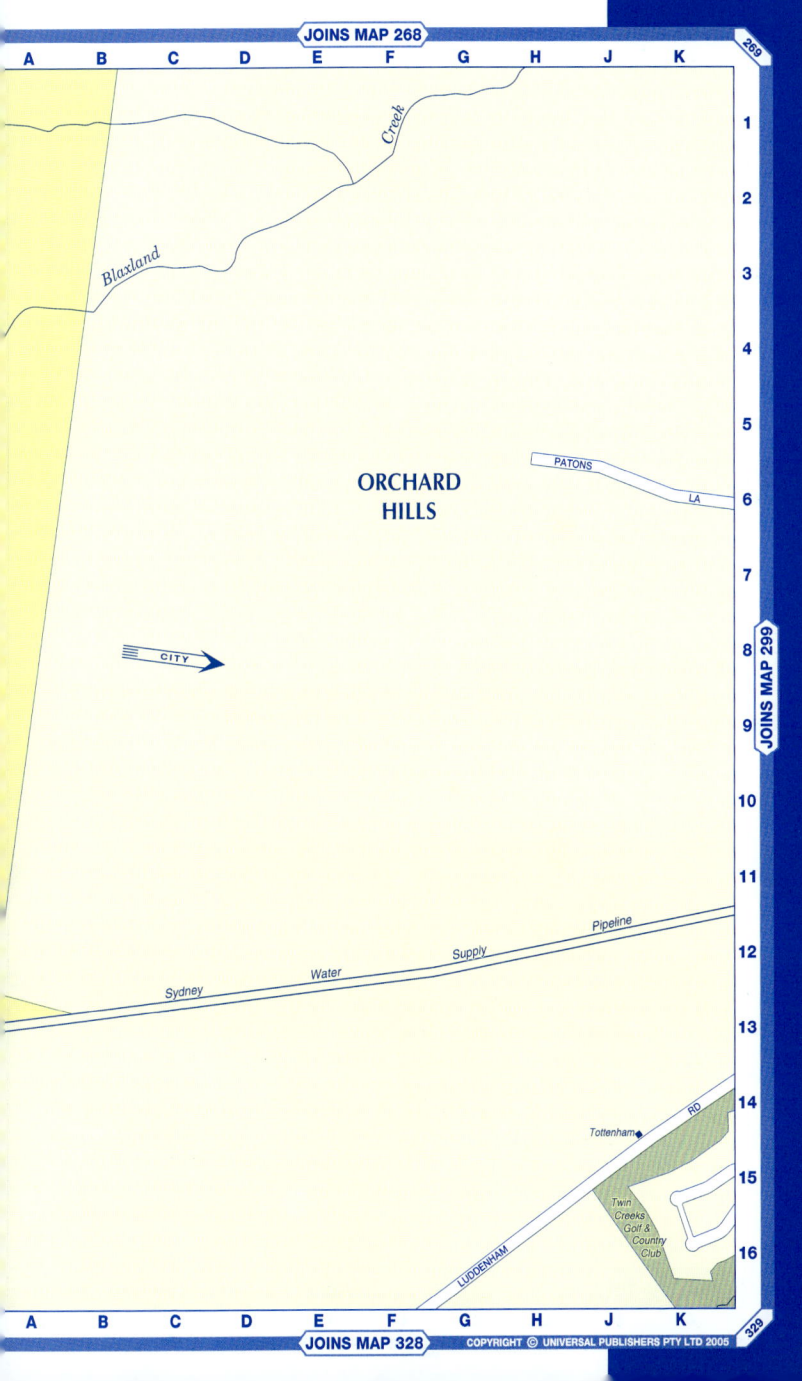

ORCHARD HILLS

Blaxland Creek

PATONS LA

CITY

Sydney Water Supply Pipeline

Tottenham RD

Twin Creeks Golf & Country Club

LUDDENHAM

MAP 299

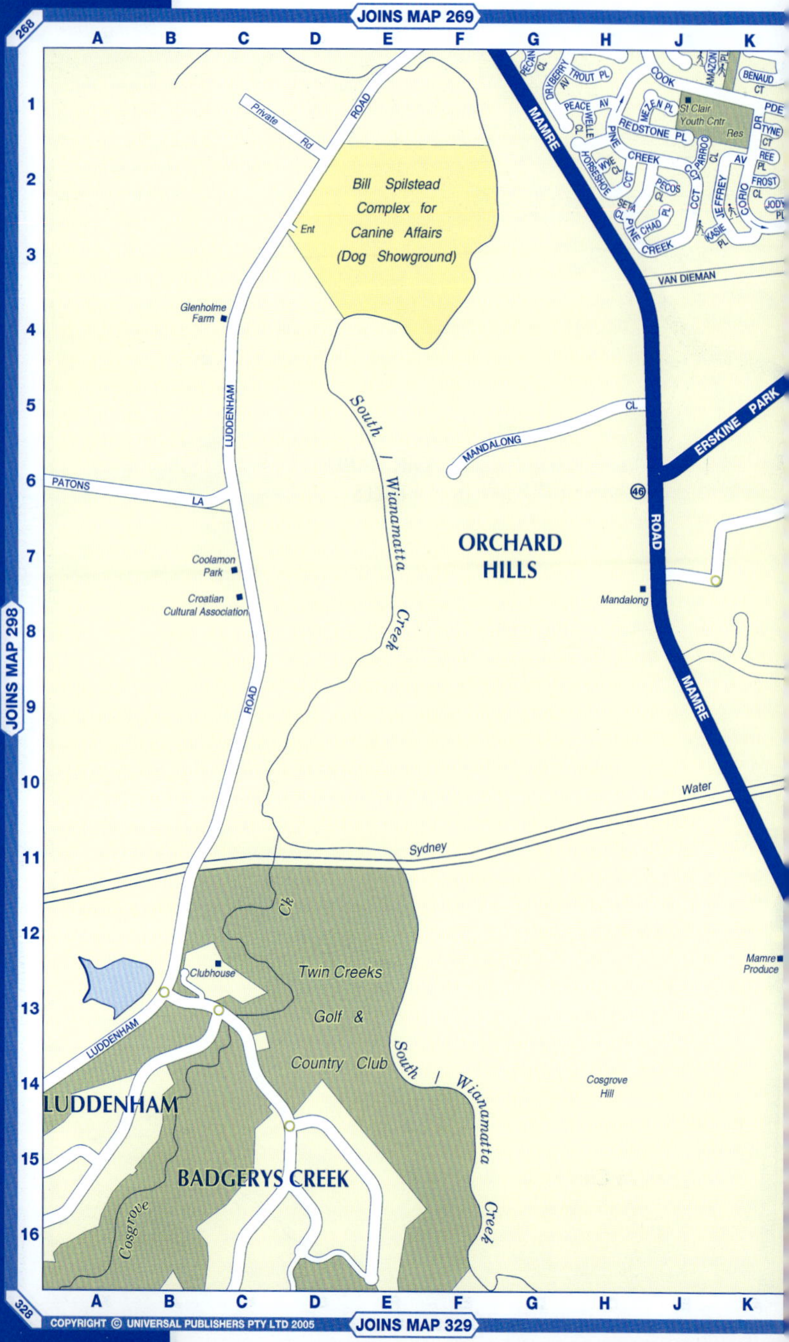

JOINS MAP 269
JOINS MAP 298
JOINS MAP 329
268
328
Private Rd
ROAD
Bill Spilstead Complex for Canine Affairs (Dog Showground)
Ent
Glenholme Farm
LUDDENHAM
PATONS LA
Coolamon Park
Croatian Cultural Association
ROAD
South Wianamatta Creek
MANDALONG CL
ORCHARD HILLS
MAMRE ROAD
ERSKINE PARK
46
Mandalong
VAN DIEMAN
TROUT PL
COOK
BENAUD CT
PEACE AV
DRYBERRY AV
WELLE CL
PINE CREEK
REDSTONE PL
St Clair Youth Cntr
Res
PDE
DR
TYNE
REE PL
FROST CL
HORSESHOE
WYE CL
CCT
PARROO CL
PECOS CL
SETA CL
CHAD PL
CREEK
JEFFREY
CORIO
KASIE PL
AV
Sydney Water
Ck
Clubhouse
Twin Creeks Golf & Country Club
LUDDENHAM
BADGERYS CREEK
Cosgrove
Cosgrove Hill
Mamre Produce

MAP 300

ERSKINE PARK

- ST CLAIR
- Peppertree Reserve
- James Erskine Pwy
- Erskine Park High
- Enviroguard Cmnty Waste Management
- Emmaus Village
- Mamre Christian College
- Trinity Catholic Primary
- Emmaus Catholic College
- Playing Field
- KEMPS CREEK
- MT VERNON
- Ropes Creek

JOINS MAP 270 (top)
JOINS MAP 330 (bottom)
JOINS MAP 301 (right)

COPYRIGHT © UNIVERSAL PUBLISHERS PTY LTD 2005

MAP 301

JOINS MAP 271

ERSKINE PARK

Sennar Dr, Weaver Rd, Ohio Pl, Gibbons Pl, Otter Pl, Sirius St, Adhara Ct, Swallow, Pegasus St, Indus St, Aquila, Weaver, Cetus St

Creek

CITY →

Sydney West Substation

Ent

Sydney Water Supply Pipeline

Ropes

Brickworks

Old Wallgrove Road

Gate
PGH — BURLEY — RD

KEMPS CREEK

Greenway Pl

Delaware

MT VERNON

JOINS MAP 300 / JOINS MAP 331

COPYRIGHT © UNIVERSAL PUBLISHERS PTY LTD 2005

MAP 302

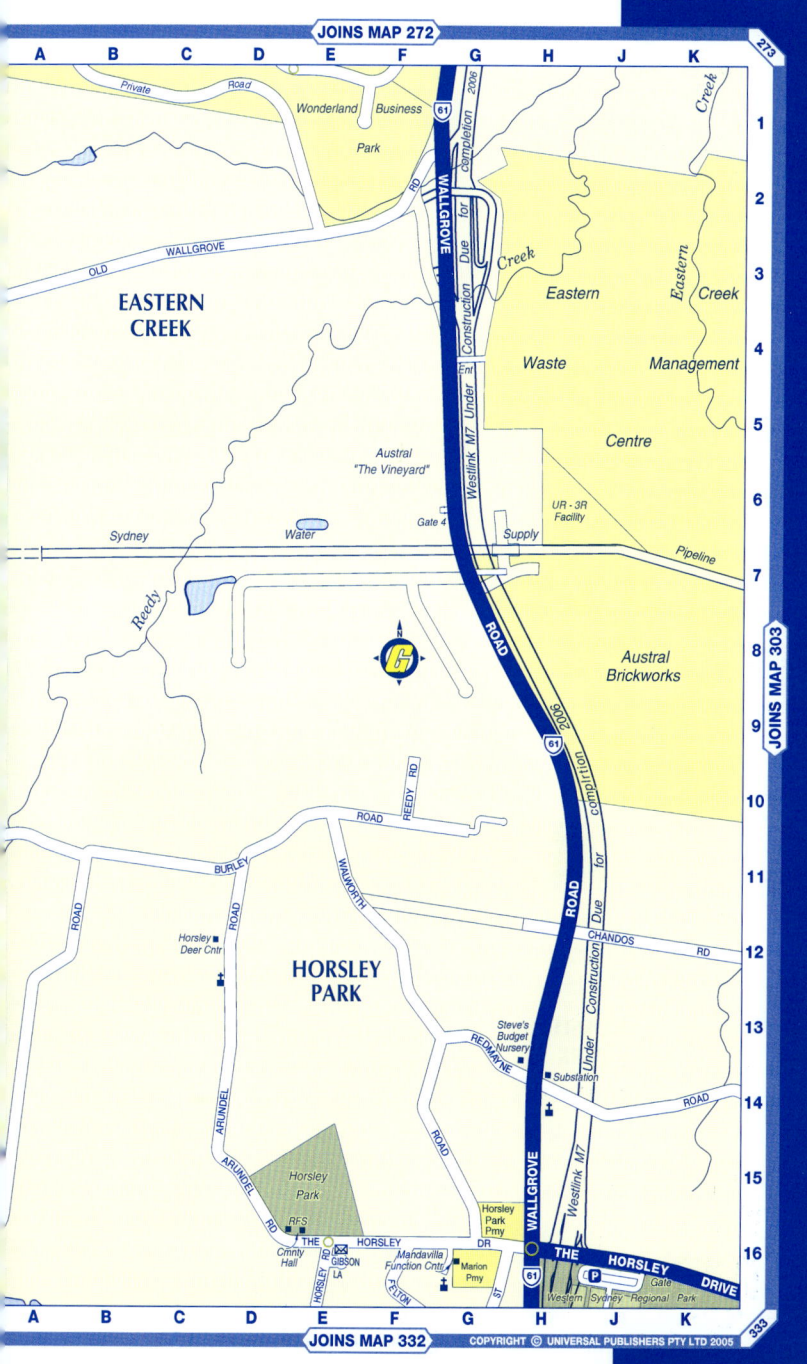

MAP 303

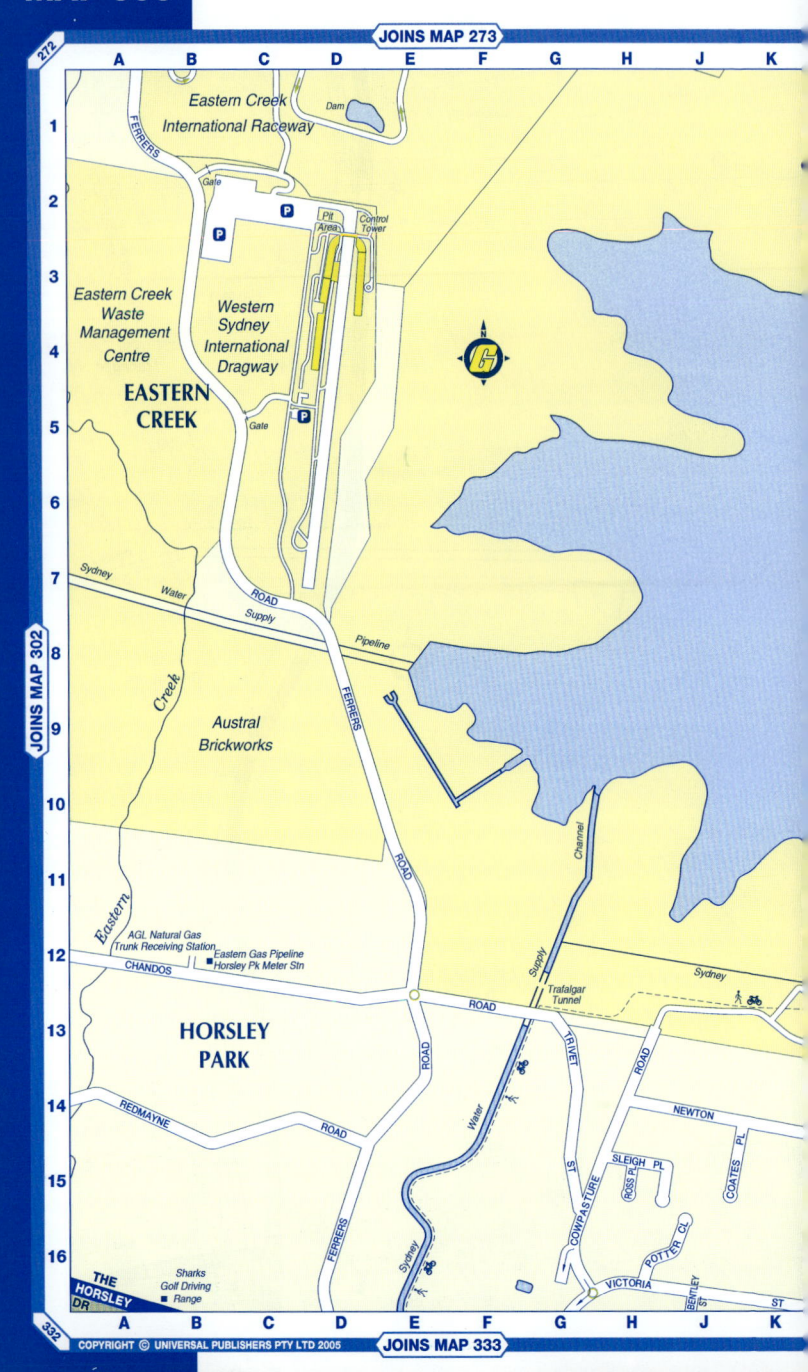

JOINS MAP 273

- Eastern Creek International Raceway
- Dam
- Gate
- P / P
- Pit Area
- Control Tower
- Eastern Creek Waste Management Centre
- Western Sydney International Dragway
- **EASTERN CREEK**
- Gate
- Sydney Water Supply Pipeline
- Creek
- Austral Brickworks
- FERRERS ROAD
- Eastern
- AGL Natural Gas Trunk Receiving Station
- Eastern Gas Pipeline
- Horsley Pk Meter Stn
- CHANDOS
- Supply Channel
- Trafalgar Tunnel
- Sydney
- ROAD
- TRIVET ROAD
- **HORSLEY PARK**
- REDMAYNE ROAD
- NEWTON
- Water
- SLEIGH PL
- ROSS PL
- COATES PL
- COWPASTURE
- BENTLEY ST
- POTTER CL
- Sharks Golf Driving Range
- Sydney
- VICTORIA
- THE HORSLEY DR

JOINS MAP 333

COPYRIGHT © UNIVERSAL PUBLISHERS PTY LTD 2005

MAP 304

PROSPECT

Open 10am - 4:45pm
(Closes 6:45pm Daylight Savings, Weekends & Public Holidays)

Peckys
Andrew Campbell Res
Prospect History Cottage

Reservoirs
Water Transport & Treatment HQ
Maintenance Office

Quarry
Gate Closes 4:45pm
Conf Cntr
George Maunder Lookout
Walder Park

PROSPECT RESERVOIR

Prospect

Boral Recycling

Creek

Water Supply Pipeline

Albright Wilson & Banfield
Waste Transfer Station

DAVIS ROAD
Gate

Road Material Recycling Centre

WETHERILL PARK

HEDHAM ROAD
BUSHELLS PL
NEWTON
ARNOTT PL
MUIR PL
WENBAN PL
DENOCI CL
KELLAWAY
ELIZABETH ST
HARGRAVES PL
CENTRE PL
CSR
FRANK ST
Industrial Area
Substn
Hassall
HASSALL ST
Industrial Area
WALLER ST
WIDEMERE RD
REDFERN ST

RECONCILIATION RD
WATCH HOUSE RD
MANNING ST

JOINS MAP 274
JOINS MAP 334
JOINS MAP 305

MAP 305

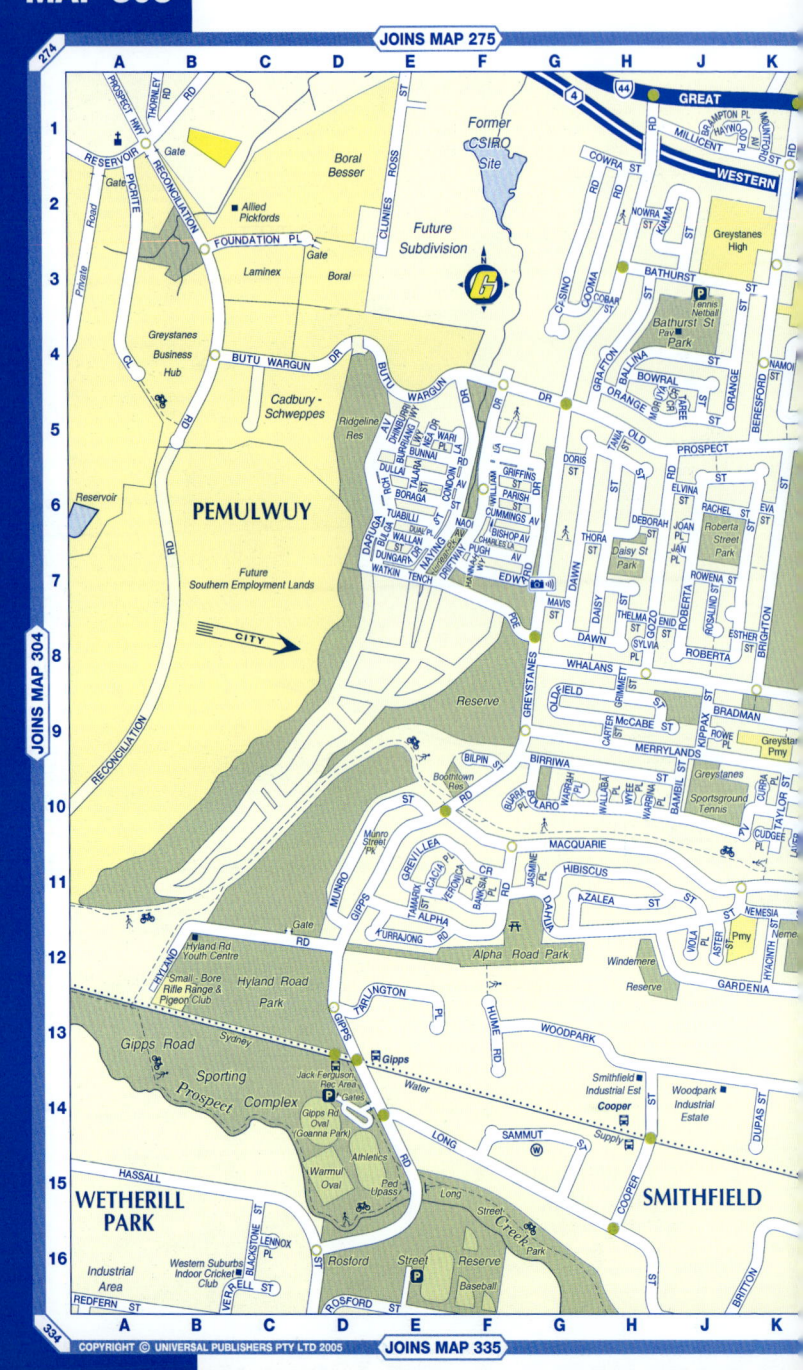

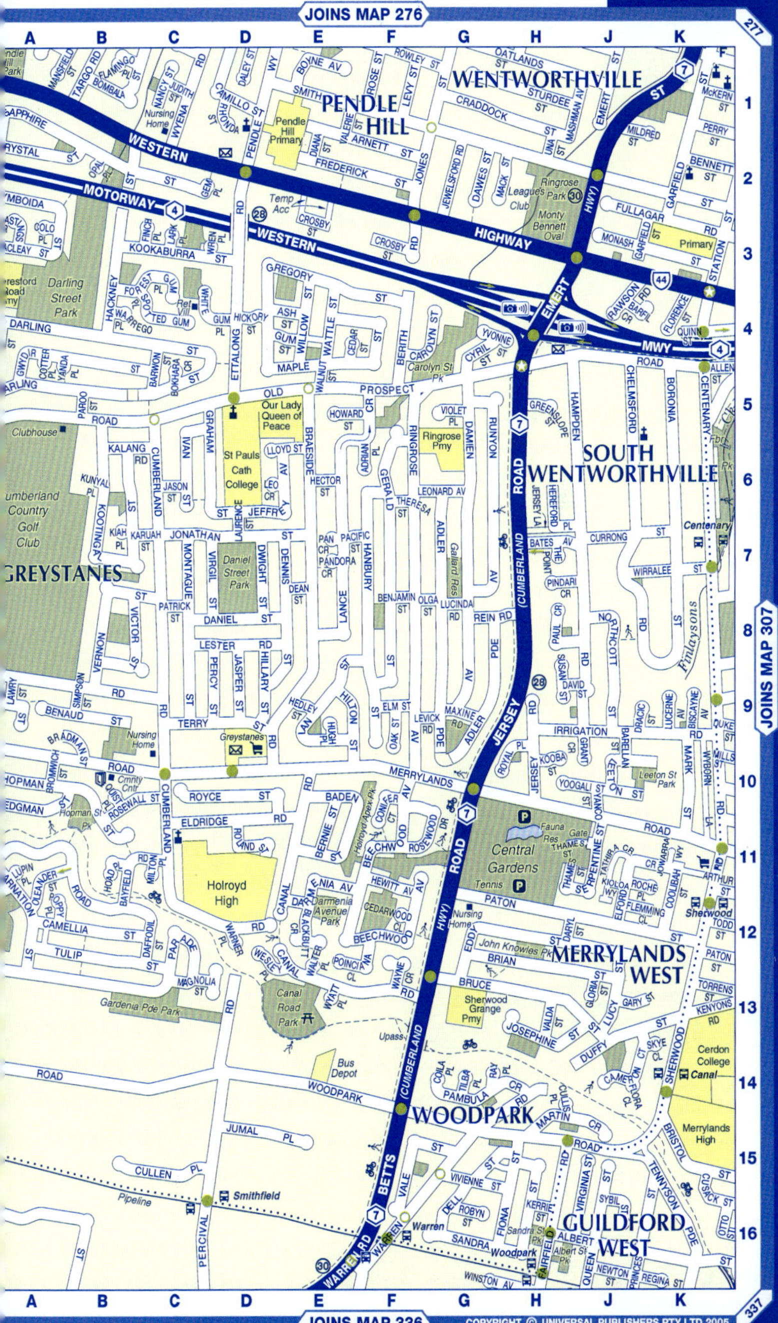
JOINS MAP 276
JOINS MAP 307
JOINS MAP 336
277
337
WENTWORTHVILLE
PENDLE HILL
SOUTH WENTWORTHVILLE
GREYSTANES
MERRYLANDS WEST
WOODPARK
GUILDFORD WEST
WESTERN HIGHWAY
MOTORWAY
WESTERN MWY
CUMBERLAND HWY
JERSEY ROAD
BETTS RD
WARREN RD
MERRYLANDS ROAD
OLD PROSPECT ROAD
WOODPARK ROAD
PATON ST
IRRIGATION RD
Pendle Hill Primary
Our Lady Queen of Peace
St Pauls Cath College
Ringrose Pmy
Holroyd High
Cerdon College
Merrylands High
Central Gardens
Cumberland Country Golf Club
Darling Street Park
Daniel Street Park
Canal Road Park
Sherwood Grange Pmy
Bus Depot
Smithfield
Warren
Woodpark
Sherwood
Centenary
Canal
Ringrose Park
Monty Bennett Oval
Carolyn St Pk
Leeton St Park
John Knowles Pk
Gardenia Pde Park
Darmenia Avenue Park
Hopman St Pk
Pipeline

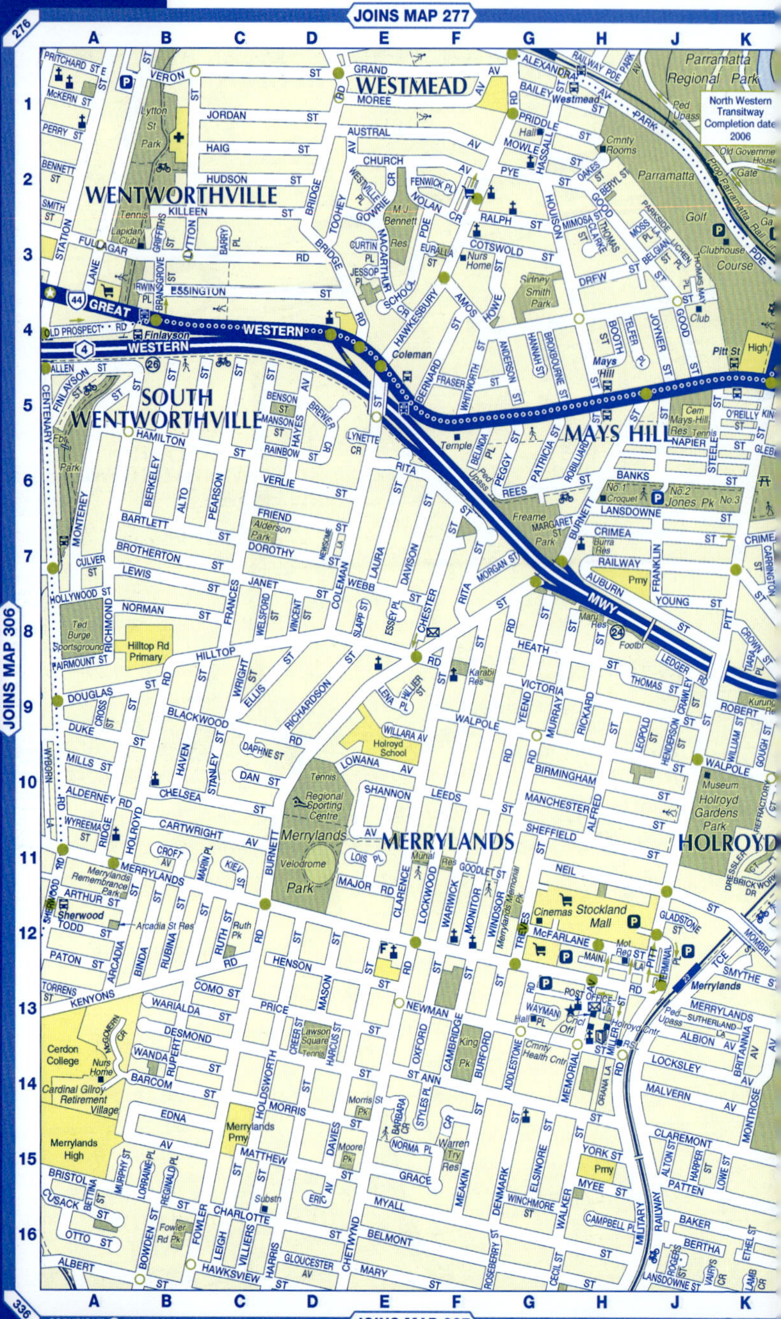
JOINS MAP 277
JOINS MAP 306
JOINS MAP 337
276
336
A B C D E F G H J K
1 2 3 4 5 6 7 8 9 10 11 12 13 14 15 16
WESTMEAD
WENTWORTHVILLE
SOUTH WENTWORTHVILLE
MAYS HILL
MERRYLANDS
HOLROYD
Parramatta Regional Park
North Western Transitway Completion date 2006
Parramatta Golf Course
Lytton St Park
Sirdney Smith Park
Coleman
Finlayson
GREAT WESTERN
WESTERN
MWY
Alderson Park
Hilltop Rd Primary
Ted Burge Sportsground
Holroyd School
Regional Sporting Centre
Merrylands Velodrome Park
Stockland Mall
Cinemas
Holroyd Gardens Park
Museum
Jones Pk
Freame Margaret St Park
Cerdon College
Cardinal Gilroy Retirement Village
Merrylands High
Merrylands Pmy
King Pk
Lawson Square
Merrylands Remembrance Park
Sherwood
Arcadia St Res
Fowler Rd Pk
Warren Try Res
Moore Pk
Morris St Pk
Merrylands
Holroyd Cntr
Cmnty Health Cntr
Post Office
ALEXANDRA AV
GRAND AV
AUSTRAL AV
CHURCH ST
HUDSON ST
JORDAN ST
HAIG ST
KILLEEN ST
FULLAGAR RD
ESSINGTON ST
VERON ST
HILLTOP RD
DOUGLAS ST
BLACKWOOD ST
MERRYLANDS RD
KENYONS RD
PRICE ST
NEWMAN ST
ST ANN ST
MORRIS ST
MYALL ST
BELMONT ST
MARY ST
HAWKSVIEW ST
CHARLOTTE ST
ALBERT ST
BURNETT ST
WALPOLE ST
BIRMINGHAM ST
MANCHESTER ST
SHEFFIELD ST
NEIL ST
MCFARLANE ST
MERRYLANDS RD
MILITARY RD
RAILWAY ST
PITT ST
BANKS ST
LANSDOWNE ST
CRIMEA ST
AUBURN ST
YOUNG ST
HEATH ST
VICTORIA ST
ROBERT ST
BAKER ST
PATTEN ST
MALVERN AV
LOCKSLEY ST
CLAREMONT ST

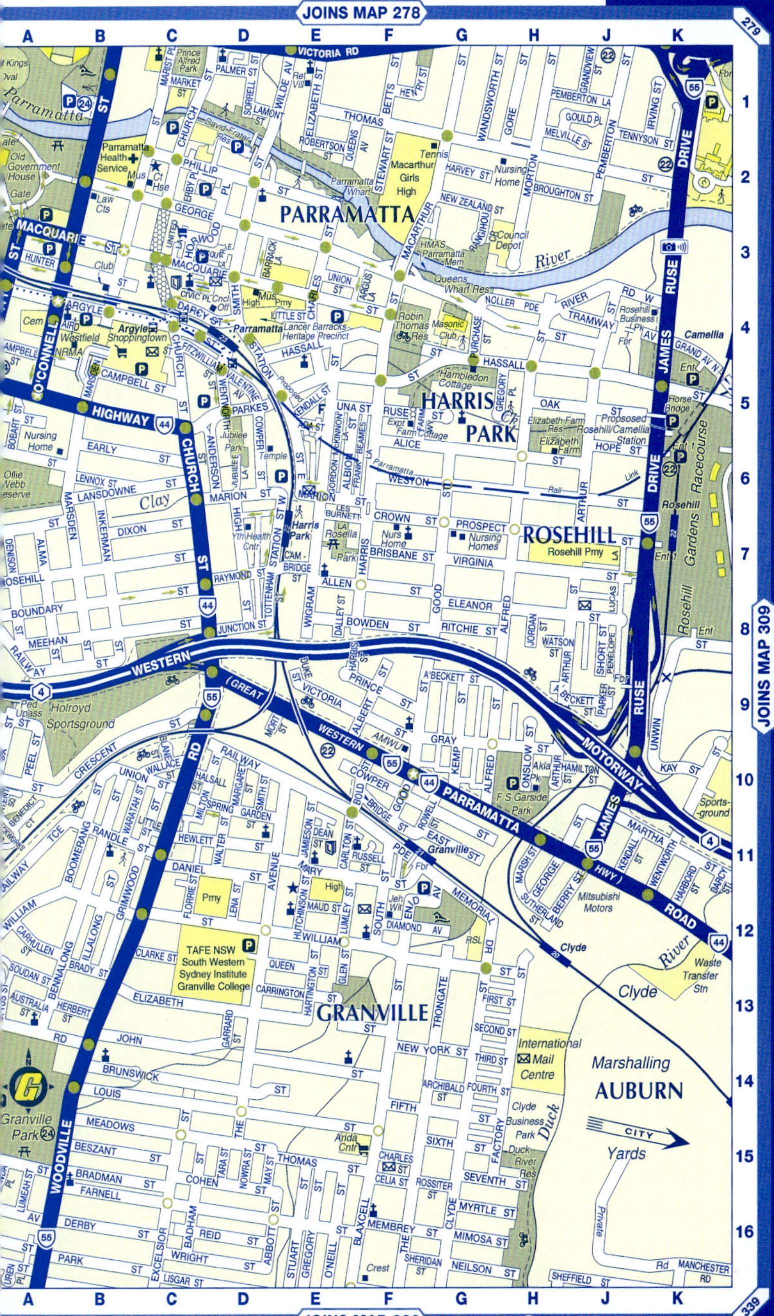
JOINS MAP 278
JOINS MAP 309
JOINS MAP 338
279
339
A B C D E F G H J K
1 2 3 4 5 6 7 8 9 10 11 12 13 14 15 16
PARRAMATTA
HARRIS PARK
ROSEHILL
GRANVILLE
AUBURN
Parramatta River
River
Clay
Duck River
VICTORIA RD
MACQUARIE ST
GEORGE
PHILLIP
CHURCH ST
O'CONNELL
WESTERN HIGHWAY
(GREAT WESTERN HWY)
WESTERN MOTORWAY
PARRAMATTA ROAD
JAMES RUSE DRIVE
WOODVILLE RD
HASSALL ST
Parramatta Health Service
Old Government House
Law Cts
Westfield Argyle Shoppingtown
Parramatta Wharf
Macarthur Girls High
Tennis
Nursing Home
Council Depot
HMAS Parramatta Mem
Queens Wharf Res
Robin Thomas Res
Masonic Club
Lancer Barracks Heritage Precinct
Hambledon Cottage
Elizabeth Farm Res
Elizabeth Farm
Rosehill Pmy
Rosehill Gardens Racecourse
Proposed Rosehill/Camellia Station
Camellia
Jubilee Park
Harris Park
Rosella Park
Holroyd Sportsground
F S Garside Park
Sports-ground
Mitsubishi Motors
Waste Transfer Stn
Clyde
TAFE NSW South Western Sydney Institute Granville College
International Mail Centre
Clyde Business Park
Duck River Res
Marshalling Yards
CITY
Granville Park
Arida Cntr
Crest
Nursing Homes
Ruse Expt Farm Cottage
Yth Health Cntr
Temple
Cem
Nursing Home
Ollie Webb Reserve
Kings Oval
Prince Alfred Park

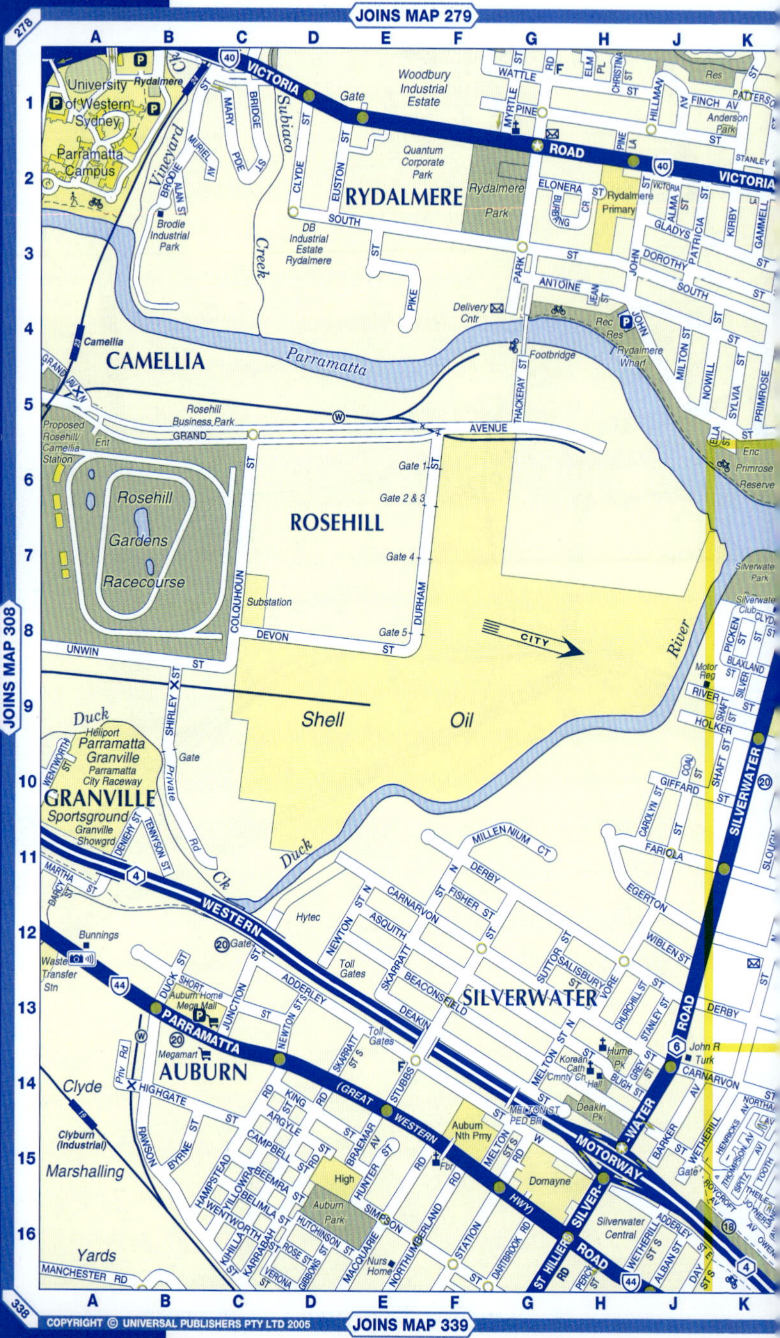
JOINS MAP 279
278
A B C D E F G H J K
1 2 3 4 5 6 7 8 9 10 11 12 13 14 15 16
JOINS MAP 308
338
JOINS MAP 339
University of Western Sydney
Parramatta Campus
Rydalmere
Vineyard
BRODIE
ALAN ST
MURIEL AV
MARY PDE
BRIDGE ST
VICTORIA
Subiaco
Creek
Brodie Industrial Park
Woodbury Industrial Estate
Gate
Quantum Corporate Park
CLYDE ST
EUSTON ST
RYDALMERE
Rydalmere Park
SOUTH
DB Industrial Estate Rydalmere
PIKE
Delivery Cntr
WATTLE ST
MYRTLE
PINE
RD
ELM PL
CHRISTINA ST
HILLMAN
FINCH AV
PATTERSON
Anderson Park
ROAD
STANLEY
VICTORIA
ELONERA
BURBANG
CR
Rydalmere Primary
ALMA ST
GLADYS
PATRICIA
KIRBY
GAMMELL
DOROTHY
PARK
ANTOINE
JEAN ST
JOHN
SOUTH ST
Rec Res
Rydalmere Wharf
MILTON ST
NOWILL
SYLVIA
PRIMROSE
Footbridge
THACKERAY ST
Parramatta
Camellia
CAMELLIA
GRAND AV N
Rosehill Business Park
GRAND
AVENUE
Proposed Rosehill/ Camellia Station
Ent
Eric Primrose Reserve
ELLA ST
Gate 1
Gate 2 & 3
Gate 4
Gate 5
Rosehill Gardens Racecourse
ROSEHILL
COLQUHOUN
DURHAM ST
Substation
DEVON
ST
UNWIN
ST
CITY
River
Silverwater Park
Silverwater Club
CLYDE
PICKEN ST
BLAXLAND ST
Motor Reg
RIVER
SILVER
SHAFT ST
HOLKER
Duck
Heliport
Parramatta Granville
Parramatta City Raceway
SHIRLEY ST
WENTWORTH ST
Shell
Oil
Gate
Private
Rd
GRANVILLE
Sportsground
Granville Showgrd
DENIEHY ST
TENNYSON ST
Duck
Ck
COAL ST
GIFFARD
CAROLYN ST
SILVERWATER
MILLENNIUM CT
FARIOLA
EGERTON
DERBY
FISHER ST
CARNARVON
ASQUITH
NEWTON ST N
MARTHA
DARCY ST
ST
WESTERN
Hytec
Bunnings
Waste Transfer Stn
20 Gate
Toll Gates
SKARRATT
BEACONSFIELD
SUTTOR ST
SALISBURY ST
VORE
WIBLEN ST
SILVERWATER
DERBY
DUCK ST
SHORT
Auburn Home Mega Mall
JUNCTION
ADDERLEY
ST
DEAKIN
PARRAMATTA
NEWTON ST S
Toll Gates
SKARRATT ST S
CHURCHILL ST
STANLEY ST
Megamart
AUBURN
STUBBS
MELTON ST N
Hume Pk
Korean Cath Cmnty Ch
Hall
GREY ST
BLIGH ST
ROAD
John R Turk
CARNARVON
Clyde
Priv Rd
HIGHGATE
KING ST
RD
(GREAT WESTERN
ARGYLE
BRAEMAR
AV
MELTON ST PED BR
Deakin Pk
WATER
NORTHAM
Clyburn (Industrial)
RAWSON
BYRNE ST
CAMPBELL
ST RD
HUNTER ST
Auburn Nth Prmy
MELTON ST S
RD
W
MOTORWAY
BARKER ST
WETHERILL ST
HENRICKS AV
THOMPSON AV
Marshalling
HAMPSTEAD
YILLOWRA
BEEMRA
BELIMLA
WENTWORTH ST
High
Auburn Park
SIMPSON
Fbr
Domayne
HWY)
SILVER-
Gate
ROYCROFT AV
SPITZ AV
TOOTH
THEILE
JOYNER
Yards
KIHILLA ST
KARRABAH ST
ROSE ST
HUTCHINSON ST
VERONA ST
GIBBONS ST
MACQUARIE
Nurs Home
NORTHUMBERLAND
STATION ST
DARTBROOK RD
ST HILLIERS RD
PERCY ST
ROAD
Silverwater Central
WETHERILL ST S
ALBAN ST
ADDERLEY
DAY ST S
OWEN
MANCHESTER RD

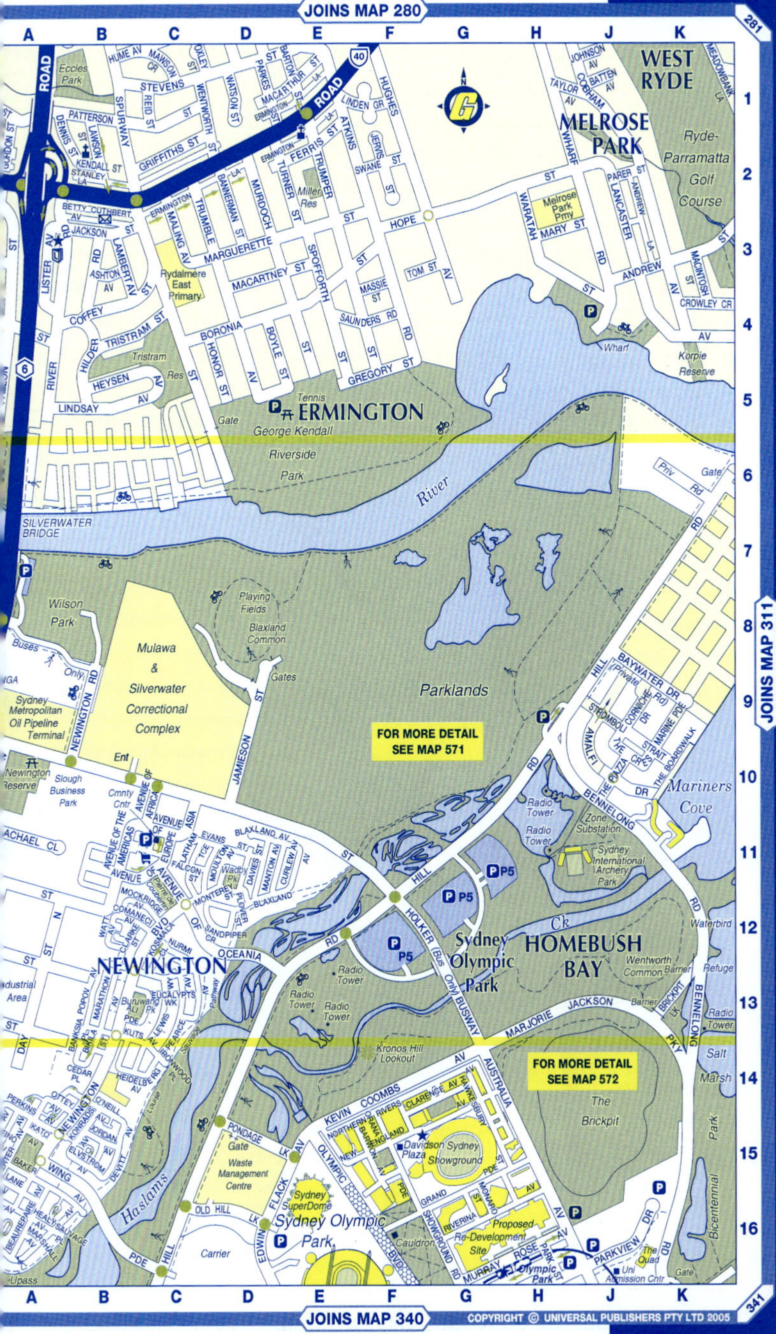

MAP 311

INDEX OF STREETS AT C14
1. BREWER AV — C14
2. BRUNSWICK AV — C14
3. COLE CR — C16
4. CONNER CL — C15
5. DONNELLY CL — C15
6. ELIZA AV — C15
7. FRAZIER CL — C15
8. HEWIN CL — C14
9. JOSEPH CL — C14
10. NEWTON CL — C14
11. POWELL CL — C15
12. ROBERTS CL — C15
13. SIMEON PL — C15
14. THORPE AV — C15
15. WEBB AV — C14
16. WENTON AV — C15
17. WILLIAM CL — C14
18. WILTSHIRE CL — C15

JOINS MAP 282
JOINS MAP 313
JOINS MAP 342
283
343
A B C D E F G H J K
1 2 3 4 5 6 7 8 9 10 11 12 13 14 15 16
RYDE
PUTNEY
GLADESVILLE
TENNYSON POINT
MORTLAKE
BREAKFAST POINT
CABARITA
ABBOTSFORD
VICTORIA ROAD
BLAXLAND RD
Field of Mars Cemetery
Field of Mars Reserve
Strangers Ck
Buffalo Creek
Pidding Park
Ryde Secondary Coll
Holy Cross College
Burrows Park
Ryde Park
Ryde Pmy
Top Ryde
Royal Rehabilitation Centre
Retirement Village
Nurs Home Moorong
St Charles Pmy
Ryde Aquatic Leisure Centre
Tennis Olympic Pk
Enterprise Park
Bus Depot
Glade View Business Park
Westminster Park
Monash Pk Grandstand
Tyagarah Park
Mallee Res
Bremner Park
Cudal Res
Parry Park
Coorabel
Putney Pmy
Donnelly Pk
Frank Downing Sportsgrd
Morrison Bay Park
Peel Park
Putney Park
Putney Pt
Kissing Point Bay
Morrisons Bay
Glades Bay
Glades Bay Park
Bill Mitchell Park
Tennyson Pk
Raven Pt
Breakfast Pt
PARRAMATTA RIVER
Looking Glass Bay
Looking Glass Pt
Looking Glass Bay Park
Gladesville Hospital
Childrens Cochlear Implant Centre
Bedlam Bay
Bedlam Pt
Kendall Bay
Cabarita Wharf
Cabarita Pt
Cabarita Park
Swimming Pool
Hen & Chicken Bay
Village Green
Village Cntr
Country Club
Proposed Marina
Scots Coll Rowing Shed
SGS Rowing Shed
Shore School Rowing Shed
Parramatta River Sailing Club
d'Albora (Westport) Marina
Abbotsford Wharf
Sydney Rowing Club
Sydney Womens Rowing Club
Sydney High School Rowing Shed
12' Flying Squadron
Newington Rowing Shed
Punt Park
Howse Pk
RTA
SES
Boyla Reserve
Weemala

JOINS MAP 283
JOINS MAP 312
JOINS MAP 343
282
342
A B C D E F G H J K
1 2 3 4 5 6 7 8 9 10 11 12 13 14 15 16
RYDE
Field of Mars Reserve
Field Studies Centre
Buffalo
Ck
Strangers
EAST RYDE
Sugarloaf Hill
Lane Cove National Park
LANE COVE
Buffalo Creek Reserve
LANE COVE WEST
Blackman Park
Lane Cove Industrial Estate
Lane Cove Substation
Council Depot
Skate Pk
Tennis Courts
Lovetts Reserve
Boronia Park
Boronia Park
Tipperary Falls
Brickmakers Ck
Montefiore Jewish Home
Synagogue
Cunninghams Reach
Burns Bay
LINLEY POINT
Linley Pt
RIVERVIEW
St Ignatius (Riverview) College
St Ignatius Junior
Metro Inn Riverview Apartments
Museum
Linley Point Res
Aged Care
St Josephs College Sportsground
Villa Maria Pmy
St Josephs College
Catholic Theological Union
Heydon Pk
Tarban Ck
PILKINGTONS BRIDGE
FIG TREE BRIDGE
HUNTERS HILL
Hunters Hill High
Ferdinand St Res
St Malo Res
HUNTLEYS COVE
Riverglade Reserve
Mental Health Review Tribunal
St Josephs Coll Rowing Shed
Uni NSW Rowing Ct
TARBAN CREEK BRIDGE
Huntleys Point Res
Huntleys Pt
Lukes Bay
Lyndhurst Res
Gladesville Hospital
Bedlam Bay Reg Pk
Gladesville Henley Reserve
Riverside Girls High
Betts Park
HUNTLEYS POINT
Gladesville Wharf
GLADESVILLE BRIDGE
HENLEY
Baths
Wallumatta Bay
PARRAMATTA
Five Dock Pt
Howley Park
Marina
Wrights Pt
Rea Res
Drummoyne Bay
DRUMMOYNE
Wolseley St Wharf
Three Brothers Rocks
Searles Monument
Chiswick Wharf
Blackwall Pt Res
Armitage Res
CHISWICK
Abbotsford Bay
Five Dock Bay
Chambers Park
VICTORIA ROAD
BURNS BAY RD
CENTENNIAL ROAD
PITTWATER RD
HIGH ST
BARONS CR
BORONIA AV
RYDE RD
GLADESVILLE RD
JOLY PDE
CHURCH ST
ALEXANDRA ST
WRIGHTS RD
THE ESPLANADE
WOLSELEY ST
21
40
8

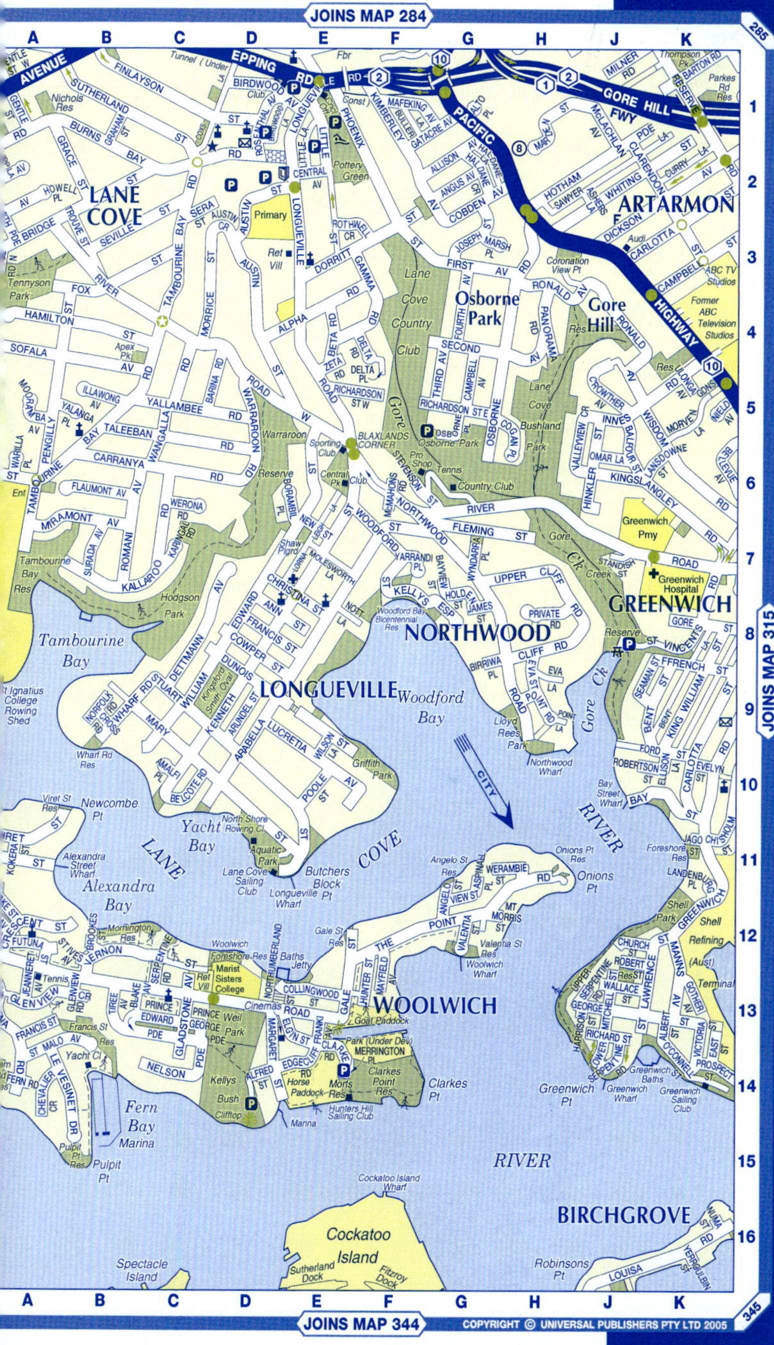
JOINS MAP 284
JOINS MAP 315
JOINS MAP 344
285
345
A
B
C
D
E
F
G
H
J
K
1
2
3
4
5
6
7
8
9
10
11
12
13
14
15
16
LANE COVE
ARTARMON
Osborne Park
Gore Hill
GREENWICH
NORTHWOOD
LONGUEVILLE
WOOLWICH
BIRCHGROVE
AVENUE
EPPING RD
PACIFIC HIGHWAY
GORE HILL FWY
FINLAYSON
SUTHERLAND
BURNS
GRACE
BAY
LONGUEVILLE RD
KIMBERLEY
PHOENIX
MAFEKING
CENTRAL
Primary
Ret Vill
Lane Cove Country Club
Tennyson Park
HAMILTON
SOFALA
FOX
RIVER RD
TAMBOURINE BAY RD
MORRICE
AUSTIN
ALPHA
GAMMA
BETA
DELTA
RICHARDSON
FIRST AV
SECOND
THIRD AV
FOURTH
RONALD AV
PANORAMA
Coronation View Pt
ABC TV Studios
Former ABC Television Studios
Res
HOTHAM
CARLOTTA
CAMPBELL
DICKSON
WHITING
CLARENDON
YALLAMBEE
TALEEBAN
CARRANYA
FLAUMONT AV
MIRAMONT AV
WERONA
KALLAROO
Tambourine Bay
Hodgson Park
Warraroon Reserve
BLAXLANDS CORNER
Sporting Club
Central Pk
Osborne Park
Pro Shop
Tennis
Country Club
Lane Cove Bushland Park
NORTHWOOD RD
RIVER
FLEMING ST
UPPER CLIFF
Gore Ck
Greenwich Pmy
Greenwich Hospital
Woodford Bay Bicentennial Res
Woodford Bay
CITY
Lloyd Rees Park
Northwood Wharf
Bay Street Wharf
ST VINCENTS
KING WILLIAM
Griffith Park
Kingsford Smith Oval
St Ignatius College Rowing Shed
Wharf Rd Res
Newcombe Pt
Yacht Bay
North Shore Rowing Cl
Aquatic Park
Lane Cove Sailing Club
Longueville Wharf
Butchers Block Pt
LANE
COVE
RIVER
Alexandra Bay
Alexandra Street Wharf
Angelo St Res
WERAMBIE
Onions Pt
Valentia St Res
Woolwich Wharf
Marist Sisters College
Woolwich Foreshore Res
Baths Jetty
Goat Paddock
Park (Under Dev)
MERRINGTON PL
Clarkes Point Res
Clarkes Pt
Horse Paddock
Morts Res
Hunters Hill Sailing Club
Kellys Bush
Clifftop
Marina
Fern Bay Marina
Pulpit Pt
Yacht Cl
Shell Park
Shell Refining (Aust)
Terminal
Greenwich Baths
Greenwich Wharf
Greenwich Sailing Club
Greenwich Pt
Cockatoo Island
Cockatoo Island Wharf
Sutherland Dock
Fitzroy Dock
Spectacle Island
Robinsons Pt
LOUISA

JOINS MAP 285

284

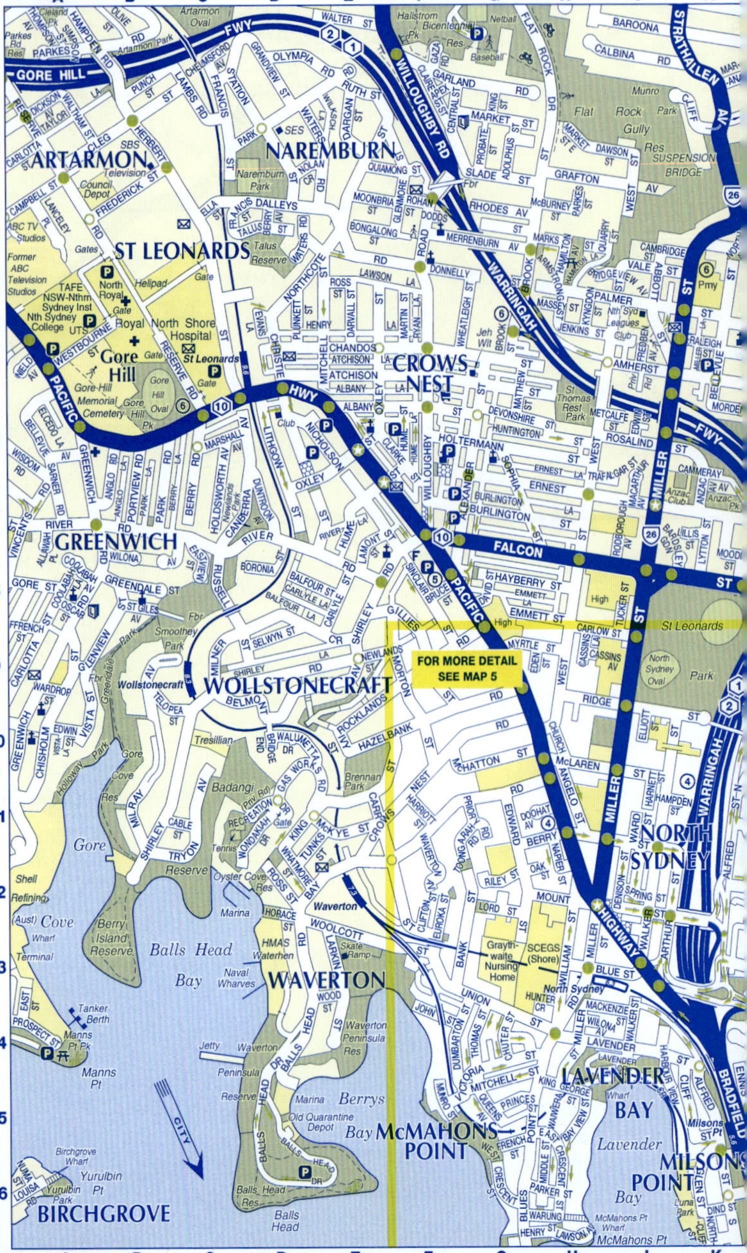

JOINS MAP 314

344

JOINS MAP 345

MAP 316

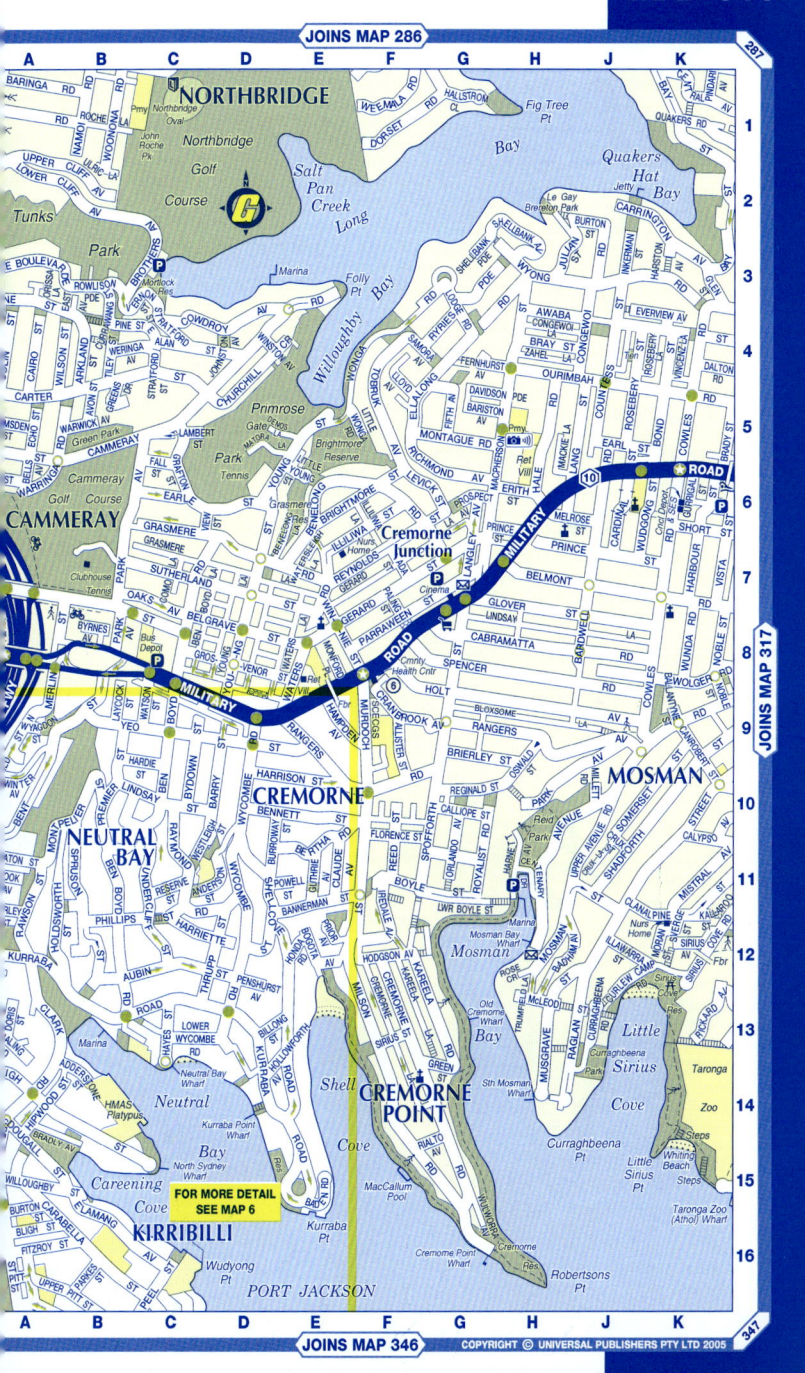

MAP 317

JOINS MAP 287

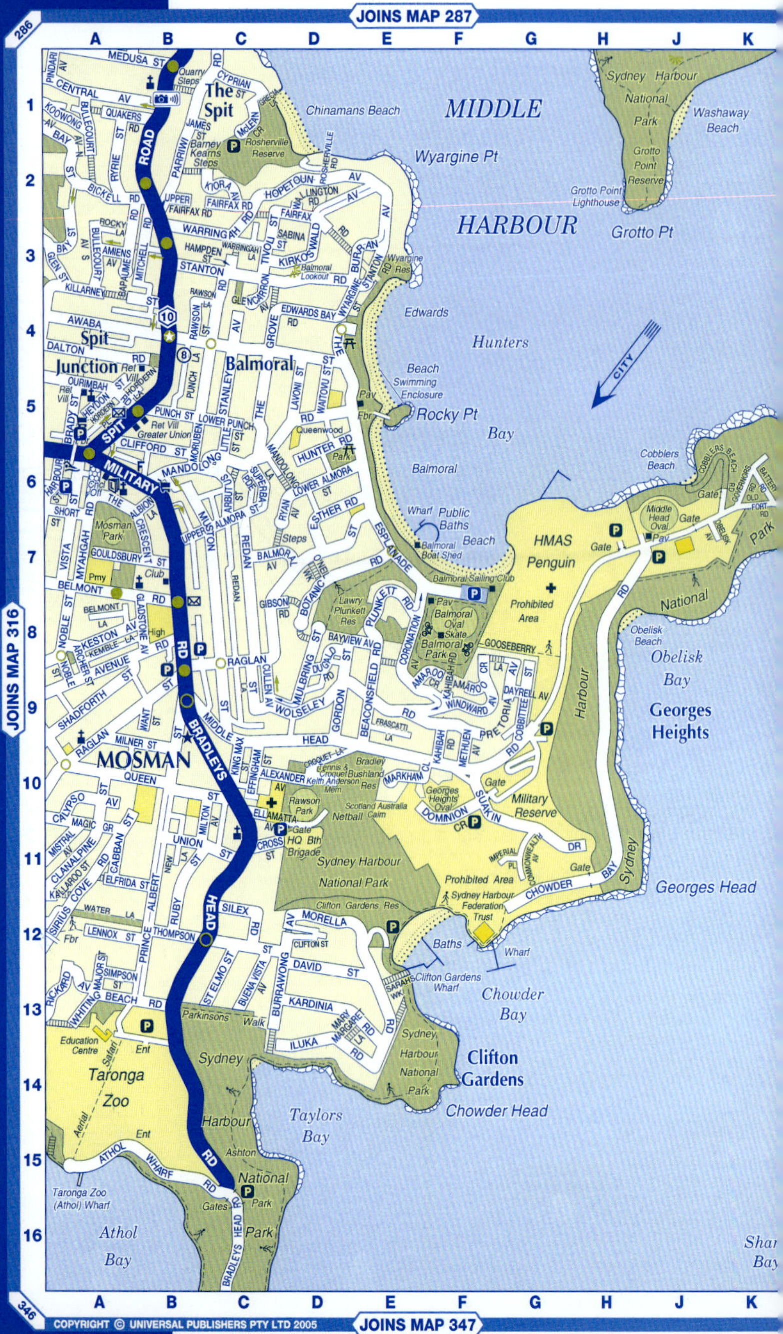

JOINS MAP 347

MAP 318
MAP 323 FOLLOWS

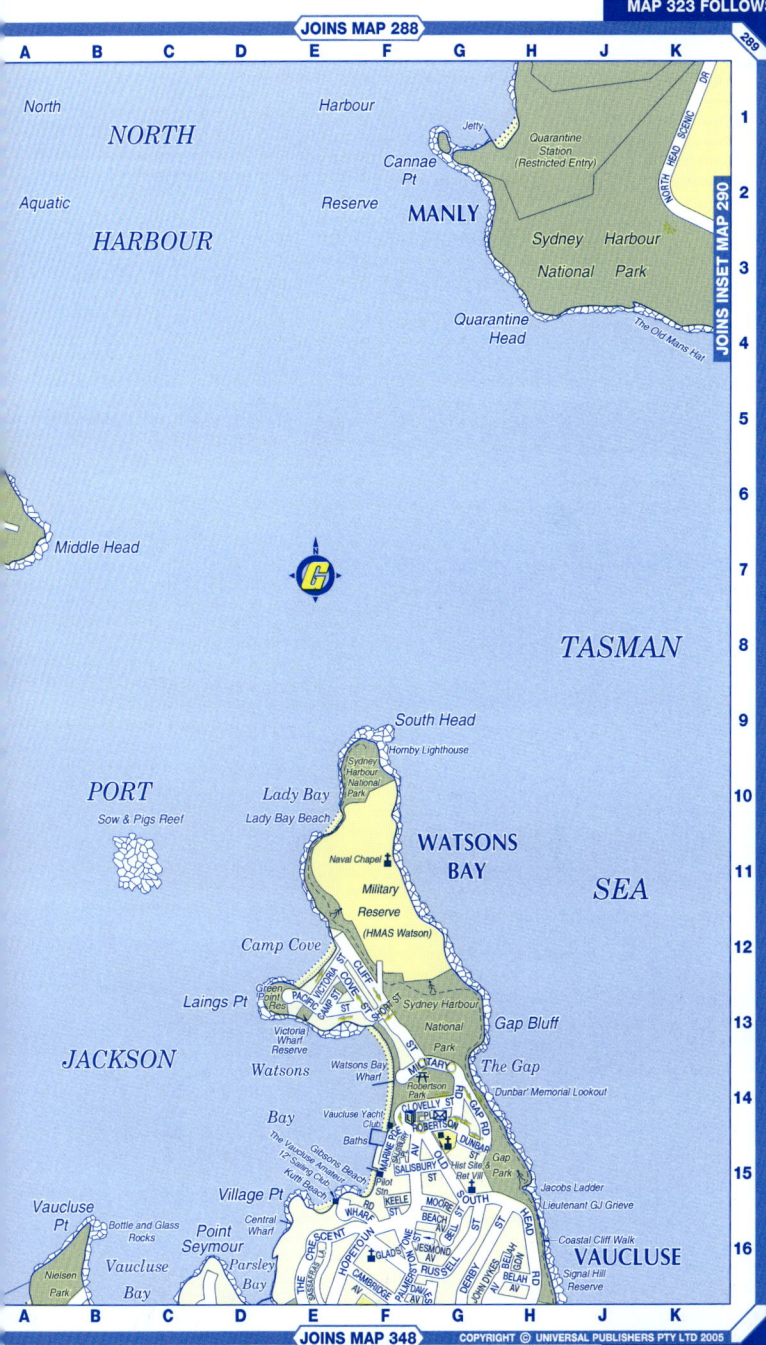

JOINS MAP 288

JOINS MAP 348

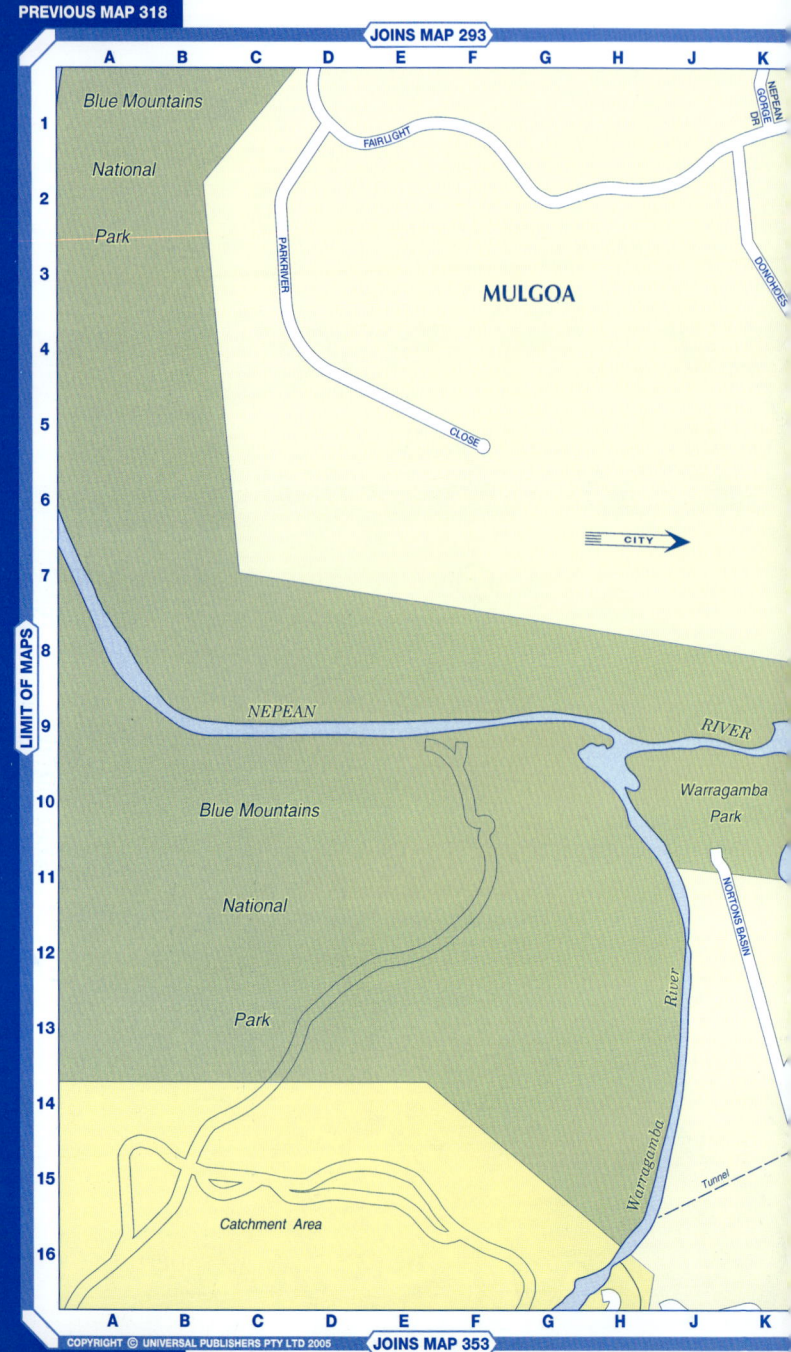

MAP 323
PREVIOUS MAP 318

JOINS MAP 293

Blue Mountains National Park

FAIRLIGHT

PARKRIVER

MULGOA

CLOSE

NEPEAN GORGE DR

DONOHOES

CITY

NEPEAN RIVER

Blue Mountains National Park

Warragamba Park

NORTONS BASIN

Warragamba River

Tunnel

Catchment Area

LIMIT OF MAPS

JOINS MAP 353

COPYRIGHT © UNIVERSAL PUBLISHERS PTY LTD 2005

MAP 324

- Mt Schoenstatt Retreat Cntr
- Henry Cox Dr
- Glenleigh Rd
- Schoenstatt Shrine
- Mt Henry 189m
- Oberug Cl
- Glenleigh Av
- Pipeline
- Supply
- Water
- Sydney
- Nepean
- Nortons Basin
- Jerrys Ck
- Weir
- Blaxland Crossing Reserve
- Water St
- Mulgoa Rd
- Wallacia Golf Course
- Blaxlands Crossing
- Gate
- Alwyn
- Clubhouse
- RFS
- St Charles
- **WALLACIA**
- Road
- Park Rd
- Goleview Dr
- Green St
- Lark Pl
- Ret Vill
- Shelley Rd
- Byron
- Greendale
- Eagle St
- Crossman Pl
- Fowler Reserve
- Peter Pan Av
- Roma Av
- Downes Pl
- Murroobin
- Denton Pl
- Quarry
- Deandar
- Bents Basin Rd
- Creek
- River
- Silverdale Rd
- Baines
- Davenport Dr
- Hopewood Health Centre
- Saladillo Gr

JOINS MAP 294 (top)
JOINS MAP 295 (right top)
JOINS MAP 325 (right bottom)
JOINS MAP 354 (bottom)
JOINS MAP 355 (right bottom corner)

COPYRIGHT © UNIVERSAL PUBLISHERS PTY LTD 2005

MAP 325

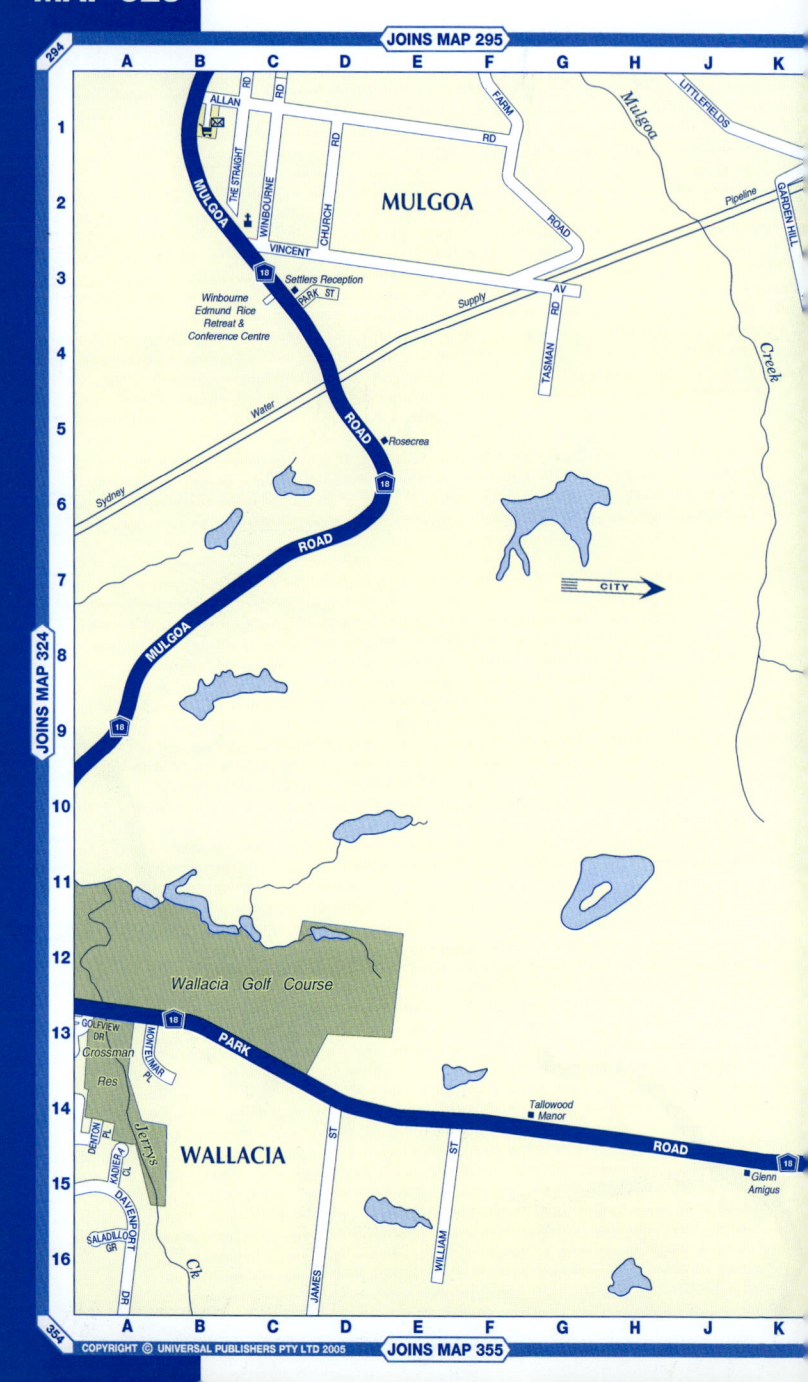

JOINS MAP 295

MULGOA

- Allan
- Mulgoa Rd
- The Straight
- Winbourne Rd
- Vincent
- Church Rd
- Farm Rd
- Mulgoa Rd
- Littlefields
- Garden Hill
- Park St
- Settlers Reception
- Winbourne Edmund Rice Retreat & Conference Centre
- Supply
- Tasman Rd
- AV
- Pipeline
- Creek
- Water Road
- Rosecrea
- Sydney
- Mulgoa Road
- CITY

JOINS MAP 324

WALLACIA

- Wallacia Golf Course
- Golfview Dr
- Crossman
- Montelimar Pl
- Park Road
- Denton Pl
- Kanera Cl
- Jerrys
- Davenport Dr
- Saladillo Gr
- Res
- James St
- William St
- Tallowood Manor
- Glenn Amigus
- Ck

JOINS MAP 355

MAP 326

JOINS MAP 296

LUDDENHAM

Labels visible on map:
- Sydney Water Supply Pipeline
- Gates Rd
- The Northern Road
- Oaky Rd
- Queens Hill Dr
- Galaxy Rd
- Pleasant View
- Baiada
- Park Road
- Nursery
- Nalla Boarding Kennels
- Luddenham Showground
- Campbell St
- Hawkins Av

JOINS MAP 296 (top) · JOINS MAP 297 (right top) · JOINS MAP 327 (right bottom) · JOINS MAP 356 (bottom) · JOINS MAP 357 (bottom right)

COPYRIGHT © UNIVERSAL PUBLISHERS PTY LTD 2005

MAP 327

JOINS MAP 297

LUDDENHAM

Blackford 101m

Hillview

Sydney Society of Model Engineers "Model Park"

Ent

Luddenham Lodge

LUDDENHAM ROAD

ELIZABETH

Creek

Creek

52

DRIVE

Cosgrove ROAD

Ferndale Produce

Oaky

ADAMS

ANTON RD

Gate

Hubertus Country Club

JOINS MAP 326
JOINS MAP 296
JOINS MAP 356
JOINS MAP 357

COPYRIGHT © UNIVERSAL PUBLISHERS PTY LTD 2005

MAP 328

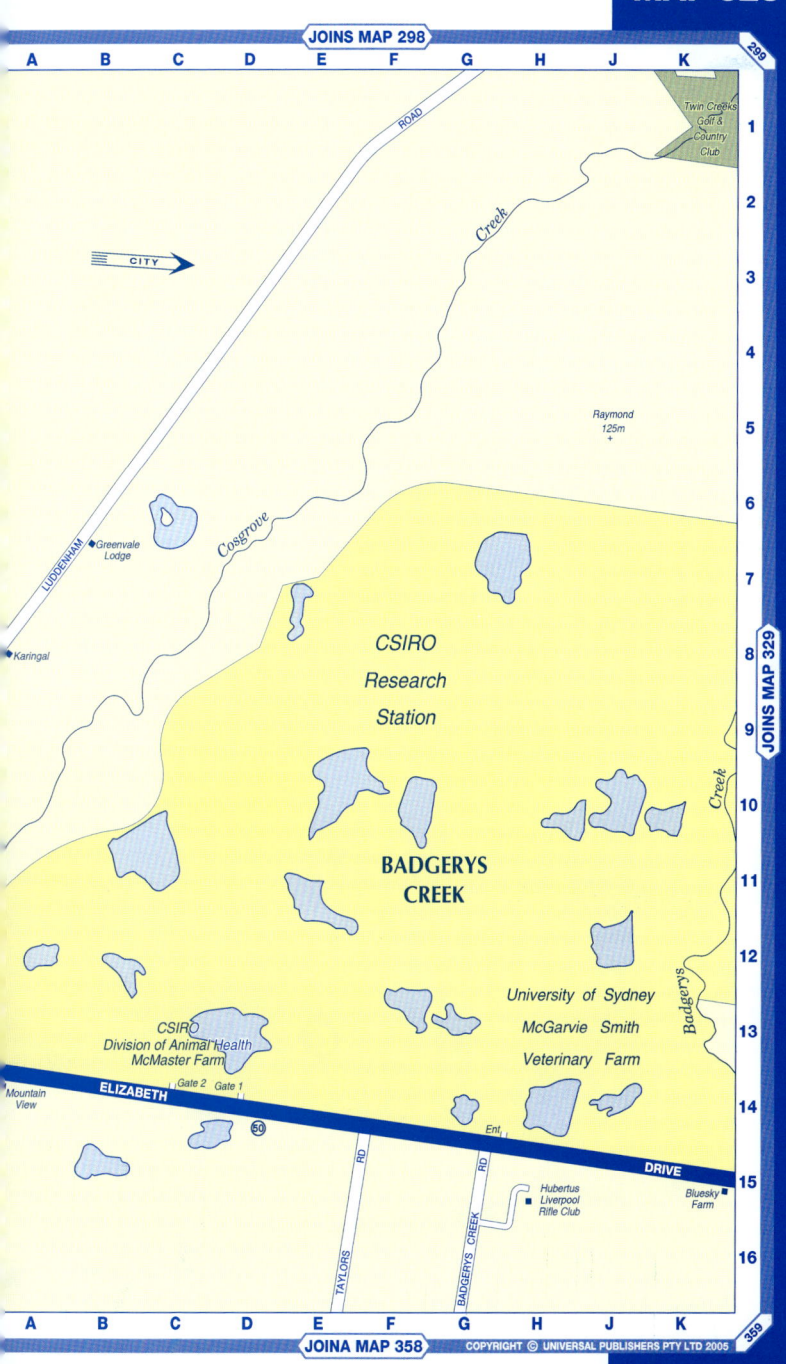

JOINS MAP 298

Twin Creeks Golf & Country Club

CITY

Creek

Cosgrove

Raymond 125m

Ludenham
Greenvale Lodge

Karingal

CSIRO Research Station

Badgerys Creek

BADGERYS CREEK

CSIRO Division of Animal Health McMaster Farm

University of Sydney McGarvie Smith Veterinary Farm

Mountain View

ELIZABETH   Gate 2 Gate 1   Ent.   DRIVE

TAYLORS RD

BADGERYS CREEK RD

Hubertus Liverpool Rifle Club

Bluesky Farm

JOINS MAP 358

JOINS MAP 329

COPYRIGHT © UNIVERSAL PUBLISHERS PTY LTD 2005

MAP 329

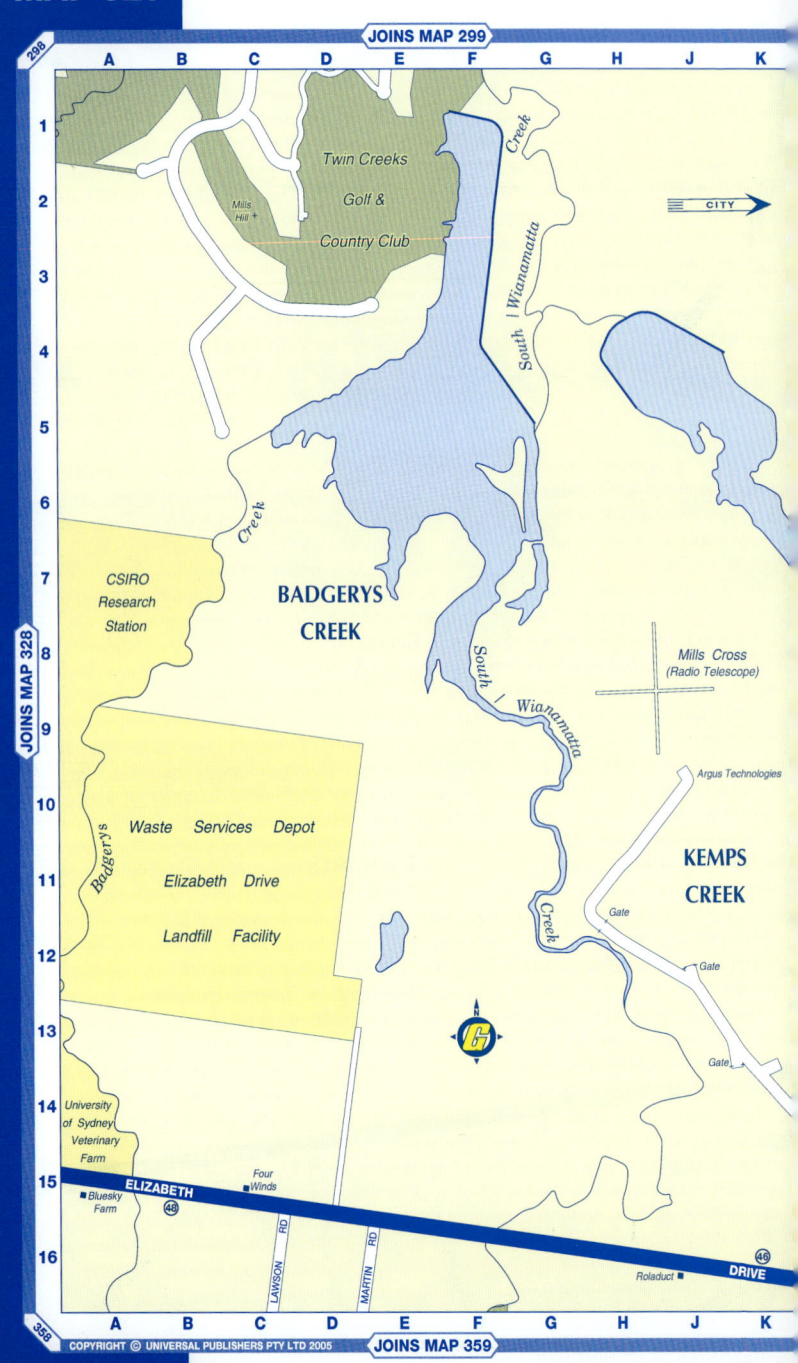

- Twin Creeks Golf & Country Club
- Mills Hill
- South Wianamatta Creek
- CSIRO Research Station
- BADGERYS CREEK
- Mills Cross (Radio Telescope)
- Argus Technologies
- KEMPS CREEK
- Badgerys Creek
- Waste Services Depot Elizabeth Drive Landfill Facility
- University of Sydney Veterinary Farm
- Bluesky Farm
- Four Winds
- ELIZABETH DRIVE
- LAWSON RD
- MARTIN RD
- Roladuct

JOINS MAP 299 (top)
JOINS MAP 328 (left)
JOINS MAP 359 (bottom)

MAP 330

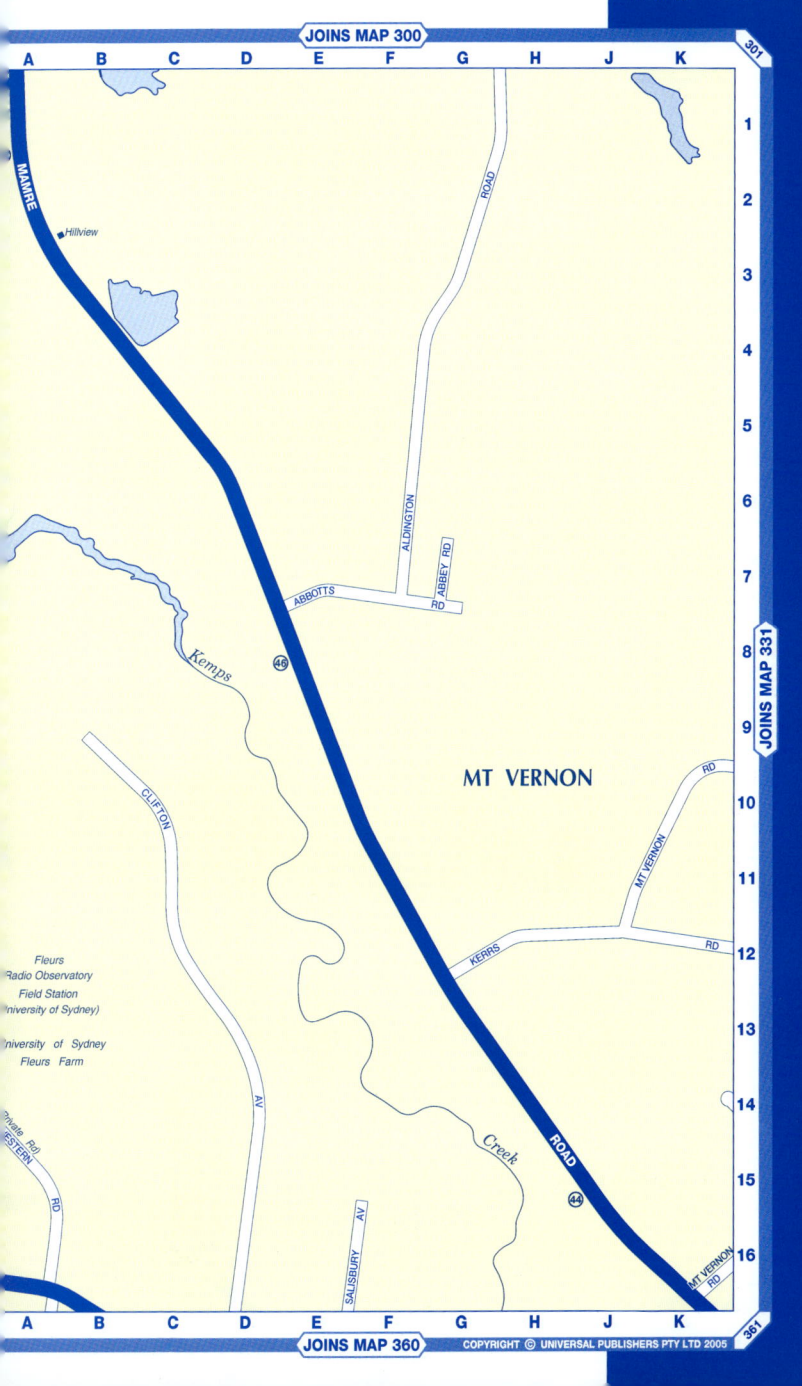

JOINS MAP 300

MAMRE

Hillview

ALDINGTON ROAD

ABBEY RD

ABBOTTS RD

Kemps

MT VERNON

CLIFTON AV

MT VERNON RD

KERRS ROAD

Fleurs
Radio Observatory
Field Station
(University of Sydney)

University of Sydney
Fleurs Farm

WESTERN RD

SALSBURY AV

Creek

MT VERNON RD

JOINS MAP 360

JOINS MAP 331

COPYRIGHT © UNIVERSAL PUBLISHERS PTY LTD 2005

MAP 331

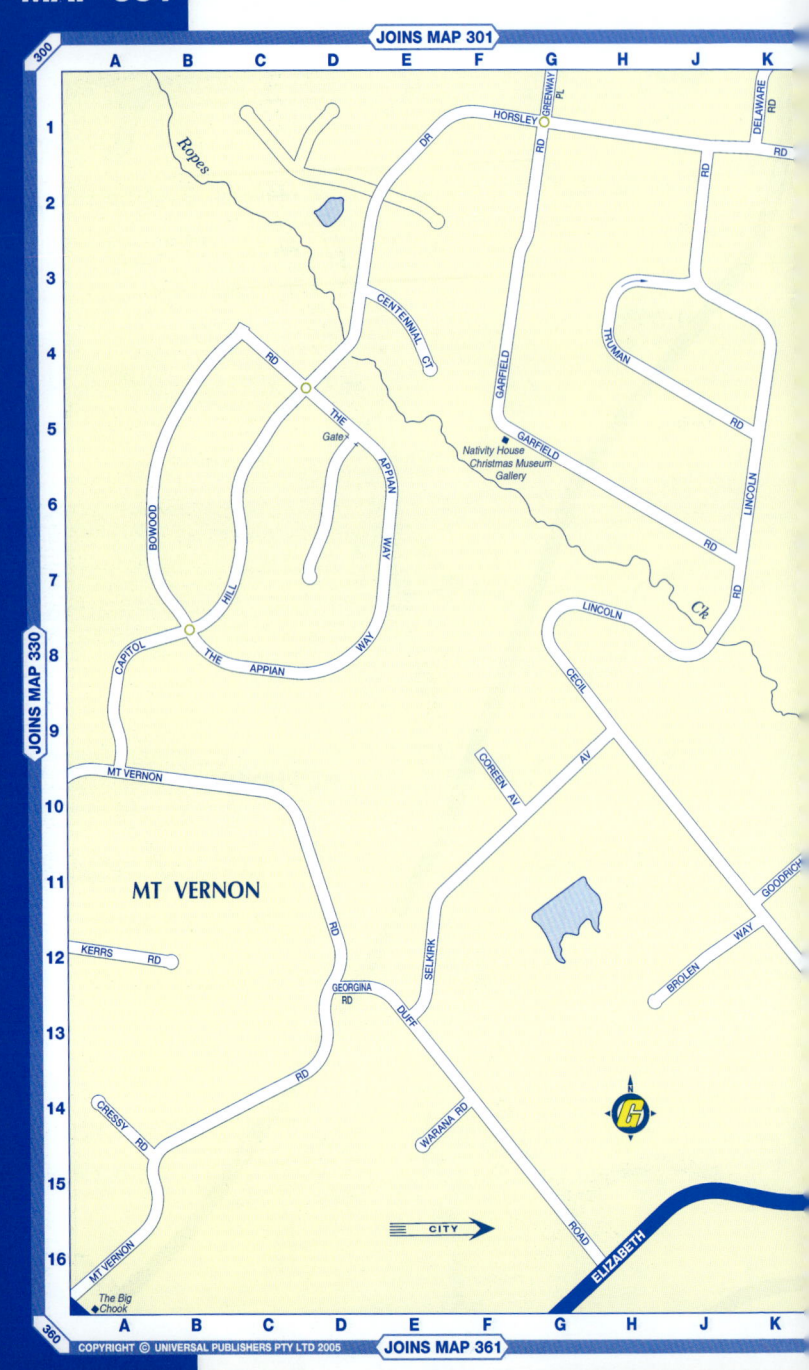

MAP 332

Key features

- Horsley Park
- Cecil Park
- Abbotsbury
- Sydney International Equestrian Centre
  - Main Ent Gate
  - Stables
  - Indoor Arena
  - Practice Arenas
  - Main Stadium
  - Steeple Chase
- Western Sydney Regional Park
- Wallgrove Garden Centre
- Fairfield City Farm
- Sugarloaf Ridge
- Reservoir
- Devils Back Tunnel
- Channel Tunnel
- Cecil Hills Tunnel

Roads and streets

- JAMIESON CL
- BARBARO LA
- COBHAM ST
- FELTON ST
- HORSLEY WAY
- KOALA WAY
- KOALA DR
- ABBOTSBURY RD
- CALMSLEY PL
- ALAINE PL
- FARLEY RD
- VILLIERS RD
- WALLGROVE RD
- Westlink M7 (Under Construction / Due for completion 2006)
- Sydney – Cecil Hills Tunnel (Proposed)
- SAXONY Gate
- SOUTHDOWN RD
- BORDER RD
- COTSWOLD RD
- Supply Hills
- Water
- TRIGON RD
- BALSON CL
- LEWERS CL
- WHITLEY PL
- USHER CL
- ASHINGTON WY
- DRIVE
- ROAD 61
- 40
- M7
- Mountain bike Track

JOINS MAP 302 (top)
JOINS MAP 362 (bottom)
JOINS MAP 303 (right top)
JOINS MAP 333 (right bottom)

COPYRIGHT © UNIVERSAL PUBLISHERS PTY LTD 2005

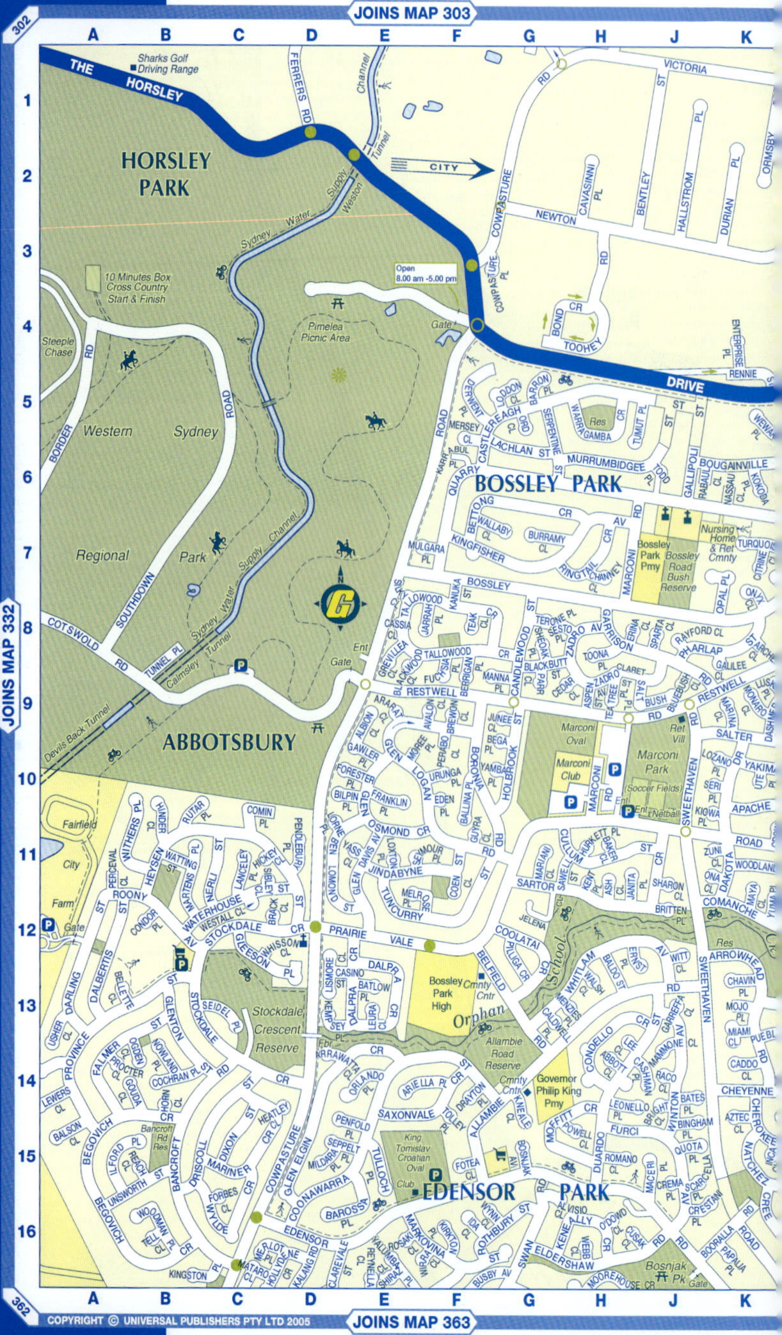
JOINS MAP 303
JOINS MAP 332
JOINS MAP 363
302
362
A B C D E F G H J K
1 2 3 4 5 6 7 8 9 10 11 12 13 14 15 16
THE HORSLEY DRIVE
Sharks Golf Driving Range
HORSLEY PARK
CITY
BOSSLEY PARK
ABBOTSBURY
EDENSOR PARK
Western Sydney Regional Park
Sydney Water Supply Channel
Weston Tunnel
Channel Tunnel
10 Minutes Box Cross Country Start & Finish
Steeple Chase
Pimelea Picnic Area
Open 8.00 am -5.00 pm
Gate
Ent
Devils Back Tunnel
Calmsley Tunnel
TUNNEL PL
COTSWOLD RD
SOUTHDOWN ROAD
BORDER RD
FERRERS RD
COWPASTURE RD
VICTORIA
NEWTON
CAVASINNI PL
BENTLEY ST
HALLSTROM PL
DURIAN PL
ORMSBY
BOND CR
TOOHEY
ENTERPRISE PL
RENNIE
RESTWELL RD
BOSSLEY
PRAIRIE VALE
Marconi Oval
Marconi Club
Marconi Park (Soccer Fields)
Netball
Ret Vill
Bossley Park Pmy
Bossley Road Bush Reserve
Nursing Home & Ret Cmnty
Bossley Park High
Cmnty Cntr
Orphan School Ck
Allambie Road Reserve
Governor Philip King Pmy
King Tomislav Croatian Oval
Club
Stockdale Crescent Reserve
Fairfield City Farm
Bancroft Rd Res
Bosnjak Pk
SWEETHAVEN RD
MARCONI RD
SAXONVALE
EDENSOR RD
ELDERSHAW
STOCKDALE CR
WATERHOUSE ST
CANDLEWOOD ST
BUSBY AV
KINGSTON
BOORALLA ROAD
ALLAMBIE
BOSNJAK AV

JOINS MAP 304
JOINS MAP 335
JOINS MAP 364
305
365
A B C D E F G H J K
1 2 3 4 5 6 7 8 9 10 11 12 13 14 15 16
WETHERILL PARK
PRAIRIEWOOD
WAKELEY
ST JOHNS PARK
GREENFIELD PARK
THE HORSLEY DRIVE
VICTORIA ST
CSR Industrial Area
Industrial Area
Victoria
Elizabeth
Wetherill
Wetherill Park Business Cntr
Buddhist Temple
Abruzzi Sports Club
Slovenian Social Club
Greenway Plaza
Mot Reg
Reservoir
Horsley
Wetherill Park
TAFE NSW - South Western Sydney Institute Wetherill Park College
Wetherill Park Shopping Centre
Tenpin Bowl
Skate Pk
Tennis
Emerson Street Reserve
William Stimson Pmy
Cinemas
Stockland Shopping Centre
Prairiewood
Fbr
NRMA
Prairiewood High
Fairfield
Gate
Fairfield Golf Course
Braeside
Terone Park
Calabria Cmnty Club (Soccer)
Youth & Cmnty Cntr
NSW Spastic Assoc
Leisure Centre
Choma Pk
Clubhouse
Flora Park
Dog Training Area
Steam Train Rides
Hall
Fairfield Showground
Parklands Function Cntr
Deerbush Park
Prairievale Primary
Orphan School
Orphan School Ck
Mary McKillop College
Esperance Res
Innisfail Res
Wylde Pk
Greenfield
Cmnty Cntr
St Johns Park High
St Johns
Club
Nurs Home
Clear Paddock
Clear Paddock Ck
Paddock
King Park
King Park Pmy
Hampshire Res
Canley Heights RSL
COPYRIGHT © UNIVERSAL PUBLISHERS PTY LTD 2005

JOINS MAP 305
JOINS MAP 334
JOINS MAP 365
304
364
WETHERILL PARK
SMITHFIELD
FAIRFIELD WEST
CANLEY HEIGHTS
CANLEY VALE
THE HORSLEY DRIVE
SMITHFIELD (CUMBERLAND HWY)
PALMERSTON RD
NEW CAMBRIDGE ST
CAMBRIDGE (CUMBERLAND HWY) ST
Prospect Creek
Brenan Park
Endeavour Sports Reserve
Westfields Sports High
Fairvale High
Smithfield Primary
Smithfield West Pmy
Queens Square
Vehicle Inspection Station
TAFE NSW
Orphan School Creek
Green Valley Creek
King Park
Avery Park
Prospect View Park
Charles Park
Gipps Park
Victoria St Pk
Smithfield Cemetery
Brian Wunsch Centre
Council Office
Assyrian Club
Aldi
Mosque
Cmnty Hall
Baseball
Soccer
Tennis
Netball
RSL
Thorley Park
Museum & Gallery

MAP 336

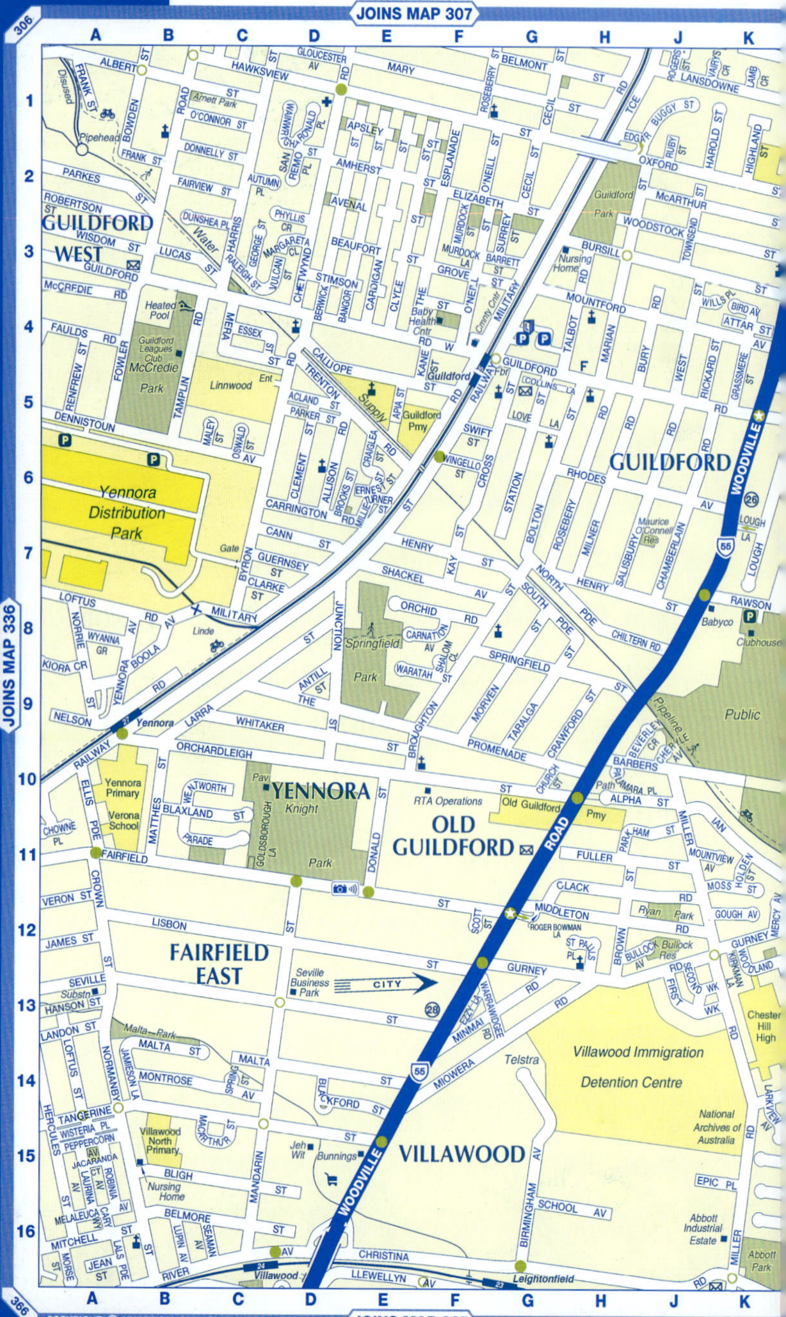

JOINS MAP 367

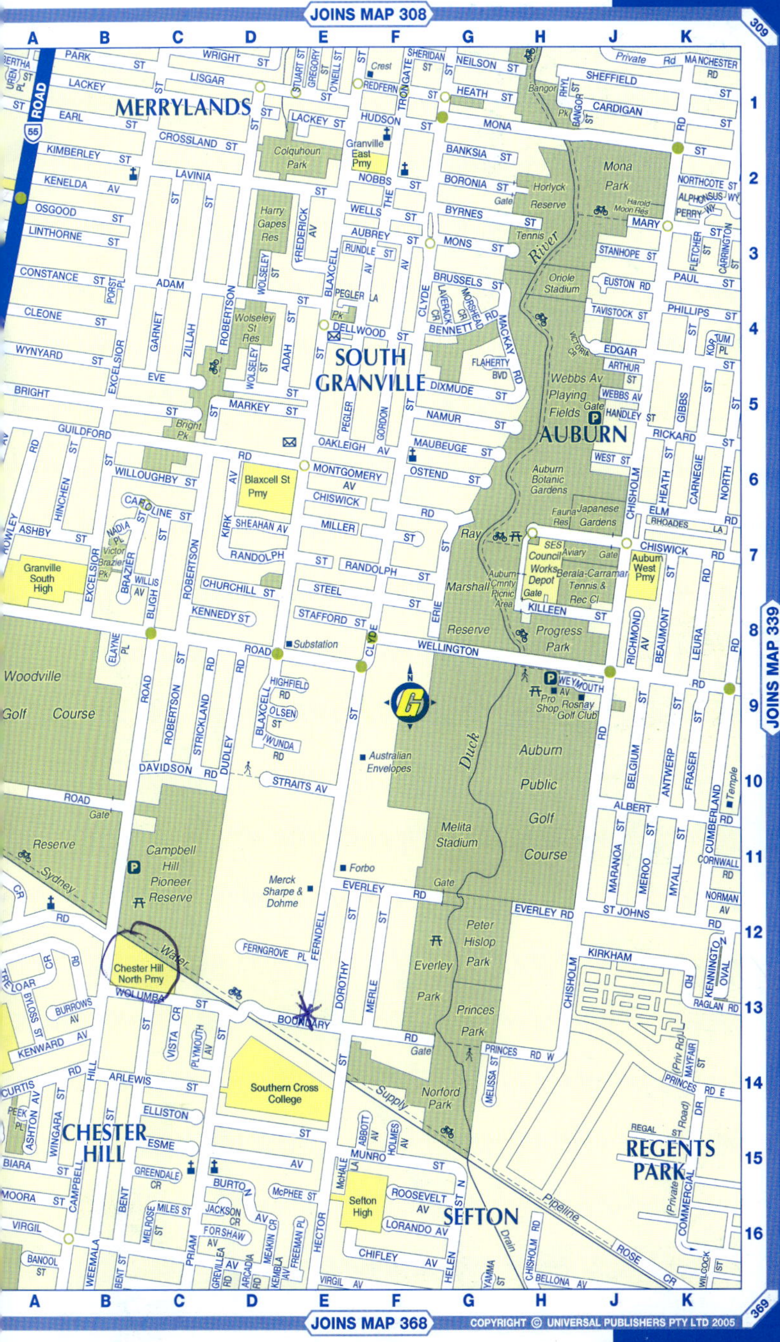
JOINS MAP 308
JOINS MAP 339
JOINS MAP 368
309
369
A B C D E F G H J K
1 2 3 4 5 6 7 8 9 10 11 12 13 14 15 16
MERRYLANDS
SOUTH GRANVILLE
AUBURN
CHESTER HILL
SEFTON
REGENTS PARK
PARK ST
WRIGHT ST
LISGAR
LACKEY ST
EARL ST
CROSSLAND ST
KIMBERLEY ST
LAVINIA
KENELDA AV
OSGOOD ST
LINTHORNE ST
CONSTANCE ST
PORST PL
ADAM
CLEONE ST
WYNYARD ST
BRIGHT
EVE
MARKEY ST
GUILDFORD
WILLOUGHBY ST
CAROLINE ST
ASHBY ST
GARNET
ZILLAH
ROBERTSON
WOLSELEY ST
ADAH
EXCELSIOR
Colquhoun Park
Harry Gapes Res
Wolseley St Res
Bright Pk
FREDERICK AV
BLAXCELL
PEGLER
GORDON
Granville East Pmy
HUDSON
NOBBS
WELLS
AUBREY
RUNDLE
PEGLER LA
DELLWOOD
OAKLEIGH AV
MONTGOMERY AV
CHISWICK
MILLER
RANDOLPH ST
STEEL
STAFFORD ST
Substation
Blaxcell St Pmy
SHEAHAN AV
KIRK
CHURCHILL ST
KENNEDY ST
ROAD
Granville South High
Victor Brazier Pk
NADIA PL
WILLIS AV
BLIGH
ELAYNE PL
Woodville Golf Course
HIGHFIELD RD
OLSEN ST
WUNDA RD
DAVIDSON RD
STRICKLAND
DUDLEY
STRAITS AV
Australian Envelopes
Reserve
Gate
Sydney Water Supply Pipeline
Campbell Hill Pioneer Reserve
Chester Hill North Pmy
Merck Sharpe & Dohme
Forbo
FERNGROVE PL
FERNDELL
EVERLEY RD
DOROTHY
MERLE
BOUNDARY RD
WOLUMBA
VISTA CR
PLYMOUTH AV
Southern Cross College
ARLEWIS ST
ELLISTON
ESME
GREENDALE CR
BURTON
McPHEE ST
JACKSON CR
MILES ST
FORSHAW AV
MELROSE
PRIAM
GREVILLEA RD
ARCADIA RD
KEMBLA AV
MEAKIN CR
FREEMAN PL
HECTOR
VIRGIL AV
MUNRO ST
ABBOTT AV
HOLMES AV
McHALE LA
Sefton High
ROOSEVELT AV
LORANDO AV
CHIFLEY AV
HELEN
Norford Park
TRELOAR
BYLOSS ST
BURROWS AV
KENWARD AV
CURTIS RD
PEEK PL
ASHTON AV
WINGARA
HILL
BIARA ST
CAMPBELL
BENT
MOORA ST
VIRGIL
BANOOL ST
WEEMALA
BENT ST
SHERIDAN ST
NEILSON ST
Crest
REDFERN
TRONGATE
HEATH ST
MONA
BANKSIA ST
BORONIA ST
BYRNES
MONS ST
BRUSSELS ST
LAVERACK CR
MORSHEAD CR
BENNETT
MACKAY RD
FLAHERTY BVD
DIXMUDE ST
NAMUR ST
MAUBEUGE ST
OSTEND ST
CLYDE
ERIE
WELLINGTON
Ray Marshall Reserve
Duck River
Horlyck Reserve
Tennis
Oriole Stadium
Webbs Av Playing Fields
Auburn Botanic Gardens
Fauna Res
Japanese Gardens
SES Council Works Depot
Aviary
Auburn Cmnty Picnic Area
Berala-Carramar Tennis & Rec Cl
KILLEEN ST
Progress Park
WEYMOUTH AV
Pro Shop
Rosnay Golf Club
Auburn Public Golf Course
Melita Stadium
Peter Hislop Park
Everley Park
Princes Park
PRINCES RD W
MELISSA ST
YAMMA ST
CHISHOLM RD
BELLONA AV
Drain
Private Rd
MANCHESTER RD
SHEFFIELD
Bangor Pk
RHYL
BANGOR ST
CARDIGAN
Mona Park
Harold Moon Res
NORTHCOTE ST
ALPHONSUS WY
PERRY WY
MARY
STANHOPE ST
FLETCHER ST
CARRINGTON ST
PAUL ST
EUSTON RD
TAVISTOCK ST
PHILLIPS ST
KORTUM PL
VICTORIA CR
EDGAR
ARTHUR ST
WEBBS AV
HANDLEY ST
GIBBS
RICKARD
WEST ST
CHISHOLM
HEATH ST
CARNEGIE
NORTH
ELM
RHOADES LA
CHISWICK RD
Auburn West Pmy
RICHMOND AV
BEAUMONT
LEURA
BELGIUM
ANTWERP
FRASER
CUMBERLAND RD
Temple
ALBERT
MARANOA ST
MEROO
MYALL ST
CORNWALL RD
NORMAN AV
ST JOHNS
KIRKHAM
KENNINGTON OVAL
RAGLAN RD
MAYFAIR ST
(Priv Rd)
PRINCES RD E
REGAL ST
(Private Road)
COMMERCIAL DR
ROSE CR
WILCOCK ST
55
COPYRIGHT © UNIVERSAL PUBLISHERS PTY LTD 2005

MAP 339

JOINS MAP 309
JOINS MAP 338
JOINS MAP 369
308
368
A B C D E F G H J K
1 2 3 4 5 6 7 8 9 10 11 12 13 14 15 16
AUBURN
LIDCOMBE
BERALA
REGENTS PARK
PARRAMATTA RD
ST HILLIERS ROAD
BOOREA ST
OLYMPIC DRIVE
JOSEPH ST
MANCHESTER RD
SHEFFIELD ST
CARDIGAN
NORTHCOTE
MARY
HAPP ST
PAUL
PHILLIPS ST
LILY ST
LANGTRY AV
EDGAR
PROVINCIAL RD
RICKARD ST
UNION
CHESTNUT
PINE
ELM
CHISWICK
WELLINGTON RD
VAUGHAN
NORMAN
MT AUBURN
ALBERT
CORNWALL
CLARKE
ST JOHNS
LIDBURY
YORK
RAGLAN
PRINCES RD E
JENKINS
WALTERS
St Josephs Hospital
Auburn Central
Westside Hearing Clinic
Cncl Off
Mosque
Jnr
Snr
Auburn
Tooheys
Haslams
Tiger-Wests Athletic Club
Gate Netball
Anne Clark Netball Centre
Basketball Centre
Wyatt Park
Lidcombe Oval & Velodrome
Youth Cntr
Auburn Swim Cntr
Tennis
Chadwick Res
Civic Pk
Dudley Pk
Norman Pk
York Pk
Grey Box Gum Res
Nursing Home
Temple
Lidcombe
Cath Club
RSL
Berala
Baseball
Coleman Park
Carnarvon Golf Course
Clubhouse
M S Centre
Norman May Park
TAFE NSW Southern Sydney Institute Lidcombe College
Former Lidcombe Hospital
Uni of Sydney Cumberland Campus
Hardware House
Cinemas
Spencer St Res
Kibo Res
Christian Cmnty High
Guilfoyle Pk
Stormwater Channel
NECROPOLIS
RAILWAY

JOINS MAP 310

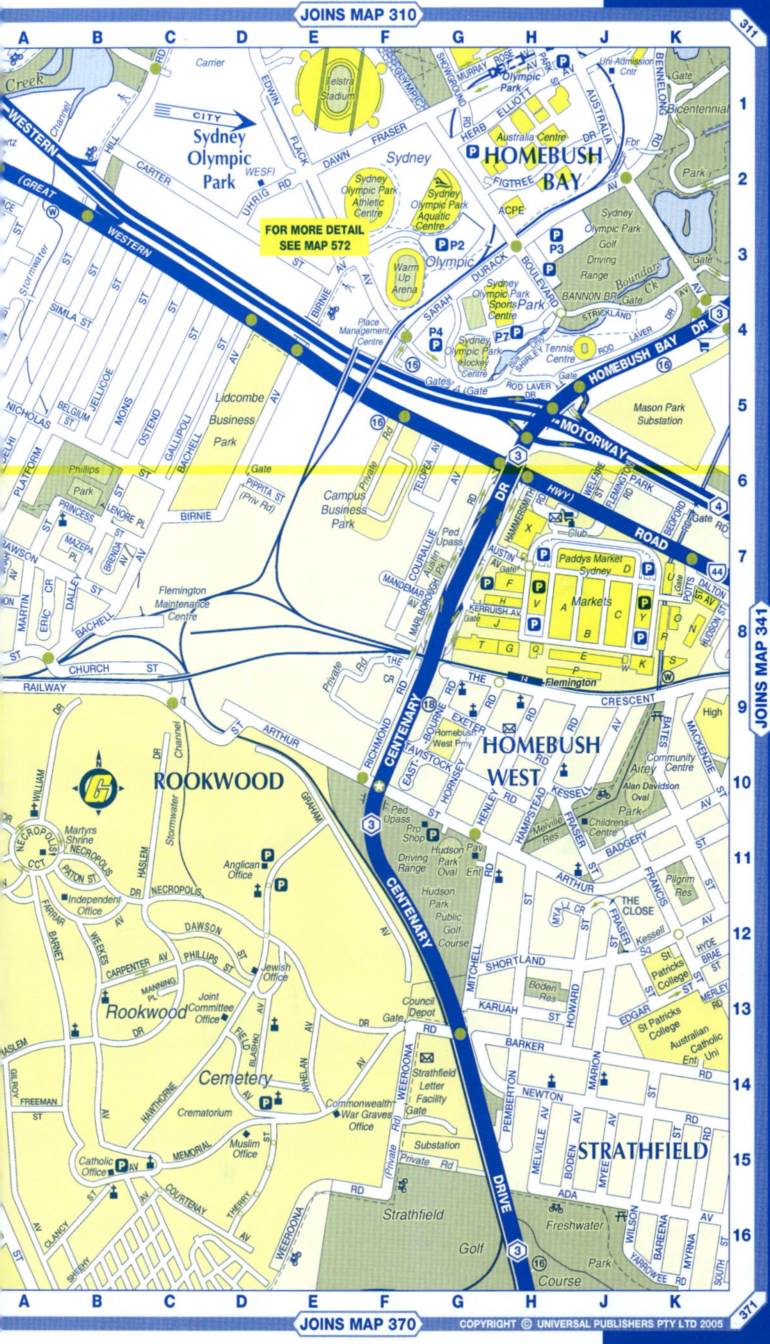

JOINS MAP 370

JOINS MAP 311
JOINS MAP 340
JOINS MAP 371
310
370
HOMEBUSH
CONCORD WEST
CONCORD
NORTH STRATHFIELD
STRATHFIELD
Concord Golf Course
Clubhouse
CITY
Bicentennial Park
Treillage
Radio Tower
Tea House
Bressington Park
Mason Park
Homebush Wetlands
Mason Park Substn
FOR MORE DETAIL SEE MAP 572
Homebush Substation
Stormwater Channel
Bill Boyce Res
Majors Bay Res
Central Park
Henley Park
Goddard Park
Homebush Boys High
Seminary of The Good Shepherd
Fitzgerald Pk
Catholic Theological College
Strathfield Girls High
SDA College
Australian Catholic Uni
Mt Royal Reserve
Chalmers Rd Special
Trinity Gram Prep
Santa Sabina College
Santa Maria Del Monte
Burwood Pmy
Burwood Plaza
Strathfield Plaza
TAFE (OTEN)
Meth Ladies Coll
MLC
Burwood Park
Strathfield Nth Pmy
Homebush Pmy
Concord West
St Ambroses Cath
HOMEBUSH BAY DR
CONCORD RD
PARRAMATTA RD
WESTERN MOTORWAY
THE BOULEVARDE
LEICESTER AV
REDMYRE RD
PATTERSON ST
GIPPS
COPYRIGHT © UNIVERSAL PUBLISHERS PTY LTD 2005

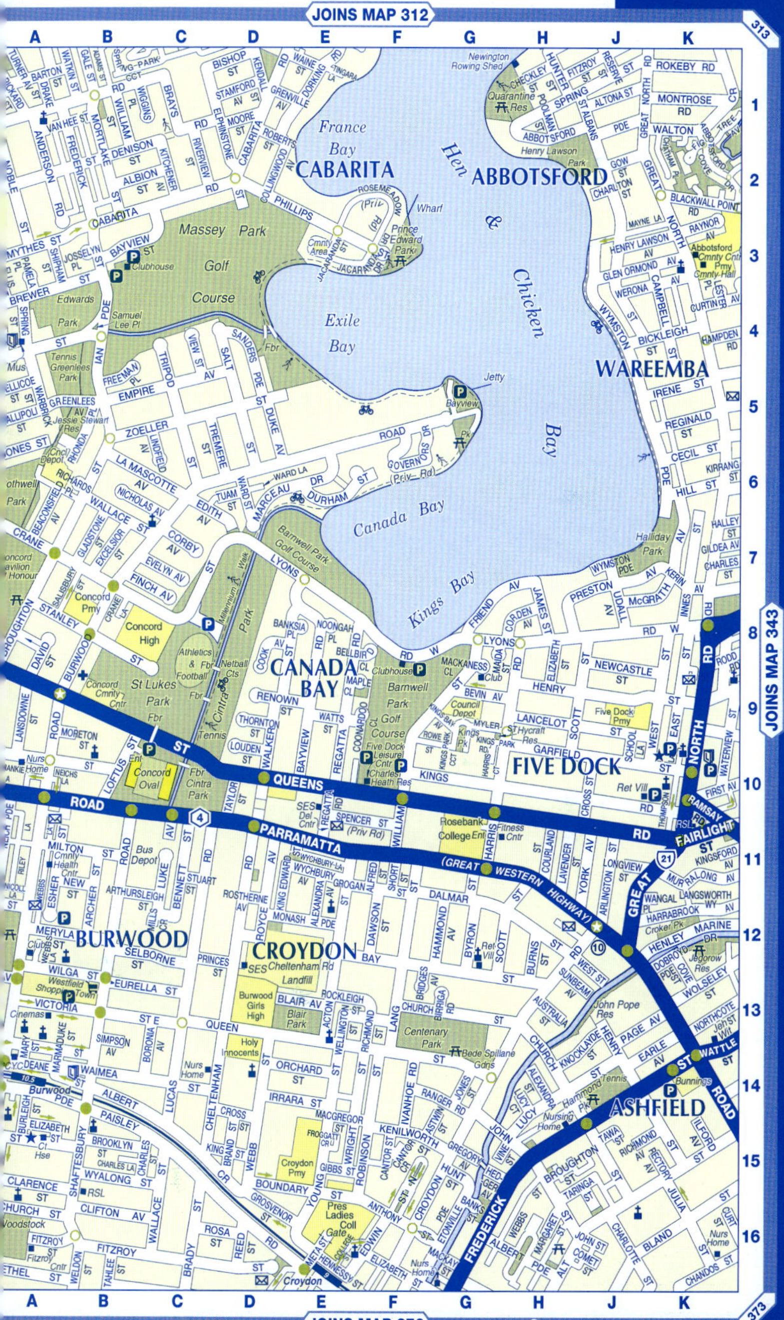

MAP 343

COPYRIGHT © UNIVERSAL PUBLISHERS PTY LTD 2005

JOINS MAP 373

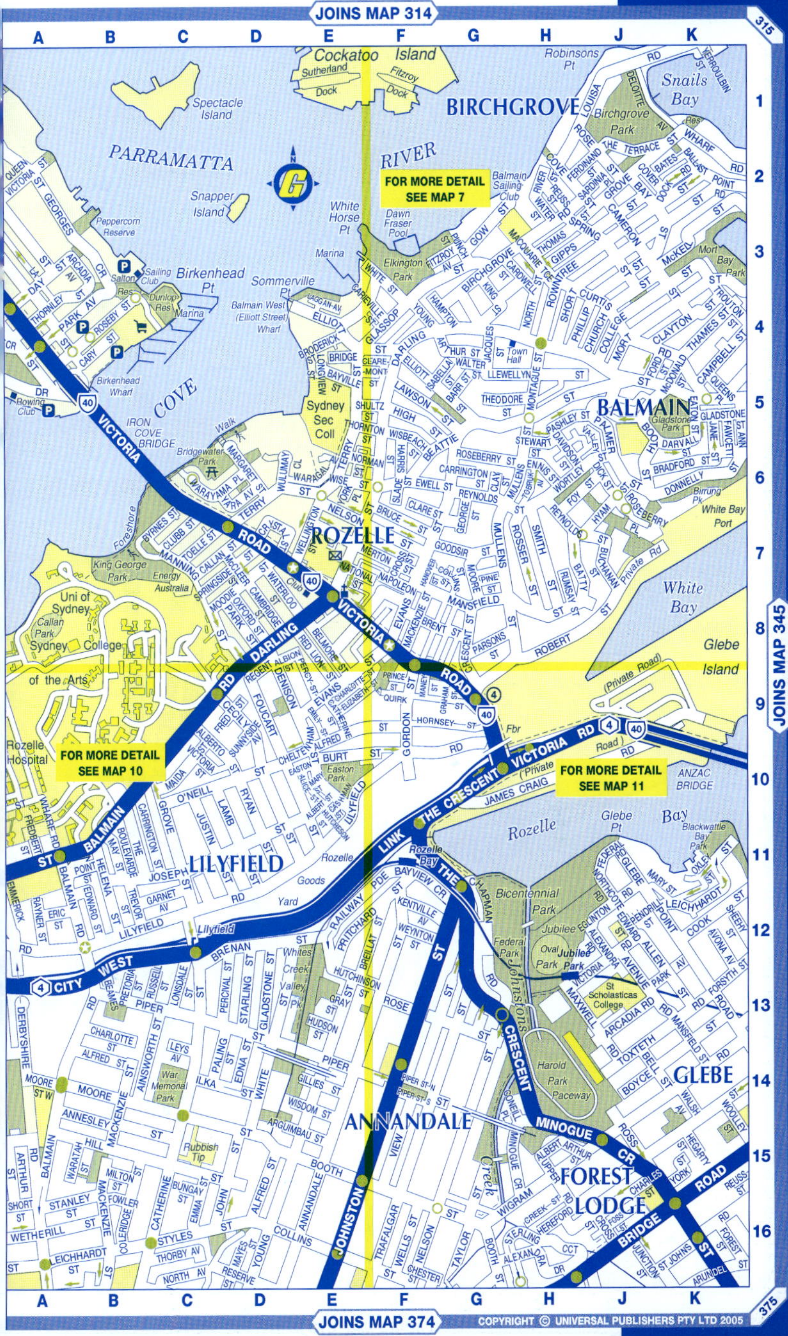
JOINS MAP 314
JOINS MAP 345
JOINS MAP 374
315
375
A B C D E F G H J K
1 2 3 4 5 6 7 8 9 10 11 12 13 14 15 16
Cockatoo Island
Sutherland Dock
Fitzroy Dock
Spectacle Island
PARRAMATTA RIVER
Snapper Island
Robinsons Pt
BIRCHGROVE
Birchgrove Park
Snails Bay
FOR MORE DETAIL SEE MAP 7
White Horse Pt
Dawn Fraser Pool
Balmain Sailing Club
Elkington Park
Peppercorn Reserve
Birkenhead Pt
Sailing Club
Dunlop Res
Marina
Sommerville Pt
Balmain West (Elliott Street) Wharf
Birkenhead Wharf
Rowing Club
IRON COVE BRIDGE
COVE
VICTORIA ROAD
Bridgewater Park
Sydney Sec Coll
Town Hall
BALMAIN
Gladstone Park
Birrung Pk
White Bay Port
ROZELLE
King George Park
Energy Australia
Foreshore Walk
Uni of Sydney
Callan Park
Sydney College of the Arts
White Bay
Glebe Island
(Private Road)
Fbr
Rozelle Hospital
FOR MORE DETAIL SEE MAP 10
Easton Park
VICTORIA RD
THE CRESCENT
JAMES CRAIG
FOR MORE DETAIL SEE MAP 11
ANZAC BRIDGE
Rozelle Bay
Glebe Pt
Blackwattle Bay Park
LILYFIELD
Rozelle Goods Yard
CITY WEST LINK
Lilyfield
Bicentennial Park
Jubilee Oval
Jubilee Park
Federal Park
Johnstons Creek
St Scholasticas College
Harold Park Paceway
War Memorial Park
Rubbish Tip
Whites Creek Valley Pk
ANNANDALE
JOHNSTON ST
CRESCENT
MINOGUE CR
GLEBE
FOREST LODGE
BRIDGE ROAD

MAP 345

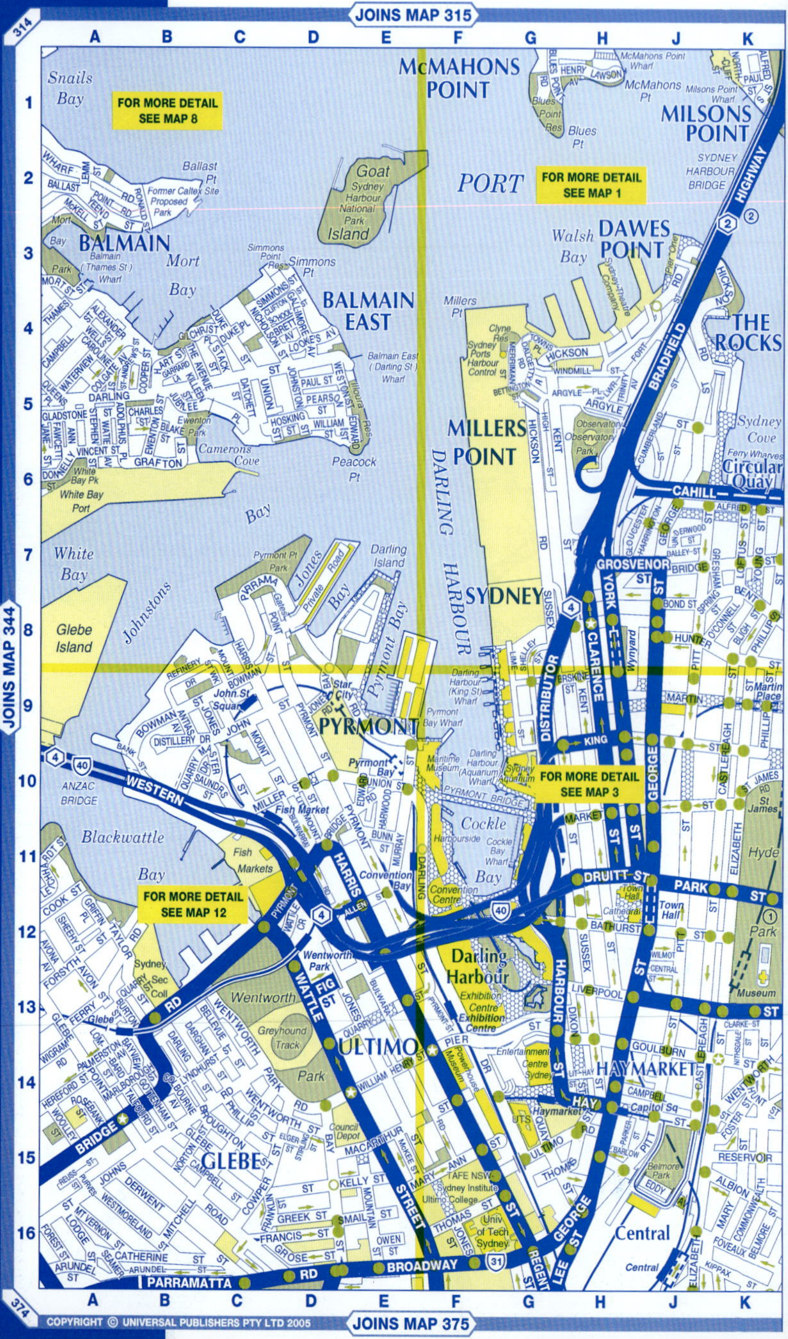
JOINS MAP 315
JOINS MAP 344
JOINS MAP 375
McMAHONS POINT
MILSONS POINT
Snails Bay
FOR MORE DETAIL SEE MAP 8
FOR MORE DETAIL SEE MAP 1
FOR MORE DETAIL SEE MAP 3
FOR MORE DETAIL SEE MAP 12
Goat Island
Sydney Harbour National Park
PORT
DAWES POINT
Walsh Bay
BALMAIN
Mort Bay
BALMAIN EAST
THE ROCKS
MILLERS POINT
DARLING HARBOUR
SYDNEY HARBOUR BRIDGE
Sydney Cove
Circular Quay
White Bay
Glebe Island
Johnstons Bay
Jones Bay
Pyrmont Bay
SYDNEY
PYRMONT
ANZAC BRIDGE
WESTERN
Blackwattle Bay
Cockle Bay
Darling Harbour
Hyde Park
Wentworth Park
ULTIMO
HAYMARKET
GLEBE
Central
BROADWAY
PARRAMATTA RD
GEORGE ST
HARRIS ST
WATTLE ST
BRADFIELD HIGHWAY
CAHILL
PARK ST
DRUITT ST
KING
MARKET

JOINS MAP 316
JOINS MAP 347
JOINS MAP 376
KIRRIBILLI
Kirribilli Wharf
Kirribilli House
Admiralty House
Kirribilli Point
Jeffrey Street Wharf
Milsons Point
Beulah St Wharf
Speed Cameras & Emergency Phones throughout tunnel
SYDNEY HARBOUR TUNNEL
FOR MORE DETAIL SEE MAP 2
Fort Denison
JACKSON
Robertsons Point
Bennelong Point
Sydney Opera House
Man O'War Jetty
Mrs Macquaries Point
Mrs Macquaries Chair
Garden Island
ADI Naval Dockyard
Government House
Farm Cove
Royal Botanic Gardens
Sydney Conservatorium of Music
The Andrew (Boy) Charlton Pool
Woolloomooloo Bay
Fitting out Wharf
Finger Wharf
Captain Cook Graving Dock
HMAS Kuttabul
CAHILL EXP
EXPRESSWAY
Parliament House
The Domain
Art Gallery
FOR MORE DETAIL SEE MAP 4
FOR MORE DETAIL SEE MAP 13
Darling Point Wharf
Elizabeth Bay
ELIZABETH BAY
Elizabeth Point
POTTS POINT
DARLING POINT
Macleay Point
Rushcutters Bay
RUSHCUTTERS BAY
Rushcutters Bay Park
W'MOOLOO
Cathedral
Museum
Kings Cross
WILLIAM ST
NEW SOUTH HEAD RD
SGS Weigall Sportsground
NSW LTA Tennis Courts
Ascham
Girls Sch
Edgecliff
EDGECLIFF
Trumper Park
DARLINGHURST
Sydney Police Centre
SURRY HILLS
PADDINGTON
OXFORD ST
Victoria Barracks

MAP 347

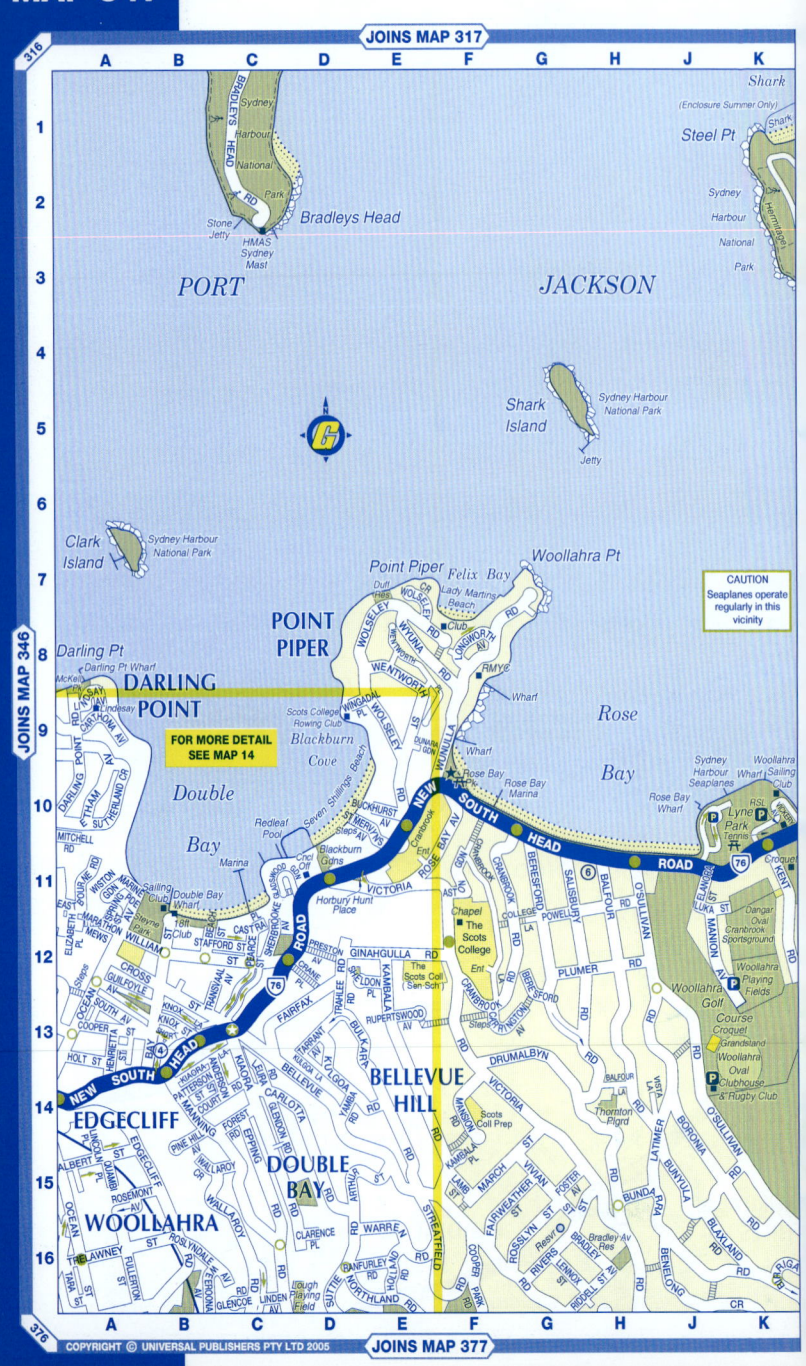

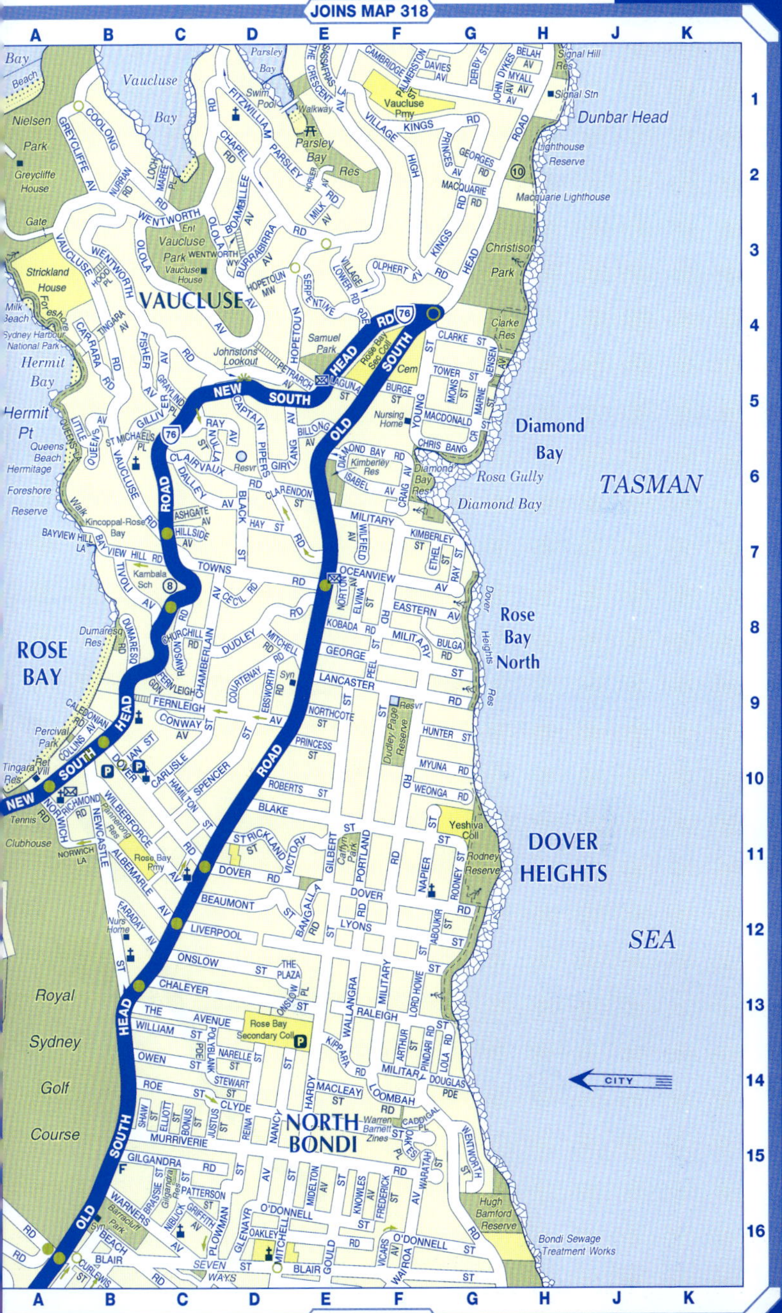

MAP 353
PREVIOUS MAP 348

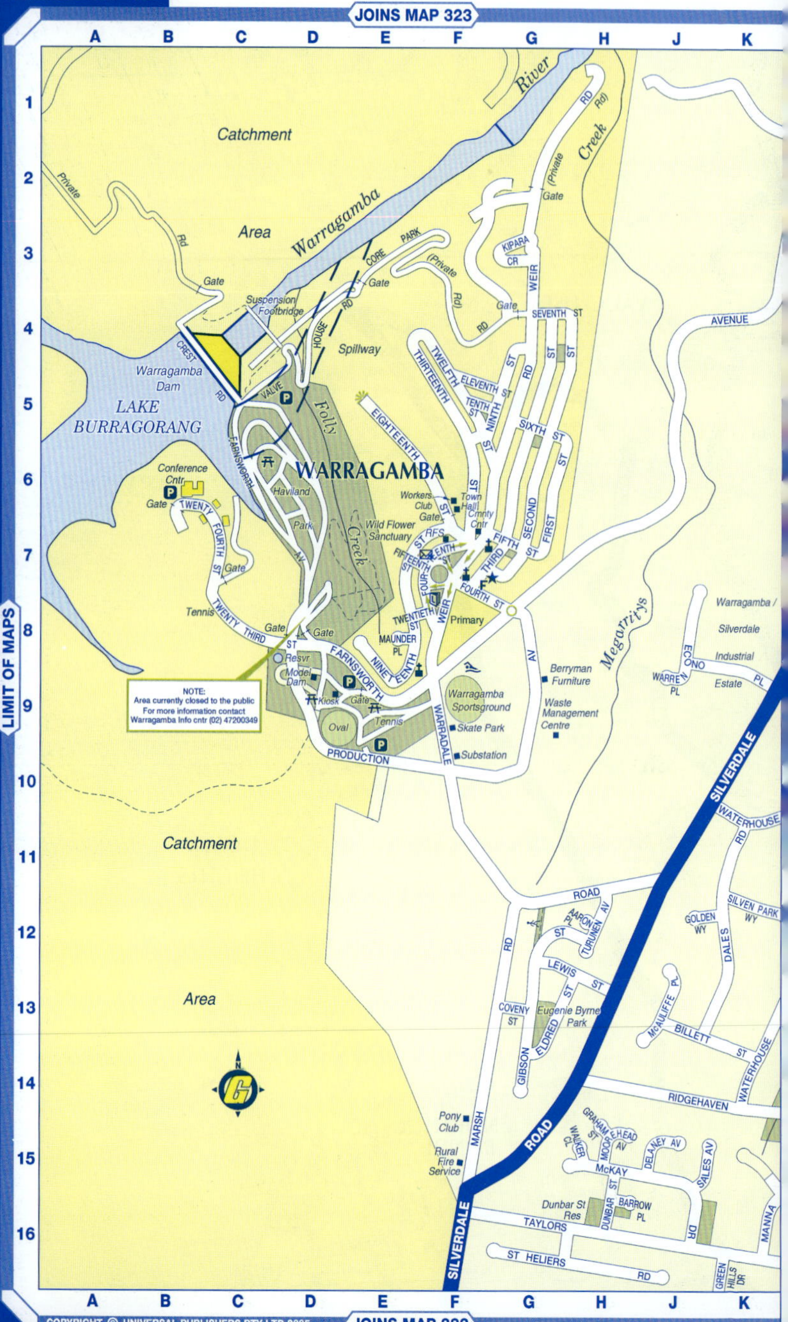

MAP 354

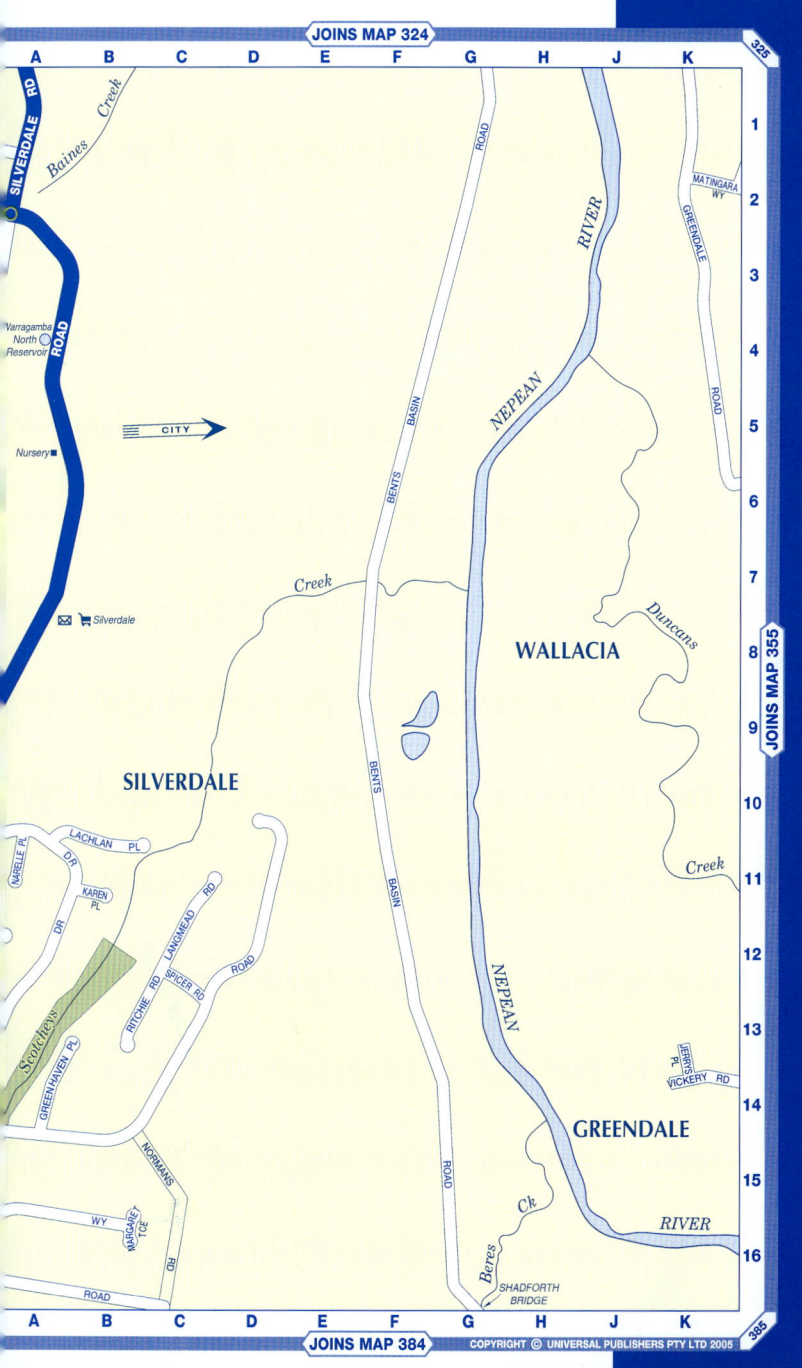

JOINS MAP 324

SILVERDALE

WALLACIA

GREENDALE

Baines Creek
Silverdale Rd
Warragamba North Reservoir
Road
Nursery
Silverdale
Bents Basin
Nepean River
Duncans Creek
Creek
Matingara Wy
Greendale Road
Nepean
Beres Ck
Shadforth Bridge
River

Lachlan Pl, Narelle Pl, Karen Pl, Ritchie Rd, Langmead Rd, Spicer Rd, Greenhaven Pl, Scotcheys, Normans, Margaret Tce, Wy, Road, Jerns Pl, Vickery Rd

CITY →

JOINS MAP 384

MAP 355

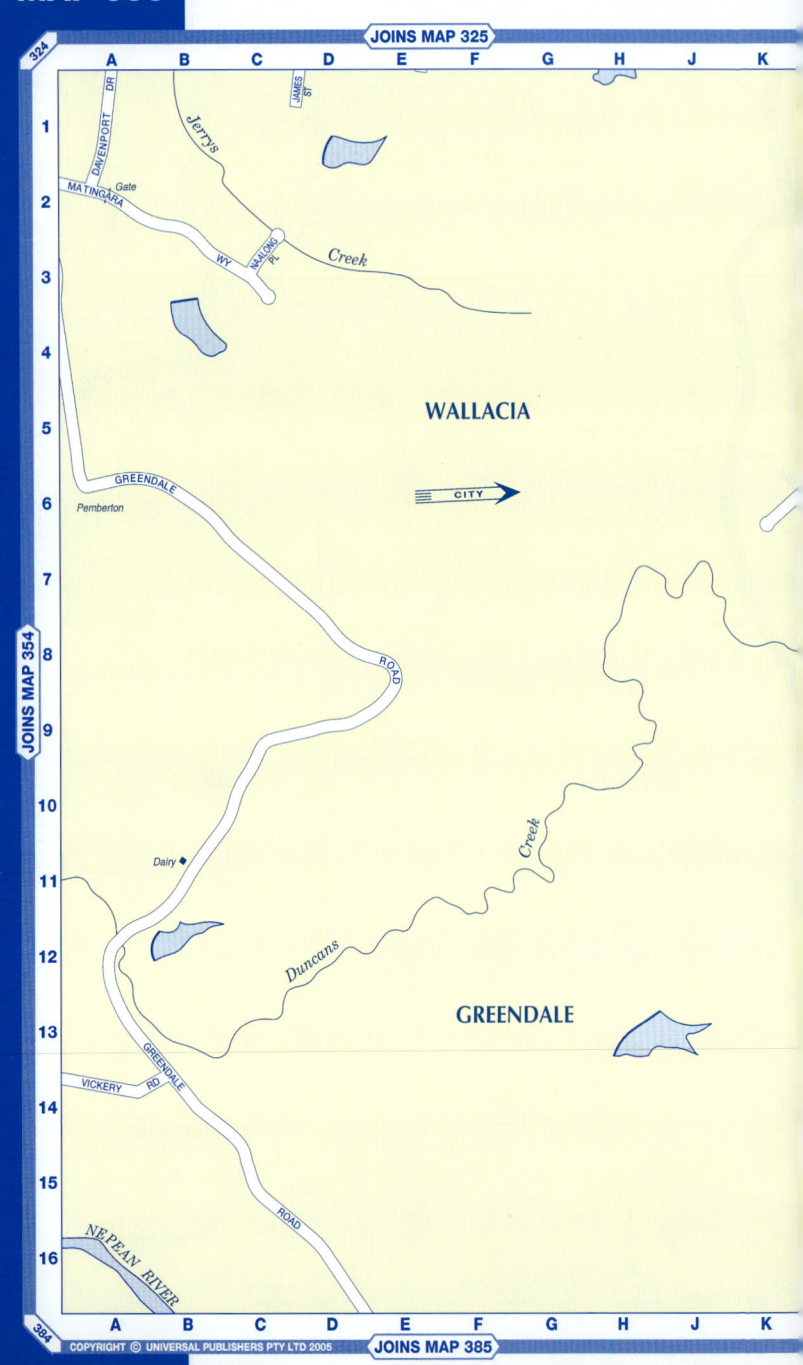

JOINS MAP 325

DAVENPORT DR
MATINGARA
Gate
Jerrys Creek
JAMES ST
WALONG PL
WY

WALLACIA

CITY

GREENDALE
Pemberton

ROAD

Dairy

Creek

Duncans Creek

GREENDALE

GREENDALE RD
VICKERY RD

ROAD

NEPEAN RIVER

JOINS MAP 354
JOINS MAP 385

MAP 356

JOINS MAP 326

LUDDENHAM

Luddenham Showground
Hawkins Av
Michel Av
Freeburn Pk
Blaxland Av
Jamison
Roots Av
Campbell St
Holy Family Pmy
Luddenham Robert Hall Green Oval / Sales Park
The Northern
RFS
Luddenham Pmy
Adams St
Eaton Rd
Road
Willowdene Av
Silverwood Av
Willowdene Av
Duncans Creek
Proposed Airport Site
Vicary's Winery
Private Rd
Vicar Park La
Tagalong Performance Horses & Equestrian Centre

JOINS MAP 386

COPYRIGHT © UNIVERSAL PUBLISHERS PTY LTD 2005

MAP 357

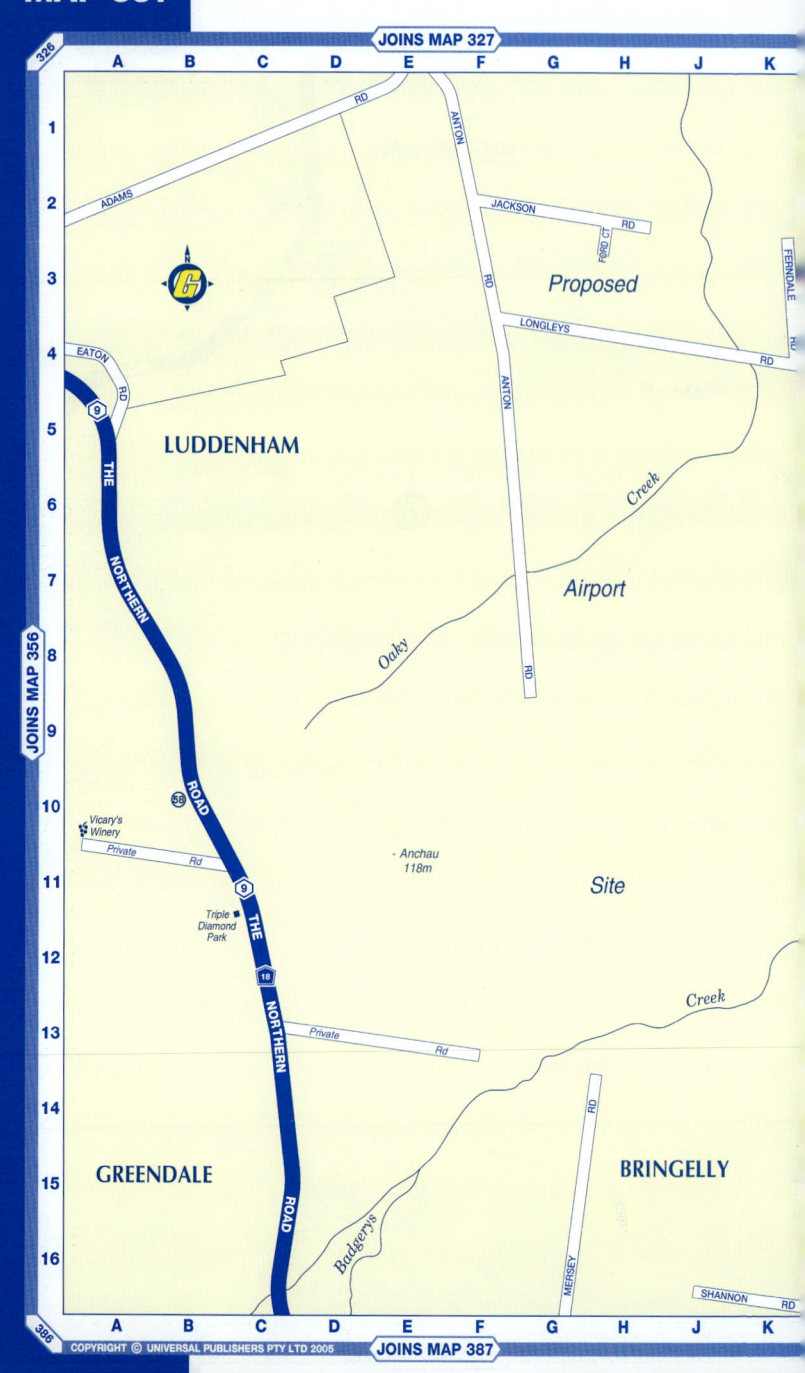

JOINS MAP 327

Labels

- ADAMS RD
- EATON RD
- LUDDENHAM
- JACKSON RD
- FORD CT
- FERNDALE RD
- ANTON RD
- LONGLEYS RD
- Proposed
- Oaky Creek
- Airport
- THE NORTHERN ROAD
- Vicary's Winery
- Private Rd
- Triple Diamond Park
- Anchau 118m
- Site
- Creek
- Private Rd
- GREENDALE
- BRINGELLY
- Badgerys
- MERSEY RD
- SHANNON RD

JOINS MAP 387
JOINS MAP 356

COPYRIGHT © UNIVERSAL PUBLISHERS PTY LTD 2005

MAP 358

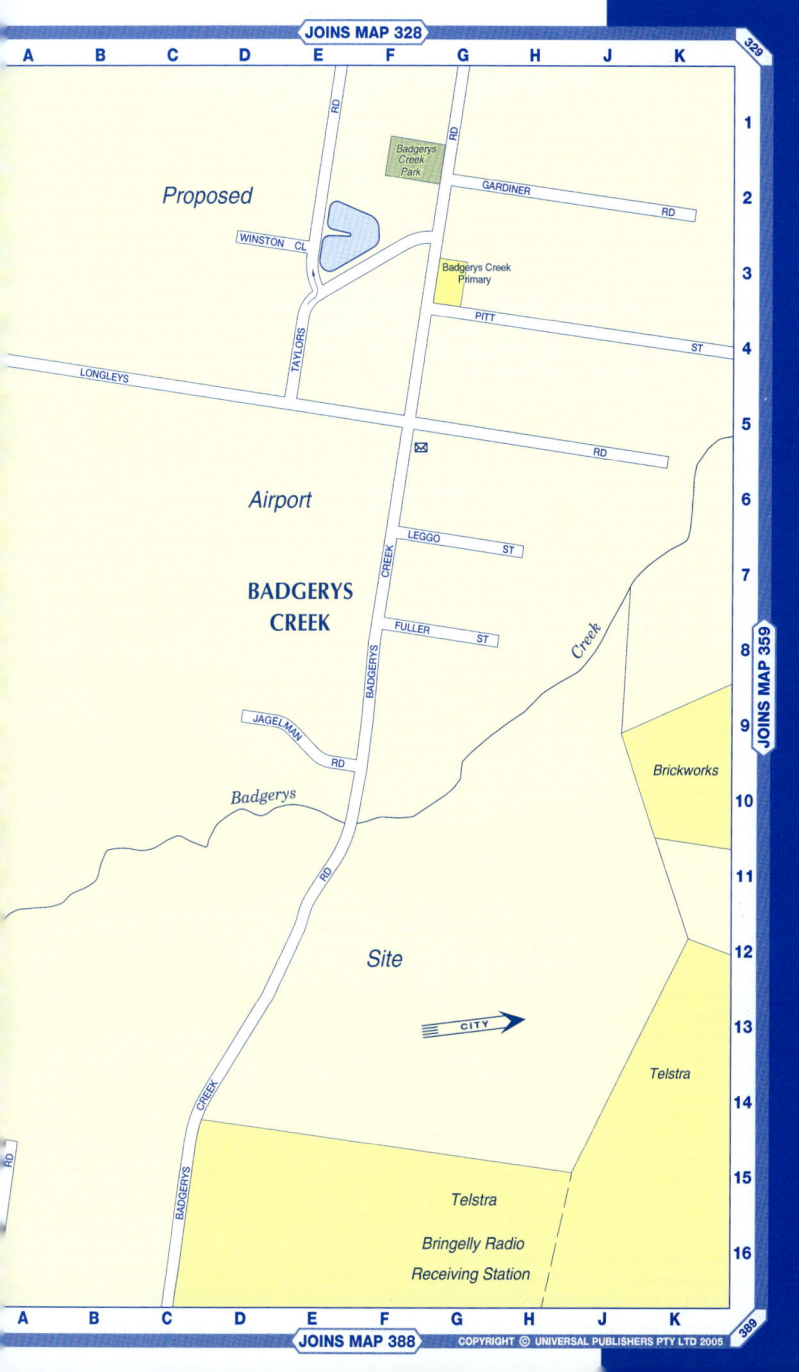

BADGERYS CREEK

- Badgerys Creek Park
- Badgerys Creek Primary
- Gardiner Rd
- Winston Cl
- Taylors Rd
- Longleys
- Pitt St
- Badgerys Creek Rd
- Leggo St
- Fuller St
- Jagelman Rd
- Badgerys Creek
- Brickworks
- Site
- CITY
- Telstra
- Telstra
- Bringelly Radio Receiving Station
- Proposed Airport

JOINS MAP 328
JOINS MAP 359
JOINS MAP 388

COPYRIGHT © UNIVERSAL PUBLISHERS PTY LTD 2005

MAP 359

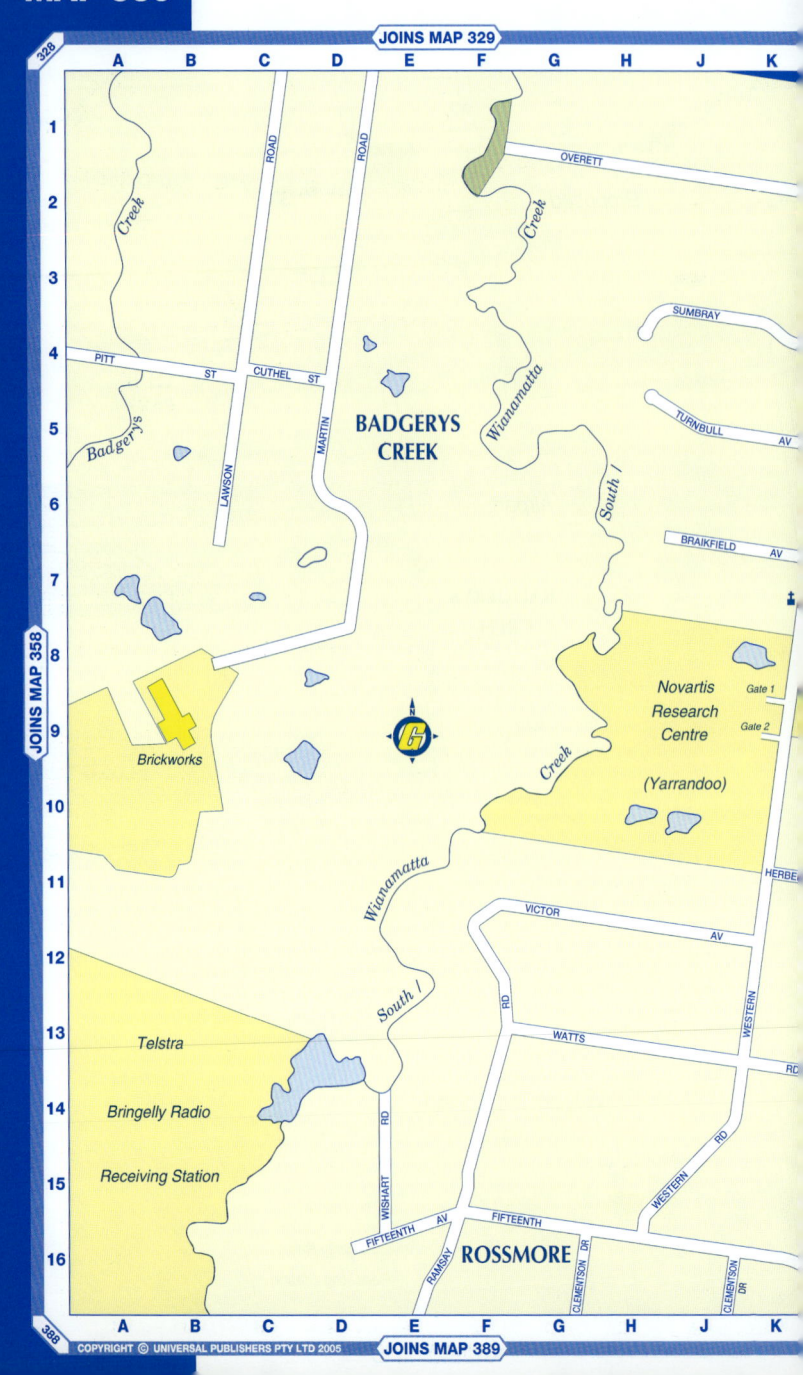

JOINS MAP 329

OVERETT
Creek
SUMBRAY
PITT ST
CUTHEL ST
TURNBULL AV
Badgerys Creek
LAWSON
MARTIN ROAD
BADGERYS CREEK
Wianamatta
South I
BRAIKFIELD AV

Brickworks
Novartis Research Centre
Gate 1
Gate 2
(Yarrandoo)

HERBE...
Wianamatta
VICTOR AV

South I
WATTS
WESTERN RD
Telstra
Bringelly Radio
Receiving Station
WISHART RD
RAMSAY
FIFTEENTH AV
FIFTEENTH
CLEMENTSON DR
WESTERN RD
CLEMENTON DR
ROSSMORE

JOINS MAP 389
JOINS MAP 358
COPYRIGHT © UNIVERSAL PUBLISHERS PTY LTD 2005

JOINS MAP 330

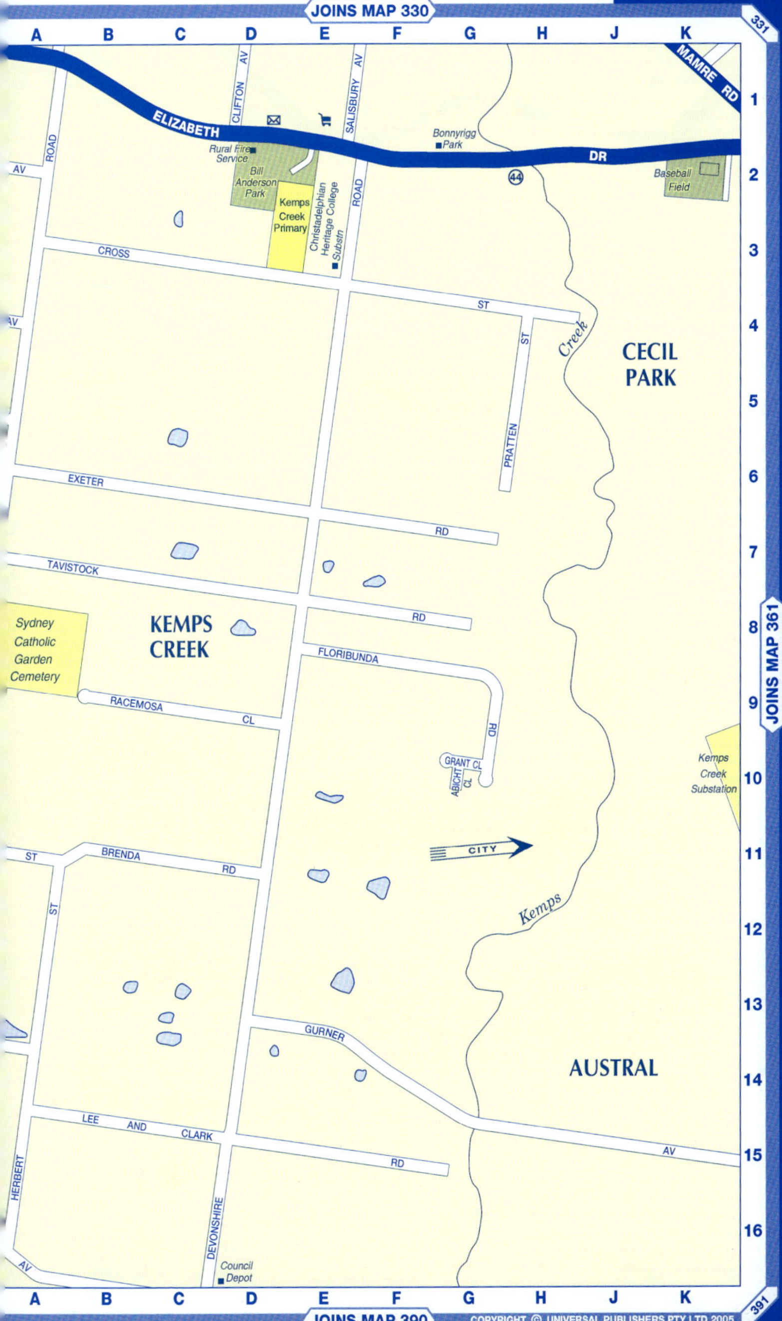

JOINS MAP 361

JOINS MAP 390

MAP 361

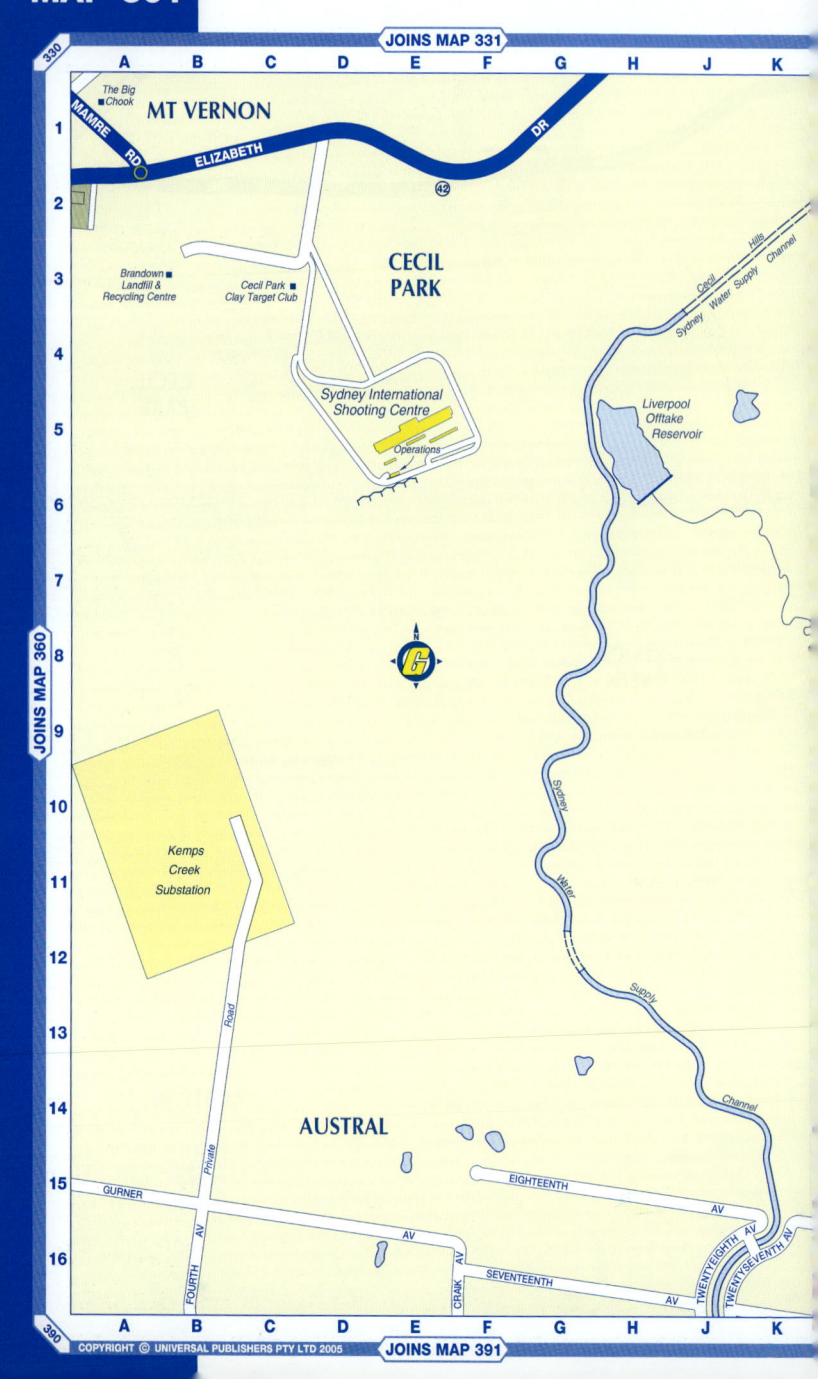

JOINS MAP 331

MT VERNON

The Big Chook

MAMRE RD

ELIZABETH DR

CECIL PARK

Brandown Landfill & Recycling Centre

Cecil Park Clay Target Club

Sydney International Shooting Centre

Operations

Cecil Hills

Sydney Water Supply Channel

Liverpool Offtake Reservoir

Kemps Creek Substation

Sydney Water Supply Channel

AUSTRAL

Private Road

GURNER

FOURTH AV

CRAIK AV

EIGHTEENTH AV

SEVENTEENTH AV

TWENTYEIGHTH AV

TWENTYSEVENTH AV

JOINS MAP 360
JOINS MAP 391

COPYRIGHT © UNIVERSAL PUBLISHERS PTY LTD 2005

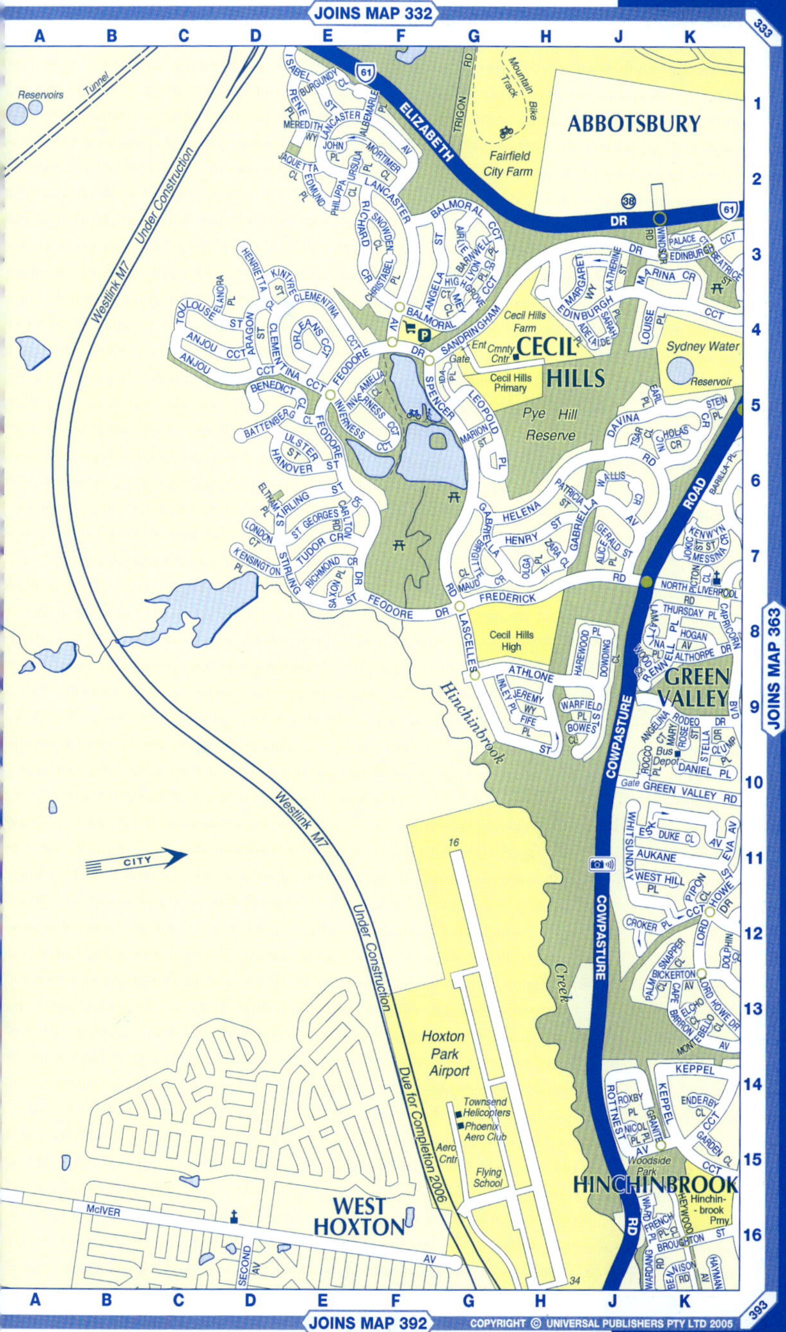
JOINS MAP 332
JOINS MAP 363
JOINS MAP 392
333
393
A B C D E F G H J K
1 2 3 4 5 6 7 8 9 10 11 12 13 14 15 16
ABBOTSBURY
CECIL HILLS
GREEN VALLEY
HINCHINBROOK
WEST HOXTON
ELIZABETH DR
COWPASTURE RD
COWPASTURE ROAD
Westlink M7 Under Construction
Westlink M7 Under Construction Due for Completion 2006
Reservoirs
Tunnel
CITY
Mountain Bike Track
Fairfield City Farm
Cecil Hills Farm
Cmnty Cntr
Ent
Gate
Cecil Hills Primary
Pye Hill Reserve
Sydney Water Reservoir
Cecil Hills High
Hinchinbrook Creek
Hoxton Park Airport
Townsend Helicopters
Phoenix Aero Club
Aero Cntr
Flying School
Bus Depot
Woodside Park
Hinchin-brook Pmy
TRIGON RD
FEODORE DR
SANDRINGHAM DR
BALMORAL CCT
BALMORAL AV
LANCASTER AV
FREDERICK RD
LASCELLES RD
ATHLONE ST
GREEN VALLEY RD
NORTH LIVERPOOL RD
McIVER AV
SECOND AV
KEPPEL CCT
BROUGHTON ST
CLEMENTINA CCT
ANJOU CCT
BENEDICT CL
BATTENBERG CL
ULSTER ST
HANOVER ST
STIRLING ST
ST GEORGES RD
TUDOR CR
RICHMOND CR
KENSINGTON PL
LONDON CT
ELTHAM PL
CARLTON CR
INVERNESS CCT
SPENCER ST
LEOPOLD ST
MARION ST
HELENA ST
HENRY ST
GABRIELLA AV
DAVINA RD
WALLIS CR
GERALD ST
EDINBURGH CCT
MARINA CR
HAREWOOD PL
DOWDING CL
WARFIELD PL
JEREMY WY
FIFE PL
THURSDAY PL
HOGAN AV
ALTHORPE DR
CAPRICORN BVD
RODEO DR
DANIEL PL
WHITSUNDAY CCT
AUKANE ST
DUKE CL
ESK AV
WEST HILL PL
CROKER PL
LORD HOWE DR
BICKERTON AV
MONTEBELLO AV
ROTTNEST AV
ROXBY PL
ENDERBY CL
GARDEN CL
HEYWOOD
BENISON RD
HAYMAN AV
16
34

MAP 363

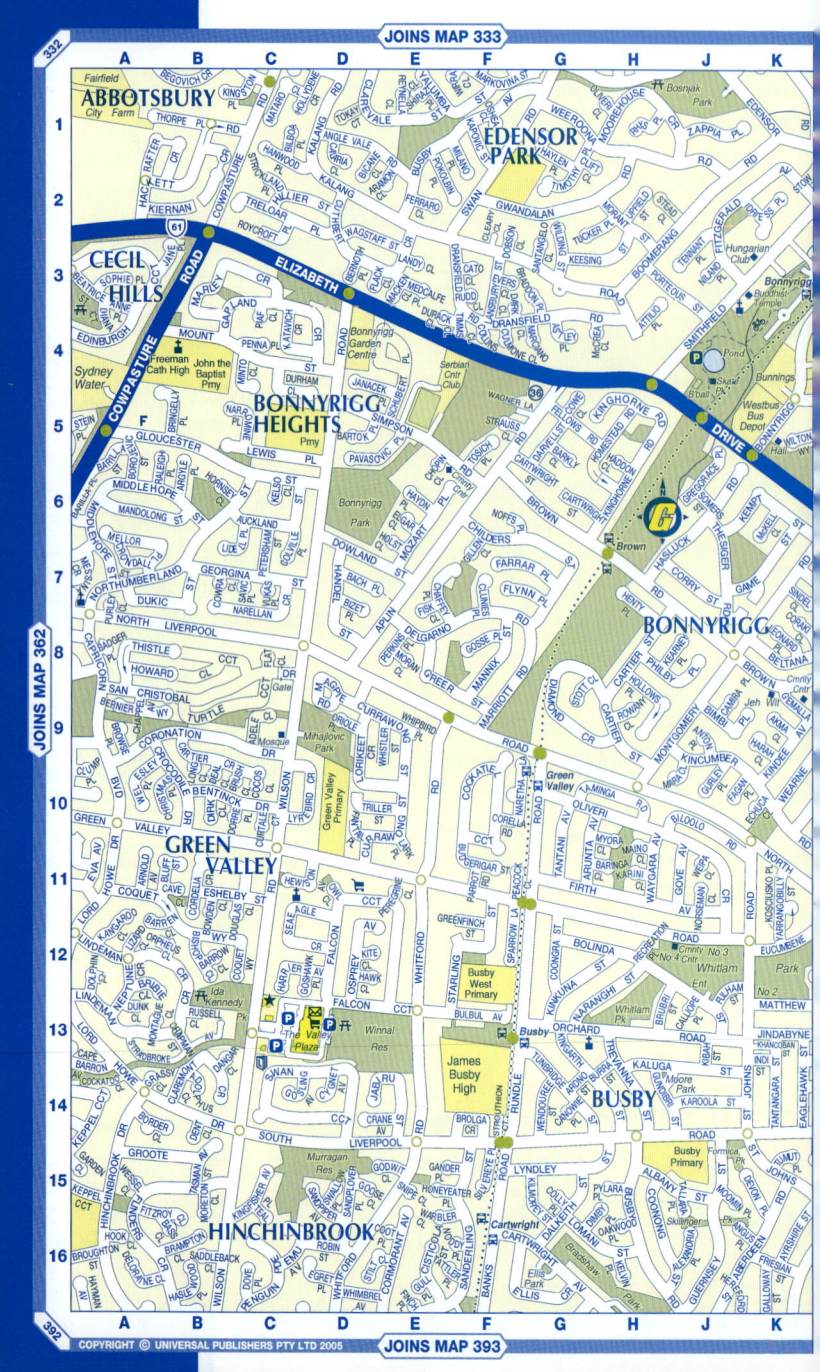

JOINS MAP 334

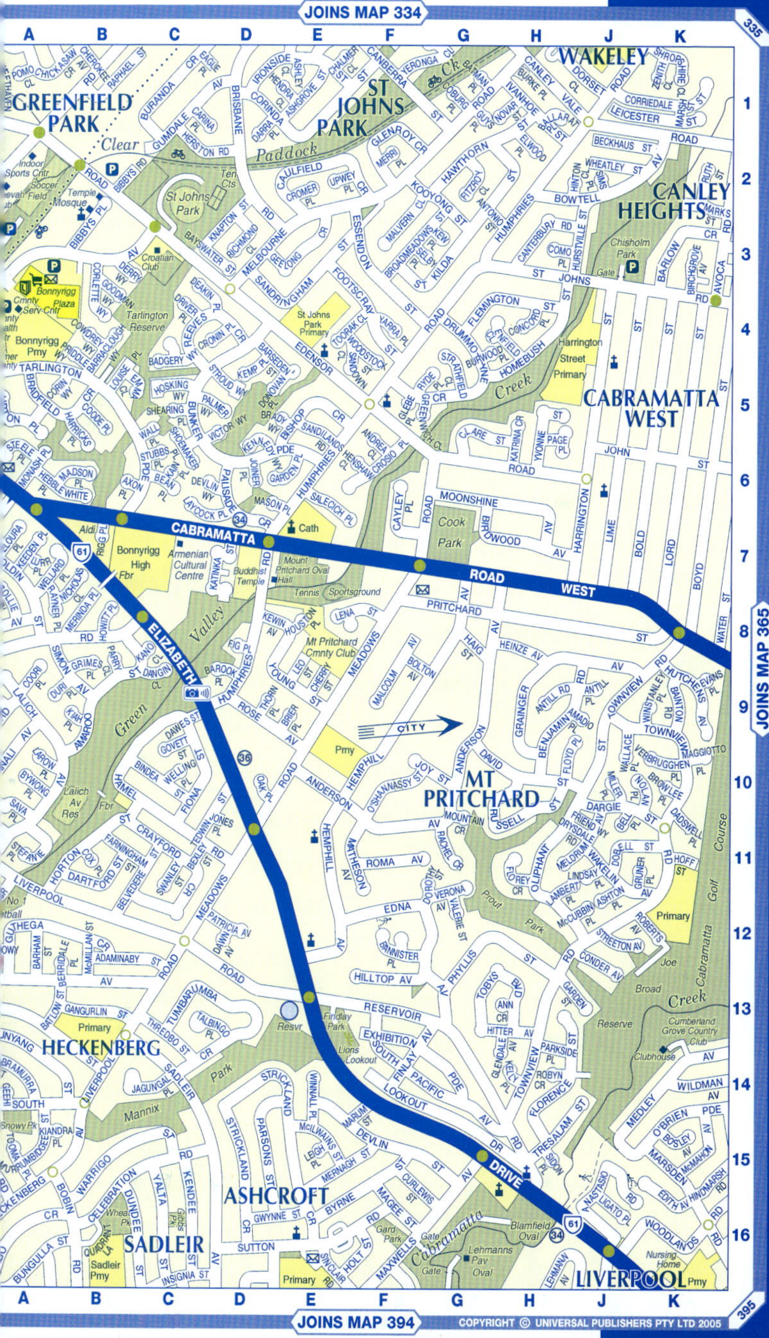

JOINS MAP 394

JOINS MAP 335
JOINS MAP 364
JOINS MAP 395
334
394
A B C D E F G H J K
1 2 3 4 5 6 7 8 9 10 11 12 13 14 15 16
CANLEY HEIGHTS
CABRAMATTA WEST
CABRAMATTA
WARWICK FARM
LIVERPOOL
CAMBRIDGE ST
CUMBERLAND HWY
JOSEPH ST
ORANGE GROVE RD
HUME HWY
SYDNEY RD
CABRAMATTA RD WEST
CANLEY VALE RD
JOHN ST
HUGHES ST
McBURNEY RD
GILBERT RD
BROAD ST
Canley Heights Pmy
Cabramatta West Primary
Cabramatta High
Canley Vale Pmy
Warwick Farm Primary
Mekong Panthers Club
Aust Lao-Chinese Assoc
St Sergius Nursing Home
Cabramatta Golf Course
Cumberland Grove Country Club
Megacenta Liverpool
Officeworks
Don Dawson Oval
Dwyer Oval
Freeman Oval
Durrant Oval
Cabramatta Creek
Warwick Farm Recreation Reserve
Jacqui Osmond Softball Centre
Hargrave Park
Schell Park
Cabra-Vale Park
Cabra-Vale Ex-servicemens Club
Adams Park
Avenel Park
Peter Warren
Masterton Homes
Liverpool Substation
Campbells Cash & Carry
Brickmakers
Homepride Pk
Cabramatta Rugby League Club
Kampuchea Krom Cultural Centre
Werriwa AB Dog Training Club
Lawrence Hargrave
Rosedale Oval
Mosque
Function Cntr

MAP 366

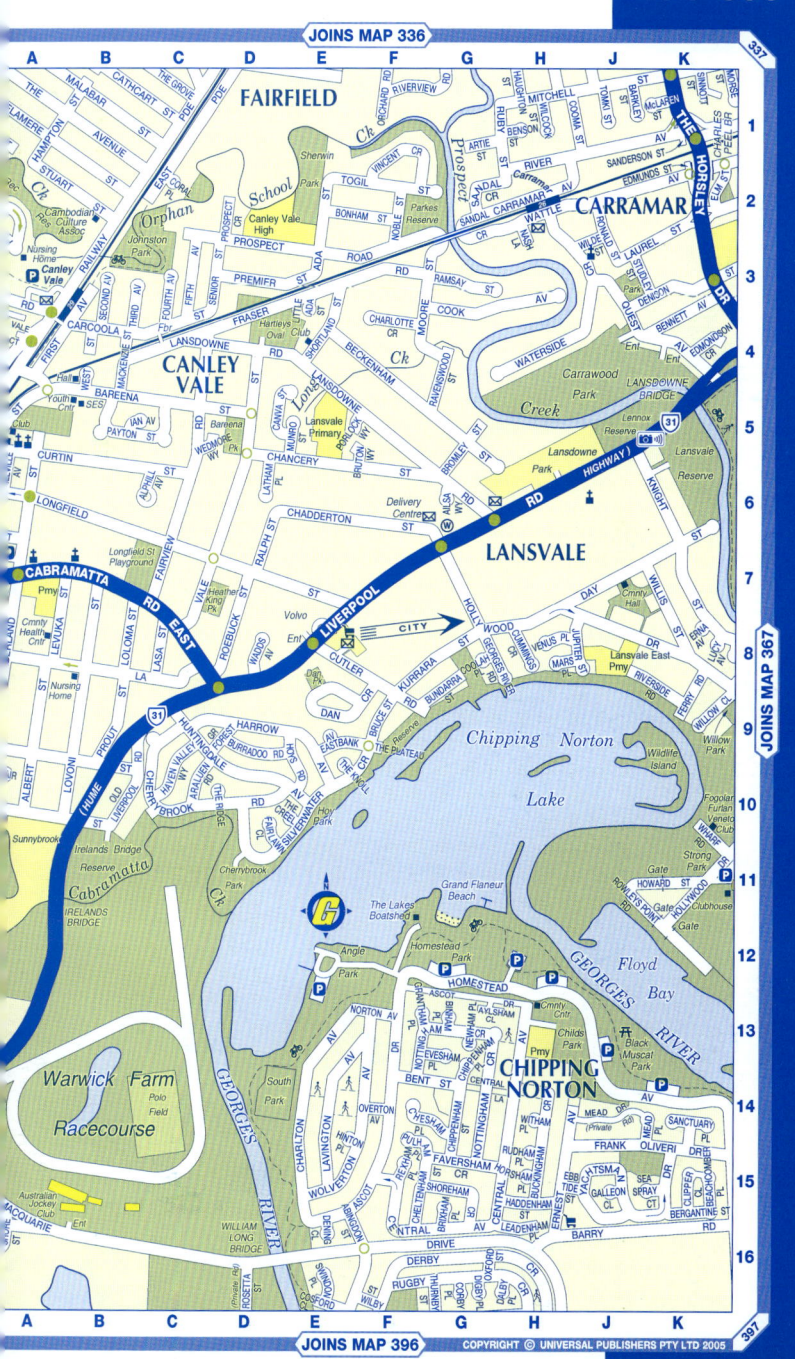

JOINS MAP 337

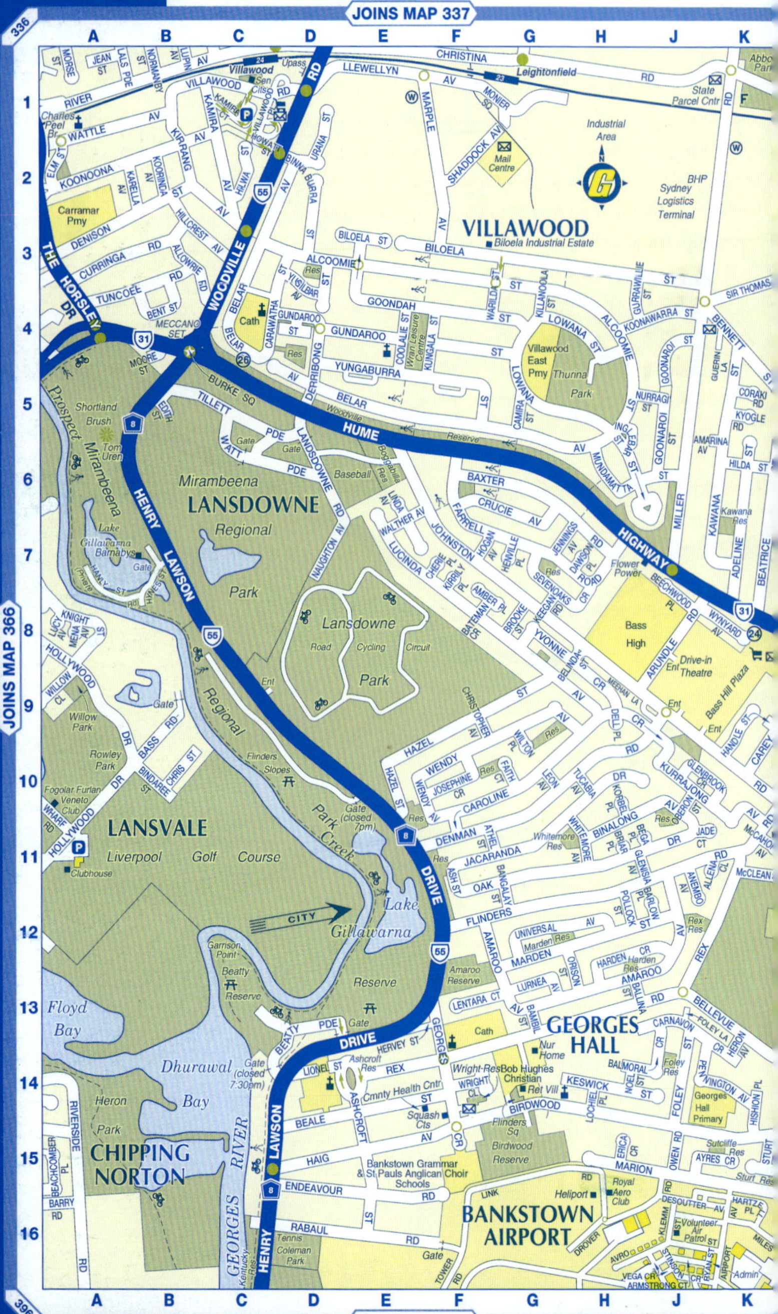

JOINS MAP 397

JOINS MAP 338

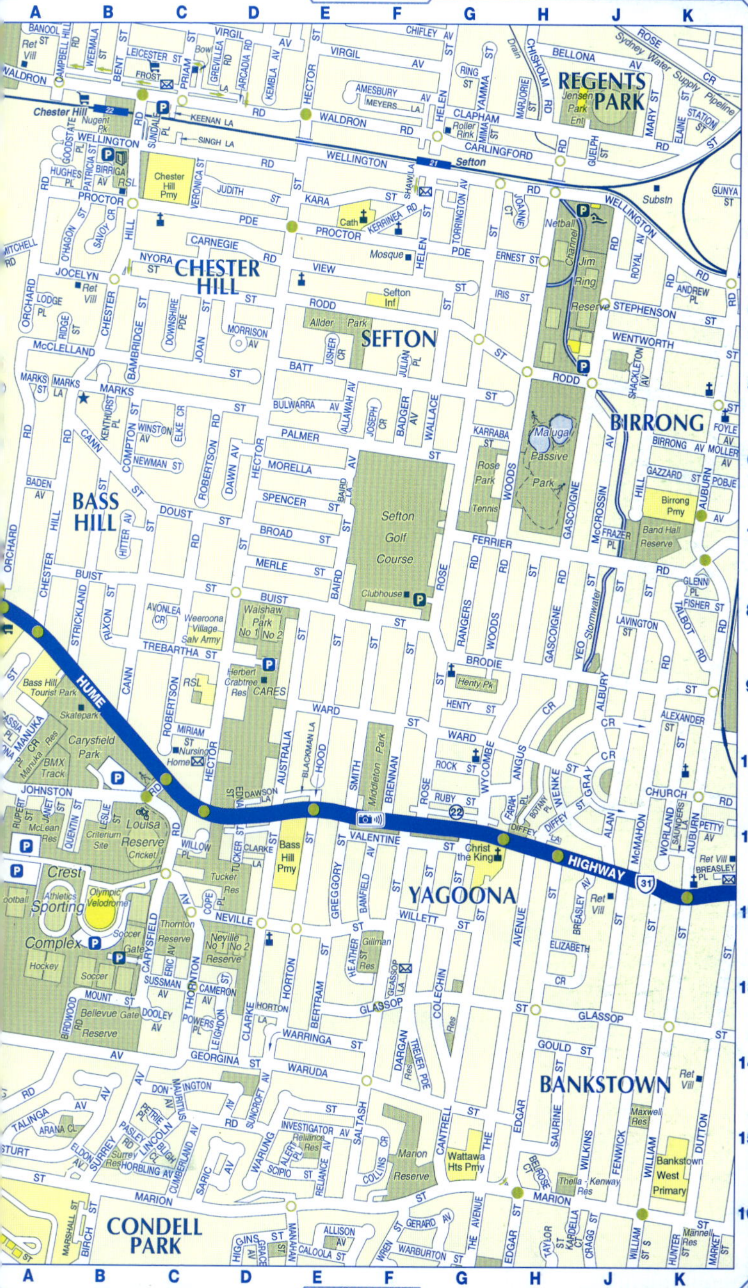

JOINS MAP 369

JOINS MAP 398

JOINS MAP 339
JOINS MAP 368
JOINS MAP 399
338
398
A B C D E F G H J K
1 2 3 4 5 6 7 8 9 10 11 12 13 14 15 16
BERALA
REGENTS PARK
Regents Pk
LIDCOMBE
POTTS HILL
BIRRONG
Birrong
YAGOONA
Yagoona
BANKSTOWN
MT LEWIS
Carnarvon Golf Course
Former Lidcombe Hospital
Motor Vehicle Testing Laboratory
EPA
Minali Special School
Railfast Centre
Potts Hill Switching Station
Chullora Railway Workshops
TAFE NSW-Southern Sydney Institute Bankstown College (Appex)
RSPCA Animal Shelter
Waste Service Recycling Centre
Reservoir No 1
Reservoir No 2
Reservoirs
Potts Hill
Sydney Water Critical Inventory Centre
Sydney Water Hydrographic Services
Potts Park
Greyhound Social Club
Chullora Business Park
Toll Fleet
Industrial Area
Christian Community High
Guilfoyle Park
Sp Sch
Pmy
Water Supply Pipeline
Birrong Girls High
Birrong Boys High
Aurora Rec Clubhouse
Sydney Water Depot
Resvr
O'Neill Park
Graf Park
George Green Oval
Gazzard Park
Nurs Home
Ret Vill
Yagoona Pmy
Pullen Reserve
Alice Pk
McLeod Res
LaSalle Catholic College
TAFE NSW Southern Sydney Inst Bankstown Coll
Yagoona Business Park
Bankstown North Pmy
Wood Pk
Apex Res
Winsor Park
Tennis Gosling Park
SES
Hume Nursing Home
Nissan
Leo Res
Greenacre Heights Res
R M Campbell Res
Jeh Wit
PCYC
Mosque
Town Hall
Paul Keating Pk
Civic
Cin
Mall
Bankstown Square
Mot Reg
NRMA
Cncl Off
Cncl Ch
RSL
Depot
Bankstown
Sydney
Private
Gate
Ent
Exit
Ped U'Pass
JOSEPH ST
ROOKWOOD RD
BRUNKER RD
HUME HWY
STACEY ST
BORONIA RD
CHULLORA
WEEROONA
PHILLIPS AV
COLEMAN AV
GREATREX AV
WHITING ST
DOWNING AV
CLAUDE AV
JAMES CR
CLUCAS RD
NOTTINGHILL RD
WYATT
WILGA ST
LARCOMBE ST
AMY
MIMULUS LA
EDWIN ST
KINGSLAND RD
BERRY ST
DUNBAR AV
YUKKA RD
MAUNDER ST
SMITH ST
DAWES AV
CUTCLIFFE AV
CLIFFE ST
KERSLAKE AV
LEWIS ST
ROSE CR
CARLINGFORD ST
CORLISS ST
GUNYA ST
BAGDAD ST
MAGNEY AV
HOPE ST
MAUDE ST
KITCHENER
REGENT ST
TERRENE ST
MORRIS
KERRIE
DANA PDE
TEWINGA RD
NEUTRAL AV
WENTWORTH ST
AVALON ST
MAGDELLA ST
MARMION ST
HOLLAND ST
TERESA
AUBURN RD
RODD
FOYLE AV
MOLLER AV
POBJE AV
HUDSON PDE
LARIEN CR
COOPER RD
BOARDMAN ST
GRAF AV
MUIR RD
DASEA
ELCAR PL
WORTH
ALLDER ST
HOUSTON RD
QUARRY CL
NOBBS RD
RUDELLE CR
TERPENTINE PL
MCMILLAN
SUTHERLAND ST
ANTHONY ST
LAMBERT ST
PATIENCE AV
POWELL ST
BOWDEN BVD
LITHGOW AV
JOSEPH LA
LLOYD AV
MERLEN CR
CHARLTON ST
AVOCA ST
RYAN LA
EMERY AV
ASHBY
ARNOLD AV
FARNELL RD
MARTHA ST
DALEY RD
VENTURE CR
CALDWELL
WOODBINE
AVOCA
CLAREMONT AV
BERESFORD AV
ROSEDALE AV
ANZAC ST
RAWSON
CHISWICK
WALSH LA
HILLCREST AV
ISLINGTON CR
BELFORD PL
RESERVOIR AV
DAVIS LA
CHURCH
RITCHIE RD
DURANT
PETTY LA
BREASLEY PL
PALOMAR PDE
GEORGE ST
BLUDE
JOHN WALL LA
KEARNS
THOMPSONS LA
O'DONNELL AV
ORANA PL
BURRANEER CR
BANKSIA
MARINA CR
STILLER PL
MIMOSA
CORBETT ST
REMI ST
FREDERICK ST
YAGOONA LA
THE CRESCENT
BENNY LA
MULLA RD
AVON ST
PRICE LA
HEATH ST
NIOKA PL
GREENACRE RD
HIGHVIEW
MELANIE ST
BRANCOURT
GLASSOP
CARMEN ST
RAW AV
CONWAY
BANKS
MILTON ST
KONRAD AV
SUVA
DUTTON
BOWER ST
BRAUNBECK ST
FRENCH AV
JACOBS
SIR JOSEPH BANKS
MYRTLE RD
OLD KENT
HILLVIEW AV
COLEMAN AV
MITCHAM RD
REYNOLDS
CAIRDS
RICKARD RD
RESTHAVEN RD
HAROLD
HIGHLAND
GORDON ST
WEIGAND
KITCHENER
CHAPEL
FETHERSTONE ST
THE APPIAN WY
CIVIC DR
LADY CUTLER AV
PRAIRIE VALE RD
SEALY ST
LITTLE
GAIL PL
ALLUM
BUNGALOW CR
MEREDITH
COLE LA
WATTLE
FRANK
MARION ST
NORTH TCE
SOUTH TCE
WEST TCE
EAST TCE
OLYMPIC PDE
DEPOT PL
MARKET ST
CLARENCE ST
PRINGLE AV
OXFORD AV
EGAN ST
WINSPEAR AV
20
31
6
18
19

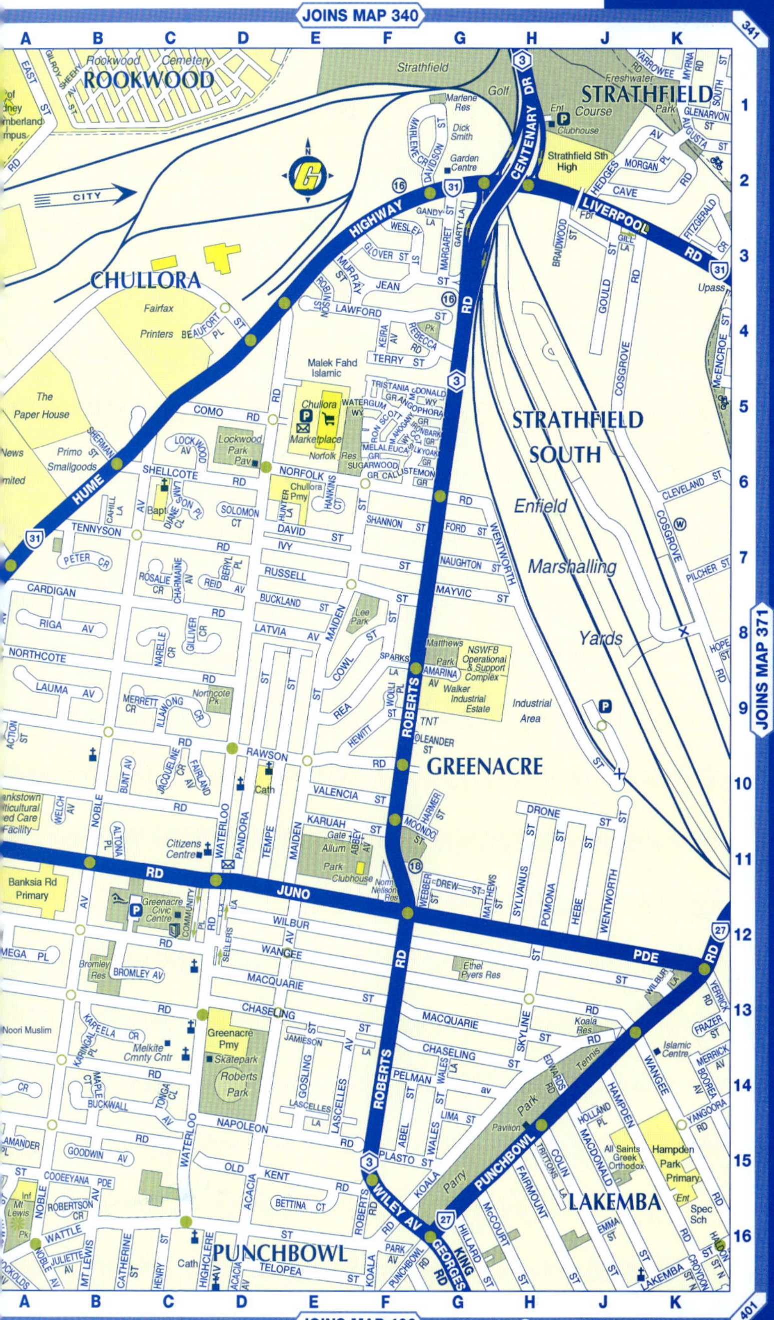

JOINS MAP 341
JOINS MAP 370
JOINS MAP 401
STRATHFIELD
BURWOOD
STRATHFIELD SOUTH
ENFIELD
Enfield South
BELFIELD
BELMORE
LAKEMBA
LIVERPOOL
HUME
THE BOULEVARDE
CORONATION PDE
GEORGES RIVER RD
PUNCHBOWL RD
Strathfield Park
Henley Park
Ford Park
Bark Huts Reserve
Begnell Park
Cooke Park
Rudd Park
Flockhart Park
Belmore Sportsground
Cooks River
Coxs Ck
Channel

JOINS MAP 342
JOINS MAP 373
JOINS MAP 402
343
403
A B C D E F G H J K
1 2 3 4 5 6 7 8 9 10 11 12 13 14 15 16
CROYDON
ASHFIELD
CROYDON PARK
ASHBURY
CANTERBURY
CAMPSIE
HURLSTONE PARK
EARLWOOD
LIVERPOOL (HUME HIGHWAY) RD
FREDERICK ST
MILTON ST
BRIGHTON AV
CANTERBURY RD
BEAMISH ST
NEW CANTERBURY RD
Canterbury Park Racecourse
Canterbury Park
Croydon Park
Picken Oval
Pratten Park
Peace Pk
W H Wagener Oval
Tasker Park
Little Tasker Park
Ewen Park
Sutton Reserve
Cooks River
Boys High
Girls High
The Sydney Private Hospital
Trinity Grammar
Cardinal Freeman Village & Nurs Home
Ashfield Pmy & High
Ashbury Pmy
Special Sch
De La Salle Coll
Bethlehem Coll
Sugar Works
Simpson Res
Heynes Res
Gough Res
Yeo Park
Footbridge
Ice Rink
Petanque
Croydon
Canterbury
Ashfield
Viewing Tower
CITY
31
54
10

MAP 373

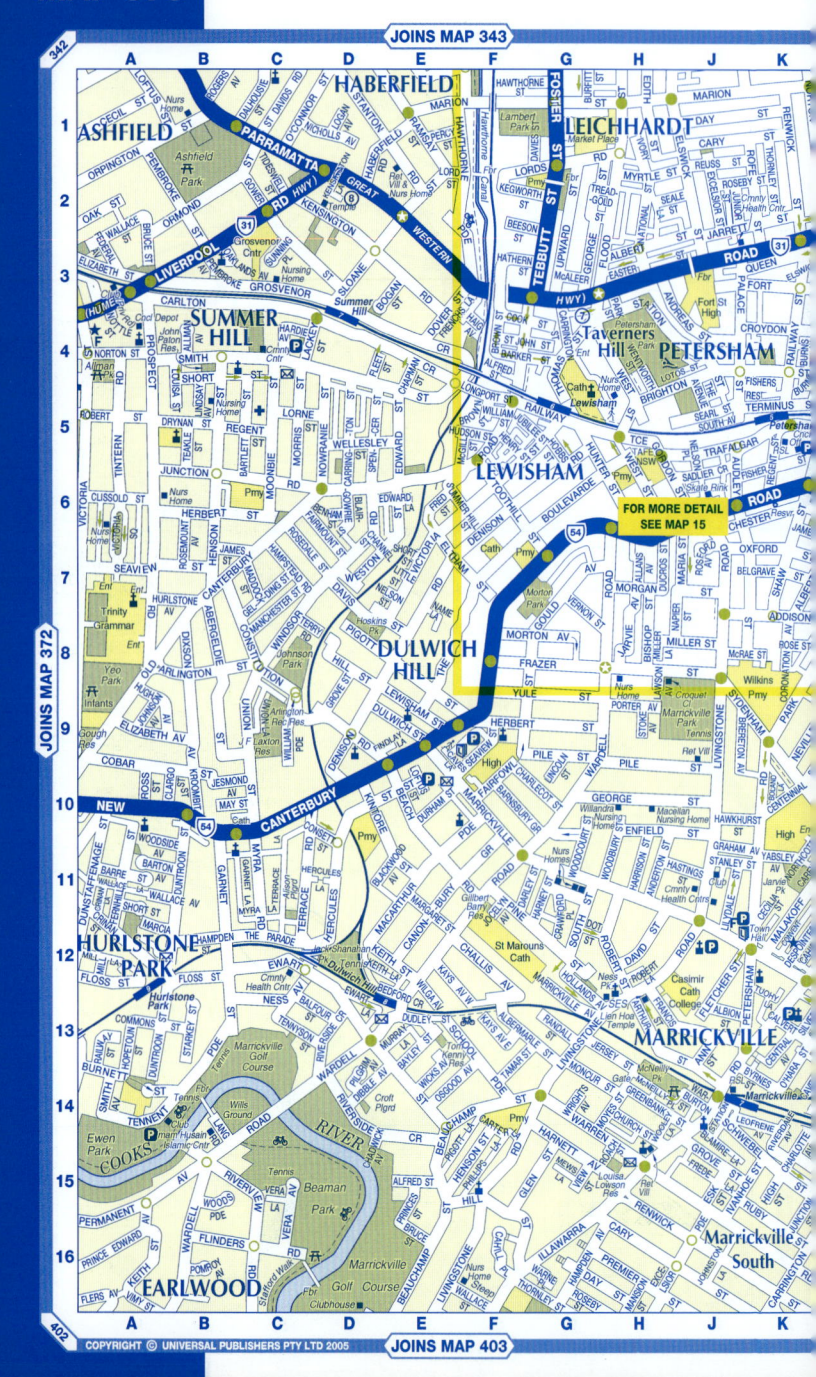

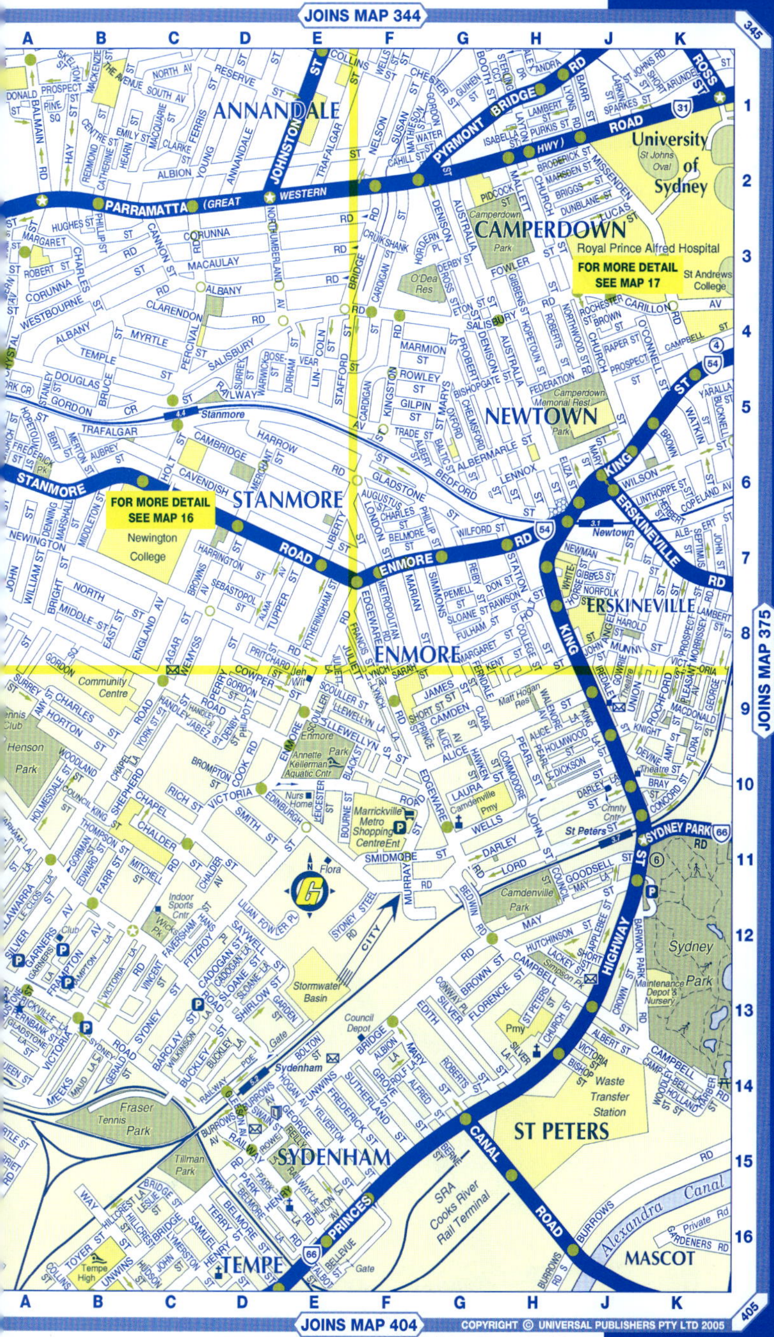
JOINS MAP 344
JOINS MAP 375
JOINS MAP 404
345
405
A B C D E F G H J K
1 2 3 4 5 6 7 8 9 10 11 12 13 14 15 16
ANNANDALE
CAMPERDOWN
NEWTOWN
STANMORE
ENMORE
ERSKINEVILLE
SYDENHAM
ST PETERS
TEMPE
MASCOT
University of Sydney
St Johns Oval
Royal Prince Alfred Hospital
St Andrews College
FOR MORE DETAIL SEE MAP 17
FOR MORE DETAIL SEE MAP 16
Newington College
Camperdown Park
Camperdown Memorial Rest Park
O'Dea Res
Stanmore
Newtown
Sydenham
St Peters
PARRAMATTA (GREAT WESTERN HWY)
PYRMONT BRIDGE RD
CITY RD
STANMORE ROAD
ENMORE RD
KING ST
ERSKINEVILLE RD
PRINCES HIGHWAY
CANAL ROAD
SYDNEY PARK RD
JOHNSTON ST
MISSENDEN RD
Community Centre
Henson Park
Annette Kellerman Aquatic Cntr
Enmore Park
Marrickville Metro Shopping Centre
Camdenville Park
Camdenville Pmy
Matt Hogan Res
Sydney Park
Maintenance Depot & Nursery
Stormwater Basin
Council Depot
Indoor Sports Cntr
Wicks Pk
Fraser Tennis Park
Tillman Park
Tempe High
Waste Transfer Station
SRA Cooks River Rail Terminal
Alexandra Canal
Simpson Pk
Flora
Theatre

MAP 375

JOINS MAP 345
JOINS MAP 374
JOINS MAP 405
344
404
A B C D E F G H J K
1 2 3 4 5 6 7 8 9 10 11 12 13 14 15 16
GLEBE
C'DALE
University of Sydney
Camperdown Campus
Victoria Park
Darlington Campus
St Andrews College
FOR MORE DETAIL SEE MAP 18
FOR MORE DETAIL SEE MAP 19
Carlton & United Breweries
Central
Prince Alfred Park
SURRY HILLS
DARLINGTON
EVELEIGH
NEWTOWN
REDFERN
Redfern Park
Oval
Eveleigh Railway Workshops
Australian Technology Park
WATERLOO
Waterloo Park
Alexandria Park
ERSKINEVILLE
Erskineville Oval
ALEXANDRIA
Perry Park
Basketball Stadium
Green Square
Sydney Park Village
Sydney Park
Sydney Park Business Centre
ZETLAND
South Sydney Council Office
BEACONSFIELD
ROSEBERY
Australia Post State Mail Centre
South Sydney Corporate Park
Schweppes Cottees
Alexandra Canal
Mascot Techpark
Bunnings
Meadow Lea Foods
Gardeners Rd Pmy
Crete Res
PARRAMATTA RD
BROADWAY
CLEVELAND ST
CITY RD
KING ST
REGENT ST
BOTANY RD
SWANSON ST
COPELAND ST
FOUNTAIN ST
McEVOY ST
EUSTON RD
SYDNEY PARK RD
GARDENERS RD
O'RIORDAN ST
WYNDHAM ST
GIBBONS ST
ABERCROMBIE ST

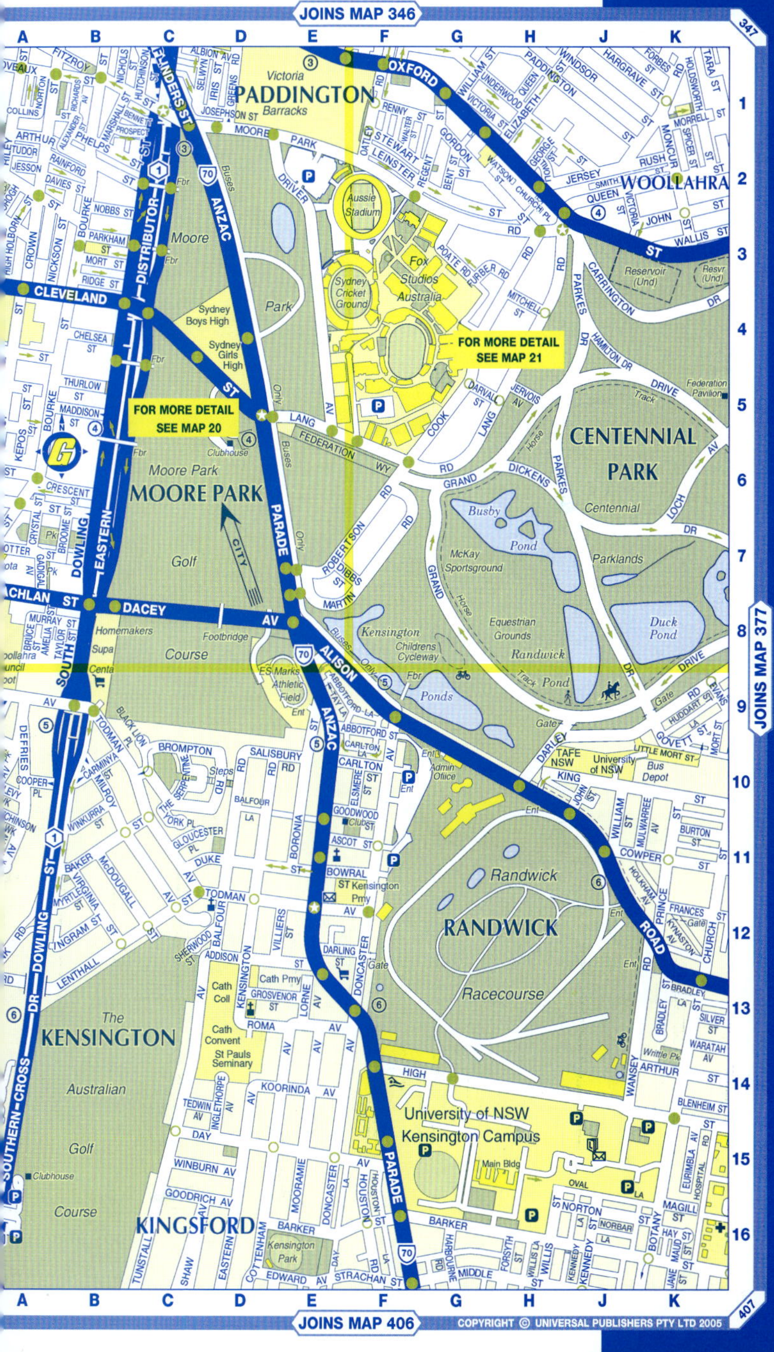
JOINS MAP 346
JOINS MAP 377
JOINS MAP 406
347
407
A B C D E F G H J K
1 2 3 4 5 6 7 8 9 10 11 12 13 14 15 16
PADDINGTON
Victoria Barracks
WOOLLAHRA
OXFORD ST
Aussie Stadium
Sydney Cricket Ground
Fox Studios Australia
FOR MORE DETAIL SEE MAP 21
FOR MORE DETAIL SEE MAP 20
CENTENNIAL PARK
Centennial Parklands
Busby Pond
Duck Pond
McKay Sportsground
Equestrian Grounds
Kensington Ponds
Randwick Pond
Federation Pavilion
Reservoir (Und)
Moore Park
MOORE PARK
Moore Park Golf Course
Sydney Boys High
Sydney Girls High
CLEVELAND ST
DACEY AV
SOUTH DOWLING ST
EASTERN DISTRIBUTOR
ANZAC PARADE
ALISON RD
FLINDERS ST
LANG RD
FEDERATION WY
GRAND DR
DICKENS DR
PARKES DR
CARRINGTON DR
CITY
ES Marks Athletic Field
Homemakers Supa Centa
TAFE NSW
University of NSW
Bus Depot
RANDWICK
Randwick Racecourse
KENSINGTON
The Australian Golf Course
KINGSFORD
Kensington Park
University of NSW Kensington Campus
Main Bldg
Cath Coll
Cath Convent
St Pauls Seminary
SOUTHERN CROSS DR
HIGH ST
BARKER ST
ROAD
STRACHAN ST
Clubhouse

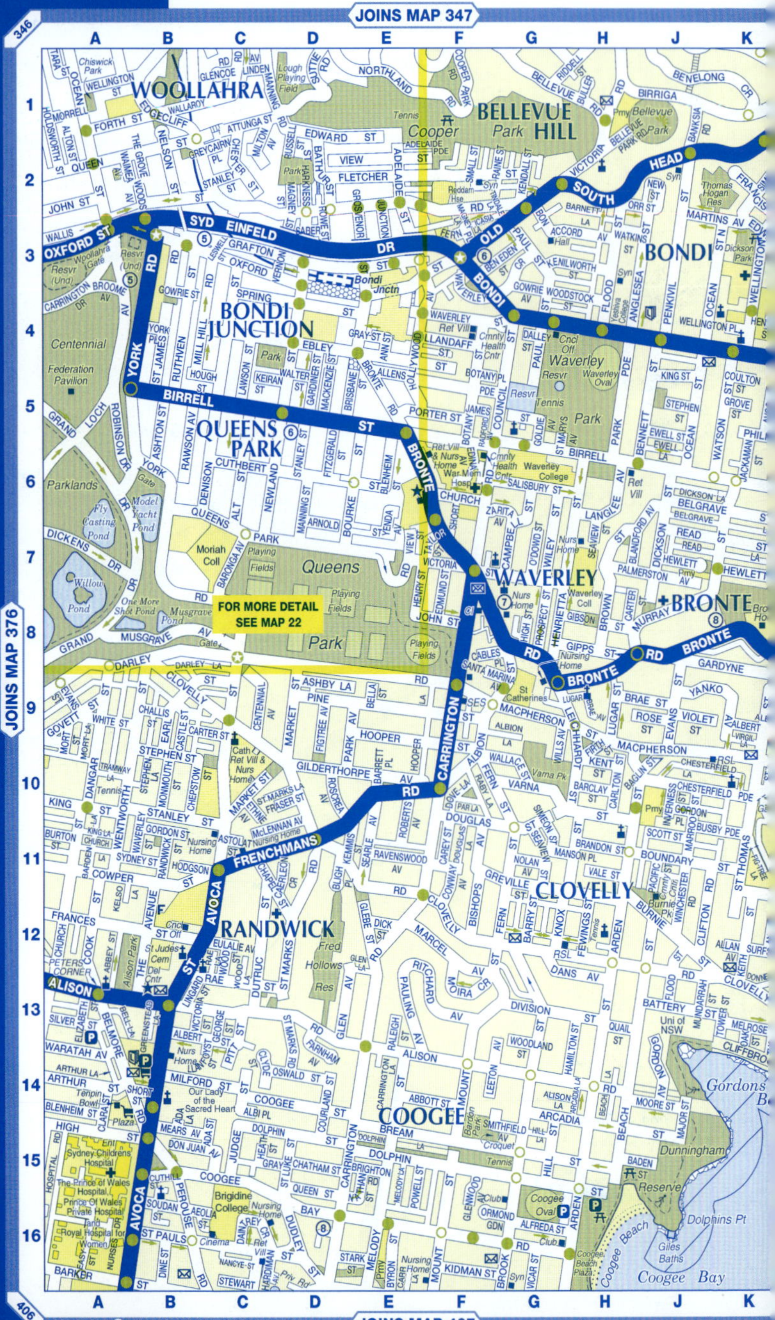
JOINS MAP 347
JOINS MAP 376
JOINS MAP 407
346
406
A B C D E F G H J K
1 2 3 4 5 6 7 8 9 10 11 12 13 14 15 16
WOOLLAHRA
BELLEVUE HILL
BONDI
BONDI JUNCTION
QUEENS PARK
WAVERLEY
BRONTE
CLOVELLY
RANDWICK
COOGEE
Centennial
Federation Pavilion
Parklands
Queens Park
Cooper Park
Bellevue Park
Waverley Oval
Fred Hollows Res
Coogee Oval
Coogee Beach
Coogee Bay
Gordons Bay
Dunningham Reserve
Dolphins Pt
Giles Baths
FOR MORE DETAIL SEE MAP 22
OXFORD ST
SYD EINFELD DR
OLD SOUTH HEAD RD
BONDI RD
YORK RD
BIRRELL ST
BRONTE RD
CARRINGTON RD
FRENCHMANS RD
AVOCA ST
ALISON RD
GRAND DR
MUSGRAVE AV
Moriah Coll
Brigidine College
Sydney Childrens Hospital
The Prince of Wales Hospital
Prince Of Wales Private Hospital
Royal Hospital for Women
Uni of NSW
Waverley College

MAP 378
MAP 383 FOLLOWS

JOINS MAP 348

NORTH BONDI
- Bondi Sewage Treatment Works
- Bondi Golf Course
- Williams Park
- Clubhouse Bondi Diggers Club
- Murriverie Pass
- Ben Buckler

BONDI BEACH
- Bondi Park
- Bondi SLSC & Pavilion
- North Bondi SLSC
- Bondi Baths & Bondi Icebergs Club
- Bondi Bay
- Mermaid Rocks
- Ray O'Keefe Res

TAMARAMA
- Marks Park
- Mackenzies Pt
- Mackenzies Bay
- Tamarama Bay
- Bronte Beach
- Nelson Bay
- Bronte Park
- Bronte Baths

Waverley Cemetery

- Burrows Park
- Shark Pt
- Clovelly Bay
- Bronte - Coogee Aquatic Reserve

TASMAN SEA

← CITY

JOINS MAP 408

COPYRIGHT © UNIVERSAL PUBLISHERS PTY LTD 2005

MAP 383
PREVIOUS MAP 378

JOINS MAP 353

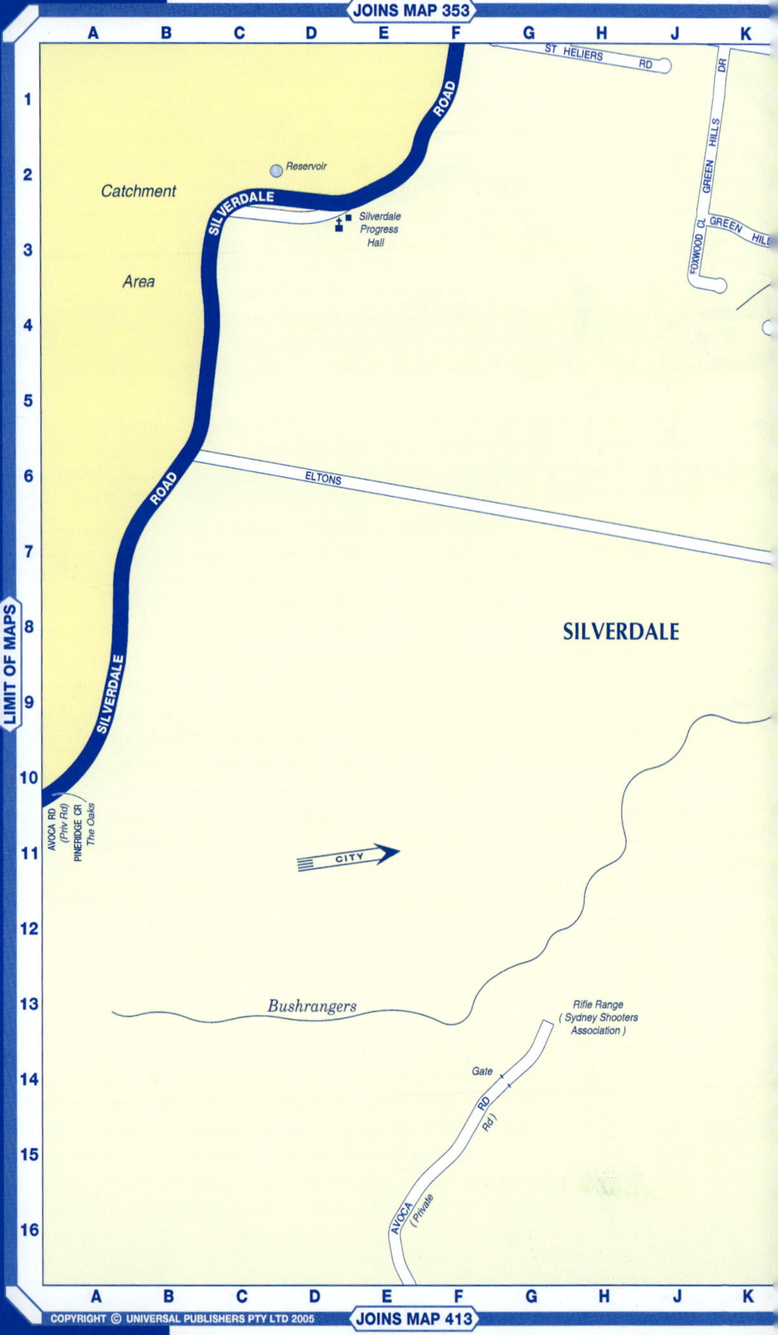

ST HELIERS RD
GREEN HILLS DR
FOXWOOD CL
GREEN HILL

Reservoir
Catchment Area
SILVERDALE ROAD
Silverdale Progress Hall

ELTONS

SILVERDALE ROAD

SILVERDALE

LIMIT OF MAPS

AVOCA RD (Priv Rd)
PINERIDGE CR
The Oaks

CITY →

Bushrangers

Rifle Range
(Sydney Shooters Association)

Gate
AVOCA RD (Private Rd)

JOINS MAP 413

COPYRIGHT © UNIVERSAL PUBLISHERS PTY LTD 2005

MAP 384

JOINS MAP 354

WALLACIA

Taylors Road
Beres Dr
James Beres Bridge
Barrington Rd
Pipers La
Taylors Road
Shadforth Bridge
Bents Creek
Bents Basin Road

Tara Guides Camp
Creek
Bushrangers Cave
Gate
Bents Basin
Bents
Kiosk
River
Ellis Bent Rd
Wolstenholme Av
Gate
Brumby Cl

GREENDALE

Basin
State
Recreation
Area
Nepean

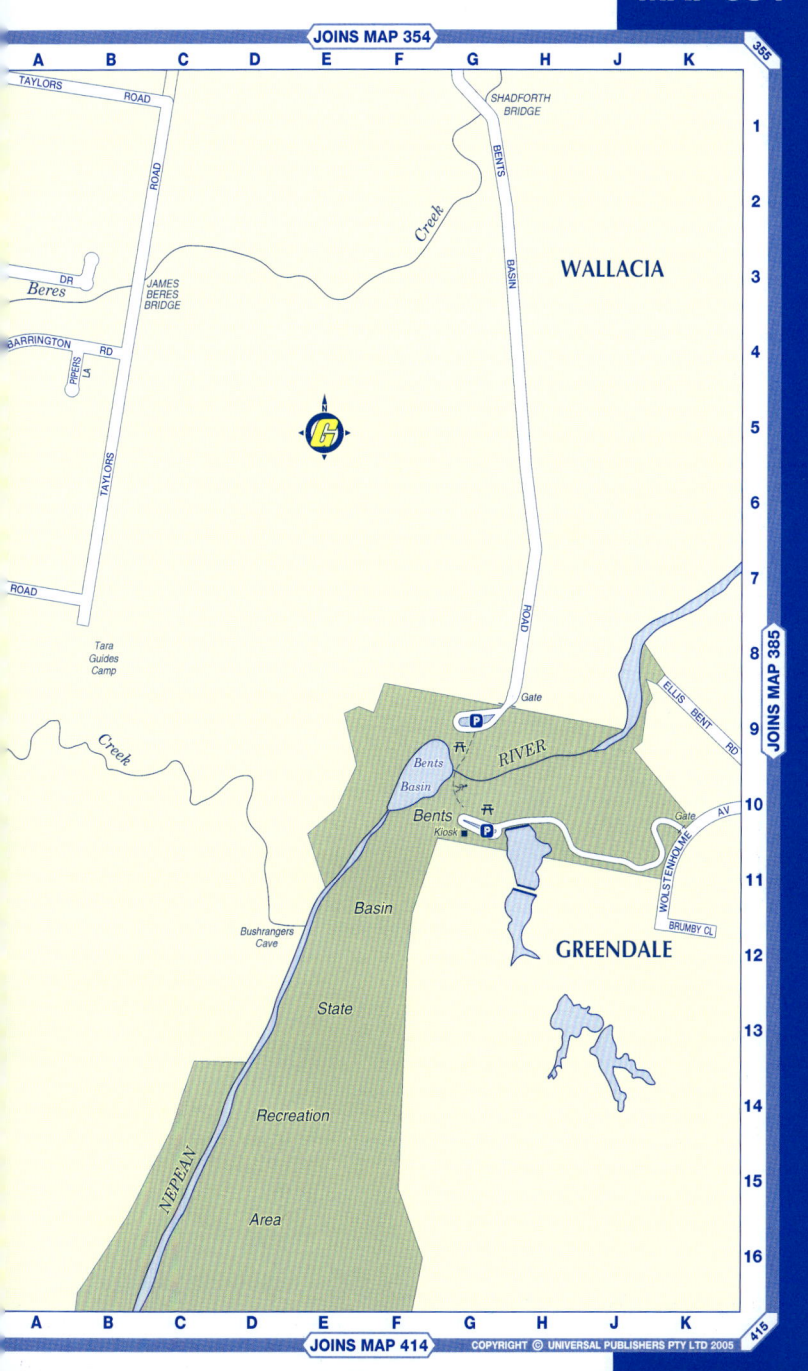

JOINS MAP 414
JOINS MAP 385

COPYRIGHT © UNIVERSAL PUBLISHERS PTY LTD 2005

MAP 385

WALLACIA

NEPEAN RIVER

Cemetery

GREENDALE ROAD

WOLSTENHOLME AVENUE

GREENDALE

ELLIS BENT RD

WOLSTENHOLME

ORIENT ROAD

CITY →

University

John Bruce Pye Farm

Bringelly

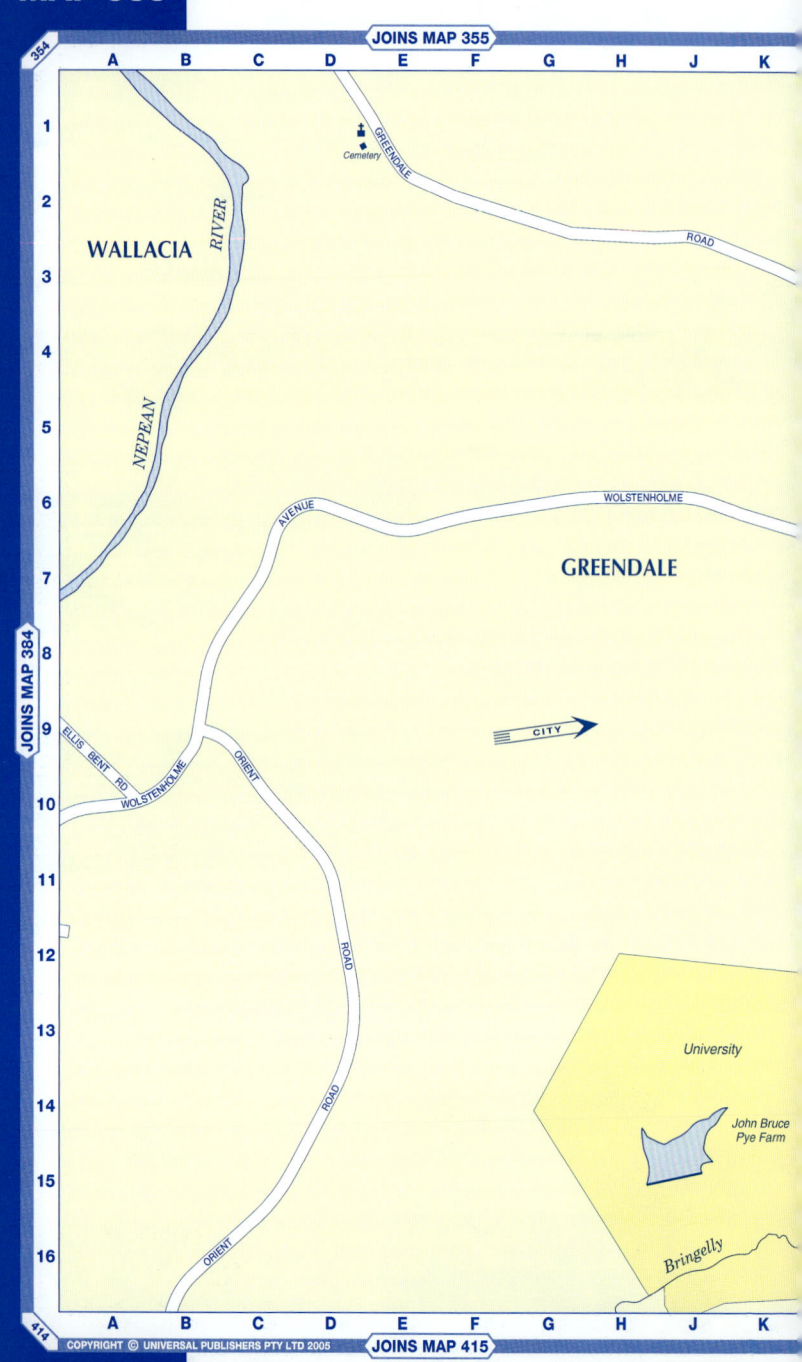

JOINS MAP 355
JOINS MAP 384
JOINS MAP 415

COPYRIGHT © UNIVERSAL PUBLISHERS PTY LTD 2005

MAP 386

Proposed Airport Site

+ Cadia Mtn

GREENDALE AV ROAD

FINDLEY RD

BRINGELLY

Gate
Road GREENDALE ROAD
of Private Sydney Gate
Private Road
Wolverton Farm

COBBITTY

Creek

JOINS MAP 356 (top)
JOINS MAP 387 (right)
JOINS MAP 416 (bottom)

MAP 387

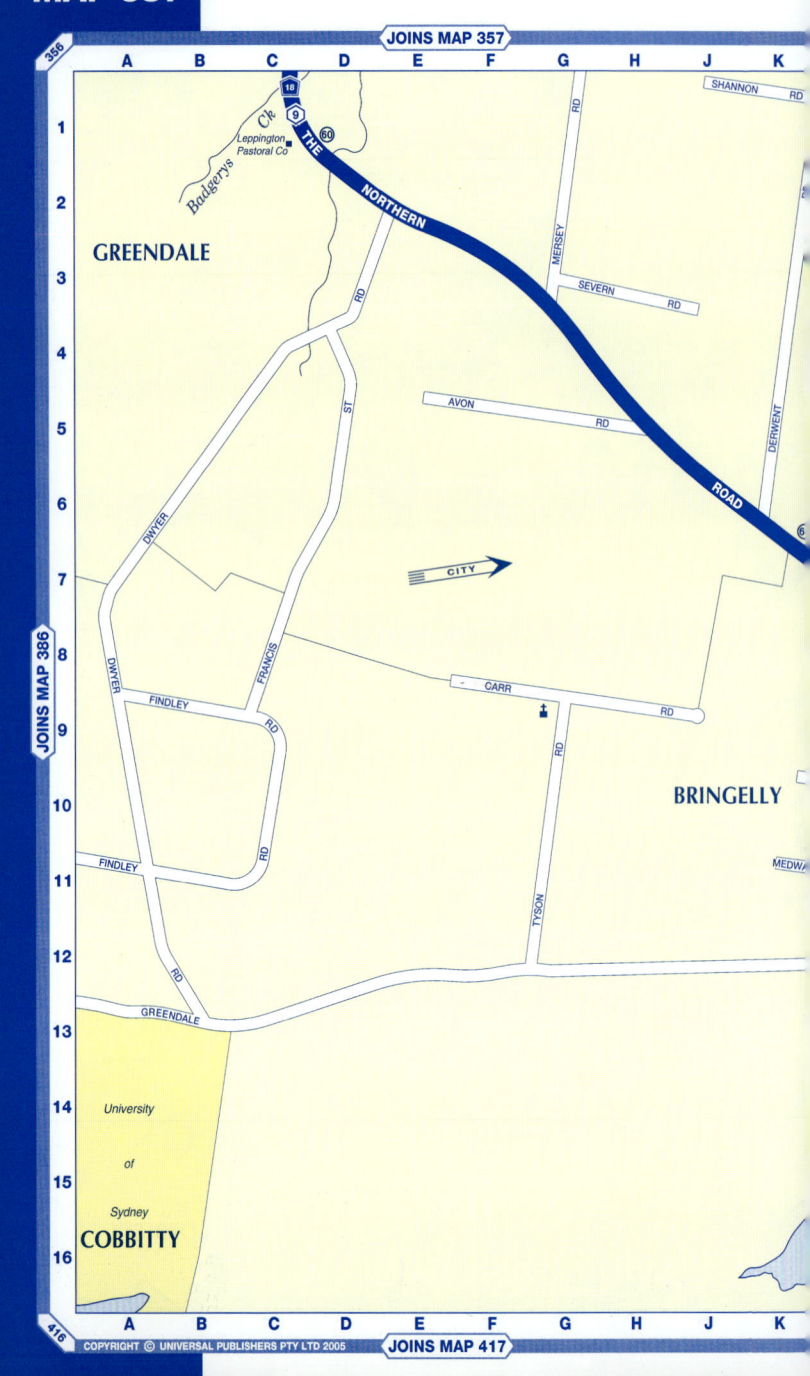

JOINS MAP 357

GREENDALE

Badgerys Ck
Leppington Pastoral Co
THE NORTHERN ROAD
SHANNON RD
MERSEY RD
SEVERN RD
DERWENT RD
AVON RD
CITY
DWYER
FRANCIS ST
FINDLEY RD
CARR RD
TYSON RD
MEDWA
BRINGELLY
FINDLEY RD
GREENDALE RD

University of Sydney
COBBITTY

JOINS MAP 417
JOINS MAP 386

MAP 388

Telstra Bringelly Radio Receiving Station

Royal Australian Air Force Telecommunications Unit

Bringelly Remote Receiving Station

Thompsons Creek

THE RETREAT DR
KELVIN PARK DR
THOMAS LAYCOCK PL
MEDICH PL
KELVIN PARK
KELVIN PARK
BRINGELLY ROAD
JERSEY RD
LOFTUS RD
ROBINSON ROAD
BELMORE RD
SOLWAY RD
MEDWAY RD
THAMES RD
NORTHERN RD
DART RD (Private Road)
BADGERYS CREEK RD
LEA RD
Private Road
Private Rd

Hi-Tech Homes
Boral Brickworks
Bringelly Park
Bringelly Pmy
Nursery
Australian Koi Farm

JOINS MAP 358
JOINS MAP 418
JOINS MAP 389

MAP 389

JOINS MAP 359

Telstra Bringelly Radio Receiving Station

Thompsons Ck

South Wianamatta

Creek

MANDINA PL

KELVIN PARK DR

BRINGELLY

RAMSAY RD

EMMETTS FARM

BELLEVUE CL

GOODSIR CL

CLEMENTSON DR

Gates

WHITAKER RD

ROSSMORE

WYNYARD

MAY AV

BELLFIELD

AV

ROSSMORE

BRINGELLY

CHURCH ST

Cemetery

AV W ROSSMORE

NORTH ROAD

South Wianamatta Creek

MASTERFIELD ST

ALLENBY RD

Rossmore Park

Rossmore P.wy

McCANN RD

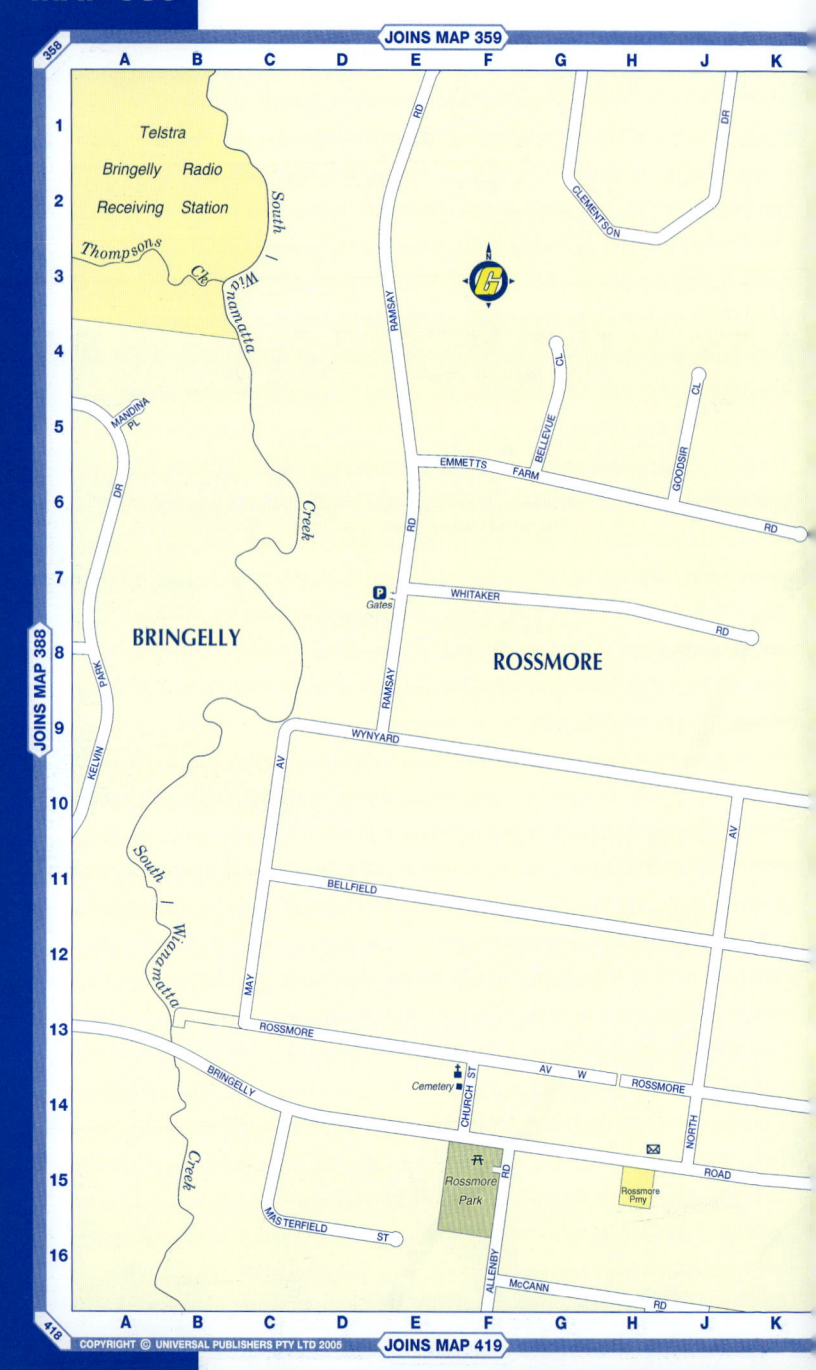

JOINS MAP 388
JOINS MAP 419

COPYRIGHT © UNIVERSAL PUBLISHERS PTY LTD 2005

MAP 390

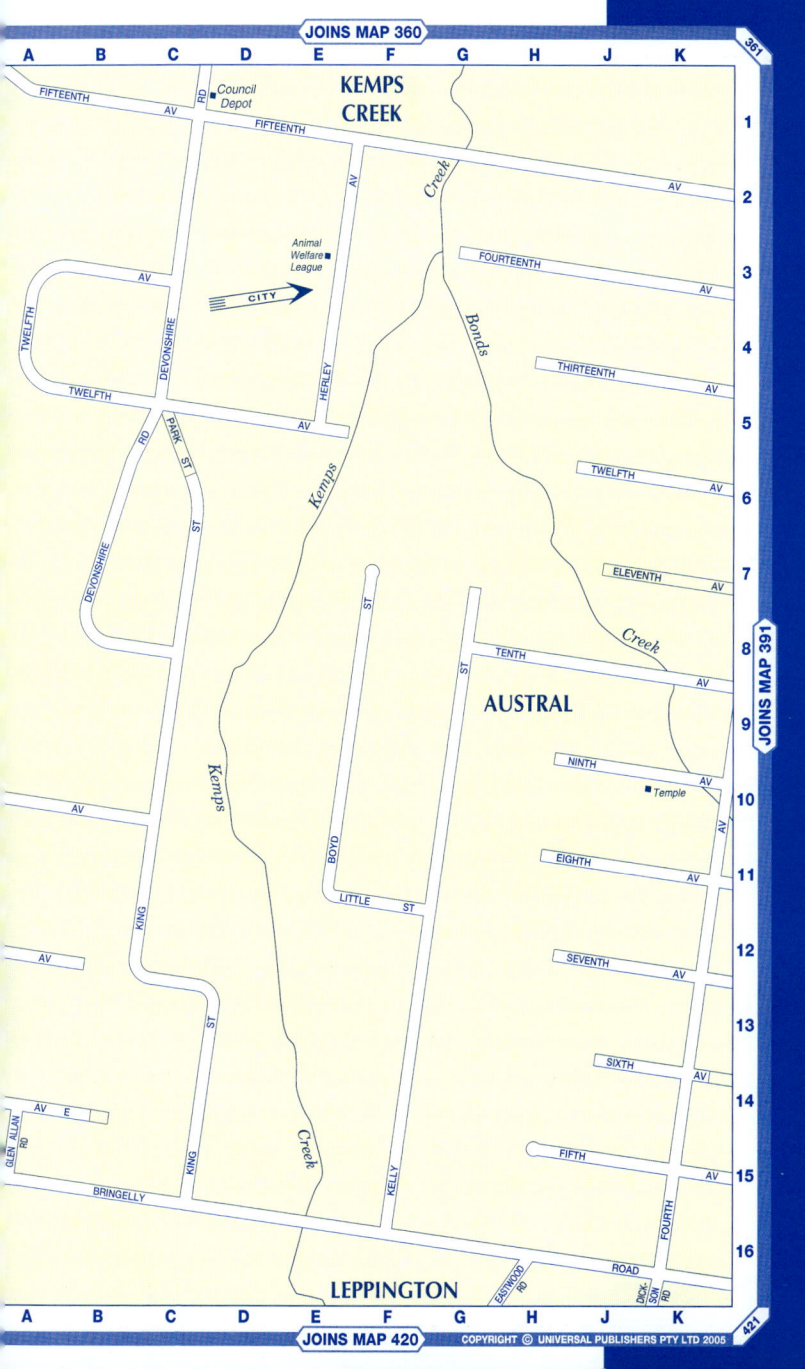

KEMPS CREEK

AUSTRAL

LEPPINGTON

Streets and features:
- Fifteenth Av
- Council Depot
- Fifteenth Av
- Twelfth Av
- Devonshire Av
- Herley Av
- Animal Welfare League
- City
- Twelfth Av
- Park St
- Devonshire Rd
- Kemps Creek
- Fourteenth Av
- Bonds Creek
- Thirteenth Av
- Twelfth Av
- Eleventh Av
- Tenth Av
- Boyd St
- Ninth Av
- Temple
- Eighth Av
- Little St
- Seventh Av
- Sixth Av
- King St
- Glen Allan Av E
- Bringelly
- Fifth Av
- Kelly St
- Eastwood Rd
- Dickson Rd
- Fourth Road

MAP 391

JOINS MAP 361

AUSTRAL

Streets and features:
- SEVENTEENTH AV
- SIXTEENTH AV
- FIFTEENTH AV
- FOURTEENTH AV
- THIRTEENTH AV
- TWELFTH AV
- ELEVENTH AV
- TENTH AV
- NINTH AV
- EIGHTH AV
- SEVENTH AV
- SIXTH AV
- FIFTH AV
- FOURTH AV
- CRAIK AV
- EDMONDSON AV
- BROWNS RD
- TWENTIETH AV
- TWENTYFIRST
- TWENTYSECOND
- TWENTYTHIRD
- TWENTYFOURTH
- TWENTYFIFTH
- TWENTYSIXTH
- TWENTYSEVENTH AV
- TWENTYEIGHTH AV
- THIRTYSECOND
- THIRTYTHIRD AV
- STOREY AV
- BAILEY
- LOWRY AV
- THOM RD
- AMOS
- GODFREY
- KIRKPATRICK
- FOSTER
- HOPKINS PL
- CARNE CL
- STUART
- BRINGELLY

Features and places:
- Camp Austral
- Craik Park
- Skate Ramp
- Tennis
- Youth Centre
- Austral Pmy
- RFS
- Petanque
- Bonds Creek
- Sydney Water Supply Channel
- Scalabrini Village
- Pavilion
- W.V. Scott Memorial Park
- Renbury Farm Animal Shelter
- One Lane Bridge
- Resvr
- Wellards Nurseries
- Gas Receiving Station
- Grow Community

Wingate area:
- COBLE CCT
- PROUT DR
- WINGATE AV
- LYCETT
- GARLING
- DOWLING ST
- GOULD ST
- HARRADEN
- WAINEWRIGHT
- BIRD PL
- LARMER
- FERRARO

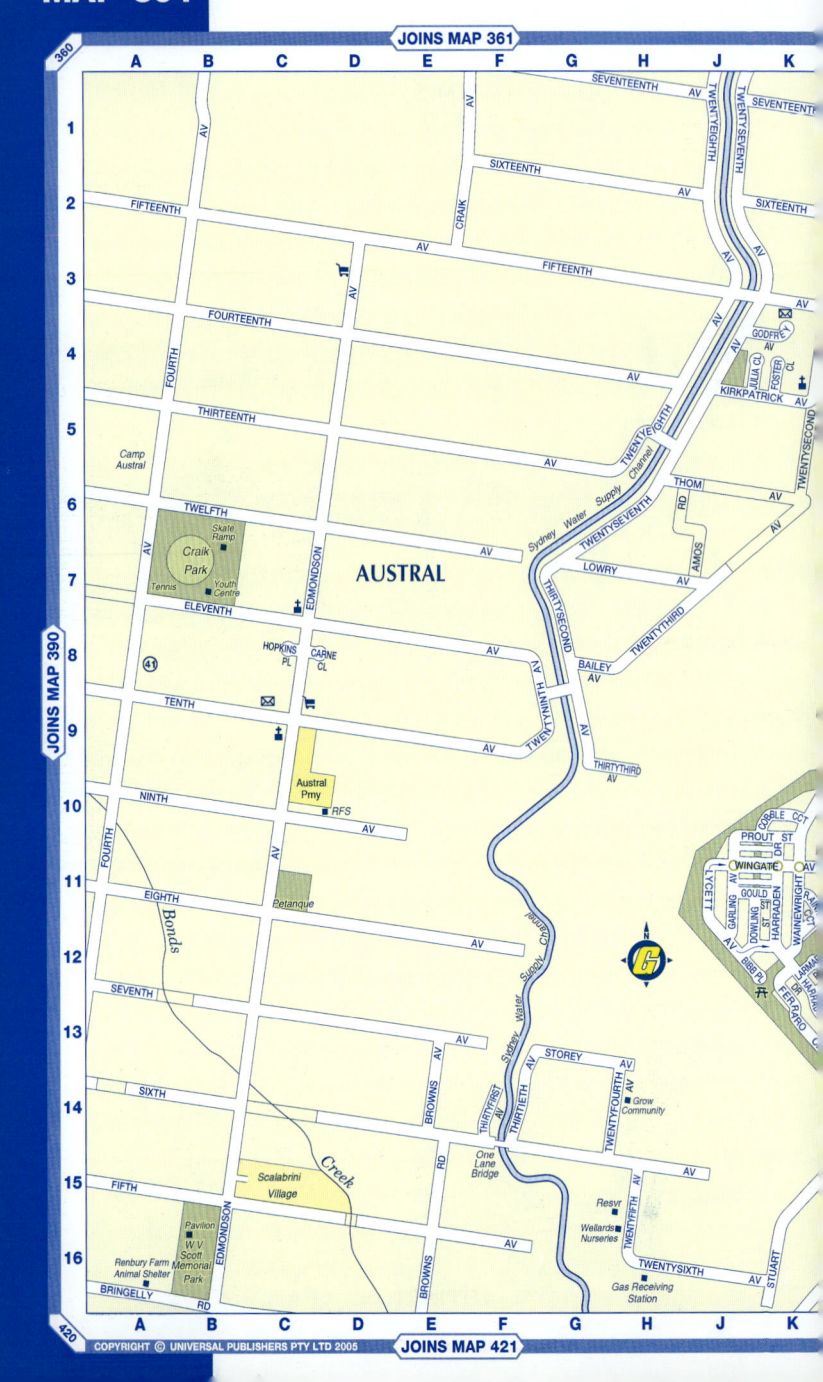

JOINS MAP 390
JOINS MAP 421

COPYRIGHT © UNIVERSAL PUBLISHERS PTY LTD 2005

JOINS MAP 362

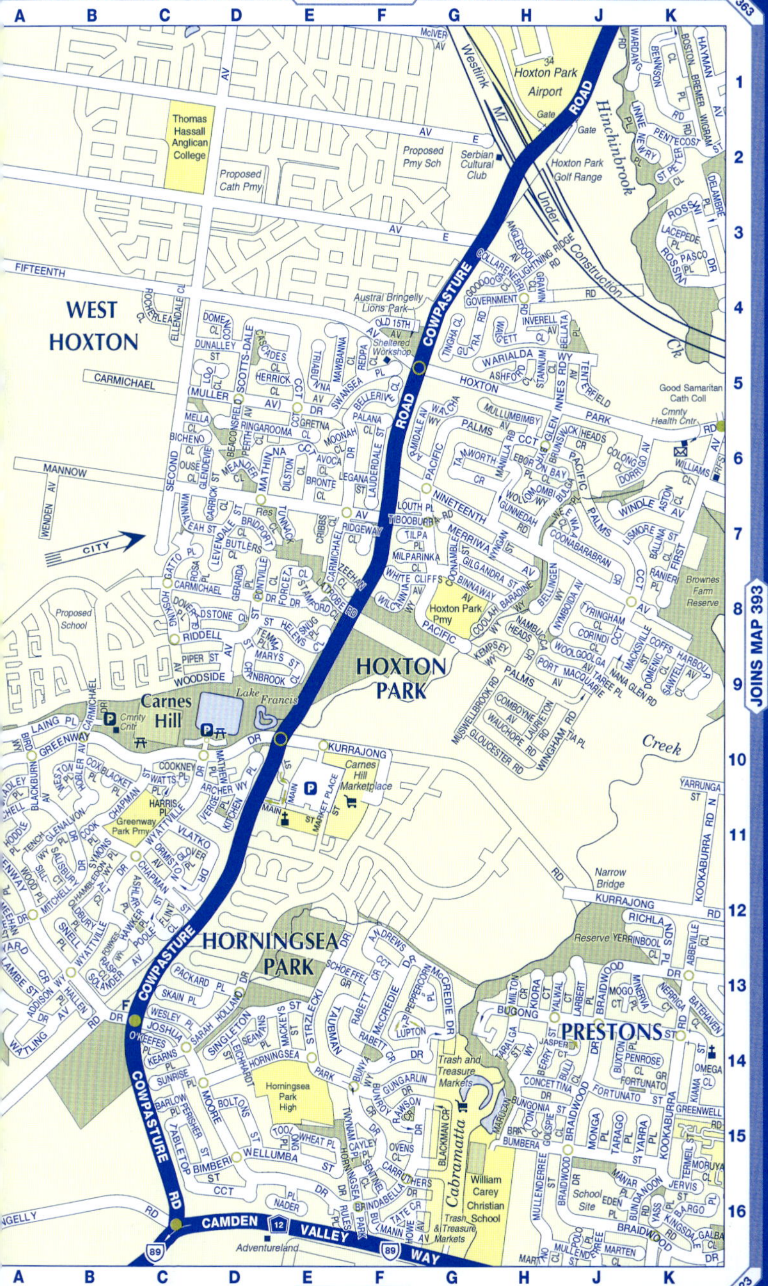

JOINS MAP 422

MAP 393

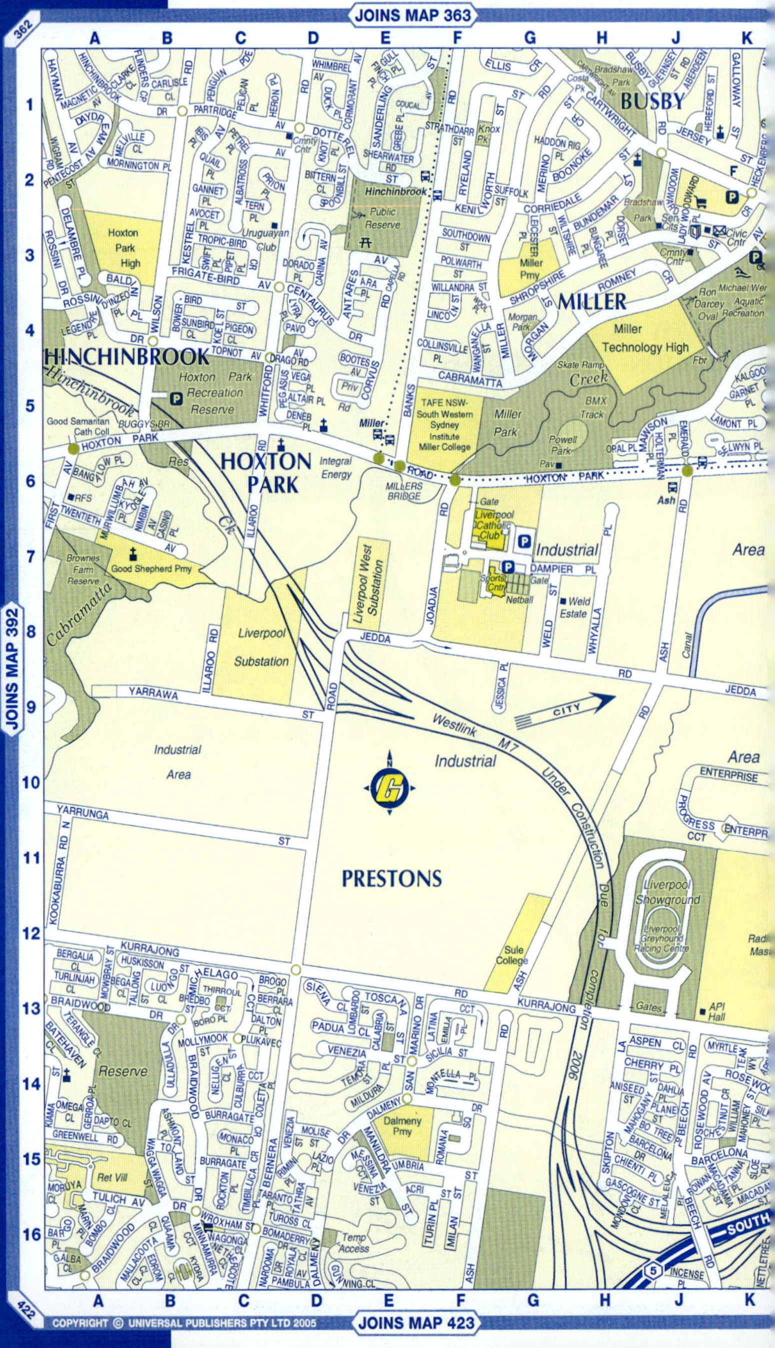
JOINS MAP 363
JOINS MAP 392
JOINS MAP 423
362
422
A B C D E F G H J K
1 2 3 4 5 6 7 8 9 10 11 12 13 14 15 16
BUSBY
MILLER
HINCHINBROOK
HOXTON PARK
PRESTONS
Hoxton Park High
Hoxton Park Recreation Reserve
Good Samaritan Cath Coll
Good Shepherd Pmy
Brownes Farm Reserve
Cabramatta
Hinchinbrook Ck
Hinchinbrook Public Reserve
Uruguayan Club
Miller Pmy
Miller Technology High
Miller Park
Powell Park
Skate Ramp
BMX Track
Ron Darcey Oval
Michael Wenden Aquatic Recreation
Bradshaw Park
Cartwright Av Costa Pk
Knox Pk
Morgan Park
TAFE NSW-South Western Sydney Institute Miller College
Integral Energy
MILLERS BRIDGE
Liverpool Catholic Club
Sports Cntr
Netball
Weld Estate
Industrial Area
Liverpool Substation
Liverpool West Substation
Westlink M7 Under Construction Due for completion 2006
CITY
Liverpool Showground
Liverpool Greyhound Racing Centre
Sule College
API Hall
Dalmeny Pmy
Ret Vill
Reserve
Temp Access
HOXTON PARK ROAD
CABRAMATTA RD
JEDDA RD
YARRAWA ST
YARRUNGA ST
KURRAJONG RD
JOADJA RD
ASH RD
BANKS RD
WHITFORD RD
ILLAROO RD
KOOKABURRA RD N
ENTERPRISE
PROGRESS CCT
SOUTH

JOINS MAP 364

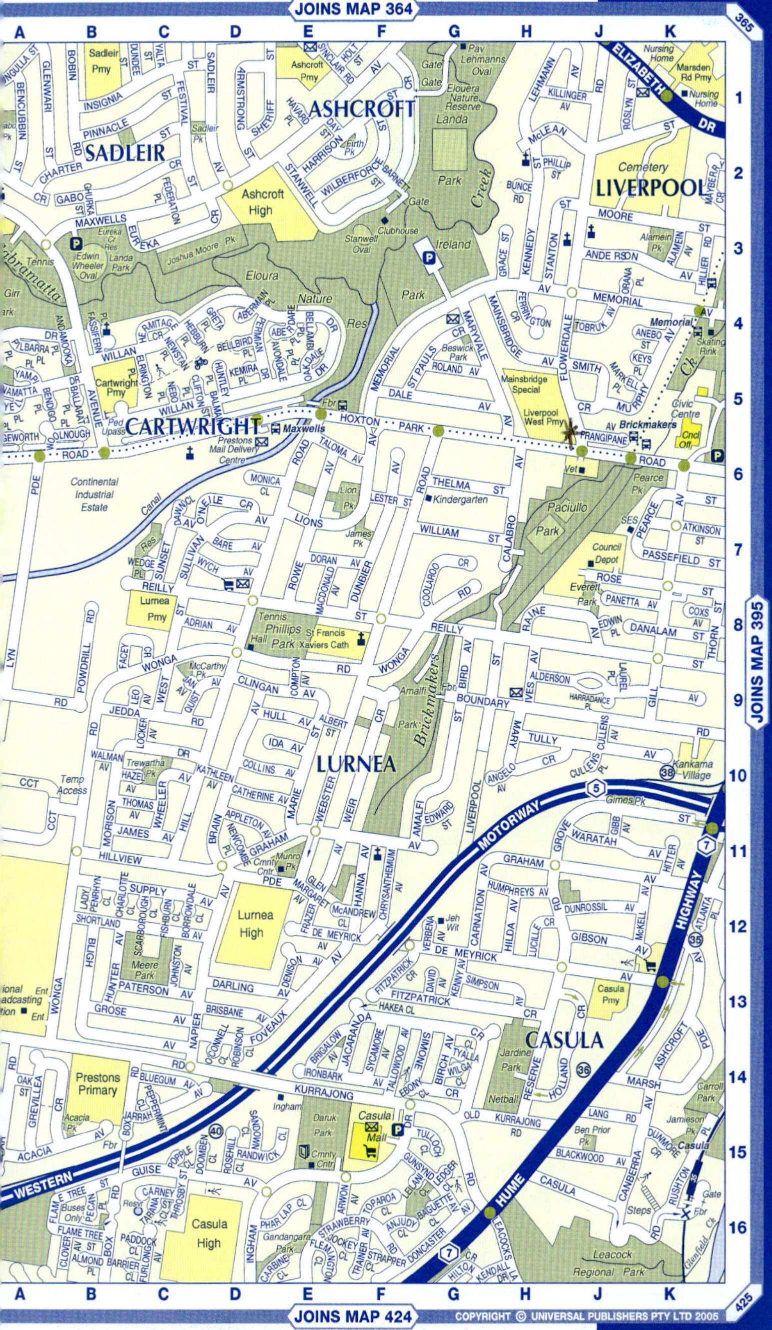

JOINS MAP 395

JOINS MAP 424

JOINS MAP 365
JOINS MAP 394
JOINS MAP 425
364
424
A B C D E F G H J K
1 2 3 4 5 6 7 8 9 10 11 12 13 14 15 16
WARWICK FARM
LIVERPOOL
MOOREBANK
CASULA
Chatham Village
Military Reserve
Liverpool Boys High
Liverpool Girls High
Liverpool Hospital
(Private Rd)
TAFE NSW Sth Western Sydney Institute
Westfield Complex
Cinemas
Macquarie Club
All Saints Boys
Bigge Park
Liverpool Bus Terminus
Liverpool
Weir
RIVER
GEORGES
Haigh Park
Wetland Wildlife Refuge
Bill Morrison Park
Light Horse Park
Woodward Park
Whitlam Leisure Centre
Hillier Oval
Memorial Skating Rink
Ten Cts
Collimore Park
Netball
Barbara Long Pk
Brickmakers Ck
Marsden Rd Pmy
Apex Pk
Dunbier Pk
Discovery Pk
Liverpool Regional Museum
Collingwood Hse
Mill Pk
Helles Park
Archery
Radio Controlled Car Raceway
Barefoot Waterski
Rifle Range Park
M Five Industrial Park
Stegbar
Buttercup
Industrial Area
Seton Rec Cntr
Clinchs Pond Res
Titalka Pk
Orara Pk
Substation
Defence Estate Organisation
Corporate Services & Infrastructure Centre
Defence National Storage & Distribution Centre
Carroll Pk
Casula Powerhouse Arts Centre
Kankama Village
Motor Reg
2GLF
Cmnty Health Cntr
ELIZABETH DR
HUME HWY
COPELAND ST
MEMORIAL AV
SCOTT ST
TERMINUS ST
MACQUARIE ST
NEWBRIDGE ROAD
HEATHCOTE RD
MOOREBANK AV
SOUTH WESTERN MOTORWAY
ANZAC RD
CHURCH RD
MOORE ST
HOXTON PARK RD
PEARCE ST
ATKINSON ST
PASSEFIELD ST
ROSE ST
CHRISTIE ST
REILLY ST
ALDERSON AV
BOUNDARY RD
CONGRESSIONAL DR
DEERWOOD AV
MONTECLAIR AV
PHOENIX CR
ST. ANDREWS CR
WESTCHESTER AV
COLONIAL PL
BOULEVARDE
BUCKLAND RD
JORDAN RD
BULLDOG RD
LONG HAI RD
BAPAUME RD
YPRES RD
GREENHILLS AV
CUNNINGHAM ST
MITCHELL RD
SCRIVENER ST
PRIDDLE ST
HENDRA
LACHLAN ST
CAMPBELL ST
BATHURST ST
NORTHUMBERLAND ST
GEORGE ST
BIGGE ST
GOULBURN ST
FORBES ST
COLLEGE ST
NAGLE ST
SPEED ST
RIVERPARK DR
SHEPHERD ST
CHARLES ST
McGOWEN CR
HELLES AV
COOPER ST
KING ST
MARKET ST
BRADSHAW AV
SWAIN ST
KALESKI ST
BRIDGES RD
FIELD CL
DEADMAN RD
SETON RD
CENTENARY AV
7 61 5 34 35 36
CITY
N

JOINS MAP 366
367
A B C D E F G H J K
1 2 3 4 5 6 7 8 9 10 11 12 13 14 15 16
JOINS MAP 397
JOINS MAP 426
427
CHIPPING NORTON
Industrial Area
Industrial Area
Moore
Chauvel Park
Nursing Home
Thomas Moore Pk
Quota Pk
McMillan Park
NEWBRIDGE
ROAD
Flower Power
Regan Pk
Skate Ramp
EWINS RIDGE
Kelso
Park
Cmnty Health Cntr
Edgecombe Pk
Moorebank Shopping Village
Nuwarra Pmy
Boral Brickworks
Molly Moore Park
Moorebank High
Newbridge Hts Pmy
Williams Pk
Cowan Pk
Field Pk
Cath
Cole Pk
Paine Park
RIVER
GEORGES
Ernie Smith Recreation Area
(Liverpool City Hockey Complex)
Metcalfe Pk
Syme Pk
Hillcrest Pk
Topin Pk
Wilkes Pk
Only Pk
Renton Pk
Josephine Pk
Freda Pk
New Brighton Golf Course
Clubhouse
Resvr
Clyde Pk
Vasta Pk
SOUTH-WESTERN MOTORWAY
HEATHCOTE ROAD
NUWARRA ROAD
JUNCTION ROAD
Anzac Village
WATTLE GROVE
HOLSWORTHY
HAMMONDVILLE
Hammondville Pmy
Nursing Home
Hammond Village Nursing Home
Lieutenant Cantello Reserve
Peter Pan Park
Brallos Pk
Sananando Pk
Wattle Grove Pk
Lakeside Park

JOINS MAP 367
JOINS MAP 396
JOINS MAP 427
366
426
CHIPPING NORTON
Baseball
Fields
Joshua Allen Diamond
Blake Rimmer Diamond
CHILDS RD
ALFRED RD
RIVERSIDE RD
ARTHUR ST
RICKARD RD
Peterson Pk
Kentucky Res
GEORGES
HENRY LAWSON DRIVE
Clubhouse
Riverwood Golf Course
Gate
ROAD
Control Tower
BANKSTOWN AIRPORT
NPWS Flight Operations
TOWER
STARKEY
Australian Aviation Museum
DR
RUNWAY
TAXIWAY
Helipad
Airport Admin
AVRO ST
ARMSTRONG
KESTREL PL
TERMINAL CT
Hawker de Haviland Aircraft
MURRAY JONES DR
NEWBRIDGE ROAD
Beveridge Pk
Flower Power
ROBINSON DR
DAVY
Davy Robinson Pk
Hind Pk
MILPERRA BR
Airport
MILPERRA
Ashford Res
Res
Vale of Ah Res
Park
AULD AV
Gate
Gordon Parker Reserve
Bankstown Golf Course
BLAXLAND PL
WORKS PL
MILPERRA
Tennis
Milperra Sports Centre
Driving Range
KEYS
PDE
Clubhouse
BORELLA RD
RUTHVEN AV
INGRAM AV
WHITTLE AV
KEYSOR PL
BULLECOURT AV
SADLIER AV
PEELER PL
Newland Res
PIPER CL
LINKS
MARTIN CR
NEWLAND AV
DUNSTAN AV
STRATTON CR
GRIEVE CR
POZIERES AV
JOYNT AV
TREADGOLD ST
COWPER CT
OAKLEIGH AV
GOOLAGONG CT
GANMAIN CR
FROMELLES AV
BEATHAM PL
ARMENTIERES
BAPAUME PL
MESSINES AV
MERRIS PL
LILLE PL
SINAI AV
ZONNEBEKE CR
HERMIES AV
HAMEL CL
SOMME
ASHFORD AV
DERNANCOURT PDE
PROYART
Thompson Res
FLANDERS
Milperra Res
University of Western Sydney Bankstown Campus
IAN SMITH DR
Mount St Joseph Girls Sec
Riverlands Golf Course
Wetlands
LONE PINE AV
RALEIGH PL
CAMBRAI
Vesta Res
Milperra Pmy
CHAUVEL AV
PRESCOT
Gate
WARLENCOURT PDE
MACTIER AV
MAYGAR
METEREN CL
Toll Gate
MOTORWAY
BRANSGROVE RD
Council Depot
Gate
Clubhouse
Toll Gate
Former Bankstown Tip
New Brighton Golf Course
SOUTH WESTERN
Toll Gates
Former Blue Gum Farm Zoo
MAXWELL AV
Gate
CITY
Ck
Deepwater Park
Lieutenant Cantello Reserve
HAMMONDVILLE
RIVER
Deepwater Motor Boat Club
Gate
WEBSTER ST
Kelso Park Nth Sporting Complex
Georges River Softball Complex
Kelso Park
Kelso
HOMELEA AV
KERRIE CR
MARCO
CAMMARLIE

JOINS MAP 368
JOINS MAP 399
JOINS MAP 428
369
429
CONDELL PARK
REVESBY
PANANIA
Condell Park High
Bankstown Basketball Stadium
Kinch Res
Deverall Park
Netball
Tennis
Bankstown City Paceway
Function Cntr
Bankstown Trotting Recreational Club
Telstra
Industrial Area
Bankstown-Lidcombe Hospital
Sir Joseph Banks High
Broderick Gillawarra Special
Revesby Pmy
Panania North Primary
Condell Pk Pmy
Beechwood Nursing Home
Temple
Revesby Workers Club
Amour Park
Johnstone Res
Killara Reserve
Toby Res
Wall Res
Gowland Res
Tracey Res
Greenway Res
Eldridge Res
O'Brien Pk
Wattawa Res
Dalton Res
Rotary Park
Putt Putt Golf
Milperra Business & Delivery Cntr
Bunnings
Toll Gate
WESTERN MOTORWAY
SOUTH
CANTERBURY RD
ROAD
HORSLEY ROAD
BEACONSFIELD
CARRINGTON ST
GORDON PARKER
ALLINGHAM
RAILWAY
TOWNSEND
YANDERRA
ELDRIDGE
LANCELOT
NORMAN
AUGUSTA
BIRDSALL
WINIFRED
HARRIS ST
ILMA ST
MAVIS
TURVEY
BISHOP ST
DOVE ST
ANNE ST
LANGDALE AV
DOYLE
THORN ST
LINTON AV
VAUGHAN AV
BUCKLEY AV
FLOOD AV
SPHINX AV
HORSLEY
LAWSON
BRANSGROVE
ELLESMERE
GOWLAND
GLENVIEW
HARRISON ST
ILUKA
ROBB ST
MARONG ST
MARCO
HENDY AV
BRAESMERE
COPYRIGHT © UNIVERSAL PUBLISHERS PTY LTD 2005

JOINS MAP 369
JOINS MAP 398
JOINS MAP 429
368
428
A B C D E F G H J K
1 2 3 4 5 6 7 8 9 10 11 12 13 14 15 16
CONDELL PARK
BANKSTOWN
PADSTOW
REVESBY
MARION ST
MARKET ST
YORK ST
NORMAN ST
BRANDON
CAMBRIDGE
CHELMSFORD
CHERTSEY
LANCELOT ST
CLARENCE
PRINGLE
OXFORD
KOONYA AV
OGMORE CT
AUGUSTA ST
GALLIPOLI ST
SHENTON
SUNSET AV
TUMUT CL
HIGH
Bankstown City Sports Complex
OSTEND ST
ANTWERP
B'town Senior College
EDWARD
IRVINE
ARTHUR ST
ELDRIDGE
Bankstown-Lidcombe Hosp
ARTEGALL ST
NORTHAM
CALIDORE ST
CLARIBEL
HERBERT ST
CHAPEL
Home Central
Homemaker City
SES
Bob Jane T-Mart
CANTERBURY
Flood Res
Caroline Chisholm Special Sch
GIBSON
NELSON AV
LACHLAN ST
NAPOLI
REIBA CR
SNOWSILL
STILES AV
ATKINSON AV
GOW
Sydney Water
Padstow Industrial Estate
CITY
WORDIE PL
Roller Skate Rink
TURVEY
Sir Joseph Banks High
WOLAROI CR
SOUTH WESTERN MOTORWAY
Toll Gate
BRYANT
LAUREL CR
LOUIE
BISHOP ST
DRAVET
DOVE ST
MACKINNON
ANNE ST
RONALD
LANGDALE AV
ARCHIBALD
MAHNKEN AV
MACKENZIE
CAROOTA
LESTER
BLACKALL ST
DOYLE
TAFE NSW Southern Sydney Institute Padstow College
Playford Park
CAHORS RD
PYRAMID
ROBYN
PIVETTA
ENGLISH
BARROW ST
WILBERFORCE RD
RHONDA
RAINE
CAIRO
SPHINX
ARAB
CORY
HENDRICK
ALICE ST
VANNAN
SHEARER LA
MEMORIAL DR
Little Res
Padstow
STEPHENS RD
SHOULTS LA
PADSTOW PDE
SEGERS AV
GLOUCESTER AV
HOWARD
CRUSADE AV
RSL
MONTGOMERY
WYREEMA AV
McGIRR
TONY CR
CORAL AV
BADDELEY ST
SPRING ST
Pmy
OLYMPIC PDE
DALE PDE
DEPOT PL
Bankstown
SOUTH TCE
STEWART LA
GREENFIELD
Club
McDONALD LA
SWEETHAVEN
MONA ST
RAYMOND ST
LOPEZ LA
WEST TCE
EAST TCE
Tenpin Bowl
CROSS ST
Girls High
Bankstown Primary
Bankstown Oval
Memorial Park
St Brendans Cath
STANLEY
ROSS ST
Cmnty Hlth Cntr
RESTWELL
VIMY ST
LEONARD
PERCY
Stevens Res
MACAULEY
Temple
DUDLEY AV
DELLWOOD ST
WHITE AV
JUNE ST
DE WITT LA
DE WITT
NOUMEA AV
MARSHALL ST
HIXSON
ARCHER CR
HOSKINS
TOPAZ PL
CLEMENTS
COTTAM
EXCELLER
MEGAN AV
Ruse Park
Bankstown Football Centre
ADEPT LA
GARTMORE AV
SEDDON
STACEY ST
ARKLEY
WARREN AV
FORT AV
ROAD
STACEY ST
FAIRFORD RD
DAVIES RD
SOUTH
CARNATION AV
GRIFFITHS
GARDENIA
SALVIA AV
VERBENA
PETUNIA AV
DAPHNE AV
ASTER AV
MARCELLA ST
JAMES
LAVENDER AV
SALADINE AV
Arthur Pk
MICHAELS CR
BOYLEY CR
Infants
HOMEDALE RD
LANCASTER CR
NEVADA ST
JOHN
JAMES ST
SUNNY CR
COLUMBINE
PRATTEN LA
LANCASTER
WARWICK
MAWSON
GOWRIE
WILGA
Salmon Res
MULGA
WATTLE
STANSFIELD
Sidings
Dorothy Park
SCOTT
GILLIAN PL
McPHERSON
WYLEENA PL
VIOLA
PUNCHBOWL
Punchbowl Park
Croatian Cl
MOXON
WEYLAND ST
VERNON ST
BRAMHALL AV
SEPTIMUS AV
LYON AV
CARLTON
JOYCE
CRAIG ST
KYLIE
Craig St Res
WIGGS
Bunnings
SHORT ST
Bankstown Substation
Salt Pan Reserve
Salt Pan Ck
Baseball
McLaughlin Oval
LUPIN AV
LILY AV
IRIS AV
Fbr
Ped Upass
Industrial Area
GWANDALAN RD
HALCYON AV
BEAMISH ST
LIBERA AV
MORO AV
NEWEY AV
Padstow North Primary
ENTERPRISE AV
STUART ST
Clubhouse
Stuart St Reserve
Steps
WATSON
JAYELEM CR
McEVOY ST
KURANDA AV
IBERIA
Mot Reg
Sen Cits
STEPHANIE
JEANETTE ST
NIGEL PL
Padstow Park
BANKS
BRIDGE ST
MEAGER AV
MAL AV
RYAN RD
PARKER LA
LOCK AV
TREVONE ST
TRURO PDE
MONTANA
MICHIGAN
KENTUCKY
IDAHO PL
Sports Field
Riverwood Pmy
MARY ST
UNION
COLERIDGE
Riverwood Park
Lillian Rd Res
WILLIAM
HENRY RD
LILLIAN
WEBB
BASIL ST
WEEMALA ST
SHENSTONE RD
TURNER

JOINS MAP 370
A B C D E F G H J K
PUNCHBOWL
WILEY PARK
LAKEMBA
ROSELANDS
RIVERWOOD
NARWEE
BEVERLY HILLS
PEAKHURST
JOINS MAP 401
JOINS MAP 430
KING GEORGES ROAD
CANTERBURY ROAD
SOUTH WESTERN MOTORWAY
TELOPEA ST
BOUVARDIA ST
LILAC ST
WARATAH ST
PUNCHBOWL RD
URUNGA PDE
THE BOULEVARDE
STANLEA PDE
RAILWAY PDE
Punchbowl Boys High
Punchbowl Primary
Wiley Pk Girls High
Wiley Pk Pmy
Lakemba Pmy
Wiley Park
Scott Res
Roselands
Bennett Park
Wise Res
Rotary Park
Lance Hutchinson Oval
Bland Oval
Hannans Rd Pmy
Spicers Paper Ltd
Daihatsu
Retirement Village
Nursing Home
Richard Podmore Res
Robert Gardner Res
Windarra Res
John Mountford Res
Bev Hills Nth Pmy
Narwee Pmy
Frappell Res
Progress Pk
Rasdall Park
Legion Club
Sen Cits
Riverwood
Narwee
Punchbowl
Wiley Park
BELMORE RD
HANNANS RD
BONDS RD
MARTIN AV
WERONA AV
SHORTER AV
WESTON AV
GROVE AV
WINDARRA ST
METHUEN PDE
EARLS AV
NIRIMBA
BROAD ARROW RD
JOSEPHINE ST
THURLOW ST
CAIRNS ST
ELDON ST
SHORT RD
MEADOWLAND RD
MILFORD RD
OLIVE CR
CHAMBERLAIN RD
MOUNTVIEW AV
BALFOUR RD
EDGBASTON RD
BRYANT ST
PENSHURST RD
STATION LA
MIDLOTHIAN AV
WELFARE AV
WOODLANDS AV
ROSELANDS DR
PAYTEN AV
FARNHAM AV
CHARLESCOTTE AV
BELAIR AV
MITCHAM ST
CULLENS RD
HEATH ST
VIOLA ST
LANCELOT ST
LINDEN ST
ROSSMORE AV
HILLCREST AV
BROADWAY
CANTERBURY
DENMAN AV
FERGUSON AV
TUCKER ST
HAIGH AV
CANARYS RD
STODDART ST
NICOLL ST
BERRING AV
SYLVESTER AV
ALPHA AV
HILTON AV
CHICK ST
ROSEVIEW AV
ROBIN PL
ROSEANNE AV
SHIRLEY AV
RAYMOND AV
HALIFAX ST
DIANA AV
CENTRE AV
KENT ST
FENWICK AV
DUNLOP ST
EWEN ST
PENTLAND AV
FAIRVIEW AV
MOUNT ST
DRAPER AV
HIGHLAND AV
SPRINGFIELD AV
AUGUSTA RD
VICTORIA RD
MAJOR ST
CHRISTIAN RD
LUMEAH AV
DEBORAH PL
PARKLAND AV
PEAKHURST
BEVERLY HILLS

JOINS MAP 371

A B C D E F G H J K

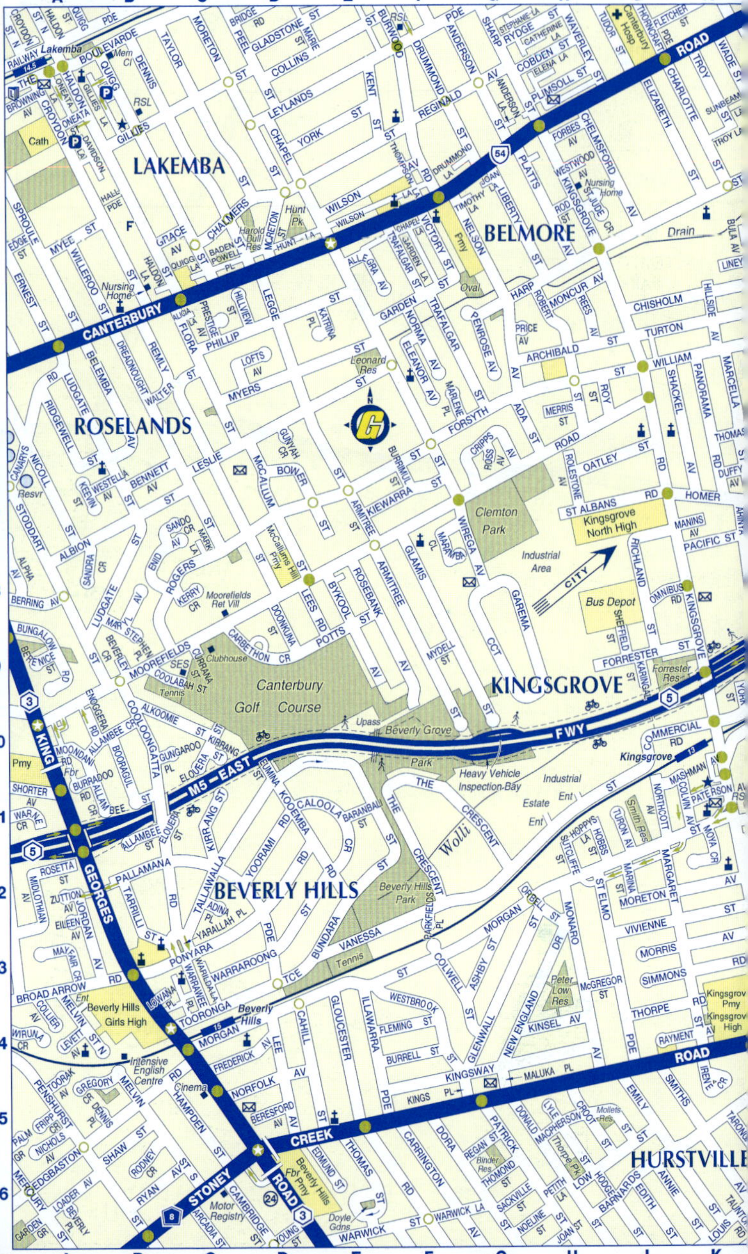

1 2 3 4 5 6 7 8 9 10 11 12 13 14 15 16

JOINS MAP 400

A B C D E F G H J K

JOINS MAP 431

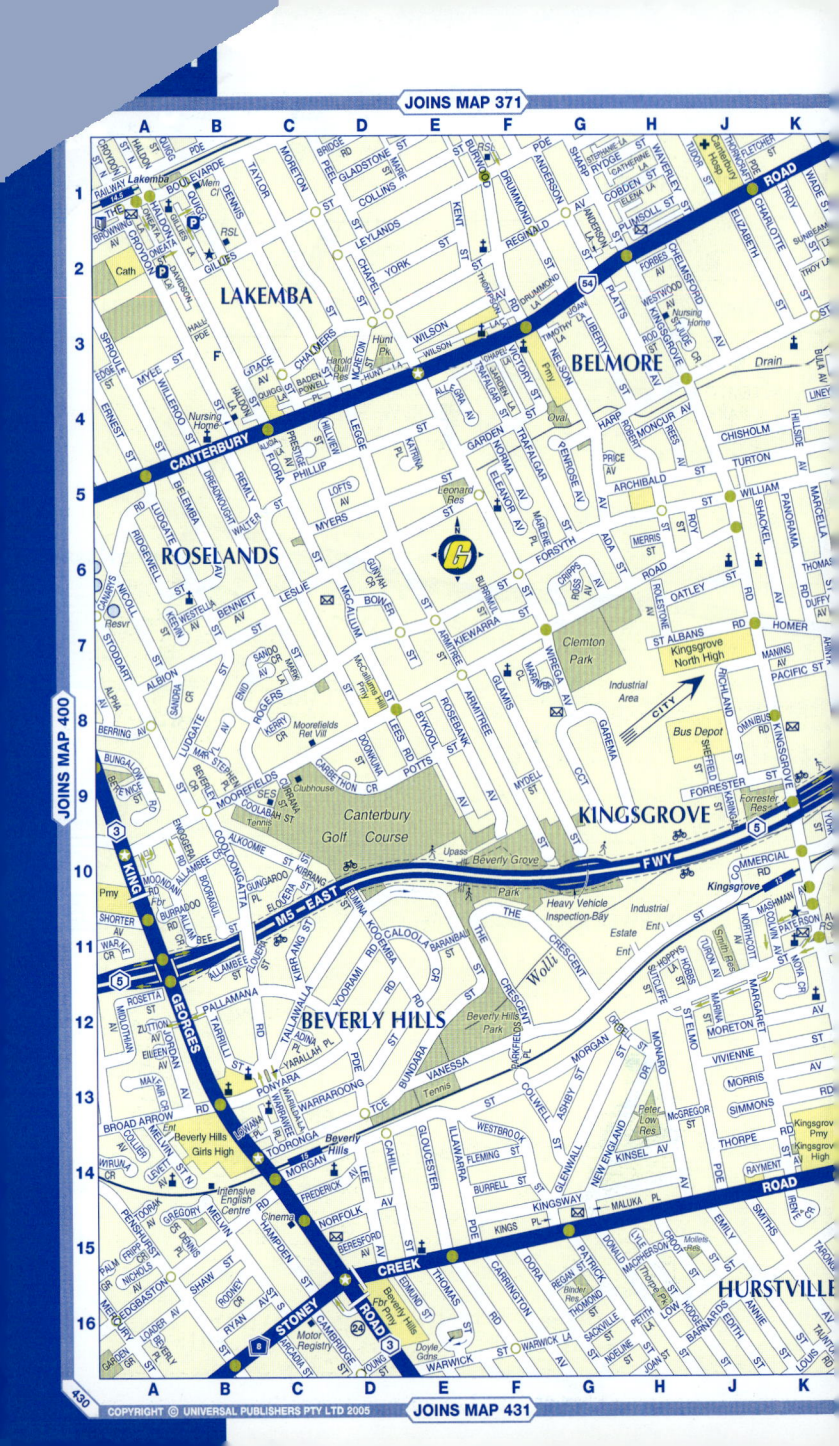

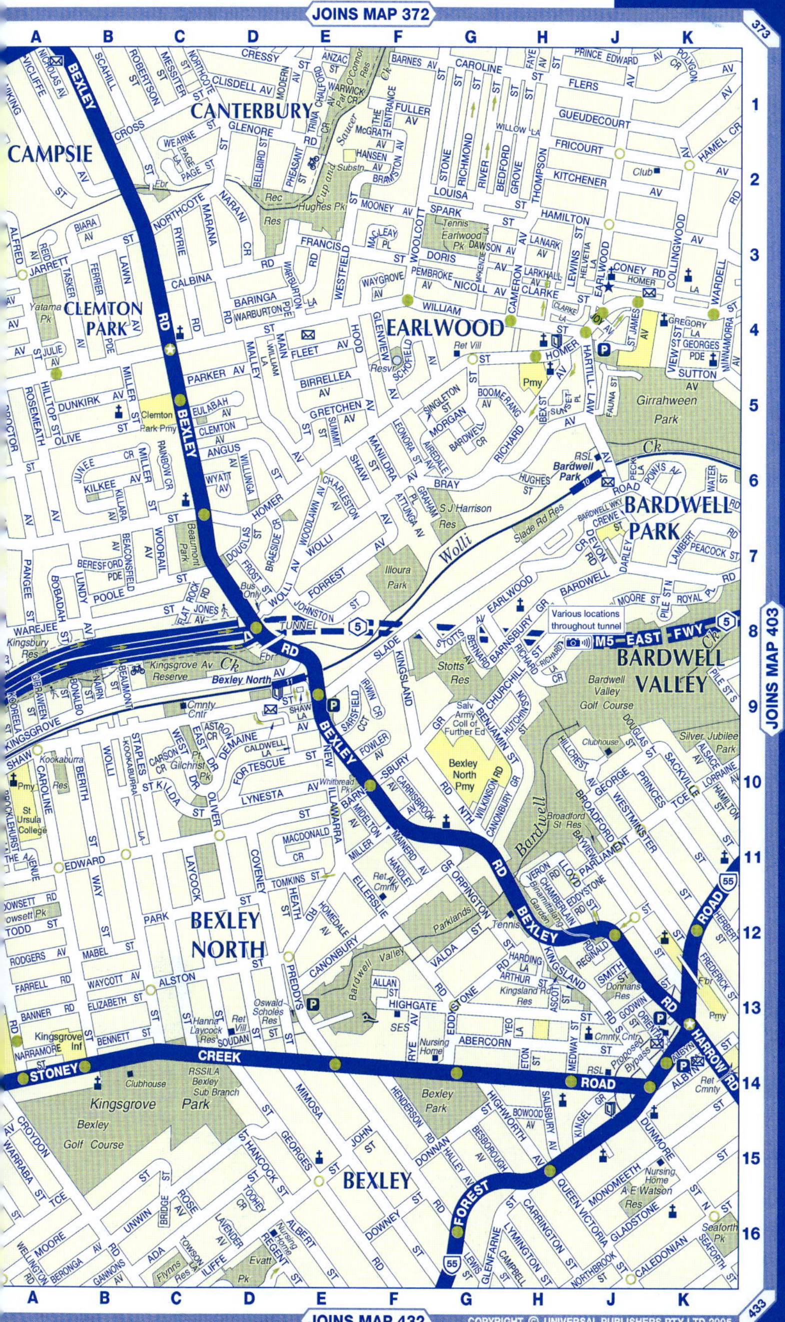
JOINS MAP 372
JOINS MAP 403
JOINS MAP 432
373
433
CAMPSIE
CANTERBURY
CLEMTON PARK
EARLWOOD
BARDWELL PARK
BARDWELL VALLEY
BEXLEY NORTH
BEXLEY
BEXLEY RD
STONEY CREEK ROAD
FOREST RD
HARROW RD
M5-EAST FWY
TUNNEL
Various locations throughout tunnel
Kingsgrove Bexley Golf Course
Bardwell Valley Golf Course
Girrahween Park
Bexley Park
Wolli Ck
Bardwell Ck
Cooks River

MAP 403

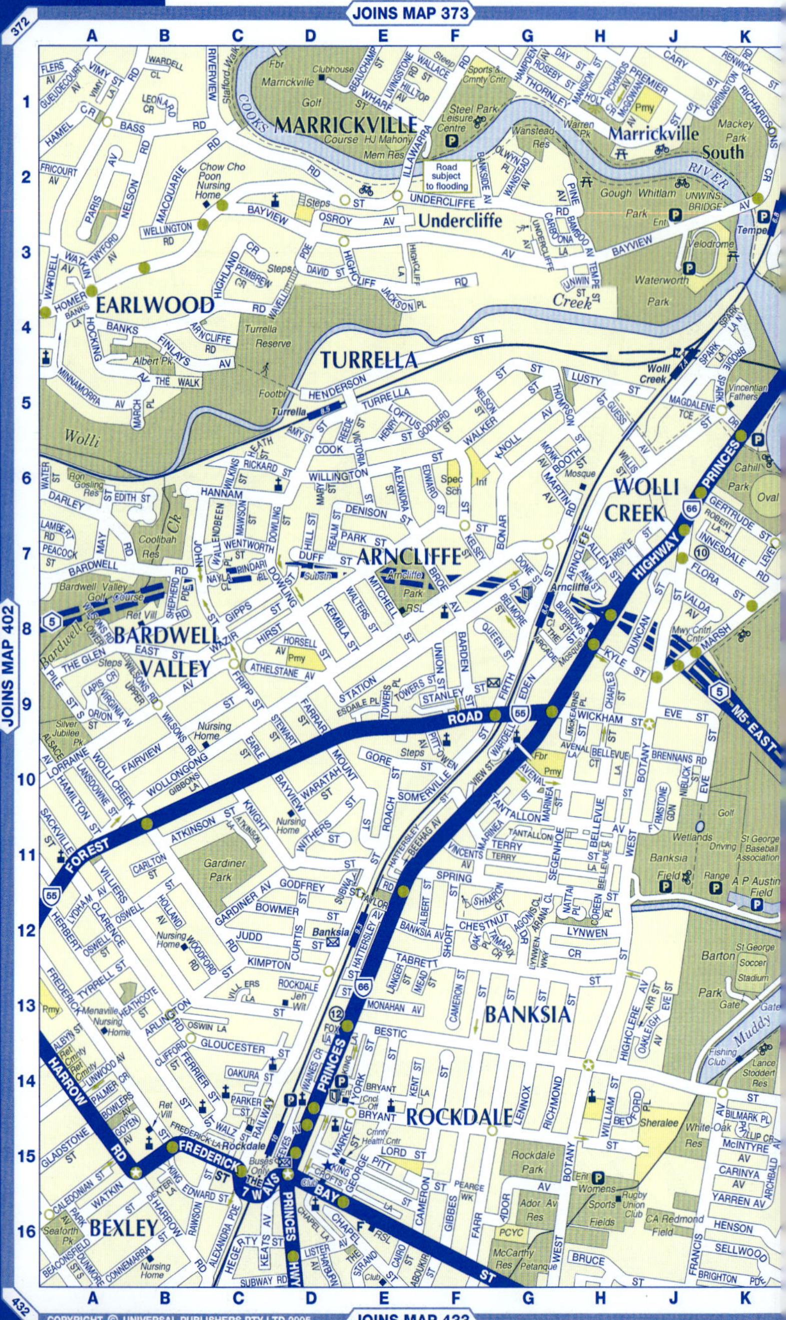
JOINS MAP 373
JOINS MAP 402
JOINS MAP 433
372
432
A B C D E F G H J K
1 2 3 4 5 6 7 8 9 10 11 12 13 14 15 16
MARRICKVILLE
Marrickville South
Undercliffe
EARLWOOD
TURRELLA
ARNCLIFFE
BARDWELL VALLEY
WOLLI CREEK
BANKSIA
ROCKDALE
BEXLEY
COOKS RIVER
Wolli Creek
Marrickville Golf Course
Steel Park Leisure Centre
Road subject to flooding
Gough Whitlam Park
Waterworth Park
Turrella Reserve
Bardwell Valley Golf Course
Gardiner Park
Rockdale Park
Barton Park
Banksia Field
Muddy Creek
FOREST ROAD
PRINCES HIGHWAY
HARROW RD
M5 EAST
THE 7 WAYS

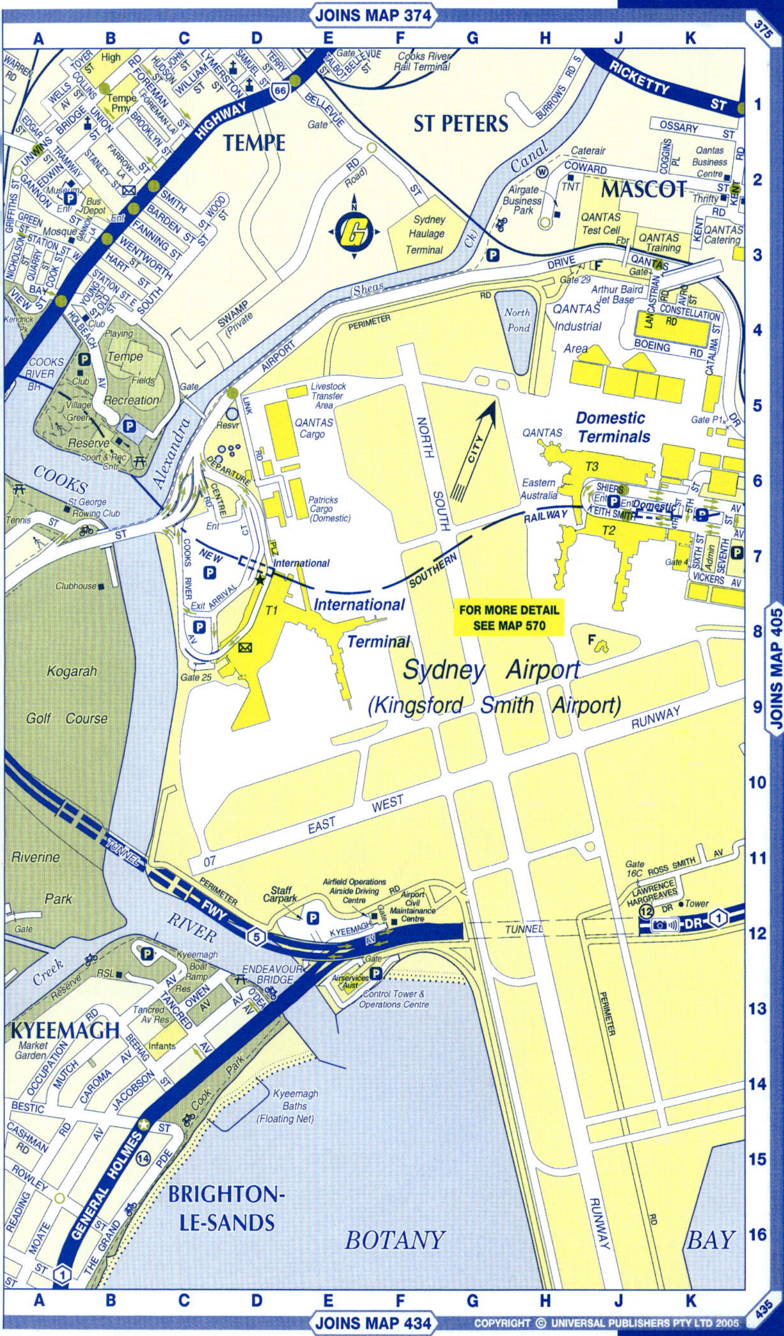
JOINS MAP 374
JOINS MAP 405
JOINS MAP 434
375
435
A B C D E F G H J K
1 2 3 4 5 6 7 8 9 10 11 12 13 14 15 16
TEMPE
ST PETERS
MASCOT
KYEEMAGH
BRIGHTON-LE-SANDS
BOTANY
BAY
Sydney Airport
(Kingsford Smith Airport)
International Terminal
Domestic Terminals
T1
T2
T3
FOR MORE DETAIL SEE MAP 570
QANTAS Industrial Area
QANTAS Cargo
Livestock Transfer Area
Patricks Cargo (Domestic)
Sydney Haulage Terminal
Cooks River Rail Terminal
Airgate Business Park
Qantas Business Centre
QANTAS Test Cell
QANTAS Training
QANTAS Catering
Arthur Baird Jet Base
North Pond
Tempe Recreation Reserve
Kogarah Golf Course
Riverine Park
Kyeemagh Baths (Floating Net)
Airfield Operations Airside Driving Centre
Airport Civil Maintainance Centre
Control Tower & Operations Centre
Staff Carpark
ENDEAVOUR BRIDGE
COOKS RIVER
Alexandra Canal
RICKETTY ST
HIGHWAY
GENERAL HOLMES DR
EAST WEST RUNWAY
NORTH SOUTH RUNWAY
SOUTHERN RAILWAY
AIRPORT DR
SHEAS CK
TUNNEL
FWY

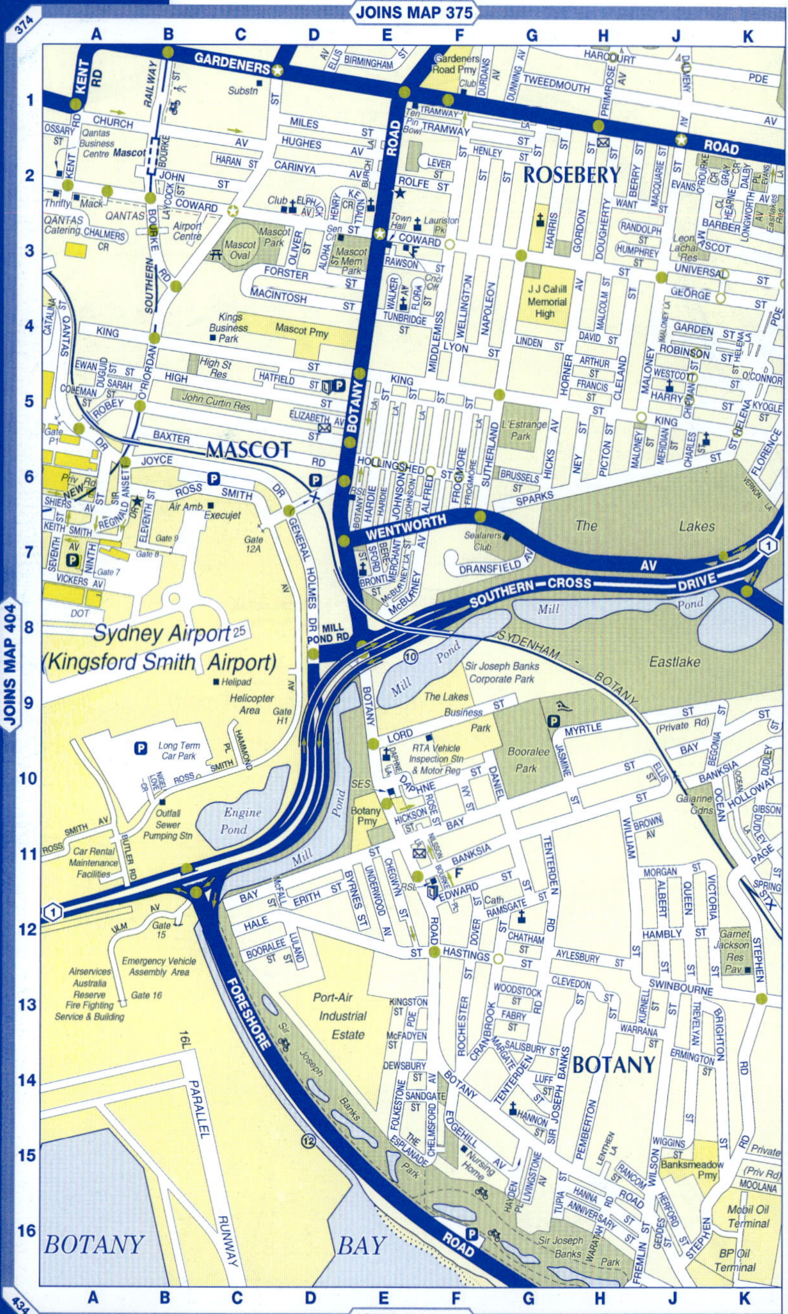
JOINS MAP 375
JOINS MAP 404
JOINS MAP 435
374
434
A B C D E F G H J K
1 2 3 4 5 6 7 8 9 10 11 12 13 14 15 16
ROSEBERY
MASCOT
BOTANY
Sydney Airport
(Kingsford Smith Airport)
The Lakes
Eastlake
Mill Pond
Engine Pond
BOTANY BAY
GARDENERS RD
KENT RD
BOTANY ROAD
SOUTHERN CROSS DRIVE
WENTWORTH AV
FORESHORE ROAD
GENERAL HOLMES DR
MILL POND RD
SYDENHAM - BOTANY
J J Cahill Memorial High
Mascot Oval
Mascot Park
Mascot Pmy
Kings Business Park
John Curtin Res
L'Estrange Park
Booralee Park
Botany Pmy
Banksmeadow Pmy
Port-Air Industrial Estate
Sir Joseph Banks Corporate Park
The Lakes Business Park
Sir Joseph Banks Park
Qantas Business Centre
Long Term Car Park
Helicopter Area
Car Rental Maintenance Facilities
Outfall Sewer Pumping Stn
Emergency Vehicle Assembly Area
Airservices Australia Reserve Fire Fighting Service & Building
RTA Vehicle Inspection Stn & Motor Reg
Mobil Oil Terminal
BP Oil Terminal
Garnet Jackson Res
Gaiarine Gdns
PARALLEL RUNWAY
16L

JOINS MAP 376
JOINS MAP 407
JOINS MAP 436
377
437
A B C D E F G H J K
1 2 3 4 5 6 7 8 9 10 11 12 13 14 15 16
KENSINGTON
RANDWICK
DACEYVILLE
KINGSFORD
EASTLAKES
PAGEWOOD
MAROUBRA
EASTGARDENS
BANKSMEADOW
HILLSDALE
MATRAVILLE
The Australian Golf Course
GARDENERS ROAD
SOUTHERN CROSS DRIVE
RAINBOW ST
ANZAC PDE
BUNNERONG ROAD
WENTWORTH AV
DENISON ST
THE NINE WAYS
Astrolabe Park
Rowland Park
Jellicoe Park
Snape Park
Mutch Park
Heffron Park
Nagle Park
Wills Pagewood Park (Industrial Estate)
Westfield Eastgardens
Ampol Terminals
Mobil Oil Terminal
ORICA
RAILWAY
CITY
Southpoint Shop Cntr
Matraville Park
Hockey Fields
South East Sydney High
Cath High
Daceyville Pmy
Eastlakes Pmy
Matraville Pmy
Maroubra Jnctn Pmy
R'wick Boys High
Girls Tech High
Paine Res
Shaw Res
COPYRIGHT © UNIVERSAL PUBLISHERS PTY LTD 2005

JOINS MAP 377

376

A B C D E F G H J K

1 2 3 4 5 6 7 8 9 10 11 12 13 14 15 16

JOINS MAP 406

A B C D E F G H J K

436

JOINS MAP 437

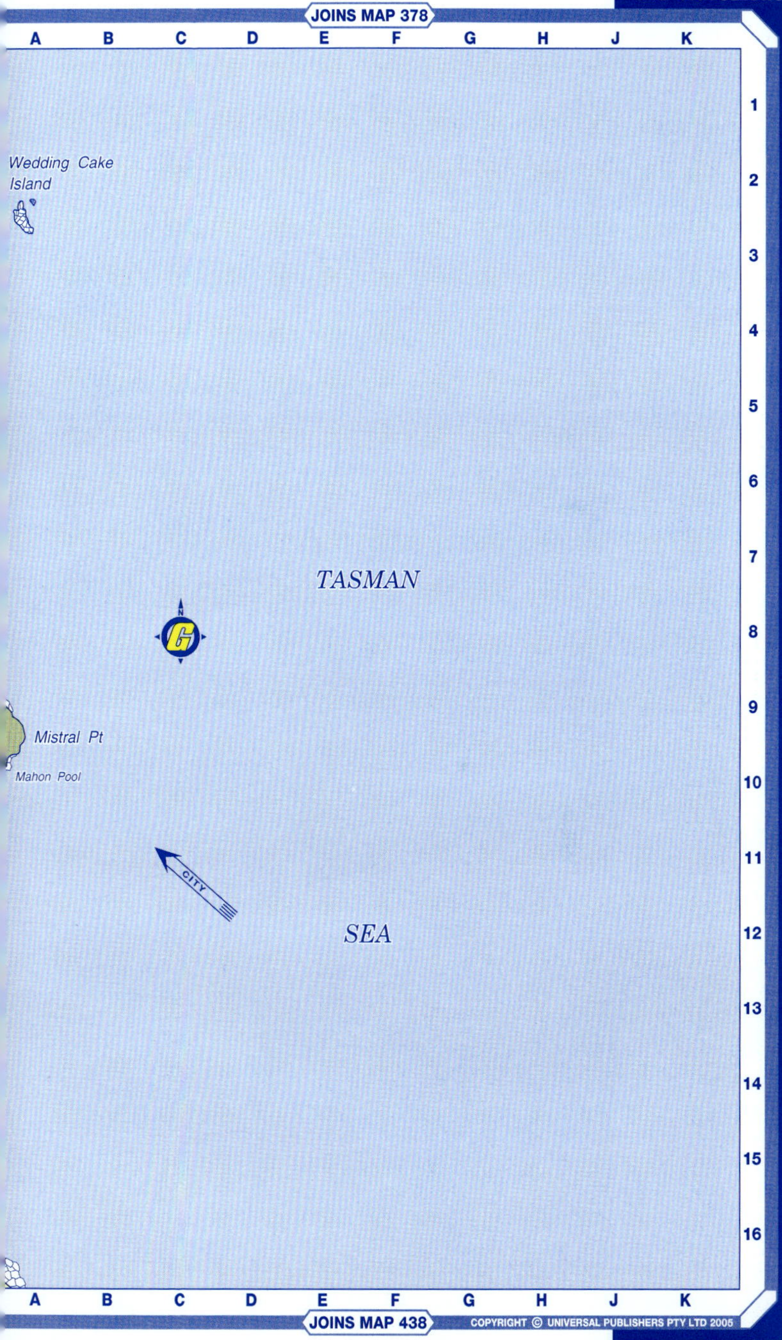

MAP 408
MAP 413 FOLLOWS

JOINS MAP 378

Wedding Cake Island

TASMAN

Mistral Pt
Mahon Pool

CITY

SEA

JOINS MAP 438

MAP 413
PREVIOUS MAP 408

JOINS MAP 383

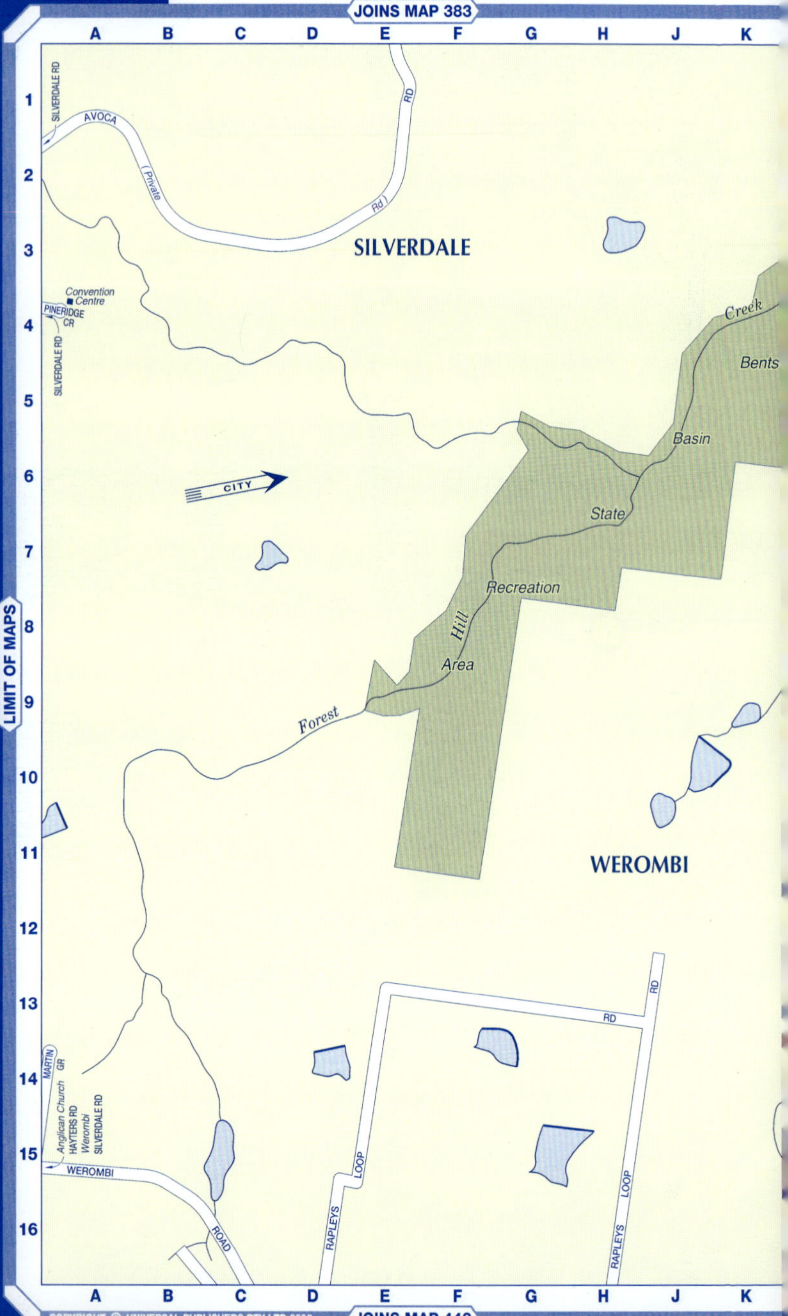

SILVERDALE

WEROMBI

JOINS MAP 443

MAP 414

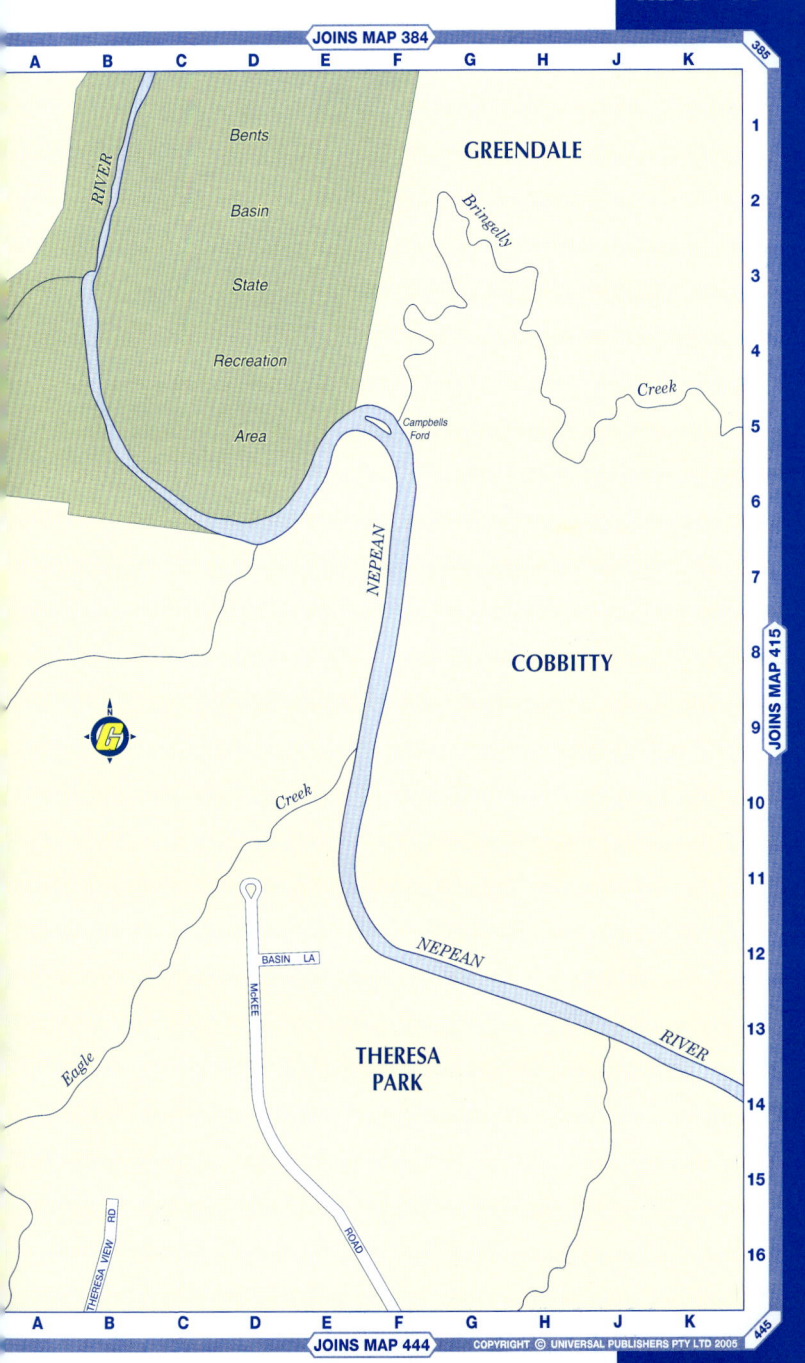

JOINS MAP 384

GREENDALE

Bents Basin State Recreation Area

Bringelly Creek

Campbells Ford

Nepean River

COBBITTY

Creek

BASIN LA
McKEE ROAD

NEPEAN RIVER

THERESA PARK

Eagle Creek

THERESA VIEW RD

JOINS MAP 444
JOINS MAP 415

MAP 415

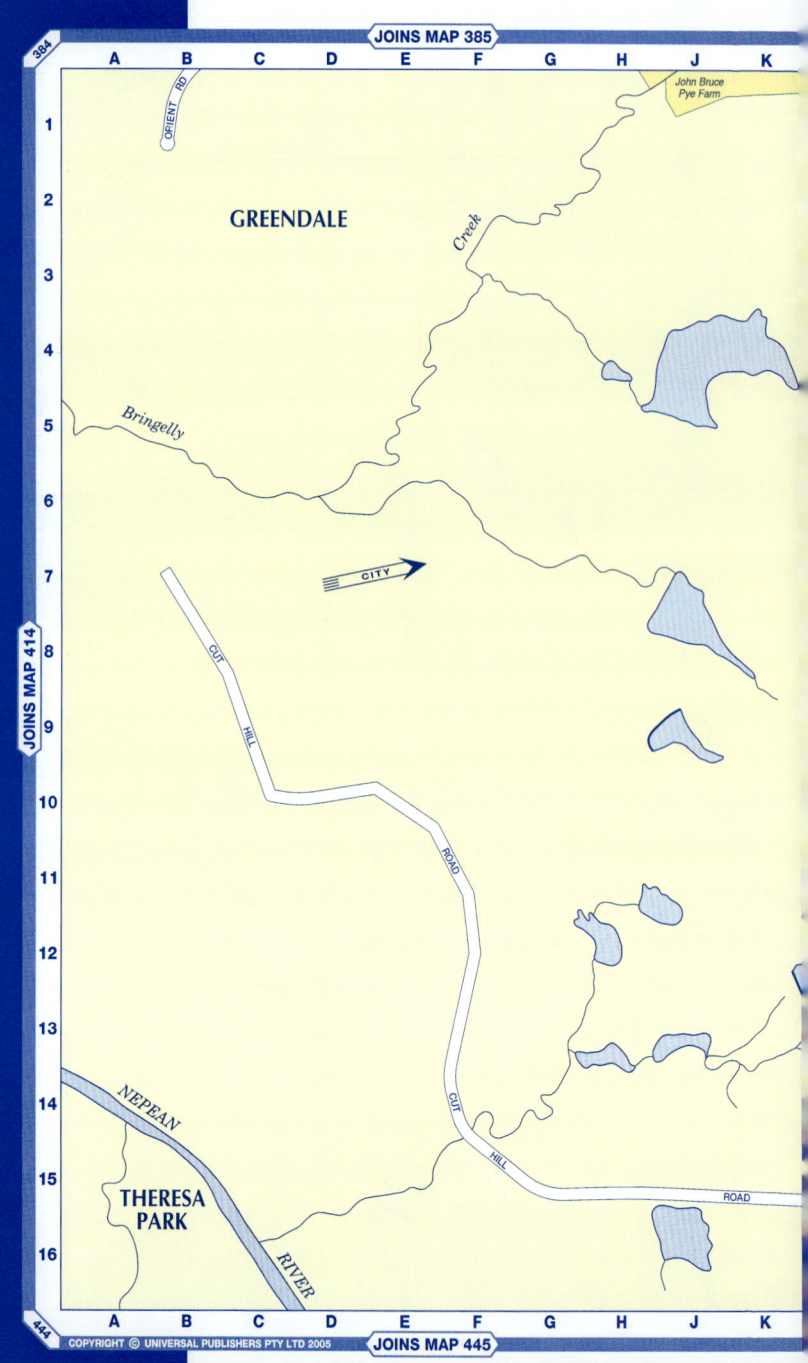

GREENDALE

Creek

John Bruce Pye Farm

ORIENT RD

Bringelly

CITY

CUT HILL ROAD

CUT HILL ROAD

NEPEAN RIVER

THERESA PARK

MAP 416

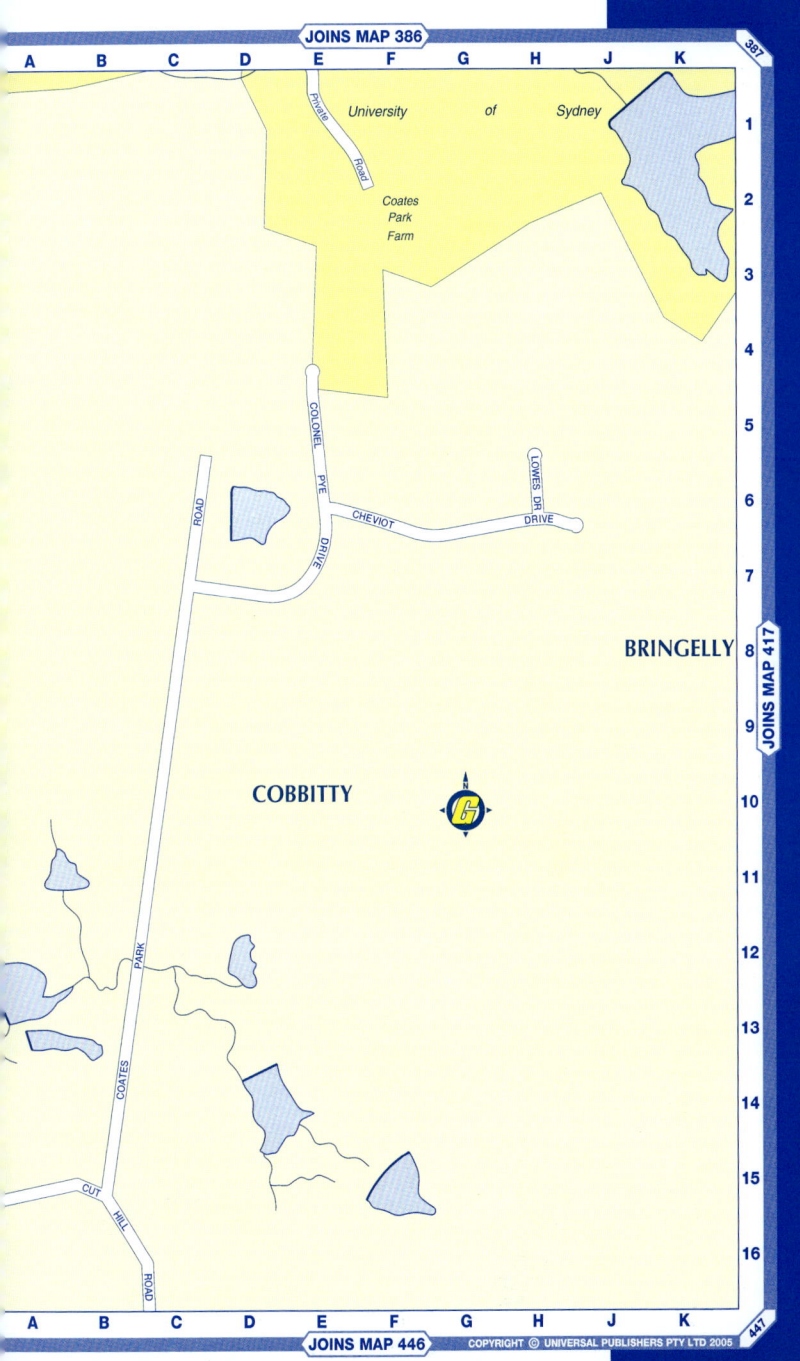

JOINS MAP 386

University of Sydney
Private Road
Coates Park Farm

COLONEL PYE DRIVE
CHEVIOT
LOWES DR DRIVE

PARK ROAD
COATES
CUT HILL ROAD

COBBITTY

BRINGELLY

JOINS MAP 446

MAP 417

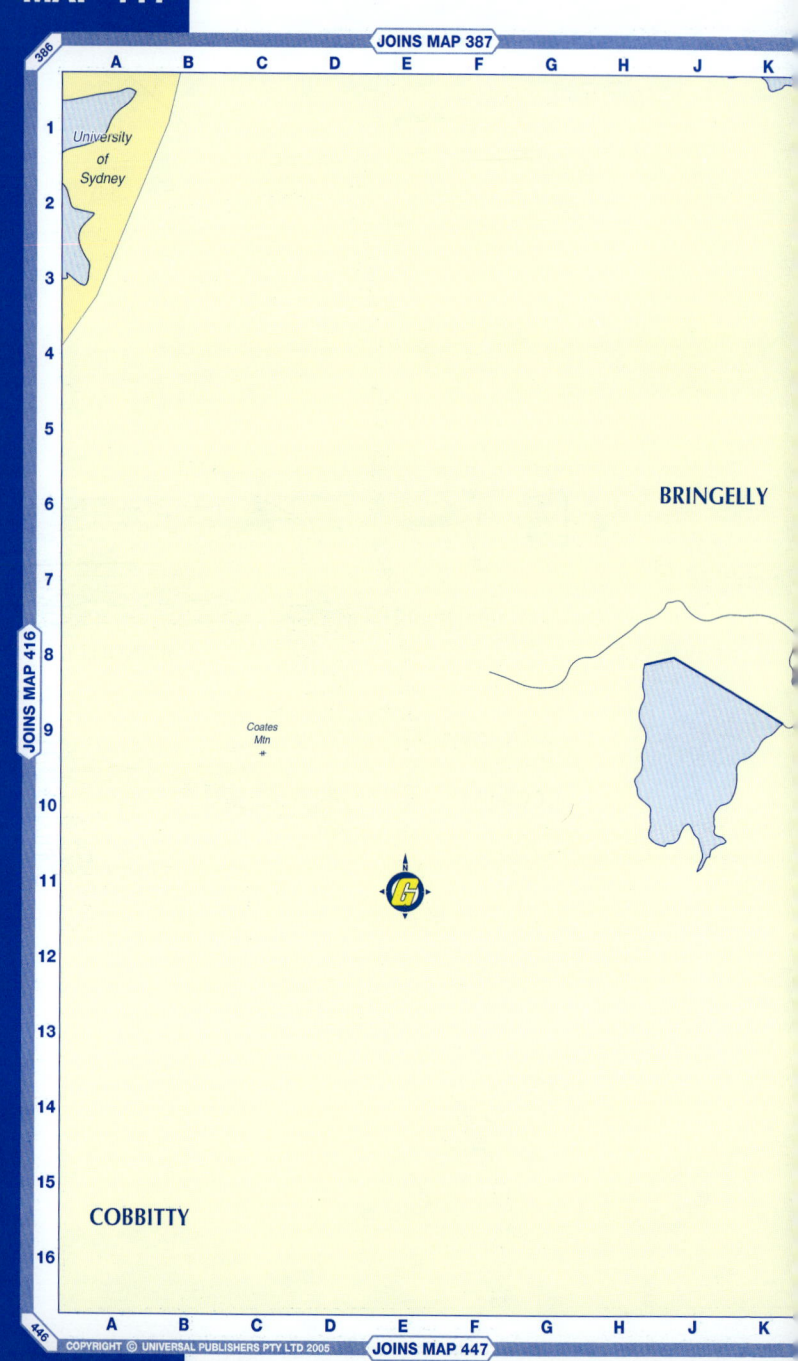

University of Sydney

BRINGELLY

Coates Mtn

COBBITTY

MAP 418

JOINS MAP 388

BELMORE ROAD
JERSEY ROAD
CARRINGTON ROAD
THE NORTHERN ROAD
Lowes
Creek
Leppington Pastoral Company
Greenway
CITY
ORAN PARK
Private Road
Cobbitty Pony Club
THE NORTHERN ROAD

JOINS MAP 448

COPYRIGHT © UNIVERSAL PUBLISHERS PTY LTD 2005

MAP 419

JOINS MAP 389

BRINGELLY

ROSSMORE

- McCann Road
- Allenby
- Barry
- Rossmore
- Karen
- Polo
- Mark
- Graham
- Rileys
- Gregory
- Roberts Cr
- Anthony
- Causeway
- Alma

ORAN PARK

- South Wianamatta Creek
- Lowes Creek

CATHERINE FIELD

- Catherine
- Deepfields
- Eastwood
- Dwyer
- Creek
- Road

JOINS MAP 418 / JOINS MAP 449

COPYRIGHT © UNIVERSAL PUBLISHERS PTY LTD 2005

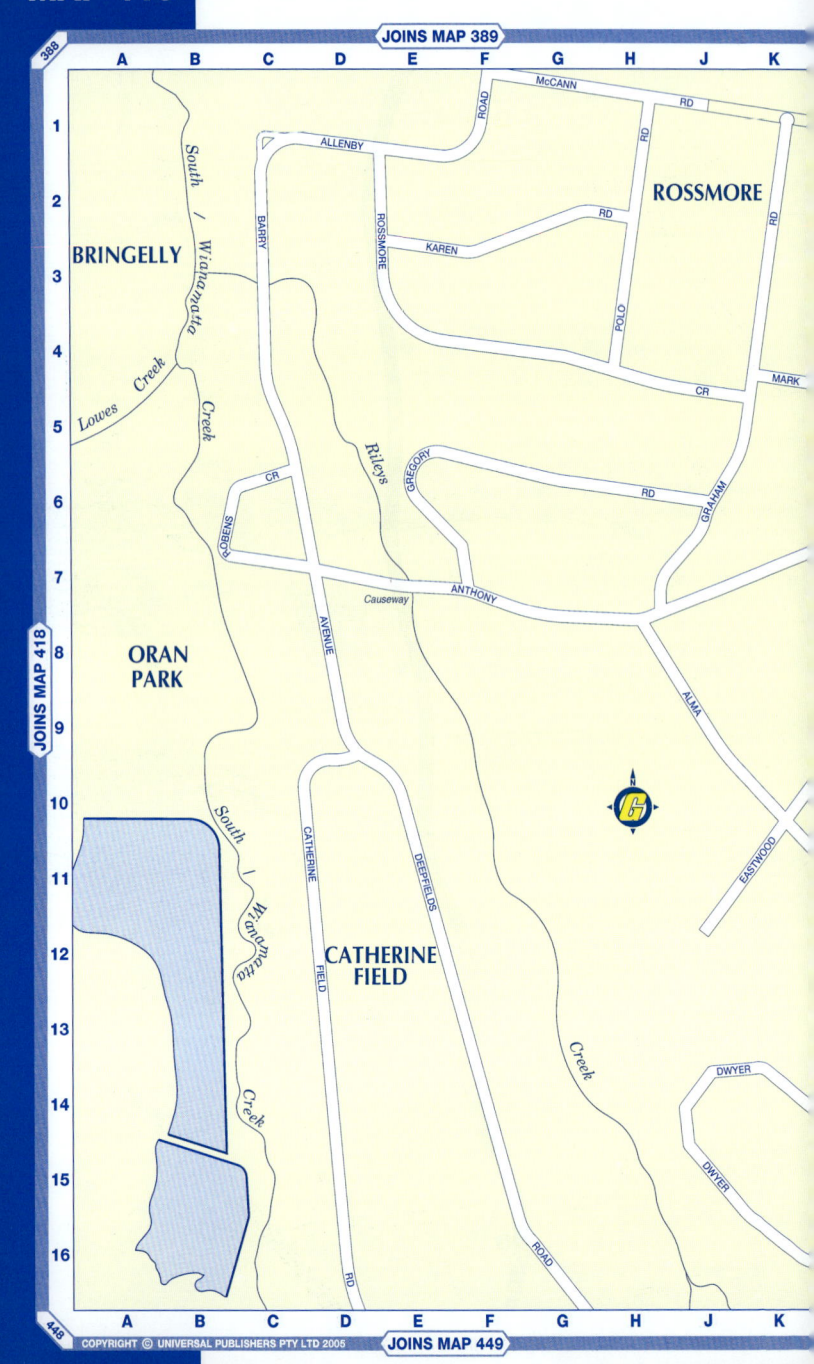

MAP 420

MAP 421

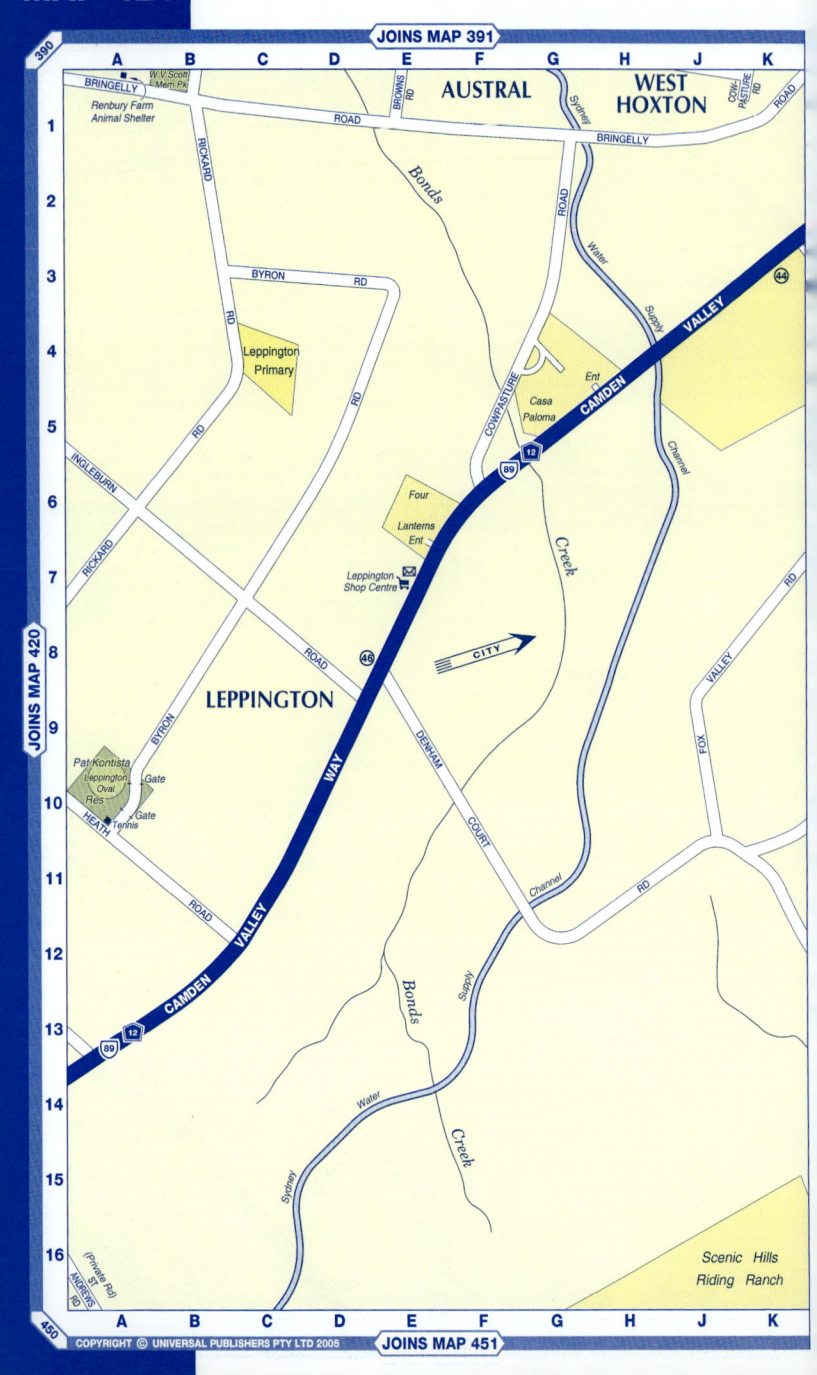

JOINS MAP 392
393
A B C D E F G H J K
1 2 3 4 5 6 7 8 9 10 11 12 13 14 15 16
Adventureland
CAMDEN
VALLEY
WAY
Trash & Treasure Markets
William Carey Christian Sch
PRESTONS
MARTINO
MULLENDERREE
GUNDARY
WEJA
MARTEN
KIANGA
CORFIELD RD
BROOMAN ST
BRAIDWOOD DR
DURRAS ST
CAMPI CT
Ent
Exit
Forest Lawn
Memorial Gardens
Cemetery
Creek
EDMONDSON
PARK
RYNAN
JARDINE
DR
AV
BUCHAN
DALMATIA AV
CASSIDY
ST
CULVERSTON
CUBITT
WHIDDON CL
PEMBURY CL
Cabramatta
ZOUCH
SPRINGMEAD
HUNTINGDALE
JOINS MAP 423
BLAXLAND RD
BURKE RD
CUNNINGHAM
BASS RD
OXLEY RD
Gate
STEVENS RD
ROAD
Pmy
DENHAM
COURT
Jeh Wit
INGLEBURN
ENGLAND
HOWELL RD
BATMAN RD
HENTY RD
HUME RD
LEICHHARDT
MACDONALD RD
DENHAM
COURT
Cottage
Ck
CHURCH RD
CAMPBELLTOWN
DICKSON RD
BLOMFIELD RD
KEATING PL
HUME HWY
453
JOINS MAP 452

MAP 423

JOINS MAP 393
JOINS MAP 422
JOINS MAP 453
392
452
PRESTONS
EDMONDSON PARK
INGLEBURN
MACQUARIE LINKS
CAMDEN VALLEY WAY
CAMPBELLTOWN ROAD
HUME HIGHWAY
SOUTH WESTERN MWY
Westlink M7 Under Construction
St Catherine of Siena Pmy
Temp Access
Prestons Substn
Clubhouse
Driving Range
Tree Valley Golf Course
Crossroads Homemaker Centre
Fire Control Cntr
Bunnings
Ajuga Sch
Glenfield Park School
Campbell House School
ROY WATTS (Private Road) RD
Gate
QUARTER SESSIONS RD
Proposed Hotel
Macquarie Field House
Golf Course
Macquarie Links International Golf Course
Tennis
Clubhouse
Gatehouse
Bunbury Curran Ck
Canal
Macquarie Fields
Bus Depot
Pmy
DALMATIA AV
CROATIA AV
BRAIDWOOD DR
MINNAMURRA PL
MALLACOOTA CL
EDROM CL
KHORA CL
YERONA ST
NETHERCOTE CL
NAROOMA DR
BERNERA RD
PAMBULA AV
GERALDTON ST
DALMENY DR
GUNNING CL
LARNE ST
DEE CL
BROULEE ST
ASH RD
PARKERS FARM PL
BEECH RD
CREEKSIDE PL
PINE RD
INCENSE PL
HASSARATI PL
LAVENDER CL
BOTTLEBRUSH AV
FOX GROVE AV
MAPLE ST
WATTLE CL
VALLEY CL
NATALIE Gate CL
CEDAR
BOAB PL
TLETREE
WILLOW ST
MARJORIE CL
DARCY ST
ERIN PL
DURANTA CL
PAPERBARK CCT
LAWSON
BLAXLAND RD
CUNNINGHAM RD
STURT RD
WENTWORTH RD
FLINDERS CR
EYRE AV
BASS RD
OXLEY RD
LEICHHARDT RD
MACDONALD RD
MACQUARIE LINKS DR
STRATHWALLEN CL
LOCHBURIE WY
GOVERNORS CCT
GOVERNORS WY
LAIRD CT
REBELLION PL
LORD
CASTLEREAGH
BARRACK
JAMES MEEHAN WY
ELIZABETH CCT
HENRIETTA
JANE JARVIS WY
SCARANISH AV
QUARTERMASTER ROW
HEBRIDES
HOMESTEAD
FORBES AV
LINKS DR
WILLIAMSON RD
HENDERSON RD
GARNER PL
(Private Road)
RAILWAY PDE
ALEXANDER CR
WARATAH CR
SAYWELL RD
EDWARD ST
VICTORIA
CLARENCE ST
GLOUCESTER ST
WINDSOR ST
ARGYLE PL
ATCHISON
CEDRIC ST

JOINS MAP 394
JOINS MAP 425
JOINS MAP 454
395
455
A B C D E F G H J K
1 2 3 4 5 6 7 8 9 10 11 12 13 14 15 16
CASULA
The Cross Roads
GLENFIELD
MACQUARIE FIELDS
HUME HIGHWAY
GLENFIELD ROAD
CAMBRIDGE AV
7
38
Casula High
All Saints Senior High
Maple Grove Retirement Village
Materials in the Raw
Leacock Regional Glenfield Park
GEORGES RIVER
CITY
Proposed Bus Link
Substn
Glenfield Waste Disposals
(Subject to Flooding) Causeway
Department of Education Regional Centre
Hurlstone Agricultural High
Glenfield
Glenfield Pmy
Blinman Park
Trobriand Park
Glenwood Primary
Frank Whiddon Masonic Homes
Glenfield Park
Seddon Park
Kennett Baseball Park
Georges River Nature Reserve
Bunbury Curran
Curran Park
Youth Cntr
TAFE NSW
Glenquarie Town Centre
James Meehan High
Cmnty Cntr
Guise Primary
Flinders Field
Sewage Treatment Works
Military Reserve
MYALL ST
LEACOCKS LA
CANTERBURY RD
VICTORIA RD
BELMONT RD
HARROW RD
FAWCETT ST
OWEN STANLEY RD
TRAFALGAR ST
GOODENOUGH ST
TROBRIAND CR
CHAMPION ST
MONCKTON PL
WOODLARK PL
PROPOSED PARKWAY

MAP 425

MAP 426

HAMMONDVILLE

HOLSWORTHY

Holsworthy Barracks

- Tobruk Lines
- Kapyong Lines
- Coral Lines
- Malaya Lines
- Jordan Lines
- Johore
- Gallipoli Lines
- Old Holsworthy Camp
- Military Reserve
- Harris Creek Oval
- Holsworthy Sewage Treatment Plant
- Holsworthy High
- Holsworthy Primary
- Moorebank Sports Club
- Hammondville Park
- Lieutenant Cantello Res
- Peter Pan Park
- 142 SIG SQUADRON
- HQ 5 BDE
- 5 CSSB
- 4/3 Battalion
- Sydney Field
- Brisbane Field
- Melbourne Field 1
- Adelaide Field 2
- Hobart Field 3
- Playing Field

JOINS MAP 396 (top) · JOINS MAP 456 (bottom) · JOINS MAP 427 (right) · 397 (top right)

COPYRIGHT © UNIVERSAL PUBLISHERS PTY LTD 2005

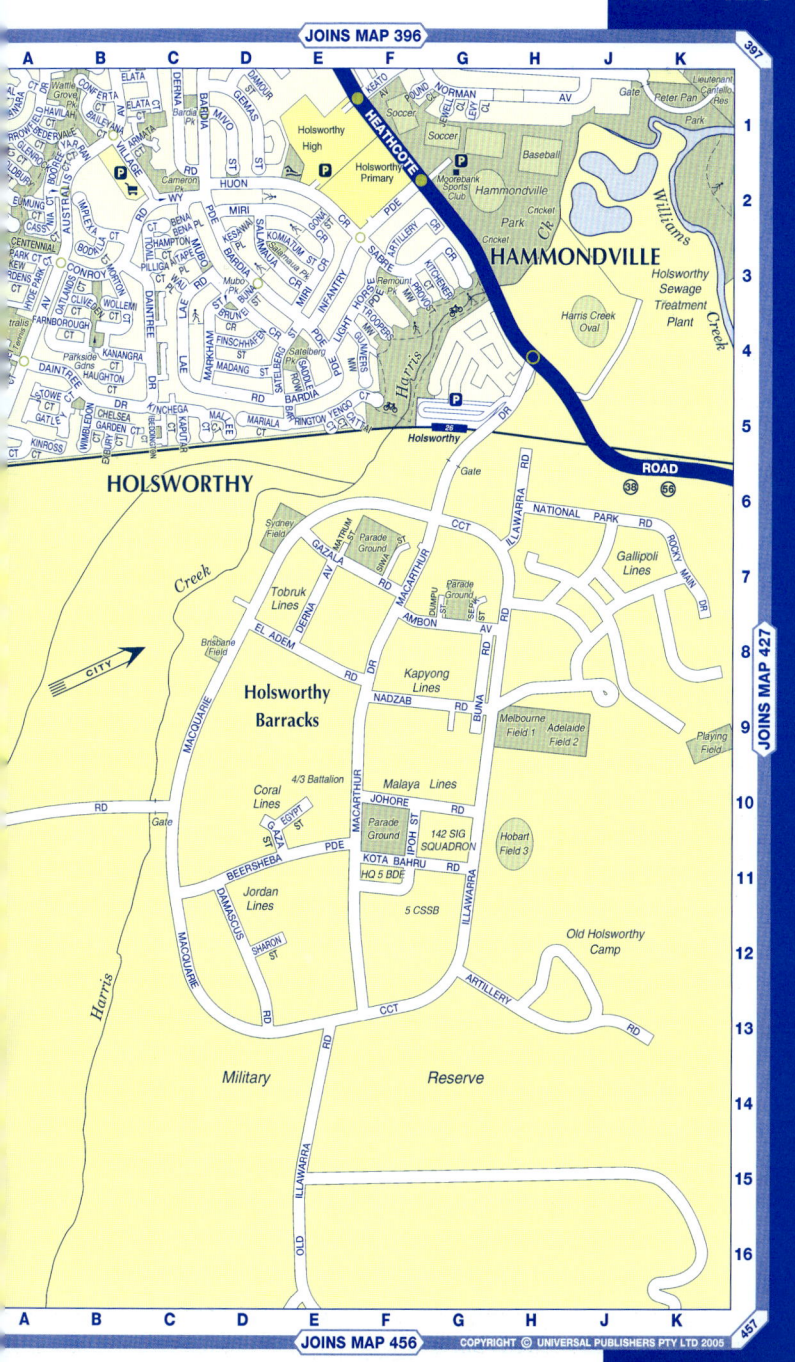

JOINS MAP 397

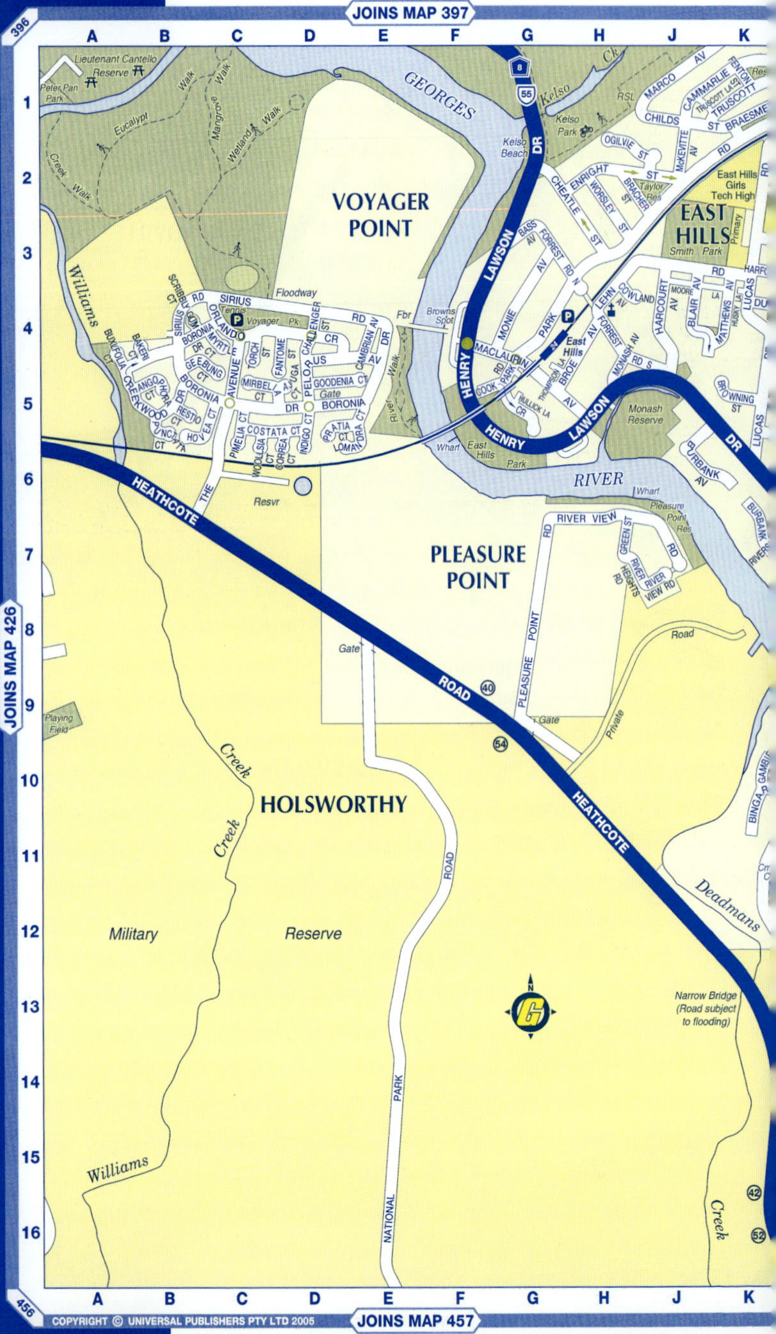

JOINS MAP 426

JOINS MAP 457

JOINS MAP 398

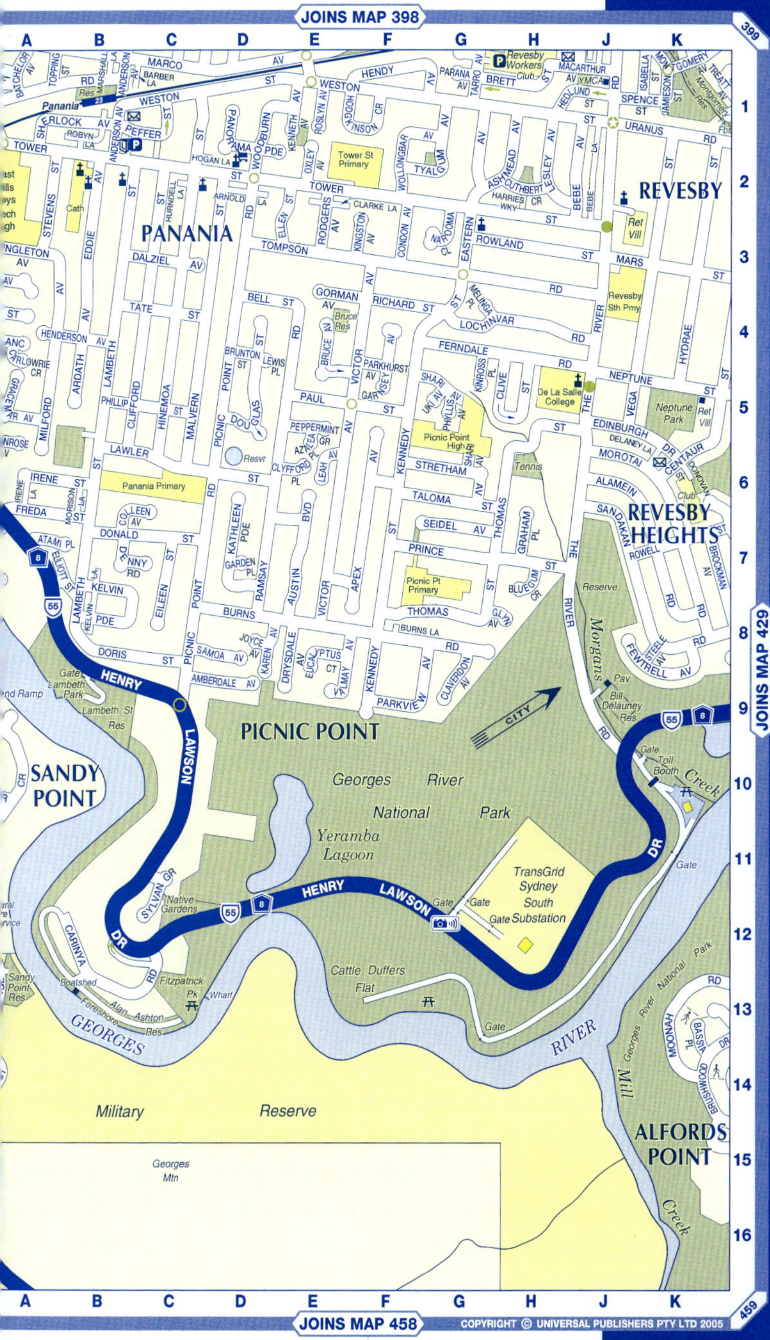

MAP 429

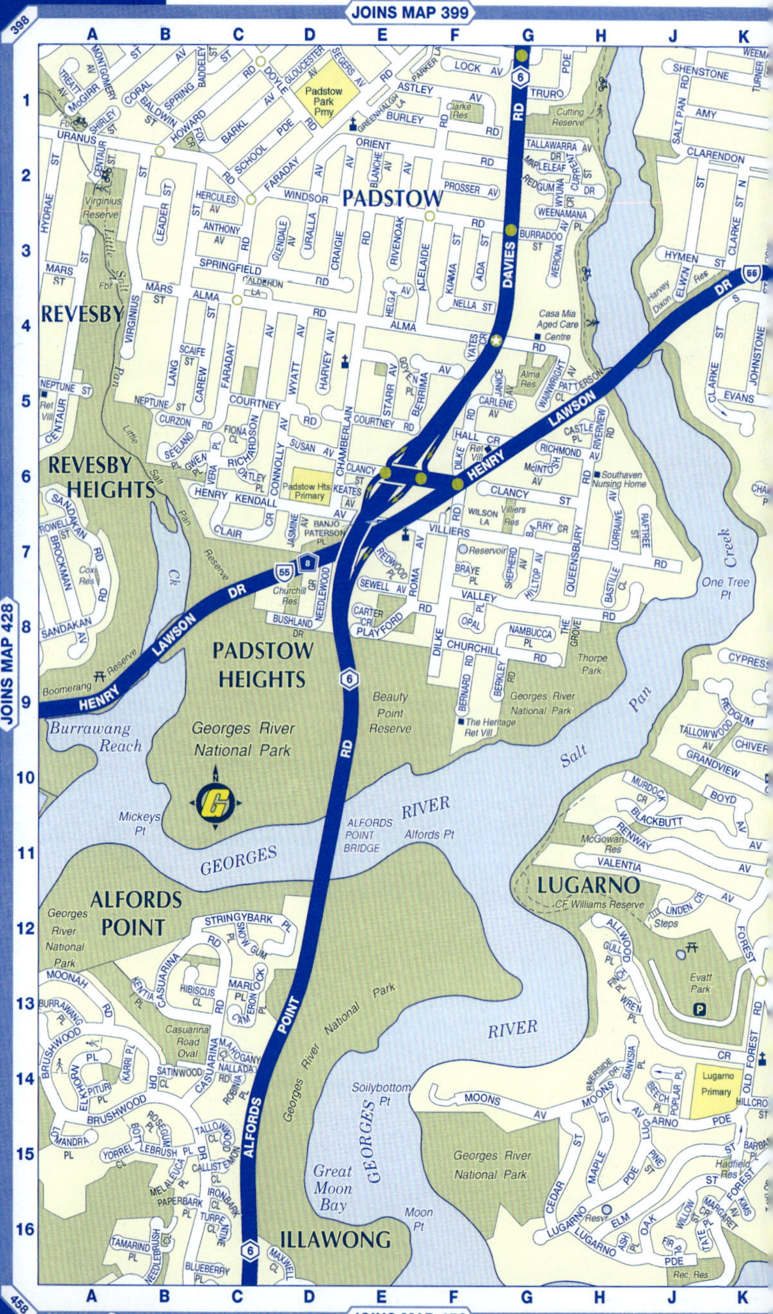
JOINS MAP 399
JOINS MAP 428
JOINS MAP 459
398
458
A B C D E F G H J K
1 2 3 4 5 6 7 8 9 10 11 12 13 14 15 16
PADSTOW
REVESBY
REVESBY HEIGHTS
PADSTOW HEIGHTS
ALFORDS POINT
LUGARNO
ILLAWONG
Padstow Park Prmy
Padstow Hts Primary
Lugarno Primary
Georges River National Park
GEORGES RIVER
Salt Pan
Salt Pan Ck
Burrawang Reach
Mickeys Pt
Alfords Pt
ALFORDS POINT BRIDGE
Beauty Point Reserve
Great Moon Bay
Moon Pt
Soilybottom Pt
One Tree Pt
Thorpe Park
Evatt Park
CE Williams Reserve
Casuarina Road Oval
Virginius Reserve
Cutting Reserve
Casa Mia Aged Care Centre
Southaven Nursing Home
The Heritage Ret Vill
Boomerang Reserve
DAVIES RD
HENRY LAWSON DR
ALFORDS POINT RD
ALMA RD
UURANUS RD
PADSTOW
HYMEN ST
CLARENDON
SHENSTONE
MOONS AV
LUGARNO PDE
FOREST RD

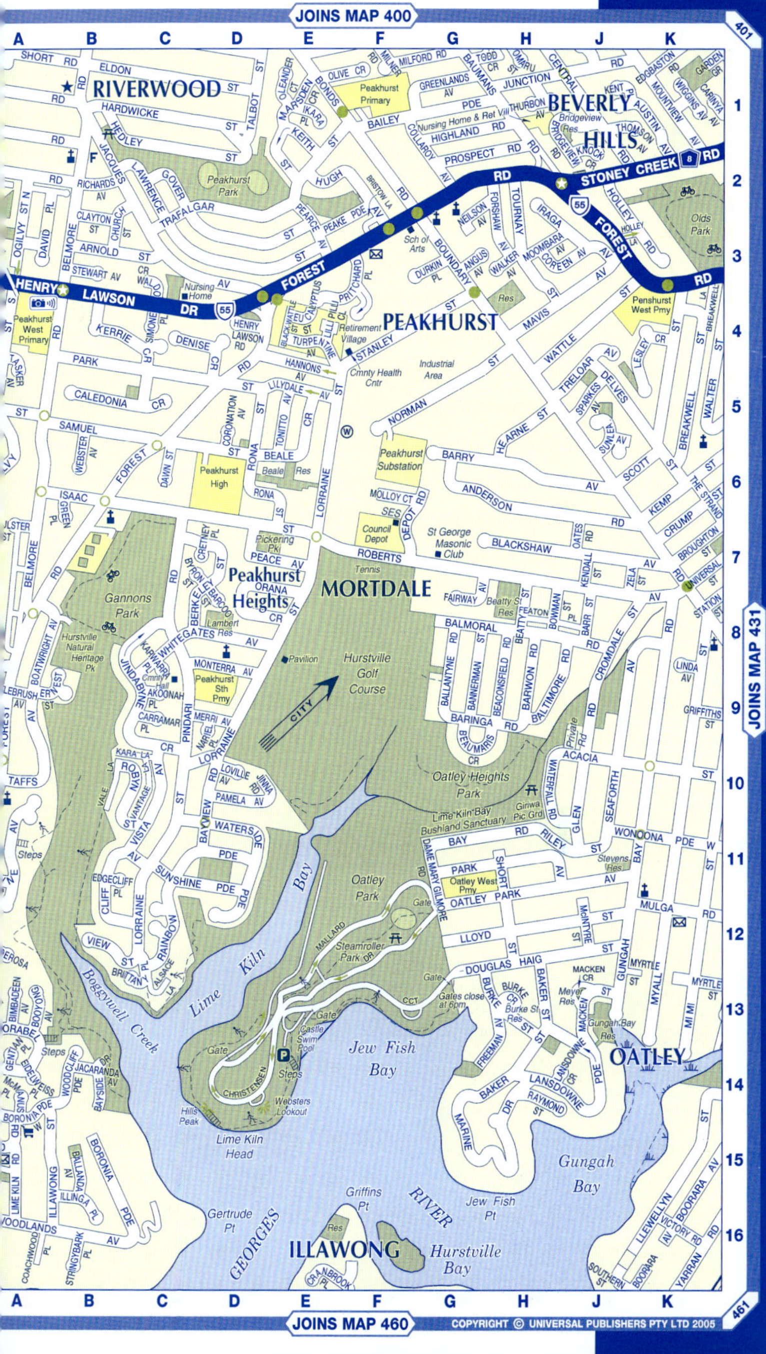
JOINS MAP 400
JOINS MAP 431
JOINS MAP 460
401
461
A B C D E F G H J K
1 2 3 4 5 6 7 8 9 10 11 12 13 14 15 16
RIVERWOOD
BEVERLY HILLS
PEAKHURST
MORTDALE
Peakhurst Heights
OATLEY
ILLAWONG
HENRY LAWSON DR
FOREST RD
STONEY CREEK RD
Peakhurst Park
Peakhurst Primary
Peakhurst West Primary
Penshurst West Pmy
Peakhurst High
Peakhurst Substation
Peakhurst Sth Pmy
Council Depot
St George Masonic Club
Retirement Village
Cmnty Health Cntr
Industrial Area
Sch of Arts
Nursing Home
Nursing Home & Ret Vill
Bridgeview Res
Olds Park
Gannons Park
Hurstville Natural Heritage Pk
Hurstville Golf Course
Pavilion
CITY
Pickering Pk
Beale Res
Lambert Res
Beatty St Res
Oatley Heights Park
Lime Kiln Bay Bushland Sanctuary
Giriwa Pic Grd
Oatley Park
Oatley West Pmy
Steamroller Park DR
Castle Swim Pool
Websters Lookout
Hills Peak
Lime Kiln Head
Lime Kiln Bay
Boggywell Creek
Jew Fish Bay
Jew Fish Pt
Gungah Bay
Gungah Bay Res
Meyer Res
Burke St Res
Stevens Res
Gates close at 6pm
Griffins Pt
Gertrude Pt
GEORGES RIVER
Hurstville Bay
Steps
Gate
Tennis
NORMAN ST
ROBERTS AV
BLACKSHAW AV
ANDERSON RD
BARRY AV
BOUNDARY RD
LORRAINE ST
BELMORE RD
SAMUEL ST
ISAAC ST
CALEDONIA CR
KERRIE RD
DENISE CR
PARK RD
WONOONA PDE W
MULGA RD
DOUGLAS HAIG ST
OATLEY PARK AV
LLOYD ST
BAY RD
PARK RD
BALMORAL ST
BARINGA RD
ACACIA ST
LANSDOWNE ST
BAKER ST
MARINE DR
RAYMOND ST
CHRISTENSEN
MALLARD
SUNSHINE PDE
WATERSIDE PDE
VIEW ST
BOORARA AV
LLEWELLYN
VICTORY RD
YARRAN RD
SOUTHERN ST

MAP 431

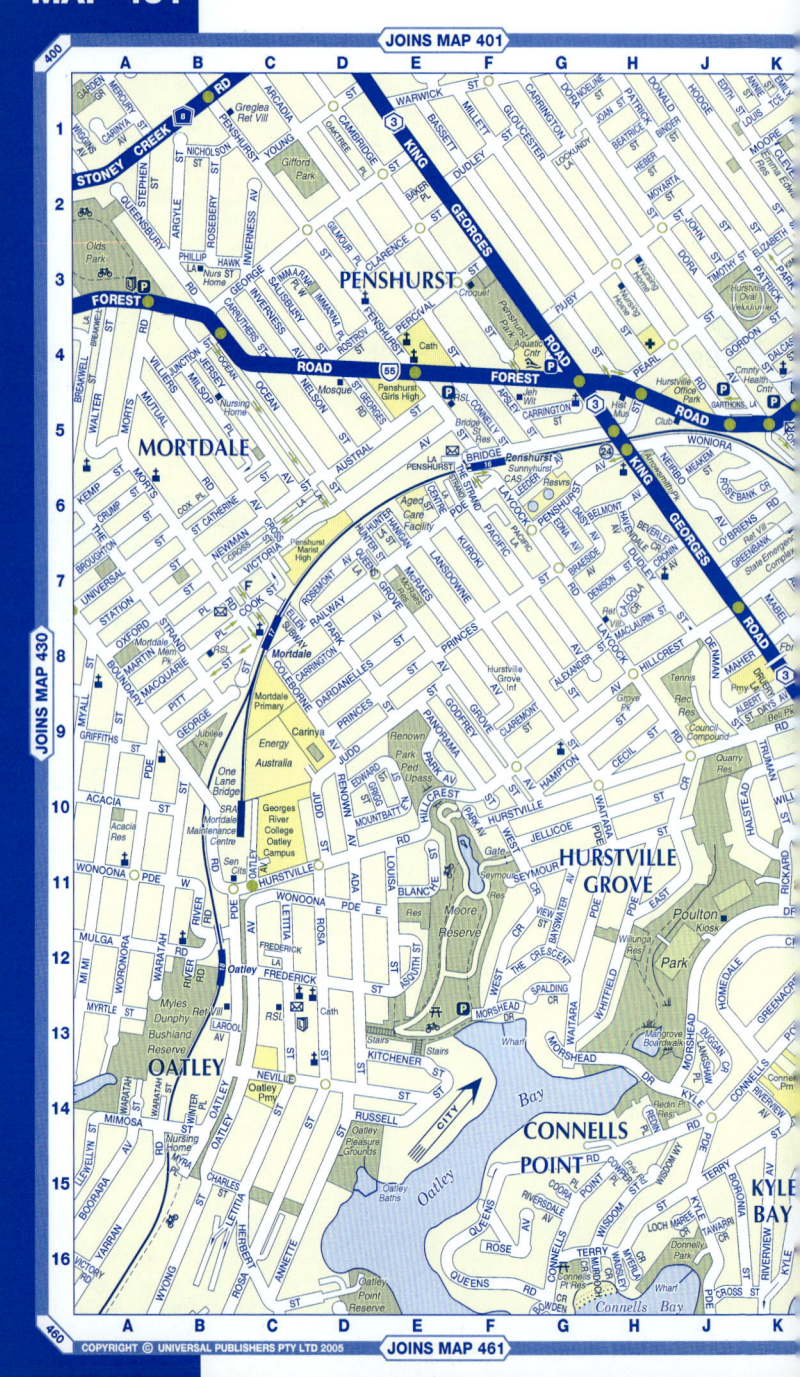

JOINS MAP 402
403
A B C D E F G H J K
1 2 3 4 5 6 7 8 9 10 11 12 13 14 15 16
HURSTVILLE
BEXLEY
CARLTON
ALLAWAH
STH HURSTVILLE
BEVERLEY PARK
CARSS PARK
BLAKEHURST
KOGARAH BAY
Kogarah Bay
Kyle Bay
FOREST RD
CROYDON RD
KING GEORGES ROAD
PRINCES HIGHWAY
Hurstville
Allawah
Carlton
Kempt Field
Sydney Technical High
Bethany College
Hurstville Boys High
Hurstville Pmy
Blakehurst High
Carss Bush Park
Kogarah War Memorial Olympic Pool
Todd Park
Tidal Baths
Carss Cottage
Carss Pt
JOINS MAP 433
JOINS MAP 462
463

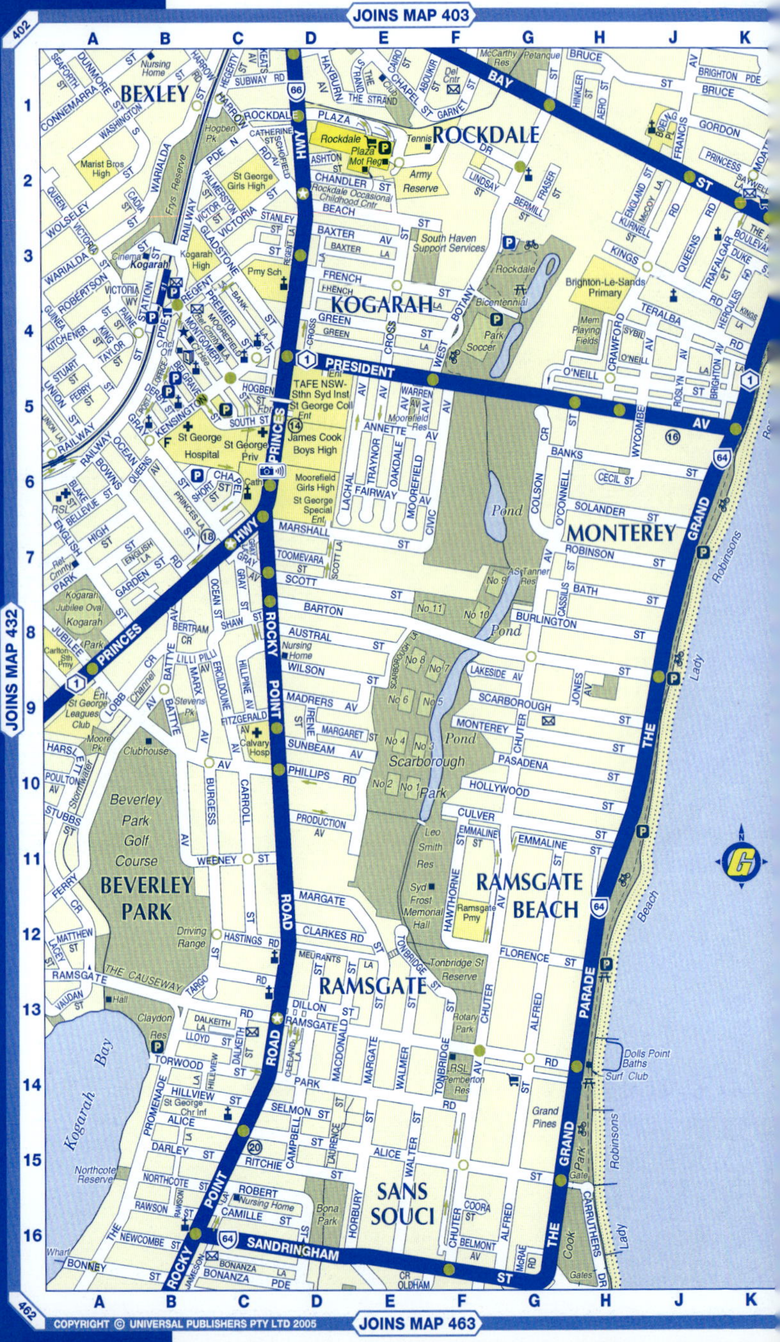
JOINS MAP 403
JOINS MAP 432
JOINS MAP 463
402
462
A B C D E F G H J K
1 2 3 4 5 6 7 8 9 10 11 12 13 14 15 16
BEXLEY
ROCKDALE
KOGARAH
MONTEREY
BEVERLEY PARK
RAMSGATE BEACH
RAMSGATE
SANS SOUCI
PRINCES HWY
ROCKY POINT ROAD
PRESIDENT AV
BAY ST
THE GRAND PARADE
SANDRINGHAM ST
Rockdale Plaza
Mot Reg
Army Reserve
Tennis
Rockdale Occasional Childhood Cntr
South Haven Support Services
Rockdale Bicentennial Park
Soccer
Brighton-Le-Sands Primary
Mem Playing Fields
Marist Bros High
St George Girls High
Kogarah High
Pmy Sch
Cinema
Nursing Home
Hogben Pk
Frys Reserve
St George Hospital
St George Priv
TAFE NSW-Sthn Syd Inst St George Coll
James Cook Boys High
Moorefield Girls High
St George Special
Moorefield Res
Kogarah Jubilee Oval
Carlton Sth Pmy
St George Leagues Club
Stevens Pk
Moore Pk
Calvary Hosp
Clubhouse
Beverley Park Golf Course
Driving Range
Pond
AS Tanner Res
Scarborough Park
Leo Smith Res
Syd Frost Memorial Hall
Ramsgate Pmy
Tonbridge St Reserve
Rotary Park
RSL
Pemberton Res
Grand Pines
Claydon Res
Kogarah Bay
Northcote Reserve
St George Chr Inf
Bona Park
Dolls Point Baths
Surf Club
Cook Park
Robinsons Beach
Lady Robinsons Beach
THE CAUSEWAY
Hall
Wharf

MAP 434

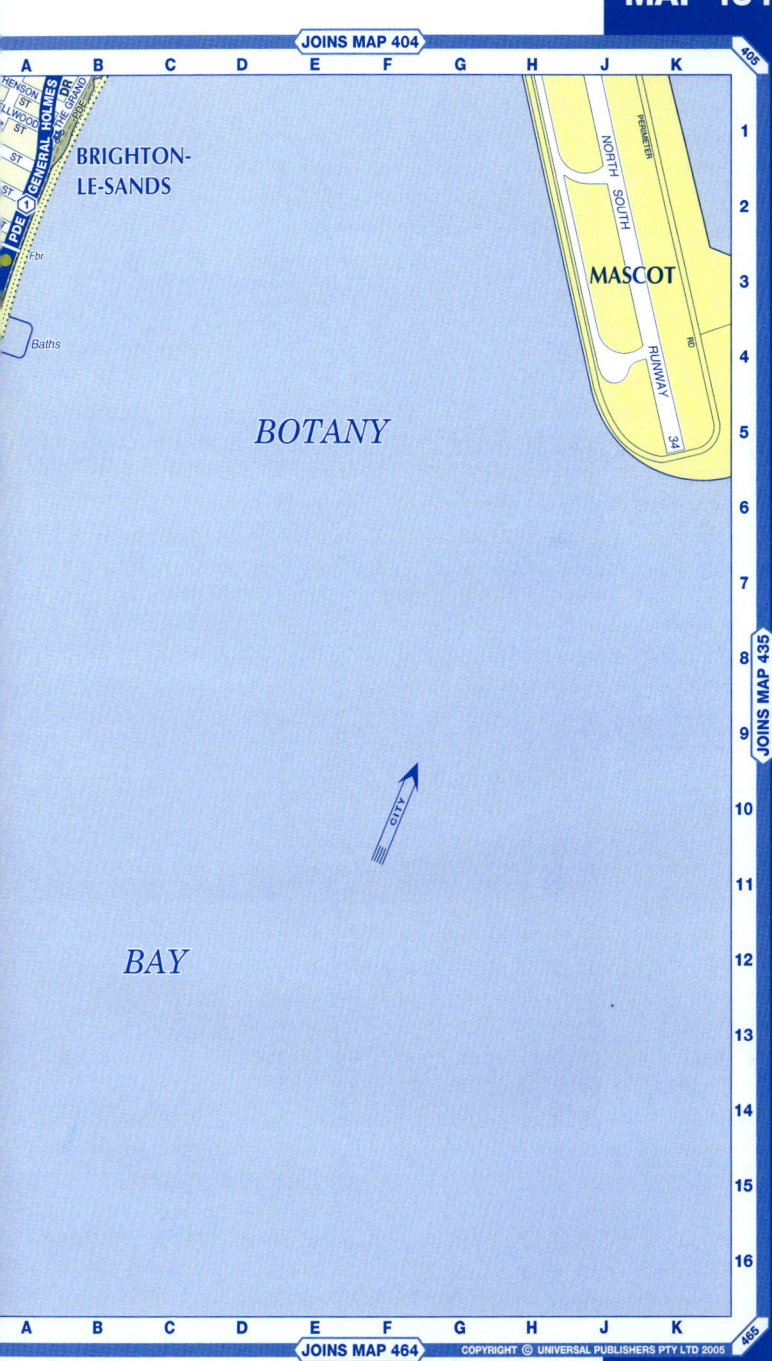

BRIGHTON-LE-SANDS

MASCOT

BOTANY

BAY

MAP 435

JOINS MAP 405

BOTANY

PARALLEL RUNWAY

PENRHYN
B117
Gate B118
B119

BOTANY

Port of Botany Bay

CITY

BAY

BP Oil Terminal
DENT ST
BOTANY
McPHERSON
GREENFIELD
FORESHORE
Joseph Banks Park
Banksmeadow
Botany Clubhouse
Golf
Army Reserve

JOINS MAP 434
JOINS MAP 465

COPYRIGHT © UNIVERSAL PUBLISHERS PTY LTD 2005

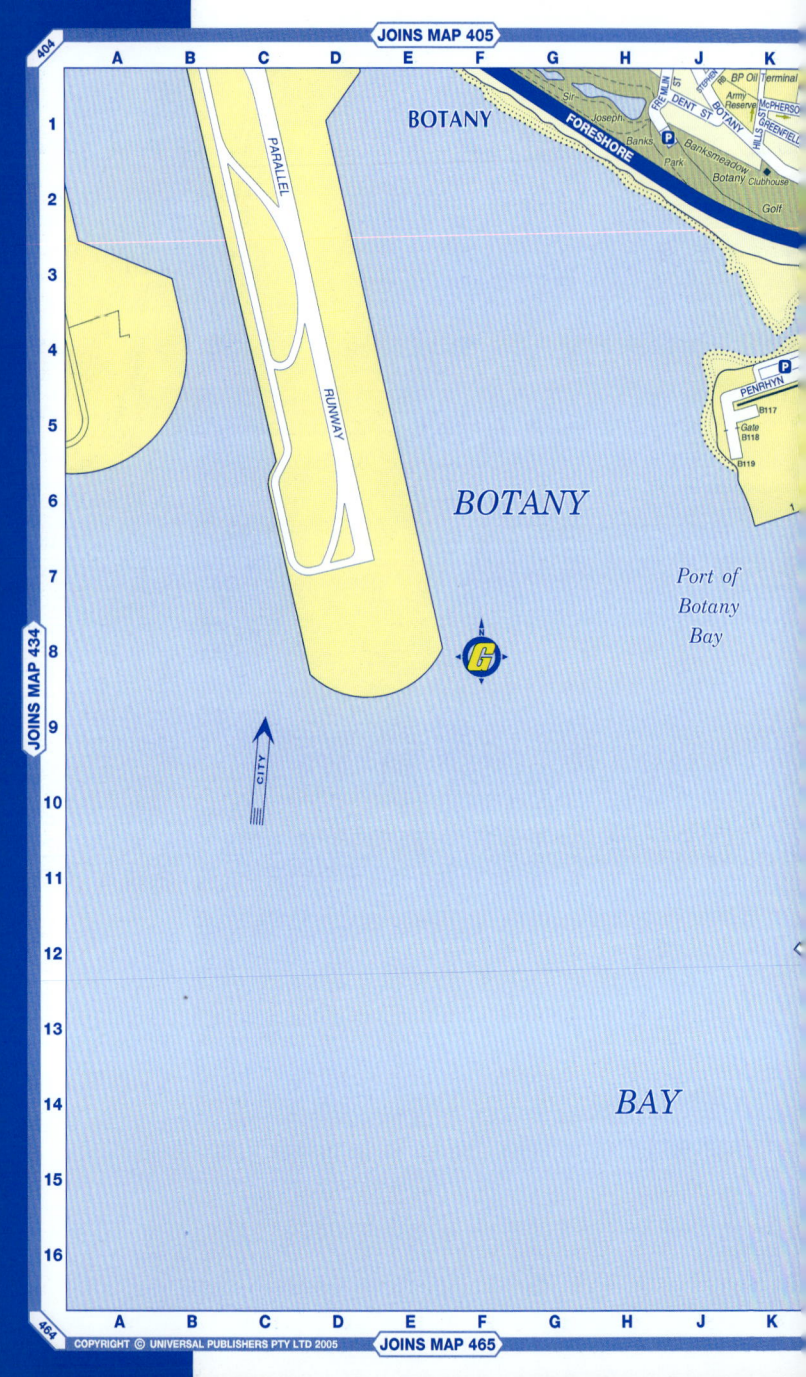

JOINS MAP 406
407
JOINS MAP 437
JOINS MAP 466
A B C D E F G H J K
1 2 3 4 5 6 7 8 9 10 11 12 13 14 15 16
BANKSMEADOW
ORICA
MATRAVILLE
PORT BOTANY
PHILLIP BAY
LA PEROUSE
BOTANY ROAD
BEAUCHAMP
DENISON ST
BUNNERONG RD
PERRY
HAROLD ST
AUSTRALIA AV
MURRABIN AV
PARTANNA AV
FRANKLIN
WINDSOR ST
DAUNT
PATERSON
JENNINGS
BAIRD
SOLANDER ST
KELLY LA
KELLY ST
RAYMOND AV
McCAULEY
McPHERSON ST
NANT ST
BARE ST
EXELL ST
Discovery Cove Industrial Estate
The Botany Bay Industrial Estate
Caltex Oil Terminal
Seafarers Centre
No vehicles over 6m permitted in McCauley St
Australian Paper
Purcell Park
BROTHERSON AV
MOORINA AV
MOONA AV
SHIRLEY
Jeh Wit
INTER - TERMINAL ACCESS
P&O Trans Australia
Alcatel
Govt Bus Depot
Smith Bros
Patrick Container Terminal
Brotherson Dock
CTAL Container Terminal
P&O Ports
Port Botany Container Park
GOLDEN GROVE
BUMBORAH POINT RD
MILITARY RD
MILLENNIUM CT
Eastern Suburbs Crematorium
Botany Cemetery
Vopak Site A
Origin
Bulk Liquids Storage Area
CHARLOTTE RD
ELGAS
Hydrocarbon Storage Terminal
FRIENDSHIP RD
SIMBLIST
Vopak Site B
Gate (Emergency Access Only)
FISHBURN
Sea Wall
PRINCE OF WALES DR
Banks Wall
Molineaux Pt
Bumborah Pt
Yarra Bay
Yarra Pt
Groyne
Yarra Bay Sailing Club
Yarra Bay House
Bicentennial Park
Frenchmans Bay
LEICHHARDT
WASSELL
DAMPIER
CARNEGIE
WARBURTON
EYRE ST
FORREST ST
BUNNERONG ST
La Perouse Pmy
Nurs Home
ANZAC PDE
ENDEAVOUR
Botany Bay National Park Information: Phone (02) 9311 3379
Museum Botany Bay National Park
Cann Pk
Botany Bay National Park
Congwong Bay Beach
Footbridge
Bare Island
Museum & Fort
Congwong Bay

MAP 437

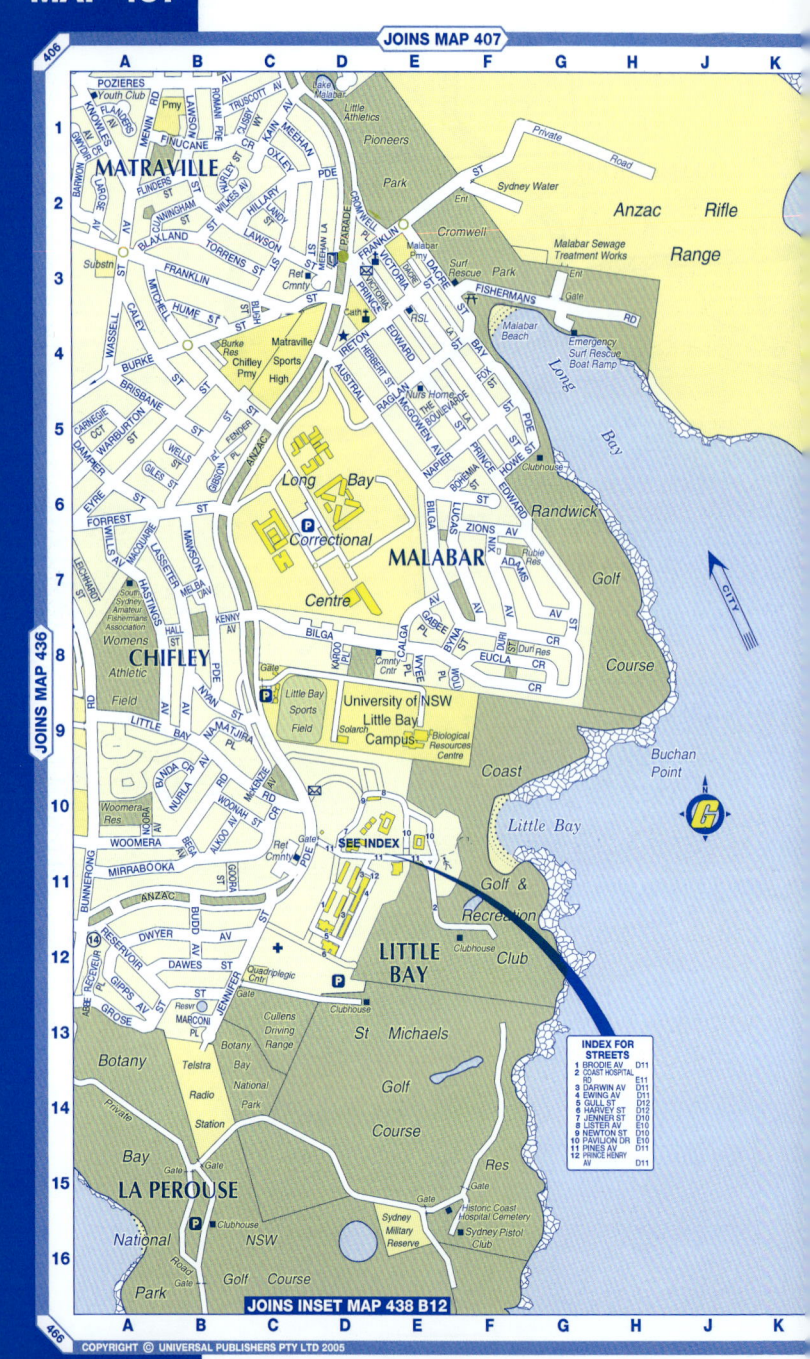

INDEX FOR STREETS

1. BRODIE AV — D11
2. COAST HOSPITAL RD — E11
3. DARWIN AV — D11
4. EWING AV — D11
5. GULL ST — D12
6. HARVEY ST — D12
7. JENNER ST — D10
8. LISTER AV — E10
9. NEWTON ST — D10
10. PAVILION DR — E10
11. PINES AV — D11
12. PRINCE HENRY AV — D11

MAP 438
MAP 443 FOLLOWS

JOINS MAP 408

Magic Pt

Boora Pt

TASMAN

SEA

INSET

JOINS MAP 437 B16

Little Congwong Beach — Clubhouse — Sydney Military Res — Sydney Pistol Club

Botany Bay — Gate — NSW Golf Course — **LA PEROUSE**

Endeavour Light — National — Park — *TASMAN*

Henry Head — Cape Banks — Cruwee Cove — *SEA*

BOTANY BAY — Aquatic Reserve — Cape Banks

MAP 443
PREVIOUS MAP 438

JOINS MAP 413

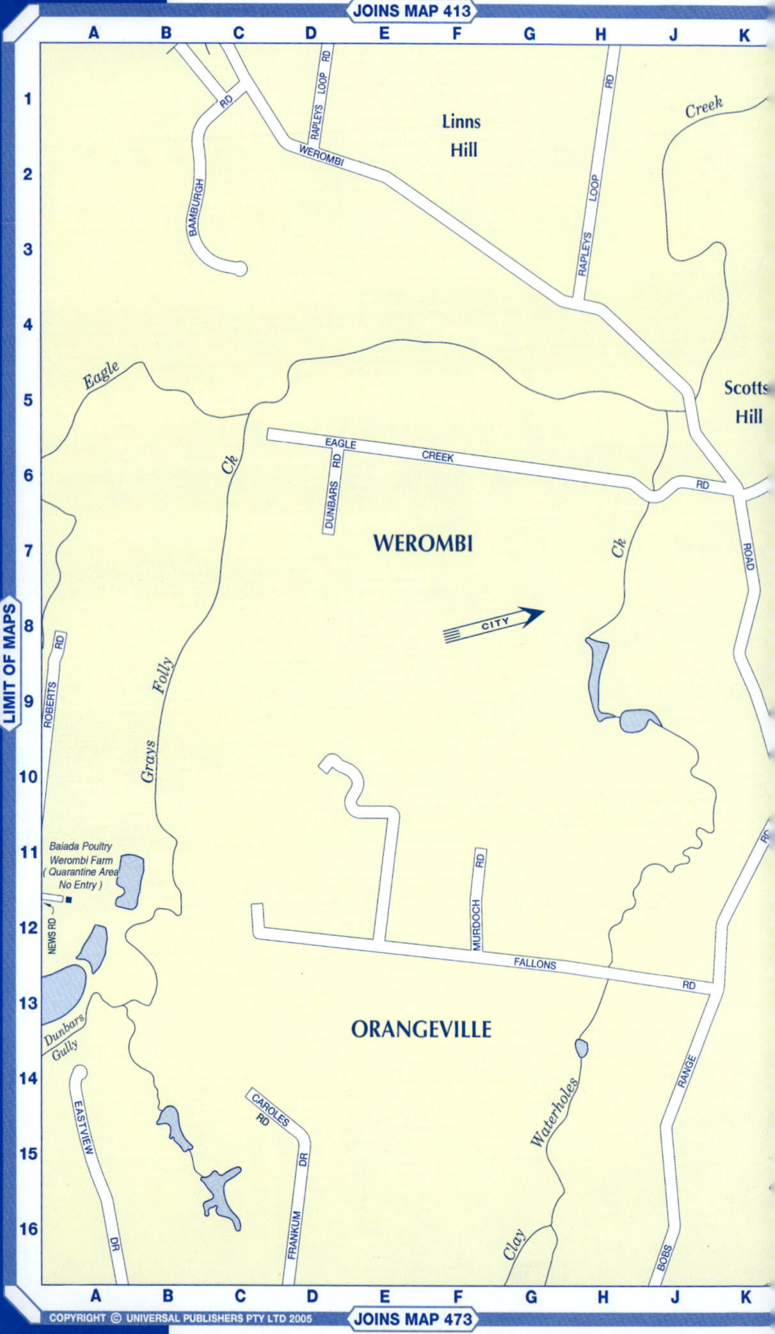

Linns Hill

Creek

Scotts Hill

BAMBURGH RD

RAPLEYS LOOP RD

WEROMBI RD

RAPLEYS LOOP RD

Eagle Ck

EAGLE CREEK RD

DUNBARS RD

WEROMBI

Ck

CITY

Grays Folly Ck

ROBERTS RD

LIMIT OF MAPS

Baiada Poultry Werombi Farm (Quarantine Area No Entry)

NEWS RD

MURDOCH RD

FALLONS RD

Dunbars Gully

ORANGEVILLE

EASTVIEW DR

CAROLES RD

FRANKUM DR

Waterholes

Clay

BOBS RANGE RD

JOINS MAP 473

COPYRIGHT © UNIVERSAL PUBLISHERS PTY LTD 2005

MAP 444

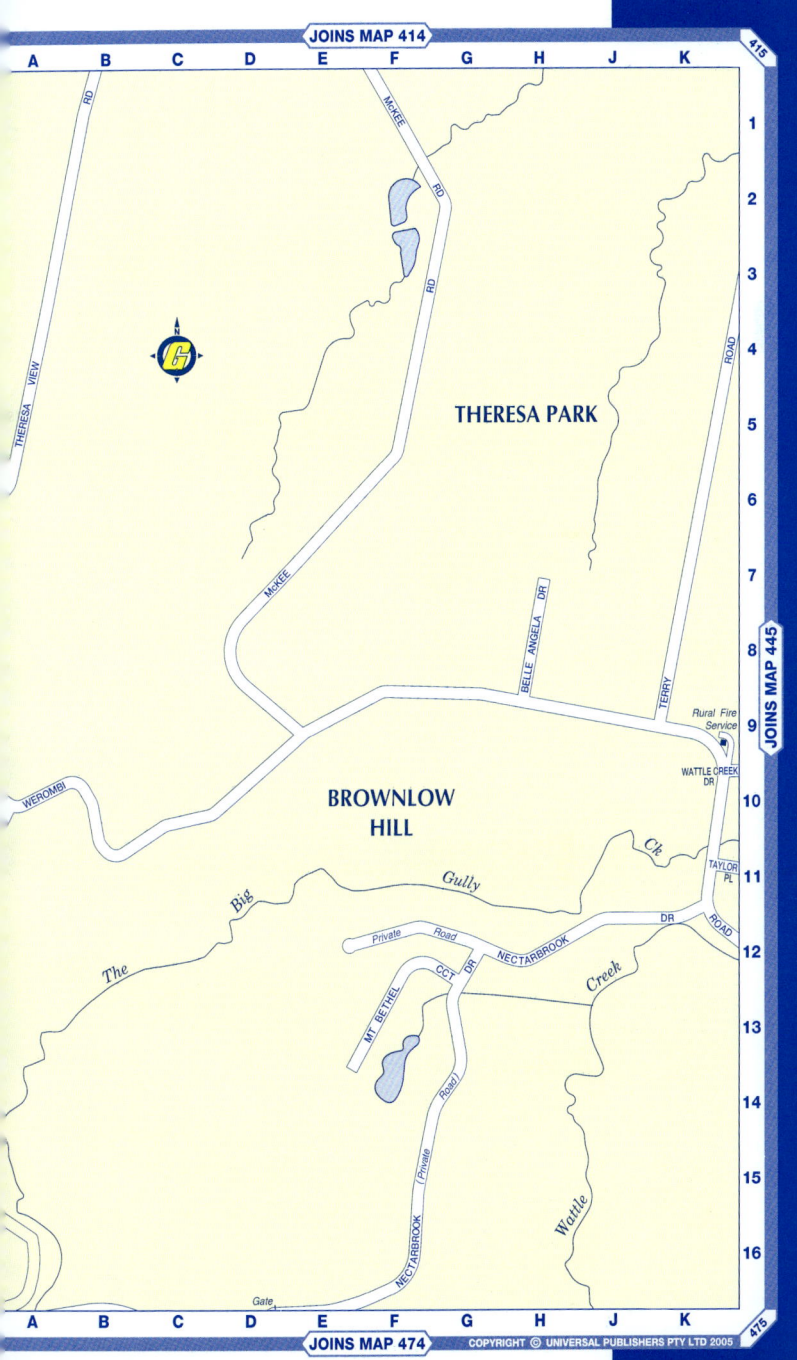

JOINS MAP 414

THERESA PARK

BROWNLOW HILL

Rural Fire Service

Wattle Creek Dr
Taylor Pl

Belle Angela Dr
Terry Road
McKee Rd
Theresa View Rd
Werombi Rd
Big Gully Ck
The Creek
Nectarbrook Dr
Mt Bethel Cct Dr
Nectarbrook (Private) Road
Wattle Creek

JOINS MAP 474

MAP 445

NEPEAN RIVER

GREENFIELDS PL
GLENWORTH PL
TERRY RD

University Of Sydney Farms

Westwood Farm

THERESA PARK

Road
Private RD

NEPEAN
CITY

Rural Fire Service
WATTLE CREEK DR
Wattle
TAYLOR PL
WEROMBI
STANHOPE
WW1

Brownlow Hill Weir

BROWNLOW HILL

Vet Faculty Horse Unit
University of Sydney Farms
Gate
Animal Reproduction Unit

ROAD

JOINS MAP 415 (top)
JOINS MAP 475 (bottom)
JOINS MAP 444 (left)
414 / 474 (corners)

COPYRIGHT © UNIVERSAL PUBLISHERS PTY LTD 2005

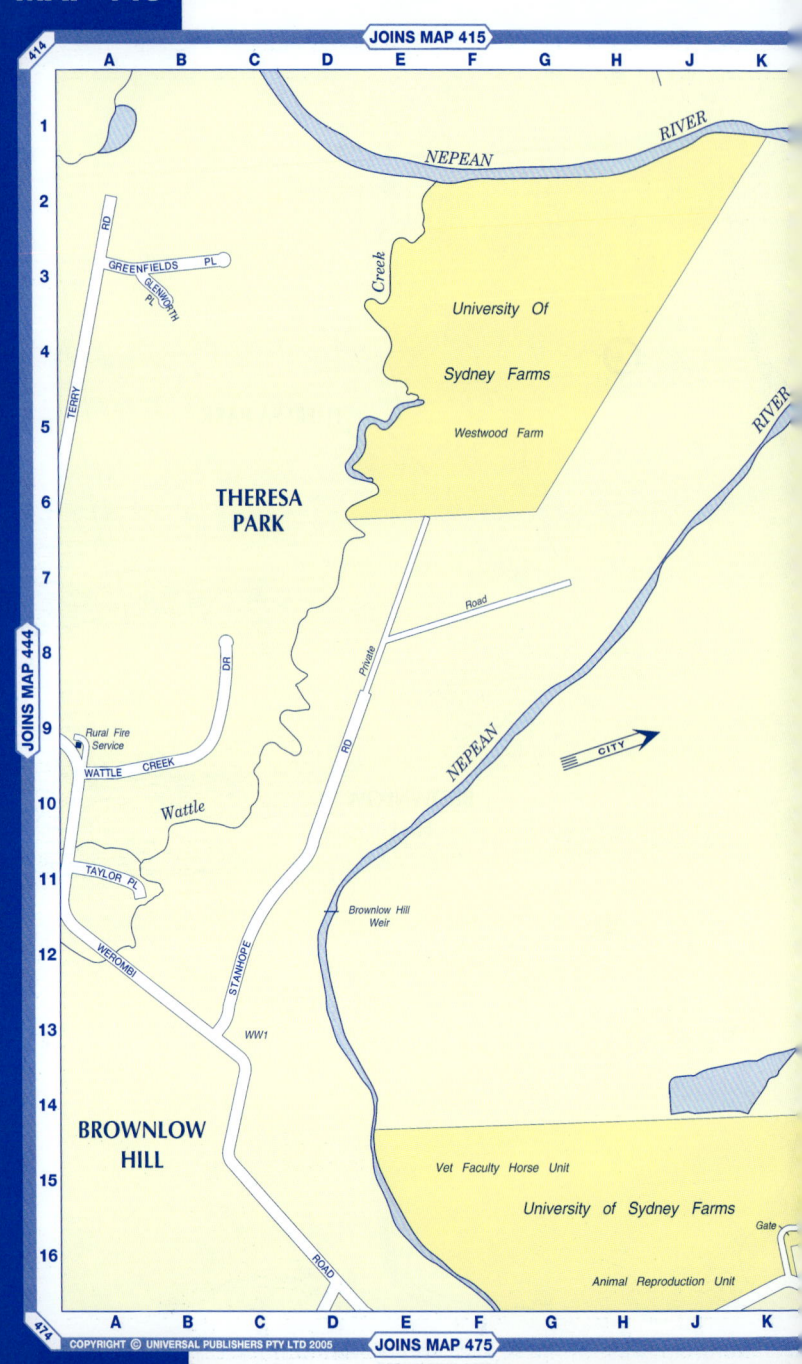

MAP 446

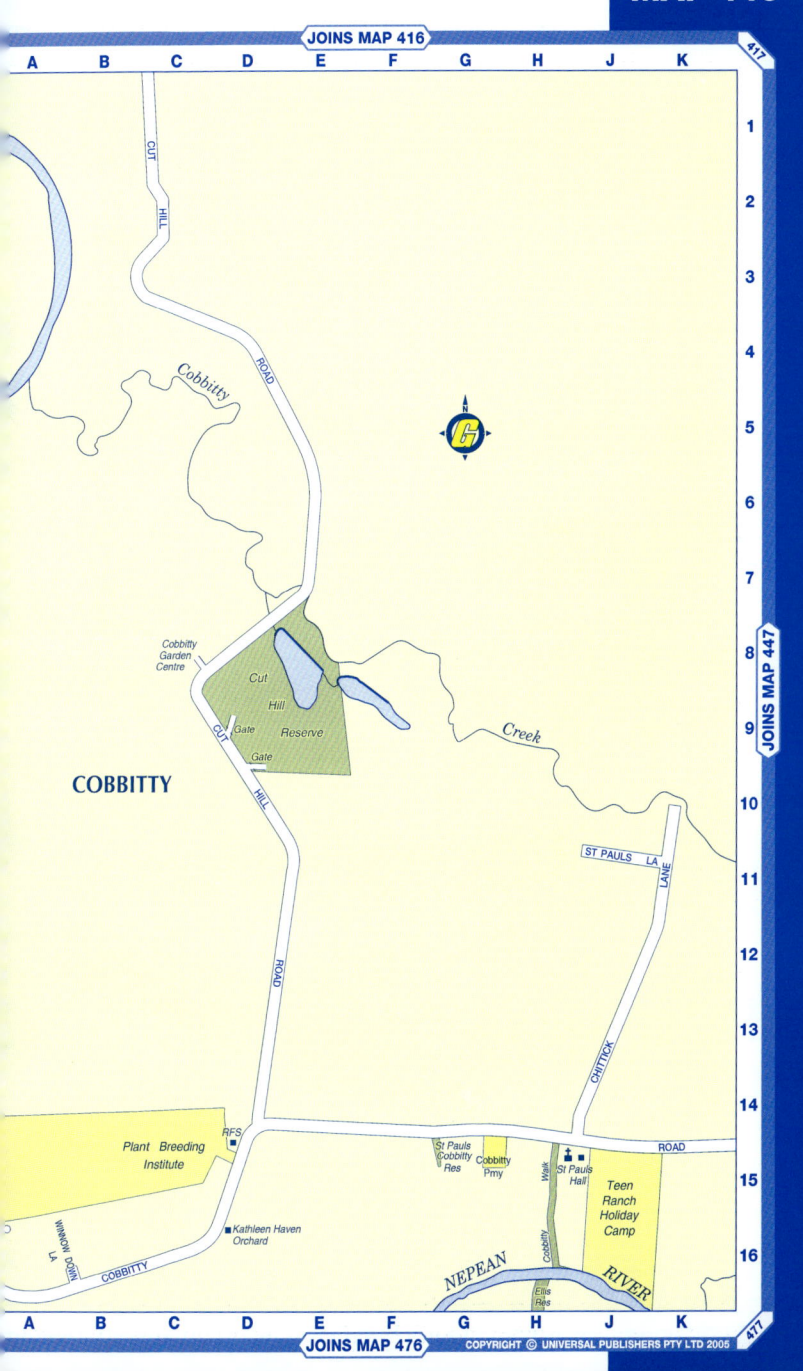

MAP 447

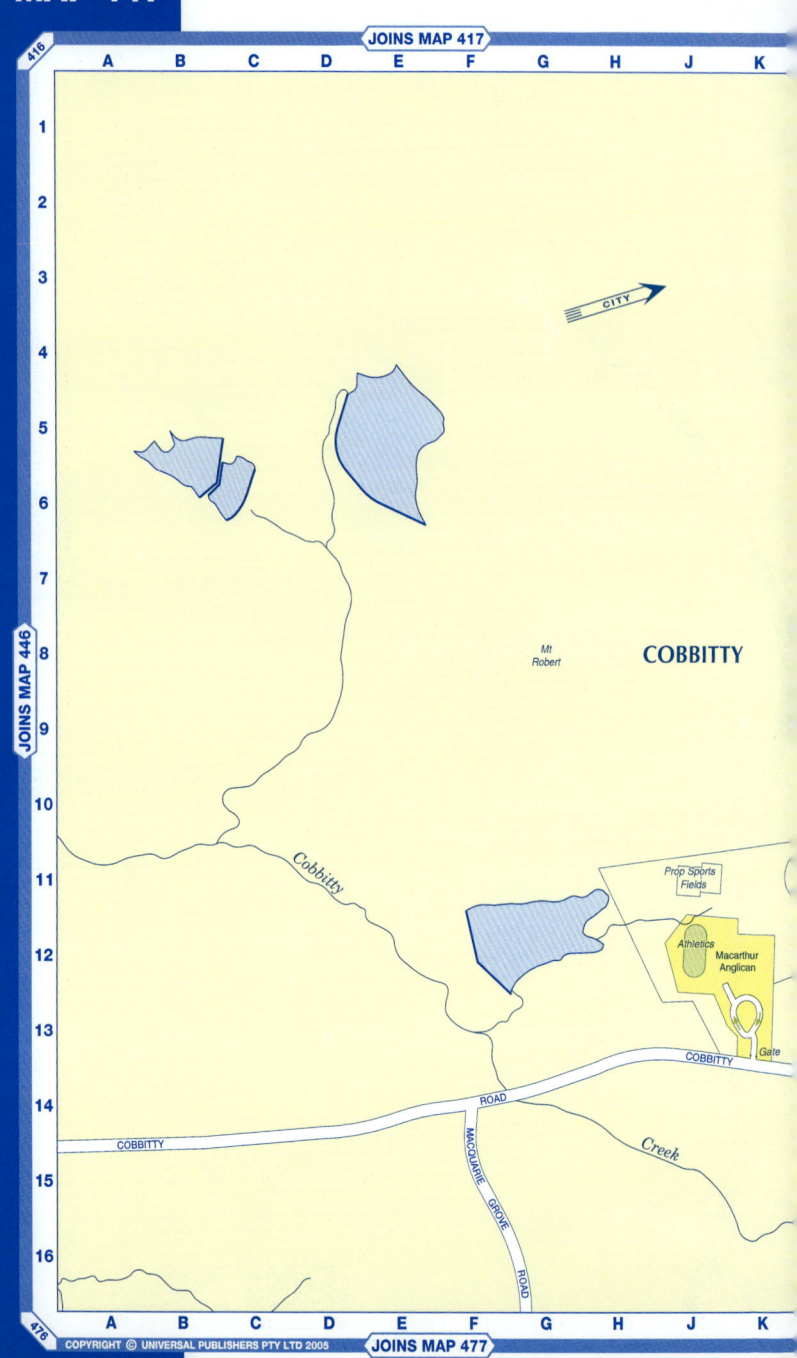

COBBITTY

Mt Robert

Cobbitty

Cobbitty Creek

COBBITTY ROAD

MACQUARIE GROVE ROAD

Prop Sports Fields

Athletics

Macarthur Anglican

Gate

JOINS MAP 417
JOINS MAP 446
JOINS MAP 477

MAP 448

JOINS MAP 418

BRINGELLY

ORAN PARK

Oran Park Motorsport

Family Hill Rd
Peter Brock Dr
Cobbitty
Gate
Cobbitty Park
Merryn Cl
Northern Road
The Northern Road

HARRINGTON PARK

Campbell Rivulet
Road

JOINS MAP 478
JOINS MAP 449
419
479

COPYRIGHT © UNIVERSAL PUBLISHERS PTY LTD 2005

MAP 449

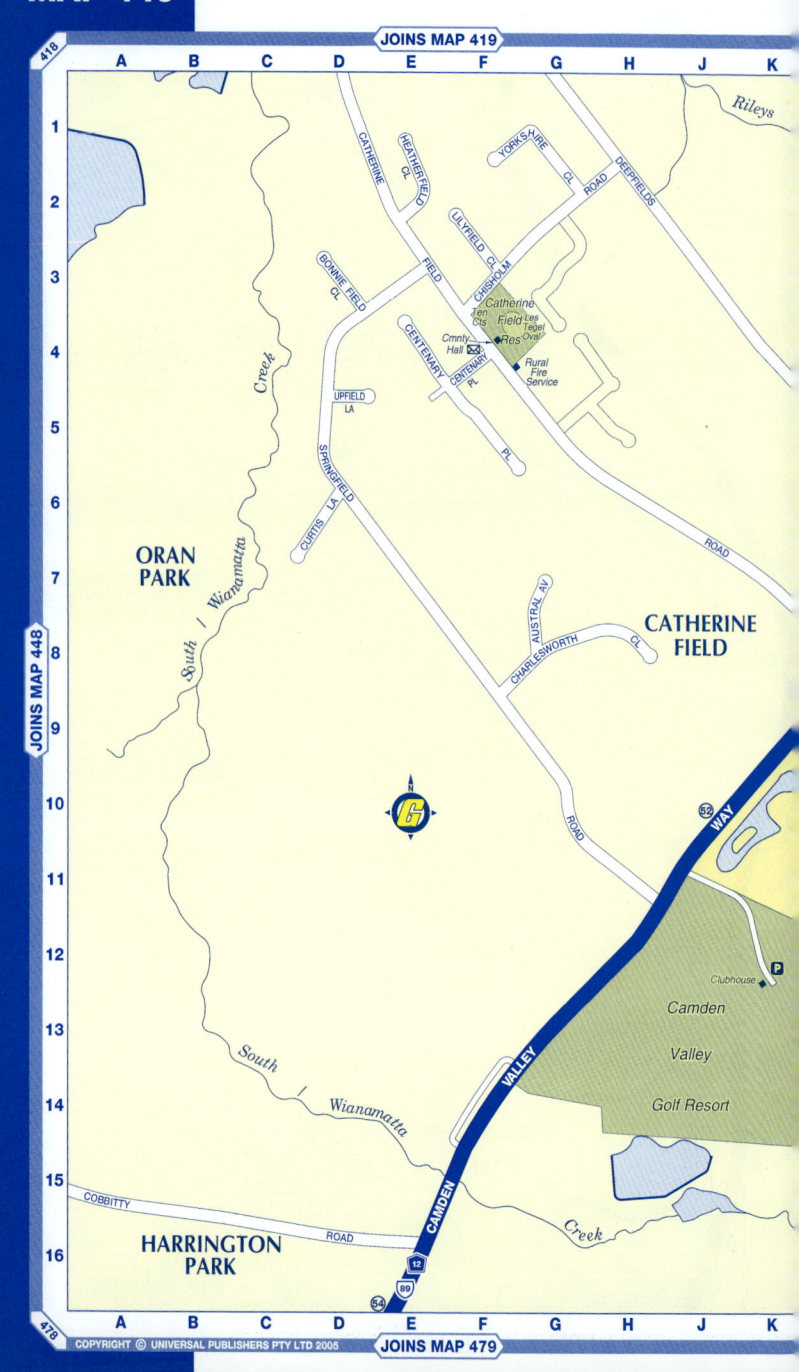

Joins Map 419 (north)
Joins Map 418 (northwest edge)
Joins Map 448 (west)
Joins Map 479 (south)

Localities:
- ORAN PARK
- CATHERINE FIELD
- HARRINGTON PARK

Roads and streets:
- Catherine Field Road
- Heatherfield Cl
- Lilyfield Cl
- Yorkshire Cl
- Deepfields Road
- Chisholm
- Bonnie Field Cl
- Centenary Pl
- Upfield La
- Springfield
- Curtis La
- Charlesworth
- Austral Av Cl
- Camden Valley Way
- Cobbitty Road

Features:
- South Wianamatta Creek
- Rileys (Creek)
- Catherine Field Res, Les Tegel Oval
- Ten Cts, Cmnty Hall
- Rural Fire Service
- Camden Valley Golf Resort, Clubhouse

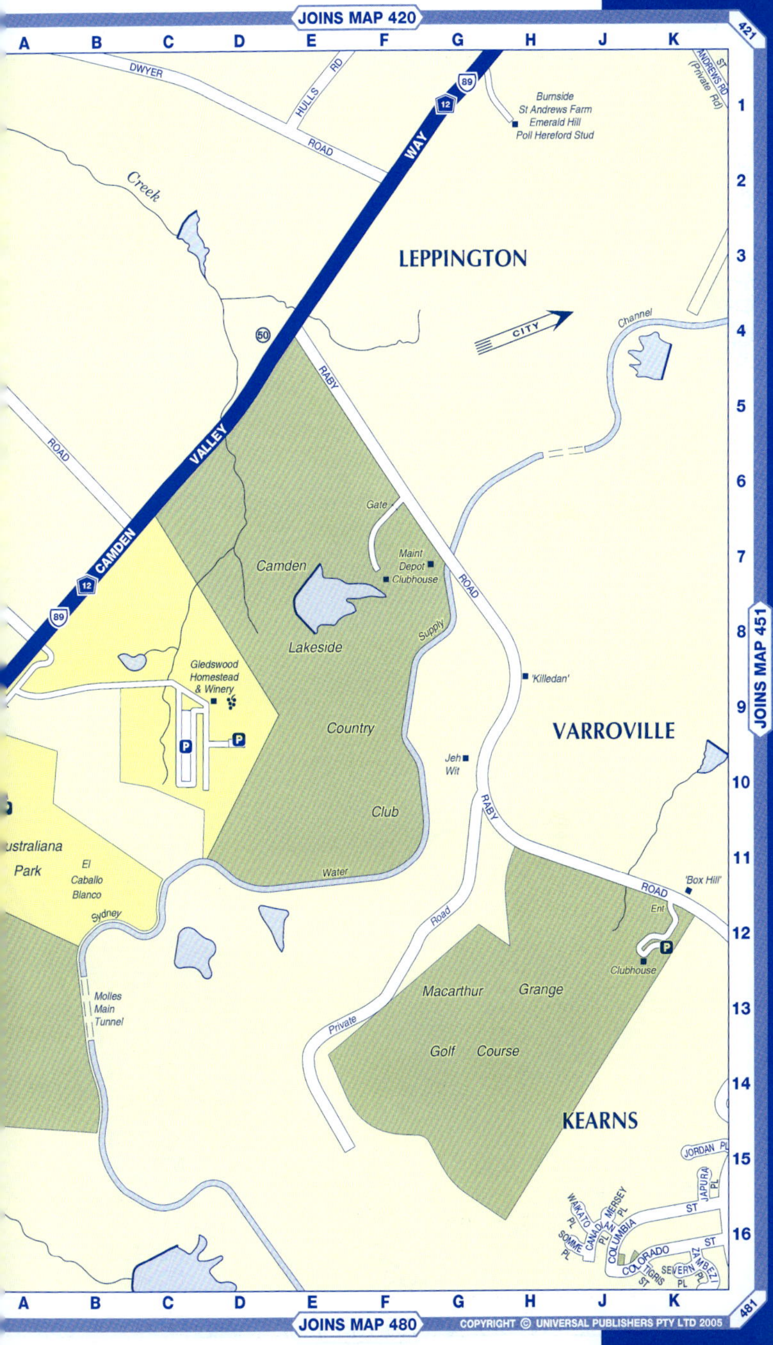
JOINS MAP 420
JOINS MAP 451
JOINS MAP 480
421
481
A B C D E F G H J K
1 2 3 4 5 6 7 8 9 10 11 12 13 14 15 16
DWYER ROAD
HULLS RD
CAMDEN VALLEY WAY
12
89
50
ST ANDREWS RD (Private Rd)
Burnside
St Andrews Farm
Emerald Hill
Poll Hereford Stud
Creek
LEPPINGTON
CITY
Channel
RABY ROAD
ROAD
Gate
Maint
Depot
Clubhouse
Camden
Lakeside
Country
Club
Supply
Water
Sydney
'Killedan'
VARROVILLE
Jeh
Wit
Gledswood
Homestead
& Winery
P
ustraliana
Park
El
Caballo
Blanco
Molles
Main
Tunnel
Private
Road
'Box Hill'
Ent
Clubhouse
Macarthur
Grange
Golf
Course
KEARNS
JORDAN PL
JAPURA PL
WAIKATO PL
CANADIAN PL
MERSEY PL
SOMME PL
COLUMBIA
ST
COLORADO
TIGRIS ST
SEVERN PL
ZAMBEZI
ST

MAP 451

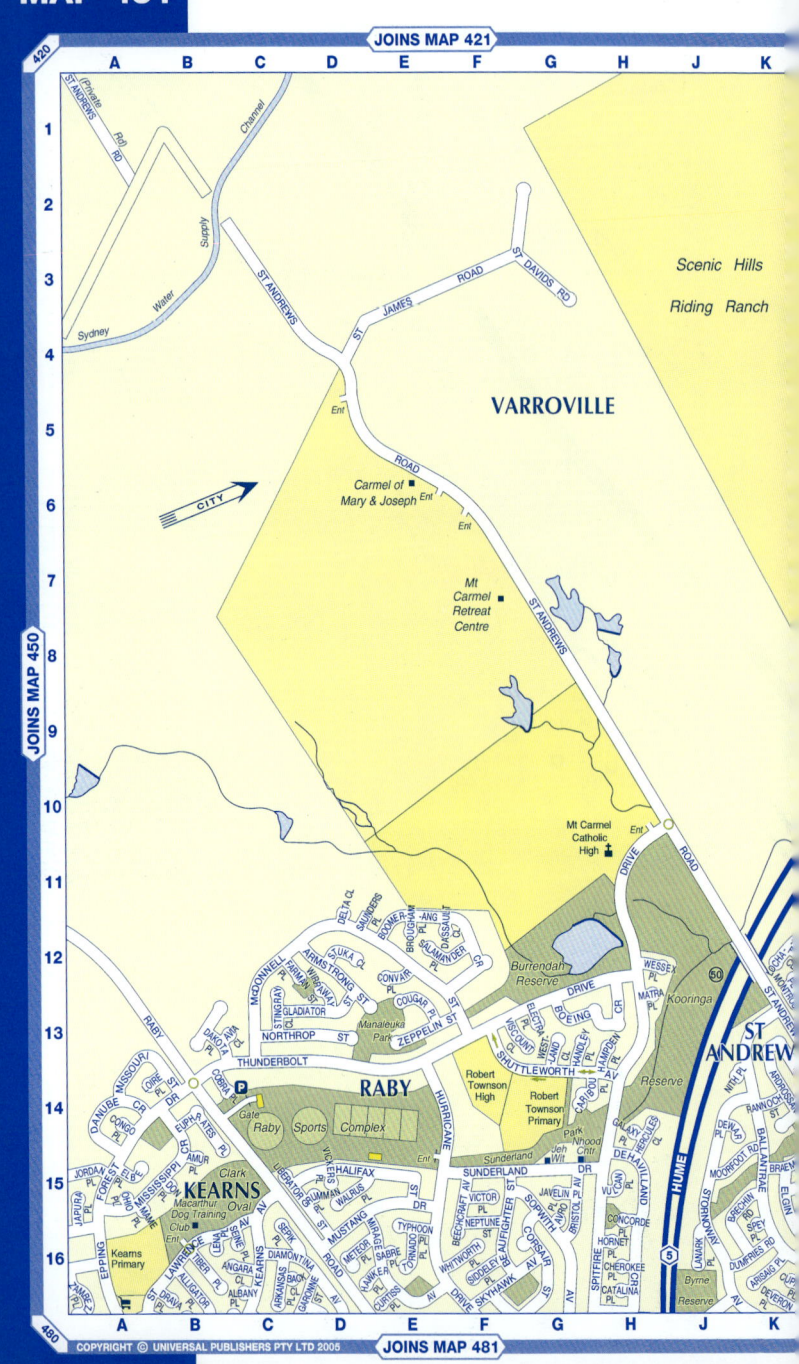

MAP 452

JOINS MAP 423

422

JOINS MAP 452

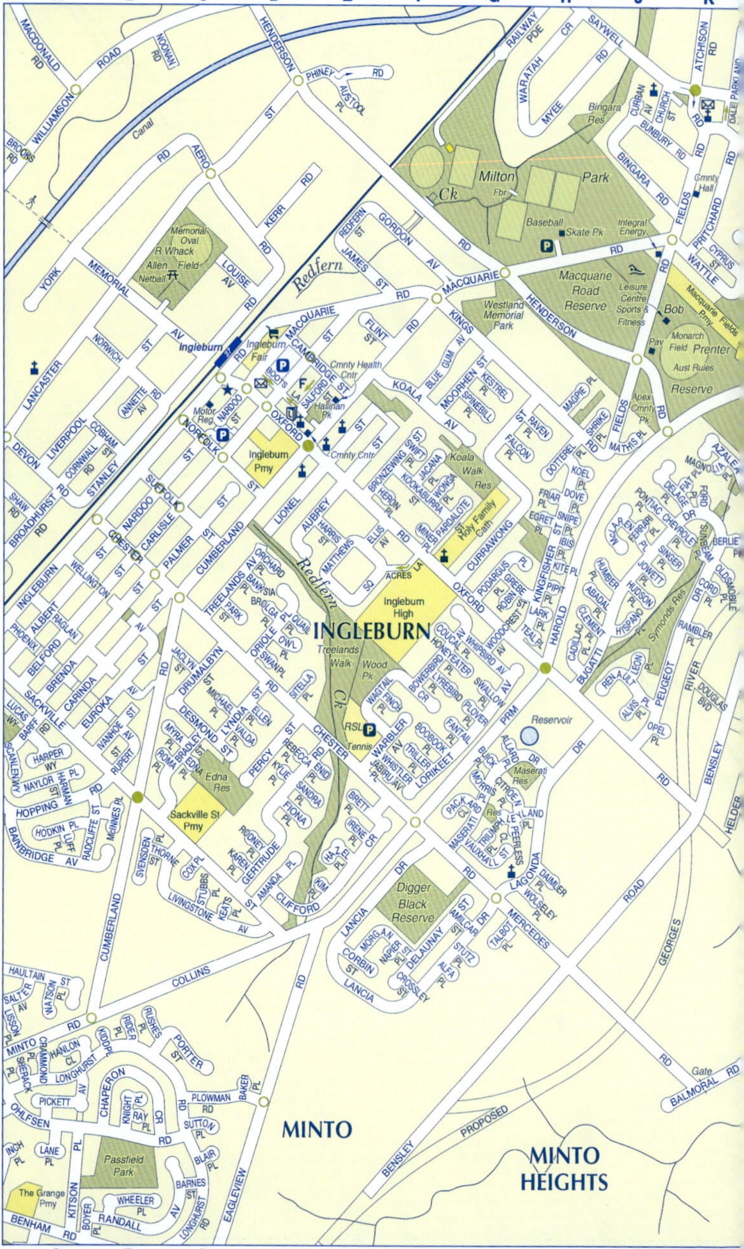

482

JOINS MAP 483

MAP 454

Macquarie Fields

Key features visible on the map:
- Macquarie Fields (suburb)
- Macquarie Fields Park
- James Meehan Pk
- James Meehan High Cmnty Cntr
- Macquarie Fields High
- Thomas Acres Walk
- Bensley Reserve (Soccer Pav.)
- Ingleburn Res, Weir
- Georges River Nature Res
- Long Point
- Simmos Beach Recreation Reserve
- Georges River
- Military Reserve
- Kingdon Pde
- Nursery
- Hazlett
- Curran Pmy
- Guise Pmy
- Bass Res
- Hyacinth Res
- Caley Pk

Joins Map 424 (north), Joins Map 484 (south), Joins Map 455 (east), Map 425 (NE corner), Map 485 (SE corner)

Selected streets: Edgar St, Parliament, Saywell, Second St, Harvey St, Alice St, Edith, Noelne Cl, Brooks Rd, Third Av, Fourth Av, Fuchsia Cr, Plume Cl, Apple, Bensley Rd, Mentha, Amaranthus, Casuarina, Hydrangea, Orchid, Loreli, Poppy, Mistletoe, Cranberry, Daisy, Lotus, Ambrosia, Evelyn Av, Wills Rd, Cook, Oakley, Picnic St, Brindale St, Georges River Pde, Regina, Macquarie Rd, Harold, Cadogan Rd, Rosemary, Yarran, Hibiscus, Magnolia, Alpine, Clematis, Gimlet, Yate, Melaleuca, Melliodora Wy, Flame, Eucalyptus Cr, Cypress, Rosewood, Blackwood, Mallee, Cassia, Tea Tree Field, Flinders, Leptospermum Pl, Hawthorne Dr, Ironbark Pl, Cottonbush, Coolabah, Laurel, Old, Beech, Elder Pl, Costata, Telopea, Box, Ebony, Starleaf Wy, Juniper Wy, Punicea Wy, Sarissa Wy, Montana Wy, Trinervis Wy, Greville, Haka, Catkin, Bundy Ct, Lutchen, Peppermint Dr, Saglan, Boree, Cestrum, Scribbly, Petunia, Towards, Hyacinth, Bramble, Gardenia, Geranium, Fifth Av, Sixth Av, Correa, Pelargonium Cr, Felicia, Knotwood Rd, Parkway, Loftus Av, Emily, Amos St, Daphne Rd, Melon, Kingdon Pde

MAP 455

JOINS MAP 425

Harris

CITY

HOLSWORTHY

GEORGES RIVER

Military

Creek

Reserve

Complete

Harris Hill

Holsworthy

Harris

Field

Firing

Range

JOINS MAP 454

JOINS MAP 485

COPYRIGHT © UNIVERSAL PUBLISHERS PTY LTD 2005

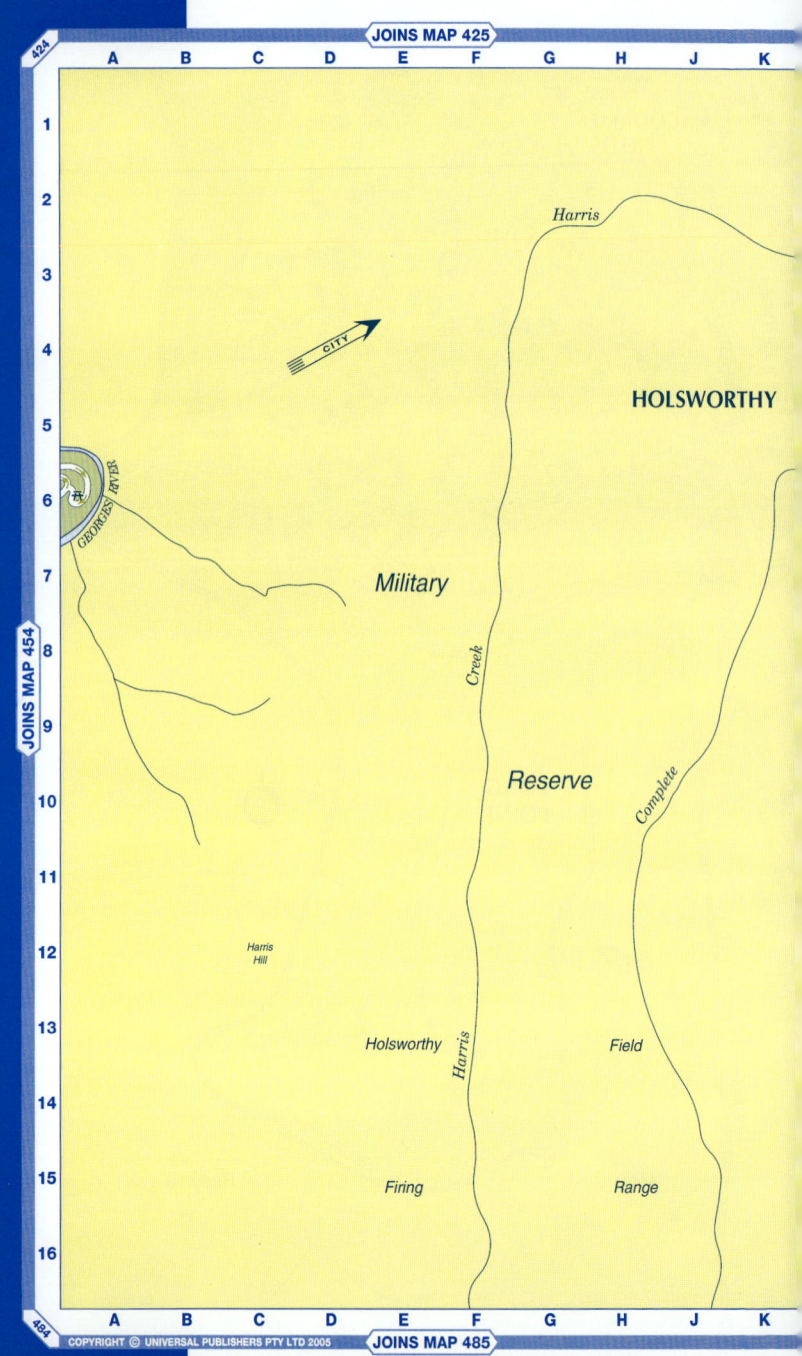

MAP 456

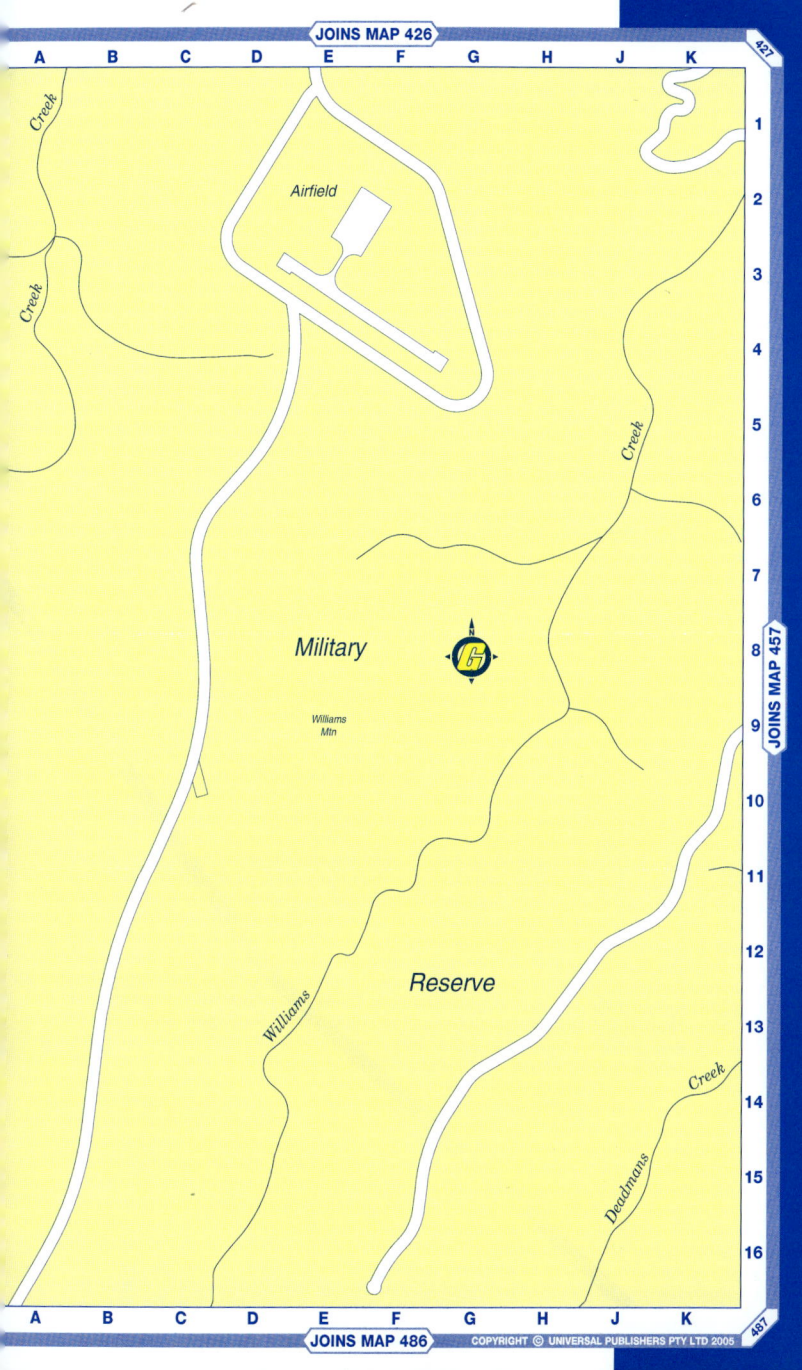

Airfield

Military

Williams Mtn

Reserve

Williams

Deadmans Creek

Creek (×3)

JOINS MAP 426 (top)
JOINS MAP 486 (bottom)
JOINS MAP 457 (right)

MAP 457

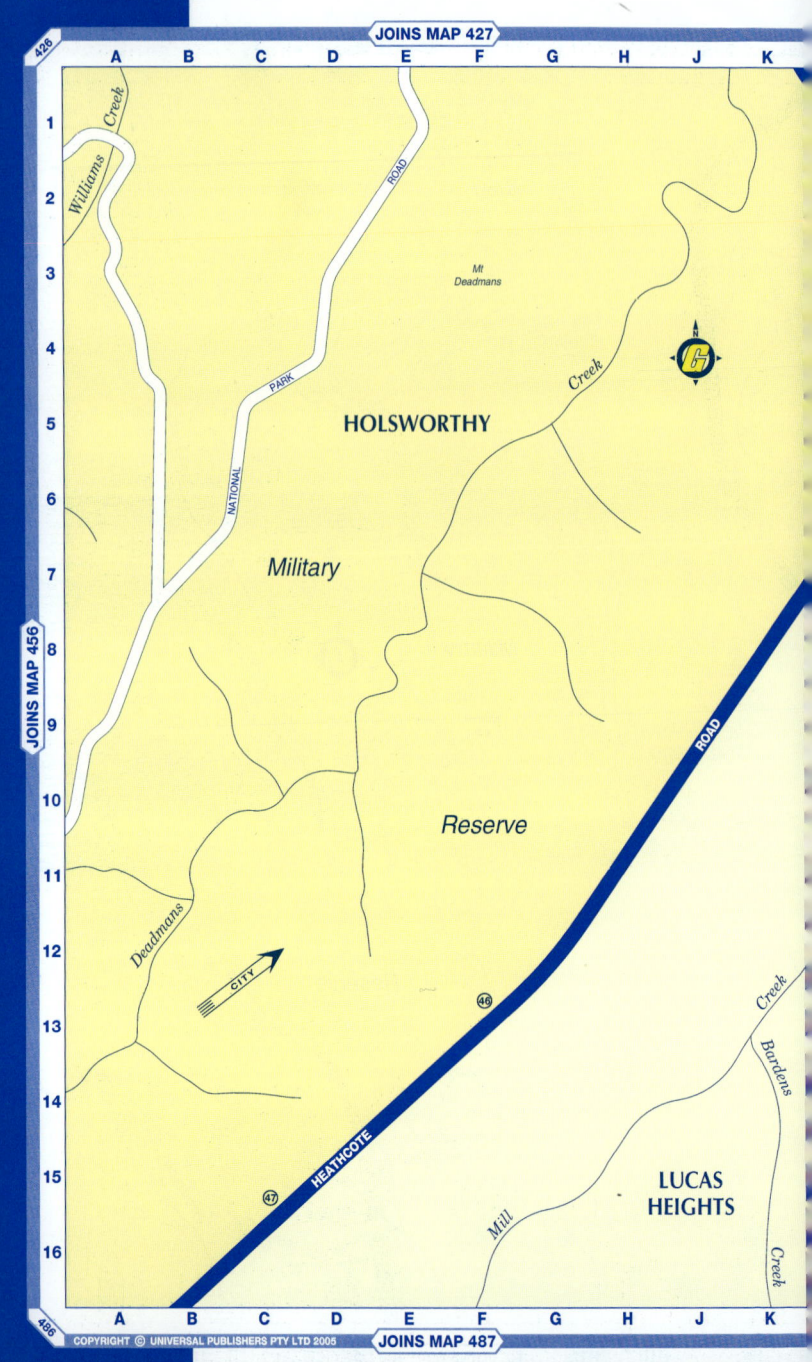

MAP 458

JOINS MAP 428

Military Reserve

ALFORDS POINT

MENAI

BARDEN RIDGE

JOINS MAP 488

COPYRIGHT © UNIVERSAL PUBLISHERS PTY LTD 2005

MAP 459

MAP 460

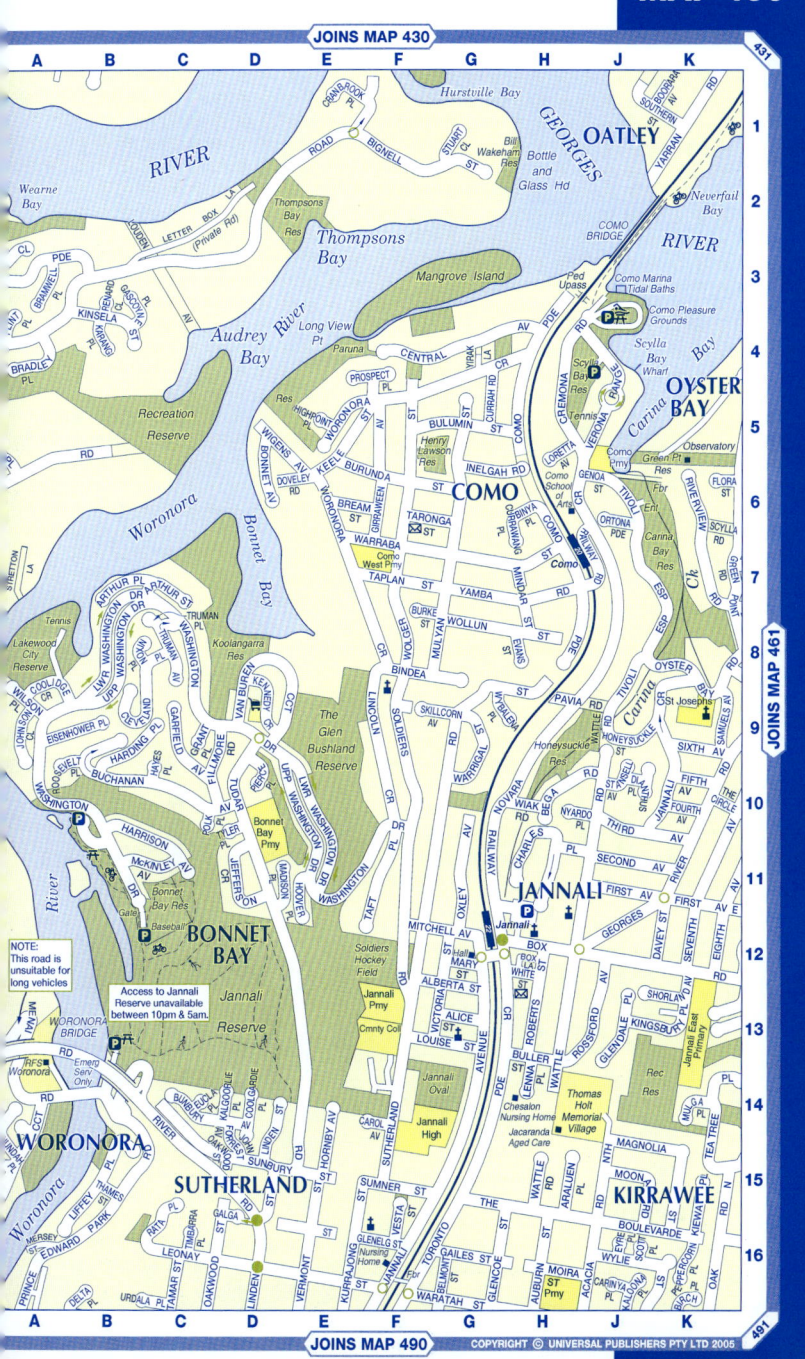

JOINS MAP 431
JOINS MAP 460
JOINS MAP 491
430
490
A B C D E F G H J K
1 2 3 4 5 6 7 8 9 10 11 12 13 14 15 16
OATLEY
CONNELLS POINT
KYLE BAY
GEORGES
OYSTER BAY
Caravan Head
KANGAROO POINT
SYLVANIA
Sylvania Heights
KAREELA
JANNALI
KIRRAWEE
GYMEA
Connells Bay
Harness Cask Pt
Oatley Pt
Connells Pt
Oatley Bay
Oatley Point Res
Neverfail Bay
Green Pt
Coronation Bay
Caravan Hd
Kangaroo Pt
Kangaroo Pt Res
Bay
Oyster
Caravan Head Bushland Res
Oyster Bay Oval
Oyster Bay Pmy
Cmnty Hall
Freya St Res
Kareela Pmy
A R Hurst Reserve
Kareela Golf & Social Club
Sylvania Heights Primary
Ret Vill
Cmnty Health Cntr
Kareela Golf & Social Club
Clubhouse
Kirinari Student Hostel
Cmnty & Youth Cntr
Sylvania Heights Reserve
Hockey
Corea Oval
Joseph Banks Native Plants Res
Bates Dr Sylvanvale Pmy
Bates Dr Oval
Football Fields
Clubhouse
Kareela Oval
Sutherland Shire Council Depot
Port Hacking Substn
Gymea Nth Pmy
Nursery
Nurs Home
Rec Res
Rec
Res
HIGHWAY
PRINCES
WYONG ST
NEVERFAIL PL
LETITIA ST
ALGERNON
DINJERRA CR
ROSA ST
HERBERT ST
CLIFTON ST
PHIPPS ST
QUEENS RD
BOWDEN CR
KYLE
CROSS ST
PDE
DISCOVERY PL
RIVER RD
JUVENIS AV
GEORGES
COOK RD
GETYUNGA RD
TIRANNA PL
ROAD
BORA
MBIL PL
CARINA
GLENHAVEN PL
FARRER PL
RICKARD RD
CONNELL RD
WARD CR
CR
SHIPWRIGHT PL
RIVERHAVEN PL
(Priv Rd)
FLORA ST
CARAVAN HEAD RD
HIGHVIEW CR
CAROLINE ST
SCYLLA
COWAN RD
COMO
DRUMMOND RD
WATERVIEW ST
GREEN POINT RD
MANNING ST
OYSTER BAY RD
SAGE AV
PHILLIP ST
SHORT
CARVERS
SAMUELS AV
LOVES AV
GEORGES RIVER
CIRCLE THE
SEVENTH AV
TENTH AV
SIANDRA DR
STRUEN MARIE
RANI PL
INGRID
TRADEWINDS PL
RIPPLE
NERIDA RD
MOONBI PL
ONDINE PL
BALANDRA
PASCHA PL
KURREWA PL
RIVAL
WESTWARD
MERCEDES PL
RAINBOW PL
SOLO ST
MORINA PL
THE PROMENADE
THE ESPLANADE
MORTY PL
BATES
CHRISTINA PL
FIRST AV E
EIGHTH
NINTH
BOX RD
SEVENOAKS
TUNBRIDGE PL
CARVERS
BUDERIM
BARANA PL
BULIMBA AV
BOONDAH
BANOOL
SELWA PL
FREYA
ANITRA
CADENCE CR
SOLVEIG
CHERANA PL
SURREY PL
ULLADULLA PL
KENDALL RD
BELLBIRD
DRYSDALE PL
EDWARD
ROCKLEA
THE
BOX RD
ALBERT AV
MACFARLANE PDE
HENRY AV
CRYSTAL ST
TARA ST
ESPLANADE
THORNTON PL
ROBVIC AV
KANGAROO POINT RD
YOUNG
BIRDWOOD
SYLVAN LA
SYLVAN
VENETIA
LISBON
HOLT
MELROSE
EASTON
SNOWDEN
TERRACE AV
HARLEY ST
TEDMAN PDE
NORTH ROAD
ALEXANDER ST
WEBBER
MURCHISON
COREA
FORMOSA
ESSINGTON
WARWICK
KELLY ST
OAKHAM
DURHAM PL
CHESTER
CRAIGHOLM
TOMAH
ADELAIDE PL
LEAVESDEN PL
ILMA AV
ALLAN ST
BOORROO ST
ANEMONE PL
ARGYLE PL
INVERNESS PL
BATH RD
BANDAIN
GARNET ST
BATES DR
KARNU ST
ALPITA
ALBANY
MANOOKA PL
TEA TREE
STIRLING
PEEBLES
PERTH
ETHELL RD
MEDIKA
MIKARIE
MEMMANG
CHAKOLA PL
MURONGA PL
KANNAN
GUNDAIN RD
MARSHALL
HOTHAM
BOULEVARDE
YALGAR RD
DUDLEY ST
OAK
MOKERA AV
RD N
THE BOULEVARDE
OPAL PL
RUBY
BATHURST ST
CAMPBELL ST
COX PL
REDFERN PL
MACQUARIE
WHALAN PL
GREENWAY
JINGARA PL
JEENGA PL
AMAROO
BYWONG PL
CALGA PL
KOBADA
SYLVANIA
VIOLET
JEAN AV
DOUGLAS
GRAHAM
JASON
DORIS
LORNA
ARGO PL
MACARTNEY
BELLINGARA
HUNTING
DALE
MEADOW PL
SEINE
PARIS
Bellingarra Netball Courts
Nur Home
THE KNOLL AV
NEWCASTLE
ARBOR HILL RD
MERCEDES
1

JOINS MAP 432
JOINS MAP 463
JOINS MAP 492
433
493
A B C D E F G H J K
1 2 3 4 5 6 7 8 9 10 11 12 13 14 15 16
BLAKEHURST
SANS SOUCI
SYLVANIA WATERS
TAREN POINT
CARINGBAH
MIRANDA
Kogarah Bay
RIVER
Shipwrights Bay
Gwawley Bay
Sylvania Bay
TOM UGLY'S BRIDGE
(GEORGES RIVER BRIDGE)
CAPTAIN COOK BRIDGE
PRINCES HIGHWAY
PORT HACKING ROAD
TAREN POINT ROAD
ROCKY POINT RD
Kyle Williams Rec Res
Bald Face Pmy
Bald Face Pt Res
Bald Face Pt
Carss Bush Pk
Carss Pt
Tidal Baths
Church St Native Flora Res
Dover Pk
Kogarah Bay Sailing Club
Shipwrights Bay Res
Marina
Tom Ugly's Pt
Horse Rock Pt
Tom Uglys Bridge Marina
Shag Pt
Sylvania Pmy
Southgate
Tenpin Bowl
Canberra Rd Oval
Sandy Pt
Botany Bay Yacht Club
Len Reynolds Res
St Kilda Pt
St George Motor Boat Club
Water Police Wharf
Olympic Pool
Sans Souci Pk
Bass & Flinders Cruises
Wharf
Rocky Pt
Taren Pt
Taren Point Res
Hawkesbury Res
Sylvania High
Frank Vickery Village
Gwawley Ck
Youth Cntr
Gwawley Oval
Flower Power
Pound
Athletics
Southern Districts Rugby Club
Forshaw Field
Tennis
Doltone House
Tabor Coll
Sydney Water
Captain Cook Golf Course
Harts
Rittal
Cronulla Carpets
CITY
OBERON ST
TARO ST
MT VERNON ST
HATFIELD PDE
STUART ST
READ ST
CENTRE ST
PLEASANT WY
THE KNOLL
COMO ST
PACIFIC ST
SUNNYSIDE PL
RIVER ST
COOGARAH ST
TOWNSON ST
EAST ST
CHURCH ST
MARIE DODD CR
RALEIGH ST
TOTTENHAM PL
TORRENS ST
BEACH ST
BLAKE AV
GOLD ST
STUART CR
STUART RAY ST
CASTLE ST
FLETCHER AV
WOODLANDS AV
ENDEAVOUR ST
BOULEVARDE
THE PROMENADE
ENDEAVOUR LA
VISTA ST
NELSON ST
PLIMSOLL ST
WELLINGTON ST
HARRIS ST
WATER ST
LAWSON ST
MERIEL ST
DOON DR
HARROW RD
KOOROOMA PL
CLARE ST
MOWBRAY ST
MURRALIN LA
MADEIRA ST
BELGRAVE ST
MARRA PL
ELLIS ST
EVELYN ST N
ENDEAVOUR RD
VERAN ST
CAPITAL PL
FLORIDA ST
PEMBROKE ST
CANBERRA RD
FORMOSA ST
JUNIPER PL
HOLTS POINT PL
LACHLAN AV
CULGOA PL
BARWON PL
BOGAN PL
NEPEAN ESP
DARLING PL
NAMOI PL
MURRAY ISLAND
DALMAN PL
EVELYN AV
RICHMOND AV
SNOWY PL
HASTINGS ST
TWEED PL
BELGRAVE ESP
CASTLEREAGH CR
MACLEAY PL
SHOALHAVEN RD
CLARENCE CR
TUMUT PL
JAMES COOK ISLAND
BURNETT PL
WARREGO AV
MACINTYRE CR
NYMBOIDA CR
HAMPTON RD
FITZROY PL
GOULBURN PL
PENINSULA
BELGRAVE ESP
ROPER RD
ORD CR
CORDEAUX CR
BELLINGER PL
PAROO AV
WOLLONDILLY PL
HAWKESBURY ESP
MURRUMBIDGEE AV
PEEL PL
BARCOO ISLAND
TUROSS AV
MORUYA AV
HOLT AV
CURTIS AV
HOLT RD
APSLEY PL
FREDERICK RD
OLD TAREN POINT ROAD
WOODLANDS AV
SMITH ST
TOORAK AV
ALEXANDER
PRODUCTION RD
BAY RD
BOX RD
ERSKINE RD
PARRAWEENA RD
KOONYA CCT
WILLARONG RD
CRAMMOND BVD
WOODFIELD BVD
CAWARRA RD
SHIRLEY RD
GWAWLEY PDE
NYNGAN PL
TEAK PL
KAREENA RD N
EDWARD AV
RENOWN AV
INGARA AV
WINSTON PL
HOLT
BEDFORD
TAIWAN
ROMA PL
LEICHHARDT
GILBERT ST
WITHYBROOK PL
WILLOWBROOK PL
BARJADDA AV
JASMINE
CLASSEN ST
MACARTHUR AV
CAMDEN ST
ONSLOW PL
MERINO PL
BELLINGARA RD
WORDSWORTH AV
TENNYSON PL
RAMU CL
QUEANBEYAN AV
QUIBEREE ST
KIAMA ST
SILVERWATER CR
WINGELLO RD
MONOMEETH
HEIGHTS RD

MAP 463

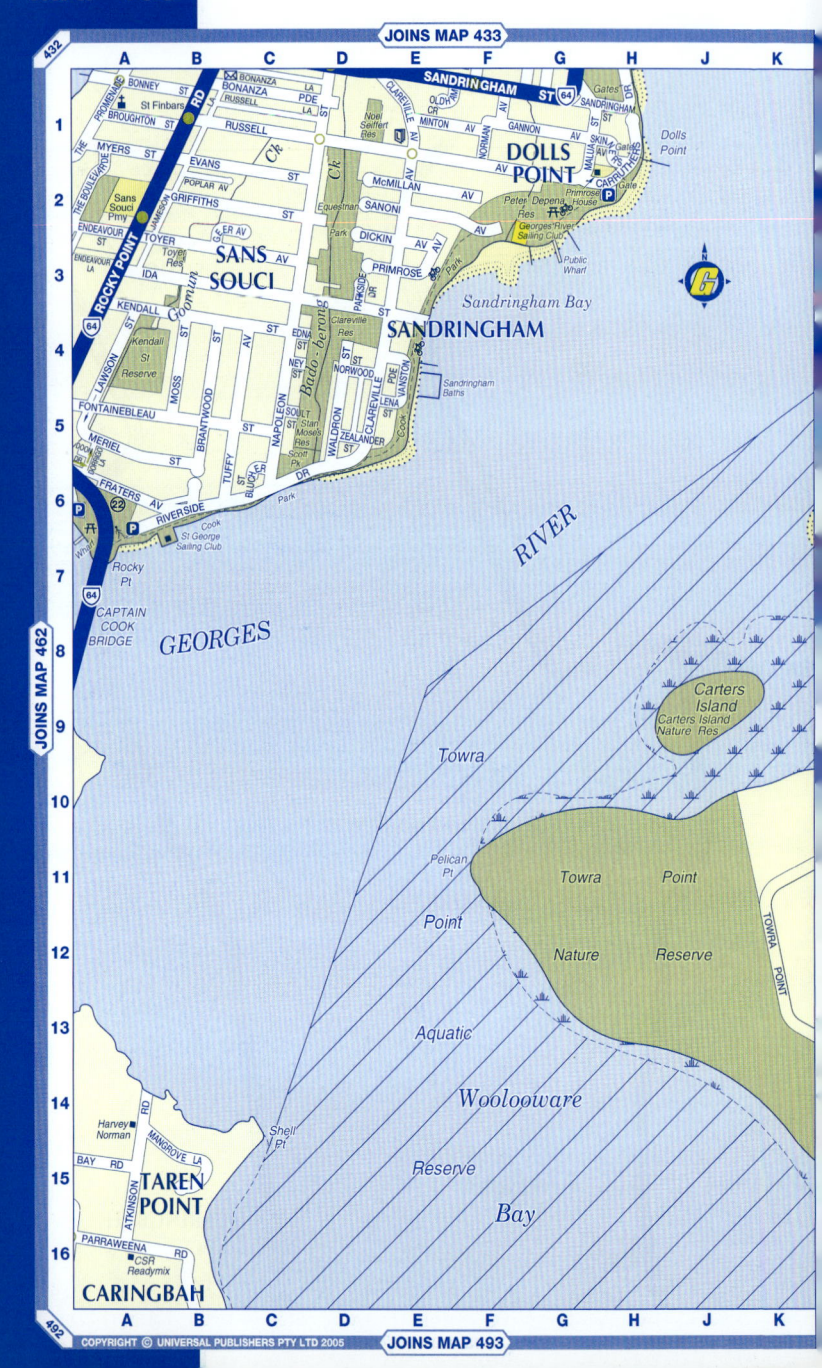

MAP 464

BOTANY BAY

- Towra
- Towra Pt
- Towra Point Aquatic Reserve
- Elephants Trunk
- Towra Spit
- Beach
- Towra Beach
- Towra Point Nature Reserve
- Weeney Bay
- Quibray Bay
- KURNELL
- Ent Landfill
- Towra Point Nature Reserve Drive
- Charlotte Breen Memorial Park
- Civil Aviation Authority Beacon
- Connell Hill
- ROAD
- COOK
- CAPTAIN
- WARSOP ST
- Ent P
- RULEY RD

JOINS MAP 434
JOINS MAP 494
JOINS MAP 465
COPYRIGHT © UNIVERSAL PUBLISHERS PTY LTD 2005

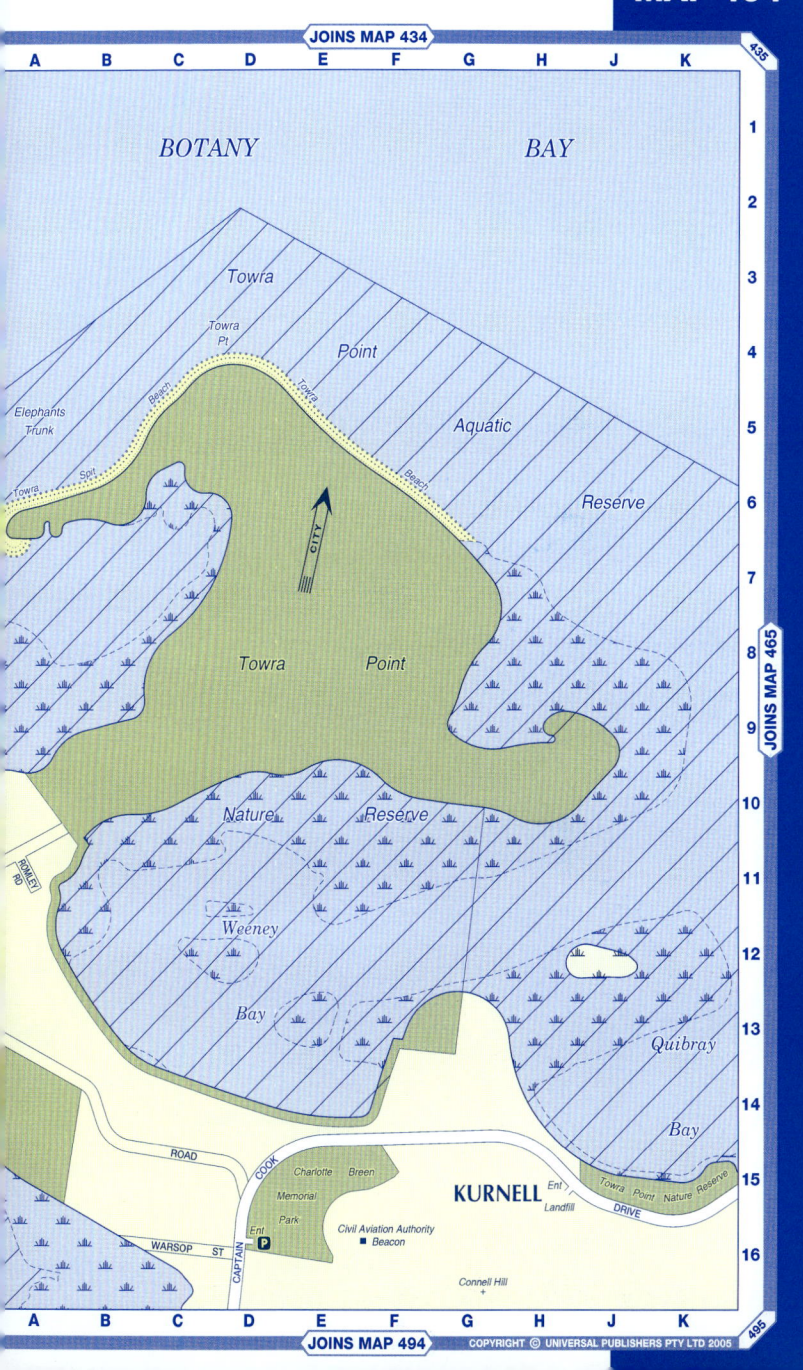

MAP 465

BOTANY

CITY

- Silver
- Swim Enclosure
- Groynes
- Tidal Baths
- Bonna Pt
- Bonna Point Reserve
- Sutherland Shire Sailing Club & Coast Guard
- Kurnell Catamaran Club
- Silver Beach Resort
- PRINCE CHARLES
- WARD ST
- BALBOA ST
- Kurnell Pmy
- KURNELL
- TORRES ST
- BRIDGES
- DAMPER ST
- Tower
- TASMAN ST
- HORNING ST
- Cmnty Sports & Rec Club
- Towra Point Aquatic Reserve
- Quibray Bay
- Kurnell Substn
- Substn
- CAPTAIN
- Serenity Cove Studios
- Abbott Laboratories
- Gate
- Kurnell Boarding Stables
- Ent
- Serenity Cove Corporate Park
- Ent
- Boat Harbour 4WD Park (Private)
- DRIVE
- Ent
- SIR JOSEPH BANKS
- Boral
- Towra Point Nature Res
- CAPTAIN COOK RD
- Ent Gate 1
- Ent Gate 3
- Rocla
- LINDUM
- Kurnell Peninsula
- Holt Land Rehabilitation For Future Resort
- Recreation Reserve

JOINS MAP 435 (top)
JOINS MAP 464 (left)
JOINS MAP 495 (bottom)
434 / 494

COPYRIGHT © UNIVERSAL PUBLISHERS PTY LTD 2005

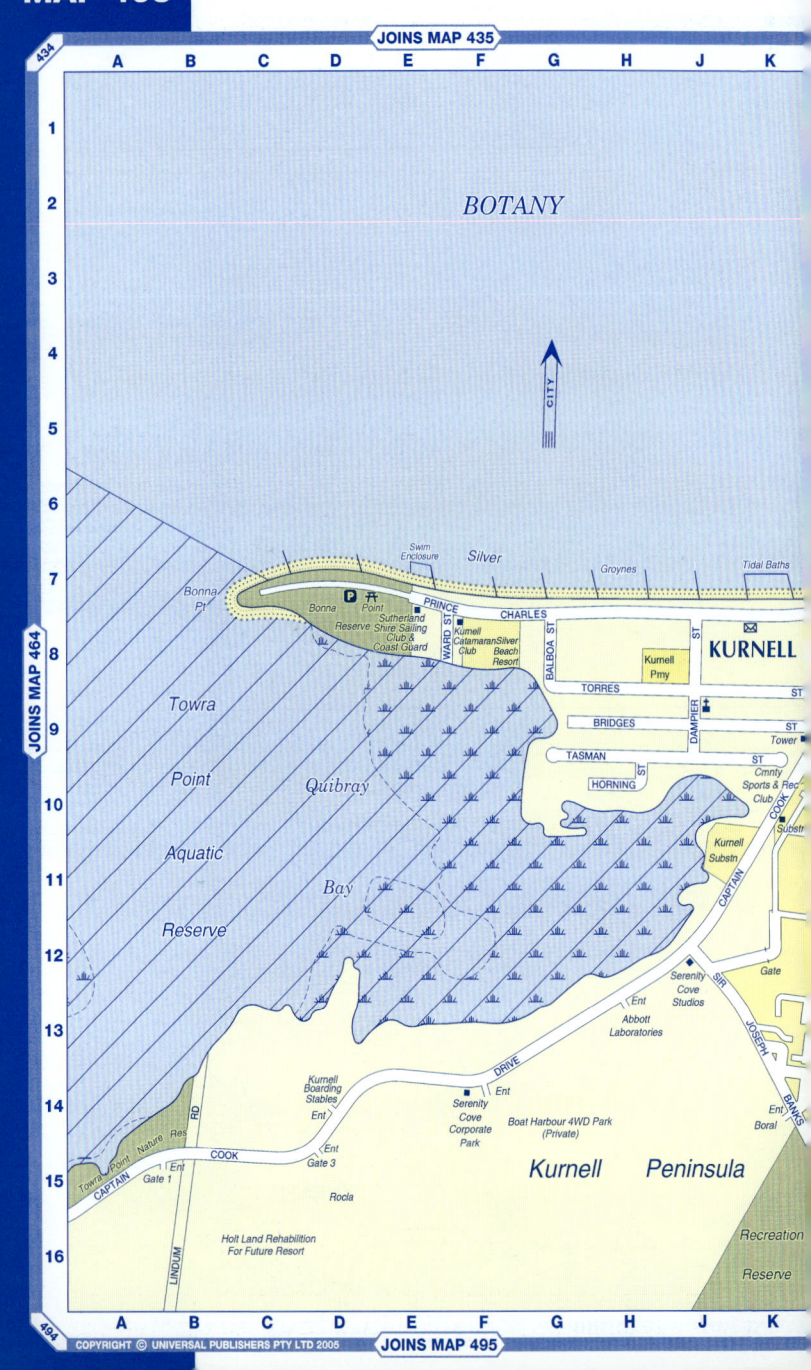

MAP 466
MAP 473 FOLLOWS

JOINS MAP 436

Bare Island

BAY

Caltex Oil Refinery Wharf

Inscription Pt
Sutherland Pt
Captain Cooks Landing Place
Solander Monument
Point Solander
Commemoration Flat Picnic Area
Sir Joseph Banks Memorial
The Discovery Centre
Cook Obelisk
Vice Regal Gate
Houston
Skeleton Cave
Groynes
Beach
Muru Fire Trail

TASMAN

PARADE
Toll Gate
Botany Bay National Park Information: Phone (02) 9668 9111
Kurnell
Botany
Bay
(The Meeting Place of Cultures)
Yena Picnic Area
Rescue Flotation Device

Marton Hall
Marton Park
RFS
SHEPHERD ST
SILVER RD
COOK ST
SOLANDER
ROAD J
Main Gate
ROAD L
ROAD 7
ROAD A
ROAD D
ROAD E
ROAD G
POLO ST
SHARK
RESERVE RD
CAPTAIN COOK DRIVE
GANNON ST

Yena Gap

Reservoir

Cape Solander

National

Caltex Oil Refinery
ROAD M
ROAD 6
ROAD N
ROAD 4
ROAD 3
ROAD 2
ROAD 1
ROAD N
ROAD Q

Civil Aviation Authority Beacon

Park

SEA

Heights

ROAD U
ROAD V
ROAD 17
ROAD 16
ROAD W

Bally Track

Tabbigai Gap

Endeavour

Cape

DRIVE

JOINS MAP 496
COPYRIGHT © UNIVERSAL PUBLISHERS PTY LTD 2005

JOINS MAP 443

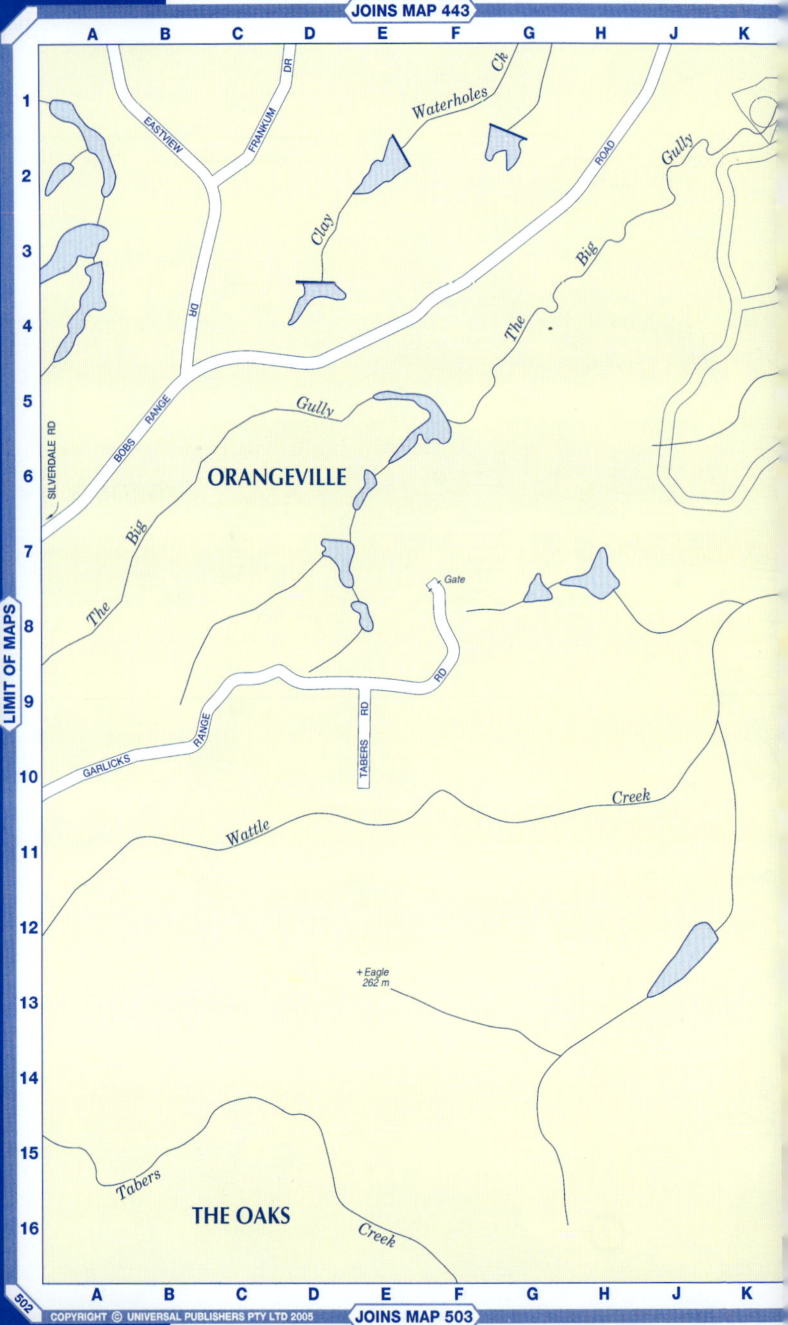

JOINS MAP 503

MAP 474

JOINS MAP 444

- John McDonald Wy
- Gate NECTARBROOK DR (Private Road)
- Private
- Creek
- + Brownlow Hill 134m
- Wattle
- **BROWNLOW HILL**
- CITY →
- Creek
- Flaggy Hill 186m +
- Flaggy
- **MT HUNTER**
- MONKS LA

JOINS MAP 475

JOINS MAP 504

COPYRIGHT © UNIVERSAL PUBLISHERS PTY LTD 2005

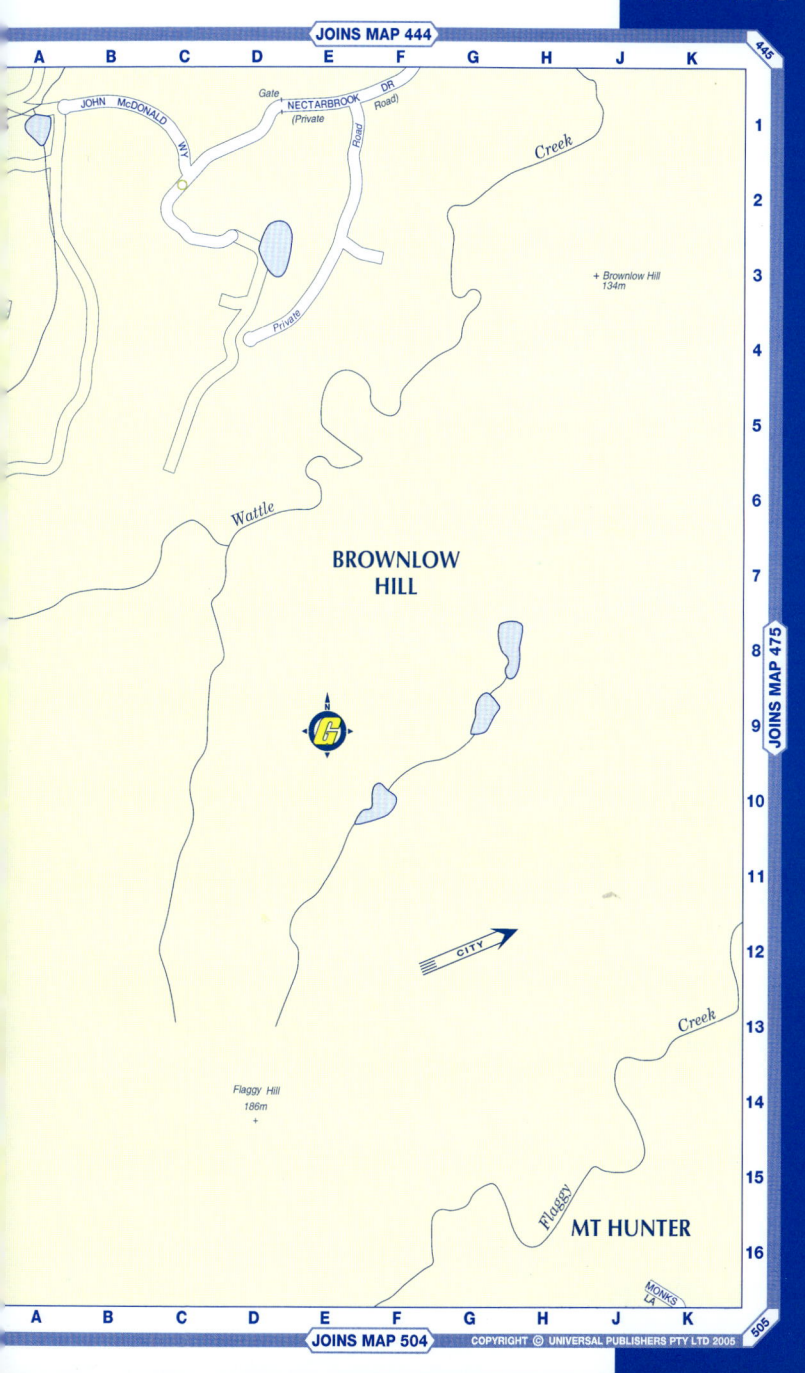

MAP 475

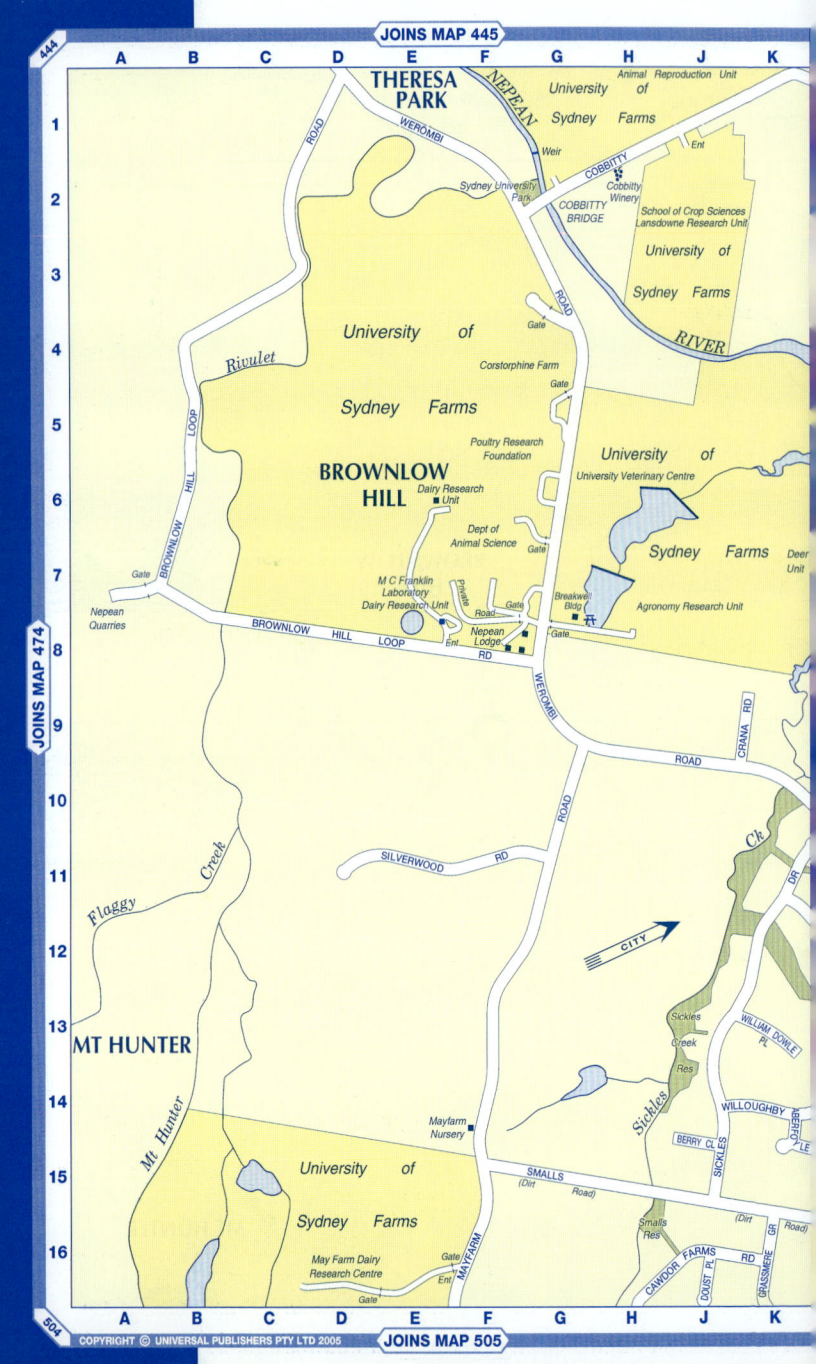

JOINS MAP 446

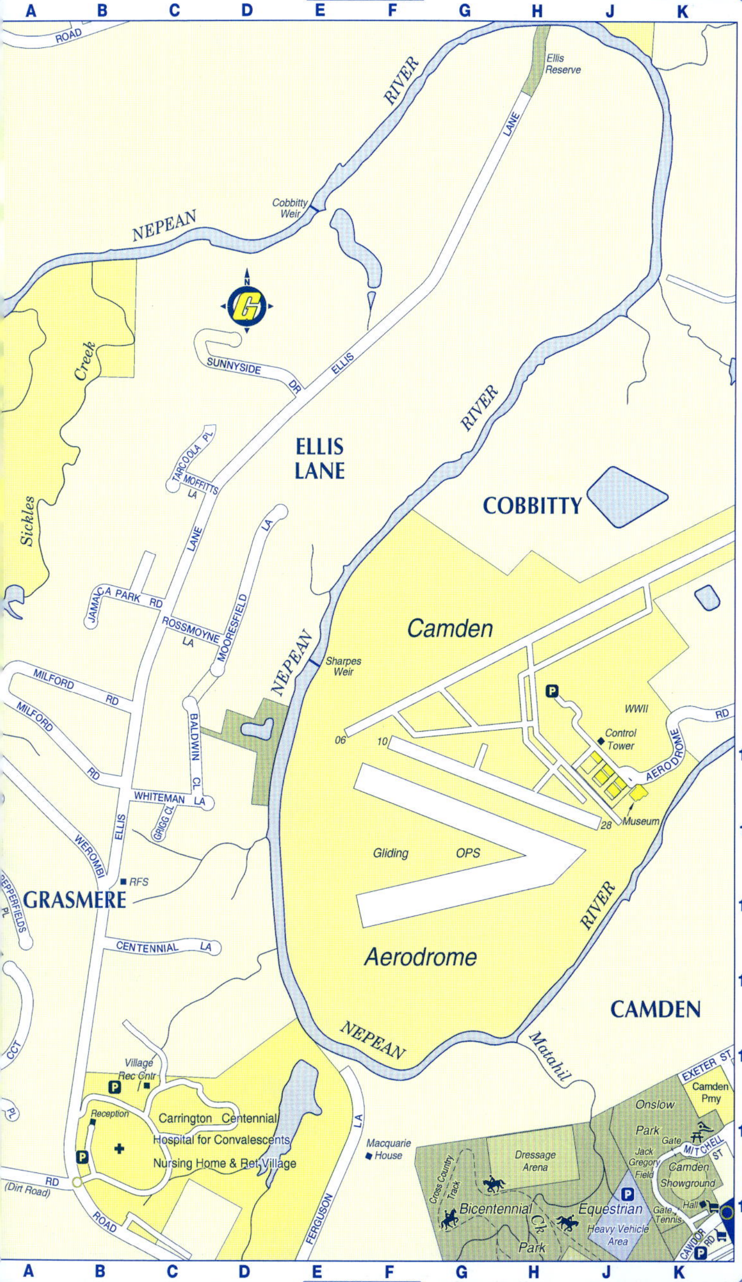

447
JOINS MAP 477
JOINS MAP 506
507

MAP 477

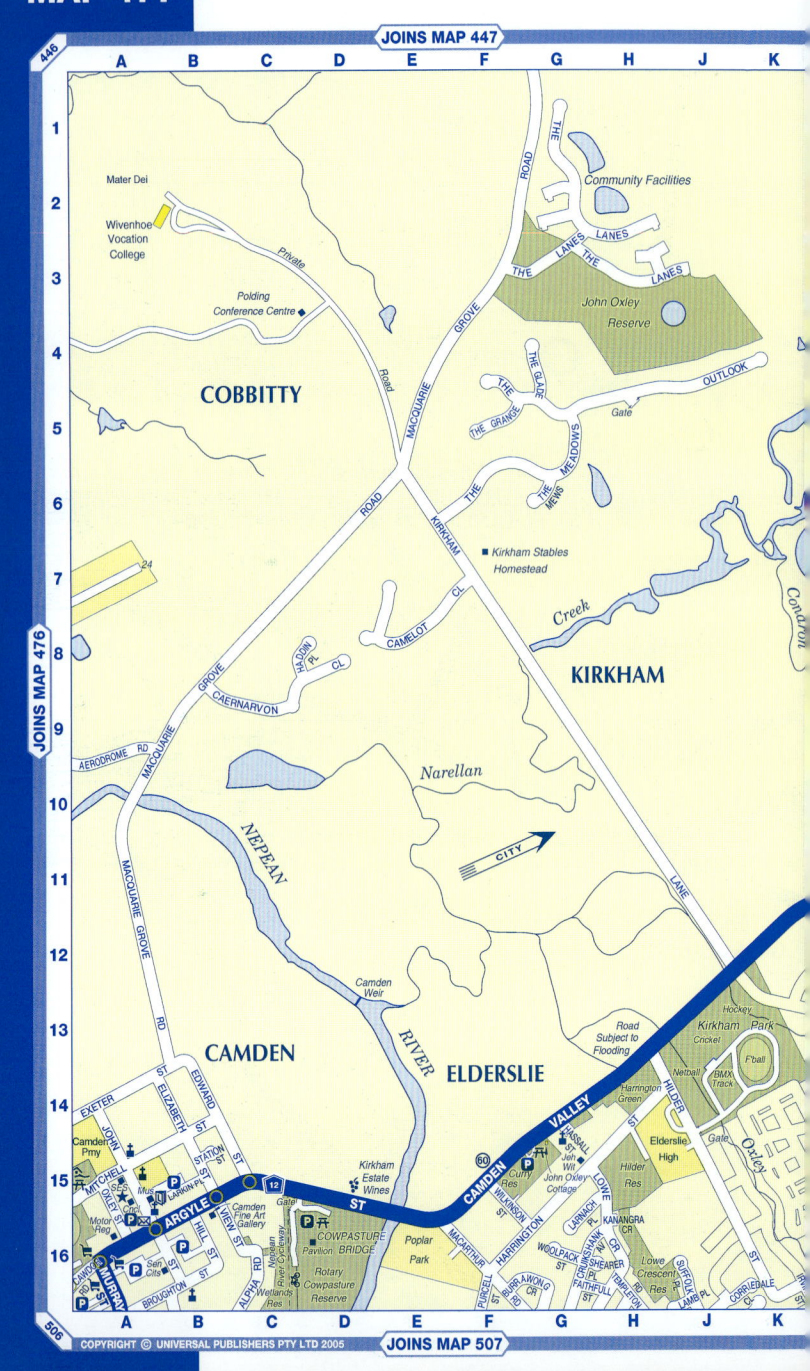

JOINS MAP 448

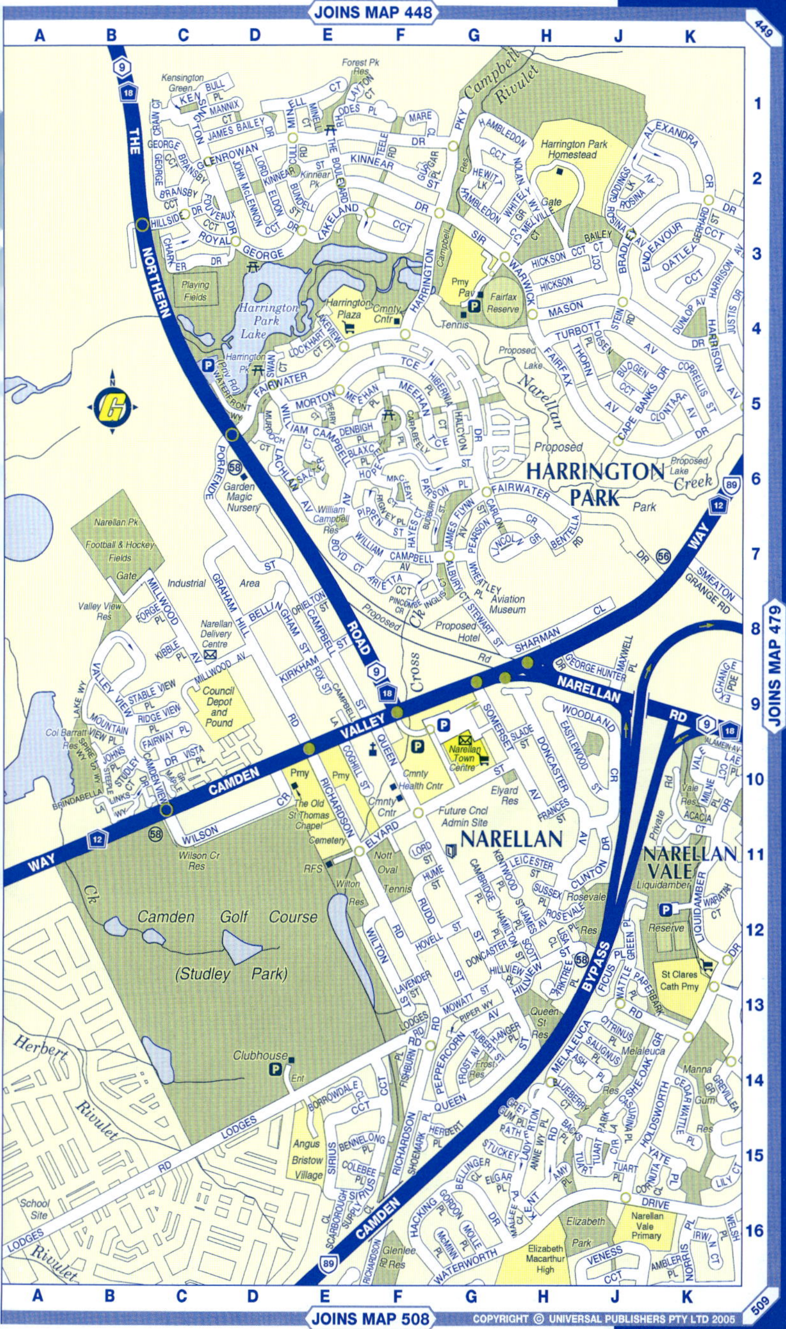

JOINS MAP 479

JOINS MAP 508

MAP 479

MAP 480

KEARNS

ESCHOL PARK

EAGLE VALE

BLAIRMOUNT

St Gregorys College
Mount Universe (Private)
Mount Annan Christian College
Mount Annan Village
Biriwiri Ck
Tunnel Channel
Badgally Water Supply
Smeeton Res

Streets/labels: COLORADO ST, TIGRIS ST, SEVERN PL, YAMBER PL, RIO GRANDE DR, YANGTZE PL, CHASSELAS AV, FRONTIGNAN ST, HARCOURT PL, ASHTON CL, BLEAREY CL, EAGLE VALE DR, FEES PL, YOUNG PL, DOBELL PL, GRIFFITHS, NEW PL, BADGALLY RD, CLYDESDALE DR, BOURKE, BARR PL, FRECHEM PL, MARYFIELD DR, ST STEPHEN PL, MONKS, CALABRESE ST, HUME HWY, KENNY HILL RD, CHURCH RD, HARRIER PL, STEAMER DR, HORSEMAN, QUARTERS PL, WOOLS PL, COMBINGS PL, CLASSERS PL, MANOKA CL, SADDLE CL, HILLTOP RD, SYDNEY, Annan 18, Gilinganadum Dam, Garden, SGA Office, Pmy, Res, Private Rd, Gate

JOINS MAP 450 (top)
JOINS MAP 510 (bottom)
JOINS MAP 451 (top right)
JOINS MAP 481 (right)
JOINS MAP 511 (bottom right)

COPYRIGHT © UNIVERSAL PUBLISHERS PTY LTD 2005

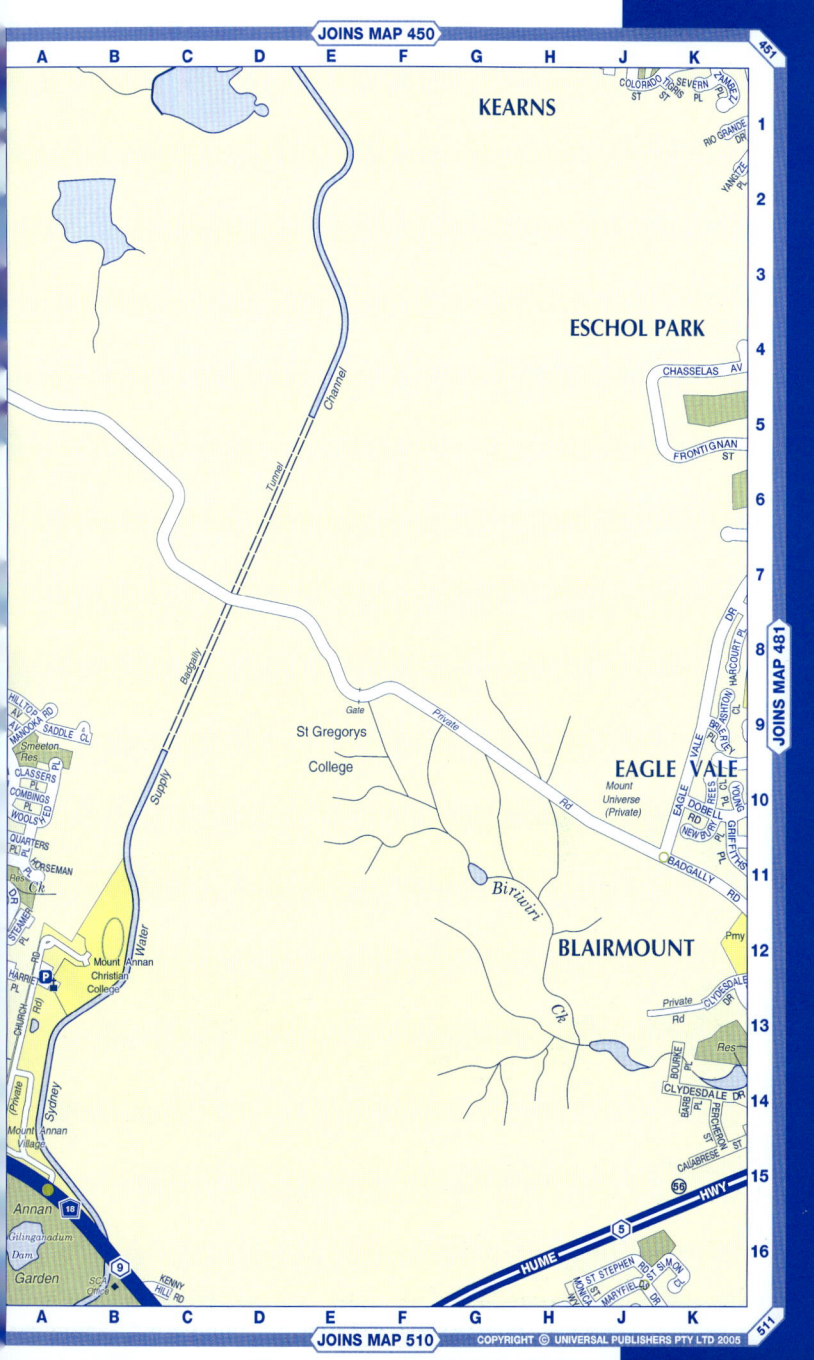

MAP 481

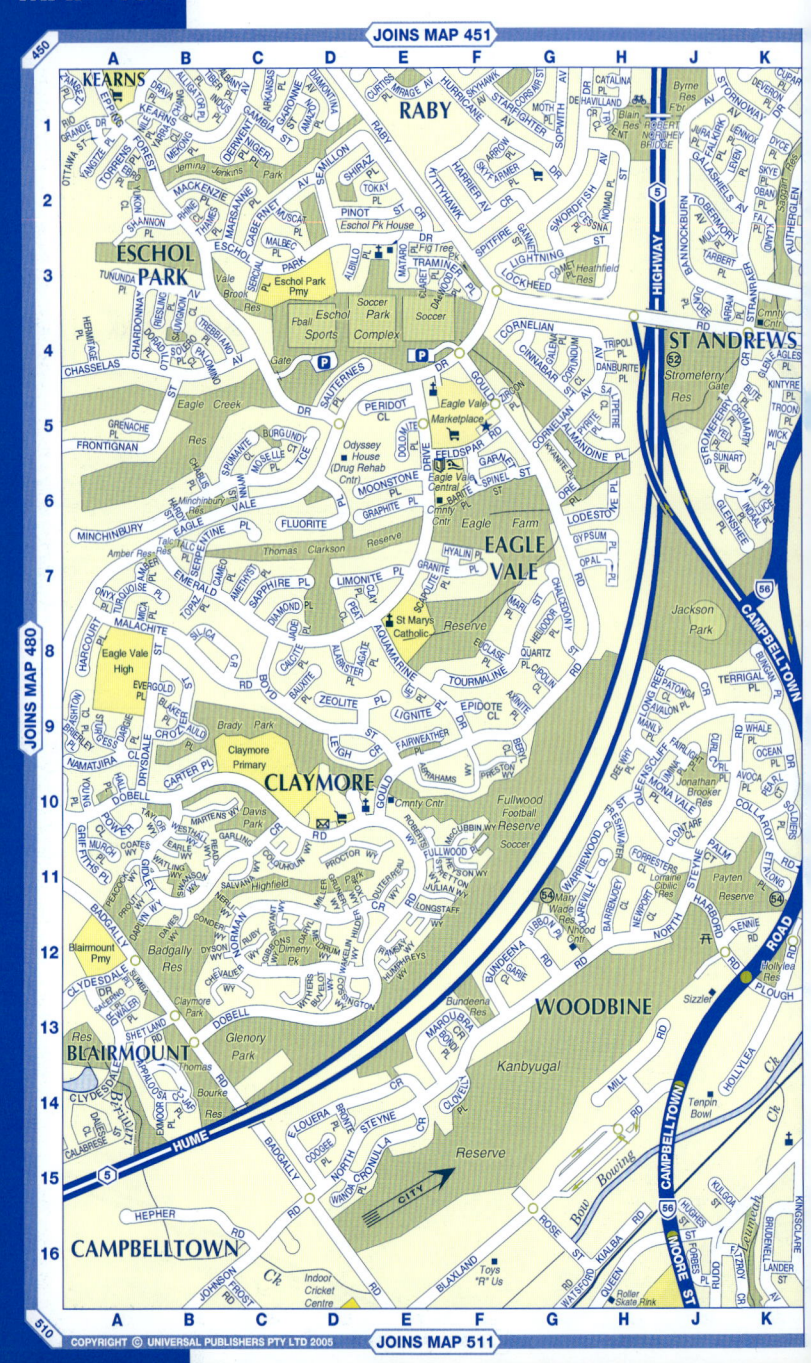

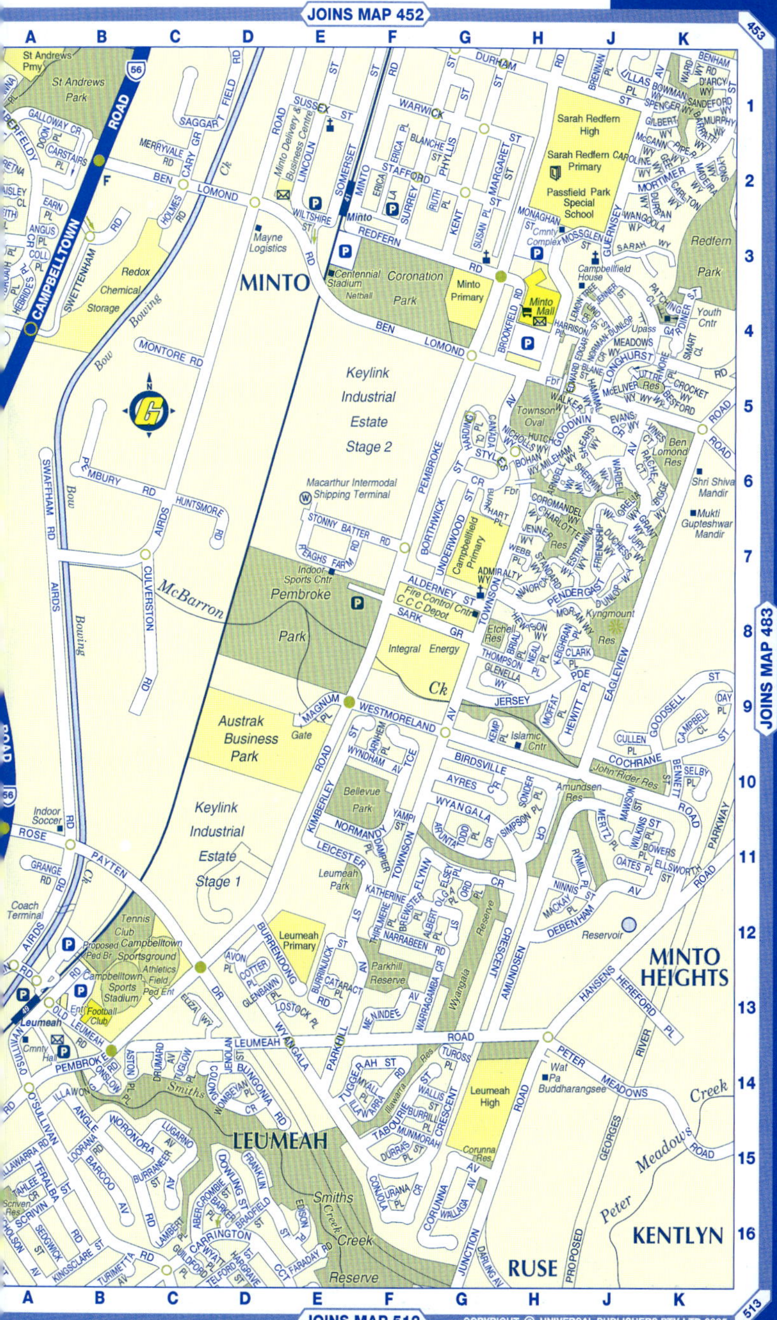
JOINS MAP 452
JOINS MAP 483
JOINS MAP 512
453
513
A B C D E F G H J K
1 2 3 4 5 6 7 8 9 10 11 12 13 14 15 16
MINTO
MINTO HEIGHTS
LEUMEAH
KENTLYN
RUSE
St Andrews Pmy
St Andrews Park
CAMPBELLTOWN ROAD
Sarah Redfern High
Sarah Redfern Primary
Passfield Park Special School
Redfern Park
Youth Cntr
Minto
Minto Delivery & Business Centre
Mayne Logistics
Redox Chemical Storage
Centennial Stadium
Netball
Coronation Park
Minto Primary
Minto Mall
Cmnty Complex
Campbellfield House
Keylink Industrial Estate Stage 2
Macarthur Intermodal Shipping Terminal
Townson Oval
Ben Lomond Res
Shri Shiva Mandir
Mukti Gupteshwar Mandir
Campbellfield Primary
Indoor Sports Cntr
Pembroke Park
Fire Control Cntr
C C C Depot
Integral Energy
Etchell Res
Kyngmount Res
Austrak Business Park
Gate
Islamic Cntr
John Rider Res
Amundsen Res
Bellevue Park
Keylink Industrial Estate Stage 1
Leumeah Park
Leumeah Primary
Parkhill Reserve
Reservoir
Indoor Soccer
Coach Terminal
Tennis Club
Proposed Ped Br
Campbelltown Sportsground
Athletics Field
Campbelltown Sports Stadium
Ped Ent
Football Club
Leumeah
Cmnty Hall
Wat Pa Buddharangsee
Leumeah High
Corunna Res
Smiths Creek Reserve
Scriven Res
McBarron Ck
Bow Bowing Ck
Peter Meadows Creek
BEN LOMOND RD
PEMBROKE RD
WESTMORELAND RD
LEUMEAH ROAD
PAYTEN AV
O'SULLIVAN RD
PETER MEADOWS ROAD
GEORGES RIVER RD
AMUNDSEN CRESCENT
TOWNSON AV
SWAFFHAM RD
AIRDS RD
CULVERSTON RD
DURHAM ST
WARWICK ST
REDFERN RD
EAGLEVIEW RD
COCHRANE ST
BIRDSVILLE ST
WYANGALA CR
JUNCTION RD
PROPOSED

MAP 483

MAP 484

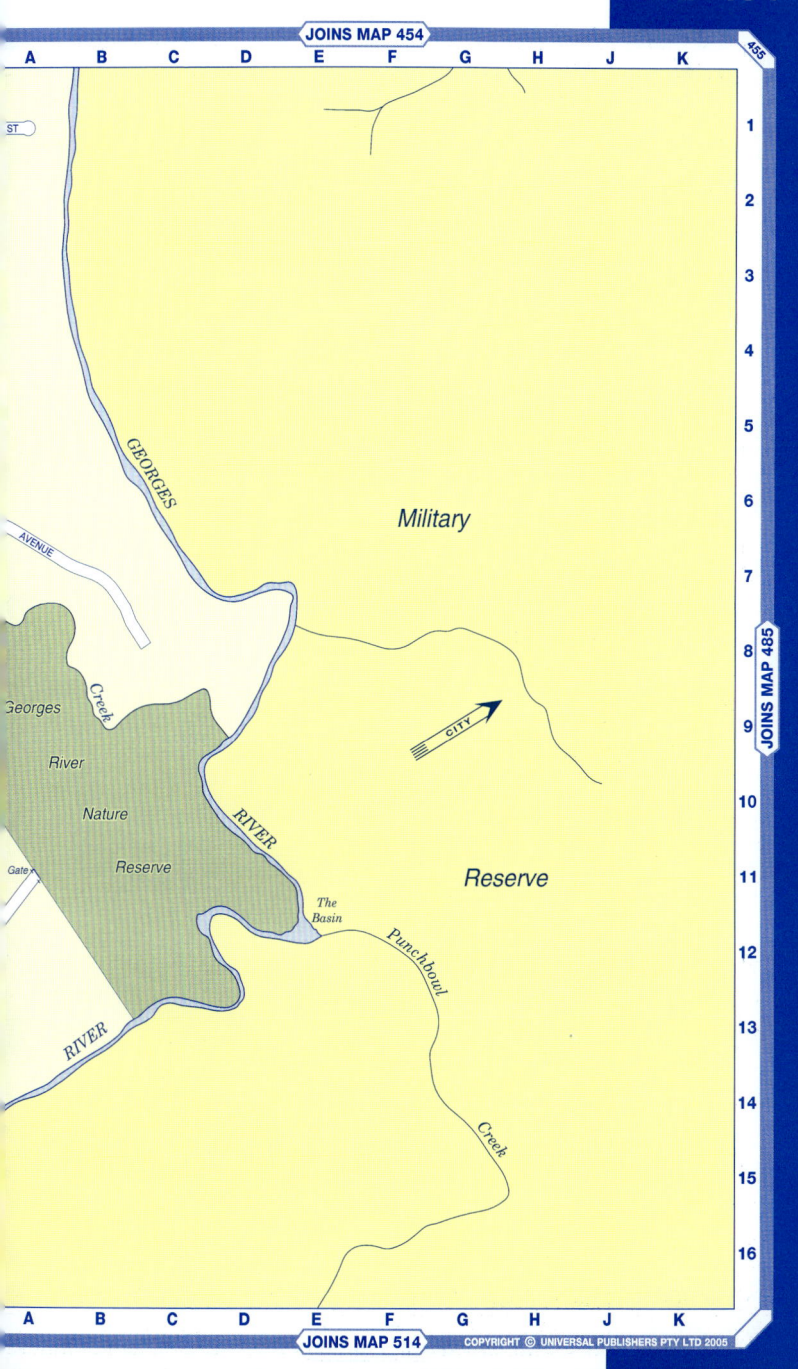

JOINS MAP 454

ST

GEORGES

AVENUE

Georges
Creek
River
Nature
Reserve
Gate
RIVER

RIVER

The Basin

Military

CITY

Reserve

Punchbowl
Creek

JOINS MAP 514

MAP 485

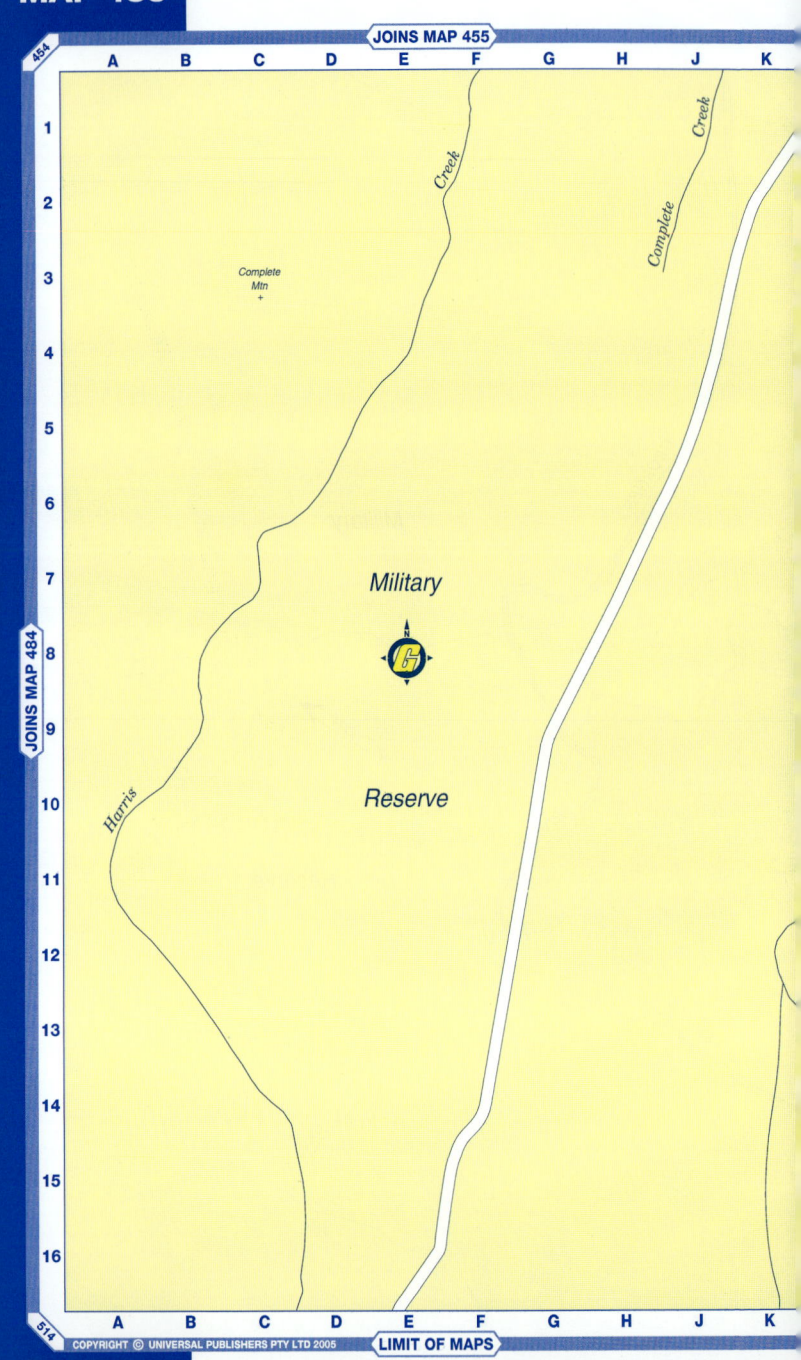

Complete Mtn

Complete Creek

Complete Creek

Military Reserve

Harris

MAP 486

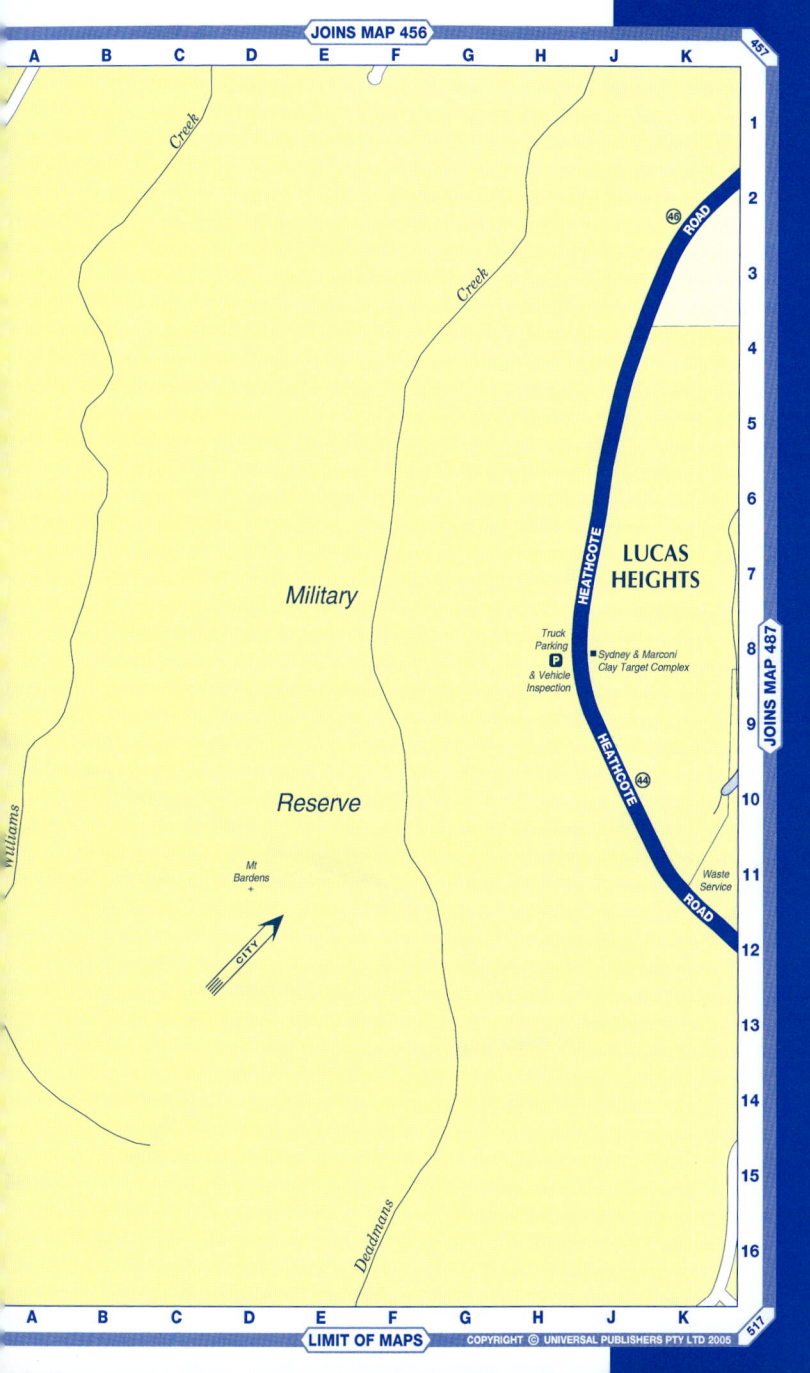

JOINS MAP 456

JOINS MAP 487

Creek

Creek

Williams

Deadmans

Military

Reserve

Mt Bardens

CITY

Truck Parking & Vehicle Inspection

Sydney & Marconi Clay Target Complex

LUCAS HEIGHTS

HEATHCOTE ROAD

Waste Service

LIMIT OF MAPS

MAP 487

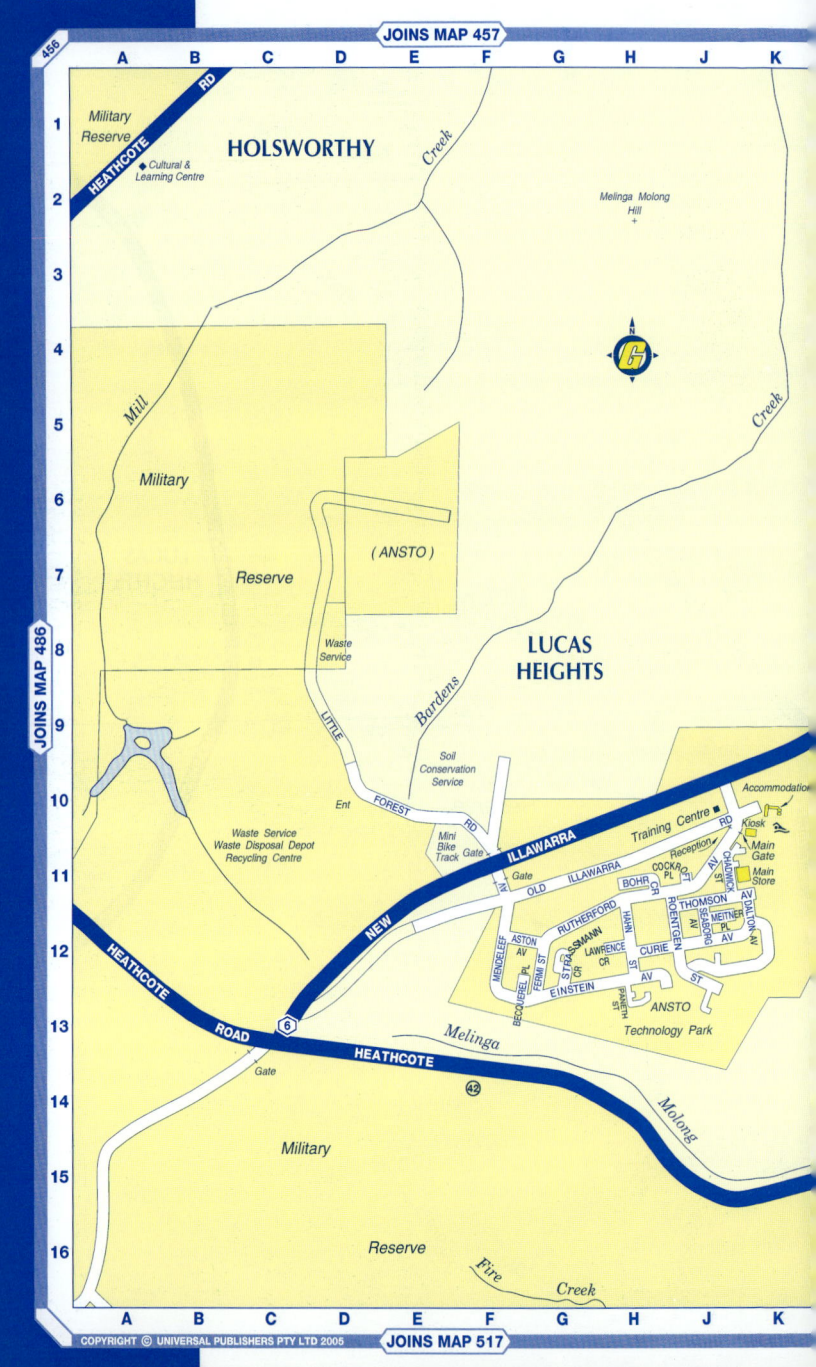

MAP 488

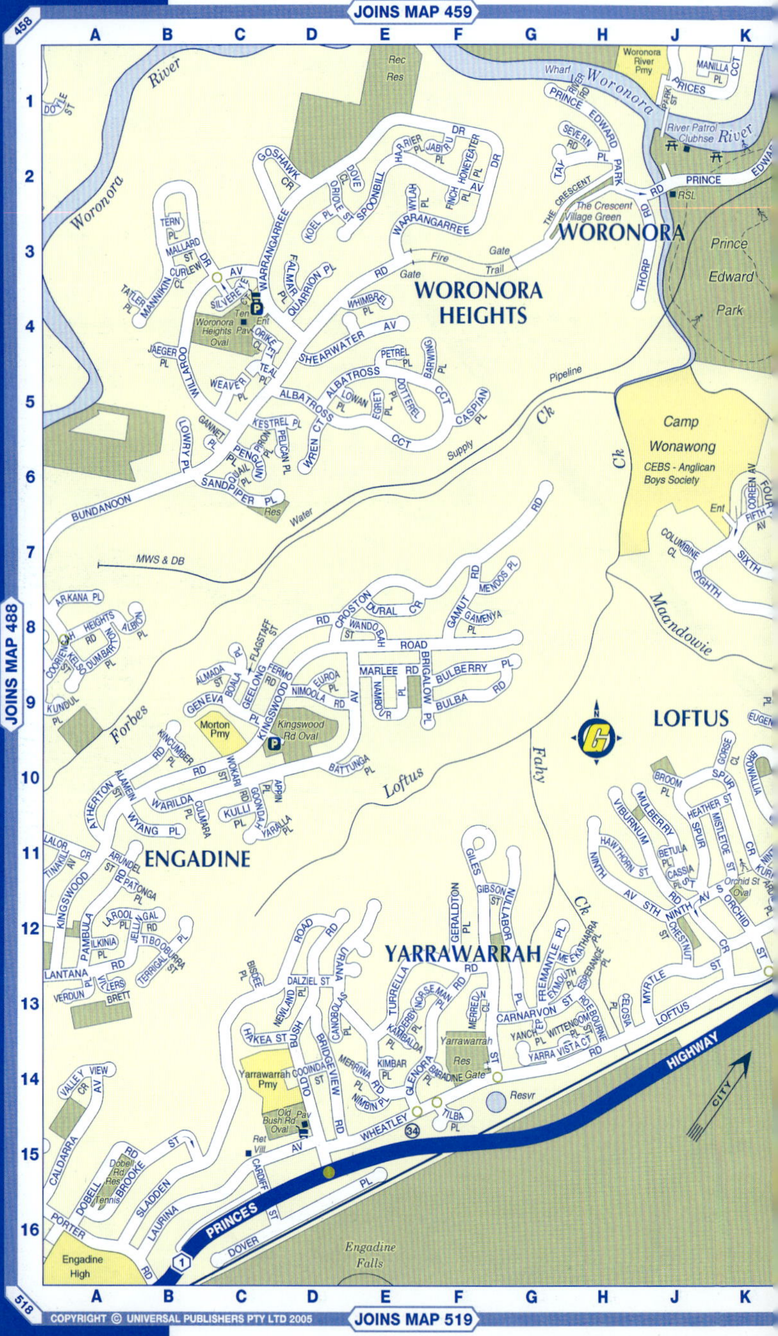
JOINS MAP 459
JOINS MAP 488
JOINS MAP 519
458
518
A B C D E F G H J K
1 2 3 4 5 6 7 8 9 10 11 12 13 14 15 16
WORONORA HEIGHTS
WORONORA
ENGADINE
YARRAWARRAH
LOFTUS
Woronora River
Prince Edward Park
Camp Wonawong
CEBS - Anglican Boys Society
The Crescent Village Green
River Patrol Clubhse
Woronora River Pmy
Woronora Heights Oval
Morton Pmy
Kingswood Rd Oval
Yarrawarrah Pmy
Old Bush Rd Oval
Yarrawarrah Res
Dobell Rd Res
Engadine High
Engadine Falls
Orchid St Oval
Rec Res
Forbes
Loftus Ck
Fahy Ck
Maandowie
Supply Water Ck
Pipeline
MWS & DB
Fire Trail
PRINCES HIGHWAY
CITY
BUNDANOON RD
WARRANGAREE DR
PRINCE EDWARD PARK RD
KINGSWOOD RD
LOFTUS AV
WHEATLEY RD
ENGADINE AV
CARNARVON ST
ALBATROSS CCT
SHEARWATER AV
HEIGHTS RD
ROAD
DUMBARTON PL
CROSTON RD
DURAL CR
BRIGALOW PL
BULBERRY PL
BULBA RD
CALDARRA AV
PORTER RD
SLADDEN ST
DOVER PL
CARDIFF ST

JOINS MAP 460

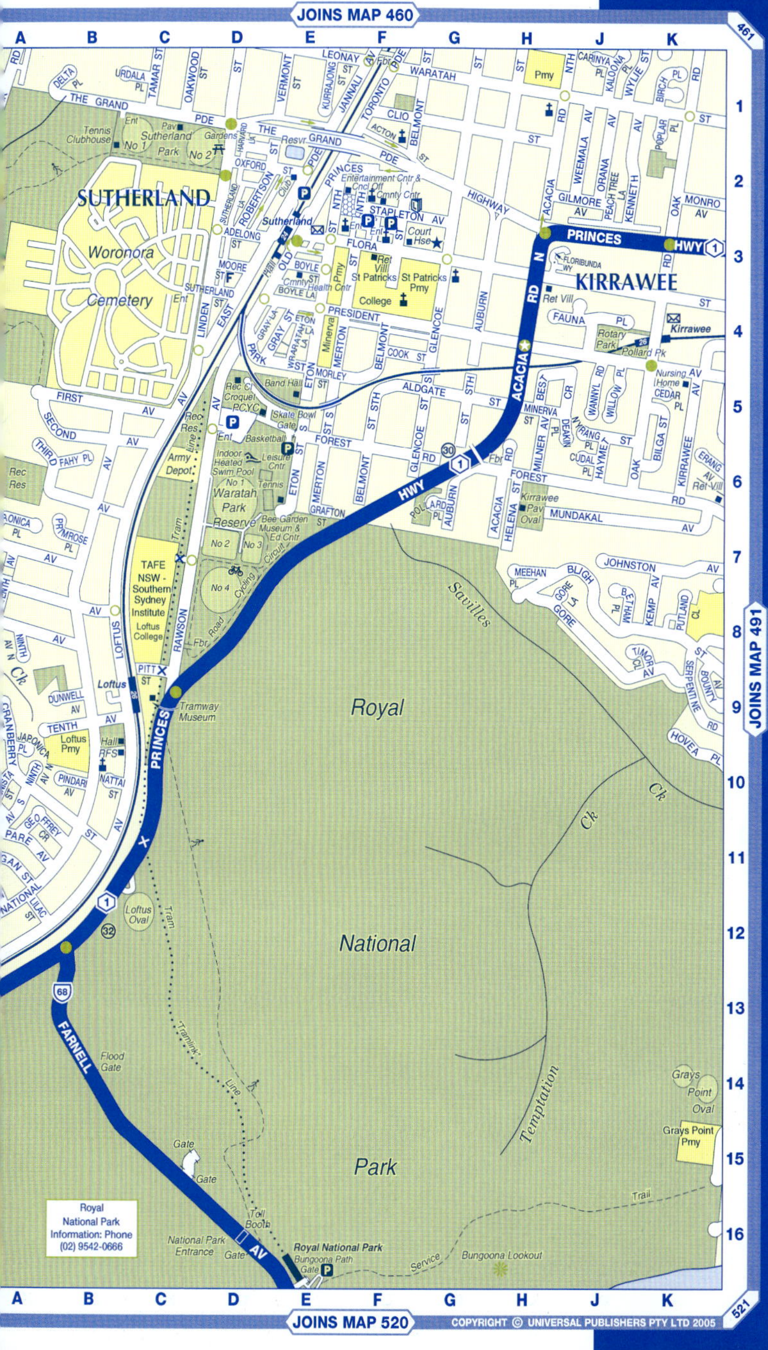

JOINS MAP 491

JOINS MAP 520

521

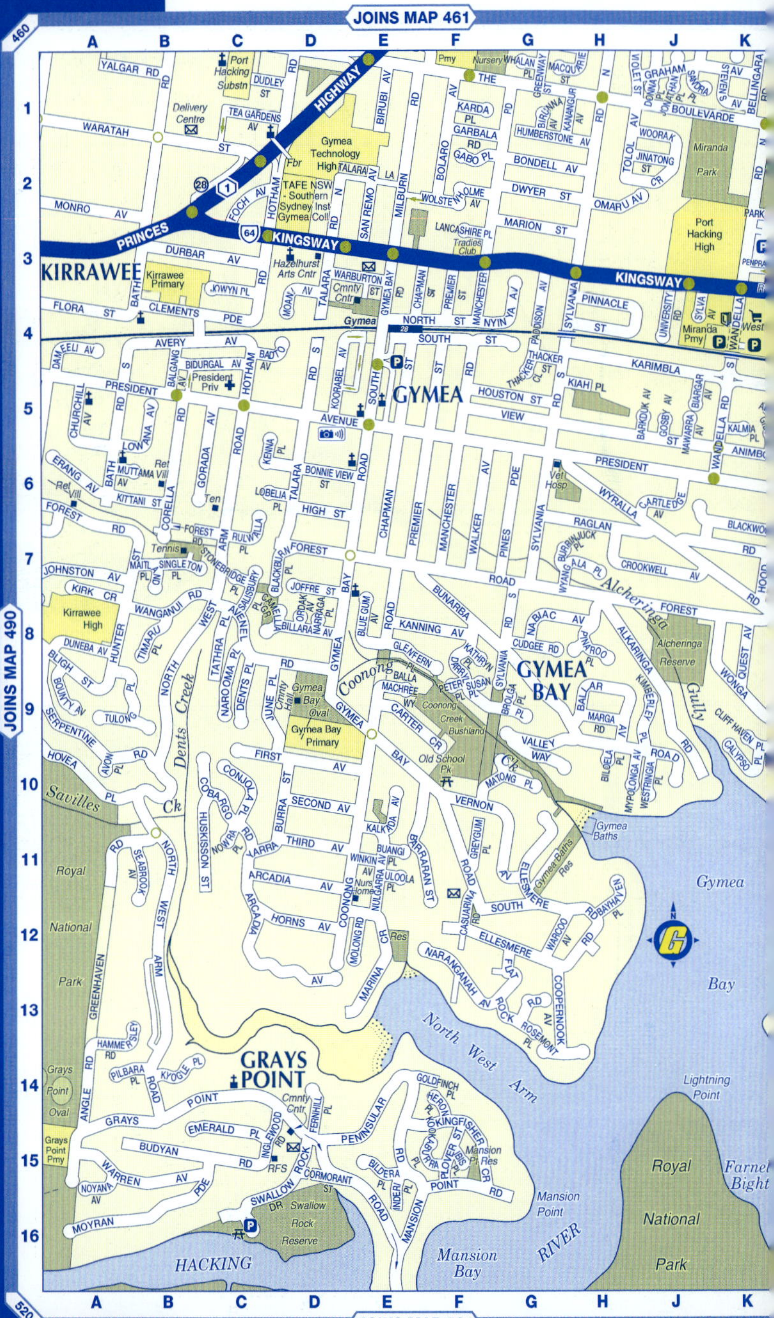

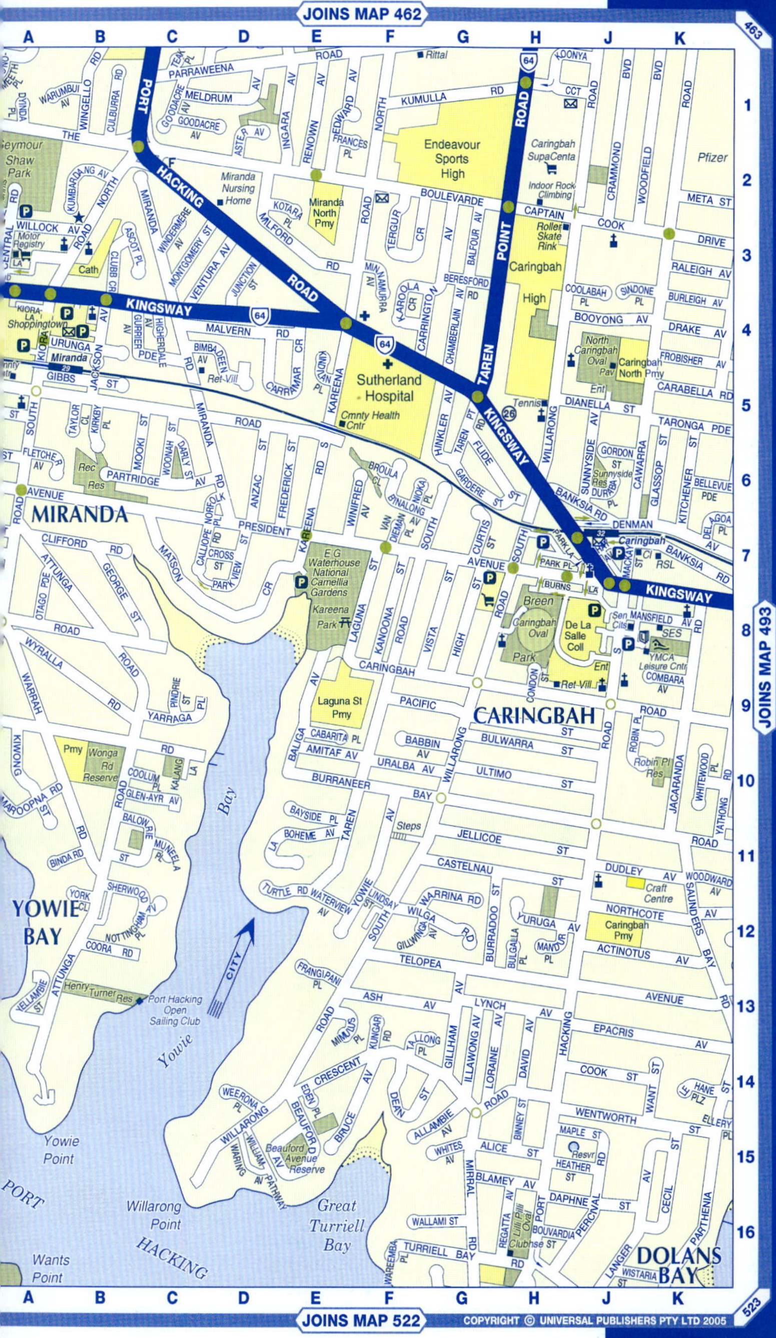

MAP 493

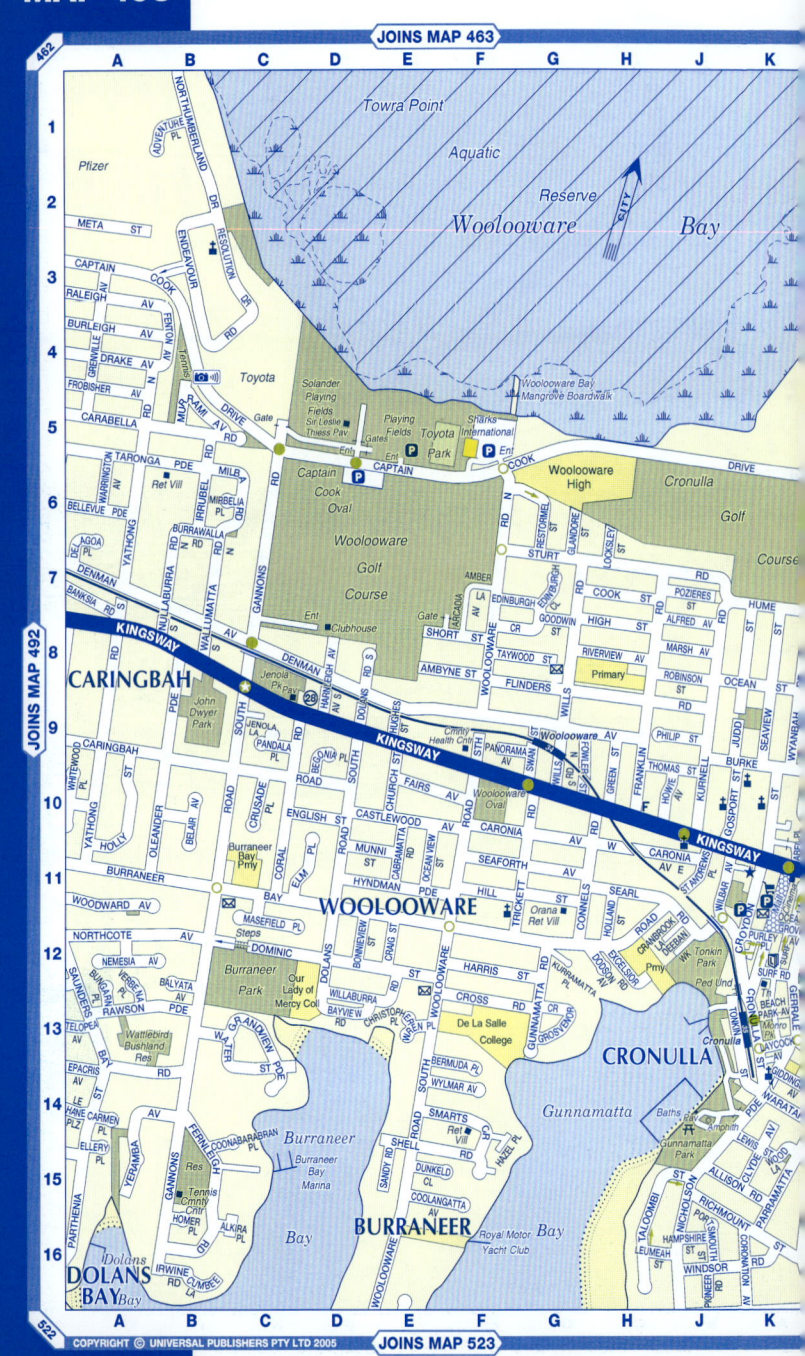

MAP 494

KURNELL

Connell Hill

Sewage Treatment Works

Gate

Cronulla Golf Driving Range

Wanda Mtn

4WD Access to Beach

Recreation Reserve

4WD Access to Beach

Beach

Cronulla High

COOK

Gate

4WD Access to Beach

CAPTAIN RD

BATE BAY RD

Gate

Gate

Lucas Res

4WD Access to Beach

Helipad

BERRY ST

SUPER AV

SANDERSON ST

MURROCK

Wanda Res

LINKS AV

LINKS AV

KIRKWOOD

JOHN DAVEY AV

MIERE ESP

Wanda SLSC

Wanda Beach

North Cronulla

Nurs Home

RD

LIMBAR RD

Elouera SLSC

Res

Elouera Beach

RD

MITCHELL

PRINCE

ELOUERA

Nth Cronulla SLSC

Dunningham Pk

FERRYMAN

McDONALD ST

Baths

Walking

North Cronulla Beach

BATE BAY

Cronulla Beach

Cronulla SLSC & Sports Complex

MENTONE

BOORIMA

ELIZABETH PL

ROKER

PDE

INGALARA

ARTHUR

The Esplanade

Cronulla Pt

Shark Island

Blackwoods Beach

Stella Maris Nursing Home & Hostel

Shelly Pk

Shelly Beach Baths

JOINS MAP 464

JOINS MAP 524

JOINS MAP 495

MAP 495

KURNELL
Kurnell Peninsula

Recreation Reserve
Boat Harbour 4WD Park (Private)
Mt Long No 105m

Recreation Reserve

Cape
Boat Harbour
Pimelwi Rocks
Boat Harbour Aquatic Reserve
The Merries Reef

BATE BAY

CITY

COPYRIGHT © UNIVERSAL PUBLISHERS PTY LTD 2005

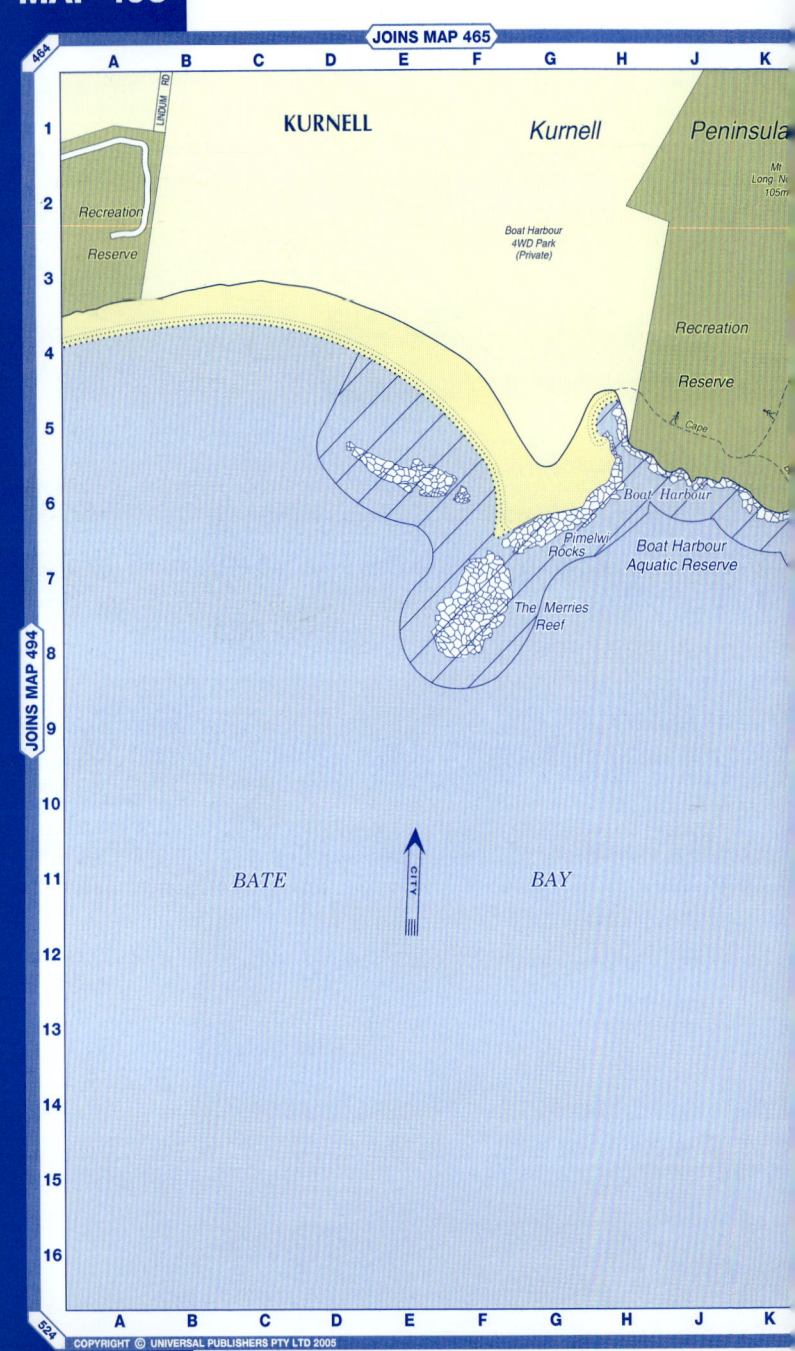

MAP 496
MAP 499 FOLLOWS

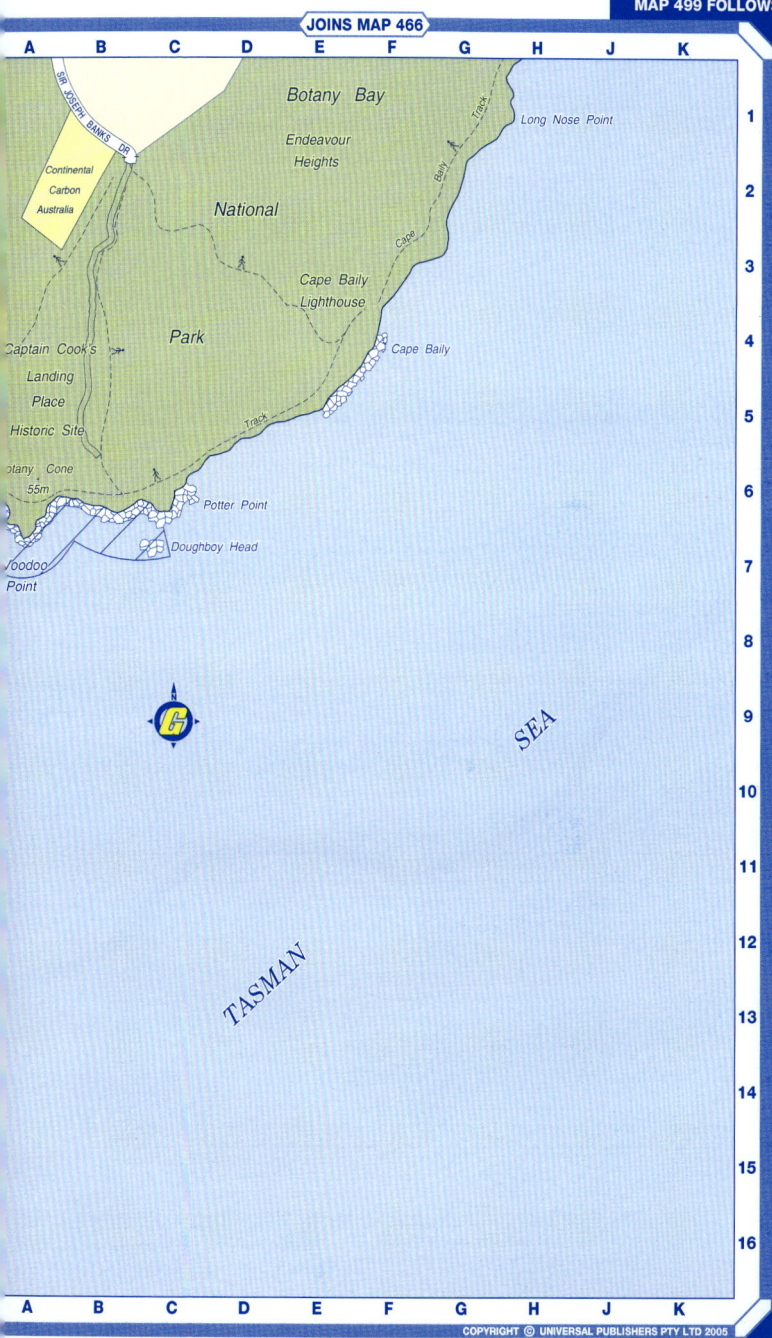

JOINS MAP 466

Botany Bay
Long Nose Point
Endeavour Heights
Continental Carbon Australia
SIR JOSEPH BANKS DR
National
Cape Baily Track
Cape Baily Lighthouse
Captain Cook's Landing Place Historic Site
Park
Cape Baily
Botany Cone 55m
Track
Potter Point
Voodoo Point
Doughboy Head

TASMAN SEA

MAP 499
PREVIOUS MAP 496

BURRAGORANG ROAD

STEVEYS FOREST RD

Club Sid Sharpe Oval

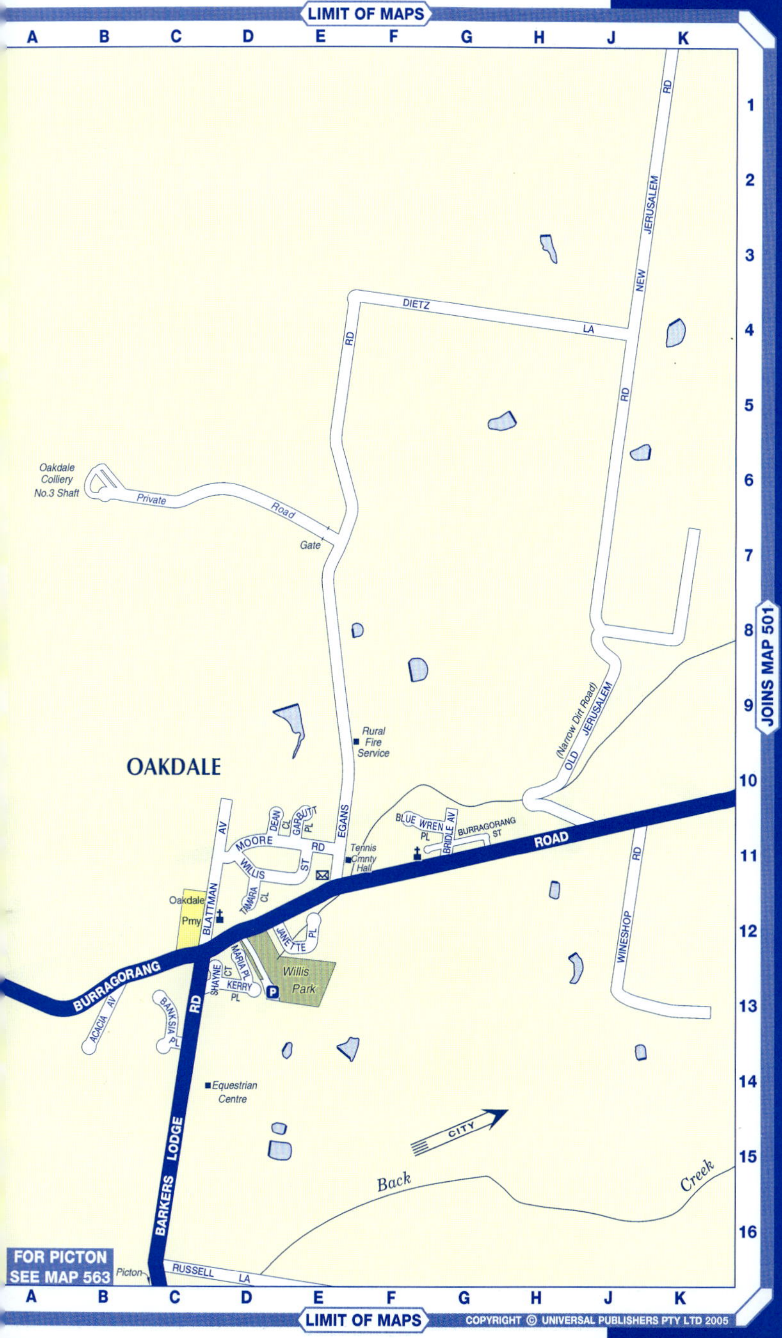
LIMIT OF MAPS
A B C D E F G H J K
1 2 3 4 5 6 7 8 9 10 11 12 13 14 15 16
JOINS MAP 501
NEW JERUSALEM RD
DIETZ LA
EGANS RD
Oakdale Colliery No.3 Shaft
Private Road
Gate
Rural Fire Service
OAKDALE
(Narrow Dirt Road)
OLD JERUSALEM
BURRAGORANG ROAD
BLUE WREN PL
BRIDLE AV
BURRAGORANG ST
WINESHOP RD
Tennis Cmnty Hall
DEAN CL
GARBUTT PL
MOORE RD
WILLIS ST
TAMARA CL
BLATTMAN AV
Oakdale Pmy
JANETTE PL
MARIA PL
SHAYNE CT
KERRY PL
Willis Park
ACACIA AV
BANKSIA PL
Equestrian Centre
CITY
Back Creek
BARKERS LODGE RD
FOR PICTON SEE MAP 563
Picton
RUSSELL LA
LIMIT OF MAPS

MAP 501

OAKDALE

BELIMBLA PARK

Back Hill

Creek

Back Creek

BURRAGORANG

DAIRY ROAD

Gundungurra Park

BINALONG ST

WALMA ST

KUNDABUNG ST

WONAWONG

DALEY CL

QUARRY

MAP 502

The Oaks

Locations and features visible on map:

- Silverdale Penrith
- "Oak Ridge"
- Big Hill Rd
- Wedgewood Rd
- Nepean Brae
- Monkey Rd
- Werriberri Creek
- Silverdale Rd
- Burragorang Road
- Cemetery
- Timothy Lacey La
- Maple Av
- North Vanderville St
- Browns Rd Res
- Danella
- Merlin St
- Russell St
- Chaseling Pl
- Mary St
- John St
- The Oaks Pmy
- William St
- South Vanderville St
- Burragorang
- RFS
- McIntosh St
- Fbr
- Badgally Rd
- Blackbutt Pl
- Glenbawn Pl
- Dudley Chesham Sportsground
- Tennis
- The Oaks Airfield
- Barralier Park
- Glendiver
- Cedar Pl
- Merlin
- Harold Noakes Res
- Wollondilly Heritage Cntr
- Edward
- Casuarina Ct
- Devitt
- Marsh Pl
- Hardwicke St
- Lugarno Pl
- Gate
- Montpelier Dr
- Jooriland Rd Picton
- Werriberri

FOR PICTON SEE MAP 563

LIMIT OF MAPS

JOINS MAP 503

COPYRIGHT © UNIVERSAL PUBLISHERS PTY LTD 2005

MAP 503

JOINS MAP 473

BROWNLOW HILL

THE OAKS

Tchers Ck

Creek

BURRAGORANG

MOORES

Splitters

GLENMORE

WAY

ROAD

Gate
Ent

Jensens Garden Cen

Gully

Sawpit Mountain

Flaggy

GLENDIVER RD

Gate

Glendiver Farm

Road

Sawpit

Creek

Creek

Private

Spring

SPRING CREEK

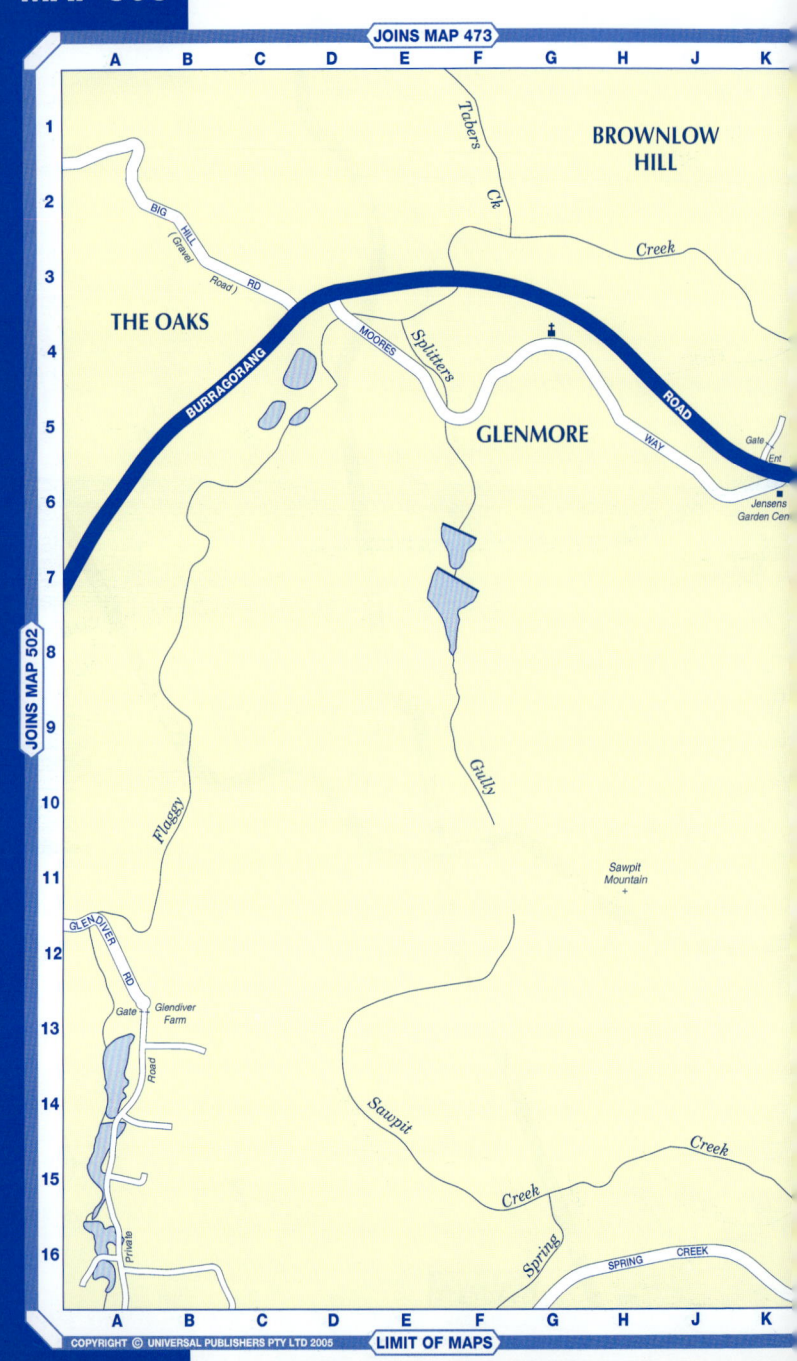

JOINS MAP 502

LIMIT OF MAPS

MAP 504

BROWNLOW HILL

Flaggy Creek

BURRAGORANG ROAD

WESTBROOK BRIDGE

MT HUNTER

Mt Hunter Pmy

Cmnty Hall
RFS

WESTBROOK RD

CLYDE PL

MONKS LANE

Rivulet

SPRING CREEK

Private Road

Mount Hunter Creek

Spring Creek

PEPPERCORN PL
LAKESIDE DR
CALF FARM RD

JOINS MAP 474
JOINS MAP 505
LIMIT OF MAPS

COPYRIGHT © UNIVERSAL PUBLISHERS PTY LTD 2005

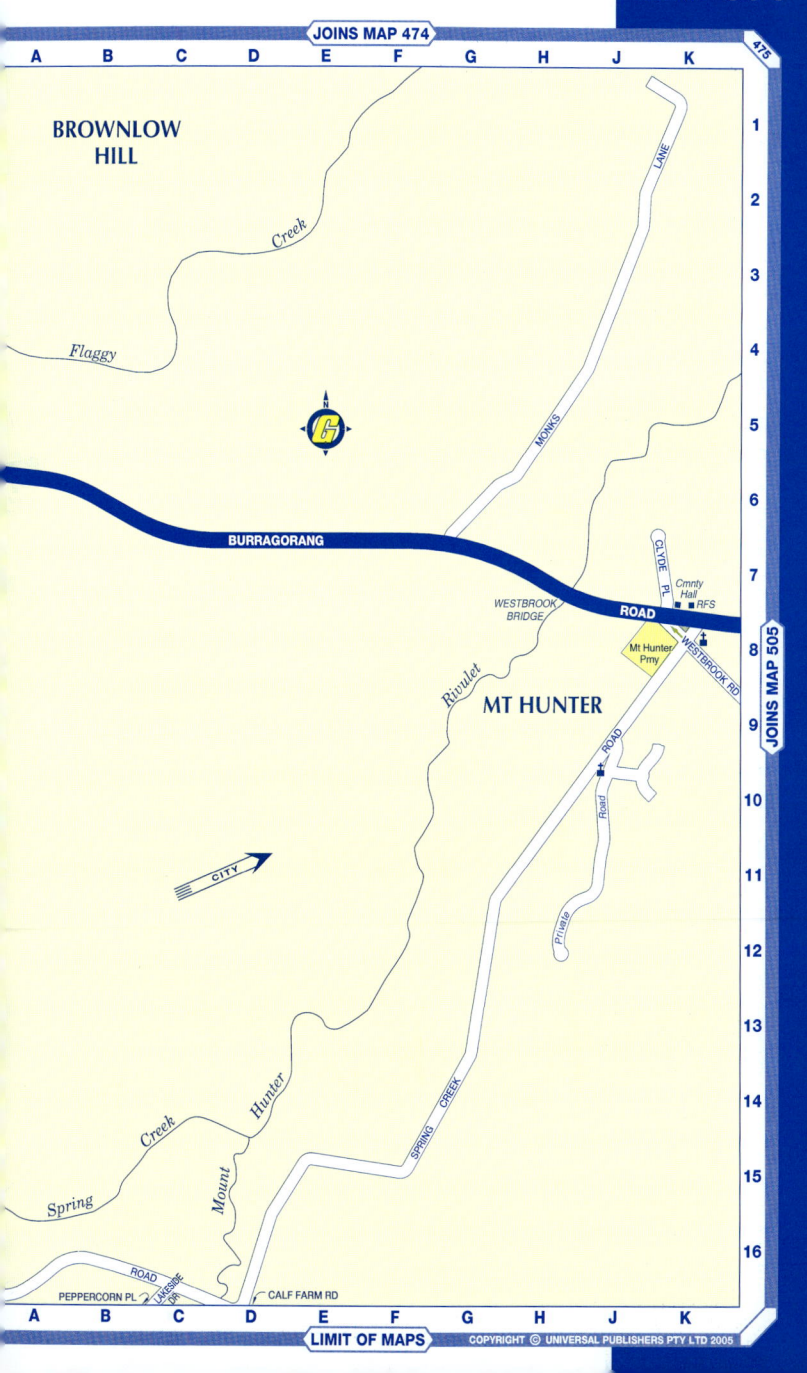

MAP 505

JOINS MAP 475

May Farm Dairy Research Centre

University of Sydney Farms

Mt Hunter Rivulet

BROWNLOW HILL

Sickles Creek

Benwerrin Res.

Mt Hunter Farm

University of Sydney Farms

BURRAGORANG RD

Peppercorn Park

MT HUNTER

BICKLEY VALE

JOINS MAP 504

LIMIT OF MAPS

COPYRIGHT © UNIVERSAL PUBLISHERS PTY LTD 2005

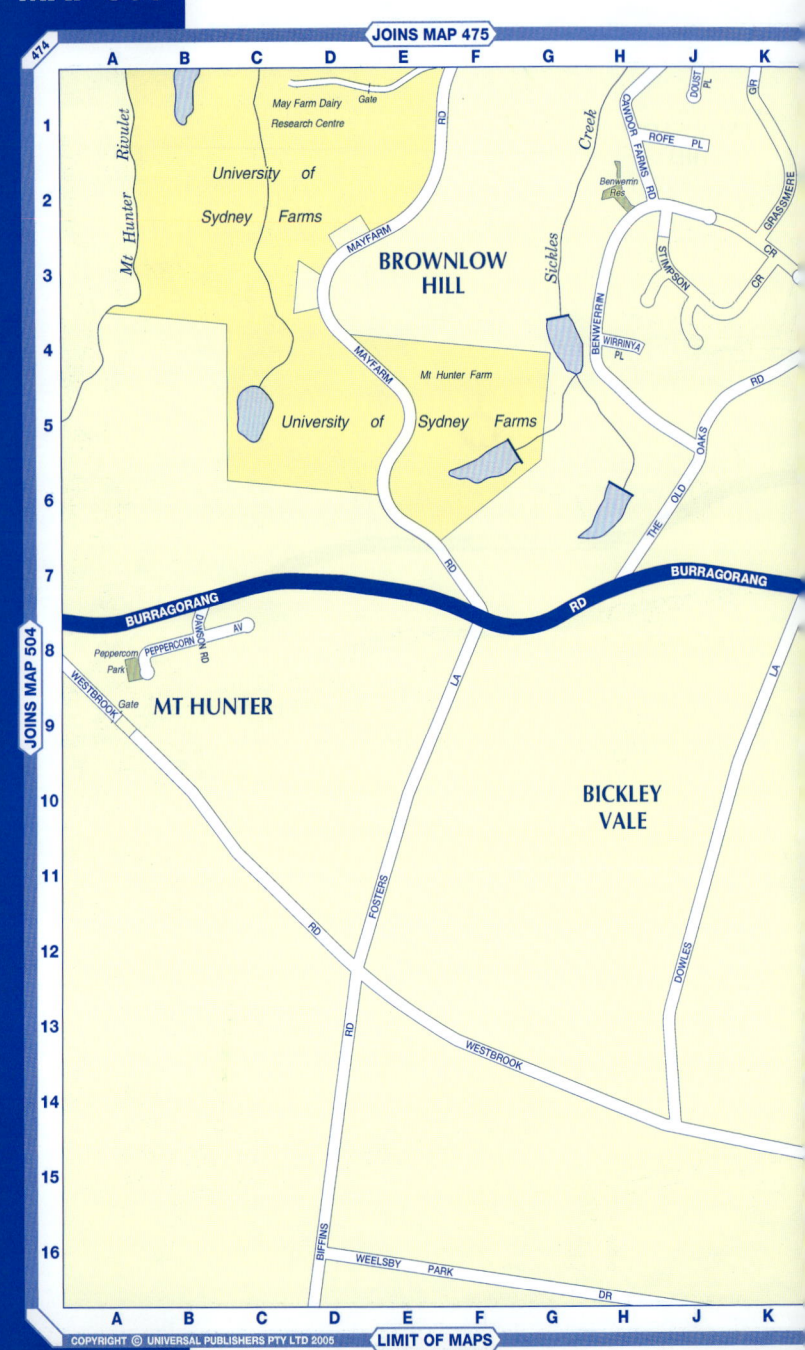

MAP 506

JOINS MAP 476

GRASMERE

Carrington Centennial Hospital Nursing Home & Ret Vill
Sydney Water West Camden STP Gate
Bicentennial Equestrian Park
Cross Country Track
Showjumping
Rodeo
Heavy Vehicle Area
Camden Apex Pk
RSL Youth Club

CAMDEN

Little Byrne St
Little Res
Barsden St
Broughton St
Pindari
Annabella Rd
Pindari Res
Engesta Reserve
Engesta Av
Byrne Pl

CAWDOR

Cem
Camden General Cemetery
(THE COAL RD) BURRAGORANG RD
Starr Reserve
Dobroyd Av
Starr Cl
Matahil Creek
Bligh Av
Johnson Dr
Tennis
King
Cowper Pl
Flinders Res
Cunningham Pl
Dine Soccer Res
Bourke Pl
Blaxland Rd
Berallier
Flinders Dr
Banks Res
McCrae
Bass Pl
Lawson Av
Lawson Res
Crookston Dr

CAMDEN SOUTH

Hayter Reserve
Camden Rugby Park
Cranfield Pl
Crookston Res
Furner Av
West Pl
Dawson Av
Hayter Pl
Huthnance Pl
Dominish Cr

Gas Treatment Facility
WIRE RD
Cemetery
DONCASTER AV
LAGOON FLATS PL
OLD RAZORBACK RD
EAGLES RD
CAWDOR RD

THE OLD OAKS
WEROMBI RD
FERGUSON LA
SHEATHER LA
CAWDOR RD
MAIN SOUTHERN RD

Camden High

→ CITY

LIMIT OF MAPS
COPYRIGHT © UNIVERSAL PUBLISHERS PTY LTD 2005
JOINS MAP 507

JOINS MAP 477
JOINS MAP 506
JOINS MAP 537
476
A B C D E F G H J K
1 2 3 4 5 6 7 8 9 10 11 12 13 14 15 16
CAMDEN
ELDERSLIE
SPRING FARM
CAMDEN SOUTH
NEPEAN
RIVER
CAMDEN BYPASS
MACARTHUR BRIDGE
CITY
MURRAY ST
BROUGHTON ST
BROUGHTON
OLD HUME HWY
CAMDEN HWY
FORMER HUME HWY
BURRAGORANG RD
PARK ST
LITTLE ST
Macarthur Park
Cmnty Health Cntr
Camden Hosp
CHELLASTON ST
FORREST CR
TINGCOMBE PL
PAUL ST CL
ALPHA RD
Rotary Cowpasture Res
Westlands Res
King Bush Res
Cycleway
John Peat Res
Fbr River Reserve
RIVER RD
VICTORY AV
LERIDA AV
WILLIAM AV
MENANGLE
GILBULLA AV
Don Moon Mem Pk
KIMBARRA AV
MURRANDAH
MACQUARIE AV
HAWKEY CR
CHRISTOPHER
ROSALIE AV
ONSLOW AV
PETER AV
BELGENNY AV
Belgenny Oval
Belgenny Reserve
Camden South Pmy
KELLOWAY AV
NEPEAN AV
Camden Nursing Home
Nepean River
ANNABELLA RD
PINDARI
Septimus Res
IRONBARK AV
BELAR RD
Busways Depot
Sq Cts
DOBROYD AV
STARR CL
PATERSON ST
Greenway Res
GROSE PL
CHISHOLM
GREENAWAY AV
WILLIAM
FAHY PL
EYRE
HUNTER ST
WATERHOUSE ST
CAROLINE
ARNDELL
BLIGH
ANTILL
BARKER CL
Barker Res
COWPER
ULMARRA AV
MYUNA PL
Elizabeth Macarthur Reserve
FLINDERS
WILLS PL
BANKS PL
Banks Res
STURT PL
BERALLIER DR
COOLALIE AV
BRIGALOW AV
MARTINE AV
MICHELE PL
ELIZABETH MACARTHUR AV
ARALUEN PL
Belgenny Farm
SELKIRK PL
ADELONG PL
BOWMAN AV
HOPSON AV
RIX PL
WENTWORTH DR
CROOKSTON
REEVE PL
Reeve Res
Ret Village
KYLIE PL
BARRATT
Barratt Res
Macarthur's Homestead
Private Road
McCALL
Bowman Res
TALINISH AV
FURNER AV
TAPLIN PL
THOMPSON PL
ARMOUR AV
SMART
ENGLISH AV
DAWSON AV
DOMINISH CR DR
SHARPE PL
DOWLE
ARNOLD
WHEELER AV
Griffiths Res
WIRE LA
Camden Valley Inn
GRIFFITHS AV
Stoney Range Res
HILLIER CL
MACARTHUR
CCT
Elizabeth Macarthur Agricultural Institute
Thurns Weir
BURRAWONG
MACARTHUR RD
CHURCH ST
GALVIN ST
LUKER ST
SILKY-OAK GR
BRITTON CL
ACORN GR
SUNSET AV
PURCELL
FELD
HYNES PL
THURN PL
FAITHFULL ST
CRUIKSHANK AV
BRUCHHAUSER CR
MARSDEN AV
TEMPLETON RD
PEPPIN PL
COX ST
MERINO
Bobbie Vile Res
MERRIMAN CL
Mawarra Pmy
SOUTHDOWN
Lowe Cr Res
LAMB PL
SUFFOLK DR
CORRIEDALE CL
LINDSEY PL
HILDER ST
LODGES RD
CASHMERE DR
POLWORTH CL
Merino Res
BORDER CL
DORSET CL
Fuchs Res
DORMER CL
COOPWORTH RD
TUKIDALE
DRYSDALE RD
Drysdale Res
CORMO CL
ELAND
RYE CL
ELLIOTDALE CL
Bates Res
BATES CL
FLETCHER
HAWDON CL
Macarthur Turf Farm
SPRINGS RD
Camden Estate Winery
Ettiesdale Res
ETTIESDALE
12
62
64
89

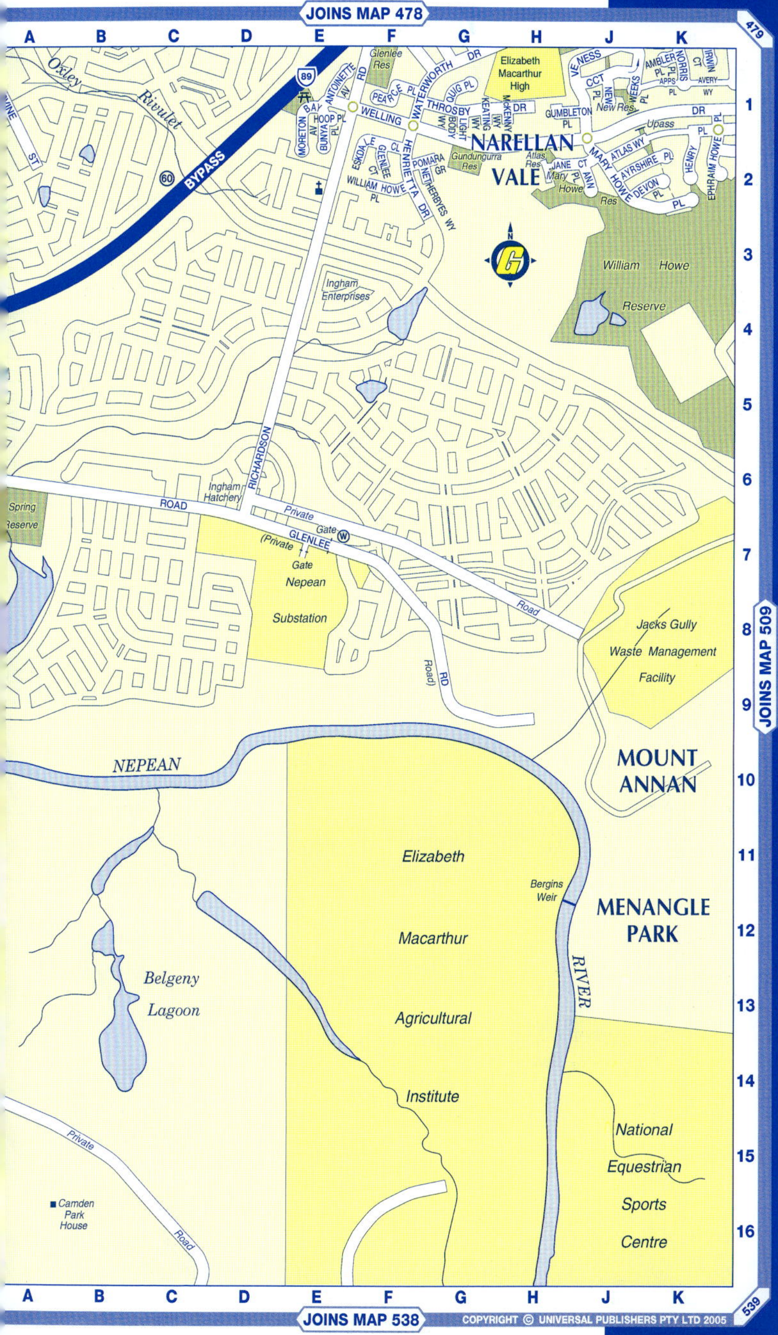
JOINS MAP 478
JOINS MAP 509
JOINS MAP 538
479
539
NARELLAN VALE
MOUNT ANNAN
MENANGLE PARK
Oxley Rivulet
BYPASS
Glenlee Res
Elizabeth Macarthur High
WELLING
WATERWORTH
THROSBY
GUMBLETON PL
DR
Upass
Gundungurra Res
Atlas Res
Mary Howe Res
WILLIAM HOWE PL
HENRIETTA DR
NETHERBYES WY
POMARA GR
ATLAS WY
AYRSHIRE PL
DEVON PL
HENRY
EPHRAIM HOWE PL
JANE CT
ANN
MARY HOWE
MORETON BAY AV
BUNYA PL
HOOP PL
ANTOINETTE AV
RD
PEARCE PL
QUIG PL
BODY WY
LIGHT WY
KEATING WY
McKENNY DR
ESKDALE CL
GLENLEE CT
AMBLER PL
NORRIS CT
IRWIN
APPS PL
AVERY WY
WEEKS PL
NEW CCT
New Res
VE NESS
William Howe Reserve
Ingham Enterprises
Ingham Hatchery
RICHARDSON
ROAD
Private
Gate
GLENLEE
(Private Road)
RD
Road
Nepean Substation
Spring Reserve
Jacks Gully Waste Management Facility
NEPEAN
RIVER
Bergins Weir
Elizabeth Macarthur Agricultural Institute
Belgeny Lagoon
National Equestrian Sports Centre
Camden Park House
Private Road
ST

MAP 509

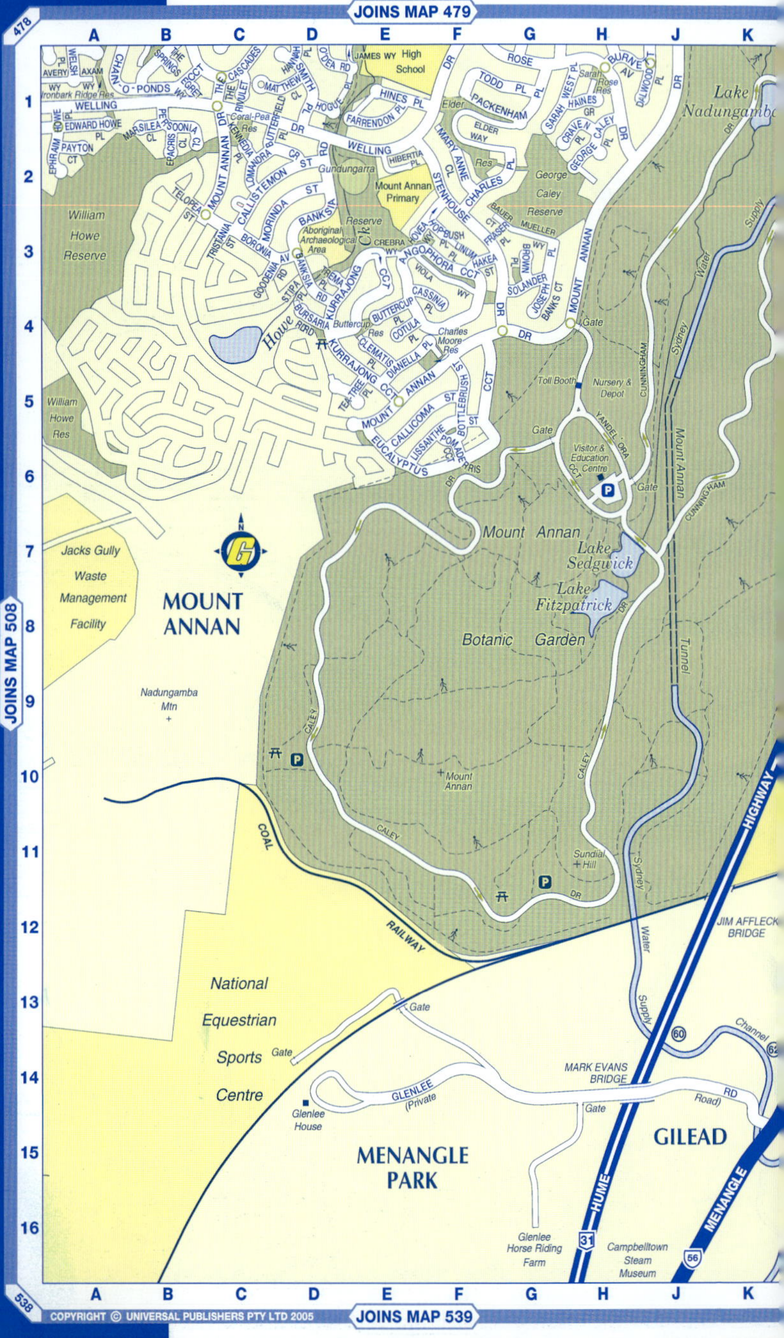

JOINS MAP 479
JOINS MAP 508
JOINS MAP 539
478
538
A B C D E F G H J K
1 2 3 4 5 6 7 8 9 10 11 12 13 14 15 16
MOUNT ANNAN
MENANGLE PARK
GILEAD
Mount Annan Botanic Garden
Lake Sedgwick
Lake Fitzpatrick
Lake Nadungamba
Jacks Gully Waste Management Facility
National Equestrian Sports Centre
Nadungamba Mtn
Mount Annan
Sundial Hill
William Howe Reserve
William Howe Res
George Caley Reserve
Aboriginal Archaeological Area
Reserve
Howe Ck
High School
Mount Annan Primary
Gundungarra
Charles Moore Res
Buttercup Res
Coral-Pea Res
Sarah Rose Res
Ironbark Ridge Res
Elder Res
Toll Booth
Nursery & Depot
Visitor & Education Centre
Gate
Glenlee House
Glenlee Horse Riding Farm
Campbelltown Steam Museum
MARK EVANS BRIDGE
JIM AFFLECK BRIDGE
HUME HIGHWAY
MENANGLE RD
GLENLEE RD (Private Road)
COAL RAILWAY
Sydney Water Supply Channel
Mount Annan Tunnel
MOUNT ANNAN DR
CALEY DR
CUNNINGHAM DR
YANDEL 'ORA CCT
WELLING DR
STENHOUSE DR
CHARLES PL
PACKENHAM DR
TODD PL
ROSE PL
BURNE AV
DALWOOD CT
SARAH WEST PL
HAINES GR
CRAVEN PL
CALEY PL
GEORGE CALEY DR
ELDER WAY
MARY ANNE CL
HINES PL
FARRENDON PL
HIBERTIA PL
HOGUE PL
SMITH PL
MATTHEW CL
HANNAH
O'DEA RD
JAMES WY
THE CASCADES
THE RIVULET
THE SPRINGS
ECCO CCT
EGRET WY
CHAN-O-PONDS WY
AVERY PL
WELSH PL
AXAM WY
EDWARD HOWE PL
EPHRAIM HOWE
PAYTON CT
MARSILEA CL
PERSOONIA CL
EPACRIS CL
KENNEDIA PL
LOMANDRA PL
BUTTERFIELD PL
CALLISTEMON CR
MORINDA ST
BANKSIA ST
BORONIA ST
TELOPEA ST
TRISTANIA
GOODENIA RD
BANKSIA AV
STIPA PL
BURSARIA RD
KURRAJONG CCT
TREMA PL
CREBRA WY
HOVEA WY
HOPBUSH PL
LINUM PL
HAKEA ST
ANGOPHORA CCT
VIOLA WY
CASSINIA PL
BUTTERCUP PL
COTULA PL
CLEMATIS PL
DIANELLA PL
TEA TREE PL
MOUNT ANNAN DR
CALLICOMA ST
BOTTLEBRUSH ST
LISSANTHE CCT
POMADERRIS
EUCALYPTUS CCT
BAUER CT
FRASER PL
MUELLER WY
BROWN PL
SOLANDER
JOSEPH BANK'S CT
60
62
31
56

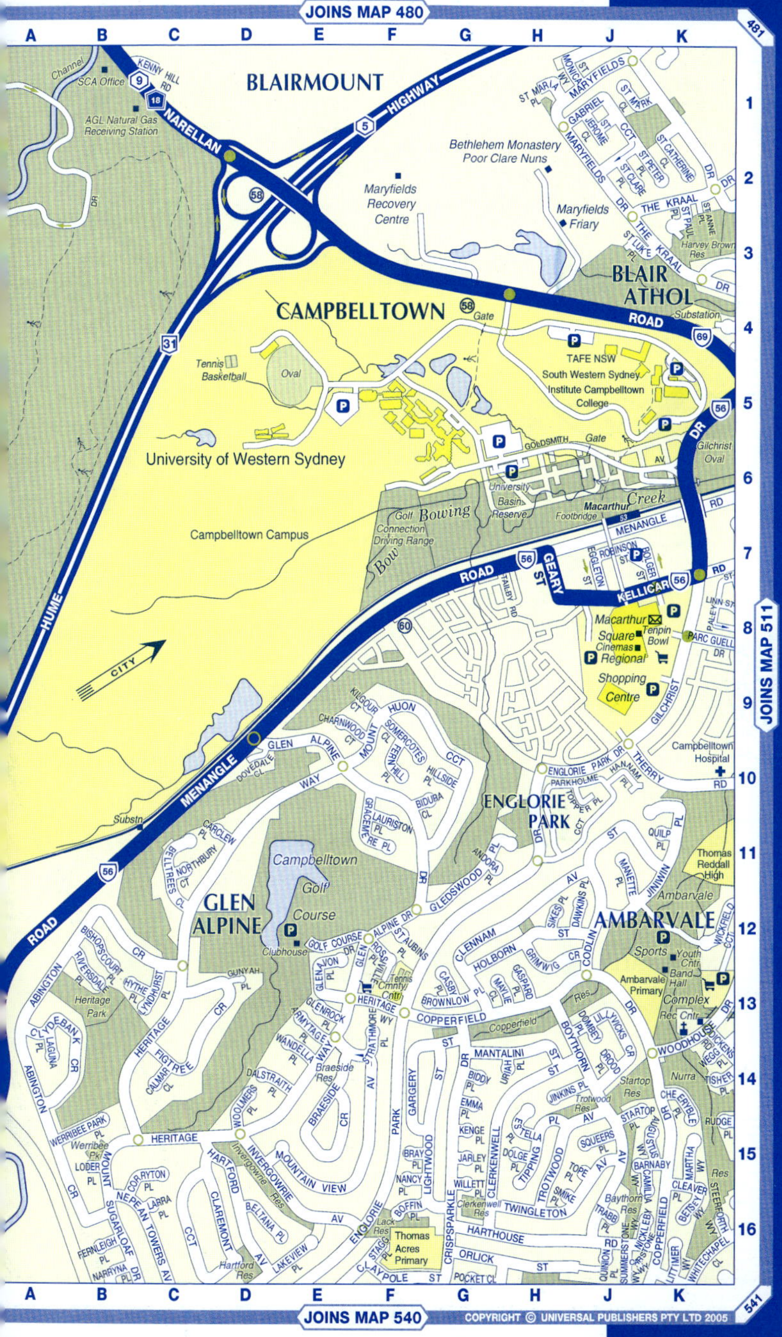
JOINS MAP 480
481
BLAIRMOUNT
CAMPBELLTOWN
BLAIR ATHOL
University of Western Sydney
Campbelltown Campus
ENGLORIE PARK
GLEN ALPINE
AMBARVALE
Campbelltown Golf Course
Macarthur Square Regional Shopping Centre
TAFE NSW South Western Sydney Institute Campbelltown College
Bethlehem Monastery Poor Clare Nuns
Maryfields Recovery Centre
Maryfields Friary
Campbelltown Hospital
Thomas Reddall High
Ambarvale Primary
Thomas Acres Primary
SCA Office
AGL Natural Gas Receiving Station
HUME HWY
NARELLAN RD
MENANGLE ROAD
JOINS MAP 511
JOINS MAP 540
541

MAP 511

JOINS MAP 481
JOINS MAP 541
JOINS MAP 510
480
540
A B C D E F G H J K
1 2 3 4 5 6 7 8 9 10 11 12 13 14 15 16
BLAIR ATHOL
CAMPBELLTOWN
BRADBURY
AMBARVALE
Indoor Cricket Centre
Roller Skate Rink
Campbelltown Performing Arts High
Campbelltown North Primary
Sp Sch
Harvey Brown Res
Aldi
Campbelltown
Cncl Off & Civic Cntr
Court Hse
Campbelltown Showground
Tennis
Mawson Park
St Peters Ang Pmy
Cmnty Health Cntr
St John Cath
Pmy
Campbelltown NRMA Mall
Cinemas
Theatre
Koshigaya Park
Catholic Club
Art Gallery
Marketfair
Gym
Motor Reg
Marsden Park
TAFE
Gilchrist Oval
Substation
Macarthur Priv
Hurley Park
St Johns Catholic Cem
Centenary Park
Bon Wrightson Res
McLEAN
Bradbury Park
Apex Park
Campbelltown Hospital
Helipad
Thomas Reddall High
Throsby Res
Fieldhouse
Ped Upass
St Patricks College
St Thomas More Pmy
Busway Depot
Baden Powell Res
Bow Bowing Res
Sherwood Hills
Bradbury Primary
Macleay Res
Airds High
Dorchester
Reiby Juvenile Justice Cntr
Briar Rd Primary
Kenny Res
Quirk Reserve
Manooka Res
Nurra Res
Shiel Res
Merino Res
Hagan Res
Resvrs
Bow Bowing Creek
Fishers Ghost Ck
Birunji Ck
NARELLAN RD
APPIN ROAD
(MOORE - OXLEY) BYPASS
QUEEN ST
MOORE ST
BROUGHTON ST
CAMDEN RD
GEORGE ST
JOHNS RD
BRIAR RD
PARKWAY AV

MAP 512

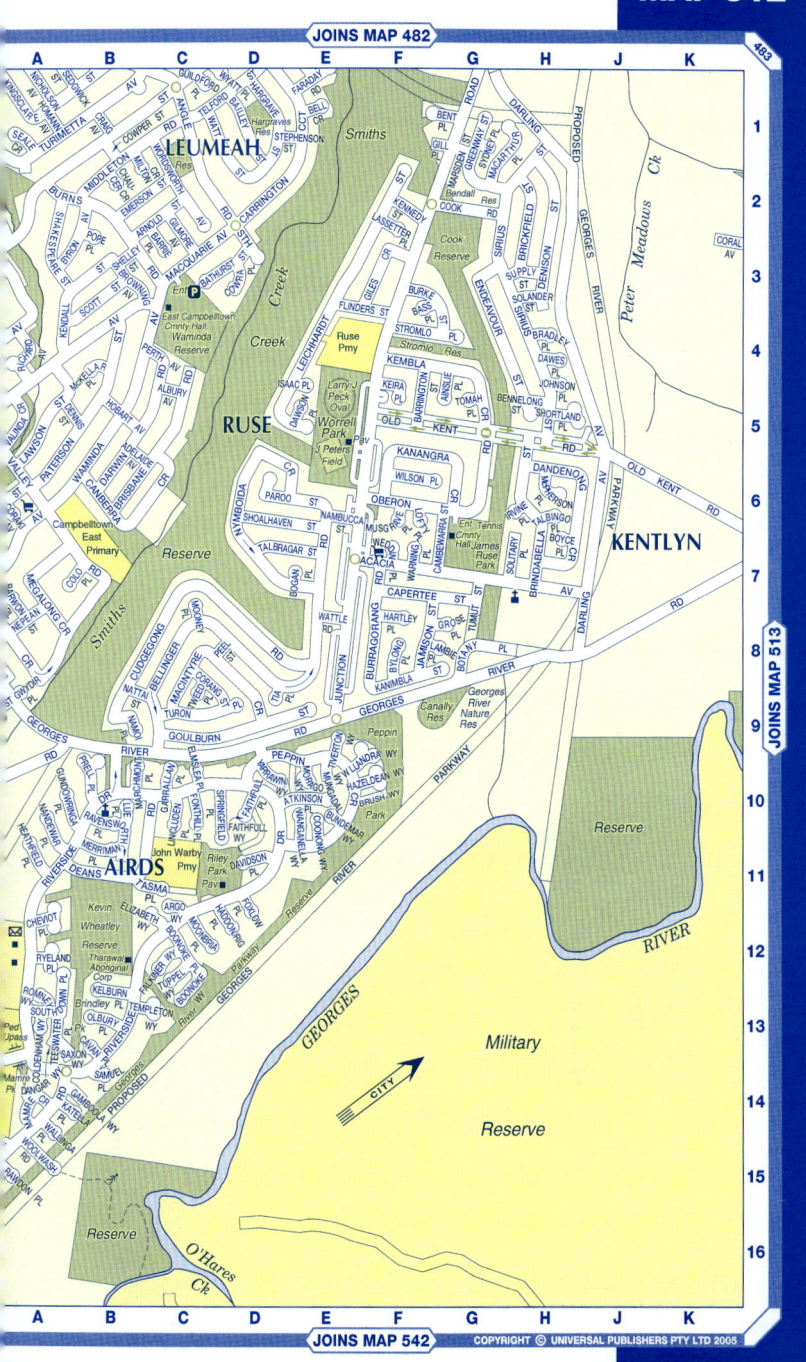

MAP 513

JOINS MAP 483

KENTLYN

- Freres Crossing Reserve
- Riverview Rd
- Coral Av
- Peter Meadows Rd
- Hamilton Rd
- Harrison Rd
- Gate
- Nurs Home
- Bus only
- Convent of Our Lady of Kazan
- Smith St
- The Fraternity of the Holy Cross
- Kentlyn Pny
- Kentlyn Res
- RFS
- Kentlyn Elevated Reservoir
- 2nd Av
- 3rd Av
- Rel Vill
- Old Kent River
- Georges River
- Reserve
- Military
- Tucker

JOINS MAP 512
JOINS MAP 483
LIMIT OF MAPS

COPYRIGHT © UNIVERSAL PUBLISHERS PTY LTD 2005

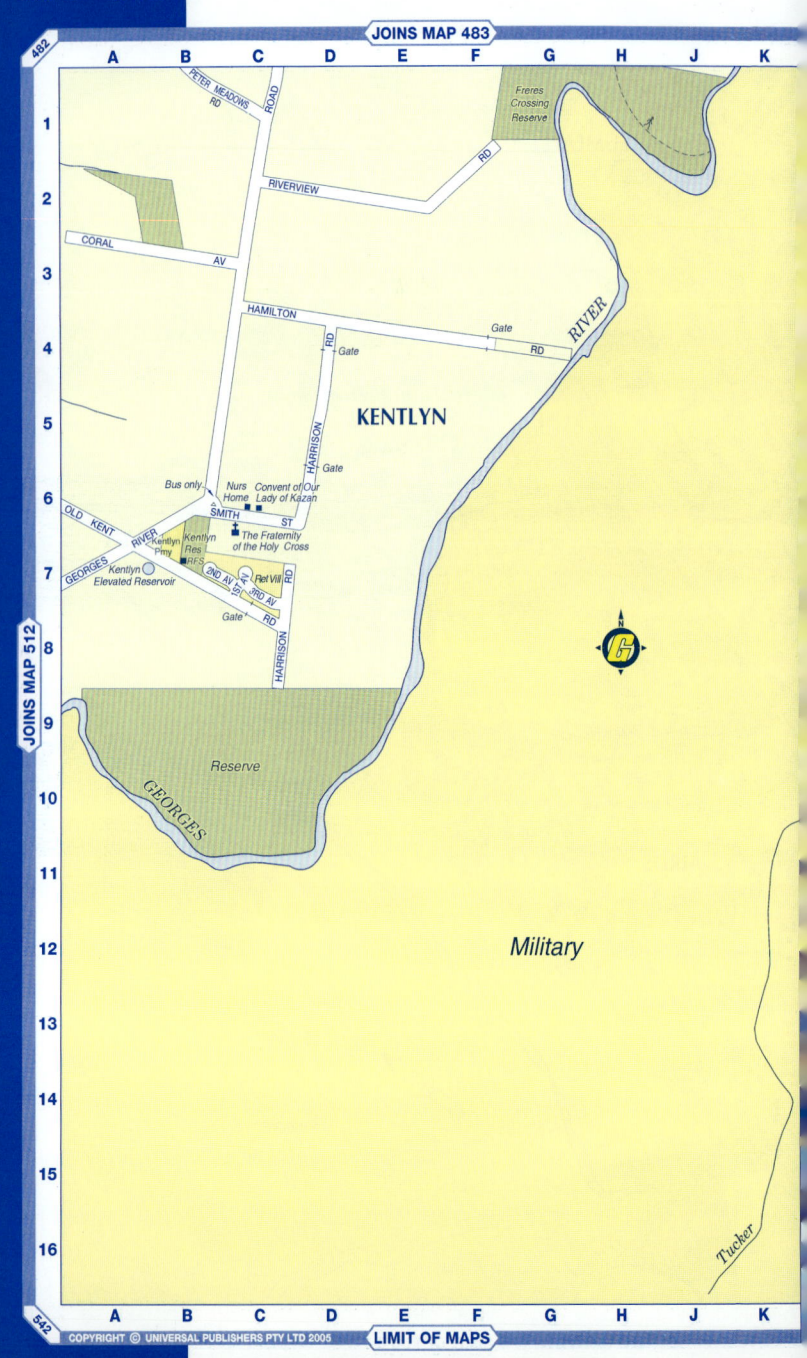

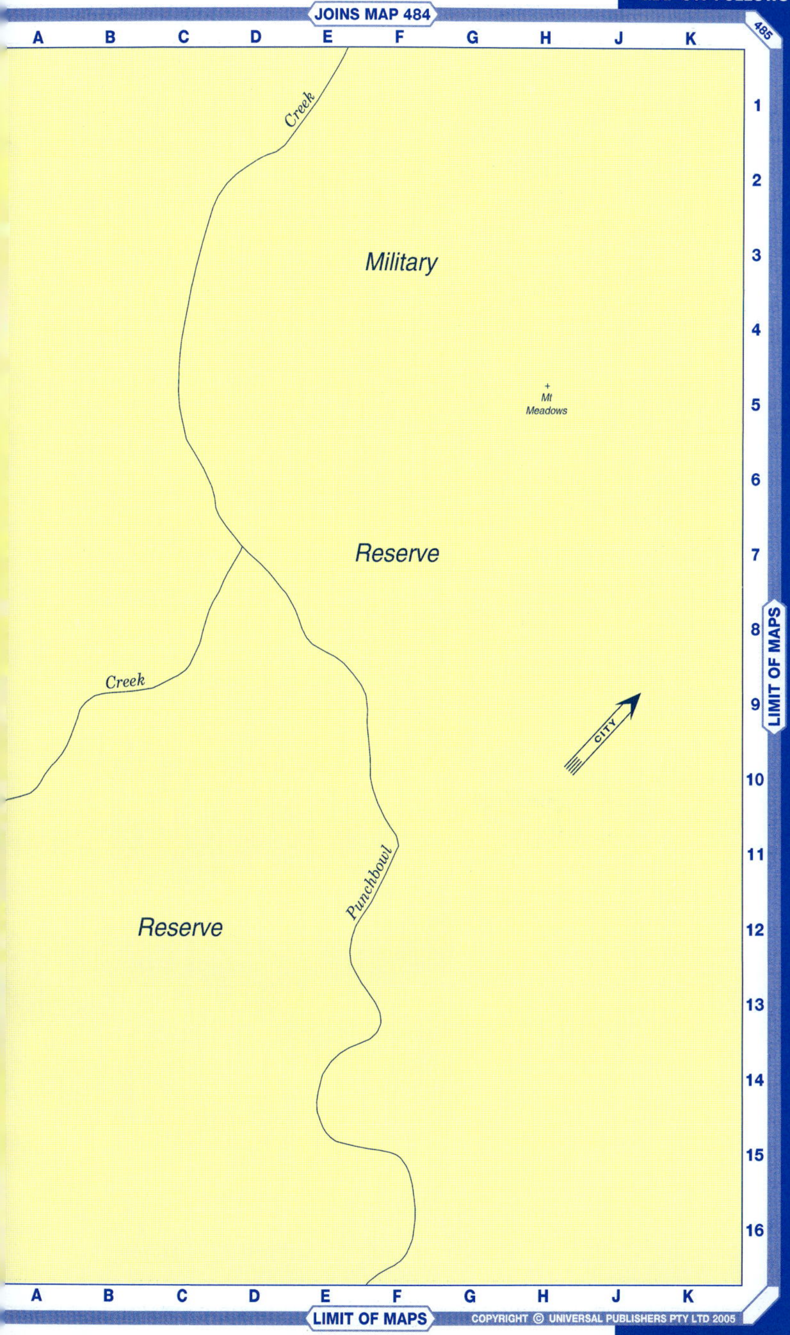

MAP 514
MAP 517 FOLLOWS

JOINS MAP 484

Creek

Military

+ Mt Meadows

Reserve

Creek

CITY

Punchbowl

Reserve

LIMIT OF MAPS

COPYRIGHT © UNIVERSAL PUBLISHERS PTY LTD 2005

MAP 517

PREVIOUS MAP 514

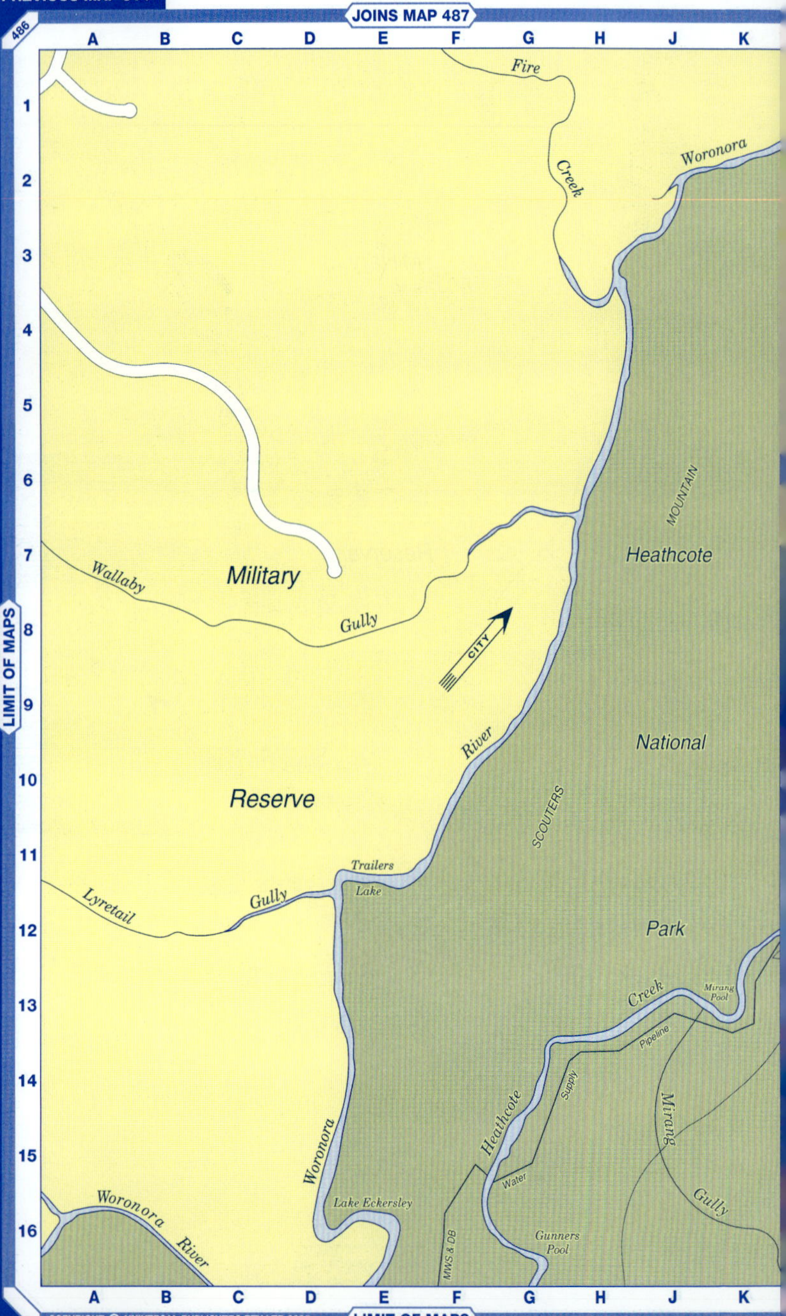

MAP 518

MAP 519

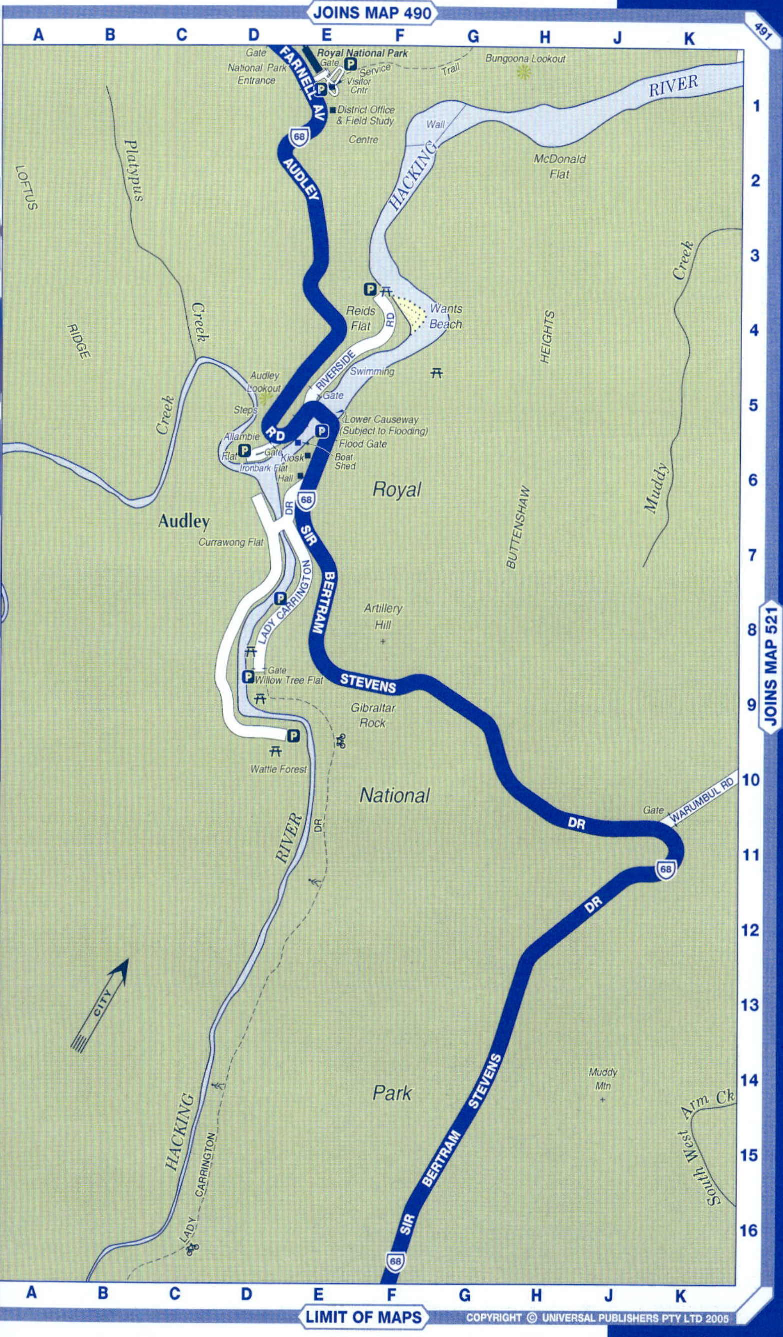
JOINS MAP 490
A B C D E F G H J K
491
1 2 3 4 5 6 7 8 9 10 11 12 13 14 15 16
Gate
National Park Entrance
Royal National Park
Gate
Service
Visitor Cntr
Trail
Bungoona Lookout
FARNELL AV
District Office & Field Study Centre
RIVER
Wall
HACKING
McDonald Flat
AUDLEY
Platypus
LOFTUS
Creek
Wants Beach
Reids Flat
RD
RIVERSIDE
HEIGHTS
RIDGE
Creek
Swimming
Audley Lookout
Gate
Steps
Lower Causeway (Subject to Flooding)
Flood Gate
Allambie Flat
Gate
Kiosk
Boat Shed
Ironbark Flat
Hall
RD
Creek
Royal
BUTTENSHAW
Muddy
Audley
Currawong Flat
DR
SIR
BERTRAM
LADY CARRINGTON
Artillery Hill
Gate
Willow Tree Flat
STEVENS
Gibraltar Rock
Wattle Forest
National
WARUMBUL RD
Gate
DR
RIVER
DR
DR
CITY
STEVENS
Muddy Mtn
Park
South West Arm Ck
BERTRAM
HACKING
LADY CARRINGTON
SIR
68
JOINS MAP 521

MAP 521

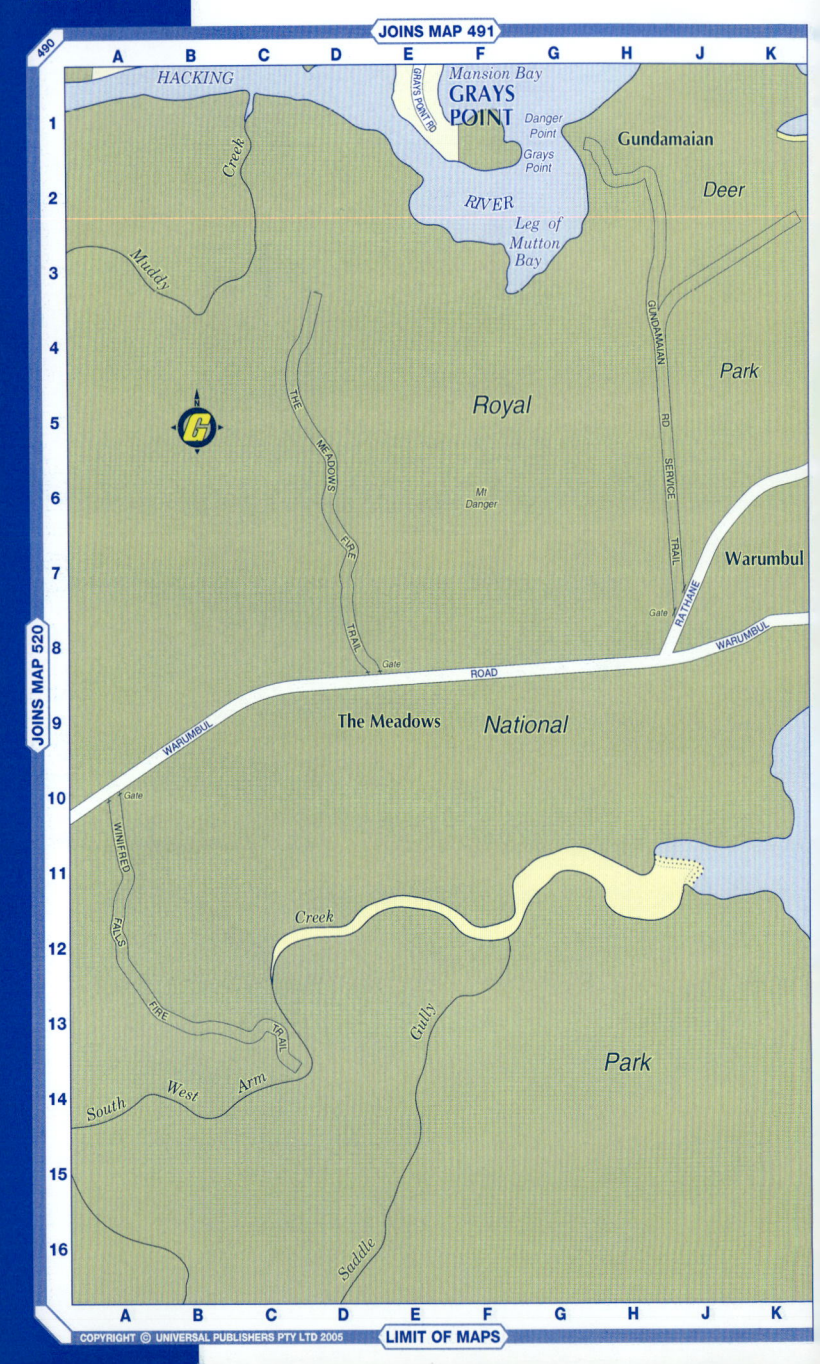

MAP 522

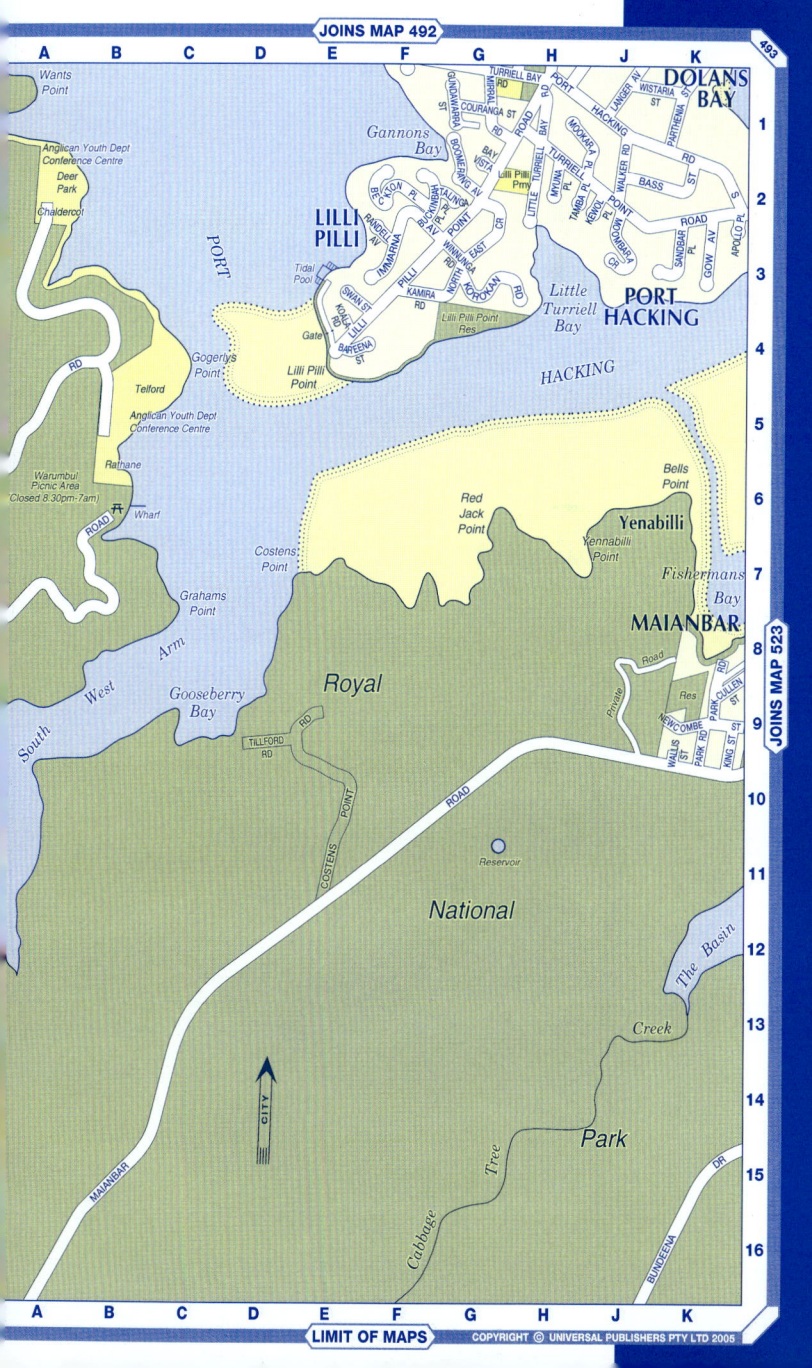

Locations and Features

Grid A-B, Row 1-3:
- Wants Point
- Anglican Youth Dept Conference Centre
- Deer Park
- Chaldercot

Grid B-C, Row 5-7:
- Telford
- Anglican Youth Dept Conference Centre
- Rathane
- Warumbul Picnic Area (Closed 8.30pm-7am)
- Wharf

Grid C, Row 3-8:
- PORT
- Gogerlys Point
- Grahams Point
- South West Arm

Grid C-D, Row 8-9:
- Gooseberry Bay

Grid D-F, Row 2-4 (LILLI PILLI area):
- Gannons Bay
- LILLI PILLI
- Tidal Pool
- Gate
- Lilli Pilli Point

Streets: BECKTON PL, RANDELL AV, MARANTA, PILLI, SWAN ST, KOOLA, BAREENA ST, KAMIRA RD, NORTH, DEALING PL, BUCKINGHAM, WANNAGA, KORONA CR, GUNDAWARA ST, BOOMERANG ST, BAY VISTA, COURANGA ST, TURRIELL BAY RD

Grid G-K, Row 1-3 (PORT HACKING / DOLANS BAY):
- DOLANS BAY
- PORT HACKING
- Little Turriell Bay
- Lilli Pilli Pny
- Lilli Pilli Point Res

Streets: TURRIELL BAY RD, PORT RD, HACKING, LITTLE TURRIELL BAY RD, MYUNA PL, TAMBA PL, KEWA, WALKER RD, ANGER RD, WISTARIA ST, PARTHENIA ST, MOOMARA, BASS, GOW AV, APOLLO ST, SANDBAR, YARMBIRA, CR

Grid E-J, Row 4-7:
- HACKING
- Costens Point
- Red Jack Point
- Bells Point
- Yenabilli Point
- Yenabilli
- Fishermans Bay
- MAIANBAR

Grid J-K, Row 8-9 (MAIANBAR area):
- MAIANBAR
- Pindie Road
- Res
- Streets: NEWCOMBE, WALLIS ST, PARK RD, PARK, CULLEN, KING ST

Grid D-J, Row 8-16:
- Royal National Park
- TILLFORD RD
- COSTENS POINT RD
- Reservoir
- The Basin
- Creek
- Cabbage Tree
- MAIANBAR RD
- CITY (arrow)
- BUNDEENA DR

Borders:
- JOINS MAP 492 (top)
- JOINS MAP 523 (right)
- 493 (top right)
- LIMIT OF MAPS (bottom)
- COPYRIGHT © UNIVERSAL PUBLISHERS PTY LTD 2005

MAP 523

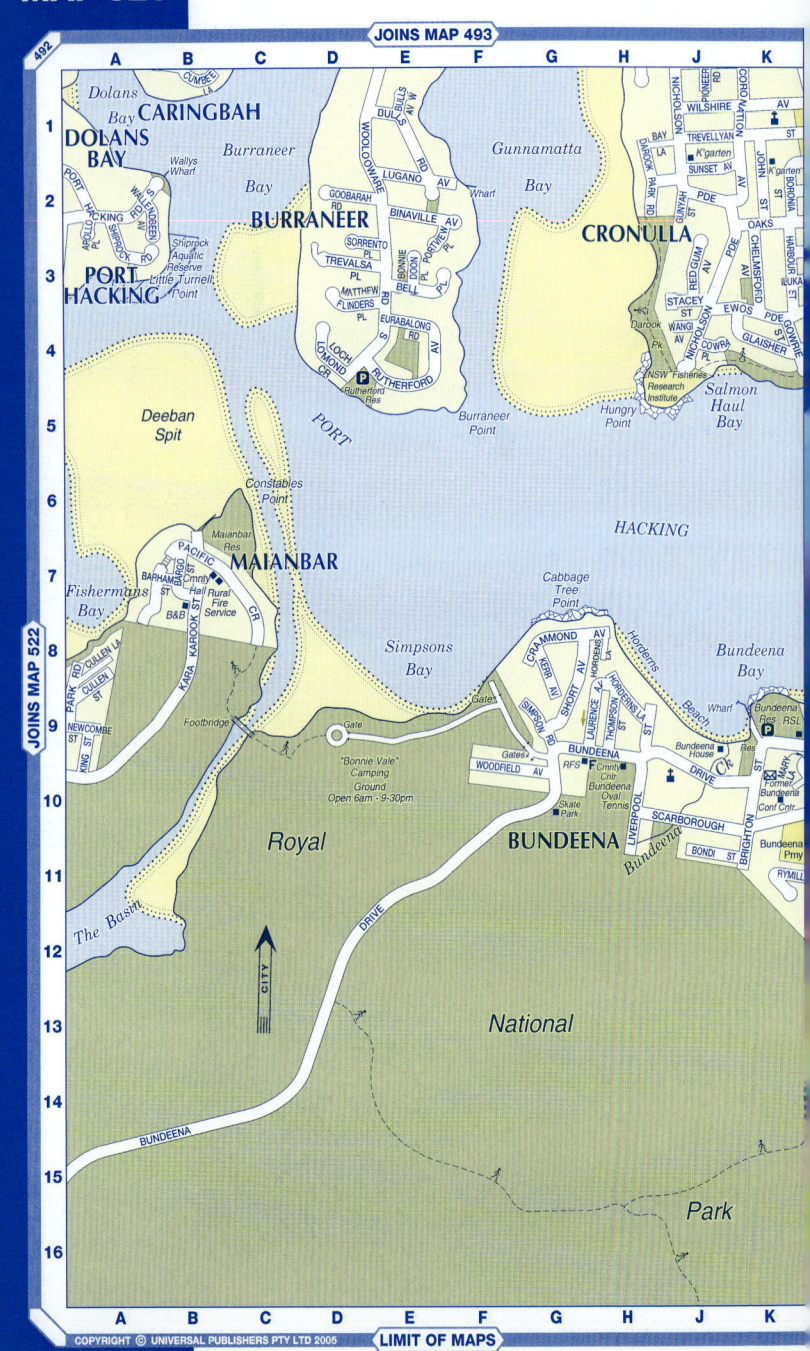

MAP 524
MAP 537 FOLLOWS

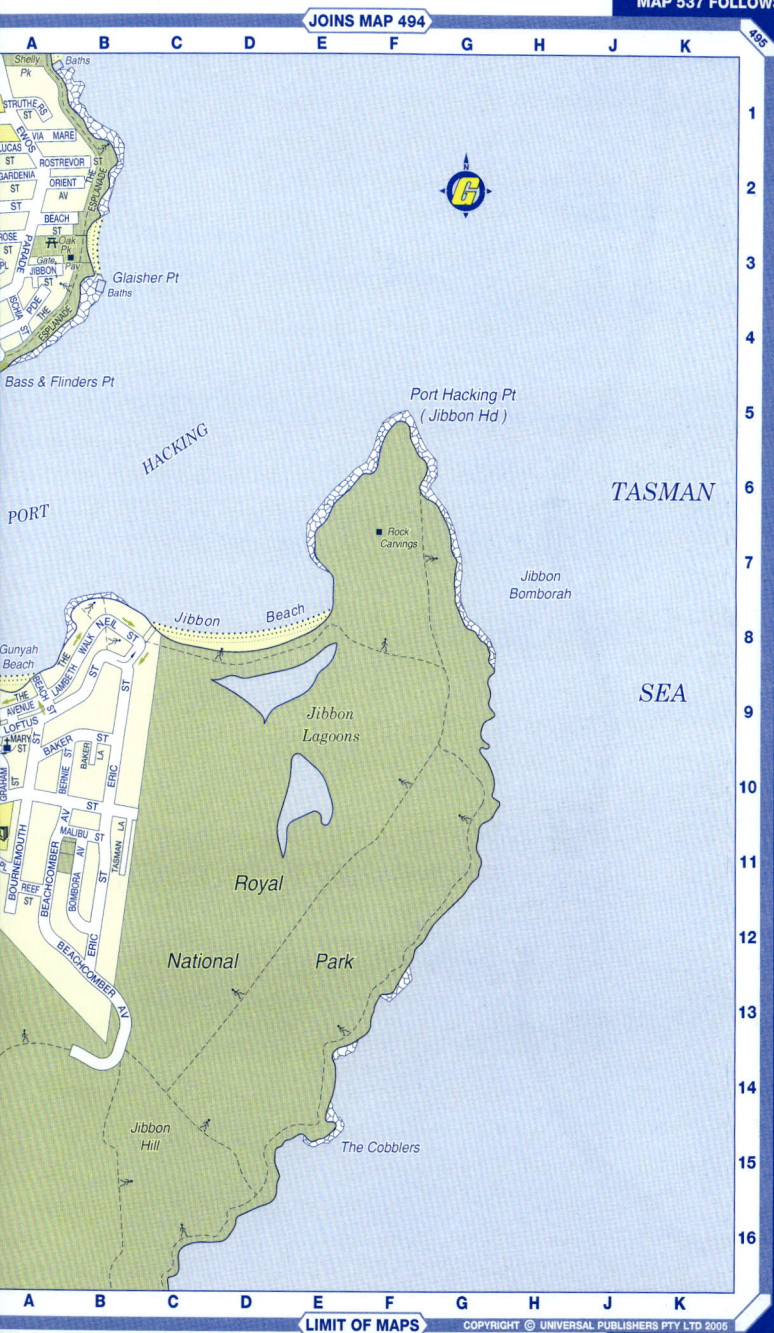

JOINS MAP 494

Shelly Pk
Baths
STRUTHERS ST
ENOS
VIA MARE
LUCAS ST
ROSTREVOR
GARDENIA ST
ORIENT AV
ROSE ST
BEACH ST
Oak
PARADE
Gable
JIBBON
Pav
ECHA
THE ESPLANADE
PDE

Glaisher Pt
Baths

Bass & Flinders Pt

PORT HACKING

Port Hacking Pt
(Jibbon Hd)

TASMAN

Rock Carvings

Jibbon Bomborah

Jibbon Beach

Gunyah Beach

SEA

NEIL ST
THE AVENUE
LAMBETH WALK
LOFTUS ST
MARY ST
BAKER ST
BERNIE ST
BAKER LA
ERIC ST
GRAHAM
BOURNEMOUTH
MALIBU AV
BOMBORA AV
TASMAN LA
REEF ST
BEACHCOMBER AV
ERIC ST

Jibbon Lagoons

Royal

National Park

Jibbon Hill

The Cobblers

LIMIT OF MAPS
COPYRIGHT © UNIVERSAL PUBLISHERS PTY LTD 2005

JOINS MAP 507

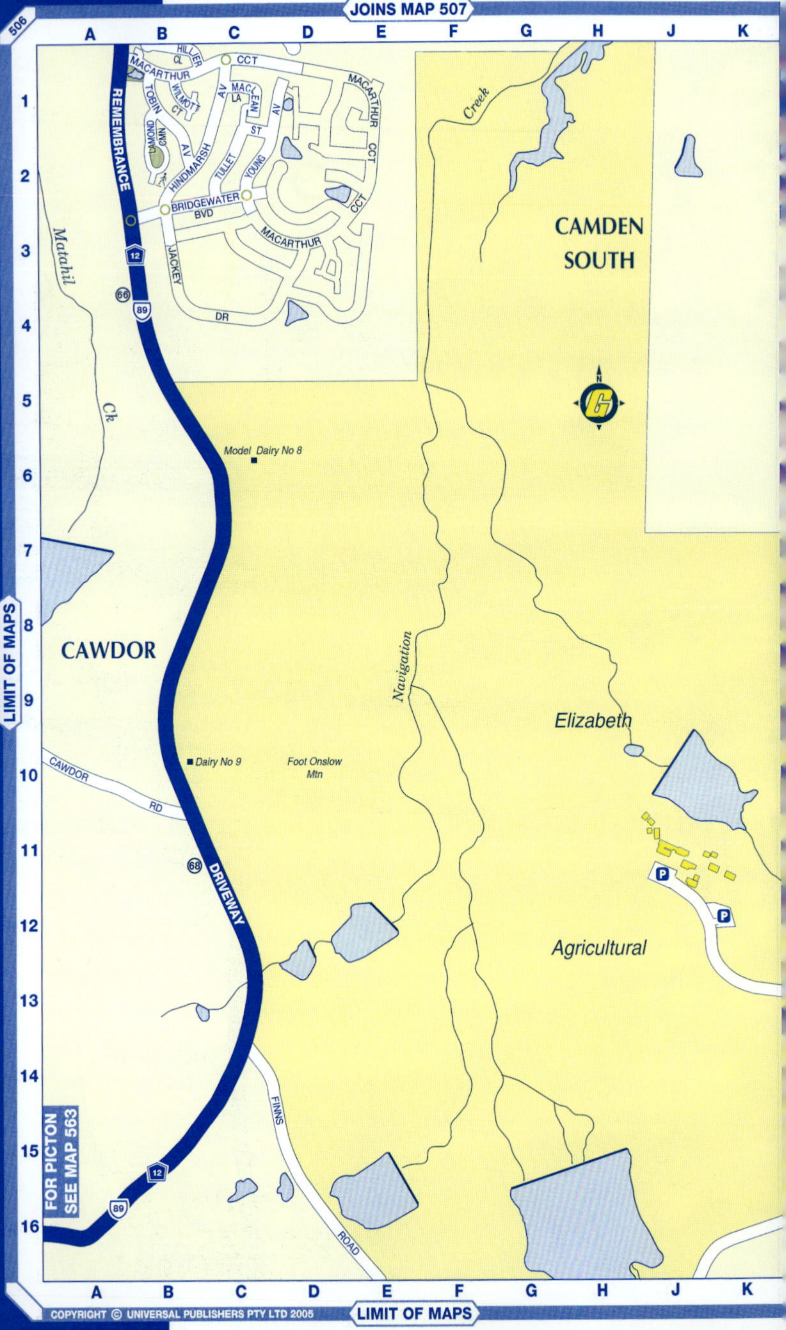

LIMIT OF MAPS

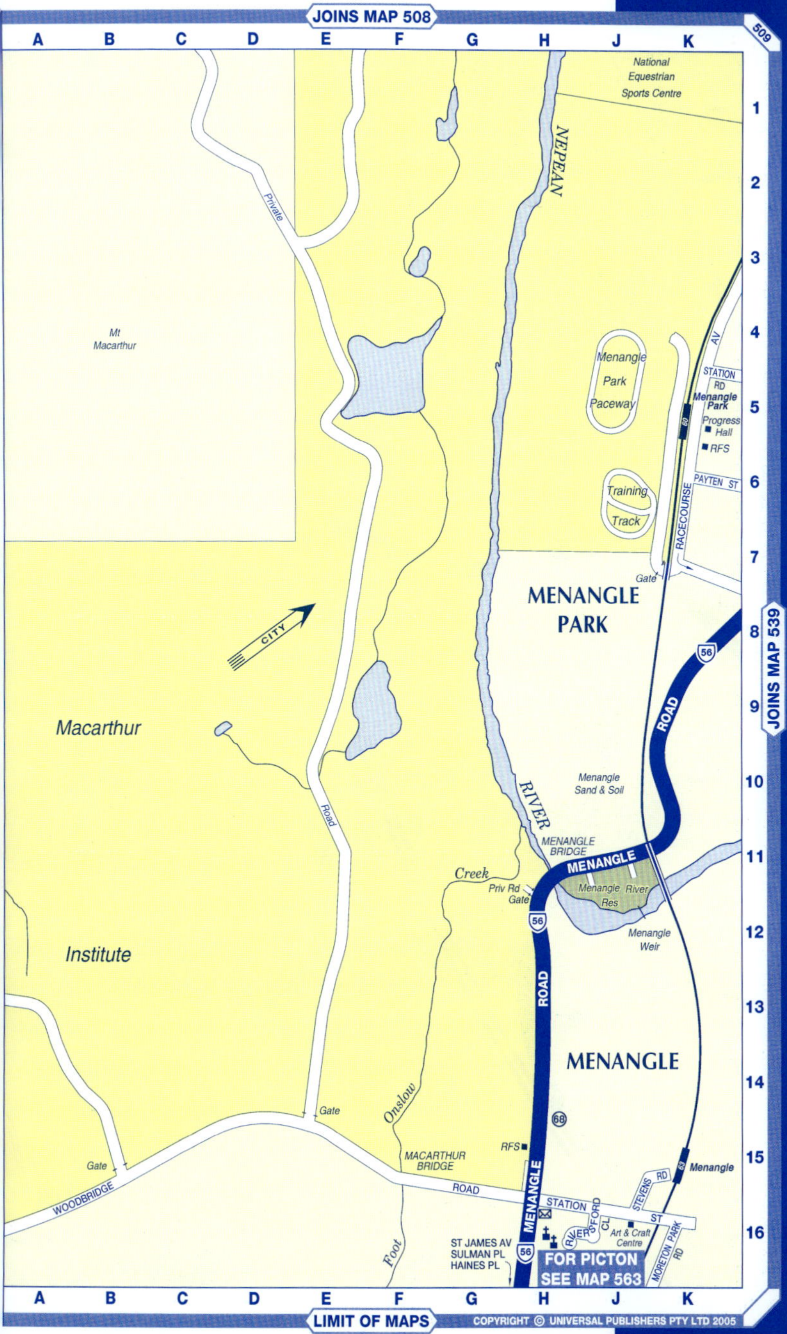
JOINS MAP 508
509
JOINS MAP 539
LIMIT OF MAPS
A B C D E F G H J K
1 2 3 4 5 6 7 8 9 10 11 12 13 14 15 16
National Equestrian Sports Centre
NEPEAN
RIVER
Private
Road
Mt Macarthur
Macarthur
Institute
CITY
Menangle Park Paceway
Training Track
STATION RD
Menangle Park
Progress Hall
RFS
PAYTEN ST
RACECOURSE
AV
Gate
MENANGLE PARK
ROAD
Menangle Sand & Soil
MENANGLE BRIDGE
MENANGLE
Menangle River Res
Menangle Weir
Creek
Priv Rd Gate
ROAD
MENANGLE
Onslow
Gate
Gate
WOODBRIDGE
ROAD
MACARTHUR BRIDGE
RFS
STATION
ST
STEVENS
RD
RIVERSFORD CL
Art & Craft Centre
Menangle
MORETON PARK RD
Foot
ST JAMES AV
SULMAN PL
HAINES PL
FOR PICTON SEE MAP 563
56
68
60
63

MAP 539

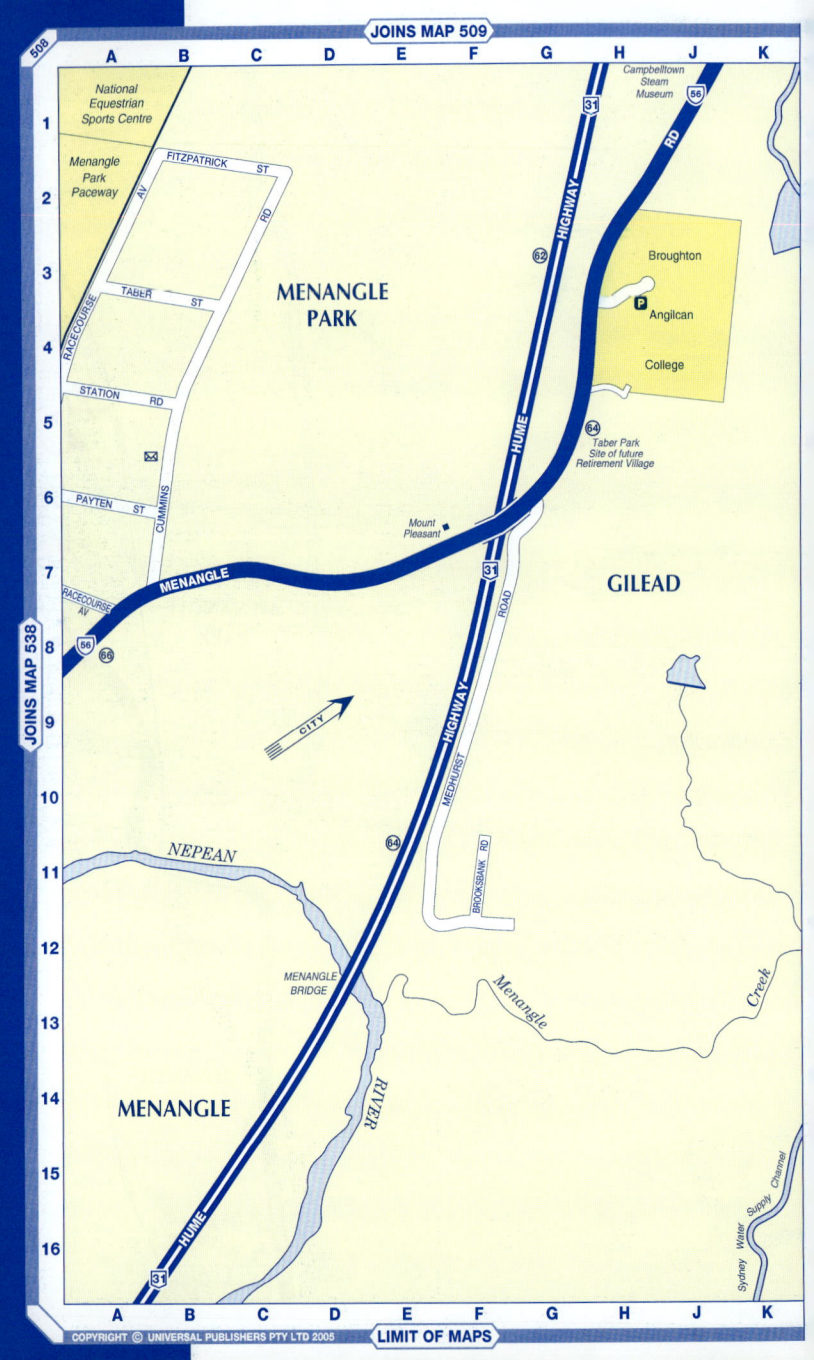

MAP 540

MAP 541

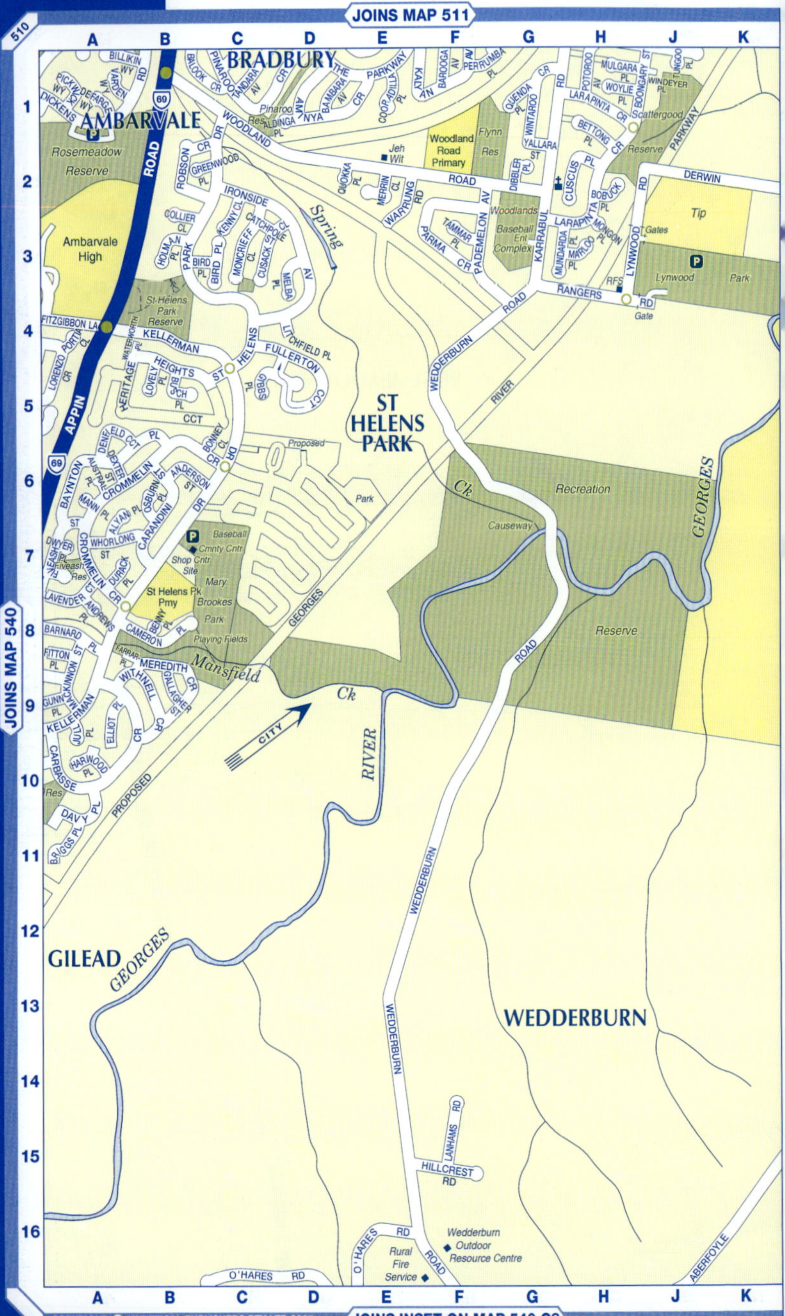
JOINS MAP 511
JOINS MAP 540
JOINS INSET ON MAP 540 C8
510
A B C D E F G H J K
1 2 3 4 5 6 7 8 9 10 11 12 13 14 15 16
BRADBURY
AMBARVALE
ST HELENS PARK
GILEAD
WEDDERBURN
APPIN ROAD
WOODLAND ROAD
WEDDERBURN ROAD
O'HARES RD
HILLCREST RD
LANHAMS RD
RANGERS RD
DERWIN
PARKWAY
ABERFOYLE
Rosemeadow Reserve
Ambarvale High
St Helens Park Reserve
Woodland Road Primary
Flynn Res
Woodlands Baseball Ent Complex
Scattergood Reserve
Tip
Lynwood Park
Gates
Gate
RFS
Baseball Cmnty Cntr
Shop Cntr Site
St Helens Pk Pmy
Mary Brookes Park
Playing Fields
Recreation Reserve
Causeway
GEORGES RIVER
Mansfield Ck
Spring Ck
CITY
PROPOSED
Proposed
Park
Fiveash Res
Wedderburn Outdoor Resource Centre
Rural Fire Service
Jeh Wit
Pinaroo Res

MAP 542
MAP 561 FOLLOWS

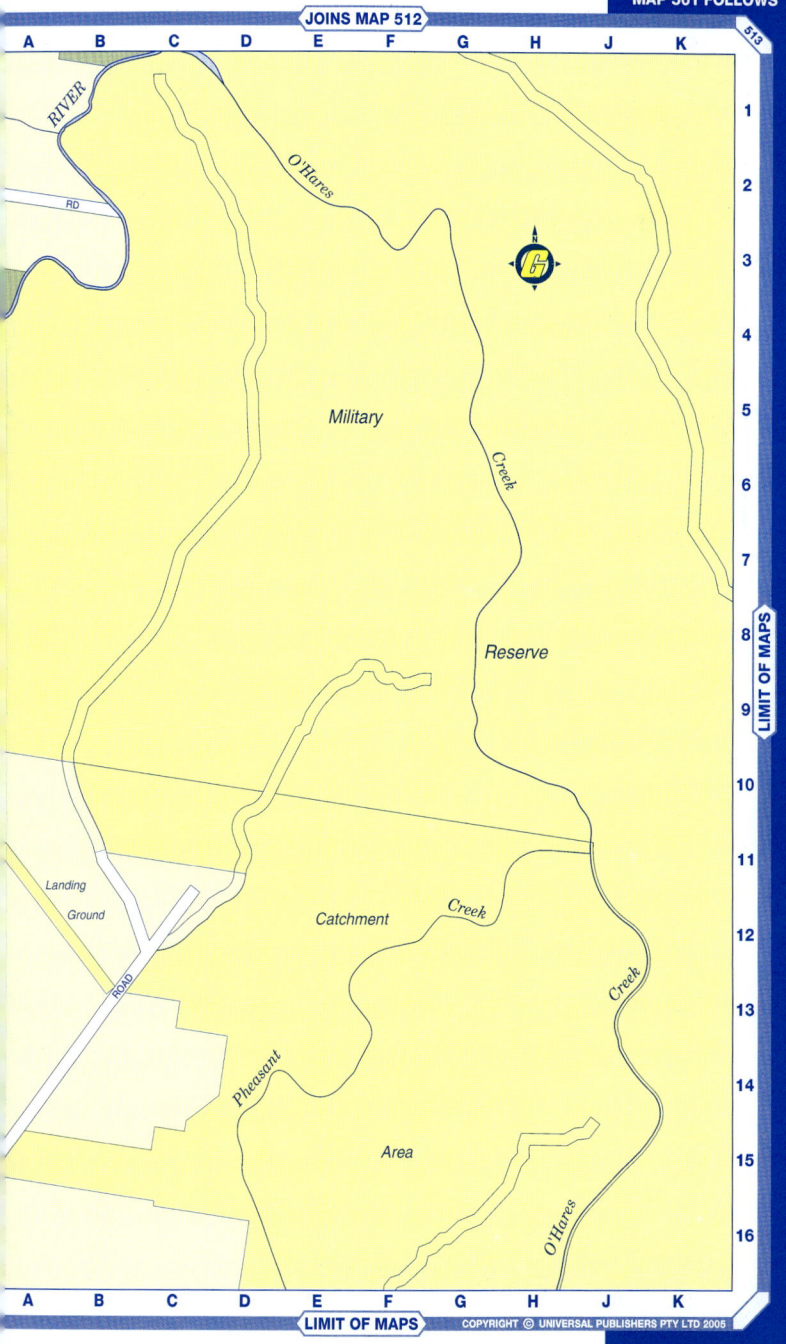

JOINS MAP 512

RIVER
RD
O'Hares
Military
Creek
Reserve
Landing Ground
ROAD
Catchment Creek
Creek
Pheasant
Area
O'Hares

LIMIT OF MAPS
LIMIT OF MAPS

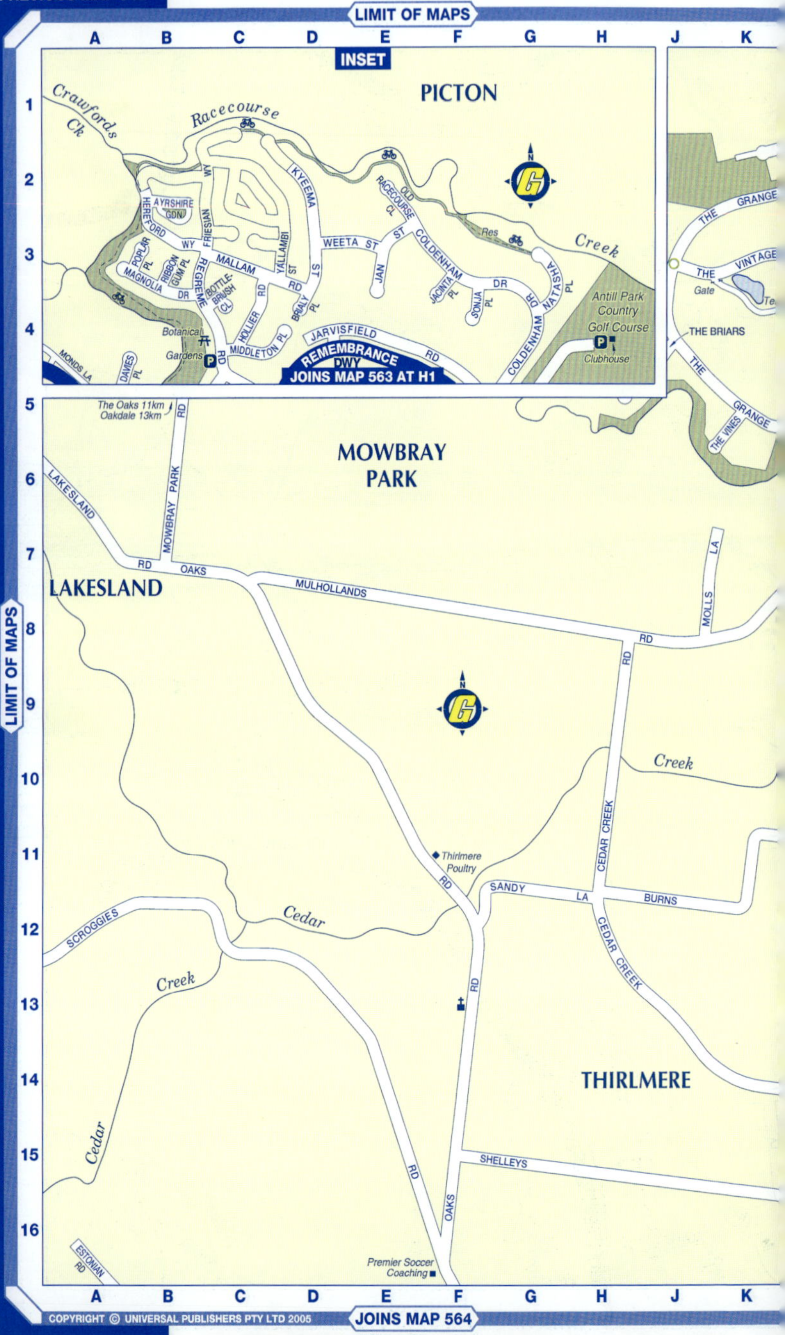

LIMIT OF MAPS
A B C D E F G H J K
1 2 3 4 5 6 7 8 9 10 11 12 13 14 15 16
INSET
PICTON
Crawfords Ck
Racecourse
Creek
Res
KYEEMA
OLD RACECOURSE CL
AYRSHIRE GDN
HEREFORD WY
FRIESIAN WY
YALLAMBI ST
WEETA ST
ST
COLDENHAM DR
JAN
POPLAR PL
RIBBON GUM PL
MAGNOLIA DR
REGREME RD
MALLAM RD
BOTTLE-BRUSH CL
ST
BRIALY PL
JACINTA PL
SONJA PL
NATASHA PL
COLDENHAM DR
HOLLIER RD
MIDDLETON PL
JARVISFIELD RD
REMEMBRANCE DWY
JOINS MAP 563 AT H1
Botanical Gardens
MONDS LA
DAVIES PL
Antill Park Country Golf Course
Clubhouse
THE GRANGE
THE VINTAGE
Gate
THE BRIARS
THE GRANGE
THE VINES
The Oaks 11km
Oakdale 13km
MOWBRAY PARK RD
MOWBRAY PARK
LAKESLAND RD
LAKESLAND
OAKS RD
MULHOLLANDS RD
MOLLS LA
Creek
CEDAR CREEK RD
Thirlmere Poultry
SANDY LA
BURNS RD
CEDAR CREEK
Cedar
SCROGGIES
Creek
THIRLMERE
Cedar
SHELLEYS
RD
OAKS
ESTONIAN RD
Premier Soccer Coaching
LIMIT OF MAPS
JOINS MAP 564

MAP 562

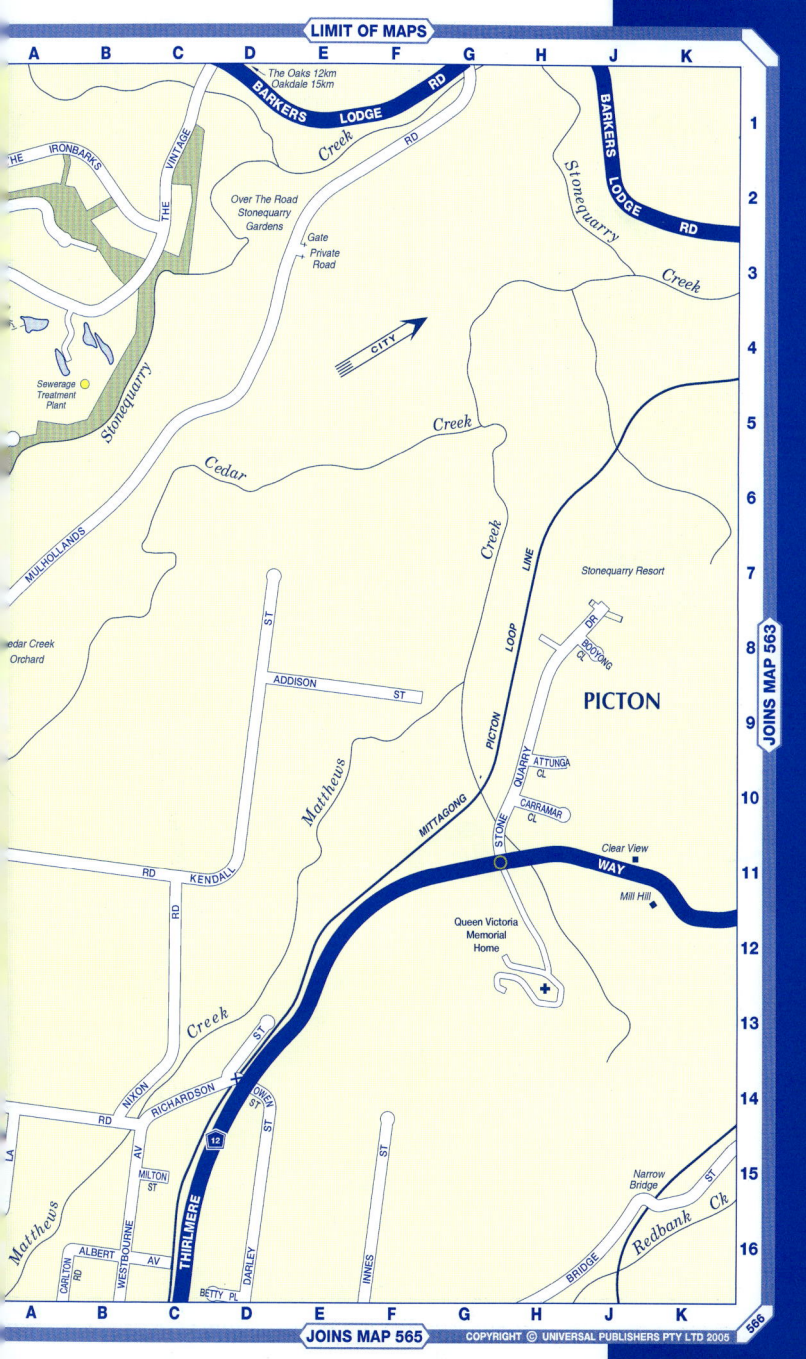

LIMIT OF MAPS

BARKERS LODGE RD — The Oaks 12km, Oakdale 15km

BARKERS LODGE RD

Stonequarry Creek

Creek

Over The Road Stonequarry Gardens
Gate Private Road

THE IRONBARKS
THE VINTAGE

Sewerage Treatment Plant

Stonequarry

CITY →

Cedar Creek

Cedar Creek Orchard

MULHOLLANDS

Matthews

Creek

PICTON LOOP LINE

Stonequarry Resort
BOOYONG CL
DR

PICTON

ADDISON ST

ATTUNGA CL
CARRAMAR CL

STONE QUARRY

MITTAGONG

Clear View
WAY
Mill Hill

KENDALL RD

Queen Victoria Memorial Home

Creek

NIXON RD
RICHARDSON
MILTON ST
OWEN ST
DARLEY ST
INNES ST

THIRLMERE
BETTY PL
12

CARLTON RD
ALBERT
WESTBOURNE AV

Narrow Bridge
BRIDGE ST
Redbank Ck

Matthews

JOINS MAP 565

JOINS MAP 563

COPYRIGHT © UNIVERSAL PUBLISHERS PTY LTD 2005

LIMIT OF MAPS
JOINS INSET MAP 561 AT D5
JOINS MAP 562
JOIN MAPS 566
565
PICTON
Valley View Estate
EQUESTRIAN DR
ABBOTSFORD RD
ABBOTSFORD BRIDGE
MONDS LA
DAVIES PL
BARKERS LODGE RD
Creek
Stonequarry
Botanical Gardens
REGREME RD
LOVE PL
RAMSAY ST
Basketball
Hume Oval
Pavilion
Tennis
DOWNING ST
RSL Memorial Park
REMEMBRANCE DWY
CITY
GOVERNORS LA
Wool-Away Woolshed
Camden 18km Map 477
CLIFFE ST
ELIZABETH ST
Ct Hse
WALTON LA
MENANGLE ST W
MARGARET ST
Council Depot
Cmnty Cntr
Hall
Cncl
COLDEN ST
EMMETT CL
SES
RFS
Cem
DAWSON LA
ARGYLE ST
NRMA
Delivery Cntr
St Anthony Cath
MENANGLE RD
BAXTERS LA
NPWS Area Office
CRAKANTHORP LA
COULL ST
PICTON AV
Fbr
LUMSDAINE ST
Showground
Ent
Clubhse
Victoria Park
Ten
WEBSTER ST
STATION ST
WHITFIELD PL
Picton Pmy
VIEW ST
Historic Viaduct
Picton
One Lane Bridge
SPELLING ST
STAR ST
PRINCE ST
VICTORIA ST
CAMPBELL ST
VICTORIA BR
HEATHCOTE ST
Gate
STONEQUARRY PL
Res
WHERRITT CL
CONNELLAN CR
COWPER ST
DUNLOP ST
Picton Cem
RSA Depot
MATTHEWS LA
RUMKER ST
THIRLMERE WAY
Redbank Cem (Unit Ch)
ANTILL ST
MAIDSTONE ST
Crown Res
HILL ST
WILD ST
TARRANT CL
Glenrock Reserve (Nature Walks)
MINERAL SPRINGS RD
PICTON RD
Picton Kart Track
Maldon
Menangle Rd
Hume Hwy 8km
Wilton 11km
Campbelltown 26km Map 511
Red Bank Res
HADDON PL
MAIN SOUTHERN RAILWAY
Wollondilly Community Leisure Centre
Stonequarry Lodge
BOLLARD PL
Industrial Area
WOOD ST
COACHWOOD CR
REDBANK PL
BRIDGE ST
HENRY ST
Picton Inducom Cntr
Picton High
Council Pound & Waste Transfer Stn
Cmnty Nursery
WONGA RD
Redbank
Not suitable for Heavy Vehicles
STILTON LA
Back Ck
89
12
88

MAP 564

THIRLMERE

- Thirlmere Reservoir
- Premier Soccer Coaching
- Estonian Village
- Wollondilly Greyhound Club Thirlmere Trial Track
- Lin Gordon Reserve
- Cemetery

Streets & Roads
- Estonian Rd
- Bonds Rd
- Oaks Rd
- Lakes St
- Dry Lakes Rd
- Mitchell St
- Matthews Creek
- Ryan St
- Mason St
- Kim Ct
- Campbell Close
- George Ping Dr
- Leonard St
- Victoria St
- Victa Pl
- Station St
- Pde
- Chanter Rd
- Tharawal Rd
- Slades Rd
- Boundary St
- West Pde
- Picton-Mittagong Loop Line
- Myrtle St
- Nattai St
- Banksia St
- Wongawilli St
- Colo St
- East St
- Meryla St
- River Pde
- Bargo River Rd
- The W.E. Middleton Dr

COURIDJAH

- Couridjah
- Tharawal Local Aboriginal Land Council
- Buxton 2km
- Buxton 3km

Thirlmere Lakes National Park

- Lake Gandangarra
- Lake Werri Berri
- Lake Couridjah
- Gate (Usually closed to motor vehicles)

CITY →

JOINS MAP 561
JOINS MAP 562
JOINS MAP 565
LIMIT OF MAPS

COPYRIGHT © UNIVERSAL PUBLISHERS PTY LTD 2005

MAP 565

THIRLMERE

COURIDJAH

MAP 566

JOINS MAP 563

PICTON

Back Ck

Sewage Treatment Plant

Carlton Stud

Not suitable for Heavy Vehicles

Myrtle

Wollondilly Abattoir

Crown Reserve

TAHMOOR

Child Care Centre

Crown Reserve

Bargo River

LIMIT OF MAPS

COPYRIGHT © UNIVERSAL PUBLISHERS PTY LTD 2005

MAP 567 BARGO

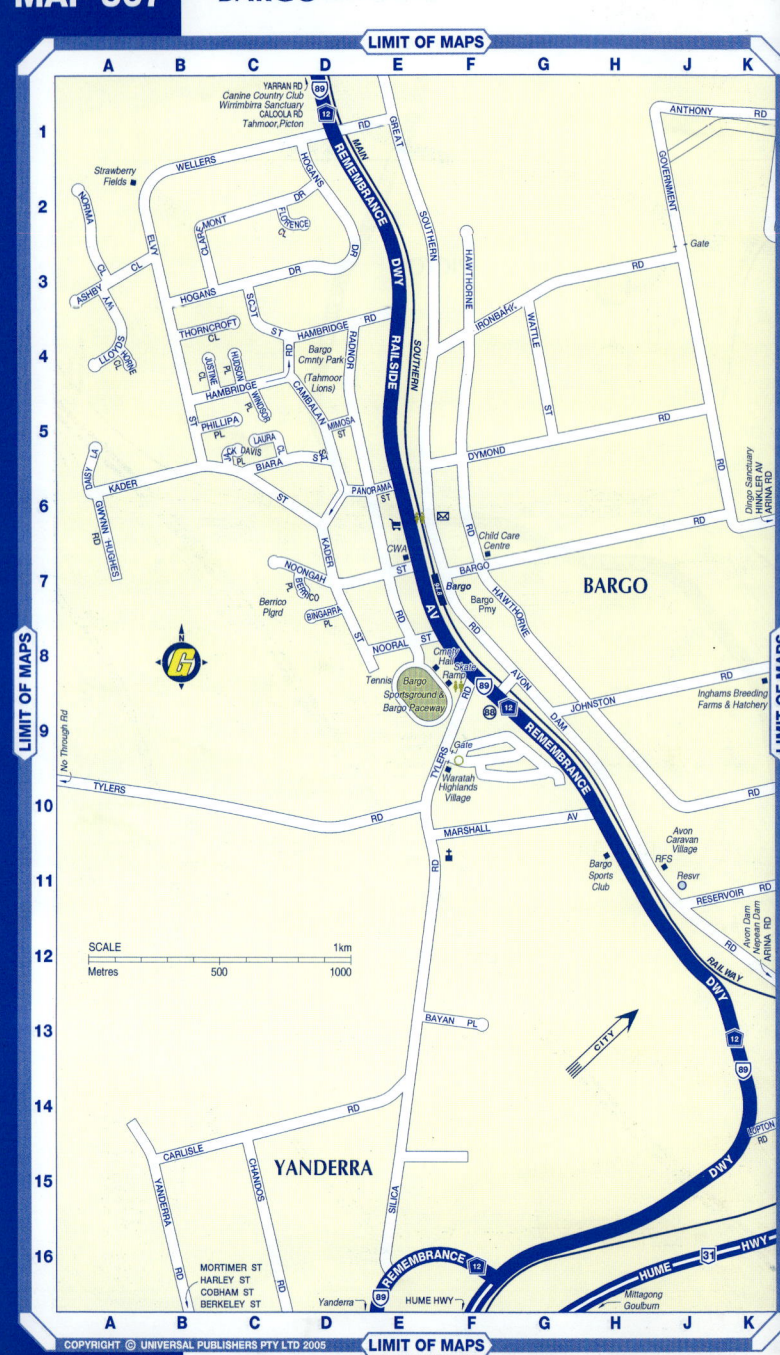

DOUGLAS PARK

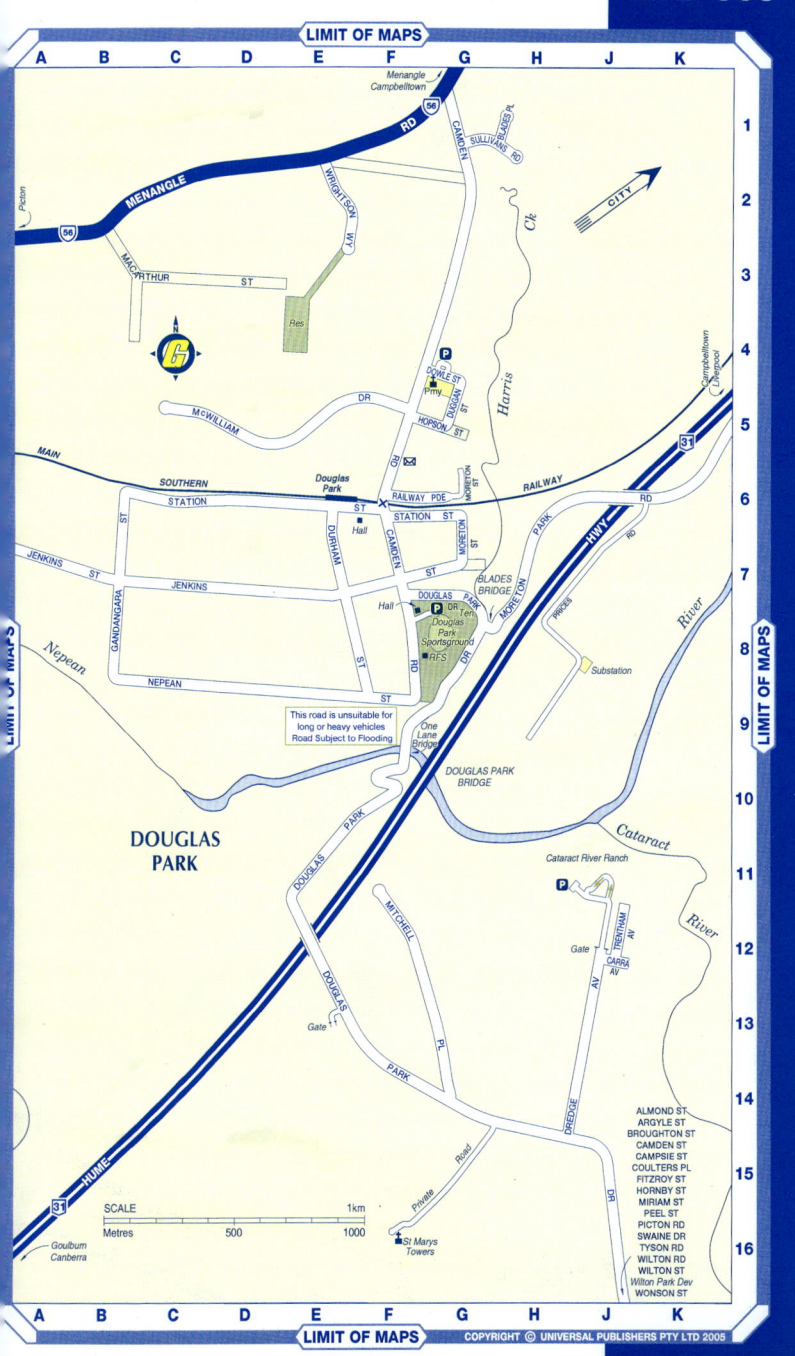

MAP 568

Street Index:
- ALMOND ST
- ARGYLE ST
- BROUGHTON ST
- CAMDEN ST
- CAMPSIE ST
- COULTERS PL
- FITZROY ST
- HORNBY ST
- MIRIAM ST
- PEEL ST
- PICTON RD
- SWAINE DR
- TYSON RD
- WILTON RD
- WILTON ST
- Wilton Park Dev
- WONSON ST

MAP 569 APPIN

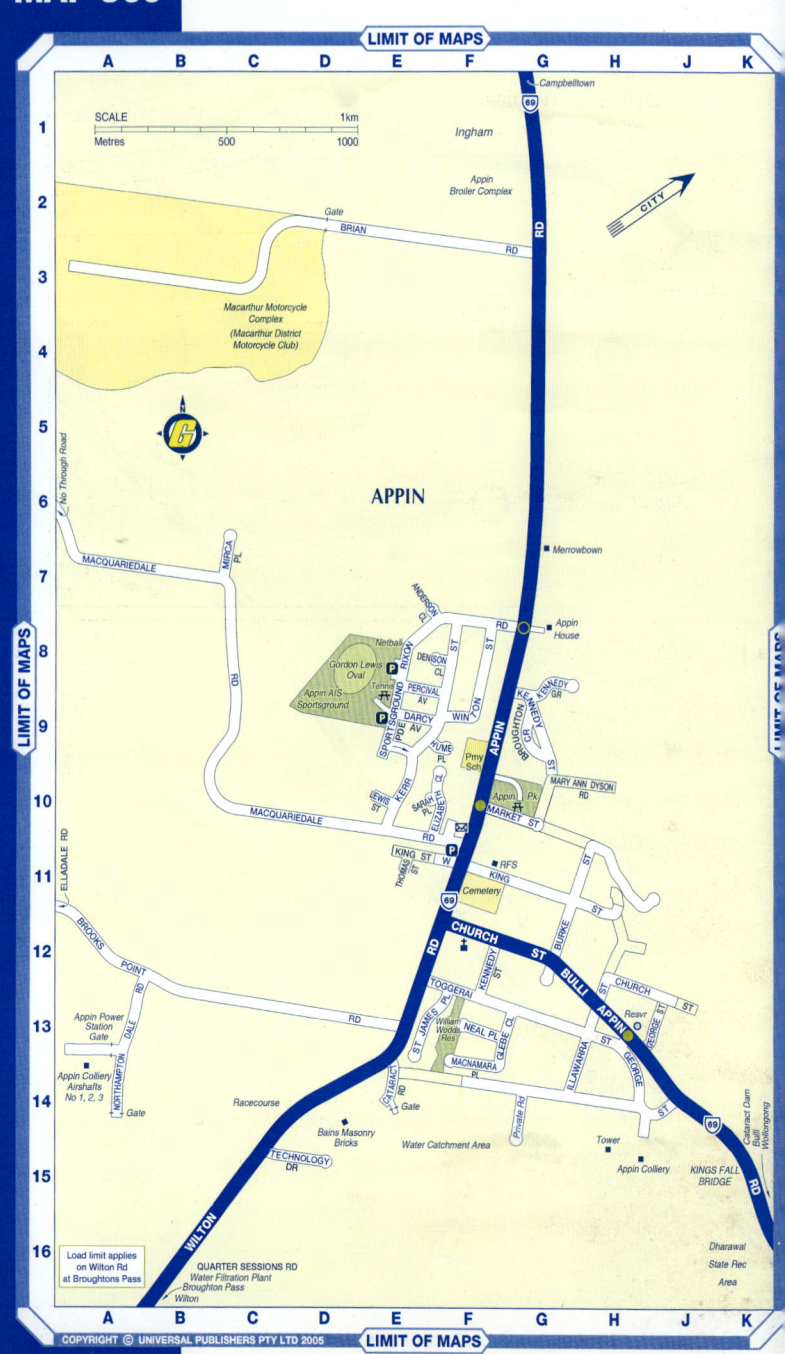

MAP 570

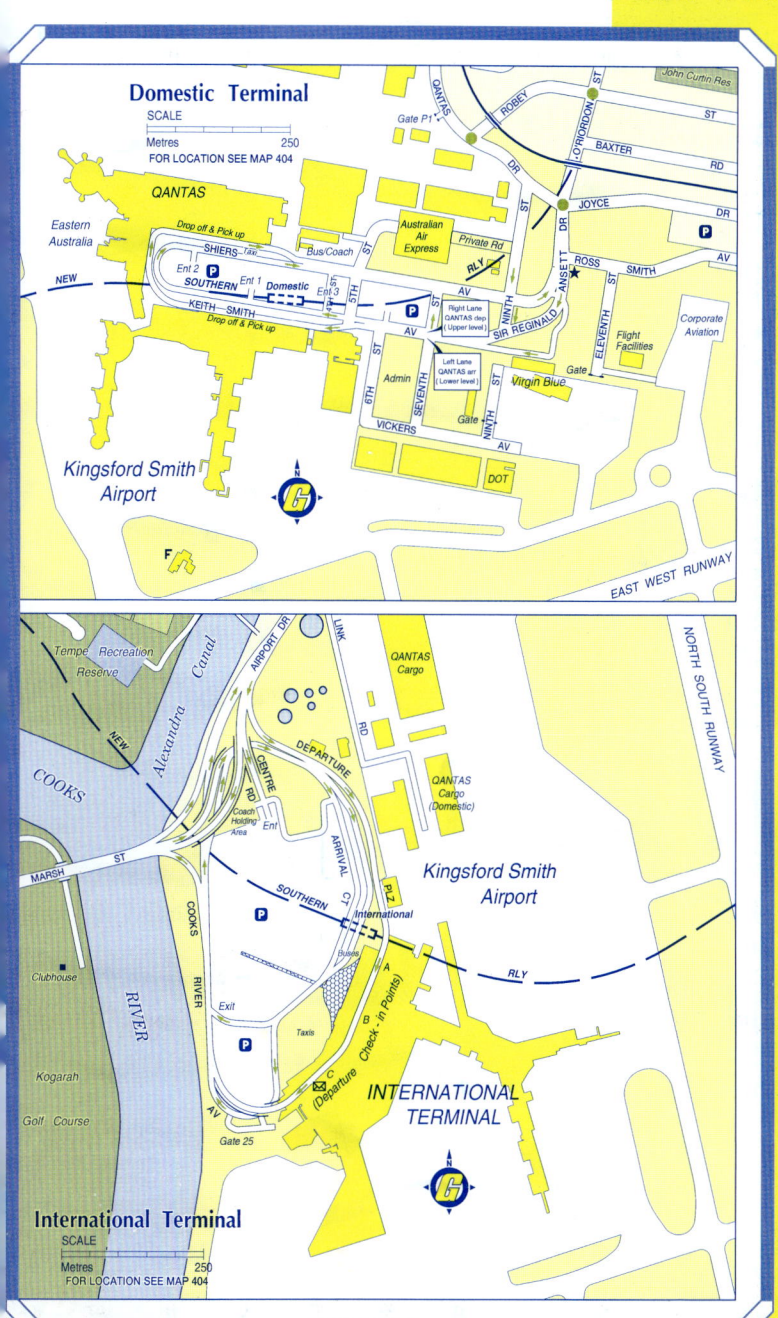

MAP 571

JOINS MAP 311
JOINS MAP 310
JOINS MAP 309
HOMEBUSH BAY
The new heart of Sydney
Homebush Bay
Mariner's Cove
Waterbird Refuge
Sydney Olympic Park
Sydney Olympic Park Ferry Terminal
Woo-la-ra (Elevation: 22m)
Silverwater Marker
Nature Reserve
Newington Armory
Blaxland Common
Playing Fields
River Marker
Mulawa & Silverwater Correctional Centre
Wilson Park
Slough Business Park
Newington Reserve
Sydney Metropolitan Oil Pipeline Terminal
ERMINGTON
George Kendall Riverside Park
PARRAMATTA RIVER
SILVERWATER BRIDGE
Eric Primrose Reserve
Silverwater Park
SILVERWATER
Duck River
Wentworth Common
Sydney International Archery Park
Kronos Hill
Brickpit
2SM/2UE Radio Tower
2SM/2UE Standby Radio Tower
2KY Radio Tower
2KY Standby Radio Tower
2AM Radio Tower
2CH/2EA Radio Tower
Viewing Tower
Zone Substation
MLLVC Office
SCALE
Metres
500
BURROWAY RD
HILL RD
HOLKER (Bus Only) BUSWAY
AVENUE OF OCEANIA
AVENUE OF EUROPE
AVENUE OF AFRICA
AVENUE OF ASIA
AVENUE OF THE AMERICAS
JAMIESON ST
NEWINGTON RD
SILVERWATER RD
BLAXLAND AV
HOLKER ST
SHAFT ST
SLOUGH AV
FARIOLA ST
DERBY ST
EGERTON ST
RACHAEL CL
CLYDE ST
PICKEN ST
RIVER ST
GIFFARD ST
JOHN ST

MAP 572

INDEX A - STREETS
REF		
1	BARRIER ST	C9
2	BROWN AV	A7
3	CLARENCE AV	A8
4	CUMBERLAND ST	A7
5	DARLING ST	B9
6	GWYDIR ST	B6
7	HUME ST	B9
8	HUNTER ST	B6
9	ILLAWARRA ST	C8
10	MACARTHUR ST	B8
11	MACQUARIE ST	B7
12	MANNING ST	B7
13	MONARO ST	B7
14	NEWELL ST	A8
15	SHOALHAVEN ST	C6

SYDNEY SHOWGROUND
INDEX B - BUILDINGS
	REF
ADI THEATRE	V C8
BADGERY PAVILION	T C7
BINNIE PAVILION HALL 3	U D6
BURING PAVILION HALL 4	D D6
CHARLES MOSES STADIUM	S C7
CLYDESDALE PAVILION	N B6
DOWNES PAVILION	E A7
FALKINER PAVILION	K A7
GRACE PAVILION	H A8
HORDERN ARENA	X C8
HORSE MARSHALLING	R B6
JEWE COMPLEX	M B7
JENO PAVILION	I A7
KELLY PAVILION	L B7
MACKAY PAVILION	A A7
McINTOSH PAVILION	F C B9
MUNRO PAVILION	B8
MURCHISON PAVILION	J B8
PADDINGTON PAVILION	P D7
ROSS PAVILION HALL 2	O D6
ROYAL AGRICULTURAL		
SOCIETY ADMINISTRATION	Z D7
SCHMIDT ARENA	W B7
SHEEP PAVILION	Y C8
SHOWRING COMPLEX	I D7
THE DOME HALL 1	C B9
WHITE PAVILION	Q B6
WYNNE PAVILION		

Info Guide

airline info

Australian Airlines	1300 799 798 or www.australianairlines.com.au
Eastern Australian Airlines	131 223 or www.qantas.com.au
Jetstar	131 538 or www.jetstar.com.au
Qantas Airways	131 313 or www.qantas.com.au
Regional Express (REX)	131 713 or www.regionalexpress.com.au
Virgin Blue	136 789 or www.virginblue.com.au

transport info line

For information on how to travel in Sydney by bus, train or ferry contact the Public Transport Info Line on **131 500** between 6am to 10pm. Alternatively, go to www.131500.com.au

taxis

ABC	13 25 22
Cumberland	13 10 17
Legion	13 14 51
Manly Warringah	13 16 68
Northern Districts	13 10 17
Premier	13 10 17
Premier Maxi Cabs	8868 4555
Premier Prestige	8868 4545
RSL Ex-Servicemens	9581 1111
Silver Service	13 31 00
South Western	13 27 88
St George	13 21 66
Taxis Combined	8332 8888
TTY	9020 3315
Western District	13 10 17
Wheelchair Accessible	8332 0200
Yellow	13 19 24

water taxis

ABC	1300 300 925
Beach Hopper	1300 306 676
Dolphin	1300 130 742
Harbour	1300 300 925
Water Taxis Bookings	1300 138 840
Water Taxis Combined	1300 666 484
Yellow	9299 0199

radio station frequencies

am
- **ABC News Radio** 630
- **ABC Radio National** 576
- **2BL (ABC Local)** 702
- **2CH** 1170
- **2GB** 873
- **2KY** 1017
- **2SM** 1269
- **2UE** 954

fm
- **ABC Classic** 92.9
- **C91.3**
- **MIX** 106.5
- **NOVA** 96.9
- **THE EDGE** 96.1
- **TRIPLE J** 105.7
- **TRIPLE M** 104.9
- **WSFM** 101.7
- **2DAY FM** 104.1
- **2MBS** 102.5
- **2RRR** 88.5

Festivals

	Month	Description	Website	Phone
Sydney Festival	January	Established over 25 years ago this is Sydney's premier cultural event and one of Australia's leading Arts festivals. Held over the month of January in the midst of Sydney's sunny summer.	sydneyfestival.org.au	8248 6500
Gay & Lesbian Mardi Gras	February/March	Enjoying international fame, Sydney's Mardi Gras attracts both international & national visitors from the conservative to the outrageous.	mardigras.org.au	9568 8600
Sydney Film Festival	June	Two weeks of day and night screenings of more than 200 recent international features.	sydneyfilmfestival.org	9280 0511
Manly Jazz Festival	October	Australia's largest and longest running International community jazz festival featuring more than 70 outdoor free performances.	manlytourism.com.au manly.nsw.gov.au	9977 1088
Homebake	December	All Australian music festival featuring contemporary new music with an edge.	homebake.com.au	